MODERN ENGLISH BIOGRAPHY

MODERN ENGLISH BIOGRAPHY

containing many thousand concise memoirs
of persons who have died between the years 1851-1900
with an index of the most interesting matter

FREDERIC BOASE

Volume I — A to H

FRANK CASS & CO. LTD.

1965

First published in 1892

This edition published in 1965 by
Frank Cass & Co. Ltd.,
10 Woburn Walk, London W.C.1

First edition, 1892
(privately printed, limited to 250 copies)

Second impression 1965

Printed in Great Britain by
Thomas Nelson (Printers) Ltd., London and Edinburgh

Introduction to the Second Impression

RESEARCH into any aspect of British life in the nineteenth century is often hampered by lack of a guide to the available biographical sources. MODERN ENGLISH BIOGRAPHY the monumental compilation by Frederic Boase provides an indispensable mine of information for this period, and much material which is not obtainable elsewhere.

Boase published his work privately, the first three volumes which were limited to 250 of each, were published in Cornwall between 1892–1901 and the three supplementary volumes which were limited to 125 of each, were published between 1901–1921. As the entire edition was so small the work has not received the wide recognition it deserves and consequently very few sets have been available during the last fifty years.

The six volumes in over 4,000 pages contain some 30,000 short biographical sketches of persons who died between 1851–1900 who achieved any public importance whatsoever. In most cases biographies are accompanied by a note of the particular sources used in each entry so that further research can be greatly facilitated. Boase made a special study of the existence of portraits and photographs of his subjects and gives details where these can be found. He also placed a great emphasis on exact detail particularly of births and deaths, a list of published works or theatre performances, and other facts which are sometimes omitted in larger works of reference, but which are all available here.

As Boase stated in the preface to the first edition his object was to cover the careers of not only the well known people such as judges, members of parliament, bishops, privy counsellors, members of the armed services, knights of the realm, stipendary magistrates and others but also to survey the lives of other interesting people such as architects, engineers, inventors, businessmen, shipbuilders, publishers, authors, actors, dramatists, physicians, surgeons, musicians, music-hall artistes, electricians, railway managers, painters, sculptors, engravers, explorers, sporting celebrities, eccentric characters and notorious criminals. . . . in fact anyone who has been well known. Additionally many foreigners living in England and nationals of British colonies have also been included.

Boase gathered his material from obituaries and reports published in the *Times, Illustrated London News* and other journals, he consulted local newspapers, the Transactions of learned societies, parish and church registers, the records of the registrar-general at Somerset House, published memoirs, correspondence with private individuals and many other sources. The whole series therefore, has a greater coverage of national and local celebrities who died in the latter part of the nineteenth century than the *Dictionary of National Biography*. MODERN ENGLISH BIOGRAPHY is an essential reference tool for anyone engaged in research in this important period of history.

Frederic Boase was born in 1843, educated at Penzance and Bromsgrove grammar schools, was admitted as a solicitor in 1857 and appointed Librarian to the Incorporated Law Society in 1877. He retired in 1903 and from then until his death he devoted himself to this great work. He was an original member of the Library Association and a contributor to *Notes and Queries* and many other journals.

Preface to the First Edition

BIOGRAPHY like other subjects seems to have its fashion; at one time it is much attended to, at another time neglected. The Historical Register from 1717 to 1739, The European Magazine from 1782 to 1826, and The Gentleman's Magazine from 1731 to 1868 furnished most useful and excellent notices of deceased worthies; then there appeared for one year only, The Register and Magazine of Biography, the first volume by Mr. Thompson Cooper, F.S.A., the second by Mr. Edward Walford, M.A. After this period there was a lull and biography was for some time at a discount; gradually however *The Times*, which hitherto had paid little attention to the subject, commenced inserting numerous obituary notices and this fashion gradually increased, until at the present day there are few numbers of that paper which do not contain interesting memoirs. Other periodicals followed suit, and now the majority of the daily and weekly journals not only give lives but many of them well engraved portraits.

In the meantime there also came out various books on biography, such as Men of the Time, Men of Mark, Eminent Women Series, English Men of Action, English Men of Letters, English Worthies, Great Artists, Great Writers, Memorable Men of the Nineteenth Century, Men worth Remembering, The Biograph and others, while various improved biographical dictionaries, more especially the Dictionary of National Biography, still in progress, were produced.

General Biography has now become so large a subject, that no one work can comprehend it, and it will, it is imagined, in future, be necessary to attack it in small sections, if anything like justice is to be done to the matter.

Impressed with these ideas, the author of this work, who had during a period of twenty years made a collection of notes relating to English persons deceased since 1850, thought it not improbable that by printing his materials, he might be able to make a useful contribution to biographical literature. The first volume of ''Modern English Biography'' is the result; in it will be found memoirs referring to the period mentioned, of all privy councillors, knights, judges, recorders, queen's counsel, serjeants, stipendiary magistrates, benchers of the inns of court, bishops, deans, archdeacons, chancellors, admirals, generals and members of parliament; other persons too, frequently omitted in biographical works, such as architects, engineers, inventors, ship builders, electricians, railway managers, publishers, actors, dramatists, musicians, music hall artistes, painters, sculptors, engravers, physicians, surgeons, sporting celebrities, eccentric characters and notorious criminals have also been inserted, in fact any one who has been well known and about whom a question might arise in general conversation. In addition, many foreigners who have spent portions of their lives in England and some few natives of the British colonies have been included.

The plan in these memoirs, of which there are nearly 8,000 in this volume, has been first to give the main facts in each life, then, in the case of authors, short though exact titles of their chief works, concluding with references to books where longer accounts are to be found. The subject of portraits has been made a speciality, and thousands of notices of likenesses in books, periodicals and newspapers have been inserted. The Transactions of the most important scientific and literary societies as well as the best known magazines and newspapers have been examined and the biographical notices extracted.

The memoirs, though short, will be found to contain many exact facts not given in larger works. Great trouble has been taken about births and deaths, the dates of births frequently cannot be obtained and the places and dates of deaths of even very well known individuals are sometimes not easily settled. Information has been sought from all printed sources, from private individuals, and from church registers; reference has been also continually made to the books of the registrar general at Somerset House.

Froude in one of his Essays says ''We want the biographies of common people;'' this adage has been acted on in Modern English Biography, and many hundred notices of the less known authors, artists, newspaper proprietors and journalists, merchants, country gentlemen and others, which can be found in no other book, are here recorded.

Some reference must be made to the Knights Bachelor, an increasing and important body of men of much repute, about whom the annual knightages do not furnish exact information. For the elucidation of their history, the columns of the London Gazette have been carefully searched and the dates and places of their knighthood extracted, information which it is believed, cannot be found concentrated in any other single volume.

The memoirs are arranged lexicographically according to the surnames, the peers however have all been inserted under their titles, for the reason that their family names are not generally known to ordinary readers.

To my father Mr. John Josias Arthur Boase and to my eldest brother the Rev. Charles William Boase, I am much indebted for their great kindness in conjointly defraying the cost of printing this work, which I claim, to be an important contribution to the English biography of the nineteenth century.

My thanks are due to Mr. William Prideaux Courtney and to my brother Mr. George Clement Boase, joint authors of the Bibliotheca Cornubiensis, as well as to my before mentioned brother the Rev. C. W. Boase, for kindly reading proofs and supplying additional facts, while to Mr. Richard Bissell Prosser late of the Patent Office and to Mr. Ralph Thomas author of The Handbook of Fictitious Names, I am under an obligation for information about inventors and other persons.

The Second Volume is in active preparation and will appear as soon as is possible, consistently with careful research.

In a biographical work arranged alphabetically an Index is not a necessity, but it was thought that one might add value to the book. A general index was not practicable, as it would have been as extensive as the work itself, but an elaborate and carefully considered compilation of the more remarkable, curious and interesting matter in the volume, has been made for me by my brother Mr. G. C. Boase. Clergy lists, Law lists and Army and Navy lists being common, the names of persons belonging to those professions have not been included. The first important heading in the index is that of Actors followed by Actors' Stage Names, a list probably unique, while Dancers, Singers and others have not been neglected. To Initialisms, Fancy Names, Changes of Names and Pseudonyms much attention has been given and the entries are very extensive. Fellows of the Royal Society, astronomers, explorers, physicians, surgeons, civil engineers, painters and sculptors are duly recorded, while sport is represented by masters of hounds, betting men, racing men, cricketers, pedestrians and pugilists.

The names of the Knights Bachelor occupy considerable space, and the article London will be found very interesting. Some amount of additional information has been inserted in the Index, to which the reader is recommended to refer when using "Modern English Biography."

FREDERIC BOASE

36, James Street,
        Buckingham Gate,
            London, S.W.,
                7 April, 1892.

Abbreviations

1 child	...	eldest child.
1 dau.	...	eldest daughter.
1 son	...	eldest son.
A.A.G.	...	assistant adjutant general.
A.D.C.	...	aide de camp.
A.G.	...	adjutant general.
A.I.C.E.	...{	associate of Institution of Civil Engineers.
anon.	...	anonymous.
A.R.	...	Annual Register.
A.R.A.	...	associate of the Royal Academy.
A.R.S.A.	...{	associate of the Royal Scottish Academy.
astronom.	...	astronomical.
Aug.	...	August.
b. ...	...	born.
B.A.	...	bachelor of Arts.
bapt.	...	baptized.
batt.	...	battalion.
B.Chir.	...	bachelor of surgery.
B.C.L.	...	bachelor of civil laws.
B.D.	...	bachelor of divinity.
B.Th.	...	bachelor of theology.
B.I. ...	...	British Institution.
biog.	...	biography.
bur. ...	...	buried.
C. ...	...	curate.
Cam. and Camb.		Cambridge.
cap.	...	chapter.
cath.	...	cathedral.
C.B.	...	companion of the Bath.
C.C.	...	Corpus Christi.
C.E.	...	civil engineer.
cemet.	...	cemetery.
ch. ...	...	church.
Ch. Ch.	...	Christ Church.
C.I.E.	...	companion of the Indian Empire.
C.M.G.	...{	companion of St. Michael and St. George.
co. ...	...	county.
col. ...	...	colonel.
coll. ...	...	college.
comr.	...	commissioner.
cr. ...	...	created.
C.S.	...	civil service.
C.S.I.	...	companion of Star of India.
d. ...	...	died.
D.A.A.G.	...	deputy assistant adjutant general.
dau.	...	daughter.
D.C.L.	...	doctor of civil laws.
D.D.	...	doctor of divinity.
Dec.	...	December.
dict.	...	dictionary.
D.I.G.	...	deputy inspector general.

ed. ...	...	editor, also educated.
Edin. and Edinb.		Edinburgh.
educ.	...	educated.
E.I.C.S.	...	East India company's service.
eld. ...	...	eldest.
Emm.	...	Emmanuel.
ex. and extraord.		extraordinary.
F.C.S.	...	fellow of Chemical Society.
Feb.	...	February.
F.G.S.	...	fellow of Geological Society.
F.L.S.	...	fellow of Linnean Society.
F.R.A.S.	...{	fellow of Royal Astronomical Society.
F.R.C.S.	...{	fellow of Royal College of Surgeons.
F.R.C.P.	...{	fellow of Royal College of Physicians.
F.R.G.S.	...{	fellow of Royal Geographical Society.
F.R.H.S.	...{	fellow of Royal Historical Society.
F.R.I.B.A.	...{	fellow of Royal Institution of British Architects.
F.R.S.	...	fellow of Royal Society.
F.R.S. Edin.	...{	fellow of Royal Society, Edinburgh.
F.S.A.	...	fellow of Society of Antiquaries.
F.S.S.	...	fellow of the Statistical Society.
G.C.B.	...	knight grand cross of the Bath.
G.C.H.	...	knight grand cross of Hanover.
G.C.I.E.	...{	knight grand commander of the Indian Empire.
G.C.M.G.	...{	knight grand commander of St. Michael and St. George.
G.C.S.I.	...{	knight grand commander of Star of India.
G.G.	...	Grosvenor gallery.
G.I.	...	Gray's Inn.
Gloucs.	...	Gloucestershire.
G.M.	...	Gentleman's Magazine.
gr. ...	...	grammar.
H.E.I.C.S.	...{	Honourable East India Co.'s service.
H.M.S.	...	Her Majesty's ship.
hon.	...	honorary and honourable.
h.p. ...	...	half pay.
I.L.N.	...	Illustrated London News.
inc. ...	...	incumbent.
instit.	...	institution.
I.T. ...	...	Inner Temple.
Jan. or Jany. ...		January.
J.P. ...	...	justice of the peace.

ABBREVIATIONS

K.C.	...	King's counsel.
K.C.B.	...	knight commander of the Bath.
K.C.H.	...	knight commander of Hanover.
K.C.I.E.	...	knight commander of the Indian Empire.
K.C.M.G.	...	knight commander of St. Michael and St. George.
K.C.S.I.	...	knight commander of the Star of India.
K.G.	...	knight of the Garter.
K.H.	...	knight of Hanover.
K.P.	...	knight of St. Patrick.
K.T.	...	knight of the Thistle.
K.T.S.	...	knight of the Tower and Sword.
L.C.P.	...	licentiate of College of Physicians.
L.G.	...	lieut. general.
L.I.	...	Lincoln's Inn.
lieut.	...	lieutenant.
Lincs.	...	Lincolnshire.
L.K.Q.C.P.I.	...	licentiate of King's and Queen's College of Physicians, Ireland.
LLB.	...	bachelor of laws.
LLD.	...	doctor of laws.
L.S.A.	...	licentiate of Society of Apothecaries.
m.	...	married.
M.A.	...	master of Arts.
mag.	...	magazine.
Magd.	...	Magdalen and Magdalene.
matric.	...	matriculated.
M.B.	...	bachelor of medicine.
M.C.C.	...	Marylebone cricket club.
M.Ch.	...	mastery of surgery.
M.D.	...	doctor of medicine.
M.G.	...	major general.
Med. & Chir. Soc.		Medical and Chirurgical Society.
mem.	...	member.
M.I.C.E.	...	member of Institution of Civil Engineers.
M.I.M.E.	...	member of Institution of Mechanical Engineers.
min.	...	minutes.
min. plen. and min. plenipo.		minister plentipotentiary.
M.L.	...	licentiate in medicine.
M.P.	...	member of parliament.
M.R.I.A.	...	member of Royal Irish Academy.
M.R.I.B.A.	...	member of Royal Institution of British Architects.
M.R.C.S.	...	member of Royal College of Surgeons.
MS. and MSS.		manuscript and manuscripts.
M.T.	...	Middle Temple.
N. and Q.	...	Notes and Queries.
N.G.	...	new gallery.
N.I.	...	native infantry.
Nov.	...	November.
N.S.W.	...	New South Wales.
N.W.	...	New water colour soc.
N.Z.	...	New Zealand.
Oct.	...	October.
O.W.	...	Old water colour soc.
Ox. and Oxf.	...	Oxford
p. and pp.	...	page and pages.
P.C.	...	perpetual curate.
P.C.	...	privy councillor.
phys.	...	physician.
P.R.A.	...	president of the Royal Academy.
preb.	...	prebendary.
pres.	...	president.
proc.	...	proceedings.
pseud.	...	pseudonyms.
pt. and prt.	...	portrait.
pub.	...	published.
Q.C.	...	Queen's counsel
R.	...	rector.
R.	...	royal.
R.A.	...	rear admiral.
R.A.	...	royal academician.
R.A.	...	royal academy.
R.A.	...	royal artillery.
R.E.	...	royal engineers.
rep.	...	representative.
R.H.A.	...	royal horse artillery.
r.l.	...	royal licence.
R.M.	...	royal marines.
R.N.	...	royal navy.
R.S.A.	...	Royal Scottish academician.
r.v.	...	rifle volunteers.
S.C.L.	...	student of civil laws.
sch.	...	school.
sec.	...	secretary.
Sep. or Sept.	...	September.
soc.	...	society.
S.P.C.K.	...	society for propagation of Christian Knowledge.
S.P.G.	...	society for propagation of the Gospel.
sq.	...	square.
S.S.	...	Sidney Sussex and Suffolk st.
st.	...	street.
ter.	...	terrace.
T.R.	...	theatre royal.
Trans.	...	Transactions.
Trin.	...	Trinity.
U.K.	...	United Kingdom.
univ.	...	university.
U.S.	...	United States.
V.	...	vicar.
V.A.	...	vice admiral.
V.C.	...	Victoria Cross.
V.P.	...	vice president.
Ven.	...	venerable.
Vict.	...	Victoria.
Wm.	...	William.
W.S.	...	writer to the signet.

ABBEY, John. b. Whilton, Northants 22 Dec. 1785; employed by James David and then by Hugh Russell organ-builders London; worked for Sebastian Erard in Paris 1826; an organ-builder in Paris; built choir organs for cathedrals of Rheims, Nantes, Versailles, and Evreux, large organs for cathedrals of Rochelle, Rennes, Viviers, Tulle, Bayeux and Amiens, many organs for South America, and an organ for the opera-house in Rue Lepelletier, Paris, destroyed by fire with the house, 28 Nov. 1873; introduced into French organs English mechanism, and the bellows invented by Alexander Cumming. d. Versailles 19 Feb. 1859.

ABBISS, James. b. Wallsworth near Hitchin in Herts 3 June 1812; tea-dealer in Gracechurch st. London 1835; chairman of City of London Union 1857 to death; alderman for ward of Bridge 1859–67; sheriff of London 1860-61. d. The Shrubbery, Chase Side, Enfield 7 July 1882. bur. Edmonton ch. yard 11 July.

ABBISS, Rev. John (son of John Abbiss of Wandsworth, Surrey). b. 12 July 1789; matric. Trin. Coll. Ox. 10 Oct. 1810, B.A. 1814, M.A 1817; R. of St. Bartholomew the Great, city of London 1819 to death. d. 41 Myddelton sq. Clerkenwell 8 July 1883. bur. Stoke d'Abernon near Leatherhead 13 July.

ABBOTT, Augustus (eld. son of Henry Alexius Abbott, of Calcutta, merchant). b. London 7 Jan. 1804; ed. at Warfield in Berks, Winchester, and Addiscombe; 2 lieut. Bengal

ABBOTT, A. (Con.)

artillery 16 April 1819; commanded the artillery in defence of Jellalabad, Nov. 1841 to April 1842; Col. 14 Nov. 1858 to death; served in Afghan war 1838-42; principal commissary of ordnance 12 Dec. 1847 to 9 Feb. 1855; inspector-general of ordnance and magazines Bengal 9 Feb. 1855–18 Jan. 1858; commander at Meerut 27 Jan. 1858; M.-G. 13 April 1860; Douranee order conferred on him Nov. 1840, but he never wore it; C.B. 11 Oct. 1842; one of the finest artillery officers of his time. d. 4 Paragon buildings, Cheltenham 25 Feb. 1867. *The Afghan War, 1838–1842, from the Journal of the late Augustus Abbott. By C. R. Low.* 1879.

ABBOTT, Rev. Edward Singleton. Preb. of St. Michael's in Ch. Ch. cathedral, Dublin 13 Aug. 1844; preb. of St. John's 11 Mch. 1845; preb. of St. Michan's 12 Feb. 1854-55; R. of St. Mary's, Dublin 1855 to death; sub.-dean of chapel royal Dublin 1858 to death; committed suicide by shooting himself at 7 North Frederick st. Dublin 12 June 1865 aged 63.

ABBOTT, Edwin. b London 12 May 1808; principal of Philological school 248 Marylebone road, London 1827-72; and secretary 1872 to death; one of the first to advocate a more thorough English training in schools; author of *A second Latin book* 1858; *Greek tragic iambics* 1864; *Complete concordance to works of Alexander Pope* 1875. d. 18 Palace sq. Upper Norwood 27 May 1882. bur. Kensal Green 31 May.

ABBOTT, JOHN *(son of Robert Abbott of Halifax, carpet manufacturer, who founded the carpet trade in Halifax with Mr. Crossley, and d. 1825).* b. Halifax 20 July 1796 ; a woolstapler there ; took a leading part in all matters of social improvement and left charitable bequests of £61,500. *d.* Halifax 13 May 1870.

ABBOTT, REV. JOSEPH. *b.* Cumberland 1789 ; ed. at Bampton sch. and Marischal coll. Aberdeen ; Missionary of the S.P.G. at St. Andrew's, Grenville, Lower Canada 1818–47, when he retired ; wrote *The Emigrant to North America from memoranda of a settler in Canada,* first published in the Quebec *Mercury* 1842, republished in many leading Canadian papers and in several English papers, including *Emigration Gazette,* and in pamphlet form by the Emigration agent. 2nd ed. 1843, it was also pub. in a more extended form by John Murray in the Home and Colonial library, under the title of *Philip Musgrave or the adventures of a Missionary in Canada ;* contributed many tales to Canadian periodicals. *d.* Montreal, Jany. 1863. *Morgan's Bibliotheca Canadensis* (1867) *pp.* 3-4.

ABBOTT, THOMAS EASTOE. *b.* East Dereham, Norfolk 1779 ; author of *Peace ; a lyric poem* 1814 ; *The triumph of Christianity* 1819 ; *The soldier's friend* 1828. *d.* Darlington 18 Feb. 1854.

ABDY, MARIA. *b* London ; wrote in the *New Monthly, The Metropolitan* and the Annuals ; privately printed *Poems* 8 series, 8 vols. 1830–62 ; *An appeal on behalf of governesses,* her longest poem gained first prize offered for literary productions on that subject. *(m.* Rev. John Channing Abdy, R. of St. John's Southwark who *d.* 27 Jany. 1845 aged 52.) *d.* 7 Upper Marine terrace, Margate 19 July 1867 aged 70. *bur.* St. Peter's church yard Isle of Thanet.

ABDY, SIR THOMAS NEVILLE, 1 Baronet *(only son of Anthony Thomas Abdy, captain R.N. who d. 9 June 1838, by Grace dau. of admiral Sir Thomas Rich).* b. 21 Dec. 1810 ; ed. at St. John's coll. Cam., B.A. 1833 ; M.P. for Lyme Regis, (lib.) 30 July 1847–1 July 1852 ; cr. baronet 8 Jan. 1850 ; sheriff of Essex 1875. *(m.* 19 Oct. 1841 Harriet 2nd dau. of Rowland Alston, M.P. of Pishobury, Herts, she *d.* 8 July 1877.) *d.* 6 Grosvenor place, London 20 July 1877.

ABDY, SIR WILLIAM, 7 Baronet. *b.* 1779 ; succeeded 21 July 1803. *d.* 20 b. Hill st. London 15 Apl. 1868.

A'BECKETT, ARTHUR MARTIN *(youngest son of Wm. A'Beckett of Golden square, London, long known as the Reform solicitor, who d. 23 Feb. 1855 aged 77, by his 1 wife Sarah who d. 25 Aug. 1817).* b. Golden square, London 1812 ; ed. at London univ. 1834 and at Paris ; M.R.C.S. 9 March 1838, F.R.C.S. 13 Dec. 1855, M.D. ; Staff surgeon to British legion in Spain ; on staff of Sir De Lacy Evans 1835–37 ; arrived in Sydney 1838 ; practised there 1838–58 ; member of legislative council of N.S.W. to 1858 ; knight of San Ferdinand ; F.R.G.S. 1860. *(m.* 15 May 1838 Emma Louisa 1 dau. of Marsham Elwin of Thirning, Norfolk, she was *b.* 26 Aug. 1814). *d.* Sydney 23 May 1871. *Medical Times and Gazette, ii,* 263 (1871); *Heads of the people, ii,* 83 (1848) *pt.*

A'BECKETT, GILBERT ABBOT (2 son of *Wm. A'Beckett of Golden sq.).* b. The Grange, Haverstock hill, London 9 Jany. 1811. ed. at Westminster school ; sole proprietor of following periodicals, *The terrific penny magazine, The Ghost, The Lover, The gallery of terrors, The Figaro* monthly newspaper, and *The Figaro* caricature gallery ; proprietor with Thomas Littleton Holt of following periodicals, *The evangelical penny magazine, Dibdin's penny trumpet, The thief, Poor Richard's journal,* and *The people's penny pictures ;* student at Gray's Inn 25 Apl. 1828 ; dramatic critic of the *Weekly Despatch ;* edited *Figaro in London* comic weekly paper, 160 numbers 1 Dec. 1831 to 27 Dec. 1834 ; joint manager with Edward Mayhew of the Fitzroy theatre, Fitzroy st. Tottenham court road, London 1834 where he produced his first burlesque Glaucus and Scylla ; edited *The Wag* 1837, and *The Squib* 1842, comic weekly papers ; one of the original staff of *Punch or the London Charivari,* which appeared 17 July 1841, wrote in it from number 4 to his death ; wrote leading articles in *The Times* one year, and in *Morning Herald ;* wrote humorous articles in *Pictorial Times ;* barrister G.I. 27 Jany 1841 ; poor Law comr. to inquire into iniquities practised in Andover union, March 1846 ; magistrate at Greenwich and Woolwich police court, Feb. 1849, and at Southwark, Dec. 1849 to death ; went to Boulogne 17 July 1856 ; author of *Scenes from the rejected comedies,* a series of parodies upon living dramatists 1844 ; *The quizziology of the British drama* 1846 ; *The comic Blackstone* 1846 ; *The comic history of England,* 2 vols. 1847–8 ; *The comic history of Rome* 1852 ; wrote more than 50 plays ; dramatised with Mark Lemon, Dickens's novel " *The Chimes,*" produced at Adelphi theatre 19 Dec. 1844. *(m.* about 1836 Mary Anne eld. dau. of Joseph Glossop, she was granted a civil list pension of £100, 23 Oct. 1856. She *m.* (2) George Jones, barrister, and *d.* 11 Dec. 1863 aged 46). *d.* of typhus fever at Rue Neuve Chaussée, Boulogne 30 Aug. 1856, body removed to Highgate cemetery. *The Critic, xv.* 436 (1856); *Mr. Punch, his origin and career* 1870; *Alfred Bunn's A word with Punch* 1847, *pp.* 5-7 *pt.*; *I.L.N. xxx,* 570 (1857), *view of his tomb in Highgate cemetery.*

NOTE.—There is a portrait of him by Leech in his two page cartoon, called " Mr. Punch's fancy ball ". in *Punch* 9 Jany. 1847, where he is represented as playing the violin in the orchestra between the double bass and the clarionet. His first contribution to *Punch,* entitled " The above bridge navy," appeared in No. 4, 7 Aug. 1841 with John Leech's earliest cartoon, " Foreign Affairs."

A'BECKETT, SIR WILLIAM (*eld. son of Wm. A'Beckett of Golden square*). *b.* London 28 July 1806; ed. at Westminster; barrister L.I. 30 June 1829; went to Sydney 1837; solicitor general of New South Wales 1841; a judge of court of N.S.W. 24 Nov. 1845; resident judge at Port Philip 3 Feb. 1846; chief justice and judge of admiralty court of Victoria 25 Aug. 1851; knighted by patent 19 Nov. 1852; returned to England 1858; author of great part of *The Georgian Era* 4 vols. 1832-34; of *Universal biography* 3 vols. 1840; and of *The Earl's choice and other poems* 1863. (*m.* (1) 1832 Emily dau. of E. Hayley, she *d.* 1 June 1841. *m.* (2) 1849 Matilda dau. of E. Hayley, she *d.* 8 Aug. 1879 aged 64). *d.* Abbotsville, Upper Norwood, Surrey 27 June 1869.

NOTE.—He edited at Sydney from 1837-38 a periodical called the Literary News, of which no copies are supposed to be now in existence.

ABELL, LUCIA ELIZABETH (2 *dau. of Wm. Balcombe, navy agent, purveyor to Napoleon Bonaparte at St. Helena, and afterwards the colonial treasurer of N.S.W. who d.* 19 March 1829). Author of *Recollections of the Emperor Napoleon during the first three years of his captivity on the island of St. Helena* 1848, including the time of his residence at her father's house, "the Briars." (*m.* Edward Abell). *d.* 18 Chester terrace, Eaton sq. London 29 June 1871. *Recollections of the Emperor Napoleon* 3rd ed. 1873, *pt.* Of Mrs. Abell.

ABERCROMBY, GEORGE RALPH ABERCROMBY, 3 Baron. *b.* Edinburgh 30 May 1800; M.P. for Clackmannan, (whig) 13 July 1824-2 June 1826, 10 Aug. 1830-23 April 1831, and 6 July 1841-18 Feb. 1842; M.P. for Stirlingshire 30 April 1838-23 June 1841; major 3

dragoon guards 22 June 1826-21 Nov. 1828; succeeded 14 Feb. 1843; lord lieutenant of Clackmannan 1843 to death; was blind. *d.* Airthney castle, Stirling 25 June 1852.

ABERCROMBY, THE HONBLE. ALEXANDER. *b.* 4 March 1784; ensign 52 foot 16 Aug. 1799; lieut. col. 28 foot 8 Dec. 1808-25 July 1814; commanded a brigade at battle of Albuera 16 May 1811; captain Coldstream guards 25 July 1814-25 Oct. 1821, when placed on half pay on reduction of regiment; C.B. 4 June 1815; K.M.T.; K.T.S.; K.S.G.; M.P. for co. Clackmannan 11 April 1817-10 June 1818. *d.* at his country seat in Scotland 27 Aug. 1853. *Napier's Peninsular War, book xii, chapters* 6 *and* 7.

ABERCROMBY, SIR GEORGE SAMUEL, 6 baronet. *b.* Edinburgh 22 May 1824; succeeded 6 July 1855. *d.* Forglen house, Turriff Banffshire 15 Nov. 1872.

ABERCROMBY, SIR ROBERT, 5 baronet. *b.* Forglen house, Banffshire 4 Feb. 1784; M.P. for Banffshire 2 Nov. 1812-10 June 1818; succeeded 18 July 1831. *d.* Forglen house 6 July 1855.

ABERDEEN, GEORGE HAMILTON GORDON, 4 Earl of (1 *son of George Gordon, styled Lord Haddo* 1764-91, *by Charlotte, youngest dau. of Wm. Baird of Newbyth, co. Haddington, she d.* 8 *Oct.* 1795). *b.* Edinburgh 28 Jany. 1784; ed. at Harrow, and St. John's coll. Cam., M.A. 1804; succeeded his grandfather 13 Aug. 1801; visited Greece, Turkey and Russia; founded Athenian society 1804, of which no one might be a member who had not visited Athens; rep. peer Scotland 15 Dec. 1806-1 June 1814; K.T. 16 March 1808; ambassador to Vienna 29 July 1813-April 1814, when he prevailed with the Emperor to join the allied sovereigns against Napoleon by treaty of Toplitz 9 Sep. 1813; present at battles of Dresden and Leipsic; signed treaty of peace at Paris 1 June 1814; created a peer of the U.K. as Viscount Gordon of Aberdeen, co. Aberdeen 1 June 1814; P.C. 23 July 1814; took name of Hamilton before that of Gordon by royal license 13 Nov. 1818; chancellor of univ. of Aberdeen 1827; chancellor of duchy of Lancaster 26 Jan. 1828-2 June 1828; sec. of state for foreign affairs 2 June 1828-2 Nov. 1830 and 2 Sep. 1841-5 July 1846; sec. of state for the colonies 5 June 1834-18 April 1835; ranger of Greenwich park 1 Feb. 1845; lord lieut. of Aberdeenshire 23 April 1846; first lord of the treasury 28 Dec. 1852-1 Feb. 1855; an elder brother of Trinity house

Nov. 1853–54; a comr. for executing office of treasurer of exchequer of Great Britain, and lord high treasurer of Ireland 6 Mch. 1854; president of Society of Antiquaries 1842–46; F.R.S. 28 April 1808, F.R.G.S. 1830, K.G. 7 Feb. 1855; visited by the Queen at Haddo house, 15 Oct. 1857; author of *Inquiry into principles of beauty in Grecian architecture,* 1822. *(m.* (1) 28 July 1805 Catherine Elizabeth, 3 dau. of John James Hamilton, 1 Marquess of Abercorn, she was *b.* 10 Jan. 1784, and *d.* 29 Feb. 1812. *m.* (2) 8 July 1815 Harriet, 2 dau. of honble. John Douglas and widow of James Hamilton, eld. son of 1 Marquess of Abercorn, she was *b.* 8 June 1792, and *d.* 26 Aug. 1833). *d.* 7 Argyll st. Regent st. London 14 Dec. 1860. *bur.* in family vault at Stanmore 21 Dec. *Correspondence of Earl of Aberdeen* 1850–53, *privately printed* 1880; *Edinburgh Review, clviii,* 547–77 (1883); *Thirty years of foreign policy* 1854; *Proc. of Royal Society of Edin. iv,* 477–83 (1862); *The British cabinet in* 1853, *pp.* 7–43, *pt.; Jerdan's National portrait gallery, vol.* 3, *pt.; I.L.N. i,* 461 (1842), *xx,* 1, (1853) *xxxvii,* 635 (1860) *pts.; A.R.* (1860) 376–83.

NOTE.—Lord Byron in his "English bards and Scotch reviewers," refers to him as "The travelled Thane, Athenian Aberdeen." He was allowed the very rare distinction of being permitted to retain the order of the Thistle, together with that of the Garter. Exclusive of royalty, 12 Knights of the Thistle (since the reestablishment of the order in 1687), have been elected to the Garter, of these 12 only 4 have retained both orders.

ABERDEEN, GEORGE JOHN JAMES HAMILTON-GORDON, 5 Earl of. *b.* Bentley priory, Stanmore 28 Sep. 1816; ed. privately. and at Trin. coll. Cam., M.A. 1837; attaché at Constantinople 1837; M.P. Aberdeenshire (lib.) 22 Aug. 1854–14 Dec. 1860, when he succeeded; went to Egypt, Sep. 1854, and June 1860; went to Madrid, May 1863 to petition Queen of Spain for a remission of sentence on Manuel Matamoros, (who was sentenced to 9 years penal servitude for preaching Protestantism, he was eventually exiled from Spain, he was *b.* Malaga, Oct. 1834 and *d.* Lausanne, 31 July 1866.) *d.* Haddo house, Aberdeenshire 22 March 1864. *bur.* Methlie churchyard 29 March. *Memoir of Lord Haddo by Rev. E. B. Elliott,* 6 *ed.* 1873; *The true nobility by Alexander Duff* 1868; *I.L.N. xxiv,* 265 (1854) *pt.*

ABERDEEN, GEORGE HAMILTON-GORDON, 6 Earl of. *b.* 10 Dec. 1841; succeeded 22 March 1864; one of the Scotch 8 in rifle competition at Wimbledon for Elcho challenge shield 1864 and 1865; dropped his title and adopted

name of George H. Osborne about 22 May 1866; sailor in American merchant service June 1866 to death; sailed from Boston for Melbourne in the ship "Hera" 21 Jany. 1870, washed overboard and drowned in latitude 40"10', longitude 58"14', 27 Jany. 1870. *Memoir of Lord Haddo, by Rev. E. B. Elliott,* 6 *ed.* 1873, 315–28; *Sir Bernard Burke's Reminiscences* (1882) 201–26.

ABERGAVENNY, REV. WILLIAM NEVILL, 4 Earl of. *b.* 28 June 1792; succeeded 12 April 1845. *d.* Birling manor near Maidstone 17 Aug. 1868.

NOTE.—His personalty was sworn under £300,000 Oct. 1868.

ABINGDON, MONTAGU BERTIE, 5 Earl of. *b.* 30 April 1784; succeeded 26 Sept. 1799; cupbearer at coronation of George iv 19 July 1821; lord lieut. of Berkshire 1828 to death. *d.* Wytham abbey, Berkshire 16 Oct. 1854. *bur.* at Rycote 24 Oct.

ABINGDON, MONTAGU BERTIE, 6 earl of. *b.* Dover st. Piccadilly 19 June 1808; ed. at Eton and Trin. coll. Cam., M.A. 1829, D.C.L. Ox. 1834; M.P. Oxfordshire (tory) 5 Aug. 1830–23 April 1831, and 17 Dec. 1832–1 July 1852, for Abingdon 3 Dec. 1852–16 Oct. 1854, when he succeeded; lord lieut. of Berkshire 13 Feb. 1855–1881. *d.* 18 Grosvenor st. London 8 Feb. 1884. *bur.* Wytham abbey 13 Feb.

ABINGER, ROBERT CAMPBELL SCARLETT, 2 Baron. *b.* London 5 Sep. 1794; barrister I.T. 27 Nov. 1818; M.P. Norwich (conserv.) 7 Jany. 1835–17 July 1837, for Horsham 28 June 1841–7 April 1844, when he succeeded; envoy ex. and min. plen. to Tuscany 13 Dec. 1859–22 March 1860, when mission was abolished on annexation of Tuscany to Sardinia. *d.* Abinger hall near Dorking 24 June 1861.

ABINGTON, LEONARD JAMES. *b.* London 27 Nov. 1785; edited *The Pottery Mercury* at Hanley Staffordshire 1824; pastor of New st. baptist chapel, Hanley 1836–63. *d.* Northwood, Hanley 7 Aug. 1867. *Personal recollections of late L. J. Abington* 1868, *pt.*

ABRAHALL, THEOPHILUS BENNETT HOSKYNS (2 *son of Rev. John Hoskyns Abrahall, C. of Badgworth, Somerset).* Barrister I.T. 25 June 1830; went western circuit; sec. of commissions of the peace to lord chancellor; revising barrister S. Lancashire and Northumberland; deputy registrar of London court of bankruptcy 1844–54, registrar 1854–14 Dec. 1861;

comr. of Newcastle district court of bankruptcy 14 Dec. 1861–31 Dec. 1869, when country district courts were abolished. *d.* Wonford house lunatic asylum, Heavitree, Exeter 2 Aug. 1874 aged 72.

ABRAHAM, GEORGE FREDERICK, admitted solicitor Nov. 1805; practised in London to death; originated with Thomas Thompson of the Stock Exchange the Home Missionary Society 11 Aug. 1819, the Congregational Union was merged in it 1827. *d.* 3 Mansfield st. Portland place, London 3 Jany. 1870 aged 88.

ABRAHAM, ROBERT. *b.* Cumberland; ed. for medical profession at Univ. of Edin.; served on the press in Cumberland; edited a leading Liverpool journal; went to Canada about 1843; Proprietor of the *Montreal Gazette*, editor to Dec. 1848, when it was sold; admitted an advocate of Lower Canada; edited the *Transcript* 1849 to death; edited the *Lower Canada Agricultural Journal* to death. *d.* Montreal 10 Nov. 1854. *Morgan's Bibliotheca Canadensis* (1867) *pp.* 4–5.

ABRAHAM, THOMAS. *b.* Bampton, Devon 1807; ed. at Blundell's gr. sch. Tiverton; apprenticed to Edward Acton at Grundisburgh, Suffolk; studied at Guy's hospital, London; L.S.A. Dec. 1833, M.R.C.S. April 1834; began practise in Old Broad st. 1834; surgeon to parish of Allhallows on the Wall for 3 years from Jany. 1835; surgeon to London infirmary for diseases of the skin 1836 to its close in 1837; member of Health of London association 1847; a comr. of sewers to his death; M.D. Erlangen 1851; M.D. Edin. 1859; a governor of Dulwich college 1861 to death and of Bridewell and Bethlehem hospitals; one of a sub committee of 4 who drew up "Report of health of London association on sanitary condition of Metropolis"; member of council of Hunterian society; helped to found Ragged school in Foster st. city of London; treasurer of London philanthropic society. *d.* Marsden villa, Haverstock hill 16 July 1864 in 57 year. *bur.* Kensal Green 21 July. *Medical Circular* i, 10, 25 (1852) *pt.*

ABYSSINIA, ALAM-AYAHU, Prince of. *(son of Theodore King of Abyssinia 1818–68). b.* Debra Tabor 23 April 1861; arrived in England 14 July 1868; ed. at Cheltenham, Rugby and Sandhurst. *d.* Headingley, Leeds 14 Nov. 1879.

ACKERLEY, CHARLES HENRY *(younger son of John Hawksey Ackerley, barrister, who d. 18 May 1842 aged 73, by Elizabeth dau. of Rev. John Chamberlayne of Maugersbury house, Gloucester)*. Entered navy 1 Feb. 1810; lieut. 20 Nov. 1822; commander on half pay 1 July 1864; presented with large silver medal of Society of arts for his safety rods for ships' boats 2 June 1828; invented a lamp which he called the lamp of life; tried at Swansea 27 Feb. 1851 for causing death of a miner named Dingle by the use of this lamp, and found not guilty; author of *A plan for the better security of vessels navigating the river Thames* 1834. *d.* at residence of his sister Mrs. Peter Brown at Dover 22 Nov. 1865.

ACKERS, GEORGE HOLLAND. *b.* 10 Aug. 1812; commodore of royal Victoria yacht club 1850-62, this club was founded at Ryde, Isle of Wight 24 May 1845, its admiralty warrant is dated 29 July 1845; sheriff of Cheshire 1852; author of *Universal yacht signals* 1847, of which he gave the copyright to Robert Henry Hunt who at his suggestion started *Hunt's Yachting Magazine* Aug. 1852. *d.* 15 Hyde park terrace, London 20 Jan. 1872.

ACKERS, JAMES. *b.* 1811; M.P. for Ludlow (conserv.) 3 July 1841–23 July 1847; purchased estate of Prinknash, Gloucestershire 1847. *d.* 27 Sep. 1868.

ACLAND, JAMES *(son of Mr. Acland of London, Government contractor). b.* city of London 21 March 1799; ed. at Alfred house academy, Camberwell; joined Phillimore's theatrical company at Chew Magna; clerk in office of Hullett Brothers & Company, South American merchants, Austin Friars; leading tragedian of Royalty theatre, Wellclose square; taught English at Calais; a penny a liner in London; sub editor of the *British Traveller;* took lodgings in Queen st. Hull 1831; started a publication called *The Portfolio, or memoirs and correspondence of an editor,* Aug. 1831; printed it himself at 23 Queen st.; erected a stall in the market place and refused to pay usual fee for it; ran a packet called the "Magna Charta" from Hull to Barton on Humber, charging less than half fares; ran a light cart over all bridges in the town and refused to pay bridge toll, great alarm being created, the Mayor swore in 800 special constables, corporation began action against him in court of King's Bench, Jany. 1832; tried at York 31 March 1832 for infringement of Barton ferry, when verdict went against him with damages one farthing, his costs amounting to £270, he barricaded his house for several

ACLAND, J. *(Con.)*

months to prevent anyone entering to arrest him, his *Portfolio* being sold through a crevice in the window ; elected churchwarden of Holy Trinity, Hull, Easter Monday 1832 ; taken to gaol for not paying his costs ; a candidate for office of chamberlain of Hull, Sep. 1832 ; a grocer at 23 Queen st., to which house he gave name of "Anti-corporate castle ;" confined in the King's Bench prison, Nov. 1832 ; sentenced to 18 months imprisonment in gaol of Bury St. Edmunds for libel ; served the full term ; contested Hull as a liberal 13 Dec. 1832, polled only 433 votes ; last number of the *Portfolio* issued 13 July 1833, a few sheets followed, which he styled *Prison Proverbs*. Proprietor with Richard and Anthony Dugdale of *Paris Sun*, "the largest continental journal and the only English paper in the world, published daily throughout the year," was director and editor of it at 7 Rue Vivienne, Paris 1 Jany. 1837 ; only number of it in British Museum library is headed "Vol. 2, No. 54, Thursday morning, Feb. 23, 1837, 10 sous," the proprietors were condemned by the president of 6th chamber of correctional police to a fine to government of 2000 francs, and to payment of 1000 francs to proprietors of an opposition paper for libel 22 Feb. 1837 ; lecturer of Anti-corn law league 1838–46 ; convened and addressed farm labourers of every village in Devon and Cornwall ; an election and parliamentary agent 1846 to death ; a very good speaker on nearly any subject ; author of *True patriotism, a poem* 1817, *The Imperial poll book of all elections from 1832 to 1864, Second ed.* 1869. *d.* 14 Ellerslie terrace, Clapham, London 21 June 1876. *The Bristolian Nos. 1–7, 23 Feb.–11 May* 1872 ; *W. A. Gunnell's Sketches of Hull celebrities* 1876, 460–64.

ACLAND, Sir Peregrine Fuller Palmer, 2 Baronet. *b.* 10 Nov. 1789 ; succeeded 23 Feb. 1831. *d.* Fairfield, Bridgwater 25 Oct. 1871.

ACLAND, Sir Thomas Dyke, 10 Baronet (1 *son of Sir Thomas Dyke Acland, 9 baronet, who d. 17 May 1794, by Henrietta Anne only dau. of Sir Richard Hoare, baronet, she d. 2 Sep. 1841*). *b.* London 29 March 1787 ; ed. at Harrow and Ch. Ch. Ox., B.A. 1808, M.A. 1814, D.C.L. 1831 ; one of the founders of Grillion's club 1812, which met at Grillion's hotel, 7 Albemarle st. London ; M.P. Devon (tory) 17 Oct. 1812–10 June 1818 and 18 March 1820–23 April 1831 ; M.P. for North Devon 29 July 1837–21 March 1857 ; head of religious party in House of Commons ; F.G.S. 1818, F.R.G.S. 1830, F.R.S. 20 June

ACLAND, Sir T. D. *(Con.)*

1839. *(m.* 7 April 1808 Lydia Elizabeth only dau. of Henry Hoare of Fleet st. London, banker, she *d.* 23 June 1856 aged 69*)*. *d.* Killerton, Broad Clyst, Devon 22 July 1871. *J. B. Sweet's Life of Henry Hoare* 1870 ; *I.L.N.* lix, 99, 116, 121, 362 (1871) *pt. Grillion's Club by P. G. E. privately printed* 1880 *pt.*

Note.—His personalty was sworn under £70,000 ; a statue of him by E. B. Stephens, A.R.A., was erected on Northernhay, Exeter 1861.

ACTON, Eliza *(eld. dau. of John Acton of Hastings, brewer*). *b.* Battle, Sussex 17 April 1799 ; published Poems 500 copies 1826, 2 ed. 1827 ; lived some time in France ; at Tunbridge 1837 ; at Hampstead ; author of *The voice of the North, a poem* 1842 ; *Modern Cookery in all its branches* 1845, 6 ed. 1855 ; *The English bread book* 1857. *d.* Snowdon house, John st. Hampstead 13 Feb. 1859.

ACTON, Marianne Lady Acton *(elder dau. of general Joseph Edward Acton*). *b.* 1782. *m.* 1796 by dispensation of the Pope, her uncle Sir John Francis Edward Acton, 6 baronet, prime minister of Naples several years, he was *b.* 1736 and *d.* 12 Aug. 1811. *d.* Buckland 18 March 1873.

ACTON, William. *b.* 1789 ; sheriff of Wicklow 1820 ; M.P. for co. Wicklow (conserv.) 17 July 1841–27 April 1848. *d.* Westaston Rathdrum, co. Wicklow 10 April 1854.

ACTON, William. *b.* Shillingstone rectory 15 Sep. 1814 ; placed under care of Dr. Mant in London 1830 ; articled pupil of Charles Wheeler, (Apothecary to St. Bartholomew's hospital) 1830–35 ; Externe at female venereal hospital Paris ; Secretary of the Parisian medical society 1839 ; returned to London Oct. 1840 ; M.R.C.S. June 1840 ; practised in George st. Hanover square 1840–43 ; removed to 46 Queen Anne st. Cavendish square March 1843 ; surgeon to Islington dispensary ; author of *A practical treatise on diseases of the urinary and generative organs* 1841, 3 ed. 1860 ; *Prostitution considered in its moral, social and sanitary aspects in London and other large cities* 1857, 2 ed. 1870. *d.* 17 Harley st. London 7 Dec. 1875. *Medical Circular i,* 11–12 (1852).

ADAIR, Sir Robert *(son of Robert Adair, sergeant surgeon to George III, who d. 16 March 1790, by Caroline Keppel, 1737–69 elder dau. of Wm. Anne 3 Earl of Albemarle*). *b.* London 24 May 1763 ; ed. at Westminster and Univ. of Gottingen ; called to the bar at L.I. 27 April 1785 ; M.P. Appleby, (whig) 18 June 1799–29 June 1802, for Camelford

ADAIR, SIR R. *(Con.)*

7 July 1802–29 Sep. 1812 ; minister to court of Vienna 7 May 1806–14 May 1807 ; minister to Constantinople 5 July 1808, and ambassador 14 April 1809 ; sent on a special mission to the Low Countries 1831–35 : P.C. 23 July 1828 ; G.C.B. 3 Aug. 1831 for negotiating peace between Great Britain and Ottoman Porte in 1809 ; author of *Historical memoir of a mission to court of Vienna in* 1806 *with a selection from despatches,* 1844 ; *The negotiations for the peace of the Dardanelles in* 1808-1809, 2 vols. 1845. *(m.* 1805 Angélique Gabrielle dau. of Marquess d'Hazincourt). *d.* 11 Chesterfield st. Mayfair, London 3 Oct. 1855. *G.M., xliv,* 535 (1855) ; *Lord John Russell's Memorials of C. J. Fox, vol. ii, appendix.*

NOTE.—At his death he was the senior knight of the order of the Bath, and the last survivor of those who were knights before its enlargement in 1814.

ADAIR, SIR ROBERT SHAFTO, 1 Baronet *(eld. son of W. Adair of Ballymena, co. Antrim* 1754–1844, *by Camilla dau. of Robert Shafto of Benwell, Northumberland, she d.* 18 *Nov.* 1787*). b.* 26 June 1786 ; created Baronet 2 Aug. 1838 ; sheriff of Suffolk 1846 ; F.S.A. 16 May 1861. *(m.* (1) 17 Sep. 1810 Elizabeth Maria dau. of Rev. James Strode of Berkhampstead, Herts, she *d.* 1 Sep. 1853. *m.* (2) 3 Oct. 1854 Jane Anne eld dau. of Rev. Townley Clarkson, V. of Hinxton, Cambs, she *d.* 18 March 1873). *d.* Flixton hall, Suffolk 24 Feb. 1869.

ADAM, SIR CHARLES *(eld. son of Wm. Adam* 1751–1839, *lord chief comr. of jury court of Scotland by Eleanora Elphinstone* 1749–1800 2 *dau. of Charles,* 10 *baron Elphinstone). b.* Brighton 6 Oct. 1780 ; entered navy 15 Dec. 1790 ; captain 12 June 1799 ; captain of Invincible, 74 guns 1811–1813 ; of Royal Sovereign yacht 15 Dec. 1814–7 Feb. 1816, and 20 July 1821–27 May 1825 ; R.A. 27 May 1825, V.A. 10 Jany. 1837 ; commander in chief, North America and West Indies 17 Aug. 1841–May 1845, when placed on half pay ; admiral 8 June 1848 ; M.P. Kinrossshire (lib.) 20 May 1831–3 Dec. 1832 ; M.P. for Clackmannan and Kinross 24 Dec. 1832–23 June 1841 ; Lord Lieut. of Kinross 1 April 1839 to death ; 1st naval Lord of Admiralty 25 April 1835–8 Sep. 1841, and 24 July 1846–20 July 1847 ; one of elder brethren of Trinity House 1839–41 ; Governor of Greenwich hospital 10 July 1847 to death ; K.C.B. 10 Aug. 1835. *(m.* 4 Oct. 1822 Elizabeth dau. of Patrick Brydone of Lennell, F.R.S., she *d.* 1871). *d.* Greenwich hospital 16 Sep. 1853, *bur.* there 21 Sep.

ADAM, SIR FREDERICK *(younger son of above named Wm. Adam* 1751–1839). *b.* 1781 ; ed. at Woolwich ; ensign 26 foot 4 Nov. 1795 ; lieut. col. 5 garrison battalion Aug. 1804 to 5 Jany 1805 ; lieut. col. 21 foot 5 Jany 1805 to 4 June 1814 ; served in Sicily 1806–11 ; Aide de camp to Prince Regent 8 Feb. 1811 ; commanded a brigade in Spain 1813 ; the third British brigade at Waterloo 1815 ; and a division at Malta 1817–22 ; K.C.B. 22 June 1815 ; G.C.B. 20 June 1840 ; G.C.M.G. 27 Dec. 1821 ; invested at Corfu 15 Jany. 1822 ; grand master ; lord high commissioner of Ionian islands 7 April 1824– 8 Sep. 1832 ; P.C. 29 June 1831 ; governor of Madras 25 Oct. 1832–4 March 1837. *(m.* (1) at Corfu 23 June 1820 Diamantino Pallatiano, she *d.* at Rome 1 June 1844. *m.* (2) at Kensington 24 July 1851, Ann Lindsay dau. of John Maberly). *d.* at Greenwich railway station 17 Aug. 1853. *Siborne's War in France and Belgium* 1848 ; *Napier's Peninsular War, book xx, chapter* 4 *and book xxi, chapter* 2.

ADAM, JAMES. *b.* Paisley 1809 ; worked at the loom ; went to London 1834 ; edited the Aberdeen Herald 1834 to death ; author of *The knowledge qualification* : a plan for the reciprocal extension of education and the franchise 1837. *d.* Old Aberdeen 10 Nov. 1862.

ADAM, WILLIAM PATRICK *(elder son of Admiral Sir Charles Adam, Governor of Greenwich Hospital). b.* 14 Sep. 1823 ; ed. at Rugby and Trin. coll. Cam., B.A. 1846 ; called to bar at Inner Temple 4 May 1849 ; went home circuit ; Sec. to Baron Elphinstone, Govenor of Bombay Dec. 1853–Sep. 1858 ; M.P. for Clackmannanshire and Kinrossshire (lib.) 2 May 1859–Oct. 1880 ; a Lord of the Treasury April 1865–July 1866, and Dec. 1868–Aug. 1873 ; first Commissioner of Works and Buildings, and Paymaster General 11 Aug. 1873–Feb. 1874, and April 1880–Nov. 1880 ; P.C. 9 Aug. 1873 ; governor of Madras 11 Oct. 1880 to death ; whip of liberal party April 1874–April 1880 ; left for India 27 Nov. 1880. *(m.* 23 Feb. 1856 Emily Eliza dau. of Sir Wm. Wyllie, K.C.B., she was raised to rank of a baronet's wife 22 May 1882). *d.* Ootacamund, Madras 24 May 1881. *bur.* there 26 May. *Fraser's Mag. civ,* 113–22 (1881) ; *Graphic xxiii,* 589 (1881) *pt.; I.L.N. lxxvii,* 564 (1880) *pt.*

ADAMS, ALEXANDER MAXWELL, L.R.C.S. Edin. 1835, F.F.P.S. Glasgow 1840 ; M.D. King's college Aberdeen 1849 ; professor of Institutes of medicine in Anderson's university Glasgow ; senior surgeon Lock hospital Glasgow ; went to Lanark about 1852 ; provost

ADAMS, A. M. *(Con.)*

of Lanark 1860 to death; author of *Essay on Scarlet Fever. d.* Bloomgate st. Lanark 24 July 1867 aged 50.

ADAMS, ANDREW LEITH (2 *son of Francis Adams of Belfield house, Banchory, co. Aberdeen).* Assistant surgeon 64 foot 22 Dec. 1848; surgeon major 20 Oct. 1868–23 Jany. 1875, when he retired with honorary rank of deputy surgeon general; professor of zoology, Royal college of science, Dublin 1873–78; professor of natural history, Queen's college, Cork, Nov. 1878 to death; F.G.S. 1870, LL.D. Aberdeen 1871, F.R.S. 6 June 1872; author of *Wanderings of a naturalist* 1867; *Notes of a Naturalist* 1870. (*m.* 26 Oct. 1859 Bertha Jane, eld. dau. of Frederick Grundy of The Avenue, Hardwick). *d.* Queenstown 29 July 1882.

ADAMS, ARTHUR. Assistant surgeon R.N. 13 Oct. 1841; surgeon 14 April 1853; employed in the Actæon on surveying service, on coast of China and Tartary, Aug. 1856; fleet surgeon 27 May 1865; retired 27 July 1871; M.R.C.S. 1848; author of *The zoology of the voyage of H.M.S. Samarang* 1850; *Travels of a naturalist in Japan and Manchuria* 1870. *d.* Stoke villa, Honor Oak Kent 16 Oct. 1878 aged 58.

ADAMS, ARTHUR ROBARTS *(fourth son of Henry Cadwallader Adams of Anstey Hall, Warwickshire 1779–1842 by Emma eld. dau. of Sir Wm. Curtis, Lord mayor of London, 1st Bart., she d. 22 June 1857 aged 76).* b. 16 Aug. 1812; ed. at Merchant Taylors' sch. 1822–30, and at St. John's coll. Ox. 1830–35; B.C.L. 1835, D.C.L. 1840; Fell. of his coll. 1835 to death; called to bar at Mid. Temple 11 Jan. 1839; went Midland circuit; Recorder of Birmingham 20 Jan. 1866 to death; Q.C. 22 June 1869, Bencher of his Inn 27 Jan. 1870; Assessor of Chancellor's court, Oxford, Nov. 1871–1876. *d.* suddenly while out shooting in Bagley Wood near Oxford 13 Dec. 1877. *bur.* Anstey near Coventry 20 Dec. 1877.

ADAMS, EDWARD MOORE. Practised as a surgeon; Sec. to proprietors of Cremorne gardens, London for 30 years before 5 Oct. 1877, when they closed; *d.* Bristol 2 June 1881 in 78 year. *bur.* Arno's Vale cemetery 6 June.

ADAMS, FRANCES MATILDA. Exhibited pictures of flowers at the Royal Academy from 1816; water colour painter extraordinary to Queen Adelaide. *d.* 24 Oct. 1863 aged 79.

ADAMS, FRANCIS. *b.* Lumphanan, co. Aberdeen 13 March 1796; ed. at Aberdeen; M.R.C.S. 1 Dec. 1815; practised at Banchory-Ternan 1816 to death; translated Paulus Ægineta, 3 vols. 1844–47, being the only English translation; *Hippocrates* 2 vols. 1849, and *Aretæus* 1856; author of *Arundines Devæ, or poetical translations on a new principle* 1853. *d.* Banchory-Ternan 26 Feb. 1861. *Scotsman 27 Feb. and 9 March 1861.*

ADAMS, FRANK. *b.* 1809; ensign 28 foot 30 Dec. 1826; lieut. col. 28 foot 16 July 1852–4 March 1866; commanded Mhow division of Bombay army 9 Jan. 1866–1869; C.B. 5 July 1855. *d.* at sea, on board the Tanjore, on his way home from India 19 Sep. 1869.

ADAMS, GEORGE, physician general Madras army 6 Feb. 1841–31 Jan. 1846. *d.* 148 New Bond st. London 11 July 1852.

ADAMS, SIR GEORGE POWNOLL *(younger son of Wm. Adams 1752–1811, of Bowdon near Totnes, Devon, M.P. for Totnes, by Anna Maria dau. of Richard Dacres of Leatherhead, Surrey, she d. Bowdon 19 April 1830).* b. Bowdon 1778; Cornet 2nd dragoon guards 5 Oct. 1795; lieut. col. 25th dragoons 8 Dec. 1804–25 Dec. 1818; commanded the troops at Bangalore 1810–1814; Colonel of 6th dragoons 26 Oct. 1840 to death; General 11 Nov. 1851; K.C.H. 1831; knighted by the king at St. James's palace 28 Sep. 1831. (*m.* (1) at Totnes, Devon 28 Nov. 1804 Elizabeth Lovelace. *m.* (2) 23 July 1821 Elizabeth 2 dau. of Sir Wm. Elford, Bart., she d. 28 Feb. 1857). *d.* Temple hill, East Budleigh, Devon 10 June 1856.

ADAMS, HENRY WILLIAM *b.* 31 Jan. 1805; ensign 12th foot 31 July 1823; Lieut. col. 18th foot 13 March 1840–12 April 1844; Lieut. col. 49th foot 12 April 1844 to death; Brigadier general 21 Feb. 1854 to death; C.B. 14 Oct. 1841. (*m.* 28 Nov. 1843 his cousin Katherine 2 dau. of Rev. Thomas Coker Adams, V. of Anstey, Warwickshire, she was raised by royal warrant to the rank of the wife of a K.C.B. for which honour her husband was named in the London gazette 10 July 1855). *d.* Scutari 19 Dec. 1854.

ADAMS, JOHN (3 *and youngest son of Simon Adams of East Haddon, Northamptonshire, Recorder of Daventry who d. 10 March 1801, by Sarah dau. of Cadwallader Coker of Bicester, she d. 17 July 1833 aged 80).* b. 1786; barrister M.T. 27 Nov. 1812; went the Midland circuit; Sergeant at law 5 July 1824, patent of precedence 24 April 1834; J.P. 14 Jan. 1836, steward of Coventry; Chairman of Middlesex magistrates March 1836; Assistant judge of Middlesex sessions 17 Aug. 1844 to death; author of *"A treatise on the principles and practice of the action of Ejectment and the remitting action of mesne profits* 1812, 4 ed. 1846. *(m.* (1) 1811 Eliza only dau. of Wm. Nation of Exeter, she *d.* 12 Aug. 1814. *m.* (2) 1817 Jane dau. of Thomas Martin of Nottingham, she *d.* 19 June 1825. *m.* (3) 28 Dec. 1826 his cousin Charlotte Priscilla only dau. of John Coker of Bicester, Oxon). *d.* 9 Hyde park st. London 10 Jany. 1856 in his 70th year.

NOTE.—He had two sons by his 1 wife, namely John Adams, author of the Doctrine of equity who *d.* 18 Sep. 1848, and Rev. Wm. Adams, author of the Shadow of the cross who *d.* 17 Jan. 1848.

ADAMS, JOHN, apprenticed to J. G. Andrews of London, surgeon; studied at the London hospital, M.R.C.S. 3 Oct. 1828, F.R.C.S. 11 Dec. 1843; assistant surgeon London hospital 1828; and lecturer there with James Luke on anatomy and physiology 1833; afterwards sole lecturer; senior surgeon, and ultimately consulting surgeon; known as "honest Jack Adams"; author of *The anatomy and diseases of the prostate gland* 1851. *d.* 2 Vanbrugh park road west, Blackheath 18 Jany. 1877 in his 72nd year.

ADAMS, ROBERT. *b.* Ireland about 1791; ed. at Trin. coll. Dublin, B.A. 1814, M.A. 1832, M.D. 1842; apprenticed to Wm. Hartigan, surgeon; L.R.C.S.I. 1815, F.R.C.S.I. 1818; surgeon to Jervis st. hospital, Dublin; surgeon to Richmond hospital, Dublin 1835–73; founded with R. Carmichael and E. Mac Dowel, the Richmond school of medicine, afterwards called the Carmichael school; where he was professor of surgery; surgeon to Richmond lunatic asylum; pres. of royal college of surgeons Ireland 3 times; surgeon to the Queen in Ireland 15 Nov. 1861; Regius professor of surgery in univ. of Dublin 1861; member of senate of Queen's univ.; member of Society of surgery Paris; author of *A treatise on rheumatic gout* 1857, which became the work on the subject; *Illustrations of the effects of rheumatic gout* 1857. *d.* 22 Stephen's Green north, Dublin 13 Jany. 1875. *bur.* Mount Jerome cemetery 19 Jany.

ADAMS, VERY REV. SAMUEL (3 *son of rev. Benjamin Adams 1756–1840, R. of Kellinick, co. Cavan by Elizabeth dau. of John Clark, she d. 28 Feb. 1833 aged 77). b.* 15 Feb. 1788; preb. of Tirbrien in Elphin cathedral 20 March 1813; dean of Cashel 10 Aug. 1829 to

death; instituted and installed dean 29 Aug.; author of *A comparative view of the Anglican and Roman Churches* 1836. *(m.* 4 Jany. 1809 Frances youngest dau. of Capt. John Hervey of Killiam castle, co. Wexford). *d.* Northlands, co. Cavan 7 Dec. 1856.

ADAMS, THOMAS. *b.* 5 Sep. 1785; studied music under Thomas Busby 1796; organist of Carlisle chapel, Lambeth 1802–14; of St. Paul's, Deptford 22 March 1814–1824; and of St. George's, Camberwell 1824 to death; St. George's - was opened 26 March 1824, when an anthem by him, for 5 voices was performed; organist of St. Dunstan in the West, Fleet st. 1833 to death; published many organ pieces, fugues and voluntaries, besides 90 interludes, several variations, and many vocal pieces. *d.* Addington place, Camberwell, London 15 Sep. 1858.

ADAMS, THOMAS. *b.* Worksop 5 Feb. 1807; apprenticed to a draper at Newark 1821-28; entered house of Messrs. Boden; a lace merchant in Stoney st. Nottingham 1830; built new warehouse in Stoney st., to which he removed, 10 July 1855; converted his business into company of "Thomas Adams & Co., limited" 1862; chairman and managing director 1862 to death; lived at Lenton Firs 1844 to death. *d.* there 16 May 1873. *bur.* in cemetery, Nottingham 24 May; *Memorials of T. Adams, by Rev. W. Milton* 1874 *portrait.*

ADAMS, WILLIAM *(youngest son of Patience Thomas Adams of Bushey Grove, Herts, Filazer of Court of King's Bench, who d.* 2 *May* 1793, *in his* 57th *year, by Martha only child of Thomas Marsh of London, she d.* 19 *Feb.* 1795 *in her* 54th *year). b.* 39 Hatton Garden, London 13 Jany. 1772; ed. at Tunbridge school; matriculated at Trinity Hall, Cam. 17 Dec. 1788; Fell. of his hall to 1803; contested the mastership, Dec. 1815; admitted to college of Advocates 4 Nov. 1799, lived there 1799–1811; one of the Comrs. to prepare tables of fees, and regulate practice of Vice Admiralty Courts abroad 14 Nov. 1811; Comr. to negociate and conclude a treaty of peace with United States 30 July 1814; Comr. of Inquiry into duties of Courts of Justice in England 9 Feb. 1815–1824; one of the Plenipotentiaries to treat of, and conclude a convention of commerce between Great Britain and United States, June 1815; one of Counsel for Queen Caroline's divorce bill 6 July 1820; retired from practice, Sep. 1825; resided at Thorpe in Surrey 1836 to death. *(m.* (1) at Kensworth, Herts 31 Aug. 1803 Sarah dau.

of Rev. Thomas Scott, R. of King's Stanley, Gloucs, she *d.* 3 Feb. 1806. *m.* (2) at Marylebone church 6 April 1811 Mary Anne 3 dau. of Hon. W. Cockayne of Rushton hall, Northamptonshire, she was raised by patent to the rank of a Viscount's daughter 4 September 1831, she *died* 16 June 1873). *d.* Thorpe, Surrey 11 June 1851. *bur.* Thorpe churchyard 17 June. *G.M. xxxvi,* 197–200 (1851).

ADAMS, WILLIAM. Member of firm of Hamilton, Adams & Co. publishers. *d.* The Limes, Clapham road 23 Feb. 1872 aged 75.

ADAMS, WILLIAM BRIDGES. *b.* London 1797; a carriage builder in Long Acre; travelled over great part of Europe and America; pupil of John Farey civil engineer; invented the fish-joint for railway rails 1847, this joint is still universally used on railways; made many valuable improvements in rolling stock; manufactured railway plant at works at Bow, London but failed; patented improvements in carriages, in ship propulsion, guns and wood carving; took out no less than 32 patents; author of *English pleasure carriages* 1837; *Railways and permanest way* 1854; *Roads and Rails* 1862, and of very many articles in scientific and technical periodicals; wrote several political pamphlets under the pseudonym of Junius Redivivus. *(m* 1834 Sarah dau. of Benjamin Flower of Great Harlow, Essex, she was *b.* 22 Feb. 1805, wrote many poems and hymns, and *d.* Aug. 1848). *d.* Broadstairs 23 July 1872. *bur.* at St. Peters. *Engineering* 26 *July* 1872 *p.* 63.

ADAMS, WILLIAM DACRES. *b.* 16 Dec. 1775; confidential sec. to William Pitt during his last administration May 1804 to Feb. 1806; a comr. of woods and forests 31 July 1810 to 23 Aug. 1834. *d.* Sydenham 8 June 1862.

ADAMS, WILLIAM HENRY *(second son of Thomas Adams of Norman Cross, Hunts, by Anna Maria dau. of W. Farr of Romsey, Hunts).* *b.* Norman Cross 1809; compositor in a printing office in London; manager of *Lincolnshire Herald* at Boston 1834; law reporter for the *Morning Herald;* barrister M.T. 24 Nov. 1843; went northern circuit; Auditor of the Poor law accounts for Lincoln, Nottingham and Rutland districts 1856; M.P. for Boston (lib. conserv.) 27 March 1857 to 23 April 1859; mayor of Boston twice; Recorder of Derby 10 Jan. 1859; Attorney General for colony of Hong Kong 19 April 1859; Mem. of legislative council there 2 Feb. 1860 and

Chief Justice 5 July 1860. *(m.* (1) 1832 Anne dau. of Thomas Walford. *m.* (2) 1 June 1864 Ellen Williams eld. dau. of Edward Cobb of Kensington). *d.* Plas Llyssyn, Carno, Montgomeryshire 29 Aug. 1865. *bur.* Carno 6 Sep. *I.L.N. xxxvii,* 467 (1860) *portrait.*

ADAMS, WILLIAM HENRY. *b.* Malta; captain 36 foot 3 July 1840 to 7 June 1844, when placed on half pay; professor of fortification at R.M. college, Sandhurst 1845–70. *d.* Athenæum st. Plymouth 20 Dec. 1883 aged 79.

ADAMS, WILLIAM JAMES. *b.* London 1809; articled to a solicitor; London agent for Bradshaw's railway map about 1838; published Bradshaw's railway guide for the proprietors at 170 Fleet st. 1841–43 and at 59 Fleet st. 1843 to death; the 1st number is dated Dec. 1841, and consisted of about 38 pages; the continental Bradshaw was started 1847. *d.* 59 Fleet st. London 21 Dec. 1873. *Athenæum 27 Dec.* 1873; 17 *Jany* 1874, *and* 24 *Jany* 1874.

ADAMS, WILLIAM PITT. *b.* 11 Dec. 1804; chargé d'affaires and consul general to republic of Peru 30 Nov. 1842 to death. *d.* Lima 1 Sep. 1852.

ADAMSON, REV. HENRY THOMAS; ed. at St. John's coll. Cam., B.D. 1864; V. of Benthall Salop 1871–77; chaplain at Turin 1877–78; at Nervi 1880; author of *The analogy of the faith* 1869; *The truth as it is in Jesus* 1878; *The three sevens* 1880; *The Millenium* 1882. *d.* Lyons 29 May 1882 in 66 year.

ADAMSON, JOHN *(3 son of Cuthbert Adamson, lieut. R.N. by his 2 wife Mary dau. of John Huthwaite of Seaton Delaval near Newcastle).* *b.* High st. Gateshead 13 Sep. 1787; ed. at Newcastle gr. sch.; articled to Thomas Davidson of Newcastle, attorney; practised at Newcastle 1808 to death; undersheriff there 1811–36; sec. to Newcastle and Carlisle railway company 1829 to death; member of Literary and philosophical society of Newcastle 1811, one of its secretaries 1825 to death; treasurer and sec. of "The Antiquarian society of Newcastle" 11 Feb. 1813 to death; one of the 4 founders of Typographical society of Newcastle; K.C. and K.T.S. of Portugal; F.L.S. 1823, F.S.A., F.R.G.S. 1830; author of *Memoirs of life and writings of Luis de Camoens* 1820, 2 vols; *Lusitania illustrata notices of the history of Portugal,* 2 parts 1842–46. *(m.* 3 Dec. 1812 Elizabeth dau. of Samuel Huthwaite of Seaton Delaval, she *d.* 5 July 1855).

ADAMSON, J. *(Con.)*
d. 9 Victoria terrace Jesmond road, Newcastle 27 Sep. 1855. *bur.* Jesmond cemetery 1 Oct. *Dibdin's Northern tour i*, 369–91 (1838); *Martin's Catalogue of privately printed books* 1834, 419–40.

NOTE.—His library which contained a probably unrivalled collection of books relating to Portugal was nearly entirely destroyed by fire 16 April 1849, the remainder was sold at Sotheby's in London 22 May 1856.

ADCOCK, JAMES. *b.* Eton 1778; chorister in St. George's chapel Windsor and Eton college chapel 1786; lay clerk in St. George's chapel 1797 and in Eton college chapel 1799; member of choirs of Trinity, St John's and King's colleges Cambridge; master of the choristers of King's college; published several of his glees and *The rudiments of singing, with about 30 solfeggi to assist persons wishing to sing at sight. d.* Union road, Cambridge 30 April 1860.

ADDAMS, JESSE *(son of Richard Addams of Rotherhithe, shipbuilder). b.* 1 Jany. 1786; ed. Merchant Taylor's sch. 1793; at St. John's coll. Ox. 1804; B.C.L. 1810, D.C.L. 1814; admitted a proctor at Doctors Commons 3 Nov. 1814; Q.C. Jany. 1858; author of *" Reports of cases argued and determined in the ecclesiastical courts at Doctors Commons and in the high court of delegates,"* 3 vols. 1823–26. *d.* 224 Marylebone road, London 25 May 1871.

ADDERLEY, ARDEN, entered navy 4 June 1796; Captain 19 July 1814; went on half pay 1 Oct. 1846; retired admiral 16 June 1862. *d.* Hams lodge, Ryde, Isle of Wight 15 Jany 1864.

ADDINGTON, HENRY UNWIN (2 *son of John Hiley Addington, M.P., P.C. who d.* 11 *June* 1818, *by Mary dau. of Henry Unwin, she d.* 3 *Sep.* 1833). *b.* Blount's Court near Henley on Thames 24 March 1790; ed. at Winchester; envoy extraord. and min. plenipo. at Madrid 10 Oct. 1829 to 2 Nov. 1833; permanent under secretary of state for foreign affairs 4 March 1842 to 9 April 1854; P.C. 15 April 1854; F.R.G.S. 1861 and member of council 1861–70. *(m.* 17 Nov. 1836 Eleanor Anne Bucknall eld. dau. of Thomas Grimston Bucknall Estcourt of Estcourt Gloucs, she *d.* 17 Oct. 1877). *d.* 78 Eaton place London 6 March 1870.

ADDIS, BERNARD. *b.* London 28 Feb. 1791; entered Society of Jesus at Hodder 14 Oct. 1817; ordained priest at Maynooth college 1 June 1822; procurator at Mount St. Mary's college, Derbyshire 1852–59; assistant missioner at Skipton, Yorkshire 1863–73. *d.* the Novitiate, Manresa house, Roehampton, Surrey 1 Oct. 1879.

ADDISON, REV. BERKELEY *(son of Rev. Joseph Addison of Weymouth);* ed. at Reading gr. sch. and St. Peter's coll. Cam., B.A. 1839, M.A. 1842; R. of Collyhurst, Manchester 1855–60; domestic chaplain to Earl Caithness 1856 to death; surrogate 1861; V. of Jesmond, Northumberland 1861 to death; member of Newcastle upon Tyne school board 25 Jan. 1871 and vice chairman; hon. canon of Durham 1877 to death. *d.* Jesmond vicarage 13 Jany. 1882 in 67 year.

ADDISON, CHARLES GREENSTREET *(youngest son of Wm. Dering Addison of Newark house, Maidstone);* barrister Inner Temple 10 June 1842; went home circuit; revising barrister for East Kent; author of *The history of the knights templars, the Temple church and the Temple* 1842, 3 ed. 1852; *A treatise on the law of contracts*, 2 vols. 1845–47, 8 ed. 1883; *Wrongs and their remedies* 1860, 5 ed. 1879. *(m.* 19 Nov. 1848 Frances Octavia 8 dau. of James Wolfe Murray, Lord Cringletie). *d.* 29 Alfred place west, Thurloe square London 19 Feb. 1866.

ADDISON, EDWARD PHILLIPS, stage name of Edward Philip Haddy. *b.* Plymouth Dock (name changed to Devonport 1 Jany. 1824) 24 Feb. 1809; acted in the provinces; first appeared in London at Lyceum theatre 1 April 1839 in "Dark Events"; acted at Drury Lane, Olympic, Prince of Wales's and Lyceum theatres; played Pickwick in Albery's dramatic version of it at Lyceum theatre 23 Oct. 1871 to Nov. 1871; lessee of Doncaster theatre many years. *d.* Plymouth 16 April 1874. *bur.* there 19 April.

ADDISON, HENRY ROBERT. *b.* Calcutta; cornet 2 dragoon guards 12 July 1827; lieut. 15 March 1831 to 21 June 1833 when placed on half pay; began writing for the stage 1830; author of about 60 dramas and farces; lessee of Queen's theatre London Aug. 1836–1837; wrote many songs and articles in monthly magazines; edited *Who's Who* 1849-50; special correspondent of a morning paper at Paris exhibition 1867; deputy chairman of London steamboat company; author of about 12 novels and stories. *d.* Albion st. Hyde park, London 24 June 1876 aged 71. *Dublin Univ. Mag. xviii*, 505 (1841) *portrait.*

ADDISON, JOHN *(son of John Addison of Preston, recorder of Clitheroe who d.* 1837 *in his* 83 *year, by Agnes dau. of Thomas Batty of Avenham house, Preston). b.* Fishergate, Preston 21 April 1791; ed. at Blanchard's school, Nottingham; articled with Aspden and Shuttleworth of Preston, solicitors; barrister Inner

ADDISON, J. *(Con.)*

Temple 6 Feb. 1818; went northern circuit; recorder of Clitheroe 1837 to death; judge of county court number 4 circuit, Lancashire March 1847 to death; his first court was held at Blackburn 7 June 1847; presented with valuable piece of plate by registrars of his circuit 1857; alderman of Preston 25 Sep. 1832, again 27 Feb. 1846; mayor 1833 and 1843; councillor for St. John's ward 1842. *d.* Winckley sq. Preston 14 July 1859. *bur.* St. Leonard's ch. Balderston 20 July.

ADDISON, JOSEPH *(youngest son of Rev. Wm. Addison, R. of Dinsdale, Durham).* *b.* 1789; ed. at gr. sch. Richmond, Yorkshire and Lincoln coll. Ox., B.A. 1811, M.A. 1813; barrister Inner Temple 28 Jany 1831; went northern circuit; bencher of his inn 1857. *(m.* 28 Dec. 1824 Jane 1 dau. of Thomas Beckett of Thornton le Moor near Northallerton). *d.* 7 Dean's yard, Westminster 10 April 1858.

ADDISON, LAURA, stage name of Laura Wilmshurst *(dau. of Thomas Wilmshurst of Colchester, grocer).* *b.* Colchester 15 Nov. 1822; first appeared on stage at Worcester theatre, Nov. 1843, as Lady Townley in *The provoked husband;* played at Glasgow, Dublin and Edinburgh; at Sadlers Wells theatre, London 26 Aug. 1846 to 1848; at Drury lane 26 Dec. 1849 to 1850; at the Haymarket 6 March 1851 to 31 July 1851; made her first appearance in New York, at the Broadway theatre 29 Sep. 1851, as Lady Teazle in *The school for scandal.* *d.* from congestion of the brain, on board the steamer Oregon, between Albany and New York 3 Sep. 1852, *bur.* in Second Avenue burying-ground, New York. *Theatrical Times, i,* 185 (1847) *portrait; Tallis's Drawing room table book* (1851) 23–24, *portrait.*

ADDISON, THOMAS *(younger son of Joseph Addison of Long Benton, near Newcastle, grocer, who d.* 1823 *aged* 67, *by Sarah dau. of Mr. Shaw of Newcastle, grocer, she d.* 1841 *aged* 80*).* *b.* Long Benton, April 1793; ed. at Newcastle gr. school, and Univ. of Edin.; M.D. 1 Aug. 1815; pres. of royal medical society of Edin. 1814; house surgeon to Lock hospital, London; L.R.C.P. 22 Dec. 1819 and F.R.C.P. 4 July 1838; a medical officer of general dispensary 8 years; assistant phys. at Guy's hospital 1824 and phys. 1837–60; lecturer on Materia Medica there 1827–37; and on practice of medicine 1837–60; pres. of royal medico-chirurgical society 1849 and 1850; discovered disease of the supra renal capsules, called after him " Addison's disease." Author of *The elements of the practice of medi-*

ADDISON, T. *(Con.)*

cine, vol. 1 only 1839; *On the constitutional and local effects of disease of the supra renal capsules* 1855. *(m.* 14 Sep. 1847 Elizabeth Catherine, widow of W. W. Hanxwell, she *d.* 30 May 1872 aged 72); placed under medical care, May 1860; attempted to destroy himself several times. *d.* 29 June 1860 at 15 Wellington villas, Brighton, from injuries caused by jumping down the area there, 27 June, buried near north eastern corner of Lanercost abbey churchyard 5 July; *A collection of the published writings of the late Thomas Addison, M.D.* 1868; *H. Lonsdale's Worthies of Cumberland, iv,* 239–72 (1873) *portrait; Munk's Roll of physicians,* 2 ed. *iii,* 205–211 (1878).

NOTE.—A bust of him by Joseph Towne, is in the pathological museum of " Guys," one of the medical wards in new portion of the hospital is named after him, and in the chapel there is a marble tablet to his memory.

ADDISON, THOMAS BATTY *(eld. son of John Addison of Preston, barrister who d. Nov. 1837 in 83 year, by Agnes dau. of Thomas Batty of Avenham house, Preston).* *b.* Fishergate, Preston 17 June 1787; ed. at Charter house; barrister Inner Temple 1 July 1808; went northern circuit; recorder of Preston 1819 to death; a magistrate for Lancashire 1821; chairman of Preston quarter sessions 1821 to March 1874; commissioner of Bankrupts for Preston district. *d.* 23 Winckley square, Preston 6 June 1874.

ADDISON, WILLIAM, L.S.A. 1824, M.R.C.S. 1825, F.R.S. 29 Jany. 1846, F.R.C.P. 1858; Gulstonian lecturer 1859; physician Brighton and Hove dispensary; author of *A dissertation on the Malvern water* 1828; *Cell therapeutics* 1856. *d.* 10 Albert road, Brighton 26 Sep. 1881 in 80 year.

ADEANE, HENRY JOHN. *b.* Babraham, Cambs. 9 June 1833; M.P. for Cambs. (lib.) 6 April 1857 to 6 July 1865. *d.* 8 Seamore place, London 17 Feb. 1870.

ADEY, REVEREND JOHN. *b.* Painswick, Gloucs. 15 May 1793; in business at Winslow, Bucks; began first voluntary Sunday school in Gloucester; founded a Sunday school at Great Horwood; ordained congregational minister there 1820; moved to Cranbrook, Kent then to Ramsgate; minister at Horselydown, Surrey 1836–58; at Bexley Heath, Kent 1858–68 when he retired; author of *The eleventh hour* 1835; *The convert from popery* 1851. *d.* Bexley Heath 16 Dec. 1869. *bur.* Abney Park cemetery.

ADIE, ALEXANDER JAMES. *b.* Edinburgh 1775; an optician there; much employed by all kinds of inventors to give their schemes a practical form; erected on his house in Merchant court an observatory, long before any public observatory existed in Edin.; invented the sympiesometer 1818 which contributed much to the safety of shipping; F.R.S. Edin. *d.* Canaan near Edinburgh 4 Dec. 1858.

ADIE, ALEXANDER JAMES *(son of the preceding). b.* Edinburgh 1808; ed. at the high school and univ.; apprenticed to James Jardine, C.E.; resident engineer of Bolton Chorley and Preston railway 1836; engineer and manager of Edinburgh and Glasgow railway to about 1863; made a series of important experiments on the expansion of stone by heat; M.R.S. Edin. 1846. *d.* Rockville near Linlithgow 1879.

ADOLPHUS, JOHN LEYCESTER *(only son of John Adolphus 1768–1845, barrister, F.S.A., by Martha Elizabeth only dau. of Rev. Ralph Leycester of White place, Berks). b.* 11 May 1795; ed. at Merchant Taylor's school 1802–11, head monitor, elected to fellowship at St. John's coll. Ox. 1811; Newdigate English verse prizeman 1814; B.A. 1815, M.A. 1819; visited Sir Walter Scott at Abbotsford; barrister Inner Temple 21 June 1822; went northern circuit; Bencher of his inn 1851; reported in Court of King's Bench, first with Richard Vaughan Barnewall 1831–35, then with Thomas Flower Ellis 1835–52; solicitor general of county palatine of Durham; judge of county courts circuit 44 Marylebone, Oct. 1852 to death; sat for the first time 14 Oct. 1852; author of *Letters to Richard Heber, Esq., containing critical remarks on the series of novels, beginning with " Waverley," and an attempt to ascertain their author;* author with Richard Vaughan Barnewall, of *Reports in court of King's Bench* 1830–34, 5 vols. 1831–35; with Thomas Flower Ellis, of *Reports in court of King's Bench and Queen's Bench* 1834–41, 12 vols. 1835–42 and *Queen's Bench reports, new series* 1841–52, 18 vols., 1842–56; *Letters from Spain* 1858, *and of many metrical jeux d'esprit. (m.* 10 Sep. 1822 Clara dau. of Rowland Richardson of Streatham, Surrey). *d.* 12 Hyde park sq. London 24 Dec. 1862. *G.M. xiv,* 246 (1863).

ADY, JOSEPH *(son of John Ady of London, recording clerk of the Society of Friends, who d.* 17 *Nov.* 1812 *aged* 68*). b.* London 1775 or 1776; a hatter and hosier at 6 Charlotte st. Wapping; hatter at 11 Circus, Minories 1831–

ADY, J. *(Con.)*

33; accountant at same address 1833; was accustomed to examine lists of unclaimed dividends, estates and bequests, and to send letters always unstamped to all persons he could find who were called by any of the names mentioned in the lists, stating to each person that on his remitting a fee of 20/- he would be informed of something to his advantage. The Lord Mayor, Sir Peter Laurie, in 1833, publicly advertised people to be cautious of him, and the Court of Aldermen the same year directed measures to be taken against him. His lucrative trade was at last stifled by a new section in the Post Office Act, which made the writers of letters that were refused, liable for the postage; he then resorted to a new device, this was to post his letters really unstamped, but bearing marks on them as of stamps removed, so as to furnish ground for his asseveration that stamps had really been put on them. In the year 1835 he was indicted by the Rev. Francis Tebbutt for a misdemeanour, under statute 7 & 8, George iv, cap. 29 sec. 53, for obtaining a sovereign by various false pretences, he was tried at the Central criminal court 7 Feb. 1835, found guilty and sentenced to 7 years transportation, which was commuted to 1 year's imprisonment in the House of Correction. He was sent to prison again in the year 1851 for a similar offence, but was released early in 1852 by order of the Home Secretary in consequence of his declining health. *d.* 89 Fenchurch st. London 17 July 1852 aged 77. *bur.* Friend's burial ground, Whitechapel 22 July. *Central criminal court minutes of evidence, by Henry Buckler, i,* 646–52 (1835); *De Quincey's Works, vi,* 258, 327 (1862). The epistle of which the following is an exact copy, was received by the Duke of Wellington 5 Dec. 1833, and sent by him to the Lord Mayor the next day:

MY LORD,
The undersigned is able to inform you of something considerably to your advantage on receipt of 20 shillings, by post office order or otherwise for his trouble.

Yours respectfully,
JOSEPH ADY, Accountant,
11 Circus, Minories,
Nov. 29th, 1833.   London.

No letters received unless postpaid.

To His Grace The Duke of Wellington,
Strathfieldsaye, Hants.

The annexed is copied from a letter of his, which was received by a gentleman in the country.

" The undersigned is able to inform you of something considerably to your advantage (value £100 and

ADY, J. *(Con.)*

upwards), on receipt of 20/- by order on Whitechapel post office as an equivalent for his trouble and costs generally.

Respectfully

JOSEPH ADY, Accountant,
No. 5 York St Charlotte St.
¼ mile East of Whitechapel Chh.
London.

Personally known to each of the Aldermen of London, having been a Freeman and Housekeeper 50 years.

April 5th, 1847.

Should you find any difficulty in getting the money, the Rt. Hon. Sir Peter Laurie, Deputy Lord Mayor, will frank you from all Expenses except Postage, which you must pay both ways. In your reply be pleased to copy the Marks of Reference, F. 1847, Page 6."

ADY, VENERABLE WILLIAM BRICE *(son of Wm. Ady, comr. of the Gun Wharf, Devonport).* *b.* 1816; ed. at Eton; entered Ex. coll. Ox. 29 Oct. 1834, B.A. 1838, M.A. 1841; V. of Little Baddow, Essex 1842–57 and Rector 1857 to death; archdeacon of Colchester Dec. 1864 to death. *(m.* 10 April 1844 Emilia 3 and youngest dau. of Rev. Brook Henry Bridges, R. of Danbury, Essex). *d.* Little Baddow 21 April 1882. *bur.* Little Baddow churchyard 27 April. *Statute 29 & 30 Vict. cap. 111, sections 15 and 16.*

AFFLECK, SIR GILBERT, 5 Baronet. *b.* 9 June 1804; succeeded 7 May 1851. *d.* Calverley park, Tunbridge Wells 18 Nov. 1854.

AFFLECK, REV. SIR ROBERT, 4 Baronet. *b.* 27 Jany. 1765; ed. at Westminster, captain of the school 1782; and at Ch. Ch. Ox.; B.A. 1787, M.A. 1790; Preb. of York cathedral 8 May 1802 to death; V. of Doncaster 1807–17; V. of Silkstone near Barnsley 1817–37; succeeded 10 Aug. 1833. *d.* Dalham hall near Newmarket 7 May 1851.

AFFLECK, SIR ROBERT, 6 Baronet. *b.* Retford Notts 28 July 1805; succeeded 18 Nov. 1854; sheriff of Suffolk 1875. *d.* Dalham hall 9 Oct. 1882.

AGAR, SIR EMANUEL FELIX, lieutenant 1 life guards 15 Nov. 1804; major 2 life guards 28 April 1814 to April 1815; M.P. for Sudbury (lib.) 5 May 1807 to 29 Sep. 1812; knighted by the Prince Regent at Carlton house 18 July 1812. *(m.* 21 Aug. 1811 Margaret youngest dau. of Edward George Lind of Stratford place, London, she *d.* 10 Aug. 1863). *d.* 6 Langham st. Marylebone, London 28 Aug. 1866 aged 85.

AGAR, HONORABLE GEORGE CHARLES (2 son of Most Rev. Charles Agar 1736–1809, 1 Earl of Normanton Abp. of Dublin, by Jane eld.

AGAR, HONORABLE G. C. *(Con.)*

dau. of *Wm. Benson of Downpatrick, she d.* 25 Oct. 1826). *b.* 1 Aug. 1780; ed. at Westminster and Ch. Ch. Ox., M.A. 1807; ensign 3 foot guards 21 Jany. 1804; lieut. 1 June 1809 to 5 Nov. 1811 when he retired; F.R.S. 7 June 1832. *d.* Ropley house Alresford, Hants 24 Jany. 1856.

AGAR, HONOURABLE AND VENERABLE JAMES *(3 son of Most Rev. Charles Agar, 1 Earl of Normanton). b.* 10 July 1781; ed. at Westminster and at Ch. Ch. Ox.; preb. of Timothan in St. Patrick's cathedral, Dublin 16 Nov. 1805; R. of St. Nicholas without, Dublin 1806; R. of Caningallen, Leitrim 1809; archdeacon of Kilmore 1810 to death. *(m.* 7 July 1829 Louisa youngest dau. of Samuel Thompson of Greenmount, co. Antrim). *d.* 6 Sep. 1866.

AGER, JOSEPH *(son of Joseph Ager of London, apothecary). b.* London; entered at Pembroke coll. Ox. 1 April 1800 aged 18, Ossulston scholar; B.A. 1803, M.A. 1807, M.B. 1807, M.D. 1810; fellow of his college; F.R.C.P. 30 Sep. 1811, Gulstonian lecturer 1812, and Censor 1815, 1825 and 1835; delivered the Materia Medica lectures 1827–28: F.R. Med. and Chir. soc. 1814; assistant phys. to Marylebone infirmary many years; greatly assisted Robert Hooper, M.D. in the formation of his pathological museum. *d.* 85 Great Portland st. London 17 July 1857 in 77 year.

AGLIO, AGOSTINO. *b.* Cremona 15 Dec. 1777; painter at Rome 1797; went to England, Dec. 1803; painted scenery at the Opera house, London 1804, and at Drury Lane theatre 1806; largely employed in decoration of country mansions in England and Ireland; decorated Pantheon in Oxford st. 1811; ceiling of R.C. chapel in Moorfields 1819 where he also executed the altarpiece; produced many easel pictures about 1820; exhibited 22 pictures at British Institution, 8 at the Suffolk st. gallery 1825–56, and 13 at the R.A. 1830–46; painted 2 portraits of the Queen; decorated the Olympic theatre, which was reopened 26 Dec. 1849; published *Mexican Antiquities* 9 vols. 1830–48; drew many works in lithography. *d.* 87 Beresford st. Walworth 30 Jany. 1857. *bur.* Highgate cemetery.

AGLIONBY, HENRY AGLIONBY. *b.* 28 Dec. 1790; M.P. for Cockermouth (lib.) 12 Dec. 1832 to death. *d.* The manor house, Caterham, Surrey 31 July 1854. *I.L.N. vi, 184 (1845) portrait.*

AGNESI, LOUIS FERDINAND LEOPOLD, stage name of L. F. L. Agniez. *b.* Erpent, Belgium 17 July 1833; ed. at the Conservatoire, Brussels; a baritone singer of the first rank; member of Italian opera company at Drury Lane; sang at the fifth triennial Handel festival at Crystal palace 19–26 June 1874. *d.* 56 Loudoun road, Hampstead 2 Feb. 1875.

AGNEW, THOMAS. *b.* Liverpool Dec. 1794; fellow student with John Gibson the sculptor; partner with Vittoria Zannetti of Market st. lane, Manchester 1816, who was then the only art dealer in the north of England except Burland of Liverpool; carried on business in Exchange st. Manchester 1826 to Oct. 1861 when he retired; published many works of art and not less than 1000 engravings; alderman of Salford from its incorporation 16 April 1844 and mayor 1850; gave many pictures and prints to the free museum and library at Peel park, Salford. *d.* Fair Hope, Eccles. Manchester 24 March 1871. *bur.* churchyard of St. Mark's Worsley 29 March.

AHMUTY, JAMES, 2 Lieut. Bengal artillery 7 Sep. 1791; colonel commandant 29 Aug. 1824 to death; general 15 Sep. 1855. *d.* 14 Chesham place, Belgrave sq. London 12 Jany. 1864 aged 89.

AIKENHEAD, MARY *(eld. child of David Aikenhead of Cork, physician who d. 28 Dec. 1801, by Mary eld. dau. of Mr. Stacpole of Cork, merchant, she m. (2) Mr. Bernard of Palace Anne and d. 1809).* *b.* Cork 19 Jany 1787; received into R. C. church 6 June 1802 and confirmed 2 July 1802; took name of Sister Mary Augustine, June 1812; superior of the first convent of sisters of charity William st. Dublin Aug. 1815 to 1827; made her perpetual vows 9 Dec. 1816; superior of convent at Sandymount 16 Aug. 1831; superior general of the Irish foundation of Sisters of charity 1843; lived at convent of Our Lady's Mount, Harold's Cross, Dublin Sep. 1845 to death. *d.* Our Lady's Mount, 22 July 1858. *Mary Aikenhead by S.A.* 2 ed. revised 1882, *portrait.*

AIKIN, ARTHUR *(1 son of John Aikin, M.D. of Warrington, Lancs. 1747–1822 by Martha dau. of Arthur Jennings of Harlington, Bedford, she d. 1830 aged 83).* *b.* Warrington 19 May 1773; ed. there and at Palgrave in Norfolk; studied classics under Gilbert Wakefield, and chemistry under Dr. Priestley; settled in London 1796; one of the founders of Geological Society of London 1807, which was incorporated 23 Apl. 1823; one of the secretaries and a member of council; lecturer on chemistry

AIKIN, A. *(Con.)*

at Guy's hospital 1816–52; secretary of Society for encouragement of arts, manufactures and commerce 1817–40, where he read more than 40 lectures; chairman of its committee of chemistry 1840; the first treasurer of Chemical Society 30 March 1841; F.L.S. 1818; the first hon. sec. of Institution of Civil Engineers 2 Jany. 1818; one of specially selected members of the Athenæum club; much employed in drawing specifications of patents for improvements in chemical manufactures, in which Lord Lyndhurst held him to excel all other persons; made many chemical analyses for patentees and public companies; lived at 19 John st. Adelphi 1817–40; at 7 Bloomsbury sq. 1840 to death; edited *The annual review* 1802–1806; author of *Journal of a tour through north Wales, and part of Shropshire* 1797; *Manual of mineralogy* 1814, 2 ed. 1815. *d.* 7 Bloomsbury sq. London 15 April 1854. *J. Kenrick's Profiles of Warrington worthies,* 2 ed. 1854, *portrait;* *European Mag. lxxv,* 387 (1819) *portrait;* *Proc. of Linnæan society, ii,* 304–306 (1855); *Minutes of proceedings of institution of civil engineers, xiv,* 120–23 (1855).

AIKIN, LUCY *(only dau. of John Aikin, M.D. of Warrington 1747–1822).* *b.* Warrington 6 Nov. 1781; author of *Epistles on women, a poem* 1810, *Lorimer, a tale* 1814, *Memoirs of the court of Queen Elizabeth,* 2 vols. 1818; *Memoirs of the court of King James I,* 2 vols. 1822; *Memoirs of the court of King Charles I,* 2 vols. 1833; *Life of Addison* 1843; lived at Church row, Hampstead, June 1822 to 1830; at 18 Church row 1830–44; in London 1844–45; at Wimbledon 1845–50; at John st. Hampstead 1850 to death. *d.* Milford house, Hampstead 29 Jany. 1864. *bur.* near east end of old churchyard of Hampstead. *Memoirs, miscellanies and letters of the late Lucy Aikin,* edited by P. H. Le Breton 1864; *J. Kendrick's Profiles of Warrington worthies,* 2 ed. 1854, *portrait.*

AIKMAN, JAMES. A bookseller in Edinburgh; author of *Poems, chiefly lyrical* 1816; *An account of the tournament at Eglinton* 1839; *The animal kingdom* 1861; editor and proprietor of a weekly paper called *The Star. d.* Edinburgh 21 May 1860 aged 81.

AILESBURY, CHARLES BRUDENELL-BRUCE, 1 Marquess of *(3 and youngest son of Thomas Bruce 1 earl of Ailesbury 1729–1814, by his 1 wife Susanna dau. of Henry Hoare of Stourhead, Wilts and widow of honble. Charles Boyle, she d. 4 Feb. 1783).* *b.* Seamore place May–

AILESBURY, C. B. B. *(Con.)*

fair, London 12 Feb. 1773 ; M.P. for Marlborough (tory) as Charles B. B. Bruce commonly called Lord Bruce 30 May 1796 to 19 April 1814, when he succeeded ; col. of Wiltshire yeomanry 1798–1811 ; col. commandant of Wiltshire militia 25 July 1811 to 1827 ; K.T. 20 May 1819 ; created Viscount Savernake of Savernake Forest co. Wilts, Earl Bruce of Whorlton co. York, and Marquess of Ailesbury co. Buckingham 17 July 1821. *(m* (1) 10 April 1793 Henrietta Maria 1 dau. of Noel Hill, 1 baron Berwick, she *d.* 2 Jany. 1831. *m.* (2) 20 Aug. 1833 Maria Elizabeth youngest dau. of honble. Charles Tollemache and widow of Charles John Clarke, she was *b.* 27 Oct. 1809). *d.* Tottenham park near Marlborough 4 Jany. 1856. *bur.* in family vault in parish church of Great Bedwyn, Wilts 12 Jany.

AILESBURY, GEORGE WM. FREDERICK BRUDENELL-BRUCE, 2 Marquess of *(elder son of the preceding).* *b.* Lower Grosvenor st. London 20 Nov. 1804 ; ed. at Ch. Ch. Ox. ; lieut. col. commandant Wilts yeomanry cavalry 30 June 1837 and col. 1 April 1876 to death ; summoned to house of Lords in his father's barony of Bruce 10 July 1838 ; kept a racing stud 1840 to death ; won the St. Leger with St. Albans 12 Sep. 1860 ; succeeded his father 4 Jany. 1856 ; aide de camp to the Queen with rank of colonel 13 March 1857 to death ; P.C. 18 June 1859 ; master of the horse to the Queen 24 June 1859 to July 1866 and 16 Dec. 1868 to Feb. 1874 ; lord lieut. of Wilts 25 March 1863 to death ; K.G. 23 May 1864 ; succeeded his cousin as 8 Earl of Cardigan 28 March 1868. *(m.* 11 May 1837 Mary Caroline 2 dau. of George Augustus Herbert, 11 Earl of Pembroke, she was *b.* 22 March 1813). *d.* Savernake park, Marlborough 6 Jany. 1878. *Baily's Mag. iv,* 217–20 (1862) *portrait.*

AILSA, ARCHIBALD KENNEDY, 2 Marquess of (1 *son of Archibald Kennedy, styled Earl of Cassilis 1794–1832, by Eleanor only dau. of Alexander Allardyce of Dunottar, co. Kincardine, she d.* 16 *Nov.* 1832). *b.* Dunottar, Aug. 1816 ; succeeded his grandfather 8 Sep. 1846 ; K.T. 7 March 1859 ; Lord. lieut. of Ayrshire 7 Dec. 1861 to death. *(m.* 10 Nov. 1846 Julia 2 dau. of Sir Richard Mounteney Jephson, 1 baronet). *d.* Culzean castle, Maybole, N.B. 20 March 1870 from injuries received in the hunting field.

AINGER, REV. THOMAS *(youngest son of William Ainger of Whittlesea, Cambs.) b.* Whittlesea 1

AINGER, REV. T. *(Con.)*

Aug. 1799 ; ed. at Norwich gr. school and St. John's Coll. Cam. ; B.A. 1821, M.A. 1824 ; C. of St. Giles ch. Reading 1 Sep. 1822 ; Asst. minister of St. Mary's, Greenwich 1825 ; P.C. of Hampstead 28 March 1841 to death ; founded in Hampstead, the Parochial Association in aid of the Society for the propagation of Gospel 1845 ; founded the Church Extension Association 1858 ; Preb. of St. Paul's Cath., Aug. 1859 ; preached his last sermon Easter day 5 April 1863. *(m.* 4 Aug. 1828 Frances only dau. of Wm. Barnard of Deptford Green). *d.* the Parsonage, Hampstead 15 Nov. 1863. *bur.* in churchyard of parish church 20 Nov. *The last sermons of the Rev. Thomas Ainger, M.A., with a memoir of the author prefixed* 1864.

AINSLIE, FREDERICK GEORGE. 2 lieut. 21 foot 24 April 1828 ; lieut. col. 23 April 1852 to death. *d.* on board the "Andes" in Scutari harbour 14 Nov. 1854 aged 45, of wounds received at battle of Inkerman 5 Nov.

AINSLIE, REV. GILBERT *(youngest son of Henry Ainslie, M.D. of Hall Garth Lancashire, he was senior wrangler 1781 and d. 1834, by Agnes dau. of Wm. Ford of Coniston Water Head) b.* 1793 ; ed. at Charterhouse and Pemb. coll. Cam. 8 wrangler and B.A. 1815, M.A. 1818 ; foundation fellow of his college 1816 ; treasurer, tutor, bursar and lecturer ; laid first stones of university library at Cam. Sep. 1837. and of the Fitzwilliam museum 2 Nov. 1837 ; Master of his college 15 Aug. 1828 to death ; Vice Chancellor of the Univ. 1828 and 1836. *(m.* 2 Dec. 1829 Emily 2 dau. of Wm. Coxhead Marsh of Park hall, Essex). *d.* Pembroke college lodge 9 Jany. 1870. *bur.* at Over Kellet, Lancs. 14 Jany.

AINSLIE, HUGH. *b.* Bargeny Mains, parish of Dailly, Ayrshire 5 April 1792 ; emigrated to New York 1822 ; established several breweries, mills and factories in the western States ; author of *A pilgrimage to the land of Burns* 1822 ; *Scottish songs, ballads and poems* 1855. *d.* Louisville Kentucky 11 March 1878.

AINSLIE, SIR ROBERT SHARP, 2 Baronet. *b.* 1777 ; M.P. for Mitchell, Cornwall 6 July 1802 to 24 Oct. 1806 ; succeeded 22 July 1812. *d.* Chingford, Essex 14 March 1858.

AINSWORTH, JAMES *(son of Jeremiah Ainsworth of Manchester). b.* Manchester 5 March 1783 ; ed. at Manchester free gr. sch. and by Rev. Joshua Brookes ; apprenticed at the infirmary Manchester 1798 ; studied at Univ. of Edin. ; surgeon to the infirmary Manchester 1806 ; the first to commence anatomical

AINSWORTH, J. *(Con.)*

lectures in Manchester; one of the ablest operators of his day, and the first who tied the internal iliac artery successfully; one of the founders of Natural history society, and of Botanical and horticultural society; member of Manchester literary and philosophical society Jany. 1805 to death; hon. F.R.C.S. 1843. *d.* Cliff point, Higher Broughton near Manchester 28 Oct. 1853. *Admission Register of Manchester school ii,* 202–204 (1868).

AINSWORTH, PETER. *b.* 24 Nov. 1790; M.P. for Bolton, (radical) 9 Jany. 1835 to 23 July 1847. *d.* Smithills hall, Bolton 18 Jany. 1870.

AINSWORTH, WILLIAM HARRISON *(elder son of Thomas Ainsworth of Manchester, solicitor 1778–1824, by Ann Harrison 1778–1842 eld. dau. of Rev. Ralph Harrison of Manchester, Presbyterian minister).* *b.* King st. Manchester 4 Feb. 1805; ed. at the free gr. sch. 1817–22; articled 1821 to Alexander Kay of Manchester, solicitor; a publisher in London 1826–27; edited *Bentley's Miscellany,* March 1839 to Dec. 1841; author of *Jack Sheppard,* 3 vols. 1839 which was produced in dramatic form simultaneously, at Adelphi, Queen's, Sadler's Wells, Victoria and Pavilion theatres in London, Oct. 1839; received £1000 from the '*Sunday Times*' for '*Old St. Paul's*' 1841, and another £1000 for the '*Lancashire Witches*' 1848; edited *Ainsworth's Magazine,* Feb. 1842 to 1854; purchased *New monthly magazine* from Henry Colburn 1845; purchased *Bentley's Miscellany* 1854 and combined with it Ainsworth's Magazine, Jany. 1855; gave the flitch of bacon at Dunmow in Essex 19 July 1855 and 25 July 1857; granted a civil list pension of £100 a year 10 Dec. 1868; entertained at a banquet in the town hall, Manchester by the mayor, Thomas Baker 15 Sep. 1881; lived at the Elms, Kilburn; at Kensal manor house; at Brighton; at Tunbridge Wells; at Reigate. *(m.* 11 Oct. 1826 Anne Frances younger dau. of John Ebers of John st. London, publisher, she *d.* 6 March 1838). *d.* St. Mary's road, Reigate 3 Jany. 1882. *bur.* Kensal Green cemetery 9 Jany. *Manchester quarterly, i,* 136–55 (1882) *portrait; Maclise portrait gallery* (1883) 256–62, *portrait; J. H. Friswell's Modern men of letters* (1870) 257–72; *Illustrated Review, ii,* 321–23 (1872) *portrait; Horne's New spirit of the age, ii,* 215–22 (1844).

NOTE.—His novel *Mervyn Clitheroe* is autobiographical; in March 1878 he presented a life size portrait of himself, painted by H. W. Pickersgill, about 1841 to the Chetham Library Manchester; the best

AINSWORTH, W. H. *(Con.)*

portrait of him is the figure in the vignette by Cruikshank, which forms the standing title to monthly editorial gossip in early numbers of Ainsworth's magazine. He was caricatured unmercifully by Thackeray in Punch. His books and the MSS. of 18 of his novels were sold by Sotheby in London for £463, 21-22 Aug. 1882. He was the author of upwards of 40 works of fiction.

AIRD, DAVID MITCHELL. Compositor at The Sun newspaper office, London; started a bimonthly magazine called *The Student* which lasted 6 months; edited *The Mirror* 1843; printed for the Countess de Brunetiere Tallien the first daily French paper published in England 1851 which failed; barrister M.T. 11 June 1867; wrote several books under pseudonym of Pamphilius. *d.* 2 Sussex gardens, Hyde park, London 15 June 1876. *Head and Heart legacy by Pamphilius* 1861, *portrait.*

AIRD, THOMAS *(2 child of James Aird of Bowden, Roxburghshire, portioner or farmer who d. aged 86, by Isabella Paisley, she d. aged 86) b.* Bowden 28 Aug. 1802; ed. there, at Melrose and at Univ. of Edinburgh; edited *Edinburgh Weekly Journal* 1833; *Dumfriesshire and Galloway herald* at Dumfries 1835–63; presided at Scott centenary at Dumfries 9 Aug. 1871; author of *The old bachelor in the Scottish village* 1845; *Poetical works* 1848, 5 ed. 1878; contributed poetry and prose to *Blackwood's Magazine. d.* Dumfries 25 April 1876. *bur.* near Robert Burns in St. Michael's churchyard 1 May. *Poetical works of T. Aird with a memoir by Rev. J. Wallace,* 5 ed. 1878, *portrait.*

AIREY, RICHARD AIREY, 1 Baron. *b.* Newcastle April 1803; ed. at Sandhurst; ensign 34 foot 15 March 1821; lieut. col. 10 Feb. 1838 to 12 Feb. 1847 when placed on half pay; military sec. to commander in chief 1 Oct. 1852 to 17 April 1854; quartermaster general in the Crimea 1 Sep. 1854 to Nov. 1855; quartermaster general of the forces 26 Dec. 1855 to 31 Oct. 1865; governor and commander in chief at Gibraltar 10 Nov. 1856 to 4 Sep. 1870; col. 17 foot 20 July 1860 to 1 May 1868; col. 7 foot 1 May 1868 to death; adjutant general 1 Oct. 1870 to 31 Oct. 1876; general 9 April 1871; pres. of commission of inquiry into results of new short service system 1879; K.C.B. 5 July 1855, G.C.B. 13 March 1867; created Baron Airey of Killingworth, Northumberland 29 Nov. 1876. *d.* the Grange, Leatherhead 13 Sep. 1881. *bur.* Kensal Green cemetery 17 Sep. *A. W. Kinglake's History of the war in the Crimea* (1863–75); *Sir A. M. Tulloch's The Crimean commission* 1881; *I.L.N. lxix,* 500, (1876), *portrait.*

AIRLIE, DAVID GRAHAM DRUMMOND, 5 or 7 Earl of. *b.* London 4 May 1826 ; succeeded 20 Aug. 1849 ; a representative peer for Scotland 18 March 1850 to death ; F.R.G.S. 1859 ; K.T. 12 March 1862 ; high comr. to general assembly of Church of Scotland 1872–73. *d.* at an hotel in Denver city, Colorado 25 Sep. 1881. *bur.* Cortachy, Forfarshire 3 Nov.

AITCHISON, GEORGE. *b.* Leyton, Essex 21 Dec. 1792 ; student at Royal academy ; clerk of the works to St. Katherine's dock company 1827, docks were opened 25 Oct. 1828 ; A.I.C.E. 1828 ; district surveyor of Woolwich 1844. *d.* Muscovy court, Trinity square, London 12 June 1861. *Minutes of proc. of Instit. of C.E. xxi*, 569–71 (1862).

AITCHISON, SIR JOHN (3 *son of Wm. Aitchison of Drummore, East Lothian, by Jane eld. dau. of James Mylne of Langridge, East Lothian*). *b.* 1789 ; ensign Scots fusilier guards 25 Oct. 1805 ; lieut. col. 11 Aug. 1837 to 23 Nov. 1841 ; commanded Mysore division of Madras army 2 June 1845 to 1851 ; col. 72 foot 29 Dec. 1851 to 27 Aug. 1870 ; general 30 July 1860 ; col. Scots fusilier guards 27 Aug. 1870 to death ; K.C.B. 21 June 1859 ; G.C.B. 13 March 1867. (*m.* 31 Oct. 1857 Ellen Elizabeth youngest dau. of Thomas Mayhew of Fairfield house, Suffolk). *d.* 4 Devonshire place, London 13 May 1875.

AITKEN, DAVID. Educ. high school and univ. of Edinburgh ; D.D. 8 July 1843 ; licensed by presbytery of Edin. 28 March 1821 ; minister of parish of Minto 14 Sep. 1827 to 16 Nov. 1864 ; lived in Edin. 1866 to death ; corresponded with Georg Hegel the German philosopher ; offered chair of church history in univ. of Edin. 1843 ; wrote an article on German literature in Edinb. Review, xlvi, 304–51 (1827) ; F.R.S. Edin. 1868. *d.* Charlotte square, Edin. 27 March 1875.

AITKEN, JOHN. Member of Manchester geological society 1863, pres. twice ; author of part of *Thomas Newbigging's History of the forest of Rossendale* 1868, and of many papers in geological periodicals. *d.* Clifton villas, Urmston 29 July 1884 aged 64.

AITKEN, REV. ROBERT (*son of Robert Aitken*). *b.* Crailing near Jedburgh 22 Jany. 1800 ; a schoolmaster in Sunderland ; ordained deacon by Bishop Van Mildert 1823 ; minister of Wesleyan Zion chapel, Waterloo road, Liverpool to 20 Dec. 1840 ; C. of Perranuthnoe, Cornwall 1842–44 ; domestic chaplain to Earl of Caithness 1844–64 ; minister of Episcopalian church, Coatbridge about Oct. 1847 to

AITKEN, REV. R. (*Con.*)

1848 or 1849 ; V. of Pendeen, Cornwall 1849 to death ; the church, of which he was the architect, was built for him by his parishioners 1854 ; domestic chaplain to Earl of Seafield 1864 to death ; well known throughout England as a preacher of almost unrivalled fervour ; author of many sermons and pamphlets. *d.* on platform of Great Western railway station, Paddington 11 July 1873. *bur.* Pendeen 18 July. *Boase and Courtney's Bibliotheca Cornubiensis i, 2 and iii,* 1025 ; *John Smith's Our Scottish clergy 2 Series 80–87 (1849)* ; *Church Times 6 Aug. to 24 Sep. 1875.*

AITKEN, ROBERT DICKSON. *b.* Hawick, Roxburghshire 8 May 1801 ; a gardener, then a horsebreaker ; left Hawick 1857 ; purchased estate of Reston Mains, Berwickshire, worth many thousands ; tried in the sheriff court at Greenlaw 31 May 1860, for making people of Dunse believe he was heir to a large estate, when found guilty and sentenced to 6 months imprisonment with hard labour ; his career was dramatised by George Duckenfield, theatrical manager ; he played the chief part in this drama at Berwick and other border towns ; delivered a lecture in Hawick 31 May 1864 entitled "How I did the Dunse dunces." *d.* the poor house, Hawick 30 April 1879.

AITKEN, WILLIAM. *b.* Dunbar 1814 ; kept a school at Ashton-under-Lyne ; went to the United States 1842 ; grand master of the Odd-fellows there 1846 ; author of *A journey up the Mississipi river ;* and of articles in the *Quarterly magazine of Odd-fellows ;* committed suicide at Ashton 27 Sep. 1869. *Quarterly magazine of Odd-fellows i,* 129–32 (1858) *portrait.*

AITKEN, WILLIAM COSTEN. *b.* Dumfries 3 March 1817 ; worked for R. W. Winfield of Birmingham, brassfounder 1844–64 ; took out a patent for ornamenting cornice poles, &c. with porcelain or glass which was much used ; manager at Skidmore's Art manufacturing company, Coventry, retired 1872 ; chief organiser of Industrial Exhibition at Bingley house, Birmingham 1849, from which Prince Albert took the idea of Exhibition of 1851 ; contributed descriptive notes signed W.C.A. to Illustrated catalogue of Great Exhibition 1851 ; wrote about a third of *Birmingham and the Midland hardware district* 1865 ; wrote in the *Art Journal. d.* Birmingham 23 March 1875. *Birmingham Daily Post 24 March 1875.*

AITON, JOHN (*youngest son of Wm. Aiton 1760–1848, sheriff substitute of Lanarkshire*). *b.*

AITON, J. (Con.)

Strathaven, June 1797; studied theology at univ. of Edinburgh; licensed by presbytery of Hamilton 30 Nov. 1819; minister of parish of Dolphington 14 April 1825 to death; D.D. Glasgow, March 1836; author of *Life and times of Alexander Henderson* 1836; *Clerical Economics* 1842, 2 ed. 1846; *The lands of the Messiah, Mahomet, and the Pope* 1852; *Manual of domestic economy* 1857. *d.* Pyrgo park, Havering, Essex 15 May 1863.

AITON, JOHN TOWNSEND. Gardener at Kensington palace 1831 to death. *d.* Kensington palace 4 July 1851 aged 74.

AKERMAN, JOHN YONGE (*son of John Akerman of St. Mary Newington, Surrey who d.* 2 *Nov.* 1835 *aged* 50). *b.* London 12 June 1806; F.S.A. 16 Jany. 1834; started the *Numismatic Journal* June 1836, the first English periodical devoted to the illustration of coins; one of the secretaries of Numismatic society 1836–60, the first regular meeting was held 22 Dec. 1836; edited *Journal of Numismatic Society* 1837–60; and *Numismatic Chronicle* 1838–60; gold medallist of French Institute; joint sec. with Sir Henry Ellis of Society of Antiquaries 2 May 1848 and sole sec. 1853–24 June 1860; lived at Abingdon 1860 to death; author of *Numismatic Manual* 1832; *Descriptive catalogue of rare Roman coins, 2 vols.* 1834; *Legends of old London* 1853 and 18 other books; author of many papers in the *Archæologia* and *Numismatic Journal*. *d.* Abingdon 18 Nov. 1873. *Numismatic Chronicle xiv*, 13–19 (1874).

AKHURST, WILLIAM. *b.* Hammersmith 29 Dec. 1822; went to Australia 1850; sub editor and musical critic on the *Argus* daily paper in Melbourne; wrote 14 pantomimes; wrote *The siege of Troy* burlesque which was performed 60 nights, a run without precedent in Australia; returned to England 1870; wrote pantomimes for Astley's, Pavilion, and Elephant and Castle theatres. *d.* on board the "Patriarch" on his voyage to Sydney 7 June 1878.

ALABASTER, HARRY. Interpreter in consulate Bangkok Siam 30 Nov. 1864 to 31 Dec. 1871; author of *The modern Buddhist, translated by H.A.* 1870; *The wheel of the law, Buddhism, illustrated from Siamese sources* 1871. *d.* Bangkok Siam 8 Aug. 1884.

ALBANO, BENEDETTO. *b.* in kingdom of Naples about 1796; fled to England at the Bourbon restoration 1815; employed by Messrs. Rennie in London; naturalised by 1 & 2 Vict. cap.

ALBANO, B. (Con.)

42, 9 May 1838; converted Covent garden theatre into an opera house at a cost of nearly £30,000, 1846; A.I.C.E. 1831, M.I.C.E. 1840. *d.* 75 Welbeck st. Cavendish sq. 7 Nov. 1881.

ALBANY, LEOPOLD GEORGE DUNCAN ALBERT, 1 Duke of (8 *child and* 4 *son of Queen Victoria*). *b.* Buckingham palace 7 April 1853. K.G. 24 May 1869, K.T. 24 May 1871; matric. at Univ. of Ox. (Ch. Ch.) 1872; D.C.L. 1876; P.C. 1874; admitted by patrimony to freedom of city of London 25 Oct. 1875; a younger brother of the Trinity House 1875; an elder brother 1878; G.C.S.I. 25 Jany. 1877; a bencher of Lincoln's Inn 18 June 1877; G.C.M.G. 24 May 1880; created Duke of Albany, Earl of Clarence, and Baron Arklow 24 May 1881. *d.* Villa Nevada, Cannes at 2 a.m. 28 March 1884. *bur.* royal tomb, St. George's chapel, Windsor 5 April. *Graphic, xxix,* 317–22 and 341–61 (1884) 2 *portraits; I.L.N. lxxxiv,* 313–29 (1884), 4 *portraits.*

ALBEMARLE, AUGUSTUS FREDERICK KEPPEL, 5 Earl of. *b.* 2 June 1794; M.P. for Arundel (whig) as Viscount Bury 8 March 1820 to 2 June 1826; succeeded as 5 Earl 30 Oct. 1849, but never took his seat in House of Lords; declared to be of unsound mind on an inquisition Dec. 1849. *d.* Blacklands house asylum, King's Road, Chelséa 15 March 1851.

ALBERT, PRINCE CONSORT OF QUEEN VICTORIA. *b.* the Rosenau near Coburg 26 Aug. 1819; baptised in the Marble hall at the Rosenau 19 Sep. 1819 when he received the following names in the order in which they are given, Franz Karl August Albrecht Immanuel; ed. at Brussels and Bonn 1836–38; invested with the order of the Garter at Gotha 23 Jany. 1840; received the title of Royal Highness by patent 6 Feb. 1840; naturalized by act of parliament 3 and 4 Vict. cap. 2, 7 Feb. 1840; Field Marshal 8 Feb. 1840. *m.* at the chapel royal, St. James's Palace, London 10 Feb. 1840 Queen Victoria; G.C.B. 6 March 1840, acting great master 31 May 1843; Colonel 11 Hussars 30 April 1840 to 25 April 1842; appointed Regent 4 Aug. 1840; admitted to the freedom of city of London 28 Aug. 1840; P.C. 11 Sep. 1840; ranger of Windsor park 6 April 1841; pres. of fine arts commission 22 Nov. 1841; lord warden of the Stannaries, and chief steward of the Duchy in Cornwall and Devon 16 April 1842; colonel Scots Fusilier guards 25 April 1842 to 25 Sep. 1852; governor and constable of Windsor castle 18 May 1843 to death; captain general and colonel of the

Artillery company 20 Sep. 1843; elected chancellor of Univ. of Cam. 27 Feb. 1847, by a majority of 112 over Earl Powis, installed chancellor 6 July 1847; organised the Great Exhibition of 1851; colonel in chief of 60th or King's Royal rifle corps 15 Aug. 1850 to 23 Sep. 1852; of the Rifle brigade 23 Sep. 1852 to death; master of the Trinity house 19 Oct. 1852 to death; colonel of Grenadier guards 23 Sep. 1852 to death; created Prince Consort by patent 25 June 1857; pres. of British Association at Aberdeen 14 Sep. 1859; G.C.S.I. 25 June 1861; composed many songs and chorales; the "Athalie" and "Œdipus" of Mendelssohn were first performed in this country at Windsor castle by his command. *d.* at Windsor castle at 10.50 p.m. 14 Dec. 1861. *The life of The Prince Consort by Theodore Martin 5 vols. 1874-80, 5 portraits; The early homes of Prince Albert by Alfred Rimmer 1883; Medical Times and Gazette ii, 638–42 (1861).*

ALCHIN, WILLIAM TURNER. *b.* St. Mary-at-Hill Billingsgate, London 1790; a solicitor at Winchester; compiled indexes to ecclesiastical registers of Winchester and Salisbury; librarian of Guildhall library, London 1845 to death; compiled indexes to the ancient records of the corporation of London; and calendar of the wills enrolled in the court of Hustings of London. *d.* Chelsea 3 Feb. 1865.

ALCOCK, THOMAS SAINT LEGER. Major 95 foot 2 Feb. 1844 to 21 April 1846 when placed on half pay; lieut. colonel 1 or royal East Middlesex militia 30 Jany. 1851 to 21 July 1871; colonel 21 July 1871 to death. *d.* 22 Somerset st. Portman sq. 7 Aug. 1882.

ALDBOROUGH, BENJAMIN O'NEALE STRATFORD, 6 Earl of. *b.* Dublin 10 June 1808; succeeded 4 Oct. 1849; took out 5 patents for Improvements in aerial navigation 1854-57. *d.* Alicante, Spain 19 Dec. 1875.

ALDER, JOSHUA *(son of Mr. Alder of Newcastle, provision merchant who d. Nov. 1808). b.* Dean st. Newcastle 7 April 1792; ed. at Tanfield school; member of Literary and Philosophical society of Newcastle Feb. 1815; a provision merchant at Newcastle to 1840; collected the large museum of shells and zoophytes which with his library was presented by Sir Wm. Armstrong to Natural history society of Northumberland and Durham; this society founded in 1839 and the Tyneside Naturalists Field Club founded in 1846 owed very much to Alder, pres. of this

club 1849; granted a civil list pension of £70 18 June 1863; author with Albany Hancock of the great monograph *On the British Nudibranchiate Mollusca* 1845-55 (Ray, Society); wrote more than 50 papers all zoological in the chief natural history periodicals. *d.* Newcastle 21 Jany. 1867. *Natural history trans. of Northumberland and Durham i,* 324–37 (1867), *portrait.*

ALDERSON, SIR EDWARD HALL *(eld. son of Robert Alderson, recorder of Norwich who d. 4 Dec. 1833 aged 80, by a dau. of Samuel Hurry of Yarmouth, she d. 1791). b.* Yarmouth 11 Sep. 1787; ed. at Scarning Norfolk, the Charterhouse, and Caius coll. Cam.; Browne's medallist 1807; senior wrangler, first Smith's prizeman and first chancellor's medallist Jany. 1809; B.A. 1809, M.A. 1812; fellow of his college 1809-23; barrister I. T. 28 June 1811; a comr. for amendment of the law 1828; sergeant at law 11 Nov. 1830; justice of court of Common Pleas 12 Nov. 1830; knighted by William iv at St. James's palace 17 Nov. 1830; baron of court of Exchequer 29 April 1834 to death; published with R. V. Barnewall *Reports of cases in court of King's Bench,* 5 vols. 1818-22. *(m.* 1823 Georgina 3 dau. of Rev. Edward Drewe of the Grange near Honiton, Devon, she *d.* 1871). *d.* Beechwood park Hemel Hempstead, Herts 27 Jany. 1857. *bur.* churchyard of Risby near Bury, Suffolk. *Selections from the charges of Baron Alderson by C. Alderson 1858.*

ALDERSON, SIR JAMES *(son of John Alderson, M.D. of Hull 1758–1829 by Sarah dau. of Christopher Scott). b.* Hull 1800; ed. at Hull and Pembroke coll. Cam.; 6 wrangler 1822; B.A. 1822, M.A. 1825; fellow of his college 1823; incorporated M.A. at Magdalen hall, Ox. 1826; B.M. 1826, D.M. 1829, D.C.L. 1870; inceptor candidate college of physicians 26 June 1826; candidate 30 Sep. 1829; fellow 30 Sep. 1830; senior censor 1848 and 1856; treasurer 1854-67; pres. 1867-70; physician at Hull 1829-45; in London 1845 to death; F.R.S. 17 June 1841; senior physician of St. Mary's hospital, Paddington 1851-67; consulting physician 1867; representative of Royal college of physicians at the general medical council 27 Jany. 1864 to 13 May 1867; knighted by the Queen at Windsor castle 11 Nov. 1869; one of Her Majesty's physicians extraordinary 30 Aug. 1875; *Lumleian* lecturer 1852 and 1853; delivered Harveian oration 1854 and 1867; author of *Diseases of the Stomach and alimentary canal* 1847. *(m.* 24 June 1828 Mary Anne dau. of Peter Berthon of Glenadda, Carnarvon, she *d.* 5 March 1877). *d.* 17 Berkeley sq. London 13 Sep. 1882. *Medical Circular i,* 27 (1852) *portrait.*

ALDHAM, WILLIAM CORNWALLIS. *b.* 21 Sep. 1809; Captain R.N. 9 May 1853; captain Greenwich hospital 12 Jan. 1863 to 1 Oct. 1865; retired V.A. 30 July 1875; C.B. 22 Sep. 1858. *d.* Assoint Upper Nile 27 Feb. 1878.

ALDIS, SIR CHARLES (7 *son and one of* 22 *children of Daniel Aldis of Hoxne, Suffolk, surgeon*). *b.* Dickleborough, Norfolk 1776; apprenticed to his father 1789; studied at Guy's and Bartholomew's hospitals; surgeon to the sick and wounded at the depôt for prisoners of war at Norman Cross, Hunts 1797–99; practised at Hertford 1800–1802; in London 1802; M.R.C.S. 1803; senior surgeon New Finsbury dispensary 1831; founded Glandular institution for the cure of cancer and scrofula in Clifford st. about 1820, surgeon there. *d.* 13 Old Burlington st. London 28 March 1863. *Biographical memoirs of Sir Charles Aldis and Dr. Aldis, privately printed* 1852, *portrait.*

ALDIS, CHARLES JAMES BERRIDGE (*eldest son and survivor of 14 infants of the preceding*). *b.* London 16 Jany. 1808; admitted into St. Paul's school 9 May 1815; exhibitioner to Trinity coll. Cam. July 1827; B.A. 1831, M.B. 1832, M.A. and L.M. 1834, M.D. 1837; studied at St. George's hospital, London; F.R.C.P. 1838, member of council, delivered Harveian oration 1859; physician to London dispensary 1839; lectured at Charlotte st. school of medicine 1841; phys. to Surrey dispensary 1843; physician to St. Paul and St. Barnabas dispensary which was founded 1848; medical officer of health for St. George's Hanover square 1855 to death; superintended Hunterian school of medicine several years; invented an instrument for examination of the chest. (*m.* 9 Nov. 1835 Emily Arabella dau. of Rev. John Brome of Trinity college Cambridge). *d.* 45b Chester sq. London 26 July 1872. *Biographical memoirs of Sir C. Aldis* 1852, *portrait.*

ALDRIDGE, IRA FREDERICK, known as the African Roscius (*son of Rev. Daniel Aldridge, minister of Calvinistic chapel, Green st. New York who d. Sep.* 1840). *b.* Bell Air, Harford, Maryland 1804; ed. at Schenectady college near New York and the Univ. of Glasgow; made his first appearance on the stage at the Royalty theatre London as Othello 1826; played 7 weeks at the Coburg theatre London

in 1826, then in the provinces Scotland and Ireland; acted Othello at Covent garden 10 April 1833; acted Aaron in Titus Andronicus at Britannia theatre 15 March 1852, first time acted since 1721; played with great success in Germany 1852-55; received large gold medal of Art and Science from the King of Prussia 25 Jany. 1853, the only other persons who had been so distinguished being Humboldt, Spontini and Liszt; played in Sweden 1857, made several tours in Russia; naturalised in England 7 Nov. 1863. *d.* Lodez, Poland 7 Aug. 1867. *Theatrical times iii,* 121–23 (1848), *portrait; Tallis's Drawing room table book* (1851) 15–16, 2 *portraits; N. and Q.* 4 *series x,* 132, 373 (1872).

ALEX, EPHRAIM. *b.* Cheltenham Dec. 1800; a dentist at 35 Brook st. Grosvenor sq. London; founded Jewish board of guardians for the relief of Jewish poor 1859; the first pres. of it 1859-69, this board was really the pioneer of charitable organisation societies in England; warden of the great synagogue. *d.* 5 Chichester st. Harrow road, London 13 Nov. 1882. *bur.* Willesden cemetery 16 Nov.

ALEXANDER, ALEXANDER (*only son of Wm. Humphrys of Birmingham, merchant, who d.* 1 *May* 1807, *by Hannah youngest child of Rev. John Alexander of Dublin, presbyterian clergyman, she d.* 12 *Sep.* 1814). *b.* 21 June 1783; went abroad with his father 1802; detained prisoner in France till 1814; kept a school called Netherton house academy near Worcester 1815; assumed name of Alexander by royal license 8 March 1824; took title of Earl of Stirling and Dovan 7 Feb. 1826; tried at Edinburgh 29 April to 4 May 1839 for forging documents to prove his title, when acquitted. (*m.* 4 Jany. 1812 Fortunata Maria Gertrude only dau. of Giovanni Bartoletti of Naples). *d.* 1859. *W. C. Townsend's Modern state trials i,* 403–68 (1859).

ALEXANDER, ANDREW. Professor of Greek in the University of St. Andrews 1820 to death; M.A. St. Andrews 1846. *d.* St. Andrews 5 June 1859.

ALEXANDER, CHARLES CARSON. 2nd lieut. R.E. 20 July 1813; superintended exhuming body of Napoleon at St. Helena 15 Oct. 1840; lieut. col. R.E. 2 Feb. 1848 to death; commanded the R.E. in the Crimea 22 Sep. 1854 to death. *d.* of apoplexy in his tent before Sebastopol 19 Oct. 1854.

ALEXANDER, CHARLES REVANS, Educ. at Eton; M.R.C.S. 1840; constructed many chess problems. *d.* 6 Cork st. London 9 Sep. 1871.

ALEXANDER, HENRY. M. R. C. S. 1805, F.R.C.S. 1844; F.R. Med. and Chir. soc. 1813; surgeon to the Eye infirmary Cork st. London; surgeon oculist to Queen Victoria 1838 to death; F.R.S. 22 April 1847. *d*. 6 Cork st. London 17 Jany. 1859 aged 76.

ALEXANDER, HENRY. *b*. 9 April 1787; a director of the H.E.I.Co. 8 March 1826; M.P. for Barnstaple (tory) 10 June 1826 to 24 July 1830. *d*. Belmont, Herts 14 Jany. 1861.

ALEXANDER, REV. JOHN *(son of Rev. Wm. Alexander)*. *b*. Lancaster 19 Dec. 1792; entered Hoxton academy 13 Aug. 1814; a chapel was built for him at Norwich which was opened 1 Dec. 1819; ordained 31 May 1820; pastor of this chapel to April 1866; chairman of Congregational Union of England and Wales 1853; author of sermons entitled *The preacher from the press*, 2 vols. 1838. *d*. Norwich 31 July 1868. *bur*. the Rosary cemetery, Norwich 4 Aug. *The Congregational year book* 1869, *pp*. 234–36.

NOTE.—He was to Norwich what John Angell James was to Birmingham and Thomas Raffles to Liverpool.

ALEXANDER, JOHN HENRY. *b*. Dunbar, July 1796; actor at Queen's theatre, Glasgow 1810; member of Murray's company in Edinburgh 1816; managed the Caledonian theatre, Edinburgh; Lessee of Dumfries and Carlisle theatres; stage manager at Newcastle; manager of Dunlop st. theatre, Glasgow and of theatres at Carlisle and Dumfries, and Adelphi theatre, Edin. 1822–29; proprietor of Dunlop st. theatre, Glasgow, the most elegant in Scotland (which he built) 1829–1851; the best actor of Scotish characters, except Charles Mackay. *d*. Glasgow 15 Dec. 1851.

NOTE.—On 17 Feb. 1849, 65 persons were killed in attempting to escape from the gallery of his theatre, an alarm having spread that it was on fire.

ALEXANDER, JOHN HOBHOUSE INGLIS. *b*. 1832; captain R.N. 16 Aug. 1863; naval aide-de-camp to the Queen 21 April 1875 to death; C.B. 30 Nov. 1864. *d*. Mentone 22 Nov. 1875.

ALEXANDER, NATHANIEL. *b*. Hillsborough, co. Down, Aug. 1815; M.P. for co. Antrim (conserv.) 14 April 1841 to 1 July 1852. *d*. Ardimersey cottage, Islay 5 Jany. 1853.

ALEXANDER, ROBERT. *b*. Paisley; ed. at Paisley gr. sch.; conducted *Clydesdale journal* at Hamilton and at Glasgow; conducted the *Western luminary* at Exeter, about 2 years; edited the *Watchman* in London; managed the *Morning journal* to 1830, when he was

ALEXANDER, R. *(Con.)*

prosecuted for libel, and condemned to one year's imprisonment in Newgate, and fined £300, 10 Feb. 1830; edited the *Liverpool Standard;* founded the *Liverpool Mail* 1836, edited it 1836 to death. *d*. Great Crosby near Liverpool 9 Feb. 1854 in his 59 year. *G.M. xli*, 429–30 (1854).

ALEXANDER, SIR ROBERT, 2 Baronet. *b*. 16 Dec. 1769; succeeded 1809. *d*. 35 St. James's place, London 1 Dec. 1859.

ALEXANDER, ROBERT. In the navy 1810–19; ensign Madras army 12 June 1819; adjutant general 24 Sep. 1839 to 15 Aug. 1849; col. 24 N.I. 16 Aug. 1851 to 1869; general 25 June 1870, retired 31 Dec. 1877. *d*. 6 Marloes road South Kensington 16 May 1879 in his 81 year.

ALEXANDER, ROBERT. *b*. 2 July 1813; in the Bengal civil service 1832–61; C.B. 18 May 1860. *d*. Schuls, Lower Engadine 16 Aug. 1882.

ALEXANDER, THOMAS. *b*. Preston-pans near Edinburgh; entered army medical service 10 Oct. 1834; served in the west Indies, Nova Scotia, Canada, Cape of Good Hope, Turkey the Crimea and Canada; had charge of the light division throughout the Crimean war; inspector general (local rank) 21 July 1856; director general of army medical department 22 June 1858 to death; hon. surgeon to the Queen 16 Aug. 1859 to death; C.B. 4 Feb. 1856. *(m*. Mary Alice eld. sister of T. Heath Haviland, lieutenant governor of Prince Edward island, she *d*. 12 April 1881). *d*. 26 Norfolk square Hyde Park, London 1 Feb. 1860.

NOTE.—A statue of him by Wm. Brodie was unveiled at Preston-pans by Lord Elcho Sep. 1862.

ALEXANDER, WILLIAM. Lieut. col. 2 Bengal light cavalry 21 Aug. 1849 to death; C.B. 9 June 1849. *d*. Dorundah, Bengal 2 Oct. 1851.

ALEXANDER, REV. WILLIAM. *b*. Chapel Rosan, parish of Stoneykirk, Wigtonshire 21 Feb. 1763; a carpenter in Lancaster 1783–1802; pastor of Independent ch. at Prescot near Liverpool 1802–10; ordained 23 Oct. 1805; pastor at Leigh 20 Jany. 1811; pastor at Church Town 1 May 1825 to death. *d*. Southport 23 Jany. 1855. *Memoir of Rev. W. Alexander, by Rev. John Alexander* 1856; *Evangelical mag. March* 1823. *portrait*.

ALEXANDER, WILLIAM. *b*. 1794; a writer to the signet in Edin. 1819; principal clerk and

ALEXANDER, W. (Con.)

registrar of Commissary Court of Edin. 21 Dec. 1849 to death; author of *Abridgment of acts of Sederunt* 1838; *An abridgment of acts of parliament of Scotland* 1841; *Plan and description of the original electro-magnetic telegraph by the inventor* 1851. *d.* 21 Dec. 1859.

ALEXANDER, WILLIAM. In Nelson's fleet 1805; surveyor of shipping to the underwriters and Mersey dock and harbour board, Liverpool nearly 50 years. *d.* 4 Mount Vernon Green, Liverpool 11 Feb. 1884, in 97 year.

ALEXANDER, SIR WILLIAM JOHN, 3 Baronet *b.* 1 April 1797; ed. at Trin. coll. Dub. and Trin. coll. Cam.; B.A. Dub. 1817, incorp. B.A. Cam. 1825, M.A. 1825; barrister M.T. 8 Feb. 1825; went Oxford circuit; Q.C. 10 July 1844; Bencher of his inn 1844; attorney general to Prince of Wales 24 June 1853; succeeded as 3 baronet 1 Dec. 1859; one of council of Prince of Wales 27 Jany. 1864. *d.* 22 St. James's place, London 31 March 1873. *I.L.N. xlii*, 400 (1863) *portrait.*

ALEXANDER, REV. WILLIAM LINDSAY. *b.* Edinburgh 24 Aug. 1808; ed. at univs. of Edin. and St. Andrew's; classical tutor in Lancashire college 1828; minister of Newington chapel, Liverpool 2 years; pastor of Augustine church, Edin.; principal of theological hall of Scottish congregational churches; member of Old Testament revision company 1870; author of the 3 articles *Moral philosophy, Scripture, and Theology* in 8 ed. of *Encyclopedia Britannica*; F.R.S. Edin. *d.* Pinkieburn near Edin. 20 Dec. 1884. *Our Scottish clergy*, 2 series 1849, *pp.* 199–204.

ALFORD, REV. HENRY (3 *son of Rev. Samuel Alford, Dean of St. Burian, Cornwall, who d.* 15 *Aug.* 1799). *b.* Curry Rivell Vicarage 3 Dec. 1782; ed. at Crewkerne, Bridgwater and Tiverton schools; entered Wad. Coll. Ox. 1800; B.A. 1804, M.A. 1811; Fellow of his college; barrister I.T. 22 Nov. 1811; ordained at Quebec chapel, Lon. to curacy of Steeple Ashton, Wilts 13 June 1813; R. of Ampton, Suffolk 1826–42; R. of Winkfield 1833–35; R. of Aston Sandford, Bucks July 1836 to 1850. (*m.* (1) 20 Dec. 1809 Sarah Eliza 3 dau. of Thomas Bradley Paget of Tamworth, Staffs. banker. *m.* (2) 11 Aug. 1831 Susanna eld. dau. of Thomas Barber of Stukeley, Hunts). *d.* Tunbridge 22 Sep. 1852. *Memorial of Rev. Henry Alford by Henry Alford, B.D.* 1855.

ALFORD, VERY REV. HENRY (*only child of the preceding by his first wife*). *b.* 25 Alfred place Bedford sq. London 7 Oct. 1810; ed. at Charmouth in Dorset and Ilminster gr. school; matric. from Trin. coll. Cam. 13 Nov. 1828; scholar 1830, Bell scholar March 1831; 34 wrangler and 8 classic 1832; B.A. 1832, M.A. 1835, B.D. 1849, D.D. 1859; ordained at Exeter Cathedral to curacy of Ampton, Suffolk 27 Oct. 1833; fellow of his college 1 Oct. 1834; ordained priest at St. Margaret's, Westminster 6 Nov. 1834; V. of Wymeswold Leics. 11 March 1835; Hulsean lecturer in Univ. of Cam. 1841–42; examiner in logic and moral philosophy in Univ. of London 1841–57; minister of Quebec chapel Portman sq. 1853; lived at 6 Upper Hamilton terrace, St. John's Wood 26 Sep. 1853 to 19 June 1857; dean of Canterbury 18 March 1857 to death; one of the revisers of the New Testament; edited *Contemporary Review* Dec. 1866; author of *Poems and poetical fragments* 1831; *Chapters on the poets of Greece* 1841; *Greek Testament* 5 vols. 1849–61, and 40 more volumes besides 104 articles in reviews. (*m.* 10 March 1835 Frances Oke dau. of Rev. Samuel Alford, P.C. of Muchelney, Somerset, she *d.* 18 Nov. 1878 aged 67). *d.* The Deanery, Canterbury 12 Jany. 1871. *bur.* churchyard of St. Martin's, Canterbury 17 Jany. *Life of Henry Alford edited by his widow* 1873, *portrait; Illustrated Review i*, 295–98, *portrait; I.L.N. xxvi*, 269 (1855), *lviii*, 67 (1871), *portrait.*

NOTE.—The statue erected to his memory in a niche of the west front of Canterbury Cathedral was unveiled 17 Oct. 1871.

ALFORD, STEPHEN SHUTE. M.R.C.S. 1843, F.R.C.S. 1858, L.S.A. 1844; hon. sec. to Society for promoting legislation for control and cure of habitual drunkards; author of *A few words on drink craving; Dipsomania its prevalence, causes and treatment. d.* 61 Haverstock hill, London 5 July 1881 aged 60.

ALICE MAUD MARY, Princess of the United kingdom of Great Britain and Ireland (3 child and 2 dau. of Queen Victoria). *b.* Buckingham palace 25 April 1843. *m.* at Osborne 1 July 1862 Frederick Wm. Louis Charles afterwards Louis iv grand duke of Hesse-Darmstadt, he was *b.* 12 Sep. 1837; founded the Women's Union for nursing the sick and wounded in war called after her name. *d.* the palace Darmstadt 14 Dec. 1878. *bur.* in the mausoleum at Rosenhohe near Darmstadt 18 Dec. *Alice grand duchess of Hesse, biographical sketch of* 1884, 2 *portraits; Martin's Life of the Prince Consort v*, 252 (1880), *portrait.*

ALISON, Sir Archibald, 1 Baronet *(younger son of Rev. Archibald Alison 1757–1839 prebendary of Sarum)*. *b.* Kenley, Salop 29 Dec. 1792; ed. at Univ. of Edin.; advocate 8 Dec. 1814; advocate depute 1823–30; wrote his History of Europe 1 Jany. 1829 to 7 June 1842; sheriff of Lanarkshire Dec. 1834 to death; lived at Possil house near Glasgow 1835 to death; lord rector of Marischal college, Aberdeen March 1845, beating Macaulay by 48 votes; lord rector of Univ. of Glasgow 15 Jany. 1852; created baronet 25 June 1852; D.C.L. at Oxford July 1852; author of *History of Europe during the French revolution*, 10 vols. 1833–42, 7 ed. 20 vols. 1847–48; in 1853 the book was stereotyped; *The military life of John Duke of Marlborough* 1848, 2 ed. 2 vols. 1852. *d.* Possil house at 11.30 p.m. 23 May 1867. *bur.* Dean cemetery, Edinburgh 30 May. *Some account of my life and writings by Sir A. Alison, edited by Lady Alison*, 2 vols. 1883, 2 *portraits*.

Note.— He is drawn by Disraeli in Coningsby as Mr. Wordy.

ALISON, Charles. Envoy extraord. and minister plenipo. at Tehran, Persia 7 April 1860; C.B. 28 Nov. 1860. *d.* Tehran 29 April 1872.

ALISON, Somerville Scott. *b.* Edin. 1812; M.D. Edin. 1833; M.R.C.P. 1844, F.R.C.P. 1859; practised at Tranent 1833–40, in London 1840 to death; author of *Inquiry into propagation of contagious poisons* 1839; *Medication of the larynx and trachea* 1853; *Morbid throat and pulmonary consumption* 1869. *d.* 85 Park st. Grosvenor sq. 11 June 1877.

ALISON, William Pulteney *(elder son of Rev. Archibald Alison 1757–1839)*. *b.* Boroughmuirhead near Edin. 1790; M.D. Edin. 1811; ascended Mont Blanc 1814; professor of medical jurisprudence in Univ. of Edin. 1820–22, of institutes of medicine 1822–42; and of practice of physic 1842–56; physician to the Queen in Scotland 3 Feb. 1847; hon. D.C.L. Oxford 1850; granted civil list pension of £100, 10 Nov. 1856; presided over meeting of British Medical Association at Edin. Aug. 1858; author of *Outlines of physiology* 1831; *Outlines of pathology* 1833; *Observations on the management of the poor in Scotland* 1840, this book caused the appointment of the Board of Supervision under the act of 1845. *(m.* 11 Aug. 1832 Margaret dau. of James Gregory, M.D. of Edinburgh). *d.* Woodville, Colington, Edinburgh 22 Sep. 1859. *Edin. Medical Journal v*, 469–86 and 597–603 (1860).

ALLAN, Alexander Stewart. *b.* 1822; employed in financial department, Bengal 1859–73; supplied many of the notes to the publications of the Grampian club; wrote many articles in *Notes and Queries*, signed A.S.A. *d.* Kincardine, Richmond, Surrey 20 Dec. 1881.

ALLAN, Bryce. *b.* Greenock; founded at Liverpool a branch of the Allan shipping company with his brothers Alexander and James (who *d.* Skelmorlie 1 Sep. 1880 aged 71). *d.* 16 Holly road Fairfield, Liverpool 24 May 1874.

Note.—His personalty was sworn under £250,000 Sept. 1874.

ALLAN, Sir Hugh (2 *son of Alexander Allan, commander of ships trading between the Clyde and Montreal)*. *b.* Saltcoats, Ayrshire 29 Sep. 1810; clerk in house of Wm. Kerr and Co. Montreal 1826–29; partner in firm of Millar and Edmonstone of Montreal, shipowners 1835; partner with Edmonstone 1 May 1839; established April 1856 a line of steamers from Montreal to Liverpool, called the Montreal Ocean steamship company, afterwards the Allan line; knighted by patent 24 July 1871. (*m.* 13 Sep. 1844 Matilda Caroline 2 dau. of John Smith of Montreal, she *d.* 11 June 1881 aged 63). *d.* 27 St. Andrew sq. Edinburgh 9 Dec. 1882. *bur.* Montreal 27 Dec. *H. J. Morgan's Sketches of celebrated Canadians* 1862, *pp.* 669–74; *W. S. Lindsay's History of merchant shipping iv*, 260–64 (1876).

ALLAN, James. Major 94 foot 20 July 1809 to 25 Dec. 1818, when placed on h. p. regiment being disbanded; served in Peninsular war 1810–14; lieut. col. 57 foot 20 March 1828 to 9 Nov. 1846; M.G. 9 Nov. 1846; col. 50 foot 11 Oct. 1852 to death; C.B. 19 July 1838. *d.* Cheltenham 17 Feb. 1853.

ALLAN, James. *b.* Aberdeen; sec. to Peninsular steam navigation company when first formed 1837; this was first company which ran steamers to distant foreign ports, the Iberia first steamer despatched with Peninsular mails in Sep. 1837; the first sec. of Peninsular and Oriental company 1840; one of the 3 managing directors 1848 to death; A.I.C.E. 4 Dec. 1849. *d.* Camp's hill, Lewisham near London 15 Sep. 1874 aged 63. *Minutes of proc. of Instit. of C.E. xxxix*, 283–85 (1875).

ALLARDICE, Robert Bridges Barclay, known as Captain Barclay *(eld. son of Robert Barclay of Ury, Kincardineshire 1731–97, founder of town of Stonehaven, who assumed name of Allardice 1776)*. *b.* Ury 25 Aug.

ALLARDICE, R. B. B. (Con.)

1779; kept a pack of fox hounds at Ury 1807; walked from London to Birmingham viâ Cambridge 150 miles in 2 days Dec. 1799; walked 100 miles in 19 hours Dec. 1801; captain 71 foot 13 March 1806; major 20 Jany. 1814 to 31 March 1814 when he resigned; lieut. col. Kincardineshire militia; walked 1000 miles in 1000 succesive hours at the rate of a mile in each and every hour at Newmarket 1 June to 12 July 1809, when about £100,000 changed hands on the result; trained Tom Cribb at Ury July–Aug. 1811 for his great fight with Tom Molineaux the Black, which Cribb won 28 Sep. 1811; a great agriculturist and cattle breeder; claimed the Earldom of Airth 1839 and the Earldoms of Strathern and Monteith 1840. (m. 19 July 1819 Mary dau. of Alexander Dalgarno of Wales st. Aberdeen, she d. 30 Aug. 1820 aged 23). found dead in his bed at Ury 1 May 1854. bur. in family burying ground called the Houff, which contains an account of the family from year 1110. H. H. Dixon's Field and fern (North) 1865 pp. 196–210; Pugilistica by H. D. Miles i, 435–39 (1880), portrait; Pedestrianism [by Walter Thom] Aberdeen 1813, portrait; The eccentric mag. i, 133–50 (1812), portrait.

NOTE.—The coach called the Defiance (of which he was one of the 5 proprietors) ran from Edinburgh to Aberdeen and was the fastest and best conducted coach in the United Kingdom, it performed the journey 126 miles in 12 hours; it ran its first journey 1 July 1829 and its last Oct. 1849. The 1000 mile feat has never been performed by any other man, although many persons are stated to have done it.

ALLASON, THOMAS. b. London 31 July 1790; architect in London 1817; employed in landscape gardening; a comr. of Board of Metropolitan Sewers; author of Picturesque views of the antiquities of Pola in Istria 1819. d. 9 April 1852.

ALLCROFT, JEREMIAH MACKLIN. b. 1791; partner in firm of Dent, Allcroft and Co. of Wood st. London and Worcester, glovers; chamberlain of Worcester 1832–33. d. Worcester 6 July 1867.

ALLEN, CHARLES, calling himself Charles Edward Lewis Casimir Stuart, Count d'Albanie (only son of Charles Manning Allen 1799–1880). Col. in the Austrian army. (m. 15 May 1874 Alice Mary Emily 3 and youngest dau. of the 17 Earl of Errol, she was b. 7 July 1835 and d. 7 June 1881.) d. 8 May 1882 aged 57, thus ending this dynasty of modern pretenders.

ALLEN, CHARLES. b. 1808; a member of Financial council, Calcutta; alderman of Tenby; mayor 2 or 3 times; sheriff of co. Pembroke 1876. d. Tenby 5 Nov. 1884.

ALLEN, CHARLES MANNING, calling himself Charles Edward Stuart, Count d'Albanie (younger son of Thomas Gatehouse Allen 1772–1851, by Katharine Matilda dau. of Rev. Owen Manning, V. of Godalming, Surrey. T. G. Allen called himself James Stuart, Count d'Albanie and affirmed that he was son of Charles Stuart the young Pretender by the Princess Louisa of Stolberg-Gädern). b. Versailles 4 June 1799; served in advanced guard of Napoleon's army at Waterloo; assumed Christian name of Stuart 1822; changed his name to Allan-Hay; changed again to Stuart; lived with his brother John at Edin. then at Glasgow then at Eile-an-Aigais near Inverness; author with his brother John of The costume of the clans 1845; Tales of the century 1847; Lays of the deer forest, 2 vols. 1848. (m. 9 Oct. 1822 Anne dau. of John Beresford, M.P. for co. Waterford, and widow of Charles Gardiner). d. on board the Rainbow steamer at Pauillac near Bordeaux 25 Dec. 1880. J. H. Ingram's Claimants to royalty (1882) 252–59; Quarterly Review lxxxi, 57–85 (1847); Edinburgh Review cxiv, 145–82 (1861); Western Antiquary Sep. 1884, 67–72; Doran's London in Jacobite times ii, 390–412 (1877).

ALLEN, GEORGE. b. London Nov. 1800; attorney and solicitor of supreme court at Sydney 1822; mayor of Sydney 1844; member of legislative council N.S.W. 1845 and 1856 to death; chairman of committees 1856–73. d. Toxteth park, Glebe, N.S.W. 3 Nov. 1877.

ALLEN, GEORGE JOHN (eld. son of Right Rev. Joseph Allen, bishop of Ely who d. 20 March 1845 aged 75). b. 1810; warden of the college of God's Gift in Dulwich 1843 to 31 Dec. 1857 when that Corporation was dissolved by 20 and 21 Vict. c. 84, and he was granted an annuity of £1015. d. The Mount, Budleigh Salterton, Devon 19 July 1883.

ALLEN, HENRY ROBINSON. b. Cork 1809; ed. at R.A. of Music; made his début at the English Opera as Elvino in La Sonnambula; A.R.A.M.; tenor vocalist and ballad composer, his song "Maid of Athens" was much sung. d. Shepherd's Bush, London 27 Nov. 1876.

ALLEN, REV. HUGH. b. Cork July 1806; ed. at Trin. coll. Dub.; scholar 1834, B.A. 1835, M.A., B.D. and D.D. 1861; minister

ALLEN, REV. H. *(Con.)*

of an episcopal chapel at Douglas, Isle of Man, Aug. 1835 ; C. of St. John's ch. Bury, Lancs. 1838–48 ; Inc. of St. Jude's Whitechapel 1848–59 ; lecturer of St. Olave's, Old Jewry 1856–59 ; R. of St. George the Martyr Southwark 1859 to death ; edited the *London Messenger* 1862. *d.* 231 New Kent road, London 20 June 1877.

NOTE.—He was the Sunday afternoon lecturer at church of St. George-in-the-East, London where disturbances began 21 Aug. 1859 in consequence of the Rector the Rev. Bryan King adopting an elaborate ritual and refusing to allow time for the lecture, the riots lasted till 25 June 1860.

ALLEN, JAMES BAYLIS. *b.* Birmingham 18 April 1803; employed by W. and E. Finden, engravers in London 1824 ; engraved many of Turner's water colour drawings 1830–45, and many large views for the Art Journal. *d.* Camden Town, London 11 Jany. 1876.

ALLEN, JAMES MOUNTFORD *(son of Rev. John Allen, V. of Bleddington, Gloucs.) b.* Crewkerne, Somerset 14 Aug. 1809; an architect in London to 1856, at Crewkerne 1856 to death ; built many churches, rectory houses and schools. *d.* 27 Feb. 1883.

ALLEN, JAMES PEARCE. Spent 5 years in India 1836–41 ; a publisher in London 1855 to death. *d.* Grove lodge, Clapham Common 2 Nov. 1878 in 61 year.

ALLEN, JOHN *(elder son of Admiral John Carter Allen who d. 2 Oct. 1800). b.* 1774; captain R.N. 29 April 1802 ; admiral on h. p. 30 July 1852. *d.* Torpoint near Plymouth 4 June 1853.

ALLEN, JOHN. *b.* Dublin ; a woollen draper at 36 College green ; committed to Tower of London on a charge of high treason 6 March 1798, tried at Maidstone 21 and 22 May 1798 when acquitted ; an associate of Robert Emmett in the insurrection of 23 July 1803 ; fled to France and became sous-lieutenant in the army Dec. 1803 ; led the storming party at capture of Cindad Rodrigo in Spain 10 July 1810 ; chef de bataillon March 1814 ; retired on half pay after the Irish regiment was disbanded Sep. 1815 ; lived at Tours then at Caen. *d.* Caen 10 Feb. 1855. *R. R. Madden's The united Irishmen, 3rd series iii,* 135–39 (1846) ; *Howell's State Trials xxvi,* 1193–1432 (1819), and *xxvii,* 1–142 (1820).

ALLEN, JOHN. *b.* Liskeard, Cornwall 26 Sep. 1790; author of *State churches and the kingdom of Christ* 1853 ; *History of the borough of Liskeard and its vicinity* 1856. *d.* Liskeard 15 Feb. 1859. *Annual Monitor for 1860 pp.* 3–26.

ALLEN, JOHN CARTER HAY, calling himself John Sobieski Stolberg Stuart *(elder son of Thomas Gatehouse Allen 1772–1851).* Said to have received cross of the Legion d' Honneur from hands of Napoleon for bravery on field of Waterloo ; lived with his brother Charles at Edinburgh, at Glasgow, at Eile-an-Aigais near Inverness; author of *Poems* 1822 ; edited the *Vestiarium Scoticum* 1842. *(m.* 29 Oct. 1845 Georgiana eld. dau. of Edward Kendall of Cheltenham). *d.* 52 Stanley st. St. George's Hanover sq. 13 Feb. 1872.

ALLEN, JOHN ROY *(elder son of John Allen of Lyngford, Somerset). b.* 1799 ; ed. at Pemb. coll. Cam. ; B.A. 1821, M.A. 1825 ; barrister I.T. 10 Feb. 1826 ; recorder of Taunton, Andover and Bridgwater. *d.* Weston super Mare 10 March 1875.

ALLEN, JOSEPH. Chairman of Brighton bench of magistrates many years ; one of the gentlemen of H.M. privy chamber 1838 to death. *d.* Podstream house Wivelsfield, Sussex 9 Dec. 1851 aged 78.

ALLEN, JOSEPH. Military superintendent of halls, &c. at Greenwich hospital 1 Sep. 1833 to death ; edited Allen's "New Navy List"; newspaper writer on professional topics. *d.* Greenwich Hospital 21 Oct. 1864 aged 54.

ALLEN, JOSEPH WILLIAM. *b.* Paradise row, Lambeth 1803; usher at a school at Taunton ; theatrical scene painter in London ; a founder of "The Society of British Artist" 1823 ; professor of drawing at city of London school from its opening 2 Feb. 1837 to death. *d.* Hammersmith 26 Aug. 1852.

ALLEN, PETER. *b.* Dec. 1826 ; M.D. Aberdeen 1849 ; L.S.A. and M.R.C.S. Eng. 1849 ; F.R.C.S. Edin. 1868 ; surgeon at Yealand Conyers 1856–68, and in London 1868 to death ; aural surgeon to St. Mary's hospital ; author of *Practical observations on deafness* 1853 ; *Aural Catarrh* 1870. *d.* 117 Harley st. Cavendish sq. London 18 Jany. 1874.

ALLEN, ROBERT (3 son of Samuel Allen of Rue St. Honoré, Paris). An actor ; a schoolmaster ; barrister G.I. 18 Nov. 1835 ; went Oxford circuit ; serjeant at law 3 July 1845, received patent of precedence. *d.* Bessborough st. London 17 Feb. 1854.

ALLEN, REV. SAMUEL JAMES. *b.* near Tower of London 16 June 1798 ; ed. at Merchant Taylor's school 1808–16 and Pemb. coll. Cam. ; B.A. 1820, M.A. 1824 ; University preacher at Cam. ; V. of Easingwold, Yorkshire 1838 to death ; completed *Whitaker's History of*

ALLEN, REV. S. J. (Con.)

Richmondshire 1823 in which some of the chapters were entirely written by him; author of *Lectures in defence of the church of England*. d. Easingwold vicarage 29 April 1856.

ALLEN, WILLIAM. b. Weymouth Nov. 1792; entered navy 2 Oct. 1805; accompanied Richard Lander's expedition up the river Niger 1832; returned to England April 1834 being one of the nine survivors; commanded steamer Wilberforce in expedition to Niger 1840–42; captain 31 Jany. 1842, retired R.A. 12 April 1862; F.R.G.S. 1835, F.R.S. 18 April 1844; author of *The narrative of expedition sent to river Niger* 1848; *The Dead Sea, a new route to India* 1855; exhibited landscape paintings at the R.A. 1828–47. d. Bank house, Weymouth 23 Jany. 1864.

ALLEN, WILLIAM FERNELEY (son of *Wm. Houghton Allen of London, publisher who d. 22 Jany. 1855 aged 67*). b. 31 Oct. 1816; a publisher in London 1855 to death; sheriff 1857–58; alderman for ward of Cheap 1858 to death, and Lord Mayor 1867–68. d. 13 Waterloo place, London 22 May 1877. bur. in family vault at Sevenoaks, Kent 26 May. *I.L.N. li*, 517 (1867), *portrait*.

ALLEN, WILLIAM HENRY. Solicitor in London 1826 to death; principal of Clifford's Inn 13 May 1833 to death. d. 20 Oct. 1854 aged 71.

ALLEN, WILLIAM PHILIP. b. near town of Tipperary April 1848; a carpenter in Cork, Dublin and Chester; helped to rescue Colonel Kelly the Fenian from a prison van at Manchester 18 Sep. 1867; in the mêlée, a police sergeant named Brett was killed; executed at the old prison Manchester 23 Nov. 1867. *Speeches from the dock. Dublin* 1868.

ALLEYNE, SIR REYNOLD ABEL, 2 Baronet. b. 10 June 1789; ed. at Eton; succeeded his father 1801; member of council in Barbados 30 years; col. of 2 regiment of militia there. d. Burton under Needwood 14 Feb. 1870.

ALLEYNE, SARAH FRANCES. b. Clifton 15 Oct. 1836; organised courses of lectures for women; member of council of Clifton high school for girls; sec. of Oxford local examination at Clifton; translated E. Zeller's *Plato and the older Academy* 1876 and M. Duncker's *History of Greece* 1883. d. London 16 Aug. 1884. bur. Redland Green churchyard 21 Aug.

ALLIES, JABEZ (2 son of *Wm. Allies of Alfrick in Lusley co. Worcester*). b. Alfrick 22 Oct. 1787; a solicitor in London; author of *The causes of planetary motion* 1838; *The antiquities*

ALLIES, J. (Con.)

and folk lore of Worcestershire 2 ed. 1852, the best work on local field names ever published. d. Tivoli house, Cheltenham 29 Jany. 1856.

ALLIOTT, REV. RICHARD (son of *Rev. Richard Alliott, pastor of congregational church in Castle Gate, Nottingham*). b. 1 Sep 1804; ed. at Homerton college and Glasgow univ.; LL.D. 1840; assistant minister to his father 1828; co-pastor with him 1830–40; ordained Jany. 1830; pastor of same church 1840; of church in York road, Lambeth, London 1843–49; pres. of Western college, Plymouth 1849–57; pres. of Cheshunt college 1857; chairman of Congregational union of England and Wales 1858; professor of dogmatic and general theology and philosophy at Spring Hill college, Birmingham, Sep. 1860 to death; pastor of church at Acock's Green near Birmingham 1860 to death; author of *Psychology and Theology* 1854. d. Acock's Green 20 Dec. 1863.

ALLMAN, THOMAS. Bookseller in Princes st. Hanover sq. 1817; at Holborn hill 1830–59, when he retired. d. 2 Clifton villas, Maida hill, London 3 Dec. 1870 aged 78.

ALLOCK, JON JUNIM. b. China; brought to England by Andrew Ducrow the equestrian about 1819; a great attraction at Astley's, London as a Chinese juggler; travelled with Ducrow all over Europe and America; fell from a horse and broke his thigh about 1841; lived at Glasgow about 1845 to death. d. Glasgow 9 Aug. 1859 aged nearly 80.

ALLOM, THOMAS. b. London 13 March 1804; articled to Francis Goodwin, architect; furnished the drawings for many illustrated works published by Virtue & Co. and Heath and Co.; exhibited drawings at the R.A.; made for Sir Charles Barry the drawings of new Houses of Parliament which were presented to Nicholas Czar of Russia. d. 1 Lonsdale road, Barnes, Surrey 21 Oct. 1872.

ALLSOP, THOMAS. b. Stainsborough hall near Wirksworth, Derbyshire 10 April 1795; a stockbroker in London; the favourite disciple of Samuel Taylor Coleridge; great friend of Charles Lamb, Robert Owen and other eminent men; author of *Letters, conversations and recollections of S. T. Coleridge*, 2 vols. 1836; *California and its gold mines in* 1852–3. d. Exmouth, Devon 12 April 1880. bur. Woking cemetery 17 April. *Dictionary of national biography i*, 337–39 (1885).

ALMOND, EMMA (dau. of *Mr. Romer*). b. 1814; first appeared on stage at Covent Garden 16 Oct. 1830 as Donna Clara in *The Duenna*;

ALMOND, E. *(Con.)*

the original Zerlina in Auber's opera *Fra Diavolo* at C.G. 3 Nov. 1831; original singer of title parts in Barnett's *Mountain Sylph* and *Fair Rosamond;* chief singer at English opera house; sang at Westminster Abbey festival 1834; sang at Drury Lane 1836; manager of the Surrey theatre 1852, where she brought out a series of operas in English. *(m.* 1836 George Almond of Bond st. hatter, he *d.* Nov. 1863). *d.* Clifton terrace, Margate 14 April 1868. *bur.* Brompton cemetery 21 April. *Actors by daylight ii,* 57 (1839), *portrait.*

ALSBURY, George. Stipendiary magistrate and pres. of island of Anguilla, Caribbee islands 26 Nov. 1863 to 28 Jany. 1868. *d.* St. Heliers, Jersey 10 Nov. 1879.

ALSTON, Edward Graham. Ed. at St. Paul's sch. and Trin. coll. Cam.; B.A. 1855; barrister L.I. 17 Nov. 1857; registrar general of Vancouver island Feb. 1861, of British Columbia 1 June 1870; attorney general of Sierra Leone 13 May 1871 to death, and Queen's advocate July 1871 to death. *d.* Sierra Leone 12 Sep. 1872 in 40 year.

ALSTON, Edward Richard. *b.* Stockbriggs near Lesmahagow 1 Dec. 1845; zoological sec. of Linnæan society 1880 to death; contributed to the *Proceedings of Zoological society* 1874–80; author of the division Mammalia in Salvin and Godman's *Biologia Centrali-Americana* 1879. *d.* 14 Maddox st. London 7 March 1881.

ALTHANS, John *(son of Henry Althans the friend of popular education).* Connected with Religious tract society 47 years and trade manager the last 6 years. *d.* West lodge, White Hart lane, Tottenham 15 Dec. 1882 aged 66.

ALVANLEY, Richard Pepper Arden, 3 Baron. *b.* the Rolls house, Chancery lane, 8 Dec. 1792; major 84 foot 26 Sep. 1822 to 30 Oct. 1823 when placed on h. p.; succeeded his brother 9 Nov. 1849. *d.* 12 Bruton st. London 24 June 1857.

Note.—His library was sold by Sotheby 15-20 Feb. 1858.

ALVES, John. *b.* Elgin 1787; captain 74 foot 2 Nov. 1830 to 17 Aug. 1841 when placed on half pay; granted a service reward 27 Jany. 1854; M.G. 5 Dec. 1856; sergeant at arms to the Queen 1855 to death. *d.* 14 King st. St. James's, London 18 Sep. 1860.

AMBROSE, George James. Lieut. col. 3 Foot 31 Dec. 1857 to death; C.B. 1 March 1861. *d.* Brislington 19 July 1862 aged 38.

AMCOTTS, Weston Cracroft. *b.* 9 March 1815; ed. at Eton; sheriff of Lincolnshire 1861; M.P. for Mid-Lincolnshire (Lib.) 1868-74. *d.* Harrogate 14 July 1883.

AMESBURY, Joseph *(youngest child of Joseph Amesbury of Huntspill, Somerset who d. about* 1802). *b.* Huntspill 15 Oct. 1795; M.R.C.S. 4 Aug. 1820; a surgeon in London 1820-58; opened a private spinal establishment at 59 Burton crescent 1838; lived at 26 Fitzroy sq. 1847–58; invented apparatus for cure of stiff joints, spinal curvature, and other deformities for which he took out 3 patents; author of *Practical remarks on nature and treatment of fractures of the trunk and extremities* 2 vols. 1831. *d.* 93 Lansdowne place, Brighton 27 March 1864.

AMEUNEY, Antonius George *(son of Georgius Ameuney of Latakia).* *b.* Latakia 1821; went to England 1840; studied at King's college; went with J. B. Thompson, M.D. on a mission to Damascus 1844; surveyed the Jordan and Dead Sea with captain Lynch of the U.S. navy 1848; worked for the London Arabic literary fund 1859; professor of Arabic at King's college, London Jany. 1865 to death; author of *Notes from the life of a Syrian, with an appeal on behalf of* 80,000,000 *of the human family* 1860. *d.* 87 Seymour st. London 16 Sep. 1881.

AMHERST, William Pitt Amherst, 1 Earl of *(only son of Wm. Amherst* 1732–81, *governor of Newfoundland).* *b.* Bath 14 Jany. 1773; ed. at Ch. Ch. Ox.; B.A. 1793, M.A. 1797; succeeded his uncle as 2 Baron Amherst 3 Aug. 1797; envoy to Naples 1809-11; P.C. 30 Dec. 1815; ambassador extraordinary to China 8 Feb. 1816 to 30 July 1817; visited Napoleon at St. Helena 1817; governor general of India 23 Oct. 1822 to 10 March 1828; declared war against Burmah 24 Feb. 1824; created Viscount Holmesdale and Earl Amherst of Arracan in the East Indies 19 Dec. 1826; appointed governor general of Canada but never took office; granted a pension of £3,000 a year; G.C.H. 1834. *d.* Knole house near Sevenoaks 13 March 1857. *bur.* in Sevenoaks church. *Jerdan's National portrait gallery vol.* 1 (1830), *portrait; Waagen's Galleries of art* (1857) 337–41; *Ellis's Journal of the proceedings of the late embassy to China* 1817; *Mill's History of British India, by H. H. Wilson, vol. iii,* 1848.

AMHERST, Right Rev. Francis Kerril *(eld. son of Wm. Kerril Amherst of Parndon, Essex, by Mary Louisa youngest dau. of Francis Fortes-*

AMHERST, RIGHT REV. F. K. *(Con.)* *cue Turvile of Bosworth hall co. Leicester). b.* London 21 March 1819; ed. at Oscott; ordained priest by bishop Wiseman 6 June 1846; professor at Oscott, Nov. 1855 to Oct. 1856; served the mission of Stafford, Oct. 1856 to May 1858; bishop of Northampton 14 May 1858 to 1879; consecrated 4 July 1858; assistant at pontifical throne 8 June 1862; preconised to titular see of Sozusa 1880; author of *Lenten thoughts* 1873, 4 ed. 1880. *d.* Fieldgate house, Kenilworth 21 Aug. 1883. *bur.* R.C. cathedral, Northampton 28 Aug.

AMHERST, G. A. *b.* London 1776; first appeared on the stage 14 July 1817 in *The blue devils* at Haymarket theatre; visited United states as director of Cooke's Equestrian company 1838; made his début in Philadelphia as the Castillian in *Mazeppa* 2 April 1838; author of many plays. *d.* in the Philadelphia Almshouse 12 Aug. 1851.

AMOS, ANDREW *(son of James Amos of Devonshire sq. London, Russian merchant). b.* India 1791; ed. at Eton and Trin. coll. Cam.; 5 wrangler 1813, B.A. 1813, M.A. 1816; fellow of his college 1815–23; barrister L.I. 24 Nov. 1818; went Midland circuit 1818–37; professor of English law in Univ. of London 1829–37; recorder of Banbury, Nottingham and Oxford; member of first criminal law commission 1834–43; 4th ordinary member of supreme council of India 11 Oct. 1837 to 15 Feb. 1843; judge of county courts for Brentford, Brompton and Marylebone, circuit 44, March 1847 to Sep. 1852; Downing professor of laws of England in Univ. of Cam. 1848 to death; author of *A treatise on the law of fixtures* 1827, 3 ed. 1883; *The English constitution in the reign of Charles ii,* 1857; *Martial and the Moderns* 1858. *(m.* 1 Aug. 1826 Margaret eld. dau. of Rev. Wm. Lax Lowndes professor of astronomy at Cambridge, she *d.* 13 April 1882). *d.* Downing college, Cambridge 18 April 1860. *Law Times* xxxv, 117–18 (1860).

NOTE.—There is a marble bust of him in University college, London.

AMOS, CHARLES EDWARDS. *b.* March, Cambs. 27 Nov. 1805; a millwright at Wandsworth, Surrey 1835–66; patented several inventions in manufacture of paper; invented dynamometer brought out and designed for Atlantic cable 1857; M.I.C.E. 22 May 1855. *d.* Cedars road, Clapham common 12 Aug. 1882. *Minutes of proc. of instit. of C.E. lxxi,* 387–95 (1883).

AMOTT, JOHN. Organist at Gloucester cathedral 1832 to death. *d* College Green, Gloucester 3 Feb. 1865 in 67 year.

AMPHLETT, SIR RICHARD PAUL *(eld. son of Rev. Richard Holmden Amphlett, R. of Hadsor, Worcs., who d. 8 March 1842 in 60 year). b.* Salop 24 May 1809; ed. at Brewood gr. sch. and St. Peter's coll. Cam.; 6 wrangler 1831, B.A. 1831, M.A. 1834; fellow of his college 1832–40; hon. fellow 6 Nov. 1882; student of L.I. 5 Feb. 1831, barrister 6 June 1834, bencher, Jany. 1858; Q.C. Jany. 1858; M.P. for East Worcester (Conserv.) 24 Nov. 1868 to Jany. 1874; pres. of Legal education association, Oct. 1872; serjeant at law, and baron of Court of Exchequer 24 Jany. 1874; knighted by the Queen at Osborne 27 Jany. 1874; judge of court of appeal 27 Oct. 1876 to Nov. 1877; P.C. 28 Nov. 1876; struck with paralysis 3 April 1877. *d.* 32 Wimpole st. London 7 Dec. 1883. *bur.* at Hadsor 13 Dec. *I.L.N. lxiv,* 120, 129 (1874) *portrait.*

NOTE.—His was the first instance of nomination of an equity practitioner to a common law judgeship since the appointment of Sir Robert Rolfe in Nov. 1839.

AMPTHILL, ODO WILLIAM LEOPOLD RUSSELL, 1 Baron *(youngest son of Lord George Wm. Russell, G.C.B.). b.* Florence 20 Feb. 1829; ed. at Westminster; attaché at Vienna 15 March 1849; employed on special service at Rome, Nov. 1860 to 9 Aug. 1870; ambassador extraord. and plenipo. at Berlin 16 Oct. 1871 to death; P.C. 5 Feb. 1872, G.C.B. 21 Feb. 1874, G.C.M.G. 24 May 1879; created Baron Ampthill of Ampthill, Beds. 7 March 1881. *d.* Potsdam 25 Aug. 1884. *bur.* in family vault in parish church of St. Michael, Chenies, Bucks 3 Sep. *I.L.N. lxxxv,* 220 (1884) *portrait.*

AMSINCK, HENRY. *b.* 1798; served in navy 1811–44; retired commander 22 March 1876; sec. to the Railway commission 1844; went to Melbourne 1853; M.P. for West Bourke. *d.* Hawthorne, Victoria 17 Dec. 1878.

ANCELL, HENRY *(son of Mr. Ancell of Carshalton, Surrey, cotton miller). b.* Croydon 23 Jany. 1802; walked through the United States 1823–25; L.S.A. 1828, M.R.C.S. 1831; surgeon to Metropolitan police; lectured at Lane's school next St. George's hospital 1837; sec. to National association of general practitioners 1845–47; author of *A treatise on Tuberculosis* 1852; *Lectures on the blood* and *Commentaries on Liebig. d.* 3 Norfolk crescent Hyde Park 19 Nov. 1863.

ANDERDON, JAMES HUGHES. *b.* 1790; collected many pictures of British School; bought Hogarth's Sigismunda for £56 (which he bequeathed to National Gallery), and his portrait of Sarah Malcolm the murderess. *d.* 23 Upper Grosvenor st. London 24 Jany. 1879.

ANDERDON, JOHN LAVICOUNT (3 *son of John Proctor Anderdon). b.* Bristol 5 April 1792; ed. at Ealing and Harrow; a West India merchant in London 1816–54; contested Penryn 1818; author of *The river Dove* 1847; *The life of bishop Ken, by a Layman* 2 vols. 1851; *The Messiah* 1861. (*m.* 4 March 1816 Anna Maria 2 dau. of Wm. Manning, M.P., she *d.* 1 May 1880 in 84 year). *d.* Brighton 8 March 1874. *Geron, the old man in search of paradise, by J. L. Anderdon with a biographical notice, by Rev. G. Williams* 1877.

ANDERDON, THOMAS OLIVER. Barrister L.I. 20 Nov. 1822; equity draftsman; Q.C. 1841; bencher of his inn 1841. *d.* Horsendon house Bucks 31 July 1856 aged 70.

ANDERSON, ADAM, Lord Anderson (2 *son of Samuel Anderson of Moredun, co. Edinburgh). b.* Edin. 1797; ed. at Univ. of Edin; advocate 1818; solicitor general Nov. 1834 to April 1835; sheriff of Perthshire 1835–1842; solicitor general for Scotland 8 Nov. 1842 to 1846; Dean of Faculty of Advocates 28 Feb. 1852; Advocate for Scotland 28 Feb. 1852; one of Lords of Session and of Justiciary 18 May 1852 to death. *d.* 55 Upper Brook st. London 28 Sep. 1853. *bur.* under St. John's episcopal chapel Edin. *B. W. Crombie's Modern Athenians* (1882) 112, *portrait.*

ANDERSON, ALEXANDER. *b.* near Stirling 1762; assistant surgeon R.N. 1784; served in North America and West Indies; surgeon 15 Oct. 1790; retired on h. p. 1803; practised at Knightsbridge, London 1803–35; the last medical officer who belonged to Lord Nelson's fleet. *d.* Clarence terrace, New Hampton, Middlesex 6 Sep. 1859.

ANDERSON, ALEXANDER. *b.* 7 May 1807; 2 Lieut. R.M. 13 May 1823; col. commandant 21 Nov. 1859 to death; general 1 April 1870; C.B. 2 June 1869. *d.* St. Alban's place, St. James's London 21 Nov. 1877.

ANDERSON, REV. ALEXANDER. *b.* Peterhead 1808; ed. at St. Andrew's; founder and head of Chanonry house school (the Gymnasium) Old Aberdeen. *d.* Aboyne 25 Oct. 1884.

ANDERSON, ALEXANDER DUNLOP (*son of Andrew Anderson of Greenock, merchant). b.* Greenock 1794; M.R.C.S. 1816, M.D. Edin. 1819; asst. surgeon 49 foot 22 June 1815 to 25 Dec. 1818, when placed on half pay; practised in Glasgow; surgeon to royal infirmary 1822 and phys. 1837; pres. of faculty of phys. and surgeons 1852–55; pres. of Med. Chir. society of Glasgow. *d.* 159 St. Vincent st. Glasgow 13 May 1871.

ANDERSON, ALFRED. Celebrated Australian pianist. *m.* at Sydney 29 Dec. 1875 Ilma de Murska, the "Hungarian nightingale." *d.* Melbourne 22 March 1876 aged 28.

ANDERSON, ANDREW. A stocking weaver. Champion draught player of Scotland; author of *The Game of Draughts* 1848, 2 ed. 1852, 3 ed. 1878. *d.* Braidwood near Carluke, Lanarkshire 1 March 1861.

ANDERSON, ARTHUR (*eld. son of Robert Anderson of Grimaster, Shetland). b.* Grimaster, Feb. 1792; midshipman R.N. 1810; a merchant in London 1823; superintended naval portion of expedition to Portugal under Don Pedro 1831–32; started a line of steamers to the Peninsula 1836; formed fishery establishment in Orkney and Shetland 1838; member of Anti-corn law league formed at Manchester 18 Sep. 1838, took an active part in it; a founder of Peninsular and Oriental steam navigation company incorporated 1840; their first boat the Hindostan was started Sep. 1842; chairman of the company; chairman of Union steamship company and of Crystal palace company; M.P. for Orkney (lib.) 1 Sep. 1847 to 1 July 1852; F.S.A.; author of *Communication with India, China, &c.* 1843; *National defence* 1852. *d.* Norwood, Surrey 28 Feb. 1868. *I.L.N. xviii,* 232 (1851), *portrait.*

ANDERSON, CHARLES ABERCROMBY. Inspector general of hospitals and fleets 12 April 1869 to death; C.B. 17 June 1871. *d.* London 25 Feb. 1872.

ANDERSON, CHRISTOPHER (*youngest son of William Anderson of Edin. ironmonger 1744–1804). b.* West Bow, Edin. 19 Feb. 1782; clerk in the Friendly Insurance Office 1800–1804; ordained pastor of English baptists in Edin. 21 Jany. 1808; originated the Edinburgh Bible Society Oct. 1810, the Gaelic School Society Nov. 1810; author of *The annals of the English bible,* 2 vols. 1845, 2 ed. 1862. *d.* Edinburgh 18 Feb. 1852. *The life and letters of Christopher Anderson, by his nephew Hugh Anderson* 1854, *portrait.*

ANDERSON, SIR GEORGE CAMPBELL (*son of John Anderson). b.* 1804 or 1805; admitted attorney in Bahama 1827; speaker of House of Assembly, Bahama 1831 to 1868; attorney general 1837; knighted by patent 16 Sep. 1874; chief justice 11 Oct. 1875; president of legislative council 1875; acting chief justice, Ceylon 1875–77; chief justice of Leeward islands 27 March 1877–1880. *d.* Kingston, Jamaica 1 March 1884.

ANDERSON, George Frederick. *b.* Carlton palace, London 1793; member of royal private band 1819, conductor 1847–48; master of the Music 1848–70; band changed by Prince Albert from a mere wind band to a full orchestra 24 Dec. 1840; treasurer of Philharmonic society, and of Royal Society of musicians. *(m.* 1820 Lucy Philpot). *d.* 34 Nottingham place, London 14 Dec. 1876. *bur.* Kensal Green 20 Dec.

ANDERSON, Sir George William *(son of Robert Anderson of London, merchant).* *b.* London 1791; ed. at Haileybury; entered Bombay civil service 1806; senior judge of the Sudder Dewanee 1833; member of council 8 March 1838; governor of Bombay 27 April 1841 to 28 July 1842, of the Manritius 9 Feb. 1849 to Oct. 1850, of Ceylon Oct. 1850 to Feb. 1855; knighted by the Queen at St. James's palace 22 Feb. 1849; C.B. 22 March 1849, K.C.B. 22 Nov. 1850. *(m.* (1) 1813 Caroline 2 dau. of John Proby Kensington of Lime Grove, Putney. *m.* (2) 1833 Jane dau. of Archibald Wight of Ormiston, East Lothian). *d.* 99 Westbourne terrace, London 17 March 1857. *G. M. ii,* 493-94 (1857).

ANDERSON, Sir Henry Lacon *(eld. son of the preceding).* *b.* Surat, East Indies 1817; ed. at St. Paul's, at St. John's coll. Ox. and Haileybury; entered Bombay civil service 1840; judge of Kandeish 1853; sec. to government of Bombay in political and judicial departments 1854; chief sec. to government 1860; mem. of council of India for making laws and regulations 1863–1865, when he retired; sec. to India Board in judicial, public and sanitary departments 1866; K.C.S.I. for long service in Bombay 24 May 1867. *(m.* 1841 Anne Grace 4 dau. of Hope Stewart of Ballechin, Perthshire, she *d.* 19 Feb. 1885). *d.* 46 Leinster gardens, London 7 April 1879 aged 62.

ANDERSON, Rev. James. *b.* Newburgh; ed. at St. Andrew's Univ.; B.D., D.D.; author of *The Course of creation* 1846; *Dura Den, a monograph* 1859. *d.* Nice 16 March 1864 aged 65.

ANDERSON, Sir James *(son of John Anderson of Stirling, merchant).* *b.* Stirling 1800; a manufacturer at Glasgow; lord provost 1848–49; knighted by the Queen at Glasgow 14 Aug. 1849; M.P. for Stirling (lib.) 13 July 1852 to 23 April 1859. *(m.* 1831 Janet only dau. of Robert Hood of Glasgow). *d.* Blairvadick, Dumbartonshire 8 May 1864.

ANDERSON, James. *b.* Cumberland; went to Rome before 1839; became well known there as a photographer under name of Isaac Atkinson. *d.* Rome 28 Feb. 1877. *Law Reports xxi Chancery division* 100-104 (1882).

ANDERSON, James. *b.* 1797; entered navy 17 Sep. 1808; captain 1 Nov. 1849; retired admiral 21 March 1878. *d.* Teignmouth, Devon 7 March 1882 in 85 year.

ANDERSON, Rev. James. ed. at Univ. of Aberdeen; lived at Morpeth 1844 to death; the first moderator of Presbyterian church of England; D.D. St. Andrew's 12 Feb. 1878. *d.* The Manse, Morpeth 17 May 1882 in 87 year.

ANDERSON, Sir James Caleb, 1 Baronet *(elder son of John Anderson of Fermoy co. Cork, merchant, by his 2 wife Elizabeth only dau. of James Semple, of Waterford, she d. 3 April 1830).* *b.* Waterford 21 July 1792; created a baronet 22 March 1813 as a mark of approbation of the services rendered to Ireland by his father, who advanced the civilization of Ireland fully 50 years; improved steam locomotion. *(m.* 1815 Caroline 4 dau. of Robert Shaw of Dublin, she *d.* 1859). *d.* London 4 April 1861. *D. O. Madden's Revelations of Ireland* (1848) 268-85.

ANDERSON, Sir James Eglinton *(eld. son of W. Anderson of Glasgow, merchant, by a dau. of James Eglinton).* *b.* 1788; ed. Univ. of Glasgow; M.D. Edin. and Dublin; entered medical department of the navy 1808; surgeon 19 Aug. 1811; Surgeon to one of royal yachts 1827 to Nov. 1833, when he retired from the service; M.R.C.P.; Physician in ord. to Lord Lieut. of Ireland; knighted by him 1829; M.R.I.A. *(m.* 1819 Jane 3 dau. of Rev. W. Learmont of Luce Abbey, she *d.* 20 Sep. 1857). *d.* 7 Harley st. London 29 Feb. 1856.

ANDERSON, Rev. James Stuart Murray. ed. at Ball. coll. Ox.; B.A. 1821, M.A. 1823; P.C. of St. George's, Brighton 1831-51; chaplain in ord. to the Queen 1844; preacher of Lincoln's Inn 1844–1859; R. of Tormarton, Gloucs. 1851; hon. canon of Bristol 1856; British chaplain at Bonn 1859; author of *The history of the church of England in the colonies and foreign dependencies of the British empire,* 3 vols. 1845–56, 2 ed. 1856; *Addresses on miscellaneous subjects* 1849, 2 ed. 1858, and many sermons. *d.* Bonn 22 Sep. 1869. *I.L.N. xxvi,* 269 (1855) *portrait.*

ANDERSON, Rev. John. b. Craig farm, parish of Kilpatrick-Durham, Galloway 23 May 1805; ed. at Univ. of Edin; ordained a minister of church of Scotland 13 July 1836; sent out to Madras as a missionary 1836; baptised his first converts 20 June 1841; joined the Free Church at the disruption 1 July 1843; the mission was then carried on in connection with that church; established many schools both for boys and girls; published the *Native Herald*, a bimonthly periodical 2 Oct. 1841. d. Madras 25 March 1855. *Rev. John Braidwood's True Yoke-fellows in the mission field* 1862, *portrait*.

ANDERSON, John. Col. 43 Madras N.I. 7 Jan. 1843 to 7 Feb. 1848; col. 37 Madras N.I. 7 Feb. 1848 to death; L.G. 23 Sep. 1857. d. Folkestone 22 July 1858.

ANDERSON, John (son of *Wm. Anderson of Green st. London, horse dealer*). Partner with his father many years; the first man to direct attention to the value of action in horses; Anderson's Steppers were known all over Europe; kept steppers in Green st., hacks in Bryanston st. and hunters at Mapesbury farm, Willesden lane, which is minutely described in Edmund Yates's first novel; *Broken to harness* 1865. d. Jany. 1864 aged 55. *Sporting Gazette* 11 *Feb.* 1865, *p.* 113.

Note.—His horses were sold 7-9 Feb. 1865 for sum of £20898 average £205 each horse, which exceeded in value any previous sale of horses in this country.

ANDERSON, John. Col. 61 Bengal N.I. 7 July 1842 to death; General 14 Jan. 1864. d. Norwood, Surrey 25 April 1866 aged 84.

ANDERSON, Rev. John Henry. b. Oakham 4 July 1841; Wesleyan Methodist minister 1862 to death. d. on board the "Lorraine" in latitude 28°31 S. longitude 61°46 E. in the Indian ocean 3 Jany. 1880. *Memorials of Rev. J. H. Anderson* 1882, *portrait*.

ANDERSON, John Henry, known as Professor Anderson the Wizard of the North (*eld. child of Mr. Anderson of Aberdeen, mason*). b. estate of Craigmyle parish of Kincardine, Aberdeenshire 14 July 1814; call boy in Ryder's theatrical company in Scotland 1824; first performed as a conjuror in small towns of north of Scotland 1831; performed in Waterloo rooms, Edinburgh 100 nights in 1837; erected a building called The Temple of Magic at Glasgow, seated for 2000 spectators, and performed in it 200 nights in 1838 and 1839; first appeared in London at Strand theatre 1840, when he displayed finest col-

ANDERSON, John Henry. (*Con.*)
lection of apparatus that had ever been seen in London, performed there 4 months; converted St. James's bazaar in St. James's street, into a Temple of Magic 1840; performed in Ireland 1840; built theatre at Glasgow which was burnt; performed at Alexandrisky theatre, St. Petersburg, and in all chief cities of central Europe; at Covent Garden 1846, at the Strand; in America 1851–53; before the Queen at Balmoral 1853; lessee of Lyceum theatre, London, Sep. 1855; of Covent Garden 24 Dec. 1855 where he produced a pantomime and the drama of Rob Roy in which he acted Rob Roy; the theatre was burnt down 5 March 1856; performed at Sadler's Wells 1856; abroad 1856–64, at St. James's hall, London 1864–65; went to India and Australia. d. Fleece hotel, Darlington 3 Feb. 1874. bur. St. Nicholas churchyard, Aberdeen 7 Feb. *Frost's Lives of the conjurors* (1876) 228–60; *The Era* 8 *Feb.* 1874, *p.* 4, *col.* 1; 15 *Feb. p.* 4, *col.* 3.

ANDERSON, Joseph Jocelyn. b. 1789; ensign 78 foot 27 June 1805; served in Peninsula 1809–12; lieut. col. 50 foot 1 April 1841 to 19 Sep. 1848 when he sold out; military commander and civil superintendent of convicts Norfolk Island; commanded a brigade in Gwalior campaign 1843; a squatter on the Goulburn Victoria; member of legislative council 1852; K.H. 1837, C.B. 2 May 1844. d. Fairlie house, South Yarra 18 July 1877. bur. St. Kilda cemetery 21 July. *I.L.N. lxxi*, 347, 348 (1877), *portrait*.

ANDERSON, Lucy (dau. of *John Philpot of Bath*). b. Bath Dec. 1790; made her début at Philharmonic Society's concerts 1822; Pianist to Queen Adelaide 1832; Pianist to Queen Victoria 1837; gave her last concert 30 May 1862 in Her Majesty's theatre; granted a civil list pension of £100 23 July 1840. (*m.* 1820 George Frederick Anderson). d. 34 Nottingham place, London 24 Dec. 1878 bur. Kensal Green cemetery 31 Dec. *I.L.N. xli*, 77 (1862), *portrait*.

ANDERSON, Paul (2 son of *James Anderson of Grace Dieu, co. Waterford, by Susanna youngest dau. of Christmas Paul*). b. 29 March 1767; ensign 51 foot 31 March 1788; lieut. col. 60 foot 14 Jany. 1808 to 25 Feb. 1817 when placed on h. p.; commander of Gravesend and Tilbury forts 1 Dec. 1827, of Pendennis castle 23 July 1832; col. 78 foot 9 Feb. 1837 to death; general 11 Nov. 1851; C.B. 4 June 1815, K.C. d. Bath 17 Dec. 1851.

ANDERSON, REV. PHILIP (*son of Mr. Anderson, captain H.E.I.Co.*) Entered St. Paul's school 7 Oct. 1824 aged 8; Pauline exhibitioner C. C. coll. Cam. 1834; B.A. 1838, M.A. 1849; chaplain at Colaba, Bombay Nov. 1849 to death; began *Bombay quarterly magazine* 1850; edited *Bombay quarterly review* Jany. 1855; author of *The English in Western India* 1854. *d.* Malabar hill, Bombay 13 Dec. 1857.

ANDERSON, REV. RICHARD. *b.* 16 Jany. 1792; ed. at Linc. coll Ox., B.A. 1815; V. of ¿Burreston, Yorkshire 1834–54; P.C. of Leeming, Yorkshire 1868–79; chairman of Leeming school board to 1879. *d.* Aisken house near Bedale 24 Oct. 1884

NOTE.—He was the survivor of the celebrated trio of hardriding Yorkshire clergymen mentioned by "Nimrod" in his *Sporting Tour* as hunting with the Earl of Darlington's hounds.

ANDERSON, ROBERT. *b.* Fettercairn, Aberdeenshire; assistant surgeon R.N. 1838; surgeon of the Investigator and Enterprise in the Arctic seas 1848–55; made a large collection illustrative of natural history of Arctic regions, zoological specimens were sent to British Museum, dried plants to Kew, and fossil remains to Geological society. *d.* June 1856 aged 38.

NOTE.—Anderson bay on Victoria land is named after him.

ANDERSON, ROBERT STERLING HORE. *b.* near Coleraine; ed. at Belfast academy and Dublin Univ.; solicitor in Dublin 1846, in Melbourne, Victoria 1854; M.P. for Emerald Hill 1855; comr. of customs 1860–61, 1862–63 and 1875–77; repres. of Eastern province in legislative council; minister for justice. *d.* Melbourne 26 Oct. 1883 aged 62.

ANDERSON, SAMUEL. *b.* London 15 Nov. 1839; secretary to American land boundary commission 1869; chief astronomer to North American boundary commission 14 June 1872; returned to England 30 June 1875; comr. for demarcation of frontier of Servia 1 April 1879; major R.E. 13 Sep. 1879 to death; C.M.G. 30 May 1877. *d.* Dalhousie grange, Bonnyrigg, Midlothian 11 Sep. 1881.

ANDERSON, THOMAS. Colonel 3 Madras light cavalry 21 Dec. 1859 to death; M.G. 21 April 1863. *d.* 9 Thurloe square, London 27 May 1864.

ANDERSON, THOMAS (*eld. son of Thomas Anderson, sec. to National bank of Scotland*). *b.* Edin. 26 Feb. 1832; M.D. Edin. 1853; in Bengal medical service 1854 to death; surgeon 20 May 1866; had medical charge of

ANDERSON, T. (*Con.*)

Hodson's Horse during the mutiny; superintendent of forest department 1864–66; director of Calcutta botanic garden 1869 to death; worked out the flora of India; author of *Florula Adenensis* 1860 and more than 20 other papers in journal of Linnæan society, &c. *d.* Edin. 26 Oct. 1870. *Trans. Bot. Soc. Edin. ii,* 41–45 (1873).

ANDERSON, THOMAS. *b.* 2 July 1819; M.D. Edin. 1841; F.R.S. Edin. 1845, Keith medallist 1855; chemist to Highland and Agricultural society of Scotland 1848–73; regius professor of chemistry in Univ. of Glasgow 1852; pres. of Glasgow philosophical society 1859; pres. of chemical section of British Association at Dundee 1867; royal medallist of Royal Society 1872. *d.* Chiswick near London 2 Nov. 1874. *Journal of chemical society of London* (1875) 1309–13.

ANDERSON, THOMAS. Ensign 78 foot 1845, served with it 18 years chiefly in India; captain 17 Aug. 1857 to 24 March 1863 when he sold out; Persian interpreter to Sir Willoughby Cotton and Sir John Grey commanders in chief at Bombay; adjutant general of militia in New Brunswick; commanded the frontier field force there during threatened Fenian invasion 1866. *d.* Westward Ho, Devonshire 11 Feb. 1876 aged 48.

ANDERSON, WILLIAM (*son of James Anderson of Oban, Argyleshire, supervisor of excise who d. 1812.*) *b.* Edin. 10 Dec. 1805; joined *Aberdeen Journal* 1831; edited *Aberdeen Advertiser* 1835; *The Western Watchman* a weekly journal at Ayr 1842; sub edited *The Witness* newspaper at Edin. 1844; chief sub editor of *North British Daily Mail* 14 April 1847 to 1849, this was first daily paper in Scotland; author of *Poetical Aspirations* 1830, 2 ed. 1833; *Landscape Lyrics* 1839, 2 ed. 1854; *The Scottish nation* 3 vols. 1860–62. *d.* London 2 Aug. 1866. *J. G. Wilson's Poets and poetry of Scotland ii,* 269–72 (1877).

ANDERSON, WILLIAM. Lieut. col. Bengal artillery 6 March 1854 to 20 Feb. 1855; C.B. 24 Dec. 1842. *d.* Albury hall, Ware, Herts 22 Sep. 1869 aged 64.

ANDERSON, REV. WILLIAM (2 *son of Rev. John Anderson, Relief minister at Kilsyth near Glasgow*). *b.* Kilsyth 6 Jany. 1799; licensed by Relief presbytery Glasgow 5 Sep. 1820; minister of John st. church Glasgow 6 March 1821 to 24 Dec. 1871, the church was pulled down in 1858 and a new church opened by him 1 Jany. 1860; LL.D. Glasgow April 1850;

ANDERSON, REV. W. *(Con).*

author of *An apology for the organ* 1829; *Discourses* 1st series 1844, 2nd series 1859; *Regeneration* 1850, 3 ed. 1875. d. Prospect house, Uddingstone near Glasgow 15 Sep. 1872. *Rev. G. Gilfillan's Life of Rev. W. Anderson* 1873, *portrait; Reunion in the heavenly kingdom by the Rev. Wm. Anderson* 1876, *portrait.*

ANDERSON, WILLIAM ACLAND DOUGLAS *(son of Joseph Jocelyn Anderson, C.B.)* b. 1829; captain 65 foot 1852–54; a comr. of gold fields in Victoria; col. commandant of all the volunteer corps in Victoria 1862; C.M.G. 25 May 1878. d. South Yarra 23 Jany. 1882.

ANDERSON, WILLIAM COCHRANE. b. East Lothian 1792; col. R.A. 20 June 1854 to 26 Oct. 1858; M.G. 26 Oct. 1858. d. Edge hill near Edin. 30 Aug. 1865 aged 73.

ANDERSSEN, ADOLF. b. Breslau 6 July 1818; gained 1st prize at London chess tournaments 1851 and 1862; 2nd prize at Manchester 1857; 1st prize at Baden 1870; 3rd prize at Vienna 1873; beaten by Paul Morphy at Paris Dec. 1858, losing 7 out of 9 games; an unrivalled player in the beauty of his combinations. d. Breslau 14 March 1879. *Westminster chess club papers x,* 39 (1878), *portrait; Chess players chronicle iii,* 73–75 (1879).

ANDERTON, JAMES. b. near Lincoln 1782; solicitor in London 1811; common councilman for ward of Farringdon Without 1836–66; undersheriff several times; projected Law life assurance society 1823; founded Solicitors benevolent institution 1858. d. Cypress lodge, Dulwich 23 Jany. 1868.

ANDRÉE, RICHARD COLLIER. Colonel 7 Bengal N.I. 20 June 1836 to 28 Sep. 1850; colonel 69 Bengal N.I. 28 Sep. 1850 to death; general 2 Nov. 1861. d. Stuttgart 27 March 1865 aged 70.

ANDREW, JAMES *(son of Rev. James Andrew, the first principal of East India college at Addiscombe, Surrey who d. 13 June 1833 in 60 year).* b. Addiscombe college 1811; ed. at Caius coll. Cam.; studied medicine at Edin. while he kept his terms at Cam.; M.D. Cam. 1839; practised at Edin.; phys to Royal infirmary 1846–56; F.R.C.P. Edin., member of council; F.R.S. Edin. d. 15 Queen st. Edin. 1 Dec. 1859.

ANDREW, JOHN WILLIAM, Captain R.N. 26 Sep. 1812; C.B. 4 June 1815; retired R.A. 1 Oct. 1846. d. Chudleigh 5 Jany. 1854.

ANDREW, WILLIAM. b. Glasgow 1804; ed. at Marischal coll. Aberdeen; professor of mathematics in Mc Gill coll. Quebec; rector of the high school Quebec; edited the *Daily Chronicle* Quebec. d. Aberdeen 1862.

ANDREWS, ALEXANDER. Author of *The eighteenth century* 1856; *The history of British journalism,* 2 vols. 1859. d. Albion grove, Stoke Newington 9 Nov. 1873 aged 50.

ANDREWS, AUGUSTUS. Entered Madras army 1793; col. of 27 N.I. 5 June 1829, of 42 N.I. 21 Feb. 1834, of 1 N.I. 5 Jany. 1837, of 8 N.I. 2 Oct. 1848, and of 39 N.I. 4 July 1856 to death; general 16 March 1855; C.B. 23 July 1823. d. Vellore, Bath 3 March 1858 aged 78.

ANDREWS, BIGGS. b. 1794; barrister M.T. 12 Nov. 1819; bencher 21 April 1837, treasurer 1846; K.C. 24 Feb. 1837; comr. of bankrupts for Exeter district 16 Dec. 1858 to 31 Dec. 1869 when granted £1,800 on abolition of his office. d. Heavitree house near Exeter 28 April 1880 in 86 year.

ANDREWS, GEORGE. b. London 1798; made his début as Lothair in *Adelgitha* at Manchester 1819; first appeared in America Oct. 1827 as Bob Acres in *The Rivals* at Federal st. theatre Boston; acted in New York 1838, in Philadelphia 1842; left the stage and managed old Chinese Buildings, New York as a ball room. d. New York 7 April 1866.

ANDREWS, HARRY. b. Monmouthshire 28 May 1831; a pedestrian; won the Four Miles champion cup at Bow; defeated the American Deer, Whitmore, Deerfoot, and many others; managed running grounds at Lillie Bridge and Surbiton. d. Cottage grove, Surbiton 7 March 1885.

ANDREWS, HENRY OGDEN *(youngest son of Charles Savery Andrews, captain 24 foot).* b. St. John's, Newfoundland 28 April 1808; ed. at Stratford on Avon, and in Canada; called to Canadian bar; Q.C. d. 37 Lansdowne crescent, Leamington 25 March 1884.

ANDREWS, JANE *(dau. of Mr. Constant).* b. 1817; vocal composer and teacher. *(m.* John Holman Andrews). d. 60 Baker st. Portman sq. London 29 March 1878.

ANDREWS, RICHARD *(son of Thomas Andrews of Bramdean, Hants, wheelwright).* b. Bishop Sutton near Alresford 18 Dec. 1798; a coachmaker at Southampton 1 Oct. 1832 to death; sold more than 300 carriages for £22,000 in 1845; built state carriages for Mehemet Ali

ANDREWS, R. (Con.)

and the Sultan ; one of first members of Anti-Corn-law league ; sheriff of Southampton 1848, mayor 1849, 1850, 1851 and 31 May 1856 to Dec. 1856 ; contested Southampton Dec. 1856 ; gave a great banquet to Louis Kossuth on his arrival in England 25 Oct. 1851. *d.* Portland st. Southampton 28 March 1859. *I.L.N. xix,* 549 (1851), *xx,* 12 (1852), *portrait.*

ANDREWS, ROBERT. Colonel R.A. 20 June 1854 to 7 June 1856 ; M.G. 7 June 1856. *d.* Sunderland terrace, Westbourne park, London 1 Nov. 1863.

ANDREWS, ROBERT. Called to Irish bar 1825 ; Q.C. 7 Feb. 1849. *d.* 1865.

ANDREWS, WILLIAM. *b.* Chichester 1802 ; made many valuable additions to the flora and fauna of south west of Ireland ; his name will be perpetuated in names of Trichomanes Andrewsii, and Galathea Andrewsii ; a founder and subsequently sec. and pres. of Natural history society of Dublin ; chairman of Natural history committee of Royal society of Dublin many years ; M.R.I.A. 10 Jany. 1842. *d.* Dublin 11 March 1880. *Journal of botany* (1880) 256–86.

ANGAS, CALEB. *b.* 1782 ; a farmer at Brancepeth and at Neswick farm, East Yorkshire about 1815 to death ; the best authority on farming in the East Riding ; wrote letters in the *Sun* newspaper on Free Trade which excited much attention and were of great service. *d.* Driffield, Yorkshire 6 Feb. 1860.

ANGAS, GEORGE FIFE. *b.* Newcastle 1 May 1789 ; senior partner of G. F. Angas & Co. shipowners and merchants 2 Jeffrey sq. London 1824–33 when he retired to Devonshire ; originated National and Provincial bank of England 1833 ; one of the first comrs. for formation of colony of South Australia 1834 ; established South Australian company 1836, Union bank of Australia 1837, and Bank of South Australia 1841 ; chairman of London boards of direction of these 3 companies down to 1850 ; arrived in Adelaide 15 Jany. 1851 ; M.P. for district of Barossa in 1st legislative council July 1851–1871 ; leading spirit in colonizing South Australia. *d.* Lindsey park Angaston, South Australia 15 May 1879.

ANGELL, ALFRED. Organist of Exeter cathedral 34 years. *d.* The Close, Exeter 24 May 1876 aged 60.

ANGELL, HELEN CORDELIA (5 *dau. of Wm. Thomas Coleman, M.D. of Horsham, Sussex).* *b.* Horsham Jany. 1847 ; exhibited drawings of flowers at Dudley Gallery 1864, afterwards called The general water colour society, and 6 flower pictures at the R.A. 1876–78 ; the only successor of Wm. Hunt. *(m.* Oct. 1875 Thomas Wm. Angell, Postmaster of the S.W. district of London). *d.* 55 Holland road, Kensington 8 March 1884. *Clayton's English female artists ii,* 261–63 (1876).

ANGELL, JOHN BENEDICT, ed. at Eton and Magd. coll. Ox. ; won first Grand national hunt steeplechase at Farndon village with Bridegroom 1860 and second with Queensferry 1861 ; won Liverpool Grand national with Alcibiade 1865 ; one of chief revivers of coaching ; commonly known as " Cherry " Angell ; the hero of C. Clarke's novel *A box for the season. d.* 36 Curzon st. London 12 May 1874. *Illust. sporting and dramatic news i,* 400 (1874), *portrait.*

ANGELO, EDWARD ANTHONY. Captain 30 foot 9 Aug. 1831 to 12 Dec. 1834 when placed on h. p. ; K.H. 1827 ; a military knight of Windsor 1854 to death. *d.* Windsor Castle 26 Aug. 1869.

ANGELO, HENRY. Superintendent of sword exercise to the army 1833 to death. *d.* Brighton 14 Oct. 1852 aged 72. *G. M. xxxviii,* 543 (1852).

ANGERSTEIN, JOHN. M.P. for Greenwich 10 Jany. 1835 to 17 July 1837. *d.* the Woodlands, Blackheath 10 April 1858 aged 85.

ANGERSTEIN, JOHN JULIUS WILLIAM. *b.* 1800 ; major Grenadier guards 27 Dec. 1850 to 20 June 1854 ; L. G. 2 Feb. 1862 ; col. 4 West India regiment 14 Jany. 1866 to death. *d.* Weeting hall near Brandon, Norfolk 23 April 1866.

ANGLESEY, HENRY WILLIAM PAGET, 1 Marquess of *(eld. child of Henry Bayly,* 1 *Earl of Uxbridge* 1744–1812). *b.* 17 May 1768 ; ed. at Westminster and Ch. Ch. Ox., M.A. 1786 ; M.P. for Carnarvon 1790–96 and 1806-10 ; M.P. for Milbourn Port 1796–1804 ; raised among his father's tenantry 80th regiment of foot or Staffordshire volunteers ; lieut. col. commandant of it 12 Sep. 1793 to 16 June 1795 ; lieut. col. 16 light dragoons 16 June 1795 ; lieut. col. 7 light dragoons 6 April 1797 and col. 16 May 1801 to 20 Dec. 1842 ; succeeded 13 March 1812 ; lord lieut. of Anglesey 21 April 1812 to death ; G.C.B. 2 Jany. 1815 ; created Marquess of Anglesey 4 July 1815 ; G.C.H. 1816 ; K.G. 19 Feb.

ANGLESEY, 1 MARQUESS OF. *(Con.)*

1818; general 12 Aug. 1819; lord high steward at coronation of George iv, 19 July 1821; master general of the ordnance 1827–28 and 1846–52; P.C. 30 April 1827; lord lieut. of Ireland 1828–29 and 1830–33; col. of royal horse guards 20 Dec. 1842 to death; field marshal 9 Nov. 1846; lord lieut. of Staffs. 31 Jany. 1849 to death. *d.* 1 Old Burlington st. London 29 April 1854. *bur.* in Lichfield cathedral 6 May. *J. W. Cole's British generals i,* 109–44 (1856), *portrait; N. and Q. 3rd series ii,* 249, 320, 339; *H. Martineau's Biographical sketches,* 4 *ed.* 1876 57–63.

NOTE.—In a garden close to the church at Waterloo is a monument to his right leg lost in the battle; he refused a pension of £1,200 per annum granted him for this loss, thus saving his country nearly £47,000.

ANGLESEY, HENRY PAGET, 2 Marquess of *(eld. son of preceding). b.* 6 July 1797; M.P. for Anglesey 1820–32; summoned to House of Lords as Baron Paget of Beaudesert 15 Jany. 1833; col. in the army 28 June 1838, retired 1843; lord chamberlain of the Queen's household 6 May 1839 to 14 Sep. 1841; P.C. 22 May 1839; succeeded 29 April 1854; lord lieut. of Anglesey 18 May 1854 to death; kept a racing stud 1831–35 and 1854 to death; made on the high ground above Beaudesert near Lichfield one of best cricket grounds in England. *d.* Beaudesert 6 Feb. 1869. *Baily's Mag. v,* 51–54 (1863), *portrait.*

ANGLESEY, HENRY WILLIAM GEORGE PAGET, 3 Marquess of. *b.* 9 Dec. 1821; lieut. col. 2 Staffordshire militia 5 Jany. 1853 to 29 Sep. 1855; M.P. for south Staffs 1854–57; succeeded 6 Feb. 1869. *d.* 10 Albert mansions, Victoria st. London 30 Jany. 1880.

ANGUS, GEORGE. Surgeon Bengal medical service 1836; sec. to medical board at Calcutta; superintending surgeon at Benares, and at Cawnpore; retired 1854; pres. of Medical society of Aberdeen 2 years; manager of royal infirmary and general dispensary, Aberdeen. *d.* 13 Golden sq. Aberdeen 7 April 1872 in 78 year.

ANGUS, REV. HENRY. *b.* Inverkeithing, Fifeshire 18 Oct. 1794; minister of St. Nicholas' lane united presbyterian church, Aberdeen 1813; author of *Works of fiction, their use and abuse* 1853. *d.* Aberdeen 28 June 1860. *Sermons by the late Rev. Henry Angus, edited with a memoir by his son Rev. Robert Angus* 1861.

ANNESLEY, WILLIAM RICHARD ANNESLEY, 4 Earl *(eld. son of 3 Earl Annesley 1772–1838). b.* Rutland sq. Dublin 21 Feb. 1830;

ANNESLEY, 4 EARL. *(Con.)*

succeeded 25 Aug. 1838; M.P. for Grimsby 1852–57; established his claim as a peer 24 July 1855; representative peer for Ireland 15 Oct. 1867. *d.* Cowes, Isle of Wight 10 Aug. 1874. *I.L.N. lxv,* 188 (1874), *portrait.*

ANSELL, CHARLES *(eld. son of Thomas Ansell of Lewisham, Kent). b.* 1794; actuary of Atlas insurance office 1823–64; published *A treatise on friendly societies* 1835, when a large professional practice at once fell to his share; completed the Bonus investigation of National provident office; F.R.S. 10 April 1834; F.S.A. 21 June 1828. *d.* 7 Eastern terrace, Brighton 14 Dec. 1881.

ANSELL, GEORGE FREDERICK. *b.* Carshalton, Surrey 4 March 1826; assistant to A. W. Hofman at Royal School of mines; scientific director at Royal Panopticon, Leicester sq. London 1854; employed at Royal mint 12 Nov. 1856 to 31 Dec. 1868; an analyst in London 1869 to death; patented the firedamp indicator 9 March 1865, which was adopted in many foreign collieries. *d.* 6 Hartham road, London 21 Dec. 1880. *The royal mint by G. F. Ansell,* 3 *ed.* 1871.

ANSELL, THOMAS. M.R.C.S. Eng. and L.S.A. 1820; M.D. St. Andrews 1843; surgeon at Bow, London; chairman of Society of Apothecaries 1861 to death; officer of health for Bow; F.L.S. *d.* of cholera at Harley place, Bow road 24 July 1866 in his 68 year.

ANSON, AUGUSTUS HENRY ARCHIBALD. *b.* 5 March 1835; captain 84 foot 1855–58; aide de camp to general Grant in Indian mutiny 1857–58; received Victoria cross for bravery at Bolundshawm and Lucknow 24 Dec. 1858; M.P. for Lichfield 1859–68, and for Bewdley 1869–74. *d.* Cannes 17 Nov. 1877. *Mrs. Fairlie's Portraits of the children of the nobility, 3rd series* 1841, *portrait.*

ANSON, VERY REV. FREDERIC *(youngest son of George Adams of Orgrave, Staffs.* 1731–89 *who assumed name of Anson). b.* 23 March 1779; ed. at Eton, Rugby and Ch. Ch. Ox.; student 1796, B.A. 1801, M.A. 1804, B.D. and D.D. 1839; fellow of All soul's coll. 1799–1803; R. of Sudbury, Derbyshire 1803–36; canon of Southwell, Notts. 7 Oct. 1826; dean of Chester 9 May 1839 to death; R. of Doddleston, Cheshire 1843 to death. *(m.* 2 May 1807 Mary Anne only dau. of Rev. Richard Levett of Milford, Staffs., she *d.* 15 Oct. 1862). *d.* The deanery, Chester 8 May 1867. *bur.* Chester cemetery.

ANSON, GEORGE (2 son of Thomas Anson, 1 Viscount Anson 1767–1818). b. Shugborough near Stafford 13 Oct. 1797; captain 14 dragoons 1823–25 when placed on h.p.; clerk of the Ordnance 1846–52; M.G. 11 Nov. 1851; commanded a division in Bengal 1853 and the Madras army 1854; commander in chief in India 20 Nov. 1855 to death; col. 55 foot 19 Dec. 1856 to death; M.P. for Great Yarmouth 1818–34, for Stoke upon Trent 1836–37, and for South Staffs. 1837–53; a great friend of Duke of York; crack shot of Red House Club, Battersea when pigeon shooting mania was at its height 1828; was never excelled as a judge of racing. d. of cholera at Karnál during the mutiny 27 May 1857. *Fortnightly Review xxxix*, 541–44 (1883).

ANSON, JOHN WILLIAM. b. Marylebone, London 31 July 1817; made his début at T.R. Bath as Lissardo in *The Wonder* 1842; acted in north of England and Ireland 1843–49; manager of Scotch theatres 1849–53; acted at Astley's 1853–59; founded Dramatic, equestrian and musical sick fund 4 July 1855, Dramatic burial ground at Woking 1856, Dramatic college at Woking 1859, (opened by Prince of Wales 5 June 1865) and the G. V. Brooke lifeboat fund 1866; treasurer and acting manager of Adelphi theatre 1858–78; published *Dramatic almanac* 1857–72. d. 50a Lincoln's Inn Fields 6 Feb. 1881. *The Players i*, 185 (1860), *portrait; Anson's dramatic almanac* 1872, *portrait.*

ANSON, SIR JOHN WILLIAM HAMILTON, 2 Baronet. b. London 26 Dec. 1816; ed. at Eton and Trin. coll. Cam.; succeeded 13 Jany. 1847. d. Royal hotel Wigan 2 Aug. 1873 2 hours after accident at Wigan junction station of London and North Western railway. *I.L.N. lxiii*, 134, 135 (1873).

ANSTEAD, THOMAS. b. Twickenham 9 Aug. 1840; a fast round-armed bowler; engaged at the Oval, London 1866; and at Oatlands park club, Weybridge 1869 to death. d. Weybridge 21 July 1875.

ANSTED, DAVID THOMAS (son of Wm. Ansted). b. London 5 Feb. 1814; ed. at Jesus coll. Cam. 32 wrangler 1836; B.A. 1836, M.A. 1839; Ley fellow of his college 1840–1851; professor of geology in King's college London April 1840–1853; professor of geology at college of Civil Engineers Putney 1845; consulting geologist and mining engineer 1850 to death; F.G.S. 1838, Sec. 1844–1847; F.R.S. 11 Jany. 1844; edited *Quarterly Journal of Geological Society;* author of *An elementary course of geology* 1850, 2 ed. 1856; *Physi-*

cal geography 1867, 5 *ed.* 1871 and many other books. (m. 24 June 1848 Augusta Dorothea Hackett youngest dau. of Alexander Baillie of Green st. Grosvenor sq.) d. Melton near Woodbridge 20 May 1880. *Proc. of Royal society xxxi*, 1 (1881).

ANSTER, JOHN (eld. son of John Anster of Charleville, Cork). b. Charleville 1793; ed. at Trin coll. Dublin; scholar 1814, B.A. 1816, LL.B. and LL.D. 1825; barrister 1824; registrar of high court of admiralty Ireland 1837 to death; granted civil list pension of £150 30 Aug. 1841; regius professor of civil law Trin. coll. Dub. 1850 to death; M.R.I.A. 12 Feb. 1838; vice pres. 1849–52; author of *Faustus from the German of Goethe*, 2 parts 1835–64 the first English translation and thrice reprinted in Germany. *Xeniola, poems including translations from Schiller and De la Motte Fouqué* 1837. (m. 1832 Elizabeth eld. dau. of Wm. Blacker Bennett of Castle Crea, co. Limerick, she was granted a civil list pension of £50 3 Aug. 1870). d. Dublin 9 June 1867. *Dublin Univ. Mag. xiv*, 544–46 (1839), *portrait.*

ANSTEY, THOMAS CHISHOLM (2 son of Thomas Anstey of Anstey Barton, Tasmania, sheep farmer and member of legislative council who d. 23 May 1851 aged 73). b. London 1816; ed. at Wellington Somerset, and Univ. college London; articled to J. A. Frampton of 10 New Inn, London, solicitor; one of the first affected by the Oxford tractarian movement who went over to Rome; barrister Middle Temple 25 Jany. 1839; equity draftsman; professor of law and jurisprudence at colleges of St. Peter and St. Paul, Prior park, Bath. some years; comr. for insolvent debtors in Van Diemen's Land a short time; member of the Irish confederation which first met 13 Jany. 1847; M.P. for Youghal (lib.) 7 Aug. 1847 to 1 July 1852; contested Bedford 9 July 1852; signalized himself as the special adversary of Lord Palmerston, moved a kind of general impeachment of him in a speech of 5 hours length during which he never referred to a note for a date, figure or fact 8 Feb. 1848; introduced bills for repeal of Roman catholic penal laws 1848 and 1849; a comr. to revise the statutes March 1853; attorney general at Hong Kong Oct. 1855 to 30 Jany. 1859; poisoned by Ah-lum the Chinese baker there 15 Jany. 1857 but recovered; joined the Bombay bar 1860, became leader of it 1862; acting judge of high court of Bombay as deputy for Sir Joseph Arnould 1865 to 30 Dec. 1865; went

ANSTEY. T. C. *(Con.)*

to England 1866; revising barrister in England 1868; rejoined the Bombay bar 1869; author of *A guide to the laws of England affecting Roman Catholics* 1842; *Guide to the history of the laws and constitutions of England* 1845. (*m.* 1840 Harriet 2 dau. of Gerard Edward Strickland of Loughlin house, co. Roscommon). *d.* Bombay 12 Aug. 1873. *Law mag. and law review* xxi, 136–40 (1866), *xxiii*, 145–55 (1867), *xxvi*, 121–40 (1868); *Law Times lv*, 316–17 and 352–54 (1873); *I.L.N. xvi*, 85 (1849), *portrait; Hansard's Debates xcvi*, 291–311 (1848).

ANSTICE, WILLIAM REYNOLDS. *b.* Shropshire 1807; a solicitor at Iron Bridge; partner in Madeley Wood iron company 1858; manager of the works 1867 to death; devoted much attention to manufacture of cold-blast pig iron; member of Iron and steel institute 1869. *d.* Madeley 28 July 1881.

ANSTIE, FRANCIS EDMUND *(youngest child of Paul Anstie of Devizes, manufacturer). b.* Devizes 11 Dec. 1833; M.R.C.S. and L.S.A. 1856, M.B. London 1857, M.D. 1859; M.R.C.P. 1859, F.R.C.P 1865; assistant phys. Westminster hospital 1860–73, phys. 1873 to death; edited the *Practitioner* 1868 to death, wrote a great deal of it; originated with Ernest Hart inquiry into workhouse system, which resulted in Gathorne Hardy's Metropolitan poor act 1867; author of *Stimulants and narcotics* 1864; *Notes on epidemics* 1866; *Neuralgia and the diseases which resemble it* 1871. *d.* 16 Wimpole st. Cavendish square, 12 Sep. 1874. *Graphic x*, 298, 309 (1874), *portrait; Practitioner xiii*, 241, 305 (1874), *xvi*, 1–43 (1876), *portrait.*

ANSTIE, GEORGE WASHINGTON. *b.* 1800; admitted attorney 1822; practiced at Devizes; worked energetically for parliamentary reform, negro emancipation, corn law repeal and the temperance movement. *d.* Park dale, Devizes 17 July 1882.

ANSTRUTHER, PHILIP. *b.* 12 Sep. 1807; served in China 1841; a prisoner there 6 months; served in Punjab and Kaffir wars; major Madras artillery 1853–58; M.G. 4 Nov. 1858; C.B. 24 Dec. 1842. *d.* Pitcorthie near Fife 18 Feb. 1884.

ANSTRUTHER, PHILIP ROBERT. *b.* 30 June 1841; ensign 94 foot 31 Dec. 1858; lieut. col. 7 Aug. 1880 to death. *d.* Transvaal of wounds received in action 26 Dec. 1880. *I.L.N. lxxviii*, 205 (1881) *portrait.*

ANSTRUTHER, SIR RALPH ABERCROMBIE, 4 baronet. *b.* Grosvenor place, London 1 March 1804; succeeded 2 Aug. 1818; rector of univ. of St. Andrews 1859. *d.* Balcaskie, Fifeshire 18 Oct. 1863.

ANSTRUTHER, SIR WYNDHAM CARMICHAEL, 4 Baronet. *b.* Lincoln's Inn Fields, London 6 March 1793; succeeded Nov. 1831. *d.* Boulogne 10 Sep. 1869.

ANTHONY, CHARLES. Founded the Hereford Times 1832; mayor of Hereford 6 times. *d* The Elms, Hereford 5 Feb. 1885 in 82 year.

ANTRIM, HUGH SEYMOUR MacDONNELL, 4 Earl of. *b.* Portman square, London 7 Aug. 1812; succeeded 26 Oct. 1835. *d.* Glenarm castle, Larne, co. Antrim 18 July 1855.

ANTRIM, MARK MacDONNELL, 5 Earl of. *b.* Portman square, London 3 April 1814; established his claim as an Irish peer 15 July 1858; captain R.N. 1 July 1864. *d.* Glenarm castle 19 Dec. 1869.

ANTROBUS, SIR EDMUND, 2 Baronet. *b.* St. Martin's in the Fields London 17 May 1792; succeeded 6 Feb. 1826. *d.* 146 Piccadilly 4 May 1870.

NOTE.—His personalty was sworn under £300,000 25 June 1870.

ANTROBUS, GIBBS CRAWFURD. *b.* 27 May 1793; sec. of legation to the United States of America 18 June 1816, at Turin 8 Feb. 1823, and at court of the two Sicilies 1 Oct. 1824 to May 1826; M.P. for Aldborough, Yorkshire 1820–26 and for Plympton, Devon 1826–32. *d.* Eaton hall, Congleton 21 May 1861.

APLIN, JOHN GUISE ROGERS. *b.* 7 Nov. 1819; ensign 28 foot 7 Oct. 1837; lieut. col. 48 foot 23 Nov. 1860 to 12 Nov. 1870 when placed on h. p.; L.G. 1 July 1881. *d.* 10 Edith road, West Kensington, London 10 April 1883.

APPERLEY, WILLIAM WYNNE *(son of Charles James Apperley 1778–1843, author of sporting works under pseudonym of Nimrod).* Cornet Bengal cavalry 1823; in charge of Poosah stud in Behar 1840–43 and 1845–52; superintended central division of stud department in Bengal 1854–55; major 3 European light cavalry 1854–61; remount agent at Cape of Good Hope 1857–60; left the service Dec. 1861. *d.* Morben near Machynlleth, Montgomeryshire 25 April 1870 aged 62. *Baily's Mag. xviii*, 253–55 (1870).

APPLEBY, JOHN FREDERICK *(son of John Appleby of Soberton, Hants, farmer)*. *b.* 18 Nov. 1795; captain R.N. 29 Jany. 1838; retired admiral 10 Sep. 1869. *d.* Blackbrook lodge, Fareham 3 Feb. 1878.

APPLEGATH, AUGUSTUS *(son of Augustus Joseph Applegath, captain of H.E.I. Co.'s ship Europa)*. *b.* parish of St. Dunstan, Stepney 17 June 1788; a printer in Nelson sq. Blackfriars road; constructed machines for printing bank notes 1818; erected a printing office in Duke st. Stamford st.; invented the composition ball and roller, and the steam printing press; the first book printed by steam was Waterton's Wanderings; invented with Edward Cowper the four-cylinder machine, and erected it at the Times office 1827; patented vertical machine 1846; erected one at Times office, May 1848, which produced 10,000 impressions per hour; invented a machine for printing 6 colours at once; took out 18 patents for improvements in letterpress and silk printing; established large silk and print works at Crayford, and printing works at Dartford. *d.* Dartford 9 Feb. 1871. *Bohn's Pictorial handbook of London* (1854) 76–86; *N. and Q.* 4 series iii, 485 (1869) vii, 153 (1871); *Dartford Chronicle* 25 Feb. 1871, *p.* 3, *col.* 1.

NOTE.—In the year 1818 Messrs. Applegath and Cowper constructed machines for the Bank of England to print in several colours in perfect register designs for the prevention of forgery; some millions of £1 notes were printed by them in the Bank, but were never issued, in consequence of the resumption of cash payment 1 May 1821.

APPLETON, CHARLES EDWARD CUTTS BIRCHALL *(son of Rev. Robert Appleton, Head master of Reading school who d. 5 Feb. 1875 aged 73)*. *b.* Reading 16 March 1841; Tunbridge fellow of St. John's coll. Ox. 1864 to death; B.A. 1863, D.C.L. 1871; studied at Heidelberg and Berlin; lecturer in philosophy at his college Oct. 1867; lived at Hampstead 1872–77; founded *The Academy* monthly literary paper 9 Oct. 1869, edited it to his death; took an active share in agitation that resulted in passing of Universities act 1877; wrote in the *Theological, Fortnightly* and *Contemporary Reviews;* edited *Essays on the endowment of research* 1876. *d.* Luxor, Upper Egypt 1 Feb. 1879. *Dr. Appleton his life and literary relics, by J. H. Appleton and A. H. Sayce* 1881, *portrait.*

APPLEYARD, GEORGE. Of Westbourne place, Eaton square, London; many years secretary and librarian to the Earls Spencer. *d.* Walmer 30 Aug. 1855.

APPOLD, JOHN GEORGE *(son of Christian Appold of Wilson st. Finsbury, London, fur skin dyer, who was naturalized by 45 George iii, cap. 83)*. *b.* Wilson st. 14 April 1800; a fur skin dyer there 1822; a manager of the London Institution 1844; invented Centrifugal rotary pump which was a prominent feature in International Exhibitions of 1851 and 1862; invented a break used in laying first Atlantic cable 1857; A.I.C.E. May 1850; F.R.S. 2 June 1853. *d.* Clifton Down hotel, Clifton 31 Aug. 1865. *Proc. of Royal society xv,* 1–6 (1867); *Minutes of proc. of instit. of C.E. xxv,* 523–25 (1866).

APTHORP, EAST. Entered Madras army 1820; commandant at Hyderabad 18 March 1859 to 18 April 1860; retired M.G. 31 Dec. 1861; C.B. 16 Nov. 1858. *d.* Amherst lodge, Tunbridge Wells 3 March 1875 aged 69.

ARBUCKLE, BENJAMIN HUTCHESON VAUGHAN. *b.* 1788; captain R.A. 1825–46; L.G. 24 Aug. 1866. *d.* Little Heath, Old Charlton 11 Oct. 1874.

ARBUTHNOT, SIR ALEXANDER DUNDAS YOUNG *(only son of Robert Arbuthnot, lieut. col. 31 foot, who d. 10 July 1796)*. *b.* 1796; captain R.N. 1824–46 when he retired on h.p.; gentleman of Privy Chamber 2 Nov. 1824 to death; col. commandant of depôt at Santander, Spain 26 Oct. 1835; led forlorn hope at storming of Irun; brigadier general in service of Queen of Spain 1838; knighted by Queen Victoria at St. James's palace 25 June 1859; retired admiral 30 Nov. 1863; lord prior of English language of Knights of Malta 16 July 1860 to death. *(m.* 25 May 1827 Catherine Maria 3 dau. of Rev. Charles Eustace of Robertstown co. Kildare). *d.* Shenton hall, Nuneaton, Leics. 8 May 1871.

ARBUTHNOT, CHARLES GEORGE JAMES *(eld. son of Right Hon. Charles Arbuthnot of Woodford house, Thrapstone, who d. 18 Aug. 1850 aged 82)*. *b.* 1801; ed. at Westminster; ensign grenadier guards 26 Dec. 1816; lieut. col. of 72 foot 25 Sep. 1826; of 90 foot 17 May 1831, and of 72 foot 23 Feb. 1838 to 14 April 1843, when placed on h.p.; col. of 89 foot 9 July 1857, and of 91 foot 4 July 1864 to death; general 25 Nov. 1864; M.P. for Tregony 1831–32. *d.* Folkestone 21 Oct. 1870.

ARBUTHNOT, GEORGE. *b.* 1802; clerk in the Treasury 1820 to death; private secretary to 6 successive secretaries of the Treasury; private sec. to Sir Robert Peel when prime minister Feb. 1843; and to Sir Charles Wood when chancellor of the exchequer July 1846;

ARBUTHNOT, G. *(Con.)*

auditor of the civil list 1850 to death. *d.* Surbiton, Surrey 28 July 1865. *Dictionary of national biography ii,* 61 (1885).

ARBUTHNOT, GEORGE BINGHAM. Lieut. col. 8 Madras light cavalry 1 Feb. 1856 to 31 Dec. 1861; retired M.G. 31 Dec. 1861. *d.* Bath 30 May 1867 aged 63.

ARBUTHNOT, SIR ROBERT (4 *son of John Arbuthnot of Rockfleet castle co. Mayo). b.* 1773; captain Coldstream guards 25 July 1814 to 19 July 1821, when placed on h. p.; L.G. 23 Nov. 1841; col. 76 foot 31 May 1843 to death; K.C.B. 2 Jan. 1815, K.T.S. *(m.* Harriot only child of Wm. Vesey of Farmill, Ireland, she *d.* 5 Dec. 1861). *d.* Bonchurch, Isle of Wight 6 May 1853. *Household Words v,* 519 (1852).

ARBUTHNOT, SIR ROBERT KEITH, 2 Baronet. *b.* Edinburgh 9 Sep. 1801; in Bombay civil service 1819-47; succeeded 18 Sep. 1829. *d.* Florence 4 March 1873.

ARBUTHNOT, WILLIAM URQUHART (5 *son of Sir Wm. Arbuthnot,* 1 *Bart.* 1766–1829). *b.* 24 March 1807; ed. at high sch. Edin. and Haileybury college; in the Madras civil service 1826-46; member of firm of Arbuthnot and Co. Madras 1846; returned to England 1858; member of Indian council 21 Sep. 1858 to death; chairman of its finance committee. *(m.* 2 June 1834 Eliza only dau. of Gen. Sir Henry George Andrew Taylor, G.C.B.) *d.* Eaton place, London 11 Dec. 1874. *Graphic xi,* 68 (1875), *portrait.*

ARBUTHNOTT, JOHN, 8 Viscount Arbuthnott *(eld. son of John Arbuthnott,* 7 *Viscount Arbuthnott, who d. 27 Feb.* 1800). *b.* 16 Jany. 1778; Rep. Peer Scotland 1818-47; lord rector of Univ. of Aberdeen; lord lieut. of Kincardineshire to 1847. *d.* Berlin 10 Jany. 1860.

ARBUTHNOTT, SIR HUGH (2 *son of 7 Viscount Arbuthnott). b.* 1780; lieut. col. 52 foot 9 May 1811 to 8 April 1813, when placed on h.p.; col. 38 foot 4 April 1843 to 14 March 1862; col. 79 foot 14 March 1862 to death; general 20 June 1854; M.P. for co. Kincardine 1826-65; C.B. 8 Dec. 1815; K.C.B. 10 Nov. 1862. *d.* 11 July 1868.

ARBUTHNOTT, WILLIAM. *b.* 1786; lieut col. R.A. 23 Nov. 1841 to 1 April 1844 when retired on full pay; general 29 March 1873. *d.* 20 Gloucester road, London 14 Dec. 1876.

ARCEDECKNE, ANDREW *(only son of Andrew Arcedeckne of Glevering hall, Suffolk* 1780–1849). *b.* 1822; ed. at Ch. Ch. Ox.; sent out a cargo of tobacco pipes to our soldiers in the Crimea; sheriff of Suffolk 1856, paid fine of £100 for not having javelin men; commodore of royal London yacht club 18 years. *(m.* 1870 Jane Elsworthy, an actress, she *d.* 5 Oct. 1879 aged 54). *d.* 45 Marlborough hill, St. John's Wood, London 31 May 1871 in 49 year.

NOTE.—Thackeray depicted him in language, manner and gesture as Harry Foker in Pendennis, where there is also an exact woodcut portrait of him.

ARCH, JOHN *(son of William Arch of* 163 *Fenchurch st. London, linen shirt maker).* Apprenticed to George Robinson of 25 Paternoster row, the great publisher of his day; bookseller at corner of Lombard st. and Gracechurch st. 1792, with his brother Arthur Portsmouth Arch who *d.* 9 April 1839; at 61 Cornhill 1810–38; collected the Henry Perkins library, the George Hibbert library, also the London institution library; published many valuable books. *d.* Vassal road, Kennington 1853 aged 87.

ARCHBOLD, JOHN FREDERICK. Barrister L.I. 5 May 1814; author of *The practice of the court of King's Bench in personal actions and ejectment,* 2 vols. 1819, 14 ed. 1885; *A summary of the law relating to pleading and evidence in criminal cases,* 19 ed. 1878; *The parish officer* 1852, 6 *ed.* 1881, and many other legal works. *d.* 15 Gloucester st. Regent's park, London 28 Nov. 1870 aged 85. *J. G. Marvin's Legal bibliography* (1847) 66–70.

ARCHBOLD, ROBERT. M.P. for co. Kildare (radical) 11 Aug. 1837 to 23 July 1847. *d.* Davidstown house near Castle Dermot, co. Kildare 9 March 1855.

ARCHDALL-GRATWICKE, REV. GEORGE. *b.* Derbyshire 21 April 1787; ed. at Em. coll. Cam.; B.A. 1815, M A. 1818, B.D. 1825, D.D. 1835; fellow of his college; dean, bursar, prœlector and steward; master May 1835 to death; vice chancellor of Cambridge 1835 and 1841; canon of Norwich 1842–67; took additional surname of Gratwicke by royal license 28 April 1863. *(m.* 1835 Jemima Elizabeth eld. dau. of Rev. Wm. Kinleside of Angmering, Sussex). *d.* the Lodge, Em. coll. Cambridge 16 Sep. 1871.

NOTE.—His personalty was sworn under £180,000 Oct. 1871, he left £6000 to his college.

ARCHER, FREDERICK SCOTT (2 son of Mr. Archer, of Bishop Stortford, butcher). b. 1813; assistant to Massey of Leadenhall st. London, silversmith; a sculptor; applied collodion to photography successfully 1850, first account of this process was in the Chemist, March 1851, it was in general use for 30 years till the gelatine process was discovered; photographer at 105 Great Russell st. Bloomsbury 1852 to death; invented a camera and a liquid lens; the first to use a triplet lens. d. 105 Great Russell st. 1 May 1857. Report of the jurors on class xiv (photography) of the International Exhibition 1862; N. and Q. 1 series vi, 277, 396, 426 (1852), vii, 92, 218 (1853).

ARCHER, GEORGINA (sister of James Archer). Went to Berlin 1859; Victoria Lyceum there was founded in 1867, mainly through her efforts. d. Montreux, Switzerland 22 Nov. 1882.

ARCHER, HENRY. Invented and patented machine for perforating postage stamps 1848. d. Pau, France 2 April 1863.

ARCHER, JOHN WYKEHAM. b. Newcastle 1808; apprenticed to John Scott of Coppice row, London, animal engraver; Engraver in London 1831 to death; Associate of New Society of Painters in Watercolours; author of Vestiges of old London 1851; Posthumous Poems 1873. d. Kentish town, London 25 May 1864. Pinks's Clerkenwell (1865) 639–41.

ARCHER, THOMAS CROXEN. Clerk in Customs at Liverpool; collected, arranged and named the specimens of the imports into Liverpool for the Great Exhibition of 1851; a professor in the Liverpool institution; superintendent of Technological museum Edin. 26 June 1860, and director Jany. 1866 to death; joint executive comr. from Great Britain to American Centennial Exhibition 1876; F.R.S. Edin. d. London 19 Feb. 1885. Athenæum 28 Feb 1885, p. 283. Graphic xiii, 542, 552 (1876), portrait.

ARCHIBALD, CHARLES DICKSON (eld. son of Samuel George Wm. Archibald, Speaker of Assembly, Nova Scotia). b. Truro, Nova Scotia 31 Oct. 1802; author of A look towards the future of the British colonies 1854; F.R.S. 26 Nov. 1840. (m. 16 Sep. 1832 Bridget only child of Myles Walker of Rusland hall, Lancashire). d. 1868.

ARCHIBALD, SIR EDWARD MORTIMER (brother of the preceding). b. 10 May 1810; chief clerk and registrar of supreme court of Newfoundland 8 Nov. 1832; attorney general 5 Nov. 1846; advocate general 15 April 1847 to May 1855; consul in state of New York 1 Oct. 1857; judge in mixed court New York

ARCHIBALD, SIR E. M. (Con.)

for suppression of African slave trade 14 Oct. 1862 to 1 Oct. 1870; consul general for states of New York, &c. 9 Feb. 1871 to 1 Jany. 1883; C.B. 17 March 1865; K.C.M.G. 12 Aug. 1882. (m. 1834 Katherine dau. of A. Richardson of Halifax, Nova Scotia). d. 11 St. John's terrace, Brighton 8 Feb. 1884.

ARCHIBALD, SIR THOMAS DICKSON (brother of the preceding). b. Truro, Nova Scotia 1817; attorney and barrister province of Nova Scotia 1837; a special pleader in London 1844–52; student of M.T. 11 Nov. 1840, barrister 30 Nov. 1852; drew Petition of Right act usually called Bovill's act 1860; junior counsel to Treasury otherwise called Attorney general's Devil Feb. 1868 to Nov. 1872; serjeant at law 20 Nov. 1872; judge of Court of Queen's Bench 22 Nov. 1872 to Feb. 1875; knighted by the Queen at Osborne 5 Feb. 1873; judge of Court of Common Pleas Feb. 1875 to death. (m. 1841 Sarah only dau. of Richard Smith of The Priory Dudley). d 7 Porchester gate, Hyde Park 18 Oct. 1876 in 60 year. Law magazine and law review ii, 177–88 (1877); I.L.N. lxii, 11, 13 (1873), portrait.

ARDEN, HENRY THOMAS, the assumed name of Henry Thomas Arnold; author of Princess Charming, The belle of the Barley-mow, The armourer's daughter, The right-fall heir and many other burlesques and extravaganzas. d. 25 Nov. 1876 aged 36.

ARDEN, JOSEPH (eld. son of Joseph Arden of Islington) b. 10 May 1799; ed. at Merchant Taylors; barrister G.I. 18 Nov. 1840, bencher 1 March 1875; principal of Cliffords Inn 5 Feb. 1855 to death; F.S.A. 10 June 1847; author of The orations of Hyperides for Lycophron and Euxenippus now first printed in facsimile with a short account of the discovery of the original manuscript at Western Thebes in Upper Egypt in 1847. Cambridge 1853. d. 1 Cliffords Inn 30 Jany. 1879.

ARGUIMBAU, LAWRENCE. Captain 1 foot 1809–16 when placed on h.p.; Col. 80 foot 30 April 1853 to death; L.G. 20 June 1854; C.B. 22 June 1815. d. Mahon, Minorca 18 Aug. 1854.

ARKWRIGHT, GEORGE. b. 20 Aug. 1807; barrister L.I. 22 Nov. 1833; M.P. for Leominster 1842 to death. d. 2D The Albany Piccadilly, London 5 Feb. 1856.

ARKWRIGHT, HENRY. b. 16 Dec. 1837; captain 84 foot 18 April 1865 to death; killed by fall of an avalanche when ascending Mont Blanc 13 Oct. 1866.

ARKWRIGHT, Rev. Joseph. *b.* 9 Aug. 1791; ed. at Eton and Trin. coll. Cam., B.A. 1812; master of Essex foxhounds 1861 to death; built new kennels at Harlow; a celebrated horseman; one of largest farmers in Essex. *d.* 29 Feb. 1864. Personalty sworn under £400,000 April 1864.

ARKWRIGHT, Peter. *b.* 17 April 1784; sheriff of Derbyshire 1855. *d.* Willersley, Derbyshire 19 Sep. 1866. Personalty sworn under £800,000 Nov. 1866.

ARMENI, Sir Peter Braila. Greek envoy extraord. and min. plenipo. in London 24 April 1882 to death; G.C.M.G. 1882. *d.* 18 Queen's gate terrace, South Kensington 15 Sep. 1884.

ARMISTEAD, Wilson. Author of *A tribute for the Negro* 1848; *Select Miscellanies*, 2 vols. 1851; *The Anti-slavery pilot*, 22 numbers 1855; *Tales and legends of the English lakes and mountains, by Lorenzo Tuvar* 1855. *d.* Virginia house, Leeds 18 Feb. 1868 aged 49. *Joseph Smith's Friends books i*, 124–31 (1867); *Annual Monitor for* 1869 *pp.* 2–8.

ARMITAGE, Sir Elkanah (*3 son of Elkanah Armitage of Newton, Lancs.*) *b.* Failsworth Sep. 1794; a handloom weaver; founded firm of Armitage and Co. of London and Manchester, cotton spinners 1827, retired 1873; member of the first town council Manchester 1838; alderman 1841–65; mayor 1846–48; knighted by the Queen at Buckingham Palace 31 Jany. 1849 for his services during Chartist riots 1848; contested Salford March 1857; sheriff of county palatine of Lancaster 1866. *d.* Hope hall, Pendleton near Manchester 26 Nov. 1876. *Graphic xiv*, 592, 595 (1876), *portrait*.

ARMITAGE, George. Took a point net machine to Antwerp 1801, introducing manufacture of point net lace into Belgium; went to Paris where he effected many alterations in the stocking frame; invented the circular hose frame; went to Prussia then to Cambray; sent or took lace machines to Moscow; went to Australia about 1850. *d.* Australia 1857 aged 89.

ARMITAGE, Rev. Robert. R. of Easthope, Salop 1843 to death; published anonymously *Doctor Hookwell or the Anglo-Catholic family*, 3 vols. 1842; *The Penscellwood papers comprising essays on the souls and future life of animals*, 2 vols. 1846; *Ernest Singleton* 1848; *Dr. Johnson his religious life and his death* 1850. *d.* Easthope 2 Feb. 1852 aged 47.

ARMSTRONG, Alexander. 2 Lieutenant Royal Irish Artillery 7 July 1783; major 24 July 1800 to 1 April 1801 when he retired on full pay; general 30 June 1854. *d.* Green park, Bath 2 Dec. 1861 aged 94.

ARMSTRONG, Sir Andrew, 1 Baronet (*eld. son of Edmund Armstrong of Gallen, King's county* 1754–1827). *b.* Gallen Priory 19 Oct. 1786; sheriff of King's county 1811 and 1836; receiver general of stamps in Ireland 1831–41; M.P. for King's county 1841–52; created baronet 18 Sep. 1841. *d.* Chester 27 Jany. 1863.

ARMSTRONG, Edmund John. *b.* Mornington house, Upper Merrion st. Dublin 23 July 1841; ed. at Trin. coll. Dublin; took 1st prize in Latin and Greek verse; pres. of the Undergraduate philosophical society; received gold medal of Royal historical society Nov. 1864; author of *Poems* 1865, new ed. 1877. *d.* Kingstown near Dublin 24 Feb. 1865. *Life and letters of E. J. Armstrong, edited by G. F. Armstrong* 1877, *portrait*.

ARMSTRONG, James Wells. Lieut. col. 4 depôt battalion 2 Oct. 1855 to 16 Oct. 1860 when placed on h. p.; deputy adjutant general 1 Nov. 1871 to 25 Nov. 1876; deputy adjutant general for auxiliary forces 25 Nov. 1876 to death; C.B. 2 Jany. 1857. *d.* 98 St. George's sq. Westminster 12 April 1880.

ARMSTRONG, John. *b.* Ingram, Northumberland 13 Oct. 1775; a millwright and engineer at Bristol, city surveyor there 1831 to death; A.I.C.E. 1828. *d.* 17 March 1854.

ARMSTRONG, Right Rev. John (*eld. son of John Armstrong of London, M.D.*) *b.* Bishopwearmouth 22 Aug. 1813; ed. at Charterhouse 1827; Crewe exhibitioner at Linc. coll. Oxf. 1832; B.A. 1836; M.A. 1850; C. of Clifton 1838–41; priest vicar of Exeter cathedral 1841; R. of St. Paul's, Exeter 1843; V. of Tidenham, Gloucs. 1845; originated female penitentiary which was opened at Clewer 1849; founded *National Miscellany* a monthly religious periodical 1853, it was united with the *Illustrated London magazine* 1855; bishop of Grahamstown, South Africa 25 October 1853; consecrated in St. Mary's, Lambeth 30 Nov. 1853; suffragan to bishop of Cape Town 6 Dec. 1853; arrived at Grahamstown 26 Oct. 1854; author of *Sermons on the festivals* 1845; *Parochial sermons* 1854; wrote many and edited all the *Tracts for the Christian seasons*, 2 series 1848–50. (*m.* 22 Feb. 1843 Frances eld. dau. of Edward Whitmore). *d.* Grahamstown 16 May 1856. *A memoir of John Armstrong,*

ARMSTRONG, RIGHT REV. J. (Con.)

D.D. by Rev. T. T. Carter 1857, portrait; G.M. i, 376–82 (1856); Guardian 20 Dec. 1882 p. 1809.

ARMSTRONG, VERY REV. JOHN (brother of Sir Andrew Armstrong). b. June 1791; archdeacon of Clonfert 24 June 1845; dean of Kilfenora Jany. 1847 to death. d. 16 June 1856.

ARMSTRONG, JOHN. Provisional ensign Cape mounted rifles 19 March 1835; formed and commanded a corps of irregular horse known as "Armstrong's Horse" during Kaffir war 1852–53; C.B. 13 March 1867, M.G. 6 July 1867. d. Stoulgrove house, near Chepstow 28 June 1874 aged 55.

ARMSTRONG, JOHN WARNEFORD. b. King's county 28 Aug. 1770; captain King's county militia 19 Jany. 1798; betrayed Henry and John Sheares barristers of Dublin to the Government 1798; they were hung for high treason 14 July 1798; received pension of £500 per annum 1798 to death. d. 1858. Howell's State trials xxvii, 255–398 (1820).

ARMSTRONG, JOSEPH. b. Bewcastle Cumberland 21 Sep. 1816; engine driver on Liverpool and Manchester railway 1836–40; superintendent of locomotive carriage and wagon departments of Great Western Railway June 1864 to death; M.I.M.E. 1857, M.I.C.E. 1877. d. Matlock Bath 5 June 1877. Minutes of proc. of Instit. of C.E. xlix, 255–58 (1877).

ARMSTRONG, REV. NICHOLAS. Rector of St. James's, Dublin; an agent of the Reformation society 1831; the most powerful of Irish declaimers; an Irvingite apostle 18 Jany. 1834; apostle to Ireland and Greece 1838; author of Two letters to a friend in answer to the inquiry What is the use of the gifts of the spirit 1832; Sermons preached in the Catholic Apostolic church Gordon Square 1857; Homilies on the Epistles and Gospels 1870; Sermons on various subjects, 1870–79. d. Albury heath, Surrey 9 Oct. 1879 in 78 year. Rev. Edward Miller's History and doctrines of Irvingism, vol. i; R. S. Brooke's Recollections of the Irish church (1877) 25–27.

ARMSTRONG, SIR RICHARD (only son of lieut. col. Richard Armstrong of Lincoln.) b. 1782; ensign 24 foot 23 June 1796; served in Peninsula 1808–14; lieut. col. 1 foot 18 Oct. 1821, and of 26 foot 24 Jany 1829 to 13 Feb. 1835 when placed on h. p.; colonel 95 foot 29 March 1848 and of 32 foot 25 June 1850 to death; commander in chief at Madras 29 Sep. 1851 to 27 Oct. 1853; L.G. 11 Nov. 1851; C.B. 4 June 1815, K.C.B. 7

ARMSTRONG, SIR R. (Con.)

April 1852, K.T.S.; Knighted by Wm. IV. at St. James's palace 28 Sept. 1831. d. on board the ship Barham on his voyage home from Madras 3 March 1854.

ARMSTRONG, RICHARD (eld. son of Wm. Armstrong, of Roxborough, co. Armagh, engineer.) b. Armagh 1815; ed. at Trin. coll. Dublin; called to Irish bar 1839, went Leinster circuit; Q.C. 28 Jany. 1854, bencher of King's Inns 1861; third sergeant at law 1861–65, second 1865, and first 1866 to death; M.P. for Sligo 1865–68. (m. 1847 Elizabeth dau. of Edward Meurant.) d. 32 Stephen's Green, Dublin 26 Aug. 1880. Irish law times xiv, 452 (1880.)

ARMSTRONG, ROBERT ARCHIBALD (eld. son of Robert Archibald of Kenmore, Perthshire). b. Kenmore 1788; ed at Univs. of Edin. and St. Andrews; Gaelic lexicographer in ordinary to George iv 1826; head master of South Lambeth gr. sch. 1830–52; author of A Gaelic dictionary 1825, which was the first ever published; wrote many scientific papers in the Arcana of science and art 1837 et seq. d. Choumert road, Peckham Rye 25 May 1867.

ARMSTRONG, ROBERT BAYNES (eld. son of John Armstrong of Lancaster, merchant). b. Lancaster 1785; ed. at Clitheroe and Sedbergh schools and St. John's coll. Cam., B.A. 1807, M.A. 1810, fellow of his college; barrister I.T. 23 June 1814, bencher 1840, reader 1851; treasurer 1852; Q.C. 1840; recorder of Hull 1836–37, of Leeds 1837–39 and of Manchester and Bolton May 1848 to May 1865; M.P for Lancaster 1848–53. (m. Dec. 1842 Frances youngest dau. of Richmond Blamire of Thackwood, Cumberland, she d. 19 March 1862.) d. 29 Chester sq. Pimlico, London 15 Jany. 1869.

ARMSTRONG, THOMAS WILLIAM DE BUTTS. b. 1826; resident engineer on several important works in Mayo 1848–53; one of the first engineers sent to India in government service 1855; chief engineer of Central Provinces 1869 to death; M.I.C.E. 10 April 1866. d. on board P. and O. steamer Travancore off the Malabar coast 1 May 1877. Minutes of proc. of Instit. of C.E. li, 261–65 (1878).

ARMSTRONG, WILLIAM. Called to Irish bar 1819; Q.C. 17 Aug. 1841; chairman of quarter sessions co. Londonderry. d. 1866.

ARNEY, SIR GEORGE ALFRED (6 son of Wm. Arney of The Close, Salisbury). b. Salisbury 3 Jany. 1806; ed. at Winchester and Brasn. coll. Ox., B.A. 1832; barrister L.I. 5 May

1837; recorder of Winchester Dec. 1856–1857; chief justice of New Zealand 1858–75; knighted by patent 18 July 1862. *(m.* 13 June 1833 Harriet dau. of Thomas Parr, captain R.N., she *d.* 18 April 1844). *d.* 17 Devonshire place, Portland place, London 7 April 1883.

ARNOLD, REV. CHARLES THOMAS. *b.* 26 Oct. 1817; ed. at Rugby and Magd. hall, Ox., B.A. 1840, M.A. 1843; Assistant master at Rugby 1841–78. *d.* Rome 13 May 1878.

ARNOLD, REV. EDWARD PENROSE (3 *son of Rev. Thomas Arnold 1795–1842, head master of Rugby*). *b.* 28 Oct. 1826; ed. at Rugby and Ball. coll. Ox., B.A. 1848, M.A. 1851; Fellow of All Soul's coll. Ox. 1852; assistant inspector of schools 15 April 1854; inspector 1866–77. *d.* Fox How, Ambleside 6 April 1878.

ARNOLD, JAMES ROBERTSON (2 *son of general Benedict Arnold 1741–1801*). *b* New York 28 Aug. 1781; 2 Lieut. R.E. 29 Aug. 1798; served in the wars against France 1800–15; aide de camp to the Sovereign 1830–41; col. R.E. 1837–41; L.G. 11 Nov. 1851; K.H. 1831; K.C. *(m.* 21 March 1807 Virginia 4 dau. of Bartlett Goodrich of Saling Grove, Isle of Wight). *d.* Onslow sq. London 27 Dec. 1854. *I. N. Arnold's Life of Benedict Arnold* (1880) 407–17.

ARNOLD, REV. JOHN MÜEHLEISEN. *b.* Zell, Wurtemberg 1817; C.M.S. missionary in Abyssinia and India; Chap. to Bishop of Gibraltar; Chap. to St. Mary's hospital, Paddington 1852–61; founded Moslem mission society in England 1859, hon. sec. 1860–65; C. of East Ham, Essex 1861–65; Consular Chap. at Batavia 28 Oct. 1865, resigned 6 Aug. 1870 but continued his services till 30 June 1871; R. of St. Mary's, Papendorf, Capetown, March 1876. *d* Papendorf 9 Dec. 1881. *Guardian 29 March 1882 p.* 448, *vol.* 3.

ARNOLD, SAMUEL JAMES (*only son of Samuel Arnold 1740–1802, organist and composer to George 3*). *b.* 1774; exhibited portraits at the R.A. 1800–1806; brought out a musical play called Auld Robin Gray at Haymarket theatre 1794; exhibited a panorama in Spring gardens; member of "Sublime society of beefsteaks" 15 April 1809; opened Lyceum theatre as an English opera house 26 June 1809; built new theatre on same site and opened it as the English opera house 15 June 1816, it was burnt down 16 Feb. 1830, he rebuilt it and opened it 14 July 1834; manager of Drury

Lane theatre 1812–15; author of *The Creole or haunted island* 3 *vols.* 1796; *The shipwreck,* a comic opera in 2 acts 1796; *Man and wife, comedy in 5 acts* 1809, 8 ed. 1809. *(m.* 18 May 1802 Matilda Catherine younger dau. of Henry James Pye, poet laureate). *d.* Walton upon Thames 16 Aug. 1852 in 78 year. *G.M. xxxviii,* 538 (1852).

ARNOLD, THOMAS JAMES (*eld. son of the preceding*). *b.* Downing st. Westminster 1803; ed. at St. Paul's school and univ. of Gottingen; barrister L.I. 24 Nov. 1829; commissioner of bankruptcy at Liverpool; stipendiary magistrate at Worship st. police court 27 Jany. 1847 and at Westminster police court Aug. 1851 to death; member of Numismatic Society 1862; F.S.A. 1869; author of *A treatise on the law relating to municipal corporations* 1852, 3 ed. 1883; *Anacreon in English* 1869; *Faust, a tragedy translated in the original metres* 1877. *d.* 1 Greville place, Kilburn priory 20 May 1877. *Numismatic Chronicle xvii,* 13–15 (1877).

ARNOLD, REV. THOMAS KERCHEVER (*eld. son of Thomas George Arnold of Stamford, M.D.*) *b.* 1800; ed. at Trin. coll. Camb.; B.A. 1821; M.A. 1824; fellow of his college; R. of Lyndon, Rutland 1830 to death; projected and edited *Churchman's Quarterly magazine* 1837, *Churchman's Monthly Companion* 1844 *and Theological Critic* 1851; author of *Henry's first Latin book* 1839, 26 ed. 1883; *The first Greek book* 1849, new ed. 1883; *The first Hebrew book* 1851, 7 ed. 1883; *Anticleptic gradus ad Parnassum* 1852 and many other educational books. *d.* Lyndon rectory 9 March 1853. *Fraser's Mag. xlvii,* 173–83 (1853); *G.M. xxxix,* 667 (1853).

ARNOLD, WILLIAM DELAFIELD (2 *son of Rev. Thomas Arnold, D.D. 1795–1842, head master of Rugby*). *b.* Laleham 7 April 1828; ed. at Rugby; student of Ch. Ch. Ox. 1847; ensign 58 Bengal N.I. 2 Dec. 1848; principal director of public education in the Punjab 1857 to death, where his name is perpetuated by an annual distribution of medals, bearing his likeness, to the best pupils in schools which he founded; author of a novel entitled *Oakfield or fellowship in the East, by Punjabee,* 2 vols. 1853; translated *Wiese's Letters on English education* 1854. *d.* Gibraltar 9 April 1859. *Prospective Review x,* 274–303 (1854).

ARNOLD, WILLIAM MUNNINGS (2 *son of Rev. Richard Arnold.*) *b.* Ellough, Suffolk 1820; arrived in New South Wales 1839; settled near Maitland on the Paterson river; member

ARNOLD, W. M. *(Con.)*

of legislative assembly 1856 ; chairman of committees 1858 ; minister for public works 1860–63 ; speaker of the assembly 3 Oct. 1865 to death ; drowned in the floods at Stradbroke, his estate on the Paterson river 2 March 1875.

ARNOT, REV. WILLIAM *(7 and youngest child of Robert Arnot of Scone, farmer.)* b. New Mains farm near Scone 6 Nov. 1808 ; matric. at Univ. of Glasgow 10 Oct. 1829 ; licensed as a preacher by presbytery of Glasgow 4 Oct. 1837 ; minister of Free Saint Peter's Church, Glasgow 1 Jany. 1839 to 6 Oct. 1864 ; ejected from his church by a decision of the Court of Session Feb. 1849 ; opened a new church in Main st. Glasgow 26 May 1850 ; minister of Free high church Edinburgh 11 Oct. 1864 to death ; author of *Illustrations of the Book of Proverbs, 2 series* 1856 ; *Roots and fruits of Christian life* 1860, 2 ed., 1864 ; *This present world* 1873. d. Edinburgh 3 June 1875 ; *Autobiography of Rev. W. Arnot* 1877, *portrait.*

ARNOT, WILLIAM. b. Falkirk ; a chemist ; employed purifying the river North Esk 1868 ; opened large chemical works at Kirkintilloch 1873 ; delivered a course of 6 Cantor lectures on *The technology of the paper trade* at the Society of Arts 1877. d. Bridge of Allan 9 Feb. 1881 aged 38.

ARNOTT, ARCHIBALD. b. Kirkconnell hall, Ecclefechan, co. Dumfries 1771 ; surgeon 20 foot 23 Aug. 1799 to 25 Dec. 1826, when placed on h.p. ; medical attendant of Napoleon at St. Helena 1 April 1821 to 5 May 1821, when he died at 5.49 p.m. with his right hand in that of Dr. Arnott ; author of *An account of the last illness decease and post mortem appearances of Napoleon Bonaparte* 1822. d. Kirkconnell hall, 6 July 1855.

ARNOTT, FRANCIS SHORT. b. 1805 ; surgeon Bombay army 5 June 1845 ; hon. surgeon to the Queen 1861 to death ; C.B. 21 March 1859. d. Kirkconnell hall 16 Oct. 1879.

ARNOTT, GEORGE ARNOTT WALKER *(son of David Walker Arnott of Arlary near Kinross who d. 1822).* b. Edinburgh 6 Feb. 1799 ; ed. at the High school and Univ. of Edin., M.A. 1818, LL.D. Aberdeen 1837 ; advocate 1821 ; visited France, Spain and Russia ; F.R.S Edin. 1822, F.L.S. 1825 ; worked with William Hooker the botanist at Glasgow 1830–40 ; member of Botanical society of Edin. 1836 ; professor of botany in Univ. of Glasgow 1845 to death ; published descriptions of many new

ARNOTT, G. A. W. *(Con.)*

plants from Asia and America in various periodicals 1830–40 ; author of the article *Botany* in the *Encyclopedia Britannica, 7 ed. vol. 5. d.* Glasgow 17 June 1868. *Trans. Botanic Society of Edin. ix,* 414–26 (1868).

ARNOTT, NEIL. b. Arbroath, Angusshire 15 May 1788 ; surgeon in H.E.I. Co's. naval service 1807–11 ; practised in London 1811–55 when he retired ; M.R.C.S. 1813 ; M.D. Aberdeen 15 Sep. 1814 ; L.R.C.P. 31 March 1817 ; invented his hydrostatic or water bed 1832 ; and Arnott stove and the ventilator ; one of senate of Univ. of London 1836 ; founded an exhibition there for experimental physics 1875 ; phys. extraordinary to Queen Victoria 8 Aug. 1837 ; F.R.S. 25 Jany. 1838, Rumford medallist 1854 ; F.G.S. 1847 ; founded scholarships of natural philosophy at the 4 Scottish universities 1869 ; author of *Elements of physics* 1827, 7 ed. 1876 ; *A survey of human progress* 1861. d. Cumberland terrace, London 2 March 1874. *Proc. of Royal Society xxv,* 14–18 (1877) ; *Medical Circular i,* 92, 149 (1852), *portrait ; Graphic ix,* 314, 328 (1874), *portrait.*

ARNTZ, ROBERT RICHARD. b. Erefeldt, Prussia 1815 ; taken to England 1819 ; articled to W. Herbert of London, builder 1831 ; naturalised 15 May 1848 ; surveyor to Westminster district board of works ; A.I.C.E. 1856 ; F.S.A. 18 Dec. 1862. d. 17 Feb. 1882.

ARRAN, PHILIP YORKE GORE, 6 Earl of. b. Dublin castle 23 Nov. 1801 ; chargé d'Affaires at Buenos Ayres 17 Oct. 1832 to 18 Oct. 1834 ; succeeded his uncle 20 Jany. 1837 ; K.P. 6 May 1841. d. 27 Chesham st. London 25 June 1884.

ARRINDELL, SIR WILLIAM. b. in one of the Virgin islands 1796 ; ed. in England ; attorney general British Guiana 10 May 1845 to 1852 ; chief justice of Demerara 1852 to death ; C.B. 30 Nov. 1858 ; knighted by patent 13 Dec. 1858. d. Demerara 27 Dec. 1862.

ARROW, SIR FREDERICK *(2 son of Wm. Arrow, captain Indian Navy.)* b. Calcutta 1818 ; ed. at Bath gr. sch. ; in mercantile marine service June 1834 to Feb. 1859 ; an elder brother of Trinity House Feb. 1859, and deputy master June 1865 to death ; knighted by patent 29 Aug. 1868 ; F.R.G.S. 1871 ; *(m.* 1850 Harriet 5 dau. of R. Stileman of the Friars, Winchelsea.) *d.* Pilgrims hall, South Weald, near Brentwood 17 July 1875 ; *I.L.N. lxvi* 95, 100 (1875) *portrait.*

ARROWSMITH, JOHN. b. Winston near Barnard Castle, Durham 23 April 1790; joined his uncle Aaron Arrowsmith of Soho Square London, geographer 14 Feb. 1810; one of founders of Royal geographical society 1830, gold medallist 1862; produced *London atlas of universal geography* 1834, 3 ed. 1858; illustrated with maps *Leichhardt's journal of an overland expedition in Australia* 1847, and many other books; bought 10 Soho Square 1839, carried on business there down to 1861 when he retired; F.R.A.S. d. 35 Hereford sq. Old Brompton 2 May 1873. *Journal of geographical society xliii*, 161–63 (1873.)

ARTHINGTON, MARIA. Author of *The little scholar's first grammar* 1828; *Rhymes for Harry and his nursemaid* 1851; *Poetry of bye-gone days and other selected pieces not published* 1861. d. 5 Oct. 1863.

ARTHUR, SIR FREDERICK LEOPOLD, 2 Baronet. b. West Indies 20 Dec. 1816; captain 4 foot 8 June 1838 to 13 Dec. 1850, when placed on h.p.; retired from the army 1863; succeeded 19 Sep. 1854. d. United Service club Pall Mall London 1 June 1878.

ARTHUR, SIR GEORGE, 1 Baronet (3 *and youngest son of John Arthur of Plymouth* 1733–88.) b. 21 June 1784; governor of Honduras 1814–1822; lieut. col. 7 West India foot 1 June 1815; lieut. col. 5 West India foot 29 Aug. 1816, and lieut. col. York Chasseurs 8 May 1817 to 25 Oct. 1819, when placed on h.p.; governor of Van Diemen's Land 14 May 1824 to 30 Oct 1836; lieut. governor of Upper Canada 23 March 1838 to April 1841; suppressed the rebellion Nov. 1838; governor of Bombay 27 April 1841 to 6 Aug. 1846; M.G. 9 Nov. 1846; col. 50 foot 28 Feb. 1853 to death; K.C.H. 1837; knighted by the Queen at St. James's palace 19 July 1837; created baronet 5 June 1841; P.C. 17 June 1847; hon. D. C. L. Ox. 5 July 1848. d. Gloucester square, Hyde Park, London 19 Sep. 1854. *J. Mac Mullen's History of Canada* 2 ed. 1868, *pp.* 461–94.

ARTHUR, REV. JOHN. b. Houston, Renfrewshire 1794; ed. at Univ. of Glasgow; Congregational minister at Helensburgh 1824 to 1866, this district was the scene of several movements that attracted much attention, such as "The Speaking with Tongues," "Miraculous healing," and the "Row Heresy case." d. 17 May 1884.

ARTHUR, RICHARD. b. 10 Jany. 1779; captain R.N. 11 Jany. 1810; superintendent of Sheerness dockyard 23 Sep. 1844 to 9 Nov. 1846; V.A. 17 Sep. 1853; C.B. 28 July 1838. d. Plymouth 26 Oct. 1854.

ARTLETT, RICHARD AUSTIN. b. 9 Nov. 1807; pupil of Robert Cooper and James Thomson; engraved in the dotted manner a few figure subjects and several portraits; distinguished as an engraver of sculpture, his plates of which in the *Art Journal* are executed with great taste and delicacy. d. 1 Sep. 1873.

ARTOIS, The Flying Wonder, stage name of John Lilley. b. Liverpool 12 July 1848; a performer on the flying trapeze 1866 to death; held a foremost rank in his profession; fell from his trapeze at the Star music hall Dublin 21 March 1882 and fractured his skull. d. Mercer's hospital Dublin 21 March 1882. bur. Mount Jerome cemetery 24 March.

ARTOM, REV. BENJAMIN. b. Asti near Pimont, Genoa 1835; minister of Jewish synagogues at Saluzzo, Genoa and Naples; Haham of Spanish and Portugese congregation of London 9 Aug. 1866 to death; inducted 16 Dec. 1866. (m. 10 Feb. 1875 Henrietta Hahaba widow of Solomon David of Bombay). d. 3 Marine parade Brighton 6 Jany. 1879. *Jewish Chronicle* 10 Jany. 1879 9–12; *Graphic xix*, 52 (1879), *portrait.*

ARUNDALE, FRANCIS. b. London 9 Aug. 1807; articled to A. Pugin the elder; spent nine years in the East 1831–40; author of *Edifices of Palladio* 1832; *Illustrations of Jerusalem and Mount Sinai* 1837. d. Brighton 9 Sep. 1853.

ARUNDELL, HENRY BENEDICT, 11 Baron Arundell of Wardour. b. Irnham hall, co. Lincoln 12 Nov. 1804; the only R.C. peer who voted against the Reform bill 1832; succeeded 21 June 1834; a count of the Holy Roman Empire. d. Wardour castle, Wilts 19 Oct. 1862.

ARUNDELL, REV. THOMAS, formerly called Thomas Arundell Tagg. Ed. at Merchant Taylor's, St. Bees and St. John's coll. Cam., B.D. 1868; C. of Ch. Ch. Blackfriars 1853–54; C. of All Saint's Gordon square and Reader of Ch. Ch. Newgate st. Lond. 1854–56; P.C. of St. Peter Hammersmith 1856–60; V. of Hayton with Bielby, Yorks 1860; V. of St. John's, Whetstone, Finchley Feb. 1876; author of *Historical reminiscences of the City of London* 1869; and of sermons and articles in periodicals. d. the vicarage Whetstone 5 Nov. 1880 in his 64 year.

ASBURY, JACOB VALE (*son of Mr. Asbury of Stone, Staffs.*) Surgeon at Enfield 1820 to death; invented a surgical instrument for puncture of the tympanum; took out patents for railway buffers 1853 and 1855. (m. 1820

Dorothy 3 dau. of Charles Jacomb of Guildford st. Russell square). *d.* Enfield 21 June 1871 in his 80 year. *Medical times and gazette ii*, 87 (1871).

NOTE.—Charles Lamb his friend and patient bore witness to his successful treatment of cholera in a witty acrostic on his name.

ASCHER, JOSEPH. *b.* London 1831; pupil of Ignaz Moscheles; court pianist to Empress Eugénie in Paris; composed above 100 mazurkas, gallops, nocturnes, études, and transcriptions. *d.* London 3 June 1869.

ASH, EDWARD. A minister of Society of Friends; M.D.; lived at Bristol; author of *An inquiry into some parts of Christian doctrine and practice* 1841; *Four lectures on the Apocalypse* 1848; *Explanatory notes and comments on the New Testament,* 3 *vols.* 1849-50. *d.* Cotham, Bristol 23 Dec. 1873 aged 76.

ASHBROOK, HENRY FLOWER, 5 Viscount. *b.* 17 June 1806; succeeded his father 4 May 1847. *d.* Castle Durrow, co. Kilkenny 3 Aug. 1871.

ASHBROOK, HENRY JEFFERY FLOWER, 6 Viscount. *b.* 26 March 1829; ed. at Eton; sheriff of Queen's county 1856; succeeded 3 Aug. 1871. *d.* Castle Durrow 14 Dec. 1882.

ASHBURNER, JOHN *(son of Mr. Ashburner of Bombay 1769-98, member of supreme council).* *b.* Bombay 10 Jany. 1793; ed. at Dublin, Glasgow and Edin.; M.D. Edin. 1 Aug. 1816; physician in London 1816; L.R.C.P. 1818; physician to Small pox hospital 1818-24, when he went to India; lecturer on Midwifery at St. Thomas's hospital; a great believer in Mesmerism; author of *Dentition* 1834; *Notes and studies on the philosophy of animal magnetism and spiritualism* 1867. *d.* 59 Cambridge place, London 13 Nov. 1878. *Munk's Roll iii*, 181 (1878); *Medical Circular i*, 93 (1852).

ASHBURNHAM, BERTRAM ASHBURNHAM, 4 Earl of *(eld. son of George Ashburnham, 3 Earl of Ashburnham 1760-1830).* *b.* 23 Nov. 1797; succeeded his father 27 Oct. 1830; sold his pictures at Christie's 20 July 1850. *d.* Ashburnham place near Battle 22 June 1878.

NOTE.—He was the collector of an extensive library of early and rare books and of a vast assemblage of MSS. which comprised 4 divisions, the Libri collection, the Barrois collection, the Stowe collection and a portion known as The Appendix comprising his miscellaneous collections. In July 1883 the Government purchased the Stowe collection for £45,000; and in May 1884 the Italian Government bought for the Laurenzian library at Florence the larger portion of the

Libri collection and the Dante MSS. from the Appendix for the sum of £23,000. A very full account of the contents of the whole of the Ashburnham MSS. will be found in the 8th Report of the Historical Manuscript Commission (1881) Appendix part 3 pp. 127.

ASHBURNHAM, REV. SIR JOHN, 7 Baronet. *b.* Scotland Yard Westminster 26 Dec. 1770; ed. at Clare hall Cam.; B.D. 1815; R. of Guestling, Sussex 1795 to death; Preb. of Chichester 2 May 1796 to death; Chancellor of Chichester 4 May 1796 to death; V. of Pevensey, Sussex 1816 to death; succeeded his brother the 6 Bart. 22 March 1843. *d.* Guestling rectory 1 Sep. 1854.

ASHBURNHAM, THOMAS *(4 son of George Ashburnham, 3 Earl of Ashburnham 1760-1830.)* ensign Coldstream guards 30 **Jany.** 1823; lieut. col. 62 foot 7 Jan. 1842 to 21 Sep. 1847; commanded a brigade in Sutlej campaign 1845-46; aide de camp to the Queen 3 April 1846 to 20 June 1854; lieut. col. 29 foot 22 Nov. 1849 to 20 June 1854; col. 82 foot 13 Dec. 1859 to death; general 19 April 1868; C.B. 3 April 1846. *d.* 104 **Park** st. Grosvenor sq., London 3 March 1872.

ASHBURTON, WILLIAM BINGHAM BARING, 2 Baron. *(eld. son of Alexander Baring, 1 Baron Ashburton 1774-1848.)* *b.* June 1799; ed. at Oriel coll. Ox.; B.A. 1821, M.A. 1836, hon. D.C.L. 1856; M.P. for Thetford 1826-30, for Callington 1830-31, for Winchester 1832-37, for North Staffs. 1837-41, and again for Thetford 1841-48; sec. of board of control 8 Sep. 1841 to 17 Feb. 1845; paymaster general of the forces and treasurer of the navy 25 Feb. 1845 to 12 July 1846; P.C. 30 June 1845; succeeded his father 13 May 1848; F.R.S. 27 April 1854; Commander of Legion of Honour 1855; pres. of geographical society 1860-62, vice pres. 1862 to death. *d.* the Grange, Alresford Hants 23 March 1864. *Monographs by Lord Houghton* (1873) 225-55; *Waagen's Treasures of art in Great Britain ii*, 97-112 (1854).

ASHBURTON, FRANCIS BARING, 3 Baron. *b.* 20 May 1800; M.P. for Thetford 1832-41 and 1848-57; succeeded 23 March 1864. *d.* Hazlewood near Watford 6 Sep. 1868.

ASHBURY, JOHN. *b.* 31 Jany. 1806; a wheelright at Manchester; began the large works at Openshaw near Manchester for building railway carriages and wagons 1847; constructed a railway wagon in 13 hours for the great exhibition of 1862; sold his works to a limited liability company 1862. *d.* 9 Sussex place, Hyde Park, London 2 Sep. 1866. Personalty sworn under £400,000 27 Oct. 1866.

ASHBY, Rev. John Eyre. *b.* 22 Jany. 1820; ed. at Univ. coll. school London, B.A. London 1840; a congregational minister in Arundel, Brighton and London; lectured on the higher mathematics in same places; kept a school at Enfield 1856 to death; F.R.A.S. 1843, LL.D. Jena 1858. *d.* 22 Dec. 1863.

ASHER, Adolphus. *b.* Stettin 3 Sep. 1801; spent 5 years in England 1820–25; diamond merchant at St. Petersburgh; bookseller in Russia 1827–30, at Berlin 1830 to death; introduced the English annuals into Germany and Russia; foreign bookseller to British museum 1841 to death; published *Travels of Benjamin of Tudela, Berlin* 1840. *d.* Venice 2 Oct. 1853.

ASHLEY, Anthony John (4 *son of Cropley Ashley, 6 Earl of Shaftesbury*). *b.* 24 Grosvenor square, London 21 Dec. 1808; ed. at Ch. Ch. Ox., B.A. 1829; barrister I.T. 10 June 1836; Q.C. 9 Jany. 1866. (*m.* 17 March 1840 Julia eld. dau. of Henry John Conyers of Copt hall, Essex). *d.* Upper Brook st. London 1 Jany. 1867.

ASHLEY, Anthony William (*brother of preceding*). *b.* 24 Grosvenor square 4 Oct. 1803; attaché to embassy at Vienna 31 March 1830; treasurer and vice chamberlain to Queen Adelaide 28 Oct. 1834 to her death 2 Dec. 1849; master governor and keeper of royal hospital of St. Katherine in the Regents' Park, London 23 May 1859 to death. (*m.* 8 March 1831 Maria Anne eld. dau. of Col. Hugh Duncan Baillie, M.P. of Tarradaile). *d.* Mentone 18 April 1877.

ASHLEY, Henry. *b.* 1790; an attorney in London 1816 to death; one of the 4 privileged attorneys of Lord Mayor's court to 1853 when he received compensation on abolition of the privilege; erected independent chapel afterwards called Maberly chapel in Ball's Pond road, Islington 1826; author of *Doctrine and practice of attachment in Mayor's court* 1818. *d.* Greenhithe, Kent 20 May 1867.

ASHMORE, Charles. Lieut. col. 36 foot 22 May 1845 to 15 May 1857 when placed on h. p.; col. 30 foot 6 Jany. 1867 to death; general 19 Oct. 1875. *d.* 10 Granville place, Portman sq. 2 March 1881 in 88 year.

ASHPITEL, Arthur (*eld. son of the succeeding*). *b.* Hackney 15 Dec. 1807; ed. at Homerton; commenced practice as an architect in Crown Court Old Broad st. 1842; built church of St. Barnabas at Homerton 1845; partner with John Whichcord 1850; elected F.S.A. 7 Jan. 1847; F.R.I.B.A. 1841, Vice Pres. 1862;

ASHPITEL, A. (*Con.*) published with John Whichcord "*Observations on baths and wash-houses with an account of their history* 1855; *Town dwellings an essay on the erection of fire proof houses in flats* 1855. *d.* 2 Poet's Corner, Westminster Abbey 18 Jany. 1869. *Reg. and Mag. of Biog. i*, 212–15 (1869); *Proc. of Soc. of Antiq.* 2 series iv, 299–301.

ASHPITEL, William Hurst. *b.* 1776; pupil of Daniel Asher Alexander the architect of prisons at Dartmoor and Maidstone; assisted him in designs for the London docks; a pupil of John Rennie; largely concerned in Kenneth and Avon canal; partner with James Savage; J.P. for Middlesex; designed the first new church and extensive schools at South Hackney and many other buildings, besides several large engineering works. *d.* Clapton sq. London 23 April 1852 in 76 year.

ASHTON, Henry. *b.* London 1801; employed by Sir Jeffrey Wyattville to 1840; erected stables at Windsor and kennels at Frogmore; erected summer palace at the Hague for king of Holland; architect for Victoria st. improvements in London, and designed Victoria st. opened 6 Aug. 1851. *d.* 18 March 1872.

ASHTOWN, Frederick Mason Trench, 2 Baron. *b.* 25 Dec. 1804; succeeded 1 May 1840; his claim to the peerage was allowed 12 July 1855. *d.* Clonodfoy, co. Limerick 12 Sep. 1880. Personalty sworn under £350,000 April 1881.

ASHURST, William (*son of the succeeding*). *b.* 1819; admitted solicitor Jany. 1843; partner with his father; partner with John Morris about 1855–62; solicitor to the Post Office 1862 to death; a great friend of Garibaldi and Mazzini. *d.* 7 Prince of Wales's Terrace, Kensington, London 14 July 1879 in 60 year.

ASHURST, William Henry. *b.* London 11 Feb. 1792; a solicitor in London; belonged to a small sect called 'Freethinking Christians'; member of common council of city of London; undersheriff; a founder of the society of the 'Friends of Italy,' 1851 and of the 'Peoples International League,' 1852; took an active part in agitation against church rates; author of *The Corporation Register* 1832, which advocated reforms in the city. *d.* Wimbledon Park, Surrey 13 Oct. 1855.

ASHWELL, Rev. Arthur Rawson. *b.* Cheyne Walk Chelsea 9 Dec. 1824; ed. at Trin. coll. Cam.; scholar of Caius coll. 1846; 15 Wr. 1847, B.A. 1847, M.A. 1850; C. of Speldhurst Kent 1848–49; C. of St. Mary

ASHWELL, REV. A. R. *(Con.)*

the less, Cam. 1849–50 ; vice principal of St.
Mark's college Chelsea Jany. 1851 to Nov.
1852 ; principal of Oxford diocesan training
college at Culham Nov. 1852 to 1862 ; minister
of Holy Trinity church Hanover square London 1862–64 ; principal of Durham training
college 1865–70 ; canon res. of Chichester
and principal of Chichester theological college
1870 ; R. of St. Andrew's Chichester 1871–
75 ; R. of St. Martin's Chichester 1872–75 ;
chancellor of Chichester cath. 1879 to death,
installed 19 June 1879 ; edited the *Literary
Churchman* 1864–76 and Sep. 1879 to death,
and the *Church quarterly review* 1876. (*m.* 20
April 1854 Elizabeth eld. dau. of J. F. Fixsen
of Blackheath.) *d.* Chichester 23 Oct. 1879.
Literary Churchman xxv, 443–45, 501 (1879).

ASHWELL, JAMES. *b.* Nottingham 1799. One
of the six founders of the society afterwards
known as the Institution of Civil engineers
2 Jany. 1818, it obtained a royal charter 3
June 1828 ; a fellow commoner at Jesus coll.
Cam. ; managing director and engineer in
chief of the Great Luxembourg railway company 1847–52. *d.* Mildmay lodge, Weston-
super-Mare 2 July 1881. *Minutes of proc. of
Instit. of C.E. lxvi,* 372–75 (1881.)

ASHWELL, SAMUEL. *b.* Nottingham 1798 ;
studied at Guy's Hospital, London 1817–
20 ; general practitioner in Lime st. square
1821–30 ; obstetric asst. to Guy's Hosp. 1820 ;
obstetric physician and lecturer May 1834 to
1846 ; M.R.C.P. 1835 ; removed to the West
end 1840 ; author of *Practical treatise on par-
turition* 1828 ; *A practical treatise on the diseases
peculiar to women* 1848. *d.* 30 Brook st. Grosvenor sq. 21 Dec. 1857. *Medical Circular i,*
109–111 (1852), *portrait.*

ASHWORTH, EDMUND. *b.* Birtwhistle near
Bolton ; partner with his brother Henry as
spinners at Egerton Mill near Bolton ;
member of Anti-Corn-Law League 1839 ;
member of Manchester chamber of commerce,
a director 1868–78, pres. 1874–77 ; said to
be original of Mr. Millbank in '*Coningsby*' ;
a magistrate for Bolton April 1847 to death ;
one of founders of Cotton supply association
1857 ; the first pres. of Bolton British school
union. *d.* Southport 21 March 1881 in 81
year. *Manchester Guardian 22 March 1881 p.
5, col. 4, and 26 March p. 11, col. 4.*

ASHWORTH, SIR FREDERICK (2 *son of Robert
Ashworth of Dublin*). *b.* Dublin 1783 ; ensign
58 foot 6 July 1799 ; major 22 Nov. 1810
to 20 Feb. 1817 when placed on h. p. ;
knighted by lord lieut. 1850 ; lieut. general

ASHWORTH, SIR F. *(Con.)*

20 June 1854 ; colonel of 44 foot 8 Feb. 1855
to death. (*m.* 29 Oct. 1833 Harriet eld. dau.
of Sir Bellingham Reginald Graham, 7 Bart.,
she was *b.* 1815 and *m.* (2) 26 Feb. 1862 George
Hamilton Chichester, 3 Marquess of Donegal).
d. 5 St. George's place, Hyde park corner,
London 1 Aug. 1858.

ASHWORTH, HENRY. *b.* Birtwhistle near
Bolton 4 Sep. 1794 ; ed. at Ackworth school ;
partner with his brother Edmund ; a founder
of "Anti-Corn Law Association" 10 Jany.
1839, afterwards called "The National Anti-
Corn-Law League" ; great friend of Bright
and Cobden, the three were known as the
A, B, C of the League, the final meeting of
which was held in Manchester town hall 2
July 1846 ; author of *Statistical illustrations
of Lancashire* 1842 ; *A tour in the United
States, Cuba and Canada* 1861. *d.* Florence
17 May 1880. *Recollections of Richard Cobden,
by H. Ashworth,* 2 ed. 1878, *portrait.*

ASHWORTH, JOHN. Preached his trial sermon
8 Oct. 1837 ; founded a chapel for the destitute in Baillie st. Rochdale 4 Oct. 1858 ; representative of United Methodist Free churches
at the Conference of Evangelical Christians
held in New York Oct. 1873 ; author of
Strange tales from humble life, 5 series 1863–74,
these 61 tales were also published singly,
upwards of 3,000,000 copies have been circulated. *Simple Records,* 2 series 1871–72. *d.*
Broadfield, Rochdale 26 Jany. 1875. *Life
and labours of John Ashworth, by A. L.
Calman* 1875, *portrait.*

ASHWORTH, REV. JOHN HARVEY (*younger
son of John Ashworth*). *b.* Elland, Yorkshire
1795 ; ed. at Manchester gr. sch. and Univ.
coll. Ox., scholar 1815, B.A. 1819, M.A. 1825 ;
R. of Hethe, Oxon 1820–21 ; C. of St. Mary's,
Rochdale 1821 ; bought old castle of Craggan,
co. Clare which he restored ; V. of St. Mary's,
Staveley-in-Cartmel 1874 to death ; author of
Hurstwood, a tale 3 vols. 1823 ; *Scenes and
thoughts from secluded life* 2 vols. 1827 ; *The
Saxon in Ireland* 1851 ; *The young curate or the
quicksands of life* [anon.] 1859, and *Rathlynn*
[anon.] 3 vols. 1864. *d.* 4 Aug. 1882.

ASKEW, RICHARD CRASTER (5 *son of John
Askew of Pallinsburn, Northumberland who d.
28 Oct. 1794*). *b.* 5 Sep. 1778 ; barrister L.I.
13 June 1807 ; recorder of Newcastle upon
Tyne 1833–34. *d.* Pallinsburn 30 July 1851.

ASKEY, JAMES ROBERT ROPER. Chief clerk
of the divorce registry 1858 to death. *d.* 14
Park village West, Gloucester gate, Regents'
park, London 30 Jany. 1866.

ASLETT, THOMPSON. 2 Lieut. R.M. 1 June 1796; col. commandant 9 Nov. 1846 to 17 Aug. 1848 when he retired on full pay. *d.* 27 Aug. 1851 aged 75.

ASLETT, WILLIAM STRATTON. 2 Lieut. R.M. 26 July 1837; brigade major in Crimean war; col. commandant 13 Feb. 1867 to death; M.G. 6 March 1868. *d.* Cury road, Gosport 28 July 1876.

ASPINALL, BUTLER COLE (*son of Rev. James Aspinall, R. of Althorpe, Lincs.*) *b.* Liverpool 7 Nov. 1830; ed. at Merchant Taylor's; connected with *Morning Chronicle;* barrister M.T. 17 Nov. 1853; arrived in Victoria 1854; law reporter to the *Argus* paper 1854; practised at Melbourne 1854; M.L.A. for Talbot 1856; M.L.A. for Portland to 1870; member of the Heales government 1861, of the Macpherson government 1869; defended the Eureka stockade rioters 1855; defended H. J. O'Farrell who was tried 30–31 March 1868 for shooting Prince Alfred (Duke of Edinburgh) at Clontarf 12 March 1868; became insane 1871. *d.* England 4 April 1875.

ASPINALL, REV. JAMES (*son of J. B. Aspinall of Cleongar hall, Cheshire*). *b.* Liverpool; ed. at St. Mary hall Ox., B.A. 1820, M.A. 1823; C. of Rochdale 5 years; P.C. of St. Luke's, Liverpool 1830 where he preached 5 June 1831 a remarkable sermon called *The Crisis or the signs of the times with regard to the Church of England;* R. of Althorpe, Lincs. 2 June 1839 to death; author of *Roscoe's library or old books and old times* 1853; *Parish sermons* 2 series 1854–59. *d.* Althorpe rectory 15 Feb. 1861 aged 65.

ASPLAND, ALFRED (*son of Rev. Robert Aspland 1782–1845, pastor of the Unitarians at Hackney 40 years*). *b.* 1815; ed. at King's college, London; studied at Guy's hospital; L.S.A. 1837, M.R.C.S. 1838, F.R.C.S. 1859; practised at Dukinfield, Cheshire till about 1870; editor of the Holbein Society publications; pres. of Manchester statistical society 1863–65; his large collection of books and drawings was sold at Sotheby's Jany. 1885; author of *Crime in Manchester* 1868; edited for Holbein Society *H. Burgmair's Triumph of the Emperor Maximilian* 1875; and *The golden legend* 1878. *d.* St. Helen's Field, Dukinfield 24 Oct. 1880. *Book-lore March* 1885 *p.* 119.

ASPLAND, REV. ROBERT BROOK (*brother of the preceding*). *b.* Newport, Isle of Wight 19 Jany. 1805; Unitarian pastor of Crook's lane chapel, Chester Aug. 1826; copastor with Lant Carpenter of Lewin's Mead chapel, Bristol 1833; kept a boarding school at

ASPLAND, REV. R. B. (*Con.*)
Bristol 1833–36; pastor at Dukinfield 1 Jany. 1837 and at Hackney 1858 to death; edited the *Christian Reformer* Jany. 1845 to Dec. 1863 when it ceased; one of secretaries of Manchester college 1846–57, which was moved from Manchester to London 1853; secretary to British and Foreign Unitarian Association 1859 to death. (*m.* 21 Oct. 1833 Jane dau. of Robert Hibbert of Brookside Godley, Cheshire). *d.* Well st. Hackney 21 June 1869. *John Evans's Lancashire authors* (1850) 4–8; *The Inquirer* 3 *July* 1869 427–28.

ASPULL, WILLIAM. *b.* Nottingham 1798; tenor singer; composed many vocal pieces. *d.* 192 Clapham road, London 16 Jany. 1875.

ASTLEY, SIR FRANCIS DUGDALE, 2 Baronet (*only son of Sir John Dugdale Astley, 1 Baronet 1778–1842*). *b.* 5 Nov. 1805; succeeded 19 Jany. 1842. *d.* Eastleigh lodge, Warminster 23 July 1873.

ASTLEY, REV. RICHARD. *b.* Chesterfield 12 March 1785; Unitarian minister at Rochdale 1810, at Halifax 1812–26, at Gloucester 1826–31 and at Shrewsbury 1831–53; author of *A selection of 500 hymns for public and private worship.* *d.* Stourbridge 19 March 1855. *The Christian Reformer xi*, 265–73 (1855).

ASTON, SIR ARTHUR INGRAM (*younger son of Henry Hervey Aston of Aston, Cheshire, who d. Madras 23 Dec. 1798 aged 37 from a wound received in a duel with major Allen*). *b.* London 23 Dec. 1798; ed. at Brasen coll. Ox., created M.A. 18 June 1817; sec. of embassy at Paris 11 Jany. 1833; min. plenipo. there for short periods 9 times between 19 April 1833 and 14 Sep. 1838; envoy extraord. and min. plenipo. at Madrid 13 Feb. 1840 to 13 Nov. 1843; G.C.B. 10 Nov. 1843; pensioned 8 March 1846; sheriff of Cheshire 1850. *d.* Aston hall, near Runcorn 5 May 1859.

ASTON, JAMES JONES (2 *son of Benjamin Richard Aston of 71 Banner st. Finsbury, coal merchant*). *b.* 71 Banner st. 12 Dec. 1822; barrister M.T. 6 Nov. 1846; went Northern circuit; Q.C. for county palatine of Lancaster 1867; Q.C. 24 March 1880; author of *Chancery practice of the county palatine of Lancaster* 1852. (*m.* 7 Sep. 1854 Sarah Margaret eld. dau. of Thomas Eccles of Walton-le-dale, Lancs.) *d.* 13 Pembroke gardens, Kensington 17 Jany. 1885.

ASTON, JOHN PARTINGTON (*son of John Aston of Manchester, liquor merchant.*) *b.* Manchester 9 Nov. 1805; ed. at Manchester gr. sch.; solicitor at Manchester 1829 to death; one

ASTON, J. P. *(Con.)*

of leading conveyancing and patent lawyers; solicitor and sec. of Owens college, Manchester; contributed prose and verse to periodicals; author with W. H. Ainsworth of *Sir John Chiverton* 1826. *d.* Higher Broughton, Manchester 11 May 1882. *Admission register of Manchester school iii,* 112 (1874).

ATHERLEY, MARK KER (2 *son of Arthur Atherley M.P. for Southampton who d. 21 Oct. 1844 aged 74*). Ensign 15 foot 28 Aug. 1823; lieut. col. 92 foot 23 Nov. 1849 to 5 June 1863 when placed on h.p.; commanded a brigade in the Crimea 4 Nov. 1855 to 13 March 1856; brigadier general Malta 1863–68; col. of 109 foot 14 Feb. 1873, of 93 foot 30 Jany. 1880 and of 92 foot 5 April 1880 to death; general 1 Oct. 1877. *d.* 11 March 1884 in 80 year.

ATHERSTONE EDWIN. *b.* Nottingham 17 April 1788; author of *The fall of Nineveh, a poem,* 2 vols. 1828–68; *The Sea Kings in England, an historical romance,* 3 vols. 1830; *The handwriting on the wall, a story* 3 vols. 1858; *Israel in Egypt* 1861 a poem of nearly 20,000 lines; granted civil list pension of £75 Oct. 4 1858 and another of £25 Jany. 16 1860. *d.* 19 Macaulay buildings, Bath 29 Jany. 1872.

ATHERTON, CHARLES (3 *son of Nathan Atherton of Calne, Wilts attorney*). *b.* Calne 1805; ed. at Queen's coll. Cam.; 33 wrangler 1828, B.A. 1828; resident engineer of river Clyde 1832–34; manager of business of Claud Girdwood and Co. of Glasgow, ironfounders 1834–37; chief engineer at Woolwich dockyard 6 April 1847 to 31 Dec. 1848 and 8 Sep. 1851 to 26 July 1862; at Devonport dockyard 1 Jany. 1849 to 7 Sep. 1851; consulting engineer in London 1862–70; M.I.C.E. 19 Feb. 1828. *d.* Sandown, Isle of Wight 24 May 1875. *Min. of proc. of Instit. of C.E. xlii,* 252–55 (1875).

ATHERTON, SIR WILLIAM (*only son of Rev. Wm. Atherton of Battle Bridge Middlesex, Wesleyan minister* 1775–1850). *b.* Glasgow October 1806; special pleader 1832–39; barrister I.T. 22 Nov. 1839, bencher 1851; went northern circuit of which he became leader; Q.C. July 1851; Q.C. for duchy of Lancaster 1851–60; M.P. for Durham 9 July 1852 to death; judge advocate of the fleet and counsel to the Admiralty 1854 to 16 Dec. 1859; solicitor general 16 Dec. 1859 and attorney general 4 July 1861 to Sep. 1863; knighted by the Queen at St. James's palace 23 Feb. 1860. (*m.* 15 April, 1843 Agnes

ATHERTON, SIR W. *(Con.)*

Mary younger dau. of Thomas James Hall, chief magistrate at Bow st. London, she *d.* 26 March 1866). *d.* 13 Westbourne terrace, Hyde Park 22 Jany. 1864.

ATHLUMNEY, WILLIAM MEREDYTH SOMERVILLE, 1 Baron. *b.* 1802; ed. at Harrow; paid attaché at Berlin 1829–32; M.P. for Drogheda 1837–52 and for Canterbury 1854–65; under sec. of state for Home department 5 July 1846 to 22 July 1847; chief sec. for Ireland 22 July 1847 to Feb. 1852; P.C. 22 July 1847; raised to peerage of Ireland as Baron Athlumney 14 Dec. 1863 and to peerage of United Kingdom as Baron Meredyth 3 May 1866. *d.* Dover 7 Dec. 1873.

ATHOLE, GEORGE AUGUSTUS FREDERICK JOHN MURRAY, 6 Duke of. *b.* Great Cumberland place, London 20 Sep. 1814; took part in the Eglinton tournament 28–30 Aug. 1839; grand master mason of Scotland 1843–63; succeeded his uncle as 6 Duke of Athole 14 Sep. 1846; K.T. 28 Oct. 1853; pres. of Highland and Agricultural Societies 1858–62; kept Otter hounds at Dunkeld. *d.* Blair castle, Perthshire 16 Jany. 1864.

ATKINS, EDWARD. *b.* 1818; played at T. R. Birmingham 1851–61; made his début in London at Drury Lane 28 Oct. 1861; played Jem Dalton in Tom Taylor's drama *The Ticket of leave man* at Olympic theatre 27 May 1863 to 16 Sep. 1864 406 times, and more than 600 times afterwards in different theatres; played Autolycus in *A winter's tale* at Drury Lane 28 Sep. 1878. *d.* 5 Carlton road west, Peckham 8 April 1883. *Tallis's Drawing room table book part 16, portrait.*

ATKINS, EDWIN. Manager with his brother John Atkins of Zoological gardens situated between Farnworth st. and Butler st. Liverpool which were established in 1832 by Thomas Atkins, keeper of a travelling menagerie, the gardens were eventually turned into a limited liability company, and in 1863 the place was dismantled and the land sold; started for interior of Africa 1852. *d.* on a small island of the White river, a branch of the Nile Jany. 1854.

ATKINS, EDWIN MARTIN (*eld. son of Atkins Edwin Martin-Atkins of Walcot in Bath*). *b.* 1808; ed. at Rugby; matric. Magd. coll. Ox. 26 July 1825 aged 17, B.A. 1829; sheriff of Berkshire 1844; F.S.A. 10 Dec. 1857; the original of the Squire depicted by Tom Hughes in *The scouring of the White Horse* 1859. *d.* Weston super Mare 5 May 1859.

ATKINSON, CHARLES CALEB (*eld. son of Caleb Atkinson of Hillingdon, Middlesex*). *b.* 1793; barrister M.T. 6 June 1834; sec. of University college London 1835 to July 1867; sub editor of *The Sphinx;* owner of *The Athenæum* for short time. (*m.* 1831 Harriet dau. of George Swimley of Henley on Thames). *d.* Alexandra road, Kilburn, London 11 Jany. 1869.

ATKINSON, FENTON ROBINSON. *b.* Leeds 12 Nov. 1784; admitted attorney May 1810; practised at Manchester; a leading bankruptcy lawyer; sold his library Dec. 1817 and his other library of 13,000 volumes May 1858 a ten days sale; member of Chetham, Camden, Hakluyt, Shakspere and Percy Societies and Warton club; contributed to *Bibliographiana*, originally published in the *Manchester Exchange Herald* 1815–16 and afterwards as a small vol. of which only 24 copies were issued 1817. *d.* The Grove, Withington, Lancs. 9 June 1859. *Law Times xxxiii*, 212, 257 (1859).

ATKINSON, SIR HENRY ESCH (3 *son of Henry Wm. Atkinson 1753–1834 provost of Company of moneyers). b.* 1792; entered navy 2 Feb. 1807; commander 30 April 1827; employed in the Coast Guard 1835–38; retired captain 1 April 1856; knighted by lord lieutenant of Ireland 1836; superintendent of convicts in Van Diemen's Land 1846. (*m.* 1819 Sarah dau. of John Randall of the Isle of Wight, she *d.* 1873). *d.* Hobart Town 1857.

ATKINSON, JAMES. *b.* county of Durham 9 March 1780; assistant assay master at Calcutta mint 1813–28; superintendent of the government Gazette 1817–28; surgeon to 55 Bengal N.I. 1833; superintending surgeon to the army of the Indus 1838–41; a member of Bengal medical board 1845–47; author of *The Shâh Nâmah translated and abridged* 1832, which won gold medal of Oriental translation fund; *The expedition into Afghanistan* 1842; *Sketches in Afghanistan* 1842. *d.* 18 Dorset sq. London 7 Aug. 1852. *Journal of Royal Asiatic Society xv, vi–ix*, (1855).

ATKINSON, JAMES. Perfumer in Old Bond st. London; lived at Village park, Ealing. *d.* 27 June 1853 aged 71.

ATKINSON, JAMES CHARLES. *b.* Middlesex 1 May 1783; served in merchant service 1796–1803; joined R.N. as a volunteer 1803; master 29 Jany. 1814; staff commander on h.p. 11 June 1863. *d.* Southampton 27 Oct. 1882 aged 99 years and six months.

ATKINSON, SIR JASPER (*son of Henry Wm. Atkinson 1753–1834, provost of Company of moneyers). b.* Dulwich 1790; employed in the Mint 1804–51; provost of Company of moneyers 1 April 1848 to July 1851 when it was dissolved; knighted by patent 28 Nov. 1842 for services rendered to Ottoman, Russian and French governments. (*m.* 12 May 1819 Louisa Jane Grace only dau. of Wm. Gyll of Wyrardisbury house, Bucks, she was *b.* 21 July 1800 and *m.* (2) 1863 Percy Honey of Exchequer Office, Lincolns Inn). *d.* North Frith Haddow near Tonbridge Wells 6 Oct. 1856.

ATKINSON, RICHARD. *b.* Dublin 1796; a poplin manufacturer there 1820 to death; alderman of Dublin 1857 to death; mayor 1856 and 1861; gave a grand ball to Prince of Wales 11 Sep. 1861; a great philanthropist. *d.* 1867. *I.L.N. xxxviii*, 83 (1861) *portrait.*

ATKINSON, SOLOMON. *b.* Cumberland; ed. at Trin coll. Cam.; senior wrangler and 2 Smith's prizeman 1821; B.A. 1821; barrister L.I. 21 May 1827; author of *County court extension act*, 1850; *Law and practice of county courts* 1853. *d.* Mornington crescent, Hampstead road 12 Feb. 1865.

ATKINSON, THOMAS WITLAM. *b.* Cawthorne, Yorkshire 6 March 1799; employed in rebuilding St. Mary's church Barnsley 1819 where he carved some very fine work; architect in London 1827–42 when he went to Hamburg; engaged in reconstruction of St. Nicholas church Hamburg 1845; went to Russia 1846; granted by Emperor of Russia rare privilege of a blank pass throughout his Asiatic dominions; travelled in Siberia and Mongolia; F.R.G.S. 1858, F.G.S. 1859; author of *Explorations in Oriental and West Siberia* 1857; *Travels in the regions of the Upper and Lower Amoor* 1860; (*m.* 1847 Lucy authoress of *Recollections of Tartar Steppes* 1863, she was granted a civil list pension of £100 18 June 1863). *d.* Lower Walmer, Kent 13 Aug. 1861.

ATKINSON, WILLIAM GREENE. *b.* Darlington 1810; barrister M.T. 19 Nov. 1841; librarian of the Great seal patent office, London Jany. 1854 to death; prepared manuscript of catalogue of the library which was printed in 2 vols. 4°. 1882–83; edited the Commissioners of patents journal Jany. 1854 to death. *d.* 59 Rowan road, Hammersmith 18 Sep. 1881.

ATKINSON, WILLIAM STEPHEN (*eld son of Rev. T. D. Atkinson Rector of Rugeley, Staffs.*) director of public instruction for Bengal. *d.* Rome 15 Jany. 1876 aged 55.

ATTHILL, REV. WILLIAM LOMBE. *b.* 11 July 1807; scholar of Caius coll. Cam. 1825; B.A. 1830, M.A. 1851; sub-dean, canon and commissary of collegiate church of Middleham, Yorkshire 1839-51; P.C. of Horsham Norfolk 1851-63; V. of Horsford, Norfolk 1851-63; married 4 times; author of *The way of Catechising* 1840; *History and antiquities of the collegiate church at Middleham* 1847 and of articles in Burke's *Historic Lands of England* 1849. *d.* Brandiston hall, Alderford, Norfolk 11 Dec. 1884.

ATTREE, WILLIAM WAKEFORD. *b.* 1805; ed. at Eton and Trin. coll. Cam., B.A. 1829, M.A. 1832; barrister M.T. 7 June 1833; assistant tithe comr.; recorder of Hastings and of Seaford about 1842 to death; author of *Report of Braintree church rate case* 1853. *d.* Queen's Park, Brighton 28 Jany. 1862.

ATTWOOD, BENJAMIN *(son of Matthias Attwood of Hales Owen, founder of bank of Attwoods in London and Birmingham).* a manufacturer at Birmingham; came into a large fortune from his nephew Matthias Attwood; gave with greatest secrecy for many years sums of £1000 each to all manner of charities to amount of £375,000. *d.* Pengelly house, Cheshunt 22 Nov. 1874. *I.L.N. lxvi* 57 (1875) *portrait; Graphic xi* 67 (1875) *portrait.*

ATTWOOD MATTHIAS *(brother of the preceeding).* partner in bank of Attwoods; chairman of General steam navigation co.; M.P. for Callington 14 March 1820, for Boroughbridge 2 Aug 1830, and for Whitehaven 15 Dec. 1832 to 23 July 1847. *d.* Dulwich hill 11 Nov. 1851. *G.M. xxxvii* 192-93 (1852).

ATTWOOD, THOMAS *(brother of the preceding).* *b.* Howe house, Hales Owen, 6 Oct. 1783; a banker and manufacturer at Birmingham and London; opposed orders in council of 1807 and 1809 prohibiting all trade between England and the ports occupied by the French, the orders were partly revoked June 1812; originated abolition of East India monopoly 1813; one of the 3 founders of Birmingham Political Union 1829 which contributed largely towards passing of the Reform bill; presented with freedom of city of London 23 May 1832; M.P. for Birmingham 12 Dec. 1832 to Jany. 1840; presented to House of Commons the Chartist petition signed by 1280000 people, 14 June 1839; author of *Letters of a Scotch banker,* first published anonymously in *The Globe* 1828. *d.* Great Malvern 6 March 1856. *Dents Old and new Birmingham, section* 2, (1880) 349-52.

ATTWOOD, T. *(Con.)*

NOTE.—There is a statue of him in Stephenson place New st. Birmingham, which was unveiled 7 June 1858. He is the "King Tom" of Cobbett's Weekly Register.

ATWOOD, REV. HENRY ADAMS SERGISON. *b.* St. Margaret's Westminster 13 Jany. 1800; ed. at Queen's coll. Ox., B.A. 1822, M.A. 1824; F.R.A.S. 1827; R. of Ashelworth, Gloucs. 1839 to death; author of *A new version of the Book of Psalms in verse by H. A. S. A.* 1834. *d.* Ashelworth rectory 22 June 1877.

AUBIN, JOHN. One of the 11 judges of the Royal Court in Jersey 17 May 1862 to death. *d.* 27 Midvale road, St. Heliers 28 Jany. 1874 aged 78.

AUBREY, THOMAS. *b.* Cefn-coed-y-cymer near Merthyr-Tydvil 13 May 1808; Wesleyan minister 1826 to death; chairman of North Wales district 1854-65. *d.* Rhyl 15 Nov. 1867. *Wesl. Meth. Mag. xci, pt.* 2 *p.* 845 (1868).

AUBREY, SIR THOMAS DIGBY, 7 Baronet. *b.* Llanblythian, Glamorganshire 2 Dec. 1782; barrister L.I. 11 Feb. 1811; sheriff of Bucks 1815; succeeded 1 March 1826; chairman of Bucks quarter sessions some years. *d.* Oving house near Aylesbury 2 Sep. 1856.

AUCHMUTY, SIR SAMUEL BENJAMIN (2 *son of Samuel Auchmuty of Bryanstown).* *b.* Ireland 1781; major 7 foot 28 Oct. 1813 to 1 Aug. 1822 when placed on h. p.; aide de camp to the Sovereign 1831-41; granted service reward 3 Aug. 1845; col. of 65 foot 31 Jany. 1851 and of 7 foot 18 Jany. 1855 to death; general 19 June 1860; C.B. 4 June 1815, K.C.B. 2 Jany. 1857, G.C.B. 28 June 1861. (*m.* 1817 Mary Anne Buchanan, she *d.* 2 Jany. 1869 aged 69). *d.* Pau 30 April 1868.

AUCKLAND, RIGHT REV. ROBERT JOHN EDEN, 3 Baron. *b.* Eden farm Beckenham, Kent 10 July 1799; ed. at Eton and Magd. coll. Cam., M.A. 1819, D.D. 1847; R. of Eyam 1823; R. of Huntingfordbury 1825; V. of Battersea 1835; chaplain to William iv 1831-37 and to Victoria 1837-47; Bishop of Sodor and Man 7 May 1847; consecrated 23 May 1847; installed at Castletown 29 June 1847; translated to see of Bath and Wells 2 June 1854; resigned his episcopal functions Oct. or Nov. 1869; succeeded his brother as 3 Baron 1 Jany. 1849. *d.* The palace, Wells 25 April 1870. *I.L.N. lvi,* 489, 490 (1870), *portrait.*

AUDLEY, GEORGE EDWARD THICKNESSE TOUCHET, 20 Baron. *b.* 26 Jany. 1817; succeeded 14 Jany. 1837. *d.* Homburg 18 April 1872. *Burke's Portrait gallery ii,* 41 (1833).

AUDUBON, JOHN JAMES. *b.* New Orleans 4 May 1780; arrived at Liverpool 20 July 1826; lived in England 1826–29, 1830–31, 1834–36 and 1838–39; author of *Birds of America* published in 87 parts, elephant folio at price of 1000 dollars; F.L.S. 1828, F.R.S. 18 March 1830. *d.* New York Island 27 Jany. 1851 *R. Buchanan's Life of J. J. Audubon* 1868, 2 *portraits.*

AUDUS, JAMES (*only son of John Audus of Selby, Yorkshire, merchant 1752–1809*). *b.* 28 July 1781; captain in York city militia 1808–33; began a coasting trade between Selby and London 1826, had 18 schooners so employed 1830; chairman of Yorkshire banking company 1843; erected and endowed St. James's church Selby at cost of about £14000, laid the foundation stone 6 May 1866. *d.* Selby 14 May 1867. *W. W. Morrell's History of Selby* (1867) 186, 254–58.

NOTE.—He was the oldest railway director in England, having been one of original board of Leeds and Selby railway which obtained its act 1830.

AULDJO, JOHN. Ascended Mont Blanc 8 Aug. 1827, being the 14th ascent ever made; F.R.G.S. 1832; F.R.S. 7 May 1840; author of *Ascent of Mont Blanc* 1827; *Sketches of Vesuvius* 1832; *Journal of a visit to Constantinople* 1835. *d.* 1857.

AULSEBROOK, RICHARD. M.R.C.S. 1834, L.S.A. 1835; surgeon to Lambeth workhouse; resident medical officer of Hanwell lunatic asylum; author of *An inquiry into the physical condition of the working classes in the parish of St. James's Westminster.* *d.* 50 King sq., Goswell road London 1855.

AURIOL, REV. EDWARD. Ed. at Ch. Ch. Ox., B.A. 1828, M.A. 1832; R. of Newton Valence, Hants 1838; R. of St. Dunstan in the West, London 1841 to death; Preb. of St. Paul's April 1865 to death; commissary for Bishop of Nelson 1866. *d.* 35 Mecklenbergh sq. London 10 Aug. 1880 aged 75.

AUSTEN, CHARLES JOHN. *b.* 1779; captain R.N. 10 May. 1810; captain of Bellerophon 80 guns 1838–40; awarded good service pension 1840; R.A. 9 Nov. 1846; commander in chief in East Indies 14 Jany. 1850 to death; C.B. 18 Dec. 1840; *d.* Prome, Burmah 8 Oct. 1852.

AUSTEN, SIR FRANCIS WILLIAM (4 *son of Rev. George Austen R. of Steventon, Hants*). *b.* Steventon 23 April 1774; captain R.N. 13 May 1800; served in action off St. Domingo 1805, for which he received thanks of houses of parliament; colonel R.M. 27

AUSTEN, SIR F. W. (*Con.*)
May 1825; commander in chief on north American and West Indian station 27 Dec. 1844 to 12 Jany. 1848; admiral 1 Aug. 1848; R.A. of United Kingdom 5 June 1862; V.A. of U.K. 11 Dec. 1862; admiral of the fleet 27 April 1863 to death; C.B. 4 June 1815, K.C.B. 28 Feb. 1837, G.C.B. 18 May 1860. *d.* Portsdown lodge, Portsmouth 10 Aug. 1865.

AUSTEN, SIR HENRY EDMUND (*only son of Robert Austen of Shalford, Surrey who d. 3 Nov. 1797*). *b.* Shalford 20 May 1785; ed. at Harrow and Oriel coll. Ox., M.A. 1807; sheriff of Surrey 1810; a gentleman of the Privy Chamber 26 Jany. 1832 to death; knighted by the king at St. James's Palace 22 Feb. 1832. *d.* 2 Suffolk place Cheltenham 1 Dec. 1871.

AUSTEN, REV. JOHN THOMAS. Ed. at St. John's coll. Cam.; senior Wr. and senior Smith's prizeman 1817; B.A. 1817, M.A. 1820, B.D. 1827; fellow of his college 1817; V. of Aldworth, Berks 1832–48; R. of West Wickham, Kent 1848 to death; hon. canon of Canterbury cathedral 1873. *d.* West Wickham rectory 10 June 1876 aged 82.

AUSTEN, REV. ROBERT (*only son of Venerable Robert Austen 1723–92, archdeacon of Cork*). Treasurer of Cloyne 24 July 1810 to 10 June 1833 when he resigned. *d.* Southsea, Hants 4 Nov. 1854 in 83 year.

AUSTEN, THOMAS. Lieut. col. of 60 regiment of foot 20 June 1805 to 1817; M.P. for West Kent 1845–47. *d.* Kippington, Sevenoaks 23 July 1859 aged 84.

AUSTIN, ALFRED. *b.* 1805; assistant poor law comr. 1843–1854; sec. to Office of Works 1854–1868; C.B. 11 Oct. 1869. *d.* 67 Queen's gardens, Bayswater 19 May 1884 in 79 year.

AUSTIN, CHARLES (2 *son of Jonathan Austin of Creeting Mill, Suffolk, government contractor*). *b.* 26 March 1799; ed. at Bury St. Edmund's gr. sch. and Jesus coll. Cam., B.A. 1824, M.A. 1827; pupil of Sir Wm. Follett; barrister M.T. 25 May 1827; bencher 1841; Q.C. 1841; practised chiefly before committees of Houses of Parliament where he was the leading counsel; retired with a large fortune 1848; high steward of Ipswich; chairman of quarter sessions for East Suffolk. (*m.* 10 June 1856 Harriet Jane elder dau. of Ralph Mitford Preston Ingilby). *d.* Brandeston hall, Wickham Market 21 Dec. 1874. Personalty sworn under £140,000 19 Feb. 1875. *J. S. Mill's Autobiography* (1873) 76–79; *Fortnightly Review xxiii,* 321–38 (1875); *Public men of Ipswich* (1875) 90–96.

AUSTIN, SIR HORATIO THOMAS. Entered navy 8 April 1813; took part in Parry's second Arctic expedition 1824–1825; commanded Salamander one of first steamers in the navy 1832–34; captain 28 June 1838; served in the Syrian war 1839–1843; commanded a squadron in search of Sir John Franklin 1850–1851; superintendent of Deptford dockyard 18 Oct. 1854 to 28 Nov. 1857; admiral superintendent of Malta dockyard 6 April 1863 to 26 Nov. 1864; V.A. 20 Oct. 1864; C.B. 18 Dec. 1840, K.C.B. 28 March 1865. (m. 8 Nov. 1831 Anne Eliza only dau. of Thomas Hawkins of Pennance, Creed, Cornwall and widow of Rev. J. Rawlinson, she d. 7 July 1876). d. Leinster gardens, London 16 Nov. 1865 in 65 year. *O'Byrne's Naval biography* (1861) 30.

NOTE.—Austin channel between Byam Martin and Bathurst Isles and Cape Austin on the west coast of Cornwallis Isle are named after him.

AUSTIN, JOHN (*eld son of Jonathan Austin of Creeting Mill, Suffolk*). b. 3 March 1790; in the army 1806–11 when he sold out; served in Sicily; barrister I.T. 5 June 1818; gave up practice 1825; professor of jurisprudence in Univ. of London 1826, lectured there 1828 to June 1832; member of Criminal law commission 1833; delivered a course of lectures on jurisprudence at Inner Temple 1834; went to Malta as Royal Comr. to inquire into grievances of which the natives complained 1836; lived in Paris 1844–48 and at Weybridge, Surrey 1849 to death; corresponding member of moral and political class of French Institute; author of *The province of jurisprudence determined* 1832, 2 ed. 1861; *A plea for the Constitution* 1859. (m 1820 Sarah Taylor.) d. Weybridge 17 Dec. 1859. *Dict. of national biography* ii, 265–68 (1885).

AUSTIN, SARAH (*youngest child of John Taylor of Norwich, yarn maker*). b. Norwich 1793; translated *The story without an end* by Carové 1834; *Ranke's History of the Popes of Rome*, 2 vols. 1840, 4 ed. 3 vols. 1866; author of *Germany from 1760 to 1814, or sketches of German life* 1854; granted civil list pension of £100 13 Oct. 1849. (m. 1820 John Austin). d. Weybridge, Surrey 8 Aug. 1867.

AVELAND, GILBERT JOHN HEATHCOTE, 1 Baron. b. Normanton park, Stamford 16 Jany. 1795; ed. at Westminster, Edinburgh and Trin. coll. Cam.; M.P. for Boston 1820–30 and 1831–32, for Lincolnshire 1832–41 and for Rutlandshire 1841–56; created Baron Aveland of Aveland, county Lincoln 26 Feb. 1856; lord lieutenant of Lincolnshire 12

AVELAND, G. J. H. (*Con.*)

March 1862. d. 12 Belgrave sq. London 6 Sep. 1867; Personalty sworn under £400,000 26 Oct. 1867.

AVELING, THOMAS. b. Elm, near Wisbech 11 Sep. 1824; a farmer at Ruckinge in Romney Marsh; agricultural implement maker at Rochester; an engine builder there 1860 to death; the first to build a traction engine with a single cylinder; invented steam road rollers, now to be found in nearly every town in the kingdom; A.I.C.E. 1871; M.I.C.E. 1877; M.I.M.E. 1869; member of Iron and Steel institute; chevalier of Legion of Honour; knight of order of Francis Joseph. d. Boley hill house Rochester 7 March 1882. *Graphic xxv* 289 (1882) *portrait*; *Min. of proc. of Instit. of C.E. lxxiii* 350–55 (1883).

AVELING, REV. THOMAS WILLIAM BAXTER. b. Castletown, Isle of Man 11 May 1815; usher in a school at Wisbech; studied at Highbury college 1834–38; Congregational minister at Kingsland 10 June 1838 to death; hon. sec. to Asylum for fatherless children at Reedham, Surrey 1847–83, the chapel there is called after him, the "Aveling Memorial Chapel"; chairman of Congregational Board 1873 and of Congregational Union of England and Wales 1874; author of *Naaman or Life's shadows and sunshine* 1853; *Memorials of the Clayton family* 1867; edited *the Jewish Herald* 5 years. d. Reedham orphanage asylum 3 July 1884. *Congregational year book* (1885) 176–79.

AVERY, JOHN. M.R.C.S. 1829, F.R.C.S. 1843; M.D. Paris 1831; surgeon in chief to the 5th Polish ambulance in Polish army; a prisoner many months; a consulting surgeon in London; surgeon to Charing Cross hospital; invented an apparatus for exploring internal cavities of the body which gained large silver medal of Society of Arts; a successful operator in cases of cleft palate. d. 3 Queen st. Mayfair 5 March 1855. *Medical directory* 1856, 722–24.

AVONMORE, BARRY JOHN YELVERTON, 3 Viscount. b. 21 Feb. 1790; succeeded 28 Nov. 1814; principal registrar of court of chancery in Ireland to 1826 when granted pension of £4,200 on abolition of office. d. Raglau road, Dublin 24 Oct. 1870.

AVONMORE, WILLIAM CHARLES YELVERTON, 4 Viscount (*elder son of the preceding*). b. 27 Sep. 1824; ed. at Woolwich; captain R.A. 16 July 1850 to 1 April 1861 when placed on h.p.; suspended from all military duties March 1861. (m. 26 July 1858 Emily Mari-

AVONMORE, W. C. Y. *(Con).*

anne youngest dau. of Sir Charles Ashworth, K.C.B. and widow of Edward Forbes, F.R.S.) *d.* Biarritz 1 April 1883. *The Yelverton correspondence by the Hon. Theresa Yelverton 1863, portrait ; J. J. Macqueen's Reports in House of Lords iv,* 743–912 (1866).

NOTE.—He went through marriage ceremonies with Maria Theresa eld, dau of Thomas Longworth of Manchester, manufacturer (1) at 1 St. Vincent st. Edinburgh on 12 April 1857 and (2) in chapel of Kilbroney near Rostrevor, Ireland on 15 Aug. 1857. A great deal of litigation took place between them to settle the point whether they were married or not, the end of which was that on 28 July 1864, House of Lords decided in favour of Lord Avonmore and against the marriage, thus reversing the judgment of the Court of Session in Edinburgh which had decided in her favour.

AVONMORE, BARRY NUGENT YELVERTON, 5 Viscount. *b.* 1 Randolph cliff, Edinburgh 11 Feb. 1859 ; 2 lieut. 37 foot 30 Jany. 1878 ; lieut. 20 Feb. 1879 to death ; succeeded 1 April 1883. *d.* of enteric fever at Kerbekan in the Soudan 13 Feb. 1885. *I.L.N. lxxxvi,* 431 (1885) *portrait.*

AVORY, HENRY. *b.* 1826 ; articled to John Clark of London, solicitor ; clerk of indictments home circuit 1845 ; admitted a solicitor Nov. 1857 ; deputy clerk of assize home circuit 1858 to death ; clerk of arraigns at central criminal court May 1860 to death. *d.* 26 Ladbroke gardens, London 5 April 1881.

NOTE.—He figures in W. P. Frith's series The race for wealth in the 4th picture " Judgment."

AWDRY, SIR JOHN WITHER (2 *son of John Awdry of Notton house, Chippenham* 1766–1844). *b.* Swindon 21 Oct. 1795 ; ed. at Winchester and Ch. Ch. Ox., B.A. 1817, M.A. 1820, D.C.L. 1844 ; fellow of Oriel coll. 1820–1830 ; barrister M.T. 22 Nov. 1822 ; puisne judge and comr. of insolvent debtor's court Bombay 1830–1839 ; knighted by patent 18 June 1830 ; chief justice of supreme court of Bombay 1839–1841 when he resigned ; chairman of Wilts quarter sessions 1848 to 1866. *d.* Notton house 31 May 1878.

AYCKBOURN, HUBERT *(youngest son of Thomas Harman Ayckbourn, barrister who d. 31 Dec. 1870 aged 94).* author of *The practice of the high court of Chancery* 1844, 9 ed. 1870 ; *The jurisdiction and practice of the supreme court of judicature* 1874 2 ed. 1876 ; committed suicide 2 or 3 May 1880 aged 56.

AYLEN, JONATHAN *(son of John Aylen of Portsea). b.* Portsmouth 22 May 1798 ; entered navy 13 Feb. 1813 ; master 5 Sep. 1823 ; master attendant at Sheerness dock-

AYLEN, J. *(Con.)*

yard 25 May 1849 to March 1856 ; examiner in navigation and seamanship at Hull May 1856 ; retired captain 25 May 1858 ; made several important inventions in anchors, his improvement on the Admiralty anchor was successfully tested at trial of anchors of all nations 1852. *d.* Welton near Brough, Yorkshire 9 Oct. 1874. *O'Byrne* (1861) 31–32.

AYLES, JOHN GEORGE AUGUSTUS. *b.* 1808 ; 2 lieut. R.M. 13 May 1828 ; col. commandant 16 May 1862 to 4 Nov. 1864 ; M.G. 4 Nov. 1864 ; *d.* Clevelands Basset, Southampton 25 Nov. 1883.

AYLESFORD, HENEAGE FINCH, 5 Earl of, *(eld son of Heneage Finch 4 Earl of Aylesford 1751–1812). b.* 24 April 1786 ; succeeded 20 Oct. 1812. *d.* Packington hall, Coventry 3 Jany. 1859.

AYLESFORD, HENEAGE FINCH, 6 Earl of. *b.* Packington hall, 24 Dec. 1824 ; M.P. for south Warwickshire 7 June 1849 to 21 March 1857. *d.* Grosvenor st. London 10 Jany. 1871.

AYLESFORD, HENEAGE FINCH, 7 Earl of. *b.* Upper Brook st. London 21 Feb. 1849 ; entertained Prince of Wales at Packington hall Nov. 1874 ; a prize fight and a cock fight took place there in 1876 ; effected 56 policies of insurance on his life to amount £204,830. *d.* the Big Springs cattle ranche, Texas 13 Jany. 1885.

AYLMER, FREDERICK WHITWORTH AYLMER, 6 Baron. *b.* Twyford near Southampton 12 Oct. 1777 ; captain R.N. 18 May 1805 ; commanded Severn 50 guns at battle of Algiers 27 Aug. 1816 ; naval aide-de-camp to Wm. iv 1830–37 ; V.A. 9 Nov. 1846, pensioned 1 July 1851 ; admiral on half pay 11 Sep. 1854 ; C.B. 19 Sep. 1816, K.C.B. 5 July 1855, K.F.M. ; succeeded as 6 Baron 23 Feb. 1850. *d.* 20 Dawson place, Westbourne grove 5 March 1858. *O'Byrne* (1861) *p.* 32.

AYLMER, SIR GERALD GEORGE, 9 Baronet. *b.* Carnarvon 15 Sep. 1798 ; succeeded 23 May 1816. *d.* Donadea castle Kilcock, co. Kildare 8 Feb. 1878.

AYLMER, SIR GERALD GEORGE, 10 Baronet. *b.* Dublin 26 May 1830. *d.* 25 June 1883.

AYLMER, SIR JUSTIN GERALD, 11 Baronet. *b.* 17 Nov. 1863 ; ed. at Harrow and Trin. coll. Cambridge. *d.* Trinity college 15 March 1885 the result of a fall from a bicycle 3 days before.

AYLMER, SIR ARTHUR PERCY, 12 Baronet. *b*. 31 Aug. 1801; ed. at Trin. coll. Dublin, B.A. 1823, M.A. 1826; student L.I. *d*. Cork 7 May 1885.

AYLMER, THOMAS BRABAZON. Ensign 20 foot 9 Aug. 1797; major 9 foot 4 Sep. 1807 to 25 Feb. 1816 when placed on h.p.; general 25 Sep. 1856; colonel 45 foot 25 Sep. 1856 to death. *d*. Worthing 19 July 1858 aged 76.

AYLWARD, WILLIAM. A student at R.A. of Music, gained a King's scholarship; professor of violoncello there; member of Philharmonic society and of Royal Italian opera band; taught music at Slough. *d*. 12 March 1878.

AYRE, REV. JOHN. *b*. Feb. 1801; ed. at Caius coll. Cam., B.A. 1823, M.A. 1827; Incumbent of St. John's chapel, Downshire hill Hampstead; dom. chap. to Earl of Roden; general secretary and librarian of Parker Society 1840–53; edited for Parker Society *Sermons of Edwin Sandys, archbishop of York* 1841; *Works of Thomas Becon* 3 vols. 1843–44; *Works of John Jewel, bishop of Salisbury* 4 vols. 1845–50; *Works of John Whitgift, archbishop of Canterbury* 3 vols. 1851–53; author of *Treasury of Bible knowledge* 1866. *d*. Church row, Hampstead 20 May 1869.

AYRE, JOSEPH. *b*. Lynn, Norfolk 1781; sent to sea 1800; studied medicine at Guy's hospital and Univ. of Edin.; M.D. 24 June 1807; practised at Hull 1808–24, in London 1824–31, and at Hull again 1831 to death; L.R.C.P. 1824, F.R.C.P. 1859; author of *Practical observations on bilious complaint* 1821; *Researches into the nature and treatment of dropsy* 1825. *d*. Hull 15 Jany. 1860.

AYRES, JOHN. *b*. 1807; clerk of the Royal Society of Literature more than 30 years. *d*. 4 St. Martin's place, London 9 July 1881.

AYRES, PHILIP BURNARD. *b*. Thame, Oxon 12 Dec. 1813; entered Univ. college London Oct. 1833; L.S.A. 1836, M.R.C.S. 25 April 1836; M.D. London 9 Dec. 1841 where he won 7 medals; practised nearly 10 years at Thame; lecturer on chemistry at Charing Cross hospital; phys. to Islington dispensary 1851; edited *Pharmaceutical Times;* patented a method of utilising sewage as manure 1847; superintendent of quarantine in Mauritius 5 Jany. 1856 to death. *d*. Champ de Mars, Port Louis, Mauritius 30 April 1863.

NOTE.—His widow presented his herbarium of Mauritius plants to royal gardens at Kew.

AYRIS, HENRY. *b*. 12 Dec. 1805; whipper-in to the Berkeley hounds 1826; huntsman of same pack down to Dec. 1865, when presented with a purse of 500 guineas, and granted an annuity of £100 by Lord Fitzhardinge; the best huntsman of his day. *d*. Ham near Berkeley 28 April 1874.

AYRTON, EDWARD NUGENT. *b*. Richmond, Surrey 1815; ed. at Ealing and Trin. coll. Cam., B.A. 1836, M.A. 1840; barrister L.I. 20 Nov. 1845; wrote in the Law Times. *d*. Bexhill, Sussex 28 Nov. 1873.

AYRTON, FREDERICK *(elder brother of preceding.) b*. London 20 March 1812; ed. at Ealing and Addiscombe; 2 lieut. Bombay artillery 1828; captain June 1843 to 11 Sep. 1843, when he retired on a pension; barrister M.T. 30 Jany. 1846; sec. to Abbas Pasha viceroy of Egypt 1851 to 13 July 1854 when he died, educated Ilhami Pasha his only son, sec. to him 1854 to his death 1861; A.I.C.E. 9 June 1835; received title of Bey from the Khedive. *d*. Arundel gardens, Notting hill London 20 June 1873. *Min. of proc. of Instit. of C.E. xxxviii*, 306–308 (1874).

NOTE.—He formed a magnificent collection of Arabic calligraphs and MSS. which he bequeathed to to the nation, but unfortunately the conditions with which the bequest was accompanied, prevented the Trustees of the British Museum accepting it.

AYRTON, MATILDA *(dau. of Mr. Chaplin.) b*. Honfleur 1846; passed preliminary examination at the Apothecaries' Hall 1869 but was refused admission to the later examination on ground of her sex; matriculated at Univ. of Edin.; completed her education at Paris; lived in Japan 1873–77; taught midwifery to a class of Japanese women; M.D. Paris Dec. 1879; a licentiate of the King and Queen's College of Physicians in Ireland, when she came out first in the examination; author of *Child life in Japan* 1879; contributed many articles to periodicals. *(m.* 1872 Wm. Edward Ayrton professor in Imperial college of engineering, Japan). *d*. Sloane st. London 19 July 1883. *The Englishwoman's Review* 15 *Aug*. 1883.

AYRTON, WILLIAM *(younger son of Edmund Ayrton 1734–1808, Master of the chapel royal to George iii). b*. London 22 Feb. 1777; Captain in Queen's royal volunteers Westminster; musical and literary critic of the *Morning Chronicle* 1813–1826; chief originator of Philharmonic society 1813; **manager of** Opera house London 1817 **and** 1821; **pro**duced Mozart's Don Giovanni **for first time in**

AYRTON, W. *(Con.)*

England 12 April 1817; edited and wrote much in the *Harmonicon* 1823–33; wrote the musical articles in the *Penny Cyclopædia* 1833–44; edited the *Sacred Minstrelsy* 1834–35 and the *Musical library* 1834–36; one of the original members of Royal institution and of the Athenæum club; F.R.S. 1 June 1837; *d.* 9 Bridge st. Westminster 8 May 1858.

AYRTON, WILLIAM SCROPE *(only son of the preceding)*. *b.* 28 April 1804; ed. at Loughborough house school; barrister M.T. 26 Nov. 1830; a registrar of Court of Bankruptcy Aug. 1838 to July 1847; comr. of Leeds district Court of Bankruptcy 5 July 1847 to 31 Dec. 1869 when granted sum of £1800 on abolition of his office; F.S.A. 21 May 1840; author with Basil Montagu of *Reports of cases in Bankruptcy* 3 vols. 1834–39 and of *The law and practice in Bankruptcy* 2 vols. 1837. *d.* Cliffden, Saltburn-by-the-Sea 3 May 1885.

AYSCOUGH, JOHN *(son of John Ayscough, Capt. R.N.)* *b.* on board H.M.S. "Swan" during an action on the way from North America 1775; captain R.N. 18 April 1806; protected Sicily against invasion of Joachim Murat 1810; superintended the ordinary at Plymouth 1822–25; Comr. of dockyards at Jamaica and Bermuda; admiral 3 Oct. 1855; awarded good service pension. *d.* Norwood, Surrey 2 Dec. 1863. *O'Byrne* (1861) 33–34.

AYTOUN, ROBERT. *b.* Edinburgh 1799; ed. at Univ. of Edin.; a writer to the Signet; member of Royal Scottish society of arts 1826; read many papers; A.I.C.E. 1839; invented a safety cage for mines exhibited at great exhibition 1862. *d.* 9 Sep. 1876.

AYTOUN, WILLIAM EDMONDSTOUNE. *b.* 21 Abercromby place, Edin. 21 June 1813; ed. at academy and univ. of Edin.; M.A. 1849; a writer to the Signet 1835; an advocate 1840; on the staff of Blackwood's magazine 1839 to death, contributed more than 120 articles; professor of Rhetoric and Belles Lettres in Univ. of Edin. 22 Oct. 1845 to 1864, during which time he raised number of students from 30 to 1850; sheriff of Orkney and Zetland 29 May 1852; delivered 6 lectures on poetry and dramatic literature at Willis's Rooms, London 1853; presided at Burns centenary festival at Ayr 25 Jany. 1859; hon. pres. of associated societies of Univ. of Edin. 1860; author of *Poland, Homer and other poems* [*anon.*] 1832; *Lays of the Scottish cavaliers and other poems* 1848, 29 ed.

AYTOUN, W. E. *(Con.)*

1883; *Firmilian or the student of Badajoz, a spasmodic tragedy by T. Percy Jones* [*pseud.*] 1854; *Bon Gaultier ballads* (with T. Martin) 1855, 13 ed. 1877; *Bothwell, a poem in six parts* 1856; edited *The ballads of Scotland* 2 vols. 1858, 4 ed. 1870. *d.* Blackhills near Elgin 4 Aug. 1865. *Theodore Martin's Memoir of W. E. Aytoun* 1867, *portrait; Crombie's Modern Athenians* 1882, *portrait.*

B

BABBAGE, BENJAMIN HERSCHELL *(eld. son of the succeeding)*. Geologist of colony of South Australia; examined the country north and east of Adelaide for gold 1856; commanded an exploring party sent by Parliament of South Australia to Lake Torrens Feb. 1858 to 5 Nov. 1858. *d.* Adelaide 22 Oct. 1878 aged 63. *W. Howitt's History of discovery* ii, 311–24 (1865); *Rev. J. E. T. Wood's History of discovery* ii, 260–79 (1865).

BABBAGE, CHARLES *(son of Benjamin Babbage of London, banker)*. *b.* near Teignmouth, Devon 26 Dec. 1792; ed. at Enfield and Trinity and Peterhouse colleges Cam., B.A. 1814, M.A. 1817; F.R.S. 14 March 1816; a founder of Royal Astronomical Society 1820, one of its secs. 1820–24, vice pres., foreign sec and member of council successively; began his calculating machine 1823, suspended its construction 1833, after spending on it about £6,000 besides £17,000 granted him by Government; Lucasian professor of mathematics at Cambridge 1828–39 but delivered no lectures; a founder of British Association 1831, a trustee 1832–38, originated the statistical section at Cambridge meeting 1833; contested Finsbury as a radical Dec. 1832 and June 1834; chief founder of Statistical Society 15 March 1834, chairman 1835; author of *Table of logarithms of the natural numbers from 1 to 108,000,* 1827; *The decline of science in England* 1830; *On the economy of manufactures* 1832, 4 ed. 1835; *The ninth Bridgewater treatise* 1837, 2 ed. 1838. *d.* 1 Dorset st. Portman sq. 18 Oct. 1871. *Babbage's Passages from the life of a philosopher* 1864; *Monthly notices of R. Astronom. soc.* xxxii, 101–109 (1872); *C. R. Weld's History of royal society* ii, 369–91 (1848); *Edinburgh Review* lix, 263–327 (1834); *Journal of statistical soc.* xxxiv, 411–15 (1871); *I.L.N.* lix, 423 (1871), *portrait; Graphic* iv, 495 (1871), *portrait.*

BABER, Rev. Henry Hervey (*son of Thomas Baber of London, barrister*). *b.* 22 Aug. 1775; ed. at St. Paul's sch. and All Soul's coll. Ox., B.A. 1799, M.A. 1805; sub librarian of the Bodleian 1796; assistant librarian at British Museum 1807 and keeper of Printed books 1812–37; vice principal of St. Mary's hall Ox. 1805; C. of St. Mary the Virgin Ox. 1805; R. of Stretham with Thetford, Cambridge 1827; F.R.S. 23 May 1816; one of founders of Royal society of literature 2 June 1823 which received a charter 13 Sep. 1826; editor of *Vetus testamentum Græcum e codice MS. Alexandrino*, 4 vols. 1816–28. *d.* Stretham rectory 28 March 1868.

BABINGTON, Benjamin Guy (*son of Wm. Babington of London, physician* 1756–1833). *b.* Guy's Hospital 1794; ed. at the Charterhouse 1803–1807; midshipman R.N., served at Walcheren and Copenhagen 1809; in the Madras medical service 1812–19; studied at Guy's Hospital and Pemb. coll. Cam., M.B. 1825, M.L. 1827, M.D. 1830, F.R.C.P. 1831; delivered Croonian and Lumleian lectures; F.R.S. 13 March 1828, on the council 1861–63; assistant phys. to Guy's Hospital 1837 and phys. 1840–55; a founder of Sydenham Society 1843, treasurer 1843–58 when society was dissolved; chief founder of Epidemiological society Aug. 1850, pres. 1850–64; pres. of Royal Medical and Chirurgical society 1861; invented the Laryngoscope, made for him by an optician called Elsworthy and exhibited at Hunterian Society 18 March 1829; took out patents for pens 1843, and for preventing incrustation of boilers 1850; author of *Passing thoughts in sonnet* [*anon.*] 1855. *d.* 31 George st. Hanover sq. 8 April 1866 in 73 year. *Trans. of Epidemiological Society ii*, 160–67 *and* 471–76 (1865–67).

BABINGTON, Cornelius Metcalfe Stuart. *b.* India 1816; M.R.C.S. 1838, M.R.C.P. 1849, F.R.C.P. 1857; surgeon accoucheur to St. George's and St. James's dispensary London; phys. to Queen Charlotte's Lying-in-hospital 1850 to death; a founder of Obstetrical Society 16 Dec. 1858, vice pres. 2 Jany. 1861. *d.* Hertford st. London 25 Jany. 1862. *Proc. of Royal Med. and Chir. society iv*, 86–88 (1864).

BABINGTON, David. Entered Madras army 1820; brigadier general in command of Malabar and Canara 17 Jany. 1862 to 3 Feb. 1865; L.G. 16 May 1872. *d.* Clifton 12 Aug. 1874.

BABINGTON, George Gisborne. *b.* 22 Jany. 1794; M.R.C.S. 1816, F.R.C.S. 1843; practised at Golden sq. London; surgeon to St. George's hospital; delivered Hunterian oration at Royal college of surgeons 14 Feb. 1842. *d.* 13 Queen's gardens, Hyde park 1 Jany. 1856.

BABINGTON, William Knox. Brigadier general commanding northern district of Madras 29 Nov. 1867 to 1 Dec. 1868; L.G. 1 Oct. 1877. *d.* 48 Oxford terrace, Hyde Park 31 July 1878.

BABY, Daniel. Ensign 24 foot 9 Nov. 1797; captain 6 Aug. 1806 to 1 June 1826 when placed on h.p.; M.G. 31 Aug. 1855. *d.* 15 April 1858.

BACHE, Francis Edward (*eld. child of the succeeding*). *b.* Birmingham 14 Sep. 1833; pupil of Alfred Mellon; played violin in orchestra at Birmingham festivals 1846 and 1847; organist at All Saint's Church Gordon sq. London Oct. 1850 to Oct. 1853; his first Overture was performed at Adelphi theatre Nov. 1850; composed many pianoforte pieces and songs; designed the organ in Hope st. church, Liverpool. *d.* Frederick st. Edgbaston, Birmingham 24 Aug. 1858. *The Christian Reformer xiv*, 713–19 (1858).

BACHE, Rev. Samuel. *b.* Bridgnorth 24 Dec. 1804; assistant in school of Rev. Lant Carpenter at Bristol; ed. at Manchester college, York 1826–29; unitarian minister at the old meeting Dudley 1829–32 and at the new meeting Moor st. Birmingham 1832–62 when it was sold and congregation moved to Church of the Messiah, Broad st. where he was minister 1862–68; kept a school at Birmingham many years; author of *Harmony of science and revelation* 1839; *Exposition of Unitarian views of Christianity* 1854; *Miracles the credentials of the Christ* 1863 and 19 other publications, none of which are mentioned in *The English catalogue of books*, or *Allibone's Dictionary*. *d.* Gloucester 7 Jany. 1876. *Beale's Memorials of old meeting house Birmingham* 1882.

BACHHOFFNER, George Henry. *b.* London 13 April 1810; originated and suggested scheme of Royal Polytechnic Institution, which was opened 6 Aug. 1838, principal in department of natural and experimental philosophy there, Aug. 1838 to Aug. 1855; one of district registrars of Marylebone parish 1837, and superintendent registrar

BACHHOFFNER, G. H. (Con.)
1853 to death ; lessee and manager of Royal Colosseum, Dec. 1856 to 16 Feb. 1864, when it closed for ever; professor of natural philosophy at Elizabeth college, Guernsey ; invented the Polytechnic gas fire 1850 ; author of *Chemistry as applied to the fine arts* 1837. *d.* 78 The Grove, Hammersmith 22 July 1879.

BACK, SIR GEORGE (*son of John Back of Stockport, Cheshire*). *b.* Stockport 6 Nov. 1796 ; midshipman R N. Sep. 1808 ; a prisoner at Verdun in France 1809–14 ; went with Franklin to the Spitzbergen seas 1818, along Arctic coast of America 1819–22, and to Mackenzie river 1825–27 ; conducted overland Arctic expedition 1833–35, when he travelled 7500 miles, and discovered the Back or Great Fish river ; captain by order in council 30 Sep. 1835, an honour which no other officer in the navy had received except William iv ; commanded the Terror in expedition to the frigid zone 1836–37 ; knighted by the Queen at St. James's palace 6 March 1839 ; F.R.G.S. 1836, Founder's gold medallist 1836 ; F.R.S. 7 Jany. 1847 ; gold medallist of Geographical Society of Paris ; pres. of the Raleigh club 1844 ; awarded good service pension 21 Jany. 1854 ; D.C.L. Oxford 28 June 1854 ; admiral on h.p. 18 Oct. 1867 ; author of *Narrative of the Arctic land expedition to the mouth of the Great Fish river* 1836 ; *Narrative of an expedition in H.M.S. Terror* 1838. (*m.* 13 Oct. 1846 Theodosia Elizabeth, widow of Anthony Hammond of Savile row, London, she *d.* 6 Jany. 1861). *d.* 109 Gloucester place, Portman sq. 23 June 1878. *Geographical mag. v*, 179–81 (1878) ; *I.L.N. lxxii*, 4 (1878) *portrait*; *Graphic xviii*, 116 (1878) *portrait*.

BACK, WILLIAM. *b.* Surrey ; ed. at Guy's hosp. and Univ. of Edin. ; M.D. 24 June 1808 ; L.C.P. 22 Dec. 1814 ; Physician to Guy's hosp. 17 March 1819 to 1840. *d.* New Park road, Clapham park 6 Nov. 1856 aged 74.

BACKHOUSE, EDWARD (*son of Edward Backhouse of Darlington*). *b.* Darlington 1808 ; a banker at Sunderland, and a partner in colleries ; an Elder of Society of Friends 1854 to death ; erected a large mission hall at Sunderland ; author of *The religious society of Friends* 1870. *d* Hastings 22 May 1879. *Early church history compiled by the late E. Backhouse, edited by C. Tylor* 1884, *portrait*.

BACKHOUSE, GEORGE CANNING. Clerk in the Foreign Office 5 April 1838 ; commissary judge at Havannah 16 Dec. 1852 to death ; murdered at Havannah 30 Aug. 1856 aged 37 ; a civil list pension of £100 granted his widow 15 Nov. 1856.

BACKHOUSE, JAMES. *b.* 8 July 1794 ; ed. at Leeds ; minister of Society of Friends 1824 ; missionary to Australia and South Africa 1831–41 ; author of *A narrative of a visit to the Australian colonies* 1843 ; *A narrative of a visit to the Mauritius and South Africa* 1844 and many small books. *d.* Holdgate house, York 20 Jany. 1869. *Memoir of James Backhouse by his sister* 1870 ; *Smith's Friends' Books i*, 152–56 (1867).

BACON, ANTHONY. Cornet 16 Lancers 13 Aug. 1812 ; lieut. 13 Dragoons 1818–1821 when placed on h.p. ; commanded the whole cavalry of Queen Dona Maria of Portugal 1832–34 ; created General on field of battle at Loures by Emperor Don Pedro in person 12 Oct. 1833 ; K.T.S. *d.* Crondall near Farnham 2 July 1864 aged 68. *Sketches in Portugal by J. E. Alexander* (1835) 120, 245.

BACON, CHARLOTTE MARY (2 *dau.* of *Edward Harley, 5 Earl of Oxford* 1773–1848). *b.* Harley st. London 12 Dec. 1801 ; Lord Byron dedicated his *Childe Harold* to her under name of Ianthe 1812. (*m.* 1823 general Anthony Bacon). *d.* 13 Stanhope place, Hyde park 9 March 1880. *Finden's Illustrations of Lord Byron vol. ii*, (1833), *portrait*; *I.L.N. lxxvi*, 292 (1880), *portrait*.

BACON, SIR EDMUND, 9 Baronet of Redgrave and 10 Baronet of Mildenhall. *b.* Raveningham, Beccles, Norfolk 16 July 1779 ; succeeded his father as Premier Baronet of England 5 Sep. 1820. *d.* Raveningham 30 May 1864.

BACON, GEORGE PETER (*younger son of R. M. Bacon of Norwich, editor of the Norwich Mercury*). Bought the Sussex Advertiser 1843, wrote all the leading articles and edited the paper to his death ; sec. of Hop excise duty repeal association 1858 to April 1862 when duty which yielded £750,000 a year was taken off. *d.* 64 High st. Lewes 15 March 1878 in 72 year. *I.L.N. xlii*, 641 (1863).

BACON, SIR HENRY HICKMAN, 10 and 11 Baronet. *b.* Blundeston near Lowestoft 5 April 1820 ; succeeded 30 May 1864 ; sheriff of Lincoln 1867. *d.* Thonock hall, Gainsborough 14 Nov. 1872.

BACON, JOHN (2 *son of John Bacon, R.A. sculptor* 1740–99). *b.* Newman st. Oxford st. London March 1777 ; completed his father's works ; exhibited 64 sculptures at the R.A. 1792–1824 ; executed statue of Wm. iii in St. James's sq. 1808 ; 6 monuments in St. Paul's and 11 monuments in Westminster Abbey. *d.* Bathwick hill near Bath 14 July 1859.

BACON, Rev. Robert. ed. at Univ. of Glasgow LL.D. 1800, and Em. coll. Cam. LL.B. 1806; C. of Hunstanton 1802-42; C. of Sedgeford 1809-32; P.C. of Fring, Norfolk 16 Feb. 1809 to death; R. of Wolverton, Norfolk 1836 to death; author of *Poems*, 1790; *Treatise on Baptism* 1827; *Theological essays* 1829. *d.* 1861.

BACOT, John. *b.* 29 May 1781; M.R.C.S. 1801, F.R.C.S. 1843; assistant surgeon Grenadier Guards 1803-20; practised in London 1820; edited with Roderick Mc Cleod *Medical and Physical journal;* chairman of Court of examiners of Society of Apothecaries 1832-38, master of the company 1845-46; member of General board of Health 1854; author of *Observations on the use and abuse of friction* 1822 and *A treatise on Syphilis* 1829. *d.* 4 Portugal st. Park lane 4 Sep. 1870. *Medical Circular i*, 130 (1852).

BADDELEY, John. *b.* at sea in Bay of Bengal 22 Jany. 1846; taken to England 1851; ed. at Bonn and Univ. of Edin.; M.B. 1867; founded Athletic club of Univ. of Edin. May 1867, pres. 1867-68; fellow of Botanical society of Edin. 14 Dec. 1865; member of Royal Medical Society 23 Nov. 1866. *d.* Royal Infirmary Edin. 29 Feb. 1868. *Transactions of Botanical Society ix*, 304-12 (1868).

BADDELEY, William. Civil engineer; made many improvements in manual fire engines 1820-62; invented portable cistern used by London Fire Brigade. *d.* March 1867 aged 61.

BADELEY, Edward Lowth (*son of John Badeley M.D. of Leighs hall, near Chelmsford 1742-1831*). *b.* 1803; ed. at Brasen. coll. Ox.; B.A. 1823, M.A. 1828; barrister I.T. 29 Jany. 1841; counsel for Bishop of Exeter in Gorham case before judicial committee of P. C. 17-18 Dec. 1849; joined Church of Rome 1850; author of *The privilege of religious confessions in English courts of justice* 1865. *d.* 29 March 1868. *Memoir of J. R. Hope Scott* 2 *vols.* 1884.

BADELEY, John Carr (*brother of the preceding*). *b.* 1794; ed. at the Charterhouse and Caius coll. Cam.; M.B. 1817, M.D. 1822; F.R.C.P.; phys. to Asylum for health Lisson Grove, London; phys. to Chelmsford dispensary 20 years; inspecting phys. to lunatic asylums of Essex; Harveian orator 1849; poisoned himself accidentally at Guy Harlings, Chelmsford 22 Sep. 1851.

BADEN, Maudit or Mardit. *b.* Pewsey, Wilts Feb. 1763 or 1773. *d.* Oare, parish of Wilcot, Wilts 11 May 1869. *Human longevity by W. J. Thoms* (1873) 129-31.

BADGER-EASTWOOD, Thomas Smith (*eld son of Thomas Badger of Rotherham, solicitor 1793-1862*). *b.* 1823; ed. at Doncaster gr. sch. and Trin. hall Cam., B.A. 1846, M.A. 1849; barrister M.T. 29 Jany. 1847; reader on real property law to 4 Inns of Court 1856 to death; assumed surname of Eastwood 1863; edited *Concise forms of wills by W. Hayes and T. Jarman* 5 *ed.* 1860. *d.* 28 Gloucester place, Hyde park gardens 30 May 1866.

BADGLEY, Francis. L.R.C.S. Edin. 1827, M.D. Edin. 1829, L.S.A. 1830; M.R.C.P. London 1860; a phys. at Kensington 1829-42, at Montreal 1842-59 and at Malvern 1860 to death; fellow of Royal medical and chirurgical society 1838; M.D. Univ. of Toronto 1851; professor of medical jurisprudence in Mc Gill college; professor of medicine in medical school of Montreal; professor of medicine in Univ. of Toronto 1851; founded *Montreal Medical Gazette* 1844, edited it 1844-45. *d.* Holyrood house, Great Malvern 24 Dec. 1863 aged 56.

BADGLEY, W. *b.* Montreal 1801; called to Canadian bar 1823; sec. of Constitutional Association of Montreal district 1836-38; one of three delegates of this Association to England 1837-38; comr. of bankrupts for district of Montreal 1840 to April 1847; circuit judge July 1844 to April 1847; attorney general for Lower Canada April 1847; member of the provincial parliament May 1847 to 1855; puisne judge Lower Canada Jany. 1855 to 1876; Grand master of Freemasons for Montreal. *d.* 1876. *H. J. Morgan's Sketches of eminent Canadians* (1862) 492-97.

BADHAM, Rev. Charles. ed. at Em. coll. Cam., B.A. 1839, M.A. 1846; V. of All Saints Sudbury, Suffolk 1847 to death; author of *Selections from Robert Hall* 1840; *Aids to devotion* 1843; *History of All Saints, Sudbury* 1852. *d.* All Saints vicarage, Sudbury 15 April 1874.

BADHAM, Rev. Charles (*son of Charles Badham 1780-1845, Regius professor of physics in Univ. of Glasgow*). *b.* Ludlow 18 July 1813; ed. by Jean Henri Pestalozzi; at Eton 1826; scholar of Wadham coll. Ox. 1830, B.A. 1837, M.A. 1839; studied in Germany and Italy 7 years; incorporated M.A. at Cam. as member of St. Peter's college 1847, D.D. Cam. 1852; headmaster of Birmingham proprietary school 1854-67; professor of classics and logic in Univ. of Sydney 1867 to death; one of greatest scholars of his time; author of *Criticism applied to Shakespeare* 1846; published editions with notes of the *Ion of*

Badham, Rev. C. *(Con.)*

Euripides 1851, 1853 and 1861; and of the *Philebus of Plato* 1855 and 1878. *d.* Sydney 26 Feb. 1884. *Saturday Review lvii*, 540 (1884).

BADHAM, Rev. Charles David *(brother of preceding).* *b.* London 1806; ed. at Eton and Em. coll. Cam., B.A. 1826; incorporated B.A. at Ox. as mem. of Pemb. coll. 1829, M.A. 1829, M.B. 1830, M.D. 1833; travelling fellow of Univ. of Ox. 1829; M.R.C.P., F.R.C.P.; practised at Rome and Paris long time; returned to England 1845; ordained deacon at Norwich by Bishop Stanley; C. of East Bergholt, Suffolk 1849–55; author of *Insect life* 1845; *The esculent funguses of England* 1847; *Prose Halieutics or ancient and modern fish tattle* 1854; contributed much to *Blackwood* and *Fraser. d.* East Bergholt 14 July 1857 in 52 year. *Fraser's Mag. lvi*, 162–63 (1857).

BAGEHOT, Walter *(only son of Thomas Watson Bagehot of Herds Hill Langport, Somerset 1796–1881).* *b.* Langport 3 Feb. 1826; ed. at Bristol and Univ. coll. London, B.A. 1846, M.A. 1848, mathematical scholar 1846, gold medallist 1848; barrister L.I. 17 Nov. 1852; edited the *National Review* with R. H. Hutton July 1855 to Nov. 1864; edited the *Economist* 1860 to death; examiner in political economy in Univ. of London; author of *Estimates of some Englishmen and Scotchmen* 1858; *The English constitution* 1867; *Physics and Politics* 1872. *(m.* 21 April 1858 Eliza eld. dau. of James Wilson, M.P.) *d.* Herds Hill 24 March 1877. *Literary studies by the late W. Bagehot, edited by R. H. Hutton*, 3 ed. i, ix–lxvii (1884), *portrait; Dictionary of Nat. Biog. ii*, 393–96 (1885).

BAGG, William. Surgical artist; illustrated many medical books. *d.* 20 Dec. 1869 in his 66 year.

BAGGE, Rev. Henry Theodore James *(only son of the succeeding).* *b.* 28 Feb. 1824; ed. at Rugby and Downing coll. Cam., B.A. 1851; C. of Weyhill, Hants 1851–54; author of *Toleratio intolerabilis or the free development of the Romish system* 1851; *St. Paul's Epistle to the Galatians, the text revised and illustrated* 1856. *d.* Munich 19 Nov. 1861.

BAGGE, Rev. James. ed. at St. John's coll. Cam.; B.A. 1814, M.A. 1818; R. of Crux-Easton near Newbury 1843 to death; author of *Twelve sermons* 1835; *The Gawthorne correspondence and the Rev. W. B. Barter* 1852, and other Sermons and Pamphlets. *d.* 1877.

BAGGE, Sir William, 1 Baronet *(eld son of Thomas Philip Bagge of Stradsett hall, Norfolk 1771–1827).* *b.* Stradsett hall 17 June 1810; ed. at the Charterhouse and Ball coll. Ox.; M.P. for West Norfolk 1837–57 and 1865 to death; created baronet 13 April 1867. *d.* Stradsett hall 12 Feb. 1880.

BAGGE, Sir William Henry Ernest, 2 Baronet. *b.* Stradsett hall 9 Aug. 1840. *d.* Heatherside, Woking 23 Oct. 1881.

BAGLEY, James. *b.* Ireland 1822; went to the U.S.; commanded 69th Regiment 1862–66; alderman of New York; Sachem of the Tammany society to death. *d.* New York 21 Dec. 1876.

BAGLEY, John Woodhouse. made many important improvements in the bobbin net machine for which he took out patents 1844, 1850 and 1851; his productions were shewn in the London exhibition of 1851 and the Paris exhibition of 1855. *d.* 1859 aged about 50. *W. Felkin's History of hosiery* (1867) 371–75.

BAGNALL, Charles. *b.* West Bromwich, Staffs. 1827; an ironmaster; M.P. for Whitby 1865–68. *d.* Brighton 25 Feb. 1884.

BAGNALL, John Nock. *b.* Hateley Heath, West Bromwich 30 May 1826; member of firm of John Bagnall and Sons of the Gold's Hill Iron works (where most of the rails used on foreign lines were made) 1844–61; captain of Bilston rifle corps which he raised 26 Jany. 1860, commanded Wolverhampton battalion 9 Nov. 1868 to March 1884; pres. of South Staffordshire branch of the English Church Union; licensed by Bishop Selwyn as a lay deacon in diocese of Lichfield 1872, took charge of St. Mary's, Hateley Heath; sheriff of Staffs. 1875–76; author of *A history of Wednesbury in the county of Stafford* [anon.] 1854. *d.* The Moss Shenstone, Staffs. 18 Oct. 1884. *John Nock Bagnall A memoir by his daughter Mary Willett* 1885, *portrait.*

BAGNOLD, Michael. Entered Bombay army 1803; colonel 29 Bombay N.I. 21 Jany. 1846 to death; M.G. 20 June 1854. *d.* Upper Hamilton terrace, St. John's Wood, London 1 Dec. 1857 aged 71.

BAGOT, William Bagot, 2 Baron (3 *son of Wm. Bagot,* 1 *Baron Bagot* 1728–98). *b.* Bruton st. London 11 Sep. 1773; ed. at Westminster and Ch. Ch. Ox.; succeeded 22 Oct. 1798; author of *Memorials of the Bagot family* 1823. *d.* Blithfield near Stafford 12 Feb. 1856. *Memorials of the Bagot family* 1823, *portrait.*

BAGOT, ALAN (2 *son of the succeeding*). *b.* 1 June 1856; M.I.M.E., F.C.S., F.S.A.; invented several apparatus for saving life and preventing accidents in mines; author of *Accidents in mines* 1878; *The principles and practice of colliery ventilation* 1879, 2 ed. 1882; *Principles of civil engineering* 1885. *d.* Bournemouth April 1885.

BAGOT, CHARLES. *b.* 20 May 1808; captain grenadier guards 15 May 1840; lieut. col. 3 Stafford militia 5 April 1853 and col. 27 March 1858 to death; assistant master of ceremonies in Royal household 1861 to death. *d.* 49 Cadogan place, London 20 Feb. 1881.

BAGOT, REV. CHARLES WALTER (3 *son of Right Rev. Richard Bagot* 1782–1854). *b.* 11 Feb. 1812; ed. at Ch. Ch. Ox., B.A. 1834, M.A. 1842; fellow of All Souls college 1842–46; R. of Castle-Rising, Norfolk 1846 to death; chancellor of diocese of Bath and Wells 1851 to death. *d.* 10 Sep. 1884.

BAGOT, HENRY. *b.* 12 July 1810; entered navy 13 May 1823; admiral on h.p. 22 Jany. 1877. *d.* Brewood hall, Stafford 30 Nov. 1877.

BAGOT, RIGHT REV. RICHARD (6 *son of Wm. Bagot, 1 Baron Bagot* 1728–98). *b.* Daventry 22 Nov. 1782; ed. at Rugby and Ch. Ch. Ox. B.A. 1803, M.A. 1806, D.D. by diploma 30 Nov. 1829; fellow of All Souls college 1804–1806; R. of Leigh, Staffs. 1806; R. of Blithfield 1807; canon of Worcester 16 July 1817; canon of Windsor 25 March 1822; dean of Canterbury 2 Sep. 1827 to Nov. 1845; elected Bishop of Oxford 13 July 1829, confirmed 22 and consecrated 23 Aug.; Bishop of Bath and Wells 6 Nov. 1845 to death; his see was administered for a time by Right Rev. James Henry Monk, bishop of Gloucester and Bristol. *d.* Brighton 15 May 1854. *Rev. W. Palmer's Events connected with publication of Tracts for the times* 1883.

BAGSHAW, HENRY RIDGARD (2 *son of Sir Wm. Chambers Darling afterwards Bagshaw of Sheffield, physician* 1771–1832). *b.* 1 Nov. 1799; ed. at Oakham and Richmond gr. schs. and Trin. coll. Cam., B.A. 1822; barrister M.T. 25 Nov. 1825, bencher Dec. 1854, treasurer 1864–65; Q.C. Dec. 1854; judge of county courts of Cardigan, Carmarthen and Pembroke (circuit 31) 30 Oct. 1861 and of Clerkenwell district (circuit 41) June 1868 to death. *d.* 21 Fellow's road, Eton park south Hampstead 16 May 1870.

BAGSHAW, JOHN. *b.* 1784; ed. at Rugby; a banker and merchant at Calcutta; M.P. for Sudbury 1835 to 1837 and for Harwich 1847 to 1852 and 1853 to 1859; high steward of Harwich. *d.* Norwood 20 Dec. 1861.

BAGSHAW, ROBERT JOHN. *b.* 1803; a merchant at Calcutta; M.P. for Harwich 9 Dec. 1857 to 23 April 1859; sheriff of Essex 1873 *d.* 42 Gloucester square, London 11 Aug. 1878.

BAGSHAWE, WILLIAM LEONARD GILL. *b.* 18 Oct. 1828; ed. at Eton and Trin. coll. Cam., B.A. 1851; rowed No. 5 in Cambridge boat against Oxford 29 March 1849 and 15 Dec. 1849; the best oarsman on the river Cam.; killed by poachers at Wormhill hall, near Tideswell 20 July 1854. *Annual Register* (1854) 430–34.

BAGSTER, SAMUEL (2 *son of George Bagster of Beaufort buildings, Strand, London*). *b.* 26 Dec. 1772; bookseller in the Strand 1794–1816, in Paternoster Row 1816 to death; published *The English version of the polyglott Bible* 1816; *Biblia sacra polyglotta Bagsteriana*, 4 vols. 1817–28; *The English Hexapla* 1841 giving six most important English versions of New Testament; and many Bibles and Prayer Books in foreign languages. (*m.* 19 Dec. 1797 Eunice Birch, she was *b.* 23 Aug. 1777 and *d.* 22 Aug. 1877). *d.* Old Windsor 28 March 1851.

BAGWELL, JOHN (*eld son of Very Rev. Richard Bagwell, dean of Clogher who d.* 25 Dec. 1825). *b.* Clogher, co. Tyrone 3 April 1811; ed. at Winchester; sheriff of Tipperary 1834; M.P. for Clonmel 30 March 1857 to 26 Jany. 1874; a lord of the treasury June 1859 to July 1861. *d.* Marlfield, Clonmel 2 March 1883.

BAIGRIE, ROBERT (*son of John Baigrie of Fearn, Rossshire*). Entered Bombay army 3 Feb. 1848; major staff corps 3 Feb. 1868; quartermaster general Bombay army to 1874; commandant 28 N.I. 20 May 1876 to death; C.B. 24 May 1873. *d.* Poona 25 Sep. 1877. *I.L.N. lxxi* 481, 482 (1877), *portrait.*

BAIKIE, WILLIAM BALFOUR (*eld son of John Baikie captain R.N.*) *b.* Kirkwall, Orkney 27 Aug. 1825; ed. at Kirkwall gr. sch. and Univ. of Edin., M.D.; assistant surgeon R.N. 1848; surgeon and naturalist to expedition to the river Niger 1854; commanded expedition to river Niger 1 April 1857; author of *Narrative of an exploring voyage up the river Niger* 1856. *d.* at house of Charles Heddle, Sierra Leone 12 Dec. 1864. *Journal of royal geographical society xxxv*, 123 (1865); *I.L.N. xlvi*, 88 (1865), *portrait.*

BAILES, WILLIAM HAIGH. *b.* 1821; solicitor at Boston 1843 to death; member of Boston town council 1863-72, alderman 1872, mayor 1873. *d.* 14 April 1885.

BAILEY, REV. BENJAMIN. V. of Dallington, Northampton 1819; senior chaplain in Ceylon; archdeacon of Colombo 1852 to death. *d.* Nottingham place, Marylebone 25 June 1853 aged 62.

BAILEY, CRAWSHAY. *b.* Wenham, Suffolk 24 Oct. 1789; an ironmaster in South Wales; sheriff of Brecon 1835, of Monmouth 1850; took out a patent for railway rails 1843; M.P. for Monmouth 1852-68. *d.* Llanfoist near Abergavenny 9 Jany. 1872.

BAILEY, FANNY *(dau. of John Mitchell of Ferring, Sussex, farmer).* *b.* Ferring 7 Aug. 1777. *d.* Christchurch schools, Worthing 6 April 1881 aged 103 years and 8 months. *I.L.N. lxxviii* 440 (1881), *portrait; N. and Q. 5 S. viii,* 265 (1877), *xii,* 407 (1879), 6 *S. iii,* 485 (1881).

BAILEY, JAMES. Ed. at Trin. coll. Cam., B.A. 1814, M.A. 1823; head master of Perse's Free school Cam.; granted a Civil list pension of £100, 30 Oct. 1850; edited *Forcellini's Latin dictionary* 2 vols. 1826; author of *Comicorum Græcorum fragmenta* 1840. *d.* London 13 Feb. 1864.

BAILEY, SIR JOSEPH, 1 Baronet *(elder son of Joseph Bailey of Wakefield* 1747-1813). *b.* Great Wenham priory, Suffolk 21 Jany. 1783; an ironmaster in Brecknock and Monmouth; chairman of Birkenhead docks company; sheriff of Monmouth 1823; M.P. for Worcester 1835-47 and for Brecknockshire 1847 to death; created a baronet 5 July 1852. *d.* Glanusk park, Brecknockshire 20 Nov. 1858.

BAILEY, SAMUEL. *b.* Sheffield 1791; one of the trustees of Sheffield 1828; a founder of Sheffield Banking company 1831, and chairman; contested Sheffield 14 Dec. 1832 and 12 Jany. 1835; his supporters founded a Bailey club; pres. of Sheffield Literary and Philosophical society several times; author of *Essays on the formation and publication of opinions* 1821, 3 ed. 1831; *Critical dissertation on the nature, measure, and causes of Value* 1825; *Maro or poetic irritability in four cantos* [anon.] 1845; *The theory of reasoning* 1851, 2 ed. 1852; *Letters on the philosophy of the human mind, 3 series,* 1855-1863. *d.* Norbury near Sheffield 18 Jany. 1870, left about £90,000 for benefit of that town. *English*

psychology translated from the French of T. Ribot (1873) 315-22; *British Controversialist July* 1868 *pp.* 1-25; *N. and Q. 5 S. ix* 182-85, 216 (1878).

BAILEY, THOMAS. *b.* Nottingham 31 July 1785; a silk hosier there, then a wine merchant; contested Nottingham July 1830; member of town council 26 Dec. 1835 to 1843; proprietor and editor of *Nottingham Mercury* 1846-52; author of *What is life, and other poems* 1820; *Recreations in retirement* 1836; *Annals of Nottinghamshire* 4 vols. 1852-55, originally published in 32 shilling parts; *Records of Longevity* 1857, and 9 other books. *d.* Old Bassford near Nottingham 23 Oct. 1856. *C. Brown's Nottinghamshire Worthies* (1882) 341-50.

NOTE.—While connected with the Independents, he was one of three individuals chosen to take part in a public disputation arranged to be held in Nottingham between the friends of Christianity and Richard Carlisle, the champion of infidelity who *d.* 10 Feb. 1843 aged 52.

BAILHACHE, REV. CLEMENT. *b.* St. Heliers Jersey 11 Dec. 1830; ed. at Stepney college 1851; minister of Baptist chapel, South parade, Leeds 1855; minister at Watford 1859, at Cross st. Islington 1864; association sec. of Baptist mission Oct. 1870; sec. of Baptist missionary society 1876 to death. *d.* 6, Leigh road, Highbury 13 Dec. 1878. *Baptist handbook* (1879) 296-98.

BAILLIE, ALFRED. *b.* London 22 June 1830; hon. sec. of Marylebone cricket club May 1858 to 12 Feb. 1863. *d.* May or June 1867.

BAILLIE, AGNES *(elder sister of Joanna Baillie).* *b.* 24 Sep. 1760. *d.* Hollybush hill, Hampstead 27 April 1861 aged 100 years and 7 months.

BAILLIE, EDWARD. *b.* Gateshead; a glass painter; exhibited at Great Exhibition of 1851 "Shakespeare reading a play to Queen Elizabeth." *d.* London 21 Sep. 1856 aged 43.

BAILLIE, GEORGE ALEXANDER. *b.* 1804; ensign 15 Madras N.I. 6 April 1820; lieut. col. of 52 N.I. 9 June 1853, of 14 N.I. 15 Sep. 1855, and of 26 N.I. 1857-64; col. 15 N.I. 9 June 1865 to 1 Oct. 1877; general 1 Oct. 1877. *d.* 92 Westbourne park road, London 3 March 1882.

BAILLIE, HUGH DUNCAN. *b.* 1777; M.P. for Rye 1830-31 and for Honiton 1835-47; Lieutenant and sheriff principal of Rossshire 22 March 1843 to death. *d.* 65 Rutland gate, London 21 June 1866.

BAILLIE, JOANNA *(youngest child of Rev. James Baillie, minister of Bothwell, Lanarkshire).* *b.* Manse of Bothwell 11 Sep. 1762; lived with her only brother Matthew Baillie in London 1783–91; lived at Hampstead 1802 to death; published anonymously *A Series of plays in which it is attempted to delineate the stronger passions of the mind,* 3 vols. 1798–1812, of these plays *De Montford, a tragedy* on hatred was produced at Drury Lane theatre 29 April 1800 and ran 11 nights, *The Election, a comedy* was produced as an opera at English Opera house June 1817, *Constantine Paleologus, a tragedy* produced at Surrey theatre as a melodrama under title of *Constantine and Valeria The Family legend, a tragedy* produced at T. R. Edin. 1810 and at Drury Lane 29 May 1815, *The Separation* and *Henriquez* have been also acted; author of *Miscellaneous Plays,* 3 vols. .1836. *d.* Hollybush hill, Hampstead 23 Feb. 1851. *The songstresses of Scotland by Tytler & Watson* ii, 180–334 (1871); *Chambers Biog. dict. of eminent Scotsmen* i, 53 (1868), portrait; *W. Howitt's Homes and haunts of the most eminent British poets* ii, 248–56 (1847); *T. H. Ward's English poets,* 2 ed. iv, 221–26 (1883); *The living and the dead by a country curate,* i.e. Rev. Erskine Neale (1827) 177–91.

BAILLIE, SIR WILLIAM, 1 Baronet. *b.* Edinburgh July 1784; created Baronet by patent dated 14 Nov. 1823. *d.* Perth 28 Jany. 1854.

BAILLIE-HAMILTON, CHARLES (2 son of *George Baillie-Hamilton, M.P. of Mellerstain, Berwickshire* 1763–1841). *b.* Mellerstain 3 Nov. 1804; admitted advocate at Scottish bar 1830; advocate depute 1844 to 1846 and 1852; sheriff of Stirlingshire 2 March 1853; solicitor general for Scotland 17 March 1858; Lord advocate for Scotland 10 July 1858; raised to rank of an Earl's son 5 July 1859; M.P. for Linlithgowshire 7 Feb. 1859 to 15 April 1859; a judge of Court of Session 15 April 1859 to April 1874; assumed courtesy title of Lord Jerviswood 1859; assessor of Univ. of St. Andrew's 1861; a lord of justiciary 17 June 1862 to April 1874. *d.* Dryburgh house, St. Boswell's 23 July 1879.

BAILLIE-HAMILTON, CHARLES JOHN. *b.* 4 Jany. 1800; M.P. for Aylesbury 31 July 1839 to 23 July 1847. *d.* Ronco near Genoa 25 Aug. 1865.

BAILLIÈRE, HIPPOLYTE. Came to London about 1827; opened first shop in London for sale of French medical works at 219 Regent st. 1830; collected books for royal college of surgeons; publisher. *d.* 219 Regent st. 11 May 1867 aged 58.

BAILY, CHARLES. *b.* 10 April 1815; assistant to the City Architect, London; built St. John's church East Dulwich; restored Barnard's Inn Hall and Leigh church Kent; F.S.A. 1844; master of the Ironmongers Company 1874–75; author with G. R. French of *Catalogue of the Antiquities and works of art exhibited at Ironmongers hall London in 1861,* 2 vols. 1869. *d.* Reigate 2 Oct. 1878.

BAILY, EDWARD HODGES. *b.* Bristol 10 March 1788; pupil of Flaxman in London 1807–14; student of R.A. 1809, gained silver and gold medals 1809 and 1811, A.R.A. 1817, R.A. 1821, retired 1863; executed the bassi-relievi on the south or park side of the Marble Arch 1821; executed sculptures of Apollo 1815, Eve at the fountain 1818, Eve listening to the voice 1841, The Graces seated 1849 and statues of Sir Richard Fletcher and Thomas Telford in Westminster Abbey. *d.* 99 Devonshire road, Holloway 22 May 1867. *Scott's British school of sculpture* (1871) 123–28; *Sandby's History of Royal Academy* ii, 57–59 (1862); *Walford's Photographic portraits of living celebrities* (1859), portrait.

BAILY, JOHN *(eld. son of John Baily of Blandford sq. Marylebone).* *b.* London April 1805; ed. at Merchant Taylor's sch. and St. John's coll. Cam., 2 wrangler and junior Smith's prizeman 1828; fellow of his college 29 March 1830; barrister L.I. 10 May 1832, bencher 3 Nov. 1851; Q.C. 11 July 1851; leader in V. C. Kindersley's Court to 1867; counsel to Univ. of Cam. *d.* Stoney Hills, Esher Surrey 19 June 1877.

BAILY, JOHN WALKER. *b.* Kent road, London 9 Jany. 1809; head of firm of Wm. Baily and Sons, ironmongers 71 Gracechurch st.; master of the Ironmongers company 1862–63; member of British Archæological Association 6 Dec. 1865, on the council May 1869; formed an important collection of Romano-British and mediæval remains found in London 1862–72, this collection was purchased by Corporation of London 1881; his collection of arms and armour was bought by Baron de Cosson of Chertsey 1881. *d.* 4 March 1873. *Journal of British Archæological Association* xxx, 349–51 (1874).

BAIN, ALEXANDER. *b.* Thurso 1810; a journeyman clockmaker in London 1837; made electrical experiments on the Serpentine; invented electrical clocks, patented 11 Jany. 1841 and exhibited at Royal Polytechnic 28 March 1841; constructed the earth battery 1843; patented apparatus for **registering** progress of ships 1844, and **electro-chemical**

BAIN, A. (Con.)

telegraph 1846; invented automatic method of transmitting signals; devised electrical methods of playing keyed instruments at a distance. *d.* in the Home for incurables Kirkintilloch near Glasgow 2 Jany. 1877. *J. Finlaison's An account of some remarkable applications of the electric fluid to the useful arts by Mr. Alexander Bain 1843.*

BAIN, DONALD. *b.* Fordyce, Banffshire; author of *The patriot or Wallace, a historical tragedy* 1806; *Olden times, a comedy* 1841, 2 ed. 1845. *d.* April 1865.

BAIN, EDWIN SANDYS (*eld. son of Lieut. Col. William Bain of Livelands near Stirling*). *b.* 1804; barrister M.T. 19 June 1829; went northern circuit; serjeant at law 12 Nov. 1845. *d.* Livelands 30 Dec. 1874.

BAIN, HENDERSON. Entered navy 4 Sep. 1793; captain 6 April 1813; retired admiral 11 Feb. 1861. *d.* Esher, Surrey 18 Jany. 1862 aged 86.

BAIN, JAMES. A bookseller at the Mews Gate, Charing Cross, London 1819; at 1 Haymarket 1831 to death. *d.* Highgate 10 Dec. 1866 aged 72.

BAIN, SIR WILLIAM. *b.* Culross, Perthshire 1771; Master R.N. 1811; commanded steamers for general steam navigation company; harbour master of Granton on the Firth of Forth 10 years; knighted by the Queen at St. James's palace 20 March 1844; author of *An essay on the variation of the compass* 1817. *d.* The Grange, Romford 11 Sep. 1853.

BAINBRIDGE, EDWARD THOMAS. *b.* 1798; a banker in London; M.P. for Taunton 6 Aug. 1830 to Feb. 1842. *d.* 30 Medina villas Brighton 30 Sep. 1872.

BAINBRIDGE, JOHN NATHAN. Studied at St. Thomas' and Guy's hospitals; M.R.C.S. 1820, F.R.C.S. 1852, L.S.A. 1821; bought a practice in St. Martin's lane 1824; medical officer of St. Martin's-in-the-Fields workhouse 1835; M.D. St. Andrew's 1842; prescribed for 1669 cases with only 27 deaths during prevalence of cholera 1849 for which, Board of Guardians gave him £200; surgeon to London Friendly Institution. *d.* 86 St. Martin's lane 16 April 1863 aged 63. *Medical Circular i* 131, 169 (1852) *portrait.*

BAINBRIDGE, WILLIAM (*only son of Wm. Bainbridge of Alston, Northumberland, solicitor*). Barrister I.T. 23 Nov. 1838; author of *A*

BAINBRIDGE, W. (Con.)

treatise on the law of mines and minerals 1841, 4 ed. 1878; *Lionel Merval a novel* [*anon.*] 3 vols. 1866. *d.* Cliffe house, Cullercoats 13 Dec. 1869 aged about 60.

BAINBRIGGE, JOHN HANKEY (*2 son of Philip Bainbrigge of Ashbourne, Derbyshire 1756-99*). *b.* 1791; ensign 20 foot 25 March 1808; lieut. 9 March 1809 to 25 Dec. 1814; town major Guernsey 29 Nov. 1839 to 30 May 1861; general 1 Oct. 1877; *d.* Robais manor, Guernsey 15 March 1881.

BAINBRIGGE, SIR PHILIP (*brother of the preceding*). *b.* London 1786; entered navy 1799; ensign 20 foot 30 June 1800; permanent assistant quartermaster general 15 Oct. 1812 to 23 Nov. 1841; deputy quartermaster general Ireland 23 Nov. 1841 to 9 Nov. 1846; commanded the forces in Ceylon 1852-54; col. of 26 foot 31 March 1854 to death; general 24 Aug. 1861; granted service reward 15 Nov. 1848; C.B. 19 July 1838, K.C.B. 18 May 1860; invented a protracting pocket sextant 1809. *d.* St. Margaret's Litchfield, Hants 20 Dec. 1862. *G.M. xiv.* 236-37 (1863); *Annual Register* (1850) 323-31.

BAINES, REV. EDWARD. *b.* Cainham vicarage, Shropshire 1 Aug. 1801; ed. at Shrewsbury head præpositor; at Christ's coll. Cam., Bell Univ. scholar, and Browne medallist for Latin and Greek epigrams 1821, B.A. 1824, M.A. 1827; fellow classical lecturer and tutor of his college; R. of Clipston 1840-43; R. of Bluntisham, Hants 1843-59; V. of Yalding, Kent 1859 to death; author of *First form Latin grammar* 1855; *Visit to the Vaudois of Piedmont* 1855. *d.* San Remo 20 April 1882. *Sermons by the late Rev. Edward Baines edited with memoir by Alfred Barry, D.D.* 1883.

BAINES, REV. JOHN. Ed. at St. John's coll. Ox., B.A. 1843; V. of Little Marlow, Bucks 1859 to death; author of *Tales of the Empire* 1851; *Life of Archbishop Laud* 1855; *Twenty sermons* 1857; *Hints for harvest services* 1866. *d.* 63 Abingdon villas Kensington, London 20 May 1880 aged 58.

BAINES, MATTHEW TALBOT (*eld. child of Edward Baines 1774-1848, M.P. fo Leeds*). *b.* Leeds 17 Feb. 1799; ed. at Richmond gr. sch. and Trin. coll. Cam. scholar, B.A. 1820; barrister I.T. 6 May 1825, bencher 1841, reader 1854, treasurer 1855; recorder of Hull 1837-47; Q.C. 1841; M.P. for Hull 1847-1852 and for Leeds 1852-1859; pres. of Poor law board 1 Jany. 1849 to 2 March 1852 and 1 Jany. 1853 to 13 Aug. 1855;

BAINES. M. T. *(Con.)*

P.C. 30 July 1849; mem. of committee of council on education 10 March 1855; chancellor of Duchy of Lancaster with a seat in the cabinet 7 Dec. 1855 to 26 Feb. 1858. *d.* 13 Queen's square, Westminster 22 Jany. 1860. *Taylor's Biographia Leodiensis* (1865) 482–86; *Illust. News of the World* 24 Nov. 1860, *portrait.*

NOTE.—He was the first dissenter admitted to a seat in the Cabinet.

BAINES, THOMAS. *b.* Kings Lynn 1822; went to Cape Colony 1842; painted pictures and taught drawing; went through Kafir wars 1846–54; explored North West Australia under Augustus Gregory 1855–56; artist and store keeper to the Livingstone Zambesi Expedition 1858, his series of pictures of scenes on the Zambesi has been exhibited at the Crystal palace, Dublin exhibition and Alexandra palace; lectured in England 1864–68; F.R.G.S. 1857; author of *Explorations in South Western Africa* 1864. *d.* D'Urban, Port Natal 8 April 1875. *The gold regions of South Eastern Africa, by the late Thomas Baines* 1877, *portrait; Illust. News of the World* i, 64 (1858), *portrait.*

BAINES, THOMAS (3 *son of Edward Baines 1774–1848 M.P. for Leeds*). *b.* Leeds 1806; edited *Liverpool Times* 1829–59; a parliamentary agent in London 1859; author of *History of commerce and town of Liverpool* 1852; *Lancashire and Cheshire past and present* 1867; *Yorkshire past and present* 1875. *d.* Seaforth hall near Liverpool 31 Oct. 1881.

BAIRD, ANDREW WOOD. *b.* Colchester; ed. at Univ. of Edin., M.D. 1823; L.R.C.S. Edin. 1821, M.R.C.P. 1827; a phys. at Ipswich 1824–52, at Dover 1852 to death; phys. to Dover hospital. *d.* 7 Camden Crescent, Dover 10 Jany. 1882.

BAIRD, SIR DAVID, 2 Baronet. *b.* 1795; succeeded 18 Aug. 1829. *d.* 9 Jany. 1852.

BAIRD, FRANCIS (2 *son of Charles Baird, founder of the 'Baird Works' at St. Petersburg who d. 10 Dec. 1843 in his 77 year*). *b.* 16 Feb. 1802; ed. at Univ. of Edin.; joined his father's Works 1819; sole proprietor 1843 to death; M.I.C.E. 25 Feb. 1823; executed the 4 bas-reliefs, eagles and candelabra, and colossal figure of the angel on the Alexander column in the Winter Palace St. Petersburg, also the St. Nicholas bridge, first permanent bridge across the Neva. *d.* St. Petersburg 25 March 1864; *Min. of proc. of Instit. of C.E. xxx* 428 (1870).

BAIRD, JAMES (4 *son of Alexander Baird of Kirkwood, Lanarkshire farmer 1765–1833*). *b.* Kirkwood 5 Dec. 1802; an ironmaster at Gartsherrie works near Airdrie 1829 which became largest iron works in the world except those at Dowlais; largely assisted J. B. Neilson in perfecting his invention of the hot blast; M.P. for Falkirk burghs 1851–57; bought estate of Muirkirk Ayrshire 1863 for £135,000; founded Baird lectures for defence of orthodoxy 1871, and Baird Trust in connection with Church of Scotland at cost of £500,000 July 1873. *d.* Cambusdoon near Ayr 20 June 1876. Personalty sworn under £1190,000 Aug. 1876. *Practical Mag.* i, 241–48 (1873) *portrait; Burke's Vicissitudes of families* 2 ed. 1859, *pp.* 40–46; *Graphic xiv,* 12 (1876), *portrait.*

BAIRD, REV. JOHN (*eld son of Rev. James Baird, minister of Swinton, Berwickshire who d. 11 Feb. 1814*). *b.* Manse of Eccles 17 Feb. 1799; ed. at Whitsome and Kelso and Univ. of Edin.; founded the Plinian Society at Edin. 1823, which was eventually incorporated with Botanical Society of Edin.; minister of Yetholm near Kelso June 1829 to death; established a school at Yetholm for Gipsies 1843, this was the first ragged school in Scotland; a founder of Berwickshire Naturalists' Club 22 Sep. 1831, pres. 1837; author of *Scottish Gipsies Advocate* 1839; *Account of the parish of Yetholm* in the *New Statistical account of Scotland* iii, 159–76 (1845). *d.* Yetholm 29 Nov. 1861. *Memoir of the late Rev. John Baird by W. Baird M.D.* 1862.

BAIRD, ROBERT. *b.* 1806; an ironmaster at Glasgow; lord dean of guild Glasgow 1855. *d.* Cawdor house, Glasgow 7 Aug. 1856.

BAIRD, THOMAS. Wrote much in *Western Times* Exeter newspaper under pseudonym of Nathan Hogg; author of *Letters in the Devonshire dialect in verse by Nathan Hogg* 1847. *d.* St. Thomas's hospital London May 1881.

BAIRD, WILLIAM (*elder brother of James Baird*). *b.* 1796; senior partner in Gartsherrie iron works; M.P. for Falkirk 1841–45; bought estate of Elie, Fifeshire for £145,000. *d.* Edinburgh 8 March 1864, leaving a fortune of £2,000,000 sterling.

BAIRD, WILLIAM (*younger brother of Rev. John Baird*). *b.* the Manse of Eccles Berwickshire 1803; ed. at Edin. Dublin and Paris; surgeon H.E.I. Co's. navy 1823–33; practised in London 1833–41; assistant in Zoological department of the British Museum Sep. 1841 to death; F.R.S. 6 June 1867; author

BAIRD, W. (Con.)

of *The natural history of the British Entomostraca* published by Ray Society 1850; *Cyclopædia of natural sciences* 1858. *d.* 38 Burlington road, Westbourne park 27 Jany. 1872.

BAIRD, REV. WILLIAM. Ed. at Linc. coll. Ox., B.A. 1859, M.A. 1861; V. of St. Barnabas, Homerton 1870 to death; author of *Hallowing of our common life, sermons* 1867, 3 ed. 1874; *Inheritance of our fathers, the book of common prayer* 1868; *Days that are past, early church history* 1870. *d.* Coleshill st. Eaton sq. London 5 Dec. 1875.

BAKER, ANNE ELIZABETH. *b.* 16 June 1786; wrote the geological and botanical part of her brother George Baker's *History and antiquities of Northamptonshire;* author of *Glossary of Northamptonshire words and phrases* 2 vols. 1854. *d.* Gold st. Northampton 22 April 1861.

BAKER, ANTHONY ST. JOHN. Consul general in the U.S. of America 6 Jany. 1816 to 5 Jany. 1832 when office abolished. *d.* Mount Calverley lodge, Tunbridge Wells 16 May 1854.

BAKER, B. B. Director of the college at Corfu; professor of English literature in the Ionian University. *d.* Malta 20 Feb. 1868.

BAKER, REV. DAVID BRISTOW. Ed. at St. John's coll. Cam., B.A. 1829, M.A. 1832; Inc. of Claygate, Surrey 1841–52; author of *A treatise on the nature of doubt in religious questions* [by *D.B.B.*] 1831; *Discourses and Sacramental addresses to a village congregation* 1832. *d.* Parliament st. Westminster 24 July 1852 aged 49.

BAKER, D. S. Deaf and dumb heraldic artist; drew for many years the arms for the obituary notices in the Illustrated London News; painted heraldic paintings on panels and doors of state carriage of Lord Mayor of London. *d.* 1 Sep. 1877 aged 53.

BAKER, SIR EDWARD BAKER, 2 Baronet. *b.* Dublin 4 Nov. 1806; ed. at Ch. Ch. Ox.; succeeded 4 March 1825. *d.* 51 Upper Brook st. London 29 March 1877.

BAKER, REV. FRANKLIN. *b.* Birmingham 1801; M.A. Univ. of Glasgow; minister of Presbyterian chapel Bolton 14 Dec. 1823; ordained 23 Sep. 1824; author of *The rise and progress of Nonconformity in Bolton* 1854. *d.* Birmingham 25 May 1867.

BAKER, GEORGE. *b.* Northampton; mayor 1837; issued proposals for a history of Northamptonshire 1815; published the first

BAKER, G. (Con.)

part 1822, the second 1826, the third completing the first volume 1830, the fourth part 1836 and about one third of the fifth part 1841, the manuscripts were eventually purchased by Sir Thomas Phillipps. *d.* May Fair, Northampton 12 Oct. 1851 aged 70. *G.M.* xxxvi, 551–52, 629 (1851).

BAKER, GEORGE. *b.* 8 Jany. 1794; cornet 16 light dragoons 6 July 1809; captain 19 Oct. 1820 to 18 July 1826, when placed on h.p.; English comr. for defining boundary frontier between Turkey and Greece 1830; F.R.G.S. 1830. *d.* Grosvenor place, Bath 22 Dec. 1859. *Journal of Royal Geographical society* xxx, c–cii (1860).

BAKER, GEORGE. *b.* Cobham near Gravesend 31 May 1838; a bowler at Lord's cricket ground, London 1862–64; started the United north and south of England Eleven 1866, sec. to that body which soon became extinct; kept a cricket and newspaper shop at Stratford, Essex about 1864 to death; a left handed bowler and batsman. *d.* Lydd, Kent 2 June 1870.

BAKER, SIR HENRY LORAINE, 2 Baronet. *b.* Nancy in Lorraine 3 Jany. 1787; captain R.N. 13 June 1815; retired V.A. 9 July 1857; succeeded as 2 Bart. 4 Feb. 1826; C.B. 4 June 1815. *d.* Dunstable house, Richmond 2 Nov. 1859.

BAKER, REV. SIR HENRY WILLIAMS, 3 Baronet *(elder son of the preceding)*. *b.* London 27 May 1821; ed. at Trin. coll. Camb., B.A. 1844, M.A. 1854; C. of Great Horkesley Essex 1842–51; V. of Monkland, Hereford 1851 to death; originated the most popular hymn book ever compiled, *Hymns ancient and modern* 1860, of which 20 million copies have been sold, author of several of these hymns. *d.* Horkesley house, Monkland 12 Feb. 1877.

BAKER, REV. JAMES. *b.* Lincoln; ed. at Winchester; fellow of New college Ox. 1807–18, B.A. 1811, M.A. 1815; chancellor of diocese of Durham 1818 to death; R. of Nuneham Courtenay, Oxon 1825 to death. *d.* Nuneham Courtenay 6 Sep. 1854 aged 66.

BAKER, JAMES. *b.* York 4 Oct. 1851; the first editor of a periodical entitled *Bachelors' Papers* Liverpool 1870; studied at Univ. of Edin. 1872; M.B. 1876; resident phys. Royal infirmary Edin. 1876; pres. of Royal medical society. *d.* Royal infirmary Edin. 17 April 1877. *The annual monitor for 1878 pp.* 15–29.

BAKER, JAMES VASHON. *b.* 1798; entered navy 1811; captain 10 July 1843; admiral on h.p. 30 July 1875. *d.* Neen-Sollars rectory, Shropshire 14 Oct. 1875.

BAKER, JOHN. One of the pioneers of South Australia; one of its foremost public men; member of Legislative Council. *d.* Morialta, South Australia 18 May 1872 aged 59.

BAKER, JOSEPH. *b.* Great new st. Fetter lane London about 1766; map engraver; employed by the Board of Ordnance; a liveryman of company of stationers 1787, one of the court of assistants 1825, master of the company 1832 and 1833, a stockkeeper for management of business concerns of the company 1840 to death. *d.* Warren st. Pentonville, London 2 March 1853.

BAKER, SIR RICHARD (*eld. son of John Baker of Cott house, New Totnes, Devon*). *b.* Cott house 1782; army and navy clothier Dublin; sheriff of Dublin 1833; knighted by Marquess Wellesley 1833; alderman of Dublin 1838–41. *d.* Mount Errol, Donnybrook, co. Dublin 1 June 1853.

BAKER, ROBERT. *b.* Terling, Essex Nov 1793; a tenant farmer at Writtle; founded Society for protection of agriculture 17 Feb. 1844; author of *A lecture on the economy of farming* 1852; edited J. S. Bayldon's *Art of valuing rents and tillages* 1856. *d.* 24 Dec. 1859.

BAKER, ROBERT. Member of medical profession; sub-inspector of factories 1834; inspector 18 June 1858; C.B. 27 Oct. 1877. *d.* Leamington 6 Feb. 1880 in 77 year.

BAKER, REV. ROBERT GEORGE. Ed. at Trin. coll. Cam., B.A. 1810, M.A. 1813; V. of Fulham 1834–71; Preb. of St. Paul's 1846 to death; rural dean 1851–71; author of *Account of benefactions and charities of Fulham; The olden characters of Fulham* 1847. *d.* Ivy cottage, Fulham 21 Feb. 1878 in 90 year.

BAKER, THOMAS. *b.* 8 Oct. 1809; landscape painter in Midland counties; known as Baker of Leamington; exhibited at the R.A. 1831. *d.* 10 Aug. 1869.

BAKER, THOMAS (*son of a farmer at Old Park, Durham*). A civil engineer; invented method of laying down railway curves; laid out Stockton and Darlington railway the first line in the kingdom, opened 27 Sep. 1825; laid out atmospheric line from Dublin to Kingstown, opened 17 Dec. 1834; author of *Rudimentary treatise on mensuration* 1850;

BAKER, T. *(Con.)*
Principles and practice of statics and dynamics 1851; *The mathematical theory of the steam engine* 1862. *d.* Charter house hospital London Sep. or Oct. 1871.

BAKER, THOMAS ELD. *b.* Margate 1791; M.R.C.S. 1813; surgeon Bengal army 1814 to 23 Aug. 1838 when he retired; treasurer of Royal humane society; author of *The art of preserving health in India* 1829; *An appeal to the common sense of the people of England in favour of anatomy* 1832. *d.* 76 Porchester Terrace, London 23 July 1868.

BAKER, THOMAS PALMER. Chief engineer Chatham dockyard 11 Nov. 1856 to Dec. 1868 when office abolished; chief inspector of machinery afloat 6 July 1866; C.B. 2 June 1869. *d.* 170, Lewisham high road, Newcross 6 Oct. 1876 in 69 year.

BAKER, WILLIAM (*son of Mr. Baker of Eastover, Bridgwater, butcher*). *b.* Eastover 3 March 1787; apprenticed to Mr. Tuthill of Bridgwater, currier Sep. 1800; worked in London and Glasgow 1807–1809; a currier in Fore st. Bridgwater 1809; alderman; F.G.S. Nov. 1842; sec. to Somersetshire Archæological and natural history society. *d.* Bridgwater 8 Oct. 1853. *A brief memoir of Wm. Baker by John Bowen* 1854.

BAKER, WILLIAM (*elder son of George Wingfield of Cotham who d. 1774*). Barrister L.I. 23 Nov. 1797, bencher 1818 to death; M.P. for Bodmin 1 Nov. 1806 to 29 April 1807; chief justice of Brecon circuit; a comr. of bankrupts; K.C. 1818; master in Chancery 19 March 1819 to March 1849; assumed surname of Baker in lieu of Wingfield by R. L. 29 Dec. 1849. *d.* Sherborne castle, Dorset 21 March 1858.

BAKER, WILLIAM. *b.* 1784; an attorney in London; coroner for east division of Middlesex; author of *A practical compendium of the recent statutes, cases and decisions affecting the office of coroner* 1851. *d.* 12 Chester terrace, Regent's Park 22 Feb. 1859.

BAKER, WILLIAM. *b.* 19 May 1817; articled to G. W. Buck, C.E. 1834–39; engineer upon southern division of London and north western railway 1852–59, chief engineer of that line Oct. 1859–1878, during which time he carried out a great extent of railway works; M.I.C.E. 7 May 1848; member of council 1877 to death. *d.* 7 March 1878. *Minutes of proc. of Instit. of C.E. lv*, 315–17 (1879).

BAKER, SIR WILLIAM ERSKINE *(son of Joseph Baker, capt. R.N.) b.* Leith 1808; 2 lieut. Bengal engineers 15 Dec. 1826. col. commandant 10 March 1857; military sec. at India office 1858; member of council of India 1861–1875; general 1 Oct. 1877; placed on retired list 29 Nov. 1878; K.C.B. 1 Feb. 1870. *(m.* 1837 Frances Gertrude 3 dau. of major general A. Duncan). *d.* the Castle, Banwell 16 Dec. 1881.

BAKER, REV. WILLIAM RICHARD. *b.* Waltham abbey, Essex 3 Sep. 1798; agent of Home missionary society at Ramsey, Isle of Man 1822–28; minister of independent chapel at Shepton Mallet, Somerset 1828–38; sec. of New British and Foreign Temperance Society 1838–41; minister of Portland chapel St. John's Wood, London 1841–51; a founder of United Kingdom temperance and general provident Institution 1840, resident director 1852; author of *The curse of Britain* 1838; *The idolatry of Britain* 1840; *Our state church* 1850; *Anti-mysticism* 1855. *d.* Down house near Sutton, Surrey 28 Sep. 1861. *Life of the late Rev. W. R. Baker, edited by his sister Mrs. E. L. Edmunds* 1865.

BALD, ROBERT. *b.* Culross, Perthshire 1776; engaged in the Mar collieries; a mining engineer at Edin. about 1820; much employed in Scotland, England and Wales; reported on coalfields of Sweden for the Swedish government; F.R.S. Edin. 1817; author of *A general view of the coal trade of Scotland* 1812; of the article *Mine* in the *Edinburgh Encyclopædia* and of many papers. *d.* Alloa 28 Dec. 1861.

BALD, WILLIAM. *b.* Burnt Island, Fifeshire; a civil engineer 1803; made a territorial survey of co. Mayo about 1810, his map on a scale of 4 inches to a mile was one of the finest maps ever constructed; a draftsman at the Admiralty; resident engineer to trustees of the river Clyde 1839–45; examined the river Seine 1845. *d.* 1857. *Quarterly journal of Geological Society xiv,* 42–43 (1858).

BALDERS, CHARLES WILLIAM MORELY *(eld. son of Charles Morely Balders of West Barsham, Norfolk). b.* Sunderland 4 Feb. 1804; cornet 3 dragoons 10 Nov. 1825, and major 1845–48; major 5 dragoon guards 1848–54; lieut. col. 12 lancers 8 Jany. 1858 to 31 Aug. 1860; col. 17 lancers 4 Feb. 1867 to death; L.G. 28 Oct. 1869; C.B. 24 May 1847. *d.* 11 Adelaide crescent, Brighton 21 Sep. 1875.

BALDERSON, ABRAHAM THOMAS. *b.* 1804; ed. at Guy's hospital; L.S.A. 1826; assistant to Sir Astley Cooper 1825–41; examiner of lunatics, parish of St. James, Westminster. *d.* 37 Woburn sq. London 3 Feb. 1872

BALDOCK, EDWARD HOLMES. *b.* 1812; M.P. for Shrewsbury 30 July 1847 to 21 March 1857. *d.* 8 Grosvenor place, London 15 Aug. 1875 from effect of walking through a plate glass window in Alexander Collie's house, 12 Kensington palace gardens.

BALDOCK, ROBERT *(youngest son of Thomas Baldock of Burwash Sussex, surgeon). b.* Burwash July 1789; bookseller at 85 High Holborn, London 1814 to death. *d.* 85 High Holborn 5 Nov. 1861.

BALDOCK, THOMAS. Midshipman R.N. 25 Oct. 1806; superintended packet service at Dover 19 Aug. 1846 to Sep. 1852; captain on h.p. 9 Jany. 1854; retired R.A. 10 Sep. 1869; K.T.S. 1 May 1837. *d.* Hastings 11 March 1871 aged 81.

BALDWIN, AUGUSTUS. Entered navy May 1794; captain 1 Jany. 1817; retired admiral 10 Nov. 1862. *d.* Toronto 5 Jany. 1866.

BALDWIN, CHARLES *(3 son of Henry Baldwin of London, printer, who founded the St. James's Chronicle* 1761). *b.* 1774; sole proprietor of *St. James's Chronicle* and *Morning Herald;* founded the *Standard* evening paper 21 May 1827, published in it the news of the surrender of Varna 11 Oct. 1828 a fortnight before arrival of the Government couriers; contested Lambeth Aug. 1837 and July 1841; master of the Stationers' company 1842 and 1843; retired from business 1844; probably oldest volunteer in the kingdom. *d.* 27 Sussex gardens, Hyde park, London 18 Feb. 1869 in 95 year. *Reg. and mag. of biog. i,* 313–15 (1869).

BALDWIN, CHARLES BARRY *(eld. son of Charles Baldwin, lieut. col. of Kings county militia). b.* 1789; barrister I.T. 26 Nov 1824; secretary to comrs. for claims on France, sole comr. to 1830; M.P. for Totnes 1830–32 and 1839–52. *d.* Paris 13 April 1859.

BALDWIN, CONNELL JAMES *(son of James Baldwin of Clohina, co. Cork). b.* Clohina; ensign 87 foot 23 July 1807; captain 50 foot 10 Feb. 1820 to 22 Feb. 1827 when placed on h.p.; served in the Peninsula for which he received a medal and 10 clasps; raised a regiment at Cork for Emperor of Brazil but

BALDWIN, C. J. (Con.)

brought the men back again on being ordered to the interior of Brazil as settlers; went to Canada about 1828; raised a regiment of Militia for defence of the frontier in troubles of 1837–38. *d.* Toronto 14 Dec. 1861. *H. J. Morgan's Sketches of eminent Canadians* (1862) 733–35.

BALDWIN, EDWARD. *b.* Waterford; a pugilist 6 feet 5 inches in height; beaten by Andrew Marsden 21 Oct. 1863; beat George Iles 19 Feb. 1866; beat A. Marsden 25 Sep. 1866; matched to fight Joseph Wormald for Championship 29 April 1867 but forfeited his stakes; matched to fight James Mace for Championship 15 Oct. 1867 but Mace was arrested; fought J. Wormald at Lynnfield Massachusetts 1868 for Championship and 2,500 dollars when police interfered, he was awarded the stakes as Wormald declined to renew the fight; shot dead in the United States Sep. 1875. *Modern Boxing by Pendragon* (1879) 83–89; *Illust. Sporting News v,* 97 (1866), *portrait.*

BALDWIN, GEORGE WALTER. Major 31 foot 1863–64; major 20 foot 1864 to death; murdered by Japanese at Kamahura, about 17 miles from Yokohama 21 Nov. 1864. *R. Lindau's Erzählungen und Novellen i,* 15–54 (1871); *F. O. Adams's History of Japan i,* 485–98 (1874), *ii,* 1–5 (1875).

BALDWIN, HENRY. Called to bar in Ireland 1826; Q.C. 17 Aug. 1841; law adviser of the Castle during state trials 1848–49; comr. of insolvent court 1850 to death. *d.* Dublin 24 May 1854.

BALDWIN, MARTIN. *b.* Coalbrookdale Shropshire 22 Nov. 1788; an engine factor at Bradley near Bilston 1809; carried on the Lower Bovereux colliery; invented many improvements in the construction of engines and machinery. *d.* Newbridge crescent, Wolverhampton 16 Feb. 1872.

BALDWIN, ROBERT (*only son of Benjamin Baldwin of Faringdon, Berkshire surgeon*). Printer and bookseller in Bridge st. Blackfriars 1806–10, and in Paternoster row 1810; united his business with that of another firm under name of Baldwin, Cradock and Joy; started the *London Magazine* Jany. 1820, in opposition to *Blackwood's Mag.* transferred it to Messrs. Taylor and Hessey 1821; became insolvent; a stock keeper of Company of Stationers 1834 to death. *d.* Cumberland place, Westbourne grove north, 29 Jany. 1858 aged 78.

BALDWIN, ROBERT (*son of Wm. Warren Baldwin of Toronto, lawyer who d. 8 Jany. 1844*). *b.* Toronto 1804; partner with his father 1825–48; member of Assembly of Upper Canada 1829; executive councillor 18 Feb. 1836 for short time; solicitor general 1840; attorney general for Upper Canada Sep. 1842 and Feb. 1848 to July 1851; C.B. 23 June 1854. *d.* Spadina near Toronto 9 Dec. 1858. *H. J. Morgan's Sketches of eminent Canadians* (1862) 397–405.

BALDY, JOHN PATEY. M.R.C.S. 1814; private teacher of anatomy and surgery. *d.* 23 Pembroke st. Devonport 6 Sep. 1861 aged 67.

BALE, CHARLES SACKVILLE. Made a splendid collection of pictures at 71 Cambridge terrace, Edgeware road, London. *d.* 71 Cambridge terrace 28 Nov. 1880 aged 89. *Waagen's Treasures of art ii,* 329–32 (1854); *Waagen's Galleries of art* (1857) 116–21.

BALFE, MICHAEL WILLIAM (*only son of Balfe of Dublin, violinist 1783–1823*). *b.* 10 Pitt st. Dublin 15 May 1808; played the violin at a concert in Royal Exchange, Dublin, May 1816; first violinist in Drury Lane orchestra 1823; chief baritone at Italian opera, Paris 1827–29; sang in Italy 1829–35; lessee of English opera house Lyceum 9 March 1841 to 13 May 1841; conductor at Her Majesty's theatre 3 March 1846 to 1852 when house closed; went to St. Petersburg 1852; purchased Rowney Abbey, Ware, Herts and turned gentleman farmer 1864; chevalier of Legion of honour 22 March 1870; composed *Rivals* 1829, *Siege of Rochelle* 1835, *Bohemian Girl* 1843 (produced at Drury Lane 27 Nov. 1843, performed in almost every European country), *Rose of Castille* 1857, *Puritan's daughter* 1861, *Il Talismano* produced at Her Majesty's theatre 1874; arranged *Moore's Irish Melodies* as duets and quartets. (*m.* Lina Rozer a Hungarian prima donna). *d.* Rowney Abbey 20 Oct. 1870. *Balfe, his life and work by W. A. Barrett 1882, portrait; A memoir of M. W. Balfe by C L. Kenny 1875; Illust. Review v,* 671–77, *portrait; Recollections of J. R. Planché i,* 241 (1872), *portrait by Thackeray.*

NOTE.—A statue of him was placed in the vestibule of Drury Lane theatre 24 Sep. 1874, his memorial window in St. Patrick's cathedral, Dublin, was uncovered 14 April 1879, and his memorial tablet in Westminster Abbey was unveiled 20 Oct. 1882.

BALFE, VICTOIRE (*2 dau. of the preceding*). *b.* Rue de la Victoire, Paris 1 Sep. 1837; made her first appearance in London at Lyceum Theatre 28 May 1857 as Amina in opera of *La Sonnambula;* sang with great

BALFE, V. *(Con.)*

success in England, Italy and at St. Petersburg 1857–59. *(m.* (1) 31 March 1860 Sir John Fiennes Twisleton Crampton 2 Baronet, marriage was annulled on her petition 20 Nov. 1863, she *m.* (2) 1864 Duc de Frias and *d.* Madrid 22 Jany. 1871. *bur.* Burgos cathedral. *Illust. news of the world iii,* 328 (1859), *portrait; I.L.N. xxxi,* 116 (1857), *portrait, lviii,* 115 (1871).

BALFOUR, BLAYNEY TOWNLEY. *b.* 28 May 1769; sheriff of Louth 1792; M.P. for Belturbet in Irish parliament 1797–98. *d.* Townley hall near Drogheda 22 Dec. 1856.

BALFOUR, BLAYNEY TOWNLEY *(eld son of the preceding). b.* 1799; lieutenant governor of the Bahamas 1833 to 1834; sheriff of co. Louth 1841. *d.* Townley hall 5 Sep. 1882.

BALFOUR, CLARA LUCAS *(dau. of Mr. Liddell). b.* in the New Forest 21 Dec. 1808; signed the pledge at a chapel in St. George's road, Pimlico 16 Oct. 1837 being the 9th person to do so in Chelsea district; edited *Temperance Beacon* and *Teetotal Magazine;* a public lecturer 1841–70; author of *Women of Scripture* 1850; *Happy evenings* 1851, 3 ed. 1877; *Sketches of English literature* 1852; *Moral heroism* 1854, new ed. 1877; *Family Honour* 1880; wrote in many periodicals. *(m.* 1828 James Balfour). *d.* London road, Croydon 3 July 1878. *Home makers by the late Mrs. C. L. Balfour with a biographical sketch of the author by the Rev. C. Bullock* 1878, *portrait.*

BALFOUR, FRANCIS MAITLAND *(3 son of James Maitland Balfour of Whittingham, East Lothian 1820–56). b.* Queen st. Edinburgh 11 Nov. 1851; ed. at Harrow 1865–70 and Trin. coll. Cam.; natural science scholar 1871; B.A. 1873, M.A. 1877; studied at Professor Dohrn's Zoological station, Naples; fellow of his college Oct. 1874 and lecturer on natural science 1875; F.R.S. 1878, member of council 1881 to death, royal medallist 1881; pres. of Cambridge Philosophical society Nov. 1881; professor of Animal Morphology in Univ. of Cam. 31 May 1882 to death; LLD. Glasgow 1880; edited with E. R. Lankester *The quarterly journal of Microscopical science;* author of *Monograph on the development of Elasmobranch fishes* 1878; *Treatise on Comparative Embryology* 2 vols. 1880–81; left Courmayeur 18 July 1882 to ascend Aiguille Blanche a peak of Mont Blanc his body was found 23 July on Fresnay glacier at foot of the Penteret. *bur.* at Whittingham 5 Aug. 1882. *Fortnightly Review xxxii,* 568–80 (1882); *I.L.N. lxxxi,* 197 (1882), *portrait; Report of British Assoc.* 1882 *meeting pp.* 555–58.

BALFOUR, JAMES. *b.* Russell st. Covent Garden 16 Oct. 1796; served in the navy 5 years; a temperance advocate in London many years; employed in the Ways and Means office of House of Commons 1853. *(m.* 1828 Clara Lucas Liddell). *d.* London road, Croydon 22 Dec. 1884.

BALFOUR, JAMES MELVILLE *(youngest son of Rev. Lewis Balfour, minister of Colinton near Edin. who d.* 24 *April* 1860 *aged* 82.) *b.* Manse of Colinton 2 June 1831; ed. at high school and Univ. of Edin; marine engineer to province of Otago, New Zealand 1863–65 and to government of N.Z. 1865 to death; invented the Refraction Protractor for lighthouses; designed many lighthouses in N.Z., also the dry dock at Port Chalmers; M.I.C.E. 15 May 1866; drowned off Timaru N.Z. 18 Dec. 1869. *Min. of proc. of Instit. of C.E. xxxi,* 200–202 (1871.)

BALFOUR, JOHN HUTTON. *b.* 15 Buccleuch place, Edin. 15 Sep. 1808; ed. at high school and Univ. of Edin., M.D. 1832, M.A., LL.D.; apprenticed to Sir George Ballingall; a pres. of Royal Medical Society 1831–33; LL.D. Glasgow and St. Andrew's; M.R.C.S. Edin. 1833, F.R.C.S. 1835; practised at Edin. 1834–41; Botanical Society of Edin. was founded at his house 15 Dundas st. 8 Feb. 1836; a lecturer on botany in Surgeon sq. 1840; professor of botany in Univ. of Glasgow 1841, and in Univ. of Edin. 22 Oct. 1845 to Feb. 1879; regius keeper of Royal botanic garden, and Queen's botanist for Scotland 1845–79; F.R.S. Edinburgh 1835, F.L.S. 1844, F.R.S. 5 June 1856; dean of the Medical faculty; an editor of *Annals of natural history* 1842–57 and of *Edinburgh New philosophical journal* 1855–66; author of *Class book of botany* 1854, 5 ed. 1875; *Introduction to study of Palæontological botany* 1872. *d.* Inverleith house, Edin. 11 Feb. 1884. *The Biograph i,* 430–38 (1882).

BALFOUR, LOWRY VESEY TOWNLEY. *b.* 1819; secretary of the order of St. Patrick 1853 to death. *d.* Dublin 12 Feb. 1878.

BALFOUR, ROBERT FREDERICK. *b.* Balbirnie Fifeshire 30 April 1846; ensign Grenadier guards 9 Aug. 1865; major 1 April 1882 to death; served in Egypt 1882; wounded at battle of Tel-el-Kebir 9 Sep. 1882. *d.* 24 Belgrave sq. London 23 Oct. 1882. *I.L.N. lxxxi,* 497 (1882), *portrait; Graphic xxvi,* 605 (1882), *portrait.*

BALGUY, JOHN *(eld. son of John Balguy of Darwent hall, Derbyshire, recorder of Derby who d.* 14 *Sep.* 1833). *b.* 14 Sep 1782; barrister M.T. 14 June 1805, bencher 1833; recorder of Derby 1830 to death; Q.C. 1833; chairman of Derbyshire quarter sessions 1837; bankruptcy comr. at Birmingham 21 Oct. 1842 to death. *d.* Duffield hall near Derby 16 Dec. 1858.

BALL, CHARLES ASHBY. *b.* Albury, Surrey 1809; entered the paper business 1826; purchased with his father the Guerres works near Dieppe 1829; founded the Doullens works 1836; purchased the Valvernes works near Dieppe; manufactured paper from esparto and bleached straw; founded the Fort Andemer works 1844; sold his business to La Compagnie des Establishments de la Risle 1869; perfected many important improvements in manufacture of paper. *d.* Sainte Addresse near Havre 27 March 1885.

BALL, FRANCES (6 *and youngest child of John Ball of Dublin, merchant who d.* 1808). *b.* Eccles st. Dublin 9 Jany. 1794; joined the Institute of the Blessed Virgin Mary at Mickle Bar convent York 11 June 1814; introduced this Institution into Ireland 1821; assumed name of Sister Mary Theresa 8 Sep. 1814; founded in various parts of the world 37 convents tenanted by about 800 nuns. *d.* Rathfarnham Abbey near Dublin 19 May 1861. *Life by H. J. Coleridge* 1881, *portrait; Life by Wm. Hutch, D.D.* 1879.

BALL, NICHOLAS *(son of John Ball of Dublin, silk mercer). b.* Dublin 1791; ed. at Stonyhurst and Trin. coll. Dub., B.A. 1812; called to Irish bar 1814; K.C. 1830; bencher of King's Inns 1836; M.P. for Clonmel 1836–39; third Serjeant at law 10 Nov. 1836 to 11 July 1838; attorney general 11 July 1838 to 23 Feb. 1839; P.C. Ireland 1838; justice of Irish Court of Common Pleas 23 Feb. 1839 to death. *d.* 85 Stephens Green, Dublin 15 Jany. 1865.

BALL, RICHARD. Lived at Bridgewater, Bristol and Taunton successively; a Friend; joined the Plymouth Brethren; author of *Holy Scripture the test of truth* 1835; *Christianity in China* 1850; *Horæ Sabbaticæ or the Sabbatic cycle the divine chronometer* 1853. *d.* Aberdeen terrace, Clifton 10 May 1862 aged 68. *Smith's Friends' Books i,* 161–63 (1867).

BALL, ROBERT *(son of Bob Stawel Ball). b.* Cove of Cork 1 April 1802; clerk in under secretary's office in Dublin 1827–52; F.R.S. Dublin 1834; M.R.I.A. 23 Feb. 1835, treasurer 1845 to death; member of Geol. soc. of

BALL, R. *(Con.)*
Ireland 1835, pres. 1852; sec. to Zoological society of Dub. 1837 to death; director of museum of Trinity college Dub. 1844, presented his valuable private collection to the college; hon. LL.D. Dub. 1850; sec. to Queen's Univ. in Ireland 1851; founded University zoological and botanical association 1853. *(m.* 21 Sep. 1837 Amelia Gresley dau. of Thomas Hellicar of Bristol, merchant, she was granted a civil list pension of £100 4 Oct. 1858). *d.* Dublin 30 March 1857. *Natural history review v,* 1–34 (1858), *portrait.*

BALL, SAMUEL. Member of East India Company's establishment at Canton 1804–26; author of *Observations on expediency of opening a second port in China* 1817; *An account of the cultivation and manufacture of tea in China* 1848. *d.* Sion house, Wolverley 5 March 1874 in 94 year.

BALL, THOMAS GERRARD *(son of Abraham Ball of Chester). b.* Chester 24 Jany. 1791; served in navy 1801–1807; ensign 34 foot 17 Sep. 1807; lieut. col. 8 foot 2 Oct. 1835 to 25 Oct. 1842 when placed on h.p.; col. 46 foot 24 April 1860 and of 8 foot 17 June 1861 to death; general 10 Jany. 1870. *d.* 7 Stanley place, Chester 18 Dec. 1881.

BALL, WILLIAM *(son of Richard Ball of Bridgwater who d.* 1834). *b.* Bridgwater 1 Jany. 1801; solicitor at Bristol 1828–35; a minister of Society of Friends 1846 to death. *(m.* 1834 Anne Dale, she *d.* 1861). Author of *Nugæ Sacræ or psalms and hymns and spiritual songs* [anon.] 1825; *The Transcript and other poems* 1855; *Hymns or lyrics* 1864; *Verses composed since* 1870, 1875. *d.* at an hotel in Aberdeen 30 July 1878. *Annual Monitor for* 1879 *pp.* 8–54.

BALL, WILLIAM. *b.* 1785; composed hundreds of comic and sentimental songs, his song *Jack's lament for the loss of his tail* was one of the most popular songs of the day ever written; his Drawing room concerts in 1829 were very successfull; adapted to English words librettos of Masses of Haydn, Mozart and Beethoven, Mozart's *Requiem,* Spohr's *God thou art great,* Rossini's *Stabat Mater* and Mendelssohn's *St. Paul* and *Lobgesang;* edited with N. Mori *The musical gem,* 2 vols. 1831–32; edited *The London Spring annual lyrical and pictorial* 1834. *d.* London 14 May 1869.

BALL, SIR WILLIAM KEITH, 2 Baronet *(only child of Sir Alexander John Ball, 1 Baronet). b.* Greenwich 27 Oct. 1791; succeeded 25 Oct. 1809. *d.* Spernall hall, **Warwickshire 9 March 1874.**

BALL-HUGHES, EDWARD HUGHES *(said to be son of a slop seller in Ratcliffe highway, London). b* 1799. Ed. at Eton and Trin. coll. Cam. ; cornet 7 hussars 28 Aug. 1817 to 11 Feb. 1819 when placed on h.p. ; took additional name of Hughes by royal license 7 Aug. 1819 on coming into a fortune of £40,000 per annum from his uncle Admiral Sir Edward Hughes ; one of the leading dandies of his day, known as the Golden Ball ; lost £45,000 in one night at Wattier's club, Piccadilly 1819, lost three quarters of his fortune at play, the greatest gambler of his day ; bought Oatlands near Weybridge 1827, which he sold to Lord Francis Egerton ; lived at St. Germain near Paris for some years before his death. *(m.* 22 March 1823 Mercandotti the opera dancer, natural dau. or protégée of 4 Earl of Fife, she was then aged 16). *d.* St. Germain 13 March 1863. *R. H. Gronow's Celebrities* (1865) 112–17.

BALLANTINE, JAMES. *b.* The West Port, Edinburgh 11 June 1808 ; a house painter at Edin. 1830 ; one of the first to revive the art of glass painting ; executed the 12 stained glass windows in the House of Lords, Westminster, representing kings and queens both regnant and consort of the U.K. ; sec. of committee of Burns centenary 1859 ; grand bard of Scottish Grand lodge of Freemasons about 1862 to death ; contributed about 50 songs to *Whistle-Binkie or the piper of the party* 1832 ; author of *The Gaberlunzie's wallet* 1843 ; *A treatise on painted glass* 1845 ; *Poems* 1856 ; *Chronicle of the hundredth birthday of Robert Burns* 1859, which contains reports of 872 Burns' centenary meetings held all over the world 25 Jany. 1859 ; *The Provost's daughter,* a musical farce in 2 acts performed at T.R. Edin. 1855 ; *The Gaberlunzie,* a drama in 3 acts 1858. *d.* Warrender lodge, Edinburgh 18 Dec. 1877. *Whistle-Binkie ii, xiv–xxvii* (1878) ; *History of the lodge of Edinburgh by D. M. Lyons* (1873) 50, 363, *portrait.*

BALLANTINE, WILLIAM. Barrister I.T. 5 Feb. 1813 ; magistrate at Thames police court 1821–48. *d.* 89 Cadogan place, Chelsea 14 Dec. 1852 in 74 year. *I.L.N. ix,* 317 (1846), *portrait.*

BALLANTYNE, JAMES ROBERT. *b.* Kelso 13 Dec. 1813 ; ed. at Edinburgh new academy and college ; teacher of Hindi and Sanskrit at Naval and military academy Edin. 1839 ; principal of College of Benares 1845–61 ; librarian of India office library Cannon row, Westminster 1861 to death ; author of *Lectures on the sub-divisions of knowledge, Sanskrit and*

BALLANTYNE, J. R. *(Con.)*
English 1848 ; *The Mahabhashya or great commentary on the aphorisms of Panini* 1856 ; *Christianity contrasted with Hindu philosophy* 1859 and 14 other works. *d.* 16 Feb. 1864. *Journal of Royal Asiatic Society i, v–vii* (1865).

BALLANTYNE, ROBERT MICHAEL. *b.* Edinburgh 24 April 1825 ; in the Hudson Bay Company's service 1841–47 ; author of *Hudson's Bay or every day life in the wilds of North America* 1848, 3 ed. 1859 ; *Coral island, a tale of the Pacific ocean* 1857 ; *Deep down, a tale of the Cornish mines* 1868, and many other tales. *d.* **1894.**

BALLANTYNE, THOMAS. *b.* Paisley 1806, a weaver there ; edited *Bolton Free Press;* edited *Manchester Guardian;* printer, publisher and one of the 4 original proprietors of *Manchester Examiner;* editor of *Liverpool Journal* and *Liverpool Mercury;* edited the *Leader* in London ; started the *Statesman,* edited it till its close ; edited *St. James's Chronicle;* author of *Passages selected from writings of T. Carlyle* 1855 ; *Essays in mosaic* 1870. *d.* Tufnell park, Holloway 30 Aug. 1871.

BALLARD, EDWARD GEORGE *(only child of Edward Ballard, alderman of Salisbury who d.* 6 *March* 1827). *b.* Salisbury 29 April 1791 ; clerk in the Stamp and Excise offices London 1809–17 ; wrote most of the poetry and critiques for the *Weekly Review;* author of *A new series of original poems* [anon.] 1825 ; *Microscopic amusements* 1829 ; wrote part of a continuation of Strype's *Ecclesiastical annals* in *The Surplice* weekly paper 1848. *d.* Compton terrace, Islington 14 Feb. 1860.

BALLARD, JOHN ARCHIBALD. *b.* 1829 ; 2 lieut. Bombay Engineers 8 Dec. 1848 and lieut. col. 10 Nov. 1869 to 31 Dec. 1878 ; lieut. col. Turkish army 1854 ; served in campaigns on the Danube 1854–55, in Crimea 1855, and in Mingrelia 1855–56 ; assistant quartermaster general of Persian expeditionary force 1856–57, and of Rajpootana field force and Malwa division in Indian mutiny 1858–59 ; C.B. 10 May 1856 ; mint master Bombay 1862–78 ; general 31 Dec. 1878. *d.* Pass of Thermopylæ near Livadia Greece 1 April 1880.

BALLARD, THOMAS. *b.* Mayfair London ; studied at St. George's hospital ; fellow of Royal Med. and Chir. society 1849 ; author of *New and rational explanation of the diseases peculiar to infants and mothers* 1860 ; *On the convulsive diseases of infants* 1863 ; *An enquiry into constitutional syphilis in the infant* 1874. *d.* 10 Southwick place, Hyde park 11 Sep. 1874 aged 56.

BALLINGALL, DAVID JAMES. Midshipman R.N.; served at Copenhagen 1801; 2 lieut. R.M. 1 July 1803; col. commandant 19 Nov. 1851 to 10 Jany. 1852 when he retired on full pay. *d.* Southsea 31 March 1854.

BALLINGALL, SIR GEORGE *(son of Rev. Robert Ballingall, minister of Forglen, Banffshire).* *b.* in the manse of Forglen 2 May 1780; ed. at Univs. of St. Andrews and Edin.; M.D. Edin. 1803, M.R.C.S. Edin. 15 Aug. 1820; assistant surgeon 1 foot 10 July 1806; surgeon of 33 foot 1815–18 when placed on h.p., retired 1831; professor of military surgery in Univ. of Edin. 18 Jany. 1823 to death; knighted by Wm. iv at St. James's palace 4 Aug. 1830; F.R.S.; author of *Introductory lectures to a course of military surgery* 1830; *Outlines of military surgery,* 5 ed. 1855. *d.* Altamont near Blairgowrie 4 Dec. 1855.

BALNEAVIS, HENRY. Ensign 16 foot 3 Jany. 1797; captain 27 foot 1805–24 when placed on h.p.; L.G. 20 June 1854; colonel 65 foot 18 Jany. 1855 to death; C.M.G. 17 July 1833; K.H. 1836. *d.* Malta 17 July 1857 aged 77.

BALVAIRD, WILLIAM. Major Rifle brigade 1814–18; major 99 foot 1824–26, retired from the army 27 Aug. 1841; C.B. 26 Sep. 1831. *d.* Edinburgh 7 Sep. 1853.

BALY, WILLIAM. *b.* Lynn, Norfolk 1814; L.S.A. 1834, M.R.C.S. 1834; studied in Paris, Heidelberg and Berlin; M.D. Berlin 1836; practised in London 1836; L.R.C.P. 1841, F.R.C.P. 1846, a censor 1858; phys. to Milbank penitentiary 1841–60; lecturer on forensic medicine at St. Bartholomew's hospital 1841–54, assistant phys. there 1854 and lecturer on medicine 1855; Gulstonian lecturer Feb. 1847; F.R.S. 15 April 1847; phys. extraordinary to the Queen 18 April 1859; member of general council of medical education and registration 1 Aug. 1860 to death; author with W. S. Kirke of *Advances in physiology of motion* 1848, and with W. G. Gull of *Reports on epidemic cholera* 1854; killed in the train on the South Western railway about 7 miles from London at the junction with the Epsom line 28 Jany. 1861. *Medical Critic ii,* 334–40 (1861); *I.L.N. xxxviii,* 111, 122 (1861), *portrait.*

BAMFORD, SAMUEL. *b.* Middleton 28 Feb. 1788; ed. at Manchester gr. sch.; a hand-loom weaver at Middleton; secretary to the Hampden club at Middleton 1816; examined before Privy Council on a charge of high

BAMFORD, S. *(Con.)*
treason April 1817 when set free with a warning; took part in reform meeting at Peterloo 16 Aug. 1819, tried at York assizes March 1820 when found guilty of a seditious misdemeanour, sentenced in Court of King's Bench, London 15 May 1820 to 1 year's imprisonment in Lincoln gaol; employed in Inland Revenue Office London 1849–58; author of *Miscellaneous poetry* 1821; *Passages in the life of a Radical* 2 vols. 1840–44; *Early days* 1849 2 ed. 1859; *Walks in South Lancashire* 2 vols.; *Talk o Seawth Lankeshur by Samhul Beamfort* 1850, in this volume he professes to correct the dialect in Tim Bobbin; *Life of Amos Ogden of Middleton* 1853. *d.* Moston, Harpurhey near Manchester 13 April 1872; monument in Middleton cemetery, unveiled 6 Oct. 1877. *F. Espinasse's Lancashire Worthies 2 series* 1877, *pp.* 462–91; *Procter's Memorials of bygone Manchester* (1881) 220–25.

BAMFORD, WILLIAM. Surgeon at Rugely Staffs 1803 to death; one of principal witnesses at trial of Wm. Palmer the poisoner 1856. *d.* Rugely 17 April 1859 in 84 year.

BAMPTON, AUGUSTUS HAMILTON. *b.* London 13 March 1823; civil engineer at Plymouth 1844; chief surveyor to the corporation 1849–54; engineer to South Devon and Tavistock railway 1852 to death; M.I.C.E. 1849; author of *The drainage of towns* 1849. *d.* North hill Devon 4 March 1857. *Min. of proc. of Instit. of C.E. xvii,* 92–94 (1858).

BANCALARI, PETER. *b.* 1806; a noted cricket, umpire at Oxford many years. *d.* Oxford 31 Oct. 1869.

BANDINEL, REV. BULKELEY *(eld. son of Rev. James Bandinel V. of Netherbury Dorset who d. 25 Nov. 1804 aged 92).* *b.* Oxford 21 Feb. 1781; ed. at Reading and Winchester; scholar of New college Ox. 1800, fellow, B.A. 1805, M.A. 1807, B.D. and D.D. 1823; chaplain in the Victory 1808; under librarian Bodleian library Ox. 1810, librarian 25 Aug. 1813 to Sep. 1860; published Catalogue of the printed books 4 vols. 1843–50; proctor Univ. of Ox. 1814; R. of Haughton-le-Skerne, Durham 1823–60; author of *Catalogue of books relating to British topography and Saxon and Norman literature bequeathed to the Bodleian library by Richard Gough* 1814; author with John Caley and Henry Ellis of new editions of *Dugdale's Monasticon Anglicanum* 1817–30 crown folio 6 vols. in 8, and 1846, folio, 8 vols; edited *Clarendon's History of the rebellion* 1826. *d.* Oxford 6 Feb. 1861.

BANDON, JAMES BERNARD, 2 Earl of *(eld. son of Francis Bernard 1 Earl of Bandon 1755–1830). b.* Castle Bernard, Bandon co. Cork 14 June 1785; ed. at St. John's coll. Cam.; M.A. 1806; M.P. for Bandon 1820–26 and 1830; succeeded as 2 Earl 26 Nov. 1830; recorder of Bandon; a representative peer of Ireland 31 July 1835; lord lieutenant of Cork 1842; F.R.S. 5 June 1845. *d.* Castle Bernard 31 Oct. 1856.

BANDON, FRANCIS BERNARD, 3 Earl of *(eld. son of the preceding). b.* Grosvenor st. London 3 Jany. 1810; ed. at Eton and Oriel coll. Ox., B.A. 1830, M.A. 1834; M.P. for Bandon 1831–32 and 1842–56; a representative peer of Ireland 21 Aug. 1858; lord lieutenant of Cork 2 Nov. 1874. *d.* Castle Bernard 17 Feb. 1877.

BANGOR, EDWARD WARD, 4 Viscount. *b.* London 23 Feb. 1827; succeeded 1 Aug. 1837; ed. at Eton and Trin. coll. Cam., M.A. 1848; representative peer for Ireland 9 Jany. 1855. *d.* Brighton 14 Sep. 1881.

BANIM, MICHAEL *(eld. son of Michael Banim of Kilkenny, shopkeeper). b.* Kilkenny 5 Aug. 1796, postmaster there 1852–73; contributed *Crohoore, The Croppy, The ghost hunter, The mayor of Windgap, Father Connell* and other tales to *The tales by the O'Hara family* 24 vols. *d.* Booterstown, co. Dublin 30 Aug. 1874. *P. J. Murray's Life of John Banim* 1857.

BANKES, GEORGE *(3 son of Henry Bankes of Kingston hall, Dorset 1757–1834). b* 1788. Ed. at Westminster and Trin. hall, Cam.; fellow; LL.B. 1812; bankruptcy comr. 1822; recorder of Weymouth 25 Aug. 1823; cursitor Baron of the Exchequer 6 July 1824 to death when office abolished; M.P. for Corfe Castle 1816–23 and 1826–32 and for Dorset 1841 to death; sec. to Board of control 2 May 1829 to 16 Feb. 1830 and comr. of same board 24 Feb. 1830 to 6 Dec. 1830; a junior lord of the Treasury 24 April to 24 Nov. 1830; P.C. 27 Feb. 1852; judge advocate general 28 Feb. to Dec. 1852; author of *The story of Corfe Castle and of many who have lived there* 1853. *d.* 5 Old palace yard Westminster 6 July 1856. *Waagen's Galleries of art* (1857) 374–83; *I.L.N. xxiv,* 97 (1854).

BANKES, WILLIAM JOHN *(elder brother of the preceding).* Ed. at Trin. coll. Cam., B.A. 1808, M.A. 1811; M.P. for Truro 1810–12, for Cambridge Univ. 1821–25, for Marlborough 1829–32 and for Dorset 1833–34; a great friend of Lord Byron; travelled in the East with Giovanni Finati whose life he translated from the Italian 2 vols. 1830. *d.* Venice 15 April 1855. *A. R.* 1826 49–56.

BANKHEAD, CHARLES. *b.* Antrim; ed. at Londonderry and Univ. of Edin., M.D. 24 June 1790; surgeon to the Londonderry militia; L.C.P. 25 June 1807; practised at Brighton; physician extraordinary to Prince Regent 24 Feb. 1816, removed to London; physician extraordinary to George 4th 30 March 1821; practised many years at Florence. *d.* Florence 26 Nov. 1859 in 92 year.

BANKHEAD, CHARLES. Minister plenipotentiary to Mexican republic 24 Nov. 1843 to 6 April 1851. *d.* 8 St. James's st. London 11 March 1870.

BANKS, GEORGE LINNÆUS *(4 son of John Banks of Birmingham, horticulturist). b.* Bull Ring, Birmingham 2 March 1821; began lecturing 29 Dec. 1846; promoted Mechanics' Institutes in Yorkshire and Durham; edited the Advertiser at Harrogate 1848, Mercury at Birmingham, Daily Express at Dublin, Chronicle at Durham, Royal Standard at Windsor, and the Sussex Mercury 1864; wrote the popular negro melody *Dandy Jim of Caroline;* author of *Blossoms of poesy* 1841; *Staves for the human ladder, poems* 1850; *All about Shakspere* 1864; *The Swiss father* a drama produced at T.R. Liverpool 1846 and *Better late than never* a comedy produced at Durham theatre 1858. *d.* Dalston, London 3 May 1881. *Illustrated Review vi,* 261–63, portrait.

BANKS, JOHN. *b.* 1 Sep. 1752 at 11.30 p.m., a period marked by the change of style which conducted him 11 days onward in his journey half an hour after his birth. *d.* Easingwold 24 Nov. 1852.

BANKS, JOHN SHERBROOKE. *b.* 1811; ensign 33 Bengal N.I. 1829, major 1857 to death; succeeded Sir Henry Lawrence as chief comr. of Lucknow; shot through the head while examining an outpost at Lucknow 21 July or 1 Aug. 1857.

BANKS, THOMAS CHRISTOPHER *(eld. child of Thomas Banks one of the gentlemen pensioners).* Genealogist at 5 Lyons Inn London 1813–20, at the dormant peerage office John st. Pall Mall 1820; sent to North America by Alexander Humphrys to publish his rights as Earl of Stirling and to search for evidence 1826, returned 1828, sent to Ireland 1828–29, created baronet by Humphrys 1831 but resigned the rank about 1834; knight of holy order of St. John of Jerusalem; author of *Dormant and extinct baronage of England* 3 vols. 1807–1809; *History of the ancient noble family of Marmyun* 1817; *Stemmata Anglicana* 1825. *d.* Greenwich 30 Sep. 1854 in 90 year. *T. C.*

BANKS, T. C. *(Con.)*

Banks's Baronia Anglica vol. i, (1844), *preface; S. Warren's Miscellanies ii,* 169–291 (1855); *G. M. xliii,* 206–208 (1855).

BANKS, WILLIAM STOTT. *b.* Wakefield, March 1820; admitted solicitor Jany. 1851; partner with J. M. Ianson at Wakefield 1853; clerk to the borough justices March 1870 to death; author of *List of provincial words in use at Wakefield* 1865; *Walks in Yorkshire* 2 vols. 1866–72. *d.* Northgate, Wakefield 25 Dec. 1872. *Yorkshire Archæol. and Topog. Journal ii,* 459–60 (1873).

BANNAN, JOSEPH. A schoolmaster at Plymouth down to 1832 when his school was ruined by the cholera; edited the *South Devon Monthly Museum* 7 vols., Plymouth 1833–36; cashier and chief accountant of the *Western Times* newspaper at Exeter 1836 to death. *d.* Exeter 28 May 1865 aged 60.

BANNATYNE, ANDREW *(eld. son of Dugald Bannatyne of Glasgow, merchant).* *b.* 1798; ed. at Univs. of Glasgow and Heidelberg; member of faculty of procurators in Glasgow; dean of the faculty; member of University court Glasgow. *d.* 1871.

BANNATYNE, REV. ARCHIBALD. *b.* Rothesay; licensed by presbytery of Ayr 1835; minister at Oban 1842–53 and at John Knox's Free church Glasgow 1853 to death. *d.* 18 May 1863. *Truth in love, a few memorials of the Rev. Archibald Bannatyne* 1864.

BANNER, REV. BENJAMIN HOLFORD. *b.* 26 Nov. 1798; ed. at Merchant Taylor's and St. John's coll. Ox., B.A. 1821, M.A. 1824; precentor of Cashel 26 Aug. 1826 to death; chancellor of Emly, Tipperary 2 April 1835 to death. *d.* 1874.

BANNERMAN, SIR ALEXANDER *(son of Thomas Bannerman of Aberdeen, wine merchant who d. Jany. 1820 aged 77).* *b.* Aberdeen 7 Oct. 1788, shipowner, merchant and banker there; M.P. for Aberdeen 1832–47; dean of faculty in Marischal college Aberdeen 1837; a comr. of Greenwich hospital 1841; governor of Prince Edward island 3 Feb. 1851, of the Bahamas 8 May 1854 and of Newfoundland 9 Feb. 1857 to 1863; knighted by the Queen at Buckingham palace 3 Feb. 1851. *d.* Louth cottage, Chorley 30 Dec. 1864. *I.L.N. xix,* 236 (1851), *portrait.*

BANNERMAN, SIR ALEXANDER, 9 Baronet. *b.* Aberdeen 6 April 1823; succeeded 18 June 1851. *d.* 46 Grosvenor place, London 21 April 1877.

BANNERMAN, SIR CHARLES, 8 Baronet. *b.* 18 Aug. 1782; succeeded 31 May 1840. *d.* Clarges st. Piccadilly, London 18 June 1851.

BANNERMAN, REV. JAMES *(son of Rev. James Patrick Bannerman, minister of Cargill, Perthshire).* *b.* manse of Cargill 9 April 1807; ed. at Univ. of Edin., M.A. 1826; minister of Ormiston, Midlothian 1833–43 when he left the Established for the Free church; professor of apologetics and pastoral theology in New college Edin. 1849 to death; took a leading part in Free church movement; D.D. Princeton college New Jersey 1850; author of *The prevalent forms of unbelief* 1849; *Apologetical theology* 1851; *Inspiration* 1865; *The Church* 2 vols. 1868. *d.* Edinburgh 27 March 1868.

BANNISTER, CHARLES WILLIAM *(son of Charles George Bannister of London, solicitor 1796–1858).* *b.* 1826; ed. at Charterhouse; captain 2 Bombay light cavalry 24 April 1854 to 10 April 1861; governor of Maidstone gaol. *d.* 20 April 1874.

BANNISTER, REV. JOHN *(son of David Bannister of York 1788–1854).* *b.* York 25 Feb. 1816; ed. at Trin. coll. Dub., B.A. 1844, M.A. 1853, LL.B. and LL.D. 1866; P.C. of Bridgehill, Derbyshire 1846–57; P.C. of St. Day, Cornwall 13 Dec. 1857 to death; author of *A glossary of Cornish names,* 20,000 Celtic and other names now or formerly in use in Cornwall with derivations and significations (1871). *d.* St. Day 30 Aug. 1873. *Bibl. Cornub. i,* 9 (1874), *iii,* 1047 (1882).

BANNISTER, SAXE. *b.* Bidlington house Steyning, Sussex 27 June 1790; ed. at Lewes, Tunbridge and Queen's coll. Ox., B.A. 1813, M.A. 1815; raised a company and volunteered for the army 1813; captain on h.p. 25 Dec. 1813; barrister L.I. 25 Nov. 1819; attorney general of New South Wales 5 April 1824 to April 1826 when removed from office; printed a statement of his 'claims' 1853 after presenting many petitions to the Government; gentleman bedel of Royal College of Physicians London 1849–50; author of *Records of British enterprise beyond sea vol.* 1 1849; *William Paterson, his life and trials* 1858; *The writings of Wm. Paterson* 3 vols. 1859; *Classical and prehistoric influences upon British history,* 2 ed. 1871. *d.* Thornton lodge, Thornton Heath 16 Sep. 1877. *Dict. of Nat. Biog. iii,* 142 (1885).

BANON, AWLY PATRICK. F.R.C.S. Ireland 1844, vice president June 1866 to death; M.D. St. Andrew's 1851; F.R.C.P. Edin.

BANON, A. P. (Con.)

1852; author of *Observations on hermaphroditism illustrated by a remarkable case* 1852. *d.* 37 Fitzwilliam sq. Dublin 28 May 1867.

BANTING, WILLIAM. *b.* 1797; an undertaker at 27 St. James's st. Piccadilly, London 1820–70; made Duke of Wellington's funeral car Oct. 1852; reduced his weight from 202 lbs. to 156 lbs. in 12 months Aug. 1862 to Aug. 1863 by abstaining from bread, butter, milk, sugar, beer, and potatoes; author of *Letter on corpulence addressed to the public* 1863 4 ed. 1869; Thousands of people adopted the course he advised, which became known as "banting." *d.* 4 The Terrace, Kensington 16 March 1878. *Blackwood's Mag. xcvi*, 607–17 (1864); *Tanner's Practice of medicine i*, 148 (1875).

BANTRY, RICHARD WHITE, 1 Earl of (eld. son of Simon White of Bantry). *b.* 6 Aug. 1767; created a peer of Ireland as Baron Bantry 31 March 1797 on account of exertions in repelling the French invasion at Bantry bay 27 Jany. 1797, Viscount Bantry 29 Dec. 1800 and Viscount Berehaven and Earl of Bantry 22 Jany. 1816. *d.* Glengariffe lodge, co. Cork 2 May 1851.

BANTRY, RICHARD WHITE, 2 Earl of. *b.* St. Finbar, Cork 16 Nov. 1800; a representative peer for Ireland 1 July 1854. *d.* Exbury house, Hants 16 July 1868.

BANTRY, WILLIAM HENRY HARE WHITE, 3 Earl of. *b.* Dublin 16 Nov. 1801; ed. at St. John's coll. Cam., M.A. 1823; sheriff of Cork 1848; lieut. col. commandant West Cork artillery militia 1854–73; a representative peer for Ireland 6 July 1869. *d.* Bantry house, Cork 15 Jany. 1884.

BAPTIST, JOHN THOMAS. A well known florist at Sydney N.S.W. *d.* The Gardens, Surrey hills, Sydney 15 Sep. 1873 aged 69.

BARBER, CHARLES. *b.* Birmingham; teacher of drawing in Royal Institution, Liverpool; assisted to found the Architectural and Archæological association; a landscape painter; exhibited 3 pictures at the R.A. and many pictures at local exhibitions; pres. of the Liverpool Academy. *d.* Liverpool Jany. 1854.

BARBER, CHARLES CHAPMAN. ed. at St. John's coll. Cam., 9 wrangler 1833, B.A. 1833, M.A. 1836; pupil of Lewis Duval the conveyancer; barrister L.I. 3 May 1833; member of chancery procedure commission 1853; junior counsel for defendant in ejectment action of Tichborne v. Lushington 11

BARBER, C. C. (Con.)

May 1871 to 6 March 1872; junior counsel for the Crown in prosecution of Roger Tichborne for perjury 23 April 1873 to 28 Feb. 1874; engaged in court 103 days in the ejectment case, and 188 days in the perjury case; judge of county courts for circuit No. 6 East Riding of Yorkshire Feb. 1874 to March 1874 when he resigned and resumed practice. *d.* 71 Cornwall gardens London 5 Feb. 1882.

BARBER, FAIRLESS (2 son of Joseph Barber of Brighouse, solicitor). *b.* Castle hill, Rastrick 11 Jany. 1835; ed. at St. Peter's school York; admitted a solicitor 1859; practised at Brighouse; member of Huddersfield Archæological and Topographical Association 1866, sec. Sep. 1866, it became mainly through him in 1870 the Yorkshire Archæological and Topographical Association; F.S.A. 26 May 1870; edited *The Yorkshire Archæological and Topographical journal* 6 vols. 1876–81. *d.* Pinner 3 March 1881. *Yorkshire Arch. and Topog. journal vii*, 1–5 (1882).

BARBER, JAMES. A very extensive proprietor of coaches between London and Edinburgh; senior partner in firm of Barber and Co. of York, wholesale jewellers; sheriff of York 1826; lord mayor 1833, elected again 1844 but paid the fine to be excused serving. *d.* Tang hall near York 10 March 1857 aged 73.

BARBER, JAMES (son of a cutlery manufacturer at Sheffield.) made a large sum of money by cards and billiards at Manchester; went to Paris, where he purchased famous race horse Chanticleer which won the Northumberland plate, Goodwood stakes, and Doncaster cup 1848; in partnership with Joseph Saxon as racing men; won Great Northern handicap at York with Ben Webster 1860, and the Oaks with Brown Duchess 1861; at one period one of richest men on the turf. *d.* Sheffield 18 April 1885 in 69 year.

BARBER, JOHN. *b.* West Runham, Norfolk; drayman in firm of Truman and Co., London 8 years; purveyor of pigeons and sparrows at 27 Sclater st. Bethnal Green 1821 to death; attended all the chief shooting matches in England for 40 years; his blue rock pigeons well known all over the world. *d.* 27 Sclater st. 18 June 1860 aged 71.

BARBER, JONATHAN. Frame work knitter at Nottingham; leader of the infidels there, held public discussions with Rev. J. W. Brooks of Nottingham. *d.* Nottingham 17 Jany. 1859. *The apology for renouncing infidel opinions of Jonathan Barber* 1859.

BARBER, JONATHAN. *b.* England 1784; M.R.C.S.; practised in Scarborough and London; went to United States about 1820; taught elocution in Yale and Harvard Univs., became the best teacher in America; lectured on phrenology; went to Montreal 1836; resumed medical practice as a homœopath about 1845; professor of oratory in McGill univ. Montreal down to 1862; author of *The Elocutionist* 1829; *A grammar of elocution* 1830. *d.* near Montreal 11 May 1864.

BARBER, MARY ANN SERRETT *(daughter of Thomas Barber)*. Wrote many articles in the *Church of England Magazine* and *Charlotte Elizabeth's Christian lady's magazine;* edited *Children's Missionary magazine* afterwards called *The Coral Missionary mag.* 1847 to death; author of *Redemption in Israel or narratives of conversions among the Jews* 1844, *The sorrows of the streets* 1855, *Castle Rag and its dependencies or the sins and sorrows of the poor* 1858, *Du Bourg or the Mercuriale* 1851 and many other books. *d.* 9 Sussex sq. Brighton 9 March 1864 aged 63. *Breadwinning or the Ledger and the Lute an Autobiography by M. A. S. Barber* 1865.

BARBER, WILLIAM HENRY. *b.* about 1807; clerk to Messrs. Scoones of Tonbridge, Kent, solicitors 1819–36; established Literary and Scientific institution there 1837; solicitor in London 1837; partner with Merrick Bircham; founded The legal discussion society, sec. and treasurer; founded with Lord Brougham and George Birkbeck, Adult instruction society; tried at Central Criminal Court April 1844 for uttering a will of one Anne Slack knowing same to be a forgery when sentenced to be transported for life; arrived at Norfolk Island 9 Nov. 1844; moved to Tasman's Peninsula March 1847 on breaking up of Norfolk Island establishment; granted conditional pardon by royal warrant dated 12 Nov. 1846 and a free pardon 3 Nov. 1848; arrived in Paris May 1848 and in London Nov. 1848; applied for his annual certificate as a solicitor 31 Jany. 1849, certificate refused him 6 July 1850; petition for inquiry and redress presented to House of Commons 5 April 1852; granted a certificate 21 Nov. 1855; practised in London, ceased to practice 1862. *The case of Mr. W H. Barber,* 8 ed. 1853; *Central criminal court, minutes of evidence by H. Buckler xix,* 778–850 (1844); *I.L.N. iv,* 80, 249 (1844), 2 *portraits.*

BARBOUR, ROBERT. *b.* Renfrewshire 1797; one of the merchant princes of Manchester down to about 1864 when he retired; member of the first Synod of English Presbyterian

BARBOUR, R. *(Con.)*
church about 1834; endowed at cost of £12,000 a chair which bears his name in Presbyterian college; purchased Bolesworth castle near Chester 1857; sheriff of Cheshire 1866. *d.* Bolesworth castle 17 Jany. 1885, will proved at Chester 14 April 1885, value of personalty upwards of £472,000.

BARCLAY, ANDREW WHYTE *(son of John Barclay, captain R.N.)* *b.* Dysart, Fifeshire 17 July 1817; ed. at high sch. and univ. of Edin.; M.D. 1839; studied at Caius coll. Cam. 1843, and St. George's hospital, London; M.B. 1847, M.D. 1852; medical registrar at St. George's many years; F.R.C.P. 1851, examiner, councillor and censor, Lumleian lecturer 1864, Harveian orator 1881, treasurer 1884; fellow of Royal Med. and Chir. soc., pres.; assistant phys. at St. George's 1857, phys. 1862–82; the first medical officer of health at Chelsea 1856; author of *Manual of medical diagnosis* 1857 3 ed. 1870. *d.* Whitney Wood, Stevenage, Herts 28 April 1884. *British Medical Journal i,* 932 (1884).

BARCLAY, ARTHUR KETT *(eld. son of Charles Barclay of Bury hill near Dorking, Surrey 1780–1855)*. *b.* 20 June 1806; ed at Harrow; head of firm of Barclay, Perkins and Co., brewers; built an observatory at Bury hill 1848; F.R.G.S. 1840, F.R.S. 3 June 1852; paralysed 1855. *(m.* 20 Dec. 1836 **Maria Octavia** dau. of Ichabod Wright of Mapperley, Notts). *d.* 20 Nov. 1869.

BARCLAY, CHARLES. *b.* 26 Dec. 1780; M.P. for Southwark 1815–1818, for Dundalk 1826–1830 and for west Surrey 1835–1837; head of firm of Barclay, Perkins and Co.; pres. of Guy's hospital; sheriff of Surrey 1842; F.R.G.S., F.S.A. *d.* Bury hill, Surrey 5 Dec. 1855.

BARCLAY, HUGH *b.* Glasgow 18 Jany. 1799; member of Glasgow faculty of procurators 1820; sheriff substitute of West Perthshire 1829, and of Perthshire 1833; sheriff of Perthshire 1883 to death; author of *A digest of the law of Scotland* 2 vols. 1852–53 4 ed. 1880; *Thoughts on Sabbath schools* 1855; *The Sinaitic inscriptions* 1866. *d.* Early bank Craigie near Perth 1 Feb. 1884.

BARCLAY, RIGHT REV. JOSEPH *(only son of John Barclay of Strabane, co. Donegal who d.* 9 *Dec.* 1845). *b.* Strabane 12 Aug. 1831; ed. at Trin. coll. Dublin 16 Oct. 1849 to 1854, B.A. 1854, M.A. 1857, LL.D. 1865, D.D. 1880; C. of Bagnalstown 1854-58; missionary at Constantinople 1858–61; incumbent of Ch.

BARCLAY, RIGHT REV. J. *(Con.)*
Ch. Jerusalem 1861–70; R. of Stapleford,
Herts 29 March 1873; bishop of Jerusalem
June 1879 to death, consecrated in St. Paul's
25 July 1879, installed 24 Feb. 1880; held
2 ordinations and 5 confirmations; author of
*Talmud, Selection of treatises translated from the
Mishna* 1878. *d.* the bishop's palace, Jerusalem 23 Oct. 1881. *Joseph Barclay a missionary
biography* 1883, *portrait.*

BARCLAY, LYDIA ANN *(dau. of Robert Barclay
of Clapham.)* Edited *Selections from the
writings of Patrick Livingstone* 1847; *Memoirs
and letters of Richard and Elizabeth Shackleton*
1849; *A journal of the life and gospel labours
of John Conran* 1850. *d.* Cockermouth 31
Jany. 1855 aged 55. *A short memoir of L. A.
Barclay by Wm. Hodgson, junior* 1855; *A
selection from the letters of L. A. Barclay* 1862.

BARCLAY, SIR ROBERT, 9 Baronet. *b.* Dungannon 1819; succeeded 14 Aug. 1839. *d.*
Dungannon 19 May 1859.

BARCLAY, ROBERT *(younger son of John Barclay, a minister in Society of Friends who d. 11
May* 1838 *aged* 41.) *b.* Croydon 4 Aug. 1833;
a manufacturing stationer in London 1855;
patented March 1860 an indelible writing
paper for prevention of forgery; author of
*The inner life of the religious societies of the
Commonwealth* 1876, reissued 1877 and 1878.
d. Hillside, Reigate 11 Nov. 1876. *Sermons
by Robert Barclay with a brief memoir edited by
his widow* 1878, *portrait.*

BARCLAY, VERY REV. THOMAS *(son of Rev.
James Barclay, minister of Unst, Shetland).*
b. Unst June 1792; ed. at King's coll. Aberdeen, M.A. 1812; taught elocution at Aberdeen; a parliamentary reporter for the *Times*
1818–22; licensed by presbytery of Lerwick
27 June 1821; ordained 12 Sep. 1822 to
parish of Dunrossness, Shetland; minister of
Lerwick 13 Dec. 1827; clerk of the synod of
Shetland 27 Apl. 1831; minister of Peterculter Sep. 1843, and of Currie July 1844;
principal of Univ. of Glasgow 13 Feb. 1858
to death; one of the best Scandinavian
scholars. *d.* the college, Gillmore hill, Glasgow 23 Feb. 1873. *Scott's Fasti Ecclesiæ Scoticanæ pt. v,* 422, 426.

BARCLAY, WILLIAM. *b.* London 1797; miniature painter; made many copies from works
of Italian masters in the Louvre Paris; exhibited portraits and copies in water-colours
at the Salon 1831–59 and at Royal Academy
1832–56. *d.* 1859.

BARDELIN, AUGUSTE DE. *b.* Aix in Provence;
member of the Garde-du-Corps of Louis xvi;
emigrated to Italy, Germany and Belgium;
taught French and Italian at Norwich about
1792–1814; accompanied Louis xviii to Paris
1814; lived there till 1848 when he went to
Provence. *(m.* 1815 or 1816 Miss Sutton).
d. Nice 8 May 1852 in 85 year.

BARDIN, GEORGE GREGORY. Chief inspector
of machinery afloat 6 Aug. 1870; C.B. 15
Aug. 1868. *d.* about May 1875.

BARDSLEY, SIR JAMES LOMAX (2 son of
Edward Bardsley of Nottingham). *b.* Nottingham 7 July 1801; ed. at Univs. of Glasgow
and Edin.; M.D. Edin. 1823; physician at
Manchester 1823 to death; physician to Manchester royal infirmary 1824–43; member of
Manchester medical society 1834, pres. 1838–
42 and 1845–47; knighted by the Queen at
Buckingham palace 8 Aug. 1853; F.R.C.P.
1859; lecturer on principles and practice of
physic at Royal school of medicine Manchester 1825–43; author of *Hospital facts
and observations* 1830 and of the articles
Diabetes and Hydrophobia in the *Cyclopædia
of practical medicine* 1833. *d.* The Orchard
Greenheys, Manchester 10 July 1876. *Photographs of eminent medical men ii,* 95–98 (1868),
portrait.

BARDSLEY, SAMUEL ARGENT. *b.* Kelvedon,
Essex 27 April 1764; apprenticed to a surgeon at Nottingham; studied at Leyden Univ.
1786–89; M.D. 1789; physician at Manchester 1790; phys. to Manchester infirmary
1790 to Aug. 1823; author of *Critical remarks
on the tragedy of Pizarro* 1800; *Medical reports
of cases and experiments* 1807. *d.* near Hastings
25 May 1851.

BAREZ, REV. HENRY. Minister of the French
protestant episcopal church of St. Martin
Orgars formerly in Cannon st. London;
granted civil list pension of £100 23 July
1840 in consideration of having taught Queen
Victoria German. *d.* Leicester square, London 26 Dec. 1867 aged 79.

BARFF, SAMUEL. *b.* England? about 1793;
lived at Zante 1816 to death, an eminent
merchant and banker there; took an active
part in the struggle for independence carried
on by the Greek nation 1823–24. *d.* Zante 1
Sep. 1880 aged 87. *Moore's Life of Lord
Byron; Trikoupes'* Ἱστορια τῆς Ἑλληνικῆς
Ἐπαναστασεως 4 vols. 1853–57.

BARHAM, CHARLES FOSTER (4 son of *Thomas
Foster Barham of Penzance, Cornwall* 1766–
1844). *b.* Truro 9 March 1804; ed. at

BARHAM, C. F. (Con.)

Queen's coll. Cam.; foundation scholar May 1823; studied in Paris and Italy 1825-28; M.B. Cam. 1827, M.D. 1860; physician Tavistock dispensary 1832-35; phys. at Truro Aug. 1837 to death; senior phys. Royal Cornwall infirmary 1838-73; pres. Royal Instit. of Cornwall 1859-61; mayor of Truro 1862; author of *Report on the sanitary state of the labouring classes in the town of Truro* 1842 and of many papers on meteorology and other subjects in *Reports* and *Journal of Royal Instit. of Cornwall* and other publications. *d.* 11 Strangways terrace, Truro 20 Oct. 1884. *Boase and Courtney's Bibl. Cornub. i,* 10 (1874), *iii,* 1048 (1882).

BARHAM, REV. CHARLES HENRY *(youngest son of Joseph Foster Barham, M.P.) b.* London 1808; ed. at Charterhouse and Ch. Ch. Ox., B.A. 1831, M.A. 1834; M.P. for Appleby 24 May 1832 to 3 Dec. 1832; R. of Barming, Kent about 1838-47; R. of Kirkby Thore, Westmoreland 1847-52. *d.* Trecwn, Pembrokeshire 15 Aug. 1878.

BARHAM, FRANCIS FOSTER *(5 son of Thomas Foster Barham, of Penzance). b.* Leskinnick, Penzance 31 May 1808; solicitor in London 1831; joint proprietor and editor with J. A. Heraud of *The new monthly Magazine and humorist* 1 July 1839 to 26 May 1840; lived at Clifton 1844-54, and at Bath 1854 to death; member of Anglo Biblical Instit. 1852; a vegetarian many years; author of *The Adamus Exul of Grotius or the prototype of Paradise lost, now first translated from the Latin* 1839; *The ecclesiastical history of Great Britain by Jeremy Collier, new ed. with a life of the author* 9 vols. 1840; *The Alist or divine, a message to our times* 1840; *The political works of Cicero translated* 2 vols. 1841-42; *Socrates, a tragedy in 5 acts* 1842; *The life and times of John Reuchlin or Capnion* 1843; *The new Bristol guide, a poem* 1850 and many other books. *d.* 8 St. Mark's place, Bath 9 Feb. 1871. *A memorial of Francis Barham, edited by Isaac Pitman* 1873 *pp. lv.* and 495 printed in the phonetic character; *Boase and Courtney's Bibl. Cornub. i,* 11, *iii,* 1048.

NOTE.—He advocated at one period the formation of a religious association to be called Alists or Godists, some of his works on this subject have A. F. Barham or Alist Francis Barham on the title page.

BARHAM, THOMAS FOSTER *(eld. son of Thomas Foster Barham of Penzance). b.* Hendon, Middlesex 10 Sep. 1794; ed. at Queen's coll. Cam., M.B. 1820; phys. at Penzance 1820 and at Exeter about 1830-49; lived at New-

BARHAM, T. F. *(Con.)*

ton Abbot, Devon 1849 to death; author of *Introduction to Greek grammar* 1829; *Greek roots in English rhymes* 1837; *Philadelphia or claims of humanity* 1858; contributed to transactions of Cornish scientific societies. *d.* Castle Dyke, Highweek, Newton Abbot 3 March 1869. *Boase and Courtney's Bibl. Cornub. i,* 13, *iii,* 1050.

BARING, RIGHT REV. CHARLES THOMAS *(youngest son of Sir Thomas Baring, 2 Baronet 1772-1848). b.* 11 Jany. 1807; ed. privately and at Ch. Ch. Ox.; double first class 1829, B.A. 1829, M.A. 1832; student of his college; C. of St. Ebbe Ox. 1830-44; select preacher before Univ. of Ox. 1846 and 1855; R. of All Souls Marylebone 28 Sep. 1847; chaplain in ord. to the Queen 7 Feb. 1851; R. of Lympsfield Surrey 1855-56; Bishop of Gloucester and Bristol July 1856, consecrated at Lambeth 10 Aug. 1856, translated to Durham 6 Nov. 1861, resigned 2 Feb. 1879; 102 new parishes were formed and 119 new churches built in diocese of Durham 1861-78. *d.* Cecil house, Wimbledon 14 Sep. 1879. *Durham Diocesan calendar* 1880 *pp.* 184-89.

BARING, HENRY BINGHAM. *b.* York place, London 4 March 1804; ed. at Ch. Ch. Ox., B.A. 1825; M.P. for Callington 31 July 1830 to 3 Dec. 1832, and for Marlborough 11 Dec. 1832 to 11 Nov. 1868; a lord of the treasury 6 Sep. 1841 to 6 July 1846. *d.* Nice 25 April 1869.

BARING, THOMAS *(2 son of Sir Thomas Baring 2 Baronet 1772-1848). b.* 7 Sep. 1800; ed. at Winchester; joined banking house of Hope and Co. at Amsterdam; entered house of Baring Brothers and Co. merchants 8 Bishopgate st. London 1828, head of the firm to 1871; chairman of Lloyds 1830 to March 1868; pres. of London institution 1835 to death; M.P. for great Yarmouth 1835-37 and for Huntingdon 1844 to death; a director of Bank of England 1848-67; declined Chancellorship of the Exchequer offered him by Earl of Derby 1852 and 1858; one of the 5 comrs. of Great Exhibition 1862. *d.* Fontmell lodge, Bournemouth 18 Nov. 1873, personalty sworn under £1,500,000 Dec. 1873. *I.L.N. iii,* 265 (1843), *portrait, xl,* 215 (1862), *portrait, lxiii,* 501, 639 (1873); *Waagen's Treasures of art ii,* 174-92, *iv,* 93-100.

BARKER, ALEXANDER. Lived at 103 Piccadilly, London; made a fine collection of pictures chiefly by great painters of 15th century which was sold at Christie's 6 June 1874 for sum of £38,591, **his library was**

BARKER, A. *(Con.)*

sold 24–25 June 1874 for £4,019. *d.* Hatfield near Doncaster 24 Oct. 1873. *Waagen's Treasures of art ii*, 125–29, *iv*, 71–79.

BARKER, BERNARD. Editor of literary portion of *The Bazaar*; author of a novel called *Elliot the younger* 3 vols. 1878. *d.* 13 Sep. 1882.

BARKER, FRANCIS. *b.* Waterford; ed. at Univs. of Dublin and Edinburgh, B.A. Dublin 1793, M.B. and M.D. 1810; practised at Waterford 5 years, where he opened the first fever hospital in Ireland; professor of chemistry Univ. of Dublin 1808; started first medical paper in Ireland with Dr. Todd; sec. of Irish board of health 1820–52; published with Dr. Cheyne a treatise on *Epidemic fevers in Ireland* 2 vols. 1821; edited the *Dublin Pharmacopœia* 1826. *d.* Wellington road, Dublin 8 Oct. 1859 aged 86.

BARKER, RIGHT REV. FREDERIC (5 *son of Rev. John Barker, V. of Baslow, Derbyshire who d. 6 June* 1824). *b.* Baslow 17 March 1808; ed. at Grantham and Jesus coll. Cam., B.A. 1831, M.A. 1839, D.D. 1854; P.C. of Upton, Cheshire 24 April 1831 to 28 Sep. 1834; P.C. of St. Mary's Edge hill, Liverpool 1835–54; V. of Baslow Jany. 1854; bishop of Sydney Aug. 1854 to death; created Metropolitan of Australia 19 Oct. 1854, consecrated at Lambeth 30 Nov. 1854, arrived in Sydney May 1855; pres. of the Synod of the diocese of Sydney which first met 5 Dec. 1866; author of *Thirty-six psalms with commentary* 1854. *d.* San Remo, Italy 6 April 1882. *bur.* Baslow 18 April. *I.L.N. lxxx*, 452 (1882), *portrait*; *Graphic xxv*, 448 (1882), *portrait*.

BARKER, GEORGE. Entered navy 1 June 1771; captain 8 June 1799; admiral on h.p. 27 Dec. 1847. *d.* Spring Vale, Isle of Wight 25 Dec. 1851 in 92 year.

BARKER, GEORGE ARTHUR. *b.* 1812; Tenor singer and vocal composer; his song "The White Squall" 1835 has passed through many editions and is still frequently sung. *d.* Aylestone near Leicester 2 March 1876.

BARKER, SIR GEORGE ROBERT (*youngest son of John Barker, deputy storekeeper general*). *b.* London 1817; ed. at Woolwich; 2 lieut. R.A. 21 June 1834; lieut. col. 1 June 1855 to death; served in Crimean war and Indian mutiny; C.B. 5 July 1855, K.C.B. 16 May 1859 for capturing stronghold of Birwah. *d.* Simla, India 27 July 1861.

BARKER, HENRY ASTON (*younger son of Robert Barker of Leicester square, London, reputed inventor of panoramas* 1739–1806). *b.* Glasgow 1774; pupil at Royal Academy; assisted his father in his panoramas 1789–1806; carried on the business in Leicester square 1806–20; opened a building occupying site of present Strand theatre as Reinagle and Barker's New Panorama 1820; exhibited a series of panoramas here with his pupil John Burford to 1826; realised £10,000 by his panorama of battle of Waterloo 1842. (*m.* 1802 Harriet Maria eld. dau. of Wm. Bligh, admiral R.N., she *d.* 26 Feb. 1856). *d.* Bitton near Bristol 19 July 1856. *G.M. i*, 515–18 (1856); *Art Journal ix*, 47 (1857).

BARKER, JOHN. Ed. at Trin. coll. Dublin, M.B. 1846, M.D. 1863; L.R.C.S. Ireland 1846, M.R.C.S. 1863; demonstrator of anatomy Univ. of Dublin; curator of museum of Royal college of surgeons Dublin; M.R.I.A. and F.R.S. Dublin; author of Cryptogamic part of Steele's *Handbook of field botany* 1847. *d.* 83 Waterloo road, Dublin 2 Feb. 1879 aged 63.

BARKER, JOHN HENRY. *b.* Ashford hall, Derbyshire 1806; ed. at Ch. Ch. Ox., B.A. 1829, M.A. 1834; barrister L.I. 3 May 1836; magistrate at Worship st. police court, London July 1860 and at Clerkenwell police court Jany. 1863 to 3 Aug. 1874. *d.* East lodge, Bakewell Derbyshire 28 Jany. 1876.

BARKER, JOSEPH. *b.* Bramley near Leeds 11 May 1806; a travelling preacher of Methodist new connexion at Hanley 1829; stationed on Sheffield and Mossley circuits successively; edited *Evangelical Reformer* a weekly periodical 1837–40; expelled from the above Society 1841 on ground that he had denied divine appointment of baptism; pastor of a congregation of Barkerites at Newcastle; edited *The Christian Investigator* 2 vols. 1842–43; became a Unitarian 1845; presented with a steam press at Wortley, Leeds 6 July 1846; issued a library of 300 volumes being cheapest books then ever issued; edited *The People* 1846, 20,000 copies of which were sold weekly; a town councillor at Leeds 1848; tried as a Chartist but acquitted 1848; emigrated to Central Ohio 1851; a leading abolitionist; lectured in United States 1857–59; sailed for England 11 Jany. 1860; edited *Barker's Review* 3 vols. 1862–63; joined the Primitive Methodists at Tunstall; a local preacher to 1868 when he went to America; author of many books. *d.* Omaha, Nebraska 15 Sep.

1875. *Life of Joseph Barker* 1880, *portrait; Methodist new connexion mag. July* 1842, *Sep.* 1843 *and Dec.* 1875.

BARKER, PETER. *b.* 10 July 1808; lost his sight 1812; a skilful performer on the violin; a carpenter at Hampsthwaite, Yorkshire; sang in the church choir; one of the bell ringers, curfew bell is rung at Hampsthwaite at 8 every evening. *d.* in his cottage near churchyard gate, Hampsthwaite 18 Feb. 1873. *Life of Peter Barker, Pately Bridge* 1873; *S Baring-Gould's Yorkshire Oddities i,* 177–82 (1874).

BARKER, REV. RALPH. Ed. at St. Peter's coll. Cam., B.A. 1821; V. of Pagham near Chichester 1850 to death; rural dean of Chichester 1858 to death; co-editor of *The Protestant Guardian* 1827–29, and of *The Quarterly educational magazine* 2 vols. 1847–49; author of sermons, pamphlets and reviews. *d.* 1871.

BARKER, THOMAS. *b.* Carlton near Nottingham 15 Nov. 1798; a lace maker there; professional cricketer at Cambridge 1822 and 1841–45; a practice bowler at Lord's cricket ground, London about 1835–41; an umpire at Cambridge 1846 and in London 1856. *d.* Nottingham 2 March 1877.

BARKER, THOMAS HERBERT. *b.* Dunstable 31 Oct. 1814; studied at Univ. coll. London 1834–35; L.S.A. 1837, M.R.C.S. 1842, F.R.C.S. 1851; M.B. London 1845, M.D. 1847; practised at Bedford; one of the very best general practitioners in England; recorded for many years a series of meteorological observations which were incorporated in reports of the Registrar General; F.R.S. Edin.; author of *Practical observations on the diet of infancy and childhood* 1850; *On the hygienic management of infants and children* 1859. *d.* Harpur place, Bedford 24 Oct. 1865. *Photographs of eminent medical men i,* 117–23 (1866), *portrait; British Medical Journal ii,* 481–84 (1865).

BARKER, THOMAS JONES (*eld. son of Thomas Barker of Bath, painter* 1769–1847). *b.* Bath 1815; pupil of Horace Vernet in Paris; exhibited many pictures at the Salon where he gained 3 gold medals; painted several pictures for Louis Philippe; returned to England 1845; gained appellation of the 'English Horace Vernet'; exhibited 29 pictures at the R.A., 34 at British Institution and 15 at Suffolk st. gallery 1844–76; painted many pictures in France during the German war

1870. *d.* Avon house, Steele's road, Haverstock hill, London 27 March 1882. *Times* 29 *March* 1882, *p.* 10, *col.* 1.

BARKER, THOMAS RAWSON. *b.* Bakewell, Derbyshire 9 April 1812; a lead merchant at Sheffield; mayor of Sheffield 1848; played in many great cricket matches; a right-handed batsman but a left round-armed bowler. *d.* The Edge, Sheffield 26 April 1873.

BARKER, THOMAS RICHARD. *b.* London 30 Nov. 1799; ed. at Christ's Hospital 1807–16; entered Homerton old college 1821; independent minister at Alresford Hants 1822, at Harpenden Herts 1824 and at Uxbridge 1833–38; tutor in classics at Spring Hill college Birmingham 1838 to death. *d.* near the College 12 Nov. 1870. *Congregational year book* 1871 *pp.* 302–304.

BARKER, WILLIAM (*only son of Francis Barker, M.D., professor of chemistry in Univ. of Dublin*). Assistant to his father many years; prof. of natural philosophy to Royal Society of Dublin 1848; prof. of chemistry R.C.S. Ireland 1850 to death; edited *Parkes's Chemical Catechism* 1837 and 1854; M.R.I.A. 25 Jany. 1836. *d.* Hatch st. Dublin 11 Sep. 1873 aged 63.

BARKER, WILLIAM BURCKHARDT (*son of John Barker* 1771–1849, *British consul general in Egypt*). *b.* Aleppo about 1810; taken to England 1819; resided at Tarsus in an official capacity many years; professor of the Arabic Turkish, Persian and Hindustani languages at Eton; chief superintendent of British land transport depot at Sinope 1855 to death; author of *Lares and Penates or Cilicia and its governors* 1853; *Odessa and its inhabitants* 1855; *A short historical account of the Crimea* 1855. *d.* Sinope 28 Jany. 1856 aged 45. *E. B. Barker's Syria and Egypt* 2 vols. 1876.

BARKER, WILLIAM GIDEON MICHAEL JONES *b.* 27 Aug. 1817; author of *The three days of Wensleydale, the valley of the Yore* 1854. *d.* Leeds 10 April 1855.

BARKLEY, JOHN TREVOR. *b.* Yetminster, Dorset 12 Oct. 1826; resident engineer on Whitehaven and Furness railway; manager of coalfields of Heraclea in Turkey 1850–55; constructed Danube and Black Sea railway 40 miles long (which was sold to Roumanian government Nov. 1882) and several other lines in east of Europe, also upwards of 20 bridges chiefly on the Bucharest and Varna

BARKLEY, J. T. (Con.)

line; returned to England about 1869; member of Iron and Steel Institute 1873. d. 8 Jany. 1882. *Journal of Iron and Steel institute No. 2, 1882 651–53.*

BARLEE, SIR FREDERICK PALGRAVE *(son of Rev. Edward Barlee 1788–1853, R. of Worlingworth, Suffolk). b.* 1827; served in ordnance department 1844–55; colonial sec. of Western Australia 1855–77; member of legislative council to Nov. 1875; lieut. governor of British Honduras 1877–1883; left England to administer the government of Trinidad 2 June 1884; C.M.G. 30 May 1877, K.C.M.G. 24 May 1883. *(m.* 2 April 1851 Jane youngest dau. of Edward Oseland of Coleraine). *d.* Trinidad 8 Aug. 1884.

BARLING, JOHN. *b.* Weymouth 11 Aug. 1804; congregationalist minister at Square Chapel, Halifax 1829–34; Unitarian minister at Northgate end, Halifax Jany. 1854 to Jany. 1858; author of *A review of Trinitarianism* 1847; *Leaves from my writing desk by an old student* 1872. *d.* Leeds 20 Aug. 1883.

BARLOW, CHARLES ANSTRUTHER. *b.* 5 Feb. 1800; entered navy 1812; commanded the Nimrod 20 guns 1839–41; captain 8 June 1841; C.B. 14 Oct. 1841. *d.* Hammersmith 31 Dec. 1855.

BARLOW, REV. EDWARD WILLIAM *(only son of Dr. Barlow, M.D. of New Sydney Place, Bath).* ed. at Ex. Coll. Ox., B.A. 1834, M.A. 1836, D.D. 1865; C. of Rochford, Essex; author of *A brief manual on writing Latin* 1834; *A treatise on the state of the soul* 1843; *The Apocrypha, its use and abuse* 1850; *Clerical manual* 2 parts 1852; *A compilation on Dilapidations* 1853. *d.* Cleveland villa, Bath 13 Feb. 1869 aged 57.

BARLOW, GEORGE HILARO (4 *son of Rev. Thomas Wm. Barlow 1760–1821 preb. of Bristol). b.* 2 May 1806; midshipman R.N.; ed. at Trin. coll. Cam., B.A. 1829, M.A. 1832, M.D. 1841; studied at Univ. of Edin. and Guy's hospital; M.R.C.P. 1834, F.R.C.P. 1842; assistant phys. to Guy's hospital 1840, phys. 1843; one of editors of *Guy's hospital reports*; chairman of New Equitable life assurance company 1856, and of the Briton medical and general life association 1862. *d.* Longton lodge, Sydenham 13 Oct. 1866. *Lancet ii,* 454–55 (1866).

BARLOW, HENRY CLARK *(only child of Henry Barlow of Newington Butts, London 1783–1858). b.* 6, Churchyard row, Newington Butts 12 May 1806; studied at Royal Academy and

BARLOW, H. C. (Con.)

Univ. of Edin., M.D. 3 Aug. 1837; spent 5 years in Italy 1841–45; F.G.S. 1864; took a prominent part in Dante festival at Florence 14–16 May 1865; Cavalier of order of the Saints Maurice and Lazarus June 1865; author of *Industry on Christian principles* 1851; *Francesca da Rimini her lament and vindication* 1859 2 ed. 1875; *Essays on Symbolism* 1866. *d.* Salzburg 8 Nov. 1876. *A brief memoir of H. C. Barlow, privately printed* 1868; *Quarterly journal of Geological society xxxiii,* 60–62 (1877).

NOTE.—He left by will £1,000 consols to University College London for the endowment of an annual course of lectures on the 'Divina Commedia' as well as all the books and prints in his library which related to Dante and Italian history and literature; he also left £500 consols to the Geological Society for the furtherance of geological science.

BARLOW, JOHN. *b.* the Oak farm, Chorley, Cheshire 20 Sep. 1815; studied at Veterinary college Edin. 1842; assistant professor and lecturer on Zootomy at same college 1845 to death; member of Physiological Society. *d.* 1 Pilrig st. Edin. 29 Jany. 1856. *A memoir of John Barlow* 1858.

BARLOW, REV. JOHN. Ed. at Trin. coll. Cam., B.A. 1820, M.A. 1823; F.R.S. 18 Dec. 1834; sec. of Royal Institution 1842–60; chaplain in ordinary at Kensington palace 12 Oct. 1854 to Sep. 1867. *d.* 5 Berkeley st. Piccadilly 8 July 1869 aged 70.

BARLOW, MAURICE. Ensign 85 foot 21 July 1814; lieut. col. 14 foot 25 Dec. 1847 to 27 Jany. 1857 when placed on h.p.; brigadier general in the Crimea 30 July 1855; col. of 3 West India regiment 8 June 1863 and of 14 foot 9 Aug. 1870 to death; general 21 March 1874. *d.* Florence 12 April 1875.

BARLOW, PETER. *b.* parish of St. Simon, Norwich 13 Oct. 1776; mathematical master at Royal military academy Woolwich 1801; mathematical professor there to 1847 when he retired on full pay; gold medallist of Society of Arts 1821; F.R.S. 29 May 1823, Copley medallist 1825 for his discoveries in magnetism; F.S.A. 1829, F.R.A.S. 1829; a corresponding member of Academies of Brussells and Paris; one of Irish railway comrs. 19 Oct. 1836; invented method of compensating compass errors in ships whereby difficulty of navigation was in a great measure overcome, for which he received from board of longitude a grant of £500; contributed largely to *Encyclopædia Metropolitana* and *Rees's Encyclopædia;* author of *A new mathematical and philosophical dictionary* 1814;

Essay on the strength of timber and other materials 1817, 6 ed. 1867; Essay on magnetic attractions 1820, 2 ed. 1823. d. Old Charlton, Kent 1 March 1862. Proc. of Royal Society xii, 33–34 (1863); Min. of proc. of Instit. of C.E. xxii, 615–18 (1863).

BARLOW, PETER WILLIAM (elder son of the preceding). b. 1800; A.I.C.E. 1826, M.I.C.E. 1845, Telford medallist 1845; engaged upon construction of Liverpool and Birmingham canal and the New London docks; resident engineer on London and Dover since called South Eastern railway; planned and executed Reading and Reigate and Tonbridge and Hastings branches 1841–46; designed and constructed Lambeth bridge opened 11 Nov. 1862, cheapest bridge in London, cost only £30,000; planned the Tower Subway opened Feb. 1870; F.R.S. 20 Nov. 1845. d. 56 Lansdowne road, Notting hill, London 20 May 1885.

BARLOW, SIR ROBERT, 2 Baronet. b. Calcutta 24 Sep. 1797; in the Bengal civil service 1817 to death; succeeded 18 Dec. 1846. d. Hanover square, London 21 Jany. 1857.

BARLOW, THOMAS WORTHINGTON (only son of Wm. Worthington Barlow of Cranage, Cheshire). barrister G. I. 14 June 1848; practised at Manchester; Queen's advocate at Sierra Leone April 1856 to death; F.L.S. April 1848; author of The mystic number, a glance at the system of nature 1852; Memoir of W. Broome 1855; edited The Cheshire and Lancashire historical collector 2 vols. 1853–55. d. Freetown, Sierra Leone 10 Aug. 1856 aged 33.

BARLOW, SIR WILLIAM OWEN, 8 Baronet (only son of Wm. Owen, a brigadier general). b. 11 April 1775; barrister M.T. 22 Nov. 1799, bencher 1838; tubman of Court of Exchequer 1809, postman 1815–1837; succeeded his uncle 4 Jany. 1817; attorney general for Carmarthen circuit many years; took name of Barlow 1844; lived in Fig tree court Temple 1799 to death. d. 5 Fig tree court 25 Feb. 1851. G.M. xxxv, 433 (1851).

BARMBY, JOHN GOODWYN. b. Yoxford, Suffolk 1820; associated with revolutionists in London 1837; went to Paris 1840; founded the Communist Propaganda Society 1841, afterwards known as the the Universal Communitarian Association; a practical preacher of Christian Socialism; Unitarian minister at Southampton, Topsham and Lancaster successively and at Wakefield 1858–79; edited a periodical called The Promethean

1842; author of The poetry of home and childhood 1853; The return of the swallow and other poems 1864; Aids to devotion 1865; wrote many tracts and hymns and articles in periodicals. d. The Vines, Yoxford 18 Oct. 1881. Frost's forty years recollections (1880) 54–75; Unitarian Herald xxi, 358 (1881).

BARNARD, SIR ANDREW FRANCIS (son of Rev. Dr. Henry Barnard of Bovagh, co. Londonderry). b. Fahan, co. Donegal 1773; ensign 90 foot 26 Aug. 1794; lieut. col. Rifle brigade 29 March 1810; commanded 2 brigade of light division in the Peninsula 16 Feb. 1814; commanded British division in Paris 1815; col. of 1 battalion Rifle Brigade 25 Aug. 1822 to death; clerk marshal of the King's household 1830–37, of the Queen Dowager's household 1837–49; lieut. governor of Chelsea hospital 26 Nov. 1849 to death; general 11 Nov. 1851; K.C.B. 2 Jany. 1815, G.C.B. 20 June 1840, G.C.H. 1834. d. Royal hospital Chelsea 17 Jany. 1855. Cope's History of the rifle brigade 1877; Lord W. P. Lennox's Celebrities I have known, 2 series i, 250–79.

BARNARD, CHARLOTTE ALINGTON. b. 23 Dec. 1830; composed about 100 popular ballads under pseudonym of Claribel 1858–69 two of the best known are "Come back to Erin" and "Wed better bide a wee"; author of Thoughts, verses and songs. (m. 18 May 1854 Rev. Charles Cary Barnard, R. of Brocklesby, Lincs.) d. Dover 30 Jany. 1869. The Choirmaster March 1869.

BARNARD, EDWARD. b. 14 March 1786; ed. at Eton; in the colonial office 1804 to death; agent general for Crown colonies 1825 to death; F.L.S. 17 Feb. 1818. d. 13 Dec. 1861.

BARNARD, EDWARD. Entered navy 12 May 1797; captain 4 July 1817; retired admiral 22 Nov. 1862. (m. Aug. 1811 Mary Parkins). d. Hipswell lodge, Richmond, Yorkshire 5 Oct. 1863 aged 82. O'Byrne 1861 p. 48.

BARNARD, EDWARD GEORGE. A shipbuilder at Deptford; M.P. for Greenwich 14 Dec. 1832 to death; purchased Gosfield hall, Essex from the Marquess of Buckingham. d. Gosfield hall 14 June 1851 aged 73. Wright's Essex ii, 1 (1836).

BARNARD, FREDERICK LAMPORT. b. 20 Feb. 1813; entered navy 3 June 1827; captain 10 Oct. 1855; captain of the Mœander 10 guns 23 Feb. 1861 to 14 June 1864; retired V.A. 30 Jany. 1879. d. 28 July 1880.

BARNARD, SIR HENRY WILLIAM *(son of Rev. Wm. Barnard of Water Stratford, Bucks).* *b.* Westbury, Bucks 1799; ed. at Westminster and Sandhurst; ensign 1 foot guards 9 June 1814, captain 1831–49 when placed on h.p.; commanded South Wales district 1852–54 and one of the brigades in Crimea 1854–55; chief of the staff in Crimea 28 June 1855; commanded 2nd division of British army in Crimea; commanded troops before Delhi June 1857 to death; C.B. 27 July 1855, K.C.B. 3 May 1856. *(m.* 17 Jany. 1828 Isabella Letitia 2 dau. of James Catlin Craufurd, brigadier general, she was granted a civil list pension of £200 15 Feb. 1858). *d.* of cholera before Delhi 5 July 1857. *Kaye's Sepoy war in India ii,* 513–70, 678 (1870).

BARNARD, JOHN. Fellow of King's coll. Cam. 1818 to death; F.S.A. 3 May 1855. *d.* King's coll. Cam. 16 Nov. 1878 aged 84.

BARNE, GEORGE HUXLEY (2 *son of John Barne of Tiverton.)* ed. at Magd. coll. Ox; barrister L.I. 17 Nov. 1866; attorney general of Jamaica March 1874 to death. *d.* Kingston, Jamaica 8 March 1876.

BARNES, CHRISTOPHER HEWETSON. *b.* 7 Feb. 1833; 2 lieut. Bengal artillery 9 Dec. 1852; lieut. col. R.A. 31 Dec. 1878 to death; commanded R.A. in Egypt to death. *d.* Cairo 28 Sep. 1884. *I.L.N. lxxxv,* 373 (1884), *portrait.*

BARNES, GEORGE CARNAC *(eld. son of Ven. George Barnes 1784–1847, archdeacon of Barnstaple).* ed. at Westminster 1833–35; comr. of the Cis-Sutlej States; foreign sec. at Calcutta 1861 to death; C.B. 18 May 1860. *d.* Hazareebagh, Bengal 13 May 1861.

BARNES, JAMES. Lieutenant Royal horse guards 29 Aug. 1811 to 3 Nov. 1814 when he retired; major in command of Radnor Militia 15 Feb. 1828 to 21 March 1846. *d.* Portishead near Bristol June 1853 aged 64.

BARNES, JAMES HINDMARSH. ed. at Charing Cross and Westminster Ophthalmic hospitals; M.R.C.S. and L.S.A. 1857; L.R.C.P. Edin. 1860; practised in London; visiting surgeon to the workhouse hospital, Liverpool 1874; superintendent registrar 1874 to death; author of *Notes on surgical nursing.* *d.* 57 Pembroke place, Liverpool 19 March 1880 aged 47. *Medical Times and gazette i,* 387 (1880).

BARNES, JOHN *(son of Thomas Barnes of Newcastle, coal viewer, who d.* 1801.) *b.* Walker colliery near Newcastle 12 Aug. 1798; in the Soho works of Boulton and Watt 1813–15; studied at univ. of Edin. 1815–17; manu-

BARNES, J. *(Con.)*
facturing engineer with Joseph Miller in London 1822–35, made many engines for French steamers; constructed the Sophia Jane the first steam vessel ever employed in Australia 1831; manager of the works at La Ciotat near Marseilles 1845 to death; much improved the French steam navy; M.I.C.E. 1823. *d.* La Ciotat 24 Sep. 1852. *bur.* Long Benton near Newcastle. *Min. of proc. of Instit. of C.E. xii,* 140–48 (1853).

BARNES, MARY *(dau. of Mr. Greenhill).* *b.* London; acted in the provinces as Miss Simpson; acted at Haymarket and Drury Lane; made her first appearance in America at the Park theatre New York 17 April 1816 as Juliet; a great actress in tragedy, melodrama and pantomime; took farewell of the stage 2 Nov. 1841. *(m.* John Barnes a comedian who *d.* 28 Aug. 1841 aged 60). *d.* Vandam st. New York 26 Aug. 1864 in 84 year.

BARNES, RALPH (4 *son of Rev. Ralph Barnes, archdeacon of Totnes, Devon who d. 20 May 1820 aged 87).* *b.* 14 July 1781; ed. at Exeter gr. school; admitted attorney 25 Nov. 1802; practised at Exeter 1802 to death; chapter clerk there 15 Sep. 1810; sec. to bishops of Exeter April 1830 to death; author of *An inquiry into equity practice* 1827; *The papal brief considered with reference to the laws of England* 1850; edited *Bishop Lacy's Liber pontificalis* 1847. *d.* Bellairs, Topsham road, Exeter 22 Feb. 1869. *Reg. and mag. of biog. i,* 306–308 (1869); *Law Journal iv,* 140–42 (1869).

BARNES, REV. RICHARD WILLIAM. *b.* Comercolly, Bengal; matric. from Edmund hall Ox. 27 June 1829, B.A. of Queen's coll. 1834, M.A. 1841; R. of Dunchideock, Devon 1841–45; P.C. of East and West Looe, Cornwall 1845–49; V. of Probus, Cornwall 1849 to death; Preb. of Exeter Nov. 1853 to death; author of *Public opinion considered in letters between one of his friends and R. W. Barnes* 1855; *Let well alone or removal of blemishes from church and state, by Alazon* 1860 *and many sermons.* *d.* The Sanctuary, Probus 27 May 1885 aged 74.

BARNES, ROBERT. *b.* Manchester 1800; cotton spinner there with his brother Thomas Barnes; mayor 1851; gave £10,000 to Royal infirmary Sep. 1869; founded Convalescent hospital at Cheadle at cost of £40,000, and a certified industrial school at Heaton Mersey at cost of £20,000. *d.* Oakley, Fallowfield Manchester 25 Dec. 1871.

BARNES, SAMUEL C. *b.* Ireland; went to the United States 1830; principal of a school at Brooklyn 1830–67; originator and secretary of East Brooklyn savings bank. *d.* Brooklyn 18 Feb. 1873 aged 60.

BARNES, THOMAS. *b.* Wigton, Cumberland 1793; ed. at Univ. of Edin., M.D. 1817; M.R.C.S. 1815; physician at Carlisle 1817; leading phys. in north of England down to 1850; founded Cumberland infirmary and Carlisle fever hospital; F.R.S. Edin. 1830. *d.* Bunker's hill near Carlisle 31 March 1872.

BARNES, THOMAS WILSON. The best chess player in London for a short period; an original whist player; reduced his weight from 16 stone to 7 stone 8 lbs. in 10 months Aug. 1873 to June 1874 by banting. *d.* Cambridge st. Eccleston sq. London 20 Aug. 1874 aged 49. *Westminster Papers vii*, 99–100 (1874), *portrait.*

BARNES, WILLIAM AUGUSTUS. Pantomimist in London; made his first appearance in America at Philadelphia 4 Dec. 1846 as Grimaldi in pantomime of Magic Pills; played clown in pantomime of William the Conqueror at Olympic theatre London 26 Dec. 1848; pantaloon at Drury Lane theatre; photographer at 6 North st. Smith sq. Westminster; committed suicide at 6 North st. by taking cyanide of potassium 17 May 1868 in 59 year.

BARNETT, CHARLES (*only son of major general Charles Barnett 1758–1804*). *b.* Stratton, Beds. 31 Oct. 1796; ed. at Putney and Em. coll. Cam., fellow commoner 1815; sheriff of Beds. 1821; master of Cambridgeshire hounds many years from 1829; a great short horn breeder. *d.* Stratton park, Beds. 20 June 1876. *Baily's Mag. xi*, 55–58 (1866), *portrait.*

BARNETT, CHARLES JAMES. M.P. for Maidstone 1832–1835. *d.* 12 Chichester terrace, Brighton 31 Dec. 1882 in 85 year.

BARNETT, CHARLES JOHN. Captain 3 Foot Guards 26 Oct. 1820 to 26 Oct. 1826; consul at Warsaw 31 May 1833; consul general in Egypt May 1841 to 17 Aug. 1846. *d.* Round Oak, Englefield 4 Aug. 1856 aged 66.

BARNETT, EDWARD. *b.* 1799; entered navy 3 Feb. 1811; captain 20 June 1846; admiral on h.p. 1 Aug. 1877. *d.* 14 Woburn square, London 7 Sep. 1879.

BARNETT, HENRY N. Dramatist and critic; edited *Sunday Times* 13 years; occupied at

BARNETT, H. N. (*Con.*)
one time the pulpit in South place vacated by J. W. Fox, M.P. *d.* Hammersmith 6 Jany. 1872 aged 42.

BARNETT, HUMPHREY. Acting manager at Lyceum theatre London 1862; acting manager for J. C. M. Bellew at St. George's hall, Regent's st. *d.* 24 Londoun road, St. John's Wood 30 April 1874.

BARNETT, JOHN. Ensign 71 foot 25 Nov. 1813; lieut. 23 foot 1819–22; lieut. col. of 3 West York militia 28 Feb. 1846 to death. *d.* the Linen hall barracks Dublin 24 Feb. 1855.

BARNETT, MORRIS. *b.* London 16 Aug. 1799; lived in Paris; acted at Brighton and Bath; made his first appearance in London at Drury Lane 1833 as Captain O'Cutter; wrote and performed title rôle in *Monsieur Jacques*, a musical piece which created a furore at St. James's theatre 1837; played at Princess's theatre; musical critic of *Morning Post* and *The Era* nearly 7 years; gave a series of farewell performances at Adelphi theatre 1854; wrote many dramas best known being *The Serious family, Lilian Gervais* and *Married and unmarried*. *d.* Montreal, Canada 18 March 1856. *Actors by gaslight* (1838) *p.* 137, *portrait; I.L.N. xxv*, 305 (1854), *portrait.*

BARNETT, ROBERT. *b.* Macclesfield 1818; an industrious arranger of instrumental music. *d.* Windsor Oct. 1875.

BARNHAM, HILDEBRAND BARRY. Ensign 15 foot 19 Nov. 1807; captain 28 Dec. 1832 to 1839 when he retired. *d.* 13 Camberwell park, London 12 July 1885 in 95 year.

BARNINGHAM, WILLIAM. *b.* Arkingarthdale near Richmond, Yorkshire 1826; a blacksmith; employed on Paris and Rouen railway 1843; began a foundry at Manchester with 3 of his brothers which failed; a manufacturer of railway switches and crossings at Middlesborough; founded ironworks at Pendleton and Albert hill, Darlington; the latter were transferred to a limited liability company 1873. *d.* Pendleton 3 Nov. 1881. *Journal of iron and steel institute*, No. 2, 1882 657–58.

BARNSTON, JAMES. M.D. Edin.; professor of botany in McGill college Montreal. *d.* Montreal 28 May 1858 aged 28.

BARON, JAMES. *b.* Blackburn 1817; ed. at Stonyhurst; held professorships at Prior Park Bath and the Luso-British college Lisbon; kept a school at Lytham in the Fylde, Lancashire for many years from 1849. *d.* St. Helens 23 Feb. 1883.

BARON, JOHN. *b.* St. Andrews 26 May 1786; ed. at Univs. of St. Andrews and Edin., M.D. Edin. July 1805; physician at Gloucester 1807–33; phys. of Gloucester infirmary 1809 to 21 Feb. 1833; lived at Cheltenham 1833 to death; F.R.S. 13 Feb. 1823; author of *Enquiry illustrating the nature of tuberculated accretions of serous membranes* 1819 and 2 other books on Tubercle *Life of Edward Jenner, M.D.* 2 vols. 1838. *d.* 1 St. Margaret's terrace, Cheltenham 2 Oct. 1851. *Pettigrew's Medical portrait gallery vol. 2 (1840) 12 pages, portrait; Taylor's National portrait gallery iii, 43–44 (1847), portrait.*

BARON, JOHN. *b.* Blackpool 2 Sep. 1807; entered the Society of Jesus at Hodder 21 Sep. 1827, master of the school in London 1831–32 and 1833–35; ordained priest at Stonyhurst 19 Sep. 1841; vice rector of Mount St. Mary's college 17 Oct. 1848 and rector 17 Oct. 1851–1854; missioner at Wakefield 1854–70. *d.* Holywell 11 July 1878.

BARR, DAVID. Entered Bombay army 1803; col. 24 Bombay N.I. 4 July 1844 to death; L.G. 11 Nov. 1851. *d.* Cheltenham 21 Nov. 1862 aged 78.

BARR, HENRY JAMES. *b.* 8 April 1815; ensign 8 Bombay N.I. 22 May 1834; lieut. col. Bombay staff corps 18 Feb. 1861 to death; L.G. 1 Oct. 1877. *d.* Apsleytown, East Grinstead 17 May 1881.

BARR, REV. HUGH. *b.* Bridge of Weir, Renfrewshire 2 April 1825; an apprentice tailor; studied at Univ. of Glasgow; an agent of Glasgow city mission; minister of United Presbyterian church at Kingskettle 28 Sep. 1854 to death. *d.* Kingskettle 9 Nov. 1873. *Too late for martyrdom Memorials of the Rev. Hugh Barr by Rev. T. Dunlop 1875, portrait.*

BARR, JAMES. *b.* Kilbarchan near Paisley 1779; a friend of Robert Tannahill the poet who has immortalized him as "Blithe Jamie Barr"; harmonized a few airs as glees; well known at various glee clubs in Glasgow; went to America 1834; living at Govan near Glasgow 1859.

BARR, ROBERT. *b.* 3 Sep. 1794; attorney at Leeds 1823; coroner of Leeds 1824; clerk to the Leeds borough magistrates 3 Dec. 1836 to death. *d.* Mount Pleasant, Leeds 18 Oct. 1871.

BARR, SAMUEL. *b.* Glasgow 1807; a self taught musician of strong native genius; his song "Naebody kens ye" possesses much merit; author of *Art of singing at first sight simplified* 1847. *d.* Glasgow 16 May 1866.

BARRALLIER, FRANCIS LOUIS. Ensign in New South Wales corps (afterwards 102nd foot) 14 Aug. 1800; surveyed Bass's Straits in the Lady Nelson schooner 1801–1803; attempted to cross the Blue Mountains 1802; captain 101 foot 6 July 1809 to 7 Jany. 1817 when placed on h.p.; made an elaborate survey of island of Barbadoes 1812–17; captain 73 foot 4 Oct. 1831 to 9 Aug. 1833 when placed on h.p.; brevet lieut. col. 9 Nov. 1846. *d.* 24 Bedford square, Commercial road, London 11 June 1853 aged 80. *New South Wales general orders 1791–1806; Sydney 1802–1806 the first book printed in Australia; United Service Mag.* 1853 part 2, p. 632.

BARRATT, ALFRED *(eld. son of James Barratt of Manchester, solicitor).* *b.* Heald Grove near Manchester 12 July 1844; ed. at Sandbach and Rugby where he gained 29 prizes; a commoner of Balliol college Ox. 1862; won the first Balliol scholarship 1862; gained unprecedented distinction of 5 first classes 2 classical, 2 mathematical and 1 law and modern history; fellow of Brasenose coll. 1867; Eldon law scholar 1870; barrister L.I. 26 Jany. 1872; sec. to the Oxford university commission 1880; author of *Physical Ethics or the science of action* 1869. *d.* 18 May 1881. *Physical Metempiric by the late A. Barratt* 1883, *portrait.*

BARRAUD, HENRY. *b.* 1811; painted many portraits with horses and dogs, also subject pictures such as 'The Pope blessing the animals' 1842; exhibited at British Institution and Society of British Artists 1831–68 and at R.A. 1833–59; his pictures 'We praise thee O God'; 'The London Season'; 'Lord's cricket ground'; and 'The lobby of the House of Commons' have all been engraved or autotyped. *d.* London 17 June 1874.

BARRELL, JUSTINIAN. Entered navy Aug. 1791; commander 21 March 1815; captain 19 March 1852; the last surviving officer of Lord Howe's victory of 1 June 1794. *d.* Holloway 23 Nov. 1869 aged 87. *O'Byrne* (1861) *p.* 52.

BARRETT, APOLLON MARIE ROSE. *b.* South of France 1804; pupil of Vogt at Conservatoire, Paris 1823; solo oboe player at the Odéon, and at Opéra Comique 1827, and at Italian Opera in London 1829–74; professor of the oboe at R.A. of music; author of *A complete method for the Oboe. d.* Paris 8 March 1879.

BARRETT, Rev. Basil Richard (7 *child of John Briant Barrett of Milton house near Abingdon*). *b.* Milton house 11 May 1781; sent to St. Omer's college Aug. 1790; joined the refugees from Douay college at Crook hall, Durham June 1795; ordained priest about July 1806; lived at Froidemont in Belgium an establishment for the care of invalid priests; author of *Pretensions to a final analysis of the nature and origin of sublimity, style, beauty, genius and taste* 1812; *The life of Cardinal Ximenes* 1813 and of a work in manuscript entitled *A mathematical treatise showing how the circle can be squared*. *d.* Froidemont 3 May 1858. *Gillow's English Catholics i*, 144 (1885).

BARRETT, George. *b.* Exeter 9 June 1794; made his début on the stage at Park theatre New York as one of the children in Dunlap's version of The Stranger 10 Dec. 1798; stage manager of Bowery theatre N.Y. 1828; acting manager of Broadway theatre N.Y. 1847; the best light comedian in America, known as "Gentleman George"; took farewell of the stage at Academy of Music N.Y. 20 Nov. 1855. *d.* New York 5 Sep. 1860.

BARRETT, Henry Michael. Member of company of T.R. Liverpool; made his début in London at Drury Lane theatre as Falstaff in Henry the Fourth 31 Dec. 1850; played at Sadlers Wells, Drury Lane and Princess's theatres; played Polonius in Hamlet at the Princess's 15 June 1871. *d.* in a cab on his way home from the theatre 15 June 1871 aged 68.

BARRETT, James William (*brother of Rev. Basil Richard Barrett*). The first Roman catholic admitted a solicitor after passing of the act by which Roman catholics were enabled to practise as solicitors in England; one if not the last of the survivors of the English college at Douay. *d.* Speen hill near Newbury, Berks. 20 Feb. 1864 in 88 year.

BARRETT, Rev. John Casebow. Ed. at Ch. Ch. Ox.; B.A. 1833, M.A. 1837; P.C. of St. Mary's district parish, Birmingham 1837 to death; author of *God's claims upon youth's obedience* 1838; *Minister's trials* 1846; *Papal aggression* 1850; *Psalms and hymns for the church service* 1853. *d.* St. Mary's vicarage, Birmingham 26 Feb. 1881 aged 70.

BARRETT, Lucas (*eld. son of George Barrett, of London, ironfounder.*) *b.* London 14 Nov. 1837; ed. at Royston, Univ. college school, Ebersdorf in Germany and Trin. coll. Cam.; curator of Woodwardian museum. Cam. 1855; delivered many lectures for Professor Sedg-

BARRETT, L. (*Con.*)
wick at Cam. 1856–58; director of geological survey of Jamaica March 1859 to death; comr. for Jamaica at International Exhibition 1862; F.G.S. 1855 when only 18; F.L.S. 5 April 1860; author of 11 papers on natural history and geology; drowned while diving at the Caps outside Port Royal harbour, Jamaica 19 Dec. 1862. *Proc. of Linnæan Society* (1863) 31–34; *I.L.N. xlii*, 188 (1863), portrait.

BARRETT, Michael. A stevedore; lived in Glasgow; member of Fenian brotherhood; fired a barrel of gunpowder close to the wall of the Clerkenwell House of Detention, London 13 Dec. 1867 which killed 4 persons and injured about 40; arrested at Glasgow 14 Jany. 1868; tried at Central Criminal Court 20–25 April 1868 for murder of Sarah Ann Hodgkinson at Clerkenwell, when found guilty and sentenced to death; hanged at Newgate by Calcraft 26 May 1868 aged 27, being last person publicly executed in England. *Central Criminal Court, Minutes of evidence by Barnett and Buckler lxvii*, 486–542 (1868).

BARRETT, Richard. A brewer in Ireland; journalist in Dublin; established the *Pilot* daily evening newspaper 1827 which became principal organ of Daniel O'Connell; it was suppressed by Government, but Barrett continued it by changing the title to *The Morning Register, the Pilot having been suppressed;* sentenced to six months imprisonment 1833 for publishing a letter of O'Connell's; prosecuted frequently and imprisoned 3 times. *d.* Dublin 19 Oct. 1854.

BARRETT-LENNARD, Sir Thomas, 1 Baronet (*natural son of Thomas Barrett-Lennard, 17 Baron Dacre who d. 12 Jany. 1786*). *b.* 6 Jany. 1761; assumed by r. l. surname of Barrett-Lennard instead of Thomas 13 March 1786; created baronet 30 June 1801. *d.* 40 Bryanston sq. London 25 June 1857.

BARRINGTON, William Keppel Barrington, 6 Viscount. *b.* London 1 Oct. 1793; ed. at Westminster and Ch. Ch. Ox., B.A. 1814; succeeded his father 5 March 1829; M.P. for Berkshire 1837–57. *d.* Beckett house, Faringdon Berks 9 Feb. 1867. *Burke's Portrait gallery ii*, 61 (1833).

BARRINGTON, Lady Caroline (3 *dau. of Charles Grey, 2 Earl Grey 1764–1845*). *b.* 30 Aug. 1799. (*m.* 15 Jany. 1827 Hon. George Barrington, captain R.N. he was *b.* 20 Nov. 1794 and *d.* 2 June 1835); governess to children of Queen Victoria Jany. 1851 to death. *d.* 28 April 1875.

BARRINGTON, SIR MATTHEW, 2 Baronet. *b.* Limerick 21 May 1788; crown solicitor for province of Munster 1832 to death; succeeded 10 Jany. 1846. *d.* Dublin 1 April 1861.

BARRINGTON, SIR WILLIAM HARTIGAN, 3 Baronet. *b.* Dublin 6 Oct. 1815; sheriff of Limerick 1846; succeeded 1 April 1861. *d.* Glenstal, Limerick 14 July 1872.

BARRITT, JAMES LITTLER. Formerly senior partner of firm of Barritt & Co. wholesale bible warehouse 173 Fleet st. *d.* St. Margaret's Rochester 18 Aug. 1863 aged 62.

BARRON, ARTHUR. ed. at Trin. coll. Cam.; B.A. 1820, M.A. 1823; fellow of his college; barrister I.T. 24 Nov. 1826; author with Alfred Austin of *Reports of cases of controverted elections in the 14th Parliament of the United Kingdom* 1844. *d.* 13 June 1856 aged 55.

BARRON, RIGHT REV. EDWARD. *b.* Ireland 1801; studied at college of the Propaganda, Rome, D.D.; pastor of St. Mary's church, Philadelphia; pres. of theological seminary of St. Charles Borromeo; vicar general of diocese of Philadelphia; missionary to Liberia, Africa; embarked from Baltimore 21 Dec. 1841; bishop of Constantine and vicar apostolic of the two Guineas 1843–45; missionary priest at Philadelphia, St. Louis and in Florida. *d.* Savannah 12 Sep. 1854. *R. H. Clarke's Lives of deceased bishops ii,* 595–60 (1872).

BARRON, EDWARD ENFIELD *b.* Norwich; L.S.A. 1832; F.R.C.S. 1844; M.D. London 1850, M.R.C.P. 1851; assistant demonstrator at Grainger's school Southwark, then the largest in London, Oct. 1834, and demonstrator May 1836 to date when school was transferred to St. Thomas's hospital; Post-mortem demonstrator at St. Thomas's; a medical and surgical tutor. *d.* St. John's, Woking 25 Dec. 1878 aged 67.

BARRON, SIR HENRY WINSTON, 1 Baronet *(eld. son of Pierse Barron of Ballyneal co. Waterford 1752–1811). b.* Ballyneal 15 Oct. 1795; ed. at Trinity coll. Dublin; M.P. for city of Waterford 1832–47, 1848–52, 1865–68 and 22 Nov. 1869 to 20 Jany. 1870, when his election was declared void; created baronet 23 Aug. 1841; sheriff of Waterford 1857; author of *Notes on education in Holland and Germany. d.* 2, Halkin st., Belgrave sq., London 19 April 1872. *O'Malley and Hardcastle's Reports of election petitions ii,* 1–5 (1875).

BARRON, WILLIAM. Formerly of the Strand; master of Stationers company 1837 and 1841. *d.* Highgate 5 April 1851 aged 82.

BARROW, REV. ANDREW. *b.* Manchester 27 Jany. 1804; entered Society of Jesus at Rome 2 Nov. 1821; prefect of studies at Stonyhurst 1831; ordained priest 20 Dec. 1834; rector of Stonyhurst college 14 July 1842; chaplain at Broughton hall, Yorkshire 17 July 1845 to death; rector of the Yorkshire district 14 April 1860. *d.* Broughton hall 20 Oct. 1865.

BARROW, SIR GEORGE, 2 Baronet *(eld. son of Sir John Barrow, 1 Baronet 1764–1848). b.* London 22 Oct. 1806; ed. at the Charterhouse; clerk in the colonial office July 1825; chief clerk and sec. of order of St. Michael and St. George July 1870 to 29 Sep. 1872; C.M.G. 28 May 1874; author of *Ceylon past and present* 1857. *d.* 24 Addison road, Kensington 27 Feb. 1876. *I.L.N. lxviii,* 263, 407 (1876), *portrait.*

BARROW, JOHN HENRY. Edited the *Mirror of Parliament;* author of *Characteristic sketches of animals principally from the Zoological gardens, Regent's Park* 1832; *Emir Malek, prince of the assassins an historical novel of the thirteenth century* [anon.] 3 vols. 1837. *d.* Newington, Surrey 30 March 1858.

BARROW, LOUSADA. Lieutenant col. Madras staff corps 18 Feb. 1863 to death; chief comr. of Oude 1869–74; M.G. 26 March 1870. *d.* Southlands, Ryde, Isle of Wight 1 Oct. 1877 aged 61.

BARROW, RICHARD (3 *son of Rev. Richard Barrow, 64 years vicar choral of collegiate church of Southwell who d. 23 Feb. 1838 aged 90). b.* 20 July 1787; a merchant trading with Spain and Portugal; took over the Staveley coal and iron works 1840 which he greatly extended; sold the collieries and works to a limited liability company for £600,000 in 1864; chairman of board of directors of this company 1864 to death; made greater part of iron work for Great Exhibition of 1862 and iron tubes for London Pneumatic despatch company 1862. *d.* London 10 Jany. 1865. *I.L.N. xxxvi,* 596, 610 (1860), *portrait.*

BARROW, WILLIAM HODGSON *(elder brother of the preceding). b.* 1 Sep. 1784; ed. at collegiate school Southwell; practised as an attorney 1806–33; sheriff of Notts 1845; M.P. for South Notts 17 Feb. 1851 to 26 Jany. 1874. *d.* Southwell 29 Jany. 1876.

BARRY, SIR CHARLES (4 son of *Walter Edward Barry of Westminster, stationer who d.* 1805). *b.* Bridge st. Westminster 23 May 1795; travelled in France, Italy, Greece, Turkey, Egypt, Palestine, Syria and Sicily 1817–20; architect in Ely place, Holborn Aug. 1820, removed to 27 Foley place, Cavendish sq. 1827 and to 32 Great George st. 1841; erected Traveller's club 1829–31, Reform club 1837–39 and Bridgwater house 1847; awarded the prize for design of Houses of Parliament 29 Feb. 1836, first stone laid 27 April 1840 opened by the Queen 3 Feb. 1852; A.R.A. 1840, R.A. 1842; F.R.S. 7 June 1849; knighted at Windsor Castle 11 Feb. 1852. (*m.* 7 Dec. 1822 Sarah dau. of Samuel Rowsell, stationer, she *d.* 7 April 1882 in 83 year). *d.* Elm house, Clapham Common 12 May 1860. *bur.* nave of Westminster Abbey 22 May. *Memoir by Alfred Barry, D.D.,* 2 ed. 1870, *portrait; Sandby's History of Royal Academy ii,* 203–209 (1862).

BARRY, EDWARD MIDDLETON (3 *son of Sir Charles Barry*). *b.* 27 Foley place, London 7 June 1830; ed. at King's college school; pupil of Thomas Henry Wyatt; student at the R.A. 1848; assisted his father to 1860; reconstructed Covent Garden theatre in short space of 8 months, opened 15 May 1858; designed the Floral hall opened 7 March 1860; architect to Houses of Parliament 1860 to death; A.R.A. 29 Jany. 1861, R.A. July 1869; professor of architecture at the R.A. 16 May 1873 to death and treasurer March 1874 to death. *d.* at council table of Royal Academy 27 Jany. 1880. *Lectures on architecture with memoir* 1881, *portrait; Min. of proc. of Instit. of C.E. lxiii,* 322–26 (1881); *I.L.N. xxxviii,* 178 (1861), *portrait.*

BARRY, GEORGE. *b.* Cork 1825; a merchant; M.P. for co. Cork 29 July 1865 to death. *d.* St. Leonards on Sea 31 Jany. 1867.

BARRY, JAMES. A woman; ed. Univ. of Edin.; M.D. 1812; entered army dressed like a man as a hospital assistant at Plymouth 5 July 1813; served at Malta many years and at Cape of Good Hope where she fought a duel with another officer; inspector general of hospitals 7 Dec. 1858 to 19 July 1859 when placed on h.p.; maintained assumption of manhood down to her death. *d.* 14 Margaret st., London 25 July 1865 aged 73. *Medical times and gazette ii,* 227, 293, 350 (1865).

BARRY, JAMES (*brother of Sir Charles Barry, R.A.*) Head of firm of Barry and Hayward

BARRY, J. (*Con.*)
of Queenhithe wholesale stationers about 1830 to death. *d.* Eliot Bank, Forest Hill 3 Jany. 1885 in 93 year.

BARRY, JAMES HUGH SMITH. *b.* 1816; sheriff of Cheshire 1846; formed a fine collection of antique sculpture and more than 300 pictures at Marbury hall near Northwich. *d.* Dec. 1857. *Waagen's Galleries of art* (1857) 406–13.

BARRY, JAMES REDMOND. *b.* 1789; one of foremost of southern Irish leaders in struggle for Catholic emancipation; inspector general of Irish fisheries; a comr. of Irish fisheries about 1830–75; claimed ancient title of Viscount Buttevant 1825. *d.* Glandore co. Cork 18 June 1879.

BARRY, RIGHT REV. JOHN. *b.* Barony of Forth, co. Wexford about 1799; studied at Charleston; ordained in cathedral of St. Finbar 24 Sep. 1825; pastor of church of the Holy Trinity at Augusta, Georgia 1826–54; vicar general of diocese of Charleston and superior of the theological seminary 1844; vicar general of diocese of Savannah 1853; bishop of Savannah 1857 to death; consecrated in Baltimore cathedral 2 Aug. 1857; sailed from New York 2 July 1859. *d.* Convent of the Brothers' Hospitalers of St. John of God at Paris 19 Nov. 1859. *R. H. Clarke's Lives of deceased bishops ii,* 551–54 (1872).

BARRY, JOHN O'BRIEN MILNER. *b.* 1815; B.L. Univ. of Paris 1834; M.D. Edin. 1837; L.R.C.S. Edin. 1838; M.R.C.P. 1859, F.R.C.P. 1876; physician at Laugharne, at Totnes and at Tunbridge Wells 1852 to death; author of essays on 'Cystine' and 'Leucocythemia' in the *Medical Archives* 1858–60. *d.* Tunbridge Wells 15 Sep. 1881.

BARRY, JOHN THOMAS. *b.* 1789; entered house of Allen Hanbury and Barry of Plough court, Lombard st., chemists and druggists about 1804, one of the managers; introduced method of evaporation in vacuo for preparation of medicinal extracts; an original member of Pharmaceutical Society 15 April 1841. *d.* Hornsey March 1864.

BARRY, MARTIN (*brother of the preceding*), *b.* Fratton, Hants 28 March 1802; studied medicine in Univs. of Edin. Paris, Erlanger, Heidelberg and Berlin; M.R.C.S. Edin.; M.D. Edin. 1833; F.R.S. Edin.; F.R.C.P. Edin.; ascended Mont Blanc 16 Sep. 1834 being 16th ascent then made; F.R.S. 13 Feb. 1840; royal medallist 30 Nov. 1839; made important discovery of presence of Spermatozoa within the ovum 1843; house surgeon Royal maternity hospital Edinburgh 1844; lived abroad 1849–53; author of *Ascent to the summit of Mont Blanc* 1836; *Researches in embryology* 3 · series. 1839–40. *d.* Beccles, Suffolk 27 April 1855. *Edinburgh Medical journal i,* 81–91 (1856); *Proc. of Royal Society viii,* 577–82 (1855); *Annual Monitor for* 1856, *pp.* 13–18.

BARRY, PHILIP. *b.* 1789; 2nd lieut. R.E. 10 Feb. 1809; col. R.E. 17 Feb. 1854 to 13 Jan. 1855; M.G. 13 Jany. 1855. *d.* Guernsey 17 April 1869.

BARRY, SIR REDMOND (3 *son of major general Henry Green Barry of Ballyclough, co. Cork who d.* 14 *May* 1838 *aged* 68). *b.* Air hill, co. Cork 1813; ed. at Hall place Kent and Trin. coll. Dublin, B.A. 1837, LL.D. 1876; called to Irish bar 1838; went to Sydney 1839; comr. of court of requests at Melbourne 1842; solicitor general of Victoria 1850; judge of supreme court of Victoria 25 Aug. 1851; chancellor of univ. of Melbourne 7 May 1853; pres. of trustees of Melbourne public library 1856; knighted by patent 24 May 1860; represented colony of Victoria at great exhibitions in London 1862 and in Philadelphia 1876; LL.B. and M.A. univ. of Melbourne 1863; administered government of Victoria 3 Jany. 1875 to 10 Jany. 1875; K.C.M.G. 30 May 1877. *d.* Melbourne 23 Nov. 1880. *Men of the time in Australia* (1878) 10–11.

BARRY, THOMAS. *b.* Ireland; performed with Samwell's circus 1842; clown to the ring in Astley's amphitheatre London 1843–48 and 1851–56; kept the Clown tavern 40 Bridge road, Lambeth 1848–50 and March 1856 to 1857. (*m.* Mrs. Campbell of City of London theatre). *d.* 26 March 1857 aged 47. *bur.* Norwood cemetery. *Autobiography of Baron Nicholson* (1860) 348–52; *H. Valentine's Behind the curtain* (1848) 76–78; *I.L.N. v,* 193 (1844), *portrait, xxiii,* 460 (1853), *portrait.*

BARRY, WILLIAM WHITTAKER (3 *son of Rev. Henry Barry, R. of Draycott Cerne, Wilts who d.* 10 *Aug.* 1850 *aged* 60). Gained first law studentship awarded by the Inns of Court Jany. 1853; barrister L.I. 30 April 1853; author of *A treatise on the statutory jurisdiction of the Court of Chancery* 1861; *A walking tour round Ireland in* 1865 *by an Englishman* 1867; *A walking tour in Normandy* [*anon*] 1868. *d.* on the Krimmler Tavern pass in the Tyrol 1 Oct. 1875.

BARRY, WILLIAM WIGRAM (*brother of Sir Redmond Barry*). *b.* 28 May 1827; 2 lieut. R.A. 1 May 1846; col. 1 Oct. 1877 to death; brigadier general Bombay 23 July 1877 to 4 April 1879; M.G. 1 May 1880; granted service reward 1 Oct. 1882; C.B. 28 Feb. 1861. *d.* Hotel Royal, Naples 19 April 1883.

BARRYMORE, MRS. (*dau. of Mr. Adams*). *b.* 1783; dancer at the old Royal Circus now Surrey Theatre, London 1803; the most graceful dancer in London for some years; her power of pantomimic expression as the dumb girl Finella contributed much to success of Auber's opera Massaniello when first produced at Drury Lane 4 May 1829; made her début in America at the Park Theatre, New York 21 Aug. 1831; taught dancing at Boston to 1846. (*m.* William Barrymore of London, dramatist who *d.* Boston 16 Feb. 1845). *d.* London 6 Jany. 1863.

BARSTOW, JAMES PULTENEY (*eld son of Nathaniel Barstow, of Wetherby, Yorkshire*). Barrister G.I. 18 Nov. 1824; bencher 1 May 1854; treasurer 30 Jan. 1856. *d.* Sandgate, Folkestone 8 Sep. 1873.

BARTER, CHARLES. Worked in Royal botanic gardens, Kew 1849–51; foreman of Royal botanic society Regents Park 1851–57; botanist to Niger expedition under W. B. Baikie 1857 to death; author of *The Dorp and the Veld or six months in Natal* 1852. *d.* Rabba on the Niger 15 July 1859.

BARTER, RICHARD. *b.* Cooldaniel, co. Cork 1802; M.R.C.S. 1828; Physician of Dispensary Inniscana, Cork; opened St. Anne's water cure establishment at Blarney; set up the first hot-air baths in Ireland, also the first hot-air baths without vapour—the so-called Turkish bath. *d.* Blarney 3 Oct. 1870. *Recollections of the late Dr. Barter; Dublin* 1875.

BARTER, REV. ROBERT SPECCOTT (*youngest son of Rev. Charles Barter V. of Cornworthy near Totnes, Devon, 71 years who d.* 26 *April* 1846 *aged* 97). *b.* Cornworthy 3 July 1790; ed. at Tiverton gr. sch. Winchester and New coll. Ox.; B.C.L. 1815; commoner tutor at Winchester to Dec. 1814; tutor of New college 1815–30 when he resigned; Bursar 1817, Poser 1817, Sub-warden 1820; Warden of Winchester 18 May 1822 to death. *d.* College st. Winchester 8 Feb. 1861. *Rev. H. C. Adams's History of Winchester college* (1878) *pp.* 322–42.

BARTER, REV. WILLIAM BRUDENELL (*elder brother of the preceding*). *b.* Jany. 1788; ed. at Tiverton, Westminster and Ch. Ch. Ox.,

B.A. 1809, M.A. 1813; Fellow of Oriel coll.
1811; tutor in family of Lord Carnarvon;
R. of Highclere, Hants 1825 to death; R. of
Burghclere, Hants 1825 to death; published
many letters and pamphlets on the topics of
the day. *d.* Burghclere 16 Nov. 1858.

BARTH, HEINRICH. *b.* Hamburg 16 Feb. 1821;
ed. at Univ. of Berlin; a lecturer in the
Univ.; went with James Richardson to
Central Africa 1849, returned 1855; C.B. 17
Nov. 1858; foreign associate of Royal Geographical Society; pres. of Geographical
society of Berlin; professor extraordinary at
Univ. of Berlin; author of *Travels in North
and Central Africa* 1857. *d.* Berlin 25 Nov.
1865. *Journal of Royal Geog. Soc. xxxvi,* 134–
36 (1866); *Allgemeine Dentsche Biographie ii,*
96–99 (1875).

BARTHELÉMY, EMANUEL. Shot a gensdarme
in Paris; condemned to the galleys for life,
set free 1830; greatly distinguished himself
in revolution of June 1848; fled to England
1848; shot Cournet a French political exile
in a duel at Englefield Green near Egham 19
Oct. 1852; murdered George Moore and
Charles Collard at 73 Warren st. Fitzroy
square, London 8 Dec. 1854; tried at Central
criminal court 4 Jany. 1855, found guilty and
sentenced to death; executed at Newgate 22
Jany. 1855. *A.R.* (1852) 170, (1854) 206–
212, (1855) 14–16; *Central criminal court
trials xli,* 298–307 (1855).

BARTHOLOMEW, ANNE CHARLOTTE *(dau.
of Arnol Fayerman) b.* Loddon, Norfolk 28
March 1800; member of Society of Female
artists and of Society of Water colour
painters; exhibited 29 pictures at the R.A.
and 39 at Suffolk st. gallery 1841–62;
author of *Its only my aunt,* a farce 1825, first
acted at Marylebone theatre May 1849;
Songs of Azrael 1840 and *The ring or the
farmer's daughter,* a drama 1845. *(m.* (1)
1827 Walter Turnbull, musical composser, he
d. 1838. *m.* (2) 30 July 1840 Valentine
Bartholomew). *d.* 23 Charlotte st. Rathbone
place 18 Aug. 1862. *E. C. Clayton's English
female artists i,* 398–400 (1876).

BARTHOLOMEW, VEN. JOHN *(son of Rev.
John Bartholomew, head master of Exeter Gr.
Sch.) b.* Exeter Oct. 1790; ed. at Exeter
Gr. Sch., Winchester and C. C. Coll. Ox.;
Scholar, B.A. 1813, M.A. 1820; P.C. of
Withycombe Rawleigh, Devon 1817; P.C. of
Sowton 1819; R. of Lympstone 1820; R. of
Morchard Bishop, Devon 1831; Preb. of

Exeter Cath. 9 May 1831; Canon Res.
of Exeter Cath. Sep. 1840 to death; Archdeacon of Barnstaple 3 Aug. 1847 to death.
d. Morchard Bishop Rectory 24 Sep. 1865.

BARTHOLOMEW, VALENTINE *(son of Josiah
Bartholomew of Clerkenwell, watchmaker* 1766–
1847). *b.* 18 Jany. 1799; flower painter;
member of Water Colour Society 1835 to
death; exhibited 20 pictures at the R.A. and
27 at Suffolk st. gallery 1826–56; flower
painter in ordinary to Duchess of Kent and
to Queen Victoria. *(m.* (1) 1827 Evelina
Charlotte Adelaide only dau. of Joseph
Nicholas Hullmandel, musician, she *d.* 1
Jany. 1839. *m.* (2) 30 July 1840 A. C.
Turnbull). *d.* 23 Charlotte st. Rathbone
place 21 March 1879.

BARTHOLOMEW, WILLIAM. *b.* London 1793;
chemist, violin player and flower painter;
translated or adapted the words of most of
Mendelssohn's vocal works; received gold
medal of merit from king of Prussia for the
Antigone; wrote English words for Méhul's
Joseph, Spohr's Jessonda, and Costa's Eli,
Naaman, and The Dream. *(m.* 1853 Ann
Sheppard Mounsey, vocal composer). *d.* Lon-
don 18 Aug. 1867.

BARTLETT, JOHN SHERREN. *b.* Dorset;
surgeon R.N. 1812; a prisoner of war at
Boston U.S. 1812–13; surgeon at Boston
1813; removed to New York; founded *The
Albion* weekly paper 1822; edited it 1822–
47; founded *The Anglo-Saxon* weekly paper
at Boston 1847; published *The European* at
Liverpool; British consul at Baltimore 1857.
d. New Jersey 24 Aug. 1863 aged 73.

BARTLETT, LAVINIA STRICKLAND. *b.* Preston
Andover 27 Nov. 1806; a baptist 26 Oct.
1828; a teacher of the New Park st. chapel
Sunday schools London 1859 to death. *d.* 2
Aug. 1875. *Mrs. Bartlett and her cluss by her
son E. H. Bartlett* 1877, *portrait.*

BARTLETT, ROBERT. *b.* Patcham near Brighton 1782; huntsman to the Brookside
harriers, to Duke of Dorset's hounds at
Knowle in Kent, on the Duke's death in
1815 they were sold to Charles Shard of
Winkfield, Berks where Bartlett was huntsman several seasons; huntsman to Colonel
Wyndham at Singleton, Sussex to 1825;
whip to the Royal hounds 1825–53. *d.* near
the royal kennels, Ascot Heath 12 Nov. 1856.

BARTLETT, REV. SYMEON TAYLOR. Ed. at
Clare coll. Cam., LL.B. 1840, LL.D. 1846;
R. of Everley, Wilts 1857 to death; edited

Cicero's Letters to his friends, Xenophon's Anabasis, Horace's Satires, Cicero de Oratore and *Cicero de Senectute.* d. 1877.

BARTLETT, THOMAS. *b.* 7 July 1818; worked under Thomas Brassey the railway contractor; constructed the Victor Emmanuel railway between France and Italy; executed works on Bilboa railway, Spain; invented an antomatic tunnel boring machine, preceding in date that used in the Mont Cenis tunnel; A.I.C.E. 1845, M.I.C.E. 1852. *d.* Lisbon 23 July 1864.

BARTLETT, REV. THOMAS. *b.* 1789; ed. at St. Edmund's hall Ox.; B.A. 1813, M.A. 1816; R. of Kingstone, Kent 1816–51; R. of Chevening, Kent 1851–54; V. of Luton, Beds. 1854–57; R. of Burton Latimer 1857 to death; author of *Memoir of Bishop Butler* 1839; *An index to Butler's Analogy* 1842, and of many pamphlets, letters and sermons maintaining evangelical tenets. *d.* Burton Latimer 28 May 1872.

BARTLETT, WILLIAM HENRY. *b.* Kentish town, London 26 March 1809; articled to John Britton the architext 1822–29; made 6 journeys to the East 1834–54, and 4 journeys to America 1836–52; edited *Sharpe's London Magazine* March 1849 to June 1852; author of *Forty days in the desert on the track of the Israelites* 1848 3 ed. 1849; *The Nile boat, or glimpses of the land of Egypt* 1849 2 ed. 1850; *Gleanings pictorial and antiquarian on the overland route* 1851. (*m.* 6 July 1831 Susanna Moon, she was granted a civil list pension of £75 4 Oct. 1858). *d.* on board French steamer Egyptus off Malta 13 Sep. 1854. *bur.* in the sea 14 Sep. *Brief memoir by Wm. Beattie M.D.* 1855, *portrait; Notice by J. Britton in Art journal* 1855, *pp.* 24–26, *reprinted privately* 1855.

BARTLEY, GEORGE (*younger son of Mr. Bartley, box-keeper of the Bath theatre*). *b.* Bath 1782; a strolling player; made his début in London at Drury Lane as Orlando in As you like it 18 Dec. 1802; joined Incledon in his entertainment at the Lyceum theatre called A voyage to India 24 April 1807; manager at Glasgow theatre 1809–11, also at Dundee and Perth; made his début in New York as Falstaff 18 Nov. 1818; played at Covent Garden and Lyceum; stage manager of former house about 1830–40; took his farewell of the stage at Princess's theatre 18 Dec. 1852. *d.* 11 Woburn sq., London 22 July 1858. *bur.* in St. Mary's churchyard Oxford 30 July. *Metropolitan Mag. xvii,* 366–69 (1836); *I.L.N. i,* 405 (1842), *portrait xxii,* 141 (1853), *portrait.*

BARTON, CHARLES JAMES. 2 Lieut. Bombay artillery 12 Dec. 1845; lieut. col. 26 April 1866 to 1 Aug. 1872; M.G. 1 Aug. 1872. *d.* Norfolk, Virginia, U.S. 19 Nov. 1879 aged 52.

BARTON, EZEKIEL. Entered Bengal army 1799; col. 71 N.I. 11 March 1841 to 8 Feb. 1843; col. 46 N.I. 8 Feb. 1843 to death; L.G. 11 Nov. 1851. *d.* Irthlingborough house near Higham Ferrers 4 June 1855 aged 73.

BARTON, RALPH. Entered navy 2 March 1812; captain 9 Nov. 1846; retired admiral 1 Aug. 1877. *d.* South hill cottage, Southport 14 Jany, 1881 aged 83.

BARTON, RICHARD BOLTON (*eld. son of John Barton of Dublin*). *b.* 1819; ed. at Trin. coll. Dublin, B.A. 1844, LL.D. 1868; barrister G.I. 30 Jany. 1850; went to India about 1855; chief magistrate, coroner and chief comr. of insolvency at Bombay. *d.* Stour lodge, Bradfield Essex 27 Dec. 1882.

BARTON, SIR ROBERT (5 *son of Wm. Barton of Grove, co. Tipperary*). *b.* Fethard, co. Tipperary 1770; volunteer in French national guard 1790; major 2 life guards 14 June 1805 to 28 April 1814; major 60 foot 28 April 1814 to 25 March 1816 when placed on h.p.; general 11 Nov. 1851; K.C.H. 1 March 1837. *d.* 2 Montague place, Montague sq. London 17 March 1853.

BARTON, SAMUEL. *b.* 23 April 1789; pupil of Abernethy at St. Bartholomew's hospital; surgeon at Manchester 1811; surgeon to the Eye hospital 1815; made a splended collection of pictures and engravings. *d.* Whalley Range near Manchester 18 April 1871. Personalty sworn under £100,000 May 1871.

BARTON, WILLIAM HENRY (*eld son of Sir John Barton, treasurer to Queen Adelaide, he d. 25 Aug. 1834 aged 63*). *b.* 1802; connected with the Mint 38 years; deputy master and comptroller 1851 to death. *d.* the Cottage, Bushey park, Teddington 25 Aug. 1868.

BARTON, WILLIAM WHITTLE. *b.* Liverpool; pastor of Methodist new connexion at Rochdale, the chapel in Zachary Rochdale was opened 2 June 1822; town surveyor of Rochdale 1818–58. *d.* 1859.

BARWELL, LOUISA MARY (*dau. of Richard Mackenzie Bacon of Norwich, journalist 1775–1844*). *b.* parish of St. Peter, Mancroft, Norwich 4 March 1800; assisted her father to edit *Quarterly Musical Magazine* 1818; contributed frequently to *Quarterly journal of Education* from about 1831; great friend of Lady Noel Byron; author of *Little lessons for*

BARWELL, L. M. (Con.)

little learners 1833 (in monosyllables) and 14 subsequent editions; The value of time 1834 and 14 other books. (m. John Barwell of Norwich, wine merchant 1798–1876.) d. Norwich 2 Feb. 1885.

BASDEN, JAMES LEWIS. Ensign Scotch brigade 12 Jany. 1800; lieut. col. 89th foot 6 July 1838 to 16 June 1843 when he retired on full pay; C.B. 26 Dec. 1818. d. Newton villa, Westbourne grove, London 22 May 1856.

BASEVI, JAMES PALLADIO (son of George Basevi of London, architect 1794–1845). b. 23 Feb. 1832; ed. at Rugby, Cheltenham and Addiscombe; 2 lieut. R.E. 12 Dec. 1851, captain 15 Feb. 1861; assistant in great trigonometrical survey of India 18 Jany. 1856, surveyor 1st grade 1 April 1866 to death. (m. Charlotte Louisa, she was granted a civil list pension of £100 29 April 1874). d. at east end of Changchenmo valley in the Himalayas 17 July 1871. Journal of Royal Geog. soc. xlii, 163–67 (1872); Monthly notices of Royal astron. soc. xxxii, 109–11 (1872).

BASHAM, WILLIAM RICHARD. b. Diss, Norfolk 1804; clerk in a bank; studied at Westminster hospital; M.D. Edin. 1834; M.R.C.P. 1838, F.R.C.P. 1850, Censor 1864–66 and 1873 and Croonian lecturer 1864; phys. to Westminster hospital 1843, and lecturer on medicine 1849–71; author of On dropsy connected with disease of the kidneys 1858, 2 ed. 1862; Renal diseases 1870; Aids to the diagnosis of diseases of the kidneys 1872. d. 17 Chester st. Belgrave sq. 16 Oct. 1877.

BASIRE, JAMES. b. 1796; engraver; engraved some pretty plates of Sussex country houses. d. London 17 May 1869.

BASS, CHARLES (first cousin to Wm. Evans Burton the comedian). b. London 5 March 1803; manager of Caledonian theatre Edinburgh about 1829; acted at the old Park theatre New York 1844–45; director of the American Dramatic fund; resided at Hamilton, Upper Canada; published Lectures on Canada 1863. d. Hamilton 5 May 1863. Morgan's Bibliotheca Canadensis (1867) 20–21.

BASS, MICHAEL THOMAS (eld. son of Michael Thomas Bass of Burton-on-Trent, brewer 1760–1827). b. Burton-on-Trent 6 July 1799; brewer at Burton; M.P. for Derby 1848–83; introduced and carried a bill by which householders might require street musicians to quit neighbourhood of their houses; built and

BASS, M. T. (Con.)

endowed church of St. Paul at Burton; gave to town of Derby a large recreation ground, public swimming baths, a free library opened 28 June 1879 and an art gallery d. Rangemoor Burton-on-Trent 29 April 1884. Fortunes made in business ii, 407–50 (1884); Graphic xxix, 457 (1884), portrait; I.L.N. lxxxiv, 440 (1884), portrait.

BASSANO, ALFRED. b. 25 June 1826; ensign 32 foot 3 April 1846; commanded the troops in China 28 July 1877 to 3 June 1878; M.G. 12 Dec. 1877; C.B. 24 May 1873. d. 2 Inverness place, Bayswater 12 Sep. 1882.

BASSET, FRANCES BASSET, Baroness. b. 30 April 1781; succeeded 5 Feb. 1835. d. Tehidy park, Redruth, Cornwall 22 Jany. 1855.

BASTARD, JAMES STOKES. 2 Lieut. R.A. 15 Nov. 1800; col. 9 Nov. 1846 to 20 June 1854; L.G. 24 Jany. 1857. d. Charlton 10 June 1871 aged 87.

BATCHELDOR, THOMAS (2 son of Robert Batcheldor of Cholesbury, Bucks, farmer). b. 23 July 1796; student of Gray's Inn 14 Nov. 1827; practised as a conveyancer; registrar of Eton College 1827 to death; chapter clerk to dean and canons of Windsor 1843 to death; steward of the courts of Eton College; F.S.A. 21 June 1855. d. The Cloisters, Windsor Castle 24 July 1866.

BATE, WILLIAM THORNTON (son of Wm. Bate, governor of Ascension island). b. 1820; ed. at royal naval college Portsmouth 1833–35; midshipman R.N. 1835; mate of the Blenheim 74 guns 19 March 1841; captain of the Actæon surveying vessel 6 Feb. 1857 to death; F.R.A.S. 9 March 1849; killed at storming of Canton 29 Dec. 1857. Memoir by Rev. John Baillie, 3 ed. 1862, portrait.

BATEMAN, CHARLES PHILIP BUTLER (son of Nathaniel Bateman, Captain R.N.) b. Wormley Herts 1776; Captain R.N. 25 Sep. 1806; Admiral on h.p. 18 June 1857. d. Corston near Bath 23 Nov. 1857.

BATEMAN, COLTHURST. b. 2 Oct. 1780; sheriff of co. Kerry 1832–40. d. Sherborne 2 Aug. 1859.

BATEMAN, HEZEKIAH LINTHICUM. b. Baltimore 6 Dec. 1812; an actor 1832; played in the leading juvenile business; manager of the St. Louis theatre 1855–59; first appeared in England at Adelphi theatre, London 12 June 1865 as David of Ruthin in Geraldine; lessee of Lyceum theatre, London 11 Sep.

1871 to death; produced *The Bells* a version by Leopold Lewis of Erckmann-Chatrian's *Le Juif Polonais* 25 Nov. 1871, and Hamlet 30 Oct. 1874 which ran till 29 June 1875, the longest run on record. (*m.* 10 Nov. 1839 Sidney Frances Cowell). *d.* Rutland lodge, South place, Knightsbridge, London 22 March 1875.

BATEMAN, JAMES. *b.* Lancaster 9 Oct. 1805; entered Society of Jesus at Mont-Rouge, France 7 Sep. 1826; ordained priest 24 Sep. 1836; a Spiritual Coadjutor 2 Feb. 1845; rector of St. Aloysius' college Lancs. 13 March 1858 to Nov. 1861; missioner at Blackpool 1865, at Bournemouth 1874 and at Newhall 1877 to death. *d.* Newhall 17 June 1879.

BATEMAN, JOHN. *b.* 1792; Sheriff of Kerry 1820; M.P. for Tralee 7 Aug. 1837 to 12 March 1838. *d.* 1863.

BATEMAN, JOSEPH (*son of William Bateman of Selby, sailor*). *b.* Selby 4 March 1797; clerk in Board of Excise, London 1829–46; assistant solicitor to the Excise 4 July 1846 to 6 Jany. 1849 when department of stamps and taxes was amalgamated with the Excise; barrister L.I. 27 Jany. 1847; author of *The general turnpike acts* 1828, 4 ed. 1852; *Precedents of private acts of Parliament* 1829; *A practical treatise on the law of auctions* 1838, 6 ed. 1882; *The laws of Excise* 1843, 3 ed. 1865. *d.* Walthamstow, Essex 10 Nov. 1863.

BATEMAN, SIDNEY FRANCES (*dau. of Joseph Cowell of New York, comedian 1792–1863*). *b.* New York 29 March 1823; author of a drama called '*Self*' produced at People's Theatre St. Louis 6 April 1857; *Geraldine or the master passion* produced at Philadelphia 1859, afterwards at Adelphi theatre London 12 June 1865; lessee of Lyceum theatre 22 March 1875 to Aug. 1878, of Sadlers Wells theatre 1879 to death, rebuilt the interior and opened it 9 Oct. 1879. (*m.* 10 Nov. 1839 Hezekiah Linthicum Bateman). *d.* Taviton st. Gordon sq. London 13 Jany. 1881.

BATEMAN, THOMAS (*only child of Wm. Bateman of Middleton by Youlgreave, Derbyshire 1787–1835*). *b.* Rowsley 8 Nov. 1821; made an extensive series of excavations in the tumuli of Yorkshire, Staffordshire and Derbyshire; fellow of Ethnological society; author of *Vestiges of the antiquities of Derbyshire* 1848; *Ten years diggings in Celtic and Saxon gravehills* 1861; contributed largely to antiquarian periodicals. *d.* Lomberdale house near Bake-

well 28 Aug. 1861. *Reliquary ii*, 87–97 (1862), *portrait*; *Journal Brit. Archaol. Assoc. xviii*, 362–7 (1862).

BATEMAN, THOMAS HUDSON. Barrister M.T. 24 Nov. 1815; comr. of bankrupts for Halifax; judge of borough court, Lancaster. *d.* 1881.

BATEMAN, THOMAS OSBORNE (4 *son of Richard Bateman, sheriff of Derbyshire who d. 1821*). *b.* Foston hall, Derbyshire 1 March 1809; ed. at Newark gr. sch., Harrow and St. John's coll. Cam.; B.A. 1834; student at Lincoln's Inn; restored ancient stained glass windows in Morley church 1847; bought Hartington hall Derbyshire from Duke of Devonshire 1857; built mansion of Breadsall Mount 1864; author of many pamphlets and letters. *d.* 14 Jany. 1874. *Reliquary xv*, 97–101 (1875).

BATES, REV. JOHN ELLISON. Ed. at Ch. Ch. Ox.; student of Ch. Ch.; rowed No. 3 in Oxford boat against Cambridge 1829; B.A. 1831, M.A. 1833; P.C. of Ch. Ch. Litherland Jany. 1842; P.C. of Ch. Ch. Hougham in Dover 1844 to death. *d.* Priory Gate 17 Feb. 1856.

BATES, JOSHUA (*only son of Colonel Joshua Bates of Weymouth near Boston U.S.*) *b.* Weymouth 1788; merchant at Boston 1809–12; sent to London 1812 by W. R. Gray of Boston, largest shipowner in America; banker with John Baring in London 1826–28 when they became partners in bank of Baring brothers; naturalised by private act of parliament 5 and 6 Vict. c. 49.; gave sum of 50,000 dollars to Boston public library 1852, also nearly 27,000 books, library was opened 1854 and the large hall named after him, the Bates hall. *d.* New lodge, Windsor Forest 24 Sep. 1864. Personalty sworn under £600,000 Jany. 1865.

BATES, THOMAS. *b.* 1810; ed. at Jesus coll. Cam., 8 Wrangler 1834; fellow of his college; barrister L.I. 3 May 1839. *d.* Heddon, Northumberland 30 Jany. 1882.

BATES, REV. WILLIAM (4 *son of John Moore Bates of Heddon, Northumberland*). Ed. at Ch. coll. Cam., B.A. 1836, M.A. 1839, B.D. 1847, D.D. 1858; fellow, dean, lecturer and tutor of his college; R. of Burnham Westgate, Norfolk 1849 to death; author of *College lectures on ecclesiastical history* 1844, 2 ed. 1848; *College lectures on Christian antiquities and the ritual of the English church* 1845, 2 ed. 1852. *d.* Burnham rectory 22 Nov. 1877.

BATES, WILLIAM. B.A. London 1857; a teacher of languages; professor of classics in Sydenham medical college Birmingham; professor of classics in Queen's college Birmingham to death; M.R.C.S. 1874; medical officer to Birmingham borough fever hospital 1875–84; author of *George Cruikshank the artist* 1878; *The Maclise portrait gallery of illustrious literary characters with memoirs* 1873, new ed. 1883. *d.* 19 The Crescent, Birmingham 24 Sep. 1884 aged about 60. *Edgbastonia Oct.* 1884, *portrait.*

BATESON, SIR ROBERT, 1 Baronet *(only son of Thomas Bateson 1752–1811).* *b.* 13 March 1780; sheriff of county Down 1809; created a baronet 18 Dec. 1818; M.P. for Londonderry 16 Aug. 1830 to May 1842. *d.* Belvoir park, Belfast 21 April 1863.

BATESON, SIR ROBERT HARVEY, 2 Baronet. *b.* 1787; succeeded his uncle 1825. *d.* Castruse, co. Donegal 15 April 1870.

BATESON, REV. WILLIAM HENRY *(son of Richard Bateson of Liverpool, merchant).* *b.* Liverpool 3 June 1812; ed. at Shrewsbury and St. John's coll. Cam., B.A. 1836, M.A. 1839, B.D. 1846, D.D. 1857; fellow of his college Feb. 1837, senior bursar 1846 to 2 Feb. 1857, master 2 Feb. 1857 to death; V. of Madingley, Cambs. 1843–47; public orator 26 Oct. 1848 to 2 Feb. 1857; sec. of a commission to inquire into state of Univ. of Cam. 1850; vice chancellor 1858. *d.* St. John's college lodge, Cambridge 27 March 1881. *The Eagle, No. lxv,* (1881); *Cambridge Review ii,* 258 (1881).

BATHER, LUCY ELIZABETH *(dau. of Right Rev. Charles James Blomfield 1786–1857 bishop of London).* *b.* Fulham 31 March 1836; author of *Footprints on the sands of time, Biographies for young people* 1860 and a number of stories for children under pseudonym of Aunt Lucy. *(m.* 29 Aug. 1861 Arthur Henry Bather of Meole Brace, Shropshire). *d.* The hall Meole Brace 5 Sep. 1864.

BATHGATE, REV. WILLIAM *(youngest son of Wm. Bathgate of Buckholmside, Galashiels, engineer).* *b.* Buckholmside 28 Sep. 1820; studied at Glasgow Univ. and Theological academy 1840–44; expelled from the academy May 1844 for opinions supposed to be heretical; minister of Independent church at Stair 6 Dec. 1844, of Bridgeton church Glasgow 1846, of church at Ayr 1847, of church at Forres 1849, of Evangelical Union church Clerk's lane, Kilmarnock Aug. 1847 to Nov. 1860 and of Winton place ch. Kil-

BATHGATE, REV. W. *(Con.)*

marnock 11 Nov. 1860 to death; author of *The moral character of God* 1849; *Æternitas* 1851; *The Soul's Arena* 1852; *Essays on a superior popular literature* 1854; *Christ and man* 1865. *d.* Kilmarnock 28 Dec. 1879. *Progressive religion, Sermons and selections from the manuscripts of Wm. Bathgate, D.D.* 1884.

BATHURST, HENRY GEORGE BATHURST, 4 Earl *(eld. child of Henry Bathurst, 3 Earl Bathurst 1762–1834).* *b.* Apsley house, Piccadilly 24 Feb. 1790; comr. of the India board 1812–18; M.P. for Weobley 15 Jany. 1812 to 29 Sep. 1812 and for Cirencester 12 Oct. 1812 to 27 July 1834, when he succeeded as 4 Earl. *d.* Cirencester 25 May 1866.

BATHURST, WILLIAM LENNOX BATHURST, 5 Earl. *b.* George st. Westminster 14 Feb. 1791; ed. at Eton and All Souls coll. Ox., B.A. 1812, M.A. 1817; fellow of All Souls college 1812; M.P. for Weobley 1812–16; barrister L.I. 6 Feb. 1821; joint sec. to Privy Council 1827–60; succeeded his brother as 5 Earl 25 May 1866. *d.* 38 Half Moon st. Piccadilly 24 Feb. 1878. *I.L.N. lxxii,* 245 (1878), *portrait.*

BATHURST, REV. WILLIAM HILEY. *b.* 28 Aug. 1796; author of *Roman antiquities found at Lydney park, Gloucestershire* 1879. *d.* Lydney park 25 Nov. 1877.

BATTERSBY, GEORGE *(eld. son of Thomas Battersby of Newcastle, co. Meath 1767–1839).* *b.* 8 Sep. 1802; ed. at Trin. coll. Dublin, B.A. 1824, LL.B. and LL.D. 1832; called to Irish bar 1826; Q.C. 2 Nov. 1844, bencher of King's Inns 1861; judge of Consistorial court of Dublin 1862–67, and of Provincial court of Dublin 1867–71; chancellor of archdiocese of Dublin 1871 to death. *d.* 20 Lower Leeson st. Dublin 9 June 1880.

BATTHYANY, GUSTAVUS THEODORE ANTHONY, Count. *b.* Hungary 8 Dec. 1803; naturalised in England by private act of parliament 1 and 2 Vict. cap. 48 (1838); won the Derby with Galopin 1875. *d.* in the grand stand at Newmarket 25 April 1883. *bur.* Highland road cemetery Portsmouth 2 May. *Graphic xxvii,* 477 (1883), *portrait; I.L.N. lxxxii,* 432 (1883), *portrait; Baily's Mag. xl,* 371–72 (1883).

BATTINE, WILLIAM. Lieut. col. Bengal artillery 1 Dec. 1834, colonel 6 July 1843 to death; M.G. 23 Nov. 1841; commander at Barrackpore 26 April 1850 to death; C.B. 20 July 1838. *d.* Lahore 21 July 1851 aged 63.

BATTLEY, RICHARD (2 son of John Battley of Wakefield, architect). b. Wakefield about 1770; studied at St. Thomas's and Guy's hospitals; assist. surgeon in the Navy; apothecary in St. Paul's churchyard, London; assisted in founding the London Infirmary for curing diseases of the Eye 1804; Pharmaceutical chemist in Fore st. Cripplegate about 1812; introduced many important improvements in pharmaceutical operations. d. Reigate 4 March 1856. G.M. xlv, 534 (1856).

BATTY, GEORGE. Proprietor of a menagerie, retired about 1859; lived in Jersey. d. Raune, France 5 June 1867 aged 64.

BATTY, WILLIAM (only brother of the preceding). Proprietor of a large circus with which he travelled all over Great Britain and Ireland; converted Lambeth baths, London, into a circus which he opened Nov. 1841 as the Olympic Arena; opened the Surrey theatre Whitsuntide 1842; re-built Astley's and opened it 17 April 1843, lessee 1843–55 and 1861–62. d. Neville lodge, Grove end road, St. John's Wood 7 Feb. 1868 in 68 year. H. Valentine's Behind the curtain (1848) 73–76; I.L.N. ii, 222 (1843).

BATTYE, JAMES. b. Huddersfield 1803; composer of glees and anthems; published a set of Twelve glees 1854. d. Huddersfield 10 Oct. 1858.

BATTYE, WIGRAM (8 son of George Wyngard Battye of Bengal civil service). b. Kensington, London 13 May 1842; ensign 6 Bengal European regiment 1859; wing officer, adjutant and commandant of cavalry of the Corps of Guides successively 1863 to death; accompanied as a noncombatant the army led by Crown prince of Germany against the French 1870; killed at Futtehabad, Afghanistan when leading the Guides against the Kugiani Afghans 31 March 1879. S. H. Shadbolt's Afghan campaigns (1882) 12–14, portrait.

BAUDERET, FRANCIS HENRY ABRAM. Master of Brooks's club London 50 years. d. Brooks's club 31 Jany. 1880 in 83 year.

BAUGH, THOMAS FOLLIOT. Entered navy 1784; captain 21 Oct. 1810, retired R.A. 1 Oct. 1846. d. 3 Higher Mount Radford terrace, Exeter 19 Aug. 1857 aged 84.

BAUMANN, JEAN FRANCOIS. b. Belgium; lived in London for 25 years before his death; the best player on the bassoon. d. Albert st. Regent's park, London 25 Aug. 1856 aged 52. I.L.N. iv, 29 (1844), portrait.

BAUME, PIERRE HENRI JOSEPH. b. Marseilles 1797; private secretary to Ferdinand I, king of the two Sicilies 1815; went to London about 1825; naturalised 1832; a preacher of doctrine of reforming optimism; a theatrical manager; proprietor of some model experimental gardens near Holloway, and a promoter in Manchester of public houses without intoxicating drinks about 1850; bought a large estate at Colney Hatch valued at £40,000; organised Sunday lectures in Manchester; lived at Douglas Isle of Man 1857 to death. d. Duke st. Douglas 28 Oct. 1875. Left all his property in trust for philanthropic purposes in Isle of Man. G. J. Holyoakes History of co-operation i, 349–51 (1875), ii, 400–405 (1879).

BAUMGARDT, JOHN GREGORY. Ensign 91 foot 1 Aug. 1798; lieut. col. of 31 foot 12 Jany. 1826 and of 2 foot 24 Dec. 1829 to 1 Jany. 1847; inspecting field officer of Bristol recruiting district 1 Jany. 1847 to 11 Nov. 1851; M.G. 11 Nov. 1851; C.B. 6 June 1840. d. Rue de L'Oratoire, Champs Elysées, Paris 7 May 1855 aged 72.

BAXENDALE, JOSEPH (eld. son of Josiah Baxendale of Lancaster, surgeon who d. 1834). b. Lancaster Sep. 1785; partner in firm of Pickford & Co. carriers 1817 to death; chairman of South eastern railway to 1844; A.I.C.E. 8 Feb. 1839. d. Woodside, Whetstone, Middlesex 24 March 1872.

BAXTER, CHARLES. b. Little Britain, London March 1809; a painter chiefly of miniatures and portraits; exhibited 45 pictures at the R.A, 1834–72; member of Society of British Artists 1842, exhibited 127 pictures there 1842–79. d. Lewisham 10 Jany. 1879. Art Journal (1864) 145–7, (1879) 73; I.L.N. lxxiv, 72 (1879), portrait.

BAXTER, CRICHTON M. Poet, painter and chess problem composer; lived at Dundee. d. Feb. 1881. Chess problems by the late C. M. Baxter 1883, portrait.

BAXTER, SIR DAVID (2 son of Wm. Baxter of Balgavies, Forfarshire, export merchant). b. Dundee 13 Feb. 1793; partner in linen manufacturing firm of Baxter brothers 1825 which became one of largest houses in the world; purchased estates of Kilmaron 1856 and Balgavies 1863; created baronet 1 Jany. 1863; founded 4 scholarships in the Univ. of Edin. and a chair of engineering which he endowed with sum of £6,000; gave with his sisters Eleanor and Mary Ann the Baxter park to Dundee opened 9 Sep. 1863. d. Kilmaron castle 13 Oct. 1872. Personalty sworn under £1,098,000 Dec. 1872. *W. Norrie's Dundee Celebrities* (1873) 400–407; *J. Thomson's History of Dundee* (1874) 385–90.

BAXTER, EDWARD. Merchant at Manchester; took a prominent part in every movement in favour of popular rights; brought up the great Manchester address on the Reform bill to Lord Grey; offered the first seat in Parliament for new borough of Manchester but declined; retired from business about 1834. *d.* 27 July 1856 aged 77.

BAXTER, EDWARD *(eld. son of Wm. Baxter of Balgavies, export merchant)*. *b.* 3 April 1791; partner with his father about 1813–26; export merchant at Dundee 1826 to death; vice consul for the U.S. at Dundee 9 Oct. 1818; dean of guild 1831; one of the merchant princes of Dundee. *d.* Kincaldrum, Forfarshire 26 July 1870. *W. Norrie's Dundee Celebrities* (1873) 368–74.

BAXTER, EVAN BUCHANAN *(son of James Baxter, director of the English school at St. Petersburg)*. *b.* St. Petersburg 1844; ed. at King's college London; gained an open scholarship at Lincoln coll. Ox. 1862; became a positivist; entered medical department of King's college London Oct. 1864; L.S.A. 1868, M.R.C.S. 1869; house phys. King's college hospital 1868–69, and Sambrooke medical registrar 1870–71; B.A. London 1865, M.B. 1869, M.D. 1870; medical tutor at King's college 1871–74, and professor of materia medica and therapeutics 1874–84; M.R.C.P. 1872, F.R.C.P. 1877; phys. to Royal free hospital 1881; translated for the New Sydenham Society, *Rindfleisch's Pathological histology* 2 vols. 1872–73; edited *Garrod's Essentials of materia medica* 4 ed. 1874. *d.* 28 Weymouth st. Portland place, London 14 Jany. 1885. *Lancet* 24 *Jany.* 1885 *p.* 181.

BAXTER, FRANCIS WILLOUGHBY *(younger son of Wm. Edward Baxter of Dundee, merchant)*. *b.* Dundee; partner in mercantile firm of Guthrie and Baxter; contributed to *Tait's Magazine* and other periodicals; edited the *Dundee Advertiser*; author of *Percy Lockhart or the hidden will* 2 vols. 1872. *d.* Broughty Ferry, near Dundee June 1870 aged 64. *W. Norrie's Dundee Celebrities* (1873) 358–60.

BAXTER, GEORGE *(2 son of John Baxter of Lewes* 1781–1858). A wood engraver in London; invented oil colour picture printing 1836, employed 20 different blocks in some of the illustrations to the "Pictorial Album" 1836. *d.* The Retreat Sydenham 11 Jany. 1867 aged 62.

BAXTER, GEORGE R. WYTHEN. Author of *Modern refinement* 1834; *Humour and pathos* 1838; *The book of the Bastiles* 1841; edited *Don Juan Junior, a poem by Byron's Ghost* 1839. *d.* Bryn, Montgomeryshire 17 Jany. 1854.

BAXTER, JOHN. *b.* Rickhurst Surrey 21 Oct. 1781; printer and publisher at Lewes down to Jany. 1858; the first printer in England who used the inking roller; made paper from the common nettle; published *Library of practical agriculture* 1846, 4 ed. 2 vols. 1851; wrote first book laying down rules of cricket published as *Lambert's Cricketer's Guide*; established *Sussex Agricultural Express* 1837. *d.* Lewes 12 Nov. 1858. *M. A. Lower's Worthies of Sussex* (1865) 283–84, *portrait.*

BAXTER, JOHN BOYD *(son of Wm. Baxter of Balgavies, merchant)*. *b.* 1796; pres. of general council of procurators for Scotland several times; dean of faculty of procurators and solicitors at Dundee 1825 to death. *d.* Craig Tay, Dundee 4 Aug. 1882.

BAXTER, MARY ANN. Gave with the preceding in 1881 sum of £130,000 for founding a college in Dundee which was opened 5 Oct. 1883. *d.* Ellangowan, Dundee 19 Dec. 1884. Personalty amounted to upwards of £283,000.

BAXTER, ROBERT DUDLEY *(eld. son of Robert Baxter of Westminster, solicitor)*. *b.* Doncaster 3 Feb. 1827; ed. at Trin. coll. Cam., B.A. 1849, M.A. 1852; admitted a solicitor 1852; partner in firm of Baxter, Rose and Norton, Westminster; A.I.C.E. 4 Dec. 1866; author of *The national income* 1868; *The taxation of the United Kingdom* 1869; *English parties and conservatism* 1870; *The national debts of the various states of the world* 1871. *d.* 13 Oak hill, Frognal, Hampstead 20 May 1875. *Min. of Proc. of instit. of C.E. xlii,* 259–61 (1875); *I.L.N. lxvi,* 547 (1875), *portrait.*

BAXTER, WILLIAM. Curator of botanic garden at Oxford 1813–54; established a library for the use of Oxford gardeners; F.L.S. 1817; author of *British phænogamous botany, or figures and descriptions of the genera of British flowering plants* 6 vols. 1834–43. *d.* Oxford 1 Nov. 1871 in 84 year.

BAXTER, WILLIAM RALEIGH. L.R.C.S. 1840, LL.D. Aberdeen 1843; senior surgeon Osmanli horse artillery 1854; volunteer surgeon major in French army at Constantinople; author of *A treatise on certain abnormal sounds of the heart; A handbook of chemistry* 1851; edited *Medical Record. d.* Emsworth, Hants 26 Oct. 1875 aged 63.

BAYES, CORDELIA *(dau. of Thomas Williams of Cambridge). b.* Cambridge 1797 ; admitted into membership with Society of Friends 1825 ; a Minister 1837 ; laboured amongst the very poor in the lowest parts of London 1840–45 ; visited United States and Canada 1851–53. *(m.* 1820 James Kirbell Bayes he *d.* 1842*). d.* Stoke Newington, London 11 April 1865. *Annual Monitor for 1866 pp.* 8–34.

BAYLEE, REV. JOSEPH. Ed. at Trin. coll. Dublin ; B.A. 1834, M.A. 1848, B.D. and D.D. 1852 ; P.C. of Holy Trinity, Birkenhead, Liverpool 1842–64 ; founder of St. Aidan's theological college Birkenhead 1846, and principal 1846–69, present college building opened 1856 ; V. of Shepscombe, Gloucs. 1871 to death ; author of *The institutions of the Church of England are of divine origin,* 3 *ed.* 1838 ; *Unitarianism a rejection of the word of God* 1852 ; *The intermediate state of the blessed dead* 1864 ; *Introduction to the study of the Bible* 2 *ed.* 3 *vols.* 1870 ; *The Apocalypse with an exegetical commentary* 1876. *d.* Shepscombe vicarage 7 July 1883 in 76 year.

BAYLEY, CHARLES JOHN. Ed. at Eton and Trin. coll. Cam. ; scholar 1839, B.A. 1839, M.A. 1844 ; barrister I.T. 26 Jany. 1844 ; colonial sec. of Mauritius 1849 ; governor of Bahama islands Feb. 1857 to 1864 ; C.B. 23 July 1862. *d.* 6 July 1873.

BAYLEY, SIR EDWARD CLIVE *(son of Edward Clive Bayley of St. Petersburg). b.* St. Petersburg 17 Oct. 1821 ; entered Bengal civil service 1841 ; barrister M.T. 12 June 1857 ; sec. to government of India, home department March 1862 to 1872 ; vice chancellor of Univ. of Calcutta 1869–74 ; member of council of Governor general of India 19 April 1873 to April 1878 when he retired upon the annuity fund ; pres. of Bengal Asiatic Society 5 times, and of Royal Asiatic Society 3 years ; K.C.S.I. 1 Jany. 1877. *(m.* 6 March 1850 Emily Anne Theophila, eld. dau. of Sir Theophilus Metcalfe, Baronet). *d.* Wilmington lodge, Keymer Sussex 30 April 1884. *Annual report of Royal Asiatic Society* 1884.

BAYLEY, FREDERICK WILLIAM NAYLOR. *b.* Ireland ; went to Barbadoes 1825, returned 1829 ; literary dramatic and musical critic on the *Morning Post* about 1831 ; started and edited the *National Omnibus,* a penny weekly paper ; edited the *Illustrated London News* May 1842 to 1848 ; author of *Four years residence in the West Indies* 1830 ; *Scenes and stories by a clergyman in debt* 3 *vols.* 1835 ; *Tales of the late revolutions* 1831 ; issued a series of songs set to music under the title of *The Nosegay*

1832 ; wrote many popular songs including *The Newfoundland dog* ; author of *New tale of a tub* 1841 ; *Comic nursery rhymes* 1842 ; *The model of the earth* 1851. *d.* from delirium tremens New Bull's Head Inn, Digbeth, Birmingham 1 Dec. 1852 aged 40. *Rev. J. Richardson's Recollections of the last half century* ii, 197–203 (1855).

BAYLEY. HENRY VINCENT *(eld. son of Wm. Butterworth Bayley, who d. 29 May 1860 aged 78). b.* 1815 ; ed. at Eton ; entered Bengal civil service 1834 ; judge of high court of judicature at Calcutta 13 May 1862 to death. *d.* Calcutta 2 Feb. 1873.

BAYLEY, JOHN. *b.* Upper Green, Mitcham, Surrey 17 May 1794 ; a tailor there ; a practice bowler at Lord's cricket ground London 1823–54 ; played in many great matches ; a slow round-armed bowler ; lived at Mitcham all his life. *d.* Upper Green, Mitcham 7 Nov. 1874.

BAYLEY, SIR JOHN EDWARD GEORGE, 2 Baronet. *b.* London 23 Dec. 1793 ; barrister M.T. 6 May 1835 ; clerk of assize northern circuit 1836 to death ; succeeded 10 Oct. 1841. *d.* Stanhope lodge, Kensington Gore, London 23 Dec. 1871.

BAYLEY, JOHN WHITCOMB *(2 son of John Bayley of Hempstead, Gloucs., farmer).* A junior clerk in Record office, Tower of London, chief clerk 1819 ; sub-commissioner on the public records to May 1834 ; edited *Calendars of the proceedings in Chancery in the reign of Queen Elizabeth* 3 *vols.* fol. 1827–32, for which he received £2,739 ; student of Inner Temple Aug. 1815 ; author of *History and antiquities of the Tower of London* 2 *parts* 1821–25 ; F.S.A. 1819, F.R.S. 1823. *d.* Paris 25 March 1869.

BAYLEY, ROBERT. Ed. at Highbury theological college ; independent minister at Howard st. chapel Sheffield 1835–45, at Ratcliff Highway, London 1845–57 and at Hereford 1857 to death ; started a monthly periodical called *The people's college journal* 1846 ; author of *A history of Louth* ; *Nature considered as a revelation* 1836 ; *Lectures on the early history of the Christian church* ; *A new concordance to the Hebrew Bible juxta editionem Hooghtianam. d.* Hereford 14 Nov. 1859.

BAYLEY, WILLIAM. *b.* 1810 ; vicar choral at St. Paul's and organist of St. John's Southwark ; composed some beautiful cavatinas including *Softly ring ye gay bluebells* and *Come sister come. d.* London Nov. 1858.

BAYLEY, WILLIAM BUTTERWORTH (6 son of Thomas Butterworth Bayley of Hope hall, Eccles 1744–1802). b. 1782; ed. at Eton, and the college Fort William, Calcutta; sec. in revenue and judicial department 1814; chief sec. to supreme government of India 1819–25; member of the council 1825 to 11 Nov. 1830; governor general of India 13 March to 4 July 1828; a director of East India company 23 July 1833, deputy chairman 1839, chairman 1840. d. St. Leonard's on Sea 29 May 1860.

BAYLIS, ALEXANDER JOHN. b. 1812; under-sheriff of London 1846 and 1869; solicitor to Comrs. of Sewers Dec. 1862 to death. d. at an hotel near Redhill railway station 16 May 1882.

BAYLIS, CHARLES OLIVES. b. Jany. 1815; M.R.C.S. Edin. 1837, F.S.A. 1839, M.R.C.S. England 1843; practised at Birkenhead; medical officer of health there 1866–73; medical officer for new combined district of West Kent 1873–83. d. 62 Windsor road, Southport, Lancs. 12 Dec. 1884.

BAYLIS, EDWARD. Clerk in Alliance insurance office; founded between 1838 and 1854 a series of life offices all of which have disappeared except the English and Scottish Law office; went to Cape of Good Hope about 1859; author of The arithmetic of annuities and life assurances or compound interest simplified 1844. d. Cape of Good Hope 12 Sep. 1861 aged about 70.

BAYLIS, THOMAS HUTCHINSON (son of the preceding). Manager of the Trafalgar life insurance office 1850; founded Unity general life insurance office and the Unity bank about 1852, manager of them both to Oct. 1856; founded British foreign and colonial insurance association 1857 and the Consols life association 1858; invented the Positive life assurance, an ingenious form of life policy 1869. d. 17 Vere st. Cavendish sq. 17 Nov. 1876 aged 53.

BAYLY, SIR HENRY (2 son of Zachary Bayly of Bideford). b. Bath 1790; ensign 51 foot 30 April 1807; captain 24 April 1817 to 15 Aug. 1826 when placed on h.p.; K.H. 1835; knighted by the Queen at St. James's palace 18 July 1838. d. Burly, Lyme Regis, Dorset 31 Jany. 1867.

BAYLY, THOMAS DAVIS (4 son of Charles Bayly of Frome Selwood, Somerset, solicitor). b. 1805; barrister G.I. 27 Jany. 1836; comr. in Court of bankruptcy Dorset and Somerset 1838–43; bencher of his inn 1 March 1875. d. 20 Aug. 1879.

BAYNES, SIR EDWARD STUART. Deputy assistant commissary general 16 Dec. 1813; secretary general of Ionian islands April 1828–1838; Consul at St. Petersburgh 24 April 1838 to Sep. 1849; British agent and consul general in regency of Tunis 25 Oct. 1849 to death; C.M.G. 9 Feb. 1833, K.C.M.G. 26 June 1833. d. Tunis 23 July 1855 aged 64.

BAYNES, EDWIN DONALD. b. 1828; colonial sec. and treasurer of Montserrat 1850–54; colonial sec. of Antigua 1863; acting lieut. governor of Dominica 1871; colonial sec. of Leeward islands, and pres. of Antigua 1872; lieut. governor of Leeward islands 1876–84; C.M.G. 1877. d. St. John's, Antigua 1 Nov. 1884 in 57 year.

BAYNES, SIR ROBERT LAMBERT (youngest son of Thomas Baynes, commander R.N. who d. 1818). b. 1796; entered navy 19 April 1810; captain 8 July 1828; commander in chief on Pacific station 8 July 1857 to 5 May 1860; admiral 5 May 1865; C.B. 13 Nov. 1827, K.C.B. 18 May 1860. (m. 8 July 1846 Frances 4 dau. of Thomas Denman 1 Baron Denman she was b. 17 Sep. 1812). d. Upper Norwood 7 Sep. 1869.

BAYNES, SIMCOE. Midshipman R.N. 1810; ensign royal Corsican rangers 24 June 1812; lieut. col. royal Malta fencible regiment 23 July 1852 to 26 Oct. 1858; colonel 35 foot 27 March 1863 to death; general 14 Dec. 1873. d. Tarxien Malta 10 Sep. 1875 aged 77.

BAYNES, SIR WILLIAM, 2 Baronet. b. 28 Nov. 1789; succeeded 16 March 1837. d. 25 Portland place London 1 Jany. 1866.

BAYNING, REV. HENRY WILLIAM POWLETT, 3 Baron. b. London 8 June 1797; ed. at Eton and St. John's coll. Cam.; succeeded 2 Aug. 1823. d. Honingham hall near Norwich 5 Aug. 1866.

BAYS, PETER PAYNE. b. Cambridge; a sailing master in the merchant service; a school-master at Cambridge; auditor of Cambridge Union; author of A narrative of the wreck of the Minerva whaler of Port Jackson 1831. d. New York 7 Feb. 1864 aged 80.

BAZLEY, SIR THOMAS (eld. son of Thomas Bazley of Gilnow near Bolton, Lancs. 1773–1845). b. Gilnow 27 May 1797; ed. at Bolton gr. sch.; cotton spinner and merchant at Bolton 1818–26 when he removed to Manchester, retired from business 1862; member of the Anti-Corn Law Assoc. and of the Council of the League; director of Manchester Chamber of Commerce, vice pres.,

BAZLEY, SIR T. *(Con.)*

pres. 1845–59; one of Royal comrs. of Great Exhibition 1851; M.P. for Manchester 17 Nov. 1858 to 24 March 1880; created Baronet 7 Oct. 1869. *d.* Riversleigh Lytham, Lancs. 18 March 1885. *I.L.N. xix*, 487, 508, 523 (1851), *portrait; Touchstone* 19 *April* 1879, *portrait.*

BEACH, SIR MICHAEL HICKS, 8 Baronet. *b.* Netheravon house, Wilts 25 Oct. 1809; succeeded 23 Oct. 1834; lieut. col. of North Gloucester militia 10 Feb. 1844 to death; M.P. for East Gloucs. 9 Jany. 1854 to death. *d.* Williamstrip park, Gloucs. 29 Nov. 1854.

BEACH, WILLIAM. *b.* 24 July 1783; M.P. for Malmesbury 13 Oct. 1812 to Feb. 1817. *d.* Oakley hall near Basingstoke 22 Nov. 1856.

BEACONSFIELD, BENJAMIN DISRAELI, 1 Earl of *(eld. son of Isaac Disraeli of London 1766–1848). b.* London 21 Dec. 1804; baptised in parish church of St. Andrew, Holborn 31 July 1817; articled to Wm. Stevens of 6 Frederick's place Old Jewry, solicitor 10 Nov. 1821; student of Lincoln's Inn 18 Nov. 1824 to 25 Nov. 1831; M.P. for Maidstone 1837–1841, for Shrewsbury 1841–1847 and for Bucks. 1847–1876; chancellor of the exchequer Feb. 1852 to Dec. 1852, Feb. 1858 to June 1859 and July 1866 to Feb. 1868; P.C. March 1852; introduced and carried Representation of the people act 1867; first lord of the Treasury 29 Feb. 1868 to 2 Dec. 1868 and 21 Feb. 1874 to 27 April 1880; lord rector of Glasgow University 1871–1875, installed 19 Nov. 1873; F.R.S. 10 Feb. 1876; lord privy seal 12 Aug. 1876 to Feb. 1878; created Earl of Beaconsfield and Viscount Hughenden of Hughenden Manor, Bucks. 21 Aug. 1876; first British plenipotentiary at Berlin congress 13 June to 13 July 1878; K.G. 22 July 1878; admitted to freedom of City of London 3 Aug. 1878; author of *Vivian Grey* 4 vols. 1827; *The young duke* 3 vols. 1831; *Alroy* 3 vols. 1833; *Contarini Fleming* 1833; *The Revolutionary Epick, a poem* 1834; *Henrietta Temple* 3 vols. 1836; *Venetia* 3 vols. 1837; *Alarcos a tragedy* 1839 which was produced on the stage at Astley's; *Coningsby or the new generation* 3 vols. 1844; *Sybil or the two nations* 3 vols. 1845; *Tancred or the new crusade* 3 vols. 1847; *Political biography of Lord George Bentinck* 1851; *Lothair* 3 vols. 1870; *Endymion* 3 vols. 1880. *d.* 19 Curzon st. Mayfair London 19 April 1881. *bur.* Hughenden churchyard 26 April. *Maclise Portrait gallery by W. Bates* (1883) 164–72, *portrait; Lord*

BEACONSFIELD, EARL OF. *(Con.)*

Beaconsfield, a biography by *T. P. O'Connor,* 6 ed. 1884; *The public life of Lord Beaconsfield* by *F. Hitchman,* 3 ed. 1884; *An appreciative life of Lord Beaconsfield,* edited by *C. Brown,* 2 vols. 1882, *portrait.*

NOTE.—He is the hero of 'Vivian Grey' the first edition of which novel has whole chapters not found in subsequent editions; he figures almost by name in Lady Bulwer Lytton's novel "Behind the Scenes" 3 vols. 1854. His statue in Parliament sq. was unveiled 19 April 1883, Primrose day.

BEACONSFIELD, MARY ANNE DISRAELI, Viscountess *(only dau. of John Viney Evans, Captain R.N. of Branceford park, Devon). b.* 1795. *(m.* (1) 1811 Wyndham Lewis, M.P. for Maidstone who *d.* 14 March 1838, *m.* (2) 28 Aug. 1839 Benjamin Disraeli, 1 Earl of Beaconsfield). Created Viscountess Beaconsfield of Beaconsfield 30 Nov. 1868. *d.* Hughenden, Bucks 15 Dec. 1872. *Heath's Book of beauty* 1841 p. 236, *portrait.*

BEADON, SIR CECIL *(youngest son of Richard Beadon who d. 6 April 1858 aged 76). b.* Wells 1816; ed. at Eton and Shrewsbury; under secretary to government of Bengal 1843 and secretary 1852; secretary to government of India home department 1854 and foreign department 1859; member of Governor general's council 1860; lieutenant governor of Bengal 1862–1866; K.C.S.I. 24 May 1866. *d.* Latton, Wilts 18 July 1880. *Fortnightly Review viii*, 180–91 (1867).

BEADON, REV. FREDERICK *(3 son of Rev. Edward Beadon, R. of North Stoneham, Hants who d. 17 Dec. 1810). b.* London 6 Dec. 1777; ed. at Charter house and Trin. coll. Ox., B.A. 1800, M.A. 1804; R. of Weston-super-Mare 1801–11; preb. of Wells cathedral 26 May 1809, canon residentiary 1812–1875 and chancellor 13 Aug. 1823 to death; V. of Titley near Hereford 1811–1876; R. of Sulham, Berks 1814–1823; R. of North Stoneham Jany. 1811 to death. *d.* North Stoneham rectory 10 June 1879 aged 101 years and 6 months. *Norman's Memoir privately printed* 1879; *Graphic xx*, 108 (1879), *portrait.*

BEADON, WILLIAM FREDERICK *(eld. son of Richard Beadon who d. 6 April 1858). b.* 1808; ed. at Eton and St. John's coll. Cam., B.A. 1829, M.A. 1833; barrister I.T. 1 May 1835; police magistrate at Wandsworth and Hammersmith 1847, and at Marlborough st. police court 1856 to death. *d.* Stratford place, Cavendish sq. 30 March 1862.

BEAGLEY, THOMAS. *b.* Farringdon near Alton, Hants 5 Oct. 1789; a builder there to Nov. 1850; professional cricketer; a splendid bat and long-stop; played for his county many years. *d.* 27 Alfred road, Harrow road, London 21 Feb. 1858.

BEAL, ABRAHAM. *b.* Chatham about 1803; a great advocate of total abstinence; acquired title of "the Prisoner's friend"; emigrated to the United States 1848; general agent of New York prison association 1863 to death; more than 10000 prisoners were released or pardoned through his active agency. *d.* Brooklyn New York 25 Feb. 1872. *American Annual Cyclopædia xii*, 59–60 (1873).

BEAL, REV. WILLIAM. *b.* Devonport 4 May 1785; Wesleyan minister 1808 to death; at Liskeard, Cornwall 1857 to death; the first sunday school teacher in Cornwall; author of *The fathers of the Wesley family and references to their times* 1833, 2 ed. 1862; *Britain and the Gael* 1855 2 ed. 1860. *d.* Liskeard 18 June 1872.

BEAL, REV. WILLIAM *(eld. son of the preceding).* *b.* Sheffield 9 Dec. 1815; ed. at King's coll. London and Trin. coll. Cam., B.A. 1841, LL.D. Aberdeen 1845, F.S.A. 1850; head master of Tavistock gr. sch. 1837–47; V. of Brooke Norfolk 1847 to death; originated at Brooke the Parochial harvest home 1854; diocesan inspector of schools 1855 to death; edited the *West of England magazine* 1840–47; author of *First book in chronology* 1840; *Church Unions* 1848; *Peoples Colleges* 1851. *d.* Aigle, canton Vaud Switzerland 20 April 1870.

BEALE, LIONEL JOHN. *b.* Falmouth Oct. 1796; M.R.C.S. 1815; practised in London about 1831 to death; medical officer of health to parish of St. Martin-in-the-Fields 1856 to death; author of *On spinal diseases* 1830; *The laws of health in relation to mind and body* 1851; *Health and longevity* 1854; *On personal and domestic hygiene* 1855. *d.* 108 Long Acre London 23 June 1871. *Medical Times and gazette ii*, 24 (1871).

BEALE, SAMUEL *(son of William Beale of Camphill, Birmingham).* *b.* Birmingham 1803; an iron master; M.P. for Derby 28 March 1857 to 6 July 1865; chairman of Midland railway 1858–1864. *d.* Warfield grove, Bracknell Berkshire 11 Sep. 1874. Personalty sworn under £350,000 Oct. 1874.

BEALE, THOMAS WILLIAM. Clerk in office of Board of Revenue at Agra many years; author of *Miftahu-t-Tawarikh or Key of history*

lithographed at Agra 1849; *The Oriental biographical dictionary edited by the Asiatic Society of Bengal* 1881. *d.* summer of 1875 very old. *Sir H. M. Elliott's History of India viii*, 441–44 (1877).

BEALE, WILLIAM. *b.* Landrake Cornwall 1 Jany. 1784; a chorister of Westminster Abbey; Midshipman R.N.; member of Royal Society of Musicians 1 Dec. 1811; gained by his madrigal *Awake sweet muse* prize cup given by Madrigal Society 12 Jany. 1813; one of gentlemen of Chapel Royal 30 Jany. 1816 to 13 Dec. 1820; organist at Trinity college Cambridge 1 Nov. 1820 to Dec. 1821; organist of Wandsworth parish church 1822, afterwards of St. John's church Clapham Rise; published *A first book of madrigals, glees, &c. for 3, 4, and 5 voices* 1815; *Collection of glees and madrigals* 1820. *d.* Paradise Row, Stockwell, London 3 May 1854.

BEALE, WILLIAM JOHN *(son of Wm. Beale of Camphill, Birmingham).* Solicitor at Birmingham; legal adviser to Midland railway; chairman of orchestral committee of musical festivals 1870–76. *d.* Bryntirion near Dolgelly 21 May 1883 in 76 year.

BEALES, EDMOND *(son of Samuel Pickering Beales of Newnham, Cambridge, merchant).* *b.* Newnham 3 July 1803; ed. at Eton and Trin. coll. Cam., scholar, B.A. 1825, M.A. 1828; barrister M.T. 25 June 1830; revising barrister for Middlesex 1862–66; president of National league for independence of Poland 1863; chairman of the Circassian committee; pres. of Reform league 1865 to 10 March 1869, league was dissolved 13 March 1869; contested Tower Hamlets Nov. 1868; judge of county courts for Beds. and Cambs. 17 Sep. 1870 to death. *d.* Osborne house Bolton gardens south, Brompton 26 June 1881. *Annual Register* (1866) 98–102.

BEAMAN, GEORGE. *b.* near London 1803; apprenticed to Mr. Holland of Knutsford, surgeon; L.S.A. and M.R.C.S. 1822, F.R.C.S. 1852; M.D. St. Andrews 1854; partner with Mr. Hewson, apothecary in James street, Covent Garden 1824; founded with Thomas Wakley, the new Equitable life assurance office; medical officer of London and South Western railway about 1840 to death; a leading general practitioner. *d.* 3 Caversham road, Kentish Town 15 Jany. 1874. *Medical times and gazette i*, 142 (1874).

BEAMES, JOHN. Barrister L.I. 25 May 1811, bencher 1832; comr. of lunatics 1821–23; comr. of bankrupts 1823–30; K.C. Nov. 1832; author of *The elements of pleas in equity* 1818; *A brief view of the writ Ne exeat regno as an equitable process*, 2 ed. 1824; *A summary of the doctrine of the Court of Equity with respect to costs* 1822, 2 ed. 1840; *Sketch of the doctrine relative to commitments in bankruptcy* 1827. *d*. 17 Oct. 1853 aged 72.

BEAMES, REV. THOMAS. Educ. at Lincoln coll. Oxf., B.A. 1837, M.A. 1838; C. of St. Bride's Fleet st. London 1844–46; C. of St. James's Westminster 1846 to death; author of *Rookeries of London* 1850, 2 ed. 1852; *Plea for educational reform* 1856. *d*. Godolphin road, Shepherds Bush 6 Aug. 1864.

BEAMISH, FRANCIS BERNARD (6 son of *Wm. Beamish of Cork, porter brewer* 1760–1828). *b*. Beaumont near Cork 5 April 1802; ed. at Rugby; M.P. for Cork 1837–1841, and 1853 to 1865; mayor of Cork 1843, sheriff of co. Cork 1852; chairman of Reform club London to death. *d*. Totnes, Devon 1 Feb. 1868.

BEAMISH, REV. HENRY HAMILTON. Minister of Holy Trinity chapel, Conduit st. London 1832–62; V. of Old Cleeve, Somerset 1862–65; V. of Wimbish 1865–69; R. of Lillingstone Dayrell, Bucks 1869 to death; author of *Romanism and Tractarianism refuted* 1853; *Lectures, Who is Antichrist* 1854. *d*. Lillingstone Dayrell rectory 23 Feb. 1872.

BEAMISH, NORTH LUDLOW (*brother of Francis Bernard Beamish*). *b*. 31 Dec. 1797; ed. at Sandhurst; cornet 4 dragoon guards 7 Nov. 1816, captain 1823–26 when placed on h.p.; F.R.S. 15 Nov. 1827; K.H. 1837; lieut. colonel in Hanoverian service 1852; sheriff of city of Cork 1855; author of *Peace campaigns of a cornet* [anon.] 3 vols. 1829; *History of the King's German legion* 2 vols. 1832–37; *The discovery of America by the Northmen in the tenth century* 1841; *On the uses and application of cavalry in war* 1855. *d*. Ann Mount near Glanmire, Cork 27 April 1872.

BEAMISH, RICHARD (*brother of the preceding*). *b*. 16 July 1798; ensign Coldstream Guards 1814–18 when placed on h.p.; assistant engineer on the Thames tunnel Aug. 1826 and resident engineer Dec. 1834 to Aug. 1836; engineer for Cork and other counties in Ireland 1828–34; resident engineer of Gloucester and forest of Dean railway to 1850; M.I.C.E. 27 Jany. 1829; F.R.S. 24 March 1836; author of *Popular instruction on the calculation of probabilities translated from*

BEAMISH, R. (*Con.*)

the French of *A. Quetelet* 1839; *A treatise on elocution* 1854; *A memoir of the life of Sir Marc Isambard Brunel* 1866; *The Psychonomy of the hand*, 2 ed. 1865. *d*. Bournemouth 20 Nov. 1873. *Min. of Proc. of Instit. of C.E. xl*, 246–51 (1875).

BEAMONT, REV. WILLIAM JOHN (*only son of Wm. Beamont of Warrington, solicitor*). *b*. Warrington 16 Jany. 1828; ed. at Warrington, Eton and Trin. coll. Cam.; chancellor's medallist 1850, B.A. 1850, M.A. 1853; fellow of his college 1852 to death; C. of St. John's the Evangelist, Drury lane, London 1855; P.C. of St. Michael's Cambridge 1857 to death; chief founder of Cambridge School of art 1858 and the Church Defence Association 1859; originator of the Church Congress 1861; author of *Catherine the Egyptian slave* 1852; *Concise grammar of the Arabic language* 1861; author with Rev. W. M. Campion of *The prayer-book interleaved* 1868, 7 ed. 1880. *d*. Trinity college, Cambridge 6 Aug. 1868.

BEAN, WILLIAM. Began riding with the Queen's stag hounds 1792; a great steeplechase rider; rode 24 steeplechases and won 17 of them. *d*. Notting hill London about 31 March 1867 aged about 86. *Scott and Sebright by the Druid* (1885) 282–89; *Illust. sporting news vi*, 241 (1867), *portrait*.

BEARD, REV. JOHN RELLY. *b*. Southsea, Portsmouth 4 Aug. 1800; ed. at Unitarian college, York; minister at Salford, Manchester 1825; kept a school at Salford 1826; D.D. Univ. of Giessen 1838; minister at Strangeways, Manchester 1848–64; started a scheme for educating young men for home missions, which originated Unitarian home missionary board or college, of which he was the first principal; minister at Sale near Ashton-on-Mersey 1865–73; the first editor of the *Christian Teacher* 1835; started the *Unitarian Herald*; author of *Voices of the church in reply to Dr. Strauss* 1845; *Historical and Artistic illustrations of the Trinity* 1846; *Illustrations of the divine in Christianity* 1849; *Latin dictionary* 1854; *Christ the interpreter of scripture* 1865; *Christian evidence, an antidote to materialism* 1868; *Autobiography of Satan* 1872. *d*. Ashton upon Mersey 21 Nov. 1876. *J. Evans's Lancashire authors* (1850) 13–17.

BEARD, WILLIAM (*son of a farmer at Banwell, Somerset*). *b*. Banwell 24 April 1772; a small farmer; dug out a cavern in Banwell hill and found many bones of the bear, buffalo, reindeer and wolf about 1826; let his land and spent all his time searching for bones;

BEARD, W. (*Con.*)

his collection of bones was bought by the Somersetshire Archæological and natural history society and is now in the museum at Taunton Castle. *d.* Banwell 9 Jany. 1868. *J. Rutter's Delineations of north western division of Somerset* (1829) 147–60, *portrait.*

BEARDMORE, NATHANIEL (2 son of *Joshua Beardmore of Nottingham*). *b.* Nottingham 19 March 1816; partner with James Meadows Rendel C.E. in London and Plymouth to 1848; took out a patent for piers and breakwaters 1848; one of the first hydraulic engineers; engineer to Public works loan comrs. and River Thames Conservancy board; M.I.C.E. 3 May 1842; F.R.A.S. 8 Jany. 1858; F.M.S. pres. 1861 and 1862; F.R.G.S. 1852; author of *Manual of hydrology* 1852, *new ed.* 1867, which became the text book of the profession for hydraulic engineering. *d.* Broxbourne, Herts. 24 Aug. 1872; *Min. of Proc. of Instit. of C.E. xxxvi,* 256–64 (1873).

BEARDMORE, WILLIAM. *b.* Greenwich 6 May 1824; partner with Wm. Rigby in the Parkhead rolling mill and forge near Glasgow 1861–71, and partner with his brother 1871 to death, these works became largest of their kind in Scotland and achieved an European reputation; A.I.C.E. 6 March 1860; inventor and patentee. *d.* Brighton 11 Oct. 1877. *Min. of Proc. of Instit. of C.E. li,* 268–70 (1878).

BEASLEY, JOSEPH NOBLE. *b.* 30 March 1832; lieut. col. Royal Irish Fusiliers 21 June 1880 to death. *d.* Ismaila, Egypt 20 Sep. 1882.

BEATRICE, MADEMOISELLE, stage name of Marie Beatrice Binda (*dau. of Chevalier Binda, British consul at Florence*). *b.* Lucca, Italy 5 Aug. 1839; acted at Theatres de l'Odeon and Vaudeville, Paris; made her début in London under name of Lucchesini at Haymarket theatre 3 Oct. 1864; played at Lyceum theatre 1865 and in the provinces 1866–68; organised a company 1870 with which she travelled to her death; played in London summers of 1872, 74, 75 and 78; produced and acted chief parts in *Our Friends, The Sphinx, Frou-Frou* and other translations from the French. *d.* 102 Earl's Court road, London 22 Dec. 1878. *bur.* Père Lachaise cemetery Paris 2 Jany. 1879. *The Stage i,* 61, 63 (1874), *portrait; Pascoe's Dramatic list* (1880) 388–90.

BEATSON, REV. BENJAMIN WRIGGLESWORTH (son of *Anby Beutson*). *b.* 24 Jany. 1803; ed. at Merchant Taylors' school and Pemb. coll. Cam., 16 wrangler 1825, B.A. 1825, M.A. 1828; fellow of his college 1827 to death;

BEATSON, REV. B. W. (*Con.*)

author of *Progressive exercises on the composition of Greek Iambic verse* 1836, 10 *ed.* 1871; *Exercises on Latin prose composition* 1840; *Lessons in ancient history* 1853; edited *Demosthenes' Oration against Leptines* 1864. *d.* Charles st. City road, London 20 July 1874.

BEATSON, GEORGE STEWART (3 son of *Henry Duncan Beatson of Campbelltown, Argyleshire*). *b.* Greenock May 1814; ed. at Glasgow Univ., M.D. 1836; L.R.C.S. Edin. 1836; assistant surgeon army medical department 1838; surgeon general 1 May 1863; principal medical officer of British troops in India 1863–68 and 1871 to death; in charge of Royal Victoria hospital Netley 1868–71; honorary phys. to the Queen 13 March 1866; C.B. 2 June 1869. *d.* Knollswood, Simla 7 June 1874. *I.L.N. lxv,* 229 (1874), *portrait.*

BEATSON, WILLIAM FERGUSON. *b.* about 1804; entered Bengal army 1820; served with British legion in Spain 1835–36; commander of the 10 regiment in Spain 13 July 1836; commanded the Nizam of Hyderabad's division of cavalry to March 1851; organised a corps of 4000 Bashi Bazouks in Crimean war 1854–55, resigned command of the corps Sep. 1855; served in Indian mutiny 1857–58 when he raised and organised two regiments of cavalry in 6 months; M.G. 3 Oct. 1866; created a knight of San Fernando by Queen Regent of Spain. *d.* The vicarage New Swindon 4 Feb. 1872. *Nolan's Russian war ii,* 753 (1857), *portrait; The war department and the Bashi Bazouks by W. F. Beatson* 1856, *privately printed.*

BEATTIE, JAMES. *b.* parish of Rayne, Scotland 27 Jany. 1781; a shoemaker at Gordonstown in Auchterless; conducted a school of from 30 to 40 pupils for 60 years for which he would never take any payment; known as "the Auchterless John Pounds" after the Portsmouth cobbler of that name who founded ragged schools and died 1839. *d.* Gordonstown July 1867.

BEATTIE, JOSEPH HAMILTON (son of *George Beattie of North of Ireland, architect*). *b.* 12 May 1808; assistant engineer on London and Southampton railway 1837; assistant engineer and locomotive superintendent of London and south western railway 1851 to death; took out many patents for improvements in railway rolling stock and effected great saving in consumption of fuel in working locomotives; M.I.C.E. 1 Dec. 1857. *d.* South Bank, Surbiton, Surrey 18 **Oct. 1871.** *Min. of Proc. of Instit. of C.E. xxxiii,* 204–206 (1872).

BEATTIE, WILLIAM *(son of James Beattie of Dalton, Annandale who d.* 1809). *b.* Dalton 1793; ed. at Clarencefield academy 1807–13 and Univ. of Edin. 1813-20, M.D. 1818; studied in France, Italy and Germany 1823–26; physician to Duke of Clarence 8 years and private secretary to him 3 years; L.R.C.P. 1827; practised at Hampstead 1827–45; foreign sec. to British Archæological Society; lost £7,000 in Albert Assurance Office Aug. 1869; author of *Journal of a residence in Germany* 2 vols. 1831; *Scotland illustrated* 2 vols. 1838; *The Waldenses illustrated* 2 vols. 1838; *The Danube* 1844; *Life of Thomas Campbell* 3 vols. 1848. *d.* 13 Upper Berkeley st. London 17 March 1875. *Madden's Literary life of Countess of Blessington iii,* 255–76 (1855).

BEATTY, GEORGE. Second lieutenant R.M. 16 May 1795, colonel commandant 12 Feb. 1842 to 9 Nov. 1846; general 20 June 1855. *d.* Dublin 27 June 1857 aged 79.

BEATTY, THOMAS EDWARD *(son of John Beatty, M.D.)* Ed. at Trin. coll. Dublin; M.D. Edin. 1820, M.R.C.S. Ireland 1821, F.R.C.S. 1824; master of South-Eastern Lying-in hospital, Dublin; professor of medical jurisprudence at Royal college of surgeons Dublin, pres. 1850; helped to found City of Dublin hospital 1832; pres. of Dublin Pathological Society 1859; fellow of King and Queen's college of physicians 2 May 1862, pres. 1864–65; M.D. Dublin 1863. *d.* 3 May 1872.

BEAUCHAMP, JOHN REGINALD PYNDAR, 3 Earl (2 son of *Wm. Lygon,* 1 *Earl Beauchamp* 1747–1816). Assumed name of Pyndar 22 Oct. 1813: succeeded 12 May 1823. *d.* 37 Portman sq. London 22 Jany. 1853 in 71 year.

BEAUCHAMP, HENRY BEAUCHAMP LYGON, 4 Earl *(brother of the preceding). b.* 5 Jany. 1784; cornet 13 Dragoons 9 July 1803; lieut. col. 1 Life Guards 17 July 1821 to 10 Jany. 1837; colonel 10 Hussars 23 June 1843 to death; general 20 June 1854; M.P. for Worcestershire 1816–1831 and for West Worcestershire 1832–1853; succeeded 22 Jany 1853. *d.* Madresfield Court, Great Malvern 8 Sep. 1863.

BEAUCLERK, AUBREY WILLIAM. *b.* 20 Feb. 1801; M.P. for East Surrey 15 Dec. 1832 to 17 July 1837. *d.* Ardglass castle, co. Down 1 Feb. 1854.

BEAUFORT, JOHN HENRY SOMERSET, 7 Duke of *(eld. child of Henry Charles Somerset,* 6 *Duke of Beaufort* 1766–1835). *b.* 5 Feb. 1792; **cornet 10 Hussars 1811; aide de camp to**

BEAUFORT, DUKE OF. *(Con.)*

Duke of Wellington in the Peninsula; captain 37 Foot 2 Dec. 1819 to 25 Oct. 1821 when placed on h.p.; M.P. for Monmouth 30 Dec. 1813 to 3 Dec. 1832 and for West Gloucs. 12 Jany. 1835 to 23 Nov. 1835 when he succeeded as 7 Duke; junior lord of the Admiralty 1816–1819; lieut. colonel commandant of Gloucestershire yeomanry April 1834 to death; K.G. 1842; master of the Badminton fox hounds 1835 to death. *d.* Badminton, Gloucs. 17 Nov. 1853. *Lord W. P. Lennox's Celebrities I have known* 2 series i, 118–30 (1877); *Sporting Review xxxi,* 69–70 (1854); *I.L.N. xxiii,* 448, 476 (1853), *portrait.*

BEAUFORT, SIR· FRANCIS *(younger son of Rev. Daniel Augustus Beaufort* 1739–1831, *V. of Collon, co. Louth). b.* Collon 1774; entered navy 21 June 1787; engaged in the action off Brest 1 June 1794; constructed with R. L. Edgeworth a telegraph from Dublin to Galway 1804; captain R.N. 30 May 1810; conducted survey of coast of Asia Minor 1810–12; granted pension for wounds 2 Dec. 1815, retired R.A. 1 Oct. 1846; F.R.S. 30 June 1814; one of founders of Royal Astronomical Society 1820 and of Royal Geographical Society 1830; corresponding member of Institute of France; hydrographer of the Admiralty July 1832 to 30 Jany. 1855; K.C.B. 27 April 1848; author of *Karamania or a brief description of the south coast of Asia Minor* 1817 which was the chief book of travels of its day. *d.* Hove near Brighton 17 Dec. 1857 in 84 year. *H. Martineau's Biographical sketches,* 4 ed. (1876) 213–30; *Quarterly Journal of Geological Soc. xiv,* 47–54 (1858); *Proc. of Royal Soc. ix,* 524–27 (1858).

BEAUFORT, FRANCIS LESTOCK *(son of the preceding). b.* 1815; in Bengal civil service 1837–76 when he retired upon the annuity fund; judge of the 24 Purgunnahs beyond the suburbs of Calcutta 1863–76; author of *Digest of the criminal law procedure in Bengal* 1850. *d.* 1879.

BEAUFOY, HENRY BENJAMIN HANBURY *(eld. son of Mark Beaufoy of London, astronomer* 1764–1827). Established 4 scholarships at Univ. of Cam.; gave city of London school £10,000; erected at cost of £10,000 Lambeth Ragged schools opened 5 March 1851, and invested £4,000 in perpetual trust for their maintenance; formed a library of 25000 volumes; privately printed his father's *Nautical and hydraulic experiments* 1834; F.R.S. 14 Dec. 1815, F.L.S. *d.* South Lambeth 12 July 1851 in 66 year. *H. Mayhew's Shops of* **London i,** 7–12 (1865).

BEAULIE, BARON A. DE. Belgian envoy extraordinary and minister plenipotentiary in London 1 March 1869 to death. *d.* 43 Upper Brook st. Grosvenor sq. 11 Oct. 1872 aged 66.

BEAUMONT, MILES THOMAS STAPLETON, 8 Baron *(eld. son of Thomas Stapleton of Carlton hall, Yorkshire 1778–1839). b.* Richmond, Yorkshire 4 June 1805; fought a duel with major general Lorenzo Moore on Wimbledon Common 13 Feb. 1832 when he received a bullet in his breast which was never extracted; summoned to House of Lords by writ as one of the coheirs of barony of Beaumont 16 Oct. 1840; col. commandant of 4 West York Militia 18 May 1853 to death; author of *Austria and Central Italy* 1849; *The late edict of Court of Rome; Lord Beaumont's letter to Lord Zetland* 1850, 7 ed. 1850. *d.* 17 Bruton st. Berkeley sq. London 16 Aug. 1854.

BEAUMONT, EDWARD BLACKETT. *b.* 1802; F.R.S. 4 June 1835, F.R.A.S. *d.* 33 Norland sq. Notting hill, London 7 June 1878.

BEAUMONT, SIR GEORGE HOWLAND, 9 Baronet. *b.* Addington park, Surrey 12 Sep. 1828; succeeded 7 June 1845; sheriff of Leicestershire 1852. *d.* Cole Orton hall, Ashby-de-la-Zouch 8 June 1882.

BEAUMONT, REV. JOSEPH. *b.* Castle Donington, Leics. 19 March 1794; Wesleyan minister 1813 to death; minister in Edinburgh 1821–23 and 1833–35, in London 1831–32, 1836–38 and 1845–50, in Liverpool 1839–44; M.D. Edin. 1836; an eloquent and popular preacher; author of *Memoir of Mrs. Mary Tatham* 1838. *d.* in the pulpit of Waltham chapel, Hull 21 Jany. 1855. *Life by his son Joseph Beaumont* 1856, *portrait; The lamps of the temple,* 3 ed. 1856, 381–403.

BEAUMONT, THOMAS *(brother of the preceding). b.* 1 July 1795; L.S.A. 1822; surgeon at Bradford 1822 to death; pres. of Bradford Medical Association; alderman of Bradford; one of the founders of Bradford Temperance Society the first in England 2 Feb. 1830; author of *An essay on the nature and properties of alcoholic liquors* 1837. *d.* Bradford 16 Oct. 1859.

BEAUMONT, WILLIAM RAWLINGS. *b.* London 1803; studied at St. Bartholomews hospital and in Paris; M.R.C.S. 1826, F.R.C.S. 1844; surgeon to Islington dispensary; went to Toronto 1841; professor of surgery in Toronto Univ. 1843; surgeon to general hospital; M.D. Toronto 1850; emeritus professor of surgery in Trinity college; invented many surgical

BEAUMONT, W. R. *(Con.)*
instruments, especially one for the making of deep sutures 1837, which suggested invention of the Singer sewing machine. *d.* 12 Oct. 1875. *Canadian Lancet 1 Nov. 1875.*

BEAUREGARD, ELIZABETH, Countess de *(dau. of Joseph Hargett).* Known as Miss Howard; remarkable for her beauty; mistress of Louis Napoleon to 1853 when he created her Countess de Beauregard. *(m.* 16 May 1854 Clarence Trelawney, Hussar officer in the Austrian army, he was *b.* 20 Dec. 1826 and obtained a divorce in Court of appeal Paris Feb. 1865). *d.* Chateau of Beauregard near Versailles 20 Aug. 1865 aged 42.

BEAVAN, CHARLES *(son of Hugh Beavan of Llowes, Radnorshire). b.* March 1805; ed. at Aldenham and Caius coll. Cam., 22 wrangler 1829; B.A. 1829, M.A. 1832; barrister M.T. 25 June 1830, bencher 6 May 1873; practised in Chancery courts; an official examiner of Court of Chancery June 1866 to Jany. 1884 when office abolished; author of *Reports of cases in Chancery argued and determined in the Rolls Court* 36 vols. 1840–69, being the longest series of authorized reports ever published. *d.* 91 St. George's road, Pimlico, London 18 June 1884. *Solicitor's Journal xxviii,* 173, 592, 601 (1884).

BEAVAN, EDWARD *(younger brother of the preceding). b.* 1814; ed. at Hounslow; practised as special pleader; barrister M.T. 3 May 1844; recorder of Chester 1864–66. *d.* 15 Feb. 1870.

BEAZLEY, SAMUEL *(son of Samuel Beazley of Whitehall, London, army accoutrement maker). b.* Whitehall 1786; served as a volunteer in the Peninsula; designed St. James's, Lyceum and City of London theatres, also 2 theatres in Dublin, 2 in Belgium, 2 in India and 1 in Brazil; erected London Bridge railway station, most of the stations on North Kent line and Lord Warden hotel at Dover; wrote and arranged more than 100 dramatic pieces chiefly farces and short comedies; author of *The Roué* [anon.] 3 vols. 1828; *The Oxonians, a glance at society* 3 vols. 1830. *d.* Tunbridge Castle 12 Oct. 1851 in 66 year. *Lord W. P. Lennox's Celebrities, I have known,* 2 series ii, 70–90 (1877); *Lord W. P. Lennox's Percy Hamilton* 1851 in which he is drawn to the life.

BECHER, ALEXANDER BRIDPORT *(eld. son of Alexander Becher, captain R.N. who d.* 1827). *b.* 12 June 1796; midshipman R.N. 28 Nov. 1812; captain on h.p. 20 March 1856, retired R.A. 11 June 1874; assistant in Hydrographic office 12 May 1823 to 1865,

BECHER, A. B. (Con.)

arranged and methodised all documents preserved there 1823–26; sec. to board of visitors of royal observatory; F.R.A.S. 1830, member of council; edited the *Nautical magazine* from its commencement in 1832 to 1871; author of *The landfall of Columbus on his first voyage to America* 1856. *d.* 46 Upper Gloucester place, London 15 Feb. 1876. *Dunkin's Obituary notices of astronomers* (1879) 1–6.

BECHER, Lady Eliza (*eld. dau. of John O'Neill, stage manager of the Drogheda theatre*). *b.* Drogheda 1791; made her début in Dublin at Crow street theatre as The widow Cheerly in the *Soldier's daughter* 1811 and in London at Covent Garden theatre as Juliet 6 Oct. 1814; the favourite actress in London both in comedy and tragedy 1814–19; said to have made £12,000 a year; acted for the last time 13 July 1819. (*m.* 18 Dec. 1819 Wm. Wrixon, M.P. for Mallow, he was *b.* 31 July 1780, assumed name of Becher, was created a baronet 1831 and *d.* 23 Oct. 1850). *d.* Ballygiblin near Mallow 29 Oct. 1872. *Mrs. C. B. Wilson's Our actresses i, 33–74 (1844), portrait; Theatrical inquisitor vi, 243 (1815), portrait.*

BECHER, John Reid. *b.* 3 July 1819; 2 lieut. Bengal Engineers 6 March 1838; colonel 13 Oct. 1863; colonel commandant 15 Sep. 1881 to death; served in Affghan campaign 1842 and Sutlej campaign 1846; general 29 July 1878; C.B. 18 May 1860. *d.* Southampton 9 July 1884.

BECHER, Martin William (*son of Wm. Becher of Norfolk, farmer who d. 1816*). *b.* Norfolk; served in the Store-keeper general's department; an officer in Buckinghamshire yeomanry cavalry 1821; won the Northampton steeple chase 4 April 1834; beat the Marquis of Waterford in a match for 1000 guineas a side 1834; won the St. Albans steeple chase 1835 and 1836 and many other races; the best steeple chase rider in England. *d.* 21 Maida hill, St. John's Wood, London 11 Oct. 1864 aged 67. *Sporting Review lii, 400–404 (1864); Scott and Sebright by the Druid (1885) 292–303, portrait.*

BECK, Baroness Von, assumed name of Wilhelmina Racidula; passed herself off as a Hungarian exile who had rendered good service to the cause of independence; came to Birmingham with her secretary Constant Derra July 1851, where she was assisted by many of the Liberal leaders; arrested as an impostor and confined in Moor st. police court 29 Aug.; author of *Personal adventures during*

BECK, Baroness Von. (Con.)

the late war of independence in Hungary 2 vols. 1850. *d.* in the ante-room of the Court at Moor st. Birmingham 30 Aug. 1851 aged about 54. *The persecution and death of the Baroness Von Beck at Birmingham in August 1851,* 8°. 1852; *Athenæum* (1852) 578, 629, 653, 701, 846 *and* 869; *The facts of the case as to the pretended Baroness Von Beck by J. T. Smith* 1852.

BECK, Edward. Commanded a merchant ship; a slate merchant at Isleworth, Middlesex; constructed the great waterworks at Hampton; one of most successful growers of Pelargoniums in the kingdom, long unrivalled as an exhibitor; author of *A treatise on the cultivation of the Pelargonium* 1847; edited *The florist and garden miscellany* 4 vols. 1848–61. *d.* Worton cottage, Isleworth 15 Jany. 1861 aged 57. *The Florist Feb.* 1861, pp. 36–38.

BECK, Richard. Manufacturing optician at 31 Cornhill, London; author of *A treatise on the construction, proper use and capabilities of Smith, Beck and Beck's achromatic microscopes* 1865 and of 9 papers read before the Microscopical Society 1859–66. *d.* Stamford hill, London 30 Sep. 1866 aged nearly 39.

BECK, Thomas Snow. *b.* Newcastle-upon-Tyne; ed. at gr. school there, and in Cumberland; apprenticed to a surgeon at Newcastle; student at Univ. college London 1836; M.R.C.S. 1839, F.R.C.S. 1847; walked the Paris hospitals 1839–40; visited universities of Switzerland, Italy and Germany 1840–41; M.D. London 1849; M.R.C.P. 1852; practised in London 1841; phys. to Farringdon general dispensary 1850; F.R.S. 5 June 1851, royal medallist 1845. *d.* 7 Portland place, London 6 Jany. 1877 aged 63. *Medical Circular i,* 209–211 (1852).

BECKER, Carl Ludwig Christian. *b.* Ratzeburg in Mecklenberg Strelitz 16 July 1821; manager for Elliott brothers of London electrical engineers 1858; member of the firm 1873 to death; F.R.A.S. Jany. 1874. *d.* 55 St. Paul's Road Canonbury 3 April 1875.

BECKET, Thomas. M.R.C.S. 1794, F.R.C.S. 1843; surgeon 1 Foot Guards 8 July 1795 to 1809; surgeon to the Savoy 28 Sep. 1809. *d.* 5 Russell place, Fitzroy sq. London 21 July 1856 aged 82.

BECKETT, Sir Edmund, 4 Baronet. *b.* Gledhow hall, Leeds 29 Jany. 1787; M.P. for west riding Yorkshire 12 July 1841 to 23

BECKETT, SIR E. (Con.)

July 1847, and 11 Dec. 1848 to 23 April 1859; succeeded 17 Nov. 1872. *d.* Doncaster 24 May 1874. Personalty sworn under £300,000 Aug. 1874. *I.L.N. lxiv,* 547 (1874) *lxv,* 236 (1874).

BECKETT, JOHN STANIFORTH *(son of Joseph Beckett, of Barnsley 1751–1840).* Presented a dispensary to Barnsley, to which he also left sum of £5000. *d.* Wombwell near Barnsley 9 Nov. 1868 in 75 year. Personalty sworn under £350,000 Jany. 1869.

BECKETT, SIR THOMAS, 3 Baronet. *b.* Leeds 1 Jany. 1779; succeeded 31 May 1847. *d.* Somerby park near Gainsborough 17 Nov. 1872. Personalty sworn under £350,000 March 1873.

BECKETT, WILLIAM *(5 son of Sir John Beckett, 1 Baronet 1743–1826).* *b.* Leeds 3 March 1784; principal partner in the eminent banking firm of Beckett and Co. of the Leeds "Old Bank"; M.P. for Leeds 1841 to 1852 and for Ripon 1852 to 1857. *d.* Brighton 26 Jany. 1863. *Rev. R. V. Taylor's Biographia Leodiensis* (1865) 506–509.

BECKWITH, JOHN CHARLES *(eld. child of John Beckwith of Halifax, Nova Scotia).* *b.* Halifax 2 Oct. 1789; ensign 50 Foot 1803, exchanged into 95 Foot 1804, captain 1808 to 20 Jany. 1820 when place on h.p.; served in Hanover, Denmark and Sweden, and in the Peninsula 1809–14; lost his left leg at Waterloo where 4 horses were killed under him 18 June 1815; C.B. 22 June 1815, M.G. 9 Nov. 1846; visited the Vaudois valleys Piedmont Oct. 1827 and 5 succeeding years, lived at St. Jean 1834–39 and at La Tour 1841–51, established 120 schools in the Vaudois valleys all of which he frequently inspected; knight of Sardinian order of St. Maurice and St. Lazarus 15 Dec. 1848. *(m.* 20 June 1850 Caroline Volle of the Vaudois). *d.* La Tour 19 July 1862. *bur.* in the cemetery of Tour Pellice. *General Beckwith, his life and labours among the Waldenses of Piedmont by J. P. Meille 1873.*

BECKWITH, JOSEPH. An early member of the Corresponding Society which was founded 1791; a contemporary of Hardy aud Thelwall; lived in Clerkenwell nearly 60 years. *d.* 3 Dec. 1860 aged 84.

BECKWITH, WILLIAM *(eld. son of Wm. Beckwith of Trimdon, co. Durham 1772–1847).* *b.* 20 Aug. 1795; cornet 16 Dragoons 7 Jany. 1813; major 14 Dragoons 14 Feb. 1828 to 6 Dec. 1833 when placed on h.p.; colonel 15

BECKWITH, W. (Con.)

Hussars 17 July 1859 to death; general 9 April 1868; K.H. 1832; sheriff of Durham 1858. *d.* Silkworth near Sunderland 23 Feb. 1871.

BEDDOME, JOHN REYNOLDS. M.R.C.S. 1811; M.D. Erlangen; surgeon at Romsey 1811 to death; mayor of Romsey 6 times. *d.* Romsey 26 Dec. 1859. *I.L.N. xxxiv,* 385 (1859), *portrait.*

BEDFORD, FRANCIS RUSSELL, 7 Duke of *(eld. child of John Russell 6 Duke of Bedford 1766–1839).* *b.* 13 May 1788; ed. at Westminster and Trin. coll. Cam., M.A. 1808; M.P. for Beds. 1812 to 1832; summoned to House of Lords as Baron Howland 15 Jany. 1833; succeeded as 7 Duke 20 Oct. 1839; P.C. 6 July 1846; K.G. 26 March 1847; lord lieutenant of Beds 29 Nov. 1859; high steward of Cambridge 1860; master of the Oakley hounds to 1828 when he sold the pack to Lord Southampton for £2,000, master again 1836–39. *d.* Woburn Abbey, Beds 14 May 1861. *Baily's Mag. i,* 57–59 (1860), *portrait; Waagen's Treasures of Art ii,* 283–86, *iii,* 463–74 *and iv.* 331–37.

BEDFORD, WILLIAM RUSSELL, 8 Duke of. *b.* Grosvenor square London 1 July 1809; M.P. for Tavistock 10 Dec. 1832 to 23 June 1841; succeeded 14 May 1861. *d.* 6 Belgrave sq. London 26 May 1872. Personalty sworn under £600,000 June 1872. *I.L.N. lx,* 555, 592, 623 (1872), *portrait.*

BEDFORD, FRANCIS. *b.* 1799; apprenticed to Finlay a bookbinder 1814; worked under Charles Lewis, foremost of English bookbinders; carried on business for benefit of Lewis's widow; partner with John Clarke who was unrivalled in tree marbled calf; afterwards in business alone at 91 York st. Westminster; the best binder in England or perhaps Europe. *d.* 12 Coningham road, Shepherd's Bush 8 June 1883. His library was sold by Sothebys 21, 22, 24 and 25 March 1884 for £4,876 16s. 6d.

BEDFORD, GEORGE AUGUSTUS. *b.* 8 Feb. 1809; entered navy 23 Dec. 1823; Captain 2 Jan. 1854; retired V.A. 22 March 1876; F.R.G.S. 1859. *d.* The Elms, Sydenham hill 11 Feb. 1879.

BEDFORD, REV. JOHN *(son of John Bedford of Wakefield).* *b.* Wakefield 27 July 1810; Wesleyan minister at Glasgow 1831; at Manchester 1855 to death; sec. to general chapel committee 1860–72; pres. of conference 1867; author of *Correspondence with*

BEDFORD, REV. J. (*Con.*)

the Rev. *Wm. Sutcliffe relative· to the doctrines, ministry and system of the Wesleyan Methodists* 1842. *d.* Chorlton-cum-Hardy near Manchester 20 Nov. 1879. *I.L.N. li,* 232 (1867), *portrait.*

BEDFORD, PAUL JOHN. *b.* Bath 24 Jany. 1792; made his début on the stage at Bath 1815; acted in Ireland and Scotland; made his début in London at Drury Lane 2 Nov. 1824 as Hawthorn in opera of *Love in a village;* played at Adelphi theatre 1838–67; had one of the deepest and richest bass voices ever heard, his best parts were Blueskin in *Jack Sheppard* 1839, Jack Gong in *The green bushes* 1845 and the Kinchin cove in *The flowers of the forest* 1847; took his farewell of the stage at the Queen's theatre 16 May 1868; sang at Weston's Music hall London and The hall by the sea Margate 1869; author of *Recollections and wanderings* 1864; *Drawing room dramas* 1874. (*m.* (1) Miss Green of Dublin, an actress who *d.* April 1833 aged 32. (*m.* (2) Miss Verinder, a pianist and harpist, she *d.* 1864). *d.* Lindsey place, Chelsea 11 Jany. 1871. *Theatrical times i,* 129 (1847), *portrait; Illust. sporting news ii,* 180 (1863), *portrait, v.* 133 (1866), *portrait.*

BEDINGFELD, FELIX WILLIAM GEORGE RICHARD (*youngest son of Sir Richard Bedingfeld, 5 Baronet 1767–1829*). *b.* 12 Aug. 1808; crown comr. of Turk's Island in the Bahamas 1842–49; barrister L.I. 26 April 1849; master of supreme court of Trinidad 1849–54; colonial sec. for and member of council of Mauritius 1860–68; C.M.G. 1869. *d.* Pilgrim, Lymington, Hants 7 Dec. 1884.

BEDINGFELD, SIR HENRY RICHARD PASTON, 6 Baronet. *b.* Oxburgh, Norfolk 10 May 1800; succeeded 22 Nov. 1829. *d.* Oxburgh 4 Feb. 1862.

BEDSON, GEORGE. *b.* Sutton Coldfield, Warwick 3 Nov. 1820; manager of business of Messrs. Johnson of Manchester 1851; manager of Bradford iron works 1858 to death; initiated and perfected many inventions in the iron and wire trades; propounded theory of continuous brakes for railway trains about 1864; lived at Bradford 1858–72 and 1882 to death, and at Marple, Cheshire 1872–82. *d.* Bradford house, Manchester 12 Dec. 1884.

BEECH, REV. HUGH. *b.* Chesterton, Staffs. 3 June 1787; Wesleyan minister 1811 to death. *d.* Cheedle, Staffs. 22 Feb. 1856. *The good soldier, a memoir of Rev. Hugh Beech* 1856.

BEECHAM, REV. JOHN. *b.* Barnoldby-le-Beck near Great Grimsby 1787; became a Wesleyan preacher 1815; general secretary of Wesleyan Missionary Society 1831 to death; pres. of Wesleyan conference 1850; author of *An essay on the constitution of Wesleyan Methodism* 1829, 3 ed. 1851; *Ashantee and the Gold Coast* 1841. *d.* Canonbury, London 22 April 1856. *Wesleyan Meth. Mag. lxxix, pt.* 2, 577–605 (1856).

BEECHEY, FREDERICK WILLIAM (2 *son of Sir Wm. Beechey R.A.* 1753–1839). *b.* 17 Feb. 1796; entered the navy 7 July 1806; went with Sir John Franklin to Spitzbergen on his first expedition 1818; with Edward Parry in the Hecla 1819; helped to survey north coast of Africa Nov. 1821 to July 1822; commanded the Blossom in the Pacific 1825–28; captain 8 May 1827; surveyed coast of Ireland 1837–47; superintendent marine department of Board of Trade 1850 to death; aide de camp to the Queen 18 July 1851 to 11 Sep. 1854; R.A. 11 Sep. 1854; F.R.G.S. 1833, pres. 1855 to death; F.R.S. 23 Dec. 1824, vice pres. 1854; author of *Narrative of a voyage to the Pacific and Behring's Strait* 2 vols. 1831; *A voyage of discovery towards the north pole* 1843. *d.* 8 Westbourne crescent, Hyde Park, London 29 Nov. 1856. *Proceedings of Royal Society viii,* 283–87 (1856).

BEECHEY, GEORGE D. (*brother of the preceding*). Portrait painter; exhibited 24 portraits at the R.A. 1817 to 1832; went to Calcutta about 1830; court painter and controller of the household to King of Oudh. (*m.* an Indian Lady called Hinda, whose portrait he sent to the R.A. 1822). Supposed to have died in India 1856.

BEECHEY, HENRY WILLIAM (*brother of the preceding*). travelled with Belzoni in Egypt 1816–17; examined and reported on antiquities of the Cyrenaica for Colonial Office 1821–22; F.S.A. 1825; exhibited a picture at the R.A. 1829, and another at British Institution 1838; emigrated to New Zealand 1855; wrote a memoir of Sir Joshua Reynolds prefixed to his Literary works published in 2 vols. 1835 and reprinted 1852. Supposed to have died in New Zealand in or about 1870.

BEECHING, JAMES. *b.* Bexhill near Hastings 1788; apprenticed to a boat builder; boat builder at Great Yarmouth; introduced the handsome build of fishing vessel now used there; invented the self righting lifeboat for which he gained the prize of £105, 13 Aug. 1851 when 280 models were sent in from all parts of the world, his boat slightly modified

BEECHING, J. (Con.)

has served as the model for all the boats of the Royal National Lifeboat institution. *d.* 7 June 1858. *Rev. John Gilmore's Storm-warriors* (1874) 32–47.

BEECROFT, GEORGE SKIRROW. *b.* Outwood house, Horsforth near Leeds 16 Nov. 1809; proprietor of Kirkstall forge near Leeds; M.P. for Leeds 5 June 1857 to 11 Nov. 1868; seconded address of House of Commons in reply to speech from the throne 3 Feb. 1859. *d.* 4 Gloucester terrace, Regent's park, London 18 March 1869. *I.L.N. xxxiv*, 189 (1859), *portrait.*

BEECROFT, JOHN. Explored the Niger and other rivers falling into the Gulf of Guinea 1832 to death; governor of Fernando Po; consul general for West Aprica 1850. *d.* Clarence, West coast of Aprica 10 June 1854.

BEER, JOHN (*eld. son of John Beer of Devonport, coal merchant*). *b.* Devonport about Dec. 1806; solicitor at Devonport 1827 to death; clerk to the Devonport comrs. 1838–82; an able advocate, engaged in all the chief local trials; member of Devonport town council many years and mayor 1849 and 1850; recorder of Saltash 1871 to death. *d.* 2 Albemarle villas, Stoke 14 April 1883.

BEER, JULIUS. *b.* Frankfort 1836; proprietor of *The Observer* London weekly paper 1870 to death; F.R.G.S. 1870. *d.* Mentone 29 Feb. 1880 in 44 year. *bur.* Highgate cemetery 8 March. Personalty sworn under £400,000 March 1880.

BEETE, ROBERT CROSBY. First puisne judge British Guiana 1853 to Jany. 1869 when he retired on a pension. *d.* Charing Cross hospital London 2 Nov. 1878 aged 68.

BEETON, SAMUEL ORCHART. Bookseller and publisher at 148 Fleet st. London; published the first English edition of *Uncle Tom's Cabin* 1852; went a voyage to America to present Mrs. Stowe with a voluntary payment of £500; published *Beeton's Christmas Annuals* 1860–65; sold his stock and copyrights for £1,900 to Ward, Lock and Tyler Sep. 1866; a publisher again 1877 to death; author with Doughty and Emerson of *The coming K.* 1872; *The Siliad* 1873 *and Jon Duan* 1874. *d.* Sudbrook park, Richmond, Surrey 6 June 1877 aged 46. *The law reports Equity cases xix*, 207–22 (1875).

BEEVOR, SIR THOMAS BRANTHWAYT, 3 Baronet. *b.* Old Buckenham, Norfolk 7 April 1798; succeeded 10 Dec. 1820. *d.* Yarmouth 6 April 1879.

BEEVOR, SIR THOMAS, 4 Baronet. *b.* Hargham Norfolk 23 Aug. 1823; ed. at Univ. coll. London; barrister L.I. 29 Jany. 1850; chairman of Norwich Union life assurance society; succeeded 6 April 1879. *d.* Hingham, Attleborough, Norfolk 18 Aug. 1885.

BEGBIE, JAMES. *b.* Edinburgh 18 Dec. 1799; ed. at high school and Univ. of Edin.; M.D. 1821; F.R.C.S. Edin. 1822; F.R.C.P. Edin. 1847, pres. 1854–56; pres. of Medico Chirurgical Society 1850–52; one of Her Majesty's physicians in ordinary in Scotland 6 June 1853; author of *Contributions to practical medicine* 1862, and of many papers in medical journals. *d.* 10 Charlotte sq. Edinburgh 26 Aug. 1869. *Proc. of Royal Society of Edin. vii*, 2–6 (1872).

BEGBIE, JAMES WARBURTON (2 son of the preceding). *b.* 19 Nov. 1826; ed. at Edinburgh academy and univ., M.D. 1847, LL.D. Aug. 1875; pres. of Royal Medical Society 1847–49; practised at Edinburgh 1852; F.R.C.P. Edin. 1852; phys. to the Cholera hospital 1854; phys. to Royal Infirmary 1855–65; lectured on practice of physic there 10 winter sessions 1855–65; had the largest consulting physician's practice in Scotland 1869 to death; author of *A handy book of medical information and advice by a physician* 1860, 2 ed. 1872; wrote 13 articles in *J. R. Reynolds's System of medicine 3 vols.* 1871 and many reviews and notices in *Edinburgh Medical Journal. d.* 16 Great Stuart st. Edinburgh 25 Feb. 1876. *Selections from the works of the late J. W. Begbie, edited by Dyce Duckworth, The New Sydenham Society London* 1882, *portrait.*

BEGG, REV. JAMES. *b.* Manse of New Monkland, Lanarkshire 31 Oct. 1808; ed. at Univ. of Glasgow, M.A.; licensed as a preacher June 1829; minister at Maxwelltown, Dumfries 18 May 1830; minister of Middle parish church Paisley 1831, and of Liberton near Edin. 25 June 1835 to 5 July 1843 when he was declared no longer a minister having joined in the Free Secession; minister of Newington Free church near Edin. 1843 to death; sent by his church to Canada on public duty 1844–45; moderator of Free general assembly 18 May 1865; a sum of £4,600 was presented to him by his friends 1875; author of *Are you prepared to die* 1845; *How to promote and preserve the beauty of Edinburgh* 1849; *A handbook of Popery* 1852; *The art of preaching* 1863. *d.* George sq. Edinburgh 29 Sep. 1883. *Memoirs by Professor Thomas Smith* (1885); *John Smith's Our Scottish clergy, 3 series* (1851) 127–33.

BEHAN, THOMAS LAWRENCE. Connected with the *Hampshire Independent;* on the staff of the *Observer* and other London newspapers; editor, manager, and publisher of the *London Gazette* 1 Oct 1854 to death. *d.* Southampton 27 Aug. 1869 aged 66.

BEHNES, WILLIAM. *b.* London 1794; learnt drawing in Dublin; gained 3 silver medals at Royal Academy; a portrait draughtsman in London, afterwards a sculptor; executed busts of many of the most eminent men of his time; executed statues of Lady Godiva 1844, Europa 1848 and The startled nymph 1849; exhibited 215 sculptures at the R.A. 1815–63; bankrupt on his own petition 25 Nov. 1861. *d.* Middlesex hospital London 8 Jany. 1864. *Cornhill Mag. ix,* 688–701 (1864); *Lectures on art by Henry Weekes* (1880) 294–317; *W. B. Scott's British school of sculpture* (1871) 99–102.

BEHRENS, LOUIS. *b.* Hamburg 1801; joined his brother Jacob in business as merchants at Bradford 1836; founded a business in Manchester 1840; established it as a separate concern 1870. *d.* Southport 1 June 1884.

BEKE, CHARLES TILSTONE *(son of James Beck, of Hackney, London, commissioner of sewers).* *b.* Stepney, London 10 Oct. 1800; student at Lincoln's Inn; changed spelling of his name from Beck to Beke 1834; acting consul at Leipzig 1837–38; Ph. Doc. Univ. of Tubingen 6 Aug. 1837; travelled in Abyssinia 1840–43 and 1865–66; received gold medals of Royal Geographical Societies of London and Paris 1845 and 1846; sec. to National Association for protection of industry and capital throughout British empire 1849–53, when association was dissolved; granted a civil list pension of £100 14 Dec. 1870; went to Palestine to determine position of Mount Sinai Dec. 1873; F.S.A. 1835; author of *Origines Biblicæ* 1834; *The sources of the Nile* 1860; *The British captives in Abyssinia* 1865; *The idol in Horeb* 1871 and other books. *d.* Bromley, Kent 31 July 1874. *Summary of the late Dr. Beke's published works and of his inadequately requited public services By his widow* 1876; *Dictionary of national biography iv,* 138–41 (1885); *I.L.N. lxv,* 140 (1874), *portrait; Graphic x,* 174 (1874), *portrait.*

BELCHER, SIR EDWARD *(2 son of Andrew Belcher, of Clarence lodge, Roehampton, Surrey).* *b.* Nova Scotia 1799; entered navy 9 April 1812; one of original fellows of Royal Geog. Soc. 1830; sailed round the world in H.M.S. Sulphur 1836–42; captain 6 May 1841; engaged surveying in East Indies 1842–47;

C.B. 14 Oct. 1841, K.C.B. 13 March 1867; knighted by patent for his services in China 21 Jany. 1843; granted pension for wounds 13 March 1847; commanded expedition in search of Sir John Franklin 10 Feb. 1852 to Oct. 1854; admiral 20 Oct. 1872; F.R.A.S. Dec. 1837; claimed to be the inventor of water-tight bulkheads and compartments; granted a Greenwich hospital pension of £150 per annum 7 Dec. 1874; author of *A treatise on nautical surveying* 1835; *Narrative of a voyage round the world* 2 vols. 1843; *Narrative of the voyage of H.M.S. Samarang* 2 vols. 1848; *Horatio Howard Brenton a naval novel* 3 vols. 1856; *The last of the Arctic voyages* 2 vols. 1855. *(m.* 11 Sep. 1830 Diana dau. of George Jolliffe, captain H.E.I.C.S.) *d.* 6 Melcombe place, Dorset sq. London 18 March 1877. *Army and Navy mag. iv,* 1–5 (1882), *portrait; I.L.N. xxi,* 321 (1852), *portrait, lxx,* 299 (1878), *portrait; Journal of Royal Geog. Soc. xlvii,* 136–42 (1877); *Monthly notices of Royal Astron. Soc. xxxviii,* 141–43 (1878); *Transactions of Instit. of naval architects xi,* 12–19, 197–211 (1870).

BELCHER, REV. JOSEPH. *b.* Birmingham 5 April 1794; Baptist divine; went to United States 1844; author of *Pastoral recollections* 1837; *The clergy of America* 1849; *George Whitfield, a biography* 1860; said to have written more religious works than any other author of the century. *d.* Philadelphia 10 July 1859.

BELCHER, THOMAS. *b.* St. James's churchyard Bristol 14 April 1783; went to London 1803; fought and beat Jack Ware in Tothill Fields, Westminster 26 June 1804; beaten by Wm. Ryan at Willesden Green 30 Nov. 1804, but beat him near Chertsey 4 June 1805; beat Jack O'Donnell at Shepperton 27 April 1805; fought Dutch Sam (Elias Samuels) for 100 guineas at Moulsey Hurst 8 Feb. 1806, when beaten; fought him again 20 July 1807, when fight was declared drawn; beaten by him 21 Aug. 1807; beat Dogherty 14 April 1808, Cropley 25 Oct. 1808, Farnborough 1 Feb. 1809, Silverthorne 6 June 1811; fought Dogherty again for 100 guineas on the Curragh of Kildare 23 April 1813, when he won again; landlord of the Castle Tavern Holborn 1814–28; one of the 18 pugilists selected by Jackson to act with him as pages at coronation of George IV. in Westminster Abbey 19 July 1821, one gold coronation medal was given to the boxers which they raffled for, when Belcher won it and held the trophy until his death. *d.* Peckham,

BELCHER, T. *(Con.)*

d. of apoplexy at 19 Trafalgar sq. Peckham, Surrey 9 Dec. 1854. *Pugilistica by H. D. Miles i*, 153–66 (1880), *portrait ; The Fancy by An Operator i*, 297–300 (1826), *portrait ; Every night book* (1827) 37–44 ; *Boxiana by P. Egan ii*, 28–45 (1818).

BELDAM, JOSEPH (3 *son of Wm. Beldam of Royston, Herts who d.* 20 *June* 1827 *aged* 64). *b.* 26 Dec. 1795 ; ed. at St. Peter's coll. Cam. ; barrister M.T. 12 May 1825 ; standing counsel for Anti slavery party ; F.S.A. 1 May 1856 ; author of *Il pastore incantato, a drama ; Pompeii and other poems by a student of the Middle Temple* 1823 ; *A summary of the laws peculiarly affecting Protestant dissenters* 1827 ; *Recollections of scenes and institutions in Italy and the East* 2 vols. 1851. *d.* Royston 6 June 1866.

BELDHAM, WILLIAM. *b.* Wrecclesham near Farnham, Surrey 5 Feb. 1766 ; professional cricketer ; the "crack" batsman of England many years, excelled also in bowling, fielding, wicket keeping and single wicket playing ; played in the Gentlemen versus Players match 1787 to 1821 ; the last surviving member of the once far famed Hambledon cricket club ; had 39 children, 28 by his first wife, all of whom died young leaving no issue. *d.* Tilford near Farnham 20 Feb. 1862. *Nyren's Cricketer's Tutor* (1833) 93–96.

BELFORD, WILLIAM ROWLES. *b.* Easton near Bristol Dec. 1824 ; made his début in London at Sadler's Wells theatre 22 Dec. 1851 as Sir Charles Cropland in *The poor Gentleman ;* played prominent parts in 32 Shakespearian revivals at same house 1852–63 ; acted with S. Phelps in Germany 1859 ; played at Strand theatre about 1863–69 ; created leading role in W.S. Gilbert's comedy *Randall's Thumb* at Court theatre 25 Jany. 1871 ; played Henry the 8th in the provinces 1876 ; last appeared on the stage at Imperial theatre London April 1879 in comic drama of *A rough diamond ;* acted at nearly every west-end theatre in London ; sum of £1,100 was raised for him Dec. 1879. *d.* 43 Grand parade, Brighton 3 June 1881. *Pascoe's Dramatic list* (1880) 42.

BELFOUR, EDMUND. Secretary of Royal college of surgeons 1814 to death. *d.* 37 Lincoln's Inn Fields 30 Jany. 1865 in 76 year.

BELHAVEN AND STENTON, ROBERT MONTGOMERY HAMILTON, 8 Baron *(eld. child of Wm. Hamilton, 7 Baron Belhaven and Stenton* 1765–1814.) *b.* Wishaw house, Lanarkshire 1793 ; succeeded 29 Oct. 1814 ; created Baron

BELHAVEN AND STENTON, 8 BARON. *(Con.)*

Hamilton of Wishaw in peerage of U.K. 10 Sep. 1831 ; lord high comr. to general assembly of Church of Scotland 1831–41, 1847–51, 1853–57 and 1860–66 ; lieut. col. commandant 1 Lanarkshire militia 21 Nov. 1833 to death ; lord lieut. of Lanarkshire 10 Aug. 1863 to death. *d.* Wishaw house 22 Dec. 1868.

BELL, ALEXANDER. *b.* Cupar Fife 1775 ; ed. at Univ. of Edin. ; pupil of Sir Astley Cooper in London, M.R.C.S. ; served in Ireland as surgeon of 1st Regiment of Dundee Volunteers (Loyal Tay Fencibles) during rebellion of 1798 until May 1802 when regiment was disbanded ; practised in village of Errol 1802–1807, and at Dundee 1807–50 surgeon to Dundee infirmary 30 years ; performed operation of lithotomy many times with great success. *d.* Dundee 28 March 1852.

BELL, ALEXANDER. Professor of elocution in London ; author of *Practical elocutionist* 1835 ; *The tongue, a poem* 1846 ; *The Bride, a play* 1847 ; *Stammering and other impediments of speech* 1849. *d.* Harrington sq. London 23 April 1865.

BELL, ALEXANDER MONTGOMERIE *(son of John Bell of Paisley, manufacturer).* *b.* Paisley 4 Dec. 1809 ; ed. at Paisley gr. sch. and Univ. of Glasgow ; a writer to the Signet 1835 ; partner of Messrs. Dundas and Wilson ; professor of conveyancing in the Univ. of Edin. 1856 to death ; author of *Lectures on conveyancing* 1867, 3 ed. 2 vols. 1882. *d* East Morningside house, Edinburgh 19 Jany. 1866.

BELL, ARCHIBALD. *b.* 1775 ; member of faculty of advocates 1798 ; sheriff depute of Ayrshire 18 Feb. 1815 ; author of *The Cabinet, a series of essays moral and literary* [*anon.*] 2 vols. 1835 ; *Count Clermont, a tragedy, Caius Toranius, a tragedy with other poems* 1841 ; *Melodies of Scotland* 1849. *d.* Edinburgh 6 Oct. 1854.

BELL, BENJAMIN *(son of Joseph Bell of Edinburgh, surgeon* 1786–1848). *b.* Edinburgh 13 April 1810 ; ed. in Edin. and London ; L.R.C.S. Edin. 1832, F.R.C.S. 1835, pres. 1864 ; M.R.C.S. 1833 ; founded with Robert Hamilton the Eye infirmary Edin. 1834 ; vice pres. of Medico-Chirurgical society of Edin. 1856, pres. 1859–61 ; author of *A probationary essay on injuries of the male urethra* 1835 ; *The life of Benjamin Bell by his grandson* 1868. *d.* Coates crescent, Edinburgh 13 June 1883. *Edinburgh Medical Journal xxix*, 91–95 (1884).

BELL, CATHERINE DOUGLAS. Author of *Arnold Lee, or rich children and poor children by cousin Kate* 1852 ; *Help in time of need* 1856, 2 ed. 1866; *Self mastery* 1857; *Home sunshine* 1859, 2 ed. 1866; *Hope Campbell, or know thyself* 1866 and other books for children. d. Edinburgh 15 Nov. 1861. *Last hours with cousin Kate [C. D. Bell]* 1862, portrait.

BELL, CHARLES. b. London 1805; partner in firm of Thomson, Bonar & Co. of London and St. Petersburg, merchants; M.P. for City of London 16 Nov. 1868 to death. d. Terrace house, Richmond, Surrey 9 Feb. 1869. Personalty sworn under £300,000 April 1869.

BELL, CHRISTOPHER. Entered navy June 1796; captain 7 Feb. 1812, retired R.A. 1 Oct. 1846; C.B. 4 July 1840. d. Aigburth Ash near Liverpool 16 Oct. 1853 aged 70.

BELL, EDWARD WELLS. Lieutenant 7 Foot 16 May 1811 ; major 19 Dec. 1826 to 29 June 1830 when placed on h.p. ; colonel 66 Foot 26 Dec. 1859 to death; general 12 July 1868. d. Kempsey, Worcester 9 Oct. 1870.

BELL, EDWARD WILLIAM DERRINGTON. b. 1824; 2 lieut. 23 Foot 15 April 1842 ; lieut. col. 8 Jany. 1858 to 1 Sep. 1869; served in Russian war 1854–55 and in Sepoy mutiny 1857–58; personally captured and secured the first gun taken at battle of the Alma; M.G. 6 March 1868; commanded Belfast district 28 Feb. 1875 to death; C.B. 13 March 1867; V.C. 26 June 1856. d. Fort William park, Belfast 10 Nov. 1879.

BELL, SIR GEORGE (*son of George Bell of Belle Vue on Lough Erin Fermanagh*). b. Belle Vue 17 March 1794; ed. at Dublin; ensign 34 Foot 11 March 1811 ; served in the Peninsula 1811–14; lieut. col. 1 Foot 5 Dec. 1843 to 1 May 1855; commanded 1 brigade of third division in Crimean war 1854–55; inspecting field officer at Liverpool 1 May 1855 to 4 April 1859; colonel 104 Foot 23 Oct. 1863, of 32 Foot 2 Feb. 1867 and of 1 Foot 3 Aug. 1868 to death; general 8 March 1875; C.B. 5 July 1855, K.C.B. 13 March 1867. d. 156 Westbourne terrace, London 10 July 1877. *Rough notes by an old soldier Sir G. Bell* 2 vols. 1867, portrait.

BELL, HENRY GLASSFORD (*eld. son of James Bell, Town clerk of Greenock*). b. Glasgow 8 Nov. 1805 ; ed. at Glasgow high school and Univ. of Edin. ; admitted advocate 20 Nov. 1832; sheriff substitute of Lanarkshire 1 July 1838; sheriff principal 8 June 1867 to death; started *Edinburgh Literary Journal* 1828, edited it to 14 Jany. 1832 when it was

merged in *Edinburgh Weekly Chronicle* ; he is sketched under name of Tallboys in *Noctes Ambrosianæ* ; author of *Life of Mary Queen of Scots* 2 vols. 1828 ; *Summer and winter hours* 1831 ; *Romances and minor poems* 1866. d. Glasgow 7 Jany. 1874. *Journal of jurisprudence xviii*, 92–103 (1874).

BELL, JACOB (*son of John Bell of 338 Oxford st. London, chemist who d. 14 Jany. 1849 aged 74*). b. 338 Oxford st. 5 March 1810 ; apprenticed to his father 1827–32; chemist in Oxford st. 1832 to death, his drugs earned a European reputation ; founder of Pharmaceutical Society 1841, on which he spent a large sum; edited *Pharmaceutical Journal* July 1841 to death; M.P. for St. Albans 24 Dec. 1850 to 1 July 1852; contested Great Malvern 1852 and Marylebone 1854 ; collected at his house 15 Langham place, London a gallery of pictures many by Sir Edwin Landseer, the 13 best of which he bequeathed to the nation ; F.L.S. 6 March 1832; author of *Chemical and pharmaceutical processes and products* 1852. d. Tunbridge Wells 12 June 1859. *J. Bell and T. Redwood's Historical sketch of progress of pharmacy* (1880) 280–92 ; *I.L.N. xviii*, 299 (1851), portrait, *xxxi*, 4, 24 (1859), portrait.

BELL, JAMES SPENCER. b. 1818; M.P. for Guildford 7 July 1852 to 21 March 1857. d. 1 Devonshire place, Portland place, London 22 Feb. 1872.

BELL, JOHN (*only son of John Bell of Thirsk*). b. 1809 ; M.P. for Thirsk 1 July 1841 to death ; declared insane by a commission July 1849. d. Thirsk 5 March 1851.

BELL, REV. JOHN. b. Snaith, Yorkshire ; ed. at Douay, France; ordained priest at Crook hall, co. Durham 23 Dec. 1794; prefect general of Douay college Durham and professor of rhetoric and poetry 1794–1817, the college was moved from Crook hall to Ushaw 1808 ; appointed to mission of Samlesbury near Preston 1817 and to Kippax park Yorkshire 1828; author of *The wanderings of the human intellect, or a new dictionary of sects* 1814, 2 ed. 1838. d. Selby 31 May 1854 aged 87.

BELL, JOHN. Lived in Abyssinia 1842 to death; general in army of Ras Ali the ruler of Abyssinia 1848 who gave him the province of Diddim ; taken prisoner by Kasai 1853 who deposed Ali and took title of Theodorus ; minister and general in chief to Theodorus 1853 to death; killed in a battle fought against Garred at Waldabba near the western bank of the Taccazy river 31 Oct. 1860 after he had himself killed Garred.

BELL, JOHN. *b.* Newcastle 1782; Bookseller at Newcastle; land surveyor at Gateshead; one of founders of Society of antiquaries of Newcastle on Tyne, treasurer 6 Feb. 1813; author of *Rhymes of northern bards* 1812; contributed to *Gent. Mag. d.* Bentinck crescent, Newcastle 30 Oct. 1864.

BELL, JOHN. *b.* Ireland 1796; went to the United States 1810; author of *On baths and mineral waters* 1831; *Practical dictionary of materia medica* 1841; *On regimen and longevity* 1842; *Dietetical and medical hydrology* 1850. *d.* Philadelphia 1872.

BELL, SIR JOHN *(son of David Bell of Bonytoun, Fifeshire). b.* Bonytoun 1 Jany. 1782; ensign 52 Foot 15 Aug. 1805; served in Peninsular war; permanent assistant quartermaster general to 10 Nov. 1814; chief sec. of government at Cape of Good Hope 1828–41; aide de camp to the sovereign 6 May 1831 to 23 Nov. 1841; lieut. governor of Guernsey 24 Jany. 1848 to 30 June 1854; col. of 95 Foot 25 June 1850 and of 4 Foot 26 Dec. 1853 to death; general 15 June 1860; C.B. 4 June 1815, K.C.B. 6 April 1852, G.C.B. 18 May 1860. *d.* 55 Cadogan place, London 20 Nov. 1876. *I.L.N. lxix,* 541 (1876), *portrait.*

BELL, JOHN DAVID *(youngest son of George Joseph Bell, professor of law at Univ. of Aberdeen). b.* 1823 or 1824; barrister M.T. 12 May 1848; practised at Calcutta 1850–58; founder and chairman of Positive Life Assurance Company 1870; standing counsel to government of India at Calcutta 1878 to death. *d.* Calcutta 15 Aug. 1880 in 57 year.

BELL, JOHN GRAY *(son of Thomas Bell of Newcastle* 1785–1860). *b.* Newcastle 21 Sep. 1823; a bookseller in London 1848–54 and in Manchester 1854 to death; published a valuable series of *Tracts on the topography history and dialects of the counties of Great Britain* 1850; author of *A descriptive and critical catalogue of works illustrated by Thomas and John Bell* 1851; privately printed *A genealogical account of the descendants of John of Gaunt* 1855. *d.* Manchester 21 Feb. 1866.

BELL, JOHN MONTGOMERIE. *b.* Paisley 1804; advocate in Edinburgh 1825; advocate depute 1847; sheriff of Kincardine 7 May 1851 to death; author of *Treatise on law of arbitration in Scotland* 1861; *The martyr of liberty, a poem* 1863. *d.* Linnhouse 16 Oct. 1862.

BELL, JONATHAN ANDERSON *(2 son of James Bell, advocate). b.* Glasgow 1809; ed. at Univ. of Edin.; spent some years with

BELL, J. A. *(Con.)*

Messrs. Rickman and Hutcheson of Birmingham, architects; an architect in Edinburgh 1838 to death; sec. to Royal Association for the promotion of the fine arts in Scotland May 1839 to death; author of *Poems. Privately printed* 1865. *d.* Edinburgh 28 Feb. 1865. *Poems by J. A. Bell* (1865) *v–xi.*

BELL, SIR JOSHUA PETER. *b.* co. Kildare 1826; owner with his father and brothers of a splendid station called Jimbour near Dalby, Queensland where they became great wool growers; M.P. for Dalby in Queensland parliament 1863 to March 1879; colonial treasurer 1871–74; pres. of legislative council March 1879 to death; K.C.M.G. 24 Nov. 1881. *d.* Brisbane 20 Dec. 1881. *Illust. sporting and dramatic news xvi,* 405 (1882), *portrait.*

BELL, LADY MARION *(2 dau. of Charles Shaw of Ayr). b.* Edinburgh 1787. *(m.* 3 June 1811 Sir Charles Bell, F.R.S., celebrated physiologist *b.* Nov. 1774 *d.* 28 April 1842). Granted a civil list pension of £100 for her husband's services to science 14 Sep. 1843; published *The letters of Sir Charles Bell* 1870. *d.* 47 Albany st. Regent's park, London 9 Nov. 1876.

BELL, MATTHEW. *b.* 18 April 1793; ed. at Eton and Ch. Ch. Ox.; sheriff of Northumberland 1816; M.P. for Northumberland 1826–31 and for South Northumberland 1832–52; lieut. col. of Northumberland and Newcastle yeomanry cavalry 1826–63. *d.* Woolsington near Newcastle 28 Oct. 1871.

BELL, OSWALD HOME. M.R.C.S. Edin. 3 Feb. 1863; professor of medicine in Univ. of St. Andrews 1863 to death; dean of the medical faculty. *d.* The Scores, St. Andrews 24 June 1875 in 39 year.

BELL, REV. PATRICK *(son of George Bell of Mid Leoch farm, parish of Auchterhouse near Dundee). b.* Mid Leoch farm April 1799; ed. at Univ. of St. Andrews, LL.D. 1867; ordained 1843; minister of Carmyllie, Arbroath Dec. 1843 to death; invented a reaping machine 1826 being 7 or 8 years before the earliest American inventors; presented by Highland Society with sum of £1000 1868. *d.* The manse of Carmyllie 22 April 1869. *Reg. and mag. of biog. i,* 473 (1869); *I.L.N. lii,* 225 (1868), *portrait.*

BELL, ROBERT *(son of Benjamin Bell, surgeon). b.* 1782; ed. at high school Edinburgh; advocate 1809; sheriff of Berwickshire 1842–60; procurator to Church of Scotland 1842

BELL, R. *(Con.)*

to death; member of Bannatyne club; made a fine collection of Rembrandt etchings. *d.* 15 Great Stuart st. Edinburgh 27 April 1861. *Crombie's Modern Athenians* (1882), *portrait.*

BELL, ROBERT *(youngest son of John Bell of Cork).* *b.* Cork 16 Jany. 1800; ed. at Trin. coll. Dublin where he originated the Dublin Historical Society; settled in London 1828; edited the *Atlas* weekly paper many years, the *Monthly Chronicle* and the *Home News* a monthly journal; author of *History of Russia* 3 vols. 1838; *Lives of the English poets* 2 vols. 1839; *Wayside pictures through France, Belgium and Holland* 1849, 2 ed. 1858; *Hearts and altars* 3 vols. 1852; *The ladder of gold* 3 vols. 1856; *The annotated edition of the English poets* 24 vols 1854–57, and of 3 five-act comedies, *Marriage* 1842; *Mothers and daughters* 1843, 2 ed. 1845 and *Temper* 1847. *d.* 14 York st., Portman sq. London 12 April 1867.

BELL, VENERABLE ROBERT. Ordained 1831; Inc. of Tipperary 1866 to death; archdeacon of Cashel 1872 to death; canon of St. Patrick's cathedral, Dublin. *d.* rectory Tipperary 10 Jany. 1883 in 75 year.

BELL, ROBERT CHARLES. *b.* Edinburgh 1806; Engraved a series of Scottish views and a number of vignette portraits, also many plates for the Royal Scottish Association; his largest and most important work was an engraving of Sir William Allan's Battle of Preston Pans which he completed in 1872; several of his best plates appeared in the *Art Journal* 1850–72. *d.* Edinburgh 5 Sep. 1872. *Art Journal* (1872) 284.

BELL, SIR SYDNEY SMITH *(9 son of Wm. Bell, of London, banker).* *b.* 1805; ed. at Univs. of Edin. and Glasgow; barrister I.T. 3 May 1839; puisne judge at Cape of Good Hope 7 Feb. 1851, and first puisne judge May 1858; chief justice of supreme court and pres. of legislative council of Cape of Good Hope 16 Dec. 1868 to 1879; knighted by patent 9 Oct. 1869; author of *Cases decided in the House of Lords on appeal from the courts of Scotland* 7 vols. 1843–52; *Colonial administration of Great Britain* 1859. *d.* 42 Kensington park road, London 13 Sep. 1879.

BELL, THOMAS *(son of Richard Bell of Newcastle).* *b.* Newcastle 16 Dec. 1785; land valuer and surveyor; an antiquary, assisted the local topographical authors in their works especially Rev. John Hodgson in his *History of Northumberland* 6 vols. 1827–40; one of the founders of Newcastle Literary and

BELL, T. *(Con.)*

Philosophical Society and of Society of antiquaries of Newcastle 1813. *d.* Newcastle 30 April 1860.

BELL, THOMAS *(only son of Thomas Bell of Poole, Dorset, surgeon).* *b.* Poole 11 Oct. 1792; studied at Guys and St. Thomas's hospitals; M.R.C.S. 1815, F.R.C.S 1844, F.L.S. 1815, pres. 1853–61; dental surgeon to Guy's hospital 1817–61 where he lectured on comparative anatomy; F.R.S. 10 Jany. 1828, junior secretary 1848–53; professor of Zoology at King's college London 1836 to death; pres. of the Ray Society 1843–59; purchased in 1866 from the grandnieces of Gilbert White The Wakes, Selborne where he lived to his death; author of *Monograph of Testudinata, parts 1–8,* 1832–37, *folio*; *History of British quadrupeds* 1837, 2 ed. 1874; *History of British reptiles* 1839; *History of British Stalk-eyed Crustacea* 1853; edited White's *Natural history of Selborne* 2 vols. 1877. *d.* The Wakes, Selborne 13 March 1880. *Nature xxi,* 473, 499 (1880).

BELL, SIR WILLIAM *(son of Wm. Bell of Ripon, Yorkshire).* *b.* 1788; ed. at Woolwich; 2 lieut. R.A. 23 Nov. 1804; served through Peninsular war; colonel R.A. 18 March 1852, colonel commandant 26 Dec. 1865 to death; general 31 Jany. 1872; K.C.B. 13 March 1867. *d.* South lodge, Ripon 28 March 1873.

BELLAIRS, REV. HENRY *(3 son of Abel Walford Bellairs of Uffington, Lincolnshire 1755–1839).* *b.* 29 Aug. 1790; midshipman on board H.M.S. Spartiate; wounded twice at Trafalgar; cornet 15 Hussars 25 Nov. 1808; lieut. 26 May 1809 to 1811; ed. at St. Mary hall Ox., B.A. 1820, M.A. 1823; R. of Bedworth, Warws 1830; V. of Hunsingore, Yorkshire 1832 to death; hon. canon of Worcester Sep. 1853 to death. *d.* Paignton near Torquay 17 April 1872.

BELLAIRS, SIR WILLIAM *(younger brother of the preceding).* *b.* Uffington 1793; cornet 15 Hussars 2 May 1811; captain 10 April 1817 to 10 Feb. 1820 when he sold out; exon of Yeomen of the Guard 19 Sep. 1837 to Dec. 1848; knighted by the Queen at St. James's Palace 17 May 1848. *(m.* 1822 Cassandra dau. of Edmund Hooke of Mulbarton lodge, Norfolk, she *d.* 1876). *d.* London 2 Oct. 1863.

BELLAMY, GEORGE. *b.* Plymouth 15 Nov. 1773; surgeon's mate R.N. Feb. 1793; surgeon 19 May 1795; surgeon to the Bellerophon 74 guns 1796–1800; served at battle of the Nile; placed on retired list 1817; M.R.C.P.; mayor of Plymouth 1811–12. *d.* Plymouth 10 Oct. 1863.

BELLAMY, REV. JAMES WILLIAM *(son of John Bellamy).* *b.* 25 Nov. 1788; ed. at Merchant Taylors' school and Queen's coll. Cam., B.A. 1811, M.A. 1816; Norrisian and Seatonian prizeman 1815; incorporated at St. John's coll. Ox. 1820, B.D. 1821; head master of Merchant Taylors' school 6 April 1819 to 23 July 1845; V. of Sellinge, Kent 1822 to death; preb. of St. Paul's cathedral 10 March 1843 to death; F.R.S. 18 Dec. 1834; edited *A concordance to the Holy Bible* 1818. *d.* Sellinge 2 March 1874.

BELLAMY, JOHN CREMER. *b.* Plymouth 7 Dec. 1812; L.S.A. 1833, M.R.C.S. 1834; Curator of Plymouth Institute and Devon and Cornwall Nat. Hist. Society; author of *The natural history of South Devon* 1839; *The housekeeper's guide to the fish market for each month of the year* 1843, new ed. 1862; *A thousand facts in the histories of Devon and Cornwall* 1850. *d.* George st. Plymouth 12 May 1854.

BELLAMY, WILLIAM HOARE. *b.* Cork 5 Aug. 1800; made his debut at Elmsworth 1825 as Sir Simon Rochdale in *John Bull*; went to the United States; made his début in New York 1838. *(m.* Mrs. A. W. Penson she was *b.* Scotland and acted in the United States 1838 to her death May. 1857). *d.* Greenpoint, Long Island 15 April 1866.

BELLARS, HENRY JOHN. *b.* Chester; a schoolmaster; sec. and curator of Chester Natural History Society; photographic artist in London 1862 to death; the best facsimilist in England; author of *Illustrated catalogue of British land and freshwater shells* 1858; *The historical numismatic atlas of the Roman emperors.* *d.* 12 Bedford court, Covent Garden 22 June 1868 aged 44.

BELLASIS, EDWARD *(only son of Rev. George Bellasis, V. of Basildon, Berkshire who d.* 1814). *b.* Basildon vicarage 14 Oct. 1800; ed. at Christ's Hospital 1808–15; barrister I.T. 2 July 1824; employed in parliamentary practice 1836–66, counsel in 342 important cases; serjeant at law 10 July 1844; received into Roman Catholic Church 28 Sep. 1850; trustee with J. R. Hope-Scott Q.C. of Earl of Shrewsbury 1853–56; steward of manors of Duke of Norfolk in Norfolk and Suffolk 1863; one of the 3 comrs. who reported on College of Arms 1870; author of several anonymous pamphlets. *d.* Hyères, France 24 Jany. 1873. *The Tablet* 1 Feb. 1873 *p.* 138.

BELLEW, PATRICK BELLEW, 1 Baron *(elder son of Sir Edward Bellew, 6 baronet who d.* 15 March 1827). *b.* London 29 Jany 1798;

succeeded 15 March 1827; lord lieut. of co Louth 1832 to death; col. of Louth militia 17 Nov. 1843 to death; M.P. for Louth 1831–1832 and 1834–1837; P.C. Ireland 1838; created a peer of Ireland by title of Baron Bellew of Barmeath co. Louth 17 July 1848. *d.* Barmeath 10 Dec. 1866.

BELLEW, REV. SIR CHRISTOPHER, 2 Baronet. *b.* 1818; succeeded 26 June 1855. *d.* at house of the Jesuit Fathers, Gardiner st. Dublin 18 March 1867.

BELLEW, JOHN CHIPPENDALL MONTESQUIEU *(only child of Robert Higgin, lieutenant 12 Foot who d.* 24 Jany. 1853). *b.* Lancaster 3 Aug. 1823; ed. at Lancaster gr. sch. and St. Mary hall Ox.; assumed his mother's name of Bellew Aug. 1844; C. of St. Andrew's Worcester 1849; C. of Prescot Lancs. 1850; assistant chaplain in Bengal 1851; chaplain of St. John's cathedral Calcutta Dec. 1852 to 1855; edited the *Bengal Hurkaru;* assistant minister of St. Philip's Regent's st. London 1855–57; P.C. of St. Mark's St. John's Wood 1857–62; minister of Bedford chapel Bloomsbury 26 Oct. 1862 to 1868; one of the most popular preachers in London; received into Church of Rome Oct. 1869; executed deed of relinquishment of holy orders 13 Aug. 1870; very successful as a public reader in England and the United States; author of *Shakespeare's house at New Place* 1863; *Blount Tempest a novel* 3 vols. 1866; *Poets Corner, a manual for students* 1868. *d.* 16 Circus road, St. John's Wood 19 June 1874. *Bentley's Quarterly Review i,* 476–92 (1859); *Traits of character by a contemporary i,* 285–312 (1860); *Cartoon portraits* (1873) 50–51, *portrait; Graphic x,* 15 (1874), *portrait; E. Yates's Recollections ii,* 66–69 (1884).

BELLEW, SIR MICHAEL DILLON, 1 Baronet *(son of Christopher Dillon Bellew of Mount Bellew, co. Galway 1763–1826). b.* 29 Sep. 1796; created a baronet 15 Aug. 1838. *d.* Greenville lodge, Rathmines near Dublin 26 June 1855.

BELLEW, RICHARD MONTESQUIEU *(younger son of Sir Edward Bellew 6 baronet who d.* 1827). *b.* 12 Feb. 1803; M.P. for co. Louth 21 Dec. 1832 to 1 July 1852 and 16 May 1859 to 6 July 1865; a lord of the treasury 6 Aug. 1847 to 1852; member of Local government board, Ireland. *d.* Dublin 8 Jany. 1880.

BELLEW, THOMAS ARTHUR GRATTAN. *b.* 1824; M.P. for co. Galway 26 July 1852 to

BELLEW, T. A. G. *(Con.)*

21 March 1857; assumed additional surname of Grattan by r.l. 19 March 1859. *d.* Mount Bellew, Duleek, co. Galway 24 July 1863.

BELLHOUSE, EDWARD TAYLOR *(eld. son of David Bellhouse of Manchester).* *b.* Manchester 10 Oct. 1816; started firm of E. T. Bellhouse and Co., engineers, Eagle foundry, Hunt st. Manchester 1 July 1842; erected the Gas works for Buenos Ayres, Pernambuco and Athens; erected many large bridges for various railways and many iron buildings; pres. of Manchester Mechanics' Institute; M.I.M.E. 1857. *d.* Southport 13 Oct. 1881. *Proc. of Instit. of M.E.* (1882) 1–2.

BELLINGHAM, O'BRYEN *(3 son of Sir Alan Bellingham, 2 baronet 1776–1827).* *b.* 12 Dec. 1805; ed. at Feinagle's school; M.D. Univ. of Edin. and L.R.C.S. Edin. 1830; professor of botany, Royal college of surgeons Ireland to 1850, a surgical examiner 1850, chairman of the court 1856; sec. of Surgical society of Ireland to death; surgeon to St. Vincent's hospital 1835 to death; author of *Observations on aneurism and its treatment by compression* 1847; *Treatise on diseases of the heart* 1857. *d.* The Castle, Castle Bellingham, co. Louth 11 Oct. 1857. *Dublin Journal of medical science lxiv,* 469–75 (1877).

BELLOC, ANNE LOUISE *(dau. of Colonel James Swanton, commandant of Rocroi, France who was b. Ireland).* *b.* La Rochelle 1 Oct. 1796; assisted Lafayette in establishing public libraries; founded a choice circulating library; translated many English books into French. *(m.* 1823 Jean Hilaire Belloc, Director of Royal School of Design, Paris who *d.* 1866). *d.* Paris 6 Nov. 1881. *S. J. Hale's Woman's record,* 2 ed. 1855 *p.* 583, *portrait.*

BELLOT, JOSEPH RENÉ. *b.* Paris 18 March 1826; served in French navy 1843–50; went as a volunteer with captain Kennedy in the Prince Albert in search of Sir John Franklin 1851–52; sailed in the Phœnix for the Arctic regions 10 May 1853; left the ship to carry dispatches to Sir Edward Belcher 12 Aug. 1853; author of *Journal d'un voyage aux Mers Polaires* 1854; fell into a crack in the ice near Cape Bowden and drowned 18 Aug. 1853; an obelisk was erected to his memory by public subscription in front of Greenwich hospital 1857. *Memoirs of J. R. Bellot* 2 vols. 1855, *portrait.*

BELLOT, THOMAS *(elder son of Thomas Bellot of Manchester, surgeon).* *b.* Manchester 16 March 1806; ed. at Manchester gr. sch.;

BELLOT, T. *(Con.)*

pupil of Joseph Jordan, surgeon; M.R.C.S. 15 Feb. 1828, F.R.C.S. 6 Aug. 1844; assistant surgeon H.M. sloop Harrier 1831; surgeon R.N. 1835; surgeon H.M. flag ship Britannia Nov. 1854; author of translations of the *Aphorisms of Hippocrates and of Galen On the hand* 1850; *Sanscrit derivation of English words* 1856; arranged two collections of Chinese coins, one of which he presented to the Natural history society of Manchester; collected many ancient Chinese bronzes and a library of Chinese works. *d.* 37 Greek st. Stockport 25 June 1857. *Manchester school register iii,* 118 (1874); *Medical directory* (1858) 849–50.

BELMORE, GEORGE, stage name of George Belmore Garstin. Made his début in London at Marylebone theatre 26 Dec. 1856 as Bokes in *The Creole;* acted at Princess's and Drury Lane theatres; played Nat Gosling in Boucicault's drama *Flying Scud* at Holborn theatre more than 200 nights from 6 Oct. 1866; acted in the provinces and at Adelphi theatre where he played Newman Noggs in *Nicholas Nickleby* 20 March 1875 to July 1875; acted in New York Aug. to Oct. 1875. *(m.* 16 April 1862 Alice Maude dau. of Wm. Cooke proprietor of Astley's Amphitheatre). *d.* New York 15 Nov. 1875 aged 47. *Entr'acte* 27 *Nov.* 1875, *portrait.*

BELOE, CHARLES *(2 son of Rev. Wm. Beloe 1756–1817, Prebendary of St. Paul's).* A clerk in the London Twopenny post office; sec. to the Alfred club. *d.* Reading 23 Oct. 1855 aged 69.

BELPER, EDWARD STRUTT, 1 Baron *(only son of Wm. Strutt of St. Helen's house Derby, manufacturer 1756–1830).* *b.* Derby 26 Oct. 1801; ed. at Trin. coll. Cam.; B.A. 1823, M.A. 1826, L.L.D. 1862; M.P. for Derby 1830–1848 when unseated for bribery; M.P. for Arundel 1851–1852 and for Nottingham 1852–1856; chief comr. of railways 29 Aug. 1846 to March 1848; P.C. 30 Oct. 1846; sheriff of Notts. 1850; chancellor of Duchy of Lancaster 30 Dec. 1852 to 21 June 1854; chairman of Notts. quarter sessions 1855; created Baron Belper of Belper, county Derby 29 Aug. 1856; lord lieutenant of Notts. 6 Dec. 1864; pres. of Univ. coll. London 29 July 1871. *d.* 75 Eaton square, London 30 June 1880.

BELSHES, JOHN MURRAY. Captain 59 Foot 4 Sep 1812 to 25 May 1816 when placed on h.p.; L.G. 12 Nov. 1862. *d.* Inverary 12 Jany. 1863. *P. R. Drummond's Perthshire in bygone days* (1879) 81–85.

BELSON, GEORGE JOHN. Second lieutenant R.A. 29 Sep. 1804; lieut. col. 23 Nov. 1841 to 7 April 1842 when he retired on full pay; L.G. 27 Feb. 1866. *d.* Woolwich 22 April 1868 aged 80

BELT, THOMAS (*son of Mr. Belt of Newcastle, seedsman*). *b.* Newcastle 1832; member of Natural history society of Northumberland June 1850; went to Australia 1852; a mining engineer in London 1860; travelled all over Asia and America; superintendent of Nova Scotian gold company's mines in Nova Scotia 1863–65; examined the quartz rocks of North Wales; superintendent of the Chontales Gold mining company in Nicaragua 1868–72; travelled in Russia 1873–76; F.G.S.; author of *Mineral veins, an enquiry into their origin* 1861; *The naturalist in Nicaragua* 1874; *The glacial period in North America. d.* Denver, Colorado 21 Sep. 1878 in 46 year. *Natural history transactions of Northumberland vii*, 235–40 (1880).

BELZONI, SARAH. Remarkable for her size and strength; married in London about 1804 Giovanni Baptista Belzoni, acrobat, engineer and traveller who was *b.* Padua 1778 and *d.* at Gato, Benin, Africa 3 Dec. 1823; performed feats of strength with her husband in the streets, at fairs and at Astley's Amphitheatre; travelled in Egypt with him 1815–19; granted civil list pension of £100 6 Feb. 1851; author of *Account of the women of Egypt, Nubia and Syria. d.* Belozanne valley, Jersey 12 Jany. 1870 aged 87.

BENBEY, SADI OMBARK. Came to England with Mungo Park whom he taught Arabic language. *d.* 11 Feb. 1854 aged more than 80.

BENBOW, JOHN. Solicitor in London; M.P. for Dudley 8 Aug. 1844 to death. *d.* Hastings 24 Feb. 1855 aged 86.

BENDIGO. cognomen of WILLIAM THOMPSON (*son of Mr. Thompson of Nottingham, cabinet maker*). *b.* Nottingham 11 Oct. 1811, being one of 3 children at a birth; fought and beat Ben. Caunt 1 July 1835; beat Brassey (John Leechman) 24 May 1836; beat young Langan 24 Jany. 1837; beat Looney 13 June 1837; beaten by Ben. Caunt 3 April 1838; beat Deaf Burke at Heather, Leicestershire 12 Feb. 1839 in presence of 15000 persons; presented with a "Champion's belt" by James Ward at Queen's theatre, Liverpool; beat Ben. Caunt near Sutfield Green Oxon, 9 Sep. 1845 when they fought for £200 a side and the championship; fought Tom Paddock for £200 a side at Mildenhall 5 June 1850 when he won

again; a preacher and leader of revivalist services at the Cabmen's Mission hall, King's Cross, London. *d.* Beeston, Notts. 23 Aug. 1880. *H. D. Miles's Pugilistica iii*, 1–46 (1880), *portrait*; *J. Greenwoods Low life deeps* (1876) 86–94, *portrait*; *Rev. C. M. Davies's Unorthodox London 2 series* 156–64.

NOTE.—His curious name Bendigo was a contraction of Abednego, his first challenge in Bell's Life in London in 1835 is signed Abednego of Nottingham; the town of Bendigo in Victoria, Australia (since called Sandhurst) was named after him.

BENEDICT, SIR JULIUS (2 *son of M. Benedict of Stuttgart, banker*). *b.* Stuttgart 27 Nov. or 24 Dec. 1804; pupil of Hummel at Weimar and of Weber at Dresden; conductor at the Kärnthnerthor theatre Vienna 1823–25 and at the San Carlo and Fondo theatres Naples 1825–35; went to London 1835; conducted a series of Italian comic operas at Lyceum theatre 1836; conductor of English opera at Drury Lane 1838, where he produced *The gipsy's warning* 19 April 1838; *The brides of Venice* 22 *April* 1844, *and The Crusaders* 1846; travelled with Jenny Lind in the United States and Havannah and directed all her 122 concerts 1850–52; formed a choral society called The vocal association; conductor of Italian opera at Drury Lane and Her Majesty's theatres 1859–60; conducted the Norwich Musical Festivals 1845–78 where he produced *Undine* 1860, *Richard Cœur de Lion* 1863 and *St. Cecilia* 1866; conducted the Monday Popular Concerts; his best known opera *The Lily of Killarney* was produced at Covent Garden 8 Feb. 1862; conductor of Liverpool Philharmonic society 9 April 1867 to Feb. 1879; wrote for Birmingham musical festivals *St. Peter* 1870 and *Graziella* 1873; knighted at Windsor Castle 24 March 1871. *d.* 2 Manchester sq. London 5 June 1885. *I.L.N. lviii*, 377 (1871), *portrait*, *lxvi*, 494 (1875), *portrait*; *Scribner's Monthly xiii*, 480–84 (1877); *Graphic xxix*, 184 (1884), *portrait*.

BENETT, JOHN (2 *son of Thomas Benett of Pyt house Tisbury, Wilts. who d.* 16 *May* 1797 *aged* 68). *b.* 20 May 1773; sheriff of Wilts. 1798; M.P. for Wilts. 19 July 1819 to 3 Dec. 1832 and for South Wilts. 17 Dec. 1832 to 1 July 1852; author of some essays on agricultural subjects. *d.* Pyt house 1 Oct. 1852. *G.M. xxxviii*, 636–37 (1852).

BENHAM, JAMES ERLE. Ed. at St. Mary hall Ox.; student Middle Temple 20 Nov. 1875; author of *The student's guide to the preliminary examination for attorneys and solicitors* 1868;

BENHAM, J. E. *(Con.)*

edited *The preliminary examination Journal* 1871. *d.* Abercorn house, Baron's court, Kensington, London 11 July 1885 aged 34.

BENHAM, WILLIAM. Author of *English ballads for school reading* 1862; *St. Matthew, authorised version* 1862; *Epistles for the Christian year, with notes* 1864; *Companion to the Lectionary* 1873. *d.* 14 Arley hill, Bristol 16 Sep. 1885 aged 69.

BENIOWSKI, BARTHOLOMEW. Educ. at Ecole d'etat major of Paris 1832–33; major in Polish army; attempted to revolutionise art of printing by use of short words cast into one such as, and, but, the; teacher of memory at the Royal Adelaide gallery, Strand, London 1842; took out patents for machinery for printing and composing type 1846, 47 and 49; author of *Phrenotypics* 1842; *A French vocabulary* 1843; *The Anti-absurd or phrenotypic alphabet and orthography* 1844. *d.* 8 Bow st. Covent Garden 29 March 1867 aged 66.

BENISCH, ABRAHAM. *b.* Drosan, Bohemia 1811; ed. at Univ. of Vienna; settled in England 1841; edited the *Jewish Chronicle* 1854 to death; one of chief founders of Society of Hebrew Literature 1870, and of the Anglo Jewish Association 1871; author of *A translation of the Old Testament* 1851; *An essay on Colenso's criticism of the Pentateuch and Joshua* 1863; *Judaism surveyed* 1874. *d.* 13 Brownswood park, Green Lanes, London 31 July 1878.

BENJAMIN, GEORGE. *b.* Sussex 15 April 1799; went to Canada; founded the *Intelligencer* at Belleville 1834, edited it to 1848; member of legislative assembly Canada 1856–61; grand master of the Orangemen of British North America 1848; author of *Short lessons for members of Parliament compiled from English and other publications* 1862. *d.* Belleville 6 July or 7 Sep. 1864.

BENJAMIN, JUDAH PHILIP. *b.* St. Croix, West Indies 1811; ed. at Yale college, Connecticut 1825–28; called to the bar in New Orleans 16 Dec. 1832; member of firm of Slidell, Benjamin and Conrad 1840; counsellor of the supreme court New Orleans Dec. 1848; practised chiefly in Washington; a senator for Louisiana to the Senate 1852 to 4 Feb. 1861 when he withdrew, expelled the Senate 14 March 1861; attorney general of the Southern Confederacy Feb. 1861; acting secretary of war Aug. 1861 to Feb. 1862; sec. of state Feb. 1862 to April 1865 when the members of the cabinet left

BENJAMIN, J. P. *(Con.)*

Richmond; a student L.I. 13 Jany. 1866, called to bar at L.I. 6 June 1866, bencher 15 April 1875; Q.C. for county palatine of Lancaster July 1869; Q.C. with patent of precedence 29 July 1872; made £15,000 a year for several years; entertained on his retirement, at a banquet in hall of Inner Temple 30 June 1883; author of *Digest of decisions of supreme court of New Orleans* 1834; *Treatise of the law of sale of personal property* 1868, 3 ed. 1883. *d.* Avenue de Jena, Paris 6 May 1884. *J. Davis's Rise and Fall of the Confederate government i,* 242 (1881), *portrait; Law Journal* (1883) 100–103; *I.L.N. lxxx* 465 (1884), *portrait; Graphic xxix,* 484 (1884), *portrait.*

BENN, ANTHONY. *b.* 1814; 2 lieut. R.A. 20 Dec. 1832; col. 27 June 1864 to 6 March 1868; M.G. 6 March 1868. *d.* Plumstead 22 Dec. 1875.

BENN, EDWARD *(son of John Benn of Belfast, brewer* 1767–1853). *b.* 1798; purchased with his brother George, an estate at Glenravel near Ballymena where they tried to create a new industry by manufacture of potato spirit; formed a fine archæological collection now in the Belfast Museum; contributed papers to Irish antiquarian journals; founded 3 hospitals in Belfast, the Eye Ear and Throat, the Samaritan and the Skin Diseases. *d.* 1874.

BENN, GEORGE *(brother of the preceding). b.* Tanderagee co. Armagh 1 Jany. 1801; entered Belfast Academical institution 1816; took gold medals in logic 1817 and moral philosophy 1818; author of *The history of the town of Belfast* [*anon.*] 1823; *A history of the town of Belfast* 2 vols. 1877–80. *d.* 8 Jany. 1882.

BENN, PIERCY. *b.* 1800; 2 lieut. R.A. 3 Feb. 1821; col. 7 June 1856 to 16 July 1862; M.G. 16 July 1862. *d.* Farringdon, Hants. 17 June 1876.

BENNETT, CHARLES FOX, formerly of Clifton, Bristol, late premier of Newfoundland. *d.* St. John's, Newfoundland 5 Dec. 1883.

BENNETT, CHARLES HENRY. Draughtsman on wood; contributed sketches signed in the corner with the figure of an owl to *Diogenes* comic weekly paper 1853 and portraits of members of Parliament to *Illustrated Times;* contributed sketches to *Fun* down to 1866 and to *Punch* 1866 to death; published *Fables of Æsop and others translated into human nature* 1858; *Proverbs with pictures* 1858; *London people sketched from life* 1863; *Adventures of Young Munchausen* 1864. *d.* Caversham road, Kentish Town 2 April 1867 in 38 year. *Punch* 13 *April* 1867 *p.* 151.

BENNETT, GEORGE (2 *son of John Bennett, Judge of Irish court of King's Bench who d.* 25 *Dec.* 1791). *b.* Cork 20 Sep. 1777; called to Irish bar 1800; went Munster circuit; K.C. 18 Feb. 1822; crown prosecutor for Munster circuit Feb. 1832; bencher of King's Inns Dublin 1836, retired about 1849. *d.* Sodylt hall, Shropshire 26 May 1856. *Dublin univ. mag. xxxiv,* 526–32 (1849), *portrait.*

BENNETT, GEORGE JOHN *(son of George Bennett of Norwich, comedian).* *b.* Ripon 9 March 1800; served in the navy 1813–17; first appeared on the stage at Lynn 1818, and in London at Covent Garden 27 Jany. 1823 as Richard iii; acted at Covent Garden 1830–38, at Drury Lane 1841–43 and at Sadler's Wells 27 May 1844 to 15 March 1862 when he left the stage, his best parts were Bossola in the *Duchess of Malfi,* and Caliban in *The Tempest;* author of a five act play called *Retribution or love's trials* produced at Sadlers Wells 11 Feb. 1850, and of a drama called *The Justice* produced at Birmingham. *d.* Edmonton 21 Sep. 1879. *Theatrical times i,* 241 (1847), *portrait; Tallis's Drawing room table book, parts* 8, 10, 17 *and* 21, 4 *portraits; The Players iv,* 17 (1861), *portrait.*

BENNETT, JAMES. *b.* Falfield, Thornbury, Gloucs. 10 May 1785; apprenticed to George Robbins of Bath, printer; printer and bookseller in Tewkesbury 1810–52; published *History of Tewkesbury* 1830; *Tewkesbury Register and Magazine* 1830–49. *d.* Tewkesbury 29 Jany. 1856.

BENNETT, REV. JAMES. *b.* London 22 May 1774; preached his first sermon 24 Dec. 1792; Congregational minister at Romsey Feb. 1796; ordained 5 April 1797; theological tutor and pastor at Rotherham 22 Aug. 1813; pastor of Silver st. church, London Nov. 1828, and of Falcon sq. church, London 1843 to Nov. 1860; one of foreign secs. to London Missionary society May 1830 to 1832; chairman of Congregational Board 1840; author of *Lectures on preaching of Christ* 1836; *Lectures on Acts of the Apostles* 1846; author with Rev. David Bogue of *History of dissenters from the Revolution in* 1688 *to the year* 1808 4 *vols.* 1808, 2 *ed.* 3 *vols.* 1833; wrote much in the *Eclectic Review* and *Evangelical Mag. d.* 49 Gibson sq. Islington 4 Dec. 1862. *Memorials of the late Rev. James Bennett* 1863.

BENNETT, JAMES. Member of company of T.R. Birmingham many years; made his début in London at Lyceum theatre 18 March 1859 as Iago in *Othello;* acted in the provinces. *d.* London 9 March 1885. *Tallis's Drawing room table book* (1851) 41, *portrait.*

BENNETT, JAMES GORDON. *b.* New Mill, Keith, Banffshire 1 Sep. 1800; went to Halifax, Nova Scotia 1819; a printer's reader, bookseller's clerk and assistant in a newspaper office at Boston; went to New York about 1822; started the *New York Globe* Oct. 1832 a two cent paper which lived only 30 days; partner with Messrs. Anderson and Smith of New York, printers 1835; founded the *New York Herald* a one cent daily paper 6 May 1835 all of which he wrote; in 1841 the circulation was 20,000 and the receipts 100,000 dollars, during the civil war its circulation doubled; sent Henry M. Stanley to Central Africa in search of Dr. Livingstone at cost of £10,000 in 1871. (*m.* 6 June 1840 Henrietta Agnes Crean, she *d.* 31 March 1873). *d.* New York 1 June 1872. *Memoir of J. G. Bennett by a Journalist* 1855, *portrait; F. Hudson's Journalism in the United States* 1873; *J. Parton's Famous Americans of recent times* (1867) 259–305; *Democratic Review xxxi,* 409–19 1853, *portrait; C. F. Wingate's Views and interviews* (1875) 275–86; *Graphic v,* 600, 611 (1872), *portrait.*

BENNETT, JOHN HUGHES. *b.* London 31 Aug. 1812; ed. at Exeter gr. sch. and Univ. of Edin., M.D. 1837, LL.D. Aug. 1875; founded in Paris the Parisian Medical Society 1837, pres. 1837; pathologist to Royal infirmary Edin. 1843; discovered a remarkable disease of the blood which he called Leucocythemia or white cell blood 1845; editor of *Edinburgh Monthly Journal of medical science* 1846; professor of Institutes of medicine in Univ. of Edin. July 1848 to July 1874; F.R.S. Edin. 1842, F.R.C.P. Edin. 1842; author of *An introduction to clinical medicine* 1849, 4 *ed.* 1862; *The pathology and treatment of pulmonary tuberculosis* 1853, 2 *ed.* 1859; *Clinical lectures on principles and practice of medicine* 1852, 5 *ed.* 1868 which was translated into French, Russian and Hindoo. *d.* The Wilderness, Bracondale, Norwich 25 Sep. 1875. *bur.* Dean cemetery Edin. 30 Sep. *Edinburgh Medical Journal xxi,* 466–74 (1875); *British Medical Journal ii,* 473–78 (1875).

BENNETT, JOHN JOSEPH. *b.* Tottenham 8 Jany. 1801; ed. at Enfield and at Middlesex hospital; assistant keeper of the Banksian herbarium and library British Museum Nov.

BENNETT, J. J. *(Con.)*

1827, keeper 1828-70; F.L.S. 1828, sec. 1840-60; F.R.S. 16 Dec. 1841; wrote part of T. Horsfield's *Plantæ Javanicæ Rariores* 1852—53. *d.* Maresfield, Sussex 29 Feb. 1876; bust by Weekes in botanical department British Museum. *Journal of botany British and Foreign v,* 97-105 (1876), *portrait.*

BENNETT, SAMUEL. *b.* Cornwall 20 March 1815; went to Sydney 1841; superintendent of a printing office there 1842-59; purchased with Wm. Hanson the *Empire* newspaper 1859, conducted it as a daily and weekly paper; started the *Evening News* 29 July 1867, the *Australian town and country journal* 8 Jany. 1870; author of *The history of Australian discovery and colonisation* 1867. *d.* Mundarrah towers, Little Coogee, Sydney 2 June 1878.

BENNETT, SAMUEL JAMES. Founder of the Mercantile Association; founded the *Commercial Gazette* weekly paper 1853. *d.* The Firs, Staplecross, Sussex 23 May 1881.

BENNETT, THOMAS. *b.* Hereford 22 Feb. 1785; captain R.N. 16 Sep. 1828; commodore on North America and West India station 7 Feb. 1848 to 29 April 1851; granted a service pension 2 Nov. 1863; admiral on h.p. 12 Sep. 1865; mayor of Hereford 1842. *d.* Broomy hill, Hereford 12 June 1870.

BENNETT, THOMAS RANDLE *(youngest son of John Bennett of Manchester, timber merchant). b.* Manchester 1821; ed. at the gr. sch. and Ch. Ch. Ox., B.A. 1843, M.A. 1846, special pleader 1848; barrister I.T. 17 Nov. 1855; lectured on law and history at London Working men's college Bloomsbury; an original member of English Church Union 1859, one of its central council; examiner to the Inns of Court 1877-78; author of *A popular manual of the constitutional history of England* 1862 and of several political pamphlets. *d.* Shrewbridge hall, Nantwich 23 Feb. 1885. *Law Times lxxviii,* 343 (1885).

BENNETT, WILLIAM. *b.* Newmarket; enlisted into Cambridge militia 10 Oct. 1797 aged 20; enlisted into 46 Foot 18 March 1799, and into 32 Foot 15 June 1803, discharged 18 Aug. 1814; assisted at burial of Sir John Moore Jany. 1809. *d.* Inchicore, Ireland 23 Jany. 1872 aged 95, but generally reputed to be 105. *W. J. Thoms's Human longevity* (1873) 235-36.

BENNETT, WILLIAM. *b.* 1798; made his début in London at Haymarket theatre as Jack Junk in *The birthday* 15 May 1812; member of English opera company; played old men at Drury Lane about 1829; secretary to Drury Lane theatrical fund. *d.* Bellevue cottage, Walthamstow 8 Aug. 1875. *The Oddfellow i,* 77 (1839), *portrait.*

BENNETT, WILLIAM. *b.* 1796; solicitor at Chapel en le Frith, Derbyshire 1819 to death; clerk to county magistrates 1834 to death; author under pseudonym of Lee Gibbons of *The Cavalier* 3 *vols.* 1821; *Malpas* 3 *vols.* 1822; *The King of the Peak* 3 *vols.* 1823; *Owain Goch a tale of the Revolution* 3 *vols.* 1827; these books are also attributed to Thomas Roscoe jun.; contributed to the *Reliquary* many papers on archæology of Derbyshire 1862-72. *d.* Chapel en le Frith 20 April 1879.

BENNETT, WILLIAM MINEARD. *b.* Exeter 1778; pupil of Sir Thomas Lawrence; a painter of portraits and miniatures; exhibited at the R.A. 1812-16 and 1834-35; lived many years in Paris; lived at Exeter 1844 to death; composed many glees and songs which were popular in Paris and Naples. *d.* Hill's buildings, St. Sidwell's, Exeter 17 Oct. 1858.

BENNETT, SIR WILLIAM STERNDALE *(youngest child of Robert Bennett of Sheffield, organist of the parish church who d. 3 Nov.* 1819*). b.* 8 Norfolk Row, Sheffield 13 April 1816; ed. at Royal Academy of Music, London 1826-36, and at Leipsic 1836-37; member of Royal Society of Musicians 1838; taught music in London; founded the Bach Society 1849; professor of music at Univ. of Cam. 4 March 1856; Mus. Doc. Cam. 1856, M.A. 1867; D.C.L. Ox. 1870; a life member of St. John's coll. Cam. 26 Sep. 1856; conductor of Philharmonic Society concerts 1856-68, Beethoven gold medallist 7 July 1867; principal of Royal Academy of Music 22 June 1866 to death; knighted at Windsor Castle 24 March 1871; composed *The Naiads,* overture produced at Society of British Musicians 25 Jany. 1837; *The wood nymphs,* overture produced at the Gewandhaus concerts Leipzig 24 Jany. 1839; *The May Queen,* pastoral produced at Leeds musical festival 8 Sep. 1858; *The woman of Samaria,* oratorio produced at Birmingham musical festival 27 Aug. 1867. (*m.* 9 April 1844 Mary Anne only dau. of James Wood, commander R.N., she *d.* 17 Oct. 1862 aged 37.) *d.* 66 St. John's Wood road London 1 Feb. 1875. *bur.* north aisle of choir Westminster Abbey 6 Feb.

BENNETT, SIR W. S. *(Con.)*

Grove's Dictionary of music i, 224–29 (1879); *W. A. Barrett's English Church composers* (1882) 163–65; *Academy vii*, 154, 179, 388, 466 (1875); *I. L. N. xl*, 551 (1862), *portrait, lxvi*, 152, 326 (1875), *portrait.*

BENNIS, GEORGE GEARY. *b.* Corkamore, Limerick 1790 or 1793; a grocer at Limerick; settled at Liverpool where he became a Quaker; went to Paris 1823; director of a libraire des étrangers in Paris 1830–36; an insurance agent and librarian to the British embassy, Paris; edited *Galignani's Messenger;* chevalier of the Legion d' Honneur 1854; author of *The principles of the one faith professed by all Christians, Liverpool* 1816, 3 ed. Paris 1826; *Traveller's pocket diary and Student's journal; Treatise on life assurance. d.* Paris 1 Jany. 1866, left over 10,000 volumes to found a free library at Limerick. *J. Smith's A descriptive catalogue of Friends books i*, 246 (1867).

BENSON, CHARLES. Ed. at Trin. coll. Dublin, scholar 1818, B.A. 1819, M.A. and M.B. 1822, M.D. 1840; L.R.C.S. Ireland 1821, F.R.C.S. 1825, pres. 1854; professor of practice of medicine in school attached to the college; M.R.I.A. 30 Nov. 1825; physician to City of Dublin hospital; contributed 4 articles to *Todd's Cyclopædia of anatomy* and a course of lectures on the Diseases of the digestive organs to *Dublin Medical Press* 1840–42. *d.* 42 Fitzwilliam sq. Dublin 21 Jany. 1880 in 83 year.

BENSON, REV. CHRISTOPHER *(son of Thomas Benson of Cockermouth, solicitor). b.* Cockermouth 1788; ed. at Trin. coll. Cam., scholar, B.A. 1809, M.A. 1815; select preacher 1817; Hulsean lecturer (the first) 1820–22; fellow of Magd. coll. Cam. 1820; preb. of Worcester cathedral 27 Dec. 1825 to death; R. of St. Giles's-in-the-Fields, London 1824–26; V. of Cropthorne, Worcs 1826–40; master of the Temple London 1827–45; author of *Discourses on powers of the clergy* 1841; *Baptism and baptismal regeneration* 1843. *d.* Woodfield, Ross, Hereford 25 March 1868. *The living and the dead by a country curate (Rev. E. Neale)* 1827 *pp.* 81–98; *E. M. Roose's Ecclesiastica* (1842) 413–15.

BENSON, SIR JOHN *(only son of John Benson of Collooney, co. Sligo). b.* Collooney 1812; architect and civil engineer; county surveyor to east riding of co. Cork 8 April 1846; surveyor of city of Cork 29 Jany. 1851; architect and builder of Dublin exhibition 12 Aug. 1852 which was opened 12 May 1853,

BENSON, SIR J. *(Con.)*

knighted by Earl of St. Germans at the opening; engineer of Cork waterworks which cost £80,000; built 48 bridges in co. Cork; M.I.C.E. 4 March 1862. *d.* 15 Alexander sq. Brompton London 17 Oct. 1874. *Min. of Proc. of Instit. of C.E. xl*, 251–53 (1875).

BENSON, RICHARD. Entered Bengal army 1805; colonel 11 Bengal N.I. 16 July 1849 to death; C.B. 3 April 1846; M.G. 28 Nov. 1854. *d.* at his residence on lake of Buttermere, Cumberland 26 Aug. 1858.

BENSON, REV. SAMUEL. Ed. at St. John's coll. Cam.; B.A. 1823, M.A. 1826; lecturer at St. John's Horsleydown 1823–33; chaplain of Horsemonger lane gaol 1833–43; V. of St. Saviour's Southwark 1868 to death; author of several sermons and tracts. *d.* 34 Borough high st. London 22 Feb. 1881 aged 82. *I. L. N. xxiv*, 401 (1854), *portrait.*

BENT, JEFFERY HART *(eld. son of Robert Bent of Lancashire).* Ed. at Trin. coll. Cam., B.A. 1804, M.A. 1807; barrister M.T. 7 Feb. 1806; chief justice of New South Wales 1814, of Grenada 1820 to 1833, of St. Lucia 1833 to 1836 and of British Guiana 1836 to death. *d.* George Town Demerara 29 June 1852 aged 72. *I.L.N. xxi*, 155 (1852).

BENT, SIR JOHN *(eld. son of Wm. Bent of Stoneyfield near Newcastle under Lyne). b.* Newcastle under Lyne 1793; ed. at Newcastle gr. sch.; a large brewer at Liverpool; alderman of Liverpool, mayor 1850–51; knighted by the Queen at Liverpool 9 Oct. 1851. *d.* Edge hill near Liverpool 13 Aug. 1857.

BENT, JOHN. Assistant surgeon in the army 11 Sep. 1838; served in the Crimea 30 April 1855 to end of the war; deputy surgeon general 28 Jany. 1862; surgeon general 11 July 1874 to death. *d.* The Camp Aldershot 23 Nov. 1874 aged 57.

BENT, ROBERT *(son of Wm. Bent who founded Bent's Literary Advertiser* 1802). Edited *The London Catalogue of books* 1839. *d.* 6 Dec. 1859.

BENTHAM, GEORGE. *b.* June 1787; entered navy 1795; captain 16 Sep. 1816; retired V.A. 9 July 1857; knight of Sardinian order of St. Maurice and St. Lazare. *d.* Barton fields, Canterbury 24 Feb. 1862.

BENTHAM, GEORGE (2 *son of Sir Samuel Bentham, naval architect* 1757–1831). *b.* Stoke near Plymouth 22 Sep. 1800; lived in France 1814–26; managed his father's estate of

BENTHAM, G. *(Con.)*

2000 acres near Montpellier; student at Lincoln's Inn; worked for his uncle Jeremy Bentham 1826-32; F.L.S. 1828, vice pres. 1858, pres. 1861-74: hon. sec. of Horticultural Society 1829-40 which he raised to a flourishing condition; presented his collections and books valued at £6,000 to Kew Gardens 1854; F.R.S. 5 June 1862, royal medallist 1859; LL.D. Cambridge 4 June 1874; C.M.G. 1878; author of *Outlines of a new system of logic* 1827 which set forth for the first time doctrine of quantification of the predicate, the most fruitful discovery in abstract logical science since Aristotle; *Handbook of the British flora* 1858, 2 vols. 1865; *Flora Hong-Kongensis* 1861; *Flora Australiensis* 7 vols. 1863-78; author with Sir Joseph Hooker of *Genera Plantarum*, 6 parts in 3 vols. 1862-83 which marks an epoch in botany. *d.* 25 Wilton place, London 10 Sep. 1884. *Nature xxx*, 539-43 (1884); *G. C. Wallich's Eminent men of the day* (1870), *portrait.*

BENTINCK, ADOLPHE BARON VON. Secretary of legation for the Netherlands at Copenhagen, Stockholm, Berlin and Vienna successively; councillor of the legation in London 7 years; envoy extraord. and minister plenipo. in London 25 Aug. 1851 to death. *d.* 26 Eaton sq. London 2 March 1868 aged 70.

BENTINCK, ARTHUR CAVENDISH. *b.* 9 May 1819; ensign 84 Foot 2 Nov. 1838; lieut. col. 7 Dragoon guards 8 Dec. 1854 and 4 Dragoon guards 30 Aug. 1859 to 30 May 1862 when placed on h.p.; L.G. 1 Oct. 1877; *d.* Thomas's hotel, 25 Berkely sq. London 11 Dec. 1877.

BENTINCK, CHARLES ANTHONY FERDINAND. *b.* 4 March 1792; ensign Coldstream guards 16 Nov. 1808, lieut. col. 9 Nov. 1846 to 25 April 1848 when placed on h.p.; colonel 12 Foot 14 April 1857 to death; L.G. 15 Jany. 1858. *d.* Bergheim in principality of Waldeck 28 Oct. 1864.

BENTINCK, SIR HENRY JOHN WILLIAM *(youngest son of Major general John Charles Bentinck 1763-1833).* *b.* 8 Sep. 1796; ensign Coldstream guards 25 March 1813, lieut. col. 22 Aug. 1851 to 20 June 1854; aide de camp to the Queen 23 Nov. 1841 to 20 June 1854; commanded the brigade of Guards in the Crimea 22 Feb. to 8 Nov. 1854 and the fourth division 1 June to 10 Oct. 1855; colonel 28 Foot 11 Oct. 1854 to death; K.C.B. 5 July 1855; groom in waiting to the Queen Nov. 1859 to June 1867; general 8 Dec. 1867. *d.* 35 Grosvenor st. London 29 Sep. 1878.

BENTINCK, HENRY WILLIAM CAVENDISH *(youngest son of 4 Duke of Portland 1768-1854).* *b.* 9 June 1804; ed. at Ch. Ch. Ox.; M.P. for North Notts. 6 March 1846 to 21 March 1857; invented the call for trumps at whist, known as Blue Peter, at Graham's club house 87 St. James's st. about 1836, an explanation of which first appeared in print in *The laws and practice of whist by Cœlebs, M.A. [E. A. Curlyon],* 2 ed. 1856; master of the Rufford hounds 1835-36, of the Burton hounds 1842-64, when he sold the pack for £3,500, had over 100 horses in his stable at one time. *d.* Tathwell hall near Louth 31 Dec. 1870. *Baily's Mag. xix,* 288-93 (1871).

BENTINCK, VENERABLE WILLIAM HARRY EDWARD. *(elder son of Lord Edward Charles Bentinck 1744-1819).* *b.* 2 Feb. 1784; ed. at Westminster and Ch. Ch. Ox.; B.A. 1805, M.A. 1808; R. of Sigglesthorne near Hull 1808 to death; Canon of Westminster 7 Oct. 1809 to 1864 and Archdeacon 1854-64; rural dean 1842 to death; built at his own expense church of Holy Trinity, Vauxhall bridge 1852. *d.* Sigglesthorne rectory 29 Sep. 1868. *I.L.N. xxiv,* 401 (1854), *portrait.*

BENTLEY, CHARLES. Member of the old watercolor Society 1844; painted many pictures chiefly of coast and river scenery, four of which are in the South Kensington Museum. *d.* of cholera at Mornington place London 4 Sep. 1854 aged 48.

BENTLEY, EDWARD *(eld. son of John Bentley 1786-1860).* *b.* 31 Dec. 1817; an operative chemist; gained credit for his method of obtaining the more powerful vegetable preparations for medical use; studied at Guy's Hospital; L.R.C.P. 1845; M.D. St. Andrews 1845; very instrumental in founding City of London hospital for diseases of the chest 1848; hon. sec. to Pathological Society of London. *d.* 8 St. Thomas sq. Hackney 2 Feb. 1861.

BENTLEY, JAMES. *b.* 1785; purchased Wood Green park, Cheshunt, Herts 1839 and the manor of the rectory of Cheshunt 1855; sheriff of Herts 1860; treasurer of St. Bartholomew's hospital 1841-55. *d.* Wood Green park 26 Oct. 1880 in 96 year.

BENTLEY, JOHN *(son of Edward Bentley, principal of accountants office bank of England who d. 24 July 1838 aged 85).* *b.* 12 Nov. 1786; ed. at St. Paul's school; secretary to Bank of England 1850-60. *d.* Park crescent, Brighton 20 Dec. 1860.

BENTLEY, JOSEPH. Lecturer and writer on education; promoted two assurance companies 1855-56; author of *Manual of life insurance* 1862; *Financial position of life offices* 1865. *d.* Feb. 1872 aged 67.

BENTLEY, JOSEPH CLAYTON. *b.* Bradford, Yorkshire 1809; a landscape painter; went to London 1832; exhibited landscapes chiefly views in Yorkshire at Royal Academy and other exhibitions; a line engraver; executed many plates for publications of Messrs. Fisher and Messrs. Virtue especially for the *Gems of European Art 2 vols.* 1847; some of his best works are in the Vernon Gallery at the National Gallery. *d.* Sydenham, Kent 9 Oct. 1851.

BENTLEY, RICHARD *(brother of John Bentley 1786-1860).* *b.* Oct. 1794; ed. at St. Paul's sch.; publisher with his brother Samuel in Salisbury st. Fleet st. Jany. 1819 to 1829; publisher with Henry Colburn 1829-32; started *Bentley's Miscellany* 1837; founded with George Smythe and the Young England party a newspaper called *Young England* Jany. 1845 which collapsed April 1845; started with John Douglas Cook *Bentley's Quarterly Review* 1859 of which only 4 numbers appeared; published *Standard Novels* 127 volumes the copyright and stock of which he sold 27 Feb 1856 for £11,000; publisher in ordinary to the Queen 1838 to death. *d.* Ramsgate 10 Sep. 1871. *Graphic iv, 375, 381 (1871), portrait.*

BENTLEY, SAMUEL *(brother of the preceding).* *b.* 10 May 1785; ed. at St. Paul's school; apprenticed to John Nichols, printer and publisher; partner in firm of Nichols, Son and Bentley April 1812 to Dec. 1818; publisher with his brother Richard Jany. 1819 to 1829; carried on business at Bangor house, Shoe lane under firm of Samuel and John Bentley, Wilson and Fley 1829 to April 1853 when he retired; an antiquary, musician and artist; edited the *Concio de puero Jesu of Erasmus* 1816; author of *Excerpta Historica* 1831; indexed *Nichols's Literary anecdotes* and *Surtees's History of Durham. d.* Croydon 13 April 1868. *G.M. i, 127 (1868).*

BENTLEY, WILLIAM *(brother of the preceding).* *b.* 1788; ed. at St. Paul's school; principal of the Bank stock office, Bank of England; master of the Leathersellers Company 1857-58. *d.* Colfe lodge, Lewisham 28 Jany. 1877.

BENTON, MARY *(dau. of Ralph Lodge).* *b.* Raby Moor house near Keverstone, Durham 12 Feb. 1751. *(m.* John Benton of Long-

BENTON, M. *(Con.)*

newton, butcher). Lived at hamlet of Elton near Stockton on Tees many years. *d.* Elton 7 Jany. 1853 aged 102. *I.L.N. xviii,* 324 (1851), *portrait.*

BEOR, HENRY ROGERS *(4 son of Richard White Beor of Swansea).* Barrister M.T. 26 Jany. 1870; admitted to Queensland bar 7 Dec. 1875; member of Queensland parliament for Bowen; attorney general for Queensland 1880. *d.* on his voyage from Sydney to Auckland 25 Dec. 1880.

BERE, MONTAGU BAKER. *b.* 15 July 1798; barrister L.I. 21 June 1825; commissioner of Court of bankruptcy at Leeds 21 Oct. 1842 to 1844 and at Exeter 1844 to death. *d.* Barley near Exeter 13 Dec. 1858.

BERENS, VENERABLE EDWARD *(son of Joseph Berens of Hextable, Kent).* Matric. from Ch. Ch. Ox. 17 Jany. 1794 aged 17; B.A. 1798, M.A. 1801; fellow of Oriel coll.; V. of Shrivenham, Berks. 1804 to death; R. of Englefield, Berks. 1818-55; Preb. of Salisbury 23 Oct. 1829 to death; archdeacon of Berks. 7 Sep. 1832 to 1855; author of *A discourse on parochial psalmody* 1825; *Advice to a young man upon first going to Oxford* 1832, 6 ed. 1853; *The history of the Prayer Book of the Church of England* 1839, 2 ed. 1854; *A memoir of the life of Bishop Mant* 1849; *Lectures on the Liturgy* 1850 *and other books. d.* Shrivenham vicarage 7 April 1859.

BERENS, HENRY HULSE *(son of Joseph Berens of Kevington, Kent).* *b.* 1804; deputy chairman of Public works loan office 1849-52; a director of Bank of England many years. *d.* Sidcup, Kent 23 Aug. 1883 aged 78.

BERENS, OTTO ALEXANDER. Linen draper in St. Paul's churchyard, London; originated the fancy trade; moved to Cannon st. 1854. *d.* Raleigh hall, Brixton-rise London 15 April 1860 aged 63.

BERESFORD, WILLIAM CARR BERESFORD, 1 Viscount *(natural son of George de la Poer Beresford, 1 Marquis of Waterford 1735-1800).* *b.* Ireland 2 Oct. 1768; ed. at Strassburg; ensign 6 Foot 27 Aug. 1785; lieut. col. of 124 or Waterford Foot (a regiment raised by his father) 11 Aug. 1794; lieut. col. 88 Foot 1 Sep. 1795 to 9 Feb. 1807; commanded first brigade in Egypt June 1801 to 1802 and first brigade at Cape of Good Hope 1806; captured Buenos Ayres 27 June 1806 but lost it 12 Aug.; colonel 88 Foot 9 Feb. 1807 to 11 March 1819; governor of Madeira 24

BERESFORD, VISCOUNT. (Con.)

Dec. 1807 to July 1808; marshal commanding Portugese army 1 March 1809 to 1819; captain general of Spain 1811; commander in chief at battle of Albuera 16 May 1811; voted the thanks of Parliament 7 June 1811; received a cross with 7 clasps for 12 actions July 1815; governor of Jersey 29 Jany. 1820 to death; col. 69 Foot 11 March 1819 to 15 March 1823; col. 16 Foot 15 March 1823 to death; lieutenant general of the ordnance 8 Feb. 1823 to 3 May 1824, master general 29 Jany. 1828 to 22 Nov. 1830; general 27 May 1825; col. in chief 60 Rifles 23 Sep. 1852 to death; K.C.B. 18 Oct. 1810, G.C.B. 2 Jany. 1815; knighted at Whitehall 23 Oct. 1810; Conde de Trancoso in peerage of Portugal 1810; Duke of Elvas in peerage of Spain; M.P. for co. Waterford 28 June 1811 to 17 May 1814 but never took his seat; created Baron Beresford of Albuera and Dungarvan, co. Waterford 17 May 1814; G.C.H. 1818; P.C. 6 Feb. 1821; created Viscount Beresford of Beresford, co. Stafford 22 April 1823. d. Bedgebury park, Goudhurst Kent 8 Jany. 1854. *J. W. Cole's Memoirs of British generals i*, 165–217 (1856); *W. C. Taylor's National portrait gallery iv*, 96 (1848), *portrait; I.L.N. xxi*, 545 (1852), *portrait, xxiv* 38, 58 (1854), *portrait; Napier's Peninsular War vol. iii.*

BERESFORD, DENIS WILLIAM PACK. *b.* London 7 July 1810; M.P. for co. Carlow 7 Aug. 1862 to 11 Nov. 1868. *d.* 28 Dec. 1881.

BERESFORD, SIR GEORGE DE LA POER, 2 Baronet. *b.* 1 March 1811; M.P. for Athlone 8 July 1841 to 13 June 1842; succeeded 2 Oct. 1844. *d.* Glasgow 11 Feb. 1873.

BERESFORD, MOST REV. JOHN GEORGE (2 *son of George Beresford, 1 Marquis of Waterford 1735–1800). b.* Tyrone house, Dublin 22 Nov. 1773; ed. at Eton and Ch. Ch. Ox., B.A. 1793, M.A. 1796, D.D. 1805; ordained deacon 1795, priest 1797; R. of Clonegam and Newtown Lenan; dean of Clogher 23 Dec. 1799; R. of Termonmaguirk 1801; bishop of Cork and Ross 20 Feb. 1805; consecrated 24 March 1805; translated to Raphoe 10 Aug. 1807; translated to Clogher 25 Sep. 1819; created Archbishop of Dublin 21 April 1820; enthroned 6 May 1820; P.C. Ireland 23 May 1820; archbishop of Armagh and primate of all Ireland 17 June 1822; vice chancellor of Univ. of Dublin 1829, chancellor 19 Nov. 1851; founded the chair of Ecclesiastical history 1853; gave £6000 to college of St. Columba; restored Armagh

BERESFORD, MOST REV. J. G. (Con.)

cathedral at expense of nearly £30,000. *d.* Woburn near Donaghadee 18 July 1862. *bur.* in crypt of Armagh cathedral 30 July. *Creasy's Memoirs of eminent Etonians new ed.* 1876, 568–89; *I.L.N. xli*, 128, 138 (1862), *portrait; Dublin Univ. Mag. xvi*, 86–89 (1840), *portrait.*

NOTE.—He presided over the church in Ireland for 40 years, a longer period than any primate for nearly 1000 years; on completing the 50th year of his episcopate, 29 March 1855 he received an address of congratulation signed by all the Irish bishops and by 1980 out of the entire body of 2100 Irish clergy.

BERESFORD, MARCUS (2 *son of Hon. George Beresford 1776–1842). b.* 28 July 1800; 2 lieut. 21 Foot 4 Sep. 1817; lieut. col. 3 Foot 25 Dec. 1835 to 13 May 1842 when placed on h.p.; colonel 20 Foot 22 Sep. 1858 to death; general 4 March 1866. *d.* Leamington 16 March 1876.

BERESFORD, WILLIAM *(younger son of Marcus Beresford 1764–97, M.P. for Dungarvan). b.* 17 April 1797; ed. at Eton and St. Mary's hall Ox., B.A. 1819, M.A. 1824; captain 12 Lancers 6 April 1826 to 16 July 1830 when placed on h.p.; served in Portugal 1827; master of the Tennis Court, Hampton Court 1823 to death; contested Waterford 1837; M.P. for Harwich 1841–1847 and for North Essex 1847–65; secretary at war 28 Feb. 1852 to Dec. 1852; P.C. 27 Feb. 1852. *d.* Eccleston sq. London 6 Oct. 1883. *I.L.N. xx*, 267 (1852), *portrait.*

BERGENROTH, GUSTAVE ADOLPH. *b.* Oletzko, East Prussia 26 Feb. 1813; ed. at Univ. of Königsberg 1833–36; assessor to the high court at Berlin 1843 and 1846–49; studied English history in London 1857–60; examined the Spanish Archives at Simancas, Spain Aug. 1860 to death, deciphering more than 12 ciphers of exceeding difficulty; author of *Calendar of letters, despatches and state papers relating to the negotiations between England and Spain 1485–1525*, 3 vols. 1862–68. *d.* Fonda de los Principes, Puerta del Sol, Madrid 13 Feb. 1869. *W C. Cartwright's G. Bergenroth a memorial sketch* 1870.

BERGER, GEORGE. *b.* London; a journeyman compositor; wholesale newsagent and bookseller in Holywell st. Strand 1834; the largest retailer of papers and periodicals in London; publisher in Newcastle st. Strand 1864 to death. *d.* Friern house, Finchley 1 Feb. 1868 aged 72.

BERGNE, John Brodribb. *b.* Kensington, London 1800; clerk in the Foreign Office 1815 to death; superintendent of treaty department 1 July 1854 to 1 Dec. 1870 when foreign office agencies were abolished; member of commission to revise Slave trade instructions 1865; an original member of Numismatic Society 1837, treasurer July 1843 to 1857; contributed 16 papers to *Numismatic Chronicle;* F.S.A. 1844; made a fine collection of coins which was sold at Sotheby's in an 11 day sale May 1873 for above £6000. *d.* 21 Thurloe sq. London 16 Jany. 1873. *Numismatic Chronicle xiii,* 13–15, 304–308 (1873).

BERKELEY, Thomas Moreton Fitzhardinge Berkeley, 6 Earl of. *b.* 19 Oct. 1796; ed. at C. C. coll. Ox.; succeeded 8 Aug. 1810, but never assumed the title or took his seat in House of Lords though he received usual summons to do so. *d.* Hartington lane, Cranford, Hounslow 27 Aug. 1882.

BERKELEY, Charles Assheton Fitzhardinge. *b.* 10 Oct. 1818; ensign 11 Foot 27 May 1836; lieut. col. 32 Foot 24 July 1857 to death; C.B. 24 March 1858. *d.* on board the "Simla" off the island of Socotra 25 Sep. 1858.

BERKELEY, Craven Fitzhardinge *(brother of 6 Earl of Berkeley).* *b.* Berkeley house, Spring Gardens London 28 July 1805; ensign 85 Foot 13 Feb. 1823; captain 2 Life Guards 22 March 1831 to 25 Aug. 1837 when placed on h.p.; M.P. for Cheltenham 10 Dec. 1832 to 23 July 1847, 28 July 1848 to 24 Aug. 1848, when election declared void and 8 July 1852 to death; fought a duel with Henry George Boldero M.P. for Chippenham, in Osterly park 15 July 1842. *d.* Frankfort upon Main 1 July 1855. *Godings History of Cheltenham* (1863) 85–94, 365–8.

BERKELEY, Francis Henry Fitzhardinge *(brother of the preceding).* *b.* 7 Dec. 1794; gentleman commoner at Ch. Ch. Ox. 1814; M.P. for Bristol 22 July 1837 to death; leader in House of Commons of the ballot question 8 Aug. 1848 to death, the ballot bill was passed 13 July 1872; chief opponent of the Temperance cause in House of Commons, presented by the licensed victuallers with a testimonial of £1,050 at Bristol 24 Sep. 1856. *d.* 1 Victoria sq. Pimlico London 10 March 1870. *Burn's Temperance dictionary* (1861) 300–303; *Illust. News of the world iii,* 84 (1859), *portrait.*

BERKELEY, George Charles Grantley Fitzhardinge *(brother of the preceding).* *b.* Cranford house, Hounslow 10 Feb. 1800; ed. at Sandhurst; ensign Coldstream Guards 1821–23 when placed on h.p.; heir presumptive to Earldom of Berkeley 1810 to death; kept a pack of stag hounds at Cranford 1824–29 and at Harrold hall Beds. from 1829; M.P. for West Gloucs. 24 Dec 1832 to 1 July 1852; fought a duel with Wm. Maginn editor of *Fraser's Mag.* in a field near the Harrow road 5 Aug. 1836 when Maginn was slightly wounded; author of *Berkeley Castle an historical romance* 3 *vols.* 1836; *Sandron Hall or the days of Queen Anne* 3 *vols.* 1840; *Reminiscences of a huntsman* 1854; *Love and the lion, a poem* 1857; *The English sportsman in the western prairies* 1861; he is depicted in C. J. Collins's novel *Sackville Chase* 3 *vols.* 1863; he was the last person who wore the flat cocked hat known as the chapeau bras. *d.* Longfleet, Poole 23 Feb. 1881. *My life and recollections by G. C. G. F. Berkeley* 4 *vols.* 1865–66, *portrait; Fraser's Mag. xiv,* 242–7 (1836), *xv,* 100–143 (1837); *I.L.N. lxxviii,* 253 (1881), *portrait.*

BERKELEY, Sir George Henry Frederick *(elder son of Admiral Sir George Cranfield Berkeley, G.C.B. 1753–1818).* *b.* 9 July 1785; cornet Royal horse guards 21 Jany. 1802; captain 3 Foot guards 22 Feb. 1821 to 16 Nov. 1826 when placed on h.p.; col. 81 Foot 15 Jany. 1844 and of 35 Foot 11 July 1845 to death; surveyor general of the ordnance 28 June to Dec. 1852; general 20 June 1854; M.P. for Devonport 7 July 1852 to death; K.C.B. 2 Jany. 1815. *d.* Richmond, Surrey 25 Sep. 1857.

BERKELEY, Robert James. Called to bar in Ireland 1830; Q.C. 9 Nov. 1852. *d.* 6 Trafalgar terrace, Monkstown, Ireland 31 Oct. 1873.

BERKELEY, Sackville Hamilton. Ensign 16 Foot 1 May 1800, captain 25 Dec. 1804 to 26 Feb. 1824 when placed on h.p.; deputy adjutant general in West Indies 20 June 1811 to 15 March 1827; col. of 75 Foot 16 Sep. 1845 and of 16 Foot 22 March 1858 to death; general 20 June 1854. *d.* 4 York terrace, Regent's Park, London 12 Feb. 1863.

BERKLY, James John. *b.* Holloway near London 21 Oct. 1819; pupil of Robert Stephenson 1839; chief resident engineer of Great Indian Peninsula railway 1850–58; first 20 miles of the line from Bombay to Tanna were opened 16 April 1853 thus ini-

tiating the Indian railway system; comr. of
Bombay municipal board 1857; member of
senate of Bombay Univ. 1858; M.I.C.E. 4
Dec. 1855, Telford medallist 1860. d. Syden-
ham, Kent 25 Aug. 1862. *Min. of Proc. of
Instit. of C.E. xxii*, 618–24 (1863).

BERNAL, RALPH (*only son of Jacob Bernal of
7 Fitzroy square, London who d. 10 Nov.* 1811).
ed. at Christ's coll. Cam., B.A. 1806, M.A.
1809; student L.I. 13 June 1804, barrister 8
Feb. 1810; M.P. for Lincoln 1818–20, for
Rochester 1820–41 and 1847–52 and for
Weymouth 1841–47; spent sum of £66,000
in election contests; chairman of committees
of House of Commons 1830–50; pres. of
British Archæological association 1853 to
death; made a splendid collection of works
of art from the Byzantine period to that of
Louis Seize and of furniture and plate which
was sold for £63,000 in a 32 day sale 1855.
d. 93 Eaton sq. London 26 Aug. 1854.
Annual Register (1855) 41–44; *G.M. xlii*,
628 (1854).

BERNAL OSBORNE, RALPH (*eld. son of the
preceding*). b. 26 March 1808; ed. at the
Charterhouse; matric. from Trin. coll. Cam.
Oct. 1829; ensign 71 Foot 8 June 1830;
captain 7 Foot 27 July 1838 to 1841 when
he sold out; M.P. for Chipping Wycombe
1841–47, for Middlesex 1847–57, for Dover
1857–59, for Liskeard 1859–65, for Nottingham 1866–68 and for Waterford city
1870–74; took surname of Osborne in lieu
of Bernal 19 Aug. 1844 but always known
as R. Bernal Osborne; presided at banquet
given to Lord Palmerston at Reform club
20 July 1850; secretary of the Admiralty
Dec. 1852 to Feb. 1858; author of 2
poems called *The chaunt of Achilles* 1838 and
A voice from Palace yard. d. Bestwood lodge
near Nottingham 4 Jany. 1882. *Bagenal's
Life of R. Bernal Osborne privately printed*
1884; *Temple Bar, lxxii*, 34–49 (1884);
Fortnightly Review xxxvi, 535–44 (1884);
I.L.N. xiv, 397 (1849), *portrait, lxxx*, 61 (1882),
portrait; Graphic xxv, 45 (1882), *portrait*.

BERNARD, HERMANN. b. Uman or Human
Poland 1785; a banker; went to England 1825;
Hebrew teacher in Univ. of Cambridge 1830
to death; author of *The creed and ethics of the
Jews* 1832; edited *Guide of the Hebrew student*
1839; author with Rev. P. H. Mason of *An
easy practical Hebrew grammar;* in the title
pages of all his works the name of Hedwig
being that of a departed sister whom he
wished to commemorate is joined to his own.
d. Cambridge 15 Nov. 1857. *The book of Job
as expounded to his Cambridge pupils by the late*

H. H. Bernard edited by Frank Chance vol. i,
(1864) *lxxvii–ciii*, (1864), *portrait*.

BERNARD, MOUNTAGUE (3 *son of Charles
Bernard of Eden, Jamaica*). b. Tibberton
Court, Gloucs. 28 Jany. 1820; ed. at Sherborne and Trin. coll. Ox., B.A. 1842, B.C.L.
1845, D.C.L. 1871; Vinerian scholar and
fellow of his college; barrister L.I. 1 May
1846; Chichele professor of international law
and diplomacy in Univ. of Oxford 1859 to
9 May 1874; assessor of the Chancellor's
Court, Oxford 1859 to Nov. 1871; sec. to
royal commission on Cattle plague 1866;
member of royal commissions on Naturalisation 1868, Fugitive slaves 1876 and Univ. of
Ox. 1877; fellow of All Souls coll. Ox. 1870;
curator of Taylor institution at Ox. 9 Feb.
1871; one of high comrs. for treating with
the United States of America 16 Feb. 1871,
signed treaty of Washington 8 May 1871;
P.C. 29 June 1871, member of its Judicial
committee 24 Nov. 1871; an original member of the Institut de droit international
1873, pres. at the Oxford meeting 1880; one
of founders of *Guardian* newspaper 1846,
wrote the weekly summary of events in it
for some years. d. Overross, Ross, Herefordshire 2 Sep. 1882.

BERNARD, THOMAS. b. Sep. 1816; sheriff of
King's county 1837 and lord lieutenant 5
Dec. 1867 to death; colonel of King's county
militia 23 March 1871 to death. d. Castle
Bernard, Kinnetty, King's county 13 Dec.
1882.

BERNARD, SIR THOMAS TYRINGHAM, 6
Baronet. b. Bolton st. Piccadilly London 15
Sep. 1791; ed. at Eton and Ch. Ch. Ox.;
sheriff of Bucks. 1816; M.P. for Aylesbury
28 March 1857 to 6 July 1865; succeeded
22 Jany. 1876. d. Cadogan lodge, Carlyle
sq. London 8 May 1883. *I.L.N. lxxxii*, 525
(1883), *portrait*.

BERNARD, WILLIAM BAYLE (*son of John
Bernard, English comedian* 1756–1828). b.
Pleasant st. Boston U.S. 27 Nov. 1809;
came to England 1820; clerk in Army
accounts office 1826–30 when office was
abolished; wrote much dramatic and other
criticism for the press; author of *The free-
booter's bride 5 vols.* 1828; *Life of Samuel
Lover 2 vols.* 1874 and of 114 plays, best
known being *Rip Van Winkle* 1832; *The nervous
man* 1833; *The man about town* 1836; *Marie
Ducange* 1837; *His last legs* 1839; *The
boarding school* 1841; *The round of wrong* 1846.
d. Brighton 5 Aug. 1875. *The Era Almanac*
(1868) 17–18.

BERNARD, WILLIAM SMYTH (4 *son of 1 Earl of Bandon* 1755–1830). *b.* Castle Bernard, King's County 14 Nov. 1792; sheriff of Cork 1820; M.P. for Bandon 15 Dec. 1832 to death. *d.* Queenstown 6 Feb. 1863.

BERNAYS, ADOLPHUS. Professor of German language and literature at King's College London 1831–63; F.R.G.S. 1858; author of *German poetry for beginners* 1836; *German poetical anthology* 1843; *German historical anthology* 1846 and 6 other school books. *d.* The rectory, Great Stanmore 22 Dec. 1864.

BERNAYS, REV. LEOPOLD JOHN *(eld. son of the preceding).* *b.* 28 Dec. 1820; ed. at Merchant Taylors and St. John's coll. Ox., B.A. 1843, M.A. 1846, fellow of his college; head master of Elstree school 1847–60; R. of Great Stanmore, Middlesex 1860 to death; author of *Translation of Goethe's Faust, part 2 and other poems* 1839; *Manual of family prayers and meditations* 1845; *The church in the schoolroom* 1851. *d.* The rectory, Great Stanmore 25 Oct. 1882.

BERNCASTLE, JULIUS. Educ. at Univ. of Paris and Guy's hospital London; assistant colonial surgeon Van Diemen's Land 1841–42; surgeon at Croydon, Surrey 1842–48; surgeon to Croydon union and infirmary 1842–48 when presented by medical profession with a purse of gold; practised in London 1851–54; an oculist and aurist at Sydney 1854 and at Melbourne 1867 to death; author of *A voyage to China 2 vols.* 1850; *The revolt of the Bengal Sepoys* 1857; *The defenceless state of Sydney* 1865; *Australian snake bites; The use and abuse of tobacco* [*Two lectures*] 1868. *d.* Greville place, Prahran, Victoria 30 June 1870 in 51 year.

BERNERS, REV. HENRY WILSON, 5 Baron. *b.* 1 Oct. 1762; R. of Alexton, Leics. 1814 to death; R. of Kirby-Cane, Norfolk 1820 to 1845; succeeded 25 March 1838. *d.* Kirby-Cane 26 Feb. 1851.

BERNERS, HENRY WILLIAM WILSON, 6 Baron. *b.* Kirby-Cane hall, Norfolk 23 Feb. 1797; ed. at Eton and Em. coll. Cam.; built Keythorpe hall, co. Leicester 1842; succeeded 26 Feb. 1851; pres. of Royal agricultural society 1859 and of Smithfield club 1860 and 1861; a successful breeder of sheep and shorthorns; a great hawker and hunter. *d.* Keythorpe hall 27 June 1871. *Illust. news of the world ii,* (1858), *portrait; I.L.N. xxviii,* 74 (1858), *portrait.*

BERNERS, VENERABLE HENRY DENNY (2 *son of Charles Berners of Woolverstone park, Suffolk* 1740–1815). *b.* 18 Sep. 1769; ed. at St. Mary hall Ox., B.C.L. 1794; R. of Erwarton, Suffolk 1801–35; archdeacon of Suffolk 27 Feb. 1819 to 12 Jany. 1846. *d.* Woolverstone park, 24 Jany. 1852.

BERNEY, SIR HANSON. 8 Baronet. *b.* Kirby-Bedon, Norfolk 3 Dec. 1780; succeeded 4 Oct. 1825. *d.* 7 Sep. 1870.

BERNSTORFF, ALBRECHT GRAF VON, BARON. *b.* Dreilükow, Mecklenburg 22 March 1809; Prussian minister in London 1 May 1854; minister for foreign affairs at Berlin July 1861 to Oct. 1862; Prussian ambassador in London Oct. 1862; ambassador of North German confederation Feb. 1867 and of German empire 24 Feb. 1871 to death. *d.* 9 Carlton house terrace, London 26 March 1873. *Illust. news of the world i,* 10 (1858), *portrait.*

BERRI, AMY D'ARTOIS, Duchesse de *(dau. of Rev. Joseph Brown of Maidstone, Kent who d. 8 April 1824 aged 77 by Mary Anne Deacon who d. 10 March 1806 aged 59).* *b.* Maidstone 8 April 1783   *m.* at the Catholic church King st. Portman sq. London 1806, Charles Ferdinand d'Artois Duc de Berri son of Comte d'Artois afterwards Charles x, he was *b.* 24 Jany. 1778 and was assassinated by Louvel on the steps of the Opera house Paris 13 Feb. 1820, the marriage was annulled by Louis xviii in 1815. *d.* Château de la Contrie, commune de Couffé, Loire-Inférieure France 7 May 1876. *Les secrets des Bourbons par C. Nauroy* (1882) 5–62; *Bingham's Marriages of the Bonapartes ii,* 198–200 (1881).

BERRIDGE, JAMES SAMUEL. *b.* 1806; Educ. at the Charter House and Trin. hall Cam.; pres. of legislative council St. Christopher 1846, puisne judge Court of Queen's Bench and Common Pleas 1847, chairman of Board of Health 1860, postmaster 1860, pres. of legislative assembly 1870; pres. of St. Christopher April 1872 to death; member of executive council of Leeward Islands 1872. *d.* Limekiln, St. Kitts 5 Nov. 1885.

BERRY, JAMES MIDDLETON. Librarian to the Queen 1839 to death. *d.* Manchester 25 Oct. 1875 aged 72.

BERRY, AGNES *(younger dau. of Robert Berry of London, merchant who d. 18 May 1817).* *b.* Kirkbridge, Yorkshire 29 May 1764; travelled on the Continent with her sister Mary 1783–85 and 1802. *d.* 8 Curzon st. London 29

BERRY, A. (*Con.*)

Jany. 1852. *Extracts from the Journals of Miss Berry, edited by Lady T. Lewis, 2 ed. vol. 1* (1866), *portrait.*

BERRY, ALEXANDER. *b.* Fifeshire 30 Nov. 1781; member of legislative council of New South Wales 1829; member of the upper house 1856–61. *d.* Sydney 17 Sep. 1873.

BERRY, REV. CHARLES (3 *son of Rev. John Berry, Independent minister at Romsey, Hants who d. about 1821*). *b.* Romsey 10 Nov. 1783; ed. at Homerton college; Unitarian minister of the Great meeting Leicester 1803–59; kept a school at Leicester 1808–38, had many distinguished pupils; one of founders of Leicester literary and philosophical society and of Leicester town museum; author of *The duty of national thanksgiving* 1812; *Funeral sermon for Queen Caroline* 1821; *Remarks on Popery* 1851. *d.* Olive Mount, Wavertree, Liverpool 4 May 1877. *Remembrance of Rev. C. Berry by J. C. (James Clephan)* 1877.

BERRY, REV. CORNELIUS (*brother of the preceding*). *b.* Romsey 23 July 1788; ed. at Homerton college; Independent minister at Ware, Herts 1 Oct. 1809 to 30 Sep. 1810, at Hatfield Heath, Essex 31 March 1811 to death; ordained 9 Oct. 1811. *d.* 5 Mathon place, Richmond road, Barnsbury, London 8 Sep. 1864. *Biographical sketch of the Rev. C. Berry by John Hayden* 1865.

BERRY, MARY (*sister of Agnes Berry*). *b.* Kirkbridge, Yorkshire 16 March 1763; travelled on the Continent 1783–85 and 1802; became acquainted with Horace Walpole 1788 who left her at his death 2 March 1797 sum of £4000 and house called Little Strawberry Hill; engaged to General O'Hara 1796; edited *The works of Horace Walpole 5 vols.* 1798 on which her father's name appears as editor; author of *Fashionable Friends*, a comedy in 5 acts produced at Drury Lane theatre 22 April 1802; *A comparative view of the social condition of England and France* 1828; *Social life in England and France from the French revolution in 1789 to that of July 1830* [*anon.*] 1831. *d.* 8 Curzon st. London at midnight 20 Nov. 1852. *H. Martineau's Biographical sketches, 4 ed.* (1876) 293–98; *Extracts from the Journals of Miss Berry, edited by Lady T. Lewis, 2 ed. 3 vols.* 1866, 3 *portraits; I.L.N. xxi,* 517 (1852), *portrait.*

BERRY, WILLIAM. Writing clerk to Registrar of College of arms 1793–1809; lived in Guernsey some years then at Doddington place, Kennington, Surrey; author of *Intro-*

BERRY, W. (*Con.*)

duction to heraldry 1810; *History of the island of Guernsey* 1815; *Genealogica antiqua or mythological and classical fables* 1816; *Encyclopædia heraldica 4 vols.* 1828; *Pedigrees of the families in the County of Kent* 1830, *Sussex* 1830, *Hampshire* 1833, *Berkshire, Buckinghamshire and Surrey* 1837, *Essex* 1839, *Hertfordshire* 1842, the 3 last of these books were produced by means of lithography. *d.* Spencer place, Brixton 2 July 1851 in 77 year. *G.M. xcix; pt. 2, 99-101* (1829), *c, pt. 2, 409–16* (1830), *xxxviii,* 101 (1852).

BERTINI, HENRI JERÔME. *b.* London 28 Oct. 1798; celebrated pianist, excelled in phrasing and execution; gave concerts in the Netherlands 1811; made a professional tour through England and Scotland; settled in Paris 1821, retired about 1855; composed nearly 200 pieces of music. *d.* Meylan near Grenoble 1 Oct. 1876.

BERWICK, RICHARD NOEL NOEL HILL, 5 Baron. *b.* Betton, Shropshire 21 Nov. 1800; succeeded 28 Sep. 1848. *d.* Cronkhill near Shrewsbury 12 April 1861.

BERWICK, WILLIAM NOEL NOEL HILL, 6 Baron. *b.* 6 July 1802; ensign 3 Foot 13 Nov. 1817; major 69 Foot 4 Dec. 1835 to 30 Oct. 1840 when placed on h.p.; colonel 20 June 1854; succeeded 12 April 1861. *d.* Attingham hall near Shrewsbury 24 Nov. 1882.

BERWICK, EDWARD. Called to Irish bar 1832; pres. of Queen's college Galway 1845 to death. *d.* Queen's college, Galway 7 March 1877.

BERWICK, WALTER (*son of Rev. Edward Berwick, R. of Esker Lucan, co. Dublin*). Called to Irish bar 1826; chairman of quarter sessions for Waterford 1835–47, for east riding of co. Cork 1847–59; Q.C. 6 Feb. 1840, bencher of King's Inns 1856; serjeant at law 1855; judge of Irish Bankruptcy court 1859 to death; burned alive in the train at Abergele, Denbighshire 20 Aug. 1868 the most terrible railway accident that ever happened in this country. The Berwick Art Club was established in Dublin to perpetuate his memory Oct. 1868. *Irish law times ii,* 477 (1868); *I.L.N. liii,* 205, 234 (1868).

BESEMERES, JOHN. (*eld. son of Mr. Besemeres of City of London*). Merchant at Calcutta; author of following plays, all written under pseudonym of John Daly, *Broken Toys*, produced at Sadlers Wells 1850; *Young husbands* comedy, at same house Aug. 1852 ; *The Times* drama, at Olympic July 1853 ; *Old Salt* drama, at Strand 12 Jany. 1868 ; *Dotheboys Hall* drama, at Court 26 Dec. 1871 ; *Marriage lines* drama, at Court 17 March 1873 and *Forget and Forgive* comedy, at Charing Cross 5 Jany. 1874. *d.* Islington infirmary London 19 Nov. 1879 aged 57.

BESLEY, ROBERT. *b.* Exeter 14 Oct. 1794 ; member of firm of Messrs. Thorogood of city of London, type founders 1829 ; member for Aldersgate ward of Court of common council 1852, alderman of the ward 1861 to death ; sheriff 1864–65, lord mayor 1869–70. *d.* Victoria road, Wimbledon park 18 Dec. 1876. *I.L.N. lv*, 461 (1869), *portrait*.

BESLY, REV. JOHN. Ed. at Balliol coll. Ox., fellow 1823, B.A. 1821, M.A. 1826, D.C.L. 1835 ; tutor in Rugby school 1823–28 ; sub librarian Bodleian library 1828–31 ; V. of Long Benton near Newcastle 1830 to death ; R. of Aston-sub-edge, Gloucs. 1831 to death ; proctor in Convocation of York 1836–45 and 1855–64 ; author of *A translation of Aristotle's Rhetoric with analysis by Hobbes* 1833 ; *Desultory notices of the church and vicarage of Long Benton* 1843 and of *Sermons. d.* Long Benton 17 April 1868 aged 68.

BESSBOROUGH, JOHN GEORGE BRABAZON PONSONBY, 5 Earl of *(eld. son of John Wm. Ponsonby, 4 Earl of Bessborough 1781–1847). b.* London 4 Oct. 1809 ; ed. at the Charterhouse ; attaché to embassy at St. Petersburgh 3 July 1832 ; M.P. for Bletchingley 5 May 1831 to July 1831, for Higham Ferrers 6 Oct. 1831 to 3 Dec. 1832 and for Derby 8 Jany. 1835 to 16 May 1847 when he succeeded ; lord lieutenant of co. Carlow 5 Sep. 1838 to death ; master of the buckhounds 16 May 1848 to Feb. 1852, 30 Dec. 1852 to 26 Feb. 1858 and 18 June 1859 to 20 Jany. 1866 ; P.C. 30 June 1848 ; lord steward of the household 20 Jany. 1866 to July 1866 and 9 Dec. 1868 to 2 March 1874. *d.* Bessborough house near Piltown, co. Kilkenny 28 Jany. 1880. *Baily's Mag. vi*, 163–64 (1863), *portrait*.

BESSONET, JAMES. Called to Irish bar 1807 ; K.C. 13 July 1830 ; chairman of sessions for county Waterford. *d.* 21 Lower Leeson st. Dublin 3 Oct. 1859 aged 76.

BEST, SAMUEL. Second lieut. Madras Engineers 16 Dec. 1825 ; captain 9 May 1842 to death ; planned fortifications of Singapore ; superintendent of roads in Madras, Presidency 1845 to death ; his principal works are the Southern

Trunk road and the Goolcheroo pass ; contributed many papers to *Madras Literary transactions* and *Madras Engineering papers. d.* of jungle fever at Chittoor 5 Oct. 1851.

BEST, REV. SAMUEL (3 son of 1 *Baron Wynford* 1767–1845). *b.* 2 Dec. 1802 ; ed. at King's college Cam., fellow, B.A. 1826, M.A. 1830 ; R. of Abbots-Anne, Andover 1831 to death ; rural dean of Andover ; author of *Parochial sermons* 1836 ; *Manual of parochial institutions* 1849 ; *Catechism on collects* 1850 ; *Discourses on collects, epistles and gospels* 1853. *d.* The rectory, Abbots-Anne 20 Jany. 1873.

BEST, THOMAS *(brother of the preceding). b.* 12 Aug. 1799 ; entered navy 3 Nov. 1812 ; captain 22 July 1830 ; V.A. on h.p. 10 Nov. 1862. *d.* 19 Hyde park sq. London 4 Sep. 1864.

BEST, WILLIAM MAWDESLEY *(eld. son of Thomas Best, captain 26 Foot who d. 8 Oct. 1813). b.* 24 Dec. 1809 ; ed. at Trin. coll. Dub., B.A. 1831, LL.B. 1832, M.A. 1834 ; barrister G.I. 11 June 1834, bencher 16 Jany. 1867 ; author of *Right to begin and right to reply in law courts* 1837 ; *Treatise on circumstantial proof in criminal cases* 1844 ; *Principles of the law of evidence* 1849, 7 ed. 1883. *d.* 17 Nov. 1869.

BESTOW, WILLIAM *(son of Wm. Bestow of 124 Wood st. Cheapside, London, web manufacturer). b.* 14 Feb. 1789 ; partly founded several papers ; founded *Theatrical Journal, a weekly record of the English drama* 1840, edited it to Nov. 1872, 33 vols., it ceased 16 April 1873 ; wrote several political pamphlets. *d.* 20 Frederick st. King's Cross, London 30 April 1873.

BETHAM, MARY MATILDA *(eld. dau. of Rev. Wm. Betham 1749–1839, master of endowed school at Stonham Aspal, Suffolk 1784–1833). b.* 1776 or 1777 ; gave Shakespearian readings in London about 1803 ; author of *Elegies* 1797 ; *Biographical dictionary of celebrated women* 1804 ; *Poems* 1808 ; *The lay of Marie, a poem* 1816. *d.* 36 Burton st. Burton crescent, London 30 Sep. 1852 aged 76. *Six life studies of famous women by M. Betham-Edwards* (1880) 231–303, *portrait ; Fraser's Mag.* July 1878, 73–84.

BETHAM, SIR WILLIAM *(brother of the preceding). b.* Stradbroke, Suffolk 22 May 1779 ; clerk to Sir Chichester Fortescue, Ulster king of arms 1805 ; genealogist attendant on order of St. Patrick 15 July 1812 ; knighted by Lord lieutenant of Ireland 15 July 1812 ;

BETHAM, SIR W. (*Con.*)

Ulster king of arms 1820; keeper of parliamentary records of Ireland 1830; F.S.A. 6 May 1824; M.R.I.A. 22 Jany. 1827, foreign sec. to March 1840; author of *Irish antiquarian researches* 1827; *Dignities feudal and parliamentary* 1830, reissued as *The origin and history of the constitution of England* 1834; *Etruria Celtica* 2 vols. 1832; *The Gael and Cimbri* 1834; made an index of 40 folio volumes to the names of all persons mentioned in the wills at the Prerogative office in Dublin; his manuscripts were sold at Sotheby's in London 1860. *d.* Rochford house, Blackrock near Dublin 26 Oct. 1853. *G.M. xl*, 632–35 (1853), *xlii*, 145 (1854).

BETHELL, RIGHT REV. CHRISTOPHER (2 *son of Rev. Richard Bethell, R. of St. Peter's, Wallingford who d.* 12 *Jany.* 1806). *b.* Isleworth, Surrey 21 April 1773; ed. at Eton and King's coll. Cam., B.A. 1796, M.A. 1799, D.D. 1817, fellow of his college; R. of Kirby Wiske, Yorkshire 1808–30; dean of Chichester 5 April 1814 to March 1824; bishop of Gloucester 24 March 1824, consecrated 11 April 1824; bishop of Exeter 8 April 1830; preb. of Exeter 22 June 1830; bishop of Bangor 28 Oct. 1830 to death; author of *A general view of the doctrine of regeneration in baptism* 1821, 4 ed. 1845. *d.* The palace, Bangor 19 April 1859. *bur.* Llandegai church yard 27 April.

BETHELL, REV. GEORGE. Educ. at Eton; assistant at Eton 1802; fellow of Eton 21 Sep. 1818 to death; R. of Worplesdon, Surrey 1833 to death. *d.* Eton college 16 March 1857 aged 78.

BETHELL, JOHN (*son of Richard Bethell M.D. of Bristol*). *b.* 1804; solicitor in London 1825–54; patented a complete system of diving apparatus 1835; patented a process for preserving timber from decay by impregnating it with creosote oil 11 July 1838, this invention has been adopted on a large scale, in marine works it is almost indispensable, the idea was taken from the embalming of mummies; patented many other inventions; carried on a distillery of beetroot spirit in Berkshire; A.I.C.E. 20 March 1838. *d.* Cleveland sq. Hyde Park London 22 Feb. 1867. *Minutes of proc. of Instit. of C.E. xxvii*, 597–99 (1868).

BETHELL, RICHARD. *b.* 10 May 1772; ed. at King's coll. Cam., B.A. 1795, fellow of his college; owner of large estates in Yorkshire 1799; M.P. for Yorkshire 5 Aug. 1830 to 23

BETHELL, R. (*Con.*)

April 1831, and for the East Riding 18 Dec. 1832 to 23 June 1841; chairman of East Riding quarter sessions many years; author of 2 Latin poems in second series of *Musæ Etonenses* 2 vols. 1797. *d.* Rise near Hull 25 Dec. 1864.

BETHUNE, CHARLES RAMSAY DRINKWATER (2 *son of John Drinkwater of Thorncroft, Surrey, C.B., F.S.A.* 1762–1844). *b.* 27 Dec. 1802; entered navy 2 Aug. 1815; captain 22 July 1830; served in Chinese war 1840–41; V.A. 10 Nov. 1862, admiral 2 April 1866; retired 1 April 1870; assumed additional name of Bethune 1837; C.B. 29 June 1841, F.R.G.S. 1842. *d.* 4, Queensbury place South Kensington 21 Feb. 1884. *M. F. Conolly's Biog. dict. of eminent men of Fife* (1866) 56.

BETHUNE, SIR HENRY LINDESAY (*eld. child of Martin Eccles Lindesay Bethune, commissary general in Scotland who d.* 1813). *b.* Hilton near Perth 12 April 1787; lieut. Madras Horse artillery 18 July 1804; captain 3 Sep. 1813 to 1 Sep. 1822 when he retired; drilled and disciplined the Persian army 1811–21, his lofty stature, 6 feet 7 inches, and great personal strength gained for him in Persia the epithet of "Rustum" the Hercules of ancient Persian story; knighted at St. James's Palace 20 July 1832; sent to Persia as British agent 1834; commanded advanced guard of the Shah's army 1834–35; returned home Sep. 1835; created baronet 7 March 1836. *d.* Tabreez, Persia 19 Feb. 1851. *M. F. Conolly's Biog. dict. of eminent men of Fife* (1866) 57.

BETHUNE, JOHN ELLIOT DRINKWATER (*brother of C. R. D. Bethune*). Ed. at Trin. coll. Cam., B.A. 1823; barrister M.T. 4 May 1827; one of municipal corporation comrs.; counsel to the Home Office 1833–47; drew the Municipal reform, Tithe commutation and County courts bills; legislative member of Supreme council of India 11 April 1848 to death; pres. of council of education at Calcutta 1848; established a school for native females of the higher classes at Calcutta which he endowed by his will with property in Calcutta. *d.* Calcutta 12 Aug. 1851 aged 50. *G. M. xxxvii*, 94–96, 434 (1852).

BETTINGTON, CLAUDE (2 *son of Albemarle Bettington of Halsey house, Cheltenham*). Commanded Bettington's Horse in Zulu war 1879–80; C.M.G. 30 Oct. 1880. *d.* Elmina, Gold Coast 29 Dec. 1880.

BETTRIDGE, Rev. William Craddock. *b.* 30 Aug. 1791; ensign 81 Foot 7 April 1813; lieutenant 31 Aug. 1815 to 25 Feb. 1816 when placed on h.p.; town major of Brussels 1815; entered Univ. of Jena Saxony 1818; walked from Jena to Naples; entered Neapolitan army 1822; aide-de-camp to Sir Richard Church 1822; accorded by Government a continuance for life of his half pay by a special mandamus; studied at St. John's coll. Cam., B.D. 1837; ordained deacon 1824; C. of Elvington near York 1824; C. of Ecclesfield 1828; Inc. of St. Paul's, Southampton 1828–34; R. of Woodstock, Ontario, Upper Canada 1834 to death; obtained a grant of 400 acres of land for each of the 57 rectories of Upper Canada; canon of Huron; declined bishopric of Huron 1857; author of *A brief history of the church in Upper Canada* 1838. *d.* Woodstock 21 Nov. 1879.

BETTS, Edward Ladd *(eld. son of Wm. Betts of Sandown, Kent).* *b.* Buckland near Dover 5 June 1815; constructed Midland railway from Rugby to Leicester and many other lines; partner with Sir S. M. Peto; constructed the line from Balaclava to English camp before Sebastopol; constructed with Brassey the grand trunk railway of Canada including Victoria tubular bridge, and with Crampton the London, Chatham and Dover railway; chairman of Eastern counties railway co. 1851 and 1852; sheriff of Kent 1858; contested Maidstone 1865; A.I.C.E. 26 June 1849. *d.* Assouan, Upper Egypt 21 Jany. 1872. *bur.* at Aylesford, Kent. *Minutes of proc. of Instit. of C.E. xxxvi,* 285–88 (1873); *I.L.N. lx,* 187, 207, 611 (1872)

BETTY, William Henry West *(only child of William Henry Betty, M.D. of Lisburn, Ireland who d. 1811).* *b.* Shrewsbury 13 Sep. 1791; made his début at Belfast theatre 16 Aug. 1803 as Osman in tragedy of *Zara,* and at Crow st. theatre Dublin 29 Nov. 1803 as Douglas; engaged at Covent Garden for 12 nights at £50 per night and a clear benefit, and at Drury Lane on intervening nights on same terms 1 Dec. 1804, after 3 nights his salary was raised to £100 per night; known as the young Roscius; fellow commoner of Christ's college, Cambridge July 1808 to 1811; returned to the stage 1812 when he failed to draw; made his last appearance in London June 1813; took his farewell benefit at Southampton 9 Aug, 1824. *d.* 37, Ampthill sq. London 24 Aug. 1874. *Roscius in London Biographical Memoirs of W. H. W. Betty* 1805, *portrait; Tinsley's Mag. xv,* 415–23 (1874); *Temple Bar xlii,* 346–61 (1874); *Theatrical*

Betty, W. H. W. *(Con.)*
Inquisitor xii, 227 (1818), *portrait; Graphic x,* 227 (1874), *portrait; The dawn of the 19th century in England by J. Ashton ii,* 118–29 (1886), *portrait.*

BEVAN, Charles Dacres *(son of Charles Bevan, Lieut. col. 4 Foot who d. 12 July 1811).* *b.* 7 Nov. 1805; ed. at Charterhouse and Ball. coll. Ox., B.A. 1827, M.A. 1829; barrister M.T. 21 May 1830; recorder of Dartmouth 1845–55, of Truro 1848–49, of Falmouth 1850–56, of Helston 1850–56 and of Penzance Dec. 1855 to Jany. 1857; judge of county courts for Cornwall (circuit 59) 22 Jany. 1857 to death. *d.* near Fowey, Cornwall 24 June 1872.

BEVAN, Edward. *b.* London 8 July 1770; apprenticed to a surgeon at Hereford; studied at St. Bartholomew's hospital; M.D. St. Andrews 1818; physician at Mortlake 5 years, at Stoke-upon-Trent, at Congleton 12 years and at Mortlake again 2 years; lived at Bridstow near Ross, then at Hereford 1849 to death; one of founders of Entomological Society 1833; author of *The Honey-Bee, its natural history, physiology and management* 1827, 3 ed. 1870, which was the best book on the subject; *Hints on the history and management of the Honey-Bee* 1851. *d.* Hereford 31 Jany. 1860. *The Naturalist,* ed. by Neville Wood iv, 142–46 (1838), *portrait.*

BEVAN, Hannah Marishall *(dau. of Wm. Bevan of London, tea merchant).* *b.* London 1 Feb. 1798; joined the Newgate prison committee; worked with Elizabeth Fry and others; a minister of Society of Friends 1828. *(m.* 1827 Thomas Bevan, M.D. who *d.* 1847 aged 43). *d.* Penge 8 Nov. 1874. *Annual Monitor for 1876 pp.* 3–19.

BEVAN, Philip. Ed. at Trin. coll. Dub., M.A. and M.B. 1843, M.D. 1845; F.R.C.S. Ireland 1837; lecturer on anatomy Dublin School of medicine; surgeon to Mercers hospital to about 1870; M.R.I.A. 13 April 1846; professor of practical anatomy Royal college of surgeons to death. *d.* 33 Pembroke road, Dublin 6 Dec. 1881.

BEVAN, Venerable Thomas. Ed. at Jesus coll. Ox., B.A. 1823, M.A. 1828; V. of St. Peter's, Carmarthen 1833 to death; archdeacon of St. David's 11 June 1833 to death; preb. of Brecon 1853 to death. *d.* 28 Dec. 1863 aged 63.

BEVERIDGE, THOMAS. *b.* Dunfermline 7 Oct. 1775; deputy clerk in the court of session, Edinburgh; author of *A practical treatise on the forms of process containing the new regulation before the Court of Session...2 vols.* 1826; *A guide to the judicial records of the court of session* 1852. *d.* near Edinburgh 27 May 1858.

BEVERLEY, CHARLES JAMES. *b.* Fort Augustus, Scotland Aug. 1788; assistant surgeon R.N. 1810; served in Sir Edward Parry's first Arctic expedition 1819-20; went with him to Spitzbergen as surgeon and naturalist 1827; practised in London; F.R.S. 5 May 1831. *d.* Derman Terrace. Great Yarmouth 16 Sep. 1868.

BEVERLEY, EDWARD, stage name of Edward Dickenson. *b.* Beverley, Yorkshire; a chorister in choir of York minster; sang at Weston's music hall London; principal tenor of Madame Bodda-Pyne's opera company, and of John Russell's opera bouffe company; played at Gaiety and Opera Comique theatres London; in the United States; leading tenor at St. Mark's church New York May 1880 to death. *d.* Flushing, Long island, New York Aug. 1880.

BEVERLEY, HENRY, stage name of Henry Roxby. *b.* 1797; made his début at West London theatre; chief low comedian at Adelphi theatre Oct. 1838; lessee of Victoria theatre 16 Sep. 1839 to 1840; manager of Sunderland and other theatres in north of England. *d.* 26, Russell sq. London 1 Feb. 1863.

BEWES, THOMAS. M.P. for Plymouth 11 Dec. 1832 to 23 June 1841. *d.* Beaumont, Plymouth 18 Nov. 1857 aged 79.

BEWICK, JANE (*eld. child of Thomas Bewick, painter in water colours* 1753-1828). *b.* 29 April 1797; edited *Memoir of Thomas Bewick written by himself* 1862. *d.* 19, West st. Gateshead 7 April 1881.

BEWICK, WILLIAM (3 *son of Wm. Bewick of Darlington, upholsterer*). *b.* Darlington 20 Oct. 1795; pupil of B. R. Haydon in London 1817-20; portrait painter at Darlington 1824; copied pictures in Rome 1826-29; exhibited 4 pictures at the R.A., 8 at the B.I. and 9 at Suffolk st. exhibition 1822-48; competed for decorations of Houses of Parliament 1843; a skilful copyist especially of Rembrandt. *d.* Haughton house near Darlington 8 June 1866. *Life and letters by T. Landseer* 2 *vols.* 1871, *portrait.*

BEXFIELD, WILLIAM RICHARD. *b.* Norwich 27 April 1824; chorister at Norwich cathedral 1832-39; organist to parish church of Boston 1846; Mus. Bac. Ox. 1846; Mus. Doc. Cam. 1849; organist at St. Helens, Bishopsgate, London Feb. 1848; composed oratorio of *Israel restored*, performed by Norwich choral society Oct. 1851 and at Norwich musical festival 22 Sep. 1852. *d.* 12 Monmouth road, Bayswater, London 28 Oct. 1853. *W. A. Barrett's English church composers* (1882) 162-63.

BEXLEY, NICHOLAS VANSITTART, 1 Baron (*younger son of Henry Vansittart* 1732-70, *governor of Bengal*). *b.* 29 April 1766; ed. at Cheam, Surrey and Ch. Ch. Ox., B.A. 1787, M.A. 1791, D.C.L. 1841; barrister L.I. 26 May 1791, bencher 12 Nov. 1812; M.P. for Hastings 1796-1802, for Old Sarum 1802-12 and for Harwich 1812-23; joint sec. of the Treasury 1801-1804 and 1806-1808; lord of the Treasury in Ireland 1804; P.C. 14 Jany. 1805; chief sec. for Ireland 23 March 1805 to Sep. 1805; chancellor of the Exchequer 9 June 1812 to Jany. 1823; created Baron Bexley of Bexley, Kent 1 March 1823; chancellor of Duchy of Lancaster 31 Jany. 1823 to Jany. 1828; author of many political and financial pamphlets 1793-1818. *d.* Footscray place, Kent 8 Feb. 1851. *W. C. Taylor's National portrait gallery i,* 91 (1846), *portrait; G.M. xxxv,* 431-32 (1851); *S. Walpole's History of England,* 2 *ed. vols.* 1 *and* 2 (1879).

BEYER, CHARLES FREDERICK. *b.* Plauen, Saxony 14 May 1813; head of the mechanical works of Messrs. Sharp, Roberts & Co. of Manchester, engineers 1843-53; naturalised in England 5 Nov. 1852; established with Richard Peacock locomotive works of Beyer, Peacock & Co., Gorton foundry Manchester 1854; designed and adapted many special tools for making locomotive engines; one of founders of Institution of Mechanical engineers 1847; M.I.C.E. 7 March 1854; left a large bequest for foundation and endowment of professorships of science at Owen's college Manchester. *d.* Llantysilio hall, Denbighshire 2 June 1876. *Minutes of proc. of Instit. of C.E. xlvii,* 290-97 (1877).

BIANCONI, CARLO (2 *son of Pietro Bianconi of Tregolo, Lombardy, farmer who d.* 1833). *b.* Tregolo 24 Sep. 1786; went to Ireland as a picture seller 1802; opened a carver and gilder's shop at Carrick-on-Suir 1806, removed to Waterford and then to Clonmel; started a one-horse two-wheeled car for conveyance of passengers from Clonmel to Cahir 6 July 1815; started cars all over Ireland

Bianconi, C. (Con.)

where they were known as "Bians"; in 1864 his passenger traffic realised £27,700 and his mail contracts £12,000; gave up his shop at Clonmel 1826 and his car business 1865; received letters of Naturalisation from Irish Privy Council 31 Aug. 1831; mayor of Clonmel 1844–46; purchased Longfield, Tipperary for £22,000 23 March 1846, where he lived 16 Sep. 1846 to death; D.L. for Tipperary June 1863. (m. 14 Feb. 1827 Eliza, dau. of Patrick Hayes of Dublin, stockbroker). d. Longfield 22 Sep. 1875. *Charles Bianconi, a biography 1786–1875 by his daughter Mrs. Morgan John O'Connell 1878, portrait; Dublin univ. mag. lxxxv 16–24 (1875), portrait.*

BIBBY, Thomas. b. Kilkenny 1799; ed. at Kilkenny gr. sch. and Trin. coll. Dublin scholar 1814, B.A. 1816; one of the best Greek scholars of his day; author of two dramatic poems, *Gerald of Kildare* 1854 and a sequel to it called *Silken Thomas* 1859; confined by his relations in a private lunatic asylum in Dublin but released by his literary friends. d. St. Canice's Steps, Kilkenny 7 Jany. 1863.

BIBER, Rev. George Edward. b. Ludwigsburg, Würtemberg 4 Sep. 1801; ed. at Univs. of Tubingen and Gottingen; Ph. Doc. Tubingen 1839; LL.D. Gottingen 1839; settled in England 1826; head of a classical school at Hampstead, afterwards at Coombe Wood; naturalised by private act of parliament 2 and 3 Vict., cap. 51 June 1839; ordained to curacy of Ham, Surrey July 1839; V. of Roehampton, Surrey 1842–72; R. of West Allington Lincs. 1872 to death; edited *John Bull* weekly paper 1848–56; author of *Henry Pestalozzi and his plan of education* 1831; *The Standard of Catholicity* 1840, 2 ed. 1844; *Vindication of the Church* 1844; *The life of St. Paul* 1849; *Bishop Blomfield and his times* 1857. d. West Allington 19 Jany. 1874.

BICHENO, James Ebenezer (son of Rev. James Bicheno of Newbury, Berks, baptist minister who d. 9 April 1831 aged 80). b. Newbury 1785; F.L.S. 7 April 1812, secretary 1825–32; barrister M.T. 17 May 1822; comr. to inquire into expediency of introducing Poor Law into Ireland 1833–36; colonial sec. in Van Diemen's Land Sep. 1842 to death, arrived out there 10 April 1843; a founder of Royal Society of Van Diemen's Land 1844; author of *An inquiry into the nature of benevolence* 1817; *Observations on the philosophy of criminal jurisprudence* 1819; *Ireland and its economy* 1830. d. Hobart Town 25 Feb. 1851. *Proc. of Linnæan Soc ii, 180 (1855).*

BICKERS, Henry. b. near Leicester square, London; bookseller in Noel st. Soho, in Leicester square 1833 to death; partner with H. J. Bush 1847–63; published many standard works 1863 to death. d. 83 Cumberland road, London 6 Aug. 1875 aged 69.

BICKERS, Henry (son of the preceding). Head of firm of Bickers and Son, publishers Leicester square, London 1875 to death. d. Dulwich 1 Dec. 1884 aged 49. His copyrights were sold at Hodgson's Chancery lane for £8,500 March 1885.

BICKERSTETH, Robert (youngest son of Henry Bickersteth of Kirkby Lonsdale, Westmoreland, surgeon). b. Kirkby Lonsdale 1787; M.R.C.S. 1806, F.R.C.S. 1843; practised at Liverpool 1807 to death; surgeon to Liverpool infirmary 1810–50. d. 2 Rodney st. Liverpool 17 April 1857. *Lancet i, 441 (1857).*

BICKERSTETH, Right Rev. Robert (4 son of Rev. John Bickersteth, R. of Sapcote. co. Leicester who d. 2 Sep. 1855 aged 74). b. Acton, Suffolk 24 Aug. 1816; ed. at Queen's coll. Cam., B.A. 1841, M.A. 1848, D.D. 1857; ordained deacon 1841, priest 1842; C. of Sapcote 1841–43; C. of St. Giles's Reading 1843–45; Inc. of St. John's church Clapham 1845–51; R. of St. Giles's in the Fields, London 1851–56; canon residentiary of Salisbury April 1854–56; bishop of Ripon 30 Nov. 1856 to death, consecrated in Ripon Minster 18 June 1857; pres. of Church Congress at Leeds 8 Oct. 1872; edited *The weekly visitor* 1851; author of *Bible landmarks* 1850; *Means of grace* 1851 and many charges and sermons. d the palace Ripon 15 April 1884. bur. in south end of Cathedral churchyard 19 April. *Our bishops and deans by Rev. F. Arnold ii, 103–16 (1875); Orthodox London by Rev. C. M. Davies, 2 series (1875) 135–42, 394–95; Illust. news of the world iii, (1859), portrait; I.L.N. xxx, 43 (1857), portrait, lxxxiv, 401 (1884), portrait; Graphic xxix, 400 (1884), portrait.*

BICKERTON, Thomas. Educ. at Andersonian Univ. of Glasgow; L.R.C.S. Edin. 1851, L.S.A. 1851; house surgeon to Warrington dispensary; surgeon to the Emigration service; practised at Liverpool 1854 to death; surgeon to the Eye and Ear infirmary; consulting surgeon to London and North Western railway company; a skilful operator in ophthalmic surgery. d. Mount Pleasant, Liverpool 13 April 1872 aged 45. *British Medical journal i, 459 (1872).*

BICKMORE, REV. CHARLES. Ed. at Trin. coll. Cam., B.A. 1840, M.A. 1843; ad eund. Ox. 1853; Incorp. at Trin, coll. Ox. 1857, B.D. and D.D. 1857; C. of Bebbington, Cheshire 1840–43; asst. Min. at Temple Church Balsall, Warwick 1848–54; Min. of Christ Church Leamington 1856–70; author of *A course of historical and chronological instruction; A series of questions and answers on Dr. Smith's History of Greece.* d. Highlands, Leamington 12 May 1880 aged 73.

BICKNELL, ELHANAN *(son of Wm. Bicknell of London, serge manufacturer who d. 21 Nov. 1825 aged 77).* b. Blackman st. London 21 Dec. 1788; joined a firm at Newington Butts engaged in the sperm whale fishery 1809 retired from business 1859; lived at Herne hill, Surrey 1819 to death where he formed a splendid collection of pictures by Gainsborough, Turner, Roberts and other modern British painters, this collection was sold at Christie's 25–29 April 1863 for sum of £74,380. *d.* Herne hill 27 Nov. 1861. *Waagen's Treasures of art ii,* 349–54 (1854).

BICKNELL, HENRY EDGEWORTH *(younger son of John Bicknell of Lincoln's Inn, barrister).* b. 1787; ed. at Greenwich; clerk to the registrars of high court of Chancery June 1809; senior registrar to 11 July 1859 when he retired on a superannuation allowance of £2,250; served under 14 Lord Chancellors. *d.* 28 Upper Bedford place, Russell sq. London 20 Feb. 1879 in 92 year.

BICKNELL, HERMAN (3 *son of Elhanan Bicknell 1788–1861).* b. Herne hill 2 April 1830; ed. at Paris, Hanover, Univ. coll. London and St. Bartholomew's hospital; M.R.C.S. 1854; assistant surgeon of 81 Foot 16 May 1855 and of 84 Foot 15 Feb. 1861; served during Indian mutiny; explored parts of Java, Thibet and the Himalayas; went to Cairo 1862; joined the annual pilgrimage to the shrine of. Mohammed at Mecca May 1862, a dangerous exploit which no other Englishman had achieved without disguise of person or nationality; climbed nearly all the chief mountains in Switzerland; travelled over nearly the whole globe; author of *Hafiz of Shiraz, selections from his poems translated from the Persian by H. Bicknell* 1875. *d.* 48 Seymour st. Portman sq. London 14 March 1875. *bur.* at Ramsgate. *H. Bicknell's Hafiz of Shiraz* (1875) ix–xii, 365–68.

BIDDER, GEORGE PARKER *(son of Mr. Bidder of Moreton Hampstead, Devon, stonemason).* b. Moreton Hampstead 14 June 1806; was ex-

hibited about England as the 'calculating phenomenon'; ed. at Camberwell gr. sch. 1818–19 and Univ. of Edin. 1819–24; engaged on the ordnance survey 1824–25; civil engineer in London 1825–77; A.I.C.E. 1825, M.I.C.E. 1837, member of. council 1847 to death, vice pres. 1854, pres. 1860 and 1861; a founder of Electric Telegraph company 1846; constructed Victoria docks, London 100 acres for less than £870,000 in 1853; engineer of Royal Danish railway opened 1855; originator of railway swing bridge, the first of which was erected at Reedham in Norfolk; lieut. col. commandant of Engineer and railway volunteer staff corps 1865. *d.* Ravensbury, Dartmouth 20 Sep. 1878. *I.L.N. xxviii,* 267–68 (1856), *portrait; Min. of Proc. of Instit. of C.E. xv,* 251–80 (1856), *lvii,* 294–309 (1879), his contributions to these proceedings embrace the whole range of engineering and require no less than 16 columns of the general indexes for citation.

BIDDER, SAMUEL PARKER. *b.* 10 Nov. 1843; assistant manager to Victoria Docks graving company; took out 2 patents for apparatus for breaking down coal, shale, stone and other minerals 1868; took out a patent for safety lamps 1869, which have come into very general use in South Wales; A.I.C.E. 1 Dec. 1868. *d.* Southsea 10 Jany. 1878.

BIDDLE, RICHARD JUNIUS (3 *son of Richard Biddle, of Wooton under Edge, co. Gloucester).* b. 9 Nov. 1832; a marine artist; exhibited 6 sea pieces at Suffolk st. exhibition, and Royal Academy 1877–80. *d.* 30 Nov. 1882.

BIDDLECOMBE, SIR GEORGE *(son of Thomas Biddlecombe of Sheerness dockyard, who d. 12 Sep. 1844).* b. Portsea 5 Nov. 1807; officer in H.E.I. Co's. navy 1825–28; second master R.N. May 1828; master of 6 different ships 1836–50; master of the Baltic fleet on board Duke of Wellington 14 March to 27 Dec. 1854; assistant master attendant in Keyham yard, Devonport 26 Feb. 1855 to 5 Nov. 1864; master attendant of Woolwich yard 5 Nov. 1864 to Jany. 1868; C.B. 13 March 1867; staff captain 1 July 1867; knighted at Windsor Castle 26 June 1873; granted a Greenwich hospital pension 29 May 1874; author of *Art of rigging* 1848; *Remarks on the English Channel* 1850, 6 *ed.* 1863; *Naval tactics and trials of sailing* 1850; *Steam fleet tactics* 5 Nov. 1857. *d.* 68 Granville park, Lewisham 22 July 1878. *Autobiography of Sir George Biddlecombe* 1878.

BIDDULPH, EDWARD. Second lieutenant Bengal artillery 1806; lieut. col. 6 Dec. 1839 to 6 Oct. 1846; C.B. 22 May 1843. *d.* Fitzroy terrace, Regent's park, London 3 Dec. 1858 aged 70.

BIDDULPH, ROBERT. *b.* 1801; ed. at Harrow and Brasenose coll. Ox.; M.P. for city of Hereford 12 Dec. 1832 to 17 July 1837; sheriff of Hereford 1857. *d.* 31 Eaton place, London 28 Feb. 1864.

BIDDULPH, ROBERT MYDDELTON. *b.* Manchester sq. London 20 June 1805; ed. at Eton and Ch. Ch. Ox.; M.P. for Denbigh 1830–32, for Denbighshire 1832–34 and 1852–68; colonel of Denbigh militia 3 March 1840 to death; lord lieut. of Denbighshire 1841 to death; aide-de-camp to the Queen 1869 to death. *d.* 35 Grosvenor place, London 21 March 1872.

BIDDULPH, SAMUEL. *b.* Hyson Green near Nottingham 23 Dec. 1840; a lace maker; professional cricketer; a good batsman and bowler and a firstrate wicket keeper; employed by the Marylebone Club at Lord's cricket ground, London 1863 to death. *d.* Mornington st. Nottingham 7 March 1876.

BIDDULPH, SIR THEOPHILUS, 6 Baronet. *b.* East Barnet, Herts 25 March 1785; succeeded 30 July 1841; sheriff of Warwickshire 1849. *d.* Birdingbury hall, Rugby 15 July 1854.

BIDDULPH, SIR THEOPHILUS WILLIAM, 7 Baronet. *b.* Nursling, Hants 18 Jany. 1830; succeeded 15 July 1854. *d.* Mentone 1 March 1883.

BIDDULPH, SIR THOMAS MYDDELTON (2 *son of Robert Biddulph of Ledbury, Herefordshire who assumed name of Myddelton and d.* 1843). *b.* 29 July 1809; ed. at Eton; cornet 1 Life Guards 7 Oct. 1826; captain 16 May 1834 to 31 Oct. 1851 when placed on h.p.; Master of the Queen's household 16 July 1851 to 3 March 1866 and 16 July 1878 to death; one of joint keepers of Queen's privy purse 3 March 1866, sole keeper 30 April 1867; receiver general of Duchy of Cornwall 31 March 1866; general 1 Oct. 1877; K.C.B. 27 March 1863; P.C. 22 Dec. 1877. *d.* Abergeldie Mains near Balmoral 28 Sep. 1878. *bur.* churchyard of Clewer near Windsor 7 Oct. *Queen Victoria's More leaves from the journal of a life in the Highlands* (1884) 375–78; *Graphic* xviii, 392 (1878), *portrait.*

BIDWELL, JOHN. Superintendent of consular department in Foreign Office 15 Jany. 1826 to 30 Sep. 1851 when he retired on pension. *d.* Park place, St. James's st. London 31 Oct. 1853 aged 70.

BIDWELL, JOHN CARNE (*eld. child of Joseph Bidwell of Exeter, merchant*). *b.* Exeter 1815; a merchant at Sydney N.S.W. 1838; made an exploring voyage to New Zealand 1839; comr. of crown lands and chairman of bench of magistrates for district of Wide Bay N.S.W.; discovered the Bunya Bunya tree (afterwards named after him Araucaria Bidwelli) and the Nymphœa gigantea; author of *Rambles in New Zealand* 1841. *d.* Tinana. Maryborough, Australia March 1853.

BIGG, HENRY HEATHER (*son of Mr. Bigg of London, surgical instrument maker*). *b.* Dean st. Southwark 23 July 1826; studied at St. George's hospital; a surgical instrument maker in London; made the substitutes for lost limbs of our soldiers wounded in Crimean war; A.I.C.E. 4 March 1862; author of *On artificial limbs* 1855; *Orthopraxy the mechanical treatment of deformities* 1865, 3 ed. 1877; *The gentle treatment of spinal curvature* 1875. *d.* 56 Wimpole st. Cavendish sq. London 30 April 1881. *Min. of Proc. of Instit. of C.E.* lxviii, 317–20 (1882).

BIGG, JOHN STANYAN. *b.* Ulverston, Lancashire 14 July 1828; editor of the *Ulverston Advertiser* 1848 to about 1854 and 1860 to death, and proprietor 1863 to death; editor of the *Downshire Protestant* about 1854–60; author of *The sea King, a metrical romance in* 6 cantos 1848; *Night and the Soul, a dramatic poem* 1854; *Alfred Staunton, a novel* 1860; *Shifting scenes and other poems* 1862. *d.* 7 Hoad terrace, Ulverston 19 May 1865. *Ulverston Advertiser 25 May* 1865 *p.* 4. *col.* 5.

BIGGAR, WILLIAM. Editor and proprietor of *The railway times* weekly paper. *d.* Thorpe banks, Willow vale, Shepherd's Bush 27 Dec. 1872 in 64 year.

BIGGE, ARTHUR (7 *son of Charles Wm. Bigge of Linden, Northumberland*). *b.* 18 May 1818; ed. at Rugby and Univ. coll. Ox., B.A. 1840, M.A. 1843; fellow of All Soul's college, bursar 1848–58; barrister I.T. 7 June 1844; stipendiary magistrate for Brighton (the first) 3 Feb. 1855 to 3 May 1884; started the plan of presenting to the deserving aged poor of Brighton on St. Thomas's day annually sum of 10/- each. *d.* 23 Cambridge road Hove, Brighton 28 Aug. 1885.

BIGGE, REV. JOHN FREDERIC. Educ. at Univ. coll. Durham, B.A. 1840, M.A. 1843; V. of Ovingham 1841–47; V. of Stamfordham 1847 to death; author of many articles in *Transactions of Tyneside Naturalists field club.* *d.* Newcastle 28 Feb. 1885 in 71 year.

BIGGS, JAMES. *b.* Canterbury; bookseller at 18 Strand, London, removed to 421 Strand; started 13 May 1843 *The Family Herald or useful information and amusement for the million* in weekly numbers and monthly parts, this paper in a few years attained a circulation of 260,000 copies per week; founded Biggs's Charity 1863 for granting pensions of £10 a year to printers and their widows over 55 years of age. *d.* 421 Strand, London 22 May 1859 aged 64, leaving nearly £50,000 in legacies to about 300 charities and individuals.

BIGGS, JOHN. *b.* Leicester 1801; manufacturer at Leicester; mayor 1840, 1847 and 1855; M.P. for Leicester 1856-1862; took out a patent for lacemaking 1844. *d.* Leicester 4 June 1871.

BIGGS, WILLIAM. *b.* Leicester 1805; mayor of Leicester 1842 and 1849; M.P. for Newport, Isle of Wight 9 July 1852 to 21 March 1857. *d.* Upper Parliament st. Liverpool 3 Oct. 1881 in 77 year.

BIGLAND, WILSON BRADDYLL. *b.* Bigland hall, Holker, Lancashire 20 July 1788; entered navy 21 Oct. 1801; captain 6 March 1821; retired V.A. 2 Oct. 1857; K.H. 25 Jany. 1836. *d.* Lansdowne place, Leamington 19 Nov. 1858.

BIGNOLD, SIR SAMUEL *(youngest son of Thomas Bignold of Norwich, banker).* *b.* Norwich 13 Oct. 1791; secretary of Norwich Union Fire insurance company 1814 and of Norwich Union Life insurance company 1818; sheriff of Norwich 1830 and mayor 1833, 1848, 1853 and 1873; knighted by the Queen at St. James's Palace 3 May 1854; M.P. for Norwich 1854–1857. *(m.* 1815 Elizabeth only child of Wm. Atkins of Ridlington, Norfolk, she *d.* 30 March 1860). *d.* Surrey st. Norwich 2 Jany. 1875. *I.L.N. lx,* 181, 189 (1872), *portrait.*

BIGSBY, JOHN JEREMIAH *(eld. son of John Bigsby of Nottingham, physician 1760–1844).* *b.* Nottingham; baptised at St. Peter's church 14 Aug. 1792; ed. at Univ. of Edin., M.D. 1814; assistant surgeon in the army 14 March 1816; physician at Newark 1827–46; lived in London 1846 to death; F.G.S. 1823, Murchison medallist 1874, founded Bigsby gold medal 1877; F.R.G.S. 1850; F.R.S. 3 June 1869; author of *The shoe and canoe, or pictures of travel in the Canadas* 2 vols. 1850; *Thesaurus Siluricus the flora and fauna of the Silurian period* 1868; *Thesaurus Devonico-Carboniferus the flora and fauna of the Devonian and Carboniferous periods* 1878. *d.* 89 Gloucester place, Portman sq. London 10 Feb. 1881. *Quarterly Journal of Geol. Soc. xxxvii,* 39–41 (1881).

BIGSBY, ROBERT *(only son of Robert Bigsby 1764–1825, registrar of archdeaconry of Nottingham).* *b.* Castle gate, Nottingham 11 April 1806; ed. at Repton school; a virtuoso or collector of relics and memorials of illustrious characters; author of *The triumph of Drake, a poem* 1839; *Miscellaneous poems and essays* 1842; *Visions of the times of old, or the antiquarian enthusiast* 3 vols. 1848; *Ombo, a dramatic romance in 12 acts* 1853; *Historical and topographical description of Repton* 1854; *Irminsula, or the great pillar, a mythological research* 1864; *Memoir of the order of St. John of Jerusalem* 1869 and 10 other books; granted civil list pension of £100 16 Jany. 1860; member of order of St. John of Jerusalem; F.S.A., F.R.S.; a knight of St. James of Portugal. *d.* 4 Beaufort terrace, Peckham Rye, London 27 Sep. 1873. *The Freemason* 18 Oct. 1873 *p.* 677.

BILBY, THOMAS. *b.* Southampton 1794; musical composer; best known as composer of the hymn tune called "Joyful." *d.* Islington, London 24 Sep. 1872.

BILLER, GEORGE. *b.* 20 Nov. 1811; solicitor in London; wrote many letters to *The Church Advocate* and other papers on Priestly Absolution; author of *Rhymes, reasons and recollections from the common-place books of a Sexagenarian* 1876; *A few suggestions on Prayer book reform* 1878. *d.* 43 Agate road, Hammersmith 24 April 1885.

BILLING, ARCHIBALD *(son of Theodore Billing of Cromlyn, co. Dublin).* *b.* Cromlyn 10 Jany. 1791; ed. at Trin. coll. Dub., B.A. 1811, M.B. 1814, M.A. and M.D. 1818; incorporated M.D. at Oxford 22 Oct. 1818; physician in London 1818 to death; F.R.C.P. 22 Dec. 1819, Censor 1823, Consiliarius 1852 and 1855–57; the first in London to organise a system of practical teaching at the bedside and to give it full effect by regular clinical lectures; physician to London Hospital 2 July 1822 to 4 June 1845; member of senate of Univ. of London 1836 to death; F.R.S. 6 June 1844; author of *First principles of medicine* 1831, 6 ed. 1868; *On the treatment of Asiatic cholera* 1848; *Practical observations on diseases of the lungs and heart* 1852; *The science of gems, jewels, coins and medals* 1867. *d.* 34 Park lane, London 2 Sep. 1881. *Medical Circular i,* 243–45 (1852), *portrait; I.L.N. lxxix,* 272 (1881), *portrait; Graphic xxiv,* 389 (1881), *portrait.*

BILLING, RICHARD ANNESLEY. *b.* 1814; called to bar in Ireland Nov. 1839; practised at Dublin; admitted to bar at Melbourne 23 Oct. 1856; lecturer in law at Melbourne

BILLING, R. A. *(Con.)*

Univ.; Q.C. 1878; county court judge for western division of Victoria April 1882 to death. *d.* Melbourne 21 June 1882.

BILLINGE, MARY *(dau. of Charles Billinge of Eccleston near Prescot).* *b.* Eccleston 6 Nov. 1772. *d.* Edge lane, Liverpool 20 Dec. 1863 aged 91, but generally reputed to be 112 and so recorded in the 26th report of the Registrar General. *W. J. Thoms's Human longevity* (1873) 34–37, 105–13.

BILLINGS, ELKANAH *(2 son of Bradish Billings, of Gloucester near Ottawa, then called Bytown, farmer).* *b.* Gloucester 5 May 1820; ed. at Ottawa and Potsdam in state of New York; admitted attorney at Toronto 1844; called to bar at Toronto 1845; practised at Ottawa 1845–48, and at Renfrew 1849–52; edited the *Citizen* paper at Ottawa 1852–55; palæontologist to Geological survey of Canada at Montreal 1 Aug. 1856 to death; visited Europe 1858; F.G.S. April 1858; published the *Canadian Naturalist* Feb. 1856, edited the first vol. and wrote 55 out of the 63 papers in it; contributed to *Silliman's Journal;* presented his fine collection of Star fishes, Cystideans and Crinoids to museum of Geological survey of Canada. *d.* Montreal 14 June 1876. *Canadian Naturalist viii,* 251–61 (1878); *Quarterly journal of Geol. Soc. xxxiii,* 48–50 (1877).

BILLINGS, ROBERT WILLIAM. *b.* London 1813; pupil of John Britton, topographical draughtsman 1813–20; illustrated Godwin's *History of St. Paul's Cathedral* 1837; *Illustrations of the Temple Church, London,* 1838; *Baronial and ecclesiastical antiquities of Scotland* 240 *illustrations* 4 vols. 1845–52; restored the chapel of Edinburgh Castle; built Castle Wemyss, Renfrewshire. *d.* The Moulinère, Putney, Surrey 14 Nov. 1874. *Builder xxxii,* 982, 1035 (1874).

BILLINGTON, WILLIAM *(son of a contractor for road making).* *b.* the Yew Trees, Samlesbury near Blackburn 1827; worked in cotton mills at Blackburn 1839; a beerseller at Blackburn; wrote a ballad called *Th' Shurat Weyvur* 14,000 copies of which were sold at time of Lancashire cotton famine; author of *Sheen and shade* 1861; *Lancashire poems with other sketches* 1883, some copies of which have a portrait of him. *d.* 2 Bradshaw st. Blackburn 3 Jany. 1884 aged 56.

BINDLEY, CHARLES. *b.* 1796; author of following books all written under pseudonym of Harry Hieover; *Stable talk and table talk,* 2

BINDLEY, C. *(Con.)*

vols. 1845–46, *portrait; The pocket and the stud* 1848, *portrait; The stud for practical purposes and practical men* 1849; *Practical horsemanship* 1850; *The hunting field* 1850; *Bipeds and quadrupeds* 1853; *Sporting facts and sporting fancies* 1853; *The world how to square it* 1854; *Hints to horsemen* 1856; *Precept and practice* 1857; *The sportsman's friend in a frost* 1857; *The sporting world* 1858 and *Things worth knowing about horses* 1859. *d.* at house of Sir Thomas Barrett-Lennard, 7 Lewes crescent, Brighton 12 Feb. 1859.

BINDON, SAMUEL HENRY. *b.* Ireland 1812; ed. at Trin. coll. Dublin, B.A. 1835; called to Irish bar Nov. 1838; practised at Dublin; went out to Victoria 1855; called to bar at Melbourne 22 May 1855; member of legislative assembly of Victoria 1864–69; minister of justice 1866–1869; county court judge at Sale, Victoria 1869 to death except a short time, during which the Berry ministry took all the judges of county courts off the bench, the day when this was done 9 Jany. 1878 was known as *Black Wednesday;* had a prominent share in establishment of technological classes in large places. *d.* Melbourne 1 Aug. 1879 in 67 year.

BINFIELD, JOHN BILSON *(son of Mr. Binfield of Reading, organist who d.* 1839). *b.* Reading 1805; organist of St. Giles's church Reading many years; author of *The choral service of the Church* 1846; editor and compiler of *The Reading psalmody* 1847; set Dean Milman's *Martyr of Antioch* to music. *d.* Devizes 28 June 1875.

BINGE, JOHN BULL *(son of a Sheffield cutler).* First appeared in London May 1839 at Strand theatre in Lee's adaptation of Aubers opera *The fairy lake;* sang at Covent Garden theatre 1840–42; known as The singing mouse from his small voice; kept a toyshop in the Lowther Arcade; sec. to Covent Garden theatrical fund 1869 to death. *d.* New Malden, Surrey 21 Nov. 1878 aged about 63.

BINGHAM, CHARLES. *b.* 1 June 1815; 2 lieut. R.A. 20 June 1832; brigade major at Woolwich 1849–54; deputy adjutant general to R.A. 1 April 1858 to death; colonel R.A. 20 Jany. 1863 to death. *(m.* 13 March 1841 Williamina Henrietta dau. of John Mackintosh, M.D. of Edinburgh, she was granted a civil list pension of £150, 19 June 1865). *d.* Brighton 6 April 1864.

BINGHAM, Rev. Charles William *(youngest son of Rev. Wm. Bingham 1771-1810, R. of Cameley Somerset).* *b.* 28 Sep. 1810; ed. at New coll. Ox., fellow, B.A. 1833, M.A. 1836; V. of Sydling St. Nicholas Dorset 1838–46; R. of Melcombe Horsey, Dorset 23 Feb. 1842 to death; preb. of Salisbury 1876 to death; author of *Commentaries on the four last books of the Pentateuch translated from the Latin of John Calvin 4 vols.* 1852–55; a frequent contributor to *Notes and Queries* 1850 to death. *d.* Bingham's Melcombe 1 Dec. 1881.

BINGHAM, Henry. Second lieut. 60 Rifles 30 April 1827, lieut. col. 19 June 1857 to 1865; inspecting field officer 1865–70; M.G. 6 March 1868. *d.* Wolverton house, co. Dublin 1 Oct. 1878.

BINGHAM, Peregrine *(elder son of Rev. Peregrine Bingham 1754–1826, R. of Edmundesham, Dorset).* *b.* 1788; ed. at Winchester and Magd. coll. Ox., B.A. 1810; barrister M.T. 27 Nov. 1818; recorder of Southampton 5 Nov. 1830 to July 1840; contested Southampton 9 Jany. 1835; police magistrate at Worship st. London 1841, at Great Marlborough st. 1846–60; lived at 35 Gordon square, London 1842 to death; author of *The law and practice of judgments and executions* 1815; *The law of infancy and coverture* 1816; *A system of shorthand* 1821; *Reports of cases in Court of Common Pleas and other courts* 10 vols. 1824–34; *New cases in the Court of Common Pleas and other courts 6 vols.* 1835–41; one of chief contributors to *Westminster Review*, wrote 5 articles in the first number Jany. 1824. *d.* 35 Gordon sq. London 1 Nov. 1864.

BINGHAM, Rev. Richard *(son of Rev. Isaac Moody Bingham, R. of Runwell, Essex who d. 1807).* *b.* 1 April 1765; ed. at Winchester and New coll. Ox., fellow, B.A. 1787, B.C.L. 1801; P.C. of Trinity church, Gosport 1790 to death; V. of Great Hale, Lincs. 1796 to death; preb. of Chichester cathedral 22 July 1807 to death; sentenced to 6 months imprisonment in county gaol at Winchester 26 Nov. 1813 for having illegally obtained a license for a public house when no such house was in existence; published by subscription third ed. of Joseph Bingham's *Origines Ecclesiasticæ* 1829. *d.* Newhouse, Gosport 18 July 1858. *Proceedings in a trial, the King against Rev. Richard Bingham* 1814.

BINGHAM, Rev. Richard *(eld. son of the preceding).* *b.* 1798; ed. at Magd. hall Ox., B.A. 1821, M.A. 1827; C. of Trinity church, Gosport 1821–43; P.C. of Ch. Ch. Harwood,

BINGHAM, Rev. R. *(Con.)*
Bolton 1844–52; C. of St. Mary's Marylebone 1853–56; P.C. of Queenborough, Kent 1856–70; edited *The works of the Rev. Joseph Bingham* 10 vols., *Clarendon Press Oxford* 1855; author of *Liturgia Recusa or suggestions for revising the services of the United church of England and Ireland* 1860; *Liturgiæ recusæ exemplar, The Prayer book as it might be* 1863; *The Gospel according to Isaiah* 1870; *Hymnologia Christiana Latina* 1871. *d.* Sutton, Surrey 22 Jany. 1872.

BINGHAM, Richard Camden. *b.* 2 May 1801; chargé d'affaires at Venezuela 23 Nov. 1852 to 31 Aug. 1858. *d.* 23 Jany. 1872.

BINNEY, Edward William. *b.* Morton, Notts. 1812; solicitor at Manchester 1836; conducted the case for the Claimant in the great Chadwick law suit Nov. 1847; a paraffin oil manufacturer in Scotland; chief founder and sec. of Manchester geological society Oct. 1838, pres. 1857–59 and 1865–67, contributed 33 papers to the Transactions 1839–72; member of Manchester literary and philosophical society Jan. 1842, president to death; F.G.S. 1853, F.R.S. 5 June 1856; possessed the most exact knowledge of coal fields of Lancashire and Cheshire and of the geology of the whole district. *d.* Cheetham hill, Manchester 19 Dec. 1881. *Trans. of Geol. Soc. of Manchester xvi*, 256–59 (1882); *Proc. of Manchester Lit. and Philos. Soc. xxi*, 142–48 (1882).

BINNEY, Rev. Thomas. *b.* Newcastle-on-Tyne April 1798; apprenticed to Mr. Angas of Newcastle, bookseller 1813–20; ed. at Wymondley college Herts 1820–23; minister of the New meeting, Bedford 1823; minister of St. James's st. chapel Newport, Isle of Wight Aug. 1824 to July 1829; ordained 29 Dec. 1824; minister of King's Weighhouse Chapel Eastcheap, London July 1829 to 4 July 1869, where foundation stone of new chapel was laid 16 Oct. 1833; went to the United States and Canada 1845 and to Australia 1857; LL.D. Univ. of Aberdeen 1852; chairman of Congregational Union of England and Wales 1848; founded the Colonial Missionary Society 1836; author of *Illustrations of the practical power of faith* 1830, 3 ed. 1856; *Conscientious clerical nonconformity* 1839, 5 ed. 1860; *Is it possible to make the best of both worlds, a book for young men* 1853, this book sold at the rate of 100 a day for many months, it was translated into several languages; *St. Paul his life and ministry* 1866; author of three Letters under pseud. of *Fiat Justitia*

1831, and of *The Great Gorham case* 1850, and several other pamphlets under pseud. of *John Search;* author of a pamphlet called *Leicester Gaol by A. Balance, Esq. of the Middle Temple* 1841. *d.* Doric lodge, High road, Upper Clapton 24 Feb. 1874. *Sermons by T. Binney second series, edited by Henry Allon* (1875) *xiii–lxvi, portrait; A memorial of the late Rev. T. Binney, edited by Rev. J. Stoughton* 1874; *T. Binney, his mind, life and opinions by Rev. E. P. Hood* 1874; *The lamps of the temple* 3 *ed.* (1865) 146–87; *Contemporary Review xxiii,* 884–97 (1874); *Graphic ix,* 218 (1874), *portrait;* He is introduced as Canon Burney into the novels called *The master of Marton* 1864 and *Diary of a novelist* 1870 *by Eliza Tabor.*

BINNS, EDWARD. M.D.; author of *The anatomy of sleep or the art of procuring sound and refreshing slumber at will* 1842; *Prodromus towards a philosophical inquiry into the intellectual powers of the negro* 1844. *d.* Lucca, Jamaica 10 Feb. 1851.

BINNS, JOHN (*son of Mr. Binns of Dublin, ironmonger who d.* 1774). *b.* Dublin 22 Dec. 1772; apprenticed to a soapboiler 1786; a member of the London Corresponding Society 1794 which became the greatest political association in Great Britain, chairman of its general committee 6 months in 1795; connected with the United Irishmen; left London for France 21 Feb. 1798 but arrested at Margate 27 Feb. and after an examination by the Privy Council committed to Tower of London; tried for high treason at Maidstone May 1798 when acquitted; confined in Clerkenwell prison, then in Gloucester prison till March 1801; sailed for America July 1801; started a newspaper called *The Republican Argus* at Northumberland, Pennsylvania March 1802; edited at Philadelphia March 1807 to 1829 *Democratic Press* which soon became leading paper in the state; alderman of Philadelphia Dec. 1822 to 1844. *d.* Philadelphia 16 June 1860. *Recollections of the life of John Binns* 1854, *portrait.*

BINNS, THOMAS. Head master of the Friends' school, Grove house, Tottenham 1828; member of Committee of British and Foreign Bible Society 1852–68, chairman of the Editorial Sub-Committee. *d.* Rockley near Bristol 2 Dec. 1872 aged 74. *Annual Monitor for* 1874 6–10.

BINSTEAD, CHEESMAN HENRY. *b.* 1797; entered navy 10 June 1810; agent for trans-

ports afloat 1828–34; captain 7 March 1853; retired V.A. 30 July 1875. *d.* South parade, Wakefield 26 Nov. 1876.

BINYON, EDWARD. *b.* Manchester 1828; landscape painter both in oil and water colours; contributed to exhibitions of Royal Academy and Dudley Gallery 1857–76; his picture 'The bay of Mentone' has frequently been reproduced; lived in island of Capri many years. *d.* 5 Via Piazza, Capri 18 July 1876.

BIRCH, REV. HENRY MILDRED (*eld. son of Rev. Wm. Henry Rous Birch, R. of Southwold, Suffolk*). *b.* Bedfield rectory, Suffolk 1820; ed. at Eton and King's coll. Cam., scholar 1839, Craven scholar 1841, B.A. 1843, M.A. 1846; fellow of his college 1843, members prizeman 1844; assistant master at Eton; tutor to Prince of Wales 6 Aug. 1848 to 1851; R. of Prestwich, Lancs. 1852–84; chaplain in ordinary to the Queen 27 Feb. 1852; B.D. Lambeth 1862; hon. chaplain to Prince of Wales 16 Feb. 1863; canon of Ripon 29 June 1868 to death; proctor in convocation 1868, 1874 and 1880 to death. *d.* St. Leonard's lodge, Windsor 29 June 1884. *I.L.N. xlii,* 456 (1863), *portrait.*

BIRCH, JAMES WHEELER WOODFORD (*eld. son of Rev. James Wheeler Birch, V. of All Saint's, Hertford*). member of Ceylon civil service 1846–70; colonial sec. of the Straits Settlements May 1870; British resident in Malay state of Perak Nov. 1874 to death; assassinated by the Malays at Perak 2 Nov. 1875.

BIRCH, JOHN FRANCIS. Second lieut. R.A. 18 Sep. 1793; second lieut. R.E. 1 Jany. 1794, colonel R.E. 29 July 1825, colonel commandant 19 Oct. 1847 to death; C.B. 26 Sep. 1831; general 20 June 1854; served in Flanders, Holland, Egypt and Spain. *d.* Folkestone 29 May 1856 aged 79.

BIRCH, SIR RICHARD JAMES HOLWELL (*son of Richard Comyns Birch, of Bengal civil service*). *b.* Calcutta 1803; entered Bengal army 1821; studied at Trin. coll. Cam. 1823–24; judge advocate general to the forces in Bengal 1841–52; military secretary to government of India 1854 to 31 Dec. 1861 when he retired; M.G. 4 May 1858; C.B. 5 June 1849, K.C.B. 18 May 1860. *d.* Venice 25 Feb. 1875. *I.L.N. lxvi,* 259 (1875).

BIRCH, ROBERT HENRY. *b.* 1771; second lieut. R.A. 9 March 1795; colonel 10 Jany. 1837 to 9 Nov. 1846, col. commandant 12 Aug. 1849 to death; M.G. 9 Nov. 1846. *d.* Dublin 29 June 1851.

BIRCH, SAMUEL (*eld. son of Rev. Samnel Birch, R. of St. Mary Woolnoth, City of London who d. 1848*). *b.* London 3 Nov. 1813; ed. at Merchant Taylors' school 1826–31; employed in Public record office 1834; assistant in department of Antiquities of British Museum Jany. 1836, assistant keeper 1844; keeper of the Oriental Mediæval and British antiquities and Ethnographical collections 1861 to death; corresponding member of Archæological Institute of Rome 1839, of Berlin Academy 1851, of Academy of inscriptions of French Institute 1861; LL.D. St. Andrews 1862; determined the ancient Cypriote to be a Greek language 1872; presided over Congress of Orientalists held in London 14 Sep. 1874; received German order of the Crown Nov. 1874; Rede lecturer Univ. of Cam. for 1876; LL.D. Cam. 1875; hon. fellow of Queen's coll. Ox. 1875; D.C.L. Ox. 1876; author of *Gallery of antiquities* 1842; *Introduction to the study of hieroglyphics* 1857; *History of ancient pottery* 1857, 2 ed. 1873; edited *Records of the past* 12 vols. 1873–77; *The manners and customs of the ancient Egyptians by Sir J. G. Wilkinson, new ed.* 3 vols. 1878. *d.* 64 Caversham road, Kentish Town, London 27 Dec. 1885. *Times 29 Dec. 1885 p. 8, col. 3; Athenæum 2 Jany. 1886 pp. 34–35; Dublin Univ. Mag. xc, 53–60 (1877), portrait; I.L.N. lxxxviii, 64 (1886), portrait.*

BIRCH, SYLVESTER DOUGLAS. A writer in Madras civil service 1830; secretary and treasurer of Bank of Madras 1843; accountant general at Bombay, pres. of the mint committee and government director of Bank of Bombay 1859 to 28 Feb. 1865 when he retired on an annuity. *d.* San Remo, Italy 4 Feb. 1881.

BIRCH, SIR THOMAS BERNARD, 2 Baronet. *b.* 18 March 1791; succeeded 22 Aug. 1833; sheriff of Lancs. 1841; M.P. for Liverpool 30 July 1847 to 1 July 1852. *d.* The Hazles Prescot near Liverpool 3 March 1880.

BIRCH, THOMAS JACOB (*2 son of Wyrley Birch of Wretham hall near Thetford, Norfolk 1781–1866*). *b.* 15 Oct. 1806; ed. at Eton and Brasenose coll. Ox., B.A. 1828, M.A. 1831; barrister I.T. 18 Nov. 1831; recorder of Thetford March 1839 to Dec. 1866; judge of Norfolk county courts (circuit 32) March 1847 to death. *d.* Ballycroy, Mayo 26 April 1868.

BIRCHALL, REV. JOSEPH (*son of John Birchall of Prescot, watchmaker*). *b.* Prescot 1805; ed. at Manchester school and Brasn. Coll. Ox., Somerset scholar 1825, B.A. 1828, M.A. 1830; C. of Newbury, Berks. 1831–38; R.

BIRCHALL, REV. J. (*Con.*)
of Church, Lancashire 1840 to death; proctor in Convocation for Archd. of Manchester; author of *Occasional Sermons* 1840; *Ecclesiastical Synods* 1868. *d.* Church rectory 27 Oct. 1878.

BIRCHAM, FRANCIS THOMAS (*youngest son of Samuel Bircham of Booton hall, Norfolk*). *b.* Booton hall 1810; admitted solicitor 1833; practised in London to 1882; solicitor to London and South Western railway 1834–82; pres. of Incorporated law society 1874–75. *d.* Burhill near Walton-on-Thames 25 Nov. 1883. Personalty sworn upward of £161,000 3 March 1884; his correct name was Thomas Francis Bircham, but he always called himself Francis Thomas Bircham.

BIRD, REV. CHARLES SMITH (5 *child of William Bird of Liverpool, West Indian Merchant, who d. 1814*). *b.* Union st. Liverpool 28 May 1795; articled to Stanistreet and Eden of Liverpool, solicitors Feb. 1812, released from articles 1814; entered Trin. coll. Cam. 1816, scholar 1818, 3 Wr. and 2 Smith's prizeman 1820, Fell. of his coll. Sep. 1820; C. of Burghfield, Berks. 1823–44; took pupils 1823–44; F.L.S. 4 March 1828; C. of Sulhamstead 1840; V. of Gainsborough 1843–59; preb. of Lincoln 16 June 1843; chancellor of Lincoln June 1859 to death, instituted and installed 16 July 1859; edited a monthly periodical called *The Reading church guardian* 1839–40; author of *For ever and other devotional poems* 1833; *Transubstantiation tried by Scripture and reason* 1839; *The baptismal privileges, the baptismal vow, and the means of grace considered in 6 Lent lectures* 1841, 2 ed. 1843; *The eve of the Crucifixion* 1858. *d.* The Chancery, Lincoln 9 Nov. 1862. *Sketches from the life of Rev. Charles S. Bird by Rev. Claude S. Bird* (1864), *portrait.*

BIRD, EDWARD JOSEPH (*son of Rev. Godfrey Bird, R. of Little Waltham, Essex*). Entered navy 9 Sep. 1812; attempted to reach North Pole from Spitzbergen in the Hecla 1825, penetrated a little beyond 82° 45′ a latitude more northern than had ever been attained; 1 lieut. of the Erebus in Antarctic expedition 1839–43; captain of the Investigator 1848–49; admiral on h.p. 11 Dec. 1875. *d.* The Wilderness, Witham 3 Dec. 1881 in 83 year.

BIRD, FREDERIC. *b.* Colchester 23 Jany. 1818; ed. at Guy's Hospital; surgeon in Craven st. Strand 1841; performed operation of ovariotomy for ovarian dropsy 26 June 1843, being one of the pioneers of that treatment; lectured on forensic medicine at Westminster

BIRD, F. *(Con.)*

Hospital, obstetric physician there 1861; phys. to the Maternity Charity; edited *Provincial (now British) Medical Journal.* d. 13 Grosvenor st. London 28 April 1874. *Medical Circular i*, 229 (1852); *Medical times and gazette i*, 519 (1874).

BIRD, GEORGE. Writer Madras civil service 1821; judge and criminal judge of Canara 1835–38 and 1839–42; civil and session judge Coimbatore 1844–47 and 1850–51; resigned the service 25 Feb. 1851. *d.* England 20 July 1880.

BIRD, GOLDING. *b.* Downham, Norfolk 9 Dec. 1814; studied at Guy's hospital London 1832; lecturer on natural philosophy there 1836–43; L.S.A. 21 Jany. 1836, M.D. St. Andrews 24 April 1838 being only place where a degree could be obtained without residing, M.A. 18 April 1840; physician to Finsbury dispensary 1838–43; L.R.C.P. 1840, F.R.C.P. 1845; assistant phys. at Guy's hospital and lecturer on materia medica 1843 to 4 Aug. 1853; F.L.S. 1836, F.R.S. 22 Jany. 1846; author of *The elements of natural philosophy* 1839, 6 ed. 1867; *Urinary deposits their diagnosis pathology and therapeutical indications* 1844, 5 ed. 1857. *d.* Camden park, Tunbridge Wells 27 Oct. 1854. *Biographical sketch by J. H. Balfour* 1855; *Medical Circular iii*, 129 (1853), *portrait.*

BIRD, JAMES. Ed. at King's college Aberdeen 1810, M.A. 1814; apprenticed to his maternal uncle Dr. Scott of Elgin 1812–15; studied at Guy's and St. Thomas's hospitals; M.R.C.S. Sep. 1816; assistant surgeon H.E.I. Co's. Bombay service 2 Aug. 1818; residency surgeon at Sattara 1826–32; superintending surgeon of Belgaum division of the army 1840–43 and of Presidency division 1843–44; physician general to Bombay medical board 1844 to 1 Dec. 1847 when he retired. *d.* Fern acre lodge, Gerrards Cross, Bucks. 10 July 1864 aged 67.

BIRD, JAMES. Solicitor in London; coroner for West Middlesex 9 July 1862 to death. *d.* Phœnix lodge, Brook Green, Hammersmith 7 Jany. 1868.

BIRD, JAMES. *b.* Cardiff Feb. 1802; ed. at St. Bartholomew's hospital; L.S.A. 1821, M.R.C.S. 1825; surgeon at Cardiff 1825–32; surgeon in London 1832 to 1856; joint sec. with Henry Ancell to the British medical association; author of *Private devotions for girls* 1874. *d.* 80 Seymour st. Portman sq. London 4 June 1874. *Medical Circular i*, 263 (1852).

BIRD, REV. JOHN. *b.* Betchworth, Surrey 14 Sep. 1783; ed. at Stonyhurst college; ordained priest 10 Dec. 1808; professed of the 4 vows 2 Feb. 1819; rector of St. Aloysius' college 26 June 1832 to 18 May 1839 and 15 Sep. 1841; missioner at Pontefract 1842–48; superior of St. George's Residence, Worcester Nov. 1850 to death. *d.* 8 June 1853.

BIRD, LOUIS SAUNDERS. Ensign Bengal Infantry 26 Nov. 1808; col. 23 Bengal N.I. 17 April 1856–1869; L.G. 22 Feb. 1870. *d.* Clevedon, Somerset 17 April 1874 aged 81.

BIRD, ROBERT MERTTINS. *b.* 1788; Bengal civil servant; assistant to registrar of Court of Sadr Diwàni Adàlat at Calcutta 9 Nov. 1808; comr. of revenue and circuit for the Gorakhpur division 1829; member of board of revenue at Allahabad 1832; revised settlement of land revenue of North western provinces 1833–41, the most complete settlement that had yet been made in India; retired to England 1842; active member of committee of the Church Missionary Society. *d.* Torquay 22 Aug. 1853. *Dict. of nat. biog. v*, 78 (1886).

BIRD, ROBERT NICHOLAS. Ensign 20 Foot 30 Aug. 1859; lieut. 2 Dec. 1862 to death; murdered by Japanese at Kamahura about 17 miles from Yokohama 21 Nov. 1864. *R. Lindau's Erzählungen und Novellen i*, 15–54 (1871); *F. O. Adams's History of Japan i*, 485–98 (1874), *ii*, 1–5 (1875).

BIRD, WILLIAM WILBERFORCE *(eld. son of Wm. Wilberforce Bird of the Spring, Kenilworth, M.P. for Coventry).* *b.* 1784; ed. at Warwick and Geneva; writer in H.E.I. Co.'s civil service at Calcutta 11 July 1803; third ordinary member of council of India 21 March 1838; senior member of board of customs salt and opium and of the marine board 17 Sep. 1838; deputy governor of Bengal 4 times; pres. of the council 1840–44; governor general of India 15 June 1844 to 23 July 1844; very instrumental in abolition of suttee and suppression of slavery; retired to England 1844. *d.* 22 Sussex sq. Hyde Park, London 1 June 1857.

BIRDWOOD, CHRISTOPHER. *b.* 1806; ensign 3 Bombay N.I. 3 May 1825; commissariat officer of Malwa field force 1839–41; colonel Bombay staff corps 9 Nov. 1868; general 1 Oct. 1877. *d.* Pucklechurch near Bristol 4 July 1882 in 76 year. *Graphic xxvi*, 221 (1882), *portrait.*

BIRKETT, REV. GEORGE WILLIAM. Educ. at St. John's coll. Cam., scholar, B.A. 1823,

BIRKETT, REV. G. W. (*Con.*)

M.A. 1827; V. of St. Florence near Tenby 1829 to death; author of *The trial of creation and other poems* 1848. *d.* Tenby 26 Nov. 1877 aged 78.

BIRKIN, RICHARD (*eld. son of Richard Birkin of Belper, calico weaver*). *b.* Belper 6 July 1805; lace manufacturer at New Basford, Nottingham with Mr. Biddle 1826–47; juror on behalf of Nottingham for lace goods in International Exhibitions 1851 and 1862; mayor of Nottingham 1850, 55, 62 and 63; used mohair as a material for lace being the first to do so either in England or France. *d.* Aspley hall, Radford, Nottingham 10 Oct. 1870. *J. B. Robinson's Derbyshire gatherings* (1866) 70–72, *portrait; W. Felkin's History of hosiery* (1867) 368–71.

BIRKINSHAW, JOHN CASS. *b.* Bedlington iron works Durham 1811; the first articled pupil of Robert Stephenson at Newcastle; engineer of London end of London and Birmingham railway 1835; engineer of Birmingham and Derby railway 1837–42; engineer of many railways projected but not made; engineer of Danish land company 1865; M.I.C.E. 2 March 1847; took out a patent 1820 for wrought or malleable iron rails instead of cast iron as used up to that time. *d.* March 1867 in 56 year. *Min. of proc. of Instit. of C.E. xxxi*, 202–207 (1871).

BIRKS, REV. THOMAS RAWSON (*younger son of Mr. Birks of Staveley, Derbyshire, farmer*). *b.* Staveley 28 Sep. 1810; ed. at Chesterfield, Mill Hill and Trin. coll. Cam., scholar, fellow 1834–44, 2 wrangler and 2 Smith's prizemen Jany. 1834; R. of Kelshall, Herts 1844 to 1864; hon. sec. to Evangelical Alliance 1850–71; P.C. of Holy Trinity Cam. 1865–77; hon. canon of Ely cathedral 1871 to death; professor of moral theology, casuistical divinity and moral philosophy at Cambridge 30 April 1872 to death; published an edition of Paley's *Horæ Paulinæ* with notes and a supplementary treatise entitled *Horæ Apostolicæ* 1850; author of *Horæ Evangelicæ* 1852; *The Bible and modern thought* 1861; *Commentary on the book of Isaiah* 1871, 2 ed. 1878; *First principles of moral science* 1873; *Modern Utilitarianism* 1874; *Supernatural revelation* 1879 and many other books. *d.* 6 Salisbury villas, Cambridge 19 July 1883. *Record* 27 July 1883 *p.* 741.

BIRLEY, HUGH. *b.* Blackburn 21 Oct. 1817; ed. at Winchester; a partner in firm of Macintosh and Co. indiarubber manufacturers;

BIRLEY, H. (*Con.*)

chairman of National educational union; M.P. for Manchester 1868 to death. *d.* Moorland, Withington, Manchester 9 Sep. 1883.

BIRMINGHAM, JOHN. *b.* 1816; lived at Millbrook near Tuam; discovered a remarkable new star in Corona Borealis 12 May 1866; author of *Catalogue of red stars* in *Transactions of Royal Irish Academy xxvi*, 249 (1879); Cunningham medallist of the Academy 1884; discovered 22 May 1881 a deep red star in Cygnus which proved strikingly variable and became known by his name; author of a small poetical work entitled *Anglicania or England's mission to the Celt* 1863. *d.* Millbrook 7 Sep. 1884.

BIRMINGHAM, VERY REV. PATRICK. Dean of the lay college and professor of humanity Carlow college 1851 to July 1854 when he went to Australia; vice pres. and professor of theology at Carlow college Sep. 1864 to July 1871 when he went again to Australia. *d.* Fitzroy sq. London 9 Sep. 1883.

BIRNIE, ALEXANDER. *b.* Morayshire 1826; a baptist minister at Preston; walked to Falkirk 1860; a painter at the Carron works Falkirk; wrote articles in *Falkirk Advertiser* under signature of Cock of the Steeple; started the *Falkirk Liberal* a penny weekly paper 1861 which soon collapsed; having been without food or drink for a fortnight, he entered the workhouse Morpeth where he *d.* March 1862.

BIRRELL, DAVID. *b.* 15 Sep. 1800; entered Bengal army 1817; commanded a brigade at battle of Sobraon 10 Feb. 1846; lieut. col. 51 N.I. 1851, of 52 N.I. 1852 and of 72 N.I. 1857 to 1858; M.G. 25 April 1858; general 23 July 1876. *d.* 28 Oct. 1878.

BIRT, WILLIAM RADCLIFF. *b.* 15 July 1804; employed by Sir John Herschel in the reduction and arrangement of his barometric observations; investigated subject of atmospheric waves for the British Association; reduced and discussed electrical observations made at Kew 1848; F.R.A.S. 14 Jany. 1859; the first pres. of the Selenographical society 1877 or 1878 to death; author of *Hurricane and Sailor's guide* 1850; *Handbook of the law of storms* 1854, new ed. 1878. *d.* Leytonstone, Essex 14 Dec. 1881. *Monthly notices of Royal Astronom. Soc. xlii*, 142–43 (1882).

BIRTWHISTLE, JOHN. Ensign 32 Foot 14 April 1813; major 19 Jany. 1839 to 12 March 1841 when placed on h.p; M.G. 28 Aug. 1865. *d.* Cheltenham 6 Oct. 1867 aged 75.

BISHOP, ANNE *(dau. of Daniel Riviére of London, artist)*. *b.* London 1814; student at Royal academy of music June 1824 to June 1828; a singer at Philharmonic concerts 1831; one of chief singers at Vauxhall gardens, the Oratorio concerts and country festivals; went abroad with R. N. C. Bochsa the harpist 1839; sang at 260 concerts in chief cities of Europe Sept. 1839 to May 1843; sang with great success at St. Petersburg 1840–41 and in Italy 1843–46; appeared in 20 operas at the San Carlo, Naples; went to America 1846 where she appeared at Park theatre New York 4 Aug. 1847 as Linda; went to Australia 1855; sang at the Crystal palace London 1858; gave her farewell concert at Surrey music hall 17 Aug. 1859; sang in Canada, Mexico and Havana 1859–65; went to California 1865; wrecked on her way from Honolulu to China Feb. 1866; arrived in India 1867; sang in Australia 1868; re-appeared at Steinway hall New York Jany. 1881. *(m.* (1) 1832 Sir Henry Rowley Bishop 1786–1855. *m.* (2) at New York 30 April 1858, Martin Schultz). *d.* New York 18 March 1884. *Drawing room portrait gallery of eminent personages, third series* 1860, *portrait; N. P. Willis's Hurrygraphs, 2 ed.* (1851) 200–203.

BISHOP, REV. DANIEL GODFREY. Head master of Buntingford gr. sch. Herts. 1841–74; V. of Tibshelf near Alfreton, Derbyshire 1874 to death; author of numerous articles upon biblical criticism, classical literature, and general biography in *Penny Cyclopœdia*. *d.* Briston vicarage, Norfolk 14 April 1880 in 86 year.

BISHOP, REV. FRANCIS. *b.* Dorchester 27 July 1813; Unitarian minister at Cheltenham 1840, at Warrington 1841, at George's meeting Exeter 1844–47, at Liverpool 1847–56, at Manchester 1856–58 and at Chesterfield 1858 to death; edited *The Christian Investigator;* author of *The atonement, or God's way of speaking and man's way of speaking* 1843. *d.* Chesterfield 5 Aug. 1869. *The Inquirer* (1869) 533.

BISHOP, GEORGE. *b.* Leicester 21 Aug. 1785; a maker of British wines in London, being the largest maker in England; erected an observatory at South Villa, Regent's Park 1836 where 11 planets were discovered 1847–54, after his death the dome and the instruments were removed by his son George Bishop to his house at Twickenham; F.R.A.S. 1830, sec. 1833–39, treasurer 1840–57, pres. 1857–59; F.R.S. 9 June 1848; published in 1852

BISHOP, G. *(Con.)*
Astronomical observations during the years 1839–51. *d.* South villa, Regent's Park, London 14 June 1861. *Monthly notices of Royal Astronomical Soc. xxii,* 104–106 (1862).

BISHOP, SIR HENRY ROWLEY *(son of Mr. Bishop of London, Watch-maker)*. *b.* Great Portland st. London 18 Nov. 1786; pupil of Francesco Bianchi the composer; composer of ballet music at Italian opera house 1806; produced his opera of *The Circassian bride* at Drury Lane theatre 23 Feb. 1809, theatre was burnt down the next night; musical director and composer at Covent Garden theatre 1810–23, where he produced 50 musical dramas; director of music at King's theatre, Haymarket 1816–17; received freedom of city of Dublin 2 Aug. 1820; composer at Drury Lane theatre 1825–28; musical director of Vauxhall gardens 1830–33; director of Her Majesty's concerts of ancient music 1840–48; Reid professor of Music in Univ. of Edin. Nov. 1841 to Dec. 1843; knighted at St. James's palace 1 June 1842, being the first musician who ever received that honour; professor of music in Univ. of Ox. Jany. 1848 to death; Mus. Bac. Ox. 1848, Mus. Doc. 1853; author of many songs and glees, best known being *Bid me discourse, Should he upbraid, The winds whistle cold, My pretty Jane, Mynheer Van Dunck* and of the trio and chorus *The chough and crow. d.* 13 Cambridge st. Edgware road, London 30 April 1855. *I.L.N. xix,* 669–70 (1851), *portrait; Charles Mackay's Forty years recollections ii,* 165–217 (1877); *Illust. news of the world iv,* 381 (1859), *portrait.*

BISHOP, JAMES. *b.* Trowbridge, Wiltshire 1793; a cloth worker 1813; partner with Atkins and Gillman, proprietors of a menagery which became a formidable opponent to George Wombwell's menagery; attended all the great fairs in England; proprietor of various exhibitions; father of 20 children; the oldest showman in England. *d.* Plymouth 19 Feb. 1881.

BISHOP, JOHN (4 *son of Samuel Bishop of Pimperne, Dorset)*. *b.* 15 Sep. 1797; studied at St. Bartholomew's Hospital; M.R.C.S. 1824, F.R.C.S. 1843, member of council 1851, Hunterian orator 1859; member of Medical society of London 1839, councillor, trustee, orator and Lettsomian lecturer successively, and pres. 1852; F.R.S. 9 May 1844; very successful in treatment of impediments of speech; author of *On articulate sounds and on the causes and cure of impediments*

BISHOP, J. (*Con.*)

of speech 1851; *Researches into the pathology and treatment of deformities in the human body* 1852; *The Lettsomian lectures on Bones* 1855; *On the construction of hearing and speaking instruments* 1856. *d.* Strangeways-Marshall, Dorset 29 Sep. 1873. *Proc. of royal society xxi,* 5–6 (1873); *British medical journal ii,* 450 (1873)

BISHOP, WILLIAM. Agent at 170 New Bond st. London for Westley Richards the gunmaker 1820 to death; brought into public notice by Vincent Dowling, who rarely wrote a report of a prize fight without bringing him on the scene; got the Dog Stealers act passed which is known as Bishop's act; well known in London as "the Bishop of Bond st." *d.* 170 New Bond st. 16 March 1871 in 74 year. *Illust. sporting news ii,* 164 (1863), *portrait.*

BISSET, REV. JAMES (*2 son of George Bisset of Udny, Aberdeenshire, schoolmaster who d. 1812*). *b.* Udny 20 April 1795; ed. at Marischal coll. and Univ. of Aberdeen; kept a school at Udny 1812–25 which became celebrated; licensed by presbytery of Ellon 31 March 1819; minister of parish of Bourtie, Aberdeenshire June 1825 to death; ordained 19 April 1826; D.D. Aberdeen 23 Feb. 1850; moderator of general assembly 22 May 1862. *d.* Bourtie 8 Sep. 1872.

BISSET, SIR JOHN. *b.* Perth 1777; commissary general 31 July 1811 to 1819 when placed on h.p.; served through Peninsular war; K.C.H. 1832; knighted at St. James's Palace 6 Nov. 1832; K.C.B. 16 Aug. 1850; granted pension of £550; author of *Memoranda regarding the duties of the Commissariat on field service abroad* 1846. *d.* Perth 3 April 1854.

BISSHOPP, CECIL (*son of Harry Bisshopp, colonel in the army*). Cornet 14 Dragoons 10 Dec. 1799; major 11 Foot 6 Sep. 1834 to 17 May 1844 when placed on h.p.; M.G. 11 Nov. 1851; colonel 16 Foot 16 May 1857 to death; C.B. 26 Dec. 1818. *d.* Stoke, Plymouth 21 March 1858.

BISSHOPP, SIR EDWARD CECIL, 11 Baronet. *b.* 23 Feb. 1826; succeeded 15 Dec. 1865. *d.* 27 Jany. 1870.

BISSHOPP, SIR GEORGE CURZON, 10 Baronet. *b.* 10 April 1823; succeeded 23 Jany. 1849. *d.* Parham park near Hastings 15 Dec. 1865.

BISSON, EDWARD LEONARD (*son of Rev. Amias Bisson, R. of St. Laurens, Jersey*). *b.* St. Laurens 1797; jurat or judge of the royal

BISSON, E. L. (*Con.*)

court Jersey 1832 to death; lieutenant bailiff 1839 to death. *d.* St. Heliers, Jersey 1 April 1884 in 88 year.

BLAAUW, WILLIAM HENRY (*only son of Wm. Blaauw of Beechland, Newick, Sussex 1748–1808*). *b.* Queen Anne st. London 25 May 1793; ed. at Eton and Ch. Ch. Ox., B.A. 1815, M.A. 1818; chief founder of Sussex Archæological Society 18 June 1846, sec. 1846–58, edited Society's Collections 1846–56; elected F.S.A. 30 May 1850, admitted 27 Feb. 1851; member of council of Camden Society 1848–65, treasurer 1861–65; sheriff of Sussex 1859; author of *The barons' war, including the battles of Lewes and Evesham* 1844, 2 ed. 1871. *d.* Beechland 26 April 1870 *Sussex Archæological Collections xxii,* 9–11 (1870), *portrait.*

BLACHFORD, AUGUSTUS GEORGE. Ensign 24 Foot 12 Nov. 1825; lieut. col. 30 March 1858 to 9 March 1860 when he retired on full pay with hon. rank of major general. *d.* Sheringham near Cromer 13 Nov. 1884 aged 78.

BLACHFORD, JOHN. *b.* 1790; solicitor in City of London 1818 to death; head of firm of Blachford, Riches and Wood of 25 Abchurch lane to death; vestry clerk of parish of St. James Aldgate 40 years. *d.* 4 Jany. 1886.

BLACHLEY, HENRY. 2 Lieutenant R.A. 10 Aug. 1804; lieut. col. 23 Nov. 1841 to 4 April 1843 when he retired on full pay; L.G. 27 Feb. 1866. *d.* Banwell, Somerset 13 Aug. 1868.

BLACK, ADAM (*son of Charles Black of Edinburgh, builder*). *b.* Charles st. Edin. 20 Feb. 1784; ed. at high sch. Edin.; opened a bookseller's shop at 57 North bridge, Edin. 1808; published *Edinburgh Review* 1827 to death, and *Encyclopædia Britannica,* 7 ed. 22 vols. 1830–42, 8 ed. 22 vols. 1853–61, wrote many articles in it; master of the Merchant Company Edin. 1831; a member of the town council 1832; lord provost 1843–48; pres. of Philosophical Institution 1845; bought works of Sir Walter Scott on behalf of an association of 60 persons for £27,000 March 1851; M.P. for Edinburgh 9 Feb. 1856 to 6 July 1865; retired from business 1865. *d.* 38 Drummond place, Edin. 24 Jany. 1874. A bronze memorial statue of him in East Prince's st. gardens was unveiled 3 Nov. 1877. A fine portrait of him by Sir J. W. Gordon is in the council room Edinburgh. *Life of A*

BLACK, A. *(Con.)*

Black by A. Nicolson 1885 ; *Crombie's Modern Athenians* (1882) 179–83, *portrait; Proc. of Royal Soc. of Edin. viii,* 467 (1865).

BLACK, REV. ALEXANDER *(son of John Black of Aberdeen, gardener).* b. Aberdeen 1789 ; ed. at Aberdeen gr. sch. and Marischal college, B.A. 1807, D.D. May 1824 ; licensed by presbytery of Aberdeen 9 Feb. 1814 ; minister of Tarves Nov. 1817 to 27 June 1832 ; ordained 1 April 1818 ; professor of divinity in Marischal college Aberdeen April 1832 to 1843 when he joined the Free church at the Disruption ; sent to the East to make enquiries as to expediency of beginning a mission to the Jews 1839 ; professor of exegetical theology in New college Edinburgh about 1844–1856. *d.* Edinburgh 24 or 27 Jany. 1864 in 75 year.

BLACK, JAMES. *b.* Scotland 1787 ; L.R.C.S. Edin. 1808 ; assistant surgeon R.N. 1809 ; practised at Bolton to 1839 and 1848–56, at Manchester 1839–48, and at Edin. 1856 to death ; M.D. Glasgow 1820, L.R.C.S. Eng. 1823, F.R.C.P. 1860 ; an original member of British Association 1831 ; pres. of British medical association 1842 ; pres. of Provincial medical association 1853 ; pres. of Manchester Geological Society ; F.G.S. 1838, F.G.S. of France 1848 ; F.R.S. Edin. 1857 ; author of *An inquiry into the capillary circulation of the blood* 1825 ; *A comparative view of the more intimate nature of fever* 1826 ; *A manual of the bowels* 1840 ; *A medico-topographical, geological and statistical sketch of Bolton and its neighbourhood,* a paper of 100 pages in the *Transactions of Provincial medical and surgical association. d.* 2 George sq. Edin. 30 April 1867 in 80 year. *Proc. of Royal Society of Edin. vi,* 188 (1869).

BLACK, JOHN *(only son of Ebenezer Black of Burnhouses near Dunse, Berwickshire, farm labourer). b.* Burnhouses 1783 ; articled to a writer at Dunse 1796–1800 ; clerk in an accountant's office Edinburgh ; engaged on the *Morning Chronicle* daily paper in London 1810, principal editor 1819–44 ; fought a harmless duel with John Arthur Roebuck, M.P. 19 Nov. 1835 ; sold his library of 30,000 volumes 1844 ; translated Humboldt's *Political essay on the kingdom of New Spain* 4 *vols.* 1811–12 and other books. *d.* Birling, Kent 15 June 1855. *C. Mackay's Forty years' recollections i,* 70–95, *ii,* 177–78 ; *I.L.N. xxvii,* 13–14 (1855), *portrait.*

BLACK, JOHN. *b.* Glenrinnes, Upper Banff 1834 ; professor of humanity in University of Aberdeen 1868 to death. *d.* at his college residence Old Aberdeen 17 Nov. 1881.

BLACK, NEIL *(son of Archibald Black of Cowal Argyleshire, sheep farmer). b.* Cowal 1804 ; sailed for Adelaide April 1839 ; bought a station near Glenormiston, Victoria ; bought the Sisters station ; his annual sales of cattle attracted buyers from all parts of Australia ; member of legislative council of Victoria for the Western province 1856 to death. *d.* Mount Noorat, Victoria 15 May 1880. *Men of the time in Australia, Victorian series* (1878) *p.* 16.

BLACK, PATRICK (2 son of *colonel Patrick Black of the Bengal cavalry who d. about* 1819). *b.* Aberdeen 1813 ; ed. at Eton 1828–30 and Ch. Ch. Ox., B.A. 1834, M.D. 1836 ; F.R.C.P. 1845, censor 3 times, Croonian lecturer 1855 ; assistant phys. to St. Bartholomew's hospital 1842, warden of the medical school 1851–56, physician and clinical lecturer 1860–78, lecturer on medicine 1861–78 ; author of *Chloroform how shall we ensure safety in its administration* 1855 ; *Essay on the Spleen* 1876 ; revised the Latin part of the *Nomenclature of diseases* for Royal College of Phys. 1867. *d.* 11 Queen Anne st. Cavendish sq. London 12 Oct. 1879. *St. Bartholomew's hospital reports xv, pp. xxix–xl* (1879).

BLACK, THOMAS. *b.* Wemyss 1819 ; surgeon at Anstruther 1839 to death ; his body was found floating in the harbour of Anstruther 29 Feb. 1864. *Conolly's Biog. dict. of eminent men of Fife* (1866) 64.

BLACK, WILLIAM. *b.* Anstruther 1770 ; entered navy 13 April 1793 ; captain 7 June 1814 ; retired R.A. 9 Oct. 1846. *d.* Ormsby, Norfolk 6 Nov. 1852 in 82 year. *Conolly's Biog. dict. of eminent men of Fife* (1866) 62.

BLACK, REV. WILLIAM. *b.* Auchinairn parish of Cadder 1801 ; ed. at Univ. of Glasgow ; licensed by presbytery of Hamilton Aug. 1824 ; minister of Shettleston April 1826 ; minister of Barony church Glasgow Sep. 1828 to death ; D.D. Glasgow April 1834. *d.* Florence 15 Jany. 1851 in 50 year. *Smith's Our Scottish clergy, 2 series* (1849) 17–26.

BLACK, WILLIAM HENRY *(eld. son of John Black of Kintore, Aberdeenshire). b.* 7 May 1808 ; a tutor among families residing at and near Tulse Hill, Surrey 1825 ; clerk in the Public Record Office, assistant keeper ; founder and sec. of Chronological institute of London Dec. 1850, registrar 21 Dec. 1853 ; founded Palestine archæological association 13 Sep. 1853 and Anglo-biblical institute ; F.S.A. 9 Dec. 1858 ; pastor of the Seventh Day Baptists (one of smallest sects in England) in Mill yard, Leman st. Whitechapel 1840 to death ; prepared an edition of the

BLACK, W. H. (Con.)

British part of the *Itinerary of Antoninus* (never issued); contributed to Samuel Bentley's *Excerpta Historica* 1831; catalogued the manuscripts of the Ashmolean Museum at Oxford, the Arundel MSS. in the library of the Heralds' College, and Colfe's library at Lewisham. *d.* 15 Mill yard, Whitechapel 12 April 1872. *Rev. C. M. Davies's Unorthodox London* (1872) 227–37; *J. E. Ritchie's Religious life of London* (1870) 159–66.

BLACKADDER, ROBERT BARNES. *b.* Scotland; came to London 1834, employed by Roake and Varty and other booksellers; edited and published *Chronological Bible* 1867 and *Chronological New Testament* 1867. *d.* Booksellers' provident retreat Abbot's Langley 26 June 1883 aged 71.

BLACKALL, JOHN (*6th son of Rev. Theophilus Blackall, Preb. of Exeter cath. who d. 4 Aug. 1781*). *b.* St. Paul's st. Exeter 24 Dec. 1771; ed. at Exeter gr. sch. and Baliol coll. Ox.; B.A. 1793, M.A. 1796, M.B. 1797, M.D. 1801; studied medicine at St. Bartholomew's hosp. London; practised at Exeter 1797–1801 and 1807–52; physician to Devon and Exeter hosp. 1 June 1797–1801 when he resigned, and June 1807; practised at Totnes 1801–1807; physician to St. Thomas's lunatic asylum Exeter 1812; candidate of R.C.P. 22 Dec. 1814; fellow 22 Dec. 1815; the chief physician in the West of England 1822–52; author of *Observations on the nature and cure of dropsies* 1813 4 *ed.* 1818 which at once placed him in the rank of the first physicians of his day and acquired for him an European reputation. *d.* Southernhay Exeter 10 Jany. 1860. *Munk's Roll of royal college of physicians iii*, 138–41 (1878), abridged from *British Medical Journal i*, 75–76 (1860).

BLACKALL, ROBERT. Entered Bengal army 1805; colonel of 43 N.I. 18 July 1848, of 2 European Fusiliers 7 April 1851, and of 13 N.I. 19 Aug. 1859 to death; L.G. 18 Dec. 1860. *d.* 20 April 1863.

BLACKALL, SAMUEL WENSLEY (*eld. son of Robert Blackall of Colamber manor, co. Longford who d. 1855*). *b.* 1809; ed. at Trin. coll. Dublin; ensign 85 Foot 26 June 1827, lieut. 17 Feb. 1832 to 1 Feb. 1833 when he sold out; sheriff of co. Longford 1833, of co. Tyrone 1862; M.P. for co. Longford 13 Aug. 1847 to April 1851; lieutenant governor of Dominica 1 April 1851 to 1857; governor of Sierra Leone 1862; governor of West African Settlements 23 Feb. 1866; governor of Queensland 4 May 1868 to death. *d.* Brisbane 21 Jany. 1871.

BLACKBOURN, JOHN (*son of James Blackbourn of Billingsgate, London, fish salesman*). One of the singing boys of St. Paul's cathedral 1800–1808, apprenticed to John Sale the master of the boys 1811; organist of Wandsworth parish church 1818–21 and of Clapham parish church 1821 to death; member of Royal Society of Musicians 1818, of the Madrigal Society 1819, of the Glee Club 1819, and secretary to 1825. *d.* Clapham 18 Dec. 1854 aged 62.

BLACKBURN, REV. JOHN. *b.* the Minories, London 1791; ed. at Stepney and Hoxton; a missionary in the Irish Evangelical society; pastor of Church of Christ at Finchingfield, Essex 25 Sep. 1815 to 1822; pastor of Claremont chapel Pentonville, London 1822 to death; editor of *Congregational Magazine*; originated and edited *Congregational Calendar*, afterwards merged in the *Congregational year book*; a projector and sec. of Congregational Union of England and Wales 1831; originator of the Christian Instruction society 1825; edited *The Biblical educator*. *d.* 17 Holford sq. Pentonville 16 June 1855. *Congregational year book* (1856) 208–10; *J. Waddington's Congregational history v*, 198–202 (1870).

BLACKBURN, PETER (*eld. son of John Blackburn of Killearn near Glasgow*). *b.* Levenside, Dumbartonshire 1811; ed. at Eton; cornet 2 Life Guards 29 Jany. 1830, lieut. 4 May 1832 to 1836; M.P. for Stirlingshire 5 March 1855 to 6 July 1865; a lord of the Treasury 15 March 1859 to June 1859; chairman of Edinburgh and Glasgow railway Sep. 1846 to death. *d.* Killearn house, Killearn 20 May 1870.

BLACKBURNE, FRANCIS (*eld. son of Richard Blackburne of Great Footstown, co. Meath who d. 1798*). *b.* Great Footstown 11 Nov. 1782; entered Trinity college Dublin July 1798, scholar 1801, B.A. 1803, LL.B. and LL.D. 1852; called to bar in Ireland Jany. 1805; went the Home circuit; K.C. 1822; administered the Insurrection act in Limerick and Clare 1822–24; serjeant at law July 1826, king's second serjeant at law 19 April 1830 to Jany. 1831; attorney general in Ireland 11 Jany. 1831 to April 1835 and 23 Sep. 1841 to Oct. 1842; P.C. Ireland 1831; master of the Rolls 1 Nov. 1842 to 23 Jany. 1846; chief justice of Queen's Bench 23 Jany. 1846 to Feb. 1852; lord chancellor of Ireland Feb. 1852 to Dec. 1852 and 24 July 1866 to March 1867; vice chancellor of Univ. of Dub. Dec. 1851; one of Commissioners of National education 1852–53; lord justice of Appeal in Ireland Oct. 1856 to July 1866; offered the Lord Chancellorship by Earl of

BLACKBURNE, F. (Con.)

Derby 24 Feb. 1858 but declined; refused a Baronetcy May 1867. d. Rathfarnham Castle near Dublin 17 Sep. 1867. *Life of the Right Hon. Francis Blackburne by his son Edward Blackburne 1874, portrait; O. J. Burke's History of lord chancellors of Ireland (1879) 277–93; Dublin univ. mag. xxiv, 470–78 (1844), portrait; I.L.N. xii, 323 (1848), portrait.*

BLACKBURNE, JOHN GEORGE. b. London 4 June 1815; articled to Wm. Dunn of Oldham, surveyor 31 May 1828, partner with him 5 June 1835 to 27 June 1840 when he died; practised at Oldham 1835 to death; M.I.C.E. 1 May 1855; F.G.S. 1835; pres. of Manchester district society of surveyors and valuers 1866. d. Dryclough, Oldham 30 Sep. 1871. *Minutes of proc. of Instit. of C.E. xxxiii, 206–209 (1872).*

BLACKBURNE, JOHN IRELAND. b. 26 May 1783; M.P. for Newton, Lancashire 8 May 1807 to 10 June 1818 and for Warrington 7 Jany. 1835 to 23 July 1847. d. Hale hall near Warrington 27 Jany. 1874.

BLACKER, REV. GEORGE (*elder son of James Blacker of Dublin, police magistrate*). b. 1791; ed. at Trin. coll. Dublin; scholar 1809, B.A. 1811, M.A. 1858; C. of St. Andrew's, Dublin 1811–38; V. of Maynooth 1838 to death; Preb. of St. Patrick's cathedral 28 Dec. 1840 to death; author of *Castle of Maynooth* 1853, 2 ed. 1860; *Castle of Kilkea* 1860; *A record of the history of Maynooth church* 1867, all privately printed. d. the Rectory, Maynooth 23 May 1871 in 80 year. *Irish Ecclesiastical Gazette xiii, 131 (1871).*

BLACKER, WILLIAM. Ensign 60 Foot 3 July 1801; lieut. col. Armagh militia 5 Nov. 1812 to 6 May 1846; vice treasurer of Ireland 1817–1829. d. Carrick house, Armagh 25 Nov. 1855 aged 80.

BLACKETT, SIR EDWARD, 6 Baronet. b. London 23 Feb. 1805; ed. at Eton and Ch. Ch. Ox.; succeeded 27 Oct. 1816; sheriff of Northumberland 1833; married 4 times. d. Matfen hall, Northumberland 23 Nov. 1885.

BLACKETT, HENRY. Publisher in London with Daniel Hurst (who d. 6 July 1870 aged 67). d. The Green, Ealing 7 March 1871 in 45 year.

BLACKIE, JOHN (*son of John Blackie of Glasgow, publisher who d. 17 June 1874 aged 92*). b. Glasgow 29 Sep. 1805; ed. at the high school; head of the publishing firm of Blackie and Son in Glasgow and London, with

BLACKIE, J. (Con.)

branches in every important town in Scotland; member of Glasgow town council 1857; lord provost 1863; originated the City Improvement scheme. d Hillhead, Lillybank, Glasgow 11 Feb. 1873. *Bookseller 1873 p. 205.*

BLACKLEY, REV. WILLIAM. Ed. at St. John's coll. Cam.; B.A. 1835, M.A. 1852; chaplain to Viscount Hill 1837 to death; V. of Stanton-upon-Hine-Heath, Salop 1855–72; author of *Expository lectures on the first four chapters of St. Matthew's Gospel* 1842; *Diplomatic correspondence of the Right Hon. Richard Hill 2 vols.* 1845; *Scriptural teaching* 1847; *The Gospel history between the death of Christ and the day of Pentecost* 1855. d. Garforth house, Upper Sydenham 29 March 1885 aged 87.

BLACKLOCK, AMBROSE. b. Dumfries 1816; Assistant surgeon Madras 8 Feb. 1840; professor of surgery and surgeon of the General hospital Madras 1851, and professor of medicine and physician 1858 to 28 April 1867; went to England on sick leave 29 Aug. 1865; returned to Madras 1868; deputy inspector general of Presidency, Circle and Northern divisions 4 Aug. 1870 to death; author of *A treatise on sheep* 1838, 12 ed. 1853. d of enteritis at Chittoor, Madras 11 Feb. 1873.

BLACKLOCK, WILLIAM JAMES. b. Cumwhitton near Carlisle about 1815; landscape painter; exhibited pictures at Royal Academy, British Institution and Society of British Artists 1836–55. d. Dumfries 12 March 1858 aged 42. *Carlisle Journal 19 March 1858.*

BLACKMAN, WILLIAM. b. Arundel 27 Nov. 1862; ed. at Ardingley college, captain of the cricket eleven 1880, an assistant master 1880; in the Sussex county eleven 17 July 1881 to 1884; one of the best all-round cricketers in South of England. d. 4 Royal terrace, Fitzroy, Melbourne 2 June 1885. *Cricket 28 Jany. 1886 p. 1, portrait.*

BLACKMORE, REV. RICHARD WHITE. Educ. at Merton coll. Ox., B.A. 1813; chaplain to the Russia company 1819–47; R. of Donhead St. Mary near Salisbury 1847 to death; author of *History of the church of Russia* 1842; *The doctrine of the Russian church* 1845. d. Donhead St. Mary rectory 28 June 1882 in 91 year.

BLACKMORE, WILLIAM. b. Salisbury; admitted solicitor 1849; practised at Liverpool 1856–69; presented his very valuable collection of stone implements and other objects of art of aboriginal **inhabitants of**

America to city of Salisbury 1863 which formed nucleus of the Blackmore museum, Salisbury; member of Ethnological society of London 1866; member of council of Anthropological society 21 Jany. 1871 on its amalgamation with Ethnological society, and vice pres. 1872. *d.* Belgrave mansions, Grosvenor gardens, London 12 April 1878.

BLACKSTONE, WILLIAM SEYMOUR. *b.* 30 Oct. 1809; M.P. for Wallingford, Berkshire 11 Dec. 1832 to 1 July 1852. *d.* 6 Jany. 1881.

BLACKWALL, JOHN *(son of Mr.·Blackwall of Manchester, importer of Irish linen).* *b.* St. Anne's square, Manchester 20 Jany. 1790; partner with his father to 1833; lived at Llanrwst, North Wales 1842 to death; member of Manchester literary and philosophical society; F.L.S. April 1827; author of *Researches in Zoology* 1834, 2 ed. 1873; *A history of the spiders of Great Britain and Ireland,* 2 *parts* 1861–64, published by the Ray Society; wrote 82 papers in natural history periodicals 1821–71. *d.* Hendre house, Llanrwst 11 May 1881. *Entomologist xiv,* 145–50, 190 (1881).

BLACKWELL, THOMAS. Partner with E. Crosse as oilmen at 11 King st. Soho, London 1829, this was oldest house of the kind in London having been founded 1706; moved to Soho square 1840; began manufacture of jams 1841 and of table jellies 1850. *d.* Brookshill, Harrow Weald 16 Dec. 1879. Will proved 6 March 1880, Personalty sworn under £160,000. *H. Mayhew's Shops of London i,* 174–88 (1865).

BLACKWELL, THOMAS EVANS *(son of John Blackwell, civil engineer who d.* 1840). *b.* Devizes 28 July 1819; engineer to Kennet & Avon canal co. 1840; engineer to Bristol docks 1852–57; vice pres. and general manager of grand trunk railway 1857–62; F.G.S., F.R.G.S.; A.I.C.E. 1843, M.I.C.E. 1849. *d.* 25 June 1863.

BLACKWOOD, ARTHUR JOHNSTONE (2 *son of Sir Henry Blackwood, admiral R.N.,* 1 *Baronet* 1770–1832). *b.* 25 April 1808; clerk in Colonial office April 1824 to May 1867; groom of the privy chamber 1836 to death. *d.* Oakham, Rutland 2 Jany. 1874.

BLACKWOOD, FRANCIS PRICE *(brother of the preceding).* *b.* 25 May 1809; entered navy 6 Dec. 1821; captain 28 June 1838; commanded the Fly surveying vessel on East India station 17 Nov. 1841 to 1846; F.R.A.S.

d. of cancer in the throat at Richmond 22 March 1854. *Journal of Royal Geog. Soc. xxiv,* 80–81 (1854).

BLACKWOOD, GEORGE FREDERICK (2 *son of Wm. Blackwood, major in Bengal army).* *b.* Moradabad, Bengal 1838; ed. at Edinburgh academy and Addiscombe; 2 lieut. Bengal artillery 11 Dec. 1857; commanded the artillery in the Lushai expedition Nov. 1871; major 10 Feb. 1875; commanded E. battery B. brigade of Royal Horse Artillery in the Afghan campaign 1879 to death; killed at battle of Maiwand 27 July 1880, being one of the 11 officers and men who fought till they were all killed. *Shadbolt's Afghan campaign* (1882) 20–22, *portrait.*

BLACKWOOD, SIR HENRY, 3 Baronet. *b.* 7 May 1828; succeeded 7 Jany. 1851. *d.* Athens 26 May 1854.

BLACKWOOD, SIR HENRY MARTIN, 2 Baronet *(only son of Sir Henry Blackwood,* 1 *baronet* 1770–1832). *b.* 11 June 1801; entered navy 22 July 1814; captain 28 April 1827; succeeded his father 14 Dec. 1832; commodore on East India station 29 June 1844; captain of the Fox 14 Oct. 1843 to 5 Aug. 1848. *d.* Portsmouth 7 Jany. 1851. *I.L.N. xviii,* 37 (1851).

BLACKWOOD, JOHN (6 *son of William Blackwood of Edinburgh, publisher* 1776–1834). *b.* Edinburgh 7 Dec. 1818; ed. at high school and Univ. Edin.; superintended London branch of his brother Robert's publishing business 1840–45; partner in the firm 1845; head of the firm 1852 to death; editor of *Blackwood's Mag.* 1845 to death; published in it George Eliot's *Scenes of clerical life,* published all her books except *Romola. d.* Strathtyrum, St. Andrews 29 Oct. 1879. *The Critic xxi,* 6, 38, 102, 128, 192 *and* 225 (1860); *George Eliot's Life by J. W. Cross* 3 vols. 1885; *I.L.N. lxxii,* 461 (1879), *portrait; Graphic xx,* 525 (1879), *portrait.*

BLAGDEN, ISA JANE. Lived at Florence 1849 to death; great friend of Mrs. Theodosia Trollope and of Mrs. E. B. Browning both of whom she nursed in their last illnesses; author of *Agnes Tremorne* 2 vols. 1861; *The cost of a secret* 3 vols. 1863; *The woman I loved and the woman who loved me* 1865; *The crown of a life* 1869. *d.* Florence 26 Jany. 1873. *Poems by the late Isa Blagden with a memoir* 1873.

BLAGDEN, RICHARD *(youngest son of Richard Bragg Blagden of Petworth, Sussex, surgeon).* M.R.C.S. 1811, F.R.C.S. 1843; surgeon in

BLAGDEN, R. *(Con.)*

London 1814–54; surgeon to Duchess of Kent 1828 to death; surgeon accoucheur to Queen Victoria 1840 to death; F.R. Med. and Chir. Soc. 1839, served on the council 1847–48. *d.* Percy place, Bath 31 March 1861 aged 72.

BLAGDEN-HALE, Edward. *b.* 14 Aug. 1814; ensign 82 Foot 2 Aug. 1833, lieut. col. 7 Sep. 1855 to 10 Nov. 1856 and 6 Feb. 1857 to 1 June 1861 when placed on h.p.; brigadier general Bengal 16 Oct. 1858 to 14 Feb. 1859; L.G. 1 Oct. 1877; C.B. 24 March 1858. *d.* Alderley, Wotton under Edge 17 May 1881.

BLAGROVE, Henry Gamble *(eld. son of Mr. Blagrove of Nottingham, professor of music).* *b.* Nottingham 20 Oct. 1811; appeared as a violinist at Drury Lane theatre in an entertainment called *The Lilliputians* 1817; played at concerts at Exhibition rooms in Spring Gardens 1817; studied at Royal Academy of Music 1823; solo violinist in royal private band 1830–37; pupil of Spohr at Cassel 1832–34; played at Vienna and elsewhere with great success; leader of a string quartett party which gave a series of concerts at the Hanover square rooms 1836; led the State band at the Coronation of Queen Victoria; principal violin in Jullien's band, at both opera houses, at most of the provincial festivals, the Handel festivals at Crystal Palace, and leading musical societies in London; taught the violin at R.A. of music; published some valuable exercises for the violin, and a few solos. *(m.* 17 Aug. 1841 Etheldred dau. of Henry Combe, she *d.* 8 Jany. 1869). *d.* 224 Marylebone road, London 15 Dec. 1872. *Rev. W. W. Cazalet's History of royal academy of Music* (1854) 285–87; *I.L.N. lxi,* 633 (1872), *portrait.*

BLAIKIE, Francis *(son of Andrew Blaikie, tenant of Holydean, Scotland).* Went to England about 1789; agent to Earl of Chesterfield, and then to Earl of Leicester; introduced the turnip drill and other improvements in agriculture; author of papers on science of agriculture; retired about 1832. *d.* St. Helens Sep. 1857.

BLAIKIE, Sir Thomas *(4 son of John Blaikie, of Aberdeen).* *b.* Aberdeen 1802; ed. at gr. sch. and Marischal coll.; merchant at Aberdeen; lord provost 5 times; knighted at St. James's palace 20 Feb. 1856. *d.* Bonacord terrace, Aberdeen 25 Sep. 1861.

BLAINE, Delabere Roberton. *b.* Woodbridge, Suffolk; solicitor in Lincoln's Inn

BLAINE, D. R. *(Con.)*

Fields London; barrister M.T. 8 May 1846; revising barrister for Essex 1866–71; judge of Northumberland county court (circuit No. 1) April 1871; transferred to London (circuit No. 43) Nov. 1871; F.R.G.S. 1854; author of *Laws of Artistic copyright and their defects* 1853; *Suggestions on the copyright bill* 1861; *d.* Southwick place, Hyde park sq. London 13 Dec. 1871 aged 64.

BLAIR, Charles Edward. L.S.A. 1836, M.R.C.S. 1836; army surgeon in a Portugese regiment during war between Dom Miguel and Dom Pedro 1833–34; reported in the *Lancet* the first cases of cholera in London 1832; author of *Lectures on the anatomy and physiology of the teeth;* K.C., K.T.S. *d.* East hill, Colchester 28 Aug. 1855 aged 45.

BLAIR, James Kennedy *(eld. son of James Blair of Weatfield, Belfast).* *b.* Weatfield 9 Dec. 1807; ed. at Univ. of Edin.; barrister L.I. 27 Jany. 1835; judge of Court of record for hundred of Salford, Lancashire; joint judge of county courts for circuit No. 6 comprising Liverpool, Ormskirk and St. Helens 22 Oct. 1857 to 28 Feb. 1872 when he resigned. *d.* New Brighton, Cheshire 1 Oct. 1879.

BLAIR, Stephen. *b.* Bolton 1804; Merchant and bleacher at Bolton; M.P. for Bolton 12 Sep. 1848 to 1 July 1852. *d.* 5 July 1870.

BLAKE, Barnett. Edited *Exeter and Plymouth Gazette* 1843–52; secretary of Exeter Literary and Scientific Institution 5 years; editor and manager of *Liverpool Standard;* secretary of Yorkshire Union of Mechanics' Institutes 1856 to death. *d.* of typhus fever at Beeston near Leeds 14 March 1866 aged 54.

BLAKE, Edward Samuel. Colonel in Bombay artillery 29 May 1861 to death; C.B. 21 March 1859. *d.* 18 Princes sq. Bayswater, London 26 June 1862 aged 51.

BLAKE, Sir Francis, 3 Baronet. *b.* Heston, Middlesex 1774; succeeded 22 May 1818; M.P. for Berwick 29 March 1827 to 29 Dec. 1834. *d.* 10 Sep. 1860.

BLAKE, Frederick Rodolph *(son of Wm. Blake of Danesbury who d. 24 Nov. 1852).* *b.* 15 Aug. 1808; ensign 85 Foot 30 June 1825; lieut. col. 33 Foot 3 Oct. 1848 to death; served at battle of the Alma and before Sebastopol; C.B. 5 July 1855. *d.* Rottingdean, Sussex 23 Aug. 1855.

BLAKE, Rev. George Bannerman. *b.* Aberdeen; *ed.* at Marischal college Aberdeen; studied theology at New college Edinburgh; M.A. 1854; licensed by Presbytery of Edin. 1855; assistant pastor of St. George's presbyterian church Sunderland July 1856, junior minister 9 July 1857 to death, ordained 9 July 1857; founded Ropery lane mission, Sunderland March 1859. *d.* Sunderland 29 Aug. 1863 aged 32. *A memorial sketch of the late Rev. G. B. Blake with a selection from his sermons* 1864, *portrait.*

BLAKE, George Charles. Entered navy 2 July 1799; inspecting commander in Coast Guard 1832–35; captain 28 June 1838; gentleman usher to Prince Albert 1841; retired captain 15 Oct. 1852; retired admiral 10 Sep. 1869. *d.* Bury near Gosport 14 Nov. 1872 aged 84.

BLAKE, Sir Henry Charles, 4 Baronet. *b.* 23 Nov. 1794; succeeded 21 April 1832. *d.* Ashfield lodge, Great Ickworth, Suffolk 22 Jany. 1880.

BLAKE, Martin Joseph (*elder son of Walter Blake of Ballyglunin park, Athenry, co. Galway*). *b.* 1790; M.P. for co. Galway 1833–57. *d.* Ballyglunin park March 1861.

BLAKE, Patrick John (2 *son of Sir James Henry Blake, 3 baronet who d. 21 April 1832*). *b.* 1797; entered navy April 1813; captain 6 May 1841; commanded the Juno 26 guns in the Pacific 3 Sep. 1845 to 14 Feb. 1849; admiral on h.p. 20 Oct. 1872. *d.* Thurston, Bury St. Edmunds 29 Sep. 1884.

BLAKE, Sir Thomas Edward, 13 Baronet. *b.* Killagh, co. Galway 25 May 1805; succeeded Jany. 1847. *d.* 2 Jany. 1875.

BLAKE, William. Bought estate of Danesbury near Welwyn Herts. 1820; sheriff of Herts. 1836; formed a valuable collection of modern water colour paintings; F.R.S. 14 May 1807. *d.* Danesbury 24 Nov. 1852 aged 78.

BLAKE, William Hume (*son of Rev. Dominick Edward Blake, R. of Kiltegan, co. Wicklow*). *b.* Kiltegan 10 March 1809; *ed.* at Trin. coll. Dublin; emigrated to Canada and settled in township of Adelaide 1832; called to Canadian bar 1835; a bencher of Canadian law society Nov. 1845; solicitor general 1848; chancellor of Upper Canada 30 Sep. 1849 to 1862; judge of court of appeal; chancellior of Univ. of Toronto; professor of law in Univ. of Toronto. *d.* Toronto 15 Nov. 1870. *Law Journal vi,* 23–24 (1871).

BLAKE, William John (*eld. son of Wm. Blake of Danesbury, Herts. who d. 24 Nov. 1852*). *b.* 12 May 1805; *ed.* at Ch. Ch. Ox.; double first class 1826, B.A. 1827, M.A. 1829; barrister L.I. 10 June 1831; M.P. for Newport, Isle of Wight 26 July 1837 to 23 June 1841, defeated by one vote only 31 July 1847; F.R.S. 20 Jany. 1831. *d.* Danesbury 15 Sep. 1875.

BLAKE, William Williams. Cornet 20 Dragoons 26 April 1797; major 21 March 1805 to Dec. 1818 when placed on h.p.; C.B. 4 June 1815. *d.* Brighton 21 Feb. 1863 aged 83.

BLAKELY, Rev. Fletcher (*youngest son of Joseph Bleakly of Ballyroney, co. Down, farmer*). *b.* Ballyroney 13 May 1783; *ed.* at Glasgow college; Presbyterian minister of Moneyrea, co. Down 19 Sep. 1809; the first avowed humanitarian preacher in Ulster from which arose the proverb 'Moneyrea, where there is one God and no devil'; joined with his whole congregation the remonstrant secession from the Synod of Ulster 1829; assisted Henry Montgomery leader of the New Light party in forming remonstrant synod; joint editor of the *Bible Christian* 1830–33; resigned ministry of Moneyrea 22 Sep. 1857; author of several tracts and sermons. *d.* Cradley, Worcestershire 25 Feb. 1862. *bur.* at Moneyrea. *Inquirer* 15 *March* 1862; *Christian Unitarian* (1862), *p.* 123.

BLAKELY, Very Rev. Theophilus. Educ. at Trin. coll. Cam., B.A. 1794; alternate morning preacher at Berkeley and Fitzroy chapels London; dean of Connor 4 May 1811 to 6 Dec. 1824; dean of Achonry 6 Dec. 1824 to 11 May 1839; dean of Down 11 May 1839 to death; one of the first advocates of the Irish National system of education. *d.* Clare st. Dublin 1 Dec. 1855 aged 85. *G.M. xlv,* 309 (1856).

BLAKENEY, Sir Edward (4 *son of colonel Wm. Blakeney M.P. for Athenry in Irish parliament*). *b.* Newcastle 1778; Cornet 8 Light dragoons 28 Feb. 1794; lieut. col. 7 Foot 20 June 1811 to 2 June 1825; served in the Peninsula 1811–14; commanded first brigade in army sent to Portugal 1825; colonel 7 Foot 20 Sep. 1832 to 21 Dec. 1854; commanded troops in Ireland 1838–55; general 20 June 1854; colonel 1 Foot 21 Dec. 1854 to death; lieutenant governor of Chelsea hospital 6 Feb. 1855, governor 25 Sep. 1856 to death; field marshal 9 Nov. 1862; colonel in chief of Rifle brigade 28 Aug. 1865 to death; K.T.S. 1812, K.C.B. 2 Jany. 1815,

BLAKENEY, SIR E. (Con.)

G.C.B. 7 May 1849; G.C.H 7 May 1836; P.C. Ireland 7 May 1836. d. Chelsea hospital 2 Aug. 1868.

BLAKENEY, REV. RICHARD PAUL. b. Roscommon 2 June 1820; ed. at Trin. coll. Dublin, B.A. 1842, LL.B. and LL.D. 1852, D.D. Edin. 1868; C. of St. Paul's, Nottingham 1843–44; P.C. of Hyson Green, Notts. 1844–52; P.C. of Ch. Ch. Claughton, Cheshire Jany. 1852 to 1874; V. of Bridlington 1874 to death; rural dean of Bridlington 1876 to death; canon of York 1882 to death; author of Translation of the Moral theology of Alphonsus Liguori 1845, 2 ed. 1852; A manual of Romish controversy 1851; Protestant Catechism 1854; History and interpretation of the Book of common prayer 1865, 3 ed. 1878. d. Bridlington 31 Dec. 1884. Church portrait journal May 1880, portrait.

BLAKESLEY, VERY REV. JOSEPH WILLIAMS (son of Jeremiah George Blaksly of City of London, factor who d. 1817 or 1818). b. 38 Coleman st. city of London 6 March 1808; ed. at St. Paul's school 1819–27 (captain 1826–27) and C. C. coll. Cam., migrated to Trinity college 1830, foundation scholar 1830, 21 wrangler and 3 classic 1831, B.A. 1831, M.A. 1834, B.D. 1850; fellow of Trinity 1831, assistant tutor 1834, tutor 1839–45; member of the celebrated Apostles club at Cambridge; select preacher 1840 and 1843; V. of Ware, Herts. 30 May 1845 to 1872; canon of Canterbury 27 June 1863 to 4 July 1872; dean of Lincoln 4 July 1872 to death; master of the Mercers Company 1864; an active member of the committee for revision of translation of New Testament; author of Thoughts on the recommendations of the Ecclesiastical commission 1837; Life of Aristotle 1839; Conciones Academicæ 1843; Herodotus with a commentary 2 vols. 1852–54; Four months in Algeria, with a visit to Carthage 1859; wrote under signature of "A Hertfordshire Incumbent" many letters on social questions to The Times which attracted general attention. d. The deanery, Lincoln 18 April 1885. Saturday Review lix, 533 (1885); Guardian 22 April 1885, p. 596.

BLAKEY, ROBERT (son of Robert Blakey of Morpeth, Northumberland, mechanic who d. Feb. 1796 aged 22). b. Manchester lane, Morpeth 18 May 1795; wrote for the Black Dwarf a London paper 1817–21 and for the Newcastle Mag., Durham Chronicle and Cobbett's Register 1822–32; mayor of Morpeth 1836–37; purchased the Newcastle Liberator 1 Jany. 1838 which was amalgamated with the

BLAKEY, R. (Con.)

Champion a London weekly paper 1840; started the Politician a London weekly paper of which only 6 numbers were issued; professor of logic and metaphysics in Queen's college Belfast Aug. 1849 to 1851; a great proficient in the art of angling; granted civil list pension of £100, 20 Jany. 1860; author of An essay towards an easy and useful system of logic 1834, 2 ed. 1848; Hints on angling by Hackle Palmer 1846; History of the philosophy of the mind 4 vols. 1848; The anglers complete guide to the rivers and lakes of England 1854; The history of political literature from the earliest times 2 vols. 1854, and of a number of minor works. d, 20 Blomfield road, Shepherds Bush, London 26 Oct. 1878. Memoirs of R. Blakey edited by Rev. H. Miller 1879.

BLAKISTON, ANNE (elder dau. of John Rochfort of Clogrenane, co. Carlow). m. Sep. 1782 Sir Matthew Blakiston, 2 baronet, who was b. 1760 and d. 20 Sep. 1806, she d. Lymington, Hants. 27 Nov. 1862 in 102 year.

BLAKISTON, SIR MATTHEW, 3 Baronet. b. Athlone 13 May 1783; succeeded 20 Sep, 1806. d. Sandybrooke hall, Ashbourne, Derbyshire 23 Dec. 1862.

BLAKISTON, SIR MATTHEW, 4 Baronet. b. Bath 15 Jany. 1811; ed. at the Charterhouse and Trin. coll. Dub.; succeeded 23 Dec. 1862. d. Sandybrooke hall 3 Dec. 1883.

BLAKISTON, PEYTON (youngest child of Sir Matthew Blakiston, 2 baronet 1760–1806). b. 6 Sep. 1801; ed. at Eton and Trin. coll. Cam.; migrated to Em. coll., a Dixie fellow; B.A. 1823, M.A. 1827, M.L. 1837, M.D. 1841; C. of Bilton, co. Warwick; V. of Lymington, Hants. 1830–33; studied medicine at Cambridge and Paris; practised at Birmingham, phys. to general hospital 1841; F.R.S. 21 Jany. 1840; F.R.C.P. 1843; practised at St. Leonard's on Sea 1848–71; author of On diseases of the Chest 1848; Clinical observations on diseases of the heart 1865; Clinical reminiscences 1878. d. 140 Harley st. London 17 Dec. 1878. Proc. of Med. and Chir. Soc. viii, 397–99 (1880); Proc. of Royal Soc. xxix, 1–2 (1879).

BLAMIRE, GEORGE. Barrister L.I. 25 June 1819; owner of large estates in Cumberland and Glamorganshire; occupied 3 rooms on first floor of 1 Adam st. Adelphi, London 1847 to death; slept in an arm chair last 16 years of his life; found dead in his chair at 1 Adam st. 17 Sep. 1863, having probably died 13 or 14 Sep. aged 75.

BLAMIRE, JANE CHRISTIAN (2 dau. of Wm. Blamire of The Oaks near Dalston, Cumberland, surgeon who d. 29 Jany. 1814). b. The Oaks 20 March 1788; housekeeper to her brother at Thackwood, Cumberland 1813 to 1831; a great philanthropist. d. Thackwood 20 Sep. 1857. H. Lonsdale's Worthies of Cumberland iv, 117–39 (1873).

BLAMIRE, WILLIAM (only brother of the preceding). b. The Oaks 13 April 1790; ed. at Carlisle and Westminster; entered Ch. Ch. Ox. Oct. 1808, B.A. 1811; a great stock breeder, went to all the fairs in Scotland and North England; sheriff of Cumberland 1828; M.P. for Cumberland 9 May 1831 to 3 Dec. 1832, for East Cumberland 17 Dec. 1832 to Aug. 1836; made a great speech in House of Commons on Tithe Commutation bill 25 March 1836; Tithe comr. for England and Wales 22 Aug. 1836 to 8 Aug. 1851 when the commission expired after having converted tithes into rent charges amounting to more than £4,000,000 per annum; Copyhold and Tithe comr. 22 June 1841; Inclosure comr. 21 Aug. 1845 to 1860. d. Thackwood near Carlisle 12 Jany. 1862. A biographical sketch of the late W. Blamire by H. Lonsdale, M.D. 1862

BLANC, JEAN JOSEPH LOUIS. b. Madrid 28 Oct. 1813; clerk in a lawyer's office in Paris 1830; edited a journal called Le Bon Sens 1836–38; founded La revue du progrès 1838 in which he advocated socialistic ideas; published The organisation of labour 1841; Histoire des dix ans 1841 which helped to precipitate the revolution of 1848; a member of the Provisional government 1848; pres. of the Labour commission; declined the Dictatorship; a member of the National Assembly; proscribed by the Assembly; lived in exile in England 1849–70; correspondent to several French journals; published Letters on England, 2 series 2 vols. 1867; a member of French National Assembly Feb. 1871 to death. d. Cannes 6 Dec. 1882. Louis Blanc, sa vie, ses œuvres, par C. Robin 1851, portrait; Louis Blanc, par C. Edmond 1882, portrait; I.L.N. xii, 182 (1848), portrait, xiii, 189 (1848), portrait, lxxxi, 629 (1882), portrait.

NOTE.—When an attempt was made to assassinate him in Paris 15 Aug. 1839 his brother Charles Blanc had a vivid presentiment of the scene, an incident on which Dumas founded the play of the Corsican Brothers.

BLANCHARD, EDMUND FORSTER (youngest son of Samuel Laman Blanchard of London, author 1804–45). contributed to many periodicals; connected with Lloyd's Newspaper

BLANCHARD, E. F. (Con).
some time; author with Edward Wilberforce of Poems 1857; published The poetical works of Oliver Goldsmith with a notice of his life and genius 1867. d. 20 Air st. Piccadilly, London 25 July 1870 aged 38.

BLANCHARD, SIDNEY LAMAN (elder brother of the preceding). Author of The Ganges and the Seine 2 vols. 1862; Yesterday and to-day in India 1867; Riddles of love or the knave of hearts 3 vols. 1871. d. Brighton 9 Nov. 1883.

BLANCHARD, THOMAS. Pantaloon at Covent Garden theatre 26 Dec. 1827; acquired considerable repute as a broadswordsman; obtained great fame at the old Coburg theatre London for the celebrated drunken combat with Thomas Bradley in The Maid of Genoa 1828; said to be original inventor of the "one two three and under" style of using the broadsword; last appeared as pantaloon at Victoria theatre 1845; built some cottages at back of Victoria theatre which still bear his name d. London 20 Aug. 1859 aged 72.

BLAND, VENERABLE GEORGE (2 son of Michael Bland F.R.S. who d. 19 April 1851 aged 74). b. 1804; ed. at Caius coll. Cam., B.A. 1828, M.A. 1831; R. of Slinfold Sussex 1836–44; archdeacon of Lindisfarne 7 May 1844 to 1853; archdeacon of Northumberland 1853 to death; R. of St. Mary-le-Bow Durham 1856–59. d. The college, Durham 17 Feb. 1880.

BLAND, HUMPHREY. b. England 1812; an actor at Surrey theatre London 1834; went to America 1844; made his début at Park theatre New York 1 Sep. 1845 as Lewson in The Gamester; first appeared in Philadelphia 4 March 1850 at the Arch st. theatre as Joseph Surface in The school for scandal. d. New York 17 Jany. 1869.

BLAND, JAMES (2 son of George Bland of London, actor by Maria Theresa Romanzini of London, vocalist 1769–1838). b. 5 March 1798; made his first appearance in London at English opera house 1 July 1822 in an operetta called Love among the roses; comedian at Drury Lane and Haymarket; at Olympic 1831, at Covent Garden 1839, at Lyceum and Adelphi, and at Strand theatre down to his death. d. at stage door of Strand theatre, Surrey st. London 17 July 1861.

BLAND, LOFTUS HENRY (3 son of John Bland of Blandsfort, Queen's county who d. 11 Nov. 1810). b. Blandsfort Aug. 1805; ed. at Trin. coll. Cam.; B.A. 1825, M.A. 1828; called to Irish bar 1829; M.P. for King's county 26 July 1852 to 23 April 1859; Q.C. 28 Jany.

BLAND, L. H. *(Con.)*

1854; chairman of quarter sessions co. Cavan 1862. *d.* 33 Merrion sq. Dublin 21 Jany. 1872.

BLAND, MICHAEL *(only child of Thomas Bland of Norwich, merchant who d. 28 Aug. 1818 in 79 year).* Partner in firm of Whitbread and Co. of London, brewers; F.R.S. 8 Feb. 1816, F.S.A., F.G.S. *d.* 65 Cambridge terrace, Hyde park, London 19 April 1851 aged 74.

BLAND, REV. MILES *(son of Thomas Bland).* *b.* Sedbergh 11 Oct. 1786; ed. at Sedbergh sch. and St. John's coll. Cam., 2 wrangler and Smith's prizeman 1808, B.A. 1808, M.A. 1811, B.D. 1818, D.D. 1826, fellow of his college 5 April 1808, assistant tutor 1809, tutor to 1823; R. of Lilley, Herts. 16 May 1823 to death; preb. of Wells cathedral 18 April 1826 to death; F.R.S. 12 April 1821, F.R.A.S., F.S.A.; author of *Algebraical problems* 1812, 9 *ed.* 1849; *Geometrical problems* 1819, 3 *ed.* 1827; *Annotations on the historical books of the New Testament* 2 vols. 1828–29; *Mechanical and philosophical problems* 1830. *d.* 5 Royal crescent, Ramsgate 27 Dec. 1867.

BLAND, WILLIAM *(younger son of Robert Bland of London, physician who d. 29 June 1816 aged 76).* *b.* London 5 Nov. 1789; surgeon's mate on board a man-of-war; fought a duel with the purser of his ship in the Persian gulf when he shot his opponent dead; fought another duel with Lieut. Wm. Randall, tried at Calcutta and sentenced to 7 years transportation 1814, exiled to Sydney 1814, obtained a free pardon; surgeon at Sydney 1815 to death; fined £50 with 12 months in Paramatta gaol for libelling Governor Macquarie; a naval surgeon 7 July 1826; member for Sydney to first elective legislature of New South Wales 15 June 1843 to 1848; presented with a testimonial of £1000 by people of Sydney 14 Sep. 1858. *d.* 28 College st. Sydney 21 July 1868. *Carlisle's History of family of Bland* (1826) 235–47; *Illust. news of the world iv*, 68 (1859), *portrait; Heads of the people ii*, 67 (1848), *portrait.*

BLANE, ARCHIBALD WILLIAM. *b.* 29 March 1788; member of council Mauritius; discovered the wealth of the Peel river district Australia; deputy governor of Australian Agricultural company 1845 to death. *d.* Booral, Port Stephens 6 Nov. 1852.

BLANE, DAVID ANDERSON. *b.* 1801; entered Bombay civil service 1819; member of council at Bombay 1 March 1849 to 1854 when he retired on annuity. *d.* 21 Prince's gardens, South Kensington, London 17 June 1879.

BLANE, SIR HUGH SEYMOUR, 2 Baronet. *b.* 29 July 1795; ed. at the Charterhouse 1803–7; ensign 3 Foot guards 31 March 1814, captain 30 Aug. 1831 to 1835; succeeded 27 June 1834. *d.* The Pastures near Derby 14 April 1869.

BLANE, ROBERT. Cornet 2 Life Guards 1 Nov. 1831; assistant adjutant general and military sec. 1854–55; military attaché at St. Petersburgh 21 July 1866 to death; colonel 11 April 1860; C.B. 2 Jany. 1857. *d.* 11 Eaton terrace, Eaton sq. London 30 May 1871.

BLANSHARD, THOMAS. Second lieut. R.E. 28 Sep. 1807, colonel 5 July 1851 to 16 Dec. 1854, M.G. 16 Dec. 1854; C.B. 19 July 1838. *d.* Grove house, Hampton, Middlesex 19 June 1859 aged 70.

BLANSHARD, WILLIAM *(eld. son of Richard Blanshard of Northallerton).* *b.* 29 June 1802; served in East India company's navy 1817–19; barrister I.T. 16 May 1828; recorder of Ripon 1830–35; revising barrister 1832–63; advocate in all the Courts of Archbishop of Canterbury, who created him M.A. 18 Feb. 1839; recorder of Doncaster June 1857 to July 1870; judge of Northumberland county court (circuit No. 1.) 10 Jany. 1863 to Oct. 1871; author of *A treatise on the statutes of limitations* 1826. *d.* Scarborough 28 Nov. 1872.

BLANTYRE, LADY EVELYN *(2 dau. of 2 Duke of Sutherland* 1786–1861). *b.* 2 Hamilton place, Piccadilly, London 8 Aug. 1825. *(m.* 4 Oct. 1843 Charles Stuart, 12 Baron Blantyre who was *b.* 21 Dec. 1818). *d.* Nice 24 Nov. 1869. *Sir. H. Nicolas's Court of Queen Victoria* (1845) 13–18, *portrait; Illust. News of the world ix*, (1862), *portrait.*

BLASIS, CARLO *(son of Francesco Antonio Blasis of Naples, ballet composer).* *b.* Naples 4 Dec. 1803; a principal dancer at Marseilles, Bordeaux, Paris and Milan 1816–26; dancer and ballet composer at the King's theatre London 1826; finishing master of the Imperial Academy of dancing at Milan 1 Dec. 1837; ballet composer at Royal Italian opera Covent Garden 1846; composed the Spanish dances which were performed at the public breakfasts given by the Duchess of St. Albans; wrote more than 50 ballets; wrote the chapters upon private dancing in *The young lady's book* 1828–29; author of *The code of Terpsichore* 1830. *d.* Cernolio near lake of Como Jany. 1878. *Notes upon dancing by C. Blasis* (1847) 36–148, *portrait.*

BLAXLAND, GREGORY. *b.* Kent 1771; emigrated to Sydney 1806; crossed the Blue Mountains with W. C. Wentworth May 1813 after several unsuccessful attempts had been made to do so; introduced cultivation of oaten hay into colony of New South Wales. *d.* 3 Jany. 1853.

BLAYNEY, CADWALLADER DAVIS BLAYNEY, 12 Baron. *b.* Dover st. Piccadilly, London 19 Dec. 1802; M.P. for Monaghan 18 Aug. 1830 to 8 April 1834, when he succeeded; an Irish representative peer 12 June 1841 to death. *d.* 18 Jany. 1874.

BLECKLEY, THOMAS MACDOUGALL *(son of Rev. John Bleckley).* *b.* 13 Dec. 1828; assistant surgeon in the army 6 Jany. 1854; surgeon major 1 March 1873 to 24 Jany. 1880; C.B. 31 March 1874. *d.* Lorne house, Central hill, Upper Norwood 23 Nov. 1882.

BLEECK, ARTHUR HENRY. *b.* about 1829; employed in the British Museum; held a post in connection with the land transport corps at Sinope during Crimean war; author with W. B. Barker of *A practical grammar of the Turkish language* 1854; author of *A concise grammar of the Persian language* 1857; *Catalogue of the Napoleon library in the possession of Mr. Joshua Bates privately printed* 1858; *Avesta, the religious books of the Parsees, from Spiegel's German translation of the original manuscripts* 3 vols. 1864. *d.* 56 Bevington road, Kensington 27 Jany. 1877 aged 47.

BLEEK, WILHELM HEINRICH IMMANUEL *(son of Friedrich Bleek of Berlin, biblical critic 1793–1859).* *b.* Berlin 8 March 1827; ed. at Bonn and Berlin; studied habits and language of the Kaffirs in Natal 1855–57; interpreter to Sir George Grey at Cape Town 1857; librarian of the valuable collection of rare books presented by Sir G. Grey to the colony at Cape Town 1 Feb. 1862 to death; granted civil list pension of £150, 18 June 1870. *(m.* Jemima Charlotte, she was granted a civil list pension of £100, 13 June 1877); author of *The languages of Mozambique* 1856; *The library of Sir George Grey* 2 vols. 1858–59; *Comparative grammar of South African languages,* 2 *parts* 1862–69; *Reynard the Fox in South Africa, or Hottentot tales and fables* 1864; *Bushman folklore* 1875. *d.* Cape Town 17 Aug. 1875. *Cape Monthly Mag. xi,* 167–69 (1875).

BLENKINS, WILLIAM BAZETT GOODWIN. Captain 6 Bombay native infantry 26 April 1842 to death; C.B. 4 July 1843. *d.* Bombay 12 June 1852.

BLENKIRON, WILLIAM *(son of Mr. Blenkiron of Marrick near Richmond, Yorkshire, farmer).* *b.* Marrick 1807; a general agent at 78½ Wood st. Cheapside, London 1834–48; a breeder of race horses at Dalston 1848, at Middle park near Eltham 1852 to death; his breeding stud gradually became the largest in England; held his first sale of blood stock at Middle park June 1856, held two annual sales there 1867 to death; bred Hermit winner of the Derby 1867, and Gamos winner of the Oaks 1870; gave 5000 guineas for Blink Bonny, 5000 guineas for Blair Athol, and 5800 guineas for Gladiateur; founded the great two year old race at Newmarket, namely The Middle Park Plate 1866. *d.* Middle Park 25 Sep. 1871 in 64 year. *Rice's History of the British turf ii,* 338–44 (1879); *Gent. Mag. iii,* 451–62 (1869); *I.L.N. lix,* 377 (1871), *portrait; Illust. sporting and dramatic news i,* 181 (1874), *portrait; Sporting life* 27 Sep. 1871, *p.* 2, cols. 1, 5, 4 Oct. *p.* 2, col. 6.

BLEWITT, JONATHAN *(son of Jonas Blewitt of London, organist who d.* 1805). *b.* about 1781; organist in London, at Haverhill and at Brecon; organist of St. Andrew's Dublin; composer and director of music at T. R. Dublin; grand organist to Freemasons of Ireland; wrote pantomime music for most of the London theatres 1826–52; director of music at Sadler's Wells Theatre 1828–29, at Vauxhall gardens 1838 and at Tivoli gardens Margate; wrote a few light operas and upwards of 2000 pieces of vocal music, most of them comic songs, the best known are *Barney Brallaghan's Courtship* and *The merry little fat grey man* 1845, which he used to sing inimitably; composed the tune of *The Perfect Cure* 1844 which was associated with a now forgotten song called *The monkey and the nuts,* 20 years afterwards it was utilised by James Hurst Stead who became known as The Perfect Cure, and cleared more than £2000 by linking the tune with other words. *d.* London 4 Sep. 1853 in 73 year.

BLEWITT, OCTAVIAN *(son of John Edwards Blewitt of London, merchant* 1784–1860). *b.* St. Helen's place, Bishopsgate, London 3 Oct. 1810; ed. at Plymouth gr. sch.; travelled in Italy, Egypt, Greece, Turkey and other countries 1837–39; secretary of Royal literary fund in London 13 March 1839 to death; elected a member of the Athenæum club 1848 by a majority of 112 votes to 2; F.G.S. 1835; a knight of order of Leopold of Belgium 1872; edited the newspaper portion of the *Gardener's Chronicle* 1840–69; author of *A panorama of Torquay* 1830; *A sketch of the*

BLEWITT, O. *(Con.)*

district comprised between the Dart and the Teign 1832 ; *Treatise on the happiness arising from the exercise of the Christian faith* 1832 ; *Handbook for travellers in Central Italy* 1843 *(anon)* 2 ed. *(with the author's name)* 1850 ; *Handbook for travellers in Southern Italy* 1853. *d.* 133 Elgin crescent, London 4 Nov. 1884. *Biograph v,* 170–85 (1881).

BLEWITT, REGINALD JAMES (2 *son of Edward Blewitt of Llantarnam abbey, Monmouthshire who d.* 8 March 1832 *in* 70 *year).* b. 26 May 1799 ; ed. at Rugby ; solicitor at 8 New square Lincoln's Inn London 1821–27 ; M.P. for borough of Monmouth 24 July 1837 to March 1852 ; established the *Monmouthshire Merlin* a liberal paper 1829, edited it 1829–32 ; manager of Monmouthshire bank which failed for a very large sum. *d.* The Priory, Putney 11 Sep. 1878. *Law Times lxv,* 405 (1878).

BLIGH, SIR JOHN DUNCAN (2 *son of John Bligh,* 4 *Earl of Darnley* 1767–1831). b. London 11 Oct. 1798 ; ed. at Eton. and Ch. Ch. Ox., B.A. 1821, B.C.L. 1828, D.C.L. 1836 ; paid attaché in Paris 9 May 1828 ; sec. of legation at Florence 30 July 1829 ; sec. of embassy at The Hague 1 Nov. 1830 ; Min. plenipo. at The Hague 3 July 1832, at St. Petersburg 7 Sep. 1832, at Stockholm 28 Oct. 1835, and at Hanover 17 April 1838 to 14 June 1856 when he retired ; C.B. 1 March 1851, K.C.B. 30 Sep. 1856. *d.* Sandgate, Kent 8 May 1872.

BLIGHT, WILLIAM. Entered navy 9 May 1793 ; captain 22 July 1830 ; retired R.A. 27 Sep. 1855. *d.* Stonehouse, Plymouth 22 July 1862 aged 77.

BLISS, HENRY (4 *son of Jonathan Bliss of New Brunswick).* b. New Brunswick ; barrister I.T. 9 Feb. 1827, bencher 1850, reader 1863, treasurer 1864 ; Q.C. 1850 ; agent in England for Nova Scotia many years ; author of *On colonial intercourse* 1830 ; *Statistics of the trade, industry and resources of Canada* 1833 ; *State trials, specimen of a new edition by N. T. Moile, pseud.* 1838 ; *Cicero, a drama by N. T. Moile,* 1847 ; *Robespierre, a tragedy* 1854. *d.* Folkestone 31 July 1873 aged 76.

BLISS, REV. PHILIP. *(son of Rev. Philip Bliss* 1742–1803 *R. of Frampton Cotterell, Gloucs).* b. Chipping Sodbury, Gloucs. 21 Dec. 1787 ; ed. at Merchant Taylors' 1797–1806 and St. John's coll. Ox., scholar 1806, law fellow 1809, B.C.L. 1815, D.C.L. 1820 ; assistant librarian Bodleian library 1810, under librarian July 1822 to Dec. 1828 ; prepared the first

BLISS, REV. P. *(Con.)*

136 pages of the catalogue issued 1814 ; C. of Newington, Oxon. 1817 to Feb. 1830 ; registrar of the University 1824 to April 1853 ; chaplain at Studley Priory 1830–55 ; registrar of the University Court 1831 ; principal of St. Mary hall Ox. April 1848 to death ; edited Bishop Earle's *Microcosmography* 1811 ; Anthony à Wood's *Athenæ Oxonienses and Fasti* 4 vols. 1813–20 ; *Reliquiæ Hearnianæ the remains of Thomas Hearne* 2 vols. 1857, 2 ed. 1869 and many other books. *d.* the Lodgings St. Mary Hall, Oxford 18 Nov. 1857. *Dict. of Nat. Biog. v,* 221–22 (1886).

BLITZ, ANTONIO. b. Deal, Kent 21 June 1810 ; made his first appearance on the stage as a ventriloquist and conjurer at Hamburg Sep. 1823 ; performed in all the cities of North Europe ; first appeared in England at Dover Dec. 1825, and in London at Coburg theatre, Lent 1828 ; sailed for New York 1 Aug. 1834 ; in 1870 there were 13 conjurers travelling in America under assumed name of Blitz. *d.* Philadelphia 28 Jany. 1877. *Fifty years in the magic circle by Signor Blitz* (1871), *portrait.*

BLOCHMANN, HENRY. b. Dresden 7 Jany. 1838 ; landed at Calcutta Sep. 1858 ; professor of mathematics at the Doveton college Calcutta 1862–65 ; M.A. Calcutta Univ. 1865 ; assistant professor of the Calcutta Madrassa 1865, principal 1875 to death ; member of Asiatic Society of Bengal 6 April 1864, sec. 1868 to death ; author of *The Prosody of the Persians* 1872 ; *School geography of India* 1873 ; *English and Urdu school dictionary Romanized,* 8 ed. 1877 ; *The first geography,* 17 ed. 1879. *d.* Calcutta 13 July 1878. *Proc. of Asiatic Society of Bengal* (1878) 164–67.

BLOCKLEY, JOHN. b. 1801 ; Music publisher at 3 Argyll st. Regent st. London ; composed many ballads, several of which were very popular namely the duet *List tis music stealing* and the songs *Love not* and *The Englishman. d.* 6 Park road, Haverstock hill, London 24 Dec. 1882.

BLOIS, SIR CHARLES, 7 Baronet. b. Sway, Hants. 1794 ; lieut. col. East Suffolk militia 1844 to 1853 ; succeeded 20 Aug. 1850. *d.* Cockfield hall, Suffolk 12 June 1855.

BLOMEFIELD, REV. SIR THOMAS EARDLEY WILMOT, 3 Baronet. b. Peamore near Exeter 3 Aug. 1820 ; succeeded 30 June 1858 ; V. of All Saint's Pontefract 1859–72 ; master of Archbishop Holgate's hospital near Hemsworth 1872 to death. *d.* Holgate lodge, Pontefract 21 Nov. 1878.

BLOMEFIELD, SIR THOMAS WILLIAM, 2 Baronet. *b.* Arlington st. Piccadilly, London 24 March 1791; succeeded 24 Aug. 1822. *d.* Egremont lodge, Brighton 30 June 1858.

BLOMFIELD, RIGHT REV. CHARLES JAMES *(eld. son of Charles Blomfield of Bury St. Edmunds, school master who d. 28 Sep. 1831 in 69 year).* *b.* Bury St. Edmunds 29 May 1786; ed. at Bury gr. sch. and Trin. coll. Cam.; scholar 1805, fellow Oct. 1809, Craven Univ. scholar 1806, 3 wrangler and Chancellor's classical medallist 1808; B.A. 1808, M.A. 1811, B.D. 1818, D.D. 1820; R. of Dunton, Bucks. Dec. 1811; V. and R. of Great and Little Chesterford July 1817; R. of Tuddenham, Suffolk 1817; R. of St. Botolph, Bishopsgate May 1820; archdeacon of Colchester 15 Jany. 1822 to 4 June 1824; bishop of Chester 8 June 1824, consecrated in Whitehall chapel 20 June; bishop of London 15 Aug. 1828 to 30 Sep. 1856 when he resigned on a pension of £6000; P.C. 31 July 1828; admitted dean of chapels royal 12 Dec. 1828, enthroned in St. Paul's cathedral 16 Jany. 1829; member of Ecclesiastical commission 1836 of which he was the moving spirit; published editions of *Prometheus Vinctus* 1810, *Septem contra Thebas* 1812, *Persæ* 1814, *Choephoræ* 1821; an edition of *Callimachus* 1815 and of *Euripides* 1821; wrote on classical subjects for *Edinburgh* and *Quarterly Reviews*, and for the *Museum Criticum* a journal established by himself and James Henry Monk 1813 *d.* Fulham palace 5 Aug. 1857. *A memoir of C. J. Blomfield edited by his son Alfred Blomfield, 2 ed. 1864; Rev. G. E. Biber's Bishop Blomfield and his times 1857; H. Martineau's Biographical sketches, 4 ed. (1876) 167–74; I.L.N. xxiv, 401 (1854), portrait.*

BLOOD, BINDON. *b.* Cranacher, Ireland; lived at 22 Queen st. Edinburgh 1829–42; an original member of the Abbotsford Club 20 March 1833; a great collector of books which were piled in great heaps in his garrets, cellars and warerooms like unsorted goods; known as The Vampire and The Dragon. *d.* Ireland 1855. *Crombie's Modern Athenians (1882) 11–14, portrait; J. H. Burton's The bookhunter, new ed. (1882) 55–58.*

BLOOD, CLEMENTS. Lieutenant Bombay artillery 10 June 1821; major Bombay artillery 10 Nov. 1854; brigadier in command at Ahmednuggur 12 March 1855 to 18 Feb. 1858, and at Hydrabad 18 Feb. 1858 to 12 May 1859 when he retired with rank of M.G. *d.* Chiswick, Middlesex 10 April 1869 aged 63.

BLOOD, RICHARD. Lieutenant 6 Bombay N.I. 20 April 1819, lieut. col. 1 European regiment 1 Nov. 1852 to 18 May 1858; M.G. 1 Dec. 1858. *d.* 6 Circus road, St. John's Wood, London 8 July 1877 aged 74.

BLOOMFIELD, JOHN ARTHUR DOUGLAS BLOOMFIELD, 2 Baron *(eld. child of Benjamin Bloomfield, 1 Baron Bloomfield 1768–1846).* *b.* 12 Nov. 1802; attaché at Vienna 16 Feb. 1818; envoy extraord. and min. plenipo. at St. Petersburgh 3 April 1844, at Berlin 28 April 1851, at Vienna 22 Nov. 1860 to 28 Oct. 1871 when he retired on a pension; succeeded 15 Aug. 1846; C.B. 27 April 1848, K.C.B. 1 March 1851, G.C.B. 3 Sep. 1858, P.C. 17 Dec. 1860; created Baron Bloomfield of Ciamhaltha in the United Kingdom 7 Aug. 1871. *(m.* 4 Sep. 1845 Georgiana 16 and youngest child of 1 Baron Ravensworth, she was *b.* 13 April 1822). *d.* Ciamhaltha, Newport, Tipperary 17 Aug. 1879. *Reminiscences of court and diplomatic life by Georgiana Baroness Bloomfield ii, 310 (1883), portrait.*

BLOOMFIELD, HENRY KEANE. Ensign 59 Foot 30 Sep. 1813; lieut. col. 11 Foot 27 June 1845 to 1 April 1859 when placed on h.p.; colonel 64 Foot 20 Jany. 1867 to death; L.G. 13 Aug. 1868. *d.* 108 Jermyn st. Piccadilly, London 11 Feb. 1870 aged 72.

BLOOMFIELD, SIR JOHN *(son of Patrick Bloomfield of Sligo).* *b.* 1793; ed. at Woolwich; 2 lieut. R.A. 28 April 1810, colonel 28 Nov. 1854, colonel commandant 5 April 1866 to death; aide-de-camp to the Queen 20 June 1854 to 25 Sep. 1859; inspector general of artillery 1 May 1859 to 30 June 1864; general 26 Nov. 1876; K.C.B. 13 March 1867, G.C.B. 24 May 1873. *d.* 108 Jermyn st. London 1 Aug. 1880.

BLOOMFIELD, REV. SAMUEL THOMAS. Educ. at Sid. Sus. coll. Cam., B.A. 1808, M.A. 1811, D.D. 1829; V. of Bisbrooke, Rutland 1814 to death; hon. canon of Peterborough cath. 1854 to death; granted civil list pension of £200, 30 June 1846; author of *Recensio synoptica annotationis sacræ, being a critical digest of the most important annotations on the New Testament* 8 vols. 1826–28; *Translation of Thucydides* 3 vols. 1829; *The Greek Testament with English notes* 2 vols. 1832, 12 ed. 1870; *A Greek and English lexicon to the New Testament* 1840, 2 ed. 1845. *d.* Hone house, Wandsworth common near London 28 Sep. 1869 aged 85.

BLORE, EDWARD *(eld. son of Thomas Blore of Derby, topographer 1764–1818).* *b.* Derby 13 Sep. 1787; architect and artist; designed

BLORE, E. *(Con.)*

exterior of Abbotsford for Sir Walter Scott 1816 ; designed organ-screen and choir fittings of Peterborough cathedral ; restored Glasgow cathedral and Merton college chapel ; special architect to Wm. iv and Victoria ; completed erection of Buckingham Palace for £100,000, 1837 ; architect at Westminstel Abbey ; declined honour of knighthood ; F.S.A. 27 Nov. 1823 ; D.C.L. Oxford 1834 ; F.R.S. 10 June 1841 ; a founder of Royal Archæological Institute Dec. 1843 ; author of *The monumental remains of noble and eminent persons comprising the sepulchral antiquities of Great Britain* 1825. *d.* 4 Manchester sq. London 4 Sep. 1879. *Proc. of Soc. of Antiq. viii,* 347–52 (1881) ; *I.L.N. lxxv,* 280 (1879), *portrait.*

BLORE, Rev. Edward William *(elder son of the preceding).* *b.* London 24 Jany. 1828 ; ed. at Eton 1842–47, member of the cricket eleven ; began residence at Trin. coll. Cam. Oct. 1847, scholar 1849, fellow Oct. 1853 ; in the Cambridge eleven 1848–51 ; 37 wrangler 1851, B.A. 1851 ; assistant tutor of his college 1857, tutor 1862, senior tutor 1868–75, senior dean 1860–66 ; prime mover in restoration of Trin. coll. chapel, only important building in England founded by Queen Mary. *d.* Trinity college, Cambridge 24 June 1885 *The little journal i,* 77–88 (1884).

BLORE, Robert. Manufacturer of small porcelain biscuit figures in Bridge gate, Derby 1830 ; very clever in making pastes and glazes ; an assistant at Mason's factory at Lane Delph ; superintended a pot-works at Middlesbrough until his death. *d.* about 1866.

BLOUNT, Sir Edward, 8 Baronet. *b.* Mawley hall, Cleobury Mortimer, Salop 3 March 1795 ; succeeded 31 Oct. 1803 ; sheriff of Worcestershire 1835. *d.* Mawley hall 28 April 1881.

BLOXAM, Rev. Andrew *(4 son of Rev. Richard Rouse Bloxam, assistant master of Rugby school 38 years who d. 28 March 1840).* *b.* Rugby 22 Sep. 1801 ; ed. at Rugby 1808–20 and Worcester coll. Ox., B.A. 1824, M.A. 1827 ; fellow of his college ; naturalist on board the Blonde frigate (which conveyed bodies of King and Queen of Sandwich Islands to their native land) 1824–26 ; P.C. of Twycross, Leics. 1839–71 ; R. of Harborough Magna 1871 to death ; wrote on conchology, ornithology and plants ; author of *A guide to Bradgate park with natural history of Charnwood Forest* 1829. *d.* Harborough Magna 2 Feb. 1878. *Midland Naturalist, April* 1878 *pp.* 88-90.

BLOXAM, Rev. A. *(Con.)*

Note.—A water-colour drawing by Turner in the National Gallery represents A. Bloxam and his five brothers attending the funeral of their uncle Sir T. Lawrence, R.A.

BLOXAM, Charles John. Admitted solicitor Trinity term 1821 ; practised in London to death, probably oldest solicitor in practice on the rolls ; senior member of court of Clothworkers' Company, served as master when the new hall was opened by Prince Albert 27 March 1860. *d.* 16 Bedford place, Russell sq. London 25 Feb. 1885 in 85 year.

BLOXAM, Rev. Richard Rowland *(elder brother of Rev. A. Bloxam).* *b.* Jany. 1798 ; ed. at Rugby and Worcester coll. Ox., B.A. 1819 ; master of Guilsborough gr. sch. 1821– 24 ; chaplain of Pembroke dockyard 1845 ; domestic chaplain to Earl Ferrers 1848 ; R. of Harlaston, Tamworth 1850 to death ; author of *A voyage to the Sandwich Islands in H.M.S. Blonde. d.* Leamington 23 Jany. 1877.

BLOXAM, Thomas. *b.* London 1836 ; ed. at city of London school and King's college ; chemist to Industrial museum of Scotland 1860 to date when office was abolished ; lecturer on chemistry at St. George's hospital London ; lecturer in experimental and natural science at Cheltenham college 1862 to death ; F.C.S. 1859, F.G.S. 1869. *d.* London July 1872. *Cheltenham College Mag. iii,* 258–59 (1872).

BLUNDELL, Frederick. Second lieutenant Madras artillery 1813, colonel 4 May 1858 to death ; C.B. 24 Dec. 1842 ; M.G. 28 Nov. 1854. *d.* Cheltenham 5 July 1860 aged 62.

BLUNDELL, James. *b.* London 27 Dec. 1790 ; ed. at United Borough hospitals and Univ. of Edin., M.D. 24 June 1813 ; physician in London 1813 to death ; L.R.C.P. 25 June 1818, F.R.C.P. 6 Aug. 1838 ; lecturer at Guy's hospital 1819 to 1836 ; his class on Midwifery was largest in London ; author of *Researches, physiological and pathological* 1825 ; *Principles and practice of Obstetricy* 1834 ; *Observations on some of the more important diseases of women* 1837 ; *d.* 80 Piccadilly, London 15 Jany. 1878. Personalty sworn under £350,000, 9 Feb. 1878. *Pettigrew's Medical portrait gallery vol.* 1 (1840), *portrait ; W. C. Taylor's National portrait gallery ii,* 59 (1846), *portrait ; Medical Circular i,* 283 (1852).

BLUNT, John Elijah. Ed. at Trin. coll. Cam. ; B.A. 1819, M.A. 1822 ; barrister L.I. 24 June 1822 ; a comr. in lunacy 1833–42 ; master in chancery 26 Nov. 1849 to death ;

BLUNT, J. E. (Con.)

author of *A history of the establishment and residence of the Jews in England with an enquiry into their civil disabilities* 1830. *d.* 45 Dover st. Piccadilly, London 28 June 1856 aged 59.

BLUNT, REV. JOHN HENRY. *b.* Chelsea 25 Aug. 1823; a manufacturing chemist in London; entered Univ. coll. Durham 1850, L. Th. 1852, hon. M.A. 1855, hon. D.D. June 1882; C. of Tynemouth, Northumberland 1853–54; C. of Breamore, Hants. 1867–68; V. of Kennington near Oxford 1868–73; R. of Beverstone, Gloucs. 20 Jany. 1873 to death; F.S.A. 7 June 1866; author of *The Atonement* 1855; *Three essays on the Reformation* 1860; *Key to the Bible* 1865; *Annotated book of Common Prayer* 1866, new ed. 1884; *History of the Reformation* 1868; *Dictionary of theology* 1870, 2 ed. 1872; *The book of church law* 1872; *Dictionary of sects and heresies* 1874; *Annotated Bible* 1878 and many other books. *d.* London 11 April 1884. *Church Times* 18 *April* 1884 p. 303.

BLUNT, REV. JOHN JAMES *(son of Rev. John Blunt V. of Lilleshall, Shropshire who d. 14 June 1843 aged* 77). *b.* Newcastle-under-Lyme 1794; entered St. John's coll. Cam. 1812, first Bell scholar 1813, 15 wrangler 1816, B.A. 1816, M.A. 1819, B.D. 1826, fellow of his college 1816; travelling bachelor 1818, travelled in Italy and Sicily; C. of Hodnet, Shropshire 1823; C. of Chetwynd, Shropshire; Hulsean lecturer at Cam. 1831–32; R. of Great Oakley, Essex 1834–39; Lady Margaret professor of divinity at Cambridge 9 May 1839; offered the bishopric of Salisbury 1854; author of *Vestiges of ancient manners and customs discoverable in modern Italy and Sicily* 1823; *Sketch of the Reformation in England* 1832, 29 *ed.* 1875; *The acquirements and principal obligations and duties of the parish priest* 1856, 6 *ed.* 1872; *A history of the Christian church during the first three centuries* 1856, 4 *ed.* 1869; *On the right use of the early fathers, two series of lectures* 1857, 2 *ed.* 1858. *d.* Cambridge 17 June 1855. *Rev. J. J. Blunt's Two introductory lectures on the study of the early Fathers, 2 ed.* 1856 *v–xii; Quarterly Review civ,* 151–70 (1858); *Guardian* 10 *May* 1882 *pp.* 665–66; *Cambridge Chronicle* 23 *June* 1855.

BLUNT, RICHARD. Ensign 3 Foot 31 Jany. 1787; lieut. col. 23 Aug. 1799 to 1814; colonel 66 Foot 25 March 1835 to death; general 23 Nov. 1841. *d.* Barnfield house, Southampton 25 Dec. 1859 aged 90.

BLYTH, BENJAMIN HALL *(son of Robert Brittain Blyth of Edinburgh, iron merchant). b.* Edinburgh 14 July 1819; civil engineer at Edin. 1850 to death; engineer in chief to Great North of Scotland railway 1852; acted as adviser and engineer at various times to most of the principal railway companies in Scotland; constructed many important lines; extensively employed as a parliamentary engineer; A.I.C.E. 1844, M.I.C.E. 1851. *d.* North Berwick near Edin. 21 or 22 Aug. 1866. *Min. of proc. of Instit. of C.E. xxvi,* 556–60 (1867).

BLYTH, EDWARD. *b.* London 23 Dec. 1810; a druggist at Tooting 1832; contributed to *Magazine of natural history* from 1833; curator of museum of Asiatic Society of Bengal at Calcutta Sep. 1841 to 1862; contributed to the *Indian Field, India sporting review* and *Calcutta Review;* contributed to *Land and Water* and the *Field* under nom de plume of Zoophilus; one of the first zoologists of his time, and founder of the study of that science in India. *d.* 27 Dec. 1873. *Memoir prefixed to Catalogue of mammals and birds of Burma by E. Blyth in Journal of Asiatic Society of Bengal extra number Aug.* 1875, *portrait.*

BLYTHE, DAVID *(son of Charles Blythe of Yetholm, Roxburghshire, king of the gipsies who d.* 1861). *b.* Wooler, Northumberland 1795; king of the gipsies at Yetholm 1861 to death. *d.* 17 Feb. 1883. *bur.* in Chirnside churchyard. *David Blythe the gipsy king, a character sketch by Charles Stuart, M.D.* 1883, *portrait; All the year round vi,* 69–72 (1861).

BLYTHE, JOHN DEAN *(son of Peter Dean Blythe of Ashton-under-Lyne). b.* Ashton-under-Lyne 12 April 1842; worked in a factory; reporter on a local paper; learned Latin, French and Spanish; edited a manuscript magazine circulated amongst members of a self-improvement society at Manchester; killed by accidental discharge of a revolver 5 Feb. 1869. *A sketch of the life and a selection from the writings of J. D. Blythe* 1870.

BOAG, JOHN. *b.* Highgate in parish of Beith, Ayrshire 7 Jany. 1775; matric. at Univ. of Glasgow 1797; joined the body of independents or congregationalists who in 1812 formed themselves into Congregational Union of Scotland; held small charges in Isle of Man and Helensburgh; pastor in village of Blackburn, Linlithgowshire; author of *A popular and complete English dictionary 2 vols.* 1848; *The imperial lexicon of the English language 2 vols.* 1853, and of a number of pamphlets on questions of the day. *d.* Craigton house, Linlithgowshire 15 Sep. 1863.

BOAG, SIR ROBERT (*son of the preceding*). *b.* 22 Aug. 1809; alderman of Belfast; knighted at Dublin Castle 30 Jany. 1877. (*m.* 1834 Violet only dau. of John Stevens of Glasgow). *d.* Glenorchy house, Newington, Edinburgh 7 Nov. 1877.

BOASE, CHARLES WILLIAM (3 *son of Henry Boase* 1763–1827, *managing partner in banking house of Ransom, Morland and Co. Pall Mall, London*). *b.* 6 Knightsbridge, London 8 June 1804; ed. at Helston gr. sch.; entered Dundee New Bank 1821, manager 1828; cashier of Dundee Banking company 13 March 1838, manager 1840 to 20 Feb. 1864 when it was merged in Royal bank of Scotland, managed the branch to 21 Dec. 1867 when he retired on a pension; secretary and treasurer of Watt Institution Dundee 1824–36, founded the museum to which he largely contributed; received freedom of Dundee 1 Sep. 1831 for his exertions in aiding to procure it a liberal constitution; one of the trustees elected by the creditors when town of Dundee became bankrupt 1842; a member of the Catholic Apostolic or Irvingite church 1836, erected a little chapel in Bell st. Dundee which the congregation used until 30 Nov. 1867 when church in Constitution road was opened; ordained to the priesthood Oct. 1836 and to the Episcopate Aug. 1851; had charge of the Evangelistic work throughout Scotland Dec. 1867 to death; author of *Tithes and Offerings* 1865; *A century of banking in Dundee* 1867; *The Elijah ministry* 1868; *Notes on doctrines and ecclesiastical facts* 1868; *Physical a part of theological science*, 2 ed. 1874. *d.* Albury, Surrey 7 June 1872. *W. Norrie's Dundee Celebrities* (1873) 397–99; *An account of the families of Boase or Bowes privately printed* (1876) 13–14.

BOASE, GEORGE CLEMENT (*brother of the preceding*). *b.* 127 Sloane st. Chelsea 25 Aug. 1810; ed. at Exeter gr. sch. and Queen's coll. Cam. 1828–29; cashier of Dundee Banking company April 1840 to Feb. 1864; submanager of Dundee branch of Royal Bank of Scotland Feb. 1864 to 21 Dec. 1867 when he retired on a pension; a member of the Catholic Apostolic church 1836, ordained to the priesthood Oct. 1836, had charge of the church at Brighton 1868 to death; author of *To husbands, father and brothers specially those of the labouring classes being a warning against prevailing delusions by a brother* [G. C. Boase] 1848; *The restoration of Apostles* 1867; *Thoughts and memories in verse by G. C. B[oase]* 1876. *d.* Fairlie house, Bridge of Allan near Stirling 23 July 1880. *An account of the families of Boase* 15–16.

BOASE, HENRY SAMUEL (*brother of the preceding*). *b.* 6 Knightsbridge, London 2 Sep. 1799; ed. at Tiverton gr. sch.; studied chemistry in Dublin 1815–17 and medicine in Univ. of Edin. 1817–21, M.D. 1821; sec. to Royal Geological Society of Cornwall at Penzance 1822 to 1829; collected from every part of Cornwall specimens of the rocks 1829–31 which were deposited in Geological Museum at Penzance; a partner in the Penzance Union Bank 1823 to April 1838 when bank was dissolved; lived in Burton crescent, London 1837–38; F.R.S. 4 May 1837; managing partner in firm of Turnbull Brothers of the Claverhouse Bleachfield, Dundee June 1838, this firm became Boase & Co.; took out a patent for 'improvements in the process of drying organic substances' 17 July 1855; author of *A treatise on primary geology* 1834; *The philosophy of nature* 1860; *An essay on human nature* 1865; *The second Adam, the seed of the woman. Anon.* 1876; *A few words on evolution and creation* 1883; wrote a minute geological account of each parish in *The parochial history of Cornwall by D. Gilbert* 4 vols. 1837. *d.* 5 Magdalen place, Dundee 5 May 1883. *Dict. of Nat. Biog. v,* 282–3 (1886); *An account of the families of Boase* 8–10.

BOATE, EDWARD WELLINGTON (*eld. son of George Boate of Waterford*). Edited the Waterford *Chronicle* and Wexford *Guardian*; a reporter for the *Times* in the House of Commons; went to New York; worked on the *Irish American, Evening Express,* and other journals; joined the 42nd New York Volunteers 1863; taken prisoner at battle of Bristo station and sent to Belle Island; comr. and chairman of delegation of 95000 men to negotiate with Abraham Lincoln for an exchange of prisoners; a reporter on the *Sunday Mercury* to Sep. 1871. *d.* King's county hospital, Flatbush, Pittsburgh, Philadelphia 4 Oct. 1871 aged 49.

BOAZ, THOMAS (*eld. son of Richard Boaz of Scarborough, ship-carpenter*). *b.* Scarborough 10 Aug. 1806; studied at Theological seminary Newport Pagnel 1829–33; ordained at Manchester 18 June 1834; Congregational minister of Union chapel Calcutta Dec. 1834 to Dec. 1858; LL.D. King's college Aberdeen 1849; sole editor and proprietor of *Calcutta Christian Advocate*, May 1839 to 1853; one of editors of *Calcutta Christian Observer* 1835–47. *d.* 6 Priory grove, West Brompton, London 13 Oct. 1861. *The Mission pastor, memorials of Rev. T. Boaz by his widow* (1862), *portrait*.

BOCHSA, ROBERT NICOLAS CHARLES. *b.* Montmédi, France 9 Aug. 1789; harpist to Emperor

Bochsa, R. N. C. (Con.)

Napoleon 1813; may fairly be said to have revolutionised harp playing; fled to London having been detected in extensive forgeries 1817; tried in his absence and condemned to 12 years imprisonment; joint manager with Sir G. Smart of the Lent Oratorios 1822, sole manager 1823; professor of the harp and general sec. at R.A. of Music 24 March 1824 to 1827; conductor at the King's theatre 1826–32; ran away with Sir H. R. Bishop's wife 1839; visited every country in Europe except France; went to United States 1847; appeared at Prince of Wales's theatre Sydney 22 Dec. 1855; wrote an oratorio called *Le déluge universel*, 8 operas, a Method and many solo pieces. *d.* Sydney 7 Jany. 1856.

BODDAM, EDWARD TUDOR. Entered Madras army 11 Dec. 1841; lieut. col. staff corps 11 Dec. 1867; M.G. 16 June 1876. *d.* 12 Feb. 1880 aged 55.

BODDINGTON, HENRY JOHN (2 son of *Edward Williams of London, artist*). *b.* London 1811; exhibited pictures at the R.A. 1837 to death; member of Society of British artists 1842, exhibited about 10 pictures every year at their gallery in Suffolk st. 1842 to death, his paintings are mostly taken from quiet English country life. (*m.* 1832 Clara Boddington whose name he adopted). *d.* Barnes, Surrey 11 April 1865.

BODE, REV. JOHN ERNEST (*son of Wm. Bode of the General Post Office, London*). *b.* 1816; ed. at Eton, the Charterhouse and Ch. Ch. Ox., Hertford scholar (the first) 1835, B.A. 1837, M.A. 1840; student and tutor of his college 1841–47, censor 1844; R. of Westwell Oxon. 1847–60; select preacher 1848; surrogate 1850–60; Bampton lecturer 1855; contested chair of poetry in Univ. of Ox. 1857; R. of Castle Camps, Cambridge 1860 to death; author of *Ballads from Herodotus* 1853, 2 ed. 1854; *Lecture on the English formularies* 1855; *Short occasional poems* 1858; *Hymns from the Gospel of the day* 1860. *d.* Castle Camps rectory 6 Oct. 1874.

BODEN, GEORGE (*youngest son of John Boden of Edmaston lodge, Derbyshire*). *b.* 22 Jany. 1816; ed. at Rugby and Trin. coll. Cam., B.A. 1841, M.A. 1845; barrister I.T. 30 April 1841, bencher 30 April 1862, treasurer 1876; recorder of Stamford Feb. 1855; recorder of Derby 7 May 1859 to death; Q.C. 6 Feb. 1862. *d.* 7 Queen's gardens, Hyde park, London 16 Feb. 1880.

BODEN, SAMUEL STANDIGE. *b.* Hull 11 April 1826; clerk in South Eastern railway office at Nine Elms, London 1849; edited *British Chess review* 1854–55, contributing a large portion of its contents; conducted chess department of *The Field* 24 April 1858 to Jany. 1869; exhibited 5 landscapes at Suffolk st. gallery 1865–73. *d.* Tavistock st. Bedford sq. London 13 Jany. 1882. *Westminster Papers ix*, 89 (1876), *portrait; Illust. news of the world viii*, 164 (1861), *portrait.*

BODENHAM, CHARLES THOMAS (*only son of Charles Bodenham of Rotherwas park, near Hereford 1758–1826*). *b.* 15 Feb. 1783; a member of the Roman Catholic board; chief supporter with Rev. Thomas Weld, afterwards Cardinal, of Dr. Milner in opposing the concessions which it was proposed to make in regard to the oath. (*m.* 25 Nov. 1810 Elizabeth Mary 5 dau. of Thomas Weld of Lulworth Castle, Dorset, she was *b.* 2 July 1789, and was author of *Mrs. Herbert and the villagers or familiar conversations on the principal duties of Christianity* 2 vols. 1853, 10 ed. 1878). *d.* 5 Dec. 1865.

BODINGTON, GEORGE. Ed. at Magdalen coll. sch. Oxford; studied at St. Bartholomew's hospital; L.S.A. 1825; surgeon at Erdington near Birmingham to 1843; proprietor of Driffold house asylum, Sutton Coldfield, Warws. 1836–68; warden of Sutton Coldfield 1852–54; author of *A letter on a case of Asiatic cholera addressed to Central board of health*, London 1831; *Essay on the treatment and cure of pulmonary consumption* 1840, in which he anticipated by many years the modern views on the treatment of Phthisis. *d.* Sutton Coldfield 5 Feb. 1882 in 83 year. *Medical times and gazette i*, 241 (1882).

BODKIN, JOHN JAMES (*eld. son of Thomas Bodkin of Kilcloony, co. Galway*). *b.* 1801; M.P. for town of Galway 6 May 1831 to Dec. 1832, and for co. Galway 15 Jany. 1835 to 23 July 1847. *d.* Calais Jany. 1882.

BODKIN, SIR WILLIAM HENRY (*only son of Peter Bodkin of Northampton sq. London, auctioneer*). *b.* Islington, London 5 Aug. 1791; ed. at Islington academy; hon. sec. Society for suppression of mendicity 1821; barrister G.I. 15 Nov. 1826, bencher 2 July 1857, treasurer 30 Jany. 1858; counsel to the Treasury; recorder of Dover 1834 to Jany. 1874; M.P. for Rochester 1841–47; carried a bill making relief of irremovable poor, chargeable on common fund of unions, which is foundation of present system; assistant judge of Middlesex sessions court 6

June 1859 to Jany. 1874; chairman of Metropolitan assessment sessions; knighted at Osborne 3 Aug. 1867; member of Society of Arts 1823 on the council till 1874; author of *Brief observations on the bill now pending in Parliament to amend the laws relative to the relief of the poor in England* 1821. *d.* West hill, Highgate 26 March 1874. *I.L.N. xxxv,* 82 (1859), *portrait, lxiv,* 331 (1874), *portrait.*

BODMER, JOHN GEORGE. *b.* Zurich 6 Dec. 1786; partner with Baron d' Eichtal in a cotton mill at St. Blasien, Black forest 1806–21; director general of iron works of Grand Duke of Baden to 1822; lived in England 1824-28 and 1833-48, established a factory for machines and machine tools at Manchester; made great improvements in cotton-spinning machines; invented what is now called the travelling crane about 1826; took out 13 patents in England for his inventions; lived at Vienna 1848-60 and at Zurich 1860 to death; M.I.C.E. 15 Feb. 1835. *d.* Zurich 29 May 1864. *Min. of Proc. of Instit. of C.E. xxviii,* 573–608 (1869).

BOGLE, SIR ARCHIBALD *(son of J. A. Bogle).* *b.* 1805; ed. at Harrow; entered Bengal army 1823; superintendent of Arracan 1827, and comr. 1837; comr. Tenasserim province 20 April 1849 to 1859; M.G. 2 Aug. 1862; knighted by patent 9 Dec. 1853. *d.* 90 Westbourne terrace, London 12 June 1870.

BOGUE, DAVID. Assistant to Thomas Ireland of Edinburgh bookseller to 1836; assistant to Charles Tilt of London publisher 1836-40, partner with him 1840–43; bookseller and publisher at 86 Fleet st. London 1843 to death; wrote several children's books anonymously; one of principal proprietors of *Illustrated Times. d.* 76 Camden road villas, Camden town, London 17 Nov. 1856 aged 44.

BOHLER, JOHN. *b.* South Wingfield near Alfreton, Derbyshire 31 Dec. 1797; a stocking weaver; collector of medicinal plants for the doctors; an expert field botanist and microscopist; explored Snowdon and adjacent mountains about 1860; a great collector of rare fungi and other curious plants; published *Lichenes Britannici or specimens of the Lichens of Britain* 16 *monthly parts* 1835-7; author of *A Flora of Roche Abbey* in Aveling's *Roche Abbey Yorkshire* 1870; *The Flora of Sherwood Forest* in R. White's *Worksop, the Dukeries and Sherwood Forest* 1875. *d.* Sheffield 24 Sep. 1872. *Reliquary xi,* 212–13 (1871); *R. White's Worksop* (1875) 303–26.

BOHN, HENRY GEORGE *(eld. son of John Henry Martin Bohn of Soho, London, bookbinder* 1758–1843). *b.* 4 Jany. 1796; assisted his father; bookseller at 4 York st. Covent Garden 1831; brought out *A Catalogue of books* 1841 containing 1948 pages and 23208 articles; built up a trade in remainder books in which he had no rival; published Standard library 1845, Scientific and antiquarian 1847, Classical 1848, Illustrated 1849, Shilling series 1850, Ecclesiastical 1851, Philological 1852 and British classics 1853, the whole numbering 617 volumes some of which he compiled and edited; author of *A dictionary of quotations from the English poets* 1882; published *The bibliographer's manual of English literature by W. T. Lowndes, new ed. revised, corrected and enlarged by H. G. Bohn* 4 *vols.* 1864; sold his Libraries to Bell and Daldy in 1864 for about £40,000 and his copyrights and plates to Chatto and Windus in Dec. 1874 for £20,000; his art collections were sold for £45,000 1875–78 and March 1885. *d.* North end house, Twickenham 22 Aug. 1884. *Bookseller Sep.* 1884 *pp.* 907–909.

BOHN, JAMES GEORGE STUART BURGES *(brother of the preceding). b.* London 20 Dec. 1803; ed. at Winchester and Gottingen; assisted his father some years; bookseller at 12 King William st. Strand, London Feb. 1834, and at 66 St. James's st. 1845-47; published a catalogue of 792 pages 1840; republished *Dugdale's Monasticon* 8 *vols, folio* 1846; contributed to *Family Herald;* assistant editor of the *Reader;* prepared a catalogue of theological books of 704 pages for David Nutt 1857; compiled catalogues of foreign books for Nicholas Trubner for many years before his death. *d.* Peckham 4 Jany. 1880. *Bookseller Feb.* 1880, *pp.* 105–106.

BOILEAU, ALEXANDER HENRY EDMONSTONE. *b.* 3 Feb. 1807; colonel Bengal engineers 8 June 1856 to death; M.G. 18 Oct. 1861. *d.* Cawnpore 30 June 1862.

BOILEAU, SIR JOHN PETER, 1 Baronet *(eld. son of John Peter Boileau of Tacolnestone hall, Norfolk* 1747–1837). *b.* Hertford st. Mayfair, London 2 Sep. 1794; 2 lieut. Rifle corps 6 Sep. 1813, lieut 1816–17 when placed on h.p.; bought estate of Ketteringham, Norfolk 1839 and Burgh Castle, Suffolk the ancient Gariononum most remarkable example of Roman masonry in England; created baronet on coronation of Queen Victoria 24 July 1838; F.R.S. 1 June 1843; sheriff of Norfolk 1844; Vice pres. of Norfolk and Norwich Archæological Society from its formation Dec. 1845,

BOILEAU, SIR J. P. *(Con.)*
pres. 1849; F.S.A. 9 Dec. 1852, vice pres.
1858–62, 1863–67 and 1868 to death. *d.*
Torquay 9 March 1869. *bur.* at Ketteringham.
Reg. and Mag. of Biog. i, 292–4 (1869).

BOILEAU, SAMUEL BRANDRAM. *b.* 15 June
1801; ensign 31 Foot 18 Sep. 1823; lieut.
col. 22 Foot 18 Dec. 1840 to 25 Sep. 1857
when placed on h.p.; M.G. 26 Oct. 1858.
d. Hillsborough, Monkstown co. Dublin 23
Dec. 1860.

BOILEAU, THOMAS EBENEZER JOHN. Writer
in Madras civil service 1815; civil and session
judge at Masulipatam 1844; at Chingleput
1847–51 and at Guntoor 1851 to 15 April
1851 when he resigned on an annuity. *d.*
Brighton 8 Feb. 1853 aged 56.

BOISRAGON, THEODORE WALTER ROSS. *b.*
19 May 1830; ensign 36 Bengal N.I. 20 July
1847; lieut col. Bengal staff corps 2 Sep.
1872 to 2 Sep. 1881 when he retired with
hon. rank of M.G.; C.B. 22 Feb. 1881. *d.* 4
Albert terrace, Bedford 21 Sep. 1882. *Graphic
xxvi*, 536 (1882), *portrait.*

BOISSIER, REV. GEORGE RICHARD. Educ. at
Magd. coll. Cam., B.A. 1828; lived at Oakfield, Penshurst Kent; published anonymously
Notes on the Cambridgeshire churches 1827. *d.*
23 June 1858 aged 67.

BOLCKOW, HENRY WILLIAM FERDINAND
*(eld. son of Heinrich Bolckow of Varchow in
grand duchy of Mecklenburg). b.* Sulten,
Mecklenburg 8 Dec. 1806; came to England
1827; naturalised by acts of parliament 4
and 5 Vict. c. 48 and 31 and 32 Vict. c. 10;
partner with John Vaughan as iron makers
at Middlesbrough 1841; a Tees conservancy
comr. 1851; took the oath of allegiance 27
Feb. 1853; mayor of Middlesbrough (the
first) 1853; donor of the Albert park at a
cost of £20,000 opened 11 Aug. 1868; erected
the St. Hilda's schools opened 22 Sep. 1869;
A.I.C.E. 14 April 1863; M.P. for Middlesbrough 16 Nov. 1868 to death; chairman of
Bolckow, Vaughan and Co., limited (with a
capital of £3,500,000) 1871 to death; collected a fine gallery of pictures by modern
French and English artists. *d.* Ramsgate 18
June 1878. *Practical Mag. i*, 81–90 (1873),
portrait; Athenæum 22 Nov. 1873 *pp.* 664–6.

BOLD-HOGHTON, SIR HENRY, 8 Baronet.
b. Walton hall near Preston 3 Jany. 1799;
sheriff of Lancashire 1829; succeeded 27
Nov. 1835. *d.* Anglesey near Gosport 19 July
1862. *G.M. xiii*, 360–62 (1862).

BOLDEN, SAMUEL EDWARD *(younger son of
John Bolden of Hyning near Lancaster, breeder
of shorthorn cattle 1776–1855). b.* 1812; one
of promoters of Lancaster and Carlisle railway opened 1846; one of the most successful
breeders and soundest judges of shorthorn
cattle; the first breeder to realise £1,000 for
one animal; sold his herd 1862. *d.* Derby
22 March 1880. *Saddle and Sirloin by the
Druid* (1885) 384–9.

BOLDERO, HENRY GEORGE *(son of Rev. John
Boldero, R. of Ampton, Suffolk). b.* 1797;
captain 10 Foot 1828–30 when placed on h.p.;
M.P. for Chippenham 1831–32 and 1835–59;
clerk of the ordnance 9 Sep. 1841 to 1846;
fought a duel in Osterley park with Craven
Fitzhardinge Berkeley, M.P. for Cheltenham,
15 July 1842. *d.* Charles st. St. James's sq.
London 9 April 1873.

BOLENO, HARRY, stage name of Henry Boleno
Mason *(son of S. Mason, a clerk in the Victualling
office, Somerset house, London). b.* April 1821;
learnt from Andrew Ducrow the Grecian
Statues; played in the first pantomimes
produced at Lyceum, Strand, Standard and
City of London theatres; a dancer at White
Conduit house and Eagle tavern; clown at
T.R. Dublin 10 years; landlord of The Clown
tavern in Williamson sq. Liverpool and of
The Catherine Wheel, Great Windmill st.
London; kept the Opera Stores Covent
Garden; clown at Drury Lane theatre 1860–
70 and at Surrey theatre 1874–75; landlord of the Swan tavern Windsor; author of
several burlesques and ballets. *(m.* about
1849 Emma dau. of Thomas Davie of Hoddesdon, Herts. maltster, she was *b.* 27 Jany.
1832 and *d.* 18 Oct. 1867, as a columbine she
has never been excelled). *d.* The Swan tavern,
Windsor 25 Jany. 1875. *The Players ii*, 287
(1860), *portrait; Illust. Sp. and Dr. News ii*,
268 (1874), *portrait.*

BOLINGBROKE, HENRY ST. JOHN, 4 Viscount. *b.* 6 March 1786; succeeded 18 Dec.
1824. *d.* North college, Elgin 1 Oct. 1851.
I.L.N. xix, 450, 663 (1851).

BOLINGBROKE, HENRY *(son of Nathaniel
Bolingbroke of Norwich). b.* Norwich 25 Feb.
1785; sailed for Demerara 28 Nov. 1798,
returned to England 21 Oct. 1805; deputy
vendue master at Surinam in Guiana 1807–13;
in business at Norwich; published *A voyage to
the Demerary* 1807. *d.* Norwich 11 Feb. 1855.

BOLLAERT, WILLIAM. *b.* 1807; chemical
assistant at Royal Institution, London;
assayer and chemist in survey of silver mines

BOLLAERT, W. (Con.)

in Peru; made a survey of province of Tarapaca 1827; one of the first white men who crossed the desert of Atacama; served as a volunteer under Sir J. M. Doyle in Portugese war 1832–33; created a knight of Order of the Tower and Sword of Portugal; explored Texas, New Granada, Ecuador, Peru and Chili; author of *Antiquarian and other researches in New Granada* 1860; *Wars of succession of Portugal and Spain* 2 vols. 1870. *d.* 15 Nov. 1876 in 69 year. *Journal of Royal Geog. Soc. xlvii*, 148–50 (1877).

BOLLAND, WILLIAM PROCTOR (2 *son of Sir Wm. Bolland 1772–1840, Baron of Court of Exchequer).* Educ. at Eton; barrister I.T. 6 May 1842; the original of Fred. Bayham in Thackeray's *The Newcomes*, and of Wm. Bowker in Yates's *Land at last. d.* Clifton 10 June 1863 aged 47.

BOLOGNA, SIR NICHOLA, Count Delle Catene *(son of Baron Paolo Sceberras).* C.M.G. 1833, K.C.M.G. 4 Dec. 1868. *d.* Valetta, Malta 1875.

BOLTON, DANIEL. Second lieut. R.E. 14 Dec. 1811, colonel 13 Dec. 1854 to 20 June 1859; M.G. 20 June 1859. *d.* Capetown, Cape of Good Hope 16 May 1860 aged 66.

BOLTON, GEORGE *(son of Mr. Bolton of Piccadilly, London, tailor).* b. 9 May 1824; Manager of Olympic theatre 1846–47, of Marylebone and Queen's theatres, and of Drury Lane theatre 1852; brought out about 1846 a comic weekly paper called *Nonsuch a farrago of something, nothing, everything and many things besides;* author of *Nothing, in rhyme and prose* 1845; *All about love and jealousy, an original comedy in 5 acts produced at Olympic theatre* 13 *April* 1846. *d.* 13 Philadelphia terrace, Mount gardens, Lambeth 25 May 1868.

BOLTON, REV. JAMES JAY (5 *son of Rev. Robert Bolton of Henley on Thames, dissenting minister).* b. Southdown college near Weymouth 11 Feb. 1824; went to the United States 1836; ed. at College Point New York and C. C. coll. Cam., scholar, B.A. 1848; C. of Saffron Walden, Essex 1849–51; C. of St. Michael's, Chester sq. Pimlico, London 1851–52; Minister of St. Paul's chapel, Kilburn 1852 to death; chaplain to Earl Ducie 1852; has never been surpassed as a childrens' preacher; author of *Fragments of the great diamond set for young people, being a variety of addresses for children* 1856, 3 ed.

BOLTON, REV. J. J. (Con.)

1861; *Life lessons, scripture truths for the young* 1862. *d.* Kilburn parsonage 8 April 1863. *Selected sermons of Rev. James Bolton* 1863, *portrait.*

BOLTON, JASPER. *b.* Ballykisteen, co. Tipperary; land agent to Earl of Derby's estates in Ireland 1862 to death. *d.* Limerick 19 Nov. 1871 aged 30. *Quickly ripened or recollections of the late Jasper Bolton* (1872), *portrait.*

BOLTON, JOHN HENRY. *b.* Dec. 1795; in the commissariat department; solicitor at 1 New sq. Lincoln's Inn, London 1828 to death; president of Incorporated law society 1868–69. *d.* Lee terrace, Blackheath, Kent 13 Oct. 1873.

BOLTON, REV. WILLIAM JAY. Educ. at Caius coll. Cam., Hulsean prizeman 1852, B.A. 1853, M.A. 1857; V. of St. John's Stratford, Essex 1866–81; V. of St. James's, Bath 1881 to death; author of *Evidences of Christianity from the early Fathers* 1853; *Fireside preaching* 1856; *Footsteps of the flock* 1860; *The great Anti-Christ* 1870. *d.* Pelham, Oldfield park, Bath 28 May 1884 in 68 year.

BONAPARTE, JEROME NAPOLEON *(elder son of Jerome Bonaparte 1784–1860, king of Westphalia).* b. Camberwell, London 7 July 1805. *d.* Baltimore 17 June 1870. *Bingham's Marriages of the Bonapartes ii,* 191–94 (1881).

BONAPARTE, NAPOLEON EUGÈNE LOUIS JEAN JOSEPH *(only child of Charles Louis Napoleon Bonaparte 1808–73, Napoleon iii Emperor of France).* b. Palace of the Tuileries, Paris 16 March 1856; went with his father to the seat of war 1870, present at capture of Saarbrück 2 Aug. 1870; landed at Dover 8 Sep. 1870; lived at Camden house, Chislehurst, Kent 10 Dec. 1870 to 12 Oct. 1871 and 1874–79; a cadet at Royal military college Woolwich 12 Oct. 1871 to 1874 where a statue of him by Count Gleichen was unveiled 13 Jany 1883; left Southampton 27 Feb. 1879; killed by Zulus in valley of Ityolyozi, Zululand 1 June 1879, buried in St. Mary's church Chislehurst 12 July 1879. *Life of the Prince Imperial of France by Ellen Barlee* 1880, *portrait: Graphic xix,* 633, 637, 644 (1879), 3 *portraits, xxvii,* 53 (1883); *I.L.N.* 16 *July* 1879, *portrait; The life of Napoleon iii by Blanchard Jerrold iv,* 427 (1882), 2 *portraits.*

BONAR, REV. JOHN *(son of Rev. Archibald Bonar of Cramond, Midlothian).* b. Cramond; ed. at Univ. of Edin.; licensed by presbytery of Edin. 30 April 1823; ordained 11 July 1826; minister of Larbert and Dunipace March 1826 to 24 May 1843 when he joined in the free secession; Convener of committee for colonial and continental missions in the Free church 1846; minister at Aberdeen Dec. 1846 and at the Renfield st. church, Glasgow 1848–54; D.D. Edin. 1857; author of *The established church of Scotland as it was and as it is* 1845. *d.* Edinburgh 20 Dec. 1863 in 63 year. *Our Scottish Clergy, second series* (1849) 149–55.

BONAR, WILLIAM (3 son of *Andrew Bonar of Edinburgh, banker*). *b.* Edin. 3 Jany. 1798; ed. at high school and Univ. Edin.; a partner in bank of Ramsay, Bonar and Co. 1817 to date when bank was merged in Bank of Scotland; employed a missionary to look after the ignorant and neglected poor in Edin.; F.R.S. Edin. 1822; author of several religious tracts. *d.* Chatsworth house, Malvern 9 Nov. 1866.

BOND, HENRY JOHN HAYLES (son of *Rev. Wm. Bond, R. of Whitacre, Norfolk*). *b.* Whitacre Dec. 1801; ed. at Norwich gr. sch.; studied medicine at Cambridge, London, Edinburgh and Paris; M.B. Cam. 1825, M.D. 1831; F.R.C.P. 1835; practised at Cam.; Regius professor of physic in Univ. of Cam. 27 Jany. 1851 to Jany. 1872; a member of General medical council 29 Oct. 1858 to 29 Oct. 1863; author of *Analysis of an elementary course of lectures on Pathology* 1866. *d.* Regent st. Cambridge 3 Sep. 1883.

BOND, JOHN JAMES (son of *Andrew Bond of Ashford, Kent*). *b.* 9 Dec. 1819; Clerk in public record office at Royal riding school, Carlton House 1841, senior assistant keeper to death; author of *Handy book of rules and tables for verifying dates with the Christian Era* 1866, *new ed.* 1874. *d.* 96 Philbeach gardens, Earl's Court, London 9 Dec. 1883.

BOND, R. SEBASTIAN. *b.* Liverpool 1808; landscape painter; exhibited 7 pictures at Royal Academy, 13 at British Institution, and 5 at Suffolk st. gallery 1846–72. *d.* Jany. 1886.

BOND, STEPHEN. *b.* St. Columb, Cornwall 24 March 1826; ed. at Stonyhurst; entered Society of Jesus at Hodder 7 Sep. 1843; Matric. at Univ. of London July 1846, B.A. 1848; superior of the seminary adjoining Stonyhurst college Aug. 1861; professed of the four vows 2 Feb. 1862; vicar general to Bishop Etheridge in Demerara 1864–69. *d.* Wigan 10 Jany. 1871.

BONE, HENRY PIERCE (*eld. son of Henry Bone of London, enamellist* 1755–1834). *b.* Islington, London 6 Nov. 1779; exhibited 210 pictures, miniatures and enamels at the R.A. 1799–1855; painted classical subjects 1806–33, and enamels 1833–55: enamel painter to Duchess of Kent 1834, to Queen Victoria 1837, to Prince Albert 1841; his collection of 172 enamels was sold at Christies 13–14 March 1856. *d.* 22 Percy st. Bedford sq. London 21 Oct. 1855. *Notice of H. Bone R.A. and his works together with those of his son H. P. Bone by J. Jope Rogers* 1880.

BONE, HUGH. *b.* Ayrshire 1777; ed. at Univ. of Glasgow, M.D. 26 April 1815; L.R.C.P. London 26 June 1815; inspector general of hospitals 2 Oct. 1843 to 24 Nov. 1845 when placed on h.p. *d.* Picardy place, Edin. 13 Feb. 1858.

BONER, CHARLES (*only son of Charles Boner of Bath, who d. 14 Aug. 1833 aged 74*). *b.* Weston near Bath 29 April 1815; ed. at Bath and Tiverton; lived with John Constable the painter as tutor to his sons 1831–37; lived with Prince Thurn and Taxis at St. Emeran, Ratisbon as tutor 1840–60; settled at Munich, March 1860; corresponded with Mary Russell Mitford 1845–55; special correspondent to *Daily News* at Vienna Aug. 1865 to Aug. 1866; author of *Chamois hunting* 1853, *new ed.* 1860; *The new dance of death and other poems* 1857; *Transylvania its products and its people* 1865 and other books. *d.* 5 Louisen Strasse, Munich 7 April 1870. *Memoirs and letters of C. Boner, edited by R. M. Kettle* 2 *vols.* 1871.

BONHAM, EDWARD WALTER (2 son of *Henry Bonham of Titness park, Berkshire, M.P. for Rye who d. 9 April* 1830). *b.* 24 Nov. 1809; consul at Tabreez, Persia 11 May 1837; transferred to Calais 2 Feb. 1846, and to Naples 14 Jany. 1859; consul general at Naples 5 May 1862 to 5 April 1872 when he retired on a compensation allowance; C.B. 13 Oct. 1865. *d.* the British consulate Boulogne 15 March 1886.

BONHAM, HENRY FREDERIC (*brother of the preceding*). *b.* 2 June 1808; ed. at the Charterhouse; Cornet 10 Hussars 22 May 1829, lieut. col. 28 April 1846 to 27 Feb. 1852 when placed on h.p.; appointed to the Brighton and Canterbury cavalry depôt June 1854. *d.* 28 Brunswick sq. Hove, Brighton 16 Feb. 1856.

BONHAM, PINSON (*eld. son of Samuel Bonham of Great Warley place, Essex who d. 25 Jany.* 1821). Clerk in Court of Chancery 10 years;

ensign 60 Foot 24 April 1789; served in West Indies 22 years; deputy quartermaster general 10 years; governor of Surinam or Dutch Guiana to 1814 when colony was surrendered to the Dutch; major 69 Foot 30 March 1797 to 1814, general 10 Jany. 1837. *d.* Great Warley, Essex 19 April 1855 aged 92.

BONHAM, SIR SAMUEL GEORGE, 1 Baronet *(only son of George Bonham, captain H.E.I. Co.'s navy who d. 1810). b.* Faversham, Kent 7 Sep. 1803; governor of Prince of Wales Island, Singapore and Malacca 1837–47; chief superintendent of British trade in China, and governor and commander in chief of Hong Kong 27 Nov. 1847 to 24 Dec. 1853; C.B. 27 April 1848, K.C.B. 22 Nov. 1850; created baronet 27 Nov. 1852. *d.* Paddington, London 8 Oct. 1863. *The Chinese Repository vols. xvii–xx.*

BONHAM-CARTER JOHN *(son of John Carter of Petersfield, M.P. for Portsmouth who assumed additional name of Bonham). b.* 13 Oct. 1817; ed. at Trin. coll. Cam.; M.P. for Winchester 1847–74; a lord of the Treasury 1866–68; chairman of committees of House of Commons 1872–74. *d.* Adhurst St. Mary's, Petersfield 26 Nov. 1884. *I.L.N. lx,* 601, 607 (1872), *portrait.*

BONNAR, WILLIAM *(son of Mr. Bonnar of Edinburgh, house-painter). b.* Edin. June 1800; foreman at a leading decorative painters; member of Royal Scottish Academy; painted many pictures which became popular when engraved; very successful in rural scenes and pictures of child life; painted portraits latterly, many of which were engraved by his sons. *d.* London st. Edin. 27 Jany. 1853.

BONNER, JOHN GEORGE. Major Madras artillery 9 June 1825 to 4 July 1829; M.G. 4 July 1829; inspector general of military stores for India; F.R.S. 18 June 1840. *d.* 17a Great Cumberland st. Hyde park, London 3 March 1867 aged 79.

BONNEY, FRANCIS AUGUSTUS BURDETT *(son of John Augustus Bonney of London, solicitor who d. 30 Dec. 1813). b.* 1804; ed. at Ealing; made many contributions chiefly in verse to literary journals especially *European Magazine;* studied medicine in Edin. and Paris; L.R.C.S. Edin. 1829, L.S.A. 1833; practised at Brentford 1833, Chichester and London; author of *Nugæ or poetic trifles* 1821, and of some valuable papers in medical journals. *(m. Miss*

Elliott, proprietress of Elm house lunatic asylum, Queen's Elm, Brompton, London). *d.* Elm house 13 Oct. 1877. *Medical Circular i,* 303 (1852).

BONNEY, VENERABLE HENRY KAYE *(son of Rev. Henry Kaye Bonney, R. of King's Cliffe, Northamptonshire who d. 20 March 1810). b.* Tansor, Northamptonshire 22 May 1780; ed. at the Charterhouse and Em. coll. Cam; migrated to Christ's coll., B.A. 1802, M.A. 1805, D.D. 1824; Preb. of Lincoln cathedral 8 Jany. 1807; R. of King's Cliffe March 1810 to death; V. of Nassington 1810–29; archdeacon of Bedford 10 Dec. 1821, installed 2 Feb. 1822; archdeacon of Lincoln 22 Feb. 1845 to death; canon residentiary of Lincoln 1845 to death; author of *The life of the Right Rev. Father in God, Jeremy Taylor* 1815; *Historic notices in reference to Fotheringay* 1821; *The life and remains of Bishop Middleton* 1824. *d.* King's Cliffe rectory 24 Dec. 1862.

BONNEY, VENERABLE THOMAS KAYE *(brother of the preceding). b.* Tansor, Northamptonshire 20 June 1782; ed. at Clare coll. Cam., B.A. 1803, M.A. 1806; R. of Coningsby Lincs. 1814 to death; R. of Normanton, Rutland 1814 to death; Preb. of Lincoln 17 Oct. 1823 to death; archdeacon of Leicester 22 Jany. 1831 to death. *d.* Normanton rectory 7 April 1863.

BONOMI, JOSEPH *(son of Giuseppe Bonomi of London, architect 1739–1808) b.* 76 Great Titchfield st. London 9 Oct. 1796; ed. at Carshalton, Surrey; studied drawing at Royal Academy and sculpture under Nollekens; fellow Student with John Gibson in Rome; lived in Egypt and Syria 1824–32 and 1842–44; went to the Holy Land 1833; illustrated the Egyptological works of Wilkinson and Birch and nearly all those of Samuel Sharpe; curator of Sir John Soane's Museum, Lincoln's Inn Fields, London 1861 to death; F.R.A.S, 8 Feb. 1861; author of *Nineveh and its palaces* 1852, new ed. 1869. *d.* The Camels, Wimbledon park, Surrey 3 March 1878. *Monthly notices of Royal Astronom. Soc. xxx,* 216–19 (1879); *The Proportions of the human figure by J. Bonomi,* 5 ed. 1880, *portrait; I.L.N. lxxii,* 245 (1878), *portrait.*

BONTEIN, JAMES *(younger son of John Pitt Bontein, captain 1 Life guards).* Groom of the privy chamber 1874 to death. *d.* Ambassadors' court, St. James's palace 16 Oct. 1884 aged 63.

BOOKER, THOMAS *(son of Thomas Booker of 56 New Bond st. London, publisher who d. 26 Feb. 1826).* Printer at 37 Ranelagh st. Liver-

BOOKER, T. *(Con.)*

pool 1840; printer and publisher at 9 Rupert st. Leicester sq. London 1848, and at 75 Great Queen st. to death; published *The weekly register* 4 Aug. 1849 to 26 Jany. 1850; *The Catholic register and magazine* 1850; *Booker's Pocket-Book directory*. *d.* Richmond 9 Nov. 1859 aged 37.

BOOKER-BLAKEMORE, THOMAS WILLIAM *(son of Rev. Luke Booker 1762–1836, V. of Dudley).* *b.* Dudley 28 Sep. 1801; ed. at Hartlebury, Worcs.; tin plate manufacturer; took out patents for tin plate making 1837 and for manufacturing iron 1841; sheriff of Glamorganshire 1848; M.P. for Herefordshire 18 Oct. 1850 to death; took an active part on protectionist side in free trade controversy; A.I.C.E. 1850; assumed by r.l. additional name of Blakemore Sep. 1855; author of *Treatise on the mineral basin of South Wales* 1848. *d.* Kingston-upon-Thames 7 Nov. 1858.

BOOLE, GEORGE *(son of Mr. Boole of Lincoln, tradesman).* *b.* Lincoln 2 Nov. 1815; opened a school at Lincoln 1835; professor of mathematics in Queen's college Cork 1849 to death; public examiner for degrees in Queen's University of Ireland; LL.D. Dublin 1852; Keith medallist of Royal Society of Edinburgh 1857; F.R.S. June 1857, Royal medallist 1844; hon. D.C.L. Oxford 1859; author of *Mathematical analysis of logic* 1847; *Investigation of the laws of thought* 1854, a work of astonishing originality and power; *Treatise on differential equations* 1859, 3 ed. 1872; *Treatise on the calculus of finite differences* 1860, *new ed.* 1880. *(m.* 1855 Mary dau. of Rev. Thomas Roupell Everest, R. of Wickwar, Gloucs., she was granted a civil list pension of £100, 19 June 1865). *d.* Blackrock near Cork 8 Dec. 1864. There are memorial windows to him in Lincoln cathedral and the college hall at Cork. *Proc. of Royal Society* xv, 6–11 (1867); *Athenæum* 23 Aug. 1884 *pp.* 237–39; *G.M.* xviii, 247–49 (1865); *I.L.N.* xlvi, 59, 61 (1865), *portrait.*

BOONE, REV. JAMES SHERGOLD *(son of Thomas Boone of Sunbury, Middlesex).* *b.* 30 June 1799; ed. at Charterhouse 1812–16; student at Ch. Ch. Ox. 1816; Craven scholar 1817; won Chancellor's prize for Latin verse, and Newdigate prize for English verse 1817; published anonymously a satire on Oxford University life called *The Oxford Spy* 2 parts 1818–19, which created a great sensation; chancellor's prizeman 1820; B.A. 1820, M.A. 1823; edited *The Council of Ten* a monthly periodical June 1822 to May 1823, wrote nearly all of it; Incumbent of St. John's

BOONE, REV. J. S. *(Con.)*

church Paddington June 1832 to death; edited *The British Critic* from Jany. 1827; author of *An essay on the study of modern history* 1821; *Men and things in 1823, a poem in three epistles with notes* 1823; *The educational economy of England* 1838; *Sermons on various subjects and occasions* 1853. *d.* 2 Stanhope st. Hyde park, London 24 March 1859. *Mozley's Reminiscences* ii, 200–204 (1882); *Notes and Queries* 3rd series iii, 510, iv, 35, 98, 138, 153, 299.

BOONE, WILLIAM. Bookseller at 480 Strand, London 1815-30 with his brother Thomas Boone who *d.* 21 April 1873 aged 83; moved to New Bond st. 1830; buyer of books for British Museum on death of Thomas Rodd 1849, retired 1860. *d.* 26 Nov. 1870 aged 75.

BOORMAN, JAMES. *b.* Kent 1785; partner with Divie Bethune in New York 1805–13; founded with John Johnson firm of Boorman, Johnson and Co. leading mercantile house in New York, which was dissolved 1855; pres. of Hudson River railroad to 1863; founded the Bank of Commerce 1839. *d.* New York 24 Jany. 1866.

BOOSEY, THOMAS. Foreign bookseller at 28 Holles st. Cavendish sq. London; published Italian operas of Bellini, Donizetti and Verdi down to 1854, when deprived of all his foreign copyrights by a decision of the House of Lords. *d.* 27 Notting hill sq. London 25 Oct. 1871 aged 76. *C. Clark's House of Lords Cases* iv, 815–996 (1855).

BOOTH, REV. GEORGE *(youngest son of Wm. Booth of Masbrough, Yorkshire).* Ed. at Eton and Trin. coll. Cam., pensioner; matric. from Lincoln coll. Ox. 16 May 1811 aged 19, B.A. 1813, M.A. 1816, B.D. 1823; fellow of Magdalen coll., vice pres. 1830, dean of divinity 1832; V. of Findon, Sussex 1833 to death; privately printed a quarto vol. of Latin poetry entitled *Nugæ Cunoræ* 1826; composed a school song entitled *Sicut lilium, carmen hortativum* which is regularly sung by boys of Magdalen school on their breaking up. *d.* Findon vicarage 21 June 1859 in 68 year.

BOOTH, HENRY *(eld. son of Thomas Booth of Liverpool, corn merchant).* *b.* Rodney st. Liverpool 4 April 1788; a corn merchant; one of chief promoters of scheme for making a railway between Liverpool and Manchester 1822, sec. and treasurer of the company 1826, managing director, the line was begun June 1826 and opened 15 Sep. 1830; suggested the multitubular boiler, coupling

BOOTH, H. (Con.)

screws, spring buffers, and lubricating material for carriage axles, all of which are still used; sec. for northern section of London and North-Western railway July 1846, a director of the company October 1848 to 18 May 1859, presented by the Company with 3000 guineas 12 Oct. 1846 and 5000 guineas 9 April 1859; author of *Sebastian a tragedy* 1823; *The rationale of the currency question* 1847; *Master and man a dialogue* 1853, and many other small books. *d.* Eastbourne, Princes park, Liverpool 28 March 1869. *Memoir of the late Henry Booth by Robert Smiles* (1869).

BOOTH, REV. JAMES *(eld. son of John Booth of Lava, co. Leitrim).* *b.* Lava 25 Aug. 1806; ed. at Trin. coll. Dub., scholar 1829, B.A. 1832, LL.B. and LL.D. 1842; principal of Bristol college 1840–43; vice principal of Collegiate institution Liverpool 1843–48; pres. of Literary and philosophical institution Liverpool 1848–51; lectured in London for Society of Arts 1848–54, fellow 1852, treasurer and chairman of the council 1855–57; C. of St. Anne's Wandsworth, London 1854–59; V. of Stone, Bucks. 1859 to death; F.R.S. 22 Jany. 1846, F.R.A.S. 10 June 1859; author of *Education and educational institutions* 1846; *Examination the province of the state* 1847; *A treatise on some new geometrical methods* 2 vols. 1873–77. *d.* Stone vicarage 15 April 1878. *Monthly notices of Royal Astronom. Soc. xxxix,* 219–25 (1879).

BOOTH, JAMES *(4 son of Thomas Booth of Toxteth lodge near Liverpool).* *b.* 1796 or 1797; ed. at St. John's coll. Cam.; barrister L.I. 10 Feb. 1824; member of Royal commission for inquiring into municipal corporations of England and Wales 1833; counsel to the speaker and examiner of recognizances Sep. 1839; prepared the Companies, Lands, and Railways Clauses Consolidation acts 1845, and 8 other consolidation acts 1847; secretary to Board of trade 10 Oct. 1850 to 1865; member of Royal commission for inquiring into trades unions 12 Feb. 1867, which made 11 reports 1867–69; C.B. 6 July 1866; author of *The problem of the world and the church reconsidered in three letters to a friend by a Septuagenarian* 1871, 3 ed. 1879. *d.* 2 Princes gardens, Kensington, London 11 May 1880.

BOOTH, JOHN *(son of Thomas Booth of Killerby near Catterick, Yorkshire, cattle breeder who d. 1835).* Breeder of shorthorns at Killerby 1819 to 1852; judged a great deal at cattle shows in England and Ireland; sold all his

BOOTH, J. (Con.)

stock 21 Sep. 1852; master of the Bedale hunt 3 seasons. *d.* Killerby 7 July 1857 in 70 year. *W. Carr's History of rise and progress of Killerby herds of shorthorns* 1867; *Saddle and Sirloin by the Druid* (1870) 195–207.

BOOTH, JOHN KAY *(eld. son of John Booth of Brush house, Ecclesfield).* *b.* Yorkshire; ed. at Univ. of Edin., M.D. 24 June 1805; L.C.P. 30 Sep. 1809; fellow Royal Med. and Chir. Soc. 1810; settled at Birmingham; physician to general hospital there 1812–35; physician to Queen's hospital there; principal of Queen's college Birm. 1856; one of founders of Medical school of Birmingham, and the first lecturer there on practice of physic. *d.* Brush house, Ecclesfield 14 Jany. 1859 aged 80.

BOOTH, JUNIUS BRUTUS *(son of Richard Booth of Queen st. Bloomsbury, London, attorney who d. 1840 aged 76).* *b.* St. Pancras, London 1 May 1796; made his début on the stage at Peckham as Campillo in *The Honeymoon* 13 Dec. 1813; played in Belgium and Holland 1814 and 1826, and at Covent Garden 1815; acted in the provinces 1818 and at Drury Lane 7 Aug. 1820 to 13 Jany. 1821; went to the United States April 1821; appeared at Park theatre New York 2 Oct. 1821; managed the Camp theatre New Orleans 1828; played at Drury Lane, Surrey and Sadler's Wells theatres 1836–7; lived on his farm at Bel Air 30 miles from Baltimore 1842 to death; made his last appearance at St. Charles theatre New Orleans 19 Nov. 1852. *d.* on board the J. S. Chenoweth between New Orleans and Cincinnati 30 Nov. 1852. *bur.* in Greenmount cemetery Baltimore 11 Dec. *The elder and the younger Booth by A. B. Clarke* (1882) 1–116, 3 *portraits*; *Memoirs of J. B. Booth* (1817), *portrait*; *The tragedian by T. R. Gould* (1868), *portrait*; *Phelps's Players of a century* (1880); *T. A. Brown's History of the American stage* (1870) 40, *portrait*.

NOTE.—His son John Wilkes Booth shot Abraham Lincoln, pres. of the U.S. at Ford's theatre, Washington, Good Friday 14 April 1865, he was himself shot near Bowling Green 26 April.

BOOTH, RICHARD *(brother of John Booth who d. 7 July 1857).* Breeder of shorthorns at Studley farm, Yorkshire 1814–34 when he sold his herd; breeder at Warlaby, Yorkshire 1835 to death; gained many medals and prizes at cattle shows. *d.* Warlaby 31 Oct. 1864 aged 76. *Saddle and Sirloin by the Druid* (1870) 195–207.

BOOTH, SIR ROBERT GORE, 4 Baronet. *b.* Bath 25 Aug. 1805; succeeded 23 Oct. 1814;

BOOTH, SIR R. G. *(Con.)*

sheriff of Sligo 1830; M.P. for Sligo 12 March 1850 to death; chairman of the Musical Union; lord lieutenant of Sligo 7 Dec. 1868. *d.* Lissadell, co. Sligo 21 Dec. 1876. *Burke's Portrait gallery ii*, 129 (1833).

BOOTH, SARAH. *b.* Birmingham early in 1789; a dancer at Manchester about 1804; first appeared in London at Surrey theatre 1810 as Cherry in a burletta founded on the *Beaux Stratagem;* played at Covent Garden 23 Nov. 1810, at the Olympic 19 Dec. 1821, at Drury Lane 2 Feb. 1822, at Haymarket and Adelphi theatres; retired about 1828, last appeared for a benefit at Marylebone theatre 1841. *d.* 39 Queen's sq. Bloomsbury, London 30 Dec. 1867. *Mrs. C. B. Wilson's Our actresses i*, 121–7 (1844); *Oxberry's Dramatic biography iv*, 55–65 (1826), *portrait; Theatrical Inquisitor ii*, 69–74 (1813), *portrait.*

BOOTH, WILLIAM. Ensign 53 Foot 8 May 1806; lieut. col. 41 Foot 11 July 1837 to 12 Sep. 1843 when placed on h.p.; colonel 15 Foot 10 Nov. 1861 to death; L.G. 27 March 1863. *d* London 20 April 1868 aged 77.

BOOTH, WILLIAM. Deputy commissary general 18 Dec. 1818 to 1824 when placed on h.p.; served in Spain, Portugal and the Netherlands; principal clerk of survey at Dublin 1824 to 1856; C.B. 17 Aug. 1849. *d.* 17 Lansdowne crescent, Cheltenham 4 May 1880 in 88 year.

BOOTH, SIR WILLIAMSON, 2 Baronet. *b.* Stanstead Abbots, Herts. 15 July 1810; ed. at Eton; succeeded 24 Jany. 1850; sheriff of Cambridge and Hunts 1855. *d.* Paxton park, St. Neots 26 Aug. 1877.

BOOTHBY, BENJAMIN *(eld. son of Benjamin Boothby of Cornwall place, Holloway, London).* *b.* Doncaster 5 Feb. 1803; barrister G.I. 28 April 1841; revising barrister for West Riding of Yorkshire 1845–52; judge of Court of Record of Pontefract and recorder 1848–53; second judge of supreme court of South Australia Feb. 1853, sworn in 17 Oct. 1853, presided as senior judge Dec. 1856 to July 1858; deputy judge of Court of Vice Admiralty 1856–61; removed from judgeship of Supreme Court by South Australian parliament July 1867 owing to his objections to the Real Property or Torrens act. *d.* Adelaide 21 June 1868.

BOOTHBY, REV. SIR BROOKE WILLIAM ROBERT, 10 Baronet. *b.* Winchester 21 Jany. 1809; ed. at Charterhouse and Ch. Ch. Ox., B.A. 1829, M.A. 1833; fellow of All Souls'

BOOTHBY, REV. SIR B. W. R. *(Con.)*

college 1829; R. of Elmley, Kent 1846–52; R. of Welwyn, Herts. 17 Sep. 1852 to death; succeeded 21 April 1846. *d.* Tunbridge Wells 21 Sep. 1865.

BOOTHBY, LADY LOUISA CRANSTOUN *(eld. dau. of Frederick Hayes Macnamara, ensign 52 Foot).* *b.* 1 April 1812; a juvenile theatrical wonder under name of Louisa Mordaunt, made her first appearance in London at Drury Lane theatre 16 Oct. 1829 as the Widow Cheerly in Cherry's comedy of *The Soldier's Daughter;* acted at the Haymarket 1830, 1837–39 and 1840–44; re-appeared at Drury Lane Oct. 1832; acted at the Queen's 1835 and Strand; played Constance in *The love chase* nearly 100 nights from 9 Oct. 1837 and Lady Gay Spanker in *London Assurance* 4 March 1841 in both of which parts she was unequalled; played leading parts in genteel comedy at Covent Garden 1839–40. *(m.* (1) Jany. 1831 John Alexander Nisbett of Brettenham hall, Suffolk, Cornet 1 Life Guards, he *d.* 2 Oct. 1831. *m.* (2) 15 Oct. 1844 Sir Wm. Boothby, 9 baronet of Ashbourne hall, Derbyshire, he was *b.* 25 March 1782 and *d.* 21 April 1846). *d.* Rose Mount, St. Leonard's on Sea 16 Jany. 1858. *C. B. Wilson's Our actresses ii*, 66–88 (1844), *portrait; Theatrical Times ii*, 121, 130 (1847), *portrait; Dramatic and musical review iii*, 498, 527 (1844); *I.L.N. x*, 256 (1847), *portrait.*

BOOTT, FRANCIS *(son of Kirk Boott of Boston, Massachusetts).* *b.* Boston 26 Sep. 1792; ed. at Univs. of Harvard and Edinburgh, M.D. Edin. 1824; surgeon in London 1825–31; lecturer on botany in Webb st. school of medicine 1825–31; member of senate and council of Univ. coll. London; F.L.S. 1819, sec. 1832–39, treasurer Nov. 1856 to May 1861; wore a blue coat with brass buttons and a yellow waistcoat the costume of 1830 down to his death; author of *Memoir of the life and medical opinions of John Armstrong, M.D.* 2 vols. 1833–34; *Illustrations of the genus Carex* 4 parts 1858–67. *d.* 24 Gower st. London 25 Dec. 1863. *Proc. of Linnæan Society* (1864) 23–27.

BORCHARDT, LOUIS. *b.* Landsburg on Warthe, Prussia 1813; ed. at Univ. of Berlin, M.D. 1838; practised as a physician at Zorbich and then at Breslau; imprisoned in fortress of Glatz 1848–50; practised at Bradford, Yorkshire 1850–52, and at Manchester 1852 to death, phys. to Childrens' Dispensary June 1853, pres. of Manchester Medical Society. *d.* Swinton house, Fallowfield, Manchester 15 Nov. 1883.

BORLAND, JAMES. *b.* Ayr April 1774; surgeon's mate 42 Foot 20 Dec. 1792; surgeon to the forces in St. Domingo 1796–8; deputy inspector of army hospitals 5 Dec. 1799; established existing system of regimental hospitals 1805; inspector general 22 Jany. 1807; head of medical department of the army in Mediterranean 1810–16 during which time he organised the hospitals of the Anglo-Sicilian contingent; retired on h.p. 25 May 1816; received order of St. Maurice and St. Lazare of Savoy; phys. extraord. to Duke of Kent. *d.* Bridgeman house, Teddington 22 Feb. 1863. *G.M. xiv*, 666 (1863).

BOROUGH, SIR EDWARD RICHARD, 2 Baronet. *b.* Merrion sq. Dublin 20 June 1800; ed. at Westminster and Ch. Ch. Ox.; army agent in Dublin; succeeded 22 Jany. 1837. *d.* 61 Fitzwilliam sq. north, Dublin 3 Dec. 1879.

BORRADAILE, EDWARD SIDNEY *(son of the succeeding).* *b.* Littlehampton 30 March 1845; assistant engineer Launceston and Western railway Tasmania 1868–9; wrote for the Press 1870–3; lost whilst exploring in North Australia June 1874, two mountains are named after himself and his companion Mr. Permain in memory of the event.

BORRADAILE, HARRY *(son of Henry Borradaile of London 1759–1822).* *b.* 19 July 1800; in the Bombay civil service 1819–44; compiled for publication by Government *Reports of select suits decided in the Suddur Adawluts* 1825; translated the *Muyook* (Sanscrit Law book) into Mahratta and Goozerattee 1827; author of *Collection of the rules and customs of various castes as affecting civil rights;* and of *A table of a decimal system of accounts* 1853; a member of the India law commission at Calcutta under T. B. Macaulay. *d.* London 7 Oct. 1876.

BORRELL, HENRY PERIGALL. Learnt business in London; merchant at Smyrna 1818 to death; very successful in discovery of inedited Greek coins; author of *Notice sur quelques médailles grecques des Rois de Chypre, Paris* 1836 and of papers in *Revue Numismatique, Numismatic Chronicle* and various German numismatic periodicals; his collection of coins, antiquities and gems was sold in London 1851. *d.* Smyrna 2 Oct. 1851 aged 56.

BORRER, WILLIAM *(eld. son of Wm. Borrer of Parkyns manor, Hurstpierpoint 1753–1832).* *b.* Henfield, Sussex 13 June 1781; endeavoured to cultivate every critical British species and all the hardy exotic plants he could obtain, having no less than 6660 species;

BORRER, W. *(Con.)*
wrote descriptions of species of Myosotis, Rosa, and nearly all of Rubus for Sir W. Hooker's *British Flora* 1830 and subsequent editions; several plants were named after him and the genus Borreria of Acharius amongst lichens; his herbarium of British plants is kept at the Royal gardens, Kew; F.L.S. 1805, F.R.S. 4 June 1835. *d.* Barrow hill, Henfield 10 Jany. 1862. *Proc. of Linnæan Society* (1862) 85–90; *Lower's Worthies of Sussex* (1865) 71–73.

BORRIE, JOHN *(son of Peter Borrie, proprietor of the Dundee foundry).* *b.* Dundee 27 Nov. 1837; employed by Bolckow and Vaughan of Middlesbrough, engineers 1856–61; resident engineer at Cleveland iron works Eston 1866–71; a consulting engineer 1871 to death; designed and set to work the hopper-and-spout kilns for calcining ironstone 1869, which have become general, reducing cost of labour very considerably; M.I.M.E. 1869. *d.* Stockton-on Tees 8 Feb. 1884. *Engineering 26 Nov.* 1869.

BORROW, GEORGE HENRY *(younger son of Thomas Borrow, captain in West Norfolk militia who d.* 1823). *b.* East Dereham, Norfolk 5 July 1803; ed. at Norwich gr. sch. 1815–18; articled in office of Simpson and Rackham solicitors Norwich 1818–23; worked for Sir Richard Phillips the publisher in London; travelled in France, Germany, Russia, the East and Spain 1833–39, acting as agent for the British and Foreign Bible Society; sent letters to the *Morning Herald* 1837–39, being the first of the newspaper correspondents; travelled in Albania, Wallachia, Hungary and Turkey 1844; author of *Romantic ballads translated from the Danish* 1826; *Targum or metrical translations from 30 languages and dialects* 1835; *The Zincali, or an account of the Gypsies of Spain* 2 vols. 1841, 4 ed. 1846; *The Bible in Spain* 3 vols. 1843, *new ed.* 1873; *Lavengro the scholar, the gypsy, the priest* 3 vols. 1851, 3 ed. 1872 which is in a great degree an autobiography; *The Romany Rye* 2 vols. 1851, 3 ed. 1872; *Wild Wales* 3 vols. 1862, 2 ed. 1865. *d.* Oulton near Lowestoft, Norfolk 26 July 1881. *Lavengro vol. i,* (1851), *portrait; The Norvicensian April* 1882, *pp.* 109–14.

BORROWES, REV. SIR ERASMUS DIXON, 8 Baronet. *b.* Portarlington, Queen's county 21 Sep. 1799; ed. at Trin. coll. Dublin; succeeded 7 March 1834; R. of parish of Ballyroan, Queen's county. *d.* Lauragh near Portarlington 27 May 1866.

BORROWS, Rev. William. *b.* Derby 15 Nov. 1781; ed. at Quorn, Derbyshire, Winkfield, Wilts. and St. Edmund Hall Ox., B.A. 1812, M.A. 1815; C. of Over, Oxon 1812–15; P.C. of St. Paul's chapel, Clapham 1815 to 1 July 1851; author of *Reformation from Popery two sermons* 1818; *Sacred maxims collected from the discourses of W. B. by an attached member of his congregation* 1852. *d.* 3 April 1852. *bur.* Derby churchyard 10 April. *Select sermons by the late Rev. Wm. Borrows, with a brief memoir edited by Rev. Philip Gell* (1852).

BORTHWICK, Cunninghame Borthwick, 12 Baron (2 *son of Patrick Borthwick who d.* 12 *April* 1840 *aged* 60). *b.* Edinburgh 6 June 1813; ed. at high school and univ. of Edin.; head of firm of Borthwick, Wark and Co. of London, stock-brokers; established his claim to this barony (which had been dormant since 1772) before a committee of House of Lords 5 May 1870; bought Ravenstone castle, Wigtonshire in 1874 for £85,000; a representative peer for Scotland April 1880. *d.* Ravenstone castle 24 Dec. 1885. *P. H. M'Kerlie's Lands in Galloway ii,* 445–50 (1877).

BORTHWICK, Michael Andrews. *b.* Dunbar, East Lothian 30 Oct. 1810; A.I.C.E. 1833, M.I.C.E. 1845; resident engineer of Northern and Eastern railway 1837 and subsequently manager; engaged with Stephenson carrying out Egyptian railway between Alexandria and Cairo. *d.* Pernambuco 3 June 1856. *Min. of Proc. of Instit. of C.E. xvi,* 108–13 (1857).

BORTHWICK, Peter *(only son of Thomas Borthwick of Edinburgh). b.* Cornbank, parish of Borthwick, Mid Lothian 13 Sep. 1804; ed. at Univ. of Edin.; entered Jesus coll. Cam.; fellow commoner of Downing coll.; contested Evesham 1832 and St. Ives, Penryn and Falmouth 1847; M.P. for Evesham 6 Jany. 1835 to 23 July 1847; barrister G.I. 28 April 1847; edited the *Morning Post* 1850 to death; author of *A brief statement of Holy Scriptures concerning the second Advent* 1836; *A Lecture on slavery* 1836. *d.* 11 Walton villas, Brompton, London 18 Dec. 1852. *G.M. xxxix,* 318–20 (1853); *I.L.N. ii,* 8 (1843), *portrait, xxi,* 563 (1852), *xxii,* 11 (1853).

BORWICK, Rev. W. B. *b.* Orkney; ed. at Univ. of Edin.; licensed to preach 1834; pastor of the United Secession church in the Overgate, Dundee May 1835, and of United presbyterian church in Bell st. Dundee 1850 to May 1866. *d.* Newport 15 June 1870 aged 62. Monument erected in Western cemetery Dundee Jany. 1871. *W. Norrie's Dundee Celebrities* (1873) 355–7.

BOSANQUET, Augustus Henry (2 *son of Wm. Bosanquet of London, banker who d.* 21 *June* 1800 *aged* 43). *b.* 1 March 1792; ed. at Harrow and Haileybury; in Bengal civil service 1811–17; one of founders of Universal Life insurance company 1842, director 1842–77. *d.* 19 Feb. 1877.

BOSANQUET, George William (4 *son of Rev. Robert Wm. Bosanquet* 1800–80, *R. of Bolingbroke, co. Lincoln). b.* 4 July 1845; ensign 85 Foot 19 April 1864 to 1866; clerk in the Exchequer and audit department. *d.* 2 Brunswick terrace, Kensington 24 Jany. 1869. *Essays and stories by the late G. W. Bosanquet, with an introductory chapter by Captain C. B. Brackenbury, R.A.* 1870.

BOSANQUET, James Whatman (2 *son of Samuel Bosanquet of Forest house, Waltham forest, Essex* 1768–1843). *b.* 26 Jany. 1804; ed. at Westminster school; taken into his father's bank 1822; F.R.A.S.; author of *Chronology of the times of Daniel, Ezra and Nehemiah* 1848; *Messiah the Prince* 1866, 2 ed. 1869; *Hebrew chronology from Solomon to Christ* 1867. *d.* Claysmore, Enfield 22 Dec. 1877.

BOSANQUET, Samuel Richard *(brother of the preceding). b.* London 1 April 1800; ed. at Eton and Ch. Ch. Ox., B.A. 1822, M.A. 1829; barrister I.T. 5 May 1826; a revising barrister 1832; chairman of Monmouth quarter sessions 35 years; wrote many leading articles for *The Times;* author of *New system of logic* 1839, 2 ed. 1870; *The rights of the poor vindicated* 1841; *Principia, a series of essays* 1843; *Prophecies of Zechariah interpreted* 1877; *Select interpretations of Scripture* 1878. *d.* Dingestow court, Monmouth 27 Dec. 1882.

BOSIO, Angiolina. *b.* Turin 22 Aug. 1830; made her début at Teatro Rè, Milan in *I Due Foscari* July 1846; sang in Paris 1848, in America 1849–51; sang at Covent Garden theatre London during seasons 1852 to 1855 and 1858; sang at the Lyceum theatre 1856 and 1857; première cantâtrice to Imperial Court of St. Petersburg 1858 being the first singer to obtain that honour. *d.* St. Petersburg 12 April 1859. *E. C. Clayton's Queens of song ii,* 317–29 (1863).

BOSSEY, Peter *(eld. child of Francis Bossey, constructor in royal carriage department of Woolwich arsenal). b.* Woolwich 3 April 1806; apprenticed to Thomas Bayles of Woolwich; studied at United Borough hospital; L.S.A. 1826, M.R.C.S. 1828, F.R.C.S. 1852; surgeon to Convict hulk establishment at Wool-

wich to 1848 when he retired on pension;
fellow of Med. and Chir. Soc. 1846; gave up
practice 1857; author of many statistical
reports and papers on diseases and mortality
of prisoners printed in *Reports of Superintendent of Convict establishment at Woolwich. d.*
Worthing 22 Dec. 1862. *Proc. of Royal Med.
and Chir. Soc. iv,* 203–7 (1864).

BOSTOCK, JAMES. Proprietor of Bostock and
Wombwell's menagerie. *d.* 12 April 1878
aged 63.

BOSTON, FLORANCE GEORGE HENRY IRBY, 5
Baron. *b.* Florence 9 March 1837; sheriff of
Anglesea 1865; succeeded 22 Dec. 1869. *d.*
Porthamel Anglesey 4 Jany. 1877.

BOSTON, GEORGE IRBY, 3 Baron. *b.* Grosvenor st. London 24 Dec. 1777; Cornet 1
Dragoons 1794, major 13 Light Dragoons
22 Jany. 1801 to 14 Aug. 1801; succeeded
23 March 1825. *d.* Hedsor lodge near
Maidenhead 12 March 1856.

BOSTON, GEORGE IVES IRBY, 4 Baron. *b.*
Grosvenor st. London 14 Sep. 1802; succeeded
12 March 1856. *d.* Wilton crescent, London
22 Dec. 1869.

BOSWELL, SIR JAMES, 2 Baronet *(son of
Sir Alexander Boswell, 1 Baronet b. 1775
and killed by James Stuart in a duel 26
March 1822). b.* Dec. 1806. *d.* Auchinleck,
Ayrshire 4 Nov. 1857.

BOSWORTH, REV. JOSEPH. *b.* Derbyshire
early in 1789; ed. at Repton gr. sch., Univ.
of Aberdeen, and Trin. coll. Cam., B.A.,
M.A., and LL.D. Aberdeen; B.D. at Cam.
1834, D.D. 1839; incorp. D.D. of Ch. Ch.
Ox. 1858; V. of Horwood Parva, Bucks.
1817–29; chaplain at Amsterdam 1829–32
and at Rotterdam 1832–40; V. of Waith,
Lincs. 1841–45 and 1848–58; R. of Water
Stratford, Bucks. 1858–75; F.R.S. 4 June
1829; professor of Anglo Saxon in Univ. of
Oxford 4 Nov. 1858 to death; made over to
Univ. of Cam. by deed of gift in 1867 sum
of £10,000 towards professorship of Anglo
Saxon which was founded May 1878; author
of *The elements of Anglo-Saxon Grammar* 1823,
earliest English work of the kind; *Anglo-
Saxon dictionary* 1838, 2 ed. 1882; *Scandinavian
literature* 1839; *A compendious dictionary of
Anglo-Saxon* 1848, 5 ed. 1882. *d.* 20 Beaumont
st. Oxford 27 May 1876. *Academy 3. and 10
June* 1876; *Times 29 May* 1876, *p.* 10, *col.* 4.

BOTFIELD, BERIAH *(eld. son of Beriah Botfield
of Norton hall, Northamptonshire* 1768–1813).
b. Earl's Ditton, Salop. 5 March 1807; ed. at
Harrow and Ch. Ch. Ox., B.A. 1828, M.A.
1847; sheriff of Northamptonshire 1831;
M.P. for Ludlow 23 May 1840 to 23 July
1847 and 27 March 1857 to death; F.R.S.
17 Jany. 1839; F.S.A. 1839; a chevalier of
order of Albert the Brave of Saxony; knight
of order of Leopold of Belgium; member of
Abbotsford, Bannatyne, Maitland, and Roxburgh clubs, and of Surtees Society, for all
of which he edited books; set up a private
printing-press at Norton hall, where he printed
*Journal of a tour through the Highlands of
Scotland anon.* 1830; *Stemmata Botevilliana*
1843; *Bibliotheca Hearneiana* 1848; published
Notes on cathedral libraries of England 1849;
*Prefaces to first editions of Greek and Roman
classics* 1861. *d.* 5 Grosvenor sq. London 7
Aug. 1863. *Stemmata Botevilliana* (2 ed. 1858)
84–7, 156, *App.* 33, 479–96; *G.M. xv.* 645–7
(1863); *Numismatic Chronicle iv,* 17–18 (1864).

BOTT, THOMAS. *b.* near Kidderminster 1829;
a portrait painter at Birmingham; one of
principal artists of the Royal Porcelain works
Worcester 1852; gained many prizes at
Worcester School of Art; obtained distinction
for his work in Worcester enamel, at Paris
Exhibition 1855 and London Exhibition
1862; one of his best works is now in South
Kensington Museum. *d.* Worcester 13 Dec.
1870. *Jewitt's History of the Ceramic art in
Great Britain* (1883) 143–4 *and* 150.

BOTTRELL, WILLIAM *(son of Wm. Vingoe
Bottrell of Raftra, St. Levan, Cornwall, farmer
1790–1876). b.* Raftra 7 March 1816; learnt
farming under his father; English master in
the Seminary of Quebec, Canada Sep. 1847
to 1851; author of *Traditions and hearthside
stories of West Cornwall* 1870, 2 series 1873;
communicated upwards of 50 of the "Drolls"
to Robert Hunt for his *Popular romances of
the west of England* 2 vols. 1865. *d.* Dove st.
St. Ives 27 Aug. 1881.

BOUCH, SIR THOMAS *(3 son of Wm. Bouch,
captain in merchant service). b.* Thursby,
Cumberland 22 Feb. 1822; manager and
engineer of Edinburgh and Northern railway
1849; made floating railways for goods trains
over rivers Forth and Tay; constructed a
number of remarkable bridges chiefly railway,
in all of which he made use of the lattice
girder; designed railway bridge over river
Tay, completed 22 Sep. 1877, opened 31 May
1878, the central portion of this bridge fell
into the river carrying with it an entire

train and its load of about 70 passengers 28
Dec. 1879; designed railway bridge over
river Forth begun 30 Sep. 1878, work was
stopped after above accident; A.I.C.E. 3 Dec.
1850, M.I.C.E. 11 May 1858; presented
with freedom of Dundee 31 May 1878;
knighted at Windsor Castle 26 June 1879.
d. Moffat, Dumfriesshire 30 Oct. 1880. *Min.
of Proc. of Instit. of C.E. lxiii*, 301–308 (1881);
I.L.N. lxxvii, 468 (1880), *portrait*.

BOUCHER, REV. JOHN (*son of Mr. Boucher of
Moneyrea, near Belfast, tenant-farmer*). *b.* 1819;
ed. at Belfast academy 1837–42; Unitarian
minister at Southport 1842, at Glasgow to
1848 and at the New Gravel Pit chapel
Hackney, London 1848–53 when he entered
at St. John's coll. Cam. to read for orders in
Church of England, B.A. 1857; one of
trustees of Dr. Williams's library: a member
of the presbyterian board; published a sermon on *The present religious crisis* 1850. *d.*
Chesterton near Cambridge 12 March 1878.
The Inquirer 23 March 1878 *p.* 190.

BOUCHIER, REV. BARTON (*son of Rev. Jonathan Boucher 1738–1804, V. of Epsom, Surrey*).
b. 1794; ed. at Baliol coll. Ox., B.A. 1822,
M.A. 1827; changed his name from Boucher
to Bouchier; C. of Cheam, Surrey about 1832
to 1858; R. of Fonthill Bishops, Wilts. 1858
to death; author of *Manna in the house or
daily expositions of the Gospels* 4 vols. 1852–58;
*Manna in the heart or daily comments on the
book of Psalms* 2 vols. 1855–56; *My Parish*
1856, *second series* 1857. *d.* Fonthill Bishops
20 Dec. 1865.

BOUDIER, REV. JOHN. Educ. at Sid. Sus.
coll. Cam., B.A. 1809, M.A. 1813; V. of
Warwick 1815–72; hon. canon of Worcester
1852 to death; author of *Plain and practical
sermons* 1818; *Attendance on daily public worship the Christian's duty* 1854; *Congregational
psalmody and church choirs* 1857; *The two holy
sacraments of the Christian church necessary to
salvation* 1859. *d.* 7 Nov. 1874 aged 88.

BOUGH, SAMUEL (*3 child of Mr. Bough of
Carlisle, shoemaker*). *b.* Carlisle 8 Jany. 1822;
executed the illustrations to Jefferson's *History
of Cumberland* 2 vols. 1840–2; assistant scene
painter in T.R. Manchester about 1845;
exhibited pictures at Manchester Institute,
where Heywood gold medal was awarded
him; principal scene painter at T.R. Glasgow
1848; A.R.S.A. 1856, R.S.A. 10 Feb. 1875;
a collection of his works was exhibited at
Glasgow Institute 1880 and another at Edin-

burgh 1884. *d.* Edinburgh 19 Nov. 1878.
Portfolio x, 114 (1878); *Academy 30 Nov.*
1878 *and 5 July* 1884.

BOUGHEY, SIR THOMAS FLETCHER FENTON,
3 Baronet. *b.* Betley, Staffs. 22 Jany. 1809;
succeeded 27 June 1823; sheriff of Staffs.
1832. *d.* Aqualate, Newport, Staffs. 6 Oct.
1880.

BOUGHTON, SIR WILLIAM EDWARD ROSE,
10 and 2 Baronet (*only son of Sir Charles Wm.
Rose Boughton, 9 and 1 Baronet who d 26 Feb.
1821*). *b.* Lower Grosvenor st. London 14
Sep. 1788; F.R.S. 5 May 1814; M.P. for
Evesham 6 March 1820 to 2 June 1826. *d.*
Downton hall near Ludlow 22 May 1856.

BOULT, SWINTON. *b.* 1809; local agent in
Liverpool for insurance offices 1831; founded
Liverpool fire and life insurance company
1836 which became largest fire insurance
office in the world, it was renamed in 1848
Liverpool and London insurance office and in
1864 Liverpool, London and Globe, secretary
1836–65, managing director 1865 to death;
originated Liverpool Salvage committee, first
combination of the kind ever introduced;
devised a uniform policy for tariff offices;
author of *Law and practice relating to assurance,
banking and other joint-stock companies* 1841;
Trade and partnership 1855. *d.* suddenly in
the Aigburth road, Liverpool 8 July 1876. *C.
Walford's Insurance Cyclopædia i*, 353–5 (1871).

BOULTBEE, FREDERICK MOORE. Entered
navy 17 March 1811; captain 23 Nov. 1841;
admiral on h.p. 30 July 1875; chief constable
for Bedfordshire. *d.* Emery Down, Lyndhurst
23 Nov. 1876.

BOULTBEE, REV. THOMAS POWNALL (*eld.
son of Rev. Thomas Boultbee, V. of Bidford,
Warwickshire who d. 23 March 1883*). *b.* 7
Aug. 1818; ed. at Uppingham school 1833–7,
captain 1836–7; exhibitioner at St. John's
coll. Cam. 1837, 5 wrangler 1841, B.A. 1841,
M.A. 1844, LL.D. 1872; fellow of his college
March 1842; C. of St. Mary's Cheltenham,
and then of St. Luke's; theological tutor of
Cheltenham college 1853–63; principal of
London College of divinity at Kilburn 1863,
and at St. John's hall Highbury 1865 to
death; preb. of St. Paul's cathedral Oct.
1883; author of *A commentary on the Thirty
nine articles* 1871; *A history of the Church of
England, pre-reformation period* 1879. *d.*
Bournemouth 30 Jany. 1884. *Quiet strength,
a memorial sketch of the life and works of the
late Rev. T. P. Boultbee by Rev. Gordon
Calthrop* (1884).

BOURCHIER, CLAUD THOMAS. 2 Lieutenant Rifle brigade 10 April 1849, major 4 Aug. 1865 to 20 May 1868 when placed on h.p.; aide-de-camp to the Queen 30 April 1869 to 1876; V.C. 26 June 1856. d. 38 Brunswick road, Brighton 19 Nov. 1877 aged 46.

BOURCHIER, HENRY. Entered navy 28 Aug. 1797, Captain 22 Aug. 1811, superintendent of quarantine establishment at Milford Jany. 1827 to 1 Oct. 1846, retired R.A. 1 Oct. 1846. d. Lille, France 14 Oct. 1852.

BOURCHIER, JAMES CLAUD. Cornet 28 Dragoons 28 Sep. 1797; major 11 Dragoons 5 Nov. 1818 to 25 Sep. 1820, when placed on h.p.; colonel 3 Dragoon Guards 9 Jany. 1851 to death; L.G. 20 June 1854. d. Buxton vicarage, Norfolk 12 Feb. 1859 aged 78.

BOURDILLON, JAMES DEWAR (2 son of Rev. *Thomas Bourdillon. V. of Fenstanton, Hunts. who d.* 11 *March* 1854 *aged* 82). b. 1811; ed. at Ramsgate and Haileybury college; writer in Madras civil service 1829; secretary to Board of revenue 1843; third member of Board of revenue 1855; secretary to Government revenue department 1859–60 when he became an annuitant on the Fund, resigned the service 1861; wrote report of commission which reported upon system of public works in Madras presidency; author of *A short account of the measures proposed by the late Colonel J. T. Smith for the restoration of the Indian exchanges by an Ex-Madras civilian* 1882. d. Tunbridge Wells 21 May 1883.

BOURKE, OLIVER PAGET. b. 1817; Ensign 17 Foot 11 Dec. 1835, lieut. col. 7 Sep. 1855 to 10 Nov. 1856, when placed on h.p.; Exon of yeomen of the guard 17 July 1862 to Nov. 1873; L.G. 1 Oct. 1877. d. 3 Breffin terrace, Kingstown near Dublin 28 April 1880.

BOURKE, SIR RICHARD (*only son of John Bourke of Dromsally, Ireland*). b. Dublin 4 May 1777; ed. at Westminster and Ch. Ch. Ox.; ensign 1 Foot 22 Nov. 1798; captain 1 Garrison battalion 5 Dec. 1805; quartermaster general South America 1806; served in the Peninsula 1809-14; governor of eastern district of Cape of Good Hope 1825, conducted the government of the colony to Nov. 1829; governor of New South Wales 3 Dec. 1831 to 5 Dec. 1837; colonel 64 Foot 29 Nov. 1837 to death; general 11 Nov. 1851; C.B. 4 June 1815, K.C.B. 26 Jany. 1835; sheriff of Limerick 1839; edited with

BOURKE, SIR R. (*Con.*)

Earl Fitzwilliam *The correspondence of Edmund Burke* 1829. d. Thornfield, Castle Connell, co. Limerick 12 Aug. 1855. *R. Therry's Reminiscences*, 2 ed. (1863) 129–89.

NOTE.—The people of New South Wales erected a magnificent bronze statue by Westmacott to his memory in the Domain Sydney, which was unveiled 11 April 1842, this was the first statue in New South Wales.

BOURKE, WALTER (*eld. son of Joseph Bourke of Carrowkeel, co. Mayo who d.* 1820). b. 1808; ed. at Trin. coll. Dublin, B.A. 1824; called to Irish bar 1827; Q.C. 7 Feb. 1849. d. Carrowkeel 26 Dec. 1870.

BOURKE, WALTER MCWILLIAM (2 *son of Isidore Bourke of Curraghleagh Claremorris, co. Mayo, a crown solicitor for Ireland who d.* 1866). b. 1838; ed. at Stonyhurst and Clongowes Wood colleges and Trin. coll. Dublin, B.A. 1859, M.A. 1863; called to Irish bar 1858, practised in Dublin and then in high court at Calcutta; purchased Rahassane park, co. Galway 1880; contributed to Dublin literary magazines; published a volume of Indian law reports; assassinated at Castle Taylor near Ardrahan, co. Galway 8 June 1882. *Irish law times xvi*, 298 (1882).

BOURNE, HUGH (*son of Joseph Bourne of Fordhays farm in parish of Stoke-upon-Trent, farmer*). b. Fordhays farm 3 April 1772; a carpenter and builder at Bemersley, Staffs.; joined Wesleyan methodists June 1799; built a chapel at Harrisehead 1802; held a camp meeting on the mountain at Mowcop near Harrisehead 31 May 1807, first of many held in Staffordshire; expelled from Wesleyan Methodist Society 27 June 1808; formed first class of a new community at Standley near Bemersley 14 March 1810, first general meeting was held at Tunstall 26 July 1811, name Primitive Methodist was finally adopted 13 Feb. 1812, first annual conference was held at Hull May 1820, and a deed poll of the Primitive Methodist was enrolled in Court of Chancery 10 Feb. 1830; purchased land and built at Tunstall their first chapel 1811; travelled in United States 1844-6; author of *Remarks on the ministery of women* 1808; *History of the Primitive Methodist* 1823; *A treatise on Baptism* 1823; edited *The Primitive Methodist Magazine* 1824 to about 1844. d. Bemersley 11 Oct. 1852. bur. at Englesea Brook, Cheshire. *J. Walford's Memoirs of H. Bourne* 1855, *portrait; J. Petty's Primitive Methodist connexion* 1864, *portrait; Simpson's Recollections of H. Bourne* 1859.

BOURNE, JAMES. *b.* Dalby near Spilsby, Lincolnshire 1773; teacher of drawing in London; made numerous sketches in Cumberland and in Devon and Cornwall; Huntingtonian minister at Sutton Coldfield, Warwickshire May 1845 to death. *d.* Sutton Coldfield 11 June 1854 in 82 year. *W. Benson's Life and letters of J. Bourne 1875, portrait.*

BOURNE, JAMES (*brother of Hugh Bourne*). *b.* Feb. 1781; joined Wesleyan Methodists 1799; co-operated with his brother in establishment of Camp meetings 1807; the first general book steward of Primitive Methodist connexion 1820; chairman at the annual conferences many times. *d.* Bemersley, Staffs. Jany. 1860. *J. Petty's History of Primitive Methodist connexion, (new ed. 1864).*

BOURNE, SIR JAMES, 1 Baronet (*2 son of Peter Bourne of Hackinsall, Lancs. 1783–1846). b.* 8 Oct. 1812; ed. at Shrewsbury; lieut. col. commandant royal Lancashire artillery 13 April 1863 to 27 July 1881, hon. col. 27 July 1881 to death; M.P. for Evesham 12 July 1865 to 24 March 1880; created baronet 10 May 1880; C.B. 24 May 1881. *d.* Heathfield house, Wavertree near Liverpool 14 March 1882.

BOURNE, SIR JAMES DYSON, 2 Baronet (*eld. child of the preceding). b.* 29 July 1842; cornet 5 Dragoon guards 21 Dec. 1860, lieut. col. 1 July 1881 to 1883. *d.* Brook st. Grosvenor sq. London 11 Nov. 1883.

BOURNE, STEPHEN. Edited the *World* newspaper which was incorporated with the *Patriot* 1831; an active promoter of the Protestant Society, of the Ecclesiastical Knowledge Society, and of the Test and Corporation agitation; stipendiary magistrate in Jamaica; registrar of Berbice; a cotton grower in Jamaica. *d.* Brixton, London 29 March 1868 aged 76.

BOUSFIELD, NATHANIEL GEORGE PHILIPS. *b.* Dublin 1829; M.P. for Bath 4 Feb. 1874 to 24 March 1880. *d.* Grosvenor place, London 21 May 1883.

BOUTELL, REV. CHARLES (*son of Rev. Charles Boutell, P.C. of Repps, Norfolk who d. 26 July 1855 in 84 year). b.* St. Mary Pulham, Norfolk 1 Aug. 1812; ed. at St. John's coll. Cam., B.A. 1834, incorp. at Trin. coll. Ox. 1836, M.A. 1836; R. of Downham Market, Norfolk 1847–50; V. of Wiggenhall, St. Mary, Norfolk 1847–55; Reader at St. Luke's Lower Norwood, Surrey 1860–67; assistant minister at St. Stephen's Portland town London 1872–73; one of founders of London

BOUTELL, REV. C. (*Con.*)
and Middlesex Archæological society 14 Dec. 1855, sec. 23 July 1857 to 27 Nov. 1857; sec. of St. Alban's Architectural Society; author of *Monumental brasses and slabs of the Middle ages* 1847; *A manual of British Archæology* 1858; *A manual of heraldry historical and popular* 1863, 3 ed. 1864; *English heraldry, illustrated* 1867, 4 ed. 1879; *A Bible Dictionary* 1871, republished as *Haydn's Bible Dictionary* 1879. *d.* 18 Portsdown road, London 31 July 1877. *London and Middlesex Arch. Soc. Trans. i, 209, 316.*

BOUTFLOWER, REV. HENRY CREWE (*son of John Johnson Boutflower of Salford, Manchester, surgeon). b.* Salford 25 Oct. 1796; ed. at Manchester school 1807–15, and St. John's coll. Cam., Hulsean theological prizeman 1816, B.A. 1819, M.A. 1822; C. of Elmdon near Birmingham 15 April 1821; head master of Bury sch. Lancs. 6 May 1823 to 1857; P.C. of St. John's Bury 1832–57; R. of Elmdon 1857 to death; author of *The doctrine of atonement is agreeable to reason* 1817, and of sermons; collected materials for a history of Bury. *d.* West Felton vicarage, Salop 4 June 1863. *Admission register of Manchester school iii, 13–15 (1874).*

BOUTFLOWER, VENERABLE SAMUEL PEACH (*eld. son of Charles Boutflower of Colchester, surgeon). b.* 1815; ed. at St. John's coll. Cam., scholar, 22 wrangler 1838, B.A. 1838, M.A. 1841; P.C. of Brathay 1839–42 and 1856–67; C. of Seaforth 1842–56; V. of St. Lawrence Appleby 1867 to death; archdeacon and canon res. of Carlisle 1867 to death. *d.* The Abbey, Carlisle 22 Dec. 1882.

BOUVERIE, REV. EDWARD (*2 son of hon. Bartholomew Bouverie 1753–1835, M.P. for Downton). b.* 15 Aug. 1783; ed. at Ch. Ch. Ox., B.A. 1804, M.A. 1807; V. of Coleshill, Berks. 1808 to death; chaplain in ord. to the Sovereign 1819 to death; preb. of Preston in Sarum cathedral 16 Feb. 1826 to death. *d.* Coleshill vicarage 22 July 1874.

BOUVERIE, EVERARD WILLIAM (*eld. son of Edward Bouverie of Delapré abbey near Northampton 1767–1858). b.* 13 Oct. 1789; ed. at Harrow and St. John's coll. Cam., B.A. 1812, M.A. 1816; cornet Royal horse guards 2 April 1812, lieut. col. 16 Sep. 1845 to Sep. 1853 when placed on h.p.; colonel 15 Hussars 17 July 1859 to death; general 9 April 1868; author of *The horse-buyer's guide, shewing the tricks of dealers* 1853. *d.* Delapré abbey 18 Nov. 1871. *Annual Register (1862) 149–53.*

BOUVERIE, Rev. Frederick William Bryon. Educ. at College Bourbon, Paris 1844 ; C. of St. Peter Port, Guernsey 1850–57 ; Incumb. of St. Paul, Aberdeen 1858–69 ; Incumb. of French Anglican church of St. John. Bloomsbury st. London 1869 to death ; author of *Force et Faiblesse* 1859 ; *Life and its lessons, a tale* 1859 ; *Six short stories for short people* 1861, *new ed.* 1868 ; *Herbert Lovell* 1862. *d.* 1884.

BOUVERIE, Sir Henry Frederick *(youngest son of Edward Bouverie 1738–1810, M.P. for New Sarum). b.* 11 July 1783 ; ed. at Eton ; ensign 2 Foot Guards 23 Oct. 1799, major 18 Jany. 1820 to 27 May 1825 ; assistant adjutant general to 4 division of the army 1810 ; governor of Malta 1 Oct. 1836 to 14 June 1843 ; L.G. 28 June 1838 ; col. of 1 West India regiment 13 May 1842 and of 97 Foot 21 Nov. 1843 to death ; K.C.B. 5 Jany. 1815, G.C.B. 6 April 1852, G.C.M.G. 28 Sep. 1836. *d.* Woolbeding house near Midhurst, Sussex 14 Nov. 1852.

BOUVERIE, Venerable William Arundell *(brother of Rev. Edward Bouverie). b.* 6 Feb. 1797 ; ed. at Eton and Ch. Ch. Ox., B.A. 1817, M.A. 1820, B.D. 1829 ; fellow of Merton coll. ; R. of West Tytherley, Hants. 1829–39 ; R. of Denton, Norfolk 1839 to death ; hon. canon of Norwich 1847 to death ; archdeacon of Norfolk 20 Dec. 1850 to 1869. *d.* Denton rectory 23 Sep. 1877.

BOUVIER, Augustus Jules *(son of Jules Bouvier of London, painter 1800–67).* Painter of figure subjects in water colours in London ; member of New Society of Painters in water colours 1853 ; exhibited 55 pictures at Suffolk st. gallery 1845–65. *d.* 56 Alexandra road, St. John's Wood, London 20 Jany. 1881 aged 54.

BOVILL, George Hinton *(son of Benjamin Bovill of Durnsford lodge, Wimbledon who d. 1864). b.* London 1821 ; member of firm of Swayne and Co. of Millwall, makers of railway wheels and machinery ; introduced important improvements in grinding of corn by use of an air blast and exhaust between the millstones 1849 ; connected with Millwall iron works ; constructed the iron forts at Plymouth ; took out a patent dated 5 June 1849 for 'Improvements in the manufacture of flour,' there was a very long litigation about this patent which lasted 12 years 1856–68 and cost £60,000, the judges not being able to settle meaning of the words "my invention relates only to sucking away the

BOVILL, G. H. *(Con.)*
plenum of dusty air forced through the stones." *d.* Malvern 9 May 1868. *W. W. Wynne's The Bovill patent* 1873.

BOVILL, Sir William *(brother of the preceding). b.* Allhallows, Barking, London 26 May 1814 ; articled in office of Willis and Co. solicitors Tokenhouse yard ; pupil of Wm. Fry Channell ; practised as special pleader ; barrister M.T. 15 Jany. 1841, bencher 1855, treasurer 1866 ; went the Home circuit ; largely engaged in commercial cases in which he was unsurpassed ; Q.C. 1855 ; M.P. for Guildford 28 March 1857 to 29 Nov. 1866 ; Petition of right act 23 and 24 Vict. cap. 34 and Partnership law amendment act 28 and 29 Vict. cap. 86 are known as Bovill's acts ; solicitor general 10 July 1866 ; knighted at Osborne 26 July 1866 ; serjeant at law 29 Nov. 1866 ; lord chief justice of Court of Common Pleas 29 Nov. 1866 to death ; P.C. 28 Dec. 1866 ; F.R.S. 9 May 1867 ; hon. D.C.L. Ox. 1870 ; tried ejectment case of Tichborne *v.* Lushington 11 May 1871 to 6 March 1872 when he ordered the plaintiff to be indicted for perjury ; he is one of the three clerks drawn by John Oxenford in his first dramatic piece *My fellow clerks* 1835. *d.* Combe house, near Kingston on Thames 1 Nov. 1873. *I.L.N. xlix,* 569 (1866), *portrait, lxiii,* 447, 614 (1873).

BOVILL, William John *(only son of Wm. Bovill of Upper Tooting, Surrey, solicitor.) b.* Dec. 1810 ; solicitor at Upper Tooting 1833–5 and at 24 Essex st. Strand, London 1835–46 ; barrister M.T. 29 Jany. 1847 ; admitted ad eundem at L.I. 31 Jany. 1850 ; Q.C. 8 Feb. 1872 ; bencher of L.I. 8 May 1872. *d.* Bath 3 March 1882.

BOWATER, Sir Edward *(only son of Edward Bowater of Hampton Court Middlesex, admiral R.N.) b.* St. James's palace, London 13 July 1787 ; ed. at Harrow ; ensign 3 Foot Guards 31 March 1804, major 12 Oct. 1826 to 10 Jany. 1837 ; served in Peninsula and at Waterloo ; equerry to William iv, 1831–37 ; equerry to Prince Albert 1840–46 ; groom in waiting in ordinary to the Queen 3 March 1846 ; colonel 49 Foot 24 April 1846 to death ; general 20 June 1854, K.C.H. 1837. *d.* Cannes, France 14 Dec. 1861. *Miscellanea geneal. et herald. n.s. ii,* 177–9 ; *Martin's Life of the Prince Consort v,* 405, 417.

BOWDEN, Hannah *(dau. of John Finch Marsh of Croydon). b.* London 1823 ; wrote poetry in *The Peace Advocate. (m.* Sep. 1857 James Bowden, recording clerk of Society of

Friends). *d.* Croydon 3 July 1859. *Poetical remains of Hannah Bowden edited by her sister [Priscilla Marsh]* 1860.

BOWDEN, REV. JOHN EDWARD (*eld. son of John Wm. Bowden, of Wimbledon, Surrey who d. 15 Sep. 1844 aged 46*). *b.* London 24 April 1829; ed. at Eton 1841-6 and Trin. coll. Ox.; joined Church of Rome 1848; novice at Oratory of St. Wilfrid's Cotton hall, Staffs. 2 Feb. 1849, went to King Wm. st. Strand, London with the other Fathers May 1849; ordained priest 1852; edited *Notes on doctrinal and spiritual subjects by F. W. Faber* 2 vols. 1866; *The spiritual works of Louis of Blois* 1871; author of *The life and letters of Frederick Wm. Faber* 1869. *d.* the Oratory, Brompton, London 14 Dec. 1874.

BOWDICH, EDWARD HOPE SMITH (*son of Thomas Edward Bowdich, African traveller 1791-1824*). *b.* 16 Feb. 1822; ed. at Merchant Taylors' school 1829-38; entered Bombay army 1838; served in Persian campaign under Sir James Outram 1856-7, and Indian mutiny 1857-9; commandant 7 Bombay N.I. 1 Jany. 1862 to 31 Dec. 1874 when he retired on full pay; M.G. 23 Jany. 1875. *d.* 58 Harley st. London 5 Feb. 1882.

BOWDLER, HENRY. Entered Madras army 1797; col. 21 N.I. 24 Dec. 1835 to death; M.G. 28 June 1838. *d.* Dublin 6 June 1851.

BOWDLER, REV. THOMAS (*eld. son of John Bowdler of Eltham, Kent 1746-1823*). *b.* 13 March 1780; ed. at Hyde Abbey sch. near Winchester and St. John's coll. Cam., B.A. 1803, M.A. 1806; C. of Leyton, Essex 1803-6; Incumbent of Hopton-Wafers, Salop 1806, of Ash, Kent 1809, of Ridley, Kent 1809, of Addington, Kent to 1832, and of St. Bartholomews, Sydenham 1832-43; sec to Incorporated Church building society 1846 to death; preb. of St. Paul's 7 Dec. 1849 to death; author of *A pastor's address to his flock* 1818, 4 ed. 1822; *Sermons on the nature, offices and character of Jesus Christ* 2 vols. 1818-20; *Quid Romæ faciam* 1841, 2 ed. 1842; *Sermons on the privileges, responsibilities and duties of members of the Gospel covenant* 2 vols. 1845-46. *d.* 2 Onslow sq. Brompton, London 11 Nov. 1856. *An account of a memorial to the late Rev. T. Bowdler with memoir* 1858; *G.M. ii,* 241-2 (1857).

BOWEN, FRANCIS NATHANIEL BURTON (*son of Edward Bowen, chief justice of Canada*). *b.* Canada 1822; ed. at Univ. of Edin., M.B. 1854; assistant surgeon Coldstream Guards

22 Dec. 1854 to 2 Dec. 1859 when placed on h.p.; surgeon in Military school Dublin; practised in London 1862 to death; assisted Spencer Wells in his private practice; published some interesting papers 1866 on *Cancer of the Peritoneum* and *Fatty degeneration of the walls of Ovarian Cysts. d.* 28 Oct. 1868.

BOWEN, HERBERT. Entered Bengal army 1795; lieut. col. commandant 51 N.I. 28 Nov. 1826; col. 34 N.I. 5 Jany. 1829 to 2 April 1834; col. 55 N.I. 2 April 1834 to 1842 and col. 19 N.I. 1842 to death; M.G. 28 June 1838; C.B. 20 July 1838. *d.* Montagu sq. London 16 Oct. 1851 aged 70.

BOWEN, REV. JEREMIAH. Educ. at All Souls' coll. Ox., B.A. 1825; R. of West Lynn, Norfolk 1830-63; R. of Walton-Lewes, Norfolk 24 Feb. 1863 to death; author of *The Resurrection defended against the objections of the Mental improvement society* 1838; *The war abroad and the Church at home* 1854; *Starlight and other poems by Walton-Lewes pseud.* 1869; *St. Cross and other poems by Walton Lewes* 1872. *d.* 1875.

BOWEN, RIGHT REV. JOHN (*son of Thomas Bowen, captain 85 Foot who d. 1844.*) *b.* Court near Fishguard, Pembrokeshire 21 Nov. 1815; ed. at Haverfordwest; went to Canada April 1835; farmed land at Dunville on shores of Lake Erie 1835-42; entered at Trin. coll. Dublin Jany. 1843, B.A. 1847, LL.B. and LL.D. 1857; ordained deacon in Ripon Cathedral 20 Sep. 1846, and priest 19 Sep. 1847; C. of Knaresborough 1848-50; R. of Orton Longueville, Hunts. 1853-57; Bishop of Sierra Leone 10 Aug. 1857 to death; consecrated at Lambeth 21 Sep. 1857; sailed for his diocese 26 Nov. 1857. *d.* Freetown, Sierra Leone 28 May 1859. *Memorials of John Bowen compiled from his letters and journals by his sister* 1862; *G. M. vii,* 187-8 (1859).

BOWER, GEORGE HENRY KERR. *b.* 1817; entered navy March 1828; commanded the Osborne yacht 1856-64; master attendant Gosport victualling yard 1 Dec. 1864 to 1869; retired captain 15 June 1870; knight of the Legion of Honour; C.B. 13 March 1867; author of *Drops from the ocean, or life under the Pennant* 1879. *d.* York crescent Lower Norwood 26 Aug. 1883.

BOWER, HAROLD ELYOTT. Paris correspondent of *Morning Post* 1848 to 1852 and of *Morning Advertiser* 1852 to death; killed Saville Morton, Paris correspondent of *Morning Advertiser* by stabbing him in Paris

BOWER, H. E. *(Con.)*

1 Oct. 1852, tried in Paris for murder 27 Dec. 1852 when acquitted. *d.* 142 Rue de la Tour, Passy, Paris 8 Dec. 1884 aged 69. *Annual Register* (1852) 402–407.

BOWER, JOSHUA. Crown and bottle glass manufacturer at Hunslet near Leeds; one of the largest toll farmers in England, having at one time nearly all turnpikes between Leeds and London besides numerous others: took a conspicuous part in most of the political movements of his time; contested Leeds 17 Feb. 1834; a member of Leeds town council 1835 to death, and alderman Nov. 1844 to death; proprietor of extensive coal mines. *d.* Hillidge house Hunslet 7 Sep. 1855 aged 82.

BOWERBANK, JAMES SCOTT *(son of Edward Bowerbank of Bishopsgate, London, rectifying distiller).* *b.* Bishopsgate July 1797; rectifying distiller in Bishopsgate 1817–47; a founder of London Clay Club 1836, Microscopical Society 1839, Ray Society 1844 and Palæontographical Society 1847; F.R.S. 17 Nov. 1842; built a museum at Highbury 1846; his magnificent natural history collection was sold to British Museum 1864; author of *A history of the fossil fruits and seeds of the London clay* 1840; *A monograph of the British Spongiadæ* 3 vols. 1864, and of 45 papers in scientific periodicals. *d.* 2 East Ascent, St. Leonards-on-Sea 9 March 1877. *Monthly notices of Royal Astronom. Soc. xxxviii,* 144–7 (1878).

BOWERS. CHARLES ROBERT. Cornet 13 Dragoons 18 Jany. 1810; captain 23 Foot 30 Dec. 1818 to 5 April 1820 when placed on h.p.; L.G. 10 March 1866. *d.* Little Tew Lodge, Oxfordshire 9 Oct. 1870.

BOWERS, VERY REV. GEORGE HULL *(son of Francis Bowers).* *b.* Staffordshire 1794; ed. at Pembroke gr. sch. and Clare coll. Cam., B.A. 1819, B.D. 1829, D.D. 1849; P.C. of Elstow Beds. 1819–32; select preacher to Univ. of Cam. 1830; R. of St. Paul's Covent Garden, London 1831–47; joint founder with Rev. Charles Eaton Plater of Marlborough college 1843; dean of Manchester 19 June 1847 to 24 Sep. 1872; author of *Sermons preached before the University of Cambridge* 1830; *A scheme for the foundation of schools for the sons of clergymen and others* 1842; *Pew rents injurious to the Church* 1865. *d.* Leamington 27 Dec. 1872 in 79 year. *R. Parkinson's Old church clock* 5 ed. 1880 *p.* lxxiv.

BOWERS, REV. JOHN. *b.* Chester 19 July 1796; Wesleyan minister in London 1834–40; a chief founder of Theological college at

BOWERS, REV. J. *(Con.)*

Didsbury near Manchester 1842, and governor 1843–64; Pres. of Wesleyan conference 1858–59. *d.* Southport 30 May 1866. *Wesl. Meth. Mag. lxxxix, pt.* 2, 942–3 (1866); *J. Evan's Lancashire authors* (1850) 38–42.

BOWERYEM, GEORGE. *b.* England; went to United States 1854; a correspondent of *The Tribune* at Charleston and subsequently of *Philadelphia Press* with the army of the Potomac; published melodies of considerable merit; drowned near Newport News 12 July 1864 aged about 33.

BOWES, JAMES STUART. Edited *Galignani's Messenger* in Paris 40 years; wrote *Deeds of dreadful note* and many other dramatic pieces for the London stage under pseudonym of Alfred Dubois. *d.* Paris 24 May 1864 aged 75.

BOWES, JOHN *(son of John Bowes of Swineside Coverdale, parish of Coverham, Yorkshire 1779–1853).* *b.* Swineside 12 June 1804; joined Wesleyan Methodists 1817, and Primitive Methodists Dec. 1821; went from town to town preaching in the open air; pastor of the first church of Christian Mission in Dundee 20 April 1831; one of English representatives at Brussels peace congress 20–21 Sep. 1848; published two monthly magazines entitled *The Christian Magazine* and *The truth promoter;* author of *Treatise on Christian Union* 1835; *The New Testament translated from the purest Greek* 1870, and 220 Gospel and other tracts to instruct Christians. *d.* Westfield house, Dundee 23 Sep. 1874. *The autobiography or history of the life of John Bowes* 1872, *portrait.*

BOWES, JOHN *(natural son of John Bowes–Lyon 10 Earl of Strathmore 1769–1820).* *b.* 19 July 1811; ed. at Eton; M.P. for South Durham 24 Dec. 1832 to 23 July 1847; began racing 1834, won Derby with Mundig 1835, gaining £19,000 besides stakes of £6,000, won Two thousand guineas with Meteor 1842, same race and Derby with Cotherstone 1843, Derby with Daniel O'Rourke 1852, and Two thousand guineas Derby and St. Leger with West Australian 1853, won Ascot cup with same horse 1854; the luckiest man on the turf and one of best judges of yearlings; oldest member of Jockey club; sheriff of Durham 1854; erected at Barnard Castle, Durham in memory of his first wife the "Josephine and John Bowes museum and park" at cost of £80,000 and gave art treasures to the museum. *(m.* (1) 1872 Josephine Benoite, Countess of Montalbo who *d.* 1874, *m.* (2) 1877 Alphonsina Marie de St. Amand,

Bowes, J. *(Con.)*

Comtesse de Courten of the Valais, Switzerland). *d.* Streatlam Castle near Gateshead 9 Oct. 1885. *Sporting Review xl*, 114–8 (1858); *Illust. sp. and dr. news xxiv* 107, 114 (1885).

BOWES, ROBERT AITKEN *(son of John Bowes 1804–74).* Editor of the *Bolton Guardian. d.* 7 Nov. 1879 aged 42.

BOWIE, JAMES. *b.* London; entered service of Royal gardens, Kew 1810; botanical collector to the gardens 1814; collected plants and seeds in Brazil 1815–17, and in South Africa 1817–23; enriched gardens of Europe with greater variety of succulent plants than had ever been discovered by any traveller; gardener to Baron Ludwig of Ludwigsberg, Cape of Good Hope about 1829–41; made journeys into interior of South Africa to collect plants for sale. *d.* 1853.

BOWLBY, THOMAS WILLIAM *(eld. child of Thomas Bowlby, captain R.A.) b.* Gibraltar about 1817; articled to Russell Bowlby of Sunderland solicitor; member of firm of Lawrence, Crowdy and Bowlby solicitors 25 Old Fish st. Doctors Commons London 1846–54; arranged performances abroad for L. G. Jullien the musician; special correspondent of *Times* at Berlin 1848 and in China 1860 to death; shipwrecked in the Malabar at Point de Galle 22 May 1860; went with Admiral Hope to Tang-chow Aug. 1860; captured by Tartar general Sanko-lin-sin 18 Sep. 1860; died from effects of torture inflicted by Chinese, 22 Sep. 1860. *bur.* in Russian cemetery outside Antin gate of Pekin 17 Oct. *Boulger's History of China iii*, 499–521 (1884); *I. L. N. xxxvii*, 615–6 (1860), *portrait.*

BOWLER, THOMAS WILLIAM *b.* in the Vale of Aylesbury; assistant astronomer under Sir T. Maclear at Cape Town 1833–7; an artist and teacher of drawing at Cape Town; painted a panorama of the district; made a number of drawings in Mauritius 1866; published *Four views of Cape Town* 1844; *South African sketches* 1854; *The Kafir wars a series of 20 views* 1865. *d.* England 24 Oct. 1869. *Art Journal ix*, 107 (1870).

BOWLES, SIR GEORGE *(2 son of Wm. Bowles of Heale house, Wilts.) b.* Heale house 1787; Ensign Coldstream Guards 20 Dec. 1804, major 31 Dec. 1839 to 30 May 1843 when placed on h.p.; served in the Peninsula 1808–14, in Flanders and France 1814–18, in the West Indies 1820–25, and in Canada 1837–

Bowles, Sir G. *(Con.)*

43; commanded the troops in Lower Canada during rebellion of 1838; comptroller of household of Viceroy of Ireland 1843–5; master of the Queen's household 4 April 1845 to July 1851; lieutenant of Tower of London 16 July 1851 to death; K.C.B. 22 July 1851, G.C.B. 24 May 1873; col. of 1 West India regiment 9 Sep. 1855 to death; general 9 Nov. 1862. *d.* 9 Berkeley st. Piccadilly London 24 May 1876. *I.L.N. lxviii*, 551 (1876), *lxix*, 255.

BOWLES, REV. HENRY MATTHEW JOHN. Educ. at Trin. coll. Dublin, B.A. 1846, M.A. 1851, M.A. Ox. 1856; C. of St. John Cheltenham 1851–54; R. of Framilode Gloucs. 21 Sep. 1854 to 1867; R. of St. Aldate's Gloucester 15 April 1867 to death; author of *Prayers for the dead* 1873; *Fasting communion* 1873; *Lawlessness* 1874. *d.* Cathedral house, College gardens, Gloucester 6 Jany. 1884.

BOWLES, REV. JOSEPH. Educ. at Magd. hall Ox., B.A. 1835, M.A. 1836, LL.D. 1837, D.D. 1841; R. of Woodstock 1841–7; V. of Stanton-Lacey, Shropshire 1847 to death; author of *Elegy on the death of the Princess Charlotte; Monody on the death of Sir John Throckmorton; Letters in vindication of the appointment of the Bishop of Hereford. d.* 1879.

BOWLES, SIR WILLIAM *(eld. son of Wm. Bowles of Heale house, Wilts.) b.* Heale house 1780; entered navy 9 Sep. 1796, captain 13 Oct. 1807; commander in chief on South American station 1816–20; comptroller general of the Coastguard July 1822 to Nov. 1841; a lord of the Admiralty 13 May 1844 to 13 July 1846; M.P. for Launceston 20 May 1844 to 1 July 1852; admiral 28 Nov. 1857; commander in chief at Portsmouth 1 March 1859 to 1 March 1860; admiral of the fleet 15 Jany. 1869 to death; C.B. 18 April 1839, K.C.B. 10 Nov. 1862, F.R.G.S. 1833; author of *Thoughts on national defence; Considerations on the late naval war* 1856. *d.* 8 Hill st. Berkeley sq. London 2 July 1869. *Journal of Royal Geog. Soc. xl, pp. cxl–cxlii,* (1870).

BOWLEY, ROBERT KANZOW *(son of Mr. Bowley of Charing Cross, London, bootmaker). b.* 13 May 1813; brought up to the bootmaking business; conductor of Benevolent society of musical amateurs; organist of an independent chapel near Leicester sq. about 1834; joined the Sacred harmonic society 1834, librarian 1837–54, treasurer 1854–70; originated in 1856 plan of the gigantic Handel festivals which have been held every three years at

BOWLEY, R. K. (*Con.*)

Crystal Palace since 1857 ; general manager of Crystal Palace 8 April 1858 to death ; committed suicide by jumping into the Thames from a steamboat at Greenwich 25 Aug. 1870.

BOWLY, SAMUEL (*son of Mr. Bowly of Bibury, Gloucs., miller*). *b.* Cirencester 23 March 1802 ; a cheese factor at Gloucester 1829 ; chairman of many local companies ; took a prominent part in agitation against the corn laws and against slavery ; a founder of British and ragged schools in Gloucester ; formed a teetotal society at Gloucester 30 Dec. 1835 ; pres. of National temperance league. *d.* Gloucester 23 March 1884. *Sessions's Life of S. Bowly* 1884, *portrait ; The Public Good, Sep. and Oct.* 1851, *portrait.*

BOWMAN, EDDOWES (*eld. son of John Eddowes Bowman of Wrexham, bank manager* 1785–1841). *b.* Nantwich 12 Nov. 1810 ; ed. at Hazelwood near Birmingham ; sub-manager of Varteg iron works near Pontypool about 1835–40 ; studied in Univ. of Glasgow and at Berlin ; professor of classical literature and history in Manchester New College 1846 to 1853 when college was removed to London as a purely theological institution ; F.R.A.S. 1864 ; built an observatory at Manchester ; author of *Arguments against the divine authority of the Sabbath considered and shown to be inconclusive* 1842 ; *On the Roman governors of Syria at the time of the birth of Christ* 1855 and of many papers in the *Christian Reformer. d.* Victoria park, Manchester 10 July 1869. *Unitarian Herald* 16 *July* 1869 ; *Hall's History of Nantwich* (1883) 505.

BOWMAN, HENRIETTA (*dau. of Rev. John Bowman, P.C. of Burscough near Ormskirk Lancs.*) *b.* Cumberland 1838 ; taught Bible classes for young ladies at Clifton and Southport ; author of *Life, its duty and discipline* 1859 ; *Christian daily life* 1860, *new ed.* 1877 ; *Our village girls* 1863 ; *Thoughts for workers and sufferers* 1868 ; *The autobiography of Elsie Ellis* 1869, in which she describes her own childhood and girlhood ; *Lily Hope and her friends* 1885. *d.* Southport 13 Feb. 1872. *Songs amid the shadows by the late Hetty Bowman* 2 ed. 1872 ; *Woman's Work in the great harvest field i,* 137–40 (1872).

BOWMAN, JOHN EDDOWES (*brother of Eddowes Bowman* 1810–69). *b.* Welchpool 7 July 1819 ; ed. at King's college London ; demonstrator of chemistry at the college 1845 and professor of practical chemistry there 1851 to death ; one of founders of Chemical society of London 1841 ; author of *A lecture on steam*

BOWMAN, J. E. (*Con.*)

boiler explosions 1845 ; *An introduction to practical Chemistry* 1848, 6 *ed.* 1871 ; *A practical handbook of medical chemistry* 1850, 4 *ed.* 1862. *d.* 10 Feb. 1854. *Chem. Soc. Journ. ix,* 159 (1857).

BOWNESS, WILLIAM. *b.* Kendal 1809 ; portrait and figure painter in London 1830 ; exhibited his 'Keepsake' at Royal Academy 1836 and about one picture annually until his death ; exhibited 26 pictures at British Institution and 86 pictures at Suffolk st. gallery ; author of *Rustic studies in the Westmoreland dialect with other scraps from the sketch-book of an artist* 1868. *d.* Charlotte st. Fitzroy sq. London 27 Dec. 1867.

BOWRING, ALGERNON CHARLES. *b.* Hackney, London 19 March 1828 ; ed. at London Univ. and Trin. coll. Cam. ; joined Church of Rome 1850 ; entered Society of Jesus at Hodder 24 March 1850 ; professor of rhetoric at Stonyhurst college 1854 ; studied theology at St. Beuno's college and then in the Roman college at Rome 1855 to death. *d.* the Roman College 18 Nov. 1857.

BOWRING, SIR JOHN (*eld. son of Charles Bowring of Larkbear Devon, serge manufacturer*). *b.* Exeter 17 Oct. 1792 ; set up in business in London 1815 ; travelled abroad 1819–20 ; joint editor of *Westminster Review* 1824 and then sole editor ; examined and reported on public accounts of Holland 1828 and France 1831 ; LL.D. Univ. of Groningen 31 Jany. 1829 ; sec. to Commission for inspecting accounts of United Kingdom 1831 ; contested Blackburn 1832, M.P. for Kilmarnock 1835–37 and for Bolton 1841–49 ; British consul at Canton 10 Jany. 1849 ; plenipotentiary to China 24 Dec. 1853 to 17 April 1857 ; governor of Hong Kong 10 Jany. 1854 ; sent on special mission to Siam 12 March 1855 ; retired on a superannuation allowance 17 July 1859 ; knighted at Buckingham Palace 16 Feb. 1854 ; F.R.S. 5 June 1856 ; one of greatest linguists on record ; author of *Specimens of the Russian poets translated* 1820 ; *Minor morals for young people illustrated in tales and travels* 2 vols. 1834–35 ; *The kingdom and people of Siam* 2 vols. 1857 ; *The Oak, original tales and sketches* 1869 and many other books. *d.* Claremont near Exeter 23 Nov. 1872. *Bowring, Cobden and China a memoir by L. Moor* 1857 ; *Autobiographical recollections of Sir J. Bowring with a brief memoir by L. B. Bowring* 1877 ; *Sir J. Bowring's The kingdom and people of Siam vi,* 248–340 (1857), *portrait ; Illustrated Review i,* 161–65, *portrait ; Dict. of Nat. Biog. vi,* 76–80 (1886).

BOWSTEAD, REV. JOHN. Educ. at St. John's coll. Cam., B.A. 1832, M.A. 1835; V. of Messingham, Lincs. 1840–62; R. of St. Olave's Southwark, London 1862 to death; author of *The village wake* 1846; *Practical sermons 2 vols.* 1856; *Regeneration not salvation, a letter to Mr. Spurgeon* 1864. *d.* 29 Jany. 1875 aged 64.

BOWYER, CORNELIUS. Entered Bengal army 1799, lieut. col. 9 July 1825, retired 20 May 1829; C.B. 26 Dec. 1826. *d.* Ostend 12 Feb. 1855.

BOWYER, SIR GEORGE, 6 and 2 Baronet. *b.* Radley house near Abingdon, Berkshire March 1783; ed. at Ch. Ch. Ox., B.A. 1804, M.A. 1807; succeeded his father 6 Dec. 1799; M.P. for Malmesbury 8 May 1807 to Jany. 1810, for Abingdon 24 June 1811 to 10 June 1818; author of *The resolution of the House of Commons in the last session of the late Parliament relative to the adjustment of the claims of the Roman Catholics considered* 1813. *d.* Dresden 1 July 1860.

BOWYER, SIR GEORGE, 7 and 3 Baronet *(eld. son of the preceding)*. *b.* Radley house 8 Oct. 1811; barrister M.T. 7 June 1839, reader 1850; hon. M.A. Ox. 1839, hon. D.C.L. 1844; contested Reading 1849; M.P. for Dundalk 1852–68, and for co. Wexford 1874–80; expelled from Reform Club by a vote of two-thirds at a general meeting 23 June 1876 for his frequent voting against Liberal party; joined Church of Rome 1850; chamberlain to Pope Pius ix; built church of St. John of Jerusalem Great Ormond st. Bloomsbury, London; a knight of Malta; knight grand cross of order of St. Gregory the Great; author of *A dissertation on the statutes of the cities of Italy* 1838; *Commentaries on the modern civil law* 1848; *Lombardy, the Pope and Austria* 1848; *Commentaries on universal public law* 1854; *Friends of Ireland in council—Sir George Bowyer, W. H. Wilberforce, J. P. Hennessey* 1864; *Introduction to the study and use of the civil law* 1874; found dead in his bed at 13 King's Bench Walk Temple, London 7 June 1883. *Rev. T. Mozley's Reminiscences ii,* 231–5 (1882); *I.L.N. xxxvi,* 548 (1860), *portrait.*

BOWYER, HENRY GEORGE *(brother of the preceding)*. *b.* 3 Jany. 1813; inspector of schools 28 Sep. 1847. *d.* Leamington 26 Sep. 1883.

BOWYER, JAMES. Member of many private clubs in London such as the Blenheim, the Socials, the Watsonians' and the Hollywoods'; a well known whist player of the very old school. *d.* 17 Tavistock sq. London 11 Jany. 1871 aged 72.

BOWYER, JOHN. *b.* Mitcham, Surrey 18 June 1790; a print cutter at Mitcham where he lived all his life; came out as a professional cricketer in the match Surrey against England at Lords 16–18 July 1810 where he played in many great matches till 1828; played in 6 matches of England against an eleven whose names all began with B.; played at Mitcham till 1838. *d.* Mitcham 3 Feb. 1880. *F. Gale's Echoes from old cricket fields* (1871) 20–29; *Illust. sporting and dramatic news ix,* 483 (1878), *portrait.*

BOWYER, WILLIAM BOHUN. *b.* 1 Aug. 1789; entered navy 9 May 1803; inspecting commander in coast guard 14 Feb. 1817 to April 1828; captain 17 Feb. 1830; retired R.A. 9 July 1855. *d.* Southampton 8 Oct. 1859.

BOX, THOMAS. *b.* Ardingly, Sussex 7 Feb. 1809; played cricket 1825–54, 30 seasons; first played at Lords 25 June 1832 in Sussex against England; played in 43 great matches 1851; the best wicket keeper in England; kept the Hanover Arms and Ground in Lewes road Brighton, then the Egremont hotel in Western road Brighton, then Brunswick cricket ground and hotel at Hove; ground keeper at Prince's cricket ground London from date of formation of that club to death. *d.* suddenly on Prince's cricket ground 12 July 1876. *W. Denison's Cricket* (1846) 16–17; *I.L.N. iii,* 45 (1843), *portrait.*

BOXALL, SIR WILLIAM *(son of Thomas Boxall of Oxford, Clerk to the Collector of Excise)*. *b.* Oxford 29 June 1800; ed. at Abingdon gr. sch. and Royal Academy 1819–27; lived in Italy 1827–9; exhibited 86 pictures at R.A. 1823–80; designed several illustrations for Waverley novels; painted portraits of many literary and artistic celebrities; many of his portraits of females were engraved in art publications; A.R.A. 1851, R.A. 1863; director of National Gallery Dec. 1865 to Feb. 1874; knighted at Windsor Castle 24 March 1871. *d.* 14 Welbeck st. Cavendish sq. London 6 Dec. 1879. *Fortnightly Review xxvii,* 177–89 (1880); *Waagen's Galleries of art* (1857) 196–8; *I.L.N. xliii,* 80, 94 (1863), *portrait.*

BOXER, EDWARD. *b.* Dover 1784; entered navy 1 July 1798; captain 23 June 1823; C.B. 18 Dec. 1840; agent for transports and harbour master at Quebec 24 Aug. 1843 to 5 March 1853; R.A. 5 March 1853; admiral superintendent in the Bosphorus 7 April 1854 and at Balaklava 18 Dec. 1854 to death; gazetted K.C.B. 10 July 1855. *d.* of cholera on Board H.M.S. Jason outside harbour of

BOXER, E. (Con.)

Balaklava 4 June 1855 in 72 year. *I.L.N.
xxvi*, 644 (1855).

BOYCE, REV. JAMES. *b.* Ardagh, co. Longford;
ed. at St. John's coll. Fordham New York,
ordained priest 1854; pastor of St. Mary's
Roman Catholic church N.Y. 1854–63 and of
St. Teresa's church 21 June 1863 to death;
founded St. Teresa's Male academy at 10
Rutgers st. N.Y. 1865 and established a con-
vent for girls at 139 Henry st. 1872. *d.* New
York 9 July 1876 aged 50. *J. G. Shea's
Catholic churches of New York city* (1878) 674-8.

BOYCE, JOSEPH (3 *son of James Boyce of
Kilcason, Ferns, co. Wexford*). *b.* 1795; a
merchant at Dublin; lord mayor of Dublin
1855; sheriff of city and county of Dublin
1865. *d.* 1875.

BOYD, VERY REV. ARCHIBALD *(son of
Archibald Boyd of Gortlee and Derry, treasurer
of Donegal).* *b.* Londonderry 1803; ed. at
diocesan college Londonderry and Trin. coll.
Dub., B.A. 1825, M.A. 1832, B.D. and D.D.
1868; C. and preacher in Derry Cathedral
1827–42; P.C. of Ch. Ch. Cheltenham
1842–59; hon. canon of Gloucester cath.
1857–67; P.C. of Paddington 1859–67;
rural dean 1860–67; dean of Exeter 11 Nov.
1867 to death; author of *Sermons on the
Church* 1838; *Episcopacy and Presbytery* 1841;
The history of the Book of Common Prayer
1850; *Turkey and the Turks* 1853; *Baptism
and baptismal regeneration* 1865. *d.* the
deanery Exeter 11 July 1883. Bequeathed
nearly £40,000 to societies and institutions
in diocese of Exeter. *A golden decade of a
favoured town by Contem Ignotus* (1884) 70–102.

BOYD, BENJAMIN (2 *son of Edward Boyd of
Merton hall, Wigtonshire who d.* 1846). *b.*
about 1796; a stockbroker in City of London
1824–39; went out to Sydney to organise
various branches of Royal Banking Company
of Australia 1840–41; speculated largely in
whaling also in shipping cattle to Tasmania
and New Zealand; founded Boyd Town,
Twofold Bay N.S.W.; the largest squatter
in Australia having in 1847 estates of his
own amounting to 381,000 acres; went to
California 1850; murdered by the natives at
Gaudalcanar one of the islands in the Solomon
Group 1851. *Heads of the people i*, 21 (1847),
*portrait; J. H. Heaton's Australian dictionary
of dates* (1879) 23-4.

BOYD, CHARLES. Commissioner of customs
in Ireland; surveyor general of customs for
the United Kingdom 1840 to 1855. *d.* Brixton, London 7 May 1857 aged 76.

BOYD, DAVID. Superintending surgeon Madras
army 8 Dec. 1837, surgeon genl. 19 Aug.
1846 to 1 Aug. 1850 when he retired. *d.* 26
Drummond place, Edin. 25 Oct. 1854 aged 61.

BOYD, SIR HARLEY HUGH, 5 Baronet. *b.*
Drumawillen house, co. Antrim 2 Nov. 1853;
succeeded 7 Aug. 1857. *d.* 2 June 1876.

BOYD, REV. JAMES *(son of Mr. Boyd of Paisley,
glover)*. *b.* Paisley 24 Dec. 1795; ed. at Paisley
and Univ. of Glasgow; licensed to preach
by Presbytery of Dumbarton May 1822;
House Governor of Heriot's hospital Edinburgh 1825 to 29 Aug. 1829; one of Classical
masters in high sch. Edin. 19 Aug. 1829 to
death; sec. to Edinburgh Society of teachers
many years. *d.* George sq. Edinburgh 18
Aug. 1856. *W. S. Dalgleish's Memorials of
the high school of Edinburgh* (1857) 31, 46-7,
*portrait; History of Dr. Boyd's fourth High
school class with biographical sketch of Dr. Boyd
by James Colston*, 2 ed. 1873.

BOYD, REV. JAMES. Licensed by Presbytery
of Edinburgh 28 June 1815; ordained 11
Feb. 1818; minister of Auchinleck 24 Nov.
1818, of Ochiltree 27 March 1833 and of
Tron church Glasgow 28 March 1844 to
death; D.D. Glasgow 1845. *d.* 27 March
1865 in 79 year. *Our Scottish Clergy*, (2 series
1849) 51–58.

BOYD, JAMES. *b.* Drogheda, Ireland; proprietor and editor of the *Panama Star and
Herald* 1865 to death. *d.* Panama 25 April
1882 aged 43.

BOYD, SIR JOHN, 3 Baronet. *b.* 5 June 1786;
ensign 5 Foot 8 July 1808; lieut. 1 Garrison
battalion 1811–1814 when placed on h.p.;
succeeded 30 May 1815. *d.* Boulogne 19
Jany. 1855.

BOYD, JOHN *(son of John Boyd of Belle Isle,
co. Antrim)*. *b.* Rose-yard, co. Antrim 1789;
M.P. for Coleraine 18 Feb. 1843 to March
1852 and 30 March 1857 to death. *d.* 2
Jany. 1862.

BOYD, SIR JOHN AUGUSTUS HUGH, 4 Baronet.
b. 30 July 1819; succeeded 19 Jany. 1855.
d. 7 Aug. 1857.

BOYD, JOHN M'NEILL *(brother of Very Rev.
Archibald Boyd).* *b.* Londonderry 1812;
entered navy 1825; second captain of Royal
George 120 guns 1853-6; served in the
Baltic campaign; captain 10 May 1856,
captain of Ajax 60 guns coastguard ship at
Kingstown 1 Feb. 1858 to death; author of
A manual for naval cadets 1857. *drowned
while attempting to rescue crew of a vessel*

wrecked near Kingstown harbour 9 Feb. 1861. *Life in death a sermon preached on board H.M.S. Ajax on Sunday Feb.* 17, 1861 *by the Lord Bishop of Labuan with a memoir of J. M. Boyd by his brother* 1861.

BOYD, MARK (4 son of Edward Boyd of Merton hall, Wigtonshire who d. 1846). b. Surrey 1805; director in London of a Scotch Insurance Office; engaged in colonization of Australia and New Zealand 1843–53; author of *Reminiscences of fifty years* 1871; *Social Gleanings* 1875. (m. 23 Sep. 1848 Emma Anne widow of Robert Coates, better known as Romeo Coates the eccentric actor, she d. 1872). d. 16 St. George's place, Hyde park, London 12 Sep. 1879.

BOYD, MOSSEM. Entered Bengal army 1795; lieut. col. commandant 65 N.I. 13 May 1825; colonel of 5 N.I.; colonel of 53 N.I. to death; general 9 April 1856. d. 6 Dawson place Bayswater, London 8 April 1865 aged 84.

BOYD, PERCY. Great friend of Dickens and Thackeray; author of *A book of ballads from the German* 1848. d. London 1 Jany. 1876.

BOYD, ROBERT. M.R.C.S. 1830, M.D. Edin. 1831, L.R.C.P. 1836, F.R.C.P. 1852; resident phys. at Marylebone workhouse infirmary; phys. and superintendent of Somerset county lunatic asylum; proprietor and manager of Southall Park private asylum; pres. of Med. Psychol. Assoc. 1870; contributed 16 papers to the *Journal of Mental Science* and papers to *Royal medical and chirurgical transactions, Edinburgh Medical Journal* and the *Lancet;* lost his life in a fire which destroyed his asylum at Southall Park 14 Aug. 1883. *Lancet ii,* 352–3 (1883); *Medical times and gazette ii,* 249–50 (1883).

BOYD, WILLIAM. Called to Irish bar 1818; Q.C. 7 Feb. 1849; recorder of Londonderry to death. d. 1855.

BOYD, WILLIAM (3 son of Richard Keown of Downpatrick). b. Dublin March 1816; sheriff of co. Down 1849; M.P. for Downpatrick 5 Aug. 1867 to 26 Jany. 1874; assumed name of Boyd 1873. d. Carrowdore castle, co. Down 19 Jany. 1877.

BOYES, JOHN FREDERICK (son of Benjamin Boyes of Charterhouse sq. London). b. 10 Feb. 1811; entered Merchant Taylors' school Oct. 1819; scholar of Linc. coll. Ox. 1828; Andrews' civil law exhibitioner at St. John's coll. 1829, B.A. 1833, M.A. 1835; second master of proprietary school Walthamstow,

then head master; author of *Illustrations of tragedies of Æschylus and Sophocles from the Greek, Latin and English poets* 1844; *English repetitions in prose and verse* 1849; *Life and Books, a record of thought and reading* 1859; *Lacon in council* 1865. d. 10 St. James's terrace, Harrow road, London 26 May 1879. *Preface and appendix to Sermon by Rev. J. G. Tanner* 1879.

BOYLE, ALEXANDER (2 son of David Boyle lord chief justice of Scotland). b. 9 March 1810; entered navy 4 Sep. 1823; commander of Thunderbolt steam sloop at Cape of Good Hope 27 Dec. 1845, lost his ship in Algoa Bay Feb. 1847 for which he was dismissed service 4 May 1847 but restored Jany. 1849; captain 8 Aug. 1857; retired V.A. 2 Aug. 1879. d. 17 Prince's Gardens London 8 June 1884.

BOYLE, CAROLINE COURTENAY. b. 26 May 1803; maid of honour to Queen Adelaide many years; granted civil list pension of £100, 30 Oct. 1850. d. 23 Jany. 1883.

BOYLE, COURTENAY EDMUND WILLIAM. b. 3 Aug. 1800; entered navy 7 Sep. 1816; captain 27 May 1830; groom of the chamber to Prince Albert 1840; retired captain 1 Oct. 1850; retired R.A. 27 Sep. 1855. d. Rue Faubourg St. Honoré Paris 11 Feb. 1859.

BOYLE, DAVID (2 son of Patrick Boyle of Shewalton, Ayrshire who d. 26 Feb. 1798.) b. Irvine, Ayrshire 26 July 1772; ed. at Univ. of Edin; member of Faculty of Advocates 14 Dec. 1793; solicitor general for Scotland 9 May 1807; M.P. for Ayrshire 5 June 1807 to Feb. 1811; a lord of Session and Justiciary 23 Feb. 1811; lord justice clerk 15 Oct. 1811; P.C. 11 April 1820; lord justice general of Scotland and lord president of Court of Session 9 Oct. 1841 to May 1852; distinguished for his personal appearance, there are full-length portraits of him by Sir J. W. Gordon at Faculty of Advocates and at Society of Writers to the Signet Edinburgh. d. Shewalton 30 Jany. or 6 Feb. 1853. *I.L.N. xxii,* 76, 134 (1853), *portrait.*

BOYLE, JOHN (2 son of Edmund Boyle 8 Earl of Cork 1767–1856). b. Wimpole st. London 13 March 1803; ed. at Winchester and Ch. Ch. Ox., B.A. 1824, M.A. 1827; M.P. for co. Cork 4 Dec. 1827 to 24 July 1830, and for Cork city 11 Aug. 1830 to 3 Dec. 1832. d. Rock Wood, Torquay 6 Dec. 1874.

BOYLE, ROBERT (son of Mr. Boyle of Hamilton Lanarkshire, surgeon). b. Hamilton 1821; started a bakery for manufacture of pure bread at Glasgow; lectured for missionary purposes in Scotland; invented a new description of detonating powder 1866 which was reported upon favourably by principal military authorities; invented an ink which is perfectly inerasable; invented the Self-Acting Air-pump ventilator which was awarded highest and only prize given to roof ventilators by judges at International Medical and Sanitary Exhibition 1881. d. 2 Sep. 1878. Robert Boyle inventor and philanthropist a biographical sketch by L. Saunders 1885, portrait.

BOYLE, ROBERT EDWARD (brother of John Boyle 1803-74). b. London March 1809; ensign 68 Foot 14 Nov. 1826; captain Coldstream guards 10 Dec. 1847 to death; secretary to Order of St. Patrick 1837-53; groom in waiting to the Queen 1846-52 and 1853 to death; secretary to master general of the Ordnance Dec. 1853 to death; M.P. for Frome 30 July 1847 to death. d. Varna 3 Sep. 1854.

BOYLE, ROBERT FREDERICK. b. 13 June 1841; ed. at Ball. coll. Ox., B.A. 1864, M.A. 1866; fellow of All Souls' coll.; barrister M.T. 17 Nov. 1866; inspector of schools 16 May 1871. d. Florence 15 May 1883.

BOYLE, WILLIAM. b. 25 Jany. 1821; ensign 15 Foot 6 Dec. 1838; lieut. col. 89 Foot 13 Oct. 1858 to death; C.B. 20 May 1871. d. 10 Craven hill gardens, London 14 Feb. 1874.

BOYLE, WILLIAM GEORGE. b. Dublin 12 Aug. 1830; 2 lieut. 21 Foot 9 Feb. 1849; captain Coldstream guards 24 Nov. 1863 to 1867; lieut. col. 2 Somerset militia 23 March 1868 to 12 Sep. 1870; M.P. for Frome 23 July 1856 to 21 March 1857; F.C.S., F.G.S. d. San Francisco 22 April 1880.

BOYLE, WILLIAM ROBERT AUGUSTUS. Barrister L.I. 24 Nov. 1835; author of A practical treatise on the law of charities 1837; Inspiration of book of Daniel 1863; The tribute of Assyria to biblical history 1868; Literature under the shade of Great Britain 1870, 2 ed. 1870. d. 7 Church st. Kensington 20 May 1875.

BOYNE, GUSTAVUS HAMILTON, 6 Viscount. b. 12 April 1777; succeeded 29 Feb. 1816. d. 22 Belgrave sq. London 30 March 1855.

BOYNE, GUSTAVUS HAMILTON-RUSSELL, 7 Viscount (son of the preceding). b. Downton hall near Ludlow 11 May 1797; assumed

BOYNE, G. H. R. (Con.)
name of Russell by r.l. 1850; created Baron Brancepeth of Brancepeth, co. palatine of Durham 31 Aug. 1866. d. Brancepeth castle, co. Durham 29 Oct. 1872.

BOYNTON, SIR HENRY, 9 Baronet. b. St. James's st. Westminster 22 March 1778; succeeded 17 Nov. 1832. d. Burton Agnes, Yorkshire 29 Aug. 1854.

BOYNTON, SIR HENRY, 10 Baronet. b. Nafferton hall, Yorkshire 2 March 1811; succeeded 29 Aug. 1854. d. Burton Agnes 25 June 1869.

BOYS, EDWARD (son of John Boys of Betteshanger, Kent, agriculturist 1749-1824). b. 1785; entered navy 1796; a prisoner in France 1803-9; superintendent of Deal dockyard 16 Sep. 1837 to 1841; retired captain 1 July 1851; author of Narrative of a captivity and adventures in France and Flanders 1827, which is the source from which Captain Marryat in his novel Peter Simple drew much of the account of his hero's escape; Remarks on the practicability and advantages of a Sandwich or Downs harbour 1831. d. 14 Blomfield terrace, Harrow road, London 6 June 1866 in 82 year.

BOYS, HENRY. b. 1806; composed a few glees and songs, best known being Friar Tuck a glee for 3 voices 1842. d. Margate 1851.

BOYS, REV. RICHARD (brother of Edward Boys 1785-1866). b. 1783; ed. at King's school Canterbury and C. C. coll. Cam., B.A. 1807, M.A. 1818; chaplain at St. Helena 1811-29; P.C. of Platt, Kent 1849-54; P.C. of Loose, Kent 1854 to death; author of Elements of Christian knowledge 1838; Primitive obliquities 1851. d. Loose 13 Feb. 1866.

BOYS, REV. THOMAS (son of Thomas Boys of Sandwich, Kent, rear admiral R.N.). b. Sandwich 1792; ed. at Tonbridge gr. sch. and Trin. coll. Cam., B.A. 1813, M.A. 1817; attached to the military chest in the Peninsula under Wellington 1813; wounded in 3 places at battle of Toulouse 10 April 1814; teacher of Hebrew to Jews at Hackney college 1830-2; professor of Hebrew at Missionary college Islington 1836; Inc. of Holy Trinity, Hoxton 22 Feb. 1848 to death; translated the Bible into Portugese 1813, his version has been adopted both by Protestants and Roman Catholics; author of Tactica Sacra 1824; Plain exposition of the New Testament 1827. d. 23 Leighton road, Kentish town, London 2 Sep. 1880.

BOYS, THOMAS SHOTTER. *b.* Pentonville, London 2 Jany. 1803; articled to George Cooke, engraver; a member of Institute of Painters in water colours; exhibited 2 pictures at Royal Academy and 14 at Suffolk st. gallery 1824–58; lithographed the works of David Roberts and Clarkson Stanfield 1837; published *Picturesque architecture in Paris* 1839 which was much admired; *Original views of London as it is* 1843; drew illustrations to Blackie's *History of England;* etched some plates for Ruskin's *Stones of Venice. d.* of paralysis at 30 Acacia road, Marylebone, London 10 Oct. 1874.

BRABAZON, LUKE (*elder son of Hugh Higgins of Brabazon park, co. Mayo who d. 26 April 1864 aged 63*). *b.* 23 March 1832; 2 Lieut. R.A 20 June 1849; second captain 23 Aug. 1855 to death; deputy assistant quartermaster general; changed his name to Brabazon 1854; author of *Soldiers and their science* 1860; went with admiral Hope to Tang-chow, China Aug. 1860, captured by Tartar general San-ko-lin-sin 18 Sep. 1860; executed by the Chinese on the bridge at Palikao 21 Sep. 1860. *Boulger's History of China iii,* 499–521 (1884).

BRACEBRIDGE, CHARLES HOLTE (*only son of Abraham Bracebridge of Atherstone hall, Atherstone, Warws. who d. 21 Aug. 1832*). *b.* 19 March 1799; ed. at Merton coll. Ox.; went with Florence Nightingale to Constantinople Oct. 1854; author of *A letter on the affairs of Greece* 1850; *Shakespeare no deerstealer, or a short account of Fulbroke park near Stratford-on-Avon* 1862. *d.* of heart disease at Atherstone hall 13 July 1872.

BRACKENBURY, SIR EDWARD (2 *son of Richard Brackenbury of Aswardby, co. Lincoln*). *b.* 1785; ensign 61 Foot 1803, served in Peninsula 1809–14; attached to Portuguese and Spanish army 1814–16; major 28 Foot 1 Nov. 1827 to 31 Jany. 1828 when placed on h.p.; lieut. col. 10 Jany. 1837; retired from the service 1847; K.T.S. 1824, K.S.F.; knighted at Windsor Castle 26 Aug. 1836. *d.* Skendleby hall near Spilsby, co. Lincoln 1 June 1864.

BRACKENBURY, REV. JOSEPH. *b.* Langton, Lincolnshire 1788; a student at C. C. coll. Cam. 28 Oct. 1808, B.A. 1811, M.A. 1819; chaplain Madras establishment 1812–19; chaplain and secretary to Magdalen hospital Blackfriars road London 1828–56; R. of Quendon, Essex 1862 to death; author of *Natale solum and other poetical pieces* 1810. *d.* Quendon rectory 31 March 1864.

BRACKENRIDGE, GEORGE WEARE (*eld. son of George Brackenridge of Brislington near Bristol, merchant*). *b.* Hanover county, Virginia 4 Jany. 1775; ed. at Dr. Estlin's school Bristol, England; partner in a leading West India firm; lived at Brislington 1824 to death; formed a good collection of Coleoptera and organic remains; gave greater portion of building fund for Christchurch, Clevedon, also a permanent endowment for church which was consecrated 1839. *d.* Brislington 11 Feb. 1856. *Quarterly Journal of Geol. Soc. of London xiv,* 60–62 (1858).

BRADBURY, HENRY (*eld. son of the succeeding*). A pupil at Imperial printing office Vienna 1850 where he learnt process of Nature printing which he claimed afterwards to have invented; founded a business in Fetter lane, London which he moved to Farringdon st. and carried on under name of Bradbury, Wilkinson and Co.; produced nature printed plates to Moore and Lindley's *Ferns of Great Britain and Ireland* 1855 and Johnstone's *British sea weeds* 4 vols. 1860–1; author of *Printing, it's dawn, day, and destiny* 1858; *Autotypography or art of nature printing* 1860; *Specimens of bank note engraving* 1860; committed suicide by drinking prussic acid in Cremorne gardens, London 1 Sep. 1860 aged 30.

BRADBURY, WILLIAM. Printer at 76 Fleet st. London 1824; publisher with F. M. Evans in Whitefriars st. 1830; published *The Christmas carol* 1843; *Punch* 1843 to death, the *Daily News* 1846 to death; joint proprietor with C. Dickens, J. Forster and W. H. Wills of *Household Words* 1850–59; proprietor of *Gent. Mag.* 1866–70. *d.* 13 Upper Woburn place, London 11 April 1869 in 70. year. *Reg. and mag. of biog. i,* 485 (1869); *C. Beavan's Reports of cases in chancery xxvii,* 53–61 (1861).

BRADDYLL, EDWARD STANLEY BAGOT RICHMOND GALE. *b.* 1803; contested North Durham 21 Dec. 1832; fought a duel with Russell Bowlby at Offerton lane near Herrington, Durham 27 Sep. 1832 and another with Sir Hedworth Williamson, Bart. at the Hare and Hounds on the Sedgefield road same day. *d.* Windermere Bank, Bowness, Ambleside 2 Sep. 1874 aged 71. *Sykes's Local Records ii,* 397–8 (1833).

BRADEN, REV. WILLIAM. *b.* Marylebone, London 22 Nov. 1840; ed. at Maida Hill gr. sch. and Cheshunt coll.; Congregational minister at St. Alban's 1861 at Hillhouse chapel Huddersfield 1866 and at the King's

BRADEN, REV. W. *(Con.)*

Weigh house chapel, London Jany. 1871 to death; edited the *English Independent;* author of *The beautiful gleaner, A Hebrew pastoral story* 1872; *Our social relationships* 1876. *d.* Clapton, London 20 July 1878. *Sermons by the Rev. W. Braden, edited by Agnes Braden* 1880; *J. Waddington's Congregational history v,* 598-602 (1878).

BRADFIELD, HENRY JOSEPH STEELE *(son of Thomas Bradfield of Derby st. Westminster, coal merchant).* *b.* Derby st. Westminster 18 May 1805; left England in the schooner Unicorn as surgeon under Lord Cochrane 26 April 1826; sous lieutenant in Bataillon Etranger of Belgium 1 Sep. 1832; stipendiary magistrate in Tobago 31 Dec. 1835, removed to Trinidad 13 May 1836, reappointed to the Southern or Cedros district 13 April 1839; private sec. to Lieutenant Governor of Dominica 1841, colonial sec. in Barbados 1842; author of *Waterloo or the British minstrel a poem* 1825; *The Athenaid or modern Grecians a poem* 1830; *Tales of the Cyclades and other poems* 1830; committed suicide by drinking a bottle of prussic acid in coffee room of St. Albans hotel, 12 Charles st. St. James's sq. London 11 Oct. 1852. *G.M. xxxix,* 102 (1853); *Morning Post* 13 Oct. 1852 *p. 4 and 15 Oct. p. 6.*

BRADFORD, GEORGE AUGUSTUS FREDERICK HENRY BRIDGEMAN, 2 Earl of. *b.* 23 Oct. 1789; ed. at Trin. coll. Cam., M.A. 1810; succeeded 7 Sep. 1825. *d.* Weston park Shiffnal, Salop 22 March 1865.

BRADFORD, SIR THOMAS *(son of Thomas Bradford of Ashdown park, Sussex).* *b.* 1 Dec. 1777; ensign of an Independent company 20 Oct. 1793; commanded a brigade of Portuguese army 1810-13, and a division 1813-14; lieut. col. of 34 Foot 18 May 1809, and of 82 Foot 21 Dec. 1809 to 1815; commanded seventh division of the army of occupation in France 1815-17; commanded the troops in Scotland 1819-25; colonel of 94 Foot 1 Dec. 1823, of 30 Foot 16 April 1829 and of 4 Foot 7 Feb. 1846 to death; commander in chief in Bombay 20 July 1825 to 17 May 1829, assumed command 3 May 1826; general 23 Nov. 1841; K.C.B. 5 Jany. 1815; G.C.B. 15 Feb. 1838; G.C.H. 1831. *d.* 13 Eaton sq. London 28 Nov. 1853. *United Service Mag.* 1854 *part 1 p.* 157.

BRADFORD, REV. WILLIAM. R. of Storrington, Sussex 1811 to death; chaplain in ordinary to the Sovereign 1821 to death. *d.* Storrington rectory 13 June 1857 aged 77.

BRADLEY, REV. CHARLES *(elder son of Thomas Bradley of Wallingford).* *b.* Halstead, Essex Feb. 1789; took pupils 1810-25; a member of St. Edmund hall Ox.; C. of High Wycombe, Bucks. 1812-25; V. of Glasbury, Brecknockshire 1825 to death; P.C. of St. James's Clapham, London 1829-53; very eminent as a preacher; author of *Sermons* 1818, 11 ed. 1854; *Sermons* 1825, 9 ed. 1854; *Practical sermons* 2 vols. 1836-8; *Sacramental sermons* 1842; *Sermons on the Christian life* 1853. *d.* Cheltenham 16 Aug. 1871 aged 82. *A selection from the sermons of Rev. C. Bradley, edited by Rev. G. J. Davies* 1884; *Guardian* 22 March 1882, 421-2.

BRADLEY, GEORGE. *b.* Whitby, Yorkshire 1816; a reporter on *York Herald;* editor of *Sunderland and Durham County Herald;* editor and one of proprietors of *Newcastle Guardian* about 1848 to death; author of *A concise and practical system of short-hand writing* 1843. *d.* Newcastle 14 Oct. 1863.

BRADLEY, REV. RICHARD BEADON. *b.* Minehead, Somerset 1803; P.C. of Ash Priors near Taunton 1834 to death; P.C. of Cothelstone, Somerset 1835 to death; author of *The portion of Jezreel, a sacred drama* 1843; *Pauperism. Whence does it arise? how may it be remedied* 1846; *The expected budget, or how to save more than twelve millions a year* 1850. *d.* Teignmouth 22 March 1851 aged 48.

BRADLEY, ROBERT GREENE *(only son of Robert Bradley of Slyne near Lancaster who d.* 1825). *b.* 14 April 1788; barrister G.I. 22 June 1814, bencher 26 April 1837, treasurer 30 Aug. 1839; comr. of bankrupts for Lancaster. *d.* of paralysis at Slyne 16 Oct. 1869.

BRADLEY, SAMUEL MESSENGER. *b.* 2 June 1841; ed. at Manchester school of medicine, M.R.C.S. 1862, F.R.C.S. 1869; demonstrator of anatomy at Manchester school of medicine 1865, and lecturer on anatomy 1866; professor of physiology at Stonyhurst college several years; assistant surgeon to Manchester Royal infirmary 1873 and surgeon 1876 to death; lecturer on practical surgery at Owens college school of medicine 1876 to death; author of *Manual of comparative anatomy and physiology* 1869, 3 ed. 1875; *Notes on Syphilis* 1872; *Injuries and diseases of the lymphatic system* 1879. *d.* Ramsgate 27 May 1880. *Medical times and gazette i,* 625-6 (1880).

BRADLEY, WILLIAM. *b.* Manchester 16 Jany. 1801; a painter and teacher of drawing at Manchester 1817; a portrait painter in London 1822-47; exhibited 13 portraits at

BRADLEY, W. (*Con.*)

Royal Academy, 21 at Free Society of artists, and 8 at British Institution 1823–46. *d.* Manchester 4 July 1857.

BRADSHAW, GEORGE (*only son of Thomas Bradshaw of Windsor Bridge, Pendleton, Salford*). *b.* Windsor Bridge 29 July 1801; an engraver and printer at Belfast 1820–21, and at Manchester 1821; projected engraved and published maps of the English counties 1827; published *Bradshaw's Railway map* 1838; *Railway time tables* 1839; *Monthly railway guide* Dec. 1841 *to death; Continental railway guide June* 1847 *to death; General railway directory* 1849–53; attempted to establish an ocean penny postage; A.I.C.E. Feb. 1842. *d.* of Asiatic cholera near Christiania, Norway 6 Sep. 1853. *Min. of Proc. of Instit. of C.E. xiii,* 145–9 (1854); *Manchester Guardian* 17 *Sep.* 1853, *p.* 7.

BRADSHAW, HENRY (*son of J. H. Bradshaw of London*). *b.* London 2 Feb. 1831; ed. at East Sheen and Eton; scholar of King's coll. Cam. 1847, fellow 1854 to death, B.A. 1854, M.A. 1857; assistant master at St. Columba's college near Dublin for a year; principal library assistant in Cambridge Univ. library March 1857 to Dec. 1858, superintendent of the manuscripts 1859–67, librarian 8 March 1867 to death; pres. of Library Association at the Cambridge meeting 5–8 Sep. 1882; F.S.A. 26 March 1860; author of 17 papers in *Antiquarian Communications* of Cambridge Antiquarian Society, and of a series of pamphlets which he called *Memoranda*, most important being *The University library* 1881; found dead in his rooms at King's coll. Cam. 11 Feb. 1886, having died about 11 p.m. 10 Feb. *The library chronicle iii,* 25–36 (1886); *Book-lore April* 1886, *pp.* 141–5.

BRADSHAW, JAMES HILL (*eld. son of J. F. Bradshaw, manager of Quebec branch of Bank of Upper Canada*). *b.* Hillsborough, co. Down 21 Aug. 1834; ed. at Quebec; ensign 52 Foot 29 Feb. 1856, lieutenant 11 July 1856 to death; shot through the heart at Delhi 14 Sep. 1857. *H. J. Morgan's Sketches of celebrated Canadians* (1862) 712–19.

BRADSHAW, JOSEPH. Ensign 37 Foot 12 May 1825; lieut. col. 60 Rifles 9 May 1845 to death; C.B. 9 June 1849. *d.* Kussowlie, North Western provinces of India 18 Oct. 1851.

BRADSHAW, LAWRENCE. Ensign 46 Foot 25 Sep. 1780; lieut. col. 13 Foot 1 Sep. 1795 to 2 Feb. 1803; major 1 Life Guards 2 Feb.

BRADSHAW, L. (*Con.*)

1803 to 1 March 1812 when he sold out; a comr. of military inquiry 1806–12; M.G. 25 July 1810, retired 1826. *d.* Harley st. London 10 Jany. 1853 aged 84.

BRADSHAW, THOMAS JOSEPH CAVENDISH (*eld. son of Joseph Hoare Bradshaw of London, banker who d.* 24 *May* 1845 *aged* 61). *b.* 17 Oct. 1824; ed. at Eton and Ch. Ch. Ox.; barrister L.I. 17 Nov. 1853; secretary to Royal commission on judicature 1867–71; judge of county courts of Northumberland (Circuit No. 1) 27 Oct. 1871 to death. *d.* in a room adjoining town hall, Newcastle 17 Dec. 1884.

BRADSTREET, SIR SIMON, 4 Baronet. *b.* Upper Leeson st. Dublin 25 Nov. 1772; succeeded March 1791; a member of Repeal association many years. *d.* Clontarf near Dublin 25 Oct. 1853.

BRADWELL, EDMUND (*son of Wm. Bradwell of Covent Garden theatre London, mechanician who d.* 4 *Aug.* 1849). Theatrical decorator and mechanician in London; introduced some extraordinary mechanical changes into Tom Dibdin's pantomime of *Guy, Earl of Warwick* at Victoria theatre Dec. 1833; mechanician at Olympic, Lyceum, Her Majesty's and other theatres. *d.* 11 Magdala terrace, Lordship lane Dulwich 25 July 1871 aged 72. *Era* 30 *July* 1871, *p.* 11, *col.* 4.

BRADY, SIR ANTONIO (*eld. son of Anthony Brady, storekeeper at Royal William victualling yard, Plymouth*). *b.* Deptford 10 Nov. 1811; junior clerk in Royal Victoria victualling yard Deptford 29 Nov. 1828; clerk in accountant general's office London 26 June 1844; registrar of contracts 1864; superintendent of purchase and contract department 13 April 1869 to 31 March 1870 when he retired on a special pension; knighted at Windsor Castle 23 June 1870; promoted the Plaistow mission and East London museum; pres. of Inventors' Institute; a judge in Verderer's Court for forest of Epping; made a collection of fossil Mammalia which is now in Natural history museum Kensington; author of *The Church's work and its hindrances with suggestions for church reform* 1869; *Catalogue of Pleistocene Mammalia from Ilford, Essex* 1874. *d.* Maryland point, Forest lane, Stratford Essex 12 Dec. 1881. *Geological Mag.* 1882, *p.* 93.

BRADY, ELIZABETH (2 *dau. of Jacob Hutchinson of Islington, London*). *b.* Islington 1803; ed. at Islington school where she was successively

BRADY, E. *(Con.)*

apprentice, teacher, and governess, head mistress there 1838–42; superintendent of the York Girls' school 1842–46; conducted a school for daughters of Friends at Edgbaston Birmingham 1848–69. *(m.* 1828 Edward Foster Brady head master of Islington school who *d.* 1838). *d.* Edgbaston 22 May 1874. *The Annual Monitor for* 1876, *pp.* 20–25.

BRADY, SIR FRANCIS *(son of James Brady of Navan, Meath). b.* 1809; ed. at Trin. coll. Dub., B.A. 1835; called to Irish bar 1836; chief justice of Newfoundland and judge of vice admiralty court 15 Oct. 1847 to 1865; knighted by patent 24 May 1860. *(m.* 1839 Kate dau. of David Lynch of Dublin, she *d.* 16 Jany. 1880). *d.* 59 Burlington road, Bayswater London 29 Dec. 1871.

BRADY, SIR MAZIERE, 1 Baronet *(2 son of Francis Tempest Brady of Dublin, gold and silver thread manufacturer* 1763–1821). *b.* Dublin 20 July 1796; ed. at Trin. coll. Dub. 1812–16, scholar 1814, B.A. 1816; called to Irish bar 1819; barrister I.T. 1835; solicitor general for Ireland 1837; attorney general 1839; P.C. Ireland 1839; chief baron of Court of Exchequer 11 Aug. 1840 to 1846; lord chancellor of Ireland 1846 to Feb. 1852, Jany. 1853 to 1858 and 1859 to 28 June 1866; vice chancellor of Queen's Univ. Ireland 1850 to death. *d.* 26 Upper Pembroke st. Dublin 13 April 1871. *O. J. Burke's Lord chancellors of Ireland* (1879) 270–7.

BRAE, ANDREW EDMUND. Practised as dentist at Leeds to 1872; lived in Guernsey 1872 to death; author of *Literary cookery with reference to matter attributed to Coleridge and Shakespeare* 1855; *Electrical communication in railway trains* 1865; *The treatise on the Astrolabe of G. Chaucer, edited by A. E. B.* 1870; wrote many papers on Shakespeare and Chaucer in first series of *Notes and Queries* under signature of A. E. B. *d.* London 10 Dec. 1881. *bur.* Mont Durand, Guernsey. *Notes and Queries,* 6 *series vi,* 323 (1882).

BRAGGE, WILLIAM *(3 son of Thomas Perry Bragge of Birmingham, manufacturing jeweller). b.* Birmingham 31 May 1823; a civil engineer; constructed the first railway line in Brazil namely from Rio Janeiro to Petropolis; knighted and made a chevalier by Emperor of Brazil; partner with John Brown in Atlas Steel works, Sheffield 1858–64 when works were sold to a limited company and he received sum of £50,000, managing director of the company 1864–72; established works at Birmingham for manufacture of watches

BRAGGE, W. *(Con.)*

by machinery 1876 which became English Watch company in 1882; M.I.M.E. 1854, F.S.A. 1870; sold his collection of illuminated manuscripts for £12,272, June 1878, and his collection of 13000 pipes and smoking apparatus for £4,000 Feb. 1882; author of *Bibliotheca Nicotiana, a catalogue of books about tobacco* 1880. *d.* 59 Hall road, Handsworth, Birmingham 6 June 1884.

BRAHAM, CHARLES BAMPFYLDE *(son of the succeeding). b.* 20 Dec. 1823; made his first appearance on stage at Princess's theatre London 26 Oct. 1848 as Adelmar in Leoline; sang in Italy and Portugal with great success. *d.* 103 Ebury st. Pimlico, London 11 June 1884.

BRAHAM, JOHN *(son of John Abraham of Goodman's Fields, London, a German Jew). b.* Goodman's Fields 20 June 1773; pupil of Myer Lyon otherwise Leoni; made his début at Bagnigge Wells assembly rooms; changed his name to Braham 1787; sang at Bath 1794–6, Drury Lane 1796, in Paris 1797 and Italy 1798–1801, at Covent Garden 1801–5 and Drury Lane 1805–24; sang in Italian opera at King's theatre London 1804–6 and 1816; made £14,000 per annum 1801–24; built St. James's theatre London in 14 weeks at cost of £36,000 Sep.–Dec. 1835, managed it 1835–9; sang in New York Nov. 1840; composed music to *The Cabinet* 1801; *Family Quarrells* 1802 and 10 other dramas. *d.* The Grange, Brompton, London 17 Feb. 1856. *Oxberry's Dramatic Biography iii,* 145-59 (1825), *portrait; Metropolitan Mag. xviii,* 130–42 (1837); *Stirling's Old Drury Lane ii,* 91–5 (1881); *I.L.N. xx,* 245–6 (1852), *portrait; P. Fitzgerald's Life of C. Lamb iii,* 226, *vi,* 145.

BRAID, GEORGE ROSS. *b.* May 1813; made his first appearance in London at Adelphi theatre 29 Sep. 1843; acted at Haymarket theatre many years. *d.* Holly house, Kennington road London 18 Feb. 1878.

BRAID, JAMES *(son of Mr. Braid of Rylaw, Fifeshire). b.* Rylaw about 1795; ed. at Univ. of Edin.; M.R.C.S. Edin.; surgeon at Manchester; investigated subject of mesmerism 1841; author of *Neurypnology or the rationale of nervous sleep* 1843; *The power of the mind over the body* 1846; *Magic, witchcraft, animal magnetism, hypnotism and electro-biology* 3 ed. 1852. *d.* 25 March 1860. *Med. Times and Gaz. i,* 355, 386 (1860); *Manchester Courier* 31 *March* 1860.

BRAIDWOOD, JAMES *(son of Mr. Braidwood of Edinburgh, builder). b.* Edinburgh 1800; ed. at the High sch.; engaged in his father's

BRAIDWOOD, J. (*Con.*)

business; superintendent of Edinburgh fire engines 1823; published his work "*On the construction of Fire Engines and Apparatus, the training of firemen and the method of proceeding in cases of Fire*" 1830; superintendent of London Fire Engine establishment formed by 8 of the Insurance companies 1 Jany. 1833; A.I.C.E. 1833; read many papers on subject of fires at Institute of Civil Engineers and Society of Arts; killed in great fire at Cotton's wharf, Tooley st. London 22 June 1861 which continued burning for a month and destroyed property of the value of £2,000,000. *J. Braidwood's Fire prevention with memoir of the author* (1866), *portrait; Min. of Proc. of Instit. of C.E. xxi*, 571–8 (1862).

BRAITHWAITE, REV. GEORGE. *b.* Kendal 15 April 1818; ed. at Sedbergh sch. and Queen's coll. Ox., B.A. 1840, M.A. 1843; C. of Perry Barr, Staffs. 1847–51; V. of St. Peter the Great, Chichester 1851–68; subdean of Chichester cathedral 1853–68; author of *Sonnets and other poems* 1851, 2 ed. 1875. *d.* Beechfield, Carnforth, Lancashire 2 April 1875. *Sonnets by the late Rev. G. Braithwaite*, 2 ed. 1875 *preface*.

BRAITHWAITE, JOHN (3 son of *John Braithwaite of London, engineer who d. June* 1818). *b.* 1 Bath place, New road London 19 March 1797; engineer in London 1818–44; ventilated House of Lords by means of air pumps 1820; constructed the first practical steam fire engine; engineer of Eastern Counties railway 1836–43; joint founder with J. C. Robertson of the *Railway Times* 1837, sole proprietor 1837–45 when his affairs were wound up; surveyed lines in France 1844–46; F.S.A. 1819, M.I.C.E. 1838; author of *Supplement to Capt. Sir John Ross's Narrative of a second voyage in search of a North-West passage* 1835. *d.* 8 Clifton gardens, Paddington London 25 Sep. 1870. *Mechanic's Mag. xiii*, 235–7, 377–88, 417–9 (1830), *portrait; Min. of Proc. of Instit. of C.E. xxxi*, 207–11 (1871).

BRAME, BENJAMIN. Attorney at Ipswich 1798 to death; bailiff of Ipswich 1820 and 1822; the first mayor of Ipswich 1835. *d.* 21 July 1851 aged 78. *G.M. xxxvi*, 332 (1851).

BRAMSTON, THOMAS WILLIAM (*elder son of Thomas Gardiner Bramston of Skreens, Essex* 1770–1831, *M.P. for Essex*). *b.* 30 Oct. 1796; ed. at Winchester and Ch. Ch. Ox., B.A. 1819, M.A. 1823; fellow of All Souls' college; M.P. for South Essex 19 Jany. 1835 to 6 July 1865. *d.* 30 Eccleston sq. London 21 May 1871.

BRAMWELL, JOHN (*son of Rev. Wm. Bramwell, Wesleyan minister who d.* 1818). *b.* 24 April 1794; attorney at Durham 1815; alderman of Durham 1835–52; mayor 1840, 41, 45, 52 and 1853; undersheriff of co. Durham 1840; recorder of Durham and steward of Court Leet and Court Baron of city of Durham March 1860 to death. *d.* Framwell gate, Durham 25 Nov. 1882.

BRANCKER, SIR THOMAS (*eld. child of Peter Whitfield Brancker of Liverpool* 1750–1836). *b.* Liverpool 17 Sep. 1783; sugar refiner at Liverpool; mayor of Liverpool 1830; knighted at St. James's palace, London 13 Sep. 1831. *d.* Mount Pleasant, Liverpool 13 Feb. 1853.

BRANCKER, WILLIAM GODEFROY (*son of W. Brancker of Erbstock hall, Ruabon*). *b.* 27 March 1834; ed. at Em. coll. Cam.; lieut. R.A. 6 March 1856; lieut. col. 4 Oct. 1882 to death; instructor in artillery at Woolwich 1872–80; C.B. 18 Nov. 1882. *d.* Ipswich 22 May 1885.

BRAND, SIR CHRISTOFFEL JOSEPH (*son of Johannes Henricus Brand, member of Court of Justice in Cape Colony*). *b.* 1797; ed. at Leyden, doctor in philosophy and law 1820; admitted advocate in Court of Justice, Cape of Good Hope 1821; member of legislative council 1850; speaker of house of assembly 1854 to death; knighted by patent 24 May 1860. *d.* 20 May 1875.

BRAND, FERDINAND. Comptroller of Bridge house estates, City of London 1839 to Dec. 1878, and of the Chamber, City of London 1854 to Dec. 1878. *d.* Craigmillar, Avenue road, Crouch End 1 Nov. 1880 in 80 year.

BRAND, GEORGE. *b.* Arbuthnott, Aberdeenshire 1816; ed. at King's coll. Aberdeen, B.A., M.A.; vice consul at Loanda 27 Dec. 1844 to 31 July 1856; author of various Reports including a very able one on the Decree of the Portuguese government for registration and emancipation of slaves in the Colonial possessions of Portugal; consul at Lagos, West Africa 10 June 1859 to death. *d.* on board H.M.'s steamer Alecto 16 June 1860.

BRAND, JOHN. *b.* Armenia; lived some time there; compiled a dictionary of the Armenian language, shutting himself up in a convent for that purpose; had an estate at Sutton near Ipswich; a successful batsman for about 15 seasons in great cricket matches, played his first match at Lords 31 May 1815; one of the very best amateur boxers and chessplayers. *d.* in a private lunatic asylum at Ticehurst, Sussex April 1856 aged 66.

BRAND, WILLIAM ALLAN. Editor of the *Montrose Review*. *d.* Inchbridge near Montrose 7 Feb. 1869 aged 31.

BRAND, WILLIAM. *b.* Blackhouse parish of Peterhead 1807; a writer to the signet 1834; partner in firm of Scott and Balderston of Edinburgh; secretary to Union Bank of Scotland, Edin. 1846 to death; a founder of Botanical Society of Edin. 8 Feb. 1836, treasurer 17 March 1836, contributed many papers, enriched its herbarium with many thousand specimens of plants; discovered several rare and new plants in Scotland. *d.* Edinburgh 15 Oct. 1869. *Trans. of Botanical Soc. of Edin. x*, 284–8 (1870).

BRANDARD, ROBERT. *b.* Birmingham 1805; landscape engraver in London 1826 to death; engraved plates for Turner's *England* and *Rivers of England* and other books, also for the *Art Journal*; produced some etchings from his own designs, one series of which was published by the Art Union 1864; painted both in oils and water-colours; exhibited 3 pictures at R.A., 21 at British Institution and 32 at Suffolk st. gallery 1831–58. *d.* Campden hill, Kensington, London 7 Jany. 1862.

BRANDE, EVERARD AUGUSTUS *(eld. son of Augustus Everard Brande of Arlington st. London, apothecary to George iii.) b.* Arlington st. 1776; ed. at Westminster sch.; studied at St. George's hospital 1795; apothecary to George iii and Queen Charlotte 1801; apothecary to William iv and Queen Adelaide 1830–33 when he retired from practice; a member of first Court of Examiners of Society of Apothecaries 1815; presented to College of Phys. valuable collection of Materia Medica made by Dr. Burgess. *d.* Sulhamstead house, Turnham-Green, London 11 Dec. 1868. *Reg. and mag. of biog. i*, 312 (1869).

BRANDE, GEORGE WILLIAM *(brother of the preceding)*. Chief clerk of the Treasury many years. *d.* Exeter 18 June 1854 aged 69.

BRANDE, WILLIAM THOMAS *(brother of the preceding). b.* Arlington st. 11 Jany. or Feb. 1788; ed. at Westminster; began lecturing on chemistry 1808; F.R.S. 13 April 1809, Copley medallist 1813, one of secretaries 1816–26; professor of chemistry to Apothecaries company 4 Nov. 1812 and professor of materia medica 1813, master of the Company 1851; professor of chemistry at Royal Institution May 1813 to 1854; superintendent of die department of Mint 1825 and of

BRANDE. W. T. *(Con.)*

coining department 1854; edited with M. Faraday *Quarterly journal of science and arts* 1816–36; author of *Outlines of geology* 1817, 2 *ed.* 1829; *A manual of chemistry* 1819, 6 *ed.* 2 vols. 1848; *A manual of pharmacy* 1825, 3 *ed.* 1833; edited *A dictionary of science literature and art* 1842, 3 *ed.* 1853. *d.* Tunbridge Wells 11 Feb. 1866. *Proc. of Royal Society xvi*, 2–6 (1868); *S. Muspratt's Chemistry* vol. 1 (1853), *portrait*.

BRANDLING, JOHN JAMES. Second lieut. R.A. 19 March 1839; lieut. col. 8 March 1860 to death; C.B. 5 July 1855. *d.* Woodsley house, Leeds 16 April 1860 aged 39.

BRANDON, JOHN RAPHAEL. *b.* 1817; articled to W. Parkinson, architect 1836; practised at Beaufort buildings, Strand, London with his brother Joshua Arthur Brandon 1841–7 when the latter died; joint architect with Robert Ritchie of Catholic Apostolic church, Gordon sq. London, opened 1 Jany. 1854; architect of St. Peter's church, Great Windmill st. Piccadilly 1861; one of the 11 architects who competed for Royal Courts of Justice, London 1867; author with his brother of *Analysis of Gothick architecture* 2 vols. 1847; *Views of English ecclesiastical structures* 1848, *new ed.* 2 vols. 1858; *Open timber roofs of the middle ages* 1849; *Railways and the Public* 1868, 8 *ed.* 1871; shot himself at his chambers 17 Clement's Inn, Strand, London 8 Oct. 1877.

BRANDRETH, THOMAS ALSTON. Second lieut. R.A. 19 July 1797; colonel 23 Nov. 1841 to death; served in the Peninsula 1812–14; C.B. 26 Sep. 1831. *d.* Chudleigh, Devon 24 Sep. 1851 aged 72.

BRANDRETH, THOMAS SHAW (2 *son of Joseph Brandreth M.D. of Liverpool, physician* 1746–1815). *b.* 24 July 1788; ed. at Eton and Trin. coll. Cam., 2 wrangler, 2 Smith's prizeman and chancellor's medallist 1810, B.A. 1810, M.A. 1813; fellow of his college 1811; barrister I.T. 5 June 1818; revising barrister for Liverpool, Bolton and other towns in Lancashire many years; invented a logometer or ten-foot gunter, a friction wheel, and a double-check clock escapement, all of which he patented; invented a machine in which the weight of a horse was utilised on a moving platform, this invention was used where steam power proved too expensive as in Lombardy and in some parts of the United States where it is still employed; F.R.S. 8 March 1821; author of *Homer's Iliad with notes* 2 vols. 1841 in which the Digamma was

BRANDRETH, T. S. (Con.)

restored throughout for sake of the metre; *A dissertation on the metre of Homer* 1844; *Homer's Iliad, translated* 2 vols. 1846. *d.* The Steyne, Worthing 27 May 1873.

BRANDT, FRANCIS FREDERICK (*eld. son of Rev. Francis Brandt R. of Gawsworth Cheshire who d.* 1870). *b.* Gawsworth rectory 1819; ed. at Macclesfield gr. sch.; practised as special pleader; barrister I.T. 30 April 1847; leader of Chester and Knutsford sessions; reported for the *Times* in Court of Common Pleas; contributed to *Bells Life in London;* author of *Habet, a short treatise on the law of the land as it effects pugilism* 1857; *Fur and feathers* 1859; *Frank Marland's Manuscripts* 1859; *Games, gaming and gamester's law* 1871, 2 *ed.* 1873. *d.* 8 Fig tree court, Temple London 6 Dec. 1874.

BRANDT, ROBERT. Barrister L.I. 1 June 1821; went northern circuit; commissioner in Bankruptcy for Manchester; judge of Bury Court of Requests; judge of Manchester county court March 1847 to death. *d.* Pendleton near Manchester 15 April 1862. *Law Times xxxvii,* 321 (1862).

BRANKS, REV. WILLIAM. Minister of parish of Torpichen; published anonymously *Heaven our Home* 1861, *new ed.* 1864, sale of which reached considerably over 100,000 copies; *Zion's King* 1859; preserved anonymous character of his works to the last. *d.* Torpichen 18 Feb. 1879.

BRANSON, WILLIAM SCHOLES. Member of company of T.R. Liverpool 1847 or before; manager of Adelphi theatre Liverpool; author of many plays. *d.* Fairfield, Liverpool Jany. 1884 aged 74.

BRANT, JAMES. Vice consul at Trebizond 31 March 1830; consul at Erzeroom 27 April 1836 and at Damascus Sep. 1856 to 2 Nov. 1860 when he retired on a pension; C.B. 31 Oct. 1860. *d.* Cliftonville, Brighton 24 Nov. 1861.

BRANT, REV. WILLIAM HOLT. Consular chaplain at St. Michael's in the Azores 11 Nov. 1834 to 25 April 1865. *d.* Lisbon 20 April 1867 aged 90.

BRANWHITE, CHARLES (*son of Nathan Branwhite of Bristol, miniature painter*). *b.* Bristol 1817; landscape painter especially of frost scenes; exhibited 9 pictures at R.A., 25 at British Institution and 2 at Suffolk st. gallery 1845-57. *d.* Bramford house, Westfield park, Redland, Bristol 15 Feb. 1880. *I.L.N. lxxvi,* 285 (1880), *portrait.*

BRASIER, JAMES. Entered navy 3 Dec. 1799; captain 10 Jany. 1837; V.A. on h.p. 14 Nov. 1863. *d.* Bradney near Bridgnorth 28 July 1864 aged 80.

BRASSEY, THOMAS (*son of John Brassey of Buerton, Aldford, Cheshire, farmer*). *b.* Buerton 7 Nov. 1805; land surveyor at Birkenhead 1826; railway contractor in London 1836; made line from Paris to Rouen 1841-3 and from Rouen to Havre 1843-5; contractor for Great Northern railway 1847-51, railways in Italy 1850-3, Grand Trunk railway of Canada 1852-9 and railways in Australia 1859-63; established with E. T. Betts and M. Peto Canada works at Birkenhead 1853. *d.* Hastings 8 Dec. 1870. *Life by Arthur Helps* 1872, *portrait; J. Devey's Life of Joseph Locke* (1862) 145-54; *Work and wages practically illustrated, by T. Brassey, M.P.* 1872.

NOTE.—He laid out £78,000,000 of other people's money and upon that outlay retained £2,500,000 being as nearly as possible three per cent.; he had in his employ at one time upwards of 30,000 men on railways in Europe; his will was proved in London 7 Feb. 1871, personalty being sworn under £3,200,000.

BRAVO, CHARLES DELAUNEY TURNER (*only son of Charles Turner of the Isle of Jersey*). *b.* 39 Upper Charlotte st. Tottenham Court road, London 30 Nov. 1845; ed. at King's coll. London and Trin. coll. Ox., admitted gentleman commoner 16 Jany. 1864, B.A. 1866, M.A. 1868; barrister M.T. 30 April 1870, went Home circuit; changed his name to Bravo 1868 or 1869. (*m.* 7 Dec. 1875 Florence eld. dau. of Robert Campbell of Buscot park near Reading, she was *b.* 5 Sep. 1845, *m.* (1) 21 Sep. 1864 Alexander Lewis Ricardo, Ensign Grenadier Guards (who *d.* 19 April 1871), she *d.* at Lumps villa Southsea 17 Sep. 1878 and was *bur.* at Farringdon, Berkshire 21 Sep.) C. D. T. Bravo *d.* suddenly and mysteriously from taking tartar emetic at The Priory Bedford hill road, Balham Surrey 21 April 1876. *bur.* Lower Norwood cemetery 1 May. *The Balham mystery or the Bravo poisoning case 7 numbers 56 pages* (1876), *portraits.*

NOTE.—There was a coroner's inquest held at which no conclusion was arrived at as to how the poison was administered, a renewed inquest was opened by the Coroner for East Surrey 11 July 1876 which lasted till 11 Aug. when the coroner's jury returned the following verdict, "We find that the deceased did not commit suicide, but that he was wilfully murdered by the administration of tartar emetic, but there is not sufficient evidence to fix the guilt upon any person or persons." In consequence of this decision the Government offered a reward of £250 for information leading to the conviction of the murderer, but nothing more was ever found out.

BRAY, ANNA ELIZA *(only dau. of John Kemp of the Mint, London, bullion porter 1748–1823).* *b.* St. Mary Newington, Surrey 25 Dec. 1790; author of *Traditions, legends, superstitions and sketches of Devonshire, the Tamar and the Tavy* 3 *vols.* 1838; *Trelawnie of Trelawne or the prophecy* 3 *vols.*, 2 ed. 1845; *Henry de Pomeroy or the eve of St. John* 3 *vols.* 1842, *new ed.* 1846; *Handel, his life personal and professional* 1857; *Joan of Arc* 1874. *(m.* (1) Feb. 1818 Charles Alfred Stothard, historical draughtsman who *d.* 28 May 1821, *m.* (2) 1822 Rev. Edward Atkyns Bray, V. of Tavistock who *d.* 1857). She *d.* 40 Brompton Crescent, London 21 Jany. 1883. *Mrs. Bray's Autobiography* 1844, *portrait; Library Chronicle* i, 126–9 (1884); *I.L.N. lxxxii,* 197 (1883), *portrait.*

BRAY, CHARLES *(son of Mr. Bray of Coventry, ribbon manufacturer who d. 1835). b.* Coventry 31 Jany. 1811; ribbon manufacturer at Coventry 1835–56; helped to establish Coventry Labourers' and Artisans' Society 1843 which developed into a co-operative society of which he was president; started a working man's club 1845; purchased *The Coventry Herald and Observer* 1846 which he sold to J. M. Scott 1874; author of *Education of the feelings* 1838, 4 ed. 1872; *Philosophy of necessity* 2 vols. 1841, 2 ed. 1863; *Outlines of social systems and communities* 1844; *A manual of anthropology* 1871, 2 ed. 1883; *Psychological and ethical definitions on a physiological basis* 1879 and a number of pamphlets. *d.* 5 Oct. 1884. *C. Bray's Phases of opinion and experience during a long life* (1884), *portrait; George Eliot's Life, by J. W. Cross* 1885.

BRAY, REV. EDWARD ATKYNS *(only son of Edward Bray of Tavistock, solicitor). b.* the Abbey house, Tavistock 18 Dec. 1778; a student at M.T. 1801, barrister M.T. 1806; ordained by bishop of Norwich about 1811; entered at Trin. coll. Cam. 1812, B.D. 1822; V. of Tavistock 1812 to death; P.C. of Brent Tor, Devon 1812 to death; author of *Sermons from the works of the most eminent divines* 1818; *Discourses from tracts and treatises of eminent divines* 1821; *Discourses on Protestantism* 1829; *Poetical remains* 2 vols. 1859. *d.* Tavistock 17 July 1857. *Poetical remains of the late E. A. Bray* i, pp. ix–lii, (1859), *portrait.*

BRAY, EDWARD WILLIAM. Ensign 67 Foot 12 Jany. 1805; major 39 Foot 9 Nov. 1841 to 7 Aug. 1846 when he retired on full pay; C.B. 2 May 1844. *d.* Montpellier villas, Brighton 3 Dec. 1859 aged 70.

BRAY, GEORGE FREDERICK CAMPBELL. *b.* 23 April 1826; ensign 39 Foot 22 March 1844; lieut. col. 96 Foot 14 Sep. 1870 to 13 March 1878 when placed on h.p.; assistant adjutant general second division Abyssinian expedition 11 Nov. 1867 to 7 June 1868; deputy A.A.G. Bombay 20 Sep. 1872 to 15 Nov. 1873; A.A.G. and Q.M.G. southern district 15 March 1878 to 31 March 1883; hon. M.G. 26 Sep. 1883. *d.* 16 Kidbrook Green, Blackheath 26 Sep. 1884.

BRAY, REGINALD *(son of Edward Bray of Shere near Guildford 1768–1814, treasurer of Society of Antiquaries). b.* 26 Jany. 1797; solicitor in London 1818 to death; F.S.A. 26 Nov. 1829; printed many papers on reforms of the law; author of *Concise directions for obtaining Lord Chancellors orders for election and removal of coroners of counties* 1831. *d.* Shere 9 Sep. 1879.

BRAYBROOK, RICHARD GRIFFIN NEVILLE, 3 Baron *(eld. son of Richard Aldworth Neville Griffin, 2 Baron Braybrook 1750–1825). b.* Stanlake, Berks. 26 Sep. 1783; ed at Sunbury, Eton and Magd. coll. Cam., M.A. 1811, D.C.L. Ox. 1810; M.P. for Thirsk 1805–1806, for Saltash 1806–1807, for Buckingham 1807–1812 and for Berkshire (after a 15 days poll) 12 Oct. 1812 to 28 Feb. 1825 when he succeeded as 3 Baron; recorder of Saffron Walden to 1835; pres. of Camden Society and of Surtees Society; edited *Diary and correspondence of Samuel Pepys* 2 vols. 1825, 4 ed. 4 vols. 1854; *Life of Jane Lady Cornwallis* 1842; author of *History of Audley End and Saffron Walden* 1835. *d.* Audley End 13 March 1858.

BRAYBROOK, RICHARD CORNWALLIS NEVILLE, 4 Baron *(eld. son of the preceding). b.* St. George's parish, Hanover sq. London 17 March 1820; ed. at Eton; ensign Grenadier guards 2 June 1837, lieut. 31 Dec. 1841 to 1842 when he sold out; F.S.A. 25 March 1847; succeeded 13 March 1858; author of *Saxon Obsequies discovered in Cambridgeshire* 1852. *d.* Audley End 22 Feb. 1861.

BRAYBROOKE, SAMUEL. Second lieut. 1 Ceylon regiment 17 Dec. 1812, lieut. col. 26 Jany. 1844 to 11 June 1859; col. 99 Foot 26 Jany. 1866 to death; general 16 April 1875. *d.* 3 Gledhow gardens, South Kensington, London 7 Oct. 1880 aged 84.

BRAYBROOKE, WILLIAM LEMAN *(2 son of the preceding).* Ensign 90 Foot 29 **March** 1844; ensign 15 Foot 6 June 1845; **ensign** Ceylon Rifles 11 July 1845, lieut. **10 Jany.**

BRAYBROOKE, W. L. *(Con.)*

1847 to death, adjutant 7 April 1848 to 1854 ; served with and carried colours of 95 Foot in Crimean war 1854. *d.* on board H.M.S. Vulcan in Black Sea 21 Sep. 1854 from wounds received at battle of the Alma 20 Sep. *The diary of the late W. L. Braybrooke* 1855.

BRAYE, SARAH OTWAY-CAVE, Baroness. *b.* July 1767. *(m.* 25 Feb. 1790 Henry Otway who was *b.* 1769 and *d.* 13 Sep. 1815) ; barony of Braye in abeyance since 1557 was revived in her favour 3 Oct. 1839. *d.* 14 Great Stanhope st. London 21 Feb. 1862.

BRAYLEY, EDWARD WEDLAKE. *b.* Lambeth, Surrey 1773 ; apprenticed to an enameller at Clerkenwell ; prepared enamel plates for Henry Bone ; edited with John Britton *The beauties of England and Wales* 10 vols. 1801– 14 ; sec. and librarian to Russell Institution 55 Great Coram st. London 1826 to death ; F.S.A. 1823 ; author of *The history and antiquities of the abbey church of St. Peter Westminster* 2 vols. 1818 ; *Historical and descriptive account of the theatres of London* 1826 ; *Londiniana, or reminiscences of the British metropolis* 4 vols. 1829 ; *The graphic and historical illustrator*, a periodical July 1832 to Nov. 1834 ; *A topographical history of the county of Surrey* 5 vols. 1841–8 and many other books. *d.* 55 Great Coram st. London 23 Sep. 1854. *Memoir by John Britton privately printed* 1855 ; *G.M. xlii*, 538, 582 (1854).

BRAYLEY, EDWARD WILLIAM *(eld. son of the preceding).* *b.* London 1801 ; studied science at London and Royal Institutions ; joint librarian of the London Institution 1834 where he also lectured, sole librarian 1865 to death, and professor of physical geography and meteorology 1865 to death ; an original member of Zoological society 1826 and of Chemical society of London 1841 ; F.R.S. 1 June 1854 ; F.R.A.S. Nov. 1866 ; one of the editors 1822–45 of *Annals of philosophy, Zoological journal*, and *Philosophical Magazine* to all of which he contributed papers ; author of *Ancient castles of England and Wales* 2 vols. 1825. *d.* 53 Oakley road, London 1 Feb. 1870. *Monthly notices of Royal Astronom. Soc. xxxii*, 111 (1872).

BREADALBANE, JOHN CAMPBELL, 2 Marquis of *(only son of John Campbell, 1 Marquis of Breadalbane 1762–1834).* *b.* Nethergate, Dundee 26 Oct. 1796 ; ed. at Glasgow college ; M.P. for Okehampton 1820–26 ; M.P. for Perthshire 29 Dec. 1832 to 29 March 1834 when he succeeded as 2 Marquis ; F.R.S. 5 June 1834 ; K.T. 21 March 1838 ; lieut. and

BREADALBANE, J. C. *(Con.)*

sheriff principal of Argyllshire 5 Dec. 1839 ; presided over meeting of British Association at Glasgow 1840 ; lord rector of Univ. of Glasgow 1841 ; received Queen Victoria at Taymouth Castle, Perthshire on her first visit to Scotland 8 Sep. 1842 ; lord chamberlain of the household 1848–52 and 1853–58 ; P.C. 4 Sep. 1848 ; colonel of Argyll and Bute militia 18 Sep. 1854 to death. *d.* Lausanne 8 Nov. 1862. *P. R. Drummond's Perthshire in bygone days* (1879) 6–17.

BREADALBANE, JOHN ALEXANDER GAVIN CAMPBELL, 6 Earl of. *b.* London 30 March 1824 ; ensign 79 Foot 2 Aug. 1842 ; captain 1 Foot 4 Aug. 1854 to 12 Jany. 1855 when he sold out ; succeeded 8 Nov. 1862, confirmed as 6 Earl by Court of Session 1866 and by House of Lords 1867 ; a frequent correspondent of *The Field* ; a great salmon fisher. *d.* 4B The Albany, Piccadilly, London 20 March 1871. *J. Paterson's Breadalbane succession case* 1863.

BREEKS, JAMES WILKINSON. *b.* Edengate, Warcop, Westmoreland 5 March 1830 ; entered Madras civil service 1849, private sec. to Sir W. T. Denison governor of Madras 1861–64 ; comr. of the Nilagiris, principal sanatorium of South of India to death ; made a complete collection of arms, ornaments, dresses and implements in use among four aboriginal tribes of the Nilagiris and of contents of many cairns and cromlechs ; author of *An account of the primitive tribes and monuments of the Nilagiris* 1873. *(m.* 19 Feb. 1863 Susan Maria eld. dau. of Sir. W. T. Denison). *d.* Madras 6 June 1872.

BREEN, JAMES 2 *son of Hugh Breen who superintended Lunar reductions at Royal Observatory, Greenwich).* *b.* Armagh 5 July 1826 ; a calculator at Royal Observatory, Greenwich Aug. 1842 to Aug. 1846 and at Cambridge Observatory Aug. 1846 to Dec. 1858 ; observed the total eclipse of the sun at Camuesa in Spain 18 July 1860 ; F.R.A.S. 10 June 1862 ; author of *The Planetary Worlds, the topography and telescopic appearance of the sun, planets, moon and comets* 1854 ; contributed to *Popular Science Review* and other periodicals generally anonymously. *d.* 25 Aug. 1866. *Monthly notices of Royal Astronom. Soc. xxvii*, 104 (1867).

BREESE, EDWARD. *b.* 13 April 1835 ; ed. at Lewisham, Kent ; admitted solicitor 1857 ; practised at Dolgelly to death ; clerk of the peace for Merionethshire ; F.S.A. 21 March 1872 ; author of *Kalendars of Gwynedd, or chronological lists of lords-lieutenant, sheriffs*

BREESE, E. *(Con.)*

and knights of the shire for the counties of Angle-sey, Caernarvon and Merioneth 1873. *d.* Morva lodge, Portmadoc, Carnarvonshire 10 March 1881. *Law Times lxx,* 357, 413 (1881).

BREFFIT, EDGAR. *b.* Cromford near Mat-lock 12 June 1810; founded a glass bottle manufactory in City of London which became the leading house, trading as Aire and Calder glass bottle company at Castleford Yorkshire and Free trade wharf London; took out patents for stoppered bottles and for making large bottles with taps for drawing off the contents; member of court of common council for Dowgate ward 1865; sheriff of London 1875-6; alderman of ward of Cheap 1877 to death. *d.* The Glebe, Lee Kent 18 Oct. 1882. *I.L.N. lxvii,* 475 (1875), *portrait; Graphic xi,* 446 (1875), *portrait.*

BREMNER, JAMES. *b.* Keiss, parish of Wick, Caithnessshire 25 Sep. 1784; shipbuilder at Wick 1809 to death; designed and constructed many harbours and piers on north coast of Scotland; raised 236 wrecked vessels between Aberdeenshire and Isle of Skye; removed steamer Great Britain off strand in Dundrum bay 1847, she was stranded 22 Sep. 1846 and floated 27 Sep. 1847; author of *Treatise on the planning and constructing of harbours in deep water* 1845. *d.* Harbour place, Pulteney Town, Wick 20 Aug. 1856. *Min. of Proc. of Instit. of C.E. xvi,* 113-20 (1857).

BREMRIDGE, RICHARD. *b.* Barnstaple 1803; solicitor at Barnstaple 1825; M.P. for Barnstaple 1847-52, re-elected 8 July 1852 but election declared void; M.P. for Barnstaple 1863-65. *d.* Exmouth 15 June 1878.

BRENNAN, VERY REV. PATRICK. *b.* Carlow; one of the Superiors of Carlow college 1812-20; priest of parish of Kildare 1820; Peni-tentiary of dioceses of Kildare and Leighlin. *d.* Kildare 1864.

BRENT, JOHN *(eld. son of John Brent of Rother-hithe, Kent, shipbuilder 1786-1867).* *b.* Rother-hithe 21 Aug. 1808; a miller at Canterbury; alderman; city treasurer; F.S.A. 7 April 1853; author of *The sea wolf, a romance* 1834; *Lays and legends of Kent* 1840, 2 ed. 1851; *The battle cross, a romance of the fourteenth century* 3 vols. 1845; *Canterbury in the olden time* 1860, 2 ed. 1879; *Village bells and other poems* 1865, 2 ed. 1868 and of many papers in antiquarian magazines. *d.* 8 Dane John grove, Canterbury 23 April 1882. *C. R. Smith's Retrospections i,* 259, 303 (1883); *Journal of Brit. Archæol. Assoc. xxxviii,* 235-6 (1882).

BRENT, WILLIAM BRENT. Barrister L.I. 19 Nov. 1813; comr. of bankrupts to 1831; steward of Marshalsea Court and Palace Court, Great Scotland yard, Westminster 16 Sep. 1825 to 31 Dec. 1849 when they were abolished by 12 & 13 Vict. c. 101, s. xiii; probably dead.

BRENTON, JOHN. *b.* 28 Aug. 1782; entered navy 28 Aug. 1798; captain 26 Dec. 1822; retired V.A. 5 Jany. 1858; knight of Russian order of St. Vladimir. *d.* Ryde, Isle of Wight 17 Sep. 1859.

BRENTON, SIR LANCELOT CHARLES LEE, 2 Baronet *(younger son of Vice Admiral Sir Jahleel Brenton, 1 Baronet 1770-1844).* *b.* 1807; ed. at Hyde abbey sch. Winchester, and Oriel college Oxford; ordained 1830; seceded from Church of England Dec. 1831; took a small chapel at Bath and set up a new sect which died out with its founder; succeeded 21 April 1844; author of *The Sep-tuagint version of the Old Testament according to the Vatican text translated into English* 2 vols. 1844; *Cardiphonia Latina,* 3 ed. 1850; *Diaconia, or thoughts on the subject of Ministry* 1852; *Psalms: Bible and Prayer book version, parallel* 1860. *d.* Montagu house, Ryde 13 June 1862. *Memoir of Sir Jahleel Brenton re-edited by his son [Rev. L. C. L. Brenton]* 1855, *preface vii–cxxv; Rev. T. Mozley's Reminiscences ii,* 114-20 (1882).

BRERETON, REV. CHARLES DAVID *(eld. son of Rev. Charles David Brereton, R. of Little Massingham, Norfolk).* *b.* 19 April 1820; ed. at Trin. coll. Cam., B.A. 1843, M.A. 1846; C. of St. James Piccadilly 1848–49; R. of St. Edmund Norwich 1849-52; consular chaplain at Malaga, Spain 27 Aug. 1850 to 30 April 1859; R. of Bixley with Framling-ham Earl, Norfolk 1863 to death; author of *Lectures for travellers* 1854; *Verses and lectures* 1868. *d.* Lowestoft 15 April 1876.

BRERETON, SIR WILLIAM *(son of major Robert Brereton who fought at Culloden).* *b.* 1789; 2 lieut. R.A. 10 May 1805; lieut. col. 17 Aug. 1843 to 16 Dec. 1854; served in Spain, France and the Netherlands; granted service reward 1 April 1856; head of Irish con-stabulary short time; K.H. 1837; C.B. 19 July 1838; K.C.B. 28 June 1861; L.G. 27 June 1864; author of *The British fleet in the Black Sea while under the command of Vice Admiral J. W. D. Dundas,* privately printed 1857. *d.* 3E Albany, Piccadilly, London 27 July 1864. *I.L.N. xlv,* 154, 299 (1864).

BRERETON, WILLIAM WESTROPP (4 son of Arthur Brereton of Ballyadams Queen's county). b. 1810; ed. at Trin. coll. Dublin, B.A. 1832, M.A. 1856; called to Irish bar 1836; went Munster circuit; Q.C. 9 Nov. 1852; assistant barrister for co. Kerry 1858; chairman of quarter sessions for co. Galway 1858 to death. d. Fitzwilliam sq. north, Dublin 13 Dec. 1867. Law mag. and law review v, 260 (1855).

BRETT, HARRY AUGUSTUS. Writer Madras civil service 1831; collector of Salem 1860; member of Board of Revenue 1862–65; pres. of Income tax commission 1862–67; resigned the service 27 May 1867. d. 20 Dec. 1867.

BRETT, JOHN WATKINS (son of Wm. Brett of Bristol, cabinet maker). b. Bristol 1805; Telegraphic engineer; laid a gutta percha wire between Dover and Cape Grisnez 1850 by which the first submarine message was sent from England to France; laid cables between Dover and Calais 1851, Dover and Ostend 1853, and Sardinia and France 1854; mainly instrumental in forming Atlantic Telegraph Company 1856; director of Submarine Telegraph Co.; made a splendid collection of works of art; author of On the origin and progress of the Oceanic telegraph 1858. d. Lunatic asylum, Coton Hill, Stafford 3 Dec. 1863 bequeathing one tenth of his large property to charity. Notes and Queries 3 S. viii, 203 (1865).

BRETT, ROBERT. b. at or near Luton Beds. 11 Sep. 1808; ed. at St. George's hospital London, M.R.C.S. and L.S.A. 1830; assistant to Samuel Reynolds of Stoke Newington surgeon, partner with him 1860 to death; founded the Guild of St. Luke, a band of medical men who co-operate with the clergy; vice pres. of London Union on church matters 1850; one of founders and vice pres. with Dr. Pusey of English Church Union 1860; author of The Churchman's guide to faith and piety by R. B. 1862, 5 ed. 1871; Scripture history for the young 1845; Devotions for the sick room 1843; Companion for the sick room 1844; Thoughts during sickness, 4 ed. 1870 and 11 other books. d. Stoke Newington 3 Feb. 1874. Robert Brett. In memoriam reprints from the principal church journals including a sermon by Rev. J. W. Belcher 1874.

BRETT, WILLIAM FREELAND. b. 19 Oct. 1821; ensign 54 Foot 1 April 1842, major 14 Aug. 1857; major 61 Foot 27 Sep. 1861; lieut. col. brigade depot 26 Jany. 1876; M.G. 1 Oct. 1877; placed on retired list 1 July 1881. d. Colchester 10 Nov. 1884.

BRETT, REV. WILLIAM HENRY. b. Dover; left Dover on his first journey to Demerara as missionary from S.P.G. 10 Feb. 1840; ordained deacon 1843 and priest 1844; chaplain to Bishop of Guiana and R. of Holy Trinity Essequibo 1851–79; author of The Indian tribes of Guiana 1852; Legends and myths of the aboriginal Indians of British Guiana 1880; Mission work among the Indian tribes in the forests of Guiana 1881. d. Bowruma, Totnes road, Paignton, Devon 10 Feb. 1886 aged 67.

BRETTELL, REV. JACOB (only son of Rev. Jacob Brettell, Independent minister at Sutton-in-Ashfield, Notts who d. 19 March 1810). b. Sutton-in-Ashfield 16 April 1793; ed. at Manchester college York 1809–14; Unitarian minister at Cockey Moor (now called Ainsworth) Lancs. July 1814 and at Rotherham Sep. 1816 to June 1859; author of The country minister, a poem in 4 cantos 1821; The country minister part second, a poem in 3 cantos 1825; The country minister, a poem in 7 cantos with additional poems and notes 1827; contributed hundreds of hymns and political and patriotic pieces to Christian Reformer, Sheffield Iris, and other periodicals. d. Rotherham 12 Jany. 1862. Christian Reformer xviii, 128, 191 (1862).

BRETTLE, ROBERT. b. Portobello near Edinburgh 6 Dec. 1831; a glassblower in the hardware districts; fought B. Malpas for £50 a side 14 Feb. 1854 when stakes were drawn; fought Sam. Simmonds for £200 a side 3 June 1856, and Job Cobley for £100 a side 4 Aug. 1857 and beat them both; fought Bob Travers for £100 a side 26 Jany. 1858 when he won after 100 rounds in 2 hours; fought James Mace for £100 a side 21 Sep. 1858 when he won; fought Tom Sayers who staked £400 to Brettle's £200, 20 Sep. 1859 when Sayers won; fought James Mace again 9 Sep. 1860 when Mace won; fought Jack Rooke for £200 a side 31 Dec. 1861, 1 Jany. 1862 and 11 March 1862 when stakes were drawn; kept the White Lion, Digbeth, Birmingham 1857 to about 1868 when he went to the United States; trained and brought out some of the best light-weight pugilists. d. 56 Upper Windsor st. Birmingham 7 April 1872. The championship of England by the editor of Bell's Life in London [Francis Dowling] 1860 pp. 70–4; Illust. sporting news 1862 p. 9, portrait; H. D. Miles's Pugilistica iii, 451–60 (1881).

BREWER, GEORGE. b. Gosport 7 Aug. 1773; entered navy 19 March 1793; joined the 'Robust' 15 Feb. 1795; discharged incurable

BREWER, G. (Con.)

17 May 1799 ; a waterman at Gosport. *d.* in a court in Havant st. Portsea 7 Sep. 1871 aged 98 but generally reputed to be 106. *Thoms's Human longevity* (1873) 185–6.

BREWER, REV. JOHN SHERREN (*eld. son of John Sherren Brewer of Eaton, Norwich, schoolmaster*). *b.* 1810; ed. at Queen's coll. Ox., B.A. 1833, M.A. 1835 ; chaplain of workhouse of St. Giles's in the Fields and St. George's Bloomsbury 17 Dec. 1837 to July 1845 ; lecturer in classical literature at King's college London 1839–60, professor of English language and literature there 1855 and of English literature and modern history 1865–77 ; reader at the Rolls chapel Chancery lane 1857–62, and preacher 1862 to death; hon. fellow of Queen's coll. Ox. Nov. 1870 ; head of Working mens' college in Great Ormond st. 1872 ; R. of Toppesfield Essex 16 Sep. 1876 to death; edited the *Standard* for short time in 1860 ; edited *Aristotle's Ethics* 1836 ; *Book of the Church by R. Field* 3 vols. 1843 ; *Lectures to ladies on practical subjects* 1855 ; and *Letters and papers foreign and domestic of the reign of Henry viii,* 4 vols. *d.* Toppesfield rectory 16 Feb. 1879. *Rev. J. S. Brewer's English Studies* (1881) vii–xl.

BREWER, THOMAS. *b.* 1807 ; entered office of Town Clerk of City of London 1823 ; secretary of City of London school 1837 to death; a founder of Sacred Harmonic Society 1832, secretary 1832–70, pres. Nov. 1870 to death; author of *Memoir of John Carpenter, town clerk of London* 1836, 2 ed. 1856 ; *Memoir of Walter Scott, citizen and plaisterer of London* privately printed 1858. *d.* City of London school, Milk st. London 25 Dec. 1870.

BREWER, WILLIAM (*brother of Rev. John Sherren Brewer*). Ed. at Univ. of Edin., M.D., L.R.C.S. Edin. 1834; M.D. St. Andrew's 1834 ; M.R.C.P. London 1841, F.R.C.P. 1872 ; M.P. for Colchester 18 Nov. 1868 to 26 Jany. 1874; member of Metropolitan Board of Works for St. George's Hanover square 1870 ; chairman of Metropolitan Asylums Board ; author of *The family medical reference book* 1840 ; *Beatrice Sforza or the progress of truth* 3 vols. 1863 ; translated *A. Tavernier's Treatise on the treatment of deformities of the spine* 1842. *d.* 21 George st. Hanover sq. London 3 Nov. 1881.

BREWSTER, ABRAHAM (*eld. son of Wm. Bagenal Brewster of Ballinulta, co. Wicklow*). *b.* Ballinulta April 1796; ed. at Kilkenny coll. and Univ. of Dublin, B.A. 1817, M.A. 1847 ; called to Irish bar 1819, went Leinster

BREWSTER, A. (Con.)

circuit ; K.C. 13 July 1835, legal adviser to lord lieut. of Ireland 10 Oct. 1841 ; bencher of King's Inns Dublin 1846 ; solicitor general for Ireland 2 Feb. 1846 to 16 July 1846; attorney general 10 Jany. 1853 to 10 Feb. 1855 ; P.C. Ireland Jany. 1853 ; lord justice of Court of Appeal in Ireland July 1866 ; lord chancellor of Ireland March 1867 to 17 Dec. 1868. *d.* 26 Merrion square south, Dublin 26 July 1874. *Burke's Lord Chancellors of Ireland* (1879) 307–11 ; *I.L.N. lxv,* 115, 427 (1874).

BREWSTER, SIR DAVID (2 *son of James Brewster, rector of Jedburgh gr. sch. who d.* 1815). *b.* Canongate, Jedburgh 10 or 11 Dec. 1781 ; ed. at Jedburgh gr. sch. and Univ. of Edin. ; licensed by Presbytery of Edin. 1804 ; LL.D. Aberdeen 1807, M.A. Cam. 1807 ; F.R.S. Edin. 1808, pres. 1864 ; F.R.S. 4 May 1815, Copley medallist 1815, Rumford medallist 1818, Royal medallist 6 times ; founded Scottish Society of Arts 1821 ; invented polyzonal lens for lighthouses 1811, Kaleidoscope 1816 and lenticular stereoscope ; procured establishment of British Association 1831 ; K.H. 1831 ; knighted at St. James's Palace 8 March 1832 fees of £109 were never demanded from him; principal of Univ. of St. Andrew's Jany. 1838 to Oct. 1859 ; a chevalier of Order of Merit 1847 ; one of the 8 foreign associates of French Institute 1849 ; president of Peace congress at Exeter hall London 22–24 July 1851 ; principal of Univ. of Edin. 28 Oct. 1859 to death; author of *Treatise on the Microscope* 1837, *new ed.* 1851 ; *Lives of Galileo, Tycho Brahe, and Kepler* 1841, *new ed.* 1874 ; *More worlds than one* 1854, *new ed.* 1874 ; *History of the Stereoscope* 1856 and many other books. *d.* Allerley near Melrose 10 Feb. 1868, centenary of his birth celebrated at Jedburgh 10 Dec. 1881. *The home life of Sir D. Brewster by his daughter Mrs. Gordon* 1869, *portrait ; Proc. of Royal Soc. xvii,* 69–74 (1869); *Min. of Proc. of Instit. of C.E. xxvi,* 194–200 (1871) ; *Grant's Story of Univ. of Edin. ii,* 274–8 (1884), *portrait ; Maclise Portrait Gallery* (1883) 143–7, *portrait ; I.L.N. xvii,* 121 (1850), *portrait, lii,* 189 (1868), *portrait.*

BREWSTER, REV. PATRICK *brother of the preceding*). *b.* 20 Dec. 1788 ; licensed by Presbytery of Fordoun 26 March 1817; minister of Abbey church Paisley Aug. 1817 to death; ordained 10 April 1818 ; had but few equals as a preacher for elegance of style and purity of diction ; took an active share in chartist agitation ; author of *An essay on*

BREWSTER, REV. P. (Con.)

passive obedience 1836; The rights of the poor of Scotland vindicated against the misrepresentations of the editor of the Glasgow Post and Reformer 2 parts; The seven Chartist and military discourses libelled by the Marquis of Abercorn and other heritors of the Abbey parish 1843. d. Craigie Linn near Paisley 26 March 1859, monument to his memory erected by public subscription in Paisley cemetery 1863. John Smith's Our Scottish clergy, 2 series 1849, 162–6.

BREWSTER, WILLIAM BAGENAL. Educ. at St. John's coll. Ox., B.A. 1846; rowed No. 4 in Oxford boat against Cambridge 1842 when Oxford gained her first victory on the Putney to Mortlake course; ensign 1 battalion Rifle brigade 7 July 1846, captain 29 Dec. 1854 to 1858 when he sold out; served in Kaffir war 1852–3; lieut. col. 23 Middlesex Volunteers (Inns of Court) 9 April 1860 to death. d. 75 Warwick sq. Belgrave road, London 7 July 1864 in 45 year. Saturday Review xviii, 81–2 (1864).

BRICE, EDWARD. Second lieut. Madras Artillery 16 June 1826, colonel 25 Sep. 1861 to death; C.B. 1 March 1861. d. Harley st. London 9 June 1868.

BRIDELL, FREDERICK LEE (son of Mr. Bridell of Southampton, builder). b. Southampton 7 Nov. 1831; apprenticed to a picture dealer 1846–53; studied painting at Munich 1854-7; his chief works are 'Sunset on the Atlantic,' exhibited at Liverpool Nov. 1857; 'Temple of Venus' painted in emulation of Turner 1858 and 'The Coliseum by moonlight' painted at Rome 1858, exhibited at the R.A. 1859 and at International Exhibition 1862; his patron James Wolff of Southampton acquired so many of his works that he formed a 'Bridell gallery' which was sold for nearly £4,000. d. Aug. 1863. Art Journal n.s. iii, 12 (1864).

BRIDGE, REV. JOHN BRICE. b. Liverpool 2 Nov. 1793; ed. at Stonyhurst college; admitted to Society of Jesus at Hodder 7 Sep. 1814; ordained priest at Dublin July 1819; spiritual father and superior of seminary Stonyhurst June 1838; minister of Stonyhurst college Nov. 1841; superior of residence of St. Michael, Yorkshire many years; missioner at Allerton Park, Yorkshire 18 July 1842 to death; compiler of the Ordo S. J. 1844 to death. d. Allerton park 20 Feb. 1860.

BRIDGEMAN, CHARLES ORLANDO (2 son of 1 Earl of Bradford 1762-1825). b. 5 Feb. 1791; entered navy 18 June 1804; captain 2 Sep.

BRIDGEMAN, C. O. (Con.)

1819, captain of the Rattlesnake in Mediterranean 1827–30; retired captain 1 Oct. 1846; retired V.A. 10 Sep. 1857. d. Knockin near Oswestry 13 April 1860.

BRIDGER, CHARLES. Clerk in Heralds' College London; assistant of Stephen Tucker, Somerset Herald; author of An index to printed pedigrees contained in county and local histories 1867; The family of Leete edited by J. C. Anderson privately printed 1881. d. 17 Selwood terrace, South Kensington, London 27 May 1879 in 54 year.

BRIDGER, WILLIAM. Solicitor at Guildford, Surrey 1854 to death; travelled in Australia; formed one of the best known collections of birds eggs; F.R.Z.S. d. Stoke near Guildford 15 Oct. 1870 aged 38.

BRIDGER, WILLIAM MILTON. Educ. at Winchester and Ch. Ch. Ox., B.A. 1814, M.A. 1818; barrister M.T. 20 June 1817; recorder of Chichester 1821 to death; recorder of Petworth d. from an accident in London 12 Aug. 1863.

BRIDGES, REV. CHARLES. Educ. at Queen's coll. Cam., B.A. 1818, M.A. 1831; V. of Old Newton, Suffolk 1823–49, rural dean 1844–9; R. of Melcombe Regis, Dorset 1849–55; R. of Hinton Martell, Dorset 1855 to death; author of An exposition of Psalm cxix, 1827, 27 ed. 1873; The Christian ministry 1830, 7 ed. 1849; Memoir of Miss M. J. Graham 1832, 3 ed. 1833; An exposition of the book of Proverbs 1846; Scriptural studies 9 ed. 1884. d. Hinton Martell rectory 2 April 1869 aged 75. Reg. and mag. of biog. i, 399 (1869).

BRIDGES, SIR HENRY (son of Alexander Bridges of Ewell, Surrey). b. Ewell 1786; sheriff of Surrey 1813–14; knighted on presenting an address to Prince Regent at Carlton house 11 May 1814. (m. 1808 Frances dau. of general Wm. Tombes Dalrymple, she d. 6 Feb. 1859). d. Beddington house near Croydon 29 Oct. 1861.

BRIDGMAN, FREDERICK (eld. son of Frederick Horatio Bridgman). b. 1837; barrister I.T. 17 Nov. 1860; went South Eastern circuit 1860–82; Queen's Advocate for Gold Coast Colony 7 Oct. 1882 to death, acting chief justice 1883 to death. d. Cape Coast 5 May 1883.

BRIDPORT, SAMUEL HOOD, 2 Baron. b. Catherington, Hants. 7 Dec. 1788; ed. at Trin. coll. Cam., M.A. 1809; succeeded 3 May 1814. d. Cricket St. Thomas, Chard, Somerset 6 Jany. 1868.

BRIDSON, THOMAS RIDGWAY (*son of Paul Bridson of Douglas, Isle of Man who d.* 1820). *b.* 1795; owner of bleach works near Bolton foremost establishment of the kind in the world; invented the patent "stenter" or elastic finishing machine which much advanced mechanism of the trade; mayor of Bolton 1847–8. *d.* 24 Jany. 1863. *H. Mayhew's Shops of London i,* 127–38 (1865).

BRIGGS, AUGUSTUS. *b.* 7 May 1813; member of House of Assembly, Barbados many years, speaker 1868–75; member of Legislative council 1878 and president 1881 to death. *d.* Maynards, Barbados 17 May 1882.

BRIGGS, GEORGE. Second lieut. Madras artillery 16 Dec. 1824; colonel 18 Feb. 1861 to 6 May 1867; M.G. 6 May 1867. *d.* Cambridge st. Pimlico, London 29 July 1875 in 80 year.

BRIGGS, RIGHT REV. JOHN. *b.* Manchester 20 May 1788; ed. at St. Cuthbert's college Ushaw; sub-deacon 1812, deacon 1813 and priest 1814; had charge of Chester 1818–32; pres. of Ushaw 28 March 1832 to 11 Aug. 1836; co-adjutor of Bishop Penswick in Northern district Jany. 1833; consecrated as Bishop of Trachis in Thessalia 29 Jany. 1833; vicar apostolic of Northern district Feb. 1836 and of Yorkshire district July 1840; bishop of Beverley 29 Sep. 1850 to 7 Nov. 1860 when he resigned; enthroned in St. George's church York 13 Feb. 1851; a Count of the Holy Roman empire. *d.* at his house York 4 Jany. 1861. *Brady's Episcopal succession iii,* 396–8 (1877); *The Lamp iii,* 163 (1851), *portrait.*

BRIGGS, JOHN (*eld. child of James Briggs, physician general Madras, who d. about* 1830). *b.* Madras 18 Sep. 1785; ed. at Eton 1794–9; lieut. 15 Madras N.I. 10 July 1801; resident at Sattara Jany. 1823 to Jany. 1827; senior comr. in Mysore 1831 to 13 Nov. 1832; resident at Nagpore Dec. 1832 to March 1835; colonel 13 Madras N.I. 16 Nov. 1836 to 1869; general 6 Feb. 1861; took the chair at meeting of Anti-corn-law league in Covent Garden theatre 22 May 1844; contested Exeter April 1844 and July 1845; F.R.S. 22 Nov. 1838. *d.* Bridge Lodge, Burgess Hill, Sussex 27 April 1875. *Memoir of John Briggs by Evans Bell* 1885, *portrait.*

BRIGGS, JOHN JOSEPH (*son of John Briggs of King's Newton near Melbourne, Derbyshire, farmer* 1777–1864). *b.* King's Newton 6 March 1819; apprenticed to W. Bemrose of Derby, printer 1834; farmer at King's

BRIGGS, J. J. (*Con.*)
Newton about 1840 to death; originated 'The Naturalists' column' in the *Field* newspaper 1855; author of *Melbourne, a sketch of its history and antiquity* 1839; *History of Melbourne* 1852; *The Trent and other poems* 1857; *The Peacock at Rowsley* 1869; *Guide to Melbourne* 1871; *History and antiquities of Hemington, Leicestershire,* 12 *copies privately printed* 1873. *d.* King's Newton 23 March 1876. *Reliquary xvii,* 49–54 (1877).

BRIGGS, SIR JOHN THOMAS (*son of Wm. Briggs*). *b.* London 4 June 1781; sec. to Commission for revising civil affairs of navy 1806; assistant sec. of Victualling Board 1809–30; private sec. to Sir James Graham, first lord of Admiralty 1830; comr. of Victualling Board 1831–2; accountant general of navy 1832 to Feb. 1854; knighted at St. James's Palace 26 Feb. 1851; author of several pamphlets on naval administration. *d.* 4 Royal Crescent, Brighton 3 Feb. 1865. *Morning Post 8 Feb.* 1865 *and 3 Jany.* 1874; *Daily Telegraph 6 Jany.* 1874.

BRIGGS, SIR THOMAS (7 *son of Stephen Briggs, chief surgeon at Madras*). *b.* Southampton 1780; entered navy 10 Sep. 1791; captain of Queen Charlotte 100 guns 1818–21; resident comr. of naval yard at Bermuda 1823 and at Malta 1829–32; superintendent of Malta dockyard 1832–38; G.C.M.G. 26 June 1833; admiral 2 Sep. 1850; commander in chief at Portsmouth 18 Sep. 1851 to death. *d.* Admiralty house, Portsmouth 16 Dec. 1852.

BRIGHAM, REV. HENRY. *b.* Manchester 23 June 1796; ed. at Stonyhurst college; entered Society of Jesus at Hodder 7 Sep. 1813; ordained priest 1 June 1822; missioner at Hereford 10 Dec. 1827; removed to Preston 2 Oct. 1834 and to Bury St. Edmunds 23 July 1836; superior of College of Holy Apostles 1842–3; served missions of Pontefract, Teignmouth and Ugbrooke; professor of elocution at St. Stanislaus' college Beaumont near Windsor 1865. *d.* St. Stanislaus' college 26 May 1881.

BRIGHT, HENRY (*son of Richard Bright of Bristol, merchant*). West India Merchant at Bristol; M.P. for Bristol 1820–30. *d.* Malvern 26 March 1869 aged 83.

BRIGHT, HENRY (*son of Jerome Bright of Saxmundham, Suffolk who d.* 1846). *b.* Saxmundham 1814; apprenticed to a chemist at Woodbridge; studied painting in London; a member of Institute of Painters in Water Colours and of the Graphic Society; very

BRIGHT, H. *(Con.)*

popular as a teacher of painting; exhibited 12 pictures at R.A., 26 at B.I. and 7 at Suffolk st. gallery 1836–73. *d.* Ipswich 21 Sep. 1873. *Art Journal Oct.* 1873; *I.L.N. lxiii,* 389 (1873), *portrait.*

BRIGHT, HENRY ARTHUR *(eld. son of Samuel Bright of Liverpool, shipowner 1799–1870.)* *b.* Liverpool 9 Feb. 1830; ed. at Rugby and Trin. coll. Cam., B.A. 1857 (being with James Heywood first non-conformist to take a degree at Cam.) M.A. 1860; partner in firm of Gibbs, Bright and Co. shipowners 1857; contributed largely to *Athenæum* 1871 to death; published *A year in a Lancashire garden* 1879, which he wrote in *Gardeners' Chronicle* 1874, and privately printed 50 copies 1875; *The English flower garden* 1881 and 5 other books. *d.* Ashfield, Knotty Ash near Liverpool 5 May 1884. *H. A. Bright's The Brights of Colwall* (1872), *p.* 11; *Christian Life* 10 *and* 17 *May* 1884; *N. Hawthorne and his wife ii,* 21–7 (1885).

BRIGHT, JACOB *(youngest son of Jacob Bright).* Learnt handloom weaving at New Mills Derbyshire 1790–6; bookkeeper to J. and W. Holme of Rochdale, partner with them; cotton spinner at Hanging road factory Rochdale, at Greenbank mill Cronkeyshaw 1809, had 7000 spindles at work 1823; retired from business 1839. *d.* 7 July 1851 aged 76. *Fortunes made in business ii,* 181–97 (1884).

BRIGHT, JOHN. *b.* Derbyshire 1782; ed. at Wad. coll. Ox., B.A. 1801, M.A. 1804, M.B. 1806, M.D. 1808; practised at Birmingham; removed to London; candidate of R.C.P. 30 Sep. 1808, Fellow 30 Sep. 1809, Censor 1813, 1822, 1833 and 1840, Harveian orator 1830, Consiliarius 1839, an Elect 25 June 1839; Physician to Westminster hospital 1822–43; a Metropolitan Commissioner in Lunacy 1 Sep. 1836. *d.* 19 Manchester sq. London 1 Feb. 1870. *Munk's Roll of physicians iii,* 79 (1878).

BRIGHT, REV. MYNORS *(son of John Bright, physician 1783–1870).* *b.* 1818; ed. at Shrewsbury; entered Magd. coll. Cam. 3 July 1835, B.A. 1840, M.A. 1843, Tyrwhitt Hebrew scholar 1843, foundation fellow, and tutor of his college, president 1853 to 1873; proctor of Univ. of Cam. 1853; re-edited Lord Braybrook's edition of *Pepys's Diary* published simultaneously in 4°. and 8°. 6 vols. 1879 for which he redeciphered the whole of Pepys's Diary from the original M.S. in Magd. coll. library. *d.* 23 Sussex place, Regent's Park, London 23 Feb. 1883.

BRIGHT, RICHARD *(3 son of Richard Bright of Bristol, merchant).* *b.* Queen sq. Bristol 28 Sep. 1789; ed. at Univ. of Edin., M.D. 13 Sep. 1813; L.R.C.P. 23 Dec. 1816; assistant phys. to Guy's hospital 1820–4, phys. 1824–43; F.R.S. 8 March 1821; F.R.C.P. 25 June 1832, Gulstonian lecturer 1833, Lumleian lecturer 1837, Censor 1836 and 1839, Consiliarius 1838 and 1843; phys. extraordinary to Queen Victoria 8 Aug. 1837; the leading consulting phys. in London; discovered several affections of the kidney, dependent upon an altered condition of the blood, called after him Bright's disease or nephritis; author of *Travels from Vienna through Lower Hungary* 1818; *Reports of medical cases, selected with a view of illustrating the symptons and cure of diseases by a reference to morbid anatomy* 3 parts 1827–31. *d.* 11 Savile Row, London 16 Dec. 1858. *Munk's Roll of physicians iii,* 155–60 (1878); *Pettigrew's Medical portrait gallery vol.* 2 (1840), *portrait; Proc. of Royal Soc. x,* 1–4 (1860); *Morbus Brighti von Joseph Buchner, Leipzig* 1870.

BRIGHT, RICHARD *(son of the succeeding).* *b.* Abbots Leigh near Bristol 14 April 1822; ed. at Rugby and Ch. Ch. Ox., B.A. 1843; barrister I.T. 21 Nov. 1851; M.P. for East Somerset 19 Nov. 1868 to death. *d.* 28 Feb. 1878.

BRIGHT, ROBERT *(brother of Richard Bright 1789–1858).* *b.* 1795; partner in great mercantile house of Gibbs and Bright of Bristol, Liverpool and London, owners of the Eagle line of packets and of Great Britain steamship; took chief part in freeing port of Bristol from heavy dues levied on its commerce 1848 for which he was presented with a service of plate worth £1,000 at Bristol March 1855. *d.* Abbots Leigh near Bristol 19 Sep. 1869. *I.L.N. xxvi,* 325–6 (1855).

BRIGHTWELL, CECILIA LUCY *(eld. child of the succeeding).* *b.* Thorpe near Norwich 27 Feb. 1811; pupil of John Sell Cotman, etcher; etched many landscapes and subjects; author of *Memorials of the life of Amelia Opie* 1854, 2 ed. 1855; *Palissy, the Huguenot potter a true tale* 1858, 2 ed. 1877; *Heroes of the laboratory and the workshop* 1859, 2 ed. 1860 and 18 other books. *d.* Norwich 17 April 1875.

BRIGHTWELL, THOMAS *(son of Thomas Brightwell of Ipswich, tanner).* *b.* 18 March 1787; articled to S. Daniell of Colchester, attorney; practised at Norwich 1810; partner with Thomas Bignold; mayor of Norwich 1837; F.L.S. 1821; made a fine collection of Insects especially Coleoptera, which he gave to the

BRIGHTWELL, T. (Con.)

Norwich museum about 1844; author of *Notes on the Pentateuch selected from the exegetical parts of Rosenmuller's Scholia* 1840. *d.* Norwich 17 Nov. 1868. *Memorials of the life of Mr. Brightwell of Norwich by his daughter C. L. Brightwell 1869, portrait.*

BRIGSTOCKE, THOMAS. *b.* 1809; studied at Sass's drawing school London; pupil of H. P. Briggs, R.A. and J. P. Knight, R.A.; spent 8 years in Paris and Italy; made a copy of Raphael's 'Transfiguration' in the Vatican which was purchased for Christ Church, Albany st. Regent's Park; went to Egypt 1847; painted an historical picture entitled 'The prayer for victory'; exhibited 16 pictures at R.A. and 2 at B.I. 1843–65; author of *The mutual scourges, or France and her neighbours, an historical drama in 4 acts* 1871. *d.* 11 March 1881.

BRIMLEY, GEORGE (*son of Mr. Brimley of Cambridge*). *b.* Cambridge 29 Dec. 1819; ed. at Totteridge, Herts. 1830–5; entered at Trin. coll. Cam. Oct. 1838, scholar 1841, librarian 4 June 1845 to 1857; contributed articles to the *Spectator* and *Fraser's Mag.* 1851 to death; one of the finest critics of his day. *d.* Cambridge 29 May 1857. *Essays by the late G. Brimley edited by W. G. Clark, 3 ed. 1882, portrait.*

BRINCKMAN, SIR THEODORE HENRY LAV-INGTON, 1 Baronet (*eld. son of Theodore Henry Broadhead of Holly grove, Windsor, M.P. 1767–1820.*) *b.* London 17 Jany. 1798; ed. at Eton and Trin. coll. Cam.; M.P. for Yarmouth 17 Jany. 1821 to 2 June 1826; created baronet 30 Sep. 1831; assumed by royal licence original family surname of Brinckman 5 July 1842. *d.* St. Leonards near Windsor 9 Feb. 1880.

BRIND, FREDERICK. Colonel Bengal army 20 June 1854; C.B. 9 June 1849. *d.* Sealkote Bengal 10 July 1857 aged 55.

BRINDLE, VERY REV. THOMAS. *b.* Walton-le-Dale, Lancs. 18 Dec. 1791; ed. at Bene-dictine coll. Ampleforth, Yorks.; ordained priest Sep. 1815; administrator of Western diocese and Grand Vicar March 1829 to 1830; regent of college at Prior park, Bath 1830 to Nov. 1849; vicar general of diocese of Clif-ton 1850 an office which he held at various periods for 21 years; provost of the Cathe-dral Chapter 1852; domestic prelate to Pope Gregory xvi, 1854; received many persons into R.C. church during Tractarian movement. *d.* Bath 13 Dec. 1871. *Tablet 23 Dec.* 1871.

BRINE, GEORGE (3 *son of James Brine, admiral R.N. who d.* 1814). Entered navy Feb. 1797; captain 7 Dec. 1818; retired 1 Oct. 1846; retired admiral 23 March 1863. *d.* Richmond, Surrey 16 Nov. 1864 aged 79.

BRINTON, WILLIAM (2 *son of Henry Brinton of Kidderminster, carpet manufacturer who d. about* 1856). *b.* Kidderminster 20 Nov. 1823; matric. at Univ. of London 1843, M.B. 1847, M.D. 1848; M.R.C.P. 1849, F.R.C.P. 1854, Croonian lecturer 1859; medical tutor at King's college, London 1850–3; lecturer on forensic medicine at St. Thomas's hospital 1853; phys. to Royal free hospital 1852–60 and to St. Thomas's hospital 1860 to Nov. 1864; member of Alpine Club; F.R.S. 1864; author of *Bürger's Leonora, Englished* [*by W.B.*] 1850; *On the medical selection of lives for insurance* 1856, 3 ed. 1861; *The diseases of the stomach* 1859. *d.* 24 Brook st. Grosvenor sq. London 17 Jany. 1867. *Proc. of Royal Soc. xvi, 6–8 (1865).*

BRISBANE, SIR THOMAS MACDOUGALL (*eld. son of Thomas Brisbane of Largs, Ayrshire who d.* 1812 *aged* 92). *b.* Brisbane house, Largs 23 July 1773; ensign 38 Foot 9 April 1789; lieut. col. 69 Foot 4 April 1800 to 30 May 1805 when placed on h.p.; commanded 1 brigade of 3 division in Peninsula 1812 to end of the war; commanded brigade in Canada 1813 and a brigade in army of occupation in France and afterwards the second division there; governor of New South Wales 1 Dec. 1821 to 1 Dec. 1825; colonel 34 Foot 16 Dec. 1826 to death; general 23 Nov. 1841; fought in 14 general actions and 23 other battles; erected an observatory near Brisbane house 1808, another at Paramatta near Sydney opened 2 May 1822 and a third at Makerstown near Kelso 1826 to which he added a magnetic station 1841 only one in Scotland; F.R.S. 10 May 1810; F.R.S. Edin. 1811, pres. 1832; gold medallist of Royal Astronom. Soc. 1828; F.G.S. 1833; pres. of British Assoc. at Edin. 1834; G.C.H. 1831; baronet 22 Feb. 1836; G.C.B. 6 Feb. 1837. *d.* Brisbane house 27 Jany. 1860. *Reminiscences of Sir T. M. Brisbane privately printed* 1860; *Proc. of Royal Soc. xi, 3–7* (1860); *Monthly notices of Royal Astronom. Soc. xxi, 98–100* (1861); *G.M. viii, 298–302* (1860).

BRISCO, SIR ROBERT, 3 Baronet. *b.* Crofton hall, Carlisle 17 Sep. 1808; succeeded 1 Oct. 1862; became a pledged **abstainer** 1858, vice pres. of United Kingdom Alliance, lectured frequently on **temperance**. *d.* Crof-ton hall 23 Dec. 1884.

BRISCO, Sir Wastell, 2 Baronet. *b.* 17 May 1778; succeeded 27 Dec. 1806; sheriff of Cumberland 1813. *d.* Crofton hall 1 Oct. 1862.

BRISCOE, John Ivatt (*son of John Briscoe of Cross Deep, Twickenham*). *b.* Twickenham 1791; ed. at Ealing and Univ. coll. Ox., B.A. 1812, M.A. 1815; M.P. for Surrey 1830–32, for East Surrey 1832–34, for Westbury 1837–41 and for West Surrey 1857 to death. *d.* 60 Eaton place, London 16 Aug. 1870.

BRISCOE, Joseph. *b.* Wilmount, co. Kilkenny; ed. at Trin. coll. Dublin; went to United States 1854; connected as civil engineer with many important public works in Pennsylvania coalfields; enlisted in First New York Volunteers at outbreak of the civil war; chief of the staff of Tenth army corps; colonel of 199 regiment Pennsylvania volunteers; commanded a brigade at capture of Petersburg; stormed Fort Gregg for which he was brevetted general; pres. of Examining board for officers in regular army. *d.* New York 24 May 1869 aged 35.

BRISTOL, Frederick William Hervey, 1 Marquis of (*younger son of Right Rev. Frederic Augustus Hervey, bishop of Derry, 4 Earl of Bristol 1730–1803*). *b.* 2 June 1769; ed. at St. John's coll. Cam., M.A. 1788, LL.D. 1811; ensign 1 Foot Guards 1788–92; M.P. for Bury St. Edmunds 27 May 1796 to 8 July 1803 when he succeeded; under sec. of state for foreign affairs 20 Feb. 1801 to 8 Nov. 1803; F.R.S. 23 May 1805; created Marquis of Bristol and Earl Jermyn of Horning's Heath, Suffolk 30 June 1826. *d.* 6 St. James's sq. London 15 Feb. 1859. *Doyle's Official baronage of England i*, 242 (1886), *portrait.*

BRISTOL, Frederick William Hervey, 2 Marquis of (*eld. son of the preceding*). *b.* Portland place, London 15 July 1800; ed. at Trin. coll. Cam., M.A. 1822, LL.D. 1862; M.P. for Bury St. Edmunds 12 June 1826 to 15 Feb. 1859 when he succeeded; treasurer of Royal household 9 Sep. 1841 to 6 July 1846; P.C. 6 Oct. 1841; colonel of West Suffolk militia 25 March 1846 to death. *d.* Ickworth park, Bury St. Edmunds 30 Oct. 1864.

BRISTOW, Alfred Rhodes (*youngest son of Isaac Bristow of Greenwich, government contractor*). *b.* Greenwich 20 Dec. 1819; ed. at King's college London; admitted solicitor 1842, head of firm of Bristow and Tarrant of London and Greenwich; represented Greenwich and Deptford at Metropolitan Board of Works 1856–62; solicitor to the Admiralty 1862 to death;

Bristow, A. R. (*Con.*) barrister G.I. 17 Nov. 1868; M.P. for Kidderminster 30 April 1859 to May 1862; treasurer of Westminster Chess Club Oct. 1870 to death; fell down dead on leaving railway station at Sydenham 5 April 1875. *Westminster Papers viii*, 14 (1876), *portrait.*

BRISTOW, Henry. *b.* 1786; cornet 1 Life Guards 14 Feb. 1805; major 11 Foot 20 Jany. 1814 to 27 April 1815 when placed on h.p.; M.G. 20 June 1854. *d.* Madrid 22 Nov. 1874.

BRISTOWE, Edmund (*son of Mr. Bristowe of Windsor, heraldic printer*). *b.* Windsor 1 April 1787; made sketches of public characters in Eton and Windsor; exhibited 7 pictures at R.A., 12 at B.I. and 8 at Suffolk st. gallery 1809–38; some of his works are in the royal collection at Windsor. *d.* Eton 12 Feb. 1876.

BRITTAIN, Thomas. *b.* Sheffield 2 Jany. 1806; a professional accountant; lived at Manchester about 1842 to death; lectured on natural science at mechanics' and similar institutions; vice. pres. of Manchester Microscopical Society 1879, then pres.; author of *Half a dozen songs by Brittannicus* 1846 privately printed; *Micro-fungi, when and where to find them* 1882; *Whist, how to play and how to win* 1882. *d.* Manchester 23 Jany. 1884. *Axon's Field Naturalist* (1882), *p.* 148; *Unitarian Herald* 1 Feb. 1884.

BRITTON, John (*eld. son of Mr. Britton of Kington St. Michael near Chippenham Wilts., farmer*). *b.* Kington St. Michael 7 July 1771; author of *The beauties of Wiltshire* 3 vols. 1801–25; *The architectural antiquities of Great Britain* 4 vols. 1805–14; *Cathedral antiquities of England* 14 vols. 1814–35; *Dictionary of the architecture and archæology of the middle ages* 4 parts 1830–8; edited with E. W. Brayley *The beauties of England and Wales* 10 vols. 1801–14; granted civil list pension of £75, 5 April 1852. *d.* Burton cottage Burton st. London 1 Jany. 1857. *Autobiography of John Britton* 1850; *G.M. ii*, 126, 185–92, 258 (1857).

BRIZZI, Signor, stage name of Francesco Achille Scipione Bisteghi (*son of Giovanni Bisteghi, general in army of Napoleon I*). *b.* Milan 16 April 1810; pupil at Royal Academy of Music, London Sep. 1828 to Dec. 1831; fought in Piedmontese army against the Austrians 1848; greatly assisted Benjamin Lumley in organising new company for Her Majesty's theatre London 1855, director of the company on its Continental tour 1856. d. 47 Grove road, Regent's park, London 24 Aug. 1884. *Illust. sporting and dramatic news xxii*, 27 (1884).

BROADBRIDGE, WILLIAM. b. Duncton near Petworth, Sussex 1 Oct. 1790; a farmer there; played in cricket matches 1813–40; played his first match at Lords (Sussex *v.* Epsom) 2–6 July 1817 when 1047 runs were made altogether, being largest number ever made down to 1861 or later; a good batsman and wicket keeper; in a match Sussex *v.* Hampshire and Surrey 7 Aug. 1826 he performed extraordinary feat of stumping 7 men and catching 2. d. Duncton 19 April 1860.

BROADHEAD, HENRY (6 *son of Theodore Henry Broadhead of Holly Grove, Windsor, M.P.* 1767–1820). b. 25 April 1806; entered navy 6 April 1820; captain 27 June 1846; admiral on half pay 1 Aug. 1877. d. Walton on Thames 20 May 1878.

BROADHEAD, WILLIAM. Secretary of Saw Grinders Union at Sheffield from 1848 in connection with which a great many outrages were committed; treasurer of United Kingdom Alliance of organised trades; kept an inn in Carver st. Sheffield to 22 Aug. 1867 when magistrates refused to renew his license; went to America Nov. 1869 but failed to find employment there; lectured upon his own career; a grocer in Meadow st. Sheffield to death; he is the villain under name of Grotait of Charles Reade's novel *Put yourself in his place.* d. Meadow st. Sheffield 15 March 1879 aged about 60. *Sheffield Daily Telegraph 17 March 1879 p. 4, col. 2; Trades unions commission, Sheffield outrages inquiry vol. 2 Minutes of evidence* (1867) 222–51.

BROADLEY, HENRY. b. 1793; chairman of Hull and Selby railway 1836–43; M.P. for east riding of Yorkshire 10 Aug. 1837 to death. d. 3 Charles st. St. James's square, London 8 Aug. 1851 in 58 year. *bur.* Holy Trinity church Hull 16 Aug.

BROCK, THOMAS SAUMAREZ. Entered navy 9 Feb. 1815; captain 13 Nov. 1850; held possession of Eupatoria against the Russians 15 Sep. 1854 to 25 Dec. 1854; superintendent agent of transports at Genoa 15 March 1855; retired R.A. 20 March 1867; C.B. 5 July 1855; knight of St. Maurice and Lazare 1856. d. The hermitage, Guernsey 28 April 1873 in 73 year.

BROCK, REV. WILLIAM (*eld. child of Wm. Brock of Honiton, Devon, Unitarian baptist who d.* 20 *June* 1811). b. Honiton 14 Feb. 1807; ed. at Culmstock and Honiton; apprenticed to a watchmaker at Sidmouth Sep. 1820 to March 1828; a journeyman watchmaker at Hertford 1828–29; studied at Derby and Stepney baptist college; pastor of baptist chapel in parish of St. Mary's Norwich 1833–48; pastor of Bloomsbury chapel London 5 Dec. 1848 to 30 Sep. 1872; D. D. Harvard 1859; held his first service in London theatres, at the Britannia theatre Hoxton 18 Dec. 1859; pres. of London Baptist association Nov. 1865; went to the United States 1866; pres. of Baptist Union of Great Britain and Ireland 1869; author of *Fraternal appeals to young men; Sacramental religion* 1850; *A biographical sketch of Sir Henry Havelock* 1858; *Midsummer morning sermons* 1872. d. Orwell house, St. Leonards 13 Nov. 1875. *Life of W. Brock by C. M. Birrell* 1878, *portrait; W. Brock by G. W. M'Cree* 1876; *Rev. C. M. Davies's Unorthodox London* (1873) 81–88; *I.L.N. lxvii*, 537, 590 (1875), *portrait; Graphic xi*, 518, 533 (1875), *portrait.*

BROCK, REV. WILLIAM JOHN (*eld. son of John Brock of George st. Portman sq. London*). b. about 1818; ed. at Magd. hall Ox.; C. of St. George's, Barnsley 1852; P.C. of Hayfield, Derbyshire 1856 to death; author of *Wayside verses* 1848; *Twenty seven sermons* 1855, 2 ed. 1858; *The rough wind stayed* 1867; *The bright light in the clouds* 1870. d. Hayfield 27 April 1863 aged 45.

BROCKEDON, WILLIAM (*only child of Mr. Brockedon of Totnes, Devon, watchmaker who d. Sep.* 1802). b. Totnes 13 Oct. 1787; watchmaker at Totnes 1802–7; studied at R.A. London 1809–15; painted "The resurrection of the widow's son" which obtained premium of £105 from British Institution 1818 and was presented by him to Dartmouth church; patented plan of using drilled gems in wire drawing 1819 universally adopted; founded Graphic Society 1831 an association of 100 artists of reputation; F.R.S. 18 Dec. 1834; exhibited 36 pictures at R.A. and 29 at B.I. 1812–37; author of *Illustrations of the passes of the Alps* 2 vols. 1828–9; *Journals of excursions in the Alps* 1833; *Italy classical historical and picturesque* 1842–4; edited *Illustrated road book from London to Naples* 1835. d. 29 Devonshire st. Queen sq. Bloomsbury, London 29 Aug. 1854. *G.M. xlii*, 521–3 (1854); *Journal of Royal Geog. Soc. xxv*, 84 (1855).

BROCKET, STANES BROCKETT (*eld. son of Stanes Chamberlayne of the Ryes, Essex who d. 12 April 1834 in 89 year*). *b.* 9 April 1782; barrister M.T. 29 May 1812, bencher 1841 to death; assumed surname of Brocket, May 1834; sheriff of Essex 1844. *d.* Spain's hall near Ongar 2 March 1873.

BROCKETT, WILLIAM HENRY (*youngest son of John Brockett of Newcastle*). *b.* Jany. 1804; merchant at Gateshead; mayor of Gateshead 1839; sole proprietor of *Gateshead Observer*; sec. to Newcastle and Gateshead Chamber of commerce; author of *The tradesmens tokens of Durham and Northumberland* 1851; *The tradesmens tokens of Cumberland and Westmoreland* 1853; *The tradesmens tokens of Derbyshire* 1857. *d.* Gateshead 15 Jany. 1867. *G.M. iii*, 264 (1867).

BROCKLEHURST, JOHN (*son of John Brocklehurst of Jordan gate house Macclesfield*). *b.* 30 Oct. 1788; a silk manufacturer and banker at Macclesfield; pres. of Macclesfield institution; M.P. for Macclesfield 14 Dec. 1832 to 11 Nov. 1868. *d.* London 13 Aug. 1870. Personalty sworn under £800,000, 22 Oct. 1870.

BROCKMAN, EDWARD DRAKE (*youngest child of James Drake Brockman of Beachborough near Hythe, Kent who d. 28 June 1832*). Barrister I.T. 29 June 1819; recorder of Folkestone 1833; M.P. for Hythe 31 July 1847 to 21 March 1857. *d.* Beachborough 7 Nov. 1858.

BROCKY, CHARLES. *b.* Temeswar in the Banat Hungary 1807; studied painting in Vienna and Paris; portrait and subject painter in London; exhibited 43 picturers at R.A. and 16 at B.I. 1839–54; painted portraits of the Queen, Prince Consort, Lord Melbourne and other celebrities; left 5 pictures to his native country which are in the Musée at Pesth. *d.* London 8 July 1855. *N. Wilkinson's Sketch of the life of C. Brocky* 1870.

BRODERIP, FRANCES FREELING (2 *dau.* of *Thomas Hood the poet* 1798–1845). *b.* Winchmore Hill, Middlesex 1830; granted civil list pension of £50, 4 Oct. 1847; author of *Wayside Fancies* 1857; *Funny fables for little folks* 1860; *Chrysal, or a story with an end* 1861 and many other childrens' books. (*m.* 10 Sep. 1849 Rev. John Somerville Broderip R. of Cossington Somerset, he was *b.* 1814 and *d.* 10 April 1866). *d.* Clevedon, Somerset 3 Nov. 1878.

BRODERIP, WILLIAM JOHN (*eld. child of Wm. Broderip of Bristol, surgeon*). *b.* Princes st. Bristol 21 Nov. 1789; ed. at Bristol and Oriel coll. Ox., B.A. 1812; pupil of Godfrey Sykes; barrister L.I. 12 May 1817; magistrate at Thames police court 1822–46, and at Westminster police court 1846 to Dec. 1855; bencher of Grays Inn 30 Jany. 1850, treasurer 29 Jany. 1851; F.L.S. 1824; F.G.S. 1825, co-secretary to 1830; a founder of Zoological Society 1826; F.R.S. 14 Feb. 1828; his unrivalled conchological cabinet was purchased by British Museum; edited with P. Bingham *Reports of cases in the Court of Common Pleas and other courts* 3 vols. 1820–2; author of *Zoological recreations* 1847; *Leaves from the note book of a naturalist* 1852. *d.* 2 Raymond's buildings, Grays Inn, London 27 Feb. 1859. *Berger's W. J. Broderip, ancien magistrat, naturaliste, litterateur*, Paris 1856; *Fraser's Mag. lix*, 485–8 (1859); *I.L.N. ix*, 317 (1846) *portrait, xxviii*, 253 (1856), *portrait*; *Law mag. and law review viii*, 174–8 (1859).

BRODIE, ALEXANDER (*son of Wm. Brodie of Chesterhill, Roxburghshire*). Author of *A history of the Roman government* 1810; *The prophetess, a tale of the last century in Italy* 3 vols. [*anon.*] 1826. *d.* The Whim house, Peebleshire 13 March 1858.

BRODIE, ALEXANDER (*younger son of John Brodie of Aberdeen, mariner*). *b.* Aberdeen 1830; apprenticed in foundry of Messrs. Blaikie Brothers of Aberdeen brass-finishers; sculptor at Aberdeen about 1858 to death; very successful in bust-portraiture and medallions; his best known statues are those of Duke of Richmond at Huntly and Queen Victoria at Aberdeen. *d.* Aberdeen 30 May 1867.

BRODIE, SIR BENJAMIN COLLINS, 1 Baronet (3 *son of Rev. Peter Bellinger Brodie* 1742–1804, *R. of Winterslow, Wilts.*) *b.* Winterslow 9 June 1783; studied at St. George's hospital London 1803–5, assistant surgeon 1808 and surgeon 1822 to Jany. 1840; teacher of anatomy in Windmill st. school 1805–12 and lecturer on surgery 1808–29; F.R.S. 15 Feb. 1810, Copley medallist 1811 and pres. 1858–61; professor of comparative anatomy and physiology at College of Surgeons 1819–23 and pres. 1844; surgeon to George iv, 11 Aug. 1828; serjeant surgeon to Wm. iv, 5 Sep. 1832; presented his pathological museum to St. George's hospital 1829; created baronet 30 Aug. 1834; author of *Pathological and surgical observations on diseases of the joints* 1818, 3 ed. 1834; *Lectures on the diseases of*

BRODIE, SIR B. C. *(Con.)*

the urinary organs 1832, 4 *ed.* 1849 and many other books. *d.* Broome park, Surrey 21 Oct. 1862. *Autobiography of the late Sir B. C. Brodie* 1865; *Proc. of royal society xii,* 42–56 (1863); *Pettigrew's Medical portrait gallery ii,* (1840), *portrait; Taylor's National portrait gallery i,* 41 (1846), *portrait.*

BRODIE, SIR BENJAMIN COLLINS, 2 Baronet *(eld. son of the preceding). b.* Sackville st. Piccadilly, London 5 Feb. 1817; ed. at Harrow and Ball. coll. Ox., B.A. 1838, hon. D.C.L. 1872; studied chemistry at Giessen 1845; propounded doctrine of polarity of chemical elements 1847; sec. of Chemical Soc. of London 1850–4, pres. 1859–61; F.R.S. 7 June 1849, Royal medallist 1850; lecturer at Royal Institution 1851; Aldrichian prof. of chemistry at Ox. 1855–66 when professorship was suppressed, and Waynflete prof. of chemistry 1865–72; discovered graphitic acid. *d.* Torquay 24 Nov. 1880. *Journal of Chemical Soc. xxxix,* 182–5 (1881).

BRODIE, GEORGE *(youngest son of Wm. Brodie of Chesterhill, East Lothian, farmer). b.* Chesterhill 1786; ed. at high sch. and Univ. of Edin.; member of faculty of advocates 1811; historiographer royal of Scotland 1836 to death; author of *A history of the British empire from the accession of Charles I to the Restoration* 4 vols. 1822, new ed. 3 vols. 1866; edited *Stair's Institutes of the law of Scotland.* *d.* Percy house, Randolph road, London 22 Jany. 1867.

BRODIE, JAMES CAMPBELL JOHN. *b.* 26 March 1848; ed. at Rugby and St. Andrew's; lord lieutenant of Nairnshire 26 June 1873 to death. *d.* Moss close, Manor road, Bournemouth 25 Feb. 1880.

BRODIE, JOHN. *b.* Edinburgh; served at hospital Scutari during Russian war; went to New York 1869; city editor of *New York Dispatch;* contributed largely to columns of the *Spirit of the Times. d.* New York 29 Jany. 1873 aged 32.

BRODIE, PETER BELLINGER *(brother of Sir B. C. Brodie, 1 Baronet). b.* Winterslow, Wilts. 20 Aug. 1778; pupil of Charles Butler; a conveyancer; barrister I.T. 5 May 1815; drew charter of King's College London 1829; a real property comr. 1828, drew the part relating to Fines and Recoveries of first report made May 1829, the part relating to Probate of wills of second report made June 1830, and the part relating to Copyhold and Ancient Demesne made April 1833; drew bill for abolishing Fines and Recoveries

BRODIE, P. B. *(Con.)*

which became law 1833; author of *A treatise on a tax on successions to real as well as personal property* 1850. *d.* 49 Lincoln's Inn Fields, London 8 Sep. 1854. *Law Review xxi,* 348–54 (1855).

BRODIE, WILLIAM. *b.* 2 July 1799; ed. at King's coll. Aberdeen; lord lieutenant of Nairnshire 1824 to death. *d.* Brodie castle, Forres, Morayshire 6 June 1873.

BRODIE, WILLIAM *(brother of Alexander Brodie 1830–67). b.* Banff 22 Jany. 1815; studied in the Trustees school of design, Edinburgh 1846–52; an associate of Royal Scottish Academy 1857, member 1859, sec. 8 Nov. 1876; executed portrait busts of most of the celebrities of his day; executed 4 busts of the Queen, colossal statue of Prince Consort at Perth, and one of the representative groups in bronze, for Scottish memorial to Prince Consort in Edin. *d.* Douglas lodge, Edin. 30 Oct. 1881. *Biograph ii,* 218 (1879).

BRODIE, WILLIAM BIRD. *b.* 26 Sep. 1780; a banker at Salisbury; M.P. for Salisbury 14 Dec. 1832 to April 1843. *d.* Swanage, Dorset 24 Oct. 1863.

BRODRIBB, WILLIAM PERRIN. Pupil of Abernethy at St. Bartholomew's hospital London; L.S.A. 1822, M.R.C.S. 1823, L.R.C.P. Edin. 1859; surgeon to Magdalen hospital, London; chairman of court of examiners of Society of Apothecaries 1860–1, sec. to the court 1865 to death. *d.* 7 Bloomsbury sq. London 8 Jany. 1869 aged 68.

BROGDEN, REV. JAMES. Educ. at Trin. coll. Cam., B.A. 1830, M.A. 1833; R. of Great Henny, Essex 1841–5; C. of St. Michaels, St. Albans 1845–8-; V. of Deddington, Oxon 1848 to death; author of *Illustrations of the liturgy and ritual of the united church of England and Ireland* 3 vols. 1842; *Catholic safeguards against the errors, novelties, and corruptions of the church of Rome* 3 vols. 1851. *d.* Deddington 11 Feb. 1864 aged 58.

BROKE, SIR ARTHUR BROOKE DE CAPELL, 2 Baronet *(elder son of Sir Richard Brooke-Supple, 1 baronet 1758–1829). b.* Bolton st. Piccadilly, London 22 Oct. 1791; ed. at Magd. coll. Ox., B.A. 1813, M.A. 1816; captain 17 Dragoons 26 Feb. 1818 placed on h.p. same date; changed his name from Brooke to Broke; F.R.S. 29 May 1823; founded the Raleigh Club, (forerunner of Royal Geographical Society), first regular meeting took place at the Thatched house 7 Feb. 1827, in 1854 the name of Raleigh was dropped and it became

BROKE, SIR A. B. DE C. *(Con.)*

Geographical club; succeeded 27 Nov. 1829; sheriff of Northamptonshire 1843; author of *Travels through Sweden, Norway and Finmark to the North Cape* 1823; *A winter in Lapland and Sweden* 1827; *Sketches in Spain and Morocco* 2 vols. 1831. *d.* Oakley hall near Kettering 6 Dec. 1858. *C. Markham's Fifty years work of the Royal Geographical Society* (1881) 15–18.

BROKE, CHARLES ACTON. *b.* 30 June 1818; 2 lieut. R.E. 18 June 1836, captain 17 Feb. 1854 to death; quartered in island of Zante; well known to all H.M.'s ships, merchantships and yachts as "Signal Broke" as he challenged all vessels passing Zante from the signal posts and extracted news from them; supported 40 or 50 starving families in Zante during winters of 1852–54. *d.* Ayr 7 Sep. 1855.

BROKE, HORATIO GEORGE. *b.* 4 June 1790; captain 58 Foot 18 March 1813 to 25 Feb. 1816 when placed on h.p.; permanent assistant quartermaster general 4 July 1823; deputy quartermaster general Nova Scotia 20 July 1830 to 12 Sep. 1834; aide-de-camp to the Queen 23 Nov. 1841 to 20 June 1854; colonel 88 Foot 24 Dec. 1858 to death; L.G. 15 June 1860. *d.* Gloucester place, Portman sq. London 30 Aug. 1860.

BROKE, SIR PHILIP VERE, 2 Baronet. *b.* 15 Jany. 1804; entered navy Dec. 1819; captain 12 Sep. 1835; succeeded 2 June 1841; sheriff of Suffolk 1844. *d.* Broke hall near Ipswich 24 Feb. 1855.

BROKE, SIR WILLIAM DE CAPELL, 3 Baronet. *b.* Deal, Kent 12 June 1801; ed. at Rugby and Brasn. coll. Ox., B.A. 1822, M.A. 1835; barrister I.T. 25 May 1827; sheriff of Rutland 1852; succeeded 6 Dec. 1858. *d.* The Elms, Market Harborough 8 March 1886. *Law Times lxxx,* 364 (1886).

BROMBY, REV. JOHN HEALEY. *b.* 1771; ed. at Hull gr. sch. and Sid. Suss. coll. Cam., 17 wrangler 1792, B.A. 1792, M.A. 1795, fellow of his coll.; V. of Trinity, Hull 1797–1866; V of Cheswardine, Salop 1821–67; master of the Charterhouse, Hull 1849 to death; author of various sermons, essays and lectures published in Hull. *d.* Hull 25 March 1868, the oldest clergyman in Church of England.

BROME, FREDERICK. Governor of military prison on Windmill hill, Gibraltar 1846 to Dec. 1868, and of military prison at Weedon Northampton 1869 which was abolished same year; well known as a palæontologist. *d.* 4 March 1870. *Nature i,* 509 (1870).

BROMEHEAD, REV. WILLIAM CRAWFORD *(youngest son of Rev. A. C. Bromehead of Newbold, Warws.)* Educ. at Repton and Trin. coll. Cam., scholar, B.A. 1849, M.A. 1853, B.D. 1879, chaplain of his college 1857–9; chaplain in Bengal 1859–79; one of founders of Indian church aid association and the first hon. sec.; chaplain in ord. at Kensington palace, London 8 July 1879 to death; author of *A short account of the lives of the bishops of Calcutta* 1876; *Step by step or the devout communicant led through the Church to the vision of God* 1878. *d.* Kensington palace 6 May 1884 aged 59.

BROMFIELD, WILLIAM ARNOLD *(son of Rev. John Arnold Bromfield of Boldre in the New Forest who d. 1801).* *b.* Boldre 1801; entered Univ. of Glasgow 1821, M.D. 1823; travelled through Germany, Italy and France 1826–30; went to West Indies 1844 and to North America 1846; embarked for the East, Sep. 1850; author of *List of plants likely to be found wild in the Isle of Wight* 1840; *Botanico-topographical map of the Isle of Wight* 1850; *Letters from Egypt and Syria* 1856. *d.* of malignant typhus fever at Damascus 9 Oct. 1851. *Hooker's Kew garden miscell. iii,* 373–82 (1851); *Proc. of Linnæan Soc. ii,* 182–3 (1855); *W. A. Bromfield's Flora Vectensis* 1856, *portrait.*

BROMHEAD, SIR EDMUND GONVILLE, 3 Baronet. *b.* Birch grove, Ballinasloe 22 Jany. 1791; ensign 8 Foot 18 Jany. 1808; lieut. 54 Foot 23 March 1809; captain 19 Foot 21 Nov. 1822 to 13 May 1826 when placed on h.p. as major; served in Walcheren expedition, the Peninsula and at Waterloo; led the forlorn hope at Cambray 24 June 1815; succeeded 14 March 1855. *d.* Thurlby hall near Lincoln 25 Oct 1870.

BROMHEAD, SIR EDWARD THOMAS FFRENCH, 2 Baronet *(eldest son of Sir Gonville Bromhead, 1 baronet 1758–1822).* *b.* Dublin 26 March 1789; ed. at Gonville and Caius. coll. Cam., B.A. 1812, M.A. 1815; barrister I.T. 28 May 1813; succeeded 11 May 1822; F.R.S. 13 March 1817, F.L.S. 1844. *d.* Thurlby hall 14 March 1855.

BROMLEY, SIR RICHARD MADOX *(2 son of Samuel Bromley, Surgeon R.N. who d. 1835).* *b.* 11 June 1813; ed. at Lewisham gr. sch.; entered Admiralty department of Civil service 1829; sec. to Comrs. for auditing public accounts 6 June 1848 to Feb. 1854; accountant general of the Navy Feb. 1854 to March 1863; comr. of Greenwich hospital 28 March 1863 to death; C.B. 13 Sep. 1854, K.C.B. 6 Sep. 1858. *d.* The Marina, St. Leonard's-on-Sea 30 Nov. 1865.

BROMLEY, Sir Robert Howe, 3 Baronet *(only son of Sir George Smith, 2 baronet 1753– 1808, who assumed surname of Bromley 1778). b.* Stoke near Newark 28 Nov. 1778; entered navy 26 Dec. 1791; captain 28 April 1802; placed on h.p. 1809; admiral 17 Aug. 1851; succeeded his father 17 Aug. 1808. *d.* Stoke 8 July 1857.

BROMLEY, Valentine Walter *(eld. son of Wm. Bromley of St. John's Wood, London). b.* London 14 Feb. 1848; contributed many illustrations to *Illustrated London News;* an associate of Institute of painters in water colours; exhibited 5 pictures at R.A. and 22 at Suffolk st. gallery 1865–77; his picture of Troilus and Cressida is engraved in *Art Journal* 1873. *d.* Fallows Green, Harpenden 30 April 1877. *I.L.N. lxx*, 469 (1877), *portrait.*

BROMLEY-DAVENPORT, William *(eld. son of Rev. Walter Davenport-Bromley of Wooton hall, Staffs.* 1787–1862). *b.* Capesthorn near Crewe 20 Aug. 1821; ed. at Harrow and Ch. Ch. Ox.; lieut. col. Staffordshire yeomanry cavalry 13 July 1864 to death; M.P. for North Warwickshire Dec. 1864 to death; assumed name of Bromley-Davenport in lieu of Davenport-Bromley 1868; aide-de-camp to the Queen 15 Aug. 1883 to death; author of many hunting songs and of an article entitled *Fox hunting* in *The Nineteenth Century* June 1883. *d.* Lichfield 15 June 1884. *Waagen's Treasures of art iii*, 371–80 (1854); *I.L.N. lxxxv*, 629 (1884), *portrait; Baily's Mag. xlii*, 385 (1884).

BRONTE, Charlotte Mary Hood, Duchess of *(only dau. of Wm. Nelson, 1 Earl Nelson* 1757–1835). *b.* 20 Sep. 1787; succeeded her father as Duchess of Bronte in Sicily 28 Feb. 1835. *(m.* 3 July 1810 Samuel Hood, 2 Baron Bridport 1788–1868). *d.* Cricket, St. Thomas 29 Jany. 1873. *Earl Nelson v. Lord Bridport, 6 Beavan, Reports in Chancery* 295– 305 (1845); 7 *Beavan* 195–202 (1846); 8 *Beavan* 527–74 (1847).

BRONTE, Charlotte *(3 child of the succeeding). b.* Hartshead 21 April 1816; ed. at Cowan's Bridge, Yorkshire 1824–5, and at Miss Wooler's school Roehead, Yorkshire 1831–2 where she was teacher 29 July 1835 to Dec. 1837; learnt French in Brussels 1842–3. *(m.* 19 June 1854 Rev. Arthur Bell Nicholls, C. of Haworth); author with her sisters Emily and Anne of *Poems by Currer, Ellis and Acton Bell* 1846; *Jane Eyre an autobiography edited by Currer Bell* 3 vols. 1847; *Shirley, a tale by Currer Bell* 3 vols. 1849; *Villette by Currer Bell* 3 vols. 1853; *The professor, a tale* [edited

Bronte, C. *(Con.)*
by *A. B. Nicholls*] 2 vols. 1857. *d.* Haworth parsonage 31 March 1855. *Mrs. Gaskell's Life of C. Bronte 2 vols.* 1857, *portrait; C. Bronte, a monograph by T. W. Reid* 1877; *The Bronte family by F. A. Leyland* 1886; *G. B. Smith's Poets and novelists* (1875) 207–50; *W. Smith's Old Yorkshire* (1883) 124–30, *portrait; P. Bayne's Two great Englishwomen* (1881) 155– 340; *Illust. Review iv*, 257–65, *portrait.*

BRONTE, Rev. Patrick *(son of Hugh Prunty of Ahaderg, Downshire). b.* Ahaderg 17 March 1777; opened a school at Drumgooland, Downshire 1793; changed his name to Bronte about 1801; entered St. John's coll. Cam. Oct. 1802, B.A. 1806; ordained to a curacy in Essex; C. of Hartshead, Yorkshire 1811; P.C. of Thornton near Bradford 1814–20; Inc. of Haworth near Bradford 25 Feb. 1820 to death; author of *Cottage poems* 1811; *The rural minstrel* 1813 and of a tract called, *The cottage in a wood, or the art of becoming rich and happy* 1818 *reprinted* 1859, he is partly represented as Mr. Helstone in his daughter's novel *Shirley. d.* Haworth parsonage 7 June 1861. *Dict. of nat. biog. vi*, 406–13 (1886).

BROOK, Charles *(son of James Brook of Huddersfield, banker and cotton spinner at Meltham). b.* Upperhead row, Huddersfield 18 Nov. 1814; partner with his father 1840; made many improvements in machinery; founded Convalescent Home at Huddersfield at cost of £40,000 where there is a portrait of him by Samuel Howell; purchased Enderby hall near Leicester 1865 at cost of £150,000; rebuilt Enderby church 1865. *d.* Enderby hall 10 July 1872.

BROOKE, Sir Arthur Brinsley, 2 Baronet. *b.* 1797; succeeded 24 March 1834; M.P. for co. Fermanagh 30 April 1840 to death. *d.* Colebrooke, co. Fermanagh 20 Nov. 1854.

BROOKE, Charles. *b.* in the Mint Exeter 8 Aug. 1777; ed. at English academy Liege; took part in emigration to Stonyhurst 1794; ordained at Maynooth 12 June 1802; entered Society of Jesus at Hodder Place near Stonyhurst 26 Sep. 1803; missioner at Clayton, Enfield Sep. 1817; provincial 1826–32; superior of Seminary adjacent to Stonyhurst college 30 July 1834; visitor of Ireland June 1842 to July 1843; rector of St. Aloysius' college 1843–5; sent to Exeter 11 Sep. 1845 to gather materials for continuation of history of English province of Society of Jesus from 1635. *d.* in same room in which he had been born at Exeter 6 Oct. 1852.

BROOKE, CHARLES *(son of Henry James Brooke 1771–1857). b.* 30 June 1804 ; ed. at Chiswick, Rugby and St. John's coll. Cam., 23 wrangler 1827, B.A. 1827, B.M. 1828, M.A. 1853 ; M.R.C.S. 1834, F.R.C.S. 1844 ; pres. of Meteorological and Microscopical Societies ; invented the bead suture, a great improvement in treatment of deep wounds ; invented self recording meteorological instruments which register their variations by means of photography ; fellow of Royal Med. and Chir. Soc. 1844, councillor, librarian and vice. pres. successively ; F.R.S. 4 March 1847 ; author of *A synopsis of the principal formulæ and results of pure mathematics* 1829 ; edited Golding Bird's *Elements of natural philosophy* 4 ed. 1854, 5 ed. 1860, *and* 6 ed .1867. *d.* Weymouth 17 May 1879. *Proc. of Royal Soc. xxx*, 1–2 (1880).

BROOKE, EDWARD BASIL. *b.* 1799 ; 2 lieut. R.A. 15 Dec. 1817 ; lieut. col. 67 Foot 9 Nov. 1846 to 31 Dec. 1858 ; inspecting field officer 31 Dec. 1858 ; M.G. 1 May 1861. *d.* London 1 Dec. 1868.

BROOKE, EDWIN HARCOURT, stage name of Edward James Macdonald Brook. *b.* Buckinghamshire 12 June 1843 ; ed. at City of London School ; made his first appearance in London at Princess's theatre 10 July 1862 as Lord Chamberlain in *Henry the Eighth* ; acted at Sadlers Wells theatre, Prince's theatre Manchester, Glasgow 2 seasons, Alexandra theatre Liverpool nearly 3 years ; played Bassanio in *The Merchant of Venice* at Prince of Wales's theatre London April 1875 ; played at Lyceum theatre 2 years where he acted Simon Renard in Tennyson's *Queen Mary* April 1876 ; played title role in *The Silver King* in the provinces more than 400 times 1883–4 ; author of *Gustave* produced at Alexandra theatre Liverpool about 1876 ; of a comedietta called *Bessie* produced at Royalty theatre ; and of an adaptation of *David Copperfield. d.* 1 Bullen road, Clapham Junction, London 30 Nov. 1884. *Biograph vi*, 582–4 (1881).

BROOKE, FRANCIS CAPPER *(only son of Rev. Charles Brooke of Ufford, Suffolk 1765–1836). b.* 18 Sep. 1810 ; ed. at Harrow and Ch. Ch. Ox., B.A. 1831 ; sheriff of Suffolk 1869 ; one of earliest contributors to *Notes and Queries* under initials F.C.B. ; collected a fine library of 20,000 volumes at Ufford ; author of *Sepulchral memorials of the Cobham family* 1874. *d.* Ufford 13 Jany. 1886.

BROOKE, SIR GEORGE. *b.* 1793 ; 2 lieut. Bengal artillery 8 Sep. 1808, col. com-

BROOKE, SIR G. *(Con.)*
mandant 21 July 1851 to 1 Oct. 1877 when placed on retired list ; general 24 May 1870 ; C.B. 3 April 1846, K.C.B. 13 March 1867. *d.* Charles st. St. James's London 31 Dec. 1882. *I.L.N. lxxxii*, 149 (1883), *portrait.*

BROOKE, GEORGE WILLIAM. Secretary of London, Chatham and Dover railway company 1868 to death. *d.* West hill, Sydenham 21 Feb. 1876.

BROOKE, GUSTAVUS VAUGHAN *(son of Gustavus Vaughan Brooke of Dublin). b.* Hardwick place, Dublin 25 April 1818 ; ed. at Edgeworthstown ; first appeared on the stage, at T.R. Dublin 9 April 1833 as William Tell ; played in Ireland and Scotland ; first appeared in London, at Victoria theatre as Virginius 1837 ; acted in United States 1851–3 ; manager of Astor opera house New York May 1852 ; played in Australia and New Zealand at large salary of £100 a night 1855–7 ; partner with George Coppin in T.R. Melbourne and Melbourne Cremorne in which he lost all his money, they dissolved partnership Feb. 1859 ; drowned in the London in Bay of Biscay on his way to Australia 10 Jany. 1866. *Longman's Mag. March* 1885, 490–501 ; *Theatrical times iii*, 18, 49 (1848), *portrait* ; *Tallis's Drawing room table book* (1851) 41–2, 2 *portraits* ; *Tallis's Illust. Life in London* (1864) 120, 126, 2 *portraits* ; *I.L.N. xii*, 12, 91 (1848), 2 *portraits.*

BROOKE, HENRY FRANCIS *(eld. son of George Brooke of Ashbrooke, co. Fermanagh). b.* 3 Aug. 1836 ; ensign 48 Foot 6 June 1854 ; served in Crimea and China ; adjutant general Bombay army 23 Nov. 1877 to 28 March 1880 ; brigadier general in command of second infantry brigade in Kandahar 28 March 1880 to death ; killed at Maiwand in a sortie from Kandahar 16 Aug. 1880, *bur.* in family vault at Colebrooke 14 Dec. *Shadbolt's Afghan campaign* (1882) 24–6, *portrait* ; *I.L.N. lxxvii*, 289 (1880), *portrait.*

BROOKE, HENRY JAMES *(son of Mr. Brooke of Exeter, broadcloth manufacturer). b.* Exeter 25 May 1771 ; a trader in Spanish wool in London 1802 ; established companies to work mines of South America ; actuary and sec. to London Life association to 1843 ; F.G.S. 1815 ; F.L.S. 1818 ; F.R.S. 22 April 1819, member of council 1842–44 ; his unrivalled collection of minerals was presented to Univ. of Cam. ; discovered 13 new mineral species ; author of *A familiar introduction to Crystallography* 1823 ; edited with extensive alterations and additions *An elementary introduction*

BROOKE, H. J. *(Con.)*

to *Mineralogy by W. Phillips* 1852. *d.* Clapham Rise, Surrey 26 June 1857. *Proc. of Royal Soc. ix*, 41–4 (1857); *Quarterly Journal of Geological Soc. xiv*, 44–45 (1858).

BROOKE, HENRY VAUGHAN. *b.* 11 Nov. 1808; ensign 32 Foot 12 July 1827, lieut. col. 13 Sep. 1848 to 24 July 1857; C.B. 9 June 1849; aide-de-camp to the Queen 20 June 1854 to death. *d.* Holyhead 15 Sep. 1858.

BROOKE, SIR JAMES (2 *son of Thomas Brooke of Widcombe crescent, Bath who d.* 1835). *b.* Secrole now called Secrore the European suburb of Benares 29 April 1803; ed. at Norwich gr. sch.; in the Bengal army 1819–30; sailed for Borneo in a schooner of his own 16 Dec. 1838; subdued insurrection in Borneo 1840–1; created Rajah of Sarawak 24 Sep. 1841, formerly installed at Kuching 18 Aug. 1842; suppressed piracy in Malayan Archipelago 1843–9; founded settlement of Labuan in Borneo 2 Dec. 1846; comr. and consul general in Borneo 23 July 1847 to 9 Aug. 1855; admitted to freedom of City of London 29 Oct. 1847; governor of Labuan 27 Nov. 1847 to Feb. 1856; D.C.L. Ox. 25 Nov. 1847; K.C.B. 27 April 1848; left Sarawak April 1863. *d.* Burrator, close to Sheepstor, Dartmoor, Devon 11 June 1868 an estate which was purchased for him by public subscription 1859. *The private letters of Sir J. Brooke edited by J. C. Templer 3 vols.* 1853; *The life of Sir J. Brooke by S. St. John* 1879, *portrait; G. L. Jacob's Rajah of Sarawak 2 vols.* 1876, *portrait; Illust. news of the world ii,* 380 (1858), *portrait; I.L.N. xi,* 233 (1847), *portrait.*

BROOKE, JAMES CROFT. Ensign 31 Foot 31 Oct. 1831; major 8 Foot 2 Oct. 1849 to 15 Oct. 1861 when placed on h.p.; M.G. 6 March 1868; C.B. 24 May 1873. *d.* Hastings terrace, Jersey 27 April 1875.

BROOKE, JOHN. Called to Irish bar 1819; Q.C. 1 July 1837; bencher of King's Inns 1859. *d.* 1877.

BROOKE, JOHN BROOKE JOHNSON *(eld. son of Rev. Francis Charles Johnson, V. of White Lackington, Somerset who d.* 22 Dec. 1874 *aged* 78). Ensign 88 Foot 11 Oct. 1839, captain 18 Jany. 1848 to Jany. 1853 when he retired; joined his uncle Sir James Brooke in Sarawak 1848; took his uncle's name of Brooke 1848; member of council of state Sarawak 1855–63; carried on government of Sarawak as Rajah Muda during his uncle's illness 1858; distin-

BROOKE, J. B. J. *(Con.)*

guished for energy with which he suppressed piracy on coast of Borneo. *d.* Hounslow 1 Dec. 1868 aged 45. *Reg. and mag. of biog. i,* 128 (1869).

BROOKE, RICHARD *(son of Richard Brooke of Liverpool who d. 15 June 1852 aged 91). b.* Liverpool 1791; solicitor and notary at Liverpool 1814; member of Liverpool Literary and Philosophical society 12 Nov. 1855, member of council 1860 to death; F.S.A.; author of *Observations illustrative of the accounts given by the ancient historical writers of the battle of Stoke Field* 1825; *A treatise on the office and practice of a Notary of England* 1839, 4 ed. 1876; *Liverpool as it was during the last quarter of the eighteenth century* 1853; *Visits to fields of battle in England of the fifteenth century* 1857. *d.* Liverpool 14 June 1861.

BROOKE, SIR RICHARD, 6 Baronet. *b.* Norton Priory, Cheshire 18 Aug. 1785; succeeded 6 March 1795; sheriff of Cheshire 1817. *d.* Norton Priory 11 Nov. 1865.

BROOKE, REV. RICHARD SINCLAIR. Educ. at Trin. coll. Dublin, B.A. 1827, M.A. 1858, B.D. and D.D. 1860; minister of Mariners' church Kingstown, Dublin 1835–62; R. of Wyton, Hunts. 1862–77; author of *The sheaf of corn, or mornings with a scripture class* 1850; *Poems illustrative of Grace-Creation-Suffering* 1852; *Recollections of the Irish church* 1877. *d.* 11 Herbert st. Dublin 6 Aug. 1882 aged 80.

BROOKE, THOMAS (2 *son of Sir Richard Brooke, 6 Baronet* 1785–1865). *b.* Norton Priory 2 April 1816; ensign 12 Foot 31 Oct. 1834, lieut. col. 19 May 1854 to 22 Feb. 1861 when placed on h.p.; col. 28 Foot 30 Sep. 1878 to death; general 27 April 1879. *d.* 13 Manson place, Queen's gate, London 4 Nov. 1880.

BROOKE, WILLIAM. *b.* Burnham Market, Norfolk 1 Aug. 1795; kept a school at Norwich 1820–65; supplied records of his meteorological observations to local papers and scientific journals 1829 to death; F.R.A.S. 1849. *d.* Upper Surrey st. Norwich 1 Aug. 1867. *Monthly notices of Royal Astronom. Soc. xxviii,* 77 (1868).

BROOKE, WILLIAM *(eld. son of Wm. Brooke, M.D. of Dublin). b.* Dublin 22 July 1796; ed. at Trin. coll. Dublin, scholar 1812, B.A. 1814; called to Irish bar 1817; Q.C. 7 Feb. 1835; bencher of King's Inns 1846; a master in court of chancery 1846–74; a comr. of the Great Seal Feb. 1874; P.C. June 1874. *d.* Taney hill house, **Dundrum, co. Dublin** 19 Aug. 1881.

BROOKE, William Henry. b. 1781; clerk in bank of John Trotter in London who established first bazaar in this country namely in Soho sq. 1816; pupil of Samuel Drummond, A.R.A. who in his etching from his own painting of "The death of Nelson" has introduced a portrait of Brooke as one of the sailors; exhibited 9 pictures at the R.A., 6 at the B.I. and 9 at Suffolk st. gallery 1808–33; portrait painter in London 1798; contributed drawings to the *Satirist* 1812 to Sep. 1813; illustrated *Moore's Irish Melodies* 1822; *Keightley's Greek and Roman Mythology* 1831 and many other popular books; many of his drawings on wood were engraved by Thomson, Branston and other eminent xylographers. d. Chichester 12 Jany. 1860. *C. R. Smith's Collectanea Antiqua v,* 273–6 (1861); *C. R. Smith's Retrospections i,* 281–5 (1883).

BROOKES, Warwick. b. Birtles' sq. Greengate, Salford 1806; entered print works of John Barge near Broughton Bridge, Salford; artist at Manchester. d. Egerton grove, Stretford new road, Manchester 11 Aug. 1882. *Manchester City News 26 Aug. 1882 and following weeks.*

BROOKFIELD, Rev. William Henry (2 son of Charles Brookfield of Sheffield, solicitor). b. Sheffield 31 Aug. 1809; ed. at Sheffield, Leeds and Trin. coll. Cam., B.A. 1833, M.A. 1836; C. of Maltby near Bawtry Dec. 1834; C. of St. Luke's Berwick st. London 1841; inspector of elementary church schools 11 Feb. 1848 to 1865; R. of Somerby near Grantham 1861 to death; hon. chaplain in ord. to the Queen 24 March 1862, chaplain in ord. 1 Jany. 1867 to death; chaplain of Rolls chapel, Chancery lane 1866 to death; preb. of St. Paul's cath. 1868 to death; he is described in Thackeray's *Curates Walk* as Frank Whitestock; author of *Paris exhibition Reports on classes. Printing and books, class vi,* (reprinted in *Illustrated London News* 17 *Aug.* 1867). d. 16 Hereford sq. West Brompton, London 12 July 1874. *Sermons by the late Rev. W. H. Brookfield edited by Mrs. Brookfield 1875, portrait.*

BROOKS, Charles William Shirley (son of Wm. Brooks of London, architect who d. 11 Dec. 1867 aged 80). b. 52 Doughty st. London 29 April 1816; articled to his uncle Charles Sabine of Oswestry, solicitor 1832–7; wrote parliamentary summary in *Morning Chronicle* 1848–52, special correspondent for it in Russia, Syria and Egypt 1853; contributed to *Punch* 1851 to death, editor June 1870 to death, wrote *Punch's Essence of parliament;* edited *Literary Gazette* 1858–9 and *Home*

News 1867; author of *The Creole or love's fetters,* produced at Lyceum theatre 8 April 1847; *The daughter of the stars,* produced at New Strand theatre 5 Aug. 1850; *Aspen Court, a story of our own time* 3 vols. 1854; *The gordian knot* 1859; *The silver cord* 3 vols. 1861. d. 6 Kent terrace, Regent's park, London 23 Feb. 1874. *G.M. xii,* 561–9 (1874); *Illust. review iii,* 545–50 (1872), *portrait;* E. Yates's *Recollections ii,* 143–9 (1884); *Cartoon portraits* (1873) 128–33, *portrait.*

BROOKS, George Benjamin. Entered Bombay army 1799; colonel 20 Bombay N.I. 8 Oct. 1839 to death; commanded the field force in Upper Scinde 1840; general 30 Aug. 1860. d. Clewer hill, Windsor 4 Oct. 1862. *The memorial of G. B. Brooks to the Honorable the Court of directors of the East India Company* 1842.

BROOKS, John (only son of Rev. John Brooks, R. of Walton-le-Dale, Lancs.) b. 7 April 1856; ed. at Harrow and Merton coll. Ox., B.A. 1878; barrister I.T. 29 June 1881; M.P. for Altrincham division of Cheshire 27 Nov. 1885 to death. d. Eaton place, London 8 March 1886.

BROOKS. Ven. Jonathan (son of Mr. Brooks of Liverpool, merchant). b. Oldhall st. Liverpool 1 Sep. 1775; ed. at Macclesfield sch. and Trin. coll. Cam., B.A. 1798, M.A. 1802; C. of Walton on the hill, C. of St. James's Liverpool, and C. of St. George's Liverpool successively; senior R. of Liverpool 7 Oct. 1829 to death; archdeacon of Liverpool 29 Sep. 1848 to death; chairman of Liverpool quarter sessions many years. d. Everton road, near Liverpool 29 Sep. 1855. *G.M. xlv,* 543–4 (1855).

BROOKS, Rev. Joshua William. Curate of East Retford 1821–7; V. of Clareborough 1827–43; R. of Grove 1837–43; V. of St. Mary's Nottingham 1843–64; rural dean 1855–64; preb. of Linc. cath. 1858 to death; R. of Great Ponton 1864 to death; author of *Elements of prophetical interpretation* 1836; *History of the Hebrew nation* 1841; edited *Abdiel's Essays on the Advent of Christ* 1844; *Proverbs of Solomon* 1860. d. 17 Feb. 1882 aged 92.

BROOKS, Robert. b 1799; merchant and shipowner in London; M.P. for Weymouth 30 April 1859 to 11 Nov. 1868. d. 5 June 1882. Personalty sworn under £370,000, 15 July 1882.

BROOKS, SAMUEL *(son of Wm. Brooks of Manchester, banker who d. about* 1846). *b.* Great Harwood 1792; calico printer in Manchester; opened a bank at Manchester as a branch of Cunliffe's bank Blackburn; a great land improver, purchased estates at Moss Side, Baguley, Sale, Timperley and Partington; chairman of original meeting of promoters of Lancashire and Yorkshire railway 18 Oct. 1830. *d.* Whalley house, Whalley range, Manchester 7 June 1864. *L. H. Grindon's Manchester Banks* (1877) 197–214.

BROOKS, VINCENT. Purchased large establishment of Day and Sons, lithographers, Gate st. Lincoln's Inn Fields, London 1867, carried on the business under style of Vincent Brooks, Day and Son 1867 to death. *d.* of apoplexy in counting house of Spalding and Hodge, Drury Lane 29 Sep. 1885 in 70 year.

BROOKS, WILLIAM ALEXANDER *(son of Wm. Brooks of London, architect). b.* London 25 March 1802; engineer officer with Sir Robert Wilson in Spain 1822; resident engineer to Tees Navigation company 1828; engineer to corporation of Newcastle 1842–58; practised in London 1858 to death; made 4 journeys to Honduras 1870–6; sent out to investigate feasibility of a ship canal across Isthmus of Darien 1876; M.I.C.E. 10 June 1834, Telford medallist 1852; author of *Treatise on the improvement of the navigation of rivers* 1841; *Honduras and the Inter-Oceanic railway* 1874. *d.* Paya, in the Isthmus of Darien 26 Jany. 1877. *Min. of Proc. of Instit. of C.E. l,* 172–5 (1877).

BROOM, HERBERT *(only son of Herbert Broom of Kidderminster). b.* Kidderminster 1815; ed. at Trin. coll. Çam., 40 wrangler 1837, B.A. 1837, M.A. 1854, LL.D. 1864; barrister I.T. 20 Nov. 1840; professor of common law to council of legal education Jany. 1873 to 1875; author of *Practical rules for determining parties to actions* 1843, 2 ed. 1846; *A selection of legal maxims* 1845, 6 ed. 1884; *Commentaries on the common law* 1856, 7 ed. 1884; *Constitutional law* 1866, 2 ed. 1885, and of 2 novels *The missing will* 3 vols. 1877 and *The unjust steward* 2 vols. 1879. *d.* The Priory, Orpington, Kent 2 May 1882.

BROOME, ARTHUR. Second lieut. Bengal artillery 13 Dec. 1827, colonel 29 April 1861 to death; controller general of military expenditure Bengal 1 April 1864 to death; M.G. 6 March 1868; C.S.I. 1869. *d.* at sea on passage from India 27 March 1871.

BROOME, HENRY ALFRED. *b.* Birmingham 1826; beat Fred. Mason (the Bulldog) £50 a side 11 Oct. 1843; fought Joe Rowe £50 a side 10 Dec. 1844, beat him at renewed fight 13 May 1845; fought Ben Terry £100 a side 3 Feb. 1846; fought Wm. Perry (the Tipton Slasher) £200 a side and the championship at Mildenhall near Newmarket 29 Sep. 1851 and beat him; fought Harry Orme near Brandon 18 April 1853 £250 a side when Broome won after 31 rounds in 2 hours 18 minutes, this was the best fight for the championship ever seen; paid £180 forfeit to Tom Paddock 20 Feb. 1855 who beat Broome £200 a side 19 May 1856; landlord of the Opera tavern, Haymarket London 1851–56; kept the Albion tavern, Warblington st. Portsmouth 1856; kept the Crown and Cushion, Little Russell st. London; a public caterer at principal race meetings. *d.* 30 Frith st. Soho, London 2 Nov. 1865. *H. D. Miles's Pugilistica iii,* 308–39 (1881), *portrait; Fights for the championship by Francis Dowling* (1860) 234–55; *Illust. sporting news iv,* 561 (1865), *portrait.*

BROOME, JOHN *(brother of the preceding). b.* Birmingham 14 March 1818; fought 7 prize fights all of which he won 1834–40; fought Jack Hannan £500 a side at New park farm Oxfordshire 26 Jany. 1841 when he beat him after 47 rounds; fought Bungaree the Australian £300 a side at Mildenhall 27 April 1842 when Broome won after 42 rounds; presented with a golden belt at Castle tavern Holborn, London 27 Jany. 1842; landlord of the Rising Sun, Air st. Piccadilly 1841; invented a gun capable of carrying a ball of 50lb. weight 2 miles; cut his throat at the Wrekin tavern, Broad Court, Bow st. London 31 May 1855. *Fights for the championship by Francis Dowling* (1860) 370–8; *The new Tom Spring's Life in London* (1844) 137, *portrait.*

BROPHEY, REV. GEORGE *(son of Mr. Brophey who was executed after battle of Vinegar Hill* 1798). *b.* near Kilkenny Aug. 1775; ed. at Carlow college; studied theology in Paris; ordained priest 1798; went to America 1843; pastor of St. Paul's R.C. church Harlem, New York 1853–66; settled in Iowa 1866. *d.* Mercy hospital, Davenport, Iowa 16 Oct. 1880 in 106 year.

BROS, THOMAS. Educ. at St. John's coll. Cam., B.A. 1825, M.A. 1831; barrister L.I. 22 Nov. 1831; recorder of Abingdon 30 March 1852 to April 1878. *d.* Springfield, Upper Clapton, London 16 May 1883 aged 79.

BROTHERHOOD, ROWLAND. Railway contractor; proprietor of large iron and wagon works at Chippenham where some of the best iron bridges ever sent to India were made; constructed Bristol and South Wales Union railway and piers; Assoc. Inst. C.E. 1 May 1866. *d.* Everton villa, Chertsey road, Bristol 5 March 1883.

BROTHERTON, EDWARD. *b.* Manchester 1814; engaged in the silk trade; wrote letters on popular education in *Manchester Guardian* which led to formation of Education Aid Society and paved the way for Education Act of 1870; author of *Mormonism its rise and progress* 1846; *Spiritualism, Swedenborg and the New Church* 1860; editor and chief writer of first vol. of a monthly periodical *The Dawn* (Manchester 1861-2); wrote *Outlines of my mental history* in the *Intellectual Repository* 1849 and many articles under pseudonyms of Libra and Pilgrim in Swedenborgian periodicals. *d.* Cornbrook, Manchester 23 March 1866.

BROTHERTON, JOSEPH *(son of John Brotherton of Manchester, cotton spinner).* *b.* Whittington, Derbyshire 22 May 1783; cotton spinner at Manchester 1802-19; joined Bible Christian church 1805, pastor about 1818; M.P. for Salford (the first) 20 Dec. 1832 to death, his expences being paid by his constituents; chairman of private bills committee; active member of Anti-Corn law league. *d.* suddenly while travelling in an omnibus from his residence Rosehill, Pendleton into Manchester 7 Jany. 1857, his statue by M. Noble in Peel park was uncovered 6 Aug. 1858. *J. B. Robinson's Derbyshire gatherings* (1866) 42-4, *portrait; Book-lore ii*, 78-82 (1885); *Illust. news of the world ii*, 117 (1858), *portrait; I.L.N. viii*, 309 (1846), *portrait, xxxiii*, 210 (1858).

BROTHERTON SIR THOMAS WILLIAM. *b.* 1785; ensign Coldstream Guards 24 Jany. 1800; captain 14 Dragoons 4 June 1807, major 26 March 1812 to Oct. 1820; served in Egypt 1801, in Germany 1805 and during Peninsular war 1808-14; lieut. col. 12 Lancers 26 Oct. 1820 to 24 May 1827 when placed on h.p.; aide-de-camp to the Sovereign 22 July 1830 to 23 Nov. 1841; lieut. col. 16 Lancers 10 Feb. 1832 to 23 Nov. 1841; inspector general of cavalry 1844; colonel of 15 Hussars 18 May 1849, and of 1 Dragoon Guards 17 July 1859 to death; general 1 April 1860; C.B. 3 Feb. 1817, K.C.B. 5 July 1855, G.C.B. 28 June 1861; received the war medal with 8 clasps. *d.* at his son's house near Esher 20 Jany. 1868.

BROUGH, ANNIE *(dau. of Thomas Romer of Liverpool).* *b.* Liverpool 19 Dec. 1827; ed. at Royal academy of Music Sep. 1843 to June 1846; made her first appearance in London at Princess's theatre as Adalgisa in *Norma* 1847; sang at Haymarket theatre; prima donna at the Surrey theatre 1850. *(m.* April 1851 Wm. Brough the dramatist 1826-70). *d.* 71 Gower st. London 1 Feb. 1852. *Musical World xxx,* 94 (1852).

BROUGH, BARNABAS. Brewer and wine merchant at Pontypool; one of the principal witnesses for the Crown in trial of John Frost the Chartist 1840, which made him very unpopular and ruined his business; auctioneer and accountant at Manchester 1843-5; accountant in office of *Illustrated London News* London 1845 to death; author under name of Barnard de Burgh of several dramatic pieces, one of which *I wont go or how to keep a place* was acted in London by Tyrone Power. *d.* 4 South Lambeth place, Lambeth, London 30 Oct. 1854 aged 59.

BROUGH, JOHN CARGILL *(son of the preceding).* *b.* Pontypool, Monmouthshire 11 Feb. 1834; clerk in audit office of London and South Western railway 1852-8; wrote articles in many periodicals; an original member of the Savage club 1857; edited *The Chemist and Druggist* 1860-70; F.C.S. 1864; started *The Laboratory, a weekly record of scientific research* April 1867; published with two friends *Exeter Change* a humourous brochure during meeting of British Association at Exeter Aug. 1869; librarian and superintendent of London Institution, Finsbury Circus July 1870 to death, started and edited *Journal of London Institution*, gave a course of lectures there on Philosophy of Magic 1871-2; author of *The fairy tales of science* 1858, 2 ed. 1865; one of the editors of *England's Workshops* 1864 and of *Year book of Pharmacy* 1870-2. *d.* Esher 7 Sep. 1872. *Chemist and Druggist* (1872) 287, 305, 340.

BROUGH, MARY ANN. Nurse to Prince of Wales; murdered 6 of her children at Esher 9 June 1854 and attempted to destroy herself; tried for murder at Guildford assizes 9 Aug. 1854, when found not guilty on ground of insanity. *d.* Bethlem hospital, London about 20 March 1861. *Annual Register* (1854) 93-7;

BROUGH, REDMOND WILLIAM. Ensign 56 Foot 10 March 1807, lieut. 15 July 1808 to 10 Jany. 1822 when placed on h.p.; captain 2 Foot 7 Oct. 1824, lieut. col. 27 Nov. 1841 to 2 March 1846 when placed on h.p.; M.G. 26 Oct. 1858. *d.* Charles st. St. James's London 29 Feb. 1860 aged 68.

BROUGH, RICHARD SECKER. First lieut. R.A. 2 Sep. 1794, colonel 21 Nov. 1833 to 1841, col. commandant 17 Aug. 1846 to death; general 16 Dec. 1856. *d.* Onslow sq. London 15 Jany. 1859 aged 85.

BROUGH, RICHARD SECKER (*younger son of Thompson Brough, M.D. of Kiltegan, co. Wicklow*). *b.* Kiltegan 17 Oct. 1846; a fourth grade assistant superintendent Indian telegraph service 30 Oct. 1869; assistant to superintendent electrician at Calcutta March 1871 to death; author of *Telegraph construction;* edited Schwendler's *Instructions for testing lines, batteries and instruments.* *d.* from cholera at Calcutta 3 April 1879. *Min. of Proc. of Instit. of C.E. lix*, 315–17 (1880).

BROUGH, ROBERT BARNABAS (*brother of John Cargill Brough*). *b.* London 10 April 1828; ed. at Newport; started the *Liverpool Lion* comic weekly paper 1847, edited it 1847–8; wrote burlesques with his brother William first of which *The enchanted isle* was produced at Amphitheatre Liverpool 1848 and reproduced at Adelphi theatre London 20 Nov. 1848; edited the *Atlas* a short time and the *Welcome Guest;* author of *Life of Sir John Falstaff* 1858; *Miss Brown, a romance and other tales* 1860. *d.* Boundary st. Manchester 26 June 1860. *Marston Lynch by R. B. Brough with portrait, and a memoir of the author by G. A. Sala* 1860 this work contains the story of Brough's own life; *E. Yates's Recollections i*, 312–18 (1884).

BROUGH, WILLIAM (*brother of the preceding*). *b.* London 28 April 1826; apprenticed to a printer at Brecon; author of a series of papers called *Hints upon heraldry* in the *Liverpool Lion;* wrote with his brother Robert the Christmas and Easter pieces for Adelphi and Haymarket theatres 1848–54; author of many "Entertainments" for Mr. and Mrs. German Reed and John Parry; wrote many burlesques including *The field of the cloth of gold* which was produced at Strand theatre 11 April 1868 and played till 27 March 1869, 298 times. *d.* 37 Maitland park road, Haverstock hill 13 March 1870.

BROUGH, WILLIAM FRANCIS. *b.* Wexford 1798; made his first appearance on the stage in Sussex 1818; acted at Haymarket theatre London 3 years; first appeared in America at Park theatre New York 4 Sep. 1835; made his début in Philadelphia 18 Jany. 1836, at Chestnut st. theatre as Cedric in opera of *The Maid of Judith.* *d.* while on his passage to England 21 May 1867. *bur.* in Brooklyn cemetery New York Feb. 1868.

BROUGHAM, HENRY PETER BROUGHAM, 1 Baron (*eld. son of Henry Brougham of Brougham near Penrith 1742–1810*). *b.* 19 St. Andrew's sq. Edin. 19 Sep. 1778; ed. at high sch. and univ. Edin.; admitted advocate 10 June 1800; one of founders of *Edinburgh Review* Oct. 1802, chief contributor to it; F.R.S. 3 March 1803; barrister L.I. 22 Nov. 1808; M.P. for Camelford 1810–12, for Winchelsea 1815–30 and for West Riding of Yorkshire 5 Aug. 1830 to 23 Nov. 1830; attorney general to Queen Caroline 22 April 1820 to her death 7 Aug. 1821; lord rector of Univ. of Glasgow 1825; K.C. 1827, received patent of precedence 1827; lord chancellor 22 Nov. 1830 to 22 Nov. 1834; created Baron Brougham and Vaux of Brougham, Westmoreland 22 Nov. 1830 and by another patent dated 22 March 1860, created Baron Brougham and Vaux of Brougham and of Highhead Castle, Cumberland; foreign associate of Institute of France 1833; pres. of Social science association 1857 and 1860–5; chancellor of Univ. of Edin. 1859. *d.* Chateau Eleanor Louise, Cannes 7 May 1868. *Life and times of Lord Brougham 3 vols.* 1871, *portrait; Lord Campbell's Lives of the Chancellors viii*, 213–596; *Law mag. and law review xxiv*, 177–236 (1868); *W. C. Taylor's National portrait gallery i*, 62–5 (1846), *portrait; Maclise Portrait gallery* (1883) 81–7, *portrait; A bibliographical list of Lord Brougham's publications, by the author of The handbook of fictitious names* [*Ralph Thomas*] 1873.

NOTE.—The result of Queen Caroline's trial made him extraordinarily popular and the Brougham's Head became a common tavern sign; at time of passing of the Reform bill plaster casts of his head were sold by tens of thousands. His quarrel with Canning in the House of Commons 17 April 1823 was paraphrased by Dickens in the opening chapter of Pickwick. All the morning papers except the Times of Tuesday 22 Oct. 1839 contained leading articles on the sudden death of Lord Brougham with biographical sketches of him. He is depicted by Disraeli as 'Foaming Fudge' in Vivian Grey 1827, and by T. L. Peacock as 'the learned friend' in Crotchet Castle 1831.

BROUGHAM, WILLIAM BROUGHAM, 2 Baron (*brother of the preceding*). *b.* 26 Sep. 1795; ed. at Edin. and Jesus coll. Cam., B.A. 1819, M.A. 1822; barrister L.I. 9 May 1823; master in chancery 29 March 1831 to 2 Nov. 1852, when granted pension of £3225 on abolition of his office by 15 and 16 Vict. cap. 80; M.P. for Southwark 29 April 1831 to 29 Dec. 1834; contested Leeds 9 Jany. 1835; succeeded 7 May 1868. *d.* Brougham hall near Penrith 3 Jany. 1886. *Law Times lxxx*, 175 (1886).

BROUGHAM, JOHN. *b.* Dublin 9 May 1814; ed. at Trin. coll. Dub.; made his début at

BROUGHAM, J. (*Con.*)

Tottenham st. theatre London in extravaganza of *Tom and Jerry* July 1830; played at Olympic and Covent Garden; manager of Lyceum 1840–2; managed Niblo's Garden New York; opened a new theatre in Broadway N.Y. called Brougham's Lyceum 15 Oct. 1850; lessee of Bowery theatre N.Y. 7 July 1856; played in London 1860–5 and in America 1865–79; opened Brougham's theatre 25 Jany. 1869; edited a comic paper in New York called *The Lantern* 1852; author of nearly 80 dramatic pieces; said to have been original of Harry Lorrequer in Lever's novel. *d.* 60 East Ninth st. New York 7 June 1880. *Life of J. Brougham edited by W. Winter* 1881, *portrait; Ireland's Records of New York stage ii*, 178, 210, 384, 594, 655 (1867); *The Oddfellow i*, 65 (1839), *portrait.*

BROUGHTON, JOHN CAM HOBHOUSE, 1 Baron (*eld. son of Sir Benjamin Hobhouse, 1 baronet 1757–1831*). *b.* Redland near Bristol 27 June 1786; ed. at Westminster and Trin. coll. Cam., B.A. 1808, M.A. 1811; visited Greece and Turkey with Lord Byron 1809–10 who dedicated to him fourth canto of *Childe Harold* for which he wrote the explanatory notes; F.R.S. 19 May 1814; imprisoned in Newgate 14 Dec. 1819 to 29 Jany. 1820 for publishing a pamphlet called *The trifling mistake;* M.P. for Westminster 1820–33 for Nottingham 1834–47 and for Harwich 1848–51; active member of the Greek Committee in London 1823–24; one of the 6 founders of Royal Geographical Society 1830; sec. of state for war 1 Feb. 1832 to 4 April 1833; chief sec. for Ireland 28 March to 17 May 1833; first comr. of woods and forests 19 July to 31 Dec. 1834; pres. of Board of control 29 April 1835 to 9 Sep. 1841 and 10 July 1846 to Feb. 1852; P.C. 6 Feb. 1832; colonel of Wilts militia 8 Feb. 1840 to death; created Baron Broughton of Broughton de Gyfford, Wilts. 26 Feb. 1851; G.C.B. 23 Feb. 1852; author of *Imitations and translations from the classics, with original poems* 1809; *Journey through Albania and other provinces of Turkey with Lord Byron* 1812, 2 ed. 1818; *Substance of some letters written by an Englishman resident at Paris during the last reign of Napoleon* 2 vols. 1816. *d.* 42 Berkeley sq. London 3 June 1869. Personalty sworn under £250,000 14 Aug. 1869. *Recollections of a long life by the late Lord Broughton De Gyfford* 5 vols. *privately printed* 1865; *Edinburgh Review cxxxiii*, 287–337 (1871); *Maclise Portrait gallery* (1883) 372–8, *portrait; I.L.N. liv*, 602, 624 (1869), *portrait.*

BROUGHTON, REV. SIR HENRY DELVES, 8 Baronet. *b.* 10 Jany. 1777; ed. at Jesus coll. Cam., B.A. 1801, M.A. 1805; P.C. of Broughton Staffs. 1803 to death; succeeded 9 Aug. 1847. *d.* Broughton hall, Staffs. 3 Nov. 1851.

BROUGHTON, ROBERT EDWARDS. Barrister I.T. 6 May 1825; police magistrate at Worship st. London 1827–54, and at Marylebone 1854 to death; F.R.S. 17 Feb. 1842. *d.* 33 Dorset sq. London 29 June 1860 aged 79.

BROUGHTON, WILLIAM EDWARD DELVES (*2 son of Thomas Broughton of Ham Common, Surrey who d.* 24 *Jany.* 1846). *b.* 30 April 1802; 2 Lieut. R.E. 6 Aug. 1825; comr. to survey northern boundaries of British possessions in North America June 1840 to 31 March 1845; colonel R.E. 18 April 1860; colonel commandant 19 June 1872 to death; general 1 Oct. 1877. *d.* 8 Crescent, Surbiton, Surrey 5 April 1880.

BROUGHTON, RIGHT REV. WILLIAM GRANT (*eld. son of Grant Broughton*). *b.* Bridge st. Westminster 22 May 1788; ed. at Barnet gr. sch. and King's sch. Canterbury; clerk in treasury department of East India house 1807–12; resident member of Pemb. hall Cam. Oct. 1814, 6 wrangler 1818, B.A. 1818, M.A. 1823, D.D. 1836; C. of Hartley Wespall, Hants. 1818–27; C. of Farnham 1827; chaplain of Tower of London 6 Oct. 1828 to 24 June 1829; archdeacon of New South Wales 7 Dec. 1828, sworn into office 17 Sep. 1829; bishop of Australia 18 Jany. 1836, consecrated in Lambeth palace chapel 14 Feb. 1836; installed in St. James's church Sydney 2 June 1836; bishop of Sydney and metropolitan of Australasia 25 June 1847 to death. *d.* 11 Chester st. Belgrave sq. London 20 Feb. 1853. *bur.* south aisle of Canterbury cath. 26 Feb. *Sermons on the Church of England by the Right Rev. W. G. Broughton edited with prefatory memoir by B. Harrison* 1857; *G.M. xxxix*, 431–6 (1853); *J. Bonwick's Curious facts of old colonial days* (1870) 34–56.

BROUN, JOHN ALLAN (*son of Mr. Broun of Dumfries, schoolmaster who d. about* 1837). *b.* Dumfries 21 Sep. 1817; ed. at Univ. of Edin.; director of Sir T. M. Brisbane's magnetic observatory at Makerstoun, co. Dumfries 1842–9; director of observatory at Trevandrum, South India Jany. 1852 to April 1865; built an observatory on the Agustia Malley 6200 feet above the sea 1855; discovered that changes in daily mean horizontal force are nearly the same all over the globe, his researches contributed largely to establish meteorology on a scientific basis; F.R.S. 2 June 1853, Royal medallist 1878; author of *Observations of magnetic declination made at Trevandrum and Agustia Malley* 1873 and of more than 50 papers in scientific journals. *d.* 9 Abercorn place, London 22 Nov. 1879. *Proc. of Royal Soc. xxx,* 3–6 (1880).

BROUN, SIR RICHARD, 8 Baronet (*eld. son of Sir James Broun of Colston park, Lochmaben, Dumfriesshire, 7 Baronet who d. 30 Nov. 1844*). *b.* Lochmaben 22 April 1801; a knight of St. John of Jerusalem 28 July 1835, registrar 8 March 1837, sec. of the Langue of that order in England 24 June 1839, K.C.J.J. and G.C.J.J. 24 June 1841; hon. sec. of Committee of the baronetage for sustaining rights and privileges of the Order 15 July 1840 to death; demanded inauguration as a knight on account of being eldest son of a baronet, on the Lord Chamberlain's refusal to present him to the Queen for this purpose, he assumed title of Sir and addition of "Eques auratus" June 1842; projected The London Necropolis and national mausoleum at Woking 1849 which was incorporated 1852. *d.* Sphinx lodge, Chelsea, London 10 Dec. 1858.

BROUN, SIR WILLIAM, 9 Baronet. *b.* July 1804; ed. at Univ. of Edin.; admitted procurator 1829; dean of Faculty of procurators for county of Dumfries; succeeded 10 Dec. 1858. *d.* 7 Irving st. Dumfries 10 June 1882.

BROWELL, REV. WILLIAM ROBERT. Educ. at Pemb. coll. Ox., B.A. 1828, M.A. 1831, fellow and tutor of his college; public examiner 1834; R. of Beaumont-cum-Mose Essex 1839 to death; translated *Count Carnot's Reflexions on the metaphysical principles of the infinitesimal analysis* 1832; edited *Carwithen's History of the Church of England* 1849. *d.* Beaumont rectory 15 Aug. 1867.

BROWN, REV. ANDREW MORTON. *b.* parish of Loudown, Ayrshire 12 March 1812; ed. at Univs. of Glasgow and Edin.; Congregational minister at Overton, Hants.; minister at Poole 1837–43; minister of Highbury chapel Cheltenham 8 Jany. 1843 to death; chairman of Congregational Union of England and Wales 1854; author of *The leader of the the Lollards, his times and trials* 1848; *Salvation and the way to secure it,* 3 ed. 1851; *Evenings with the prophets, a series of memoirs and meditations* 1854; *Peden the prophet a tale of the covenanters founded on fact* 1859. *d.*

Bridport 17 July 1879. *Waddington's Congregational history v,* 596–8 (1880); *Congregational year book* (1880) 310–12.

BROWN, CHARLES PHILIP (*son of Rev. David Brown 1763–1812, provost of Calcutta College*). *b.* Calcutta 1798; ed. at Haileybury college; entered Madras civil service 1817; Persian translator to Madras government 1838; postmaster general and Telugu translator 1846–55; presented his fine collection of manuscripts including over 2000 Sanskrit and Telugu works to Madras Literary Society 1845; one of the foremost South Indian scholars; author of *Prosody of the Telugu and Sanskrit languages* 1826; *Dictionaries of Telugu-English and English-Telugu* 2 vols. Madras 1852; *Grammar of the Telugu language* 1840, 2 *ed.* 1857, and many other works some of which were translated into Tamil, Canarese and Hindustani. *d.* 22 Kildare gardens, Paddington, London 12 Dec. 1884. *Some account of the literary life of C. P. B. privately printed* 1866.

BROWN, ELEANOR (*dau. of Mr. Fairlam of city of London, jeweller*). *b.* near Regent's Park London 22 March 1829; landscape painter; exhibited 1 picture at B.I. and 2 at Suffolk st. gallery 1857–72; author of a fairy tale entitled *Muriel's Dreamland* 1871. (*m.* 22 March 1849 J. W. Brown of London, estate agent). *d.* 17 Feb. 1878. *E. C. Clayton's English female artists ii,* 177–83 (1876).

BROWN, GEORGE. *b.* Stoughton, Sussex 27 April 1783; a tailor at Emsworth, Hants.; moved to Brighton 1825; lessee of Royal Brighton Cricket ground 1831 to about 1840; kept a lodging house at 71 Middle st. Brighton to Sep. 1856; played his first cricket match at Lords 30 July 1818; the fastest bowler who ever played in great cricket matches; threw a cricket ball 137 yards on Walderton Common about 1819, the longest throw on record; one of the Sussex eleven till about 1838. *d.* Sompting, Sussex 25 June 1857.

BROWN, SIR GEORGE (3 *son of George Brown, provost of Elgin*). *b.* Linkwood near Elgin 3 July 1790; ensign 43 Foot 23 Jany. 1806; lieut. col. Rifle brigade 5 Feb. 1824 to 23 Nov. 1841; deputy adjutant general 23 Nov. 1841; adjutant general 8 April 1850 to 12 Dec. 1853; colonel 77 Foot 11 April 1851 to 22 Dec. 1854; commanded Light division during Crimean war 1854–55, invalided home 28 June 1855; colonel commandant Rifle brigade 18 Jany. 1855, colonel in chief

BROWN, SIR G. (Con.)

18 April 1863 to death; general 7 Sep. 1855;
commander of the forces in Ireland 1 April
1860 to April 1865; P.C. Ireland 1860;
colonel 32 Foot 1 April 1863 to death; K.H.
1831, C.B. 19 July 1838, K.C.B. 6 April
1852, G.C.B. 5 July 1855. d. Linkwood 27
Aug. 1865. E. H. Nolan's Russian war i, 203,
384 (1857), portrait; G. Ryan's Our heroes of
the Crimea (1855) 58–61; Kinglake's Invasion
of the Crimea, 6 ed. vols. 2–7 (1877–83).

BROWN, GEORGE (son of Peter Brown 1784–
1863). b. Edinburgh 29 Nov. 1818; went
to New York 1838 and to Toronto 1843;
founded the Daily Globe at Toronto 1844 and
the Canada Farmer 1864; member of legislative assembly of Canada for county Kent
Dec. 1851, for Lambton 1854, for city of
Toronto 1857, and for South Oxford March
1863 to the Union 27 May 1867; formed a
ministry in Aug. 1858 which only lasted 2
days; member of the Senate 16 Dec. 1873 to
death; joint plenipotentiary with Sir E.
Thornton at Washington to arrange a commercial treaty with United States 1874;
gazetted K.C.M.G. 24 May 1879 but declined
the honour. d. Toronto 9 May 1880 having
been shot by a discharged employé 25 March
1880. Morgan's Sketches of eminent Canadians
(1862) 769–73; Dominion annual register
(1879) 210, 352, (1880) 393–5; I.L.N. xlv,
496 (1864), portrait.

BROWN, GEORGE GRANVILLE (son of Charles
Ferdinand D'Artois Duc de Berri 1778–1820
by his first wife Amy dau. of Rev. Joseph Brown
1784–1876, V. of All Saints church Maidstone,
Kent). b. London 1805; brought up at
Ouchy near Lausanne; served in army of
King of Naples; naturalised in France about
1843; lived at Mantes-sur-Seine near Paris
about 1843 to death. d. Mantes 5 July
1882. Illust. Lon. News lxxxi, 62 (1882).

BROWN, RIGHT REV. GEORGE HILARY (son
of Wm. Brown of Clifton in the Fylde, Lancs.)
b. 13 Jany. 1786; entered St. Cuthbert's
college Ushaw 25 Sep. 1799, left it 8 April
1819; ordained deacon 1808, priest 1810; in
charge of mission at Lancaster 1819–40;
Vicar Apostolic of Lancashire district 1840;
consecrated Bishop of Bugia in partibus, at
Liverpool 24 Aug. 1840; translated to Tloa
in partibus 1842; assistant at Pontifical
throne 1843; bishop of Liverpool 29 Sep.
1850 to death; author of A supplement
to the Diurnal adapted to the English mission
1833. d. Catherine st. Liverpool 25 Jany.
1856.

BROWN, HENRY. Educ. at London hospital,
London; L.S.A. 1827, M.R.C.S. 1832;
surgeon at Windsor; medical attendant on
the Queen and royal household at Windsor
1838 to death. d. Neet st. Windsor 24 Oct.
1868 aged 66.

BROWN, HUGH. Hand loom weaver in
Ayrshire; a schoolmaster 1828–70; author of
a poem to the memory of Lord Byron in the
Scots Magazine 1825; published The Covenanters
and other poems 1838. d. Glasgow 27 Aug. 1885
aged 85.

BROWN, ISAAC BAKER (son of Mr. Brown
of Colne Engaine, Essex). b. Colne 8 June
1812; studied at Guy's Hospital; L.S.A. and
M.R.C.S. 1834, F.R.C.S. 1848; partner with
Samuel Griffith of Edgware road London
1834–40; removed to Oxford sq. 1845; gave
up general practice for that of surgeon
accoucheur 1847; surgeon and accoucheur to
St. Mary's hospital, Paddington 1850–8;
founded London Surgical Home 1858; fellow
of Obstetrical Society 1859 to 3 April 1867;
pres. of Medical Soc. of London 1865;
author of On Scarlatina and its successful
treatment by the Acidum aceticum dilutum of
the Pharmacopœia 1846, 2 ed. 1857; On some
diseases of women admitting of surgical treatment
1854, 3 ed. 1866; On ovarian dropsy 1862, 2
ed. 1868. d. 88 Albany st. Regent's park
London 3 Feb. 1873. J. F. Clarke's Autobiographical recollections of the medical profession
(1874) 495–503; Medical Circular i, 261,
301–3 (1852), portrait; British Medical Journal
i, 395–410 (1867).

BROWN, JAMES. b. near Montrose; mate of
the brig Pomona, built by him and his elder
brother; taken by a French privateer 1808
and imprisoned at Verdun 1808–14; ship
builder at Perth 1814; built 99 vessels including the steam-boat Tourist one of the first
sea-going steamers constructed; raised many
sunken ships in all parts of Europe including
the Comet, boiler of which exploded in the
Clyde off Greenock 1820; inspector of steam
vessels for Dundee district. d. Dundee 19
Jany. 1861 in 77 year. W. Norrie's Dundee
Celebrities (1873) 194–6.

BROWN, JAMES. Flax spinner in Dundee;
dean of Guild 1824; the first pres. of Watt
institution 1824; provost of Dundee 1844–7;
contributed many articles to the Caledonian
and other periodicals; author of a small
volume of poetry privately printed. d. 6
Jany. 1869 in 82 year.

BROWN, JAMES (*only son of James Brown of Leeds, merchant*). *b.* 12 April 1814; ed. at Trin. coll. Cam., B.A. 1836, M.A. 1840; sheriff of Yorkshire 1852; M.P. for Malton 1857–68. *d.* 43 Upper Grosvenor st. London 19 April 1877. Personalty sworn under £250,000, 14 July 1877.

BROWN, RIGHT REV. JAMES. *b.* Wolverhampton 11 Jany. 1812; ed. at Sedgley park school 1820–6 and St. Mary's college Oscott 1826–37; ordained priest 18 Feb. 1837; professor and prefect of studies at Oscott 1837–44; pres. of Sedgley park school 1844–51; bishop of Shrewsbury 27 June 1851 to death, consecrated in St. George's cath. Southwark 27 July 1851; one of bishops assistant at Pontifical throne 17 April 1870; silver jubilee of his episcopate celebrated in Shrewsbury cath. 27 July 1876. *d.* St. Mary's Grange near Shrewsbury 14 Oct. 1881. *A sermon preached on the occasion of the silver jubilee of the Bishop of Shrewsbury by the Rev. John Morris 1876.*

BROWN, REV. JAMES BALDWIN (*elder son of James Baldwin Brown 1785–1843, judge of court of requests at Oldham*). *b.* 10 Harcourt buildings, Inner Temple, London 19 Aug. 1820; ed. at Univ. coll. London, B.A. London 1839; student at Inner Temple 1839–41; studied at Highbury college 1841; minister of London road independent chapel Derby 1843; minister of Clayland's chapel Clapham road London 1846, removed to new chapel built for him at Brixton July 1870; chairman of Congregational union of England and Wales 1878; author of *The soul's exodus and pilgrimage* 1862, 3 ed. 1867; *First principles of ecclesiastical truth* 1870; *The higher life* 1874, 5 ed. 1879; *The doctrine of annihilation* 1875, 2 ed. 1878 and many other works. *d.* Coombe, Surrey 23 June 1884. *In memoriam James Baldwin Brown edited by Elizabeth Baldwin Brown 1884, portrait; Leisure hours by a journalist* (1878) 91–102; *Biograph v,* 154–8 (1881).

BROWN, JANE (*dau. of John Hemsworth of Strokestown, co. Roscommon*). Roman Catholic bookseller, printer and publisher with George Keating in Duke st. Grosvenor sq. London Feb. 1837 to 1840 when they dissolved partnership; in business at 10 Duke st. Manchester sq. 1840; published *The Penny Catholic Magazine* 7 Sep. 1839 to 1840; *The Laitys Directory* 1838 *and* 1839 when it ceased. (*m.* Richard Brown of Duke st. Grosvenor sq., principal R.C. publisher in London who *d.* 25 Feb. 1837 aged 60). She *d.* 23 March 1860 aged 73.

BROWN, SIR JOHN. Ensign 18 Foot 27 May 1795; lieut. col. 1 Greek light infantry 1813–15; lieut. col. 21 Dragoons 1815–20; lieut. col. 13 Dragoons 1820–30; colonel 8 Hussars 4 April 1843 to death; general 20 June 1854; K.T.S. 25 June 1813; knighted by patent 24 Aug. 1814; K.C.H. 1831. *d.* 118 Pall Mall London 16 Nov. 1855 aged 80. *bur.* at Beckenham, Kent.

BROWN, REV. JOHN (*eld. son of Rev. John Brown 1754–1832, minister of the Burgher Secession congregation in Whitburn*). *b.* Burnhead, Whitburn 12 July 1784; ed. at Whitburn parish school, and Edinburgh Univ. 1797–1800; taught a school in village of Elie, Fife 1800–1803; licensed by Presbytery of Stirling and Falkirk to preach the gospel 12 Feb. 1805; minister of Biggar 6 Feb. 1806; translated to Rose st. ch. Edinburgh 1 May 1822; inducted to Broughton place ch. Edin. 20 May 1829; received degree of D.D. from Jefferson college Pensylvania 1830; professor of exegetical theology to United Presbyterian church 1834–57; engaged with ardour in Apocrypha, Voluntary, and Atonement controversies 1835–43; promoted union of Secession and Relief bodies; jubilee of his ministry celebrated April 1856; author of *Expository discourses on 1 Peter* 2 vols. 1848, 2 ed. 1849; *Discourses and sayings of our Lord Jesus Christ* 3 vols. 1850; *Discourses suited to the Lords Supper* 1816, 3 ed. 1853; *Exposition of the Epistle to the Hebrews* 2 vols. 1862. *d.* Newington, Edinburgh 13 Oct. 1858. *John Cairns's Memoir of John Brown 1860, portrait; John Smith's Our Scottish clergy* (1848) 272–80.

BROWN, JOHN. *b.* Dover 2 Aug. 1797; in the East Indian merchant service 1811–15; wholesale goldsmith and diamond merchant in London; advocated expeditions in search of Sir John Franklin and made collections illustrative of Arctic adventure; F.R.G.S. 1837; a founder of Ethnological Soc. 1843; author of *The north west passage and the plans for the search for Sir John Franklin a review* 1858, 2 ed. 1860. *d.* Scaleby lodge, Camden road, London 7 Feb. 1861. *Journal of Royal Geog. Soc. xxxi,* 116 (1861); *G.M. x,* 571–3 (1861).

BROWN, JOHN. *b.* Barnwell near Cambridge 4 Aug. 1796; brought up as a shoemaker; entered the army but deserted; became a strolling player; served in the navy; worked as a shoemaker; acted in London and the provinces; proprietor of University billiard rooms and racket court, Ram yard, Bridge st. Cambridge for many years before his death; town councillor of Cambridge. *d.* Cambridge

22 Aug. 1863. *Sixty years gleanings from life's harvest by John Brown* 1858, *portrait*.

BROWN, JOHN (*son of Rev. John Brown* 1784–1858). *b.* Biggar, Lanarkshire 22 Sep. 1810; ed. at high sch. and univ. Edin.; apprenticed to James Syme the eminent surgeon 1828–33; M.D. Edin. 1833; physician at Edin. 1833 to death; author of *Horæ Subsecivæ* 3 vols. 1858–82. *d.* 23 Rutland st. Edin. 11 May 1882. *Good Words for* 1882 *pp.* 446–51, *portrait; Macmillan's Mag. xlvii,* 281–95 (1883); *I.L.N. lxxx,* 508 (1882), *portrait*.

BROWN, JOHN. *b.* Crathie near Balmoral, Aberdeenshire 8 Dec. 1826; personal attendant on Queen Victoria Dec. 1865 to death. *d.* Clarence tower, Windsor Castle 27 March 1883. *bur.* Crathie cemetery 5 April. *Life of J. Brown by H. L. Williams* 1883; *More leaves from the journal of a life in the Highlands* (1884) 31, *portrait; I.L.N. lxxxii,* 332 (1883), *portrait*.

BROWN, JOHN A. (3 *son of Alexander Brown of Baltimore, banker*). *b.* Ballymena, co. Antrim 21 May 1788; went to United States about 1800; manager of his father's bank at Philadelphia 1818, succeeded to the business; retired about 1839 with a large fortune; gave to charities sum of 500,000 dollars 300,000 of them to Presbyterian hospital of Philadelphia *d.* Philadelphia 31 Dec. 1872.

BROWN, JOHN CHARLES. *b.* Glasgow 1805; landscape painter in London, Glasgow and Edin.; associate of Royal Scottish Academy; drew views for John Wilson's *Scotland illustrated* 1845; his picture 'The last of the Clan' was engraved for Royal Association of Fine Arts Scotland 1851. *d.* 10 Vincent st. Edin. 8 May 1867.

BROWN, JOHN HOSKINS. Entered navy 25 July 1805; registrar general of seamen 1835 to April 1851; captain 20 March 1863; C.B. 8 April 1862; author of *The Shipmasters' guide* 1844, *new ed.* 1855; edited *The mercantile navy list* 1850 etc. *d.* Brixton, London 29 June 1864 aged 72.

BROWN, JOHN TATTON BUTLER. *b.* 1 Oct. 1833; 2 lieut. R.A. 18 June 1851, lieut. col. 9 Nov. 1876 to 29 Oct. 1881 when he retired with hon. rank of M.G.; C.B. 27 Nov. 1879. *d.* Park Mount, Kent road, Southsea 19 Aug. 1885.

BROWN, JOHN WRIGHT (*son of Rev. Charles J. Brown of Edinburgh*). *b.* Edin. 19 Jany. 1836; assistant in herbarium connected with

Botanic garden Edin.; an associate of Edinburgh Botanical Society to which he contributed a list of the plants of Elie, Fifeshire. *d.* 39 George sq. Edinburgh 23 March 1863. *Trans. Bot. Soc. Edin. vii,* 519–20 (1863).

BROWN, REV. JOSEPH. Educ. at Queen's coll. Cam., B.A. 1829, M.A. 1833; P.C. of St. Matthias, Bethnal Green, London 1844–9; R. of Ch. Ch. Southwark 1849 to death; originator of Homes for servants out of place, and the Albert Institution Blackfriars; practically created Cholera orphan house, Ham common, since called National orphan home; author of *Narratives and sermons for schools* 1856; *Hymns and psalms for divine worship* 1859. *d.* Richmond hill, Surrey 13 Aug. 1867 aged 67. *I.L.N. xxvi,* 269 (1855), *portrait*.

BROWN, JOSEPH (7 *son of George Brown of North Shields*). *b.* North Shields Sep. 1784; ed. at Univ. of Edin.; entered army medical service, attached to Wellington's staff in Peninsular war; resumed his studies at Edin., M.D. 2 Aug. 1819; practised at Sunderland 1819 to death, medical officer of the Infirmary 1822 to death; mayor of Sunderland 1840, alderman 1841; author of *Medical essays on fever, inflammation and rheumatism* 1828; *A defence of revealed religion* 1851; *Memories of the past and thoughts on the present age* 1863; *The food of the people* 1865. *d.* Villiers st. Sunderland 19 Nov. 1868. *Munk's Roll of physicians iii,* 284 (1878); *Medical times and gazette ii,* 683–4 (1868).

BROWN, LEWIS GEORGE. *b.* 23 Feb. 1838; ensign 5 Bombay N.I. 13 July 1854; wing commander 8 Bombay N.I. 30 June 1877 to death; lieut. col. staff corps 9 June 1880 to death. *d.* Sibi, Afghanistan 11 Aug. 1880. *I.L.N. lxxvii,* 309 (1880), *portrait*.

BROWN, OLIVER MADOX (*son of Ford Madox Brown of London, historical painter*). *b.* Finchley 20 Jany. 1855; ed. at Univ. coll. London; exhibited 2 water colours at Dudley Gallery 1869–70; exhibited a water colour "Exercise" at the R.A. 1870, "Prospero and the infant Miranda" at International exhibition South Kensington 1871 and "Silas Marner" at Society of French artists 1872; published a story entitled *Gabriel Denver* 5 Nov. 1873. *d.* Fitzroy sq. London 5 Nov. 1874. *O. M. Brown, a biographical sketch by H. Ingram* (1883), 2 *portraits; The Dwale Bluth and other literary remains of O. M. Brown* 2 vols. 1876, 2 *portraits; Scribner's Mag. xii,* 425–8 (1876).

BROWN, PETER. Ensign 82 Foot 7 Dec. 1799; major 23 Foot 20 July 1815 to 25 July 1816 when placed on h.p.; commandant of Royal military asylum at Chelsea 15 Dec. 1843 to 1851; M.G. 9 Nov. 1846; served in the Peninsula 1810 to end of the war. *d.* Gosport 3 Jany. 1853.

BROWN, PETER. *b.* Perth; editor of the *Dundee Advertiser* about 1835; edited the *Dundee Herald* originally called *Dundee Chronicle*; a reporter on the *Morning Post* in London to death. *d.* 5 April 1855.

BROWN, PETER. *b.* Scotland 29 June 1784; merchant in Edinburgh; went to New York 1838; editor and proprietor of the *British Chronicle*; removed to Toronto 1843 where he established *The Banner* 18 Aug. 1843 and edited it; author of *The fame and glory of England vindicated, by Libertas* 1842. *d.* Toronto 30 June 1863. *Morgan's Bibl. Canad.* (1867) *r.* 51.

BROWN, RAWDON LUBBOCK. *b.* 1803; lived at Venice 1833 to death; commissioned by Lord Palmerston to calendar Venetian state papers treating of English history 1862 for which purpose he examined twelve million packets of documents in North Italy; author of *Calendar of state papers and manuscripts relating to English affairs existing in the archives and collections of Venice and of other libraries of Northern Italy* 8 vols. 1864–84. *d.* Casa della Vida, Venice 25 Aug. 1883. *Times 29 Aug., 8 Sep. and 13 Sep. 1883; Athenæum 8 Sep. 1883 p.* 307.

BROWN, ROBERT (2 *son of Rev. James Brown, Episcopalian minister of Montrose*). *b.* Montrose 21 Dec. 1773; ed. at Marischal coll. Aberdeen and Univ. of Edin.; naturalist to H.M.S. Investigator under Flinders 1801–5 when he collected nearly 4000 species of dried plants; librarian to Linnæan Society 1805–20; custodian of library and collections of Sir Joseph Banks 1810–20; keeper of Banksian botanical collection at British Museum 1827 to death; F.R.S. 12 Dec. 1811, Copley medallist 1839; F.L.S. 1822, pres. 1849 to May 1853; one of the 8 foreign associates of French Academy of Sciences 1833; an honorary member of every academy in Europe; granted a civil list pension of £200, 14 Sep. 1843; author of *Prodromus Floræ Novæ Hollandiæ et insulæ Van Diemen* 1810; *Vermischte botanische Schriften, ed. by C. G. Nees von Esenbeck* 5 vols. 1825–34. *d.* 17 Dean st. Soho, London 10 June 1858. *Proc. of Royal Soc. ix, 527–32 (1858); Proc. of Linnæan Soc. (1859) 25–30; Journal of Royal*

BROWN, R. (*Con.*)
Geog. Soc. xxix, 115–19 (1859); *I.L.N. xxxiii,* 29 (1858), *portrait.*

BROWN, REV. ROBERT CHRISTOPHER LUNDIN (*son of Rev. Robert Brown, minister of Largo*). ed. at Univ. of Edin., M.A. 1854; missionary in British Columbia 1860–5; V. of Lineal Salop 1869–74; P.C. of Rhodes near Manchester 1874–5; author of *British Columbia* 1863; *The dead in Christ* 1868; *Klatsassan* 1873; *The life of Peace* 1876. *d.* 26 Grafton sq. Clapham, London 16 April 1876.

BROWN, SIR SAMUEL (*eld. son of Wm. Brown of Borland, co. Galloway*). *b.* London 1776; entered navy 8 June 1795; commander 1 Aug. 1811; retired captain 18 May 1842; invented iron chain cables, described in *Philosophical Magazine* Oct. 1814; built Union suspension bridge over the Tweed near Berwick 1820; erected chain pier at Brighton 1823; K.H. 13 Jany. 1835; knighted at St. James's palace 21 Feb. 1838; took out patents for chains and chain cables and ten other patents. *d.* Vanbrugh lodge, Blackheath 15 March 1852. *G.M. xxxvii,* 519–20 (1852).

BROWN, SAMUEL. Cornet 6 Dragoons 15 March 1798; assistant quartermaster general to the army in Egypt 1801; major York light infantry 25 Sep 1807 to 19 March 1817 when placed on h.p.; general 20 June 1854. *d.* Bromley, Kent 2 March 1855.

BROWN, SAMUEL (4 *son of Samuel Brown of Haddington, founder of itinerating libraries*). *b.* Haddington 23 Feb. 1817; ed. at high sch. and univ. of Edin., M.D. 1839; delivered a course of lectures on philosophy of the sciences at Edin. 1840–1, and 4 lectures on the Atomic theory 1843; contested chair of chemistry in Univ. of Edin. 1843; experimented on the atomic constitution of bodies; author of *The tragedy of Galileo Galilei in 5 acts and in verse* 1850; *Lectures on the atomic theory and essays scientific and literary* 2 vols. 1858, and of many articles in *North British Review* and other periodicals. *d.* Canaan grove, Morningside, Edin. 20 Sep. 1856. *Macmillan's Mag. xii,* 74–82 (1865); *North British Review Nov.* 1856.

BROWN, SAMUEL. *b.* 1812; actuary of Mutual life office 1850 and of Guardian insurance company 1855; advocated uniform weights and measures throughout commercial world; an active founder of Institute of Actuaries 1848, pres. 1867–70, instituted the Brown prize; joint editor of *Journal of Institute of Actuaries;* pres. over section of Economic

BROWN, S. (Con.)

Science and Statistics at British Association in Norwich 1868; author of numerous papers in *Assurance Magazine* 1850 to death and in *Journal of Statistical Society*. *d*. The Elms 42 Lark hall rise, Clapham, London 20 March 1875. *C. Walford's Insurance Cyclopedia i*, 395–6 (1871).

BROWN, THOMAS. Midshipman R.N. 1787; captain 22 Jany. 1806; commanded the Ordinary at Sheerness 1816–19; commanded Vigo 74 guns, Tartar 42 guns, Talavera 74 guns and Caledonia 120 guns, successively May 1833 to Oct. 1835 when placed on h.p.; admiral on h.p. 4 July 1855. *d*. Southampton 17 June 1857 aged 79.

BROWN, THOMAS (*son of Christopher Brown, member of firm of Longmans, publishers, London who d. 1807*). *b*. near Paternoster Row, London 1778; ed. at Christ's hospital; apprenticed in his father's firm Dec. 1792; a partner 1811 to June 1859; a liveryman of Stationers Company 1804, warden and upper warden 1856–8; gave a stained glass west window to St. Paul's cathedral which was uncovered 19 March 1867; left by his will £10,000 to Booksellers Provident Institution, £10,000 to Booksellers Retreat and £10,000 to Christ's hospital. *d*. 39 Ludgate hill, London 24 March 1869. *W. H. Blanch's Famous blue-coat boys* (1880) 59–83; *Reg. and mag. of biog. i*, 480–2 (1869).

BROWN, RIGHT REV. THOMAS JOSEPH. *b*. Bath 2 May 1798; received Benedictine habit at the college Acton Burnell near Shrewsbury 19 April 1813, removed with the college to St. Gregory's college Downside near Bath where he was professed 28 Oct. 1814, professor of theology there 1823–40, prior of the college 18 July 1834 to 3 July 1840; ordained priest in London 12 March 1823; cathedral prior of Winchester 1833–40; D.D. 24 July 1834; vicar Apostolic of newly created Welsh district 3 July 1840; consecrated in St. John's chapel Bath, Bishop of Apollonia in Archdiocese of Thessalonica 28 Oct. 1840; bishop of Newport and Menevia 29 Sep. 1850 to death; assistant at pontifical throne 29 Nov. 1854; author of various pamphlets and letters in defence of doctrines of Church of Rome. *d*. Bullingham near Hereford 12 April 1880. *M. Brady's Episcopal succession iii*, 337, 354, 424–6 (1877); *Downside Review July* 1880 *pp*. 4–16.

BROWN, REV. THOMAS RICHARD (*son of Richard Brown of Cambridge*). *b*. 1791; ed. at St. John's coll. Cam., B.A. 1815, M.A.

BROWN, REV. T. R. (Con.)

1820; V. of Southwick near Oundle, Northamptonshire 1834 to death; author of *English terminations* 1838; *Hebrew hieroglyphs* 1840; *Etymological dictionary 2 vols*. 1843; *Essentials of Sanscrit grammar* 1851. *d*. Southwick 1 Sep. 1875.

BROWN, WILLIAM (*son of a small farmer at Foxford, co. Mayo*). *b*. Foxford 22 June 1777; went to Pennsylvania 1786; commanded an English merchant ship; commodore in navy of Buenos Ayres Feb. 1814; destroyed Spanish fleets at Martin Garcia and Monte Video 1814 and in Pacific ocean and Caribbean sea 1815–18; commanded Buenos Ayres fleet in war against Brazil 12 Jany. 1826 to 1828; assumed reins of government on breaking out of civil war 1842. *d*. Barracas near Buenos Ayres 3 May 1857. *M. G. Mulhall's English in South America* (1878) 144–69, *portrait*.

BROWN, WILLIAM (4 *son of James Brown of Cononsyth, flax-spinner*). Flax-spinner with his brother James at East Ward mill Dundee 1809–56, in 1811 every mill in Dundee was stopped except their mill and the Dens mill; author of *Reminiscences of flax-spinning* 1862 and of a volume of poetry. *d*. 14 Nov. 1864 aged 73. *Norrie's Dundee Celebrities* (1873) 245–8.

BROWN, REV. WILLIAM. Professor of Biblical criticism and theology at St. Andrews University Scotland 14 June 1851 to death; author of *The scientific character of the Scottish universities viewed in connection with religious belief and their educational use* 1856. *d*. St. Andrews 19 July 1868 aged 68.

BROWN, SIR WILLIAM, 1 Baronet (*eld. son of Alexander Brown of Ballymena, co. Antrim, linen merchant 1764–1834*). *b*. Ballymena 30 May 1784; ed. at Catterick, Yorkshire; went to the United States 1800; partner in firm of Alexander Brown and Sons of Baltimore, linen merchants; founded firm of Brown, Shipley and Co. at Liverpool 1810 which became leading house in American trade; alderman of Liverpool 1831–8; M.P. for South Lancashire 21 July 1846 to 23 April 1859; raised and equipped a corps of artillery which ranks as the 1 brigade of Lancashire artillery volunteers 1859; a director of Atlantic telegraph company Dec. 1856, chairman; erected at a cost of £40,000 Free public library and Derby museum at Liverpool opened 8 Oct. 1860; created a baronet 24 Jany. 1863; sheriff of Lancashire 1863. *d*. Richmond hill, Liverpool 3 March 1864.

Personalty sworn under £900,000, 21 May 1864. *H. R. F. Bourne's English merchants ii*, 307–20 (1866); *I.L.N. xix*, 70 (1851), *portrait*.

BROWN, SIR WILLIAM (*son of Richard Brown, chief examiner of accounts at the War Office London*). *b.* 1812; a temporary clerk in office of Secretary at war Dec. 1828; a first class clerk on the consolidation of War office Jany. 1856; assistant accountant general Oct. 1857; accountant general Aug. 1860 to 1 April 1870 when he retired on a pension of £800 a year; C.B. 7 Dec. 1868; knighted at Windsor Castle 18 May 1870. *d.* Hillside, Parkstone, Dorset 19 May 1884.

BROWN, WILLIAM GUSTAVUS. *b.* 5 Feb. 1809; ensign 24 Foot 7 July 1825, lieut. col. 21 Dec. 1849 to 1 Sep. 1861 when placed on h.p.; brigadier general Bengal 28 July 1858 to 15 Nov. 1859 and 5 Sep. 1860 to 2 April 1861; brigadier general Aldershot 1 Sep. 1861 to 28 Feb. 1863; colonel 83 Foot 29 May 1873 to death; general 1 Oct. 1877. *d.* Sydenham 27 Nov. 1883.

BROWN, WILLIAM ROBERT HENRY. Projector and one of founders of Morning Advertiser, first number issued 8 Feb. 1794 and of Licensed Victuallers schools at Kennington 1794; projected Golden Lane brewery in which 600 persons were proprietors Sep. 1804; common councilman for ward of Cripplegate 1807; one of founders of Hope Life Insurance Company, the first chairman; governor of Newgate 1817 to 1822 when he resigned; warden of the Fleet prison in city of London and keeper of the old and new palaces in county of Middlesex (alias Westminster Hall) 13 April 1822 to 31 May 1842 when appointment was abolished by act of Parliament 5 and 6 Vict. c. 22 and the prisoners were transferred to Queen's Bench prison. *d.* 3 Doughty st. London 15 Feb. 1853 aged 86.

BROWN, REV. WILSE. Educ. at Em. coll. Cam., scholar; B.A. 1833; P.C. of Eggleston, Durham 1835–57; R. of Whitstone near Exeter 1857 to death; private in Exeter Rifle Corps 1862 to death being only clergyman in England serving in Volunteer Corps, gained many prizes at Wimbledon. *d.* Whitstone rectory 22 Jany. 1883 aged 72.

BROWN–GREIVE, JOHN TATTON. Second lieut. R.M. 21 May 1811, lieut. col. 13 Dec. 1852, col. commandant 30 Oct. 1855 to 1 April 1870 when he retired on full pay; granted good service pension 1 April 1857;

general 13 Feb. 1867; C.B. 2 June 1869. *d.* Orde house near Berwick-on-Tweed 4 Nov. 1880 aged 85.

BROWNBILL, REV. FRANCIS. *b.* Gillmoss, Lancs. 5 Nov. 1793; entered Society of Jesus at Hodder 7 Sep. 1813; ordained priest in Dublin Dec. 1819; superior of St. George's Residence Worcester and of College of St. Francis Xavier 1838–42; superior at the Seminary Stonyhurst 1847; missioner at Newhall, Chelmsford 1843–63; superior at the Little college Hodder Dec. 1864. *d.* Stonyhurst college 13 May 1875.

BROWNBILL, REV. JAMES (*brother of the preceding*). *b.* Gillmoss 31 July 1798; entered Society of Jesus 7 Sep. 1815; ordained priest at Stonyhurst 30 July 1829; rector of Stonyhurst college 15 May 1836; minister of Stonyhurst 29 May 1839; rector of college of St. Ignatius London 1841–54; missioner to Bury St. Edmunds 1854. *d.* Newhall, Chelmsford 14 Jany. 1880.

BROWNE, ALEXANDER. *b.* Langlands parish of Twynholm 1800; ed. at Univ. of Edin.; hospital assistant in the army 16 June 1825; assistant surgeon 23 foot 3 Aug. 1826; went on a medical mission to Emperor of Morocco 1827 whom he cured of ague; surgeon to 37 foot 22 Nov. 1839 to 2 Aug. 1850 when placed on h.p.. *d.* Langlands 15 April 1872. *Medical times and gazette i*, 613 (1872).

BROWNE, ANDREW. *b.* 6 June 1820; Ensign 28 foot 30 April 1841; lieut. col. 44 foot 10 Nov. 1869 to 27 Sep. 1871 when placed on h.p.; C.B. 28 Feb. 1861; granted a service reward 9 Sep. 1878; placed on retired list with hon. rank of L.G. 1 July 1881. *d.* Dublin 8 April 1883.

BROWNE, CHARLES ALFRED (*son of Wm. Loder Browne of Kennington, London, merchant*). Entered Madras army 1826; sec. to military department 4 Feb. 1845 to 1860; M.G. 6 April 1862; a leading member of Church Missionary Society. *d.* King's head court, St. Martin's le grand, London 14 Feb. 1866 aged 65.

BROWNE, CHARLES FARRAR. *b.* Waterford, Maine 26 April 1834; a printer in Maine, Boston and Cincinnati; wrote in the *Cleveland Plaindealer* a letter purporting to come from a travelling showman signing it with nom de plume of Artemus Ward; edited *Vanity Fair* the leading comic paper in New York 1861; gave his first lecture in New York at Clinton hall 23 Dec. 1861; went to California and

Utah 1862; went to England 1866; contributed to *Punch* 1866; lectured at the Egyptian hall, Piccadilly 13 Nov. 1866 to 23 Jany. 1867. *d.* Radley's hotel, Southampton 6 March 1867. *The genial showman by E. P. Hingston* 1871; *Essays by E. S. Nadal* 1882 16–41; *Illust. sporting news v,* 705 (1866), *portrait.*

BROWNE, CHARLES THOMAS. *b.* Wellington, Somerset 1825; ed. at Trin. coll. Dublin; engaged on a London daily paper 1857 to death; author of *Astrello or the prophet's vision* 1850; *Life of Southey* 1854; *The United States constitution and powers* 1856 and under pseudonym of Alexander de Comyne of a poem entitled *Irene* 1844. *d.* Basingstoke 7 Oct. 1868.

BROWNE, FIELDING. Ensign 40 Foot 7 March 1800; major 19 Jany. 1815 to 22 June 1820 when placed on h.p.; C.B. 22 June 1815; colonel 10 Jany. 1837. *d.* Gloucester crescent, Regent's park, London 22 July 1864 aged 79.

BROWNE, GEORGE. Captain 37 Foot 24 March 1825 to 29 Aug. 1826 when placed on h.p.; chief commissioner of Dublin Metropolitan police 1837–58; C.B. 13 June 1857. *d.* Clifton gardens, Folkestone 12 July 1879 aged 91.

BROWNE, GEORGE (2 *son of John Browne of Hall court, Herts. attorney general of Jamaica who d.* 1828). *b.* Jamaica 1825; ed. at Jesus coll. Cam., B.A. 1848; barrister I.T. 4 May 1849; a revising barrister 1868; recorder of Ludlow 22 Jany. 1873 to death; Q.C. 24 March 1880; author of *A treatise on the principles and practice of the court for divorce and matrimonial causes* 1864, 4 ed. 1880; *A treatise on the principles and practice of the court of probate* 1873, 2 ed. 1881. *d.* Calverley park, Tunbridge Wells 19 Sep. 1880.

BROWNE, RIGHT REV. GEORGE JOSEPH PLUNKET. *b.* about 1790; ed. at Maynooth; parish priest of Athlone many years; bishop of Galway 6 Aug. 1831, consecrated by Abp. of Tuam 23 Oct. 1831; translated to Elphin 26 March 1844. *d.* 1 Dec. 1858 in 68 year. *W. M. Brady's Episcopal succession ii,* 208, 231–2 (1876).

BROWNE, HABLOT KNIGHT (9 *son of Wm. Loder Browne of Kennington, London, merchant). b.* Lower Kennington lane, London 15 June 1815; apprenticed to Wm. Finden the line engraver; illustrated Dickens's *Sunday as it is, by Timothy Sparks* 1836, published at 1/- but now worth more than its weight in gold; illustrated under pseudonym of Phiz *Pickwick*

papers, Martin Chuzzlewit and many other of Dickens's novels; exhibited many watercolours at Brit. Instit. and Soc. of Brit. artists; illustrated many of Lever's and Ainsworth's novels; contributed about 350 sketches to *Judy* July 1869 to death. *d.* Hove, Brighton 8 July 1882. *D. C. Thomson's Life and labours of H. K. Browne* 1884, *portrait; Phiz, a memoir by J. G. Kitton* 1882, *portrait; Graphic xxvi,* 132 (1882), *portrait; G. Everitt's English Caricaturists* (1886) 336–54, 412–16.

BROWNE, REV. HENRY (*son of Rev. John Henry Browne, R. of Crownthorpe, Norfolk who d.* 1 *May* 1843 *aged* 75). *b.* 1804; ed. at C.C. coll. Cam.; Bell Univ. scholar 1823, B.A. 1826, M.A. 1830; V. of Rudgwick, Sussex 1831; R. of Earnley, Sussex 1833; principal of diocesan theol. coll. Chichester 1842–7; preb. of Chichester cath. 9 Dec. 1842; chaplain to bishop of Chichester 1847–70; P.C. of St. Bartholomew's Chichester 1850–4; R. of Pevensey 1854 to death; author of *Ordo sæculorum* 1844; *Remarks on Mr. Greswell's Fasti Catholici* 1852; translated with C. L. Cornish for the 'Library of the Fathers' 17 short treatises of St. Augustine. *d.* Pevensey 19 June 1875.

BROWNE, VERY REV. HENRY MONTAGUE (2 *son of 2 Baron Kilmaine* 1765–1825). *b.* 3 Oct. 1799; dean of cathedral church of St. Carthagh, Lismore 1850 to death. *d.* Bredon rectory, Worcs. 24 Nov. 1884.

BROWNE, RIGHT REV. JAMES. *b.* Mayglass, Forth, co. Wexford 1786; ed. at Maynooth college; dean of Maynooth 1814–6, professor of Sacred Scriptures 1816–27; bishop of Kilmore 20 March 1827 to death; consecrated to see of Magida *in partibus* 10 June 1827; *d.* Cavan 11 April 1865. *Battersby's Catholic directory* (1866) 389–92.

BROWNE, JAMES SOLOMON. *b.* Paddington, London 6 Aug. 1791; ed. at Eton; clerk in Prerogative office Doctors Commons 1802; played Harlequin to Grimaldi at Birmingham; played at Liverpool 1813–23 and 1826–38; first appeared in London at Drury Lane 7 Oct. 1823 as Lord Foppington in *A trip to Scarborough;* became most versatile actor of of the day; acted in America 1838, at Olympic theatre London 1845, afterwards in New York; the original Robert Macaire in the drama of that name; retired from the stage 1858. *d.* New York 28 Nov. 1869. *Oxberry's Dramatic biography ii,* 177–88 (1825), *portrait.*

BROWNE, VEN. JOHN HENRY. Educ. at St. John's coll. Cam.; R. of Cotgrave near Nottingham 1811 to death; archdeacon of Ely 23 Sep. 1816 to death; preb. of Ely 26 June 1817. *d.* Cotgrave 2 Nov. 1858 aged 79.

BROWNE, JOHN ROSS. *b.* Ireland 1817; passed his youth in state of Kentucky; went to California 1849; went to Europe as a newspaper correspondent 1851; inspector of custom houses on northen frontier of the U.S.; reported on the mineral resources of the country west of the Rocky Mountains for the Government 1866 and 1868; United States minister in China 1868–9; author of *Etchings of a whaling cruise* 1846; *Crusoe's Island* 1864; *An American family in Germany* 1866; *The land of Thor* 1867. *d.* Oakland near San Francisco 7 Dec. 1875.

BROWNE, JOHN SAMUEL (*eld. son of John Browne of London, landscape engraver who d. 2 Oct. 1801 in 60 year*). *b.* St. Saviour's, Southwark 15 Sep. 1782; clerk in the East India house 1801; author of *A catalogue of bishops containing the succession of archbishops and bishops of Canterbury and York from 1688 to the present time* 1812; contributed to *Gentlemen's Mag.* and *Morning Herald. d.* Walworth, Surrey 6 June 1858. *Gent. Mag. v,* 198 (1858).

BROWNE, PETER. *b.* 1794; M.P. for Rye 18 June 1818 to 2 June 1826; chargé d' affaires at Copenhagen 8 times during the period 1823–52; retired on a pension 6 Jany. 1853. *d.* Pallanza 7 April 1872.

BROWNE, PHILIP. *b.* 16 Sep. 1772; entered navy 1 July 1777; captain 19 June 1810; captain of the Hermes 20 guns 1811–14 when placed on h.p.; V.A. on h.p. 15 April 1854. *d.* Parkstone near Poole, Dorset 25 Jany. 1860.

BROWNE, REV. SAMUEL (*son of Rev. John W. Browne, Independent minister*). *b.* England 19 March 1788; went to Cincinnati with his father 1798; a minister of the United Brethren; joined presbytery of Cincinnati about 1868; accumulated a large fortune by the rise of real estate in Cincinnati; bequeathed sum of 150,000 dollars for establishment of a university to bear his name also land whereon to erect the building and an endowment for professorships. *d.* Harrison junction, Ohio 10 Sep. 1872.

BROWNE, THOMAS. Entered navy 5 April 1782; captain 29 April 1802; V.A. 11 Dec. 1846. *d.* Clifton 7 April 1851 in 83 year. *O'Byrne's Naval biog. dict.* (1849) 136.

BROWNE, SIR THOMAS HENRY (*elder son of George Browne of Liverpool, Tuscan consul*). *b.* Liverpool 8 Sep. 1787; ensign 23 foot 28 Oct. 1805, captain 15 April 1813 to 25 Dec. 1814 when placed on h.p.; received war medal with 8 clasps; aide-de-camp to Marquis of Londonderry at head quarters of Russian and Austrian armies 1815; L.G. 20 June 1854; colonel 80. foot 19 Aug. 1854 to death; sheriff of Flintshire 1824; K.C.H. 1826. *d.* London 11 March 1855.

BROWNE, WALTER JOHN. Ensign Bombay army 17 Sep. 1819; col. 14 N.I. 22 Aug. 1857–1869; general 29 Aug. 1873; C.B. 4 July 1843. *d.* Warkworth 31 Oct. 1881 aged 81.

BROWNE, WALTER RALEIGH (*3 son of Rev. Thomas Murray Browne, V. of Almondsbury, Gloucs.*) *b.* Standish, Gloucs. 1842; ed. at home and Trin. coll. Cam., scholar 1863, 19 wrangler and tenth classic 1865, B.A. 1865; fellow of his coll. 1867; managing director of Bridgewater Engineering company 1874–8; M.I.M.E. 1869, sec. 1878 to Jany. 1884; M.I.C.E. 27 May 1879, Telford medallist 1871 and 1876; F.G.S.; F.R.G.S.; one of founders of Society for Psychical Research 1882; lectured frequently for Christian evidence society; author of *Facts and fallacies of pauper education* 1878; *The inspiration of the New Testament* 1880; *The foundations of mechanics* 1882; *The student's mechanics* 1883. *d.* from typhoid fever in the general hospital, Montreal 4 Sep. 1884. *Min. of Proc. of Instit. of C.E. lxxix,* 362–6 (1885).

BROWNE, WILLIAM. *b.* 1 Nov. 1791; M.P. for co. Kerry 19 July 1841 to 23 July 1847. *d.* at his house in London 4 Aug. 1876.

BROWNE, WILLIAM ALEXANDER FRANCIS. *b.* near Stirling 1805; ed. in Edinburgh high school and Univ., M.D. 1826; L.R.C.S. Edin. 1826; studied in France 1826–30; physician at Stirling 1830; superintendent of Montrose lunatic asylum; superintendent of Crichton Instit. at Dumfries 1839; paid Comr. in lunacy for Scotland 23 Sep. 1857 to 1870; the first phys. in Scotland who adopted new system of treating the insane; author of *What asylums were, are, and ought to be. d.* Crindan, Dumfries 2 March 1885 aged 79.

BROWNE, WILLIAM CHESELDEN. *b.* 1805; entered navy 1816; captain 9 Jany. 1854; retired admiral 9 Jany. 1880; sec. to Royal yacht club at Cowes 1853–60. *d.* Townsend house, West Cowes 6 April 1881.

BROWNE, VEN. WILLIAM HENRY. Educ. at Trin. coll. Dublin; archdeacon of Launceston, Tasmania 1870 to death. *d.* Launceston 18 June 1877 aged 77.

BROWNE, WILLIAM HENRY JAMES (*son of Mr. Browne, harbour master at Dublin*). Served in merchant service; 2 lieut. of the Enterprise 1848–9; led a sledge party from Port Leopold to east coast of Prince Regent's Inlet; 2 lieut. of the Resolute 1850–1; his sketches of Arctic scenery at Port Leopold were published by Ackerman 1849; assisted in painting the Arctic panorama in Leicester square London; retired commander 1 July 1864. *d.* Woolwich March–June 1871.

BROWNE, WILLIAM MEREDITH. Assistant sec. of Westminster Fire Office 1831, sec. 1838 to death; a founder of Mutual Life Office 1834; founded Westminster and General Life Office 1839, actuary 1839–69; hon. sec. of London Fire Engine Establishment 1832–65, when the work was undertaken by Metropolitan Board of Works. *d.* Clarendon road, Putney 30 March 1880 aged 74.

BROWNING, COLIN ARROTT. Surgeon in the navy 8 Feb. 1817; surgeon of the Surrey, convict ship 1831 and of six other convict ships 1834–46; retired deputy inspector of hospitals 30 June 1856; author of *England's exiles* 1842; *The Convict ship* 1844; *The convict ship and England's exiles*, 6 ed. 1855. *d.* Woolwich 26 Oct. 1856.

BROWNING, ELIZABETH BARRETT (*eld. dau. of Edward Moulton of Burn hall, Durham*). *b.* Burn hall 6 March 1809; lived at 74 Gloucester place London many years; lived at Florence 1847 to death. (*m.* 9 Sep. 1846 Robert Browning the poet). author of *An essay on mind, with other poems,* anon. 1826; *Casa Guidi Windows* a poem 1851; *Aurora Leigh* 1857, 18 *ed.* 1884 and many other poems. *d.* Casa Guidi, Florence 30 June 1861. *The poetical works of E. B. Browning, complete with a memoir* 2 vols. *New York* 1871; *P. Bayne's Two great Englishwomen* (1881), 1–154; *Macpherson's Memoirs of the life of Anna Jameson* (1878) 191–263; *G. B. Smith's Poets and novelists* (1875) 57–110; *M. R. Mitford's Recollections of a literary life* (1859), 154–68; *T. H. Ward's English poets,* 2 ed. (1883) *iv,* 562–80.

BROWNING, GEORGE. Secretary of Society for promoting the fine arts; author of *Footprints, poems translated and original* 1871; *A memoir of the late Emperor Napoleon iii, and a political poem entitled Rip Van Winkle,* 2 ed.

BROWNING, G. (*Con.*)

1873; *The Edda, songs and sagas of Iceland,* a lecture, 2 ed. 1876. *d.* 21 Kildare gardens, London 20 Dec. 1878 in 65 year.

BROWNING, WILLIAM SHERGOLD (*uncle of Robert Browning the poet*). author of *Leisure hours* 1801; *The history of the Huguenots during the sixteenth century* 2 vols. 1829, *new ed.* 1845; *Hoel Morvan or the court and camp of Henry v,* 3 vols. 1844. *d.* 4 March 1874.

BROWNLOW, JOHN CUST, 1 Earl (*eld. son of Brownlow Cust, 1 baron Brownlow 1744–1807*). *b.* 19 Aug. 1779; ed. at Trin. coll. Cam., B.A. 1801, LL.D. 1835; created D.C.L. at Ox. 10 June 1834; M.P. for Clitheroe 6 July 1802 to Jany. 1808; colonel of Royal Lincoln militia; succeeded 25 Dec. 1807; lord lieut. of Lincolnshire 1 March 1809; created Viscount Alford and Earl Brownlow 27 Nov. 1815; recorder of Boston 12 Dec. 1820; G.C.H. 1834; pres. of Archæological Institute at Lincoln 1848; F.L.S. 1828, F.R.S. 8 May 1838. *d.* Belton house, Grantham 15 Sep. 1853. *Portraits and memoirs of eminent Conservatives, portrait; Waagen's Treasures of art ii,* 313–16 (1854).

BROWNLOW, JOHN WILLIAM SPENCER BROWNLOW EGERTON CUST, 2 Earl. *b.* Carlton gardens, London 28 March 1842; succeeded 15 Sep. 1853. *d.* Mentone 20 Feb. 1867. *bur.* at Belton 2 March. *Good words viii,* 373 (1867), *a poem by G. Massey; I.L.N. li,* 609 (1867), *portrait.*

BROWNLOW, EMMA SOPHIA CUST, Countess (*eld. dau. of Richard Edgcumbe, 2 Earl of Mount Edgcumbe 1764–1839*). *b.* Portugal st. London 28 July 1791; one of the 6 ladies of the bedchamber to Queen Adelaide July 1830 to 2 Dec. 1849 when the Queen died; author of *Slight reminiscences of a septuagenarian* 1867, 3 *ed.* 1868. (*m.* 17 July 1828 1 Earl Brownlow). *d.* Belton lodge, Torquay 28 Jany. 1872. *I.L.N. lxi,* 139, 434 (1872).

BROWNLOW, FRANCIS (*eld. son of Wm. Brownlow*). *b.* 19 July 1836; ed. at Harrow; ensign 72 Foot 8 Sep. 1854, lieut. col. 15 Aug. 1877 to death; C.B. 19 Nov. 1879; served in Crimean war, Indian mutiny and Afghan war; killed at battle with Ayab Khan's army in Kandahar 1 Sep. 1880. *Shadbolt's Afghan campaign* (1882) 27–8, *portrait; I.L.N. lxxvii,* 309 (1880), *portrait.*

BROWNLOW, VERY REV. JOHN. Ordained 1832; R. of Ardbraccan, Navan 1843 to death; dean of Clonmacnois, Meath 1862 to death. *d.* Ardbraccan rectory 24 May 1882 aged 77.

BROWNRIGG, CHARLES JAMES. *b.* 19 Nov. 1836; captain R.N. 18 Sep. 1873; captain of Euphrates, Indian troop ship 22 April 1878; captain of London, store ship 8 June 1880 to death; killed by the crew of a slave dhow off Zanzibar 3 Dec. 1881. *I.L.N. lxxix*, 650 (1881), *portrait; Graphic xxv*, 45 (1882), *portrait.*

BROWNRIGG, SIR HENRY JOHN *(eld. son of general Thomas Brownrigg who d. May* 1826). *b.* 18 June 1798; 2 lieut. Rifle brigade 6 Dec. 1813, lieut. 23 Dec. 1819 to 23 April 1826 when placed on h.p.; entered Irish Constabulary 1826, inspector general 1858 to 1865; C.B. 13 June 1857; knighted by Earl of Eglinton lord lieutenant of Ireland 1858. *d.* 12 Talbot sq. Hyde park, London 25 Nov. 1873.

BROWNRIGG, JOHN STUDHOLME. *b.* 17 March 1786; a merchant in London; M.P. for Boston 9 Jany. 1835 to 23 July 1847. *d.* Ashford lodge, Middlesex 21 Sep. 1853.

BROWNRIGGE, SIR ROBERT WILLIAM COLE-BROOK, 2 Baronet. *b.* Audley square, London 29 July 1817; succeeded 27 May 1833. *d.* 12 Eaton place West, London 6 Aug. 1882.

BROWNSMITH, JOHN LEMAN. *b.* Westminster 1809; chorister at Westminster Abbey; organist of St. John's church Waterloo road, London 1829–53; lay vicar of Westminster Abbey 1838; organist to Sacred harmonic society 1848; organist at Handel festivals Crystal palace 1857, 1859, 1862 and 1865; organist of St. Gabriel, Pimlico 1853 to death; published *The psalms and hymns in the morning and evening services with the pointing completed for chanting* 1839; *A course of Psalms* 1848. *d.* 104 Cambridge st. Pimlico, London 14 Sep. 1866.

BRUCE, ALEXANDER *(2 son of Henry Bruce of London).* Educ. at Univ. coll. London 1858–64; lecturer on anatomy and assistant surgeon to Wesminster hospital Dec. 1867 to death; invented the gas cautery which has proved very successful; author of *Observations in the military hospitals of Dresden* 1866; *An epitome of the Venereal diseases* 1868. *d.* 6 Albert terrace, Regent's park, London 11 April 1869 aged 27. *Reg. and mag. of biog. i*, 406 (1869).

BRUCE, DAVID. *b.* Scotland 1770; went to New York 1793; started with his brother George a book printing office at corner of Pearl st. New York 1806, removed to Sloat lane 1809 where they had 9 presses at work; learnt art of stereotyping in England 1812

BRUCE, D. *(Con.)* which he established in America, retired from business 1822; published *Specimens of printing types New York* 1815. *d.* New York 1857.

BRUCE, EYRE EVANS. Entered Madras army 1827; colonel 35 Madras N.I. 5 July 1854 to 1869; general 3 Sep. 1871. *d.* Doneraile, Ireland 10 April 1874.

BRUCE, SIR FREDERICK WILLIAM ADOLPHUS *(3 son of Thomas Bruce, 7 Earl of Elgin* 1766–1841). *b.* Broomhall, Dunfermline 14 April 1814; colonial sec. at Hong Kong 9 Feb. 1844; lieut. governor of Newfoundland 27 June 1846; consul general in Bolivia 23 July 1847; chargé d' affaires in Uruguay 29 Aug. 1851; agent and consul general in Egypt 3 Aug. 1853; principal sec. to 8 Earl of Elgin British ambassador in China April 1857; envoy extraord. and minister plenipo. to Emperor of China 2 Dec. 1858; chief superintendent of British trade in China 1 March 1859; envoy extraord. and min. plenipo. to the United States 1 March 1865 to death; C.B. 28 Sep. 1858, K.C.B. 12 Dec. 1862, G.C.B. 17 March 1865. *d.* Boston, United States 19 Sep. 1867. *bur.* Dunfermline abbey 8 Oct. *D. C. Boulger's History of China iii*, (1884); *G.M. iv*, 677–8 (1867).

BRUCE, GEORGE *(brother of David Bruce* 1770–1857). *b.* Edinburgh 26 June 1781; a type founder in New York 1816 to death; harmonised and graduated size of different bodies of type as they ranged in the 11 series from pearl to canon; introduced the body called "agate" which is largely used by American newspapers; pres. of New York Type founders association 1863 to death; invented with his nephew David Bruce type-casting machine which was in general use many years. *d.* New York 6 July 1866.

BRUCE, SIR HENRY WILLIAM *(3 son of Rev. Sir Henry Hervey Aston Bruce, 1 Baronet who d.* 17 Oct. 1822). *b.* 2 Feb. 1792; entered navy 1803; captain 16 Nov. 1821; commodore on West Coast of Africa 5 March 1851; commander in chief in the Pacific 25 Nov. 1854 to 8 July 1857 and at Portsmouth 1 March 1860 to 1 March 1863; admiral 27 April 1863; K.C.B. 28 June 1861. *d.* Fairfield near Liverpool 14 Dec. 1863.

BRUCE, HERBERT. Entered Bombay army 1842; captain 2 European regiment 27 March 1855 to death; C.B. 26 July 1858. *d.* on board Messageries Imperiales steamer, near Suez 26 Feb. 1866 aged 39.

BRUCE, James. *b.* Aberdeen 1808; editor of the *Fifeshire Journal* at Cupar; edited successively *Madras Athenæum, Newcastle Chronicle* and *Belfast Northern Whig;* author of *The black kalendar of Aberdeen* 1840; *Lives of eminent men of Aberdeen* 1841; *Table talk* 1845; *Classic and historic portraits* 1853; *Scenes and sights in the East* 1856. *d.* Belfast 19 Aug. 1861.

BRUCE, Sir James Lewis Knight (3 *son of John Knight of Fairlinch, Devon who d.* 1799). *b.* Barnstaple, Devon 15 Feb. 1791; ed. at Bath gr. sch. and Sherborne 1799–1805; articled to B. C. Williams of Lincoln's Inn Fields solicitor 1807–12; barrister L.I. 21 Nov. 1817, bencher 6 Nov. 1829, treasurer 1842–3, laid foundation stone of the new hall 20 April 1843; practised in Court of Chancery; K.C. Nov. 1829; recorder of Brecon; M.P. for Bishop's Castle 30 April 1831 to 3 Dec. 1832; contested borough of Cambridge Aug. 1837; spoke for 7 days in case of Small *v.* Attwood Nov 1831; leader in Sir Lancelot Shadwell's court 1834; made £18,000 a year 1835–41; assumed by royal license additional surname of Bruce 4 Sep. 1837; vice chancellor 28 Oct. 1841; knighted at Windsor Castle 15 Jany. 1842; P.C. 15 Jany. 1842; chief judge in bankruptcy Nov. 1842; exercised jurisdiction of the old Court of Review, after it's abolition 1847; senior lord justice of appeal in chancery 8 Oct. 1851 to Oct. 1866; F.R.S. 18 March 1829, D.C.L. Ox. 1834. *d.* The Priory, Roehampton, Surrey 7 Nov. 1866. *Law mag. and law review v,* 244–50 (1858), *xxii,* 278–93 (1867); *London Society xi,* 181–8 (1867), *portrait; The bench and the bar, part* 1, *portrait.*

BRUCE, John. *b.* London 1802; a founder of Camden Society 2 March 1838, director 19 years; edited the first and 12 other volumes for the Society; F.S.A. 1830, treasurer 1849–54; edited *Gent. Mag.* some years; edited *Calendars of state papers, domestic series Charles i* 1625–39, 12 *vols.* 1858–71; contributed many papers to the *Archæologia. d.* suddenly in Montagu sq. London 28 Oct. 1869, his library was sold at Sotheby's 27 April to 2 May 1870. *Proc. of Soc. of Antiq.* 2 *series iv,* 472–5 (1870).

BRUCE, Sir Michael, 7 Baronet. *b.* 31 March 1796; succeeded 1827. *d.* Scotstown, Aberdeen 14 Dec. 1862.

BRUCE, Michael. *b.* 16 May 1823; ensign Grenadier guards 15 Dec. 1840, lieut. col. 16 May 1865 to 22 Sep. 1875; L.G. 31 Oct.

BRUCE, M. *(Con.)*
1880; placed on retired list with hon. rank of general 1 July 1881. *d.* Glenelg, Bournemouth 29 Sep. 1883.

BRUCE, Robert (3 *son of Thomas Bruce,* 7 *Earl of Elgin* 1766–1841). *b.* 15 March 1813; ensign Grenadier guards 18 June 1830, major 16 Sep. 1856 to 7 Dec. 1858 when placed on h.p.; military secretary to his brother Lord Elgin in Jamaica 1841–47, in Canada 1847–54; surveyor general of the ordnance 1855; governor to Prince of Wales 9 Nov. 1858 to death; M.G. 7 Dec. 1859. *d.* St. James's palace, London 27 June 1862. *I.L.N. xli,* 58, 61 (1862), *portrait.*

BRUCE, Robert *(eld. son of Alexander Bruce of Kennet, co. Clackmannan). b.* 8 Dec. 1795; ed. at Eton; ensign 1 Foot guards 9 Dec. 1813, lieut. 1820–24 when he sold out; served in the Peninsula and at Waterloo; M.P. for Clackmannan 27 March 1820 to July 1824; vice lieut. and convener of Clackmannan 1853; chairman of Scottish Central railway board; claimed Scottish peerage of Balfour of Burley which was allowed to his son by committee for privileges in House of Lords 23 July 1868. *d.* Kennet house near Alloa 13 Aug. 1864. *M. F. Conolly's Biog. dict. of eminent men of Fife* (1866) 88–90.

BRUCE, Rev. William (2 *son of Rev. Wm. Bruce of Belfast, Presbyterian minister* 1757–1841). *b.* Belfast 16 Nov. 1790; entered Trin. coll. Dublin 2 July 1804, B.A. 1809; licensed by presbytery of Antrim 25 July 1811; presbyterian minister at Belfast 19 Jany. 1812 to 21 April 1867; professor of Classics and Hebrew in Belfast Academical Instit. 27 Oct. 1821 to 1825 and of classics only 1825 to Nov. 1849; moderator of northern presbytery of Antrim 4 April 1862. *d.* 25 Oct. 1868.

BRUCE, William. Captain 79 foot 14 March 1811; served in Peninsula 1812–4 and at Waterloo; major 75 foot 31 Dec. 1827 to 27 Nov. 1828 when placed on h.p.; K.H. 1837; lieut. col. 23 Nov. 1841. *d.* Grosvenor hotel, London 28 Nov. 1868.

BRUCE, William Downing *(eld. son of Samuel Barwick Bruce of Ripon, surgeon* 1786–1853). *b.* 14 Aug. 1824; barrister L.I. and M.T. 30 April 1853; consul in Scotland for Monte Video 1856; recorder of Wallingford June 1863 to 1869; counsel in Yelverton appeal case; district judge at Spanish Town, Jamaica 1869 to death; author of *Chronological tables*

BRUCE, W. D. *(Con.)*

1847 ; *An account of the ecclesiastical courts* 1852 ; *How the ecclesiastical courts rob the public* 1856. *d.* Jamaica 1875.

BRUEN, HENRY. M.P. for county Carlow 30 Oct. 1812 to 23 April 1831 ; colonel commandant of Carlow militia to death. *d.* Oak park, co. Carlow 5 Nov. 1852 in 62 year.

BRUNEL, ISAMBARD KINGDOM *(only son of Sir Mark Isambard Brunel, civil engineer 1769–1849).* *b.* Portsmouth 9 April 1806 ; engineer of Great Western Railway 7 March 1833 which was completed 30 June 1841 ; constructed the station at Paddington 1849–54 ; constructed South Devon railway 1844–6, where his system of atmospheric propulsion failed ; constructed Royal Albert bridge at Saltash 1853–9 ; designed Great Western Steamship launched 19 July 1837 and the Great Britain the first large iron steamship, launched 19 July 1843 ; designed the Great Eastern steamship 1852, she was floated 31 Jany. 1858 ; conducted experiments for Admiralty with screw propeller 1841–4 ; F.R.S. 10 June 1830. *d.* 18 Duke st. Westminster 15 Sep. 1859. *Life of I. K. Brunel by I. Brunel 1870, portrait ; Drawing room portrait gallery of eminent personages 2 series 1859, portrait ; Proc. of Royal Soc. x, 7–11 (1860) ; Min. of proc. of Instit. of C.E. xix, 169–73 (1860).*

BRUNKER, JAMES ROBERT. Ensign 91 foot 9 April 1825 ; deputy adjutant general in Ceylon 24 Aug. 1852 to 6 Aug. 1858 ; major 15 foot 2 Oct. 1854 to 2 Feb. 1855 when placed on h.p. ; M.G. 10 March 1866 ; commanded forces in China 16 Dec. 1867 to death. *d.* Hong Kong 24 March 1869.

BRÜNNOW, ERNST PHILIPP IVANOVITCH, Count de. *b.* Dresden 31 Aug. 1797 ; Russian envoy and minister in London 1840 to 8 Feb. 1854 and 4 Feb. 1861 to July 1874 ; raised to the rank of Count, April 1871. *d.* Darmstadt 11 April 1875. *Illust. News of the World iii,* (1859), *portrait.*

BRUNSWICK AND LUNEBURG, KARL FRIEDRICH AUGUST WILHELM HERZOG VON. *b.* Brunswick 30 Oct. 1804 ; lived at Vauxhall in London 1809–15 ; laid foundation stone of Vauxhall bridge 1814 ; entered on exercise of his authority as Duke of Brunswick 30 Oct. 1823 ; fled to England 7 Sep. 1830, abdicating in favour of his brother William ; was much libelled in the *Age* and *Satirist* 1843 ; crossed to France in Green's balloon the Victoria in 5 hours 31 March 1851 ;

BRUNSWICK, DUKE OF. *(Con.)*

lived in Paris at 52 Champs Elysees and in London at Brunswick house, New road ; bequeathed all his property including his collection of valuable diamonds to city of Geneva. *d.* Geneva 18 Aug. 1873, his decorations consisting of various orders of principal European courts enriched with jewels were sold at Debenhams in London 25 June 1874. *Temple Bar lxxiii,* 353–63 (1885) ; *Life of T. S. Duncombe ii,* 44–99 *and* 162–90 (1868).

BRUNTON, REV. ALEXANDER. *b.* Edinburgh 1772 ; minister of parish of Bolton 1797–1803, of New Greyfriars church Edin. 1803–9 and of the Tron church Edin. 23 Nov. 1809 to death ; professor of Oriental languages in Univ. of Edin. 19 May 1813 to death ; D.D. Edin. 17 Dec. 1813 ; moderator of General Assembly 22 May 1823 ; author of *Sermons and lectures* 1818 ; *Outlines of Persian grammar with extracts* 1822 ; *Forms for public worship in the Church of Scotland* 1848. *d.* Jordonstone house, Coupar Angus 9 Feb. 1854. *W. B. Crombie's Modern Athenians* (1882), *portrait.*

BRUNTON, ROBERT. *b.* Lockwinnock N.B. 10 Feb. 1796 ; chief assistant to his brother W. Brunton 1823 ; engaged by Banks & Co. of Bilston ; principal assistant of Isaac Dodds at the Horsley iron works Staffs. ; in service of Indian iron company 1835 to death ; constructed and managed works at Porto Nuovo on coast of Coromandel ; acting engineer of Maestaeg iron works Glamorganshire to death ; M.I.C.E. 1842 ; author of *A compendium of mechanics or text book for engineers, millwrights, machine makers* 1824, 2 ed. 1825. *d.* Maestaeg iron works 6 July 1852. *Min. of proc. of Instit. of C.E. xii,* 149 (1853).

BRUNTON, WILLIAM *(eld. son of Robert Brunton of Dalkeith, watch maker).* *b.* Dalkeith 26 May 1777 ; partner in and manager of Eagle foundry Birmingham 1815–25 ; civil engineer in London 1825–35 ; partner in Cwm Avon tin works Glamorganshire 1835–8 ; had a large share in introduction of steam navigation ; invented the Calciner used in nearly all Cornish tin mines and Mexican silver mines, and a walking machine called the Steam Horse which was used at Butterley 1813–5 when it exploded and killed 13 persons ; took out many patents. *d.* Camborne, Cornwall 5 Oct. 1851. *Min. of proc. of Instit. of C.E. xi,* 95–9 (1852).

BRUNTON, WILLIAM *(3 son of the preceding).* *b.* Birmingham 3 April 1817 ; resident engineer of West Cornwall railway 1847 ; invented the apparatus for washing and separating ores from their matrix known as "Brunton's endless cloth"; invented a fuse making machine of most ingenious construction, this process has never been divulged, its introduction at once reduced the selling price of fuse by 75 per cent.; chief engineer of the Punjab railway 1865; leaseholder of a sheep-run of 30000 acres in New Zealand; district engineer of railways in Southland, N.Z. 1871; M.I.C.E. 7 March 1854. *d.* Wellington, N.Z. 13 June 1881.

BRUSHFIELD, THOMAS (2 *son of George Brushfield of Ashford-in-the-Water, Derbyshire who d. 25 Feb. 1825 aged 52*). *b.* Ashford-in-the-Water 16 Feb. 1798; kept an oil and colour shop at 28 Union st. Spitalfields, London 1821–55; played under an assumed name at City of London theatre 1827; chairman of Whitechapel board of guardians 1839–48; member for Whitechapel of Metropolitan Board of Works 1865 to death; contributed many papers to *The Reliquary, quarterly archæological journal and review* 1861 to death. *d.* 5 Church st Spitalfields, London 1 Sep. 1875. *Reliquary xvi,* 209–16 (1876).

BRUTON, JAMES. Author of a few dramatic pieces and of many songs. *d.* Palace road, Westminster 5 March 1867 aged 52.

BRYAN, GEORGE LEOPOLD. *b.* Ballyduff house 29 Nov. 1828; sheriff of Kilkenny 1852; M.P. for co. Kilkenny 24 July 1865 to 24 March 1880. *d.* 29 June 1880.

BRYCE, DAVID. *b.* Scotland; private secretary to Benjamin D'Israeli; a publisher in Paternoster Row, London; employed by W. H. Smith the bookseller; compiled *The confessional unmasked* from Petrus Dens's *Theologia moralis et dogmatica* 8 *tomes* 1832. *d.* 1 May 1875 aged 56.

BRYCE, DAVID (*son of Mr. Bryce of Edinburgh, builder*). *b.* Edin. 3 April 1803; partner with Wm. Burn leading architect in Edin. to 1844; became leading architect in Scotland; designed important works in all styles in most of chief towns in Scotland; revived the picturesque French Gothic now naturalised in Scotland under name of Baronial; A.R.S.A. 1835, R.S.A. 1836, F.R.I.B.A., F.R.S. Edin. 1856; grand-architect to grand lodge of Masons in Scotland 1850 to death; built Fettes College, Royal Infirmary, and Bank of Scotland, all in Edinburgh. *d.* Edinburgh 7 May 1876. *Builder xxxiv,* 508 (1876); *D. M. Lyon's Lodge of Edinburgh* (1873) 30, 341, *portrait; Proc. of Royal Soc. of Edin. ix,* 216–8 (1878).

BRYCE, REV. JAMES (*son of John Bryce of Airdrie, Lanarkshire*). *b.* Airdrie 5 Dec. 1767; ed. at Univ. of Glasgow; ordained minister of Scottish Antiburgher Secession church 1795; minister of Antiburgher congregation at Killaig, co. Londonderry 1805; founded a branch of the Presbyterian church which took name of the Associate Presbytery of Ireland; this body was ultimately united with Scottish united presbyterian church. *d.* Killaig 24 April 1857.

BRYCE, REV. JAMES. Minister of Church of Scotland in Bengal 11 April 1814 to 30 May 1842; D.D. Edin. 12 Aug. 1818; author of *Sketch of the state of British India* 1810; *On the ecclesiastical establishment of the Church of Scotland* 1815; *Ten years of the Church of Scotland* 2 vols. 1850. *d.* Edinburgh 11 March 1866 in 82 year.

BRYCE, JAMES (3 *son of Rev. James Bryce* 1767–1857). *b.* Killaig 22 Oct. 1806; ed. at Univ. of Glasgow, B.A. 1828, hon. LL.D. 1858; mathematical master in Belfast academy; master in high school Glasgow 1846–74; F.G.S., F.G.S., Dublin; pres. of Philosophical Soc. of Glasgow; author of *First principles of geography and astronomy* 1848; *General gazetteer* 1859; *Library gazetteer* 1859; *Geology of Arran* 1864; killed by accident at Inverfarigaig on shores of Loch Ness 11 July 1877. *Proc. of Royal Soc. of Edin. ix,* 514 (1878).

BRYDGES, SIR JOHN WILLIAM EGERTON, 2 Baronet. *b.* Canterbury Nov. 1791; succeeded 8 Sep. 1837. *d.* Lee priory, Canterbury 15 Feb. 1858.

BRYDON, WILLIAM. *b.* London 9 Oct. 1811; assistant surgeon Bengal army 9 July 1835, surgeon 14 Nov. 1849, retired 1 Nov. 1859; C.B. 16 Nov. 1858. *d.* Westfield, Rossshire 20 March 1873. *Kaye's History of war in Afghanistan,* 3 ed. (1874) 389; *I.L.N. lxii,* 369 (1873), *portrait; J. McCarthy's A history of our own times, new ed.* (1882) i, 161–95, iii, 8.

NOTE.—He was the one solitary individual of the 13000 soldiers and camp followers composing the army of General Elphinstone who was neither killed nor taken prisoner in the terrible disaster of January 1842, it was also his singular fate to be shut up with Sir Henry Lawrence at Lucknow and to pass uninjured through that long and trying siege. Mrs. Thompson-Butler painted a portrait of him appearing under the walls of Jellalabad in her picture "Remnant of an army" exhibited at Royal Academy 1881 and engraved 1883.

BRYDSON, REV. THOMAS. *b.* Glasgow 1806; ed. at Univ. of Glasgow and Edin.; minister of Levern chapel near Paisley 1839–42; minister of Kilmalcolm 1842 to death; author of *Poems* 1829; *Pictures of the past* 1832;

BRYDSON, REV. T. (*Con.*)
contributed to *Edinburgh Literary Journal* and *Republic of letters, Glasgow. d.* Kilmalcolm 28 Jany. 1855. *The modern Scottish minstrel by Charles Rogers iv,* 172–3 (1857).

BRYMER, VEN. WILLIAM THOMAS PARR. Educ. at Trin. coll. Cam., B.A. 1820, M.A. 1823; R. of Charlton Mackrell, Somerset 1821 to death; archdeacon of Bath 6 March 1839 to death; canon res. of Wells 1840 to death; superintended affairs of the entire diocese during incapacity of Bishop Law. *d.* Charlton Mackrell 19 Aug. 1852. *G.M. xxxviii,* 544 (1852).

BRYSON, ALEXANDER. *b.* Edinburgh 12 Oct. 1816; clock and watch maker at Edin. 1840 to death; F.R.S. Edin. 1858; pres. of Royal Soc. of Arts 1860; pres. of Royal Physical Soc. 1863; F.G.S. London and Edin.; author of many papers on geology. *d.* Hawkhill 7 Dec. 1866.

BRYSON, ALEXANDER. Assistant surgeon R.N. 7 Feb. 1827; inspector general of hospitals and fleets 30 June 1855; hon. physician to the Queen 1859 to death; director general of medical department of navy 1864–9; F.R.S. 1 June 1854; C.B. 7 June 1865. *d.* The Heritage, Barnes, Surrey 12 Dec. 1869 aged 67.

BUCCLEUCH, WALTER FRANCIS MONTAGU-DOUGLAS-SCOTT, 5 Duke of. (2 *son of* 4 *Duke of Buccleuch* 1772–1819). *b.* Dalkeith house near Edinburgh 25 Nov. 1806; ed. at Eton and St. John's coll. Cam., M.A. 1827, LL.D. 1842, D.C.L. Ox. 1834; succeeded 20 April 1819; lord lieut. of Midlothian 5 March 1828 to death, of Roxburghshire 2 Dec. 1841 to death; K.T. 5 Nov. 1830; K.G. 23 Feb. 1835; pres. of Royal Archers 1837–9, captain general 1839 to death; lord privy seal 2 Feb. 1842 to 21 Jany. 1846; P.C. 2 Feb. 1842; colonel of Edinburgh militia 6 Jany. 1842 to death; lord pres. of the council 21 Jany. 1846 to 6 July 1846; chancellor of Univ. of Glasgow 24 April 1878; constructed harbour and port of Granton 1835. *d.* Bowhill house, co. Selkirk 16 April 1884, will proved in London 30 Oct. 1884, personality in England £475,000 in Scotland £435,000. *Sir H. Nicolas's Court of Queen Victoria* (1845) 55–63; *J. B. Paul's History of royal company of archers* (1875), *portrait; R. C. Dudgeon's History of Edinburgh militia* (1882), *portrait; Graphic xxix,* 400 (1884), *portrait.*

BUCHAN, HENRY DAVID ERSKINE, 12 Earl of. *b.* July 1783; succeeded 19 April 1829. *d.* 8 St. Agnes Villas, Bayswater, London 13 Sep. 1857.

BUCHAN, PETER. *b.* Peterhead 1790; a printer there 1816 to death; author of *The recreation of leisure hours being songs and verses in the Scottish dialect* 1814; *Annals of Peterhead* 1819; *Treatise proving that brutes have souls and are immortal* 1824; *Ancient ballads and songs of the North of Scotland hitherto unpublished* 2 vols. 1828 and many other works. *d.* London 19 Sep. 1854. *W. Anderson's Scottish nation iii,* 691–3 (1863).

BUCHANAN, SIR ANDREW, 1 Baronet (*only son of James Buchanan of Blairvadock Ardinconnal, co. Dumbarton* 1776–1860). *b.* 7 May 1807; attached to embassy at Constantinople 10 Oct. 1825; minister plenipotentiary to Swiss confederation 12 Feb. 1852; envoy extraordinary and min. plenipo. to king of Denmark 9 Feb. 1853; transferred to Madrid 31 March 1858; transferred to the Hague 11 Dec. 1860; ambassador extraordinary and plenipotentiary to King of Prussia 28 Oct. 1862; P.C. 3 Feb. 1863; ambassador extraord. and plenipo. to Russia 15 Sep. 1864, to Austria 16 Oct. 1871 to 16 Feb. 1878 when he retired on a pension; C.B. 23 May 1857, K.C.B. 25 Feb. 1860, G.C.B. 6 July 1866; created a baronet 14 Dec. 1878. *d.* Craigend castle near Glasgow 12 Nov. 1882.

BUCHANAN, GEORGE (3 *son of David Buchanan of Montrose, printer* 1745–1812). *b.* Montrose about 1790; ed. at Univ. of Edin.; a land surveyor about 1812 then a civil engineer; engaged in all the important salmon fishing cases in Scotland; built chimney nearly 400 feet high for Edinburgh gasworks 1848; F.R.S. Edin.; pres. of Royal Scottish Society of Arts 1847–8; author of *Report on the theory and application of Leslie's Photometer* 1824 and of the article "Furnaces" in 8 ed. of *Encyclopædia Britannica. d.* 30 Oct. 1852.

BUCHANAN, GILBERT JOHN LANE. Second lieut. R.A. 16 Dec. 1831, colonel 16 July 1862 to 2 April 1870; commanded at Fort William, Bengal 10 Sep. 1867 to 2 April 1870; M.G. 6 March 1868. *d.* Cambridge st. Hyde park sq. London 13 April 1875.

BUCHANAN, REV. JAMES. *b.* Paisley 1804; minister of Roslin near Edin. 1827; minister of North Leith 1828; attained great fame as a preacher; D.D. Princeton college, New Jersey 1844; LL.D. Glasgow; minister of high church Edin. 1840, of St. Stephens free church Edin. 1843; professor of apologetics in New college Edin. 1845 and of systematic theology 1847–68; author of *Comfort in affliction* 1837; *Faith in God and modern atheism compared* 2 vols. 1855; *Analogy considered as a guide to truth,* 2 ed. 1867. *d.* 1870.

BUCHANAN, ROBERT. *b*. Ayr 1813; a schoolmaster, a lecturer advocating socialistic views of Robert Owen and a journalist successively; author of *The religion of the past and present society* 1839; *The origin and nature of ghosts* 1840; *Concise history of modern priestcraft* 1840; *The past, the present and the future* 1840. *d*. Bexhill, Sussex 4 March 1866.

BUCHANAN, REV. ROBERT. *b*. Callander 1785; ed. at Univ. of Glasgow, LL.D. 1869; licensed as a preacher of Church of Scotland 1812; minister of parish of Peebles 1813; assistant professor of logic Univ. of Glasgow 1824, professor 1827–64, the Buchanan prizes were instituted 1866 in commemoration of his services, he bequathed by his will £10,000 for founding of Buchanan bursaries; author of *Fragments of the table round* 1860; *Vow of Glentruil and other poems* 1862; *Tragic dramas from Scottish history* 1868 and *Wallace, a tragedy* 1856 performed twice at Prince's theatre Glasgow March 1862. *d*. Ardfillayne, Dunoon 2 March 1873.

BUCHANAN, REV. ROBERT (*son of Mr. Buchanan of St. Ninians near Stirling, brewer and farmer*). *b*. St. Ninians 15 Aug. 1802; ed. at Univs. of Glasgow and Edin.; licensed by presbytery of Dunblane; minister of Gargunnock near Stirling Oct. 1826; ordained 6 March 1827; minister of Salton, East Lothian 1829; minister of Tron church Glasgow 22 Aug. 1833; D.D. Glasgow 1840; minister of Free college church Glasgow 26 December 1857; pres. of Sustentation fund committee 1847–75; moderator of the Assembly 1860; presented with sum of £4,200 in Queen's hotel, Glasgow 8 Aug. 1864; member of Glasgow school board 1872 to death; author of *History of the ten years conflict* 2 *vols.* 1849; *Notes of a clerical furlough* 1859; *Book of Ecclesiastes* 1859. *d*. 25 Via dell' Angelo Custode Rome 31 March 1875. *Robert Buchanan, D.D. an ecclesiastical biography by the Rev. L. N. Walker* 1877, *portrait*; *Good Words xix*, 15–20 (1878), *portrait*; *J. Smith's Our Scottish clergy* (1878) 17–23.

BUCHANAN, WALTER. *b*. Glasgow 1797; a merchant in Glasgow; M.P. for Glasgow 1 April 1857 to 6 July 1865. *d*. Plas Newton, Chester 21 May 1883.

BUCHANAN, WILLIAM (*son of David Buchanan of Montrose, printer aud publisher* 1745–1822). *b*. Montrose 1781; ed. at Univ. of Edin.; called to Scottish bar 1806; an elder of the Glasite church 1823 to death; Queen's advocate and solicitor of teinds or tithes 1856; author of *Reports of certain remarkable cases in*

BUCHANAN, W. (*Con.*)

the court of session and trials in the high court of justiciary 1813; *Treatise on the law of Scotland on the subject of teinds* 1862. *d*. Edinburgh 18 Dec. 1863.

BUCHANAN, WILLIAM. *b*. Glasgow 1777; picture dealer in London; author of *Memoirs of painting with a chronological history of the importation of pictures by the Great Masters into England since the French revolution* 2 vols. 1824. *d*. Glasgow 19 Jany. 1864 aged 86.

BUCHANAN, REV. WILLIAM. Licentiate of Church of Scotland; editor of *Ayr Observer* and subsequently of *Edinburgh Courant* and *Glasgow Courier;* author of *Verses serious, humorous and satirical* 1866. *d*. Ayr July 1866.

BUCK, HENRY. *b*. Yorkshire; wrote on racing in the *Sportsman* in London and on billiards under pseud. of "Spot Stroke"; wrote on racing in *Daily Telegraph* under pseud. of "Hotspur"; a large betting commission agent. *d*. 25 Jany. 1884.

BUCK, LEWIS WILLIAM (2 *son of George Stucley Buck of Moreton, Devonshire*). *b*. 1784; M.P. for Exeter 1826 to 1832, and for North Devon 1839 to 1857; sheriff of Devon 1826. *d*. 12 Norfolk st. Park lane, London 25 April 1858.

BUCK, ZACHARIAH. *b*. Norwich 10 Sep. 1798; teacher of the pianoforte; assistant organist of St. Peter Mancroft, Norwich 1818–21; organist of Norwich cathedral and master of the choristers 1819–77; Mus. Doc. by Abp. of Canterbury 1853; composed many services, anthems and chants. *d*. Newport, Essex 5 Aug. 1879.

BUCKINGHAM, RICHARD PLANTAGENET TEMPLE NUGENT BRYDGES-CHANDOS-GRENVILLE, 2 Duke of (*only child of 1 Duke of Buckingham* 1776–1839). *b*. Pall Mall, London 11 Feb. 1797; ed. at Eton; M.P. for Bucks. 22 June 1818 to 17 Jany. 1839 when he succeeded; introduced into reform act 1832 the tenant at will clause; G.C.H. 1835; lord privy seal 3 Sep. 1841 to 2 Feb. 1842; P.C. 3 Sep. 1841; K.G. 1842; D.C.L. Cam. 1842; received Queen Victoria at Stowe 15 Jany. 1845; Stowe was taken possession of by bailiffs 31 Aug. 1847; sold part of his estates 10 May 1848 for £263,000; author of *Memoirs of the court and cabinets of George iii* 3 vols. 1853–5; *Memoirs of the court of England during the Regency* 1811–20 2 *vols.* 1856; *Memoirs of the court of George iv* 2 *vols.* 1859; *Memoirs of the courts and cabinets of William iv and Victoria* 2 vols. 1861. *d*.

BUCKINGHAM, DUKE OF. (*Con.*)

Great Western railway hotel, Paddington 29 July 1861. *G. Lipscomb's History of Bucks. iii,* 87–108 (1847); *G. H. Francis's Orators of the age* (1847) 217–23; *I.L.N. i,* 496 (1842), *portrait.*

BUCKINGHAM, JAMES SILK (*youngest child of Christopher Buckingham of Barnstaple who d. 1794*). *b.* Flushing near Falmouth 25 Aug. 1786; commander of merchant ships 1807–13; established *Calcutta Journal* at Calcutta which appeared 2 Oct. 1818 to 26 April 1823 when it was suppressed and he was expelled from India; started Jany. 1824 *Oriental herald and colonial review* which ceased Dec. 1829; edited *The Sphynx* a weekly journal 1827–9; started *The Athenæum* 2 Jany. 1828; M.P. for Sheffield 15 Dec. 1832 to 17 July 1837; travelled in America 1837–41; resident director of British and foreign institute Hanover sq. London 1843–6; pres. of London temperance league 1851; granted civil list pension of £200 per annum 1 Sep. 1851; travelled through the country delivering lectures many years; author of *Travels in Palestine* 1822; *America historical descriptive and statistic* 3 vols. 1841; *The eastern and western states of America* 3 vols. 1842 and 16 other books, also about 40 pamphlets on social and political subjects. *d.* Stanhope lodge, Upper Avenue road, St. John's Wood, London 30 June 1855. *Autobiography of J. S. Buckingham* 2 vols. 1855, *portrait; Boase and Courtney's Bibl. Cornub. i,* 44–8 (1874), *iii,* 1098–9 (1882).

BUCKINGHAM, LEICESTER SILK (*youngest son of the preceding*). *b.* 11 Cornwall terrace, Regent's park, London 29 June 1825; wrote and delivered explanatory description of views of various countries at the Panopticon Leicester sq. 1854; manager of Strand theatre short time; dramatic and musical critic of the *Morning Star* 1857–67; author of Memoir of *Mary Stuart Queen of Scotland* 1844 and other books and of about 35 burlesques, comedies and farces. *d.* Margate 15 July 1867. *Boase and Courtney's Bibl. Cornub. i,* 48–9 *iii,* 1099.

BUCKINGHAMSHIRE, REV. AUGUSTUS EDWARD HOBART-HAMPDEN, 6 Earl of. *b.* Ripon 1 Nov. 1793; ed. at Westminster and Brasn. coll. Ox., B.A. 1815, M.A. 1818; R. of Bennington, co. Lincoln 14 Dec. 1817; R. of Walton-on-the-Woulds Leics. 5 July 1820 to 1847; preb. of Wolverhampton 1844 to death; succeeded 1 Feb. 1849; assumed additional name of Hampden by r. l. 5 Aug.

BUCKINGHAMSHIRE, EARL OF. (*Con.*)

1878. *d.* Hampden house, Great Missenden, Bucks. 13 Oct. 1885.

BUCKLAND, FRANCIS TREVELYAN (*eld. son of Very Rev. Wm. Buckland* 1784–1856). *b.* Christ Church, Oxford 17 Dec. 1826; ed. at Winchester 1839–44 and Ch. Ch. Ox., B.A. 1848; studied at St. George's hospital London 1848–51, house surgeon May 1852 to June 1853; assistant surgeon 2 life guards 14 Aug. 1854 to 1863; discovered coffin of John Hunter in vaults of St. Martin's church, Charing Cross 22 Feb. 1859, the remains were buried iu Westminster Abbey 28 March 1859; wrote largely in the *Field* newspaper 1856–65; started *Land and Water* 27 Jany. 1866; inspector of salmon fisheries for England and Wales 6 Feb. 1867 to death; the highest authority on subject of pisciculture; scientific referee to South Kensington Museum May 1865, where he established a large collection of fish-hatching apparatus and the like which expanded into International Fisheries Exhibition of 1883; author of *Curiosities of natural history,* 4 vols. 1857–72; *Logbook of a fisherman and zoologist* 1875; *Natural history of British fishes* 1881; edited *White's Natural history of Selbourne* with original notes 1875. *d.* 37 Albany st. Regent's park, London 19 Dec. 1880. *Life of Frank Buckland by G. C. Bompas* 1885, *portrait; Macmillan's Mag. xliii,* 303–9 (1881); *Graphic xxiii,* 45 (1881), *portrait.*

BUCKLAND, VERY REV. WILLIAM (*eld. son of Rev. Charles Buckland, R. of Templeton, Devon who d.* 1829). *b.* Axminster 12 March 1784; ed. at Tiverton, Winchester and C. C. coll. Ox., Devon scholar 1801, B.A. 1805, M.A. 1808, B.D. 1816, D.D. 1825, fellow of his college 1809–25; reader in mineralogy Univ. of Ox. 1813, and reader in geology 1819; F.G.S. 1813, pres. 1824–5 and 1840–1, Wollaston medallist 1848; F.R.S. 26 Feb. 1818, Copley medallist 1822, F.L.S. 1821; R. of Stoke Charity, Hants. 1825–46; canon of Ch. Ch. cathedral Ox. 1825–46; pres. of British Assoc. at Ox. 1832; dean of Westminster 27 Nov. 1846 to death; R. of Islip, Oxon. 1846 to death; a trustee of British Museum 1847; author of *Geology and mineralogy considered with reference to natural theology* 2 vols 1836, 4 ed. 2 vols. 1869–70; *Reliquiæ Diluvianæ* 1823, 2 *ed.* 1824. *d.* Clapham, London 14 Aug. 1856. *Geology and mineralogy by the late Very Rev. W. Buckland, edited by F. T. Buckland,* 2 vols. 1858; *Quarterly Journal of Geol. Soc. xiii,* 27–45 (1857); *Proc. of Royal Soc. viii,* 264–8 (1856); *I.L.N. vii,* 336 (1845), *portrait.*

BUCKLE, HENRY BRUGES. Assistant surgeon Bengal medical department 18 March 1844; surgeon 16 Sep. 1857; principal medical storekeeper 1866–70; deputy surgeon general 4 Oct. 1870; C.B. 29 May 1865. *d.* Clarges st. Piccadilly 12 Dec. 1874.

BUCKLE, HENRY THOMAS (*only son of Thomas Henry Buckle of London, shipowner 1779–1840*). *b.* Lee, Kent 24 Nov. 1821; travelled in Belgium, Germany, Holland, Italy and France 1840–1; lectured at Royal Instit. London on the "Influence of women on the progress of knowledge" 19 March 1858, published in *Fraser's Mag.* April 1858; author of *History of civilisation in England* 2 vols. 1857–61, republished as *History of civilisation in England, France, Spain and Scotland* 3 vols. 1869; won the chess tournament at Strand divan London 1849; one of the best chess, whist, and back-gammon players in Europe; knew 19 different languages, 7 of them well; left Southampton for Alexandria 20 Oct. 1861. *d.* from typhoid fever at Damascus 29 May 1862. *The life and writings of H. T. Buckle by A. H. Huth 2 vols. 1880, 2 portraits; Miscellaneous and post-humous works of H. T. Buckle vol. 1 (1872); Chess player's magazine ii, 33–45 (1864), portrait.*

BUCKLE, MATTHEW (*only son of Matthew Buckle, admiral R.N. who d. 7 July 1784 aged 68*). *b.* Nork house, Banstead 3 May 1770; entered navy 4 Feb. 1777; captain 29 April 1802; superintendent of Portsmouth district of Sea fencibles 2 May 1804 to Feb. 1810 when corps was discharged; captain of the Adamant 44 guns, 16 Aug. 1810 to 14 Sep. 1813; admiral on h.p. 30 July 1852. *d.* Bath 8 April 1855.

BUCKLE, WILLIAM. *b.* Alnwick Castle 1794; superintended arrangements of visit of George iv to Ireland; held a responsible post in Soho works of Boulton and Watt at Birmingham to 1851; built first locomotive engine which made journey from Liverpool to Manchester 15 Sep. 1830; an officer in coining depart-ment of Royal Mint, London 1851 to death. *d.* Royal Mint, London 30 Sep. 1863.

BUCKLER, JOHN (*son of Edward Buckler 1741–92*). *b.* Calbourne, Isle of Wight 30 Nov. 1770; an architect in London to 1826; contributed water colour drawings yearly to Royal Academy 1796–1849; F.S.A. 1810. *d.* Rockingham row, New Kent road, London 6 Dec. 1851.

BUCKLER, WILLIAM. *b.* Newport, Isle of Wight 13 Sep. 1814; studied at Royal Academy where he exhibited 1836–56, 62

BUCKLER, W. (*Con.*) pictures chiefly portraits in water-colour; lived at Emsworth, Hampshire about 1848 to death; contributed to *Entomologist's Weekly intelligencer; Weekly Entomologist* and *Ento-mologist's monthly magazine.* *d.* Lumley, Emsworth, Hants. 9 Jany. 1884. *Entomologist's Monthly Mag. xx*, 216, 229–36 (1884).

BUCKLEY, CECIL WILLIAM. Entered navy 1845; served in White Sea and Black Sea during Russian war 1854–6; landed and fired a quantity of stores at Genitchi 29 May 1855, and the stores and government buildings at Taganrog June 1855; decorated with Victoria cross on institution of that order 27 Feb. 1856; captain 16 April 1862; com-manded Pylades on Pacific station 1868–70, and Valiant coastguard ship in the Shannon Dec. 1871 to Oct. 1872. *d.* Madeira Dec. 1872.

BUCKLEY, EDWARD PERY (*eld. son of Edward Pery Buckley of New hall near Salisbury 1760–1840*). *b.* Audley sq. London 7 Nov. 1796; ed. at Harrow and Marlow; ensign 1 foot guards 24 June 1812, captain 12 April 1827 to 9 Nov. 1830 when placed on h.p.; equerry to the Queen 1837–58; colonel 83 foot 17 Aug. 1865 to death; general 17 Aug. 1865; M.P. for Salisbury 15 Nov. 1853 to 6 July 1865. *d.* 12 South Audley st. London 28 May 1873.

BUCKLEY, JOSEPH (*son of George Buckley of Maer, Staffs.*) *b.* Maer 13 May 1804; joined Society of Friends 26 June 1829; a minister 9 Feb. 1843; a cotton spinner at Preston 1834, removed to Manchester 1837; went on a mission to Norway 1856 and 1866; travelled in Germany 1863. *d.* Sale near Manchester 27 Sep. 1868. *Memoirs of Joseph Buckley edited by his daughter 1874, portrait.*

BUCKLEY, R. BISHOP. *b.* England; entered the minstrel profession in Boston, U.S. 1843 in a band organised by his father under title of Buckley's Minstrels; the chief performer in the band 1843 to death. *d.* of paralysis at Quincy, Massachusetts 6 June 1867.

BUCKLEY, REV. THEODORE ALOIS WILLIAM. *b.* 27 July 1825; servitor at Ch. Ch. Ox., B.A. 1849; chaplain of his college; translated classics for H. G. Bohn; edited and wrote numerous works for Routledge; author of *The great cities of the ancient world* 1852; *A history of the council of Trent* 1852; *The great cities of the middle ages* 1853; edited *L. Apuleii de Deo Socratis, liber singularis* 1844. *d.* Lon-don 30 Jany. 1856. *G.M. xlv*, 314–6 (1856).

BUCKLEY, WILLIAM. *b.* Moreton near Macclesfield, Cheshire 1780; brought up a bricklayer; served in the 4th Regt. the King's Own 1799; sentenced to transportation for life for mutiny, he with 6 others having turned out to shoot the Duke of Kent at Gibraltar 24 Dec. 1802; escaped from Port Phillip, Victoria 27 Dec. 1803; resided among the natives of Port Phillip without ever seeing a white man for 32 years; received a pardon from Governor Arthur 28 Aug. 1835; resided in Tasmania 1837 to death; died from being thrown out of a cart at Hobart Town 2 Feb. 1856. *Morgan's Life and adventures of Buckley, Hobart Town* 1852, *portrait*; *Labilliere's Early history of Victoria ii*, 64–87 (1878); *Progress iii*, 166, 238, 311, 273 (1884).

BUCKLEY–MATHEW, SIR GEORGE BENVENUTO *(eld. son of George Mathew of Fabians, Essex 1760–1846)*. *b.* 1807; ensign 52' foot 7 July 1825; lieut. Coldstream guards 26 July 1833; captain 85 foot 17 June 1836 to 23 Sep. 1836 when placed on h.p.; retired from army 9 April 1841; M.P. for Athlone 1835–7, for Shaftesbury 1837–41; governor of Bahama islands 1844–50; minister plenipotentiary to the republics in Central America 21 Aug. 1861, to Argentine republic 13 April 1866, to republic of Paraguay 6 Dec. 1866, to Brazil 19 Sep. 1867 to 1 April 1879 when he retired on pension; changed his Christian name from Byam to Benvenuto 1836; assumed additional surname of Buckley by r.l. 9 May 1865; C.B. 7 Aug. 1863; K.C.M.G. 24 May 1879. *d.* Suffolk st. Pall Mall, London 22 Oct. 1879 in 73 year.

BUCKMAN, JAMES *(son of John Buckman)*. *b.* Cheltenham 1814; curator and resident professor at Birmingham Philosophical Instit. 1842–8; professor of geology and botany at Royal Agricultural college Cirencester 1848–63; conducted a farm on scientific principles at Bradford Abbas near Sherborne 1863 to death; a recognised authority on all agricultural matters; presented collections of Roman antiquities and fossils to Cirencester; F.L.S.; F.G.S.; F.S.A.; author of *Remains of Roman art at Cirencester* 1851; *Science and practice in farm cultivation* 1865; edited *The practical farmer's chronicle* 1861; author of many papers on archæology, botany and geology. *d.* Bradford Abbas 23 Nov. 1884.

BUCKSTONE, JOHN BALDWIN. *b.* Hoxton, London 14 Sep. 1802; made his début in London at Surrey theatre as Ramsay in *The fortunes of Nigel* 30 Jany. 1823; acted at Coburg theatre 1824–7, at Adelphi theatre winter seasons of 1827–39 and at Haymarket

BUCKSTONE, J. B. *(Con.)*
theatre summer seasons of 1833–9; played in United States 1840–2; lessee and manager of Haymarket theatre 28 March 1853 to 1877; author of 150 comedies, dramas and farces best known being *The wreck ashore*, produced at Adelphi theatre 21 Oct. 1830, *The green bushes*, produced there 27 Jany. 1845 and *The flowers of the forest*, produced there 11 March 1847; one of the best low comedians of his time, his best parts were Sir Andrew Aguecheek, Bob Acres and Tony Lumpkin; cleared £20,000 by *Our American cousin* 1861–2; adjudicated bankrupt 27 March 1878. *d.* Bell green lodge, Lower Sydenham 31 Oct. 1879. *Maclise Portrait gallery* (1883) 411–6, *portrait*; *The Theatre iii*, 261–7 (1879); *Illust. Review n.s. i*, 161–3; *J. E. Mayall's Celebrities of the London stage*; *Cartoon portraits* (1873) 116–7, *portrait*; *Pascoe's Dramatic list*, 2 *ed.* (1880) 66–72; *I.L.N. i*, 384 (1842), *portrait*, *lxxv*, 457 (1879), *portrait*.

BUDD, CORDELIA GEORGIANA *(yonngest dau. of Wm. James Turquand of Bengal civil service)*. Composed many musical pieces under nom de plume of "Dewdrop" and afterwards under initials C.B. *(m.* 4 May 1844 Samuel Budd of Exeter, physician who *d.* 21 May 1885 in 79 year). *d.* 1 Charleville road, West Kensington, London 3 May 1886 aged 61.

BUDD, EDWARD HAYWARD. *b.* Great Missenden, Bucks. 23 Feb. 1785; a clerk in War Office 1801 to Dec. 1817 when he retired on pension of £180 a year; played his first cricket match at Lord's 13 Sep. 1802; played in all the great matches of Marylebone cricket Club 1805–25; played his last cricket match 16 June 1852; one of the best batsmen, bowlers and amateur boxers of his time; lived at Wroughton, Wilts. 1825 to death. *d.* Rose cottage Wroughton 29 March 1875. *C. A. Wheeler's Sportascrapiana*, 2 *ed.* 1868, *portrait*; *Baily's Mag. xxvii*, 9–16 (1875).

BUDD, GEORGE *(3 son of Samuel Budd of North Tawton, Devon, surgeon)*. *b.* North Tawton Feb. 1808; ed. at St. John's and Caius colleges Cam., 3 wrangler 1831, B.A. 1831, M.B. 1835, M.D. 1840; fellow of Caius coll. 1831–54, hon. fellow 1880; studied at Middlesex hospital London; practised in London 1840–67; F.R.S. 21 Jany. 1836; F.R.C.P. 1841, Gulstonian lecturer 1843, Croonian lecturer 1847, censor 1845–7; physician to Dreadnought hospital ship 1837–40; professor of medicine in King's college London 1840–63; phys. to King's college hospital 1840–63; author of *On diseases of the liver* 1845, 3 *ed.* 1857; *On the organic diseases and functional disorders of the stomach* 1855. *d.* Ashleigh, Barnstaple 14 March 1882. *Proc. of Royal Soc. xxxiv,* 1–3 (1883); *Medical Circular i,* 458–9 (1852); *Van Kaathoven's Collection vol. 2, portrait.*

BUDD, REV. HENRY *(son of Richard Budd of London, physician 1746–1821).* *b.* Newbury, Berkshire 25 Sep. 1774; ed. at St. John's coll. Cam., B.A. 1798, M.A. 1801; chaplain of Bridewell hospital 1801 to April 1831 when he resigned; R. of White Roothing, Essex 18 March 1808 to death; a founder of Prayer book and homily society 21 May 1812; author of *Infant baptism the means of national regeneration* 1827, 3 ed. 1841; *Helps for the young* 2 vols. 1832–9. *d.* White Roothing rectory 27 June 1853. *A memoir of Rev. Henry Budd* 1855; *Christian Observer lvi* 194–211 (1856).

BUDD, RICHARD. *b.* 1795; ensign 16 Madras N.I. 11 June 1812; commandant of Southern division 10 May 1857 to 1862; colonel of 2 European regiment 27 Jany. 1858, of 32 Madras N.I. 1860 to 1869; general 8 July 1874. *d.* Belfont, The Park, Cheltenham 22 Jany. 1885.

BUDD, WILLIAM *(brother of George Budd 1808–82).* *b.* North Tawton Sep. 1811; ed. in London, Edinburgh, and Paris; M.D. Edin. 1838; practised at Bristol 1842–73; physician to Bristol royal infirmary 1847–62; F.R.S. 8 June 1871; the greatest authority on zymotic diseases; author of *Scarlet fever and its prevention* 1869, 4 ed. 1870; *Typhoid fever its nature, mode of spreading and prevention* 1873 and of many articles in medical papers. *d.* Clevedon, Somerset 9 Jany. 1880. *British Med. Jour.* (1880) i, 163–6.

BUDGE, REV. EDWARD *(son of John Budge).* *b.* Devonshire 1800; ed. at Saffron Walden and Ch. coll. Cam., B.A. 1824; C. of Launcells, Cornwall 1834–9; V. of Manaccan, Cornwall 1839–46; R. of Bratton Clovelly, Devon 1846 to death; author of *The mirror of history* 1851; translated the *Homilies of St. John Chrysostom on the statues* for Dr. Pusey's Library of the Fathers; supplied many articles to Geol. Soc. and Royal Instit. of Cornwall. *d.* Bratton Clovelly 3 Aug. 1865. *Life prefixed to Rev. E. Budge's Posthumous gleanings* 1866.

BUDGETT, SAMUEL. *b.* Wrington, Somerset 27 July 1794; provision dealer at Kingswood near Bristol 1816 to about 1838 and at Bristol about 1838 to death; founded greatest house

in provision trade in West of England; gave £2,000 a year in charity for some time before his death. *d.* Kingswood 29 April 1851. *The Successful merchant by W. Arthur* 1885.

BUIST, GEORGE *(eld. son of Rev. John Buist, minister of Tannadice, Forfarshire who d. 8 Dec. 1845 in 92 year).* *b.* Tannadice 17 Nov. 1805; ed. at St. Andrew's univ. 1817–24, and at Univ. of Edin.; edited *Dundee Courier* 1834; established *Dundee Guardian* 1834; edited *Perth Constitutional* 1835, and *Fifeshire Journal* 1837–9, and *Bombay Times* at Bombay 1840–58; started *Bombay Standard* 1858; F.R.S. 29 Jany. 1846; founded Bombay Reformatory School of Industry 1850; superintendent of government printing press Allahabad 1859 to death; author of *Index to books and papers on the physical geography antiquities and statistics of India* 1852. *d.* Calcutta 1 Oct. 1860. *Memoir of G. Buist, Cupar* 1846; *W. Norrie's Dundee Celebrities* (1873) 190–2.

BULL, REV. JOHN *(eld. son of John Bull of Oxford, surgeon).* *b.* Oxford; ed. at Ruthin gr. sch. and Westminster; student at Ch. Ch. Ox. 1808, Rhetoric reader, censor, and librarian of his house; B.A. 1812, M.A. 1814, B.D. 1821, D.D. 1825; public examiner 1817–8, Proctor 1820; preb. of Fenton in York cathedral 1 June 1826 to death; V. of Staverton, Northamptonshire 1830 to death; canon of Exeter 26 March 1823 to death; archdeacon of Cornwall 6 Feb. 1826 to 6 May 1826, of Barnstaple 6 May 1826 to 10 March 1830; canon of Ch. Ch. Ox. 15 March 1830 to death; endowed vicarage of St. Mary Magdalen, Oxford with £2,000. *d.* at his lodgings in Ch. Ch. Oxford 21 Feb. 1858 aged 68.

BULLAR, HENRY *(son of John Bullar, of Basset Wood near Southampton).* *b.* 25 Feb. 1815; a special pleader 1839–53; barrister L.I. 6 June 1853; recorder of Poole Oct. 1864 to death; a judge of Court of record of Poole Oct. 1864 to death; published with Joseph Bullar *A winter in the Azores* 2 vols. 1841; *Prætors or pleaders.* *d.* Basset Wood 5 Jany. 1870.

BULLEN, SIR CHARLES *(son of John Bullen, surgeon general R.N.)* *b.* Newcastle 10 Sep. 1769; entered navy 16 Feb. 1779; captain 29 April 1802; commodore on coast of Africa 12 Dec. 1823 to 1827; superintendent of Pembroke dockyard and captain of Royal Sovereign yacht 22 July 1830 to 10 Jany.

BULLEN, SIR C. *(Con.)*

1837; admiral 30 July 1852; C.B. June 1815, K.C.B. 18 April 1839, G.C.B. 6 April 1852, K.C.H. 13 Jany. 1835; knighted at St. James's palace 25 Feb. 1835; granted 12 July 1843 good service pension of £300. *d.* Shirley near Southampton 2 July 1853. Portrait of him in painted hall at Greenwich.

BULLEN, EDWARD *(son of Robert Bullen of Taunton, solicitor).* *b.* Taunton 3 April 1813; ed. at Benedictine college, Douay; law student at Lincoln's Inn; practised in London as a certificated special pleader 1836 to death; author of *A practical treatise on the law of distress for rent and of things damage feasant* 1842; author with S. M. Leake of *Precedents of pleadings in common law* 1860, 3 ed. 1868. *d.* 82 Belsize park gardens, London 19 July 1868.

BULLEN, JOSEPH *(2 son of Rev. John Bullen, R. of Kennet, Cambs.)* *b.* 14 April 1761; midshipman on board "Pallas" 36 guns 1774; commanded Lynn Regis district of Sea Fencibles 26 Sep. 1804 to 1810 when corps was disbanded; admiral on h.p. 23 Nov. 1841. *d.* Bath 17 July 1857.

BULLER, SIR ANTHONY *(youngest son of John Buller of Morval, Cornwall 1744–90).* *b.* Antony house, Torpoint 26 July 1780; ed. at Westminster; barrister L.I. 12 May 1803; M.P. for West Looe 1812–16 and 1831–32; appointed a puisne justice at Madras 6 Sep. 1815, but was transferred to Calcutta March 1816 and it is believed never took his seat on the Madras bench; knighted by Prince Regent at Carlton house 23 April 1816. *d.* Marytavy rectory, Devon 27 June 1866.

BULLER, SIR ARTHUR WILLIAM *(2 son of Charles Buller of Bengal civil service 1774– 1848).* *b.* Calcutta 5 Sep. 1808; ed. at Edin. and Trin. coll. Cam., B.A. 1830, M.A. 1834; pupil of Thomas Carlyle; barrister L.I. 10 June 1834; Queen's advocate in Ceylon 19 Oct. 1840 to July 1848; judge of supreme court at Calcutta July 1848 to 1858 when he retired; M.P. for Devonport 17 Aug. 1859 to June 1865, and for Liskeard 21 June 1865 to death. *d.* 6 Half Moon st. Piccadilly, London 30 April 1869.

BULLER, FREDERICK WILLIAM. Ensign 37 foot 20 Jany. 1790; lieut. col. 88 foot 28 Aug. 1804 and 1 foot 27 Feb. 1806 to 1 Dec. 1808; captain Coldstream guards 1 Dec. 1808 to 1814; aide de camp to George iii, 25 July 1810 to 4 June 1813; L.G. 27 May 1825; retired 1833. *d.* Bury st. St. James's, London 8 Nov. 1855 aged 83.

BULLER, SIR GEORGE *(3 son of Frederick Wm. Buller of Pelynt, Cornwall who d. 8 Nov. 1855).* *b.* 30 May 1800; ensign 23 foot 2 March 1820; lieut. col. Rifle brigade 27 Aug. 1841 to 12 Dec. 1854, col. commandant 13 Oct. 1860 to death; commanded 2 brigade of light division in Crimea 21 Feb. 1854 to 11 Dec. 1854; commanded a brigade and then a division in first Kaffir war 1847; commanded a division in second Kaffir war 30 Aug. 1852 to 31 Oct. 1853; commanded division in Ionian Isles 1856–62 and troops at Portsmouth 1865–70; C.B. 26 Dec. 1848; K.C.B. 5 July 1855; G.C.B. 2 June 1869. *d.* 23 Bruton st. Berkeley sq. London 12 April 1884.

BULLER, JAMES WENTWORTH *(eld. son of James Buller of Downes near Crediton 1766– 1827, M.P. for Exeter).* *b.* Downes 1 Oct. 1798; ed. at Harrow and Oriel coll. Ox., B.A. 1819, B.C.L. 1824, D.C.L. 1829; fellow of All Souls coll.; M.P. for Exeter 29 July 1830 to 29 Dec. 1834, for North Devon 6 April 1857 to death; colonel 1st Devon yeomanry cavalry 5 Aug. 1842 to death; chairman of Bristol and Exeter railway. *d.* 109 Jermyn st. Piccadilly, London 13 March 1865.

BULLEY, REV. FREDERIC *(3 son of John Bulley of Reading).* Demy of Magd. coll. Ox. July 1825, probationer fellow 1837, served offices of dean of arts, bursar, vice pres., dean of divinity and college tutor successively, B.A. 1829, M.A. 1832, B.D. 1840, D.D. 1856; pres. of his college Jany. 1855 to death; author of *A tabular view of the varieties in the communion and baptismal offices of the Church of England* 1842. *d.* Marston hill near Fairford 3 Sep. 1885 aged 75.

BULLIONS, REV. PETER. *b.* Moss Side near Perth Dec. 1791; ed. at Univ. of Edin. 1810–13; licensed by presbytery of Edin. June 1817; pastor of presbyterian church at Argyle in Washington county, New York March 1818; professor of languages in Albany academy Nov. 1824 to 1848; pastor of United presbyterian church at Troy, New York 1834–52 and Dec. 1853 to death; author of *Practical lessons in English grammar* 1844, *new ed.* 1853; *An analytical and practical grammar of the English language*, 21 ed. 1853, and many other books. *d.* Troy 13 Feb. 1864.

BULLOCH, JOHN. *b.* 1805; a working brass-finisher at Aberdeen; contributed several articles on decimal coinage to the *Athenæum*; suggested a number of textual emendations which were introduced into notes of *W. G.*

BULLOCH, J. *(Con.)*

Clark's Cambridge Shakespeare 1863; author of *Studies of the text of Shakespear* 1878. *d.* Aberdeen at end of Dec. 1882.

BULLOCK, EDWARD *(eld. son of Edward Bullock of Jamaica).* Educ. at Eton and Ch. Ch. Ox., B.A. 1822, M.A. 1825; barrister I.T. 26 Nov. 1824; judge of Sheriff's Court of London and comr. at Old Bailey 1840–50; common serjeant of City of London 1850 to Dec. 1855. *d.* Upfield near Stroud, Gloucs. 27 Dec. 1857 aged 57.

BULLOCK, FREDERICK *(son of James Bullock, commander R.N.)* Entered navy 28 Nov. 1804; captain 28 June 1838; granted pension for wounds 11 Nov. 1864; admiral on half pay 10 Sep. 1869; F.R.G.S. 1830. *d.* 6 Feb. 1874 in 87 year.

BULLOCK, RALPH. *b.* Morpeth 1841; apprenticed to Thomas Dawson of Tupgill 1851; rode his first race at Harrowgate 1853; won the Derby on Colonel Townley's Kettledrum 1861; won Ascot vase and Goodwood and Doncaster cups on Tim Whiffler 1862; one of the very best jockeys in England; won 212 races 1854–62. *d.* Tupgill 23 Jany. 1863. *Sporting Review xlix,* 86, 203–5 (1863), *portrait.*

BULLOCK, REV. WILLIAM THOMAS (2 son of John Bullock of London). *b.* London 1818; ed. at Magd. Hall Ox., B.A. 1847, M.A. 1850; C. of St. Anne, Westminster 1847–50; assist. sec. S.P.G. June 1850, sec. 1865 to death; chaplain at Kensington Palace 13 Sep. 1867 to death; preb. of Oxgate in St. Paul's cathedral 1875 to death; author of *Sermons on missions and other subjects* 1879, of *Ecclesiastes* in the *Speaker's Commentary* 1880 and of about 70 articles in Smith's *Dictionary of the Bible. d.* Mentone 27 Feb. 1879.

BULMER, HENRY TAYLOR. Artist at Preston where he painted the altar-piece at St. Augustine's church 1840; decorated St. Cuthbert's, North Shields, and several other churches; painted many portraits. *d.* Brook hill, Sheffield 6 Dec. 1857 aged 46.

BULTEEL, HENRY BELLENDEN *(son of Thomas Bulteel of Plymstock, Devon).* b. Bellevue near Plymouth 1800; Educ. at Brasn. coll. Ox., B.A. 1822, M.A. 1824; fellow of Ex. coll. 30 June 1823 to 6 Oct. 1829; C. of St. Ebbe's Oxford 1826 to 10 Aug. 1831 when his license was revoked by Bishop of Oxford for fraternising with dissenters and preaching in their chapels; built a large chapel behind Pembroke college, Oxford, his congregation

BULTEEL, H. B. *(Con.)*

were called Bulteelers; preached a sermon on 1 Corinthians ii, 12 before Univ. of Ox. at St. Mary's 6 Feb. 1831 which created great excitement in Oxford and when printed went to 6 editions; author of *The doctrine of the miraculous interference of Jesus on behalf of believers* 1832 in which he narrated how by means of prayer and intercession he had cured and restored to health 3 women; *The Oxford Argo by an Oxford divine* 1845, an anonymous denunciation of the Puseyite party. *d.* The Crescent, Plymouth 28 Dec. 1866 aged 66. *Cox's Oxford* (1868) 244, 248; *Mozley's Reminiscences* (1882) *i,* 228, 350.

BUNBURY, SIR CHARLES JAMES FOX, 8 Baronet. *b.* Messina in Sicily 4 Feb. 1809; ed. at Trin. coll. Cam.; contested Bury St. Edmunds 1835 and 1837; F.R.S. 5 June 1851; succeeded 13 April 1860; sheriff of Suffolk 1868. *d.* 18 June 1886.

BUNBURY, SIR HENRY EDWARD, 7 Baronet *(younger son of Henry Wm. Bunbury the caricaturist 1750–1811). b.* London 4 May 1778; ed. at Westminster; ensign Coldstream guards 14 Jany. 1795; quartermaster general in Mediterranean 1805–9; lieut. col. Royal Newfoundland fencible infantry 1805–14; under secretary of state for war 1809–16; K.C.B. 2 Jany. 1815; L.G. 22 July 1830; succeeded his uncle as 7 Baronet 31 March 1821; M.P. for Suffolk 11 Aug. 1830 to 3 Dec. 1832, the county had been uncontested for 40 years before 1830; author of *Narrative of the campaign in North Holland* 1849; *Narrative of certain passages in the late war with France* 1852. *d.* Barton hall, Bury St. Edmunds 13 April 1860. *Memoir and literary remains, edited by his son Sir C. J. F. Bunbury P.P.* (1868).

BUNBURY, HENRY WILLIAM ST. PIERRE (3 son of the preceding). *b.* Brompton, London 2 Sep. 1812; ensign 43 foot 29 June 1830; lieut. col. 23 foot 9 March 1855 to 10 Jany. 1857 when placed on h.p.; C.B. 5 July 1855. *d.* Marchfield house, Bracknell 18 Sep. 1875.

BUNBURY, THOMAS. Ensign 46 foot 25 March 1804; lieut. col. Rifle corps 5 Feb. 1824 to 24 April 1835; lieut. col. 67 foot 24 April 1835 to 9 Nov. 1846; L.G. 20 June 1854; colonel commandant Rifle corps 9 Feb. 1855 to death; K.H. 1835. *d.* London 13 April 1857.

BUNBURY, THOMAS. Ensign 3 foot 13 Aug. 1807; major 80 foot 21 Nov. 1834 to 26 July 1844; C.B. 3 April 1846; K.T.S. *d.* 11 St. James's terrace, Regent's park, London 25 Dec. 1861.

BUNN, ALFRED. *b.* 8 April 1796; a junior clerk in army medical department; stage manager of Drury Lane theatre 1823; manager of T.R. Birmingham 1819 to May 1825; one of 7 managers of Drury Lane one season; managed Drury Lane and Covent Garden theatres 1833; introduced orchestra stalls first used at Drury Lane 5 Feb. 1833; lessee of Drury Lane 1835–48; purchased for £2,000 dignity of a gentleman at arms formerly called gentleman pensioner 14 March 1836; bankrupt 17 Dec. 1840; adapted a great number of pieces for the stage; made his début in America at Niblo's Saloon, New York in a literary and dramatic entertainment 11 Oct. 1852; said to be the original of Mr. Dolphin the manager in Thackeray's *Pendennis;* (*m.* 1819 the succeeding). author of *The stage both before and behind the curtain,* 3 vols. 1840; *A word with Punch* 1847; *Old England and New England,* 2 vols. 1853; edited *The Vauxhall papers* 1841. *d.* of apoplexy at Boulogne 20 Dec. 1860. *J. R. Planche's Reminiscenses, vol.* i, (1872); *Dent's Old and New Birmingham* (1880) 385–7, 432, *portrait; I.L.N. iv,* 220 (1844), *portrait, xvi,* 141 (1850), *portrait.*

BUNN, MARGARET AGNES (*eld. dau. of John Somerville of Marylebone, London, biscuit baker*). *b.* Lanark 26 Oct. 1799; made her first appearance on the stage at Drury Lane theatre 9 May 1816 as Imogine in Maturin's tragedy of *Bertram;* created character of Bianca in Dean Milman's *Fazio* at Bath 6 Jany. 1818; played at Drury Lane 1816–18 and 1823–24, Covent Garden 1818–19. (*m.* 1819 the preceding). *d.* Blue Earth city, Minnesota Jany. 1883. *Oxberry's Dramatic biog. v.* 163–74 ((1826), *portrait; T. Marshall's Lives of actors* (1848) 73–8.

BUNNETT, FANNY ELIZABETH. Author of *The golden balance or the false and the real* 1859; *Nature's school or lessons in the garden and the field* 1859; *Louise Juliane, Electress palatine and her times* 1862; *Linked at last* 1871; translated *Shakespeare commentaries by G. G. Gervinus* 1863, 3 ed. 1877; *W. Luebke's History of art* 1868, and many other books. *d.* Budleigh Salterton near Exmouth 19 Feb. 1875 in 43 year.

BUNNEY, JOHN COOPER. Established with Theodore Hook, *John Bull* weekly paper 1820, published it 1820–50. *d.* Clerkenwell 22 June 1867.

BUNNEY, JOHN WHARLTON. *b.* Charlotte st. Fitzroy sq. London 20 June 1828; apprenticed to a stationer in city of London; employed by Messrs. Smith and Elder, publishers to

BUNNEY, J. W. (*Con.*)
1859; gave lessons in drawing; made drawings for John Ruskin in Switzerland and Italy; painted at Florence 1863–70 and at Venice 1870 to death; painted a picture of St. Mark's Venice for J. Ruskin 1876–80; exhibited 8 pictures at the R.A., 2 at the B.I. and 10 at Suffolk st. Gallery 1853–81. *d.* Venice 23 Sep. 1882. *Catalogue of the exhibition of pictures and drawings of Venice, also a memoir of the late J. Bunney by A. Wedderburn* 1882.

BUNNING, JAMES BUNSTONE. *b.* London 6 Oct. 1802; architect in London; surveyor of Foundling hospital estates 1825; erected City of London school opened 2 Feb. 1837; surveyor to London cemetery company 1839; laid out Nunhead cemetery; clerk of the City of London's works 23 Sep. 1843 to death; built Coal Exchange 1849, City prison Holloway 1852, Billingsgate market 1853, Metropolitan cattle market Copenhagen fields opened 15 June 1855; F.S.A. 1848, F.R.I. B.A. *d.* 6 Gloucester terrace, Regent's park, London 7 Nov. 1863.

BUNNY, ARTHUR. *b.* 5 May 1825; 2 lieut. Bengal artillery 8 Dec. 1843; brigade major siege artillery Lucknow Feb. 1858 to April 1858; col. R.A. 1 Oct. 1877 to 1879; L.G. 1 Oct. 1882; C.B. 24 May 1873, placed on retired list 26 July 1883. *d.* 40 Addison gardens north, Kensington 9 Nov. 1883.

BUNSEN, FRANCES, Baroness de (*eld. dau. of Benjamin Waddington of Llanover, Monmouthshire who d. 19 Jany. 1828 in 80 year*). *b.* Dunston park, Berkshire 4 March 1791. (*m.* 1 July 1817 Christian Charles Josiah Baron de Bunsen, German ambassador in London 1841–54); published *A memoir of Baron Bunsen drawn chiefly from family papers by his widow* 2 vols. 1868, she *d.* Carlsruhe, Baden 23 April 1876. *A. J. C. Hare's Life of Baroness Bunsen* 2 vols. 1882; *F. M. Muller's Biographical essays* (1884) 311–62; *Contemporary Review xxviii,* 948–69 (1876).

BUNTING, REV. JABEZ (*only son of Wm. Bunting of Manchester, tailor*). *b.* Newton lane, Manchester 13 May 1779; Wesleyan minister at Oldham st. chapel Manchester 1803, stationed at London 1803, 1815 and 1833 to death, at Manchester 1805 and 1824, and Liverpool 1809 and 1830; sec. to the Conference 1814, president 1820, 1828, 1836 and 1844; senior sec. of Missionary Society 1833; pres. of Theological Institute 1835; M.A. Aberdeen 1818; D.D. Middleton Univ. U.S.A. 1835; superintended the Connexional

BUNTING, REV. J. (Con.)

literature 1821–4; his conduct in some of the Society's affairs gave rise to the expression "Bunting Methodism." *d.* 30 Myddleton sq. London 16 June 1858. *Life by T. P. Bunting* (1859), 2 *portraits; Rev. W. H. De Puy's Threescore years and beyond, New York* 1873; *I.L.N. ii,* 208 (1843), *portrait, xxxii,* 642 (1858); *Illust. news of the world ii,* 37 (1858), *portrait.*

BUNTING, REV. WILLIAM MACLARDIE (eld. child of the preceding). *b.* Manchester 23 Nov. 1805; Wesleyan minister at Salford 1824–7, Manchester 1827–9 and 1838–41, Huddersfield 1829–32, Halifax 1832–5, London 1835–38 and 1841 to death; edited *Select letters of Mrs. Agnes Bulmer* 1842; contributed to *Wesleyan Methodist Mag. d.* at his residence Highgate Rise 13 Nov. 1866. *Memorials of the late Rev. W. M. Bunting, edited by Rev. G. S. Rowe* 1870, *portrait.*

BURANELLI OR BURINELLI, LUIGI. *b.* Ancona, Italy; officer of dragoons in the Pope's army; valet to Stewart Drummond a monk known as the Abbé Stewart who was assassinated whilst bathing; servant to John Craufurd of 12 Grafton st. Bond st. London; a tailor at Penshurst near Tunbridge Wells; shot Joseph Latham dead at 5 Foley place, Regent st. London 7 Jany. 1855 after which he shot himself; tried for murder at Central criminal court 12 April 1855; hanged at Newgate 30 April 1855 aged 32. *The law on its trial by A. H. Dymond* (1865) 178–94; *Central criminal court trials xli,* 633–61 (1855).

BURCHAM, THOMAS BORROW. Educ. at Trin. coll. Cam., fellow 1832 to death, B.A. 1830; barrister I.T. 27 Jany. 1843; recorder of Bedford 1848–1856; magistrate of Southwark police court 1856 to death. *d.* Chingford, Essex 27 Nov. 1869 aged 62.

BURCHELL, WILLIAM JOHN (son of Matthew Burchell of Fulham, nurseryman). *b.* Fulham 1783; schoolmaster at St. Helena 1805–10; explored South Africa 1811–15; explored Brazil 1825–30; executed at Rio Janeiro a series of views from which R. Burford's panorama of that city was painted; F.L.S. 15 Feb. 1808; hon. D.C.L. Ox. 1834; lived at Fulham 1830 to death; his name is perpetuated in scientific names of many animal and plant species discovered by him; author of *Travels in Southern Africa 2 vols.* 1822. *d.* Churchfield house, Fulham 23 March 1863. *Journal of Royal Geog. Soc. xxxiii,* 124 (1864).

BURCHETT, RICHARD. *b.* Brighton 30 Jany. 1815; entered school of design at Somerset House about 1841, assistant master 1845, head master 1851 to death; exhibited 5 historical pictures at Royal Academy 1847–73; assisted in decoration of dome of Great Exhibition 1862; author of *Practical geometry* 1855; *Linear perspective* 1856. *d.* Dublin 27 May 1875. *Graphic xi,* 606, 621 (1875), *portrait.*

BURDEN, HENRY. *b.* Dunblane, Scotland 1791; went to America 1819; maker of agricultural implements; invented the first cultivator 1820; invented a machine for making hook-headed spikes 1840, which are used on every railroad in United States; devised a machine for making horseshoes June 1857 which is self-acting, and produces 60 shoes per minute from iron bars. *d.* Woodside Troy, New York 19 Jany. 1871.

BURDER, REV. GEORGE BERNARD (son of Rev. George Burder 1752–1832, editor of Evangelical magazine). ed. at Magd. coll. Ox.; C. of Ruardean, Gloucs.; received into Church of Rome at Oscott college 24 Jany. 1846; ordained priest; joined the Cistercians at Mount St. Bernard's abbey, Leics. where he filled offices of sub-prior, prior, and abbot; author of the following traslations from the French *The souls in purgatory by Bouquets* 1873; *The consoler by Lambilotte* 1873; *St. Bernard and his work by Caussette* 1874; *Confidence in the mercy of God by Languet de Villeneuve de Gergy* 1876; *The Christian life and virtues considered in the religious state by C. Gay* 1878. *d.* 26 Sep. 1881.

BURDER, REV. HENRY FORSTER (brother of the preceding). *b.* Coventry 27 Nov. 1783; ed. at Hoxton academy and Glasgow Univ.; assistant minister at Independent chapel St. Thomas sq. Hackney 31 Oct. 1811, minister 2 March 1814 to 1852; professor of philosophy and mathematics at Hoxton college 1810–30; chairman of Congregational union of England and Wales 1844; author of *Mental discipline or hints on the cultivation of intellectual and moral habits* 1822; *A collection of psalms and hymns* 1826, 3 ed. 1845 and other books. *d.* Hatcham park, Surrey 29 Dec. 1864. *Evangelical Mag. March* 1865 *pp.* 129–34.

BURDER, WILLIAM CORBETT (son of Rev. John Burder). *b.* Stroud, Gloucs. 30 Oct. 1822; connected as a meteorologist with Glaisher's corps of observers; discovered 2 new comets 28 March 1854 and 30 June 1861; author of *A motto or apophthegm for every day in the year selected by W.C.B.* 1859;

BURDER, W. C. (*Con.*)

The meteorology of Clifton 1863; published with J. Hine and W. Godwin *The architectural antiquities of Bristol and its neighbourhood* 1851. *d.* Clifton 16 Oct. 1865.

BURDETT, SIR ROBERT, 2 Baronet. *b.* Piccadilly 26 April 1796; major 10th hussars 11 Oct. 1827 to 8 March 1831, when placed on h.p.; retired from army 1846; succeeded 23 Jany. 1844; sheriff of Derbyshire 1848. *d.* G. 2 Albany, Piccadilly, London 7 June 1880. Personalty sworn under £300,000 4 Sep. 1880.

BURFORD, ROBERT. *b.* 1791; exhibited 4 landscapes at Royal Academy 1812–16; exhibited panoramas with H. A. Barker on site of present Strand theatre to 1827 when he moved to Leicester square, where he exhibited a succession of panoramas of chief places of interest in Europe. *d.* 35 Camden road villas, London 30 Jany. 1861. *T. Taylor's Leicester Square* (1874) 467–71.

BURGES, REV. GEORGE. Educ. at St. John's coll. Cam., B.A. 1787; V. of Halvergate, Norfolk 1812 to death; V. of Moulton, Norfolk 1813 to death; author of *An address to the people of Great Britain* 1798; *Remarks on the leading arguments in favour of Catholic emancipation* 1812, 2 ed. 1813; *Reflections on the nature and tendency of the present spirit of the times in a letter to the freeholders of Norfolk* 1819, 2 ed. 1820. *d.* Whittlesea 24 Jany. 1853 aged 89.

NOTE.—In Watt's Bibliotheca Britannica the classical publications of George Burges, M.A., of Trin. coll. Cam., who *d.* 11 Jany. 1864, are erroneously added to those of the Rev. George Burges.

BURGES, GEORGE. *b.* Bengal about 1786; ed. at Charter house and Trin. coll. Cam., scholar 1803, B.A. 1807, M.A. 1810; started two coaches which plied up and down the New Road London; constructed a machine for aerial conveyance of passengers from Dover to Calais; maker of a new kind of stays called 'corsets à la Vénus'; gave a series of public lectures upon ancient and modern literature; kept a lodging house at Ramsgate 1856 to death; granted civil list pension of £100 per annum 7 June 1841; author of a play in 5 acts called *The son of Erin or the cause of the Greeks by an Asiatic liberal* 1823; published the *Troades of Euripides* 1807 and the *Phœnissæ* 1809; the *Supplices and Prometheus of Æschylus* 1831 and other classical works. *d.* Ramsgate 11 Jany. 1864 aged 78.

BURGES, WILLIAM (*son of Wm. Burges of London, civil engineer*). *b.* 2 Dec. 1827; ed. at King's coll. London 1839–44; pupil of Edward Blore, architect 1844–9; gained first award in international competition for Lille cathedral 1856; Cantor lecturer at Society of Arts 1862; designed cathedral at Brisbane, Queensland 1859, cathedral at Cork 1862; rebuilt Cardiff Castle 1865; prepared designs for new law courts in Strand, London; F.R.I.B.A. 1860, A.R.A. 28 Jany. 1881; author of *Art applied to industry, a series of lectures* 1865; *Architectural drawings with descriptive letterpress* 1870. *d.* 9 Melbury road, Kensington, London 20 April 1881. *Trans. of Royal Instit. of British Architects* (1882) 17–30, 183–95; *I.L.N. lxxviii,* 429 (1881), *portrait; Graphic xxiii,* 456 (1881), *portrait.*

BURGESS, REV. HENRY. *b.* 1808; ed. at Stepney college; LL.D. Glasgow 1851; Ph. D. Gottingen 1852; P.C. of Clifton Reynes, Bucks. 1854–61; V. of St. Andrew, Whittlesea, Cambs. 1861 to death; edited *Journal of sacred literature* 1848; *Clerical journal* 1854–68; author of *Poems* 1850; *Select metrical hymns and homilies of Ephraem translated* 1853; *The festal epistles of St. Athanasius translated from the Syriac* 1852. *d.* 10 Feb. 1886.

BURGESS, JOHN CART. *b.* 1798; painter of flowers and fruit in water colours; exhibited 31 pictures at the R.A., 7 at the B.I., and 15 at Suffolk st. gallery 1812–37; taught painting in London; author of *A practical essay on the art of flower painting* 1811; *An easy introduction to perspective,* 6 ed. 1835. *d.* Leamington 20 Feb. 1863.

BURGESS, JOSEPH TOM. *b.* Cheshunt, Herts. 1828; reporter on *Leicester Journal* 1844; edited *Clare Journal* at Ennis; edited *Bury Guardian* 7 years; *Leamington Spa Courier* 1865–78; *Berrow's Worcester Journal* 5 years; F.S.A. 1 June 1876; author of *Life scenes and social sketches* 1862; *Old English wild flowers* 1868; *Harry Hope's holidays* 1871; *Historic Warwickshire* 1876; *A handbook to the cathedral of Worcester* 1884. *d.* Leamington 4 Oct. 1886.

BURGESS, REV. RICHARD. Educ. at St. John's coll. Cam, B.D. 1835; R. of Upper Chelsea 1836–69; preb. of St. Paul's cath. 1851 to death; R. of Horningsheath, Suffolk 27 Dec. 1869 to death; lectured at early meetings of British Architects in Covent Garden and Grosvenor st. London; author of *A treatise on the ludi circenses* 1828; *Topography and antiquities of Rome 2 vols.* 1831; *Greece and*

BURGESS, REV. R. *(Con.)*

the Levant 2 vols. 1835. *d.* Brighton 12 April 1881 in 85 year. *I.L.N. xxvi,* 268 (1855), *portrait.*

BURGESS, RIGHT REV. THOMAS. *b.* near Preston 1 Oct. 1791; ed. at Benedictine college, Ampleforth where he was professed 13 Oct. 1807; prior of Ampleforth July 1818 to 1830 when he left Benedictine order and became secularized in order to raise up a new collegiate establishment at Prior park, Bath; opened Portland chapel, Queen st. Bath 26 May 1832; kept a school at Monmouth; bishop of Clifton 27 June 1851 to death; consecrated in St. George's cathedral, Southwark 27 July 1851. *d.* the Convent, Westbury on Trym 27 Nov. 1854. *Catholic Directory* (1860) 258–61, *portrait.*

BURGESS, THOMAS HENRY. Educ. at Trin. coll. Dublin; M.R.C.S. England 1835; M.D. Edin. 1837; practised in London 1838 to death; phys. to Blenheim st. dispensary 1841; fellow of Med. and Chir. Soc. 1839; author of *The physiology and mechanism of blushing* 1839; *Eruptions of the face and hands* 1849; *The climate of Italy in relation to pulmonary consumption* 1852; translated Cazenave and Schedel's *Practical treatise on diseases of the skin* 1832. *d.* Southsea 17 Dec. 1865. *Medical Circular i,* 491 (1852).

BURGOYNE, HUGH TALBOT *(only son of the succeeding).* *b.* Dublin 19 July 1833; entered navy 18 Jany. 1853; captain of 'Constance' 35 guns 1867–9; captain of armour plated turret ship 'Captain' 6 guns 30 April 1870 to death; V.C. 24 Feb. 1857; lost in the 'Captain' which foundered off Cape Finisterre about 2 a.m. 7 Sep. 1870. *I.L.N. lvii,* 302, 307, 312 (1870), *portrait.*

BURGOYNE, SIR JOHN FOX, 1 Baronet *(elder natural son of John Burgoyne 1723–92, commander in chief in Ireland).* *b.* Queen st. Soho, London 24 July 1782; ed. at Eton and Woolwich 1796–8; 2 lieut. R.E. 29 Aug. 1798; commanding engineer of expedition to New Orleans 1814; chairman of board of Public works in Ireland 1831–45; a founder of Instit. of Civil Engineers of Ireland and first pres. 5 Aug. 1835; inspector general of fortifications in England July 1845 to 1 Jany. 1868 when he retired on full pay; pres. of Irish famine relief commission 10 Feb. 1847; sent to Constantinople to report on defence of Turkey Jany. 1854; conducted siege of Sebastopol Oct. 1854 to Feb. 1855; col. commandant R.E. 22 Nov. 1854 to death; general 5 Sep. 1855; created baronet 18

BURGOYNE, SIR J. F. *(Con.)*

March 1856; F.R.S. 6 June 1856; constable of Tower of London 8 April 1865 to death; field marshal 1 Jany. 1868; granted a pension of £1,500 a year; K.C.B. 19 July 1838; G.C.B. 6 April 1852; admitted to freedom of City of London 22 Oct. 1868; author of *Our defensive forces* 1869, 3 *ed.* 1870. *d.* 5 Pembridge sq. Bayswater, London 7 Oct. 1871. *bur.* in Tower of London 17 Oct. *Life and correspondence of Sir J. F. Burgoyne* 2 vols. 1873, *portrait; A sketch of the life of Sir J. Burgoyne by Sir F. Head* 1872; *Papers on subjects connected with duties of the Corps of Royal Engineers n.s. xx, ix–xlii,* (1872); *Graphic iv,* 387, 392 (1871), *portrait.*

BURGOYNE, SIR JOHN MONTAGU, 9 Baronet. *b.* Sutton park, Bedfordshire 17 Oct. 1796; ensign 68 foot 17 Oct. 1816; captain grenadier guards 5 June 1835 to 1847; succeeded 11 Aug. 1817; sheriff of Beds. 1852. *d.* 17 March 1858.

BURKE, JAMES SAINT GEORGE (2 son of John French Burke). *b.* 1804; barrister M.T. 20 Nov. 1846; counsel to London, Chatham and Dover railway; Q.C. 2 Dec. 1862; bencher of his inn 27 April 1863; retired from practice about 1869. *d.* The Auberies near Sudbury 25 Feb. 1881. Personalty sworn under £250,000, 30 April 1881.

BURKE, SIR JOHN CHARLES, 4 Baronet. *b.* 7 Feb. 1858; succeeded 9 Dec. 1875. *d.* 16 April 1880.

BURKE, SIR JOHN LIONEL, 12 Baronet. *b.* Glinsk Castle, co. Roscommon 26 Nov. 1818; succeeded 30 Oct. 1865. *d.* 21 July 1884.

BURKE, SIR JOSEPH, 11 Baronet. *b.* Ardfry, co. Galway 31 Jany. 1786; succeeded 1845. *d.* 30 Oct. 1865.

BURKE, PETER *(elder son of John Burke of London, genealogist 1787–1848).* *b.* London 7 May 1811; ed. at Caen college, Normandy; barrister I.T. 7 June 1838; Q.C. of county palatine of Lancaster 1858; serjeant at law 11 Jany. 1860; director of Society of Antiquaries of Normandy 1866–7; author of *Celebrated trials connected with the aristocracy* 1849; *The romance of the forum* 4 vols. 1852–61; *The public and domestic life of Edmund Burke* 1853; *Celebrated naval and military trials* 1866. *d.* Coleherne road, South Kensington, London 26 March 1881.

BURKE, ROBERT O'HARA. *b.* St. Cleram near Galway 1820; entered Austrian army 1840; served in Irish constabulary 1848;

BURKE, R. O. (Con.)

emigrated to Australia 1853; inspector of Melbourne police; commanded expedition fitted out to explore centre of Australia which started from Melbourne 20 Aug. 1860; reached Cooper's Creek 11 Nov. 1860; crossed the continent and reached Gulf of Carpentaria 10 Feb. 1861; returned to Cooper's Creek 21 April 1861 where he d. of starvation 28 June 1861. bur. with a public funeral at Melbourne 21 Jany. 1863. Bronze statue erected in Collins st. Melbourne 1864 at cost of £4,000. *The Burke and Wills exploring expedition* 1861; *W. Howitt's History of discovery in Australia ii*, 190–310 (1865); *Illust. news of the world ix*, 65 (1862), *portrait*.

BURKE, THOMAS. Ensign 83 foot 23 July 1794; major 4 foot 22 July 1813 to 25 Feb. 1816 when placed on h.p.; colonel 10 foot 11 April 1860 to death; L.G. 18 Jany. 1861. d. Prospect villa, Ringaskiddy, Cork 4 Feb. 1863.

BURKE, THOMAS HENRY (2 son of Wm. Burke of Knocknagur, co. Galway). b. 25 May 1829; private secretary to Sir Thomas Redington under secretary for Ireland April 1851; under secretary for Ireland May 1869 to death; stabbed to death in Phœnix park, Dublin 6 May 1882 by members of a secret society called the Invincibles; memorial window in Dominican church, Dublin erected by Earl Spencer, Viceroy of Ireland. *I.L.N. lxxx*, 453 (1882), *portrait; Graphic xxv*, 464 (1882), *portrait.*

BURKE, SIR THOMAS JOHN, 3 Baronet. b. 7 June 1813; succeeded 14 Sep. 1847; M.P. for co. Galway 17 May 1847 to 6 July 1865. d. Marble hill, Loughrea, co. Galway 9 Dec. 1875. *Burke's Portrait gallery i*, 92 (1833).

BURKE VERY REV. THOMAS NICHOLAS (son of Walter Burke of Galway who d. 29 Nov. 1872). b. Galway 8 Sep. 1830; entered order of St. Dominic at Perugia 29 Dec. 1847; ordained priest 26 March 1853; superintendent of novices at Tallaght near Dublin 1857–64; rector of Irish Dominican college of San Clemente, Rome Sep. 1864; went to America as visitor of his order Oct. 1871 where he acquired extraordinary popularity as a preacher and lecturer; author of *English misrule in Ireland* 1873; *Ireland's case stated in reply to Mr. Froude* 1873; *Lectures and sermons* 1873; *Lectures on faith and fatherland* 1874. d. Tallaght 2 July 1883. *The life of the Very Rev. T. N. Burke by W. J. Fitz-patrick* 2 vols. 1885, *portrait.*

BURKE, THOMAS WILLIAM ASTON HAVILAND. b. near London Aug. 1795; ed. at Westminster; barrister L.I. 18 Nov. 1819; chairman of Middlesex hospital 1848 to death; made a collection of prints supposed to be finest of its kind, it was very strong in works of Woollett, Strange and Sharpe, and in plates by and after Turner. d. 27 Gloucester place, Marylebone, London 3 April 1852. *G.M. xxxvii*, 624–6 (1852).

BURLTON, WILLIAM. b. 1793; entered Bengal army 1807; commissary general 12 April 1837 to 10 Feb. 1848; lieut. col. of 7 light cavalry 1843, of 10 light cavalry 1848, of 8 light cavalry 1849, of 2 light cavalry 1850 to 10 Aug. 1850; C.B. 3 April 1846; author of *A few brief comments on Sir C. Napier's letter to Sir J. Hobhouse, "On the baggage of the Indian army"* 1849. d. Oaklands, Shepherd's Bush, London 10 Nov. 1870.

BURMESTER, ARNOLD EDWARD. Ensign 59 foot 31 Aug. 1830, lieut. col. 12 Oct. 1860 to 23 Sep. 1862 when he retired on full pay with rank of M.G.; C.B. 1 March 1861. d. 11 St. Stephen's sq. Bayswater, London 3 Oct. 1877.

BURN, GEORGE. Surgeon R.N. 21 April 1829; inspector general of hospitals and fleets 17 Sep. 1858 to 1 April 1870 when he retired; C.B. 2 June 1869. d. The Cedars, Shirley, Southampton 20 Feb. 1881 aged 70.

BURN, JACOB HENRY. Assistant to Wm. Hone the bookseller in London about 1820, helped to compile *The every day book* 3 vols. 1826–7; bookseller in Maiden lane, afterwards in King st. Covent Garden; edited *Willis's Current notes* 7 vols. 1851–7; author of *A descriptive catalogue of the London traders tavern and coffee-house tokens current in the seventeenth century presented to the Corporation library by H. B. H. Beaufoy* 1853, 2 ed. 1855, these tokens were collected by him for Beaufoy; *Catalogue of a collection of early newspapers and essayists presented to the Bodleian library by Rev. F. W. Hope* 1865, formed chiefly by Burn 1830–4. d. St. Mary's hospital, Paddington, London 19 Feb. 1869 aged 76. *Reg. and mag. of biog. i*, 317–8 (1869).

BURN, JAMES. b. Darlington, Durham 15 March 1804; apprenticed to a skinman at Newcastle; fought and beat O'Neal £25 a side 26 July 1824; beaten by Ned Neale £100 a side 19 Dec. 1824 and by Philip Sampson £50 a side 14 June 1825; beat Pat Magee £100 a side 25 July 1826; beat Ned Baldwin £100 **a side 24 April 1827**, beaten

BURN, J. *(Con.)*

by him 3 July 1827 after 85 rounds in 90 minutes; beaten by Ned Neale again 13 Nov. 1827; landlord of the Red Horse, Bond st., the Queen's Head, Windmill st. Haymarket, and the Rising Sun, Air st. Piccadilly, London successively. *d.* The Rising Sun 29 May 1862. *H. D. Miles's Pugilistica ii*, 326–37 (1880); *Illust. sporting news* (1862) 265, *portrait.*

BURN, ROBERT. Second lieut. R.A. 17 Dec. 1812, colonel 6 Jany. 1855 to 27 June 1864, col. commandant 2 Aug. 1868 to death; general 1 Oct. 1877. *d.* Cheltenham 19 Dec. 1878 aged 86.

BURN, WILLIAM *(son of Robert Burn of Edinburgh, builder).* *b.* Edin. 20 Dec. 1789; pupil of Robert Smirke, architect; architect in Edin. 1816–44 and in London 1844 to death; consulting government architect for Scotland; designed mansions in nearly every county in United Kingdom. *d.* 6 Stratton st. Piccadilly, London 15 Feb. 1870.

BURNABY, CHARLES HERRICK. *b.* 28 Oct. 1800; second lieut. R.A. 9 June 1825, lieut. col. 22 July 1853 to 28 Nov. 1854 when he retired on full pay; general 1 Oct. 1877. *d.* 20 Regent's park terrace, London 11 Jany. 1879.

BURNABY, EDWYN SHERARD *(only son of Edwyn Burnaby of Baggrave hall near Leicester 1799–1867).* *b.* 22 May 1830; ed. at Eton; ensign Grenadier guards 3 Nov. 1846, lieut. col. 1 Oct. 1877 to June 1880; served in Crimea Nov. 1854 to 28 July 1855; commanded British-Italian legion of 3500 men 1855–7; went on special duty to Syria 1861; commanded Metropolitan volunteers 1877–80; M.G. 29 April 1880; M.P. for North Leics. 12 April 1880 to death; author of *An account of the right flank company of the third battalion Grenadier Guards at the battle of Inkerman* 1857; *John Bryant or the stag hunt by E. S. B.* 1868. *d.* Palmeira sq. Hove, Brighton 31 May 1883. *New monthly mag. cxviii*, 421–5 (1880), *portrait; Biograph iv*, 510–3 (1880).

BURNABY, FREDERICK GUSTAVUS *(son of Rev. Gustavus Andrew Burnaby of Somerby hall near Oakham 1802–72).* *b.* Bedford 3 March 1842; ed. at Bedford gr. sch. and Harrow; cornet Royal horse guards 30 Sep. 1859, lieut. col. 6 April 1881 to death; correspondent of the *Times* at Carlist camp in Spain Aug. to Oct. 1874; agent of Stafford house committee in Russo-Turkish war 1877–8; commanded fifth Turkish brigade at battle of Tashkesan 31 Dec. 1877; contested Birmingham April 1880; went to Egypt as a volunteer 10 Jany. 1884; made 19 balloon ascents, crossed

BURNABY, F. G. *(Con.)*

English channel in balloon Eclipse 23 March 1882; author of *A ride to Khiva* 1876, 11 ed. 1877; *On horseback through Asia Minor* 2 vols. 1877; *A ride across the channel* 1882; killed by a spear wound at battle of Abu Klea in Soudan 17 Jany. 1885; obelisk to his memory in St. Philip's churchyard, Birmingham unveiled 11 Nov. 1885. *Life and times of Col. F. Burnaby by J. R. Ware and R. K. Mann* 1885, *portrait; Vanity Fair 7 Feb.* 1885, *portrait; I.L.N. lxxxvi*, 103 (1885), *portrait.*

BURNABY, JOHN DICK *(eld. son of John Dick Burnaby of Evington, Leics. 1776–1852, captain Grenadier guards).* *b.* Billesdon Coplow, Leics. 19 April 1802; ed. at Emm. coll. Cam., LL.D. 1826; barrister I.T. 21 Nov. 1828; comr. of bankrupts for Leicester, Nottihgham and district; judge of county courts circuit 34 (Leicestershire) March 1847 to death. *d.* Torquay 29 Dec. 1855.

BURNABY, RICHARD BEAUMONT *(2 son of Rev. Thomas Burnaby 1761–1830, preb. of Lincoln).* *b.* Misterton, Leics. 22 Feb. 1793; 2 lieut. R.A. 17 Dec. 1812, captain 9 Sep. 1834 to 9 April 1849; lieut. col. commandant Hampshire artillery 30 May 1853 to death; L.G. 10 Nov. 1868. *d.* Carlton crescent, Southampton 1 June 1871.

BURNABY, SIR WILLIAM CRISP HOOD, 3 Baronet *(only son of Sir Wm. Chaloner Burnaby, 2 baronet who d. 19 Feb. 1794).* Entered navy 11 Oct. 1806; commander of Ardent prison ship at Bermuda 26 May 1814 to May 1816. *d.* Bermuda 1 Aug. 1853.

BURNABY, SIR WILLIAM EDWARD, 4 Baronet. *b.* July 1824; ed. at Exeter coll. Ox.; succeeded 1 Aug. 1853. *d.* Boulogne 19 Aug. 1881.

BURNARD, NEVILL NORTHEY *(son of George Burnard of Alternun, Cornwall, mason).* *b.* Alternun 1818; a mason; a carver in London; employed by Bailey, Marshall, Foley and other sculptors; executed statue of Richard Lander erected on the column in Lemon st. Truro about 1850, and statue of Ebenezer Elliott erected in Market place, Sheffield; executed many portrait busts of eminent men. *d.* the Infirmary, Redruth, Cornwall 27 Nov. 1878.

BURNE, JOHN. *b.* Worcestershire; ed. at Univ. of Edin.; M.D. 1 Aug. 1821; L.R.C.P. 22 Dec. 1823, a Fellow 4 July 1838; phys. to Westminster hosp. 1835–42; removed to Tiverton about 1843; removed to Bath about 1850; author of *A practical treatise on the Typhus or adynamic fever* 1828; *A treatise on*

BURNE, J. *(Con.)*

the causes and consequences of habitual constipation 1840. *d.* the United hospital, Bath 3 April 1880 aged 86.

BURNELL, ARTHUR COKE *(eld. son of Arthur Burnell of East India Company's navy). b.* St. Briavel's, Gloucs. 11 July 1840; ed. at King's college London; entered Indian civil service 1860; served in Madras 1860–80; C.I.E.; author of *Specimens of South Indian dialects collected by A. C. B.* 1873–8; *Elements of South Indian palæography* 1874, *enlarged edition* 1878; *Classified index to the Sanskrit MSS. in the palace at Tanjore* 1880. *d.* West Stratton, Hampshire 12 Oct. 1882. His library was sold at Sotheby's 14–17 Jany. 1884 for £1,566. *Hobson—Jobson being a glossary of Anglo-Indian colloquial words and phrases by H. Yule and the late A. C. Burnell* (1886) *xiii, portrait.*

BURNELL, GEORGE ROWDEN. *b.* 1814; civil engineer in America, Belgium and Holland; assistant engineer on Paris and Rouen railway 1842–8; built Equity and Law life office Lincoln's Inn Fields London; author of *The rudiments of hydraulic engineering* 1852; wrote for *Weale's Rudimentary Series,* treatises on *Acoustics; Sound in public and private buildings; Well-sinking, boring and pump-work; Hydraulic engineering; River engineering; Fluids;* and *Lines, mortars and concrete;* edited *Engineer and Architect's pocket book* and *Builder's and contractor's price book;* contributed many articles to Arts and Sciences division of *English Cyclopædia, Proc. of Instit. of British Architects, Journal of Gas-lighting* and *Builder. d.* 23 Kensington gardens terrace, Hyde park, London 23 July 1868 in 54 year.

BURNES, JAMES *(eld. son of James Burnes 1780–1852, town clerk of Montrose). b.* Montrose 12 Feb. 1801; ed. at Montrose academy and Univ. of Edin.; entered Bombay medical service 1821; garrison surgeon of Bombay 1837; physician general in Bombay 15 Sep. 1848 to 20 Nov. 1849; provincial grand master of Western India 1836–46; grand master of Scottish lodge of Masons in India 1846–9; F.R.S. 2 April 1835; K.H. 1837; author of *A narrative of a visit to the court of Scinde* 1829; *A sketch of the history of the Knights Templars* 1837. *d.* Queen's hotel, Manchester 19 Sep. 1862. *Notes on his name and family by James Burnes* 1851 *PP.*

BURNET, REV. JOHN. *b.* Methven st. Perth 13 April 1789; a shoemaker at Perth; Independent congregational minister at Cork 1815–30; pastor of Mansion house chapel

BURNET, REV. J. *(Con.)*

Camberwell, London 12 Sep. 1830, of Camberwell Green chapel 1853 to death; took an active part in agitation for abolition of slave trade; one of committee of Bible Society; chairman of congregational Union of England and Wales 1845; author of *Essay on the Deity of Christ* 1835; *The authority of pastors in the church, d.* Camberwell 10 June 1862. *W. H. Blanch's Ye parish of Camerwell* (1877) 234; *Services on occasion of the death of Rev. John Burnet* 1862.

BURNET, JOHN *(son of George Burnet, surveyor general of excise for Scotland). b.* Musselburgh near Edin. 20 March 1784; apprenticed to Robert Scott, landscape engraver 7 years; painter and engraver in London 1806–60; engraved many of Wilkie's pictures; exhibited 1 picture at the R.A., 30 at B.I. and 6 at Suffolk st. gallery 1808–62; F.R.S. 16 March 1837 to 1849 or 1850; granted civil list pension of £75, 19 April 1861; author of *A practical treatise on painting in three parts* 1822–7, *new ed.* 4 parts 1880; *An essay on the education of the eye* 1837; *Landscape painting in oil colours* 1849, 2 ed. 1861; *Turner and his works* 1852, 2 ed. 1859 and many other books. *d.* Victoria road, Stoke Newington, London 29 April 1868. *I.L.N. lii,* 504 (1868), *portrait.*

BURNETT, SIR ALEXANDER, 9 Baronet. *b.* Crathes castle near Aberdeen 17 Dec. 1789; succeeded 16 Feb. 1849. *d.* Crathes castle 20 March 1856.

BURNETT, SIR JAMES HORN, 10 Baronet. *b.* Crathes Castle 22 June 1801; succeeded 20 March 1856; lord lieut. of Kincardineshire 5 Jany. 1864 to death. *d.* Crathes castle 16 Sep. 1876.

BURNETT, SIR WILLIAM *(son of Wm. Burnett of Montrose). b.* Montrose Jany. 1779; surgeon's mate R.N. 1795, surgeon 1799; had charge of hospitals for prisoners of war at Portsmouth and Forton 1805–10; phys. and inspector of hospitals to Mediterranean fleet 26 May 1810 to 1813; a medical comr. of the navy 1822; L.R.C.P. 1825, F.R.C.P. 1836, consiliarius 1845–7; knighted at St. James's palace 25 May 1831; K.C.H. 21 June 1831; F.R.S. 18 April 1833 to 1856 or 1857 when he withdrew; phys. general to the navy 1833 this designation was changed 1840 to that of inspector general of naval hospitals and fleets which gave way in 1844 to that of director general of medical department of the navy, a post which he held down to 1855 when he retired; phys. in ordinary to Wm. iv, 13 April 1835; K.C.B. 16 Aug.

1850; invented well-known disinfecting fluid 1838 and a fluid for preserving timber 1845; author of *A practical account of the Mediterranean fever* 1816. *d.* Chichester 16 Feb. 1861. *Physic and physicians ii,* 323–5 (1839); *Munk's Roll of physicians iii,* 307–8 (1878); *Lancet ii,* 558–63 (1850), *portrait.*

BURNETT, WILLIAM FARQUHARSON. Entered navy 28 June 1838; captain 13 Nov. 1854; commodore on Australian station 21 July 1862 to death; C.B. 5 July 1855; lost in H.M.S. Orpheus off Manukan, New Zealand 7 Feb. 1863 when 190 lives were lost out of 260 on board, buried at Auckland. *Annual Reg.* (1863) 19–22.

BURNEY, VEN. CHARLES PARR *(son of Rev. Charles Burney, preb. of Lincoln who d. 25 Dec. 1817).* *b.* Chiswick, Middlesex 19 Oct. 1785; ed. by his father and at Merton coll. Ox., B.A. 1808, M.A. 1811, B.D. and D.D. 1822; kept school at Greenwich 1814–35; R. of Sible Hedingham, Essex March 1838 to 1848; archdeacon of St. Albans 16 Oct. 1840; archdeacon of Colchester 15 Aug. 1845 to death; R. of Wickham Bishops, Essex 1848 to death; gave sum of £6,000 to establish a Clergy relief fund for his diocese; F.R.S. 22 Dec. 1814; F.L.S. 21 Jany. 1823. *d.* Brighton 1 Nov. 1864.

BURNEY, JAMES. Entered navy 6 Jany. 1807; captain 10 Dec. 1835, retired 1 July 1851; retired admiral 18 Oct. 1867. *d.* 1 Montpellier terrace, Teddington, Middlesex 30 Oct. 1884 aged 91.

BURNEY, MARTIN CHARLES *(only son of James Burney, rear admiral R.N.)* *b.* 1788; solicitor in London; assisted in drawing up population and poor law returns; barrister I.T. 20 June 1828; reported in Master of the Rolls court for *The Times;* a great friend of Charles Lamb. *d.* James st. Buckingham gate, Westminster 20 Oct. 1852.

BURNEY, WILLIAM. Major Cape mounted riflemen 20 June 1834 to 16 Feb. 1844 when placed on retired full pay; K.H. 1837; colonel 28 Nov. 1854. *d.* Elgin crescent, Kensington park, London 1 Dec. 1879.

BURNS, REV. ISLAY *(6 child of Rev. Wm. Hamilton Burns 1779–1859, minister of Kilsyth, near Glasgow).* *b.* Manse of Dun, Forfarshire 16 Jany. 1817; ed. at Aberdeen gr. sch. at Marischal coll. and the Univ., D.D. 1864; ordained to charge of St. Peter's Dundee June 1843; professor of Apologetics and

systematic theology in free church college Glasgow 1864 to death; author of *History of the Church of Christ* 1862 and of a series of essays on Tractarian and other movements in Church of England in the *British and foreign evangelical review. d.* 4 Sardinia terrace, Glasgow 20 May 1872. *Select remains of Islay Burns D.D.* 1874, *portrait.*

BURNS, REV. JABEZ. *(son of Mr. Burns of Oldham, chemist).* *b.* Oldham 18 Dec. 1805; joined Methodist New Connexion 1821; pastor of Baptist congregation at Perth 1830–5; of Baptist congregation in New church st. Marylebone, London June 1835; became a pledged abstainer May 1836; delivered 35 annual temperance sermons beginning 16 Dec. 1839; one of earliest members of Evangelical Alliance formed 1845; author of *The Christian sketch book* 1828, *second series* 1835; *The golden pot of Manna* 2 vols. 1837, in the 5 ed. title was altered to *The Christian's daily portion* 1848; *Original sketches and skeletons of sermons* 11 vols.; edited *Journal of New British and Foreign Society* 1839–42 when society was dissolved; edited *Christian ministers companion* 4 vols. 1844. *d.* 17 Porteus road, Paddington, London 31 Jany. 1876. *A retrospect of 45 years Christain ministry by Jabez Burns* 1875; *D. Burns's Temperance dictionary* (1861) 527–30; *Illust. news of the world viii,* (1861), *portrait; Graphic xiii,* 182, 188 (1876), *portrait.*

BURNS, JAMES *(brother of Rev. Islay Burns 1817–72).* *b.* Manse of Dun 8 Nov. 1808; employed by Whitaker and Co. publishers in London 1832; bookseller at Duke st. Manchester sq. 1834, and at 17 Portman st.; published The Englishman's library; The Fireside library; *Poems and pictures* 1845, first of the illustrated Christmas books; joined Church of Rome 1847; edited *The Missal; The Vespers book; The paradise of the Christian soul; The path to heaven;* published *The Dublin Review* July 1863 to death; *Annals of the propagation of the faith* 1861 *to death; The Rambler* a weekly journal 1 Jany. 1848 to Nov. 1859. *d.* 17 Portman st. London 11 April 1871. *J. Gillow's English Catholics i,* 346–8 (1885); *Illustrated Catholic family annual* (1884), *portrait.*

BURNS, JAMES *(3 son of Rev. John Burns, minister of Barony church, Glasgow).* *b.* Glasgow 9 June 1789; a shipowner with his brother George Burns; began to use steam navigation 1824; founded with Samuel

BURNS, J. *(Con.)*

Cunard and David Mac Iver, Cunard company for establishing a line of ocean steamers to America, first of which sailed from Liverpool 4 July 1840. *d.* Bloomhall, Dumbartonshire 6 Sep. 1871.

BURNS, REV. JAMES DRUMMOND. *b.* Edinburgh 18 Feb. 1823; ed. at High sch. and Univ. of Edin.; minister of Free church Dunblane near Stirling Aug. 1845 to 4 Oct. 1848; spent 5 years in Madeira 1847–53; minister of English Presbyterian chapel Well walk, Hampstead 22 May 1855; author of *The vision of prophecy and other poems* 1854, 2 ed. 1858; *The heavenly Jerusalem or glimpses within the gates* 1856; contributed a series of papers on cities of the Bible to Rev. A. Cameron's *Family treasury* and article Hymns to *Encyclopædia Britannica,* 8 ed. xii, 188–90 (1856). *d.* Mentone 27 Nov. 1864. *bur.* Highgate cemetery Dec. *Rev. J. Hamilton's Memoir and remains of Rev. J. D. Burns* 1869, *portrait; Reminiscences of Rev. J. D. Burns from Weekly Review of Dec.* 17, 1864.

BURNS, ROBERT *(eld. son of Robert Burns the poet 1759–96).* *b.* Tarbolton, Ayrshire Sep. 1786; ed. at Dumfries academy; clerk in Stamp office, London 1804; an accomplished scholar, musician and artist; edited *The Caledonian musical museum* 1809. *d.* Dumfries 14 May 1857.

BURNS, REV. ROBERT. *b.* Borrowstownness West Lothian 13 Feb. 1789; ordained to charge of Low church Paisley July 1811; sec. of Glasgow colonial society 1815–30; seceded with the Protestors 1843; sent by Free church to visit churches in U.S. and Canada 1844; pastor of Knox's church Toronto 1845–56; Emeritus professor of church history in Knox college Toronto 1856; moderator of church in Canada twice; author of *A historical dissertation on the law and practice of Great Britain with regard to the poor* 1819; *On Pluralities* 1824; *The Gareloch heresy tried* 1830; edited Wodrow's *History of the sufferings of the Church of Scotland,* new ed. 4 vols. 1828; edited *Edinburgh Christian instructor* 1838–40. *d.* Toronto 19 Aug. 1869. *Morgan's Bibliotheca Canadensis* (1867) 58–9.

BURNS, WILLIAM. *b.* Saltcoats, Ayrshire Dec. 1809; a procurator in Glasgow 1844; head of firm of Burns, Alison and Aitken; engaged much in consideration of public bills and legal education; author of *What's in a name* 1861; *War of Scottish independence* 2 vols. 1874. *d.* Moffat, Dumfriesshire 2 Aug. 1876.

BURNS, REV. WILLIAM CHALMERS *(brother of Rev. Islay Burns 1817–72).* *b.* Manse of Dun 1 April 1815; licensed as a preacher by presbytery of Glasgow 27 March 1839; minister of St. Peters, Dundee; preached with great success in Scotland, north of England and Canada; sent to China as a missionary by Presbyterian church of England Nov. 1847, where he founded many native congregations of Christians; translated the *Pilgrim's Progress* and many hymns into Chinese. *d.* at port of Nieu-chwang, China 4 April 1868. *Memoir by Rev. Islay Burns,* 3 ed. 1870, *portrait; W. G. Blaikie's Leaders in modern philanthropy* (1884) 219–40, *portrait.*

BURNSIDE, HENRY EDWARD HILLMAN. Ensign 61 foot 20 Jany. 1843; chief instructor at school of musketry Hythe, Kent 1873 to 1 Aug. 1875 when placed on h.p. as lieut. col.; C.B. 29 May 1875. *d.* Stogumber, Somerset 29 Nov. 1876.

BURR, DANIEL HIGFORD DAVALL *(elder son of Daniel Burr, lieut. general H.E.I.C.S. who d. 19 Feb. 1828 aged 79).* *b.* 24 March 1811; ed. at Eton and Ch. Ch. Ox.; M.P. for Hereford 25 July 1837 to 23 June 1841; contested Salisbury 10 July 1852, and Abingdon 3 Dec. 1852; sheriff of Berks. 1851. *d.* 23 Eaton place, London 29 Nov. 1885.

BURRARD, SIR CHARLES, 2 Baronet. *b.* Dorking, Surrey 2 March 1793; succeeded 18 Oct. 1813; entered navy 13 July 1805; captain 29 Jany. 1822; flag captain in the Revenge 76 guns 20 March 1823 to April 1827; placed on retired half pay 1 Oct. 1846; retired admiral 27 April 1863. *d.* Holmefield, Lyndhurst, Hants. 12 July 1870.

BURRARD, REV. SIR GEORGE, 3 Baronet. *b.* Lymington, Hampshire 6 April 1769; R. of Yarmouth, Isle of Wight 1801–41; Chaplain in ordinary 1801 to death; V. of Middleton-Tyas, Yorkshire 1804 to death; R. of Burton-Coggles, Lincs. 1822 to death; succeeded 7 Feb. 1840. *d.* Walhampton, Lymington 17 May 1856.

BURRARD, SIR GEORGE, 4 Baronet. *b.* 13 Oct. 1805; M.P. for Lymington 31 July 1828 to 3 Dec. 1832; succeeded 17 May 1856; drowned while bathing at Lyme Regis, Dorset 7 Sep. 1870.

BURRARD, SIR HARRY, 5 Baronet. *b.* 13 Oct. 1818; succeeded 7 Sep. 1870. *d.* Hastings 15 April 1871.

BURRELL, SIR CHARLES MERRIK, 3 Baronet *(eld. son of Sir Wm. Burrell, 2 baronet 1732–96).* *b.* Golden sq. London 21 May 1774;

BURRELL, SIR C. M. *(Con.)*

succeeded 20 Jany. 1796 ; M.P. for Shoreham 4 Nov. 1807 to death, the "father" of the House for some time before his death ; Sussex agriculturists owe to him introduction of the white or Belgian carrot and valuable experiments in feeding and fattening cattle. *d.* Knepp castle, West Grinstead 4 Jany. 1862. *Sporting Review xlvii,* 108 (1862).

BURRELL, GEORGE. *b.* Long Houghton, Northumberland 26 Feb. 1777 ; ensign 15 foot 4 Feb. 1797 ; lieut. col. 18 foot 22 July 1830 to 22 Nov. 1841 ; C.B. 14 Oct. 1841 ; L.G. 11 Nov. 1851 ; colonel 39 foot 11 Feb. 1852 to death. *d.* Alnwick 4 Jany. 1853.

BURRELL, JOHN PALFREY *(youngest son of Palfrey George Burrell of Alnwick).* Barrister G.I. 2 July 1805, bencher 20 May 1829, treasurer 1833–4 ; police magistrate at Queen sq. office Westminster 1833–46 and at Vincent sq. office Westminster 1846–54. *d.* 1 Gray's Inn sq. London 11 July 1859 aged 86.

BURRELL, SIR PERCY, 4 Baronet. *b.* Grosvenor place, London 10 Feb. 1812 ; succeeded 4 Jany. 1862 ; M.P. for Shoreham 5 Feb. 1862 to death. *d.* 44 Berkeley sq. London 19 July 1876.

BURRELL, SIR WALTER WYNDHAM, 5 Baronet. *b.* 26 Oct. 1814 ; barrister L.I. 1840 ; contested East Sussex 1865 ; M.P. for Shoreham 4 Aug. 1876 to 18 Nov. 1885 ; sheriff of Sussex 1871 ; succeeded 19 July 1876. *d.* West Grinsted park, Horsham 24 Jany. 1886. *Law Times lxxx,* 236 (1876).

BURRITT, ELIHU. *b.* New Britain, Connecticut 8 Dec. 1810 ; a blacksmith at Worcester, Massachusetts 1837 ; translated all the Icelandic Sagas relating to discovery of America and obtained name of the "learned blacksmith" ; public lecturer 1841 ; started *Christian Citizen* a weekly journal 1842 ; co-operated in England with English peace advocates 1846–9 ; developed basis of an international association known as the League of universal brotherhood 1848 ; prominent organiser of first Peace Congress at Paris 22 Aug. 1849 ; editor of *Citizen of the World* in Philadelphia 1852 ; walked from London to John O'Groats 1863 and from London to Land's End 1864 ; United States consul at Birmingham 1867 to June 1869. *d.* New Britain 9 March 1879. *The world's workers by J. W. Kirton* (1885) 65–94, *portrait.*

BURROUGHES, HENRY NEGUS. *b.* 8 Feb. 1791 ; sheriff of Norfolk 1817 ; M.P. for East Norfolk 11 Aug. 1837 to 21 March 1857. *d.* 22 March 1872.

BURROUGHS, WATKINS. *b.* England 1795 ; Manager of Surrey theatre, London Oct. 1822 ; stage manager at Astley's theatre ; lessee of Belfast theatre ; first appeared in America 1825, at Park theatre, New York as Harry Dornton in *The road to ruin;* acting and stage manager of Lafayette theatre N.Y. ; acted at Philadelphia 1825. *d.* Liverpool 12 July 1869.

BURROW, VEN. EDWARD JOHN. Educ. at Magd. coll. Cam., B.A. 1805, M.A. 1808 ; incorporated M.A. at Trin. coll. Ox. 1820, B.D. and D.D. 1820 ; P.C. of Bempton, Yorkshire 1810–16 ; minister of Hampstead chapel near London 1816–23 ; domestic chaplain to bishop of Winchester 1823–35 ; principal of College school Mount Radford, Exeter July 1827 to Jany. 1828 ; civil chaplain of Gibralter 1835–42 ; archdeacon of Gibralter 1842-59 ; F.R.S. 26 Feb. 1818 ; author of *Elements of conchology* 1815, 2 *ed.* 1818 ; *The Elgin marbles with an account of Athens* 1817 ; *A summary of Christian faith and practice* 3 *vols.* 1822 ; *Questions on the memorial scripture copies* 1829, 3 *ed.* 1854. *d.* Honiton, Devon 8 Aug. 1861. *A statement of the manner in which E. J. Burrow became connected with Mount Radford and of his removal* 1828.

BURROWES, JOHN FRECKLETON. *b.* London 23 April 1787 ; pupil of William Horsley, organist ; organist of St. James's church, Piccadilly, London about 1815 to death ; an original member of Philharmonic Society 1813 ; author of *The pianoforte primer containing the rudiments of music* 1818, 48 *ed.* 1862 ; *Thorough bass primer* 1819, 37 *ed.* 1871 ; *A companion to the thorough bass primer* 1832. *d.* 13 Nottingham place, New road, London 31 March 1852.

BURROWES, ROBERT. *b.* Dublin 19 March 1810 ; sheriff of Cavan 1838 ; M.P. for co. Cavan 13 April 1855 to 21 March 1857. *d.* Stradone house, Cavan 30 Nov. 1881.

BURROWS. SIR JOHN CORDY *(eld. son of Robert Burrows of Ipswich, silversmith).* *b.* Ipswich 5 Aug. 1813 ; M.R.C.S. 1836, F.R.C.S. 1852 ; practised at Brighton 1839 to death ; projected Royal literary and scientific institution 1841, secretary 1841–57 ; mayor of Brighton 1857–9 and 1871–2 ; knighted at Osborne 5 Feb. 1873 ; a very great benefactor to town of Brighton. *d.* 62 Old Steyne, Brighton 25 March 1876. Statue of him in grounds of Royal Pavilion unveiled 14 Feb. 1878. *Lancet i,* 515, 548 (1876); *I.L.N. lxii,* 191 (1873), *portrait, lxviii,* 335 (1876), *lxxii,* 173 (1878).

BURSLEM, CHARLES. *b.* Manchester; a journalist; assistant editor of the *North Eastern Daily Gazette* some years; author of several serial tales in provincial journals; author of several successful pantomimes and of a farce entitled *Third floor lodgers* produced at Gaiety theatre West Hartlepool. *d.* Manchester Jany. 1886 aged 28.

BURSTAL, EDWARD. *b.* Devonport 1 Feb. 1818; entered navy Dec. 1832; commander 29 Sep. 1855; assisted in laying down first submarine telegraph cable between Dover and Calais 1852; laid cable from Orfordness to the Hague; secretary to conservators of river Thames 1857 to death; a member of Thames Embankment and other royal commissions; retired captain 29 Sep. 1870; F.R.G.S. 1857. *d.* Ramsgate 13 July 1886.

BURT, SIR ARCHIBALD PAUL (2 son of *George Henry Burt, speaker of house of assembly St. Christopher, West Indies*). *b.* St. Christopher 1810; barrister M.T. 21 Nov. 1845; attorney general of St. Christopher 1849–60, member of legislative and executive councils, speaker of house of assembly; comr. of civil court in Western Australia July 1860, chief justice there 1861 to death; knighted at Windsor Castle 12 Dec. 1873. *d.* Strawberry hill, Perth, Western Australia 21 Nov. 1879.

BURTON, ADOLPHUS WILLIAM DESART. *b.* 1827; ensign 82 foot 8 Aug. 1845; major 7 dragoon guards 17 Sep. 1857 to 1863; C.B. 5 July 1855. *d.* Pau 11 Feb. 1882.

BURTON, REV. CHARLES (*youngest son of Daniel Burton of Rhodes hall, Middleton, Lancs. cotton manufacturer*). *b.* Rhodes hall 18 Jany. 1793; ed. at Univ. of Glasgow and St. John's coll. Cam., L.L.B. Cam. 1822, B.C.L. and D.C.L. Ox. 1829; Wesleyan minister; built church of All Saints, Chorlton-upon-Medlock, Manchester at cost of £18,000, R. of All Saints 1820 to death, greater part of church was destroyed by fire 6 Feb. 1850; F.L.S. for discovering in Anglesea a plant new to science; author of *Horæ Poeticæ* 1815; *The Bardiad, a poem in two cantos* 1823, 2 ed. 1823; *Lectures on the Millenium* 1841; *Lectures on the world before the flood* 1844; *Lectures on Popery* 1851 and about 15 other books. *d.* Western lodge, Durham 6 Sep. 1866. *Evans's Lancashire authors and orators* (1850) 47–51.

BURTON, CHARLES EDWARD (*son of Rev. Edward Wm. Burton, R. of Rathmichael, co. Dublin*). *b.* Barnton, Cheshire 16 Sep. 1846; assistant in Lord Rosse's observatory at Parsonstown 1868–9; B.A. Dublin 1868;

joined Sicilian expedition to observe total solar eclipse of 22 Dec. 1870; photographer to transit of Venus expedition 1874; worked at observatory of Dunsink near Dublin 1876–8; devised with Howard Grubb the 'ghost micrometer' described before Royal Dublin Society 15 Nov. 1880; F.R.A.S. 8 May 1874; author of numerous papers in scientific periodicals. *d.* Castle Knock church 9 July 1882. *Astronomical Register xx,* 173–4 (1883).

BURTON, DECIMUS (10 son of *James Burton of London, builder*). *b.* 30 Sep. 1800; architect in London 1821–69; designed the Colosseum in Regent's Park 1823; carried out Hyde Park Corner improvements where he designed the facade and triumphal arch 1825; designed the Athenæum club 1827; laid out Calverley Park estate at Tunbridge Wells 1828–50; architect to Royal botanic society 1840–70; F.R.S. 6 Dec. 1832, F.R.I.B.A. *d.* The Cottage, St. Leonard's-on-Sea 14 Dec. 1881. *Proc. of Royal Soc. xxxiv,* 8–10 (1883); *Builder xli,* 779–80 (1881); *I.L.N. lxxix,* 650 (1881), *portrait*.

BURTON, EDWARD FREDERICK (*son of James Burton of London, solicitor who d. 1869*). *b.* 1818; solicitor in London 1843 to death; member of council of Incorporated law society 1865 to death, vice pres. 1876–7, pres. 1877–8; member of judicature acts (legal offices) committee 1877. *d.* Eastbourne 11 July 1879.

BURTON, JAMES RYDER. *b.* 1795; entered navy 12 May 1806; captain 23 Feb. 1824; granted good service pension 4 Nov. 1852; admiral on half pay 4 Nov. 1863; K.H. 1 Jany. 1837; invented a method for propelling ships of war during a calm 1819. *d.* 15 Park sq. east, Regent's park, London 2 Aug. 1876.

BURTON, JOHN HILL (2 son of *Wm. Kinnimont Burton of Aberdeen who d. 1820*). *b.* the Gallowgate, Aberdeen 22 Aug. 1809; ed. at Marischal coll. Aberdeen; called to Scottish bar 1831; contributed articles to *Blackwood's Mag.* 1842 to death; sec. to general board of directors of prisons in Scotland 24 July 1854; manager of Perth prison 4 Jany. 1861 to Jany. 1878; historiographer royal of Scotland 1867; author of *Law of bankruptcy in Scotland* 2 vols. 1845; *Life of D. Hume* 2 vols. 1846; *Lives of Lord Lovat and Duncan Forbes* 1847; *Narratives from criminal trials in Scotland* 2 vols. 1852; *History of Scotland* 9 vols. 1853–70, 2 ed. 9 vols. 1873; *The book hunter* 1862, *new ed.* 1882; *History of the reign*

BURTON, J. H. *(Con.)*

of *Queen Anne* 3 vols. 1880; *The Scot abroad*
2 vols. 1881. *d.* Morton house, Lothianburn
10 Aug. 1881. *The Bookhunter by J. H. Burton*
(1882) *i–civ, portrait; Blackwood's Mag. cxxx,*
401–4 (1881); *Graphic xxiv,* 269 (1881),
portrait.

BURTON, SIR RICHARD *(son of Sir John
Burton of Wakefield, Yorkshire).* b. Westminster 1773; knighted at St. James's palace
13 Sep. 1831. *d.* Sackett's hill house, Margate 3 Sep. 1855.

BURTON, WILLIAM EVANS *(son of Wm.
Burton of London, printer 1774–1825).* b.
London Sep. 1802; ed. at St. Paul's sch.;
acted in Norwich circuit 7 years; first appeared in London at Pavilion theatre Feb.
1831 as Wormwood in *The lottery ticket;* acted
at Haymarket 1833; first appeared in
America at Arch st. theatre Philadelphia 3
Sep. 1834 as Doctor Ollapod in *The Poor
gentleman;* lessee and manager of theatres in
Philadelphia and Baltimore; leased Palma's
Opera house New York 1848 which he renamed Burton's Theatre; manager of Metropolitan theatre Broadway which he renamed
Burton's New theatre Sep. 1856–8; wrote
several plays best known being *Ellen Wareham*
a domestic drama, produced May 1833 when
it was played at 5 London theatres at same
time; edited *Cambridge Quarterly Review* and
Philadelphia Literary Souvenir 1838–40; author
of *Waggaries and vagaries* 1848; *Cyclopædia
of wit and humour* 2 vols. 1857. *d.* 174
Hudson st. New York 9 Feb. 1860. *Ireland's
Records of the New York stage ii,* 235–8 (1867);
Burton's Cyclopædia (1857), *portrait; T. A.
Brown's American stage* (1870) 57, 66, *portrait.*

BURTON, WILLIAM MARTIN. Second lieut.
Madras artillery 1798, colonel 26 Feb. 1840
to death; L.G. 11 Nov. 1851. *d* at his
residence near London 13 Aug. 1853.

BURTON, WILLIAM PATON *(son of Wm.
Paton Burton, captain Indian army).* b.
Madras 1828; ed. at Edinburgh; pupil of
David Bryce, architect; a water colour
painter; exhibited many landscapes at the
R.A. and Suffolk st. gallery 1862–80. *d.*
Cults, Aberdeen 31 Dec. 1883.

BURTON-PETERS, HENRY. *b.* 1792; M.P.
for Beverley 31 July 1830 to 17 July 1837.
d. Bath 24 Nov. 1874.

BURTT, JOHN. *b.* Fulbeck, Lincs.; published
*The young patriot and other poems by J. B. a
friend of the Aborigines protection society* 1846.
d. Stockport, Cheshire 5 July 1859 aged 71.
Annual Monitor for 1860 *pp.* 66–74.

BURTT, JOHN. *b.* Knockmarlock, Ayrshire
1789; apprenticed to a weaver; pressed into
navy 1807; served on board the Magnificent
5 years; taught in Kilmarnock and Paisley
1816; went to United States; studied at
Princeton college; Presbyterian minister at
Salem; professor of theology 1835. *d* 24
March 1866.

BURTT, JOSEPH. *b.* St. Pancras, London
7 Nov. 1818; worked under Sir Francis
Palgrave at Chapter house, Westminster
Abbey 1832–40; clerk in Record Office 1840,
a second class assistant keeper of records
Aug. 1851, a first class June 1859 to death;
sec. to Royal Archæol. Instit. 1862 to death;
edited *Archæological Journal;* edited *Household expenses of John of Brabant, and of
Thomas and Henry of Lancaster* for the
Miscellany of Camden Society. *d.* Crofton
lodge, Upper Tulse hill, Surrey 15 Dec. 1876.
Archæological Journal xxxiv, 90–2 (1877).

BURY, CHARLOTTE SUSAN MARIA *(dau. of 5
Duke of Argyll 1723–1806).* b. Argyll house,
Oxford st. London 28 Jany. 1775; lady in
waiting to Princess of Wales, afterwards
Queen Caroline 1809; published anonymously
Poems on several occasions by a Lady 1797;
Love 3 vols. 1837, 2 ed. 1860; *Diary illustrative
of the times of George the Fourth* 4 vols. 1838–9;
and with her name, *The divorced* 2 vols. 1837,
2 ed. 1858. *(m.* (1) 14 June 1796 John
Campbell, M.P. for Ayr burghs who *d.* 15
March 1809. *m.* (2) 17 March 1818 Rev.
Edward John Bury, R. of Lichfield, Hants.
who *d.* May 1832 aged 42.) *d.* 91 Sloane st.
Chelsea 31 March 1861. *Burke's Portrait
gallery i,* 103 (1833), *portrait; New monthly
mag. xlix,* 76–7 (1837), *portrait.*

BURY, EDWARD. *b.* Salford near Manchester
22 Oct. 1794; manufacturer of machinery
at Liverpool; introduced a series of improved
engines for steamboats employed on river
Rhone; managed locomotive department of
London and Birmingham railway for some
years after opening Sep. 1838; managed
locomotive department of Great Northern
railway; F.R.S. 1 Feb. 1844 for great
improvements which he had introduced in
adjusting dimensions of cylinder and driving
wheels of steam engines. *d.* Scarborough 25
Nov. 1858. *Proc. of Royal Soc. x,* 12 (1860).

BURY, GEORGE BUTT. Second lieut. R.M. 10
Nov. 1804, colonel 10 Jany. 1852, col.
commandant 21 June 1854 to 1 Aug. 1854
when he retired on full pay; M.G. 20 June
1855. *d.* 25 Athenæum st. Plymouth 4 Jany.
1873 aged 87.

BURY, THOMAS TALBOT. *b.* 26 Sep. 1811; articled to Augustus Pugin, architect 1824; architect in Gerrard st. Soho, London 1830; very skilful in colouring architectural studies; designed with A. Pugin details of Houses of parliament; exhibited 18 drawings at the R.A. 1838–72; designed 35 churches and about 50 other large buildings; F.R.I.B.A. 1843, vice pres. 1876; F.S.A. 1863; author of *Remains of ecclesiastical woodwork* 1847; *History and description of the styles of architecture of various countries* 1849. *d.* 50 Welbeck st. London 23 Feb. 1877. *Sessional papers read at Royal Instit. of British Architects* (1877) 152–4.

BUSFEILD, WILLIAM. *b.* 12 Feb. 1773; M.P. for Bradford 25 July 1837 to 23 June 1841 and 16 Sep. 1841 to death. *d.* 15 Bury st. St. James's London 11 Sep. 1851.

BUSH, WILLIAM. Cornet 2 Dragoon guards 7 Jany. 1808; lieut. col. 1 West India regiment 4 Sep. 1835 to 1 Jany. 1847; inspecting field officer of Leeds recruiting district 1 Jany. 1847, of London district 17 April 1852 to death; M.G. 20 June 1854; K.H. 1835. *d.* 66 Cadogan place, London 27 Aug. 1854. *H. S. Smith's Military obituary for* 1854, 10–12.

BUSHNAN, JOHN STEVENSON (*son of Joseph Bushnan who d. 21 Feb. 1831, controller of the Chamber, City of London* 1803–31). *b.* The Guildhall, London 1810; M.R.C.S. Edin. 1830, F.R.C.S. 1839; M.R.C.P. Edin. 1830, M.D. Heidelberg 1836; practised at Castle Cary, Somerset 1837–41; travelled abroad 1841–8; practised in London 1848; edited *Medical times and gazette* 1849–52; author of *Philosophy of instinct and reason* 1847; *Miss Martineau and her master* 1851; *Homœopathy and the homœopaths* 1852 and other books. *d.* The Charterhouse, City of London 17 Feb. 1884. *Medical Circular ii,* 149–50 (1853).

BUSK, HANS (*youngest son of Sir Wadsworth Busk* 1730–1811, *attorney general of Isle of Man*). *b.* 28 May 1772; lived in Russia some years where he was a member of Empress Catherine's celebrated Chevalier Guard; sheriff of Radnorshire 1837–8; author of *Fugitive pieces in verse* 1814; *The Vestriad or the Opera, a mock epic poem* 1819; *The dessert, a poem to which is added The tea* 1820; *The lay of life, a poem* 1834. *d.* 22 Great Cumberland place, Hyde park, London 8 Feb. 1862.

BUSK, HANS (*eld. son of the preceding*). *b.* 11 May 1815; ed. at King's coll. London and Trin. coll. Cam., B.A. 1839, M.A. 1844; formed a model rifle club at Cam. 1837; bar-

BUSK, H. (*Con.*)
rister M.T. 7 May 1841; sheriff of Radnorshire 1847; joined Royal Victoria rifle club London 1858 only volunteer corps then existing, captain 1860; delivered lectures instrumental in extending volunteer movement over whole kingdom; devised a steam life boat service 1869, the Petronelle first of the class was launched 1873; founded *New Quarterly review* 1874; author of *The rifleman's manual* 1858, 7 ed. 1860; *Rifle volunteers how to organize and drill them* 1859, 7 ed. 1860; *The navies of the world their present state and future capabilities* 1859; *Handbook for Hythe* 1860; *Maiden-hours and maiden-wiles designed by Beaujolais* 1869. *d.* 21 Ashley place, Victoria st. Westminster 11 March 1882. *I.L.N. lxxx,* 284 (1882), *portrait; Graphic xxv,* 313 (1882), *portrait.*

BUSS, ROBERT WILLIAM (*son of Wm. C. Buss of 60 Jewin st. Cripplegate, London, engraver who d.* 1832). *b.* London 4 Aug. 1804; apprenticed to his father; painted 15 theatrical portraits for *Cumberland's British Drama* which were exhibited at Colosseum; exhibited 25 pictures at R.A., 20 at B.I. and 45 at Suffolk st. gallery 1826–59; contributed to Westminster competition a cartoon of Prince Henry and Judge Gascoigne; illustrated Charles Knight's *London, Chaucer, Shakespeare* and *Old England;* painted 71 pictures, 25 of which were engraved; painted large frescoes representing Origin and triumph of music for Earl of Hardwicke at Wimpole hall; privately printed *English graphic satire* 1874; edited *The fine art almanac, or artist's remembrancer* 1850–2. *d.* 14 Camden st. Camden Town, London 26 Feb. 1875. *G. Everitt's English Caricaturists* (1886) 363–6; *People's Journal vi,* 3 (1848); *Notes and Queries* 5 *S. iii,* 228, 257, 330, 419, 455, 473 (1875), *iv,* 15 (1875), *vii,* 138 (1877), 6 *S. vi,* 488 (1882), *vii,* 216 (1883).

BUTCHER, MOST REV. SAMUEL (*eld. son of Samuel Butcher* 1770–1849, *vice admiral R.N.*) *b.* Danesfort near Killarney 9 Oct. 1811; ed. at Cork and Trin. coll. Dublin, scholar 1832, B.A. 1834, fellow 1837–52, tutor and lecturer, M.A. 1839, B.D. 1848, D.D. 1849; professor of ecclesiastical history in Univ. of Dublin April 1850, Regius professor of divinity Nov. 1852 to Aug. 1866; R. of Ballymoney, Cork 1854–66; bishop of Meath Aug. 1866 to death; P.C. Ireland 1866; author of *The ecclesiastical calendar its theory and construction* 1877; cut his throat at Ardbraccan house, Navan near Dublin 29 July 1876.

BUTE, SOPHIA FREDERICA CHRISTINA CRICH-
TON-STUART, Marchioness of (2 *dau. of* 1
Marquis of Hastings 1754–1826). *b.* 1 Feb.
1809; gave the Sophia gardens to town of
Cardiff; edited *Poems of lady Flora Hastings*
1841; *Private journals of* 1 *Marquis of Hastings*
2 *vols.* 1858. (*m.* 10 April 1845, John Crich-
ton-Stuart, 2 Marquis of Bute 1793–1848).
d. 120 George st. Edinburgh 28 Dec. 1859.

BUTLER, CHARLES SALISBURY *(eld. son of*
John Butler of Hackney, London). b. 1812;
commissioner of taxes; M.P. for Tower
Hamlets 8 July 1852 to 11 Nov. 1868; chairman of Quarter sessions of Tower Hamlets
liberties to death. *d.* 48 Prince's gate, Hyde
park, London 11 Nov. 1870.

BUTLER, SIR EDWARD (5 *son of* 13 *Baron*
Dunboyne 1780–1850). *b.* 29 Oct. 1811; lieut.
of corps of gentlemen at arms 1839 to May
1845; knighted at St. James's palace 19 Feb.
1840; contested Southampton, contest was
protracted from Nov. 1856 to 11 Feb. 1857
when he was defeated by 32 votes; sheriff of
Hants 1855. *d.* Marseilles 20 Oct. 1858.

BUTLER, EDWARD. *b.* Kilkenny 1824; re-
established *The Nation* with C. G. Duffy 1849;
went to New South Wales 1853; called to
bar at Sydney 16 Oct. 1855, Q.C.; member
of legislative assembly for Argyle 1869;
attorney general 1872 to Nov. 1873; member
of legislative council Oct. 1877 to death. *d.*
Supreme court, Sydney 9 June 1879. *Times*
18 *July* 1879 *p.* 5, *col.* 6, 11 *Aug. p.* 11, *col.* 2.

BUTLER, FRANCIS *(son of Mr. Butler, trainer*
of horses to Duke of York who d. 1827). *b.*
Sep. 1817; professional jockey 1839–53;
won the Oaks on Poison 1843 at odds of 40
to 1, on Princess 1844, on Lady Evelyn 1849,
on Rhedycina 1850, on Iris 1851 and on
Songstress 1852; won St. Leger on The
Baron 1845; won Derby on Daniel O'Rourke
1852 and Two thousand guineas, Derby and
St. Leger on West Australian 1853. *d.* Newmarket 1 Feb. 1856. *Sporting Review xxxi,*
143–8 (1854), *portrait; I.L.N. xxii,* 416
(1853), *portrait.*

BUTLER, FRANCIS. *b.* England 1810; professor of languages at several educational
institutions in New York; a dog-trainer and
fancier; author of *Breeding, training, manage-*
ment and diseases of dogs 1857; *The Spanish*
teacher and colloquial phrase book, 8 *ed.* 1857.
d. from hydrophobia at Brooklyn, New York
17 June 1874.

BUTLER, VERY REV. GEORGE (2 *son of Rev.*
Weeden Butler 1742–1823, *Morning preacher at*
Charlotte st. Chapel Pimlico, London). b. Pim-
lico 5 July 1774; foundation scholar of Sid.
Sus. coll. Cam.; Senior Wr. and first Smith's
prizeman Jany. 1794; B.A. 1794, M.A. 1797,
B.D. 1804, D.D. 1805; Fellow of his college
1794, mathematical lecturer and classical
tutor; kept his terms at Lincolns Inn; one
of the 8 select preachers before Univ. of
Cam. 1805; Head master of Harrow school
April 1805 to Easter 1829; R. of Gayton,
Northampton 1814 to death; chancellor of
Peterborough 1836–42; dean of Peterborough
3 Nov. 1842 to death, admitted Dean 25
Nov. 1842; author of *Extracts from the com-*
munion service of the Church 1839, 2 *ed.* 1842;
Statutes of Peterborough cathedral translated
1853; *Harrow, a selection of the lists of the*
School 1849. *d.* the deanery Peterborough 30
April 1853. Monument erected in Harrow
church July 1854. *P. M. Thornton's Harrow*
school (1885) 215–64.

BUTLER, GEORGE SLADE *(son of Richard*
Butler of Rye, Sussex, surgeon). b. Rye 4
March 1821; solicitor at Rye 1843 to death;
town clerk 1875–81; registrar of county
court; F.S.A. 6 March 1862; author of *Topo-*
graphica Sussexiana 1866, originally printed
in *Collections of Sussex Archæological Society* to
which he contributed many papers on antiquities of Rye. *d.* Rye 11 April 1882.

BUTLER, HENRY EDWARD (2 *son of* 2 *Earl*
of Carrick 1746–1813). *b.* 3 Dec. 1780;
ensign 27 foot 15 Feb. 1800; major 2 garrison
battalion 19 March 1812 to 25 Dec. 1816
when placed on h.p.; L.G. 20 June 1854;
col. 94 foot 25 July 1854 and col. 55 foot 19
Jany. 1855 to death. *d.* Paris 7 Dec. 1856.

BUTLER, JAMES ARMAR (4 *son of the pre-*
ceding). b. 1827; ensign 90 foot 13 Oct.
1843; captain Ceylon rifle regiment 6 May
1853 to May 1854 when placed on h.p.; conducted siege of Silistria, Turkey against the
Russians May 1854 to death; gazetted brevet
major 14 July 1854 and lieut. Coldstream
guards 15 July 1854. *d.* Silistria of wounds
received during the siege 22 June 1854 in 28
year. *E. H. Nolan's War against Russia i,*
214–27 (1857); *G. Ryan's Our heroes of the*
Crimea (1855) 141–3.

BUTLER, JAMES ARTHUR. *b.* 1795; ensign
1 foot guards 23 June 1813, captain 18 April
1816 to 25 Dec. 1818, carried the colours at
Waterloo; captain 80 foot 31 July 1823 to
19 Nov. 1825 when placed on h.p.; general
5 Dec. 1871. *d.* Holt lodge, Kintbury, Berkshire 26 Feb. 1881.

BUTLER, REV. PIERCE (*brother of James Armar Butler 1827–54*). *b.* 27 Feb. 1826; ed. at Trin. coll. Cam., B.A. 1849, M.A. 1852; explored peninsula of Sinai 1853–4; R. of Ulcombe, Kent 1861 to death; translated from the Danish *Öhlenschläger's Axel and Valborg*, a tragedy in 5 acts 1874. *d.* Ulcombe rectory 8 Feb. 1868. *Journal of Royal Geog. Soc. xxxviii, pp. cxliv–cxlvi,* (1868).

BUTLER, PIERCE SOMERSET. *b.* 26 Jany. 1801; called to Irish bar 1832; M.P. for co. Kilkenny 1 Dec. 1843 to 1 July 1852. *d.* 28 July 1865. *Annual Register* (1854) 402–14.

BUTLER, VERY REV. RICHARD (*eld. son of Rev. Richard Butler, V. of Burnchurch, co. Kilkenny who d. 1841*). *b.* near Granard, co. Longford 14 Oct. 1794; ed. at Reading and Balliol coll. Ox., B.A. 1817; V. of Trim, co. Meath 1819 to death; dean of Clonmacnois Dec. 1847 to death; one of founders of Irish archæological Society 1840 (united with Celtic Society 1854), for which he edited *Clyn and Dowling's Annals of Ireland* 1849; author of *Some notices of the Castle and of the Abbies at Trim* 1835, 2 ed. 1840. *d.* 17 July 1862.

BUTLER, SIR RICHARD PIERCE, 9 Baronet. *b.* 4 March 1813; succeeded 8 Nov. 1861. *d.* 22 Nov. 1862.

BUTLER, SIR THOMAS, 8 Baronet. *b.* 23 Oct. 1783; succeeded 16 Jany. 1817. *d.* 8 Nov. 1861.

BUTLER–CLARKE–SOUTHWELL–WANDESFORD, CHARLES HARWARD (*4 son of 17 Earl of Ormonde who d. 30 Jany. 1796*). *b.* 9 Nov. 1780; M.P. for city of Kilkenny 1802–9 and 1814–20; M.P. for county Kilkenny 1820–30. *d.* Mount Juliet, Kilkenny 7 Nov. 1860.

BUTLER–JOHNSTONE, HENRY (*3 son of 13 Baron Dunboyne 1780–1850*). *b.* Dublin 28 Aug. 1809; M.P. for Canterbury 8 July 1852 to 21 Feb. 1853 when unseated on petition of the electors, M.P. again 1857–62; colonel commandant Dumfries militia 7 Feb. 1868 to 15 March 1873. *d.* 8 Seamore place, Mayfair, London 1 April 1879.

BUTT GEORGE MEDD (*2 son of John Butt of Sherborne*). *b.* Sherborne 1797; practised as special pleader; barrister I.T. 25 June 1830, bencher 1845, reader 1858, treasurer 1859; Q.C. 1845; M.P. for Weymouth 10 July 1852 to 21 March 1857. *d.* 17 Eaton square, London 11 Nov. 1860.

BUTT, ISAAC (*only son of Rev. Robert Butt R. of Stranorlar, co. Donegal*). *b.* Glenfin, co. Donegal 6 Sep. 1813; ed. at Royal school Raphoe and Trin coll. Dublin, scholar 1832, B.A. 1835, LL.B. 1836, M.A. and LL.D. 1840; Whately professor of political economy in Trin. coll. Dublin 1836–41; called to Irish bar Nov. 1838; alderman of Dublin 1840; barrister I.T. 17 Nov. 1859; carried on a counter agitation to that of the Repeal Association 1843; Q.C. 2 Nov. 1844; M.P. for Harwich 8 May 1852 to 1 July 1852, for Youghal 1852 to 1865 and for Limerick 1871 to death; leader of the Home Rule party 1871 to death; defended the Fenian prisoners 1865–9; pres. of Amnesty Association 1869; a founder of *Dublin Univ. Mag.* 1833, editor Aug. 1834 to 1838; established in Dublin a weekly newspaper called the *Protestant Guardian* afterwards amalgamated with the *Warder*; author of *Ovid's Fasti translated* 1833; *The history of Italy* 1860; *A practical treatise on the new law of compensation to tenants in Ireland* 1871; *Home government for Ireland* 1874. *d.* Roebuck cottage near Dundrum, co. Dublin 5 May 1879. *Dublin Univ. Mag. xciii,* 710–15 (1879); *Sullivan's New Ireland* (1877), *ii,* 306–10, 319; *Graphic iv,* 485 (1871), *portrait, xix,* 508 (1879), *portrait; I.L.N. iv,* 40 (1844), *portrait.*

BUTT, JAMES PALMER. Educ. at school established in Somers Town, London by Abbé Carron and at Stonyhurst college; kept a school with his brother Wm. Henry Butt at Baylis house, Salt hill near Windsor about 1828 to death. *d.* Baylis house, Salt hill 2 May 1873 aged 84.

BUTTER, DONALD. Surgeon Bengal army 28 Aug. 1833; superintending surgeon at Benares 31 Dec. 1854 to 23 April 1859 when placed on h.p. with rank of inspector general; author of *Outline of the topography and statistics of the Southern districts of Oudh* 1839; *Snake bite curable and hydrophobia preventible* 1873. *d.* Hazelwood, Upper Norwood 24 Dec. 1877 aged 78.

BUTTER, JOHN. *b.* Woodbury, Devon 22 Jany. 1791; ed. at Exeter gr. sch.; surgeon at Plymouth 1814–20, physician there 1820–56 when he became blind; M.D. Edin. 1820; originated Plymouth Eye Dispensary 1821; F.L.S. 1817; F.R.S. 21 March 1822; author of *Remarks on irritative fever commonly called the Plymouth dockyard disease* 1845. *d.* 7 Windsor villas, Plymouth 13 Jany. 1877.

BUTTERWORTH, HENRY (*son of Henry Butterworth of Coventry, timber merchant*). *b.*

BUTTERWORTH, H. *(Con.)*

Coventry 28 Feb. 1786; law publisher at 7 Fleet st. London 1818 to death; representative of ward of Farringdon Without in Court of Common Council 1823–30; law publisher to the Queen 23 Nov. 1852 to death; F.S.A. 6 Jany. 1848. *d.* Upper Tooting, Surrey 2 Nov. 1860. *Memoir of the late H. Butterworth* (1861).

BUTTERWORTH, WILLIAM JOHN. Adjutant 38 Madras N.I. 1821; lieut. col. of 2 European regiment 1841–3 and 1846–51, of 10 Madras N.I. 1843–6; col. of 5 Madras N.I. 3 Dec. 1851 to death; C.B. 20 July 1838; governor of Prince of Wales island, Singapore and Malacca 14 June 1843 to 1855, presented with piece of plate value £700 by the inhabitants 1856; general 28 Nov. 1854. *d.* Millmead house, Guildford 4 Nov. 1856 aged 55. *I.L.N. xxix,* 105–6 (1856), *portrait.*

BUXTON, BERTHA H. *(dau. of Wm. Lenpold or Leupold of London, merchant).* *b.* 26 July 1844; ed. at Queen's college, Tufnell park, London; travelled in Holland, Germany and America; published *Jennie of "The Prince's,"* a novel by B. H. B. 3 vols. 1876; *Won, by the author of Jennie of the Prince's* 3 vols. 1877: *Rosabella, a doll's Christmas story by Auntie Bee* 1877; *More dolls by Auntie Bee* 1878; the following books have her name on them *Fetterless though bound together* 3 vols. 1879, *Great Grenfell gardens* 3 vols. 1879, *Nell—On and off the stage* 3 vols. 1880, *From the wings* 3 vols. 1880, *Many loves* 3 vols. 1880, *Little Pops a nursery romance* 1881, *Sceptre and king* 1881. *(m.* at Hanwell parish church 22 Dec. 1860, Henry Buxton of Hanwell, merchant son of Edward Buxton, merchant). *d.* 12 St. Mary's terrace, Kensington, London 31 March 1881. *Biograph iv,* 159–62 (1880); *Carisbrooke Mag. April* 1881, *portrait; Tinsley's Mag. xxviii,* 499–500 (1881).

BUXTON, CHARLES (3 *son of Sir Thomas Fowell Buxton, 1 Baronet 1786–1845).* *b.* Cromer 18 Nov. 1822; ed. at Trin. coll. Cam., B.A. 1845, M.A. 1850; partner in firm of Truman, Hanbury and Co. of Spitalfields, London, brewers 1845; M.P. for Newport, Isle of Wight 1857–9, for Maidstone 1859–65, for East Surrey 1865 to death; member of the Ritual commission 1867–8; his secretary Arthur White attempted to shoot him at 7 Grosvenor crescent, Hyde Park 29 April 1870; author of *Slavery and freedom in the British West Indies* 1860; *The ideas of the day on policy Dec.* 1865. *d.* Lochearnhead hotel near Killin, Perthshire 10 Aug. 1871. Personalty sworn

BUXTON, C. *(Con.)*

under £250,000, 28 Feb. 1872. *Notes of thought by the late C. Buxton,* 2 ed. (1883) 5–52; *Graphic iv,* 219, 237 (1871), *portrait.*

BUXTON, SIR EDWARD NORTH, 2 Baronet *(brother of the preceding).* *b.* Earlham, Norfolk 16 Sep. 1812; succeeded 19 Feb. 1845; M.P. for South Essex 1847–52, for East Norfolk 6 April 1857 to death. *d.* Colne house, Cromer 11 June 1858.

BUXTON, FREDERICK. *b.* Bow lane, Cheapside, London; made his first appearance on the stage at York 1844 as Mr. Gillman in *The happiest day of my life;* made his début in London at Olympic theatre 1847 as David in *The Rivals;* first appeared in America at Louisville, Kentucky March 1850 as Peter in *The Stranger. d.* Chicago 17 Jany. 1858.

BUXTON, RICHARD (2 *son of John Buxton of Sedgley hall farm, Prestwich, farmer).* *b.* Sedgley hall farm 15 Jany. 1786; apprenticed to a bat maker 1798; botanised in Derbyshire, Yorkshire, and North Wales; frequently cited in J. B. Wood's *Flora Mancuniensis* 1840 as the authority for many localities of the rarer plants; author of *Botanical guide to the flowering plants found within 16 miles of Manchester* 1849, 2 ed. 1859. *d.* Manchester 2 Jany. 1865. *J. Cash's Where there's a will there's a way* (1873) 94–107; *Seemann's Journ. of Bot. iii,* 71 (1865).

BYAM, EDWARD *(younger son of Edward Byam of Cedar hill, Antigua 1767–95).* *b.* 1795; ensign 38 foot 11 Nov. 1811; major 15 Hussars 16 June 1825 to 26 Sep. 1826 when placed on h.p.; colonel 18 Hussars 23 Feb. 1858 to death; L.G. 16 Nov. 1858. *d.* Byam house, Brighton 9 Sep. 1864.

BYAM, SIR WILLIAM *(brother of the preceding).* *b.* 1792; ed. at Eton; lieut 15 Hussars 17 Sep. 1812 to 1817; served in Peninsula, south of France and Waterloo; pres. of local council in Antigua; colonel of regiment of dragoons raised in Antigua; knighted by patent 6 July 1859. *d.* Westwood, Southampton 5 July 1869.

BYLES, SIR JOHN BARNARD *(eld. son of Jeremiah Byles of Stowmarket, Suffolk, timber merchant).* *b.* Stowmarket 11 Jany. 1801; a special pleader; barrister I.T. 18 Nov. 1831; recorder of Buckingham 1840 to Jany. 1858; serjeant-at-law 14 Feb. 1843; leader of Norfolk circuit 1845; received a patent of precedence 1846; Queen's serjeant with serjeants Shee and Wrangham 27 Feb. 1857,

BYLES, Sir J. B. *(Con.)*

this was last appointment of queen's serjeants of whom he was the survivor; judge of Court of Common Pleas Jany. 1858 to Jany. 1873 when he retired on pension of £3,500; knighted at St. James's palace 14 April 1858; P.C. 3 March 1873; author of *A discourse on the present state of the law of England* 1829; *A practical treatise on the law of bills of exchange* 1829, 14 ed. 1885; *Observations on the usury laws* 1845; *Free trade and its so called sophisms examined by a barrister* 1850; *Foundations of religion in the mind and heart of man* 1875. *d.* Harefield house, Uxbridge 3 Feb. 1884, Will proved 25 March 1884, personalty upwards of £201,000. *A. Pulling's Order of the Coif* (1884) 41, 105, 182; *A generation of judges by their Reporter* 1886; *Law Journal xix*, 115, 255 (1884); *Times* 5 Feb. 1884 p. 7, col. 1.

BYNG, Gerald Frederick *(youngest son of 5 Viscount Torrington 1741–1813)*. Page of honour to Prince of Wales 1791; cornet 27 light dragoons 1800; ensign 53 foot 1801–2 when place on h.p.; clerk in Foreign office 5 Jany. 1801 to 5 Nov. 1839 when he retired on a superannuation allowance; ensign St. George's volunteer infantry 1803; attended on King and Queen of Sandwich Islands during their visit to England May to July 1824; one of gentlemen ushers of privy chamber 23 March 1831 to death; a comr. for inquiring into Smithfield market 28 Nov. 1849; joined ranks of Queen's rifle volunteers 1859; presented to that corps colours of the St. George's volunteer infantry 1860; generally known as Poodle Byng, a soubriquet given him by George Canning on account of his curly hair; lived at 5 Cleveland court, afterwards called 37 St. James's place, Pall Mall, London 1831 to death. *d.* there 5 June 1871 aged 87. *Life of G. Brummell by captain Jesse i*, 110 (1886), *portrait*.

BYNG, Henry Dilkes *(brother of the preceding)*. *b.* 1784; entered navy March 1798; captain 9 March 1814; held a command on lakes of Canada 15 years; captain of the Ordinary at Portsmouth 1833–6; commodore at Jamaica 1842–3; retired captain 1 Oct. 1846; retired V.A. 31 Jany. 1856. *d.* Queen's terrace, Southsea 23 Sep. 1860.

BYRES, Patrick *(younger son of Robert Byres of London, merchant)*. *b.* about 1778; entered Bengal army 1794; major 11 Bengal N.I. 5 Aug. 1816; colonel 20 Bengal N.I. 3 June 1825; colonel 33 Bengal N.I. 9 July 1840 to death; L.G. 11 Nov. 1851. *d.* Lonley, Aberdeenshire 1 Feb. 1854.

BYRNE, Right Rev. Andrew. *b.* Navan, Ireland 5 Dec. 1802; went to America 1820; deacon April 1827, priest 11 Nov. 1827; stationed at various places in Carolina; pastor of St. Mary's R.C. church at Charleston 1830; vicar general of Bishop of Charleston; pastor of St. James's church N.Y. 1 Sep. 1836, of St. Andrew's church N.Y. 19 March 1842, of Church of the Nativity N.Y. 5 June 1842; bishop of Little Rock comprising state of Arkansas 1844 to death; consecrated at St. Patrick's cath. N.Y. 10 March 1844; attended sixth provincial council at Baltimore, May 1846 and first provincial council at New Orleans 1856. *d.* 1862. *R. H. Clarke's Lives of deceased bishops ii*, 264–71 (1872).

BYRNE, John. Ensign 22 foot 1 Oct. 1808; lieut. col. 31 foot 8 Oct. 1844 to 15 April 1846; lieut. col. 53 foot 15 April 1846 to 9 May 1851 when he sold out; C.B. 3 April 1846. *d.* 21 July 1851.

BYRNE, Miles. *b.* Monaseed, co. Wexford 20 March 1780; joined society of United Irishmen 1797; joined insurgents under Rev. John Murphy at Corrigua, co. Wexford 3 June 1798; clerk in timber yard in Dublin 1798–1803; lieutenant of infantry in Napoleon's Irish legion Nov. 1803, commanded a bataillon d'elite of Irish troops 1810, chevalier of Legion of honour 18 June 1813, received cross of that order 1832; chef de bataillon in 56 regiment of the line 1830–5; served in Greece 1828–30; lived in Paris 1835 to death. *d.* Rue Montaigne, Paris 24 Jany. 1862. Monument in Montmartre cemetery. *Memoirs of Miles Byrne 3 vols.* 1863, *portrait*.

BYRNE, Oscar *(son of James Byrne, dancer who d. 5 Burton crescent, London 4 Dec. 1844 aged 85)*. Made his first appearance as a dancer in a ballet at Drury Lane theatre 1803; spent some years in Ireland and abroad; ballet master at Princess's theatre 1850–9, at Drury Lane 1862, at Her Majesty's Nov. 1866; had an inexhaustible invention in designing new dances; taught most of the English dancers who gained distinction during his time. *d.* 22 Islip st. Kentish Town, London 4 Sep. 1867 aged 72.

Note.—His father James Byrne introduced in Powell's pantomime Harlequin Amulet or the Magic of Mona at Drury Lane theatre Christmas 1799 an entirely new dress for the harlequin consisting of a white silk shape fitting without a wrinkle into which 308 variegated silk patches were woven, the whole being profusely covered with 48,000 spangles. He completely altered the manner of playing harlequin by making him a graceful and agile dancer instead of merely posturing on the stage in 5 positions. Harlequins before that time wore loose dresses.

BYRON, ANNE ISABELLA, Baroness Wentworth *(only child of Sir Ralph Milbanke, 6 Baronet who d. 19 March 1825 aged 78).* b. Ellemore hall, Durham 17 May 1792 being first child after a marriage of 15 years. *(m.* 2 Jany. 1815 George Gordon Byron, 6 Baron Byron he was *b.* 22 Jany. 1788 and *d.* 19 April 1824, they separated by mutual consent Feb. 1816). Founded an industrial school for boys at Ealing on system of Fellenberg 1834, another at Leicester, a reformatory for girls and some village schools; became baroness Wentworth at decease of her cousin Lord Scarsdale 12 Nov. 1856 when abeyance of the barony ceased. *d.* 11 St. George's terrace, Regent's park, London 16 May 1860. *Macpherson's Memoirs of the life of Anna Jameson 1878 pp. 94, 163, 187, 188, 209 and 280; H. Martineau's Biographical sketches, 4 ed. 1876 316–25; Lady Byron vindicated by H. B. Stowe 1870; Quarterly Review Oct. 1869, Jany. 1870 and July 1883.*

BYRON, GEORGE ANSON BYRON, 7 Baron *(only son of George Anson Byron 1758–93, captain R.N.).* b. Bath 8 March 1789; entered navy as a volunteer Dec. 1800; captain 7 June 1814; admiral on h.p. 20 May 1862; succeeded his cousin the poet 19 April 1824. *d.* 44 Eaton place, London 2 March 1868.

BYRON, GEORGE ANSON BYRON, 8 Baron. *b.* Cheltenham 30 June 1818; succeeded 2 March 1868. *d.* 28 Nov. 1870.

BYRON, HENRY JAMES *(eld. son of Henry Byron 1804–84, British consul at Port au Prince, Hayti).* b. Manchester 8 Jany 1835; ed. at St. Peter's College Eaton sq. London; admitted student at M.T. 14 Jany 1858; edited *Fun* from first number 21 Sep. 1861; edited *Comic News* 13 July 1863 to May 1864; edited *Mirth* Nov. 1877 to Oct. 1878 12 numbers only; manager with Marie Wilton of Prince of Wales's theatre London 15 April 1865 to 1867; manager of Alexandra theatre Liverpool 1867, of the T.R. and Amphitheatre Liverpool; manager of Criterion theatre London when it opened 21 May 1874; made his début in London at Globe theatre 23 Oct. 1869 as Sir Simon Simple in his own comedy *Not such a fool as he looks;* author of about 120 burlesques, farces and comedies produced at West-end theatres, *Cyril's success* was played at Globe theatre 28 Nov. 1868 to 27 March 1869 being longest run of any original 5 act play in modern times, and *Our Boys* a 3 act comedy was played at Vaudeville theatre from 16 Jany. 1875 to 18 April 1879 an unbroken run of 1362 times; author of *Paid in full* 3

BYRON, H. J. *(Con.)*

vols. 1865. *d.* Rockelemont, Queen's road, Clapham, London 12 April 1884. *Illustrated Review vi.* 441–3 (1874), *portrait; Pascoe's Dramatic list* (1879) 61–68; *W. Archer's English dramatists of to-day* (1882) 119–47; *London Society xxvi,* 121–9 (1874); *Biograph* (1880) 360–8; *Theatre i,* 212 (1878), *portrait, v,* 345–50 (1882), *iii,* 268–72 (1884).

C

CABBELL, BENJAMIN BOND *(4 son of George Cabbell of 17 Wigmore st. London, apothecary).* b. Vere st. Oxford st. London 1781; ed. at Westminster; matric. from Oriel coll. Ox. 19 June 1800; migrated to Exeter college 25 Feb. 1801; barrister M.T. 9 Feb. 1816, bencher 1850; F.R.S. 19 Jany 1837; contested Marylebone July 1841; M.P. for St. Albans 1846–7 and for Boston 1847–57; sheriff of Norfolk 1854; provincial grand master of freemasons of Norfolk; a well-known patron of art. *d.* 39 Chapel st. Marylebone road, London 9 Dec. 1874. *John Pye's Patronage of British art* (1845) 358, 365, *portrait.*

CABRERA, RAMON, Condé de Morella *(son of José Cabrera of Tortosa, Catalonia, mariner who d. 1812).* b. Tortosa 27 Dec. 1806; head of a body of guerillas in service of Don Carlos on breaking out of civil war in Spain 1833; commandant general of Lower Arragon Nov. 1835; mariscal de campo 15 Aug. 1836; received grand cross of S. Fernando June 1837; captured fortress of Morella Jany. 1838; created Condé De Morella by Don Carlos 1838; routed by Espartero July 1840 when he took refuge in France; lived at Lyons 1841–5; made two attempts to effect risings in Spain 1846 and 1848; created Marquis del Ter 1848; defeated at Pasteral 27 Jany. 1849 when he fled to France and thence to England; lived in London Aug. 1849, in Naples 1850–1. *(m.* 29 May 1850 Marianne Catherine only child of Robert Vaughan Richards Q.C.). *d.* Wentworth, Virginia Water, Surrey 24 May 1877. *A life in 4 vols. by Don Buenaventura de Cordoba; F. Duncan's English in Spain* (1877) 109–23; *Blackwood's Mag. lx,* 293–308 (1846); *Pall Mall Gazette 2 June 1877; Echo 29 May 1877.*

CACHEMAILLE, REV. JAMES LOUIS VICTOR. Ordained deacon 1834 and priest 1835 by bishop of Winchester; incumbent of Island of Sark 1834 to death; author of *Essai sur*

CACHEMAILLE, REV. J. L. V. *(Con.)*
la resurrection 1850 ; *Le palais de Crystal* 1852 ; *Quelques signes des dernier temps* 1853 and many other pamphlets. *d.* Sark 30 Jany. 1877 aged 71.

CADBURY, RICHARD TAPPER. *b.* Exeter 1768 or 1769 ; mercer and draper in Bull st. Birmingham 1794 to about 1828 ; overseer of Birmingham 1800, one of board of guardians 1801, a comr. of Birmingham streets acts 1822, chairman of that board 1836–51 when it was abolished by 14 and 15 Vict. cap. xciii, 24 July 1851 ; member of Society of Friends who generally spoke of him as "King Richard." *d.* 57 Calthorpe road, Birmingham 13 March 1860. *Edgbastonia i, 2–3 (1881), portrait.*

CADDELL, CECILIA MARY (2 dau. of *Richard O'Ferrall Caddell of Harbourstown, co. Meath* 1780–1856). Author of *A history of the missions in Japan and Paraguay* 1856 ; *Blind Agnese or the little spouse of the Blessed Sacrament* 1855, 5 ed. 1873 ; *Home and the homeless, a novel* 3 vols. 1858 ; *Nellie Netterville, a tale of the times of Cromwell* 1867 ; *Wild times, a tale of the days of Queen Elizabeth* 1872 and of many articles in *The Irish Monthly* 1874–7. *d.* Kingstown near Dublin 11 Sep. 1877 in 64 year. *The Irish monthly v, 772–4 (1877).*

CADELL, FRANCIS (2 *son of Hew Francis Cadell of Cockenzie near Preston Pans, Haddingtonshire* 1790–1873). *b.* Cockenzie Feb. 1822 ; ed. at Edinburgh and in Germany ; midshipman in navy of H.E.I. Co. 1835 ; served in first Chinese war 1840–1 ; proved that the river Murray in Australia was navigable by descending that river in a boat from Swan Hill station to Lake Victoria 1851 ; promoted the Murray Steam navigation company 1853, commander Company's steamers 1853–60 ; explored South Australia, discovered mouth of river Roper and fine pastoral country in latitude 14° South, Nov. 1867 ; murdered by his crew while on a voyage from Amboyna to the Kei islands June 1879. *A. Forster's South Australia* (1866) 68–74 ; *Once a week viii, 667–70 (1863) ; I.L.N. xxvi, 173 (1855), xxvii, 176 (1855) ; The Times 7 Nov. 1879 p. 5.*

CADELL, JESSIE. *b.* Scotland 23 Aug. 1844 ; went to India where she resided chiefly at Peshawur ; author of *Ida Craven* 2 vols. 1876 and of an article in *Fraser's Mag.* for May 1879, entitled *The true Omar Khayyam. d.* Florence 17 June 1884. *Athenæum 28 June 1884.*

CADELL, WILLIAM ARCHIBALD *(eld. son of Wm. Cadell of Carron park near Falkirk). b.* Carron park 27 June 1775 ; ed. at Univ. of Edin. ; member of faculty of advocates 1798 ; F.R.S. 28 June 1810 ; F.R.S. Edin. ; F.G.S. ; detained prisoner in France several years ; author of *On the lines that divide each semidiurnal arc into six equal parts* 1816 ; *A journey in Carniola, Italy and France in the years* 1817, 1818 2 *vols.* 1820. *d.* Edinburgh 19 Feb. 1855.

CADOGAN, GEORGE CADOGAN, 3 Earl (2 *son of 1 Earl Cadogan* 1728–1807). *b.* St. James's sq. London 5 May 1783 ; entered navy 15 Dec. 1795 ; captain 23 March 1807 ; commanded naval forces at destruction of Zara Dec. 1813 ; placed on h.p. 31 Dec. 1813 ; Austrian order of Maria Theresa conferred on him 22 July 1814 ; C.B. 4 June 1815 ; created Baron Oakley of Caversham 10 Sep. 1831 ; succeeded as 3 Earl 23 Dec. 1832 ; admiral 9 July 1857. *d.* 138 Piccadilly, London 15 Sep. 1864.

CADOGAN, HENRY CHARLES CADOGAN, 4 Earl *(eld son of the preceding). b.* South Audley st. London 15 Feb. 1812 ; ed. at Oriel coll. Ox., B.A. 1832 ; M.P. for Reading 1841–7, for Dover 1852–7 ; applied for the Chiltern hundreds 1 Aug. 1842 but was refused by Henry Goulburn, Chancellor of the Exchequer on account of disclosures relating to borough of Reading ; hon. colonel 3 Middlesex militia 6 Dec. 1841 to death ; succeeded as 4 Earl 15 Sep. 1864 ; captain of yeomen of guard 10 July 1866 to 22 Dec. 1868 ; P.C. 10 July 1866. *d.* Woodrising hall, Norfolk 8 June 1873.

CADOGAN, SIR GEORGE *(brother of the preceding). b.* 2 Dec. 1814 ; ed. at Eton ; ensign 1 foot guards 22 Feb. 1833, captain 6 Aug. 1847 to 17 July 1857 when placed on h.p. ; colonel 106 foot 9 Aug. 1870 to 17 May 1874 ; colonel 71 foot 17 May 1874 to death ; general 1 Oct. 1877 ; C.B. 2 Jany. 1857 ; K.C.B. 29 May 1875. *d.* 13 Park place, St. James's, London 27 Jany. 1880.

CAFFIN, SIR JAMES CRAWFORD (3 *son of Wm. Caffin of royal laboratory, Woolwich). b.* Woolwich common 1 March 1812 ; entered navy 12 Aug. 1824 ; captain 11 Oct, 1847 ; director general of naval artillery 29 Aug. 1855 to to Dec. 1868 when he retired on pension ; director of stores and clothing at War office 2 Feb. 1857 to Dec. 1868 ; a naval aide de camp to the Queen 11 April 1863 ; admiral on half pay 1 Aug. 1877 ; C.B. 5 July 1855 ; K.C.B. 7 Dec. 1868 ; the centre of a religious

CAFFIN, SIR J. C. *(Con.)*

society at Blackheath, Kent of very pronounced views. *d.* Woodlawn, Vanbrugh park, Blackheath 24 May 1883.

CAHILL, REV. DANIEL WILLIAM (3 *son of Daniel Cahill, civil engineer of Ashfield, parish of Arless, Queen's county).* *b.* Ashfield 28 Nov. 1796; ed. at Carlow and Maynooth; professor of natural philosophy in Carlow collecge 1826; kept a school at Seapoint, Williamstown 1835-41, at Prospect, Black Rock near Dublin 1841-6; edited *Dublin Telegraph;* arrived in New York 24 Dec. 1859; lectured and preached in United States and Canada. *d.* the Carney hospital, Boston 28 Oct. 1864. *bur.* Boston, body removed to Glasnevin cemetery Dublin 9 March 1885. *Comerford's Collections* (1883) 198-200; *The Lamp ii,* 361-392 (1851), *portrait.*

CAHILL, PATRICK. Ensign 56 foot 10 Aug. 1854; carried regimental colour at battle of the Alma; captain 2 Dec. 1859 to 27 April 1870 when he retired on full pay; military knight of Windsor 1874 to death. *d.* Lower ward, Windsor castle 25 March 1881.

CAIRD, ALEXANDER M'NEIL. *b.* Scotland 1814; admitted a procurator 1835; procurator fiscal of Wigtonshire about 1838; provost of Stranraer 1852-8; author of *The cry of the children,* 2 ed. 1849; *The poor law manual for Scotland,* 6 ed. 1851; *Mary Stuart, her guilt or innocence* 1866; *The land tenancy laws* 1871; *Special evils of the Scottish poor law* 1877. *d.* Genoch near Stranraer 14 Feb. 1880.

CAIRNES, JOHN ELLIOT (6 *child of Wm. Cairnes of Drogheda, brewer).* *b.* Castle Bellingham, co. Louth 26 Dec. 1823; ed. at Kingstown, Chester and Trin. coll. Dub., B.A. 1848, M.A. 1854, LL.D. 1874; called to Irish bar Nov. 1857; Whately professor of political economy in Trin. coll. Dub. 1856-61; professor of political economy and jurisprudence in Queen's college Galway 1861 to July 1870; professor of political economy in Univ. coll. London 1866-72, emeritus professor 1872 to death; author of *The character and logical method of political economy* 1857, 2 ed. 1875; *The slave power, its character, career and probable designs* 1862, 2 ed. 1863; *Political essays* 1873; *Some leading principles of political economy newly explained* 1874. *d.* Rasay, Kidbrook park road, Blackheath 8 July 1875. *Fortnightly Review xxiv,* 149-54 (1875); *Athenæum ii,* 83-5 (1875); *I.L.N. lxvii,* 70 (1875), *portrait; Graphic xi,* 99, 102, 104 (1875), *portrait; Times* 9 *July* 1875 *p.* 5, *col.* 4.

CAIRNS, HUGH MC. CALMONT CAIRNS, 1 Earl (2 *son of Wm. Cairns of Cultra, co. Down, captain* 47 *foot).* *b.* Belfast 27 Dec. 1819; ed. at Belfast academy and Trin. coll. Dublin, B.A. 1838, LL.B. and LL.D. 1862; L.L.D. Cam. 1862; D.C.L. Ox. 1863; barrister M.T. 26 Jany. 1844; M P. for Belfast July 1852 to Oct. 1866; introduced two bills 1859, one to simplify titles to real estate and another to establish a land registry; Q.C. 7 April 1856, bencher of L.I. 15 April 1856; solicitor general 26 Feb. 1858 to 18 June 1859; knighted at St. James's palace 17 March 1858; attorney general 10 July to 29 Oct. 1866; lord justice of appeal 29 Oct. 1866 to Feb. 1868; P.C. 10 Nov. 1866; created Baron Cairns of Garmoyle Antrim 26 Feb. 1867, Viscount Garmoyle and Earl Cairns in peerage of the U.K. 27 Sep. 1878; chancellor of Univ. of Dublin 20 Dec. 1867; lord chancellor 29 Feb. to 9 Dec. 1868 and 21 Feb. 1874 to 28 April 1880. *d.* Lindisfarne, Bournemouth 2 April 1885. *Law quarterly review i,* 365-8 (1885); *C. Brown's Life of Lord Beaconsfield ii,* 114 (1882), *portrait; The bench and the bar, part* 3; *Drawing room portrait gallery* 2 *series* 1859, *portrait; I.L.N. xlix,* 413 (1866), *portrait, lxiv,* 364 (1874), *portrait, lxxxvi,* 431 (1885), *portrait; Pump Court ii,* 8-9 (1884), *portrait; Belgravia xxix,* 54-9 (1867); *St. James's Mag. xxiv,* 171-6 (1869); *Law mag. and review, Feb.* 1886 *pp.* 133-53.

CAITHNESS, ALEXANDER SINCLAIR, 13 Earl of. *b.* Barrogill castle, Thurso 24 July 1790; suceeeded 16 July 1823; lord lieut. of Caithnessshire 1823 to death. *d.* Rutland square, Edinburgh 24 Dec. 1855.

CAITHNESS, JAMES SINCLAIR, 14 Earl of *(eld. child of the preceding).* *b.* 16 Dec. 1821; succeeded 24 Dec. 1855; a lord in waiting to the Queen April 1856 to Feb. 1858 and June 1859 to July 1866; lord lieut. of Caithness March 1856 to death; a representative peer of Scotland June 1858 to Dec. 1868; created Baron Barrogill of Barrogill castle, Thurso 1 May 1866; F.R.S. 20 Nov. 1862; took out patents for working stone and for machine belts 1856 and for permanent way of railways 1859; invented a steam car to travel on ordinary roads, an improved tape loom and the Caithness gravitation compass. *d.* Fifth avenue hotel, New York 28 March 1881. *bur.* chapel royal Holyrood, Edin. 19 April.

CALCRAFT, JOHN HALES *(elder son of John Calcraft of Rempstone near Wareham, Dorset* 1766-1831, *M.P. for Dorset).* *b.* Rempstone 13 Sep. 1796; M.P. for Wareham 1820-26, 1832-41 and 1857-59; sheriff of Dorset 1867. *d.* Rempstone 13 March 1880.

CALCRAFT, JOHN HALES MONTAGU *(eld. son of the preceding).* *b.* 4 May 1831; entered navy March 1844; served in Crimean war; retired commander 25 Feb. 1862; M.P. for Wareham 13 July 1865 to death. *d.* Rempstone 1 Dec. 1868.

CALCRAFT, JOHN WILLIAM, stage name of John William Cole. Second lieut. 21 foot 16 July 1807, first lieut. 1809–17 when placed on h.p.; made his début at T.R. Dublin 23 Oct. 1824 as Joseph Surface in *The school for scandal;* lessee of T.R. Dublin 21 Aug. 1830 to 1851; secretary to Charles Kean; translated *Memoirs of H. M. de Latude* 1834; author of *The bride of Lammermoor, a drama in 5 acts* 1823; *A defence of the stage* 1839; *The life of Charles Kean* 2 vols. 1859, and of articles on the drama in *Dublin Univ. Mag.* *d.* Winchfield, Hants. 12 Feb. 1870 aged 77. *History of T.R. Dublin* (1870) 59, 61, 65, 83–130.

CALCRAFT, WILLIAM. *b.* Baddow near Chelmsford 1800; a shoemaker; watchman in Reid's brewery in Liquorpond st. Gray's Inn road, London; butler to a gentleman at Greenwich; executioner to City of London 4 April 1829 to 25 May 1874 when he retired on pension of 25/- a week; hanged Greenacre 1837, Courvoisier 1840, Good 1842, Tawell 1845, Mr. and Mrs. Manning and Rush 1849, Dove 1856, Catherine Wilson 1862, the 5 Flowery Land pirates and Muller 1864; lived in Poole st. New North road, Hoxton 1854 to death, where he *d.* 13 Dec. 1879. *Life of Wm. Calcraft the celebrated hangman* 1880, *portrait; Daily Telegraph* 17 *Dec.* 1879 *p.* 5, *col.* 1.

CALCUTT, FRANCIS MACNAMARA. *b.* Limerick 1819; M.P. for co. Clare 16 April 1857 to 23 April 1859 and 13 April 1860 to death. *d.* 16 July 1863.

CALDCLEUGH, ALEXANDER. Author of *Travels in South America* 2 vols. 1825; F.R.S. 10 March 1831. *d.* Valparaiso, Chili 11 Jany. 1858.

CALDECOTT, RANDOLPH *(son of Mr. Caldecott of Chester, accountant).* *b.* Chester 22 March 1846; clerk in a bank at Whitchurch, Shropshire, afterwards at Manchester; began drawing for *London Society* and other periodicals 1872; a popular book illustrator 1876 to death; published *John Gilpin* 1878; *The house that Jack built* 1878 and 14 other childrens books; contributed illustrations to the *Graphic;* member of Institute of Painters in water colours Feb. 1882, exhibited there, at Grosvenor gallery and the R.A. *d.* St. Augustine, Florida 12 Feb. 1886. *R. Caldecott a*

CALDECOTT, R. *(Con.)*
personal memoir of his early art career by H. Blackburn 1886, *portrait; G.M. xxiv,* 629–35 (1880); *International Mag.* Oct. 1885 *pp.* 100-3; *The Queen almanack* 1887, *portrait.*

CALDECOURT, WILLIAM HENRY. *b.* Blisworth, Northamptonshire 28 Sep. 1802; played his first cricket match at Lord's 16–18 July 1821; a hard hitter and a splendid field; a practice bowler to Marylebone club 1818 to death; brought out more gentlemen cricketers from Harrow and Cambridge than any other professional; umpire in the best matches many seasons; kept a cricket bat shop many years at 14 Townsend road, St. John's Wood, London where he *d.* 21 June 1857.

CALDER, SIR HENRY RODDAM, 5 Baronet. *b.* 15 March 1790; succeeded 3 Feb. 1792. *d.* Muirtoun, Elginshire 13 Aug. 1868.

CALDER, JAMES TAIT. *b.* Castletown, Caithness about 1794; ed. at Univ. of Edin.; parish teacher at Canisbay, Wicklow; author of *Sketches from John O'Groat's in prose and verse* 1842; *The soldier's bride* 1846 a volume of poems; *Sketch of the civil and traditional history of Caithness* 1861. *d.* Elwickbank, Shapinshay, one of the Orkney islands 15 Jany. 1864.

CALDERBANK, VERY REV. LEONARD *(son of Richard Calderbank of Standish near Wigan).* *b.* Standish 3 June 1809; ed. at Ampleforth college, Yorkshire and Prior park near Bath; ordained priest at Rome 11 Nov. 1832; vice pres. of Prior park and professor of theology at St. Paul's college 1849–50; missionary rector of St. Peter's, Gloucester 9 Oct. 1850 to death; canon of Clifton 28 June 1852 to death. *d.* Gloucester 25 June 1864. *Tablet* 9 *July* 1864 *p.* 439, *col.* 1.

CALDICOTT, REV. THOMAS FORD. *b.* Buckby, Northamptonshire 1803; emigrated to Canada 1824; Baptist pastor at Hamilton, Madison, co. New York 1831, at Lockport, N.Y. Boston and Brooklyn successively; pastor of Baptist church, Bond st. Toronto 1860 to death; wrote much for periodical religious press; author of *H. Corcoran, an authentic narrative of her conversion from Romanism* 1853. *d.* Toronto 9 July 1869.

CALDWELL, GEORGE *(son of Ralph Caldwell of Hilborough hall, Norfolk, who d. 5 Jany. 1831 aged 53).* Author of many articles on sporting in *The Field* and *Bell's Life in London,* under pseudonym of Childers and in New York *Spirit of the times,* under that of Censor. *d.* Ramsgate 5 March 1863 aged 56. *Sporting Review xlix,* 463-4 (1863).

CALDWELL, HENRY *(youngest son of Charles Andrew Caldwell of New Grange, co. Meath 1785–1859). b.* 24 Feb. 1815 ; entered navy 22 April 1828 ; captain 12 Aug. 1853 ; captain of Duke of Wellington 131 guns 19 Feb. 1855 to 1857 ; captain of the Asia 16 Feb. 1864 to 9 April 1866 ; aide de camp to the Queen 2 April 1866 to death ; commodore Cape of Good Hope station 9 April 1866 to 3 Sep. 1867 ; C.B. 4 Feb. 1856. *d.* Leamington 7 April 1868.

CALDWELL, SIR HENRY JOHN, 6 Baronet. *b.* 22 Oct. 1801 ; succeeded his father as 6 baronet and as Count of Milan in the Holy Roman empire 22 Oct. 1842. *d.* Marlborough buildings, Bath 13 Oct. 1858.

CALDWELL, HUGH. Entered Bengal army 10 Sep. 1806 ; major 49 Bengal N.I. 27 May 1830 to 9 Aug. 1836 when he retired ; lived at Rome 1836 to death. *d.* Palazzo Titoni, Via Rassella, Rome 21 Feb. 1882 aged 96. *Times* 27 Feb. 1882 *p.* 5, *col.* 5 *and p.* 7, *col.* 3.

CALDWELL, JAMES H. *b.* Manchester 1793 ; made his début in America at Charleston as Belcour in *The West Indian* Nov. 1816 ; opened St. Charles theatre New Orleans 30 Nov. 1835 ; last appeared 14 Jany. 1843 as Vapid in *The Dramatist ;* introduced gas in New Orleans 1834 and in many other southern cities. *d.* New York 11 Sep. 1863.

CALDWELL, SIR JAMES LILLYMAN *(son of Arthur Caldwell, major Bengal engineers). b.* Greenwich 1770 ; 2 lieut. Madras engineers 27 July 1789 ; colonel commandant 1 May 1824 to death ; general 20 June 1854 ; served at first siege of Seringapatam 6 Feb. 1792 and at second siege and capture 4 May 1799 ; C.B. 4 June 1815, K.C.B. 10 March 1837, G.C.B. 25 Aug. 1848. *d.* Beachlands, Ryde, Isle of Wight 28 June 1863. *H. M. Vibart's Madras Engineers ii, pp. iii–vi,* (1883), *portrait.*

CALDWELL, JAMES STAMFORD *(only son of James Caldwell, recorder of Newcastle under Lyme who d.* 16 *Jany.* 1838 *aged* 78). Educ. at St. John's coll. Cam., B.A. 1808, M.A. 1811 ; barrister L.I. 11 Feb. 1813 ; author of *A treatise on the law of arbitration* 1817, 2 *ed.* 1825 ; *A digest of the laws relating to the poor* 1821 ; *Results of reading* 1843. *d.* Linley wood near Newcastle under Lyme 18 Nov. 1858 aged 72.

CALDWELL, JOHN. Opened a room for dancing at 83 Dean st. Soho, London 1840 ; removed to 19, 20 and 21 Dean st. 1845, which he rebuilt 1850 ; lessee of Royalty

CALDWELL, J. *(Con.)*
theatre ; lessee of Surrey gardens. *d.* Starcross, Devon 16 May 1880. *bur.* Kensal Green cemetery, London 24 May.

CALEDON, JAMES DUPRÉ ALEXANDER, 3 Earl of *(only child of Dupré Alexander, 2 Earl of Caledon 1777–1839). b.* London 27 July 1812 ; ensign Coldstream guards 31 May 1833, lieut. 1839–46, when he retired from army ; M.P. for co. Tyrone 7 Aug. 1837 to 8 April 1839 when he succeeded ; an Irish representative peer 10 May 1841 to death ; colonel of Tyrone militia. *d.* 5 Carlton house terrace, London 30 June 1855. *Waagen's Galleries of art* (1857) 147–52 ; *G.M. xliv,* 193–4 (1855).

CALEY, HENRY FRANCIS. Entered Bengal army 1820 ; col. 64 Bengal N.I. 7 Nov. 1854 to death ; M.G. 18 March 1856. *d.* Rawul Pindee, Punjab, India 21 Dec. 1866.

CALKIN, JAMES. *b.* London 1786 ; one of earliest members and directors of Philharmonic Society ; organist of Regent square chapel, Gray's Inn road, London 1824 ; a successful teacher of music ; his compositions include an overture and symphony for orchestra, string quartets and much pianoforte music. *d.* 12 Oakley sq. Camden Town, London 1862.

CALL, SIR WILLIAM BERKELEY, 3 Baronet. *b.* Whiteford house near Callington, Cornwall 10 May 1815 ; partner in banking house of Call, Marten and Co. Old Bond st. London ; succeeded 3 Dec. 1851 ; special deputy warden of the Stannaries 1852 ; sheriff of Cornwall 1856. *d.* 25 Old Bond st. London 22 Dec. 1864.

CALL, SIR WILLIAM PRATT, 2 Baronet. *b.* 28 Sep. 1781 ; succeeded 1 March 1801 ; sheriff of Cornwall 1807 ; partner in banking house of Call, Marten and Co. *d.* Whiteford house near Callington 3 Dec. 1851.

CALLAGHAN, JEREMIAH THOMAS FITZGERALD. *b.* about 1830 ; ed. at Trin. coll. Dublin ; called to Irish bar, Jany. 1854 ; acting consul general at Labuan 27 May 1861 ; governor of Labuan 10 April 1862 to Nov. 1866 ; administrator of government of Gambia 10 May 1871 ; governor of Falkland islands 18 May 1876 ; governor of the Bahamas 11 Sep. 1880 to death ; C.M.G. 30 May 1877. *d.* New York 9 July 1881.

CALLAGHAN, THOMAS. *b.* Dublin 18 Sep. 1816 ; ed. at Trin. coll. Dub., B.A. 1836 ; called to the Irish bar 1839 ; emigrated to New South Wales 1840 ; crown prosecutor

CALLAGHAN, T. (Con.)

1841; chairman of quarter sessions, Dec. 1844; a district court judge 1859 to death, held his first court at Yass 19 July 1859; published *Acts and ordinances of New South Wales with notes and index* 3 vols. 1844–52. *d.* Braidwood, N.S.W. 28 Nov. 1863. *Heads of the people i,* 161 (1847), *portrait.*

CALLCOTT, MARIA. Author of *Home among strangers a tale* 2 vols. 1848; *The singers alphabet* 1849; *The power of meekness* 1853; *The two firesides a tale of 90 years ago* 1859. (*m.* Wm. Hutchins Callcott 1807–82). *d.* 1 Campden house road, Kensington 19 Aug. 1881 aged 73.

CALLCOTT, WILLIAM. *b.* Kensington near London 1800; violinist in orchestra of King's theatre (now Her Majesty's), Pall Mall; repetiteur for the ballet there; musical director of Adelphi, Olympic and Astley's Amphitheatre where he composed for Andrew Ducrow music for his representation of "The Grecian Statues"; his musical compositions for pantomimes and melodramas were the best since those of Wm. Henry Ware. *d.* Gravesend 6 Nov. 1878.

CALLCOTT, WILLIAM HUTCHINS (*son of John Wall Callcott, musical composer* 1766–1821). *b.* Kensington, London 1807; member of Royal society of musicians 4 July 1830; organist of Ely place chapel; his arrangements and transcriptions for the piano amount to many hundred pieces; author of *The child's own singing book* 1843; *A few facts on the life of Handel* 1859. *d.* 1 Campden house road, Kensington 5 Aug. 1882.

CALLENDER, GEORGE WILLIAM. *b.* Clifton 24 June 1830; student of St. Bartholomew's hospital 1849, registrar 1854, assistant surgeon 1861, surgeon 1871 to death, lecturer on anatomy 1865, lecturer on surgery 1873; surgical editor of *St. Bartholomew's hospital reports* 1865–74; M.R.C.S. 1852, F.R.C.S. 1855, F.R.S. 8 June 1871; sec. of Clinical Soc. 1867-70, pres. 1877-9; author of *Anatomy of the parts concerned in femoral rupture* 1863 and of many papers in *Transactions of Medical Chirurgical, Clinical and Pathological Societies.* *d.* on board the Gallia on his way home from Australia 20 Oct. 1879. *bur.* Norwood cemetery 29 Oct. *St. Bartholomew's hospital reports xv, pp. xli-xlvii,* (1879); *Proc. of Med. and Chir. Soc. viii,* 480–2 (1880).

CALLENDER, WILLIAM ROMAINE (*eld. son of Wm. Romaine Callender of Manchester who d.* 1872). *b.* Manchester 2 June 1825; cotton

CALLENDER, W. R. (Con.)

spinner and merchant at Bolton and Manchester; member of Manchester school board 24 Nov. 1870, vice chairman Dec. 1870 to death; M.P. for Manchester 7 Feb. 1874 to death; F.S.A. 2 June 1859; author of *Education statistics of Manchester* 1852; *The commercial crisis of 1857 its causes and results* 1858. *d.* Eversfield place, St. Leonard's on Sea 22 Jany. 1876. *Graphic xiii,* 182, 188 (1876), *portrait.*

CALLOW, JOHN. *b.* London 19 July 1822; studied art in Paris 1835–44; a landscape painter in water colours; professor of drawing in royal military academy at Addiscombe, July 1855 to 1861; sub.-professor of drawing at Woolwich 1861; a teacher in London; several of his studies have since his death been printed in colours as a series of progressive lessons in art of water-colour painting; exhibited 7 pictures at R.A., 9 at B.I. and 2 at Suffolk st. gallery 1844–67. *d.* Lewisham near London 25 April 1878.

CALTHORPE, GEORGE GOUGH-CALTHORPE, 3 Baron. *b.* 22 June 1787; succeeded his brother as 3 Baron 5 June 1807. *d.* Lyons Sep. 1851.

CALTHORPE, FREDERICK GOUGH, 4 Baron (*3 son of 1 Baron Calthorpe* 1749–98). *b.* London 14 June 1790; ed. at Ch. Ch. Ox.; M.P. for Hindon, Wilts. 1818–26, for Bramber, Sussex 1826–31; a metropolitan comr. in lunacy; assumed name of Gough in lieu of Calthorpe 14 May 1845; sheriff of Staffs. 1848; succeeded Sep. 1851; gave to town of Birmingham, Calthorpe park opened 15 April 1857. *d.* Elvetham park, Winchfield, Hants. 2 May 1868.

CALVERLEY, CHARLES STUART (*younger son of Rev. Henry Blayds* 1794-1874, *V. of South Stoke near Bath* 1839-74). *b.* Martley, Worcs. 23 Dec. 1831; ed. at Harrow and Balliol coll. Ox.; scholar 25 Nov. 1850; chancellor's prizeman 1851; migrated to Christ's coll. Cam. Oct. 1852, Craven scholar 1854; B.A. 1856, M.A. 1859; fellow of his coll. 1858–63; prepared examination paper on Dickens's *Pickwick Papers* at Cam. Dec. 1857; barrister I.T. 1 May 1865; resumed 1852 old family name of Calverley which his grandfather had changed to Blayds 1807; author of *Verses and translations* 1862; *Translations into English and Latin* 1866; *Theocritus translated into English verse* 1869; *Fly leaves* 1872. *d.* 17 Devonshire terrace, Hyde park, London 17 Feb. 1884. *C. S. Calverley's Literary remains*

CALVERLEY, C. S. *(Con.)*

1885, *portrait*; *Fortnightly Review xxxv*, 736–53 (1884); *J. Payn's Some literary recollections* (1884) 180–3; *Temple Bar*, Jany. 1887.

CALVERT, CAROLINE LOUISA WARING *(youngest dau. of James Atkinson, principal clerk in Colonial secretary's office, Sydney N.S.W.)* b. Oldbury, Argyle county N.S.W. 25 Feb. 1834; author of *Gertrude the emigrant, a tale of colonial life by an Australian lady* 1857; *Cowanda the veteran's grant* 1859; wrote many articles in *Sydney Morning Herald, Sydney Mail and Town and country journal;* collected many specimens of plants, the genus Atkinsonia was named after her also the species Epacris Calvertiana. *(m.* 1870 James Snowden Calvert 1825–74). d. Sutton Forest N.S.W 28 April 1872. *G. B. Barton's Literature of N.S.W.* (1866) 111–2.

CALVERT, CHARLES *(eld. son of Charles Calvert of Glossop hall, Derbyshire, agent for Duke of Norfolk* 1754–97). b. Glossop hall 23 Sep. 1785; cotton merchant in Manchester, landscape painter there; a founder of Manchester Royal Institution 1823, Heywood gold and silver medallist. d. Bowness, Westmoreland 26 Feb. 1852. *Art Journal* (1852) 150.

CALVERT, CHARLES ALEXANDER. b. London 28 Feb. 1828; ed. at King's college school; articled to a solicitor; acted in the provinces 1852–5; first appeared in London at Surrey theatre, Sep. 1855 as Leonardo Gonzago in *The Wife;* stage manager and principal actor at T.R. Manchester 1859; manager of Prince's theatre, Manchester 1864 to Jany. 1875; produced a series of Shakespearian revivals which eclipsed all previous representations on provincial stage 1864–74; went to New York, Jany. 1875 when he reproduced play of *Henry the fifth* at Booth's theatre; returned to England 1876; produced *Henry viii* at T.R. Manchester 1877; head of a travelling company. d. at private asylum, Sussex house, Hammersmith 12 June 1879. *bur.* Brooklands cemetery near Sale, Cheshire 18 June. *Illust. sporting and dr. news v*, 609, 614 (1876), *portrait, xi*, 351, 353 (1879), *portrait.*

CALVERT, EDWARD *(son of Roland Calvert of Appledore, Devon who d.* 1811 or 1812). b. Appledore 20 Sep. 1799; midshipman R.N.; landscape painter in London 1825; exhibited 5 pictures at the R.A. 1825–36; produced many woodcuts and plates, privately printed by himself at Brixton and Paddington. d. Hackney 14 July 1883. *Athenæum ii*, 218, 250 (1883); *Gilchrist's Life of W. Blake* (1880) i, 343, 407.

CALVERT, EDWIN. A dwarf 36 inches in height (3 inches less than Tom Thumb), weighing only $24\frac{1}{2}$ pounds; clever violinist and dancer, and mimic of birds and animals. d. Skipton, Yorkshire July or Aug. 1859 aged 17.

CALVERT, FELIX. b. 16 Oct. 1790; ensign 52 foot 1 Oct. 1807; major 32 foot 11 May 1815; lieut. col. 72 foot 9 Aug. 1821 to 25 Sep. 1826 when placed on h.p.; colonel 90 foot 14 June 1853 to death; L.G. 20 June 1854; C.B. 19 July 1831. d. 30 Cavendish sq. London 3 March 1857.

CALVERT, FREDERIC BALTIMORE *(brother of Charles Calvert* 1785–1852). b. 10 April 1793; alternated leading parts with Edmund Kean, Macready and Vandenhoff; elocutionary lecturer at King's college, Aberdeen 1829; lectured in England and America on literary subjects; master of English language and literature in Edinburgh academy about 1846; lecturer on elocution to free church colleges of Edin. and Glasgow; author of *A defence of the acted drama in a letter to T. Best, Hull* 1822; *Principles of elocution by T. Ewing, revised and improved* 1852, *another ed.* 1870; translated *Cicero's De Oratore* 1870. d. 2 West Newington, Edin. 21 April 1877.

CALVERT, FREDERICK CRACE *(son of Colonel Calvert).* b. London 14 Nov. 1819; lived in France 1836–46; démonstrateur de chimie appliquée under M. E. Chevreul the eminent chemist in Paris 1841–6; consulting chemist at Manchester 1846; professor of chemistry at Royal Instit. Manchester 1846; lecturer on chemistry at School of medicine in Pine st. Manchester; the first person in this country to manufacture phenic or carbolic acid in a pure state, its use as a disinfectant is due entirely to him, established large works at Manchester for its production 1865; F.R.S.; delivered 5 courses of 'Cantor' lectures at Society of Arts on applied chemisty; contributed largely to English and French scientific literature. d. Clayton vale house near Manchester 24 Oct. 1873. *F. C. Calvert's Dying and calico printing*, 3 ed. (1878) ix–xiv; *Journal of Society of arts xxi*, 919 (1873).

CALVERT, GEORGE. b. Denholme Gate, Thornton, parish of Bradford 26 Dec. 1809; decorative painter at Huddersfield; portrait painter at Almondbury; author of *Universal restoration, a poem in ten epochs* 2 vols. 1861; *Thoughts for thoughtful minds* 1865; *Redemption, a poem in ten epochs*, 2 ed. 2 vols. 1875. d. Hall Bower near Castle hill, Almondbury 10 June 1878. *C. A. Hulbert's Supplementary annals of Almondbury* (1885) 51–3.

CALVERT, HENRY HUNTER. Clerk in R.N. 1834–5; cancellier to consulate at Erzeroom, Turkish Armenia 1837–55; acting consul at Alexandria 1859–60, 1864, 1868–9, 1870, 1872, 1876–7 and 1878–9; acting consul at Cairo 1860–2, at Jeddah 1864–5 and 1867. *d.* the Dardanelles 29 July 1882. *I.L.N. lxxxi,* 197 (1882), *portrait.*

CALVERT, JAMES SNOWDEN. *b.* on the Borders of Scotland 13 July 1825; went to New South Wales 1840; went with Ludwig Leichhardt in his expedition from Moreton Bay Settlement to Fort Essington on north coast of Australia which was reached 17 Dec. 1845 after a journey of 3000 miles extending over 15 months; awarded a silver medal at London International Exhibition 1862 for his collection of Australian paper making materials. *d.* at his residence near Sydney 22 or 29 July 1874.

CALVERT, JOHN. *b.* Preston; mechanical and consulting engineer; founded *Calvert's Mechanic's almanac and workshop companion* 1873, edited it 1873 to death; author of *Calvert's Pocket wages table* 1875; *Calvert's Mechanic's and builder's time book,* 2 ed. 1876. *d.* Cornbrook, Manchester 6 July 1883 aged 47.

CALVERT, MICHAEL. *b.* Knaresborough; baptised 2 Feb. 1770; a chemist at Knaresborough, churchwarden 1808 and 1809; author of *An account of the Knaresborough Spaw,* 2 ed. 1831; *History of Knaresborough* 1844. *d.* Knaresborough 3 Dec. 1862. *Boyne's Yorkshire library* 1869 *p.* 142.

CALVERT, REV. WILLIAM. *b.* 1819; Educ. at Pemb. coll. Cam.; B.A. 1842, M.A. 1853; C. of Longdon, Worcs. 1842–6; minor canon of St. Paul's cathedral 1848 to death; R. of St. Antholin's, city of London 1849–58; V. of St. John the Baptist's, Kentish Town, London 1858 to death; author of *The wife's manual, or prayers, thoughts and songs on several occasions of a matron's life* 1854, 4 ed. 1882; *Pneuma or the wandering soul, a parable in rhyme and outline* 1856. *d.* Ventnor, Isle of Wight 1 Feb. 1880.

CAMDEN, GEORGE CHARLES PRATT, 2 Marquis (*only son of 1 Marquis Camden 1759–1840*). *b.* Arlington st. Piccadilly, London 2 May 1799; ed. at Eton and Trin. coll. Cam., M.A. 1819, LL.D. 1835; M.P. for Ludgershall, Wilts. 1821–6, for Bath 1826–30, and for Dunwich 1831–2; a lord of the Admiralty 19 Sep. 1828 to 15 July 1829; summoned to House of Lords in his father's barony of Camden 8 Jany. 1835; succeeded as 2 Marquis 8 Oct. 1840; K.G.

CAMDEN, G. C. P. (*Con.*)

19 Jany. 1846; lord lieut. of Brecknockshire 31 Oct. 1865; pres. of British archæological society, and of Kent archæological society. *d.* Bayham abbey, Sussex 6 Aug. 1866.

CAMDEN, JOHN CHARLES PRATT, 3 Marquis. *b.* Belgrave sq. London 30 June 1840; ed. at Trin. coll. Cam., M.A. 1860; M.P. for Brecknock 27 Feb 1866 to 6 Aug. 1866, when he succeeded. *d.* 96 Eaton sq. London 4 May 1872.

CAMERON, ALEXANDER. Ensign 42 foot 24 Feb. 1842, lieut. col. 9 Oct. 1855 to death; C.B. 27 July 1858. *d.* Bareilly, Rohilcund, India 9 Aug. 1858 aged 43.

CAMERON, REV. CHARLES. Educ. at Queen's coll. Ox., B.A. 1831, M.A. 1834; Incumb. of St. James's Dudley 1840–4; Incumb. of Worsley, Manchester 1844–53; Incumb. of donative of Oxhey Watford, Herts. 1853–6; P.C. of Ch. Ch. Longlane, Trusley Derbyshire 1860 to death; author of *The tyranny of popery by an Eye Witness as seen in Italy* 1853 and of various parochial sermons and addresses; edited *The infallible way to contentment* 1849; *The British workman* 1855–62. *d.* in Heckington church during divine service 2 Dec. 1861 aged 54.

CAMERON, CHARLES DUNCAN (*son of Charles Cameron, captain 3 foot*). Ensign 45 foot 12 June 1846 to July 1851; commanded Kaffir Irregulars sent from Natal to Cape Colony 1851–2; served on staff of Sir Fenwick Williams during Russian war 1854–6; consul in Abyssinia 30 June 1860, imprisoned by King Theodore 2 Jany. 1864 to 17 April 1866 when he was handed over to Hormuzd Rassam but reimprisoned with Rassam 12 July 1866, released 11 April 1868; returned to England 25 July 1868, retired on a pension of £350 per annum 7 Dec. 1868; F.R.G.S. Nov. 1858. *d.* Geneva 30 May 1870. *C. R. Markham's History of Abyssinian expedition* 1869; *H. M. Hozier's Narrative of Abyssinian expedition* 1869; *Journal of Royal Geog. Soc. xli,* 153 (1871).

CAMERON, CHARLES HAY (*son of Charles Cameron, governor of Bahama Islands*). *b.* 11 Feb. 1795; barrister L.I. 16 June 1820; a disciple of Jeremy Bentham; a charity comr., prepared a report on poor laws April 1833; member of law commission at Calcutta 1834; fourth member of supreme council of India 1843 to 1848; pres. of council of education for Bengal 1843–8; author of *Two essays on the sublime and beautiful and on Duelling,*

CAMERON, C. H. (*Con.*)

privately printed 1835 ; *Address to Parliament on the duties of Great Britain to India* 1853. *d.* Ceylon 8 May 1880. *Mackenzie's History of the Camerons* 1884.

CAMERON, REV. CHARLES RICHARD (*eld. son of Charles Cameron, M.D. of Worcester*). *b.* 1781 ; ed. at Ch. Ch. Ox., B.A. 1800, M.A. 1803 ; P.C. of Donnington Wood, Salop 1806–50; P.C. of Wombridge, Salop 1808–56 ; R. of Swaby, Lincs. 1831 to death ; author of *The Antichrist of St. John, St. Paul's man of sin and the Little Horn of Daniel identified in their application to the Papacy in its present aspect* 1844 ; *The doctrine of infant baptism briefly stated* 1850 ; *The beginning of the end* 1854. *d.* Swaby rectory 10 Jany. 1865.

CAMERON, DONALD. Piper to Sir J. J. R. Mackenzie of Scatwell, Rossshire 1833 ; piper to Seaforth of Dingwall, Rossshire 1848 to death ; gained gold medal at Inverness 1849, and another at competition of 9 best pipers in Scotland 1850 ; gained annual champion medals given by Highland society of London at great northern meetings 1859 and 1867 ; composed *Braham Castle, Lady Anne Mackenzie* and other excellent airs; declined several offers to become Her Majesty's piper. *d.* near Dingwall 7 Jany. 1868.

CAMERON, SIR DUNCAN, 2 Baronet. *b.* 1770; succeeded Oct. 1828. *d.* Callart near Appin, Argyleshire 15 Jany. 1863.

CAMERON, GEORGE POULETT (*son of Robert Cameron, commander R.N. who d. 22 Jany. 1807*). *b.* 1805 ; entered Madras army 1821; joined expedition to Portugal organised by Don Pedro to recover throne for Queen Maria ii, 1832 ; sent on particular service to Persia, commanded garrison of Tabriz 1836–8; political agent at titular court of Nawab of Arcot 1842 ; K.T.S., K.L.S., C.B. 25 Aug. 1841 ; commandant of the Neilgherries hills 1856–8; present with Austrian army in Italian war 1859 ; author of *Personal adventures in Georgia, Circassia and Russia*, 2 vols. 1848 ; *The romance of military life* 1853. *d.* Cheltenham 12 Feb. 1882.

CAMERON, JAMES. *b.* near Dunkeld 6 Jany. 1800 ; went to Madagascar 1826 where he taught the natives principal mechanical arts and industries; lived at Cape Town 1835–53 and 1854–63; lay missionary of London Missionary Society in Madagascar 1863 to death. *d.* Antananarivo, Madagascar 3 Oct. 1875. *Cape Monthly Mag. xti*, 169–79 (1876); *Chronicle of London Missionary Soc, for* 1876 *pp.* 21, 229–34.

CAMERON, JOHN. Second lieut. R.E. 12 Dec. 1834, colonel 1 Jany. 1868 to death ; L.G. 1 Oct. 1877 ; F.R.S. 4 June 1868 ; C.B. 14 June 1870 ; director of ordnance survey of Great Britain and Ireland, Aug. 1875 to death ; edited *Ordnance survey. Meteorological observations* 1856. *d.* Ordnance house, Southampton 30 June 1878 aged 61.

CAMERON, JOHN ALEXANDER. *b.* Inverness ; a bank clerk ; contributed to *Bombay Gazette*, acting editor to 1878, special correspondent in Afghan war 1878 ; special correspondent of the London *Standard* in Afghan war 1879 ; crossed from Bombay to Natal on outbreak of Boer insurrection Dec. 1880 ; present at battles of Laing's Nek and Ingogo Jany. 1881 ; taken prisoner at battle of Majuba Hill Feb. 1881 ; special correspondent of *Standard* in Egypt 1882–3 his description of bombardment of Alexandria was best sent home ; accompanied British force in advance upon Tokar, witnessed battles of El Teb and Tamanieb ; shot by Arabs near Metemneh in Sir H. Stewart's desert march to Gubat on the Nile 18 Jany. 1885. *London Figaro 9 Dec.* 1882 ; *Graphic xxiii*, 437 (1881), *portrait ; I.L.N. lxxxvi*, 146, 218 (1885), *portrait ; Standard 29 Jany.* 1885 *pp.* 5–6.

CAMERON, JULIA MARGARET (3 *dau. of James Pattle of Bengal civil service*). *b.* Calcutta 11 June 1815 ; raised in Calcutta a large sum of money for relief of sufferers in Irish famine 1846 ; lived in England 1848–75 ; went to Ceylon 1875 ; began photographing 1865, took admirable portraits of many eminent persons, gained gold medals in America, Austria, Germany and England ; exhibited large collection of her portraits and studies at the German gallery in Bond st. London March 1868 ; wrote many poems some of them in *Macmillan's Mag. ;* translated *Burger's Leonora* 1847. (*m.* 1838 Charles Hay Cameron 1795–1880). *d.* Ceylon 26 Jany. 1879. *Sir H. Taylor's Autobiography ii*, 48–55, 184–8.

CAMERON, LUCY LYTTELTON (*youngest child of Rev. George Butt 1741–95, V. of Stanford-on-Teme, Worcs.*) *b.* Stanford-on-Teme 29 April 1781 ; ed. at Reading 1792–7 ; author of *The two lambs* 1827 ; *Addresses to children on the Beatitudes* 1828 ; *The Caskets*, 12 ed. 1833 ; *The Berkshire shepherd*, 6 ed. 1840 and many more childrens books. (*m.* 12 June 1806 Rev. Charles Richard Cameron 1781–1865). *d.* Swaby rectory 6 Sep. 1858. *The life of Mrs. Cameron by Rev. G. T. Cameron*, 2 ed. 1873, *portrait*.

CAMERON, PATRICK. Entered Madras army 1802; colonel 1 Madras light cavalry 12 April 1843 to 1869; general 24 Oct. 1858. d. Gordonston, Inverness 8 Dec. 1871 aged 87.

CAMIDGE, JOHN (3 son of Mathew Camidge 1758–1844, organist of York minster). b. York 1790; Mus. Bac. Cam. 1812, Mus. Doc. 1819; Mus. Doc. Lambeth 1855; assistant organist of York minster, organist 15 Oct. 1842 to death; paralysed while playing the evening service 28 Nov. 1848, never played again; adapted much classical music for use in the Anglican service; published Cathedral music consisting of a service, anthems and 50 double chants; Six glees for 3 and 4 voices. d. Gray's court, Chapter house st. York 21 Sep. 1859. Musical World 1 Oct. 1859, p. 634.

CAMMELL, CHARLES (son of George Cammell of Hull). b. Hull 8 Jany. 1810; steel and file manufacturer at Sheffield 1837, added manufacture of rails and railway material 1861, and of armour plates 1863; his business was converted into a limited liability company 1864, of which he was chairman to his death; acquired Yorkshire iron and steel works at Penistone 1865, and the Oaks colliery near Barnsley 1873; M.I.M.E. Oct. 1847. d. 7 Southwick crescent, Hyde park, London 12 Jany. 1879, personalty sworn under £250,000, 8 March 1879. Iron and steel institute journal 1879, p. 615.

CAMOYS, THOMAS STONOR, 3 Baron (eld. son of Thomas Stonor of Stonor near Henley-on-Thames 1766–1831). b. London 22 Oct. 1797; M.P. for Oxford 13 Dec. 1832 to March 1833, when unseated on petition; contested Oxfordshire 29 July 1837; sheriff of Oxfordshire 1835; summoned to House of Lords 14 Sep. 1839, when ancient barony of Camoys was called out of abeyance, having been dormant since 12 Aug. 1426; a lord in waiting on the Queen 1846–52, 1853–8, 1859–66 and 1868–74. d. Stonor 18 Jany. 1881. I.L.N. lxxviii, 125 (1881), portrait.

CAMPANA, A. FABIO. b. Bologna 1815; settled in London about 1850 as teacher of singing; composed 6 operas Caterina di Guisa 1838, Giulio d'Este 1841, Vannina d'Ornano 1842, Luisa di Francia 1844, Almina, produced in London 1860 and Esmeralda, produced at Covent Garden theatre London 14 June 1870; composed The little gipsy, The twilight hour, The scout and about 400 other drawing room songs. d. 15 Westbourne place, Eaton sq. London 1 Feb. 1882.

CAMPBELL, JOHN CAMPBELL, 1 Baron (younger son of Rev. George Campbell 1747–1824, minis-

CAMPBELL, LORD. (Con.)
ter of Cupar, Fifeshire). b. Springfield near Cupar 15 Sep. 1779; ed. at Cupar gr. sch. and Univ. of St. Andrews; reported in House of Commons and law courts for Morning Chronicle 1800–5; barrister L.I. 15 Nov. 1806, bencher 1827, treasurer 1834; leader of Oxford circuit 1824–7; K.C. 13 June 1827; chairman of real property commission 9 June 1828; M.P. for Stafford 1830–2, for Dudley 1832–4 and for Edinburgh 1834–41; solicitor general 23 Nov. 1832 to 22 Feb. 1834; knighted at St. James's palace 3 Dec. 1832; attorney general 22 Feb. 1834 to Nov. 1834 and 30 April 1835 to 22 June 1841; lord chancellor of Ireland 22 June 1841 to Sep. 1841; created Baron Campbell of St. Andrews 30 June 1841; P.C. 22 June 1841; chancellor of Duchy of Lancaster 6 July 1846 to 6 March 1850; serjeant at law 5 March 1850; chief justice of Court of Queen's Bench 6 March 1850 to 18 June 1859; tried Wm. Palmer the poisoner 14 to 27 May 1856; lord chancellor 18 June 1859 to death; he was the first peer ever made a serjeant at law and held the great seal at an older age than any previous lord chancellor; author of Reports of cases determined at Nisi Prius 4 vols. 1809–16; The lives of the lord chancellors 7 vols. 1846–7, 4 ed. 10 vols. 1856–7; The lives of the lord justices 3 vols. 1849–57; Lives of Lord Lyndhurst and Lord Brougham 1869. d. Stratheden lodge, Kensington, London 23 June 1861. bur. Jedburgh abbey 29 June. Life of Lord Campbell 2 vols. 1881, portrait; W. H. Bennet's Select biographicol sketches (1867) 153–76; Ballantine's Some experiences i, 184–206 (1882); O. J. Burke's Lord chancellors of Ireland (1879) 262–72; Proc. of Royal Soc. of Edin. iv, 484–91 (1862); Quarterly Review cli, 1–40 (1881); I.L.N. iv, 180 (1844), portrait, xvi, 173 (1850), portrait, xxxviii, 611 (1861), portrait; Law mag. and law rev. xi, 347–95 (1861).

CAMPBELL, ALEXANDER (eld. son of Thomas Campbell of Ballymena, co. Antrim, schoolmaster 1763–1854). b. near Ballymena 12 Sep. 1788; ed. at Glasgow univ. 1808–9; went to United States 1809; joined the Baptists 1812; organised a separate body under name of Disciples of Christ, more commonly known as Campbellites 1827; founded a college at Bethany 21 Oct. 1841; author of numerous religious books; edited "Christian Baptist" 7 vols. 1823–9, succeeded by the Millenial harbinger. d. Bethany, west Virginia 4 March 1866. Richardson's Memoirs 2 vols. 1871, portrait; Rice's Campbellism its rise and progress 1850.

CAMPBELL, SIR ALEXANDER, 2 Baronet. *b.* 15 June 1819; succeeded 2 April 1842; a sergeant at arms in Her Majesty's Household 1851 to death. *d.* 16 Ridgeway place, Wimbledon 11 Dec. 1880.

CAMPBELL, ALEXANDER CAMERON *(eld. son of lieut. gen. Alexander Campbell of Monzie, co. Argyle who d. 24 Feb. 1832).* *b.* 30 Dec. 1811; officer in 32 foot and 15 hussars 1828–32; M.P. for co. Argyle 9 July 1841 to Aug. 1843; brought in a "Bill to regulate the exercise of church patronage in Scotland" 14 April 1842; laid foundation of the John Knox memorial church Edinburgh 18 May 1846; a great promoter of interests of Free Church of Scotland. *d.* Markham house, Leamington 5 Jany. 1869. *bur.* in St. Mary's church Warwick. *J. A. Wylie's Disruption Worthies* (1881) 125–30.

CAMPBELL, ALEXANDER DUNCAN. Writer Madras civil service 1807; sec. to Board of revenue 1817; third puisne judge of Sudder Fougdarry, Adawlut 1838, second puisne judge 1840, first puisne judge 1842, resigned the service 6 May 1842; author of *A grammar of the Teloogoo language* 1816; *A dictionary of the Teloogoo language* 1821, 2 *ed.* 1848. *d.* 23 April 1857.

CAMPBELL, ANDREW VOULLAIRE, stage name of Andrew Leonard Voullaire. *b.* London 29 Sep. 1789; gave imitations at Sanspareil theatre 1808; acted at Sadler's Wells theatre 1814–38; acted at Astley's and City of London theatres; acting manager at Royal Grecian saloon to 1851; a pensioner in Royal dramatic college, Woking 1859 to death; wrote many dramas and addresses. *d.* Royal dramatic college, Woking 2 July 1870. *Actors by daylight i*, 113 (1838), *portrait.*

CAMPBELL, SIR ANGUS, 2 Baronet. *b.* Surrey 19 Aug. 1827; entered navy 10 Dec. 1840; lieut. 4 Dec. 1849; placed on h.p. Oct. 1856; succeeded 18 Oct. 1860. *d.* Dunstaffnage, Argyleshire 13 Aug. 1863.

CAMPBELL, SIR ARCHIBALD ISLAY, 3 Baronet. *b.* Garscube near Glasgow 16 May 1825; ed. at Eton and Ch. Ch. Ox.; succeeded 23 July 1846; M.P. for Argyleshire 6 June 1851 to 21 March 1857; lieut. col. of 1 Lanarkshire rifle corps 1860. *d.* Garscube 11 Sep. 1866.

CAMPBELL, REV. AUGUSTUS. *b.* London 4 April 1786; ed. at Trin. coll. Cam., B.A. 1807, M.A. 1812; R. of Liverpool 1829 to death; V. of Childwall near Liverpool 1829 to death; author of *The rights of the English clergy asserted and the probable amount of the*

CAMPBELL, REV. A. *(Con.)*
incomes estimated 1822, 2 *ed.* 1823; *Two papers on church music read before the Liverpool Ecclesiastical music society* 1854. *d.* Childwall vicarage 16 May 1870.

CAMPBELL, CHARLES STUART. Lieutenant 26 foot 14 Dec. 1797; lieut. col. 1 foot 24 Jany. 1829 to 27 Oct. 1831 when placed on h.p.; C.B. 26 Sep. 1831; M.G. 20 June 1854. *d.* Reading 30 Aug. 1854.

CAMPBELL, COLIN MINTON. *b.* Liverpool 27 Aug. 1827; member of Society of Arts 1860; invented a new method of producing durable mural paintings by fictile vitrifaction described in a paper read before Society of Arts 14 Dec. 1870; head of firm of Minton and Co. of Stoke upon Trent, manufacturers of china; sheriff of Staffs. 1869; M.P. for North Staffs. 10 Feb. 1874 to 24 March 1880. *d.* Woodseat, Uttoxeter, Staffs. 7 Feb. 1885. Bronze statue of him by T. Brock unveiled at Stoke upon Trent 1 Jany. 1887.

CAMPBELL, DAVID. *b.* Glasgow 24 Sep. 1813; resident superintendent engineer of Coloba Press company, Bombay 1843–57; engineer at Liverpool and Glasgow 1872 to death; improved machinery for pressing goods and brought out several inventions in connection with screw and side lever presses. *d.* Glasgow 11 May 1882.

CAMPBELL, DONALD. *b.* 1778; entered navy 4 June 1791; Captain 1 Aug. 1811; inspecting commander coast guard 1822–32; R.A. 1 Oct. 1846. *d.* Barbrech house, Craignish, Argyleshire 16 Dec. 1856.

CAMPBELL, SIR DONALD, 3 Baronet. *b.* Innestore, Argyleshire 5 Oct. 1829; succeeded 13 Aug. 1863. *d.* Aix les Bains, France 8 June 1879.

CAMPBELL, DUGALD JOHN PHILIP. Entered Madras army 1846; captain 7 Madras N.I. 29 Jany. 1861 to 1 Feb. 1871 when he retired; City Marshal 17 July 1873 to death. *d.* Mansion house, London 23 Dec. 1885 aged 57.

CAMPBELL, REV. DUNCAN R. *b.* Scotland; pastor of Baptist church at Georgetown, Kentucky; pres. of Georgetown college 1849 to death. *d.* Covington, Kentucky 11 Aug. 1865 aged about 63.

CAMPBELL, SIR EDWARD FITZGERALD, 2 Baronet. *b.* Cadogan terrace, London 25 Oct. 1822; second lieut. Rifle Corps 2 July 1841; major 9 Sep. 1858 to 12 Jany. 1867; succeeded 27 Jany. 1849. *d.* West Grinstead lodge, Horsham 23 Nov. 1882.

CAMPBELL, FREDERICK (7 son of John Campbell 1730–90). b. 1780; second lieut. R.A. 12 Jany. 1797, garrison quartermaster at Woolwich 1810–28; commanded R.A. in Jamaica 1833–7 and in Canada 1838–47; superintendent of royal military repository Woolwich 1847–52; col. commandant of 6 battalion of R.A. 10 March 1852 to death; general 25 Sep. 1859. d. Woolwich 4 April 1866. *A memorial history of the Campbells of Melfort by M. O. C.* (1882) 18, 26, *portrait*.

CAMPBELL, SIR GEORGE (brother of 1 Baron Campbell 1779–1861). b. Cupar, March 1778; assistant surgeon in service of H.E.I. Co. to 1823; knighted Jany. 1833 in consideration of his active services in preserving the peace during period of Reform bill. d. Edenwood near Cupar 20 May 1854.

CAMPBELL, SIR GEORGE, 4 Baronet. b. 27 April 1829; ed. at Eton and Glasgow colleges; captain 1 dragoons 1848–57; succeeded 11 Sep. 1866. d. Malta 17 Feb. 1874.

CAMPBELL, GEORGE. Ensign 52 foot 13 March 1835, lieut. col. 27 May 1853 to 31 Jany. 1860; inspecting field officer 1860–5; L.G. 8 March 1875; colonel 85 foot 19 Oct. 1875 to death; C.B. 1 Jany. 1858; granted service reward 15 Jany. 1858. d. 31 Albemarle st. Piccadilly, London 22 Dec. 1876.

CAMPBELL, GEORGE. b. 1804; second lieut. Bengal artillery 6 June 1823, colonel commandant 10 May 1874 to 1 Oct. 1877 when placed on retired list; general 21 July 1874; C.B. 13 March 1867. d. 1 Byng place, Gordon sq. London 25 April 1882. *bur.* Inverneil, co. Argyle 2 May.

CAMPBELL, GEORGE PRYSE (younger son of 1 baron Cawdor who d. 1 June 1821). b. 1793; entered navy 7 April 1803, captain 27 Jany. 1821, retired 1 Oct. 1846; retired R.A. 8 March 1852; groom of the chamber to Wm. iv, 24 Feb. 1831; M.P. for Nairnshire 1820–6 and 1830–1. d. South Audley st. London 12 Jany. 1858.

CAMPBELL, SIR HENRY FREDERICK (son of lieut. col. Alexander Campbell who d. Nov. 1785). b. 10 July 1769; ensign 1 foot guards 20 Sep. 1786, third major 21 Oct. 1813 to 25 July 1814; commanded second brigade of guards in Portugal Dec. 1808 to 1809 and April 1811 to 1812; commanded first division of army at siege of Ciudad Rodrigo, battle of Salamanca and siege of castle of Burgos 1812; colonel 88 foot 16 Jany. 1824 and of 25 foot 20 Oct. 1831 to death; general 10

CAMPBELL, SIR H. F. (Con.)
Jany. 1837; prothonotary of Palace court Westminster 1792 to 1849 when court was abolished; M.P. for Nairn and Cromarty 1796 to 1802 and 1806–7; K.C.B. 2 Jany. 1815; G.C.H. 1818. d. 8 Lowndes sq. Belgravia, London 2 Sep. 1856.

CAMPBELL, IVIE. b. Dalgig, Ayrshire about 1798; ed. at Univ. of Glasgow; a great courser 1849–65, his dog Canaradzo brought him about £1,500 in the slips and at the stud; bred cattle, horses and sheep extensively at Dalgig; gained Highland and Agricultural Society's gold medal 1833. d. 21 Nov. 1867. *Saddle and sirloin by the Druid* (1870) 7–12; *Field and fern by the Druid* (1865) 249–66.

CAMPBELL, JAMES. Ensign 91 foot 17 Sep. 1803; major 79 foot 3 June 1819 to 10 July 1824; lieut. col. 95 foot 27 Sep. 1831 to 11 Nov. 1851; served in Irish rebellion 1798–9, expedition to Hanover 1805 and to Walcheren 1809; K.H. 1836; M.G. 11 Nov. 1851. d. London 18 Nov. 1853 aged 67.

CAMPBELL, JAMES. Ensign 51 foot 12 June 1799, lieut. col. 12 July 1831 to 26 June 1838 when placed on h.p.; inspecting field officer of Coventry recruiting district Dec. 1846; M.G. 20 June 1854; K.H. 1835. d. Brislington 8 May 1856.

CAMPBELL, JAMES. Barrister L.I. 8 Feb. 1821, bencher 1851; Q.C. July 1851; charity comr. for England and Wales 6 Nov. 1855 to death. d. 10 York place, Portman sq. London 2 March 1866.

CAMPBELL, SIR JAMES (son of James Campbell of Perth). b. Inchanoch, Port of Monteith, Perthshire 3 June 1790; warehouseman at Glasgow; lord provost of Glasgow 1840–3; knighted at St. James's palace 13 April 1842 after presenting an address on birth of Prince of Wales. d. Stracathrow house, Brechin, Forfarshire 10 Sep. 1876.

CAMPBELL, REV. JAMES ROBERTSON. b. Glasgow 1814; ed. at Univ. of Glasgow, M.A. 1835, D.D. 1861; pastor of Congregational church Montrose 1835, of church in Albany st. Edinburgh 1844, of Horton lane ch. Bradford 1 July 1855 to 14 Oct. 1883; chairman of Congregational Union of England and Wales 1867; edited *Ralph Wardlaw's Systematic theology* 1856; author of *The form of sound words, A handbook of the principles of Holy Scripture* 1858; found *dead* in his bed at Cliffe house, Baildon near Bradford 1 Dec. 1884. *Congregational year book* (1886) 152–5.

CAMPBELL, SIR JOHN, 7 Baronet (only child of Sir John Campbell, 6 baronet 1767–1834). b. 27 Nov. 1807; admitted advocate at Scottish bar 1831; succeeded 7 Nov. 1834; lieutenant governor of island of St. Vincent 9 June 1845 to death. d. Kingstown, St. Vincent 18 Jany. 1853.

CAMPBELL, SIR JOHN, 2 Baronet (younger son of Sir Archibald Campbell, 1 baronet 1769–1843). b. 14 April 1806; ensign 38 foot 25 Nov. 1821, lieut. col. 7 Aug. 1840 to 21 Feb. 1854; succeeded his father 6 Oct. 1843; commanded 2 brigade of 3 division in Crimea 21 Feb. 1854; held temporary command of fourth division Nov. 1854 to 7 June 1855; M.G. 12 Dec. 1854; gazetted K.C.B. 5 July 1855; killed in attack upon the Redan 18 June 1855. I.L.N. xxvii, 373 (1855), portrait.

CAMPBELL, SIR JOHN (son of Wm. Campbell, comr. of navy board). b. Chatham dockyard 1780; ed. at Harrow; cornet 7 hussars 1800; lieut. col. Portugese cavalry 1809; col. of fourth Portugese cavalry; organised Portugese forces 1814–20; knighted 9 March 1815; lieut. col. 75 foot 9 Aug. 1821 to 23 Sep. 1824 when he sold out; espoused cause of Dom Miguel who created him L.G.; K.T.S. 14 June 1815, K.C.T.S. 5 Oct. 1825. d. 51 Charles st. Berkeley sq. London 19 Dec. 1863. G.M. xvi, 389–90 (1864).

CAMPBELL, REV. JOHN (son of Alexander Campbell of Kirriemuir near Dundee, surgeon). b. Kirriemuir 5 Oct. 1795; a blacksmith; ed. at Univs. of St. Andrews and Glasgow, D.D. St. Andrews 1841; Independent minister at Kilmarnock, Ayrshire Feb. 1827; minister of the Tabernacle Moorfields, London 1829 to Dec. 1865; contested Bible monopoly with Queen's printer 1839, result being a great reduction in price of Bibles; presented with sum of £3,000, 17 Jany. 1865, contributed by 600 persons in all parts of the world; edited Christian Witness 1844–64, Christian penny magazine 1846–64, British Banner 1848–56, British Standard 1856–66, British Ensign 1858; author of Jethro 1839; Maritime discovery and Christian missions 1840; Pastoral visitation 1841; The martyr of Erromanga 1842; Life of David Nasmyth 1844; Wesleyan Methodism 1847; Popery, ancient and modern 1865. d. Manor house, St. John's wood park, London 26 March 1867. Life by Rev. R. Ferguson and Rev. A. M. Brown (1867); Norrie's Dundee Celebrities (1873) 283–8.

CAMPBELL, JOHN. Ensign 44 foot 23 Jany. 1812; commanded Beauharnois district during rebellion in Canada 1838; col. of 97 foot 15

CAMPBELL, J. (Con.)
Dec. 1861 and of 92 foot 3 March 1869 to death; L.G. 4 July 1864. d. Lipson terrace, Plymouth 28 Dec. 1871 aged 73.

CAMPBELL, SIR JOHN (eld. son of John Campbell of Lochend, Argyleshire 1771–1827). b. Kingsburgh, island of Skye 1802; ensign 91 foot 21 Jany. 1819; lieut. 41 Madras N.I. 5 April 1820; lieut. col. 45 Madras N.I. 1850 to 2 Jany. 1854; colonel 14 Madras N.I. 1860–9; general 21 March 1872; C.B. 24 Dec. 1842; K.C.S.I. 2 June 1869 for his services in suppression of human sacrifice among the Khonds of hill tracts of Orissa, Bengal; author of Personal narrative of 13 years service among the wild tribes of Khondistan 1864. d. 1 Hampton terrace, Edinburgh 21 April 1878. A memorial history of the Campbells of Melfort by M. O. C. (1882) 60–62.

CAMPBELL, JOHN ARCHIBALD (eld. son of John Campbell of the Citadel, Leith). b. 1788; a writer to the Signet 1813; joint crown agent 1813–6; sheriff clerk of Midlothian 1843–59; helped to found some of the most thriving institutions in Edinburgh; F.R.S. Edin. 1837. d. 2 Albyn place, Edin. 7 Sep. 1866 in 78 year.

CAMPBELL, SIR JOHN EYTON, 8 Baronet. b. 22 May 1809; succeeded April 1834. d. Gibraltar 9 Dec. 1853.

CAMPBELL, JOHN FRANCIS (son of Walter Frederick Campbell 1798–1855). b. 29 Dec. 1822; ed. at Eton and Univ. of Edin.; barrister I.T. 2 May 1851; private sec. to Lord privy seal 1853; assistant sec. to general board of health 1854; sec. to Lighthouse commission 1859; groom of Privy chamber 1861; sec. to Mines commission 1863; sec. to Coal commission 1866; groom in waiting in ordinary to Victoria 1874–80; invented sunshine recorder for indicating varying intensity of sun's rays; author of Popular tales of the West Highlands orally collected 4 vols. 1860–2; Frost and fire 1865, new ed. 2 vols. 1867; Circular notes, tour round the world 2 vols. 1876; issued a series of Gaelic texts under title of Leabhair na Feinne 1872. d. Cannes 17 Feb. 1885. I.L.N. lxxxvi, 224, 294 (1885), portrait.

CAMPBELL, JOHN FRANCIS GLENCAIRN. Ensign 91 foot 25 Oct. 1827, lieut. col. 14 April 1846 to 12 Nov. 1860; colonel 79 foot 12 July 1868 to death; L.G. 3 Feb. 1870; C.B. 6 March 1858. d. Jersey 20 Aug. 1870. aged 60.

CAMPBELL, Rev. John McLeod (eld. child of Rev. Donald Campbell 1758-1843, minister of Kilninver, Argyleshire). b. Ardnaddy house near Kilninver 4 May 1800; ed. at Univs. of Glasgow 1811-20 and Edinburgh; licensed as a preacher 1821; minister of parish of Row, Dumbartonshire 8 Sep. 1825 to Aug. 1831 when deposed by General Assembly on charge of holding and teaching doctrines on assurance of faith and atonement contrary to standards of the church; minister of Blackfriars st. chapel Glasgow 17 Sep. 1833 to April 1859; D.D. Glasgow April 1868; author of. Sermons and lectures 1832; Christ the bread of life 1851, 2 ed. 1869; The nature of the Atonement 1856, 4 ed. 1873; Thoughts on revelation 1862. d. Acknashire, Rosneath 27 Feb. 1872. J. M. Campbell's Reminiscences and reflections 1873; Memorials of J. M. Campbell edited by his son Rev. Donald Campbell 2 vols. 1877, portrait; Blackwood's Mag. cxxii, 283-302 (1877).

CAMPBELL, Sir John Nicholl Robert, 2 Baronet (eld. child of Sir Robert Campbell, 1 baronet 1771-1858). b. Vizagapatam 25 May 1799; entered Madras army 1 Sep. 1818, captain 8 Dec. 1826; chargé d' affaires in Persia to 1861; knighted at St. James's palace 22 Dec. 1832; K.C.H. 1836; succeeded 28 Feb. 1858. d. Germany 11 May 1870.

CAMPBELL, Sir Louis Henry Dugald, 9 Baronet. b. 2 March 1844; succeeded 9 Dec. 1853. d. Kildalloig, co. Argyle 18 June 1875.

CAMPBELL, Patrick. b. 1779; lieut. col. R.A. 29 July 1825 to 11 Nov. 1836 when he retired on full pay; secretary of legation in Columbia 29 Dec. 1826; agent and consul general in Egypt 7 Jany. 1833 to 13 Aug. 1841 when he retired on a superannuation allowance; general 28 Nov. 1854. d. Rockstone place, Southampton 29 Aug. 1857.

CAMPBELL, Rev. Peter Colin. Principal of University of Aberdeen 1855 to death; author of The theory of ruling eldership or the position of the lay ruler in reformed churches examined 1866. d. Chanonry, Aberdeen 12 Dec. 1876.

CAMPBELL, Sir Robert, 1 Baronet (son of John Campbell of Ballyshannon, co. Donegal). b. Ballyshannon May 1771; a director of East India company 23 July 1817 to 1852; created baronet 30 Sep. 1831. d. 5 Argyle place, London 28 Feb. 1858.

CAMPBELL, Robert Calder (son of Rev. Pryce Campbell, minister of Ardeseir, Nairn). b. Scotland 1798; lieut. Madras army 2 Oct.

CAMPBELL, R. C. (Con.)

1818; served in Burmese war 1826-7; major 43 Madras N.I. 28 April 1836 to 1 Aug. 1839 when he retired; author under name of Calder Campbell of Lays from the East 1831; The palmer's last lesson and other poems 1838; Rough recollections of rambles at home and abroad 3 vols. 1847; Winter nights, a novel 3 vols. 1850; The three trials of Loide, and other poems 1851; Episodes in the war life of a soldier 1857. d. University st. London 13 May 1857.

CAMPBELL, Thomas. b. Edinburgh 1 May 1790; apprenticed to a marble cutter; a sculptor in Rome 1818-30; executed many busts and portrait statues in bronze and marble; exhibited 38 works at Royal Academy 1827-57; lived in London 1834 to death; his chief works are statue of Princess Pauline Borghese at Chatsworth, statue of the Queen at Windsor, monuments of Sir W. Hoste in St. Paul's cathedral and of Duchess of Buccleuch at Boughton. d. 16 Great Marlborough st. London 4 Feb. 1858.

CAMPBELL, Rev. Thomas Hewitt (son of Duncan Campbell of Upper Gloucester st. London, merchant). b. 7 July 1828; ed. at Merchant Taylors' and St. John's coll. Ox., junior Univ. math. scholar 1848, B.A. 1851, M.A. 1853; fellow of his college to 1862; under master at Charterhouse; head master of Wolverhampton gr. sch.; appointed principal of Otago college, New Zealand 1863; drowned off Port Chalmers, Otago 4 July 1863.

CAMPBELL, Walter Frederick. b. 10 April 1798; M.P. for Argyleshire 14 March 1822 to 3 Dec. 1832 and 13 Jany. 1835 to 23 June 1841; author of Life in Normandy 2 vols. 1863, published anonymously by his son John Francis Campbell. d. 8 Feb. 1855.

CAMPBELL, William. Cornet 2 Dragoon guards 6 Jany. 1832, lieut. col. 30 Jany. 1846 to death; C.B. 27 July 1858. d. Cawnpore 9 July 1858.

CAMPBELL, William (brother of Sir James Campbell 1790-1876). b. near Port of Monteith, Perthshire 1793; general warehouseman in Glasgow 1814; partner with his brother; active promoter of scheme for building 20 new Free churches in Glasgow and 200 additional churches in Scotland; member of Glasgow town council; proprietor of Tillichewan castle. d. 2 April 1864 in 71 year. J. A. Wylie's Disruption Worthies (1881) 131-8.

CAMPBELL, WILLIAM. *b.* Glasgow; came to Newcastle about Nov. 1877; landlord of Duke of Wellington public house High bridge, Newcastle; exhibited himself at Egyptian hall, London. *d.* Newcastle 26 May 1878.

NOTE.—He was 76 inches round the breast and weighed 52 stone.

CAMPBELL, WILLIAM GEORGE. Barrister M.T. 29 Jany. 1836; comr. in lunacy 26 Nov. 1845 to 1878; hon. comr. in lunacy 1878 to death. *d.* 50 Ennismore gardens, London 13 June 1881 in 71 year.

CAMPERDOWN, ROBERT DUNDAS DUNCAN-HALDANE, 1 Earl of *(eld. son of Admiral Adam Duncan, 1 Viscount Duncan 1731–1804). b.* 21 March 1785; succeeded as 2 Viscount 4 Aug. 1804; created Earl of Camperdown of Lundie, co. Forfar and Glenagles, co. Perth 12 Sep. 1831; K.T. 12 May 1848. *d.* 1 Wilton terrace, Belgrave sq. London 22 Dec. 1859.

CAMPERDOWN, ADAM DUNCAN-HALDANE, 2 Earl of *(elder son of the preceding). b.* Edinburgh 25 March 1812; ed. at Eton and Trin. coll. Cam., M.A. 1834; M.P. for Southampton 1837–41, for Bath 1841–52 for Forfarshire 1854 to 22 Dec. 1859 when he succeeded as 2 Earl; obtained repeal of the Window tax by 14 and 15 Vict. cap. 36, 24 July 1851 for which he was presented with freedom of Dundee Dec. 1851; a lord of the Treasury 8 March 1855 to March 1858. *d.* Weston, Warwickshire 30 Jany. 1867. *Norrie's Dundee Celebrities* (1873) 280–1.

CAMPION, GEORGE B. *b.* 1796; an original member of New Society (now Royal Institute) of painters in water colours 1834 to which he contributed landscapes; many of his views have been published; landscape drawing master at Royal Military academy Woolwich 1 Dec. 1841 to death; author of *The adventures of a chamois hunter* and of some papers on German art in *Art Journal. d,* Munich 7 April 1870.

CANDLISH, REV. ROBERT SMITH *(youngest child of James Candlish of Edinburgh, teacher of medicine who d. 29 April 1806 aged 46). b.* Nicolson st. Edin. 23 March 1806; ed. at Glasgow college 1818–23; private tutor at Eton Dec. 1823; licensed by presbytery of Glasgow 6 Aug. 1828; assistant minister at St. Andrew's Glasgow 1829, at Bonhill, Dumbartonshire 1831–3; minister of St. George's Edin. 14 Aug. 1834; D.D. Princeton coll. New Jersey 1841; left Scotch kirk 18 May 1843; had leading share in organisation of Free church; minister of St. George's

CANDLISH, REV. R. S. *(Con.)*

free church Edin. 1846 to death; convener of education committee of Free church 1846; moderator of General Assembly 1861; principal of New college Edin. 1862; D.D. Edin. 1865; author of *Contributions towards the exposition of the book of Genesis 3 vols.* 1843–62; *Scripture characters and miscellanies* 1850, 4 ed. 1872; *Life in a risen Saviour* 1858, 3 ed. 1863; *Reason and revelation* 1859, 2 ed. 1864; *The fatherhood of God* 1865, 5 ed. 1870. *d.* Melville st. Edinburgh 19 Oct. 1873. *Memorials by Wm. Wilson* 1880, *portrait; Life by J. L. Watson* 1882, *portrait; A. Beith's Three weeks with Dr. Candlish,* 2 ed. 1874; *J. A. Wylie's Disruption Worthies* (1881) 139–46, *portrait; Crombie's Modern Athenians* (1882), *portrait; Graphic viii,* 407, 412 (1873), *portrait.*

CANE, ROBERT. *b.* Kilkenny 1807; surgeon at Kilkenny 1832 to death; M.R.C.S. England 1841; F.R.C.S. Ireland 1844; M.D. Glasgow 1842; chief promoter of repeal movement at Kilkenny, mayor 1844 and 1849; originated Celtic Union a semi-political and semi-literary society 1853; edited the *Celt,* a magazine, first number appeared 1 Aug. 1857; author of *The Williamite and Jacobite wars in Ireland* 1859. *d.* William st. Kilkenny 17 Aug. 1858. *Irish quarterly review viii,* 1004–96 (1858).

CANN, ABRAHAM *(son of Robert Cann of Colebrooke near Crediton, farmer).* Baptized Colebrooke 2 Dec. 1794; wrestled with and defeated all the best wrestlers in Devonshire; beat James Warren at Eagle tavern, City road, London 21 Sep. 1826; wrestled with James Polkinghorne, champion of Cornwall for £200 a side at Tamar Green near Devonport 23 Oct. 1826 in presence of 12000 spectators when match was declared to be drawn; is the hero of H. Kingsley's novel *Recollections of Geoffrey Hamlyn* 1859. *d.* Colebrooke 7 April 1864. *Sporting Mag. lxvii,* 165 (1826), *lxix,* 55, 215, 314, 344 (1827); *London Mag.* 1 Oct. 1826 *pp.* 160–3; *Illust. sporting news iii,* 100 (1864), 2 *portraits, v,* 197 (1866), *portrait.*

CANNING, CHARLES JOHN CANNING, 1 Earl *(youngest child of George Canning 1770–1827, prime minister). b.* Gloucester lodge, Brompton, London 14 Dec. 1812; ed. at Eton and Ch. Ch. Ox., B.A. 1833; M.P. for Warwick Aug. 1836 to 15 March 1837 when on death of his mother he became Viscount Canning; under sec. of state for foreign affairs 4 Sep. 1841 to 27 Jany. 1846; first comr. of woods and forests 2 March to 6 July 1846; P.C. 18 March 1846; postmaster general 5 Jany.

CANNING, C. J. C. (Con.)

1853 to 4 July 1855; governor general of India 4 July 1855 to March 1862; the first viceroy of India 2 Aug. 1858; G.C.B. 31 March 1859; created Earl Canning 21 May 1859; ranger of Greenwich park 1860; the first grand master of order of Star of India 25 June 1861 to March 1862; K.G. 21 May 1862. d. Grosvenor sq. London 17 June 1862. bur. Westminster abbey 21 June. *Eton portrait gallery* (1876) 356–60; *Men whom India has known* (1874) 50–5; *Nolan's British empire in India ii*, 706 (1860), *portrait*; *Illust. news of the world viii*, (1861), *portrait*; *I.L.N. xxvii*, 649 (1855), *portrait, xli*, 1, 8, 22 (1862), *portrait*.

CANNON, EDWARD ST. LEGER. b. 1803; entered navy 10 Nov. 1816; captain 9 Nov. 1846; captain of Centaur 6 guns 23 July 1851 to 29 July 1853; retired admiral 1 Aug. 1877. d. The Glen, Walmer, Kent 20 Nov. 1881.

CANNON, RICHARD. b. 1779; clerk at the Horse Guards 1 Jany. 1802; principal clerk in adjutant general's office to Jany. 1854 when he retired on full pay of £800 a year; edited *The historical records of the British army* 66 *vols.* 1836–53, being records of all the regiments of cavalry (except Royal horse guards) and of 42 regiments of infantry. d. 30 Oct. 1865.

CANNON, ROBERT (son of Rev. D. Cannon, D.D.) b. 1811; entered Madras army 1826, captain 40 Madras N.I. 15 Jany. 1841 to 26 March 1846; raised 500 men in Devonshire for British auxiliary legion of Spain; major in 6th Scotch regiment 1835; lieut. col. in Auxiliary legion 5 May 1836 and in 9th regiment 26 May 1836; commanded 9th and 10th regiments, styled the Royal Irish 20 March 1837; granted license to accept cross of first class of order of St. Ferdinand 9 Oct. 1837 and of second class 1 March 1839; granted license to accept insignia of order of Charles the third 5 Feb. 1848; joined Turkish army at Shumlah as " Behram Pacha " early in 1854; took a division of Turkish army to Eupatoria Dec. 1854; present at bombardment of Sebastopol April 1855; hon. lieut. gen. (Ferik) in service of the Sultan 5 Dec. 1856. d. Folkestone 5 April 1882. *I.L.N. xxviii*, 405 (1856), *portrait, lxxx*, 396 (1882), *portrait*.

CANNON, THOMAS. b. Eton 14 March 1790; a bargeman at Windsor; fought and beat Dolly Smith at Shirley Common near Windsor 6 May 1817; fought Joshua Hudson for £100 a side at Yateley, Hants. 23 June 1824

CANNON, T. (Con.)

when Cannon won; fought Hudson again on Warwick race course for £500 a side 23 Nov. 1824 when Cannon won again; gamekeeper to "Pea-green" Hayne 1824; fought James Ward for £500 a side at Warwick 19 July 1825 when Ward won; appeared at Coburg theatre London Aug. 1825 in *The fight at Warwick;* fought Edward Neale for £100 a side at Warfield, Berks. 20 Feb. 1827 when Neale won; landlord of the Castle tavern, 16 Jermyn st. St. James's, London 1828; a swanwatcher for Corporation of London at Strand-on-the-Green Chiswick, Middlesex; *shot himself* at Strand-on-the-Green 11 July 1858. *H. D. Miles's Pugilistica ii*, 248–62 (1880), *portrait*.

CANTERBURY, CHARLES JOHN MANNERS-SUTTON, 2 Viscount (eld. son of 1 Viscount Canterbury 1780–1845). b. London 17 April 1812; succeeded 21 July 1845; comr. to inquire into local charges on shipping 1853. d. 13 Chesterfield st. London 13 Nov. 1869.

CANTERBURY, JOHN HENRY THOMAS MANNERS-SUTTON, 3 Viscount (brother of the preceding). b. Downing st. London 27 May 1814; ed. at Eton and Trin. coll. Cam., M.A. 1835; registrar of Faculty office 1841 to death; M.P. for town of Cambridge 1839–40 and 1841–7, for Newark-on-Trent 1847–57; under sec. of state for home department 3 Sep. 1841 to 5 July 1846; chairman of commission on harbour dues 1853–4; lieutenant governor of New Brunswick June 1854 to Oct. 1861; governor of Trinidad 6 Sep. 1864 to 24 April 1866; governor of Victoria 15 Aug. 1866 to 2 March 1873; K.C.B. 23 June 1866; G.C.M.G. 25 June 1873. d. 12 Queensberry place, South Kensington, London 24 June 1877. *I.L.N. xxxv*, 586 (1859). *portrait, lxxxi*, 19 (1877), *portrait*.

CANTRELL, JOSEPH THOMAS (eld. son of Joseph Cantrell of King's Newton near Derby). b. 1802; ed. at Repton gr. sch.; barrister L.I. 22 Nov. 1831; judge of Wirksworth and Staffordshire potteries court of requests; judge of county courts circuit 19, Derbyshire, March 1847 to death. d. King's Newton 4 April 1862.

CAPE, JAMES MATTHEW. b. 1796; edited *British Press;* worked on *Mirror of Parliament,* on *Morning Chronicle,* on *Times* nearly 26 years; an active leader of the old Reform party; author of many important anonymous contributions to London Journals. d. 61 Victoria road, Kentish Town, London 18 Jany. 1874.

CAPE, REV. JONATHAN. Educ. at Trin. coll. Cam., 5 wrangler 1816, B.A. 1816, M.A. 1819; professor of mathematics at Addiscombe college 1823–65; F.R.S. 3 June 1852; author of *Mathematical tables* 1838, 3 ed. 1860; *A course of mathematics* 2 vols. 1839–40, 2 ed. 1842–4. d. George st. Croydon 9 Sep. 1868 aged 75.

CAPE, LAWSON (*son of John Cape of Uldale, Cumberland*). b. 6 Dec. 1807; ed. at St. Bartholomew's hospital 1827; M.D. Edin. 1833; L.R.C.P. London 1835, F.R.C.P. 1857; phys. to Royal infirmary for children Waterloo bridge road 1836–46; asst. phys. to General lying-in hospital York road, Lambeth 1837, phys. 1844 to death; lecturer on midwifery at St. Thomas' hospital 1837–48. d. 28 Curzon st. London 22 March 1877.

CAPE, WILLIAM TIMOTHY (*eld. son of Wm. Cape of Ireby, Cumberland*). b. Walworth, Surrey 25 Oct. 1806; ed. at Merchant Taylors' school; went with his father to Van Diemen's Land 1821; head master of Sydney public school July 1829; kept a private school in King st. Sydney 1830–5 when he transferred his pupils to Sydney college; head master of Sydney college 19 Jany. 1835 to 1842; kept another school in Sydney 1842–56; member for Wollombi of legislative assembly of N.S.W. 1859; fellow of St. Paul's college Sydney; comr. of national education. d. Warwick st. Pimlico, London 14 June 1863. *J. H. Heaton's Australian dictionary of dates* (1879) 33–5.

CAPEL, JAMES. Clerk in office of Sir Edmund Antrobus and Co. of the Stock exchange London, partner in the firm; head of firm of James Capel and Co. stock brokers; chairman of board of managers of stock exchange; chairman of committee of Spanish bondholders many years. d. 62 Westbourne terrace, London 18 Nov. 1872 aged 84.

CAPEL, SIR THOMAS BLADEN (*youngest son of 4 Earl of Essex 1732–99*). b. 25 Aug. 1776; entered navy 12 April 1792; signal lieut. to Lord Nelson at battle of the Nile; captain 27 Dec. 1798; commanded Royal George and Apollo yachts 1821–5; commander in chief of East India station 30 May 1834 to July 1837; admiral 28 April 1847; C.B. 4 June 1815; K.C.B. 20 Feb. 1832; G.C.B. 6 April 1852. d. 22 Rutland gate, Hyde park, London 4 March 1853.

CAPEL, THOMAS EDWARD (*brother of the preceding*). b. 24 March 1770; ensign 1 foot guards 10 April 1793, captain 22 June 1803 to 4 June 1814; served in Flanders and the

CAPEL, T. E. (*Con.*)
Peninsula; assistant adjutant general at Cadiz 1811; general 9 Nov. 1846. d. 14 Charles st. Berkeley sq. London 3 Feb. 1855.

CAPEL, REV. WILLIAM ROBERT. b. 28 April 1775; ed. at Merton coll. Ox. B.A. 1798, M.A. 1799; chaplain to the Sovereign 1814 to death; V. of Watford, Herts. 8 June 1799 to death; R. of Rayne, Essex 1805 to death. d. Watford 3 Dec. 1854.

CAPON, SIR DAVID (*youngest son of John Capon, lieut. col. East India company's Bombay army*). b. Bombay 1793; entered military service of E.I.C. at Bombay 26 May 1810; colonel 23 Bombay light infantry 26 Feb. 1848 to 30 Sep. 1862; col. 106 foot 30 Sep. 1862 to death; general 13 Aug. 1868; C.B. 20 Oct. 1848; K.C.B. 10 Nov. 1862. d. 8 Craven hill, Hyde park, London 17 Dec. 1869.

CAPPER, CHARLES. b. 1822; goods manager of Great Eastern railway, afterwards superintendent; general manager of Victoria docks 1855; chairman of Southampton docks company 1862 to death; M.P. for Sandwich 9 May 1866 to 11 Nov. 1868; author of *The port and trade of London, historical, statistical, local and general* 1861. d. Upton, Essex 21 March 1869.

CAPPER, SAMUEL (*son of Jasper Capper of London*). b. Gracechurch st. London 2 March 1782; a linen draper at Bristol 1803–10; a farmer at Potterne, Wilts. 1810–20; a minister of Society of Friends 1817 to death; engaged in putting down practice of bull-baiting in Bristol 1825; held many tent-meetings in counties of Gloucester, Worcester, Wilts. and in London 1834–43 and in Somerset, Devon and Cornwall 1846; author of *The acknowledged doctrines of the Church of Rome, being an exposition of Roman Catholic doctrines as set forth by esteemed doctors of the said church* 2 vols. 1849–51. d. Quaker's meeting house, Weston-super-Mare, Somerset 29 Aug. 1852. *Memoir of S. Capper edited by K. Backhouse* 1855.

CAPRON, GEORGE. b. 16 June 1783; head of firm of Capron, Babrant and Capron of Savile place, New Burlington st. London, solicitors; recorder of Orford, Suffolk 1848–59. d. Southwick near Oundle 24 Aug. 1872.

CAPUA, PENELOPE, Princess of (*2 dau. of Grice Smyth of Ballynatray, co. Waterford who d. 18 Jany. 1816 aged 54*). b. 19 July 1815. m. at Rome by Cardinal Weld 1830, Charles Ferdinand Prince of Capua 2 son of Francis i King of the two Sicilies who expressly forbade the marriage, *m.* the Prince again at Madrid, *m.* him again at Gretna Green 5 April 1836, *m.* him again at St. George's Hanover sq. London 23 May 1836, he was *b.* 10 Oct. 1811 and *d.* 22 April 1862, she *d.* Royal villa of Martia near Lucca 13 Dec. 1882. *Times* 5 May 1836, 20 *Dec.* 1882 *p.* 9, *col.* 6; *Heath's Book of beauty* (1842) *p.* 10, *portrait.*

CARADORI-ALLAN, MARIA CATERINA ROSALBINA (*dau. of Baron de Munck*). *b.* Casa Palatina, Milan 1800; took her mother's name Caradori; made her début in London 12 Jany. 1822 at King's theatre as Chérubino in *Le Nozze di Figaro;* sang at same house 1822–7, her salary rising from £300 to £1,200; sang at Philharmonic and Ancient concerts and at all great festivals; took chief part in first opera produced in England by Meyerbeer *Margherita d'Anjou;* made her début in America at Park theatre New York 28 Oct. 1837; returned to Europe July 1839; sang soprano part in *Elijah* at Birmingham 26 Aug. 1846; composed several popular Italian and French airs. (*m.* 1824 Edward Thomas Allan, secretary of King's theatre, London). *d.* Elm lodge, Surbiton, Surrey 15 Oct. 1865 in 65 year. *J. Ebers's Seven years of the King's theatre* (1828) 144, 153, *portrait; Orchestra* 28 *Oct.* 1865 *p.* 74, 4 *Nov. p.* 93; *Century Mag. xxiii,* 865–6 (1882), *portrait.*

CARDALE, JOHN BATE (*eld. son of Wm. Cardale of 2 Bedford row, London, solicitor 1777–1823*). *b.* 28 Lamb's Conduit st. London 9 Nov. 1802; ed. at Rugby 1815–8; articled to his father; head of firm of Cardale, Iliffe and Russell of Bedford row, solicitors 1824–34; Irvingite apostle Oct. 1832 to death, also an Irvingite prophet; ordained Edward Irving to be minister or angel of chapel in Newman st. London 5 April 1833; retired with the 11 other. apostles and 7 prophets to Albury, Surrey 14 July 1835 where they spent 2½ years in consultation; "The Apostle for England and The Pillar of the Apostles"; author of *Readings on the Liturgy vol.* 1 1849–51, *vol.* 2 1852–78; *The doctrine of the Eucharist as revealed to St. Paul* 1856, 2 *ed.* 1876; *A discourse on the Real Presence* 1867, 2 *ed.* 1868, and 25 other books all anonymous and most of them privately printed. *d.* Cooke's place, Albury 18 July 1877. *Miller's History of Irvingism* (1878) *i,* 61, *ii,* 416; *Mrs. Oliphant's Life of E. Irving,* (4 *ed.*) 356, 396, 398; *The old church porch i,* 87, 206 (1854); *The morning watch ii,* 869–73 (1830); *Saturday Review xliv,* 104–5 (1877); *Clement Boase's Catalogue of books relating to Catholic Apostolic Church* (1885) 9–12.

CARDEN, SIR JOHN CRAVEN, 4 Baronet. *b.* Templemore house, Tipperary 1 Dec. 1819; succeeded 23 March 1847. *d.* Templemore abbey, Tipperary 23 March 1879.

CARDEN, JOHN SURMAN. *b.* 15 Aug. 1771; entered navy 28 May 1788; captain 22 Jany. 1806; commanded the Ordinary at Sheerness 1825–40; admiral on half pay 3 July 1855. *d.* Ramoan rectory, Ballycastle, co. Antrim 22 April 1858.

CARDEW, GEORGE. Second lieut. R.E. 20 Dec. 1798, colonel 10 Jany. 1837 to 9 Nov. 1846, col. commandant 1 April 1855 to death; L.G. 20 June 1854. *d.* Portland terrace, Southsea 9 May 1859 aged 76.

CARDIGAN, JAMES THOMAS BRUDENELL, 7 Earl of (*only son of 6 Earl of Cardigan 1769–1837*). *b.* Hambledon, Hants. 16 Oct. 1797; ed. at Harrow and Ch. Ch. Ox.; M.P. for Marlborough 1818–29, for Fowey 1830–2, for North Northamptonshire 21 Dec. 1832 to 14 Aug. 1837 when he succeeded; cornet 8 hussars 6 May 1824, major 3 Aug. 1830 to 3 Dec. 1830 when placed on h.p.; lieut. col. 11 hussars (which became the crack cavalry regiment) 25 March 1836 to 20 June 1854; commanded light cavalry brigade in Crimea 21 Feb. 1854 to 1855; led the charge at Balaklava 25 Oct. 1854 when out of 607 men 409 were lost; inspector general of cavalry 1 Feb. 1855 to 31 March 1860; K.C.B. 5 July 1855; commander of legion of honour 2 Aug. 1856; col. 5 dragoon guards 14 Aug. 1859; col. 11 hussars 3 Aug. 1860 to death; L.G. 13 Feb. 1861; fought a duel which arose out of what was known as the "Black Bottle Quarrel" with Captain Harvey Garnett Phipps Tuckett on Wimbledon Common 12 Sep. 1840 when Tuckett was slightly wounded; tried before House of Lords for feloniously shooting Tuckett 16 Feb. 1841 when upon a technical deficiency of proof he was unanimously declared Not Guilty; kept staghounds in Leics. 1839–42. *d.* Deene park near Wansford, Northampton 28 March 1868. *F. A. Whinyates's From Coruna to Sevastopol* (1884) 149–202; *W. C. Townsend's Modern state trials i,* 209–43 (1850); *Kinglake's Crimean war vol.* 5; *G. Ryan's Was Lord Cardigan a hero at Balaklava?* 1855; *The trial of James Thomas, Earl of Cardigan* 1841; *Baily's Mag. xv,* 55–60 (1868), *portrait; I.L.N. iv,* 216 (1844), *portrait, lii,* 353 (1868), *portrait.*

CARDWELL, EDWARD CARDWELL, 1 Viscount (*elder son of John Cardwell of Liverpool, merchant 1781–1831*). *b.* 24 July 1813; ed. at Winchester and Balliol coll. Ox., double first

CARDWELL, VISCOUNT. (Con.)

class 1835, B.A. 1835, M.A. 1838, D.C.L. 1863; scholar of his college 1832, fellow 1835; barrister I.T. 16 Nov. 1838, bencher 28 April 1868; M.P. for Clitheroe 1842–7, for Liverpool 1847–52, for city of Oxford 1852–7 and 21 July 1857 to 6 March 1874; joint sec. to Treasury Feb. 1845 to July 1846; pres. of Board of trade 28 Dec. 1852 to Feb. 1855; P.C. 28 Dec. 1852; chief sec. for Ireland June 1859 to July 1861; P.C. Ireland 5 July 1859; chancellor of duchy of Lancaster 25 July 1861 to March 1864; sec. of state for Colonies March 1864 to June 1866; sec. of state for war 9 Dec. 1868 to 21 Feb. 1874; reorganised army by abolishing purchase system 20 July 1871 and introducing short service; created Viscount Cardwell of Ellerbeach 6 March 1874; an ecclesiastical comr. to Nov. 1882; pres. of commission on Vivisection 23 June 1875 to March 1876. *d.* Villa Como, Torquay 15 Feb. 1886. *bur.* Highgate cemetery. *St. James's Mag. Jany.* 1870 *pp.* 527–32, *portrait; I.L.N. iv,* 65 (1844), *portrait, xlvi,* 251 (1865), *portrait, liv,* 436 (1869), *portrait.*

CARDWELL, REV. EDWARD (*youngest son of Richard Cardwell of Blackburn 1749–1824*). *b.* Blackburn 3 Aug. 1787; ed. at Brasn. coll. Ox., fellow 1809; B.A. 1809, M.A. 1812, B.D. 1819, D.D. 1831; select preacher 1823; Camden professor of ancient history 1825 to death; R. of Stoke Bruerne, Northamptonshire 1828–36; principal of St. Alban hall Ox. Oct. 1831 to death; published *Aristotle's Ethica* 2 vols. 1828–30; *Enchiridion theologicum Anti-Romanum* 3 vols. 1836–7; *Josephus de bello Judaico* 2 vols. 1837; *Documentary annals of the reformed church of England* 2 vols. 1839; *Synodalia, a collection of articles of religion* 2 vols. 1842. *d.* Principal's lodge, St. Alban hall Oxford 23 May 1861. *G.M. xi,* 208–11 (1861).

CAREW, ROBERT SHAPLAND CAREW, 1 Baron (*only son of Robert Shapland Carew of Castleborough, Ross, co. Wexford who d. 25 March 1835*). *b.* Dublin 9 March 1787; ed. at Eton and Ch. Ch. Ox.; M.P. for co. Wexford 19 Oct. 1812 to 13 June 1834 when he was created Baron Carew of co. Wexford in peerage of Ireland; created Baron Carew of Castleborough, co. Wexford in peerage of United Kingdom 9 July 1838; lord lieut. of Wexford 1831 to death; K.P. 1851. *d.* Castleborough 2 June 1856.

CAREW, ROBERT SHAPLAND CAREW, 2 Baron (*eld. son of the preceding*). *b.* Dublin 28 Jany. 1818; M.P. for Waterford 24 Aug. 1840 to

CAREW, BARON. (Con.)

23 July 1847; hon. col. Wexford militia 5 April 1847 to death; lord lieut. of Wexford 2 July 1856 to death; K.P. 1872. *d.* 28 Belgrave sq. London 8 Sep. 1881.

CAREW, JOHN EDWARD. *b.* Tramore, Waterford 1782; assistant to Sir Richard Westmacott the sculptor in London 1809–23; worked for Lord Egremont 1823–31; sculptor at Brighton 1831–5; executed a statue of Huskisson for Chichester Cathedral, an altarpiece for the R.C. ch. St. James's st. Brighton, statues called 'Arethusa' and 'The Falconer'; exhibited at the R.A. 1830–48; made a claim of £50,000 upon Lord Egremont's estate on his death 11 Nov. 1837, brought an action against the executors 1840 when he was nonsuited; insolvent 1841; executed statue of 'Whittington listening to the London bells'; designed bas-relief of 'The death of Nelson at Trafalgar' in south panel of Nelson column Trafalgar sq. *d.* 40 Cambridge st. Hyde park, London 30 Nov. 1868. *Report of trial of cause Carew against Burrell 1840; Report of proceedings in Court for relief of Insolvent debtors in matter of J. E. Carew 1842; Reg. and mag. of biog. i,* 227 (1869).

CAREW, MOST REV. PATRICK JOSEPH. Professor of divinity at Maynooth; R.C. bishop of Madras 1838–40; vicar apostolic of Bengal 1840 to death; archbishop of Edessa. *d.* Bengal 2 Nov. 1855.

CAREW, SIR WALTER PALK, 8 Baronet. *b.* Marley house, Buckfastleigh, Devon 9 July 1807; succeeded 31 Oct. 1830; sheriff of Devon 1846. *d.* Marley house 27 Jany. 1874.

CAREY, REV. CHARLES STOKES. *b.* London 17 Sep. 1828; ed. at Hackney college 1849–53; matric. at Univ. of London but did not take any degree; ordained a Congregational minister 15 Sep. 1853; minister at Basingstoke, Harwich, Bungay and Leytonstone 1853–75; author of *The strength of Judah and the vengeance of Asshur, A tale of the times of Isaiah* 1862; *The Bible or the Bishop? A reply to parts 1 and 2 of Dr. Colenso's attack on the Pentateuch* 1863; *Plainer words on absolution, Privately printed* 1870; *A commonplace book of epigrams analytically arranged* 1872; edited *A concordance to the Old and New Testament by A. Cruden* 1867 *and* 1880. *d.* Leytonstone 8 June 1875.

CAREY, EUSTACE (*youngest child of Thomas Carey of Paulerspury, Northamptonshire*). *b.* Paulerspury 22 March 1791; baptized 7 July 1809; studied at Olney 1809–12, at Bristol

college 1812–3 ; sailed from Portsmouth for
India 18 Feb. 1814, landed at Serampore 1
Aug. 1814 ; missionary at Calcutta Sep. 1815 ;
returned to England 1825. *d.* 3 Eastcott
place, Camden Town, London 19 July 1855.
*Eustace Carey a missionary in India a memoir
by Mrs. Eustace Carey* 1857, *portrait*.

CAREY, George Jackson. *b.* Rozel, Guernsey
5 Oct. 1822 ; ensign Cape mounted riflemen
22 July 1845 ; served in Kaffir wars 1846–7
and 1850–2 ; brigadier general in New Zealand Aug. 1863 to Aug. 1865, Wm. Thompson the Maori chief surrendered to him 27
May 1865 ; acting governor of Victoria 7 May
to 15 Aug. 1866 ; commanded 2 brigade at
Aldershot 1 Dec. 1867 and Northern district
Oct. 1871 to death ; C.B. 18 March 1865. *d.*
Westwood, Whalley Range, Manchester 12
June 1872. *bur.* at Rozel.

CAREY, James *(son of Francis Carey of Dublin,
bricklayer).* *b.* James st. Dublin 1845 ; bricklayer in Dublin 18 years ; builder in Denzille
st. Dublin ; a leading member of the Fenians
1862–78 ; treasurer of Irish Republican
Brotherhood ; a town councillor of Dublin
1882 ; took part in murder of Lord F.
Cavendish and T. F. Burke 6 May 1882 ;
turned Queen's evidence 13 Feb. 1883 ;
sailed for Cape Town 6 July 1883 ; shot by
Patrick O'Donnel a Fenian on board Melrose
Castle steamer 12½ miles from Cape Vacca
29 July 1883. *Pall Mall Gazette 31 July
1883 pp.* 10–12, *portrait; Graphic xxvii*, 200,
273 (1883), *portrait, xxviii*, 112 (1883), *portrait*.

CAREY, Ven. James Gaspard Le Marchant.
Educ. at Trin. coll. Cam., B.A. 1853, M.A.
1856 ; R. of Snodland, Kent 1866–74 ; hon.
canon of Rochester 1870–7 ; V. of Boreham,
Essex 1874 to death ; hon. canon of St.
Alban's 1877 ; archdeacon of Essex 29 June
1882. *d.* Folkestone 17 March 1885 in 54 year.

CAREY, Peter. Cornet 16 Dragoons 9 Dec.
1795 ; major 86 foot 26 March 1807 ; lieut.
col. 84 foot 18 July 1811 to 25 Feb. 1818
when placed on h.p. ; military sec. to Sir
George Beckwith, commander of forces in
Ireland 1816–20 ; general 11 Nov. 1851.
d. 44 Cadogan place, London 20 June 1852
aged 78.

CAREY, Sir Peter Stafford *(only child of
Peter Martin Carey of Taunton).* *b.* Guernsey
7 April 1803 ; ed. at Clifton and St. John's
coll. Ox., B.A. 1825, M.A. 1829 ; barrister
M.T. 25 June 1830 ; recorder of Dartmouth
1836–45 ; judge of Borough court of Wells

1838–45 ; professor of English law at Univ.
coll. London 1838–45 ; bailiff of Guernsey
1845–83 ; knighted at Windsor Castle 23
Nov. 1863 ; author of *Borough Court rules of
England and Wales* 1841 ; *The Epistle of the
Apostle Paul to the Galatians with a paraphrase
and introduction* 1867 ; *Notes sur l'Ile de
Guernesey* 1874. *d.* 17 Jany. 1886. *Biograph
iii*, 6–8 (1880).

CAREY, Robert *(son of Sir Octavius Carey
1785–1844, major general).* *b.* 12 Dec. 1821 ;
ensign 40 foot 15 Nov. 1839, major 6 Aug.
1858 to 28 Oct. 1859 when placed on h.p. ;
deputy adjutant general in Australia 12 March
1860 to 6 Aug. 1863 ; D.A.G. in New Zealand 7 Aug. 1863 to 31 March 1866 ; M.G.
22 July 1869 ; deputy judge advocate 1 Aug.
1870 to 31 March 1882 ; C.B. 2 May 1862,
granted Service reward 8 March 1875. *d.* 17
Belgrave road, London 25 Jany. 1883.

CARFRAE, John. Entered Madras army 1797 ;
colonel 50 Madras N.I. 15 May 1834 to death ;
general 5 March 1859 ; author of *The pilgrim
of sorrow being a collection of odes, lyrics, etc.*
1848. *d.* Bower house, Dunbar 29 Aug. 1860.

CARGILL, Jasper Farmer. Barrister M.T.
11 June 1841 ; a revising barrister at Kingston, Jamaica 1848 ; acting chairman of
quarter sessions there 1855 ; judge of supreme
court, Jamaica 1856 to death. *d.* Kingston
27 Nov. 1871 in 65 year.

CARINGTON, Robert John Carington, 2
Baron *(only son of Robert Smith, 1 Baron
Carington 1752–1838).* *b.* St. James's place,
London 16 Jany. 1796 ; ed. at Eton and
Christ's coll. Cam., M.A. 1815 ; M.P. for
Wendover 1818–20, for Bucks 1820–31, for
Chipping Wycombe 1831 to 18 Sep. 1838
when he succeeded his father ; F.R.S. 14
Feb. 1839 ; col. of Royal Bucks. militia 7
March 1839 to death ; took surname of
Carington in lieu of Smith by royal license
26 Aug. 1839 ; lord lieutenant of Bucks. 20
Feb. 1839 to death. *d.* Wycombe abbey,
Bucks. 17 March 1868.

CARLETON, John William. Cornet 4 dragoons 2 July 1807, lieut. 11 April 1809 to 5
June 1817 when placed on h.p. ; the first
editor of the *Sporting Review* 1839 ; edited
The sporting sketch book 1842 ; published under
pseudonym of "Craven" *Hyde Marston, or a
sportsman's life* 3 vols. 1844 which is autobiographical ; *Recreations in shooting with some
account of the game of the British isles* 1846.
d. Hayes, Middlesex 29 May 1856. *Sporting
Review iii*, 3 (1840), *portrait*.

CARLETON, JOHN WILLIAM (eld. son of Andrew Carleton of Hermitage, co. Leitrim). b. Hermitage 1812; ed. at Elphin and Trin. coll. Dublin, B.A. 1834, M.A. 1856; called to Irish bar Jany. 1839; Q.C. 4 July 1860; author of A practical treatise on the law of judgment and judgment debts in Ireland 1844; The law relating to the qualification and registration of parliamentary voters in Ireland 1852; A compendium of the practice at elections of members to serve in Parliament as regulated by the several statutes in force in Ireland 1857, 6 ed. 1865. d. Dublin 11 Nov. 1878.

CARLETON, REV. RICHARD (youngest son of 1 Baron Dorchester 1724–1808). b. Portman sq. London 10 Feb. 1792; ed. at Trin. hall Cam., M.A. 1811; R. of Boughton, co. Northampton 1819–43; R. of Nateley-Scures, Hants. 1819 to death; F.R.S. 9 Feb. 1826. d. Brighton 2 Feb. 1869.

CARLETON, WILLIAM (youngest child of Mr. Carleton of Prillisk near Clogher, co. Tyrone, farmer). b. Prillisk 20 Feb. 1798; private tutor in family of a farmer named Murphy in co. Louth; settled at Dublin 1830; granted a civil list pension of £200, 14 July 1848; author of Traits and stories of the Irish peasantry 1830, 2 series 1833, 11 ed. 1876; Tales of Ireland 1834; Fardorougha the miser 1839, dramatised and produced at a Dublin theatre; Valentine McClutchy the Irish agent 3 vols. 1845, 3 ed. 1859; The Squanders of Castle Squander 2 vols. 1852, 2 ed. 1873. d. Woodville, Sandford, Dublin 30 Jany. 1869. Dublin Univ. Mag. xvii, 66–72 (1841), portrait, xxvi, 737–47 (1845).

CARLETON, WILLIAM. b. Dublin about 1835; made his début in America 26 Feb. 1866 as a vocalist at Tony Pastor's opera house Bowery New York, and as an actor Feb. 1868 at the Worrell Sisters theatre N.Y. in drama of Pickwick; author of many Irish plays, farces and songs; committed suicide by suffocation in New York, Aug. 1885.

CARLILE, REV. JAMES. b. Paisley 1784; ed. at Glasgow Univ. D.D.; minister of the Scots church St. Mary's Abbey, Dublin 1813 to death; acted as their missionary to Parsonstown 1839–51; resident comr. to Irish Board of education 1830–9; author of Examination of arguments for Roman Catholic episcopacy 1815; Letters on the divine origin and authority of scripture 2 vols. 1833; Manual of the anatomy and physiology of the human mind 1851, 2 ed. 1859. d. Dublin 31 March 1854. Rev. J. Carlile's Station and occupation of the saints in their final glory (1854) pp. v–xxxv and 139–65.

CARLILE, REV. WARRAND (12 child of James Carlile of Paisley, thread manufacturer). b. Paisley 12 Nov. 1796; ed. at Glasgow Univ.; licensed by presbytery of Paisley; Presbyterian minister at Carlow 1836–42; missionary at Brownsville Hanover, Jamaica, Jany. 1843 to death; visited the United States 1854 and England 1858 and 1863. d. Brownsville 25 Aug. 1881. Thirty-eight years mission life in Jamaica, a brief sketch of the Rev. W. Carlile by One of his sons (1884).

CARLISLE, GEORGE WILLIAM FREDERICK HOWARD, 7 Earl of (eld. son of 6 Earl of Carlisle 1773–1848). b. Hill st. Berkeley sq. London 18 April 1802; ed. at Eton and Ch. Ch. Ox., B.A. 1823, M.A. 1827; M.P. for Morpeth 1826–30, for Yorkshire 1830–2 and for West Riding of Yorkshire 1832–41 and 4 Feb. 1846 to 7 Oct. 1848 when he succeeded; chief sec. for Ireland 22 April 1835 to 6 Sep. 1841; P.C. 20 May 1835; P.C. Ireland 30 Sep. 1835; chief comr. of woods and forests 6 July 1846 to March 1850; lord lieut. of East riding of Yorkshire 22 July 1847; F.R.S. 3 June 1847; chancellor of Duchy of Lancaster 6 March 1850 to Feb. 1852; lord rector of Univ. of Aberdeen March 1853; K.G. 7 Feb. 1855; lord lieut. of Ireland 28 Feb. 1855 to 26 Feb. 1858 and 18 June 1859 to Oct. 1864; grand master of order of St. Patrick 1855–8 and 1859–64; author of Diary in Turkish and Greek waters 1854; Daniel's second vision; paraphrase in verse 1858. d. Castle Howard, Malton, Yorkshire 5 Dec. 1864. My reminiscences by Lord Ronald Gower i, 111–95 (1883); H. Lonsdale's Worthies of Cumberland iii, 125–88 (1872); Lord W. P. Lennox's Celebrities I have known, 2 series i, 131–61 (1877); H. Martineau's Biographical sketches, 4 ed. (1876) 131–42; Orators of the age by G. H. Francis (1847) 206–16; Waagen's Treasures of art ii, 278–80 (1854), iii, 317–32 (1854); Drawing room portrait gallery, 2 series (1859), portrait; I.L.N. xxvi, 280 (1855), portrait.

CARLOS, EDWARD JOHN (only child of Wm. Carlos of Newington, Middlesex). b. Newington 12 Feb. 1798; an attorney in City of London 1820 to death; contributed to Gent. Mag. reviews of architectural books 1822–48 and a series of descriptions of new churches in London 1824–33; author of Historical and antiquarian notices of Crosby hall 1832; G. Skelton's Oxonia restaurata, 2 ed. 1843; author with W. Knight of An account of London bridge with observations on its architecture during its demolition 1832. d. York place, Walworth, London 20 Jany. 1851.

CARLYLE, JANE BAILLIE (*only child of John Welsh of Haddington, surgeon 1776–1819*). *b.* Haddington 14 July 1801; ed. at Haddington school; known from her wit and beauty as 'the flower of Haddington.' (*m.* at Templand 17 Oct. 1826, Thomas Carlyle 1795–1881); lived at 5 Cheyne row, Chelsea 10 June 1834 to death. *d.* in her carriage in Hyde park, London 21 April 1866. *bur.* at Haddington. *Letters and memorials of Jane Welsh Carlyle, edited by J. A. Froude 3 vols. 1883, portrait; Graphic xxiii, 160 (1881), portrait.*

CARLYLE, JOHN AITKEN (*2 son of James Carlyle of Ecclefechan, Dumfriesshire, mason 1757–1832*). *b.* Ecclefechan 7 July 1801; ed. at Univ. of Edin., M.D. 1825; travelling physician to Countess of Clare 1831–7, to Duke of Buccleuch 1838–43; published *Dante's Divine comedy, the Inferno with the text of the original collated from the best editions and explanatory notes 1849, 3 ed. 1882;* edited *Irving's History of Scottish poetry 1861;* made over in 1878 to acting committee of Association for better endowment of Univ. of Edin. £1,600 to found 2 medical bursaries of not less than £25 each tenable for one year. *d.* Dumfries 15 Dec. 1879. *Graphic xxiii, 160 (1881), portrait.*

CARLYLE, THOMAS (*brother of the preceding*). *b.* Ecclefechan 4 Dec. 1795; ed. at Annan school and Univ. of Edinburgh; teacher of mathematics in a school at Annan 1814–6; schoolmaster at Kirkcaldy 1816–8; studied law at Edin. and took pupils 1819–22; tutor to Arthur and Charles Buller 1822–4; lived at 21 Comely bank close to Edinburgh 1826–8, at Craigenputtock 16 miles from Dumfries 1828–34, at 5 Cheyne row, Chelsea 10 June 1834 to death; gave lectures in London, May 1837, 1838, 1839 and 1840; lord rector of Univ. of Edin. Nov. 1865, installed 29 March 1866; pres. of Edinburgh philosophical institution 1868 and 1877; pres. of London library, St. James's sq. London, July 1870 to death, having been the first person to suggest formation of the library; received Prussian order of Merit, Feb. 1874; author of *Life of Schiller 1825, 2 ed. 1845; Wilhelm Meister's apprenticeship 3 vols. 1824; Sartor Resartus 1835; History of the French revolution 3 vols. 1837; Life and letters of Oliver Cromwell 2 vols. 1845; The life of Frederick the Great 6 vols. 1858–65. d.* 5 Cheyne row, Chelsea 5 Feb. 1881, the house was renumbered 24 in Sep. or Oct. 1881. *bur.* Ecclefechan churchyard 10 Feb. *Thomas Carlyle, a history of the first 40 years of his life by J. A. Froude 2 vols. 1882, portraits; Thomas Carlyle, a history of*

his life in London by J. A. Froude 2 vols. 1884, portraits; Memoir by R. H. Shepherd 2 vols. 1881; J. B. Crozier's Religion of the future (1880) 1–104; *Obiter dicta* (1884) 1–54; *R. H. Horne's New spirit of the age ii,* 253–80 (1844) *portrait; Biographical Mag. i,* 1–22 (1877); *The Maclise portrait gallery by W. Bates* (1883) 172–8, *portrait; Dict. of national biog. ix,* 111–27 (1887).

NOTE.—On the eightieth anniversary of his birth, 4 Dec. 1875, a gold medal was struck in his honour and an address signed by upwards of 100 men and women eminent in science, literature and art was presented to him; a bronze statue of him by J. E. Boehm in the public garden at end of Great Cheyne row, Chelsea was unveiled by Professor Tyndall 26 Oct. 1882. He is drawn by Anthony Trollope in his novel *The Warden* under name of "Dr. Pessimist Anticant."

CARLYLE, THOMAS (*son of Wm. Carlyle of King's Grange, Kirkcudbrightshire*). *b.* King's Grange 17 July 1803; ed. at Annan, Dumfries and Univ. of Edin.; called to Scottish bar 1824; practised in Edin. 1824–35; counsel for Rev. J. M. Campbell in the Row heresy case 1831; claim to dormant title of Baron Carlyle devolved on him Oct. 1824; named the ninth apostle of Catholic Apostolic church, April 1835, the Apostle for North Germany 1838; author of *An essay to illustrate the foundation of Christianity By a Layman 1827; The moral phenomena of Germany 1845; A short history of the Apostolic work 1851; Our present position in spiritual chronology 1853, another ed. 1879* and 19 other books. *d.* Heath house, Albury, Surrey 28 Jany. 1855. *Miller's Irvingism i, 14, ii, 416; Athenæum 14 May 1881 p. 654.*

CARLYON, CLEMENT (*4 son of Rev. John Carlyon 1722–98, R. of Bradwell, Essex*). *b.* Truro, Cornwall 14 April 1777; ed. at Truro gr. sch. and Pemb. coll. Cam., tenth wrangler 1798, B.A. 1798, M.A. 1801, M.L. 1804, M.D. 1813; elected travelling bachelor 1798; physician at Truro 1806–61; mayor of Truro 5 times; author of *Latin letters to the Vice Chancellor of Cambridge, Gottingen 1799–1800; Observations on the endemic typhus fever of Cornwall 1827; Early years and late reflections 2 vols. 1836–43, 2 ed. 4 vols. 1856–8; Scripture notices and proofs 1838. d.* Truro 5 March 1864. *G.M. xvi, 797–8 (1864).*

CARLYON, EDWARD AUGUSTUS (*2 son of major general Edward Carlyon of Tregrehan near Par, Cornwall 1783–1854*). *b.* 3 June 1823; barrister L.I. 19 Nov. 1850; author of *The laws and practice of whist by Cœlebs [E. A. Carlyon] 1851, 3 ed. 1858. d.* Gwavas Napier, New Zealand 4 Dec. 1874.

CARMENT, Rev. David (*son of James Carment of Keiss near Wick, schoolmaster*). *b.* Keiss 28 Sep. 1772; entered King's college Aberdeen Nov. 1791, M.A. 1795; parish schoolmaster of Strath, Isle of Skye 1795–9; licensed to preach by presbytery of Skye 4 April 1799; assistant minister of Croy near Inverness March 1803; minister of Gaelic chapel in Duke st. Glasgow April 1810; minister of parish of Roskeen 14 March 1822 to 1 Aug. 1843; a member of the Assembly 1825; took an active part in the Disruption controversy 1842–3; minister of a church built for him in Roskeen 1845 to July 1852; author of *The fiery cross* 1842. *d.* 26 May 1856. *J. A. Wylie's Disruption Worthies* (1881) 147–52.

CARMICHAEL, Charles Montauban. *b.* 21 Sep. 1790; cornet Bengal army 27 March 1806; colonel 8 Bengal light cavalry 1852–8; L.G. 14 April 1862; colonel 20 Hussars 30 Sep. 1862 to death; C.B. 20 Dec. 1839. *d.* Hotel du Louvre, Boulogne 21 Nov. 1870.

CARMICHAEL, James (*son of George Carmichael of the Trongate, Glasgow, merchant*). *b.* Glasgow, 1776; millwright with his brother Charles at Dundee 1810; fitted up first twin steam-boat for ferry across the Tay at Dundee 1821; invented planing, shaping and boring machine used at Woolwich and Portsmouth; made locomotive steam engines for Dundee and Newtyle railway 1832–3 the first locomotives made in Scotland; invented fan blast or blowing machine for heating and melting iron, brought into practical use about 1829. *d.* Fleuchar Craig, Dundee 14 Aug. 1853, bronze statue of him erected in Albert sq. Dundee. *W. Norrie's Dundee Celebrities* (1873) 144–7; *I.L.N. lxix*, 245 (1876).

CARMICHAEL, Sir James Robert, 2 Baronet. *b.* Devonshire place, London 11 June 1817; ed. at Charterhouse and Sandhurst; succeeded 4 March 1838; a claimant to Scottish earldom of Hyndford; chairman of the Submarine and of the Mediterranean extension telegraph companies. *d.* 12 Sussex place, Regent's park, London 7 June 1883.

CARMICHAEL, James (or John) Wilson. *b.* Newcastle 1800; apprenticed to a shipbuilder; a marine painter; went to London about 1845; exhibited 21 sea pieces at R.A. 21 at B.I. and 6 at Suffolk st. gallery 1835–62; author of *The art of marine painting in water colours* 1859; *The art of marine painting in oil colours* 1864. *d.* Scarborough 2 May 1868.

CARMICHAEL, Sir Thomas Gibson, 12 Baronet. *b.* Castle Craig, Peebleshire 27 Oct. 1817; commander R.N. 9 Nov. 1846; succeeded 8 May 1850. *d.* Civita Vecchia, Italy 30 Dec. 1855.

CARNAC, John Rivett. *b.* 28 June 1796; Midshipman 29 April 1812; captain 10 Jany. 1837; retired V.A. 30 Nov. 1863. *d.* 34 Seymour st. Portman sq. London 1 Jany. 1869.

CARNAC, Sir John Rivett, 2 Baronet (*son of Sir James Rivett Carnac, 1 baronet 1784–1846*). *b.* Baroda, East Indies 10 Aug. 1818; succeeded 28 Jany. 1846; M.P. for Lymington 1852 to 1860. *d.* Winchester 4 Aug. 1883. *I.L.N. xxii*, 293 (1853), *portrait.*

CARNE, Elizabeth Catherine Thomas (4 *dau. of the succeeding*). *b.* Rivière house, Phillack, Cornwall 16 Dec. 1817; head of bank of Batten, Carne, and Carne at Penzance 1858 to death; gave site for Elizabeth or St. Paul's schools opened at Penzance 2 Feb. 1876; founded schools at Wesley Rock, Carfury and Bosullo all near Penzance; built a museum at Penzance for her fine collection of minerals; author of *Three months rest at Pau in the winter and spring of 1859 by John Altrayd Wittiterly pseud.* 1860; *Country towns and the place they fill in modern civilisation* 1868; *England's three wants, anon.* 1871; *The realm of truth* 1873 and of many articles in *London Quarterly Review. d.* Penzance 7 Sep. 1873. *Boase and Courtney's Bibl. Cornub.* 60, 1113; *Geol. Mag. x*, 480, 524 (1873).

CARNE, Joseph (*eld. son of Wm. Carne of Penzance, banker 1754–1836*). *b.* Truro 17 April 1782; manager of Cornish Copper company's smelting works at Hayle 1810 or 1811; partner in bank of Batten, Carne, and Carne at Penzance 1820 to death; F.R.S. 28 May 1818; pricked for sheriff of Cornwall 1837 but declined to serve; pres. of Penzance Natural history and antiquarian soc. 1849–55; author of many papers in *Transactions of Royal Geol. Soc. of Cornwall 1816–51. d.* 28 Chapel st. Penzance 12 Oct. 1858. *Boase and Courtney's Bibl. Cornub.* 61, 1114.

CARNEGIE, John William. Entered Bengal army 1833; major 15 Bengal N.I. 30 Sep. 1860 to 6 June 1862; C.B. 18 May 1860. *d.* Gipsy hill near London 6 Jany. 1874.

CARNEGIE, Swynfen Thomas (*youngest son of 7 Earl of Northesk 1758–1831*). *b.* Rosehill, Hampshire 8 March 1813; entered navy 3 Aug. 1826; served in operations connected with civil war in Spain 1833–8, received order of San Fernando; captain R.N. 10

June 1845; C.B. 5 July 1855; officer in command of defences of the Thames and superintendent of steam naval organisation at Sheerness 1852; controller general of coast guard 6 Feb. to 27 April 1863; retired admiral 18 June 1876; M.P. for Stafford 1841-7; a lord of the treasury 11 March to 6 July 1846; a lord of the admiralty 9 March 1859. *d.* 16 Pelham crescent, London 29 Nov. 1879. *I.L.N. xx,* 172 (1852), *portrait.*

CARNEGY, ALEXANDER. *b.* 25 Feb. 1793; ensign Bengal army 20 Aug. 1813; lieut. col. of 15 Bengal N.I. 5 Nov. 1841, of 27 N.I. 1843, of 36 N.I. 1849-51; col. 15 N.I. 15 Sep. 1851 to death; commissioner at Peshawar, Punjab 26 June 1852; M.G. 28 Nov. 1854; C.B. 9 June 1849. *d.* Meggetland house, Edinburgh 1 Aug. 1862.

CARNEGY, PATRICK. *b.* 20 May 1825; entered Indian civil service 1846; assistant comr. in Oude 1856; deputy comr. of Lucknow district; comr. of the Bareilly division; first civil officer who entering service in uncovenanted branch, ever attained rank of a comr.; C.I.E. 1 Jany. 1878; F.R.G.S.; author of *Kutcherry technicalities or vocabulary of law terms as used in the Mofussil courts N.W.P. Allahabad* 1853; *Notes on the land tenures and revenue assessments of Upper India* 1874. *d.* Norwood near London 12 Nov. 1886.

CARNWATH, THOMAS HENRY DALZELL, 11 Earl of. *b.* 2 Sep. 1797; succeeded 1 Jany. 1839. *d.* Bagnéres de Bigorre, Hautes Pyrénées, France 14 Dec. 1867.

CARNWATH, HENRY ARTHUR HEW DALZELL, 12 Earl of. *b.* Heidelberg 12 April 1858; succeeded 14 Dec. 1867. *d.* Harrow school 13 March 1873.

CARNWATH, ARTHUR ALEXANDER DALZELL, 13 Earl of (2 *son of* 10 *Earl of Carnwath* 1768-1839). *b.* 15 Sep. 1799; ensign 45 foot 29 April 1819; captain 48 foot 28 June 1827, lieut. col. 23 April 1841 to 13 Dec. 1853 when placed on h.p.; inspecting field officer of militia 1853-8; commanded south eastern district of England 1861-5; col. 48 foot 10 Aug. 1864 to death; general 14 April 1873; succeeded his nephew 13 March 1873. *d.* 28 Eaton place, London 28 April 1875.

CARON, RÉNÉ EDOUARD (*son of Augustin Caron of parish of St. Anne Cote of Beaupré, Lower Canada*). *b.* St. Anne, Nov. or Dec. 1800; barrister Lower Canada 1826; member of city council of Quebec 1832, mayor 1833-7;

M.P. for Upper town of Quebec 1834-6; Q.C. 1848; member of legislative council of Canada 1841-57, speaker 8 Nov. 1843 to 1847 and 11 March 1848 to 1853, member of executive council 28 Oct. 1851; puisne judge of superior court 15 Aug. 1853, of Court of Queen's Bench, Quebec 27 Jany. 1855; lieutenant governor of province of Quebec 11 Feb. 1873 to death. *d.* Quebec 13 Dec. 1876. *Morgan's Sketches of eminent Canadians* (1862) 472-3.

CARPENTER, GEORGE (*son of the succeeding*). Ensign 53 foot 1 Oct. 1818; lieut. col. 41 foot 27 Dec. 1850 to death; killed at battle of Inkerman 5 Nov. 1854 in 55 year. *G. Ryan's Our heroes in the Crimea* (1855) 70-2.

CARPENTER, GEORGE. Entered Bengal army 1791; colonel 49 Bengal N.I. 29 April 1823 to death; general 20 June 1854. *d.* 7 Great Cumberland place, London 30 Jany. 1855 aged 91.

CARPENTER, JOSEPH EDWARDS. *b.* London 2 Nov. 1813; wrote for magazines at a very early age; gave a musical entertainment called *The Road, the Rail and the River* in London and the provinces; produced *The Sanctuary* a musical drama in 2 acts 1854, *Love and Honour* a drama in 3 acts at Surrey theatre 1854 and *Adam Bede* a drama in 3 acts at same house 1862; author of upwards of 2500 songs and duets; edited *Penny Readings in prose and verse* 10 vols. 1865-7; author of *Random rhymes or lays of London* 1833; *Lays for light hearts* 1835; *Songs and ballads* 1844; *Poems and lyrics* 1845; *Border ballads* 1846; *Lays and legends of fairy land* 1849; *My jubilee volume* 1883. *d.* 20 Norland sq. Bayswater, London 6 May 1885. *Illust. news of the world ii,* 425 (1858), *portrait.*

CARPENTER, MARGARET SARAH (2 *dau. of Alexander Geddes of Alderbury, Wiltshire*). *b.* Salisbury 1793; portrait painter in London 1814; exhibited 147 pictures at the R.A. 50 at B.I. and 19 at Suffolk st. gallery 1818-66; granted civil list pension of £100 per annum 29 Nov. 1866. (*m.* 1817 Wm. Hookham Carpenter 1792-1866). *d.* 22 Upper Gloucester place, London 13 Nov. 1872. *E. C. Clayton's English female artists i,* 386-8 (1876).

CARPENTER, MARY (*eld. child of Rev. Lant Carpenter of Bristol, Unitarian minister 1780-1840*). *b.* Exeter 3 April 1807; kept a school with her mother at Bristol 1829; opened a ragged school in Bristol 1 Aug. 1846, a reformatory at Kingswood 11 Sep. 1852, a reformatory for girls in Park row, Bristol 10 Oct. 1854 and a certified industrial school there April 1859 ; took leading part in conferences on ragged schools held in Birmingham, Dec. 1851, Dec. 1853 and Jany, 1861 ; visited India 1866–7, 1868–9, 1869–70 and 1875–6 ; visited America and Canada 1873 ; read many papers at meetings of Social Science Association ; author of *Meditations and prayers anon.* 1845 ; *Our convicts, how they are made and should be treated* 2 vols. 1864 ; *Six months in India* 2 vols. 1868 and 9 other books. *d.* Bristol 14 June 1877. *Life and work of Mary Carpenter by J. E. Carpenter* 1879, *portrait ; Theological Review, April* 1880 *p. 279 ; The children of the street by M. H. Hart* 1880 ; *Fortnightly Review xxxiii,* 662–71 (1880) ; *Graphic xv,* 624 (1877), *portrait ; Times* 18 June 1877 *p. 8, cols.* 3–5.

CARPENTER, Rev. PHILIP PEARSALL *(brother of the preceding). b.* Bristol, Nov. 1819 ; ed. at Bristol and York ; B.A. London 1841 ; Presbyterian minister at Stand, then at Warrington 1846–61 ; bought a vast collection of 14 tons of shells in Liverpool for £50, 1855, a full report on these shells occupies 209 pages of *British Association report for* 1856 ; lived in Montreal 1865 to death ; formed a great collection of Chitonidæ. *d.* Montreal 24 May 1877. *Memoir of P. P. Carpenter edited by R. L. Carpenter* 1880, *portrait.*

CARPENTER, RICHARD CROMWELL *(son of Richard Carpenter of Middlesex). b.* 21 Oct. 1812 ; ed. at the Charterhouse ; architect in London ; district surveyor for East Islington ; exhibited 9 works at R.A. 1830–49 ; built churches of St. Stephen and St. Andrew at Birmingham 1844 and 1846, St. Paul at Brighton 1849, and St. Mary Magdalen, Munster sq. London 1852 where the west window was filled with stained glass to his memory at a cost of £425 ; restored Chichester cathedral, Sherborne Abbey and St. John's college, Hurstpierpoint. *d.* 40 Upper Bedford place, Russell sq. London 27 March 1855.

CARPENTER, THOMAS DAVID. Entered Madras army 1819 ; lieut. col. 1 Madras N.I. 1 Sep. 1847 to 29 Aug. 1859 ; M.G. 29 Aug. 1859. *d.* Secunderabad 17 Oct. 1860 aged 56.

CARPENTER, WILLIAM. *b.* 1797 ; apprenticed to a bookseller in Finsbury ; edited with Wm. Greenfield *Scripture Magazine* afterwards expanded into the *Critica Biblica* 4 vols. 1824–7 ; edited *Shipping Gazette* 1836, *Era* 1838, *Railway Observer* 1843, *Lloyd's Weekly News* 1844, *Court Journal* 1848, *Sunday Times* 1854, *Bed-*

fordshire Independent 1854 ; issued a publication entitled *Political Letters* 1830–1 which was unstamped for which he was tried 14 May 1831 and imprisoned in the King's Bench ; from his prison he edited *Political Mag.* Sep. 1831 to July 1832, republished as *Carpenter's Monthly political mag.* 1832 ; hon. sec. to Chancery reform association 1851–3 ; author of *Sancta Biblica* 3 vols. 1825 ; *Scripture natural history* 1828 ; *A peerage for the people* 1835, 4 ed. 1848 ; *A comprehensive dictionary of English synonyms,* 6 ed. 1865 ; *An introducto the reading and study of the Bible* 3 vols. 1867–8. *d.* Colebrooke row, Islington, London 21 April 1874.

CARPENTER, WILLIAM BENJAMIN *(brother of Mary Carpenter* 1807–77). *b.* Exeter 29 Oct. 1813 ; M.R.C.S. and L.S.A. 1835 ; lecturer on medical jurisprudence at Bristol medical school ; Fullerian professor of physiology at Royal Institution London 1844 ; edited *British and Foreign Medico-Chirurgical Review* 1847–52 ; professor of forensic medicine at Univ. college London 1849–59 ; principal of University hall London 1851–9 ; registrar of Univ. of London May 1856 to Feb. 1879, F.R.S. 1 Feb. 1844, Royal medallist 1861 ; pres. of British Association at Brighton Aug. 1872 ; corresponding member of Institute of France 1873 ; C.B. 4 Dec. 1875 ; Lyell medallist of Geological Soc. 1883 ; author of *The principles of general and comparative physiology* 1839, 4 ed. 1854 ; *Popular cyclopædia of science* 1843 ; *Manual of physiology* 1846, 4 ed. 1865 ; *Introduction to the study of the Foraminifera, Ray Society* 1862. *d.* 56 Regent's park road, London 10 Nov. 1885. *J. Timbs's Year book of facts* (1873) 1–8, 126–33, *portrait ; Medical Circular ii,* 169–71 (1853), *portrait ; T. H. Barker's Photographs of medical men* (1865), *portrait ; I.L.N. lxi,* 148, 150 (1872), *portrait, lxxxvii,* 559 (1885), *portrait.*

CARPENTER, WILLIAM HOOKHAM *(only son of James Carpenter of Old Bond st. London, bookseller who d. 30 March 1852 aged 84). b.* Bruton st. London 2 March 1792 ; bookseller and publisher in Lower Brook st. London 1817 ; keeper of prints and drawings in British Museum, March 1845 to death ; a trustee of National portrait gallery 1856 to death ; member of Academy of fine arts at Amsterdam 1847 ; F.S.A. 13 Jany. 1853 ; author of *Pictorial notices, consisting of a memoir of Sir Anthony Van Dyck, with a descriptive catalogue of the etchings executed by him* 1844 ; *A guide to the drawings and prints exhibited to*

CARPENTER, W. H. (*Con.*)

the public in the *King's library, British Museum* 1858, 3 *ed.* 1862. *d.* British Museum, London 12 July 1866. *G.M. ii*, 410–11 (1866).

CARPMAEL, WILLIAM. *b.* 90 Chancery lane, London 27 Feb. 1804; designed and erected salt works in Cheshire which he managed; patent agent and consulting engineer in London 1835; A.I.C.E. 1830, M.I.C.E. 1840, member of council 1858; M.I.M.E. 1862; member of Metropolitan Board of Works from its formation 14 Aug. 1855 to his death; author of *The law of patents for inventions explained for the use of inventors and patentees* 1832 6 *ed.* 1860; *Law reports of patent cases* 3 *vols.* 1843–52. *d.* Streatham hill near London 9 July 1867.

CARR, REV. JAMES. *b.* April 1784; P.C. of South Shields 1831–62; hon. canon of Durham 1860 to death; master of Sherburn hospital, Durham 1862 to death. *d.* Sherburn hospital 29 March 1874.

CARR, JOHN CHARLES (*eld. son of John Carr of Trinidad*). *b.* Trinidad 1810; LL.B. London 1839; barrister G.I. 6 May 1840; Queen's advocate of Sierra Leone, May 1840, chief justice 20 Aug. 1841 to 1865; declined honour of knighthood twice. *d.* Bedford house, New Barnet 2 Sep. 1880 in 71 year.

CARR, MARK WILLIAM. Assistant inspector general of Madras police 12 Sep. 1862; major Madras staff corps 16 Feb. 1870 to death; author of *A collection of Telugu proverbs together with some Sanscrit proverbs* 1868; edited *Descriptive and historical papers relating to the seven pagodas on the Coromandel coast by W. Chambers and others* 1869; lost in wreck of " General Outram " off Rutnagherry on the coast of Malabar 16 Jany. 1871.

CARR, RIGHT REV. THOMAS. *b.* Yorkshire 1788; sizar St. John's coll. Cam. 10 June 1809; B.A. 1813; D.D. Lambeth 12 Sep. 1832; chaplain at Bombay; bishop of Bombay 15 July 1837 to July 1851, consecrated at Lambeth 19 Nov. 1837; R. of St. Peter and St. Paul *i.e.* The Abbey with St. James's, Bath, April 1854 to death. *d.* Lansdown crescent, Bath 5 Sep. 1859. *Illust. news of the world iv*, 177 (1859), *portrait.*

CARR, THOMAS. *b.* Durham 23 Jany. 1824; invented a new method of drying glue, the disintegrator a machine much used in various trades and manufactures, and a flour mill on the disintegrator principle which is a good deal used in Scotland. *d.* Bristol 29 March 1874.

CARR, SIR WILLIAM OGLE (3 *son of Thomas Wm. Carr of Frognal, Hampstead, barrister*). Barrister G.I. 26 April 1826; King's advocate in Ceylon; second puisne judge of Ceylon 19 Dec. 1839, chief justice 14 Aug. 1854 to death; knighted by patent 14 Aug. 1854. *d.* Candy, Ceylon 24 April 1856 aged 53.

CARRE, ROBERT RIDDELL. *b.* Edinburgh 27 Feb. 1782; entered navy 2 June 1796; placed on half pay 15 Nov. 1816; captain 12 Aug. 1819; retired V.A. 10 Sep. 1857. *d.* Caverse Carre, Roxburghshire 1 March 1860.

CARRICK, THOMAS (2 *child of John Carrick of Carlisle, cotton-mill owner*). *b.* Upperley near Carlisle 4 July 1802; a chemist at Carlisle to about 1830; miniature painter at Newcastle 1836, in London 1839–68; exhibited annually 8 miniatures at R.A. 1841–66, Turner annuitant 1868 to death; presented by Prince Albert with a medal for his invention of painting miniatures on marble 1845. *d.* Newcastle 31 July 1875.

CARRINGTON, FREDERICK AUGUSTUS (*only son of Rev. Caleb Carrington, V. of Berkeley, Gloucs. who d. 1839*). *b.* 1801; barrister L.I. 7 Feb. 1823; recorder of Wokingham, Oct. 1858 to death; published with Joseph Payne *Reports of cases argued and ruled at Nisi Prius* 9 *vols.* 1825–41. *d.* 28 Lincoln's Inn Fields, London 30 July 1860.

CARRINGTON, FREDERICK GEORGE (3 *son of Noel Thomas Carrington of Devonport, poet 1777–1830*). *b.* about 1816; contributed to the *Bath Chronicle, Felix Farley's Bristol Journal, Cornwall Gazette, West of England Conservative, Bristol Mirror* and *Gloucester Journal;* editor and proprietor of *Gloucestershire Chronicle;* wrote treatises on *Architecture* and *Painting* for Society for Diffusion of Useful Knowledge. *d.* Gloucester 1 Feb. 1864. *G.M. xvi*, 535 (1864).

CARRINGTON, HENRY EDMUND (*brother of the preceding*). *b.* Maidstone 16 March 1806; connected with the *Plymouth Journal, Devonport Telegraph, Sherborne Mercury,* and *Western Luminary;* edited the *Bath Chronicle;* author of *The Plymouth and Devonport guide with sketches of the surrounding scenery* 1828. *d.* Bath 5 Feb. 1859.

CARRINGTON, RICHARD CHRISTOPHER (2 *son of Richard Carrington of Brentford, brewer who d. July 1858*). *b.* Chelsea 26 May 1826; ed. at Hedley and Trin. coll. Cam., 36 wrangler 1848; B.A. 1848; observer in Univ. of Durham Oct. 1849 to April 1852; built a house at Redhill near Reigate with an observatory attached 1852–4; built an observatory on top of an isolated conical hill known as the Middle Devil's Jump at Churt Surrey 1866; F.R.A.S. 14 March 1851, hon. sec. Feb. 1857 to Feb. 1862, gold medallist 1859; F.R.S. 7 June 1860; author of *A catalogue of 3735 circumpolar stars observed at Redhill 1857 printed by the Admiralty; Observations of the spots on the sun from Nov. 9, 1853 to March 24, 1861 made at Redhill* 1863; found dead in his house at Churt 27 Nov. 1875. *Monthly notices of Royal Astronom. Soc. xxxvi,* 137–42 (1876); *I.L.N. lxviii,* 119 (1876), *portrait; Times* 22 Nov. 1875 *p.* 5, *col.* 3, 7 *Dec. p.* 11, *col.* 6.

CARROLL, SIR GEORGE. Stockbroker at 26 Oxford st. London 1811; contractor for state lotteries having offices in Cornhill, Oxford st. and Charing Cross, lotteries were abolished Oct. 1826; sheriff of London and Middlesex 1837–8; knighted at the Guildhall 9 Nov. 1837; an original director of London Joint Stock bank 1836; alderman of Candlewick ward 23 Dec. 1839 to death; lord mayor 1846–7; president of St. Bartholomew's hospital. *d.* Loughton, Essex 19 Dec. 1860 aged 76. *bur.* Norwood cemetery 27 Dec. *I.L.N. ix,* 295, 309 (1846), *portrait; City Press* 22 *Dec.* 1860 *p.* 5.

CARROLL, REV. RICHARD. *b.* Dublin 14 July 1807; entered Society of Jesus at Cheiri 18 Sep. 1825; ordained priest 20 Dec. 1834; professed of the four vows 2 Feb. 1845; superior of Seminary at Stonyhurst Sep. 1845 to Sep. 1849; sent to mission of St. Francis Xavier, Liverpool Sep. 1849 where he became distinguished as a preacher. *d.* Liverpool 14 Feb. 1858.

CARROLL, SIR WILLIAM FAIRBROTHER (3 *son of Daniel Carroll of Uskane, co. Tipperary, barrister*). *b.* Glencarrig, co. Wicklow 28 Jany. 1784; entered navy 5 Dec. 1795; captain 6 Dec. 1813; head of Bath police several years; R.A. 24 Jany. 1849; commander in chief at Cork 28 July 1853 to 13 Aug. 1855; lieutenant governor of Greenwich hospital 13 Aug. 1855 to death; C.B. 4 June 1815, K.C.B. 6 April 1852; was in action with the enemy 67 times. *d.* Greenwich hospital 8 April 1862.

CARROW, JOHN MONSON *(eld. son of Rev. Richard Carrow, R. of Broxholme, Lincs. who d. 20 Feb. 1847 aged 72).* Ed. at Trin. coll. Cam., B.A. 1831; barrister I.T. 31 Jany. 1834; judge of county courts, circuit 57, (Somerset) 13 March 1847 to death; recorder

of Wells 1852 to death; one of the authors of *Cases relating to railways and canals* 4 vols. 1840–8; and of *New Sessions cases* 3 vols. 1845–9. *d.* Weston-super-Mare 8 May 1853. *G.M. xxxix,* 668–9 (1853).

CARRUTHERS, RIGHT REV. ANDREW. *b.* Glenmillan near New Abbey in stewartry of Kircudbright 7 Feb. 1770; ed. at Scotch college, Douay; ordained priest 1795; stationed at Balloch, Perthshire, then at Traquair, Peebleshire, afterwards at Munchies and Dalbeattie; vicar apostolic of eastern district of Scotland 28 Sep. 1832 to death; consecrated at Edinburgh as bishop of Ceramis *in partibus infidelium* 13 Jany. 1833. *d.* Edinburgh 24 May 1852. *Gordon's Catholic church in Scotland* 474, *portrait.*

CARRUTHERS, RICHARD. Ensign 26 foot 19 May 1814; major 2 foot 19 Feb. 1836 to 23 July 1839 when he retired; C.B. 6 June 1840. *d.* 1 Brunswick gardens, Kensington, London 17 Feb. 1864 aged 63.

CARRUTHERS, ROBERT *(son of Mr. Carruthers of Mouswald, Dumfries, farmer).* *b.* Dumfries 5 Nov. 1799; master of national school at Huntingdon; edited *Inverness Courier,* April 1828 to death, he made it the most popular paper in North of Scotland, proprietor 1831; hon. LL.D. Edin. 21 April 1871; published *History of Huntingdon* 1824; *The Highland note book or sketches and anecdotes* 1843; *The poetical works of Alexander Pope* 4 vols. 1853; wrote with Robert Chambers most of the original matter in *Chambers's Cyclopædia of English literature* 2 vols. 1843–4. *d.* Inverness 26 May 1878. *G.M. Nov.* 1884 *pp.* 448–51; *I.L.N. lxii,* 557 (1878), *portrait.*

CARSON, RIGHT REV. THOMAS *(elder son of Rev. Thomas Carson 1763–1816, R. of Kilmahon, Cloyne).* *b.* Kilmahon rectory 27 Aug. 1805; ed. at Glanmire school and Trin. coll. Dublin; B.A. 1826, LL.B. and LL.D. 1832; V. of Urney, co. Cavan 1838; R. of Cloon and vicar general of Kilmore 1854; dean of Kilmore 1860; bishop of Kilmore, Elphin and Ardagh 1870 to death; consecrated at Armagh 2 Oct. 1870. *d.* Portrush, co. Antrim 7 July 1874.

CARSWELL, SIR ROBERT. *b.* Paisley 3 Feb. 1793; studied at Glasgow, Paris and Lyons; M.D. Marischal college, Aberdeen 1826; made a series of 2000 water-color drawings of diseased structures in Paris for University college, London 1828–31; professor of pathological anatomy at the college 1831–40; phys. to King of the Belgians at Lacken near

Brussells 1840 to death; knighted at St. James's palace 3 July 1850; author of *Illustrations of the elementary forms of disease, with coloured plates* 1837; and of 7 articles in *Cyclopædia of practical medicine* 4 vols. 1833–5. *d.* Lacken 15 June 1857.

CARTE, JOHN ELLIOT. Assistant surgeon in army 31 Dec. 1841; surgeon 14 foot 26 Jany. 1858; deputy inspector general 22 June 1870 to 17 Feb. 1872 when placed on h.p.; C.B. 5 July 1865. *d.* Portland place, Brighton 19 April 1876.

CARTER, GEORGE. *b.* Bromfield near Ludlow, Salop 29 Nov. 1792; whip to the Warwickshire hounds 1823–5, to Mr. West's harriers 1825–7; whip to Duke of Grafton 1827–31 and huntsman 1833–5; huntsman to Grantley Berkeley 1831–3; huntsman of the Tedworth hounds 1842–65; had few equals and no superiors whether in the kennel or in the field. *d.* Milton, Pewsey Vale, Wilts. 21 Nov. 1884. *Hound and horn or the life and recollections of George Carter the great huntsman by I. H. G.* (1885), *portrait.*

CARTER, HARRY WILLIAM (eld. son of Wm. Carter, M.D. of Canterbury who d. 1822). *b.* Canterbury 7 Sep. 1787; ed. at Kings sch. Canterbury and Oriel coll. Ox., B.A. 1807, M.A. 1810, M.B. 1811, M.D. 1819; Radcliffe travelling fellow 1812; F.R.C.P. 1825; phys. at Canterbury 1825–35; author of *A short account of some of the principal hospitals of France, Italy, Switzerland and the Netherlands with remarks on the climate and diseases of these countries* 1821, and of some essays in *Cyclopædia of practical medicine. d.* Kennington hall near Ashford, Kent 16 July 1863.

CARTER, HENRY LEE. Gave an entertainment called "The two lands of gold" at the Marionette theatre previously known as the Adelaide gallery, Adelaide st. Strand, London April 1853. *d.* Kensington house asylum, Kensington, London 3 Oct. 1862 aged 37.

CARTER, JAMES. *b.* Colchester 5 July 1792; tailor at Colchester 1819; removed to London 1836; author of *Lectures on taste; A lecture on the primitive state of man; Memoirs of a working man* 2 vols. 1845–50. *d.* St. John's place, Camberwell 1 June 1853. *G.M.* xl, 96 (1853).

CARTER, JAMES. *b.* parish of Shoreditch, London 1798; a landscape and figure engraver; engraved many plates for the

annuals especially *Jennings's Landscape Annual* 1830–40; engraved plates after Goodall, Nasmyth and Richard Wilson for *Art Journal* and E. M. Ward's pictures of 'The South Sea Bubble' and 'Benjamin West's First essay in art.' *d.* 6 Fleur de Lis street, Norton Folgate, London 23 Aug. 1855.

CARTER, SIR JAMES (son of James Carter of Portsmouth). *b.* 1805; ed. at Trin. coll. Cam.; barrister I.T. 27 Jany. 1832; judge of supreme court of New Brunswick 1834, chief justice 20 Dec. 1850 to 1865 when he retired on a pension; knighted by patent 12 Oct. 1859. *d.* Mortimer lodge near Reading 10 March 1878 in 74 year.

CARTER, JOHN (2 son of Thomas Carter of Castle Martin, co. Kildare). Entered navy 14 Jany. 1798; captain 7 Dec. 1815; superintendent of royal hospital at Haslar 2 Dec. 1841 to Dec. 1846; R.A. 8 April 1851; admiral on h.p. 4 Oct. 1862. *d.* 12 Devonport st. Portsmouth 2 April 1863.

CARTER, JOHN (2 son of Wm. Carter of Southwark, London). *b.* Southwark 8 March 1804; Cadet H.E.I.Co.'s service; chronometer maker at 207 Tooley st. London 1827 and at 61 Cornhill 1840 to death; his chronometers obtained prizes and pecuniary rewards from government; a common councilman of London, alderman of Cornhill ward 1851 to death, sheriff 1852–53, lord mayor 1859–60; colonel London rifle brigade; F.R.A.S. 1830; F.S.A. 3 March 1853; juror in section of mechanics at Imperial exhibition Paris 1855. *d* Stamford hill, London 8 May 1878. *Illust. news of the world* iv, 289, 308 (1859), *portrait; I.L.N.* xxxv, 437, 463, 472, 490 (1859), *portrait.*

CARTER, OWEN BROWNE. Architect at Winchester; lived at Cairo, Egypt about 1830 where he executed many drawings, a selection of which was published in a folio vol. entitled *Illustrations of Cairo* 1840; author of *Picturesque memorials of Winchester* 1830, *Some account of the church of St. John the Baptist at Bishopstone* 1845, and of articles in *Weale's Quarterly Papers on Architecture. d* Salisbury 30 March 1859 aged 53.

CARTER, ROBERT MEEK (eld. son of John Carter of Bridlington, Yorkshire). *b.* Skeffling, Holderness 1814; a coal merchant and cloth finisher at Leeds; alderman of Leeds; M.P. for Leeds 17 Nov. 1868 to Aug. 1876. *d.* The Grange, Burley near Leeds 9 Aug. 1882.

CARTER, SAMUEL *(son of Samuel Carter of Coventry)*. *b.* Coventry 15 May 1805; solicitor in partnership with his uncle Josiah Conder at Birmingham 1827 to 16 Aug. 1839 when Conder died; solicitor to London and Birmingham railway co. (afterwards London and North Western) 1831–60; solicitor to Birmingham and Derby railway co. (afterwards the Midland) 1835–68; had control of 40 bills promoted by the two companies in one parliamentary session; practised in London 1850–68; M.P. for Coventry 26 March to 11 Nov. 1868, contested Coventry Nov. 1868 and Feb. 1874. *d.* 3 Clifton place, Hyde park, London 31 Jany. 1878. *bur.* Kenilworth parish churchyard. *Solicitors' Journal xxii*, 302 (1878).

CARTER, THOMAS. Clerk at the Horse Guards, Whitehall, London April 1839, first class clerk in Adjutant general's office to death; author of *Curiosities of war and military studies* 1860, 2 ed. 1871; *Medals of the British army and how they were won* 1860–61; *Historical record of the Forty-fourth foot* 1864; edited *Historical record of the Thirteenth regiment of light infantry* 1867; *Historical record of the Twenty-sixth regiment* 1867; a constant contributor to *Notes and Queries. d.* 11 Lorrimore sq. Walworth, London 9 Aug. 1867.

CARTER, REV. THOMAS. *b.* 1774; ed. at Eton and King's coll. Cam., B.A. 1798, M.A. 1802; fellow of Eton 14 April 1829; V. of Burnham, Bucks. 1833 to death; vice provost of Eton 1857 to death. *d.* Burnham vicarage 8 Oct. 1868.

CARTER, THOMAS WREN. *b.* Nov. 1789; entered navy 29 March 1800, captain 25 April 1831; captain of Britannia 120 guns 9 Aug. 1852 to 13 March 1855; R.A. 31 Jany. 1856, retired admiral 20 Nov. 1876; C.B. 5 July 1855. *d.* Ryde, Isle of Wight 1 Feb. 1874.

CARTHEW, GEORGE ALFRED *(only son of George Carthew of Harleston, Norfolk, solicitor)*. *b.* 20 June 1807; solicitor at Framlingham, Suffolk, and at Harleston 1830–9, at East Dereham 1839 to death; F.S.A. 2 Feb. 1854; author of *The hundred of Launditch and deanery of Brisley in the county of Norfolk*, 3 parts 1877–9; *A history of the parishes of West and East Bradenham* 1883; *The origin of family or surnames* 1883, and of many papers in antiquarian periodicals; found *dead* in his chair at Millfield, East Dereham 21 Oct. 1882. *Athenæum* 4 Nov. 1882 p. 598.

CARTHEW, JAMES. *b.* Liskeard, Cornwall Jany. 1770; entered navy 8 Dec. 1780, captain 11 July 1801; admiral 14 Jany. 1850; placed on half pay 1853; pensioned 21 Jany. 1854. *d.* Tredudwell near Fowey 28 Nov. 1855.

CARTIER, SIR GEORGE ETIENNE, 1 Baronet *(youngest son of Jacques Cartier 1774–1841, lieut. col. Canadian militia)*. *b.* St. Antoine, Lower Canada 6 Sep. 1814; called to bar in L.C. Nov. 1835; Q.C. 1854; provincial sec. of L.C. 25 Jany. 1856; attorney general of L.C. 1856–8, 1858–62, and 1864 to 1 July 1867; premier of Canadian government 6 Aug. 1858 to May 1862; C.B. 29 June 1867; member of Canadian privy council July 1867; minister of militia and defence 1867–73; created baronet 24 Aug. 1868. *d.* 47 Welbeck st. Cavendish sq. London 21 May 1873. *H. J. Morgan's Eminent Canadians* (1862) 603–8; *I.L.N. xlv*, 496 (1864), *portrait*.

CARTLITCH, JOHN. *b.* in or near Manchester 1793; chief tragedian of Richardson's theatre at all the great fairs in England; the original Mazeppa at Astley's Amphitheatre Easter 1831, played the part more than 1500 times; landlord of King of Prussia public house Fair st. Horsleydown, London 1836, of Spread Eagle 137 Whitecross st. 1837–8; played at Franklin theatre, New York 1839; made his début in Philadelphia, at Museum Masonic hall 10 July 1849 as Rivers in *His last legs;* last appeared on the stage at Arch st. theatre, Philadelphia 25 June 1860; kept a café in Fourth st. Philadelphia. *d.* Philadelphia 12 Dec. 1875. *The Era 9 Jany.* 1876 *p.* 5, *col.* 4.

NOTE.—John Richardson the famous showman who died 14 Nov. 1836 aged 70, left him a legacy of £1000 because he was "such a bould speaker and might be heard from one end of the fear to the other when the trumpets were going."

CARTMELL, REV. JAMES. *b.* 1810. Educ. at Em. coll. Cam; 7 wrangler 1833, B.A. 1833, M.A. 1836, B.D. 1846, D.D. 1849; fellow of Christ's coll. 1836, master 13 Feb. 1849 to death; vice chancellor of Univ. of Cam 1849, 1865, and 1866; a member of council of the senate to Nov. 1880; chaplain in ord. to the Queen 7 Feb. 1851 to death. *d.* The lodge, Christ's college, Cambridge 23 Jany. 1881.

CARTTAR, CHARLES JOSEPH *(son of Joseph Carttar of Greenwich, solicitor)*. Solicitor at Greenwich 1830 to death; coroner for West Kent 1832 to death; conducted 14 Nov. 1878 inquest upon the 640 bodies found after sinking of the Princess Alice in the Thames 3 Sep. 1878; managed several elections at Greenwich for Conservative party. *d.* Catherine house, Blackheath road, Greenwich 19 March 1880 aged 71.

CARTWRIGHT, EDMUND. Entered Bengal army 1795; brigadier in command at Delhi 1826–34, and at Agra 1834; colonel 10 Ben-

CARTWRIGHT, E. *(Con.)*

gal N.I. 5 June 1829; col. 57 Bengal N.I. 1834 to death; L.G. 11 Nov. 1851. *d.* Piccadilly, London 31 March 1853.

CARTWRIGHT, FAIRFAX WILLIAM *(eld son of Wm. Cartwright 1797–1873). b.* London 14 May 1823; ed. at Ch. Ch. Ox., B.A. 1844; fellow of All Souls' college; served in Austrian army; major 2 hussars British German legion 7 Nov. 1855; M.P. for South Northamptonshire 25 Nov. 1868 to death. *d.* 7 New Burlington street, London 2 Feb. 1881.

CARTWRIGHT, FRANCES DOROTHY *(youngest child of rev. Edmund Cartwright 1743–1823 inventor of the power loom). b.* Goadby Marwood, Leics. 28 Oct. 1780; author of *The life and correspondence of Major Cartwright* 2 vols. 1826; *Poems, chiefly devotional, privately printed* 1835; her translations of the Spanish poet Nunez Riego's poems appeared with her initials in his *Obras postumas poeticas* 1844. *d.* Brighton 12 Jany 1863.

CARTWRIGHT, SAMUEL. *b.* Northampton 1789; an ivory turner; mechanical assistant to Charles Dumergue of Piccadilly, London, dentist; a dentist at 32 Old Burlington st. London 1811–57; at the head of his profession, made more than £10,000 a year for some years; dentist in ordinary to George IV.; the first pres. of Odontological Soc. 1856–7; F.R.G.S. 1830, F.L.S. 19 Nov. 1833, F.R.S. 11 Feb. 1841. *d.* Nizell's house near Tunbridge 10 June 1864. *British journal of dental science* vii, 287 (1864); *Proc. of Linnœan Soc.* 1865, *p.* 84; *Proc. of Med. and Chir. Soc.* v, 42–4 (1867).

CARTWRIGHT, WILLIAM *(2 son of Wm. Ralph Cartwright of Aynhoe 1771–1847, M.P. for Northamptonshire). b.* 22 Feb. 1797; ed. at Eton and Sandhurst; ensign 61 foot 2 July 1812; captain 8 hussars 2 July 1823 to 19 May 1825 when placed on h.p.; general 19 Nov. 1871. *d.* 16 Green st. Grosvenor sq. London 5 June 1873.

CARVOSSO, REV. BENJAMIN *(son of Wm. Carvosso of Mousehole near Penzance, Wesleyan preacher 1750–1834). b.* Gluvias parish, Cornwall 29 Sep. 1789; admitted as a probationer by Wesleyan conference 1814; a missionary at Hobart Town in Van Diemen's Land 1820 and 1825–30, in New South Wales 1820–5; Wesleyan minister in various parts of England 1830 to death; author of *The great efficacy of simple faith, a memoir of William Carvosso* 1835; *Drunkenness, the enemy of Britain,*

CARVOSSO, REV. B. *(Con.)*

arrested by the hand of God 1840; *An account of Miss Deborah B. Carvosso* 1840; *Attractive piety or memorials of Wm. B. Carvosso* 1844. *d.* Tuckingmill, Cornwall 2 Oct. 1854. *G. Blencowe's Memoir of Rev. B. Carvosso* 1857.

CARY, FRANCIS STEPHEN *(son of Rev. Henry Francis Cary 1772–1844, translator of Dante). b.* Kingsbury, Warws. 10 May 1808; studied art in London, Paris, Italy, and Munich; manager of Art school, Streatham st. Bloomsbury, London 1842–74; a candidate for decoration of houses of parliament in competitions held at Westminster Hall 1844 and 1847; exhibited 34 pictures at R.A. 8 at B.I. and 19 at Suffolk st. gallery 1834–76. *d.* Abinger, Surrey 5 Jany 1880.

CARY, GEORGE HUNTER *(eld. son of Wm. Henry Cary of Woodford, Essex, surgeon). b.* Woodford Dec. 1831; ed. at St. Paul's sch. and King's college, London; pupil of Sir Hugh Cairns; barrister I.T. 13 June 1854; Attorney General of British Columbia 21 March 1859; Attorney General of Vancouver Island 1861 to Nov. 1865 when he resigned; Leader of Government party in House of Assembly, Vancouver Island. *d.* 1 Upper George st. Bryanston sq. London 15 July 1866. *Law Times xli*, 684 (1866).

CARY, REV. HENRY *(brother of Francis Stephen Cary 1808–80). b.* 12 Feb. 1804; ed. at Merchant Taylors and Worcester coll. Ox., scholar 1821, B.A. 1824, M.A. 1827; barrister L.I. 15 Nov. 1827; retired from practice 1832; ordained deacon 1834; P.C. of St. Paul's, Oxford 1839–44; C. of Drayton, Berks 1847–9; went to New South Wales 1849; district court judge at Sydney 1861–70; author of *A practical treatise on the law of partnership* 1827; *Memoir of the Rev. H. F. Cary* 2 vols. 1847; edited *Memorials of the great civil war in England* 2 vols. 1842; *The works of Plato vol.* 1, 1848. *d.* Sydney 30 June 1870; *Law Times xlix*, 496 (1870).

CARYSFORT, JOHN PROBY, 2 Earl of *(2 son of 1 Earl of Carysfort 1751–1828). b.* Elton hall near Oundle 1780; ed. at Rugby; ensign 10 foot 3 June 1795; major 1 foot 25 March 1802; captain 1 foot guards 25 May 1803 to 4 June 1814; commanded brigade of guards in Flanders 1813–4; general 9 Nov. 1846; M.P. for Buckingham 1805–6, for Hunts 1806–7 and 1814–8; succeeded 7 April 1828 but never took his seat in House of Lords; insane for some years before his death. *d.* Westbury near Bristol 11 June 1855.

CARYSFORT, GRANVILLE LEVESON PROBY, 3 Earl of *(brother of the preceding)*. *b.* 1781; ed. at Rugby; midshipman R.N. 21 March 1798; present at battles of the Nile and Trafalgar; captain 28 Nov. 1806; admiral on h.p. 9 July 1857; M.P. for co. Wicklow 13 Feb. 1816 to 22 July 1829; succeeded 11 June 1855. *d.* Elton hall 3 Nov. 1868.

CARYSFORT, GRANVILLE LEVESON PROBY, 4 Earl of *(son of the preceding)*. *b.* Bushy park, co. Wicklow 14 Sep. 1825; ensign 43 foot 8 Feb. 1842; captain 74 foot 14 March 1851 to 1853; M.P. for co. Wicklow 25 Feb. 1858 to 3 Nov. 1868, when he succeeded; controller of Queen's household 25 June 1859 to July 1866; P.C. 6 July 1859; K.P. 1869. *d.* Florence 18 May 1872.

CASAMAJOR, ARSENE AUGUSTUS JOSEPH. Winner of junior sculls at Barnes regatta 1852, of senior sculls 1853; won diamond sculls at Henley on Thames 1855, 1856-7-8 and 1861; won Wingfield challenge sculls at Henley 1855, thus becoming amateur champion of the Thames a title he retained until July 1861; rowed upwards of 50 public races winning more than 40 of them Aug. 1852 to June 1861, he was never beaten in a sculler's race; an early member of London rowing club; aquatic editor of *The Field*. *d.* from breaking a blood vessel Belmont terrace, Wandsworth road, London 7 Aug. 1861 aged 27. *Rowing Almanac* (1862) *xiii-xvi, portrait; The Field* 10 *Aug.* 1861 *p.* 132, 17 *Aug. p.* 147.

CASSAL, HUGUES CHARLES STANISLAS *(son of a solicitor at Altkirch, département du Haut-Rhin, France, who d.* 1845*)*. *b.* Altkirch 1 April 1818; LL.B. Univ. of France 1839, LL.D. 1840; practised at French bar 1840-5; member for Altkirch in Assemblée Nationale 1848; went to England, Jany. 1852; taught French at University college school, London 1856 to death; professor of French at Univ. college, London 1860 to death; created Chevalier de la Légion d' Honneur 12 July 1880; author of *The graduated course of translation from English into French* 2 parts 1875-6, *new ed.* 1880; *Anthology of modern French poetry* 2 vols. 1876; *A glossary of idioms Gallicisms and other difficulties contained in the senior course of the modern French reader* 1881. *d.* 105 Adelaide road, South Hampstead, London 11 March 1885. *Athenæum* 21 *March* 1885 *p.* 375.

CASSELL, JOHN *(son of Mark Cassell, landlord of the Ring o' Bells in old churchyard, Manchester, who d.* 1830*)*. *b.* the Ring o' Bells 23

Jany. 1817; apprenticed to a joiner in Salford; went to London, Oct. 1836; a temperance lecturer; a tea and coffee dealer and patent medicine agent at 14 Budge Row, city of London 1847, at 80 Fenchurch st. 1849; started a paper called *The Teetotal Times;* a publisher in London 1850, took into partnership G. W. Petter and T. D. Galpin 1859; published *Working Man's Friend* 1850; *Popular Educator* 1852; *Cassell's Illustrated Family Paper* 31 Dec. 1853 to death; *Cassell's Illustrated Family Bible* 2 vols. 1860-66. *d.* 25 Avenue road, Regent's park, London 2 April 1865. *T. Frost's Forty years recollections* (1880) 226-38; *Cassell's Illust. family paper* 20 *May* 1865 *pp.* 262-4, *portrait; Le Livre, Juin* 1885 *pp.* 163-73.

CASSELLS, ANDREW. *b.* 1811; member of council of India 1874-84. *d.* 2 Aug. 1886.

CASSERLY, EUGENE. *b.* Ireland 1822; admitted to New York bar 1844; corporation attorney 1846-7; practised at San Francisco 1850-69 and 1873 to death; edited a paper at San Francisco; elected a senator in congress from California for the term 1869-75 but resigned before expiration of his term. *d.* San Francisco 14 June 1883.

CASSIDY, JAMES. Composed many pieces of dance music; member of orchestra of T.R. Dublin many years. *d.* Dublin 28 March 1869.

CASSIE, JAMES. *b.* Keith hall, Aberdeenshire 1819; pupil of James Giles R.S.A.; a landscape painter at Aberdeen, then at Edin. 1869 to death; exhibited 21 pictures at R.A., London 4 at B.I. and 2 at Suffolk st. gallery 1854-79; A.R.S.A. 1869, R.S.A. 10 Feb. 1879. *d.* Edinburgh 11 May 1879.

CASTLE, WILLIAM LANGFORD. *b.* 31 March 1800; entered navy 19 March 1813; captain 23 Nov. 1841; V.A. on half pay 24 May 1867. *d.* New lodge, Lymington 6 Aug. 1874.

CASTLEMAINE, RICHARD HANDCOCK, 3 Baron *(eld. child of Richard Handcock, 2 baron Castlemaine 1767-1840)*. *b.* Dublin 17 Nov. 1791; M.P. for Athlone 15 July 1826 to 3 Dec. 1832; succeeded 18 April 1840; a representative peer for Ireland 6 July 1841 to death. *d.* 4 July 1869.

CASTLESTUART, ROBERT STUART, 2 Earl of *(elder son of 1 Earl of Castlestuart 1723-1809)*. *b.* Dublin 19 Aug. 1784; succeeded 26 Aug. 1809. *d.* Stuart hall, Tyrone 10 June 1854.

CASTLESTUART, EDWARD STUART, 3 Earl of. *b.* Lower Brook st. London 11 Sep. 1807. succeeded 10 June 1854. *d.* East Cliff, Dover 20 Feb. 1857.

CASTLESTUART, CHARLES ANDREW KNOX STUART, 4 Earl of. *b.* Clifton 23 April 1810; succeeded 20 Feb. 1857. *d.* Stuart hall 12 Sep. 1874.

CASTLETOWN, JOHN WILSON FITZPATRICK, 1 Baron (*natural son of John Fitzpatrick 2 Earl of Upper Ossory 1745–1818*). *b.* London 23 Sep. 1811; ed. at Eton; M.P. for Queen's county 1837–41, 1847–52, and 1865–9; P.C. Ireland 1848; lord lieutenant of Queen's county 15 Nov. 1855 to death; created baron Castletown of Upper Ossory, Queen's county 10 Dec. 1869. *d.* 32 Hertford st. London 22 Jany. 1883. *I.L.N. lxxxii,* 149 (1883), *portrait.*

CASWALL, REV. EDWARD (*son of Rev. Robert Clarke Caswall, V. of Yateley, Hampshire*). *b.* Yateley 15 July 1814; ed. at Marlborough and Brasenose coll. Ox., B.A. 1836, M.A: 1838; P.C. of Stratford-sub-Castle, Wilts 1840–6; received into R.C. church by Cardinal Acton at Rome Jany. 1847; admitted into congregation of the Oratory at Edgbaston, Birmingham 29 March 1850 where he was ordained priest; author of *A new art teaching how to be plucked, being a treatise after the fashion of Aristotle, writ for the use of students in the Universities, to which is added a synopsis of drinking by Scriblerus Redivivus, Oxford* 1835, 7 ed. 1837, often reprinted; *Sermons on the seen and the unseen* 1846; *Lyra Catholica containing all the breviary and missal hymns translated* 1849 adopted in most R.C. prayer books; *The Masque of Mary and other poems* 1858; *A May pageant, a tale of Tintern, and other poems* 1865. *d.* The Oratory, Edgbaston 2 Jany. 1878. *Gillow's English catholics i,* 429–31 (1885).

CASWALL, REV. HENRY (*brother of the preceding*). *b.* Yateley 1810; ed. at Chigwell gr. sch. and Kenyon coll. Ohio, B.A. 1830, M.A. 1834; ordained deacon by Bishop of Ohio 1831, being the first ordained graduate of Kenyon college; returned to England 1842, obtained a private act of parliament 6 and 7 Vict. c. 32, removing disabilities attaching to his ordination in the U.S. 31 May 1843; V. of Figheldean, Wilts. 1848–70; preb. of Salisbury 1 Feb. 1860–1870; author of *America and the American church* 1839, 2 ed. 1851; *Mormonism and its author* 1852; *Scotland and the Scottish church* 1853; *The Western world revisited* 1854. *.d.* Franklin, Panama 17 Dec. 1870.

CATER, THOMAS ORLANDO. Second lieut. R.A. 1 April 1809; colonel 28 Nov. 1854 to 26 May 1857 when he retired on full pay; M.G. 26 May 1857. *d.* Blomfield road, Maida hill, London 5 June 1862 aged 71.

CATES, JAMES. Appointed an attendant at British Museum, London 19 July 1810, attendant in the reading room 20 Jany. 1815, superintendent 1824 to death. *d* 38 Alfred st. St. Giles's, London 22 Dec. 1855 aged 78. *R. Cowtan's Memories of the British Museum* (1871) 200–208; *Report on British Museum* (1850) 310–312.

CATHCART, CHARLES MURRAY CATHCART, 2 Earl (*eld. son of 1 Earl Cathcart 1755–1843*). *b.* Walton, Essex 21 Dec. 1783; cornet 2 life guards 2 March 1800; permanent assistant quartermaster general 28 July 1814 to 26 June 1823; lieut. col. royal staff corps at Hythe 1823–30; governor of Edinburgh Castle 1837–42; col. 11 hussars 30 Aug. 1842 to 19 Nov. 1847; succeeded as 2 Earl 17 June 1843; governor and commander in chief in British North America 16 March 1846 to 1 Oct. 1849; col. 3 dragoon guards 19 Nov. 1847 to 9 Jany. 1851; commanded northern and midland district of England 1849–54; col. 1 dragoon guards 9 Jany. 1851 to death; general 20 June 1854; C.B. 4 June 1815, K.C.B. 19 July 1838, G.C.B. 21 June 1859; discovered a new mineral, a sulphate of cadmium 1841 which was named Greenockite. *d.* St. Leonard's on Sea 16 July 1859. *H. J. Morgan's Eminent Canadians* (1862) 448–57; *Proc. of Royal Soc. of Edin. iv,* 222–4 (1862).

CATHCART, FREDERICK MAC ADAM (*brother of the preceding*). *b.* 28 Oct. 1789; cornet 2 dragoons 12 Jany. 1805, captain 12 Jany. 1808 to 18 May 1820 when placed on h.p.; sec. of embassy at St. Petersburg 26 May 1820; minister plenipotentiary to the Diet at Frankfort 15 Jany. 1824 to 1826; colonel of Ayrshire militia 6 April 1852; Knight of Russian order of St. Anne. *d.* Clarendon sq. Leamington 5 March 1865.

CATHCART, SIR GEORGE (*brother of the preceding*). *b.* Albemarle st. London 12 May 1794; ed. at Eton and Univ. of Edin.; cornet 2 Life Guards 25 May 1810; lieut. 6 dragoon guards 1811 to 1818 when placed on h.p.; captain 7 hussars 1819 to 1826 when placed on h.p.; lieut. col. 8 foot 20 March 1828 to 25 Sep. 1835 when placed on h.p.; lieut col. 1 dragoon guards 11 May 1838 to 19 Jany. 1844 when placed on h.p.; deputy lieut. Tower of London 13 Feb. 1846 to 13 Feb. 1852; M.G. 11

CATHCART, SIR G. (Con).

Nov. 1851; governor and commander in chief of Cape of Good Hope 20 Jany. 1852 to April 1854; granted distinguished service reward 13 July 1853; adjutant general 12 Dec. 1853; commanded fourth division of British army in the Crimea 1854 to death; knight of Russian order of St. Wladimir 3 June 1814; K.C.B. 31 May 1853; author of *Commentaries on the war in Russia and Germany in 1812 and 1813, London* 1850; shot through the heart at battle of Inkerman 5 Nov. 1854; *Correspondence of Sir G. Cathcart* 1856; *Kinglake's Invasion of the Crimea vol.* 5 (1875); *I.L.N. xx,* 125 (1852), *portrait.*

CATHCART, SIR JOHN ANDREW, 5 Baronet (*son of Hugh Cathcart*). b. 18 Feb. 1810; succeeded his grand uncle 1828. d. Edinburgh 25 March 1878.

CATHERWOOD, FREDERICK. Artist and traveller; drew views of city of Thebes, city of Jerusalem and temples of Baalbec from which Burford painted his pictures of these places published with descriptions 1834–44; travelled in Central America 1839–40; explored Peninsula of Yucatan 1841; took charge of the works for the railway across Isthmus of Panama 1851; author of *Views of ancient monuments in Central America, Chiapas and Yucatan* 1841; left Liverpool for New York on board the "Pacific" 23 Jany. 1856 which steamship has never since been heard of.

CATOR, BERTIE CORNELIUS (*son of Joseph Cator of Beckenham, Kent who d.* 1818). b. Beckenham 26 Sep. 1787; entered navy April 1800; captain 7 June 1814; retired 1 Oct. 1846; retired admiral 12 April 1862. d. London 23 July 1864.

CATOR, SIR WILLIAM (*brother of the preceding*). b. Beckenham 1785; ed. at Westminster and Woolwich; second lieut. R.A. 7 May 1803, col. 9 Nov. 1846 to 1854, col. commandant 1 April 1860 to death; brigadier general 21 Feb. 1854; L.G. 25 Sep. 1859. granted distinguished service reward 1 April 1856; C.B. 5 July 1855, K.C.B. 28 March 1865. d. 6 Eaton place, London 11 May 1866.

CATT, WILLIAM (*son of John Catt of Sussex, farmer*). b. 1780; miller at Lamberhurst, afterwards at Bishopstone near Seaford where he constructed largest watermill in Sussex; his mills became so influential as to govern the flour trade in South of England. d. Newhaven 4 March 1853 in 73 year. *M. A. Lower's Worthies of Sussex* (1865) 217–19, *portrait.*

CATTERALL, JOSEPH (*son of Paul Catterall of Preston, cotton spinner*). b. 10 July 1812; barrister M.T. 23 May 1845; district registrar at Preston of Court of Chancery of county palatine of Lancaster 1 March 1854 to 21 Dec. 1876; recorder of Wigan 19 May 1862 to April 1880. d. Fleetwood, Lancs. 6 March 1882.

CATTERALL, PETER (*brother of the preceding*). b. 1796; attorney at Preston 1817–52; principal registrar of Duchy of Lancaster 10 Feb. 1846 to death. d. Winckley square, Preston 14 July 1873. *Law Times lv,* 281, 317 (1873).

CATTERMOLE, GEORGE. b. Dickleborough near Diss, Norfolk 8 Aug. 1800; placed with John Britton the antiquary; a water colour painter; an Associate exhibitor of Society of painters in water colours 1822, a Member 1833–50; refused offer of knighthood, July 1839; received at French International exhibition 1855, one of the two grandes médailles d' honneur awarded to English artists; a member of Royal Academy of Amsterdam 1856; published *Cattermole's Historical annual* 1841; *Cattermole's Portfolio of original drawings;* illustrated many books and annuals. (*m.* 20 Aug. 1839 Clarissa Hester dau. of James Elderton, deputy remembrancer of Court of exchequer, she was granted civil list pension of £100, 28 Jany. 1875). d. 4 The Cedars road, Clapham common, London 24 July 1868. *John Sherer's Gallery of British artists i,* 97–106.

CATTERMOLE, REV. RICHARD (*brother of the preceding*). b. about 1795; secretary to Royal Society of Literature 17 June 1823 to 1852; studied at Christ's coll. Cam., B.D. 1831; V. of Little Marlow, Bucks. 1848 to death; one of the editors of the *Sacred Classics or select library of divinity* 30 vols. 1834–6; author of *Becket and other poems,* anon., 1832; *The book of the cartoons of Raphael* 1837; *The literature of the Church of England* 2 vols. 1844; *Evenings at Haddon hall* 1850. d. Boulogne 6 Dec. 1858.

CAULFIELD, RIGHT REV. CHARLES (*eld. son of Rev. Hans Caulfield, R. of Kilmanagh, co. Kerry, who d. June* 1854). Educ. at Trin. coll. Dublin, B.A. 1826, M.A., B.D. and D.D. 1858; ordained deacon 1827, priest 1828; P.C. of Clamantagh, Ossory 1832; R. of Kilcock, Kildare 1832–43; R. of Creagh, Ross 4 Aug. 1843 to Jany. 1858; archdeacon of the Bahamas 2 Feb. 1858; bishop of Nassau, New Providence, Bahamas (the first) 6 Nov. 1861 to death; consecrated at Lambeth 24 Nov. 1861; author of *The fall of Babylon* 1839. d. Nassau 4 Sep. 1862.

CAULFIELD, HENRY (son of 1 Earl of Charlemont 1728–99). b. 29 July 1779; M.P. for co. Armagh 17 July 1802 to 29 April 1807, 23 Sep. 1815 to 10 June 1818 and 22 March 1820 to 24 July 1830. d. Hockley near Armagh 4 March 1862.

CAULFIELD, JAMES (son of Ven. John Caulfield, archdeacon of Kilmore). b. 30 Jany. 1782; entered Bengal army 1798; col. 10 Bengal light cavalry 10 March 1841 to death; C.B. 26 Sep. 1831; L.G. 11 Nov. 1851; a director of East India company 1848 to death; M.P. for Abingdon 8 July 1852, but did not take his seat dying on day parliament met. d. Copswood, co. Limerick 4 Nov. 1852.

CAULFIELD, RICHARD. b. city of Cork 23 April 1823; ed. at Trin. coll. Dublin, B.A. 1845, M.A. and L.L.D. 1866; librarian of Royal Institution, Cork 1864 to death; librarian of Queen's college, Cork 1876 to death; F.S.A. 13 Feb. 1862; edited for Camden Society *Diary of Rowland Davies, D.D. dean of Cork* 1857; published *Life of St. Finn Barre* 1864 the MS. of which he discovered in Bodleian library, Oxford 1862; edited *Council book of corporation of Cork* 1876 and other valuable works. d. city of Cork about 20 Feb. 1887.

CAUNT, BENJAMIN. b. Hucknall-Torkard, Notts. 22 March 1815; pugilist; beaten by Wm. Thompson known as Bendigo 21 July 1835, fought him again 3 April 1838 when Caunt won; beat John Leechman known as Brassey after 101 rounds 26 Oct. 1840 and became champion of England; beaten by Nicholas Ward 2 Feb. 1841, beat him 11 May 1841; went to the United States Sep. 1841; proprietor of Coach and Horses public house, 90 St. Martin's lane, London 1843 to death; fought Bendigo near Sutfield green, Oxfordshire for £200 a side and the championship 9 Sep. 1845 when referee decided in favour of Bendigo in the 93rd round; fought Nat. Langham 23 Sep. 1857 when after 60 rounds no decision was given. d. 90 St. Martin's lane, London 10 Sep. 1861. bur. Hucknall-Torkard churchyard 14 Sep. *H.D. Miles's Pugilistica iii,* 47–93 (1880), *portrait; Fights for the championship by the Editor of Bell's Life in London* (1860) 135–42, 158–209; *Modern Boxing by Pendragon i.e. H. Sampson* (1879) 2–9.

CAUNTER, REV. JOHN HOBART. b. Dittisham, Devon 21 July 1794; went to India as a cadet about 1809; studied at Peterhouse coll. Cam., B.D. 1828; incumbent of St. Paul's chapel, Foley place, London 1825–44; V. of Hailsham, Sussex 1844–6; minister of St.

CAUNTER, REV. J. H. (Con.)
James's chapel, Kennington 1846–8; C. of Prittlewell, Essex 1848 to death; edited *The Oriental Annual* 1830–9; author of *The Cadet* 2 vols. 1814, a poem; *The romance of history, India* 3 vols. 1836 republished 1872; *The fellow commoner, a novel, anon.,* 3 vols. 1836; *The poetry of the Pentateuch* 2 vols. 1839; *Illlustrations of the five books of Moses* 2 vols. 1847. d. Edward st. Portman sq. London 14 Nov. 1851. *G.M. xxxvii,* 627–8 (1852); *Notes and Queries* 4 S. vi, 274, 353, 445 (1870).

CAUSTON, SIR JOSEPH (son of R. Causton of St. Albans). b. St. Albans 1815; wholesale stationer at 47 Eastcheap, London 1837 to death; common councilman for Billingsgate 1848; alderman for Bridge within 1867 to death; sheriff of London and Middlesex 1868–9; knighted at Windsor Castle 11 Dec. 1869 after the Queen's visit to the city to open Blackfriars bridge and Holborn viaduct. d. Champion hill near London 27 May 1871. bur. Norwood cemetery 3 June. *City Press* 3 June 1871 p. 5 and 10 June p. 5.

CAUTLEY, SIR PROBY THOMAS (son of Rev. Thomas Cautley, R. of Roydon, Suffolk who d. 13 July 1817). b. Roydon 1802; ed. at Charterhouse and Addiscombe; 2 lieut. Bengal artillery 1819, lieut. col. 5 May 1849 to 17 May 1854; constructed Ganges canal works 1843–54, canal opened 8 April 1854; director of canals in North West Provinces 1848; member of council of India 1858–68; chairman of public works committee 1860; gave to British Museum extensive collection of fossil mammalia from Sivalik hills in North West Provinces of India; F.G.S. 1836, Wollaston medalist 1837; F.R.S. 2 April 1846; K.C.B. 29 July 1854; wrote an elaborate report on construction of Ganges canal consisting of 3 vols. with a large atlas of plans 1860. d. The Avenue, Sydenham park, Kent 25 Jany. 1871 in 69 year.

CAUTLEY, REV. WILLIAM GRAINGER (son of Rev. J. Cautley of Messing, Essex). Educ. at Christ's hospital and Pemb. hall, Cam., 15 wrangler and 2 chancellor's medallist 1805, member's prizeman 1806 and 1807, B.A. 1805, M.A. 1809; fellow of Clare hall 1808–31; chaplain to the forces 25 Dec. 1809 to 21 April 1818; present at battle of Waterloo; R. of Earsham, Norfolk 1831 to death. d. Earsham 26 March 1855 aged 72.

CAVAGNARI, SIR PIERRE LOUIS NAPOLEON (eld. son of Major the Count Adolphe Cavagnari, private secretary to Prince Lucien Buonaparte). b. Stenay, department of the Meuse, France

CAVAGNARI, SIR P. L. N. *(Con.)*

4 July 1841; ed. at Christ's hospital, London; granted a certificate of naturalisation 7 Dec. 1857; ensign 1 Bengal Fusiliers, 9 April 1858; held political charge of the Kohat district, April 1866 to May 1877; deputy comr. of Peshawar, May 1877; negotiated treaty of Gandamuck with Yakub Khan, Ameer of Afghanistan 26 May 1879; British resident at Cabul 24 July 1879; C.S.I. 1 Jany. 1877, K.C.B. 19 July 1879; killed by Afghans in citadel, Cabul 3 Sep. 1879. *Kaliprasanna's Life of sir L. Cavagnari 1881, portrait; Shadbolt's Afghan campaign (1882) 37–41, portrait; Graphic xx, 4, 29, 261, 304 (1879), portraits.*

CAVE, SIR STEPHEN *(eld. son of Daniel Cave of Cleve hill near Bristol 1789–1872).* *b.* Clifton 28 Dec. 1820; ed. at Harrow and Ball. coll. Ox., B.A. 1843, M.A. 1846; barrister I.T. 20 Nov. 1846; M.P. for New Shoreham 29 April 1859 to 24 March 1880; paymaster general and vice pres of board of trade 10 July 1866 to Dec. 1868; P.C. 10 July 1866; judge advocate and paymaster general 25 Feb. 1874 to Nov. 1875; paymaster general Nov. 1875 to 24 March 1880; went on a special mission to Egypt, Dec. 1875; chairman of West India committee; G.C.B. 20 March 1880. *d.* Chambéry, Savoy 6 June 1880, personalty sworn under £350,000 21 Aug. 1880. *I.L.N. lxvii,* 581 (1875), *portrait; Graphic xi,* 574, 589 (1875), *portrait.*

CAVE-BROWNE-CAVE, SIR JOHN ROBERT, 10 Baronet. *b.* Stretton-en-le-Field near Ashby-de-la-Zouch 4 March 1798; succeeded 22 Aug. 1838; sheriff of Derbyshire 1844. *d.* Stretton hall 11 Nov. 1855.

CAVENDISH, FREDERICK CHARLES (2 *son of* 7 *Duke of Devonshire, b.* 1808). *b.* Compton place, Eastbourne 30 Nov. 1836; ed. at Trin. coll. Cam., B.A. 1858; private sec. to Earl Granville, pres. of the council 1859–64; M.P. for north division of west riding of Yorkshire 15 July 1865 to death; private sec. to W. E. Gladstone, July 1872 to Aug. 1873; a lord of the treasury, Aug. 1873 to Feb. 1874; financial sec. to the treasury, April 1880 to May 1882; chief sec. to Earl Spencer, lord lieutenant of Ireland, May 1882, sworn in at the Castle, Dublin 6 May; stabbed to death in Phœnix park, Dublin by assassins calling themselves "the Invincibles" 6 May 1882. *bur.* in churchyard of Edensor near Chatsworth 11 May, a memorial window placed in St. Margaret's church, Westminster at cost of members of House of Commons 22 Feb. 1883,

CAVENDISH, F. C. *(Con.)*

statue of him at Barrow in Furness uncovered 2 June 1885. *C. Brown's Life of Lord Beaconsfield ii,* 237 (1882), *portrait; I.L.N. xlviii,* 144 (1866), *portrait, lxxx,* 456, 477, 502 (1882), *portrait.*

CAVENDISH, GEORGE HENRY *(*2 *son of hon. Wm. Cavendish 1783–1812). b.* 19 Aug. 1810; M.P. for North Derbyshire 27 May 1834 to 24 March 1880; raised to rank of an Earl's son 1837 and to that of a Duke's son 1858. *d.* Ashford hall near Bakewell 23 Sep. 1880.

CAVENDISH, HENRY FREDERICK COMPTON (3 *son of* 1 *Earl of Burlington* 1754–1834) *b.* 5 Nov. 1789; lieut. 10 hussars 22 June 1808; lieut. col. 1 life guards 10 Jany. 1837 to 9 Nov. 1846; colonel 2 dragoon guards 2 June 1853 to death; general 9 Nov. 1862; M.P. for Derby 17 June 1818 to 29 Dec. 1834. *d.* Burlington gardens, London 5 April 1873.

CAW, JOHN YOUNG. *b.* Perth about 1810; ed. at St. Andrew's and Trin. coll. Cam.; connected with Bank of Manchester, then with Manchester and Salford bank; member of Literary and Philosophical Society of Manchester 1841, librarian 1854–6; F.S.A.; author of *The necessity and advantage of a bankers clearing house* 1847; *Some remarks on the deserted village of Oliver Goldsmith* 1852. *d.* Fountain villa, Cheetham hill near Manchester 22 Oct. 1858.

CAWDOR, JOHN FREDERICK CAMPBELL, 1 Earl of *(elder son of John Campbell* 1 *baron Cawdor who d.* 1 *June* 1821 *aged* 71). *b.* London 8 Nov. 1790; ed. at Ch. Ch. Ox., B.A. 1812, D.C.L. 1841; F.R.S. 11 June 1812; M.P. for Carmarthen 20 Dec. 1813 to 1 June 1821; created Viscount Emlyn of Emlyn and Earl of Cawdor 5 Oct. 1827; lord lieut. of Carmarthenshire 15 May 1852 to death. *d.* Stackpoole court, Pembrokeshire 7 Nov. 1860.

CAWLEY, CHARLES EDWARD *(son of Samuel Cawley of Gooden house, Middleton near Manchester). b.* Gooden house 7 Feb. 1812; civil engineer in London and Manchester; engineer to Manchester, Bury, and Rossendale railway; M.I.C.E. 30 June 1846; alderman of Salford 1859 to death; arbitrator to Board of Trade 1868; M.P. for Salford 17 Nov. 1868 to death. *d.* The Heath, Kersal near Manchester 2 or 9 April 1877. *Min. of proc. of Instit. of C.E. l,* 175–7 (1877); *Graphic xv,* 356 (1877), *portrait.*

CAY, JOHN *(eld. son of Robert Hodshon Cay of North Charlton, Northumberland, judge admiral of Scotland). b.* Edinburgh 31 Aug. 1790;

CAY, J. (Con).

ed. at high school and univ. of Edin.; admitted advocate 1812; sheriff of Linlithgowshire 1822 to death; F.R.S. Edin. 1821; member of Royal Scottish Society of Arts; author of *An analysis of the Scottish reform act* 2 parts 1837-40; *Analysis of the burgh registration act; Outlines of the procedure at elections for members of parliament.* d. Edinburgh 13 Dec. 1865. *Journal of Jurisprudence x,* 24 (1866).

CAYLEY, CHARLES BAGOT (*younger son of Henry Cayley of St. Petersburg, merchant 1768 -1850*). b. near St. Petersburg 9 July 1823; ed. at King's coll. London and Trin. coll. Cam., B.A. 1845; published *Dante's Divine comedy, translated in the original ternary rhyme* 4 vols. 1851-5; *Psyche's Interludes* 1857 a small vol. of poems; *The Psalms in metre* 1860; *Filippo Malincontri or student life in Venetia, an autobiography translated from the Italian* 2 vols. 1861; *The Iliad of Homer, homometrically translated* 1877; author with F. Garrido of *History of political and religious persecutions* 2 vols. 1876. d. suddenly of heart disease at 4 South crescent, Bloomsbury, London, night of 5-6 Dec. 1883. *Athenæum ii,* 776, 817 (1883).

NOTE.—An accurate likeness of him exists in Ford Madox Brown's fresco in the Manchester town hall, of Wm. Crabtree of Broughton watching the transit of Venus over the sun 24 Nov. 1639. He was the original of Oliver Serpleton in Oliver Madox Brown's story *The Dwale Bluth* (in his *Literary Remains* 1876).

CAYLEY, SIR DIGBY, 7 Baronet. b. York 13 March 1807; succeeded 15 Dec. 1857. d. Brompton near Scarborough 22 Dec. 1883.

CAYLEY, EDWARD STILLINGFLEET (*only son of John Cayley of Low hall near Brompton, who d.* 16 *June* 1846). b. Newbold hall near Market Weighton 13 Aug. 1802; ed. at Rugby and Brasenose coll. Ox.; M.P. for North Riding of Yorkshire 17 Dec. 1832 to death; chairman of committees on Hand-loom weavers 1834-5 and on Agricultural distress; edited *Agricultural and Industrial Mag.* 25 numbers 1 Oct. 1834 to 1 Dec. 1835. d. 11 Dean's yard, Westminster 25 Feb. 1862. *Farmer's Mag. x,* 81-4 (1844), *portrait, xxi,* 354-5 (1862).

CAYLEY, EDWARD STILLINGFLEET (*elder son of the preceding*). b. 30 July 1824; ed. at Eton and Trin. coll. Cam.; barrister I.T. 13 June 1851; author of *The European revolutions of 1848* 2 vols. 1856; *The war of 1870 and the peace of 1871,* 1871. d. Wydale, Brompton 10 Sep. 1884.

CAYLEY, SIR GEORGE, 6 Baronet (*only son of sir Thomas Cayley, 5 baronet 1732–92*). b. 27 Dec. 1773; succeeded 15 March 1792; in-

CAYLEY, SIR G. (Con.)

vented an instrument for testing purity of water by abstraction of light, and another for obtaining and applying electric power to machinery; carried out a system of arterial drainage in Yorkshire on a principle previously unknown in England; the first promoter and adopter of cottage allotment system; chairman of the Polytechnic Institution, Regent st. London 1838; chairman of the Whig club at York. d. Brompton 15 Dec. 1857. *The Times* 18 Dec. 1857 p. 7, col. 6.

CAYLEY, GEORGE JOHN (*younger son of Edward Stillingfleet Cayley 1802–62*). b. 26 Jany. 1826; ed. at Eton; barrister I.T. 17 Nov. 1852; author of *Some account of the life and adventures of Sir Reginald Mohun, Baronet, done in verse* 1850; *Las alforjas or the bridle roads of Spain* 2 vols. 1853, 2 ed. 1860. d. Hunton rectory, Kent 11 Oct. 1878.

CAZALET, EDWARD. b. Brighton 1827; author of *The Berlin conference and the Anglo-Turkish convention* 1878; *The Eastern congress an address to working men* 1878, 2 ed. 1879; *Bimetallism and its connection with commerce* 1879. d. Hotel d'Angleterre, Constantinople 21 April 1883.

CAZALET, REV. WILLIAM WAHAB. b. 1808; ed. at Charterhouse and Trin. coll. Cam.; B.A. 1833, M.A. 1837; ordained deacon 1834, priest 1836; teacher of elocution in London; chaplain to the union, Watford, Herts.; author of *The history of the Royal Academy of music* 1854; *On the right management of the voice in speaking and reading* 1855; *Stammering its cause and cure* 1858; *The voice or the art of singing* 1861. d Watford 24 April 1875.

CAZENOVE, JOHN (*son of James Cazenove of Old Broad st. London, merchant, who d.* 20 *Oct.* 1827 *aged* 83). b. 1788; one of a club of 35 members formed to promote views of political economy 1821; president of London Chess Club; author of *A selection of games at chess* 1817; *An elementary treatise on political economy* 1840; *Thoughts on a few subjects of political economy* 1859. d. 13 Middleton road, Battersea Rise, London 15 Aug. 1879.

CAZENOVE, PHILIP (*brother of the preceding*). b. Nov. 1798; ed. at the Charterhouse; member of Stock Exchange, London; head of firm of P. Cazenove and Co. stockbrokers Threadneedle st.; a munificent supporter of Church societies, hospitals and charities of every kind. d. Clapham Common, London 20 Jany. 1880, personalty sworn under £250,000 Feb. 1880. *Guardian* 28 Jany. 1880 p. 106, *col.* 1.

CECIL, REV. WILLIAM (*son of Rev. Richard Cecil*). *b.* 1792; ed. at Magd. coll. Cam.; Bell's Univ. scholar 1811; 17 wrangler 1814; B.A. 1814, M.A. 1817; fellow of his college; R. of Longstanton St. Michael near Cambridge 1823 to death; author of *The church choir, a collection of psalm and hymn tunes* 1846; *Recollections suitable for confirmation and other solemn seasons* 1856, 3 ed. 1873; *Spanish metres illustrated in music and English verse* 1866. *d.* Longstanton rectory 10 Feb. 1882.

CELESTE, MADAME, stage name of Celeste Elliott (*dau. of Monsieur Keppler of Paris*). *b.* Paris 6 Aug. 1811; ed. at Academie Royale de Musique; made her first appearance at Bowery theatre, New York as a dancer 27 June 1827; first appeared in London at Drury Lane theatre 1830 in ballet of *La Bayadère;* played in Italy, Germany and Spain 1832-3; played in United States 1834-7 clearing sum of £40,000; manager with B. Webster of T.R., Liverpool Christmas 1843; directress of Adelphi theatre, London 1844-8; manager of Lyceum theatre, London 28 Nov. 1859 to Aug. 1860; re-appeared in New York 23 Aug. 1865; sailed for Australia Oct. 1866 and returned to England early in 1868; made her last appearance 15 May 1878 at Drury Lane; her best characters were Mathilde in *The French Spy* and Miami in *The green bushes*. (*m.* 1828 Henry Elliott of Baltimore who *d.* 1842). *d.* 18 Rue Chapeyron, Paris 12 Feb. 1882. *H. P. Phelps's Players of a century* (1880) 122, 189, 198, 265, 278; *C. E. Pascoe's Dramatic List* (1879) 74-83; *Tallis's Drawing room table book* (1851) 27-8, *portrait; Brown's American stage* (1870) 65, 74, *portrait; Illust. news of the world, viii* (1861), *portrait.*

CHABOT, CHARLES. *b.* Battersea, London 1815; a lithographer and engraver in Skinner st. Snowhill, Holborn; an expert in handwriting; gave evidence at trial of Wm. Roupell, M.P. for Lambeth, who was sentenced to penal servitude for life for forgery 24 Sep. 1862; examined handwriting of letters of Junius and compared it with handwriting of persons to whom letters had been attributed 1871. *d.* 26 Albert sq. Clapham, London 15 Oct. 1882 in 68 year. *Cornhill Mag. Feb.* 1885, *pp.* 148-62; *I.L.N. lxxxi*, 549 (1882), *portrait.*

CHABOT, PHILIP JAMES (*son of Mr. Chabot of Spitalfields, London, dyer who d. 1832*). *b.* Spitalfields 1801; ed. at St. John's coll. Cam., B.A. 1825, M.A. 1828; barrister L.I. 11 May 1830; a dyer in Fashion st. Spitalfields 1832-56; originator of the Silk Conditioning Society, secretary and manager to death;

CHABOT, P. J. (*Con.*)
member of Spitalfields Mathematical Soc. 1834, F.R.A.S. 1845; member of Cavendish, Philological and Chemical Societies; made several improvements in dyeing. *d.* 41 Claremont sq. Pentonville, London 11 Jany. 1868.

CHAD, SIR CHARLES, 2 Baronet. *b.* 21 April 1779; ensign 92 foot 15 March 1798; cornet royal horse guards 3 May 1800; lieut. 2 life guards 2 April 1803 to 7 Nov. 1805 when he retired; succeeded 24 Nov. 1815. *d.* 1 Gloucester sq. Hyde park, London 30 Sep. 1855.

CHADS, SIR HENRY DUCIE (*eld. son of Henry Chads, captain R.N. who d. 10 Oct.* 1799). *b.* 1788; entered navy Sep. 1803, captain 25 July 1825; captain of Andromache 28 guns 1834-7 and 1841-5; commodore in East Indies 3 Feb. 1844 to 29 June 1844; superintendent of royal naval college at Portsmouth and captain of Excellent 28 Aug. 1845 to 12 Jany. 1854; fourth (afterwards third) in command of Baltic fleet on board Edinburgh 6 Feb. to Dec. 1854; commander in chief at Cork 1 April 1856 to 24 Nov. 1858; chairman of committee on coast defence 1859; admiral 3 Dec. 1863; C.B. 26 Dec. 1826, K.C.B. 5 July 1855, G.C.B. 28 March 1865; granted good service pension 4 May 1865. *d.* Southsea 7 April 1868. *Memoir of Sir H. D. Chads by an Old follower (M. Burrows)* 1869, *portrait; James's Naval history v,* 409-23 (1860).

CHADS, JOHN CORNELL (*brother of the preceding*). Second lieut. R.M. 4 May 1809; captain 1 West India Regiment 27 Jany. 1820, major 22 April 1836 to 3 March 1843 when he retired on full pay; president of British Virgin Islands 1852 to death. *d.* Government house, Tortola 28 Feb. 1854 aged 60.

CHADWICK, REV. FRANCIS (*son of Francis Chadwick of Burgh hall, Lancs.*). *b.* 14 Sep. 1801; entered Society of Jesus 7 Sep. 1818; prefect of studies and professor of rhetoric at Stonyhurst college 1827, minister of Stonyhurst 12 March 1833; went to Rome 14 Jany. 1834; sailed from Portsmouth for Calcutta 31 May 1834; served Mission at Calcutta 1834-8 and 1839-42; served Missions of Worcester 1842, Holywell 1844-6, London 1851. *d.* Oxford 5 March 1857.

CHADWICK, RIGHT REV. JAMES (3 *son of John Chadwick of Drogheda*). *b.* Drogheda 24 April 1813; entered St. Cuthbert's college, Ushaw 26 May 1825, ordained priest 17 Dec. 1836, general prefect, professor of humanities, mental philosophy and pastoral theology successively 1837-50; professor again 1856-**9** and 1863; served missions in North of England 1850–6; chaplain to Lord Stourton 1859–63; bishop of Hexham and Newcastle 31 Aug. 1866 to death; consecrated at St. Cuthbert's 28 Oct. 1866. *d.* Newcastle 14 May 1882. *Gillow's English Catholics i*, 444–6 (1885).

CHADWICK, SAMUEL TAYLOR. L.S.A. 1831, M.R.C.S. 1831, F.R.C.S. 1858; M.D. Edin. 1848; surgeon at Wigan 1831, at Bolton 1837 to May 1863 when he was presented by 7000 working men with a full-length portrait of himself; made over to trustees sum of £22,000 to build and maintain an orphanage for children in the Bolton union 1868–9, orphanage was opened Dec. 1874; a bronze statue of him in Town hall square, Bolton, was unveiled 1 Aug. 1873. *d.* Peel house, Southport 3 May 1876 aged 66. *I.L.N. lxiii*, 127, 129, (1873).

CHADWICK, WILLIAM *(2 son of John Chadwick of Pentonville, London, mason, who d. 1821).* *b.* 1797; statuary and mason in Southwark 1818; built St. Peter's church, Newington; erected bridges on Great Western railway; carried out line of railway from Didcot to Oxford 1844; chairman of London and Richmond railway which line was opened 27 July 1846. *d.* 8 Jany. 1853.

CHAINE, JAMES. *b.* Ballycragie, co. Antrim 1841; sheriff of Antrim 1873; M.P. for co. Antrim 16 Feb. 1874 to death. *d.* Larne, co. Antrim 4 May 1885.

CHALK, SIR JAMES JELL *(2 son of James Chalk of Queenborough, Kent).* *b.* Queenborough 1803; articled to an attorney 1819, admitted 1824; a strolling actor; entered Ecclesiastical commission office 4 Oct. 1836; barrister M.T. 22 Nov. 1839; assistant sec. to Ecclesiastical commissioners Sep. 1849, sec. Dec. 1850 to 4 Oct. 1871 when he resigned; knighted at Osborne 28 July 1871; F.S.A. 30 May 1872; *d.* 80 Warwick sq. Pimlico, London 23 Sep. 1878.

CHALLICE, ANNIE EMMA *(dau. of Mr. Armstrong).* *b.* London 1821; author of *The village school fête* 1847; *The sister of charity* 1857; *The secret history of the court of France under Louis XV*, 1861 *anon.; French authors at home* 1864; *Illustrious women of France* 1873. *(m. the succeeding). d.* of cancer of the liver at 7 Upper Wimpole st. Cavendish sq. London 11 Jany. 1875.

CHALLICE, JOHN. *b.* Horsham, Sussex 1815; L.S.A. 1836, M.D. King's college, Aberdeen 1850, F.R.C.P. Edin. 1860; deputy coroner

for East Middlesex to 1860; medical officer of health for Bermondsey 1856 to death; author of *Should the Cholera come what ought to be done?* 1848; *Medical advice to mothers* 1851; *Letter to Lord Palmerston on sanitary reform* 1854. *d.* 13 Great Cumberland st. London 11 May 1863.

CHALLIS, REV. JAMES *(4 son of John Challis of Braintree, Essex).* *b.* Braintree 12 Dec. 1803; ed. at Mill Hill school, London and Trin. Coll. Cam., scholar 1824, senior wrangler and first Smith's prizeman 1825, B.A. 1825, M.A. 1828; fellow of his college 1826–31; re-elected fellow May 1870; R. of Papworth Everard 1830–52; examiner for the Smith prizes 1836–78; Plumian professor of astronomy and experimental philosophy in Univ. of Cam. 2 Feb. 1836 to death; director of Cambridge observatory 1836–61; invented the Meteoroscope 1848 and the Transit reducer 1849; F.R.A.S. 8 April 1836, F.R.S. 9 June 1848; author of *Notes on the principles of pure and applied calculation and applications of mathematical principles to theories of the physical forces* 1869; *Lectures on practical astronomy and astronomical instruments* 1879. *d.* 2 Trumpington st. Cambridge 3 Dec. 1882. *Monthly notices of Royal Astronom. Soc. xliii*, 160–79 (1883).

CHALLIS, THOMAS *(son of Thomas Challis of 92 Fore st. Cripplegate, London, butcher).* *b.* 92 Fore st. 1 or 2 July 1794; a skin broker in Finsbury, a hide and skin salesman in Leadenhall and Bermondsey markets; alderman of Cripplegate ward 17 Oct. 1843; sheriff of London and Middlesex 1846–7; lord mayor 1852–3, there was no procession or dinner in consequence of recent death of Duke of Wellington; M.P. for Finsbury 9 July 1852 to 20 March 1857. *d.* Baker st. Enfield 20 Aug. 1874. *I.L.N. xxi*, 396 (1852), *portrait; City Press 22 Aug.* 1874 p. 5, 29 *Aug. p.* 4.

CHALMER, JAMES ARCHIBALD. Second lieut. R.A. 10 Aug. 1804, assistant director general 17 Jany. 1843, colonel 11 Nov. 1851 to 15 May 1855; M.G. 15 May 1855. *d.* 17 Queen Anne st. Cavendish sq. London 9 Dec. 1856 aged 69.

CHALMERS, GEORGE PAUL *(son of Mr. Chalmers of Montrose, master of a small coasting vessel).* *b.* Montrose 1833; apprenticed to a ship-chandler; ed. at Trustees school, Edin. 1853–5; painter in Edin. of portraits, subject pictures and landscapes; A.R.S.A. 1867, R.S.A. 1871; exhibited 58 pictures at R.S.A. 1855–78, 20 at Glasgow 1862–78, and 6 at

CHALMERS, G. P. (Con).

R.A. 1863–76 ; found insensible in an area in Charlotte st. Edin. 16 Feb. 1878. d. Royal infirmary, Edin. 20 Feb. 1878. *George Paul Chalmers, R.S.A.* 1879, *portrait ; Good Words xix,* 285–8 (1878).

CHALMERS, JAMES. b. Arbroath 2 Feb. 1782 ; bookseller in Castle st. Dundee ; convener of the Nine Incorporated Trades ; member of town council, Dundee, treasurer several years ; vice consul for Sweden and Norway at Dundee Sep. 1827 ; suggested a uniform rate of postage and exhibited a sample of an adhesive postage stamp in Dundee, Aug. 1834 ; competed for premium of £200 offered by the Government for best design of a postage stamp, there were 2000 candidates, but the premium was never awarded. d. Comley bank, Dundee 26 Aug. 1853. *James Chalmers the inventor of the adhesive stamp by Patrick Chalmers* 1884 ; *Philatelic Record iii,* 194–201, *iv,* 27, 68, 167, 169–72, 184–6.

CHALMERS, JAMES. b. Perthshire ; an engineer in America ; practised in London 1861 to death ; invented Chalmers target for defence of ships of war, it was tried at Shoeburyness 1863 and nearly completed at Atlas works, Sheffield for War Office at time of his death ; made a design for a wrought-iron railway tunnel across the English channel ; his Indian problem at chess baffled some of the best players ; author of *Channel railway connecting England and France* 1861, 2 ed. 1867 ; *England's danger, the Admiralty policy of naval construction* 1864 ; *Armour for ships and forts* 1865. d. 22 Southampton road, Haverstock hill, London 26 Dec. 1868 aged 49.

CHALMERS, PATRICK (eld. son of Patrick Chalmers of Auldbar castle near Brechin who d. 1826). b. Auldbar castle 31 Oct. 1802 ; cornet 3 dragoon guards 12 June 1823, captain 1826–27 when he sold out ; M.P. for Forfar district of burghs 15 Jany. 1835 to April 1842 ; F.S.A. 24 Jany. 1850 ; author of *The ancient sculptural monuments of Angus* 1848 ; *The Cartulary of the abbey of Arbroath,* vol. 2, 1856. d. Rome 23 June 1854. bur. churchyard of Auldbar church which he had just rebuilt. *Journal of British Archœol. Assoc. xi,* 164–70 (1855).

CHALMERS, REV. PETER. Licensed by presbytery of Glasgow 11 Sep. 1814 ; minister of Dunfermline (second charge) 17 March 1817, ordained 18 July 1817 ; minister of Dunfermline (first charge) 5 Oct. 1836 to death ; joined Free Secession 18 May 1843 but changed his

CHALMERS, REV. P. (Con.)

mind and was received back 21 June 1843 ; D.D. 5 Feb. 1855 ; author of *Two discourses on the sin, danger and remedy of duelling* 1822 ; *An historical and statistical account of Dunfermline* 2 vols. 1844–59. d. the Abbey church manse, Dunfermline 11 April 1870 in 80 year.

CHALMERS, SIR WILLIAM (eld. son of Wm. Chalmers, town clerk of Dundee). b. Castle st. Dundee 1785 ; ensign 52 foot 9 July 1803, captain 27 Aug. 1807 to 2 Oct. 1817 when placed on h.p. ; brigade major of various infantry brigades in Peninsular campaigns 1810–14 ; colonel of 20 foot 28 Feb. 1853, of 78 foot 30 Sep. 1853 to death ; L.G. 20 June 1854 ; K.C.H. 1837, C.B. 19 July 1838 ; knighted by patent 17 April 1844 ; principal clerk of the peace for the county of Forfar and keeper of Sasines about 1830 to death. d. Glenericht, Perthshire 21 June 1860. *Norrie's Dundee celebrities* (1873) 179–81.

CHALON, ALFRED EDWARD (younger son of Jean Chalon, professor of French at Royal military college at Sandhurst). b. Geneva 15 Feb. 1780 ; student at R.A. London 1797 ; exhibited 363 pictures at R.A. and 21 at B.I. 1801–60 ; A.R.A. 1812, R.A. 1816 ; founded with 7 other artists the Evening Sketching Society 1808 which lasted 40 years ; the most fashionable portrait painter in water colours ; painted the first portrait of Queen Victoria after her accession and many portraits of the female aristocracy ; painter in water colours to the Queen ; exhibited at Society of Arts a collection of 120 of his brother's works with some of his own 1855. d. El Retiro, Campden hill, Kensington, London 3 Oct. 1860. *Athenœum ii,* 487, 756, 792 (1860) ; *Art Journal* (1860) 337, (1862) 9 ; *A memoir of T. Uwins with his correspondence with A. E. Chalon* 1858.

CHALON, JOHN JAMES (brother of the preceding). b. Geneva 27 March 1778 ; a student at Royal Academy, London 1796 ; member of Watercolour society 1808–13 ; A.R.A. 1827, R.A. 1841 ; exhibited 86 pictures at R.A. and 49 at B.I. 1801–54 ; painted landscapes, figure and animal subjects, and marine pictures with equal facility ; author of *Sketches of Parisian manners* 1820. d. El Retiro, Campden hill, Kensington 14 Nov. 1854. *Redgrave's Century of painters ii,* 468–73 (1866) ; *Sandby's History of Royal Academy ii,* 167–9 (1862).

CHALON, THOMAS BARNARD. Judge advocate general Madras army 21 Aug. 1840 to 17 June 1859 ; retired M.G. 17 June 1859. d. Stuttgard 28 Jany. 1867 aged 67.

CHALONER, THOMAS (*son of Robert Chaloner of Guisborough*). *b.* 6 Feb. 1815; entered navy 2 Aug. 1827; captain 6 April 1853, retired 31 March 1866; retired admiral 2 Aug. 1879; C.B. 24 May 1881. *d.* Long Hull, Guisborough 20 Oct. 1884.

CHALONER, THOMAS (*son of a baker at Manchester*). *b.* Manchester 2 June 1839; won the St. Leger by a head on Caller Ou 1861 when betting was 100 to 1 against him, on The Marquis 1862, Achievement 1867, Formosa 1868, and Craigmillar 1875; won the Oaks on Feu de Joie 1862, the Two thousand guineas and Derby on Macaroni 1863; won 409 races 1855–63; combined coolness with great ability and a patience excelled by no other jockey; a trainer at Newmarket 1879 to death. *d.* Osborne house, Newmarket 3 April 1886. *Sporting Review lii,* 61–3 (1864), *portrait. Illust. sp. and dr. news i,* 16 (1874), *portrait, iii,* 261 (1875), *portrait, and* 17 *April* 1876, *portrait; Sporting Life* 5 *Feb.* 1887 *p.* 5, *portrait.*

CHAMBERLAIN, CHARLES FRANCIS FALCON *youngest son of Sir Henry Chamberlain 1 baronet 1773–1829). b.* 11 Oct. 1826; major Bombay staff corps 13 June 1866 to death; C.B. 14 Aug. 1868. *d.* Umballa, Punjab, India 31 Oct. 1870.

CHAMBERLAIN, SIR HENRY ORLANDO ROBERT, 3 Baronet (*elder son of Sir Henry Chamberlain, 2 baronet 1796–1843). b.* 15 Dec. 1828; succeeded 8 Sep. 1843; member of Corps of Gentlemen-at-arms Oct. 1857 to 1860. *d.* Bruges 30 Dec. 1870.

CHAMBERLAIN, JOHN HENRY (*son of Rev. Joseph Chamberlain, minister of Calvinistic Baptists at Leicester). b.* Leicester 26 June 1831; architect at Birmingham 1856 to death; partner with Wm. Martin 13 April 1864 to death; built Institute buildings in Paradise st. and Free Libraries in Edmund st; member of council of Midland Institute 1867, hon. sec. 1868 to death; member of Society of Artists March 1861, professor of architecture 1861, vice pres. 1879. *d.* at house of Lawson Tait, The Crescent, Birmingham 22 Oct. 1883. *Edgbastonia iii,* 161–6 (1883), *portrait; The Architect* 27 *Oct.* 1883 *pp.* 254–5.

CHAMBERLAIN, WILLIAM CHARLES (*brother of Charles Francis Falcon Chamberlain). b.* 21 April 1818; entered navy June 1831, captain 21 Feb. 1856; superintendent of Chatham dockyard 30 Nov. 1868 to 19 Jany. 1874; R.A. 19 Jany 1874, superintendent of Devonport dockyard 5 Aug. 1875 to 1 May 1876. *d.* Brighton 27 Feb. 1878.

CHAMBERLAYNE, THOMAS (*only son of Rev. Thomas Chamberlayne, R. of Charlton, Kent). b.* 1805; ed. at Magd. coll. Ox.; purchased the old hull of a celebrated cutter called the Arrow, and from her midship section built a cutter of 84 tons called the Arrow which won cups and prizes worth several thousands, she beat the America and the Mosquito at Ryde 22 July 1852, and the Volante and 6 other yachts at Ryde 4 Aug. 1869; made a beautiful cricket ground at Cranbury near Winchester 1834, and got together an Eleven second to none in England; pres. of Marylebone Cricket Club; a great coursing, hunting and coaching man; built stables at Cranbury at an expense of £20,000 which are matchless in style; sheriff of Hampshire 1835. *d.* Cranbury park 21 Oct. 1876. *Baily's mag. xii,* 55–59 (1867), *portrait; Hunt's yachting mag. i,* 103 (1853), *xviii,* 30–5, 381–91, *xxv,* 699 (1876).

CHAMBERLAYNE, WILLIAM. *b.* The Ryes, Essex 12 Aug. 1788; ed. at Westminster; captain 2 dragoon guards 9 May 1811 to 30 Dec. 1826 when placed on h.p.; general 14 Jany. 1866. *d.* Orford house, Oakley, Essex 21 July 1869.

CHAMBERS, REV. JOHN CHARLES (*son of John Chambers of The Tything, Worcester, topographer 1780–1839). b.* The Tything 23 Nov. 1817; ed. at Norwich gr. sch. and Em. coll. Cam., B.A. 1840, M.A. 1843; Tyrwhitt Hebrew scholar 1842; founded the first Sunday schools in Cambridge; C. of Sedbergh, Yorkshire 1842–6; missionary priest at Perth 1846–50; canon and chancellor of St. Ninian's cathedral, Perth 1850–5; V. of St. Mary Magdalene, Harlow 1855–6; Inc. of St. Mary the Virgin, Crown st. Soho, London 1856 to death, this was the first parish in which church guilds were set on foot; warden of House of Charity, Soho Nov. 1856 to death; author of *Sermons* 1857; *Reformation not deformation* 1864; *The destruction of Sin, being thirteen addresses delivered in Advent* 1872, *edited by J. J. Elkington* 1874. *d.* London 21 May 1874.

CHAMBERS, JOHN GRAHAM (*eld. son of Wm. Chambers of Hafod, Cardiganshire* 1809–75). *b.* Llanelly, Carmarthenshire 12 Feb. 1843; ed. at Eton and Trin. coll. Cam., B.A. 1865; the best walker in the University; rowed against Oxford 1862 and 1863; won the 7 mile walking championship March 1866; founded the Amateur Athletic Club at Beaufort house grounds, Walham green, 1866; pres. of Cambridge University Boat Club 1864–6; won the Colquhoun sculls at Cam. 1863, and the senior sculls at Barnes 1865

CHAMBERS, J. G. (Con.)

and 1866; coached the Cambridge crew at Putney 1871–4; edited *Land and Water* 1871 to death. *d.* 10 Wetherby terrace, Earl's court, London 4 March 1883. *Sporting Mirror* **v**, 121–3 (1883), *portrait; Land and Water* **xxxv**, 175–6, 249–50 (1883); *Illust. sporting and dr. news* i, 136 (1874), *portrait*.

CHAMBERS, MONTAGU (5 son of George Chambers of Harford, Hunts.) *b.* 1799; ensign Grenadier Guards 9 Nov. 1815 to 1 Oct. 1818 when placed on h.p.; barrister L.I. 8 Feb. 1828, bencher 3 Nov. 1845, treasurer 1868; Q.C. 3 July 1845; M.P. for Greenwich 8 July 1852 to 20 March 1857 and for Devonport 22 May 1866 to 26 Jany. 1874; edited the *Law Journal Reports* 1835 to death. *d.* 394 Uxbridge road, London 18 Sep. 1885.

CHAMBERS, ROBERT. *b.* Walker near Newcastle 14 June 1831; worked as a puddler at a forge on banks of the Tyne; won sculler's prize at Thames national regatta 1856 and 1858; beat T. White of Bermondsey for £200 on the Tyne 19 April 1859; sculled H. Kelley for the championship 29 Sep. 1859 when he won easily; beat White again 18 Sep. 1860, and G. W. Everson of Greenwich 14 April 1863; beat R. A. W. Green the Australian 16 June 1863; beaten by Cooper of Newcastle 28 July 1863 but beat him 7 Sep. 1864 and 12 June 1865; beaten by H. Kelley for the championship 8 Aug. 1865; beat J. H. Sadler of Putney 22 Nov. 1866; introduced the long slow stroke in rowing; rowed 112 races 90 of which he won. *d.* of consumption, result of overtraining, at The King's Arms, St. Anthony's, Newcastle 4 June 1868. *Rowing Almanac* (1861), *portrait*, (1862) 105–6, (1886) 163; *Illust. Sporting news* i, 141 (1862), *portrait*, ii, 64, (1863), *portrait*, iv, 361 (1865), *portrait*, v, 745 (1866), *portrait; I.L.N.* lv, 513 (1869); *Bell's Life in London* 13 June 1868 p. 9.

CHAMBERS, ROBERT (2 son of James Chambers of Peebles, cotton manufacturer). *b.* Peebles 10 July 1802; bookseller at Leith 1818–22, at Edin. 1822; partner with his brother William as publishers in Edin. 1832 to death; F.R.S. Edin. 1840; F.G.S. 1844; hon. LL.D. St. Andrews 1868; author of *Traditions of Edinburgh* 2 vols. 1823, *new ed.* 1868; *History of the rebellion of 1745*, 1828, 7 ed. 1869; *Biographical dictionary of eminent Scotsmen* 4 vols. 1832–4; *Vestiges of the natural history of creation* 1844, *anon.* 12 ed. 1884; *The book of days* 2 vols. 1862–4. *d.* St. Andrews 17 March 1871. *Memoir of W. and R. Chambers by W. Chambers*, 12 ed. 1883, *portrait; Illust. Review* **i**, 423–7 (1871), *portrait*.

CHAMBERS, WILLIAM (brother of the preceding). *b.* Peebles 16 April 1800; bookseller at Leith 1819–23, at Broughton st. Edin. 1823; edited *Chambers's Edinburgh Journal* 4 Feb. 1832 to death; partner with his brother Robert 1832; lord provost of Edin. 1865–9; LL.D. Edin. 1872; presented town of Peebles with a library (10,000 volumes) and other buildings called the Chambers Institution opened Aug. 1859; spent about £25,000 on St. Giles's church, Edin., re-opened 23 May 1883; accepted offer of a baronetcy May 1883 but died before receiving the honour. *d.* Chester st. Edinburgh 20 May 1883. *Dublin Univ. Mag. xxxvii*, 177–90 (1851); *Drawing room portrait gallery of eminent personages, fourth series* 1860, *portrait*.

CHAMBERS, WILLIAM FREDERIC (eld. son of Wm. Chambers of H.E.I.Co's civil service who d. 1793). *b.* India 1786; ed. at Westminster and Trin. coll. Cam., scholar, B.A. 1808, M.A. 1811, M.D. 1818; physician to St. George's hospital, London 20 April 1816 to 1839; F.R.C.P. 30 Sep. 1819, censor 1822, 1836, consilarius 1836, 1841, 1845, an Elect 1847; F.R.S. 13 March 1828; phys. in ord. to Queen Adelaide 25 Oct. 1836; phys. to Wm. IV. 4 May 1837; created K.C.H. by Queen Victoria at St. James's palace 8 Aug. 1837 but allowed to decline assumption of the prefix Sir; the leading phys. in London 1836–48, being the last who to any extent monopolised consulting practice among the rich and noble; phys. in ord. to Queen Victoria 8 Aug. 1837. *d.* Hordle Cliff near Lymington, Hants. 16 Dec. 1855. *Lives of British physicians* 2 ed. 1857 *pp.* 388–402; *Munk's Roll of physicians* iii, 196–200 (1878); *Medical Circular* i, 373 (1852), *portrait*.

CHAMBRE, WILLIAM (younger son of Meredith Calcott Chambre of Hawthorn hill, co. Armagh, who d. 8 Feb. 1812). Lieut. York light infantry volunteers 27 May 1812; captain 11 foot 10 Jany. 1822 to 30 July 1844 when placed on h.p.; L.G. 26 Jany. 1874. *d.* 1 Duncairn terrace, Bray, co. Dublin 24 Oct. 1876.

CHAMIER, FREDERICK (4 son of John Chamier, member of council for Madras presidency, who d. 23 Feb. 1831). *b.* London 1796; midshipman R.N. 24 June 1809; served in United States war 1812; commander 9 Aug. 1826; placed on reserved list July 1851; retired captain 1 April 1856; author of *The life of a sailor* 3 vols. 1832; *Ben Brace* 3 vols. 1836; *Jack Adams* 3 vols. 1838; *Tom Bowling* 3 vols. 1841; *My travels, or an unsentimental journey through France, Switzerland and Italy* 3 vols. 1855, and of many papers in *New Monthly Mag.*; edited

W. James's Naval history of Great Britain, 3 ed. 6 vols. 1837. *d.* 29 Warrior sq. St. Leonard's on Sea 31 Oct. 1870. *New Monthly Mag. lii*, 508–10 (1838), *portrait.*

CHAMIER, HENRY. Writer Madras civil service 1812; chief sec. to Madras government 1837–43; member of council 1843–8; pres. of the revenue, marine and college boards 1843 to 14 Jany. 1867 when he resigned the service. *d.* 9 Waterloo crescent, Dover 4 Feb. 1867 aged 71.

CHAMPAIN, SIR JOHN UNDERWOOD BATEMAN (2 son of *Agnew Champain*, major 9 foot, who *d.* 1876). *b.* Gloucester place, London 22 July 1835; ed. at Cheltenham and Addiscombe; 2 lieut. Bengal Engineers 11 June 1853, lieut. col. 31 Dec. 1878 to death; director in chief of Indo-European government telegraph department 1869 to death; granted special permission to accept a sword of honour from Shah of Persia 1885 an honour quite unprecedented; K.C.M.G. 31 Dec. 1885; assumed additional name of Bateman 1870. *d.* San Remo 1 Feb. 1887. *Sir F. J. Goldsmid's Telegraph and Travel* (1874) 206–388, 639.

CHAMPION, JOHN GEORGE. *b.* Edinburgh 5 May 1815; Ensign 95 foot 2 Aug. 1831, major 11 Nov. 1851 to death; served at Hongkong 1847–50; brought a collection of dried plants to England 1850, most of his novelties were described in *Hooker's Journals;* placed last set of his plants in the Kew herbarium 1854, his name is commemorated in the genus Championia and by the splendid plant Rhodoleia Championi. *d.* Scutari hospital 30 Nov. 1854 of wounds received at battle of Inkerman 5 Nov. *G. Bentham's Flora Hongkongensis* (1861) 8*–9*; *Gardener's Chronicle* (1854) 819–20; *G. Ryan's Our heroes of the Crimea* (1855) 93–5.

CHAMPNEYS, VERY REV. WILLIAM WELDON *(eld. son of Rev. Wm. Beyton Champneys).* *b.* Camden Town, London 6 April 1807; matric. from Brasenose coll. Ox. 3 July 1824, scholar of his college, fellow 1831; B.A. 1828, M.A. 1831; C. of St. Ebbe's, Oxford 1831–7; R. of St. Mary's, Whitechapel, London 1837–60; canon residentiary of St. Paul's cath. 3 Nov. 1851 to 11 Nov. 1868; V. of St. Pancras, London 1860–8; dean of Lichfield and R. of Tatenhill, Staffs. 11 Nov. 1868 to death; author of *Images or allegories for the young* 1849, 8 ed. 1868; *Six lectures on Protestantism* 1852; *The Sunday school teacher*, 3 ed. 1857; *The Spirit in the word* 1862, 4 ed. 1866; *Facts and Fragments* 1864. *d.* the Deanery, Lichfield 4 Feb. 1875. *Rev. W. W. Champ-*

neys's Story of the tentmaker (1875) 7–14, *portrait; Drawing room portrait gallery (4th series* 1860) 1–2, *portrait.*

CHANCE, HENRY *(youngest son of Wm. Chance of Birmingham).* *b.* Newhall st. Birmingham 1794; a certificated conveyancer 1819; barrister L.I. 21 May 1824; practised as conveyancer 1819–66 when he retired; author of *A treatise on Powers* 2 vols. 1831. *d.* 7 North villas, Camden sq. London 16 Feb. 1876.

CHANDLER, VERY REV. GEORGE. Educ. at Winchester and New coll. Ox.; B.C.L. 1804, D.C.L. 1824; R. of Southam, Warws. 1815–30; R. of All Souls, St. Marylebone, London 1825–47; Bampton lecturer 1825; dean of Chichester 20 Feb. 1830 to death, installed 18 March 1830; R. of Felpham, Sussex 1832 to death; F.R.S. 7 Feb. 1833; author of *The Bampton lectures* 1825. *d.* The Deanery, Chichester 3 Feb. 1859 aged 80.

CHANDLER, JOHANNA. *b.* 1820; called a meeting at Mansion House, London 2 Nov. 1859 when sum of £800 was collected for a National hospital for the paralysed and epileptic, which was opened in Queen's square, Bloomsbury, May 1860; founded Samaritan society to give aid to out-door patients and Home for convalescent women patients at East Finchley. *d.* 43 Albany st. Regent's Park, London 12 Jany. 1875. *Facta non verba by the author of Contrasts [Wm. Gilbert]* (1874) 101–25; *Good Words vii*, 537–42 (1866).

CHANDLESS, THOMAS *(eld. son of Thomas Chandless of York place, Portman square, London).* *b.* 1798; barrister G.I. 19 June 1822, practised in court of chancery; bencher of his inn 5 May 1847, treasurer 1850–51; Q.C. 11 July 1851. *d.* 45 Harewood sq. London 22 Feb. 1883 in 85 year.

CHANNELL, SIR WILLIAM FRY *(son of Pike Channell, an officer in the navy, afterwards a merchant in London).* *b.* 31 Aug. 1804; barrister I.T. 25 May 1827, went Home circuit; serjeant at law 19 Feb. 1840; shared with Serjeant Talfourd leading business of Court of Common Pleas 1840–6 when practice was thrown open to the bar generally; obtained patent of precedence 1844; leader of Home circuit 1845–57; Baron of Court of Exchequer 12 Feb. 1857 to Jany. 1873; knighted at St. James's palace 18 June 1857; issued an address to Beverley at general election July 1852 but withdrew before the election; nominated a P.C. Feb. 1873 but did not live to be sworn in. *d.* 2 Clarendon place, Hyde park gardens, London 26 Feb. 1873. *Law mag. and law review ii*, 351–4 (1873); *I.L.N. lxii*, 234, 249, 318 (1873), *portrait.*

CHAPLIN, CHARLES. *b.* 21 April 1786; M.P. for Lincolnshire 25 June 1818 to 23 April 1831. *d.* London 24 May 1859.

CHAPLIN, EDWARD. *b.* Ryhall, Rutland 28 March 1842; ed. at Harrow; captain Coldstream guards 1871; M.P. for Lincoln 4 Feb. 1874 to 24 March 1880; master of the Blankney hounds 1872-6; a member of the Four-in-hand club 1877. *d.* 25 Charles st. Berkeley sq. London 23 Dec. 1883. *Baily's mag. xxxi*, 311-2 (1878), *portrait*.

CHAPLIN, WILLIAM JAMES *(son of Wm. Chaplin of Rochester). b.* Rochester 1787; one of the largest coach proprietors in' the kingdom, being owner of 64 stage coaches worked by 1500 horses; chairman of London and South western railway company to death; sheriff of London 1845-46; M.P. for Salisbury 1847-1857. *d.* 2 Hyde Park gardens, London 24 April 1859 aged 71.

CHAPMAN, REV. BENEDICT. Educ. at Gonville and Caius coll. Cam., 6 Wr. 1792, B.A. 1792, M.A. 1795, D.D. 1840; fellow of his college, tutor, master, May or June 1839 to death; R. of Ashdon, Essex 1818 to death. *d.* Ashdon rectory 23 Oct. 1852 in 83 year. *bur.* in chapel of his college 30 Oct.

CHAPMAN, HENRY SAMUEL. *b.* Kennington, London, July 1803; went to Canada 1823; founded at Montreal 1833 *Daily Advertiser* first daily newspaper published in Canada, edited it 1833-4; barrister M.T. 12 June 1840; a judge of supreme court of New Zealand, June 1843 to March 1852; colonial sec. of Van Diemen's Land, March 1852 to Nov. 1852; attorney general of Victoria 11 March 1857 to 29 April 1857 and March 1858 to 27 Oct. 1859; formed a ministry, March 1858; acted as judge of supreme court of Victoria 1862 to March 1863; judge of supreme court of New Zealand 1865-77; author of *Thoughts on the money and exchanges of Lower Canada* 1832; *The New Zealand portfolio* 1843. *d.* Dunedin, N.Z. 27 Dec. 1881.

CHAPMAN, HENRY THOMAS *(elder son of Thomas Chapman of Ampthill, Beds. who lived to be 94). b.* Ampthill 1806; studied at St. Bartholomew's hospital, London, house surgeon; surgeon in Lower Seymour st. London; lecturer on surgery in school next St. George's hospital; fellow of Med. and Chir. Soc. 1837; author of *A brief description of surgical apparatus* 1832; *The treatment of obstinate ulcers and cutaneous eruptions of the leg without confinement* 1848, 3 ed. 1859; *Varicose veins, their nature, consequences and treatment* 1856. *d.* Cheltenham 19 Nov. 1874.

CHAPMAN, RIGHT REV. JAMES. *b.* 1799; ed. at Eton and King's coll. Cam., B.A. 1823, M.A. 1826, D.D. 1845; Fell. of his coll.; deacon 1824, priest 1825; assistant master at Eton; R. of Dunton Waylett, Essex 1834-45; Bishop of Colombo 24 April 1845-1861; Fell. of Eton, April 1862; R. of Wootton Courtney, Somerset 1863 to death; Preb. of Wells cath. 1868. *d.* Wootton Courtney 20 Oct. 1879.

CHAPMAN, JOHN *(son of John Chapman of Loughborough, clockmaker). b.* Loughborough 20 Jany. 1801; manufacturer with his brother Wm. of machinery required for the bobbinnet trade technically called insides 1823-34 when completely ruined by the protection laws; wrote for the *Mechanics Magazine* which he edited short time 1835; sec. to Safety cabriolet and two-wheel carriage company in London 1836; invented all the valuable improvements found in the modern 'Hansom cab,' a patent for his cab was granted 31 Dec. 1836; laid before Board of Trade a project for constructing Great Indian Peninsular railway 1844; prepared a great scheme for irrigation of India which was formally sanctioned by the government just after his death; author of *The cotton and commerce of India, published* 1 Jany. 1851; *Principles of Indian reform* 1853, and of many articles in periodicals and newspapers. *d.* London 11 Sep. 1854. *General Baptist Mag. iii*, 169-76, 209-17, 292-8, 329-32 (1856); *Nottingham Review* 11 *Sep. to* 3 *Dec.* 1833.

CHAPMAN, JOHN *(son of John Chapman of Ashton, Lancs. who d. 19 May 1819 aged 55). b.* Ashton 1810; sheriff of Cheshire 1856.; M.P. for Great Grimsby 14 Feb. 1862 to 6 July 1865 and 5 Feb. 1874 to death. *d.* Hill End, Mottram in Longdendale, Cheshire 18 July 1877 in 67 year.

CHAPMAN, MARY FRANCIS *(dau. of Mr. Chapman of Dublin, custom house officer). b.* Dublin 28 Nov. 1838; ed. at Staplehurst, Kent; published following novels under pseud. of J. C. Ayrton, *Mary Bertrand* 1856, *Lord Bridgnorth's Niece* 1862, *A Scotch Wooing* 1875, *Gerald Marlowe's Wife* 1876; wrote with her father in *Churchman's family magazine* 1869 an historical tale called *Bellasis or the fortunes of a cavalier;* her last work *The gift of the Gods* 1879 appeared under her own name. *d.* Old Charlton, Kent 18 Feb. 1884.

CHAPMAN, MATTHEW JAMES. Educ. at Univ. of Edin. and Trin. coll. Cam.; M.D. Edin. 1820; B.A. Cam. 1832, M.A. 1835; published *Barbadoes and other poems* 1833; *Jephtha's*

CHAPMAN, M. J. (Con.)

Daughter a dramatic poem 1834; *Theocritus, Bion and Moschus, translated* 1836. *d.* 25 Albemarle st. Piccadilly, London 15 Nov. 1865 aged 69.

CHAPMAN, SIR MONTAGUE LOWTHER, 3 Baronet *(eld. son of Sir Thomas Chapman, 2 baronet 1756–1837). b.* 10 Dec. 1808; M.P. for Westmeath 12 Aug. 1830 to 23 June 1841; succeeded 23 Dec. 1837; sheriff of Westmeath 1844; sailed from Melbourne for Sydney May 1852 but his ship was never heard of again; *death* announced as having occurred on the coast of Australia 17 May 1852. *Annual Register* 1853 p. 229.

CHAPMAN, SIR STEPHEN REMNANT *(son of Richard Chapman of Tainfield house, Taunton). b.* Tainfield house 1776; second lieut. R.E. 18 Sep. 1793; sec. to Lord Mulgrave, master general of the ordnance 1810 to 29 July 1825; civil sec. at Gibraltar 1825–31; col. R.E. 29 July 1825 to 10 Jany. 1837; governor, vice admiral and commander in chief at Bermuda 23 April 1831 to 8 Feb. 1839; carried into effect emancipation of the slaves there 1834; L.G. 9 Nov. 1846; col. commandant R.E. 9 March 1860 to death; C.B. 4 June 1815; knighted at St. James's palace 8 June 1831; F.R.S. 21 Nov. 1816. *d.* Tainfield house 6 March 1851.

CHAPPELL, EDWARD. *b.* 10 Aug. 1792; entered navy, May 1804; captain 27 Dec. 1838; retired R.A. 20 Jany. 1858; secretary to Royal mail steam packet company, Feb. 1842; author of *Narrative of a voyage to Hudson's Bay* 1817; *Voyage to Newfoundland and the southern coast of Labrador* 1818. *d.* Charlwood st. west, Warwick sq. London 21 Jany. 1861.

CHAPPLE, JAMES. *b.* Exeter; Won the Derby on Dangerous 1833 on Amato 1838; won the Oaks on Vespa 1833; won Cesarewitch on Glauca 1850 and Cambridgeshire on Landgrave 1850; rode many years for Sir Gilbert Heathcote; had no superior for a knowledge of pace and fineness of hand. *d.* Newmarket, 10 June 1858 in 63 year. *Sporting Review xxvii,* 58–61 (1852), *portrait; Bell's Life in London* 13 *June* 1858 *p.* 4.

CHAPPLE, JOHN. *b.* 10 Jany. 1826; worked under I. K. Brunel the civil engineer and G. G. Scott the architect; restored churches at Frinstead, Kent and Chesham, Bucks.; clerk of the works for restoration of St. Albans Abbey 1870–6 and 1877 to death; supervised restoration of great church of St. Nicholai, Hamburg 1876–7; member of council of St. Albans 1877, mayor 1879, alderman 1883 to death. *d.* Torrington hall, St. Albans 6 Feb. 1887. *The Herts Advertiser* 12 *Feb.* 1887.

CHARLEMONT, FRANCIS WILLIAM CAULFIELD, 2 Earl of *(eld. son of 1 Earl of Charlemont 1728–99). b.* 3 Jany. 1775; M.P. for Armagh in Irish House of Commons 1797 to 4 Aug. 1799 when he succeeded; one of representative peers for Ireland 22 Nov. 1806 to death; K.P. Oct. 1831; P.C. Ireland 1832; lord lieut. of Tyrone 1839 to death; created Baron Charlemont in peerage of the U.K. 13 Feb. 1837. *d.* Clontarf 26 Dec. 1863.

CHARLES, REV. JOHN *(sŏn of John Charles of Laurencekirk, Kincardineshire). b.* 1770; M.A. Marischal college and Univ. of Aberdeen 26 March 1792; schoolmaster of Glenbervie; minister of Garvock 7 June 1821 to death; author of *A sermon preached in the church of Glenbervie* 1814; *The Protestant's Hand Book* 1855. *d.* 17 Nov. 1868 aged nearly 99.

CHARLES, THOMAS *(younger son of Wm. Charles of Maidstone, felter and blanket cleaner, who d.* 1832). Apprenticed to his father, became his partner, succeeded to the business 1832 which he sold 1840; author of a translation of *Boethius's Consolations of philosophy;* bequeathed his valuable collections to the town of Maidstone which purchased his house and opened The Charles Museum in it, Jany. 1858. *d.* Chillington house, Maidstone 29 April 1855 aged 77. *C. R. Smith's Retrospections i,* 141–6 (1883); *J. M. Russell's History of Maidstone* (1881) 357–62.

CHARLESWORTH, EDWARD PARKER *(son of Rev. John Charlesworth, R. of Ossington, Notts.) b.* 1783; ed. at Univ. of Edin., M.D. 1807; physician at Lincoln 1807 to death; visiting phys. to Lincoln lunatic asylum 1820 to death, where he substituted moral control and kindness in place of physical control and coercion; author of *Remarks on the treatment of the insane* 1828. *d.* Lincoln 20 Feb. 1853. *G.M. xxxix,* 548–50 (1853).

CHARLESWORTH, REV. JOHN *(brother of the preceding). b.* Ossington parsonage 1782; practised with a surgeon at Clapham, London 1804; ordained deacon by Bishop of Norwich 1809; R. of Flowton, Suffolk 1814–44; kept his terms at Queen's coll. Cam. 1820–3, B.D. 1826; R. of St. Mildred's, Bread st. London 1844 to death. *d.* Islington, London 22 April 1864. *bur.* churchyard of Limpsfield, Surrey. *J. P. Fitzgerald's The quiet worker for good, a sketch of the late John Charlesworth* 1865.

CHARLESWORTH, JOHN CHARLESWORTH DODGSON. *b.* Chapelthorpe hall near Wakefield 1815; ed. at Sedbergh, Yorkshire and St. John's coll. Cam., B.A. 1837, M.A. 1840; M.P. for Wakefield 27 March 1857 to 23 April 1859. *d.* 21 March 1880.

CHARLESWORTH, MARIA LOUISA *(dau. of Rev. John Charlesworth 1782–1864). b.* rectory of Blakenham Parva near Ipswich 1 Oct. 1819; lived at Nutfield, Surrey 1864 to death; author of *The female visitor to the poor, by a Clergyman's daughter* 1846; *A book for the cottage* 1848; *The light of life* 1850; *Ministering Children* 1854 which had a very large circulation; *Where dwellest thou? or the Inner home* 1871. *d.* Nutfield 16 Oct. 1880. *Woman's Work in the great harvest field x*, 45–7 (1881).

CHARLETON, ROBERT *(eld. son of James Charleton, who d. Ashley hill, Bristol 1847). b.* Bristol 15 April 1809; pin manufacturer at Kingswood near Bristol 1833–52; one of the deputation of 3 Friends, to Emperor of Russia Feb. 1854; went with Robert Forster as a deputation to governments of Northern Europe to present the "Plea for liberty of conscience" issued by Society of Friends 1858; lectured in England and Ireland 1860 to death; author of *Opposition to the war, an address* 1855; *A brief memoir of Wm. Forster* 1867; *Thoughts on the Atonement* 1869. *d.* Ashley Down, Bristol 5 Dec. 1872. *Memoir of Robert Charleton edited by his sister-in-law Anna F. Fox* 1873, *portrait.*

CHARLEVILLE, CHARLES WILLIAM BURY, 2 Earl of *(only son of 1 Earl of Charleville 1764–1835, by Catherine Maria dau. of Thomas Townley Dawson and widow of James Tisdall, she was b. 22 Dec. 1762 and d. 24 Feb. 1851). b.* 29 April 1801; M.P. for Carlow 15 June 1826 to 3 Dec. 1832, for Penryn and Falmouth 11 Dec. 1832 to 29 Dec. 1834; succeeded as 2 Earl 31 Oct. 1835; representative peer of Ireland 13 April 1838 to death. *d.* near London 14 July 1851. *Burke's Portrait gallery of distinguished females i*, 5 and *ii*, 8 (1833); *G.M. xxxv*, 429–30 (1851).

CHARLEVILLE, CHARLES WILLIAM GEORGE BURY, 3 Earl of. *b.* Geneva 8 March 1822; succeeded 14 July 1851. *d.* Charleville forest, Tullamore, King's county 19 Jany. 1859.

CHARLEVILLE, CHARLES WILLIAM FRANCIS BURY, 4 Earl of. *b.* Charleville Forest 16 May 1852; succeeded 19 Jany. 1859. *d.* Staten island, New York 3 Nov. 1874.

CHARLEVILLE, ALFRED BURY, 5 Earl of. *b.* 19 Feb. 1829; succeeded 3 Nov. 1874. *d.* Brighton 26 June 1875.

CHARLTON, EDWARD *(2 son of Wm. John Charlton of Hesleyside, Northumberland 1784–1846). b.* 23 July 1814; M.D. Edin. 1836; M.D. Durham 1856, D.C.L. 1870; practised at Newcastle; pres. of Royal Med. Soc. of Edin.; pres. of British Medical Assoc. 1870; author of *An account of the late epidemic of*

scarlatina in Newcastle 1847; *Memorials of North Tyndale and its four surnames* 1871. *d.* 7 Eldon sq. Newcastle 14 May 1874. *Medical times and gazette i*, 632, (1874).

CHARLTON, JOHN. *b.* Hartlepool, Durham 1828; Jockey to Baron Rothschild 1851; won the One thousand guineas on Mentmore Lass 1853, Oaks on Mincemeat 1854, Derby and Oaks on Blink Bonny 1857, Ascot cup on Skirmisher 1857. *d.* Malton 27 July 1862. *Sporting Review xxxviii*, 17–19 (1857), *portrait; I.L.N. xxii*, 416 (1857), *portrait; Bell's Life in London* 3 Aug. 1862 p. 5.

CHARLTON, REV. WILLIAM HENRY. Educ. at Magd. hall, Ox., B.A. 1819, M.A. 1822; V. of Felmingham, Norfolk 1834 to death; P.C. of parish chapel of St. Marylebone, London 1851 to death; author of *Poems and translations* 1834; *Sacred sonnets and other poems* 1854. *d.* 11 July 1866 aged 79.

CHARNOCK, RICHARD *(2 son of James Charnock of Islington, London). b.* 1799; student of Gray's Inn 28 July 1813; admitted solicitor 1820; barrister I.T. 12 June 1840; one of Her Majesty's gentlemen at arms 1837–41; author of *A digest of all the new rules as to practice and pleading in all the courts* 1836, 2 ed. 1845; *Digest of the various decisions since the new pleading rules came into operation* 1837; *The act for abolishing arrest on mesne process in civil actions* 1838; *The police guide, containing the Metropolitan and City of London police acts* 1841; edited *J. Story's Commentaries on the law of Bailments* 1839. *d.* 5 King's Bench Walk, Temple 26 May 1864.

CHARRETIE, ANNA MARIA *(dau. of Mr. Kenwell of Vauxhall, London, architect). b.* Vauxhall 5 May 1819; studied drawing under Valentine Bartholomew; miniature and oil painter; exhibited 40 pictures at R.A., 4 at B.I. and 32 at Suffolk st. Gallery 1843–75. *(m.* 1841 John Charretie, captain H.E.I.Co., he *d.* 18 Nov. 1868). *d.* 8 Hornton st. Kensington, London 5 Oct. 1875. *E. C. Clayton's English female artists i*, 415–9 (1876).

CHARRINGTON, HAROLD *(son of Spencer Charrington of Hunsden house, Ware, Herts.)* Naval cadet 13 April 1869; lieut. 23 June 1880; flag lieut. of Euryalus 16 guns 15 April 1882; went with E. H. Palmer and Wm. Gill to Egypt for the purpose of detaching the Arabs from Arabi Pacha; shot by the Arabs near Gaza 11 Aug. 1882. *bur.* in crypt of St. Paul's cathedral, London 6 April 1883. *Graphic xxvi*, 469 (1882), *portrait; I.L.N. lxxxi*, 461 (1882), *portrait.*

CHART, HENRY NYE (eld. son of John Chart of London, who d. 1863 aged 76). b. 1822; acted at Sadler's Wells theatre under name of Henry Nye; low comedian and stage manager at Brighton theatre, July 1850 and acting manager 1852 to 28 Feb. 1854; lessee of Brighton theatre 29 July 1854 to 7 May 1866 when he purchased theatre and opened a new house on same site 15 Oct. 1866. (m. 27 July 1867 Ellen Elizabeth Rollason, leading actress at Brighton theatre). d. 9 New road, Brighton 18 June 1876. Era 25 June 1876 p. 5, col. 1, 2 July p. 10, col. 4.

CHARY, CHINTAMANNY RAGOONATHA. Attached to the Madras observatory nearly 40 years, first assistant 1863 to death; took a chief share in making 38,000 observations with transit-circle for the star catalogue; member of expeditions to observe total eclipses of the sun 18 Aug. 1868 and 11 Dec. 1871; discovered 2 new variable stars; F.R.A.S. 12 Jany. 1872; edited for 12 years astronomical portion of Asylum Press Almanac; published 1874 a pamphlet on the Transit of Venus, which appeared in 6 Indian languages as well as in English. d. Madras 5 Feb. 1880. Monthly notices of Royal Astronom. Soc. xli, 180 (1881).

CHASE, ANN (dau. of Mr. M'Clarnonde, who d. 1818). b. North of Ireland 1807; went to New York 1824; m. 1836 Franklin Chase, consul general at Tampico, Mexico; in the Mexican war 1846 city of Tampico was surprised and taken by the American forces, through her instrumentality, without loss of life, the fortress of the city was named Fort Ann in her honour, and the ladies of New Orleans presented to her a service of plate; lived at Tampico 1834–71 and at Brooklyn, New York 1871 to death. d. Brooklyn 24 Dec. 1874. S. J. Hale's Woman's Record 2 ed. 1855 pp. 859–61, portrait.

CHASE, JOHN. b. John st. Fitzroy sq. London 26 Feb. 1810; landscape water-colour painter; member of New Society of painters in watercolours 1835; exhibited 11 pictures at R.A. and 8 at Suffolk st. gallery 1826–70; author of A practical treatise on landscape painting and sketching from nature in water-colours, edited by Rev. James Harris 1861. d. 113 Charlotte st. Fitzroy sq. London 8 Jany. 1879.

CHASLES, VICTOR EUPHÉMION PHILARÈTE. b. Mainvilliers near Chartres 8 Oct. 1798; fled to England soon after the Bourbon restoration 1815; a proof reader at Valpy's printing office in Took's Court, Chancery lane, London; wrote in the Athenæum 1832 to death; keeper of Mazarin library, Paris 1837; professor in

CHASLES, V. E. P. (Con.)
Collége de France, Paris; translated many books from English into French. d. Venice 19 July 1873.

CHASSELS, REV. DAVID. b. Glasgow 30 April 1787; went with his parents to United States 1795; graduated at Dartmouth college, Vermont 1810; principal of the academy in Peacham, Vermont, and then of academy in Cambridge, New York; ordained by Presbytery of Troy 1820; took charge of the Fairfield academy 1821 and then of academy at Herkimer; a good teacher and fine classical scholar. d. Holland Patent, Oneida county, New York 10 Jany. 1870.

CHATELAIN, CLARA DE (dau. of M. de Pontigny). b. London 31 July 1807; wrote a number of fugitive pieces in English under pseudonyms of Leopold Wray, Baronne Cornelie de B., Rosalia Santa Croce and Leopoldine Ziska; wrote and composed many ballads; translated upwards of 400 songs; author of The Silver Swan 1847; A handbook of the four elements of vocalization 1850; The sedan chair 1866; Truly noble 1870; her name and her assumed names are attached to 140 original tales, 50 fairy tales and 16 handbooks. (m. 13 April 1843 the succeeding, they received the Dunmow flitch of bacon from W. H. Ainsworth 19 July 1855). d. insane in London 30 June 1876; bur. in Lyndhurst churchyard, Hants. 7 July. In Memoriam of Clara de Chatelain with a catalogue of her works 1876; Fleurs et fruits, souvenirs de feu Madame C. de Chatelain 1877, portrait; Andrews's History of the Dunmow flitch (1877) 18, 27–31.

CHATELAIN, JEAN BAPTISTE FRANÇOIS ERNEST DE. b. Paris 19 Jany 1801; published a weekly paper in London called Le petit Mercure 1825 which he changed to Le Mercure de Londre 1826; went on foot from Paris to Rome to study sayings and doings of Pope Leo XII, 1827; edited Le propagateur de la Gironde at Bordeaux 1830 for which he was condemned to 6 month's imprisonment and fined 1320 francs 5 May 1831; published many works in France 1833–8; assumed title of Chevalier 1840; lived in England 1842 to death, naturalised 6 June 1848; author of Rambles through Rome 1852; Ronces et Chardons 1869 and 50 other works, the chief being Beautés de la poesie Anglaise, 5 tomes 1860–72 containing over 1000 translations of poems from Chaucer to Tennyson; received Prussian order of Merit 1835. d. 20 Warwick crescent, Regents park, London 15 Aug. 1881. bur. in Lyndhurst churchyard 22 Aug. Catalogue des Ouvrages du Chevalier De Chatelain 1875.

CHATTERLEY, LOUISA *(dau. of Madame Simeon of St. James's st. Piccadilly, London, milliner).* b. St. James's st. 16 Oct. 1797; made her début on the stage at Bath, Nov. 1814 as Juliet; first appeared in London at Lyceum theatre 9 July 1816 as Harriet in *Is he jealous;* acted at Surrey theatre 1817, Olympic 1820, Covent Garden 1821; the best representative of a Frenchwoman on the English stage. *(m. 11 Aug. 1814 Wm. Simmonds Chatterley, actor 1787–1822, she m. (2) 13 Feb. 1830 Mr. Place).* d. 37 Brompton sq. London 3 Nov. 1866. *Oxberry's Dramatic biography v, 271–82 (1826), portrait; British Stage iv, 237 (1820), portrait; The Era 18 Nov. 1866 p. 11.*

CHATTERTON, FREDERICK BALSIR *(eld. son of Edward A. Chatterton of London, box book-keeper at many theatres who d. 5 Dec. 1875 in 65 year).* b. Euston sq. London 17 Sep. 1834; amateur actor at Cabinet and Soho theatres 1852; acting manager at Lyceum theatre 1857 and 1861–2; lessee of St. James's theatre 1859–60; joint lessee with Edmund Falconer of Drury Lane theatre 12 Sep. 1863, sole lessee 22 Sep. 1866 to 4 Feb. 1879 when he closed the theatre being £36,000 in debt; joint manager with B. Webster of Princess's and Adelphi theatres 1871; made his début as a reciter at St. James's hall, London 14 March 1883. d. 18 Feb. 1886. *E. Stirling's Old Drury Lane i, 273–317 (1881); Illust. sporting news v, 593 (1866), portrait; Touchstone, March 1879 p. 3, portrait.*

CHATTERTON, LADY HENRIETTA GEORGIANA MARCIA *(only child of Rev. Lascelles Iremonger, prebendary of Winchester, who d. 6 Jany. 1830).* b. 24 Arlington st. Piccadilly, London 11 Nov. 1806; author of *Aunt Dorothy's Tales,* 2 vols. 1837 anon.; *Rambles in the South of Ireland* 1839, 2 ed. 1839; *Home sketches and foreign recollections* 1841; *Allanston or the Infidel* 1843; *Compensation,* 2 vols. 1856 anon.; *The reigning beauty* 3 vols. 1858; *Memorials of Admiral Lord Gambier* 2 vols. 1861; *Leonore a tale and other poems* 2 vols. 1864; *Won at last* 3 vols. 1874 and 20 other books; received into Church of Rome, Aug. 1875. *(m. (1) 3 Aug. 1824 Sir W. A. Chatterton 1787–1855. m. (2) 1 June 1859 Edward Heneage Dering 2 son of Rev. John Dering, R. of Pluckley, Kent, he was b. 15 March 1827).* d. Malvern Wells 6 Feb. 1876. *Memoirs of Georgiana, Lady Chatterton with some passages from her diary by E. H. Dering 1878; J. Gillow's English Catholics i, 478–80 (1885).*

CHATTERTON, SIR JAMES CHARLES, 3 Baronet *(youngest son of Sir James Chatterton, 1 baronet, who d. 9 April 1806).* b. 1792;

cornet 12 light dragoons 23 Nov. 1809; lieut. col. 4 dragoon guards 9 Dec. 1831 to 3 Oct. 1848 when placed on h.p.; col. 5 lancers 23 Feb. 1858 to 22 Nov. 1868; general 31 March 1866; col. 4 dragoon guards 22 Nov. 1868 to death; M.P. for co. Cork 1831–5 and 1849–52; sheriff of co. Cork 1851–2; a gentleman of the privy chamber; succeeded his brother 7 Aug. 1855; K.S.F.; K.H. 1832; K.C.B. 10 Nov. 1862, G.C.B. 24 May 1873. d. Albemarle st. Piccadilly, London 5 Jany. 1874. *I.L.N. xvi, 133 (1850), portrait; Graphic ix, 52, 59 (1874), portrait.*

CHATTERTON, JOHN BALSIR *(son of John Chatterton of Portsmouth, professor of music).* b. Portsmouth 1802; pupil of Robert Bochsa the harpist; professor of the harp at R.A. of Music, London 1827; harpist to the Queen 1842 to death; published numerous transcriptions from popular operas for the harp. *(m. Eliza Davenport only dau. of Thomas Davenport Latham of Coombe hill, Croydon, she d. 9 Jany. 1877 in 71 year).* d. 32 Manchester st. Portman sq. London 9 April 1871. *Wm. Ball's Musical Gem (1831) 50–1, portrait.*

CHATTERTON, SIR WILLIAM ABRAHAM, 2 Baronet. b. 6 Aug. 1787; succeeded 9 April 1806. d. Rolls park, Chigwell, Essex 7 Aug. 1855.

CHATTO, WILLIAM ANDREW *(only son of Wm. Chatto of Newcastle, merchant, who d. 1804).* b. Newcastle 17 April 1799; wholesale teadealer in Eastcheap, London 1830–4; edited *New Sporting Magazine* 1839–41; projected *Puck a journalette of fun,* a penny daily comic illustrated paper 22 numbers 6 May 1844 to 29 June 1844; author of *Scenes and recollections of fly-fishing by Stephen Oliver the younger* 1834; *The angler's souvenir by P. Fisher* 1836, 2 ed. 1871; *A treatise on wood engraving* 1839, 3 ed. 1877; *Facts and speculations on the origin and history of playing cards* 1848. d. The Charterhouse, London 28 Feb. 1864.

CHAVASSE, PYE HENRY. b. Cirencester 1810; L.S.A. 1833; M.R.C.S. 18 Jany. 1833, F.R.C.S. 12 Aug. 1852; practised at Birmingham 1834–74; pres. of Queen's college medical chirurgical society 1856–8; author of *Advice to mothers on the management of their offspring* 1839, 14 ed. 1885; *Advice to a mother on the management of herself* 1869, 4 ed. 1879; *Counsel to a mother* 1869, 4 ed. 1879; *Aphorisms on mental culture of a child* 1872, 2 ed. 1877; his books were translated into nearly every European language and several Asiatic. d. 214 Hagley road, Edgbaston, Birmingham 21 Sep. 1879.

CHAYTOR, SIR WILLIAM RICHARD CARTER, 2 Baronet. *b.* 7 Feb. 1805; M.P. for city of Durham 23 March 1831 to 29 Dec. 1834; succeeded 28 Jany. 1847. *d.* Scrafton lodge, Middleham, Yorkshire 9 Feb. 1871.

CHEAPE, DOUGLAS *(younger son of John Cheape of Rossie, Fifeshire 1757–1838).* *b.* 1797; member of Faculty of Advocates, Edin. 1819; professor of civil law in Univ. of Edin. 1827–42, substituted English for Latin in class examinations; author of *Res Judicata* and other squibs published in the *Court of Session Garland* 1839, his other squibs were *The book of the chronicles of the city, being a Scriptural account of the election of a member for the city of Edinburgh in May* 1834, and probably *La festa d'Overgroghi* (Over Gogar near Edinburgh) a burlesque opera in Italian and English. *d.* Trinity grove, Trinity near Edin. 1 Sep. 1861. *Blackwood's Mag. cix,* 111–2 (1871).

CHEAPE, SIR JOHN *(brother of the preceding).* *b.* 1792; second lieut. Bengal engineers 3 Nov. 1809, col. commandant 19 Feb. 1844 to death; general 6 Dec. 1866; C.B. 20 July 1838, K.C.B. 5 June 1849, G.C.B. 28 March 1865; served in the 3 campaigns of first Burmese war 1824–6; second in command in second Burmese war 1852–3. *d.* Old park, Ventnor, Isle of Wight 30 March 1875. *W. F. B. Laurie's Second Burmese war* 1853.

CHEEKE, ALFRED. *b.* Evesham, Worcs. 1811; barrister M.T. 29 Jany. 1836; went to Sydney, Oct. 1837; comr. of Court of Claims, March 1841; crown prosecutor at quarter sessions, June 1841; chairman of quarter sessions 1844–5 and 1851–7; comr. of Court of requests for county of Cumberland, Jany. 1845; district court judge 1858 to June 1865; puisne judge of supreme court, June 1865 to death. *d.* Darling point, Sydney 14 March 1876. *Heads of the people ii,* 151–2 (1848), *portrait.*

CHEETHAM, JOHN *(son of George Cheetham of Stayleybridge).* *b.* Stayleybridge 1802; a merchant and manufacturer; M.P. for South Lancashire 14 July 1852 to 23 April 1859, and for Salford 11 July 1865 to 11 Nov. 1868. *d.* 18 May 1886.

CHELMSFORD, FREDERICK THESIGER, 1 Baron *(youngest son of Charles Thesiger, collector of customs in island of St. Vincent, who d. 18 Feb. 1831).* *b.* 1 Fowkes buildings, Tower st. London 15 July 1794; midshipman R.N. 1807; student of G.I. 5 Nov. 1818, of I.T. 2 March 1824, barrister I.T. 21 May 1824; went Home circuit, became leader; K.C. 7 July 1834; ben-

CHELMSFORD, F. T. 1 Baron *(Con.)*
cher of I.T. 18 Nov. 1834, reader 1842, treasurer 1843; solicitor general 17 April 1844 to July 1845; knighted at Buckingham palace 23 May 1844; attorney general 29 June 1845 to 3 July 1846 and Feb. 1852 to Dec. 1852; lord chancellor 26 Feb. 1858 to 18 June 1859 and 6 July 1866 to 29 Feb. 1868, when he resigned office; P.C. 26 Feb. 1858; M.P. for Woodstock 20 March 1840 to April 1844, for Abingdon 11 May 1844 to 1 July 1852 and for Stamford 10 July 1852 to 1 March 1858; F.R.S. 19 June 1845; created baron Chelmsford of Chelmsford, Essex 1 March 1858. *d.* 7 Eaton sq. London 5 Oct. 1878. *Illust. news of the world, vol.* 1 (1858), *portrait; London Society xi,* 87, 95 (1867), *portrait.*

CHENERY, THOMAS. *b.* Barbados 1826; ed. at Eton and Caius coll. Cam., B.A. 1854, M.A. 1868; correspondent of *Times* at Constantinople 1854–6, wrote leading articles and reviews in *Times;* barrister L.I. 10 June 1859; Lord Almoner's professor of Arabic at Oxford, April 1868 to Nov. 1877; member of Ch. Ch. Ox., incorporated M.A. 1868; member of 2 class of Imperial order of Medjidie, July 1869; secretary to Royal Asiatic Society; one of the revisers of Old Testament 1870–83; editor of *Times* Nov. 1877 to death, worked on it to 1 Feb. 1884; published *The six assemblies of El Hariry translated* 1867; edited the *Machberoth Ithiel of Jehudah ben Shelomo Alkharizi.* *d.* 16 Serjeant's Inn, Fleet st. London 11 Feb. 1884. *Journal of Royal Asiatic Soc. xvi, pp. xii–xv* (1884); *Times* 12 *Feb.* 1884 *p.* 6, *cols.* 5–6; *I.L.N. lxxxiv,* 180 (1884), *portrait; Graphic xxix,* 148 (1884), *portrait.*

CHEPMELL, REV. HAVILLAND LE MESURIER. Educ. at Pembroke coll. Ox., Townsend scholar, B.A. 1833, M.A. 1836, B.D. and D.D. 1851; chaplain to Royal military college, Sandhurst 1841–67; translated *Lectures on Roman History by B. G. Niebuhr* 1849; author of *Course of history, Greek, Roman and English,* 10 ed. 1874, 2nd series 2 vols. 1857. *d.* The hermitage, St. Martin's, Guernsey 21 March 1887.

CHERMSIDE, HENRY LOWTHER *(2 son of the succeeding).* *b.* 1825; second lieut. R.A. 19 June 1844, colonel 8 Sep. 1875 to 16 Nov. 1878 when he retired with hon. rank of major general; commanded R.A. at Poona 1876–8; C.B. 29 May 1875. *d* Regia house, Teignmouth 2 Jany. 1886.

CHERMSIDE, SIR ROBERT ALEXANDER *(3 son of Dr. Chermside of Portaferry, co. Down).* *b.* Portaferry 1787; Assist. surgeon to 7th Hussars 16 Aug. 1810; Surgeon to 10th Hussars

CHERMSIDE, SIR R. A. (Con.)
29 June 1815 to 30 Oct. 1823; graduated
M.D. at Edin. 1817; L.R.C.P. London 16
April 1821, F.R.C.P. 27 April 1843; phys.
to British embassy at Paris; physician extra-
ordinary to Duchess of Kent; K.C.H. 31
July 1835; Knight of St. John of Jerusalem;
Knight of Red Eagle of Prussia; Knight of
Legion of Honour. d. Oxford 8 Sep. 1860.

CHERRY, FREDERICK CLIFFORD. Veterinary
surgeon of 11 light dragoons 12 Oct. 1803,
of Waggon Train 16 July 1807 to 25 Sep.
1819 when placed on h.p.; Vet. surgeon 2
life guards 10 May 1833; principal vet. surgeon in the army 17 Sep. 1839 to death. d.
Clapham, London 11 July 1854.

CHESHAM, CHARLES COMPTON CAVENDISH, 1
Baron (4 son of 1 Earl of Burlington 1754–
1834). b. Savile row, London 28 Aug. 1793;
M.P. for Newtown, Hants. 1821–6 for Yarmouth, Isle of Wight 1831–2, for East Sussex
1832–41, for Youghal 1841–7, for Bucks
1847–57; created Baron Chesham of Chesham,
Bucks. 15 Jany. 1858. d. 19 Grosvenor sq.
London 10 Nov. 1863.

CHESHAM, WILLIAM GEORGE CAVENDISH, 2
Baron. b. 20 Oct. 1815; ed. at Eton; M.P.
for Peterborough 30 July 1847 to 1 July
1852, for Bucks. 23 Dec. 1857 to 10 Nov.
1863 when he succeeded. d. Latimer, near
Chesham, Bucks. 26 June 1882.

CHESHAM, SARAH. Tried at Chelmsford
assizes 1847 upon a charge of poisoning the
illegitimate child of Lydia Taylor but acquitted; tried 1848 for poisoning two of her
children but acquitted; tried at Chelmsford
assizes 6 March 1851 for poisoning with
arsenic her husband Richard Chesham, who d.
May 1850, when she was found guilty and
sentenced to death; known as 'Arsenic Sal';
executed at Chelmsford 25 March 1851. A.R.
(1850) 109, (1851) 396–400; A. H. Dymond's
The law on its trial (1865) 211–19.

CHESNEY, CHARLES CORNWALLIS (son of
Charles Cornwallis Chesney, captain Bengal artillery who d. 1830). b. Packolet, near Kilkeel,
co. Down 29 Sept. 1826; second lieut R.E.
18 June 1845, lieut col. 1 March 1868 to
death; commanded R.E. in home district
1873 to death; professor of military history
at Sandhurst 1858–68; the best military critic
of his day; member of royal commission on
military education 1868–70; sent by government to report on Franco-German war 1871;
author of A military view of recent campaigns

CHESNEY, C. C. (Con.)
in Virginia and Maryland 1863, 2 ed. 1864;
Waterloo lectures, a study of the campaign of
1815, 1868, 3 ed. 1874; Essays in military
biography 1874. d. 11 Grosvenor mansions,
Victoria st. London 19 March 1876. Graphic
xiii, 342, 348 (1876), portrait.

CHESNEY, FRANCIS RAWDON (2 son of Alexander Chesney 1755–1843, coast-officer in the
district of Mourne, co. Down). b. Ballyvea
Mourne 16 March 1789; 2 lieut. R.A. 9
Nov. 1804, commanded R.A. at Hong Kong
1843–7, col. 11 Nov. 1851 to 6 Jany. 1855,
col. commandant 27 June 1864 to death;
general 1 Jany. 1868; explored Syrian route
to India 1830–1; commanded expedition for
examining route to India by the Euphrates
1835–6; explored the Tigris and Karūm
1836–7; surveyed Euphrates route again 1857;
F.R.G.S. 1838, gold medallist 1838; F.R.S.
6 Feb. 1834; author of Expedition for survey
of Euphrates and Tigris 2 vols. 1850; Observations on past and present state of fire arms 1852;
The Russo-Turkish campaign of 1828 and 1829,
1854; Narrative of Euphrates expedition 1868.
d. Packolet 30 Jany. 1872. The Life of F. R.
Chesney, by his wife and daughter, edited by S.
Lane-Poole (1885), portrait; Dublin Univ. mag.
xviii, 574–80 (1841), portrait; Journal of
Royal Geog. Soc. xlii, 159–61 (1872).

CHESSAR, JANE AGNES. b. Edinburgh 1835;
had charge of a class in Home and Colonial
training college, London 1852–66; lecturer
and private tutor in London 1866–75; member for Marylebone of London school board 27
Nov. 1873 to 1875; edited Mrs. Somerville's
Physical geography 1877; W. Hughes's Manual
of geography 1880; wrote much for the Queen
and other newspapers. d. Brussels 3 Sep.
1880. Graphic ix, 30 (1874), portrait.

CHESTER, HARRY (youngest son of sir Robert
Chester of Bush hall, Herts. 1768–1848). b. 1
Oct. 1806; ed. at Charterhouse, Westminster
and Trin. coll. Cam.; clerk in Privy Council
office May 1826 to 1 Jany. 1859; assistant
sec. to Committee of Privy Council on education 1840–58; author of The lay of the Lady
Ellen, a tale of 1834, London 1835, and of an
article entitled The food of the people in Macmillan's Mag. Oct. and Nov. 1868. d. 63
Rutland gate, London 5 Oct. 1868.

CHESTER, JOSEPH LEMUEL (son of Joseph
Chester of Norwich, Connecticut, grocer, who d.
1832). b. Norwich 30 April 1821; a merchant's clerk in New York 1840, in Phila-

CHESTER, J. L. *(Con.)*

delphia 1845 ; a temperance lecturer in many
of the states ; musical editor of *Godey's Lady's
Book* 1845–50 ; one of the editors of *Philadelphia Inquirer* and of the *Daily Sun* 1852 ; member of council of Philadelphia 1854 ; one of
aide-de-camps of governor of Pennsylvania
with rank of colonel 1855–8 ; lived in London
1859 to death ; made most extensive extracts
from parish registers, and at his death left 87
folio vols. of such extracts ; copied the matriculation register of the university of Oxford
1866–9 ; D.C.L. Ox. 22 June 1881 ; one of
founders of Harleian Society 1869 ; a member
of first council of Royal Historical Society
1870 ; published *Greenwood cemetery and other
poems* 1843 ; *The registers of the abbey of St.
Peter, Westminster* 1876, (Harleian Society) also
Privately Printed for the author ; *The parish
registers of St. Michael, Cornhill, London* 1882.
d. 124 Southwark park road, London 26 May
1882. *Latting's Memoir of Colonel Chester* 1882 ;
Dean's Memoir of Colonel Chester 1884, *portrait ;
Marshall's Genealogist vi,* 189*–92* (1882) ;
New Monthly Mag. June 1881 *pp.* 626–30,
portrait.

CHESTERFIELD, GEORGE AUGUSTUS FREDERICK STANHOPE, 6 Earl of *(only son of 5 Earl
of Chesterfield* 1755–1815). *b.* Bretby hall,
Burton-on-Trent, Derbyshire 23 May 1805 ;
ed. at Eton and Ch. Ch. Ox. ; succeeded 29
Aug. 1815 ; lord of the bedchamber to George
iv, 11 Aug. 1828 to 26 June 1830 ; master of
the Buckhounds 30 Dec. 1834 to April 1835 ;
P.C. 29 Dec. 1834 ; began racing 1826, won
Ascot cup with Zinganee 1829, the Oaks with
Industry 1838 and Lady Evelyn 1849 and
St. Leger with Don John 1838 ; master of
Pytchley hounds 1838–40 ; the yellow gossamer overcoat known as a Chesterfield was
called after him ; he is depicted under name
of Earl of Chesterlane in *D'Horsay, or the
follies of the day by A man of fashion* 1844. *d.*
3 Grosvenor sq. London 1 June 1866. *bur.* at
Bretby church 8 June. *Rice's History of the
British turf i,* 284–6 (1879) ; *Sporting Review
xxix,* 450–2 (1858), *lvi,* 10, 79 (1866) ; *Baily's
Mag. ii,* 55–8 (1861), *portrait ; Sporting Times
7 March* 1885 ; *Doyle's Official baronage i,* 374,
(1886), *portrait.*

CHESTERFIELD, GEORGE PHILIP CECIL
ARTHUR STANHOPE, 7 Earl of. *b.* 28 Sep.
1831 ; ed. at Eton ; cornet Royal horse guards
21 Aug. 1849, lieut. 2 Sep. 1853 to 1860 ;
M.P. for south Notts. 18 Dec. 1860 to 1 June
1866 when he succeeded. *d.* Bretby hall 1
Dec. 1871.

CHESTERFIELD, GEORGE PHILIP STANHOPE,
8 Earl of. *b.* 29 Nov. 1822 ; succeeded 1 Dec.
1871, his claim was admitted by House of
Lords 7 July 1873. *d.* Killendanagh near
Lifford, co. Donegal 19 Oct. 1883.

CHESTERFIELD, HENRY EDWYN CHANDOS
SCUDAMORE STANHOPE, 9 Earl of *(eld. son of
Sir Edwyn Francis Scudamore Stanhope, 2 baronet* 1793–1874). *b.* Teignmouth, Devon 8
April 1821 ; ed. at Balliol coll. Ox., B.A.
1841 ; succeeded as 3 baronet 8 Feb. 1874,
as 9 Earl 19 Oct. 1883. *d.* St. Leonard's on
Sea 21 Jany. 1887.

CHETHAM-STRODE, SIR EDWARD (4 *son of
Thomas Chetham of Mellon hall, Derbyshire). b.*
5 July 1775 ; entered navy 29 April 1786 ;
captain 13 Oct. 1807 ; captain of the Leander
50 guns 1 May 1816 to July 1819 ; superintendent of Haslar hospital and Royal Clarence
Victualling yard 5 April 1838 to 23 Nov.
1841 ; R.A. on h.p. 23 Nov. 1841 ; C.B. 8
Dec. 1815 ; K.C.H. 1 Jany. 1837 ; knighted
by Wm. iv, at St. James's palace 1 March
1837 ; K.C.B. 8 May 1845 ; assumed additional surname of Strode 1845 ; granted good
service pension 18 June 1857 ; admiral of the
white 22 Aug. 1857. *d.* Southill house, Shepton-Mallet, Somerset 1 April 1862.

CHETWODE, SIR JOHN NEWDIGATE LUDFORD,
5 Baronet. *b.* Oakley near Mucklestone,
Staffs. 12 Nov. 1788 ; succeeded 17 Dec.
1845 ; sheriff of Warwick 1852. *d.* Oakley 8
Sep. 1873.

CHETWYND RICHARD WALTER CHETWYND,
6 Viscount. *b.* Bolton row, London 14 Dec.
1800 ; succeeded 27 Feb. 1821. *d.* Marpool
near Exmouth 6 Dec. 1879.

CHETWYND, SIR GEORGE, 3 Baronet. *b.*
Grendon hall near Atherstone, co. Warwick
6 Sep. 1809 ; succeeded 24 May 1850. *d.*
Grendon hall 25 March 1869.

CHETWYND, GEORGE *(son of W. J. Chetwynd,
captain 52 foot). b.* 1824 ; receiver and accountant general, Post Office, London 1864 to
death ; C.B. 16 May 1881. *d.* Hyde Vale,
Blackheath, London 3 Dec. 1882.

CHETWYND, WILLIAM FAWKENER. *b.* 15
Oct. 1788 ; M.P. for Stafford 11 Dec. 1832 to
23 June 1841. *d.* Brocton hall near Stafford
25 April 1873.

CHEVALLIER, REV. TEMPLE *(eld. son of Rev.
Temple Fiske Chevallier, R. of Badingham,
Suffolk). b.* Badingham 19 Oct. 1794 ; ed. at

CHEVALLIER, REV. T. *(Con.)*

Pemb. coll. Cam., fellow 1819; 2 wrangler and 2 Smith's prizeman 1817; B A. 1817, M.A. 1820, B.D. 1833; fellow and tutor of St. Cath. hall, Cam.; V. of St. Andrew the Great, Cam. 1821–34; Hulsean lecturer 1826–7; P.C. of Esh near Durham 1835–69; registrar of Univ. of Durham 1835; professor of mathematics in Univ. of Durham 1835–71 and professor of astronomy 1841–71; hon. canon of Durham cathedral 2 Oct. 1846, canon res. Sep. 1865 to death; F.R.A.S. 13 Dec. 1839; author of *A translation of the epistles of Clement of Rome, Polycarp, and Ignatius and of the Apologies of Justin Martyr and Tertullian* 1833, 2 *ed.* 1851 and of 18 papers in journals of Royal Astronom. Soc. *d.* at house of his son-in-law, the vicarage, Harrow-Weald, Middlesex 4 Nov. 1873. *Monthly notices of Royal Astronom. Soc. xxxiv,* 137–39 (1874).

CHEVERS, NORMAN *(son of Forbes Mackbean Chevers, surgeon R.N.) b.* Greenhithe on the Thames 1818; ed. at Guy's hospital; assistant surgeon Bengal army 1 Aug. 1848; secretary to Medical Board, Calcutta 1855–61; principal of Calcutta medical college, professor of medicine and first phys. of the college hospital 27 April 1861 to 1876; deputy surgeon general to 1876; C.I.E.; Co-editor of the *Indian annals of medical science* 1853–72; author of *Management of the diseases of the heart* 1851; *Removable and mitigable causes of death* 1852; *Medical jurisprudence in India* 1855, 3 *ed.* 1861 for which he was awarded the Swiney prize by Royal coll. of phys.; *Preservation of the health of seamen* 1864, 2 *ed.* 1866; *Commentary on the diseases of India* 1886. *d.* 32 Tavistock road, Bayswater, London 2 Dec. 1886. *British medical journal* 18 *Dec.* 1886 *p.* 1245; *Biograph vi,* 129–31 (1881).

CHEYNE, CHARLES HARTWELL HORNE *(eld. son of Rev. Charles Cheyne, second master at Christ's hospital, who d. 1867). b.* 1 May 1838; ed. at Merchant Taylor's, and St. John's coll. Cam., foundation scholar, June 1859, 18 wrangler 1861, B.A. 1861, M.A. 1864; second mathematical master of Westminster school, March 1863 to Dec. 1876; F.R.A.S. June 1868; author of *An elementary treatise on the planetary theory* 1862, 3 *ed.* 1883; *The Earth's motion of rotation, including the theory of precession and nutation* 1867. *d.* Torquay 1 Jany. 1877. *Monthly notices of Royal Astronom. Soc. xxxvii,* 147 (1877).

CHICHESTER, HENRY THOMAS PELHAM, 3 Earl of *(eld. son of 2 Earl of Chichester 1756–1826). b.* Stratton st. Piccadilly, London 25

CHICHESTER, H. T. P. *(Con.)*

Aug. 1804; ed. at Westminster and Trin. coll. Cam.; cornet 6 dragoons 24 June 1824; lieut. Royal horse guards 28 April 1827; succeeded as 3 Earl 4 July 1826; pres. of Church Missionary Society 1835; an ecclesiastical comr. for England 22 Feb. 1841 to death; joint comr. to consider state of bishoprics in England and Wales 30 Jany. 1847; chief comr. for management of ecclesiastical estates 24 Aug. 1850 to Oct. 1878; lord lieut. of Sussex 21 Nov. 1860 to death. *d.* Stanmer park near Lewes 16 March 1886. *Sunday at home* (1885), 296–300, *portrait.*

CHICHESTER, SIR ALEXANDER PALMER BRUCE, 2 Baronet. *b.* Malta 24 Dec. 1842; succeeded 10 Dec. 1851; sheriff of Devon 1868. *d.* Arlington court, Barnstaple 25 Jany. 1881.

CHICHESTER, FREDERICK RICHARD, called by courtesy, Earl of Belfast *(younger son of 3 Marquis of Donegall 1797–1883). b.* 25 Nov. 1827; ed. at Eton; pres. of Classical harmonist's society established at Belfast 1852; author of *Two generations or birth parentage and education, a novel* 2 vols. 1851; *Poets and poetry of the nineteenth century, a course of lectures* 1852. *d.* Naples 15 Feb. 1853.

CHICHESTER, JOHN LUDFORD (6 *son of 2 Marquis of Donegall* 1769–1844). *b.* 12 Nov. 1811; M.P. for Belfast 20 Aug. 1845 to 1 1 July 1852. *d.* Cambridge house, Twickenham 22 April 1873.

CHICHESTER, SIR JOHN PALMER BRUCE, 1 Baronet *(eld. son of John Palmer Bruce Chichester 1769–1823, colonel of Royal Cardigan rifle corps). b.* 1794; served in the navy 1810–20; M.P. for Barnstaple 3 May 1831 to 23 June 1841; created baronet 7 Sep. 1840. *d.* 20 Eaton sq. London 10 Dec. 1851.

CHIFNEY, SAMUEL *(younger son of Samuel Chifney, jockey* 1753–1807). *b.* 1786; rode for Prince of Wales at Stockbridge races 1802; won the Oaks on Briseis 1807, on Sorcery 1811, on Landscape 1816, on Shoveller 1819 and on Wings 1825; won the Derby on Sam a horse called after himself 1818 and on Sailor 1820; won the One thousand guineas on Extempore 1843; a trainer at Newmarket to 1843; had a stud of his own there 1843–51. *d.* Hove, Brighton 29 Aug. 1854. *Sporting Review vii,* 416 (1842), *portrait, xxxii,* 231–5, 312–6 (1854) *xxxiii,* 31–5, 89–95, 162–7, 231–6, 309–14, 401–6 (1855) *xxxiv,* 5–10, 75–8 (1855).

CHIFNEY, WILLIAM (*brother of the preceding*). *b.* Newmarket 1784; a trainer near Newmarket; owner with his brother of a small stud of horses at Newmarket to June 1834; publicly thrashed on 31 May 1803 Lieut. col. George Leigh, an equerry to Prince of Wales, for abusing his father, imprisoned for the assault 6 months at Cambridge. *d.* Pancras sq. Pancras road, London 14 Oct. 1862. *H. Corbett's Tales of sporting life* (1864) 176–82.

CHILD-VILLIERS, FREDERICK WILLIAM (3 *son of 5 Earl of Jersey 1773–1859*). *b.* Berkeley sq. London 20 July 1815; ed. at Eton; lieut. Coldstream Guards 1838 to 24 May 1844 when placed on h.p.; M.P. for Weymouth 15 Dec. 1847 to 1 July 1852; lieut. col. commandant of 5 Middlesex militia 16 May 1853 to 4 May 1855; sheriff of Northamptonshire 1869. *d.* Berkeley sq. 24 May 1871.

CHILDE, HENRY LANGDON. *b.* 1782; made his first magic lantern 1797; painted on glass and produced slides illustrating natural history and astronomy; invented dissolving views 1807 which he exhibited at Adelphi theatre, London 1818 and at Her Majesty's theatre 1837–40; connected with the Polytechnic Institution, Regent st. from date of opening 6 Aug. 1838 for nearly 20 years; invented the chromatrope, a lantern slide by which beautiful effects of colour were produced. *d.* Mostyn road, Brixton, London 15 Oct. 1874.

CHILDE, JAMES WARREN. Landscape and Miniature painter in London 1798 to death; most of his exhibited works were portraits of popular actors and actresses; exhibited 76 pictures at R.A. and 16 at Suffolk st. gallery 1798–1853. *d.* 27 Scarsdale villas, Kensington, London 19 Sep. 1862 aged 82.

CHILDE, WILLIAM LACON. *b.* 3 Jany. 1786; ed. at Harrow and Ch. Ch. Ox.; M.P. for Wenlock 9 March 1820 to 2 June 1826; sheriff of Salop 1828. *d.* 15 Dec. 1880.

CHILDERS, JOHN WALBANKE. *b.* 27 May 1798; ed. at Eton and Ch. Ch. Ox., B.A. 1825, M.A. 1834; M.P. for Cambridgeshire 21 Dec. 1832 to 30 Dec. 1834, for Malton 12 Feb. 1836 to April 1846 and 28 July 1847 to 1 July 1852. *d.* Cantley hall, Doncaster 8 Feb. 1886. *Times* 9 *Feb.* 1886 *p.* 10 *col.* 4.

CHILDERS, MICHAEL. Ensign 2 West India regiment 25 Feb. 1799; lieut. col. 11 light dragoons 21 Sep. 1820 to 25 March 1836 when placed on h.p.; C.B. 26 Dec. 1818; colonel 10 Jany. 1837; retired 8 June 1838. *d.* Sandhutton near York 9 Jany. 1854.

CHILDERS, ROBERT CÆSAR (*son of Rev. Charles Childers, chaplain at Nice*). *b.* 1838; ed. at Wadham coll. Ox., Hebrew scholar; a writer in Ceylon civil service 1860, private secretary to the governor Sir Charles McCarthy 3 years; office assistant to government agent in Kandy to March 1864 when he returned home; sub-librarian at India office, London 1872; professor of Pali and Buddhist literature at Univ. coll. London, July 1873 to death; published Pali text of the *Khaddaka Patha* with English translation and notes in *Journal of Royal Asiatic Society, Nov.* 1869 being the first Pali text printed in England; *Dictionary of the Pali language 2 vols.* 1872–5, awarded by the Institute of France the Volney prize, July 1876 as the best philological work of the year. *d.* Weybridge, Surrey 25 July 1876. *Annual report of Royal Asiatic Society, June* 1877 *pp. viii-x.*

CHILDREN, JOHN GEORGE (*only child of George Children of Ferox hall, Tunbridge, Kent 1742–1818*). *b.* Ferox hall 18 May 1777; ed. at Eton and Queen's coll. Cam.; established gunpowder mills at Ramhurst 1813; a librarian in department of antiquities at British Museum 1816, keeper of the Zoological collections 1823 to 25 March 1840; F.R.S. 12 March 1807, one of the secretaries 1826–7 and 1830–7, vice pres. 1837–8; F.R.S. of Edin. 1812; F.S.A. 1816; pres. of Entomological Soc. 1834–5; discovered a method for extracting silver from its ore without the use of mercury 1824; published translations of *Thenard's Traité de Chymie* 1819, and of *Berzelius's Use of the blowpipe in chemical analysis* 1822. *d.* Halstead place, Kent 1 Jany. 1852. *Memoir of J. G. Children, privately printed* 1853; *Min. of proc. of Instit. of C.E. xii,* 137–40 (1853); *G.M. xxxvii,* 622–4 (1852).

CHILDS, CHARLES (*son of the succeeding*). *b.* 1807; head of firm of John Childs and Son of Bungay, Suffolk, printers 1853 to death; gave evidence before select committee of House of Commons on the Queen's printers' patent 1859; wrote several articles in the *Westminster Review. d.* Bungay 26 Dec. 1876.

CHILDS, JOHN. *b.* Bungay 1783; printer at Bungay 1806 to death; projected with Joseph Ogle Robinson the series known as '*Imperial octavo editions of standard authors;* a pioneer of movement for cheap and good literature for the million. *d.* Bungay 12 Aug. 1853 in 70 year.

CHILDS, JOSEPH. Second lieut. R.M. 21 April 1809, col. commandant 14 July 1855 to 31 March 1857 when he retired on full pay; M.G. 31 March 1857. *d.* Liskeard, Cornwall 2 Jany. 1870 aged 83.

CHILTON, GEORGE *(eld. son of George Chilton of Chancery lane, London, solicitor).* Educ. at Queen's coll. Ox., B.A. 1818; barrister I.T. 16 June 1820, bencher 1837, reader 1848, treasurer 1849; recorder of Gloucester, March 1837 to death; Q.C. 1837; judge of county courts for Greenwich and Lambeth (circuit 48), July 1847 to death; edited *R. B. Comyn's A treatise on the law of landlord and tenant*, 2 ed. 1830. *d.* Boulogne 1 Nov. 1852 aged 56.

CHINNERY, REV. SIR NICHOLAS, 3 Baronet *(only son of Sir Brodrick Chinnery, 2 baronet 1779–1840).* *b.* Bath 7 July 1804; ed. at Queen's coll. Cam., B.A. 1826, M.A. 1829; succeeded 17 Jany. 1840; C. of Trinity chapel, Conduit st. London 1855–6; author of *Anglican formalism* 1862; *The design of heresies* 1867; killed in a railway accident between Abergele and Llandulas stations on Chester and Holyhead railway 20 Aug. 1868, when 33 persons were literally burned alive. *A.R.* (1868) 106–11; *I.L.N. liii*, 234 (1868).

CHIOSSO, JAMES. Opened gymnasia and schools of arms at 21 New road, Marylebone, London 1853, and at 123 Oxford st. 1854; professor of gymnastics at University college school, London, where he erected one of the earliest gymnasia in London about 1838; invented the Calisthenic and Gymnastic Polymachinon 1855; author of *Remarks on physical education* 1845; *Gymnastics an essential branch of national education* 1854; *The gymnastic polymachinon* 1855. *d.* 11 Norfolk villas, Bayswater, London 14 March 1864 aged 75. *Illust. Sporting news i*, 116 (1862), *portrait.*

CHIPP, EDMUND THOMAS *(eld. son of the succeeding).* *b.* London 25 Dec. 1823; a member of Society of British Musicians 1842; organist of St. John's chapel, Hampstead 1843–6; a violinist in Queen's private band 1843–55; organist at St. Olave, Southwark 1847–52 and at St. Mary-at-Hill 1852–6; organist at Panopticon, Leicester sq. 1855 and at Holy Trinity church, Paddington 1856–62; Mus. Bac. Cam. 1859, Mus. Doc. 1861; organist of St. George's ch. and Ulster Hall, Belfast 1862–6, and of Ely cathedral, Nov. 1866 to death; composed *Job an oratorio; Naomi a sacred idyll*, several songs, services, and organ and pianoforte music. *d.* Nice 17 Dec. 1886. *Biograph vi*, 563–5 (1881); *Graphic xxxv*, 100 (1887), *portrait.*

CHIPP, THOMAS PAUL. *b.* London 25 May 1793; teacher of the harp; harpist in orchestra of Covent Garden theatre 1818, of Her Majesty's theatre 1826; a member of all chief

CHIPP, T. P. *(Con.)*

London orchestras 1813–66; played at coronations of George iv, Wm. iv, and Victoria. *d.* Camden Town, London 19 June 1870.

CHISHOLM, CAROLINE *(dau. of Wm. Jones of Wootton, Northamptonshire).* *b.* Wootton, May 1808; went to Madras 1832 where she established Female school of industry; went to Sydney 1839 where she opened an office for the use of emigrants, Jany. 1841; promoted emigration of families from England 1846–54; laboured in Australia 1854–66; granted civil list pension of £100, 19 June 1867; author of *The A.B.C. of colonisation* 1850, *Emigration and transportation relatively considered.* (*m.* 1830 Archibald Chisholm, captain 13 Madras N.I. who *d.* Rugby 17 Aug. 1877 aged 82). *d.* 43ª Barclay road, Walham Green near London 25 March 1877. *bur.* Northampton 31 March. *Mackenzie's Memoirs of C. Chisholm* 1852, *portrait; Michelet's La Femme* (1860) 398–406; *I.L.N. xx*, 301 (1852), *portrait, xxiv*, 337 (1854), *portrait, lxx*, 349 (1877), *portrait.*

CHISHOLM, WALTER *(son of Mr. Chisholm of Easter Harelaw near Chirnside, Berwickshire, shepherd).* *b.* Easter Harelaw 21 Dec. 1856; wrote poems signed 'Wattie' in the *Haddington Courier* and in the *People's Friend;* his poem entitled *Scotia's Border Land* gained second prize in competition promoted by *People's Journal* Christmas 1876. *d.* of pleurisy at Dowlaw farm 1 Oct. 1877. *Poems by the late Walter Chisholm*, edited by *W. Cairns* 1879 pp. ix-xvi.

CHITTY, EDWARD (3 son of Joseph Chitty of the Middle Temple, London, barrister 1776–1841). *b.* 1804; barrister L.I. 7 July 1829; went to Jamaica 1840; author of *An index to all the reported cases of equity and bankruptcy* 2 vols. 1831, 3 ed. 4 vols. 1853; author with E. E. Deacon of *Reports of cases in bankruptcy* 4 vols. 1833–7; with Basil Montagu of *Reports of cases in bankruptcy* 1840; with F. Forster of *A digested index to all the common law reports relating to conveyancing and bankruptcy* 1841. *d.* Cambridge lodge, Walham green near London 28 Sep. 1863.

CHITTY, THOMAS *(brother of the preceding).* *b.* 1801; practised in London as a special pleader below the bar 1820–77; taught many men who became judges and leading counsel; author of *Forms of practical proceedings in the courts of Queen's Bench Common Pleas and Exchequer of Pleas* 1834, 12 ed. 1883; edited *J. F. Archbold's Practice of the Court of King's Bench*, 4 ed. 2 vols. 1835, 5 ed. 2 vols. 1836, 6 *ed.* 2 vols. 1838, 7 *ed.* 2 vols. 1840, *and* 8 *ed.* 2 vols. 1845–7. *d.* 47 Lancaster gate, Hyde park, London 13 Feb. 1878.

CHITTY, Tompson. Barrister M.T. 31 Jany. 1851 ; edited *Joseph Chitty's A practical treatise on the law of contracts, not under seal,* 3 *ed.* 1841 ; author with Leofric Temple of *A practical treatise on the law of carriers of goods and passengers* 1856. *d.* Stockwell Surrey 4 Feb. 1863.

CHOLMELEY, Sir Montagu John, 2 Baronet. *b.* Grantham 5 Aug. 1802 ; M.P. for Grantham 14 June 1826 to 23 April 1831, for North Lincolnshire 12 Jany. 1847 to 1 July 1852, and 31 March 1857 to death ; succeeded 10 March 1831. *d.* Easton hall, Grantham 18 Jany. 1874.

CHOLMLEY, Sir George, 7 Baronet. *b.* Welburn, Kirkby Moorside, Yorkshire 26 Nov. 1782 ; M.P. for Yorkshire 6 May 1831 to 3 Dec. 1832, for west riding of Yorkshire 20 Dec. 1832 to 23 June 1841, for Preston 29 June 1841 to 21 March 1857 ; succeeded 8 Jany. 1834 ; assumed name of Cholmley in lieu of Strickland by royal licence 17 March 1865. *d.* Newton hall near Malton 23 Dec. 1874.

CHOLMONDELEY, George Horatio Cholmondeley, 2 Marquis of. *b.* Paris 16 Jany. 1792 ; M.P. for Castle Rising, Norfolk 21 Feb. 1817 to 24 Dec. 1821 ; summoned to House of Peers in his father's barony of Newburgh 24 Dec. 1821 ; succeeded 10 April 1827 ; Joint hereditary grand chamberlain of England 10 April 1827 to death ; P.C. 19 July 1830. *d.* Cholmondeley castle, Nantwich, Cheshire 8 May 1870.

CHOLMONDELEY, William Henry Hugh, 3 Marquis of. *b.* Piccadilly, London 31 Aug. 1800 ; ed. at Eton and Ch. Ch. Ox. ; M.P. for Castle Rising 1 Feb. 1822 to 3 Dec. 1832, for South Hants. 14 July 1852 to 21 March 1857 ; succeeded 8 May 1870 ; joint hereditary grand chamberlain of England 8 May 1870 to death. *d.* Houghton hall, Rougham, Norfolk 16 Dec. 1884.

CHORLEY, Charles *(son of John Chorley, lieutenant 1 Somerset militia, who d. 22 Feb. 1839 aged 66).* *b.* Taunton about 1810 ; sub-editor of *Cornwall Gazette* at Truro 30 years ; sec. to Truro Public Rooms company ; sub-manager of Truro Savings' bank ; edited *Journal of the Royal Institution of Cornwall* 1863–74 ; published *Jephtha or the Vow   tragedy by [George]*

Buchanan, translated from the Latin by C. C[horley] 1854 ; *The Baptist or calumny, a tragedy by [George] Buchanan, translated from the Latin by C. C[horley]* 1864, *Verse by C. C.* 1867. *d.* 24 Lemon st. Truro 22 June 1874. *Journal of Royal Instit. of Cornwall, Oct.* 1874 *pp. iii, iv, vii.*

CHORLEY, Henry Fothergill (3 *son of John Chorley of Blackley Hurst, Lancs. lock maker, who d.* 15 *April* 1816). *b.* Blackley Hurst 15 Dec. 1808 ; started with his brother W. B. Chorley, M.D. an annual called *The Winter's Wreath* 1828 ; a reviewer on the Athenæum 1833–66, musical critic of it 1833–68 ; author of *Sketches of a Sea-port town* 3 vols. 1835 ; *Conti the discarded, a novel* 3 vols. 1835 ; *Memorials of Mrs. Hemans* 2 vols. 1836 ; *Modern German music* 3 vols. 1854 ; *Thirty years musical recollections* 2 vols. 1862 ; *Prodigy, a tale of music* 3 vols. 1866 ; librettos for Wallace's *Amber Witch,* and Bennett's *May Queen.* *d.* 13 Eaton place west, London 16 Feb. 1872. *H. F. Chorley, autobiography, memoir and letters,* compiled by H. G. Hewlett 2 vols. 1873, *portrait ; Musical cynics of London, a satire by George Linley* 1862 a satirical poem on H. F. Chorley.

CHORLEY, John Rutter *(brother of the preceding).* *b.* Blackley Hurst about 1807 ; secretary to Grand Junction railway between Liverpool and Birmingham ; formed a fine collection of Spanish plays which he gave to British Museum ; principal reviewer of German, Italian and Spanish books for the *Athenæum* 1846–54 ; author of *The Wife's Litany, and other poems* 1865. *d.* 29 June 1867. *H. F. Chorley's Autobiography* ii, 254–92 (1873).

CHOWN, Rev. Joseph Parbery. *b.* Kingsthorpe, Northamptonshire 9 Dec. 1821 ; ed. at Horton (now Rawdon) college ; pastor of Sion baptist chapel, Bradford 1848–75 ; pastor of Bloomsbury chapel, London 1875–85 ; pres. of London baptist association 1879 ; pres. of Baptist union of Great Britain and Ireland 1883 ; author of many circular letters written for the Yorkshire Baptist Association and of sermons, which had a wide circulation ; one of the most popular Baptist preachers. *d.* 24 Marlborough hill, St. John's Wood, London 8 July 1886. *The Baptist* 16 *July* 1886 *pp.* 42–4 ; *The Freeman* 16 *July* 1886 *pp.* 464–5 ; *John Taylor's Bibliotheca Northamtonensis.*

CHOWNE, William. M.R.C.S. 1813 ; M.D. Edin. 1827, L.R.C.P. 1833, F.R.C.P. 1857 ; practised in Holland, Lincs. 1813–27, moved to London 1833 ; assistant phys. to Charing Cross hospital, lecturer on medicine, obstetrics

CHOWNE, W. *(Con.)*

and diseases of women and children ; pres. of Westminster Medical Soc. ; pres. of Harveian Soc. 1850–1 ; author of *An oration delivered before the Medical Society of London, with an appendix on coroners' inquests* 1846. *d.* 17 Sep. 1870 aged 79. *Medical Circular i*, 261–3, 301 (1852), *portrait.*

CHRISTIAN, RICHARD. *b.* Cottesmore, Rutland, March 1779 ; head groom to Sir Wm. Heathcote 1799–1809 ; a farmer at Luffenham, Rutland 1809–17 ; whip to Lord Scarborough at Rufford 1820–35. *d.* 5 June 1862. *Post and Paddock by the Druid pp.* 336–67 ; *Silk and Scarlet by the Druid pp.* 1–69, *portrait.*

CHRISTIE, ALEXANDER *(eld. son of David Christie of Edinburgh). b.* Edin. 1807 ; ed. at Edin. academy and univ.; apprenticed to a writer to the signet ; studied art in Edin. London and Paris ; an assistant in ornamental department of School of Art, Edin. 1843, director 1845 ; A.R.S.A. 1848, where he exhibited pictures for some years ; painted a large picture 'The apparition of the Cross to Constantine,' as an altar-piece for the chapel at Murthley Castle ; delivered lectures on art at Philosophical Instit. of Edin. *d.* 5 May 1860.

CHRISTIE, JAMES ROBERT (2 son of *Samuel Hunter Christie* 1784–1865). *b.* Woolwich 9 Feb. 1814 ; mathematical master at Royal military academy, Woolwich 1837–47, first mathematical master 1847–65 ; F.R.S. 18 March 1847 ; F.R.A.S. 13 Jany. 1854 ; author of *Introduction to practical astronomy* 1853 ; *Test questions in pure and mixed mathematics* 1866. *d.* Arundel house, South Norwood park near London 28 Feb. 1879. *Monthly notices of Royal Astronom. Soc. xl*, 188 (1880).

CHRISTIE, JOHN. Entered Bengal army 1822 ; captain 1 European light cavalry 1 Jany. 1846 to 21 Feb. 1861 ; aide-de-camp to the Queen 7 March 1856 to 21 Feb. 1861 ; C.B. 13 March 1867. *d.* San Remo, Italy 7 May 1869.

CHRISTIE, JONATHAN HENRY. Educ. at Balliol coll. Ox., B.A. 1813, M.A. 1815 ; barrister L.I. 21 May 1824 ; fought a duel with John Scott editor of the *London Magazine* at Chalk farm near London at 9 p.m. 16 Feb. 1821 when at the second fire Scott fell mortally wounded and died at Chalk farm tavern 4 March ; tried at the Old Bailey for murder 13 April 1821 when acquitted. *d.* 9 Stanhope st. Hyde park gardens, London 15 April 1876 aged 83. *J. G. Millingen's History of duelling ii*, 244–52 (1841) ; *A. Steinmetz's Romance of duelling ii*, 253–9 (1868).

CHRISTIE, SAMUEL HUNTER *(youngest son of James Christie of 90 Pall Mall, London, auctioneer 1730–1803). b.* 90 Pall Mall 22 March 1784 ; admitted sizar at Trin. coll. Cam. 7 Oct. 1800, scholar 1803, 2 wrangler and bracketed 1 Smith's prizeman 1805 ; B.A. 1805, M.A. 1808 ; founded Cambridge university boat club ; captain of Grenadier company of Cambridge volunteers ; mathematical assistant at Royal military academy, Woolwich 1806, professor of mathematics 1838–54 ; F.R.S. 12 Jany. 1826, sec. of Royal Soc. 1837–54, contributed to the Transactions many papers on magnetism and kindred subjects ; author of *An elementary course of mathematics 3 parts* 1845–7. *d.* Ailsa villa, Twickenham 24 Jany. 1865. *Proc. of Royal Soc. xv*, 11–14 (1867).

CHRISTIE, SAMUEL TOLFREY. Ensign 80 foot 22 Jany. 1836, lieut. col. 5 March 1858 to Nov. 1865 ; C.B. 14 May 1859 ; L.G. 5 April 1876. *d.* Roehampton, Surrey 5 Oct. 1876.

CHRISTIE, WILLIAM DOUGAL *(eld. son of Dougal Christie, M.D. of the H.E.I.Co.'s Bombay medical service). b.* Bombay 3 Jany. 1816 ; ed. at Trin. coll. Cam., B.A. 1838, M.A. 1862 ; barrister I.T. 16 June 1840 ; M.P. for Weymouth 1842–7 ; sec. of legation at Berne 25 Feb. 1851 ; chargé d' affaires in Argentine Republic 10 Oct. 1854, minister plenipotentiary 15 Jany. 1856 ; envoy extraord. to Emperor of Brazil 2 Sep. 1859 to 20 Oct. 1863 when he retired ; C.B. 24 July 1871 ; author of *Notes on Brazilian questions* 1865 ; *Life of the First Earl of Shaftesbury 2 vols.* 1871 ; *Ballot and corruption and expenses at elections* 1872. *d.* 32 Dorset sq. Marylebone, London 27 July 1874. *Fraser's Mag. xxxiv*, 661–3 (1846) ; *I.L.N. lxv*, 140, 355 (1874).

CHRISTIE, WILLIAM HARVEY *(son of Thomas Christie, M.D. of Cheltenham). b.* Ceylon 2 Aug. 1808 ; ed. at Rugby and Woolwich ; ensign 80 foot 8 April 1825, major 9 Nov. 1838 to 17 Jany. 1840 ; police magistrate at Hyde park barracks, Sydney to 1842 ; agent for church and school estates, Sydney 1842–52 ; postmaster general of N.S.W. 1852–1865. *d.* Pyrmont, Sydney 19 March 1873.

CHRISTISON, JOHN. *b.* 18 Nov. 1788 ; sheriff of Ayrshire 13 March 1854 to death. *d.* 11 June 1862.

CHRISTISON, SIR ROBERT *(son of Alexander Christison, professor of humanity in Univ. of Edin., who d. 25 June 1830). b.* Edin. 18 July 1797 ; ed. at Univs. of Edin. and Paris ; M.D. Edin. 1819, LL.D. 1872 ; F.R.C.P. Edin. 1823, pres. 1839 and 1848 ; professor of

CHRISTISON, SIR R. *(Con.)*·

medical jurisprudence in Univ. of Edin. 23 Feb. 1822 to 1832, professor of clinical medicine 1832–55, professor of materia medica 1832 to April 1877; medical witness in almost every important case in Scotland 1829–66; one of the Queen's phys. in ord. in Scotland 1848–82; a crown representative in general medical council 1858–77; pres. of Royal Soc. of Edin. 1868–73; created baronet 20 Nov. 1871; pres. of British medical assoc. 1875; author of *A treatise on poisons* 1829, 4 ed. 1845; *On granular degeneration of the kidneys* 1839; *A dispensatory or commentary on the pharmacopœias of Great Britain* 1842, 2 ed. 1848. *d.* 40 Moray place, Edin. 27 Jany. 1882. *Life of Sir R. Christison edited by his sons 2 vols.* 1885–6, *2 portraits; S. Muspratt's Chemistry vol.* 1 (1853), *portrait.*

CHRISTMAS, REV. HENRY, afterwards Noel-Fearn *(only son of Robert Noble Christmas of Taunton).* *b.* London 1811; ed. at St. John's coll. Cam., B.A. 1837, M.A. 1840; librarian and sec. of Sion college, London 1841–8; minister of Verulam chapel, Lambeth 1843–56; lecturer at St. Peter's church, Cornhill 1852–66; C. of St. James's, Thames st. 1866; professor of English history and archæology in·Royal Society of Literature 1854–9; joint hon. sec. of Numismatic Society of London 1844–7, his collection of coins was sold at Sotheby's for £1260, 1–5 Feb. 1864; edited *Churchman* 1840–3, *Church of England Quarterly review* 1840–3 and 1854–8, *British Churchman* 1845–8, *Literary Gazette* 1859–60; F.R.S. 14 April 1842; F.S.A.; author of *The Voyage, a poem* 1833; *The cradle of the twin giants, science and history 2 vols.* 1849; *The shores and islands of the Mediterranean 3 vols.* 1851 and 15 other books; took name of Noel-Fearn 1866. *d.* suddenly of apoplexy in a cab in the Haymarket, London 11 March 1868.

CHRISTOFF, GEORGE, stage name of George Christopher. One of the best tight rope dancers in England; performed at the New Queen's theatre, London in *The last days of Pompeii,* drama in 5 acts by John Oxenford 8 Jany. 1872, and several months afterwards. *d.* Lambeth infirmary, London 13 June 1881 aged about 55.

CHRISTOPHER-NISBET-HAMILTON, ROBERT ADAM *(elder son of Philip Dundas, governor of Prince of Wales Island, who d.* 1807). *b.* 9 Feb. 1804; ed. at Univ. of Edin.; advocate 1826; M.P. for city of Edin. 1831–2, for North Lincolnshire 1837–57; F.R.S. 18 April 1833; P.C. 27 Feb. 1852; chancellor of Duchy

CHRISTOPHER-NISBET-HAMILTON, R. A. *(Con.)* of Lancaster 1 March to 30 Dec. 1852; assumed surname of Christopher in lieu of Dundas 20 Jany. 1836, took additional surname of Nisbet-Hamilton 1854. *d.* 23 Chesham place, London 9 June 1877.

CHRISTY, HENRY (2 son of W. Miller Christy of Woodbines, Kingston upon Thames, banker 1778–1858). *b.* 26 July 1810; partner in firm of Messrs. Christy's of Bermondsey and Stockport, manufacturers; succeeded his father as a director of London joint stock bank 1858; travelled in Scandinavia 1852–3; explored with Edward B. Tylor all parts of Mexico; examined the caves in valley of the Vezere, south of France, finding thousands of specimens of remains; F.G.S. 1858; selected by council of Royal society to be elected a fellow 1 June 1865; author with E. Lartet of *Reliquiæ Aquitanicæ, being contributions to the archæology and palæontology of Perigord and the adjacent provinces of Southern France* 1865–70. *d.* La Palisse, Allier, France 4 May 1865. *Proc. of Linnæan Soc.* (1865) 85–90.

NOTE.—By his will he bequeathed his magnificent collections illustrating the history of early man, with the equally large series of articles representing the habits of modern savages, to the nation; the trustees of the British Museum secured the suite of rooms at 118 Victoria st. Westminster (in which Christy himself had lived) and here the collection was exhibited until 1884 when it was moved to the British Museum.

CHUBB, JOHN *(son of Charles Chubb of London, locksmith, who d.* 16 May 1845). Locksmith in St. Paul's churchyard, London, afterwards in Queen Victoria st.; M.I.C.E. 1845, read a valuable paper on locks and keys before that institution 1850 for which he was awarded Telford silver medal; patented various improvements in locks and safes. *d.* Radcliffe house, Brixton Rise, London 30 Oct. 1872 in 57 year. *Min. of Proc. of Instit. of C.E. ix,* 310–43 (1850).

CHURCH, SIR RICHARD (2 son of Matthew Church of Cork). *b.* 1784; ensign 13 foot 3 July 1800; major 1 Greek light infantry 9 Sep. 1809; lieut.-col. 2 Greek light infantry 19 Nov. 1812 to 1815 when both regiments (which he had raised) were disbanded; commander in chief in Sicily 1820; generalissimo of Greek army 1827–8 and 1832–43 when he joined the revolutionary party; C.B. 4 June 1815; knighted at Carlton house 12 June 1822; G.C.H. 1837. *d.* Athens 20 March 1873.

CHURCHILL, FRANCIS GEORGE SPENCER, 2 Baron. *b.* Blenheim 6 Oct. 1802; ed. at Harrow and Ch. Ch. Ox.; attaché at Vienna 10 Aug. 1823, at Lisbon 12 Jany. 1828; succeeded his father 7 March 1845; commanded Oxfordshire yeomanry 1857–74. *d.* 32 Albemarle st. London 24 Nov. 1886.

CHURCHILL, ALFRED B. *b.* Constantinople; succeeded his father as editor and proprietor of Turkish semi-official paper the *Jeride Hawades;* much improved character of Turkish printing; attended the Sultan on his visit to England, July 1867 as official historiographer. *d.* Constantinople, Nov. or Dec. 1870 aged 45.

CHURCHILL, FLEETWOOD. *b.* Nottingham, Feb. 1808; studied in London, Dublin and Paris; M.D. Edin. 1831; practised at Dublin 1832–75; fellow of King and Queen's college of Phys. 27 Oct. 1851, censor 1855–7,-vice pres. 1856, professor of midwifery in school of physic 1856–64, pres. 1867–8; pres. of Obstetrical Soc. of Dublin 1856 and 1864; author of *Diseases of females* 1838; *Operative Midwifery* 1841; *Diseases of Children* 1850. *d.* Ardtrea rectory near Stewartstown 31 Jany. 1878. *Dublin Journal of medical science lxv,* 285–8 (1878).

CHURCHILL, HENRY ADRIAN (*son of Wm. Nosworthy Churchill*). *b.* 1828; attaché at Teheran 22 April 1852; attached as secretary and interpreter to staff of General Williams in Asia 18 July 1854 to 28 Nov. 1855 when taken prisoner at capitulation of Kars; consul general in Syria 1862, at Algiers 1863–7; political agent and consul at Zanzibar 15 June 1867 to 12 Feb. 1872 when he retired on a pension; consul in Sicily 1 Oct. 1879 to death; C.B. 19 June 1856. *d.* Palermo 12 July 1886.

CHURCHILL, JOHN SPRIGGS MORSS (3 *son of Rev. James Churchill, Independent minister at Ongar, Essex*). *b.* Ongar 4 Aug. 1801; medical bookseller at 16 Princes st. Soho, London 1830–54, at New Burlington st. 1854 to 31 Dec. 1870 when he retired; published *British and foreign medical review* 1838, *Lancet* 1842–7, *Medical Times* 1850 and nearly all the medical books; projected and edited a series of medical manuals. *d.* Tunbridge Wells 3 Aug. 1875. *H. Curwen's History of booksellers* (1873) 339–45; *Medical times and gazette ii,* 197–200 (1875).

CHURSTON, JOHN YARDE-BULLER, 1 Baron (2 *son of Sir Francis Buller-Yarde 2 baronet* 1767–1833). *b.* Dilhorne hall, Staffs. 12 April 1799; ed. at Oriel coll. Ox.; succeeded 17 April 1833; M.P. for South Devon 13 Jany. 1835 to 2 Aug. 1858 when created Baron Churston of Churston Ferrers and Lupton, Devon; lieut.-col. of South Devon militia 1845; special deputy warden of the stannaries 1852;

changed his name from Buller-Yarde to Yarde-Buller by royal license 13 Feb. 1860. *d.* Lupton near Brixham 4 Sep. 1871. *I.L.N. xxxvii,* 191, 208 (1860), *portrait, lix,* 259, 530 (1871).

CHURTON, VENERABLE EDWARD (2 *son of Ven. Ralph Churton* 1754–1831, *archdeacon of St. David's*). *b.* Middleton Cheney, Northamptonshire 26 Jany. 1800; ed. at Charterhouse 1810–18 and Ch. Ch. Ox., B.A. 1821, M.A. 1824; head master of Hackney church of England school 1830–4; R. of Crayke, Yorkshire 1835 to death; preb. of York cath. 1841 to death; archdeacon of Cleveland 21 Jany. 1846 to death; edited with Rev. W. Gresley *The Englishman's Library,* for which he wrote *The early English Church* 1840; author of *Lays of faith and loyalty* 1847; *The book of Psalms in English verse* 1854; *Gongora, an historical and critical essay on the times of Philip iii and iv of Spain with translations* 2 vols. 1863. *d.* Crayke 4 July 1874. *Poetical remains of Edward Churton* 1876, *portrait.*

CHURTON, EDWARD. Bookseller and publisher as 26 Holles st. Cavendish sq. London many years. *d.* Wanganui, New Zealand 24 July 1885 aged 73.

CHUTE, JAMES HENRY. *b.* Gosport 4 July 1810; played at Bristol theatre as Mr. Chew; performed on the York and Lincoln circuits; played at T.R. Dublin 7 years; joined the Bristol stage about 1842; lessee of the Old theatre, King st. Bristol, Sep. 1853 to death, of the new theatre Bristol to death; made his last appearance 6 April 1876. *d.* Bristol 23 July 1878. *Era 28 July* 1878 *p.* 4, *col.* 4, 4 *Aug. p.* 10, *col.* 1.

CHUTE, SIR TREVOR (3 *son of Francis Chute of Chute hall, Tralee, co. Kerry, who d.* 12 *Aug.* 1849). *b.* Spa, Tralee 31 July 1816; ensign Ceylon rifle regiment 10 Aug. 1831; captain 70 foot 8 Nov. 1839, lieut. col. 14 Dec. 1849 to 12 May 1863 when placed on h.p.; brigadier general Bengal 1858–9 and 1860–1; brigadier general Australia 1863–5; major general New Zealand 1865–7; major general Australia 1867–70; col. 22 foot 6 May 1873 to death; general 1 Oct. 1877; placed on retired list 1 July 1881; C.B. 3 April 1846, K.C.B. 13 March 1867. *d.* Egmont, Bracknell, Berks. 12 March 1886. *Sir J. E. Alexander's Bush fighting* (1873) 267–305.

CHUTE, WILLIAM LYDE WIGGETT. *b.* 16 June 1800; sheriff of Norfolk 1832; M.P. for West Norfolk 29 July 1837 to 23 July 1847. *d.* The Vyne near Basingstoke 6 July 1879.

CIANCHETTI, Pio (*2 son of Francesco Cianchetti of Rome*). *b.* London 11 Dec. 1799; performed a sonata of his own composition in the opera concert room, London 1805; performed in Germany, Holland and France; spoke the English, French, German and Italian languages at 8 years old; composed instrumental pieces including a grand concerto which he executed at a concert in London 1809; acted as composer and conductor of Madame Catalani's concerts in England 1822; composed concertos, pianoforte music and songs; edited an edition in score of symphonies and overtures by Mozart and Beethoven. *d.* Cheltenham 21 July 1851.

CLAIRMONT, Clara Mary Jane (*dau. of Mr. Clairmont, who d. about May 1798, by Mary Jane, who m.* (2) *Wm. Godwin the author*). *b.* 27 April 1798; ed. at Walham Green; went to France with her half sister Mary Godwin, when she eloped with the poet Shelley 28 July 1814; introduced herself to Lord Byron early in 1816, became his mistress, her daughter Allegra was born at Bath 12 Jany. 1817 and *d.* in the convent of Bagna-Cavallo near Ravenna 19 April 1822; a governess in Russia about 1823-9; lived in Italy and Paris. *d.* Florence 19 March 1879. *C. K. Paul's Life of Wm. Godwin ii,* 108, 213, 217, 247-8, 280 (1876); *Moore's Life of Lord Byron* (1847) 389, 557, 567. *Dowden's Life of P. B. Shelley i,* 439-522 (1886).

CLANCARTY, William Thomas Le Poer Trench, 3 Earl of. *b.* Castletown, co. Kildare 21 Sep. 1803; lieut.-col. of Galway militia 1830-65; succeeded 24 Nov. 1837. *d.* Salt hill near Dublin 26 April 1872.

CLANMORRIS, John Charles Robert Bingham, 4 Baron (*eld. son of Denis Arthur Bingham, 3 Baron Clanmorris* 1808-47). *b.* Moyode castle, co. Galway 28 Nov. 1826; ed. at Rugby; succeeded his father 24 Feb. 1847. *d.* at his seat in West of Ireland 5 April 1876.

CLANRICARDE, Ulick John De-Burgh, 1 Marquis of (*only son of 13 Earl of Clanricarde* 1744-1808). *b.* Belmont, Hants. 20 or 28 Dec. 1802; succeeded as 14 Earl 27 July 1808; created a marquis in peerage of Ireland 6 Oct. 1825; created Baron Somerhill in peerage of the U.K. 13 June 1826; under sec. of state for foreign affairs 2 Jany. 1826 to 17 Aug. 1827; captain of yeomen of the guard 1 Dec. 1830 to 3 Dec. 1834; P.C. 1 Dec. 1830; lord lieut. of Galway 1831; K.P. 7 Oct. 1831; colonel of Galway militia 1 Jany. 1838, hon. colonel 12 Feb. 1873 to death; ambassador at St. Petersburgh 6 Oct. 1838 to 28 March

CLANRICARDE, Marquis of (*Con.*)
1840; postmaster general 7 July 1846 to 27 Dec. 1852; lord privy seal 3 Feb. 1858 to 26 Feb. 1858. *d.* 17 Stratton st. Piccadilly, London 10 April 1874. *bur.* Portumna, Galway. *Baily's Mag. xi,* 333-7 (1866), *portrait; I.L.N. iv,* 332, (1844), *portrait; Graphic ix,* 433 (1874), *portrait.*

CLANWILLIAM, Richard Charles Francis Meade, 3 Earl of (*elder son of Richard Meade, 2 Earl of Clanwilliam* 1766-1805). *b.* 15 Aug. 1795; succeeded 3 Sep. 1805; private sec. to Marquess of Londonderry 5 Jan. 1817 to 11 July 1819; under sec. of state for foreign affairs 22 Jan. 1822 to 12 Aug. 1822; envoy extraord. and minister plenipo. at Berlin 1 Feb. 1823 to 25 Dec. 1827; G.C.H. 1826; created a peer of the U.K. by title of Baron Clanwilliam of Clanwilliam, co. Tipperary 28 Jany. 1828; created D.C.L. Ox. 11 June 1834. *d.* 32 Belgrave square, London 7 Oct. 1879. Personalty sworn under £250,000 Jany. 1880.

CLAPHAM, Robert Calvert (*son of Anthony Clapham, who established soda and alkali works on the Tyne*). *b.* Newcastle 15 Sep. 1823; manager of the Walker alkali works; chief founder of Newcastle Chemical society 1868, pres. 1878; sec. of Newcastle literary and philosophical society 21 years; M.I.M.E. 1869; F.C.S.; author of the article on Soda in *Chemistry as applied to arts and manufactures. d.* Winchelsea 22 Dec. 1881. *Proc. of Instit. of Mechanical Engineers* (1882) 2-3.

CLAPHAM, William. Entered Madras army 1796; colonel 47 Madras N.I. 5 April 1831 to death; M.G. 28 June 1838. *d.* Widcombe house, Bath 29 Aug. 1851 aged 70.

CLARE, John Fitzgibbon, 2 Earl of (*elder son of John Fitzgibbon, 1 Earl of Clare* 1749-1802, *lord chancellor of Ireland*). *b.* 10 June 1792; succeeded as 2 Earl 28 Jany. 1802; ed. at Ch. Ch. Ox., B.A. 1812, M.A. 1819; lord lieutenant of Limerick; governor of Bombay, Aug. 1830 to 17 March 1835, took his seat 21 March 1831; P.C. 25 Aug. 1830; G.C.H. 1835; K.P. 17 Sep. 1845. *d.* Brighton 18 Aug. 1851.

CLARE, Richard Hobart Fitzgibbon, 3 Earl of (*brother of the preceding*). *b.* Dublin 2 Oct. 1793; registrar of affidavits in Irish court of Chancery 1797-1836 when office was abolished; ensign 1 foot guards 18 Aug. 1808; captain 2 Ceylon regiment 1811-14; M.P. for co. Limerick 1818-41; lord lieut. of Limerick 1851; succeeded as 3 Earl 18 Aug. 1851. *d.* Kensington palace gardens, London 10 Jany. 1864.

CLARE, JOHN *(son of Parker Clare of Helpstone near Stamford, labourer)*. *b.* Helpstone 13 July 1793; cottage farmer at Helpstone 1827-32, at Northborough 1832-7; confined at High Beech private lunatic asylum, Epping Forest 1837-41, at county asylum, Northampton 1841 to death; author of *Poems descriptive of rural life and scenery* 1821·; *The village minstrel and other poems* 2 vols. 1821; *The rural muse* 1835. *d.* Northampton asylum 20 May 1864. *bur.* Helpstone 25 May. *F. Martin's Life of J. Clare* 1865; *J. L. Cherry's Life of J. Clare* 1873; *M. R. Mitford's Recollections of a literary life* (1859) 103-14; *J. Clare's Village Minstrel vol.* 1 (1821), *portrait.*

CLARE, JOHN. Nautical inventor; one of the persons who suggested protection of war vessels by means of iron plates; made a claim on the Government for a sum of about a million for compensation, which claim was rejected; author of *Mechanical defects of things resembling iron ships, but constructed upon the tin-pot principle* 1856; *Life preserving ships hydrodynamically developed upon metallic principles* 1868. *d.* 1 West bank road, Liverpool 12 Oct. 1885 aged 65.

CLARE, PETER *(son of Peter Clare of Manchester, clockmaker, who d. 30 July 1799)*. *b.* Manchester 1781; member of Manchester literary and philosophical society 1810, sec. 1821-42; F.R.A.S. 1841; a zealous member of Antislavery committee. *d.* Manchester 24 Nov. 1851. *Monthly notices of Royal Astronom. Soc. xii*, 89-90 (1852).

CLARENDON, GEORGE WILLIAM FREDERICK VILLIERS, 4 Earl of *(eld. son of hon. George Villiers* 1759-1827). *b.* London 12 Jany. 1800; ed. at St. John's coll. Cam.; attaché of embassy at St. Petersburg 1820-23; a comr. of the Excise 1823-33; envoy extraord. and min. plenipo. to Madrid 16 Aug. 1833 to 18 Oct. 1839; G.C.B. 19 Oct. 1837; succeeded his uncle as 4 Earl 22 Dec. 1838; P.C. 3 Jany. 1840; lord keeper of privy seal 15 Jany. 1840 to 3 Sep. 1841; chancellor of Duchy of Lancaster 31 Oct. 1840 to 23 June 1841 and 7 April 1864 to Nov. 1865; pres. of board of trade 6 July 1846 to 22 July 1847; lord lieut. of Ireland 20 May 1847 to 2 March 1852; grand master of order of St. Patrick 26 May 1847 to 1852; K.G. 23 March 1849; sec. of state for foreign department 21 Feb. 1853 to 26 Feb. 1858, 3 Nov. 1865 to 5 July 1866 and 9 Dec. 1868 to death; ambassador extraord. and plenipo. to congress of Paris 15 Feb. to April 1856; ambassador extraord. at coronation of King Wm. i of Prussia 2 Oct.

CLARENDON, 4 Earl of *(Con.)*
1861; chancellor of Queen's Univ. of Ireland 8 Oct. 1864. *d.* 1 Grosvenor crescent, London 27 June 1870. *bur.* at Watford, Herts. 1 July. *W. H. Bidwell's Imperial Courts of France and England, New York* (1863) 157-61; *Men of the time, British Statesmen* (1854) 287-317; *D. O. Maddyn's Chiefs of parties* (1859) 136-53; *Waagen's Treasures of art ii*, 454-58 (1854); *Macmillan's mag. xxii*, 292-6 (1870); *St. James's mag. Feb.* 1870 *pp.* 676-85, *portrait; The British cabinet in* 1853 *pp.* 287-317.

CLARGES, SIR RICHARD GODDARD (2 *son of Rev. James Hare of Stratton, Wilts.*) *b.* Chingford -hall, Essex; ed. at Rugby, entered at Oxford but never resided; lieut. 30 foot 6 July 1796; major 12 foot 1 July 1813 to 27 Aug. 1825 when placed on h.p.; colonel 73 foot 18 May 1849 to 29 July 1852; colonel 12 foot 29 July 1852 to death; L.G. 11 Nov. 1851; served in Egypt, Hanover, Spain and the Peninsula; assumed surname of Clarges 18 June 1844; C.B. 4 June 1815; K.C.B. 5 Feb. 1856. *d.* Bitchfield near Grantham 13 April 1857.

CLARIDGE, SIR JOHN THOMAS *(eld. son of John Fellowes Claridge of Sevenoaks, Kent)*. *b.* 1792; ed. at Harrow and Ch. Ch. Ox., B.A. 1813, M.A. 1818; barrister M.T. 6 Feb. 1818; recorder of Prince of Wales Island, Singapore and Malacca 30 Sep. 1825 to 1829; knighted at Windsor Castle 30 Sep. 1825. *d.* Stoke villa, Leamington 20 June 1868.

CLARIDGE, WILLIAM. Succeeded James Edward Mivart (who *d.* 5 Jany. 1856 aged 75) as owner of Mivart's hotel, Brook st. Hanover sq. London 1851 the hotel par excellence for princes and foreign ambassadors; sold the hotel to a company for £60,000 March 1881. *d.* Cragthorne, Grove park, Kent 12 April 1882 aged 68.

CLARINA, EYRE MASSEY, 3 Baron. *b.* Cork 6 May 1798; succeeded Jany. 1810; a representative peer for Ireland 16 April 1849 to death. *d.* Elm park, Clarina, co. Limerick 18 Nov. 1872.

CLARIS, JOHN CHALK *(son of Mr. Claris of Canterbury, bookseller)*. *b.* Canterbury about 1797; edited the *Kent Herald* 1826-65; published under pseudonym of Arthur Brooke following poetical works; *Juvenile Pieces* 1816; *Poems* 1817; *Durovernum, The curse of Chatterton and other poems* 1818; *Thoughts and feelings* 1820; *Retrospection (with portrait)* 1821; *Elegy on the death of Pery Bysshe Shelley* 1822. *d.* Best lane, Canterbury 10 Jany. 1866. *Notes and Queries, Fourth series, x*, 29, 95 (1872).

CLARK, BRACY. b. Chipping Norton, Oxon 7 April 1771; a veterinary surgeon in London 1800; F.L.S. 15 Jany. 1793; author of *An essay on the bots of horses and other animals* 1815; *Hippodonomia, or the true structure laws and economy of the horse's foot* 1829; *Treatise on the bits of horses*, 2 ed. 1835; and many other small books on veterinary subjects. d. Giltspur st. London 16 Dec. 1860. *Proc. of Linnœan Society* (1861) 21–4; *J. Smith's Catalogue of Friends' books i*, 417–22 (1867).

CLARK, CHARLES. b. Heybridge, Maldon, Essex 1806; lived at Great Totham hall near Witham where he composed and printed with his own hands numerous broadsides consisting chiefly of satirical songs and parodies; printed *A history of the parish of Great Totham by G. W. Johnson* 1831; contributed to the *Literary Gazette, Family Herald* and *Sportsman*. d. of heart disease at Heybridge 21 March 1880. *W. T. Lowndes's Bibliographer's Manual by H. G. Bohn iv, appendix pp.* 216–17 (1864).

CLARK, CHARLES. Barrister M.T. 21 May 1830; official reporter to House of Lords 1840; secretary to Channel Islands' criminal law commission 1846; revising barrister for South Essex 1863–4, for Herts 1864–73; sec. to Juridical Society 1855–8; bencher of his inn 15 Jany. 1872; Q.C. 9 Feb. 1874; author of *A summary of colonial law* 1834; *House of Lords cases* 11 vols. 1849–66; author with Patrick Dow of *Reports in the House of Lords* 2 vols. 1827–32, with William Finnelly of *Reports in the House of Lords* 12 vols. 1835–47. d. 10 Albert road, Regent's park, London 28 June 1881.

CLARK, EDWARD RAWSON. b. Yorkshire; employed at Crockford's, St. James's st. London; kept a racing stud from about 1834; a finance agent in London to 1856; a member of Tattersall's 52 years; commonly known as D'Orsay Clark. d. 147 Church st. Chelsea 12 April 1885 aged 81. *Sporting Review xl*, 434–7, (1858); *Sporting Times 2 May* 1885 p. 5.

CLARK, FRANCIS WILLIAM (*eld. son of Francis Wm. Clark of Kilpatrick, Argyllshire*). b. Stirling 1827; ed. at Stirling gr. sch. and Univ. of Edin., hon. LL.D. 1877; advocate 1851; sheriff substitute for Glasgow 1867–76; sheriff of Lanarkshire 1876 to death; author of *A treatise on the law of partnership and joint-stock companies according to the law of Scotland* 1866. d. Kelvinside, Glasgow 19 Nov. 1886.

CLARK, REV. FREDERICK SCOTSON (*eld. son of Michael Clark of Southwark, London*). b. Southwark 16 Nov. 1840; organist of Regent

CLARK, REV. F. S. (*Con.*)
Square church, London 1854; studied at Royal academy of music; founded the London Organ school 1865; matriculated from Exeter coll. Ox. 13 Oct. 1865; organist of Ex. coll. 1865–7; Mus. Bac. 1867; head master of St. Michael's gr. sch. Brighton 1867; C. of St. Michael's, Lewes 1868–9; assistant chaplain at Stuttgart 1870–4, at Amsterdam 1874–8; chaplain at Paris 1879; the English official representative organist at Paris Exhibition 1878 when he was awarded a gold medal; composed many pieces for the organ, harmonium and piano. d. the London organ school 3 Prince's st. Cavendish sq. 5 July 1883.

CLARK, VENERABLE GEORGE. Educ. at Univ. coll. Ox., Bennett scholar, B.A. 1831, M.A. 1833; C. of Alton, Hants 1835–42; C. of Tawstock, Devon 1843–5; V. of Cantley, Yorkshire 1845–54; preb. of Hereford 12 Dec. 1848 to death; R. of Tenby 1854–67; archdeacon of St. David's 21 Jany. 1864 to death. d. Lampeter Velfrey rectory 11 Dec. 1874.

CLARK, GEORGE AITKEN (*son of John Clark of Paisley, thread manufacturer*). b. Paisley 9 Aug. 1823; shawl manufacturer with Robert and John Ronald at Paisley to 1851; started with Peter Kerr a thread business at Linside Mill, Paisley 1851; established a branch factory at Newark, New Jersey 1864; bequeathed £20,000 for erection of a town hall at Paisley which was opened 30 Jany. 1882, and £20,000 to found 4 scholarships of £300 a year each, tenable for 3 years in Glasgow Univ. d. Newark 13 Feb. 1873. *The inauguration of the George A. Clark town hall, Paisley* 1882, *portrait; I.L.N. lxxx*, 133 (1882).

CLARK, SIR JAMES, 1 Baronet (*son of David Clark of Findlater, who d. 15 Aug. 1836*). b. Findlater 14 Dec. 1788; ed. at Fordyce gr. sch. and King's coll. Aberdeen; M.R.C.S. Edin. 1809; assistant surgeon R.N. 1809–16 when placed on h.p.; M.D. Edin. 1 Aug. 1817; physician at Rome 1819–26, in London 1826–60; L.R.C.P. 26 June 1826; F.R.S. 7 April 1832; first phys. in ord. to the Queen 8 Aug. 1837; created baronet 11 Nov. 1837; member of senate of Univ. of London 1838–65; physician to Prince Albert 1840–60; served on general medical council 1858–60; lived at Bagshot park, lent to him by the Queen 1860 to death; K.C.B. 6 July 1866; author of *The influence of climate in the prevention and cure of chronic diseases* 1829, 3 ed. 1841; *Remarks on medical reform* 1843; *A memoir of John Conolly, M.D.* 1869. d. Bagshot park 29

June 1870. *Proc. of Royal Soc. xix*, 13–19 (1871); *Physic and Physicians ii*, 254–60 (1839); *Barker's Photographs of medical men, portrait; I.L.N. lvii*, 48, 61, 70 (1870), *portrait.*

CLARK, JOHN *(son of Thomas Clark of Greinton, Somerset, minister of Society of Friends, who d. 16 June 1850 aged 91).* b. Greinton 21 Nov. 1785; projected an electric telegraph; took out a patent for construction of Air Beds and cushions by use of a solution of india rubber which he disposed of to Mackintosh; constructed a machine for composing hexameter Latin verses 1848; author of *The Avalonian guide to the town of Glastonbury and its environs* 1810, 10 ed. 1855; *Tales of the convent of St. Clair* 1823; *Don Juan, Canto xvii published by John Clark* 1827. d. Bridgwater 23 May 1853. *J. Smith's Friends' books i*, 425–7 (1867).

CLARK, JOHN. Race judge for 30 years at Newmarket, Doncaster, Ascot, Epsom 1822–52. d. Newmarket 15 July 1853 aged 74.

CLARK, JOHN. Attorney in London; clerk of the Central criminal court, Old Bailey 1829 to death; clerk of the peace for City of London and borough of Southwark 1829–42 and 1843 to death. d. London 28 July 1858. bur. Datchet 5 Aug. *City Press 31 July 1858 p. 2, col. 2, and p. 3, col. 2.*

CLARK, JOHN. Artist and illustrator of books; inventor and executant of the Myriorama, Urania's Mirror and other ingenious art-toys; known as 'Waterloo Clark' from his sketches of some of the incidents of the field of Waterloo taken by himself on the spot immediately after the battle. d. Edinburgh, Oct. 1863 aged 92.

CLARK, JOHN. Ensign 55 foot 2 June 1814; commandant royal military asylum 2 April 1852 to 26 Oct. 1858; M.G. 26 Oct. 1858; col. 59 foot 9 March 1863 to death. d. Brighton 22 March 1865.

CLARK, RICHARD. b. Datchet, Bucks. 5 April 1780; lay clerk at St. George's chapel, Windsor and Eton college 1802–11; secretary of the Glee club 1805; member of Royal Society of musicians 3 July 1814; a gentleman of the Chapels Royal 1 Oct. 1820; a vicar choral of St. Paul's cathedral 1827; a lay clerk at Westminster abbey 1828; published *Words of the most favourite pieces performed at the Glee club, Catch club and other societies* 1814, 2 ed. 1824; *An account of the national anthem, God save the king* 1822, which he at first attributed to Carey but afterwards claimed for Bull;

Reminiscences of Handel 1836; *Reading and playing from score simplified* 1838; composed glees, anthems and chants. d. the Littlington tower, Westminster abbey cloisters 5 Oct. 1856.

CLARK, REV. SAMUEL *(youngest child of Joseph Clark of Southampton, brush maker).* b. Southampton 19 May 1810; publisher with John Maw Darton at Holborn hill, London 1836 to 11 June 1843; entered Magd. hall, Ox. 7 Jany. 1839, B.A. 1845, M.A. 1846; vice principal of St. Mark's training college, Chelsea, May 1846–1851; principal of National Society's training college, Battersea 1851–63; V. of Bredwardine, Hereford 1863–71; R. of Eaton Bishop, Hereford, June 1871 to death; inspector of schools for diocese of Hereford 1872 to death; published *Peter Parley's Tales of the sun, moon and stars* 1837; *Maps illustrative of physical and political history of the British empire* 1849; contributed to the Speaker's Commentary, Leviticus, the latter part of Exodus and Micah; one of revisers of the Old Testament. d. Cosham house, East Cosham, Hants. 17 July 1875. *Memorials of Samuel Clark edited by his wife* (1878), *portrait.*

CLARK, SARAH *(6 child of John Davies of Caerwys, Flintshire).* Baptized in Caerwys church 1 March 1767. *(m.* 3 March 1790 Wm. Clark of Hawarden parish, labourer, who d. 20 Jany. 1844). buried at Hawarden 21 April 1871. *W. J. Thoms's Human longevity* (1873) 268–72.

CLARK, THOMAS. b. Canterbury 1775; composed several anthems and many hymn tunes, a few of which continue in use as "Queenborough," "Burnham" and "Pembroke." d. Canterbury 30 May 1859.

CLARK, THOMAS. b. Ayr 1801; lecturer on chemistry at Glasgow Mechanics' Institution 1836; discovered the pyrophosphate of soda 1836; studied at Glasgow Univ. 1827–31, .M.D. 1831; apothecary to Glasgow infirmary 1829; professor of chemistry in Marischal college and univ. Aberdeen 1833–60 when the coll. and univ. was fused with King's college and univ.; best known by his water tests and by his process for softening chalk waters; contributed to *Westminster Review* articles on weights and measures and on the patent laws 1834–5. d. 27 Nov. 1867.

CLARK, THOMAS *(son of Wm. Clark, sheriff-substitute of Clackmannanshire).* b. Whiteside, Stirlingshire 14 Nov. 1820; landscape painter in oil and water colours at Edinburgh; A.R.S.A. Nov. 1865. d. Dundaroch, Aberfoyle 7 Oct. 1876.

CLARK, THOMAS JAMES (2 son of Wm. Clark of St. John st. London and of Edmonton, hop merchant). b. 1822; ed. at Univ. coll. London; B.A. London 1842; barrister I.T. 21 Nov. 1845; went Home circuit; Q.C. 13 Dec. 1866; bencher of his inn 25 Jany. 1867. d. Myrtle cottage, Catford bridge, Kent 17 March 1877.

CLARK, REV. WILLIAM (2 son of John Clark, M.D. of Newcastle 1744–1805). b. Newcastle 5 April 1788; entered Trin. coll. Cam. Oct. 1804, scholar 1807, fellow 1809; 7 wrangler 1808, B.A. 1808, M.A. 1811, M.D. 1827; licensed to practise by Univ. of Cam. 5 July 1813; professor of anatomy at Cam. 1817–66, ordained deacon 1818; V. of Arrington, Cambs. 1824–5; R. of Guiseley near Leeds 1825–59; F.R.C.P. 25 June 1830; F.R.S. 28 Jany. 1836; author of *Analysis of a course of lectures on the anatomy and physiology of the human body* 1822; *Handbook of zoology translated from the Dutch of J. Vander Hoeven* 2 vols. 1856–68. d. Cambridge 15 Sep. 1869. *Macmillan's Mag. xxi*, 267–72 (1870).

CLARK, WILLIAM. b. Colchester 17 March 1821; ed. at King's coll. London; engineer to municipality of Calcutta 1855–74 where he devised a complete system of drainage and waterworks; M.I.C.E. 2 Feb. 1864; M.I.M.E. 1867; partner with W. F. Batho in London 1874, joint patentee with him of steam road roller; invented a tied brick arch; author of *The drainage of Calcutta* 1871. d. Surbiton, Surrey 22 Jany. 1880. *Min. of Proc. of Instit. of C.E. lxiii*, 308–10 (1881).

CLARK, WILLIAM GEORGE. b. Barford hall, Darlington, March 1821; ed. at Shrewsbury and Trin. coll. Cam.; second in the classical tripos and second chancellor's medallist 1844, B.A. 1844, M.A. 1847; fellow of Trin. coll. 1844 to death, tutor 1856–66, vice master 9 Oct. 1868 to 1871; public orator of Univ. of Cam. 1857 to Oct. 1869; ordained deacon 1853, priest 1854; relinquished holy orders by deed inrolled in chancery 2 Sep. 1870; F.S.A. 15 June 1865; one of founders and editors of *Journal of Philology* 1868; author of *Gazpacho, or summer months in Spain* 1850; *Peloponnesus, notes of study and travel* 1858; edited with Glover and Wright *The Cambridge Shakespeare* 9 vols. 1863–6; left £300 a year to endow a lectureship of English literature at Trinity coll. Cam. d. York 6 Nov. 1878. *C. A. Bristed's Five years at an English University* (1873) 215–7, 219; *Academy ii*, 472, 496 (1878); *Notes and Queries 5 S. x*, 400, 438 (1878), *xi*, 55 (1879).

CLARK, WILLIAM H. Pupil of John Loder the violinist; played the violin in orchestra of Bath theatre; made his first appearance on the stage at Weymouth 1833 and in London at Surrey theatre 3 April 1837 in *Jack's Alive* and *The loadstone of the earth*; acted at Haymarket theatre 17 April 1838 to 1877; always known as Little Clark. d. 3 June 1887 in 72 year. *bur.* Tooting cemetery 8 June.

CLARK, SIR WILLIAM STEPHENSON (son of Wm. Clark, sheriff of York in 1786). b. York, Aug. 1782; studied medicine in London 1803 to 1806; practised at York 1806 to death; one of the city chamberlains 1809, member of common council for Micklegate ward 1813–20 and 1835–39, one of city sheriffs 1820, alderman 1839–49, mayor 1839–40, one of the city magistrates 1842 to death; knighted at St. James's palace 1 July 1840. (m. Oct. 1811 Anne 3 dau. of John Audus of Selby, Yorkshire, she d. 16 July 1883 aged 95). d. York 2 May 1851.

CLARK, WILLIAM TIERNEY (son of Thomas Clark of Sion house, Somerset). b. Bristol 23 Aug. 1873; employed by John Rennie in London 1808–11; resident engineer of West Middlesex water works 1811 where he constructed reservoirs to contain 40,000,000 gallons of water; erected Hammersmith suspension bridge 1824–7; constructed Gravesend town pier 1834–5; erected great suspension bridge over Danube between Pesth and Buda 1839–49 at cost of £622,042; M.I.C.E. 1823; F.R.S. 4 May 1837; author of *An account of the suspension bridge across the river Danube* 1852–3. d. Hammersmith 22 Sep. 1852. *Min. of proc. of Instit. of C.E. xii*, 153–7 (1853).

CLARK-KENNEDY, SIR ALEXANDER KENNEDY (eld. son of John Clark of Nunland). b. Dumfries 1782; cornet 6 dragoon guards 8 Sep. 1802; captured single-handed at Waterloo the eagle of the 105th regiment of French infantry; lieut.-col. 7 dragoon guards 11 June 1830 to 22 Dec. 1843 when placed on h.p.; A.D.C. to the Queen 1841–54; colonel 6 dragoon guards 14 June 1858 to 17 July 1860; L.G. 3 June 1860; colonel 2 dragoons (Scots Greys) 17 July 1860 to death; K.H. 1831; C.B. 19 July 1838; K.C.B. 10 Nov. 1862; assumed additional name of Kennedy 1839. d. 69 Oxford terrace, Hyde park, London 30 Jany. 1864. *bur.* St. Michael's churchyard, Dumfries.

CLARK-KENNEDY, JOHN (eld. son of the preceding). b. Knockgrey, Kirkcudbright 21 Sep. 1817; cornet 7 dragoon guards 25 Oct. 1833;

CLARK-KENNEDY, J. *(Con.)*

took additional name of Kennedy 1839; captain 18 foot 4 March 1842, lieut.-col. 22 June 1855 to 10 Nov. 1856 when placed on h.p.; served in second Sikh war 1848–9 and in Crimean war 1854–6; C.B. 2 Jany. 1857; col. commandant military train 10 Feb. 1860 to death. *d.* Cairo 18 Dec. 1867.

CLARKE, SIR ARTHUR *(son of Arthur Clarke)*. *b.* Dublin 1778; M.R.C.S. 7 April 1807, F.R.C.S. 26 Aug. 1844; surgeon to Dublin police; knighted 1811; author of *An essay on diseases of the skin* 1821; *A practical manual for the preservation of health* 1824. *d.* Dublin 9 Nov. 1857.

CLARKE, AUGUSTUS. Entered Madras army 1817; colonel 8 Madras N.I. 4 July 1856 to 1869; general 23 April 1872. *d.* Glebeland house, Lee 24 Jany. 1878 aged 76.

CLARKE, REV. CHARLES. Educ. at Trin. coll. Ox., B.A. 1837; C. of Norton by Daventry 1844–54; chaplain to Earl of Stamford 1864; author of *Letters to an undergraduate of Oxford* 1848; *Charlie Thornhill* 3 vols. 1863; *A box for the season, a sporting sketch* 2 vols. 1864; *Crumbs from a sportsman's table, by A Sportsman* 1865; *The Beauclercs, father and son* 3 vols. 1867 and other novels; wrote articles in *Baily's Mag.* under pseudonym of The Gentleman in black. *d.* from tumor of the abdomen at Esher 23 July 1870 aged 55.

CLARKE, CHARLES COWDEN *(son of John Clarke of Enfield, Middlesex, schoolmaster, who d. Dec. 1820)*. *b.* Enfield 15 Dec. 1787; bookseller and publisher in London 1820; music publisher with Alfred Novello; lectured on Shakespeare and other dramatists and poets in the provinces and London 1834–56, many of his lectures were published; lived at Nice 1856–61, at Genoa 1861 to death; author of *Readings in natural philosophy* 1828; *Tales from Chaucer* 1833, 2 *ed.* 1870; *Riches of Chaucer* 2 vols. 1835, 3 *ed.* 1877; *Carmina Minima a poem* 1859; *Shakespeare characters, chiefly those subordinate* 1863; *Molière characters* 1865; edited with his wife *The works of Shakespeare* 1864 and 1869, reissued 1875 and under title of *Cassell's Illustrated . Shakespeare* 1886. *(m.* 5 July 1828 Mary Victoria eld. child of Vincent Novello the composer, she was *b.* 22 June 1809). *d.* Villa Novello, Genoa 13 March 1877. *I.L.N. lxx,* 291, 292 (1877), *portrait.*

CLARKE, SIR CHARLES MANSFIELD, 1 Baronet *(son of John Clarke of Chancery lane, London, surgeon)*. *b.* London 28 May 1782; ed. at St.

CLARKE, SIR C. M. *(Con.)*

Paul's school and St. George's hospital; M.R.C.S. 1802; lectured on midwifery 1804–21; surgeon to Queen Charlotte's Lying-in-hospital; M.R.C.P.; F.R.C.P.; F.R.S. 9 June 1825; M.D. Lambeth 1827; physician to Queen Adelaide 1830; created baronet 30 Sep. 1831; hon. M.A. Cam. 1842; hon. D.C.L. Ox. 1845; founded the Milton prize for an English poem at St. Paul's school 1851; author of *Observations on those diseases of females which are attended by discharges* 2 parts 1814–21, 2 *ed.* 1821–6, translated into German 1818–25. *d.* Brighton 7 Sep. 1857. *Physic and physicians ii,* 329–31 (1839); *W. C. Taylor's National portrait gallery i,* 16 (1846), *portrait; T. J. Pettigrew's Medical portrait gallery i,* (1840), *portrait; R. B. Gardiner's St. Paul's school* (1884) 199, 433–8.

CLARKE, HARRIET LUDLOW *(4 dau. of Edward Clarke of London, solicitor)*. Engraver on wood about 1837; executed some of the illustrations for Mrs. Jameson's *Sacred and legendary art* 1848; a designer and painter on glass; executed windows in St. Martin's church, Canterbury and Sidcup church, Kent 1851–4; executed for the Queen a large window in church of North Marston, Bucks.; designed a large window representing history of St. Thomas à Becket, which was put up in Canterbury cathedral, May 1863. *d.* Cannes 19 Jany. 1866. *G.M. i,* 436 (1866).

CLARKE, JACOB AUGUSTUS LOCKHART. *b.* 1817; studied at Guy's and St. Thomas's hospitals; L.S.A. 1842, M.R.C.S. 1860; practised in London to death; F.R.S. 1 June 1854, royal medallist 1864; F.K.Q.C.P. Ireland 1867; M.D. St. Andrew's 1869; M.R.C.P. 1871; physician to the hospital for epilepsy and paralysis, London; author of many articles in medical journals. *d.* 21 New Cavendish st. London 25 Jany. 1880 in 64 year.

CLARKE, JAMES. *b.* London 1793; teacher of music; author of *A catechism of wind instruments* 1845; *Instruction book for children on the pianoforte; The child's alphabet of music; Catechism of the rudiments of music; New School of music;* composed popular song *The maid of Llangollen. d.* Leeds 1859.

CLARKE, JAMES. *b.* 1798; member of British Archæological Assoc. 1847; a frequent exhibitor at its meetings of coins and other antiquities of which he contributed short notices to the journal; author of *The Suffolk Antiquary* 1849. *d.* 25 Sep. 1861. *Journal of British Archæol. Assoc. xviii,* 367–8 (1862).

CLARKE, JAMES FERNANDEZ (*son of Mr. Clarke of Olney, Bucks. lace merchant*). *b.* Olney 1812; aided Ryan in the *London medical and surgical journal*; reported at hospitals and medical societies for the *Lancet* 1834–64; M.R.C.S. 1837; practised in Gerrard st. Soho 1837 to death; author of *Autobiographical recollections of the medical profession* 1874, reprinted from *Medical times and gazette*. *d.* 23 Gerrard st. Soho 6 July 1875 in 63 year. *Medical Circular ii*, 310 (1853); *Medical times and gazette ii*, 82–3 (1875).

CLARKE, JAMES LANGTON (2 son of *Andrew Clarke of Belmont, co. Donegal*). *b.* 1801; ed. at Queen's coll. Cam., B.A. 1829, M.A. 1833; barrister M.T. 30 Jany. 1835; practised as a conveyancer; admitted to bar of Victoria, Australia 7 June 1855; judge of county courts for district of Ararat 1867, for district of Maryborough to about 1874. *d.* Mentone 16 Feb. 1886 aged 85.

CLARKE, JOHN. *b.* about 1830; photographer in Farringdon st. London; first appeared on stage in London at Strand theatre, Jany. 1852, chief comedian there 1852–5 and 1858–62; thrown from a horse and lamed for life, Jany. 1863; played at Prince of Wales's theatre 15 April 1865 to 1867; acted John Chodd in Robertson's comedy *Society* 11 Nov. 1865 to Sep. 1866, Hugh Chalcot in Robertson's comedy *Ours* 15 Sep. 1866 to April 1867, Sarah Gamp in H. Wigan's drama *Martin Chuzzlewit* at Olympic 2 March 1868, Quilp in A. Halliday's drama *Nell or the old curiosity shop* at Olympic 19 Nov. 1870; acted at nearly all the west-end theatres; last appeared on the stage at Globe theatre 8 June 1878. (*m.* 10 Aug. 1873 Theresa Elizabeth, dau. of Charles Furtado of London, professor of music, leading actress at Adelphi theatre, she *d.* 9 Aug. 1877 aged 32). *d.* 15 Torriano avenue, Camden road, London 20 Feb. 1879. *Pascoe's Dramatic list* (1880) 390–2; *The Players i*, 129 (1860), *portrait*; *Illust. sporting and dramatic news, x*, 572 (1879), *portrait*.

CLARKE, JOHN RANDALL (*son of Joseph Clarke of Gloucester*). *b.* about 1828; an architect; author of *Architectural history of Gloucester* 1850; and of two novels, *Gloucester Cathedral, or last days of the Tudors* 1856, and *Manxley Hall*; contributed to *Gent. Mag., Le Follet, The Era* and other periodicals. *d.* College Green, Gloucester 31 March 1863.

CLARKE, REV. JOSEPH. *b.* about 1811; ed. at St. John's coll. Cam., B.A. 1837, M.A. 1841; R. of Stretford, Manchester 1850 to death; rural dean of Manchester 1854 to

CLARKE, REV. J. (*Con.*)
death; wrecked in the Orion steamer between Liverpool and Greenock 17 June 1850; author of *The wreck of the Orion, tribute of gratitude* 1851; *Trees of righteousness*; made collections for history of parish of Stretford which were used by Rev. F. R. Raines in his *History of the chantries within the county of Lancaster* 1862. *d.* Stretford 25 Feb. 1860. *G.M. viii*, 463 (1860), *xv*, 243 (1863).

CLARKE, MARCUS ANDREW HISLOP (*only son of Wm. Hislop Clarke of Lincoln's Inn, London, barrister*). *b.* 11 Leonard place, Kensington 24 April 1846; went to Victoria 1863; joined staff of the *Argus*, Melbourne daily paper 1867, wrote the dramatic criticism some years; contributed to all principal Melbourne journals; secretary to trustees of public library, Melbourne 1872, assistant librarian 1876 to death; author of a novel called *Long Odds* 1868; produced at T.R. Melbourne pantomimes of *Little Bo-Peep* 1870 and *Twinkle Twinkle, Little Star* 1873; author of *His natural life* 1874 a novel republished in London, New York and Germany; *Holiday Peak* a collection of stories. *d.* Melbourne 2 Aug. 1881. *Men of the time in Australia, Victorian series* (1878) *p.* 36; *Heaton's Australian dictionary of dates* (1879) *p.* 39.

CLARKE, MARY ANN (*dau. of Mr. Thompson*). *b.* Ball and Tin alley, White's alley, Chancery lane, London 1776; eloped at 15 years of age with Joseph Clarke (son of a builder on Snow hill, London) who married her 1794; the kept mistress of Frederick Duke of York at Gloucester place 1803–1806 when discharged with pension of £400; published *The rival princes or a faithful narrative of facts relative to the acquaintance of the author with Colonel Wardle* 2 vols. 1810; *A letter to the Right Hon. William Fitzgerald, chancellor of the Irish Exchequer* 1813, for which she was prosecuted for libel and sentenced to 9 months imprisonment. *d.* Boulogne 21 June 1852. *Biographical Memoir* 1809, *portrait*; *The investigation of the charges brought against the Duke of York ii*, (1809), *portrait*; *The rival princes vol. i* (1810), *portrait*; *Gronow's Reminiscences*, 2 ed. (1862) 35–42; *G.M. xxxviii*, 208–9 (1852); *Marmion travestied, a tale of modern times by Peter Pry* 1809, in which her history is given in rhyme.

NOTE.—After the inquiry into the Duke of York's conduct, Mrs. Clarke announced her intention of publishing a narrative of circumstances relating to her connection with him, this book was actually printed but was suppressed by her in consideration of receiving the sum of £7,000 and an annuity of £400 for life, and an annuity of £200 for each of her daughters; the printer received £1,500 of the above sum of £7,000, the whole edition of 10,000 copies was burnt except one copy which was deposited in Drummond's bank.

CLARKE, NATHANIEL RICHARD (eld. son of Nathaniel Gooding Clarke of Handsworth, Staffs. recorder of Walsall). b. Duffield, Derbyshire 11 May 1785 ; ed. at Ashbourne gr. sch. and Trin. coll. Cam., B.A. 1808, M.A. 1811 ; barrister M.T. 22 Nov. 1811 ; recorder of Lincoln, Newark, Northampton and Walsall to death ; serjeant at law 6 Feb. 1843 ; judge of county courts, circuit 25 (Wolverhampton, Oldbury and Walsall) March 1847 to death. d. Wolverhampton 31 July 1859.

CLARKE, SIR ROBERT BOWCHER (eld. son of Robert Bowcher Clarke of Eldridge, Barbados). b. 1802 ; ed. at Codrington coll. Barbados and Trin. coll. Cam., LL.B. 1827 ; barrister I.T. 9 Feb. 1827 ; solicitor general at Barbados 1837–42, chief justice 1842–74 ; chief justice of St. Lucia 19 June 1850 to 1859 ; knighted by patent 20 March 1840 for his services in relation to emancipation of the slaves ; C.B. 27 April 1848. d. Eldridge, Chislehurst, Kent 9 May 1881 in 79 year.

CLARKE, SEYMOUR (2 son of Frederic Clarke of Streatham, Surrey). b. Streatham 1814 ; superintendent of London division of Great Western railway, Oct. 1837, in charge of the line from London to Swindon 1840–50 ; general manager of Great Northern railway, May 1850 to Sep. 1870 ; a comr. to inquire into Irish railways 1867, the report of the commission was chiefly written by him ; A.I.C.E. 5 Dec. 1865. d. Walthamstow 15 March 1876. Min. of proc. of Instit. of C.E. xliv, 225–7 (1876).

CLARKE, THOMAS. b. 14 July 1789 ; admitted an attorney 1810 ; practised in Craven st. Strand, London 1810–45 ; solicitor to Board of Ordnance 1845 to death ; sec. of the Lowtonian club ; member of council of Incorporated Law Society, July 1843, vice-pres. 1848–9, pres. 1849–50. d. Highgate hill, Kentish town, London 15 July 1854.

CLARKE, REV. THOMAS TRACY. b. Dublin 4 July 1802 ; ed. at Stonyhurst and Maynooth colleges ; entered Society of Jesus 1823 ; master at Hodder School 1825–9 ; ordained priest 24 Sep. 1836 ; professor of history and librarian at Stonyhurst college 1840–5 ; master of novices at Hodder 1845–60, by his exertions the novitiate was removed to Beaumont lodge, Old Windsor 4 Sep. 1854. d. the Residence of St. Ignatius' college, Hill st. London 11 Jany. 1862.

CLARKE, TREDWAY. b. July 1764 ; Second lieut. Madras artillery 20 Oct. 1780, colonel 25 July 1810 to death ; head commissary of ordnance and stores at Fort St. George 1798–

CLARKE, T. (Con).

1811 ; declined command of artillery at Madras 1820 ; general 23 Nov. 1841 ; lived in England 1811 to death. d. Upper Charlotte st. Fitzroy sq. London 3 May 1858.

CLARKE, WILLIAM. b. Nottingham 24 Dec. 1798 ; a bricklayer ; landlord of the Bell Inn, Nottingham to 1847 ; proprietor of the Trent Bridge cricket ground, Nottingham 1838–47 ; played in the Nottingham Eleven from 1816 ; played his first match at Lord's 11 July 1836 ; a practice bowler at Lord's 1846 ; originated the All England matches 1846 ; the best slow underhand bowler of his day ; a great fives player, at which game he lost his right eye by accident. d. Priory lodge, Wandsworth road, London 25 Aug. 1856. Denison's Cricket (1846) 21–6 ; Pycroft's Cricket Field (1862), portrait.

CLARKE, WILLIAM. Private soldier ; quartermaster 14 light dragoons 15 Sep. 1837, major 23 Nov. 1848 to 30 Dec. 1853 ; granted distinguished service reward 18 March 1868 ; L.G. 1 Oct. 1877. d. 2 Notting hill terrace, Bayswater, London 17 Oct. 1881.

CLARKE, REV. WILLIAM BRANWHITE. b. East Bergholt, Suffolk 2 June 1798 ; ed. at Dedham gr. sch. and Jesus coll. Cam., B.A. 1821, M.A. 1824 ; presented to a living in Dorset 1833 ; chaplain to Bishop of Salisbury 1837–9 ; V. of St. Thomas's, Willoughby, N.S.W. 1846 to 1 Oct. 1870 ; made geological researches in N.S.W. 1839 to death ; ascertained auriferous nature of the country 1841, ten years before the popular date 1851 ; voted sum of £1,000 by legislature of N.S.W. 1853 but £5,000 was afterwards given to him ; F.G.S. 1826. Murchison medallist 1877 ; F.R.S. of N.S.W. 1867 ; F.R.S. 1 June 1876 in recognition of his discovery of gold in Australia ; author of Lays of leisure 1822 ; Recollections of a visit to Mont Blanc 1839 ; Remarks on the sedimentary formations of N.S.W., 4 ed. 1878 and of many scientific papers. d. North Shore, Sydney 17 June 1878. Journal and proc. of Royal Soc. of N.S.W. xiii, 4–23 (1880) ; Therry's Reminiscences, 2 ed. (1863) 363–8 ; Proc. of Royal Soc. xxviii, 1–4 (1879) ; Quarterly Journal of Geol. Soc. xxxv, 44–6 (1879) ; Phillips's Mining and metallurgy of gold and silver (1867).

CLARKE, WILLIAM FAIRLIE (son of Wm. Fairlie Clarke of Bengal civil service, who d. Calcutta 23 Sep. 1835 aged 47). b. Calcutta 1833 ; ed. at high school, Edin., Rugby and Ch. Ch. Ox., B.A. 1856, M.A. and M.B. 1862, M.D. 1876 ; studied medicine at King's coll. Lon. 1858 ; M.R.C.S. 1862, F.R.C.S. 1863 ; practised in London 1863–76, and at Southborough

CLARKE, W. F. (*Con.*)

near Tunbridge Wells 1876 to death; assistant surgeon at Charing Cross hospital 1871; author of *A manual of the practice of surgery* 1865, 3 ed. 1879; *A treatise on the diseases of the tongue* 1873. *d.* Bonchurch, Isle of Wight 8 May 1884. *bur.* Elvington churchyard 14 May. *Life and letters of W. F. Clarke edited by E.A.W.* (1885), *portrait.*

CLARKE-JERVOISE, REV. SIR SAMUEL, 1 Baronet *(youngest son of Jervoise Clarke 1734–1808, M.P. for Hampshire). b.* Albemarle st. Piccadilly, London 25 Nov. 1770, ed. at C.C. coll. Ox., B.A. 1792, M.A. 1795; R. of Chalton with Idsworth 1794–1834; R. of Blendworth, Hants. 1795–1835; took additional surname of Jervoise by royal license 9 Nov. 1808; created baronet 13 Nov. 1813. *d.* 1 Oct. 1852.

CLARKE-TRAVERS, SIR WILLIAM HENRY ST. LAWRENCE, 2 Baronet. *b.* 3 Aug. 1801; succeeded 7 Feb. 1808; assumed by royal license additional name of Travers 20 March 1853. *d.* 3 Queen's gardens, Hyde park, London 31 Aug. 1877.

CLARKSON, EUGENE COMERFORD (3 *son of Frederick Clarkson of Doctor's Commons, London, proctor). b.* 1831; ed. at King's college, London; barrister L.I. 26 Jany. 1854; practised in court of Admiralty about 1858 to death; Q.C. 21 March 1881. *d.* from hydrophobia at East end lodge, Pinner 19 Aug. 1881.

CLARKSON, WILLIAM. Barrister I.T. 7 Feb. 1823; recorder of Faversham 1844 to death. *d.* Westfield lodge, Brighton 24 Oct. 1856 aged 61. *J. Grant's Portraits of public characters i,* 232–8 (1841); *I.L.N. iv,* 228 (1844), *portrait.*

CLASON, REV. PATRICK *(youngest child of Rev. Robert Clason, minister of Logie near Stirling). b.* Manse of Dalziel on the Clyde 13 Oct. 1789; ed. at college of Glasgow; D.D. Glasgow, March 1836; licensed to preach the gospel 1811; minister of Carmunock near Glasgow 1815, of St. Cuthbert's Chapel of Ease (now Buccleuch ch.), Edin. 16 April 1824; joint clerk of the free church general assembly 18 May 1843 to death; moderator of general assembly 1848 and 1864. *d.* 22 George sq. Edin. 30 July 1868. *J. A. Wylie's Disruption Worthies* (1881) 161–4, *portrait; Crombie's Modern Athenians* (1882) 17–19, *portrait.*

CLASPER, HENRY *(son of Robert Clasper of Dunston near Newcastle). b.* Dunston 1812; a putter at Hetton colliery; a coke burner at Derwenthaugh; sculled his first race, June

CLASPER, H. (*Con.*)

1841; beaten by R. Coombes at Newcastle 18 Dec. 1844; beat Carroll on the Mersey 29 Sep. 1845; beat W. Pocock at Newcastle 25 Nov. 1845; beaten by Candlish for the championship of the Tyne 9 Sep. 1851; beat Robert Campbell of Glasgow for championship of the Clyde and £200, 22 July 1858, beat him again on Loch Lomond 6 Oct.; beaten by T. White on the Thames 9 Nov. 1858; rowed with three of his brothers many four-oared races in England and Scotland; a boat builder on the Tyne; brought his first outrigger boat to London 1844, generally said to have invented the outrigger boat, but he only brought it to perfection; rowed on every river between the Thames and Clyde; presented by the public with a freehold house. *d.* Newcastle 12 July 1870. *Illust. sporting news* (1862) 77, 139, 141, 2 *portraits; Illust. news of the world ii,* 267, 269 (1858), *portrait; Rowing almanac* (1863) 95–104.

CLATER, THOMAS (3 *son of Francis Clater of East Retford, Notts., farrier* 1756–1823). Baptised at East Retford 9 June 1789; painter; exhibited 43 pictures at the R.A., 91 at B.I. and 194 at Suffolk st. gallery 1819–59; fellow of Society of British Artists 1843. *d.* 1 Hemus terrace, South Chelsea, London 24 Feb. 1867.

CLAUDET, ANTOINE FRANÇOIS JEAN. *b.* Lyons 12 Aug. 1797; opened a warehouse at 89 High Holborn, London for sale of French glass 1829; invented machine for cutting cylindrical glass 1833; photographer at Adelaide gallery, London 1840–51, at 107 Regent st. 1851 to death; one of the first to adopt the collodion process; F.R.S. 2 June 1853; invented many new photographic processes; photographer in ordinary to the Queen 1858; author of upwards of 40 papers; received awards of 11 medals; a chevalier of the Legion of Honour 1863. *d.* 11 Gloucester road, Regent's park, London 27 Dec. 1867. *Scientific Review, August* 1868 *pp.* 151–4; *Proc. of Royal Soc. xvii, pp. lxxxv-lxxxvii* (1869).

CLAUGHTON, RIGHT REV. PIERS CALVELEY *(son of Thomas Claughton of Haydock Lodge, Winwick, Lancs., M.P. for Newton, Lancs., who d.* 1842). *b.* Haydock lodge 8 Jany. 1814; ed. at Repton and Brasn. coll. Ox., B.A. 1835, M.A. 1838, D.D. 1859; fell. and tutor of Univ. coll. Ox. 1837–42; R. of Elton, Hunts. 1845–59; select Pr. in Univ. of Ox. 1843 and 1850; bishop of St. Helena 3 June 1859 to May 1862; bishop of Colombo 13 May 1862 to Dec. 1870; archdeacon of London with canonry of St. Paul's annexed Dec. 1870 to

CLAUGHTON, RIGHT REV. P. C. *(Con).*

death ; rural dean of Hackney 1874 to death ; chaplain general to the forces 7 April 1875 to death ; assistant bishop of London 1879 to death ; author of *A brief examination of the Thirty nine articles* 1843 ; *A catechism for the Sundays in Lent* 1847. *d.* 2 Northwick terrace, Maida hill, London 11 Aug. 1884. *bur.* Elton churchyard 15 Aug., a tablet to his memory containing a medallion portrait of him was placed in the crypt of St. Paul's cathedral.

CLAVELL, RICHARD. Second lieut. R.M.L.I. 21 Nov. 1837, col. commandant 13 Feb. 1872 to death ; L.G. 25 Dec. 1877. *d.* Gosport 1 Sep. 1878 in 59 year.

CLAVERING, SIR THOMAS JOHN, 8 Baronet. *b.* 6 April 1771 ; succeeded 14 Oct. 1794 ; raised at his own expense a troop of yeomanry 1798 ; sheriff of Northumberland 1817–18. *d.* Clifton 18 Nov. 1853.

CLAVERING, SIR WILLIAM ALOYSIUS, 9 Baronet. *b.* 1800 ; succeeded 18 Nov. 1853 ; sheriff of Durham 1859. *d.* St. George's hospital, London 8 Oct. 1872.

CLAXTON, MARSHALL *(son of Rev. Marshall Claxton of Bolton, Lancs., Wesleyan minister).* *b.* Bolton 12 May 1813 ; entered Royal Academy, Jany. 1831 ; awarded gold medal of Society of Arts 1835 ; competed in the Cartoon exhibitions at Westminster hall 1843, 1844 and 1847 ; took out to Australia about 200 pictures by himself and others, which he exhibited gratis 1850, this being the first exhibition of works of art in Australia ; went to India where he sold most of the pictures ; painted for the Queen, 'General view of Sydney' and 'Portrait of the last Queen of the Aborigines'; exhibited 32 pictures at R.A., 31 at B.I. and 25 at Suffolk st. gallery. *d.* 155 Carlton road, Maida vale, London 28 July 1881.

CLAY, ALFRED BORRON (2 *son of Rev. John Clay* 1796–1858). *b.* Walton near Preston 3 June 1831 ; articled to a solicitor at Preston ; studied art in Liverpool and London ; exhibited 19 pictures at R.A., 1 at B.I. and 2 at Suffolk st. gallery 1852–70 ; his chief pictures were 'The imprisonment of Mary Queen of Scots at Lochleven Castle,' 'Charles ix and the French court at the massacre of St. Bartholomew,' 'The return to Whitehall 29 May 1660,' now in the Walker gallery at Liverpool. *d.* Rainhill near Liverpool 1 Oct. 1868.

CLAY, SIR GEORGE, 3 Baronet. *b.* 14 Aug. 1831 ; ensign 19 foot 1849, captain 29 Dec. 1854 to 1 May 1866 when placed on h.p. ; succeeded 14 Oct. 1876. *d.* 17 Cavendish square, London 30 June 1878.

CLAY, JAMES *(son of James Clay of Old Broad st. London, merchant).* *b.* London 1804 ; ed. at Winchester and Balliol coll. Ox., B.A. 1827 ; took the leading parts in operas performed by amateurs at Florence when Lord Burghersh was British minister there 1821–30 ; travelled in the Holy Land with B. Disraeli 1830 ; a merchant in London ; contested Beverley, July 1837, and Hull, June 1841 ; M.P. for Hull 1847–53 and 1857 to death ; chairman of committee to settle laws of whist 1863, by his book on whist and influence made the game popular and intelligible ; the finest whist and piquet player of his time ; he is described under name of Castlemaine in G. W. Lawrence's novel *Sans Merci, or kestrels and falcons* 3 vols. 1866 ; author of *A treatise on the game of whist by J. C.,* affixed to J. L. Baldwin's *Laws of short whist* 1864. *d.* 30 Regency sq. Brighton 26 Sep. 1873. *W. A. Gunnell's Sketches of Hull celebrities* (1876) 473–7 ; *Westminster Papers vi,* 117–8 (1873) ; *Graphic viii,* 362, 376 (1873), *portrait; Power, Rodwell and Dew's Controverted elections ii,* 96–100 (1857).

NOTE.—He was unseated March 1853 for bribery by his agents, in Feb. 1857 he was again returned and his election is the only instance on record of a member unseated on petition taking his seat a second time for the same place in the same parliament, the case would have been tried before a committee of the House of Commons had not a dissolution occurred 20 March 1857.

CLAY, REV. JOHN (5 *son of Thomas Clay of Liverpool, ship and anchor smith, who d. 1821).* *b.* Liverpool 10 May 1796 ; invented an improved bow and arrow which long bore his name ; assist. chap. of Preston gaol 11 Aug. 1821 ; entered Em. coll. Cam. as a ten years man 1822, B.D. 1835 ; chap. of Preston gaol, Aug. 1823 to Jany. 1858 ; issued annual reports 1824–57, in 1836 his annual reports were reprinted in a parliamentary blue book ; author of *Twenty five sermons* 1827 ; *Burial clubs and infanticide in England* 1854 ; *A plain address to candidates for confirmation* 1866. *d.* Lansdowne crescent, Leamington 21 Nov. 1858. *The prison chaplain by Rev. W. L. Clay* (1861), *portrait.*

CLAY, RICHARD. *b.* Cambridge ; apprenticed to John Smith at the Pitt Press, Cambridge ; printer near Devonshire square, Bishopsgate, London ; printer to the S.P.G. ; head of firm of Clay Sons and Taylor, Bread st. hill, London, retired Oct. 1868. *d.* Hornsey 10 Dec. 1877 in 89 year. *Bookseller, January* 1878 *p.* 7.

CLAY, SIR WILLIAM, 1 Baronet *(son of George Clay of London, merchant* 1757–1836). *b.* London 15 Aug. 1791 ; merchant and shipowner with his father ; M.P. for Tower Hamlets 12 Dec. 1832 to 20 March 1857 ; author of the

CLAY, SIR W., 1 Baronet *(Con.)*

Small tenements rating act 1850 ; one of foremost holders of advanced radical views ; secretary to Board of Control 30 Sep. 1839 to 8 Sep. 1841 ; created baronet 20 Sep. 1841 ; chairman of Grand Junction and Southwark and Vauxhall water companies ; author of *Speech on moving for a committee to inquire into the act permitting the establishment of joint-stock banks*, 2 ed. 1837 ; *Remarks on the water supply of London*, 2 ed. 1849 and 3 other pamphlets. *d.* Cadogan place, London 13 March 1869.

CLAY, WILLIAM. *b.* Liverpool 15 May 1823 ; manager of ironworks near Glasgow ; invented a method of rolling taper bars 1848 ; manager of Mersey Forge, Liverpool ; designed and forged the "Monstre" gun which weighed 22 tons and threw a projectil of 300 lbs. to a distance of 5 miles, it was mounted at Tilbury Fort ; partner in Mersey Forge to 1864 when the works were transferred to a company ; the first maker of puddled steel on a large scale ; established with C. A. Inman and captain McNeile the Birkenhead Forge 1864 ; M.I.M.E. 1859 ; formed in 1861 Eighth Lancashire artillery volunteer corps, lieut.-col. commandant 9 May 1861, hon. col. 1 May 1880 to death. *d.* Liverpool 28 Feb. 1881. *Proc. of Instit. of M.E.* (1882) 3–5.

CLAY, SIR WILLIAM DICKASON, 2 Baronet. *b.* London 21 Dec. 1828 ; succeeded 13 March 1869. *d.* 9 Lowndes sq. London 14 Oct. 1876.

CLAY, REV. WILLIAM KEATINGE. *b.* 1797 ; C. of Greenwich 1823 ; C. of Paddington 1830 ; C. of Blunham, Beds. 1834 ; B.D. Cam. (Jesus coll.) 1835 ; minor canon of Ely 1838–54 ; P.C. of Holy Trinity, Ely 1842–54 ; V. of Waterbeach, Cambs. 1854 to death ; author of *Explanatory notes on the Prayer book version of the Psalms* 1839 ; *The book of Common Prayer illustrated* 1841 ; *An historical sketch of the Prayer Book* 1849 ; *History of the Parish of Waterbeach* 1859, *Landbeach* 1861, and *Horningsey* 1865, these 3 histories printed separately by the Cambridge Antiquarian Soc. were collected into one vol. 1865. *d.* Waterbeach 26 April 1867. *A history of the parish of Milton by the late W. K. Clay* (1869) v–vi.

CLAYTON, REV. CHARLES. *b.* Cambridge 13 July 1813 ; ed. at Caius coll. Cam., 21 wrangler 1836, B.A. 1836, M.A. 1839 ; C. of St. John's, Chatham 1837–45 ; fellow and tutor of his college to 1855 ; London sec. to Church Pastoral aid soc. 1845–8 ; V. of Holy Trinity, Cam. 1851–65 ; hon. canon of Ripon cath. 1864 to death ; R. of Stanhope, Durham 1865

CLAYTON, REV. C. *(Con.)*

to death ; rural dean of Stanhope 1880 to death ; author of *Sermons preached at Cambridge* 1859, *Second series* 1865 ; *Letters from abroad* 1878. *d.* Stanhope rectory 21 Oct. 1883. *Church of England photographic portrait gallery* (1859) part 57, *portrait*.

CLAYTON, REV. GEORGE (2 *son of Rev. John Clayton* 1754–1843, *pastor of King's Weigh House chapel, London*). *b.* London 9 April 1783 ; ed. at Reading and Hoxton college ; Independent minister at Southampton 1802, at Walworth, Surrey 1804 to death ; ordained 6 June 1804 ; the Clayton jubilee memorial schools were opened 27 June 1855. *d.* Gaines 14 July 1862. *T. W. Aveling's Memorials of the Clayton family* (1867), *portrait*.

CLAYTON, JOHN. *b.* Hereford ; architect at Hereford, where many public buildings were erected from his designs ; practised in London about 1839 to death ; A.R.I.B.A. 13 June 1842, F.R.I.B.A. 2 Nov. 1857 ; exhibited architectural designs at the R.A. 1844–7, 1853 and 1856 ; author of *A collection of the ancient timber edifices of England* 1846 ; *The parochial churches of Sir Christopher Wren erected in the cities of London and Westminster* 1848. *d.* Teignmouth, Devon 14 Sep. 1861 aged 41.

CLAYTON, REV. JOHN *(brother of Rev. George Clayton* 1783–1862). *b.* London 13 May 1780 ; ordained congregational minister at Kensington 21 Oct. 1801 ; pastor of the congregation in Camomile st. London 4 April 1805 which migrated to the Poultry 1819, where he was pastor 17 Nov. 1819 to 1847 ; frequently called on to undertake services in all parts of the country at openings of chapels and other special occasions ; joint sec. of London Missionary Soc. 1830–2 ; author of *The choice of books* 1811. *d.* Bath 3 Oct. 1865. *bur.* Abney park cemetery, London. *T. W. Aveling's Memorials of the Clayton family* (1867), *portrait*.

CLAYTON, RICE RICHARD. *b.* 15 Nov. 1798 ; sheriff of Bucks 1838 ; M.P. for Aylesbury 28 June 1841 to 23 July 1847. *d.* Hedgerley park near Slough 4 May 1879.

CLAYTON, SIR WILLIAM ROBERT, 5 Baronet *(eld. child of Sir Wm. Clayton* 4 *baronet* 1762–1834). *b.* Harleyford, Bucks 28 Aug. 1786 ; ed. at Eton and Trin. coll. Cam. ; cornet Royal horse guards 28 Sep. 1804, captain 27 April 1809 to 25 Feb. 1816 when placed on h.p. ; served in the Peninsula, Netherlands and at Waterloo ; M.P. for Great Marlow 1831–42 ; succeeded 26 Jany. 1834 ; sheriff of

CLAYTON, SIR W., 5 Baronet (Con.)

Bucks 1846; general 12 Jany. 1865. d. South-sea 19 Sep. 1866. bur. Marlow parish church 27 Sep.

CLEASBY, SIR ANTHONY (youngest son of Stephen Cleasby of London, Russian broker, who d. 31 Aug. 1844). b. 27 Aug. 1804; ed. at Eton and Trin. coll. Cam., 3 wrangler 1827, B.A. 1827, M.A. 1830; fellow of his coll. 1828–36; barrister I.T. 10 June 1831; contested East Surrey 1852 and 1859, and Univ. of Cam. 1867; Q.C. 22 Feb. 1861; bencher of I.T. 1861–8; serjeant at law 25 Aug. 1868, admitted 2 Nov.; baron of Court of Exchequer 25 Aug. 1868 to 9 Jany. 1879 when he retired on a pension; knighted at Windsor Castle 9 Dec. 1868. d. Pennoyre near Brecon 6 Oct. 1879. Cleasby and Vigfusson's Icelandic-English dictionary (1869) pp. lxi-civ; Law mag. and review v, 113–27 (1880); A generation of Judges by Their Reporter (1886) 54–9; I.L.N. liv, 93 (1869), portrait.

CLEBURNE, PATRICK. b. near Queenstown, Cork 17 March 1828; a private in British army 1847–50; went to the United States 1850; studied law at Helena, Arkansas; a private in Confederate army 1861; brigadier general, March 1862; commanded a division at battle of Stone River 2 Jany. 1863, and at Chickamauga 21 Sep. 1863; killed at battle of Franklin, Tennessee 30 Nov. 1864.

CLEGG, SAMUEL. b. Manchester 2 March 1781; apprenticed to Boulton and Watt; invented lime purifiers for purifying gas; engineer of Chartered gas company, London 1814; invented and patented a water meter 1816; an engineer at Liverpool where he lost all his money; reconstructed the mint at Lisbon; M.I.C.E. 1829. d. Fairfield house, Adelaide road, Haverstock hill, London 8 Jany. 1861. Min. of proc. of Instit. of C.E. xxi, 552–4 (1862).

CLEGG, SAMUEL (only son of the preceding). b. Westminster 2 April 1814; made a trigonometrical survey of part of the Algarves in Portugal 1836; resident engineer of Southampton and Dorchester railway 1844–5; M.I.C.E. 1848; professor of civil engineering and architecture at Putney college, Surrey 1849; lecturer on civil engineering to Royal Engineers at Chatham 1849 to death; author of A practical treatise on the manufacture and distribution of coal gas 1841, 4 ed. 1866. d. Putney 25 July 1856. Min. of proc. of Instit. of C.E. xvi, 121–4 (1857).

CLEGHORN, THOMAS (son of Alexander Cleghorn, collector of customs at Edinburgh). b. Edinburgh 3 March 1818; ed. at Edin. academy and univ.; called to Scottish bar 1839; advocate depute; registrar of friendly societies; sheriff of Argyleshire 19 Feb. 1855 to death; legal adviser of Free church of Scotland 1871; founded Wellington school for reformation of young criminals; author with Robert Balfour of History of the Speculative Society; wrote many articles in early numbers of North British Review; revised Journal of Lord Cockburn 2 vols. 1874. d. Edin. 13 June 1874. Proc. of Royal Soc. of Edin. viii, 468–9 (1875); Journal of jurisprudence xviii, 385–6 (1874).

CLELAND, ROBERT STEWART (3 son of Samuel Cleland of Stormont castle, co. Down). b. 24 June 1840; ed. at Eton and Harrow; cornet 7 dragoon guards 7 July 1857; lieut. 9 lancers 6 Nov. 1860, lieut.-col. 27 June 1879 to death. d. at Murree, Bengal 7 Aug. 1880 from wounds received in the action of Killa Kazi 11 Dec. 1879. Shadbolt's Afghan campaign (1882) 46–7, portrait.

CLEMENT, WILLIAM INNELL. Newsvendor in London; purchased a share of the Observer 1815, conducted it 1815 to death; published Cobbett's Register; bought the Morning Chronicle 1822 for £42,000, sold it to John Easthope 1834 for £16,500; bought Bell's Life in London 1825, conducted it 1825 to death, raised circulation from 3000 to 30,000. d. Hackney, London 24 Jany. 1852 bur. Kensal green 31 Jany. G.M. xxxvii, 306–7 (1852); A. Andrews's British Journalism ii, 85, 93, 172–3, 206 (1859); J. Grant's Newspaper Press iii, 28–33 (1872).

CLEMENT, WILLIAM JAMES (eld. son of Wm. Clement of Shrewsbury, surgeon, who d. 15 Jany. 1853). b. Shrewsbury 1804; a surgeon at Shrewsbury; M.R.C.S. 3 Dec. 1824, F.R.C.S. 26 Aug. 1844; obtained Fothergillian gold medal; mayor of Shrewsbury 1863, 64 and 65; M.P. for Shrewsbury 11 July 1865 to death; author of Observations in surgery and pathology 1832. d. The council house, Shrewsbury 29 Aug. 1870.

CLEMENTS, FRANK, stage name of Robert Menti. b. Aberdeen 8 July 1844; ed. at King's coll. Aberdeen; appeared on the stage for the first time at New theatre, Birmingham 1861; leading actor at T.R. Birmingham 1867–9 and 1870 to Dec. 1873; manager and leading actor at T.R. Nottingham 1869–70; first appeared in London at Lyceum theatre, July 1874 as Lord Moray in Charles the First;

CLEMENTS, F. *(Con.)*

played nearly every leading legitimate and Shakespearian character in the provinces 1875–7; played Philip de Comines in *Louis xi* at Lyceum theatre, March 1878; member of the companies of Miss Genevieve Ward and Madame Modjeska in the United States; killed by a railway train passing over him at Newark, New Jersey 8 May 1886.

CLEMENTS, JOHN. Bookseller and stationer at 21 Little Pulteney st. Golden sq. London; one of the first to attempt publication of cheap serial works among which were *The romancist and novelist library* issued in weekly parts; obtained contract for first supply of envelopes ever used by the Stationery office; the first to introduce sale of note paper in 5 quire packets. *d.* Tunbridge Wells 10 Nov. 1878 in 73 year.

CLEMO, EBENEZER. *b.* London about 1831; went to Toronto, Canada 1858; patented a mode of using nitric acid in the conversion of straw and grasses into pulp, and for treating this pulp with a solution of hydrate of an alkali to reduce it to a fibrous pulp for making paper 1860; author of *The life and adventures of Simon Seek, or Canada in all shapes, by Maple Knot, Montreal* 1858; *Canadian homes or the mystery solved, Montreal* 1858. *d.* Morristown 1860.

CLEMONS, CLEMENT. Entered Madras army 1819; major 20 Madras N.I. 21 Oct. 1842, lieut.-col. 23 March 1849 to 1855; lieut.-col. 12 N.I. 1855–6, 21 N.I. 1856–7, 43 N.I. 1857 to 3 Dec. 1857, 38 N.I. 3 Dec. 1857 to 7 Oct. 1860; L.G. 31 Dec. 1861. *d.* 4 St. Stephen's crescent, Bayswater, London 27 Jany. 1885 in 82 year.

CLERK, SIR GEORGE, 6 Baronet *(elder son of James Clerk, who d. 1793).* *b.* Edinburgh 19 Nov. 1787; succeeded his uncle Sir John Clerk 24 Feb. 1798; entered Trin. coll. Ox. 21 Jany. 1806, D.C.L. 1810; called to Scottish bar 1809; M.P. for Midlothian 1811–32 and 1835–7, for Stamford 1838–47 and for Dover 1847–52; a lord of the Admiralty 1819–27 and 1828–30; clerk of the ordnance, May 1827; under sec. of state for home department 5 Aug. to 22 Nov. 1830; sec. to the Treasury 19 Dec. 1834 to 21 April 1835 and Sep. 1841 to Feb. 1845; vice pres. of Board of Trade 5 Feb. 1845 to 6 July 1846; P.C. 5 Feb. 1845; master of the Mint 12 Feb. 1845 to 14 July 1846; F.R.S. 27 May 1819; chairman of Royal academy of music. *d.* Penicuik house near Edin. 23 Dec. 1867. *G.M. v,* 246–7 (1868).

CLERK, SIR JAMES, 7 Baronet. *b.* London 17 July 1812; succeeded 23 Dec. 1867. *d.* St. Vincent's hall, Clifton, Bristol 17 Nov. 1870.

CLERK, ROBERT. Writer Madras civil service 1816; secretary to Government in military department 1831–2, in civil department 1835–6 and 1837–44, in secret political and public departments 1836–7; resigned the service 22 Feb. 1844. *d.* Westholme house, Pilton, Shepton Mallet 3 April 1873 aged 75.

CLERKE, VENERABLE CHARLES CARR (3 *son of Rev. Sir Wm. Henry Clerke, 8 Bart. 1751–1818).* *b.* 30 Dec. 1798; ed. at Ch. Ch. Ox., student, B.A. 1818, M.A. 1821, B.D. 1830, D.D. 1847; select preacher 1826; V. of St. Mary Magdalene, Oxford 1827; archdeacon of Oxford 9 March 1830 to death; R. of Milton, Berks. 1836–75; canon of Ch. Ch. Ox. 24 March 1845 to death; sub-dean of Ch. Ch. 1853 to death; author of *Duty of churchwardens* 1864; *Daily devotions for a churchman's household* 1868. *d.* Ch. Ch. Oxford 24 Dec. 1877.

CLERKE, SAINT JOHN AUGUSTUS *(son of Jonathan Clerke).* *b.* 1795; ensign 94 foot 13 Oct. 1808; major 77 foot 26 May 1825 to 30 Dec. 1828 when placed on h.p.; colonel 75 foot 22 March 1858 to death; general 8 March 1867; K.H. 1832. *d.* 66 Mountjoy sq. Dublin 17 Jany. 1870.

CLERKE, SIR WILLIAM HENRY, 9 Baronet *(brother of Ven. Charles Carr Clerke 1798–1877).* *b.* London 13 Sep. 1793; ensign 89 foot 10 Jany. 1811; lieut. 52 foot 19 Sep. 1811, captain 25 April 1822 to 2 May 1823 when placed on h.p.; succeeded 10 April 1818; sheriff of Flintshire 1848. *d.* Heath house, Aston on Clun, Salop 16 Feb. 1861.

CLERKE, SIR WILLIAM HENRY, 10 Baronet. *b.* Clonmel 17 Nov. 1822; a principal clerk in the Treasury, London; succeeded 16 Feb. 1861. *d.* 10 Eaton place south, London 8 Feb. 1882.

CLEUGH, VENERABLE JOHN. Educ. at Trin. hall, Cam., B.D. 1824; civil chaplain at Malta 1824 to 1865; archdeacon of Malta 1865 to death. *d.* Valetta, Malta 25 March 1881 aged 88.

CLEVELAND, HENRY VANE POWLETT, 2 Duke of *(eld. child of 1 Duke of Cleveland 1766–1842).* *b.* London 16 Aug. 1788; M.P. for co. Durham 1812–18, for Tregony 1818–26, for Totnes 1826–30, for Saltash 1830–1, for South Shropshire 24 Dec. 1832 to 29 Jany. 1842 when he succeeded; cornet 7 hussars 6 July 1815;

CLEVELAND, 2 Duke of *(Con.)*

major 2 Ceylon regiment 3 July 1823 ; major 75 foot 11 Dec. 1823 to 6 July 1826 when placed on h.p. ; colonel 1 Durham militia 1842–60 ; general 23 Oct. 1863 ; K.G. 11 April 1842. *d.* Raby castle, Durham 18 Jany. 1864. *Doyle's Official baronage i,* 415 (1886), *portrait.*

CLEVELAND, WILLIAM JOHN FREDERICK POWLETT, 3 Duke of *(brother of the preceding). b.* London 3 April 1792 ; ed. at Brasenose coll. Ox., M.A. 1812 ; M.P. for Winchelsea 1812–15, for co. Durham 1815–31, for St. Ives, Cornwall 1846–52, for Ludlow 1852–57 ; kept racehorses from 1843 but was very unlucky, his only good horse being Tim Whiffler which won the Goodwood and Doncaster cups ; succeeded 18 Jany. 1864. *d.* Raby castle 6 Sep. 1864. *W. Day's Reminiscences of the turf,* 2 ed. (1886) 328–42.

CLEVELAND, JOHN WHEELER. Entered Madras army 1808 ; commandant of Trichinopoly 26 Nov. 1844 to 26 April 1850 ; col. 18 Madras N.I. 1 Oct. 1846 to 30 June 1853 ; commandant of Southern division of the army 17 Feb. 1852 to 10 May 1857 ; col. 38 N.I. 30 June 1853 to 1869 ; general 6 March 1868 ; placed on retired list 1 Oct. 1877. *d.* Cleveland house, Bangalore 1 Nov. 1883 aged 92.

CLIAS, PETER HENRY. An officer in Swiss artillery ; introduced gymnastics into Swiss army 1814 ; professor of gymnastics in academy of Bern ; came to London 1822, introduced his system of gymnastics into British army and navy ; professor of gymnastics in Royal military academy, Woolwich 20 March 1823 to 4 Sep. 1825 ; author of *Elementary course of gymnastic exercises* 1824. *d.* Bern about Dec. 1854, left a considerable sum of money to city of Bern under condition that his skeleton should be exhibited in the Natural history museum as a palpable confirmation of beneficial effects of gymnastics.

CLIFDEN, HENRY AGAR-ELLIS, 3 Viscount *(eld. son of 1 Baron Dover 1797–1833). b.* Spring gardens, London 25 Feb. 1825 ; succeeded his father 10 July 1833 ; succeeded his grandfather as 3 Viscount Clifden 13 July 1836 ; won the Derby and St. Leger with Surplice 1848 no horse having won both these races since 1800 ; won the Great Northamptonshire stakes 1852 with Poodle carrying the extraordinary feather weight of 4 st. 5 lb. *d.* Dover house, Whitehall, London 20 Feb. 1866. *Illust. sporting news v,* 136 (1866), *portrait ; G.M. i,* 584–5 (1866).

CLIFFE, CHARLES FREDERICK. Edited *Gloucestershire Chronicle ;* author of *The book of South Wales, the Bristol Channel, Monmouthshire an*' *the Wye* 1847, 3 ed. 1854 ; *The book of North Wales, scenery, antiquities, highways and byeways, lakes, streams and railways* 1850, 2 ed. 1851. *d.* Clifton, Bristol 7 Oct. 1851 aged 42.

CLIFFORD, HUGH CHARLES CLIFFORD, 8 Baron. *b.* New park, Somerset 29 May 1790 ; ed. at Stonyhurst ; travelled in south of Europe where he made a large collection of all the catechetical works of instruction authorized by the several religious communities of the continent ; succeeded 29 April 1831. *d.* Rome 28 Feb. 1858. *buried* Rome 2 March by the side of Cardinal Weld. *Gillow's English Catholics i,* 509–11 (1885).

CLIFFORD, CHARLES HUGH CLIFFORD, 9 Baron. *b.* 27 July 1819 ; succeeded 28 Feb. 1858. *d.* Ugbrook park, Chudleigh, Devon 5 Aug. 1880.

CLIFFORD, SIR AUGUSTUS WILLIAM JAMES, 1 Baronet. *b.* 26 May 1788 ; ed. at Harrow ; midshipman R.N. May 1800, captain 23 July 1812, R.A. 23 March 1848, admiral 7 Nov. 1860 ; M.P. for Bandon Bridge 1818–20, for Dungarvan 1820–2, for Bandon Bridge again 1831–2 ; gentleman usher of the black rod 24 July 1832 to death ; deputy lord great chamberlain of England several times between 1843 and 1866 ; C.B. 8 Dec. 1815 ; knighted by Wm. iv at St. James's palace 4 Aug. 1830 ; created baronet 4 Aug. 1838. *d.* House of Lords, Westminster 8 Feb. 1877, personalty sworn under £250,000, 28 April 1877. *Graphic xv,* 172, 179 (1877), *portrait ; I.L.N. lxx,* 171, 181 (1877), *portrait.*

CLIFFORD, SIR HENRY HUGH (3 *son of 8 Baron Clifford* 1790–1858). *b.* 12 Sep. 1826 ; 2 lieut. rifle brigade 7 Aug. 1846 ; A.Q.M.G. China 20 Aug. 1857 to 24 Aug. 1859 ; A.Q.M.G. Aldershot 18 Feb. 1860 to 31 Dec. 1864 ; A.Q.M.G. at head quarters 1 Jany. 1865 to 25 Nov. 1868 ; A.D.C. to commander in chief 1 April 1870 to 4 Dec. 1873 ; A.A.G. at head quarters 5 Dec. 1873 to 31 Oct. 1875 ; M.G. Cape of Good Hope 6 April 1879 to 14 Nov. 1880 ; M.G. eastern district 1 April 1882 to 15 Sep. 1882 ; V.C. 24 Feb. 1857 ; C.B. 2 June 1869 ; K.C.M.G. 19 Dec. 1879 ; granted pension of £100 for distinguished service 7 Oct. 1874. *d.* Ugbrook 12 April 1883. *C. R. Low's Soldiers of the Victorian age i,* 208–21 (1880) ; *Graphic xix,* 372 (1879), *portrait.*

CLIFFORD, HENRY MORGAN *(only son of Morgan Morgan Clifford of Penystone, co. Hereford, who d.* 1814). *b.* 1806 ; ed. at Eton and Ch.

CLIFFORD, H. M. *(Con.)*

Ch. Ox.; chairman of Herefordshire quarter sessions 1845; M.P. for Hereford 1847–65; a comr. of lunacy 1853; col. of Monmouthshire militia 5 March 1858. *d.* St. Ronan's, Torquay 12 Feb. 1884 in 78 year.

CLIFFORD, SIR WILLIAM JOHN CAVENDISH, 2 Baronet. *b.* London 12 Oct. 1814; ed. at Eton; entered navy 24 Feb. 1829, captain 18 Aug. 1847, V.A. 1 Oct. 1871, retired 7 May 1872, retired admiral 1 Aug. 1877; C.B. 5 July 1855; succeeded 8 Feb. 1877. *d.* Bournemouth 11 April 1882.

CLIFFORD, WILLIAM KINGDON *(son of Wm. Clifford of Exeter, bookseller, who d. Feb. 1878). b.* Exeter 4 May 1845; ed. at King's coll. London and Trin. coll. Cam., a minor scholar, Oct. 1863; 2 wrangler and 2 Smith's prizeman 1867; B.A. 1867, M.A. 1870; fellow of his college, Oct. 1868; took part in English eclipse expedition 1870, wrecked in the Psyche off Catania; professor of applied mathematics at Univ. coll. London 1871; F.R.A.S. 12 Dec. 1873; F.R.S. 4 June 1874; a prominent member of Metaphysical Soc. 1874; author of *Mathematical fragments* 1881; *Mathematical papers edited by R. Tucker* 1882; *Common sense of the exact sciences edited by K. Pearson* 1885. *(m.* 7 April 1875 Sophia Lucy Jane dau. of John Lane of Barbadoes, she was granted civil list pension of £80, 13 Oct. 1880). *d.* Madeira 3 March 1879. *bur.* Highgate cemetery. *Lectures and essays by the late W. K. Clifford edited by Leslie Stephen and Frederick Pollock vol.* 1 (1879), *portrait; Edinburgh Review cli,* 474–511 (1880).

CLIFTON, SIR ARTHUR BENJAMIN *(youngest son of Sir Gervase Clifton, 6 baronet, who d.* 1815). *b.* 1772; ed. at Rugby; cornet 3 dragoon guards 6 June 1794, major 17 Dec. 1803 to 22 Nov. 1810; lieut.-col. 1 dragoons 22 Nov. 1810 to 11 June 1829 when placed on h.p.; col. 17 lancers 25 Aug. 1839 to 30 Aug. 1842; col. 1 dragoons 30 Aug. 1842 to death; general 20 June 1854; C.B. 22 June 1815, K.C.B. 19 July 1838, G.C.B. 28 June 1861; K.C.H. 1832. *d.* 52 Old Steyne, Brighton 7 March 1869. *bur.* Clifton, Notts. 12 March, personalty sworn under £140,000, May 1869.

CLIFTON, HENRY ROBERT, known as Harry Clifton. *b.* Hoddesdon, Herts.; apprenticed to John Clark, circus proprietor, who taught him riding and clowning; comic and motto vocalist at music halls in London and the provinces, many of his songs obtained great popularity; organised a concert company with

CLIFTON, H. R. *(Con.)*

which he visited every town in Great Britain and Ireland 1864–72. *d.* of hepatic disease at 26 St. Stephen's road, Hammersmith, London 15 July 1872 aged 40. *The Era* 21 *July* 1872 *p.* 12, *col.* 3.

CLIFTON, JOHN TALBOT. *b.* London 5 March 1819; M.P. for North Lancs. 1844–7; col. 1 royal Lancashire militia 8 Oct. 1852–1870; sheriff of Lancs. 1853. *d.* on board his steam yacht Taurus at Algiers 16 April 1882.

CLIFTON, SIR JUCKES GLANVILLE JUCKES, 8 Baronet. *b.* Aug. 1769; succeeded his brother 28 April 1837. *d.* Clifton hall near Nottingham 1 Oct. 1852.

CLIFTON, REV. ROBERT COX. *b.* Gloucester 4 Jany. 1810; ed. at Worcester and Worcester coll. Ox., B.A. 1831, M.A. 1834; fellow of his coll. 1833; clerk in orders at Manchester collegiate church 1837, elected to a fellowship by the collegiate chapter 6 Dec. 1843; R. of Somerton, Oxon 1840 to death; canon of Manchester, Dec. 1843 to death; a trustee of Owen's college, Manchester; author of several sermons and pamphlets. *d.* Somerton rectory 30 July 1861.

CLIFTON, SIR ROBERT JUCKES, 9 Baronet. *b.* 24 Dec. 1826; ed. at Eton; lost heavily on the turf during his minority; succeeded 1 Oct. 1852; M.P. for Nottingham 26 Dec. 1861 to May 1866 (when unseated on petition) and 18 Nov. 1868 to death. *d.* Clifton hall 30 May 1869.

CLINT, ALFRED *(youngest son of the succeeding). b.* Alfred place, Bedford sq. London 22 March 1807; painted portraits and landscapes; member of Society of British artists 1843, secretary 1853–9, pres. 1869–81; best known as a marine painter; exhibited 24 pictures at R.A., 35 at B.I. and 343 at Suffolk st. gallery 1828–79; drew and etched illustrations to Bennett's *Pedestrian's guide through North Wales* 1838; author of *Landscape from nature* 1855. *d.* 54 Lancaster road, Notting hill, London 22 March 1883, *I.L.N. lxxxii,* 332 (1883), *portrait.*

CLINT, GEORGE *(son of Michael Clint of Lombard st. London, hairdresser). b.* Brownlow st. Drury Lane, London 12 April 1770; a house painter, painted the stones of the arches in nave of Westminster abbey; a miniature painter in Leadenhall st.; made copies in colours from prints after Morland and Teniers; painted a series of dramatic scenes; exhibited 99 pictures at R.A., 9 at B.I. and 15 at Suffolk st.

CLINT, G. (Con.)

gallery; A.R.A. 1821–36. d. 10 Pembroke sq. London 10 May 1854. *Sandby's History of Royal Academy ii*, 66–8 (1862).

CLINTON, CHARLES RODOLPH TREFUSIS, 18 Baron. b. South Brent, South Devon 9 Nov. 1791; ed. at Eton and Oriel coll. Ox.; B.A. 1814, M.A. 1817; fellow of All Souls coll.; M.P. for Callington 4 March 1813 to 10 June 1818; a comr. of excise 29 Sep. 1823; succeeded 7 Oct. 1832; lieut.-col. commandant of North Devon yeomanry cavalry 1842. d. Heanton Satchville house, North Devon 10 April 1866.

CLINTON, REV. CHARLES JOHN FYNES (3 *son of Rev. Charles Fynes 1748–1827, preb. of Westminster, who took name of Clinton 1821*). b. 16 April 1799; ed. at Westminster and Oriel coll. Ox., B.A. 1822, M.A. 1825; V. of Orston, Notts 1827–55; R. of Cromwell, Notts 1828 to death; author of *An address to all classes on the first visitation of cholera* 1832; *Plain doctrinal and practical sermons* 1842; edited H. F. Clinton's *Epitome of chronology of Rome and Constantinople* 1853; *Literary remains of H. F. Clinton* 1854. d. of pleurisy at 3 Montague place, St. George's, Bloomsbury, London 10 Jany. 1872.

CLINTON, HENRY FYNES (*brother of the preceding*). b. Gamston, Notts. 14 Jany. 1781; ed. at Westminster and Ch. Ch. Ox., student Dec. 1802 to June 1809, B.A. 1803, M.A. 1805, one of the few who passed an examination for the M.A. degree; M.P. for Aldborough 3 Nov. 1806 to June 1826; a candidate for librarianship of British Museum, Dec. 1827; author of *Fasti Hellenici* 4 vols. 1824–34; *Fasti Romani* 2 vols. 1845–50. d. Welwyn, Herts. 24 Oct. 1852. *Literary remains of H. F. Clinton edited by Rev. C. J. F. Clinton* 1854; *C. Brown's Lives of Nottinghamshire worthies* (1882) 338–41; *G.M. xxxix*, 315–6 (1853).

CLISSOLD, REV. AUGUSTUS (*son of Augustus Clissold of Stonehouse near Stroud, Gloucs.*) b. 1797; matric. from Exeter coll. Ox. 6 Dec. 1814, B.A. 1818, M.A. 1821; C. of St. Martin-in-the-Fields, London; C. of St. Mary, Stoke Newington; pres. of Swedenborg Association 1845; purchased in 1854 for use of the Swedenborg Society a 70 years lease of 36 Bloomsbury st. London; author of *Principles of Apocalyptical interpretation* 3 vols. 1845; *Spiritual exposition of the Apocalypse* 4 vols. 1851; *Transition or the passing of ages* 1868; *Prophetic spirit in relation to wisdom and madness* 1870; *The creeds of Athanasius, Sabellius and*

CLISSOLD, REV. A. (Con.)

Swedenborg examined 1873, 2 ed. 1873 and 17 other books. d. 4 Broadwater Down, Tunbridge Wells 30 Oct. 1882.

CLISSOLD, REV. HENRY. Educ. at Ex. coll. Ox., B.A. 1818, M.A. 1821; R. of Chelmondiston, Suffolk 1830–58; author of *Last hours of eminent Christians* 1848; *Lamps of the church, lives of eminent Christians* 1862. d. 19 Talbot sq. Sussex gardens, London 10 Jany. 1867.

CLISSOLD, REV. STEPHEN. b. about 1790; ed. at Clare coll. Cam., B.A. 1819, M.A. 1822; R. of Wrentham, Suffolk 1830–53; hon. canon of Norwich cathedral 1848 to death; author of *Letters of Cincinnatus* 1815; *Considerations on the trade, manufacture and commerce of the British Empire* 1820. d. Wrentham 12 May 1863.

CLITHEROW, JOHN (*eld. son of Christopher Clitherow of Bird's Place, Essendon, Herts*). b. 13 Dec. 1782; ensign 3 foot guards 19 Dec. 1799, lieut.-col. 15 Sep. 1825 to 22 July 1830; L.G. 23 Nov. 1841; administered government of Canada after decease of Lord Sydenham 1841; col. 67 foot 15 Jany. 1844 to death. d. Boston house, Middlesex 14 Oct. 1852.

CLIVE, CAROLINE (2 *dau. of Edmund Meysey Wigley of Shakenhurst, Worcs.*) b. Brompton Grove, London 24 June 1801; author of *ix Poems by V.* 1840, 2 ed. 1841; *The valley of the Rea, a poem by V.* 1851; *Paul Ferroll, a tale by the author of, ix Poems by V.* 1855; *Why Paul Ferroll killed his wife* 1860; *John Greswold* 2 vols. 1864. (m. 10 Nov. 1840 Rev. Archer Clive, preb. of Hereford, he was b. 16 March 1800·and d. 17 Sep. 1878). d. by an accident from fire at Whitfield near Hereford 13 July 1873. *Contemporary Review xxiii*, 197–217 (1874).

CLIVE, GEORGE (3 *son of Edward Bolton Clive of Whitfield, Herefordshire, who d. 22 July 1845 in 81 year*). b. Verdun, France, Oct. 1806; ed. at Harrow and Brasenose coll. Ox., B.A. 1826, M.A. 1829; barrister L.I. 29 June 1830; assistant poor law comr. 1836–9; police magistrate for Kensington and Wandsworth 1840–7; judge of county courts circuit 47 Southwark, March 1847 to 1858; recorder of Wokingham 1849–58; M.P. for city of Hereford 14 Feb. 1857 to 9 March 1869 (when unseated on petition) and 3 Feb. 1874 to March 1880; under sec. of state for home department, June 1859 to Nov. 1862; chairman of Herefordshire quarter sessions, Jany. 1871 to death. d. Perrystone near Ross 8 June 1880. *O'Malley and Hardcastle's Reports of election petitions i*, 194–7 (1870).

CLIVE, HENRY BAYLEY (4 *son of Wm. Clive of Leigh hall, Salop 1745–1825*). *b.* Styche, Market Drayton 1800; M.P. for Ludlow 1847–52. *d.* Styche 26 Feb. 1870.

CLIVE, ROBERT HENRY (2 *son of Earl of Powis 1754–1839*). *b.* 15 Jany. 1789; ed. at St. John's coll. Cam., M.A. 1809, LL.D. 1835; M.P. for Ludlow 1818 to 1832, for South Shropshire 1832 to death; under sec. of state for home department 21 April 1818 to 17 Jany. 1822; pres. of Cambrian archæological assoc. 1852; author of *Documents connected with the history of Ludlow and the Lords Marchers* 1841 preface signed R. H. C. *d.* Shrewsbury 20 Jany. 1854.

CLIVE, ROBERT WINDSOR (*son of the preceding*). *b.* Grosvenor st. London 24 May 1824; M.P. for Ludlow 1852–1854, for South Salop 1854 to death. *d.* 53 Lower Grosvenor st. London 4 Aug. 1859.

CLIVE, VENERABLE WILLIAM (*brother of Henry Bayley Clive 1800–1870*). *b.* 14 March 1795; ed. at St. John's coll. Cam., B.A. 1817, M.A. 1820; V. of Welshpool 1819–65; archdeacon of Montgomery 29 Feb. 1844–1861; preb. of St. Asaph 25 July 1849; hon. canon of St. Asaph 1854 to death; R. of Blymhill, Staffs. 1865. *d.* Blymhill rectory 24 May 1883.

CLOËTÉ, SIR ABRAHAM JOSIAS (2 *son of Peter Laurence Cloëté, member of council at Cape of Good Hope*). *b.* Cape of Good Hope 7 Aug. 1794; cornet 15 hussars 29 Jany. 1809; deputy quartermaster general at Cape of Good Hope 1840–54; commanded forces in West Indies 1855–61; colonel 19 foot 10 March 1861 to death; general 25 Oct. 1871; placed on retired list 1 Oct. 1877; C.B. 23 Sep. 1847, K.C.B. 10 Nov. 1862; knighted at St. James's palace 9 June 1854. *d.* 88 Gloucester terrace, London 26 Oct. 1886.

CLONCURRY, VALENTINE BROWNE LAWLESS, 2 Baron (2 *son of 1 Baron Cloncurry 1735–99*). *b.* Merrion sq. Dublin 19 Aug. 1773; ed. at Portarlington, Chester and Trin. coll. Dublin; member of Society of United Irishmen; member of executive directory of United Irish Society 1797; arrested 31 May 1798, again 14 April 1799, confined in the Tower of London 8 May 1799 to March 1801; succeeded as 2 Baron 28 Aug. 1799; P.C. for Ireland 1831; created a Baron of the United Kingdom 14 Sep. 1831. *d.* Maretimo, Blackrock near Dublin 28 Oct. 1853. *W. J. Fitzpatrick's Life of Lord Cloncurry* 1855; *G.M. xli*, 82–7 (1854); *Personal recollections of Lord Cloncurry* (1849).

CLONCURRY, EDWARD LAWLESS, 3 Baron. *b.* Lyons house, co. Kildare 13 Sep. 1816; ed. at Eton and Ball. coll. Ox., B.A. 1861; succeeded 23 Oct. 1853; killed by falling from a window of Lyons house whilst of unsound mind and unaccountable for his acts 3 April 1869. *Morning Post 6 April 1869 p. 5.*

CLONMELL, JOHN HENRY SCOTT, 3 Earl of. *b.* Hertford st. London 4 Jany. 1817; succeeded 18 Jany. 1838. *d.* Bishop's court, Naas, co. Kildare 7 Feb. 1866.

CLOSE, VERY REV. FRANCIS (*youngest son of Rev. Henry Jackson Close, R. of Bentworth, Hants. who d. April 1806*). *b.* near Frome 11 July 1797; ed. at Merchant Taylors' and St. John's coll. Cam. Scholar 1817, B.A. 1820, M.A. 1826, D.D. 1857; C. of Church Lawford, Warws. 1820–22; C. of Willesden and Kingsbury 1822–24; P.C. of Cheltenham 1826–56; Dean of Carlisle 24 Nov. 1856 to Aug. 1881 when he resigned; P.C. of St. Mary, Carlisle 1865–68; a most popular evangelical preacher; author of upwards of 70 books. *d.* Morrab house, Penzance 18 Dec. 1882. *buried* Carlisle cemetery 23 Dec. *The Christian cabinet illustrated almanack for 1861, 32–33, portrait; Illust. news of the world viii, (1861), portrait; Congregationalist iv, 562–72 (1875); A golden decade of a favoured town by Contem Ignotus (1884) 11–69; E. M. Roose's Ecclesiastica (1842) 429–30; I.L.N. lxxxii, 45 (1883), portrait.*

CLOSE, THOMAS (*son of John Close of Manchester, merchant*). *b.* Manchester 12 Feb. 1796; a founder and original member of Reform club, London 1836; auditor of the London and South Western railway many years; F.S.A. 10 May 1855; author of *St. Mary's church, Nottingham, its probable architect and benefactors* 1866, drew up elaborate pedigrees of the Tattershall and Wake families and many illuminated pedigrees of royal, noble and illustrious houses. *d.* Nottingham 25 Jany. 1881. *Manchester school register iii, 66–8 (1874).*

CLOUGH, ARTHUR HUGH (2 *son of James Butler Clough of Liverpool, cotton merchant 1784–1844*). *b.* Liverpool 1 Jany. 1819; ed. at Rugby and Balliol coll. Ox., scholar Nov. 1836, B.A. 1841, M.A. 1843; fellow of Oriel coll. 1842 to Oct. 1848, tutor 1843–8; principal of University hall, Gordon sq. London, Oct. 1849 to 1851; professor of English language and literature at Univ. coll. London, Nov. or Dec. 1850; sec. to commission on military education 1856; author of *The Bothie of Toperna-Fuosich, a long vacation pastoral* 1848;

Clough, A. H. (Con.)

Plutarch's lives, the translation called Dryden's Corrected from the Greek and revised 1859; author with Thomas Burbidge of *Ambarvalia, poems* 1849. *d.* Florence 13 Nov. 1861. *Poems and prose remains of A. H. Clough edited by his wife* 2 vols. 1869; *Poems by A. H. Clough with a memoir* [by F. T. Palgrave], 2 ed. 1863; *A. H. Clough a monograph by S. Waddington* 1883; *J. C. Shairp's Balliol scholars, a remembrance* 1873; *T. H. Ward's English poets*, 2 *ed. iv,* 589–607 (1883).

CLOUGH, Very Rev. Charles Butler (4 *son of Rev. Roger Clough, canon of St. Asaph*). *b.* 1793; ed. at St. John's coll. Cam., B.A. 1815, M.A. 1825; V. of Mold, Flintshire 1824–54; archdeacon of St. Asaph 20 Feb. 1844–1854, hon. canon of St. Asaph 25 July 1849–1854, dean and chancellor of St. Asaph 1854 to death. *d.* the Deanery, St. Asaph 4 Sep. 1859.

CLOWES, George (*son of Wm. Clowes of London, printer* 1779–1847). *b.* 1814; ed. at Tooting and London Univ. college; partner with his father 1846; printed the official publications of the Great Exhibition 1851; auditor to the Guild of Literature many years; printed and published *The Law Reports* 1865 to death. *d.* Oak hill, Surbiton 3 Nov. 1886. *London Figaro* 20 Nov. 1886 p. 6, col. 2, *portrait.*

CLOWES, Thomas Ball (*son of Mr. Clowes of Canterbury, surgeon*). *b.* Wingham, Kent 30 June 1787; entered navy 17 June 1801; captain 16 May 1823, retired 1 Oct. 1846; retired admiral 24 Sep. 1863. *d.* Upton, Slough 31 March 1864.

CLOWES, Rev. William (*son of Wm. Clowes of Burslem, Staffs., potter*). *b.* Burslem 12 March 1780; a working potter; attended the first camp meeting ever held in England, which was at Mow Hill near Harrisehead 31 May 1807; a local Wesleyan preacher, Oct. 1808; one of founders of Primitive Methodist connection 14 March 1810; preached in most of the northern counties of England, also in London and Cornwall. *d.* Hull 2 March 1851. *Davison's Life of W. Clowes* (1854), *portrait; Petty's Primitive Methodist connection* (1864), *portrait.*

CLOWES, William (*brother of George Clowes* 1814–86). *b.* 15 May 1807; entered his father's business 1823, partner with him 1846; trustee of Printers' pension corporation 1844, treasurer 1853. *d.* Gloucester terrace, Hyde park, London 19 May 1883.

CLULOW, Rev. William Benton. *b.* Leek, Staffs.; ed. at Hoxton academy; pastor of Congregational chapel at Shaldon, Devon 1823–35; classical tutor of Airedale college, Bradford 1835–43; author of *Aphorisms and reflections, a miscellany of thought and opinion* 1843; *Sunshine and Shadows, or Sketches of thought, philosophic and religious* 1863; *Essays of a recluse, or traces of thought, literature and fancy* 1865. *d.* Leek 16 April 1882.

CLUTTERBUCK, Henry (5 *child of Thomas Clutterbuck of Marazion, Cornwall, attorney, who d. 6 Nov.* 1781). *b.* Marazion 28 Jany. 1767; M.R.C.S. 7 Aug. 1790; practised at Walbrook, city of London 1790–1802; projected *The Medical and Chirurgical Review* 1795, edited it 1795–1807; M.D. Glasgow 16 April 1804; licentiate of College of Physicians 1 Oct. 1804; physician in Bridge st. Blackfriars 1808 to death; physician to general dispensary, Aldersgate st. 1809; lectured on materia medica and the practice of physic; author of *Remarks respecting venereal disease* 1799; *An enquiry into the seat and nature of fever* 1807, 2 *ed.* 1825; *An essay on Pyrexia, or symptomatic fever* 1837; *A series of essays on inflamation* 1846. *d.* 1 Crescent, New Bridge st. Blackfriars, London 24 April 1856. *Lives of British physicians* (1857) 403–16; *T. J. Pettigrew's Medical portrait gallery* ii, (1840), *portrait; W. C. Taylor's National portrait gallery* ii, 88–9 (1846), *portrait; Medical Circular* ii, 495–7 (1853), *portrait.*

CLUTTERBUCK, Rev. James Charles (2 *son of Robert Clutterbuck of Watford, Herts.* 1772–1831). *b.* Watford 11 July 1801; ed. at Ex. coll. Ox., fellow 26 Dec. 1822 to 19 Jany. 1831; B.A. 1826, M.A. 1827; C. of Watford; V. of Long Wittenham, Berkshire 14 Jany. 1830 to death; rural dean of Abingdon 1869 to death; great authority on all questions relating to water; member of Board of Thames Conservancy. *d.* Long Wittenham 8 May 1885.

CLYDE, Colin Campbell, 1 Baron (*eld. child of John McLiver of Glasgow, cabinet maker, who d. 22 Dec.* 1859, *by Agnes Campbell*). *b.* Glasgow 20 Oct. 1792; ed. at Glasgow high sch. and Gosport; gazetted ensign 9 foot under name of Campbell 26 May 1808; lieut.-col. 98 foot 19 June 1835 to 1 April 1853; aide-de-camp to the Queen 23 Dec. 1842 to 20 June 1854; commanded third division of army under Lord Gough in Punjaub campaigns of 1848–49; commanded the Peshawur district 1851–52; commanded Highland brigade in the Crimea 1854; commandant at Balaklava 1854; colonel 67 foot 24 Oct. 1854 to 15

CLYDE, Baron (Con.)

Jany. 1858; commanded first division of British army in the Crimea, Dec. 1854 to 3 Nov. 1855; inspector general of infantry, Sep. 1856; commander in chief in India 11 July 1857; stormed Lucknow, Nov. 1857, captured it 19 March 1858, left India 4 June 1860; colonel 93 foot 15 Jany. 1858 to 4 June 1860; general 14 May 1858; colonel Coldstream guards 22 June 1860 to death; field marshal 9 Nov. 1862; admitted to freedom of city of Glasgow 1856, of London 20 Dec. 1860; granted pension of £2,000 by the H.E.I.Co. 1858; created Baron Clyde of Clydesdale 16 Aug. 1858; C.B. 24 Dec. 1842, K.C.B. 9 June 1849, G.C.B. 5 July 1855; K.S.I. June 1858, K.C.S.I. 25 June 1861. d. the Government house, Chatham 14 Aug. 1863. bur. Westminster abbey 22 Aug., statue of him by Marochetti erected in Carlton gardens, Pall Mall 1867, and a statue by Foley at Glasgow 1868. *Shadwell's Life of Lord Clyde* 2 vols. 1881, *portrait; C. R. Low's Soldiers of the Victorian age* ii, 372–446 (1880); *A personal narrative of the siege of Lucknow by L. E. R. Rees,* 3 ed. 1858; *Illust. news of the world* i, (1858), *portrait.*

COATS, THOMAS (4 *son of James Coats of Paisley, thread manufacturer*). b. Paisley 18 Oct. 1809; thread manufacturer with his brother Peter, at the Ferguslie thread works, Paisley, one of the largest in the world; pres. of Paisley Philosophical Institution 1862–4, to which he gave an observatory on Oakshaw hill 1882; presented to town of Paisley a public park called the Fountain's Gardens 1868; chairman of Paisley school board 1873 to death; made valuable collection of Scottish coins. d. 15 Oct. 1883, statue of him erected at Paisley.

COBBE, GEORGE (2 *son of Charles Cobbe of Newbridge house, co. Dublin* 1756–98). b. 1782; second lieut. R.A. 9 Oct. 1799, col. commandant 29 Aug. 1857 to death; general 15 Dec. 1864. d. 9 Sydney place, Onslow sq. Brompton London 8 Feb. 1865.

COBBE, HENRY CLERMONT (*eld. son of Thomas Alexander Cobbe* 1788–1836, *col. H.E.I.C.S.*) Ensign 86 foot 15 Feb. 1831; lieut.-col. 2 West India regiment 26 May 1844 to 14 April 1854; lieut.-col. 4 foot 14 April 1854 to death; C.B. 5 July 1855. d. in the camp before Sebastopol 6 Aug. 1855.

COBBETT, JOHN MORGAN (2 *son of Wm. Cobbett, political writer* 1762–1835). b. 1800; barrister L.I. 26 Nov. 1830; M.P. for Oldham 9 July 1852 to 6 July 1865 and 5 June 1872

COBBETT, J. M. (Con.)

to death; author of *Letters from France, containing observations on that country during a journey from Calais to the South as far as Limoges* 1825. d. 20 Brompton crescent, South Kensington, London 13 Feb. 1877.

COBBETT, RICHARD BAVERSTOCK BROWN (*brother of the preceding*). b. 1804; attorney at Manchester 1838 to death; defended some of the Chartists; sec. to the council of Manchester Political Union which got up the great demonstration on Kersal Moor to demand the six points of the Charter 24 Sep. 1838; author of some legal pamphlets. d. Wilmslow, Manchester 3 June 1875.

COBBETT, WILLIAM (*brother of the preceding*). Brought actions against several of the judges in connection with an attempt on his part to obtain release of the Tichborne claimant by means of a writ of habeas corpus. d. the watchman's room, central hall of Houses of Parliament, Westminster 12 Jany. 1878.

COBBIN, REV. INGRAM. b. London, Dec. 1777; ed. at Hoxton academy 1798–1802; Independent minister at South Molton 1802; assist. sec. to British and Foreign school society; first sec. of Home Missionary society 1819; Owing to weak health he did not hold any pastorate for more than a short period; author of *Elements of English grammar* 1828, *thirty three editions; Elements of Arithmetic for children* 1828, *fifteen editions; Evangelical Synopsis* 1833; *The Condensed Commentary* 1837; *The Portable Commentary* 1843; *Domestic Bible* 1844; *Bible Remembrancer* 1848; *Scripture light on Popish Darkness* 1851; and about 30 other works. d. of phthsis at Denmark cottage, Cold Arbour lane, Kennington, London 10 March 1851. *Congregational year book* 1851 p. 212.

COBBOLD, JOHN CHEVALIER (*eld. child of John Cobbold of Ipswich, brewer* 1774–1860). b. Ipswich 24 Aug. 1797; banker and merchant at Ipswich and Harwich; chairman of Eastern union railway co. and of Ipswich and Bury St. Edmunds railway co.; M.P. for Ipswich 30 July 1847 to 11 Nov. 1868. d. Holywells, Ipswich 6 Oct. 1882. *Public men of Ipswich* (1875) 57–63; *Graphic* xxvi, 412 (1882), *portrait.*

COBBOLD, JOHN PATTESON (*eld. son of the preceding*). b. Ipswich 12 July 1831; a banker and brewer at Ipswich; M.P. for Ipswich 6 Feb. 1874 to death. d. the Cliff, Ipswich 10 Dec. 1875. *Licensed victualler's year book* (1876), *portrait; I.L.N.* lxvii, 614, 629 (1875), *portrait; Public men of Ipswich* (1875) 274.

COBBOLD, Rev. Richard (20 *child of John Cobbold of Ipswich, brewer*). *b.* Ipswich 1797; ed. at Bury St. Edmunds and Caius coll. Cam., scholar, B.A. 1820, M.A. 1823; R. of Wortham, Suffolk 1826 to death; rural dean of Hartismere, Suffolk 1844–69; author of *History of Margaret Catchpole* 2 vols. 1845 of which 100,000 copies were sold; *Mary Ann Wellington* 3 vols. 1846; *The young man's home* 1848 and other books. *d.* Wortham rectory 5 Jany. 1877. *Public men of Ipswich* (1875) 170.

COBBOLD, Thomas Clement (3 *son of John Chevalier Cobbold* 1797–1882). *b.* Ipswich 22 July 1833; ed. at Charterhouse; served in diplomatic service abroad 5 Sep. 1855 to 22 Dec. 1875; M.P. for Ipswich 1 Jany. 1876 to death; C.B. 2 Sep. 1879. *d.* Ipswich 21 Nov. 1883. *Graphic xiii*, 75, 84 (1876), *portrait*.

COBBOLD, Thomas Spencer (*youngest son of Rev. Richard Cobbold* 1797–1877). *b.* Ipswich 26 May 1828; ed. at the Charterhouse and Edin. univ., M.D. and gold medallist 1851, curator of the anatomical museum 1851–7; lecturer on botany at St. Mary's hospital, London 1857–61, at Middlesex hospital 1861 where he lectured on comparative anatomy 13 years; practised in London 1865; Swiney lecturer on geology at British Museum, May 1868 to May 1873; professor of botany at Royal Veterinary college 1873 of helminthology 1874; F.R.S. 2 June 1864; author of *Entozoa, an introduction to the study of Helminthology* 1864; *Tapeworms* 1866, 4 ed. 1883; *Parasites, a treatise on the Entozoa of man and animals* 1879. *d.* 74 Portsdown road, Maida hill, London 20 March 1886. *Barker's Photographs of eminent medical men ii*, 77–81 (1868), *portrait; Lancet 27 March 1886 p.* 616.

COBDEN, Richard (2 *son of Wm. Cobden of Dunford, Heyshott near Midhurst, Sussex, farmer, who d. 15 June* 1833). *b.* Dunford 3 June 1804; calico printer at Manchester 1829–39; M.P. for Stockport 1841–7, for West riding of Yorkshire 1847–57, for Rochdale 1859 to death; member of Anti-Corn law league Oct. 1838 to 1846, repeal of the corn law was chiefly due to him, sum of nearly £80,000 was raised for him by subscription 1846; negotiated commercial treaty with France signed 23 Jany. 1860; presented with sum of £40,000 by about 100 friends 1860; admitted to freedom of city of London 6 June 1861; author of the following pamphlets *England, Ireland and America by a Manchester manufacturer* 1835; *Russia by a Manchester manufacturer* 1836; *1792 and 1853 in three letters* 1853; *How wars are got up in India* 1853;

COBDEN, R. (*Con*).

What next? and next? 1856; *The three panics of 1848, 1853 and 1862*, 1862. *d.* 23 Suffolk st. Pall Mall, London 2 April 1865; *bur.* West Lavington churchyard near Midhurst 7 April. J. Morley's *Life of R. Cobden* 2 vols. 1881, *portrait*; W. C. Taylor's *National portrait gallery iii*, 51–4 (1847), *portrait*; H. R. F. Bourne's *English merchants ii*, 365–84 (1866); J. H. Jennings's *Anecdotal history of the British parliament* (1880) 332–8; *Fagan's Reform club* (1887) 41, *portrait*.

COCHET, John. *b.* Rochester 3 Aug. 1760; entered navy 22 Dec. 1775, captain 9 Dec. 1796, placed on h.p. 30 May 1799; principal agent for transports in the Mediterranean 2 May 1805 to June 1810; admiral 23 Nov. 1841. *d.* Bideford 10 June 1851.

COCHRANE, Charles (*natural son of hon. Basil Cochrane, lieut. col. 36 foot who d. 14 May* 1816). Traversed the United Kingdom dressed in Hungarian costume and sang songs while playing the guitar 1825–6; the farce of *The Wandering Minstrel* by Henry Mayhew produced at Fitzroy theatre, London 16 Jany. 1834 was founded on his eccentricities; pres. of National philanthropic instit. in Leicester sq. London 1842–50; contested city of Westminster July 1847; author of *Journal of a tour made by Senor Juan de Vega, a character assumed by an English gentleman* 2 vols. 1830. *d.* Nelson sq. Blackfriars road, London 13 June 1855 in 48 year. *G.M. xliv*, 324–5 (1855).

COCHRANE, Sir James (4 *son of Thomas Cochrane, speaker of house of assembly at Nova Scotia*). *b.* Nova Scotia 1798; barrister I.T. 6 Feb. 1829; attorney general of Gibraltar 1837, chief justice 1841 to May 1877; knighted at St. James's palace 12 March 1845; *d.* Glenrocky, Gibraltar 24 June 1883.

COCHRANE, John George (*son of Mr. Cochrane of Glasgow*). *b.* Glasgow 1781; bookseller and publisher with John White in Fleet st. London; manager of foreign bookselling house of Messrs. Treuttel and Wurtz, Soho sq.; acting editor of *Foreign quarterly review* 1827–35; edited *Caledonian Mercury* at Edin.; catalogued Sir Walter Scott's library at Abbotsford; edited a newspaper at Hertford; sec. and librarian of London library, London 17 Feb. 1841 to death, library was opened 3 May 1841; compiled two catalogues of the library 1842 and 1847. *d.* London library, St. James's sq. London 11 May 1852. *Catalogue of the London library by R. Harrison* 1875 *pp. vii-xi*.

COCHRANE, SIR THOMAS JOHN *(eld. child of Sir Alexander Forester Inglis Cochrane, G.C.B. 1758–1831)*. *b.* Edinburgh 5 Feb. 1789; entered navy 15 June 1796; captain 23 April 1806; second in command on East India station 1842 to 1845; commander-in-chief 1845 to 1847; commander-in-chief at Portsmouth 18 Dec. 1852 to Jany. 1856; admiral 31 Jany. 1856; admiral of the fleet 12 Sep. 1865; knighted by Prince Regent at Carlton house 29 May 1812; governor of Newfoundland 16 April 1825 to 1834; M.P. for Ipswich 1837–41; C.B. 18 April 1839, K.C.B. 29 Oct. 1847, G.C.B. 18 May 1860. *d.* Ryde, Isle of Wight 19 Oct. 1872. *bur.* Kensal Green cemetery 25 Oct.

COCHRANE, WILLIAM GEORGE. Ensign 40 foot 13 Feb. 1805; lieut.-col. 10 foot 16 Sep. 1836 to 10 July 1837 when placed on h.p.; deputy adjutant general in Ireland 11 Dec. 1846 to 1 April 1852; colonel 11 foot 23 June 1856 to death; L.G. 26 Sep. 1856. *d.* 127 Piccadilly, London 4 Sep. 1857.

COCK, HENRY. Entered Bengal army 1802; col. 64 Bengal N.I. 1849 to death; C.B. 20 July 1838. *d.* Hopton hall near Lowestoft 17 Feb. 1851.

COCK, REV. THOMAS ASTLEY. Educ. at Trin. coll. Cam., 27 wrangler 1834, B.A. 1834, M.A. 1839; mathematical tutor King's coll. London and professor of mathematics Queen's coll. London many years. *d.* 18 Rodney st. Pentonville, London 3 July 1885 in 74 year.

COCKAYNE, REV. THOMAS OSWALD *(son of Mr. Cockin)*. *b.* 1807; ed. at St. John's coll. Cam., 10 wrangler 1828, B.A. 1828, M.A. 1835; a master at King's college sch. London 1842–69; member of Philological and Early English Text Societies; author of *The civil history of the Jews from Joshua to Hadrian* 1841, 2 ed. 1845; *Greek Syntax* 1846; *Life of Marshal Turenne* 1853; *Leechdoms, Wort-cunning and Starcraft of early England* 3 vols. 1858; *Spoon and Sparrow, or English roots in Greek, Latin and Hebrew* 1861. Shot himself at Carrackdew, St. Ives 2 or 3 June 1873. *Cornish Telegraph* 18, 25 *June* 1873.

COCKBURN, ALEXANDER (4 son of Sir James Cockburn 6 baronet 1729–1804). *b.* 20 Aug. 1776; envoy extraord. and min. plenipo. to Wurtemburg 6 March 1820 to 8 Feb. 1823, to Columbia, South America 28 Feb. 1826 to 21 Sep. 1829. *d.* St. Heliers, Jersey 14 Oct. 1852.

COCKBURN, SIR ALEXANDER JAMES EDMUND, 10 Baronet *(only son of the preceding)*. *b.* 24 Dec. 1802; ed. at Trin. hall, Cam., fellow

COCKBURN, SIR ALEXANDER *(Con.)*

commoner 1825, fellow 1829; LL.B. 1829, LL.D. 1874; barrister M.T. 6 Feb. 1829, bencher 1841, treasurer 1853; recorder of Southampton 26 July 1840 to Aug. 1846; Q.C. Oct. 1841; M.P. for Southampton 31 July 1847 to Nov. 1856; solicitor general 11 July 1850; knighted at Buckingham Palace 14 Aug. 1850; attorney general 28 March 1851 to Feb. 1852 and 28 Dec. 1852 to 21 Nov. 1856; recorder of Bristol, April 1854 to Nov. 1856; led the prosecution of Wm. Palmer the Rugeley poisoner who was hanged 14 June 1856; lord chief justice of court of Common Pleas 21 Nov. 1856; lord chief justice of court of Queen's bench 24 June 1859, of England 2 Nov. 1874 to death; P.C. 2 Feb. 1857; succeeded his uncle as 10 baronet 30 April 1858; arbitrator for Her Majesty under treaty of Washington 1 Sep. 1871; G.C.B. 12 Feb. 1873; presided at trial of The Queen *v* Castro (Tichborne claimant) 1873–4, 188 days, longest trial upon record except that of Warren Hastings; admitted to freedom of city of London 9 March 1876; chairman of Cambridge University commission 1877–8; presided in court of crown cases reserved 20 Nov. 1880. *d.* from angina pectoris 40 Hertford st. Mayfair, London 20 Nov. 1880. *A generation of Judges by Their Reporter* (1886) 1–20; *Ballantine's Some experiences of a barrister ii,* 113–19 (1882); *Lord W. P. Lennox's Celebrities I have known, second series i,* 162–83 (1877); *E. Yates's Recollections ii,* 129–38 (1884); *Law Mag. xlvi,* 193–213 (1851); *Law Mag. and Review i,* 50–3, 896–903 (1872); *The Englishman xiv,* 88–90 (1880), *portrait; I.L.N. xvii,* 121 (1850), *portrait, lxvi,* 287 (1875), *portrait, lxxvii,* 521 (1880), *portrait.*

NOTE.—He was the first legally styled Lord chief justice of England; Sir Edward Coke assumed that title which most of his successors also did, but it was not until the Supreme Court of Judicature act 1873 that the title was fully recognised.

COCKBURN, SIR FRANCIS *(brother of Alexander Cockburn 1776–1852)*. *b.* 10 Nov. 1780; cornet 7 dragoon guards 16 Oct. 1800; lieut. col. New Brunswick Fencibles 27 Oct. 1814 to 25 April 1816 when placed on h.p.; lieut. col. 2 West India regiment 30 July 1829 to 9 Nov. 1846; governor of Honduras 1830–7, of the Bahamas 1837–44; knighted by patent 8 Sep. 1841; colonel 95 foot 26 Dec. 1853 to death; general 12 Nov. 1860. *d.* East Cliff, Dover 24 Aug. 1868.

COCKBURN, SIR GEORGE, 8 Baronet *(brother of the preceding)*. *b.* London 22 April 1772; entered navy as captain's servant 12 March

1781; captain 20 Feb. 1794; suggested and planned capture of Washington 1813; commander-in-chief at St. Helena Oct. 1815 to June 1816; conveyed Napoleon Buonaparte from Plymouth to St. Helena in the Northumberland 8 Aug. to 16 Oct. 1815; commander-in-chief on North America and West India station 6 Dec. 1832 to Feb. 1836; admiral 10 Jany. 1837; rear admiral of the U.K. 10 Aug. 1847; admiral of the fleet 1 July 1851 to death; first naval lord of the Admiralty 8 Sep. 1841 to 13 July 1846; major-general of marines 5 April 1821; M.P. for Portsmouth 1818–20, for Weobley, co. Hereford 1820–6, for Plymouth 1826–32, for Ripon 1841–7; K.C.B. 2 Jany. 1815, G.C.B. 20 Feb. 1818; F.R.S. 21 Dec. 1820; P.C. 30 April 1827; succeeded 26 Feb. 1852. *d.* Leamington Spa 19 Aug. 1853. *J. Allen's Battles of the British Navy ii*, 420 (1852), *portrait; G.M. xl*, 406–10 (1853); *I.L.N. xxiii*, 165, 166 (1853), *portrait.*

COCKBURN, HENRY THOMAS *(4 son of Archibald Cockburn, a baron of Court of Exchequer in Scotland). b.* in or near Edin. 26 Oct. 1779; ed. at Edin. high school and college; called to Scotch bar Dec. 1800; advocate depute 1806–10; leader with Jeffrey of the Scottish bar; solicitor general for Scotland 3 Dec. 1830 to 1834; lord rector of Univ. of Glasgow 1831; one of lords of Court of Session as Lord Cockburn 5 Nov. 1834; a lord comr. of justiciary 14 June 1837 to death; author of *Life of Lord Jeffrey* 2 vols. 1852. *d.* Bonaly near Edin. 26 April 1854. *Memorials of his time by H. T. Cockburn* 1856, *portrait; Journal of H. T. Cockburn* 1831–44, 2 vols. 1874; *Crombie's Modern Athenians* (1882), *portrait.*

COCKBURN, SIR JAMES, 7 Baronet *(brother of Sir Francis Cockburn* 1780–1868). *b.* 21 March 1771; succeeded his father 26 July 1804; under sec. of state for department of war and colonies 1806–7; governor and commander-in-chief of Curaçoa 10 April 1807 to 1811; governor and commander-in-chief of Bermuda islands 26 April 1811 to 1 July 1819; inspector general of Royal marines; major general 22 Feb. 1831; sheriff of Carmarthenshire 1847. *d.* Portman sq. London 26 Feb. 1852.

COCKBURN, JAMES HORSFORD; entered navy 1 Dec. 1829; captain 7 April 1850; R.A. 6 April 1866; commander-in-chief East Indies 6 Sep. 1870 to death. *d.* Government house, Calcutta 10 Feb. 1872 aged 56.

COCKBURN, VERY REV. SIR WILLIAM, 9 Baronet *(brother of Alexander Cockburn* 1776–

1852). *b.* 2 June 1773; ed. at St. John's coll. Cam., 12 wrangler 1795, B.A. 1795, M.A. 1798, B.D. and D.D. 1832; fellow of his college 1796–1806; Christian advocate to Univ. of Cam. 1803–10; dean of York 17 Oct. 1822 to death; R. of Kelston near Bath 1832 to death; succeeded his brother Sir George Cockburn 19 Aug. 1853. *d.* Kelston rectory 30 April 1858.

COCKBURN, SIR WILLIAM SARSFIELD ROSSITER, 6 Baronet. *b.* 11 June 1796; ed. at Ex. coll. Ox., B.A. 1819, M.A. 1823; succeeded 19 March 1835. *d.* Downton near Kington, Herefordshire 12 April 1858.

COCKBURN-CAMPBELL, SIR ALEXANDER THOMAS, 2 Baronet. *b.* Madras 1803; succeeded 11 Dec. 1824; assumed additional name of Campbell by royal licence 19 July 1825; superintendent of police in Western Australia, Sep. 1857; resident magistrate of Albury 1861. *d.* 23 April 1871.

COCKERELL, CHARLES ROBERT *(son of Samuel Pepys Cockerell, architect* 1754–1827). *b.* London 28 April 1788; ed. at Westminster school; explored Greece, Asia Minor and Sicily 1810–11; discovered Æginetan and Phigaleian marbles 1811; surveyor to St. Paul's cath. 1819; A.R.A. 1829, R.A. 1836; architect of Bank of England 1833; prof. of architecture, Royal academy 1840–57; one of the 8 foreign assocs. of French Instit. 1841; built the Taylor buildings at Oxford 1841–2; member of academy of St. Luke, Rome 1843; D.C.L. Ox. 20 June 1844; pres. of R.I.B.A. 1860–1, gold medallist 1848; author of *Antiquities of Athens* 5 parts, *fo.* 1830; *Iconography of the West front of Wells Cathedral* 1851; *Illustrations of the genius of M. A. Buonarotti, fo.* 1857 and other works. *d.* 13 Chester terrace, Regent's Park, London 17 Sept. 1863. *bur.* St. Paul's cath. 24 Sept. *Sandby's History of Royal academy ii*, 199–201 (1862); *G.M. xv*, 785–91 (1863); *I.L.N. xliii*, 341, 342 (1863), *portrait.*

COCKERELL, FREDERICK PEPYS *(2 son of the preceding). b.* 87 Eaton sq. London, March 1833; ed. at Winchester and King's coll. Lon.; pupil of Philip Hardwick, R.A. 1854–5; exhibited 54 designs at the R.A. 1854–77; designed Freemasons' hall in Great Queen st. 1861; A.R.I.B.A. 1860, F.R.I.B.A. 30 May 1864, sec. 1871; his design for the Albert Memorial was selected by the judges, but the Queen preferred the Gothic design of Sir G. G. Scott. *d.* Paris 4 Nov. 1878. *Builder* 16 *Nov.* 1878 p. 1194, 23 *Nov.* p. 1230, 20 *Dec.* p. 1393 and 27 *Dec.* p. 1433.

COCKS, ARTHUR HERBERT (3 *son of Philip James Cocks of Stepple hall, Salop* 1774–1857). *b.* 18 April 1819; entered Bengal civil service 1837; retired on annuity fund 1863; C.B. 18 May 1860. *d.* Ashburn place, Cromwell road, London 29 Aug. 1881.

COCKS, ROBERT. *b,* 1796; established music publishing business. in London 1823 which became one of the largest; published many valuable theoretical works including translations of foreign authors; built and endowed 10 almshouses at Old Buckenham, Norfolk, completed Aug. 1861. *d.* May 1887.

COCKTON, HENRY. *b.* London 7 Dec. 1807; lost his money in a malting speculation at Bury St. Edmunds; author of *Valentine Vox the Ventriloquist* 1840 published in monthly numbers; *George St. George Julian, the Prince* 1841; *Stanley Thorne* 3 vols. 1841; *Sylvester Sound the Somnambulist* 1844; *The love match* 1845; *The Steward* 1850; *The sisters, or the fatal marriage* 1851; *Lady Felicia* 1852; *Percy Effingham* 3 vols. 1853. *d.* Bury St. Edmunds 26 June 1853. *Cockton's George St. George Julian* 1841, *portrait.*

CODD, EDWARD. Entered navy 11 Sep. 1820; captain 1 May 1851; admiral 26 Sep. 1878. *d.* 23 Hanover sq. London 14 April 1887 aged 82.

CODRINGTON, CHRISTOPHER WILLIAM. *b.* 12 March 1805; M.P. for East Gloucs. 1834 to death. *d.* Dodington, Gloucs. 24 June 1864.

CODRINGTON, SIR EDWARD (*youngest son of Edward Codrington of London* 1732–75). *b.* 27 April 1770; entered navy 18 July 1783; captain 6 April 1795; captain of the Orion at Trafalgar 1805; colonel of Marines 4 Dec. 1813; commander-in chief of Mediterranean squadron 1 Nov. 1826 to April 1828 when recalled; commanded allied fleets of England, France and Russia at battle of Navarino 20 Oct. 1827; commanded Channel fleet 7 June 1831 to 24 Oct. 1831; admiral 10 Jany. 1837; commander-in-chief at Portsmouth 22 Nov. 1839 to 10 Dec. 1842; K.C.B. 2 Jany. 1815, G.C.B. 13 Nov. 1827, declined to pay the fees which amounted to £386 7s. 2d.; G.C.M.G. 23 April 1827, resigned 1828 but reinstated by Wm. iv, 17 Aug. 1832; M.P. for Devonport 1832–39; groom in waiting in Queen's household July 1846; F.R.S. 21 Nov. 1822. *d.* 110 Eaton sq. London 28 April 1851. *Memoir by his daughter Lady Bourchier* 2 *vols.* 1873, 2 *portraits; J. Allen's Battles of the British navy ii,* 514, (1852); *portrait.*

CODRINGTON, SIR HENRY JOHN (*youngest son of the preceding*). *b.* Preston Candover, Hants. 17 Oct. 1808; ed. at Harrow; entered navy 21 Feb. 1823; captain 20 Jany. 1836; employed in the Baltic during Russian war 1854–6; admiral superintendent of Malta dockyard 1858–63; admiral 18 Oct. 1867; commander-in chief at Plymouth 1869–72; admiral of the fleet 22 Jany. 1877 to death; C.B. 18 Dec. 1840, K.C.B. 13 March 1867; his portrait is in the Painted Hall at Greenwich. *d.* 112 Eaton sq. London 4 Aug. 1877. *Selections from the letters of Sir H. Codrington edited by his sister Lady Bourchier* 1880.

CODRINGTON, SIR WILLIAM JOHN (*brother of the preceding*). *b.* 26 Nov. 1804; ensign 88 foot 22 Feb. 1821; ensign Coldstream guards 24 April 1823, captain 8 July 1836; commanded first brigade of light division in the Crimea 1 Sep. 1854; commanded the light division 30 July 1855 to 10 Nov. 1855; commander-in-chief in the Crimea 11 Nov. 1855 to 12 July 1856; col. of 54 foot 11 Aug. 1856, of 23 foot 27 Dec. 1860 and of Coldstream guards 16 March 1875 to death; M.P. for Greenwich 9 Feb. 1857 to 23 April 1859; contested Westminster, Feb. 1874 and Lewes, April 1880; governor of Gibraltar, May 1859 to Nov. 1865; general 27 July 1863, placed on retired list 1 Oct. 1877; K.C.B. 5 July 1855, G.C.B. 28 March 1865. *d.* Danmore cottage, Hackfield near Winchfield, Hants. 6 Aug. 1884. *Army and navy mag. iii,* 358–60 (1882), *portrait; I.L.N. xxvii,* 520 (1855), *portrait, xxx,* 479 (1857), *portrait.*

CODRINGTON, SIR WILLIAM RAIMOND, 4 Baronet. *b.* Rennes, Brittany 25 Jany. 1806; succeeded 1816. *d.* Château de la Boullaye near Montfort, Brittany 7 or 17 Dec. 1873.

NOTE.—On the death of the 3rd baronet the title was assumed by the grandson of the 1st baronet on the ground that the 3rd baronet left no legitimate issue, but the Heralds' College confirmed Sir W. R. Codrington in the baronetcy.

COEY, SIR EDWARD (*son of James Coey of Larne, co. Antrim*). *b.* Larne 1805; mayor of Belfast 1861, alderman 1861; knighted by Earl of Carlisle, lord lieut. of Ireland 1861; sheriff of Antrim 1867. *d.* Merville, Belfast 26 June 1887.

COFFEY, JAMES CHARLES (2 *son of Edmund Coffey of co. Kerry*). *b.* Dublin 1815; called to Irish bar, Trinity term 1843; went Munster circuit; Q.C. 13 June 1864; county court judge for Westmeath, transferred to Leitrim, transferred to Londonderry, retired 1879; edited the *Monitor* a whig anti-repeal paper. *d.* Sea Point, co. Dublin 31 July 1880.

COFFIN, SIR EDWARD PINE (*youngest son of Rev. John Pine of East Down, Devon 1736–1824, who assumed name of Coffin 1797*). *b.* East Down 20 Oct. 1784; entered commissariat service 25 July 1805; deputy commissary general 4 Aug. 1814; commissary general 1 July 1840 to 1 April 1848 when placed on h.p.; had charge of relief operations at Limerick and on west coast of Ireland during famine, Jany. to Aug. 1846; knighted by patent 16 Sep. 1846; one of comrs. of inquiry into working of royal mint 1 April 1848. *d.* Gay st. Bath 31 July 1862.

COFFIN, HENRY EDWARD. *b.* 1794; entered navy 1 Oct. 1805; captain 23 Nov. 1841; retired admiral 30 July 1875. *d.* Springfield house, Caversham near Reading 31 Aug. 1881 in 88 year.

COFFIN, SIR ISAAC CAMPBELL (*eld. son of Francis Holmes Coffin, admiral R.N.*) *b.* 1801; entered Madras army 3 June 1818; commanded Hyderabad subsidiary force 6 Nov. 1855; commanded southern division of Madras army 28 March 1859 to 28 March 1864 for which he was created K.C.S.I. 24 May 1866; col. 12 Madras N.I. 23 July 1858 to 1869; L.G. 18 July 1869. *d.* 9 St. John's park south, Blackheath, Kent 1 Oct. 1872.

COFFIN, JOHN TOWNSEND. *b.* 1789; entered navy 7 Nov. 1799; captain 26 Dec. 1822, retired 1 Oct. 1846; retired admiral 26 June 1863. *d.* Holgate hill, York 29 April 1882.

COFFIN, RIGHT REV. ROBERT ASTON. *b.* Brighton 19 July 1819; ed. at Harrow and Ch. Ch. Ox., B.A. 1841, M.A. 1843; V. of St. Mary Magdalene, Oxford 1843; received into Church of Rome 3 Dec. 1845; ordained priest at Rome 1847; superior of St. Wilfrids, Cotton hall, Staffs. 1848–9; entered novitiate of Redemptorist Fathers at St. Trond in Belgium and made his profession 2 Feb. 1852; R. of St. Mary's, Clapham 1855; provincial 1865–82; bishop of Southwark, April 1882 to death; consecrated at Rome 11 June 1882, enthroned at St. George's cathedral, Southwark 27 July 1882; author of *The oratory of the faithful soul translated from F. L. Blosius* 1848, and of translations of many of the works of St. Alphonsus de Liguori. *d.* house of the Redemptorists, Teignmouth 6 April 1885. *Gillow's English Catholics i*, 523–6 (1885).

COFFIN, WILLIAM FOSTER. *b.* Bath 1808; ed. at Eton; called to Lower Canadian bar 1835; comr. of police 1840; raised and commanded Montreal field battery 1855; comr.

of ordnance and admiralty lands for dominion of Canada; author of *Memorial to Sir E. W. Head* 1855; *1812, The war and its moral* 2 vols. 1864; *Three chapters on a triple project; Thoughts on defence from a Canadian point of view; Quirks of diplomacy. d.* 1878.

COGAN, REV. ELIEZER (*son of John Cogan of Rothwell, Northamptonshire, surgeon who d.* 1784). *b.* Rothwell 1762; ed. at Daventry; Presbyterian minister at Cirencester 1787–9, at Walthamstow 1801–16; kept a school at Higham Hill, Walthamstow 1801–28; author of *An address to the Dissenters on classical literature* 1789; *Reflections on the evidences of Christianity* 1796; *Sermons chiefly on practical subjects* 2 vols. 1817; edited *Moschi Idyllia tria, Grece* 1795. *d.* Higham Hill 21 Jany. 1855. *Christian Reformer xi*, 237–59 (1855); *Dict. of Nat. Biog. xi*, 219–20 (1887).

COGHLAN, SIR WILLIAM MARCUS (*son of Jeremiah Coghlan, captain R.N.*) *b.* Plymouth 31 May 1803; ed. at Addiscombe; Second lieut. Bombay Artillery 19 Dec. 1820, colonel 28 Nov. 1854, col. commandant 8 May 1859 to death; political resident and commandant at Aden 1854–63; general 1 Oct. 1877; K.C.B. 6 June 1864. *d.* Ramsgate 26 Nov. 1885.

COGSWELL, JOHN. *b.* March 1827; a printer and stationer at Bath to 1833; reporter on the *Hastings News* 1833–50; edited the *Hastings Chronicle* 1850, the *Hastings and St. Leonards Times*, the *West Surrey Times* 1880–3 and 1886 to death. *d.* 13 April 1887.

COHEN, LIONEL LOUIS (*son of the succeeding*), *b.* London 2 June 1832; foreign banker with his father under name of Louis Cohen and Sons 1852; senior partner 1882–5 when he retired; a trustee and manager of Stock Exchange 1870 to death; a founder and vice-pres. of United Synagogue; pres. of Jewish Board of Guardians 1869 to death; M.P. for North Paddington 25 Nov. 1885 to death. *d.* 9 Hyde park terrace, London 26 June 1887. *Vanity Fair* 24 *April* 1886, *portrait.*

COHEN, LOUIS (*son of Joseph Cohen*). *b.* Sep. 1799; entered the Stock Exchange, London 1819, member of its committee 15 years; warden of Great Synagogue, London 1837; member of committee of the Seven Elders; member of Board of Deputies 25 years, the main author of new constitution of the Board. *d.* 84 Gloucester place, Portman sq. London 15 March 1882, personally sworn £623,000, 22 April 1882. *Jewish Chronicle* 17 *March* 1882 *p.* 12, 24 *March p.* 12.

COLBORNE, NICHOLAS WILLIAM RIDLEY-COLBORNE, 1 Baron *(2 son of Sir Matthew White Ridley of Blagdon, Northumberland, 2 baronet 1745–1813). b.* St. Marylebone, London 14 April 1779; ed. at Westminster and Ch. Ch. Ox., B.A. 1800; entered at G.I. 12 Dec. 1795 but withdrew 26 April 1809 without being called; assumed additional name of Colborne 21 June 1803; M.P. for Appleby 1807–12, for Thetford 1818–26, for Horsham 1827–32, for Wells 1834–7; created Baron Colborne of West Harding, Norfolk 15 May 1839; member of Fine Arts commission 1841, of Metropolitan improvements commission 1842. *b.* 19 Hill st. Berkeley sq. London 3 May 1854.

COLBRAN, JOHN. *b.* 1809; a bookseller at Tunbridge Wells; started in 1833 the *Tunbridge Wells Visitor*, the first newspaper there; started the *Tunbridge Wells Gazette* 1851; retired 1874. *d.* Tunbridge Wells 20 Sep. 1884.

COLBURN, HENRY. Kept circulating library in Conduit st. London 1816; publisher in New Burlington st. 1817; partner with Richard Bentley 1830 to Aug. 1832; publisher at Windsor; publisher in Great Marlborough st. London 1853, retired in favour of Hurst and Blackett; chief publisher of novels many years; published *Colburn's Modern Standard Novelists* 19 *vols.* 1835–41; originated *New Monthly Mag.* 1814; with Wm. Jerdan *Literary Gazette* 25 Jany. 1817, *Court Journal* 1828, *United Service Mag.* 1829. *d.* Bryanston sq. London 16 Aug. 1855, his copyrights were sold for £14,000, 26 May 1857. *H. Curwen's History of booksellers* (1873) 279–95.

COLBY, THOMAS FREDERICK *(eld. child of Thomas Colby, major R.M. who d.* 1813). *b.* St. Margaret's-next-Rochester 1 Sep. 1784; ed. at Northfleet school and R.M.A. Woolwich; second lieut. R.E. 2 July 1801; lost his left hand by explosion of a pistol, Dec. 1803; F.R.S. 13 April 1820; surveyed Ireland 1824–46; col. R.E. 10 Jany. 1837 to 9 Nov. 1846; M.G. 9 Nov. 1846. *(m.* 1828 Elizabeth Hester 2 dau. of Archibald Boyd, treasurer of Londonderry, she was granted a civil list pension of £100, 10 Feb. 1853). *d.* New Brighton near Liverpool 9 Oct. 1852. *J. E. Portlock's Life of General Colby* 1869; *Min. of Proc. of Instit. of C.E. xii,* 132–7 (1853).

COLCHESTER, CHARLES ABBOT, 2 Baron *(elder son of 1 baron Colchester* 1757–1829). *b.* St. James's, Westminster 12 March 1798; entered navy 8 April 1811; captain 26 Jany. 1826, placed on h.p. Jany. 1833; admiral on

COLCHESTER, C. A. *(Con.)*
h.p. 11 Jany. 1864; succeeded as 2 Baron 7 May 1829; vice pres. of Board of Trade and paymaster general 28 Feb. to Dec. 1852; P.C. 27 Feb. 1852; postmaster general, Feb. 1858 to June 1859. *d.* 34 Berkeley sq. London 18 Oct. 1867. *Walford's Photographic portraits of living celebrities* 1859, *portrait; I.L.N. xxxii,* 312 (1858), *portrait.*

COLDSTREAM, JOHN *(only son of Robert Coldstream of Leith, merchant). b.* Leith 19 March 1806; ed. at Leith, High sch. Edin. and Univ. of Edin.; apprenticed to Dr. Charles Anderson of Leith 1823; entered Royal Medical Society 19 Nov. 1824; studied in Paris 1827–28; practised at Leith 1828–47; mem. of Wernerian Society 9 Jany. 1830; enrolled as Fellow for life of Botanical Soc. 9 Dec. 1858, date of dissolution of Wernerian Soc.; F.R.C.P. 1845; removed to Edinburgh 1847; mem. of Royal Physical Society 17 Feb. 1849, one of the presidents 4 Dec. 1850. *d.* Irthing house near Carlisle 17 Sept. 1863. *J. H. Balfour's Biography of the late John Coldstream* (1865), *portrait.*

COLE, REV. ARTHUR RAGGETT. Ed. at Wad. coll. Ox., B.A. 1864, M.A. 1866, B.D. 1874; C. of St. Luke, Southampton 1864–68; C. in charge of Hurstbourne Priors, Hants. 1868 to death; author of *A short liturgy for the school room service,* 2 *ed.* 1870; *Drawing near with faith* 1872; *A book of family prayers for a month* 1875; edited the *Etcetera,* monthly mag. 1872–4. *d.* Hurstbourne Priors 23 Sep. 1877.

COLE, GEORGE. *b.* 1810; portrait painter at Portsmouth; painted a canvas show-cloth 20 feet square for Wombwell's menagerie; studied animal painting in Holland; exhibited 16 pictures at the R.A., 35 at B.I. and 209 at Suffolk st. gallery 1838–80; member of society of British Artists 1850. *d.* of heart disease at 1 Kensington crescent, London 7 Sep. 1883. *I.L.N. lxxxiii,* 307, 309 (1883), *portrait.*

COLE, GEORGE WARD. *b.* Lumley castle, Durham 15 Nov. 1793; in the navy 1807–17 when placed on h.p.; in the merchant service 1817–39; arrived in Melbourne 4 July 1840; built Cole's Wharf on the Yarra 1841; built the "City of Melbourne" 1851 the 1st screw steamer ever seen south of the equator, she traded between Melbourne and Launceston and was finally wrecked on King's Island, Bass's Straits 1853; introduced sugar-beet into Victoria from Holland 1863; member for Gipps Land of Victorian legislative council, July 1853–1855; member for the Central

COLE, G. W. *(Con.)*

province of legislative council 1859 to death; an executive councillor 1867; wrote several pamphlets in support of protection. *d.* 26 April 1879. *Men of the time in Australia, Victorian series* (1878) 37–39.

COLE, SIR HENRY *(son of Henry Robert Cole, captain 1 dragoon guards).* *b.* Bath 15 July 1808; ed. at Christ's hospital; clerk to Francis Palgrave of the Record Commission 1824–9; one of the 4 senior assistant keepers of the Records 1838–41; edited *Guide* newspaper 1837, *Post Circular* 1838; sec. of committee on penny postage 1838; edited *Journal of Design* March 1849 to Feb. 1852; member of Society of Arts 1846; member of executive committee of Great Exhibition 1851, 3 Jany. 1850; general adviser to Exhibition of 1862 with a fee of £1500; sec. to royal commission at Paris exhibitions 1855 and 1867; chief manager of Exhibitions in London 1871–4; sec. of School of Design 31 Oct. 1851; sec. of Department of practical art Jany. 1852 to April 1873; C.B. 25 Oct. 1851, K.C.B. 25 March 1875; published under the pseudonym of Felix Summerly, the following books, *The Home Treasury.* A series of children's books. Lond. printed by J. Cundall 1843–44; *Pleasure excursions to Croydon* 1846; *Heroic tales of ancient Greece, translated from the German of B. G. Niebuhr* 1849, and the following handbooks, *Westminster Abbey* 1842, *Picture galleries* 1842, *Canterbury* 1843, *Hampton Court* 1843, *National gallery* 1843, *Temple Church* 1843; *Shall we keep the Crystal palace, by Denarius* 1851; edited *Works of T. L. Peacock* 3 vols. 1875. *(m.* 28 Dec. 1833 Marian Fairman 3 dau. of Wm. Andrew Bond of Ashford, Kent, she was granted a civil list pension of £150, 10 June 1882, author of *The Mother's Primer, by Mrs. Felix Summerly* 1844). *d.* 96 Philbeach gardens, Earl's Court, London 18 April 1882. *Fifty years of public work of Sir H. Cole* 2 vols. 1884, *portrait; Practical Mag. vii, 321, portrait; I.L.N. xix, 487, 509 (1851), portrait, lxiii, 36, 38 (1873), portrait, lxxx, 417 (1882), portrait.*

NOTE.—He originated the idea of Christmas cards, the first of which was issued by Joseph Cundall at 12 Old Bond st, 1846. the drawing was made by J. C. Horsley printed in lithography by Jobbins of Warwick court, Holborn and coloured by hand, about 1000 copies were sold of the card which was the usual size of a lady's calling card.

COLE, HENRY THOMAS *(2 son of George Cole, captain Cornwall militia).* *b.* Bath 2 Feb. 1816; barrister M.T. 4 Nov. 1842, bencher Jany. 1867, treasurer 1883–4; became leader of Western circuit; recorder of Penzance April

COLE, H. T. *(Con.)*

1862 to April 1872; Q.C. 13 Dec. 1866; recorder of Plymouth and Devonport April 1872 to death; M.P. for Falmouth and Penryn 6 Feb. 1874 to 24 March 1880. *d.* 4 Glendower place, South Kensington, London 5 Jany. 1885.

COLE, HENRY-WARWICK *(3 son of Wm. Nicholas Cole of Islington, solicitor).* *b.* 12 Oct. 1812; ed. at Univ. coll. London; barrister I.T. 10 June 1836, bencher 1861, reader 1873, treasurer 1874; Q.C. 22 Feb. 1861; judge of county courts, circuit 21 Warwickshire 11 Sep. 1872 to death; author of *The law of domicile of Englishmen in France* 1857; *St. Augustine a poem in 8 books* 1877; contributed to *Quarterly Review* and *Fraser's Mag. d.* 23 High st. Warwick 19 June 1876.

COLE, JOHN LOWRY *(3 son of 2 Earl of Enniskillen 1768–1840).* *b.* 8 June 1813; sheriff of Fermanagh 1842. M.P. for Enniskillen 21 Feb. 1859 to 11 Nov. 1868. *d.* Florence court, co. Fermanagh 29 Nov. 1882.

COLE, PENNEL. Second lieut. R.E. 1 Feb. 1810, col. 20 June 1854 to 11 Aug. 1856 when he retired on full pay; M.G. 11 Aug. 1856. *d.* Boulogne 25 March 1862 aged 70.

COLE, WILLIAM JOHN. *b.* London; entered navy 5 Jany. 1802; captain on h.p. 28 June 1838; K.H. 1 Jany. 1837. *d.* Lechlade, Gloucs. 15 May 1856.

COLE, WILLIAM ROBERT. Barrister M.T. 23 Nov. 1838; went north-eastern circuit; author of *Law and practice on criminal information* 1843; *Law and practice in ejectment* 1856. *d.* Warrington gardens, Maida hill, London 27 Dec. 1881.

COLEBROOKE, SIR WILLIAM MACBEAN GEORGE *(son of Paulette Welbore Colebrooke, lieut.-col. R.A. who d. 28 Sep. 1816).* *b.* 1787; Second lieut. R.A. 17 Aug. 1803; served in Mahratta war 1817–8; comr. of Eastern inquiry 1823–31; lieut. governor of Bahamas 9 Sep. 1834; governor general of Leeward islands 11 Jany. 1837; knighted by Wm. iv at Windsor castle 31 March 1837; lieut. governor of New Brunswick 25 March 1841–1848; governor of British Guiana 28 April 1848; governor of Barbados, Grenada, St. Vincent, Tobago and St. Lucia 11 Aug. 1848 to 1856 when he retired on pension of £750; col. commandant R.A. 25 Sep. 1859 to death; general 26 Dec. 1865; K.H. 1834, C.B. 1 May 1848. *d.* Salthill, Bucks. 6 Feb. 1870.

COLEMAN, REV. WILLIAM HIGGINS. Educ. at St. John's coll. Cam., B.A. 1836, M.A. 1839; a master at Christ's hospital, Hertford 1840–7; at Ashby-de-la-Zouch gr. sch. 1847 to death; author with Rev. H. R. Webb of *Flora Hertfordiensis* 1849; published in *Journal of Biblical Literature*, July 1863 an elaborate paper on The Eighteenth chapter of Isaiah, which was reprinted with others under title of *Biblical papers, being remains of the Rev. W. H. Coleman* 1864. *d.* Burton on Trent 12 Sep. 1863.

COLENSO, FRANCES ELLEN (2 *dau. of the succeeding*). *b.* 30 May 1849; befriended Cetywayo 1881; author with Col. Edward Durnford of *History of the Zulu war* 1880; *The ruin of Zululand* 1884. *d.* Ventnor, Isle of Wight 29 April 1887.

COLENSO, RIGHT REV. JOHN WILLIAM (*son of John Wm. Colenso of Lostwithiel, mineral agent for Duchy of Cornwall, who d. 23 Dec. 1860 aged 82*). *b.* St. Austell 24 Jany. 1814; ed. at Devonport and St. John's coll. Cam.; second wrangler and Smith's prizeman 1836; B.A. 1836, M.A. 1839, B.D. and D.D. 1853; fellow of his college 13 March 1837 to 1846; mathematical master at Harrow 1839–42; private tutor at Cam. 1842–6; V. of Forncett St. Mary, Norfolk 1846–53; bishop of Natal 23 Nov. 1853, consecrated in St. Mary's, Lambeth 30 Nov.; suffragan to bishop of Cape Town 6 Dec. 1853, who pronounced sentence of deposition against him 16 April 1864, he appealed to the Crown, and the judicial committee of the privy council pronounced all the legal proceedings null and void in law; publicly excommunicated at Maritzburg cathedral 5 Jany. 1866; author of *The elements of Algebra designed for the use of schools* 1841, and numerous other works on mathematics; *Village sermons* 1854; *Ten weeks in Natal* 1855; *First steps in Zulu-Kaffir* 1859 and many other works concerning, and in that language; *The Pentateuch and Book of Joshua critically examined* 1862–65, 5 volumes, with other editions of the whole work and of parts of it; *Natal sermons, a series of discourses in the cathedral church of St. Peter's, Maritzburg* 1866; *Lectures on the Pentateuch and the Moabite stone* 1873; *The treatment by the Natal government of Langalibalele and the Amahlubi tribe* 1874. *d.* Pieter-Maritzburg, Natal 20 June 1883. *Dict. of Nat. Biog. xi,* 290–3 (1887); *Boase and Courtney's Bibl. Cornub. i,* 76–9, *iii,* 1125–7; *J. F. Hurst's History of rationalism* (1867) 401–409; *Churchman's Family Mag. v,* 395–408 (1865); *Boase's Collectanea Cornubiensia* 153–4;

COLENSO, RIGHT REV. J. W. (*Con.*) *Graphic xxvii,* 652 (1883), *portrait; Bookseller 30 July 1863 pp.* 356–8.

NOTE.—Part i of The Pentateuch an edition of 10,000 copies excited much comment and gave rise to the publication of upwards of 130 works in which its principles were adversely criticised. Of the Bishop's Arithmetic designed for Schools, more than 400,000 copies were sold.

COLERIDGE, REV. DERWENT (*younger son of Samuel Taylor Coleridge the Poet 1772–1834*). *b.* Greta hall, Keswick 14 Sep. 1800; ed. at St. John's coll. Cam., B.A. 1824, M.A. 1829; master of Helston gr. sch. 1827–41; principal of St. Mark's college, Chelsea 1841–64; preb. of St. Paul's 28 Feb. 1846 to death; R. of Hanwell 1864–80; edited works of Hartley Coleridge, S. T. Coleridge, J. Moultrie and W. M. Praed; author of *The scriptural character of the English Church* 1839; *Life of Hartley Coleridge* 1849. *d.* Eldon lodge, Torquay 28 March 1883. *The church of England photographic portrait gallery* 1859 *pt.* 9, *portrait; Illust. news of the world viii,* (1861), *portrait; Guardian 18 April 1883 p.* 569.

COLERIDGE, HERBERT (*only son of Henry Nelson Coleridge, chancery barrister 1798–1843*). *b.* Hampstead 7 Oct. 1830; ed. at Eton and Balliol coll. Ox., Balliol scholar 1847, Newcastle scholar 1848, double first class 1852; barrister L.I. 17 Nov. 1854; member of Philological Soc. Feb. 1857, hon. sec. of a special committee 'for collecting words and idioms hitherto unregistered,' this scheme developed into J. A. H. Murray's 'New English dictionary' published by Clarendon Press 1884 etc.; author of *Glossarial index to the printed English literature of the thirteenth century* 1859. *d.* 10 Chester place, London 23 April 1861. *Macmillan's Mag. v,* 56 (1862).

COLERIDGE, REV. JAMES DUKE (*eld. son of James Coleridge of Heath's Court, Ottery St. Mary, Devon 1760–1836*). *b.* 13 June 1789; ed. at Balliol coll. Ox., B.C.L. 1821, D.C.L. 1835; V. of Kenwyn and Kea, Cornwall 1823–8; R. of Lawhitton, Cornwall 1826–39; V. of Lewannick, Cornwall 1831–41; V. of Thorverton, Devon 1839 to death; preb. of Exeter cath. 5 Aug. 1825 to death; author of *A selection of family prayers* 1820, 3 *ed.* 1831; *Observations of a Parish Priest in scenes of sickness and death* 1825; *A companion to first lessons for the services of the Church on Sundays and the fasts and festivals* 1838. *d.* Thorverton 26 Dec. 1857. *Boase and Courtney's Bibl. Cornub. i,* 79, 313, *iii,* 1128.

COLERIDGE, SIR JOHN TAYLOR *(brother of the preceding).* *b.* Tiverton 9 July 1790; ed. at Ottery St. Mary, Eton and C.C. coll. Ox., scholar, April 1809; took both Bachelors' prizes for English and Latin essays 1813; B.A. 1815, M.A. 1817, hon. D.C.L. 1852; Vinerian law scholar 1812; fellow of Exeter coll. 30 June 1812 to 7 Aug. 1818; a certificated special pleader; barrister M.T. 25 June 1819; a bankruptcy comr. 1827; recorder of Exeter, Feb. 1832; serjeant-at-law 14 Feb. 1832; a justice of Court of King's Bench 27 Jany. 1835 to 28 June 1858; knighted at St. James's Palace 18 Feb. 1835; member of Inns of Court commission 1834, and of Law Courts commission 1858; P.C. 5 June 1858, member of judicial committee; edited *Blackstone's Commentaries* 4 vols. 1825; author of *Memoir of the Rev. John Keble* 1869, 4 *ed.* 1874. *d.* Heath's Court, Devon 11 Feb. 1876. *Law Mag. and law review vii,* 263–84 (1859), *i,* 486–99 (1876); *I.L.N. vi,* 245 (1845), *portrait, xxxiii,* 142 (1858), *portrait, lxviii,* 190, 213 (1876), *portrait.*

COLERIDGE, SARA *(only dau. of Samuel Taylor Coleridge the poet 1772–1834).* *b.* Greta hall near Keswick 22 Dec. 1802; published a translation of Martin Dobrizhoffer's *Account of the Abipones* 3 vols. 1822; *Pretty lessons for good children* 1834; *Phantasmion* 1837 a fairy tale; edited with her husband, S. T. Coleridge's *Biographia Literaria* 1847; one of the three maidens celebrated in Wordsworth's *Trias* 1828. *(m.* 3 Sep. 1829 her cousin Henry Nelson Coleridge, barrister, he was *b.* 25 Oct. 1798 and *d.* 26 Jany. 1843). *d.* Chester place, Regent's park, London 3 May 1852. *Memoir of Sara Coleridge edited by her daughter Edith Coleridge,* 4 *ed.* 1874; *G.M. xxxviii,* 540–2 (1852).

COLES, COWPER PHIPPS *(3 son of Rev. John Coles 1787–1865, R. of Silchester, Hants.)* *b.* 9 July 1819; entered navy 15 Dec. 1831; captain on h.p. 27 Feb. 1856; C.B. 23 March 1867; carried out an elaborate series of experiments on the methods of applying armour to vessels and mounting guns, the ship 'Captain' was built from drawings by Coles and Messrs. Laird 1866–70; author of *Our national defences* 1861, 4 *ed.* 1862. *(m.* 11 March 1856 Emily 3 dau. of Henry S. Pearson, she was granted civil list pension of £150, 11 Feb. 1871, and *d.* 11 Jany. 1876). *drowned* in the Captain, off Cape Finisterre 7 Sep. 1870 when nearly all the crew perished. *Journal of Royal United Service Instit. iv,* 280, *vii,* 110, *xi,* 434; *I.L.N. xl,* 399 (1862), *lvii,* 307, 329, (1870), *portrait.*

COLES, HENRY BEAUMONT. *b.* London 1794; barrister G.I. 30 Jany. 1837; M.P. for Andover 29 July 1847 to 20 March 1857. *d.* Portman sq. London 23 Nov. 1862.

COLES, ROBERT BARTLETT. *b.* 1785; cornet 8 dragoons 20 Aug. 1803; major 76 foot 24 Oct. 1821 to 19 Sep. 1826 when placed on h.p.; col. 65 foot 25 July 1857 to death; general 31 May 1865. *d.* Glencot, Wilts. 27 Oct. 1869.

COLES, WILLIAM COWPER. Ensign 40 foot 31 Oct. 1805; major 2 Life Guards 21 March 1829 to 20 Jany. 1832 when placed on h.p.; L.G. 9 March 1861. *d.* Woodcote, Salop 26 Aug. 1867 aged 77.

COLLARD, FREDERICK WILLIAM *(son of Wm. Collard of Wiveliscombe, Somerset).* baptized Wiveliscombe 21 June 1772; employed by Longman, Lukey and Broderip, music publishers at 26 Cheapside, London 1786; piano forte maker with Muzio Clementi in London 1799 to 24 June 1831, with his brother W. F. Collard to 24 June 1842, with his two nephews 1842 to death; took out many patents for improvements in pianos; supplied bugles, fifes and drums to regiments of East India Co. to 1858. *d.* 26 Cheapside, London 31 Jany. 1860.

COLLARD, WILLIAM FREDERICK *(brother of the preceding).* baptized at Wiveliscombe 25 Aug. 1776; member of firm of Muzio Clementi and Co. pianoforte makers 26 Cheapside down to 24 June 1831; partner with his brother 1831–42; invented many improvements in pianos. *d.* Folkestone 11 Oct. 1866.

COLLEDGE, THOMAS RICHARDSON. *b.* 1796; pupil of Sir Astley Cooper; practised in Canton and Macao; founded Medical missionary society in China 1837, pres. 1837 to death; surgeon to consulate at Canton to May 1841 when the office was abolished; M.D. King's coll. Aberdeen 1839; F.R.C.P. Edin. 1840; F.R.S. Edin. 1844; F.R.C.S. England 1853; lived at Cheltenham 1841 to death. *d.* Lauriston house, Cheltenham 28 Oct. 1879.

COLLEN, GEORGE WILLIAM. Portcullis pursuivant of arms 6 Nov. 1841 to death; author of *Britannia Saxonica, a map of Britain* 1833; *Debrett's Peerage continued* 1840. *d.* 52 Camden sq. London 9 Jany. 1878 in 79 year.

COLLETON, SIR ROBERT AUGUSTUS FULFORD GRAVES, 8 Baronet. *b.* 19 Sep. 1824; succeeded 29 July 1848. *d.* Fermoy, Ireland 28 Oct. 1866.

COLLETTE, JOHN HICKEY. Entered Madras army 1797; col. 7 Madras light cavalry 12 Aug. 1839 to death; L.G. 11 Nov. 1851. *d.* Nice 23 Oct. 1858 aged 77.

COLLEY, SIR GEORGE POMEROY POMEROY-*(youngest son of Hon. George Francis Colley of Ferney, co. Dublin 1797–1879, commander R.N.)* *b.* 1 Nov. 1835; ed. at R.M.A. Sandhurst; ensign 2 foot 28 May 1852, major 12 May 1875 to 24 April 1880 when placed on h.p.; professor at the staff college 1 July 1871 to 30 Nov. 1873; commanded the transport in Ashanti expedition, Dec. 1873 to Feb. 1874; military sec. to Viceroy of India 13 April 1876 to 12 April 1878, private sec. to him 13 April 1878 to 19 Feb. 1880; C.B. 31 March 1874; K.C.S.I. 29 July 1879; assumed additional surname of Pomeroy by r.l. 8 May 1880; author of the article *Army in Encyclopædia Britannica, 9 ed., ii, 559–619 (1875)*; governor and commander in chief Natal 24 April 1880 to death. Shot by the Boers on Majuba hill at Laing's Nek, North Natal 27 Feb. 1881. *Army and navy mag. i, 554–61 (1881), ii, 673–89 (1881), portrait; A narrative of the Boer war by T. F. Carter 1883; T. H. S. Escott's Pillars of the Empire (1879) 44–50; I.L.N. lxxiv 576 (1879), portrait, lxxviii, 224 (1881), portrait.*

COLLIER, SIR EDWARD *(son of Edward Collier of Blockley, Worcs.)* *b.* Blockley 1783; entered navy, Feb. 1796; captain 18 Nov. 1814; V.A. 18 June 1857; retired on a pension 27 Nov. 1857; admiral 4 Oct. 1862; C.B. 18 Dec. 1840; K.C.B. 7 June 1865. *d.* Blockley 5 Aug. 1872.

COLLIER, HENRY THEODOSIUS BROWNE. *b.* 1791; entered navy 28 April 1800; captain on half pay 26 Dec. 1822; retired admiral 26 June 1863. *d.* 25 Ryder st. St. James's, London 10 Sep. 1872.

COLLIER, JOHN PAYNE *(son of John Dyer Collier of London, writer on the press 1762–1825).* *b.* Broad st. London 11 Jany. 1789; reporter on *The Times* 1809–21, on the *Morning Chronicle* 1821–47; summoned before House of Commons 15 June 1819 for misreporting a speech of Joseph Hume, and committed to custody of the serjeant-at-arms; barrister M.T. 6 Feb. 1829; deputy licenser of plays; a founder of the Camden Society 1838; sec. of Royal commission on British Museum 1847–50; accused of having committed many literary frauds in connection with Shakespearian and other documents; granted civil list pension of £100, 30 Oct. 1850; author of *Criticisms on the Bar, by Amicus Curiæ* 1819; printed privately and anonymously *The Poet's Pilgrimage* 1822; pub-

lished a new ed. of *Dodsley's Old Plays* 12 vols. 1825–7; *Punch and Judy* 1828, anon.; *History of English dramatic poetry and annals of the stage* 3 vols. 1831, new ed. 1879; *Shakespeare's Library* 2 vols. 1843; *Shakespeare's Works* 8 vols. 1844, 6 vols. 1858; *Notes and emendations to the text of Shakespeare's plays from the folio in the possession of J. P. C.* [*i.e. the Perkin's folio*] 1853; *The works of Edmund Spenser* 5 vols. 1862. *d.* Riverside, Maidenhead 17 Sep. 1883. *bur.* Bray churchyard 20 Sep. *J. P. Collier's An old man's diary 4 parts 1871–2; Wheatley's Notes on the life of J. P. Collier 1884; Literary Cookery 1855, anon. by E. A. Brae; Antiquarian Mag. iv, 272–5 (1883); I.L.N. lxxxiii, 309 (1883), portrait; N. E. S. A. Hamilton's Genuineness of Collier's Annotated Shakespeare 1860.*

COLLINGS, JOHN ELIAS *(son of lieut.-col. Joseph Collings).* *b.* 11 Sep. 1821; ensign 33 foot 21 June 1839, lieut.-col. 17 Nov. 1857 to 28 Oct. 1868 when placed on h.p.; lieut.-col. brigade depôt 1 April 1873 to 24 Jany. 1874 when placed on h.p.; L.G. 18 Sep. 1879; placed on retired list with hon. rank of general 1 July 1881; C.B. 14 Aug. 1868. *d.* Grange hill, Guernsey 10 Dec. 1886.

COLLINGS, SIR WILLIAM *(2 son of John Collings of St. Peter port, Guernsey).* *b.* St. Peter port 1781; jurat of royal court of Guernsey 1822; knighted at St. James's palace 2 May 1838; colonel of Royal Guernsey militia to death. *d.* Guernsey 18 June 1854.

COLLINS, CHARLES ALLSTON *(younger son of Wm. Collins the painter 1788–1847).* *b.* Hampstead 25 Jany. 1828; practised as a painter 1848–58; contributed to *Household Words*; art critic to the *Echo*; author of *A new sentimental Journey* 1859; *The eye-witness, seeing is believing* 1860; *A cruise upon wheels* 2 vols. 1862; *The bar sinister* 2 vols. 1864; *Strathcairn* 2 vols. 1864; *At the bar, a tale* 2 vols. 1866. *d.* Thurloe place, Brompton, London, about midnight 9–10 April 1873. *Illustrated Review v, 423–8 (1873), portrait; Graphic vii, 312, 318 (1873), portrait.*

COLLINS, CHARLES JAMES. On the parliamentary staff of the *Sun, Daily Telegraph* and *Standard*; edited *Comic News* 1 May 1847; projected and edited the *Racing Times* 1861; author of *Kenilworth* and other burlesques; *Life and adventures of Dick Diminy* 1854; *Sackville Chase* 3 vols. 1863; *Matilda the Dane, a romance of the affections* 1863; *The man in chains* 3 vols. 1864; *Singed Moths, a city romance* 3 vols. 1864. *d.* 9 Manor terrace, Brixton, London 31 Dec. 1864.

COLLINS, EDWARD FRANCIS. *b.* North of Ireland 1807 ; came to London 1832 and became private secretary to Joseph Hume, M.P. ; sub-editor of the *Sun ;* edited the *Hull Advertiser* 1842–66 ; sub-editor of *The Tablet* 1868 ; author of *A form of reciting the most holy rosary, compiled for the nuns of the convent of our Lord of Mercy at Hull* 1859, *anon. d.* Upper Clapton near London 3 Jany. 1872.

COLLINS, FRANCES *(dau. of Wm. Dunn of London, engineer). b.* 1840 or 1841 ; author with Mortimer Collins of the novels entitled *Frances* 3 vols. 1874, *another ed.* 1880, her name is not on the original ed. ; *Sweet and twenty* 3 vols. 1875, *another ed.* 1877 ; *The village comedy* 3 vols. 1878 ; *You play me false* 3 vols. 1878 ; author of *Mortimer Collins, his letters and friendships* 2 vols. 1877 ; *A broken lily* 3 vols. 1882 ; author with her cousin F. Percy Cotton of *Mudge and her chicks by a Brother and Sister* [*F.P.C. and F.C.*] 1880 ; *The Woodleighs of Amscote by F. Percy Cotton and F. Collins* 1881 ; edited with Tom Taylor *Pen sketches by a Vanished Hand, from papers of M. Collins* 1879 ; edited with Edmund Yates *Thoughts in my garden by M. Collins* 2 vols. 1880. (*m.* 4 May 1868 Mortimer Collins 1827–76). *d.* Pinetree hill, Camberley, Surrey 16 March 1886, cremated at Woking cemetery 20 March.

COLLINS, HENRY POWELL. M.P. for Taunton 8 Oct. 1812 to 29 Feb. 1820 ; sheriff of Somerset 1827. *d.* Weston-super-Mare 22 Aug. 1854 aged 78.

COLLINS, JOHN *(eld. son of John Collins, landlord of the Lucan Spa house near Dublin). b.* Lucan, Sep. 1804 ; a cook in his father's hotel ; first appeared in London at Haymarket theatre 29 Aug. 1832 as Captain Macheath in *The Beggar's Opera*, chief tenor singer there ; original actor of Paul Clifford at Covent Garden 1835 ; first appeared Park theatre, New York 17 Aug. 1846, the best singer of Irish ballads and humorous songs in America ; acted in United States 1846–64, at Adelphi theatre, London, Oct. 1864, in Australia 1866. *d.* Philadelphia 13 Aug. 1874. *Actors by daylight ii,* 153 (1839), *portrait ; Belgravia xvi,* 443 (1872) ; *Ireland's New York Stage ii,* 464–5 (1867).

COLLINS, MORTIMER, whose full names were Edward James Mortimer Collins *(only child of Francis Collings of Kingsbridge, Devon, who d.* 1839). *b.* Plymouth 29 June 1827 ; reading boy at Gilbert and Rivingtons, St. John's sq. London 5 May to 29 June 1838 ; assistant in a shop in Holborn 1838 ; usher in Rev. Richard Harris's school at Westbury, Wilts. 1843–5 ;

COLLINS, M. *(Con.)*

his first poem, signed E. J. M. C. printed in *Bath and Cheltenham Gazette* 10 April 1844 ; contributed to *Felix Farley's Journal* at Bristol 1847–9, Paris correspondent 1848 ; private tutor at Windermere 1847–8 ; usher at Rev. J. H. Crump's school, Lechlade, Gloucs. Jany. to June 1849 ; tutor at Rothwell, Northamptonshire 1849 ; editor of the *Lancaster Gazette,* May 1850 ; master of a school at Launceston for 3 months in 1851 ; head master of lower school, Elizabeth college, Guernsey 1852–5 ; contributed to *Dublin Univ. Mag.* 1851 and to *Punch* 1853 ; started the *Channel Islands Mag.* 1 May 1853, 3 numbers only ; opened a private school in Guernsey 1855–6 ; edited the *Leamington Mercury* 1856–7 ; private tutor at Carlisle 1858 ; edited the *Plymouth Mail* 1859, *Nottingham Guardian* 1860–1 ; contributed to *Temple Bar* 1861–7 ; editor of and contributed to *The Owl* 1864–6 ; joint editor of *The Globe* 1866 ; author of *Windermere a poem and Sonnets, Kendal* 1848 ; *Idyls and Rhymes* 1855 ; *Summer songs* 1860 ; *Who is the heir ?* 3 vols. 1865 ; *A selection from the works of Sir Walter Scott* in Moxon's Miniature Poets 1866 ; *Sweet Anne Page* 3 vols. 1868 ; *The Ivory gate* 2 vols. 1869 ; *Letter to the Right Hon. B. Disraeli* 1869 in verse, anon. ; *The Vivian romance* 3 vols. 1870 ; *The Inn of strange Meetings, and other Poems* 1871 ; *The secret of long life* 1871 anon., 5 *ed.* 1879 ; *Marquis and Merchant* 3 vols. 1871 ; *The British birds, a communication from the Ghost of Aristophanes* 1872, 2 *ed.* 1878 ; *The Princess Clarice* 2 vols. 1871 ; *Two plunges for a pearl* 3 vols. 1872 ; *Squire Sylvester's Whim* 3 vols. 1873 ; *Miranda a Midsummer madness* 3 vols. 1873 ; *Mr. Carington, a tale of love and conspiracy by Robert Turner Cotton* 3 vols. 1873, *pseud. ; Transmigration* 3 vols. 1874 ; *Blacksmith and Scholar, and from Midnight to Midnight* 3 vols. 1876 ; *A fight with fortune* 3 vols. 1876, *another ed.* 1880. (*m.* (1) 9 May 1850 at Wargrave, Berks., Susan dau. of William Hubbard, and widow of Rev. J. H. Crump, chaplain of the Mill Hill school, Middlesex, who *d.* 14 Feb. 1849 aged 46, she *d.* 5 Aug. 1867 aged 59. *m.* (2) 4 May 1868 at St. Martins in the Fields, London, Frances dau. of Wm. Dunn of London, engineer, she *d.* 16 March 1886 aged 45). *d.* Nightingale hall, Richmond 28 July 1876. *bur.* Petersham churchyard 1 Aug. *Mortimer Collins his letters and friendships, edited by Frances Collins* 2 vols. 1877 ; *Dublin Univ. Mag. xc,* 340–56, 474–98, 561–93 (1877) ; *I.L.N. lxix,* 205, 206 (1876), *portrait.*

COLLINS, SAM, stage name of Samuel Thomas Collins Vagg *(son of Samuel Vagg who d. Uxbridge 13 Feb. 1868).* Comic singer at Mogul music hall, Drury lane, London where he made a great hit with the song *Paddy's Wedding* ; proprietor of Marylebone music hall, London and Welsh harp, Hendon ; became bankrupt on his own petition 2 July 1861 ; sang at all the chief music halls in London and the provinces ; proprietor of Lansdowne music hall, Islington green, London, afterwards known as Collins's music hall 1862 to death. *d.* 10 Paradise row, Islington 25 May 1865 aged 39. *Illust. Sporting news iv*, 217 (1865), *portrait ; Era* 28 *May* 1865 *p.* 10, 4 *June p.* 11.

COLLINS, SAMUEL (*son of a hand-loom weaver*). *b.* Hollinwood near Manchester 1 Dec. 1802 ; a hand-loom weaver ; a follower of Henry Hunt and Wm. Cobbett ; took part in the meeting at Peterloo 1819 ; wrote homely verses, some of them in the Lancashire dialect which were collected in a small vol. entitled *Miscellaneous poems and songs of S. Collins with a biographical notice by B. Brierley* 1859. *d.* Hale Moss, Chadderton near Manchester 8 July 1878.

COLLINS, THOMAS (2 son of *Rev. Thomas Collins, V. of Farnham, Yorkshire who d.* 7 *May* 1870 *aged* 89). *b.* 1825 ; ed. at Charterhouse and Wadham coll. Ox., B.A. 1847 ; barrister I.T. 4 May 1849 ; M.P. for Knaresborough 1851–2, 1857–65 and 12 May 1881 to death ; M.P. for Boston 1868–74. *d.* Harrogate 26 Nov. 1884 in 59 year.

COLLINS, WILLIAM. *b.* Eastwood, Renfrewshire 12 Oct. 1789 ; elder of Tron. ch. Glasgow 1814, and chief mover in appointment of Rev. Thomas Chalmers to that ch. 1815 ; opened first local Sabbath sch. Glasgow 1816 ; publisher and bookseller ; lecturer on Temperance in Scotland and England 1829–34 ; founder of British and Foreign Temperance Soc. London 1830 ; founder of 20 new churches in Glasgow 1834 etc. ; joined the Free ch. movement in 1843 and aided in erecting many Free churches. *d.* Rothesay 2 Jany. 1853. *Wylie's Disruption Worthies* (1881) 165–72 ; *Burns's Temperance Dictionary* (1864) *pp.* 433–43.

COLLINS, WILLIAM ANTHONY (2 son of *Charles Collins of Brixworth hall, Northamptonshire*). *b.* London 1801 ; ed. at Ch. coll, Cam, B.A. 1824, M.A. 1827 ; barrister L.I. 17 Nov. 1829, bencher 1861 ; Q.C. 22 Feb. 1861. *d.* Warrior sq. St. Leonard's on Sea 30 March 1875. *bur.* Tonbridge, Kent.

COLLINS, REV. WILLIAM LUCAS (*only son of Rev. John Collins of Axwich, Glamorgan*). Educ.

at Jesus coll. Ox., B.A. 1838, M.A. 1841 ; C. of Great Houghton, Northamptonshire 1835–62 ; R. of Cheriton, Glamorganshire 1863–7 ; V. of Kilsby 1867–73 ; R. of Lowick 1873 to death ; V. of Slipton 1876 to death ; hon. canon of Peterborough 1871 to death ; editor of *Ancient classics for English readers* 1870, wrote the vols. on *Homer's Iliad and Odyssey, Aristophanes, Lucian, Virgil, Plautus, Terence, Cicero, Livy and Thucydides ;* author of *The luck of Ladysmede* 1860 ; *The education question* 1862 ; *Etoniana ancient and modern* 1865 ; *The public schools by W. L. C.* 1867 ; *Montaigne* in Mrs. Oliphant's *Foreign classics for English readers* 1879 ; *Butler* in Knight's *Philosophical classics for English readers* 1881 ; *La Fontaine and other French fabulists* in *Foreign Classics* 1882 ; contributed to *Blackwood's Mag.* from 1843. *d.* Lowick rectory 24 March 1887 aged 70. *Blackwood's Mag. cxli*, 734–6 (1887).

COLLINSON, JAMES (*son of Mr. Collinson of Mansfield, Notts. bookseller*). *b.* Mansfield about 1825 ; ed. at Royal Academy school ; exhibited a picture called 'The charity boy's début' at the R.A. 1847 ; one of the original 7 brothers of the Pre-Raphaelite brotherhood ; contributed a devotional poem in blank verse entitled *The Child Jesus* to the Pre-Raphaelite periodical *The Germ* 1850 ; lived in seclusion at Stonyhurst 1851–4 ; fellow of Society of British Artists. *d.* of pneumonia at 16 Paulet road, Camberwell, London 24 Jany. 1881. *Fraser's Mag. May* 1882 *pp.* 568–80.

COLLINSON, REV. JOHN (*son of Rev. Richard Collinson of Bristol*). Educ. at Winchester and Queen's coll. Ox., B.A. 1803, M.A. 1806 ; one of Select Preachers 1809, Bampton Lecturer 1813 ; R. of Gateshead 1810–40 ; R. of Boldon, Durham, 1840 to death ; hon. canon of Durham 1844 to death ; author of *Analysis of Hooker's eight books of ecclesiastical polity* 1810 ; *Life of Thuanus with account of his writings* 1807 ; *Key to the writings of the Fathers of the Christian church* 1813 ; *Observations on the history of the gospel from Solomon's temple to first Christian century* 1830 ; *History of Reformation, from the French of A. Ruchat* 1845. *d.* Boldon 17 Feb. 1857. *G.M. ii*, 492–93 (1857).

COLLINSON, SIR RICHARD (*son of the preceding*). *b.* Gateshead 7 Nov. 1811 ; entered navy 2 Dec. 1823 ; captain 23 Dec. 1842 ; captain of the Enterprise 14 Dec. 1849 to 6 May 1855 during the expedition to Behring strait in search of Sir John Franklin ; granted good service pension 4 Dec. 1857 ; an elder brother of the Trinity House 1862,

COLLINSON, SIR R. (Con).

deputy master 7 Sep. 1875 to death; V.A. 17 March 1869; retired admiral 30 July 1875; C.B. 24 Dec. 1842, K.C.B. 29 May 1875; F.R.G.S. gold medallist 1848; edited for the Hakluyt Society *The three voyages of Martin Frobisher in search of a passage to Cathaia and India by the Northwest* 1867. *d.* Haven Green, Ealing 12 Sep. 1883. *Proc. of Royal Geog. Soc. v,* 606–9, 734 (1883); *I.L.N. xxvi,* 472 (1855), *portrait, lxxxiii,* 309 (1883), *portrait.*

COLLIS, REV. JOHN DAY *(eld. son of Rev. Robert Fitzgerald Collis 1790–1863, preb. of Kilconnel, co. Galway). b.* 24 Feb. 1816; ed. at Rugby and Worcester coll. Ox., Eaton scholar 1835, B.A. 1838, M.A. 1841, B.D. and D.D. 1860; Kennicott Hebrew scholar 1839; Pusey and Ellerton Hebrew scholar 1841; fellow of his college; head master of Bromsgrove gr. school Dec. 1842–1867, tercentenary of the school was celebrated 31 March 1853, the chapel was built at cost of £1500, 1856; hon. canon of Worcester 1854 to death; Grinfield lecturer on Septuagint in Univ. of Ox. 1863–65; V. of Stratford-on-Avon 1867 to death; founded Trinity college school at Stratford-on-Avon 27 Jany. 1872; author of *The chief rules of Greek accentuation* 1849 and other Greek school books; *The chief tenses of Latin irregular verbs* 1854 and other Latin school books; *Historical notes on the church of St. John the Baptist, Bromsgrove* 1859; *Ponticulus Latinus, History of Rome to destruction of Carthage* 1860. *d.* Shottery hall, Stratford-on-Avon 1 April 1879. *bur.* Bromsgrove cemetery 4 April.

COLLIS, MAURICE HENRY *(brother of the preceding). b.* 1824; ed. at Trin. coll. Dub., B.A. 1847, M.B. 1849, M.D. 1867, L.R.C.S.I. 1847, F.R.C.S.I. 1850; surgeon to Meath Hosp. 1851 to death; pres. of council of Irish Medical Assoc.; author of *On the diagnosis and treatment of cancer and the tumours analogous to it* 1864. *d.* Dublin 28 March 1869. *Reg. and mag. of biog. i,* 404–5 (1869).

COLLS, REV. JOHN FLOWERDEW. *b.* 15 Aug. 1801; ed. at Merchant Taylors' and Trin. coll. Cam., B.D. 1834, D.D. 1842; R. of Laindon, Herts. 1853 to death; author of *Vindication of infant baptism* 1829; *Utilitarianism unmasked* 1844. *d.* 9 Hanover st. Hanover square, London 19 Nov. 1878.

COLLYER, JOHN *(eld. child of the succeeding). b.* 15 July 1801; ed. at Charterhouse and Clare coll. Cam., fellow, B.A. 1822, M.A. 1825; barrister L.I. 9 Feb. 1827; commissary of Norwich 1842; judge of county courts, circuit 35, Cambridgeshire, March 1847 to death;

COLLYER, J. *(Con.)*

author of *A practical treatise on the law of Partnership* 1832, 2 ed. 1840; *Reports of cases decided in the court of Chancery by Sir J. L. Knight Bruce* 1844–6, 2 vols. 1845–7; author with Edward Younge of *Reports of cases in the court of Exchequer in Equity* 1833–41, 4 vols. 1836–46; *Reports of cases decided in the court of Chancery by Sir J. L. Knight Bruce* 1841–4, 2 vols. 1843–4. *d.* Hackford hall, Reepham, Norfolk 1 Sep. 1870.

COLLYER, VENERABLE JOHN BEDINGFELD (2 *son of Rev. Daniel Collyer of Wroxham hall, Norfolk). b.* 26 Jany. 1777; ed. at Clare coll. Camb., B.A. 1798, M.A. 1808; V. of Wroxham, Norfolk 1801 to death; archdeacon of Norwich 23 Sep. 1844 to death; author of Charges and Sermons 1838–56. *d.* Hackford hall, Norfolk 29 March 1857.

COLLYER, REV. WILLIAM BENGO *(son of Thomas Collyer of Deptford, builder). b.* Deptford 14 April 1782; ed. at the Old college, Homerton; Congregational minister at Peckham 1800 to death, his chapel was rebuilt and reopened under name of Hanover chapel 1816; ordained Dec. 1801, D.D. Edin. 1808; minister at Salter's hall chapel, Islington 1813 to death; author of *Fugitive pieces for the use of schools* 1803; *Hymns designed as a substitute for Dr. Watts* 1812; *Services suited to the solemnisation of matrimony with original hymns* 1837, and several series of popular lectures on scripture subjects. *d.* May 1854. *European Mag. lxxii,* 407–10 (1817), *portrait; Waddington's Congregational history iv,* 136–42 (1878); *The Unique, vol. 2* (1825), *portrait; Some of Dr. Collyer's errors stated and corrected* 1821.

COLNAGHI, DOMINIC PAUL *(eld. son of Paul Colnaghi of London, print dealer 1751–1833). b.* London 15 July 1790; head of the firm of Paul and Dominic Colnaghi, print dealers 14 Pall Mall East 1833; had a European reputation as an authority on prints; a connoiseur in ancient armour, original possessor of a large portion of the Meyrick collection; retired from business 1865; published *Colnaghi's Patriotic fund almanac* 1854; *Colnaghi's Crimean almanac* 1855. *d.* 62 Margaret st. Cavendish sq. London 19 Dec. 1879.

COLOMB, GEORGE THOMAS. Ensign 96 foot 8 Dec. 1808; captain 5 dragoon guards 17 March 1825 to 27 April 1827 when placed on h.p.; col. 4 West India regiment 24 April 1866 to 3 March 1869; L.G. 31 March 1866; col. 97 foot 3 March 1869 to death. *d.* Dalkey, co. Dublin 20 March 1874.

COLONSAY, DUNCAN M'NEILL, 1 Baron *(2 son of John Mc. Neill of Colonsay, Argyllshire, who d. 1846).* *b.* Colonsay 20 Aug. 1793 ; ed. at Univs. of St. Andrews and Edin. ; called to Scottish bar 1816 ; advocate depute 1820–4 ; sheriff of Perthshire, Dec. 1824 to Dec. 1834 ; solicitor general for Scotland Nov. 1834 to April 1835 and Sep. 1841 to 26 Oct. 1842 ; Her Majesty's advocate for Scotland 26 Oct. 1842 to July 1846 ; dean of faculty of advocates 1843–51 ; a lord of session 15 May 1851 ; a lord of justiciary 30 May 1851 ; lord justice general and pres. of court of session 15 May 1852 to Feb. 1867 ; P.C. 8 Aug. 1853 ; M.P. for Argyllshire 1843–51 ; created baron Colonsay of Colonsay and Oransay in the co. of Argyle 26 Feb. 1867. *d.* Pau, France 31 Jany. 1874.

COLQUHOUN, FRANCES SARA *(dau. of Edward Fuller Maitland of Park place, Stansted hall, Essex).* Completed Henry Kirke White's fragment beginning ' Much in sorrow, oft in woe' which completion has been universally accepted for use in the Church of England ; author of *Rhymes and Chimes* 1876. *(m.* 29 Jany. 1834 John Colquhoun 1805–85). *d.* 27 May 1877.

COLQUHOUN, SIR JAMES, 4 Baronet. *b.* Edinburgh 7 Feb. 1804 ; ed. at Geneva ; succeeded 3 Feb. 1836 ; lord lieutenant of Dumbartonshire 1837 ; M.P. for Dumbartonshire 1837–1841. drowned in Loch Lomond 18 Dec. 1873.

COLQUHOUN, JAMES NISBET. *b.* parish of St. Pierre, Guernsey 23 June 1791 ; Second lieut. R.A. 1 June 1808, lieut. col. 9 Nov. 1846 to death ; inspector of carriage department at Woolwich 1845 ; raised, organized, equipped and commanded corps of artillery attached to British auxiliary legion under De Lacy Evans for service of Queen of Spain in war against Don Carlos 1835–6 ; A.I.C.E. 1843, member of council 1846 ; F.R.S. *d.* Woolwich barracks 17 Sep. 1853. *Min. of proc. of Instit. of C.E. xiii,* 149–56 (1854).

COLQUHOUN, JOHN *(brother of Sir James Colquhoun, 4 baronet 1804–73).* *b.* Charlotte sq. Edin. 6 March 1805 ; ensign 33 foot 1828 ; lieut. 4 dragoon guards 1829 to 1834 when he sold out ; author of *The moor and the loch* 1840, 6 ed. 1884 ; *Rocks and Rivers* 1849 ; *Salmon casts and stray shots* 1858 ; *Sporting Days* 1866, and of 2 lectures, *The feræ naturæ of the British islands* 1873, *Instinct and Reason* 1874. *d.* Royal Terrace, Edinburgh 27 May 1885. *The moor and the loch,* 6 ed. 1884 ; *The Chiefs of Colquhoun by W. Fraser,* 2 vols. *privately printed Edin.* 1869.

COLQUHOUN, JOHN CAMPBELL *(5 son of Sir James Colquhoun, 2 Baronet).* *b.* Edinburgh 31 Jany. 1785 ; studied at Göttingen ; called to bar in Scotland 7 June 1806 ; sheriff depute of Dumbartonshire 1815–84 ; author of *Isis Revelata, an inquiry into the origin, progress and present state of animal magnetism* 1836 and of a translation of Wienholt's *Seven lectures on Somnambulism* 1845. *d.* Edinburgh 21 Aug. 1854.

COLQUHOUN, JOHN CAMPBELL *(eld. son of Archibald Campbell, lord registrar of Scotland, who took name of Colquhoun and d.* 1820). *b.* Edinburgh 23 Jany. 1803 ; ed. at Edin. high sch. and Oriel coll. Ox., B.A. 1823 ; M.P. for Dumbartonshire 1832–4, for Kilmarnock 1837–41, for Newcastle under Lyme 1842–7 ; author of *Short sketches of some notable lives* 1855 ; *Life in Italy and France in the olden times* 1858 ; *William Wilberforce his friends and his times* 1866, 2 ed. 1867 ; *Memorials of H. M. Colquhoun* 1870, and numerous other works. *d.* Chesham st. London 17 April 1870.

COLQUHOUN, SIR ROBERT GILMOUR *(eld. son of Robert Colquhoun of Camstroden, Dumbarton).* *b.* Glasgow 9 Jany. 1803 ; ed. at Pemb. coll. Ox. ; British consul at Bucharest 17 Nov. 1834, consul general there 15 Dec. 1837, agent and consul general 18 Nov. 1851 ; consul general and agent in Egypt 13 Dec. 1858 to 14 Aug. 1865 ; C.B. 5 Dec. 1859, K.C.B. 30 May 1865. *d.* Fincastle, Perthshire 10 Nov. 1870.

COLT, REV. SIR EDWARD HENRY VAUGHAN, 6 Baronet. *b.* Lescroft, Staffs. April 1808 ; ed. at Queen's coll. Ox., B.A. 1836 ; V. of Hill, Gloucs. 1839 to death ; succeeded 9 June 1849. *d.* Hill vicarage 15 Oct. 1882.

COLTHURST, SIR GEORGE CONWAY, 5 Baronet. *b.* 1824 ; ed. at Harrow ; succeeded 22 June 1829 ; M.P. for Kinsale 8 June 1863 to Jany. 1874. *d.* Buxton 24 Sep. 1878.

COLVILE, CHARLES ROBERT *(eld. son of Sir Charles Henry Colvile of Duffield hall, Derbyshire, who d.* 28 *Sep.* 1833). *b.* London 30 March 1815 ; ed. at Eton and Ch. Ch. Ox. ; M.P. for South Derbyshire 1841–59 and 1865–8 ; sheriff of Derbyshire 1874. *d.* Lullington hall, Burton-on-Trent 10 March 1886.

COLVILE, REV. FREDERICK LEIGH *(eld. son of Frederick Charles Colvile of Marylebone, London).* Educ. at Trin. coll. Ox., B.A. 1840, M.A. 1843 ; V. of Leek Wootton near Warwick 1842–80 ; chaplain of Stoneleigh abbey 1853–80 ; rural dean of Coventry 1856–80 ; author of *Catechism on the liturgy of the Church of England,* 9 ed. 1850 ; *Stoneleigh Abbey from*

COLVILE, REV. F. L. *(Con.)*

its foundation by F. L. C., privately printed 1850; *Worthies of Warwickshire* 1870. *d.* Kempsey, Bournemouth 28 March 1886.

COLVILE, HENRY ROBERT (4 *son of Robert Colvile of Newton hall, Cambs.* 1763-99). *b.* 1795; ed. at Eton; ensign 3 foot guards 29 Dec. 1813, lieut.-col. 25 March 1852 to Feb. 1854; col. 12 foot 29 Oct. 1864 to death; general 27 March 1868. *d.* Kempsey hall near Worcester 1 Nov. 1875.

COLVILE, SIR JAMES WILLIAM *(eld. son of Andrew Wedderburn, afterwards Colvile, of Crombie, Fifeshire, who d.* 1856). *b.* London 12 Jany. 1810; ed. at Eton and Trin coll. Cam., B.A. 1831, M.A. 1834; barrister I.T. 30 Jany. 1835, bencher; advocate general at Calcutta 1845-8; puisne judge of supreme court of Bengal 1848-55, chief justice 1855-9; knighted by patent 9 Dec. 1848; P.C. 6 July 1859; assessor of judicial committee of privy council on Indian appeals 1859; member of judicial committee 20 Nov. 1865 to Nov. 1871, one of the 4 paid judges Nov. 1871 to death; pres. of Asiatic Society of Calcutta; F.R.S. 29 April 1875. *d.* 8 Rutland gate, London 6 Dec. 1880. *bur.* Craigflower near Dunfermline 11 Dec. *Proc. of Royal Soc. xxxiv, page x* (1883); *Graphic iv,* 531 (1871), *portrait.*

COLVIN, JOHN. Lieut. col. Bengal Engineers 20 April 1835; C.B. 2 July 1838; retired col. Bengal army 4 Sep. 1839. *d.* Lintwardine, Herefordshire 27 April 1871.

COLVIN, JOHN RUSSELL (2 *son of James Colvin of London and Calcutta, merchant).* *b.* Calcutta May 1807; ed. at St. Andrew's, Fifeshire and Haileybury; went to Bengal 1826; assistant to Registrar of the Sudder Court 1826, to Resident at Hyderabad 14 Dec. 1827; assistant sec. in Revenue and Judicial department at Calcutta 4 Jany. 1831; Sec. to Board of Revenue in Lower Provinces 13 March 1835; private sec. to Lord Auckland the Governor General 1836-42; resident in Nepaul 1845; commissioner of Tenasserim provinces 1846; judge of Sudder Court at Calcutta 1849; lieut. governor of north western provinces 1853. *d.* Agra 9 Sep. 1857. *G.M. iv,* 212-19 (1858).

COMBE, BOYCE (2 *son of Harvey Christian Combe of Cobham park, Surrey* 1752-1818). *b.* London 1789; ed. at Harrow; barrister L.I. 19 Nov. 1813, bencher; magistrate at Thames police court 1833, at Lambeth st. near Whitechapel 1838, at Hatton garden 1839, at Clerkenwell 1842, at Southwark 1851 to death. *d.* 43 Upper Seymour st. Portman sq. London 7 Jany. 1864. *I.L.N. x,* 332 (1847), *portrait.*

COMBE, GEORGE *(son of George Combe of Edinburgh, brewer, who d.* 29 *Sep.* 1815 *in* 60 *year.)* *b.* Livingston's yards, Edin. 21 Oct. 1788; studied at Univ. of Edin. 1802-4; admitted a writer to the signet 31 Jany. 1812, practised in Edin 1812-36; a founder of Phrenological Society, Feb. 1820; delivered 158 lectures on phrenology and education in United States 1838-40; author of *Elements of phrenology* 1824, 8 ed. 1855; *Outlines of phrenology* 1824, 9 ed. 1854; *The constitution of man considered in relation to external objects* 1828, 9 ed. 1860; *Notes on the United States* 3 vols. 1841, and numerous other works. *d.* Moor Park, Farnham, Surrey 14 Aug. 1858. *bur.* in the Dean cemetery, Edin. *The life of George Combe by Charles Gibbon* 2 vols. 1878, *portrait; Charles Mackay's Forty years recollections* (1877) *ii,* 241-70; *H. Martineau's Biographical sketches,* 4 ed. (1876) 265-77; *R. Capen's Reminiscences of Spurzheim and Combe* 1881; *Crombie's Modern Athenians* (1882) 161-6, *portrait.*

COMBE, RICHARD THOMAS (2 *son of John Maddison of Alvingham, Lincs. who d.* 1849). *b.* 1813; ed. at Winchester and Univ. coll. Ox., B.A. 1835; barrister M.T. 1840; assumed name of Combe in lieu of Maddison by royal license 18 Dec. 1849; chairman of Ilminster bench of magistrates; recorder of Langport; sheriff of Somerset 1867. Shot himself 8 May 1880.

COMBE, THOMAS *(son of Thomas Combe of Leicester, bookseller).* *b.* June 1796; assistant to Joseph Parker of Oxford bookseller to 1823, to M. A. Nattali of London 1823-7; partner with his father 1827; senior partner in University press, Oxford; manager of classical side of Clarendon press, Ox.; architypographer to Univ. of Ox.; managing partner of the Bible press, Ox.; built and endowed church of St. Barnabas's, Jericho, Oxford 1869; built chapel attached to Radcliffe infirmary, Ox.; owner of Holman Hunt's picture 'The light of the world' which his widow gave to Keble college, Ox. *d.* The Clarendon press, Oxford 29 Oct. 1872.

COMBERMERE, STAPLETON STAPLETON COTTON, 1 Viscount (2 *son of Sir Robert Salusbury Cotton,* 5 *baronet, who d.* 24 *Aug.* 1809). *b.* Llewenny hall, co. Denbigh 14 Nov. 1773; ed. at Westminster; 2 lieut. 23 foot 26 Feb. 1790; lieut.-col. 25 light dragoons 9 March 1794 to 14 Feb. 1800; lieut.-col. 16 light dragoons 14 Feb. 1800 to 27 Jany. 1813; succeeded 24 Aug. 1809; M.P. for Newark 1806-1814; commanded a brigade of cavalry in Portugal 1808; commanded whole allied cavalry under Duke of Wellington 1810-14;

COMBERMERE, 1 Viscount *(Con.)*

col. 20 light dragoons 27 Jany. 1813–1819 when regiment was disbanded; created Baron Combermere of Combermere Abbey 17 May 1814 for his brilliant services during Peninsula war, with an annuity of £2000 for two generations; commanded allied cavalry in France 1815–16, the forces in West Indies 21 Dec. 1816 to 9 Feb. 1821; governor of Barbados 14 Feb. 1817 to 2 March 1821; commander in chief in Ireland 1822–5; col. 3 light dragoons 25 Jan. 1821 to 16 Sep. 1829; governor of Sheerness 25 Jany. 1821 to 11 Oct. 1852; commander in chief in India 9 Feb. 1825 to 1 Jany. 1830, captured city of Bhurtpoor, Hindostan 18 Jany. 1826; created Viscount Combermere 2 Dec. 1826; col. 1 life guards 16 Sep. 1829 to death; P.C. 15 Dec. 1834; constable of Tower of London 11 Oct. 1852 to death, sworn in 21 Feb. 1853; field marshal 2 Oct. 1855; G.C.B. 21 Aug. 1813, G.C.H. 24 July 1817, K.S.I. 19 Aug. 1861; portrait in National portrait gallery. *d.* Clifton 21 Feb. 1865. *bur.* Wrenbury ch. where is a monument; statue by Marochetti at Chester castle. *Memoirs 2 vols. 1866, 2 portraits; Army and navy mag. iii, 481–5 (1882), portrait.*

COMER, JOHN. Popular singer at concerts in Bath 1821; sang in principal cities in Italy 1830–5; Mus. Doc. Bologna 1832; principal bass singer in Italian opera at Her Majesty's theatre, London 1835; lived at Taunton from 1836 to death; leader of the Taunton Madrigal Soc. many years. *d.* Ilchester 17 March 1886 aged 86.

COMER, THOMAS *(brother of the preceding).* *b.* Bath 19 Dec. 1790; first appeared on stage at Bath theatre 1803 as Don Cæsar in *The castle of Andalusia;* first appeared in London 1816 as the Officer in *The Slave;* went to United States 1827; director of music at Tremont theatre, Boston 1828 and at other houses there. *d.* Bromfield house, Boston 27 July 1862. *Ireland's New York Stage i, 224, 556 (1866).*

COMPTON, HENRY, stage name of Charles Mackenzie (6 *child of John Mackenzie of Huntingdon).* *b.* Huntingdon 22 March 1805; clerk in office of Mr. Symonds of Aldermanbury, London, cloth merchant; acted on the Bedford, Lincoln and York circuits 1826–37; first appeared in London at Lyceum theatre 24 July 1837 as Robin in *The Waterman;* played at Drury Lane 1837–8, 1839 and 1843–4, at Lyceum 1838–9, at Princess's 1844–7, at Olympic 1847–50 and 1850–3, at Strand 1849–50, at Haymarket 1853–70, at

COMPTON, H. *(Con.)*

Globe 1871, at Lyceum 1874; went on a tour with the Vezin-Chippendale company; last appeared at Prince of Wales's theatre, Liverpool 14 July 1877; the best Shakespearean clown of his time. *d.* 12 Stanford road, Victoria road, Kensington 15 Sep. 1877. *Memoir of H. Compton edited by C. and E. Compton 1879, portrait; Actors by daylight i, 289 (1838), portrait; Tallis's Drawing room table book, part 11, portrait as Launce; The Players ii, 25 (1860), portrait; Theatrical times ii, 1 (1847), portrait.*

COMPTON, HENRY COMBE. *b.* 6 Jany. 1789; ed. at Eton and Merton coll. Ox; M.P. for South Hants. 1835–57. *d.* Minstead manor house, Lyndhurst, Hants. 27 Nov. 1866.

COMYN, SIR ROBERT BUCKLEY (3 son of Rev. Thomas Comyn, V. of Tottenham, Middlesex who *d.* 16 Feb. 1798). *b.* Tottenham 26 June 1792; ed. at Merchant Taylors' school; commoner of St. John's coll. Ox. 1809; B.A. 1813, M.A. 1815, D.C.L. 1842; barrister L.I. 24 Nov. 1814; puisne judge of supreme court of Madras 19 Aug. 1825, chief justice 31 Dec. 1835 to Jany. 1842 when he resigned; knighted at Carlton house 9 Feb. 1825; bencher of M.T. 1844; author of *Treatise on law of Usury* 1817; *Treatise on the law of landlord and tenant* 1830; *History of Western Europe from the birth of Charlemagne to the accession of Charles v,* 1841. *d.* 9 New st. Spring gardens, London 23 May 1853.

CONDER, JOSIAH (4 son of Thomas Conder of London, engraver, who *d.* June 1831 aged 84). *b.* Falcon st. Aldersgate, London 17 Sep. 1789; lost his right eye by small pox 1795; assisted his father in a bookselling business at 30 Bucklersbury 1802–11, carried on the business alone 1811–19; edited *Eclectic Review* 1814–37; edited *Patriot* newspaper, Jany. 1833 to death; edited *Modern Traveller* 30 vols. 1825–9; author of *Gloria in excelsis Deo, a poem* 1812; *The law of the Sabbath* 1830, 2 ed. 1852; *Italy* 3 vols. 1831; *A dictionary of geography* 1834; *An analytical view of all religions* 1838. *d.* 28 Belsize road, St. John's Wood, London 27 Dec. 1855. *Josiah Conder, a memoir by E. R. Conder 1857.*

CONDY, NICHOLAS. *b.* Torpoint, Cornwall 1793; ensign 43 foot 9 May 1811, lieut. 24 Feb. 1813 to 25 Dec. 1818 when placed on h.p.; a painter at Plymouth; chiefly produced small water-colours on tinted paper about 8 inches by 5, which he sold at prices ranging from fifteen shillings to one guinea each; exhibited 2 landscapes at R.A., 4 at B.I. and 1 at Suffolk st. gallery 1830–45; published

CONDY, N. *(Con.)*

Cotehele on the banks of the Tamar with a descriptive account by the Rev. F. V. J. Arundell, 17 plates. d. 10 Mount Pleasant terrace, Plymouth 8 Jany. 1857 aged 64.

CONDY, NICHOLAS MATTHEWS *(son of the preceding). b.* Union st. Plymouth 1818; a painter at Plymouth; exhibited three sea pieces at R.A. 1842–5, which gave hopes of his becoming a distinguished artist. *d.* The Grove, Plymouth 20 May 1851. *Reminiscences of a yachting cruise by Mrs. N. M. Condy with drawings by T. G. Dutton from sketches by N. M. Condy 1852, portrait.*

CONGLETON, JOHN VESEY PARNELL, 2 Baron *(eld. son of 1 Baron Congleton 1776–1842). b.* Baker st. London 16 June 1805; ed. at Edin.; received a commission in the army which he never took up; became acquainted with A. N. Groves in Dublin 1827, conveyed him to Russia in the yacht The Osprey 1829; took a room in Aungier st. Dublin for The Brethren 1829; travelled in the East 1830–4 and in India 1834–7; resided at Teignmouth where he lived with great simplicity, preached to The Brethren congregations and spent nearly all his capital in good works 1837–42; succeeded 8 June 1842; resided at Islington 1842–6, at Brighton 1846–9, in London 1849 to death; minister in the Orchard st. chapel, London 1849–60, in the Welbeck st. chapel 1860 to death; gave one half his income in charity; author of *The resurrection life, a tract* 1845, 13 *editions; The true idea of Baptism* 1850; *The Psalms, a new version* 1860, *another ed.* 1875, and of many tracts. *d.* 53 Great Cumberland place, London 23 Oct. 1883. *bur.* Kensal Green cemetery where upwards of 1000 Plymouth Brethren attended. *Memoir of Lord Congleton by H. Groves* 1884, *portrait.*

CONGREVE, GEORGE. Ensign 29 foot 8 April 1825, lieut.-col. 11 Feb. 1846 to 29 Sep. 1859 when placed on h.p.; C.B. 24 May 1847; quartermaster general East Indies 28 Nov. 1854 to 1860; M.G. 20 July 1860. *d.* Simla 30 April 1861.

CONGREVE, SIR WILLIAM AUGUSTUS, 3 Baronet *(eld. son of Sir Wm. Congreve 2 baronet 1772–1828). b.* 1827; succeeded 16 May 1828; last heard of in 1860 when he was in Sydney and proposed going to Omaha in Fiji islands; advertised for in *The Times* 17 Feb. 1882 p. 1 col. 2. Sir James Hannen judge of the Court of Probate directed letters of administration to issue 30 Nov. 1882, presuming that his death took place 14 Feb. 1860 when he wrote his last letter home.

CONINGHAM, HENRY. Entered Madras army 1819; col. 7 Madras light cavalry 24 Oct. 1858 to death; L.G. 6 Nov. 1866. *d.* Nice 21 April 1868 aged 70.

CONINGHAM, WILLIAM *(son of Rev. Robert Coningham of Londonderry). b.* Rose hill near Penzance 1815; cornet 1 dragoons 1834–6; contested Brighton, July 1847 and Westminster, July 1852; M.P. for Brighton 28 March 1857 to Jany. 1864; published *Twelve letters by John Sterling* [to William Coningham] 1851, 3 ed. [1872]; *Lord Palmerston and Prince Albert…Letters by W. Coningham, together with "The suppressed pamphlet," entitled "Palmerston, what has he done?" by "One of the people"* 1854, and other books. *d.* 6 Lewes crescent, Kemp Town, Brighton 20 Dec. 1884.

CONINGTON, FRANCIS THIRKILL *(3 son of Rev. Richard Conington, Minister of chapel of ease, Boston, Lincs. who d. 25 Sep. 1861 aged 65).* Matric. from C.C. coll. Ox. 12 June 1846 aged 18; fellow of his coll. 1849 to death; B.A. 1850, M.A. 1853; examiner in science in Univ. of Ox. 1860–1; author of *Handbook of chemical analysis* 1858; contributed to periodicals 1860 to death. *d.* Boston 20 Nov. 1863 aged 35.

CONINGTON, JOHN *(brother of the preceding). b.* Boston 10 Aug. 1825; ed. at Beverley gr. sch., Rugby and Magd. coll. Ox., demy, June 1843; Hertford and Ireland scholar 1844; scholar of Univ. coll. March 1846, fellow May 1847 to 1855; sec. of Union Society 1845, pres. 1846, librarian 1847; B.A. 1847, M.A. 1850; Eldon law scholar for 6 months 1849; student at L.I. June 1849 but not called to bar; contributed to *Morning Chronicle* 1849–50; Corpus professor of Latin in Univ. of Ox. June 1854 to death; published *The Agamemnon of Æschylus translated into English verse* 1848; *On the academical study of Latin* 1855; *The works of Virgil with a commentary* 3 vols. 1858–70; *The odes and carmen seculare of Horace translated into English verse* 1863, 4 ed. 1870; *The Æneid of Virgil translated into English verse* 1866, 3 ed. 1870. *d.* Boston 23 Oct. 1869. *bur.* Fishtoft churchyard 26 Oct. *Miscellaneous writings of John Conington edited by J. A. Symonds with a memoir by H. J. S. Smith* 2 vols. 1872; *Memoirs of Mark Pattison* (1885) 245–52.

CONNELL, ARTHUR *(eld. son of Sir John Connell, judge of the admiralty court of Scotland). b.* Edinburgh 30 Nov. 1794; ed. at High sch. and Univ. of Edin.; Snell exhibitioner at Univ. of Glasgow; matric. from Balliol coll. Ox. 20 March 1812; passed advocate at Scotch bar

CONNELL, A. (*Con.*)

1817 but never practised; professor of chemistry in Univ. of St. Andrews 1840–56; F.R.S. Edin. 1829, F.R.S. 1855; established several new mineral species; author of *A treatise on the election laws in Scotland* 1827, many papers in *Trans. of Royal Soc. of Edin.* and in *Edin. Philos. Journal.* *d.* St. Andrew's, Fife 31 Oct. 1863.

CONNELLAN, OWEN. *b.* co. Sligo 1800; employed as a scribe in Royal Irish academy more than 20 years; Irish historiographer to George iv and William iv 1821–37; professor of Irish in Queen's college, Cork 1849 to death; author of *The gospel according to St. John, in Irish with an English translation* 1830; *A Dissertation on Irish grammar* 1834; *The annals of Ireland translated from the original Irish of the Four Masters* 1846; *The proceedings of the Great Bardic Institution* 1854 being vol. 5 of *Transactions of Ossianic Society.* *d.* Dublin 1869.

CONNELLAN, THADDEUS. Author of *The two first books of the Pentateuch, the types cut from Irish MSS.* 1820; *The Irish-English guide to the Irish language* 1824; *The King's Letter translated into Irish* 1825; *The Irish-English spelling book* 1825; *The Irish-English primer* 1825; *Easy lessons on money matters, commerce, trade, wages etc.* 1835; *Psalma Daibi* 1836; *The Gospel of St. Matthew in Irish* 1840; *The Acts of the Apostles in Irish* 1840. *d.* Sligo 25 July 1854.

CONNOLLY, WILLIAM HALLETT. Second lieut. R.M. 8 May 1795, lieut.-col. 16 April 1832, col. commandant of Woolwich division 10 July 1837 to 1842 when he retired on full pay; general 20 June 1855. *d.* King's terrace, Southsea 20 June 1861 aged 79.

CONNOP, RICHARD. Ensign 93 foot 30 Dec. 1813, captain 25 Sep. 1817 to 19 Sep. 1826 when placed on h.p.; L.G. 31 March 1866. *d.* Dawlish 5 Feb. 1867 aged 75.

CONNOR, VERY REV. GEORGE HENRY (*eld. son of George Connor, master in chancery in Ireland*). *b.* 21 Dec. 1822; ed. at Trin. coll. Dublin, B.A. 1845, M.A. 1851; M.A. at Ox. 1859; V. of Newport, Isle of Wight 1852–82; hon. chaplain to the Queen 11 Oct. 1872, chaplain in ord. 8 Feb. 1875, resident chaplain in ord. 2 Nov. 1882 to death; dean of Windsor 30 Oct. 1882, installed 10 Nov. 1882. *d.* The deanery, Windsor castle 1 May 1883. *Church portrait journal i, 93* (1880), *portrait; Graphic xxvi, 412* (1882), *portrait.*

CONNOR, SKEFFINGTON. *b.* Dublin 1810; ed. at Trin. coll. Dublin, B.A. 1828, LL.B. and

CONNOR, S. (*Con.*)

LL.D. 1845; called to Irish bar 1838; called to Canadian bar at Toronto 1842; bencher of Canadian law society 1850, Q.C. 1850; represented South Oxford in legislative assembly 1856–63; solicitor general for Upper Canada 1858; puisne judge of Court of Queen's Bench, Upper Canada 1 Feb. 1863. *d.* Toronto 29 April 1863.

CONOLLY, HENRY VALENTINE (*son of Valentine Conolly of 37 Portland place, London, who d. 2 Dec. 1819*). *b.* 5 Dec. 1806; ed. at Rugby; a writer in Madras civil service 19 May 1824; collector and magistrate in Malabar 1841 to death; murdered by some Mopla fanatics in his house at Calicut 11 Sep. 1855; there is a monument to him in the cathedral Madras, and a scholarship was founded in his memory at the Madras University.

CONOLLY, JAMES. *b.* 19 Feb. 1818; cornet 5 dragoon guards 17 June 1836; deputy adjutant general Canada 6 Dec. 1861 to 20 May 1865; assistant quartermaster general at Aldershot 7 Nov. 1867 to 31 Aug. 1869; military attaché at Vienna 1869–71, at Paris 5 April 1871 to 30 Dec. 1880; L.G. 26 Dec. 1880; placed on retired list with hon. rank of general 19 Feb. 1885; C.B. 29 May 1875. *d.* Wiesbaden 22 June 1885.

CONOLLY, JOHN (*son of Mr. Conolly of Market Rasen, Lincs. who d. 1799*). *b.* Market Rasen 27 May 1794; ensign in Cambridgeshire militia 1812–16; studied at Univ. of Edin. 1817–21, M.D. 1821; physician at Chichester 1822–23, at Stratford-on-Avon 1823–7; professor of practice of medicine in Univ. coll. London 1828–30; practised at Warwick 1830–8; resident phys. to Middlesex county asylum at Hanwell 1 June 1839 to 1844, where he entirely abolished restraint; kept a private asylum at Lawn house near Hanwell 1852 to death; an original member of British medical Assoc. 1832, of Ethnological Soc. 1843; author of *The construction and government of lunatic asylums* 1847; *The treatment of the insane without mechanical restraints* 1856; *A study of Hamlet* 1863. *d.* Lawn House near Hanwell 5 March 1866. *Sir James Clark's Memoir of J. Conolly* 1869; *Medical Circular ii, 469–70* (1853), *portrait; I.L.N. xlviii, 317* (1866), *portrait.*

CONOLLY, THOMAS. *b.* Kilcooly abbey, Tipperary 23 Feb. 1823; ed. at Harrow and Ch. Ch. Ox.; sheriff of Donegal 1848; M.P. for Donegal 20 Feb. 1849 to death. *d.* Castletown house, Celbridge, Kildare 10 Aug. 1876.

CONQUEST, BENJAMIN OLIVER, stage name of Benjamin Oliver. *b.* near St. Michael's church, Cornhill, London 1805; first appeared on the stage as a witch in *Macbeth* at Lyceum theatre; acted at Pavilion theatre 1827; sang song of *Billy Barlow* 4 times every night for 28 weeks; projected and opened with Wyman and Freer the Garrick theatre, Whitechapel 1830, proprietor of it with Gomersal to 4 Nov. 1846 when it was burned down; landlord of "The Hampshire Hog" tavern 410 Strand, London 1847–51; lessee of Grecian theatre, City road, London at rent of £1300, 4 March 1851 to death. *d.* New north road, London 5 July 1872. *Actors by daylight i,* 337 (1839) *portrait.*

CONQUEST, JOHN TRICKER. *b.* Chatham, Kent 1789; assistant surgeon military depot, Chatham 1808; studied at Univ. of Edin., M.D.1813; L.C.P. London, Dec. 1819; gave 4 courses of lectures on midwifery yearly at his house 4 Aldermanbury Postern, London about 1820–4; lecturer on midwifery at St. Bartholomew's hospital 1825; noted for his operation of tapping for hydrocephalus; author of *Outlines of midwifery* 1820, 6 ed. 1854; *The Holy Bible with twenty thousand emendations* 1841; *Letters to a mother on the management of herself and her children in health and disease* 1848, 4 ed. 1852. *d.* The Oaks, Plumstead common 24 Oct. 1866 aged 77. *Medical Circular iii,* 51–53 (1853), *portrait; Physic and physicians ii,* 265–67 (1839).

CONRAN, GEORGE. Second lieut. Madras artillery 27 July 1811, col. commandant 15 May 1851 to death; general 14 Dec. 1868. *d.* Bath 28 Aug. 1869 aged 76.

CONROY, SIR EDWARD, 2 Baronet *(eld. son of Sir John Conroy 1 baronet 1786–1854). b.* Dublin 6 Dec. 1809; ed. at Ch. Ch. Ox., B.A. 1830, M.A. 1834; attaché to special mission to Brussels 1831–8; deputy registrar of births, deaths and marriages in London 1836–42. *d.* Arborfield near Reading 3 Nov. 1869.

CONROY, RIGHT REV. GEORGE *(son of Nicholas Conroy).* Professor of dogmatic theology, All Hallow's college, Dublin 1857–66; sec. to Cardinal Cullen, and professor of dogmatic theology in Holy Cross college, Clonliffe 1866–7; bishop of Ardagh 1871 to death; consecrated in St. Mel's cathedral, Longford 11 April 1871; author of *Occasional sermons, addresses and essays* 1884. *d.* St. John's, Newfoundland 4 Aug. 1878.

CONROY, SIR JOHN, 1 Baronet *(eld. son of John Ponsonby Conroy of Bettyfield, co. Roscommon 1759–97). b.* Caerhyn, Carnarvonshire 21 Oct.

CONROY, SIR JOHN *(Con.)*
1786; second lieut. R.A. 8 Sep. 1803, second captain 13 March 1811 to 17 June 1822 when placed on permanent h.p.; K.C.H. 17 Aug. 1827; comptroller of the household to Duchess of Kent to 1837 when he retired on pension of £3000; created baronet.7 July 1837; comr. of Colonial audit board; sheriff of Montgomeryshire 1843; col. of Montgomeryshire militia 30 Aug. 1852. *d.* Arborfield near Reading 2 March 1854.

CONSTABLE, HENRY *(son of a small tradesman). b.* Birmingham 10 April 1851; taught riding by T. Stevens on the Ilsley Downs; apprenticed to Wm. Reeves at Epsom 1867–71; first rode at Wye meeting on Skittles 1870; headed list of winning jockeys 1873, taking 110 races out of 395 mounts; won the Derby on Mr. W. S. Crawfurd's Sefton 1878; first jockey and trainer to Lord Rosebery. *d.* Epsom 17 Feb. 1881. *Illust. sporting and dramatic news i,* 61 (1874), *portrait, iii,* 261 (1875), *portrait, xiv,* 563, 572 (1881), *portrait; Baily's Mag. xxv* (1874), *portrait.*

CONSTABLE, THOMAS *(younngest son of Archibald Constable of Edinburgh, publisher 1774–1827). b.* Craigcrook near Edin. 29 June 1812; learned printing with C. Richards of St. Martin's lane, London; printer and publisher in Edin. to 1860; Her Majesty's printer and publisher 7 Sep. 1839; issued *Constable's Miscellany of foreign literature* 10 vols. 1854–5; issued *Constable's Educational series* 36 vols. 1857–72; published *The works of Dugald Stewart edited by Sir W. Hamilton* 10 vols. 1854; author of *Archibald Constable and his literary correspondents* 3 vols. 1873; *Memoir of Lewis D. B. Gordon* 1877, *privately printed; Memoir of Rev. C. A. C. de Boinville* 1880. *d.* Marston Biggot rectory, Frome, Somerset 26 May 1881.

CONSTABLE, SIR THOMAS ASTON CLIFFORD, 2 Baronet. *b.* Tixall hall, Staffs. 3 May 1806; succeeded 25 Feb. 1823. *d.* Burton Constable, Yorkshire 22 Dec. 1870.

CONWAY, FREDERICK B. *(son of Wm. A. Conway, actor 1780–1828). b.* London 10 Feb. 1819; made his first appearance at Princess's theatre 4 Oct. 1847; went to the United States 1850 where he acted with Edwin Forrest playing Iago to his Othello, De Mauprat to his Richelieu aud other companion parts; opened Pike's opera house Cincinnati 1859; played at Sadler's Wells theatre, London 1861; played leading parts at New Brooklyn theatre, New York 1864–73. *d.* Manchester, Massachusetts 6 Sep. 1874.

CONWAY, THOMAS SYDENHAM. *b.* 7 June 1810; ensign 22 foot 14 Feb. 1828 ; deputy adjutant general Bombay 1849–51 ; captain Grenadier guards 14 July 1854 to 8 March 1864 when placed on h.p. ; placed on retired list with hon. rank of general 7 June 1880 ; C.B. 4 July 1843. *d.* 19 Bury st. St. James's, London 7 June 1885.

CONY, BARKHAM. *b.* Ely 5 Nov. 1802 ; made his first appearance in London 1828 at Coburg theatre in *Love me, love my dog ;* first appeared in America 1835 with a number of well-trained dogs who assisted in the performance which consisted of *Forest of Bondy* and *Cherokee Chief;* played successful engagements all over the United States and Great Britain ; styled the " Dog Star." *d.* Chicago 1 Jany. 1858.

CONYBEARE, VERY REV. WILLIAM DANIEL *(son of Rev. Wm. Conybeare, R. of St. Botolph, Bishopsgate, London, who d. 5 April 1815 aged 76).* *b.* London 7 June 1787 ; ed. at Westminster and Ch. Ch. Ox., B.A. 1808, M.A. 1811 ; founded with Sir Henry de la Beche, Bristol Philosophical and Literary Institution 1817 ; corresponding member of French Institute ; V. of Sully, Glamorganshire 1821–36 ; V. of Axminster 1836–44 ; Bampton lecturer 1839 ; dean of Llandaff 29 Sep. 1844 to death ; F.R.S. 9 Dec. 1819, F.G.S. 1821 ; gave the name of Plesiosaurus to a new genus of reptilia forming an intermediate link between the Ichthyosaurus and Crocodile ; author of *Elementary course of theological lectures* 1836 ; *Geological memoir of the landslip in Devon* 1840 ; author with Wm. Phillips of *Outlines of the geology of England and Wales* 1822. *d.* Itchenstoke near Portsmouth 12 Aug. 1857. *Quarterly Journal of Geol. Soc. xiv,* 24–32 (1858) ; *Proc. of Royal Soc. ix,* 50–2 (1857) ; *G.M. iii,* 335–7 (1857) ; *I.L.N. xxxi,* 309 (1857), *portrait.*

CONYBEARE, REV. WILLIAM JOHN *(eld. son of the preceding).* *b.* 1 Aug. 1815 ; ed. at Westminster and Trin. coll. Cam., fellow, 15 wrangler and 3 classic 1837, B.A. 1837, M.A. 1840 ; Whitehall preacher 1841 ; principal of the newly founded Liverpool Collegiate Institution 1842–8 ; V. of Axminster 1848–54 ; author of *Essays ecclesiastical and social* 1855 ; *Perversion, or the causes and consequences of infidelity, a tale for the times* 3 vols. 1856 *anon. ;* author with Rev. J. S. Howson of *The life and epistles of St. Paul* 2 vols. 1852. *d.* of consumption at Weybridge 22 July 1857.

CONYNGHAM, FRANCIS NATHANIEL CONYNGHAM, 2 Marquis (2 *son of* 1 *Marquis Conyngham* 1766–1832). *b.* Dublin 11 June 1797; cornet 2 life guards 21 Sep. 1820, lieut. 13

CONYNGHAM, 2 Marquis *(Con.)*
Dec. 1821 to 12 June 1823 when placed on h.p. ; under sec. of state for foreign affairs 6 Jany. 1823 to 2 Jany. 1826 ; M.P. for co. Donegal 1825 to 1832 ; a lord of the treasury 30 April 1826 to 30 April 1827 ; succeeded 28 Dec. 1832 ; postmaster general 5 July to 31 Dec. 1834 and 8 to 30 May 1835 ; lord chamberlain of the household, May 1835 to 6 May 1839 ; G.C.H. 1823 ; K.P. 27 March 1833 ; P.C. 20 May 1835 ; lord lieut. of co. Meath 27 May 1869 to death ; general 21 March 1874. *d.* 5 Hamilton place, Piccadilly, London 17 July 1876, personalty sworn under £500,000, 9 Sep. 1876. *I.L.N. lxix,* 113, 119, 255 (1876), *portrait ; Graphic xiv,* 102, 108 (1876), *portrait.*

CONYNGHAM, GEORGE HENRY CONYNGHAM, 3 Marquis. *b.* London 3 Feb. 1825 ; cornet 2 dragoons 31 Dec. 1844 ; major 1 life guards 24 Aug. 1861 to 13 June 1868 when placed on h.p. ; equerry to the Queen 30 Sep. 1872 to death ; succeeded 17 July 1876 ; col. Royal East Kent yeomanry cavalry 16 Jany. 1878 to death ; placed on retired list with hon. rank of L.G. 1 July 1881. *d.* Belgrave sq. London 2 June 1882.

CONYNGHAM, FRANCIS NATHANIEL *(brother of the preceding).* *b.* Goodwood 24 Sep. 1832 ; served in R.N. 1846–60 ; M.P. for Clare 1857–9 and 1874–80. *d.* The Muirshiel, Lockwinnock, Renfrewshire 14 Sep. 1880.

COODE, GEORGE *(eld. son of Manners Benson Coode of St. Helier's, Jersey).* *b.* 1807 ; barrister I.T. 7 June 1833 ; assistant sec. to Poor law commission 18 Aug. 1834 to 13 June 1846 ; drafted the Irish poor law act, 1 & 2 Vict. c. 56 ; comr. for consolidating the statute law 1853 ; comr. for inquiry into state of education in England 1859 ; author of *Report on the law of settlement and removal of the poor* 1851 ; *On legislative expression* 1853 ; article on the *Poor laws* in Encyclopædia Britannica, 8 ed. xviii, 295–316 (1859) ; *Report of local taxation and digest of the laws relating to* 24 *local taxes* 1862 ; *Report on the fire insurance duties* 1862. *d.* Roselands, Walmer, Kent 27 Sep. 1869. *Law mag. and law review xxviii,* 178, 318–25 (1870).

COODE, SIR JOHN HENRY *(son of Edward Coode of Penryn, Cornwall).* *b.* Penryn 11 Feb. 1779 ; entered navy 16 June 1793 ; captain 21 Oct. 1810 ; R.A. 26 June 1847 ; V.A. on h.p. 27 May 1854, pensioned 10 Dec. 1855 ; C.B. 19 Sep. 1816, K.C.B. 5 July 1855. *d.* Plymouth 19 Jany. 1858.

COOK, ALEXANDER SHANK *(son of Rev. George Cook, professor of moral philosophy at St. Andrews). b.* 9 Dec. 1810; ed. at St. Andrews; advocate at Edin. 1834; procurator for church of Scotland 1861 to death; advocate depute; sheriff of Ross and Cromarty 22 March 1858 to death. *d.* Edinburgh 16 Jany. 1869.

COOK, EDWARD DUTTON *(eld. child of George Simon Cook of Tudor st. Blackfriars, London, solicitor, who d.* 12 Sep. 1852). *b.* 9 Grenville st. Brunswick sq. London 30 Jany. 1829; articled to his father; pupil of Rolt the painter; dramatic critic of *Pall Mall Gazette* 1867 to Oct. 1875, of *The World* Oct. 1875 to death; edited *Cornhill Mag.* 1868–71; wrote all the lives of dramatists and actors in letter A of *Dictionary of national biography* 1885; author of *Paul Foster's Daughter* 3 vols. 1861; *Leo* 3 vols. 1863; *Hobson's Choice, a story* 1867; *Art in England, notes and studies* 1869; *A book of the play* 2 vols. 1876; *Hours with the players* 2 vols. 1881; *On the stage* 1883 and 9 other books. *d.* suddenly outside his house 69 Gloucester crescent, Regent's park, London 11 Sep. 1883. *Longman's Mag. Dec.* 1883 *pp.* 179–87; *Theatre, Nov.* 1883, 212, 272, *portrait; Graphic xxviii,* 321 (1883), *portrait.*

COOK, HENRY DAVID. Writer Madras civil service 1835; civil and sessions judge, Calicut 1857–66; civil and sessions judge, Coimbatore 1866 to 18 Sep. 1870 when he retired on annuity. *d.* England 16 June 1882.

COOK, JAMES. Edited *Paisley and Renfrewshire Gazette* from its commencement Oct. 1864 to his death; author of *Bibliography of the writings of Charles Dickens* 1879. *d.* Paisley 25 Oct. 1882 aged 65.

COOK, REV. JOHN *(eld. son of Rev. John Cook 1771–1824, professor of biblical criticism in Univ. of St. Andrews). b.* St. Andrews 1 Sep. 1807; ed. at Univ. of St. Andrews, A.M. 1823, D.D. 9 Dec. 1848; licensed for ministry of Church of Scotland 13 Aug. 1828; minister of Laurencekirk 1829–45; minister of St. Leonard's in St. Andrews 1845–63; moderator of General Assembly 19 May 1859, convener of many of its important committees; Emeritus professor of ecclesiastical history in Univ. of St. Andrews 19 June 1860 to 30 July 1868; a dean of the chapel royal, Sep. 1863; author of *Evidence on church patronage* 1838; *Six lectures on the Christian evidences* 1852. *d.* St. Andrews 17 April 1869.

COOK, REV. JOHN *(eld. son of Rev. George Cook 1772–1845, leader of the 'moderate' party in the*

COOK, REV. J. *(Con.)*
Church of Scotland). b. 12 Sep. 1807; ed. at St. Andrews Univ., A.M. 1823, D.D. 1843; licensed for ministry of Church of Scotland 17 Sep. 1828; minister of Cults, Fifeshire 1832; translated to second charge at Haddington 1833, to the first charge 1843; sub-clerk of the Assembly 25 May 1859, principal clerk 22 May 1862, moderator 24 May 1866; author of *Styles of writs and forms of procedure in the church courts of Scotland* 1850, 4 *ed.* 1870. *d.* Haddington 11 Sep. 1874.

COOK, JOHN DOUGLAS. *b.* Banchory-Ternan, Aberdeenshire 25 March 1811; held an appointment in India; sec. of commission to inquire into revenues of Duchy of Cornwall; private sec. to Lord Lincoln, governor of Ionian Islands; reported in parliament for *The Times;* edited *Morning Chronicle* 1852–5; edited *Saturday Review* from first number 3 Nov. 1855 to death, joint owner of it with A. J. B. Beresford Hope, M.P. *d.* G1 The Albany, Piccadilly, London 10 Aug. 1868. *bur.* Tintagel churchyard. *James Grant's The Saturday Review its origin and progress* 1873.

COOK, PAUL *(son of Charles Cook of Jersey, Wesleyan minister).* President of French Methodist Conference; considered the founder of French Sunday schools. *d.* Paris 2 May 1886 aged 59.

COOK, RICHARD. *b.* London 1784; ed. at Royal Academy; gold medallist of Society of Arts 1832; A.R.A. 1816, R.A. 1822; exhibited pictures chiefly historical; illustrated *Scott's Lady of the Lake* 1810. *d.* Cumberland place, Hyde park, London 11 March 1857. *Sandby's History of Royal Academy ii,* 34 (1862).

COOK, SAMUEL. *b.* Camelford, Cornwall 1806; apprenticed to a woollen manufacturer at Camelford 1815; a painter and glazier at Plymouth; exhibited pictures chiefly coast scenes at New Water-Colour Society in Pall Mall, London about 1830–59, a member of the Society 1850; his "Early morning at the Lizard" was sold to Rev. Henry Tozer for 137 guineas at Plymouth 7 Feb. 1882. *d.* near Plymouth 7 June 1859. *Hayle Miscellany vol.* 2 (1860), *portrait.*

COOK, THOMAS. Entered navy 17 July 1807; lieutenant 1 June 1818; professor of fortification and artilley at H.E.I. Co.'s military academy, Addiscombe, Jany. 1837 to death; F.R.S. 4 June 1840. *d.* Abbey road, St. John's Wood, London 11 Dec. 1858.

COOKE, EDWARD. Barrister M.T. 12 Nov. 1819; judge of county courts, circuit 11, Bradford 1854 to 1861 when he resigned; author of *The real cause of the high price of gold* 1819; *A treatise on the law of insolvent debtors* 1827, 2 *ed.* 1839. *d.* 2 Taviton st. Gordon sq. London 6 Feb. 1862 aged 70.

COOKE, EDWARD WILLIAM (*son of George Cooke of London, line engraver* 1781–1834). *b.* Pentonville, London 27 March 1811; painted sign of the "Old Ship Hotel" at Brighton 1825; etched 2 series of plates entitled "Coast sketches" and "The British Coast"; made 70 drawings of new London bridge 1825–31, most of which were engraved and published 1833; executed a series of pencil drawings for Earl de Grey 1832; travelled abroad 1832–44; A.R.A. 1851, R.A. 1864; exhibited 129 pictures at R.A., 115 at B.I. and 3 at Suffolk st. gallery; 2 of his pictures are in the National Gallery, "Dutch boats in calm" and "The Boat house"; F.R.S. 4 June 1863; published *Views in London and its vicinity* 1834; *Grotesque animals invented, drawn and described* 1872; *Leaves from my sketch book* 2 series 1876–7. *d.* Glen Andred, Groombridge near Tunbridge Wells 4 Jany. 1880. *I.L.N. xlv*, 173 (1864), *portrait; Graphic xxi*, 252 (1880), *portrait.*

COOKE, GEORGE. *b.* Manchester 7 March 1807; first appeared on the stage at Walsall, March 1828; acted at Strand theatre, London 1837, at Drury Lane 1839, at Marylebone 1847; played at Strand theatre 1848, at Olympic theatre to death. (*m.* 1840 Eliza Stuart, she *d.* 13 June 1877 aged 74); committed suicide 4 March 1863. *Theatrical Times iii*, 376, 397 (1848), *portrait.*

COOKE, REV. GEORGE LEIGH (*son of Rev. Samuel Cooke, V. of Great Bookham, Surrey, who d.* 30 *March* 1820). Matric. from Ball. coll. Ox. 26 Jany. 1797 aged 17; scholar of C.C. coll. 1797, fellow 1800–15, tutor; B.A. 1800, M.A. 1804, B.D. 1812; Sedleian professor of natural philosophy in Univ. of Ox. 1818–26; keeper of the Univ. archives 1818–26; V. of Cubbington, Warws. 1820 to death; V. of Rissington Wick, Gloucs. 1820 to death; P.C. of Hunningham, Warcs. 1820 to death; founded the Literary Dining Club, sec. of it many years; author of *The three first sections aud part of the seventh section of Newton's Principia* 1850. *d.* Cubbington 29 March 1853 aged 73.

COOKE, GEORGE WINGROVE (*eld. son of T. H. Cooke of Bristol*). *b.* Bristol 1814; ed. at Jesus coll. Ox., B.A. 1834; barrister M.T. 30 Jany. 1835; contested Colchester, Feb. 1860,

Marylebone, April 1861; special correspondent of *The Times* in China 1857–8; copyhold and inclosure comr. Dec. 1862 to death; author of *Memoirs of Lord Bolingbroke* 1835, 2 *ed.* 1836; *The history of party from the rise of the Whig and Tory factions to the passing of the Reform bill* 3 vols. 1836–37; *Act for the enclosure of commons with a treatise on the law of rights of common* 1846, 4 *ed.* 1864; *Treatise on agricultural tenancies* 1850, *new ed.* 1882; *A treatise on the law and practice of copyhold enfranchisement* 1853; *Inside Sebastopol* 1856; *China and Lower Bengal* 1858; *Conquest and colonisation in North Africa* 1860. *d.* 25 Cheyne Walk, Chelsea 18 June 1865.

COOKE, REV. HENRY (*youngest child of John Cooke of Grillagh near Maghera, co. Londonderry, farmer*). *b.* in farm house of Grillagh 11 May 1788; matric. at Glasgow college, Nov. 1802; licensed by the presbytery of Ballymena; pastor at Duneane near Randalstown, co. Antrim 1808–10; minister at Donegore, co. Antrim 1811–18; studied at Glasgow and Trin. coll. Dublin 1815–18; pastor of Killyleigh, co. Down 1818–29; moderator of general synod of Ulster, June 1824; pastor of May st. chapel, Belfast 24 Nov. 1829 to Feb. 1868; D.D. Jefferson college, U.S. 21 Oct. 1829; LL.D. Dublin 9 Feb. 1837; granted freedom of city of Dublin 6 Feb. 1839; challenged O'Connell to a public discussion in Belfast 6 Jany. 1841, which he declined; moderator of the general assembly 1841; agent for distribution of *Regium Donum* 29 Nov. 1845 to death; professor of sacred rhetoric, assembly's college, Belfast, Sep. 1847 to death, pres. of the college 1848 to death; dean of residence for presbyterian church, Queen's college, Belfast 1849; author of *Translations and paraphrases in verse for the use of the Presbyterian church, Killyleigh* 1821; edited *J. Brown's Self-interpreting Bible* 1855, 2 *ed.* 1873. *d.* Ormean road, Belfast 13 Dec. 1868, statue of him erected at Belfast, Sep. 1875. *J. S. Porter's Life of Rev. Henry Cooke* (1871), *portrait.*

COOKE, JAMES (*son of Thomas Taplin Cooke, circus proprietor, who d.* 19 *March* 1866 *aged* 84). Leading rider of his father's company; the only real rival of the great Andrew Ducrow; proprietor of a circus about 1837–49 and 1850–56; resided in Edinburgh 1856 to death. *d.* Portobello, Edin. 5 Sep. 1869 aged 59.

COOKE, SIR JOHN HENRY. *b.* 1791; ensign 43 foot 15 March 1809; captain 25 foot 27 July 1838 to 15 Dec. 1840 when placed on h.p.; conducted Louis xviii from Ghent to Paris, June to July 1815; sub officer of corps of gentlemen at arms 2 Oct. 1844 to 16 Sep. 1862; ensign of Yeomen of the guard 16 Sep. 1862, lieut. 2 Feb. 1866 to death; knighted at Windsor Castle 11 Dec. 1867. *d.* Albion villa, Upper heath, Hampstead 31 Jany. 1870.

COOKE, JOHN P. *b.* Chester 31 Oct. 1820; leader of the orchestras at Adelphi, Strand and Astley's, London successively; leader at Burton's theatre, New York 1850; musical director at several New York theatres; composed and arranged music for the *Winter's Tale, Midsummer Night's Dream* and other Shakespearean plays; wrote melodies for the *Sea of Ice. d.* New York 4 Nov. 1865.

COOKE, RICHARD HARVEY. Ensign 1 Foot Guards 20 Feb. 1798, captain 7 Nov. 1811 to 26 March 1818; C.B. 22 June 1815. *d.* 45 Upper Brook st. London 8 Oct. 1856.

COOKE, REV. ROBERT. *b.* Waterford about 1820; joined the Congregation of Oblates of Mary Immaculate in France, ordained priest; stationed at Grace Dieu, Leics., at Everingham park, Yorkshire 1847–51; founded mission at Howden; restored mission at Pocklington; stationed at Leeds 1851; introduced the Oblates into Ireland, result being establishment of a mission at Inchicore; established a house of his order at Kilburn, London where a new church was erected 1879; founded church of the English Martyrs, Tower Hill, London; author of *Pictures of youthful holiness* 1872; *Catholic memories of the Tower of London* 1875, translated into French 1875; *Sketches of the life of Mgr. de Mazenod, bishop of Marseilles and founder of the Oblates of Mary Immaculate* 2 vols. 1879–82. *d.* London 18 June 1882. *Gillow's English Catholics i, 557–8(1885).*

COOKE, THOMAS (*son of Mr. Cooke of Allerthorpe in the East Riding of Yorkshire, shoemaker*). *b.* Allerthorpe 8 March 1807; kept a school at Allerthorpe 1823–9; optician at York about 1836 to death; made a telescope of 25 inches aperture 1863–8 which was mounted at Gateshead 1869, it is still the largest and best in the United Kingdom; invented an automatic engine for the graduation of circles, perfected the astronomical clock, and built nearly 100 turret clocks for public institutions and churches; F.R.A.S. 1859. *d.* 19 Oct. 1868.

COOKE, THOMAS POTTER (*son of Mr. Cooke of London, surgeon, who d.* 1793). *b.* Titchfield st. Marylebone 23 April 1786; served in navy 1796–1802, present in battle off Cape St. Vincent 1797; made his début at Royalty

theatre, Wellclose sq. Jany. 1804; stage manager of Surrey theatre 1809–16; acted at Lyceum 1820–2, at Covent Garden 1822–5; played Le Monstre (Frankenstein) 80 nights, at Porte Saint Martin theatre, Paris 1825–6; played at Adelphi 1828–9; his best known part was William in Douglas Jerrold's drama *Black-eyed Susan*, which he acted over 100 nights from 6 June 1829 at Surrey theatre; acted at Covent Garden 1829–34 and 1836, at Drury Lane 1834–6; made his last appearance on the stage 2 May 1861 at Princess's theatre; he is described by Christopher North in *Noctes Ambrosianæ* as 'the best sailor out of all sight and hearing that ever trod the stage.' *d.* 37 Thurloe sq. London 4 April 1864. *Oxberry's Dramatic Biography iii* 109 (1825), *portrait; Stirling's Old Drury Lane ii,* 105–11 (1881); *Tallis's Illustrated life in London* (1864) 33, 36, 40, 41, 3 *portraits; Actors by daylight* 11 *Aug.* 1838 *pp.* 185–87, *portrait.*

NOTE.—He left by his will £2000 to the Dramatic College, the interest of which was to be paid for a prize nautical drama, in compliance with the terms of the grant 'True to the core, a story of the Armada,' a drama by Angiolo Robson Slous was produced at Surrey theatre, London 8 Sep. 1866, the prize having been awarded to him at Maybury college, Surrey 23 April 1866.

COOKE, THOMAS TAPLIN. Proprietor of a circus, his company consisted of his 19 sons and daughters; built the first circus in Edinburgh 1835; chartered a vessel and shipped all his circus to the United States 1837, where he performed to 1839 when his circus and all his horses were burnt at Baltimore. *d.* 2 Barossa place, Brompton, London 19 March 1866 aged 84.

COOKE, REV. WILLIAM. *b.* 1806; minister in the Methodist New Connexion body 1827 to death; filled in succession all the important offices of his denomination; author of *Christian theology explained and defended* 1846, new ed. 1879; *Discourses illustrative of sacred truth* 1871; *Explanations of difficult portions of holy scripture; A survey of the unity, harmony and growing evidence of sacred truth; The Shekinah, or the presence and manifestation of Jehovah under the several dispensations,* and other works including a number of polemical treatises in connexion with Roman Catholicism. *d.* Burslem house, Forest Hill 25 Dec. 1884.

COOKE, WILLIAM. Lessee and manager of Astley's Amphitheatre, Westminster bridge road, London 1855–60; took his farewell benefit 30 Jany. 1860. *d.* 149 Acre lane, Brixton 6 May 1886.

COOKE, WILLIAM BERNARD (*brother of George Cooke, engraver 1781–1834*). *b.* London 1778; pupil of Wm. Angus the engraver; published *The Thames* 1811 for which he engraved nearly all the plates; published with his brother George Cooke *Picturesque views on the Southern coast of England* 1814–26, chiefly from drawings by Turner; illustrated 10 other works 1812–40. *d.* Camberwell, London 2 Aug. 1855.

COOKE, SIR WILLIAM BRYAN, 8 Baronet (*younger son of Sir George Cooke 7 baronet, who d. 2 June* 1823). *b.* 3 March 1782; ed. at Ch. Ch. Ox., B.A. 1803, M.A. 1806; ensign 1 foot guards 15 Oct. 1803 to 1808 when he sold out; lieut.-col. 3 West York militia 26 Oct. 1811, col. 23 Feb. 1812 to 7 Dec. 1819; contested city of York 1818; banker at Doncaster, Retford and Worksop 1 Jany. 1819; succeeded 2 June 1823; the first mayor of Doncaster 1836, alderman 1837–8; sheriff of Yorkshire 1845; author of *The seize Quartiers of the family of Bryan Cooke* 1857. *d.* Wheatley hall near Doncaster 24 Dec. 1851. *G.M. xxxvii*, 185–6 (1852).

COOKE, SIR WILLIAM FOTHERGILL (*eld. son of Wm. Cooke, professor of medicine at Durham Univ.*) *b.* Ealing near London 1806; ed. at Durham school and Univ. of Edin.; ensign 39 Madras N.I. 8 Jany. 1826, resigned his commission 1836; partner with Charles Wheatstone, Nov. 1837, they patented magnetic needle telegraph 12 June 1837; laid down a telegraph between Paddington and West Drayton 1838–9, and from West Drayton to Slough 1842; invented with Wheatstone the single needle apparatus 1845; one of founders of Electro telegraph company 1846; received with Wheatstone the 4th royal Albert gold medal 1867; A.I.C.E. 21 May 1867; knighted at Windsor Castle 11 Nov. 1869; granted civil list pension of £100, 25 July 1871; author of *Telegraphic Railways* 1842. (*m.* 1838 Anna Louisa dau. of Joseph Wheatley of Treeton, Yorkshire, she was granted civil list pension of £50, 19 June 1880). *d.* 31 Castle st. Farnham, Surrey 25 June 1879. *W. T. Jeans's Lives of the electricians i*, 134, 323 (1887); *W. F. Cooke's The electric telegraph, was it invented by professor Wheatstone?* 2 vols. 1857; *Authorship of the practical electric telegraph of Great Britain by Rev. T. F. Cooke* 1868; *Minutes of proc. of Instit. of C.E. lviii*, 358–64 (1879).

NOTE.—The merit of initiating the idea of an international exhibition has been often warmly contested, but there is no doubt that the original proposition was made to the Committee of the Society of Arts in 1844 by Sir W. F. Cooke.

COOKE, WILLIAM JOHN. *b.* Dublin 11 April 1797; pupil of his uncle George Cooke the engraver; received from Society of Arts a gold medal for improvements in engraving upon steel 1826; employed upon the Annuals and other illustrated publications to about 1840 when he left England and settled at Darmstadt; engraved several pictures after Turner, Cox and Landseer. *d.* Darmstadt 6 April 1865.

COOKESLEY, JOHN. Entered navy 29 Jany. 1791; captain 7 Dec. 1818, retired 1 Oct. 1846; retired R.A. 8 July 1851; invented a very simple and efficacious species of raft fully described and illustrated in the *Nautical Mag. iv*, 73–77 (1835). *d.* Rackley, Portishead near Bristol 25 Nov. 1852 aged 78.

COOKESLEY, REV. WILLIAM GIFFORD. *b.* Brasted, Kent 1 Dec. 1802; ed. at Eton and King's coll. Cam., B.A. 1826, M.A. 1829; assistant master of Eton 1825–55; V. of Hayton, Yorkshire 1857–60; P.C. of St. Peter's, Hammersmith 1860–8; R. of Tempsford, Beds. 22 Oct. 1868 to death; published *Selections from Pindar* 1838; *Pindari Carmina* 1844 2 vols. 1851; *Selecta e Catullo* 1845; *A revised translation of the New Testament* 1859, and 13 other works. *d.* Tempsford rectory 16 Aug. 1880.

COOKSON, REV. HENRY WILKINSON (6 *son of Thomas Cookson of Kendal*). *b.* Kendal 10 April 1810; ed. at Kendal, Sedbergh and St. Peter's coll. Cam., 7 wrangler 1832, B.A. 1832, M.A. 1835, B.D. and D.D. 1848; tutor of his college, Master 3 Nov. 1847 to death; R. of Glaston, Rutland 1847–61; vice-chancellor of Univ. of Cam. 1848, 1863, 1864, 1872, 1873; member of council of the Senate almost continuously from institution of that body 1856; pres. of Cambridge Philosophical Soc. 1865–6; declined bishopric of Lichfield 1867. *d.* St. Peter's college lodge, Cambridge 30 Sep. 1876.

COOKSON, ISAAC. *b.* 1776; a glass manufacturer at Newcastle to 1845; sheriff of Newcastle 1801, alderman 22 Sep. 1807, mayor 1809–10; bought Meldon park, Northumberland for 56,900 guineas 19 April 1832; sheriff of Northumberland 1838. *d.* Munich 8 Oct. 1851.

COOLEY, WILLIAM DESBOROUGH. F.R.G.S. 1830, hon. free member 1864; granted civil list pension of £100, 4 Oct. 1858; wrote for Lardner's 'Cabinet Cyclopœdia' *The history of maritime and inland discovery* 3 vols. 1830–1; published *The world surveyed in the xix century* 2 vols. 1845–8; *Inner Africa laid open* 1852;

COOLEY, W. D. *(Con.)*
Physical geography, or the terraqueous globe and its phenomena 1876 and other works. *d.* 56 Crowndale road, Somers Town, London 1 March 1883. *Proc. of Royal Geog. Soc. v,* 232–3 (1883).

COOMBES, ROBERT. *b.* Vauxhall, London 1808; a waterman on river Thames; sculled his first race 4 July 1836; beat J. Kelly 4 Oct. 1838; stroke in the winning four at Liverpool regatta 1840 beating 5 crews; beat H. Clasper on the Tyne 18 Dec. 1844; beat C. Campbell 19 Aug. 1846 when he became champion of the Thames; presented with a champion belt 28 Oct. 1846; raced T. Cole for £200 a side 24 May 1852 when Cole won; won the pairs with Wilson at Thames regatta 1845; with his brother Tom Coombes beat Richard and Harry Clasper on the Thames 1847; trained the Cambridge crew 1852; never surpassed in speed and style during his time; author of *Hints on rowing and training* 1852. *d.* Kent lunatic asylum, Maidstone 25 Feb. 1860. *bur.* Brompton cemetery, London 7 March. *I.L.N.* 29 May 1852 *p.* 436, *portrait.*

COOPE, OCTAVIUS EDWARD (3 son of John Coope of London, sugar refiner). *b.* Leyspring, Essex 1814; a sugar refiner in London; a partner in brewing firm of Ind, Coope and Co. at Romford, Essex 1846, established a branch brewery at Burton-on-Trent 1856 the third largest brewing firm in Burton; M.P. for Great Yarmouth 29 July 1847 to June 1848 when unseated on petition; contested Tower Hamlets, Nov. 1868; M.P. for Middlesex 14 Feb. 1874 to 18 Nov. 1885, for Brentford division of Middlesex, Dec. 1885 to death; gave £15,000 towards rebuilding Whitechapel church 1875. *d.* 41 Upper Brook st. Grosvenor sq. London 27 Nov. 1886, personalty sworn upwards of £542,000. *Licensed Victuallers' year book* (1876) 80–81, *portrait; Morning Advertiser* 29 Nov. 1886 *p.* 5 and 3 Dec. *p.* 2.

COOPER, ABRAHAM *(son of Mr. Cooper of Red Lion st. Holborn, London, tobacconist).* *b.* Red Lion st. 8 Sep. 1787; member of the Artists' fund 1812, chairman; awarded premium of 150 guineas by British Institution for his picture of the 'Battle of Waterloo' 1816; A.R.A. 1817, R.A. 1820–66; exhibited 332 pictures at R.A. and 74 at British Institution 1812–69; pre-eminent as a painter of battle pieces; furnished the illustrations to *Sporting, by Nimrod* 1838, and other works. *d.* Woodbine cottage, Woodlands, Greenwich 24 Dec. 1868. *bur.* Highgate cemetery. *J. Sherer's Gallery of British artists ii* 4–7; *Reg. and mag. of biog. i,* 131–2 (1869).

COOPER, SIR ASTLEY PASTON, 2 Baronet. *b.* Great Yarmouth 13 Jany. 1797; succeeded 12 Feb. 1841; sheriff of Herts 1864. *d.* Gadesbridge, Hemel Hempstead 6 Jany. 1866.

COOPER, BRANSBY BLAKE *(eld. son of Rev. Samuel Lovick Cooper 1763–1817, R. of Bacton, Norfolk).* *b.* Great Yarmouth 2 Sep. 1792; midshipman in the navy; second assistant surgeon R.A. 2 Dec. 1811 to 1 April 1816 when placed on permanent h.p.; M.R.C.S. 1823, hon. fellow 1843, member of the council 1848; brought an action against Thomas Wakley editor of *The Lancet* for defamation of character, and obtained £100 damages 12 Dec. 1828; surgeon of Guy's hospital, London to death; F.R.S. 18 June 1829; author of *The life of Sir Astley Cooper baronet* 2 vols. 1843; *Lectures on the principles and practice of surgery* 1851. *d.* Athenæum club, Pall Mall, London 18 Aug. 1853. *J. F. Clarke's Autobiographical recollections of the medical profession* (1874) 520–6; *Medical Circular ii,* 511–14 (1853).

COOPER, SIR CHARLES (3 son of Thomas Cooper of Henley-on-Thames). *b.* Henley-on-Thames, March 1795; barrister I.T. 9 Feb. 1827; judge of supreme court of South Australia 1839–56, chief justice June 1856 to 1861; knighted at St. James's palace 18 June 1857; Cooper's Creek in Queensland was named after him. *d.* 12 Pulteney st. Bath 24 May 1887.

COOPER, CHARLES HENRY *(eld. son of Basil Henry Cooper of Great Marlow, solicitor, who d. 1813).* *b.* Great Marlow 20 March 1808; resided at Cambridge 1826 to death; coroner of borough of Cambridge 1 Jany. 1836; admitted solicitor, Nov. 1840; town clerk of Cambridge 1849 to death; F.S.A. 10 April 1851; author of *A new guide to the university and town of Cambridge* 1831 anon.; *The annals of Cambridge* 5 vols. 1842–53; *The memorials of Cambridge* 3 vols. 1858–66; *Memoirs of Margaret, Countess of Richmond and Derby* edited by Rev. J. E. B. Mayor 1874; author with his eldest son Thompson Coooper of *Athenæ Cantabrigienses* 2 vols. 1858–61; contributed to *Gent. Mag., Notes and Queries,* and other antiquarian publications. *d.* 29 Jesus lane, Cambridge 21 March 1866. *Dict. of Nat. Biog. xii,* 139–40 (1887); *Reliquary vii,* 34–40 (1866).

COOPER, CHARLES PURTON *(son of Charles Cooper of St. Dunstan's, London).* *b.* 1793; ed. at Wad. coll. Ox., double first class 1814, B.A. 1814, M.A. 1817; barrister L.I. 18 Nov. 1816; obtained leading practice in V.C. Knight-Bruce's court, quarrelled with him and left the court; Q.C. 1837; bencher of his Inn

COOPER, C. P. *(Con.)*

1836, treasurer 1855, master of the library 1856 to which he presented 2000 vols. on civil and foreign law 1843; secretary to Record Commission 12 March 1831 to 20 June 1837 when it lapsed on the king's death; Queen's serjeant in Duchy of Lancaster 1834 to death; F.R.S. 6 Dec. 1832; F.S.A.; contested Canterbury 18 Aug. 1854 and 28 March 1857; author of *Notes in French on the Court of Chancery* 1828, 2 ed. 1830; *An account of the public records of the United Kingdom* 2 vols. 1832; *Reports of cases decided by Lord Brougham* 1835; *Reports of cases decided by Lords Cottenham and Langdale and by V. C. Shadwell* 1841; *Reports of Lord Cottenham's decisions* 2 vols. 1847; wrote, edited or printed 52 pamphlets on political topics 1850–57. *d.* Boulogne 26 March 1873. *Report from the select committee on record commission* (1836) 1–275; *Sir Henry Cole's Fifty years of public work* (1834) i, 7, ii, 20, 23.

COOPER, EDWARD JOSHUA *(eld. son of Edward Synge Cooper of Dublin, who d.* 1830). *b.* Stephens Green, Dublin, May 1798; ed. at Armagh, Eton and Ch. Ch. Ox.; erected an observatory at Markree castle, co. Sligo 1831 where he kept meteorological registers 1833 to death; M.R.I.A. 1832, Cunningham gold medallist 1858; M.P. for co. Sligo 1830–41 and 1857–9; F.R.S. 2 June 1853; author of *Views in Egypt and Nubia* 1824 privately printed; *Catalogue of Stars near the Ecliptic observed at Markree* 4 vols. 1851–6 printed at Government expense, and *Cometic Orbits* 1852. *d.* Markree castle 23 April 1863. *Proc. of Royal Soc. xiii*, 1–3 (1864).

COOPER, FREDERICK FOX *(son of Mr. Cooper of London, editor of John Bull). b.* 4 Jany. 1806; called Fox after his godfather C. J. Fox, M.P.; articled to Isaac Cooper a stockbroker; managed successively Olympic, Marylebone, Victoria, City of London and Strand theatres; sec. to Duke of Cumberland as grand master of the Orange lodges in England; examined 4 days before House of Commons on subject of Orangeism 1835; proprietor of the *Nelson Examiner*, New Zealand 1841; started with The Chisholm, *The Cerberus*, a newspaper which under 4 heads advocated 4 different lines of politics, No. 1, 17 June 1843, it was published at 164 Strand, London down to 18 Nov. 1843; author of *The sons of Thespis*, produced at Surrey theatre, *Jenny Jones, Fleet Prison, Master Humphrey's Clock, Black Sentinel, Rejected Addresses, The deserted village*, and many travesties and dramatic sketches. *d.* 56 Prince's Road, Lambeth, London 4 Jany. 1879. *Theatrical Times ii*, 177 (1847), *portrait*; *Era* 19 Jany. 1879 *p.* 12, *col.* 2.

COOPER, FREDERICK HENRY *(younger son of Rev. Allen Cooper, incumbent of St. Mark's, North Audley st. London).* Entered Bengal civil service 1847; comr. at Lahore to death; C.B. 18 May 1860; author of *The Crisis in the Punjaub* 1858; *The handbook for Delhi* 1863. *d.* Trent rectory near Sherborne 22 April 1869 aged 42.

COOPER, GEORGE *(son of Mr. Cooper, assistant organist at St. Paul's cathedral, who d.* 1843). *b.* Lambeth 7 July 1820; organist of St. Benet's, Paul's wharf, London 1834, of St. Anne and St. Agnes 1836; assistant organist of St. Paul's cathedral, March 1838 to death; organist of St. Sepulchre's 1843 to death, of Christ's hospital 1843, of the Chapel Royal, St. James's, Sep. 1856 to death; author of *The organist's assistant; The organist's manual* 1851, 26 numbers; *Organ arrangements* 3 vols. 1864 etc.; *Classical extracts for the organ* 1867–69, seven numbers; *Introduction to the organ; Maud Irving or the little orphan, An operetta in 5 acts* 1872. *d.* 2 Oct. 1876. *Musical Standard* 7, 14, 21, 28 *Oct.* 1876, 18, 25 *Nov.*, 9, 23 *Dec.*

COOPER, HENRY. Ensign 62 foot 26 Feb. 1829; lieut. col. 45 foot 19 July 1848 to 1 May 1861; inspecting field officer 1861–2; col. 79 foot 21 Aug. 1870 to 17 March 1876; col. 45 foot 17 March 1876 to death; general 1 Oct. 1877. *d.* Bottesham hall, Cambs. 24 Aug. 1878.

COOPER, HENRY CHRISTOPHER. *b.* Bath 1819; solo violinist at Drury Lane theatre 1830; principal violinist at Royal Italian opera; leader at Philharmonic Society; violinist at provincial festivals; conductor at Gaiety theatre, Glasgow to death; one of the foremost of English school of violinists. *d.* 220 Hope st. Glasgow 26 Jany. 1881.

COOPER, JOHN *(son of Mr. Cooper of Bath, locksmith). b.* Bath 1790; apprenticed to a brush maker at Bath; first appeared on the stage at Bath theatre 14 March 1811 as Inkle in Colman's drama *Inkle and Yarico*; first appeared in London at Haymarket theatre 15 May 1811 as Count Montalban in *The honeymoon* and received £4 a week; played at Liverpool some years as the rival of Vandenhoff; played at Drury Lane theatre 1820–45, stage manager; played at Princess's theatre to 1859; had studied 200 parts and was ready at very short notice to undertake any of them; the last actor of the Kemble school; lived at 6 Sandringham gardens, Ealing. *d.* Tunbridge Wells 13 July 1870. *Oxberry's Dramatic biog.* v, 73–86 (1826), *portrait*; *Metropolitan Mag. xviii*, 74–80 (1837); *Jerrold's Bride of Ludgate (Lacy's ed.* 1872), *portrait*.

COOPER, John Ramsay. Chemist and druggist at 17 High st. Canterbury; a prominent promoter of the blue riband movement; invented phonic system of teaching reading, which was adopted in many of the principal elementary schools in England 1885; bankrupt on his own petition, June 1885; died at the police station, Canterbury 5 July 1885 from taking a solution of strychnia and about 15 or 20 grains of the salt; coroner's jury returned a verdict that he committed suicide while of unsound mind.

COOPER, John Wilbye, always known as Wilbye Cooper. Tenor vocalist to 1870; composed songs entitled *Ah where are now those happy hours* 1852; *The old cottager* 1852; author of *The voice, the music of language and the soul of song, a short essay on the art of singing* 1874; edited *Cramer's Educational Course* consisting of *Cramer's Vocal Tutor* 2 parts 1867, and *Cramer's New Singing Method* 4 parts 1872-74. d. 20 Castellain road, Maida hill, London 19 March 1885.

COOPER, Joseph Thomas. *b.* London 25 May 1819; organist of St. Michael's, Queenhithe 1837, of St. Paul's, Balls Pond, London 1844, of Ch. Ch. Newgate st. 1866 to death, of Christ's hospital 1876 to death; musical editor of *Evening Hours*, monthly mag. March 1871; F.R.A.S. 1845. d. 113 Grosvenor road, Highbury 17 Nov. 1879.

COOPER, Robert. Educ. at Charter house school; went to Canada; edited *British Canadian* paper at Toronto 1846; edited *Herald* paper at London, Upper Canada; county judge of united counties of Huron and Bruce 1856; published *Rules and practice of the Court of Chancery of Upper Canada*, Toronto 1851. d. Goderich, Upper Canada 19 June 1866.

COOPER, Thomas Thornville (8 son of John J. Cooper of Bishopwearmouth, coalfitter). *b.* Bishopwearmouth 13 Sep. 1839; made several journeys into interior of Australia; clerk in house of Arbuthnot and Co. at Madras 1859-61; joined Shanghai volunteers and helped to protect that city against Taiping rebels 1863; attempted to penetrate from China through Tibet to India 1868; attempted to enter China from Assam 1869; political agent at Bamo; attached to political department of India office, London; sent to India with despatches and presents to the viceroy in connection with imperial durbar of Delhi 1876; re-appointed political agent at Bamo; author of *Travels of a pioneer of commerce in pigtail and petticoats* 1871; *Mishmee hills, an account of a journey*

Cooper, T. T. *(Con.)*

1873; murdered by a sepoy at Bamo 24 April 1878. *W. Gill's River of Golden sand, new ed.* 1883 *introduction p. 108, portrait and p. 323.*

COOPER, Rev. William. R. of Wadingham, Lincs. March 1808 to death; R. of West Rasen, Lincs. 1809 to death; chaplain in ord. to the Sovereign 1830 to death. d. West Rasen rectory 24 Aug. 1856 aged 86.

COOPER, William (son of Charles Cooper of Norwich, barrister, who d. 21 July 1836). *b.* 6 Jany. 1810; ed. at Norwich gr. sch. and Linc. coll. Ox., B.A. 1830; barrister L.I. 10 June 1831; comr. of bankruptcy for Norwich 1832-42; a revising barrister for Leics. 1839 to death; standing counsel to Metropolitan police; one of counsel to the Treasury; recorder of Ipswich, Dec. 1874 to death; author of *A sketch of the life of H. Cooper and of C. Cooper* 1856 and of 3 dramas *The student of Jena* 1842, *Mokanna* 1843 and *Zopyrus* 1856. d. 25 Great Russell st. Bedford sq. London 17 Sep. 1877.

COOPER, William Durrant (eld. son of Thomas Cooper of Lewes, solicitor 1789-1841). *b.* High st. Lewes 10 Jany. 1812; solicitor at Lewes 1833-7; on parliamentary staff of *Morning Chronicle* and *Times* 1837; solicitor to Reform club 1837; solicitor to vestry of St. Pancras 20 Dec. 1858; F.S.A. 11 March 1841; author of *The parliamentary history of the county of Sussex* 1834; *A glossary of the provincialisms in use in Sussex*, privately printed 1836 which he published 1853; *Seven letters by Sterne and his friends* 1844; *The history of Winchelsea* 1850; edited several books for the Camden and Shakespeare Societies; author of many papers in *Sussex Archæological Collections vols. ii, to xxvi.* d. 81 Guilford st. Russell sq. London 28 Dec. 1875. *Sussex Archæological Collections xxvii, 117-32 (1877).*

COOPER, William Ricketts. *b.* 1843; a designer of carpet patterns; a London missionary; assistant curator of Sir John Soane's museum, Lincoln Inn Fields; one of chief founders of Society of biblical archæology 1870, sec. 1870-6; F.R.A.S. Jany. 1875; author of *Serpent myths of Ancient Egypt* 1873; *The resurrection of Assyria* 1875; *Heroines of the past* 1875; *Egypt and the Pentateuch* 1875; *An Archaic dictionary* 1876; *The Horus myth and Christianity* 1877; *A short history of the Egyptian obelisk* 1877, 2 ed. 1878; *Christian evidence lectures* 1880; translated *Lenormant's Chaldean magic* 1877. d. Ventnor, Isle of Wight 15 Nov. 1878.

COOPER, WILLIAM WHITE (*youngest son of George Fort Cooper*). *b.* Holt, Wiltshire 17 Nov. 1816; ed. at St. Bartholomew's hospital; M.R.C.S. 1838, F.R.C.S. 1845; one of original staff of North London Eye Infirmary 1841; ophthalmic surgeon to St. Mary's hospital, Paddington 1851; surgeon oculist in ordinary to the Queen 4 March 1859 to death; it was announced that he was to be knighted 29 May 1886; author of *Invalid's guide to Madeira* 1840; *Practical remarks on near sight, aged sight and impaired vision* 1847, 2 *ed.* 1853; *Observations on conical cornea* 1850; *On wounds and injuries of the eye* 1859; *Zoological notes and anecdotes by Sestertius Holt* 1852, pseud. of which a second ed. appeared under the title *Traits and anecdotes of animals* 1861. *d.* of acute pneumonia at 19 Berkeley sq. London 1 June 1886. *Medical Circular iii*, 383–85 (1853), *portrait*.

COOTE, CHARLES. *b,* Waltham abbey, Essex 1807; sang in English opera at Lyceum theatre; pianist to Duke of Devonshire 30 years, travelling with him abroad and at home; organised the quadrille band 1848 which has become celebrated in aristocratic circles; composed upwards of 150 pieces of music chiefly quadrilles, waltzes, galops, polkas and dances on airs from popular operas. *d.* 42 New Bond st. London 14 March 1879.

COOTE, SIR CHARLES HENRY, 9 Baronet. *b.* 2 Jany. 1792; succeeded 2 March 1802; M.P. for Queen's county 1821–47 and 1852–59; col. Queen's co. militia 20 Nov. 1824 to death. *d.* 5 Connaught place, London 5 Oct. 1864.

COOTE, ELIZABETH PHILLIS (*granddau. of Charles Coote* 1807–79). *b.* 19 Oct. 1862; acted in America 1870; sang at Canterbury and Pavilion music halls, London 1871–3; played Hop o' my Thumb in pantomime at T.R. Brighton, Dec. 1873; played at Adelphi and Princess's theatres 1877–8; made a great hit at Brighton in pantomime of Little Boy Blue, Dec. 1882. *d.* Ducie st. Chorlton-on-Medlock, Manchester 18 Feb. 1886. *Illust. sporting and dramatic news viii*, 401, 422 (1878), *portrait, xvi*, 569, 574 (1882), *portrait*.

COOTE, HENRY CHARLES (*son of Charles Coote of London* 1761–1835, *member of college of advocates*). *b.* 1814; admitted proctor in Doctors' Commons 1840; practised in the Probate court; admitted solicitor 1857; F.S.A. 17 May 1860; a founder of the Folklore Society 1878; author of *Practice of the ecclesiastical courts* 1846; *The common form practice of the Court of Probate* 1858, 9 *ed.* 1883; *Practice of the high*

COOTE, H. C. (*Con.*)
court of *Admiralty* 1860, 2 *ed.* 1869; *A neglected fact in English history* 1864; *The Romans in Britain* 1878. *d.* 13 Westgate terrace, Redclyffe sq. West Brompton, London 4 Jany. 1885. *Athenæum* 17 *Jany.* 1885 *p.* 87, *col.* 3.

COOTE, HOLMES (*2 son of Richard Holmes Coote of London, conveyancer*). *b.* London 10 Nov. 1817; ed. at Westminster; F.R.C.S. 1844; assistant surgeon St. Bartholomew's 1852, surgeon 1863 to death; civil surgeon in charge of the wounded soldiers at Smyrna 1855; author of *The Homologies of the human skeleton* 1849; *A report on some of the more important points in the treatment of Syphilis* 1857; *On diseases of the joints* 1867. *d.* 22 Dec. 1872. *Medical Circular iii*, 31 (1853); *St. Bartholomew's hospital reports ix, pp. xxxix–xliii* (1873).

COPE, REV. EDWARD MEREDITH. *b.* Birmingham 28 July 1818; ed. at Ludlow, Shrewsbury and Trin. coll. Cam., B.A. 1841, M.A. 1844; fellow of Trin. coll. 1842 to death, and lecturer on Greek 1845–69; contested professorship of Greek at Cam 1867; wrote a criticism of Grote's Dissertation on the sophists in the *Cambridge Journal of classical philology* 1854–6; author of *Review of Aristotle's System of ethics, a prelection* 1867; *The Rhetoric of Aristotle with a commentary by the late E. M. Cope, revised and edited by J. E. Sandys* 3 vols. 1877. *d.* 5 Aug. 1873. *bur.* Birmingham cemetery.

COPE, SIR JOHN, 11 Baronet (*younger son of Wm. Cope of Bridges place, Kent, chapter clerk to dean and chapter of Westminster abbey*). *b.* 22 July 1768; practised as a solicitor to 1806; succeeded his elder brother 12 Dec. 1812; kept a pack of foxhounds to year of his death. *d.* Bramshill park, Hants. 18 Nov. 1851. *G.M. xxxvii*, 184–5 (1852).

COPE, REV. RICHARD. *b.* near Craven chapel, Regent st. London 23 Aug. 1776; kept a boarding school at Launceston 1800–20; Independent minister at Launceston 21 Oct. 1801 to 24 June 1820; minister of Salem chapel, Wakefield 1822–29, of Quebec chapel, Abergavenny 1829–36, of New st. chapel, Penryn, Cornwall 1836 to death; M.A. Marischal coll. Aberdeen 1819; F.S.A. 13 Feb. 1824; author of *Adventures of a religious tract* 1820 anon.; *Robert Melville or characters contrasted* 1827; *Pulpit synopsis, outlines of sermons* 1837; *Entertaining anecdotes* 1838; *Pietas privata, family prayers* 1857. *d.* Penryn 26 Oct. 1856. *Autobiography and select remains of Richard Cope edited by his son R. J. Cope* 1857.

COPE, THOMAS. *b.* London 1793; apprenticed to Joseph Smith, printer; worked under W. Clowes of Northumberland court, Strand, printer 1818–22; started a newspaper at Southampton 1822; returned to Clowes's; printer and publisher of *The Representative* 1826; managed John Wm. Parker's printing office; publisher of *The Times* 1848–63. *d.* Salisbury st. Strand, London 13 March 1877.

COPE, THOMAS. *b.* Liverpool; commenced with his brother George Cope the manufacture of cigars in Liverpool 1848 and the manufacture of tobacco 1860, employed about 1300 people at his works Lord Nelson st. Liverpool and was the first person in England to engage women in making cigars; founded with J. R. Jeffery and Robert Gladstone, Financial Reform Association 1848; speaker of Liverpool Parliamentary debating society; aided Hugh Shimmin in founding *The Porcupine* 1860; *Cope's Tobacco plant, a monthly periodical, price 1d. No.* 1 *issued* 21 *March* 1870, was brought out by Cope Brothers & Co. for about 14 years. *d.* Parkside cottage, Huyton near Liverpool 18 Sep. 1884 in 57 year. *Liverpool Daily Post* 19 *Sept.* 1884 *p.* 5.

COPE, WILLIAM (*only son of Wm. Henry Cope of Holbeach, Staffs.*) *b.* 20 Oct. 1813; ed. at Trin. coll. Ox., B.A. 1836, M.A. 1839; barrister I.T. 20 Nov. 1840; district registrar of Court of Probate, Shrewsbury 1858 to death; recorder of Bridgnorth 10 March 1871 to death. *d.* Shawbury, Shropshire 8 Jany. 1885.

COPELAND, THOMAS (*son of Rev. Wm. Copeland* 1747–87, *C. of Byfield, Northamptonshire*). *b.* May 1781; M.R.C.S. 6 July 1804, hon. F.R.C.S. 1843; assistant surgeon 1 foot guards 1804–9; surgeon to Westminster general dispensary; F.R.S. 6 Feb. 1834; surgeon extraordinary to Queen Victoria 1837; author of *Observations on some of the principal diseases of the Rectum* 1810, 3 *ed.* 1824; *Observations on the symptoms and treatment of the diseased spine* 1815, 2 *ed.* 1818 which was translated into several European languages. *d.* Brighton 19 Nov. 1855, personalty sworn under £180,000. *Medical Circular iii*, 31 (1853); *Pettigrew's Medical portrait gallery iv*, (1840), *portrait.*

COPELAND, REV. WILLIAM JOHN (*son of Wm. Copeland of Chigwell, Essex, surgeon*). *b.* Chigwell 1 Sep. 1804; ed. at St. Paul's sch. and Trin. coll. Ox., Pauline exhibitioner 1824, scholar, fellow 1830–49; B.A. 1829, M.A. 1831, B.D. 1840; C. of St. Olave, Jewry, London 1829, C. of Hackney 1829–32; R. of Farnham,

Essex 1849 to death; rural dean of Newport 1849–81; edited Newman's *Parochial and plain sermons* 8 vols. 1868; translated the *Homilies of St. John Chrysostom on the Epistle to the Ephesians* in vol. 5 of the *Library of the Fathers. d.* Farnham rectory 26 Aug. 1885, part of his library is now in the National Liberal Club, Whitehall place, London.

COPELAND, WILLIAM ROBERT. *b.* Deal; apprenticed to a chemist; lessee and manager of T.R. Liverpool and proprietor of royal amphitheatre 1843; manager of Strand theatre, London which he called "Punch's Playhouse," May 1851 to May 1852. *d.* New Brighton, Cheshire 29 May 1867 aged 68. *bur.* Smithdown lane cemetery, Liverpool 8 June. *Era* 2 *June* 1867 *p.* 4, *col.* 4.

COPELAND, WILLIAM TAYLOR (*only son of Wm. Copeland of the Stoke potteries, porcelain manufacturer, who d.* 1826). *b.* 24 March 1797; manufacturer of porcelain at Stoke upon Trent 1833; sheriff of London and Middlesex 1828–29, alderman for ward of Bishopsgate 1829 to death, lord mayor 1835–36; M.P. for Coleraine 1833–37, for Stoke upon Trent 1837–52 and 1857 to 6 July 1865; pres. of Bridewell and of Bethlehem hospitals many years; bred racehorses and kept a stud. *d.* Russell farm, Watford, Herts. 12 April 1868. *John Ward's Borough of Stoke upon Trent* 1843 *pp.* 64, 497–504, 582; *Sporting Review lix*, 309 (1868); *Art Journal* (1868) *p.* 158; *I.L.N. xxxii*, 561 (1858), *portrait.*

COPLAND, JAMES. *b.* in the Orkneys, Nov. 1791; ed. at Lerwick and Univ. of Edin., M.D. 1 Aug. 1815; Medical officer of the African company on the Gold Coast 1817; practised in London 1820–69; edited *The London medical repository* 1822–27; L.R.C.P. London 26 June 1820, fellow 3 July 1837, censor 1841, 1842 and 1861, Gulstonian lecturer 1838, Croonian lecturer 1844–46, Lumleian lecturer 1854–55, Harveian orator 1857, Consiliarius 1844, 1849–51, 1861–63; F.R.S. 5 Dec. 1833; pres. of Pathological Soc.; author of *A dictionary of practical medicine* 3 vols. 1858 brought out in parts Sep. 1832–1858; *The forms, complications, causes, prevention and treatment of consumption and bronchitis* 1861. *d.* Hertford house, Brondesbury road, Kilburn near London 12 July 1870. *Physic and physicians ii*, 285–89 (1839); *T. J. Pettigrew's Medical portrait gallery i*, 109 (1840), *portrait; J. F. Clarke's Autobiographical recollections of the medical profession* (1874) 410–20; *Medical Circular iv*, 299, 317 *and* 353 (1854).

COPLEY, Sir Joseph William, 4 Baronet. *b.* London 27 July 1804; succeeded 21 May 1838; sheriff of Yorkshire 1843. *d.* Sprotborough hall, Doncaster 4 Jany. 1883.

COPPOCK, James *(eld. son of Wm. Coppock of Stockport, Cheshire, mercer).* *b.* Stockport 2 Sep. 1798; partner in a silk firm in London; admitted attorney 1836; sec. to Liberal Registration Society with a residence in the Society's rooms 3 Cleveland row, St. James's 1835; treasurer of county courts, Aug. 1857 to death; sec. of the Reform Club, London, May to June 1836 when he was elected an hon. life member and appointed solicitor to the club; author of *The electors' manual* 1835. *d.* 3 Cleveland row, St. James's, London 19 Dec. 1857.

CORBALLIS, John Richard *(2 son of Richard Corballis of Rosemount, Roebuck, co. Dublin).* *b.* Dublin 1796; ed. at the Lay college of Maynooth and Trin. coll. Dublin, B.A. 1816, LL.B. and LL.D. 1832; barrister King's Inns, Dublin 1820; Q.C. 17 Aug. 1841; bencher of King's Inns; comr. of charitable bequests for Ireland 18 Sep. 1845; law adviser to the Crown in Ireland 1853–58 and 1859–64; crown prosecutor on the Home circuit; chairman of quarter sessions for co. Kilkenny to 1862. *d.* Rosemount 13 Feb. 1879 in 83 year.

CORBALLY, Matthew Elias. *b.* 1797; sheriff of Meath 1838; M.P. Meath 1840–41 and 1842 to death. *d.* Corbalton hall, Tara, co. Meath 25 Nov. 1870.

CORBAUX, Marie Françoise Catherine Doetter, usually called Fanny Corbaux *(dau. of François Corbaux, F.R.S. who d. 1 May 1843 aged 74).* *b.* 1812; studied at National Gallery and British Institution; gained gold medal of Society of Arts for a portrait in miniature 1830; hon. mem. of Society of British Artists 1830; mem. of New Soc. of Painters in Water colours; granted civil list pension of £30, 26 Sep. 1871; wrote in the *Athenæum, Letters on the physical geography of the Exodus;* wrote in the *Journal of sacred literature* a series of papers giving the history of a remarkable nation called 'the Rephaim" in the Bible; wrote an historical and chronological introduction to *The Exodus Papyri by D. I. Heath* 1855. *d.* Brighton 1 Feb. 1883. *E. C. Clayton's English female artists ii,* 68–70.

CORBET, Sir Andrew Vincent, 2 Baronet. *b.* Shawbury park, Shropshire 15 June 1800; succeeded 5 June 1835; sheriff of Shropshire 1843. *d.* Brancepeth castle, Durham 13 Sep. 1855.

CORBETT, Panton *(2 son of Ven. Joseph Plymley, archdeacon of Salop, who took surname of Corbett 1806 and d. 22 June 1838 aged 79).* *b.* Bank house, Longnor, Salop, April 1785; barrister L.I. 21 June 1806; M.P. for Shrewsbury 1820–1830; high steward of borough of Welshpool; sheriff of Shropshire 1849; chairman of Shropshire quarter sessions 1850 to June 1855. *d.* Longnor hall, Shropshire 22 Nov. 1855.

CORBETT, Sir Stuart *(son of Ven. Stuart Corbett, archdeacon of York, who d. 25 Aug. 1845 aged 71).* *b.* Tankersley, Yorkshire 1802; entered Bengal army 1814; lieut. col. 25 Bengal N.I. 26 Dec. 1846 to 1854; colonel 16 Bengal N.I. 18 May 1856 to death, M.G. 4 Feb. 1859; commanded Benares division 6 July 1863 to death; C.B. 9 June 1849, K.C.B. 28 Jany. 1862. *d.* Nynee Tal, India 1 Aug. 1865.

CORBETT-WINDER, Uvedale *(brother of the preceding).* *b.* 15 Nov. 1792; ed. at Pemb. coll. Ox.; barrister L.I. 11 Feb. 1815; comr. of bankruptcy in Wolverhampton district; recorder of Bridgnorth 1844–71; recorder of Wenlock to 1871; judge of county courts, circuit 27, Shropshire, March 1847 to Sep. 1865 when he resigned; assumed additional surname of Winder 2 June 1869. *d.* 36 Princes gardens, London 7 Feb. 1871.

CORCORAN, Michael. *b.* Carrowkeal, co. Sligo 21 Sep. 1827; emigrated to United States 1849, clerk in the post office there; colonel of 69 New York militia, Aug. 1859; taken prisoner at battle of Bull Run 21 July 1861, released 15 Aug. 1862; brigadier general 21 July 1861; organised the Corcoran legion which took part in the battles of Nansemond river and Suffolk, April 1863 and held in check advance of the enemy upon Norfolk, the legion was attached to army of the Potomac, Aug. 1863. *d.* of injuries received by a fall from his horse near Fairfax courthouse, Virginia 22 Dec. 1863. *The captivity of General Corcoran* 1862; *Bramhall's Military souvenir* (1863), memoir and portrait No. 45.

CORDER, Susanna. Author of *Memorials of deceased members of the Society of Friends* 1837, 6 ed. 1845; *A brief outline of the origin, principles and church government of the Society of Friends* 1841, translated into French 1845; *Life of Elizabeth Fry* 1853; *Christian instruction in the history, types and prophecies of the Old Testament* 1854, 2 ed. 1855; edited *Memoir of Priscilla Gurney* 1856. *d.* Chelmsford 28 Feb. 1864 aged 76.

CORDNER, WILLIAM JOHN. *b.* Dungannon, co. Tyrone 1826 ; teacher of music at Armagh ; the best tenor singer in north of Ireland ; organist of St. Patrick's church, Sydney 1854–56, of St. Mary's cathedral, Sydney 1856 to death. *d.* Sydney 15 July 1870.

CORFE, ARTHUR THOMAS (3 son of *Joseph Corfe 1740–1820, organist of Salisbury cathedral*). *b.* Salisbury 9 April 1773 ; a chorister of Westminster abbey 1783 ; organist of Salisbury cathedral 1804 to death ; organised and undertook a musical festival at Salisbury 19 to 22 Aug. 1828 ; wrote a service, a few anthems and some piano-forte pieces ; author of *A collection of anthems used in cathedral church, Canterbury* 1830. Found dead at his bedside in his house The Close, Salisbury 28 Jany. 1863. *F. Lear's Sermon on death of Archdeacon Drury and A. T. Corfe* 1863.

CORFE, CHARLES WILLIAM (*son of the preceding*). *b.* 13 July 1814 ; organist of Ch. Ch. cath. Ox. 1846–81 ; Mus. Bac. Ox. 1847 ; choragus of univ. of Ox. 1860 to death. *d.* 14 Beaumont st. Oxford 16 Dec. 1883. *bur.* Ch. Ch. cathedral 19 Dec.

CORFE, JOHN DAVIS (*brother of the preceding*). *b.* 1804 ; organist of Bristol cathedral more than 50 years ; conductor for many years of the Bristol Madrigal Society one of the most famous choirs in England. *d.* of heart disease at 31 Richmond terrace, Clifton 16 Jany. 1876.

CORFIELD, FREDERICK BROOKE. Ensign 28 Bengal N.I. 3 April 1820 ; lieut.-col. of 20 Bengal N.I. 3 Sep. 1849, of 49 B.N.I. 1852, of 17 B.N.I. 1853, of 55 B.N.I. 1854, of 2 B.N.I. 1855, of 6 B.N.I. 1857, of 5 B.N.I. 1858 ; col. 5 European infantry 26 April 1859 to 1869 ; general 1 Oct. 1877. *d.* Knowle house, Upper Norwood 2 Sep. 1884 aged 81. *I.L.N. lxxxv,* 292 (1884), *portrait.*

CORFIELD, WILLIAM ROBERT. Ensign 15 Bengal N.I. 3 Dec. 1821 ; general on retired list 1 Oct. 1877. *d.* 128 Lexham gardens, London 30 Nov. 1882. *Graphic xxvii,* 225 (1883), *portrait.*

CORK and ORRERY, EDMUND BOYLE, 8 Earl of (2 son of *7 Earl of Cork and Orrery 1742–98*). *b.* 21 Oct. 1767 ; ensign 22 foot 13 April 1785 ; lieut. col. 87 foot 29 March 1794 to 7 Jany. 1795 ; lieut. col. 11 foot 7 Jany. 1795 to 17 May 1796 ; captain Coldstream Guards 17 May 1796 to 17 Sep. 1802, commanded first battalion in Egypt 1801 ; succeeded his father Oct. 1798 ; col. of 16 battalion of Reserve 9 July 1803 to 1804 ; general 27 May 1825 ; K.P. 22 July 1835. *d.* 3 Hamilton place, London 29 June 1856.

CORKRAN, JOHN FRAZER. *b.* Dublin ; a dramatic writer in Dublin ; wrote many articles in *Dublin Univ. Mag.* ; Paris correspondent of *Morning Herald* and *Evening Standard* about 1836 ; author of *History of the national constituent assembly* 2 vols. 1849 ; *An hour ago, or time in dreamland, a mystery* 1858 ; *East and West, or once upon a time* 3 vols. 1861 ; *Bertha's Repentance* 1863. *d.* 9 Clairville grove, Old Brompton, London 3 Feb. 1884.

CORMACK, SIR JOHN ROSE (*only son of Rev. John Cormack, minister of Stoke near Edinburgh*). *b.* Edin. 1815 ; ed. at Univ. of Edin., M.D. 1837 ; F.R.C.P. Edin. 1841 ; phys. to Royal infirmary, Edin. ; edited *Edinburgh Monthly Journal* 1841–46 ; F.R.S. Edin. ; M.D. Paris 1870 ; surgeon to Ambulance Anglaise during both the sieges of Paris 1870–71 ; chevalier of Legion of honour 1871 ; F.R.C.P. London 1872 ; knighted at Buckingham palace 14 March 1872 ; author of *Treatise on the properties of Creosote* 1836 ; *Pathology of fever in Edinburgh* 1844 ; *Clinical studies illustrated by cases* 2 vols. 1876. *d.* 364 Rue st. Honore, Paris 13 May 1882. *Medical Circular iii,* 109–110 (1853).

CORNER, ARTHUR BLOXHAM (2 son of *Richard Corner of Southwark, London, solicitor, who d. 1820*). *b.* parish of St. Olave's, Southwark 29 Jany. 1803 ; clerk in the Crown office, Temple 1822, assistant master, May 1847 ; Queen's coroner and attorney 26 April 1859 to death ; published with his brother Richard James Corner *The practice of the Crown side of the Court of Queen's Bench* 1844. *d.* Laurel cottage, Lee road, Blackheath 17 Jany. 1861.

CORNER, GEORGE RICHARD (*brother of the preceding*). *b.* parish of Ch. Ch. Blackfriar's road, London 1801 ; admitted an attorney 1824 ; vestry clerk of parish of St. Olave, Southwark about 1835 ; F.S.A. 28 Nov. 1833, contributed papers to the *Archæologia* 1834–60 ; an original member of Numismatic Society of London 1836 and of British Archæol. Assoc. 1843 ; author of *A concise account of the local government of the borough of Southwark* 1836 ; *The rental of St. Olave and St. John, Southwark* 1838, 2 ed. 1851. *d.* Queen's Row, Camberwell 31 Oct. 1863. *C. R. Smith's Collectanea Antiqua vi,* 324–26 (1868) ; *Journal of British Archeol. Assoc. xx,* 181–6 (1864).

CORNER, JULIA (*dau. of John Corner of London, engraver*). *b.* 1798 ; author of *Historical Library* 14 vols. 1840–48 ; *Pictorial history of China and India* 1846 ; *Children's own Sunday book* 1850 ; *History of the United Kingdom* 1852 ; *Little plays for little actors* 2 vols. 1855, *new ed.*

CORNER, J. *(Con.)*

1870; *Calverley Rise, a tale* 3 vols. 1861; *No Relations* 3 vols. 1864, and about 50 other books. *d.* 92 Clarendon road, Notting hill, London 16 Aug. 1875.

CORNER, RICHARD JAMES *(brother of George Richard Corner 1801–63).* *b.* Lambeth 1805; barrister I.T. 1840; chief justice of the Gold Coast 13 March 1858; chief justice of British Honduras 3 July 1862 to 1872 when he resigned; one of the authors of *Reports of cases in all the superior courts of common law 1853–55, 3 vols. in 5, 1853–55. d.* East Moulsey, Surrey 27 Feb. 1876.

CORNEWALL, SIR VELTERS, 4 Baronet. *b.* Moccas court, Weobly, co. Hereford 20 Feb. 1824; succeeded 27 Dec. 1835; sheriff of co. Hereford 1847; joint master of the Herefordshire hunt; a breeder of hunters. *d.* 14 Oct. 1868.

CORNEY, BOLTON. *b.* Greenwich 28 April 1784; ensign 28 foot 1803; first clerk in Steward's department at Greenwich hospital 16 April 1834 to Dec. 1844; lived at Barnes, Surrey 1848 to death; a member of council of Shakespeare Soc. and of Camden Soc.; had a long controversy with Isaac D'Israeli respecting statements in his writings; author of *Researches and conjectures on the Bayeux tapestry* 1836; *Curiosities of literature by I. D'Israeli illustrated* 1837, 2 ed. to which are added *Ideas on controversy, deduced from the practice of a Veteran* 1838; *The sonnets of William Shakspere, a critical disquisition* 1862 *privately printed,* and many other works; his library was sold at Sotheby's in June 1871 for £3539 9s. 6d. *d.* 29 The Terrace, Barnes 30 Aug. 1870. *F. Hitchman's Eighteenth century studies* (1881), 254–71; *Notes and Queries* 4 series vi, 206 (1870), 6 series ii, 123 (1880), iv, 291 (1881).

CORNISH, REV. HENRY HUBERT (2 *son of Charles Cornish of Gatcombe house, Totnes).* Matric. from Magd. hall, Ox. 19 Feb. 1835 aged 23, B.A. 1841, M.A. 1842, B.D. and D.D. 1866; chaplain of C.C. coll. 1845–50; tutor of New Inn hall 1858, principal 1866 to death, when the hall ceased to possess an independent existence having been made over to Balliol college by the University Commission. *d.* Oxford 9 June 1887.

CORNWALLIS, JAMES MANN, 5 Earl. *b.* 20 Sep. 1778; ed. at St. John's coll. Cam., M.A. 1798; M.P. for Eye, Suffolk 30 Oct. 1799 to 29 April 1807; succeeded 20 Jany. 1824. *d.* Linton place near Maidstone 21 May 1852.

CORNWALLIS, CAROLINE FRANCES *(younger dau. of Rev. Wm. Cornwallis 1751–1827, R. of Elham, Kent).* *b.* 12 July 1786; learnt Latin, Greek, Hebrew and German; shared with Micaiah Hill prize of £200 given by Lady Byron for best essay on 'Juvenile Delinquency' 1853; chief projector of a series of 22 vols. entitled *Small books on great subjects edited by some well-wishers to knowledge* 1841, author of many of the vols. including the first which was entitled *Philosophical theories and philosophical experience by a Pariah* 1841; published *Pericles, a tale of Athens in the 83rd Olympiad* 2 vols. 1846, anon.; *An exposition of the vulgar and common errors adapted to the year of grace, MDCCCXLV, by Thomas Brown redivivus* 1846. *d.* Lidwells near Goudhurst, Kent 8 Jany. 1858. *Selections from the letters of C. F. Cornwallis* (1864).

CORRI, HAYDN *(son of Domenico Corri, Italian musical composer 1746–1825).* *b.* Edinburgh 1785; teacher of music at Dublin; composed a few glees and songs, one of which his vocal arrangement of *The harmonious blacksmith* used to be much sung; organist to the cathedral, Great Marlborough st. Dublin; arranged for the organ under Cherubini's instruction that composer's famous mass in D (written for coronation of Charles X) and added an additional voice part; wrote the music to *There grows a bonny briar bush* 1815, *Can you love me, lady fair* 1820, *Music can guide the soul* 1821, *O fly to the woods* 1821; his wife was chief singer at all the great concerts in Dublin many years, and *d.* Leeds 10 April 1867 in 68 year, he *d.* Dublin 19 Feb. 1860. *Era 26 Feb.* 1860 *p.* 11, *col.* 2.

CORRI, PATRICK ANTHONY *(son of the preceding).* *b.* 1820; chorister in churches in Dublin; first appeared in London at Princess's theatre about 1845 as a baritone singer; sang at Manchester; sang in operas at Grecian theatre, London 1849; musical director at Weston's music hall, Holborn, London 1857 to death, the name was changed from Weston's to The Royal 1868; composed some vocal music. *d.* Bradford 1 June 1876. *bur.* Scholemore cemetery 3 June. *Entr'acte 10 June* 1876 *p.* 8, 17 *June p.* 7, *portrait; Era 11 June* 1876, *p.* 6.

CORRIE, ARCHIBALD. *b.* Perthshire 1777; held a horticultural post near Edinburgh about 1797–1807; manager of the estate of Annat near Errol in Perthshire 1807–57; contributed agricultural reports to Scottish papers; contributed many papers on agriculture and horticulture to Loudon's and other magazines. *d.* Annat cottage near Errol 1857 in 80 year.

CORRIE, REV. GEORGE ELWES *(son of Rev. John Corrie, C. of Colsterworth, co. Lincoln).* *b.* Colsterworth 28 April 1793; entered Catharine hall, Cam., Oct. 1813, 18 wrangler 1817, B.A. 1817, M.A. 1820, B.D. 1831, D.D. 1853; fellow of his college 1818, assistant tutor, dean and steward 1820, tutor 1821–49; Norrisian professor of divinity in Univ. of Cam. 1838–54; exam. chaplain to bishop of Ely 1845–64; master of Jesus coll. Cam. Dec. 1849 to death; vice chancellor 1850; R. of Newton, Isle of Ely 1851 to death; rural dean of Wisbech 1851–78; a founder of Cambridge Antiquarian Soc. 1840; leader of Conservative party in Univ. of Cam.; published *Catalogue of the original library of St. Catharine's hall* 1840; *The sermons and remains of Hugh Latimer* 2 vols. 1844; *History of the Reformation by G. Burnet* 1847; edited *A concise history of the church and state of England during the reign of Henry VIII* 1874; edited for the University Press *An Historical Vindication of the Church of England by Sir R. Twysden* 1847; *The Homilies* 1850; and *A rational illustration of the book of Common Prayer, by C. Wheatley* 1858. *d.* The lodge, Jesus college, Cambridge 20 Sep. 1885.

CORRIE, WILLIAM. *b.* Wellingborough 1806; practised as solicitor; barrister I.T. 10 June 1836; magistrate at Clerkenwell police court, London 1851–60, at Bow st. 1860–64; remembrancer of city of London 1864 to June 1878; author of *An analysis of the Municipal Boroughs bill* 1870. *d.* 26 Cleveland sq. London 24 March 1881.

CORRIGAN, SIR DOMINIC JOHN, 1 Baronet (2 son of *John Corrigan of Dublin, merchant, who d. 1838). b.* 91 Thomas st. Dublin 1 Dec. 1802; M.D. Edin. 1825, M.D. Dublin 1849; lecturer on medicine in Carmichael school, Dublin 1833; phys. to the House of Industry hospitals 1840–66; M.R.C.S. London 1843; phys. in ord. to Queen in Ireland 23 Nov. 1847; medical comr. under Medical Charities Act 1851; fellow of King and Queen's college of phys. in Ireland 27 Oct. 1856, pres. 1859–64; created baronet 5 Feb. 1866; M.P. for city of Dublin 1870 to 1874; vice chancellor of Queen's univ. Dublin, June 1871; author of *On famine and fever in Ireland* 1846; *Lectures on the nature and treatment of fever* 1853; *Ten days in Athens with notes by the way* 1862. *d.* Merrion sq. Dublin 1 Feb. 1880. *Irish Monthly viii,* 160–71 (1880); *I.L.N. xlviii,* 252 (1866), *portrait.*

CORRY, ARMAR LOWRY. Entered navy 1 Aug. 1805, captain 23 July 1821; admiralty superintendent of packet service at Southampton

CORRY, A. L. *(Con.)*
1850–52; R.A. 8 March 1852; commanded western squadron on the Home and Lisbon stations 1852–54; second in command of English fleet in the Baltic, March to July 1854; named a K.C.B. in London Gazette 10 July 1855. *d.* Paris 2 May 1855 aged 62.

CORRY, HENRY THOMAS LOWRY *(younger son of 2 Earl of Belmore* 1774–1841). *b.* Dublin 9 March 1803; ed. at Eton and Ch. Ch. Ox., B.A. 1823, M.A. 1829; M.P. for co. Tyrone 20 June 1826 to death; comptroller of the household 29 Dec. 1834 to 1835; P.C. 23 Feb. 1835; a lord of the Admiralty 8 Sep. 1841 to 12 Feb. 1845, sec. to the Admiralty 13 Feb. 1845 to 13 July 1846, and March 1858 to June 1859; vice pres. of committee of privy council for education 12 July 1866 to March 1867, fourth charity comr. 18 July 1866; first lord of the Admiralty, March 1867 to Dec. 1868; author of *Naval promotion and retirement* 1863; *The Navy, Speeches in House of Commons* 1872. *d.* Bournemouth 6 March 1873. *I.L.N. lxii,* 259, 280, 282 (1873), *portrait.*

CORSER, REV. THOMAS (3 *son of George Corser of Whitchurch, Salop, banker). b.* Whitchurch 1793; ed. at Manchester gr. sch. and Balliol coll. Ox., B.A. 1815, M.A. 1818; C. of Prestwich, Lancs. 1823–6; R. of Stand near Manchester 8 Sep. 1826 to death; V. of Norton by Daventry, Northamptonshire 1828 to death; rural dean of Prestwich 1852–68; F.S.A. 1850; one of projectors of Chetham Society 1843; edited for the Society *Chester's Triumph* 1844, *Iter Lancastrense by R. James* 1845, *Robinson's Golden Mirror* 1850, and *Collectanea Anglopoetica* 5 parts 1860–80 being a description of the rare books in his own library which realised upwards of £20,000 when sold in London in 7 portions 1868–74. *d.* Stand rectory 24 Aug. 1876. *Manchester school register iii,* 32–36 (1874).

CORYTON, JOHN RAWLINS. Second lieut. R.M. 6 July 1803; col. commandant of Plymouth division 23 Dec. 1851 to 20 June 1855; granted good service pension 5 Sep. 1858; general 8 Sep. 1858. *d.* Woolwich 12 Sep. 1867 aged 77.

COSTA, SIR MICHAEL ANDREW AGNUS *(son of Cavaliere Pasquale Costa, who d. 1845). b.* Naples 4 Feb. 1810; accompanist at San Carlo theatre, Naples 1828; sang at Birmingham musical festival, Oct. 1829; director of music at King's theatre, London 1832–46; the first person in England to conduct with a baton instead of a violin bow 1832; naturalised in England 28 July 1845; director of music at

COSTA, SIR M. A. A. *(Con.)*

Covent Garden 1846–66; conductor of the Philharmonic concerts 1846–54; conductor of Sacred harmonic society 22 Sep. 1848; directed triennial musical festivals at Birmingham 1849–79 and at Leeds 1874–80; directed Handel festivals at Crystal palace 1857–77; knighted at Windsor castle 14 April 1869; director of Her Majesty's opera 1871–79; the first master of the art of conducting in England; composed oratorios of *Eli* and *Naaman* produced at Birmingham musical festivals 29 Aug. 1855 and 7 Sep. 1864, opera of *Malek Adhel* produced in Paris 1837 and in London 1838, and opera of *Don Carlos* produced at Her Majesty's opera 1844; wrote many songs and other music. *d.* 13 Seafield, West Brighton 29 April 1884. *bur.* Kensal Green cemetery 6 May. *Illust. Review* i, 385–6 (1874), *portrait; Touchstone* 15 Feb. 1879, *p.* 3, *portrait; Illust. news of the world* iii, 385 (1859), *portrait; I.L.N.* i, 124 (1842), *portrait,* iv, 404 (1844), *portrait, xxx,* 13 (1857), *portrait, lxxxiv,* 440 (1884), *portrait.*

COSTELLO, DUDLEY *(only son of James Francis Costello, captain 14 foot).* *b.* Sussex 1803; ensign 34 foot 1821–23 when placed on h.p.; ensign 96 foot 1824–28 when placed on h.p.; served on the staff in North America and West Indies; contributed to many periodicals 1835 to death; foreign correspondent of *Morning Herald* 1838, of *Daily News* 1846; connected with the *Examiner* 1845 to death; granted civil list pension of £75 a year 19 April 1861; author of *A tour through the valley of the Meuse* 1845; *Stories from a screen* 1855; *The joint-stock bank* 1856; *The millionaire of Mincing lane* 1858; *Faint heart never won fair lady* 1859; *Piedmont and Italy from the Alps to the Tiber* 2 vols. 1859–61; *Holidays with Hobgoblins* 1861. *d.* 54 Acacia road, St. John's Wood, London 30 Sep. 1865. *Bentley's Miscellany* lviii, 543–50 (1865); *The Examiner* 7 Oct. 1865 *p.* 637.

COSTELLO, LOUISA STUART *(only sister of the preceding).* *b.* 1799; a miniature painter in Paris and London; copied many curious illuminated MSS. in Paris and London; granted civil list pension of £75, 9 Aug. 1852; lived at Boulogne 1865 to death; author of *The maid of the Cyprus Isle and other poems* 1815; *Songs of a stranger* 1825; *A summer among the Bocages and the vines* 1840; *Memoirs of eminent Englishwomen* 1844; *The falls, lakes and mountains of North Wales* 1845; *The lay of the stork, a poem* 1856 and 12 other books. *d.* of cancer in the mouth, at Boulogne 24 April 1870.

COSTELLO, WILLIAM BIRMINGHAM. *b.* Dublin 1800; a surgeon in London about 1832; proprietor of Wyke house asylum, Sion hill, Brentford; edited *Cyclopedia of practical surgery* 12 parts 1841–3. *d.* Paris 15 Aug. 1867.

COTES, JOHN. *b.* 17 July 1799; sheriff of Shropshire 1826; M.P. for North Shropshire 21 Dec. 1832 to 29 Dec. 1834. *d.* Woodcote hall, Newport, Shropshire 10 Jany. 1874.

COTHER, CHARLES. Ensign 71 foot, Feb. 1800, lieut. col. 13 Oct. 1814; lieut. col. 83 foot 24 Oct. 1816 to 25 Dec. 1818 when placed on h.p.; retired 3 Dec. 1829; C.B. 8 Dec. 1815. *d.* York buildings, Gloucester 24 Jany. 1855.

COTMAN, JOSEPH JOHN *(2 son of John Sell Cotman, landscape painter 1782–1842).* *b.* 1814; a drawing master at Norwich 1836; an artist of much original power; produced a large number of good drawings; underwent an operation for cancer of the tongue, Feb. 1878. *d.* Norfolk and Norwich hospital, Norwich 15 March 1878.

COTMAN, MILES EDMUND *(brother of the preceding).* *b.* 5 Jany. 1810; drawing master at Norwich to 1836; assistant drawing master at King's college, London 1836, drawing master 1843; painted and taught at North Walsham latterly; exhibited 4 landscapes at R.A., 10 at B.I. and 19 at Society of British Artists 1835–56; published *Eleven original etchings, Norwich* 1846. *d.* Norfolk and Norwich hospital, Norwich 23 Jany. 1858.

COTON, WILLIAM. Pyrotechnic artist at 4 Elizabeth place, Westminster bridge, London; supplied the fireworks for Vauxhall gardens; killed by an explosion of fireworks at his factory 6 March 1854, his widow was killed by an explosion at same place 12 July 1858. *Annual Register* (1854) 40, (1858) 120–2.

COTTENHAM, CHARLES CHRISTOPHER PEPYS, 1 Earl of *(2 son of Sir Wm. Weller Pepys, 1 baronet 1740–1825, master in chancery).* *b.* Wimpole st. London 29 April 1781; ed. at Harrow and Trin. coll. Cam., LL.B. 1803; barrister L.I. 23 Nov. 1804; practised in court of chancery; K.C. 24 Aug. 1826; solicitor general to Queen Adelaide, Nov. 1830; M.P. for Higham Ferrers 14 July 1831 to Sep. 1831, for Malton 30 Sep. 1831 to Jany. 1836; solicitor general 22 Feb. 1834; knighted at St. James's Palace 26 Feb. 1834; Master of the Rolls 29 Sep. 1834; P.C. 1 Oct. 1834; first comr. of the Great Seal 23 April 1835; lord chancellor 16 Jany. 1836 to 3 Sep. 1841 and 6 July 1846 to 19 June 1850 when he

COTTENHAM, 1 Earl (Con.)

resigned; created Baron Cottenham of Cottenham, co. Cambridge 20 Jany. 1836; succeeded his brother as 3 baronet 5 Oct. 1845 and his cousin Rev. Sir H. L. Pepys as 4 baronet 9 Dec. 1849; created Viscount Crowhurst and Earl of Cottenham 11 June 1850; the act 10 & 11 Vict. c. 96 whereby trustees are authorised to pay trust moneys into court is known as Lord Cottenham's act. *d.* Pietra Santa, Duchy of Lucca 29 April 1851. *bur.* Totteridge, Herts. *Doyle's Official baronage i, 464 (1886), portrait; Law Mag. xlvi, 280–8 (1851); Law Review xiv, 353–9 (1851); Law mag. and law review xxvii, 264–72 (1869); Lord Cottenham's Earldom, 2 ed. 1850.*

COTTER, GEORGE SACKVILLE. Second lieut. Madras artillery 15 June 1827, lieut. col. 1 Sep. 1860 to 15 Nov. 1861 when he retired; commanded at siege and capture of Lucknow, July 1857 to March 1858; C.B. 1 March 1861. *d.* 25 June 1878.

COTTER, SIR LUDLOW *(eld. son of Sir James Laurence Cotter, 4 baronet of Rockforest, Mallow, Cork, b. 1828).* *b.* Dublin 11 June 1853; knighted by the Queen at Windsor castle 12 Dec. 1874 in accordance with a special privilege contained in the patent as the eldest son of a baronet. *d.* Rockforest 24 Nov. 1882.

COTTERILL, RIGHT REV. HENRY *(son of Rev. Joseph Cotterill, R. of Blakeney, Norfolk, who d. 14 Feb. 1858 aged 78).* *b.* Ampton, Suffolk 1812; ed. at St. John's coll. Cam., Bell's scholar, fellow 1835; senior wrangler and first Smith's prizeman 1835, B.A. 1835, M.A. 1836, D.D. 1857; chaplain at Madras 1836–47; vice principal of Brighton college 1847–51, principal 1851–56; bishop of Grahamstown 4 Nov. 1856 to 26 April 1871 when he was elected co-adjutor bishop of Edinburgh; bishop of Edin. April 1872 to death; author of *The Seven ages of the Church* 1849; *The Genesis of the Church* 1872; *Does science aid faith in regard to creation* 1883 and many other works. *d.* Manor place, Edin. 16 April 1886.

COTTINGHAM, NOCKALLS JOHNSON *(elder son of Lewis Nockalls Cottingham, architect 1787–1847).* *b.* 1823; an architect; assisted his father, especially in restoration of Hereford cathedral where he designed the reredos 1847; a designer for stained glass. Lost in the steamship Arctic which foundered about 50 miles from Cape Race on her way from Liverpool to New York 27 Sep. 1854.

COTTLE, JOSEPH. *b.* 1770; bookseller at Bristol 1791–99; published several of the works

COTTLE, J. (Con.)

of the Lake poets Coleridge, Southey and Wordsworth; author of *Malvern Hills* 1798, 4 ed. 1829; *Alfred, an epic poem* 1800, 2 ed. 2 vols. 1804; *John the Baptist, a poem* 1801; *The fall of Cambria, a poem* 2 vols. 1808, 2 ed. 1811; *Early recollections chiefly relating to Samuel Taylor Coleridge* 2 vols. 1837–39, 2 ed. 1847. *d.* Fairfield house, Knowle near Bristol 7 June 1853. *Pen and ink sketches,* 2 ed. (1847) 165–74; *J. Cottle's Early recollections* (1837), *portrait.*

COTTON, CORBET. *b.* 10 Aug. 1808; ensign 19 foot 9 April 1825; assistant adjutant general of cavalry at head quarters 21 Aug. 1854 to 4 Oct. 1859; colonel 101 foot 29 Dec. 1873 to death; general 1 Oct. 1877. *d.* 65 Warwick sq. Belgravia, London 30 April 1885.

COTTON, FRANCIS VERE *(son of Henry Calveley Cotton of Woodcote, Oxfordshire, who d. 15 May 1831 aged 81).* *b.* 16 June 1799; entered navy, May 1814; captain 23 Nov. 1841; placed on retired list 4 June 1855; retired admiral 30 July 1875. *d.* Alport house, Whitchurch, Salop 30 Jany. 1884.

COTTON, RIGHT REV. GEORGE EDWARD LYNCH *(only son of Thomas D'Avenant Cotton, captain 7 fusiliers, who was killed at Nivelle near Bayonne 13 Nov. 1813).* *b.* Chester 29 Oct. 1813; ed. at Westminster and Trin. coll. Cam., fellow 1838, B.A. 1836, M.A. 1839, D.D. 1858; assistant master at Rugby 1837–52, 'the young master' of *Tom Brown's School Days*; master of Marlborough 1852–58 which he completely reorganised; bishop of Calcutta 29 March 1858 to death; consecrated in Westminster abbey 13 May 1858, installed 14 Nov. 1858; established schools in Bengal for educating the middle classes; author of numerous sermons, charges and other works; drowned at Kushtiâ on the Gorai river 6 Oct. 1866, body never found. *Memoir of G. E. L. Cotton edited by Mrs. Cotton, new ed. (1872); Macmillan's Mag. xv, 102–111 (1866); I.L.N. xxxii, 525 (1858), portrait.*

COTTON, VERY REV. HENRY. *b.* Bucks 1790; ed. at Westminster and Ch. Ch., Ox., reader in Greek 1810, B.A. 1811, M.A. 1813; sublibrarian at the Bodleian library 1814–22; a student of Ch. Ch.; domestic chaplain to archbishop of Cashel 1823; preb. of Killardriffe, Cashel 1 Oct. 1823 to 19 June 1824; archdeacon of Cashel 19 June 1824; treasurer of Ch. Ch. cathedral, Dublin 12 June 1832; dean of Lismore 16 Dec. 1834 to 1850; author of *A list of editions of the Bible in English*

from 1505 *to* 1820, *with specimens of translations*
1821, 2 *ed.* 1852; *A typographical gazetteer
attempted* 1824, 2 *ed.* 1831, *second series* 1866;
The five books of Maccabees in English 1833;
Fasti ecclesiæ Hibernicæ 5 *vols.* 1845–78; *The
four gospels and the acts of the apostles with short
notes* 1857, *and many other works. d.* Lismore
3 Dec. 1879.

COTTON, VERY REV. JAMES HENRY (2 *son of
Very Rev. George Cotton* 1742–1805, *dean of
Chester). b.* the deanery, Chester 8 Feb. 1781;
ed. at Chester and St. John's coll. Cam.,
LL.B. 1804; V. of Bangor 1819–38; precentor
of Bangor 31 March 1810 to 31 March 1838;
R. of Llanllechyd, Carnarvonshire 1821 to
death; dean of Bangor 31 March 1838 to
death; author of sermons, pamphlets and addresses. *d.* the deanery, Bangor 28 May 1862.

COTTON, JOHN. Writer Madras civil service
1801; principal magistrate of Tangore 1821–
27; annuitant on the fund 1 May 1830; a
director of East India Co. 30 April 1833,
deputy chairman of Court of directors 1842,
chairman 1843–45. *d.* Westbourne terrace,
Hyde Park, London 16 July 1860 aged 76.

COTTON, REV. RICHARD LYNCH *(brother of
Francis Vere Cotton* 1799–1884). *b.* Woodcote
14 Aug. 1794; ed. at Charterhouse and Worcester coll. Ox., B.A. 1815, M.A. 1818, B.D.
and D.D. 1839; scholar of Worcester coll. 8
May 1815, fellow 7 May 1816, tutor, dean
and bursar, provost Feb. 1839 to death, resided
continuously in Worcester coll. 1815 to 1880;
V. of Denchworth near Wantage 1823–39;
vice chancellor of Univ. of Ox. 1852–57;
promoted building of Shippon, Dry Sandford
and Headington Quarry churches; author of
Scriptural view of the Lord's Supper 1837; *The
way of salvation plainly and practically traced*
1837; *Lectures on the holy sacrament of the
Lord's Supper* 1849. *d.* Oxford 8 Dec. 1880.
bur. Holywell cemetery 14 Dec. *Guardian* 29
Dec. 1880 *p.* 1, 819.

COTTON, SIR SAINT VINCENT, 6 Baronet *(eld.
son of admiral Sir Charles Cotton,* 5 *baronet*
1753–1812). *b.* Madingley hall, Cambs. 6
Oct. 1801; succeeded 24 Feb. 1812; ed. at
Westminster and Ch. Ch. Ox.; cornet 10 light
dragoons 13 May 1827, lieut. 13 Dec. 1827
to 19 Nov. 1830 when placed on h.p.; distinguished himself in the hunting, shooting,
racing and pugilistic world; played in Marylebone cricket matches 1830–35; a great
player at hazard; dissipated all his property;
drove the 'Age' coach from Brighton to Lon-

don and back for some years from 1836. *d.*
5 Hyde park terrace, Kensington road, London
25 Jany. 1863. *New sporting mag. xii,* 81,
421 (1837), *portrait.*

COTTON, SIR SYDNEY JOHN *(brother of Rev.
Richard Lynch Cotton* 1794–1880). *b.* 2 Dec.
1792; cornet 22 dragoons 19 April 1810;
lieut. col. 28 foot 8 Jany. 1843; lieut. col. 22
foot 2 Dec. 1847; lieut. col. 10 foot 14 Dec.
1854 to 26 Oct. 1858; commanded the troops
on north west frontier of India during Indian
mutiny 1857–58; col. 10 foot 5 Feb. 1863 to
death; L.G. 20 April 1866; governor of
Chelsea hospital 10 May 1872 to death;
K.C.B. 24 March 1858, G.C.B. 24 May 1873;
author of *Remarks on drill* 1857; *Nine years
on the north west frontier of India* 1868; *The
Central Asian question, a prophecy fulfilled* 1869,
reprinted 1878. *d.* Chelsea hospital 20 Feb.
1874. *F. Brodigan's Historical record of* 28
Foot (1884) 94–9; *Kaye's Sepoy Mutiny ii,*
453, *et seq.; I.L.N. xxxii,* 489 (1858), *portrait;
Graphic ix,* 314, 328 (1874), *portrait.*

COTTON, WILLIAM *(son of Wm. Cotton of the
Customs, who d. Balham hill near London* 27
Oct. 1816 *aged* 58). *b.* 1794; made a special
study of Sir Joshua Reynolds's works; F.S.A.;
author of *A graphic and historical sketch of the
antiquities of Totnes* 1850; *Sir Joshua Reynolds'
Gleanings from his diary* 1856; *Some account
of the ancient borough town of Plympton St.
Maurice or Plympton Earl* 1859; gave a fine
collection of books, prints and drawings to the
Plymouth public library which erected a building for their reception and opened it to the
public 1 June 1853. *d.* 8 West Hoe terrace,
Plymouth 22 Jany. 1863. *G.M. xiv,* 520–22
(1863).

COTTON, WILLIAM (3 *son of Joseph Cotton of
Leyton, Essex* 1745–1825, *deputy master of the
Trinity house). b.* Leyton 12 Sep. 1786;
partner in firm of Huddart and Co. manufacturers of registered cables at Limehouse,
London 1807; one of founders of National
Society 1811; a director of Bank of England
1821–66, governor 1843–45, invented automatic weighing machine for gold 1844, still
in use and called after him 'the governor';
member of S.P.C.K. 50 years, treasurer;
F.R.S. 21 May 1821; sheriff of Essex 1837;
built and endowed St. Thomas's church,
Bethnal Green 1844 and St. Paul's church, Bow
Common 1847. *d.* Walwood house, Leytonstone, Essex 1 Dec. 1866, a painted memorial
window to his memory was placed by public
subscription in St. Paul's cathedral. *G.M. iii,*
111–13 (1867); *I.L.N. v,* 20 (1844), *portrait.*

COTTON, Sir Willoughby *(only son of Rowland Cotton, admiral R.N., who d. 3 Nov.* 1794). *b.* Upper Grosvenor st. London 1783; ed. at Rugby where he was leader of a rebellion Nov. 1797; ensign 3 foot guards 31 Oct. 1798; lieut. col. 47 foot 17 May 1821, lieut. col. 14 foot 13 Oct. 1828 to 22 July 1830; commanded forces in Jamaica 1829–34 where he put down an insurrection of the slaves 1831; commanded first division of Bengal army in Afghan war 1838–39; commander in chief at Bombay 8 April 1847 to 30 Dec. 1850; colonel of 98 foot 1 Aug. 1839 to 17 April 1854, and of 32 foot 17 April 1854 to death; general 20 June 1854; C.B. 26 Dec. 1826, K.C.B. 19 July 1838, G.C.B. 21 Jany. 1840; K.C.H. 1830; knighted at St. James's palace 17 July 1830. *d.* 15 Lowndes sq. London 4 May 1860.

COUCH, Jonathan *(only child of Richard Couch of Polperro, Cornwall* 1739–1823). *b.* Polperro 15 March 1789; surgeon at Polperro 1810 to death; F.L.S. 6 April 1824; contributed to T. Bewick's *British Quadrupeds* and W. Yarrell's *British Fishes;* author of *Cornish Fauna 3 parts* 1838–44; *Illustrations of instinct deduced from the habits of British animals* 1847; *A history of the fishes of the British islands 4 vols.* 1860–65; translated *Pliny's Natural history 3 vols.* 1847–50, published by the Wernerian Club. *d.* Polperro 13 April 1870. *The history of Polperro by the late Jonathan Couch, with a short account of his life by T. Q. Couch* 1871; *Life of a Scotch naturalist Thomas Edward* (1877) 292, 296, 333–49.

COUCH, Richard Quiller *(eld. son of the preceding). b.* Polperro 14 March 1816; ed. at Guy's hospital, London; M.R.C.S. 1838, L.S.A. 1839; surgeon at Polperro; practised at Penzance 1843 to death; a sec. and curator of Penzance Natural history and antiquarian soc. 1845 to death; curator of Royal Geol. Soc. of Cornwall 1848 to death; contributed the third part (on the Zoophytes) to his father's *Cornish Fauna* 1844, and an account of natural history of West Cornwall to J. S. Courtney's *Guide to Penzance* 1845. *d.* Penzance 8 May 1863. *G.M. xv,* 106–8 (1863).

COUCH, Thomas Quiller *(brother of the preceding). b.* Polperro 28 May 1826; L.S.A. and M.R.C.S. 1852; surgeon at Bodmin 1855 to death; F.S.A. 26 March 1870; a constant contributor to *Notes and Queries,* from which two series of his articles *The folklore of a Cornish village* 1855 and 1857 have been incorporated in his father's *History of Polperro* 1871; published in the *Journal of the Royal instit. of Cornwall* 1864 and 1870 lists of local

Couch, T. Q. *(Con.)*
words afterwards included in a *Glossary of words in use in Cornwall* issued by the English Dialect Society 1880. *d.* Bodmin 23 Oct. 1884.

COULSON, Walter *(2 son of Thomas Coulson, master painter in Devonport dockyard, who d.* 1845). *b.* Torpoint, Cornwall 1794; amanuensis to Jeremy Bentham; parliamentary reporter on the *Morning Chronicle;* editor of the *Traveller* 1822, of the *Globe and Traveller* 1823; barrister G.I. 26 Nov. 1828, bencher, Nov. 1851; recorder of Penzance 18 July 1836 to Jany. 1838; Q.C. July 1851; parliamentary draughtsman for the home office; member of Political Economy club, June 1821; a registration and conveyancing comr. 1847; member of royal commission for Great Exhibition 1851. *d.* North bank, St. John's Wood, London 21 Nov. 1860. *Leigh Hunt's Correspondence i,* 98, 120, 126–34.

COULSON, William *(brother of the preceding). b.* Torpoint, Cornwall 15 Sep. 1801; studied in Berlin 1824–26; M.R.C.S. 1826, F.R.C.S. 1843, member of council 1851, Hunterian orator 1861; a founder of Aldersgate st. school of medicine 1826; surgeon to Aldersgate st. dispensary 1828–32; consulting surgeon to City of London Lying-in hospital 1830; senior surgeon to St. Mary's hospital, Paddington 1843; sheriff of Cornwall 1863; F.S.A. 19 June 1856; accumulated £200,000, one of the largest fortunes ever made in practice; author of *On deformities of the chest* 1836, 2 ed. 1837; *On diseases of the hip joint* 1837, 2 ed. 1841; *On diseases of the bladder and prostate gland* 1838, 6 ed. 1865; *On lithotrity and lithotomy* 1853; *Lectures on diseases of the joints* 1854. *d.* 1 Chester terrace, Regent's park, London 5 May 1877. *Medical Circular ii,* 329–32, 349–51 (1853), *portrait; Beattie's Life of T. Campbell ii,* 448–52 (1849).

COULTON, David Trevena. *b.* Devizes 1810; contributed to *Quarterly Review;* founded the *Britannia,* a weekly journal of news, politics and literature 13 April 1839 which he sold 1850; edited the *Press and St. James's Chronicle,* weekly paper 1854 to death; invented a plan for an atmospheric railway; author of *Fortune, a romance of life 3 vols.* 1853; and of *An inquiry into the authorship of the letters of Junius. d.* Brighton 8 May 1857.

COUPER, Sir George, 1 Baronet *(elder son of Robert Couper, M.D. of Fochabers, Morayshire). b.* 21 June 1788; ensign 69 foot 2 Nov. 1797; major 92 foot 30 Dec. 1819 to 20 March 1823 when placed on h.p.; principal equerry and comptroller of the household to Duchess of

COUPER, SIR GEORGE *(Con.)*
Kent 1839 to death; K.H. 1831, C.B. 19 July 1838; created baronet 23 June 1841. *d.* Frogmore near Windsor 28 Feb. 1861.

COURTAULD, SAMUEL *(eld. son of George Courtauld the first to introduce silk throwing into Essex), b.* Albany in the State of New York 1 June 1793; brought to England in his infancy; developed the business of a silk throwster into that of a manufacturer of crape; head of firm of Courtauld & Co. crape manufacturers, Bocking, Essex; in the Consistory court 8 Nov. 1837 raised question of legality of a church rate in Braintree, case settled in house of lords in his favor 12 Aug. 1853; presented with a testimonial worth 700 guineas at Braintree 25 Sept. 1855; F.R.A.S. 8 Nov. 1867. *d.* Gosfield hall, Essex 21 March 1881, personalty sworn under £700,000, 7 May 1881. *I.L.N. 13 Oct. 1855 pp. 445–46 with view of testimonial; Monthly Notices of R.A.S. xlii, 144 (1882); The Braintree church rate case, Gosling v. Veley, by W. W. Attree 1853.*

COURTENAY, FRANCIS BURDETT *(son of Mr. Courtenay of Ryde, Isle of Wight, surgeon).* M.R.C.S. 13 July 1833; settled in London as a specialist in urethral diseases 1833; surgeon to hospital for stricture of the urethra, London; author of *Enlargement of the prostate gland in old people* 1839; *Pathology and cure of stricture of the urethra* 1843; *On Spermattorrhea and the professional fallacies which prevail in relation to its nature* 1858, 13 *ed.* 1884; *Revelations of quacks and quackery, by Detector, pseud.* 1865, 11 *ed.* 1886. *d.* 2 Chandos st. Cavendish sq. London 15 March 1886 in 76 year. *Medical Circular iii, 71, 72 (1853).*

COURTENAY, GEORGE WILLIAM CONWAY. *b.* Beach hall near Chester 1795; entered navy 26 Sep. 1805; captain 14 April 1828; consul general at Hayti 1832–42; V.A. 29 July 1861. *d.* 1E The Albany, Piccadilly, London 31 March 1863.

COURTHOPE, WILLIAM *(only son of Thomas Courthope of Rotherhithe). b.* Rotherhithe 6 May 1808; private clerk to Francis Townsend, Rouge Dragon 1824; clerk to the College of Arms 1833; Rouge Croix pursuivant of arms Feb. 1839; sec. to Garter King of arms 1842; barrister I.T. 31 Jany. 1851; Somerset Herald 31 Jany. 1854; registrar of College of arms, Nov. 1859; author of *Synopsis of extinct baronetage* 1835; *Memoir of Daniel Chamier* 1852, privately printed; *A pictorial history of the Earls of Warwick by John Rows* dated 1845 but not published until 1859; edited Sir N. H. Nicolas's *Historic peerage of England* 1853. *d.* Hastings 13 May 1866. *bur.* Wadhurst.

COURTNEY, JOHN SAMPSON *(eld. son of James Courtney of the Excise 1778–1860). b.* Ilfracombe 10 Oct. 1803; clerk in Mount's Bay bank, Penzance 1829, manager 1856 to death; author of *A guide to Penzance and its neighbourhood, including the Islands of Scilly* 1845; and of several papers in *Transactions of Royal Cornwall Polytechnic Society* 1838–42. *d.* Alverton, Penzance 10 Feb. 1881. *Half a century at Penzance (1825–1875) from notes by J. S. Courtney, written by Louise Courtney 1878; Times 12 Feb. 1881 p. 9, col. 6.*

COUSEN, JOHN. *b.* Mirashay near Bradford 19 Feb. 1804; one of the best landscape engravers, retired from practice about 1864; engraved book plates after Turner for *The Rivers of France,* and after Stansfield for *Heath's Picturesque Annual* 1833 and 1834; engraved plates for the Royal, Vernon and Turner galleries issued in the *Art Journal. d.* Holmesdale road, South Norwood near London 26 Dec. 1880. *bur.* Croydon cemetery.

COUSINS, SAMUEL. *b.* Exeter 9 May 1801; apprenticed to S. W. Reynolds the engraver, Sep. 1814, assistant to him; a mezzotint engraver at 104 Great Russell st. London 1826; A.R.A. Nov. 1835, associate engraver 1854, the first academician engraver 10 Feb. 1855; presented an almost complete set of his engravings to British Museum 1872; gave £15,000 to R.A. for benefit of poor artists about 1872; T. Agnew and Sons held an exhibition of his works at Manchester 1877; another exhibition took place at the Fine Art Society 148 New Bond st. London 1883 and a third was held at H. Graves and Co.'s, Pall Mall 1887. *d.* 24 Camden sq. London 7 May 1887. *G. Pycroft's Memoir of S. Cousins (1887) privately printed; Artists at home 1 April 1884 pt. ii, p. 19; Sandby's History of Royal Academy ii, 322–4 (1862).*

COVENTRY, THOMAS. Barrister L.I. 1 July 1824; author of *Concise forms in conveyancing* 1827; *On conveyancers' evidence* 1832; *A readable edition of Coke upon Littleton* 1830; author with Samuel Hughes of *Analytical digested index to the common law reports* 2 vols. 1827. *d.* Nice 19 April 1869 aged 72.

COWAN, CHARLES *(son of Rev. Thomas Conolly Cowan, who d. Reading* 1856). M.D. Edin. and L.R.C.S. Edin. 1833, M.D. Paris 1834; pres. of Hunterian Soc.; an early exponent of the science and art of auscultation; practised at Bath 1835–9, at Reading 1839 to death; senior phys. Royal Berkshire hospital 1839, the best speaker in the profession; author of *A Bedside*

COWAN, C. (Con.)

manual, or a physical diagnosis of the lungs, &c. 1836; *Phrenology consistent with science and revelation* 1841, and many other works *d.* Reading 6 Dec. 1868 aged 62. *Barker's Photographs* (1868), *ii,* 9–13, *portrait*

COWAN, JOHN *(son of Hugh Cowan of Ayr).* *b.* Ayr 1798; ed. at Ayr academy and Univ. of Edin.; called to Scotch bar 1822; sheriff of Kincardineshire 10 Jany. 1848; solicitor general for Scotland 18 April 1851; lord of session and lord of justiciary 23 June 1851 to Jany. 1874 with courtesy title of Lord Cowan. *d.* Elmbank, Edinburgh 1 Aug. 1878.

COWARD, JAMES. *b.* London 25 Jany. 1824; a chorister in Westminster abbey; obtained 13 prizes for glees 1845–67; organist of Lambeth parish church; organist at Crystal palace 1857 to death; conductor of the Western Madrigal Society, Oct. 1864 to March 1872; organist of St. George's church, Bloomsbury 1866–69, of the Sacred Harmonic Society and of Grand lodge of Freemasons; organist of St. Magnus the Martyr, London Bridge to death; published *O Lord correct me* an anthem, *Sing unto God* a canon, *Airy fairy Lilian* and other part songs. *d.* 38 Lupus st. Pimlico, London 22 Jany. 1880.

COWELL, JOSEPH LEATHLEY. *b.* near Torquay 7 Aug. 1792; midshipman R.N. 1805–8; made his debut 23 Jany. 1812 at Devonport as Belcour in *The West Indian;* first appeared in London at Drury lane theatre 1812 as Samson Rawbold in Colman's *Iron Chest,* acted there till 1818; composed and acted on the Lincoln circuit a three hours olio called 'Cowell alone or a trip to London'; played at Adelphi, Drury Lane and Astley's; first appeared in America at Park theatre, New York, Oct. 1821 in *The foundling of the forest;* left the Park theatre 24 July 1823; opened Philadelphia theatre at Wilmington, Delaware, Sep. 1827; acted at Adelphi and other London theatres; author of *Thirty years passed among the players in England and America* 2 vols. 1845. *d.* Vauxhall, London 14 Nov. 1863. *J. N. Ireland's Records of New York stage i,* 394–5 (1866); *Era* 22 *Nov.* 1863 p. 10, col. 1.

COWELL, SAMUEL HOUGHTON *(son of the preceding).* *b.* Craven buildings, Drury lane, London 5 April 1819; first appeared on the stage at Boston, U.S. 1829 as Crack in T. Knight's *Turnpike Gate;* acted in all chief theatres in the U.S.; played Alessio in *La Sonnambula* at Surrey theatre, London 15 July 1844; acted at T.R. Edinburgh 4 years, then in London at

COWELL, S. H. (Con.)

Olympic, Princess's and Covent Garden, at Glasgow, Belfast and Dublin; one of the leaders of the Monte Christo row at Drury Lane theatre 12 June 1848; the leading comic singer at chief music halls in London and the provinces 1851–60; sang in United States 1860–62; his best songs were *Billy Barlow, Lord Lovel, The ratcatcher's daughter, Alonzo the brave and Richard the Third;* sang *The Ratcatcher's Daughter* at Canterbury Arms 12 Feb. 1855 and more than 50 nights afterwards; sang *Lord Lovel* 600 times; composed music to his own ballads *Clara Cline, The Yellow Busha-Belle, In Westminster* 1855, &c. *d.* Crown hotel, Blandford, Dorset 11 March 1864. *Rambles by Patricius Walker* [*W. Allingham*] 1873, *pp.* 252–55; *Tallis's Illustrated life in London* (1864) 86, 88, 89, 2 *portraits; Theatrical times iii,* 241–2 (1848), *portrait; Illust. sporting news iii,* 92 (1864), *v,* 268 (1866), *portrait; Era* 20 *March* 1864 *p.* 6, *col.* 2; *S. Cowell's New illustrated pocket songster* 4 vols. 1856.

COWELL, WILLIAM. *b.* Dublin 1820; connected with Broadway theatre, New York 1847; travelled with Barry Sullivan the actor as business manager 1858; wrote pamphlets in defence of the stage against attacks of Rev. Dr. Hatfield of Chicago; his pamphlets were considered as able a defence of the profession as ever written. *d.* Philadelphia 24 Feb. 1868.

COWELL-STEPNEY, SIR JOHN STEPNEY, 1 Baronet *(elder son of Andrew Cowell of Coleshill, Bucks., general who commanded brigade of guards in Irish rebellion, and d. 21 Sep. 1821).* *b.* 23 Feb. 1791; ensign Coldstream guards 18 May 1809, captain 15 June 1830 to 22 May 1832 when he sold out; served in 6 campaigns under Duke of Wellington and Lord Lynedoch; assumed additional surname of Stepney 29 Dec. 1857; sheriff of Carmarthen 1862; M.P. for Carmarthen 1868–74; K.H. 1832; created baronet 22 Sep. 1871; author of *Leaves from the diary of an officer of the Guards* 1854. *d.* 5 St. George's place, London 15 May 1877. *T. Nicholas's County families of Wales i,* 282 (1872).

COWEN, SIR JOSEPH *(eld. son of John Cowen of Winlaton, Durham).* *b.* Greenside, Durham, Feb. 1800; a fire brick and clay retort manufacturer; alderman of Newcastle; chairman of Gateshead Board of Guardians; appointed by act of parliament a life member of Tyne improvement commission, chairman of this commission; M.P. for Newcastle upon Tyne, July 1865 to death; knighted at Buckingham palace 14 March 1872. *d.* Stella hall near Blaydon-on-Tyne 19 Dec. 1873. *I.L.N. lxiv,* 22, 36 (1874), *portrait, lxviii,* 35 (1876).

COWEN, WILLIAM. *b.* Rotherham, Yorkshire; landscape painter; exhibited at Society of Artists 1811, at British Institution 1823–60, at the R.A. 1824–39; published *Yorkshire scenery from drawings by W. Cowen* 1826; a series of 12 etchings of Corsica 1843 included in his *Six weeks in Corsica* 1848; contributed view of Kilchurn castle, Loch Awe to fresco competition in Westminster hall 1844. *d.* about 1860.

COWIE, HUGH *(eld. son of Alexander Cowie of Auchterless, co. Aberdeen). b.* June 1829; ed. at King's coll. London and Trin. coll. Cam., scholar, 26 wrangler 1851; B.A. 1851, M.A. 1860; barrister G.I. 27 Jany. 1862, bencher 26 May 1880; a revising barrister for home circuit 1868; recorder of Maldon and of Saffron Walden 11 Aug. 1873 to death; admitted barrister M.T. 13 April 1875; chancellor of diocese of Durham, Jany. 1876; sec. to Criminal code commission 1878; Q.C. 16 Dec. 1882; reporter in Court of Exchequer for the *Law Journal Reports* 1864–71. *d.* Ythandale, Wimbledon park near London 20 July 1886.

COWIE, ROBERT. *b.* Lerwick, Shetland Islands 1842; ed. at Univs. of Aberdeen and Edin; M.A. Aberdeen; M.D. Edin. 1866; author of *Shetland descriptive and historical* 1871, 3 ed. 1879. *d.* 8 May 1874.

COWLE, WILLIAM. *b.* 6 Feb. 1802; played with success leading characters at various London theatres from 1822; a favourite actor at Birmingham; a founder of Royal general theatrical fund 7 Nov. 1838, one of its annuitants Feb. 1862 to death. *d.* 92 Camden st. London 22 March 1885.

COWLEY, HENRY RICHARD CHARLES WELLESLEY, 1 Earl *(eld. child of Henry Wellesley, 1 baron Cowley 1773–1847). b.* Hertford st. London 17 July 1804; attaché of embassy at Vienna 1 Oct. 1824; succeeded 27 April 1847; minister plenipotentiary to Berne 29 Feb. 1848; envoy extraord. and min. plenipo. at Frankfort 8 Feb. 1849; to Germanic confederation 7 June 1851; P.C. 2 Feb. 1852; ambassador extraord. and plenipotentiary to French republic 5 Feb. 1852 to July 1867; joint plenipo. with Earl of Clarendon at conference of Paris Feb. to March 1856; signed treaty of peace with Russia 30 March 1856, with Persia 4 March 1857; created Earl Cowley and Viscount Dangan 11 April 1857; employed on a confidential mission to Vienna Feb. to March 1859; signed at Paris, treaty of commerce between England and France 23 Jany. 1860; retired on a pension of £1700 16 July 1867;

COWLEY, H. R. C. W. *(Con.)*
C.B. 27 April 1848, K.C.B. 1 March 1851, G.C.B. 21 Feb. 1853; K.G. 3 Feb. 1866. *d.* 20 Albemarle st. London 15 July 1884. *bur.* parish church, Draycot near Chippenham 19 July. *Times 16 July 1884 p.* 9, *col.* 5.

COWLING, JOHN. *b.* 1802; educ. at St. John's coll. Cam., senior wr. and 1st Smith's prizeman 1824, B.A. 1824, M.A. 1827, fellow of St. John's coll. 6 April 1824; barrister M.T. 9 Nov. 1827; deputy high steward of Univ. of Cam. 1839 to death; standing counsel to Univ. of Cam. 1845 to death. *d.* 28B Albemarle st. London 12 Dec. 1855.

COWPER, GEORGE AUGUSTUS FREDERICK COWPER, 6 Earl *(eld. son of 5 Earl Cowper 1778–1837). b.* George st. Hanover sq. London 26 June 1806; cornet Royal horse guards 28 April 1827, lieut. 1830; lieut. 31 foot 13 Feb. to 6 March 1835; M.P. for Canterbury 31 July 1830 to 29 Dec. 1834; under secretary of state for foreign department 13 Nov. to 17 Dec. 1834; succeeded 21 June 1837; lord lieut. of Kent 21 April 1849 to death. *d.* at house of governor of the gaol, Maidstone 15 April 1856. *Waagen's Treasures of art in Great Britain iii,* 7–17 (1854).

COWPER, SIR CHARLES *(son of Ven. Wm. Cowper 1780–1858). b.* Drypool, Yorkshire 26 April 1807; secretary of Church and school lands corporation at Sydney 1826–33 when corporation was dissolved; sheep breeder on the Murray river 1833; member for co. Cumberland of legislative council 1843–50, for Durham 1851–56, for Sydney 1856–59, for Liverpool Plains 1869–70; colonial sec. N.S.W. 26 Aug. 1856 to 2 Oct. 1856, 7 Sep. 1857 to 26 Oct. 1859, 9 March 1860 to 15 Oct. 1863, 3 Feb. 1865 to 21 Jany. 1866 and 13 Jany. 1870 to 15 Dec. 1870; agent general for N.S.W. in London 6 Dec. 1870 to 31 May 1871; C.M.G. 23 June 1869, K.C.M.G. 23 Feb. 1872. *d.* Eldon road, Kensington, London 19 Oct. 1875. *Heaton's Australian dictionary of dates* (1879) 44–7.

COWPER, EBENEZER. Articled to Mr. Lloyd, engineer, Gravel lane, Southwark, London; partner with his brother Edward Cowper; spent his life in putting up printing presses in England, Scotland, Ireland and on the Continent on the Cowper-Applegath model; the first edition of the Waverley novels was printed at Edinburgh off a Cowper machine; erected 12 machines at Imprimerie Royale, Paris 1830; Cowper machines although superseded by the Walter press for printing newspapers are still

COWPER, E. (Con.)

used for printing books ; erected the printing machinery in the Bank of England. d. Harbourne road, Edgbaston, Birmingham 14 Sep. 1880 aged 77. *Engineering 24 Sep. 1880 p. 257 ; Iron 24 Sep. 1880 p. 244.*

COWPER, EDWARD *(brother of the preceding).* b. 1790 ; ironmonger at St. Mary, Newington Butts 1816 ; printer in Nelson sq. 1818 ; partner with his brother-in-law Augustus Applegath ; they jointly invented the four-cylinder printing machine and erected it at the Times office 1827 ; partner with his brother Ebenezer as machine makers, their machines were widely used throughout Europe ; invented an ink distributing machine ; professor of manufacturing art and machinery at King's college, London 1846 to death. d. 9 Kensington park road, London 17 Oct. 1852. *Wyman's Bibliography of printing* (1880), 14, 146.

COWPER, HENRY FREDERICK (2 *son of 6 Earl Cowper* 1806-56). b. 18 April 1836 ; ed. at Harrow and Ch. Ch. Ox.; contested Tamworth, Oct. 1863 and Herts. March 1864 ; M.P. for Herts. 24 July 1865 to Nov. 1885. d. Panshanger, Hertford 10 Nov. 1887. *I.L.N. liv,* 213 (1869), *portrait.*

COWPER, JOHN CURTIS, stage name of John Curtis *(son of David Curtis of Manchester, painter).* b. Port st. Piccadilly, Manchester 7 June 1827 ; first appeared at T.R. Manchester as Romeo ; played star engagements with G. V. Brooke ; leading tragedian at T.R. Liverpool ; first appeared in London at Adelphi theatre, 17 Dec. 1862 as Duke Aranza in *The Honeymoon ;* played leading parts at Drury Lane, Princess's, Holborn and other London theatres. d. Barnes, Surrey 30 Jany. 1885. *bur.* Brompton cemetery, London 4 Feb.

COWPER, VEN. WILLIAM. b. Whittington, Lancs. 28 Dec. 1780 ; C. of Rawdon near Leeds ; senior assistant colonial chaplain 1 Jany. 1808 ; arrived in Sydney 18 Aug. 1809 ; Inc. of St. Philip's ch. Sydney, Aug. 1809 to death, ch. was consecrated 25 Dec. 1810 ; organised the Benevolent 1818, Bible and Religious tract societies in N.S.W. ; sec. of diocesan committees of the S.P.C.K. and S.P.G. ; archdeacon of Cumberland and Camden 1848 to death ; special commissary during Bishop Broughton's absence in Europe 1852. d. Sydney 6 July 1858.

COX, DAVID *(only son of Joseph Cox of Birmingham, whitesmith, who d. about* 1830). b. Heath mill lane, Deritend, Birmingham 29 April 1783 ; scene painter at Birmingham theatre

COX, D. (Con.)

1800-4 ; came to London 1804 ; member of Soc. of painters in water colours 1813 ; drawing master in schools at Hereford 1814-26 ; exhibited 136 pictures at Pall Mall gallery 1844-54 ; made his first sketching visit to Bettws-y-coed then nearly unknown 1844, painted sign of the Royal Oak Inn there 1847 which he re-touched and varnished 1849 ; the greatest English water colour painter except Turner, his picture 'The Hayfield' fetched £2950 at the Quilter sale, April 1875, a price unparalleled for any water-colour ; the best collections of his works were exhibited in Liverpool, Nov. 1875 numbering 448 pictures insured for about £100,000, and at Manchester Exhibition 1887 ; illustrated various works ; author of *The young artist's companion* 1825 ; *A treatise on landscape painting* 1841. d. Greenfield house, Harborne near Birmingham 7 June 1859. *A biography of D. Cox by W. Hall* (1881), *portrait ; Memoirs of D. Cox by N. N. Solly* (1875) ; *Sherer's Gallery of British artists, i,* 124-6 ; *Redgrave's Century of painters ii, 479-86* (1866) ; *I.L.N. xxxv, 28, 42*(1859), *portrait.*

COX, DAVID *(only child of the preceding).* b. Dulwich Common, summer of 1809 ; pupil of his father ; a water-colour painter ; exhibited at the R.A. 1827 ; associate of Soc. of painters in water-colours 1849. d. Chester house, Mount Ephraim road, Streatham, Surrey 4 Dec. 1885.

COX, REV. EDWARD *(son of Edward Cox, who d. 27 Dec.* 1849 *aged* 73). b. about 1806 ; ed. at Old hall near Ware, Herts.; assistant priest at Chelsea ; pres. of St. Edmund's college at Old hall green, Aug. 1840 to Aug. 1851 ; missioner at Southampton, Aug. 1851 to death; a member of the Southwark chapter, vicar general ; canon of Southwark ; published *The history of the church translated from the German of the Rev. J. J. von Döllinger 4 vols.* 1840-2 ; *A treatise on the church, translated from the German of the Rev. H. Klee* 1847 ; *The Our Father, or illustrations of the Lord's prayer, from the German of J. E. Veith* 1849. d. Southampton 9 Nov. 1856.

COX, EDWARD TOWNSEND *(son of Rev. Thomas Cox, chaplain of St. John's, Deritend, Birmingham).* b. Deritend 1769 ; surgeon at Stratford-on-Avon, surgeon to the infirmary at Birmingham 40 years; took an active part in founding and conducting Royal school of medicine ; a most successful accoucheur ; disliked travelling so much that he had never seen the sea. d. 26 Nov. 1863. *W. S. Cox's Annals of Queen's college, iv,* 149-54 (1873).

COX, EDWARD WILLIAM (*eld. son of Wm. Charles Cox of Taunton, manufacturer*). *b.* Taunton 1809; barrister M.T. 5 May 1843; recorder of Helston and Falmouth, Feb. 1857 to June 1868; serjeant at law 29 May 1868; recorder of Portsmouth, June 1868; M.P. for Taunton 1868–1869 when unseated on petition; chairman of second court of Middlesex sessions, March 1870 to death; founded 22 Feb. 1875 Psychological society of Great Britain, pres. to his death, society was dissolved 31 Dec. 1879; established *Law Times* 8 April 1843; *County courts chronicle and gazette of bankruptcy* 1846; *Exchange and Mart; The country, a journal of rural pursuits* 1873; purchased from Benjamin Webster *The Field, a gentleman's newspaper devoted to sport*; proprietor of *The Queen, a lady's newspaper*; wrote or edited 1829, *A Poem* 1829; *Reports of cases in criminal law* 13 vols. 1846–78; *The magistrate* 1848; *The advocate* 1852; *The law and practice of joint-stock companies* 1855, 7 ed. 1870; *Reports of all the cases relating to the law of joint-stock companies* 4 vols. 1867–71; *What am I?* 1873; *The mechanism of man* 1876; *A monograph of sleep and dreams* 1878. *d.* Moat mount, Mill Hill, Middlesex 24 Nov. 1879. *S. C. Hall's Retrospect of a long life ii,* 121–6 (1883); *Hatton's Journalistic London* (1882) 208–11; *I.L.N.* 6 Dec. 1879 *pp.* 529, 530, *portrait.*

COX, REV. FRANCIS AUGUSTUS. *b.* Leighton Buzzard 7 March 1783; ed. at the Baptist college, Bristol and Univ. of Edin., M.A. 1802; ordained to ministry of Baptist congregation at Clipstone, Northamptonshire 4 April 1804; pastor of Baptist chapel, Hackney, London 3 Oct. 1811 to death; sec. to general body of dissenting ministers of the three denominations residing in and near London 3 years; a projector and founder of London University 1828, librarian short time; LL.D. Glasgow 1824, D.D. Waterville, U.S. 1838; author of *Female scripture biography* 2 vols. 1817; *History of the Baptist missionary society from 1792 to 1842,* 2 vols. 1842, and many other works. *d.* King Edward's road, South Hackney, London 5 Sep. 1853.

COX, REV. GEORGE VALENTINE (*son of Charles Cox of St. Martin's, Oxford*). *b.* Oxford 1786; ed. at Magdalen college sch. and New coll. Ox., B.A. 1806, M.A. 1808; master of New college school 1806 to June 1857; Esquire Bedel in law in Univ. of Ox. March 1806, in medicine and arts 29 Jany. 1815 to 1866, University coroner 1808; chaplain of New coll. 1812–20; author of *Jeannette Isabelle* 3 vols. 1837 a novel; *The Prayer book epistles* 1846; *Recollections of Oxford* 1868; translated from

COX, REV. G. V. (*Con.*)

the German Dahlmann's *Life of Herodotus* 1845, Neander's *Emperor Julian and his generation* 1850, and Ullmann's *Gregory of Nazianzum* 1851. *d.* Cowley lodge, Oxford 19 March 1875.

COX, HARRY, stage name of Oliver James Bussley. *b.* Bristol 1841; first appeared in London at Prince of Wales's theatre 15 April 1865 as Alessio in H. J. Byron's burlesque *La Sonnanbula*; acted at Strand theatre, April 1872 to day before his death. *d.* 3 Burfield st. Hammersmith 10 Jany. 1882. *Era 14 Jany.* 1882 *p.* 5, *col.* 2; *Entr'Acte* 21 *Jany.* 1882, *portrait.*

COX, HENRY CHAMBERS MURRAY. Entered Bengal army 1805; colonel 58 Bengal N.I. 5 June 1853 to 1869; general 9 Dec. 1871. *d.* St. Ann's, Burnham, Somerset 22 July 1876.

COX, JOHN. Second lieut. Rifle brigade 16 March 1808, major 19 Aug. 1828 to 17 Feb. 1837 when placed on h.p.; M.G. 18 Dec. 1855; colonel 88 foot 13 Oct. 1860 to death; K.H. 1832. *d.* Cheltenham 7 Feb. 1863.

COX, JOHN HAMILTON (*only son of Wm. Cox, K.H. who d. 13 Jany.* 1857). *b.* 1817; ensign 75 foot 10 Oct. 1834, captain 23 March 1849 to 2 Dec. 1862 when placed on h.p.; brigade major to Highland brigade during Indian mutiny; C.B. 24 May 1873; M.G. retired on full pay 5 July 1873. *d.* 37 Sterndale road, West Kensington, London 10 March 1887.

COX, JOHN LEWIS. Head of the firm of Cox and Sons (afterwards Cox and Wyman) printers to the H.E.I. Co. Great Queen st. London; master of Stationer's Co. 1849–50. *d.* Ham Common near London 1 Feb. 1856 aged 79.

COX, ROBERT (3 *son of Robert Cox of Georgie Mills, co. Edinburgh, leather-dresser*). *b.* Georgie 25 Feb. 1810; ed. at high sch. and Univ. Edin.; a writer to the signet 1832; sec. of a literary institution at Liverpool 1835–39; edited *Phrenological Journal*, numbers xxxiv to l of the first series and 1841–47; compiled index to the 22 vols. of *Encyclopædia Britannica,* 7 ed. 1842; author of *Sabbath laws and Sabbath duties* 1853; *The literature of the Sabbath question* 2 vols. 1865; bequeathed his collection of books on the Sabbath question to Advocates' library, Edin. *d.* Edinburgh 3 Feb. 1872.

COX, TALBOT ASHLEY. *b.* 9 July 1836; ensign 3 foot 29 July 1853, lieut. col. 12 July 1871 to death; C.B. 2 June 1877. *d.* Cawnpore 9 Dec. 1877.

COX, WILLIAM. Second lieut. 95 foot 6 June 1805; major 75 foot 20 June 1834 to 1 July 1843 when placed on h.p.; M.G. 20 June 1854; K.H. 1835. *d.* St. Leonard's on Sea 13 Jany. 1857.

COX, SIR WILLIAM (3 *son of John Cox of Coolcliffe, co. Wexford 1749–93*). *b.* Coolcliffe 5 Dec. 1776; ensign 68 foot 1 Oct. 1794; commanded fortress of Almeida, April 1809 to 27 Aug. 1810 when its magazine having exploded he surrendered; lieut. col. Portugese army 16 Feb. 1809 to 25 Dec. 1816 when placed on h.p.; K.T.S. 28 Aug. 1815; knighted by Prince Regent at Carlton house 13 Aug. 1816; colonel in British army 12 Aug. 1819; sheriff of King's County 1825. *d.* Longford place, Monkstown, co. Dublin 1 July 1864.

COX, WILLIAM JAMES (2 *son of Philip Cox 1779–1841, proprietor of the Royal tennis court, James st. Haymarket, London*). *b.* 2 Feb. 1806; part proprietor of the Royal tennis court many years; champion of England at game of tennis. *d.* Brantford, Canada West 30 June 1864. *J. Marshall's Annals of tennis* (1878) 100–106.

COX, WILLIAM SANDS (*eld. son of Edward Townsend Cox of Birmingham, surgeon 1769–1863*). *b.* 38 Cannon st. Birmingham 1802; L.S.A. 1823; M.R.C.S. 1824, F.R.C.S. 1843; started a medical and surgical class-room at Temple row, Birmingham 1 Dec. 1825; removed to an old chapel in Paradise st. 1830 which he named the School of Medicine, it was incorporated by royal charter as the Queen's college 1843, principal of the college 1858–9; founded Queen's hospital, Birmingham 1840–1; F.R.S. 5 May 1836; member of French Institute; hon. member of nearly every important surgical school in Europe; author of *A synopsis of the bones, ligaments and muscles, bloodvessels and nerves of the human body* 1831; *Annals of Queen's college* 4 vols. 1873. *d.* Woodside, Kenilworth 23 Dec. 1875. *Barker's Photographs of eminent medical men i*, 61–6 (1865), *portrait, reprinted in Cox's Annals iv*, 155–60 (1873); *E. Edwards's Personal recollections of Birmingham* (1877) 132–39.

COXE, REV. HENRY OCTAVIUS (8 *son of Rev. Richard Coxe, V. of Bucklebury, Berkshire*). *b.* Bucklebury 20 Sep. 1811; ed. at Westminster and Worcester coll. Ox., B.A. 1833, M.A. 1836; entered manuscript department of British Museum, May 1833; C. of Culham 1839–48, of Tubney 1848–55 both near Oxford; sub-librarian of Bodleian library 16 Nov. 1838, librarian 6 Nov. 1860 to death, catalogue of 723 folio volumes was compiled 1859–80; select preacher to Univ. of Ox. 1842;

COXE, REV. H. O. (*Con.*)
Whitehall preacher 1868; chaplain of C.C. coll. Ox. 1847–74; lecturer at St. Martin's, Carfax, Oxford 1852–59; C. of Wytham, Berks. 1861–68; R. of Wytham 1868 to death; presided at annual meeting of Library Association at Oxford 1 to 3 Oct. 1878, pres. of Association 25 Sep. 1879 to death; published *Forms of bidding prayer* 1840; *Rogeri de Wendover Chronica* 5 vols. (*English Hist. Soc.*) 1841–4; *The Black Prince, an historical poem written in French by Chandos Herald (Roxburghe club)* 1842; *Report on the Greek manuscripts yet remaining in libraries of the Levant* 1858. *d.* St. Giles's road, Oxford 8 July 1881. *bur.* at Wytham 12 July.

COXE, SIR JAMES (4 *son of Robert Coxe of Georgie, Midlothian*). *b.* Georgie 1811; ed. at Gottingen, Heidelberg, Paris and Univ. of Edin., M.D. Edin. 1835; L.R.C.S. Edin. 1835; F.R.C.P. Edin. 1837; wrote Report on management of the insane in Scotland 1855; paid comr. in lunacy for Scotland 23 Sep. 1857 to death, wrote first fifteen reports of the Commissioners; knighted by patent 10 Aug. 1863; F.R.S. Edin. *d.* Folkestone on returning from Paris 9 May 1878. *Proc. of Royal Soc. of Edin. x*, 15 (1880).

COXE, VEN. RICHARD CHARLES (*brother of Rev. Henry Octavius Coxe 1811–81*). Ed. at Reading gr. sch.; matric. from Worcester coll. Ox. 29 Nov. 1817 aged 17, scholar 1818, B.A. 1821, M.A. 1824; fellow of his coll. 1823–26; Inc. of Abp. Tenison's chapel, Regent st. London 1829–41; V. of Newcastle 1841–53; hon. canon of Durham 1843–58; archdeacon of Lindisfarne, March 1853 to death; V. of Eglingham, Northumberland, March 1853 to death; canon of Durham, Dec. 1857 to death; author of *Lectures on the evidence from miracles* 1832; *The Mercy at Marsdon rocks* 1844; *Poems scriptural, classical and miscellaneous* 1845; *Leda Tanah the martyr's child, Derwent Bank* 1851. *d.* Eglingham vicarage 25 Aug. 1865.

COXETER, ELIZABETH. *b.* Witney, Oxon. 1 Feb. 1775. *d.* Newbury, Berkshire 27 Nov. 1876 nearly 102 years of age. *Notes and Queries* 5 S. *iii*, 144 (1875), *vi*, 460 (1876).

COYNE, FREDERICK. Comic singer at principal music halls in London and the provinces 1867 to death; wrote the music to *Tuner's Opper-tuner-ty, a song* 1879. *d.* 8 Huntingdon st. Kingsland road, London 23 Feb. 1886 aged 39. *bur.* Abney park cemetery 27 Feb. *Entr'acte* 6 *March* 1886 *p.* 9, *portrait.*

COYNE, JOSEPH STIRLING (*son of Denis Coyne, port surveyor of Waterford*). *b.* Birr, King's

COYNE, J. S. (Con.)

county 1803 ; his first farce called *The Phrenologist* was produced at T.R. Dublin, June 1835 ; came to London 1836 where his farce *The queer subject* was produced at Adelphi theatre, Nov. 1836 ; author of upwards of 55 dramas, burlesques and farces produced chiefly at Adelphi and Haymarket theatres ; his drama called *Everybody's Friend* was brought out at the Haymarket 2 April 1859 it was reproduced at St. James's 16 Oct. 1867 as *The Widow Hunt ;* contributed to the first number of *Punch* 17 July 1841 ; secretary to Dramatic authors' society 1856 to death ; dramatic critic on *Sunday Times* newspaper ; author of *Scenery and antiquities of Ireland* 2 vols. 1842 ; *Pippins and pies, or sketches out of school* 1855 ; *Sam Spangle or the history of a harlequin* 1866: *d.* 61 Talbot road, Westbourne park, London 18 July 1868.

CRABB, GEORGE. *b.* Palgrave, Suffolk 8 Dec. 1778 ; classical master at Thorp-Arch school, Yorkshire ; studied German at Bremen 1801–6 ; gentleman commoner at Magd. hall, Ox. 1814, B.A. 1821, M.A. 1822 ; barrister I.T. 3 July 1829 ; author of *English synonyms explained, in alphabetical order* 1816, 7 ed. 1844 after which the book was stereotyped ; *Universal technological dictionary* 2 vols. 1823 ; *Universal historical dictionary* 2 vols. 1825 ; *History of the English law* 1829 ; *Precedents in conveyancing* 2 vols. 1835, 5 ed. 1859 ; *Digest and index of all the statutes at large* 4 vols. 1841–7 ; *Law of real property* 2 vols. 1846. *d.* Hammersmith 4 Dec. 1851.

CRABB, REV. JAMES (3 *son of James Crabb of Wilton, Wiltshire, cloth manufacturer*). *b.* Wilton 13 April 1774 ; joined the Wesleyans, Feb. 1791 ; kept a school at Romsey, and at Spring hill, Southampton ; minister of Zion chapel, Lansdowne hill, Southampton, opened 9 June 1824 ; founded infant day schools at Kingsland Place, Southampton, the earliest in England ; was popularly known as the Gipsy's friend and was the missionary referred to in Rev. Legh Richmond's *Dairyman's Daughter* as having first brought her to a sense of religion ; author of *The Gipsies Advocate* 1831, 3 *ed.* 1832 ; *An address to Irvingites in which their heresy, modes of worship, etc. are set forth* 1836. *d.* Springhill house, Southampton 17 Sep. 1851. *Memoir of Rev. James Crabb by John Rudall* 1854, *portrait ; G.M. xxxvi,* 659–60 (1851).

CRABBE, EYRE JOHN. Ensign 74 foot 11 June 1807, lieut.-col. 6 Nov. 1841 to 1 May 1846 when placed on retired full pay ; col. in the army 28 Nov. 1854 ; K.H. 1837. *d.* Highfield, Southampton 19 March 1859 aged 68.

CRABBE, REV. GEORGE (*eld. son of George Crabbe the poet* 1754–1832). *b.* Stathern, Leics. 16 Nov. 1785 ; ed. at Ipswich gr. sch. and Trin. coll. Cam., B.A. 1807 ; C. of Pucklechurch, Gloucs. 1817–34 ; V. of Bredfield and Pettistree, Suffolk 1834 to death ; author of *Life of George Crabbe* 1838 ; *Outlines of a system of natural theology* 1840. *d.* Bredfield vicarage 16 Sep. 1857.

CRACE, FREDERICK (*son of John Crace of London, architectural decorator* 1754–1819). *b.* 3 June 1779 ; architectural decorator ; employed on work at royal palaces, London, Brighton and Windsor ; a comr. of Sewers ; began to collect maps and views of London about 1818, his splendid collection was purchased by the British Museum from his son John Gregory Crace 1880, it consists of between five and six thousand prints and drawings arranged in a series of 57 portfolios, it is described in *Catalogues of maps, plans and views of London collected and arranged by F. Crace edited by J. G. Crace* 1878, a very large number of the illustrations in Thornbury and Walford's *Old and New London* are derived from this collection. *d.* Vine cottage, Blyth lane, Hammersmith 18 Sep. 1859. *The Little journal i,* 136–42 (1884)

CRACKANTHORPE, WILLIAM (*son of Christopher Cookson who assumed name of Crackanthorpe, and d.* 1800). *b.* 25 Feb. 1790 ; ed. at St. John's coll. Cam., B.A. 1811, M.A. 1816 ; had an interview with Napoleon at Elba 25 Feb. 1815 the day before he escaped to France ; sheriff of Cumberland 1826 ; chairman of Westmoreland poor law board 40 years ; rebuilt parish church of Newbiggin and the rectory house at his own expense. *d.* Newbiggin hall, Westmoreland 10 Jany. 1888.

CRACKLOW, HENRY. Ensign Bombay army 23 Dec. 1819 ; colonel 2 Bombay N.I. 1855–69 ; M.G. 22 Aug. 1855 ; general 28 March 1874 ; placed on retired list 1 Oct. 1877. *d.* Castle hill, Inverness 15 May 1886 in 83 year.

CRACROFT, PETER (2 *son of Robert Cracroft of Hackthorne, Lincs.* 1783–1862). *b.* 15 March 1816 ; entered navy 4 June 1830, lost the Reynard on the Pratas shoal, China 1846 ; captain 20 Nov. 1854 ; commodore in charge at Jamaica 31 March 1863 to death ; C.B. 7 Oct. 1862. *d.* Admiralty house, Port Royàl, Jamaica 2 Aug. 1865. *Journal of Royal Geog. Soc. xxxvi, p. cxlviii,* (1866).

CRADOCK, REV. EDWARD HARTOPP (3 *son of Edward Grove of Shenstone park, Staffs.*) *b.* 26 April 1810 ; ed. at Brasenose coll. Ox., B.A. 1831, M.A. 1834, B.D. and D.D. 1854 ; fellow

CRADOCK, REV. E. H. *(Con.)*

of Brasenose to 1845, principal 27 Dec. 1853 to death ; R. of Tedstone Delamere, Herefordshire 1845–54 ; canon of Worcester 31 Jany. 1848 to 1854 ; assumed name of Cradock by r.l. 22 May 1849. *d.* Oxford 27 Jany. 1886.

CRAIG, JAMES THOMSON GIBSON (2 *son of Sir James Gibson Craig, 1 baronet 1765–1850). b.* 12 March 1799 ; ed. at high school and univ. Edin. ; a writer to the signet ; an original member of the Bannatyne club 1823, for which he edited *Papers relating to the marriage of King James Sixth* 1828 ; issued in an edition of 25 copies a series of facsimiles of historic and artistic bookbindings in his collection 1882 ; issued in 1883 a facsimile reprint of the *Shorte summe of the whole catechism* 1583 *by John Craig ;* a first part of his valuable library was sold in London, June 1887. *d.* Edinburgh 18 July 1886.

CRAIG, RICHARD DAVIS *(eld. son of Rev. Thomas Craig of Bocking, Essex), b.* Bocking 2 Nov. 1810 ; studied at London Univ. ; drew Boundary Act which became part of Reform act 1832 ; private sec. to E. J. Littleton chief sec. for Ireland 1833 ; barrister L.I. 18 Nov. 1834, bencher 3 Nov. 1851 ; one of the 2 revising barristers for London and Westminster 1835–40 ; Q.C. 11 July 1851 ; retired from practice 1867 ; published with J. W. Mylne *Reports of cases in Chancery* 1835–41, 5 *vols.* 1837–48 ; with T. J. Phillips *Reports of cases in Chancery* 1840–41, 1 *vol.* 1842 ; author of *Legal and equitable rights and liabilities as to trees and woods* 1866. *d.* Liss, Hampshire 8 May 1884.

CRAIG, WILLIAM. *b.* Dublin 1829 ; water-colour painter ; exhibited at R.A. Dublin 1846 ; went to United States 1863 ; an original member of American Society of water-colour painters. Drowned in Lake George, New York 1875.

CRAIG, SIR WILLIAM GIBSON, 2 Baronet *(brother of James Thomson Gibson Craig 1799-1886). b.* 2 Aug. 1797 ; admitted advocate 1820 ; M.P. for co. Edinburgh 1837–41, for city of Edin. 1841–52 ; a lord of the treasury 6 July 1846 to Feb. 1852 ; succeeded his father 6 March 1850 ; lord clerk register and keeper of signet of Scotland 3 July 1862 to death ; P.C. 8 Dec. 1863. *d.* Riccarton near Edin. 12 March 1878. *Proc. of Royal Soc. of Edin. x,* 24 (1880).

CRAIGIE, DAVID. *b.* Leith near Edinburgh 6 June 1793 ; ed. at Univ. of Edin., M.D. 1816 ; F.R.C.P. Edin. 1832, pres. Dec. 1861 ; phys. to Edin. Royal infirmary 1833 ; editor of *Edinburgh Medical and Surgical Journal* 1820–32, sole proprietor and editor 1832–55 ; F.R.S.

CRAIGIE, D. L. *(Con.)*

Edin. 1833 ; author of *Elements of general and pathological anatomy* 1828, 2 *ed.* 1848 ; *Elements of anatomy, general, special and comparative* 1838 ; *Elements of the practice of physic* 2 *vols.* 1840, and of 30 separate papers on medical subjects. *d.* 17 May 1866. *Proc. of Royal Soc. of Edin. vi,* 15–16 (1869).

CRAIGIE, DAVID. Navigating lieutenant R.N. 17 Aug. 1838 ; staff commander 11 June 1863 ; retired captain 20 Jany. 1864 ; C.B. 2 June 1869. *d.* London 8 April 1883.

CRAIGIE, SIR PATRICK EDMONSTONE (3 *son of Laurence Craigie of Glasgow). b.* 1794 ; ed. at Glasgow school and college ; ensign 52 foot 3 June 1813 ; lieut. col. 55 foot 21 Nov. 1834 to 11 Aug. 1844 when placed on h.p. ; aide de camp to the Queen 23 Dec. 1842 to 20 June 1854 ; commanded centre division of Madras army 7 Jany. 1855 to 23 April 1860 ; col. of 31 foot 20 Feb. 1859, of 55 foot 1 June 1862 to death ; general 21 Jany. 1868 ; C.B. 24 Dec. 1842, K.C.B. 13 March 1867. *d.* Warrior terrace, St. Leonards 13 Dec. 1873.

CRAIGIE, ROBERT. Entered navy 22 March 1811 ; captain 7 Nov. 1839 ; admiral on h.p. 1 April 1870. *d.* Dawlish 2 March 1873 in 73 year.

CRAIGIE, WILLIAM. *b.* Belnaboth, Aberdeenshire 11 March 1799 ; studied for medical profession at Marischal college, Aberdeen and at Univs. of Edin. and Dublin ; settled at Ancaster, Canada West 1834, removed to Hamilton 1845 ; held a high position as a scientific authority on meteorology, botany, horticulture and agriculture ; a member of Board of arts and manufactures of Canada West. *d.* Hamilton, Aug. 1863.

CRAIK, GEORGE LILLIE *(eld. son of Rev. Wm. Craik, assistant minister of parish of Kennoway, Fifeshire, who d.* 1830*). b.* Kennoway 1798 ; ed. at St. Andrew's Univ. ; edited the *Star* local paper 1817 ; came to London 1826 ; professor of English literature and history at Queen's college, Belfast 1849 to death ; examiner for Indian civil service in London 1859 and 1862 ; author of *The pursuit of knowledge under difficulties* 2 *vols.* 1830–31 ; *Sketches of the history of literature and learning in England* 6 *vols.* 1844–45 expanded into *A Compendious History of English literature and of the English language* 2 *vols.* 1861 ; *Spenser and his poetry* 3 *vols.* 1845 ; *Bacon, his writings and his philosophy* 3 *vols.* 1846–7 ; *Romance of the peerage* 4 *vols.* 1848–50 ; author with C. Macfarlane of *The*

CRAIK, G. L. *(Con.)*

pictorial history of England 4 vols. 1837–41. *d.* 2 Chlorine place, Belfast 25 June 1866. *Certificates in favour of G. L. Craik for the office of one of the Latin masters in the new Edinburgh Academy.*

CRAIK, HENRY *(brother of the preceding). b.* Prestonpans, East Lothian 8 Aug. 1805; ed. at Univ. of St. Andrews; tutor in family of Anthony Norris Groves of Exeter 1826, in family of John Synge of Buckridge house near Teignmouth 1828–31; pastor of Baptist chapel, Shaldon, Devon 1831–32; laboured in Bristol with George Muller (founder of the New orphan houses, Ashley Down) 1832 to death, founded with him a society at Bristol similar to the Plymouth Brethren 1832; author of *The Hebrew language, its history and characteristics* 1860; *Principia Hebraica* 1863. *d.* Hampton park, Redland near Bristol 22 Jany. 1866. *W. E. Tayler's Passages from the diary and letters of H. Craik* 1866.

CRAMER, JOHANN BAPTIST *(eld. son of Wilhelm Cramer of London, violinist 1745–99). b.* Mannheim 24 Feb. 1771; taken to London 1774; made his first appearance as a pianist 1781; travelled abroad 1788–91, 1798 and 1816–18; a member of board of management of Royal Academy of Music 1822; founded firm of music publishers J. B. Cramer and Co. in Regent st. London 1828 from which he retired 1835; occupied the foremost rank of his day as a pianist; composed, adapted and arranged 250 pieces of music; his *Eighty four Studies* are still very popular. *d.* Kensington terrace, London 16 April 1858. *The Harmonicon i,* 179–81 (1823), *portrait.*

CRAMP, REV. JOHN MOCKETT *(son of Rev. Thomas Cramp, founder of Baptist church at St. Peter's, Isle of Thanet, who d. 17 Nov. 1851 aged 82). b.* St. Peter's 25 July 1796; ed. at Stepney college, London; pastor of baptist chapel, Dean st. Southwark 1818; assistant pastor at St. Peter's 1827–42; pastor of baptist chapel, Hastings 1842–44; pres. of baptist college, Montreal 1844–49; pres. of Acadia college, Nova Scotia 1851–69; edited *The Register* a Montreal weekly religious journal 1844–49; edited with Rev. W. Taylor *The Colonial Protestant* a monthly mag. 1848–49; general editor of *The Pilot* Montreal newspaper 1849–51; author of *A text book of Popery* 1831; *Baptist history from the foundation of the Christian church to the eighteenth century* 1868 and many other books. *d.* Wolfville, Nova Scotia 6 Dec. 1881.

CRAMPTON, SIR JOHN FIENNES TWISLETON, 2 Baronet *(elder son of the succeeding). b.* Dawson st. Dublin 12 Aug. 1805; ed. at Eton and Trin. coll. Dublin; attached to mission at Turin 1826, to embassy at St. Petersburg 1828; paid attaché at Brussels 1834, at Vienna 1839; sec. of legation to Confederated states of Swiss Cantons 1844, in the United States 1845, chargé d' Affaires there 1847–49 and 1850–52; envoy extraord. and min. plenipo. to U.S. 19 Jany. 1852, the pres. of the U.S. discontinued official intercourse with him 28 May 1856 on account of his recruiting soldiers in the U.S. for the British army, when he returned to England but he held the appointment to 20 Jany. 1857; K.C.B. 20 Sep. 1856; envoy extraord. and min. plenipo. to King of Hanover 2 March 1857, at St. Petersburg 31 March 1858, at Madrid 11 Dec. 1860 to 1 July 1869 when he retired on pension; succeeded his father 10 June 1858. *d.* Bushey park, Enniscorthy, co. Wicklow 5 Dec. 1886.

CRAMPTON, SIR PHILIP, 1 Baronet *(3 son of John Crampton of Merrion sq. Dublin 1732–92). b.* Dublin 7 June 1777; assistant surgeon in army; surgeon to Meath hospital, Dublin 1798; M.D. Glasgow 1800; taught anatomy in private lectures and maintained a dissecting room behind his own house; surgeon general to the forces in Ireland to his death, the last who held that appointment; surgeon in ord. to the Queen for Ireland; a member of senate of the Queen's Univ.; pres. of Royal college of surgeons, Dublin 3 times; F.R.S. 16 April 1812; created baronet 14 March 1839. *d.* Merrion sq. Dublin 10 June 1858. *Dublin Univ. Mag. xv,* 613 (1840), *portrait; Proc. of Med. and Chir. Soc. iii,* 52–53 (1861).

CRAMPTON, PHILIP CECIL *(4 son of Rev. Cecil Crampton 1733–1819, R. of Headford, co. Galway). b.* May 1782; ed. at Trin. coll. Dublin, scholar 1800, fellow 1807, B.A. 1802, M.A. 1807; LL.B. 1809, LL.D. 1810; called to Irish bar 1810; professor of common and feudal law in Univ. of Dublin 1816–34; solicitor general for Ireland 23 Dec. 1830; bencher of King's Inns, Dublin 1831; justice of Court of Queen's Bench, Ireland 21 Oct. 1834 to Jany. 1859; M.P. for Milborne, Port, Somerset 15 July 1831 to 3 Dec. 1832; contested Univ. of Dublin, Dec. 1832 and Dungarvan, Feb. 1834; P.C. 1858. *d.* St. Valente, Bray, co. Wicklow 29 Dec. 1862. *Address on Judge Crampton's retirement with some of his charges to Juries* 1859; *O. J. Burke's Anecdotes of Connaught circuit* (1885) 299–302.

CRAMPTON, THOMAS. *b.* Sheerness 1817; organist at Staines 1840, afterwards at Brentford and Ealing; government lecturer at Knel-

CRAMPTON, T. *(Con.)*

ler Hall training college 1854; composed anthems, glees and instrumental music; purchaser of music to the British Museum 1875; published *The church psalter* 1854; *The part singer* 1868; *Twenty-four school songs with lessons on musical notation* 1873; *Forty school songs* 1882; *Music for the New Code staff notation* 1884; composed and printed upwards of 35 pieces of music; some of his duets and trios appeared under the non de plume of J. Karl Bernhardt. *d.* 2 Devonshire gardens, Chiswick 13 April 1885.

CRANE, LUCY *(dau. of the succeeding.)* *b.* Liverpool 22 Sep. 1842; ed. in London; wrote the original verses and rhymed versions of nursery legends for her brother Walter Crane's Coloured Toybooks 1869–75; delivered lectures in London and the North on Art and the formation of taste; author of *Household stories from the Brothers Grimm, translated* 1882; *Art and formation of taste, Six lectures* 1882. *d.* Bolton-le-Moors 31 March 1882.

CRANE, THOMAS *(son of Mr. Crane of Chester, bookseller).* *b.* Chester 1808; artist at Chester 1825; associate of Liverpool Academy 1835, member 1838, treasurer 1841; lived at Torquay 1844–57; his principal works were portraits in oil, water-colour and crayon; exhibited 9 subject pictures at the R.A.; illustrated various books. *d.* Lambton terrace, Bayswater, London 15 July 1859.

CRANWORTH, ROBERT MONSEY ROLFE, 1 Baron *(elder son of Rev. Edmund Rolfe, R. of Cockley Cley, Norfolk, who d. 24 July 1795).* *b.* Cranworth, Norfolk 18 Dec. 1790; ed. at Bury school, Winchester and Trin. coll. Cam., 17 wrangler 1812, B.A. 1812, M.A. 1815; fellow of Downing coll. Cam.; barrister L.I. 21 May 1816, bencher 1832; recorder of Bury St. Edmunds about 1830; K.C. Aug. 1832; M.P. for Penryn 1832–39; solicitor general 6 Nov. to 20 Dec. 1834 and 30 April 1835 to 11 Nov. 1839; baron of Court of Exchequer 11 Nov. 1839 to 2 Nov. 1850; one of comrs. of the Great Seal 19 June to 15 July 1850; vice chancellor 2 Nov. 1850; P.C. 13 Nov. 1850; created Baron Cranworth of Cranworth, co. Norfolk 20 Dec. 1850 being the first and only instance of a vice chancellor receiving dignity of a peer; one of the two lords justices of appeal in chancery 8 Oct. 1851; lord chancellor 28 Dec. 1852 to 26 Feb. 1858 and 7 July 1865 to 6 July 1867. *d.* 40 Upper Brook st. London 26 July 1868. *bur.* Keston churchyard. *Men of the time British statesmen* (1854) 251–58; *Law mag. and law review xxvi,* 278–84 (1869); *The British cabinet in* 1853 *pp.* 251–58; *I.L.N. xvii,* 357 (1850), *portrait, xxx,* 109 (1857), *portrait, liii,* 114, 153 (1868), *portrait.*

CRAUFURD, EDWARD HENRY JOHN *(eld. son of John Craufurd* 1780–1867, *secretary to senate of Ionian islands).* *b.* 9 Dec. 1816; ed. at Trin. coll. Cam., scholar 1840, B.A. 1841, M.A. 1844; barrister I.T. 21 Nov. 1845; admitted barrister M.T. 10 April 1854; edited *The Legal Examiner* 1852; M.P. for Ayr district 22 July 1852 to 26 Jany. 1874; author of *Advocacy in county courts.* *d.* Portencross, Ayrshire 29 Aug. 1887.

CRAUFURD, JAMES *(eld. son of Archibald Clifford Blackwell Craufurd of Ardmillan, Ayrshire).* *b.* Havant, Hants. 1805; ed. at Ayr academy and at Univs. of Glasgow and Edin.; admitted advocate 1829; sheriff of Perthshire 14 March 1849; solicitor general for Scotland 16 Nov. 1853; lord of session 10 Jany. 1855 to death with courtesy title of Lord Ardmillan; lord of justiciary 16 June 1855 to death. *d.* 18 Charlotte sq. Edinburgh 7 Sep. 1876. *Journal of jurisprudence xx,* 538–9 (1876); *Graphic xiv,* 308 (1876), *portrait.*

CRAVEN, LOUISA, Countess of *(youngest dau. of John Brunton* 1750–1832, *manager of the Norwich theatre).* *b.* Norwich 21 Jany. 1779; made her first appearance on the stage at Covent Garden 25 Oct. 1803 as Lady Townley in the *Provoked Husband;* made her last appearance at Covent Garden 21 Oct. 1807 as Clara Sedley in *The Rage.* *(m.* 12 Dec. 1807 Wm. Craven 1 Earl of Craven, he was *b.* 1 Sep. 1770 and *d.* 30 July 1825). *d.* Hampstead Marshall, Newbury 27 Aug. 1860. *Mrs. C. B. Wilson's Our actresses i,* 94–102 (1844), *portrait; British Stage ii,* 241 (1818), *portrait; Theatrical Inquisitor xiii,* 3 (1818), *portrait; Bentley's Miscellany xviii,* 249–51 (1845).

CRAVEN, WILLIAM CRAVEN, 2 Earl of. *b.* 18 July 1809; ed. at Eton and Ch. Ch. Ox.; succeeded 30 July 1825; knight of the griffin at the Eglinton tournament 28 to 31 Aug. 1839; lord lieut. of Warws. 29 March 1854 to 1856; devoted great attention to coursing and held spring and autumn meetings at Ashdown hills on his own property. *d.* Royal hotel, Scarborough 25 Aug. 1866. *Baily's Mag. viii,* 327–9 (1864), *portrait; Nixon and Richardson's Eglinton tournament* (1843), *portrait.*

CRAVEN, GEORGE GRIMSTON CRAVEN, 3 Earl of. *b.* Charles st. Berkeley sq. London 16 March 1841; ed. at Harrow; succeeded 25 Aug. 1866; high steward of Newbury, Berkshire 14 Jany. 1869; lord lieut. of Berks. 11 Aug. 1881 to death; master of the old Berkshire hounds, a steeple chaser, continued the Ashdown coursing meeting. *d.* Ashdown park, Berks. 7 Dec. 1883. *bur.* Binley churchyard near Coventry 13 Dec. *Baily's Mag. xxii,* 187 (1872), *portrait.*

CRAVEN, FULWAR *(elder son of Rev. John Craven of Chilton house, Wiltshire, who d. 19 June 1804).* *b.* 25 June 1782; captain 1 dragoons 1803–1806; owner of race horses; won the Oaks with Deception 1839; one of the most notable and eccentric characters on the turf. *d.* Brockhampton park, Gloucs. 14 April 1860. *H. Corbet's Tales of sporting life* (1864) 99–108; *W. Day's Reminiscences,* 2 ed. (1886) 138–42.

CRAVEN, KEPPEL RICHARD *(youngest child of 6 Baron Craven 1737–91).* *b.* 1 June 1779; ed. at Harrow; resided with his mother at Naples 1805; chamberlain to Princess of Wales 1814–15; purchased a large convent in the mountains near Salerno, South Italy, and lived there 1834; author of *A tour through the southern provinces of the kingdom of Naples* 1821; *Excursions in the Abruzzi and northern provinces of Naples* 2 vols. 1838. *d.* Naples 24 June 1851. *Memoirs of the Margravine of Anspach* (1826), i, 72, 85, 364, ii, 74, 84, 95, 173, *portrait; Madden's Literary life of Countess of Blessington,* ii, 124–39 (1855).

CRAWFORD and BALCARRES, JAMES LINDSAY, Earl of. *b.* Balcarres, Fifeshire 24 April 1783; succeeded as 7 Earl of Balcarres 27 March 1825; created Baron Wigan in peerage of United Kingdom 5 July 1826; had Earldom of Crawford (dormant since 1808) confirmed to him by House of Lords 1848 and thus became 24 Earl of Crawford and premier Earl on union roll of Scotland; claimed Dukedom of Montrose 1855. *d.* Dunecht house, Aberdeen 15 Dec. 1869.

CRAWFORD and BALCARRES, ALEXANDER WILLIAM CRAWFORD LINDSAY, Earl of *(eld. child of the preceding).* *b.* Muncaster Castle 16 Oct. 1812; ed. at Eton and Trin. coll. Cam., M.A. 1833; succeeded 15 Dec. 1869; collected from all parts of the world the famous Crawford library consisting of more than 50,000 books and MSS., the first portion of which was sold for £19,000 in 1887, one book the Mazarin Bible fetched £2650; author of *Letters on Egypt, Edom and the Holy Land* 2 vols. 1838; *Lives of the Lindsays* 3 vols. 1840, 3 ed. 1858; *Ballads, songs and poems translated from the German* 1841; *Progression by antagonism, a theory* 1846; *Sketches of the history of Christian art* 3 vols. 1847, new ed. 2 vols. 1885; *Scepticism, a retrogressive movement in theology* 1861; *Etruscan inscriptions analysed* 1872; *The Earldom of Mar in sunshine and in shade during five hundred years* 2 vols. 1882. *d.* Villa Eualenina, Florence 13 Dec. 1880. *bur.* at Dunecht house, April 1881, personalty sworn under £300,000 April 1881. *Athenæum* 25 Dec. 1880 p. 865; *I.L.N.* lxxxi, 124 (1882).

CRAWFORD, Earl of *(Con.)*
NOTE.—His body was stolen April 1881 by Charles Soutar a ratcatcher, but the theft was not discovered until Dec. 1881, the body was found on the farm of Dumbreck near Dunecht house 18 July 1882 and buried in family vault under Wigan parish church 26 July 1882. C. Soutar was sentenced to 5 years penal servitude 24 Oct. 1882.

CRAWFORD, ABRAHAM *(youngest son of Rev. Thomas Crawford, V. of Lismore, co. Waterford).* *b.* Lismore, Oct. 1788; entered navy 19 May 1800; captain 5 Jany. 1829; retired captain 5 Jany. 1849; retired admiral 12 Sep. 1865. *d.* Teignmouth, Devon 17 Jany. 1869. *Reminiscences of a naval officer by Capt. A. Crawford, R.N.* 2 vols. 1851.

CRAWFORD, EDMUND THORNTON *(son of Mr. Crawford of Cowden near Dalkeith, land surveyor).* *b.* Cowden 1806; landscape and marine painter; A.R.S.A. 1839, R.S.A. 1848; one of the greatest landscape painters in Scotland; contributed many pictures to Royal Scottish Academy 1831–77; lived at Lasswade near Edinburgh 1858 to death. *d.* Lasswade 27 Sep. 1885. *bur.* in new cemetery at Dalkeith.

CRAWFORD, GEORGE MORLAND. *b.* Chelsfield court lodge, Kent 1816; barrister I.T. 5 May 1837; Paris correspondent of *Daily News* 1850 to death; a severe censurer of the Imperial government; very intimate with Thiers, Gambetta and Floquet; stung by a wasp in the carotid artery, Oct. 1885. *d.* from blood poisoning in Paris 23 Nov. 1885. *Daily News* 26 Nov. 1885 p. 3, 28 Nov. p. 3; *Pall Mall Gazette* 26 Nov. 1885 p. 11, 27 Nov. p. 3, portrait 9 Dec. p. 5.

CRAWFORD, JOHN. *b.* Greenock 31 Aug. 1816; a house painter at Alloa 1834 to death; author of *Doric lays, being snatches of song and ballad* 2 vols. 1850–60; committed suicide at Alloa 13 Dec. 1873. *Memorials of the town and parish of Alloa, by the late John Crawford with memoir of the author by Rev. Charles Rogers* 1874.

CRAWFORD, JOSEPH TUCKER. Consul general in Island of Cuba, April 1842 to death; C.B. 6 Dec. 1859. *d.* Havannah 21 July 1864.

CRAWFORD, REV. THOMAS JACKSON *(son of Wm. Crawford, professor of moral philosophy in United college, St. Andrews).* *b.* St. Andrews; ed. at Univ. of St. Andrews, B.D. 1831, D.D. 1844; minister of parish of Cults 1834, of parish of Glamis 1838, of St. Andrews parish Edin. 1844; professor of theology in Univ. of Edin. 1859 to death, being the last person appointed by the town to any chair in the Univ.; chaplain in ord. to the Queen 1861; a dean of the chapel royal; moderator of general

CRAWFORD, REV. T. J. (Con.)

assembly 1867 ; author of *Reasons of adherence to the Church of Scotland* 1843 ; *Presbyterianism defended against the exclusive claims of prelacy as urged by the Romanists and Tractarians* 1853, 2 ed. 1867 ; *The Fatherhood of God* 1866, 3 ed. 1870 ; *The mysteries of Christianity* 1874. *d.* Genoa 11 Oct. 1875. *Scott's Fasti iii, pt. 2, p. 772 ; Proc. of Royal Soc. of Edin. ix*, 17 (1878).

CRAWFORD, WILLIAM (2 *son of Archibald Crawford of Ayr, poet* 1779–1843). *b.* Ayr 1825 ; teacher of drawing at Royal Institution, Edinburgh ; exhibited pictures at Royal Scottish Academy, many of which were bought by Royal Assoc. for Promotion of fine arts in Scotland ; his portraits in crayons of children and ladies were much sought after ; A.R.S.A. 1860. *d.* Lynedoch place, Edinburgh 1 Aug. 1869. *Reg. and mag. of biog. ii*, 146 (1869).

CRAWFORD, WILLIAM THOMAS. Second lieut. R.A. 21 June 1833, lieut. col. 1 April 1855 to death ; C.B. 24 March 1858. *d.* Rome 6 March 1862.

CRAWFURD, ANDREW. *b.* St. John's hill, Lochwinnoch, Renfrewshire ; ed. at Univ. of Glasgow, M.D. 1813 ; surgeon at Rothesay, Isle of Bute ; professor of natural philosophy in the Dollar Institution a short time ; author of a voluminous Eik or Supplement to John Jamieson's *Etymological dictionary of the Scottish language* 2 vols. 1840, and of a supplement of 80 pages dated 1853 to *The Laird of Logan* 1841 ; collected 44 quarto manuscript volumes relating to Renfrewshire. *d.* St. John's hill, Lochwinnoch 27 Dec. 1854 aged 67.

CRAWFURD, JOHN (*son of Mr. Crawfurd of Islay, Hebrides islands, surgeon*). *b.* Islay 13 Aug. 1783 ; assistant surgeon H.E.I. Co. 1803 ; filled some of chief civil and political posts in Java 1811–17 ; envoy to courts of Siam and Cochin China 1821–23 ; governor of Singapore 1823–26 ; comr. to Pegu 1826 ; made a collection of fossil mastodon and other animals which were described by Buckland and Clift ; sent on a mission to court of Ava 1827 ; F.R.S. 7 May 1818 ; contested Glasgow, Dec. 1832, Paisley, March 1834 and Sterling, Jany. 1835 ; pres. of Ethnological Soc. 1861, contributed 38 papers to the Journal 1861–68 ; author of *History of the Indian Archipelago* 3 vols. 1820 ; *Journal of an embassy to Ava* 1828 ; *A grammar and dictionary of the Malay language* 2 vols. 1852 ; *A descriptive dictionary of the Indian islands and adjacent countries* 1856. *d.* Elvaston place, South Kensington, London 11 May 1868. *Journal of Royal Geographical Soc. xxxviii, pp. cxlviii-clii*, (1868).

CRAWLEY, GEORGE BADEN (2 *son of George Abraham Crawley of London, solicitor* 1795–1862). *b.* 4 Sep. 1833 ; ed. at Harrow, was in cricket eleven ; one of the best tennis players ; a railway contractor ; planned and carried out two railways in Belgium, two railways in Spain, a railway from Vera Cruz to Mexico and a railway of nearly 300 miles from Tiflis to Poti ; his last work was a railway from Ploesti in Roumania to Cronstadt in Hungary but this was interrupted by the war 1878 ; accidentally killed on board a steamer off Progreso coast of Mexico 23 Nov. 1879. *bur.* Highgate cemetery, London 1 Jany. 1880.

CRAWLEY, PETER. *b.* Newington Green 5 Dec. 1799 ; fought Richard Acton for £50 at Blindlow heath 6 May 1823 when Crawley won after 13 rounds ; fought James Ward for £200 at Royston heath 2 Jany. 1827 when Crawley won in 26 minutes ; landlord of Queen's head and French horn, Duke st. West Smithfield, London 1827 to death. *d.* at his house 12 March 1865. *Miles's Pugilistica ii*, 233–47 (1880), *portrait ; Illust. sporting news iii*, 37 (1864), *portrait.*

CRAWLEY, THOMAS ROBERT. *b.* 30 April 1818 ; ensign 45 foot 19 Dec. 1834 ; lieut. col. 15 dragoons 23 Sep. 1859 to 18 Sep. 1860 ; lieut. col. 6 dragoons 18 Sep. 1860 to 2 Dec. 1868 when placed on h.p. ; M.G. 6 Feb. 1870 ; tried by a court martial at Aldershot 17 Nov. to 23 Dec. 1863 for falsely arresting Sergeant Lilley at Mhow in Hindustan, who died from effects of treatment he suffered after a month's close confinement, honourably acquitted 23 Dec. 1863, the trial formed subject of several inquiries in House of Commons 1864 it cost the country £18,378 17s. 6d. *d.* 9 York terrace, Regent's park, London 2 July 1880. *British quarterly Review xxxix*, 389–408 (1864); *Annual Register* (1863) 312–28 ; *Illust. Times 28 Nov.* 1863 p. 345, *portrait.*

CRAWSHAY, ROBERT THOMPSON (*youngest son of the succeeding*). *b.* Cyfarthfa ironworks near Merthyr Tydvil 8 March 1817 ; manager of the ironworks ; head of the business 1867 ; known as the 'iron king of Wales.' *d.* Queen's hotel, Cheltenham 10 May 1879, personalty sworn under £1,200,000, 21 June. *Practical Mag.* (1873) 81–4, *portrait ; Journal of iron and steel instit.* (1879) 328–30.

CRAWSHAY, WILLIAM (*eld. son of Wm. Crawshay of Stoke Newington, Middlesex*). *b.* 1788 ; sole proprietor of Cyfarthfa ironworks ; had 10 mines in active work turning out iron ore, 9 shafts and collieries, a domain with a railway 6 miles long and large estates in Berks and

CRAWSHAY, W. (*Con.*)

Gloucestershire; sheriff of Glamorganshire 1822. *d.* Caversham park, Reading 4 Aug. 1867, personalty sworn under £2,000,000, 7 Sep. *Red Dragon v,* 289–92 (1884), *portrait; G.M. Sep.* 1867 *pp.* 393–95.

CREAGH, JAMES. Ensign 86 foot 1 Jany. 1810, lieut. col. 30 April 1852 to 24 Jany. 1860; L.G. 26 Jany. 1874; colonel 34 foot 7 Oct. 1874 to death. *d.* 16 St. Stephen's road, Westbourne park, London 1 Aug. 1875.

CREAGH, JASPER BYNG. Ensign 81 foot 9 April 1825, captain 5 Oct. 1832 to 5 Sep. 1834; captain 54 foot 20 Sep. 1839 to 12 Dec. 1843 when placed on h.p.; served with British auxiliary legion in north of Spain 1836–37; L.G. 1 Oct. 1877. *d.* Richmond road, Bayswater, London 9 March 1881 in 68 year.

CREAGH, SIR MICHAEL (5 *son of John Creagh of Limerick*). *b.* 1788; ensign 86 foot 9 May 1802, major 24 Oct. 1821 to 31 Dec. 1830 when placed on h.p.; lieut. col. 86 foot 24 Feb. 1832 to 7 Jany. 1842; lieut. col. 11 foot 7 Jany. 1842 to 27 June 1845; M.G. 20 June 1854; col. 73 foot 11 Jany. 1860 to death; knighted at St. James's palace 1 Aug. 1832; K.H 1832. *d.* Boulogne 14 Sep. 1860.

CREASY, SIR EDWARD SHEPHERD (*son of Edward Hill Creasy of Bexley, Kent, land agent*). *b.* Bexley 1812; ed. at Eton, Newcastle scholar 1831; scholar of King's coll. Cam. 1832, fellow 1834, B.A. 1835, M.A. 1838; barrister L.I. 26 Jany. 1837; professor of ancient and modern history in Univ. coll. London 1840–60; chief justice of Ceylon 19 March 1860 to 1875 when he retired on pension of £1600; knighted at St. James's palace 28 March 1860; professor of jurisprudence to the four Inns of Court, London; author of *Memoirs of eminent Etonians* 1850, 2 ed. 1876; *The fifteen decisive battles of the world from Marathon to Waterloo* 2 vols. 1851, 28 ed. 1877; *The history of the rise and progress of the English constitution* 1853, 14 ed. 1888; *History of the Ottoman Turks* 2 vols. 1854, new ed. 1877; *History of England* 2 vols. 1869–70; *The old love and the new* 3 vols. 1870. *d.* 15 Cecil st. Strand, London 27 Jany. 1878. *I.L.N. lxxii,* 133 (1878), *portrait.*

CRESSWELL, ADDISON JOHN BAKER (*son of Francis Easterby of Blackheath, Kent who assumed name of Cresswell and d. 1820*). *b.* 1 Oct. 1788; ed. at C.C. coll. Ox., M.A. 1810; sheriff of Northumberland 1821; M.P. for North Northumberland 12 July 1841 to 23 July 1847. *d.* Cresswell near Morpeth 5 May 1879.

CRESSWELL, SIR CRESSWELL (*brother of the preceding*). *b.* Biggmarket, Newcastle 1794; ed. at Charterhouse and Em. coll. Cam., B.A. 1814, M.A. 1818; admitted at M.T. 1810, at I.T. 1815, barrister I.T. 25 June 1819, bencher 1834; went Northern circuit of which he became joint leader with Robert Alexander; recorder of Hull 1830; K.C. 1834; M.P. for Liverpool 26 July 1837 to Jany. 1842; justice of Court of Common Pleas 22 Jany. 1842 to 11 Jany. 1858; serjeant-at-law 27 Jany. 1842; knighted at St. James's Palace 4 May 1842; judge of Court of Probate and Divorce (established by 20 & 21 Vict. c. 77) 11 Jany. 1858 to death; adjudicated upon 1000 cases in only one of which was his judgment reversed; P.C. 3 Feb. 1858; published with R. V. Barnewall *Reports of cases in the Court of King's Bench* 1822–1830, 10 vols. 1823–32; thrown from his horse on Constitution hill and his kneepan fractured 17 July 1863. *d.* from heart disease at 21 Prince's gate, Hyde park, London 29 July 1863. *Law Mag. and law review xx,* 179–88 (1866); *Law Times xxxviii,* 535–7 (1863).

CRESSWELL, SAMUEL GURNEY (3 *son of Francis Cresswell of Lynn, Norfolk*). Entered navy 1842; lieut. of the Investigator 17 Dec. 1849, searched for Sir John Franklin in the Polar sea 1850–53; explored 170 miles of Banks island in sledges 18 April to 20 May 1851, arrived in London 7 Oct 1853 being the first person who actually effected the North-west passage; presented with an address in the guildhall, Lynn 26 Oct. 1853; captain 17 Sep. 1858; received Baltic and Arctic medals and a portion of the £10,000 awarded to officers and crew of the Investigator for discovery of N.W. passage; published *Eight sketches in colours of voyage of Investigator* 1854; illustrated *R. J. le M. M'Clure's Discovery of north west passage* 1856. *d.* Bank house, King's Lynn 14 Aug. 1867 aged 39. *I.L.N. xxiii,* 389 (1853).

CRESTADORO, ANDREA. *b.* Genoa 1808; ed. at Univ. of Turin, Ph. Doc., professor of natural philosophy; came to England 1849; patented certain improvements in impulsoria 1852; a model of his metallic balloon was shown at Crystal Palace, June 1868; compiled catalogues for Sampson Low and Co. 1859–61; chief librarian of Manchester free libraries, Dec. 1862 to death; originated index catalogues, generally adopted as models by English municipal libraries; naturalised in England 16 April 1866; received order of Crown of Italy 1878; author of *The art of making catalogues or a method to obtain a most perfect printed catalogue of the British Museum library, by A Reader therein* 1856; *Du pouvoir temporel et de*

CRESTADORO, A. (Con.)
la souveraineté Pontificale, Paris 1861; *Catalogue of books in the Manchester free library, Reference department* 1864; *Taxation reform, or the best way of raising the revenue* 1878. *d.* 155 Upper Brook st. Manchester 7 April 1879. *Momus* 20 *March* 1879, *portrait.*

CRESWICK, THOMAS. *b.* Sheffield 5 Feb. 1811; landscape painter in London 1828; exhibited 139 pictures at R.A., 80 at B.I. and 46 at Suffolk st. gallery 1828-70; A.R.A. 1842, R.A. 11 Feb. 1851; largely employed as a designer of book illustrations; 109 of his paintings were collected together at London International Exhibition 1873; many of his pictures were in Manchester Exhibition 1887. *d.* The Limes, Linden grove, Bayswater, London 28 Dec. 1869. *I.L.N. xviii*, 219 (1851), *portrait, lvi*, 53 (1870), *portrait; A catalogue of the works of T. Creswick by T. O. Barlow* 1873.

CRESY, EDWARD. *b.* Dartford, Kent 7 May 1792; walked through England to study, measure and draw the cathedrals and most interesting buildings 1816; walked through France, Switzerland, Italy and Greece 1817-20; architect and civil engineer in London 1820 to death; superintending inspector under general board of health; author of *A practical treatise on bridge building* 1839; *Illustrations of Stone church, Kent* 1840; *An encyclopædia of civil engineering* 1847, 2 ed. 1856; author with George Ledwell Taylor of *The architectural antiquities of Rome* 2 vols. folio 1821-2, new ed. 1874; *Architecture of the middle ages in Italy* 1829. *d.* South Darenth, Kent 12 Nov. 1858. *G. L. Taylor's Autobiography of an octogenarian architect* 2 vols. 1870-72.

CREWDSON, JANE (2 *dau.* of George Fox of *Perran-arworthal, Cornwall*). *b.* Perran-arworthal 22 Oct. 1808; author of *Aunt Jane's Verses for children* 1851, 3 ed. 1871; *Lays of the Reformation and other lyrics* 1860; *A little while and other poems* 1864, 3 ed. 1872. (*m.* Oct. 1836 Thomas Dillworth Crewdson of Manchester, manufacturer). *d.* Summerlands, Whalley Range, Manchester 14 Sep. 1863.

CREWE, REV. HENRY ROBERT (2 *son* of Sir *Henry Harpur, 7 baronet* 1763-1818 *who assumed name of Crewe* 1808). *b.* Stourfield house 4 Sep. 1801; ed. at Trin. coll. Cam., B.A. 1825, M.A. 1830; R. of Breadsall, Derbyshire 1830 to death; author of *The Church of England, Pro. and Con.* 1843; *Repeal of the corn laws by One who fears God and regards man* 1846; *The war of Satan and the battle of God, remarks on Turkey and the East* 1854; *The war of prophecy* 1854. *d.* Breadsall rectory 29 Sep. 1865.

CREYKE, VEN. STEPHEN (*youngest son of Richard Creyke* 1746-1826, *commissioner of the Victualling office*). *b.* 24 Sep. 1796; ed. at C.C. coll. Ox., B.A. 1816, M.A. 1820, fellow of his college 1821-23; R. of Wigginton near York 1834-44; V. of Sutton-on-the-Forest near York 1837-44; preb. of York 28 Sep. 1841 to death; R. of Beeford, Yorkshire 1844-65; archdeacon of York 16 Oct. 1845 to 1867; canon res. of York 1857-73; R. of Bolton-Percy, Yorkshire 1865 to death. *d.* Bolton-Percy 11 Dec. 1883.

CRICHTON, SIR ALEXANDER (2 *son of Alexander Crichton of Woodhouselee and Newington, Midlothian*). *b.* Edinburgh 2 Dec. 1763; came to London 1784; M.D. Leyden 29 July 1785; studied at Paris, Stuttgart, Vienna and Halle; member of Corporation of surgeons, May 1789, got himself disfranchised 1 May 1791; L.R.C.P. 25 June 1791; physician to Westminster hosp. 1794; phys. in ord. to Alexander I Emperor of Russia 1804; head of Russian civil medical department; F.R.S. 8 May 1800; F.G.S. 1819; received grand cross of the Red Eagle 27 Dec. 1820, grand cross of St. Anne, Aug. 1830; knighted at the Pavilion, Brighton 1 March 1821; author of *Inquiry into the nature and origin of mental derangement* 2 vols. 1798; *A synoptical table of diseases designed for the use of students* 1805; *Account of experiments with vapour of tar in cure of pulmonary consumption* 1817; *On the treatment and cure of pulmonary consumption* 1823. *d.* The Grove near Sevenoaks, Kent 4 June 1856. *bur.* Norwood cemetery. *Proc. of Royal Soc. viii*, 269-72 (1856); *Quarterly Journal of Geog. Soc. xiii, pp. lxiv-lxvi* (1857).

CRICHTON, REV. ANDREW. *b.* parish of Kirkmahoe, Dumfriesshire Dec. 1790; engaged in teaching at Edinburgh and North Berwick; edited *North Briton* 1830-32, *Edinburgh Advertiser* 1832 to June 1851; member of presbytery of Edin.; elder for burgh of Cullen in general assembly of Church of Scotland 1852 to death; LL.D. St. Andrew's 1837; author of *Converts from infidelity* 2 vols. 1827; *History of Arabia* 2 vols. 1833; with H. Wheaton of *Scandinavia ancient and modern* 2 vols. 1838. *d.* 33 St. Bernard's crescent, Edinburgh 9 Jany. 1855.

CRICHTON, REV. ANDREW (*son of Rev. David Crichton, English master at Madras college, St. Andrews*). *b.* St. Andrews 22 May 1837; bursar at Univ. of Edin. 1852, B.A. 1857; licensed as a preacher by free presbytery of Arbroath June 1860; co-pastor of New North free church, Edinburgh Dec. 1860 to March

CRICHTON, REV. A. *(Con.)*

1866; pastor of free church, Chapelshade, Dundee 30 March 1866 to death; most popular preacher in Dundee; contributed many articles to *Family Treasury,* *London Review* and *Sunday Mag.*; author of *The confessions of a wandering soul.* *d.* Liberton, Edinburgh 13 July 1867. *bur.* in Grange cemetery, Edin. where is monument. *Memorials of the late Rev. A. Crichton, edited by W. G. Blaikie* (1868).

CRICHTON, SIR ARCHIBALD WILLIAM *(eld. son of Patrick Crichton, captain 47 foot). b.* 1791; ed. at Univ. of Edin.; physician to Emperor of Russia and his family; member of Russian medical council; councillor of state in Russia; received star of legion of honour 1814; D.C.L. Ox. 11 Jany 1817; knighted by Prince Regent at Carlton house 13 March 1817; received grand cross of Red Eagle of Prussia 1829, of St. Stanislaus 1832, of St. Anne 1834 and of St. Vladimir 1836. *d.* St. Petersburg 27 Feb. 1865.

CRICHTON, JOHN (*7 child of Thomas Crichton of Dundee, merchant who was b. in Queen Anne's reign). b.* Dundee 22 Feb. 1772; ed. at Univs. of St. Andrew's and Edin; M.R.C.S. Edin. 1790; surgeon at Dundee 1791; became an eminent lithotomist; performed operation of lithotomy 200 times, being unsuccessful in 14 cases only; surgeon to Royal Infirmary, Dundee 1836, his full-length portrait by John Gibson was placed in the Infirmary 14 June 1841; a reader in the Glasite church, Dundee 60 years; never went out of Scotland. *d.* Tay st. Dundee 3 July 1860. *W. Norrie's Dundee Celebrities* (1873) 182-4.

CRICHTON, WILLIAM HINDLEY. Entered Madras army 19 Aug. 1839, lieut. col. Madras staff corps 19 Aug. 1865 to 22 July 1871; hon. M.G. 17 Feb. 1872; C.B. 18 May 1860. *d.* Beaconside, North Devon 7 Dec. 1885 aged 66.

CRINNON, RIGHT REV. PETER FRANCIS. *b.* Cullen, co. Louth 1817 or 1818; went to Canada 1850; studied at St. Sulpice coll. Montreal; ordained in Toronto 1854; priest successively at London, St. Mary's, Biddulph, and Kintora; priest at Stratford 1858 where he built St. Mary's church; vicar general of London; R.C. bishop of Hamilton, Canada 1874 to death, during his administration of the diocese the number of Roman Catholics was doubled. *d.* Jacksonville, Florida 25 Nov. 1882. *Dominion Annual Register* 1883 *p.* 337.

CRIPPS, JOHN MARTEN *(son of John Cripps). b.* 1780; Fellow commoner at Jesus coll. Cam. 27 April 1798, M.A. 1803; travelled in the East with Edward Daniel Clarke 3 years;

CRIPPS, J. M. *(Con)*.

introduced from Russia the Khol-rabi for the use of dairy farms; F.L.S. 1803, F.S.A. 1805; presented part of his large collection of statues, antiques and oriental flora to Univ. of Cam. and other public institutions. *d.* Novington near Lewes 3 Jany. 1853. *Proc. of Linnæan Soc. ii*, 231-2 (1855); *M. A. Lower's Worthies of Sussex* (1865) 271-73.

CRITCHETT, GEORGE. *b.* Highgate 25 March 1817; ed. at London hospital; M.R.C.S. 1839, F.R.C.S. 1844, member of council 1870; demonstrator of anatomy at London hospital, assistant surgeon 1846, surgeon Aug. 1861 to 1863; one of the best operators on the eye; pres. of Hunterian Soc. 2 years; pres of International congress of Opthalmology held in London 1872; ophthalmic surgeon and lecturer at Middlesex hospital 1876; author of *Lectures on ulcers of the lower extremities* 1849. *d.* 21 Harley st. London 1 Nov. 1882. *I.L.N. lxxxi*, 497 (1882), *portrait.*

CRIVELLI, DOMENICO FRANCESCO MARIA *(son of Gaetano Crivelli 1774-1836 tenor singer at King's theatre, London). b.* Brescia 1794; came to England with his father 1817; taught singing in London 1817 to death; principal professor of singing at Royal Academy of Music 1823 to death; taught many of the best English singers. *d.* 71 Upper Norton st. Fitzroy sq. London 31 Dec. 1856.

CROCKER, CHARLES. *b.* Chichester 22 June 1797; shoemaker at Chichester 1809-39; employed by W. H. Mason the publisher 1839-45; sexton of Chichester cathedral 1845 to death; author of *The vale of obscurity, the Lavant and other poems* 1830, 3 ed. 1841; *A visit to Chichester cathedral* 1848; *Poetical works of C. Crocker* 1860. *d.* South st. Chichester 6 Oct. 1861. *M. A. Lower's Worthies of Sussex* (1865) 87-8; *Lives of illustrious shoemakers by W. E. Winks* (1883) 321; *Sketches of obscure poets* (1833) 102-112.

CROCKETT, JAMES *(son of Mr. Crockett, a showman by Miss Cross of Nottingham who was 6 feet 8 inches in height). b.* Prestyn, Radnorshire 9 May 1835; cornet player in circus of Messrs. Sanger, lion tamer with them 1857; performed in chief capitals of Europe; returned to England 1863; went to United States 1864; travelled in western states with Howes and Cushing's European circus at a salary of £20 a week; fell down dead in the circus at Cincinnati 6 July 1865. *Illust. Sporting news ii*, 377, 437 (1864), *portrait;* *Era 30 July 1865 p. 10, col. 1, 6 Aug. p. 11, col. 4;* *I.L.N. xxxviii*, 90 (1861).

CROFT, Sir Archer Denman, 8 Baronet (2 son of Sir Richard Croft, 6 baronet 1762–1818). b. Old Burlington st. London 7 Dec. 1801; ed. at Westminster; succeeded his brother 29 Oct. 1835; barrister L.I. 30 April 1839; a master of Court of Queen's Bench 1838 to death. d. 1 Sussex place, Hyde park, London 10 Jany. 1865.

CROFT, Ven. James (eld. son of Rev. Robert Nicholas Croft 1754–1831, canon res. of York cath.) b. 2 July 1784; ed. at Eton and Peterhouse Cam.; B.A. 1807, M.A. 1812; R. of Saltwood near Hythe 1812 to death; preb. of Ely 3 Nov. 1815; R. of Cliffe-at-Hoo, Kent 1818 to death; canon of Canterbury 26 April 1822; archdeacon of Canterbury 18 June 1825 to death. d. Saltwood rectory 9 May 1869.

CROFT, Sir John, 1 Baronet (eld. son of John Croft of Oporto, merchant, who d. 11 Feb. 1805). b. 21 March 1778; comr. to distribute parliamentary grant of £100,000 to the Portugese sufferers by Marshal Massena's invasion 1811–12; chargé d' affaires at Lisbon 1815; F.R.S. 5 March 1818; created baronet 17 Dec. 1818 for services during Peninsular war; K.T.S. 10 Dec. 1821; D.C.L. Ox. 1822. d. 53 Queen Anne st. London 5 Feb. 1862.

CROFT, William (2 son of Stephen Croft of Stillington hall, Yorkshire 1744–1813). b. 2 April 1782; entered navy 1 Sep. 1795; captain 13 Oct. 1807; admiral on half pay 28 Nov. 1857. d. Stillington 6 May 1872.

CROFTON, Edward Crofton, 2 Baron. b. Clarges st. London 1 Aug. 1806; succeeded his father as 4 baronet 8 Jany. 1816, and his grandmother as 2 baron 12 Aug. 1817; a representative peer of Ireland 20 Jany. 1840 to death; a lord in waiting to the Queen, Feb. to Dec. 1852, Feb. 1858 to June 1859 and July 1866 to Dec. 1868. d. Mote park, Roscommon 27 Dec. 1869.

CROFTON, Edward Walter. 2 lieut. R.A. 26 July 1831, col. 30 May 1862 to death; C.B. 1 March 1861. d. Malta 26 June 1863.

CROFTON, George Alfred. b. 1785; entered navy March 1798; captain 1 Feb. 1812; V.A. on h.p. 9 July 1855. d. Clifton 23 Feb. 1858.

CROFTON, John Ffolliott. b. 9 Oct. 1802; ensign 6 foot 18 Dec. 1824, lieut. col. 7 Aug. 1846 to 21 July 1848; col. of 95 foot 25 Aug. 1868, of 6 foot 5 Sep. 1869 to death; general 23 Aug. 1877. d. 29 Sussex gardens, Hyde park, London 17 July 1885.

CROGGAN, John William. 2 lieut. Madras artillery 18 Dec. 1823, col. commandant 14 Dec. 1868 to death; L.G. 10 April 1876; author of Miscellaneous exercises on artillery 1856; A treatise on Mortar practice, velocity, time of flight and range 1865. d. 35 Tregunter road, London 2 May 1877.

CROKAT, William. b. near Edinburgh 1788; ensign 20 foot 9 April 1807, captain 31 March 1814 to 7 Nov. 1826 when placed on h.p.; witnessed the death of Napoleon at St. Helena 5 May 1821, being the original of the "Officer on guard" in Steuben's well known engraving; general 25 Oct. 1871. d. 52 Inverkeith's row, Edinburgh 6 Nov. 1879 in 92 year.

CROKER, John Wilson (son of John Croker, surveyor general of customs and excise in Ireland). b. Galway 20 Dec. 1780; ed. at Portarlington and Trin. coll. Dublin, B.A. 1800, LL.B. and LL.D. 1809; student at L.I. 1800; called to Irish bar 1802; M.P. for Downpatrick 1807–12, for Athlone 1812–18, for Yarmouth, Isle of Wight 1819–20, for Bodmin 1820–26, for Aldeburgh, Suffolk 1826–27 and 1830–32, for Univ. of Dublin 1827–30; one of chief opponents of the Reform bill; sec. of the Admiralty 9 Oct. 1809 to Nov. 1830 when he retired on a pension of £1500; P.C. 16 June 1828; one of founders of Quarterly Review 1809 in which he wrote about 260 articles 1809–64; F.R.S. 5 July 1810; friend and factotum of 3 Marquis of Hertford (the Marquis of Steyne of Vanity Fair) who left him £21,000 and his cellar of wine 1842; author of Familiar epistles to F. J[one]s, Esq. on the present state of the Irish stage 1804 anon. 5 ed. 1804; Talavera 1809; Essays on the early period of the French revolution 1857 and other books; edited The new Whig guide 1819; Boswell's Life of Dr. Johnson 4 vols. 1831 and other books. d. at house of Sir Wm. Wightman, St. Alban's Bank. Hampton, Middlesex 10 Aug. 1857. bur. at West Moulsey. Memoirs, diaries and correspondence of J. W. Croker edited by L. J. Jennings, 2 ed. 3 vols. 1885, portrait; Quarterly Review cxlii 83–126 (1876); D. O. Madden's Chiefs of parties ii, 81–112 (1859); J. Grant's Memoir of Sir G. Sinclair (1870) 213–28; Mrs. Houston's A woman's memories i, 1–18 (1883); H. Martineau's Biographical Sketches, 4 ed. (1876) 376–85; Maclise Portrait gallery (1883) 72–4, portrait.

Note.—D'Israeli ridiculed him very successfully in Coningsby under name of Rigby, also in Vivian Grey under name of Vivida Vis; Lady Morgan depicted him in her novel Florence Macarthy as Councillor Crawley, and Lord Brougham in his novel Albert Lunel as La Croasse.

CROKER, MARIANNE *(dau. of Francis Nicholson of Whitby, Yorkshire, artist 1753–1844). b.* Whitby; produced her first drawing upon stone 1816; wrote *The adventures of Barney Mahoney* 1832, and *My village versus our village* 1832, both of which have the name of Thomas Crofton Croker on their title pages; *(m.* 1830 T. C. Croker 1798–1854). *d.* 3 Gloucester road, Old Brompton, London 6 Oct. 1854.

CROKER, THOMAS CROFTON *(only son of Thomas Croker, major in the army who d. 22 March* 1818). *b.* Buckingham sq. Cork 15 Jany. 1798; clerk in the Admiralty, London 1818 to Feb. 1850 when he retired as senior clerk of the first class on a pension of £580, introduced lithography into the Admiralty; F.S.A. 1827; M.R.I.A. 1827; founder and pres. of Society of Noviomagus 11 Dec. 1828 to his death; helped to found Camden Soc. 1839, Percy Soc. 1840 and British Archæological Assoc. 1843; edited *Willis's Current Notes* Jany. 1851 to death; author of *Researches in the South of Ireland* 1834; *Fairy legends and traditions of the South of Ireland* 3 parts 1825–28, *several editions*; *Legends of the Lakes, or sayings and doings at Killarney* 2 vols. 1829, *new ed.* 1874; *The popular songs of Ireland* 1839 another ed. in Morley's Universal Library vol. 40; *The Keen of the South of Ireland illustrative of Irish history, Percy Soc. vol.* 13 (1842); *A walk from London to Fulham* 1860, and many other works and translations. *d.* 3 Gloucester road, Old Brompton, London 8 Aug. 1854. *Fairy Legends of the South of Ireland by T. C. Croker with a memoir of the author by his son T. F. D. Croker* 1862; *Dublin Univ. Mag. xxxiv*, 203–16 (1849), *portrait; Fraser's Mag. iii,* 67 (1831), *portrait; Mrs. Balmanno's Pen and pencil* (1858) 156–71, *portrait; C. R. Smith's Retrospections i,* 251–57 (1883); *Numismatic Chronicle xviii*, 20–1 (1856); *Maclise Portrait Gallery* (1883) 49–53, *portrait; G.M. xlii,* 397–401 (1854).

CROKER, WILLIAM. Ensign 17 foot 27 March 1803, lieut. col. 1 April 1836 to 5 Nov. 1847 when he sold out; C.B. 20 Dec. 1839; colonel in the army 9 Nov. 1846. *d.* Cheltenham 11 Aug. 1852 aged 64.

CROLL, ALEXANDER ANGUS *(youngest son of George Croll of Perth). b.* Perth 1811; civil engineer in London; a pioneer in extension of telegraphy; chairman of United Kingdom electric telegraph company; publicly presented with a testimonial of plate worth 1000 guineas 1871; originated and erected the Wool Exchange in city of London; colonel 2 Tower Hamlets volunteers 1869–85; sheriff of London and Middlesex 1853. *d.* Dunblane, Scotland 7 June 1887. *bur.* Woking cemetery, Surrey 11 June. *I.L.N. xxiii,* 195 (1853).

CROLL, FRANCIS. *b.* Musselburgh about 1826; line engraver. *d.* Edinburgh 12 Feb. 1854. *Art Journal* (1854) 119.

CROLY, REV. GEORGE. *b.* Dublin 17 Aug. 1780; ed. at Trin. coll. Dublin, scholar 1798, B.A. 1800, M.A. 1804, hon. LL.D. 1831; came to London about 1810; dramatic critic to the *New Times;* took charge of parish of Romford, Essex 1832–35; R. of St. Benet Sherehog with St. Stephen's, Walbrook, London 1835 to death; afternoon preacher at Foundling hospital 1847–48; wrote poems in the *Literary Gazette* from 1817; edited *The Graces* 1824, *The Literary Souvenir* 1825–34; author of *Paris in* 1815, 1817; *The Beauties of the British poets* 1828; *Tales of the Saint Bernard* 1829; *Salathiel, A story of the past, the present and the future* 1829, *new ed.* 1855; *The life and times of George the Fourth* 1830, *2 ed. 2 vols.* 1841; *Divine providence, or the three cycles of Revelation* 1834; *A memoir of Edmund Burke 2 vols.* 1840; *Historical sketches, speeches and characters* 1842; *Marston, or the soldier and statesman 3 vols.* 1846, *3 ed.* 1861; *Scenes from Scripture with other poems* 1851; *The book of Job* 1863, and numerous other books and single sermons. *d.* suddenly whilst walking in Holborn, London 24 Nov. 1860. *bur.* St. Stephen's, Walbrook where a bust of him was placed. *The book of Job by Rev. G. Croly with a biographical sketch by his son* 1873; *A few personal recollections of Rev. G. Croly by Richard Herring* 1861; *James Grant's Metropolitan pulpit i,* 239–56; *G. Gilfillan's A second gallery of literary portraits* (1850) 145–59; *G.M. x,* 104–7 (1861); *I.L.N. iv,* 248 (1844), *portrait, xxiv,* 401 (1854), *portrait.*

CROMBIE, THOMAS. Ensign 79 foot 12 Aug. 1824; major Rifle corps 16 Nov. 1841 to 20 Oct. 1848 when placed on h.p.; captain Coldstream guards 22 June 1849 to 9 Feb. 1855 when placed on h.p.; col. 96 foot 10 May 1872 to death; general 1 Oct. 1877. *d.* 33 Half Moon st. Piccadilly, London 14 Oct.1877.

CROMMELIN, THOMAS LAKE. *b.* 1805; executed commissions for gentlemen on the chief public races 1835–52; a butcher in Melbourne, Australia 1853; police magistrate Victoria gold fields 1854; commissioner of crown lands Riverina district, New South Wales 1860, resigned 1869; sec. to Union club, Sydney for one month only 1869. *d.* in house of his friend hon. John Bowie Wilson at Sydney 7 April 1877. *Sporting Times 2 May* 1885 *pp.* 2–3.

CROMMELIN, WILLIAM ARDEN *(son of Charles Barker Crommelin of Garruckpore). b.* 1823; second lieut. Bengal engineers 10 Dec. 1841,

CROMMELIN, W. A. *(Con).*

colonel 1 Jany. 1870 to 31 Dec. 1878 when he retired with hon. rank of L.G.; C.B. 26 July 1858; inspector general of military works 2 Aug. 1865 to 1877, granted service reward 12 Jany. 1875. *d.* Brightlands, Barnes, Surrey 30 Oct. 1886.

CROMPTON, SIR CHARLES JOHN (3 *son of Peter Crompton, M.D. of Derby*). *b.* Derby 12 June 1797; ed. at Trin. coll. Dublin, B.A. 1818, M.A. 1821; barrister I.T. 23 Nov. 1821, bencher 1851; tub-man in Court of Exchequer, postman; contested Preston, Dec. 1832 and Newport, Isle of Wight, July 1847; assessor of Court of Passage, Liverpool 1836–52; a comr. of inquiry into Court of Chancery, Dec. 1850; justice of Court of Queen's Bench, Feb. 1852 to death; serjeant-at-law Feb. 1852; knighted at St. James's palace 26 Feb. 1852; author with John Jervis of *Reports in the Court of Exchequer 1830–32,* 2 vols. 1832–33; with Roger Meeson of *Reports in the Court of Exchequer 1832–34,* 2 vols. 1834–35; with R. Meeson and Henry Roscoe of *Reports in the Court of Exchequer 1834–36,* 2 vols. 1834–36. *d.* 22 Hyde park sq. London 30 Oct. 1865. *Law mag. and law review xxiii,* 1–30 (1867); *I.L.N. xxi,* 356 (1852), *portrait.*

CROMPTON, JOSHUA SAMUEL *(son of Joshua Crompton of York, who d.* 1832). *b.* 17 Sep. 1799; M.P. for Ripon 1832 to 1834. *d.* Azerley hall, Ripon 17 June 1881.

CROMPTON, THOMAS BONSOR *(youngest son of John Crompton of Farnworth mills, Lancashire, paper maker).* *b.* Farnworth 20 May 1792; partner with his brother John Crompton in Farnworth Mills, sole proprietor 1835 to death; contrived several mechanical appliances for utilising fibres hitherto considered unsuitable for being made into paper; became an extensive newspaper proprietor; proprietor of the *Morning Post;* erected very large cotton mill at Prestolee near Farnworth about 1833. *d.* the Hassels, Sandy, Beds. 3 Sep. 1858.

CROMPTON-STANSFIELD, WILLIAM ROOKES *(brother of Joshua Samuel Crompton 1799–1881).* *b.* 3 Aug. 1790; ed. at Harrow and Jesus coll. Cam., B.A. 1813, M.A. 1816; barrister I.T. 22 May 1819; M.P. for Huddersfield 1837 to 1853; took additional name of Stansfield 1819. *d.* Frimley park, Surrey 5 Dec. 1871.

CROMWELL, REV. THOMAS. *b.* 14 Dec. 1792; entered Literary department of Longman & Co. of London, publishers; minister of Unitarian chapel, Stoke Newington Green 1839–64; minister of old presbyterian chapel at

CROMWELL, REV. T. *(Con.)*

Canterbury 1865 to death; F.S.A. Dec. 1838; author of *The school boy with other poems* 1816; *Honour, or arrivals from college, privately printed* 1820, a comedy played at Drury Lane 17 and 18 April 1819; *Oliver Cromwell and his times* 1821, 2 ed. 1822; *History of the town and borough of Colchester* 2 vols. 1825; *History and description of the parish of Clerkenwell* 1828; *The Druid, a tragedy* 1832; *Walks through Islington* 1835; *The soul and the future life* 1859. *d.* Canterbury 22 Dec. 1870. *Notes and Queries 4th series, ix,* 198, 267, 347 (1872).

CRONYN, RIGHT REV. BENJAMIN *(son of Thomas Cronyn, mayor of Kilkenny).* *b.* Kilkenny 1802; ed. at Trin. coll. Dublin, B.A. 1822, M.A. 1825, B.D. and D.D. 1855; held curacies in Ireland 1826–32; R. of St. Paul's, London, Canada West 1832–57; bishop of Huron 14 Oct. 1857 to death, consecrated at Lambeth 28 Oct. 1857. *d.* London, Ontario 21 Sep. 1871. *I.L.N. xli,* 576, 587 (1862), *portrait.*

CROOK, JOSEPH *(eld. son of Joshua Crook of Whitebank, Bolton).* *b.* 1809; cotton manufacturer at Bolton; M.P. for Bolton 9 July 1852 to Jany. or Feb. 1861. *d.* Oakfield, Heaton, Bolton 8 Dec. 1884 in 76 year.

CROOKS, JAMES. *b.* Kilmarnock, Scotland 1778; one of earliest settlers in Upper Canada, lived at Niagara 1794; established first paper mill in and sent first load of wheat and flour from Upper Canada to Montreal; served with distinction during war of 1812; member of Canadian legislative assembly and council. *d.* West Flamborough, Ontario 1860.

CROOKSHANK, ALEXANDER CROWDER. Deputy controller Dublin district 11 Dec. 1872 to death; C.B. 24 May 1873. *d.* 20 Upper Mount st. Dublin 14 April 1877. *Graphic xv,* 408 (1877), *portrait.*

CROPPER, JOSEPH ALMOND. *b.* Loughborough; barrister G.I. 11 Feb. 1823; devised property to Westminster hospital worth £800 per annum, to St. George's hospital worth £700, and to Middlesex hospital property worth £600 per annum and the sum of £4000, these 3 hospitals are enabled by special acts of parliament to receive lands notwithstanding the Statute of Mortmain. *d.* Fulwood house, Gray's Inn London 27 Sep. 1862 aged 79.

CROSBY, ALLAN JAMES *(only son of James Crosby of Streatham).* Matric. from Worcester coll. Ox. 9 Nov. 1854 aged 18, B.A. 1858, M.A. 1873; barrister I.T. 1 May 1865; employed in the public record office about 1860

CROSBY, A. J. (Con.)

to death; edited *Accounts and papers relating to Mary Queen of Scots, Camden Soc.* 1867; *Calendar of foreign state papers of the reign of Queen Elizabeth* 4 vols. 1871–80. *d.* Holmbush, Ide near Exeter 5 Dec. 1881. *Antiquarian Mag.* i, 152 (1882).

CROSBY, JAMES. *b.* 1806; ed. at Greenwich and Trin. coll. Cam., B.A. 1826; barrister M.T. 25 June 1830; police magistrate at Kingston, St. Vincent, May 1844; member of house of assembly St. Vincent many years, speaker 1853; stipendiary magistrate British Guiana, March 1857, immigration agent general British Guiana 1 Oct. 1862 to death. *d.* Georgetown, Demerara 30 Aug. 1880.

CROSKERY, REV. THOMAS (son of Mr. Croskery of co. Down, tradesman). *b.* Carrowdore near Belfast 26 May 1830; licensed to preach by presbytery of Down 6 May 1851; a reporter and subsequently editor of the *Banner of Ulster;* ordained minister of Creggan, co. Armagh 17 July 1860, translated to Clonakilty, co. Cork 24 March 1863; minister of chapel at Waterside, city of Londonderry 1866–75; professor of logic and belles lettres in Magee college, Londonderry 1875–79, professor of theology 1879 to death; author of *A catechism on the doctrines of the Plymouth brethren; Plymouth brethrenism, a refutation of its principles and doctrines* 1879; *Irish Presbyterianism, its history, character, influence and present position* 1884. *d.* 3 Oct. 1886.

CROSLAND, THOMAS PEARSON. *b.* Crosland near Huddersfield 29 Dec. 1815; a merchant at Huddersfield; M.P. for Huddersfield 14 July 1865 to death. *d.* Gledholt near Huddersfield 8 March 1868.

CROSLEY, ALEXANDER. *b.* Camberwell 1827; a solicitor in London 1850 to death; common councilman for Langbourn ward 1857–61; under sheriff for London and Middlesex 8 times. *d.* 76 Camberwell grove, London 14 Jany. 1876 in 49 year.

CROSLEY, SIR CHARLES DECIMUS (son of Henry Crosley). *b.* the Grove, Camberwell, Surrey 21 Feb. 1820; ed. at Camberwell; a stock and share broker in city of London 1846 to death; sheriff of London and Middlesex 1854–55; knighted at Buckingham palace 1 May 1855 after visit of Emperor of the French; chevalier of legion of honour; a comr. of inland revenue for Middlesex. *d.* Eastbourne 12 Oct. 1882.

CROSMOND, ROSA, stage name of Helen Turner (dau. of Sarah Rachael Leverson known as Madame Rachel of 47 New Bond st. London, enameller of ladies faces, who d. 12 Oct. 1880 c jed 60). Member of Carter's choir at Albert hall, London about 1873; studied at Royal Academy of Music; sang at Her Majesty's theatre 1878–79 and with Mapleson's company in the United States; secured a high position at Milan particularly for her representation of Aida about 1881. (m. Edmund Turner of London, silk merchant who d. about 1879). d. St. George's hospital, London 27 April 1888, having shot herself in a cab in Piccadilly Circus the night before.

CROSS, EDWARD. Superintendent of the Royal Menagerie, Exeter Change, Strand ¹ ondon 1794 to 1814, Chunee the elephant sh t there 9 March 1826, proprietor 1814 to 16 June 829 when it was taken down and he removed his menagerie to the King's Mews, Charing C ss; originated the Surrey Zoological gardens om-prising 15 acres at Walworth, opened 12 ¹ ug. 1831, proprietor 1831–44, the conservatory 300 feet in circumference was the largest in England; exhibited the Indian one-horned rhinoceros which cost £800, 1834, three giraffes 1836, picture of Mount Vesuvius painted by Danson 1837 reproduced 1846, Iceland and its volcanoes 1839, Jullien conducted promenade concerts here 1849–51. *d.* 48 Newington place, Kennington road, London 26 Sep. 1354 aged 80. *Hone's Every-day book* ii, 321–36 (1838); *Brayley's Surrey* iii, 409–11 (1850).

CROSS, JOHN. *b.* Tiverton, May 1819; studied painting at St. Quentin and Paris; exhibited a cartoon of 'The death of Thomas à Becket' at Westminster Hall 1844, and a large oil painting called 'The clemency of Richard Cœur-de-Lion towards Bertrand de Gourdon' 1847 which gained a first premium of £300 and was purchased by the comrs. for £1000; an exhibition of his principal works was held at Society of Arts, Adelphi 1861; his widow Mary Cross was granted civil list pension of £100, 19 June 1862. He *d.* 38 Gloucester road, Regent's Park, London 27 Feb. 1861.

CROSS, JOHN (2 son of James Cross of Mortfield near Bolton, Lancs. solicitor and banker, who d. 1 Nov. 1850 aged 79). *b.* Mortfield 18 Jany. 1807; ed. at Bolton gr. school; articled to his father; solicitor at Bolton 1829–33; barrister G.I. and M.T. 8 June 1836; serjeant at law 17 May 1858; chairman of board of directors of Londonderry and Coleraine railway; author of *A treatise on the law of lien and stoppage in transitu* 1840. *d.* 2 Avenue road, Regent's park, London 1 June 1861.

CROSS, JOHN HENRY. *b.* London; connected with the Religious tract society more than 40 years; wrote for it 609 separate publications (majority being small books for children), total circulation of which amounted to nearly 80,000,000 copies, selections from them have been translated into 30 languages; edited the *Child's Companion* 33 years, the *Tract magazine* 6 years. *d.* Loughborough road, Brixton 5 Feb. 1876 aged 72.

CROSS, JOHN KYNASTON (*son of John Cross of Gartside house, Bolton*). *b.* 13 Oct. 1832; a merchant at Manchester and a cotton spinner at Bolton; M.P. for Bolton 4 Feb. 1874 to 18 Nov. 1885; under sec. of state for India, Jany. 1883 to July 1885; author of *Imports, exports and the French treaty* 1881 in Cobden Club Papers; hanged himself at Fernclough, Heaton, Bolton 20 March 1887.

CROSS, MARY ANN (*youngest child of Robert Evans 1773–1849, surveyor to Sir Roger Newdigate of Arbury hall, Warws.*) *b.* Arbury farm, parish of Chilvers Coton, Warws. 22 Nov. 1819; ed. at Nuneaton and Coventry; removed with her father to Foleshill road, Coventry, March 1841; lived at 142 Strand, London as assistant editor of *Westminster Review* Sep. 1851 to Oct. 1853; lived with George Henry Lewes at Holly lodge, Wandsworth 1859–60, at 16 Blandford sq. Regent's park 1860–63, and at The Priory 21 North bank, St. John's Wood 1863–78, G. H. Lewes *d.* 28 Nov. 1878, she proved his will 16 Dec. 1878; founded George Henry Lewes studentship worth nearly £200 a year to be held for 3 years by some student occupied in physiological investigation 1879; published *The life of Jesus critically examined by D. F. Strauss, translated from the fourth German edition* 3 vols. 1846 anon.; *The essence of Christianity by Ludwig Feuerbach translated from the second German edition by Marian Evans* 1854; author of the following works under pseudonym of George Eliot *Scenes of clerical life* 2 vols. 1858, *Adam Bede* 3 vols. 1859, *The mill on the Floss* 3 vols. 1860, *Silas Marner the weaver of Raveloe* 1861, *Romola* 3 vols. 1863, *Felix Holt the Radical* 3 vols. 1866, *The Spanish Gypsy, a poem* 1868, *Agatha, a poem* 1869, *Middlemarch a study of provincial life* 4 vols. 1871–72, *The legend of Jubal and other poems* 1874, *Daniel Deronda* 4 vols. 1876, *Impressions of Theophrastus Such* 1879, *How Lisa loved the King* 1883, *Essays and leaves from a Note-Book* 1884. (*m.* 6 May 1880 under name of Mary Ann Evans Lewes, John Walter Cross of Weybridge, Surrey). *d.* 4 Cheyne walk, Chelsea 22 Dec. 1880. *bur.* by side of G. H. Lewes in Highgate cemetery 29 Dec.

CROSS, M. A. (*Con.*)
portrait of her by Sir Frederick Burton in National portrait gallery. *The life of George Eliot by J. W. Cross* 3 vols. 1884, 2 *portraits; George Eliot by Mathilde Blind* 1883; *G. W. Cooke's George Eliot, critical story of her life* 1883; *Our living poets by H. B. Forman* (1871) 467–500; *Biographical sketches by C. K. Paul* (1883) 141–70; *Westminster Review, Jany.* 1882 *pp.* 65–71.

CROSS, PHILIP HENRY EUSTACE. L.R.C.S. Ireland 1848; assistant surgeon 1 West India regiment 3 April 1849; surgeon 97 foot 7 Sep. 1855; surgeon 13 foot 16 June 1857 to 19 Nov. 1858; staff surgeon 19 Nov. 1858; served in the Crimean war; surgeon major 27 Feb. 1872 to 14 April 1875 when he retired; slowly murdered his first wife Mary Lawson Cross by giving her doses of arsenic and strychnine, she *d.* at Shandy hall, Cork 2 June 1887, (*m.* (2) 17 June 1887 his governess Miss Skinner); found guilty of murder 17 Dec. 1887, hanged in Cork gaol 10 Jany. 1888. *Pall Mall Gazette* 10 *Jany.* 1888 *p.* 7, *col.* 2.

CROSSE, ANDREW (*elder son of Richard Crosse of Fyne court, Broomfield, Somerset*). *b.* Fyne court 17 June 1784; ed. at Rev. Mr. Seyer's school, The Fort, Bristol 1793–1802, caned on an average 3 times a day for 7 years; gentleman commoner at Brasenose coll. Ox. 1802, B.A. 1806; experimented on electrocrystallisation; observed appearance of insect life in metallic solutions supposed to be destructive to organic life 1837, the publication of this discovery gained him great notoriety. *d.* in the room in which he was born at Fyne Court 6 July 1855. *Memorials scientific and literary of Andrew Crosse the electrician by C. A. H. Crosse* 1857; *H. M. Noad's Manual of Electricity,* 4 *ed.* (1855) 173–77, 256, 378–83, 390, 401; *Letters of H. G. Atkinson to Harriet Martineau* (1851) 361–67.

CROSSE, THOMAS BRIGHT (*only son of Thomas Ikin*). *b.* 1796; ed. at Trin. coll. Cam., B.A. 1817; assumed surname of Crosse 8 Sep. 1828; sheriff of Lancashire 1837; M.P. for Wigan 1 July 1841 to April 1842 when unseated on petition. *d.* 75 Cambridge terrace, Hyde park, London 21 March 1886.

CROSSLEY, SIR FRANCIS, 1 Baronet (*youngest son of John Crossley of Halifax, carpet manufacturer, who d.* 17 *Jany.* 1837). *b.* Halifax 26 Oct. 1817; carpet manufacturer at Dean Clough mills, Halifax, the largest concern of the kind in the world; M.P. for Halifax 1852–59, for west riding of Yorkshire 1859–65, for north west riding 1865–68, for north division of west riding 1868 to death; mayor of Halifax

CROSSLEY, SIR F. *(Con.)*

1849 and 1850; founded 21 almshouses at Halifax 1855; donor of the People's park, Halifax at cost of £41,300, opened 14 Aug. 1857, where a statue of him was erected 14 Aug. 1860; created baronet 23 Jany. 1863; author of *Canada and United States* 1856. *d.* Belle Vue, Halifax 5 Jany. 1872, personalty sworn under £800,000, 27 May 1872. *Thrift by S. Smiles* (1875) 205–17; *Enoch Mellor's A true life* 1872; *Illust. news of the world iii* (1859), *portrait*; *Family Friend* 1 *March* 1870 *pp.* 39–43, *portrait*; *I.L.N. lx,* 55, 57, 587 (1872), *portrait.*

CROSSLEY, JAMES *(son of James Crossley of Halifax, clothing merchant* 1767–1831). *b.* The Mount, Halifax 31 March 1800; articled to Thomas Ainsworth of Manchester, attorney 1817; partner in firm of Ainsworth, Crossley and Sudlow at Manchester 1823–24 when Ainsworth died, partner in firm of Crossley and Sudlow 1824–60 when he retired; pres. of Incorporated Law Assoc. of Manchester 1840 and 1857; pres. of Manchester Athenæum 1847–50; pres. of Chetham Soc. Dec. 1847 to death, this society was mooted at his house in Booth st. Piccadilly early in 1843 and founded at the Chetham library 23 March 1843; F.S.A. 16 Dec. 1852; member of Surtees Soc. 1858, vice pres. 1861; pres. of Spencer Soc. 1866; the first pres. of Record Soc. 1878; one of chief contributors to *Retrospective Review* 1820; collected a library of 100,000 volumes, part of which was sold at Manchester, May 1884, and the remainder in London, July 1884 and June 1885; edited for the Chetham Soc. *Potts's Discovery of witches in the county of Lancaster* 1845; *The diary and correspondence of Dr. John Worthington* 2 vols. 1847–55; author of *Vade-Mecum to Hatton* 1867 privately printed. *d.* the Stocks house, Cheetham hill road, Manchester 1 Aug. 1883. *bur.* Kersal church 6 Aug. *Palatine note book iii,* 221–29 (1883), *portrait*; *J. Evans's Lancashire authors and orators* (1850) 67–72; *W. Smith's Old Yorkshire iii,* 49, *portrait*; *Antiquarian Mag. iv,* 198–202 (1883); *Bibliographer, Sep.* 1883, *pp.* 97–9; *Manchester Guardian* 2 *Aug.* 1883, *p.* 6, *cols.* I–5; *Momus* 11 *March* 1880, *portrait.*

NOTE.—He is described under the initial C in an article called The Theatre in W. H. Ainsworth's "December Tales" 1823 pp. 165-79, the article was written by J. P. Aston author of Sir John Chiverton.

CROSSLEY, JOHN *(brother of Sir Francis Crossley* 1817–72). *b.* Halifax 16 May 1812; mayor of Halifax 1849, 1850, 1861 and 1862; M.P. for Halifax 3 Feb. 1874 to Feb. 1877; built with his brothers Sir F. Crossley and Joseph Crossley (who *d.* 14 Sep. 1868) the Crossley

CROSSLEY, J. *(Con).*

Orphan house and school on Skircoat Moor about 1861. *d.* Broomfield, Halifax 16 April 1879. *Weekly Welcome* (1879) 357–8, *portrait.*

CROSSLEY, JOHN SYDNEY. *b.* Loughborough 25 Dec. 1812; engineer to Leicester Canal company 1832; resident engineer to Midland Railway company 1857, engineer in chief 1858 to April 1875; M.I.C.E. 1 March 1859. *d.* Barrow upon Soar 10 June 1879. *Min. of proc. of Instit. of C.E. lviii,* 341–43 (1879).

CROWDER, SIR RICHARD BUDDEN *(eld. son of Wm. Henry Crowder of Montagu place, London).* *b.* London 1796; ed. at Eton and Trin. coll. Cam.; barrister L.I. 25 May 1821; went Western circuit; Q.C. 1837; recorder of Bristol, Aug. 1846 to April 1854; counsel of the Admiralty and judge advocate of the Fleet, Aug. 1849 to March 1854; M.P. for Liskeard 3 Jany. 1849 to March 1854; justice of Court of Common Pleas, March 1854 to death; serjeant at law, March 1854; knighted at St. James's palace 3 May 1854. *d.* 17 Carlton house terrace, London 5 Dec. 1859. *Traits of character by a contemporary i,* 251–82 (1860); *Eton portrait gallery* (1876) 445–47.

CROWDY, CHARLES (3 *son of James Crowdy of Highworth, Wilts. solicitor).* *b.* Highworth, March 1786; entered navy 7 Sep. 1799; captain 13 Jany. 1834; placed on retired list 1 July 1851; retired admiral 18 Oct. 1867. *d.* Pittville lawn, Cheltenham 17 May 1870.

CROWDY, JOHN. *b.* Lewknor, Oxon. 6 Jany. 1834; foreign editor of the *Guardian* 1854 to death; editor successively of *The Choirmaster, The Musician, The Musical Standard,* and *The Artist* from its commencement 15 Jany. 1880; published *The church choirmaster* 1864; *A free chant service* 1865; *A recitative service* 1865; *A short commentary on Handel's The Messiah* 1875; author of a system of recitative for psalms and canticles in Congregational worship called 'Free Chant,' designed to provide for an undisturbed delivery of the words with suitable musical chords or cadences without necessity of signs. *d.* Addlestone, Surrey 12 Jany. 1883. *The Artist* 1 *Feb.* 1883 *pp.* 45, 48.

CROWE, CATHERINE ANN *(dau. of John Stevens of Clarges street, Piccadilly, London).* *b.* Englefield Green, Kent 1790; lived in Edinburgh many years; a disciple of George Combe; one of the persons to whom authorship of *The Vestiges of Creation* was attributed 1841; author of *Aristodemus, a tragedy* 1838, anon.; *The adventures of Susan Hopley* 3 vols. 1841, a dramatic version of this novel entitled *Susan*

CROWE, C. *(Con.)*

Hopley or the vicissitudes of a servant girl by Dibdin Pitt was produced at the Victoria theatre, London 31 May 1841 and played more than 300 nights; *Men and women, or manorial rights* 3 vols. 1843; *The Seerest of Prevorst, translated from Kerner* 1845; *The story of Lilly Dawson* 2 vols. 1847; *The night side of nature, or Ghosts and ghost seers* 2 vols. 1848, *several eds.; Light and darkness or mysteries of life* 3 vols. 1850; *The adventures of a beauty, a novel* 3 vols. 1852; *The cruel kindness, a drama in 5 acts performed at Haymarket theatre, June 6, 1853; Linny Lockwood* 2 vols. 1853; *Spiritualism and the age we live in* 1859; *Adventures of a monkey* 1861 and many books for children. *(m.* Oct. 1822 in London, lieut.-col. John Crowe who *d.* 7 March 1860). Resided at 22 Sandgate road, Folkestone, where she became bedridden and *died* of natural decay on 14 June 1872; Her son and only child Capt. John William Crowe is resident Leonard lodge, Dover road, Folkestone 1888. *Victoria Mag. xxxiii,* 35-44 (1879); *Colburn's New monthly mag. xcvi,* 439-45 (1852).

CROWE, EYRE EVANS *(son of David Crowe, captain in H.E.I.Co.'s army). b.* Redbridge, Southampton 20 March 1799; ed. at Carlow and Trin. coll. Dublin; Paris correspondent of *Morning Chronicle* 1832-44, joined staff of *Daily News* 1846, editor 1849-51; author of *The pleasures of Melancholy, and a Saxon tale* 1819; *To-day in Ireland* 1825; *Yesterday in Ireland* 1829; *The History of France* 3 vols. 1830-31 and *Lives of Foreign Statesmen* 1833 both in Lardner's Cabinet Cyclopœdia; *Connemara* 1843; *Charles Delmer, a story of the day* 1853; *The Greek and the Turk or powers and prospects in the Levant* 1853; *History of the reigns of Louis xviii and Charles x* 2 vols. 1854; *The History of France* 5 vols. 1858-68. *d.* 56 Beaumont st. Marylebone, London 25 Feb. 1868.

CROWE, JOHN. Ensign 32 foot 7 Aug. 1800, captain 30 May 1805 to 4 May 1826; major on h.p. 4 May 1826; served in Peninsula, July 1811 to end of the war 1814; lieut.-col. 10 Jany. 1837; retired 1846; K.H. 1837. *d.* Fairlea villa near Bideford 7 March 1860 aged 77.

CROWE, SIR JOHN RICE. Served in the Russian navy 6 years; British vice-consul at Hamerfest in Norway, May 1824, consul there 14 March 1837; consul general in Norway 16 Aug. 1843 to 2 April 1875 when he retired on a pension; C.B. 5 Dec. 1859; knighted at Windsor Castle 7 July 1874. *d.* near Christiania 10 Jany. 1877 aged 84. *Times 24 Jany. 1877 p. 6, col. 4.*

CROWFOOT, REV. JOHN RUSTAT *(son of Wm. Henchman Crowfoot of Beccles, Suffolk, surgeon). b.* Beccles, 21 Feb. 1817; ed. at Eton and Caius coll. Cam., 12 wrangler 1839, B.A. 1839, M.A. 1842, B.D. 1849, fellow of his college 1840-52; C. of Eynesbury, Hunts. 1840-47; C. of St. Mary the Great, Cam. 1852-54; P.C. of Southwold, Suffolk 1854-60; V. of Wangford-cum-Reydon, Suffolk 1860 to death; published *Remarks on the University of Cambridge* 1848; *Academic notes on Holy Scripture 1st series* 1850; *Plea for a colonial college at Cambridge* 1854; *Fragmenta Evangelica* 1870; *Observations on the collation in Greek of Cureton's Syriac Fragments of the Gospels* 1872. *d.* Wangford vicarage 18 March 1875.

CROWLEY, ABRAHAM. Head of brewing firm of A. Crowley and Co. at Alton, Hants.; many refreshment houses were established in London and other places which especially supplied Crowley's ales; built and supported a British school for 150 girls at Alton 1845. *d.* Alton 6 May 1864 aged 70. *Hampshire Chronicle 14 May 1864 p. 5.*

CROWLEY, NICHOLAS JOSEPH (3 *son of Peter Crowley of Dublin). b.* Dublin 6 Dec. 1819; a pupil of Royal Dublin Society; exhibited 46 pictures at the R.A. 1835-57; member of Royal Hibernian academy 1838; painted several portraits of Daniel O'Connell 1844; painted 'Taking the Veil' for St. Vincent's hospital, Dublin 1845, in the background of this picture there is a portrait of himself; many of his pictures were engraved and lithographed. *d.* 13 Upper Fitzroy st. London 4 Nov. 1857.

CROWLEY, PETER O'NEILL *(son of Mr. Crowley of Ballymacoda, co. Cork, tenant farmer). b.* Ballymacoda 23 May 1832; a farmer; joined the Fenian movement; one of the party who attacked Knockadoon coastguard station 5 March 1867; mortally wounded in a fight with the constabulary in Kilclooney wood, co. Cork 31 March 1867. *d.* Mitchelstown 31 March 1867. *bur.* at Ballymacoda 2 April. *John Savage's Fenian heroes and martyrs* (1868) 262-66, 273-80.

CROWTHER, REV. JONATHAN *(son of Rev. Timothy Crowther of St. Austell, Cornwall, methodist minister 1757-1829). b.* St. Austell 31 July 1794; ed. at Kingswood school, Gloucs.; head master Woodhouse Grove school near Bradford 1814-16; head master of Kingswood sch. 1823; general superintendent of Wesleyan missions in India 1837-43; classical tutor in Wesleyan Theological Institution at Didsbury, Lancs. 1849; edited *London Quarterly Review;*

CROWTHER, REV. J. (Con.)

author of *The Methodist manual* 1810, 2 ed. 1811; *A defence of the Wesleyan Theological institution*, 3 ed. 1834; *Sermons* 1839. *d.* at house of Rev. Wm. Williams at Leeds 16 Jany. 1856. *The Pulpit iv*, (1825), *portrait; Slugg's Woodhouse Grove school* (1885) 92-6.

CROZIER, RICHARD *(eld. son of Rawson Bodham Crozier of West hill, Freshwater, Isle of Wight 1775-1849).* *b.* 26 Aug. 1803; entered navy 1 Nov. 1813; captain 20 March 1839; admiral on h.p. 1 April 1870; K.T.S. May 1824. *d.* Westhill 3 Feb. 1880.

CROZIER, WILLIAM. Studied at St. Bartholomew's hospital; M.R.C.S. 1839, F.R.C.S. 1862; assistant surgeon H.E.I. Co. 1842; professor of anatomy and physiology at the Medical college, Calcutta 1855 to death. *d.* on board P. and O. steamer Simla on his way to England 19 Nov. 1862 aged 45.

CRUCHLEY, GEORGE FREDERICK. Publisher, mapseller, engraver and printer at 38 Ludgate st. London to 1833, at 81 Fleet st. 1833-76; sold his entire stock at Hodgsons 16 Jany. 1877. *d.* 65 Grand parade, Brighton 16 June 1880 in 84 year.

CRUICKSHANK, BRODIE. Author of *Eighteen years on the gold coast of Africa* 2 vols. 1853. *d.* Lisbon 17 Nov. 1854.

CRUICKSHANK, GEORGE *(younger son of Isaac Cruikshank of London, caricaturist, who d.* 1810 *or* 1811). *b.* Duke st. Bloomsbury, London 27 Sep. 1792; employed to complete the plates left unfinished by Gillray 1811; illustrated the political pamphlets of Wm. Hone 1819-21; published *Illustrations of phrenology* 1826; *Illustrations of time* 1827; illustrated Fielding, Smollett and Goldsmith for *Roscoe's Novelist's Library* 17 vols. 1831-2; illustrated the *Comic Almanac* 1835-53; *Bentley's Miscellany* 14 vols. 1837-41; *Ainsworth's Magazine* 1842-45; published *The Bottle* 8 plates 1847 and *The Drunkard's Children* 8 plates 1848 many thousands of which were sold in a few days, the subject was represented at 8 London theatres at once; a student at the R.A. 22 April 1853; produced the Worship of Bacchus 1862, presented to National gallery by public subscription 1869; granted civil list pension of £95, 19 June 1867; many of his works were purchased by the Westminster Aquarium for £2500 July 1876. *d.* 263 Hampstead road, London 1 Feb. 1878. *bur.* Kensal Green cemetery 9 Feb., removed to St. Paul's cathedral 29 Nov. 1878. *Life by W. B. Jerrold*, 2 ed. 1883; *George Cruikshank the artist by W. Bates*, 2 ed. 1879; *G. W. Reid's Descriptive catalogue of the works*

CRUIKSHANK, G. (Con.)

of *G. Cruikshank* 3 vols. 1871; *W. Thornbury's British Artists ii*, 55-69 (1861); *W. M. Rossetti's Fine Art* (1867) 277-82; *P. G. Hamerton's Etching and etchers* (1876) 316-23; *James Grant's Public characters ii*, 236-51 (1841); *G. Cruikshank's Omnibus* (1842) 1-8, *portrait; Temple Bar lii*, 499-516 (1878); *Illustrated Review iii*, 385-91 (1873), *portrait.*

CRUIKSHANK, ISAAC ROBERT *(brother of the preceding).* *b.* Duke st. Bloomsbury, London 27 Sep. 1789; a midshipman in H.E.I. Co.'s service; made water colour drawings for private patrons; caricaturist and miniature painter; insolvent Dec. 1826; illustrated Pierce Egan's *Life in London* 1821 (the 3 chief characters in which Tom, Jerry and Logic he designed from himself, his brother George and Pierce Egan) and *The Finish* 1831; Westmacott's *English Spy* 1825; Cumberland's *British theatre* 39 *vols.* 1823-31 and many other books. *d.* of bronchitis at 206 Pentonville road, Islington, London 13 March 1856. *George Daniel's Love's last labour not lost* (1863) 173-76.

CRUM, WALTER (2 *son of Alexander Crum of Thornliebank near Glasgow, merchant manufacturer).* *b.* Glasgow 1796; scientific chemist and manufacturer at Glasgow; member of Philosophical Soc. of Glasgow 1834, pres. 1852; F.R.S. 29 Feb. 1844; pres. of Anderson's Univ. Glasgow; best known for his successful efforts to place the arts of dyeing and calico printing on a scientific basis; the first person to give the true formula for gun cotton. *d.* The Ronken, Thornliebank near Glasgow 5 May 1867. *Proc. of Royal Soc. xvi*, 8-10 (1868).

CRUMMER, JAMES HENRY. *b.* Birr, King's county; ensign 28 foot July 1805, captain 20 July 1815 to 1 March 1839 when placed on h.p.; served in Peninsular war 1809-14; commandant of Island of Calamo 1822-27; police magistrate and superintendent of convicts at Newcastle, N.S.W. 1837-49; police magistrate of Maitland 1849-58 and of Port Macquarie 1858-64. *d.* Port Macquarie 29 Dec. 1867.

CUBBON, SIR MARK *(son of Rev. Thomas Cubbon).* *b.* 1785; lieut. 15 Madras N.I. 20 July 1801; joint comr. of Mysore 1831-34, sole comr. 17 May 1834 to Feb. 1861; col. of 15 Madras N.I. 8 Oct. 1839 to death; L.G. 11 Nov. 1851; C.B. 4 Feb. 1856, K.C.B. 26 May 1856. *d.* at Suez on his way home 23 April 1861 in 77 year, there is a fine equestrian statue of him at Bangalore where the Cubbon park is named after him. *Rice's Mysore and Coorg* 1877 *passim; J. F. Higginbotham's Men whom India has known*, 2 ed. (1874) 96-7.

1/26

CUBITT, JOSEPH (*only son of Sir Wm. Cubitt 1785–1861*). *b.* Horning, Norfolk 24 Nov. 1811; assistant to his father 1832–43; constructed great part of London and South Western railway 1838–41, Great Northern railway 1846–50 and London, Chatham and Dover railway 1855–64; built new Blackfriars bridge, London 1865–69 opened by the Queen 6 Nov. 1869; M.I.C.E. 1840, vice pres. 1865. *d.* 7 Dec. 1872. *Min. of proc. of Instit. of C.E. xxxix*, 249–51 (1875).

CUBITT, THOMAS (*son of Jonathan Cubitt of Buxton near Norwich, who d. 1807*). *b.* Buxton 25 Feb. 1788; a master carpenter in London 1809; built London Institution, Finsbury Circus 1815–19; built over large portion of the Five Fields, Chelsea 1824–29; covered with mansions, district between Eaton sq. and the Thames since known as Pimlico; built over Clapham park about 250 acres 1824; constructed about 1000 yards of embankment above Vauxhall bridge at his own expense; built large factory at Thames Bank, burnt down 17 Aug. 1854; church of St. Barnabas, Ranmore near Dorking was built at his cost 1859; A.I.C.E. 1839. *d.* Denbies near Dorking 20 Dec. 1855. *Min. of proc. of Instit. of C.E. xvi*, 158–62 (1857); *J. S. Bright's Dorking* (1884) 133–6; *G.M. xlv*, 202–205 (1856).

NOTE.—His will the longest on record extended to 386 Chancery folios of 90 words each and covered 30 skins of parchment; the personalty exceeding £1,000,000 the probate duty was £15,000.

CUBITT, SIR WILLIAM (*son of Joseph Cubitt of Bacton Wood near Dilham, Norfolk, miller*). *b.* Dilham 1785; a millwright at Horning, Norfolk; invented and patented self regulating windmill sails 1807; employed by Ransome and Son of Ipswich, agricultural implement makers 1812–21, a partner 1821–26; invented the treadmill 1817, at once adopted in chief gaols of the U.K.; a civil engineer in London 1826–58; designed the Oxford canal and Liverpool junction canal; constructed South Eastern railway 1836–46, blew down face of the Round Down Cliff with a monster charge of 18,000 pounds of gunpowder which he exploded by galvanism 26 Jany. 1843; superintended construction of Great Exhibition 1851 for which he was knighted at Windsor Castle 23 Oct. 1851; M.I.C.E. 1823, member of council 1831, vice pres. 1836, pres. 1850–52; F.R.S. 1 April 1830. *d.* Clapham Common, London 13 Oct. 1861 in 77 year. *Min. of proc. of Instit. of C.E. xxi*, 554–58 (1862); *Our iron roads by F. S. Williams*, 2 ed. (1883) 123–26; *I.L.N. ii*, 76–7 (1843).

CUBITT, WILLIAM (*brother of Thomas Cubitt 1788–1855*). *b.* Buxton near Norwich 1791; served in the navy 4 years; builder in Gray's Inn road, London to 1851; M.P. for Andover 29 July 1847 to July 1861 and 17 Dec. 1862 to death; contested City of London 29 July 1861; sheriff of London and Middlesex 1847–49; alderman of Langbourn ward 1851–63, lord mayor 1860–62; pres. of St. Bartholomew's hospital; prime warden of Fishmongers' Company; A.I.C.E. 22 Jany. 1833, member of council 1842–43. *d.* Penton lodge, Andover 28 Oct. 1863. *G.M. xvi*, 120–2 (1864); *I.L.N. xxxvii*, 435 (1860), *portrait.*

CUFF, JAMES DODSLEY (*son of Mr. Cuff of Corsley near Warminster, Wilts. yeoman*). Clerk in Bank of England about 1805 to death, clerk in bullion office there 1825 to death; an original member of Numismatic Society of London 1836; collected coins for 40 years which were sold for £7054, 29 June 1854; F.S.A.; contributed descriptions of coins to a supplement to Ainslie's *Illustrations of the Anglo-French coinage* 1830. *d.* Prescott lodge, Clapham new park, London 28 Sep. 1853 in 73 year. *Numismatic Chronicle xvii*, 15 (1855); *Journal of British Archæol. Assoc. x*, 122 (1855).

CUFFE, SIR JONAH DENNY WHEELER, 1 Baronet (*elder son of Sir Richard Wheeler, knight, who took name of Cuffe*). *b.* 1765 or 1766; student at Lincoln's Inn 17 May 1790; created a baronet of Ireland 1 Oct. 1799. *d.* Leyrath, co. Kilkenny 9 May 1853.

CUITT, GEORGE (*only son of George Cuitt of Richmond, Yorkshire, painter 1743–1818*). *b.* Richmond, Oct. 1779; a landscape painter; a drawing master at Chester 1804; resided at Masham, Yorkshire 1820 to death; published *Etchings of ancient buildings in Chester, castles in North Wales etc.* 1816; *Wanderings and pencillings amongst the ruins of the olden time, a series of 23 etchings* 1848, reissued 1855 and many other etchings. *d.* Belle Vue, Masham 15 July 1854. *G.M. xlii*, 311 (1854).

CULLEN, HIS EMINENCE CARDINAL PAUL (*son of Hugh Cullen of Prospect near Ballytore, co. Kildare, farmer*). *b.* Prospect 29 April 1803; ed. at Ballytore and Carlow college; entered Urban college of the Propaganda at Rome 29 Nov. 1820; ordained priest 1829; vice rector of the Irish college in Rome 1829, rector 1832–48; rector of the Propaganda college, May 1848 to Jany. 1849; archbishop of Armagh 19 Dec. 1849; consecrated in church of St. Agatha of the Goths, Rome 24 Feb. 1850; presided over national synod held in the college at Thurles, Aug. 1850 being first

CULLEN, HIS EMINENCE C. P. *(Con.)*

held in Ireland since convention of Kilkenny 1642; translated from Armagh to Dublin 3 May 1852; created a cardinal priest with title of San Pietro in Montorio 22 June 1866 being first Irishman raised to that rank; founded Catholic University of Ireland at Drumcondra 20 July 1862; presided at synod of Maynooth Sep. 1875; author of *Pastoral Letters* 1852–56. *d.* 59 Eccles st. Dublin 24 Oct. 1878. *bur.* beneath high altar in chapel of Clonville college 29 Oct. *P. J. O'Byrne's Lives of the Cardinals* (1879) 13–28, *portrait; Sir C. G. Duffy's League of North and South* (1886) 136, 171–75, 301–81; *M. Comerford's Collections* (1883) 188–91; *J. E. Cairnes's Political Essays* (1873) 263 *etc.; I.L.N. lxxiii,* 421 (1878), *portrait.*

CULLEN, WILLIAM. Second lieut. Madras artillery 1804, colonel 1 Oct. 1842 to death; L.G. 11 Nov. 1851. *d.* Alleppey, Madras 1 Oct. 1862.

CULLENFORD, WILLIAM. *b.* Halesworth, Suffolk, Jany. 1797; acted in the provinces; first appeared in London at Adelphi theatre 30 Sep. 1836 as Wharton in *The Christening;* acted chiefly at Adelphi and Haymarket to July 1864 when he retired; a founder of Royal general theatrical fund 16 Feb. 1839, sec. of the fund 16 Feb. 1839 to death. *d.* Jasmine cottage, New Malden, Surrey 6 Sep. 1874.

CULLIMORE, ISAAC. *b.* Ireland 1791; an original member of Numismatic Society 1836; he devoted his whole life to study of Egyptian antiquities, one of the first Orientalists who made use of astronomy to fix important dates in ancient history; published 174 plates of oriental cylinders or seals from collections in British Museum, in parts 1842–52; author of *Pharoah and his Princes* in *Syro-Egyptian Soc. Papers vol.* 1, 1845. *d.* Clapham, London 8 or 12 April 1852. *Numismatic Chronicle xv,* 22 (1853); *W. H. Ward's article on Babylonian seals in Scribner's Mag. Jany.* 1887.

CULSHA, REV. EDWARD WIDT *(only son of Edward Culsha of Islington, London).* Matric. from Magd. hall, Ox. 20 May 1846 aged 19, B.A. 1850, M.A. 1854; C. of Little Malvern, and Head Master of Colwall gram. sch. Herefordshire 1855 to death; author of *Antar and other poems* 1852; *Eastern lands and Eastern people* 1861. *d.* Colwall 11 Jany. 1863.

CULVERWELL, ROBERT JAMES. *b.* 13 July 1802; L.S.A. 1824, M.R.C.S. 1827, M.D. Giessen 1841; edited a monthly periodical entitled *Leisure Moments* from April 1850 to

CULVERWELL, R. J. *(Con.)*

1852, 3 vols.; had a museum of 1000 specimens of morbid pathology; proprietor of The Argyll Baths, 10 Argyll place and 5 New Broad st. London; author of *A practical treatise on bathing* 1829; *On consumption* 1834, 2 *ed.* 1842; *The Confessional* 1841; *Guide to health and long life* 1844, 2 *ed.* 1852; *The enjoyment of life* 1850; *Fragments from the mountains* 2 vols. 1855; *What to eat, drink and avoid,* and many other medical books. *d.* 10 Argyll place, Regent st. London 9 Dec. 1852. *The life of Dr. Culverwell written by himself* (1852), *portrait.*

CUMBERBATCH, ABRAHAM CARLTON. Attached to consulate at Paris 1825–28; vice consul at Constantinople 24 Aug. 1830, consul general there 3 May 1845 to 30 Nov. 1864 when he retired; C.B. 7 April 1866. *d.* Heron court, Richmond, Surrey 25 Oct. 1875.

CUMBERLAND, CHARLES BROWNLOW. *b.* 1801; ensign 35 foot 21 Dec. 1820; lieut.-col. 96 foot 22 July 1842 to 8 July 1856 when he retired on full pay with hon. rank of M.G. *d.* 21 Milverton crescent, Leamington 27 Nov. 1882.

CUMBERLAND, FREDERIC WILLIAM. *b.* London 1820; ed. at collegiate school, Dublin and King's college, London; appointed to engineering department of the Admiralty 1844; architect at Toronto, Canada 1847 to death; constructed Ontario, Simcoe, and Huron railway 1852–54; designed University of Toronto 1859 said to be finest specimen of Norman Gothic architecture in America; organized in Toronto a regiment afterwards called Royal Grenadiers 1861, colonel 1861–64; represented Algoma district in legislature of Ontario 1867 and in Dominion parliament 1871. *d.* Toronto 5 Aug. 1881.

CUMBERLAND, JOHN. Publisher in London; published *Cumberland's British Theatre, printed from the acting copies as performed at the Theatres Royal, London,* 39 *vols.* 1823–31; *Cumberland's Minor Theatre* 14 *vols.* 1831–32, these two series were republished in 64 or 65 vols. 1838; foreman of the jury at coroner's inquest on body of Colonel Fawcett killed by Lieut. Munroe in a duel 1 July 1843. *d.* 185 Camden road, London 13 June 1866 in 79 year.

CUMBERLAND, OCTAVIUS. *b.* 1810; entered navy 16 April 1825; captain 29 Sept. 1855; retired R.A. 25 Aug. 1873; C.B. 2 June 1869. *d.* New hall, Penicuik, Edinburgh 6 Aug. 1877.

CUMBERLAND, RICHARD FRANCIS *(son of Richard Cumberland, officer in 3 foot guards).* *b.*

CUMBERLAND, R. F. *(Con.)*

1792; a page of honour; ensign 3 foot guards 27 Jany. 1809, lieut. 25 Dec. 1813 to 1825 when he sold out; aide-de-camp to Duke of Wellington in principal actions in Peninsular war 1812–14; wounded at repulse of French sortie from Bayonne. *d.* Royal Mint, London 9 March 1870.

CUMBERLEGE, EDWARD ALTHAM. Colonel Bengal infantry 4 Feb. 1861; L.G. 17 Sep. 1871. *d.* 23 Burlington road, Westbourne park, London 28 Dec. 1873 aged 70.

CUMING, HUGH. *b.* West Alvington, Kingsbridge, Devon 14 Feb. 1791; apprenticed to a sail maker; went to South America 1819; in business at Valparaiso 1819–26; cruised in the South Pacific and along Western coast of America collecting plants and shells 1826–29; cruised among islands of Philippine group where he collected 130,000 specimens of dried plants 1835–39; his collection of shells the largest and most valuable private one in existence contained 30,000 species and varieties; G. B. Sowerby named a genus of bivalved shells Cumingia after him 1833; F.L.S. *d.* 13 Gower st. London 10 Aug. 1865. *Athenæum* 19 *Aug.* 1865 *pp.* 247–8; *Proc. of Royal Linnæan Soc.* (1865–6) 57–9.

CUMING, RICHARD. *b.* London 20 March 1777; one of first members of Aurelian Soc. 1801 afterwards known as Entomological Soc. of London; member of Lambeth Chemical Soc. established 1801; invented the Phantasmagoria 1801 which was shown by Philipstal at Lyceum theatre 1802; made purchases from all celebrated collections of curiosities and natural history which were sold 1806–70; Assoc. British Archæol. Soc. 1858; translated greater part of Cuvier's Règne Animal to which Edward Pidgeon's name is attached. *d.* 63 Kennington park road, London 15 Feb. 1870. *bur.* Norwood cemetery 22 Feb. *Journal of British Archæol. Assoc. xxvii,* 542–4 (1871).

CUMMING, SIR HENRY JOHN. *b.* 1772; cornet 11 light dragoons 12 May 1790, lieut.-col. 17 Feb. 1803 to 20 Jany. 1837; present at every engagement in the Peninsula except siege of Badajoz; col. 12 lancers 20 Jany. 1837 to death; general 9 Nov. 1846; K.C.H. 13 March 1833. *d.* 15 Upper Grosvenor st. London 28 Nov. 1856.

CUMMING, REV. JAMES. *b.* St. James's, Westminster 23 Oct. 1777; ed. at Trin. coll. Cam., 10 wrangler 1801, B.A. 1801, M.A. 1804, fellow of his college 1803–15; professor of chemistry in Univ. of Cam. 1815 to death;

CUMMING, REV. J. *(Con.)*·

made important modifications and simplifications of electric methods; pres. of Cambridge Philosophical Soc.; F.R.S. 4 Jany. 1816, F.G.S. 1816; R. of North Runcton, Norfolk 1819 to death; author of *A manual of Electro-Dynamics* 1827. *d.* North Runcton 10 Nov. 1861.

CUMMING, REV. JOHN. *b.* parish of Fintray, Aberdeenshire 10 Nov. 1807; ed. at Aberdeen gr. sch. and univ.; M.A. 1827; licensed to preach by Aberdeen presbytery 3 May 1832; minister of National Scottish church, Crown court, Covent Garden, London 18 Aug. 1832 to 21 July 1879, church was rebuilt at cost of £5000, 1847–8; a prominent controversialist; opposed the Free church of Scotland in many pamphlets and lectures; took part in the Maynooth controversy 1845; became widely known by his writings on the interpretations of prophecy; lectured against Bishop Colenso 1863; his letters to the *Times* signed a 'Beemaster' attracted much notice and were the basis of a work called *Beekeeping* 1864; his admirers raised a sum of £3000 for him 1879 which bought an annuity of £300; author of *Lectures for the times, or an exposition of Tridentine and Tractarian Popery* 1844; *Is Christianity from God? a manual of Christian evidence* 1847, 11 *ed.* 1871; *Apocalyptic Sketches* 3 series 1848–50; *Prophetic studies, or lectures on the book of Daniel* 1850; *Signs of the times, or present, past and future* 1854; *The great tribulation, or things coming on the earth* 1859; *Popular lectures on the Essays and Reviews* 1861; *The Millenial rest, or the world as it will be* 1862; *Moses right and Bishop Colenso wrong* 1863; *Driftwood, seawood and fallen leaves* 2 vols. 1863, and more than 90 other books. *d.* Chiswick 5 July 1881. *In memoriam Rev. John Cumming, D.D. printed for private distribution n.d.*; *Rev. C. M. Davies's Unorthodox London* (1875) 201–17; *Westminster Review n.s. viii,* 436–62 (1855); *Essays by George Eliot* (1884) 145–99; *Illust. news of the world iii* (1859), *portrait*; *Graphic xxiv,* 149 (1881), *portrait.*

CUMMING, REV. JOSEPH GEORGE (2 *son of Joseph Notsall Cumming of Matlock*). *b.* Matlock 15 Feb. 1812; ed. at Oakham gr. sch. and Em. coll. Cam., B.A. 1834, M.A. 1837; C. of North Runcton, Norfolk 1835–38; vice principal of King William's college, Isle of Man 1841–55; master of Lichfield gr. sch. 1855–58; warden and professor of classical literature and geology in Queen's college, Birmingham 1858–62; R. of Mellis, Suffolk 1862–67; V. of St. John's, Bethnal Green, London 1867 to death; F.G.S. 1846; author of *The Isle of*

CUMMING, REV. J. G. (Con.)

Man, its history, physical, ecclesiastical, civil and legendary 1848; *A chronology of ancient, sacred and profane history* 1853; *The great Stanley, or James VIIth Earl of Derby* 1867. *d.* St. John's vicarage, Bethnal Green 21 Sep. 1868. *Reg. and mag. of biog.* i, 219–20 (1869).

CUMMING, WILLIAM. *b.* about 1822; M.R.C.S. 1844, L.S.A. 1847; a surgeon in London; the pioneer of modern ophthalmology; the first to demonstrate that rays of light falling on the human retina might be reflected back to the eye of an observer, this important fact was communicated by him to the Medico-Chirurgical Soc. of London, June 1846 in a paper *On a luminous appearance of the human eye. d.* 15 Warkworth terrace, Commercial road, London 5 June 1855 aged 33.

CUMMING-BRUCE, CHARLES LENNOX (2 *son of Sir Alexander Penrose Cumming-Gordon* 1 *baronet, who d.* 10 *Feb.* 1806). *b.* 20 Feb. 1790; ed. at Winchester and C.C. coll. Ox., M.A. 1810; M.P. for Inverness district of burghs 17 May 1833 to 17 July 1837, for Elgin and Nairnshire 25 April 1840 to 11 Nov. 1868; joint sec. of board of control Feb. to Dec. 1852; assumed additional surname of Bruce on his marriage 1820. *d.* Broom hall near Dunfermline 1 Jany. 1875.

CUMMING–GORDON, ROUALEYN GEORGE GORDON (2 *son of the succeeding*). *b.* Altyre, co. Elgin 15 March 1820; ed. at Eton; cornet Madras cavalry 1838–40; ensign royal Newfoundland companies 3 Nov. 1843; ensign Cape Mounted rifles 23 Feb. 1844 to 22 July 1845 when he sold out; hunted in interior of South Africa 1845–50; exhibited his trophies at Great Exhibition 1851; lectured in London and the provinces 1855–58; kept a museum of his trophies at Fort Augustus on the Caledonian canal 1858 to death; author of *Five years of a hunter's life in the far interior of South Africa* 2 *vols.* 1850 which had an immense success; *The lion hunter of South Africa* 1856. *d.* Fort Augustus 24 March 1866. *I.L.N. xx*, 512 (1852), *portrait*.

CUMMING–GORDON, SIR WILLIAM GORDON, 2 Baronet. *b.* Altyre 20 July 1787; succeeded his father 10 Feb. 1806; M.P. for Elgin district of burghs 23 May 1831 to 3 Dec. 1832. *d.* Altyre 23 Nov. 1854.

CUNARD, SIR EDWARD, 2 Baronet (*son of the succeeding*). *b.* Halifax, Nova Scotia 1 Jany. 1816; agent of Cunard line of steamers at New York 1835–65; head of firm of Cunard, Burns

CUNARD, SIR E. (Con.)

and Mac Iver 1865 to death. *d.* suddenly at New York 6 April 1869, personalty sworn under £300,000, 5 June 1869.

CUNARD, SIR SAMUEL, 1 Baronet (*son of Abraham Cunard of Philadelphia, mechanic*). *b.* Halifax, Nova Scotia 21 Nov. 1787; a merchant at Halifax; established with George Burns of Glasgow and David Mac Iver of Liverpool the British and North American Royal mail steam packet company 1838; contracted with the government 4 May 1839 for conveyance of the mails between Liverpool and Halifax, Boston and Quebec for 7 years at £60,000 per annum, the first voyage across the Atlantic was made by the Britannia 4–18 July 1840; F.R.G.S. 1846; created baronet 9 March 1859. *d.* 26 Prince's gardens, Kensington, London 28 April 1865, personalty sworn under £350,000, 27 May. *W. S. Lindsay's Merchant Shipping* iv, 178–86, 217–20, 226–50 (1876); *Fortunes made in business* ii, 325–71 (1884); *London Society xxxviii*, 33–47 (1880).

CUNDY, THOMAS (*eld. son of Thomas Cundy of London, architect* 1765–1825). *b.* 1790; an architect in London; surveyor to Earl Grosvenor's London estates Dec. 1825 to death; erected Holy Trinity, Paddington, St. Paul's, Knightsbridge, and other churches in west end of London. *d.* Bromley, Kent 15 July 1867.

CUNINGHAM, ALEXANDER (2 *son of Charles Cuningham of Newholm, Lanarkshire*). *b.* Edinburgh 1805; ed. at high school and univ. of Edin.; a writer to the signet 1827; joint sec. with his father to comrs. of northern lighthouses 1842, sec. 1846–75; fellow of royal Scottish society of arts before whom he read many papers on subjects connected with lighthouse service. *d.* Palmerston place, Edinburgh 16 June 1883.

CUNINGHAM, DAVID. Entered Bombay army 1816; brigadier in command at Aden 18 Sep. 1848 to 9 Jany. 1851; col. 1 Bombay light cavalry 19 Oct. 1849 to death; M.G. 28 Nov. 1854. *d.* Cluny house near Dunkeld 4 Sep. 1861 aged 59.

CUNINGHAM, JOHN (*eld. son of John Cuningham of Port Glasgow, merchant*). *b.* Port Glasgow 1782; admitted advocate at Scotch bar 1807; deputy to Lord Advocate Jeffery, Dec. 1830; sheriff of Morayshire 1831; solicitor general for Scotland 22 April 1835; judge of supreme court with courtesy title of Lord Cuningham 9 Feb. 1837 to May 1853 when he resigned. *d.* 23 Moray place, Edinburgh 26 Oct. 1854. *Crombie's Modern Athenians* (1882), 47–48, *portrait*.

CUNLIFFE, Sir Robert Henry, 4 Baronet (2 son of Sir Foster Cunliffe, 2 baronet 1755–1834). b. Chester 22 April 1785; entered Bengal army 1798; major 1 Bengal N.I. 17 Oct. 1818; col. 4 Bengal N.I. 30 May 1828 to death; knighted by patent 16 Sep. 1829; succeeded 15 June 1834; C.B. 28 July 1838; general 13 Oct. 1857. d. Acton park near Wrexham, Denbighshire 10 Sep. 1859.

CUNNINGHAM, Francis (youngest son of Allan Cunningham the poet 1784–1842). b. 1820; ensign 23 Madras light infantry 1838; field engineer at defence of Jellalabad; Mysore comr. at Bangalore 1850–61; retired with rank of lieut.-col. 31 Dec. 1861; published an edition of Marlowe 1870, of Massinger 1871, and of Ben. Jonson 1871; a frequent contributor to Saturday Review. d. 18 Clarendon road, South Kensington, London 3 Dec. 1875.

CUNNINGHAM, Rev. John William. b. London 3 Jany. 1780; ed. at St. John's coll. Cam., 5 wrangler 1802, B.A. 1802, M.A. 1805, fellow of his college; C. of Ripley, Surrey 1802; C. of Clapham to 1811; a prominent member of the evangelical party; edited Christian Observer 1850–58; V. of Harrow 1811 to death; author of World without souls 1805, 6 ed. 1816; The Velvet Cushion 1814, 10 ed. 1816; Sancho or the Proverbialist 1817, anon. and other books. d. Harrow 30 Sep. 1861.

CUNNINGHAM, Joseph Davey (eld. son of Allan Cunningham the poet 1784–1842). b. Lambeth 9 June 1812; ed. at Addiscombe and Chatham; sailed for India, Feb. 1834; 2 lieut. Bengal engineers, captain 13 Nov. 1849 to death; lived among the Sikhs as political assistant to col. Wade and other officers 1837–45; political agent at Bhopal 7 March 1846 to 26 Oct. 1849; author of History of the Sikhs 1849. d. suddenly near Umballa, Punjab 28 Feb. 1851. J. D. Cunningham's History of the Sikhs (1849), preface.

CUNNINGHAM, Peter (brother of the preceding). b. Pimlico, London 7 April 1816; ed. at Christ's hospital; clerk in Audit office 1834, chief clerk 1854–60; art critic of Pictorial Times; treasurer of Shakespeare Society; author of Songs of England and Scotland 1835; The handbook of Westminster Abbey 1842; The life of Inigo Jones 1848; The handbook of London 2 vols. 1849, 2 ed. 1850; The story of Nell Gwynn 1852; edited many books. d. Ureulam road, St. Albans 18 May 1869. G. Hodder's Memories of my time (1870) 384–93; I.L.N. xxviii, 205, 206 (1856), portrait.

CUNNINGHAM, Peter Miller (5 son of John Cunningham of Dalswinton near Dumfries, farmer). b. Dalswinton, Nov. 1789; ed. at Univ. of Edin.; assistant surgeon in royal navy 10 Dec. 1810, surgeon 28 Jany. 1814; surgeon superintendent of convict ships, left the sea May 1841; published Two years in New South Wales 2 vols. 1827; On the motions of the earth and on the conceptions, growth and decay of man 1834; Hints for Australian emigrants 1841. d. Greenwich 6 March 1864. Rev. D. Hogg's Life of Allan Cunningham (1875) 12–14, 360–8.

CUNNINGHAM, Rev. William (eld. son of Charles Cunningham of Hamilton, Lanarkshire, merchant, who d. 1811). b. Hamilton 2 Oct. 1805; ed. at Dunse and Univ. of Edin. 1820–28; assistant minister of Middle church, Greenock 15 Oct. 1830; minister of Trinity college church, Edin. Jany. 1834; D.D. Princeton college, New Jersey 1842; professor of theology in New college, Edin. 1843, professor of church history there 1845 to death, principal June 1847 to death; the ablest defender of Calvinism of his time; edited British and Foreign Evangelical Review Oct. 1855 to Oct. 1860; moderator of general assembly 19 May 1859 to death; the sum of £7000 was presented to him 1859; author of The reformers and the theology of the Reformation 1862; Historical theology, a review of the principal doctrinal discussions in the Christian church from the Apostolic age 1863, 2 ed. 1864; Discussion on church principles, Popish, Erastian, Presbyterian 1863. d. Edinburgh 14 Dec. 1861. Life of W. Cunningham by R. Rainy and J. Mackenzie 1871, portrait; Wylie's Disruption Worthies (1881) 193–200, portrait; Sermons from 1828 to 1860 by the late W. Cunningham, edited by Rev. J. J. Bonar 1872.

CUNYNGHAME, Sir Arthur Augustus Thurlow (3 son of Sir David Cunynghame, 5 baronet 1769–1854). b. 2 Aug. 1812; 2 lieut. royal rifles 2 Nov. 1830; lieut.-col. 13 foot 3 Nov. 1846; captain Grenadier guards 1 Dec. 1846; lieut.-col. 20 foot 27 April 1849; lieut.-col. 27 foot 2 April 1852 to 16 Dec. 1853 when placed on h.p.; assistant quartermaster general of first division in the Crimea 1854–55; commanded a division of Turkish contingent May 1855; col. of 36 foot 2 Dec. 1868 to 2 Feb. 1876; commanded forces in South Africa 5 Nov. 1873 to 1 March 1878; col. commandant of first battalion royal rifles 2 Feb. 1876 to death; lieut. governor of Cape of Good Hope 5 March 1877 to 1878; general 1 Oct. 1877, placed on retired list 1 July 1881; C.B. 5 July 1855, K.C.B. 2 June 1869, G.C.B. 13

CUNYNGHAME, SIR A. A. T. (Con.)

June 1878; author of *An Aide-de-camp's recollections of service in China* 2 vols. 1844; *A glimpse at the Great Western republic* 1851; *Travels in the Eastern Caucasus* 1872; *My command in South Africa* 1879. *d.* on board ship at Aden on his way home from India 10 March 1884. *I.L.N. lxxii*, 273 (1878), *portrait*.

CUPPAGE, SIR BURKE (*son of lieut. gen. Wm. Cuppage, who d. 7 Jany. 1848 aged 87*). *b.* Charlton, Kent 1794; 2 lieut. R.A. 17 Dec. 1812; commanded R.A. in south western district 1857–63; col. commandant 2 Feb. 1868 to death; governor of Jersey 23 Oct. 1863 to 1 Oct. 1868; K.C.B. 29 May 1875. *d.* 4 Cranley place, Onslow sq. London 19 April 1877.

CURETON, REV. WILLIAM (*2 son of Wm. Cureton of Westbury, Shropshire*). *b.* Westbury 1808; ed. at Newport and Ch. Ch. Ox., B.A. 1830, M.A. 1833, B.D. and D.D. 1858; chaplain of his college 1831–38; C. of Oddington, Oxon. 1831; sub librarian of Bodleian library, Oxford 1834–37; assistant keeper of MSS. in British Museum 1837–50; F.R.S. 25 Jany. 1838; select preacher at Ox. 1840; chaplain in ord. to the Queen 18 June 1847; canon of Westminster and R. of St. Margaret's, Westminster 5 Dec. 1849 to death; corresponding member of French Institute 1855; foreign associate 1860; crown trustee of British Museum 1859; chairman of committee of Oriental translation fund 1863; author of *Vindiciæ Ignatianæ, the writings of St. Ignatius vindicated from heresy* 1846; *Corpus Ignatianum* 1849; *Spicilegium Syriacum with an English translation* 1855; *Remains of an ancient recension of the Gospels in Syriac* 1858. *d.* Westbury 17 June 1864. *The church of England photographic portrait gallery, part* 21 (1859), *portrait*; *G.M. xvii*, 520–23 (1864); *I.L.N. xxiv*, 400 (1854) *portrait*.

CURIE, PAUL FRANCIS. M.D. Aberdeen 1815; member of Gallican Society; coeditor of *Archives de la médicine homœopathique* 1836–37; author of *Principles of Homœopathy* 1837; *Annals of the London homœopathic dispensary* 1844; *A treatise on cholera, English and Asiatic* 1849; *Domestic practice of homœopathy* 1850. *d.* 17 Hanover sq. London 5 Oct. 1853.

CURLING, HENRY. Ensign 25 foot 25 Oct. 1827 to 20 Aug. 1829 when placed on h.p.; lieut. 91 foot 6 Jany. 1832 to 30 Dec. 1834 when placed on h.p.; retired 1854; author of *The soldier of fortune* 3 vols. 1843; *John of England, a romance* 3 vols. 1846; *Shakespeare the poet, the lover, the actor* 3 vols. 1848; *Non-*

CURLING, H. (Con.)

pareil House 3 vols. 1855; *Recollections of the mess table and the stage* 1855; *Camp club in the Crimea* 1856; *Edith Frankheart or the baronet's daughter* 3 vols. 1857; *The Self divorced or the school for wives* 2 vols. 1861; *Geraldine Maynard* 3 vols. 1864 and 12 other books. *d.* Weardale villas, Earl's court terrace, Kensington, London 10 Feb. 1864.

CURLING, THOMAS BLIZARD (3 *son of Daniel Curling, F.S.A. who d.* 1824). *b.* London, Jany. 1811; M.R.C.S. 1832, F.R.C.S. 1843, mem. of council 1864, pres. 1873; assistant surgeon to London hospital 1834, lecturer on surgery 1846, surgeon 1849 to Aug. 1869; F.R.S. 6 June 1850; pres. of Royal Med. and Chir. Soc. 1871; retired from practice 1879; author of *Treatise on Tetanus* 1836; *Observations on diseases of the Rectum* 1851, 4 ed. 1876; *Treatise on diseases of the Testis* 1873, 4 ed. 1878. *d.* Cannes 4 March 1888. *Medical Circular iii*, 439 (1853), *portrait*; *Barker's Photographs* (1865) *pp.* 131–32, *portrait*.

CURRAN, WILLIAM HENRY (*son of John Philpot Curran* 1750-1817, *master of the Rolls in Ireland*). Called to bar in Ireland 1816; insolvency comr. in Ireland; bencher of King's Inns, Dublin 1848; author of *Life of John Philpot Curran* 2 vols. 1819; *Sketches of the Irish bar, with essays* 2 vols. 1855. *d.* 9 Fitzwilliam place, Dublin 25 Aug. 1858 in 69 year.

CURRER, FRANCES MARY RICHARDSON (*only child of Rev. Henry Richardson* 1758–84, *R. of Thornton in Craven, who took name of Currer, June* 1784). *b.* Eshton hall near Skipton on Craven 3 March 1785; the greatest female book collector in Europe, principal part of her library of 20,000 vols. was sold at Sotheby's for nearly £6000, Aug. 1862; privately printed *Catalogue of the library of Miss Currer at Eshton hall by Robert Triphook* 1820, 2 ed. by *C. J. Stewart* 1833; *Extracts from the literary and scientific correspondence of Richard Richardson, M.D., F.R.S. of Bierley, Yorkshire* 1835. *d.* Eshton hall 28 April 1861. *Nichols's Illustrations i*, 225–52 (1817); *T. F. Dibdin's Reminiscences of a literary life ii*, 949–57 (1836); *T. F. Dibdin's Bibliographical tour ii*, 1081–90 (1838).

CURREY, FREDERICK (*son of Benjamin Currey, clerk of the Parliaments*). *b.* Norwood, Surrey 19 Aug. 1819; ed. at Eton and Trin. coll. Cam., B.A. 1841, M.A. 1844; barrister L.I. 7 May 1844; F.L.S., sec. 1860–80, vice pres. and treasurer 1880 to death; F.R.S. 3 June 1858, member of council; his collection of fungi is now in the Kew Herbarium, the genus of fungi, Curreya, was founded by Saccardo as

CURREY, F. (Con.)

a momento of Currey; edited *The natural history review* 1861 *etc.*; translated Hofmeister's *On the germination of the higher Cryptogamia* 1862; edited C. D. Badham's *Esculent funguses* 1863. *d.* 2 Vanbrugh park road, Blackheath 8 Sep. 1881. *Journal of botany n.s. x*, 310–12 (1881).

CURREY, REV. GEORGE (son of Rev. James Currey, preacher of the Charterhouse, London). *b.* Charterhouse sq. London 7 April 1816; ed. at Charterhouse and St. John's coll. Cam., scholar 1834, Bell's Univ. scholar 1835, 14 wrangler 1838, B.A. 1838, M.A. 1841, B.D. 1850, D.D. 1864; fellow of his college 1839, lecturer 1840, tutor 1844, Hulsean lecturer 1851 and 1852; preacher of the Charterhouse 1849–71, master 17 Jany. 1871 to death; preb. of St. Paul's 1872; published *Hulsean Lectures* 1851–52; edited *Tertulliani libri tres De Spectaculis* 1854; author of *An English grammar* 1856; a commentary on Ezekiel in the Speaker's Commentary and Commentaries on Ecclesiastes and Revelations in the S.P.C.K. Commentary. *d.* The master's lodge, Charterhouse 30 April 1885. *I.L.N. lxxxvi*, 583 (1885), *portrait.*

CURRIE, AUGUSTUS ARTHUR (4 son of John Currie 1797–1873). *b.* 21 Jany. 1831; ensign 45 Bengal N.I. 20 Oct. 1849; major Bengal staff corps 1869, lieut.-col. 2 March 1875 to 31 Dec. 1880 when he retired on full pay with hon. rank of M.G.; C.B. 19 Nov. 1879. *d.* St. Leonard's 23 May 1884.

CURRIE, CLAUD. Entered medical service of Madras army 1806; inspector general of hospitals 31 Jany. 1846, phys. general 19 Aug. 1846 to 31 Jany. 1851. *d.* 3 Westbourne terrace, London 8 Aug. 1854 aged 65.

CURRIE, SIR FREDERICK, 1 Baronet (3 son of Mark Currie of Cobham, Surrey). *b.* 3 Feb. 1799; ed. at Charterhouse and Haileybury; entered Bengal civil service 1817; judge of court of Sudder Adawlut of the north western provinces 1840–42; one of secs. of government of India 1842–49; chief sec. to Lord Hardinge during campaign of 1845–46; created baronet 11 Jany. 1847; a member of supreme council of India 1 April 1847 to 14 Jany. 1848, an ordinary member of council 12 March 1849 to 1853 when he retired on the annuity fund; a director of East India Co. April 1854, chairman 1857–58 being the last chairman; one of the 6 members of first council of sec. of state for India elected by the E.I. company; vice pres. of council of India 21 Sep. 1858. *d.* St. Leonard's 10 Sep. 1875. *I.L.N. lxviii*, 295, 434 (1875).

CURRIE, HENRY. *b.* Westminster 1798; ed. at Eton; member of firm of Glyn and Co. bankers, London; M.P. for Guildford 29 July 1847 to 1 July 1852. *d.* West Horsley place near Guildford 26 May 1873.

CURRIE, JOHN. *b.* 28 May 1797; M.P. for Hertford 30 April 1831 to 3 Dec. 1832. *d.* Queen's sq. Bath 19 May 1873.

CURRIE, MARK JOHN. *b.* London 21 June 1795; entered navy 29 April 1808; captain 23 Nov. 1841; V.A. on half pay 24 May 1867. *d.* Collington house, Thicket road, Anerley 1 May 1874.

CURRIE, RAIKES. *b.* 15 April 1801; member of firm of Glyn and Co. bankers, London; M.P. for Northampton 26 July 1837 to 21 March 1857. *d.* Minley manor, Farnborough, Hants. 16 Oct. 1881, personalty sworn under £280,000, 17 Dec. 1881.

CURRIE, SIR WALTER. *b.* 1819; commandant of armed mounted police at Cape of Good Hope 1855 to death; knighted by patent 24 May 1860. *d.* 7 June 1872.

CURRY, RICHARD (son of Thomas Curry of Gosport, Hants.) *b.* 1772; entered navy 22 March 1780; captain 7 Jany. 1802, R.A. 10 Jany. 1837, V.A. 9 Nov. 1846; admiral on h.p. 1 July 1851; C.B. 26 Sep. 1831. *d.* Stoke, Devonport 27 Dec. 1855.

CURSETJEE, ARDASEER. *b.* Bombay 6 Oct. 1808; in charge of shipbuilding yard at Mazagon 1828, assistant builder there 1833; introduced gas lighting into Bombay 1835, sewing machines, photography and electroplating; chief engineer at Bombay steam factory, July 1840 to July 1858 being the first Indian native placed over Europeans; A.I.C.E. 24 March 1840; F.R.S. 27 May 1841. *d.* Lowjee house, Marsh Gate, Richmond, Surrey 16 Nov. 1877. *Min. of proc. of Instit. of C.E. li*, 271–4 (1878).

CURSHAM, MARY ANN. Resided at Sutton, Notts; author of *Emanuel Swedenborg and other poems by M. A. C.*; *Martin Luther a poem by M. A. C.* 1828; *Norman Abbey a tale of Sherwood forest, by a Lady* 1832; *Poems, sacred, dramatic and lyric* 1833; *The infant's decalogue or a metrical version of the ten commandments by M. A. C.* 1836. *d.* 1 North bank, Derby 17 Dec. 1881.

CURTEIS, SIR THOMAS ISAAC HORSLEY (son of John Curteis of Norfolk). *b.* 1780; Exon of Yeomen of the Guard 31 May 1805 to May 1839; knighted at St. James's palace 27 June 1833. *d.* Twyford, Norfolk 26 Dec. 1858.

CURTIS, CHARLES BERWICK *(youngest son of Sir Wm. Curtis, 1 baronet 1752–1829)*. *b.* Culland's grove, Southgate 18 March 1795; ed. at Harrow; gunpowder manufacturer with Thomas Curtis and W. G. Harvey near Hounslow 1820–69; at time of his death the firm owned six factories in Middlesex, Kent, South Wales and Argyleshire; A.I.C.E. 1 March 1842; invented a self acting signal for railways 1842 which was used for some time. *d.* 105 Eaton sq. London 26. Oct. 1876.

CURTIS, JAMES GRAY WILLIAM. Entered Bengal army 1826; captain 37 Bengal N.I. 13 Jany. 1842 to 8 Dec. 1850: deputy assistant commissary general 27 March 1849 to 8 Dec. 1850; C.B. 9 June 1849; retired colonel 28 Nov. 1854. *d.* Oaklands, Shepherd's Bush, London 16 Nov. 1870.

CURTIS, JOHN. *b.* Norwich 3 Dec. 1791; F.L.S. 1822; made entomological tours in Scotland 1825, France 1829, Italy 1843, 1850 and 1851; entomological editor of *Gardener's Mag.* 1841–47; granted civil list pension of £100, 25 Nov. 1842 and another of £50, 19 April 1861; published *British entomology illustrated* with 770 *plates*, 16 *vols.* which came out in numbers 1 Jany. 1824 to 1 Dec. 1839; *A guide to an arrangement of British insects* 1829, 2 ed. 1837. *d.* Belitha villas, Barnsbury park, London 6 Oct. 1862. *Proc. of Linnœan Soc.* (1863) 35–41.

CURTIS, JOHN CHARLES. Principal of the British and Foreign School society's training college, Borough road, London many years before his death; author of *A School and college history of England* 1860; *Chronological and genealogical tables of English history* 1863; *An English grammar for schools* 1876 and many other school books. *d.* 24 Villa road, Brixton 10 May 1888 aged 61.

CURTIS, JOHN HARRISON. A dispenser in the navy and at Haslar hospital; lived at 18 Soho sq. London and advertised himself in the newspapers and by pamphlets as an aural surgeon 1815; founded Royal dispensary for diseases of the Ear, Carlisle st. Soho 1816; employed Hume Weatherhead and other persons to write his books; made £5000 a year for many years; had a tube from his consulting room to his waiting room by which he could hear what the patients said of themselves; always received his patients in full dress of time of George iv; gambled away his earnings at Junior United Service Club; retired to Isle of Man 1848 where he became insane; published *A treatise on the physiology and diseases of the ear* 1817, 5 ed. 1831; *An essay on the deaf and*

CURTIS, J. H. *(Con.)*
dumb 1829; *A treatise on the physiology and diseases of the eye* 1833; *Observations on the preservation of hearing and on hearing trumpets* 1834, 11 ed. 1839; *On the Cephaloscope and its uses* 1842; *Advice to the deaf* 1841, 5 ed. 1845 and other works. *d.* in an asylum in the Isle of Man about 1860. *J. F. Clarke's Autobiographical recollections of the medical profession* (1874) 358–73.

CURTIS, SIR LUCIUS, 2 Baronet *(son of admiral Sir Roger Curtis, K.C.B. 1 baronet 1746–1816)*. *b.* 3 June 1786; entered navy 2 June 1795; captain 22 Jany. 1806; R.A. 28 June 1838; admiral superintendent at Malta 8 March 1843 to 8 March 1848, admiral 9 July 1855; succeeded 14 Nov. 1816; C.B. 4 June 1815, K.C.B. 10 Nov. 1862. *d.* Portsdown hill near Portsmouth 14 Jany. 1869. *Reg. and Mag. of Biog. i,* 201, 355 (1869).

CURTIS, MATTHEW. Machine maker at Manchester, employing 1000 persons, his cotton machinery was sent all over the world; elected a member of the first town council of Manchester after the charter was granted in 1839; mayor of Manchester 1860–1 and 1875–6. *d.* Manchester 9 June 1887.

CURTIS, SAMUEL. *b.* Walworth, London 1779; nurseryman in Essex; proprietor of *Botanical Mag.* 1801–46; F.L.S. 20 Nov. 1810; built a house called La Chaise at Rozel in Jersey, where he *d.* 6 Jany. 1860. *Proc. of Linnœan Soc.* (1860) *p.* 22.

CURTIS, REV. THOMAS. *b.* England about 1780; publisher in London; published the Encyclopædia Metropolitana 59 parts 1817–45; went to the United States 1829; pastor of Baptist church in Wentworth st. Charleston some years; established a young ladies school at Limestone Spring; a very powerful preacher. *d.* in a burning steamer on the Potomac river 1858.

CURTIS, REV. THOMAS F. *(son of the preceding)*. *b.* England 26 Sep. 1815; pastor of a baptist church near Boston, U.S.; professor of theology in Lewisbury Univ. Panama to 1865; lived at Cambridge, Mass. 1867 to death; author of *Progress of Baptist principles in the last hundred years* 1857; *The human element in the inspiration of the Sacred Scriptures* 1867 in which he repudiated inspiration and authenticity of much of the Old Testament and part of the New. *d.* Cambridge 9 Aug. 1872.

CURTIS, WILLIAM FREDERICK *(eld. child of Timothy Abraham Curtis 1786–1857, governor*

CURTIS, W. F. (Con.)

of Bank of England 1838). b. 4 May 1810; cornet 1 Bombay light cavalry 26 July 1833; deputy judge advocate general 17 July 1851 to 12 Jany. 1857; lieut.-col. 21 hussars 4 April 1860 to 4 March 1868 when placed on h.p.; placed on retired list 4 May 1880; L.G. 8 May 1881. d. Upper Norwood, Surrey 2 Sep. 1882.

CURWEN, REV. JOHN (eld. son of Rev. Spedding Curwen 1790–1856, Independent minister). b. Hurst house, Heckmondwike, Yorkshire 14 Nov. 1816; assistant pastor independent chapel, Basingstoke 1838; co-pastor at Stowmarket, Suffolk 1841; pastor at Plaistow, Essex 1844–64; invented the 'Look and say' method of learning to read 1839; advocated Tonic Sol-fa system of teaching music in a series of articles in Independent Mag. 1842, lectured on the system 1853–56; started The Tonic Sol-fa Reporter 1853; sided ardently with the North on outbreak of American civil war 1861, published various tracts on the subject and organised the first Freed slaves aid society in England; Euing · lecturer at Anderson's college, Glasgow 1866–1867; member of West Ham school board 1871–73; founded Tonic Sol-fa college at Forest Gate, Essex, incorporated 1875, opened 1879 where there is a portrait of him; author of Singing for schools and congregations, a grammar of vocal music 1848; Pupils' manual of the Tonic Sol-fa method of singing 1852; Peoples service of song 1863. d. Heaton house, Heaton Mersey, Lancs. 26 May 1880. bur. Ilford cemetery 3 June. Memorials of John Curwen (1882), portrait; Grove's Dict. of Music iv, 144–50 (1884).

CURZON, EDWARD. b. 9 Dec. 1789; entered navy 7 Nov. 1804; captain 8 Feb. 1823; captain of the Asia 84 guns 1826–28; retired V.A. 5 Jany. 1858; C.B. 18 Nov. 1827. d. St. Anne's, Derby 7 March 1862.

CURZON, EDWARD CECIL (younger son of the succeeding). b. 8 Nov. 1812; ed. at Harrow and Ch. Ch. Ox., B.A. 1834, M.A. 1840; barrister L.I. 7 May 1840; registrar of copyright of designs 1842–63; registrar of joint stock companies 1863–76. d. Scarsdale house, Wright's lane, Kensington, London 12 Feb. 1885.

CURZON, ROBERT (2 son of 1 Viscount Curzon 1733–1820). b. 13 Feb. 1774; ed. at Westminster and Ch. Ch. Ox., B.A. 1795; M.P. for Clitheroe, Lancs. 1 June 1796 to 23 April 1831. d. Parham park near Steyning, Sussex 14 May 1863.

CUSACK, JAMES WILLIAM (3 son of Athanasius Cusack of Laragh house, co. Kildare 1749–1813). b. 1788; ed. at Trin. coll. Dublin; M.R.C.S. 1812; resident surgeon in Steevens's hospital, Dublin 1812, visiting surgeon to 1857; surgeon to Swift's hospital for the insane; an original projector of Park st. school of medicine; M.D. Dublin 1850; professor of surgery in Univ. of Dublin 1852 to death; surgeon in ord. to Queen in Ireland, July 1858 to death; sec. to Royal college of surgeons Ireland long time, pres. 3 times; famous as a lithotomist. d. 7 Merrion sq. north Dublin 25 Sep. 1861 in 74 year. Dublin Quarterly Journal of medical science xxxiii, 255–58 (1862).

CUSHMAM, SUSAN WEBB (dau. of Elkanah Cushman of Boston, U.S. merchant). b. Boston 17 March 1822; made her début 8 June 1839 at Park theatre, New York as Laura Castelli in Epes Sargent's play The Genoese; made a remarkable success in Satan in Paris; came to England 1846; played Ophelia and Juliet (200 nights) at Haymarket theatre, London with great success 1846; retired from the stage 1847. (m. 22 March 1848 James Sheridan Muspratt of Liverpool, chemist 1821–71). d. Liverpool 10 May 1859. Tallis's Drawing room table book, part 8, portrait; Ireland's New York Stage ii, 271 (1867).

CUST, CHARLES HENRY (2 son of 1 Earl Brownlow 1779–1853). b. 27 Sep. 1813; ed. at Ch. Ch. Ox., B.A. 1836; cornet royal horse guards 14 March 1834, captain 4 July 1845 to 1847 when he sold out; sheriff of Northamptonshire 1859; M.P. for North Shropshire 13 July 1865 to Aug. 1866. d. 19 May 1875.

CUST, SIR EDWARD, 1 Baronet (youngest son of 1 Baron Brownlow 1744–1807). b. 30 Hill st. Berkeley sq. London 17 March 1794; ed. at Eton and Sandhurst; cornet 16 dragoons 15 March 1810; major 55 foot 24 Oct. 1821 to 27 July 1822 when placed on h.p.; M.P. for Grantham 1818–26, for Lostwithiel 1826–32; equerry to Prince Leopold of Saxe Coburg for many years from 1816, master of his household to 1865; knighted at St. James's palace 3 Aug. 1831; K.C.H. 1831; assistant master of ceremonies to the Queen 18 Dec. 1845, master 1 Jany. 1847 to Feb. 1876; colonel 16 lancers 9 April 1859 to death; general 12 Jany. 1866; created baronet 23 Feb. 1876; author of Noctes Dominicae, or Sunday night readings 1848; Family reading, The New Testament narrative 1850; Annals of the wars of the eighteenth century 5 vols. 1857, 3 ed. 1862; Annals of the wars of the nineteenth century 4 vols. 1862–

CUST, Sir E. (Con.)

63; *Warriors of the thirty years war 2 vols.*
1865; *Warriors of the civil wars of France and
England 3 vols.* 1867–69. *d.* 8 Jermyn st.
Piccadilly, London 14 Jany. 1878. *bur.* at
Belton near Grantham.

CUST, Henry Francis Cockayne (*eld. son of
hon. and Rev. Henry Cockayne Cust 1780–1861,
canon of Windsor*). *b.* Cockayne, Hatley, Beds.
15 Sep. 1819; ed. at Eton; ensign 25 foot 30
March 1838; captain 8 hussars 19 Feb. 1847
to 24 Feb. 1854 when he sold out; private
sec. to Earl of Eglinton while lord lieut. of
Ireland 1852; assumed additional name of
Cockayne 14 Dec. 1861; sheriff of Beds. 1869;
M.P. for Grantham 1874–80. *d.* 5 April 1884.

CUST, Peregrine Francis (5 *son of 1 Baron
Brownlow 1744–1807*). *b.* 13 Aug. 1791; M.P.
for Honiton 1818–26; M.P. for Clitheroe
1826–32. *d.* 15 Sep. 1873.

CUSTANCE, William Neville (2 *son of Hambleton Thomas Custance of Weston house near
Norwich 1779–1845*). *b.* 24 Oct. 1811; ensign
95 foot 11 Oct. 1831; lieut.-col. 6 dragoon
guards 1 Aug. 1856 to 27 July 1861 when
placed on h.p.; commandant cavalry depot,
Canterbury 1 Oct. 1862 to 9 July 1866 when
placed on h.p.; col. 11 Hussars 8 March 1875
to death; general 7 Sep. 1880; placed on
retired list 1 July 1881; C.B. 21 Jany. 1858.
d. Brookheath, Salisbury 7 Feb. 1886.

CUTTS, Maria. *b.* Loughborough, Leics. 1811;
entered novitiate of Society of the Sacred
Heart in Paris 1828; a professed nun 1836;
superior of the convent at Grand Coteau,
St. Landry parish, Mississippi; superior of all
the convents of her order in the west of the
United States. *d.* Grand Coteau 1853.

CUYLER, Jacob Glen. Ensign 69 foot 26
Oct. 1799; major Cape Regiment 26 Jany.
1806 to 25 May 1817 when placed on h.p.;
L.G. 11 Nov. 1851. *d.* 14 April 1854.

CYPLES, William. *b* Longton, Staffs. 31 Aug.
1831; edited several provincial newspapers;
contributed to many leading periodicals; lived
at Nottingham long time, lived in London
1877 to death; author of *Pottery Poems; Satan
restored, a poem* 1859; *Philip the Dreamer 3
vols.* 1866; *An inquiry into the process of human
experience* 1880; *Hearts of gold* 1883. *d.* Hammersmith 24 Aug. 1882. *Church quarterly
review xiii,* 107–28 (1881); *Mind v,* 273, 390
(1880), *viii,* 150 (1882).

D

DACRE, Thomas Brand, 20 Baron. *b.* The
Hoo, Kimpton, Herts. 15 March 1774; barrister L.I. 25 June 1800; M.P. for Herts. 11
May 1807 to 3 Oct. 1819 when he succeeded
his mother. *d.* The Hoo 21 March 1851.

DACRE, Barbarina Brand, Baroness (3 *dau.
of Admiral Sir Chaloner Ogle, who d. 27 Aug.
1816 aged 89*). *b.* 9 May 1767; one of the
most accomplished women of her time; an
excellent amateur painter and sculptor; Ugo
Foscolo dedicated to her his *Essays on Petrarch*
1823 the last 45 pages of which contain her
translations from Petrarch; her tragedy in 5
acts entitled *Ina* was produced at Drury Lane
theatre 22 April 1815; privately printed
Dramas, translations and occasional poems 2 vols.
1821; *Translations from the Italian* 1836; edited
Recollections of a Chaperon 1833 and *Tales of
the peerage and the peasantry* 1835, both by her
only dau. Mrs. Arabella Jane Sullivan who *d.*
27 Jany. 1839 aged 42. (*m.* (1) Valentine
Henry Wilmot of Farnborough, Hants. *m.* (2)
4 Dec. 1819 Thomas Brand, baron Dacre 1774–
1851). *d.* 2 Chesterfield st. May Fair, London
17 May 1854. *G.M. xlii,* 296–97 (1854).

DACRE, Henry Otway Brand-Trevor, 21
Baron (*brother of 20 Baron Dacre 1774–1851*).
b. 17 July 1777; ensign Coldstream guards
27 April 1793, lieut.-col. 25 July 1814 to 19
July 1821; served in Flanders 1793–95;
assumed additional name of Trevor 18 Nov.
1824; colonel 31 Foot 12 July 1847 to death;
general 11 Nov. 1851; C.B. 4 June 1815;
succeeded 21 March 1851. *d.* Great Cumberland place, London 2 June 1853.

DACRES, James Richard (*son of Vice admiral
James Richard Dacres 1749–1810*). *b.* Lowestoft 22 Aug. 1788; entered navy 1796; captain 14 Jany. 1806; commander in chief at
Cape of Good Hope 9 Aug. 1845 to 3 Aug.
1848; V.A. 20 March 1848. *d.* Catesfield
lodge near Fareham, Hants. 3 Dec. 1853. *bur.*
in family vault at Tetbury, Gloucs.

DACRES, Sir Richard James (*son of Vice admiral Sir Richard Dacres 1761–1837*). *b.* 1799;
ed. at R.M.A. Woolwich; 2 lieut. R.A. 15
Dec. 1817, lieut.-col. 23 Feb. 1852; served in
Crimean war 1854–5; col. commandant 28
July 1864; commandant at Woolwich, May
1859 to 1865; general 2 Feb. 1868; placed
on retired list 1 Oct. 1877; constable of Tower

DACRES, SIR R. J. *(Con.)*

of London 2 July 1881 to death; K.C.B. 5 July 1855, G.C.B. 2 June 1869. *d.* Palmeira sq. Brighton 6 Dec. 1886. *I.L.N. lxxix,* 181 (1881), *portrait.*

DACRES, SIR SIDNEY COLPOYS *(brother of the preceding). b.* Totnes, Devon 9 Jany. 1805; entered navy 8 Feb. 1817; captain 1 Aug. 1840; captain of the Sans Pareil 70 guns, 3 June 1852 to Nov. 1855; embarked the sick and wounded after battles of Alma and Inkermann; took charge of the port of Balaklava 27 Oct. 1854; superintendent of packet service at Southampton, Feb. to July 1856; superintendent of Royal Clarence victualling yard and Royal hospital, Haslar 7 July 1856 to 25 June 1858; granted good service pension 7 Feb. 1856; captain of the fleet in Mediterranean 25 Aug. 1859, second in command Dec. 1861 to April 1863; commanded channel fleet April 1863 to 17 Nov. 1865; a lord of the admiralty July 1865, first sea lord Dec. 1868 to Nov. 1872; admiral 1 April 1870; visitor and governor of Greenwich hospital 30 Nov. 1872 to death; K.L.H. 1828, K.T.S. 1865; C.B. 5 July 1855, K.C.B. 28 March 1865, G.C.B. 20 May 1871. *d.* 47 Brunswick sq. Brighton 8 March 1884. *I.L.N. lxii,* 319, 321 (1873), *portrait.*

D'AETH, GEORGE WILLIAM *(only son of Wm. Hughes of Betshanger, Kent, who d. April* 1786). *b.* April 1786; entered navy June 1799; assumed name of D'Aeth 4 June 1808; captain 13 June 1815; retired captain 1 Oct. 1846; retired admiral 4 Oct. 1862. *d.* Knowlton court, Kent 28 April 1873.

DAFFORNE, JAMES. Contributed to the *Art Journal* 1845 to death; wrote 7 books 1872–77 on the pictures by C. R. Leslie, C. Stanfield, J. Phillip, Sir A. W. Callcott, Sir E. Landseer, W. Mulready and J. M. W. Turner; author of *The pictorial table book* 1873; *The Albert memorial Hyde Park, its history and description* 1877; *The life and works of E. M. Ward, R.A.* 1879. *d.* Brodrick road, Upper Tooting 8 June 1880.

DAFT, THOMAS BARNABAS. *b.* Birmingham 1816; an iron founder and manufacturer of metallic hot houses 1835; maker of philosophical apparatus 1839; manager of india rubber works of Charles Mackintosh and Co. at Manchester many years; took out 28 patents 1839–77; A.I.C.E. 7 Feb. 1860. *d.* 95 Clapham road, London 4 Dec. 1878.

DAGLISH, ROBERT. *b.* 21 Dec. 1779; engineer to Lord Balcarres at Wigan 1804; manager

DAGLISH, R. *(Con.)*

of Orrell colliery near Wigan; projected Bolton and Leigh railway 1825 which has no embankments or cuttings but undulates with natural surface of the land; invented best form of parallel rail and pedestals which gained premium of £100 given by London and Birmingham railway 1834 for which there were 72 competitors, this invention was generally adopted; projector of and partner in St. Helen's foundry; M.I C.E. 30 March 1830. *d.* Orrell near Wigan 28 Dec. 1865. *Min. of proc. of Instit. of C.E. xxvi,* 561–63 (1867).

DAGLISH, ROBERT (3 *son of the preceding). b.* Wigan 1809; partner in firm of Lee, Watson & Co. iron founders, St. Helens 1830; with John Smith worked the traffic of the St. Helen's and Runcorn Gap railway 1839–48; erected his first cotton mill at Wigan 1845; built many railway bridges in Lancashire and Yorkshire 1846–49; constructed Preston extension of East Lancashire railway 1850; sole proprietor of the foundry from 1851 until 1869 when joined by his nephew George H. Daglish, M.I.C.E.; erected coal drops at Garston near Liverpool 1852; extended his foundry works so that they covered an area of 22,400 square yards in 1882; assoc. of Instit. of C.E. 1852 and member 1874. *d.* 6 May 1883. *Min. of proc. of Instit. of C.E. lxxiv,* 283–5 (1883).

D'AGUILAR, SIR GEORGE CHARLES *(son of Joseph D'Aguilar, captain 2 dragoon guards). b.* Winchester, Jany. 1784; ensign 86 foot 24 Sep. 1799; major 1 Greek light infantry 1 April 1813 to 24 Feb. 1816 when regiment was disbanded and he was placed on h.p.; major Rifle brigade 6 March 1817 to 25 Dec. 1818 when placed on h.p.; major 3 foot 22 June 1820 to 13 Sep. 1821 when placed on h.p.; deputy adjutant general in Ireland 22 July 1830 to 23 Nov. 1841; commanded troops in China 1843–48; col. of 58 foot 5 Feb. 1848, col. of 23 foot 31 Jany. 1851 to death; L.G. 11 Nov. 1851; C.B. 19 July 1838, K.C.B. 6 April 1852; author of *The practice and forms of Courts Martial* 1843, 5 ed. 1867. *d.* Lower Brook st. Grosvenor sq. London 21 May 1855. *United Service Mag. Aug.* 1847 *pp.* 622–27.

DAINTREE, RICHARD. *b.* Hemingford Abbotts, Hunts, Dec. 1831; ed. at Bedford gr. sch. and Ch. coll. Cam.; went to Melbourne 1852; assistant geologist of colony of Victoria 1854–56; field geologist on geological survey of Victoria 1858–64; government geologist for North Queensland 1869–72; entrusted with

DAINTREE, R. *(Con.)*

collection sent to Exhibition at South Kensington 1871 but steamer "Queen of the Thames" containing collection was wrecked near Cape Agulhas about 200 miles from Cape Town 18 March 1871; agent general in London for colony of Queensland, March 1872 to 1876; C.M.G. 1875. *d.* Holyrood house, Beckenham, Kent 20 June 1878. *Quarterly Journal of Geol. Soc. xxxv,* 51–3 (1879); *Geol. Mag. v,* 336, 429–32 (1878).

D'ALBERT, CHARLES *(son of a captain of cavalry in French army). b.* Nienstellen near Hamburg 1808 or 1809; pupil in London of F. W. M. Kalkbrenner the pianist; studied music and dancing at Académie Royale, Paris; maître de ballet and first dancer at Covent Garden theatre; teacher of music in London; wrote various musical albums 1848–53; an exceedingly popular composer of innumerable waltzes, polkas and galops. *d.* 14 Alexander sq. South Kensington, London 26 May 1886 in 78 year. *Illust. news of the world viii* (1861), *portrait.*

DALE, JAMES. *b.* Brancepeth near Durham; succeeded his father as head gardener to 6 Viscount Boyne at Brancepeth Castle 1854; a great judge of fruit and flowers; kept a splendid stock of plants and fruit but never exhibited; known as "The King of Pine growers"; a clever naturalist and ornithologist; it is stated in Loudon's *Natural History* that Mr. Dale was the only man in England who ever took a siskin's nest, which he did in a pine tree; left a valuable collection of stuffed animals and preserved fish. *d.* Brancepeth 1 April 1882 aged 66.

DALE, JAMES MURRAY *(son of Very Rev. T. Dale 1797–1870). b.* 20 July 1822; ed. at Merchant Taylors' school; a solicitor in London 1843–73; author of *Clergyman's Legal handbook* 1858, 6 ed. 1881; *Church extension law* 1864; *Legal ritual, Judgments of privy council and dean of arches* 1871. *d.* Cromer 2 March 1877.

DALE, JOHN. *b.* Settle, Yorkshire 1 March 1803; articled to Reay and Collison, surgeons, Liverpool; played under Samuel Russell's management in the provinces 1823; first appeared in London at Haymarket theatre as Rob Roy 5 Oct. 1825; went to Paris with the Kean, Macready, Kemble company 1827; the original Adrastus in Talfourd's tragedy *Ion* at Covent Garden, May 1836; played Cromwell to Macready's Wolsey at Covent Garden; acted at Surrey and Victoria theatres; one of his best characters was Creve Cœur in *The Bohemians. d.* Manchester 25 Oct. 1872. *Theatrical Times iii,* 137, 146 (1848), *portrait.* ·

DALE, JOSEPH. Gardener to Society of the Middle Temple, London 1843 to decease, where he arranged annual exhibitions of chrysanthemums in November; greatly assisted and encouraged the plantation of trees in various parts of London; presented with a testimonial at the Salutation tavern, Newgate st. London 31 Jany. 1878; author of *On the cultivation of the chrysanthemum* 1856. *d.* Vicarage road, Leyton 31 Dec. 1878 aged 65. *Gardener's Magazine xxi,* 59 (1878), *xxii,* 7, 80 (1879).

DALE, VERY REV. THOMAS *(son of William Dale of Pentonville, London). b.* Pentonville 22 Aug. 1797; ed. at Christ hospital 1805–17 and C.C. coll. Cam., B.A. 1823, M.A. 1826, D.D. 1870; C. of St. Michael's, Cornhill, London 1822–26; professor of English language and literature at London Univ. 1828–30, at King's coll. London 1836–39; minister of St. Matthew's chapel, Denmark hill 1830–35; V. of St. Bride's, Fleet st. London 3 Jany. 1835 to 1846; Golden lecturer at St. Margaret's, Lothbury 1840–1849; preb. of St. Paul's, March 1843 to Feb. 1846; canon of St. Paul's 20 Oct. 1843 to 1870; V. of St. Pancras, July 1846 to March 1861 when that parish was subdivided into 20 incumbencies; R. of Therfield, Herts. 26 March 1861 to 1870; declined deanery of Ely 1869; dean of Rochester 23 Feb. 1870 to death, installed April 1870; author of *The widow of Nain and other poems* 1817; *The outlaw of Taurus* 1818; *The tragedies of Sophocles translated into English verse* 2 vols. 1824; *Poetical works* 1836; *The sabbath companion being essays on first principles of Christian faith and practice* 1844, 3 ed. 1853 and about 70 other books. *d.* 2 Amen corner, St. Paul's, London 14 May 1870. *Palmer's St. Pancras* (1870) 43, 142, 159–61; *Drawing room portrait gallery of eminent personages, fourth series* (1860), *portrait; Church of England photographic portrait gallery* 1859, *portrait* 24; *I.L.N. xxxv,* 647 (1859), *portrait, lvi,* 563, 643 (1870).

DALGAIRNS, REV. JOHN DOBREE *(son of Wm. Dalgairns). b.* Guernsey 21 Oct. 1818; ed. at Elizabeth coll. Guernsey and Ex. coll. Ox., scholar 27 May 1837; B.A. 1839, M.A. 1842; joined J. H. Newman's band of disciples at Littlemore; received into R.C. church 29 Sep. 1845, ordained at Langres in France 1846; a preacher and confessor at the London Oratory King William st. Strand 1849 to 1853 and 1856 to 1863, at Birmingham Oratory 1853–56; superior of London Oratory, Brompton 1863–65; wrote some of the lives in J. H. Newman's *Lives of the English saints;* author of *The devotion to the heart of Jesus with an introduction on the history of Jansenism* 1853, 2 ed. 1854;

DALGAIRNS, REV. J. D. *(Con.)*

The German mystics of the fourteenth century 1858; *The Holy Communion, its philosophy, theology and practice* 1861 frequently reprinted, and of many articles in the *British Critic, Dublin Review* and *Contemporary Review. d.* in monastery of the Cistercians at Burgess hill, near Brighton 6 April 1876. *bur.* in private cemetery of the Fathers of the Brompton oratory at Sydenham. *Gillow's English Catholics ii,* 3–5 (1885).

DALGLISH, ROBERT *(son of Robert Dalglish, provost of Glasgow). b.* Glasgow 1808; a calico printer at Glasgow; M.P. for Glasgow 1 April 1857 to 26 Jany. 1874. *d.* Lennox-mill cottage, Lennoxtown near Glasgow 20 June 1880.

DALHOUSIE, JAMES ANDREW BROWN-RAMSAY, 1 Marquis of *(youngest child of 9 Earl of Dalhousie* 1770–1838). *b.* Dalhousie castle, co. Edinburgh 22 April 1812; ed. at Harrow and Ch. Ch. Ox., B.A. 1833, M.A. 1838; contested city of Edin. Jany. 1835; M.P. for East Lothian 1837–38; succeeded as 10 Earl of Dalhousie 21 March 1838; P.C. 10 June 1843; vice pres. of Board of Trade 10 June 1843, pres. 5 Feb. 1845 to 6 July 1846; lord clerk register of Scotland 12 Dec. 1845; an elder brother of Trinity house 1846; governor general of India 4 Aug. 1847, arrived at Calcutta 19 Jany. 1848, left there 6 March 1856; annexed the Punjaub 1849, Pegu 1852, Nagpore 1853 and Oudh 1856; K.T. 12 May 1848; created Marquis of Dalhousie of Dalhousie castle and of the Punjaub 25 Aug. 1849; constable of Dover castle and lord warden of the Cinque Ports 13 Jany. 1853. *d.* Dalhousie Castle 19. Dec. 1860. *Sir C. Jackson's Vindication of the policy of Dalhousie's Indian administration; J. J. Higginbotham's Men whom India has known* (1874) 98–104; *I.L.N. xiv,* 36 (1849), *portrait, xxii,* 61 (1853), *portrait.*

DALHOUSIE, FOX MAULE-RAMSAY, 11 Earl of *(eld. son of* 1 *Baron Panmure* 1771–1852). *b.* Brechin castle, Forfarshire 22 April 1801; ed. at the Charterhouse; ensign 79 foot 3 June 1819, captain 31 Oct. 1826, sold out 1831; M.P. for Perthshire 1835–37, for Elgin district of burghs 1838–41, for Perth 1841–52; under sec. of state for home department 18 April 1835 to 15 June 1841; vice pres. of board of trade 28 June to 3 Sep. 1841; P.C. 28 June 1841; sec. of state for war 6 July 1846 to Feb. 1852 and 8 Feb. 1855 to Feb. 1858; lord rector of Univ. of Glasgow, Nov. 1842; lord lieut. of Forfarshire 16 June 1849; keeper of privy seal of Scotland 25 May 1853; K.T. 28 Oct. 1853; G.C.B. 29 Oct. 1855; succeeded

DALHOUSIE, 11 Earl of *(Con.)*

as 2 baron Panmure 13 April 1852 and as 11 Earl of Dalhousie 19 Dec. 1860. *d.* Brechin castle, Forfarshire 6 July 1874. *The statesmen of England* (1862), *portrait; Illust. news of the world, i,* (1858), *portrait; I.L.N. xvi,* 245 (1850), *portrait, xxvi,* 152 (1855), *portrait, lxv,* 61, 67, 115, 523 (1874), *portrait.*

DALHOUSIE, GEORGE MAULE-RAMSAY, 12 Earl of *(2 son of hon. John Ramsay* 1775–1842, *col. of* 79 *foot). b.* 26 April 1806; entered navy Dec. 1820; captain 20 March 1843; C.B. 4 Feb. 1856; superintendent of Pembroke dockyard 27 July 1857 to 1 Sep. 1862; commander in chief on South American station 7 May 1866 to 17 March 1869; succeeded as 12 Earl 6 July 1874; created Baron Ramsay of Glenmark, co. Forfar in peerage of the U.K. 12 June 1875; retired admiral 30 July 1875. *d.* Dalhousie castle 20 July 1880.

DALHOUSIE, JOHN WILLIAM RAMSAY, 13 Earl of *(son of the preceding). b.* 29 Jany. 1847; naval cadet Jany. 1861; commander 4 March 1874, commanded the Britannia 1877–79, retired 26 July 1884; contested Liverpool 6 Feb. 1880; M.P. for Liverpool, March 1880 to 20 July 1880 when he succeeded his father; a lord in waiting to the Queen, Sep. 1880 to June 1885; K.T. Nov. 1881; P.C. 3 April 1886; sec. of state for Scotland 5 April 1886 to 26 June 1886. *d.* Havre 25 Nov. 1887. *bur.* parish church of Cockpen, co. Edinburgh 1 Dec. 1887. *London Figaro* 3 *Dec.* 1887 *p.* 5, *col.* 2, *portrait.*

DALLAS, REV. ALEXANDER ROBERT CHARLES *(2 son of Robert Charles Dallas, miscellaneous writer* 1754–1824). *b.* Colchester 29 March 1791; clerk in commissariat office of Treasury 1805–10, deputy assistant commissary general 5 June 1810 to 1 July 1814 when placed on h.p., retired 1820; gentleman commoner of Worcester coll. Ox. 29 Feb. 1820; C. of Radley, Berks. 17 June 1821, of Highclere Hants. 1821, of Woburn 1824, of Burford, Oxon. 1826; V. of Yardley, Herts. 22 Sep. 1827; R. of Wonston, Hants. 14 Sep. 1828 to death; chaplain to bishop of Winchester 1828 to death; founded Society for Irish church missions to the Roman Catholics 1848, hon. sec. 1848 to death; author of *Cottager's guide to the New Testament* 6 vols. 1837–43; *A Guide to the Acts of the Apostles by A. D.* 1847; *Revelation readings* 3 vols. 1848 and upwards of 50 other books. *d.* in house of Mr. Annesley, Blackheath, Kent 12 Dec. 1869. *bur.* Wonston churchyard 17 Dec. *Incidents in the life and ministry of Rev. A. R. C. Dallas by his widow* (1871), *portrait.*

DALLAS, CHARLES. Ensign 32 foot 23 March 1815; governor of St. Helena 14 Feb. 1828 to 1836. *d.* Trefusis house, Exmouth 26 April 1855 in 88 year.

DALLAS, ELMSLIE WILLIAM (2 *son of Wm. Dallas of 'Lloyds,' London*). *b.* London 27 June 1809; studied at the R.A. London 1831–34; painted a series of views of Scotland for garden pavilion at Buckingham palace; exhibited at Royal Scottish Academy; F.R.S. Edin. 1851; author of *The Elements of plane practical geometry* 1855. *d.* 26 Jany. 1879. *Proc. of Royal Soc. of Edin. x,* 340 (1880).

DALLAS, ENEAS SWEETLAND (*elder son of John Dallas of Jamaica, physician*). *b.* Jamaica 1828; ed. at Univ. of Edin.; a journalist on the *Times* many years, special correspondent at Paris 1867 and 1870; contributed to *Daily News, Saturday Review, Pall Mall Gazette* and *The World;* edited *Once a Week* 1868; author of *Poetics, an essay on poetry* 1852; *The gay science* 2 vols. 1866; edited an abridgment of Richardson's *Clarissa Harlowe* 1868; published *Kettner's Book of the table, a manual of cookery* 1877 anon. (*m.* in Scotland, Dec. 1853 and in London 12 July 1855 the well-known actress Isabella Glyn (widow of Edward Wills), marriage was dissolved in the divorce court, London on her petition 10 May 1874). *d.* 88 Newman st. Oxford st. London 17 Jany. 1879. *I.L.N.* 8 Feb. 1879 *pp.* 78, 129, 131, *portrait; Law Journal Reports xlvi, pt. 1, pp.* 51–3 (1876).

DALLIN, THOMAS FRANCIS (*eld. son of Thomas James Dallin of Plumstead, Kent*). Matric. from Merton coll. Ox. 10 June 1858 aged 17, B.A. 1863, M.A. 1865; student at L.I. 23 Nov. 1861; fellow of Queen's coll. Ox. 1864–71, tutor 1866; professor of rhetoric at Gresham college, London, Aug. 1875; public orator Univ. of Ox. 8 May 1877 to death; one of secs. of Oxford Univ. commission 1880 to death; author with J.Y. Sargent of *Materials and models for Greek and Latin prose composition* 1870, 2 *ed.* 1875; *Materials for Greek prose composition* 1878. *d.* Brighton 11 Nov. 1880. *bur.* in Holywell cemetery, Oxford 16 Nov. *Times* 13 *Nov.* 1880 *p.* 5, *col.* 6, 15 *Nov. p.* 9, *col.* 4, 17 *Nov. p.* 9, *col.* 6.

DALLING and BULWER, WILLIAM HENRY LYTTON EARLE BULWER, Baron (2 *son of Wm. Earle Bulwer 1757–1807, col.* 106 *foot*). *b.* 31 Baker st. Portman sq. London 13 Feb. 1801; ed. at Sunbury and Harrow; entered Trin. coll. Cam. 1819, migrated to Downing coll.; went to the Morea as agent of the Greek committee in London 1824; attaché at Berlin 1827, at Vienna 1829, at the Hague,

DALLING and BULWER, Baron (*Con.*) 1830; M.P. for Wilton, Wilts. 1830–31, for Coventry 1831–34, for Marylebone 1835; chargé d'affaires at Brussels 1835–36; sec. of embassy at Constantinople 1837–39, at Paris 1839–43; ambassador at Madrid 14 Nov. 1843, arbitrator between Spain and Morocco 1844; P.C. 30 June 1845; K.C.B. 27 April 1848, G.C.B. 1 March 1851; ambassador at Washington 27 April 1849; minister plenipotentiary at Florence 19 Jany. 1852 to 26 Jany. 1855; granted a pension 25 April 1855; ambassador at Constantinople 10 May 1858 to Aug. 1865; M.P. for Tamworth 17 Nov. 1868 to 21 March 1871 when created baron Dalling and Bulwer of Dalling in the county of Norfolk; said to be the original of George Sand's 'Mauprat' 1836; author of *An autumn in Greece* 1826; *France, social, literary and political* 2 vols. 1834, being the first half of a work called *The monarchy of the middle classes* 1836; *Historical characters* 3 vols. 1867–73; *Life of Viscount Palmerston* 3 vols. 1870–74. *d.* Naples 23 May 1872. A. *Hayward's Biographical essays ii,* 320–40 (1870); *Madden's Life of Countess of Blessington iii,* 63–74 (1855); *Illust. Review iv,* 97–103 (1872), *portrait; I.L.N. ix,* 245 (1846), *portrait, lxi,* 168 (1872).

DALLMEYER, JOHANN HEINRICK (2 *son of Wm. Dallmeyer of Loxten near Versmold, Westphalia*). *b.* Loxten 6 Sep. 1830; apprenticed to an optician at Osnabruck 3 years; came to England 1851; a manufacturer of telescopes in London 1859; naturalised 17 Sep. 1859; F.R.A.S. 1861; supplied photographic lenses to photographers in all parts of the world; patented a single wide-angle lens 1864 largely used for photographing landscapes; received highest awards at Dublin, Berlin, Paris and Philadelphia exhibitions; author of *On the choice and use of photographic lenses,* 6 *editions. d.* on board ship off coast of New Zealand 30 Dec. 1883. *Monthly notices of Royal Astronom. Soc. xlv,* 190–91 (1885).

DALMER, THOMAS. Second lieut. 23 foot 22 May 1797, major 10 Dec. 1807 to 24 July 1817 when placed on h.p.; col. 47 foot 16 April 1847 to death; L.G. 11 Nov. 1851; C.B. 4 June 1815. *d.* Hawkhurst, Kent 26 Aug. 1854.

DALRYMPLE, SIR ADOLPHUS JOHN, 2 Baronet (*elder son of Sir Hew Whiteford Dalrymple,* 1 *baronet, who d.* 9 *April* 1830 *in* 80 *year*). *b.* parish of Marylebone, London, Feb. 1784; ed. at Harrow; ensign 37 foot 25 Oct. 1799; major 19 light dragoons 17 Nov. 1808 to Dec. 1814 when placed on h.p.; aide-de-camp to the Sovereign 1830–41; general 11 April 1860;

DALRYMPLE, SIR A. J. (Con.)

M.P. for Weymouth 1817–18, for Appleby 1819–26, for Haddington district of burghs 1826–31, for Brighton 1837–41. *d.* Delrowe house near Watford, Herts. 3 March 1866.

DALRYMPLE, DONALD (4 son of *Wm. Dalrymple of Norwich, surgeon* 1772–1847). *b.* Norwich 1814; ed. at Norwich gr. sch. and Guy's hospital; F.R.C.S. 1854; M.R.C.P. 1859; a surgeon at Norwich 1835–62; sheriff of Norwich 1860–61; M.P. for Bath 17 Nov. 1868 to death; author of *Meteorological observations on the climate of Egypt* 1861. *d.* Coldecot near Southampton 19 Sep. 1873.

DALRYMPLE, JOHN (brother of the preceding). *b.* Norwich 1803; ed. at Univ. of Edin.; a surgeon at 8 New Broad st. City of London 1827–39 when he moved to 6 Holles st. Cavendish sq.; assistant surgeon to Royal London Ophthalmic hospital 1832, surgeon 1843, consulting surgeon 1849; a founder of Royal college of Chemistry 1845; F.R.S. 7 June 1849; author of *The anatomy of the human eye* 1834; *The pathology of the human eye* 1852. *d.* 60 Grosvenor st. London 2 May 1852 in 49 year. *Proc. of Royal Soc. vi*, 250 (1852).

DALTON, CHARLES JAMES (youngest son of *Rev. James Dalton, R. of Croft, Yorkshire*). *b.* 13 May 1812; Second lieut. R.A. 18 Dec. 1829, col. 25 Sep. 1859 to 23 April 1868, col. commandant 20 April 1877 to death; L.G. 1 Oct. 1877. *d.* Percy house, Twickenham park, Twickenham 7 Nov. 1880.

DALTON, JOHN (son of *Wm. Dalton of Bessville, co. Westmeath*). *b.* Bessville 29 June 1792; ed. at Trin. coll. Dublin; called to Irish bar 1813; comr. of Irish loan fund board 1835; granted a civil list pension of £50, 4 March 1856; gained prize of £80 and Cunningham gold medal of Royal Irish Academy for best essay on social and political state of Irish people 1827; author of *History of the county of Dublin* 2 vols. 1838; *The history of Drogheda* 2 vols. 1844; *History of Ireland to the year 1245,* 2 vols. 1845 and other books. *d.* 48 Summer hill, Dublin 20 Jany. 1867.

DALTON, REV. JOHN. Educ. at Oscott college; engaged in R.C. missions at Northampton, Norwich and Lynn; elected a member of the chapter of see of Northampton; published *Christianity in Europe by Novalis translated from the German* 1844; *The art of dying well, translated from the Latin of Bellarmine* 1846 and many other translations from German, Latin and Spanish. *d.* St. John's, Maddermarket, Norwich 15 Feb. 1874 in 60 year.

DALTON, JOHN STUART. Librarian of free public library, William Brown st. Liverpool 1852 to death; author of many poems. *d.* Low hill, Liverpool 2 Aug. 1868 aged 72.

DALTON, WILLIAM HENRY. Bookseller in Cockspur st. London about 1833–63; founded Booksellers Protection Association about 1851; member of Metropolitan Board of Works for parish of St. Martin in the Fields 1855 to death, being the last survivor of the original members. *d.* 30 Coleherne road, South Kensington, London 23 June 1884.

DALY, CUTHBERT FEATHERSTONE. Entered navy 17 Feb. 1794; captain 18 Aug. 1808; R.A. on h.p. 9 Nov. 1846; C.B. 20 July 1838. *d.* Hayes place, Lisson grove, London 6 Dec. 1851.

DALY, SIR DOMINIC (3 son of *Dominic Daly of Benmore, co. Galway, who d.* 1841). *b.* Ardfry, co. Galway 11 Aug. 1798; went to Canada as private sec. to Sir Francis Burton 1822; assistant sec. to province of Lower Canada 1825–27, sec. 1827–40, sec. of province of Canada on union of the two provinces 1840–48; lieut. governor of Tobago 16 Sep. 1851, of Prince Edward's Island 8 May 1854 to 1859; knighted by patent 2 July 1856; governor and commander in chief of South Australia 28 Oct. 1861 to death, assumed office March 1862. (*m.* 20 May 1826 Caroline Maria 2 dau. of Ralph Gore of Barrowmount, co. Kilkenny, she was granted a civil list pension of £100, 17 Nov. 1868 and *d.* 1872), he *d.* Government house, Adelaide 19 Feb. 1868. *J. P. Stow's South Australia* (1883) 37–42.

DALY, ELLEN. *b.* Kidderminster 1806; acted in melodrama at Adelphi theatre, London 1820–21; acted at Covent Garden and Haymarket, at Surrey theatre 14 years, at Standard theatre 1848–49; at Princess's theatre under Charles Kean 1850–59. *d.* Notting hill, London 18 Jany. 1883. *Actors by daylight i,* 89 (1838), *portrait; Dramatic Mirror* (1847) *p.* 37, *portrait; Theatrical Times iv,* 1–2 (1849), *portrait.*

DALY, RIGHT REV. ROBERT (younger son of *Denis Daly of Dunsandle, co. Galway* 1747–91, *P.C.*) *b.* Dunsandle 8 June 1783; fellow commoner at Trin. coll. Dublin 1799, gold medallist 1803, B.A. 1803, M.A. 1832, B.D. and D.D. 1843; preb. of Holy Trinity, Cork 1809–43; preb. of Stagonill, Dublin 1809–43; R. of Powerscourt 1809–43; dean of St. Patrick's, Dublin, elected 8 Dec. 1840, declared dean 1842 by court of delegates appointed to try validity of the election; bishop of united

DALY, RIGHT REV. R. *(Con.)*
dioceses of Cashel, Emly, Waterford and Lismore 12 Jany. 1843 to death; an eminent leader of the Evangelical party; edited O'Brien's *Focaloir Gaoidhilge-Sags-Bhéarla, or an Irish-English dictionary* 1832; *Letters and papers of Viscountess Powerscourt* 1838, 9 ed. 1874. *d.* See house, Waterford 16 Feb. 1872. *Personal recollections of Right Rev. Robert Daly by An old parishioner i.e. Mrs. H. Madden* 1872.

DALYELL, SIR JOHN GRAHAM, 6 Baronet (2 *son of Sir Robert Dalyell, 4 baronet, who d. 1791*). *b.* Binns, Linlithgowshire, Aug. 1775; lamed for life when an infant; ed. at Univs. of St. Andrews and Edin.; advocate at Scottish bar 1796; knighted by patent 22 Aug. 1836; pres. of Society of Arts for Scotland 1839–40; succeeded his elder brother as 6 baronet 1 Feb. 1841; author of *Fragments of Scottish history* 1798; *Scottish poems of the sixteenth century* 1801; *Journal of Richard Bannatyne* 1806; *Darker superstitions of Scotland* 1834; *Musical memoirs of Scotland* 1849. *d.* 14 Great King st. Edinburgh 7 June 1851. *Sir J. G. Dalyell's The powers of the creator displayed in the creation to which is prefixed a memoir of the author, vol. iii,* 1858.

DALYELL, SIR ROBERT ALEXANDER OSBORNE, 8 Baronet *(eld. son of the succeeding).* *b.* 1821; ed. at Trin. coll. Cam., M.A. 1847; barrister M.T. 23 Nov. 1849; employed in the consulate at Bucharest 1855–57; consul at Erzeroum 1859–65; consul for the Vilayet of the Danube 17 Oct. 1865 to 1 July 1874 when he retired on a pension. *d.* The Binns, Linlithgow 21 Jany. 1886.

DALYELL, SIR WILLIAM CUNNINGHAM CAVENDISH, 7 Baronet. *b.* 27 April 1784; entered navy 1793; a prisoner in France 1805–14; commander of Greenwich hospital 27 Aug. 1840 to death; retired captain 1 July 1864; succeeded 7 June 1851. *d.* Royal hospital, Greenwich 16 Feb. 1865.

DALZELL, NICOL ALEXANDER. *b.* Edinburgh 21 April 1817; ed. at high sch. and Univ. of Edin., M.A. 1837; assistant comr. of customs, Bombay 1841; forest ranger of Scinde; conservator of forests Bombay, retired on a pension 1870; F.R.S. Edin.; author of *A review of Plowden's Report on salt revenue of Bombay* 1855; *The Bombay Flora* 1861. *d.* Edinburgh, Jany. 1878.

DAMES, WILLIAM LONGWORTH. Ensign 66 foot 26 July 1826, major 12 Oct. 1841 to 6 Nov. 1846 when placed on h.p.; col. 5 foot 12 Jany. 1865 to death; L.G. 4 Feb. 1867. *d.* 23 East Cliff, Dover 20 Feb. 1868 aged 61.

DAMPIER, JOHN LUCIUS (2 *son of Sir Henry Dampier 1758–1816, justice of Court of King's Bench*). *b.* 19 Bloomsbury sq. London 23 Dec. 1792; ed. at Eton and King's coll. Cam., B.A. 1816, M.A. 1819; fellow of his coll.; barrister L.I. 22 May 1819; recorder of Portsmouth 1837–38; a comr. to enquire into rights and claims connected with New Forest and Waltham forest 1849; a comr. for investigating state of Univ. of Ox. 1850; vice warden of Stannaries in county of Devon 16 Dec. 1850 to death. *d.* 33 Pulteney st. Bath 24 May 1853. *G.M. xl,* 94–5 (1853).

DANBY, FRANCIS (3 *son of James Danby of Common near Wexford, farmer*). *b.* Common 16 Nov. 1793; landscape painter especially of sunsets; exhibited 48 pictures at R.A., 17 at B.I. and 2 at Suffolk st. gallery 1820–60; A.R.A. 7 Nov. 1825; lived in Paris and on the lake of Geneva 1829–41, at Lewisham, Kent 1841–47, and at Exmouth 1847 to death; his picture 'The Deluge' exhibited in London 1840 was chief artistic feature of Dublin Exhibition 1853. *d.* Shell house, Exmouth 17 Feb. 1861. *Sandby's History of the royal academy ii,* 68–71 (1862); *Redgrave's Century of painters ii,* 437–49 (1866); *W. Stokes's Life of George Petrie* (1869) 7–10.

DANBY, JAMES FRANCIS *(eld. son of the preceding).* *b.* Bristol 1816; member of Soc. of British Artists; exhibited 35 landscapes at R.A., 42 at B.I. and 46 at Suffolk st. gallery 1842–76. *d.* 54 Park road, Haverstock hill, London 22 Oct. 1875. *Graphic xii,* 518 (1875), *portrait.*

DANBY, THOMAS *(brother of the preceding).* *b.* about 1817; copied pictures at the Louvre, Paris for his living 1830–41; exhibited 30 pictures at R.A. and 42 at B.I. 1842–76; associate of Soc. of Painters in Water-colours 1867, member 1870, his landscapes were among the chief ornaments of the Society's exhibitions. *d.* 11 Park road, Haverstock hill, London 25 March 1886.

DANCE, CHARLES *(son of George Dance of London, architect 1740–1825).* *b.* about 1794; clerk in Court for relief of Insolvent Debtors, London, registrar and auditor 1851, taxing officer 1853, chief clerk May 1858 to Oct. 1861 when he retired on pension of £800 a year; wrote many extravaganzas alone and with J. R. Planché; called the founder of modern burlesque; of his 30 dramatic pieces the *Bengal Tiger, Delicate Ground, A morning call, Who speaks first,* and *Naval Engagements* are still sometimes played. *d.* Lowestoft 5 Jany. 1863. *Planche's Extravaganzas ii,* (1879), *portrait.*

DANCER, JOHN BENJAMIN. *b.* London 1812; optician at Manchester 1835 to death; suggested application of photography in connexion with the magic lantern; constructed the optical chromatic fountain since further developed at South Kensington exhibitions; constructed the first perfectly accurate thermometer in England; produced the first cheap good microscopes; member of Manchester literary and philosophical society; F.R.A.S. *d.* Manchester about 6 Dec. 1887.

DANELL, RIGHT REV. JAMES (*son of Mr. Danell of London*). *b.* Fitzroy st. Fitzroy sq. London 14 July 1821; ed. at St. Edmund's college near Ware and St. Sulpice, Paris; ordained priest 6 June 1846; served mission at St. George's, Southwark 1846–70; canon of Southwark 27 Jany. 1857, vicar general 16 May 1862, vicar capitular 2 June 1870; bishop of Southwark 10 Jany. 1871 to death, consecrated by Abp. Manning at St. George's cathedral 25 March 1871. *d.* The Bishop's house, St. George's cathedral, Southwark 14 June 1881. *The Tablet 18 and 25 June 1881.*

DANIEL, GEORGE. *b.* City of London 16 Sep. 1789; clerk to a stockbroker in Tokenhouse yard; contributed many poems to *Ackerman's Poetical Magazine* 1808–11; author of *The Times, a prophecy* 1811 anon.; *Miscellaneous poems* 1812; *Dick Distich 3 vols.* 1812 anon.; published several squibs on royal scandals under pseud. of P—— P——, poet laureate; author of *The modern Dunciad a satire with notes, biographical and critical* 1814, 2 ed. 1816; edited *Chef d'Œuvres from French authors 2 vols.* 1821; his interlude *Doctor Bolus* was acted at English opera house 21 July 1818, and his musical farce *The disagreeable surprise* at Drury lane 1 Dec. 1819; edited *Cumberland's British Theatre with remarks, biographical and critical 39 vols.* 1823–31, for each of the plays (nearly 300) he wrote a preface under the initials D—— G——; edited *Cumberland's Minor Theatre 14 vols.* 1831–32; author of *Remarks on Miss Mitford's tragedy of Rienzi* 1828; *Ophelia Kean, a dramatic legendary tale* 1829 anon., a scurrilous attack on Edmund Kean; *Garrick in the green room* 1829; *Merrie England in the olden time 2 vols.* 1842, reprinted 1874; *The Missionary* 1847 a religious poem; *Democritus in London, to which are added Notes festivous and the Stranger Guest* 1852; *Love's last labour not lost* 1863. *d.* at his son's house, The Grove, Stoke Newington, London 30 March 1864. *Memoir of D—— G—— prefixed to Colman's Blue Devils in Cumberland's British theatre vol. xxxix (1838), pp. 3–8, portrait; G.M.* 1864 *pt.* 2, *pp.* 450–5.

DANIEL, WILLIAM SHAND. Educated at Univ. of Glasgow; contributed poetical pieces to Glasgow college Albums; wrote part of a drama which appeared in *Collections of miscellaneous poetical pieces Edin.* 1843–44; sheriff clerk depute of Dumbarton 1844 to death; edited *History of the abbey and palace of Holyrood by Duncan Anderson* 1852. *d.* 2 Dec. 1858. *R. Inglis's Dramatic writers of Scotland* 1868 *p.* 130.

DANIELL, EDMUND ROBERT (*son of George Daniell of London, barrister, who d.* 1833). Barrister M.T. 22 Nov. 1816; joint comr. with John Balguy of Birmingham court of bankruptcy 21 Oct. 1842 to death; F.R.S. 5 June 1828 to 1850; author of *Reports of cases argued on the equity side of the Court of Exchequer* 1824; *The practice of the high Court of Chancery 3 vols.* 1837–41, 6 ed., 3 vols. 1882–84; *Practical observations on the new Chancery orders* 1841, 2 ed. 1842. *d.* Meriden hall near Coventry 21 March 1854.

DANIELL, WILLIAM FREEMAN. *b.* Liverpool 1818; M.R.C.S. 1841; assistant surgeon in the army 26 Nov. 1847; served on coast of West Africa; staff surgeon 11 March 1853; wrote a paper on the frankincense tree of West Africa which led to establishment of genus *Daniellia*, Benn. called after him; author of *Medical topography and native diseases of the Gulf of Guinea* 1849; *On the Cascarilla plants of the West Indies* 1862. *d.* Southampton 26 June 1865. *bur.* Kensal Green cemetery, London 3 July.

DANSEY, CHARLES CORNWALLIS. Second lieut. R.A. 19 July 1803, col. 9 Nov. 1846 to death; C.B. 19 July 1838. *d.* London 21 July 1853.

DANSEY, REV. WILLIAM (*son of John Dansey of Blandford, Dorset*). *b.* Blandford 1792; ed. at Ex. coll. Ox., Stapledon scholar 1811–12; B.A. 1814, M.A. 1817, M.B. 1818; R. of Donhead, St. Andrew, Wilts. 1820 to death; preb. of Salisbury 10 Aug. 1841 to death; translated *Arrian on Coursing* 1831; edited *A brief account of the office of Dean Rural by J. Priaulx* 1832; author of *Horæ Decanicæ Rurales being an attempt to illustrate the name, title and functions of rural deans with remarks on the rise and fall of rural bishops 2 vols.* 1835, 2 ed. 1844. *d.* Weymouth 7 June 1856.

DANSON, GEORGE. *b.* Lancaster 4 June 1799; scene painter at theatres in London many years; exhibited 4 landscapes at R.A., 1 at B.I. and 6 at Suffolk st. gallery 1823–48; the following pictures by him were shown at Surrey Zoological gardens, Mount Vesuvius

DANSON, G. (Con.)

1837–8 reproduced 1846, Iceland and its volcanoes 1839, the City of Rome occupying 5 acres 1841 reproduced 1848, Temple of Ellora 1843, London and the great fire of 1666, 1844, Edinburgh 1845, storming of Badajoz 1849, Napoleon's passage of the Alps 1850. *d.* 711 Wandsworth road, London 23 Jany. 1881. *Daily Telegraph* 1 Feb. 1881 *p.* 5, *col.* 3.

DARBY, GEORGE (4 *son of John Darby of Markly, Sussex, who d.* 1834). *b.* 1798; ed. at Westminster and St. Cath. coll. Cam., B.A. 1820, M.A. 1823; barrister L.I. 22 Nov. 1821; M.P. for East Sussex 1 Aug. 1837 to Jany. 1846; an inclosure comr. for England and Wales 21 Aug. 1846 to 1852; a copyhold inclosure and tithe comr. 1852 to death. *d.* Down st. Piccadilly, London 16 Nov. 1877. *bur.* Markley 21 Nov.

DARBY, REV. JOHN NELSON (*brother of the preceding*). *b.* London 18 Nov. 1800; ed. at Westminster and Trin. coll. Dublin, gold medallist 1819, B.A. 1819; called to Irish bar about 1825; C. in Wicklow 1826–27; joined the 'Brethren' at Dublin 1827; worked in Switzerland 1838–40, many congregations of Darbyites were founded in cantons Vaud, Geneva and Bern; started a separate assembly at Plymouth 28 Dec. 1845, this division spread to Bristol, London and other places and Darbyism became established in England; travelled in America, New Zealand and West Indies; a most voluminous writer under his own name, his initials J. N. D., and anonymously. *d.* Bournemouth 29 April 1882. *Collected writings of J. N. Darby ed. by W. Kelly* 32 vols. 1867–83; *Herzog's Religious Encyclopœdia iii,* 1856–9, 2592–3 (1884); *Estéoule's Le Plymouthisme d'autrefois et le Darbyisme d'aujourd'hui* 1858; *A. N. Grove's Darbyism, its rise and development* 1866; *The close of 28 years association with J. N. D. by W. H. D.* 1866.

DARBY, JONATHAN GEORGE NORTON (*eld. son of George Darby* 1798–1877). *b.* 1829; ed. at Ch. Ch. Ox., B.A. 1851, M.A. 1854; barrister L.I. 9 June 1854; author with F. A. Bosanquet of *A practical treatise on the statutes of limitations in England and Ireland* 1867. *d.* 29 Westbourne park road, London 17 March 1870 in 41 year.

DARBY, JOSEPH. Second lieut. R.A. 1 July 1802, lieut.-col. 10 Jany. 1837 to 1 April 1844 when placed on retired full pay; general 1 Jany. 1868. *d.* Clifton 21 May 1869 aged 83.

DARBY-GRIFFITH, CHRISTOPHER. *b.* 1805; ed. at Eton and Ch. Ch. Ox., B.A. 1826; M.P. for Devizes 1857–68. *d.* Padworth house near Reading 19 March 1885.

D'ARCY, GEORGE ABBAS KOOLI. Ensign 94 foot 21 April 1837, adjutant 3 Aug. 1838 to 5 Jany. 1841, captain 9 Nov. 1846 to 6 July 1852; major 3 West India regiment 6 July 1852, lieut. col. 7 July 1854 to 7 May 1858 when he sold out; aide-de-camp to 5 successive governors of Bombay; governor and commander in chief of the Gambia, June 1859 to Jany. 1867 when presented with a sword of honour value £120; governor of the Falkland Islands 24 Feb. 1870 to 1876. *d.* 9 Leigham villas, Plymouth 22 Oct. 1885 aged 67.

DARELL, SIR HARRY FRANCIS COLVILLE, 3 Baronet. *b.* Lucknow 17 Nov. 1814; succeeded 13 April 1828; ensign 18 foot 1 June 1832; major 7 dragoon guards 3 Sep. 1847 to 27 June 1851 when placed on h.p. *d.* Cagliari, Sardinia 6 Jany. 1853.

DARGAN, WILLIAM (*son of Mr. Dargan of co. Carlow, farmer*). *b.* co. Carlow 28 Feb. 1799; employed by Thomas Telford in constructing Holyhead road 1820; contractor of the first railway in Ireland, from Dublin to Kingstown 1831, of the Ulster canal, of the Dublin and Drogheda railway, of the Great southern and western, and the Midland Great western; found the capital nearly £100,000 for the Irish exhibition 1853 and bore the deficit of £20,000; declined a baronetcy offered him at close of exhibition; the Irish national gallery on Leinster Lawn was erected as a monument to Dargan with a fine bronze statue of him. *d.* 2 Fitzwilliam sq. east, Dublin 7 Feb. 1867. *The Irish industrial exhibition of 1853 by J. Sproule* (1854) *ix-xiv, portrait; Irish tourist's illustrated handbook* (1853) *pp.* 12, 41, 148, *portrait.*

DARK, JAMES HENRY. *b.* Edgware road, London 24 May 1795; professional at Lord's cricket ground, Marylebone 1809–36; umpire in many great matches; purchased remainder of lease of the ground from Wm. Ward 1836, proprietor and manager of the ground 1836 to 1864 when he sold the 29½ years remainder of the lease to Marylebone club for £12,500; built a house 31 St. John's Wood road, overlooking the ground, and *d.* there 17 Oct. 1871. *bur.* Kensal Green 21 Oct. *Lillywhite's Cricket Scores i,* 350–51 (1862), *v, pp. xiii, xxii,* (1876).

DARLEY, EDWARD. Ensign 49 foot 29 Nov. 1791; major 58 foot 18 Sep. 1817 to 5 July 1831 when placed on h.p.; lieut. col. 61 foot 24 Aug. 1832 to 28 June 1838; granted distinguished service reward 1 Jany. 1843 ; L.G. 11 Nov. 1851. *d.* 24 North bank, Regent's park, London 24 March 1854 aged 78.

DARLEY, RIGHT REV. JOHN RICHARD (2 *son of Richard Darley of Fairfield, co. Monaghan*). *b.* Fairfield, Nov. 1799 ; ed. at Dungannon and Trin. coll. Dublin, foundation scholar 1819, B.A. 1820, M.A. 1827, B.D. and D.D. 1875 ; master of Dundalk gr. sch. 1826, of royal school of Dungannon 1831 ; R. of Drumgoon 1850 ; R. of Templemichael 1866 ; archdeacon of Ardagh 7 Nov. 1866 ; bishop of Kilmore, Elphin and Ardagh 23 Sep. 1874 to death ; consecrated in Armagh cathedral 25 Oct. 1874 ; author of *The Grecian drama, a treatise on the dramatic literature of the Greeks* 1840 ; *A treatise on Homer with questions* 1848. *d.* The Palace, Kilmore 20 Jany. 1884.

DARLEY, WILLIAM WALLACE. Second lieut. R.A. 16 Dec. 1816, lieut. col. 4 April 1851 to 22 April 1853 when retired on full pay ; L.G. 7 Feb. 1870. *d.* Ventnor, Isle of Wight 23 Nov. 1874.

DARLING, SIR CHARLES HENRY (*eld. son of Henry Charles Darling, governor of Barbados, who d.* 1845). *b.* Annapolis Royal, Nova Scotia 1809 ; ensign 57 foot 27 April 1827, lieut. 29 Sep. 1830 to 30 Oct. 1838 when placed on h.p., retired 1841 ; lieut. governor of island of St. Lucia 21 Dec. 1847, of Cape of Good Hope 1851, of Newfoundland, May 1855 ; captain general and governor in chief of Jamaica, Feb. 1857 ; governor of Victoria 11 Sep. 1863 to April 1866 ; K.C.B. 23 July 1862. *d.* 7 Lansdowne terrace, Cheltenham 25 Jany. 1870.

DARLING, GEORGE. *b.* Stow near Galashiels ; ed. at Univ. of Edin. ; M.D. Aberdeen 1 April 1815 ; L.R.C.P. 22 Dec. 1819 ; practised at Russell square, London 1820 to death ; much employed by artists ; author of *An essay on medical economy* 1814 anon. ; *Instructions for making unfermented bread* 1846 anon. 17 ed. 1851. *d.* Russell sq. London 30 April 1862 in 80 year.

DARLING, JAMES. *b.* Edinburgh 1797 ; apprenticed to Adam Black the publisher 1809–18 ; bookseller at 22 Little Queen st. Holborn, London 1825 to death, and at 81 Great Queen st. 1854 to death ; commenced a library for use of theological students Jany. 1840 named at first the Clerical library, afterwards the Metropolitan library ; compiled and published *Bibliotheca Clericalis* 1843 ; *Cyclopædia Bibliographica or library of theological and general literature* 2 vols. 1854–59. *d.* Fortess terrace west, Kentish Town, London 2 March 1862.

DARLING, JOHN (*younger son of George Darling, M.D. of Russell sq. London*). *b.* 16 Aug. 1821 ; ed. at Univ. coll. London, Charterhouse and Ch. Ch. Ox. ; barrister I.T. 1 May 1846 ; author of *An examination of the scriptural grounds on which the prohibition against marriage with a deceased wife's sister is based* 1849 ; *A treatise on the administration of trust funds under the Trustee Relief Act* 1855. *d.* Thornbury house, Ryde, Isle of Wight 27 Sep. 1858.

DARLING, SIR RALPH (*son of Christopher Darling, adjutant 45 foot*). *b.* 1775 ; ensign 45 foot 15 May 1793 ; lieut.-col. 69 foot 17 July 1801 to 8 May 1806 ; lieut.-col. 51 foot 8 May 1806 to 4 June 1813 ; deputy adjutant general at the Horse Guards 1814–18 ; commanded troops in Mauritius 1818–23 ; col. 90 foot 9 Oct. 1823 to 26 Sep. 1837 ; governor in chief of New South Wales 19 Dec. 1825 to 21 Oct. 1831 ; col. 41 foot 26 Sep. 1837 to 5 Feb. 1848 ; general 23 Nov. 1841 ; col. 69 foot 5 Feb. 1848 to death ; G.C.H. 2 Sep. 1835. *d.* Brunswick sq. Brighton 2 April 1858. *Braim's History of New South Wales i,* 53–74 (1876).

DARLING, WILLIAM. *b.* Belford 7 Feb. 1786 ; lighthouse keeper at the Longstone or Outer Farn or Faroe island 1815 to Dec. 1860 when he retired on full pay ; went out to the wreck of the steamboat Forfarshire (with his daughter Grace Darling 1815–43) and rescued the 9 survivors of the crew 7 Sep. 1838, the boat in which they went out was on view during the summer of 1883 at the Fisheries Exhibition, South Kensington, and on 9 Nov. it was carried through the streets of London in the Lord Mayor's show. *d.* The Wynding house, Bamburgh 28 May 1865. *Journal of W. Darling 1795–1860,* (1886) ; *I.L.N. xlvi,* 553 (1865).

DARLING, WILLIAM. *b.* Demse, Scotland ; ed. at Univ. of Edin. ; studied and taught anatomy in New York 1830–42 ; M.D. New York 1842 ; M.R.C.S. 1856, F.R.C.S. 1866 ; studied in London and Paris 1856–66 ; professor of anatomy in Univ. of New York 1867 ; censor of New York college of Veterinary surgeons 1868 ; professor of anatomy in Univ. of Vermont 1873 ; author of *Anatomography or graphic anatomy* 1879 ; author with A. L. Renney of *Essentials of anatomy* 1880. *d.* Univ. of New York 25 Dec. 1884 aged 82.

DARLING, WILLIAM LINDSAY. Ensign 99 foot 13 Dec. 1801 ; captain 51 foot 18 April 1811 to 1814 ; col. 98 foot 17 April 1854 to death ; general 15 Dec. 1861. *d.* Strote house near Chepstow 8 Oct. 1863.

DARNELL, GEORGE. Established and conducted a large day school at Islington, London; started *Darnell's Copybooks* about 1840 when he introduced plan of giving a line of copy in pale ink to be first written over by the pupil then to be imitated by him in the next line, the copy being thus always under his eye; author of *Short and certain road to reading* 1845; *Grammar made intelligible to children* 1846; *Reading lessons 6 numbers* 1855; *Arithmetic made intelligible to children* 1855, all of which had a great sale. *d.* 70 Gibson sq. Islington 26 Feb. 1857 aged 58.

DARNELL, REV. WILLIAM NICHOLAS (*son of Wm. Darnell of Newcastle, wine merchant*). *b.* Newcastle 14 March 1776; ed. at Newcastle gr. sch. and C.C. coll. Ox., Durham scholar, fellow, tutor; B.A. 1796, M.A. 1800, B.D. 1808; R. of St. Mary-le-bow, Durham 1809–15; V. of Stockton 1815–20; V. of Lastingham, Yorkshire 1815–28; preb. of ninth stall in Durham cath. 12 Jany. 1816, of sixth stall 12 Oct. 1820 to 1831; Inc. of St. Margaret's, Durham 1820–27; V. of Norham, co. Durham 1827–31; R. of Stanhope, co. Durham 1831 to death, a living worth £6000 a year; author of *Sermons* 1816; *The correspondence of Isaac Basire with a memoir* 1831; *An arrangement and classification of the Psalms, with a view to render them more useful for private devotion* 1839, and of sermons, charges and other works *d.* Stanhope rectory 19 June 1865. *bur.* Durham cathedral churchyard 24 June.

DART, JOSEPH. Deputy sec. H.E.I. Co. 1814, sec. 1818–29. *d.* Budleigh Salterton, Devon 29 Nov. 1866 aged 93.

DART, JOSEPH HENRY (*eld. son of the preceding*). *b.* India house, Leadenhall st. London 1817; ed. at Ex. coll. Ox., Newdigate prizeman for his poem *The Exile of St. Helena* 1838; B.A. 1838, M.A. 1841; barrister L.I. 28 Jany. 1841, bencher Feb. 1885; one of the six conveyancing counsel to Court of Chancery 1860; senior conveyancing counsel to high court of justice 1875–86; a verderer of New Forest 1877; author of *A compendium of the law and practice of vendors and purchasers of real estate* 1851, 6 ed. 2 vols. 1888; *The Iliad of Homer in English hexameter verse* 1862. *d.* Beech house, Ringwood, Hants. 27 June 1887. *Law Journal xxii*, 373, 381 (1887).

DARTMOUTH, WILLIAM LEGGE, 4 Earl of (*eld. son of 3 Earl of Dartmouth 1755–1810*). *b.* in parish of St. George, Hanover sq. London 29 Nov. 1784; ed. at Ch. Ch. Ox., B.A. 1805,

DARTMOUTH, Earl of (*Con.*)
D.C.L. 1834; succeeded his father 1 Nov. 1810; colonel of Staffordshire militia 15 April 1812 to death; F.R.S. 7 Nov. 1822. *d.* Patshull near Wolverhampton 22 Nov. 1853.

DARUSMONT, FRANCES, known as Fanny Wright (*dau. of Mr. Wright of Dundee, merchant, who d. 1798*). *b.* Miln's buildings, Nethergate, Dundee 6 Sep. 1795; brought up in England by her aunt; spent two years in the U.S. 1818–20; produced a tragedy 'Altorf' in New York 19 Feb. 1819; lived in Paris 1821–24; purchased 2000 acres of land on the river Nashoba in Tennessee and settled negro slaves upon it 1824, this experiment failed and the slaves were liberated and sent to Hayti; joined Robert D. Owen in his socialistic scheme at New Harmony, Indiana and edited the *New Harmony Gazette*; lectured in chief cities of U.S. on social questions 1829–30 and 1833–36, these lectures led to the formation of Fanny Wright Societies; one of the first advocates of female suffrage; author of *Views of society and manners in America* 1821; *A few days in Athens* 1822. (*m.* 1838 Phiquepal-Darusmont a French reformer, from whom she separated). *d.* Cincinnati, Ohio 14 Dec. 1852. *R. D. Owen's Threading my way* (1873) 264–72; *Mrs. Trollope's Domestic manners of the Americans* (1831) i, 96–100, ii, 76–77; *S. J. Hale's Woman's Record, 2 ed.* (1855) p. 842.

DARVALL, EDWARD. Ensign 57 Bengal N.I. 1 May 1823; lieut. col. Bengal staff corps 12 Sep. 1866 to 1 Oct. 1877 when placed on retired list; general 1 Oct. 1877. *d.* Acton place, Suffolk 20 Oct. 1885 in 80 year.

DARVALL, SIR JOHN BAYLEY (*son of Edward Darvall, captain 9 dragoons*). Ed. at Eton and Trin. coll. Cam., B.A. 1833, M.A. 1837; barrister M.T. 23 Nov. 1838, admitted to bar of N.S.W. 16 Sep. 1839; practised at Sydney, N.S.W. 1839–67; Q.C. 1853; member of senate of Univ. of Sydney 1850–67; solicitor general N.S.W. 1856–7, attorney general 1857–67; C.M.G. 23 June 1869, K.C.M.G. 30 May 1877. *d.* 23 Upper Wimpole st. Cavendish sq. London 28 Dec. 1883.

DARVILL, SIR HENRY (*eld. son of John Darvill*). *b.* 1812; solicitor at Windsor 1834 to death; mayor of Windsor 1853, town clerk 1854 to death; registrar of Windsor county court; knighted at Osborne 20 April 1883. *d.* Chirbury, Shropshire 30 Sep. 1883. *bur.* Windsor cemetery 5 Oct.

DARWIN, CHARLES ROBERT (5 child of Robert Waring Darwin of Shrewsbury, physician 1766–1848). b. The Mount, Shrewsbury 12 Feb. 1809; ed. at Shrewsbury, Univ. of Edin. and Christ's coll. Cam.; B.A. Cam. 1832, M.A. 1837, hon. LL.D. 1877; naturalist to the Beagle on her surveying voyage round the world Dec. 1831 to Oct. 1836; F.G.S., sec. 1838–41; lived at 12 Gower st. London 1839–42, at Down near Beckenham, Kent 1842 to death; F.R.S. 24 Jany. 1839, royal medallist 1853, Copley medallist 1864; author of Narrative of the surveying voyages of H.M.S. Adventure and Beagle, vol. 3, entitled Journal and Remarks; Geology of the voyage of the Beagle 3 parts 1842–46; On the origin of species by means of natural selection, or the preservation of favoured races in the struggle for life 1859; The descent of man and selection in relation to sex 1871, and other books. d. Down 19 April 1882. bur. Westminster Abbey 26 April, statue of him by J. Boehm, R.A. placed in Natural history museum, South Kensington 1885. Life and letters of C. Darwin edited by his son F. Darwin 3 vols. 1887, portrait; Charles Darwin, Nature series 1882; Illust. Review ii, 289–91 (1871), portrait; Nature x, 79 (1874), portrait; The Examiner 11 Oct. and 12 Nov. 1879, 2 portraits.

DARWIN, SIR FRANCIS SACHEVERELL (2 son of Erasmus Darwin of Derby, M.D., F.R.S. 1731–1802). b. parish of All Saints, Derby 17 June 1786; ed. at Repton and Emm. coll. Cam.; M.D. Edin.; physician at Lichfield; knighted by George iv at Carlton house 10 May 1820 on presenting an address from city of Lichfield. d. Breadsall priory near Derby 6 Nov. 1859. Proc. of Med. and Chir. Soc. iii, 195 (1861).

DASENT, JOHN BURY (eld. son of John Roche Dasent, attorney general of St. Vincent). b. 22 Dec. 1806; ed. at Westminster school and Trin. hall, Cam., LL.B. 1830; barrister M.T. 19 April 1833; judge of Bow and Shoreditch county courts (circuit No. 40) 2 Oct. 1858 to Jany. 1884 when he retired on a pension. d. 15 Warwick road, Maida hill, London 7 April 1888.

DASHWOOD, REV. GEORGE HENRY (son of Rev. James Dashwood, R. of Doddington, Isle of Ely). b. Downham Market, Norfolk 21 Oct. 1801; ed. at Linc. coll. Ox., B.A. 1824, M.A. 1825; C. of Stow Bardolph, Norfolk 1840, Vicar 1852 to death; F.S.A. 6 June 1844; printed at his private press Vice-Comites Norfolciæ, or sheriffs of Norfolk from the first year of Henry the Second to the fourth of Queen Victoria 1844; author of Sigilla Antiqua 1847, and of many papers in the Norfolk and Norwich

Archæological Society's Norfolk Archæology vols. 1–5. d. Quebec house, East Dereham, Norfolk 9 Feb. 1869. Register and mag. of biog. i, 310–12 (1869).

DASHWOOD, WILLIAM BATEMAN. b. 1 Sep. 1790; entered navy 3 Aug. 1799; lost his right arm in action 29 Nov. 1811; granted pension for wounds 4 April 1816; captain 21 Oct. 1818, retired 1 Oct. 1846; retired admiral 22 April 1862. d. suddenly at Geneva 9 May 1869.

DAUBENY, CHARLES GILES BRIDLE (3 son of Rev. James Daubeny, R. of Stratton, Gloucs. who d. 9 Feb. 1817). b. Stratton 11 Feb. 1795; ed. at Winchester and Magd. coll. Ox., demy 1810, lay fellow 1815 to death, bursar 1828, vice pres. 1830; B.A. 1814, M.A. 1817, B.M. 1818, M.D. 1821; M.D. Dublin 1835; Aldrichian professor of chemistry at Oxford, Oct. 1822–1855, professor of botany there 1834 to death, professor of rural economy 1840 to death; physician to Radcliffe infirmary 1826–30; pres. of British Association at Cheltenham 1856; F.R.S. 19 Dec. 1822; author of A description of active and extinct volcanoes 1826, 2 ed. 1848; An introduction to the atomic theory 1831, 2 ed. 1850; Lectures on Roman husbandry 1857; Lectures on Climate 1863; Miscellanies on scientific and literary subjects 2 vols. 1867. d. Botanic gardens, Oxford at 12.5 a.m. 13 Dec. 1867. Proc. of Royal Society xvii, 74–80 (1869); Quarterly Journal of Geological society xxiv, 33–36 (1868).

DAUBENY, HENRY. Ensign 84 foot 8 July 1795, lieut. col. 11 Dec. 1813 to 21 Nov. 1822 when placed on h.p.; col. 80 foot 31 Jany. 1850 to death; L.G. 11 Nov. 1851; K.H. 1832; edited C. Daubeny's Guide to the Church 1830. d. Rome 10 April 1853.

DAUBENY, HENRY. b. 1820; M.R.C.S. 1843; M.D. St. Andrews 1845; L.S.A. 1846; surgeon in London 1843–61, at San Remo, Italy 1861 to death; author of The climate of San Remo as adapted to invalids 1865. d. Hôtel des Iles Britanniques, San Remo 26 Jany. 1887.

DAUGARS, JOHN WILLIAM GUSTAVUS LEO (only son of Rev. Guillaume Gustavus Daugars, pastor of French protestant church, St. Martin's le Grand, London). b. Thurlow sq. Brompton, London 1849; ed. at Harrow and Brasenose coll. Ox., migrated to St. Alban hall, B.A. 1873; barrister M.T. 26 Jany. 1875; contributed to Temple Bar, The Graphic and other publications under nom de plume of Claude Templar. d. Hastings 20 Feb. 1885 in 36 year.

DAUGLISH, JOHN (*son of Wm. Dauglish of Bethnal Green, London, clerk in a large East India house*). *b.* Bethnal Green 10 Feb. 1824; ed. at Hackney; studied medicine at Univ. of Edin. 1852–55, bracketted gold medallist for his M.D. degree 1855; took out a patent for "An improved method of making bread" 1 Oct. 1856 and 4 other patents on same subject 1857–65, this unfermented bread which he called aerated was first made in factory of Messrs. Carr of Carlisle 1856; erected a model bakery at Islington 1859; silver medallist of Society of Arts 1860; bread sold in special shops in London and the provinces. *d.* Furze bank, Great Malvern 14 Jany. 1866. *On the healthy manufacture of bread by B. W. Richardson 1884, portrait; I.L.N. xxxvi, 259–60 (1860).*

DAUNT, VERY REV. ACHILLES (*eld. son of Achilles Daunt of Tracton abbey, co. Cork, who d. 28 Aug. 1871*). *b.* Rincurran near Kinsale 23 Aug. 1832; ed. at Kinsale and Univ. of Dublin, scholar 1852, B.A. 1854, M.A. 1866; V. of Rincurran 26 March 1856 to 11 Jany. 1867; R. of Ballymoney, co. Cork 1867; R. of Stackallen, co. Meath 1867; V. of St. Matthias, Dublin, Aug. 1867; dean of Cork and R. of St. Finbar, Cork 1875 to death; author of *The Church a lesson book for angels* 1872; *The person and offices of the Holy Ghost* 1879; *The morning of life and other gleanings from the manuscripts of the late A. Daunt* 1881. *d.* St. Anne's, Blarney near Cork 17 June 1878. *Spent in the service, a memoir of the Very Rev. Achilles Daunt by Rev. F. R. Wynne 1879, portrait; Some account of the family of Daunt by John Daunt (1881) 25–28, portrait.*

DAVENPORT, EDWARD GERSHOM. *b.* 1838; M.P. for St. Ives, Cornwall 5 Feb. 1874 to death. *d.* 28 Lancaster gate, Hyde park, London 4 Dec. 1874.

DAVENPORT, JOHN MARRIOTT. *b.* Shirburn, Oxon, Sep. 1809; solicitor at Oxford 1831 to death; clerk of the peace for co. Oxon 1831–81, undersheriff 1853–75; F.S.A. 9 March 1854; privilegiatus Univ. of Ox. 3 Nov. 1866; author of *Lords lieutenant and high sheriffs of Oxfordshire 1086–1868, 1868; Oxfordshire Annals 1869; Lord lieutenant and high sheriff, correspondence upon the question of precedence 1871; Notes upon the jurisdiction of the county justices within the city of Oxford 1872; Notes as to Oxford Castle 1877. d.* 62 St. Giles's, Oxford 31 Jany. 1882.

DAVENPORT, RICHARD ALFRED. *b.* about 1777; author of *New elegant extracts, 2nd series 12 vols.* 1823–7; wrote some of the biographical notices and critical prefaces to

DAVENPORT, R. A. (*Con.*)
Whittingham's *British poets* 100 vols. 1822; edited more than 100 vols. of miscellaneous works including the *Poetical Register* 8 vols. 1802–11. *d.* from inadvertently taking an overdose of opium at Brunswick cottage, Park st. Camberwell, London 25 Jany. 1852.

DAVENPORT, SAMUEL (*son of Mr. Davenport of Bedford, architect*). *b.* Bedford 10 Dec. 1783; articled to Charles Warren of London, line engraver; engraved in outline a large number of portraits for biographical works; engraved *The works of W. Hogarth* 1821; his best plates are in the *Forget-me-not* 1828–42; one of the earliest engravers on steel. *d.* 15 July 1867.

DAVEY, RICHARD (*youngest son of Wm. Davey of Redruth, Cornwall, solicitor, who d. 16 April 1849*). *b.* Redruth 11 Dec. 1799; ed. at Tiverton and Univ. of Edin.; M.P. for West Cornwall 1857–68. *d.* Bochym near Helston 24 June 1884. *I.L.N. xxxiii, 92, 94 (1858), portrait.*

DAVIDS, REV. THOMAS WILLIAM (*only child of William Saunders Davids of Swansea, Congregational minister, who d. Dec. 1816*). *b.* Swansea 11 Sep. 1816; minister of Congregational church, Lion walk, Colchester 3 Feb. 1841 to 1874; secretary of Essex congregational union 20 years; author of *Annals of Evangelical Nonconformity in the county of Essex from the time of Wycliffe to the restoration* 1863, and of a number of historical articles and reviews. (*m.* 1841 Louisa eld. dau. of Robert Winter of Clapham Common, London, solicitor, she was widely known by her *Essay on Sunday schools* 1847 and *Sunday school hymn book*, she *d.* Colchester 18 Nov. 1853 aged 37), he *d.* Forest Gate, Essex 11 April 1884. *Congregational year book (1885) 187–8.*

DAVIDSON, REV. ALEXANDER DYCE. *b.* Aberdeen 8 May 1807; ed. at Aberdeen Univ.; minister of the South ch. Aberdeen 3 Aug. 1832, of the West ch. 5 May 1836, of Free ch. Belmont st. 28 Jany. 1844, of a new Free ch. in Union st. 14 Feb. 1869 to death; author of *Lectures on the book of Esther* 1859; *Lectures and sermons edited by F. Edmond* 1872. *d.* Aberdeen 27 April 1872. *Wylies' Disruption Worthies (1881) 211–14.*

DAVIDSON, ARCHIBALD (*son of Rev. T. Davidson of the Tolbooth church, Edinburgh*). *b.* 1805; ed. at high sch. Edin. and Univs. of Glasgow and St. Andrews; called to Scotch bar 1827; senior advocate depute 1846; sheriff of Kincardine 1847, of Aberdeen 10 Jany. 1848, of Edinburgh 10 Oct. 1865, of the Lothians and

DAVIDSON, A. *(Con.)*

Peebles to Feb. 1886; arranged for publication Lord Cockburn's *Memorials of his time* 1856. *d.* Edinburgh 27 March 1886.

DAVIDSON, CUTHBERT. Entered Bengal army 1827; lieut. col. 49 Bengal N.I. 31 May 1857 to 1860; lieut. col. 51 Bengal N.I. 1860 to death; C.B. 18 May 1860. *d.* 2 Aug. 1862.

DAVIDSON, DUNCAN. *b.* 1800; M.P. for co. Cromarty 30 June 1826 to 24 July 1830 and 20 May 1831 to 3 Dec. 1832; lord lieutenant of co. Ross 18 Feb. 1879 to death; married five times. *d.* Edinburgh 18 Sep. 1881.

DAVIDSON, ELLIS A. Author of *Linear Drawing* 1868; *Drawing and design without instruments* 1869; *Elements of practical perspective* 1870; *Model drawing from solid forms* 1871; *Boy joiner and model maker* 1874; *House painting and graining* 1875, 3 ed. 1880; *Amateur house carpenter* 1875 and many other books. *d.* 29 Clarendon gardens, Maida hill, London 9 March 1878.

DAVIDSON, GEORGE HENRY. Music publisher at 19 Peters hill, Doctors Commons, London; published *Universal Melodist* 2 vols. 1847–9; *Instrumental Gems* 4 vols. 1851; *Davidson's Recitations and Comic songs* 1854; sold his business to the Music publishing company limited for £20,000, 1860; author of *The Thames and Thanet Guide* 1838, 6 ed. 1850. *d.* 26 Clifton road, Peckham 4 July 1875 in 75 year.

DAVIDSON, HARRIET (2 *child of Hugh Miller the geologist* 1802–56). *b.* Cromarty, Scotland 25 Nov. 1839; ed. at Edin. and London; author of *Isabel Jardine's History* 1867; *Christian Osborne's Friends* 1869; contributed poems and stories to the Adelaide newspapers and to *Chambers's Journal*. (*m.* 1863 Rev. John Davidson, minister of Chalmer's church, Adelaide, who *d.* 1881). *d.* Adelaide 23 Dec. 1883.

DAVIDSON, JAMES (*eld. son of James Davidson of Tower Hill, London, stationer*). *b.* Tower Hill 15 Aug. 1793; lived at Secktor near Axminster, Devon 1822 to death; author of *The British and Roman remains in the vicinity of Axminster* 1833; *History of Axminster church* 1835; *History of Newenham Abbey, Devon* 1843; *Axminster during the civil war* 1851; *A glossary to the obsolete and unused words and phrases of the Holy Scriptures in the authorised English version* 1850; *Bibliotheca Devoniensis, a catalogue of printed books relating to the county of Devon* 1852 *and Supplement* 1862; *Notes on the antiquities of Devonshire* 1861. *d.* Secktor house, Axminster 29 Feb. 1864. *G. P. R. Pulman's book of the Axe* (1875) 12, 47, 677.

DAVIDSON, JOHN. *b.* Old Meldrum, Aberdeenshire 29 March 1804; ed. at Marischal coll. Aberdeen; transcriber for the Spalding Club 20 years; arranged the Burgh records of Dundee 1865; wrote a number of pamphlets on various political subjects; a small vol. containing many poems and prose pieces by him was published at Aberdeen 1872. *d.* 28 Sep. 1871.

DAVIDSON, JOHN. L.R.C.S. Edin. 1838; surgeon in the navy 29 July 1839; M.D. St. Andrews 1845; M.R.C.P. 1860; inspector general of hospitals 4 July 1866 to 26 Oct. 1874 when he retired; C.B. 13 March 1867. *d.* Bosworth lodge, Willesden lane, London 31 Jany. 1881 aged 63.

DAVIDSON, THOMAS (*son of Jonah Davidson of Oxnam Row farm near Jedburgh, shepherd*). *b.* Oxnam Row 7 July 1838; entered Univ. of Edin. 1855; schoolmaster at Forres 1860–61, in Edinburgh 1861; licensed as a preacher in united presbyterian church 2 Feb. 1864; obtained second prize in rhetoric class for a poem on 'Ariadne at Naxos' 1859, one of his friends sent this poem to Thackeray who inserted it in *Cornhill Mag.* Dec. 1860; sent songs and short poems to the '*Scotsman*.' *d.* Bankend, Jedburgh 29 April 1870. *The life of a Scottish probationer, being a memoir of Thomas Davidson by James Brown* (1878), *portrait*.

DAVIDSON, THOMAS. *b.* Nottingham 28 Aug. 1828; went to Philadelphia 1832, ship builder there 1850–61; quartermaster in Philadelphia navy yard 1861, assistant naval constructor 1863, naval constructor 1866 to death; his greatest feat was the building in 70 days of the "Juanita" (1240 tons 7 guns) from the frame of a Florida frigate; executed the models and drawings for first large torpedo boats built in New York. *d.* Philadelphia 18 Feb. 1874.

DAVIDSON, THOMAS. *b.* Edinburgh 17 May 1817; ed. in France, Italy and Switzerland; pupil of P. Delaroche and H. Vernet; matric. at Univ. of Edin. 1835; hon. sec. of Geol. Soc. 1858, Wollaston gold medallist 1865, Silurian medallist 1868; F.R.S. 11 June 1857, royal medallist 1870; author of *British Fossil Brachiopoda* 6 vols. and of the article 'Brachiopoda' in 9th ed. of Encyclopædia Britannica. *d.* 16 Oct. 1885. *Proc. of Royal Soc. xxxix*, 8–11 (1886).

DAVIE, JAMES. Violinist and composer at Aberdeen; published *The music of the church of Scotland* 1841; *Caledonian Repository* 6 *vols.*; established the Aberdeen Choral Society which held a Musical Festival 1834; choir master in

DAVIE, J. (Con.)

St. Andrew's ch. Aberdeen about 1835. *d.* Aberdeen 19 Nov. 1857 aged 74. *W. Anderson's Precentors and musical professors* (1876) 85–94.

DAVIES, REV. BENJAMIN. *b.* Werne near St. Clears, Carmarthenshire 26 Feb. 1814; ed. at Baptist college, Bristol, Univ. of Glasgow, Trin. coll. Dublin and Leipzig; Ph. D. Leipzig 1838; pres. of Baptist coll. Stepney 1844–7; a professor in Mac Gill coll. Montreal 1847–57; professor of oriental and classical languages in Baptist coll. Regents park, London 1857; one of the revisers of the Old Testament; published translations of Gesenius's Hebrew Grammar and Lexicon; the Paragraph Bible issued by Religious Tract Society was chiefly his work. *d.* Frome, Somerset 19 July 1875.

DAVIES, DAVID. Ensign 62 foot 4 June 1812, lieut. 13 Feb. 1814 to 25 June 1816 when placed on h.p.; fired a pistol loaded with ball at Lord Palmerston (the sec. of state for war) at the War Office, London 8 April 1818, tried at the Old Bailey 1 May 1818 when acquitted on ground of insanity; confined in Bethlehem hospital, May 1818 to death. *d.* of apoplexy in Bethlehem hospital 30 Dec. 1861 aged 67.

DAVIES, SIR DAVID *(only son of Robert Davies of Llwyn, Cardiganshire).* *b.* 1793; physician at Hampton; domestic phys. to William iv, 1830 to 1837, and to Queen Adelaide 1837 to 1849; K.C.H. June 1837; knighted by Queen Victoria at St. James's palace 19 July 1837. *d.* Lucca 1 May 1865.

DAVIES, DAVID ARTHUR SAUNDERS. *b.* 9 June 1792; M.P. for Carmarthenshire 27 Dec. 1842 to death; chairman of Cardiganshire quarter sessions. *d.* United University club, 4 Pall Mall, East London 22 May 1857.

DAVIES, DAVID CHRISTOPHER. *b.* Oswestry 1827; a mining engineer 1852; visited Norway on business 9 times; F.G.S. 1872; contributed numerous papers to *Geological Mag.*; author of *Christ for all the ages and other lay sermons* 1871; *Treatise on slate and slate quarrying* 1878, 2 ed. 1880; *Metalliferous minerals and mining,* 2 ed. 1880; *Treatise on earthy and other minerals and mining* 1884. *d.* suddenly on board the steamer Angelo while returning from Norway to Hull 19 Sep. 1885. *Quarterly Journal of Geol. Soc. xlii,* 43 (1886).

DAVIES, REV. EVAN. *b.* Hengwm, Lledrod, county of Cardiganshire 1805; ordained at Wycliffe Congregational chapel, London as a missionary to the Chinese 1835; sent to

DAVIES, REV. E. (Con.)

Penang by London Missionary Soc. 1835, returned home 1839; superintendent of Boys' Mission school at Walthamstow 1842–44; pastor at Richmond, Surrey 1844–57; author of *China and her spiritual claims* 1845; *Memoirs of the Rev. Samuel Dyer* 1846; *Revivals in Wales* 1859. *d.* Llanstephan near Carmarthen 18 June 1864.

DAVIES, EVAN. Watchmaker at Pontypridd; known as Myfyr Morganwg, Arch-Druid of Wales, recognized head of the Druids who meet periodically around famous rocking stone at Pontypridd; published several works on Druidism which he argued was the true religion, and several others on Celtic mythology. *d.* Pontypridd 23 Feb. 1888 in 89 year.

DAVIES, FRANCIS JOHN *(youngest son of Thomas Davies of New house, co. Hereford 1751–92, advocate general Calcutta).* *b.* 1 May 1791; ensign 52 foot 3 Feb. 1808; captain Grenadier guards 30 April 1827 to 18 May 1841 when placed on h.p.; col. of 67 foot 15 Jany. 1858 to death; general 14 Jany. 1866. *d.* 8 Eaton place, London 4 Dec. 1874.

DAVIES, GEORGE. *b.* Wells 15 Dec. 1800; entered navy 23 June 1813; inspecting commander in coast guard of Banff district, July 1843, of Penzance district 3 July 1848 to 1 Jany. 1851; captain 1 Jany. 1851; saved the lives of more than 200 persons at shipwrecks; retired V.A. 29 May 1873; chief constable of Cambridgeshire, Nov. 1851 to death, and of Hunts. April 1857 to death. *d.* 10 Scrope terrace, Cambridge 24 Nov. 1876. *O'Byrne's Naval biog. dict.* (1861) 281–2; *I.L.N. xviii,* 61–2 (1851).

DAVIES, GRIFFITH *(son of Owen Davies, farmer, who d. 21 March 1854 aged 93).* *b.* parish of Llandwrog, Carnarvon 28 Dec. 1788; kept a school in London 1811; actuary to Guardian Assurance Co. 1823 to death; constructed many tables for the Reversionary Interest Soc. 1823; F.R.S. 16 June 1831; wrote 20 reports on the various Indian funds for the H.E.I.Co.; author of *Key to Bonnycastle's Trigonometry* 1814; *Tables of life contingencies containing the rates of mortality among the members of the Equitable Society* 1825. *d.* 25 Duncan terrace, Islington, London 21 March 1855. *Assurance Mag.* July 1855 pp. 337–48; *C. Walford's Insurance Cyclopædia ii,* 172–4; *Pink's Clerkenwell* (1881) 705–8.

DAVIES, HENRY. *b.* London 1782; M.R.C.S. 1803; served in army medical service; M.D. Aberdeen 26 Sep. 1823; L.R.C.P. 22 Dec.

DAVIES, H. (Con.)

1823; phys. to British Lying-in hospital; lecturer on midwifery at St. George's hospital; edited M. Underwood's *Treatise on the diseases of children* 1846; author of *The young wife's guide* 1852. *d.* London 9 Jany. 1862.

DAVIES, HENRY THOMAS. Entered navy 3 March 1794; captain 19 Feb. 1814; retired captain 1 Oct. 1846; retired admiral 11 Feb. 1861. *d.* Bath 21 Feb. 1869 aged 91.

DAVIES, HERBERT (*son of Thomas Davies of London, physician* 1792–1839). *b.* London 30 Sep. 1818; scholar of Gonville and Caius coll. Cam. 1838, migrated to Queen's coll.; 31 wrangler 1842; B.A. 1842, M.B. 1843, M.D. 1848; fellow of Queen's coll. 1844; assistant phys. to London hospital 5 Aug. 1845, phys. 1854–74; F.R.C.P. 1850; phys. to Bank of England; author of *Lectures on the physical diagnosis of the diseases of the lungs and heart* 1851, 2 *ed.* 1854, translated into German and Dutch; *On the treatment of rheumatic fever in its acute stage exclusively by free blistering* 1864. *d.* Hampstead 4 Jany. 1885. *Medical Circular iii,* 439 (1853), *portrait.*

DAVIES, REV. JAMES (2 *son of Richard Banks of Kington, Herefordshire*). *b.* Kington 20 May 1820; ed. at Repton and Lincoln coll. Ox., scholar; B.A. 1844, M.A. 1846; Inc. of Ch. Ch. Forest of Dean 1847–52; head master of Ludlow gr. sch. 1852–57; took name of Davies in lieu of Banks 1858; wrote majority of classical articles in *Saturday Review* many years; author of a remarkable essay on 'Epigrams' in *Quarterly Review* Jany. 1865; translated Hesiod, Theognis and Callimachus into prose for Bohn's Classical library; wrote vols. on Hesiod and Theognis and on Catullus, Tibullus and Propertius for Collins's Ancient Classics for English readers; revised several of Murray's Guides for the press; author of a vol. of original verse entitled *Nugæ* 1854. *d.* Moor Court, Kington 11 March 1883.

DAVIES, REV. JOHN. Educ. at Queen's coll. Cam., B.D. 1831, D.D. 1844; R. of Gateshead 1840 to death; hon. canon of Durham, Feb. 1853 to death; author of *An estimate of the human mind, a philosophical inquiry into the legitimate application and extent of its leading faculties* 1828; *The ordinances of religion practically illustrated and applied* 1832, and about 20 other works. *d.* Ilkley Wells, Yorkshire 21 Oct. 1861.

DAVIES, LUCY CLEMENTINA (*youngest child of Leon Maurice called by courtesy Lord Leon*

DAVIES, L. C. (Con.)

Maurice Drummond de Melfort 1761–1826). *b.* Château of St. Germain near Paris 21 Nov. 1795; granted precedency of an Earl's daughter by r.l. 30 Sep. 1853; author of *Recollections of society in France and England* 2 *vols.* 1872, a work which contains much of her family history. (*m.* 8 Sep. 1823 Francis Henry Davies a registrar of Court of Chancery, who *d.* 22 Oct. 1863 aged 72). *d.* 22 Palace gardens terrace, Kensington, London 27 April 1879.

DAVIES, VENERABLE RICHARD. V. of St. John's, Brecknock 1804 to death; archdeacon of Brecknock 15 Feb. 1805 to death; canon of St. Davids 1805 to death. *d.* Residentiary house, St. David's cathedral, Brecon 14 May 1859 aged 82.

DAVIES, ROBERT (*eld. son of Peter Davies of York*). *b.* York 19 Aug. 1793; solicitor at York 1814, town clerk 1827–48; F.S.A. 22 Dec. 1842; author or editor of *The freeman's roll of the city of York* 1835; *The Fawkes's of York in the sixteenth century* 1850; *Notices of the mints and coinages at York* 1854; *The life of M. Rawdon, Camden Soc.* 1863; *A memoir of the York press* 1868; *Walks through the city of York* 1880. *d.* The Mount, York 23 Aug. 1875.

DAVIES, VENERABLE ROLAND ROBERT. Educ. at Trin. coll. Dublin, B.A. 1827; archdeacon of Hobart Town, Tasmania 1855 to death. *d.* Ferndean, Hobart Town 13 Nov. 1880 aged 75.

DAVIES, SCROPE BERDMORE. Educ. at Eton 1796–99 and King's coll. Cam., fellow 1805, senior fellow 1822 to death; B.A. 1806, M.A. 1809; remarkable for his dexterity at all athletic games especially cricket and tennis, competed with Lord Byron in swimming; intimate friend of Tom Moore and Lord Byron who when on his death bed sent him a ring; Lord Byron's *Parisina* is dedicated to him; lived at Ostend 1836; a well known talker and diner out. *d.* 2 Rue Miromenil, Paris 24 May 1852. *T. C. Grattan's Beaten Paths* (1862) ii, 146–70.

DAVIES, VENERABLE THOMAS HART FRANCIS PENROSE. Educ. at Trin. hall, Cam., B.A. 1837, M.A. 1841; C. of Holbrooke, Suffolk 1837–39; C. of Knaresborough 1839–41; P.C. of Trinity, Nottingham 1841–51; archdeacon of Melbourne, Australia 1851–53; V. of Ch. Ch. Ramsgate 1853 to death. *d.* Ramsgate 5 Jany. 1873 aged 76. *Kent Coast Times* 9 *Jany.* 1873 *pp.* 2, 3.

DAVIES, THOMAS STEPHENS. *b.* 1794; F.R.S. Edin. 1831; F.S.A. 19 March 1840; professor of mathematics at R.M.A. Woolwich 1834 to death; edited many mathematical works. *d.* Broomhall cottage, Shooter's hill, Kent 6 Jany. 1851. *Westminster Review* lv, 70–83 (1851); *Mechanics' Mag.* 11 Jany. 1851 pp. 33–5; *The Expositor* i, 284 (1851), *portrait.*

DAVIES, WILLIAM EDMUND. *b.* King's Cross, London 1819; employed by Cubitt and Co. as a carpenter; originated the betting list system 1846, hung up first of his betting lists at Salisbury Arms, Durham st. Strand, betting lists were declared illegal by act of parliament 20 Aug. 1853; lost £100,000 over the Derby 1852 when Daniel O'Rourke won, and £48,000 over the Derby 1853 when West Australian won; became known as the Leviathan; retired at end of racing season 1857. *d.* at 18 Gloucester place, Brighton 4 Oct. 1879. *Rice's History of the Turf* ii, 271–80 (1879); *Sporting Review, Jany.* 1859 pp. 39–42; *Sporting Times* 30 *May* 1885 p. 2.

NOTE.—By his will he left property in railway shares valued at £60,000 to the Brighton corporation subject to the payment of certain annuities. His widow gave notice to dispute the will, but on 21 Jany. 1880 an arrangement was made by which the greater part of the property came to the corporation on her death. Preston park, Brighton which cost £50,000 was purchased with this money and opened 8 Nov. 1884.

DAVIS, CHARLES. *b.* near Hertford 15 Jany. 1788; whipper-in to his father who hunted the King's harriers 1800 and Pistol boy to George iii; whipper-in to Mr. Sharpe's staghounds 1812; huntsman to the Queen 1821–66; presented with a testimonial in London 5 Feb. 1859, which testimonial he left to the Queen. *d.* Royal Kennels, Ascot 26 Oct. 1866. *bur.* Sunninghill churchyard 2 Nov. His horse Comus, a gift from the Prince of Wales, was shot by his last wish and one ear of the horse in a small box was placed in his grave. *Lord W. P. Lennox's Celebrities I have known, second series* ii, 284–305; *J. N. Fitt's Covert side sketches* (1878) 274–78; *Sporting Review* lx, 418–20 (1866), lvi, 402–8 (1866); *Baily's Mag.* xii, 254, 326–36 (1867); *The Sportsman n.s.* ii, 277 (1837), *portrait; I.L.N.* xxxiv, 164, 165 (1859), *portrait.*

DAVIS, RIGHT REV. CHARLES HENRY. *b.* Usk, co. Monmouth 18 May 1815; professed at St. Gregory's, Downside near Bath 1834; a member of Benedictine order 1833; ordained priest Nov. 1840; pastor of Downside 1844–48; the first R.C. bishop of Maitland, Australia 1848 to death, consecrated 25 Feb. 1848; coadjutor of the archbishop of the diocese. *d.* Sydney 17 May 1854.

DAVIS, RIGHT REV. DANIEL GATEWARD *(son of Rev. Wm. Davis). b.* Island of St. Christopher, West Indies 1788; ed. at Reading and Pemb. coll. Ox.; B.A. 1814, M.A. 1823, D.D. 1842; went to the West Indies; R. of St. Paul's, Charleston, Nevis; R. of St. George's, Basseterre, St. Christophers; rural dean; archdeacon of Antigua 1837; visited England 1842; bishop of Antigua 21 Aug. 1842 to death, consecrated in Westminster Abbey 24 Aug. *d.* 3 Bryanston st. Portman sq. London 25 Oct. 1857.

DAVIS, EDWARD DEAN. *b.* near Bath 1806; manager of Taunton theatre 1835; travelled the Devonshire circuit with a company 1843–46; lessee of T.R. Newcastle 1846–70; lessee of Lyceum theatre, Sunderland 1854, theatre was entirely destroyed by fire 23 Dec. 1855, theatre was reopened 29 Sep. 1856 when Henry Irving made his first appearance on the stage, lessee of the theatre again 1870–76. *d.* Eldon square, Newcastle 19 Feb. 1887.

DAVIS, GEORGE LENOX. Ensign 9 foot 15 Sep. 1808, lieut. col. 19 Dec. 1845 to 2 April 1852; inspecting field officer of Liverpool recruiting district 2 April 1852 to death; C.B. 27 June 1846. *d.* Galway 14 April 1852.

DAVIS, HART. Commissioner of Excise 11 Aug. 1824, deputy chairman Sep. 1837 to 6 Jany. 1849; F.R.S. 20 May 1841. *d.* Bere hill house, Whitchurch 17 June 1854.

DAVIS, HENRY GEORGE *(son of Mr. Davis, master of St. Paul's parochial schools, Knightsbridge, London). b.* 4 Mills Buildings, Knightsbridge 14 Aug. 1830; clerk in a circulating library; contributed a series of articles on 'Our local associations' to *West Middlesex Advertiser;* prepared for the press *Memorials of the hamlet of Knightsbridge with notices of its immediate neighbourhood,* ed. by his brother C. Davis 1859; left in manuscript two unfinished works 'Pimlico' and 'Recollections of Piccadilly'; wrote many antiquarian papers in *Notes and Queries. d.* St. Paul's parochial school, Wilton place, Belgravia 30 Dec. 1857.

DAVIS, JAMES EDWARD *(son of Aaron Wall Davis, M.D. of Presteign, Radnorshire). b.* 1817; barrister M.T. 25 Nov. 1842; revising barrister 1854; reporter for Law Journal Reports in Court of Exchequer 1855–64; stipendiary magistrate for Stoke-upon-Trent 1864–70, for Sheffield 1870–74; legal adviser to comrs. of Metropolitan Police 1874 to death; author of *Prize essay on the laws for the protection of women* 1854; *Practice and evidence in the county courts*

DAVIS, J. E. *(Con.)*

1855, 6 *ed.* 1887; *The Criminal law consolidation statutes* 1861; *A manual of the law of registration and election* 1868, 2 *ed.* 1879. *d.* suddenly at 4 Whitehall place, London 12 July 1887 in 70 year. *Law Journal xxii*, 397, 406, 426 (1887).

DAVIS, JOHN EDWARD *(son of Henry Davis, commander R.N.) b.* 9 Aug. 1815; entered navy 5 July 1828; Second master in the Terror in Antarctic expedition 1839–43; surveyor to North Atlantic telegraph expedition in the Fox 1862; retired captain 9 Aug. 1870; naval assistant to the Hydrographer; author with his son of the *Azimuth Tables;* invented an improved sextant; drew the charts for Antarctic expedition 1839–43; the illustrations in *Narrative of Sir James Clark Ross* 1847 are from his drawings; F.R.G.S. *d.* Douglas house, Maze hill, Greenwich 30 Jany. 1877.

DAVIS, JOHN FORD. *b.* Bath 1773; ed. in London and Edin.; M.D. Edin. 24 June 1797; L.R.C.P. 30 Sep. 1808; phys. to general hospital, Bath 1817–34; author of *An inquiry into the symptons and treatment of Carditis, or inflammation of the heart* 1808. *d.* Bath 1 Jany. 1864.

DAVIS, JOHN PHILIP, called Pope Davis. Exhibited 33 pictures at the R.A., 17 at B.I. and 59 at Suffolk st. gallery 1811–57; painted at Rome 1824 a large picture of the 'Talbot family receiving the benediction of the Pope' (hence his cognomen 'Pope Davis'); awarded a premium of £50 by directors of British Institution 1825; author of *Facts of vital importance relative to the embellishment of the Houses of Parliament* 1843; *The Royal Academy and the National Gallery, What is the state of these institutions?* 1858; *Thoughts on great painters* 1866. *d.* 67 Great Russell st. Bloomsbury, London 28 Sep. 1862 in 79 year.

DAVIS, JOSEPH BARNARD. *b.* York 13 June 1801; went as a surgeon in a whaling ship to the Arctic seas 1820; L.S.A. 1823, M.R.C.S. 1843; surgeon at Shelton Hanley, Staffs. to death; M.D. St. Andrews 1862; collected a museum of skulls and skeletons of various races, larger than all the collections in British public museums, which he sold to Royal college of Surgeons 1880; F.S.A. 21 Dec. 1854; F.R.S. 4 June 1868; author of *Popular manual of the art of preserving health* 1836; *Thesaurus Craniorum* 2 vols. 1867–75; published with John Thurnam, M.D., *Crania Britannica, or delineations of the skulls of the early inhabitants of the British Islands* 1856–65. *d.* Hanley 19 May 1881. *Nature 26 May* 1881.

DAVIS, NATHAN. Lived in an old Moorish palace 10 miles from Tunis many years; edited the *Hebrew Christian Magazine* 1852; became a Nonconformist minister; engaged excavating at Carthage and Utica for the British Museum 1856–58, chief antiquities he discovered were Roman mosaic pavements; author of *Tunis, or selections from a journal during a residence in that Regency* 1841; *Evenings in my tent* 2 vols. 1854; *Carthage and her remains* 1861; *Ruined cities within Numidian and Carthaginian territories* 1862. *d.* Florence 6 Jany. 1882. *Antiquarian Mag. i,* 152 (1882); *Edwards's Lives of the founders of the British Museum* (1870) 666–8.

DAVIS, RICHARD BARRETT *(son of Mr. Davis, huntsman to the royal harriers). b.* Watford, Herts. 1782; animal painter; exhibited 70 pictures at R.A., 57 at B.I. and 141 at Suffolk st. gallery 1802–53; animal painter to William iv, 1831. *d.* 9 Bedford place, Kensington, London 13 March 1854.

DAVIS, WILLIAM. Founded a free school at Gower's walk, Whitechapel, London 1807; one of founders of National Society 1811 and of Society for promoting enlargement, building and repairing of churches and chapels 1818. *d.* 19 Nov. 1854 aged 88.

DAVIS, WILLIAM. *b.* Dublin 1812; portrait painter at Liverpool; professor of painting at Liverpool academy; exhibited 16 landscapes at the R.A. 1851–72. *d.* London 22 April 1873.

DAVISON, REV. EDWARD *(son of Rev. Edward Davison 1760–1839, Inc. of St. Nicholas, Durham).* Matric. from C.C. coll. Ox. 25 Nov. 1803 aged 15, B.A. 1807, M.A. 1810; fellow of Univ. coll. 1807–16; R. of Harlington, Middlesex 1822–56; P.C. of St. Nicholas, Durham 1825–56; author of *Tentamen Theologicum, or an attempt to assist the young clergyman of the Church of England in the choice of a subject for his sermon on any Sunday throughout the year* by E. D. 1850, and of several sets of lectures and sermons. *d.* Durham 22 May 1863.

DAVISON, SIR HENRY (4 son of *Thomas Davison of St. Bride's, Fleet st. London).* Matric. from Trin. coll. Ox. 23 Oct. 1823 aged 18, scholar 1824, B.A. 1829, M.A. 1834: barrister I.T. 6 May 1834; puisne judge of supreme court of Madras 16 March 1857, chief justice 11 March 1859 to death; knighted by the Queen at Windsor castle 28 Nov. 1856; published with H. Merivale *Reports in the Queen's Bench and upon Writs of Error* 1844. *d.* Ootacamund on the Neilgherry hills, Madras 3 Nov. 1860.

DAVISON, JAMES WILLIAM. *b.* London 5 Oct. 1813; ed. at Univ. coll. sch. and Royal Acad. of Music; wrote pianoforte music for *Bohn's Harmonist*; edited the *Musical World* to death; musical critic of the *Times* 1850–78; wrote for the *Saturday Review* and *Graphic*; contributed to *Grove's Dictionary of music and musicians*; author of *An essay on the works of Frederic Chopin* 1849. (*m.* 1860 Arabella Goddard the pianist). *d.* York hotel, Margate 24 March 1885. *bur.* Brompton cemetery, London 28 March. *Theatre v*, 230–4, 247–9 (1885); *Musical Standard* 4 *April* 1885 *pp.* 212–3; *London Figaro* 4 *April* 1885 *p.* 11, *portrait*.

DAVISON, JOHN ROBERT (2 *son of Rev. Edward Davison, R. of Harlington, Middlesex, who d. 1863*). *b.* Church st. Durham 15 April 1826; ed. at Houghton and Durham gr. schs. and C.C. coll. Ox., B.A. 1845, M.A. 1847; barrister M.T. 2 Nov. 1849; Q.C. 9 Jany. 1866; chairman of Durham quarter sessions 1868; M.P. for city of Durham, Nov. 1868 to death, advocate general 28 Dec. 1870 to death; P.C. 8 Feb. 1871. *d.* The Auberies near Sudbury 15 April 1871. *Law Journal vi*, 282–3, 287–8 (1871); *I.L.N. lviii*, 427, 444 (1871), *portrait, lix*, 98 (1871).

DAVISON, JOSEPH (*son of Thomas Davison of Sedgefield, Durham*). Solicitor at Durham 1831; deputy registrar in Episcopal registry for wills Durham 1835–57; district registrar of Court of Probate 1857 to death; clerk and deputy steward of the Halmote Court at Durham (through which all transfers of copyhold property in co. Durham pass) 25 Nov. 1850 to death; held the office of Cursitor in the Palatinate Chancery Court 25 Jany. 1836 to death when office was abolished and documents were transferred to Record Office, London; principal proprietor of Bedlington colliery on the Tyne. *d.* Greencroft hall, Durham 20 Dec. 1868.

DAVISON, MARIA REBECCA (*dau. of Mr. Duncan of Liverpool, actor*). *b.* Liverpool 1783; acted in England, Scotland and Ireland; first appeared in London at Drury Lane 8 Oct. 1804 as Lady Teazle; created the rôle of Juliana in *The Honeymoon* 31 Jany. 1805; acted at Drury Lane 1804–19 and 1825–29 and at Covent Garden 1819–21; her best parts were Maria in *The Citizen* and Miss Hardcastle in *She stoops to conquer*. (*m.* 31 Oct. 1812 James Davison, who *d.* March 1858). *d.* Brompton, London 30 May 1858. *Mrs. C. Baron Wilson's Our actresses i*, 167–88 (1844); *Oxberry's Dramatic Biography i*, 51–7 (1825), *portrait*; *J. H. Leigh Hunt's Critical essays on the performers of the London theatres* (1807) 170–79; *The London Stage vol. 3, portrait*.

DAVISON, ROBERT. *b.* Belford, Northumberland 10 May 1804; resident engineer to Truman and Co. brewers, London 1831–45; patented a process for drying wood and other substances by currents of hot air which was worked by Patent Desiccating Co. 1845 and received gold medal of Soc. of Arts; erected Findlater's brewery, Dublin 1852; designed Allsopp's new brewery at Burton; invented machinery for raising and conveying malt; patented machinery for cleansing casks by a double rotatory motion; A.I.C.E. 1834, M.I.C.E. 1840; prime warden of Blacksmiths' Co. 1857–58. *d.* Finchley 14 March 1886. *Min. of proc. of Instit. of C.E. ii*, 192 (1842), *iii*, 57 (1843), *lxxxiv*, 442–44 (1886).

DAVISON, SIR WILLIAM (*son of Alexander Davison of St. James's sq. London, government contractor 1750–1829*). *b.* 1788; ed. at Eton; captain Northumberland militia 7 July 1807; equerry to 1 Duke of Cambridge 1813–50; equerry to 2 Duke of Cambridge 1850 to death; captain on half pay of 2 Foot 25 Dec. 1813; lieut. col. in the army 10 Jany. 1837; K.H. 1824; knighted at the King's lodge, Windsor 3 Sep. 1824. *d.* London 14 Jany. 1873.

DAVY, DAVID ELISHA (*son of Mr. Davy of Rumburgh, Suffolk, farmer, who d. 1799 aged 90*). *b.* 1769; F.L.S. 17 Dec. 1793; receiver general for Suffolk 1795; collected for nearly 50 years, materials for history of Suffolk which were bought by British Museum 1852; communicated a series of notices of sepulchral monuments existing in parish churches of Suffolk to the *Topographer and Genealogist*; wrote many articles on genealogical matters to *Gent. Mag.* under initials D. A. Y.; author of *A short account of Leiston Abbey by D. E. D.* edited by *J. Bird* 1823. *d.* Ufford near Woodbridge, Suffolk 15 Aug. 1851.

DAVY, EDMUND (2 *son of William Davy of Penzance*). *b.* Penzance 1785; assistant in laboratory of Royal Institution, London 1804–13; professor of chemistry in Royal Cork Institution 1813–26 and in Royal Dublin Society 1826–1854 when he retired on full salary; gave upwards of 30 courses of lectures on chemical subjects; F.R.S. 19 Jany. 1826; author of *An essay on the use of peat or turf as a means of promoting the public health and the agriculture of the United Kingdom* 1850, and of 33 papers 1812–57. *d.* Kimmage lodge, co. Dublin 5 Nov. 1857. *H. B. Jones's Royal Institution* (1871) *pp.* 280, 360, 366.

DAVY, EDWARD *(eld. son of Thomas Davy of Ottery St. Mary, Devon, surgeon).* b. Ottery St. Mary 16 June 1806; ed. at St. Bartholomew's hospital; L.S.A. 1828, M.R.C.S. 1829; operative chemist at 390 Strand, under title of Davy and Co. 1830; invented and patented Davy's Diamond Cement 1835; laid down a mile of copper wire around inner circle of Regent's Park 1837 where he made many experiments in electricity; opened an exhibition of his telegraphic apparatus at Exeter hall 29 Dec. 1837; patented his electro-chemical recording telegraph 4 July 1838 which was bought by the Electric Telegraph Company for £600; sailed for Australia as medical superintendent of an emigrant ship 15 April 1839; edited the *Adelaide Examiner* 1843–5; manager of copper smelting works at Yatala 1848–51; head of Government Assay office at Adelaide 1852–3 and at Melbourne, July 1853 to Dec. 1854; surgeon at Malmesbury, Victoria 1855 to death; author of *An experimental guide to chemistry* 1836; *Outline of a new plan of telegraphic communication* 1836. *d.* Malmesbury 27 Jany. 1885. *Memoir of E. Davy by his nephew H. Davy* 1883; *J. J. Fahie's Edward Davy and the electric telegraph* 1836 *to* 1839 (1883).

DAVY, JOHN (2 *son of Robert Davy of Penzance, wood-carver, who d.* 1794). b. Penzance 24 May 1790; studied medicine at Edin., M.D. 1814; F.R.S. 17 Feb. 1814; hospital assistant in the army 19 May 1815; inspector general of army hospitals 22 Dec. 1848 to 3 Feb. 1849 when placed on h.p.; author of *An account of the interior of Ceylon* 1821; *Researches, physiological and anatomical* 1839; *Notes and observations on the Ionian islands* 2 vols. 1842; *Lectures on chemistry* 1849; *Discourses on agriculture* 1849; *On some of the more important diseases of the army* 1862; *The angler and his friends or piscatory colloquies and fishing excursions* 1855. *d.* Lesketh-how near Ambleside 24 Jany. 1868. *Proc. of Royal Soc. xvi,* 79–81 (1868); *Boase and Courtney's Bibl. Cornub. i,* 111 (1874), *iii,* 1152 (1882).

DAVY, SIR WILLIAM GABRIEL *(eld. son of Major Davy, Persian secretary to Warren Hastings).* b. King's Holme near Gloucester 1779; ensign 61 foot March 1797; major 60 foot 5 Feb. 1807; lieut.-col. 7 garrison battalion 28 Dec. 1809 to 1810 when placed on h.p.; C.B. 4 June 1815; K.C.H. 1836; knighted at St. James's palace 23 March 1836; col. commandant 60 foot 2 Nov. 1842 to death; general 20 June 1854. *d.* Tracy park near Bath 25 Jany. 1856 aged 77.

DAVYS, RIGHT REV. GEORGE *(son of John Davys of Rempstone, Notts.)* b. Loughborough, Leics. 1 Oct. 1780; a sizar at Ch. coll. Cam. 1799, fellow 14 Jany. 1806–1814; tenth wrangler 1803; B.A. 1803, M.A. 1806; V. of Willoughby in the Wolds, Lincs. 1811–29; educated the Princess Victoria at Kensington Palace 1827–37; R. of Allhallows on the Wall, city of London 1829–39; dean of Chester 10 Jany. 1831 to May 1839, instituted 21 Feb. 1831; bishop of Peterborough, May 1839 to death, consecrated 16 June; author of *Village conversations on the Liturgy of the Church of England* 1820, 8 ed. 1829; *Village conversations on the principal offices of the Church* 1824, 2 ed. 1849; *Letters between a father and his son on Roman history and other subjects* 1848, and of various educational works which appeared anonymously in *The cottagers' monthly visitor* and *National School Mag.* d. The palace, Peterborough 18 April 1864.

DAVYS, VENERABLE OWEN. Educ. at St. John's coll. Cam., B.A. 1817, M.A. 1820; V. of Cranwell, Lincs. 1834–46; archdeacon of Northampton 15 Sep. 1842 to death; canon of Peterborough 15 Sep. 1842 to death; R. of Fiskerton, Lincs. 1846 to death. *d.* 8 Feb. 1875.

DAWES, GEORGE *(youngest son of Thomas Dawes, who d.* 3 *Jany.* 1871). b. Angel court, Throgmorton st. London 23 Nov. 1810; solicitor at Angel court 1835 to death; solicitor to Associated fire offices and Fire office committee; settled form of fire policy generally used by insurance offices; conducted most of the leading insurance cases. *d.* Barlow, Florida, U.S. 9 Dec. 1887.

DAWES, VERY REV. RICHARD *(son of James Dawes of Hawes in Wensleydale, Yorkshire).* Baptised at Hawes 13 April 1793; entered Trin. coll. Cam. Oct. 1813; 4 wrangler 1817; B.A. 1817, M.A. 1820; fellow and tutor of Downing college 1818; V. of Tadlow, Cambs. 1819–36; R. of Kings Somborne, Hants. 1836, founded a school there opened Oct. 1842; dean of Hereford 15 May 1850 to death, installed 13 June 1850; restored the cathedral and re-opened it 1863; master of St. Catherine's hospital, Ledbury 1861; vice pres. of British association at Bath 1864; author of *Suggestive hints towards improved secular instruction making it bear upon practical life* 1849 and ten other small books. *d.* The deanery, Hereford 10 March 1867. *A biographical notice of the late Very Rev. R. Dawes by W. C. Henry, privately printed* 1867; *G.M. May* 1867 *pp.* 674–75.

DAWES, THOMAS. Attorney in City of London 1795 to death. d. Tunbridge Wells. 3 Jany. 1871 aged 98 being oldest attorney on the rolls.

DAWES, WILLIAM RUTTER (son of Mr. Dawes, mathematical master at Christ's hospital, London). b. Christ's hospital 19 March 1799; ed. at Charterhouse sch.; surgeon at Haddenham, Bucks., at Liverpool 1826; took charge of a small independent congregation at Ormskirk, Lancs. to 1839; had charge of the observatory at South villa, Regent's park, London belonging to George Bishop 1839–1844; fitted up an observatory at Camden lodge near Cranbrook, Kent 1844; invented several valuable improvements in practical astronomy; F.R.A.S. 14 May 1830, gold medallist 1855; F.R.S. 1865. d. Hopefield, Haddenham 15 Feb. 1868. Monthly notices of Royal Astronom. Soc. xxix, 116.

DAWKINS, HENRY. b. 1765; comr. of woods and forests 31 July 1810 to 1832 when he retired on pension of £800; M.P. for Aldborough, Yorkshire 12 Oct. 1812 to Aug. 1814. d. Encombe house near Sandgate, Kent 2 Nov. 1852 in 88 year.

DAWKINS, HENRY. b. 28 Nov. 1788; ed. at Harrow and Marlow; ensign Coldstream guards 10 March 1804, captain 25 July 1814 to 31 Aug. 1826 when placed on h.p.; served through Peninsular war and at Waterloo; retired from army 1846; M.P. for Boroughbridge, Yorkshire 10 March 1820 to 24 July 1830. d. Over Norton, Oxfordshire 13 Nov. 1864.

DAWSON, GEORGE (son of Jonathan Dawson of London, schoolmaster). b. 36 Hunter st. Brunswick sq. London 24 Feb. 1821; ed. at Glasgow Univ., B.A., M.A.; minister of baptist chapel at Rickmansworth, Herts. 1843; min. of Mount Zion chapel, Birmingham, 6 Oct. 1844 to Dec. 1845; min. of "The Church of the Saviour," Birmingham 8 Aug. 1847; lectured in all chief towns of the Kingdom 30 years; lectured in the U.S. 1874; edited Birmingham Morning News from 2 Jany. 1871; mem. of Birmingham sch. board 28 Nov. 1871; took an active part in English and foreign politics; friend of Mazzini and Kossuth; author of Prayers with a discourse on prayer 1877, 9 ed. 1884; Sermons on daily life and duty 1878; Three books of God, Nature, history and scripture 1882; Shakespeare and other lectures 1878. (m. 27 Aug. 1846 Susan Frances youngest dau. of J. W. Crompton of Edgbaston, merchant, she was b. Edgbaston 23 June 1820 and d. Malvern 9 Nov. 1878). d. Kingsnorton near Birmingham 30 Nov. 1876. Crosskey's

DAWSON, G. (Con.)
Memoir of G. Dawson 1876; Ireland's Recollections of G. Dawson 1882; Manchester Quarterly i, 181–204 (1882); Gilfillan's Second gallery of literary portraits (1850) 196–213; The lamps of the temple, 3 ed. (1856) 449–65; Edgbastonia i, 94–7, 114 (1881) portrait of Mrs. Dawson, ii, 140–43 (1882), portrait of G. Dawson; Nineteenth Century ii, 44–61 (1877); Illust. news of the world, ix (1862), portrait.

DAWSON, GEORGE. b. Falkirk, Stirlingshire 14 March 1813; taken to America 1818; foreman in office of Evening Journal at Albany, New York 1830–36; edited Rochester Daily Democrat 1836–39 and 1842–46; edited Detroit Advertiser 1839–42; associate editor of Albany Evening Journal 1846, editor 1862–77; postmaster of Albany 1861–67; author of The pleasures of angling 1876. d. Albany, New York 17 Feb. 1883.

DAWSON, GEORGE ROBERT (elder son of Arthur Dawson of Castledawson 1745–1822). b. Rutland sq. Dublin 24 Dec. 1790; ed. at Harrow and Ch. Ch. Ox., B.A. 1811; M.P. for co. Londonderry 1815–30, for Harwich 1830–32; under sec. of state for home department 17 Jany. 1822 to 30 April 1827; sec. of the Treasury 28 Jany. 1828 to 26 Nov. 1830; P.C. 22 Nov. 1830; sec. of the Admiralty 24 Dec. 1834 to 27 April 1835; comr. of the Customs 29 Dec. 1841, deputy chairman 1846 to death. d. Upper Grosvenor st. London 3 April 1856.

DAWSON, HENRY. b. Water st. Hull 3 April 1811; employed in a lace factory at Nottingham to 1835; landscape painter at Nottingham 1835, at Liverpool 1844–50, at Croydon 1850; competed for decoration of Houses of Parliament 1847; one of his best pictures 'The wooden walls of old England' which sold for £75 in 1853, brought £1400 at Christie's 1876; 57 of his pictures were at Nottingham exhibition 1878 and several of his large pictures at Jubilee exhibition, Manchester 1887. d. The Cedars, Chiswick 13 Dec. 1878. C. Brown's Lives of Nottinghamshire Worthies (1882) 360–66, portrait.

DAWSON, PUDSEY (son of Pudsey Dawson of Langcliff hall, Yorkshire 1752–1816). b. 2 Oct. 1778; sheriff of West Riding, Yorkshire 1845; assoc. of Archæol. assoc. 1851; Hornby castle devised to him by Admiral Tatham who d. 24 Jany. 1840, was visited by British Archæological Soc. 2 Aug. 1850. d. Hornby Castle, Lancaster 12 April 1859. Journal of British Archæol. Assoc. xvi, 170–71 (1860).

DAWSON, ROBERT. Assistant draughtsman on the ordnance survey of Great Britain 1794; a first-class draughtsman in corps of royal military surveyors and draughtsmen 1802; contributed much to bring sketching and shading of ordnance plans to degree of perfection afterwards attained; instructor in topographical drawing at Royal military college, also at H.E.I. Co.'s military seminary, Addiscombe 1810; pensioned by Board of Ordnance. *d.* Woodleigh rectory, South Devon 22 June 1860.

DAWSON, ROBERT KEARSLEY *(eld. son of the preceding). b.* 1798; second lieut. R.E. 1 March 1816, captain 18 Aug. 1837 to 1 Dec. 1853 when he retired on full pay as lieut.-col.; employed on the Scotch and Irish surveys; assistant comr. under the Tithe Act 1836; member of the first Metropolitan sewers commission 1849; A.I.C.E. 28 March 1838; C.B. 4 Feb. 1856; compiled *Plans of the cities and boroughs of England and Wales* 1832. *d.* Blackheath, Kent 28 March 1861. *Min. of proc. of Instit. of C.E. xxi,* 582–4 (1862).

DAWSON, ROBERT PEEL *(eld. son of George Robert Dawson* 1790–1856). *b.* London 2 June 1818; ed. at Harrow and Ch. Ch. Ox.; ensign Grenadier guards 8 Aug. 1837; captain 11 Hussars 9 June 1846 to 13 July 1847 when he sold out; sheriff of Londonderry 1850; M.P. for Londonderry 1859–74; lord lieut. of Londonderry 23 June 1870 to death; col. of Londonderry militia 12 April 1871 to death. *d.* Dover 2 Sep. 1877.

DAWSON, THOMAS VESEY (2 son of 2 *Baron Cremorne* 1788–1877). Ensign Coldstream guards 11 Aug. 1837, captain 22 Aug. 1851 to death; M.P. for co. Louth 1841–1847, for co. Monaghan 1847–1852; killed at battle of Inkerman 5 Nov. 1854.

DAWSON-DAMER, GEORGE LIONEL (3 son of 1 *Earl of Portarlington* 1744–98). *b.* Queen's county 28 Oct. 1788; cornet 1 dragoon guards 4 Dec. 1806, captain 31 Dec. 1812; captain 22 light dragoons 22 Jany. 1818 to 17 Aug. 1820 when placed on h.p.; captain 65 foot 8 June 1826; major 89 foot 13 Dec. to 24 Dec. 1833 when he sold out; assumed additional surname of Damer by r.l. 14 March 1829; M.P. for Portarlington 9 Jany. 1835 to 23 July 1847, for Dorchester 28 July 1847 to 1 July 1852; comptroller of H.M.'s household, Sep. 1841 to July 1846; C.B. 26 Nov. 1816; P.C. 14 Sep. 1841. *d.* 23 Wilton crescent, Belgravia, London 14 April 1856.

DAY, ALFRED *(son of John B. Day, horse trainer, who d.* 21 *March* 1860). *b.* Danebury 3 Nov.

DAY, A. *(Con.)*

1830; rode in the Cesarewitch race 1843; won the One thousand guineas on Flea 1849 and on Kate 1852; won the Two thousand guineas on Pitsford 1850, Hermit 1854 and The Promised Land 1859; won the Derby on Andover 1854. *d.* Chilbolton near Stockbridge 4 Jany. 1868. *Sporting Review xliv,* 198–203 (1860), *portrait, lix,* 78 (1868); *Baily's Mag.,* May 1860, *portrait.*

DAY, EDWARD DERRY. *b.* Kerry 1801; served in 46 foot 1820–34; police magistrate of Maitland, N.S.W. 1836–50 and at Maitland, Muswell-brook and Port Macquarie 1853–69; captured the 'Jew Boy's gang of bushrangers' at Doughboy Hollow near Murrurundi, N.S.W. 20 Dec. 1840. *d.* Maitland 5 May 1876.

DAY, GEORGE EDWARD *(son of George Day of Manorabon house, Swansea). b.* Tenby 4 Aug. 1815; entered Trin. coll. Cam. 1833; scholar of Pemb. coll. 1833 or 1834, 29 wrangler 1837; B.A. 1837, M.A. 1840; physician in London 1843; M.R.C.P. 1844, F.R.C.P. 1847; phys. to Western general dispensary; lecturer on materia medica at Middlesex hospital; Chandos professor of anatomy and medicine at St. Andrews 1849–63; M.D. Giessen 1849; F.R.S. 6 June 1850; translated J. F. Simon's *Animal chemistry* 2 vols. 1845; J. Vogel's *Pathological anatomy of the human body* 1847; author of *A practical treatise on the domestic management and most important diseases of advanced life* 1849; *Chemistry in its relations to physiology and medicine* 1860, and of many articles in medical papers and *Chambers's Encyclopædia. d.* Andersey, Torquay 31 Jany. 1872. *Medical Circular iii,* 241 (1853), *portrait; Proc. of Med. and Chir. Soc. vii,* 45–7 (1875).

DAY, GEORGE FIOTT. *b.* June 1820; entered navy Aug. 1833; captain 20 Aug. 1861; retired captain 14 Feb. 1867; C.B. 29 May 1875; V.C. 24 Feb. 1857. *d.* Weston-super-Mare 18 Dec. 1876. *O'Byrne's Naval biog. dict.* (1861) 289–90; *I.L.N. lxx,* 21 (1877), *portrait.*

DAY, REV. HENRY THOMAS. Ed. at Clare coll. Cam., LL.B. 1836, LL.D. 1841; V. of Mendlesham, Suffolk 1835 to death; author of *Sermons at Mendlesham* 1838; *Algarsife and other poems* 1848; *An ode on the liberation of Abd-el-Kader,* and letters and pamphlets in favour of the revision of the authorised version of the Scriptures. *d.* 27 Sep. 1861 aged 62.

DAY, JOHN *(son of the succeeding).* Trainer of horses at Danebury; entered an action for libel against Admiral Rous which did not come into court; trained horses for Duke of Beaufort, Lord Hastings and many others. *d.*

DAY, J. (Con.)

Danebury 3 Dec. 1882 aged 68. *Baily's Mag. xl*, 64–72, 121–2 (1883); *Illust. sp. and dr. news xviii*, 345 (1882).

DAY, JOHN BARHAM. *b.* Houghton Down 1794; won the Oaks on Turquoise 1828, Oxygen 1831, Pussy 1834, Deception 1839 and Crucifix 1840; trainer for Lord George Bentinck many years; trained many celebrated horses for Henry Padwick and John Gully, among them were Hermit winner of the Two thousand guineas, Andover winner of the Derby, and Virago who won 12 races out of 13 as a 3 year old; earned sobriquet of the "Lyndhurst of the Turf" by his habit of talking sound sense. *d.* Woodyates 21 March 1860. *Rice's British turf i*, 274–8 (1879); *Corbet's Tales of sporting life* (1864) 55–67; *Baily's Mag. i*, 228–34 (1860).

DAY, SAMUEL *(brother of the preceding). b.* 1801; won the Derby on Gustavus 1821, on Priam 1830, on Mendicant 1846; won the Oaks on Pyrrhus the First 1846; kept livery stables in London. *d.* London 17 Feb. 1866. *Bell's Life in London* 24 Feb. 1866 *p.* 4.

DAYMAN, REV. JOHN *(eld. son of John Dayman of Padstow, Cornwall* 1778–1859). *b.* St. Columb, Cornwall 1802; ed. at Tiverton and C.C. coll. Ox., B.A. 1823, M.A. 1826; scholar of his coll. 1819, fellow 1825–31; R. of Skelton, Cumberland 1831 to death; author of *An essay concerning the nature of man* 1837; *The Inferno of Dante Alighieri translated in the terza rima of the original* 1843; *The divine comedy of Dante Alighieri translated in terza rima* 1865. *d.* London 8 July 1871.

DEACON, HENRY COLINS. Entered navy 3 Nov. 1800; captain 2 April 1817, retired 1 Oct. 1846, retired admiral 10 Nov. 1862. *d.* 12 Leonard place, Kensington 9 Nov. 1869.

DEAKIN, JAMES HENRY. *b.* near Manchester, Feb. 1851; M.P. for Launceston 1874–77; barrister M.T. 1875. *d.* Werrington park near Launceston 8 Nov. 1881.

DEALTRY, RIGHT REV. THOMAS *(son of James Dealtry of Knottingley near Pontefract). b.* Knottingley 1795; usher in a school at Doncaster; ed. at Cath. hall, Cam., LL.B. 1829; C. of St. Peter's, Cam. 1828; chaplain in Bengal army 1829; hon. sec. to Church Missionary Soc. Calcutta; archdeacon of Calcutta 1835–48; Inc. of St. John's, Bedford row, London 1848–49; bishop of Madras 9 Nov. 1849 to death, installed 2 Feb. 1850; author of *The divinity of our Lord Jesus Christ proved from his own discourse* 1830. *d.* Madras 4 March 1861.

DEALTRY, RIGHT REV. T. *(Con.)*

Higginbotham's Men whom India has known, 2 ed. (1874) 106–7; *I.L.N. xv*, 376 (1849), portrait.

DEALTRY, VENERABLE THOMAS *(only son of the preceding). b.* 1825; ed. at Trin. coll. Cam., B.A. 1847, M.A. 1850; assistant chaplain Madras army 1850–71; archdeacon of Madras 1861–71; R. of Swillington, Yorkshire 1872–78; V. of Maidstone 1878 to death. *d.* Maidstone 29 Nov. 1882.

DEANE, BONAR MILLETT. *b.* 30 Sep. 1834; ensign 96 foot 12 March 1853; lieut.-col. 19 foot 14 April 1875 to 15 Jany. 1879 when placed on h.p.; D.A.G. and Q.M.G. Cape of Good Hope 2 Aug. 1880 to death; killed by the Boers at Laing's Neck, Natal 28 Jany. 1881. *I.L.N. lxxviii*, 149 (1881), portrait.

DEANE, CHARLES *(elder son of Charles Meredith Deane, captain 24 light dragoons). b.* Southampton 6 June 1791; cornet 24 light dragoons 5 Sep. 1805, captain 5 Dec. 1818 to 25 July 1819 when regiment was disbanded; captain 1 foot 14 Nov. 1822, major 19 June 1835 to death; K.H. 1836. *d.* Newport, co. Monmouth 18 March 1853.

DEANE, REV. JOHN BATHURST *(brother of the preceding). b.* Cape of Good Hope 27 Aug. 1797; ed. at Merchant Taylors; Parkin's exhibitioner to Pemb. coll. Cam. 1816, B.A. 1820, M.A. 1823; second classical and head mathematical master at Merchant Taylors 1836–55; V. of St. Helen, Bishopsgate 1855 to death; R. of St. Martin, Outwich 1855 to death; author of *The worship of the Serpent traced throughout the world and its traditions referred to the events in Paradise* 1830; *The life of Richard Deane general at sea in the service of the Commonwealth* 1870. *d.* Sion hill, Bath 12 July 1887.

DEANE, JOHN CONNELLAN *(eld. son of the succeeding). b.* 1816; called to Irish bar; poor law inspector 1846; associated with Wm. Dargan, Sir Joseph Paxton and others in the Great Exhibitions at Cork 1852, Dublin 1853, and the Crystal palace and Alexandra palace, London; originator of Great Exhibition at Manchester; closely associated with early promoters of submarine telegraphy. *d.* Naples 24 Feb. 1887.

DEANE, SIR THOMAS *(eld. son of Alexander Dean of Cork, builder). b.* Cork 1792; a builder at Cork to 1830, an architect there 1830 to death; designed Commercial buildings, old and new Savings' banks, Bank of Ireland and Queen's college, Cork; joint designer of The

DEANE, SIR T. *(Con.)*

University Museum at Oxford 1855; mayor of Cork 1830; knighted by Duke of Northumberland at Cork 1830; pres. of Institute of Irish architects many years. *d.* 26 Longford terrace, Monkstown, Dublin 2 Oct. 1871. *I.L.N. lix,* 338 (1871).

DEANE, WILLIAM WOOD (3 *son of John Wood Deane, cashier in Bank of England, who. d.* 5 *Dec.* 1854 *aged* 68). *b.* Liverpool road, Islington, London 22 March 1825; assoc. R.I.B.A. 1848; acted at Miss Kelly's theatre, London which he subsequently decorated; architect in London 1853; made designs and perspectives for architects; assoc. of Instit. of painters in water colours 1862, member 1867; assoc. of Society of painters in water colours 1870; exhibited 23 pictures at R.A., 4 at B.I. and 13 at Suffolk st. gallery 1844–72. *d.* of cancer of the liver at 64 King Henry's road, Hampstead 18 Jany. 1873.

DEARDEN, THOMAS FERRAND. Solicitor at Rochdale 1823 to death; coroner for co. of Lancaster, March 1835 to death. *d.* The Elms, Rochdale 1 Jany. 1870 aged 68.

DEAS, SIR DAVID (*son of Francis Deas, provost of Falkland, who d.* 1857). *b.* Falkland, Sep. 1807; assistant surgeon R.N. 7 June 1828; chief medical officer of naval forces engaged during Russian war, and Chinese war up to peace of Tientsin 1859; inspector general of hospitals and fleets 1 March 1855 to March 1872 when placed on retired list; granted good service pension 11 April 1869; C.B. 5 Feb. 1856, K.C.B. 13 March 1867. *d.* 32 Heriot row, Edinburgh 15 Jany. 1876.

DEAS, SIR GEORGE (*brother of the preceding*). *b.* 7 Jany. 1804; ed. at Univ. of Edin., M.A. 1826; called to Scotch bar 1828; advocate depute 1840–41 and 1846–50; sheriff of Ross and Cromarty 1850–51; solicitor general 1851–52; lord ordinary of court of session with courtesy title of Lord Deas and a judge of Exchequer 25 May 1853; a lord comr. of justiciary April 1854 to Feb. 1885; knighted at St. James's palace 18 Feb. 1858; edited *The Scottish Jurist* 1829; edited with James Anderson, *Cases in the Court of Session, Jury Court, and the High Court of Justiciary* 1829–33, 4 *vols. d.* 32 Hériot row, Edinburgh 7 Feb. 1887.

DEASE, MATTHEW O'REILLY (*son of Richard Dease, M.D. of Dublin, who d.* 1819). *b.* 1819; ed. at Univ. of Paris; sheriff of Louth 1857 and of Cavan 1861; contested co. Cavan 1867; M.P. for co. Louth 1868–74; gave by his will

DEASE, M. O. *(Con).*

remainder of his real and personal property (equal to £40,000) to be applied towards extinguishing National Debt. *d.* 17 Aug. 1887.

DEASY, RICKARD (2 *son of Rickard Deasy of Clonakilty, Cork). b.* Clonakilty 1812; ed. at Trin. coll. Dublin, B.A. 1831, M.A. 1834; called to Irish bar 1835; Q.C. 13 Feb. 1849; bencher of King's Inns 1858; third serjeant at law 1858–59; M.P. for co. Cork 1855–61; solicitor general for Ireland, June 1859 to Feb. 1860; attorney general Feb. 1860 to Jany. 1861; P.C. 1860; baron of court of Exchequer, Jany. 1861; a judge of Court of Appeal 1 Jany. 1878 to death. *d.* 41 Merrion sq. east, Dublin 6 May 1883. *O'Flanagan's Munster circuit* (1880) 254, 376–80.

DE BAR, BENEDICT. *b.* London 5 Nov. 1812; made his début at T.R. Margate 1832; went to United States 1834; opened old National theatre, New York 1837; played in London 1840; proprietor of Chatham theatre, N.Y. 1849–52, of St. Charles' theatre, New Orleans 1853, of St. Louis theatre 1855; the best Falstaff in America 1872 to death. *d.* St. Louis 14 Aug. 1877. *Era* 14 Oct. 1877 *p.* 4.

DE-BEAUVOIR, SIR JOHN EDMOND, 2 Baronet (*eld. son of Sir John Edmond Browne, 1 baronet* 1748–1835). *b.* 10 Dec. 1794; ed. at Westminster; assumed name of De-Beauvoir in lieu of Browne 1825; claimed as eldest son of a baronet, honour of knighthood which was conferred on him 1827; contested Windsor, Dec. 1832, July 1837 and June 1841; M.P. for Windsor 7 Jany. 1835 to 6 April 1835 when unseated on petition; presented coat of arms over doorway of Westminster school to replace the former escutcheon which he helped to destroy when at school; author of *Miscellaneous poetry and scraps written for ladies' albums* 1837. *d.* Upper Gloucester st. Dorset sq. London 29 April 1869.

DE BEAUVOISIN, AUGUSTE MARIOT. Professor of French in King William st. city of London 1844 to death; also taught French at St. George's and St. James's halls, London; chevalier de la Toison d' Or; author of *How to read and translate French* 1847; *French acquired in four months* 1852; *Confabulateur Français* 1855; *French reading for self instruction* 1861; *Anecdotes in French* 1866; *French verbs at a glance* 1873. *d.* 53 Carlton hill, St. John's Wood, London 30 Oct. 1879.

DE BERG, ALEXANDER. Russian attaché chamberlain and consul general in London 16 April 1862 to death. *d.* London 14 March 1884.

DE BERGUE, CHARLES LOUIS AIMÉ. *b.* Kensington, London 24 Sep. 1807; went to Paris 1819, returned to England 1834; civil engineer at Manchester 1850, at Cardiff 1861; invented several valuable machine tools; invented a new iron permanent way for the Barcelona and Tarragona line which he constructed; invented a new construction of lattice bridge uniting lightness with great strength; A.I.C.E. 6 March 1849. *d.* 17 Kensington palace gardens, London 10 April 1873.

DE BLAQUIÈRE, WILLIAM DE BLAQUIÈRE, 3 Baron (2 *son of* 1 *Baron De Blaquière* 1735–1822). *b.* 27 Jany. 1778; ensign 56 foot 31 Aug. 1791; major 25 light dragoons 1 Feb. 1798 to 22 Jany. 1801; lieut.-col. 22 light dragoons 22 Jany. 1801 to 22 Aug. 1805; lieut.-col. 2 dragoon guards 22 Aug. 1805 to 30 July 1807; lieut.-col. 71 foot 30 July 1807 to 1808; general 23 Nov. 1841; succeeded his brother as 3 Baron 7 April 1844; great alnager of Ireland; F.R.S. 21 Feb. 1805; shot himself at Beulah hill, Norwood 12 Nov. 1851.

DE BLAQUIÈRE, PETER BOYLE (*brother of the preceding*). *b.* Dublin 27 April 1784; served as a midshipman at battle of Camperdown; emigrated to Canada 1837; a member of Canadian legislative council 1838 to death; chancellor of Toronto University; a member of the Anglican synod. *d.* Yorkville (now part of Toronto) 23 Oct. 1860.

DE BURGH, ULICK CANNING (*elder son of* 1 *Marquis of Clanricarde* 1802–74). *b.* St. James's sq. London 12 July 1827; ed. at Eton; ensign Coldstream guards 27 March 1846, captain 3 Nov. 1854 to 1860; aide-de-camp to lord lieut. of Ireland 1846–52, state steward of his household Jany. 1853; served in Crimean war, taken prisoner by the Russians 22 Oct. 1854; military sec. to Lord Canning governor general of India 1856–57; M.P. for Galway 1857–65, for co. Galway 1865 to death. *d.* 17 Stratton st. Piccadilly, London 16 Aug. 1867.

DE BURGH, REV. WILLIAM (3 *son of Thomas Burgh of Oldtown, co. Kildare, who d.* 1832). Ed. at Trin. coll. Dublin, B.A. 1821, M.A. 1847, B.D. 1851, D.D. 1857; Incumbent of St. John's, Sandymount, Dublin 1852–65; R. of Ardboe, Armagh 1865 to death; author of *Lectures on the Second Advent*, 3 ed. 1841; *Discourses on the life of Christ* 1849; *The Christian Sabbath* 1856; *An exposition of the Book of Revelations*, 5 ed. 1857; *Commentary on Book of Psalms*, 2 vols. 1860. *d.* Ardboe 15 Oct. 1866.

DE BUTTS, SIR AUGUSTUS (*son of Elias De Butts of Wicklow*). *b.* 1770; second lieut. R.E. 22 Aug. 1787, col. 30 Dec. 1814, col. commandant 20 March 1827 to death; general 11 Nov. 1851; K.C.H. 1837; knighted by Wm. iv at St. James's palace 1 March 1837. *d.* 14 Cambridge sq. London 27 Nov. 1853.

DE CETTO, BARON. Bavarian minister in London to 1872. *d.* 6 Hill st. Berkeley sq. London 7 Aug. 1879 aged 84.

DE CHABOT, SIR LOUIS WILLIAM DE ROHAN CHABOT, Viscount (*eld. son of Comte de Jarnac*). *b.* 1780; cornet 18 light dragoons 30 April 1793; major 9 light dragoons 16 March 1809; deputy adjutant general in Canada 1807–8; served in expedition to Walcheren and in Portugal 1809–10; M.G. 19 July 1821; K.C.H. 1822. *d.* 10 July 1875.

DE CHAUMONT, FRANCIS STEPHEN BENNETT FRANÇOIS. *b.* Edinburgh 1833; ed. at Univ. of Edin., M.D. 1853; L.R.C.S. Edin. 1853, F.R.C.S. Edin. 1864; assistant surgeon in the army 28 April 1854; served with Rifle brigade in Crimean war; surgeon 20 June 1865; surgeon major on h.p. 11 Oct. 1876; assistant professor of hygiene at army medical school Netley hospital 1863–76, professor 1876 to death; F.R.S. 12 June 1879; author of *Different families of the human race* 1865; *Hygiene in civil and military life*, 5 ed. 1878. *d.* Woolston Lawn, Southampton 18 April 1888.

DE CLIFFORD, EDWARD SOUTHWELL RUSSELL, 23 Baron. *b.* Upton Warws. 30 April 1824; M.P. for Tavistock 2 Aug. 1847 to 1 July 1852; succeeded 3 Jany. 1874. *d.* Kirkby Mallory, Leics. 1877.

DE COLQUHOUN, JAMES (*only son of Patrick Colquhoun, lord provost of Glasgow*). *b.* Kelvin grove, Lanarkshire 7 June 1780; ed. at St. John's coll. Cam.; consul general in London for Saxony 1827 to death; chargé d' affaires in London for grand duke of Oldenburg 1848 to death; assumed designation of Chevalier; fellow of univ. of Glasgow. *d.* Stratford place, London 23 July 1855.

DE COURCY, MICHAEL (*eld. child of Nevinson De Courcy, captain R.N.* 1789–1844). *b.* 8 May 1811; entered navy 1 Feb. 1824; captain 6 Sep. 1852; R.A. 18 Oct. 1867; retired admiral 15 June 1879; C.B. 13 March 1867. *d.* Milburn, Newton Abbot, Devon 22 Oct. 1881.

DE COURCY, NEVINSON WILLOUGHBY (*brother of the preceding*). *b.* 27 Sep. 1823; 2 lieut. R.M. 17 Aug. 1841; captain 24 Feb. 1854;

De Courcy, N. W. *(Con.)*

lieut. col. 30 Oct. 1872 to 8 Oct. 1877 when he retired on full-pay; C.B. 2 June 1877. *d.* Clapham near London 30 March 1885.

DEEDES, JOHN *(5 son of Wm. Deedes of Sandling park, Kent, M.P. for Hythe).* *b.* 1803; ed. at Winchester and Trin. coll. Camb., B.A. 1825, M.A. 1826; barrister I.T. 20 Nov. 1829, bencher 1863, treasurer 1877; a revising barrister many years; recorder of Queenborough 1834, of Deal, Sandwich, and Canterbury 1845–72; assessor to the liberty of Romney, March 1858. *d.* 26 Chapel st. Belgrave sq. London 11 Jany. 1885.

DEEDES, WILLIAM *(brother of the preceding).* *b.* Sandling park, Kent 17 Oct. 1796; ed. at Winchester and C.C. coll. Ox,, B.A. 1818; Fellow of All Souls coll. 1818–33; M.P. for East Kent 1845–57 and Dec. 1857 to death; a comr. of church estates 30 April 1858 to death; chairman of Kent general sessions; major commandant of East Kent yeomanry cavalry. *d.* Eaton terrace, London 30 Nov. 1862.

DEEDES, WILLIAM *(eld. son of the preceding).* *b.* 11 Oct. 1834; ed. at Harrow; second lieut. Rifle brigade 1852; served in Crimean war and Indian mutiny; lieut.-col. commandant of East Kent militia 1865–69; M.P. for East Kent 1876–80. *d.* Saltwood Castle, Hythe, Kent 27 May 1887.

DE FOULON, JAMES FOULON, Marquis. *b.* England 1795; ed. under his godfather John Nash the architect; lived some time at Hastings where he taught the Princess Victoria perspective drawing; architect to sir Henry Meux of Oxford st. London, brewer 1831–41; his only son was killed at Lucknow during the Indian mutiny. *d.* Fulham road, London 22 Jany. 1887. *London Figaro 5 Feb. 1887, portrait.*

DE FREYNE, ARTHUR FRENCH, 1 Baron *(eld. son of Arthur French, M.P. for co. Roscommon, who d. 24 Nov. 1820).* *b.* 1795; called to Irish bar 1825; M.P. for co. Roscommon 1821–32; created baron de Freyne of Artagh 16 May 1839, and baron De Freyne of Coolavin 5 April 1851. *d.* 71 Connaught terrace, Hyde park, London 29 Sep. 1856.

DE GEX, SIR JOHN PETER *(eld. son of John De Gex of Leicester place, Leicester sq. London).* *b.* 1809; ed. at Jesus coll. Cam., fellow, hon. fellow; B.A. 1831, M.A. 1834; barrister L.I. 30 Jany. 1835; published with Basil Montagu and Edward Deacon *Cases in bankruptcy argued*

De Gex, Sir J. P. *(Con.)*

in the Court of Review and on appeal before the lord chancellor 3 vols. 1842–5, with John Smale *Reports of cases decided in Chancery by Knight-Bruce, V.C. and Parker, V.C. 5 vols. 1849–53, with Macnaghten and Gordon Cases in the Court of appeal in Chancery 8 vols. 1851–7;* Q.C. 28 March 1865; bencher of his inn 19 April 1865, treasurer 1882; knighted at Windsor Castle 7 Dec. 1882 on occasion of opening new law courts in the Strand; author with R. H. Smith of *Arrangements between debtors and creditors under the bankruptcy act 1861, and 2 supplements 3 vols. 1867–69). d.* 20 Hyde park sq. London 14 May 1887. *I.L.N. lxxxi, 656 (1882), portrait.*

DE GREY, THOMAS PHILIP DE GREY, 2 Earl *(eld. son of Thomas Robinson, 2 baron Grantham 1738–86).* *b.* Whitehall, London 8 Dec. 1781; succeeded as 3 baron Grantham 20 July 1786; ed. at St. John's coll. Cam., M.A. 1801; assumed surname of Weddell 7 May 1803; lord lieut. of Bedford 13 Feb. 1818; succeeded as 2 Earl De Grey 4 May 1833; assumed surname of De Grey in lieu of Weddell 24 June 1833; first lord of the admiralty 22 Dec. 1834 to 25 April 1835; P.C. 29 Dec. 1834; lord lieut. of Ireland 3 Sep. 1841 to 2 July 1844; grand master of order of St. Patrick 1841–44; K.G. 12 Dec. 1844; pres. of Instit. of British Architects 1834 to death; F.R.S. 29 April 1841; author of *Memoir of the life of Sir C. Lucas 1845; Characteristics of the Duke of Wellington apart from his military talents 1853. d.* 4 St. James's sq. London 14 Nov. 1859. *I.L.N. 25 Feb. 1842 p. 146, portrait, 13 Jany. 1844, 22, 24, portrait.*

DE HAMEL, FELIX JOHN *(son of Comte Jean Baptiste Augustin Bruno de Hamel).* *b.* Tamworth 1808; ed. at Repton; admitted solicitor 1835; assistant solicitor for the Customs 1845, chief solicitor for the Customs and Board of Trade 1848–78; consolidated the Acts relating to the Customs 1854 and 1876; facilitated Customs business by introducing a simpler form of bond. *d.* 70 Avenue road, Regent's park, London 31 July 1885 in 78 year.

DE HAVILLAND, THOMAS FIOTH *(eld. son of Sir Peter De Havilland of Havilland hall, Guernsey, who d. 1821).* *b.* Havilland 10 April 1775; entered Madras army 1791; superintending engineer and architect of Madras presidency 1814; constructed Madras bulwark and pier 1822; retired lieut. col. 20 April 1825; lived in Guernsey 1823 to death. *d.* De Beauvoir, Guernsey 23 Feb. 1866. *Vibart's Madras Engineers ii, 1–35 (1883).*

DE JARNAC, PHILIPPE FERDINAND AUGUSTE DE ROHAN CHABOT, Comte (*eld. son of Viscount De Chabot 1780–1875*). *b.* 2 June 1821; chief sec. of French embassy in London; lived in Kilkenny 20 years; French ambassador in London 28 Nov. 1874 to death; author of *Rockingham or the younger brother* 1849, anon.; *Love and ambition* 3 vols. 1851, anon.; *Cécile or the pervert By Sir Charles Rockingham* 1851; *Electra, a story of modern times* 3 vols. 1853, anon. *d.* French embassy, Albert Gate house, London 22 March 1875. *I.L.N. lxvi,* 321, 331 (1875), *portrait.*

DE JERSEY, HENRY. *b.* 1804; solicitor in City of London 1826 to death; vestry clerk of parishes of St. Anne, St. Agnes and St. Mary Staining; common councilman for Aldersgate ward 1840–71; chairman of Commission of Sewers 1862–71; master of the Loriners' Company 1871; secondary of City of London 1871 to Nov. 1884; under sheriff of London and Middlesex twice. *d.* 32 St. James's road, Brixton, London 1 Dec. 1884 in 81 year.

DE LA BECHE, SIR HENRY THOMAS (*son of Thomas De La Beche of Halse hall, Clarendon, Jamaica, a colonel in the army*). *b.* London 10 Feb. 1796; ed. at Ottery St. Mary, Devon and Great Marlow; F.G.S. 1817; studied geology in Dorset, Devon, Pembroke, Switzerland and France; conducted the Geological Survey under the Ordnance in Cornwall and Devon 1832, director general of Ordnance Survey 1840 to death; sec. to Geological Society 1831, foreign Sec. 1835–46, Pres. 1847 and 1848, Wollaston medallist 1855; F.R.S. 23 Dec. 1819; F.L.S. 1821; Geological museum in Jermyn st. London founded on his recommendation 1851; received order of Leopold of Belgium; created a Knight of Danish order of Dannebrog; knighted at St. James's palace 13 April 1842; C.B. 27 April 1848; author of *Researches in theoretical geology* 1834; *How to observe geology* 1835; *Report on the geology of Cornwall, Devon and West Somerset* 1839 and other books. *d.* London 13 April 1855. *Quarterly Journal of geological society xii, pp. xxxiv–viii* (1856); *Proceedings of royal society vii,* 582–86 (1855); *I.L.N. xviii,* 422 (1851), *portrait.*

DELACOMB, HENRY ISATT. Second lieut. R.M. 21 Oct. 1805; col. commandant 22 June 1855 to 1 April 1870; general 23 Aug. 1866; C.B. 2 June 1869. *d.* 19 Albion st. Hyde park, London 15 Nov. 1878 aged 89.

DELAGARDE, PHILIP CHILWELL (*son of a clergyman at Jersey*). *b.* 1797; ed. at Exeter gr. sch.; apprenticed to Peppin and Barnes,

surgeons, Exeter; house surgeon St. Bartholomew's hospital, London 25 Sep. 1818; M.R.C.S. Aug. 1819, hon. F.R.C.S. 1843; surgeon Eye infirmary, Exeter 1836; surgeon Devon and Exeter hospital, Exeter 1841, afterwards senior surgeon; ophthalmic surgeon and after the retirement of Barnes, the most popular operator in the West of England; mayor of Exeter, Nov. 1834 to 1 Jany. 1836; sheriff of Exeter 1832–33; author of *A treatise on Cataract* 1821; *A supplement to the account of the church of St. Andrew, Cullompton and its mural paintings* in Spreate's *Sketches of churches in Devon* 1842; *A brief commentary on the construction of hospitals* 1870, and *Nursing Sisterhoods*, a pamphlet. *d.* 23 Southernhay, Exeter 17 Nov. 1871 in 74 year. *Medical Times and Gazette* 2 Dec. 1871 p. 694; *Lancet* 16 Dec. 1871 p. 868.

DELAMAINE, CHARLES HENRY. Entered Bombay army 1820; retired colonel 24 April 1854; C.B. 4 July 1843. *d.* Dinan, France 19 June 1870.

DELAMERE, THOMAS CHOLMONDELEY, 1 Baron (*eld. son of Thomas Cholmondeley of Vale Royal, Northwich, Cheshire 1726–79, M.P. for Cheshire*). *b.* Beckenham, Kent 9 Aug. 1767; high sheriff of Cheshire 1792; M.P. for Cheshire 11 June 1796 to 29 Sep. 1812; created Baron Delamere on coronation of King George 4th, by patent dated 17 July 1821. *d.* 12 Hereford st. London 30 Sep. 1855.

DELAMERE, HUGH CHOLMONDELEY, 2 Baron (*eld. son of the preceding*). *b.* Vale Royal 3 Oct. 1812; ed. at Eton; M.P. for Denbighshire 1840–41 and for Montgomery 1841–47; col. 1 Royal Cheshire militia 28 Aug. 1840 to death. *d.* Vale Royal 1 Aug. 1887.

—

DE LA MOTTE, FREEMAN GAGE (*son of Wm. De La Motte 1775–1863*). Author of *Examples of modern alphabets* 1859; *Embroiderer's book of design* 1860; *Primer of the art of illumination* 1860; *Mediæval alphabets and initials for illuminators* 1861; *Book of ornamental alphabets 9th to 19th century* 1858, 5 ed. 1863. *d.* of apoplexy 15 Beaufort buildings, Strand, London 16 July 1862 aged 48.

DE LA MOTTE, PETER. Entered Bombay army 1797; col. 3 Bombay light cavalry 27 April 1826 to death; general 16 June 1860; C.B. 28 July 1838. *d.* 15 Craven hill gardens, London 5 Feb. 1861 aged 79.

DE LA MOTTE, WILLIAM ALFRED (*eld. son of Peter De La Motte of Weymouth, postal agent*).

DE LA MOTTE, W. A. (Con.)

b. Weymouth 2 Aug. 1775; pupil of Benjamin West, R.A.; drawing master at royal military colleges, Great Marlow and Sandhurst 1803–43; published *Thirty etchings of rural subjects* 1816; exhibited 53 pictures at R.A., 13 at B.I. and 7 at Suffolk st. gallery 1793–1850; author of *Smoking and Smokers* 1845, anon.; *Historical sketch of priory and hospital of St. Bartholomew* 1846. d. The lawn, St. Giles's fields, Oxford 13 Feb. 1863.

DELANE, JOHN THADEUS (2 son of the succeeding). b. South Molton st. London 11 Oct. 1817; ed. at King's college, London and Magd. hall, Ox., B.A. 1839; barrister M.T. 28 May 1847; engaged upon the *Times* 1839, editor May 1841 to Nov. 1877; organised with aid of Lieut. Thomas Waghorn a special *Times* express from Alexandria to London 1845; exposed and stopped the railway mania 1845, at an immense cost by loss of advertisements. d. Ascot Heath house near Ascot 22 Nov. 1879. *Macmillan's Mag., Jany.* 1880 pp. 267–72; *Kinglake's Crimean war, 6 ed. vol. vii, chapter ix, pp.* 214–72; *Hatton's Journalistic London* 1882 p. 81, portrait; *Times* 25 Nov. 1879 p. 7, cols. 3–5; *I.L.N. lxxv*, 548 (1879), portrait.

DELANE, WILLIAM FREDERICK AUGUSTUS. Financial manager of *Times* newspaper; barrister G.I. 26 Jany. 1831; manager of *Morning Chronicle* to 1847; treasurer of county courts of Kent and part of Surrey (circuits 47, 48, 49 and 50), March 1847 to death; author of *A collection of decisions in the courts for revising the lists of electors for the counties of Berks [and other counties, cities and boroughs]* 1834, 2 ed. 1836; *The present laws for regulating highways* 1835. d. Hellesdon, Norwich 29 July 1857 aged 64.

DELANY, MOST REV. WILLIAM. b. Bandon 25 Dec. 1803; ed. at Dunboyne; parish priest of Bandon 1845; R.C. bishop of Cork 1847 to death, during which period there was a great revival of church architecture and multiplication of religious institutions. d. Blackrock near Cork 14 Nov. 1886.

DE LA RUE, THOMAS. b. Guernsey 24 March 1793; printer there 1815; manufacturer of straw hats in London; invented bonnets of embossed paper; founded house of De La Rue and Sons, card and ornamental paper makers; introduced several new printing inks; invented embossing of bookbinder's cloths; patented fixing of iridescent films on paper; Chevalier of Legion of Honour 1855. d. 84 Westbourne terrace, Hyde park, London 7 June 1866.

DE LA SAUSSAYE, SIR RICHARD (son of Richard Sausse of Carrick-on-Suir, co. Tipperary). b. 1807; ed. at Stonyhurst and Trin. coll. Dublin; ensign in Spanish royal foot guards 1827; served with distinction during civil war 1833–40 attaining rank of brigadier general; sent on a special mission to Great Britain 1854; commanded a division in campaign in Africa against the Moors 1859–60 where he was made major general; chamberlain to Queen of Spain; military governor of fortress of Carthagena and of province of Murcia; knighted at Windsor Castle 21 Aug. 1841 for services performed while in command of British auxiliary brigade in north of Spain; received Grand Cross of order of Isabel the Catholic. d. Paris 27 Oct. 1872.

DE LASAUX, THOMAS THORPE. b. Canterbury 1797; solicitor there 1820 to death; coroner for East Kent 1820 to death being the oldest coroner in England; coroner for Canterbury many years; said to have held 4000 inquests. d. Canterbury 21 May 1884 in 87 year.

DELAWARR, GEORGE JOHN SACKVILLE WEST, 5 Earl (only son of 4 Earl Delawarr 1758–95). b. Savile row, London 26 Oct. 1791; succeeded 28 July 1795; ed. at Harrow and Brasenose coll. Ox.; chief friend of Lord Byron at Harrow; B.A. 1812, M.A. 1819; hon. D.C.L. Cam. 1828, hon. D.C.L. Ox. 1834; lord chamberlain 8 Sep. 1841 to 8 July 1846, and 26 Feb. 1858 to 18 June 1859; P.C. 14 Sep. 1841; took name of Sackville before West 6 Nov. 1843. d. Buckhurst park, Tunbridge Wells 23 Feb. 1869. *Portraits of eminent conservatives, second series* (1846), portrait.

DELAWARR, CHARLES RICHARD SACKVILLE-WEST, 6 Earl (2 son of the preceding). b. Upper Grosvenor st. London 13 Nov. 1815; ensign 43 foot 26 July 1833; lieut.-col. 21 foot 9 March 1855 to 15 Aug. 1856 when placed on h.p.; commanded a brigade in expedition to Kinburn 1855 and a brigade at Shorncliffe 1856; M.G. 29 Oct. 1864; C.B. 5 July 1855; knight of the Medjidie 2 March 1858; K.C.B. 20 May 1871; a comr. for abolition of army purchase 30 Sep. 1871; drowned himself in the river Cam at Cambridge 22 April 1873. *United Service Mag.* 1873 par* 3, 39–49; *I.L.N. lx*, 157, 158 (1872), portrait.

DELEPIERRE, JOSEPH OCTAVE (son of Joseph Delepierre, receveur-général of province of West Flanders). b. Bruges, Belgium 12 March 1802; ed. at Univ. of Ghent; an avocat; archiviste de la Flandre Occidentale, Bruges; came to London 1843; sec. of Belgian legation, Aug. 1849 to 1874; Belgian consul in London 1

Oct. 1849 to 14 April 1875; hon. sec. of the Philobiblon Society 1853, contributed 22 papers to its privately printed Miscellanies; hon. F.S.A. 1 May 1845; author of *Heures de loisir, essais poétiques* 1829; *Old Flunders, traditions and legends of Belgium* 2 vols. 1845, and of 53 other books. *d.* 29 Upper Hamilton terrace, London 18 Aug. 1879. *J. O. Delepierre In memoriam, by N. Trubner* 1880, *portrait; Le Livre, Paris, Jany.* 1880 *pp.* 22–28, 291–92; *R. Blakey's Memoirs* (1879) 208–12, 230, 239.

DELEVANTI, GEORGE, assumed name of George Crippin. *b.* London 29 July 1848; pupil of John Delevanti the clown 1854; entered the profession as an acrobat; champion somersault rider of the world at one time; performed in nearly every part of the globe; leading equestrian at Renz's circus, Berlin. *d.* 34 Headland park, Plymouth 3 May 1887.

DELF, THOMAS. *b.* London; a bookseller in Bow lane, afterwards at 168 New Bond st. 1853 to death; partner with Nicholas Trubner 1851–2; projected *The Artist, The Children's Journal* 1863, *The photographic art Journal* 1862, *The royal cook* 1858; author under pseudonym of Charles Martel of *The principles of colouring in painting* 1855; *The principles of form in ornamental art* 1856; *Love letters of eminent persons* 1859; *On the materials used in painting with remarks on varnishing and cleaning pictures* 1859; *The principles of harmony and contrast of colours by M. E. Chevreul, translated by C. Martel* 1854, 3 *ed.* 1859. *d.* 23 July 1865 aged 55.

DE LIEFDE, JACOB. *b.* Holland; *Daily News* war correspondent outside Paris 1870–71; author of *Six months among the charities of Europe* 2 vols. 1865, *new ed.* 1872; *Romance of charity* 1867; *Truth in Tales* 1870; *The great Dutch admirals* 1873, *new ed.* 1880. *d.* Twickenham 6 Feb. 1878 aged 31.

DE L'ISLE and DUDLEY, PHILIP CHARLES SIDNEY, 1 Baron (*only son of Sir John Shelley Sidney, 1 baronet* 1771–1849). *b.* 11 March 1800; ed. at Ch. Ch. Ox.; member of Sidney Sussex coll. Cam., D.C.L. Cam. 1835; M.P. for Eye, Suffolk 19 Oct. 1829 to Feb. 1831; K.C.H. 1830, G.C.H. 1831; surveyor general of Duchy of Cornwall, March 1832 to March 1849; created Baron De L'Isle and Dudley by patent dated 13 Jany. 1835; succeeded as 2 baronet 14 March 1849. (*m.* 13 Aug. 1825 Sophia eld. child of King Wm. iv, by Mrs. Jordan the actress, she *d.* 10 April 1837). *d.* Penshurst, Kent 4 March 1851.

DE LISLE, AMBROSE LISLE MARCH PHILLIPPS (*eld. son of Charles March Phillipps of Garendon park, Leics.* 1779–1862). *b.* Garendon 17 March 1809; received into R.C. church 1824; ed. at Trin. coll. Cam. 1826–28; gave 230 acres of land in Charnwood Forest for re-establishment of Cistercian order 1835, exactly 3 centuries after its suppression; received the habit of third order of St. Dominic at Rome 1837; built R.C. church at Sheepshed 1842; a principal founder of Association for the promotion of the unity of Christendon 1857; assumed name of De Lisle 1862; sheriff of Leics. 1868; translated from the Italian *The lamentations of England by Father Dominic, Passionist* 1831; *A vindication of Catholic morality by Count Alexander Manzoni* 1836 and other books. *d.* Garendon 5 March 1878. *Two sermons preached on the death of A. L. M. P. De Lisle, March 1878, preceded by a short sketch of his life, privately printed* 1878; *Gillow's English Catholics* ii, 38–47 (1885).

DE LISLE, RUDOLPH EDWARD LISLE MARCH PHILLIPPS (*son of the preceding*). *b.* Gracedieu manor 23 Nov. 1853; midshipman R.N. 28 July 1868; lieut. 24 May 1877; lieut. Alexandra 12 guns 9 Jany. 1883; served in naval brigade attached to the Upper Nile expedition, Aug. 1884 to death; killed at battle of Abu Klea 17 Jany. 1885. *Memoir of Lieut. Rudolph De Lisle by Rev. H. N. Oxenham* (1886), *portrait.*

DELLAGANA, BARTOLOMEO. *b.* Annigino canton Ticino, Switzerland; stereotyper at 61 Red Lion st. Clerkenwell, London 1855, moved to Shoe Lane 1857; effected great improvements in stereotyping by using papier mache; stereotyped the Illustrated London News, Times, Daily Telegraph and other papers; naturalised in England 7 Jany. 1867. *d.* The Terrace, Kennington park, London 26 May 1882 in 50 year.

DEMAINBRAY, REV. STEPHEN GEORGE FRANCIS TRIBOUDET (*only son of Stephen Charles Triboudet Demainbray* 1710–82, *astronomer to royal observatory at Kew*). *b.* Ealing, Middlesex 7 Aug. 1759; ed. at Harrow and Ex. coll. Ox., B.A. 1781, M.A. 1782, B.D. 1793; fell. of his coll. 30 June 1778 to 4 Feb. 1799; astronomer at Kew observatory 1782–1840 when it was given up; Whitehall preacher 1794; V. of Long Wittenham, Berks 9 Aug. 1794 to 4 Feb. 1799; R. of Broad Somerford, Wilts. 4 Feb. 1799 to death; one of His Majesty's chaplains at Kew 1801; chaplain in ord. at St. James's palace 1802; author of *The poor man's best friend* 1831. *d.* Broad Somerford rectory 6 July 1854. *G.M. xlii,* 193–94 (1854).

DE MAULEY, WILLIAM FRANCIS SPENCER PONSONBY, 1 Baron (3 *son of 3 Earl of Bessborough* 1758–1844). *b.* Cavendish sq. London 31 July 1787; M.P. for Poole 1826–31, for Knaresborough 1831–32 and for Dorset 1832–37; created baron De Mauley of Canford, Dorset 10 July 1838; chairman of Submarine electric telegraph company. *d.* 21 St. James's place, London 16 May 1855.

DEMAUS, REV. ROBERT. Educ. at Univ. of Edin., signet medallist, M.A. 1851; chaplain to bishop of Aberdeen 1860–65; C. of St. Luke, Chelsea 1865–72; principal of Whitelands training college, Chelsea 1872 to death; author of *Class book of scripture history* 1863; *English literature and composition* 1866; *William Tyndale, a contribution to history of English Bible* 1871; *The Jesuits, a historical sketch* 1873. *d.* of apoplexy 11 St. Leonard's terrace, Chelsea 15 March 1874 aged 45.

DE MORGAN, AUGUSTUS (5 *child of John De Morgan, col. in Madras army, who d.* 1816). *b.* Madura, Madras 27 June 1806; lost his right eye soon afterwards; ed. at Trin. coll. Cam.; scholar 1825, fourth wrangler 1827, B.A. 1827; student at Lincoln's Inn 1827; professor of mathematics in London University 23 Feb. 1828 to 24 July 1831; fellow of Astronomical Soc. May 1828, member of council 1830–61, hon. sec. 1831–38 and 1848–54; professor of mathematics in University college, London, Oct. 1836 to 10 Nov. 1866; pres. of Mathematical Soc. 7 Nov. 1864; granted civil list pension of £100, 21 Jany. 1870; author of *Elements of arithmetic* 1830, 6 ed. 1876; *Formal Logic* 1847; *Trigonometry and double algebra* 1849; *Book of almanacs* 1851, 2 ed. 1871; *Budget of Paradoxes* 1872, and nearly one sixth of articles in *Penny Cyclopædia* 1833–58. (*m.* 1837 Sophia Elizabeth dau. of Wm. Frend of London, she was granted civil list pension of £50, 25 July 1871). *d.* Merton road, Regent's park, London 18 March 1871. *Memoir of A. De Morgan by S. E. De Morgan* 1882, *portrait, with list of his writings at pp.* 401–17; *Monthly notices of Royal Astronom. Soc. xxx,* 11, 112–18 (1872).

DE MORGAN, CAMPBELL GREIG (*brother of the preceding*). *b.* Clovelly, Devon 1811; ed. at Univ. coll. London; M.R.C.S. 1835, F.R.C.S. 1843; assistant surgeon Middlesex hospital 1842, surgeon 1848 to death; lectured on forensic medicine there 1841, afterwards on physiology and surgery to death; professor of anatomy 1845; F.R.S. 6 June 1861; author of *The origin of Cancer* 1872, and of the article Erysipelas in Holmes's *System of surgery* 1860.

DE MORGAN, C. G. (*Con.*) *d.* 29 Seymour st. Portman sq. London 12 April 1876. *Medical Circular iv,* 67 (1854); *Medical Times and Gazette i,* 483–5 (1876).

DEMPSTER, WILLIAM RICHARDSON. *b.* Keith, Scotland 1809; went to the United States when young, and became naturalised; a successful composer and public singer; set Tennyson's *May Queen* to music; composed music for most of the songs found in Tennyson's longer poems. *d.* London 7 March 1871.

DENBIGH, WILLIAM BASIL PERCY FIELDING, 7 Earl of. *b.* Berwick house, Salop 25 March 1796; succeeded his grandfather as 7 Earl 14 July 1800; ed. at Eton and Trin. coll. Cam.; lord chamberlain to Queen Adelaide, Jany. 1833; P.C. 4 Feb. 1833; G.C.H. 1833; master of the Horse to Queen Adelaide 15 Dec. 1834 to 2 Dec. 1849 when she died. *d.* Hampstead 25 June 1865.

DENDY, WALTER COOPER. *b.* at or near Horsham, Sussex 1794; M.R.C.S. 1814; practised in City of London; fellow of Medical Soc. of London, president; senior surgeon to Royal infirmary for children, Waterloo Road; author of *Practical remarks on the diseases of the skin* 1837, 2 ed. 1854; *The philosophy of mystery* 1841; *Psyche, a discourse on the birth and pilgrimage of thought* 1853; *The beautiful islets of Britaine* 1857, 2 ed. 1860, and other books. *d.* 25 Suffolk st. Haymarket, London 10 Dec. 1871. *J. F. Clarke's Autobiographical recollections* (1874) 441–9; *Medical Circular iv,* 155–6 (1854).

DE NEMOURS, VICTOIRE AUGUSTE ANTOINETTE, Duchesse (*only dau. of Ferdinand George Augustus, Duke of Saxe Coburg* 1785–1851). *b.* Vienna 16 Feb. 1822; lived at Claremont, Surrey 1848 to death. (*m.* 27 April 1840 Duc de Nemours 2 son of Louis Phillippe King of the French, he was *b.* 25 Oct. 1814). *d.* Claremont 10 Nov. 1857. *bur.* in the Taylor vault under R.C. church of St. Charles Borromeo, Weybridge, Nov.; body removed to a mortuary chapel adjoining above church 5 Oct. 1883.

DENHAM, SIR HENRY MANGLES (*son of Henry Denham of Sherborne, Dorset*). *b.* 28 Aug. 1800; entered navy April 1809; captain 17 Aug. 1846; F.R.S. 28 Feb. 1839; a younger brother of Trinity House 1841 to death; employed in the construction of charts 1822–52; inspector of steam-boat accidents; invented a valuable contrivance for steering a ship when disabled called Denham's Jury Tiller, also Denham's Rowlocks for rowing boats; knighted at Windsor Castle 26 March 1867; retired

DENHAM, SIR H. M. (Con.)

admiral 1 Aug. 1877; A.I.C.E. 4 March 1851; author of *Sailing directions for the British Channel* 1839 and other works. *d.* 21 Carlton road, Maida vale, London 3 July 1887. *Min. Proc. I.C.E. xci*, 460-62 (1888).

DENHAM, REV. JOSHUA FREDERICK. Educ. at St. John's coll. Cam., B.A. 1827, M.A. 1830; lecturer of St. Bride's, Fleet st. London 1828; R. of St. Mary-le Strand, London 1839 to death; F.R.S. 20 May 1841; author of *Natural theology* 1828; *History of the old St. Dunstan's church* 1832; *Letters on education* 1832 and other books. *d.* 8 New Inn, Strand, London 26 Jany. 1861 aged 60.

DENHAM, MICHAEL AISLABIE. *b.* near Bowes, Yorkshire; in business at Hull; general merchant at Piercebridge, Durham; printed *Folk Lore or a collection of local rhymes, proverbs, sayings, prophecies, slogans, &c. relating to Northumberland, Newcastle-on-Tyne and Berwick-upon-Tweed* 1858 and other books on folk lore. *d.* Piercebridge 10 Sep. 1859.

DENIEHY, DANIEL HENRY. *b.* Kent st. Sydney 1828; attorney in Sydney and Goulburn; mem. for Argyle in Representative Assembly 1856-58, for East Macquarie 1858-59; published a series of obituary notices in the *Southern Cross* 1859-60; edited *The Victorian* Melbourne weekly paper 1862-64. *d.* in the hospital, Bathurst 22 Oct. 1865 in 37 year. *G. B. Barton's Poets and prose writers of New South Wales* (1866) 94-148.

DENING, EMMA GERALDINE HENRIETTA HAMILTON (*dau. of Thomas Clarence Hooper*). *b.* Paris 30 March 1841, ed. at Bath; converted by Rev. Wm. Haslam; commenced a prayer meeting at Avon st. Bath 1861; preached in Temperance hall, Widcombe, Bath to large congregations 1862; popular preacher in country districts and in tent services; preached about 4500 sermons. (*m.* 2 Oct. 1868 T. Henry Dening of Ottery St. Mary, Devon, farmer). Mr. and Mrs. Dening by their efforts built St. James's hall, Bath 1871 where they preached, hall burnt down 1878. *d.* Green park, Bath 12 Aug. 1872. *bur.* Locksbrook cemetery 16 Aug. when 6000 people were present. *Mrs. G. Guinness' She spake of Him* (1873), *portrait*; *S. D. Major's Notabilia of Bath* (1879) 90, 194.

DENISON, CHRISTOPHER BECKETT (2 son of *Sir Edmund Beckett, 4 baronet* 1787-1874). *b.* 9 May 1825; in Bengal C.S. 1845-65; M.P. eastern division of West Riding of Yorkshire 25 Nov. 1868 to 24 March 1880; deputy chairman Great Northern railway, Jany. 1880 to death. *d.* Ireland 30 Oct. 1884. *Catalogue of collection of pictures, &c. of C. B. Denison* (1885).

DENISON, RIGHT REV. EDWARD (2 *son of John Wilkinson, who took name of Denison, of Ossington, co. Nottingham, M.P. for Chichester, who d.* 6 *May* 1820). *b.* 34 Harley st. London 13 March 1801; ed. at Esher, Eton and Oriel coll. Ox., B.A. 1822, M.A. 1826, D.D. 1837; fell. of Merton coll. 1826; V. of St. Peters in the East, Oxford to 1837; select preacher before Univ. of Ox. 1834; bishop of Salisbury 13 March 1837 to death, consecrated at Lambeth 16 April 1837; author of *Sermons and charges*. *d.* The Close, Salisbury 6 March 1854. *The Eton portrait gallery* (1876) 157-62; *G.M. April* 1854 pp. 418-20.

DENISON, EDWARD (*eld. child of the preceding*). *b.* The Palace, Salisbury 8 Sep. 1840; ed. at Eton and Ch. Ch. Ox.; read law 1862-66; lived in Philpot st. Mile end road, London where he built and endowed a school 1867-68; barrister L.I. 27 Jany. 1868; M.P. for Newark 18 Nov. 1868 to death; left England for Australia, Oct. 1869. *d.* Melbourne 26 Jany. 1870. *Letters and other writings of the late Edward Denison, edited by Sir Baldwyn Leighton* 1872; *Stray studies by J. R. Green* (1876) 3-28.

DENISON, SIR WILLIAM THOMAS (*brother of Right Rev. Edward Denison* 1801-54). *b.* Portland place, London 3 May 1804; ed. at Eton and R.M.A. Woolwich; 2 lieut. R.E. 15 March 1826; lieut. governor of Tasmania 26 Jany. 1847 to 8 Jany. 1855; governor of New South Wales with title of governor general of Australia 20 Jany. 1855 to 22 Jany. 1861; col. R.E. 20 Sep. 1860 to 7 Nov. 1868; governor of Madras, March 1861 to March 1866; acted as governor general of India 20 Nov. 1863 to Jany. 1864; chairman of commission to inquire into best means of preventing pollution of rivers 6 April 1868 to death; L.G. 23 Nov. 1870; knighted at Buckingham palace 1 Aug. 1846; K.C.B. 19 July 1856; F.R.A.S. 1834; A.I.C.E. 14 March 1837, Telford medallist; F.R.S. 22 Feb. 1838; author of *Varieties of viceregal life* 2 vols. 1870, and many other works. *d.* The Observatory, East Sheen 19 Jany. 1871. *Papers on subjects connected with duties of Corps of Royal Engineers n.s. xx, pp. ix-xlii*, (1872); *Therry's Reminiscences, 2 ed.* (1863) 449-69; *Min. of proc. of Instit. of C.E. xxxiii*, 251-59 (1872); *Dunkin's Obituary notices of Astronomers* (1879) 32-34.

DENMAN, THOMAS DENMAN, 1 Baron (*only son of Thomas Denman of London, physician, 1733-1815*). *b.* Queen st. Golden sq. London 23 Feb. 1779; ed. at Eton and St. John's coll. Cam., B.A. 1800, M.A. 1803; a special pleader 1803; barrister L.I. 9 May 1806.

DENMAN, Lord (*Con.*)

bencher 1820; M.P. for Wareham, Dorset 1818; M.P. for Nottingham 1820–26 and 1830–32; solicitor general to Queen Caroline 8 Feb. 1820 to her death 7 Aug. 1821; received freedom of city of London 7 June 1821; common serjeant of city of London 26 April 1822 to Nov. 1830; K.C. Nov. 1828; attorney general 19 Nov. 1830 to 4 Nov. 1832; knighted by Wm. 4 at St. James's palace 24 Nov. 1830; lord chief justice of King's Bench 4 Nov. 1832 to 28 Feb. 1850; P.C. 9 Nov. 1832; created Baron Denman of Dovedale, Derbyshire 22 March 1834; the first chief justice of England who sat in House of Lords without his judicial robes. *d.* Stoke Albany near Rockingham, Northamptonshire 22 Sep. 1854. *Arnould's Memoir of Lord Denman* 2 *vols.* 1873, *portrait; The Eton portrait gallery* (1876) 436–45; *J. Whiteside's Early sketches of eminent persons* (1870) 21–45; *H. Martineau's Biographical sketches,* 4 *ed.* (1876) 238–46.

DENMAN, JOSEPH (3 *son of the preceding*). *b.* 23 June 1810; entered navy 7 April 1823; captain 23 Aug. 1841; captain of H.M.'s yacht Victoria and Albert 19 Oct. 1853 to 15 Jany. 1862; naval aide-de-camp to the Queen 20 March 1858; R.A. 15 Jany. 1862; commander in chief in the Pacific 10 May 1864 to 21 Nov. 1866; V.A. 20 Nov. 1866; granted Greenwich hospital pension 9 Jany. 1869; contested Manchester 2 May 1859; author of *The African squadron and Mr. Hutt's committee* 1850. *d.* 17 Eaton terrace, London 26 Nov. 1874.

DENNETT, JOHN. *b.* 1790; invented Dennett's life-saving rocket apparatus for conveying a rope from the shore to a shipwrecked crew 1832, these rockets were sent to all parts of the world, they were superseded by Boxer's rocket 1865; custodian of Carisbrook Castle, Newport, Isle of Wight to death; contributed to *Journal of British Archeol. Assoc.* vols. 1–5 accounts of various antiquities in England. *d.* Carisbrook Castle 10 July 1852.

DENNIS, SIR JAMES (*son of John Dennis, an attorney*). *b.* 1778; midshipman in navy; ensign 49 foot 2 Sep. 1796, major 25 April 1828 to 4 June 1833; lieut. col. 3 foot 4 June 1833 to 11 Nov. 1851; commanded a division of infantry at battle of Maharajpore 29 Dec. 1843; K.C.B. 30 Oct. 1844; M.G. 11 Nov. 1851. *d.* Pall Mall, London 14 Jany. 1855.

DENNIS, REV. JAMES BLATCH PIGGOT (*son of Philip Piggot Dennis*). Matric. from Queen's coll. Ox. 28 May 1835 aged 19, B.A. 1839; C. of Maxey, Northants. 1842–54; C. of St.

DENNIS, REV. J. B. P. (*Con.*)

James, Bury St. Edmunds; F.G.S., an authority on fossil bones; his collection of hawks and owls is in Bury St. Edmunds' museum; author of *An answer to the parishioners of Lawshall, telling them why he became a Catholic* 1859. *d.* Garland st. Bury St. Edmunds 12 Jany. 1861. *Bury and Norwich Post* 15 Jany. 1861 *p.* 2.

DENNIS, JAMES SAMUEL AKED. *b.* 1809; entered navy 24 Oct. 1822; captain 18 July 1857; retired V.A. 2 Aug. 1879. *d.* rectory cottage, Hanwell 9 Feb. 1881.

DENNISTOUN, ALEXANDER. *b.* Glasgow 1790; a merchant at Glasgow; M.P. for co. Dumbarton 1835 to 1837. *d.* Lagarie row, Dennistoun, Glasgow 15 July 1874.

DENNISTOUN, JAMES (*eld. son of James Dennistoun of Dennistoun, co. Dumbarton, who d. 1 June 1834*). *b.* Dumbartonshire 17 March 1803; ed. at Univs. of Edin. and Glasgow; mem. of faculty of advocates 1824; edited several publications for the Bannatyne and Maitland clubs; contributed many articles chiefly on Art to *Edinburgh* and *Quarterly Reviews;* published *Memoirs of the Dukes of Urbino* 3 vols. 1851, and *Memoirs of Sir Robert Strange, knt., engraver, and of his brother in law Andrew Lumisden, private secretary to the Stuart Princes* 2 vols. 1855. *d.* 119 George st. Edinburgh 13 Feb. 1855. *G.M. xliii,* 647–8 (1855); *Fraser's Mag. li,* 643–4 (1855).

DENNISTOUN, JOHN. *b.* 1803; M.P. for Glasgow 1837 to 1847. *d.* Armadale Row, Dumbartonshire 9 Sep. 1870.

DENNY, HENRY. Curator of museum of Literary and Philosophical Society, Leeds 1826 to death; author of *Monographia Pselaphidarum et Scydmænidarum Britanniæ, or an essay on the British species of the genera Pselaphus of Herbst and Scydmænus of Latreille* 1825, *er; Monographia Anoplurorum Britanniæ, or an essay on the British species of parasite insects belonging to the order Anoplura of Leach* 1842. *d.* Leeds 7 March 1871 aged 68.

DENNY, WILLIAM. *b.* Dumbarton 25 May 1847; educ. Edinburgh high school; Apprentice to his father a shipbuilder at Dumbarton 1864 and partner 1868; partner in engineering firm of Denny & Co., Leven shipyard on the Clyde, increased size of works from 19 to 42 acres in 1881; made great improvements in the construction and building of steam ships 1869–82; founded an Award scheme for inventions and improvements made

DENNY, W. (*Con.*)

by his workmen 1880 ; read papers on ships, etc. before Lit. and Philos. Soc. of Dumbarton, Instit. of Civil engineers, Instit of Naval Architects and other Societies 1869–82; served on the Load Line Committee 1884–5; M.I.C.E. 7 March 1876 ; his residence Bellfield with a valuable library burnt down 1882. *d.* Buenos Ayres 17 March 1887. *Min. of proc. of Instit. of C.E. lxxxix*, 457–66 (1887).

DENT, CHARLES CALMADY. *b.* 26 Sep. 1793; entered navy 9 Aug. 1810; captain 16 Feb. 1852; retired R.A. 1 April 1870. *d.* 37 Nelson road, Great Yarmouth 3 Jany. 1872.

DENT, EDWARD JOHN. *b.* London 19 Aug. 1790; employed by Vulliamy and son, and Barrauds and son, chronometer makers 1815–29; partner with John Roger Arnold at 84 Strand 1830–40; kept a shop at 82 Strand 1840; opened branch depôts at 33 Cockspur st. and 34 Royal Exchange; began manufacture of turret clocks 1843; A.I.C.E. 1833; received order for great clock at Westminster 1852, lived only to see commencement of it; author of *On the construction and management of chronometers, watches and clocks* 1846, and other works. *d.* The Mall, Kensington Gravel Pits, London 8 March 1853. *Min. of proc. of Instit. of C.E. xiii*, 156–61 (1854); *Sir E. Beckett's Clocks, watches and bells* (1883) *pp.* 181, 238, 266–68, 300, 310, 313.

DENT, JOHN (*eld. son of John Dent of Worcester, glover* 1751–1811). *b.* 1777; glove manufacturer at Worcester with his brother Wm. Dent, who *d.* 11 Oct. 1854 aged 70; they purchased from Duke of Buckingham the ruined site of Sudeley castle and chapel, Gloucestershire which they restored; sheriff of Worcs. 1849. *d.* Sudeley Castle 8 Oct. 1855.

DENTON, REV. WILLIAM (*eld. son of James Denton of Newport, Isle of Wight*). Matric. from Worcester coll. Ox. 28 May 1841 aged 26, B.A. 1844, M.A. 1848; C. of Shoreditch, London 1847–50; V. of St. Bartholomew, Cripplegate, London 1850 to death; author of *A commentary on Gospels for the Sundays and other Holy Days* 3 *vols.* 1861–63, 3 *ed.* 1875; *A commentary on the Epistles* 1869 ; *Servia and the Servians* 1862 ; *Records of St. Giles' Cripplegate* 1882 and many other books. *d.* 22 Westbourne sq. Paddington, London 2 Jany. 1888.

DENYS, SIR GEORGE WILLIAM, 1 Baronet (*only son of Peter Denys of Hans place, Chelsea, who d. 27 June* 1816). *b.* Easton Neston, Northamptonshire 20 May 1788; ed. at Trin.

DENYS, SIR G. W. (*Con.*)

coll. Cam., M.A. 1814; equerry to Duke of Sussex; M.P. for Hull 6 Oct. 1812 to 10 June 1818; created Bart. 23 Nov. 1813. *d.* 42 Onslow sq. Brompton, London 26 April 1857.

DE PORQUET, LOUIS PHILIPPE R. FENWICK (*son of Capt. Fenwick*). *b.* Paris 1796; taught English in France; adopted his mother's name; came to England about 1823 ; author of educational works in the English, French, Italian and Spanish languages, upwards of 40 in number 1823 to death. *d.* 17 Camden st. Camden Town, London 26 Aug. 1873.

DE QUINCEY, THOMAS (4 *child of Thomas Quincey of Manchester, merchant, who d.* 18 *July* 1793 *aged* 38). *b.* Manchester 15 Aug. 1785; ed. at Bath and Manchester gr. schs. ; matric. from Worcester coll. Ox. 17 Dec. 1803 where his name remained on the books till Dec. 1810; student of Middle Temple about 1808; edited Westmoreland Gazette 1819–20; wrote in the *London Mag.* 1821–24, *Blackwood's Mag.* 1826–49 and *Tait's Mag.* 1834–51; published *Klosterheim, or the masque by the English opium eater* 1832 which was dramatised for two of the London theatres; eat opium 1804–16, 1817–18, 1824–25 and 1841–44, in 1813 his dose had risen to 340 grains of opium or 8000 drops of laudanum per diem, about half what Coleridge was taking at that time; he is described in J. H. Burton's *The Book Hunter* as Papaverius; author of *Confessions of an English opium eater* 1822 first published in the *London Mag.* 1821 ; *The logic of political economy* 1844 ; the first English edition of his collected works was published in 1853–60 as *Selections grave and gay* 14 *vols.*, 4 *ed.* 16 *vols.* 1875–80, the most complete edition of his works is the American in 20 vols. 1852–55. *d.* 42 Lothian st. Edinburgh 8 Dec. 1859. *T. De Quincey by H. A. Page* 2 *vols.* (1877), *portrait; D. Masson's De Quincey* (1881); *S. Hodgson's Outcast Essays* (1881) 1–98 ; *F. Espinasse's Lancashire Worthies, second series* (1877) 378–461 ; *C. Mackay's Forty years recollections* (1877) i, 314–26 ; *H. Martineau's Biographical Sketches*, 4 *ed.* (1876) 409–17 ; *John Bull Mag.* July 1824 *pp.* 21–24.

DE RAMSEY, EDWARD FELLOWES, 1 Baron (2 *son of Wm. Henry Fellowes of Ramsey abbey, Hunts.* 1769–1837). *b.* 14 April 1809; ed. at the Charterhouse; M.P. for Hunts. 10 Aug. 1837 to 24 March 1880; chairman of the Middle Level commission; created Baron De Ramsey 5 July 1887. *d.* 3 Belgrave sq. London 9 Aug. 1887.

DERBY, EDWARD SMITH STANLEY, 13 Earl of (*only son of* 12 *Earl of Derby* 1752–1834). *b.* 21 April 1775; ed. at Eton and Trin. coll. Cam., M.A. 1795; M.P. for Preston 1796–1812 and for Lancashire 1812–32; colonel 2 Lancashire militia 1 March 1797; created Baron Stanley of Bickerstaffe, co. palatine of Lancaster 22 Dec. 1832; succeeded his father 21 Oct. 1834; K.G. 2 April 1839; F.L.S. 1807, pres. 1828–34; pres. of Zoological Soc. 1831 to death; formed at Knowsley hall collections of living animals and birds, which far surpassed any menagerie or aviary previously attempted by a private person in this country, these collections were sold 6–11 Oct. 1851 for £7000; privately printed *Gleanings from the menagerie and aviary at Knowsley hall* 2 *parts with* 76 *plates* 1846–50. *d.* Knowsley hall 30 June 1851. *P. Draper's House of Stanley* (1864) 275–82; *Law Review xvi,* 1–32 (1852); *I.L.N. xix,* 14, 405, 449 (1851).

DERBY, EDWARD GEOFFREY SMITH STANLEY, 14 Earl of (*eld. son of the preceding*). *b.* Knowsley 29 March 1799; ed. at Eton and Ch. Ch. Ox.; M.P. for Stockbridge 1822–26, for Preston 1826–30, for Windsor 1830–32, for North Lancashire 1832–44; under sec. of state for Colonies, April 1827 to Jany. 1828; chief sec. to lord lieut. of Ireland 26 Nov. 1830 to March 1833; P.C. 22 Nov. 1830, P.C. Ireland 10 Jany. 1831; sec. of state for Colonies 28 March 1833 to 5 June 1834; lord rector of Univ. of Glasgow 1834–36; sec. of state for Colonies 3 Sep. 1841 to Dec. 1845; created Baron Stanley of Bickerstaffe 4 Nov. 1844; succeeded 30 June 1851; first lord of the Treasury 27 Feb. to 28 Dec. 1852, 1 March 1858 to 18 June 1859 and 13 June 1866 to 25 Feb. 1868; chancellor of Univ. of Oxford 12 Oct. 1852; K.G. 28 June 1859; won the One thousand guineas with Canezou 1848, Goodwood Cup with Canezou 1849 and 1850, the Oaks with Iris 1851, and the Two thousand guineas with Fazzolette 1856; sold greater part of his racing stud 1858 for over £5000; privately printed *Translations of poems ancient and modern* 1862; published *The Iliad of Homer rendered into English blank verse* 2 *vols.* 1864, 10 *ed.* 1876. *d.* Knowsley 23 Oct. 1869, personalty sworn under £250,000, 9 April 1870. *P. Draper's House of Stanley* (1864) 282–97; *The Eton portrait gallery* (1876) 291–99; *W. C. Taylor's National portrait gallery iv,* 51 (1848), *portrait; G. H. Francis's Orators of the age* (1847) 101–23; *Baily's Mag. i,* 1–6 (1861), *portrait, xvii,* 227–37 (1870).

DERBY, ALFRED THOMAS (*eld. son of William Derby, water-colour painter* 1786–1847). *b.*

London 21 Jany. 1821; painted portraits and scenes from Sir Walter Scott's novels; produced many drawings from paintings of well-known masters; exhibited 22 pictures at R.A. 8 at B.I. and 6 at Suffolk st. gallery 1839–72. *d.* of jaundice 11 Hammersmith terrace, Hammersmith 19 April 1873.

DERINZY, BARTHOLOMEW VIGORS. Ensign 81 foot 26 May 1806; lieut. col. 86 foot 7 Jany. 1842 to 30 April 1852; inspecting field officer 30 April 1852 to 7 Sep. 1855 when he retired on full pay; M.G. 7 Sep. 1855; K.H. 1834. *d.* 4 Beaufort villas, Cheltenham 22 Nov. 1861 aged 73.

DE ROBECK, JOHN MICHAEL HENRY FOCK, Swedish Baron. *b.* 14 July 1790; cornet 7 Hussars, July 1808, retired 1814; sheriff of co. Kildare 1834, of co. Dublin 1838, of co. Wicklow 1839; well known for his scientific attainments; found drowned in the fall of the salmon leap in the Liffey near Dublin 11 Oct. 1856. *Annual Register* 1856 *p.* 165.

DE ROS, WILLIAM LENNOX LASCELLES FITZGERALD-DE-ROS, 23 Baron (3 *son of hon. Henry Fitzgerald* 1761–1829). *b.* Thames Ditton, Surrey 1 Sep. 1797 or 7 Sep. 1795, according to his memorial tablet in chapel of St. Peter ad Vincula in Tower of London; cornet 1 Life guards 1819, captain 1825–27 when placed on h.p.; succeeded his brother 29 March 1839; deputy lieut. of Tower of London 13 Feb. 1852 to death when the office was abolished; captain of Yeomen of the Guard 17 March 1852 to Dec. 1852 and March 1858 to June 1859; P.C. 27 Feb. 1852; Q.M.G. to army in Turkey 1854–55; col. 4 Hussars 6 Feb. 1865 to death; general 10 Nov. 1868; author of *Field movements for a division of cavalry* 1844; *Memorials of the Tower of London* 1866; edited *The young officer's companion* 1857. *d.* Old Court, Strangford, co. Down 6 Jany. 1874.

DE ROS, JOHN FREDERICK FITZGERALD. *b.* Boyle farm, co. Surrey 6 March 1804; entered navy 20 March 1818; captain 7 Feb. 1834; R.A. on half pay 14 Feb. 1857; F.R.S. 9 June 1831; author of *Narrative of travels in the United States and Canada* 1827. *d.* 122 Piccadilly, London 19 June 1861.

DE ROSAS, JUAN MANUEL. *b.* Buenos Ayres 30 March 1793; captain general of Buenos Ayres 1831; united all the Plate River States into the Argentine Confederation 1835; his government was overthrown Feb. 1852 when he came to England; lived in Rockstone place,

DE ROSAS, J. M. *(Con.)*

Carlton crescent, Southampton several years, then at Burgess street farm, Swathling near Southampton to death; corresponded with Lord Palmerston many years. *d.* Burgess st. farm, Swathling 14 March 1877.

DE ROSAZ, LE CHEVALIER FRANÇOIS. *b.* Savoy; a great supporter of the Orleans dynasty; settled in England after the revolution 1848; F.R.A.S. 8 May 1874; bequeathed his astronomical instruments to the Museum at Brighton. *d.* Upper Bedford place, Russell sq. London 21 Sep. 1876 in 76 year.

DERRY, RIGHT REV. JOHN. Roman Catholic bishop of Clonfert, Ireland 9 July 1847 to death; consecrated 21 Sep. 1847. *d.* Cams, Fuerty, co. Roscommon 28 June 1870 aged 59.

DERVILLE, ADOLPHUS. Entered Madras army 1816; col. 34 Madras light infantry 20 Aug. 1853 to 1860; col. 42 light infantry 1860 to 12 Dec. 1862; col. 31 light infantry 12 Dec. 1862 to death; general 25 June 1870. *d.* 8 The Terrace, Kensington gardens sq. Bayswater 27 March 1874 aged 72.

DERWENTWATER, AMELIA MATILDA MARY TUDOR RADCLIFFE, calling herself Countess of *(dau. of John James Radcliffe 1764–1833 by Amelia Anna Charlotte, Princess Sobieski).* Came over to England and commenced to agitate for her rights 1865; resided at Blaydon, Northumberland 1865; took possession of the old ruined castle of Dilston 29 Sep. 1868 and suspended portraits of her family on walls of the principal hall; ejected by the agent of the Lords of the Admiralty 1 Oct. 1868 who recovered £500 damages against her; adjudicated bankrupt 24 March 1871; confined in Newcastle gaol 25 Nov. 1872 to July 1873 for contempt of court. *d.* of bronchitis at 53, Cutler's hall road, Benfieldside, Lanchester near Durham 26 Feb. 1880 aged 49. *The heirs of Dilston and Derwentwater by S. S. Jones 1869; Gillow's English Catholics ii, 49–50 (1885); Monthly chronicle of north country lore and legend, April 1888 pp. 165–70, May 1888 pp. 205–212, portrait; Saturday Review 17 Oct. 1868 pp. 520–21; Celebrated Claimants (1873) 246–55.*

DE SALIS, RODOLPH. *b.* May 1811; cornet 8 Dragoons 17 Dec. 1830, lieut.-col. 2 Oct. 1856 to 21 Feb. 1865; C.B. 1 March 1861; col. 8 Hussars 22 Sep. 1875 to death; L.G. 1 Oct. 1877. *d.* 27 Ashley place, Westminster 13 March 1880.

DESANGES, SIR FRANCIS *(son of Wm. Desanges).* Sheriff of London 1817–18; knighted by Prince Regent at Carlton house 17 April 1818; sheriff of Oxon 1825. *d.* in the Queen's Bench prison, London where he had been confined 4 years 20 Sep. 1860.

DESART, OTWAY O'CONNOR CUFFE, 3 Earl of *(only son of 2 Earl of Desart 1788–1820).* *b.* Desart house, Kilkenny 12 Oct. 1818; ed. at Ch. Ch. Ox.; elected M.P. for Ipswich 3 June 1842 but unseated on petition Aug. 1842; a representative peer of Ireland 19 Jany. 1847 to death; under sec. of state for the Colonies March to Dec. 1852. *d.* Eaton sq. London 1 April 1865. *I.L.N. xx,* 321 (1852), *portrait.*

DESBOROUGH, LAURENCE. Solicitor in City of London 1818 to 1884; member of the Law Association 1823, president 1881 to death. *d.* 46 Gloucester gardens, Hyde park, London 10 Sep. 1888 aged 92.

DE SLANE, WILLIAM MACGUCKIN, French Baron. *b.* Belfast 12 Aug. 1801; went to Paris 1830; on missions at Constantinople and in Algeria for French government 1843–45; interpreter to the army of Africa; professor of modern Arabic at Ecole de langues Orientales, Paris to death; member of French institute 1862. *d.* Passy, Paris 4 Aug. 1878.

DE SOLA, REV. ABRAHAM *(son of the succeeding).* *b.* London 18 Sep. 1825; minister of Portuguese synagogue in Montreal 1847 to death; professor of Hebrew and Oriental literature at McGill Univ. 1848; LLD. 1858; pres. of Natural history soc. of Montreal; author of *Scripture Zoology; The sanitary institutions of the Hebrews; Mosaic Cosmogony,* and other books. *d.* New York 5 June 1882. *H. J. Morgan's Bibliotheca Canadensis* (1867) 103–4.

DE SOLA, REV. DAVID AARON. *b.* Amsterdam 26 Dec. 1796; student in the Medrash 1807–16; arrived in London and became Second Hazan or minister of the Sephardi congregation London 1817; preacher in English in the Spanish and Portuguese congregation, Bevis Marks, March 1831 and senior minister; instrumental in organising an Association for the promotion of Jewish Literature 1842; author with M. J. Raphall of *A new edition of the sacred scriptures* 1844, only vol. 1 completed; author of *Eighteen treatises from the Mishna* 1845; *Ancient melodies of the liturgy of the Spanish and Portuguese Jews* and other works; Revised the Jewish library a work issued at the expense of Mrs. Charlotte Montifiore. *d.* London 29 Oct. 1860. *Biography of Rev. D. A. De Sola by Rev. A. De Sola* (1865); *J. Picciotto's Sketches of Anglo Jewish history* (1875) 327, 359–61.

DESPARD, HENRY. Ensign 17 foot 25 Oct. 1799, lieut. col. 13 Aug. 1829 to 23 June 1838; lieut. col. 99 foot 27 Sep. 1842 to 20 June 1854; C.B. 2 July 1846; M.G. 20 June 1854. *d.* Baring Crescent, Heavitree, Exeter 30 April 1859 aged 74.

DE STERN, HERMAN STERN, Baron. *b.* Frankfort 1815; established with his brother Viscount de Stern a foreign banking business in London about 1848; launched many foreign loans; created a Baron by King of Portugal 1864 having been much connected with Portuguese finance. *d.* 4 Hyde park gate, London 20 Oct. 1887, personalty in England sworn over £3,540,000, Jany. 1888.

DE TABLEY, GEORGE WARREN, 2 Baron *(son of 1 Baron De Tabley 1762–1827).* *b.* Tabley house, Knutsford, Cheshire 28 Oct. 1811; ed. at Eton and Ch. Ch. Ox.; lieut.-col. commandant Cheshire yeomanry cavalry 1847–69; a lord in waiting to the Queen, Jany. 1853 to Feb. 1858 and June 1859 to July 1866; treasurer of the Queen's household, Dec. 1868 to March 1872. *d.* Tabley house 19 Feb. 1887.

DE TRAFFORD, SIR THOMAS JOSEPH, 1 Baronet *(son of John Trafford of Croston and Trafford, who d. 29 Oct. 1815).* *b.* 22 March 1778; sheriff of Lancashire 1834; created Baronet by patent dated 7 Sep. 1841; received royal license to alter his name to De Trafford 2 Oct. 1841. *d.* Trafford park, Manchester 10 Nov. 1852.

DEUTSCH, EMANUEL OSCAR MENAHEM. *b.* Neisse, Prussian Silesia 28 Oct. 1829; assistant librarian British Museum 1855 to death; author of an essay on the Talmud in *Quarterly Review* Oct. 1867, pp. 417–64 and of many articles in Smith's *Dictionary of the Bible, Chambers's Cyclopædia* and other books. *d.* of cancer of the kidneys and bladder, Prussian Deaconesses hospital, Alexandria 12 May 1873. *Literary remains of the late Emanuel Deutsch with memoir [by Lady Strangford]* 1874; *Contemporary Review xxiii,* 779–98 (1874); *Macmillan's Mag. xxviii,* 382–84 (1873).

DE VESCI, JOHN VESEY, 2 Viscount *(eld. child of 1 Viscount de Vesci, who d. 13 Oct. 1804).* *b.* 15 Feb. 1771; M.P. for Maryborough in Irish parliament 1796–97; succeeded 13 Oct. 1804; a representative peer for Ireland 19 Jany. 1839 to death; lord lieut. of Queen's county 1831 to death. *d.* Portaferry, co. Down 19 Oct. 1855.

DE VESCI, THOMAS VESEY, 3 Viscount *(son of the preceding).* *b.* Merrion sq. Dublin 21 Sep.

DE VESCI, T. V. *(Con.)*

1803; ed. at Ch. Ch. Ox., B.A. 1825; sheriff of Queen's county 1827; M.P. for Queen's county 1835–37 and 1841–52; a representative peer for Ireland 10 Jany. 1857 to death; an ecclesiastical comr. for Ireland 1868. *d.* 4 Carlton house terrace, London 23 Dec. 1875. *I.L.N. lxviii,* 43, 431 (1876).

DEVEY, GEORGE. *b.* London 1820; architect in London; exhibited 6 designs at the R.A. 1841–48; F.R.I.B.A. 1856; produced large number of sketches; added to and altered many fine old English mansions, including those of the Duke of Argyll, Lord Granville, Lord Rosebery, Lord Wolverton and others. *d.* Hastings 5 Nov. 1886.

DE VINNE, REV. DANIEL. *b.* Londonderry 1 Feb. 1793; a minister of Methodist Episcopal church 1819; minister in Louisiana and Mississippi 1819–25, in state of New York 1825 to death; author of *The Methodist Episcopal church and slavery* 1844; *Recollections of fifty years in the Ministry* 1869; *History of the Irish primitive church* 1870. *d.* Morrisania, New York 10 Feb. 1883.

DEVLIN, ANNE *(niece of Michael Dwyer, Irish insurgent leader 1771–1815).* *b.* about 1780; servant of Robert Emmett at his residence in Butterfield lane, Rathfarnham; messenger between him and his friends in Dublin when he was hiding in the Dublin mountains 1803; suffered more than two years imprisonment in Kilmainham gaol; a washerwoman in Dublin. *d.* Dublin 18 Sep. 1851 aged 70. *bur.* Glasnevin cemetery where there is a monument.

DEVON, WILLIAM COURTENAY, 10 Earl of *(eld. son of Right Rev. Henry Reginald Courtenay 1741–1803, bishop of Exeter).* *b.* Lower Grosvenor st. London 19 June 1777; ed. at Ch. Ch. Ox.; B.A. 1798, M.A. 1801, D.C.L. 1837; barrister L.I. 11 June 1799; patentee of the Subpœna office 1800–52 when office was abolished; M.P. for Exeter 1812–26; a master in Chancery 30 July 1817 to 23 March 1826; clerk assistant of the Parliaments 6 Feb. 1826 to 26 May 1835 when he succeeded his cousin as 10 Earl; high steward of Univ. of Ox. Feb. 1838 to death; an ecclesiastical comr. for England 21 Jany. 1842 to Aug. 1850. *d.* Shrivenham, Berkshire 19 March 1859. *Doyle's Official baronage i,* 583 (1886), *portrait; Portraits of eminent conservatives and statesmen, second series* (1846), *portrait.*

DEVONSHIRE, WILLAM GEORGE SPENCER CAVENDISH, 6 Duke of *(only son of 5 Duke of Devonshire 1748–1811).* *b.* Paris 21 May 1790; ed. at Harrow and Trin. coll. Cam.,

DEVONSHIRE, 6 Duke of (*Con.*)

B.A. 1810, LL.D. 1811; succeeded 29 July 1811; lord lieut. of Derbyshire 19 Aug. 1811 to death; bought library of Thomas Dampier, bishop of Ely for £10,000, 1812, and John Kemble's collection of plays for £2000, 1821; ambassador extraordinary to Russia for coronation of Emperor Nicholas 25 April 1826; received Russian orders of St. Andrew and St. Alexander Newski and St. Anne 18 Aug. 1828 for magnificence of his embassy which cost him £50,000 beyond allowance for it made by Government; P.C. 30 April 1827; K.G. 10 May 1827; lord chamberlain of the household 5 May 1827 to 18 Feb. 1828 and 22 Nov. 1830 to 15 Dec. 1834; entertained Emperor of Russia, King of Saxony and Prince Albert at Chiswick 8 June 1844. *d.* Hardwick hall, Derbyshire 18 Jany. 1858. *G.M. iv,* 209–10 (1858); *I.L.N.* 15 *June* 1844 *pp.* 384–5, 23 *Jany.* 1858 *p.* 75; *Waagen's Treasures of art in Great Britain ii,* 88–96 (1854), *iii,* 344–70 (1854); *Catalogue of the library at Chatsworth 4 vols.* 1879.

DE WALDEN, THOMAS BLAIDES. *b.* London 1811; made his début on the stage at Haymarket theatre 1841; first appeared in America at Park theatre, New York 1844 as Belmour in *Is he jealous?*; engaged in mercantile pursuits 1857; a chaplain in volunteer army of United States during the civil war; author of *The upper ten and the lower twenty* played at Burton's theatre, New York; *The Seven Sisters; The Jesuit* played at Bowery theatre, New York 1854; *The Hypochondriac;* wrote more than 100 plays. *d.* New York 26 Sep. 1873.

DEWAR, FREDERICK CHARLES (*son of James Dewar 1793–1846, musical director of theatre royal, Edinburgh*). Made his first appearance in London at St. James's theatre 29 Oct. 1860 as Tunstall in *Up at the hills;* made his first success at same house as Dr. Bland in *Friends or Foes* the English version of Sardou's *Nos Intimes* 8 March 1862; played Tom Stylus in Robertson's comedy *Society,* at Prince of Wales's theatre 11 Nov. 1865 to Sep. 1866; played Captain Crosstree in Burnand's burlesque *The latest edition of Black-eyed Susan, or the little Bill that was taken up,* at New Royalty theatre 400 times from 29 Nov. 1866 to 20 March 1868; played Bishopriggs in Wilkie Collins's drama *Man and Wife,* at Prince of Wales's 22 Feb. 1873; played Angus Mc Alister in Gilbert's comedy *Engaged,* at Haymarket 3 Oct. 1877 to 4 Jany. 1878. *d.* Chelsea workhouse, London 8 Jany. 1878 aged 46. *bur.* Brompton cemetery. *The Universal Review* 15 *Oct.* 1888 *pp.* 162, 169, 177, *portrait; The*

DEWAR, F. C. (*Con.*)

Entr'Acte 19 *Jany.* 1878 *pp.* 6, 9, *portrait; The Era* 13 *Jany.* 1878 *pp.* 6, 12.

DE WILDE, GEORGE JAMES (*son of Samuel De Wilde, portrait painter 1748–1832*). *b.* London 1804 or 1805; contributed many articles to various periodicals; edited the *Northampton Mercury* 1830 to death; author of *Rambles round about, and Poems, edited by E. Dicey* 1872; his portrait by J. E. Williams was presented by his friends to the Northampton Museum 1871. *d.* The Parade, Northampton 16 Sep. 1871 in 67 year. *bur.* Highgate cemetery 22 Sep. *Journal of British Archæol. Assoc. xxviii,* 311 (1872); *The Northampto:. Mercury 23 Sep.* 1871 *pp.* 3, 5, 8.

DIAMOND, HUGH WELCH (*eld. son of Wm. Batchelor Diamond, surgeon H.E.I.Co.'s service*). *b.* 1809; ed. at Norwich gr. sch.; studied at St. Bartholomew's and Bethlehem hospitals; L.S.A. 1829; M.R.C.S. 1834; practised in Soho, London; resident superintendent of female patients at Surrey county lunatic asylum 1848–58; kept a private asylum for female patients at Twickenham 1858 to death; invented the paper or cardboard photographic portrait; sec. of London Photographic Soc. 1853, edited its Journal vols. 5–8 (1859–64); contributed papers to first series of *Notes and Queries* on photography; F.S.A. 15 May 1834. *d.* Twickenham house, Twickenham 21 June 1886.

DIAVOLO, JOEL IL, otherwise known as Joel Benedict. Wire walker, pantomimist and ballet master; one of the original troupe of Bedouin Arabs at Surrey theatre 1839; created a great sensation under name of Joel il Diavolo at Vauxhall Gardens 1845 by descending a single wire stretched across the gardens from a platform 120 feet high to the ground at opposite end of the gardens; adopted stage name of Joel Benedict about 1850; acting manager to Charles Dillon several years from 1852 sustaining part of clown in his pantomimes; travelled with Charles Harrison's company in the provinces 1862. *d.* 3 Feb. 1887. *I.L.N. vi,* 396 (1845), *with view.*

NOTE.—There were about half a dozen performers who successively bore the name of Joel il Diavolo at Vauxhall Gardens; the last one in 1849 was John Delany who had been a miner in the Dudley coal mines.

DIBB, JOHN EDWARD. *b.* Beeston near Leeds 24 May 1812; deputy registrar of deeds and wills in West Riding of Yorkshire 1840 to death; barrister G.I. 1869; author of *A practical guide to registration of deeds and wills in the West Riding of Yorkshire* 1846; *Registries of deeds, suggestions for the improvement of the Yorkshire offices* 1851. *d.* Wakefield 17 Sep. 1872.

DIBDIN, HENRY EDWARD (*youngest son of Charles Isaac Mungo Pitt known as Charles Dibdin, dramatist 1768–1833*). *b.* Sadler's Wells, London 8 Sep. 1813; pupil of Bochsa the harpist; made his first appearance 3 Aug. 1832 at Covent Garden theatre when he played the harp at Paganini's last concert; organist of Trinity chapel, Edinburgh 1833 to death; published *The Standard Psalm tune book* 1851, and about 40 songs, piano and harp pieces and hymn tunes. *d.* Edinburgh 6 May 1866.

DICEY, THOMAS EDWARD (*only son of Thomas Dicey of Claybrook hall, Leicestershire 1742–1807*). *b.* Claybrook hall, Leics. 11 Oct. 1789; matric. at Oriel coll. Ox. 17 Oct. 1806; migrated to Trin. coll. Cam.; senior wrangler and first Smith's prizeman 1811; B.A. 1811, M.A. 1814; chairman of Midland counties railway; a director of North Staffordshire railway from its foundation 1846 to his death; proprietor of *Northampton Mercury*. *d.* Princes terrace, Hyde park, London 20 Feb. 1858.

DICK, ALEXANDER. Entered Bengal army 1803; col. 71 Bengal N.I. 8 Feb. 1843 to 1869; general 3 May 1866. *d.* Deyrah, North West provinces of India 25 Nov. 1875 aged 86.

DICK, HOPE. Ensign 23 Bengal N.I. 28 Sep. 1808; major 56 Bengal N.I. 1839–45; colonel Bengal infantry 16 Jany. 1855; general 28 April 1875. *d.* Cheltenham 24 May 1885 aged 93.

DICK, JOHN (*son of James Dick of Rochester*). *b.* Rochester; entered navy Sep. 1785; captain 28 April 1802; admiral 19 Jany. 1852; a knight of the Crescent (Turkish order) 8 Oct. 1801. *d.* Southampton 10 Sep. 1854.

DICK, ROBERT (*elder son of Thomas Dick, Excise officer, who d. May* 1846). *b.* Tullibody, Clackmannanshire, Jany. 1810 or 1811; apprenticed to Aikman of Tullibody, baker 1824–28; journeyman baker at Leith, Glasgow and Greenock 1828–30; baker at Thurso 1830 to death; accumulated an almost perfect collection of the British flora and of fossil fishes; assisted Hugh Miller in his *Old red sandstone* 1841 and *Footprints of the Creator* 1849; helped Sir Roderick Murchison and other scientific men in their researches. *d.* Thurso 24 Dec. 1866. *Robert Dick, baker of Thurso, geologist and botanist by Samuel Smiles* 1878, *portrait; H. A. Page's Leaders of men* (1880) 94–139; *J. Copner's Sketches of celibate worthies,* 2 *ed.* (1886), 351–72.

DICK, REV. THOMAS (*son of Mungo Dick of Dundee, linen manufacturer*). *b.* the Hilltown, Dundee 24 Nov. 1774; ed. at Univ. of Edin.; licensed to preach in the Secession church 1801; teacher of Secession school at Methven 1807–17, taught at Perth 1817–27; lived at Broughty Ferry, Dundee 1827 to death; LLD. Union college, Schenectady, State of New York 1832; F.R.A.S. 14 Jany. 1853; granted civil list pension of £50, 21 July 1855; author of *The Christian philosopher or the connexion of science and philosophy with religion* 1823, 8 *ed.* 1842; *Philosophy of a future state* 1828; *The mental illumination and moral improvement of mankind* 1836; *Celestial scenery or the wonders of the heavens displayed* 1837. *d.* Broughty Ferry 29 July 1857, monument in churchyard of Chapel of Ease, Broughty Ferry, erected Jany. 1860. *W. Norrie's Dundee celebrities* (1873) 167–72; *The sidereal heavens by Rev. Thomas Dick, New York* (1844), *portrait*.

DICK, WILLIAM (2 *child of John Dick of Edinburgh, blacksmith, who d.* 1844). *b.* White Horse Close, Canongate, Edin. May 1793; ed. at Univ. of Edinburgh and Veterinary coll. London, obtained his diploma 27 Jany. 1818; practised as Vet. surgeon in Edin. 1818 to death; founded Edinburgh Veterinary College 1818; professor of veterinary surgery to Highland and Agricultural Society of Scotland; vet. surgeon to the Queen for Scotland; Head inspector of cattle for co. of Edin. 1865; published *Manual of veterinary science* 1862. *d.* Veterinary College, Clyde st. Edinburgh 4 April 1866. *Occasional papers on veterinary subjects by W. Dick with a memoir by R. O. Pringle* (1869).

DICKENS, CHARLES JOHN HUFFAM (2 *child of the succeeding*). *b.* 387 Mile End terrace, Commercial road, Landport, Portsea 7 Feb. 1812; a reporter in Doctors Commons 1829–31, in the House of Commons 1831–36; lived at No. 13 Furnival's Inn 1835, at No. 15, 1836 to 1837, at 48 Doughty st. 1837–39, at 1 Devonshire terrace, Regent's park 1839–51, at 1 Tavistock villas, Tavistock sq. 1851–60 and at Gad's hill place near Rochester 1860 to death; edited *Bentley's Miscellany,* Jany. 1837 to Jany. 1839; student at Middle Temple 1839; received freedom of Edinburgh 1841; visited U.S. of America 1842 and 1867–8; edited *Daily News* 21 Jany. to 9 Feb. 1846; started *Household Words* 30 March 1850, edited it to 28 May 1859 when he merged it into *All the year round* which he edited 30 April 1859 to his death; gave 4 series of public readings of his own works 1858–9, 1861–3, 1866–7 and 1868–70 gave his last reading 5 March 1870 in St.

DICKENS, C. J. H. (Con.)

James's Hall, London; author of *Sketches by Boz* 2 vols. 1835, *2nd series* 1 vol. 1836; *The Posthumous Papers of the Pickwick Club* 1837, and 32 other works. (*m.* at St. Luke's, Chelsea 2 April 1836 Catherine Thomson eld. dau. of George Hogarth, musical and dramatic critic of the *Morning Chronicle*, from whom he separated April or May 1858, she *d.* 70 Gloucester crescent, Regent's park, London 22 Nov. 1879 aged 64). *d.* Gad's Hill Place 9 June 1870. *bur.* in Westminster abbey 14 June. *J. Forster's Life of C. Dickens* 3 vols. 1872–74, *portrait; Letters of C. Dickens* 3 vols. 1880–82; *Charles Dickens as I knew him* by G. Dolby 1885; *J. T. Fields's In and out of doors with Charles Dickens* 1876; *Charles Dickens* by *G. A. Sala* 1870; *P. Fitzgerald's Recreations of a literary man, i,* 48–171 (1882); *C. Dickens as a reader* by *C. Kent* 1872; *E. Yates's Recollections* ii, 91–128 (1884); *J. H. Friswell's Modern men of letters* (1870) 1–48; *J. C. Jeaffreson's Novels and novelists* ii, 303–34 (1858), *portrait; R. H. Horne's A new spirit of the age* i, 1–76 (1844), *portrait; Bookseller, July* 1870 pp. 573–78, *and Christmas number* 1879 pp. 15–21; *Illust. News of the world vol.* ii (1858), *portrait; Graphic* xx, 556 (1879), *portrait of Mrs. Dickens.*

NOTE.—He is drawn by Anthony Trollope in his novel *The Warden* under the name of Mr. Popular Sentiment. The portrait of him painted by Ary Scheffer 1855 exhibited at the R.A. 1856 was purchased by trustees of National portrait gallery, July 1870.

DICKENS, JOHN. Clerk in the navy pay office at Portsmouth and Chatham dockyards to 1822, at Somerset House 1822 to 9 March 1825 when he left the service; compounded with his creditors 1823; confined in King's Bench or Marshalsea prison 1824; became insolvent, applied to be discharged 15 Dec. 1831; reporter to the *Morning Chronicle* to 1839; lived at Exeter; is drawn by Charles Dickens in *David Copperfield* as Micawber. *d.* Malvern 31 March 1851 aged 66. *bur.* in Highgate cemetery 5 April, where also lie the remains of his wife Elizabeth Dickens who *d.* 12 Sep. 1863 aged 73.

DICKENSON, HENRY. Writer Madras civil service 1806; member of council and chief judge of the Sudder Dewannee and Sudder Foujdarry Adawlut 1846 to 16 Feb. 1850 when he resigned the service. *d.* Schweizenhof, Lucerne, Switzerland 29 Nov. 1859.

DICKEY, EDWARD JOHN. Entered Bengal army 1822; superintendent of Stud department 9 May 1853; lieut.-col. 57 N.I. 15 April 1854; M.G. 31 Dec. 1861. *d.* Parklands, Guildford 19 Sep. 1883 aged 79.

DICKIE, GEORGE. *b.* Aberdeen 23 Nov. 1813; ed. at Marischal coll. Aberdeen and Univs. of Aberdeen and Edinburgh; A.M. Aberdeen 1830, M.D. 1842; M.R.C.S. Lond. 1834; lecturer on botany at King's college, Aberdeen 1839–49; professor of natural history at Belfast 1849–60 and of botany in Univ. of Aberdeen 1860–77; F.L.S. 1863; F.R.S. 1881; author of *Flora Abredonensis* 1838; *The Botanist's guide to Aberdeen, Banff and Kincardine* 1860; *A Flora of Ulster* 1864; author with James Mc Cosh of *Typical forms and special ends in creation* 1856. *d.* 16 Albyn terrace, Aberdeen 16 July 1882. *Proc. of Royal Soc.* xxxiv, *pp. xii–xiii* (1883).

DICKINSON, SIR DRURY JONES (2 *son of Edgar Dickinson of Dublin*). *b.* Dawson st. Dublin 1804; a wine merchant in Dublin; high sheriff of city of Dublin 1833–34; knighted by Marquess Wellesley the lord lieut. of Ireland 1833. *d.* 10 Mountjoy place, Dublin 8 May 1869.

DICKINSON, JOHN (*eld. son of Thomas Dickinson, superintendent of shipping to Board of Ordnance 44 years, who d.* 24 May 1828 *aged* 74). *b.* 29 March 1782; paper manufacturer at Apsley hill, Hemel Hempstead to 1857; F.R.S. 6 March 1845; master of the Stationers' Company 1857 and 1858. *d.* 39 Upper Brook st. London 11 Jany. 1869.

DICKINSON, JOHN (*son of the preceding*). *b.* 28 Dec. 1815; chief founder of the India Reform Society 12 March 1853, hon. sec. 1853–61, chairman 1861; author of *Letters on the cotton and roads of Western India* 1851; *India, its government under a Bureaucracy* 1853; *Dhar not restored* 1864 and other books chiefly pamphlets on subject of India; found dead in his study at 1 Upper Grosvenor st. London 23 Nov. 1876. *J. Dickinson's Last counsels of an unknown counsellor*, edited by *Evans Bell* (1883), *portrait.*

DICKINSON, SIR JOHN NODES (*son of Nodes Dickinson, F.R.C.S., staff surgeon to H.M.'s forces*). *b.* Island of Grenada 1806; ed. at Caius coll. Cam., B.A. 1829, M.A. 1832; barrister I.T. 20 Nov. 1840; judge in supreme court of New South Wales 23 April 1844, chief justice there 1860 to 18 Feb. 1861 when he retired on pension of £1050 per annum; knighted by patent 19 June 1860; author of *A letter to the lord chancellor on law consolidation* 1861. *d.* Rome 16 March 1882 in 76 year. *Heads of the people* ii, 41 (1848), *portrait.*

DICKINSON, JOSEPH. Educ. at Trin. coll. Dublin; M.B. 1837, M.A. and M.D. 1843;

DICKINSON, J. *(Con.)*

physician to Royal infirmary, Liverpool about 1839 and subsequently to the Fever hospital, workhouse and South Dispensary, Liverpool; lectured on medicine and botany at Liverpool school of medicine; pres. of Liverpool Lit. and Phil. Soc.; L.R.C.P. 1844, F.R.C.P. 1859; F.L.S.; M.R.I.A.; F.R.S. 1 June 1854; author of *The Flora of Liverpool* 1851 *and Supplement* 1855. *d.* 92 Bedford st. south, Liverpool 21 July 1865.

DICKINSON, SEBASTIAN STEWART. *b.* Bombay 25 March 1815; ed. at Eton; barrister I.T. 7 June 1839; M.P. for Stroud 19 Nov. 1868 to 26 Jany. 1874, re-elected 5 Feb. 1874 but election declared void April 1874. *d.* Brown's hill, Stroud 23 Aug. 1878.

DICKINSON, THOMAS. *b.* Hampshire; entered navy Feb. 1796; captain 29 Nov. 1832; received gold Vulcan medal of Society of Arts 1825 for his mode of applying percussion powder to the discharge of ships guns; author of *A narrative of the operation for the recovery of the public stores and treasure sunk in H.M.S. Thetis* 1836. *d.* Greenwich hospital 30 July 1854 aged 68.

DICKINSON, THOMAS. Entered Bengal army 1805; col. 10 Bengal N.I. 10 May 1853 to death; M.G. 28 Nov. 1854. *d.* Teignmouth 24 Oct. 1859.

DICKSON, ALEXANDER. *b.* Edinburgh 21 Feb. 1836; ed. at Univ. of Edin., M.D. 1860; professor of botany in Univ. of Dublin 1866, in Univ. of Glasgow 1868–79; professor of botany in Univ. of Edin. and regius keeper of Royal botanic garden 1 April 1879 to death; pres. of Botanical Soc. of Edin. twice; F.R.S. Edin.; author of numerous papers on botany. *d.* suddenly of heart disease at Thriepland pond near Hartree, Peebleshire 30 Dec. 1887.

DICKSON, ELIZABETH *(dau. of Archibald Dalzel, governor of Cape Coast Castle).* *b.* probably at Cape Coast Castle 1793; wrote to the English press about 1809 to entreat that immediate steps might be taken to relieve the British captives in Barbary, the matter roused public feeling and resulted in the despatch of an expedition under Lord Exmouth 1816; received a gold medal from the Anti-Piratical Society of Knights and Noble Ladies; resided in Africa, chiefly at Tripoli. *(m.* John Dickson, surgeon to Lord Nelson at battle of Copenhagen). *d.* Tripoli 30 April 1862 aged about 70.

DICKSON, ELLEN *(3 dau. of general Sir Alexander Dickson).* *b.* Woolwich 1819; an invalid from

DICKSON, E. *(Con.)*

her youth; resided chiefly at Lyndhurst, New Forest; composed under pseudonym of Dolores upwards of 50 drawing-room songs which were very popular and some of which are still sung, the best known of them are *As I lay a thynkinge* 1857; *The Brook* 1857; *The Fairies; Clear and cool; The land of long ago; O my lost love; The racing river; Tell her not when I am gone.* *d.* Lyndhurst 4 July 1878.

DICKSON, JAMES A. *b.* London 1774; made his first appearance on the stage in Boston, United States 1794 as Saville in *The Belle's Stratagem;* became eminent as an actor of comic old men; manager of Boston theatre for some years from 1806; retired from the stage 14 April 1817. *d.* Boston 1 April 1853.

DICKSON, JOHN BOURMASTER. *b.* 29 April 1815; entered navy 1834; captain 17 May 1854; retired R.A. 1 April 1870; C.B. 20 May 1871. *d.* Thornborough, Ryde 11 Feb. 1876.

DICKSON, JOHN ROBINSON. *b.* Dungannon, co. Tyrone 15 Nov. 1819; went to Canada 1838; graduated at Univ. of New York 1842; visiting physician to general hospital at Kingston, Canada 1846–54, visiting surgeon 1854–56, clinical lecturer 1856–60; dean of the medical faculty and professor of surgery in Univ. of Queen's college, Kingston 1854, the name was altered in 1866 to Royal College of physicians and surgeons, of which he was pres. 1866 to death. *d.* Wolfe island, St. Lawrence river, Canada 23 Nov. 1882.

DICKSON, SIR JOSEPH RITCHIE LYON *(2 son of Elizabeth Dickson 1793–1862).* *b.* 1820; physician to British legation at Teheran, Persia 11 Sep. 1847 to death; attended the Shah for typhus fever 1849 for which he received the Commander's Star of the Lion and Sun; accompanied the Shah to England 1873; knighted at Windsor Castle 30 June 1873. *d.* St. Juliens, Malta on his way home from Persia 7 Aug. 1887.

DICKSON, ROBERT. *b.* Dumfries 1804; ed. at high sch. and univ. of Edin., M.D. 1826; a physician in London to 1866; L.R.C.P. 1831, F.R.C.P. 1855; lectured on botany at medical school in Webb st. London and afterwards at St. George's hospital; author of *A lecture on the dry rot* 1837; wrote all the articles on Materia Medica in the *Penny Cyclopædia* 1833–58 and several articles on popular science in *Church of England Mag.* *d.* Cambridge lodge, Harmondsworth near Slough 13 Oct. 1875.

DICKSON, R. *(Con.)*

Medical times and gazette ii, 509–10, 669 (1875); *Proc. of Royal Med. and Chir. Soc. viii,* 73 (1875).

DICKSON, SAMUEL. Educ. at Univ. of Edin. and in Paris; M.R.C.S. Edin. 1825; M.D. Glasgow 1833; assistant surgeon in army in India 1828–33; practised at Cheltenham 1833, then in London to his death; started *The Chrono-thermalist, or People's Medical Inquirer* 1850 all of which he wrote himself, it ceased 1852; the Penn Medical College of Philadelphia was founded to teach his doctrines; he is drawn from life by Charles Reade in his novel *Hard Cash* 1863 as Dr. Sampson; author of *The fallacy of the art of physic as taught in the schools* 1836; *Fallacies of the faculty being the spirit of the Chrono-thermal system* 1839; *What killed Mr. Drummond, the lead or the lancet?* 1843, and 6 other books. *d.* 12 Bolton st. Piccadilly, London 12 Oct. 1869 aged 67. *S. Dickson's Memorable events in the life of a London physician* (1863).

DICKSON, THOMAS. *b.* Lauder, Berwickshire 26 March 1822; went to Canada 1835; established the Dickson Manufacturing Co. for building steam engines 1856 which became one of most important locomotive works in United States; general superintendent of Delaware and Hudson Canal Co. 1864, pres. 1869 to death; organised a company for purchase of a large tract of iron land on shores of Lake Champlain 1873; a director in 20 other companies. *d.* Morristown, New Jersey 31 July 1884.

DICKSON, WILLIAM GILLESPIE (2 *son of Henry Gordon Dickson of Edinburgh, writer to the signet). b.* Edinburgh 9 April 1823; ed. at academy and univ. of Edin.; member of Faculty of Advocates 9 March 1847; procureur and advocate general of Mauritius, July 1856 to March 1868; senior sheriff substitute at Glasgow, March 1868; sheriff of Lanarkshire 21 Jany. 1874 to death; LLD. Edin. 22 April 1874; published *A treatise on the law of evidence in Scotland* 2 vols. 1855, 2 ed. 1864. *d.* Glasgow 19 Oct. 1876.

DIGBY, GEORGE STEPHEN. *b.* 7 July 1821; second lieut. R.M.A. 16 Aug. 1842, col. 23 March 1865, col. commandant 3 May 1876 to death; C.B. 2 Jany. 1857. *d.* London 19 March 1877.

DIGBY, JANE ELIZABETH *(only dau. of Admiral Sir Henry Digby, G.C.B. 1770–1842). b.* 3 April 1807. *m.* (1) 15 Sep. 1824 Edward

DIGBY, J. E. *(Con.)*

Law 1 Earl of Ellenborough, they separated 22 May 1829, he obtained a divorce in Consistory Court of Bishop of London 20 Feb. 1830 for her adultery with Felix, Prince Swartzenburgh, marriage was dissolved by private act of parliament 11 Geo. iv, cap. 51, 8 April 1830; *m.* (2) 10 Nov. 1832 Charles Theodore Herbert, Baron Venningen of Bavaria; *m.* (3) Hadji-Petros a general in the Greek army; *m.* (4) a Bedouin Arab called Midjouel. She is sketched by About under the name of Ianthe, in his *Grèce Contemporaine* (1854) *pp.* 99–111. *d.* Damascus 11 Aug. 1881.

DIGBY, JOSEPH. *b.* 15 July 1786; entered navy 12 June 1800; captain 8 Sep. 1815; retired V.A. 9 July 1857. *d.* 5 March 1860.

DIGBY, KENELM HENRY *(younger son of Very Rev. Wm. Digby 1730–1812, dean of Clonfert). b.* 1800; ed. at Trin. coll. Cam., B.A. 1823; joined Church of Rome 1823; author of *The broad stone of honour, or rules for the gentlemen of England* 1822 anon., which he rewrote and published in 4 vols. 1826–27 omitting the second title, an edition de luxe 5 vols. 1876–7; *Mores Catholici or ages of faith* 11 *vols.* 1831–40, and 16 other books. *d.* 7 The Terrace Kensington 22 March 1880. *Gillow's English Catholics, ii,* 81–3 (1885).

DIGGLE, CHARLES. Ensign 52 foot 31 Aug. 1804; captain of companies of gentlemen cadets at Royal military college 10 Aug. 1820 to 23 June 1843 when placed on h.p. with rank of major; M.G. 31 Aug. 1855; K.H. 1831. *d.* Cheltenham 18 Sep. 1862 aged 74.

DILKE, ASHTON WENTWORTH *(younger son of Sir Charles Wentworth Dilke 1810–69). b.* London 11 Aug. 1850; ed. at Trin. hall, Cam., scholar; bought *Weekly Dispatch* for £14,000 Jany. 1875, edited it to his death; M.P. for Newcastle, April 1880 to Feb. 1883; author of *I. S. Turgenev's Virgin Soil translated by A. W. Dilke* 1878. *d.* Algiers 12 March 1883. *Graphic xxvii,* 469 (1883), *portrait.*

DILKE, CHARLES WENTWORTH *(eld. son of Charles Wentworth Dilke 1742–1826, clerk in the Civil Service). b.* 8 Dec. 1789; in the Navy Pay Office to 1836 when office was abolished and he retired on a pension; edited the *London Mag.;* edited the *Athenæum* 5 June 1830 to 23 May 1846; managed the *Daily News,* April 1846 to April 1849. *d.* Alice Holt near Farnham, Hants. 10 Aug. 1864. *bur.* Kensal Green cemetery 16 Aug. *The Papers of a Critic edited by Sir C. W. Dilke* (1875) *i,* 1–91.

DILKE, Sir Charles Wentworth (*only son of the preceding*). *b.* London 18 Feb. 1810; ed. at Westminster and Trin. hall, Cam., LLB. 1834, LLM. 1860; founded with John Lindley the *Gardener's Chronicle* 1841; chairman of council of Society of Arts several years; commissioner of Exhibitions of 1851 and 1862; unpaid comr. to New York exhibition 1853 and Paris Exposition 1855; created a baronet for services as comr. 22 Jany. 1862; M.P. for Wallingford 13 July 1865 to 11 Nov. 1868; F.S.A.; F.R.G.S. *d.* Hotel de France, St. Petersburgh 10 May 1869. *The Queen, vol.* 1 (1862), *portrait; I.L.N. xix,* 487, 509 (1851), *xl,* 215, 225 (1862), *portrait.*

DILLON, Charles. *b.* Diss, Norfolk 24 May 1819; wrote magazine articles and melodramas 1836–38; acted Hamlet at City of London theatre 1840; stage manager, leading actor and dramatic author at Marylebone theatre 1842; starred in every city and important town in Great Britain and Ireland 1845–56; played at Sadlers Wells, April to Sep. 1856; lessee and manager of Lyceum, Sep. 1856 to 2 April 1857 and 20 Jany. to 22 March 1858; played at Drury Lane 1860, in the United States 1861–63 and 1866–68, in Australia 1863–66, at Sadler's Wells 1868 and Drury Lane 1869; last appeared in London at Drury Lane, when he played Belphegor for his benefit 7 Dec. 1878; last appeared on the stage at Hawick town hall as Othello 23 June 1881; dropped dead in High st. Hawick 24 June 1881. *bur.* Brompton cemetery, London 29 June. *Time, Feb.* 1883 *pp.* 213–17; *C. E. Pascoe's Dramatic List* (1880) 119–26; *The Players i,* 161 (1860), *portrait; Touchstone* 28 *Sep.* 1878, *portrait; The Era* 25 *June* 1881 *p.* 5 *col.* 4, 2 *July p.* 9 *col.* 4, *and* 9 *July p.* 14 *col.* 1.

DILLON, John Blake (3 *son of Luke Dillon*). *b.* Ballyhadenan, co. Mayo 1814; ed. at Trin. coll. Dublin; called to Irish bar 1841; agitated for the repeal of the Union; one of founders and proprietors of the *Nation* newspaper 1842; attached himself to political fortunes of Smith O'Brien 1848; escaped to France 1848; went to the United States where he practised in the New York courts 1848; returned to Ireland 1855; a leader of the National party; M.P. for co. Tipperary 24 July 1865 to death; alderman of city of Dublin; one of founders of National Association 1865 and secretary; author of *The history of Indiana* 1 vol. 1843, no more published. *d.* Druid lodge, Killiney 15 Sep. 1866. *O. J. Burke's Anecdotes of Connaught circuit* (1885) 323–5; *Sullivan's New Ireland* (1877) *i,* 148–53; *Nation* 6 *Oct.* 1866, *portrait.*

DILLON, Mr. *b.* about 1830; clerk in general post office, London; went to France about 1850; on the staff of Paris paper *Le Sport;* killed by Duc de Gramont-Caderousse in a duel with swords in Forest of St. Germain near Paris 21 Oct. 1862; his widow obtained an order in the Court of Versailles, Nov. 1862 obliging the Duke to pay her an annuity of 3600 francs. *Larouse's Grand Dictionaire* (1870) *vi,* 855–56.

DILLON, Sir William Henry (*son of Sir John Talbot Dillon, a baron of the Holy Roman empire*). *b.* Birmingham 8 Aug. 1779; entered navy May 1790; a prisoner in France 1803–6; captain 21 March 1808; naval equerry to Duke of Sussex; K.C.H. 13 Jany. 1835; knighted at St. James's palace 24 June 1835; V.A. 5 March 1853. *d.* Monaco 9 Sep. 1857. *Journal of British Archæol. Assoc. xiv,* 191 (1858).

DILLWYN, Lewis Weston (*son of Wm. Dillwyn of Higham Lodge, Walthamstow, minister of Society of Friends, who d. Sep.* 1824 *aged* 81). *b.* Ipswich 21 Aug. 1778; head of the Cambrian pottery, Swansea 1802; published *Natural history of British Confervæ* in parts 1802–1809, and other works on natural history; wrote with Dawson Turner *The Botanists Guide* 2 vols. 1805; pres. of Royal Institution of South Wales from its foundation 1835 to his death; sheriff of Glamorganshire 1818; alderman of Swansea 1835–40, mayor 1839; M.P. for Glamorganshire 17 Dec. 1832 to July 1837; F.L.S. 1800, F.R.S. 1804. *d.* Sketty hall near Swansea 31 Aug. 1855. *Proc. of Linnæan society* (1856) 36–39.

DIMOCK, Rev. James Francis. Educ. at St. John's coll. Cam., Bell's scholar 1830; 29 wrangler 1833; B.A. 1833, M.A. 1837; minor canon of Southwell 1846–63; R. of Barnborough, Yorkshire 1863 to death; preb. of Lincoln 1869 to death; author of *Explanation of the Thirtynine articles* 2 vols. 1845; *Southwell church, views with architectural description* 1854; edited *A metrical life of St. Hugh of Lincoln* 1860; *Magna vita S. Hugonis* 1864; *Giraldi Cambrensis Opera, vols.* 5 *and* 6, 1867–69. *d.* Barnborough 21 April 1876 aged 65.

DINNEFORD, William. *b.* London; first appeared in America at Chestnut st. theatre, Philadelphia 1823, leading actor there; made his début in New York at Lafayette theatre 1826; became manager of the Bowery theatre and of the Franklin theatre, New York; travelled with strolling companies all over the United States from Maine to California; an actor, author, manager, auctioneer, broker

DINNEFORD, W. (Con.)

and merchant; opened a lodging and eating house at 157 Broadway, New York called the Byron 1845. d. Panama 8 Dec. 1852. *Ireland's Records of the New York stage i*, 405 (1866).

DINORBEN, WILLIAM LEWIS HUGHES, 1 Baron (eld. son of Rev. Edward Hughes of Kinmel park near St. Asaph, who d. 1815). b. 10 Nov. 1767; M.P. for Wallingford 5 July 1802 to 10 Sep. 1831 when created Baron Dinorben of Kinmel park, co. Denbigh; militia aide-de-camp to the Queen 7 Feb. 1840 to death. d. Kinmel park 10 Feb. 1852.

DINSDALE, FREDERICK. Educ. at Chr. coll. Cam., LLB. 1829, LLD. 1835; barrister M.T. 23 May 1834; judge of Court of Requests at Oldham 1843 to March 1847; judge of county courts, circuit No. 22 (Warwickshire), March 1847 to death; changed his name from Trotter to Dinsdale 1847; author of *A glossary of provincial words used in Teesdale* 1849, anon. d. Tachbrooke house, Leamington 8 July 1872.

DIPROSE, JOHN (eld. son of John Diprose of London, bookbinder). b. Bell Alley, Temple Bar, London 1814; bookseller at Newington Butts 1837, at 312 Strand 1841, at 16 Portugal st. Lincoln's Inn Fields, at 9 Sheffield st. 1876 to death; began his career as a publisher by issuing *The royal song book* 1840; wrote or edited upwards of 30 minor works which he styled books for the non-reading public; author of *Some account of the parish of St. Clement Danes past and present* 2 vols. 1868–76, vol. 2 has the date 1876 on the title page but was not published till 1880. d. 131 Kennington park road, London 20 June 1879. *Diprose's St. Clements ii, v-xxiii* (1876).

DIRCKS, HENRY. b. Liverpool 26 Aug. 1806; a practical engineer conducting railway canal and mining works to 1842, a consulting engineer 1842–58; patented several inventions 1840–57; invented optical delusion exhibited at Polytechnic, London under name of Pepper's Ghost, July 1863; author of *Jordantype, otherwise called Electrotype* 1852; *Perpetuum mobile or search for self-motive power* 1861, *second series* 1870; *Joseph Anstey or the patron and protégé* 1863, a novel published under pseud. of D. S. Henry; *The life of the Second Marquis of Worcester* 1865 and other books. d. Brighton 17 Sep. 1873. *H. Dircks's Inventors and Inventions* 1867, *portrait; H. Dircks's Nature-Study* 1869, *portrait; H. Dircks's Naturalistic poetry* 1872, *portrait; Notes and Queries* 6 *S. xii*, 309, 477 (1885).

DISBROWE, SIR EDWARD CROMWELL (son of Col. Edward Disbrowe of Walton, Derbyshire, who d. 30 Nov. 1818). Educ. at Eton; matric. from Ch. Ch. Ox. 21 Oct. 1808 aged 18; M.P. for Windsor 11 Feb. 1823 to 2 June 1826; entered diplomatic service 1826; envoy extraordinary and minister plenipotentiary at the Hague 28 Oct. 1835 to death; G.C.H. 1831. d. The Hague 29 Oct. 1851. *The Eton portrait gallery* (1876) 406–8.

DISNEY, JOHN (eld. son of Rev. John Disney, Unitarian clergyman 1746–1816). b. Flintham hall, Notts. 29 May 1779; inherited from his father the collection of antiquities formed by Hollis and Brand in Italy 1748–53 to which he made additions; barrister I.T. 13 May 1803; recorder of Bridport 14 Sep. 1807 to Oct. 1823; contested Harwich, Dec. 1832 and North Essex, May 1835; F.R.S. 7 June 1832; F.S.A.; presented to Univ. of Cam. a collection of 83 ancient marbles 16 April 1850; founded Disney professorship of archæology in Univ. of Cam. 1851, endowed it with sum of £1000 which he increased to £3250 by a bequest in his will 1857; published *A collection of acts of parliament relative to elections* 1811; *Outlines of a penal code* 1826; *Museum Disneianum* 3 parts 1846–9. d. The Hyde, Ingatestone, Essex 6 May 1857.

DISSTON, HENRY. b. Tewkesbury 21 May 1819; went to United States 1833; manufacturer of saws in Philadelphia about 1840 to death, employed 400 workmen; invented more than 20 improvements in saw manufacture, among them the movable or inserted teeth; inventor and manufacturer of the Disston saw. d. Philadelphia 16 March 1878.

DISTIN, JOHN. b. 1793; trumpet player in Her Majesty's theatre, London; bandmaster to Marquis of Breadalbane; formed a Quintet band of wind instruments, composed of himself and his sons 1833, travelled with it in England 1833–36 and abroad 1836–44; made an improvement in the sax horn 1844; first played at Jullien's concerts, Covent Garden 3 Nov. 1844. d. Great Newport st. St. Martin's lane, London 8 July 1863. *I.L.N. v*, 384 (1844), *portraits of John Distin and his* 4 *sons*.

DITCHER, REV. JOSEPH. Educ. at Queen's coll. Cam.; P.C. of Holy Trinity, Bitton, Gloucs. 1821–35; M.A. by Abp. of Canterbury 3 Feb. 1837; judge of consistorial episcopal court of Bath and Wells 1836–41; V. of South Brent, Somerset 1841 to death; prosecuted Archdeacon G. A. Denison for his

DITCHER, REV. J. (*Con.*)

sermons on the doctrine of the Real Presence 1856; author of *A statement of the proceedings in the case of Ditcher v. Denison* 1858. *d.* South Brent 28 Nov. 1875. *S. Ditcher's Memorials of Rev. J. Ditcher* 1876.

DIVETT, EDWARD. *b.* 1797; ed. at Eton; M.P. for Exeter 12 Dec. 1832 to death. *d.* Bystock near Exmouth 25 July 1864.

DIXON, GEORGE (3 *son of John Dixon of Gledhow hall, Yorkshire* 1753–1825). *b.* 5 Aug. 1801; ensign 3 Foot guards 20 Jany. 1820, major 25 March 1853 to 20 June 1854; col. 104 Foot 2 Feb. 1867 to death; general 1 April 1870. *d.* 97 Mount st. London 15 May 1874.

DIXON, HENRY HALL (2 *son of Peter Dixon of Warwick bridge, Carlisle, cotton manufacturer*). *b.* Carlisle 16 May 1822; ed. at Rugby and Trin. coll. Cam., B.A. 1846; articled to a solicitor at Doncaster; contributed to the *Sporting Review* about 1850–60; barrister M.T. 7 May 1852; wrote *The herds of Great Britain* in the *Mark Lane Express* 1859–60; wrote the article entitled *The Farm* in the *Illustrated London News* some years; author of *The law of the farm* 1858, 4 ed. 1879; *Field and Fern* 2 vols. 1865; published under pseudonym of The Druid *Post and Paddock* 1856; *Silk and Scarlet* 1859; *Scott and Sebright* 1862; *Saddle and Sirloin* 1870. *d.* Warwick gardens, Kensington, London 16 March 1870. *Sporting Review lxiii*, 294–97 (1870); *Illust. sporting and dramatic news i*, 65–6 (1874), *portrait*; *Sporting Times* 6 Feb. 1886 *pp.* 2–3.

DIXON, REV. JAMES. *b.* King's Mills near Castle Donington, Leics. 29 Oct. 1788; joined Methodist Society 1808, licensed at quarter sessions to preach 14 Jany. 1812; appointed to Cardiff circuit 1816; pres. of the Conference 1841; D.D. of Univ. of Pennsylvania, July 1843; appointed to South London circuit 1844; pres. of Conference of Upper Canada 1848; retired from full ministry 1862; a great preacher and orator; author of *Methodism in its origin, economy and present position* 1841; *Methodism in America* 1849 and other books. *d.* Bradford 28 Dec. 1871. *R. W. Dixon's Life of James Dixon, D.D.* 1874; *Methodist Quarterly ix*, 9, (1849), *portrait*.

DIXON, HIS GRACE THE MOST REV. JOSEPH. *b.* Cole Island near Dungannon, co. Tyrone 2 Feb. 1806; entered Royal college of St. Patrick, Maynooth 1822, dean there 5 years, professor of Sacred Scripture and Hebrew 1828; R.C. archbishop of Armagh and primate of all Ireland 28 Sep. 1852 to death, consecrated

DIXON, MOST REV. J. (*Con.*)

21 Nov.; author of *A general introduction to the Sacred Scriptures in a series of dissertations* 2 vols. 1852; *The blessed Cornelius, or some tidings of an archbishop of Armagh who went to Rome in the twelfth century* 1855. *d.* Armagh 29 April 1866. *Catholic Directory, Dublin* 1867 *pp.* 421–28.

DIXON, MANLEY HALL. *b.* Stoke Damarel, Devon 8 June 1786; entered navy June 1794; captain 28 June 1811; R.A. 27 Dec. 1847; V.A. 7 Feb. 1855; pensioned 28 Dec. 1855; admiral on half pay 1 Nov. 1860. *d.* Stoke, Devonport 3 March 1864.

DIXON, REV. RICHARD (*son of Joshua Dixon of Whitehaven*). Matric. from Queen's coll. Ox. 3 May 1796 aged 16; B.A. 1799, M.A. 1803; fellow of his college to 1829, tutor 1822; F.R.S. 21 March 1811; R. of Niton, Isle of Wight 1828 to death. *d.* Niton rectory 13 May 1858.

DIXON, VENERABLE ROBERT VICKERS. Educ. at Trin. coll. Dublin; B.A. 1833, M.A. 1840, B.D. and D.D. 1862, fellow 1839; R. of Clogherney, co. Tyrone 1853 to death; archdeacon of Armagh 1883 to death. *d.* Clogherney rectory 14 May 1885.

DIXON, REV. WILLIAM HENRY (*son of Rev. Henry Dixon, V. of Wadworth near Doncaster*). *b.* Wadworth 2 Nov. 1783; ed. at Pemb. coll. Cam., B.A. 1805, M.A. 1809; V. of Bishopthorpe near York 1824 to death; chaplain to Abp. of York to death; preb. of York 1825–31, canon residentiary 1831 to death; canon of Ripon 1836; R. of Etton near Beverley, Yorkshire 1837 to death; F.S.A. 31 May 1821; author of *Synodus Eboracensis, or a short account of the convocation of the province of York* 1848. *d.* Minster yard, York 17 Feb. 1854. *Memoir of Rev. W. H. Dixon by Rev. C. B. Norcliffe, privately printed* 1860; *Rev. W H. Dixon's Fasti Eboracenses, edited by Rev. James Raine vol.* 1, 1863, *preface*.

DIXON, WILLIAM HEPWORTH (*son of Abner Dixon of Holmfirth, Yorkshire*). *b.* Newton st. Ancoats, Manchester 30 June 1821; wrote a series of articles on the literature of the lower classes and on London prisons in the *Daily News* 1846; barrister I.T. 1 May 1854; contributed to the Athenæum 1846, editor Jany. 1853 to Aug. 1869; F.S.A. 15 Jany. 1852; helped to found Palestine exploration fund 1865, chairman of executive committee; knight commander of German order of the Crown 4 Oct. 1872; member for Marylebone

Dixon, W. H. (*Con.*)

of London school board 29 Nov. 1870 to Nov. 1873; author of *William Penn, an historical biography* 1851; *The Holy Land* 2 vols. 1865; *New America* 2 vols. 1867 of which there were 8 editions in England, 3 in America and several in France, Russia, Holland, Italy and Germany, and about 20 other books. *d.* 6 St. James's terrace, Regent's park, London 27 Dec. 1879. *In Memoriam Hepworth Dixon* 1880; *Illustrated Review vi*, 225–28 (1873), *portrait; Cartoon Portraits* (1873) 227–38, *portrait; Graphic xxi,* 69 (1880), *portrait.*

DIXON, WILLIAM JERROLD (*elder son of the preceding*). *b.* 1848; ed. at Westminster and Trin. hall, Cam., B.A. 1871; in saving lives in the skating accident in Regent's Park 15 Jany. 1867 caught a cold which rendered him an invalid and cripple for life; barrister I.T. 26 Jany. 1870; hon. sec. of the Savage club, London; sec. to Dublin sanitary commission 1879; author of articles in periodicals; adapted Molière's *Le Médecin malgré lui* under title of *The Doctor in spite of himself*, comedy in 3 acts produced at Globe theatre 23 June 1877; wrote *Married another*, a comedietta; wrote in *The Theatre* and *London Society*, in *Belgravia* under name of Gerald Dixon. *d.* Dublin 20 Oct. 1879 in 31 year. *Belgravia xl*, 193–97 (1880); *Theatre iii*, 277–79 (1879).

DIXON, WILLIAM MANLEY HALL. *b.* 1817; second lieut. R.A. 18 June 1835, col. 27 Feb. 1866 to 23 Dec. 1871 when he retired on full pay; prepared plans for attack on Bomarsund and other places during Russian war; superintendent of Royal small arms factories at Enfield 1855 to 1871; C.B. 20 May 1871; M.G. 23 Dec. 1871. *d.* Tharp lodge, Hornchurch, Essex 19 March 1888.

DOBBS, CONWAY RICHARD. *b.* 1796; ed. at Eton; entered navy 4 Sep. 1810; fought at battle of Algiers 27 Aug. 1816; lieut. 16 Oct. 1821; placed on reserved list July 1851; retired commander 1 July 1864; M.P. for Carrickfergus 19 Dec. 1832 to March 1833 when unseated on petition; sheriff of Antrim 1841. *d.* 28 Feb. 1886.

DOBBS, WILLIAM CARY (*only son of Rev. Robert Conway Dobbs, who d.* 9 Dec. 1809 aged 38). *b.* 1806; ed. at Trin. coll. Cam.; B.A. 1827, M.A. 1830; called to bar in Ireland 1833; crown prosecutor on North East circuit 1851–59; Q.C. 26 May 1858; a judge of Landed Estates Court, April 1859 to death; M.P. for Carrickfergus 2 April 1857 to 23 April 1859. *d* Wimpole st. London 17 April 1869.

DOBELL, SYDNEY THOMPSON (*eld. son of John Dobell of Cranbrook, Kent, hide merchant*). *b.* Cranbrook 5 April 1824; a wine merchant at Cheltenham 1848 to death; author of *The Roman, a dramatic poem by Sydney Yendys* 1850; *Balder, part the first, By the author of the Roman* 1854; *England in time of war* 1856; a complete edition of his works was published in 3 vols. 1875-6. *d.* Barton end house, Nailsworth near Stroud 22 Aug. 1874. *The life of Sydney Dobell edited by E. J.* [*Miss E. Jolly*] 2 vols. 1878; *The golden decade of a favored town, by Contem Ignotus* (1884) 154–93; *T. H. Ward's English poets, 2 ed. iv*, 615–20 (1883); *Temple Bar lvi*, 80–91 (1879); *Graphic x*, 264 (1874), *portrait.*

DOBSON, GEORGE (*son of John Dobson of Mortimer, Berkshire*). *b.* 1795; entered navy 14 Dec. 1807; captain 5 Jany. 1844; admiral on h.p. 11 Dec. 1875. *d.* 52 Pulteney st. Bath 13 June 1877.

DOBSON, JOHN. *b.* Chirton, North Shields 1788; executed designs for damasks 1800; pupil of David Stephenson, architect, Newcastle 1803–10; architect at Newcastle 1811 to death; became most noted architect in North of England; said to be real author of modern Gothic revival in actual practice; restored many churches; designed or erected greatest part of the public buildings and finest new streets in Newcastle; pres. of Northern Architectural Assoc. 1859. *d.* New Bridge st. Newcastle 8 Jany. 1865 in 77 year. *Memoirs of John Dobson* (1885), *portrait.*

DOBSON, THOMAS. Assistant sec. of Excise, Somerset House, London 1856–60; joint sec. to Board of inland revenue 1860–63 when his services were acknowledged in a special treasury minute laid before Parliament; granted a pension of £1010 a year 1863; presented with a service of plate by 2489 officers of excise surveying department 1863; discovered with Mr. Phillips the method of testing gravities of beer, and substitution of duty free malt in distilleries in room of malt drawback; invented method of levying duties on spirits. *d.* Yarrow lodge, Sydenham 19 June 1885 in 88 year. *I.L.N.* 17 Oct. 1863 *p.* 401.

DOBSON, REV. WILLIAM. *b.* 1809; ed. at Charterhouse and Trin. coll. Cam., B.A. 1832, M.A. 1835; fellow of his coll. 1834–41; V. of Tuxford, Notts 1840–48; principal of Cheltenham college 1841–61. *d.* Cheltenham 31 Dec. 1867. *Rev. T. Mozley's Reminiscences i*, 170–74 (1882).

DOBSON, WILLIAM *(son of Lawrence Dobson of Preston, stationer)*. *b.* Preston 1820; stationer at Preston; edited the *Preston Chronicle* to March 1868; member of Preston town council 1862–72 and 1874–83; member of Chetham Society; author of *History of the parliamentary representation of Preston during the last hundred years* 1856, 2 ed. 1868; *Rambles by the Ribble* 3 series 1864–83 and other books. *d.* Churton road, Chester 8 Aug. 1884.

DOBSON, WILLIAM BURDETT. Entered navy 11 Dec. 1806; inspecting commander in coast guard 5 May 1834 to July 1837; captain on half pay 23 Nov. 1841; V.A. on half pay 24 May 1867. *d.* Lyde house, Bath 22 March 1872 aged 79.

DOCHARTY, JAMES *b.* Bonhill, Dumbartonshire 1829; a pattern designer in Glasgow to about 1862; a landscape painter about 1862 to death; A.R.S.A. 14 Nov. 1877; exhibited many pictures in Glasgow and Edinburgh; exhibited 13 landscapes at the R.A. 1865–77. *d.* Pollokshields, Glasgow 5 April 1878.

DOCKRAY, ROBERT BENSON. *b.* 13 Nov. 1811; resident engineer at Birmingham of the London and Birmingham railway 7 March 1838, engineer for the entire line 12 June 1840 to 18 Sep. 1852; M.I.C.E. 13 June 1834, Telford medallist 1849. *d.* Dalton square, Lancaster 8 Sep. 1871. *Min. of proc. of Instit. of C.E. xxxiii,* 213–15 (1872).

DOD, CHARLES ROGER PHIPPS *(only son of Rev. Roger Dodd, V. of Drumlease, Leitrim)*. *b.* Drumlease 8 May 1793; entered King's Inns, Dublin 30 July 1816; settled in London 1818; compiled summary of parliamentary debates for the *Times* and wrote nearly all the memoirs of deceased celebrities; changed spelling of his name from Dodd to Dod 1847; published *Parliamentary pocket companion* 1833–42; *Parliamentary Companion* 1843–55; *Peerage, baronetage and knightage* 1841–55; *A manual of dignities, privileges and precedents* 1842; *The annual biography* 1843; *Electoral facts from 1832 to 1852 impartially stated* 1852, 2 ed. 1853. *d.* 5 Foxley road, North Brixton, London 21 Feb. 1855.

DOD, ROBERT PHIPPS *(only son of the preceding)*. Educ. at King's coll. London; captain in Shropshire militia 26 Jany. 1858 to death; privately printed *Birth and worth, an enquiry into the practical use of a pedigree* 1849; published *Parliamentary Companion* 1856 to death; *Peerage, baronetage and knightage* 1856 to death. *d.* Nant Issa hall near Oswestry 9 Jany. 1865.

DODD, GEORGE. *b.* 1808; miscellaneous writer of books chiefly for the publishers Charles Knight and Messrs. Chambers; edited and wrote in *Cyclopædia of the industry of all nations* 1851; some of his papers were collected and published under titles of *Days at the factories* 1843 and *Curiosities of industry* 1852; author of *The textile manufactures of Great Britain* 6 vols. 1844–6; *The food of London* 1856 and many other books; contributed papers to the *Companion to the British Almanac* 30 years; found dead at Torriano avenue, Kentish Town, London 21 Jany. 1881.

DODD, REV. PHILIP STANHOPE *(son of Rev. Richard Dodd, R. of Cowley, Middlesex, who d. 17 June 1811 aged 73)*. Educ. at Tunbridge and Magd. coll. Cam., B.A. 1796, M.A. 1799; fellow of his college; minister of Lambeth chapel, London 1803–7; R. of St. Mary at Hill, London 1807–12; R. of Aldrington, Sussex 1812 to death; R. of Penshurst, Kent 1819 to death; author of *Hints to Freshmen at the University of Cambridge* 1798, 3 ed. 1807 both anon.; *A view of the evidence afforded by the life and ministry of St. Peter to the truth of the Christian revelation* 1837. *d.* Penshurst rectory 22 March 1852 aged 77. *G.M. xxxvii,* 626–27 (1852).

DODDS, REV. GEORGE THEOPHILUS *(son of Rev. Mr. Dodds, minister of free church of Lochee, a suburb of Dundee)*. *b.* Lochee 2 June 1850; ed. at Univ. of St. Andrews and New coll. Edin.; settled at Paris as a missionary of the McAll Protestant mission, Nov. 1877; went to the United States with Mr. Réveilland as a missionary 1880. *d.* Buisson Luzas, Salbrio near Orleans, France 9 Sep. 1882. *bur.* Passy cemetery near Paris 14 Sep. *Life and work of Rev. G. T. Dodds, missionary, by H. Bonar, D.D.* 1884, *portrait.*

DODDS, ISAAC (2 son of Thomas Dodds, viewer of the Felling colliery, killed 21 Oct. 1805). *b.* Felling hall, Heworth, Durham 9 July 1801; apprenticed to George Stephenson at Newcastle; invented double action air pump 1830 and machine for weighing coals in carts 1832; engineer to the Horseley iron works, Staffordshire 1832–36; built the Star locomotive for the Liverpool and Manchester railway 1833; first maker of a locomotive to ascend an incline; inventor of plan of prevention of boiler explosions by using a plug of fusible metal, now in general use; locomotive superintendent North Midland railway 1835; invented the turn table, self-acting switches and spring buffers; took his son T. W. Dodds into partnership and recommended the Holmes

DODDS, I. (Con.)

engine and railway works, Rotherham 1850, works closed 1866; introducer of steel rails. *d.* 13 Townend st. Nether Hallam near Sheffield 1 Nov. 1882. *Min. of Proc. of Instit. of C.E. lxxv*, 308-14 (1884).

DODDS, JAMES. *b.* Softlaw near Kelso 6 Feb. 1813; ed. at Univ. of Edin.; schoolmaster at Sandyknowe; articled to a lawyer at Melrose 1836-40; writer to the Signet; a solicitor in London 1846; lectured in London and Scotland; published *The fifty years struggle of the Covenanters* 1860; *Thomas Chalmers, a biographical study* 1870. *d.* Lochee, Dundee 12 Sep. 1874. *Lays of the Covenanters by James Dodds, edited by Rev. James Dodds* (1880) *pp.* 1-140.

DODDS, REV. JAMES. *b.* Annan, Dumfriesshire 1812; ed. at Univ. of Edin.; minister of the parish of Humbie, East Lothian 1841-43; minister of free church, Dunbar 1843 to death; author of *A century of Scottish church history* 1846; *A memoir of Rev. Thomas Rosie* 1862 and other books. *d.* Free church manse, Dunbar 3 Sep. 1885.

DODGSON, VENERABLE CHARLES (*eld. son of Charles Dodgson of Hamilton, Lanarkshire*). Matric. from Ch. Ch. Ox. 5 May 1818 aged 17, student 1818-28; B.A. 1822, M.A. 1824; P.C. of Daresbury, Cheshire 1827-43; R. of Croft near Darlington 20 Jany. 1843 to death; canon res. of Ripon cathedral 1852 to death; archdeacon of Richmond 1854 to death; chaplain to Abp. of Canterbury 1862 to death; published 12 charges, sermons and letters 1837-68. *d.* Croft rectory 21 June 1868.

DODGSON, GEORGE HAYDOCK. *b.* Liverpool 16 Aug. 1811; apprenticed to George Stephenson the engineer; prepared plans for Whitby and Pickering railway; settled in London 1835 where he made drawings for architects; assoc. of New Soc. of Painters in water-colours 1842, member 1844-47; assoc. of Soc. of Painters in water-colours 1848, member 1852; exhibited 1 landscape at B.I. and 9 at Suffolk st. gallery 1835-41. *d.* 28 Clifton hill, St. John's Wood, London 4 June 1880. *I.L.N. lxxvi*, 612 (1880), *portrait.*

DODSON, SIR JOHN (*eld. son of Rev. John Dodson, R. of Hurstpierpoint, Sussex, who d. July* 1807). *b.* Hurstpierpoint 19 Jany. 1780; ed. at Merchant Taylors' sch. and Oriel coll. Ox., B.A. 1801, M.A. 1804, D.C.L. 1808; advocate of college of Doctors of law 3 Nov. 1808; commissary to dean and chapter of Westminster; M.P. for Rye, July 1819 to March 1823; advocate to Admiralty Court 11

DODSON, J. (Con.)

March 1829; advocate general 18 Oct. 1834; knighted at St. James's palace 29 Oct. 1834; barrister M.T. 8 Nov. 1834, bencher 1835; master of the Faculties, Nov. 1841; Vicar-general to the lord primate 1849; judge of Prerogative Court of Canterbury, Feb. 1852 to 9 Dec. 1857 when court was abolished; dean of the Arches court, Feb. 1852 to 9 Dec. 1857; P.C. 5 April 1852; published *Reports of cases in the high court of admiralty* 1811-22, 2 *vols.* 1815-28. *d.* 6 Seamore place, Mayfair, London 27 April 1858.

DODSWORTH, REV. WILLIAM (3 *son of John Dodsworth of Carlton hall, Yorkshire*). *b.* 1798; ed. at Trin. coll. Cam., B.A. 1820, M.A. 1823; minister of Margaret st. chapel, Cavendish sq. London to 1837; P.C. of Ch. Ch. Regent's park, London 1837 to Jany. 1851 when he joined Church of Rome; author of *Discourses on the Lord's Supper* 1835; *The Priest's Companion in the visitation of the Sick* 1843; *Sermons in Advent* 1849; *Clarendon, a tale* 3 *vols.* 1850, and about 25 other books. *d.* York terrace, Regent's park 10 Dec. 1861.

DODWORTH, THOMAS. *b.* Sheffield 1790; went to New York 1826; organised the "City Band" which became the National brass band and was first independent military band in New York. *d.* Morrisania, New York 30 April 1876.

DOHERTY, HENRY EDWARD. *b.* 20 April 1817; cornet 14 light dragoons 31 Dec. 1833, lieut.-col. 23 Nov. 1848 to 25 Aug. 1857 when placed on h.p.; general 1 Oct. 1877; C.B. 9 June 1849. *d.* Vernon house, Weston park, Bath 15 Sep. 1885.

DOHERTY, SIR RICHARD (*son of Leonard O'Dogherty of Coolmoyne, co. Tipperary*). *b.* Garculea house near Golden, co. Tipperary 1785; lieut. 90 foot 22 Nov. 1804; major 21 foot 16 Sep. 1824; lieut.-col. 1 West India regt. 6 Dec. 1827 to 4 Sep. 1835; lieut.-col. 89 foot 4 Sep. 1835 to 10 Aug. 1838; lieut.-col. royal African colonial corps 10 Aug. 1838 to Oct. 1840; lieut.-col. 3 West India regt. Oct. 1840 to 1 Aug. 1845 when placed on h.p.; knighted by patent 27 Nov. 1841; inspecting field officer 1 Jany. 1847 to 11 Nov. 1851; col. 11 foot 5 Sep. 1857 to death; L.G. 26 Oct. 1858; governor of Sierra Leone 27 March 1837 to 1840; commander in chief at Jamaica 1853-55. *d.* Charles st. St. James's, London 2 Sep. 1862.

DOLBY, ANASTASIA MARICE. Embroideress to the Queen; author of *Church embroidery,* *ancient and modern* 1867; *Church vestments, their origin, use and ornament* 1868. *(m.* Edwin Thomas Dolby of London, artist). *d.* 12 Southwood terrace, Highgate 18 Feb. 1873 aged 49.

DOLBY, THOMAS *(son of Thomas Dolby of Sawtry, Hunts., ploughman).* *b.* Sawtry 6 July 1782; a woodcutter and thatcher; attendant on Brigadier General Charles William Este, April 1804 to 1808; bookseller at 34 Wardour st. London 1808, at 299 Strand 1819, and at 17 Catharine st. Strand 1824–25 when he became bankrupt; edited *Dolby's Parliamentary Register,* 67 numbers Jany. to June 1819; imprisoned for selling *Sherwin's Register* 1819; tried 21 Oct. 1822 for publishing *Political Dictionary,* required to enter into recognizances, Nov. 1823; published *Dolby's British Theatre* 84 numbers, which became *Cumberland's British Theatre* in 1823; author of *A letter to the friends of liberty* 1819; *The Shaksperian Dictionary* 1832; *The literary cyclopædia* 1834; *The school of reform in church and state* 1835; *Floreston, or the new Lord of the manor, a tale of humanity* 1839, anon. *d.* Edward st. Portman sq. London 24 June 1856. *Memoirs of T. Dolby* 5 parts 1827.

DOLLOND, GEORGE. *b.* London 25 Jany. 1774; apprenticed to his uncle Peter Dollond of St. Paul's churchyard, optician 1788, partner with him Nov. 1804 to 1819, carried business on alone 1819 to death; assumed by royal permission surname of Dollond instead of Huggins 1804; F.R.S. 23 Dec. 1819; an active founder of Astronomical Soc. 1820; F.R.G.S. 1830; invented the Atmospheric recorder for which he received council medal of Great Exhibition 1851. *d.* Camberwell terrace north, London 13 May 1852.

DOLMAN, CHARLES *(only son of Charles Dolman of Monmouth, who d.* 1807). *b.* Monmouth 20 Sep. 1807; R.C. publisher at 61 New Bond st. London 1837–58 when he formed his business into the Catholic Bookselling and publishing company which failed; published the *Catholic Mag.* April 1838 to June 1844; *Dolman's Mag., March* 1845 *to* 1849; *Lingard's History of England,* 5 ed. 10 vols. 1849 and other books. *d.* 64 Rue du Faubourg, St. Honorè, Paris 31 Dec. 1863. *Gillow's English Catholics ii,* 87–90 (1885).

DOMBRAIN, SIR JAMES *(son of Abraham Dombrain of Canterbury).* *b.* Canterbury 1793; entered navy 1808; deputy comptroller general of coast guard in England 1816; comptroller general of coast guard in Ireland 1819–49, introduced and organised that force;

knighted by Earl De Grey, lord lieut. of Ireland at Kingstown, Dublin 1844 after an inspection of the Irish squadron of revenue cruisers. *d.* Woodstock, Sandford near Dublin 24 Sep. 1871.

DOMETT, ALFRED *(son of Nathaniel Domett of Camberwell Grove, Surrey).* *b.* Camberwell Grove 20 May 1811; ed. at St. John's coll. Cam.; barrister M.T. 19 Nov. 1841; went to New Zealand 1842; colonial sec. for New Munster (the Middle island of New Zealand) 1848; sec. for New Zealand 1851; comr. of crown lands, and resident magistrate of Hawke's Bay 1853–6; M.P. for Nelson 1855; prime minister 1862–3; registrar general of lands 1865; administrator of confiscated lands 1870–71; author of *Venice* 1839 a poem; *Narrative of the Wairoan massacre* 1843; *Ordinances of New Zealand classified* 1850; *Ranolf and Amohia, a South Sea day dream* 1872, 2 ed. 1883; *Flotsam and Jetsam, rhymes old and new* 1877. *d.* 32 St. Charles sq. North Kensington, London 2 Nov. 1887. *W. Gisborne's New Zealand Rulers* (1886) 134, *portrait.*

DOMVILE, SIR JOHN COMPTON, 1 Baronet *(eld. son of Charles Pocklington, M.P. for co. Dublin, who assumed surname of Domvile and d. April* 1810). Ensign 6 Foot 23 May 1800; captain 5 garrison battalion 8 Oct. 1807; captain 68 foot 1 Dec. 1808 to 1809 or 1810; assumed name of Domvile by r.l. 25 March 1815; created baronet 22 May 1815; M.P. for Bossiney, Cornwall 18 June 1818 to 2 June 1826, for Oakhampton 10 June 1826 to 24 July 1830, for Plympton 23 Dec. 1830 to 3 Dec. 1832; custos rotulorum of co. Dublin 1823 to death. *d.* 5 Grosvenor sq. London 23 Feb. 1857.

DOMVILLE, HENRY JONES *(3 son of James Domville, M.D. of Greenwich, who d. 28 June* 1846). Assistant surgeon R.N. 18 May 1839; surgeon 9 Nov. 1846; M.R.C.S. 1844; M.D. St. Andrews 1862; deputy inspector general of hospitals 1864, inspector general 13 Feb. 1875 to 17 Dec. 1878; C.B. 13 March 1867; granted good service pension 7 Oct. 1882. *d.* South Hill, Paignton, Devon 8 July 1888.

DOMVILLE, WILLIAM THOMAS *(brother of the preceding).* Assistant surgeon R.N. 3 May 1842; surgeon 7 Feb. 1852; served in Resolute in Arctic regions in search of Sir John Franklin 1852–54; inspector general of hospitals and fleets 18 Feb. 1875; in chief control of Haslar hospital 13 Nov. 1877 to death; C.B. 2 June 1877. *d.* royal naval hospital, Haslar 21 Oct. 1879.

DON, EMILY ELIZA (eld. dau. of John Saunders of Adelphi theatre, London, actor). Acted in comedy and farce at Adelphi, Haymarket, Surrey and other theatres. (m. at Marylebone 17 Oct. 1857 Sir Wm. Henry Don 1825–62). acted in Australia 1861–2, in England 1862–7, in New York 1867; lessee of T.R. Nottingham short time; sang at music halls latterly. d. Edinburgh 20 Sep. 1875.

DON, GEORGE (eld. son of George Don, curator of royal botanic garden, Edinburgh). b. Doo Hillock, Forfarshire 17 May 1798; assistant in Botanic garden, Chelsea 1818–21; travelled as collector of Horticultural Society in Brazil, West Indies and Sierra Leone, Dec. 1821 to Feb. 1823; F.L.S. 1831; published A general system of gardening and botany 4 vols. 1832–38. d. Bedford place, Kensington, London 25 Feb. 1856. Proc. of Linnæan Soc. (1856) 39–41.

DON, SIR WILLIAM HENRY, 7 Baronet (only son of Sir Alexander Don, 6 bart. of Newtondon, Berwickshire, who d. 11 April 1826 aged 47). b. 4 May 1825; ed. at Eton 1838–41; page to Lady Montgomerie at Eglinton tournament 28–30 Aug. 1839; cornet 5 dragoon guards 3 June 1842, lieut. 14 March 1845 to 28 Nov. 1845 when he sold out; owner of steeple chase horses; sold Newtondon for £85,000; acted in America 1850–55, in Great Britain 1855–61, in Australia 1861 to death; played Queen Elizabeth in burlesque of Kenilworth at Hobart Town 15 March 1862. d. Webb's hotel, Hobart Town 19 March 1862. N. P. Willis's Hurry-graphs, 2 ed. (1851) 230–33.

DONALDSON, JOHN. Called to Scottish bar 1826; a teacher of music in Edinburgh; Reid professor of music in Univ. of Edin. 1845 to death; contributed largely to means of carrying out concerts by erection of music room and organ 1860; got rights of the professor established by process at law 1855 after 5 years litigation; granted civil list pension of £75, 19 April 1861. d. Marchfield near Edin. 12 Aug. 1865. Sir A. Grant's Story of the Univ. of Edinburgh ii, 232–3, 459–61 (1884).

DONALDSON, REV. JOHN WILLIAM (2 son of Stuart Donaldson of London, merchant). b. London 7 June 1811; ed. at Trin. coll. Cam., B.A. 1834, M.A. 1837, B.D. 1844, D.D. 1849; fellow of his college 1835–40; head master of Bury St. Edmunds school 1841–55; a tutor at Cambridge 1855 to death; author of The New Cratylus, or contributions towards a more accurate knowledge of the Greek language 1839, 3 ed. 1859; Complete Greek grammar 1848; Complete Latin grammar 1852; Jashar, fragmenta archetypa carminum Hebraicorum 1854, 2 ed. 1860;

DONALDSON, REV. J. W. (Con.) Christian orthodoxy reconciled with the conclusions of modern Biblical learning 1857 and about 20 other books. d. 21 Craven hill, Hyde park, London 10 Feb. 1861.

DONALDSON, SIR STUART ALEXANDER (brother of the preceding). b. London 26 Dec. 1815; partner in mercantile firm of Donaldson and Co. of Sydney, N.S.W. 1836–56; a territorial magistrate 1838–59; member of council and assembly 1848–59; colonial sec. 6 June to 25 Aug. 1856; colonial treasurer 3 Oct. 1856 to 7 Sep. 1857; fought a duel with Sir Thomas Mitchell 27 Sep. 1851; returned to England 1859; contested Harwich 24 April 1860; knighted by patent 23 Aug. 1860. d. Carleton hall, Cumberland 11 Jany. 1867.

DONALDSON, THOMAS LEVERTON (eld. son of James Donaldson of London, architect). b. 8 Bloomsbury sq. London 19 Oct. 1795; studied architecture in Italy and Greece; member of Academy of St. Luke at Rome 1822; architect in London; an active founder of Royal Institute of British Architects 1834, gold medallist 1851, pres. 1864; professor of architecture at Univ. coll. London 1841–65, emeritus professor July 1865 to death; district surveyor for South Kensington; exhibited 27 works at R.A. 1816–54; author of Pompeii 2 vols. 1827; A collection of the most approved examples of doorways from ancient buildings in Greece and Italy 1833 and 10 other books. d. 21 Upper Bedford place, Bloomsbury, London 1 Aug. 1885. Builder 24 July 1869 p. 586, portrait, 8 Aug. 1885 p. 179.

DONALDSON, WALTER ALEXANDER. Actor at Dublin; in Scotland; first appeared in London at Royal Coburg theatre 11 May 1818 as Second Smuggler in Trial by Battle; appeared at Bristol 1826; retired about 1852; author of Recollections of an actor 1865; reprinted under title of Fifty years of green-room gossip 1881, Theatrical portraits or the days of Shakespeare, Betterton, Garrick and Kemble 1870 with portrait of Donaldson. d. Putney near London 19 Dec. 1877 aged 84.

DONEGALL, GEORGE HAMILTON CHICHESTER, 3 Marquis of (eld. child of 2 Marquis of Donegall 1769–1844). b. Great Cumberland place, London 10 Feb. 1797; ed. at Eton and Ch. Ch. Ox.; lieut. 7 hussars 4 Oct. 1821 to 16 April 1823 when placed on h.p.; M.P. for Carrickfergus 1818–20, for Belfast 1820–30, for Antrim 1830–37, for Belfast again 1837–38; vice chamberlain of the household 1830–34; P.C. 19 July 1830; G.C.H. 1831; lord lieut. of co. Antrim 24 April 1841 to death;

DONEGALL, 3 Marquis of *(Con.)*

col. of Antrim militia 3 April 1841 to 17 Aug. 1881; created a peer of the U.K. by titles of baron Ennishowen of Ennishowen, co. Donegal and Carrickfergus of Carrickfergus, co. Antrim 18 Aug. 1841; succeeded 5 Oct. 1844; militia aide de camp to the Queen 15 April 1847 to death; captain of yeomen of the guard 16 Feb. 1848 to 1852; K.P. 1857; lieut. col. commandant of London Irish volunteers 15 May 1860 to death; col. of 4 battalion Royal Irish rifles 17 Aug. 1881 to death. *d.* Brighton 20 Oct. 1883.

DONERAILE, HAYES ST. LEGER, 3 Viscount *(elder son of 2 Viscount Doneraile 1755–1819).* *b.* Doneraile house, co. Cork 9 May 1786; succeeded 8 Nov. 1819; a representative peer of Ireland 15 March 1830 to death; colonel of South Cork militia to death. *d.* Doneraile, co. Cork 27 March 1854.

DONKIN, BRYAN. *b.* Sandoe, Northumberland 22 March 1768; apprenticed to Mr. Hall of Dartford, Kent, paper maker; practically developed paper making machines of which he constructed 191, 1802–51; introduced improvements in printing machinery; invented and first used the composition printing roller 1816; a civil engineer in London 1815 to death; received 2 gold medals from Society of Arts; a founder of Institution of Civil Engineers 1818; F.R.S. 18 Jany. 1838. *d.* 6 The Paragon, New Kent road, London 27 Feb. 1855. *W. Walker's Memoirs of distinguished men of science of Great Britain (1862) 75–7, portrait; Proc. of Royal Soc. vii, 586–89 (1855).*

DONKIN, WILLIAM FISHBURN. *b.* Bishop Burton, Yorkshire 15 Feb. 1814; ed. at St. Peter's sch. York and St. Edmund hall, Ox.; classical scholar Univ. coll. 1834, fellow 1836; double first class 1836; B.A. 1836, M.A. 1839; Savilian professor of astronomy in Univ. of Ox. 1842 to death; F.R.S. 13 Jany. 1842; F.R.A.S.; author of *A defence of voting against propositions to be submitted to convocation* 1845; *Acoustics* 1866. *d.* from phthisis 34 Broad st. Oxford 15 Nov. 1869.

DONKIN, WILLIAM FREDERICK *(eld. son of the preceding).* Educ. at Eton; matric. from Magd. coll. Ox. 17 Oct. 1864 aged 18, demy 1864; B.A. 1868, M.A. 1872; lecturer on natural science at Keble coll. 1875–77, tutor 1877–80; professor of practical chemistry at St. George's hospital, London 1880 to death; sec. of the Alpine Club, London to death; sec. of Photographic Soc. of Great Britain to death; his photographs of the higher Alps

DONKIN, W. F. *(Con).*

were quite unique in their character; went to the Caucasus on an exploring expedition, July 1888, started from Balkar in the vale of the Terch with Mr. Harry Fox and two Swiss guides 30 Aug.; all the party probably lost their lives by an accident on the mountain known as Shkara about 1 Sep. 1888.

DONNADIEU, ALEXANDER. *b.* France; served in Napoleon Bonaparte's army; decorated with the legion of honour; came to England about 1829; gained his living as a talented musician and singer; collected autographs which he sold; lived for many years in chambers at 8 Duke st. Piccadilly where he *d.* 8 Jany. 1861 aged about 70.

DONNE, WILLIAM BODHAM *(only son of Edward Charles Donne of Mattishall, East Dereham, Norfolk, who d. 1819).* *b.* 29 July 1807; ed. at Bury St. Edmunds' gr. sch. and Caius. coll. Cam.; lived at Mattishall to 1846 and at Bury St. Edmunds 1846–52; declined editorship of *Edinburgh Review* 1852; librarian of the London library, London 1852–57; deputy examiner of stage plays, Aug. 1849, examiner 27 March 1857 to June or July 1874; author of *Old roads and new roads* 1852; *Essays on the Drama* 1858, 2 ed. 1863; edited *The correspondence of George III with Lord North* 1867; contributed the *Euripides* and *Tacitus* to Lucas Collins's *Classics for English readers. d.* 25 Weymouth st. Portland place, London 20 June 1882.

DONNELLY, THOMAS LESTER. *b.* London 31 Dec. 1832; became an actor 1854; appeared at Wood's theatre, Cincinnati 1855 under stage name of Thomas Lester; managed a company in the Western States; lessee of Brooklyn Olympic, New York 1867–75; joint lessee with John F. Poole of the Grand Opera house, New York 1876 to death; one of best actors of Irish characters in America. *d.* 224 West Twenty-fourth st. New York 5 July 1880.

DONNELLY, WILLIAM. *b.* 1804; called to Irish bar 1833; registrar general of marriages in Ireland 1844, of births, deaths and marriages to 1876; superintendent of agricultural and emigration statistics 1851–1876; C.B. 13 June 1857. *d.* Auburn, Malahide, co. Dublin 25 Oct. 1879.

DONOUGHMORE, JOHN HELY-HUTCHINSON, 3 Earl of *(eld. son of Francis Hely-Hutchinson 1759–1824, collector of customs, Dublin).* *b.* 1787; ensign Grenadier guards 25 Sep. 1807, lieut. 19 Nov. 1812 to 27 May 1819 when placed on h.p.; assisted in the escape of

DONOUGHMORE, Earl of *(Con.)*

Comte Antoine de Lavalette (who had been sentenced to death as an accomplice of Napoleon Bonaparte) by secreting him in his rooms in Paris during the night of 20 Dec. 1815; tried 22 April 1816 and sentenced to 3 months imprisonment, struck off British army list but afterwards restored; M.P. for co. Tipperary 1826–30 and 1831–32; succeeded his uncle as 3 Earl 29 June 1832; lord lieut. of Tipperary 14 Aug. 1832 to death; K.P. 8 April 1834; P.C. Ireland 17 Nov. 1834; a comr. of charitable donations and bequests in Ireland 18 Dec. 1844 to 17 Feb. 1851; known by the sobriquet of Lavalette Hutchinson. *d.* Palmerston house near Dublin 12 Sep. 1851. *P. Burke's Celebrated naval and military trials* (1866) 376–99; *G.M. xxxvi,* 539–40 (1851); *The trial of Sir R. T. Wilson and captain J. H. Hutchinson for aiding the escape of general Lavalette* 1816.

DONOUGHMORE, RICHARD JOHN HELY-HUTCHINSON, 4 Earl of *(only son of the preceding).* *b.* Dublin 4 April 1823; ed. at Harrow; ensign 98 foot 18 June 1841, lieut. 1843–45; lieut. col. South Tipperary artillery 24 July 1849 to death; paymaster general and vice pres. of Board of Trade 6 April 1858, pres. 3 March 1859 to 18 June 1859; P.C. 6 April 1858. *d.* 52 South Audley st. London 22 Feb. 1856. *bur.* Knocklofty near Clonmel 2 March. *I.L.N. xxi,* 402 (1852), *portrait, xxxii,* 385 (1858), *portrait.*

DONOVAN, SIR HENRY *(son of John Donovan of Tralee, co. Kerry).* *b.* 1822; sheriff of Kerry 1873–4; knighted by Earl Spencer lord lieutenant of Ireland, at Dublin Castle 25 Feb. 1874; chairman of Tralee town commission. *d.* Seafield, Tralee 16 July 1886.

DONOVAN, MICHAEL. Chemist; invented Donovan's Solution the liquor arsenici et hydrargyri hydriodalis of the Dublin pharmacopœia 1839; author of *Observations and experiments concerning Mr. Davy's hypothesis of Electrochemical affinity* 1811; *A treatise on chemistry* 1832 (Cabinet cyclop. vol. 106); *On the extemporaneous preparation of hydrocyanic acid from cyanide of potassium,* in *Pharmaceutical Journal, March* 1843 *pp.* 573–83. *d.* April 1876. *Pharmaceutical Journal* 29 *April* 1876 *p.* 879.

DOO, GEORGE THOMAS. *b.* 6 Jany. 1800; produced his first published engraving "The Duke of York" 1824; opened an academy for study of the antique, and of the life in the Savoy, London 1826; historical engraver in ordinary to William iv 1836–37, to Queen

Doo, G. T. *(Con.)*

Victoria 1842; a member of many foreign academies; A.R.A. 1855, R.A. 1856; published many plates; pres. of Artists' Annuity fund 1861; chairman of committee of class 40 (engravings and etchings) at International Exhibition 1862; F.R.S. 5 June 1851 to 1860; granted civil list pension of £70, 19 June 1868. *d.* Sutton, Surrey 13 Nov. 1886. *Sandby's History of Royal Academy ii,* 324 (1862).

DORAN, JOHN *(only son of John Doran of London, contractor, who d. 1824).* *b.* London 11 March 1807; writer on the *Literary Chronicle* 1826–28; author of *The Wandering Jew* produced at Surrey theatre 2 Sep. 1832; Ph.D. Univ. of Marburg, Prussia; literary editor of *The Church and State Gazette* 1841–52; wrote for the *Athenæum* 1854 to death, edited it several times during Hepworth Dixon's absence; edited *Notes and Queries* 1 Oct. 1872 to death; F.S.A. 19 May 1859; author of *Lives of the Queens of England of the house of Hanover* 2 vols. 1855, 4 ed. 1874; *Monarchs retired from business* 2 vols. 1857; "*Their Majesties Servants,*" *Annals of the English stage from T. Betterton to E. Kean* 2 vols. 1864, 2 ed. 1865, new ed. by R. W. Lowe 3 vols. 1888 and 15 other works. *d.* 33 Lansdowne road, Notting hill, London 25 Jany. 1878. *J. Doran's New pictures and old panels* 1849, *portrait; London Society xlii,* 29–37 (1882), *portrait; Temple Bar lii,* 460–94 (1878); *I.L.N. lxxii,* 133 (1878), *portrait.*

DORATT, SIR JOHN. *b.* about 1779; ed. at Westminster school and Univ. of Leyden, M.D. 1805; physician to British embassy at St. Petersburgh 1835–37; physician to Earl of Durham, governor general of British North America 1838–40; knighted at St. James's palace 14 Feb. 1838. *d.* 9 North terrace, Alexander sq. Brompton, London 4 Sep. 1863.

DORIN, JOSEPH ALEXANDER. *b.* Edmonton near London 15 Sep. 1802; assistant to accountant general at Calcutta 1821; secretary to Bank of Bengal; deputy accountant general; first financial sec. Jany. 1843; a member of supreme council of India 1853 to May 1858. *d.* St. Lawrence, Isle of Wight 22 Dec. 1862.

DORNFORD, REV. JOSEPH *(only son of Josiah Dornford of Deptford, Kent).* *b.* Deptford 9 Jany. 1794; ed. at Wadham coll. Ox., commoner 4 Dec. 1813, scholar; B.A. 1816, M.A. 1820; Michel fellow of Queen's coll. 1817–19; fellow of Oriel 1819–36, tutor 1823, dean 1828, classical examiner in the schools 1826–28; proctor 1830 when nicknamed the University Corporal; ascended Mont Blanc with

DORNFORD, REV. J. (Con.)

Dr. Joseph Von Hamel 18–20 Aug. 1820 when three of the guides were lost in a crevasse and he narrowly escaped same fate; R. of Plymtree, Devon 1832 to death; hon. canon in Exeter cath. 1844 to death. *d.* Plymtree 18 Jany. 1868. *Mozley's Reminiscences ii,* 55–77 (1882); *G.M. Sep.* 1820 *p.* 365.

DORNIN, THOMAS ALOYSIUS. *b.* Ireland about 1800; midshipman United States navy 2 May 1815; sailed round the world 1829–30; commanded the "Portsmouth" 1851; prevented invasion of Nicaragua by Wm. Walker the filibuster 1851; captain 1855; commodore on the retired list 16 July 1862; in charge of the fifth light house district 1865 to death. *d.* Norfolk, Virginia 22 April 1874.

DORRIAN, MOST REV. PATRICK. *b.* Downpatrick, co. Down 29 March 1814; ed. at Downpatrick; entered Maynooth college 23 Aug. 1833; ordained priest 23 Sep. 1837; C. at Belfast 1837–47; parish priest of Loughlin island 1847–60; coadjutor bishop of Down and Connor 4 June 1860, bishop 1865 to death; consecrated in St. Malachy's ch. Belfast 19 Aug. 1860. *d.* Dublin 3 Nov. 1885.

D'ORSAY, GILLION GASPARD ALFRED DE GRIMAUD, Comte (*younger son of Albert D'Orsay, Comte D'Orsay, general in French army*). *b.* Paris 4 Sep. 1798; in the Garde du corps of Charles x, 1815–23; became acquainted with the Earl and Countess of Blessington 1822, travelled with them in South of Europe. *m.* at Naples 1 Dec. 1827 Harriett Anne Frances dau. of 1 Earl of Blessington, they separated 1829, she was *b.* 5 Aug. 1812, *m.* (2) 1 Sep. 1852 hon. Charles Spencer Cowper and *d.* 17 Dec. 1869; the leader of fashion in London 1830–49; lived at 22 Curzon st. Mayfair 1833–36, at 4 Upper Gore, Kensington 1836–45; most intimately associated with Lady Blessington, they fled to Paris to escape imprisonment for debt April 1849, where she *d.* 4 June 1849 aged 60; 120 profile sketches by him of celebrities of the day were lithographed by R. J. Lane and published by Mitchell of Bond st; the handsomest man of his time. *d.* at house of his sister Duchesse de Gramont in Paris 4 Aug. 1852. *bur.* at Chambourcy near Paris 7 Aug. next to Lady Blessington. *R. R. Madden's Literary life of the Countess of Blessington i,* 318–72 (1855), *portrait, ii,* 406–72; *J. Grant's Portraits of public characters ii,* 191–204 (1841); *Lord W. P. Lennox's Celebrities I have known, second series ii,* 198–224; *W. Bates's Maclise portrait gallery* (1883) 284–90, *portrait; Gore House, Bentley's New Monthly*

D'ORSAY, G. G. DE G. (Con.)

Mag. June 1849 *pp.* 135–51; *H. Melton's Hints on hats* (1875) 33–8, *portrait; Baily's Mag. xli,* 153–55 (1883); *Colburn's New Monthly Mag. xcvi,* 112–26 (1852); *Grantley Berkeley's My Life* (1866) *iii,* 201–31; *S. Sidney's Book of the horse* 1886 *p.* 257, *portrait.*

NOTE.—A satire on him with a portrait was published in 1844 entitled D'Horsay or the follies of the day, By A Man of Fashion. Disraeli dedicated to him Henrietta Temple 1837, which contains a flattering portrait of him as Count Mirabel. His character and peculiarities furnished Eugene Sue with the idea of the hero of his novel Le Marquis de Létorière ou L'Art de plaire 1845. He was much satirized by Gilbert A'Beckett in Figaro in London 1832–34.

DOTTIN, ABEL ROUSE (*son of Abel Dottin of Granada hall, Barbados, who d.* 1782). Matric. from Queen's coll. Ox. 24 May 1786 aged 17; M.P. for Gatton, Surrey 17 June 1818 to 29 June 1820; M.P. for Southampton 9 June 1826 to 23 April 1831, and 9 Jany. 1835 to 23 June 1841. *d.* 31 Argyll st. Oxford st. London 7 June 1852. *Portraits of eminent conservatives, first series* (1836), *portrait.*

DOUBLEDAY, HENRY (*elder son of Benjamin Doubleday of Epping, Essex, tradesman, who d.* 1848). *b.* Epping 1 July 1808; grocer at Epping 1848–70; introduced the now familiar plan of 'sugaring' for moths 1842; an original member of Entomological Soc. of London 1833; published *A nomenclature of British birds* 1838, 4 ed. 1845; *The Zoologists' Synonymic list of British butterflies and moths* 1847, 2 ed. 1859, 2 *supplements* 1865 *and* 1873; in a lunatic asylum 1871; the chief lepidopterist England has produced, his collections of lepidoptera have been at Bethnal Green museum since Feb. 1876. *d.* Epping 29 June 1875. *Entomologist x,* 53–61 (1877), *portrait.*

DOUBLEDAY, THOMAS (*son of George Doubleday of Newcastle, soap manufacturer*). *b.* Newcastle, Feb. 1790; helped forward reform agitation 1832; sec. to Northern political union; junior partner in firm of Doubleday and Easterby, soapmakers, Newcastle; became insolvent; registrar of births, marriages and deaths in St. Andrew's parish, Newcastle; secretary to the Coal trade to death; author of *The true law of population shewn to be connected with the food of the people* 1842, 3 ed. 1853; *The eve of St. Mark, a romance of Venice* 2 vols. 1857; *A Financial, monetary and statistical history of England* 1847; *On mundane moral government* 1852, and 10 other books. *d.* Bulman village (now Gosforth) near Newcastle 18 Dec. 1870. *Monthly Chronicle of north country lore, Nov.* 1888 *pp.* 485–88, *portrait.*

DOUDNEY, REV. GEORGE DAVID. *b.* 1811; a tailor at 97 Fleet st. London, retired 13 Nov. 1847; preached his first sermon at Clapham Asylum 21 Jany. 1848; matric. Corpus coll. Camb. 3 Feb. 1848; went to Ireland as a missionary and studied the Irish language; ordained by Bp. of Derry 23 Dec. 1848; Incumbent of Dunlewey, Donegal where he preached his first sermon in Irish 25 April 1849; Incumbent of Charles church, Plymouth 26 Jany. 1852 to death; preached 245 sermons 1852; author of *Sermons preached in Charles' Chapel, Plymouth* 1866–67, 2 *vols. d.* Mannamead, Plymouth 19 May 1865. *Recollections of Rev. G. D. Doudney* 1866, *portrait.*

DOUGAL, NEIL. *b.* Greenock 9 Dec. 1776; a sailor 1792 to 14 June 1794 when he lost his eyesight by an accident; kept a tavern in Greenock 1824 and then a boarding house; teacher of singing in Greenock 1799; composed about 100 psalm and hymn tunes of which 'Kilmarnock' is one of the standard melodies in Presbyterian church service; author of *Poems and Songs* 1854. *d.* Greenock 1 Dec. 1862.

DOUGLAS, ANDREW SNAPE. Secretary of legation at Court of Palermo 1809; sec. of embassy at the Hague 1 Oct. 1824, minister plenipotentiary 6 Nov. to 6 Dec. 1824 and 22 Jany. to 25 April 1825; retired from the service 5 Jany. 1829, granted a pension 15 Sep. 1829. *d.* 7 Onslow sq. Brompton 19 Nov. 1869.

DOUGLAS, SIR CHARLES EURWICKE (*natural son of Right Hon. Charles Philip Yorke* 1764–1834). *b.* 12 May 1806; ed. at Harrow and St. John's coll. Cam., B.A. 1828, M.A. 1831, private sec. to Viscount Goderich at Colonial office, Nov. 1830 to March 1833; king-at-arms of order of St. Michael and St. George 1832–59; M.P. for Warwick 1837–1852, for Banbury 1859–1865; contested Durham city 1853; comr. of Greenwich hospital 8 Aug. 1845 to July 1846; knighted at St. James's palace 12 Oct. 1832; K.C.M.G. 1859. *d.* 27 Wilton crescent, London 21 Feb. 1887.

DOUGLAS, CLAUDE. Ensign 10 Bengal N.I. 16 Aug. 1819; major 14 N.I. 10 June 1842; col. 56 N.I. 1 May 1858, col. 65 N.I. 1859–70; general on retired list 1 Oct. 1877. *d.* Bognor 11 April 1883 in 84 year.

DOUGLAS, FRANCIS WILLIAM BOUVERIE (2 *son of 7 Marquis of Queensberry* 1818–58). *b.* Harleyford near Marlow 8 Feb. 1847; ed. at Eton; came out first in examination for direct commissions in the army 1865; killed by a

DOUGLAS, F. W. B. (*Con*).

fall whilst descending the Matterhorn, Switzerland 14 July 1865. *E. Whymper's Ascent of the Matterhorn* (1880) 273–95.

DOUGLAS, RIGHT REV. HENRY ALEXANDER (5 *son of Henry Alexander Douglas of Dryfesdale, co. Dumfries* 1781–1857). *b.* Lockaby house 22 Feb. 1821; ed. at Glasgow Univ. and Balliol coll. Ox., B.A. 1845, M.A. 1848, D.D. 1868; C. of Alverstoke, Hants. 1846–48; minister of Abp. Tenison's chapel, Regent st. London 1848–49; V. of Abbotsley, Hunts. 1849–52; dean of Capetown 1852–68; bishop of Bombay, Sep. 1868 to death; consecrated in chapel royal, Whitehall 3 Jany. 1869; author of *Sermons* 1862; *Missions in India* 1877. *d.* Clifton lodge, Clifton gardens, Maida Vale, London 13 Dec. 1875.

DOUGLAS, SIR HOWARD, 3 Baronet (3 *son of Sir Charles Douglas, 1 Baronet, who d. Feb.* 1789). *b.* Gosport, Hants. 23 Jany. 1776; 2 lieut. R.A. 1 Jany. 1794; commandant of Military college senior department at High Wycombe 1804–8 and 1809, inspector general of instructions to 1820; succeeded his brother 23 May 1809; patented the reflecting circle or semicircle known by his name 2 July 1811; governor of New Brunswick 5 Sep. 1823 to 1831 where he founded University of Frederickton; lord high comr. of Ionian islands 13 March 1835 to 2 Dec. 1840; col. of 99 foot 15 March 1841, of 15 foot 6 Oct. 1851 to death; general 11 Nov. 1851; M.P. for Liverpool 1842–46; F.R.S. 25 Jany. 1816; C.B. 3 Feb. 1817, K.C.B. 18 July 1840, G.C.B. 27 Aug. 1841; G.C.M.G. 18 March 1835; author of *An Essay on the principles and construction of military bridges* 1816, 3 *ed.* 1853; *A Treatise on naval gunnery* 1820, 5 *ed.* 1860; *On naval warfare with steam* 1858, 2 *ed.* 1860 and 9 other books. *d.* Tunbridge Wells 9 Nov. 1861. *Life of Sir Howard Douglas by S. W. Fullom* (1863), *portrait.*

DOUGLAS, SIR JAMES (*eld. son of John Douglas of Glasgow*). *b.* Demerara 14 Aug. 1803; chief factor of the Hudson Bay company, chief agent for region west of the Rocky Mountains 1833; governor of Vancouver's island 9 May 1851 to 1863, of British Columbia 3 Sep. 1858 to 1863 when he retired on a pension of £500; C.B. 30 Nov. 1858, K.C.B. 11 Aug. 1863. *d.* Victoria, Vancouver's island 2 Aug. 1877.

DOUGLAS, JAMES. *b.* Brechin 20 May 1800; ed. at Univ. of Edin.; M.R.C.S. Edin. 1820; M.R.C.S. London; went to New York 1824; practised in Quebec 1826–51; one of founders of lunatic asylum at Beauport near Quebec

1845, also manager; an enthusiastic traveller and antiquarian. *d.* New York 14 April 1886.

DOUGLAS, SIR JAMES DAWES *(elder son of James Sholto Douglas 1757-1830, major in the army)*. *b.* 14 Jany. 1785; D.A.Q.G. in South America 1806 and in Portugal 1807; lieut. col. 8th Portuguese regiment 1809-11; commanded 7th Portuguese brigade 1813-14; lost his leg at battle of Toulouse 10 April 1814; commanded south west district of Ireland 1825-30; governor of Guernsey 1830-38; col. of 93 foot 15 June 1840, of 42 foot 10 April 1850 to death; general 20 June 1854; K.T.S.; K.C.B. 2 Jany. 1815, G.C.B. 18 May 1860. *d.* Clifton 6 March 1862.

DOUGLAS, JOHN. *b.* 1811; ensign 79 foot 25 June 1829; lieut. col. 11 Hussars 13 Aug. 1854 to 8 March 1859 when placed on h.p.; C.B. 5 July 1855; M.G. 6 March 1868. *d.* Aldershot 10 May 1871.

DOUGLAS, JOHN. One of a family of 24 children; *b.* Lambeth Walk, Lambeth, London 17 March 1814; played in pantomime at Covent Garden theatre 1825; manager of Gravesend and other theatres 1833-45; manager of Douglas troupe at Sans Souci theatre, Leicester sq. London; lessee of Westminster theatre; lessee of Marylebone theatre; manager of Standard theatre, Shoreditch 1845, proprietor 1852, theatre burnt down 21 Oct. 1866, reopened it 18 Dec. 1867; manager of Pavilion theatre, Whitechapel 1857-71. *d.* Castle villa, Dalston, London 31 Jany. 1874. *Theatrical Times iii*, 399, 424 (1848), *portrait*.

DOUGLAS, SIR JOHN *(son of Sir James Dawes Douglas 1785-1862)*. *b.* 5 Dec. 1836; ed. at Rugby, Cheltenham and Univ. coll. Ox., B.A. 1864; clerk in audit office, Mauritius, Feb. 1859, sec. to council 1867; poor law comr. June 1868; auditor general Ceylon, Dec. 1869 to 1876; colonial sec. Straits Settlements 1876-78; lieut. governor and colonial sec. Ceylon, July 1878 to death; K.C.M.G. 24 May 1883. *d.* Lyndhurst, Watford 23 Aug. 1885.

DOUGLAS, SIR JOHN *(son of Sir Neil Douglas 1780-1853)*. *b.* 7 July 1817; ensign 79 foot 6 Sep. 1833, lieut. col. 13 Aug. 1854 to 16 March 1860 when placed on h.p.; A.A.G. in Scotland 1860-65; commanded the forces in Scotland 1 Oct. 1870 to 30 Sep. 1875; col. 79 foot 1 Jany. 1879 to death; general 30 Jany. 1880; placed on retired list 1 July 1881; C.B. 5 July 1855, K.C.B. 14 May 1859, G.C.B. 2 June 1877. *d.* Glenfinart, Argyllshire 8 Sep. 1887.

DOUGLAS, SIR JOSEPH ABRAHAM *(son of Joseph Douglas of Whitehaven, Cumberland)*. *b.* Chepstow 17 Jany. 1799; master in the navy 30 May 1823, retired 1851; knighted at St. James's palace 24 March 1841 for having armed his ship the Cambridge and assisted the British in Hong Kong bay in June 1839 losing £10,000 for which the government would not compensate him. *d.* of epilepsy at 2 Apsley cottage, Moor terrace, Lower park road, Peckham, London 3 April 1866. *A case of individual sacrifice and of national gratitude 1847*.

DOUGLAS, SIR NEIL *(5 son of John Douglas of Glasgow, merchant)*. *b.* Glasgow 1780; 2 lieut. 21 foot 28 Jany. 1801; captain 79 foot 19 April 1804, lieut. col. 3 Dec. 1812 to 16 Aug. 1833 when placed on h.p.; aide-de-camp to George iv and William iv 27 May 1825 to 10 Jany. 1837; governor of Edinburgh Castle 1 April 1842 to 1 Jany. 1847; col. of 81 foot 11 July 1845, of 72 foot 12 July 1847, of 78 foot 29 Dec. 1851 to death; L.G. 9 Nov. 1846; C.B. 22 June 1815, K.C.B. 19 July 1838; knighted at St. James's palace 13 Sep. 1831. *d.* Brussels 1 Sep. 1853 in 74 year. *W. B. Crombie's Modern Athenians* (1882), *portrait*; *My adventures by Col. Montgomery Maxwell i, pp. v-vi* (1845), *portrait*.

DOUGLAS, ROBERT. Second lieut. R.A. 1 Nov. 1796, lieut. col. 31 Dec. 1827 to 6 May 1835 when placed on retired full pay; general 25 Sep. 1859; C.B. 4 June 1815. *d.* Claygate near Esher 10 Feb. 1871 aged 93.

DOUGLAS, WILLIAM. Second lieut. R.E. 1 July 1801, lieut. col. 23 March 1825 to 27 Jany. 1829 when placed on half pay; lieut. col. on full pay 11 Nov. 1851 to death; general 3 April 1862. *d.* Hastings 10 Feb. 1864 aged 77.

DOUGLAS, WILLIAM SCOTT. *b.* Hawick 10 Jany. 1815; ed. in Heriot's hospital, Edinburgh; sec. of Edinburgh Burns club 1877 to death; edited *The Complete poetical works of Robert Burns* 1871, *revised ed.* 1876; *Picture of the county of Ayr* 1874; *The works of Robert Burns* 6 vols. 1877-79; supplied letterpress for *Crombie's Modern Athenians* 1882; found drowned near end of the East pier, Leith 23 June 1883.

DOULTON, FREDERICK *(3 son of John Doulton of Lambeth)*. *b.* Lambeth 1824; manufacturer of earthenware goods; member of Metropolitan board of works for Lambeth 1856 to death; contested Reigate 6 Feb. 1858; M.P. for Lambeth 5 May 1862 to 11 Nov. 1868. *d.* of apoplexy at Summerhill house, Tunbridge Wells 21 May 1872. *Affaire Doulton Bruxelles 1868*.

DOVASTON, JOHN FREEMAN MILWARD (*only son of John Dovaston of Westfelton near Oswestry 1740–1808*). *b.* 30 Dec. 1782; ed. at Oswestry, Shrewsbury and Ch. Ch. Ox., B.A. 1804, M.A. 1807; barrister M.T. 12 June 1807; author of *Fitz Gwarine with other rhymes* 1812, 3 ed. called *Poems, legendary, incidental and humorous* 1825; *A selection of British melodies* 1817; *The Dove* 1822 a selection of old poems; *Lectures on natural history and national melody* 1839. *d.* Nursery villa, Westfelton 8 Aug. 1854. *G.M. xlii,* 395–6 (1854).

DOVE, PATRICK EDWARD (*son of Henry Dove, lieutenant R.N.*) *b.* Lasswade near Edinburgh 31 July 1815, lived at the Craig near Ballantrae, Ayrshire 1841–48 when he lost most of his fortune; captain of Midlothian rifle club April 1853; edited the *Witness* for 6 months in 1854; edited the *Commonwealth* newspaper at Glasgow 1858; edited first 20 numbers of *Imperial dictionary of biography* 1857; edited with M. Rankine *Imperial Journal of the arts and sciences;* invented a rifled cannon with ratchet groves which had great range and accuracy; commanded 91st Lanarkshire rifle volunteers 1859; won several prizes at Wimbledon 1860; author of *The theory of human progression and natural probability of a reign of justice* 1850, anon.; *The Elements of political science* 1854; *Romanism, Rationalism and Protestantism* 1855; *The logic of the Christian faith* 1856; *The Revolver, its description and use* 1858. *d.* Edinburgh 28 April 1873.

DOVE, THOMAS. A house painter; a marine artist of great ability; his best pictures were produced at Liverpool. *d.* in the Whitby workhouse 27 Dec. 1886.

DOVE, WILLIAM (*son of Mr. Dove of Leeds, leather manufacturer, who d. 24 Dec.* 1854). A farmer at Bramham near Tadcaster to 1855; poisoned his wife Harriet by strychnia 1 March 1856, tried at the Assizes at York 16–18 July 1856, hanged at York 9 Aug. 1856 aged 30. *G. L. Browne and C. G. Stewart's Trials for poisoning* (1883) 233–68; *Sir J. F. Stephen's History of the criminal law of England iii,* 426–37 (1883); *Observations on the trials of J. Hill and W. Dove* 1856.

DOVETON, FREDERICK LARKINS. Entered Madras army 1806; col. 8 Madras light cavalry 18 Feb. 1845 to death; L.G. 13 March 1859. *d.* Cheltenham 20 Dec. 1859 aged 68.

DOVETON, SIR JOHN (*son of Sir Wm. Webber Doveton, knt., of the H.E.I.Co.'s civil service, who d. 13 Oct. 1843 in 90 year*). *b.* St. Helena

DOVETON, SIR J. (*Con.*)

1783; cavalry cadet in H.E.I.Co.'s army, 31 Oct. 1798; aide-de-camp to Marquis Wellesley; commanded a division of the Nizam's army; commanded centre division of Madras army; lieut. col. 4 Madras Native Cavalry 19 Aug. 1813, col. 9 Nov. 1821; col. 5 Madras light cavalry 1847 to death; general 20 June 1854; C.B. 26 Sep. 1831, K.C.B. 20 July 1838. *d.* Vichy, France 23 Sep. 1857.

DOW, REV. WILLIAM (*youngest son of Rev. Anthony Dow, D.D., minister of Kirkpatrick, Irongray, Perthshire, who d. 17 July* 1834). Educ. at Univ. of Edin., M.A. 17 April 1839; licensed by Presbytery of Dumfries 6 Nov. 1821; presented by George iv to Tongland, Kirkcudbright 13 June and ordained 21 Sep. 1826; withdrew his adherence to the confession of faith, deposed by the General Assembly 23 May 1832; called to be an Apostle of the Catholic Apostolic church when at Kirkcudbright, June 1835; made a tour of the continent 1839 as the Apostle to Russia; a writer in the *Morning Watch;* author of *A series of discourses on practical and doctrinal subjects* 1847, second series 1850; *Sermons and Homilies* 1856; *First principles of the doctrine of Christ* 1856. *d.* Albury, Surrey 3 Nov. 1855 aged 56. *Miller's Irvingism i,* 157, 166, 181, 271 (1878); *Scott's Fasti,* vol. 1, pt. 2, *p.* 725.

NOTE.—His elder brother Rev. David Dow, assistant minister of Kirkpatrick, Irongray, was called to be an Apostle of the Catholic Apostolic church when at Irongray, June 1835 but declined to accept the call; he went to the Cape of Good Hope and became a farmer.

DOWBIGGIN, MONTAGU HAMILTON (*son of Wm. Henry Dowbiggin 1780–1849, lieut.* 12 *Lancers, by Georgina 5 dau. of 1 Baron Panmure*). *b.* 15 Jany. 1832; ensign 71 foot 30 June 1848; major 99 foot 22 July 1859, lieut. col. 3 March 1863 to 10 Dec. 1863 when placed on h.p.; served in Crimean war 1854–55; the object of Lord Panmure's celebrated telegram to Lord Raglan "Take care of Dowb"; retired from army June 1865; knight of the Legion of Honour 1856. *d.* Portland place, Brighton 3 Feb. 1866. *bur.* Haversham, Bucks.

DOWDESWELL, GEORGE (*youngest son of George Dowdeswell, M.D. of Gloucester, who d.* 1776). Writer Bengal civil service 7 Aug. 1783; sec. to Board of Revenue 25 Aug. 1794; sec. in judicial and revenue departments 16 March 1801; superintendent general of police 1805; chief sec. to Government 30 Oct. 1812; member of supreme council 28 Dec. 1814 to 1823 when he resigned. *d.* Down house, Redmarley, Worcs. 6 Feb. 1852 aged 86.

DOWDESWELL, JOHN EDMUND *(youngest child of Wm. Dowdeswell, M.P. for Worcs. who d. 1775).* *b.* 3 March 1772; ed. at Westminster 1779–89 and Ch. Ch. Ox., B.A. 1793, M.A. 1795; pupil of Sir Samuel Romilly; barrister I.T. 6 May 1796, bencher 1834, reader 1841, treasurer 1842; recorder for Tewkesbury 1798–1833; M.P. for Tewkesbury 1812–1832; comr. of bankrupts 1806–1820; master in Chancery 8 Feb. 1820 to 1851. *d.* Pull court near Tewkesbury 11 Nov. 1851.

DOWDESWELL, WILLIAM *(elder son of the preceding).* *b.* Oct. 1804; ed. at Westminster and Ch. Ch. Ox., B.A. 1826, M.A. 1829; contested Tewkesbury 12 Dec. 1832; M.P. for Tewkesbury 1835 to 1847; sheriff of Worcs. 1855. *d.* Pull court 6 Feb. 1887.

DOWKER, HOWARD. Entered Madras army 1813; col. 40 Madras N.I. 3 March 1848 to 1853, col. 2 Madras N.I. 1853–1869; L.G. 21 April 1863. *d.* 5 Feb. 1870.

DOWLING, ALFRED SEPTIMUS *(son of Vincent Dowling of 30 Lincolns Inn Fields, London, bookseller).* Barrister G.I. 18 June 1828; serjeant at law 12 Nov. 1842; judge of county courts circuit No. 15 Yorkshire 9 Nov. 1849 to death; a comr. for inquiring into state of county courts 20 Aug. 1853; author of *A collection of statutes passed 1830–2,* 2 vols. 1832; *A collection of statutes passed 2 Wm. iv and 3 Wm. iv,* 1833; *Reports of cases in King's Bench practice courts with the points of pleading and practice decided in the Courts of Common Pleas and Exchequer 1830–41,* 7 vols. 1833–42, *new series (with Vincent Dowling) 1841–43,* 2 vols. 1843–44; *Reports of cases in continuation of the above (with J. J. Lowndes) 1844–49,* 7 vols. 1845–51; *The practice of the superior courts* 1848. *d.* 34 Acacia road, St. John's Wood, London 3 March 1868 aged 63.

DOWLING, FRANK LEWIS *(son of Vincent George Dowling 1785–1852).* *b.* 18 Oct. 1823; barrister M.T. 24 Nov. 1848; edited *Bell's Life in London* 1852 to death; edited and published annual issues of *Fistiana, or the Oracle of the Ring* 1853–64, prepared another ed. published 1868; managed the fight between Heenan and Sayers at Farnborough, Hants. 17 April 1860. *d.* Norfolk st. Strand, London 10 Oct. 1867. *Illustrated Sporting News 19 Oct. 1867 p. 657, portrait.*

DOWLING, REV. JOHN. *b.* Pevensey, Sussex 12 May 1807; kept a boarding school near Oxford 1829–32; ordained Baptist minister in Catskill, New York 1832; minister at Newport, Rhode Island 1834–36, in New

York 1836; preached in Providence, Philadelphia, Newark and other places; D.D. Transylvania University; author of *Exposition of the prophecies* 1840; *Defence of the Protestant Scriptures* 1843; *The History of Romanism* 1845 and other books. *d.* Middletown, New York 4 July 1878. *M. H. Smith's Sunshine and shadow in New York* (1868) 589–92.

DOWLING, VINCENT GEORGE *(brother of Alfred Septimus Dowling, who d. 1868).* *b.* London 1785; contributed to the *Observer* from 1804; employed on the *Day* newspaper 1809; edited *Bell's Life in London,* Aug. 1824 to death, a service of plate value 100 guineas voted him 18 July 1833; one of the first persons to seize Bellingham when he shot Spencer Perceval in lobby of House of Commons 11 May 1812; claimed to be the author of the plan on which new police system was organised; edited and published *Fistiana or the Oracle of the Ring,* 14 editions 1840–52. *d.* Stanmore lodge, Kilburn, London 25 Oct. 1852. *I.L.N. 13 Nov. 1852 pp. 406, 408, portrait.*

DOWN, JAMES SOMERS. Entered Bombay army 1819; col. 1 Bombay N.I. 13 July 1858 to 1869; L.G. 25 June 1870. *d.* Kilburn, London 25 Sep. 1871.

DOWNALL, VENERABLE JOHN *(only son of James Downall of Liverpool).* Matric. from Magd. hall, Ox. 3 July 1822 aged 19, B.A. 1826, M.A. 1829; P.C. of St. George's, Kidderminster 1843–49; V. of Okehampton, Devon 1850 to death; preb. of Exeter cath. 1855 to death; archdeacon of Totnes, April 1859 to death; author of *Laying on of hands or Letters on confirmation* 1848; *An address after confirmation* 1848, 5 ed. 1858 and 7 charges and sermons. *d.* Bournemouth 7 April 1872.

DOWNE, WILLIAM HENRY DAWNAY, 7 Viscount. *b.* 15 May 1812; M.P. for Rutland 12 July 1841 to Jany. 1846; succeeded 23 May 1846. *d.* Torquay 26 Jany. 1857.

DOWNES, ULYSSES DE BURGH, 2 Baron *(only son of Thomas Burgh of Bert house, Athy, co. Kildare, who d. 1810).* *b.* Dublin 15 Aug. 1788; ensign 54 foot 31 March 1804; captain 92 foot 25 Nov. 1808; captain Grenadier guards 25 July 1814 to 5 July 1827 when placed on h.p.; surveyor general of the ordnance 18 March 1820 to 14 May 1827, clerk of the ordnance 1828–30; aide-de-camp to the Sovereign 27 May 1825 to 10 Jany. 1837; col. of 54 foot 4 April 1845, of 29 foot 15 Aug. 1850 to death; general 20 June 1854; succeeded his cousin 2 March 1826; Irish

DOWNES, BARON (*Con.*)

representative peer 4 April 1833 to death; reassumed ancient name of De Burgh 1848; K.C.B. 2 Jany. 1815, G.C.B. 18 May 1860. *d.* Bert house, Athy 26 July 1863.

DOWNIE, SIR ALEXANDER MACKENZIE (*youngest son of Rev. Alexander Downie, minister of Lochalsh, Rosshire*). *b.* 1811; physician to Princess Elizabeth, landgravine of Hesse Homburg; knighted at St. James's palace 1 July 1840 for his attention to the Princess; phys. to British legation at Frankfort 1834–49; phys. in ordinary to Duke of Cambridge 30 Nov. 1840; phys. extraordinary in household of Duchess of Kent 1846; author of *A short description of Kissingen* 1841; *A practical treatise on mineral waters in the cure of chronic disease* 1841. *d.* Frankfort 3 Feb. 1852.

DOWNING, DAVID. Ensign 6 Bengal N.I. 16 Aug. 1819; colonel Bengal infantry 7 May 1855; general 23 Aug. 1875. *d.* The Grange, Plaxtole, Kent 18 Dec. 1888 aged 88.

DOWNING, M'CARTHY (2 *son of Eugene Downing of Kenmare, co. Kerry*). *b.* 11 May 1814; took an active part in formation of Irish parliamentary party of 1852; M.P. for county Cork 30 Nov. 1868 to death. *d.* Prospect house, Skibbereen, co. Cork 9 Jany. 1879.

DOWNING, SAMUEL (*son of Rev. Samuel Downing, R. of Fenagh, Leighlin*). *b.* Bagenalstown, Carlow 19 June 1811; ed. at Kilkenny coll. and Trin. coll. Dublin, B.A. 1834; educ. in engineering at Edin.; employed in construction of viaduct from Portland island to mainland, and on the Coed-re-Coed curved viaduct on Taff Vale railway; assistant professor of engineering Trinity coll. 1847, professor 1852 to death; Assoc. I.C.E. 2 March 1852; author of *The elements of practical hydraulics for the use of students* 1855, 3 ed. 1875; *Elements of practical construction in engineering and architecture* 1875; *Selections and specifications of public works. d.* 21 April 1882. *Min. of proc. of Instit. of C.E. lxxii*, 310–11 (1883).

DOWNMAN, HUGH. *b.* Plymouth 29 Oct. 1765; entered navy 10 Oct. 1776; captain 26 Dec. 1798; admiral 24 April 1847; awarded pension 1 July 1851. *d.* Hambledon, Hants. 4 Jany. 1858.

DOWNMAN, SIR THOMAS CHARLES FRANCIS (*eld. son of Col. Francis Downman, Royal artillery*). *b.* St. Neots, Hunts. 1776; 2 lieut. R.A. 24 April 1793; lieut. col. R.H.A. 20 Dec. 1814, col. commandant 28 Sep. 1843 to death; commanded Woolwich district and garrison 1848 to death; aide-de-camp to the

DOWNMAN, SIR T. C. F. (*Con.*)

Sovereign 27 May 1825 to 10 Jany. 1837; L.G. 9 Nov. 1846; C.B. 8 Dec. 1815; K.C.B. 6 April 1852; K.C.H. 1831; knighted at St. James's palace 13 Sep. 1831. *d.* Royal arsenal, Woolwich 11 Aug. 1852.

DOWNSHIRE, ARTHUR WILLS BLUNDELL SANDYS TRUMBULL WINDSOR HILL, 4 Marquis of (*eld. child of 3 Marquis of Downshire 1788–1845*). *b.* Hillsborough castle, co. Down 6 Aug. 1812; ed. at Eton and Ch. Ch. Ox.; ensign Royal South Down militia 4 June 1833, col. 30 July 1845 to death; M.P. for co. Down 30 Aug. 1836 to 12 April 1845 when he succeeded; K.P. 24 May 1859. *d.* Dolphin hotel, Herne Bay 6 Aug. 1868.

DOWTON, JOHN. *b.* Uxbridge 1820; tutor at Haileybury; professor of Hindustani at University college, London and at Staff college, Sandhurst 1855–77; author of *Grammar of the Urdu or Hindustani language* 1862; *Classical dictionary of Hindu mythology and religion, history and literature* 1879; edited from the papers of Sir H. M. Elliott *History of India as told by its own historians* 8 vols. 1867–77. *d.* Sandhurst lodge, East Worthing 23 Aug. 1881.

DOWTON, WILLIAM (*son of Mr. Dowton of Exeter, Innkeeper*). *b.* Exeter 25 April 1764; joined a company of strolling players at Ashburton 1781; acted with Mrs. Baker's company in Kent 1791–96; made his first appearance in London at Drury Lane as Sheva in *The Jew* 11 Oct. 1796, continued at Drury Lane 36 years playing at the Haymarket in the summer; manager of theatres at Canterbury and Maidstone; acted in New York, June to Nov. 1836; one of the most versatile actors of his time. *d.* Brighton terrace, Brixton 19 April 1851. *Oxberry's Dramatic Biography iv*, 253–62 (1826), *portrait*; *Bentley's Miscellany xli*, 318–30 (1857); *Cumberland's British Theatre xxvii*, 7–8, *portrait*; *British Stage, Nov. 1819 pp.* 25–6, *portrait*; *Tallis's Dramatic Mag. June 1851 pp.* 235–6, *portrait*; *Illust. sporting and dramatic news 30 Oct. 1880 pp.* 160, 162, *portrait*.

DOWTON, WILLIAM (*eld. son of the preceding*). *b.* 1793; manager of the Kent circuit 1815–35; made his first appearance in London at Drury Lane theatre 3 Dec. 1832 as Tangent; a brother of the Charterhouse 1846 to death. *d.* the Charterhouse, London 19 Sep. 1883.

DOXAT, LEWIS. *b.* British West Indies 1773; employed on the *Morning Chronicle* in London 25 years; manager of the *Observer* 1804–57; manager of the *Morning Chronicle* 1821–34. *d.* 13 Queen's crescent, Haverstock hill, London 4 March 1871 aged 98.

DOYLE, ANDREW (3 son of *Andrew Doyle of Dublin, merchant*). *b.* 1809; ed. at Trin. coll. Dublin; barrister L.I. 10 June 1842; inspector of poor law board, Feb. 1848 to 1871, of local government board 1871–76, his district included nearly all Wales; prepared elaborate reports on vagrancy 1849 and 1865, on pauper education 1850 and 1862, and a detailed report on sanitary state of his district on passing of first Public Health act 1872; assistant comr. on agricultural depression in England for Western district 1879–80. *d.* Pendarren, Crickhowell, Breconshire 14 Dec. 1888.

DOYLE, SIR CHARLES HASTINGS (*eld. son of Sir Charles Wm. Doyle, C.B.* 1770–1842). *b.* 10 April 1803; ed. at Sandhurst; ensign 87 foot 23 Dec. 1819; A.A.G. in Ireland 1847; inspector general of militia in Ireland 1856–61; commanded the troops in Nova Scotia 1861–68; lieut. governor of New Brunswick Oct. 1866 to Oct. 1867; lieut. governor of Nova Scotia, Oct. 1867 to May 1873; col. of 70 foot May 1868, of 87 foot 10 Oct. 1870 to death; commanded forces in British North America 1870–74, and Southern district of England 1874–77; general 15 March 1877, placed on retired list 1 Oct. 1877; K.C.M.G. 23 June 1869. *d.* at his lodgings 18 Bolton st. Piccadilly, London 19 March 1883.

DOYLE, SIR FRANCIS HASTINGS CHARLES, 2 Baronet (*only son of Sir Francis Hastings Doyle, 1 baronet* 1783–1839). *b.* Nun Appleton, Yorkshire 22 Aug. 1810; ed. at Eton and Ch. Ch. Ox., B.A. 1832, B.C.L. 1843, hon. D.C.L. 1877; fellow of All Souls' coll. 1835–45 and 1872–77; barrister I.T. 17 Nov. 1837; assistant solicitor of the Excise 1845–46; receiver general of Customs 1846 to Nov. 1869; comr. of Customs, Nov. 1869 to 1883; professor of poetry at Oxford 20 June 1867 to June 1877; author of *Miscellaneous Verses* 1834; *Two Destinies, a poem* 1844; *Return of the guards and other poems* 1866; *Lectures delivered before the University of Oxford* 1868, second series 1877; *Reminiscences and opinions* 1886. *d.* 46 Davies st. Berkeley sq. London 8 Feb. 1888.

DOYLE, JOHN. *b.* Dublin 1797; portrait painter in London 1821; published 6 plates entitled *The life of a racehorse* 1822; issued under initials of H. B. a series of lithographed caricatures entitled *Political sketches of H. B., Nos. 1–917 a series of coloured lithographic prints* 9 vols. 1829–51, there was a key to them entitled *A Key to the political sketches Nos. 1–600 of H. B.* 11 vols. 1831–43; paid £300 by the War Office for an improved Tent 1856. *d.* 54

DOYLE, J. (*Con.*)
Clifton gardens, Maida Vale, London 2 Jany. 1868. *Everitt's English caricaturists* (1886) 238–86; *J. Paget's Paradoxes and puzzles* (1874) 461–3; *The Month viii,* 392–411 (1868).

DOYLE, SIR JOHN MILLEY (*2 son of Rev. Nicholas Milley Doyle, R. of Newcastle, co. Tipperary*). *b.* 1781; ensign 107 foot 31 May 1794; lieut. col. Portuguese army March 1809; commanded sixth Portuguese brigade 1813–14; lieut. col. on half pay 11 May 1820; retired from service as col. 27 May 1825; M.P. for co. Carlow 1831–32; served in Portuguese army 1832 to May 1834; military knight of Windsor, July 1853; serjeant at arms to the Queen, June 1854 to death; nominated K.T.S. 12 Oct. 1812, gazetted 20 March 1813; knighted by Prince Regent at Carlton house 28 July 1814; K.C.B. 2 Jany. 1815; published pamphlets and petitions 1829–46 by which he got the mixed commission appointed to liquidate claims of English officers who served in Portuguese army. *d.* Lower ward, Windsor castle 9 Aug. 1856.

DOYLE, PERCY WILLIAM (*brother of Sir Charles Hastings Doyle* 1803–83). *b.* 1806; attached to British mission at Washington 2 June 1825; sec. of legation to Mexican republic 6 Dec. 1842, minister plenipotentiary 24 Dec. 1851 to 19 Feb. 1858 when he retired on pension; C.B. 4 March 1858. *d.* 5 Half Moon st. Piccadilly, London 21 Feb. 1888.

DOYLE, RICHARD (*2 son of John Doyle* 1797–1868). *b.* London, Sep. 1824; published *The Eglinton Tournament or the days of chivalry revived* 1839; kept a manuscript 'Journal' 1840, issued in facsimile 1885; contributed sketches and cartoons to *Punch* 1843–50; designed the cover for *Punch* now used; his *Manners and customs of ye Englyshe* appeared in *Punch* 1849; published *The foreign tour of Brown, Jones and Robinson* 1854; illustrated *The Newcomes* by Thackeray 1854 and other books; contributed *Birds'-eye views of society* to *Cornhill Mag.* 1861–63; many water-colours by him were exhibited at Grosvenor gallery, London 1885; drawn by Leech in his cartoon entitled "Mr. Punch's fancy ball" in *Punch vol. xii, p. 14, Jany.* 1847, as the clarionet player in the orchestra. *d.* 7 Finborough road, South Kensington, London 11 Dec. 1883. *Everitt's English caricaturists* (1886) 381–94; *Gillow's English Catholics ii,* 101–3 (1885); *W. M. Rossetti's Fine Art* (1867) 289–91; *Blackwood's Mag. April* 1885 *pp.* 485–91; *Graphic xxviii,* 608 (1883), *portrait; I.L.N. lxxxiv,* 13 (1884), *portrait.*

DOYLE, REV. THOMAS. *b.* 21 Dec. 1793; ed. at St. Edmund's college, Ware, ordained priest 1819; priest at Royal Belgian chapel, London road, Southwark 1820, senior priest there 1829; St. George's R.C. cathedral in St. George's Fields was built owing to his exertions, consecrated 4 July 1848; Provost of cathedral chapter of Southwark 1850 to death; wrote letters in *The Tablet* and other periodicals under signature of 'Father Thomas.' *d.* St. George's Cathedral, London 6 June 1879. *Gillow's English Catholics ii,* 103–5 (1885).

DOYLE, SIR WILLIAM HENRY *(son of Edward Doyle).* *b.* Nassau, Bahamas 1823; barrister M.T. 8 May 1846; registrar of court of bankruptcy for Bahamas 1847–58; assistant justice of general court of Bahamas 1858, chief justice and pres. of legislative council 14 Sep. 1865 to 31 March 1875; knighted at Windsor Castle 12 Dec. 1873; chief justice of Leeward Islands 31 March 1875; chief justice of Gibraltar, judge of vice admiralty court and court of requests 14 May 1877 to death. *d.* 8 Montpellier villas, Cheltenham 27 April 1879.

DOYLEY, HENRY *(youngest son of Ven. Matthias Doyley, archdeacon of Lewes, who d. 13 Nov. 1815 aged 71).* *b.* 21 April 1780; ensign Grenadier guards 2 Aug. 1797, lieut. col. 10 Jany. 1837 to 28 June 1838; col. 33 foot 28 Sep. 1847 to death; general 30 Jany. 1855. *d.* Nevill park, Tunbridge Wells 26 Sep. 1855.

DOYLEY, THOMAS *(brother of the preceding).* *b.* London 16 Nov. 1774; ed. at Westminster and Ch. Ch. Ox., B.A. 1795, B.C.L. 1800, D.C.L. 1804; fellow of All Souls' college 1800–20; barrister M.T. 9 Nov. 1798; serjeant at law 9 Feb. 1819, received patent of precedence 1834; chairman of quarter sessions, West Sussex; edited with E. V. Williams *Burn's Justice of the Peace 5 vols.* 1836. *d.* Rottingdean near Brighton 14 Jany. 1855.

DOYNE, WILLIAM THOMAS (2 *son of Rev. J. Doyne, P.C. of Old Leighlin, co. Carlow).* *b.* April 1823; articled to Edward Dixon, C.E. 1840; resident engineer of Rugby and Leamington railway 1847–50; in charge of the Army works corps consisting of about 2400 navvies and artificers, at Balaclava 1855–56; practised at Melbourne 1866 to death; consulting engineer to government of Western Australia 1869; A.I.C.E. 6 March 1849, M.I.C.E. 9 Nov. 1852; author of *The causes which have retarded the construction of railways in India* 1860; *Report upon the plains and rivers of Canterbury, New Zealand* 1864. *d.* Melbourne 29 Sep. 1877. *Min. of proc. of Instit. of C.E. li,* 270–73 (1878).

DRAKARD, JOHN. Printer and bookseller at Stamford; started a weekly paper called *The Stamford News* 15 Sep. 1809; sentenced to 18 months' imprisonment in Lincoln Castle and fined £200 at Lincoln 13 March 1811 for a seditious libel, an article in his paper of 24 Aug. 1810 entitled 'One thousand lashes'; started a weekly paper called *The Champion of the East* 5 Jany. 1830, the name was changed to the *Stamford Champion;* both his papers ceased 1834; published *Drakard's Edition of the public and private life of Colonel Wardle,* Stamford n.d. ; author of *The history of Stamford* 1822. *d.* Ripon 25 Jany. 1854 aged 79. *Howell's State Trials xxxi,* 495–544 (1823).

DRAKE, CHARLES FREDERICK TYRWHITT *(younger son of Col. Wm. Tyrwhitt Drake of the Royal horse guards, who d. 21 Dec. 1848).* *b.* Amersham, Bucks. 2 Jany. 1846; ed. at Rugby, Wellington coll. and Trin. coll. Cam. but took no degree; spent winters of 1866 and 1867 in Morocco; visited Egypt, Palestine, Syria, Greece and Turkey 1868–70; engaged on survey of Palestine for Palestine exploration fund society 1870 to death; F.R.G.S.; author of *Modern Jerusalem* 1875; author with Sir R. F. Burton of *Unexplored Syria 2 vols.* 1872. *d.* Jerusalem 23 June 1874. *Literary remains of C. F. T. Drake by W. Besant* 1877; *Modern Jerusalem by the late C. F. T. Drake with a memoir* 1875; *Palestine Fund Reports* (1874) *pp.* 131–4.

DRAKE, JOHN POAD *(son of Thomas Drake of Stoke Damerel, Devon, who d. 20 May 1835).* Baptised at Stoke Damerel 20 July 1794; painted a picture of Napoleon on board the Bellerophon at Plymouth 1815 which he exhibited in New York; occupied with schemes for breechloading guns 1829–37; laid proposals before government for ironcased floating batteries and steam rams 1832–40; patented his diagonal system of shipbuilding and a screw trenail fastening 1837; failed to obtain adoption of any of his inventions. *d.* Fowey, Cornwall 26 Feb. 1883. *Dict. of Nat. Biog. xv,* 447 (1888).

DRAKE, SAMUEL, stage name of Samuel Bryant. *b.* England 15 Nov. 1768; apprenticed to a printer; ran away and became an actor; managed a theatre in West of England; acted at Boston theatre, U.S. 1809–13, and at Albany, New York 1813–15; managed theatres at Frankfort, Lexington and Louisville all in Kentucky 1815 to about 1827, afterwards managed theatres in Ohio, Tennessee, Missouri and Indiana; may properly be called the pioneer of the drama in the West. *d.* Oldham county, Kentucky 16 Oct. 1854.

DRAKE, SIR THOMAS TRAYTON FULLER-ELIOTT, 1 Baronet (3 *son of John Trayton Fuller of Ashdown house, Sussex, who d. 1812*). *b.* Heathfield park, Sussex 8 Feb. 1785; lieut. 52 foot 5 Oct. 1804, major 26 May 1814 to 25 May 1815 when placed on h.p.; assumed additional surnames of Eliott and Drake by r.l. 31 March 1813; created baronet 22 Aug. 1821; sheriff of Devon 1822; edited *Life of Sir F. Drake* 1828. *d.* Nutwell court near Exeter 6 June 1870.

DRAKE, THOMAS TYRWHITT (*eld. son of Thomas Drake of Shardeloes, Bucks., who d.* 1810). *b.* 16 March 1783; M.P. for Amersham, Bucks. 31 Jany. 1805 to 3 Dec. 1832; sheriff of Bucks. 1836; master of hounds in the Bicester country many years. *d.* Bucknell, Oxfordshire 23 March 1852.

DRAKE, SIR WILLIAM HENRY (*son of John Drake, deputy commissary general, who d.* 24 *June* 1867 *aged* 84). *b.* 1812; deputy assistant commissary general 16 April 1835, commissary general 21 June 1859; controller in Ireland 1867, in Great Britain 1869; director of supplies and transports 3 Sep. 1871 to 29 Sep. 1872; C.B. 4 Feb. 1856, K.C.B. 20 May 1871. *d.* 10 Clanricarde gardens, Bayswater, London 28 Jany. 1882.

DRAPER, REV. DANIEL JAMES. *b.* parish of Wickham, Hants. 28 Aug. 1810; became a Wesleyan Methodist 1830; minister of Chatteris circuit 1834; minister at Sydney, N.S.W. 1836–37, 1842–46, at Melbourne 1846–47 and 1855 to 1865, at Adelaide 1847–55; president of the Conference 1859; drowned with 244 other passengers in the wreck of the "London" steamship in the Bay of Biscay 11 Jany. 1866. *F. J. Jobson's Memorial tribute to D. J. Draper* 1866, *portrait.*

DRAPER, JOHN WILLIAM (*son of John C. Draper, Wesleyan minister, who d.* 1829). *b.* St. Helen's near Liverpool 5 May 1811; ed. at Woodhouse grove school, London Univ. and Univ. of Pennsylvania, M.D. 1836; professor of chemistry and natural philosophy in Hampden Sidney college, Virginia 1836–39; professor of medical department in Univ. of New York 1839, of chemistry 1840–81; pres. of New York medical college 1850–73; made first photographic portrait from life 1839 and first photograph of moon's surface 1840; LLD. Princeton 1860; first pres. of American Chemical Soc. 1876; author of *Text book of chemistry* 1846; *Text book of human physiology* 1856; *History of the intellectual development of Europe* 2 vols. 1864; *History of the American civil war* 3 vols. 1871; *History of the conflict*

DRAPER, J. W. (*Con.*)
between religion and science 1874, translated into 9 languages. *d.* Hastings on river Hudson 20 miles north of New York 4 Jany. 1882. *Barker's Memoir of J. W. Draper* 1882, *portrait; Appleton's American Biog. ii,* 226–27 (1887), *portrait; Graphic xxv,* 68, (1882), *portrait.*

DRAPER, WILLIAM HENRY (*son of Rev. Henry Draper, lecturer of St. George's ch. Southwark*). *b.* near London 11 March 1801; arrived in Cobourg, Canada 4 June 1820; called to bar in Canada 16 June 1828; reporter to the King's Bench 18 Nov. 1829 to March 1837; solicitor general of Upper Canada 23 March 1837, member of executive council, Dec. 1837, the first attorney general for Upper Canada 13 Feb. 1841 to 28 May 1847; Q.C. 1842; a legislative councillor of Canada 10 April 1843 to Jany. 1845; member of legislative assembly Jany. 1845 to 28 May 1847; a puisne judge of Queen's Bench 12 June 1847; chief justice of Common Pleas 5 Feb. 1856; chief justice of Upper Canada 22 July 1863 to 20 Oct. 1868; C.B. 23 June 1854; pres. of court of error and appeal Ontario 20 Oct. 1868; author of *Upper Canada King's Bench Reports* 1729–31, 2 *vols.* 1861–62. *d.* Yorkville, Toronto 3 Nov. 1877. *Law Magazine and law review xxvii,* 362 (1869).

DRAYTON, HENRI. *b.* Philadelphia 1822; ed. at Paris Conservatoire; primo basso in Italian opera in France and Belgium 1848–50; sang in English opera in London 1850–59; gave parlor opera entertainments with his wife in the United States 1859–61 when he returned to England; sang with Riching's English Opera company in America 1867–70; author of dramas and operas. *d.* 57 East ninth st. New York 11 Aug. 1872. *I.L.N. xxx,* 411 (1856), *portrait.*

DREW, ANDREW. *b.* 27 Nov. 1792; entered navy 4 May 1806; commodore of provincial marine of Upper Canada 1838–39; captain on h.p. 10 June 1843; agent victualler at Cape of Good Hope 16 Dec. 1850 to 30 Jany. 1863; admiral on h.p. 30 July 1875; discovered a dangerous shoal between Trinidad and Tobago 1842, afterwards called Drew's Rock. *d.* Glenwood house, Peckham Rye, Surrey 19 Dec. 1878. *A narrative of the capture of the Caroline* 1844.

NOTE.—He successfully defended Cape Coast castle in 1824 with 160 sailors against an attack by 50,000 Ashantees. During the Canadian rebellion in 1838 with only about 35 men he captured the rebel steamer Caroline and sent it burning over the falls of Niagara, one of the most daring exploits recorded in naval history.

DREW, REV. GEORGE SMITH (*son of George Drew of 11 Tottenham court road, London, tea*

DREW, REV. G. S. *(Con.)*

dealer).   *b.* Louth, Lincs. 1819 ; sizar at St. John's coll. Cam. 22 Jany. 1839; 27 wrangler 1843 ; Inc. of St. John the Evangelist, St. Pancras, London 1850–54 ; V. of Pulloxhill, Beds. 1854–58 ; V. of St. Barnabas, South Kensington, London 1858–70 ; select preacher to Univ. of Cam. 1869–70 ; R. of Avington, Hants. 1870–72 ; Hulsean lecturer at Cam. 1877 ; V. of Holy Trinity, Lambeth, London 18 Sep. 1872 to death ; F.R.G.S. ; author of *Scripture studies or readings in the Old Testament* 1855, 2 ed. 1869 ; *Scripture lands in connection with their history* 1860, 2 ed. 1862 ; *Reasons of faith or the Christian argument developed* 1862, 2 ed. 1869 and 11 other books. *d.* Holy Trinity vicarage, Lambeth 21 Jany. 1880.

DREW, JOHN. *b.* Bower Chalk, Wiltshire 1809 ; kept a school at Southampton 1826–42 ; built a small observatory there 1847 ; supplied the correct time to ships leaving Southampton many years ; Ph. D. Univ. of Basle ; F.R.A.S. 9 Jany. 1846 ; a founder of Meteorological Soc. 1850 ; author of *A manual of Astronomy* 1845, 2 ed. 1853 ; *Practical meteorology* 1855, re-edited by his son 1860 and other books and many papers. *d.* Surbiton, Surrey 17 Dec. 1857.

DREW, JOHN. *b.* Dublin 3 Sep. 1825 ; appeared at Bowery theatre, New York 1845 as Dr. O'Toole in *The Irish Tutor ;* lessee with Wm. Wheatley of Arch st. theatre, Philadelphia 20 Aug. 1853 to 1855 ; acted in England 1855, California 1858 and Australia 1859 ; returned to New York from England 9 Jany. 1862 ; best Irish comedian on American stage ; played for last time 9 May 1862. *d.* Philadelphia 21 May 1862. *T. A. Brown's History of the American stage* (1870) *p. 105, portrait.*

DREW, REV. WILLIAM HENRY. Educ. at St. John's coll. Cam., 8 wrangler 1849 ; B.A. 1849, M.A. 1856 ; mathematical master at Blackheath proprietary school 1856–73 ; C. of Crockenhill near Dartford 1866–73 ; professor of mathematics at King's college, London June 1869 to death ; author of *A geometrical treatise on conic sections* 1857, 6 ed. 1880. *d.* Park house, Maida hill west, London 14 July 1882 aged 55.

DRISCOLL, HENRY. *b.* Dublin 1792 ; ensign 67 foot 13 June 1811 ; lieut. 100 foot 3 March 1814 ; lieut. 99 foot 1815 to 1817 when removed from the army ; studied for the bar at Montreal ; edited the *Herald* newspaper ; edited the *Courant* newspaper ; called to Canadian bar May 1823 ; Q.C.; police magistrate 1840. *d.* Montreal 28 Oct. 1869.

DROOP, HENRY RICHMOND *(son of John Abraham Droop of Stamford Hill, Middlesex).*   *b.* about 1831 ; ed. at Marlborough and Trin. coll. Cam., scholar 1853, 3 wrangler 1854 ; fellow of his coll. 1855, mathematical lecturer; B.A. 1854, M.A. 1857 ; barrister L.I. 26 Jany. 1859 ; author of *North side of the table, a criticism* 1866 ; *Proportional representation as applied to election of local governing bodies* 1871; *Relations between an invading army and the inhabitants* 1871 ; *The Edwardian vestments an investigation* 1875. *d.* 11 Cleveland gardens, London 21 March 1884.

DROUGHT, THOMAS ARMSTRONG. *b.* 1798 ; Ensign 15 Foot 11 Nov. 1813, lieut. col. 21 March 1845 to 1 Oct. 1854 ; inspecting field officer 1 Oct. 1854 to 11 Jany. 1860 ; col. 45 Foot 25 June 1866 to 21 April 1868 ; col. 15 Foot 21 April 1868 to death ; general 29 May 1875. *d.* Hill house, Winchester 22 Aug. 1877.

DRUCE, CHARLES CLARIDGE *(one of the 24 children of Charles Druce of city of London, solicitor 1791–1881).*   *b.* Billiter sq. London 1819 ; solicitor in Billiter sq. 1843 to death ; vice pres. of Incorporated Law Society 1880–81, pres. 1881–82. *d.* Brighton 10 June 1885 in 66 year.

DRUCE, GEORGE *(brother of the preceding).* Educ. at Shrewsbury and St. Peter's coll. Cam., senior classic 1843, 2 chancellor's medallist 1843 ; B.A. 1843, M.A. 1846 ; fellow of his college 1846 ; barrister L.I. 19 Nov. 1846 ; Q.C. 13 Dec. 1866 ; one of standing counsel to univ. of Cam. Nov. 1867 to death. *d.* Denmark hill, Camberwell, London 15 April 1869 aged 48 in consequence of an accident while riding the day before. *Reg. and mag. of biog. i,* 470–71 (1869).

DRUITT, ROBERT. *b.* Wimborne, Dorset, Dec. 1814 ; studied at King's college and Middlesex hospital; L.S.A. 1836 ; M.R.C.S. 1837, F.R.C.S. 1845 ; F.R.C.P. 1874 ; M.D. Lambeth, Sep. 1878 ; practised in London from 1837 ; on his retirement 370 subscribers presented him with a cheque for £1215 in a silver cup ; edited *The Medical Times and Gazette* 1862–72 ; a medical officer of health for St. George's, Hanover sq. 1856–67 ; pres. of Metropolitan Association of medical officers of health 1864–72 ; author of *The Surgeon's Vade Mecum* 1839, 11 ed. 1878 ; *Report on the cheap wines, their quality, wholesomeness and price* 1865, 2 ed. 1873. *d.* 8 Strathmore gardens, Kensington, London 15 May 1883. *W. T. Robertson's Photographs of medical men* (1868) *ii,* 109–13, *portrait.*

DRUMMOND, BERKELEY. *b.* 27 May 1796; ensign 3 Foot guards 5 March 1812, lieut. col. 31 Dec. 1844 to 28 June 1850 when placed on h.p.; col. 3 Foot 12 Dec. 1857 to death; L.G. 9 April 1859. *d.* Eaglehurst, Hants. 3 May 1860.

DRUMMOND, GEORGE HARLEY. *b.* 23 Nov. 1783; M.P. for Kincardineshire 26 Feb. 1812 to 29 Feb. 1820. *d.* 23 July 1853.

DRUMMOND, SIR GORDON (4 *son of Colin Drummond, paymaster general of the forces at Quebec).* *b.* Quebec 27 Sep. 1772; ensign 1 foot 21 Sep. 1789; lieut. col. 8 foot 22 April 1794 to 28 July 1804; commanded a division in Jamaica 1805–1807; won battle of Niagara 25 July 1814; commanded forces in Canada 1814–16; col. of 97 foot 8 Feb. 1814 to 24 Nov. 1818 when regiment was disbanded; col. of 88 foot 10 March 1819, of 71 foot 16 Jany. 1824, of 49 foot 21 Sep. 1829, of 8 foot 24 April 1846 to death; general 27 May 1825; K.C.B. 2 Jany. 1815, G.C.B. 7 Jany. 1817. *d.* 25 Norfolk st. Park lane, London 10 Oct. 1854. *Historical record of King's Liverpool regiment of foot, 2 ed.* (1883) 270–71.

DRUMMOND, HENRY *(eld. son of Henry Drummond of the Grange, Hants. 1762–94).* *b.* 5 Dec. 1786; ed. at Harrow and Ch. Ch. Ox.; partner in Drummond's bank, London; M.P. for Plympton Earle, Devon 1810–13; M.P. for West Surrey 1847 to death; founded professorship of political economy at Oxford 1825; F.R.S. 19 Dec. 1839; seceded from Church of England and was immersed by Rev. James Harrington Evans about 1817, for whom he built a chapel in John st. Bedford Row, London 1818; one of founders of Catholic Apostolic or Irvingite church 1832, pastor at Albury near Guildford 20 Oct. 1832, apostle at Albury 25 Sep. 1833; took charge of Scotland and Switzerland 1833 to death, built the C.A. church at Albury 1835 at cost of £16,000; erected new parish church of SS. Peter and Paul at Albury 1841; author of *Dialogues on prophecy* 3 vols. 1828–29; *Social Duties* 1830; *Condition of Agricultural classes* 2 vols. 1842; *On Tracts for the Times* 24 parts 1843; *Histories of British families* 8 parts 1844–49 and about 90 other books and pamphlets. *d.* Albury Park near Guildford 20 Feb. 1860. *Miller's History of Irvingism* 2 vols. 1878; *London quarterly review* Oct. 1860 pp. 255–84; *Speeches of Henry Drummond edited by Lord Lovaine* 2 vols. 1860.

DRUMMOND, HENRY. Second lieut. Bengal engineers 2 Dec. 1843, col. 23 July 1874 to 1

DRUMMOND, H. *(Con.)*

June 1878 when he retired on full pay with hon. rank of M.G.; sec. of government of India public works department 1874–78. *d.* at his residence near Bedford 28 March 1883.

DRUMMOND, HENRY HOME. *b.* 28 July 1783; M.P. for co. Stirling 1820–1831, for Perthshire 1840–1852. *d.* Blair Drummond near Stirling 12 Sep. 1867. *Proc. of R. S. of Edin. vi,* 191 (1869).

DRUMMOND, JAMES. Botanical collector; in charge of Cork botanic garden to 1829; A.L.S. 1810; went to Swan River, Western Australia 1829; Lindley's *Sketch of the vegetation of the Swan River* 1839 was drawn up from his collections; *Drummondita* a genus of Diosmeæ was founded by Dr. Harvey 1855. *d.* Western Australia 27 March 1863 aged 79.

DRUMMOND, JAMES *(son of Mr. Drummond of Edinburgh, merchant).* *b.* 1810; studied in School of Design, Edin.; subject and history painter; A.R.S.A. 1846, R.S.A. 1852, librarian 1857; curator of National gallery, Edin. 1868; member of council of Royal Scottish Soc. of Antiquaries and curator of the museum; exhibited 11 pictures at R.A., 5 at B.I. and 5 at Suffolk st. gallery 1839–72; author of *Catalogue of national gallery of Scotland* 1869 many editions. *d.* Edinburgh 12 Aug. 1877.

DRUMMOND, JAMES LAWSON *(son of William Drummond, surgeon R.N.)* *b.* Larne, co. Antrim 1783; surgeon in the navy 1807 to 21 May 1813; M.D. Edin. 24 June 1814; practised in Belfast from 1814; professor of anatomy Belfast Academical Institution 15 Dec. 1818 to Nov. 1849 when collegiate part of the Instit. was merged in Queen's College; chief founder of Belfast natural history society 5 June 1821; author of *Thoughts on the study of natural history* 1820, anon.; *First steps to botany* 1823; *Letters to a young naturalist* 1831; *First steps to anatomy* 1845. *d.* 8 College sq. north, Belfast 17 May 1853. *bur.* Ahoghill, co. Antrim 19 May. *Proc. of Belfast Nat. Hist. and Philos. Soc.* (1882) 13.

DRUMMOND, JOHN *(only son of John Drummond of The Boyce Court near Ledbury, who d. 13 May 1835 aged 81).* *b.* 5 Oct. 1793; ed. at Harrow; ensign Coldstream guards 22 Nov. 1810, captain 22 June 1826 to 13 April 1832 when placed on h.p.; general 10 Feb. 1865. *d.* The Boyce court 15 April 1875.

DRUMMOND, JOHN GAVIN. Entered Bengal army 1807; lieut. col. 30 Bengal N.I. 1847 to death; quartermaster general Bengal army 8 Feb. 1850 to death; C.B. 30 Oct. 1844. *d.* Ghelum, Bengal 11 Jany. 1852.

DRUMMOND, PETER ROBERT. *b.* parish of Madderty, Perthshire 1802; kept a circulating library at 15 High st. Perth 1832; a bookseller at 32 High st. Perth and then at 46 George st.; built the Exchange hotel, Perth; a farmer at Balmblair, Perthshire; gained a medal for a churn at Great Exhibition 1851; author of *The tenants and landlords versus the free traders, By Powdavie* 1850; *Perthshire in bygone days, one hundred biographical essays* 1879; *The life of Robert Nicoll poet, edited by James Drummond* 1884. *d.* Ellengowen, Almond Bank near Perth 4 Sep. 1879 in 77 year.

DRUMMOND, REV. WILLIAM HAMILTON (*brother of James Lawson Drummond* 1783–1853). *b.* Larne, co. Antrim, Aug. 1778; ed. at Belfast academy and Glasgow college; licensed by Unitarian presbytery of Antrim 9 April 1800; second minister of Belfast 26 Aug. 1800 to 1815; kept a boarding school at Mount college, Belfast; D.D. Marischal college, Aberdeen 29 Jany. 1810; minister at Strand st. Dublin from 15 Oct. 1815; M.R.I.A. librarian, retired 1861; author of *Juvenile poems, By a Student of the University of Glasgow* [1795]; *The Man of Age* 1797, 2 ed. 1798; *The doctrine of the Trinity* 1827, 3 ed. 1831; *The life of Michael Servetus* 1848 and 20 other books. *d.* Lower Gardiner st. Dublin 16 Oct. 1865. *Sermons of Rev. W. H. Drummond with memoir by J. S. Porter* 1867, 2 *portraits*.

DRURY, BYRON (*son of Rev. Henry Drury of Harrow school*). *b.* 1815; entered navy 13 Aug. 1830; surveyed coast of New Zealand 1850–56; captain 8 Aug. 1857; retired 31 March 1866; retired admiral 7 April 1885; F.R.G.S. *d.* 4 Cambridge villas, Cheltenham 6 Nov. 1888.

DRURY, VENERABLE HENRY (*eld. son of Henry Joseph Thomas Drury* 1778–1841). *b.* Harrow 11 May 1812; ed. at Harrow and Caius coll. Cam., B.A. 1837, M.A. 1840; R. of Alderley, Gloucs. 1843; V. of Bremhill, Wilts. Jany. 1845 to death; exam. chaplain to bishop of Salisbury 1850 to death; preb. of Salisbury cath. 1855 to death; chaplain of House of Commons, Sep. 1857 to death; archdeacon of Wilts, July 1862 to death; published with some friends a collection of translations into Latin and Greek by Cambridge men entitled *Arundines Cami* 1841, 6 ed. 1865. *d.* Bremhill vicarage 25 Jany. 1863. *G.M. xiv*, 660–61 (1863).

DRURY, WILLIAM BARKER (*eld. son of Rev. Richard Drury of Dublin*). *b.* Dublin 1812; ed. at Trin. coll. Dublin; called to Irish bar 1835;

registrar of Irish Court of Chancery 1859 to death; published *Reports of cases in the Court of Chancery tempore Sugden* 1843–4, *Dublin* 1851; *Select cases in the Court of Chancery tempore Napier* 1858–9, *Dublin* 1860; published with F. W. Walsh *Reports of cases in the Court of Chancery tempore Plunket* 1837–40, 2 *vols. Dublin* 1839–42; with R. Warren *Reports of cases in the Court of Chancery tempore Sugden* 1841–43, 4 *vols. Dublin* 1843–46. *d.* Harcourt st. Dublin 9 Jany. 1885 in 73 year.

DRY, SIR RICHARD. *b.* Elphin near Launceston, Tasmania 15 June 1815; member of council of Tasmania, Feb. 1844; member for Launceston of legislative council 1851–62, for Tamar 1862 to death; speaker of council 30 Dec. 1851 to 1855; knighted by patent 12 March 1858; colonial secretary and premier 24 Nov. 1866 to death. *d.* Hobart Town 1 Aug. 1869. *Fenton's History of Tasmania* (1884) 74, 338, 459.

DUANE, WILLIAM JOHN (*son of William Duane of Philadelphia, journalist* 1760–1835). *b.* Clonmel, Ireland 1780; a printer, afterwards a paper dealer; admitted to the bar 1815; represented Philadelphia in the legislature; assistant editor of the *Aurora*, Philadelphia paper to 1822; sec. of the U.S. treasury 1833, removed by Jackson 23 Sep. 1833, for declining to remove the deposits from the United States bank; author of *The law of nations investigated* 1809; *Letters to the people of Pennsylvania, on internal improvements* 1811; *Narrative and correspondence concerning the removal of the deposits* 1838. *d.* Philadelphia 27 Sep. 1865.

DUBOURG, GEORGE (*grandson of Matthew Dubourg, violinist* 1703–1767). *b.* 1799; contributed to various newspapers especially at Brighton; author of the words of many songs, best known of which is John Parry's 'Wanted a Governess'; published *The Violin, being an account of that leading instrument and its most eminent professors* 1836, 5 ed. 1856. *d.* Maidenhead 17 April 1882.

DUCIE, HENRY GEORGE FRANCIS REYNOLDS-MORETON, 2 Earl of (*eld. son of 1 Earl of Ducie* 1775–1840). *b.* Conduit st. London 8 May 1802; M.P. for Gloucs. 1831–32, for East Gloucs. 1832–1834; succeeded as 2 Earl 22 June 1840; a lord in waiting to the Queen 1846–1852; a charity estates comr. 1849; pres. of Royal Agricultural Society; invented the Ducie cultivator and many other agricultural implements; master of Vale of White Horse hounds 1830–42. *d.* Tortworth court, Gloucs. 2 June 1853. *Sporting Review xxviii,*

DUCIE, Earl of. (*Con.*)

64 (1852), *portrait, xxx,* 140 (1853); *I.L.N. xxi,* 41 (1852), *portrait; Cecil's Records of the Chase* (1877) 199–201.

DUCKETT, SIR GEORGE (*younger son of Sir George Jackson, 1 baronet, who took name of Duckett 1797 and d. 15 Dec. 1822 aged 97*). *b.* Old palace yard, Westminster 17 July 1777; M.P. for Lymington 1807–1812; F.R.S. 8 Dec. 1808. *d.* Gloucester gardens, Hyde park, London 15 June 1856.

DUCKWORTH, SIR JOHN THOMAS BULLER, 2 Baronet. *b.* Downes, Crediton, Devon 17 March 1809; succeeded his father 31 Aug. 1817; ed. at Eton and Oriel coll. Ox., B.A. 1829; M.P. for Exeter 1845–1857; sheriff of Devon 1861; one of referees of House of Commons for private bills 1868. *d.* Wear house near Exeter 29 Nov. 1887.

DUDLEY, WILLIAM WARD, 1 Earl of. *b.* 27 March 1817; ed. at Trin. coll. Ox.; succeeded his father as 11 Baron Ward 6 Dec. 1835; created Viscount Ednam of Ednam and Earl of Dudley 17 Feb. 1860; chairman of Worcestershire quarter sessions 1858 to 28 June 1880; gave £900,000 for the Foley estate Worcs. largest sum ever paid for purchase of an estate; his life was insured for £300,000. *d.* Dudley house, Park lane, London 7 May 1885, personalty sworn upwards of £1,026,000 18 July. *Waagen's Treasures of Art ii,* 229–38 (1854); *I.L.N. xlii,* 181 (1862), *portrait.*

DUDLEY, HOWARD (*only son of George Dudley of Tipperary, who d. at Ghent 1827*). Engraver on wood in Edinburgh 1845–52, in London 1852 to death; printed *Juvenile researches, or a description of some of the principal towns in the west of Sussex and the borders of Hants.* 1835, 2 ed. 1835; *The history and antiquities of Horsham* 1836; *The history and antiquities of Midhurst* 1836. *d.* Holford square, Pentonville, London 4 July 1864 aged 44.

DUDLEY, REV. JOHN (*eld. son of Rev. John Dudley, V. of Humberstone, Leics., who d. 17 May 1794 aged 74*). *b.* 1762; ed. at Uppingham sch. and Clare hall, Cam., 2 wrangler 1785; B.A. 1785, M.A. 1788; Fellow of his coll. 1787–94, tutor 1788–94; V. of Humberstone 1794 to death; V. of Sileby, Leics. 1795 to death; author of *The metamorphosis of Sona, a Hindu tale in verse* 1810, and 4 other books. *d.* Sileby 7 Jany. 1856. *G.M. xlv,* 197–98 (1856).

DUDLEY, WILLIAM HENRY. *b.* Roscrea, Tipperary, Ireland 7 Oct. 1811; M.R.C.S. Ireland 1833; practised in Jamaica 1834–1841 in

DUDLEY, W. H. (*Con.*)

Brooklyn, New York 1841 to death; curator of New York Medical college 1851; a founder of Long Island college hospital, treasurer, president; a member of New York Academy of Medicine 1848, of King's county Medical and other societies. *d.* Brooklyn 9 Oct. 1886.

DUFF, SIR ALEXANDER (*second son of 3 Earl of Fife 1731–1811*). Ensign 66 foot 23 May 1793; lieut. col. 88 foot 14 April 1798 to 1809 when placed on h.p.; col. 92 foot 6 Sep. 1823 to 20 July 1831; col. 37 foot 20 July 1831 to death; G.C.H. 27 May 1834; general 28 June 1838; M.P. for Elginburghs 1826–1831; lord lieut. of Elginshire 17 Feb. 1848 to death. *d.* Percy cross, Walham Green, Middlesex 21 March 1851 aged 77. *bur.* in family vault, Banff.

DUFF, REV. ALEXANDER. *b.* Auchnahyle farm, parish of Moulin, Perthshire 26 April 1806; ed. at Univ. of St. Andrews, D.D. 1837; ordained Aug. 1829; sent by general assembly of Church of Scotland as their first missionary to India, reached Calcutta 27 May 1830 where he opened an English school 1830; edited the *Calcutta Review* 1845–49; moderator or pres. general assembly of Free church of Scotland 1851 and 1873; LLD. New York 1854; the virtual governor of Univ. of Calcutta 1857–63 where 4 Duff scholarships were instituted; convener of the foreign missions committee 1864; missionary professor in New college, Edin. 1867; author of *India and India missions* 1840; *The Jesuits* 1845 and 12 other books. *d.* Sidmouth, Devon 12 Feb. 1878. *Life of A. Duff by George Smith 2 vols.* (1879), *2 portraits; Wylie's Disruption Worthies* (1881) 215–22, *portrait; Hogg's Instructor viii,* 369 (1852), *portrait; Graphic xvii,* 320 (1878), *portrait.*

DUFF, ARCHIBALD. Entered navy 29 June 1788; captain 22 Jany. 1806; R.A. 17 Aug. 1840, V.A. 3 March 1849, admiral on half pay 4 July 1855. *d.* Braemoriston 9 Feb. 1858 aged 83.

DUFF, HENRIETTA ANNE (*dau. of Norwich Duff, V.A.*) Author of *Virginia, a Roman sketch* 1877; *Fragments of verse* 1880; *Honor Carmichael, a study 2 vols.* 1880; *My imperialist neighbour and other tales* 1880. *d.* of heart disease at 9 Holland road, Hove, Brighton 14 Nov. 1879 aged 37.

DUFF, JAMES. *b.* Innes house, Elgin 29 July 1831; ed. at Rugby; 2 lieut. 23 foot 15 May 1851, captain 29 Dec. 1854 to 4 Nov. 1859 when he sold out; taken prisoner at battle of Inkerman; M.P. for North Norfolk 21 April 1876 to death. *d.* 36 Upper Brook st. London 22 Dec. 1878.

DUFF, James Cuninghame Grant *(eld. son of John Grant of Kincardine, who d. about* 1799). *b.* Banff 8 July 1789; ed. at Marischal coll. Aberdeen; entered Bombay army 1805; fought against the Mahrattas 1817–18; resident of Sattara 1818–1823; lived at Eden near Banff 1825 to death; author of *History of the Mahrattas* 1826. *d.* Eden 23 Sep. 1858.

DUFF, Mary Ann *(dau. of Mr. Dyke of Kilkenny). b.* London 1795; learnt dancing from D'Egville; first appeared as an actress at Boston theatre U.S. Nov. 1810; first appeared in London at Drury Lane 3 March 1828 as Isabella in *The fatal marriage;* played leading Shakesperean parts with Edmund Kean in the United States 1821; retired from the stage at New York 1835. *(m.* (1) 1810 John Duff of Dublin, actor 1787–1831, *m.* (2) 1833 Charles Young, marriage dissolved 1833, *m.* (3) Joel G. Seaver of New Orleans, lawyer). *d.* New York 5 Sep. 1857. *Ireland's Mrs. Duff* 1883, 2 *portraits; Ireland's Records of the New York stage i,* 419–21 (1866).

DUFF, Norwich. *b.* about 1793; entered navy June 1805; captain 23 April 1822; naval aide-de-camp to the Queen, May 1849 to 7 Oct. 1852; V.A. on half pay 28 Nov. 1857. *d.* Bath 20 April 1862 aged 68.

DUFFY, Edward. *b.* Ballaghadareen, co. Mayo 1840; devoted himself to spreading Fenian principles in Connaught 1863; arrested at Fairfield house, Sandymount 11 Nov. 1865, sentenced to a term of imprisonment, liberated on bail in consequence of ill health Jany. 1866; again applied himself to the organisation; re-arrested at Boyle 11 March 1867, tried 21 May 1867 and sentenced to 15 years penal servitude; found dead in his cell at Millbank prison, London 17 Jany. 1868. *T. D. Sullivan's Speeches from the Dock,* 23 ed. part i, *pp.* 208–10.

DUFFY, John. Ensign 10 foot 21 Oct. 1795; major 43 foot 17 June 1813; lieut. col. 95 foot 21 Sep. 1815 to 25 Dec. 1818 when placed on h.p., re-appointed lieut. col. of 95 foot 12 Aug. 1819; lieut. col. 8 foot 9 Sep. 1819 to 20 March 1828 when placed on h.p.; col. 28 foot 18 May 1849, col. 8 foot 10 Oct. 1854 to death; L.G. 11 Nov. 1851; rose by his own merit without purchasing a single step; C.B. 26 Sep. 1831. *d.* Jermyn st. Piccadilly, London 17 March 1855 aged 76.

DUFTON, William *(younger son of John Dufton of Brigham, Cumberland). b.* Cumberland; educ. Borough hospitals, London and at Jervis st. hospital, Dublin; surgeon at Birmingham

1831 to death; established Institution for relief of deafness and was its sole medical officer 1844 to decease; chief consulting practitioner in midland district for deafness; author of *The nature and treatment of deafness and diseases of the ear, and the treatment of the deaf and dumb* 1844, another ed. Philadelphia 1848. *d.* of heart disease at 39 Temple st. Birmingham 17 Oct. 1859 aged 53.

DUFTON, William. *b.* Northampton 13 March 1830; kept the Philharmonic billiard saloons, Islington, London; played many billiard matches with John Roberts senior; played Edward Green for £1000 at St. James's hall, London 30 Jany. 1865 gaining by 1001 to 893; entertained at a banquet at Victoria club, London 1865 when presented with a testimonial and 200 guineas; taught the Prince of Wales and many of the nobility; the inventor of handicap billiards; author of *Practical Billiards* 1867, 3 ed. 1873; present at match between Wm. Cook and John Roberts junior at Gaiety restaurant, London 28 May 1877; poisoned himself with cyanide of potassium at Canterbury tavern, Brixton, London 29 May 1877. *bur.* Norwood cemetery 4 June. *W. Dufton's Practical billiards* 1867, *portrait; Illust. Sporting News iii,* 356 (1864), *portrait, iv,* 633 (1865), *portrait, and v,* 108, 121 (1866), *portrait; Bell's Life in London* 2 June 1877 *pp.* 3, 5.

DUGDALE, William Stratford. *b.* 1 April 1800; ed. at Westminster and Ch. Ch. Ox.; M.P. for Shaftesbury, Dorset 1830–1831, for Bramber, Sussex 1831–1832, for North Warwickshire 1832–1847. *d.* Blyth hall near Coleshill 15 Sep. 1871.

DUGGAN, Peter Paul. *b.* Ireland about 1810; went to the United States; Professor of Art New York Free Academy soon after its opening; devoted himself chiefly to crayon drawing. *d.* Paris 15 Oct. 1861.

DUGMORE, William *(younger son of John Dugmore of Swaffham, Norfolk, comr. of inclosures, who d.* 11 Feb. 1844 *aged* 87). *b.* 1800; barrister L.I. 24 June 1828; practised as conveyancer; Q.C. 22 Feb. 1861. *d.* Cannes 1 July 1872.

DUIGAN, Daniel John. L.R.C.S. Ireland 1844, F.R.C.S. 1845; M.D. Aberdeen 1857; M.R.C.P. 1860; assistant surgeon R.N. 26 July 1844, surgeon 29 Aug. 1854, fleet surgeon 31 March 1867; retired deputy inspector general of hospitals and fleets 22 April 1876; C.B. 24 May 1881. *d.* 29 Edith road, West Kensington, London 2 Dec. 1884 in 63 year.

DUKE, REV. EDWARD (2 son of Edward Duke of Lake house near Amesbury, Wilts.) b. 1779; ed. at Magd. hall, Ox., B.A. 1803, M.A. 1807; contributed to *Gent. Mag.* 1823–49; author of *Prolusiones historicæ or essays illustrative of the Halle of John Halle citizen of Salisbury vol. i*, 1837; *The Druidical temples of the county of Wilts* 1846. *d.* Lake house 28 Aug. 1852. *G.M. xxxviii*, 643–44 (1852).

DUKE, SIR JAMES, 1 Baronet (3 son of John Duke of Montrose, merchant, who d. Aug. 1822 aged 63). b. Montrose 31 Jany. 1792; secretary to Admiral Sir John Gore 1814; coal factor and insurance broker in London 1819–48; pres. of Honourable Artillery company 1868 to death; sheriff of London and Middlesex 1836; knighted by the king at St. James's palace 5 April 1837; alderman of ward of Farringdon without, city of London 1840 to death, lord mayor 1848-49; M.P. for Boston 1837–1849, for city of London 1849–1865; created a Baronet on opening of new coal exchange, London 30 Oct. 1849. *d.* Laughton lodge, Hawkhurst, Sussex 28 May 1873. *I.L.N. xiii*, 297 (1848), *portrait, lxii*, 541, 547, (1873), *portrait.*

DUKE, THOMAS ASSHETON. b. 1805; ensign Madras European regiment 13 Feb. 1821, major 2 Jany. 1843; brigadier general Madras 8 Dec. 1857 to 12 Sep. 1859; major general Madras 20 April 1864 to 19 April 1869; general 1 Oct. 1877. *d.* 7 Queen's gardens, Hyde park, London 22 Feb. 1887.

DUKINFIELD, REV. SIR HENRY ROBERT, 7 Baronet (3 son of Sir Nathaniel Dukinfield, 5 Baronet, who d. 20 Oct. 1824). b. Sulham near Reading 1 Jany. 1791; ed. at Musselburgh, Rugby, Eton and Ch. Ch. Ox., student 1810; B.A. 1813, M.A. 1816; P.C. of Ruscombe, Berkshire 1814–16; V. of Waltham, St. Lawrence, Berkshire 1816–34; V. of St. Giles, Reading 1816–34; Preb. of Salisbury 29 March 1832 to 1856; V. of St. Martin in the Fields, Westminster 1834–48; succeeded his brother 7 Dec. 1836. *d.* 33 Eaton place, London 24 Jany. 1858. *A memoir of Rev. Sir H. R. Dukinfield, privately printed* 1861.

DUMBRECK, SIR DAVID (only son of Thomas Dumbreck, collector of inland revenue at Glasgow). b. Aberdeenshire 1805; ed. at Univ. of Edin., M.D. 1830; L.R.C.S. Edin. 1825; hospital assistant in the army 3 Nov. 1825, surgeon 2 July 1841, inspector general 19 July 1859; served with the army in the Crimea as senior deputy inspector general, placed on half pay 1 May 1860; hon. physician to the Queen 21

DUMBRECK, SIR D. *(Con.)*
Nov. 1865; C.B. 4 Feb. 1856, K.C.B. 20 May 1871. *d.* 34 Via Montebello, Florence 24 Jany. 1876.

DUN, CHARLES DENIS. Entered Madras army 1804; col. 41 Madras N.I. 1854 to death; L.G. 6 Jany. 1863. *d.* the Cloisters, Bath 16 Aug. 1864 aged 77.

DUN, FINLAY. b. Aberdeen 24 Feb. 1795; ed. at Perth gr. sch. and Univ. of Edin.; studied the violin under Baillot in Paris; first viola player in orchestra of San Carlo theatre, Naples; teacher of the violin, composition and singing in Edin.; is best known by the collections of Scotch songs which he edited; composed glees, songs and dance music. *d.* suddenly at Edinburgh 28 Nov. 1853.

DUNBAR, REV. DUNCAN. b. Northern Highlands of Scotland about 1791; in business in Aberdeen 1811–17; went to New Brunswick 1817; became a Baptist, immersed in the harbour of St. John 31 Oct. 1818; pastor of Mc Dougal st. Baptist chapel, New York. *d.* New York 28 July 1864. *Life of Rev. D. Dunbar by Rev. Jeremiah Chaplin, New York* 1878.

DUNBAR, GEORGE. b. Coldingham, Berwickshire 1774; published *Herodotus cum annotationibus* 7 vols. 1806–7; *Elements of the Greek language* 1834, 2 ed. 1846; *A new Greek and English and English and Greek lexicon* 1840, 3 ed. 1850; assistant professor of Greek literature in Univ. of Edin. 1805, professor 1806 to death; F.R.S. Edin., M.A. Edin. 1807. *d.* Rose park, Trinity, Edinburgh 6 Dec. 1851. *G.M. xxxvii*, 195–96 (1852).

DUNBAR, GEORGE (son of Alexander Orr of Landmore, co. Londonderry). b. 1810; assumed name of Dunbar instead of Orr 1833; M.P. for Belfast 1835–1837 and 1838–1841. *d.* 17 Aug. 1875.

DUNBAR, JOHN. b. Cork 17 May 1827; fellow of Univ. of Bombay; M.P. for New Ross 9 Feb. 1874 to death. *d.* 19 Russell road, Kensington, London 3 Dec. 1878.

DUNBAR, ROBERT NUGENT. Lived many years in the West Indies; author of the following poems *The Cruise or a prospect of the West Indian archipelago* 1835; *The Caraguin, a tale of the Antilles* 1837; *Indian hours or passion and poetry of the Tropics* 1839; *Beauties of Tropical scenery, lyrical sketches and love songs* 1862, 3 ed. 1866, and of a song entitled *Garibaldi at the opera of 'Masaniello'* 1864. *d.* Paris, July or August 1866.

DUNCAN, ALEXANDER. Entered Bengal army 1795; col. 5 Bengal N.I. 1 May 1824 to death; general 20 June 1854. *d.* Gattonside house, Melrose 14 May 1859.

DUNCAN, DAVID *(son of James Duncan of Alyth, Perthshire).* *b.* Perthshire 1831; a merchant in Chili 10 years, then at Liverpool; M.P. for Barrow in Furness, Nov. 1885, unseated on petition for illegal employment of voters 16 March 1886; M.P. for Exchange division of Liverpool, July 1886 to death. *d.* Gayton hall, Heswall, Cheshire 30 Dec. 1886.

DUNCAN, DAVID. *b.* Perth 1823; printer at Cardiff 1858 to death; founded *Cardiff Times* 1857, *South Wales Daily News* 1872, *South Wales Echo* evening paper 1884. *d.* Penarth, Cardiff 14 Jany. 1888.

DUNCAN, EDWARD. *b.* London 1804; member of New Soc. of Painters in water colours 1831; member of Old Water colour Soc. 1848; landscape painter, etcher and lithographer; illustrated *The life of Nelson* 1849 and other works; his works were sold at Christie's 11 March 1885. *d.* 36 Upper park road, Haverstock hill, London 11 April 1882. *I.L.N. lxxx,* 404 (1882), *portrait.*

DUNCAN, FRANCIS *(son of John Duncan of Aberdeen, advocate).* *b.* Aberdeen 4 April 1836; ed. at Univ. of Aberdeen, M.A. 1855; lieut. R.A. 24 Sep. 1855, lieut. col. 1 Oct. 1882 to 1 Oct. 1887 when placed on h.p.; col. in army 15 June 1885; reorganized the Egyptian artillery 1883; in command at Wady Halfa during the Nile expedition 1885; contested Morpeth 6 Feb. 1874, Durham city 13 June 1874, and Finsbury April 1880; M.P. for Holborn division of Finsbury, Nov. 1885 to death; seconded address to Queen 9 Feb. 1888; C.B. 25 Aug. 1885; author of *History of the Royal Artillery,* 2 ed. 2 vols. 1872, 3 ed. 1879; *The English in Spain, the war of succession* 1877. *d.* The Common, Woolwich 16 Nov. 1888. *Graphic* 18 *Feb.* 1888 *p.* 132, *portrait.*

DUNCAN, GEORGE. *b.* 1791; a merchant in Dundee to 1831; M.P. for Dundee 1841–57; mainly instrumental in introducing steam navigation between Dundee and London. *d.* The Vine, Dundee 6 Jany. 1878.

DUNCAN, REV. JOHN *(eld. child of John Duncan of Gilcomston, parish of Old Machar, city of Aberdeen, shoemaker).* *b.* Gilcomston 1796; ed. at Aberdeen gr. sch. and Univ., B.A., M.A., LLD. 1840; licensed by the Presbytery 24 June 1825; min. of Persie chapel, parish of Bendochy, Sep. 1830 to July 1831; ordained

DUNCAN, REV. J. *(Con.)*

in the Barony parish church, Glasgow 28 April 1836; min. of Milton church, Glasgow 1836–42; first missionary from the Church of Scotland to the Jews at Buda-Pesth 1840–1843; joined Free church 1843; professor of Hebrew and oriental languages New coll. Edinburgh 1843 to death; edited in 1838 a British edition of E. Robinson's *Greek and English Lexicon of the New Testament.* *d.* 10 Dalrymple crescent, Edinburgh 26 Feb. 1870. *David Brown's Life of John Duncan, LL.D* (1872); *Recollections of John Duncan by A. M. Stuart* (1872); *Wylie's Disruption Worthies* (1881) 231–36, *portrait.*

DUNCAN, JOHN *(natural son of John Duncan of Drumlithie, Kincardineshire, weaver).* *b.* Stonehaven, Kincardineshire 19 Dec. 1794; weaver at Aberdeen 1816–24, a country weaver at Longfolds 1826–32, at Netherton 1836–49, at Auchleven 1849–52, at Droughsburn 1852 to death; collected a very fine herbarium which he presented to the Univ. of Aberdeen 31 Dec. 1880. *d.* Droughsburn 9 Aug. 1881. *buried* in Alford churchyard 15 Aug. *The life of John Duncan by W. Jolly* 1883, *portrait;* *H. A. Page's Leaders of men* (1880) 220–63.

DUNCAN, JONATHAN *(son of Jonathan Duncan 1756–1811, governor of Bombay).* *b.* Bombay; ed. at Trin. coll. Cam., B.A. 1821; edited *Guernsey and Jersey Mag.* 4 vols. 1836–37; wrote and spoke frequently on financial matters and other questions of reform; started *The Journal of Industry* 1850, 16 numbers only; author of *History of Russia* 2 vols. 1854 and many other books. *d.* 33 Norland sq. Notting hill, London 20 Oct. 1865 aged 65.

DUNCAN, RIGHT REV. PATRICK *(son of John Duncan of parish of Kilmactiague, co. Sligo).* *b.* parish of Kilmactiague 5 Feb. 1790; ed. at Ballaghadereen and Maynooth; ordained priest 1820; bishop of Achonry 1852 to death, elected 28 Sep. 1852, consecrated 30 Nov. 1852. *d.* Ballaghadereen 1 May 1875.

DUNCAN, PHILIP BURY *(son of Rev. John Duncan, R. of South Warnborough, Hants.)* *b.* South Warnborough 1772; ed. at Winchester and New coll. Ox., fellow 1792; B.A. 1794, M.A. 1798, D.C.L. 1855; barrister L.I. 24 May 1800; lived much at Bath 1801 to death; keeper of Ashmolean Museum, Oxford 1826 to 1855; author of *Reliquiæ Romanæ* 1836; *Essays and Miscellanea* 1840 and other books. *d.* Westfield lodge near Bath 12 Nov. 1863.

DUNCAN, REV. THOMAS. *b.* parish of Cameron, Scotland, Oct. 1777; ed. at Univ. of St.

DUNCAN, REV. T. *(Con.)*

Andrews; a preacher of the Established Church; rector of Dundee Academy 1802–20; professor of mathematics in Univ. of St. Andrews, Nov. 1820 to death; author of *Elements of plane geometry* 1848. *d.* St. Andrews 23 March 1858.

DUNCAN, WILLIAM AUGUSTINE. *b.* Aberdeenshire 1811; publisher and bookseller at Aberdeen 5 years; went to New South Wales, July 1838; a publisher in Sydney 1838; edited the *Australasian Chronicle* 3 Sep. 1839 to 1843; issued *Duncan's Weekly Register of politics, facts, and general literature* 1843; subcollector of customs at Moreton Bay 1846; collector of customs for N.S.W. Jany. 1859 to 1881; C.M.G. 1881; author of *A plea for New South Wales constitution* 1856. *d.* Aug. 1885.

DUNCOMBE, ARTHUR (4 son of 1 *Baron Feversham* 1764–1841). *b.* 24 March 1806; entered navy 1 April 1819; captain 24 Oct. 1834; R.A. on h.p. 1 Dec. 1856; admiral on h.p. 18 Oct. 1867; M.P. for East Retford 1830–31 and 1835–51, M.P. for East Riding of Yorkshire 1851–68; groom in waiting to the Queen 1841–46; lord of the Admiralty Feb. to Dec. 1852; sheriff of Yorkshire 1874; chairman of East Riding quarter sessions. *d.* Kilnwick Percy near Pocklington, Yorkshire 6 Feb. 1889.

DUNCOMBE, VERY REV. AUGUSTUS *(brother of the preceding).* *b.* Helmsley near York 2 Nov. 1814; ed. at Worcester coll. Ox., B.A. 1836, M.A. 1852, B.D. and D.D. 1859; preb. of York cathedral 18 Oct. 1841 to 1858; dean of York 28 May 1858 to death; precentor of York 1862 to death; declined Scotch bishopric of Argyll and the Isles 1874; spent a large sum of money on the cathedral; restored St. Mary's ch. Castlegate, York at cost of £4000; author of *Manual of family devotions* 1868. *d.* York 26 Jany. 1880. *bur.* in Helmsley church 30 Jany., personalty sworn under £500,000 March 1880. *A memorial of A. Duncombe, Dean of York* 1880; *The Church of England photographic portrait gallery* 1859 *pt.* 49, *portrait*; *Church Portrait Journal iii,* 41, (1879), *portrait.*

DUNCOMBE, OCTAVIUS *(brother of the preceding).* *b.* 24 Arlington st. Piccadilly, London 8 April 1817; cornet 1 Life guards 3 April 1835, lieut. 19 July 1839, retired 1839; M.P. for North Riding of Yorkshire 1841–65 and 1867–74; an original director of Great Northern railway company 1846, chairman July 1874 to death; col. of Cambridgeshire

DUNCOMBE, O. *(Con.)*

militia 2 Aug. 1852 to death; sheriff of Hunts. 1866. *d.* 84 Eaton sq. London 3 Dec. 1879.

NOTE.—It is a curious coincidence that his death should have occurred on the same day as that of Edward Shipley Ellis chairman of the Midland Railway company.

DUNCOMBE, THOMAS SLINGSBY *(eld. son of Thomas Duncombe of Copgrove, Yorkshire 1769–1847).* *b.* 1796; ed. at Harrow 1808–11; ensign Coldstream guards 17 Oct. 1811, lieut. 1815–19 when he sold out; contested Pontefract 1821 and Hertford 1823; M.P. for Hertford 15 June 1826 to 3 Dec. 1832; M.P. for Finsbury 2 July 1834 to death having sat longer for a Metropolitan borough than any former member; reputed to be best dressed man in the House; presented people's petition praying for the six points of the charter 2 May 1842; entertained by United Trades Association at the Crown and Anchor tavern, Arundel st. Strand 21 Jany. 1846; took part in plot which led to Louis Napoleon's escape from Castle of Ham near Amiens 25 May 1846. *d.* Lancing, Sussex 13 Nov. 1861 in 66 year. *bur.* Kensal Green cemetery 21 Nov. *The life of T. S. Duncombe edited by his son T. H. Duncombe* 2 vols. 1868, *portrait*; *Orators of the age by G. H. Francis* (1847) 327–37; *Fraser's Mag. x,* 494–504 (1834), *xxxiv,* 349–52 (1846); *Illust. News of the world ii* (1858), *portrait, viii,* 321 (1861), *portrait*; *I.L.N. i,* 180 (1842), *portrait, v,* 5 (1844), *portrait.*

DUNCOMBE, WILLIAM REGINALD *(eld. son of 1 Earl of Feversham b. 1829).* *b.* London 1 Aug. 1852; ed. at Eton; M.P. for North Yorkshire 2 Feb. 1874 to death. *d.* Madeira 24 Dec. 1881. *bur.* Helmsley near York 12 Jany. 1882.

DUNCUFT, JOHN. Sharebroker at Oldham 1824 to death; M.P. for Oldham 31 July 1847 to death. *d.* Frodsham, Cheshire 27 July 1852.

DUNDAS, CHARLES WILLIAM DEANS *(elder son of Sir J. W. D. Dundas 1785–1862).* Ensign 42 foot 25 Dec. 1828; ensign Coldstream guards 3 Aug. 1830, lieut. 24 Feb. to 21 April 1837; M.P. for Flint district 1837 to 1841. *d.* Edinburgh 11 April 1856 aged 45.

DUNDAS, SIR DAVID (3 son of *James Dundas of Ochtertyre, Perthshire).* *b.* Edinburgh 1799; ed. at Westminster and Ch. Ch. Ox., student 1820, B.A. 1820, M.A. 1822; barrister I.T. 7 Feb. 1823, bencher 1840, reader 1852, treasurer 1853; Q.C. April 1840; M.P. for Sutherlandshire 1840–52 and 1861–67; solicitor

DUNDAS, SIR D. *(Con.)*

general 10 July 1846 to 25 March 1848; knighted at St. James's palace 24 Feb. 1847; judge advocate general 26 May 1849 to Feb. 1852; P.C. 29 June 1849; a trustee of British Museum 1861–67; F.R.S. *d.* 13 King's Bench Walk Temple, London 30 March 1877.

DUNDAS, FREDERICK *(only son of Charles Lawrence Dundas 1771–1810, M.P. for Malton).* *b.* 14 June 1802; M.P. for Orkney and Shetland 1837–47 and 1852 to death. *d.* 24 Hanover sq. London 26 Oct. 1872.

DUNDAS, GEORGE *(brother of Sir David Dundas 1799–1877).* *b.* Edinburgh 19 Nov. 1802; ed. at high school Edin., Glasgow univ. and Ex. coll. Ox., LLD. Edin.; B.A. Ox. 1824; called to bar in Scotland 1826; vice dean of faculty of advocates; sheriff of co. Selkirk 4 Nov. 1844 to 1845; a judge of court of sessions with title of Lord Manor 14 Oct. 1868 to death. *d.* Charlotte sq. Edinburgh 7 Oct. 1869. *Law magazine and law review xxix,* 274–76 (1870).

DUNDAS, GEORGE *(eld. son of James Dundas of Dundas, co. Linlithgow 1793–1881).* *b.* Dundas castle 12 Nov. 1819; 1 lieut. rifle brigade 15 April 1842, retired Dec. 1844; M.P. for co. Linlithgow 1847–1858; lieut. governor of Prince Edward island Jany. 1859 to July 1870; lieut. governor of St. Vincent 31 Oct. 1874 to death. *d.* St. Vincent 18 March 1880.

DUNDAS, JAMES *(eld. son of George Dundas 1802–69).* *b.* Edinburgh ? 12 Sep. 1842; 1 lieut. Bengal engineers 8 June 1860, captain 3 Aug. 1872 to death; V.C. for bravery in Bhootan 1865; killed while attempting to blow up a fort at Sherpur near Cabul 23 Dec. 1879, monument to his memory erected in Edinburgh cathedral. *Shadbolt's Afghan campaign, biog. division* (1882) 72–4, *portrait.*

DUNDAS, SIR JAMES WHITLEY DEANS *(son of James Deans, M.D. of Calcutta).* *b.* Scotland 4 Dec. 1785; entered navy 19 March 1799; captain 13 Oct. 1807; assumed surname of Dundas 1808; naval aide-de-camp to Wm. iv, 5 Sep. 1831; M.P. for Greenwich 1832–35 and 1841–52; M.P. for Devizes 1836–38; a lord of the Admiralty 23 June 1841 to Sep. 1841 and July 1846 to Feb. 1852; commander in chief of Mediterranean fleet 17 Jany. 1852 to 31 Dec. 1854; admiral 8 Dec. 1857; C.B. 25 Oct. 1839, G.C.B. 5 July 1855; awarded good service pension 12 April 1862. *d.* Weymouth 3 Oct. 1862. *E. H. Nolan's History of Russian war i,* 696 (1857), *portrait; I.L.N. xxiii,* 140 (1853), *portrait.*

DUNDAS, SIR JOHN BURNET, 4 Baronet. *b.* Richmond, Surrey 17 Nov. 1794; entered navy 10 July 1807; captain 8 July 1828; R.A. on h.p. 7 Feb. 1855; admiral on h.p. 5 May 1865; succeeded 16 June 1848. *d.* Queensberry villa, Richmond 2 Sep. 1868.

DUNDAS, JOHN CHARLES *(2 son of 1 Earl of Zetland 1766–1839).* *b.* Mask hall, Cleveland 21 Aug. 1808; M.P. for Richmond, Yorkshire 1830–35, 1841–47 and 1865 to death; M.P. for York 1835–37; lord lieut. of Orkney and Shetland 1839 to death. *d.* the Villa Cessole near Nice 14 Feb. 1866.

DUNDAS, SIR RICHARD SAUNDERS *(2 son of 2 Viscount Melville 1771–1851).* *b.* Melville castle near Edinburgh 11 April 1802; ed. at Harrow; entered navy 15 June 1817; captain 17 July 1824; superintendent of Deptford dockyard 16 April 1851 to Dec. 1852; a lord of the Admiralty, Dec. 1852 to Feb. 1855 and 21 Nov. 1857 to death; commander in chief of Baltic fleet 19 Feb. 1855 to Dec. 1855; employed on Mediterranean and Home stations Feb. 1856 to March 1857; V.A. 24 Feb. 1858; C.B. 29 June 1841, K.C.B. 4 Feb. 1856; grand officer of Legion of Honour. *d.* 13 New st. Spring Gardens, London 3 June 1861.

DUNDAS, WILLIAM BOLDEN. 2 lieut. R.A. 8 Sep. 1803, col. 1 Nov. 1848 to 28 Nov. 1854; M.G. 28 Nov. 1854; C.B. 19 July 1838. *d.* Inveresk, Edinburgh 8 Aug. 1858.

DUNDAS, WILLIAM PITT *(youngest son of Robert Dundas 1753–1819, lord chief baron of court of exchequer in Scotland).* *b.* Melville castle 6 March 1801; advocate 13 June 1823; deputy keeper of privy seal of Scotland 1852; registrar general of births, deaths and marriages in Scotland 13 Sep. 1855, deputy clerk registrar 1874–80; C.B. 10 May 1876. *d.* 14 Athole crescent, Edinburgh 17 May 1883.

DUNDONALD, THOMAS COCHRANE, 10 Earl of *(eld. child of 9 Earl of Dundonald 1748–1831).* *b.* Annsfield, Lanarkshire 14 Dec. 1775; midshipman R.N. 27 June 1793, captain 8 Aug. 1801; destroyed French shipping in road of Ile d' Aix 11 April 1809; contested Honiton 1805, M.P. for Honiton 1806–1807; M.P. for Westminster 23 May 1807 to 5 July 1814 when expelled; M.P. again 16 July 1814 to 10 June 1818; lost his rank in navy 25 June 1814; sentenced to pay a fine of £1000 and to be imprisoned in King's Bench prison for a year 21 June 1814 having been convicted unjustly of a stock-jobbing fraud 8 June 1814; commanded Chilian navy Dec. 1818 to Nov. 1822, Brazilian navy 21 March 1823 to

DUNDONALD, Earl of *(Con.)*

10 Nov. 1825, Greek navy Feb. 1827 to 1828; created Marquess of Maranham by Don Pedro of Brazil 1823; reinstated in his place in the navy by Wm. iv, 2 May 1832; R.A. 8 May 1832; commander in chief on North American and West Indian stations 12 Jany. 1848 to Jany. 1851; admiral 21 March 1851; R.A. of United Kingdom 29 Oct. 1854; K.B. 26 April 1809 to 5 July 1814 when expelled, reinstated 22 May 1847; G.C.B. 25 May 1847; author of *Narrative of the liberation of Chili* 2 vols. 1858. *d.* 12 Prince Albert road, Kensington, London 31 Oct. 1860. *bur.* centre of nave of Westminster Abbey 14 Nov. *Autobiography of a Seaman* 2 vols. 1860, *portrait; Life of Lord Cochrane by T. B. Cochrane and H. R. F. Bourne* 2 vols. 1869, *portrait; W. C. Townsend's Modern state trials ii,* 1–111 (1850); *Army and navy mag. i,* 113–29 (1881), *portrait; Law mag. and law review x,* 203–35 (1861), *xi,* 188–201; *I.L.N. xxxvii,* 471, 472 (1860), *portrait.*

DUNFERMLINE, JAMES ABERCROMBY, 1 Baron (3 son of *Sir Ralph Abercromby* 1738–1801). *b.* 7 Nov. 1776; barrister L.I. 8 Feb. 1800; a comr. of bankrupts 1802–27; M.P. for Midhurst 1807–12, for Calne 1812–30, for Edinburgh 1832–39; judge advocate general 12 May 1827 to Jany. 1828; lord chief baron of exchequer in Scotland 20 Feb. 1830 to 1832 when office was abolished under statute 2 Wm. iv, cap. 54 and he was granted pension of £2000 a year; master of the Mint 1 July 1834 to Nov. 1834; speaker of House of Commons 19 Feb. 1835 elected by a majority of 10 votes, closest contest on record, retired 15 May 1839; created Baron Dunfermline of Dunfermline, co. Fife 7 June 1839; dean of faculty in Univ. of Glasgow 1841; author of *Lieutenant general Sir Ralph Abercromby, K.B. 1793–1801, a memoir* 1861. *d.* Colinton near Edinburgh 17 April 1858. *T. Murray's Biographical annals of parish of Colinton* (1863) 107–12; *J. A. Manning's Lives of the speakers* (1850) 489–93; *J. Burke's Commoners iv,* (1838), *portrait.*

DUNFERMLINE, RALPH ABERCROMBY, 2 Baron *(eld. son of the preceding).* *b.* 6 April 1803; ed. at Eton and Peterhouse coll. Cam.; précis writer in Foreign Office 1827; min. plenipo. to Germanic confederation 2 Jany. 1839 to 17 March 1840; envoy extraord. and min. plenipo. to King of Sardinia 17 March 1840 to 28 Nov. 1849, to King of the Netherlands 26 Nov. 1851 to 13 Oct. 1858; K.C.B. 1 March 1851; succeeded 17 April 1858. *d.* Colinton house near Edinburgh 12 July 1868.

DUNGANNON, ARTHUR HILL TREVOR, 3 Viscount *(elder son of 2 Viscount Dungannon 1763–1837). b.* London 9 Nov. 1798; ed. at Ch. Ch. Ox., B.A. 1820, M.A. 1825; M.P. for New Romney 1830–31; M.P. for city of Durham 1831–32 and 1835–41; succeeded his father 14 Dec. 1837; a representative peer for Ireland 11 Sep. 1855 to death; high sheriff of Flintshire 1855; published *The life and times of William the third king of England* 2 vols. 1835–36 and other works. *d.* 3 Grafton st., Bond st. London 11 Aug. 1862.

DUNGLISON, ROBLEY *(son of William Dunglison of Keswick, Cumberland). b.* Keswick 4 Jany. 1798; a surgeon apothecary in London 1819; M.D. Erlangen 1823, LLD. Yale 1825; edited the *London Medical Repository* 1823–24, and *American Medical Intelligencer* 1837–42; professor of medicine in Univ. of Virginia, U.S. 1824–33; professor of Materia medica in Univ. of Maryland 1833–36; professor of medicine in Jefferson medical college, Philadelphia 1836 to 1868; author of *A new Dictionary of medical science and literature Boston* 1833, 15 ed. 1858; *General Therapeutics* 1836, 6 ed. 1857 and upwards of 30 other books. *d.* Girard st. Philadelphia 1 April 1869. *Gross's Memoir of R. Dunglison* 1869; *H. Lonsdale's Worthies of Cumberland vi,* 262–79 (1875); *The College and clinical record, Philadelphia* 1881 vol. 2, No. 11, *portrait.*

DUNHAM, SAMUEL ASTLEY. Author of *The history of Poland* 1831; *History of Spain and Portugal* 5 vols. 1832–33 which obtained for him membership of Royal Spanish Academy, it was translated into Spanish by Alcala Galliano 1844; *A history of Europe during the Middle Ages* 4 vols. 1833–34; *Lives of the most eminent literary and scientific men of Great Britain* 3 vols. 1836–37; *History of Denmark, Sweden and Norway* 3 vols. 1839–40; *History of the Germanic empire* 3 vols. 1844–45, these 19 vols. are all in Lardner's Cabinet Cyclopœdia. *d.* suddenly of paralysis at 22 Murray st. Camden New Town, London 17 July 1858 aged 62.

DUNKIN, ALFRED JOHN *(only son of John Dunkin, topographer 1782–1846). b.* Islington, London 9 Aug. 1812; entered his father's printing business at Bromley, Kent 1831; a printer at Dartford, Kent 1837 to death; opened a branch at 140 Queen Victoria st. London; an original member of British Archæological Association 1844; author of *History of the county of Kent* 3 vols. 1856–55 and 6 other books. *d.* 110 Stamford st. Blackfriars road, London 30 Jany. 1879. *Printing Times and Lithographer* 15 *April* 1879 p. 89.

DUNKIN, CHRISTOPHER. b. London 24 Sep. 1811; ed. at Univs. of London and Glasgow; a teacher of Greek at Harvard Univ. 1834–35; went to Canada 1835; edited *Morning Chronicle* at Montreal 1837–38; admitted to Lower Canadian bar 1846; Q.C. 1867; M.P. for Drummond and Arthabaska 1857–61, for Brome 1862 to death; provincial treasurer for Canada 1867–69; minister of agriculture and statistics 1869–71; puisne judge of superior court of Quebec 1871; introduced the "Dunkin Temperance Act of 1864." d. Lakeside, Knowlton 6 Jany. 1880.

DUNLOP, ALEXANDER COLQUHOUN-STIRLING-MURRAY- (5 son of *Alexander Dunlop of Keppoch, co. Dumbarton*). b. Greenock 27 Dec. 1798; ed. at Greenock gr. sch. and Univ. of Edin.; advocate 1820; edited *Presbyterian Review* 1834; assumed name of Murray-Dunlop 1849 and name of Colquhoun-Stirling-Murray-Dunlop 1866; contested Greenock 1845 and 1847, M.P. for Greenock 1852–68; legal adviser to the free church party, 'The Claim of Right 1842 and Protest and Deed of Demission 1843' were chiefly his work; author of *The Poor laws*, 4 ed. 1834. d. 1 Sep. 1870. *Notice of the late Mr. Dunlop by D. Maclagan; Wylie's Disruption Worthies* (1881) 237–44, *portrait*.

DUNLOP, ANDREW VANS. Educ. at Univ. of Edin., M.D. 1826; L.R.C.S. Edin. 1826; a surgeon in Edin.; left residue of his estate, about £70,000 to Univ. of Edinburgh to found scholarships of £100 a year each tenable for 3 years, in all main departments of study except theology. d. 18 Rutland sq. Edinburgh 27 Feb. 1880. *Sir A. Grant's Story of the Univ. of Edinburgh ii*, 42–45 (1884).

DUNLOP, DURHAM. Volunteer surgeon in Crimean war; proprietor and editor of the *Dublin university gazette*; M.R.I.A.; author of *The philosophy of the bath, or air and water* 1868, 3 ed. 1873; *The Church under the Tudors* 1869, 3 ed. 1872. d. Norfolk hotel, Brighton 30 March 1882 aged 70.

DUNLOP, HENRY. b. Linwood, Renfrewshire 1799; merchant at Craigton, Glasgow; director of Chamber of commerce, Glasgow 1837 to death, chairman 1841, 1859 and 1862; lord provost of Glasgow 1837–40; pres. of Glasgow Bible Society 1850–61; author of *The Cotton Trade* 1862. d. Edinburgh 10 May 1867. *bur.* at Govan.

DUNLOP, HUGH (2 son of *general James Dunlop, who d. March 1832*). Naval cadet 5 April 1821; captain 3 Aug. 1850; commodore at Jamaica 1859; R.A. 6 April 1866, retired

DUNLOP, H. (*Con.*)
1 April 1870, retired admiral 21 March 1878; C.B. 14 Sep. 1861. d. 106 St. George's sq. London 15 April 1887.

DUNLOP, ROBERT HENRY WALLACE. b. 1823; ed. at Haileybury; entered Bengal civil service 1843; captured the outlaw Rundheer Singh, on the borders of Rewah 1852; magistrate and collector at Meerut 1856–62; officiating judge of Bareilly 1862–65; C.B. 18 May 1860; author of *Service with the Meerut volunteer horse* 1858; *Hunting in the Himalaya* 1860; *Plate swimming with notes on the science of natation* 1877. d. Ellerslie tower, Ealing 15 Nov. 1887.

DUNMAN, THOMAS. b. 16 Dec. 1849; taught himself Latin and Greek; clerk and book keeper to a harness maker and currier in London 1871; physical science lecturer at Working Men's coll. 1874; lecturer on physiology at Birkbeck institution 1877 and professor of animal morphology 1879; lecturer on staff of Soc. for Extension of University teaching 1879; lectured on scientific subjects in London, Chester, Rotherham and other places 1879; author of *A glossary of Biological, Anatomical and Physiological Terms* 1879; *Practical notes for students of Physiology* 1880; contributed to Popular Science Lectures, Cassell's Science for All, Ward & Lock's Universal Instructor, Amateur Work and other publications. d. 9 May 1882. *bur.* Ilford cemetery. *T. Dunman's Talks about science* (1882) *with biographical sketch by C. Welsh; Nature xxvi*, 67, 418 (1882).

DUNN, SIR DAVID. Entered navy 30 April 1800; captain 7 June 1814; knighted at St. James's palace 12 Aug. 1835; K.C.H. 1 Jany. 1837; V.A. on half pay 12 Nov. 1856. d. Rocklands, Chudleigh, Devon 16 June 1859 aged 73.

DUNN, JOHN. b. Aberdeen 1820; member of legislative council in Tasmania 1845–55; a merchant and shipowner in London; M.P. for Dartmouth 1859–60. d. Aden 10 Sep. 1860.

DUNN, JOHN, stage name of John Benjamin Donoghue (son of *Mr. Donoghue of City of London, merchant*). b. Surrey 1812; clerk in a lawyer's office; played at Sans Souci theatre, Leicester square, at the Coburg and Surrey 1836, at Sadler's Wells; sang song of *Jim Crow* at Sadler's Wells in imitation of T. D. Rice 1836; made a great hit as Newman Noggs in *Nicholas Nickleby* at City of London theatre 1838; acted at the Victoria; went to Australia 1842 where he played to his death.

Dunn, J. *(Con.)*

d. of heart disease in a cab in Melbourne on his way to the opera house to play 17 Aug. 1875. *Actors by daylight* (1838) *i*, 329–31, *portrait; Era* 31 Oct. 1875 *p.* 5, col. 2, *p.* 14, col. 1.

DUNN, ROBERT. *b.* East Brunton near Newcastle, Aug. 1799; apprentice to W. Davison at Alnwick; studied at Guy's and St. Thomas's hospitals 1824–25; L.S.A. 1825, M.R.C.S. 1828, F.R.C.S. 1852; surgeon 31 Norfolk st. Strand, London 1838; F.R.M.C. Soc. 1833 and member of council 1845; V.P. Westminster Medical Soc. 1845; V.P. of Anthropological Soc.; especially studied cerebral physiology and the statistics of midwifery; author of *An essay on physiological psychology* 1858; *Medical Psychology* 1863 and other books. *d.* 31 Norfolk st. Strand 4 Nov. 1877. *Barker's Photographs of medical men* (1868) *ii*, 69–72, *portrait.*

DUNN, REV. SAMUEL *(son of James Dunn of Mevagissey, Cornwall, who d. 8 Aug. 1842 aged 88).* *b.* Mevagissey 13 Feb. 1798; Wesleyan Methodist minister 1819; stationed in the Shetland islands 1822–25, then at Newcastle and 9 other places successively; accused with Rev. J. Everett and Rev. W. Griffith of publishing pamphlets called the 'Fly Sheets' advocating reforms in Wesleyan governing body 1848; expelled by Wesleyan conference 25 July 1849 for publishing *Wesley Banner and Revival Record*; ministered to Free church methodists at Camborne, Cornwall 1855–64; author of *A dictionary of the Gospels* 1846, 4 ed. 1846 and upwards of 70 other books. *d.* 2 St. James's road, St. Mary Usk, Hastings 24 Jany. 1882.

DUNNE, FRANCIS PLUNKETT *(eld. son of general Edward Dunne of Brittas, Queen's county 1763–1844).* *b.* 1802; ed. at Sandhurst and Trin. coll. Dublin; cornet 7 dragoon guards 29 May 1823; captain 10 foot 5 March 1829 to 18 Sep. 1840 when placed on h.p.; lieut. col. Queen's co. militia 15 Feb. 1846, hon. col. 26 April 1873 to death; clerk of the Ordnance 5 March 1852; private sec. and aide-de-camp to Earl of Eglinton when lord lieut. of Ireland 1858–59; M.G. 26 Sep. 1865; M.P. for Portarlington 1847–57, for Queen's co. 1859–68; P.C. Ireland 1866; author of *The Pope and his infallibility* 1871. *d.* 6 July 1874.

DUNNE, VERY REV. JOHN. *b.* Ballinakill, Queen's county, July 1816; ed. at Carlow college and Maynooth; professor of moral and mental philosophy at Carlow college about 1840, vice pres. 1850, pres. 1856; parish priest of Kildare, July 1864 to death. *d.* Kildare 25 July 1867.

DUNNE, JOHN. *b.* York 1834; chorister in Worcester cath. 1850, in Cashel cath. 1854; member of Ch. Ch. St. Patrick's cath. and Trinity college choirs, Dublin; Mus. Bac. Dublin 1866, Mus. Doc. 1870; composed *Myra, a cantata; The Hanging of the Crane, a cantata*, church services, anthems, glees and songs. *d.* Ashton, Killiney near Dublin 7 June 1883.

DUNPHY, HENRY MICHAEL *(youngest son of Michael Dunphy of Fleet st. Dublin, merchant).* *b.* 1821; on the staff of the *Morning Post* upwards of 40 years; barrister M.T. 26 Jany. 1861. *d.* Hillside, Willesden park, London 2 Jany. 1889 in 68 year.

DUNRAVEN and MOUNTEARL, EDWIN RICHARD WINDHAM WYNDHAM-QUIN, 3 Earl of. *b.* London 19 May 1812; ed. at Eton and Trin. coll. Dublin, B.A. 1833; M.P. for Glamorganshire 1837–51; succeeded his father 6 Aug. 1850; created baron Kenry of Kenry, co. Limerick in peerage of G.B. 12 June 1866; lord lieut. of Limerick 1864 to death; K.P. 1866; F.R.A.S. 1831; F.R.S. 10 April 1834; F.R.G.S. 1837; F.S.A. 1836; a great antiquarian and archæologist; author of *Memorials of Adare manor* 1865; *Notes on Irish architecture* edited by Margaret Stokes 2 vols. 1875–77. *d.* Imperial hotel, Great Malvern 6 Oct. 1871. *Monthly notices of Royal Astronom. Soc. xxxii*, 120–22 (1872); *Proc. of Soc. of Antiq. second series v*, 306; *I.L.N. lix*, 386 (1871).

DUNSANY, RANDAL EDWARD PLUNKETT, 15 Baron *(elder son of 14 Baron Dunsany 1773–1848).* *b.* Rome 5 Sep. 1804; ed. at Ch. Ch. Ox.; a prominent leader of the Orange party; succeeded 11 Dec. 1848; a representative peer of Ireland 19 Nov. 1850 to death. *d.* Dunsany castle, co. Meath 7 April 1852.

DUNSANY, EDWARD PLUNKETT, 16 Baron *(brother of the preceding).* *b.* Ramsgate 29 Nov. 1808; entered navy 4 Oct. 1823; captain 9 Nov. 1846; admiral on h.p. 1 Aug. 1877; author of *The past and future of the British navy, 2 ed.* 1847; *Gaul or Teuton, considerations as to our allies of the future* 1873; translated *Graviere's Naval History 2 vols.* 1848. *d.* Hastings 22 Feb. 1889.

DUNSFORD, HENRY FREDERICK. *b.* 5 Nov. 1817; ensign 59 Bengal N.I. 28 June 1836, major 1 Jany. 1862; lieut. col. Bengal staff corps 12 Sep. 1866; general 1 Oct. 1877; C.B. 17 June 1858. *d.* St. Heliers, Jersey 31 Jany. 1887.

DUNSTERVILLE, EDWARD *(son of Edward Dunsterville of Penryn, Cornwall, shipowner).* *b.*

Penryn 2 Dec. 1796; entered navy 17 July 1812, midshipman 1813–15, when discharged on reduction of the fleet; master in navy 9 Sep. 1824; hydrographer's assistant at the Admiralty, Whitehall 19 April 1842 to 30 March 1870 when superannuated on £400 per annum; retired commander 14 Nov. 1855; author of *Admiralty catalogue of charts, plans, views and sailing directions* 7 ed. 2 vols. 1859, 8 ed. 2 vols. 1864; edited *J. Horsburgh's Indian directory* 7 ed. 2 vols. 1859, 8 ed. 2 vols. 1864. *d.* 32 St. Augustine's road, Camden sq. London 11 March 1873. *The servitude of Commander E. Dunsterville* 1870.

DUNSTERVILLE, JAMES HENDERSON. Entered Bombay army 1803; col. 1 Bombay N.I. 29 Dec. 1846 to death; M.G. 20 June 1854. *d.* 12 The Crescent, Plymouth 12 July 1858 aged 70.

DUNTZE, JOHN ALEXANDER (*eld. child of James Nicholas Duntze, paymaster general of the forces in Sicily, who d. 22 Sep. 1846 aged 78*). *b.* 26 Aug. 1805; entered navy 5 Aug. 1818; captain 24 Dec. 1829; admiral 2 Dec. 1865; retired 1 April 1870. *d.* 10 Nightingale terrace, Woolwich common 15 May 1882.

DU PLAT, GEORGE GUSTAVUS CHARLES WILLIAM. Second lieut. R.E. 1 Aug. 1841, lieut. col. 21 Sep. 1850 to death; consul at Warsaw 1841–51, consul general in Poland 1851; Queen's comr. to Austrian army with rank of brigadier general 12 Aug. 1854 to death; K.H. 31 Oct. 1831. *d.* Vienna 21 Dec. 1854.

DUPPA, BALDWIN FRANCIS (*eld. son of Baldwin Francis Duppa, barrister*). *b.* Rouen, Normandy 18 Feb. 1828; ed. at Hofwyl near Berne, Eton and Trin. coll. Cam.; entered royal college of chemistry 1855; fitted up a laboratory in his country seat at Hollingbourne near Maidstone; worked with Edward Frankland at Royal institution, London 1863–67; F.R.S. 1867. *d.* Budleigh Salterton, Devon 10 Nov. 1873. *Proc. of Royal Soc. xxi*, 6–9 (1873).

DU PRÉ, CALEDON GEORGE (*eld. son of the succeeding*). *b.* 28 March 1803; ed. at Eton and Ch. Ch. and St. Mary hall, Ox., B.A. 1825; M.P. for Bucks. 18 Feb. 1839 to 26 Jany. 1874. *d.* 7 Oct. 1886.

DU PRÉ, JAMES. *b.* 10 June 1778; M.P. for Gatton, Surrey 1800–1802, for Aylesbury 1802–1806, for Chichester 1807–12; sheriff of Bucks. 1825. *d.* 40 Portland place, London 13 June 1870, personalty sworn under £250,000, 13 Aug. 1870.

DUPUIS, SIR JOHN EDWARD (*son of Rev. George Dupuis, R. of Wendlebury near Bicester, who d. 5 March 1839 aged 82*). *b.* 1800; ed. at military academy, Woolwich; 2 lieut. R.A. 13 Feb. 1825; colonel commandant 11 brigade 15 Dec. 1864 to death; general 10 Nov. 1868; commanded artillery in India, Oct. 1857 to Feb. 1859; C.B. 5 July 1855; K.C.B. 28 March 1865. *d.* George st. Hanover square, London 25 Nov. 1876.

DURAND, SIR HENRY MARION. *b.* 6 Nov. 1812; ed. at Addiscombe; 2 lieut. Bengal engineers 12 June 1828, col. 18 Feb. 1861 to 1867; comr. of Tenasserim provinces 1844–46; political agent at court of Scindia 1849–53, at Indore 1857; drove back Tantia Topee and saved Central India 1857; member of council of sec. of state of India 1859–61; foreign sec. at Calcutta 1861–65; military member of governor general's council 10 April 1865 to 1870; L.G. 1 March 1867; lieut. governor of the Punjaub 5 May 1870 to death; C.B. 24 March 1858; K.C.S.I. 8 Feb. 1867; author of *Notes on the field equipment of the Engineers* 1844; *The first Afghan war* 1879. *d.* from a fall from an elephant in the camp at Tonk 135 miles west of Peshawur 1 Jany. 1871. *bur.* at Dera Ismail Khan 5 Jany. *Life of Sir H. M. Durand by H. M. Durand* 2 vols. 1873, *portrait*; *C. R. Low's Soldiers of the Victorian age ii*, 44–79 (1880); *Good Words xiv*, 575, 706 (1873).

D'URBAN, WILLIAM JAMES. Cornet 14 Dragoons 7 Oct. 1819; deputy quartermaster general North America 1 Dec. 1848 to 1 May 1857 when placed on half pay; col. 107 Foot 13 Aug. 1868 to death; L.G. 20 June 1870. *d.* Newport house near Exeter 5 Dec. 1873 aged 73.

DURDIN, ROBERT GARDE (*son of Robert Atkins Durdin of Cranemore house, co. Carlow, who d. 5 Jany. 1841*). *b.* 1818; solicitor in Dublin; alderman of South Dockward; lord mayor of Dublin 1872. *d.* 93 Lower Bagot st. Dublin 19 Oct. 1878. *bur.* Clonegal 23 Oct.

DURHAM, GEORGE FREDERICK D'ARCY LAMBTON, 2 Earl of. *b.* Copse hill, Surrey 5 Sep. 1828; succeeded 28 July 1840; lord lieut. of Durham 11 Aug. 1854 to death; well known breeder of horses and owner of race horses. *d.* Hill st. Berkeley sq. London 27 Nov. 1879. *bur.* Bourn Moor church 3 Dec., personalty sworn under £500,000 Dec. 1879. *Mrs. Fairlie's Portraits of the children of the nobility* 2 series 1839, *portrait*; *Baily's Mag. xii*, 109–11 (1867), *portrait*; *Athenæum ii*, 247–49 (1876).

DURHAM, JOSEPH. *b.* London; pupil of E. H. Bailey; exhibited 126 pieces of sculpture at R.A. 1835–78; designed statues entitled Hermione and Alastor for the Mansion House 1856–57; designed statue of Prince Consort in gardens of the Horticultural Society, unveiled 10 June 1863; F.S.A. 12 May 1853; A.R.A. 8 May 1866. *d.* 21 Devonshire st. Portland place, London 27 Oct. 1877 in 64 year. *I.L.N. xlviii,* 560, 561 (1856), *portrait.*

DURING, LOUIS ALEXANDER, Baron. *b.* 1783; cornet York Hussars 25 Nov. 1795; captain 98 foot 28 May 1829 to 13 Dec. 1833 when placed on h.p.; general 1 Oct. 1877; received the war medal with 7 clasps. *d.* near Horneburg, Hanover 7 Jany. 1880 in 97 year.

NOTE.—He served more than 84 years, being the longest service on record.

DURNFORD, ANTHONY WILLIAM *(eld. son of the succeeding).* *b.* Manor-hamilton, co. Leitrim 24 May 1830; ed. at Dusseldorf and royal military academy; 2 lieut. R.E. 27 June 1848, lieut. col. 11 Dec. 1873 to death; served in South Africa 1871–76 and 1877 to death; killed by the Zulus at Isandhlwana 22 Jany. 1879. *bur.* in the camp cemetery at Pietermaritzburg 12 Oct. *A. Wylde's My Chief and I* 1879, *portrait; A soldier's life and work in South Africa, edited by his brother lieut. col. E. Durnford* 1882, *portrait; Graphic xix,* 212 (1879), *portrait.*

DURNFORD, GEORGE. Second lieut. R.A. 1 Nov. 1805, lieut. col. 1 April 1844 to 5 April 1845 when he retired on full pay; L.G. 24 Aug. 1866. *d.* Turner's hill, Cheshunt 23 Sep. 1870.

DURRANT, JOHN ROWLAND. Member of stock exchange, City of London; member of Drury Lane theatre committee; founded the Garrick club in King st. Covent Garden 1831; purchased in June or July 1835 for sum of £1000 Charles Mathews's gallery of theatrical portraits containing authentic likenesses of most of the theatrical celebrities of the past two centuries; he allowed the Garrick club use of pictures during his lifetime and bequeathed the collection by his will to the club. *d.* 96 Newgate st. London 13 July 1853 in 79 year. *bur.* Highgate cemetery 20 July. *G.M. May* 1877 *pp.* 561–83.

DU TERREAUX, LOUIS HENRY FRENCH. Author of *The last of the barons,* burlesque produced at Strand theatre 18 April 1872; *Vokins's Vengeance,* comic operetta, St. George's 19 June 1872; *A cabinet secret,* comedy in 2 acts, Philharmonic 19 Oct. 1872; *The broken*

DU TERREAUX, L. H. F. *(Con.)*

branch, opera in 3 acts, Opera Comique 22 Aug. 1874; author with S. Clarke of *Love wins,* comedy in 3 acts produced at T.R. Cambridge 11 Aug. 1873. *d.* Liverpool 31 March 1878 aged 37.

DUTNALL, MARTIN. Served as a British volunteer officer under Garibaldi in Italy 1860; edited a Journal in United States for several years down to 1867; wrote many pieces chiefly for the Surrey theatre, London, among which were *The Queen of Hearts; Harlequin King Pumpkin, or Richard ye Lion Hearte,* pantomime played at Surrey theatre from 26 Dec. 1864 to 30 Jany. 1865 when theatre was burnt down; *Mad Fred; Colleen drawn from an authentic source;* author of an entertainment entitled *Funny Cards* in which he performed with the Vokes family. *d.* of disease of the lungs at Eastbourne 8 Sep. 1867 aged 29. *bur.* Woking cemetery with 5 of his brothers and sisters who all died young. *The Era 15 Sep.* 1867 *p.* 10.

DUTTON, FRANCIS STACKER *(son of Henry Hampden Dutton, British consul at Cuxhaven on the Elbe, who d. 30 March 1856).* *b.* Cuxhaven 1818; went to South America 1833; discovered the Kapunda copper mine near Adelaide 1843 (the first discovery of copper in Australia) which he sold 1845; member of legislative council of South Australia 1851–57, member of house of assembly 1857–65; comr. of crown lands Sep. 1857 to June 1859 and in 1863; comr. of public works March to Sep. 1865; formed an administration in 1863 which lasted 11 days, another in 1865 which lasted 6 months; special comr. to international exhibition, London 1862; agent general in London for South Australia 1865 to death; brought out no less than 12 public loans amounting together to about £3,000,000 every loan except one being a great financial success; C.M.G. 30 Nov. 1872; K.C. Franz Joseph 1873; A.I.C.E. 6 Feb. 1866; author of *South Australia and its mines* 1846. *d.* 134 Inverness terrace, Hyde park, London 25 Jany. 1877. *Minutes of proc. of instit. of C.E. xlix,* 268–70 (1877).

DU VAL, CHARLES. *b.* Manchester; ed. for the law; Monologue entertainer; founded and edited a newspaper at Cape of Good Hope; served with D'Arcy's Carabineers at siege of Pretoria during the Boer war, Dec. 1880; performed at St. James's hall, London and toured in England and Ireland 1887; performed in South Africa, March–Dec. 1888; committed suicide by jumping overboard from

DU VAL, C. (Con.)

steamship Oceana in the Red Sea 23 Feb. 1889. *C. Du Val's With a show through Southern Africa* 2 vols. (1882), *portrait.*

DUVAL, CHARLES ALLEN. *b.* Ireland 1808; an artist at Liverpool, at Manchester about 1833 to death; exhibited 20 portraits and subject pictures at the R.A. 1836–72; exhibited 'The Giaour' 1842, 'Columbus in chains' 1855 and many others in local exhibitions; author of five pamphlets on American civil war 1863 and of papers in *North of England Mag. d.* Alderley, Cheshire 14 June 1872.

DUVAL, CLAUDE. One of the French masters at Manchester gr. sch. 9 years; author of *Fanny, Sonnets and Poems* 1880. *d.* 48 Portsmouth st. Chorlton, Manchester 22 Jany. 1884 aged 40.

DUVARD, PRIMOGENE. Author of *Poems* 1842, 2 ed. 1843; *Mary Tudor, a drama* 1844; *Devotional exercises for fourteen days* 1846, 2 ed. 1855; *The Angel of Death* 1862; *Poems and hymns* 1864. *d.* Pond farm, Borden near Sittingbourne, Kent 25 Jany. 1877 aged 53.

DWARRIS, SIR FORTUNATUS WILLIAM LILLEY (*eld. son of William Dwarris of Warwick*). *b.* Jamaica 23 Oct. 1786; ed. at Rugby and Univ. coll. Ox., B.A. 1808; barrister L.I. 28 June 1811; bencher of M.T. 1850, treasurer 1859 laid foundation stone of new library, opened 31 Oct. 1861; comr. to inquire into administration of civil and criminal justice in West Indies 1822–26; one of Municipal corporation comrs. 18 July 1834; knighted at St. James's palace 2 May 1838; recorder of Newcastle under Lyne 1837–58; master of court of Queen's Bench 1838 to death; F.R.S. 22 April 1847; author of *A general treatise on statutes* 2 parts 1830–31, 2 ed. 1848; *Alberic, consul of Rome* 1832 anon., an historical drama in 5 acts; *Some new facts and a suggested new theory as to the authorship of Junius* 1850 privately printed, and other books. *d.* 75 Eccleston sq. London 20 May 1860. *Journal of British Archæol. Assoc. xvii,* 182–3 (1861).

DWYER, THOMAS PEARD. 2 lieut. R.M.L.I. 19 Oct. 1812, second commandant at Plymouth 14 July 1855, commandant 1 April 1857 to 2 Dec. 1859; retired M.G. 2 Dec. 1859. *d.* Southsea 22 April 1863.

DYCE, REV. ALEXANDER (*eld. son of Lieut. general Alexander Dyce*). *b.* George st. Edinburgh 30 June 1798; ed. at Edin. high sch. and Exeter coll. Ox., B.A. 1819; C. of Lanteglos, Cornwall 1821–5; C. of Nayland, Suffolk

DYCE, REV. A. (Con.)

1825–7; lived at 9 Gray's Inn square, London down to 1859, at 33 Oxford terrace 1859 to death; edited the works of Richard Bentley 3 vols. 1836–8, the works of Shakespeare 9 vols. 1857, 2 ed. 9 vols. 1864–7, the works of Beaumont and Fletcher 11 vols. 1843–6 and many other English classics. *d.* 33 Oxford terrace, Oxford st. London 15 May 1869. *Fortnightly Review xviii,* 731–46 (1875); *Alexander Dyce, a biographical sketch by John Forster* in *A catalogue of the Dyce books in South Kensington museum* (1875) *pp.* 7–24.

DYCE, ARCHIBALD BROWN. *b.* Trichinopoly, Oct. 1800; ensign Madras army 26 June 1817; col. 2 European regiment 7 Sep. 1846 to 30 Sep. 1862; commanded Northern division of Madras army 16 Feb. 1847 to 16 Feb. 1852; L.G. 26 June 1860; col. 105 Foot 30 Sep. 1862 to death. *d.* Grosvenor house, Southampton 9 March 1866.

DYCE, WILLIAM (*son of William Dyce of Aberdeen, physician*). *b.* Marischal st. Aberdeen 19 Sep. 1806; ed. at Marischal coll. Aberdeen, M.A. 1822; exhibited 41 pictures at the R.A. 1827–61; originated pre-Raphaelite movement in English school of painting 1828; portrait painter in Edinburgh 1830–37; F.R.S. Edin. 1832; A.R.S.A. 1835; head master of school of design Somerset House, London 1840–43; inspector of the provincial schools 1843–44; professor of fine arts in King's coll. London 1844; A.R.A. 1845, R.A. 1848; painted cartoon 'Baptism of Ethelbert' for House of Lords 1845 and other works; founded the Motett Society; designed the florin declared to be current money 1852; author of *The book of Common Prayer with the ancient Canto Fermo set to it at the Reformation* 2 vols. 1842–3; *Theory of the Fine Arts* 1844; *The National Gallery, its formation and management* 1853. *d.* Streatham road, Streatham, Surrey 14 Feb. 1864. *Redgrave's Century of painters ii,* 550–68 (1866); *Sandby's History of Royal Academy ii,* 183–88 (1862); *I.L.N. xxx,* 418, 420 (1857), *portrait, xliv,* 224 (1864).

DYCE-SOMBRE, DAVID OCHTERLONY (*only son of George Dyce, commandant of the forces of Zerbonissa, begum of Sirdhana, Bengal*). *b.* Sirdhana 1808; inherited half a million sterling on death of his grandmother the Begum Sumroo 27 Jany. 1836; took additional name of Sombre 1836; came to England Aug. 1838 where he became the lion of London season; M.P. for Sudbury 29 June 1841, unseated on petition for bribery 14 April 1842; put under restraint as a lunatic at Clarendon hotel 169 New Bond st. March

DYCE-SOMBRE, D. O. (Con.)

1843, a commission de lunatico inquirendo was held at Hanover lodge, Regent's Park 31 July 1843 when a verdict of unsound mind from 27 Oct. 1842 was returned; escaped from his attendant Dr. Grant at Liverpool, Sep. 1843, arrived in Paris 22 Sep.; author of *Mr. Dyce-Sombre's Refutation of the charges brought against him in the Court of Chancery* 1849, and of *The Memoir* published in English, French and Italian. *d.* Davies st. Berkeley sq. London 1 July 1851. *bur.* in catacombs of Kensal Green cemetery 8 July. *G. B. Malleson's Recreations of an Indian official* (1872) 438–59; *W. H. Sleeman's Rambles of an Indian official ii*, 377–99 (1844); *Law mag. and law review i*, 356–68 (1856); *Macnaghten and Gordon's Reports i*, 116–37 (1850); *Deane's Reports i*, 22–120 (1858).

DYER, JOSEPH CHESSBOROUGH (*son of Nathaniel Dyer, captain Rhode island navy*). *b.* Stonnington Point, Connecticut 15 Nov. 1780; machine maker at Camden Town, London 1811–16, at Manchester 1816–42 where he introduced inventions which gave a great impulse to the cotton manufacture 1817; an original director of Bank of Manchester 1828 which stopped payment 31 Dec. 1842 when he lost £96,000; established machine-making works at Gamaches, Somme, France 1832 gave them up 1848 after losing £120,000; author of *Remarks on Education* 1850, and 5 other pamphlets. *d.* at house of his son Frederick Dyer near Manchester 3 May 1871. *R. A. Smith's Centenary of science in Manchester* (1883) 298–325.

DYER, THOMAS HENRY. *b.* St. Dunstan-in-the-East, London 4 May 1804; LLD. St. Andrews 1865; author of *Tentamina Æschylea* 1841; *Life of Calvin* 1850; *History of Modern Europe* 4 vols. 1861–64, 2 ed. 5 vols. 1877; *A history of the City of Rome* 1865; *The history of the Kings of Rome* 1868; *Pompeii, its history, buildings and antiquities* 1867; *Ancient Athens, its history, topography and remains* 1873; *On imitative beauty* 1882. *d.* Bath 30 Jany. 1888. *Academy 11 Feb.* 1888, *p.* 97.

DYKE, FRANCIS HART (4 son of Sir Percival Hart Dyke, 5 baronet 1767–1846). *b.* 28 Nov. 1803; admitted a proctor 1825; partner with James Bush in Doctors' Commons to 1830; deputy registrar of Dean and chapter of St. Paul's cathedral 1838 to 1845; member of firm of Jenner, Dyke & Jenner of Doctors' Commons; Queen's proctor 25 Jany. 1845 to death; thrown from his horse at Egham near Windsor 15 July 1876. *d.* from the injuries Luddington house, Egham 17 July 1876.

DYKES, REV. JOHN BACCHUS (*son of William Hey Dykes of Hull*). *b.* Hull 10 March 1823; ed. at Wakefield and St. Cath. coll. Cam.; a founder of Cambridge university musical soc.; B.A. 1847, M.A. 1851; Mus. Doc. Durham 1861; C. of Malton 1847; minor canon of Durham 1849 to death, precentor of Durham 1849–62; V. of St. Oswald's, Durham 1862 to death; author of many sermons and letters; composed many hymn tunes most of which appeared first in *Hymns ancient and modern* 1862, of which collection they are the most popular; wrote several services and anthems. *d.* St. Leonards-on-Sea 22 Jany. 1876. *bur.* St. Oswald's churchyard, Durham 28 Jany. *In Memoriam J. B. Dykes* 1876.

DYMOKE, SIR HENRY, 1 Baronet (*elder son of Rev. John Dymoke 1764–1828, R. of Scrivelsby, Lincs.*) *b.* Scrivelsby 5 March 1801; in the navy; officiated as deputy for his father the King's Champion at coronation of George the 4th, 19 July 1821; created a baronet 23 Aug. 1841; vice lieut. of co. Lincoln 1857 and 1859; grand prior of order of St. John of Jerusalem. *d.* Portman square, London 28 April 1865. *W. Jones's Crowns and Coronations* (1883) 128–40, 318 (1883); *Once a Week xii*, 593–98 (1865); *Gent. Mag. xci*, pt. 2, 109, 395 (1821), *portrait*.

DYMOND, ROBERT (*eld. son of Robert Dymond of Exeter, estate agent, who d. 1866*). *b.* St. Edmund's, Exeter 8 Sep. 1824; estate agent at Exeter; hon. sec. of Devon and Exeter Institution 1875 to death; F.S.A. 27 March 1873; author of many pamphlets, and papers on antiquarian and historical subjects in the *Herald and Genealogist*, *Transactions of the Devonshire Association*, and *Bath and West of England Journal*. *d.* Blackslade, Widecombe-in-the-Moor near Ashburton 31 Aug. 1888. *Notes and Gleanings 15 Sep.* 1888 *pp.* 129–31.

DYNELY, THOMAS. Second lieut. R.A. 1 Dec. 1801, col. 9 Nov. 1846 to 20 June 1854, col. commandant 4 Feb. 1857 to death; L.G. 16 Dec. 1856; C.B. 19 July 1838. *d.* 78 Upper Berkeley st. London 21 June 1860 aged 78.

DYNEVOR, GEORGE TALBOT RICE, 3 Baron. *b.* 8 Oct. 1765; M.P. for Carmarthenshire 28 June 1790 to 14 March 1793 when he succeeded to the peerage; lord lieut. of Carmarthenshire 1804 to death; col. of Carmarthenshire militia to death. *d.* Barrington park, Gloucs. 9 April 1852.

DYNEVOR, GEORGE RICE, 4 Baron (*eld. child of the preceding*). *b.* 5 Aug. 1795; ed. at Westminster; M.P. for Carmarthenshire 1830–31 and 1832 to 9 April 1852 when he succeeded; lieut. col. of Carmarthen militia 28

DYNEVOR, G. R. *(Con.)*

Jany. 1831, col. 12 Aug. 1861 to death; militia aide de camp to the Queen 24 April 1852 to death. *d.* Great Malvern 7 Oct. 1869. *I.L.N. xxviii,* 72 (1856), *portrait.*

DYOTT, JOHN. *b.* Dublin 1812; acted at T.R. York and other country theatres 1834–44; first appeared in America at Park theatre, New York as Iago 2 Sep. 1844; a leading actor in New York to about 1866; edited a newspaper at New Rochelle, New York to death. *d.* New Rochelle 22 Nov. 1876.

DYSART, LIONEL WILLIAM JOHN TOLLEMACHE, 7 Earl of. *b.* 18 Nov. 1794; M.P. for Ilchester 22 Feb. 1827 to 24 July 1830; succeeded 22 Sep. 1840. *d.* 34 Norfolk st. Strand, London 23 Sep. 1878, personalty sworn under £1,700,000, 14 Dec. 1878.

DYSON, REV. CHARLES *(son of Jeremiah Dyson, clerk of House of Commons, who d.* 14 Sep. 1835 *aged* 78). Educ. at Southampton; matric. from C.C. coll. Ox. 6 Dec. 1804 aged 17, scholar of his coll.; B.A. 1808, M.A. 1812; R. of Nunburnholme, Yorkshire 1818–28; V. of Nazing, Essex 1828–36; R. of Dogmersfield, Hants. 1836 to death; Rawlinsonian professor of Anglo-Saxon at Ox. 1812–1816, delivered one lecture only; contributed 4 poems under signature of D to the volume entitled *Days and Seasons* 1845. *d.* Dogmersfield rectory 24 April 1860 aged 73. *Sir J. T. Coleridge's Memoir of Rev. John Keble,* 3 ed. (1869) *i,* 19, 35–46, 74, 99, 146, 245, 464.

DYSON, DAVID. A weaver; went to the United States about 1843, crossed the country from New York to St. Louis; returned to England with upwards of 18,000 specimens of insects, birds, shells and plants 1844; twice explored Central America and made another very large collection; curator of the Museum of Earl of Derby; left a private collection of 20,000 shells. *d.* Rusholme near Manchester 10 Dec. 1856 aged 33.

DYSON, REV. FRANCIS *(brother of Rev. Charles Dyson).* Matric. from Merton coll. Ox. 13 Dec. 1802 aged 17, B.A. 1806, M.A. 1809; fellow of his college to 1817; R. of South Tedworth, Hants. 1816 to death; R. of North Tedworth 1829 to death; chaplain in ordinary to the sovereign 1819 to death; preb. of Salisbury 6 April 1847 to death. *d.* Cheltenham 30 Nov. 1858 aged 73.

DYSON, JERRY FRANCIS. Entered Bombay army 1797; col. 18 Bombay N.I. 1 May 1824 to death; general 20 June 1854. *d.* 5 Lower Berkeley st. Portman sq. London 20 Feb. 1861.

E.

EADIE, REV. JOHN. *b.* Alva, Stirlingshire 9 May 1810; ed. at Univ. of Glasgow, LLD. 1846; D.D. St. Andrews 1850; professor of hermeneutics in United Presbyterian Church of Scotland 1847; a temperance lecturer; licensed as a preacher by United Secession church 1835; minister of Cambridge st. ch. Glasgow, Sep. 1835; minister of Lansdowne ch. Glasgow, Dec. 1863 to death; professor of Biblical literature in United Secession divinity hall, Glasgow 1843 to death; moderator of the Synod 1857; edited *Voluntary church mag.* 1840; member of New Testament revision committee 1870; edited *A Biblical cyclopædia* 1849, 14 ed. 1873; author of *A commentary on the Greek text of the epistle of Paul to the Ephesians* 1854, 3 ed. 1883; *The English Bible, an external and critical history of the English translations* 2 vols. 1876 and many other books. *d.* Glasgow 3 June 1876. *J. Brown's Life of Rev. J. Eadie* (1878); *John Smith's Our Scottish clergy* (1848) 95–102; *Dublin Univ. Mag. lxxxviii,* 276–91, *portrait; Good Words xix,* 470–72 (1878).

EAGLE, FRANCIS KING (2 *son of Robert Eagle of Lakenheath, Suffolk).* Educ. at Trin. coll. Cam., LLB. 1819; barrister M.T. 24 Nov. 1809, bencher; recorder of Thetford; judge of county courts, circuit 33. (Suffolk) March 1847 to death; F.L.S. 1807; author with Edward Younge of *A collection of reports of cases relating to tithes* 4 vols. 1826. *d.* Bury St. Edmunds 8 June 1856 aged 68.

EAGLE, GEORGE BARNARDO (i.e. Barnard). Professor of Clairvoyance; known as the "Wizard of the South"; when giving a morning performance at the Assembly Rooms, St. Peters Port, Guernsey 1 May 1858 suddenly seized on the stage with vomiting of blood. *d.* at his residence Pollet st. St. Peters Port 5 May 1858 aged 51. *bur.* Abney park cemetery, London 10 May. *Era 16 May* 1858 *p.* 10.

EAGLES, REV. JOHN *(eld. son of Thomas Eagles of Bristol, merchant and classical scholar* 1746–1812). *b.* parish of St. Augustine, Bristol, baptised 8 Nov. 1783; ed. at Winchester and Wad. coll. Ox., B.A. 1812, M.A. 1818; C. of Halberton, Devon 1822–34; C. of Winford near Bristol 1834–41; contributed to *Blackwood's Mag.* 1831–55 chiefly on subjects connected with fine art; author of *The Sketcher, Edin.* 1856; *Sonnets, ed. by Z. K. Edin.* 1858; *Felix Farley, rhymes, Latin and English, by*

EAGLES, REV. J. (Con.)

Themaninthemoon, Bristol 1826. *d.* King's Parade, Clifton 9 Nov. 1855. *G.M. xliv*, 661-62 (1855) *xlv*, 148 (1856); *Bentley's Miscellany xlvi*, 594–605 (1859).

EARDLEY, SIR CULLING EARDLEY, 3 Baronet *(only son of Sir Culling Smith, 2 bart.* 1768–1829). *b.* Lower Grosvenor st. London 21 April 1805; ed. at Eton and Oriel coll. Ox.; succeeded 30 June 1829; M.P. for Pontefract 1830–31; contested Pontefract 1837, Edinburgh 1846 and West Riding of Yorkshire 1848; founded Evangelical Alliance 1846; assumed surname of Eardley in lieu of Smith 14 May 1847; pres. of London Missionary Soc.; built All Saints ch. Belvedere, Kent 1861; took a prominent part in many religious and social movements; had a gallery of paintings at Belvedere near Erith. *d.* Bedwell park, Hatfield 21 May 1863. *Waagen's Galleries of Art* (1857) 275–84.

EARDLEY-WILMOT, FREDERICK MAROW (2 *son of Sir John Eardley Eardley-Wilmot,* 1 *bart.* 1783–1847). *b.* 29 May 1812; 2 lieut. R.A. 6 Nov. 1830, colonel 1 April 1860 to 6 March 1868; M.G. 6 March 1868; F.R.S. June 1863. *d.* Fox hills near Chertsey 30 Sep. 1877.

EARLE, SIR HARDMAN, 1 Baronet (4 *son of Thomas Earle of Spekelands, Lancs., a Liverpool merchant, who d.* 9 *July* 1822). *b.* 11 July 1792; a merchant at Liverpool; created Baronet 3 Nov. 1869. *d.* Allerton Tower, Woolton, near Liverpool 25 Jany. 1877. *I.L.N. lxx*, 156 (1877), *portrait.*

EARLE, RALPH ANSTRUTHER (2 *son of Charles Earle of Everton, Lancs.* 1798–1880). *b.* Edinburgh 1835; ed. at Harrow; attaché at Paris 6 Oct. 1854; private sec. to Disraeli, when chancellor of the exchequer 1 March 1858–June 1859; M.P. for Berwick April 1859 to Aug. 1859, for Maldon July 1865 to Nov. 1868; parliamentary sec. to poor law board 14 July 1866 to 22 March 1867. *d.* Soden, Nassau 10 June 1879.

EARLE, THOMAS. *b.* Hull 1810; exhibited 57 sculptures at R.A. and 24 at B.I. 1834–73; gained gold medal and book at R.A. for best historical group 1839; designer and modeller to Sir Francis Chantrey. *d.* of grief at his great sculpture being refused admission to R.A. 1876 at 1 Vincent st. Ovington square, London 28 April 1876. *Athenæum* 13 *May* 1876 *p.* 673; *Times* 3 *May* 1876 *p.* 12, *col.* 5.

EARLE, WILLIAM (3 *son of Sir Hardman Earle* 1792–1877). *b.* 18 May 1833; ensign 49 foot

EARLE, W. (Con.)

17 Oct. 1851; served in Crimean war; lieut. grenadier guards 20 March 1857, major 21 Aug. 1878 to 1 April 1880 when placed on h.p.; military sec. in British North America 1865–70, to viceroy of India 1872–76; C.S.I. 7 March 1876; C.B. 18 Nov. 1882; commanded garrison of Alexandria 1882–84; commanded column sent up the Nile to rescue of General Gordon at Khartoum 1884 to death; shot while leading on his troops against the Arabs at Kirbekan 10 Feb. 1885. *bur.* at Allerton, statue of him by C. B. Birch, A.R.A., erected at Liverpool. *H. Brackenbury's The river column* (1885); *I.L.N.* 21 *Feb.* 1885 *p.* 200, *portrait.*

EARLY, REV. JOHN. *b.* co. Fermanagh 1814; went to United States 1832; entered Society of Jesus 1834; ordained priest 1844; professor of belles lettres in Georgetown college, Ontario; pres. of Worcester college Mass.; went to Baltimore 1852 where he built college and church of St. Ignatius; pres. of Georgetown college. *d.* Georgetown 1874.

EARNSHAW, REV. SAMUEL. *b.* Sheffield 1805; ed. at St. John's coll. Cam.; senior wrangler and first Smith's prizeman 1831; B.A. 1831, M.A. 1834; a very successful coach at Cambridge 1831–47; chaplain in church and parish of Sheffield 1847 to death; author of *Dynamics or a treatise on motion* 1833, 3 *ed.* 1844; *The theory of Statics* 1834, 4 *ed.* 1856; *The Tradition of the Elders* 1860; *The love of the world* 1861. *d.* Earnscliffe 6 Dec. 1888.

EASBY, JOHN. *b.* Deansgate, Manchester 1812; a green coat schoolboy 1820; journalist actor and local preacher; a frequent contributor to periodicals; Manchester correspondent of *The Era. d.* Lower Mosley st. Manchester 18 Nov. 1852. *J. Easby's Scenes from the life of a green-coated schoolboy* 1851. *R. W. Procter's Manchester Streets* (1874) 224–28.

EASSIE, PETER BOYD. *b.* Lochee, Dundee 17 April 1835; railway contractor at Gloucester; constructed part of Cornwall railway, opened 1859; brought out an elliptograph and other successful inventions; author of *Wood and its use, Gloucester* 1874. *d.* 26 June 1875.

EAST, SIR EAST GEORGE CLAYTON, 1 Baronet (2 *son of Sir W. Clayton, 4 Bart.* 1762–1834). *b.* 9 April 1794; ed. at Caius coll. Cam.; LLB. 1818, LLD. 1823; assumed name of East by royal sign manual 6 April 1829; created baronet 17 Aug. 1838. *d.* Hall place near Maidenhead 6 March 1851.

EAST, Sir James Buller, 2 Baronet *(only son of Sir Edward Hyde East, 1 Bart. 1764–1847).* *b.* Bloomsbury, London 1 Feb. 1789; ed. at Harrow and Ch. Ch. Ox.; B.A. 1810, M.A. 1824, D.C.L. 1834; barrister I.T. 5 Feb. 1813; succeeded 8 Jany. 1847; bencher of his Inn 15 Jany. 1856, reader 1869; M.P. for Winchester 30 July 1830 to 3 Dec. 1832, and 10 Jany. 1835 to 10 Feb. 1864. *d.* Bourton house near Moreton in the Marsh, Gloucs. 19 Nov. 1878.

EASTBURN, Right Rev. Manton. *b.* Leeds 9 Feb. 1801; graduated at Columbia, U.S. 1817; ordained 1822; assistant minister in Ch. Ch. New York 1822–27; R. of church of the Ascension, New York 1827–42; assistant bishop of Protestant episcopal diocese of Massachusetts 29 Dec. 1842, bishop, March 1843 to death; author of *Four lectures on Hebrew, Latin and English poetry* 1825; *Lectures on · the Epistles to the Philippians* 1833 and other books. *d.* Boston 11 Sep. 1872. *H. G. Batterson's sketch of American episcopate* (1878) 136–37.

EASTHOPE, Sir John, 1 Baronet *(eld. son of Thomas Easthope of Tewkesbury).* *b.* Tewkesbury 29 Oct. 1784; stockbroker at 9 Exchange buildings, city of London 1818; made £150,000 in a few years; contested St. Albans 1821, Southampton 1835, Lewes 1837 and Bridgnorth 1847; M.P. for St. Albans 1826–30, for Banbury 1831–32 and for Leicester 1837–47; purchased *Morning Chronicle* in 1834 for £16,500; created baronet 24 Aug. 1841. *d.* Fir Grove near Weybridge, Surrey 11 Dec. 1865. *J. Grant's Portraits of public characters i,* 76–86 (1841); *J. Sedgwick's Letters* (1845) *pp. i-vi.*

EASTLAKE, Sir Charles Lock *(youngest son of George Eastlake of Plymouth, solicitor, who d. 1820).* *b.* Plymouth 17 Nov. 1793; exhibited 51 pictures at R.A. and 18 at B.I. 1813–55; painted in Rome 1816–30, in London 1830–55; A.R.A. Nov. 1827, R.A. 10 Dec. 1830, librarian 1842–44, pres. Nov. 1850 to death; F.R.S. 25 Jany. 1838; sec. to commission of the Fine Arts 3 Dec. 1841 to 1861; keeper of National gallery Nov. 1843 to Oct. 1847, director 1855 to death, when the trustees bought his library for £2,100; knighted at Windsor Castle 13 Nov. 1850; author of *Materials for a history of oil painting* 2 vols. 1847–69; *History of the Gothic revival* 1871 and other books. *d.* Pisa 24 Dec. 1865. *bur.* English cemetery, Florence 27 Dec., reinterred Kensal Green cemetery 18 Jany. 1866. *Sir C. L. Eastlake's Contributions to the literature of .the fine arts, second series with a memoir by Lady*

Eastlake, Sir C. L. *(Con).* *Eastlake* 1870; *Sandby's History of Royal Academy,* ii, 225, 280–87 (1862); *W. C. Monkhouse's Masterpieces of English art* (1869) 152–56; *The drawing room portrait gallery of eminent personages, fourth series* (1860), *portrait; I.L.N.* xvii, 357 (1850), *portrait,* xxxvi, 448, 450 (1860), *portrait.*

EASTLAKE, William *(son of George Eastlake of Plymouth, solicitor).* *b.* 1820; ed. at Repton school; articled to his father; admitted 1844; partner with his father; deputy judge advocate of the fleet 1851 to death. *d.* 3 Buckland terrace, Plymouth 12 Oct. 1881 in 61 year.

EASTON, John Alexander. *b.* India 1807; ed. at Univ. of Glasgow, M.D. 1836; surgeon of Glasgow police April 1840 to Nov. 1859; professor of materia medica in Univ. of Glasgow, Oct. 1855 to death. *d.* Blythswood sq. Glasgow 11 Nov. 1865.

EASTWICK, Edward Backhouse (2 son of *Robert William Eastwick of Thurloe sq. London 1772–1865).* *b.* Warfield, Berkshire 13 March 1814; ensign Bombay army 5 June 1836; professor of Urdu at Haileybury college, Aug. 1845, librarian 1850; sec. of legation at court of Persia 1860–62; barrister M.T. 6 June 1860; private sec. to Lord Cranbourne, sec. of state for India 1866–67; M.P. for Penryn and Falmouth 18 Nov. 1868 to 26 Jany. 1874; F.R.S. 5 June 1851; F.S.A. 17 March 1853; C.B. 6 Nov. 1866; translated *Anvari Suhaili, The Fables of Pilpay* 1854 and other books; author of *Journal of a diplomate's three years residence in Persia* 2 vols. 1864 and other books. *d.* Ventnor 16 July 1883.

EASTWICK, William Joseph *(brother of the preceding).* *b.* 1808; ed. at Winchester; ensign Bombay army 1826; acting resident at Hyderabad to 1841; a director of the H.E.I. Co. 30 June 1847, deputy chairman 1858; member of council of India 21 Sep. 1858 to 1868; an original member of Cobden club 1866; author of *Lord Lytton and the Afghan war* 1879. *d.* 12 Leinster gardens, Hyde park, London 24 Feb. 1889. *bur.* Teddington churchyard 1 March.

EASTWOOD, Rev. Jonathan. Educ. at St. John's coll. Cam.; B.A. 1846, M.A. 1849; C. of Ecclesfield near Sheffield 1847–54; C. of Eckington, Derbyshire 1854–62; P.C. of Hope near Hanley 1862 to death; author of *History of the parish of Ecclesfield in the county of York* 1862; author with W. A. Wright of *Bible word-book, a glossary of old English Bible words* 1866. *d.* St. Leonards on Sea 5 July 1864 aged 40.

EASTWOOD, RICHARD *(son of Henry Eastwood, head keeper to Peregrine Edward Towneley of Towneley, Lancs).* *b.* Burnley; admitted attorney 1824; partner with Anthony Buck of Burnley 1824-62, with A. B. Creeke and J. B. Sandy 1862 to death; bred race horses and short horns; won the Oaks with Butterfly 1860. *d.* Morecambe near Lancaster 28 May 1871. *Saddle and Sirloin, By the Druid, Part North* (1870) 345-57.

EBORALL, CORNELIUS WILKES. *b.* Birmingham 1820; general manager of East Lancashire railway company 1850-56, of South Eastern railway company 1856 to death; A.I.C.E. 5 Dec. 1865. *d.* 2 Lee park, Blackheath, Kent 15 Dec. 1874. *Min. of proc. of Instit. of C.E. xxxix,* 287-89 (1875).

EBSWORTH, JOSEPH *(son of Joseph Ebsworth of Islington, London).* *b.* Islington 10 Oct. 1788; apprenticed to a watch jeweller; sec. to D. E. Morris proprietor of the Haymarket theatre; actor and prompter at T.R. Edinburgh 1826; teacher of music and singing at Edin. 1828 to death; bookseller at 23 Elm row, Edin. 1828-43; gave concerts at Hopetoun rooms, Queen st. 1830-68; leader of the choir at St. Stephen's ch. Edin.; author of *Crockery's misfortunes or transmogrifications,* a burletta produced at Royal Coburg theatre, London 11 July 1821 and 33 other dramatic pieces. *d.* Edinburgh 22 June 1868.

EBSWORTH, MARY EMMA *(dau. of Robert Fairbrother, pantomimist and fencing-master).* *b.* London 2 Sep. 1794; author of the following play published in Cumberland's acting drama, *Payable at sight, or the chaste salute,* acted at Surrey theatre; also of *The two brothers of Pisa,* acted at Royal Coburg theatre, and *The sculptor of Florence.* (*m.* 22 June 1817 the preceding). *d.* Walworth, London 13 Oct. 1881.

EBURN, WILLIAM HAWTHORN. Acted at Glasgow; acted at Edinburgh many years; first appeared in London at Haymarket theatre as Amiens in *As you like it* 6 April 1855; acted at Adelphi theatre many years. *d.* Kennington park road, London 19 Sep. 1874. *bur.* Woking cemetery 27 Sep.

ECCLES, HENRY. *b.* Bath 1817; called to bar in Canada 1842; a bencher of Canadian Law Society 1853; Q.C. 1856; very prominent in his profession. *d.* Toronto 22 Nov. 1863.

ECCLES, REV. SETH. *b.* Longridge, Lancs. 1800; admitted student at English college, Rome 1820, a medallist; R.C. priest of Weston Underwood, Bucks. 1825 to 1871; member of chapter of see of Northampton

ECCLES, REV. S. (*Con.*)

1850, provost to death; created hon. D.D. by Pius ix, 1861; author of *An explanation of the seven penitential psalms* 1844; *On justification, What saith the Scripture* 1861. *d.* Weston Underwood 10 July 1884.

ECKFORD, JAMES. Entered Bengal army 1804; col. 56 Bengal N.I. 27 Oct. 1848 to death; L.G. 29 April 1861; C.B. 9 June 1849. *d.* 33 Clarendon road, St. Heliers, Jersey 2 July 1867 aged 81.

ECKFORD, ROBERT. Surgeon Bombay army 22 Oct. 1812; pres of medical board Bombay 1830 to 1 May 1832 when he retired. *d.* Jersey 27 Feb. 1865 aged 93.

EDE, GEORGE MATTHEWS. *b.* Clayfield lodge near Southampton Common Feb. 1834; ed. at Eton; agriculturalist at Northampton; returned to Southampton; gentleman steeplechaser and hurdle rider under name of Mr. Edwards; first rode at Warwick meeting Sept. 1856, rode 9 stone without training; won 306 races 1856-70; called the Fordham of amateurs; won the Grand National on the Lamb 1868 and the Grand Annual at Warwick on Musketeer 1868; established with his twin brother Edward Lee Ede the Hampshire county cricket club, scored 1200 runs in 1863; killed when jumping at Aintree near Liverpool 13 March 1870. *Bailey's Mag. xii,* 351-55 (1867), *portrait on title page. Sporting Review lxiii,* 238-39 (1870).

EDEN, SIR ASHLEY *(3 son of 3 Baron Auckland 1799-1870).* *b.* Hertingfordbury Herts. 13 Nov. 1831; ed. at Rugby and Winchester; entered Indian civil service 1852; sec. to government of Bengal and member of Bengal legislative council 1860-71; chief comr. of British Burmah 1871-77; lieut. governor of Bengal 1877-82; a member of secretary of state's council 1882 to death; C.S.I. 30 May 1874, K.C.S.I. 1878; the Eden canal which joins the Ganges and the Tistá is called after him. *d.* 31 Sackville st. Piccadilly, London 9 July 1887. *bur.* Armthorpe near Doncaster 14 July. *T. H. S. Escott's Pillars of the empire* (1879) 70-75.

EDEN, SIR CHARLES. *(youngest son of Sir Frederick Morton Eden, 2 baronet 1766-1809).* *b.* 3 July 1808; entered navy 27 Oct. 1821; captain 11 Aug. 1841; C.B. 5 July 1855, K.C.B. 24 May 1873; controller general of coastguard 5 Dec. 1855 to 1859; a lord of the admiralty 27 June 1859 to 1866; V.A. 6 April 1866, retired 1 April 1870; retired admiral 8 Feb. 1873. *d.* 9 Queen's gate place, London 7 March 1878.

EDEN, Rev. Charles Page (3 *son of Rev. Thomas Eden, C. of St. George's, Bristol, who d. 22 July 1809 aged 57*). *b.* Whitehall St. George's near Bristol 13 March 1807; Bible clerk at Oriel coll. Ox. 25 Oct. 1825, fellow 1832–51, dean 1838; B.A. 1830, M.A. 1833; select preacher Oxford 1838 and 1853; V. of St. Mary's, Oxford 1843–50; V. of Aberford near Leeds 1850 to death; proctor in convocation of province of York 1869, 1874 and 1880; preb. of York cath. 1870 to death; edited *Gunning's Paschal, or Lent fast* 1845; *Andrewes's Pattern of catechistical doctrine* 1846; *Jeremy Taylor's Works vols. i-viii*; contributed to the 'Tracts for the times' No. 32, 'On the standing ordinances of religion.' *d.* Aberford vicarage 14 Dec. 1885. *J. W. Burgon's Lives of twelve good men* (1888) *ii*, 305–42.

EDEN, Emily (7 *dau. of 1 Baron Auckland* 1744–1814). *b.* Old palace yard, Westminster 3 March 1797; lived in India with her brother Lord Auckland 1835–42; author of *Portraits of the people and princes of India* 1844; *The semi-detached house, edited by Lady Theresa Lewis* 1859 anon.; *The semi-attached couple, By E. E.* 2 vols. 1860; *Up the country, letters written from the upper provinces of India* 2 vols. 1866, 3 ed. 1872. *d.* Fountain house, 5 Upper Hill st. Richmond, Surrey 5 Aug. 1869. *bur.* in family vault at Beckenham, Kent.

EDEN, George Morton. *b.* 9 May 1806; ensign 84 foot 18 July 1822; lieut. col. 56 foot 20 May 1836 to 5 July 1839; captain Scots fusilier guards 5 July 1839 to 20 June 1854; col. 50 foot 20 April 1861 to death; L.G. 14 March 1862. *d.* Bern, Switzerland 11 Nov. 1862.

EDEN, Henry (4 *son of Thomas Eden, deputy auditor of Greenwich hospital, who d. 1 May* 1805). *b.* 9 Aug. 1797; entered navy 15 June 1811; captain 30 April 1827; private sec. to Lord Auckland, first lord of the Admiralty 1846–48; superintendent of Woolwich dockyard 1848–53; A.D.C. to the Queen 1853–54; a lord of the Admiralty 1855–58; admiral 16 Sep. 1864, retired 1 April 1870. *d.* 45 Eaton sq. London 30 Jany. 1888.

EDEN, John (*brother of preceding*). *b.* 25 March 1789; cornet 22 light dragoons 14 Feb. 1807; major 15 foot 8 June 1826 to 31 Dec. 1830 when placed on h.p.; col. 34 foot 28 Jany. 1860 to death; general 25 Aug. 1868; C.B. 30 March 1839. *d.* Bath 6 Oct. 1874.

EDEN, Right Rev. Robert (*brother of Sir Charles Eden* 1808–78). *b.* Pall, Mall, London 2 Sep. 1804; ed. at Westminster and Ch. Ch.

EDEN, Right Rev. R. (*Con.*)
Ox.; B.A. 1827, M.A. 1839, D.D. 1851; R. of Leigh, Essex 1837–51; bishop of Moray, Ross and Caithness 1851 to death, consecrated at St. Paul's, Edin. 9 March 1851; Primus of the Episcopal church of Scotland 5 July 1862 to death; founded cathedral of St. Andrew in Inverness, foundation stone laid 17 Oct. 1866; author of many addresses and sermons. *d.* Eden court, Inverness 26 Aug. 1886.

EDEN, William (2 *son of Sir Robert Eden, governor of Maryland 1 bart. who d. 1786*). Ensign 46 foot 26 Aug. 1786; assist. quartermaster general in England 25 Dec. 1797; lieut. col. 79 foot 15 Aug 1798 to 11 Dec. 1806; lieut. col. 84 foot 11 Dec. 1806 to 1814; quartermaster general in Madras 20 June 1807: general 28 June 1838; granted reward for distinguished service 1 Dec. 1838. *d.* Ham, Surrey 24 May 1851 aged 83.

EDEN, William Hassall. *b.* 22 Feb. 1800; ensign 6 foot 81 March 1814; lieut. col. 88 foot 10 Aug. 1839 to 16 Aug. 1839; lieut. col. 56 foot. 16 Aug. 1839 to 3 Feb. 1854; commandant at Chatham 1 Sep. 1854 to 31 March 1858; col. 90 foot 24 Oct. 1862 to death; general 4 March 1872; placed on retired list 1 Oct. 1877. *d.* 5 Royal crescent, Bath 10 Dec. 1882.

EDERSHEIM, Rev. Alfred. Educ. at Univ. of Vienna and Berlin; Ph. D. Kiel 1855; D.D. New coll. Edin.; hon. M.A. Ox. 1881, M.A. by Decree of convocation 1883; ordained deacon and priest 1875; C. of Christchurch, Hants. 1875–76; V. of Loders, Dorset 1876–83; Warburtonian lecturer at Lincoln's Inn 1880–84; select preacher at Oxford 1884–85; author of *History of the Jewish nation after the destruction of Jerusalem* 1856; *True to the end, a story of Scottish life* 1871, *new ed.* 1878; *Jewish social life in the days of Christ* 1876; *The Life and times of Jesus the Messiah* 2 vols. 1883 and many other books. *d.* Mentone 16 March 1889 aged 64.

EDGAR, Edward Fisher. Made his first appearance on the stage at Victoria theatre, London, as a child in *The Stranger*; played in the provinces; appeared at Olympic theatre, as André in *Lucille or the story of a heart* 1852; lessee of Marylebone theatre; lessee with Richard Shepherd of Surrey theatre 1871–72; acted at Princess's, Lyceum, Globe, Adelphi, Royalty and other theatres; played part of Hasting in *She stoops to conquer* at Imperial theatre, April to July 1879; sec. of Royal

EDGAR, E. F. *(Con.)*
general theatrical fund 5 April 1876 to 1879.
d. 2 Powis place, Queen sq. London 2 Sep.
1884.

EDGAR, REV. JOHN *(son of Rev. Samuel Edgar pastor of Ballykine, Tipperary).* *b.* Ballykine 13 June 1798; professor of theology in secession branch of Presbyterian church 1826–48; D.D. Hamilton college U.S.A. 1836; LLD. New York 1860; a great temperance advocate in Ireland 1829–41; a founder of Religious Book and Tract Society; moderator of general assembly of United church 1842; author of 42 pamphlets published under title of select works of John Edgar. *d.* Rathgar 26 Aug. 1866. *W. D. Killen's Memoir of John Edgar* (1867), *portrait.*

EDGAR, JOHN GEORGE *(4 son of Rev. John Edgar, minister of Hutton, Berwickshire).* *b.* 1834; passed some time in a Liverpool house; visited the West Indies on mercantile affairs; published *Biography for boys; Foot-prints of famous men* 1854 and about 20 books for the young; the first editor of *Every Boy's Magazine* 1862. *d.* London 22 April 1864.

EDGELL, HARRY *(eld. son of Hippil Edgell of Beckington, Somerset).* *b.* Beckington 30 Jany. 1767; ed. at Warminster gr. sch. and Royal college, Douai; admitted student at Gray's Inn 1787; clerk of Assize of Norfolk circuit 1795 to death; clerk of the Errors in court of Exchequer; barrister G.I. 26 June 1811; clerk of the Errors in Court of Common Pleas 1837. *d.* 21 Cadogan place, Chelsea 14 May 1863. *bur.* Ruislip, Uxbridge 21 May.

EDGELL, HARRY EDMUND *(only son of Henry Folkes Edgell 1767–1846, R.A.)* *b.* 1809; entered navy 1823; captain 9 Nov. 1846; retired V.A. 14 July 1871; C.B. 20 May 1859. *d.* Chichester 4 Feb. 1876.

EDGEWORTH, MICHAEL PAKENHAM *(youngest son of Richard Lovell Edgeworth the author 1744–1817).* *b.* 24 May 1812; ed. at Charterhouse, Edinburgh and Haileybury; entered Bengal civil service 1831; one of the 5 comrs. for settlement of the Punjaub 1850–59; collected 11 new species of plants in two hours at Aden 1846; author of *Grammar of Kashmiri language* 1841; *Pollen with 446 figures* 1877, *new ed.* 1879. *d.* in the island of Eigg, Inverness 30 July 1881.

EDISON, JOHN SIBBALD *(son of J. Edison).* *b.* 1803; barrister M.T. 25 Nov. 1831; author of *Letters to the authors of the Plain tracts for critical times, By a Layman* 1839; *Remarks on Lord Brougham's character of Pitt* 1842; *Legitimate system of national education* 1855; *Question*

EDISON, J. S. *(Con.)*
of *admissibility of Jews to Parliament* 1859; *Henry of Richmond, a drama* 2 parts 1857–60; *Commentary on Lord Brougham's character of George iii,* 1860; *Jephtha, a dramatic poem* 1863; *Northumberland, a historical dramatic poem* 1866; *Divine right of rule* 1869; *Edwin, an historical poem* 1873. *d.* Stock near Ingatestone, Essex 9 Sep. 1878.

EDKINS, ROBERT PITT. Educ. at Trin. coll. Cam.; B.A. 1830, M.A. 1836; second master of Kensington proprietary school; second master of city of London school 18 years; professor of geometry in Gresham college, city of London. *d.* 28 Belitha villas, Barnsbury, London 11 Nov. 1854 aged 49.

EDMESTON, JAMES. *b.* 10 Sept. 1791; educ. Hackney; articled to an architect and surveyor 1807; architect 1816, removed to Homerton 1822; sec. of St. Barnabas, Homerton parochial schools; author of *The search and other poems* 1817; *Anston Park, a tale* 1821; *The world of spirits; The cottage minstrel,* 50 hymns 1821; *Fifty hymns on missionary subjects* 1822; *One hundred Sunday School hymns* 1822; *Patmos a fragment and other poems* 1824; *The woman of Shunem, a sketch* 1829; *Hymns for the chamber of sickness* 1844; *Closet hymns and poems* 1846; *Sacred Poetry* 1848. *d.* 15 Brooksby's Walk, Homerton 7 Jany. 1867. *Miller's Singers and songs* (1869) *pp.* 418–20.

EDMONDS, GEORGE *(3 son of Richard Edmonds 1774–1860, town clerk of Marazion, Cornwall).* *b.* Penzance 25 March 1805; admitted attorney 4 July 1827; practised in London 1829–38; author of *The tuck net retucked, or porpoises instead of pilchards* 1824; *Complete ancient classical dictionary* [1837]; *Complete English grammar* 1837; *The tri-national grammar* [1838]; *The penny gospel* 1843. *d.* Croydon 13 Sep. 1869.

NOTE.—He was while residing in London actively engaged in writing against the stamp duty on newspapers, and was so often employed by defendants in prosecutions for selling unstamped newspapers, that he was frequently called "The attorney general for unstamped newspapers."

EDMONDS, GEORGE *(son of Rev. Edward Edmonds, pastor of Baptist chapel in Bond st. Birmingham).* *b.* Kenion st. Birmingham 1788; edited Edmonds's Weekly Recorder 1819; imprisoned 12 months for taking part in a conspiracy to elect a member of parliament 1820–21; kept a school in Bond st. Birmingham 1823; clerk of the peace for Birmingham May 1839, solicitor there 1852; author of *The philosophic alphabet with an explanation of*

EDMONDS, G. (Con.)

its principles 1832; *A universal alphabet, grammar and language comprising a scientific classification of the radical elements of discourse and illustrative translations from the Holy Scriptures and principal British classics* [1856]. *d.* Abington Abbey Retreat near Northampton 1 July 1868. *E. Edwards's Personal recollections of Birmingham* (1877) 140–54, *portrait; R. K. Dent's Old and new Birmingham* (1880) 350–56, 398, 571, *portrait; Notes and Queries* 6 S. *iv*, 102, 210, 539 (1881); *Aggravating Ladies, by Olphar Hamst* (1880) *p.* 25.

EDMONDS, RICHARD *(brother of George Edmonds* 1805–69). *b.* Penzance 18 Sep. 1801; admitted attorney 4 June 1823; practised at Penzance 1823–25 and 1836–61, at Redruth 1825–36, at Plymouth 1861 to death; author of *The Land's End district, its antiquities, natural history, natural phenomena and scenery* 1862, and of numerous papers in scientific and archæological transactions. *d.* Plymouth 12 March 1886. *Boase and Courtney's Bibl. Cornub. i*, 132–34 (1874), *iii*, 1169 (1882).

EDMONDS, THOMAS ROWE *(brother of the preceding).* *b.* Penzance 20 June 1803; ed. at Trin. coll. Cam., B.A. 1826; actuary of the Legal and general life assurance society, London 1832–66; author of *Practical, moral and political economy, or the government, religion and institutions most conducive to individual happiness and to national power* 1828; *Life tables founded on the discovery of a numerical law regulating the existence of every human being* 1832; *An inquiry into the principles of population* 1832, anon. *d.* 72 Portsdown road, Maida Vale, London 6 March 1889. *C. Walford's Insurance Cyclopædia ii*, 470–74 (1873).

EDMONDSON, GEORGE *(son of John Edmondson of Lancaster, Quaker).* *b.* Lancaster 8 Sep. 1798; ed. at Ackworth sch. Yorkshire; assisted Daniel Wheeler in superintending some agricultural institutions in Russia 1817–20; lived in Russia again 1823–30; opened a school at Blackburn 1830 and then one at Tulketh hall near Preston; kept an agricultural school at Queenwood Hall, Hants. 1847 to death; an early promoter of College of Preceptors 1846. *d.* 15 May 1863. *bur.* in burial ground of Society of Friends, Southampton. *From the Lune to the Neva sixty years ago, By J. B.* [*Mrs. Davis Benson*] 1879.

EDMONDSON, THOMAS *(brother of George Edmondson* 1798–1863). *b.* Lancaster 30 June 1792; apprenticed to a cabinet maker; journeyman in firm of Gillow and Co. Lancaster;

EDMONDSON, T. (Con.)

a cabinet maker at Carlisle, became bankrupt; railway booking clerk at Milton station (since called Brampton) 14 miles from Carlisle about 1836; invented the railway ticket system 1837; founded a ticket printing establishment at Manchester. *d.* Manchester 22 June 1851. *J. B. Edmondson's To whom are we indebted for the railway ticket system?* 1878; *Household Words vi*, 31, (1852); *I.L.N. vi*, 117 (1845), *view of ticket printing machinery*.

EDMONDSTON, LAURENCE *(son of Laurence Edmonston of Lerwick, Shetland, surgeon).* *b.* Lerwick 1795; studied at Univ. of Edin., M.D. 1830; surgeon in Unst, most northerly of Shetland islands 1830 to death; a great naturalist, made many additions to list of British birds embracing the snowy owl, the Glaucus, Iceland and Ivory gulls; author of *The claims of Shetland to a separate representation in parliament* 1836 and other pamphlets. *d.* Baltasound, Shetland, March 1879. *The home of a naturalist, In Memoriam, in Chambers's Journal* 11 Feb. 1882 *pp.* 89–92.

EDMONSTONE, SIR ARCHIBALD, 3 Baronet *(eld. son of Sir Charles Edmonstone, 2 baronet* 1764–1821). *b.* 32 Great Russell st. Bloomsbury, London 12 March 1795; ed. at Eton and Ch. Ch. Ox., B.A. 1816; succeeded 1 April 1821; contested Stirlingshire 24 May 1821; author of *Journey to two of the Oases of Upper Egypt* 1822; *Tragedies* 1837; *The Christian gentleman's daily walk* 1840, 3 ed. 1850 and 8 other books. *d.* 34 Wilton place, London 13 March 1871. *Sir A. Edmonstone's Genealogical account of the family of Edmonstone* (1875) 56–7.

EDMONSTONE, SIR GEORGE FREDERICK (4 *son of Neil Benjamin Edmonstone* 1765–1841, *member of supreme council, Bengal).* *b.* April 1813; entered Bengal civil service 1831; sec to government of India in foreign, political and secret department 1856; lieut. governor of north western provinces of Bengal 20 Jany. 1859 to 7 March 1863; K.C.B. 11 Dec. 1863. *d.* Effingham hill, Dorking 24 Sep. 1864.

EDMONSTONE, SIR WILLIAM, 4 Baronet *(brother of Sir Archibald Edmonstone* 1795–1871). *b.* Hempton, Middlesex 29 Jany. 1810; entered navy Oct. 1823; inspecting commander in Coast Guard 1844–49; captain 20 Oct. 1853; A.D.C. to the Queen 1865–69; superintendent of Woolwich dockyard 1866–71; R.A. 3 July 1869, retired 1 April 1870; retired admiral 1 Jany. 1880; M.P. for Stirlingshire 1874–80; C.B. 24 March 1863. *d.* 11 Ainslie place, Edinburgh 18 Feb. 1888.

EDMUNDS, CHARLES. *b.* 1801; entered navy 19 Dec. 1813; captain 22 Nov. 1848; retired admiral 9 March 1878. *d.* 2 Park place villas, Maida hill west, London 1 Nov. 1879.

EDMUNDS, LEONARD *(eld. son of John Edmunds of Ambleside, Westmoreland, who d. 7 July 1826).* Articled to Wm. Vizard, solicitor of 61 Lincoln's Inn Fields, London; sec. to Comrs. of the Peace, Nov. 1830; purse bearer 1830; clerk of the patents 29 Aug. 1833 to July 1864; clerk of the Crown 1834–48; reading clerk of House of Lords 1848 to July 1864; clerk of comrs. of patents, Oct. 1852 to July 1864; claimed money from the Government for several years but was always unsuccessful; brought an action for libel against W. E. Gladstone the prime minister, June 1872 when he was nonsuited. *d.* 6 Culworth st. St. John's Wood, London 19 June 1887 aged 85. *Report on case of Mr. Edmunds in* House of Commons Papers *(1865)* vols. ix and xliii; Law Reports vi Equity *(1868)* 381–96; The Edmunds scandal case *1870;* T. A. Nash's Life of Lord Westbury *(1888)* ii, 112–23.

EDWARD, THOMAS *(son of a hand-loom linen weaver).* *b.* Gosport, Hants. 25 Dec. 1814; shoemaker at Banff 1835; collected nearly 2000 species of animals which he exhibited at Banff fair, May 1845 and 1846; discovered 20 new species of Sessile-eyed Crustacea; curator of museum of Banff Institution to 1882; A.L.S. 1866; collected nearly every plant in Aberdeenshire and Banffshire; granted civil list pension of £50, 24 Jany. 1877. *d.* 27 April 1886. *Life of a Scotch Naturalist by S. Smiles* 1882; *Stories of remarkable persons by W. Chambers* (1878) 158–71; *Graphic* xv, 256 (1877), *portrait.*

EDWARDES, GEORGE WARREN (3 son of 2 baron Kensington 1777–1852). *b.* 28 May 1802; ed. at Eton; auditor general St. Helena 1845–56; governor of Labuan 13 Feb. 1856 to July 1861. *d.* Chandos house 21 Feb. 1879.

EDWARDES, SIR HERBERT BENJAMIN (2 son of Rev. Benjamin Edwardes, R. of Frodesley, Salop). *b.* Frodesley 12 Nov. 1819; ed. at King's coll. London; ensign 1 Bengal fusiliers 1841; suppressed rebellion in Mooltan, June to July 1848; captain 1 European fusiliers 1 March 1850; comr. of Peshawur frontier, Oct. 1853 to 1859; comr. of Umballa 1862–65; left India 7 Feb. 1865; M.G. 22 Feb. 1868; C.B. 20 Oct. 1849, K.C.B. 18 May 1860; K.C.S.I. 24 May 1866; author of *A year on the Punjaub frontier in 1848–49, 2 vols.* 1851. *d.* Holles st. Cavendish sq. London 23 Dec. 1868, mural tablet in Westminster Abbey.

EDWARDES, SIR H. B. *(Con.)*
Memorials of the life and letters of Sir H. B. Edwardes by Emma Edwardes 2 vols. 1886, *portrait;* C. R. Low's Soldiers of the Victorian age *ii, 1–43 (1880);* I.L.N. *xiii, 213 (1848), portrait, xviii, 618 (1851), portrait.*

EDWARDES, RICHARD *(brother of G. W. Edwardes 1802–79).* *b.* 25 Oct. 1807; entered diplomatic service 1826; minister plenipotentiary to the Argentine republic 10 Aug. 1865 to death but did not leave England. *d.* 22 Dover st. Piccadilly, London 23 March 1866.

EDWARDS, REV. BARTHOLOMEW. *b.* 2 March 1789; ed. at St. John's coll. Cam., B.A. 1811, M.A. 1814; R. of Ashill, Norfolk 1813 to death; rural dean of Breckles and Thetford. *d.* Ashill rectory 21 Feb. 1889 said to be the oldest clergyman in England.

EDWARDS, SIR BRYAN *(son of Bryan Edwards).* *b.* 1799; barrister I.T. 6 May 1825; chief justice, vice chancellor and judge of vice admiralty court for Jamaica 1859–69 when he retired on a pension; knighted by patent 15 Nov. 1859. *d.* Eltham Pen, Spanish town, Jamaica 6 Dec. 1876.

EDWARDS, CHARLES. *b.* Norwich 17 March 1797; ed. at Trin. hall, Cam., LL.B. 1807; practised law in New York; counsel to British consulate, New York 25 years; author of *The Juryman's guide* 1831; *Parties to bills and other pleadings* 1832; *Feathers from my own wings* 1832; *The History and poetry of finger rings* 1855; *Pleasantries about courts and lawyers* 1865 and other books. *d.* New York 30 May 1868.

EDWARDS, CLEMENT ALEXANDER. *b.* 12 Nov. 1812; ensign 31 foot 11 June 1829; lieut. col. 18 foot 9 March 1855, lieut. col. 49 foot 3 Aug. 1860 to 4 Aug. 1863 when placed on h.p.; inspector general of recruits 6 July 1867 to 31 July 1873; col. 18 foot 25 March 1877 to death; general 20 May 1878; placed on retired list 1 July 1881. *d.* Leeson house, Blackheath 29 July 1882.

EDWARDS, EDWARD. *b.* Corwen, Merionethshire 23 Nov. 1803; a draper at Bangor to 1839; carried on a foundry and iron works at Menai Straits several years from 1840; invented a dark-water chamber slope-back tank for marine aquaria, the principle of which was adopted here and in many of the continental and American zoological schools. *d.* 13 Aug. 1879.

EDWARDS, EDWARD. *b.* probably in London 1812; supernumerary assistant in printed

EDWARDS, E. (Con.)

book department British Museum 1839–1846; one of the 5 framers of the 91 rules for the printed catalogue; librarian of the Manchester Free library 1850–58, library was opened Sep. 1852; catalogued library of Queen's college, Oxford 1870–80; author of *Napoleon medals* 1837; *Memoirs of libraries* 2 vols. 1859; *Libraries and founders of libraries* 1865; *Lives of the founders of the British Museum* 2 vols. 1870 and other books; found dead in his bed at St. Catherine's Lodge, Niton, Isle of Wight 7 Feb. 1886. *Book-Lore, April* 1886 *pp.* 135–41.

EDWARDS, EDWIN (*son of Charles Edwards of Bridgham hall, Norfolk*). *b.* Framlingham 6 Jany. 1823; admitted solicitor 1845; practised as a proctor first in Bennett's hill, then in Knightrider st. London 1845–60; exhibited 54 pictures chiefly sea pieces at R.A. 1861–79, his etchings number about 371; author of *Cases in prerogative court with respect to wills* 1847; *Treatise on jurisdiction of high court of Admiralty* 1847; *Ecclesiastical jurisdiction, succession to personal property* 1853. *d.* 26 Golden sq. London 15 Sep. 1879.

EDWARDS, GEORGE NELSON (*eld. son of George Edwards of Eye, Suffolk, surgeon*). *b.* Eye 1830; ed. at Gonville and Caius coll. Cam., M.B. 1851, M.D. 1859; assistant phys. St. Bartholomew's hospital 1860, phys. 23 Jany. 1867; lecturer on forensic medicine 1866; edited *St. Bartholomew's hospital reports* vols. 1–3 (1865–7); author of *The examination of the chest, in a series of tables* 1862. *d.* 20 Finsbury sq. London 6 Dec. 1868.

EDWARDS, HENRY. Entered navy 19 Nov. 1796; captain 2 Aug. 1826; admiral on half pay 9 Feb. 1864. *d.* Huntingdon 22 Oct. 1864 aged 80.

EDWARDS, SIR HENRY, 1 Baronet (3 *son of Henry Lees Edwards of Pye Nest near Halifax* 1775–1848). *b.* Pye Nest 20 July 1812; M.P. for Halifax 1847–52, for Beverley 1857–69; contested Halifax 1852, 1853 and 1857; lieut. col. commandant 2 West Yorkshire yeomanry cavalry 1863 to death; created baronet 3 Aug. 1866; sheriff of Yorkshire 1871; C.B. 1881. *d.* Pye Nest 23 April 1886. *I.L.N. xxiii*, 203 (1853), *portrait, lxxxvii*, 37 (1885), *portrait*.

EDWARDS, VERY REV. HENRY THOMAS (*son of Rev. William Edwards, V. of Llangollen, who d.* 1868). *b.* Llangmawddwy, co. Merioneth 6 Sep. 1837; ed. at Westminster and Jesus coll. Ox., B.A. 1860; C. of Llangollen 1861; V. of Aberdare 1866–69; V. of Carnarvon

EDWARDS, VERY REV. H. T. (*Con*).

1869; dean of Bangor, March 1876 to death; author of *The church of the Cymry, a letter to the Right Hon. W. E. Gladstone* 1870 and other small books; hanged himself at Ruabon vicarage 24 May 1884. *bur.* Glenadda cemetery, Bangor 28 May. *Church portrait journal, Aug.* 1879 *pp.* 71–3, *portrait;* C. Mackeson's *Church congress handbook* (1877) 76–7; *I.L.N.* 31 *May* 1884 *pp.* 520, 523, *portrait*.

EDWARDS, JOHN. *b.* Llanuwch-y-lynn near Bala 15 April 1806; a farmer near Utica, New York 1828–34, 1840–66, and near Rome, New York 1866 to death; a successful competitor for the prizes awarded at the Eisteddfodan in Wales; known as Eos Glan Twrch (the nightingale of the Twrch river); edited a Welsh periodical published at Utica called *Amserai;* his published poems include *The Crucifixion* 1853 and *The Omnipresence of God* 1859. *d.* near Rome, New York 20 Jany. 1887.

EDWARDS, JOHN (*eld. son of John Edwards of Lower Broughton near Manchester*). *b.* 1836; ed. at Owen's coll. Manchester; barrister G.I. 26 Jany. 1860, bencher 7 July 1874; practised as a conveyancer in Manchester; Q.C. 6 July 1874. *d.* The Rosary, Aston-on-Mersey, Cheshire 15 Sep. 1885.

EDWARDS, REV. JOSEPH. Educ. at Trin. coll. Cam., B.A. 1824, M.A. 1835; second master of King's college school, London 1833–55; chaplain to Fishmongers' Co. 1841–55; V. of Barrow-on-Trent 1855–70; author of *Introduction to English composition*, 5 ed. 1847, and many other school books. *d.* Weybridge, Surrey 1 July 1875.

EDWARDS, REV. LEWIS. *b.* Pwllcenavon, Cardiganshire 27 Oct. 1809; studied at Univ. of Edin., M.A. 1836, D.D. 1865; ordained in Welsh Calvinistic church 1837; principal of a school at Bala (which became Bala college) 1837 to death; started *Y Traethodydd (The Essayist)* a quarterly mag. Jany. 1845, edited it 10 years; started the *Geiniogwerth (Pennyworth)* 1847; most of his essays were published as *Traethodau Ilenyddol a Duwinyddol (Essays literary and theological)* 2 vols. 1867. *d.* Bala college 19 July 1887. *Rev. L. Edwards's Athrawiaeth yr Iawn (Atonement)*, 2 ed. 1887 with memoir by his son.

EDWARDS, PETER. Second lieut. 3 Ceylon regiment 1 Oct. 1807; captain 75 foot 30 April 1818 to 11 May 1826 when placed on h.p.; general 19 Nov. 1871. *d.* London 14 Dec. 1874 aged 83.

EDWARDS, REV. ROGER. *b.* Wales 1811; edited Welsh political paper called *Cronicl yr Oes* 1835–39, wrote most of it; sec. of Calvinistic Methodist Assoc. 1839–74; co-editor of *Y Traethodydd* Jany. 1845 to death; edited the *Drysorfa* 1846 to death; wrote 3 serial stories in Welsh being the first published; author of *The Welsh psalmist; Methodist Diary. d.* 1886. *Drysorfa, Sep.* and *Oct.* 1886.

EDWARDS, THOMAS. *b.* Northop, Flintshire 1779; sec. to Nathaniel M. Rothschild in London; a member of the Cymmrodorion, delivered many of their lectures; contributed frequently to Welsh magazines; author of *Analysis of Welsh orthography* 1845; *English and Welsh dictionary, Holywell* 1850, 2 ed. 1864. *d.* 10 Cloudesley sq. London 4 June 1858. *Foulkes's Geirlyfr Bywgraffiadol.*

EDWARDS, REV. THOMAS WYNNE *(son of Evan Edwards of Plas Nantylyn, Denbighshire 1724–96). b.* Plas Nantylyn 8 April 1796; ed. at Donnington school, Shropshire and Jesus coll. Ox.; pulled the stroke-oar in his college boat in the first eight-oared boat race ever rowed at Oxford, when Jesus coll. won 1815; B.A. 1817, M.A. 1863; V. of Rhuddlan, Flintshire 1827 to death; vicar choral of St. Asaph cathedral 1828 to death. *d.* Rhuddlan vicarage 28 Dec. 1877.

EDWARDS, REV. WILLIAM. *b.* Festiniog, North Wales about 1812; a quarry-man at Meirion; studied at Liverpool and Brecon colleges; Congregational minister at Ebenezer, Aberdare 1844 to death; founded many Congregational churches in Wales; temperance, social and political reformer; chairman of Welsh Congregational Union 1883, delivered his address *The Church and the age we live in,* at Festiniog 22 Aug. 1883. *d.* Aberdare 29 Aug. 1884:

EDWARDS, WILLIAM CAMDEN. *b.* Monmouthshire 1777; engraver at Bungay, Suffolk; engraved portraits and illustrations for the *Bible* and *Pilgrim's Progress* published by Brightly of Bungay; engraved plate of 'Milton and his daughters' after Romney and many portraits; a complete series of his engravings and etchings was in Dawson Turner's collection. *d.* Bungay 22 Aug. 1855.

EDWIN, ELIZABETH REBECCA *(dau. of Mr. Richards of Dublin, actor). b.* 1769; first appeared at Crow st. theatre, Dublin when aged 8; first appeared in London at Covent Garden 13 Nov. 1789; played chief characters in comedy at nearly all the west-end theatres;

EDWIN, E. R. *(Con.)*

retired about 1822. *(m.* 1791 John Edwin the younger, comedian 1768–1805). *d.* at her lodgings in Chelsea 3 Aug. 1854. *Mrs. C. B. Wilson's Our Actresses i,* 103–20 (1844); *Oxberry's Dramatic Biography iv,* 199–209 (1826), portrait; *Theatrical Inquisitor vi,* 163–65 (1815) portrait.

EFFINGHAM, HENRY HOWARD, 2 Earl of *(son of 1 Earl of Effingham 1767–1845). b.* Southampton 23 Aug. 1806; ed. at Harrow; ensign 58 foot 1825; captain 10 foot 1830–33; M.P. for Shaftesbury 2 July 1841 to 13 Feb. 1845 when he succeeded. *d.* 57 Eaton place, London 5 Feb. 1889.

EGAN, RIGHT REV. CORNELIUS *(son of Daniel Egan of Lismickfinan, Killorghan, co. Kerry). b.* Lismickfinan 24 June 1780; entered Maynooth college 14 Aug. 1799; ordained priest 26 May 1804; principal of diocesan seminary in Killarney, professor of theology there; erected from Pugin's design a church at Killarney; P.P. Tralee and vicar general Nov. 1811; coadjutor Bishop of Kerry 29 March 1824, consecrated in Tralee church 25 July 1824, bishop of the diocese Oct. 1824 to death. *d.* Tralee 22 July 1856. *W. M. Brady's Episcopal succession ii,* 62 (1876).

EGAN, DANIEL. *b.* Windsor, N.S.W. 1803; foreman of dockyards in Sydney, a merchant there; alderman of Sydney, mayor 1851; magistrate of Sydney 1848–53; member of legislative council N.S.W. 1854, of legislative assembly 1856 to death; postmaster general 27 Oct. 1868 to death. *d.* Watson's Bay near Sydney 16 Oct. 1870.

EGAN, PIERCE *(son of Pierce Egan the author 1772–1849). b.* London 19 Dec. 1814; illustrated Davidge's *Acting Drama* and his father's *The pilgrims of the Thames in search of the national* 1837; author of *Wat Tyler* 1841, new ed. 1851; *Paul Jones* 2 vols. 1842; edited the *Home Circle* 7 July 1849 to Dec. 1851; contributed novels to the *London Journal* Dec. 1857 to death, the best of them were *The flower of the flock* 1857–8, *The snake in the grass* 1858, *The poor girl* 1862–3, *Eve or the angel of innocence* 1867. *d.* Ravensbourne, Burnt Ash, Lee, Kent 6 July 1880. *bur.* Highgate cemetery 9 July.

EGERTON, WILLIAM TATTON EGERTON, 1 Baron *(eld. child of Wilbraham Egerton 1781–1856). b.* 30 Dec. 1806; M.P. for Lymington 1830, for Cheshire 1832–58; created baron Egerton of Tatton county palatine of Cheshire 15 May 1859; lord lieut. of Cheshire 29

EGERTON, W. T. E. *(Con.)*

Jany. 1868 to death. *d.* Tatton hall, Cheshire 21 Feb. 1883. *bur.* Rostherne church 27 Feb. *Graphic xxvii*, 296 (1883), *portrait.*

EGERTON, CALEDON RICHARD. *b.* 28 July 1814 ; ensign 89 foot 15 June 1832, lieut. col. 9 March 1855 to 12 Dec. 1856 ; lieut. col. of 18 depot battalion 1856–63, of 8 depot battalion 1863–65 ; assistant adjutant general in Scotland 1865–66 ; deputy adjutant general 1 April 1866 to 1 Nov. 1871 ; M.G. 6 March 1868 ; military sec. to commander in chief 1 Nov. 1871 to 20 Feb. 1874 ; col. 89 foot 20 Feb. 1874 to death. *d.* 7 Durham villas, Kensington, London 27 May 1874.

EGERTON, SIR CHARLES BULKELEY (4 *son of Philip Egerton of Oulton park, Cheshire* 1732–86). *b.* Oulton park 5 June 1774 ; ensign 29 foot 16 Nov. 1791 ; lieut. col. 44 foot 5 Jany. 1809 to 22 Aug. 1811 when placed on h.p. ; col. 89 foot 26 Sep. 1837 to death ; general 9 Nov. 1846 ; G.C.M.G. 10 May 1837. *d.* 1 Upper Portland place, London 8 July 1857.

EGERTON, CHARLES CHANDLER *(son of Rev. Charles Egerton, V. of Thorncombe, Dorset).* *b.* Thorncombe vicarage, April 1798 ; ed. at St. Thomas's and Guy's hospitals ; M.R.C.S. 1819, assistant surgeon Bengal 1823 ; oculist at the Eye hospital and afterwards at Medical college hospital, Calcutta where he was also first surgeon to 1847 when he retired. *d.* Kendal lodge, Epping, May 1885.

EGERTON, EDWARD CHRISTOPHER *(brother of* 1 *Baron Egerton* 1806–83). *b.* Tatton park, Cheshire 27 July 1816 ; ed. at Harrow and Ch. Ch. Ox., B.A. 1837, B.C.L. 1841 ; fell. of All Soul's coll. 1837–46 ; barrister I.T. 12 June 1840 ; M.P. for Macclesfield 1852 to 1868 ; M.P. for East Cheshire 1868 to death ; under sec. for foreign affairs, July 1866 to Dec. 1868. *d.* Baveno, Italy 27 Aug. 1869. *I.L.N. xxi*, 402 (1852), *portrait.*

EGERTON, HENRY. *b.* 7 July 1836 ; acting manager T.R. Dublin ; killed in the fire of the T.R. Dublin 9 Feb. 1880, body found 6 March. *bur.* Mount Jerome cemetery 9 March. *Graphic xxi*, 205 (1880), *portrait.*

EGERTON, REV. JOHN COKER *(eld. son of John Egerton of Bunbury, Cheshire).* Matric. from Brasenose coll. Ox. 3 Feb. 1848 aged 18 ; B.A. 1852, M.A. 1854 ; C. of Nunton, Wilts. 1854–57 ; C. of Burwash, Sussex 1857–62 and 1865–67 ; C. of St. Andrew Undershaft,

EGERTON, REV. J. C. *(Con)*

City of London 1862–65 ; R. and V. of Burwash 1867 to death ; a writer in *Leisure Hour* and the *Sussex Advertiser ;* author of *Sussex Folk and Sussex Ways. d.* 20 March 1888. *The Academy 31 March* 1888 *p.* 223.

EGERTON, JOHN HUME *(elder son of John Cust* 1 *Earl Brownlow* 1779–1853). *b.* Cavendish sq. London 15 Oct. 1812 ; ed. at Magd. coll. Cam., M.A. 1833 ; M.P. for Bedfordshire 13 Jany. 1835 to death ; captain North Lincolnshire militia 29 May 1833, colonel to death ; took part in the Eglinton tournament, fought in earnest with the Marquis of Waterford the last day 30 Aug. 1839 ; took name of Egerton only by r.l. 15 March 1849. *d.* Ashridge park 3 Jany. 1851.

EGERTON, SIR PHILIP DE MALPAS GREY-, 10 Baronet *(eld. son of Rev. Sir Philip Grey-Egerton,* 9 *baronet).* *b.* Malpas, Cheshire 13 Nov. 1806 ; ed. at Eton and Ch. Ch. Ox., B.A. 1828 ; collected fossil fishes in Germany, Switzerland and Italy ; M.P. for Chester 1830–32, for South Cheshire 1835–68, for West Cheshire 1868 to death ; contested South Cheshire 1832 ; F.G.S. 1829, Wollaston medallist 1873 ; F.R.S. 10 Feb. 1831 ; author of *Alphabetical catalogue of type specimens of fossil fishes* 1871, and of over 80 papers in the *Transactions, Proceedings and Journal of Geol. Soc.,* and other scientific journals. *d.* 28^B Albemarle st. Piccadilly, London 5 April 1881. *Proc. of Royal Soc. xxxiii, pp. xxii–iv* (1882) ; *Quarterly Journal of Geol. Soc. xxxviii,* 46–8 (1882).

EGERTON, RICHARD. *b.* 7 April 1783 ; ensign 89 foot 1 Dec. 1798 ; captain 34 foot 14 April 1808 to 16 Dec. 1819 when placed on h.p. ; first aide-de-camp and private sec. to Lord Hill the commander in chief 1828–42 ; col. 46 foot 24 Jany. 1853 to death ; L.G. 20 June 1854 ; C.B. 19 July 1838. *d.* Eaton Banks, Cheshire 18 Nov. 1854.

EGERTON, WILBRAHAM. *b.* 1 Sep. 1781 ; sheriff of Cheshire 1808 ; M.P. for Cheshire 1812–31. *d.* Tatton park 25 April 1856.

EGG, AUGUSTUS LEOPOLD *(son of Joseph Egg of* 1 *Piccadilly, London, gunmaker).* *b.* 1 Piccadilly 2 May 1816 ; studied at R.A. ; exhibited 28 pictures at R.A., 9 at B.I. and 9 at Suffolk st. gallery 1837–60 ; A.R.A. 1848, R.A. 1860. *d.* Algiers 26 March 1863. *Life of Charles Dickens by J. Forster iii,* 55–74 (1874) ; *Redgrave's Century of painters ii,* 358–60 (1866) ; *Art Union monthly journal* (1847) 312, *portrait; I.L.N. xxx,* 419, 420 (1857), *portrait.*

EGLEY, WILLIAM. *b.* Doncaster 1798; miniature painter in London 1824 to death; exhibited 169 miniatures at R.A. 1824–69. *d.* London 19 March 1870.

EGLINTON, ARCHIBALD WILLIAM MONTGOMERIE, 13 Earl of *(only son of major general Archibald Montgomerie 1773–1814)*. *b.* Palermo 29 Sep. 1812; succeeded his grandfather as 13 Earl, 14 Dec. 1819; ed. at Eton; began racing 1831, won the St. Leger with Blue Bonnet 1842, with Van Tromp 1847, won the Derby and St. Leger with the Flying Dutchman 1849; col. Ayrshire militia 1836–52; carried out celebrated tournament held at Eglinton castle, Ayrshire 28–30 Aug. 1839; served heir male general of George 4 Earl of Winton (who *d.* 6 March 1704) 22 Dec. 1840; lord lieut. of Ayrshire 17 Aug. 1842; lord rector of Marischal coll. Aberdeen 1852; lord lieut. of Ireland 27 Feb. to Dec. 1852 and 26 Feb. 1858 to 5 Jany. 1859; P.C. 27 Feb. 1852; lord rector of Glasgow Univ. 1852; K.T. 18 June 1853; created Earl of Winton in peerage of U.K. 23 June 1859; the most popular man in the three kingdoms. *d.* Mount Melville near St. Andrews 4 Oct. 1861. *Nixon and Richardson's Eglinton Tournament* (1843), *portrait; Eton portrait gallery* (1876) 352–56; *Sporting Review xxxix,* 452–5 (1858), *xlvi,* 320–1 (1861); *Rice's British turf* (1879) *i,* 281–3; *Sporting Times* 28 *March* 1885 *pp.* 5–6.

EGMONT, GEORGE JAMES PERCEVAL, 6 Earl of *(3 son of 2 Baron Arden 1756–1840)*. *b.* 14 March 1794; served as midshipman at Trafalgar 21 Oct. 1805, captain 7 Dec. 1818; admiral on h.p. 23 March 1863; M.P. for West Surrey 4 Aug. 1837 to 5 July 1840 when he succeeded as 3 Baron Arden; succeeded as 6 Earl of Egmont 23 Dec. 1841. *d.* North house, Epsom 2 Aug. 1874, personalty sworn under £350,000, 26 Sep. *I.L.N. lxv,* 164 (1874), *portrait.*

EKINS, SIR CHARLES *(son of Very Rev. Jeffery Ekins, dean of Carlisle, who d. 20 Nov. 1791)*. *b.* Quainton rectory, Bucks. 1768; entered navy 20 March 1781; captain 22 Dec. 1796; admiral 23 Nov. 1841; K.C.B. 8 June 1831; G.C.B. 6 April 1852; author of *Naval battles from 1744 to the peace of 1814 critically reviewed and illustrated* 2 vols. 1824, 2 ed. 1828. *d.* 69 Cadogan place, London 2 July 1855 aged 87.

ELD, GEORGE. *b.* Coventry; a miller, silk dealer and dyer successively; edited *Coventry Standard* 20 years; mayor of Coventry 1834–5, alderman to death; made many drawings of ancient buildings and other memorials of the past. *d.* Coventry 22 May 1862 in 71 year.

ELD, JOHN (3 *son of Francis Eld of Seighford hall near Stafford 1736–1817)*. *b.* 16 July 1779; elected master of the ceremonies of assemblies at Old Ship inn, Brighton, March 1828 being the third and last master, final ball held 20 Nov. 1854. *d.* Brighton 22 Dec. 1855 in 76 year. *J. G. Bishop's A Peep into the past, Brighton* (1880) 34–6, *portrait.*

ELDER, CHARLES. Historical and portrait painter; exhibited 5 pictures at B.I., 11 at R.A. and 5 at Suffolk st. gallery 1844–52. *d.* Gower st. London 11 Dec. 1851 aged 30.

ELDER, REV. EDWARD *(son of John Edward Elder of Barbadoes)*. *b.* 1 Oct. 1812; ed. at Charterhouse and Ball. coll. Ox., open scholar 1830; B.A. 1834, M.A. 1836, D.D. 1853; master of Durham cathedral gr. school 1839–53; master of Charterhouse school 1853 to death; contributed several articles to *Smith's Dictionary of classical biography and mythology.* *d.* 6 April 1858, memorial tablet in Charterhouse chapel. *G.M. iv,* 563, 673–4 (1858).

ELDER, JOHN (3 *son of David Elder of Glasgow, marine engineer 1784–1866)*. *b.* Glasgow 8 March 1824; member of firm of Randolph Elliott & Co. of Glasgow, marine engineers 1852; a shipbuilder in Glasgow 1860 to death; employed about 4000 men; adopted the compound or combined high and low pressure engines 1854; patented his round war ship 1868 and many improvements in marine machinery; pres. of Institution of engineers and shipbuilders of Glasgow 1869. *d.* London 17 Sep. 1869. *W. J. M. Rankine's Memoir of J. Elder* 1870, *portrait; Maclehose's Memoirs and portraits of a hundred Glasgow men* 1886.

ELDER, WILLIAM. *b.* Malin, Donegal 22 July 1822; ed. at Queen's coll. Belfast, and Univs. of Glasgow and Edin.; a minister in Presbyterian church; went to New Brunswick; edited the *Colonial Presbyterian,* edited the *Morning Journal* at St. John 1865; chief editor and proprietor of the *Daily Telegraph* at St. John 1871; member of legislative assembly of New Brunswick 1878 to death; provincial secretary 1882. *d.* St. John N.B. 23 July 1882. *Dominion Annual Register* 1883 *pp.* 309–11.

ELDON, JOHN SCOTT, 2 Earl of. *b.* Manchester square, London 10 Dec. 1805; ed. at Winchester and New coll. Ox.; B.A. 1828, M.A. 1831; D.C.L. 1834; LL.D. Cam. 1842; M.P. for Truro 1829–32; succeeded 13 Jany. 1838; pres. of the Pitt club 1842; declared by inquisition to be of unsound mind Jany. 1853. *d.*

Shirley park, Surrey 18 Sep. 1854. *bur.* family vault at Kingston, Isle of Purbeck 29 Sep. *Doyle's Official baronage i, 671 (1886), portrait;* *I.L.N. iv,* 65 (1844), *portrait.*

ELDRED, JOSEPH. *b.* London 1843; agent for Rev. J. M. Bellew on a reading tour through the provinces 1860; a low comedian in Dublin 1865; an actor and manager at Liverpool; first appeared in London at Olympic theatre 15 June 1868 as Major Regulus Rattan in *Ici on parle Français;* acted at Gaiety theatre from 21 Dec. 1868; played Micawber in *Little Emly* at Olympic from 9 Oct. 1869; played several starring tours in provinces; remarkably like the Earl of Beaconsfield. *d.* Sydney, New South Wales 29 Feb. 1884. *Sporting Times 25 Sep,* 1875, *pp.* 537, 540, *portrait.*

ELDRIDGE, CHARLES MONROE. Member of assembly for city of St. John's, Antigua 1852–63; pres. of Dominica 1872 and 1882; pres. of Nevis, April 1872 to May 1873; pres. of St. Christopher 1883 and of St. Kitt's and Nevis 1883. *d.* 8 Oct. 1888.

ELEN, PHILIP WEST. Landscape painter in London; exhibited 64 pictures at R.A., 57 at B.I. and 46 at Suffolk st. gallery 1838–72. *d.* Regent's park road, London 21 Feb. 1880.

ELGIN, JAMES BRUCE, 8 Earl of, and 12 Earl of Kincardine (*2 son of 7 Earl of Elgin 1766–1841). b.* Park lane, London 20 July 1811; ed. at Eton and Ch. Ch. Ox.; B.A. 1833, M.A. 1835, D.C.L. 1856; fellow of Merton coll. 1833 to 1841; M.P. for Southampton 1841–42; succeeded his father 17 Nov. 1841; governor general of Jamaica 1842–46, of Canada 1846–54; knighted by patent 19 June 1847; K.T. 12 July 1847; created baron Elgin of Elgin 13 Nov. 1849, special ambassador to China 1857–59 and 1860–61; P.C. 21 March 1857; G.C.B. 28 Sep. 1858; postmaster general 1859 to 1860; lord rector of Univ. of Glasgow, Nov. 1859; received freedom of City of London 1 March 1860; viceroy of India 21 Jany. 1862 to death. *d.* Dhurmsala, Cashmere 20 Nov. 1863. *T. Walrond's Letters and journals of James, eighth Earl of Elgin* 1872; *L. Oliphant's Narrative of Lord Elgin's Mission to China and Japan* 2 vols. 1859; *H. Martineau's Biographical sketches,* 4 ed. (1876) 108–21; *Eton portrait gallery* (1876) 360–67; *D. C. Boulger's History of China,* vol. 3 (1884).

ELIOT, REV. EDWARD (*eld. son of Rev. Richard Eliot, Vicar of Maker, Cornwall, who d. 1795). b.* Maker 22 May 1789; ed. at Lostwithiel and Ex. coll. Ox., fellow 30 June 1811 to 10

July 1826; B.A. 1814, M.A. 1815, B.D. 1825; archdeacon of Barbadoes 1825–37; V. of Norton Bavant, Wilts. 1837 to death; preb. of Salisbury 30 Dec. 1848 to death; author of *Christianity and Slavery* 1833 and other books. *d.* Norton Bavant 1 Nov. 1861.

ELIOTT, SIR DANIEL (4 *son of Sir William Eliott, 6 baronet, who d. 14 May 1812). b.* Stobs castle, Roxburghshire 3 March 1798; writer Madras civil service 1817; sec. to board of revenue 1827; member of Madras council and pres. of revenue, marine and college boards 1848; member of legislative council of India 1855–58; K.C.S.I. 24 May 1867. *d.* 12 The Boltons, West Brompton, London 30 Oct. 1872.

ELIOTT, GEORGE AUGUSTUS (*brother of the preceding). b.* 24 May 1799; entered navy 1814; captain on h.p. 27 June 1838; admiral on h.p. 10 Sep. 1869. *d.* Bath 13 May 1872.

ELIOTT, RUSSELL (*brother of the preceding). b.* Stobs castle 26 March 1802; entered navy 16 Nov. 1814; captain 28 June 1838; admiral on h.p. 10 Sep. 1869. *d.* Appleby castle, Westmoreland 28 Dec. 1881.

ELKINGTON, GEORGE RICHARDS (*son of James Elkington of Birmingham, gilt-toy maker). b.* St. Paul's sq. Birmingham 17 Oct. 1801; apprenticed to his uncles Josiah and George Richards of Birmingham, partner with them, succeeded to the business on their death; partner with his cousin Henry Elkington, who *d.* 26 Oct. 1852, they introduced industry of electro plating and electro gilding 1840; established large copper-smelting works at Pembrey, South Wales. *d.* of paralysis at Pool park, Denbighshire 22 Sep. 1865, personalty sworn under £350,000, 20 Jany. 1866.

ELKINGTON, JOHN HENRY FORD (*son of James Goodall Elkington). b.* 10 April 1830; ensign 6 foot 28 Aug. 1846, lieut. col. 27 Nov. 1867 to 24 Feb. 1877 when placed on h.p.; lieut. governor and commanding the troops Guernsey 1 Nov. 1885 to death; L.G. 1 April 1887; C.B. 24 May 1881. *d.* St. George, Guernsey 21 Feb. 1889.

ELLA, JOHN (*son of Richard Ella of Thirsk, Yorkshire). b.* Thirsk 19 Dec. 1802; violinist in orchestra of Drury Lane theatre 18 Jany. 1821, of the King's theatre 1822; member of all important orchestras in London 1826; musical editor of the *Athenæum* and other papers; established "The Musical Union" a series of morning concerts of instrumental chamber music 1845, and a similar series of concerts entitled "Musical Winter Evenings" 1850; musical lecturer to London Institution 1855; author of *Musical Sketches abroad and at home* 1869, 3 ed. 1878; *Lectures on dramatic, music and musical education abroad and at home* 1872. *d.* 9 Victoria sq. Pimlico, London 2 Oct. 1888. *I.L.N. viii*, 420 (1846), *portrait*.

ELLACOMBE, REV. HENRY THOMAS *(son of Rev. William Ellicombe, R. of Alphington near Exeter, who d. 1831).* *b.* 1790; ed. at Oriel coll. Ox., B.A. 1812, M.A. 1816; C. of Cricklade, Wilts. 1816; C. of Bitton, Gloucs. 1817–35; V. of Bitton 1835–50; R. of Clyst St. George, Devon 1850 to death; restored church of Bitton 1822 and built 3 other churches near there; the great authority on bells, invented an apparatus of chiming hammers; changed his name to Ellacombe about 1842; author of *Practical remarks on belfries and ringers*, Bristol 1850, 4 ed. 1876; *The Church bells of Devon, Somerset and Gloucestershire* 3 vols. 1872, 1875, 1881, and other books. *d.* Clyst St. George 30 July 1885. *bur.* in Bitton churchyard. *Mozley's Reminiscences* (1882) *i*, 75–81; *Church Bells 7 Aug.* 1885 *pp.* 847–8, *portrait*.

ELLENBOROUGH, EDWARD LAW, 1 Earl of *(eld. son of 1 Baron Ellenborough 1750–1818).* *b.* 8 Sep. 1790; ed. at Eton and St. John's coll. Cam., M.A. 1809; M.P. for St. Michael's, Cornwall 1813–18; lord privy seal 22 Jany. 1828 to 10 June 1829; P.C. 26 Jany. 1828; a lord of the treasury 21 Nov. 1834; pres. of Board of Control 20 Dec. 1834 to 29 April 1835, 9 Sep. 1841 to 28 Oct. 1841, and 6 March to June 1858; governor general of India 20 Oct. 1841 to 15 June 1844; created Viscount Southam of Southam, Gloucs. and Earl of Ellenborough in the county of Cumberland 22 Oct. 1844; G.C.B. 30 Oct. 1844; first lord of Admiralty 8 Jany. 1846 to 6 July 1846. *d.* Southam Delabere, Gloucs. 22 Dec. 1871. *History of the Indian administration of Lord Ellenborough, edited by Lord Colchester* 1874; *Eton portrait gallery* (1876) 371–78; *I.L.N. ii*, 92 (1843), *portrait, lix*, 643 (1871), *lx*, 36, 37 (1872), *portrait*.

ELLERTON, REV. EDWARD *(son of Richard Ellerton of Downholm, Yorkshire).* *b.* 30 Jany. 1771; ed. at Richmond sch. and Univ. coll. Ox., B.A. 1792, M.A. 1795, B.D. 1805, D.D. 1815; Usher of Magd. coll. sch. 1795, master 1798–1810; fell. of Magd. coll. 2 Nov. 1803 to death, vice pres. 1806, tutor 1810, librarian 1827; senior proctor 1804–5; P.C. of Horsepath, Oxon. 1814; P.C. of Sevenhampton,

Gloucs. 1825–51; joint founder in 1832 with Dr. E. B. Pusey and his brother Philip Pusey of the Pusey and Ellerton Hebrew scholarships, which are three in number open to all members of the university and of annual value of £30 each. *d.* Theale curacy, Berks. 26 Dec. 1851. *J. B. Bloxam's Register of Magdalene college iii*, 246–58 (1863).

ELLERTON, JOHN LODGE *(son of Adam Lodge of Liverpool).* *b.* Chester 11 Jany. 1801; ed. at Rugby and Brasenose coll. Ox., B.A. 1821, M.A. 1828; studied music at Rome where he wrote 7 Italian operas; his English opera *Domenica* produced at Drury Lane 7 June 1838 failed; wrote another English opera *The Bridal of Triermain* and a German opera *Lucinda;* published an oratorio *Paradise Lost* 1857, fifty string quartets and many other musical works; a member of the Musical Union 1847–71; assumed name of Ellerton about 1844; author of *The bridal of Salerno, a poetical romance* 1845, *The elixir of youth, a legend and other poems* 1864. *d.* Connaught place, Hyde park, London 10 Jany. 1873.

ELLESMERE, FRANCIS EGERTON, 1 Earl of *(younger son of 1 Duke of Sutherland 1758–1833).* *b.* Arlington st. Piccadilly, London 1 Jany. 1800; ed. at Eton and Ch. Ch. Ox.; M.P. for Bletchingley, Surrey 1822–26, for Sutherlandshire 1826–30, for South Lancashire 1834–46; a lord of the Treasury 1827; under sec. of state for Colonies, Jany. to May 1828; chief sec. to Marquis of Anglesey, lord lieut. of Ireland 1828–30; P.C. 28 June 1828; P.C. Ireland 9 Aug. 1828; sec. at war 30 July to 22 Nov. 1830; rector of Univ. of Aberdeen, Oct. 1838; created Earl of Ellesmere of Ellesmere, Salop, and Viscount Brackley of Brackley, Northamptonshire 1 July 1846; K.G. 7 Feb. 1855; lord lieut. of Lancashire 9 April 1856; author of *Translations from the German and original poems* 1824; *Mediterranean sketches* 1843; *The pilgrimage and other poems* 1856. *d.* Bridgewater house, St. James's, London 18 Feb. 1857. *Journal of British Archæol. Assoc. xiv*, 184–6 (1858); *Quarterly Journal of Geol. Soc. xiv, pp. xlv–xlvii* (1858); *Fraser's Mag. July* 1835 *p.* 43, *portrait; I.L.N. viii*, 60 (1846), *portrait, xxxvii*, 563, 568 (1860), *portrait*.

ELLESMERE, GEORGE GRANVILLE FRANCIS EGERTON, 2 Earl of. *b.* Albemarle st. Piccadilly, London 15 June 1823; M.P. for North Staffs. 1847–51; succeeded 18 Feb. 1857. *d.* Balbirnie, Fifeshire 19 Sep. 1862.

ELLICE, SIR CHARLES HENRY *(2 son of general Robert Ellice 1784–1856).* *b.* Florence 10 May

ELLICE, SIR C. H. (*Con.*)

1823; ed. at Sandhurst; ensign Coldstream guards 10 May 1839; lieut. col. 24 foot 8 Aug. 1851 to 8 July 1862 when placed on h.p.; quarter master general 1 April 1871 to 30 March 1876; adjutant general 1 Nov. 1876 to March 1882; col. of 49 foot 7 Sep. 1874, of 24 foot 6 April 1884 to death; general 1 Oct. 1877; placed on retired list 1 April 1887; C.B. 1 Jany. 1858, K.C.B. 24 May 1873, G.C.B. 15 April 1882. *d.* Brook house, Horringer, Bury St. Edmunds 12 Nov. 1888.

ELLICE, EDWARD (*eld. son of Alexander Ellice, managing director of the Hudson's Bay Company*). *b.* Montreal 1781; ed. at Winchester sch. and Marischal coll. Aberdeen, M.A. 1800; settled in London as member of firm of Inglis and Ellice, West India and America house; M.P. for Coventry 1818–1826 and 1830 to death; sec. to the Treasury 26 Nov. 1830 to 10 Aug. 1832 when he resigned; sec. of war 4 April 1833 to 16 Dec. 1834; P.C. 3 April 1833; original chairman of Reform club, London mainly established by his influence 1836; hon. D.C.L. St. Andrews 1862. *d.* Ardochy, Glengary 17 Sep. 1863. *Fagan's Reform club* (1887) 33, 37, 123, *portrait*; *I.L.N. xliii*, 335, 337 (1863), *portrait*.

ELLICE, EDWARD (*only son of the preceding*). *b.* London 19 Aug. 1810; ed. at Eton and Trin. coll. Cam., M.A. 1831; contested Inverness 1834; M.P. for Huddersfield 1836–37, for St. Andrew's district 1837–80; author of *A Letter in reply to A Report on the Poor Law in the Highlands* 1855. *d.* on board his yacht Ita off Portland during the night of 2 Aug. 1880. *bur.* at Tor-na-cairidh on Lochgarry, Invernessshire.

ELLICE, ROBERT (2 *son of Alexander Ellice, managing director of the Hudson's Bay Company*). *b.* 1784; cornet 12 light dragoons 8 Nov. 1798; major 6 dragoons 25 June 1812 to 30 Nov. 1820 when placed on h.p.; col. 24 foot 2 Nov. 1842 to death; general 20 June 1854. *d.* Upper Norwood, Surrey 18 June 1856.

ELLICOMBE, SIR CHARLES GRENE (*brother of Rev. H. T. Ellacombe* 1790–1885). *b.* Alphington rectory 3 Aug. 1783; first lieut. R.E. 1 July 1801, brigade major 1821 to Dec. 1842, col. commandant 30 May 1856 to death; served in Peninsula, Nov. 1811 to end of the war; general 20 April 1861; C.B. 4 June 1815, K.C.B. 10 Nov. 1862. *d.* Worthing 7 June 1871. *United Service Mag. July* 1871 *pp.* 407–409.

ELLIOT, SIR CHARLES (*youngest son of Hugh Elliot* 1752–1830, *governor of Madras*). *b.* Dresden 1801; entered navy 26 March 1815;

ELLIOT, SIR C. (*Con.*)

captain 28 Aug. 1828; protector of slaves in British Guiana 1830–33; British plenipotentiary in China 1840–41; consul general in Texas 1841–46; governor of Bermuda 1846–54; governor of Trinidad 1854–56; governor of St. Helena 20 May 1863 to 1 Feb. 1870 when he retired on pension; retired admiral 12 Sep. 1865; K.C.B. 19 July 1856; is drawn by Sir Henry Taylor in the poem *Edwin the Fair* 1845 as Earl Athulf. *d.* Withycombe near Exmouth 9 Sep. 1875. *Autobiography of H. Taylor i,* 164–69, 345–75 (1885).

ELLIOT, CHARLES MORGAN (9 *child of John Elliot, F.R.S.*) *b.* Pimlico lodge, Westminster 27 April 1815; ed. at Eton and Addiscombe; 2 lieut. Madras engineers 1832, lieut. 11 Sep. 1841 to death; superintendent of magnetic observatory at Singapore 1840–45; made a magnetic survey of Eastern Archipelago, Jany. 1846 to Oct. 1849; F.R.S. 5 June 1851. *d.* Masulipatam 4 Aug. 1852.

ELLIOT, LADY CHARLOTTE (*eld. dau. of Sir James Carnegie, 5 baronet* 1799–1849). *b.* 22 July 1839; raised to rank of an Earl's daughter 1855 on her brother becoming Earl of Southesk; author of *Stella and other poems By Florenz* 1867; *Medusa and other poems* 1878. (*m.* (1) 16 June 1860 Thomas Frederick Scrymsoure Fothringham, who *d.* 7 March 1864; *m.* (2) 17 Dec. 1868 Frederick Boileau Elliot, barrister 1826–80). *d.* 15 Jany. 1880. *Athenæum 24 Jany.* 1880 *p.* 124.

ELLIOT, SIR GEORGE (2 *son of 1 Earl of Minto* 1751–1814). *b.* Swanage, Dorset 1 Aug. 1784; entered navy 4 June 1794; a naval aide-de-camp to Wm. iv, 1830–37; a junior lord of the Admiralty 1835–37; commander in chief at Cape of Good Hope 1837–40; commander of fleet in East Indies 15 Feb. 1840 to Nov. 1840; admiral 5 March 1853; pensioned 3 Oct. 1855; C.B. 26 Sep. 1831, K.C.B. 10 Nov. 1862. *d.* 4 Prince's terrace, Knightsbridge, London 24 June 1863.

ELLIOT, SIR HENRY MIERS (*brother of Charles Morgan Elliot* 1815–52). *b.* 1808; ed. at Winchester; entered Bengal civil service 1826; sec. for foreign department to governor general in council 1847; K.C.B. for service during Sikh war 5 June 1849; author of *Supplement to the glossary of Indian terms [Compiled in 1842 by H. H. Wilson] A–J.* 1860, no more printed; *Bibliographical index to the historians of Muhammedan, India, vol. i,* 1849; *The History of India as told by its own historians, edited by J. Dowson* 8 vols. 1867–77 and other books. *d.* Simon's Town, Cape of Good Hope 20 Dec. 1853.

ELLIOT, JOHN EDMUND (*youngest son of 1 Earl of Minto 1751–1814*). *b.* 30 March 1788; in the Bengal civil service to 1830; M.P. for co. Roxburgh 1837–1841 and 1847–1859; sec. of Board of Control 26 Jany. 1849 to March 1852; author of *Letter to the Teviotside Farmer* 1841. *d.* 29 Cadogan place, London 4 April 1862.

ELLIOT, SIR THOMAS FREDERICK (*brother of Sir Charles Eliot 1801–75*). *b.* London, July 1808; ed. at Harrow; clerk in colonial office London 5 July 1825; sec. to commission of enquiry into state of Canada, July 1835; agent general of emigration April 1837; chairman of board of advice and management over colonial land and emigration 1840–1847; assistant under sec. of state for colonies 1847 to Dec. 1868 when he retired on pension; K.C.M.G. 30 June 1869. *d.* Shepherd's hotel, Cairo 12 Feb. 1880.

ELLIOT, SIR WALTER (*eld. son of James Elliot of Wolfelee, Roxburghshire*). *b.* Edinburgh 16 Jany. 1803; writer Madras civil service 1821; third member of Board of Revenue 1844, second 1848, first 1851; comr. of the Northern Circars 1848–54; member of council and pres. of revenue and marine boards 1855–56 and 1857 to 27 Dec. 1859 when he resigned the service; a scholar in the Tamil and Hundustani languages; K.C.S.I. 24 May 1866; F.R.S. 6 June 1878; hon. LLD. Edin. 22 April 1878; author of *Carnacta translation of Esop's Fables* 1840; *Flora Andhrica, a list of plants in the Telegu district* 1859, and of many papers on archæology in *Indian Antiquary, Madras Journal of Literature and Science, Journal of Royal Asiatic Society* and other periodicals. *d.* Wolfelee 1 March 1887. *Journal of Royal Asiatic Society, July* 1887 *pp.* 519–24; *Biograph i,* 251–54 (1882).

ELLIOTSON, JOHN (*eld. son of Thomas Elliotson of 106 High st. Southwark, druggist*). *b.* High st. Southwark 24 Oct. 1791; spent 5 years at Univ. of Edin. 1805–10, M.D. 24 June 1810; L.R.C.P. London 22 Dec. 1810; spent 3 years at Jesus coll. Cam. 1813–16, M.B. 1816, M.D. 4 July 1821; candidate of R.C.P. 1 Oct. 1821, a fellow 30 Sep. 1822, censor 1825, consiliarius 1836, Gulstonian lecturer 1824, Lumleian lecturer 1829–30, Harveian orator 1846; assist. phys. to St. Thomas's hospital 1817, phys. 1823–34; professor of medicine at London University 1832 to Dec. 1838; senior phys. to University hospital 1834 to Dec. 1838; began practise of Mesmerism 1837; founded Phrenological Society of London, pres.; founded London Mesmeric

ELLIOTSON, J. (*Con.*)

infirmary in Weymouth st. 1849; established *The Zoist,* a journal of cerebral physiology and mesmerism 1844 which ran to 13 vols.; broke up his establishment and quitted his house in Conduit st. 1865; pres. of Royal Med. and Chir. Soc.; author of *The principles and practice of medicine* 1839; *Treatise on human physiology, Fifth ed.* 1835–40, another ed. 1856 and other books. *d.* 2 Davies st. Berkeley sq. London 29 July 1868. *J. Ashburner's Notes and Studies* (1867) 59–68; *Medical Circular iv,* 403–4, 419–21, 432–3 (1854); *Physic and Physicians ii,* 273–85 (1839).

ELLIOTT, CHARLES. Entered Bengal civil service 1797; senior member of Board of Revenue in Bengal; agent to governor general in Western provinces, retired on annuity 1826; F.R.S. 1832; F.R.G.S.; treasurer of Asiatic Society some years; author of *The life of Hafiz-ool-Moolk Hafiz Rehmab Khan* 1831. *d.* Portland place, London 4 May 1856 aged 79.

ELLIOTT, REV. CHARLES. *b.* Greenconway, Donegal 16 May 1792; went to the U.S. about 1815; presiding elder of Wesleyan, Ohio district 4 years; professor of languages in Madison college, Uniontown, Panama 4 years; edited *Pittsburg Conference Journal;* edited *Western Christian Advocate* to 1848 and 1852–56; professor of Biblical literature in and pres. of Iowa Wesleyan Univ. 1856–60; author of *Treatise on Baptism* 1834; *Delineation of Roman Catholicism* 2 vols. 1842, third ed. 1851; *Life of Bishop Roberts* 1853 and other books. *d.* Mount Pleasant, Iowa 6 Jany. 1869.

ELLIOTT, REV. CHARLES BOILEAU (*eld. son of Charles Elliott, who d. 4 May 1856*). *b.* 1803; ed. at Harrow and Queen's coll. Cam., B.A. 1833, M.A. 1837; V. of Godalming, Surrey 1833–38; R. of Tattingstone near Ipswich 1838 to death; F.R.G.S.; F.R.S. 5 April 1832; author of *Letters from the North of Europe* 1832; *Travels in the three great empires of Austria, Russia and Turkey* 2 vols. 1838 and other books. *d.* Geneva 1 July 1875.

ELLIOTT, REV. CHARLES JOHN. *b.* 7 July 1818; ed. at St. Cath. coll. Cam., Crosse Univ. scholar 1840, Tyrwhitt Univ. scholar 1842, B.A. 1840, M.A. 1843; V. of Winkfield near Windsor 1844 to death; surrogate 1872; hon. canon of Ch. Ch. Ox. 1873; select preacher at Cambridge 1877; member of Old Testament revision company; author of *Enquiry into the doctrine of the Church of England on private confession and absolution* 1859 **and**

ELLIOTT, REV. C. J. (Con.)

other books; contributed to the *Bible Educator* 1872, *the S.P.C.K. Commentary, Smith's Dictionary of Biography and Antiquities, Edinburgh Review, &c.* d. Winkfield vicarage 11 May 1881.

ELLIOTT, CHARLOTTE (3 *dau. of Charles Elliott of Clapham and Brighton). b.* 17 March 1789; lived at Torquay 1845–57, at Brighton 1857 to death; edited *Christian Remembrancer Pocket Book* 1834–59; edited *The Invalid's Hymn book*, 6 ed. 1854, to this collection she contributed 112 hymns including "Just as I am, without one plea," a hymn dated 1836 which has been translated into almost every living language, she also wrote "My God and Father while I stray" 1834 in the same collection; author of *Hymns for a week* 1837, 40*th thousand* 1871; *Hours of Sorrow* 1836 and many later editions; *Poems by C. E.* 1863. d. 10 Norfolk terrace, Brighton 22 Sep. 1871. *Selections from the poems of Charlotte Elliott with a memoir by her sister E. B.* (*Mrs. E. Babington*) 1873, *portrait; Just as I am, by C. Elliott* 1884 *with memoir by H. L. L.* 1885; *Miller's singers and songs of the church* 1869, 461–62.

ELLIOTT, REV. EDWARD BISHOP (*brother of the preceding). b.* 24 July 1793; ed. at Trin. coll. Cam., fellow 1817–24, B.A. 1816, M.A. 1819; wrote Seatonian prize poems 1821 and 1822; V. of Tuxford, Notts. 1824–40; preb. of Salisbury 1853; P.C. of St. Mark's chapel, Brighton 1853 to death; author of *The Question "What is the image of the Beast?"* answered 1838; *Horæ Apocalypticæ, or a commentary on the Apocalypse critical and historical* 3 vols. 1844; *Vindiciæ Horariæ* 1848 and 6 other books. d. 30 July 1875.

ELLIOTT, GEORGE PERCY (*eld. son of Rev. Luther Graves Elliott of Ottery St. Mary, Devon). b.* Silverton 1800; ed. at Winchester and St. Mary hall, Ox.; B.A. 1822, M.A. 1825; barrister M.T. 29 May 1829; magistrate at Lambeth police court 1845 to 20 Sep. 1870 when he retired; author of *A practical treatise on the qualifications of Parliamentary electors* 1839; ed. for the Camden Soc. *Diary of Dr. E. Lake* and *Autobiography of Dr. Taswell.* d. Egland, Honiton, Devon 12 July 1874.

ELLIOTT, REV. HENRY VENN (*brother of Charlotte Elliott* 1789–1871). *b.* 17 Jany. 1792; ed. at Trin. coll. Cam., fellow 1 Oct. 1816; 14 wrangler and 2 chancellor's medallist 1814; C. of Ampton, Suffolk 1823–25; prior of St. John's, Wilton near Salisbury 1826–32; P.C. of St. Mary's, Brighton 18 Jany. 1827 to

ELLIOTT, REV. H. V. (Con.)

death, this chapel was built by his father for about £10,000 in 1826; founded St. Mary's hall, Brighton opened 1 Aug. 1836; author of *Psalms and Hymns* 1835, *fourteenth thousand* 1858 and of many sermons. d. 31 Brunswick sq. Brighton 24 Jany. 1865. *Life of Rev. H. V. Elliott by Josiah Bateman* 1868, *portrait.*

ELLIOTT, SAMUEL MACKENZIE. b. Inverness 9 April 1811; graduated at College of surgeons, Glasgow 1828; studied in Cincinnati and Philadelphia 1833–35; an oculist in New York 1835–74 where he gained a high reputation; lieut. col. of 79 regiment of New York volunteers in civil war 1861; raised the Highland brigade; author of *The U.S. Highland Brigade, New York* 1861. d. New Brighton, Staten Island, New York 1 May 1873.

ELLIOTT, SIR WILLIAM HENRY (*younger son of John Elliott, captain R.N.) b.* Elliott house near Ripon 1792; ensign 51 foot 6 Dec. 1809, lieut. col. 27 June 1838 to 13 Feb. 1855 when placed on h.p.; commanded Madras brigade in second Burmese war 1852–53; commandant at Rangoon 1853–55; col. of 55 foot 15 Nov. 1861, of 51 foot 1 June 1862 to death; general 25 Oct. 1871; K.H. 19 July 1837; K.C.B. 10 Nov. 1862, G.C.B. 24 May 1873. d. 20 Cambridge sq. Hyde park, London 27 March 1874. *I.L.N. lxiv,* 331 (1874).

ELLIS, REV. ARTHUR AYRES (*son of Charles Ellis of Birmingham). b.* Birmingham 1830; ed. at Trin. coll. Cam., B.A. 1852, M.A. 1855, fell. of his coll. 1854; senior classical master Liverpool coll. 1853–57; junior dean of Trin. coll. Cam. and divinity lecturer in Ch. coll. Cam. 1859–60; V. of Stotfold, Beds. 1860 to death; published *Bentleii Critica Sacra* 1862. d. 22 March 1887.

ELLIS, SIR BARROW HELBERT (*son of S. Helbert Ellis of London). b.* London 24 Jany. 1823; ed. at Univ. coll. school and Haileybury; matric. at Univ. of London 1839; entered Bombay civil service 26 July 1843; assistant comr. in Sind 1851–55; ordinary member of Bombay council 1865, member of governor general's council 2 May 1870 to 27 April 1875; member of council of secretary of state, July 1875 to 1885; K.C.S.I. 5 Oct. 1875; vice pres. of Jews' college, London where there is a portrait of him; edited G Stack's *Dictionary of Sindhi and English*, Bombay 1855. d. Evian-les-Bains, Savoy 20 June 1887. *bur.* Jewish cemetery, Willesden, Middlesex 28 June. *Journal of Royal Asiatic Soc. xix,* 688–90 (1887).

ELLIS, CHARLES WILLATS (*eld. son of Rev. Thomas Ellis, V. of Great Milton, Oxon.*) Ed. at Westminster; matric. from Ch. Ch. Ox. 22 Oct. 1807 aged 17; B.A. 1811, M.A. 1814; barrister L.I. 21 Nov. 1817; published *A treatise on the pleadings in suits for tithes in equity* 1821; *A treatise on the law of debtor and creditor* 1822; *The clergyman's assistant* ed. by C. Ellis 1822, new ed. 1828; *A collection of acts and records of parliament by Sir H. Gwillim*, second ed. with notes by C. Ellis 1825; *The law of fire and life insurance and annuities* 1832, second ed. 1846. *d.* 42 Kensington sq. London 17 July 1868.

ELLIS, EDWARD SHIPLEY (*eld. son of John Ellis 1789-1862*). *b.* 1817; chairman of Midland railway company, May 1873 to death. *d.* The Newark, Leicester 3 Dec. 1879.

ELLIS, EDWIN. Solo violinist at Cremorne Gardens, London 1841; member of orchestra of Princess's theatre; member of orchestra at Adelphi theatre 1860, conductor 1867 to death; published selections from Flotow's Alessandro Stradella, Thomas's Le Caid and Offenbach's La Belle Hélène and a few songs. *d.* St. Thomas's hospital, London 25 Oct. 1878 aged 35.

ELLIS, GEORGE CRESSALL. Director of Her Majesty's dramatic performances at Windsor castle many years. *d.* Park road east, West Brompton, London 23 June 1875 in 66 year.

ELLIS, SIR HENRY. *b.* 1777; private sec. to pres. of Bengal board of control at Calcutta 1812-14; minister plenipotentiary ad interim in Persia 18 April 1814 to 1815; clerk of the Pells 1825-1834 when office was abolished; comr. of board of control 6 Dec. 1830 to 20 Dec. 1834; P.C. 11 July 1832; a comr. for affairs of India 13 Dec. 1832; ambassador to Persia 1 July 1835 to Nov. 1836; sent on an extraordinary and special mission to the Brazils 20 Sep. 1842; K.C.B. 27 April 1848; F.R.S. 11 June 1819, F.G.S.; author of *Journal of the proceedings of the late embassy to China* 1817. *d.* Brighton 28 Sep. 1855.

ELLIS, SIR HENRY (*younger son of John Ellis, master of the free school in Primrose st. Bishopsgate st. London, who d. 1812*). *b.* Primrose st. 29 Nov. 1779; ed. at Merchant Taylor's school and St. John's coll. Ox., fellow 1802-5; B.C.L. 1802; assistant librarian at Bodleian library 1797-1800; temporary assistant in British Museum library 1800, assistant keeper of printed books 1805, keeper 1806-12, keeper of the manuscripts 1812-27, secretary 1814-27, principal librarian 20 Dec. 1827 to Feb.

ELLIS, SIR H. (*Con.*)
1856; F.S.A. 15 Jany. 1807, one of the secs. 1813 to 1 Dec. 1853, director 1 Dec. 1853 to 7 Dec. 1857; F.R.S. 30 May 1811; K.H. 21 July 1832; knighted at St. James's palace 22 Feb. 1833; author of *History of the parish of Saint Leonard, Shoreditch* 1798; edited *Original letters illustrative of English history* 3 series 1824, 1827, 1846 and other books. *d.* 24 Bedford sq. London 15 Jany. 1869. *Fagan's Life of Panizzi* i, 142-43 (1880), *portrait; Cowtan's Memories of the British Museum* (1872) 230-32; *Proc. of Soc. of Antiq.* 2 series iv, 303-305 (1869); *I.L.N.* liv, 99, 141 (1869), *portrait..*

ELLIS, JAMES. Managed Cremorne gardens, London 1845-51; arrived in Melbourne, Oct. 1852; established Salle Valentino there also Cremorne gardens. *d.* Melbourne 9 Jany. 1874 in 62 year. *Era 22 March 1874 p. 7, col. 4.*

ELLIS, JOHN (*eld. son of Joseph Ellis of Sharman's lodge near Leicester, farmer*). *b.* Frisk house near Leicester 1789; farmer at Beaumont Leyes near Leicester 1807-47; founded at Leicester firm of Ellis, Everington and Co. 1826; projected the third line of railway in England namely from Swannington to Bagworth, opened July 1832; M.P. for Leicester 1848-52; chairman of Midland railway company 1849-58. *d.* Belgrave near Leicester 26 Oct. 1862. *Charlotte Ellis's Sketch of one branch of the Ellis family, privately printed; The Midland railway by F. S. Williams* (1876) 166-68.

ELLIS, REV. ROBERT. *b.* Tyn-y-meini, Denbighshire 3 Feb. 1810; began preaching 5 Oct. 1834; baptist minister at Llanelian 1837, at Sirhowy, Monmouthshire 1847, at Carnarvon 1862-75; author of *Lectures on Baptism* 1841; *The principles of Biblical Exegesis* 1854; *Memoir of John Williams* 1871 and other books. *d.* Gartheryr 20 Aug. 1875. *Rev. J. S. James's Biography of Rev. R. Ellis* 1877.

ELLIS, REV. ROBERT. Member of St. John's coll. Cam. 9 April 1836, scholar 5 Nov. 1839, fellow 30 March 1841 to 2 April 1872; fifth wrangler 1840; B.A. 1840, M.A. 1843; B.D. 1850; chiefly known by his controversy with W. J. Law on route followed by Hannibal over the Alps; author of *A Treatise on Hannibal's passage of the Alps* 1853; *Contributions to the ethnography of Italy and Greece* 1858; *The Armenian origin of the Etruscans* 1861 and 6 other books. *d.* 3 Higher Summerlands, Exeter 20 Dec. 1885 aged 65. *The Eagle the St. John's college magazine* (1886).

ELLIS, ROBERT LESLIE (*youngest child of Francis Ellis of Bath*). *b.* Bath 25 Aug. 1817; pensioner of Trin. coll. Cam. Oct. 1836, senior wrangler 1840; B.A. 1840, M.A. 1843; fell. of his coll. Oct. 1840 to 1849; edited *Cambridge mathematical journal*; seized with rheumatic fever at S. Remo 1849. *d.* Anstey hall, Trumpington 12 May 1859. *The mathematical and other writings of R. L. Ellis, edited by W. Walton, with a biographical memoir by Very Rev. H. Goodwin* (1863) *pp. ix-xxxvi, portrait.*

ELLIS, ROBERT STAUNTON. Entered Madras civil service 1844; member of council Madras 1875 to 16 March 1877; member of India office council 1877 to death; C.B. 21 April 1875; found dead in his bed at 141 Gloucester road, Kensington, London 9 Oct. 1877 aged 52.

ELLIS, SIR SAMUEL BURDON (*son of Charles Ellis, captain R.N.*) *b.* 1787; 2 lieut. R.M. 1 Jany. 1804; commanded Chatham division of R.M. 1851-1855; col. of Portsmouth division 28 March 1863 to death; general 1862; C.B. 1841, K.C.B. 18 May 1860. *d.* Old Charlton, Kent 10 March 1865. *Memoirs and services of Sir S. B. Ellis, edited by Lady Ellis* 1866.

ELLIS, SARAH (*dau. of William Stickney of Ridgmont near Hull, farmer, who d. 9 July 1848 aged 84*). *b.* 1812; brought up as a Quaker, but became a Congregationalist 1837; author of *Pictures of private life, 3 series 3 vols.* 1833-37; *The poetry of life 2 vols.* 1835; *Home, or the iron rule, a story 3 vols.* 1836; *The women of England, their social duties and domestic habits* 1839, more than 20 eds.; *The sons of the soil, a poem* 1839; *Family Secrets, or hints to those who would make home happy 3 vols.* 1841 and numerous other books. (*m.* 1837 William Ellis 1794-1872). *d.* Rose Hill, Hoddesdon, Herts. 16 June 1872. *Fisher's Drawing Room scrap book* 1844-5, *portrait; S. Ellis's Self Deception vol. i, portrait.*

ELLIS, SYDNEY (*youngest son of Edward Shipley Ellis 1817-79*). *b.* Leicester 12 Dec. 1850; educ. at Brighton and at Tottenham; member of a firm of worsted spinners; lectured to his work people on physical and natural science; took great interest in chemistry, geology and anthropology; member of British Assoc. 1874 and of Literary and Philosophical Soc. of Leicester; author of *Leila Marston, a tale* 1861. *d.* from accidentally inhaling poisonous gas while investigating the composition of ferro-prussiate of potash 26 Oct. 1877, left legacies of £1000 each to Anthropological Instit., the Royal, Chemical and Geological societies. *Journal of Anthropological Institute ix, 441-42 (1880).*

ELLIS, THOMAS FLOWER. *b.* 1796; ed. at Trin. coll. Cam., fellow; B.A. 1818; barrister L.I. 6 Feb. 1824; Q.C. within county palatine of Lancaster; a municipal corporation comr. 1831; recorder of Leeds, May 1839 to death; attorney general of Duchy of Lancaster to death; edited with J. L. Adolphus *Reports in court of King's Bench 12 vols.* 1835-42 and *Queen's Bench reports, new series, 18 vols.* 1842-56; with Colin Blackburn *Reports in court of Queen's Bench 8 vols.* 1852-58; with C. Blackburn and F. Ellis *Reports in court of Queen's Bench* 1858; with F. Ellis *Reports in court of Queen's Bench 3 vols.* 1858-61; acted as Lord Macaulay's executor, and edited the posthumous vol. of his works. *d.* 15 Bedford place, Russell sq. London 5 April 1861. *Trevelyan's Life of Lord Macaulay* (1878) *i, 182, 253, 345, ii, 95, 220, 284; Pollock's Personal Remembrances i, 91, 100.*

ELLIS, REV. WILLIAM (*2 child of William Ellis of London*). *b.* Charles st. Long Acre, London 29 Aug. 1794; employed as a gardener at Wisbeach; removed to London 1811; missionary of the London missionary society in the South Sea Islands 1816-25; travelling agent at home 1825-31; foreign sec. of L.M.S. 1831-41; edited *The Christian Keepsake* an annual; pastor of Congregational church at Hoddesdon, Herts. 1847-52; missionary to Madagascar 1853, 1856 and 1861-65; author of *History of Madagascar 2 vols.* 1838; *Polynesian Researches 2 vols.* 1829, *second ed. 4 vols.* 1832-34, *another ed.* 1848, 4 vols. 1853 and other books. *d.* Rose hill, Hoddesdon 9 June 1872. *bur.* Abney park cemetery 14 June. *J. E. Ellis's Life of W. Ellis* 1873; *I.L.N. lx, 625, 630 (1872), portrait.*

ELLIS, WILLIAM (*son of Andrew Ellis De Vezian, an underwriter at Lloyds, London, who took name of Ellis about 1801*). *b.* Jany. 1800; assistant underwriter of Indemnity marine insurance company 1824, chief manager 1827; founded at his own expense five schools 1848-52, naming them Birkbeck after George Birkbeck; gave lectures to the royal children at Buckingham Palace; author of *Outlines of social economy* 1846; *Education as a means of preventing destitution* 1851; *Philo-Socrates* 1861 a series of papers, and other books. *d.* 6 Lancaster terrace, Regent's park, London 18 Feb. 1881. *Good Words, Aug.* 1881 *p. 543, portrait.*

ELLIS, REV. WILLIAM WEBB (*2 son of James Ellis of Manchester*). *b.* Nov. 1807; ed. at Rugby and Brasenose coll. Ox., B.A. 1829, M.A. 1831; C. of St. George's, Albemarle st. London 1836-55; R. of St. Clement Danes.

ELLIS, REV. W. W. (*Con.*)

Strand 1843–55 ; R. of Laver Magdalen, Essex 1855 to death ; author of *A concise view of prophecy which relates to the Messiah* 1832 ; *Sermons at St. George's* 1838 ; *Dangerous errors of Romanism* 1853. *d.* 24 Jany. 1872. *I.L.N. xxiv,* 400 (1854), *portrait.*

ELLIS, WYNN (*son of Thomas Ellis of Oundle, Northamptonshire*). *b.* Oundle, July 1790 ; hosier and mercer at 16 Ludgate st. City of London 1812, wholesale silk merchant 1830–71 latterly the largest in London ; M.P. for Leicester 1831–34 and 1839–47 ; sheriff of Herts. 1851–52. *d.* 30 Cadogan place, Sloane st. London 20 Nov. 1875. *bur.* at Whitstable, personalty sworn under £600,000, 8 Jany. 1876. *I.L.N. lxviii,* 35, 37, 38 (1876), *portrait.*

NOTE.—He bequeathed all his pictures by the old masters 402 in number to the National Gallery, but the trustees selected only 44 of them which have since been exhibited as the Wynn Ellis collection. Among his modern pictures was a portrait of the Duchess of Devonshire purchased by Thomas Agnew and Sons for £10,605 the largest sum ever obtained for a picture at public auction, after being exhibited for a short time at 39 B Old Bond st., it was on the night of 26 May 1876 cut out of the stretching frame and stolen.

ELLIS-MC.TAGGART, FRANCIS (*son of Thomas Flower Ellis* 1796–1861). *b.* 13 Dec. 1823 ; ed. at Trin. coll. Cam., B.A. 1846, M.A. 1849 ; barrister I.T. 4 May 1849 ; edited with T. F. Ellis and C. Blackburn *Reports in court of Queen's Bench* 1858 ; with T. F. Ellis *Reports in court of Queen's Bench* 3 vols. 1858–61 ; judge of circuit 34 (Lincolnshire and Northamptonshire) 4 May 1861 to Dec. 1871 ; judge of circuit 43 (Marylebone, London), Dec. 1871 to death ; assumed additional name of Mc Taggart 1868. *d.* 28 Norfolk sq. London 15 March 1872.

ELLIS-NANNEY, OWEN JONES. *b.* 1790 ; contested Carnarvon district 15 Dec. 1832, seated on petition 6 March 1833, unseated on counter petition 23 May 1833 ; contested Carnarvon district 12 Jany. 1835 ; sheriff of Carnarvon 1861. *d.* 27 Oct. 1870. *Perry and Knapp's Cases of controverted elections* (1833) 106–11, 435–61 ; *Cockburn and Rowe's Cases* (1833) 127–38, 550–60.

ELLISON, CUTHBERT EDWARD. Educ. at Trin. coll. Cam., B.A. 1840, M.A. 1843 ; barrister I.T. 31 Jany. 1845 ; stipendiary magistrate at Newcastle 25 Jany. 1854, at Manchester 4 May 1860, at Worship st. police court, London 14 June 1864, at Lambeth police court, Sep. 1870 to death. *d.* 7 Chester st. Grosvenor place, London 26 May 1883.

ELLISON, NATHANIEL (*son of Rev. Nathaniel Ellison, Incumbent of St. Andrew, Newcastle upon Tyne*). *b.* Newcastle 19 March 1786 ; ed. at Durham gr. sch. ; admitted commoner of Univ. coll. Ox. 18 Oct. 1802 ; B.A. 1806, M.A. 1810 ; fellow of Merton coll. 1807–23 ; barrister L.I. 22 Nov. 1811 ; one of comrs. of bankrupts in London ; comr. of court of bankruptcy at Newcastle upon Tyne 21 Oct. 1842 to death. *d.* Jesmond near Newcastle 12 Dec. 1861.

ELLISTON, HENRY TWISELTON (2 *son of Robert Wm. Elliston the comedian* 1774–1831). *b.* about 1801 ; established with his brother Wm. a library at Leamington, afterwards known as the County library ; erected the music hall in Bath st. Leamington, lessee of the royal assembly rooms, organist at the parish church to death, librarian of the free public library Sep. 1863 ; wrote four services. *d.* Leamington 19 April 1864 aged 63.

ELMES, JAMES (*son of Samuel Elmes*). *b.* London 15 Oct. 1782 ; ed. at Merchant Taylor's school ; exhibited 36 architectural designs at R.A. 1801–42 ; vice pres. of Royal Architectural Society 1809–48 ; surveyor of port of London 1809–48 ; edited *The Annals of the Fine Arts* 1816–20 ; author of *Hints for the improvement of prisons* 1817, 3 ed. 1829 ; *Lectures on Architecture* 1823 ; *Memoirs of Sir Christopher Wren* 1823, 2 ed. 1852 ; *The Arts and Artists* 3 vols. 1825 ; *Survey of the harbour and port of London* 1838. *d.* Greenwich 2 April 1862.

ELMORE, ALFRED. *b.* Clonakilty, co. Cork 18 June 1815 ; historical painter ; exhibited 72 pictures at R.A., 9 at B.I. and 9 at Suffolk st. gallery 1834–80 ; his picture 'Origin of the Guelph and Ghibelline quarrel' was sold in 1845 for £300 ; A.R.A. 1845, R.A. 1857. *d.* 1 St. Alban's road, Kensington, London 24 Jany. 1881. *Sandby's History of Royal Academy ii,* 302–4 (1862) ; *I.L.N. lxxviii,* 125, 126 (1881), *portrait ; Ottley's Dict. of painters* 1866 *p.* 61.

ELMSLEY, JOHN (*son of John Elmsley* 1762–1805, *speaker of legislative council of Lower Canada*). *b.* Elmsley house, Toronto 1801 ; entered British navy 1815, lieut. 1824 ; member of legislative council of Upper Canada until union of two provinces 1840 ; joined Church of Rome ; established House of Providence at Toronto, and the first Roman Catholic school in Upper Canada ; chief founder of College of St. Michael in Toronto. *d.* Toronto 8 Aug. 1863.

ELMSLEY, WILLIAM. *b.* 1797; ed. at Eton and Trin. coll. Cam., B.A. 1819, M.A. 1822; barrister M.T. 11 Nov. 1825; Q.C. 1851; bencher of his inn, Dec. 1851, treasurer and master of the library 1861; judge of county courts circuit 19 (Derbyshire) 16 April 1862 to death. *d.* Derby 20 Dec. 1866.

ELMSLIE, WILLIAM JACKSON (2 *child of James Elmslie*). *b.* Aberdeen 29 June 1832; a shoe-maker to 1848; at Aberdeen gram. sch. 1848, at King's coll. Aberdeen 1853, at Free ch. divinity coll. 1858; medical student in Edin-burgh 1862; M.R.C.S. 1864; medical missionary in Kashmir 1864 to death; author of *A vocabulary of the Kashmírí language* 1872. *d.* Goojerat 16 Nov. 1872. *Seed time in Kash-mir, a memoir of W. J. Elmslie* 1875, *portrait.*

ELPHINSTONE, JOHN, 13 Baron Elphinstone (*only son of* 12 *baron Elphinstone, who d.* 21 *May* 1813). *b.* Cumbernauld house, Dumbar-tonshire 23 June 1807; cornet royal horse guards 28 Jany. 1826, captain 4 Dec. 1832 to 21 Nov. 1836 when placed on h.p.; governor of Madras 6 March 1837 to 24 Sep. 1842; a lord in waiting to the Queen, Dec. 1847 to Feb. 1852 and Jany. to Oct. 1853; governor of Bombay Oct. 1853 to May 1860, took his seat 26 Dec. 1853; representative peer for Scotland; G.C.H.; P.C. 3 Aug. 1836; G.C.B. 31 March 1859; created baron of the U.K. as Baron Elphinstone of Elphinstone 21 May 1859. *d.* King st. St. James's, London 19 July 1860. *Kaye and Malleson's History of the Indian mutiny* (1888–89) i, 309 *etc.*

ELPHINSTONE, SIR JAMES DALRYMPLE HORN, 2 Baronet (*son of Sir Robert Elphinstone, 1 baronet* 1766–1848). *b.* Logie, Elphinstone, Aberdeenshire 20 Nov. 1805; captain in navy of H.E.I.Co.; M.P. for Portsmouth, April 1857 to July 1865 and Dec. 1868 to March 1880; a lord of the Treasury, Feb. 1874 to March 1880. *d.* Uplands, Bridgwater 26 Dec. 1886.

ELPHINSTONE, MOUNTSTUART (*youngest son of* 11 *baron Elphinstone* 1737–94). *b.* 6 Oct. 1779; went to Calcutta 1796; resident at Nagpur 1803–8; envoy to King of Caubool 13 Oct. 1808; political resident at Poona 1810–18; governor of Bombay 7 Oct. 1818 to 17 Jany. 1827 where a college bearing his name was founded; author of *An account of the king-dom of Caubul* 1815; *History of India* 2 vols. 1841, 5 *ed.* 1866 and other books. *d.* Hook-ward park near Limpsfield, Surrey 20 Nov. 1859. *Life of M. Elphinstone by Sir T. E. Colebrooke* 2 vols. 1884, 2 *portraits.*

ELSLEY, CHARLES HENEAGE (2 *son of Rev. Heneage Elsley* 1746–1833). *b.* 14 Aug. 1792; ed. at St. Peter's coll. Cam., B.A. 1813, M.A. 1816; barrister M.T. 29 Jany. 1819; a comr. of bankrupts for Whitby, Scarborough and Northallerton; clerk of the peace for west riding of Yorkshire 1827 to death; recorder of Richmond, Yorkshire 1827 to death, of York 1834 to death, of Scarborough 1836 to death; judge of county courts March 1847–1854 when he resigned; author of *Reports of Cases by Sir W. Blackstone, revised* 1828; *Essay on the relation between the English and French languages* 1858. *d.* York 3 Aug. 1865.

ELT, CHARLES HENRY. *b.* about 1805; a chartist; chairman of building act committee; member of Metropolitan Board of Works 1866 to death. *d.* 41 Gibson sq. Islington 20 May 1882.

ELTON, SIR ARTHUR HALLAM, 7 Baronet (3 *son of the succeeding*). *b.* Belle Vue place, Clifton 19 April 1818; lieut. 14 foot 1840–41 when he sold out; sheriff of Somerset 1857; M.P. for Bath 28 March 1857 to 23 April 1859; author of *Poems of past years* 1856; *Below the surface* 3 vols. 1857; *Herbert Chauncey, a novel* 3 vols. 1860. *d.* Clevedon court near Bristol 14 Oct. 1883. *I.L.N. xxx, 478* (1857), *portrait.*

ELTON, SIR CHARLES ABRAHAM, 6 Baronet (*eld. son of Rev. Sir Abraham Elton, 5 baronet* 1755–1842). *b.* Bristol 31 Oct. 1778; ed. at Eton; ensign 4 foot Nov. 1796, captain 1799–1802 when placed on h.p.; captain 48 foot 1803–4; retired July 1825; lieut.-col. 2 Somerset militia; author of *Poems* 1804; *Tales of romance with other poems* 1810; *The remains of Hesiod translated into English verse* 1815; *Specimen of the classic poets in a chronological series from Homer to Tryphiodorus translated into English verse* 3 vols. 1814; *A History of the Roman emperors* 1825. *d.* at house of his son-in-law Rev. E. D. Tinling at Bath 1 June 1853.

ELTON, JAMES FREDERIC (2 *son of Roberts W. Elton, lieut. col. Bengal army*). *b.* 3 Aug. 1840; entered Bengal army 1857; aide-de-camp to Sir Hugh Rose, commander in chief; captain 98 foot; served on staff of French army in Mexico 1866; vice consul at Zanzibar 15 Dec. 1874; consul for Portuguese possessions on east coast of Africa 8 March 1875 to death; F.R.G.S.; author of *With the French in Mexico* 1867. *d.* near Usekhe in Ugogo on an ex-ploring expedition to Lake Nyassa 19 Dec. 1877. *J. F. Elton's Travels and researches among the lakes and mountains of Eastern and Central Africa* 1879, *portrait.*

ELVEY, STEPHEN *(eld. son of John Elvey of Canterbury).* *b.* Canterbury, June 1805 ; lay clerk at Canterbury cathedral ; Mus. Bac. Ox. 1831, Mus. Doc. 1838 ; organist of New coll. Ox. 1830 to death ; organist of St. John's coll. Ox. 1856 to death ; deputy professor of music at Ox. to 1847 ; choragus in Univ. of Ox. 1848 to death ; published *The Oxford Psalm Book* 1852 ; *The Psalter printed for chanting upon a new principle* 1856 ; *The Canticles* 1858. *d.* Oxford 6 Oct. 1860.

ELY, JOHN HENRY LOFTUS, 3 Marquis of *(eld. son of 2 Marquis of Ely* 1770-1845). *b.* Hill st. Berkeley sq. London 19 Jany. 1814 ; contested Gloucester 29 July 1841 ; M.P. for Woodstock 1 May 1845 to 26 Sep. 1845 when he succeeded. *d.* 63 Eaton place, London 15 July 1857.

EMDEN. WILLIAM SAMUEL. Prompter at Covent Garden theatre under Madame Vestris 1839, subsequently acting manager ; partner with F. Robson at Olympic theatre 1857-64 ; acting manager of St. James's theatre ; treasurer of Covent Garden theatrical fund 1869 to death ; wrote *The evil May Day, The head of the family, Lives labyrinth* and *The rear admiral*, printed in Duncombe and Lacy's plays. *d.* 18 Upper park road, Haverstock hill, London 4 Jany. 1872 aged 71.

EMERY, SAMUEL ANDERSON *(son of John Emery, actor* 1777-1822). *b.* Hyde st. Bloomsbury, London 10 Sep. 1817 ; first appeared on the stage at Fitzroy theatre, May 1834 as Dan in *John Bull ;* played at Lyceum 1843 and 1844-47 ; stage manager at Surrey theatre 1848-9 ; played at Drury Lane 1850 ; the original Fouché in Tom Taylor's *Plot and Passion* at Olympic 17 Oct. 1853 ; manager of Marylebone theatre 1857-58 ; first appeared in America 30 March 1863, at Barnum's Old Museum, New York ; returned to England, Sep. 1863 ; played at nearly all the west end theatres ; played in Australia 1880-81. *d.* 3 King William st. Strand, London 19 July 1881. *Tallis's Drawing room table book* (1851) 45-6, *portrait ; Theatre n.s. iii,* 70-2 (1884) ; *Theatrical Times ii,* 57 (1847), *portrait ; Touchstone* 13 *July* 1878 *p.* 3, *portrait ; Illust. sp. and dr. news, xv,* 464 (1881), *portrait.*

EMMETT, ANTHONY. Educ. at Woolwich ; 2 lieut. R.E. 16 Feb. 1808, col. 11 Nov. 1851 to 21 May 1855 when placed on retired full pay as M.G. ; served in Peninsula 1809-12 ; held various commands at St. Helena 1815-21, at Bermuda and in the Mediterranean. *d.* Brighton 27 March 1872.

EMMETT, ROBERT *(son of Thomas Addis Emmett, Irish patriot* 1764-1827). *b.* Ireland about 1792 ; went to New York with his father 1804, admitted to New York bar ; a justice of state superior court ; one of the directory formed in New York for purpose of aiding contemplated Irish insurrection of 1848. *d.* New Rochelle, New York 15 Feb. 1873.

EMPSON, WILLIAM. Educ. at Winchester and Trin. coll. Cam., B.A. 1812, M.A. 1815 ; began to contribute to *Edinburgh Review* 1823, wrote more than 60 articles upon law, politics and literary topics 1823-49, editor Feb. 1847 to death ; professor of general polity and the laws of England in Haileybury college near Hertford 2 July 1824 to death. *d.* Haileybury 10 Dec. 1852 aged 62. *Cockburn's Life of Lord Jeffrey* (1852) *i,* 374, *ii,* 232, 310 *etc. ; Selections from the correspondence of Macvey Napier* (1879) *pp.* 62, 547.

ENFIELD, EDWARD (3 *son of Henry Enfield, town clerk of Nottingham). b.* Nottingham 15 May 1811 ; one of the moneyers of the Mint, London to 1851 when he retired on pension ; member of council of University college, London, and of its committee of management 1858 to death ; chairman of committee of management and treasurer of University college hospital 1867 to death ; pres. of senate of the college 1878 to death ; pres. of Manchester New college, London to death. *d.* 19 Chester terrace, Regents park, London 21 April 1880. *N. H. Nixon's North London hospital, a history* (1882) 40 ; *In Memoriam, Edward Enfield* 1880.

ENGEL, CARL. *b.* Hanover 1818 ; author of *Pianist's Handbook* 1853 ; *The music of the most ancient nations* 1864 ; *Musical myths and facts* 2 *vols.* 1876 ; hanged himself at 54 Addison road, Kensington, London 17 Nov. 1882.

ENGLAND, POOLE VALLANCEY. Second lieut. R.A. 10 May 1805, col. 17 Feb. 1854, col. commandant 27 Feb. 1866 to 1 Oct. 1877 when placed on retired list ; general 29 March 1873. *d.* 41 Marine parade, Dover 6 Nov. 1884 in 97 year.

ENGLAND, SIR RICHARD *(son of lieut. general Richard England of Lifford near Ennis, co. Clare). b.* Detroit, Upper Canada 13 May 1793 ; ed. at Winchester and Marlow ; ensign 5 foot 25 Feb. 1808 ; lieut. col. 75 foot 6 July 1826 to 7 July 1837 ; lieut. col. 4 foot 7 July 1837 to 10 July 1837 ; lieut. col. 41 foot 10 July 1837 to 22 July 1845 ; brigadier general Madras 5 Feb. 1839 to Oct. 1840 ; commanded third division in Crimea 21 Feb.

1854 to 17 Aug. 1855; col. of 50 foot 20 Sep. 1854 to 20 April 1861; major general division Curragh 15 Aug. 1856 to 31 March 1859; col. 41 foot 20 April 1861 to death; general 6 July 1863; placed on retired list 1 Oct. 1877; K.H. 1835; K.C.B. 27 Sep. 1843, G.C.B. 5 July 1855; grand officer of legion of honour 1856. *d.* St. Margaret's, Titchfield, Hants. 19 Jany. 1883. *Once a week, xxvii, 7, 39, 53 (1872); Nolan's Russian War, ii, 405, portrait.*

ENGLISH, HENRY. *b.* 1803; proprietor and editor of *The Mining Journal* 1835 to death; edited *The quarterly mining review* 4 vols. 1830–37; F.R.G.S.; author of *A compendium of information relating to companies formed for working British mines* 1826; *A Glossary of mining terms used in Mexico, Columbia, Peru and other parts of South America, also those used in the mining districts of Cornwall and Derbyshire* 1830; *The mining almanack* 3 vols. 1849–51. *d.* Islington, London 28 April 1855.

ENNIS, SIR JOHN, 1 Baronet *(only son of John Ennis of Ballinahowen court near Athlone, who d. 31 March 1834).* *b.* Dublin 15 Aug. 1800; ed. at Stonyhurst college; merchant in Dublin; sheriff of Westmeath 1837, of co. Dublin 1849; contested Athlone, April 1856, M.P. for Athlone, April 1857 to July 1865; a comr. of charitable bequests to death; governor of Bank of Ireland to death; created baronet 27 July 1866. *d.* 9 Merrion sq. east, Dublin 8 Aug. 1878.

ENNIS, SIR JOHN JAMES, 2 Baronet *(eld. son of the preceding).* *b.* 6 April 1842; ed. at Oscott and Ch. Ch. Ox.; sheriff of Westmeath 1866; M.P. for Athlone 1868–74 and 1880 to death. *d.* Curzon st. Mayfair, London 28 May 1884.

ENNISKILLEN, WILLIAM WILLOUGHBY COLE, 3 Earl of *(eld. son of 2 Earl of Enniskillen 1768–1840).* *b.* Dover st. Piccadilly, London 25 Jany. 1807; M.P. for Fermanagh 1831 to 31 March 1840 when he succeeded his father as 3 earl of Enniskillen and 2 baron Grinstead; hon. col. Fermanagh militia 1875 to death; F.R.S. 15 Jany. 1829; F.G.S. *d.* Florence court, Fermanagh 12 Nov. 1886.

EPPS, ELLEN *(dau. of John Frederick Elliott).* *b.* 1809; author of *Labour and live, a story* 1848, anon.; *Practical Observations on health and long life* 1855; *Blenham, a story, By the author of Labour and live* 1858; *Living among the dead, a story, By the author of Blenham* 1860. *(m.* 24 Aug. 1831 John Epps 1805–69), she *d.* 7 July 1876.

EPPS, GEORGE NAPOLEON *(son of John Epps of Ashford, Kent, who d.* 1835). *b.* 22 July 1815; pupil and assistant of his brother John Epps; M.R.C.S. 1845; surgeon to Homœopathic hospital in Hanover sq. London 1845; very successful in treating spinal curvatures and deformities; author of *Spinal curvature, its theory, its cure* 1849; *On deformities of the Spine and on Club Foot* 1859. *d.* 28 May 1874.

EPPS, JOHN *(half-brother of the preceding).* *b.* Blackheath, Kent 15 Feb. 1805; ed. at Mill Hill school and Univ. of Edin., M.D. 1826; practised in London 1827 to death, latterly as a homœopath; lecturer on materia medica at Homœopathic hospital 1851; joint editor of the *London Medical and Surgical Journal* 1828–9; published *The Christian physician and Anthropological magazine* 1835–9; edited *Journal of health and disease* 1845–52; *Notes of a new truth* 1856–69; contested Northampton as a Chartist 30 July 1847; author of *The Devil* 1842, anon.; *Constipation, its theory and cure* 1854; *Consumption, its nature and treatment* 1859. *d.* 89 Great Russell st. Bloomsbury, London 12 Feb. 1869. *Diary of the late John Epps, edited by Mrs. Epps* 1875; *J. F. Clarke's Autobiographical Recollections* (1874) 137–40.

ERCK, JOHN CAILLARD. Ecclesiastical comr. for Ireland; author of *The Irish ecclesiastical register for the year 1817 By J. C. E. Dublin* 1817; *Records of patent rolls of Chancery, Ireland* 2 vols. 1847–50. *d.* Dublin 2 June 1851.

ERLE, PETER *(4 son of Rev. Christopher Erle of Gillingham, Dorset).* *b.* 1795; ed. at New college, Ox., fellow 1812–25, B.A. 1816, M.A. 1821; barrister M.T. 1 June 1821; chief charity estate comr. 24 Oct. 1853 to 1872; Q.C. 10 July 1854; bencher of his inn 22 Nov. 1854, treasurer 1864; P.C. 27 Nov. 1872. *d.* 12 Park crescent, Regent's park, London 29 Jany. 1877.

ERLE, SIR WILLIAM *(brother of the preceding).* *b.* Fifehead-Magdalene, Dorset 1 Oct. 1793; ed. at Winchester and New coll. Ox.; B.C.L. 1818, D.C.L. 1857; fellow of his college 1811–34, hon. fellow 1870 to death; barrister M.T. 26 Nov. 1819; admitted barrister at I.T. 11 June 1822, bencher 18 Nov. 1834, reader 1843, treasurer 1844; K.C. 1834; M.P. for city of Oxford 26 July 1837 to 23 June 1841; counsel for Bank of England 1844; serjeant-at-law 7 Nov. 1844; justice of Court of Common Pleas 6 Nov. 1844; transferred to Court of Queen's Bench, Oct. 1846;

chief justice of Court of Common Pleas 24
June 1859 to 26 Nov. 1866; knighted 23
April 1845; P.C. 6 July 1859; F.R.S. 22
Nov. 1860; member of Trades Union com-
mission 1867–8; author of *The law relating to
Trades Unions* 1869. *d.* Bramshott Grange
near Liphook, Hants. 28 Jany. 1880. *I.L.N.
lxxvi*, 157 (1880), *portrait*.

ERLE-DRAX, JOHN SAMUEL WANLEY SAW-
BRIDGE- *(eld. son of Samuel Elias Sawbridge of
Olantigh tower, Ashford, Kent).* *b.* 6 Oct. 1800;
captain in East Kent militia 35 years; maintained a troop of yeomanry known as the Char-
borough troop; assumed name of Erle-Drax
1828; M.P. for Wareham 1841–57, 1859–65
and 1868–80; contested Wareham 1857 and
1865. *d.* Holnest park, Sherborne 5 Jany.
1887. *The book of sports ii*, 61 (1843), *portrait;
New sporting mag. xiii*, 262 (1837), *portrait*.

ERRINGTON, MOST REV. GEORGE (2 *son of
Thomas Errington of Clintz near Richmond, Yorkshire).* *b.* Clintz 14 Sep. 1804; ed. at Ushaw
1814–21 and English college, Rome 1821–24;
sub-deacon 1825, deacon 1826, priest 22 Dec.
1827; D.D. cum præmio 1827; vice rector of
English college, Rome 29 May 1832 to 1843;
travelled in France and Spain 1832–40; presided over the studies in St. Mary's coll. Oscott
1843–47; employed at Liverpool and Salford
1848–51; bishop of newly created see of Plymouth 27 June 1851 to March 1855; consecrated in church of St. John, Salford by Abp.
Wiseman 25 July 1851; coadjutor to Cardinal
Wiseman with title of Archbishop of Trebizond
in partibus March 1855 to 2 July 1862;
administrator of diocese of Clifton, Oct. 1855
to Feb. 1857; assistant at pontifical throne
5 Dec. 1869; held charge of missions in Isle
of Man 1865–8; undertook tuition of young
theological students at St. Paul's college, Prior
Park, Bath, Oct. 1870 to death; author of
*Four lectures on the hierarchy of the Catholic
Church* 1850; *The Irish land question* 1880. *d.*
Prior Park 19 Jany. 1886. *M. Brady's Episcopal Succession, iii*, 376, 436, 437, 473 (1877).

ERRINGTON, JOHN EDWARD *(eld. son of John
Errington).* *b.* Hull 29 Dec. 1806; a resident
engineer on Grand Junction railway to 1837;
joint engineer with Joseph Locke of Lancaster
and Carlisle railway 1843; constructed Caledonian railway 1848; engineer to London and
South Western railway 1856–60; A.I.C.E.
1831, M.I.C.E. 22 Jany. 1839, mem. of council
1850, vice pres. 1861–62. *d.* 6 Pall Mall east,
London 4 July 1862. *Min. of proc. of Instit.
of C.E. xxii*, 626–29 (1863).

ERSKINE, DAVID MONTAGU ERSKINE, 2 Baron
(eld. son of 1 Baron Erskine 1750–1823). Ed.
at Trin. coll. Cam., M.A. 1797, LLD. 1811;
barrister L.I. 20 Nov. 1802; M.P. for Portsmouth 19 Feb. to July 1806; min. plenipo.
to United States, July 1806 to 1809, at Stuttgard 1825–28; ambassador at Munich, Feb.
1828 to Nov. 1843 when he retired on pension. *d.* Butler's Green near Lewes 19 March
1855 aged 79.

ERSKINE, EDWARD MORRIS (4 *son of the preceding).* *b.* Brighton 28 March 1817; attaché
at Munich 25 Sep. 1835; envoy extraordinary
and minister plenipotentiary at Athens 7 May
1864 to 24 July 1872, at Stockholm 24 July
1872 to 1 May 1881 when he retired on a
pension; C.B. 25 Feb. 1873. *d.* Neville house,
Twickenham 19 April 1883.

ERSKINE, VERY REV. HENRY DAVID (2 *son of
1 Baron Erskine 1750–1823).* Ed. at Univ.
of Edin. and Trin. coll. Cam., M.A. Cam.
1809; D.D. Columbia coll. New York 1852;
R. of Swithland, Leics. 1817–41; R. of Kirby
Underdale, Yorkshire 1840 to death; preb.
of York cath. 28 Oct. 1845, dean of Ripon 23
Sep. 1847 to death. *d.* Ripon 27 July 1859
aged 72.

ERSKINE, JOHN ELPHINSTONE *(son of David
Erskine of Cardross, Stirling).* *b.* 13 July 1806;
entered navy 1819; captain 28 June 1838;
M.P. for Stirlingshire, July 1865 to 26 Jany.
1874; R.A. 4 Nov. 1857; commanded a
division of Channel Squadron 1859–61, admiral
10 Sep. 1869; author of *A short account of the
discoveries of gold in Australia* 1851; *Journal
of a cruise among the islands of the Western
Pacific* 1853. *d.* 1 Albany, Piccadilly, London
23 June 1887.

ERSKINE, THOMAS (3 *son of 1 Baron Erskine
1750–1823).* *b.* 10 Serjeant's Inn, Fleet st.
London 12 March 1788; ed. at Harrow;
entered at Trin. coll. Cam., M.A. as a peer's
son without residence or examination 1811;
secretary of presentations 1806; practised as
special pleader 1810–13; barrister L.I. 20 May
1813; K.C. Nov. 1827; chief judge of Court
of Review in Bankruptcy 2 Dec. 1831 to Nov.
1842; P.C. 1831; a judge of Court of Common
Pleas 9 Jany. 1839 to Nov. 1844; pres. of
Trinitarian Bible Society 1840. *d.* Bournemouth 9 Nov. 1864.

ERSKINE, THOMAS *(youngest son of David
Erskine of Linlathen, Forfarshire, who d. 5 April
1791).* *b.* Edinburgh 13 Oct. 1788; an advocate in Edin. 1810–16; a friend of Dr. Chalmers and Thomas Carlyle; author of *Remarks*

on the internal evidence of the truth of revealed
religion 1820, 10 ed. 1878; *An essay on faith*
1822; *The unconditional freeness of the Gospel*
1828; *The doctrine of election and its connection
with Christianity* 1837, 2 ed. 1878 and 8 other
books. *d.* Edinburgh 20 March 1870. *Letters
of Thomas Erskine of Linlathen edited by W.
Hanna* 1878.

ESCOTT, BICKHAM SWEET. *b.* 1802; barrister
M.T. 17 June 1825; M.P. for Winchester
1841–47; contested West Somerset at general
elections of 1832, 1835 and 1847; author of
A letter on the reform question 1831 and other
works on same subject. *d.* Hartrow manor,
Somerset 4 Nov. 1853.

ESDAILE, JAMES. *b.* Montrose 6 Feb. 1808;
ed. at Univ. of Edin., M.D. 1830; assistant
surgeon Bengal army 1831; presidency surgeon at Calcutta 1848, marine surgeon 1850
to 1 June 1851; began practising mesmerism
1845; author of *Letters from the Red Sea,
Egypt and the Continent, Calcutta* 1839; *Mesmerism in India and its practical application in
surgery and medicine* 1846; *Natural and mesmeric clairvoyance with the practical application
of mesmerism in surgery and medicine* 1852
and other books. *d.* Elm bank, Lawrie road,
Sydenham 10 Jany. 1859.

ESMONDE, SIR JOHN, 9 or 10 Baronet. *b.*
Kilmanock, co. Wexford 16 May 1826; ed.
at Clongowes Wood and Trin. coll. Dublin;
called to Irish bar 1850; M.P. for co. Waterford 1852 to death; sheriff of Wexford 1866,
of Wicklow 1875. *d.* 9 Dec. 1876.

ESMONDE, SIR THOMAS, 8 or 9 Baronet. *b.*
10 Dec. 1786; succeeded his uncle 19 Dec.
1803; M.P. for Wexford 1841–47; P.C. Ireland 1847. *d.* 31 Dec. 1868.

ESPINASSE, JAMES (*only son of Isaac Espinasse
of Bexley, Kent, who d. 14 Feb. 1834 aged 76*).
b. 1798; ed. at Balliol coll. Ox., B.A. 1820;
barrister G.I. 27 June 1827; recorder of
Rochester 1842 to death; judge of county
courts, circuit 49 (West Kent), March 1847
to death; author of *A treatise on the law of
bankrupts* 1823. *d.* The college, Maidstone 16
March 1867.

ESSEX, CATHARINE CAPEL-CONINGSBY, Countess of (*dau. of Edward Stephens of London,
carver and gilder*). *b.* London 18 Sep. 1791;
sang under name of Miss Young at many
concerts in the provinces; sang in Italian
opera at the Pantheon, London 1812 as Cath-

arine Stephens; first appeared at Covent
Garden as Mandane in Arne's opera *Artaxerxes*
Sep. 1813; played Polly in *The Beggar's Opera*
and Clara in *The Duenna;* sang at Drury Lane
1822–26; sang at concerts and in oratorios;
one of the finest soprano singers; her voice
reached to the high D; retired from the
stage 1831. (*m.* 19 April 1838 George
Capel-Coningsby 5 Earl of Essex 1757–1839),
she *d.* 9 Belgrave sq. London 22 Feb. 1882,
mural monument erected in Watford church,
Herts. March 1885. *Oxberry's Dramatic Biography ii,* 123–36 (1825), *portrait; Mrs. C. B.
Wilson's Our Actresses i,* 276–87 (1844), *portrait;
E. C. Clayton's Queens of song ii,* 33–44 (1865);
Theatrical Inquisitor iii, 259–61 (1813), *portrait;
Musical Gem* (1832), 2–3, *portrait.*

ESSEX, WILLIAM. Enamel painter; sole exponent of the art after death of H. P. Bone
1855; painted many miniature copies of pictures by Correggio, Guido, Wilkie and others;
exhibited 109 enamels at R.A., 20 at B.I. and
17 at Suffolk st. gallery 1818–64; enamel
painter to the Queen 1839 to death; a private
exhibition of his works was held in 1839, of
which a catalogue was printed. *d.* Brighton
29 Dec. 1869 aged 85.

ESTCOURT, REV. EDGAR EDMUND (*eld. son of
Rev. Edmund William Estcourt of Newnton,
Wilts.*) *b.* 7 Feb. 1816; ed. at Ex. coll. Ox.,
B.A. 1838, M.A. 1840; C. of Cirencester,
Gloucs. 1842–45; received into Church of
Rome at Prior Park, Dec. 1845; ordained
priest 1848; œconomus of diocese of Birmingham 1850; canon of St. Chad's cathedral,
Birmingham to death; author of *The dogmatic
teaching of the Book of Common Prayer on the
subject of the Holy Eucharist* 1868; *The question
of Anglican orders discussed* 1873; *The memoir
of Jane Dormer, Duchess of Feria, edited by Rev.
J. Stevenson* 1887. *d.* Leamington 16 April
1884. *bur.* Kenilworth.

ESTCOURT, JAMES BUCKNALL (2 *son of the
succeeding*). *b.* Edward st. Portman sq. London
12 July 1802; ed. at Harrow; ensign 44 foot
13 July 1820, second in command in Euphrates valley expedition 1834–36; major 43 foot
21 Oct. 1836 to 25 Aug. 1843 when placed on
h.p.; adjutant general in the Crimea 21 Feb.
1854 to death; granted distinguished service
reward 25 Oct. 1854; M.G. 12 Dec. 1854;
M.P. for Devizes 1848–52; named a K.C.B.
in London Gazette 10 July 1855. *d.* of cholera
in camp before Sebastopol 23 June 1855.

ESTCOURT, THOMAS GRIMSTON BUCKNALL (eld. son of Thomas Estcourt of Estcourt, Gloucs. 1748–1818). b. 3 Aug. 1775; ed. at C.C. coll. Ox., M.A. 1796; hon. D.C.L. 1827; barrister L.I. 20 June 1820; recorder of Devizes; chairman of Wiltshire general quarter sessions to 1837; M.P. for Devizes 1805–26, for Univ. of Ox. 1826–47. d. Estcourt 26 July 1853.

ESTCOURT, THOMAS HENRY SUTTON SOTHERON (eld. son of the preceding). b. 4 April 1801; ed. at Harrow and Oriel coll. Ox.; B.A. 1823, M.A. 1826, D.C.L. 1857; M.P. for Marlborough 1829–1832, for Devizes 1835–1844, for North Wilts. 1844 to 1865; pres. of Poor law board 8 March 1858 to 9 March 1859; P.C. 1858; sec. of state for home department 3 March 1859 to June 1859. d. Estcourt 6 Jany. 1876. I.L.N. xxxii, 312 (1858), portrait, lxviii, 70, 76, 83, 287 (1876), portrait.

ESTLIN, JOHN BISHOP (son of John Prior Estlin of Bristol, schoolmaster 1747–1817). b. St. Michael's hill, Bristol 26 Dec. 1785; M.C.S. 1806, F.R.C.S. 1843; surgeon at Bristol 1808 to death, where he established a dispensary for treatment of diseases of the eye 1812 which he managed 1812–49; one of the chief ophthalmic surgeons; author of On prayer and divine aid 1825; Remarks on Mesmerism 1845. d. Park st. Bristol 10 June 1855. Memoir of J. B. Estlin By W. James 1855.

ETHERIDGE, MOST REV. JAMES. b. Redmarley, Worcs. 19 Oct. 1808; ed. at Stonyhurst coll.; ordained priest 1836; rector of Mount St. Mary's coll. 1842; minister at Hodder 1842; minister of St. Wilfred's, Preston 1855; bishop of Torona and vicar apostolic of British Guiana 1858 to death; consecrated by Cardinal Wiseman in London 17 Oct. 1858. d. on his passage from Barbadoes to Georgetown, Demerara 1 Jany. 1878.

ETHERIDGE, REV. JOHN WESLEY. b. Youngwoods near Newport, Isle of Wight 24 Feb. 1804; Wesleyan minister at Hull 1827, London 1829, in Cornwall 1833–37 and 1853 to death; Ph. D. Heidelberg 1847; a scholar in many languages; author of The Syrian churches, their history, liturgies and literature with translation of the Four Gospels from the Peschito 1846; The Life of Dr. Adam Clarke 1858; The Life of Dr. Thomas Coke 1860 and other books. d. Camborne 24 May 1866. Rev. T. Smith's Memoirs of Rev. J. W. Etheridge 1871.

ETWALL, RALPH. b. in or near Andover 1804; M.P. for Andover 1831–47; kept a racing

ETWALL, R. (Con.)
stud 1832 to about 1849; one of the best known coursers in south of England. d. Connaught st. Hyde Park, London 15 Dec. 1882. William Day's Reminiscences of the turf, 2 ed. 1886, pp. 241–46.

EUING, WILLIAM. b. Partick near Glasgow 20 May 1788; ed. at Glasgow gr. sch. and univ.; an underwriter and insurance broker at Glasgow 1819; founded a music lectureship at Anderson's college, Glasgow by deed dated 1866; left his valuable musical library (of which a catalogue was printed) to Anderson's college, with £1000 for its maintenance. d. Glasgow 12 May 1874. T. Mason's Public and private libraries of Glasgow 1885 pp. 176–93, 437; Rev. C. Rogers's Leaves from my autobiography (1876) p. 331; Journal of British Archæol. Assoc. xxxi, 231–2 (1875).

EUSTACE, SIR JOHN ROWLAND (youngest son of Charles Eustace of Robertstown, co. Kildare). b. 1795; ed. at St. Peter's coll. Cam., B.A. 1816; captain Grenadier guards 5 July 1827 to 24 April 1840 when placed on h.p.; L.G. 2 April 1859; knighted 1816; K.H. 1835; sheriff of Kildare 1848. d. Bouverie sq. Folkestone 7 Aug. 1864.

EUSTACE, SIR WILLIAM CORNWALLIS (brother of the preceding). Lieut. 32 foot 27 Sep. 1783; lieut. col. Chasseurs Britanniques 23 Aug. 1810 to 1814 when placed on h.p. regiment being disbanded; captain Grenadier guards 25 March 1818 to 18 May 1826 when placed on h.p.; col. 60 Rifles 7 April 1843 to death; general 20 June 1854; C.B. 4 June 1815; K.C.H. 1832. d. Sampford hall, Essex 9 Feb. 1855 aged 73.

EVANS, REV. ALFRED BOWEN. b. Finsbury sq. London 1816; C. of Enfield, Middlesex 1854–61; R. of St. Mary-le-Strand, London 1861 to death; a powerful and original preacher; D.D. by Abp. of Canterbury 1863; author of Dissent and its inconsistences 1841; Christianity in its homely aspects 2 vols. 1852–4; Lectures on the book of Job 1856 and 30 other books. d. 23 Gloucester crescent, Regent's park, London 6 Nov. 1878. Rev. C. M. Davies's Orthodox London (1874) 176–85.

EVANS, ANNE (dau. of the succeeding). b. 4 June 1820; resided at Britwell court near Burnham, then at Bosworth, afterwards at 16 Kensington sq. London; a friend of Thackeray and his daughters; poet and musican. d. 16 Kensington sq. London 19 Feb. 1870. Anne Evans' Poems and music, with memorial preface by Anne Thackeray Ritchie 1880, portrait.

EVANS, REV. ARTHUR BENONI (2 son of Rev. Lewis Evans 1755-1827, V. of Froxfield, Wilts.) b. Compton-Beauchamp, Berks. 25 March 1781; ed. at Gloucester and St. John's coll. Ox., B.A. 1804, M.A. 1820, B.D. and D.D. 1828; C. of Hartpury, Gloucs. 1804; professor of classics and history in royal military college, Great Marlow 1805-12 when he removed with the college to Sandhurst, resigned 1822; C. of Burnham, Bucks. 1822-29; master of Market Bosworth free gr. sch. 1829 to death; C. of Bosworth Carlton and Cadeby successively 1829-41; author of Synopses for the use of the students in the royal military academy; The Curate and other poems 1810; Leicestershire words, phrases and proverbs 1848, and 16 other books. d. Market Bosworth 8 Nov. 1854. G.M. xliii, 100-102 (1855).

EVANS, BROOKE (son of Thomas Evans of Birmingham, tailor). b. Bull st. Birmingham 1797; manufacturer of fire arms in the United States; indigo planter and merchant; glass and lead merchant at Stratford-on-Avon 6 years; partner with Charles Askin as manufacturers of nickel and cobalt at Birmingham 1835-47 when Askin died, managed the business (which gained a European reputation) 1847 to death. d. Birmingham 15 Sep. 1862.

EVANS, CALEB. b. 25 July 1831; clerk in Chancery pay office, London 1852-82; collected fossils near London 1858-83; a founder of Geologists' Association of London 1857; F.G.S. 1867; author of 11 papers on geological subjects, some of which were published separately; constructed several excellent geological models or relief maps. d. 16 Sep. 1886.

EVANS, CHARLES (eld. son of Rev. Benjamin Evans, assistant master at Harrow). b. Harrow 1798; ed. at Eton and Pemb. coll. Cam., 12 wrangler 1819; B.A. 1819, M.A. 1822; fell. of his coll. 1821; barrister L.I. 4 Feb. 1823; revising barrister for Norwich 1832 to death; comr. of bankrupts for Norwich; chancellor of diocese of Norwich 1845 to death; pres. of directors of Norwich Union Fire office. d. Norwich 21 Oct. 1868.

EVANS, CHARLES JOHN. Entered British Museum 1858; compiled the catalogue of music which occupied him 15 years; wrote many articles in Grove's Dictionary of Musicians 3 vols. 1879-82; played the fagotto or bassoon in the Wandering Minstrels Orchestra. d. 150 King's road, Chelsea 8 Dec. 1884.

EVANS, DANIEL THOMAS (eld. son of Thomas Evans of Taunton). b. Cain's Cross, Gloucs.; barrister M.T. 19 Nov. 1847; sub-editor of

EVANS, D. T. (Con.)
The Law Times 1843-46; joint editor of Wise and Evans's Digest 1846-55, sole editor 1855-73 when it ceased. d. London 6 Nov. 1885 in 73 year.

EVANS, DAVID MORIER (son of Joshua Lloyd Evans of Llanidloes, Montgomeryshire). b. London, 1819; assistant city correspondent of The Times 1846-57; manager of Morning Herald 1857, of Standard 1857-72; started The Hour, daily morning paper, March 1873; became bankrupt 19 Dec. 1873; editor and part proprietor of Banker's Mag., and Banker's Almanac and Bullionist; author of The commercial crisis of 1847-48, 1849; City men and city manners 1856; Revelations of facts, failures and frauds 1861. d. Albion house, King Edward's road, South Hackney, London 1 Jany. 1874.

EVANS, EDWARD DAVID (eld. son of Edward Evans of London, printseller, who d. 24 Nov. 1835 aged 46). Printseller at 1 Great Queen st., Lincoln's Inn Fields with his mother and brother 1835-53, then at 403 Strand 1853 to death. d. 3 Circus road, St. John's Wood, London 15 Aug. 1860 aged 42.

EVANS, REV. EVAN. b. Gellillyndy, Llanddewibrefi, Cardiganshire 8 March 1804; Calvinistic preacher 1825; joined the Independents 1847; went to America 1869; collected a small Welsh church in Arkansas 1881, in charge of it to his death; author of numerous works in the Welsh language. d. 29 Oct. 1886.

EVANS, EVAN WILLIAM. b. near Swansea 1827; graduated at Yale Univ. 1851; principal of Delaware institute, Franklin, New York; a tutor in Yale 1855-57; professor of natural philosophy and astronomy in Marietta college, Ohio 1857-64; a mining engineer 1864-67; professor of mathematics in Cornell Univ. 1868-72; regarded as the best Celtic scholar in the United States. d. Ithaca, New York 22 May 1874.

EVANS, FREDERICK JOHN (son of John Evans, gas engineer). b. 1818; chief consulting engineer of Gas light and coke company, London 1863-72, the works at Beckton, opposite Woolwich, finest establishment of the kind in the world were opened 1871; this company absorbed 7 other companies 1870-76, in 1881 it made about two-thirds of the whole metropolitan supply; discovered valuable properties of oxide of iron for gas purification which revolutionised conduct of that process;

A.I.C.E. 10 March 1840; M.I.C.E. 9 Feb. 1864. d. Clayponds, Brentford 8 July 1880. Min. of proc. of Instit. of C.E. lxiii, 311–13 (1881).

EVANS, SIR FREDERICK JOHN OWEN (son of John Evans, master R.N.) b. 9 March 1815; entered navy 1828; superintendent of compass department of navy 1855; Chief Naval Assistant to the hydrographer to the admiralty 1865, hydrographer to the admiralty 1874–84; captain 1872; C.B. 8 May 1873; K.C.B. 24 May 1881; F.R.S. 5 June 1862, vice pres. 1876; author of Chart of curves of equal magnetic declination 1858; Report on compass deviations in the royal navy 1860; edited with Archibald Smith, Admiralty manual for ascertaining deviations of the compass 1862, 3 ed. 1869. d. 21 Dawson place, Bayswater, London 20 Dec. 1885. Proc. of Royal Soc. xl, 1–7 (1886).

EVANS, SIR GEORGE DE LACY (son of John Evans of Miltown). b. Moig, co. Limerick 7 Oct. 1787; ensign 22 foot 1 Feb. 1807; captain 5 West India regiment 1815–17 when placed on h.p.; M.P. for Rye 1830–31, for Westminster 1833–41 and 1846–65; contested Westminster and Rye, Dec. 1832; commanded British legion of 9,600 men in Spain, June 1835 to June 1837; col. 21 foot 29 Aug. 1853 to death; commanded 2nd division of British army in Crimea 1854–55; general 10 March 1861; K.C.B. 13 Feb. 1838, G.C.B. 5 July 1855; granted distinguished service reward 1 Sep. 1848; grand officer of Legion of Honour 1856; author of Facts relating to the capture of Washington 1829 and other books. d. 6 Great Cumberland st. Hyde park, London 9 Jany. 1870. G. Ryan's Our Heroes (1855) 13–36; G. Mackay's Leaders of the Host 1854; Diprose's St. Clements i, 64–68 (1869); E. H. Nolan's Russian war i, 661 (1857), portrait; Duncan's The English in Spain (1877) 41, 342.

NOTE.—The thanks of the House of Commons were voted to him "in his place" 2 Feb. 1855 and so the seat from which he heard the thanks read out became his all the rest of the time he sat in the House.

EVANS, GEORGE HENRY. b. Bromyard, Herefordshire 25 March 1805; went to the United States 1820, one of the earliest land reformers there; advocated inalienable homesteads, general bankrupt laws and laborers' liens; edited and published The Man, at Ithaca, New York about 1822; the Working Man's Advocate, in New York 1830; The Daily Sentinel 1837; and Young America, in New York and then at Rahway, New Jersey 1853. d. Granville, New Jersey 2 Feb. 1855.

EVANS, JOHN (only son of John Evans of Haverfordwest, Pembrokeshire). Ed. at univ. of Glasgow and Geneva; barrister I.T. 16 June 1820; Q.C. 1837; bencher of his inn 1837, reader 1849, treasurer 1850; M.P. for Haverfordwest 1847–52; F.S.A. 3 Feb. 1853. d. Buxton 17 Oct. 1864 aged 68.

EVANS, VEN. JOHN. b. Carmarthen; ed. at St. John's coll. Cam., B.D. 1830; V. of Llanboidy, Carmarthenshire 1827 to death; R. of Llanglydwen, Carmarthenshire 1832 to death; archdeacon of Carmarthen 1858 to death. d. Nantyr-Eglwys, St. Clear's 7 Feb. 1865.

EVANS, REV. JOHN. b. Ty Mawr, North Wales 23 July 1814; Welsh poet and Calvinistic methodist minister; better known as I. D. Fpaid; author of History of the Jews 1830 in Welsh; translated into Welsh Young's Night Thoughts and Milton's Paradise Lost; contributed prose and verse to Welsh periodicals. d. 4 March 1876.

EVANS, REV. JOHN (son of John Evans of Wellington, Somerset). Matric. from Ch. Ch. Ox. 13 Oct. 1814 aged 18; P.C. of Whixhall, Salop 1844 to death; author of Compendious view of the authenticity and inspiration of the Old and New Testament 1828; Statutes of the fourth general council of the Lateran 1843 and many other books. d. Whixhall vicarage 7 March 1889.

EVANS, REV. LEWIS (4 son of Thomas Simpson Evans of St. Botolphs, London). Matric. from Wadham coll. Ox. 30 June 1832 aged 17; B.A. 1836, M.A. 1842; fell. of his coll. 1839–46; head master of Sandbach free gr. sch. 1850 to death; edited Marshall's Penitential Discipline 1844; Bishop Beveridge's Sermons 8 vols.; author of The satires of Juvenal Persius, Sulpicia and Lucillius literally translated into English prose with notes 1848; author with Rev. J. G. Sheppard of Notes upon Thucydides Books i and ii, 1857. d. Gloucester 28 March 1869.

EVANS, RICHARD. Portrait painter and copyist; pupil and assistant to Sir Thomas Lawrence; lived at Rome many years; exhibited 42 pictures at R.A. 1816–59. d. Southampton, Nov. 1871 aged 87.

EVANS, ROBERT HARDING (son of Thomas Evans of London, bookseller 1742–84). Ed. at Westminster school; apprenticed to Thomas Payne bookseller at the Mewsgate; general bookseller in Pall Mall 1804–12; auctioneer at sale of Roxburghe and many other famous libraries 1812–47; edited Bishop Burnet's History of his own time 4 vols. 1808–9; Hakluyt's Collection of *early voyages of the English nation* 5 vols. 1809–12 and other books; author with Thomas Wright of *Historical account of the caricatures of James Gillray* 1851. *d.* Edward st. Hampstead road, London 25 April 1857 in 80 year. *Dibdin's Bibliographical Decameron iii,* 51 (1817), *portrait; G.M. ii,* 734–5 (1857).

EVANS, VEN. ROBERT WILSON *(2 son of John Evans, M.D. of Shrewsbury). b.* the council house, Shrewsbury 30 Aug. 1789; ed. at Shrewsbury and Trin. coll. Cam., 7th wrangler 1811; B.A. 1811, M.A. 1814, B.D. 1842; fellow of his college 1813, classical tutor 1814; V. of Tarvin, Cheshire 1836–42; V. of Heversham, Westmoreland 1842 to death; archdeacon of Westmoreland 1856 to Jany. 1865; author of *The Bishopric of Souls* 1842, 5 *ed.* 1877; *The rectory of Valehead* 1830, 12 *ed.* 1842; *Tales of the ancient British church* 1840, 3 *ed.* 1859 and 25 other works. *d.* Heversham vicarage 10 March 1866. *E. Bickersteth's ed. of Bishopric of Souls* (1877) *v-xiv, portrait; The Church of England Photographic portrait gallery* (1859), *portrait* 33.

EVANS, THOMAS. Ensign 113 foot 3 Dec. 1794; lieut.-col. 70 foot 24 Sep. 1829 to 28 June 1838; col. 81 foot 12 July 1847 to death; general 18 May 1855; C.B. 4 June 1815. *d.* Quebec 11 Feb. 1863.

EVANS, THOMAS. *b.* Cardigan 1840; a collier at Aberdare; won 20 prizes for his poems at Eisteddfodau; his poetical works were published with a short memoir in 1866. *d.* 29 April 1865.

EVANS, REV. THOMAS SAUNDERS. Educ. at St. John's coll. Cam., scholar; B.A. 1839, M.A. 1845, M.A. Durham 1862, D.D. Edin. 1885; assistant master of Rugby 1847–62; canon of Durham 1862 to death; professor of Greek in Univ. of Durham, May 1862 to death; proctor for chapter of Durham 1864 to death; author of *Tennyson's Œnone translated into Latin hexameters* 1873; *Notes on i. Corinthians* in *The Speaker's Commentary* 1881; *The Nihilist in the Hayfield, a Latin poem* 1882. *d.* Weston-super-Mare 16 May 1889.

EVANS, WILLIAM. *b.* Carana, Ireland 22 Nov. 1786; went to Canada 1819; sec. to the first Agricultural Society founded in Montreal; established the *Canadian Quarterly* and the *Agriculturalist and Industrial Magazine;* edited in Toronto *British American Cultivator* 1842; founded at Montreal the *Canadian Agricultural Journal* 1843, edited it 1843–56; sec. and treasurer of board of agriculture in Lower

Canada 1853; author of *Theory and practice of agriculture, Montreal* 1835, *supplement* 1836. *d.* Montreal 1857.

EVANS, WILLIAM. *b.* North Wales about 1810; painted scenery in North Wales down to 1852 when he went to Italy; associate member of Old Society of Painters in water-colours. *d.* Marylebone road, London 7 Dec. 1858.

EVANS, WILLIAM *(son of Samuel Evans of Flintshire, landscape painter, who d. about* 1835). *b.* Eton 4 Dec. 1798; ed. at Eton; drawing master at Eton 1818, resigned 1856; associate of Old Society of Painters in water-colours 1828, member 1830; exhibited a great number of paintings; head of one of the houses at Eton 1856 to death. *d.* Eton 31 Dec. 1877. *I.L.N. lxxii,* 103, 107 (1878), *portrait.*

EVANS, REV. WILLIAM EDWARD *(son of John Evans, M.D. of Shrewsbury). b.* Shrewsbury 8 June 1801; ed. at Shrewsbury and Clare hall, Cam., B.A. 1823, M.A. 1826; P.C. of Criggion, Montgomeryshire 1829–32; C. of Monkland, Herefordshire 1832–50; preb. and prælector of Hereford 1841–61; V. of Madley near Hereford 1850 to death; canon of Hereford 1861 to death; author of *The song of the birds, or analogies of animal and spiritual life* 1845 and other books. *d.* The Close, Hereford 21 Nov. 1869.

EVATT, HENRY. Second lieut. R.E. 11 July 1788; col. commandant 6 April 1832 to death; L.G. 28 June 1838. *d.* Fordwich near Canterbury 27 Jany. 1851 aged 83.

EVELEGH, HENRY. Second lieut. R.A. 24 April 1793, col. commandant 6 Feb. 1845 to death; general 20 June 1854. *d.* Standen, Newport, Isle of Wight 24 Sep. 1859 aged 86.

EVERARD, HARRIETTE EMILY. *b.* 12 March 1844; first appeared at T.R. Exeter about 1860; in London at royal Alfred theatre 1869; acted at Queen's, Princess's, Royalty, St. James's and Drury Lane theatres; played Little Buttercup in *H.M.S. Pinafore* at Opera Comique 25 May 1878 to March 1880. *(m.* George Wm. Darley Beswick). *d.* 22 Feb. 1882. *bur.* Highgate cemetery 28 Feb.

EVERARD, MATHIAS. Ensign 2 foot 28 Sep. 1804; led the forlorn hope at storming of Monte Video 3 Feb. 1807 when out of 32 men 22 were killed or wounded; lieut.-col. 14 foot 12 July 1831 to 25 Dec. 1847 when placed on h.p.; M.G. 11 Nov. 1851; C.B. 26 Sep. 1826; K.H. 1831. *d.* Southsea 20 April 1857.

EVEREST, SIR GEORGE (eld. son of Tristram Everest of Gwernvale, Breconshire). b. Gwernvale 4 July 1790; 2 lieut. Bengal engineers 4 April 1806; superintendent of trigonometrical survey at Hydrabad 1823–43; surveyor general of India 1830–43; retired with rank of lieut.-col. 16 Dec. 1843; C.B. 26 Feb. 1861; knighted at St. James's palace 13 March 1861; F.R.S. 8 March 1827, mem. of council 1863–65; the loftiest peak of Himalayan range is called Mount Everest after him; author of An account of the measurement of two sections of the meridional arc of India 1830 and 1847 and other books. d. 10 Westbourne st. Hyde park gardens, London 1 Dec. 1866. F. W. Stubbs' History of Bengal artillery ii, 251–54 (1877.); Proc. of Royal Soc. xvi, pp. xi-xiv (1868).

EVERETT, EDWARD (4 son of Joseph Everett of Salisbury, banker). b. 13 May 1798; ed. at Winchester and Ball. coll. Ox.; B.A. 1820, M.A. 1824; a barrister M.T. 28 May 1824; a conveyancer at Salisbury; judge of court of requests at Salisbury; judge of Dorset county courts (circuit 56), March 1847 to Dec. 1867 when he resigned. d. Clifton 24 Jany. 1870.

EVERETT, REV. JAMES (2 son of John Everett of Alnwick). b. Alnwick 16 May 1784; Wesleyan minister at Shields 1807, in Derbyshire 1808–10, in Yorkshire 1810–22, at Newcastle 1834–39, at York 1839–42; bookseller at Sheffield 1823–25, at York 1839–42; expelled from Wesleyan conference 7 Aug. 1849 being suspected of authorship of the Fly Sheets reflecting on leading men of the conference; lived at Newcastle 1853–59, at Sunderland 1859 to death; pres. of United Methodist Free Churches, July 1857; author of Adam Clarke portrayed 3 vols. 1843 and 17 other works. d. Sunderland 10 May 1872. James Everett, a biography by Richard Chew 1875; G. Gilfillan's Remoter Stars 1867 pp. 14–25; I.L.N. xv, 188 (1849), portrait.

EVERITT, ALLEN EDWARD (son of Edward Everitt of Birmingham, art dealer). b. Birmingham 1824; a painter there all his life; member of Royal Soc. of Artists of Birmingham 1857, hon. sec. 1858 to death; taught drawing in midland counties; hon. curator of Birmingham free art gallery, June 1880 to death; illustrated Davidson's History of the Holtes of Aston 1854, and History of Old St. Martin's, Birmingham 1875. d. The Grove, Frederick road, Edgbaston 11 June 1882. Edgbastonia ii, 108 (1882), portrait.

EVERSLEY, CHARLES SHAW-LEFEVRE, 1 Viscount (eld son of Charles Shaw-Lefevre, M.P.

EVERSLEY, Viscount (Con.)
for Reading, who d. 27 April 1823). b. Bedford sq., London 22 Feb. 1794; ed. at Winchester and Trin. coll. Cam.; B.A. 1815, M.A. 1819; barrister L.I. 12 May 1819; bencher 29 May 1839; M.P. for Downton, Wilts 1830–31, for Hampshire 1831–32, for North Hants. 1832–57; speaker of House of Commons 27 May 1839 to 20 March 1857; P.C. 3 June 1839; second comr. of church estates 24 Aug. 1850; created Viscount Eversley of Heckfield co. Southampton 11 April 1857; governor of Isle of Wight 31 Oct. 1857; an ecclesiastical comr. for England 2 Aug. 1859. d. Heckfield place, Winchfield, Hants. 28 Dec. 1888. bur. Kensal Green cemetery 2 Jany. 1889. J. A. Manning's Lives of the speakers (1850), 494–96; I.L.N. xxx, 109 (1857), portrait, 5 Jany. 1889, p. 8, portrait.

EWART, JOHN FREDERICK. b. Berlin 28 July 1786; ensign 52 foot 1 Nov. 1803; lieut. col. York Chasseurs 15 Sep. 1814 to 8 May 1817; lieut. col. 67 foot 5 Feb. 1818 to June 1826; inspecting field officer of Coventry recruiting district 1826–37; col. 67 foot 30 Oct. 1852 to death; L.G. 20 June 1854; C.B. 24 Oct. 1818; d. 1ᴬ Wellington road, St. John's Wood, London 23 Oct. 1854.

EWART, JOSEPH CHRISTOPHER (2 son of Wm. Ewart of Liverpool, merchant). b. Liverpool 1799; ed. at Eton; a merchant at Liverpool; a founder of Peninsular and Oriental steam navigation company; M.P. for Liverpool 1855–65. d. Broadleas near Devizes 14 Dec. 1868.

EWART, WILLIAM (brother of the preceding). b. Liverpool 1 May 1798; ed. at Eton and Ch. Ch. Ox.; Newdigate prizeman 1820; B.A. 1821; barrister M.T. 26 Jany. 1827; M.P. for Bletchingly 1828–30, for Liverpool 1830–37, for Wigan 1839–41, for Dumfries district 1841–68; author of The Temple of Diana at Ephesus 1820. d. Broadleas 23 Jany. 1869. Reg. and mag. of biography i, 209–10, 522 (1869); I.L.N. 25 July 1846, p. 53, portrait, 6 March 1869, p. 237, portrait.

EWBANK, THOMAS. b. Barnard castle, Durham 11 March 1792; maker of cases for preserved meats in London 1812–19; manufacturer of lead, tin and copper tubing in New York 1820–36; comr. of patents in Washington 1849–52; a founder and pres. of American Ethnological Society; author of A descriptive and historical account of hydraulic and other machines for raising water 1842, 17 ed. 1876; The world a workshop, or the physical

EWBANK, T. *(Con.)*

relationship of man to the earth 1855; *Life in Brazil, or the land of the cocoa and the palm* 1856 and other books all published at New York. *d.* 140 East Thirty-first st. New York 16 Sep. 1870.

EWING, RIGHT REV. ALEXANDER *(eld. son of John Ewing, advocate of Shelagreen, Aberdeenshire 1790-1827).* *b.* Castle st. Aberdeen 25 March 1814; ed. at Chelsea 1830-31, Edin. univ. 1831 and 1834-35; incumbent of Forres 1841-47; bishop of Argyll and the Isles 28 Oct. 1847 to death; provost of Cumbrae 28 June 1854 to 28 Dec. 1866; D.C.L. Ox. 1851; author of *Revelation considered as light* 1873, new ed. 1874; *The relations of the church of England with foreign churches* 1866 and 15 other books. *d.* Westmill rectory, Herts. 22 May 1873. *Memoir of Right Rev. A. Ewing by A. J. Ross* 1879, *portrait.*

EWING, JAMES *(son of Walter Ewing who assumed name of Maclae, arbitrator, d. 22 Oct. 1814).* *b.* Glasgow 7 Dec. 1775; educ. High sch. Glasgow and univ. of Glasgow, D.C.L. 1835; West India merchant; lord dean of Guild 10 Oct. 1816; helped to establish first Provident or Savings bank in Glasgow of which he was deputy governor 19 June 1815; president of the Andersonian univ. 1817; gave an annual silver medal to Glasgow high sch.; lord provost of Glasgow 1820; a founder of the Royal Exchange and the Fir park; M.P. Glasgow 19 Dec. 1832 to 30 Dec. 1834, contested Glasgow 17 Jany. 1835; author of a *History of the Merchants' House;* left £70,000 to Glasgow charities. *d.* Glasgow 29 Nov. 1853. *Mackay's Memoir of James Ewing* 1866, *portrait; Bourne's English Merchants ii,* 321-39 (1866).

EWING, JULIANA HORATIA *(2 dau. of Rev. Alfred Gatty, V. of Ecclesfield, Yorkshire b.* 1813). *b.* Ecclesfield 3 Aug. 1841; wrote many stories in *Aunt Judy's Magazine* 1861-85; author of *Melchior's Dream and other tales* 1862; *Mrs. Overtheway's Remembrances* 1868, 3 ed. 1880; *A Flat-iron for a farthing* 1873; *Passages in life of an only son* 1872; *Lob Lie-by-the-Fire and other tales* 1874 and many other books for children. *(m.* 1 June 1867 Alexander Ewing, major army pay department). *d.* Bath 13 May 1885. *J. H. Ewing and her books, by H. K. T. Gatty* (1885), *portrait.*

EXALL, WILLIAM. *b.* Godalming, Surrey, May 1808; partner with his uncle Barrett in the Katesgrove foundry, Reading; invented patent safety cylindrical horse gear, and endless-band sawing machine; the first to apply the double

EXALL, W. *(Con.)*

acting air pump or box shaped condenser to horizontal engines; the pioneer of steam cultivation, having made first set of machinery on roundabout system for H. J. Hannam of Buscot park, Oxfordshire 1849; constructed the first hand-power threshing machine 1844 of which his firm made thousands; A.I.C.E. 3 Dec. 1850; alderman of Reading 1854 to death, mayor 1854-5. *d.* Holy Bank house, Reading 14 July 1881. *Min. of proc. of Instit. of C.E. lxvii,* 405-7 (1882).

EXETER, BROWNLOW CECIL, 2 Marquis of (2 son of 1 *Marquis of Exeter* 1754-1804). *b.* Burghley house near Stamford 2 July 1795; ed. at Eton and St. John's coll. Cam., M.A. 1814, LL.D. 1835; recorder of Stamford 1816; lord lieut. of Rutland 1826; K.G. 10 May 1827; groom of the stole to Prince Albert 1841-46; P.C. 14 Sep. 1841; lord lieut. of Northampton 1842; lord chamberlain of Queen's household 27 Feb. to 28 Dec. 1852; lord steward of Queen's household 26 Feb. 1858 to 18 June 1859; bred one of largest studs in England 1815-55; won the Oaks 1821, 1829 and 1832 and Two thousand guineas 1825, 1829, 1830 and 1852. *d.* Burghley house 16 Jany. 1867. *Rice's British Turf i,* 311-17 (1879); *Baily's Mag. i,* 311-15 (1860), *portrait; Sporting Review lvii,* 82-85 (1867); *Waagen's Treasures of art iii,* 402-9 (1854).

EXLEY, THOMAS. *b.* Gowdall near Snaith, Yorkshire; a mathematical teacher at Bristol about 1811-47; author of *A vindication of Dr. Adam Clarke, Bristol* [1817]; *Principles of natural philosophy* 1829; *Physical Optics* 1834 and other books; author with Rev. W. M. Johnson of *The Imperial Encyclopædia* 4 *vols.* [1812]. *d.* Cotham, Clifton, Bristol 17 Feb. 1855 aged 80.

EYRE, CHARLES. *b.* 1784; ed. at Trin. coll. Cam., B.A. 1807; proprietor of 3 liberal newspapers printed at Colchester; managed a large farm; author of *An illustration of the Epistles of St. Paul including an entirely new translation* 2 vols. 1832; *The fall of Adam from Milton's Paradise Lost* 1852; hanged himself at his residence Upper Park, Dedham, Essex 28 Sep. 1864.

EYRE, HENRY. Ensign 98 foot 10 Dec. 1824, lieut. col. 17 March 1843 to 28 April 1843 when placed on h.p.; commandant at Chatham 1858-59; commandant of Chatham district 1859-64; col. 59 foot 23 March 1865 to death; general 23 Sep. 1874; author of *Light Infantry Drill* 1868. *d.* Middleton-Tyas, Richmond, Yorkshire 10 April 1889 aged 83.

EYRE, SIR JAMES (*eld. son of Rev. Wm. Eyre, V. of Padbury and Hillesden, Bucks., who d. 18 March 1830 aged 76*). b. 14 Feb. 1792; M.R.C.S. 20 May 1814; surgeon in Hereford 1814 to 1834, in London 1834 to death; mayor of Hereford 1829–30; knighted by Wm. 4 at St. James's palace 4 Aug. 1830 on presenting an address from city of Hereford on his accession; M.D. Edinburgh 1 Aug. 1834; physician accoucheur to St. George's and St. James's dispensary 1834–1851, consulting phys. 30 Oct. 1851; L.R.C.P. 1836; published *Practical remarks on some exhausting diseases* 1845, 2 ed. 1851; *The stomach and its difficulties* 1852, 8 ed. 1877. d. Lauriston house, Clapham 19 June 1857. *Medical Circular i,* 353–55 (1852), *portrait.*

EYRE, SIR VINCENT (3 *son of Henry Eyre*). b. Portsdown near Portsmouth 22 Jany. 1811; ed. at Norwich gr. sch. and Addiscombe; 2 lieut. Bengal Artillery 12 Dec. 1828, col. 24 Nov. 1862 to 1 Sep. 1863 when he retired on full pay; rendered great service during Indian mutiny; inspector general of ordnance at Calcutta 1861–62; retired L.G. Oct. 1863; member of army amalgamation commission 1861; C.B. 5 Feb. 1858; K.C.S.I. 24 May 1867; author of *The military operations at Cabul* 1843; *A Fortnight's tour among French ambulances* 1870; *Lays of a Knight Errant* 1874 and other books. d. Villa des Acacias, Aix les Bains 22 Sep. 1881. *bur.* Kensal Green cemetery 1 Oct. *C. R. Low's Soldiers of the Victorian age i,* 284–347 (1880); *G. B. Malleson's Recreations of an Indian official* (1872) 249–329; *Army and navy mag. iii,* 97 (1882), *portrait; I.L.N. xxxi,* 380 (1857), *portrait.*

EYRE, SIR WILLIAM (*younger son of vice admiral Sir George Eyre 1769–1839*). b. Hatfield 21 Oct. 1805; ed. at Rugby; ensign 6 foot 17 April 1823; served in both Caffre wars 1851–2; lieut. col. 73 foot 12 Nov. 1847 to 14 April 1854; A.D.C. to the Queen 1853–1854; commanded second brigade of third division in Crimea 1854, commanded third division there 1854; commanded troops in Canada 1856–59; M.G. 12 Dec. 1854; K.C.B. 5 July 1855. d. Bilton hall near Rugby 8 Sep. 1859. *Naval and military records of Rugbeians* (1865) 53–4; *Kinglake's Invasion of the Crimea* (1877) *iii,* 278, *vi* 54, *ix* 203–17, 270.

EYTON, PETER ELLIS. b. Flint 1827; solicitor at Flint 1853 to death; M.P. for district of Flint 6 Feb. 1874 to death; author of *A trip to the Isle of Man.* d. Englefield house, Rhyl, North Wales 17 or 19 June 1878.

EYTON, REV. ROBERT WILLIAM (3 *son of Rev. John Eyton, V. of Wellington, Shropshire*). b. Wellington vicarage 21 Dec. 1815; ed. at Rugby and Ch. Ch. Ox.; B.A. 1839, M.A. 1845; R. of Ryton, Shropshire 1841–63; author of *The antiquities of Shropshire* 12 vols. 1861; *A Key to Domesday, an analysis and digest of the Dorset survey* 1878; *Court, household and itineray of Henry ii,* 1878 and other books. d. Winchfield house near Basingstoke 8 Sep. 1871.

EYTON, THOMAS CAMPBELL (*son of Thomas Eyton 1777–1855, recorder of Wenlock*). b. Eyton hall near Wellington, Shropshire 10 Sep. 1809; edited the Herd book of Hereford cattle 1842–60; formed at Eyton one of the finest collections of skins and skeletons of birds in Europe; author of *History of the rarer British birds* 1836; *A history of the oyster and the oyster fisheries* 1858; *Osteologia Avium* 1871. d. Eyton hall 25 Oct. 1880.

F

FABER, REV. FREDERICK WILLIAM (7 *child of Thomas Henry Faber, who d. 1833, sec. to Dr. Barrington, bishop of Durham*). b. Calverley vicarage, Yorkshire 28 June 1814; ed. at Shrewsbury, Harrow and Ball. coll. Ox.; scholar of Univ. coll. Ox. 1834, fellow 1837, Newdigate prizeman 1836; B.A. 1836, M.A. 1839; Johnson divinity scholar 1837; R. of Elton, Hunts. 1843–45; admitted into R.C. church at Northampton by Bishop Wareing 17 Nov. 1845; entered Monastery of St. Wilfrid, Colmore terrace, Birmingham 26 May 1846; rector of oratory of St. Philip Neri, 24 and 25 King William st. Strand, London opened 31 May 1849, Father Superior 12 Oct. 1850 to death, the oratory removed to Brompton, March 1854; created D.D. 9 July 1854; edited *The Saints and Servants of God,* continued by the Congregation of the Oratory of St. Philip Neri 42 vols. 1847–56; author of *The Cherwell water lily and other poems* 1840 and about 30 other books. d. the Oratory, Brompton 26 Sep. 1863. *bur.* in burial ground of St. Mary's, Sydenham 30 Sep. *J. E. Bowden's Life and letters of F. W. Faber* 1869; *A brief sketch of the early life of F. W. Faber, by his only surviving brother [Rev. F. A. Faber]* 1869; *Gillow's English Catholics ii,* 207–18; *I.L.N. xxiv,* 289, 290 (1854), *portrait.*

FABER, REV. GEORGE STANLEY (*eld. son of Rev. Thomas Faber, V. of Calverley, Yorkshire*). b. Calverley parsonage 25 Oct. 1773; ed. at

FABER, REV. G. S. *(Con.)*

Happenholme gr. sch. and Univ. coll. Ox., B.A. 1793, M.A. 1796, B.D. 1803; fell. and tutor of Linc. coll. 1793–1803; proctor 1801; Bampton lecturer 1801; C. of Calverley 1803; 1805; V. of Stockton upon Tees 1805–1808; V. of Redmarshall, Durham 1808–11; V. of Longnewton, Durham 1811–32; Preb. of Salisbury 1831; master of Sherburn hosp. near Durham 1832 to death; author of *Horæ Mosaicæ, or a view of the Mosaical records* 2 vols. 1801, 2 ed. 1818; *Dissertation on the prophesies* 2 vols. 1807, 5 ed. 3 vols. 1814–18; *The difficulties of Romanism* 1826, 3 ed. 1853; *The sacred calendar of prophecy* 3 vols. 1828, 2 ed. 1844 and many other works. *d.* Sherburn hospital 27 Jany. 1854. *The many mansions in the house of the Father, by G. S. Faber with memoir by F. A. Faber* 1854; *Christian Remembrancer xxix*, 310–31 (1855); *H. Heaviside's Annals of Stockton on Tees* (1865) 101–104.

FABER, WILLIAM RAIKES *(son of the preceding).* Second lieut. 60 rifles 10 April 1826; lieut. col. 2 West India foot 15 Dec. 1848 to 21 Feb. 1851 when placed on h.p.; lieut. col. 53 foot 9 Jany. 1857 to 13 July 1858 when placed on h.p.; col. 17 foot 30 April 1871 to death; general 1 Oct. 1877; C.B. 29 May 1875. *d.* Staplegrove lodge, Taunton 24 June 1879 aged 73.

FADDY, PETER. Second lieut. R.A. 8 Sep. 1803; lieut. col. 10 Aug. 1839 to 3 Sep. 1845 when he retired on full pay; general 7 Feb. 1870; author of *Essay on the defence of Great Britain at home and abroad* 1848. *d.* Charleville, co. Cork 17 July 1879.

FAGAN, WILLIAM TRANT *(eld. son of James Fagan of Cork).* *b.* Cork 1801; ed. at Southall park, Middlesex; a merchant at Cork, alderman, mayor; M.P. for city of Cork 1847–1851 and 1852 to death; author of *The life and times of Daniel O'Connell* 2 vols. 1847–8. *d.* 9 or 16 May 1859. *I.L.N. xiv*, 205 (1849), *portrait; Fitzpatrick's O'Connell* (1888) *ii*, 453.

FAGGE, CHARLES HILTON *(son of Charles Fagge, surgeon).* *b.* Hythe, Kent 30 June 1838; ed. at Guy's hospital; M.D. 1863; M.R.C.P. 1864, F.R.C.P. 1870; medical registrar of Guy's hospital 1866, assistant phys. 1867, phys. 1880; edited *Guy's Hospital Reports* some years; author of *Principles and practice of medicine* 1886, 2 ed. 1888. *d.* 76 Grosvenor st. London 18 Nov. 1888.

FAHEY, JAMES. *b.* Paddington 16 April 1804; sec. of New Society of Painters in water-colours 1838–74; drawing master at Merchant

FAHEY, J. *(Con.)*

Taylor's school 1856–83; exhibited 13 landscapes at R.A., 1 at B.I. and 5 at Suffolk st. gallery 1825–36. *d.* The Grange, Shepherd's Bush Green, London 11 Dec. 1885. *I.L.N.* 26 *Dec.* 1885 *p.* 667, *portrait.*

FAIR, ALEXANDER. Entered Madras army 1792; col. 27 Madras N.I. 1837 to death; general 20 June 1854. *d.* South crescent, Bedford sq. London 29 Jany. 1861 aged 85.

FAIRBAIRN, REV. PATRICK *(son of John Fairburn of Hallyburton, Greenlaw, Berwickshire, farmer).* *b.* Hallyburton 28 Jany. 1805; ed. at Univ. of Edin.; licensed to preach 1826; minister of parish of North Ronaldshay, Orkney islands 1830–36; minister of Bridgeton, Glasgow 1836–40; minister of Salton, East Lothian 1840–43; minister of free church Salton 1843–53; professor of divinity in free church theological college, Aberdeen 1853–56; transferred to free church college, Glasgow 1856, principal 4 Nov. 1856; moderator of general assembly 1865; member of Old Testament revision company; edited *The Imperial Bible Dictionary* 2 vols. 1866; author of *The typology of Scripture* 2 vols. 1845–47, 5 ed. 1870 and 7 other books. *d.* 6 Aug. 1874. *Pastoral Theology, by Rev. P. Fairbairn, with biog. sketch by Rev. James Dodds* 1875.

FAIRBAIRN, SIR PETER *(youngest son of Andrew Fairbairn of Kelso, Roxburghshire).* *b.* Kelso, Sep. 1799; machine maker at Glasgow 1823–28, at Leeds 1828 to death; invented many new machines; member of town council Leeds 1836–42, alderman 1854 to death, mayor 1857–59; knighted by the Queen at Leeds 7 Sep. 1858; there is a portrait of him by Sir Francis Grant in the council chamber Leeds and a bronze statue by Noble in the town. *d.* Woodsley house, Leeds 4 Jany. 1861. *Fortunes made in business ii*, 252–79 (1884); *Taylor's Biographia Leodiensis* (1865) 491–96; *Illust. news of the world ii*, 181 (1858), *portrait, vii*, 29 (1861), *portrait.*

FAIRBAIRN, SIR WILLIAM, 1 Baronet *(eld. son of Andrew Fairbairn of Smailhome, co. Roxburgh 1758–1844).* *b.* Kelso, co. Roxburgh 19 Feb. 1789; manufacturing engineer at Manchester 1817 to death; M.I.C.E. 20 April 1830; established an iron shipbuilding yard at Millwall near London 1835; built and designed nearly 100 bridges; F.R.S. 6 June 1850, Royal Medallist 1860; correspondent of National Institute of France 11 May 1852; pres. of Institution of Mechanical Engineers 1854–55; pres. of Manchester literary and philosophical society 1855–60; pres. of British

FAIRBAIRN, SIR W. (*Con.*)

Association at Manchester 1861; declined knighthood 23 Oct. 1861; created Baronet 7 Oct. 1869; author of *Useful information for Engineers* 1856, 4 ed. 1864; *Iron, its history* 1861, 3 ed. 1869 and other books. *d.* Moor park near Farnham, Surrey 18 Aug. 1874. *bur.* Prestwick parish church, Manchester. *The life of Sir W. Fairbairn, edited by W. Pole* 1877; *Fortunes made in business* ii, 240–50 (1884); *Min. of proc. of Instit. of C.E. xxxix,* 251–64 (1875); *Practical Mag.* iv, 241, *portrait; I.L.N.* xl, 215, 225 (1862), *portrait, lxv,* 205, 212, 332 (1874), *portrait.*

FAIRFAX, SIR HENRY, 1 Baronet (*youngest son of vice-admiral Sir Wm. George Fairfax* 1739–1813). *b.* Edinburgh 3 Feb. 1790; ensign 49 foot 8 June 1809; major 85 foot 17 July 1823 to 6 Nov. 1827 when placed on h.p.; retired from the army 1844; created baronet in consideration of his father's distinguished naval services 21 Feb. 1836. *d.* Edinburgh 3 Feb. 1860.

FAIRFAX, JOHN. *b.* Warwick 1804; printer and bookseller at Leamington; librarian to the Australian subscription library in Sydney 26 Sep. 1838; bought the *Sydney Morning Herald* a biweekly paper 1841, converted it into a daily morning paper which soon became leading journal of New South Wales, sole proprietor of the paper 1853; member of council of education 1870; member of legislative council 1874 to death; author of *The Colonies of Australia* 1852. *d.* Ginahgulla near Rose Bay, Port Jackson 16 June 1877.

FAIRHOLT, FREDERICK WILLIAM (16 *child of a German named Fahrholz, who Anglicised his name to Fairholt*). *b.* London 1814; employed in a tobacco factory 14 years; assistant to S. Sly the wood engraver 1835; made many hundreds of drawings on wood to illustrate Charles Knight's publications; illustrated many important works; F.S.A. 1844; draughtsman to British Archæol. Assoc. 1845–52; author of *Costume in England* 1846, 3 ed. 2 vols. 1885 and 5 other books. *d.* 22 Montpelier square, Brompton 3 April 1866. *C. R. Smith's Retrospections* i, 218–26, 307–21 (1883).

FAIRLAND, THOMAS. Pupil of Charles Warren; a lithographer, afterwards a portrait painter; his best work, one of the best ever executed in lithography, was the cartoon of the Virgin and Child by Raphael known as the Rogers Madonna; published a volume of *Comic Sketches* after W. Hunt 1844 which was very popular. *d.* of consumption Oct. 1852 in 49 year. *G.M. Jany.* 1853 *p.* 102.

FAIRLIE, ROBERT FRANCIS. *b.* Scotland, March 1831; civil engineer in Gracechurch st. London; patented the double-bogie engine 1864, first of which was built for Neath and Brecon railway 1866; these engines were introduced into many foreign countries; the Czar of Russia had a special gold medal struck in honour of Fairlie; author of *Railways or no railways, narrow guage v. broad guage* 1872. *d.* the Woodlands, Clapham common, London 31 July 1885.

FALCIERI, GIOVANNI BATTISTA, the faithful servant of Lord Byron. Entered service of Isaac D'Israeli; messenger at the India office, superannuated on pension of £140. *d.* Ramsgate 22 Dec. 1874; Sarah his widow was granted civil list pension of £50, 5 March 1875.

FALCONAR, CHESBOROUGH GRANT. Ensign 36 foot 1 Sep. 1795; major 78 foot 26 June 1823 to 22 Oct. 1825 when placed on h.p.; lieut. col. 22 foot 25 Nov. 1828 to 18 Oct. 1839; inspecting field officer 18 Oct. 1839 to 11 Nov. 1851; col. 73 foot 11 Feb. 1857 to death; L.G. 20 July 1858; K.H. 1837. *d.* Hazelbank near Edinburgh 10 Jany. 1860.

FALCONER, EDMUND, stage name of Edmund O'Rourke. *b.* Dublin 1814; acted in the provinces many years; lessee with B. Webster of Lyceum theatre, London, Aug. 1858 to April 1859; played Danny Man in *The Colleen Bawn* at Adelphi theatre 231 nights from 18 July 1860; lessee of Lyceum again 1861 where his Irish drama *Peep o' Day* ran from 9 Nov. 1861 to Dec. 1862; lessee with F. B. Chatterton of Drury Lane 1863 to 26 Sep. 1866 where he lost all his money; played in America 1867–70; author of *Memories, poems* 1863; *Murmurings in the May and Summer of Manhood, O'Ruark's Bride and Man's Missions, poems* 1865 and of many dramas, librettos and songs. *d.* 28 Keppel st. Russell sq. London 29 Sep. 1879. *Pascoe's Dramatic List* (1879) 116–20; *Illust. sporting and dramatic news* 4 *Dec.* 1875 *pp.* 233–4.

FALCONER, FORBES (2 *son of Gilbert Falconer of Braeside, Fifeshire*). *b.* Aberdeen 10 Sep. 1805; ed. at Aberdeen gr. sch. and Marischal college; teacher of Oriental languages in London; professor of Oriental languages in Univ. college, London; author of *Selections from the "Bôstan of Sâdi" in Persian* 1838; *Persian Grammar, 2 ed.* 1848. *d.* 40 Dorset st. Portman sq. London 7 Nov. 1853.

FALCONER, HUGH (*youngest child of David Falconer of Forres, Elginshire*). *b.* Forres 29 Feb. 1808; ed. at Forres gr. sch. and King's

FALCONER, H. *(Con.)*

coll. Aberdeen, M.A. 1826; studied medicine at Univ. of Edin., M.D. 1829; assist. surgeon in the H.E.I.Co.'s service 1830; superintendent of Botanic garden at Suharunpoor, North Western provinces 1832; awarded Wollaston medal of Geol. Society 1837; returned to England on sick leave 1842, went out again 20 Dec. 1847; superintendent of Calcutta botanic garden, and professor of botany in the medical college, June 1847 to 1855; F.G.S. 1842, foreign sec. 1861 to death; F.R.S. 13 Feb. 1845; author of *Descriptive catalogue of the fossil remains from the Sewalik hills, Calcutta* 1859. *d.* Park crescent, London 31 Jany. 1865. *C. Murchison's Palæontological memoirs and notes of the late Hugh Falconer* (1868) *vol* 1, *pp. xxiii-liii, portrait; Proc. of Royal Soc. xv,* 14–20 (1867); *Quarterly Journal of Geol. Soc. xxi,* 45–49 (1865).

FALCONER, RANDLE WILBRAHAM *(youngest son of Rev. Thomas Falconer of Bath 1772–1839). b.* 29 Circus, Bath 1816; studied at Edin., M.D. 1839; practised at Tenby 1839–47, at Bath 1847 to death; physician of Bath united hospital 12 Feb. 1849; physician of Bath mineral water hospital 28 Feb. 1856; mayor of Bath 1857–59; author of *The baths and mineral waters of Bath,* 6 ed. 1880, and other books. *d.* Bennett st. Bath 6 May 1881.

FALCONER, THOMAS *(brother of the preceding). b.* 25 June 1805; barrister L.I. 8 Feb. 1830; revising barrister for boroughs of Finsbury, Tower Hamlets and Marylebone 1837–1840; one of arbitrators to settle boundary of Canada and New Brunswick, Oct. 1850; colonial sec. of Western Australia 29 July 1851; judge of county courts circuit 30, (Brecknock and Glamorgan) 22 Dec. 1851 to Dec. 1881 when he retired on pension; aided in abolishing Duke of Beaufort's gaol at Swansea; author of *On Surnames and the rules of law affecting their change, Cardiff* 1862 privately printed, 2 ed. London 1862, *Supplement* 1863 and 7 other books. *d.* Royal crescent, Bath 28 Aug. 1882 in 77 year. *T. Falconer's Bibliography of the Falconer family* (1866) 20–30; *The Red Dragon ii,* 193–98 (1882), *portrait.*

FALCONER, REV. WILLIAM *(brother of the preceding). b.* Corston, Somerset 27 Dec. 1801; ed. at Oriel coll. Ox.; B.A. 1823, M.A. 1827; fellow of Exeter coll. 30 June 1827 to 18 July 1839, public examiner 1832–3 and 1836–8; R. of Bushey, Herts. 26 Jany. 1839 to death; translated with H. C. Hamilton for Bohn's Classical Library *The Geography of Strabo* 3 vols. 1854–57. *d.* Bushey rectory 9 Feb. 1885.

FALKLAND, LUCIUS BENTINCK CARY, 10 Viscount *(eld. child of Charles John Cary, 9 Viscount Falkland 1768–1809). b.* 5 Nov. 1803; succeeded his father who *d.* of wounds received in a duel 2 March 1809; a lord of the bedchamber to Wm. iv, Dec. 1830; a representative peer for Scotland 1831–32; G.C.H. 1831; created Baron Hunsdon of Skutterskelfe, co. York in peerage of the U.K. 15 May 1832; P.C. 1 March 1837; governor of Nova Scotia 1840–1846; captain of yeomen of the guard 24 July 1846 to 16 Feb. 1848; governor of Bombay 1 Feb. 1848 to Dec. 1853, took his seat 1 May 1848. *d.* Montpellier, France 12 March 1884.

FALKNER, GEORGE. *b.* Edinburgh 1817; edited *Bradshaw's Manchester Journal* from first number 1 May 1841; typographer and lithographer at Manchester to death; published his own *Notes on Algiers* 1852, and *A pilgrimage to the shrine of Our Lady of Loreto* 1882. *d.* The Oaklands, Timperley near Manchester 31 Dec. 1882.

FALLON, JAMES THOMAS. *b.* Athlone 1823; went to Sydney, N.S.W. 1842; bought a vineyard at Albury about 1859; his wines took first prize at Vienna exhibition 1873 and London exhibition 1875; made champagne from Australian grapes 1876; had largest vineyards and cellars in Australia; member of legislative assembly of N.S.W. 1869–72. *d.* Manly near Sydney 27 May 1886.

FALLOON, REV. DANIEL. *b.* Ireland; minister of Church of England in Canada; author of *An historical view of the Church of England* 2 vols. Dublin 1830; *The Apostolic Church* 1837; *History of Ireland, civil and ecclesiastical from the earliest times to the death of Henry ii,* edited by Rev. John Irwin, Montreal 1863. *d.* Montreal, Sep. 1862.

FALMOUTH, GEORGE HENRY BOSCAWEN, 2 Earl of *(only child of Edward Boscawen, 1 Earl of Falmouth 1787–1841). b.* Woolhampton house near Newbury, Berks. 8 July 1811; ed. at Eton and Ch. Ch. Ox.; B.A. 1833, M.A. 1835; M.P. for West Cornwall 8 July 1841 to 29 Dec. 1841 when he succeeded his father as 2 Earl; high steward of Wallingford 1845 to death. *d.* 2 St. James's square, Westminster 28 Aug. 1852.

FALSHAW, SIR JAMES, 1 Baronet *(son of Wm. Falshaw of Leeds). b.* Leeds 21 March 1810; assisted Stephenson in construction of Caledonian and other railways; constructed with Brassey the northern lines of railway from

FALSHAW, SIR J. (Con.)

Inverness; lord provost of Edinburgh 1876; created baronet 17 Aug. 1876; deputy chairman of North British railway co. 1881, chairman 3 Aug. 1882 to 1887. d. 14 Belgrave crescent, Edinburgh 14 June 1889. *Graphic x*, 490, 501 (1874), *portrait; I.L.N. lxix*, 253 (1876), *portrait.*

FANE, HENRY EDWARD HAMLYN (eld. son of Rev. Edward Fane of Fulbeck, Lincs. 1783–1862). b. Fulbeck hall 5 Sep. 1817; ed. at Charterhouse; ensign 90 foot 1 Aug. 1834; major 4 light dragoons 1846–50 when he sold out; lieut. col. South Lincoln militia 20 April 1854 to death; assumed name of Hamlyn by r.l. 1865; M.P. for South Hants. 1865–68; author of *Five years in India* 1842. d. Avon Tyrrel, Ringwood, Hants. 27 Dec. 1868.

FANE, JOHN WILLIAM. b. 1 Sep. 1804; sheriff of Oxfordshire 1854; lieut. col. of Oxford militia 18 July 1862 to 22 May 1872; M.P. for Oxfordshire 1862–1868. d. 34 Cavendish sq. London 19 Nov. 1875.

FANE, JULIAN HENRY CHARLES (5 son of 11 Earl of Westmoreland 1784–1859). b. Florence 2 Oct. 1827; ed. at Trin. coll. Cam.; M.A. 1850; attaché at Berlin 1844; sec. of embassy at Vienna 23 Nov. 1860, at Paris 30 Dec. 1865 to 7 June 1868 when he resigned; published *Poems* 1852; *Poems by Heinrich Heine, translated by Julian Fane* 1854; author with Edward Lytton of *Tannhäuser, or the battle of the bards, a poem by Neville Temple* [J. C. Fane] and Edward Trevor [E. R. Bulwer-Lytton] 1861. d. 29 Portman sq. London 19 April 1870. *Lytton's Julian Fane, a memoir* (1871), *portrait; Jerningham's Reminiscences of an attaché* (1886) 16–20.

FANE, MILDMAY (5 son of Henry Fane 1739–1842, M.P. for Lyme Regis). b. Sep. 1794; ensign 59 foot 11 June 1812; lieut. col. 98 foot 25 March 1824 to 24 Dec. 1829; lieut. col. 54 foot 24 Dec. 1829 to 11 Nov. 1851; col. 96 foot 11 Aug. 1855 to 27 Dec. 1860; col. 54 foot 27 Dec. 1860 to death; general 27 March 1863. d. Fulbeck 12 March 1868.

FANE, ROBERT GEORGE CECIL (brother of the preceding). b. 8 May 1796; ed. at Charterhouse and Balliol coll. Ox.; B.A. 1817, M.A. 1819; a demy and fellow of Magd. coll. Ox. 1824–35; barrister L.I. 1 June 1821; a bankruptcy comr. 1823, one of the six bankrupt comrs. 2 Dec. 1831 to death; author of *Bankrupt Reform, Letters i–vii, 2 vols.* 1838 and 8 other books. d. Burdon hotel, Weymouth 4 Oct. 1864.

FANQUE, PABLO, assumed name of William Darby. b. Norwich; apprenticed to Wm. Batty, circus proprietor; a negro rope-dancer; circus proprietor 1841 to death. d. Britannia inn, Stockport 4 May 1871 aged 67 or 75. *I.L.N. x*, 189 (1847), *portrait.*

FANSHAWE, SIR ARTHUR (youngest son of Robert Fanshawe, Capt. R.N. 1740–1823). b. 1794; entered navy 8 Feb. 1804; captain 17 Oct. 1816; commander in chief North America and West Indies 23 Nov. 1853 to 25 Nov. 1856; R.A. 18 June 1851, V.A. 9 July 1857, admiral 4 Oct. 1862; C.B. 18 Dec. 1840, K.C.B. 18 May 1860. d. 32 Chester terrace, Regent's park, London 14 June 1864 aged 70.

FARADAY, MICHAEL (younger son of James Faraday of Newington, Surrey, blacksmith 1761–1810). b. Newington 22 Sep. 1791; chemical assistant at royal institution 1 March 1813; travelled as amanuensis with Sir Humphrey Davy in France, Italy and Switzerland 1813–1815; F.R.S. 8 Jany. 1824, Copley medallist 1832 and 1838, royal medallist 1835 and 1846, Rumford medallist 1846; began his lectures to children 29 Dec. 1827; began his 'Electrical researches' 29 Aug. 1831; discovered magneto-electricity 1831, electro chemical decomposition 1833; professor of chemistry at royal institution Jany. 1833 to 1865; granted civil list pension of £300 a year 1835; senator of univ. of London 1836; an elder of the Sandemanian church for 3½ years from 1840; discovered magnetisation of light 1845, diamagnetism 1845 and magnetic character of oxygen 1847; received 95 honorary titles and marks of merit; lived in one of the Queen's houses Hampton Court Green 1858 to death; author of *Chemical manipulation, instructions to students* 1827, 3 ed. 1842 and other works. d. Hampton Court Green 25 Aug. 1867. bur. Highgate cemetery 30 Aug. *Bence Jones's Life and letters of Faraday 2 vols.* 1870, *portrait; J. F. Clarke's Autobiographical recollections of the medical profession* (1874) 399–409; *Illustrated Review v*, 29–39, *portrait; Illust. news of the world i* (1858), *portrait; Proc. of Royal Soc. xvii*, 1–68 (1868).

FARDELL, JOHN. b. 4 May 1784; F.S.A. 15 June 1809; barrister M.T. 2 July 1824; M.P. for city of Lincoln 1830–1831. d. Sprotborough rectory, Yorkshire 5 Feb. 1854.

FAREY, JOHN (son of John Farey of Woburn, geologist 1766–1826). b. Lambeth 20 March 1791; ed. at Woburn; made drawings for illustrative plates of many scientific works; invented machine for drawing ellipses 1813

FABEY, J. (Con).

for which gold medal of Society of Arts was awarded him; constructed ironworks in Russia 1819–21; a lace manufacturer in Devonshire 1821–23; consulting C.E. in London 1826 to death; M.I.C.E. 1826; author of *A treatise on the steam engine vol. i,* 1827. *d.* the Common, Sevenoaks 17 July 1851. *Min. of proc. of Instit. of C.E. xi,* 100–102 (1852).

FARGUS, FREDERICK JOHN *(eld. son of Frederick Charles Fargus of Bristol, auctioneer, who d. 14 April 1868). b.* Bristol 26 Dec. 1847; auctioneer at Bristol 1868–83; author of *Called Back* 1883, 350,000 copies of it were sold and it was at once translated into 6 European languages, his dramatic version of it was played at Prince's theatre, London nearly 200 nights from 20 May 1884; all his stories were published under pseudonym of Hugh Conway. *d.* Monte Carlo 15 May 1885. *bur.* Nice cemetery 18 May. *Called Back, by H. Conway* (1885) *pp. vii-xiii, portrait; The Lute, June* 1885 *p.* 125; *I.L.N.* 30 *May* 1885 *p.* 559, *portrait.*

FARIS, WILLIAM. Second lieut. R.E. 1 Jany. 1814, lieut. col. 6 Aug. 1849 to 24 Nov. 1851 when placed on retired list; general 8 June 1871. *d.* 17 Pall Mall, London 4 Dec. 1874 aged 80.

FARLEY, CHARLES. *b.* London 1771; first appeared on the stage at Covent Garden 1782; supervised dramatic spectacles at Covent Garden 1806–34; author of *The Magic Oak, a Christmas pantomime* 1799; *Aggression, or the heroine of Yucatan* 1805 and other pieces; instructed Grimaldi to whose Orson when he made his appearance in the character 10 Oct. 1806 he played Valentine; the best theatrical machinist of his time. *d.* 42 Ampthill square, Hampstead road, London 28 Jany. 1859. *British stage ii,* 145 (1818), *portrait.*

FARLEY, JAMES LEWIS *(only son of Thomas Farley of Meiltran, co. Cavan). b.* Dublin 9 Sep. 1823; ed. at Trin. coll. Dublin; chief accountant of Beyrout branch of Ottoman Bank 1856; accountant general of state bank of Turkey at Constantinople 1860; consul for Turkey at Bristol 1870–84; author of *The massacres in Syria* 1861; *The Druses and the Maronites* 1861; *Turks and Christians, a solution of the Eastern question* 1876 and other books. *d.* Bayswater, London 12 Nov. 1885.

FARNBOROUGH, SIR THOMAS ERSKINE MAY, 1 Baron. *b.* London 8 Feb. 1815; ed. at Bedford gr. sch.; assistant librarian House of

FARNBOROUGH, Baron *(Con.)*

Commons 1831; barrister M.T. 4 May 1838, bencher 21 May 1873; taxing master in Parliament 1847–56; clerk assistant of House of Commons 1856–71, clerk Jany. 1871 to death; member of Statute law committee 1868, chairman; C.B. 1860, K.C.B. 6 July 1866; created Baron Farnborough of Farnborough in the county of Southampton 10 May 1886; author of *Constitutional history of England 1760–1860,* 2 *vols.* 1861-2, new ed. 3 vols. 1871; *Law privileges, proceedings and usage of Parliament* 1844, 9 *ed.* 1883; *Democracy in Europe* 2 *vols.* 1877. *d.* Speaker's Court, Houses of Parliament 17 May 1886. *Biograph, Jany.* 1882 *pp.* 14–20.

FARNCOMB, THOMAS. *b.* Sussex; proprietor of one of the largest wharfs on Surrey side of the Thames for about 50 years; a merchant and shipowner; one of earliest promoters of London and Westminster bank 1834, and long a director of it; sheriff of London 1840, alderman for ward of Bassishaw 1841–59, lord mayor 1849–50. *d.* Rose hill, Forest hill, Surrey 23 Sep. 1865 aged 86.

FARNHAM, HENRY MAXWELL, 7 Baron *(eld. child of Rev. Henry Maxwell, 6 Baron Farnham 1773–1838). b.* Dublin 9 Aug. 1799; M.P. for co. Cavan 1824–38; succeeded 19 Oct. 1838; an Irish representative peer 2 July 1839 to death; K.P. 1845; killed near Abergele, Denbighshire on the London and north western railway 20 Aug. 1868. *I.L.N. liii,* 210 (1868).

FARNHAM, SOMERSET RICHARD MAXWELL, 8 Baron *(brother of the preceding). b.* Dublin 18 Oct. 1803; M.P. for Cavan 1838–40; sheriff of Cavan 1844. *d.* Farnham house, Cavan 1 June 1884.

FARNHAM, EDWARD BASIL. *b.* 19 April 1799; M.P. for North Leicestershire 1837–59; sheriff of Leics. 1870. *d.* Quorndon house near Loughborough 13 May 1879.

FARNIE, HENRY BROUGHAM. *b.* Fifeshire; ed. at Univs. of St. Andrews and Cambridge; edited the *Fifeshire Journal;* edited in London a musical weekly called *The Orchestra* 1863, also the *Paris Times, Sock and Buskin* 1867 and *Cramer's Opera Bouffe Cabinet* 1874; his song *The Last Stirrup-cup* became very popular; wrote librettos of many operettas and burlesques; translated and adapted most of the more successful modern French comic operas, most popular of which were *Genevieve de Brabant* produced at Philharmonic theatre

FARNIE, H. B. (*Con.*)

11 Nov. 1871, *Nemesis* at Strand theatre 17 April 1873, *La Fille de Madame Angot* at Gaiety theatre 10 Nov. 1873 and *Les Cloches de Corneville* at Folly theatre 23 Feb. 1878; 20 of his adaptations were printed 1850–87. *d.* Paris 22 Sep. 1889. *Law Reports 5 P.D. 153, 6 P.D. 35, 8 Appeal Cases* 43.

FARQUHAR, THOMAS NEWMAN. *b.* 1809; solicitor in London 1830 to death; one of the nine purchasers of the Crystal Palace for £70,000, 24 May 1852, one of the original directors of the Co. at Sydenham. *d.* Sydenham, Kent 30 July 1866.

FARQUHARSON, FRANCIS (*son of Rev. Robert Farquharson of Allarque, co. Aberdeen*). *b.* 1787; entered Bombay army 1802; col. 9 Bombay N.I. 8 March 1845 to 1869; general 6 Jany. 1863. *d.* Clifton 20 March 1872.

FARQUHARSON, JAMES JOHN (*only son of James Farquharson of Littleton, Dorset 1728–95*). *b.* 9 Oct. 1784; ed. at Eton and Ch. Ch. Ox.; B.A. 1828; student of L.I. 1829; kept a pack of foxhounds in Dorset at his own expense 1806 to 1858 when he sold the pack; kept a small racing stud; sheriff of Dorset 1809. *d.* 9 March 1871. *Sporting Review xxxviii,* 355–58 (1857), *xxxix,* 440–42 (1858), *portrait; Baily's Mag. xi,* 113–18 (1866), *portrait.*

FARQUHARSON, ROBERT, stage name of Robert Farquharson Smith. *b.* 1820; articled to Harris of Drury Lane, chorus master; sang at coronation of William iv, 1838; sang in opera at Drury Lane and Surrey theatres, also at concerts; member of the Sims Reeves opera troupe; went to Australia 1856, sang there in opera and concerts; sang at the Opera Comique, London. *d.* 2 Wilberforce road, Finsbury park, London 12 Feb. 1880.

FARR, WILLIAM. *b.* Kenley, Shropshire 30 Nov. 1807; studied medicine in Paris 1829–31; L.S.A. 1832; practised in London 1833–38; compiler of abstracts in registrar general's office 1838; an assistant comr. for censuses of 1851 and 1861 and a comr. for that of 1871; wrote greater part of the reports on each census; F.S.S. 1839, treasurer 1855–67, vice-pres. 1869–70, pres. 1871–2; F.R.S. 7 June 1855 to 1882; C.B. 10 April 1880; gold medallist of British Association 1880; author of *A medical guide to Nice* 1841 and of many papers in the *Lancet* and other periodicals. *d.* 78 Portsdown road, Maida Vale, London 14 April 1883. *Biographical notice of W. Farr by F. A. C. Hare* 1883; *W. Farr's Vital Statistics* 1885 *with biographical sketch by N. A. Humphreys, portrait.*

FARRAR, REV. JOHN (*youngest son of Rev. John Farrar, Wesleyan minister, who d.* 1837). *b.* Alnwick 29 July 1802; Wesleyan min. Aug. 1822; resident minister successively at Sheffield, Huddersfield, Macclesfield and London; classical tutor at Wesleyan theological institution, Richmond, Surrey 1843–58; governor and chaplain of Woodhouse Grove school near Leeds 1858–68; governor of Headingley college, Leeds 1868–76; pres. of Wesleyan conference at Birmingham 1854 and at Burslem 1870; author of *The proper names of the Bible* 1839, 2 ed. 1844; *A biblical and theological dictionary illustrative of the Old and New Testament* 1851 and 3 other books. *d.* Headingley, Leeds 19 Nov. 1884. *bur.* Abney Park cemetery, London 25 Nov. *Slugg's Woodhouse Grove school* (1885) *pp.* 14, 79–84, 135, 257; *I.L.N. 6 Aug.* 1870 *p.* 149, *portrait.*

FARRE, ARTHUR (*younger son of John Richard Farre 1775–1862*). *b.* London 6 March 1811; ed. at Charterhouse sch. and Caius coll. Cam.; M.B. 1833, M.D. 1841; F.R.S. 2 May 1839; F.R.C.P. 1843, Harveian orator 1872; professor of obstetric medicine at King's college, and phys. accoucheur to King's college hospital 1841–62; examiner in midwifery to royal college of surgeons 1852–75; pres. of Royal Microsopical Society 1851–2; phys. extraordinary to the Queen 30 Aug. 1875 to death; pres. of Obstetrical Society 1875; author of *The Uterus and its appendages* forming parts 49 and 50 of Todd's *Cyclopædia of anatomy and physiology* 1858. *d.* 18 Albert Mansions, Victoria st. Westminster 17 Dec. 1887.

FARRE, FREDERICK JOHN (*brother of the preceding*). *b.* Charterhouse sq. London 16 Dec. 1804; ed. at Charterhouse, gold medallist 1821, captain 1822; foundation scholar at St. John's coll. Cam., 32 wrangler 1827; M.A. 1830, M.D. 1837; lecturer on botany at St. Bartholomew's hospital 1831–54, on materia medica 1854–76, assistant phys. 1836, phys. 1854; phys. to Royal London Ophthalmic hospital 1843 to death; F.R.C.P. 1838, lecturer on materia medica 1843–5, treasurer 1868–83, vice pres. 1885; one of the editors of first *British Pharmacopœia* 1864, and of an abridgment of Pereira's *Materia Medica* 1865, new eds. 1872 *and* 1874. *d.* 35 Elsham road, Kensington, London 9 Nov. 1886.

FARRE, JOHN RICHARD (*son of Richard John Farre of Barbadoes, surgeon*). *b.* Barbadoes 31 Jany. 1775; student at United Borough hosps. London 1792; spent two years at Edinburgh; M.D. Aberdeen 22 Jany. 1806; L.C.P. 31 March 1806; physician in London 1806;

FARRE, J. R. *(Con.)*

joint founder with J. C. Saunders of Royal London Ophthalmic hospital 1806, physician there 1806–56; edited Journal of Morbid Anatomy, ophthalmic medicine and pharmaceutical analysis 1828; author of *The morbid anatomy of the liver* 1812–15, *Pathological researches on malformations of the human heart* 1814. *d.* Pentonville road, London 7 May 1862.

FARRELL, FRANCIS. Entered Bombay army 1818; col. 28 Bombay N.I 15 March 1851 to death; M.G. 28 Nov. 1854. *d.* Hyde lodge, Winchester 17 July 1869 aged 69.

FARREN, HENRY *(eld. son of Wm. Farren 1786–1861).* *b.* 1825; made his first appearance on the stage at Haymarket theatre as Charles Surface 1848; played leading comedy parts at Strand 1847–50 and Olympic 1850–53; manager of Brighton theatre short time; played in the U.S. 1854 to death; manager of theatre at St. Louis. *d.* St. Louis 8 Jany. 1860.

FARREN, HARRIET ELIZABETH *(dau. of Mr. Diddear, provincial theatrical manager).* *b.* Penzance, Cornwall 31 July 1789; made her first appearance in London at Covent Garden theatre 7 Oct. 1813 as Desdemona; played leading characters in tragedy and comedy at Covent Garden and Drury Lane; retired about 1837. *(m.* (1) 1805 John Faucit Saville actor, he *d.* 1 Nov. 1853. *m.* (2) Jany. 1856 William Farren 1786–1861). *d.* 23 Brompton sq. London 16 June 1857. *Oxberry's Dramatic Biography iii,* 127–35 (1825), *portrait; Theatrical inquisitor x,* 83–86 (1817), *portrait.*

FARREN, WILLIAM (3 *son of Wm. Farren of Covent Garden theatre, London, actor, who d. 9 May 1795 aged 41).* *b.* 13 May 1786; made his first appearance on the stage as Sir Archy Macsarcasm in *Love à la Mode* at Plymouth theatre about 1806; played in Ireland; appeared in London at Covent Garden theatre as Sir Peter Teazle 10 Sep. 1818; played at Covent Garden winter seasons 1818–28, at the Haymarket summer seasons 1818–28; played at Drury Lane 1828–1837, at Covent Garden again 1837, at the Haymarket 1837–47; lessee of the Strand 1847–50, of the Olympic 2 Sep. 1850 to 22 Sep. 1853; took final farewell of the stage at the Haymarket theatre 16 July 1855; famous for his old men characters. *d.* 23 Brompton sq. London 24 Sep. 1861. *Oxberry's Dramatic Biography iii,* 37–47 (1825), *portrait; Metropolitan mag. xviii,* 85–91 (1837); *Theatrical inquisitor xiii,* 323 (1818), *portrait; I.L.N. i,* 188 (1842), *portrait, xxvii,* 99, 100 (1855), *portrait.*

FARRER, JAMES *(eld. son of the succeeding).* *b.* London 8 May 1812; ed. at Winchester and New coll. Ox.; M.P. for South Durham 1847–57 and 1859–65. *d.* Ingleborough near Settle, Yorkshire 13 June 1879.

FARRER, JAMES WILLIAM *(eld. son of James Farrer).* *b.* 11 May 1785; ed. at Brasenose coll. Ox., B.A. 1806, M.A. 1809; barriste L.I. 11 Feb. 1811; a master in chancery 9 March 1824 to 30 June 1852 when office was abolished by 15 & 16 Vict. c. 80, and he retired on full pay; author of *Observations on the offices of the Masters in Chancery* 1848. *d.* Ingleborough 9 Nov. 1863.

FARRIER, ROBERT. *b.* Chelsea 1796; exhibited 35 pictures at R.A., 50 at B.I. and 32 at Suffolk st. gallery 1818–72 many of which were engraved; one of his pictures 'The Parting' is in the South Kensington Museum. *d.* Holly villa, Hayes, Uxbridge 19 April 1879.

FAULKNER, GEORGE. *b.* Oldham st. Manchester about 1790; partner in a firm of silk, cotton and linen manufacturers at Manchester 1812; the first chairman of trustees of Owens college, Manchester 1851 to Aug. 1858; a liberal benefactor to the college. *d.* Limebank, Crumpsall, Manchester 21 Feb. 1862. *Thompson's Owen's College, Manchester* (1886) *pp.* 52–8; *Manchester Courier 1 March* 1862 *p.* 7.

FAULKNER, THOMAS. *b.* Fulham near London; bookseller and stationer in Paradise row, Chelsea; contributed essays and reviews to *Gent. Mag.* for more than half a century from Oct. or Nov. 1797; published histories of Chelsea, Fulham, Kensington, Hammersmith, Brentford, Chiswick and Ealing 1810–45. *d.* Smith st. Chelsea 26 May 1855 in 79 year. *G.M. xliv,* 215–16 (1855).

FAUSSETT, REV. GODFREY *(son of Henry Godfrey Faussett of Nackington near Canterbury, who d.* 1825). Matric. from C.C. coll. Ox. 7 July 1797 aged 16, scholar 1797; B.A. 1801, M.A. 1804, B.D. 1822, D.D. 1827; probationary fellow of Magd. coll. July 1802; select preacher 1809, 1813, 1824 and 1835; Bampton lecturer 1820; Lady Margaret's professor of divinity in Univ. of Ox. 1827 to death; preb. of Worcester 1827–40; canon of Ch. Ch. Ox. 1840 to death; V. of Cropthorne, Worcs. 1840 to death; author of *The claims of the established church,* Oxford 1820; *The Thirty-nine articles considered with reference to No. 90 of Tracts for the Times* 1841 and other works. *d.* Christ Church, Oxford 28 June 1853.

FAUSSETT, THOMAS GODFREY (6 *son of the preceding*). *b.* Oxford 1829; ed. at C.C. coll. Ox., B.A. 1851, M.A. 1854, fellow of his coll. 1857–64; barrister L.I. 26 Jany. 1863; chapter clerk and auditor of Canterbury cathedral 1866 to death; district registrar of Court of Probate at Canterbury 1871 to death; F.S.A. March 1859; hon. sec. of Kent Archæological Soc. 1863–73; author of many articles on antiquity and archæology; wrote the article *Canterbury* in *Encyclopædia Britannica*, 9 *ed. d.* The Precincts, Canterbury 26 Feb. 1877. *Rev. W. J. Loftie's Memorials of T. G. Faussett* 1878.

FAUVET, PIERRE ADOLPHE DUHART-. Lived in London nearly 50 years; head French master at Working men's college North London and other institutions; author of *Champ de Roses* 1847; *Poésies Françaises* 1870, 2 *ed.* 1870; wrote Soyer's *Pantropheon, or history of food and its preparations* 1853. *d.* 8 Arlingford road, Brixton, London 15 Oct. 1882 aged 75.

FAVANTI, RITA, stage name of Margaret Edwards. Educ. at Royal Academy of Music, Aug. 1836 to May 1840; appeared as Mademoiselle Favanti at Her Majesty's theatre in Cenerentola 23 March 1844; had a compass of voice of almost 3 octaves. *d.* 28 Abingdon villas, Kensington 19 Aug. 1867 aged 39. *H. F. Chorley's Thirty years musical recollections* i, 244–50 (1862); *I.L.N.* iv, 189 (1844), *portrait*.

FAWCETT, CHARLES. *b.* Leicester; acted at Hull; author of plays entitled *The Irish Farmer* and *Cousin Sophy* played by Barney Williams; *The Irish American* played by John Drew, *Roderick the King of the Goths* and *Napoleon the Third. d.* Philadelphia 23 July 1867.

FAWCETT, HENRY (*son of William Fawcett of Salisbury, draper* 1793–1887). *b.* Salisbury 26 Aug. 1833; ed. at King's coll. London and Trin. Hall, Cam., 7 wrangler 1856; B.A. 1856, M.A. 1859; student at L.I. 26 Oct. 1854; fell. of his coll. Dec. 1856; totally blinded by his father when shooting 17 Sep. 1858; professor of political economy in Univ. of Cam. 27 Nov. 1863 to death; contested Cambridge 1862, Brighton 1863 and 1874; M.P. for Brighton, July 1865 to 26 Jany. 1874, M.P. for Hackney 24 April 1874 to death; postmaster general 3 May 1880 to death, established the parcels post 1 Aug. 1883; P.C. 3 May 1880; lord rector of Glasgow Univ. 1883; a correspondent of French academy 1884; author of *Manual of political economy* 1863, 6 *ed.* 1883 and 10 other books. *d.* 18 Brookside, Cambridge 6 Nov. 1884, monument

FAWCETT, H. (*Con.*)

placed in Westminster Abbey by national subscription. *bur.* Trumpington churchyard 10 Nov. *Life of Henry Fawcett by Leslie Stephen* (1885), 2 *portraits; Times 7 Nov. 1884 p. 10, cols. 3–6.*

FAWCETT, JOHN (*son of a shoemaker at village of Wennington, Lancashire*). *b.* Wennington 8 Dec. 1789, shoemaker there to 1825; organist and professor of music at Bolton 1825 to death; his compositions are said to number 200; his chief works are *The Seraphic Choir* 1840; *The Cherub Lute* 1845; *Music for thousands* 1845; *The Lancashire vocalist* 1854; *The temperance minstrel* 1856; *Chanting made easy* 1857; *The universal chorister* 1863; *The temperance harmonist* 1864. *d.* Bolton 26 Oct. 1867. *J. Fawcett's Harp of Zion, portrait.*

FAWCETT, JOHN (3 *son of the preceding*). *b.* Bolton 1824; organist of St. John's church, Farnworth, Lancs. 1825–1842; of Bolton parish church 1842 to death; obtained degree of Mus. Bac. Ox. 3 Nov. 1852, his exercise a sacred cantata *Supplication and Thanksgiving* was published by subscription 1856. *d.* Manchester 1 July 1857.

FAWCETT, REV. JOSHUA (2 *son of Richard Fawcett of Bradford, worsted manufacturer*). *b.* Bradford 9 May 1809; ed. at Trin. coll. Cam., B.A. 1829, M.A. 1836; P.C. of Holy Trinity, Wibsey, Yorkshire 17 Feb. 1833 to death; hon. canon of Ripon, Sep. 1860 to death; edited *The Village Churchman* afterwards incorporated with *The Churchman* and continued under title of *The Churchman's Magazine* 8 vols. 1838–45; author of *A harmony of the Gospels* 1836 and other books. *d.* suddenly while walking on Low Moor, Bradford 21 Dec. 1864. *J. James's Bradford* (1866) 263–64.

FAWKNER, JOHN PASCOE. *b.* London 20 Aug. 1792; went out to Port Phillip, Australia 1803; a publican at Launceston, Van Diemen's Land; brought out the *Launceston Advertiser* 1830; founded Melbourne, Victoria 29 Aug. 1835; brought out the *Melbourne Advertiser* the first newspaper in Victoria 1 Jany. 1838, the *Port Phillip Patriot* 5 March 1838 converted it into the *Daily News;* member of first legislative council Oct. 1851; member of the upper house, Nov. 1856 to death. *d.* Melbourne 4 Sep. 1869. *Labilliere's Early history of Victoria* ii, 88–95 (1878).

FAWSITT, AMY, stage name of Mary Ann Fawsitt (*dau. of William Fawsitt of the Manchester exchange, who d.* 1843). *b.* London

FAWSITT, A. *(Con.)*

1836; ed. for a governess at Abbeville and Milan; first appeared on stage at Edinburgh 1865; first appeared in London at Holborn theatre as Flora Grainger in *The Mistress of the Mill* 1 May 1869; played Lottie in Albery's *Two Roses* at Vaudeville theatre 400 times from 4 June 1870; played Lady Teazle at same theatre 412 times from 18 July 1872; came out at· Fifth Avenue theatre New York 27 Sep. 1876. *(m.* 27 May 1871 Edward Menzies of Perth and Belgrave sq. London). *d.* 8th Avenue, New York 26 Dec. 1876. *bur.* Marble cemetery, New York 29 Dec. *Illustrated sporting and dramatic news i,* 217, 219 (1874), *portrait; London Figaro* 29 Sep. 1877, *pp.* 10–12.

FEARON, VEN. HENRY *(son of Rev. J. F. Fearon, V. of Cuckfield, Sussex).* *b.* 20 June 1802; ed. at Winchester and Em. coll. Cam., B.A. 1824, M.A. 1827; fellow of Em. coll.; R. of Loughborough 1848 to death; archdeacon of Leicester 1863–84; author of *Old Dame Walder, a tale of Suffolk life* 1847; *What to learn and what to unlearn, Lectures* 1860 and other books. *d.* Loughborough 12 June 1885.

FEARON, ROBERT BRYCE. Ensign 31 foot June 1795, lieut. col. 8 May 1823; lieut. col. 64 foot 12 Jany. 1826; lieut. col. 6 foot 1 May 1828; lieut. col. 40 foot 23 Nov. 1838 to death; commanded troops on board ship 'Kent' burnt in Bay of Biscay 1 March 1825, C.B. for his services on this occasion 2 April 1825; M.G. 9 Nov. 1846; committed suicide by shooting himself at residence of his daughter Lady Palmer at Much Hadham, Herts. 26 Jany. 1851.

FEARON, SAMUEL TURNER. M.R.C.S. 1848; M.D. St. Andrews 1851; professor of Chinese literature, King's college, London. *d.* Abercrombie house, Southampton st. Fitzroy sq. London 18 Jany. 1854 aged 35.

FEATHERSTON, ISAAC EARL *(4 son of Thomas Featherston of Cotfield house, Durham).* *b.* 21 March 1813; studied medicine at Univ. of Edin., M.D. 1836; went to New Zealand 1840; superintendent of province of Wellington 1853–71; member of general assembly for Wanganui and afterwards for city of Wellington; agent general for New Zealand in England 1871 to death. *d.* 60 York road, Brighton 19 June 1876. *W. Gisborne's New Zealand Rulers* (1886), 83, *portrait.*

FEATHERSTONHAUGH, GEORGE WILLIAM. *b.* London 1780; went to U.S. America 1807

FEATHERSTONHAUGH, G. W. *(Con.)*

where he married and resided; geologist of U.S.A. in journeys through Mexico and Arkansas 1834–5; commissioner to determine boundary between U.S.A. and British North America 1839; British consul at Havre 29 Oct. 1844 to death; instrumental in bringing Louis Philippe and his queen to England 3 March 1848; F.R.S. 2 April 1835; edited the monthly American journal of geology from 1831; author of *The Republic of Cicero, translated* 1829; *Excursion through the slave states* 2 vols. 1844; *A canoe voyage up the Minnay Sotor* 2 vols. 1847 and other books. *d.* Havre 27 Sep. 1866. *Quarterly Journal of Geological Soc. xxiii, pp. xliii-v* (1867).

FECHTER, CHARLES ALBERT *(son of Jean Maria Guillaume Fechter, sculptor).* *b.* Hanway yard, Oxford st. London 23 Oct. 1824; made his début at Comedie Française, Paris, Dec. 1844; played at St. James's theatre, London 1847; played at Vaudeville theatre, Paris 1852–58; joint director of Odeon theatre 1857; the leading jeune premier in France; appeared as Ruy Blas in Victor Hugo's drama *Ruy Blas* at Princess's theatre 27 Oct. 1860, and as Hamlet 20 March 1861 with great success; lessee of Lyceum theatre, Dec. 1862 to Nov. 1867; played at Adelphi theatre 1867–69 and 1872; first appeared in New York 10 Jany. 1870; opened Globe theatre, New York 12 Sep. 1870; opened Park theatre, New York 15 April 1874; broke his leg 1876 when he retired from the stage. *d.* at his farm, Richmond, Bucks. county, Philadelphia 5 Aug. 1879. *Kate Field's C. A. Fechter* (1882), 4 *portraits; A. Brereton's Some famous Hamlets* (1884) 45–50; *Pascoe's Dramatic List* (1879) 127–36; *Tallis's Illustrated life in London* (1864) 104, 105, 138, 2 *portraits; Theatre iii,* 70, 132 (1879), *portrait.*

FEDERICI, FREDERICK, stage name of Frederick Baker. Sang frequently in London at St. James's hall and Monday popular concerts; played all the baritone parts in Gilbert and Sullivan's comic operas in America and England; went to Australia, June 1887; played Mephistopheles in *Faust* at Princess's theatre, Melbourne 3 March 1888. *d.* in the greenroom of the theatre at 12.10 a.m. 4 March 1888. *Illustrated sporting and dramatic news* 26 *May* 1888 *pp.* 321, 322, *portrait.*

FEENEY, PATRICK. *b.* Galway 1800; ran away from home at 9 years of age; a strolling showman or performer of feats of strength and agility, he balanced coach wheels, a plank 21 feet long and a live donkey on a ladder;

FEENEY, P. (Con.)

always known as Old Malabar; made the round of all the fairs in England and Scotland; an account of his life was written and published by David Prince Miller; performed in streets of Glasgow 5 Nov. 1883. *d.* 9 M'Pherson st. Glasgow 6 Nov. 1883. *Era 10 Nov. 1883 p. 4, col. 4.*

FEENEY, PATRICK. *b.* Rosscommon 19 Nov. 1850; first appeared on the stage at Birmingham as an Irish comic singer; first appeared in London 1876; sang in all chief music halls in London and the provinces; the leading Irish comic singer for some years before his death; spent 40 weeks in the United States 1888. *d.* Kennington park road, London 13 May 1889.

FEENEY, RIGHT REV. THOMAS. Professor in Maynooth college; bishop of Ptolemais and administrator apostolic of Killala, July 1839, consecrated 13 Oct. 1839; bishop of Killala 12 Dec. 1847 to death. *d.* Killala 9 June 1873.

FEILD, RIGHT REV. EDWARD (3 *son of James Feild*). *b.* Worcester 7 June 1801; ed. at Rugby and Queen's coll. Ox., Michel scholar, Michel fellow 1827–33; B.A. 1823, M.A. 1826, D.D. 1844; R. of English Bicknor, Gloucs. 1834–44; the first inspector of schools under National Society, May 1840; bishop of Newfoundland 22 March 1844 to death; consecrated at Lambeth palace 28 April; author of addresses, sermons and charges. *d.* the bishop's palace, Bermuda 8 June 1876. *Tucker's Memoir of E. Field* (1877), *portrait.*

FEILDEN, HENRY MASTER (*eld. son of the succeeding*). *b.* Witton park, Blackburn 21 Feb. 1818; M.P. for Blackburn 30 March 1869 to death. *d.* Lytham, Lancashire 5 Sep. 1875.

FEILDEN, JOSEPH. *b.* Blackburn 1792; sheriff of Lancs. 1818; M.P. for Blackburn 15 Aug. 1865 to 16 March 1869 when unseated on petition. *d.* Wilton park near Blackburn 29 Aug. 1870.

FEIST, CHARLES (*son of Rev. Peter Feist who became a dissenting minister*). *b.* Beverley, Yorkshire 12 April 1795; educ. Beverley gram. sch.; in solicitor's office London; member of Norfolk and Suffolk circuits under David Fisher 5 years; proprietor of a sch. at Swaffham, Norfolk 7 years, of a sch. in London 1 year, of a sch. in Newmarket 18 years where he educated many of the jockeys; correspondent of *Sunday Times* at Newmarket; came to London 1842 in connection with *Sunday Times;* author of *Breathings of the*

FEIST, C. (Con.)

Woodland Lyre 1815; *Useful rhymes for youths betimes* 1837; *Spring blossoms, dialogues on subjects entertaining to children,* 4 ed. 1844. *d.* 10 Granville sq. Clerkenwell, London 10 July 1856. *Sporting Review xxxvi,* 391–4 (1856).

FEIST, HENRY MORT. Editor of *The Sporting Life* 16 March 1859 to decease, wrote in it under name of Augur; no man understood racing and racing men more thoroughly; reporter and sporting prophet for *Daily Telegraph* under pseudonym of Hotspur; amateur actor and good in the role of a clown. *d.* Croydon 18 Dec. 1874 aged 37, a fund raised for his wife and children, admiral Rous president. *Sporting Times 26 Dec. 1874 pp. 157–8, portrait; Sporting Life 19 Dec. 1874, p. 2, 26 Dec. p. 2; Illust. sporting and dramatic news ii,* 327, 333 (1875), *portrait.*

FELIX, NICHOLAS, assumed name of Nicholas Wanostrocht (*son of Vincent Wanostrocht of Camberwell, Surrey, schoolmaster, who d. 1824*). *b.* Camberwell 5 Oct. 1804; kept a school at Peckham road, Camberwell 1824–32 when he leased it to Royal Naval School; studied cricket under Harry Hampton at Camberwell; invented the Catapulta with which he practised; left hand batsman; slow underhand left hand bowler; played first match at Lord's 23 Aug. 1828; played in the Gentlemen *v.* Players matches 1831–52; kept a school at Blackheath; afterwards lived at Montpellier road, Brighton; subscription raised for him 1858; portrait, animal and landscape painter; inventor of the tubular india rubber gloves; a player of fives and billiards; author of *Felix on the bat* 1845, 3 ed. 1855. *d.* Wimborne Minster, Dorset 3 Sep. 1876. *Lillywhite's Cricket Scores ii,* 61 (1862), *vii, p. xi* (1877).

FELLOWES, CHARLES (*son of Sir Thomas Fellowes 1778–1853*). *b.* 19 Oct. 1823; entered navy 14 May 1836; captain 26 Feb. 1858; R.A. 18 June 1876; admiral superintendent of Chatham dockyard 1876–79; V.A. 31 Dec. 1880; C.B. 20 May 1871; commanded channel squadron 3 July 1885 to death. *d.* Gibraltar 8 March 1886.

FELLOWES, SIR JAMES (3 *son of Wm. Fellowes, M.D. of Leicester, physician to George iv*). *b.* Edinburgh 1772; ed. at Rugby; entered at Peterhouse, Cam., removed to Caius as a Tancred scholar; fellow of Caius; studied medicine in London and Edinburgh; M.B. Cam. 1797, M.D. 5 July 1803; F.R.C.P. 30 Sep. 1805; hospital assist. June 1794; one of phys. to the Forces 28 Oct. 1795; knighted by George 3rd at the Queen's palace 21 March

FELLOWES, SIR J. (Con.)

1810; inspector general of military hospitals 29 April 1813 to 1815 when he retired; F.R.S. 29 Feb. 1816; author of *Reports of the pestilential disorder of Andalusia which appeared at Cadiz in the years* 1800, 1804, 1810 and 1813. 1815. *d.* Langstone cottage near Havant 30 Dec. 1857.

FELLOWES, SIR THOMAS (*brother of the preceding*). *b.* Minorca 1778; midshipman in service of H.E.I.C.; master's mate R.N. 1797; C.B. 4 June 1815; K.C. 22 Feb. 1822; knighted 13 Feb. 1828; naval A.D.C. to the Queen 1841–47; superintendent of royal naval hospital and victualling yard, Plymouth 6 Feb. 1843 to 1 Sep. 1847; R.A. 26 July 1847. *d.* Great Bedwyn vicarage, Wilts. 12 April 1853.

FELLOWS, SIR CHARLES (*son of John Fellows of Nottingham*). *b.* Nottingham, Aug. 1799; made the 13th recorded ascent of Mont Blanc 25 July 1827; discovered Xanthus and Tlos, Asia Minor 1838 and 13 other ancient cities there 1840; brought home the Lycian marbles 1844; knighted at St. James's palace 7 May 1845; author of *A journal written during an excursion in Asia Minor* 1839; *An account of discoveries in Lycia* 1841 and other books. *d.* 4 Montagu place, Russell sq. London 8 Nov. 1860. *C. Brown's Lives of Nottinghamshire Worthies* (1882) 352–3.

FELLOWS, THOMAS HOWARD (*eld. son of Thomas Fellows of Moneyhill, Herts., solicitor*). *b.* 1823; ed. at Eton; barrister I.T. 17 Nov. 1852; went to Melbourne 1853; member of legislative assembly of Victoria 1855–58 and 1867–72; member of legislative council 1858–67; solicitor general 1856–57 and 1857–58; attorney general 25 Feb. 1857 to 24 March 1857; postmaster general 14 Oct. 1863 to 24 March 1864; minister of justice and leader of the Assembly, May to July 1868; judge of supreme court of Victoria 18 Dec. 1872 to death; author of *The law of costs* 1847; *Convocation, its origin, progress and authority* 1852. *d.* Melbourne 8 April 1878 in 56 year.

FENN, REV. JOSEPH FINCH (*son of Rev. Joseph Fenn, minister of Blackheath park chapel, Kent*). *b.* 1820; ed. at Trin. coll. Cam., fellow 1844–7; B.A. 1842, M.A. 1845, B.D. 1877; V. of Stotfold, Beds. 1847–60; P.C. of Ch. Ch. Cheltenham 1860 to death; chaplain to bishop of Gloucester and Bristol 1877 to death; hon. canon of Gloucester 1879 to death; proctor in convocation 1880 to death; promoter of free library system in Cheltenham; author of a vol. of sermons entitled *Lenten Teachings*. *d.* Cheltenham 22 July 1884.

FENNELL, JOHN GREVILLE. *b.* at sea between Ireland and England 1807; artist, naturalist and angler; drew pictures of tournament at Eglinton Castle for *Illustrated London News;* wrote on fishing in *The Field* 1853 to death; contributed to *Fishing Gazette* under name of Creel, and other sporting papers; author of *The Rail and the Rod* 1867; *The book of the Roach* 1870. *d.* Jessamine cottage, Henley 13 Jany. 1885. *Fishing Gazette x,* 24, 51, 61, 220, 264 (1885), *portrait.*

FENTON, CHARLES GILL (*son of James Gill Fenton, stage director to Edmund Kean, who d. 20 Aug. 1877 aged 83*). Played small parts in pantomimes 1831; played Shakesperian parts and principal parts in pantomimes at Sadler's Wells theatre 1844–59; actor and scene painter at Strand theatre about 1863–73; acted at Vaudeville theatre 1873–74. *d.* Shelburne road, Islington 15 Feb. 1877 aged 56.

FENTON, EDWARD DYNE. Ensign 53 foot 1847, lieut. 1849–57 when placed on h.p.; captain 14 foot 1858; captain 86 foot 1860–70 when he sold out; author of *Sorties from Gib in quest of sensation and sentiment* 1872; *Military men I have met* 1872; *Eve's Daughters* 1873; *B. an autobiography* 3 vols. 1874 a novel. *d.* Scarborough 29 July 1880.

FENWICK, EDWARD MATTHEW (*son of Edward James Reid of Jamaica*). *b.* Jamaica 1812; barrister M.T. 1 May 1854; assumed name of Fenwick in lieu of Reid, June 1851; contested Lancaster 30 April 1859; M.P. for Lancaster 13 April 1864, re-elected 1 Feb. 1866, election was declared void 23 April 1866 and writ was suspended till passing of Reform bill 1867 when borough was disfranchised. *d.* Burrow hill, Kirkby Lonsdale 16 Oct. 1877.

FENWICK, HENRY (*eld. son of Thomas Fenwick of Southill, co. Durham*). *b.* 1820; ed. at St. John's coll. Cam., B.A. 1842, M.A. 1845; barrister L.I. 6 May 1845; contested Sunderland, July 1852 and Durham, Dec. 1852; M.P. for Sunderland 1855–66. *d.* Lansdowne house, Richmond, Surrey 18 April 1868.

FENWICK-BISSET, MORDAUNT (*only son of Ven. Maurice George Fenwick-Bisset 1797–1879, archdeacon of Raphoe, Ireland*). *b.* Raphoe 27 Feb. 1825; ed. at Trin. coll. Cam.; master of Devon and Somerset stag hounds 1855–80; assumed additional name of Bisset 1853; sheriff of Somerset 1872; M.P. for West Somerset, April 1880 to Feb. 1884. *d.* Bagborough house near Taunton 7 July 1884. *Covert side sketches by J. N. Fitt* (1870) 219–22; *Fores's Sporting Notes,* Oct. 1884, *portrait.*

FERGUSON, SIR ADAM (*eld. son of Adam Ferguson 1723–1816, professor of moral philosophy in Univ. of Edin.*) *b.* Edinburgh 1771; ed. at Univ. of Edin.; captain 101 foot 1808–16 when placed on h.p.; prisoner of war in France 1812–14; deputy keeper of Regalia of Scotland 1818 to death, the Regalia were discovered 5 Feb. 1818; knighted by George iv at Edin. 29 Aug. 1822. *d.* Edinburgh 1 Jany. 1855 in 84 year. *Lockhart's Life of Sir Walter Scott* (1837) iv, 223, 249, 272.

FERGUSON, GEORGE. *b.* 1786; entered navy July 1798; captain 6 June 1814; admiral on half pay 11 Feb. 1861; M.P. for Banff 1832–37. *d.* 37 Charles st. Berkeley sq. London 15 March 1867.

FERGUSON, JAMES. *b.* Perthshire 31 Aug. 1797; taken to the United States 1800; assistant civil engineer on Erie canal 1817; first assistant of U.S. coast survey 1833–47; assistant astronomer of U.S. naval observatory 1847 to death; discovered three asteroids; contributed to *Gould's Astronomical Journal, Astronomische Nachrichten, Episcopal Church Review* and other magazines. *d.* Washington, D.C. 26 Sep. 1867.

FERGUSON, JAMES FREDERIC (*son of Jacques Frédéric Jaquemain, who assumed name of Ferguson 1793, deputy postmaster of Beaufort in South Carolina*). *b.* Charleston 1807; went to Dublin 1820; indexed the entire body of Exchequer records; clerk and sec. to commission for arranging records of the Irish courts 1850; in charge of the Exchequer records to death; contributed to *Gent. Mag., Notes and Queries, Topographer and Genealogist* and *Transactions of the Kilkenny archæological society;* translated *Norman French chronicle of conquest of Ireland, edited by M. Michel. d.* Dublin 26 Nov. 1855.

FERGUSON, JOHN (*son of William Ferguson of Irvine, Ayrshire, shipmaster*). *b.* Irvine 28 Feb. 1787; ed. at Ayr; in a banker's office; went to America; settled at Irvine 1810; left by his will £80,000 for educational and religious objects in Scotland, and about £375,000 called the Ferguson Bequest Fund interest of which is spent in building churches and schoolhouses, &c. *d.* 8 Jany. 1856.

FERGUSON, JOHN CREERY. Educ. at Trin. coll. Dublin, B.A. 1823, M.B. 1827, M.A. 1833; licentiate of K.Q.C.P. Ireland 1827, fellow 1829, hon. fellow 1846; professor of practice of medicine, school of physic, Trin. coll. Dublin; professor of practice of medicine Queen's college, Belfast to death. *d.* 14 Howard st. Belfast 24 June 1865.

FERGUSON, ROBERT (*son of Robert Ferguson of Indian civil service*). *b.* India 15 Nov. 1799; studied medicine in London, Heidelberg and Univ. of Edin., M.D. Edin. 1 Aug. 1823; resident medical officer of Marylebone infirmary; L.R.C.P. 22 Dec. 1824, F.R.C.P. 3 July 1837, censor 1844 and 1845, consiliarius 1857–59; phys. to Westminster Lying-in-hospital; professor of midwifery at King's coll. 1831–39 or 40; physician accoucheur to the Queen 16 July 1840; phys. extraordinary to the Queen 14 March 1857; contributed numerous articles to *Quarterly Review;* published *Essay on diseases of women, Puerperal Fever* 1839. *d.* Ascot cottage, Winkfield near Windsor 25 June 1865. *Munk's Roll of the royal college of physicians* (1878) iii, 295.

FERGUSON, SIR ROBERT ALEXANDER, 2 Baronet. *b.* Londonderry 1795; succeeded his father 1811; ed. at Trin. coll. Cam., M.A. 1817; M.P. for city of Derry 1830 to death; lord lieut. of Londonderry 1840 to death; col. of Derry militia 24 June 1839 to death. *d.* Dublin 13 March 1860.

FERGUSON, ROBERT MUNRO. *b.* 20 Aug. 1802; ed. at Eton and Univ. of Edin.; ensign 43 foot 24 Feb. 1820; lieut. col. 79 foot 13 March 1835 to 29 Oct. 1841; M.P. for Kirkaldy burghs 1841–62. *d.* Raith house near Kirkaldy 28 Nov. 1868.

FERGUSON, SIR SAMUEL (3 *son of John Ferguson of Collon house, co. Antrim*). *b.* Belfast 10 March 1810; ed. at Belfast and Trin. coll. Dublin, B.A. 1826, M.A. 1832, hon. LL.D. 1864; called to Irish bar 1838; Q.C. 16 June 1859; deputy keeper of public records of Ireland 1867; knighted 17 March 1878; pres. of Royal Irish Academy 1882; contributed from 1833 to *Dublin Univ. Mag.;* wrote many tales and poems in *Blackwood's Mag.;* author of *Lays of the Western Gael* 1865; *Congal, an epic poem in five books* 1872; *Poems* 1880; *Ogham inscriptions in Ireland, Wales and Scotland, edited by Lady Ferguson* 1887. *d.* Strand lodge, Howth, co. Dublin 9 Aug. 1886. *bur.* Donegore, co. Antrim. *O'Hagan's Poetry of Sir S. Ferguson* 1887; *A. P. Graves's Has Ireland a national poet?; Blackwood's Mag.* Nov. 1886 *pp.* 621–41.

FERGUSON, WILLIAM. Entered Ceylon civil service 1839; lived in Ceylon, Dec. 1839 to death; author of *The Palmyra Palm, Borassus flabelliformis, Colombo* 1850; *A plan of the summit of Adam's Peak; Scripture botany of Ceylon* and 4 other books. *d.* Ceylon 31 July 1887.

FERGUSON-DAVIE, SIR HENRY ROBERT, 1 Baronet. *b.* 2 May 1797; cornet 9 Lancers 18 March 1818; major 34 foot 28 Dec. 1826, lieut. col. 1828–29; captain Grenadier guards 1830, major 1844–47; col. 73 foot 17 Feb. 1865 to death; general 25 June 1866; took additional surname of Davie 9 Feb. 1846; M.P. for Haddington burghs 1846–78; created baronet 9 Jany. 1847. *d.* Creedy park near Crediton 1 Dec. 1885.

FERGUSSON, SIR JAMES *(son of Charles Fergusson).* *b.* 17 March 1787; ensign 18 foot 20 Aug. 1801; lieut. col. 3 foot 16 May 1814 to 1815 when placed on h.p.; lieut. col. of 88 foot 12 Aug. 1819, of 52 foot 2 June 1825 to 10 May 1839 when he retired on h.p.; A.D.C. to the Sovereign 1830–41; col. 62 foot 9 March 1850 to 26 March 1850; col. 43 foot 26 March 1850 to death; commanded troops at Malta, May 1852 to July 1855; governor of Gibraltar 26 July 1855 to 1859; general 13 Feb. 1860; C.B. 26 Sep. 1831, K.C.B. 5 July 1855, G.C.B. 18 May 1860. *d.* Bath 4 Sep. 1865.

FERGUSSON, JAMES (2 son of *Wm. Fergusson, M.D.* 1773–1846). *b.* Ayr 22 Jany. 1808; an indigo manufacturer in India; member of Royal Asiatic Soc. 1840; general manager of Crystal palace, Sydenham, Feb. 1856 to 1858; F.R.S. 4 June 1863; sec. to first comr. of public works 1869; inspector of public buildings 1870–74; awarded by Institute of British Architects royal gold medal for architecture 1871; author of *Illustrations of rock cut temples of India* 1845; *Illustrations of ancient architecture in Hindostan* 1847; *History of architecture in all countries from the earliest times to the present day* 3 *vols.* 1865–7 and other books. *d.* 20 Langham place, London 9 Jany. 1886.

FERGUSSON, WILLIAM. Second lieut. R.M. 10 Sep. 1798, col. 9 Nov. 1846, col. commandant of Plymouth division 25 April 1849 to 26 Feb. 1851 when he retired on full pay; L.G. 6 Feb. 1857. *d.* Princes st. Hanover sq. London 26 Dec. 1861 aged 82.

FERGUSSON, SIR WILLIAM, 1 Baronet *(youngest son of James Fergusson of Lochmaben, Dumfriesshire).* *b.* Preston-pans, East Lothian 20 March 1808; ed. at high sch. and univ. of Edin., L.R.C.S. Edin. 1828, F.R.C.S. 1829; M.R.C.S. London 1840, F.R.C.S. 1844; professor of surgery King's college, London, May 1840 to April 1870; surgeon at King's college hospital May 1840 to death; surgeon extraord. to the Queen 18 Dec. 1855, one of serjeant surgeons in ordinary 11 Oct. 1867; F.R.S. Edin. 1839; F.R.S. 9 June 1848; created

FERGUSSON, SIR W. *(Con.)*
baronet 10 Jany. 1866; the greatest operative surgeon in Great Britain or probably in Europe; author of *A system of practical surgery* 1842, 5 *ed.* 1870; *Lectures on the progress of anatomy and surgery during the present century* 1867 and other books. *d.* 16 George st. Hanover sq. London 10 Feb. 1877. *bur.* West Linton, Peebleshire 16 Feb. *H. Smith's Sir W. Fergusson* 1877; *Medical Circular i,* 395–7 (1852), *portrait; I.L.N. xlviii,* 176 (1866), *portrait; Graphic xv,* 172 (1877), *portrait.*

FERMOR-HESKETH, SIR THOMAS GEORGE, 5 Baronet. *b.* Rufford hall near Ormskirk 11 Jany. 1825; succeeded his father 10 Feb. 1843; sheriff of Lancashire 1848; colonel 2 Lancashire militia 1 March 1852 to death; M.P. for Preston 4 April 1862 to death; assumed name of Fermor by royal license 8 Nov. 1867. *d.* Rufford hall 20 Aug. 1872.

FERMOY, EDMUND BURKE ROCHE, 1 Baron *(only son of Edward Roche of Trabolgan, co. Cloyne 1771–1855).* *b.* Aug. 1815; M.P. for co. Cork 1837–55, for Marylebone 1859–65; lord lieutenant of Cork 1856; created Baron Fermoy in the county of Cork 10 Sep. 1856. *d.* Trabolgan 17 Sep. 1874. *I.L.N. xxxv,* 82 (1859), *portrait.*

FERNELEY, JOHN *(son of Mr. Ferneley of Thrussington, Leics., wheelwright).* *b.* Thrussington 18 May 1782; pupil of Ben Marshal the animal painter; painted some large hunting pictures for Assheton Smith 1806; an animal painter at Melton Mowbray 1814 to death; enjoyed an unlimited patronage for about 50 years; many of his pictures were engraved in the *Sporting Magazine* and other similar works. *d.* Thrussington 4 June 1860. *Sporting Review xliv,* 4–6 (1860).

FERREY, BENJAMIN. *b.* Christchurch, Hants. 1 April 1810; ed. at Wimborne gr. sch.; articled to Augustus Pugin 1825; practised as an architect 1832 to death; designed oldest part of present town of Bournemouth 1837; diocesan architect of Bath and Wells 1841 to death; restored Wells cathedral 1842; designed many churches mainly Gothic; F.R.I.B.A. 1839; F.S.A. 1863; author of *Recollections of A. N. W. Pugin and of A. Pugin* 1861; author with E. W. Brayley of *Antiquities of the priory church of Christchurch, Hants.* 1834. *d.* 55 Inverness terrace, Bayswater, London 22 Aug. 1880.

FERRIER, JAMES FREDERICK *(son of John Ferrier of Edinburgh, writer to the signet).* *b.* Edinburgh 16 June 1808; ed. at univ. of

FERRIER, J. F. (Con.)

Edin. and Magd. coll. Ox., B.A. Ox. 1832; called to Scottish bar 1832; prof. of civil history in univ. of Edin. 1842–45; prof. of moral philosophy and political economy in univ. of St. Andrews 1845 to death; author of *The institutes of metaphysics* 1854, 2 ed. 1856 and other books. *d.* St. Andrews 11 June 1864. *Lectures on Greek philosophy by J. F. Ferrier* 1, *pp. vii-xliv*, 1866; *G. Gilfillan's Remoter Stars* (1867) 139–46.

FERRIER, SUSAN EDMONSTONE (*youngest child of James Ferrier of Edinburgh, writer to the signet 1744–1829*). *b.* Edinburgh 7 Sep. 1782; author of *Marriage, a novel* 3 vols. 1818, anon.; *The Inheritance* 3 vols. 1824, and *Destiny, or the chief's daughter* 3 vols. 1831. *d.* at house of her brother Walter Ferrier in Edinburgh 5 Nov. 1854. *Works of S. E. Ferrier* (1881), i, 1–38; *Edinburgh Review lxxiv*, 498–505 (1842).

FESTING, BENJAMIN MORTON (5 *son of Henry Festing, commander R.N., who d.* 1807). *b.* Andover, Hants., April 1794; entered navy 2 May 1805; inspector in the coast guard 11 July 1837–1840; captain on half pay 27 Sep. 1851; K.H. 1 Jany. 1837 for services on coast of Italy in 1812–13. *d.* Weymouth 10 May 1865.

FESTING, SIR FRANCIS WORGAN (2 *son of the preceding*). *b.* High Littleton, Somerset 24 July 1833; 2 lieut. R.M. 3 July 1850; served in the Baltic 1854–5, in the China expedition 1857–9; served in Ashantee war 1873–4 for which he received thanks of both Houses of Parliament 30 March 1874; A.A.G. of R.M. 1876–1883; A.D.C. to the Queen 7 July 1879; col. commandant R.M.A. 3 Sep. 1886; C.B. 31 March 1874; K.C.M.G. 8 May 1874. *d.* Donnington lodge, Newbury 21 Nov. 1886. *bur.* Eastney cemetery, Portsmouth 26 Nov. *Brackenbury's Ashantee war* (1874) i, 72–100; *Graphic 2 May* 1874, *pp.* 413, 415, 420, *portrait.*

FESTING, ROBERT WORGAN GEORGE (*brother of B. M. Festing 1794–1865*). Entered navy 22 Feb. 1799; captain 9 Oct. 1811; retired admiral 1 Nov. 1860; C.B. 20 July 1838. *d.* Maiden Bradley near Frome 16 July 1862 aged 73.

FEVERSHAM, WILLIAM DUNCOMBE, 2 Baron. *b.* London 14 Jany. 1798; ed. at Eton and Ch. Ch. Ox., B.A. 1820, M.A. 1823; M.P. for Yorkshire 1826–30, for North riding of Yorkshire 1832 to 16 July 1841 when he succeeded to the peerage; a breeder of short horn

FEVERSHAM, Baron. (Con.)

cattle. *d.* 3 Hyde park gate, London 11 Feb. 1867. *bur.* Helmsley church 19 Feb. *Sporting Review lvii*, 158 (1867).

FEW, ROBERT (*eld. son of Charles Few of Henrietta st. Covent Garden, London, solicitor*). *b.* 1807; ed. at old gr. sch. Marlborough; solicitor in London 1828 to death; settled with Rev. John Hodgson basis of Clergy Mutual Insurance Co. 1829, member of the board 40 years, deputy chairman 1872 to death; one of the founders of Marlborough college 1843, mem. of council many years; deputy steward of Westminster 1873 to death; author of *History of St. John's house* 1884. *d.* Wolsey grange, Esher, Surrey 24 Oct. 1887 in 80 year.

FFARINGTON, WILLIAM. *b.* 1777; entered navy 13 Oct. 1785; captain 18 Sep. 1815; retired admiral 4 Oct. 1862. *d.* Woodvale, Cowes 4 May 1868.

FFENNELL, WILLIAM JOSHUA (*eld. son of Joshua William Ffennell of Ballybrado near Cahir*). *b.* Ballybrado 16 Aug. 1799; sec. of river Suir Preservation Society 1837; fishery inspector under Board of Works 1845; commissioner to enquire into salmon fisheries of England and Wales 30 July 1860; inspector of fisheries Oct. 1861 to Oct. 1864; com. under Salmon fisheries of Scotland act 1861, 25 Sep. 1862; the act commonly called 'Ffennell's act' was passed 1848 being the first modern salmon fishery act; started with F. T. Buckland *Land and Water* 27 Jany. 1866. *d.* London 12 March 1867.

FFOULKES, VEN. HENRY POWELL (2 *son of John Powell Ffoulkes of Eriviatt, co. Denbigh, who d.* 2 *Dec.* 1826 *aged* 56). *b.* 2 Jany. 1815; ed. at Ball. coll. Ox., B.A. 1837, M.A. 1840; C. of St. Matthew, Buckley, Flints. 1840–57; R. of Llandyssil, Montgomery 1857–59; R. of Whittington, Salop 1859 to death; archdeacon of Montgomery and canon res. of St. Asaph, Feb. 1861 to death. *d.* the Canonry, St. Asaph 26 Jany. 1886.

FIDDES, THOMAS. Entered Bengal army 1804; col. of 45 Bengal N.I. 9 Aug. 1843, of 1 European fusiliers 1853, of 42 Bengal light infantry 1854, of 5 Bengal N.I. 1861 to death; L.G. 15 Sep. 1856. *d.* Oakfield, Cheltenham 13 April 1863 aged 81.

FIELD, CHARLES FREDERICK. Chief inspector of Metropolitan detective police to 1851 when he retired on pension; inquiry agent at Eldon

FIELD, C. F. (Con.)

chambers, Devereux court, Strand, London; figures prominently in Dickens's novel *Bleak House* under name of Inspector Bucket. *d.* 2 Gertrude st. Chelsea, London 27 Sep. 1874. *Publisher's Circular* 1874 *p.* 738.

FIELD, EDWIN WILKINS (*eld. child of Rev. Wm. Field* 1767–1851). *b.* Leam near Warwick 12 Oct. 1804; ed. at his father's school; admitted an attorney and solicitor Nov. 1826; partner with Wm. Sharpe 1827, they became partners in firm of Taylor and Roscoe 1835; secretary to royal commission to prepare a plan for new law courts 1865; a great law reformer, also amateur artist; author of *Memoir of Edgar Taylor, privately printed* 1839; *Observations of a solicitor on defects in the system of the equity courts* 1840 and 17 other pamphlets; drowned in the Thames near Goring 30 July 1871. *bur.* Highgate cemetery 4 Aug., statue by T. Woolner at solicitors' entrance to the Law courts in Carey st. *Edwin Wilkins Field, a memorial sketch by T. Sadler* 1872, *portrait; Law magazine and law review i,* 35–50 (1872).

FIELD, FREDERICK (2 *son of Charles Field of London, candle maker*). *b.* Lambeth, London 2 Aug. 1826; an original member of Chemical Soc. of London 1846; chemist to some copper-smelting works at Coquimbo, Chili 1848, manager of the works 1852; British vice consul at Caldera near Coquimbo 1853–56; chemist and sub-manager to smelting works at Guayacan 1856–59; lecturer on chemistry at St. Mary's hospital, London 1860; professor of chemistry in London Institution 1862; a partner in firm of J. C. and J. Field, candle makers 1866 to death; F.R.S. 4 June 1863; F.R.S. Edin.; M.R.I.A.; wrote 43 papers on scientific subjects. *d.* Oakfield, Addlestone 3 April 1885.

FIELD, REV. FREDERICK (*son of Henry Field of London, apothecary* 1755–1837). *b.* London 20 July 1801; ed. at Christ's hosp. and Trin. coll. Cam.; Tyrwhitt's Hebrew scholar and tenth wrangler 1823; B.A. 1823, M.A. 1826, hon. LL.D. 1875; fell. of his coll. 1824–43, hon. fell. of his coll. 1876 to death; R. of Reepham, Norfolk 1842–63; edited *S. Joannis Chrysostomi Homiliæ in Matthæum* 3 vols. 1839; *S. Joannis Chrysostomi Interpretatio omnium epistolarum Paulinarum per homilias facta* 7 vols. 1849–62; *Origenis Hexaphorum, quæ supersunt* 2 vols. 1874–5 and many other patristic works; member of Old Testament revision company 1870 to death. *d.* Carlton terrace, Heigham, Norwich 19 April 1885. *Origenis Hexaphorum* 1874, *preface; Cambridge Review* 6 May 1885.

FIELD, GEORGE. *b.* Berkhampstead, Herts. about 1777; grew Madder in his own garden from which he produced specimens of the colouring matter more beautiful than any before seen; invented the pereolator by atmospheric pressure for reducing the madder to its finest consistence 1816; author of *Chromatography, or a treatise on colours and pigments* 1835, 3 ed. 1885; *Outlines of analogical philosophy* 2 vols. 1839; *Rudiments of the painter's art, or a grammar of colouring* 1850 and 5 other books. *d.* Syon hill, Park cottage, Isleworth, Surrey 28 Sep. 1854.

FIELD, HENRY WILLIAM (4 *son of John Field* 1764–1845, *umpire at Royal Mint, London*). *b.* 23 March 1803; entered Royal Mint 1818, probationer assayer 1836, Queen's assay master 1851 to 1871; made chemically pure gold and brought the coin of the realm up to mathematical precision; exhibited 8 designs or models for coins at R.A. 1822–27. *d.* 10 Chesham place, Brighton 9 June 1888. *bur.* Nunhead cemetery, London 14 June. *J. Waylen's House of Cromwell* (1880) *p.* 49.

FIELD, JOSEPH M. *b.* London 1810; ed. in New York; first appeared on the stage in New York 1843; performed in most of the large cities; manager of Field's Varieties, St. Louis, Mo. 1852; established at St. Louis the *Reveille* a daily paper, one of the editors and chief proprietor; dramatized and produced many local plays; wrote many humorous sketches for the New Orleans *Picayune*, signed Straws which were widely quoted; proprietor of theatre in Mobile to death; author of *The drama of Pokerville, Philadelphia* 1847. *d.* Mobile 30 Jany. 1856.

FIELD, JOSHUA (*son of Mr. Field of Lower Thames st. London, corn and seed merchant*). *b.* Hackney 1786; ed. at Harlow, Essex 1793–1802; employed by Maudslay marine engine maker 1804–22, a partner 1822; one of the 6 founders of Institution of Civil engineers and, the first chairman 6 Jany. 1818, vice pres. 1837–48, pres. 1848–50; F.R.S. 3 March 1836. *d.* Balham hill house, Surrey 11 Aug. 1863. *Pusely's Commercial Companion,* 2 *ed.* (1860) 123–4; *Min. of proc. of Instit. of C.E. xxiii,* 488–92 (1864).

FIELD, REV. WILLIAM (*son of John Field of Stoke Newington, London, surgeon*). *b.* Stoke Newington 7 Jany. 1768; ed. for Calvinist ministry at Homerton and Daventry; pastor of presbyterian chapel, High st. Warwick 1789–1843; founded the *Warwick Advertiser* 4 Jany. 1806; schoolmaster at Leam near Warwick many years; pastor of presbyterian

FIELD, REV. W. (Con.)

chapel, Kenilworth 1828–50; published *An historical account of town and castle of Warwick* 1815; *Memoirs of the life of the Rev. S. Parr* 2 vols. 1826 and many sermons, tracts, letters and pamphlets. *d.* Leam 16 Aug. 1851. *Spears's Record of Unitarian Worthies* (1877); *J. Waylen's House of Cromwell* (1880) *p.* 51.

FIELDEN, JOSHUA (*son of John Fielden 1784–1849, M.P. for Oldham*). *b.* 1827; member of firm of Fielden Brothers, cotton spinners of Todmorden and Manchester, and of firm of Fielden Brothers & Co. of London, merchants; M.P. for eastern division of West Riding of Yorkshire 1868–80; author of *A Letter showing the effects of the malt tax* 1865. *d.* Hotel Monte Huri, Cannes 9 March 1887 in 60 year, personalty declared of value of £503,598.

FIELDEN, THOMAS (4 *son of Joshua Fielden, who d.* 1811). Member of firm of Joshua Fielden and Sons, cotton spinners, Todmorden; manager of the Manchester warehouse, firm became Fielden Brothers; erected gas works 1830; firm became Fielden Brothers & Co. 1837. *d.* Manchester 7 Dec. 1869, personalty sworn under £1,300,000, 12 March 1870. *Fortunes made in business* i, 411–56 (1884).

FIELDING, ANTONY VANDYKE COPLEY (2 *son of Nathan Theodore Fielding, painter*). *b.* 1787; pupil of John Varley; member of Society of Painters in water-colours 1813, treasurer 1817, sec. 1818, pres. 1831 to death; exhibited 17 pictures at R.A. and 100 at B.I. 1811–55; awarded a medal at Paris Salon 1824. *d.* Worthing 3 March 1855 in 68 year. *Redgrave's Century of painters* ii, 509–13 (1866); *J. Sherer's Gallery of British Artists* ii, 57–8.

FIELDING, HENRY BORRON (*only son of Henry Fielding of Myerscough house near Garstang, Lancs.*) Devoted himself to study of plants; bought herbarium of Dr. Steudel 1836; bought Prescott collection of 28,000 plants 1837; F.L.S. 1838; bequeathed his herbarium to Univ. of Oxford. *d.* Lancaster 21 Nov. 1851.

FIELDING, NEWTON SMITH (*brother of Antony V. C. Fielding 1787–1855*). *b.* Huntingdon 1799; worked in water colours, etching, aquatint and lithography; best known for his paintings and engravings of animals; taught painting to family of Louis Philippe in Paris; published *Subjects after nature* 1836; *Lessons on fortification* 1853; *A dictionary of colour containing 750 tints* 1854; *How to sketch from nature, or perspective and its application,* 2 ed. 1856 and other books. *d.* Paris 12 Jany. 1856.

FIELDING, THEODORE HENRY ADOLPHUS (*brother of the preceding*). Painter and engraver; exhibited 18 pictures at R.A., 21 at B.I. and 27 at Suffolk st. gallery 1799–1837; teacher of drawing and perspective at Addiscombe college; published numerous sets of engravings in aquatint; author of *Index of colours and mixed tints* 1830; *On the theory of painting* 1836; *The art of engraving with the various modes of operation* 1844 and other books. *d.* Croydon 11 July 1851 aged 70.

FIFE, JAMES DUFF, 4 Earl of (*elder son of Alexander Duff, 3 Earl of Fife 1731–1811*). *b.* 6 Oct. 1776; served with great distinction in Spanish army during Peninsular war, major general; M.P. for Banffshire 1818–27; succeeded as 4 Earl 7 April 1811; lord lieut. of Banffshire 1811–56; vice pres. of Antiquarian society, Scotland; G.C.H. 1823; K.T. 3 Sep. 1827; created Baron Fife 27 April 1827. *d.* Duff house, Banffshire 9 March 1857. *W. C. Taylor's National portrait gallery* iv, 86 (1848), *portrait*; *Jerdan's National portrait gallery* ii, (1831), *portrait*.

FIFE, JAMES DUFF, 5 Earl of (*elder son of General Sir Alexander Duff, G.C.H. 1777–1851*). *b.* Edinburgh 6 July 1814; attached to the embassy at Paris; M.P. for Banffshire 1837 to 1 Oct. 1857 when he was created Baron Skene of Skene; lieut. and sheriff principal of Elginshire 26 May 1851; lord lieut. of Banffshire 1857 to death; succeeded his uncle as 5 Earl 9 March 1857; K.T. 2 March 1860. *d.* Mar lodge, Braemar, Aberdeenshire 7 Aug. 1879.

FIFE, GEORGE (*son of Wm. Fife of Newcastle, surgeon*). M.D. and L.R.C.P. Edin. 1827; surgeon to Northern public dispensary, Edin.; phys. to Queen's hospital and professor of clinical medicine and materia medica and therapeutics at Queen's college, Birmingham to death; translated Coster's *Manual of operative surgery* 1831; author of *Observations on Influenza* 1833; *Treatise on Cholera* 1849 and other books; died from taking morphia at his lodgings Surrey st. Strand, London 10 May 1857 aged 50.

FIFE, SIR JOHN (*brother of the preceding*). *b.* Newcastle 1795; surgeon at Newcastle 1815; member of Newcastle corporation 1835, alderman 1835, mayor 1838–9 and 1842–3; knighted at St. James's palace 1 July 1840 for his exertions in repressing Chartist disturbances 1840; F.R.C.S. 1844; senior surgeon to Newcastle infirmary; lieut. col. commandant 1 Newcastle rifle volunteers 1860–68; author

FIFE, SIR J. *(Con.)*

of *Practical remarks on the Continental cholera, Newcastle* 1831. *d.* Reedsmouth house, North Tyne 15 Jany. 1871.

FIFE, WILLIAM WALLACE *(son of Peter Fife of Dundee, baker).* *b.* Dundee 28 March 1816; one of staff of the *Dundee Warder;* edited *North British Agriculturist* short time; edited *Nottingham Daily Guardian* to death. *d.* Hound's Gate, Nottingham 25 Sep. 1867.

FIGGINS, JAMES *(son of Vincent Figgins of Smithfield, London, type founder, who d. Dec. 1860 or Jany. 1861).* *b.* West st. Smithfield, London 16 April 1811; a type founder in Smithfield; sheriff of London 1865–6; M.P. for Shrewsbury 1868–74; alderman of Farringdon without, 9 June 1873 to 1882. *d.* 12 Russell sq. London 12 June 1884.

FILDES, JOHN. *b.* Dorton, Lancs. 18 Dec. 1811; M.P. for Great Grimsby 1865–68. *d.* Stanley house, Oxford road, Manchester 6 July 1875.

FILLANS, JAMES. *b.* Wilsontown, Lanarkshire 27 March 1808; apprenticed to a stone-mason at Paisley; a sculptor at Glasgow, moved to London 1836; his best works are The Blind teaching the Blind, Grief, a Madonna, busts of Sir James Shaw and John Wilson; exhibited 25 sculptures at R.A. 1837–50. *d.* 95 Montrose st. Glasgow 27 ? Sep. 1852. *James Paterson's Memoir of James Fillans* 1854, *portrait.*

FILLEUL, REV. PHILIP *(son of Philip Filleul of Jersey).* Matric. from Pemb. coll. Ox. 6 Dec. 1813 aged 20, scholar; B.A. 1817, M.A. 1820; R. of St. Brelade, Jersey 1818–29; R. of St. Peter, Jersey 1828–48; vice dean of Jersey 1838; R. of St. Saviour, Jersey 1848–50; R. of St. Heliers, Jersey 1850 to death; author of *Defense des Missions* 1821; *Christ est-il divisé?* Guernsey 1825; *Infant baptism and confirmation, Jersey* 1855 and other books. *d.* St. Heliers, Jersey 13 Oct. 1875.

FILMER, SIR EDMUND, 8 Baronet. *b.* 14 June 1809; succeeded his uncle 15 July 1834; M.P. for West Kent 1838 to death. *d.* East Sutton place near Maidstone 8 Jany. 1857.

FILMER, SIR EDMUND, 9 Baronet *(eld. son of the preceding).* *b.* 11 July 1835; ed. at Eton; M.P. for West Kent 1859–65, for Mid Kent 1880–84; sheriff of Kent 1870. *d.* Brighton 17 Dec. 1886.

FINCH, FRANCIS OLIVER *(only child of Francis Finch of Friday st. London, merchant, who d. 25 March 1805 aged 50).* *b.* Friday st. 22 Nov.

FINCH, F. O. *(Con.)*

1802; pupil of John Varley 1814–19; studied at Sass's life academy and produced some portraits; exhibited 14 landscapes at R.A. 1817–32; associate of S.P.W.C. 11 Feb. 1822, mem. 4 June 1827; a musician and a poet; lost the use of his limbs 10 Oct. 1861; author of *An Artist's Dream; Sonnets* 1863. *d.* Highfield villas, London 27 Aug. 1862. *Memorials of the late F. O. Finch [by his widow]* 1865, *portrait.*

FINCH, GEORGE. *b.* 1794; M.P. for Lymington, Hants. 1818–19, for Stamford 1833–37, for Rutland 1846–47. *d.* 41 South st. London 29 June 1870.

FINCH, JOHN (4 son of 4 Earl of Aylesford 1751–1812). *b.* 13 March 1793; cornet 15 dragoons 5 Oct. 1809; major Royal West India Rangers 5 March 1818 to 25 June 1819 when placed on h.p.; L.G. 20 Feb. 1855; col. 24 foot 19 June 1856 to death; C.B. 26 Dec. 1818. *d.* Dover 25 Nov. 1861.

FINCHAM, JOHN. Master shipwright of Portsmouth dockyard 2 Oct. 1844 to 2 July 1852; superintendent of school of naval architecture Portsmouth; built the celebrated "Arrogant" the first screw frigate in the British navy 1850; author of *A history of naval architecture* 1851; *A treatise on masting ships* 1854. *d.* Highland lodge near Portsmouth 15 Dec. 1859 aged 74.

FINDEN, EDWARD FRANCIS. *b.* 1791; pupil and coadjutor of William Finden sharing his successes and fortunes; among his separate works were etchings for Duppa's *Miscellaneous Opinions on the Continent* 1825 and *Illustrations of the Vaudois* 1831; illustrator of annuals, books of beauty and other sentimental works; among his separate engravings were Gainsborough's Harvest Waggon, Collins' As Happy as a King, Westall's Princess Victoria. *d.* St. John's Wood, London 9 Feb. 1857 aged 65.

FINDEN, WILLIAM *(brother of the preceding).* *b.* 1787; apprentice to James Mitan engraver; he worked chiefly in conjunction with his brother E. F. Finden; made engravings illustrating the books published by Sharpe, Sutton and others; established a school of pupils who worked under their directions and executed much of the work which goes by their name, they themselves giving the finishing touches; produced illustrations to H. Ellis' ed. of Dugdale's *History of St. Paul's* 1818 and Dibdin's *Ædes Althorpianæ* 1822; with his brother engraved Elgin marbles for British museum; published on their own account the

FINDEN, W. *(Con.)*

illustrations to Moore's *Life and works of Byron* 1833; brought out The Royal Gallery of British Art 1838–1840, Nos. 1–15, an admirable work in which they lost all their money; engraved full length portrait of George iv, after Sir T. Lawrence and other important single works; the Crucifixion, after W. Hilton, Finden's last work was purchased by Art Union for £1470. *d.* 49 Camden st. Camden Town 20 Sep. 1852 in 65 year. *bur.* Highgate.

FINDLATER, ANDREW. *b.* Aberdour, Aberdeenshire 1810; educ. Aberdeen univ. LL.D. 1864; sch. master at Tillydesk; head master Gordon's hospital, Aberdeen; commenced a life long connection with W. and R. Chambers 1853; edited *Information for the People* 1857; *Chambers's Encyclopœdia* 1860; prepared for the Educational Course, manuals on language, astronomy, physical geography and physiography, edited their *Etymological Dictionary* 1882; contributed an essay on Epicurus to *Encyclopœdia Metropolitana*, and articles in the *Scotsman*. *d.* 15 Rillbank terrace, Edinburgh 1 Jany. 1885. *London Figaro 17 Jany.* 1885 *p. 4, portrait.*

FINDLAY, ALEXANDER. Entered the army as private; ensign 2 West India regiment 27 July 1814, captain 24 Oct. 1821 to 28 Dec. 1826; major royal African corps 28 Dec. 1826 to 19 March 1829 when placed on h.p.; governor of Sierra Leone; fort major at Fort George, Inverness, Feb. 1847 to death; K.H. 1836. *d.* Fort George 10 May 1851.

FINDLAY, ALEXANDER GEORGE *(son of Alexander Findlay b. London 1790, an original F.R.G.S. 1830, made an atlas sheet of environs of London 1829 to a distance of 32 miles from St. Paul's ½ inch scale, d. 1870).* *b.* London 9 Jany. 1812; geographer and hydrographer succeeding on death of John Purdy in 1843 to the first position in this business; produced six nautical directories invaluable to the maritime world; received Soc. of Arts medal for dissertation on the English lighthouse system; F.R.G.S. 1844, member of Arctic committee and instrumental in government sending out Alert and Discovery expedition 1875; succeeded to Laurie's geographical and print publishing business in 1858 and on dispersal of navigating business of Van Kenlen of Amsterdam in 1885 it became the oldest firm in Europe for charts and nautical works; foreign hon. memb. of Società Geografica Italiana 1870; author of *A directory for the navigation of the Pacific Ocean* 2 vols. 1851 and many other books. *d.* East Cliff, Dover 3 May 1875.

FINGALL, ARTHUR JAMES PLUNKETT, 9 Earl of *(only son of 8 Earl of Fingall 1759–1836).* *b.* Geneva 29 March 1791; M.P. for co. Meath 1830–32; P.C. Ireland 1834; K.P. 12 Oct. 1846; lord lieut. of co. Meath 1849 to death. *d.* 47 Montagu sq. London 21 April 1869.

FINLAISON, JOHN *(son of Donald Finlaison d. 1790).* *b.* Thurso, Caithness 27 Aug. 1783; factor to Sir B. Dunbar 1802; employed by board of naval revision London, July 1805, first clerk 1805–8, invented systems for reforming victualling department and arranging admiralty records 1809; keeper of records and librarian of admiralty 1809–22; compiled the original account of the enemy's naval forces 1811; investigated abuse of sixpenny revenue at Greenwich hospital 1811; founded a system for the salaries in the admiralty 1813; compiled first official navy list 1814 and edited it monthly to 1821; his plan for fund for widows and orphans of civil department of navy established 17 Sep. 1819; connected with London Life Assurance Co. and other offices as actuary; made improvements on Northampton tables of mortality 1829; computed the annuity for the naval and military half pay and pensions, being the only person who could do it 1823; actuary and accountant of check department national debt office 1 Jany. 1822 to Aug. 1851; president of Institution of Actuaries 1847 to death. *d.* 15 Lansdowne crescent, Notting hill, London 13 April 1860. *Assurance magazine, April* 1862, 147–69; *Walford's Insurance cyclopœdia iii,* 300–303 (1874).

NOTE.—In 1833 he computed the duration of Slave and Creole life, with reference to the emancipation of slaves on the West Indian plantations, preliminary to raising a loan of £15,000,000 to compensate the slave owners, which was carried out and 770,280 slaves became free on 1 Aug. 1834.

FINLAY, ALEXANDER STRUTHERS. *b.* 21 July 1806; ed. at Harrow and Glasgow Univ.; M.P. for Argyllshire 1857–68; author of *Our monetary system* 1864. *d.* Castle Toward, Greenock 9 June 1886.

FINLAY, FRANCIS DALZELL *(son of John Finlay, tenant farmer).* *b.* Newtownards, co. Down 12 July 1794; apprentice to a printer at Belfast; master printer 1820; founded *Northern Whig* 1824; often prosecuted for press offences; imprisoned 3 months in 1826 and his newspaper suspended Aug. 1826 to May 1827; imprisoned 3 months in 1832 and fined £50; a friend of D. O'Connell but not an advocate of repeal. *d.* Glenarm, co. Antrim 10 Sep. 1857. *Freeman's Journal 12 Sept.* 1857 *p. 4.*

FINLAY, GEORGE *(son of John Finlay, captain R.E., F.R.S., who d. 1802).* *b.* Faversham,

FINLAY, G. *(Con.)*

Kent 21 Dec. 1799; studied law in Glasgow, at univ. of Göttingen 1821; went to Greece in 1823 where he was very intimate with Byron; joined Odysseus in an expedition into the Morea 1824, fought in the war of 1824–27; purchased an estate in Attica 1828 in which he lost his money; studied the history of Greece for many years; author of *Greece under the Romans* 1844; *The history of Greece to its conquest by the Turks* 1851; *The history of Greece under the Ottoman and Venetian domination* 1856; *History of the Greek Revolution* 1861, all republished collectively as *A History of Greece*, ed. H. F. Tozer 7 vols. 1877. *d.* Athens 26 Jany. 1875.

FINLAY, SIR THOMAS *(youngest son of David Finlay).* *b.* 1803; high sheriff of co. Cavan 1837; knighted 1837. *d.* 19 Adelaide road north, Hampstead 22 Oct. 1869.

FINLAYSON, JOHN. *b.* Scotland 1770; a writer at Cupar-Fife and then in Edinburgh; a house agent in London 1798; became a believer in Richard Brothers 1797; obtained Brothers's release from Fisher house asylum Islington 14 April 1806, Brothers resided in Finlayson's house Upper Baker st. Marylebone 1815 to his decease 25 Jany. 1824; claimed from the government £5710 for Brothers's maintenance, but all he received was £270 Brothers's naval half pay 4 Mch. 1830; reduced to poverty and lived on a parish allowance; author of *An admonition to the people of all countries* [*in support of Richard Brothers*], Edin. 1797; *An essay* [*on the First Resurrection*] 1798; *The last trumpet and the flying angel, the true system as given by God to R. Brothers and myself* 1849 and other works; engraved 9 sheets of the ground plan of the New Jerusalem and 12 sheets of views of its public buildings for Brothers' publications; *found dead* 14 Paradise st. Marylebone 20 Sept. 1854. *bur.* in Brothers' grave at St. John's Wood.

FINLAYSON, REV. THOMAS *(2 son of Thomas Finlayson of Coldock, Blair Drummond, Perthshire, farmer).* *b.* Coldock 22 Dec. 1809; licensed by presbytery of Stirling and Falkirk as a preacher of the gospel April 1835; min. of Union st. congregation Greenock, Nov. 1835 to Sep. 1847; min. of Rose st. church, Edinburgh, Sep. 1847 to death; moderator of supreme court of his church 1867; D.D. Univ. of Edin. 1867 or 1868; edited *Beattie's Poems* 1864; *Goldsmith's Poems* 1871. *d.* of heart disease at Campbeltown 17 Oct. 1872. *bur.* Grange cemetery, Edinburgh 22 Oct. *Memorials of Rev. Thomas Finlayson, D.D. Edinburgh* 1873; *John Smith's Our Scottish clergy 2 series* (1849) 295–301.

FINNELLY, WILLIAM. Barrister M.T. 26 Jany. 1827; author with Charles Clark of *Reports of cases in the House of Lords on appeals and writs of error* 1831–1846, 12 vols. 1835–47, and of *House of Lords cases on appeals and writs of error, claims of peerage and divorces* 1847–1850, 2 vols. 1849–51; found dead on the floor of his sitting room at 20 Old sq. Lincoln's Inn 23 Nov. 1851 aged 52. *Law Times* 29 Nov. 1851 p. 103.

FINNIS, THOMAS QUESTED *(son of Robert Finnis of Hythe, Kent).* *b.* Hythe, Jany. 1801; partner in firm of Finnis and Fisher 79 Great Tower st. London, provision merchants; the first pioneer of commerce to port of Bussorah; alderman of Lower Ward 18 Jany. 1848; sheriff of London 1848–49, lord mayor 1856–57. *d.* Park Gate, Wanstead, Essex 29 Nov. 1883. *J. E. Ritchie's Famous city men* (1884) 96–105; *Illust. news of the world ii,* 333 (1858), *portrait; I.L.N. xxix,* 479 (1856), *portrait, lxxxiii,* 581 (1883), *portrait.*

NOTE.—His brother John Finnis, lieut. col. 11 Bengal N.I. was the first English officer killed in the Sepoy mutiny, at Meerut 10 May 1857 in 54 year, memorial tablet in church of St. Dunstan in the East, London.

FIRBANK, JOSEPH. *b.* Bishop Auckland 1819; worked in a colliery 1826; executed works for North Western railway 1848; contractor for maintenance of Monmouthshire railway 1854–61; railway contractor in South Wales 30 years; contractor for widening of London and North Western railway near London 1859–66, for Midland Company's Bedford and London extension 1864–68 and their Settle and Carlisle extension 1870; built St. Pancras goods depot for Midland 1884; promoted the interest of his workmen; J.P. and D.L. for co. Monmouth. *d.* St. Julian's, Newport 29 June 1886. *Mc. Dermott's Life of J. Firbank* (1887).

FIRTH, JOSEPH FIRTH BOTTOMLEY- *(eld. son of Joseph Bottomley of Matlock).* *b.* near Huddersfield 21 Feb. 1842; barrister M.T. 6 June 1866; pres. of Municipal reform league; assumed additional surname of Firth by r.l. Feb. 1873; LL.B. Univ. of London 1875; member of London school board (Chelsea division) 1876–79; M.P. for Chelsea 1880–85, for Dundee 1888 to death; contested North Kensington 1885, received invitations from 13 of the London boroughs to stand for parliament at general election 1886; member of London county council 17 Jany. 1889, deputy chairman 12 Feb. 1889 to death; author of *Gas supply of London* 1874; *Municipal London* 1876. *d.* whilst ascending the Flégère moun-

FIRTH, J. F. B.- *(Con.)*

tain near Chamounix 3 Sep. 1889. *Graphic xxv*, 153 (1882), 2 *portraits*; *I.L.N.* 14 *Sep.* 1889 *pp.* 325, 326, *portrait.*

FIRTH, MARK *(elder son of Thomas Firth of Sheffield, steel manufacturer, who d.* 1848*).* *b.* Sheffield 25 April 1819; worked as a steel smelter for 20/- a week; a steel manufacturer at Sheffield with his father and brother Thomas 1843, they erected the Norfolk works covering 13 acres 1849; master cutler 1867–69; mayor of Sheffield 1875; erected the Mark Firth almshouses at Ranmoor, Sheffield at cost of £30,000, 1869; gave the Firth park of 36 acres to town of Sheffield, park was opened by Prince of Wales 16 Aug. 1875; erected and fitted up Firth college, Sheffield at cost of £20,000, opened by Prince Leopold 20 Oct. 1879, he also endowed it at cost of £5000; famous for castings for gun blocks, and for their refined steel; cast the steel cores for the government great guns; supplied to Italian government a 100 ton gun. *d.* Oakbrook, Sheffield 28 Nov. 1880, personalty sworn under £600,000, Jany. 1881. *Practical mag. vi*, 289–91 (1876), *portrait*; *I.L.N. lxvii*, 208 (1875), *portrait.*

FISCHER, JOHN GEORGE PAUL. *b.* Hanover 16 Sep. 1786; pupil of John Henry Ramberg, court painter 1800 when he painted portraits and theatrical scenery; went to England 1810, painted miniatures of Queen Charlotte, produced a series of military costumes for the Prince Regent, painted Queen Victoria 1819 and 1820; exhibited 80 paintings at R.A. and 17 at Suffolk st., chiefly portraits in miniature 1817–52. *d.* 4 Upper Spring st. Marylebone 12 Sep. 1875.

FISH, THOMAS LIVERSEDGE *(son of Mr. Fish, magistrate at Union hall police office, London).* Lived at Knowle cottage, Sidmouth, Devon; known as the "Golden Fish" from his immense wealth, having no less than 400 public houses; author of *Guide to Knowle Cottage* 1837. *d.* 18 Penton row, Walworth road, Newington, London 22 March 1861 aged 79.

FISH, WILLIAM. *b.* Norwich 1775; violinist Norwich theatre; studied under Sharp oboist, and Bond pianist and organist; organist of St. Andrew's, Norwich; kept a music warehouse; he wrote *Sonata for pianoforte, Op. i*, 1800; *The Morning Star* 1842 a ballad, words by the composer, an oboe concerto and some fantasias for the harp. *d.* 90 Rose lane, Conisford, Norwich 15 March 1866.

FISHBOURNE, EDMUND GARDINER. *b.* 1811; entered navy 1 Feb. 1824; captain 25 Feb.

FISHBOURNE, E. G. *(Con.)*

1853, retired 1 March 1866; retired admiral 2 Aug. 1879; C.B. 23 June 1859; hon. sec. to Royal patriotic fund and to Naval and military Bible Soc. many years; one of most active of Lord Shaftesbury's colleagues in work of evangelizing the masses of London; author of *Current fallacies in naval architecture* 1871; *Our ironclads and merchant ships* 1874; *Stability the seaman's safeguard* 1878 and 20 other books.. *d.* 26 Hogarth road, Kensington, London 12 May 1887.

FISHER, CHARLES *(2 son of David Fisher, manager of Suffolk circuit, who d.* 6 *Aug.* 1832 *aged* 71*).* Educ. at Cambridge; trained in singing, dancing, fencing and the drama by his father; good in tragedy, comedy and melodrama, acted in Norfolk and Suffolk; appeared at Drury Lane in Lionel and Clarissa 1818; manager of theatres on Norwich circuit 1832 to 1843; violinist, violoncellist and player of double bass; a fine organist; leader of band Norwich theatre 1843; violoncellist in various theatres. *d.* Glasgow 17 April 1869 aged 76. *Theatre i*, 193–99 (1880); *Era* 25 *April* 1869, *p.* 10, *col.* 1.

FISHER, DAVID *(brother of the preceding).* *b.* 1788; manager on the Suffolk circuit; first appeared in London at Drury Lane as Macbeth 3 Dec. 1817, the original Titus in Howard Payne's *Brutus* 3 Dec. 1818, and Angelo in Buck's *Italians* 3 April 1819; played at Bath 1823; built theatres at Bungay, Beccles, Halesworth, Eye, Lowestoft, Dereham, North Walsham and other places; leader of Norwich choral concerts; retired about 1838 to Woodbridge, Suffolk. *d.* Woodbridge 20 Aug. 1858. *Theatrical Inquisitor xi*, 479, 481 (1818).

FISHER, DAVID *(son of the preceding).* *b.* East Dereham, Norfolk 1816; violinist at local concerts; acted at Prince's theatre, Glasgow 1849–53; appeared in London at Princess's theatre as Victor in *The Lancers* 2 Nov. 1853, remained at Princess's 6 years where he played in his own piece *Music hath charms* in June 1858; acted at Adelphi as Abbé Latour in *The Dead Heart* 1859; gave an entertainment *Facts and Fancies* at Hanover sq. rooms and St. James' hall 1863; played at Princess's 1863, at Haymarket 1865 and at Ampitheatre and Alexandra theatres, Liverpool 1866–68, at opening of Globe theatre, London 28 Nov. 1868 played Major Treherne in Byron's *Cyril's Success*; appeared at Drury Lane, Olympic, Globe, Opera Comique, Criterion, Mirror, Princess's and Lyceum to 1884. *d.* St. Augustine's road, Camden Town, London 4 Oct. 1887. *The Players ii*, 73 (1860), *portrait*;

FISHER, D. *(Con.)*.

Saturday Programme 5 Feb. 1876, *portrait;
London Figaro* 15 Oct. 1887 *p. 14, col. 2,
portrait.*

FISHER, VEN. EDMUND HENRY. *b.* 31 Jany.
1835; ed. at Rugby and Trin. coll. Cam.,
fellow 1860; 20 wrangler 1858; B.A. 1858,
M.A. 1861; assistant master at Marlborough
1860; V. of St. Mark, Kennington, London
1869 to death; chaplain to Abp. of Canterbury 1869 to death; hon. canon of Winchester
cathedral 1874 to death; archdeacon of
Southwark 1878 to death; author of *The Goth
and the Saracen* 1859. *d.* Monk's Eleigh rectory 6 May 1879. *bur.* Barnes cemetery 10
May.

FISHER, REV. GEORGE. *b.* Sunbury, Middlesex
31 July 1794; clerk in Westminster insurance
office 1808; entered St. Cath. coll. Cam. 1817;
B.A. 1821, M.A. 1825; astronomer to ships
Dorothea and Trent in Arctic expedition
1818; chaplain and astronomer to Parry's
expedition to discover North West passage
1821–23; C. of Stanstead, Essex 1825–27; C.
of Ampthill, Beds. 1827; F.R.S. 27 Jany. 1825;
F.R.A.S. 1827, mem. of council 1835–63;
chaplain to H.M.'s ships Spartiate and Asia
1827–32; retired on h.p. 1832; principal and
chaplain of Greenwich hospital school 2 Dec.
1834 to 4 Sep. 1863; made experiments on
pendulums, chronometers, velocity of sound,
liquefaction of gases and refraction; author
of papers in *Phil. Trans., Proc. of Royal Soc.*
and other journals. *d.* 19 Hillmorton road,
Rugby 14 May 1873. *Monthly notices of Royal
Astronom. Soc. xxxiv,* 140–44 (1875).

FISHER, SIR JAMES HURTLE *(son of James
Fisher of London, architect). b.* 1790; attorney
in partnership with Thomas Rhodes in Davies
st. Cavendish sq. London 1811–32; resident
comr. for crown lands in South Australia 1836;
the first mayor of Adelaide 1840 and 4 times
afterwards; member for West Adelaide 1853–
55; speaker of the legislative council 1855–56;
first pres. of the legislative council 1856–65
when he retired from office and parliament;
knighted by patent 24 May 1860. *d.* Adelaide
28 Jany. 1875.

FISHER, SIR JOHN WILLIAM *(son of Peter
Fisher of Perth). b.* London 30 Jany. 1787;
M.R.C.S. 1809, F.R.C.S. 1836, member of
council 1843; surgeon to Bow st. patrol 1821;
surgeon-in-chief to Metropolitan police 1829–
65; M.D. Erlangen 1841; knighted at Osborne
2 Sep. 1858. *d.* 33 Park lane, London 22
March 1876. *Proc. of Med. and Chir. Soc. viii,*
173–4 (1876); *I.L.N. lxviii,* 335, 527 (1876).

FISHER, ROBERT ALEXANDER. Barrister M.T.
25 Jany. 1850; deputy judge of City of London court; secretary of the Judicature commission 25 Nov. 1872 to Sep. 1874 when last
report was issued; judge of county courts
(circuit 54) Somerset 1 Oct. 1874 to death;
author of *Digest of the reported decisions of the
courts of common law, bankruptcy, probate,
admiralty and divorce from 1756,* 5 *vols.* 1870,
new ed. by J. Mews 7 *vols.* 1884 and other
books. *d.* Glanmorfa, Clifton 30 Sep. 1879.

FISHER, WALTER DAVID (3 *son of David Fisher
1816–87). b.* Norwich 1845; first appeared
on stage at T.R. Glasgow 1852; played in
the provinces; acted at Athenée theatre in
Paris 1873; first appeared in London at Haymarket theatre as Moses in *The school for
scandal,* July 1875; acted Potain in *Cora* at
Globe theatre March 1877; played with Doyly
Carte's provincial company 1880; acted in
Germany with the Gilbert and Sullivan réper-
toire company 1887; played Shadbolt in *The
Yeomen of the Guard* at Court theatre, Liverpool 15 May 1889. *d.* 15 Seymour st. Liverpool 25 May 1889.

FISHER, WILLIAM (2 *son of John Fisher of Yarmouth, Norfolk). b.* 18 Nov. 1780; midshipman R.N. 18 Aug. 1795; surveyed the Mozambique channel 1809–10; employed in suppression of slave trade on coast of Guinea 1816–17;
commanded Asia in Mediterranean 1836–41;
received Turkish gold medal; good service
pension awarded him 1 July 1842; R.A. 2
Dec. 1847; suggested to Admiralty plan of
watering ships generally adopted; author of
The Petrel, or love on the' ocean 1850; *Ralph
Rutherford, a nautical romance* 1851. *d.* 38
Blandford sq. London 30 Sep. 1852.

FISHER, WILLIAM RICHARD (2 *son of John
Goate Fisher of Great Yarmouth). b.* 14 Aug.
1824; barrister L.I. 13 June 1851; author
of *The law of mortgage as applied to the redemption, foreclosure and sale in equity of incumbered
property* 1856, 4 *ed.* 1884; *The forest of Essex,
its history, laws, administration and ancient customs* 1887. *d.* Guildford, Surrey 17 Nov. 1888.

FISHER, WILLIAM WEBSTER. *b.* Westmoreland
1798; studied medicine at Montpellier, M.D.
1825; of Trin. coll. Cam. 1827, of Downing
coll., fellow to 1841; Downing professor of
medicine 1841 to death; lectured 1841–68;
M.B. Cam. 1834, M.D. 1841; univ. examiner
of students in medicine and member of univ.
board of medical studies; physician to Addenbrooke hospital; had large private practice at

FISHER, W. W. *(Con.)*

Cam.; fellow of Cambridge Philos. Soc. and contributed to its Transactions. *d.* East lodge, Downing coll. 4 Oct. 1874 in 76 year. *Brit. Med. Journ.* 10 *Oct.* 1874, 481.

FISK, WILLIAM *(son of a farmer at Can hall, Essex). b.* Thorp-le-Soken, Essex 1796; educ. Colchester; in mercantile house in London 1815–25; commenced historical compositions 1834 in which he accurately reproduced portraits and costumes, among these were Lady Jane Grey in the Tower 1834, Leonardo da Vinci expiring in the arms of Francis i. 1838, Conspiracy of the Pazzi, attempt to assasinate Lorenzo de Medici 1839 for which in 1840 was awarded gold medal of Manchester Institution; painted 5 pictures connected with reign of Charles i. 1840–44; exhibited 25 paintings at R.A., 17 at B.I. and 45 at Suffolk st. 1818–48. *d.* Danbury, Essex 8 Nov. 1872.

FISK, WILLIAM HENRY *(son of the preceding). b.* 1827; pupil of his father and student of R. Acad.; anatomical draughtsman to royal coll. of Surgeons; teacher of drawing and painting at Univ. coll. sch. London; made a series of drawing of trees for the queen; lectured on art in London and the provinces; exhibited 11 landscapes at R.A., 7 at B.I. and 5 at Suffolk st. 1846–73. *d.* Hampstead 13 Nov. 1884.

FISKEN, REV. WILLIAM. *b.* Gelleyburn farm near Crieff, Perthshire; taught a school at Alyth; minister at Stamfordham near Newcastle 1847 to death; governor and sec. of endowed schools at Stamfordham; with his brother Thomas invented the steam plough; invented a potato-sowing machine, a safety steam boiler, a propeller, apparatus for heating churches and the steam tackle for the steam plough July 1855; author of *The cheapest system of steam cultivation and steam cartage; On the comparative methods of steam tackle. d.* Stamfordham manse 28 Dec. 1883 aged upwards of 70.

FITCH, WILLIAM STEVENSON. *b.* 1793; postmaster Ipswich 1838 to death; founder of West Suffolk archæological assoc.; made collections for a history of Suffolk, which were dispersed at his death, but 30 vols. of them are in Suffolk archæol. assoc. museum at Bury St. Edmunds; author of *A catalogue of Suffolk manorial registers, Great Yarmouth* 1843; *Ipswich and its early mints, Ipswich* 1848. *d.* Ipswich 17 July 1859. *C. R. Smith's Retrospections i,* 245–8 (1883).

FITTON, MICHAEL. *b.* Gawsworth, Cheshire 1766; entered navy June 1780; served in

FITTON, M. *(Con.)*

Mediterranean 1782, in West Indies 1799–1802, 1803–4; lieut. 9 March 1804 his highest rank; captured or destroyed 40 of the enemy's ships, received the thanks of the admiralty and a sword value £50 from the Patriotic Soc.; served in the Baltic 1811–15; lieut. of the ordinary at Plymouth 22 Feb. 1831 to 1834; admitted into Greenwich hospital 20 April 1835; one of the bravest and most active officers in the navy. *d.* Peckham 31 Dec. 1852.

FITTON, WILLIAM HENRY *(son of Nicholas Fitton of Dublin). b.* Dublin, Jany. 1780; ed. at Trin. coll. Dublin, senior scholar 1798, B.A. 1799; studied at Edin. Univ. 1808, in London 1809–12; M.D. Edin. 12 Sep. 1810, incorporated at Cam. 1815; candidate of royal coll. of phys. 1815, fellow 1816; practised at Northampton 1811–19 when he removed to London and devoted himself to scientific researches; F.R.S. 9 Nov. 1815; F.G.S. 18 , sec. 18 , pres. 1827, the first to deliver an annual address 15 Feb. 1828, established publication of proceedings 1827, Wollaston medallist 1852; wrote 21 papers on geological subjects 1811–57; author of *A geological sketch of Hastings* 1833; wrote many articles in *Edinburgh Review* 1817–41. *d.* Sussex gardens, London 13 May 1861. *Quarterly Journal of Geol. Soc. xviii,* 30–34 (1862); *Proc. of Royal Soc. of London xii,* 4–6 (1861).

FITZADAM, JOHN THOMPSON *(eld. son of Adam Fitz Adam of Birmingham, barrister). b.* 1833; barrister I.T. 26 Jany. 1859; recorder of Wigan, April 1880 to death; alderman of Wigan many years. *d.* 5 Phillimore gardens, Kensington, London 19 April 1886 in 53 year.

FITZBALL, EDWARD, originally called Edward Ball. *b.* Burwell, Cambs. 1792; attempted to establish a printing office at Norwich; dramatist in London many years; author of *Edda; The Pilot* 1825; *The Innkeeper of Abbeville* 1826; *The Floating Beacon* 1826; *The Inchcape Bell* 1828; *The Flying Dutchman* 1829 and many other successful dramas; wrote all the librettos of Balfe's early operas, libretto of Wallace's *Maritana,* and many librettos for other composers; wrote *My Pretty Jane* 1828 and many other songs. *d.* near Chatham 27 Oct. 1873. *E. Fitzball's Thirty five years of a dramatic author's life* 2 vols. 1859, *portrait; I.L.N. lxiii,* 445 (1873), *portrait.*

FITZCLARENCE, LORD ADOLPHUS (7 *child and* 3 *son of William iv.* 1765–1837 *by Dorothea natural dau. of Francis Bland of Kerry, she was known on the stage as Mrs. Jordan* 1762–1816).

FITZCLARENCE, LORD A. (*Con.*)

b. 18 Feb. 1802; entered R.N. 26 May 1814; captain 24 Dec. 1824; commander of Royal George yacht 1830; captain of Victoria and Albert yacht 1 Jany. 1851 to 21 Oct. 1852 and commodore of her 21 Oct. 1852 to 17 Sep. 1853; aide de camp to Victoria 12 Feb. 1848 to death; groom of the robes to Will. iv. 24 July 1830; granted rank of younger son of a marquis 24 May 1831; G.C.H. 24 Feb. 1832; a lord of the bedchamber 5 Jany. 1833; R.A. 17 Sep. 1853. *d.* Newburgh park near Easingwold, Yorkshire 17 May 1856. *Lennox's Celebrities 2 series i,* 208–12 (1877).

FITZCLARENCE, REV. LORD AUGUSTUS (*brother of the preceding*). *b.* 1 March 1805; ed. at Trin. coll. Cam., B.C.L. 1832, D.C.L. 1835; R. of Mapledurham, Oxon. 1829 to death; chaplain in ordinary to his father 1829–37, to Queen Victoria 1837 to death; granted rank of younger son of a marquis 24 May 1831. *d.* Mapledurham 14 June 1854.

FITZCLARENCE, LORD FREDERICK (*brother of the preceding*). *b.* 9 Dec. 1799; ensign Coldstream guards 12 May 1814, assisted at arrest of Cato st. conspirators 23 Feb. 1820; lieut. col. 7 foot 2 June 1825 to 24 Aug. 1832 when placed on h.p.; granted rank of younger son of a marquis 24 May 1831; G.C.H. 1831; military governor of Portsmouth 1840; col. 36 foot 23 July 1851 to death; L.G. 11 Nov. 1851; commander in chief at Bombay 1852 to death, assumed command 22 Nov. 1852; author of *A manual of out-post duties* 1851 and other works. *d.* Poorundhur near Poonah 30 Oct. 1854, body embalmed and *bur.* at Ford, Northumberland 10 Feb. 1855.

FITZGERALD, JOHN DAVID FITZGERALD, 1 Baron (*son of David Fitzgerald of Dublin, merchant*). *b.* Dublin 1816; ed. at Trin. coll. Dublin; called to bar in Ireland 1838; Q.C. 15 Feb. 1847; bencher of King's Inns 1855; leader of the Munster circuit; M.P. for Ennis 1852–60; solicitor general for Ireland, Feb. 1855 to April 1856, attorney general April 1856 to March 1858 and 1859 to Feb. 1860; P.C. Ireland 1856; comr. of national education Ireland 1863 to death; justice of Queen's Bench, Ireland, Feb. 1860 to May 1882; principal judge at great state trials of Messrs. Parnell, Biggar and others Jany. 1881; a lord of appeal in ordinary May 1882 to death; created Baron Fitzgerald of Kilmarnock, co. Dublin 23 June 1882; P.C. 29 June 1882; bencher of Gray's Inn 21 Dec. 1883; author of *Report on trial of A. M. Sullivan and R.*

FITZGERALD, Baron (*Con.*)

Pigott for seditious libels 1868. *d.* 22 Fitzwilliam place, Dublin 16 Oct. 1889. *Law magazine and law review v,* 267–69 (1858); *Graphic 16 Nov.* 1889 *p.* 597, *portrait.*

FITZGERALD and VESEY, VERY REV. HENRY VESEY-FITZGERALD, 3 Baron. *b.* 1800; ed. at Trin. coll. Dublin, B.A. 1821, M.A. 1827; dean of Emly 6 July 1818 to 1825; dean of Kilmore 16 March 1825 to death; succeeded his brother as 3 Baron 11 May 1843. *d.* Danesfort, co. Cavan 30 March 1860.

FITZGERALD, CHARLES (*son of Robert Fitzgerald of Kilkee, co. Clare*). Entered navy 1809; governor of British settlements on the Gambia 1844 to 1847; governor of Western Australia Aug. 1848 to June 1855; captain 1 April 1856; C.B. 2 Jany. 1857. *d.* Geraldine house, Kilkee, co. Clare 29 Dec. 1887 in 96 year. *I.L.N. xxx,* 59, 60 (1857), *portrait.*

FITZGERALD, EDWARD (3 *son of John Purcell who took name of Fitzgerald*). *b.* Bredfield house near Woodbridge, Suffolk 31 March 1809; ed. at Bury St. Edmund's gram. sch. and Trin. coll. Cam., B.A. 1830; a friend of Spedding, Donne and Thackeray; resided at Farlingay hall near Woodbridge (where Carlyle visited him in 1855) 1853–60, at Woodbridge 1860–74, at Little Grange 1874 to his death; issued *Euphranor, a dialogue on youth* 1851, *Polonius, a collection of Wise Saws* 1852, *Six dramas of Calderon* 1853 the only book to which he put his name, it was withdrawn from circulation; translated the Agamemnon of Æschylus 1876 and the Œdipus Tyrannus and Œdipus Coloneus of Sophocles, the Quatrains of Omar Khayyám 1859, the Salámán and Absál of Jami 1856; author of a translation of Attar's Mantik-ut-tair which he called the Bird Parliament MS.; Tennyson's poem Tiresias 1884 contains a birthday ode to Fitzgerald. *d.* while on a visit to Merton rectory, Norfolk 14 June 1883. *W. Aldis Wright's Letters and remains of E. Fitzgerald 3 vols.* 1889, *portrait.*

FITZGERALD, JAMES. Entered Madras army 1820; commandant at Malabar 19 Feb. 1858 to 17 Jany. 1862; col. 42 Madras N.I. 12 Dec. 1862 to 1869; L.G. 25 June 1870. *d.* Kildare house, Lyndall's park, Clifton 14 Nov. 1871.

FITZGERALD, SIR JOHN FORSTER (4 *son of Edward Fitzgerald of Carrigoran, co. Clare, who d.* 1815). *b.* about 1785; ensign 29 Oct. 1793; major 60 foot 1809; commandant of Quebec

FITZGERALD, SIR J. F. (*Con.*)

and afterwards of Montreal 1818–24; lieut. col. 20 foot 1824–30; commanded divisions in Madras and Bombay 1838–41; col. of 62 foot 1843, of 18 foot 1850 to death; general 20 June 1854, field marshal 29 May 1875; K.C.B. 1831, G.C.B. 10 Nov. 1862; M.P. for co. Clare 1852–57. *d.* Tours, France 24 March 1877. *bur.* with military honours in St. Symphorien cemetery, Tours 27 March. *Times 29 March 1877 p. 9, col. 6.*

FITZGERALD, OTHO AUGUSTUS (3 *son of 3 Duke of Leinster* 1791–1874). *b.* Carton, Maynooth 10 Oct. 1827; M.P. for co. Kildare 1865–74; master of the horse to viceroy of Ireland 1855 and 1858–59; gentleman of the bedchamber 1859–62; treasurer of H.M.'s household 8 May 1866 to July 1866, comptroller 1868–74; P.C. 11 June 1866. *d.* Oakley court, Windsor 19 Nov. 1882.

FITZGERALD, SIR PETER GEORGE, 1 Baronet (5 *son of Maurice Fitzgerald, P.C., M.P., knight of Kerry* 1774–1849). *b.* 15 Sep. 1808; clerk to David Digges la Touche & Co. bankers, Dublin; vice treasurer of Ireland 1841, nineteenth knight of Kerry 1849; sheriff of Kerry 1849 and of Carlow 1875; improved his estates and built better homesteads for his tenants 1849; created a baronet 8 July 1880. *d.* Glanlearn, island of Valentia 6 Aug. 1880.

FITZGERALD, ROBERT ALLAN (2 *son of Thomas Fitzgerald of Shalstone, Bucks., who d.* 1860). *b.* 1 Oct. 1834; ed. at Harrow and Trin. coll. Cam., B.A. 1858, M.A. 1861; played in Harrow and Cambridge cricket elevens; barrister L.I. 17 Nov. 1860; sec. to Marylebone cricket club 1864–76; captain of amateur eleven who visited Canada and United States 1872; author of *Jerks in from short-leg, By Quid* 1866; *Wickets in the West, or the twelve in America* 1873. *d.* Charleywood, Herts. 28 Oct. 1881. *Illust. sp. and dr. news i, 277 (1874), portrait.*

FITZGERALD, RIGHT REV. WILLIAM (*son of Maurice Fitzgerald, M.D. of Lifford, Limerick*). *b.* Lifford 3 Dec. 1814; ed. at Middleton, co. Cork and Trin. coll. Dublin, scholar 1833, B.A. 1835, M.A. 1848, B.D. and D.D. 1853, fellow of his college, professor of moral philosophy there 1847–52 and of ecclesiastical history 1852–57; C. of Lackagh, Kildare 1838–46; C. of Clontarf, Dublin 1846–48; V. and preb. of Donoghmore, Dublin 16 Feb. 1848; V. of St. Anne's, Dublin 1851–55; P.C. of Monkstown, Dublin 13 May 1855; preb. of Timothan, Dublin 1855; archdeacon

FITZGERALD, RIGHT REV. W. (*Con.*)

of Kildare 1855; bishop of Cork, Cloyne and Ross 7 Feb. 1857, consecrated at St. Patrick's cath. Dublin 8 March, enthroned 14 March; translated to Killaloe 3 Feb. 1862; edited Bishop Butler's *Analogy with notes and a life of the author, Dublin* 1849, *reprinted* 1860; chief contributor to *The Cautions for the Times,* a series of papers ed. by R. Whately 1853; author of *Episcopacy, tradition and the sacraments considered in reference to the Oxford Tracts* 1839 and 20 other works. *d.* Clarisford house, Killaloe 24 Nov. 1883. *Brady's Records i, 302, iii, 87–8; Dublin Univ. Mag. xlix, 416–26 (1857).*

FITZGERALD, SIR WILLIAM ROBERT SEYMOUR VESEY- (*eld. son of William Fitzgerald of Dublin*). *b.* 1818; matric. from Ch. Ch. Ox. 21 Feb. 1833, of Oriel coll., B.A. 1837, M.A. 1844, Newdigate prizeman 1835, D.C.L. 1863; barrister L.I. 29 Jany. 1839; M.P. Horsham 1848 but unseated, M.P. Horsham 1852 to 1865 and 1874–5; under sec. of state foreign affairs 26 Feb. 1858 to June 1859; governor of Bombay 19 Nov. 1866 to March 1872; P.C. 28 Dec. 1866; K.C.S.I. 22 Oct. 1867, G.C.S.I. 8 Dec. 1868; chief commissioner of charities 30 Nov. 1875 to 1885; took names of Seymour Vesey. *d.* 29 Warwick sq. London 28 June 1885. *I.L.N. l, 117 (1867), portrait.*

FITZ-GIBBON, ABRAHAM COATES (2 *son of lieut. Philp Fitz-Gibbon, R.N., d.* 1826). *b.* Mount Eagle, Kilworth, co. Cork 23 Jany. 1823; apprentice to Sir Charles Lanyon 1837–43; agent and manager for W. Dargan 1847–52; in U.S. America 1852–56, in Ceylon 1857–60, in New Zealand 1860–62, in Queensland 1863–68, in all these countries he surveyed and constructed railway lines; M.I.C.E. 9 Jany. 1866; adopted a 3 foot 6 in. guage in Queensland; with his brother Maurice Fitz-Gibbon published in Journal of R. Hist. and Archæol. Assoc. of Ireland "Unpublished Geraldine Documents" which with additions were reprinted in four parts by Rev. Samuel Hayman, Dublin 1870–81. *d.* Moorside, Bushey Heath, Herts. 4 April 1887. *Min. of proc. of Instit. of C.E. lxxxix, 466–70 (1887).*

FITZGIBBON, EDWARD (*son of a land agent d.* 1817). *b.* Limerick, Aug. 1803; came to London 1817; articled to a surgeon 1819–20; classical tutor in the provinces 1820–23; at Marseilles 1824–30 studying the language and literature; parliamentary reporter for *Morning Chronicle* 1830; wrote on angling for *Bell's Life* under pseudonym of Ephemera; wrote for the

Fitzgibbon, E. *(Con.)*

Observer and acted as a theatrical critic; from 1830 his writings gave great impulse to the art of fishing, were the means of improving fishing tackle and of increasing the rents of rivers; he once killed 52 salmon on the Shin river in 55 hours fishing; author of *Handbook of Angling, By Ephemera* 1847, 3 ed. 1853; *The book of the Salmon* 1850; author with W. Shipley of *A true treatise on the art of fly fishing* 1838, and with A. Young of *Natural History of the Salmon* 1854; ed. *The Compleat Angler of Walton and Cotton* 1853. *d.* 19 Nov. 1857. *bur.* Highgate cemetery 25 Nov. *Baron Nicholson's Autobiography* (1860) 334–6; *Bell's Life in London* 22 Nov. 1857 p. 8, 29 *Nov.* p. 5.

FITZGIBBON, GERALD (4 *son of Mr. Fitzgerald of co. Limerick, tenant farmer*). *b.* Glin, Limerick 1 Jany. 1793; employed in W. Jameson's distillery, Dublin 1814; entered univ. of Dublin 1817, B.A. 1825, M.A. 1832, maintained himself by teaching 1817–30; called to Irish bar Jany. 1830; Q.C. 17 Aug. 1841; counsel for Dr. John Gray in state trial of Daniel O'Connell and his 7 fellow prisoners 15 Jany. to 12 Feb. 1844 during which on 30 Jany. he was challenged to a duel by the attorney general Thos. Bury Cusack Smith, when he brought the matter under notice of the Court and Mr. Smith apologised; the greatest commercial lawyer of his day; bencher of King's Inns 1858; third serjeant at law 1859–60; receiver-master in Chancery 1860 to April 1878; author of *Ireland in 1868 the battle field for English party strife* 1868, 2 ed. 1868; *Roman Catholic priests and National Schools* 1871, 2 ed. 1872 and other works. *d.* Larkfield, Clondalkin 27 Sep. 1882. *O. J. Burke's Anecdotes of Connaught circuit* (1885) 328–30; *Irish Law Times xvi*, 494 (1882).

FITZ GIBBON, JAMES. *b.* 1780; enlisted in the army 1797; served in war against Napoleon and in American war 1812–15; captain of Glengarry light infantry fencibles 1813–16 when placed on h.p.; assistant adjutant general of militia Upper Canada; saved city of Toronto during Mackenzie rebellion 1837 for which he was awarded 5000 acres of land and received thanks of parliament, the grant of land was subsequently disallowed; chief clerk of lower house of Canadian parliament 1816–29, clerk of the upper house 1829–35; created a military knight of Windsor 1850; author of *An appeal to the people of Upper Canada, Montreal* 1847. *d.* Lower Ward, Windsor Castle 12 Dec. 1863.

FITZHARDINGE, WILLIAM FITZHARDINGE BERKELEY, 1 Earl of *(eld. son of 5 Earl of*

Fitzhardinge, Earl of *(Con.)*

Berkeley 1745–1810). *b.* 26 Dec. 1786; lieut. South Gloucestershire militia 6 July 1803, col. 22 Aug. 1810 to death; kept a pack of hounds in Gloucestershire 1808 to death, not excelled by any in England; M.P. for Gloucestershire 1810; his claim to Berkeley peerage disallowed by House of Lords 28 June 1811; created Baron Segrave of Berkeley Castle 10 Sep. 1831 and Earl Fitzhardinge 17 Aug. 1841; lord lieut. of Gloucestershire 3 Feb. 1836 to death. *d.* Berkeley Castle about midnight 10 Oct. 1857. *Sporting Review xxxviii*, 319–22, 389–95 (1857); *Cecil's Records of the Chase* (1877) 181–5; *My life and recollections by G. F. Berkeley* (1865) i, 370–83 *and vol. ii passim*.

NOTE.—He is drawn as Fitzalleyne of Berkeley in Fitzalleyne of Berkeley, a romance of the present times by Bernard Blackmantle [Charles Molloy] 2 vols. 1825, who also makes him one of the characters in his book The English Spy 2 vols. 1826.

FITZHARDINGE, MAURICE FREDERICK FITZ-HARDINGE BERKELEY, 1 Baron *(brother of the preceding)*. *b.* 3 Jany. 1788; entered navy June 1802, captain 7 June 1814, admiral 15 Jany. 1862; M.P. for Gloucester 1831–33, 1835–37 and 1841–57; contested Gloucester 1833, 1837 and 1857; a comr. of admiralty 1833–34, 1837–39, 1846–52 and 1852–57; K.C.B. 5 July 1855, G.C.B. 28 June 1861; P.C. 13 Aug. 1855; master of the Berkeley hounds 1857 to death; claimed Barony of Berkeley 1857; created Baron Fitzhardinge of city and county of Bristol 5 Aug. 1861. *d.* Berkeley castle 17 Oct. 1867. *Baily's Mag. vi*, 217–19 (1863), *portrait*; *Sporting Review lviii*, 417–20 (1867).

FITZMAURICE, JOHN G. Second lieut. 95 foot 25 April 1811; captain rifle brigade 19 Dec. 1826 to 30 March 1832 when placed on h.p.; granted service reward 13 March 1855; M.G. 7 May 1861; lieut. of Yeomen of the Guard, Dec. 1861 to death; K.H. 1831. *d.* Drayton green, Ealing 24 Dec. 1865 aged 72.

FITZMAURICE, WILLIAM EDWARD *(younger son of John Fitzmaurice, Viscount Kirkwall* 1778–1820). *b.* 22 March 1805; ed. at Oriel coll. Ox.; captain 9 lancers 26 Feb. 1828; captain 2 life guards 1831–40 when placed on h.p.; M.P. for Bucks. 1842–47; author of *A cruise to Egypt, Palestine and Greece* 1834. *d.* Brussels 18 June 1889.

FITZPATRICK, JAMES COLEMAN. *b.* Ireland about 1818; Educ. at Trin. coll. Dublin; called to Irish bar 1844; barrister L.I. 6 June 1857; chief justice of the Gold Coast 1857–61; judge of British Kaffraria 20 July 1861 to

FITZPATRICK, J. C. (*Con.*)

1872 ; judge of supreme court of Cape of Good Hope 1872–79 when he retired on pension ; author of *The Pope, his rights and duties* 1860. *d.* Wynberg, British Kaffraria 6 Feb. 1880.

FITZROY, CHARLES (2 son of 4 *Duke of Grafton* 1760–1844). *b.* 28 Feb. 1791 ; ed. at Harrow and Great Marlow ; ensign 1 foot guards 25 June 1807 ; major 55 foot 27 Jany. 1820 to 11 Jany. 1821 when placed on h.p.; sold out 1834 ; M.P. for Thetford 1818–32, for Bury 1832–47 ; vice chamberlain of the household 29 June 1835 to 2 May 1838 ; P.C. 1 July 1835. *d.* Elm lodge, Hampton 17 June 1865.

FITZROY, SIR CHARLES AUGUSTUS (*only son of general Charles Fitzroy* 1764–1829). *b.* 10 June 1796 ; attached to staff of Sir Hussey Vivian at Waterloo 1815 ; captain royal horse guards 27 April 1820 to 23 June 1825 when placed on h.p.; M.P. for Bury St. Edmunds, June 1831 to Dec. 1832 ; lieut. governor of Prince Edward Island 19 March 1837 ; governor of Leeward Islands 3 Aug. 1841 ; governor of New South Wales 3 Aug. 1846 to 17 Jany. 1855 ; his wife Lady Mary Fitzroy killed at Parramatta being thrown from her carriage 7 Dec. 1847 ; governor general of all the Australian colonies 1850 ; act for separation of Victoria passed 5 Aug. 1850 ; constitution act of N.S.W. passed 1853 ; presented with purse of 2000 guineas 28 Jany. 1856 ; knighted by Wm. iv. at St. James's palace 1 June 1837 ; K.C.B. 12 June 1854. *d.* Half Moon st. Piccadilly, London 16 Feb. 1858. *W. Gisborne's New Zealand Rulers* (1886), 36–42 ; *Rev. J. Buller's Forty years in New Zealand* (1878) 377–82 ; *Therry's Reminiscences, 2 ed.* (1863) 376–80 ; *Heads of the people i,* 65 (1847), *portrait ; I.L.N. xxix,* 479 (1856), *portrait.*

FITZROY, HENRY (*younger son of 2 Baron Southampton* 1761–1810). *b.* Great Stanhope st. London 2 May 1807 ; ed. at Magd. coll. Ox. and Trin. coll. Cam., M.A. Cam. 1828 ; M.P. Great Grimsby 10 Aug. 1831 to 3 Dec. 1832 ; contested Lewes 1835, M.P. Lewes 21 April 1837 to death ; a lord of the Admiralty 12 Feb. 1845 to 13 July 1846 ; lieut. col. of the Artillery company 1848 to death ; under sec. of state for home department Dec. 1852 to Feb. 1855 ; P.C. 8 Feb. 1855 ; chairman of committees of House of Commons 16 April 1855 to 1859 ; chief comr. of board of works 1859 to death. *d.* Sussex sq. Kemp Town, Brighton 22 Dec. 1859.

FITZROY, ROBERT (*brother of Sir C. A. Fitzroy,* 1796–1858). *b.* Ampton hall, Suffolk 5 July 1805 ; entered navy 19 Oct. 1819 ; captain 3

FITZROY, R. (*Con.*)

Dec. 1834 ; commander of Beagle on surveys of Straits of Magellan etc. 1828–30, 1831–36, when he ran a chronometric line round the world ; F.R.G.S. 1830, gold medallist 1837 ; an elder brother of Trinity house 1839 ; M.P. Durham 1841–43 ; acting conservator of river Mersey 21 Sep. 1842 to 1843 ; governor of New Zealand 3 April 1843, superseded Nov. 1845 as he did not agree with the colonists ; retired from active service 1850 ; R.A. 1857, V.A. on half pay 12 Sep. 1863 ; F.R.S. 5 June 1851 ; superintendent of Meteorological department of board of trade 1854 ; invented Fitzroy barometer ; instituted a system of storm warnings 1862 which developed into the daily forecasts of the weather 1872 ; author of *Narrative of voyages of Adventurer and Beagle and the Beagle's circumnavigation of the globe* 3 vols. 1839 ; *Weather Book, a manual of practical meteorology* 1863, 2 *ed.* 1863 and other works ; committed suicide by cutting his throat, at his residence Lyndhurst house, Norwood, Surrey 29 April 1865. *Proc. of Royal Soc. xv,* 21–23 (1867) ; *Proc. of Royal Geog. Soc. ix,* 215–8 (1865) ; *Good Words vii,* 406–13 (1866).

FITZROY, SIR WILLIAM (3 son of 3 *Duke of Grafton* 1735–1811). *b.* 1 June 1782 ; entered navy 21 April 1794 ; captain 3 March 1804 ; admiral 2 April 1853 ; C.B. 4 June 1815, K.C.B. 4 July 1840. *d.* East Sheen near Richmond 13 May 1857.

FITZWALTER, SIR BROOK WILLIAM BRIDGES, 1 Baron (*elder son of Sir Brook Wm. Bridges, 4 bart.* 1767–1829). *b.* Goodneston park, Kent 2 June 1801 ; ed. at Winchester and Oriel coll. Ox., B.A. 1822, M.A. 1827 ; succeeded his father 21 April 1829 ; M.P. for East Kent, Feb. to July 1852 and April 1857 to April 1868 ; created Baron Fitzwalter 17 April 1868. *d.* Goodneston park 6 Dec. 1875. *I.L.N. xxx,* 478 (1857), *portrait, lxvii,* 614, 629 (1875), *portrait.*

FITZWILLIAM, CHARLES WILLIAM WENTWORTH, 5 Earl (*only child of 4 Earl Fitzwilliam* 1748–1833). *b.* Grosvenor sq. London 4 May 1786 ; ed. at Trin. coll. Cam. ; M.P. for Yorkshire 20 May 1807 to 24 July 1830 as Viscount Milton ; M.P. for Northamptonshire 23 May 1831 to March 1833 ; pres. of Yorkshire Philosophical Soc. 1830 to death ; K.G. 4 Nov. 1851 ; took surname of Wentworth by r.l. 20 Aug. 1856 ; author of *First, second and third addresses on the Corn laws* 1839 and other books ; edited with Sir Richard Bourke *Correspondence of Edmund Burke* 4 vols. 1844. *d.* Wentworth house, Rotherham 4 Oct. 1857. *Waagen's Treasures of art iii,* 337–42 (1854).

FITZWILLIAM, EDWARD. *b.* near Holborn, London 8 Aug. 1788; actor at Southend, Hythe and Gosport 1806–8; first appeared in London as Hodge in *Love in a village*, at West London theatre 1812; acted at Olympic 1813 and at Royal Circus; his best parts were Leporello, Dumbiedykes in the *Heart of Midlothian*, Patch, Partridge in *Tom Jones* and Humphry Clinker; went to Drury Lane 10 Nov. 1821; became a comic vocalist at city entertainments; generally known as Little Fitz; retired on an annuity from Drury Lane theatrical fund 1845. *d.* Regent st. London 30 March 1852. *Oxberry's Dramatic Biography ii*, 267–76 (1825), *portrait; Cumberland's Minor Theatre, vol. 2, portrait.*

FITZWILLIAM, EDWARD FRANCIS *(son of the preceding). b.* Deal, Kent 2 Aug. 1824; composed a Stabat Mater performed at Hanover square rooms, London 15 March 1845; musical director of Lyceum theatre Oct. 1847 to 1849; musical director of Haymarket theatre Easter 1853 to death; composed *The Queen of the day*, a comic opera, *A summer night's love*, an operetta; author of *O Incomprehensible Creator*, a cantata 1850; *Dramatic songs for 4 voices* 1856 and other works; his music to the songs *As I laye a thynkynge* 1846, *The maid with the milking pail* 1846, and *The jug of Punch* 1845 was very popular. *d.* 9 Grove place, Brompton, London 19 Jany. 1857. *Era* 25 Jany. 1857 p. 9, col. 3.

FITZWILLIAM, ELLEN *(eld. dau. of Thomas Acton Chaplin, d. Nov.* 1859). First appeared in London at Adelphi as Wilhelm in *Die Hexen am Rheim* 7 Oct. 1841; member of Haymarket company under J. B. Buckstone 22 years; went to Australia 1877. *(m.* 31 Dec. 1853 Edward Francis Fitzwilliam 1824–57). *d.* Auckland, New Zealand 19 Oct. 1880 aged 58. *Theatrical Times* 1S Nov. 1848 *p.* 439, *portrait.*

FITZWILLIAM, FANNY ELIZABETH *(dau. of Robert Copeland, manager of Dover circuit). b.* Dover theatre 1801; was on the stage at 3 years of age; as Norah in the *Poor Soldier* played at Dover theatre 1815; first appeared in London at Haymarket as Lucy in *The Review* 1817; went to the Olympic and the Surrey; first seen at Drury Lane as Fanny in *Maid or Wife* 5 Dec. 1821; commenced engagement at Adelphi 10 Oct. 1825, the original Kate Plowden in *The Pilot* 31 Oct. 1825 and Bella in *The Wreck Ashore* 21 Oct. 1830; manager of Sadler's Wells 1832; gave a monologue *The Widow Wiggins* at Adelphi during Lent 1835; in 1837 was at Haymarket under

B. Webster; went to America and made her debut at Park theatre, New York as Peggy in *The Country Girl*, Oct. 1839; played at Adelphi, London 1844 and afterwards at Haymarket; was good in Lady Teazle, country girls and Irish peasants. *(m.* 2 Dec. 1822 Edward Fitz William, actor 1788–1852). *d.* of cholera at Richmond lodge, Putney 11 Sep. 1854. *Ireland's Records of the New York stage i*, 302–4 (1867); *Tallis's Drawing room table book* (1851) 3–5, 2 *portraits; Actors by daylight i*, 145–6 (1838), *portrait; Theatrical Times ii*, 73 (1847), *portrait; Actors by gaslight* (1838) 25, *portrait.*

FITZWILLIAM, GEORGE WENTWORTH (3 *son of 5 Earl Fitzwilliam* 1786–1857). *b.* Grosvenor place, London 3 May 1817; ed. at Eton and Trin. coll. Cam., M.A. 1838; M.P. for Richmond 1841, for Peterborough 1841–59; sheriff of Northampton 1866; master of the Fitzwilliam hounds. *d.* Milton hall, Peterborough 4 March 1874.

FITZWILLIAM, WILLIAM JOHN WENTWORTH (5 *son of 6 Earl Fitzwilliam, b.* 1815). *b.* 7 Aug. 1852; ed. at Eton and Magd. coll. Cam., B.A. 1874; M.P. for Peterborough 29 Oct. 1878 to death. *d.* Wentworth house near Rotherham 11 Sep. 1889. *Pictorial World* 3 Oct. 1889 p. 416, *portrait.*

FITZWILLIAM, WILLIAM WENTWORTH *(brother of the preceding). b.* Grosvenor sq. London 27 July 1839; ed. at Eton and Trin. coll. Cam.; M.P. for South West Yorkshire 1865–72. *d.* 17 Jany. 1877.

FLAHERTY, WILLIAM EDWARD. Apprenticed to J. G. Barnard of London, printer; worked for Messrs. Bradbury and Evans 1834; went to Harrisons 1840; assisted Thomas Duffus Hardy in various works; compiled *The annals of England* 3 vols. 1855–7, anon.; edited *The Gentleman's Magazine*, Jany. 1861 to Dec. 1865; revised several handbooks for John Murray. *d.* 33 Hassett road, Homerton 16 June 1878 aged 71. *Bookseller, July* 1878 *p.* 585.

FLANAGAN, REV. THOMAS. *b.* 1814; educ. Sedgley park sch. Staffordshire and at Oscott coll.; ordained at Oscott 1842, professor and prefect of studies there to 1851 and again July 1853 to 1854; V.P. of Sedgley park sch. 1851 and president Aug. 1851 to July 1853; canon of the chapter of Birmingham 1850; resident priest Blackmore park 1854–60; priest at St. Chad's cath. Birmingham 1860 to death; author of *A manual of British and Irish history* 1847; *A history of the church in*

FLANAGAN, REV. T. (*Con.*)
England to the re-establishment of the hierarchy in 1850, 2 *vols.* 1857 and other works. *d.* Kidderminster 21 July 1865. *bur.* in crypt of St. Chad's cathedral. *Gillow's English Catholics ii*, 291 (1885).

FLATMAN, ELNATHAN. *b.* Holton, Suffolk 1810; apprenticed to Wm. Cooper of Newmarket, trainer; won the Goodwood cup on Glencoe 1834, the One thousand guineas on Preserve 1835, the Derby on Orlando 1844, the St. Leger on Surplice 1848; won 104 races in 1848. *d.* Newmarket 20 Aug. 1860. *Sporting Times* 25 *July* 1885 *p.* 2; *Sporting Review xxx*, 10–13 (1853), *portrait, xliv*, 162, 225 (1860); *Rice's British turf i*, 263–65 (1879); *I.L.N. xxii*, 416 (1853), *portrait*.

FLEETWOOD, SIR PETER HESKETH, 1 Baronet (*son of Robert Hesketh of Rossall, Lancashire*). *b.* Wennington hall near Lancaster 9 May 1801; ed. at Trin. coll. Ox., B.A. 1823, M.A. 1826; sheriff of Lancashire 1830; M.P. Preston 1832–47; projected and commenced to build town and port of Fleetwood on river Wyre 1836; created baronet 20 July 1838; assumed name of Fleetwood by r.l. 5 March 1851; translator of Victor Hugo's *Last days of a condemned* 1840. *d.* 127 Piccadilly, London 12 April 1866.

FLEMING, ALEXANDER. *b.* Edinburgh 1824; M.D. Edin. 1844; F.R.C.P. Lond.; his essay on the physiological and medicinal properties of Aconitum Napellus 1845 led to the introduction of a tincture of aconite known as Fleming's tincture; edited *Monthly retrospect of medical science* 2 vols. 1848–9; professor of materia medica Queen's coll. Cork to 1858; hon. physician to Queen's hospital, Birmingham 1858–73. *d.* Brixton, London 21 Aug. 1875.

FLEMING, ANN CUTHBERT. *b.* Scotland; went to Canada 1815 or 1816; kept a school at Montreal several years; author of *Home, a poem, Edinburgh* 1815; *A year in Canada and other poems, By A. C. Knight, Edinburgh* 1816; *Views of Canadian scenery* and other books. (*m.* (1) Mr. Knight, *m.* (2) James Fleming). *d.* 1860.

FLEMING, CHRISTOPHER. *b.* Boardstown, co. Westmeath 14 July 1808; educ. Dublin univ., B.A. 1821, M.D. 1838; L.C.S.I. 1824, member 1826, president 1859–60; surgeon House of Industry hospitals, Dublin 1851; M.R.I.A.; author of *Clinical records of injuries and diseases of genito-urinary organs* 1877; *Remarks on application of chloroform to surgical purposes* 1851. *d.* Donnybrook near Dublin 30 Dec. 1880.

FLEMING, EDWARD CARY. Ensign 31 foot 1803; lieut. col. of 2 Ceylon regiment 12 Aug. 1819, of 53 foot 24 Feb. 1820, of 24 foot 6 Nov. 1823 to 1 March 1833; C.B. 19 July 1838; col. 27 foot 19 Sep. 1853 to death; L.G. 20 June 1854. *d.* Gloucester sq. Hyde park, London 23 April 1860.

FLEMING, HENRY. Assistant sec. poor law board 3 Feb. 1848 to 5 July 1859, permanent sec. 5 July 1859 to 19 Aug. 1871. *d.* 2 Charles st. Berkeley sq. London 28 Feb. 1876.

FLEMING, JAMES (*eld. son of Valentine Fleming of Tuam, co. Galway*). Barrister M.T. 10 June 1836; Q.C. 9 Jany. 1858; chief comr. of West Indian incumbered estates court 17 Feb. 1865 to death; chancellor of county palatine of Durham 21 March 1871 to death; author of *Rules and orders Chancery Court, Durham* 1878. *d.* 12 Dorset sq. London 23 July 1887.

FLEMING, REV. JOHN (*son of Alexander Fleming*). *b.* Kirkroads farm near Bathgate in Linlithgowshire 10 Jany. 1785; ordained 22 Sep. 1808; minister of Flisk, Fifeshire 1810; the best zoologist in Scotland; D.D. of univ. of St. Andrews 1814; minister of Clackmannan 1832–34; professor of natural philosophy in Univ. and King's coll. Aberdeen 1834; joined the Free ch. 1834; professor of natural science Free ch. coll. Edin. 1845; studied the old red sand stone and its fossils; author of *The Philosophy of Zoology* 2 vols. 1822; *The temperature of the seasons* 1851 and other books and articles in scientific journals. *d.* Llangwym, Monmouthshire 18 Nov. 1857. *Fleming's Lithology of Edinburgh, with memoir by Rev. John Duns* 1859 *pp. i-civ.*

FLEMING, JOHN GIBSON. *b.* Glasgow 1809; ed. at Univ. of Glasgow, M.D. 1830; member of faculty of phys. and surgeons Glasgow 1833, pres. 1865–71; represented the faculty in general medical council 15 years; surgeon to Royal asylum for lunatics; F.R.S. Edin.; author of *Medical statistics of life assurance, Glasgow* 1862. *d.* 155 Bath st. Glasgow 2 Oct. 1879.

FLEMING, SIR VALENTINE (*brother of James Fleming, who d. 23 July 1887*). *b.* Ashby de la Zouch 1809; ed. at Trin. coll. Dub., B.A. 1832; barrister G.I. 21 Nov. 1838; comr. of Insolvent Court for Hobart Town 1841; solicitor general of Tasmania 1844 to Jany. 1848, attorney general Jany. 1848 to Aug. 1854; chief justice of supreme court of Tasmania Aug. 1854 to May 1870 when he resigned; knighted by patent 2 July 1856. *d.* Holbrook, Redhill 25 Oct. 1884 in 75 year.

FLETCHER, Rev. Alexander *(son of Rev. Wm. Fletcher of Bridge of Teith, Downe, Perthshire, minister of the associate synod).* *b.* Bridge of Teith 8 April 1787 ; ed. at univ. of Glasgow, M.A. ; co-pastor with his father at Bridge of Teith 16 Sep. 1807 ; minister of Miles's lane chapel, London, Nov. 1811, of Albion chapel, London Wall 7 Nov. 1816 to 1824 ; prosecuted in a breach of promise case by Eliza Dick, April 1824 ; separated from the Secession church 1824, minister of Finsbury chapel, London 1824–59 ; author of *A guide to Family Devotion* 1834 of which 50,000 copies were sold in England, *The Sabbath School Preacher and Juvenile Miscellany* 1848–50, 2 vols., and other works. *d.* 4 Portland place, Lower Clapton, London 30 Sep. 1860. *Macfarlane's Altar-Light, a tribute to the memory of the Rev. A. Fletcher* 1860 ; *Blair's The prince of preachers, Rev. A. Fletcher* 1860 ; *The Christian cabinet illustrated almanack for 1860 p. 31, portrait ; Trial of the Rev. Alexander Fletcher before the United Associate synod* 1824.

FLETCHER, Eliza *(dau. of Mr. Dawson of Oxton near Tadcaster, Yorkshire, land surveyor).* *b.* Oxton 15 Jany. 1770 ; educ. Manor sch. York ; wrote her auto-biography. *(m.* 16 July 1791 Archibald Fletcher, advocate, who died at Auchindinny house near Edinburgh 20 Dec. 1828). *d.* Edinburgh 5 Feb. 1858. *Autobiography of Mrs. Fletcher, edited by Lady Richardson* 1875, 2 *portraits.*

FLETCHER, George *(son of Joseph Fletcher).* *bapt.* Clarborough, Nottinghamshire 15 Oct. 1764 ; enlisted in Welsh fusiliers 2 Nov. 1785, deserted 16 March 1792 ; enlisted 3 foot guards 14 March 1793 when he stated that his original enlistment took place in Oct. 1773 ; pensioned 18 April 1803 on 1s. 2½d. a day ; worked in West India dock 1803–39 ; local Wesleyan preacher, gave out that his birth took place on 2 Feb. 1747 and had large congregations to see him. *d.* 41 Wade st. Poplar, London 2 Feb. 1855. *Thom's Human Longevity* (1873) 64, 164–70 ; *I.L.N.* 10 *March* 1855 *p.* 221, *portrait.*

FLETCHER, Isaac (2 *son of John Wilson Fletcher of Tarnbank, Cumberland* 1788–1857). *b.* Greysowthen, Cumberland 22 Feb. 1827 ; a coal owner and ironmaster ; M.P. for Cockermouth, Nov. 1868 to death ; chairman of Cockermouth, Keswick and Penrith railway ; F.R.A.S. 11 May 1849 ; F.R.S. 7 June 1855 ; shot himself at Morley's hotel, Trafalgar sq. London 3 April 1879.

FLETCHER, John Venour. *b.* Chesterfield 14 Nov. 1801 ; entered navy 13 Feb. 1814 ;

captain 8 June 1841, went on half pay 24 Oct. 1841 ; admiral on half pay 20 Oct. 1872. *d.* Reading 5 Dec. 1877.

FLETCHER, Joseph. *b.* 1813 ; barrister M.T. 7 May 1841 ; sec. to Handloom inquiry commission 1841, to Children's employment commission 1841–3 ; inspector of schools receiving grants under Privy Council 1844 ; one of hon. secretaries of statistical society of London 15 Feb. 1841 ; edited the *Statistical Journal ;* author of *Summary of the Moral Statistics of England and Wales* 1850 ; *Statistics of the Farm School system of the Continent and the education of pauper and criminal children* 1851. *d.* Chirk, co. Denbigh 11 Aug. 1852. *bur.* Tottenham church, Middlesex 18 Aug.

FLETCHER, Rev. Joseph *(son of Rev. Joseph Fletcher 1784–1843, independent minister at Stepney).* *b.* Blackburn 7 Jany. 1816 ; in a Manchester counting house to 1833 ; at Coward coll. 1833 ; minister of Congregational ch. Hanley 1839–49, of Christchurch, Hampshire 1849–73 ; kept a school at Christchurch but the death by drowning of 7 of his pupils in May 1838 caused him to close the establishment ; author of *The works and memoirs of Rev. Joseph Fletcher, D.D.* 1846 ; *History of Independency* 4 *vols.* 1847–49 and other works. *d.* Christchurch 2 June 1876.

FLETCHER, Ralph. *b.* Gloucester ; studied at St. Bartholomews ; surgeon to Gloucester county hospital ; had one of finest consulting practices in the kingdom, extending to whole of South Wales and Bristol ; the income from his practice, which was purely surgical, exceeded £4000 for many years ; had a very fine collection of pictures ; author of *Sketches on the influence of the mind on the body* 1833 ; *Notes on cruelty to animals* 1846. *d.* Barton st. Gloucester 8 Feb. 1851 aged 70 worth more than £80,000. *Medical Directory* 1852 *pp.* 646–7.

FLEXMORE, Richard, stage name of Richard Flexmore Geatter *(son of Richard Flexmore Geatter, celebrated comic dancer).* *b.* Kennington, London 15 Sep. 1824 ; appeared at Victoria theatre as a dancer 1832 ; clown at Grecian theatre, Christmas 1844, at Olympic theatre, Christmas 1845 ; played at Princess's, Strand, Adelphi, Covent Garden and Drury Lane to 1860 ; noted for his imitations of the leading dancers of his day ; acted with his wife in chief European cities in 1849, &c. *(m.* 28 July 1849 Franciska Christophosa dau. of Jean Baptiste Auriol famous French clown, she *m.* (2) her cousin Monsieur Auriol, and *d.* Paris

FLEXMORE, R. *(Con.)*

3 Sep. 1862). *d.* 66 Hercules buildings, Lambeth, London 20 Aug. 1860. *Illust. sp. and dr. news ii,* 268 (1874), *portrait, iv,* 294 (1875), *portrait; Era* 26 *Aug.* 1860 *p.* 10, *col.* 1, *and* 2 *Sep. p.* 10, *col.* 2; *A first appearance, By Mrs. Evans Bell* (1872), *i,* 129–33, *iii,* 195–7.

FLIGHT, WALTER *(son of William P. Flight).* *b.* Winchester 21 Jany. 1841; ed. at Queenwood coll. Hampshire, D. Sci. London 1867; assistant in mineralogical department British Museum 5 Sep. 1867, resigned 1884; experimented on the constituents of meteorites; F.R.S. 7 June 1883; author of numerous papers in scientific journals, majority of them on meteorites. *d.* 4 Wildwood terrace, North End, Hampstead 4 Nov. 1885. *W. Flight's Chapter on Meteorites* 1887.

FLOOD, FREDERICK SOLLY- *(only son of Richard Solly of Walthamstow, who d.* 1803). *b.* 7 Aug. 1801; ed. at Harrow and Trin. coll. Cam., B.A. 1825, M.A. 1828; assumed by r.l. additional surname of Flood 14 Oct. 1818; barrister L.I. 6 May 1828; attorney general for city and garrison of Gibraltar 15 Feb. 1866 to 1877. *d.* Gibraltar 13 May 1888.

FLOWER, EDWARD FORDHAM *(younger son of Richard Flower, who d.* 15 *Jany.* 1862). *b.* Marden hall, Hertfordshire 31 Jany. 1805; spent his early life in Illinois; brewer Stratford on Avon 1832–62; mayor of Stratford 3 times, also in 1864 during Shakespeare tercentenary; contested Coventry 1865 and North Warwickshire 1868; removed to London 1873; endeavoured to prevent cruelty to horses in use of bearing reins and gag-bits; author of *Bits and bearing reins* 1875, 7 ed. 1886 and 3 other books. *d.* 35 Hyde park gardens, London 20 March 1883. *E. F. Flower's Bits and bearing reins* (1886) 3–15, *portrait; Victoria Mag., May* 1878 *pp.* 67–8, *portrait; I.L.N.* 7 *May* 1864 *p.* 453, *portrait.*

FLOWER, JOHN WICKHAM. *b.* London 11 Aug. 1807; studied geology and archæology; lived at Croydon about 1848 to death; F.G.S. 1863; author of *Adam's disobedience and its results,* 2 ed. 1871; *A Layman's reason for discontinuing the use of the Athanasian creed* 1872. *d.* Park hill, Croydon 11 April 1873.

FLOWER, RICHARD. *b.* Hertfordshire about 1780; went with Morris Birkbeck to the U.S. 1817 to found an English colony in Albion, Edwards co. Illinois; instrumental in securing defeat of attempt to legalize African slavery in Illinois 1823; author of *History of the English settlement in Edwards county, Illinois*

FLOWER, R. *(Con.)*

founded in 1817 *and* 1818 *by Morris Birkbeck and Richard Flower, Chicago* 1882. *d.* Grayville, White co. Illinois 15 Jany. 1862.

FLOWERS, FREDERICK *(3 son of Field Flowers, rector of Partney, Lincs.) b.* Boston, Lincs. 1810; educ. Louth gram. sch.; barrister L.I. 18 Nov. 1839; recorder of Stamford, March 1862 to July 1864; revising barrister northern division Nottinghamshire; police magistrate Bow st. London 6 July 1864 to death. *d.* Holmesdale, Tottenham lane, Hornsey, Middlesex 26 Jany. 1886. *Graphic* 8 *Jany.* 1881 *p.* 32, *portrait; Saturday Review lxi,* 145 (1886).

FLOWERS, GEORGE FRENCH *(brother of the preceding). b.* Boston 1811; studied music under Rink and Von Wartensee in Germany; of Lincoln coll. Oxf., Bac. Mus. 1839, Doc. Mus. 1865; organist British embassy chapel, Paris, St. Mark's Myddleton sq., and St. John's Paddington successively; founded Contrapuntists' Soc. 1843; introduced and developed Vogler's system of progressive cadences 1848; his most distinguished pupil in singing was Mrs. Howard Paul; joined ch. of Rome 1860; author of *Essay on the construction of fugue* 1846; *Muscular Vocalisation, a poem, Barrow on Humber* 1861; composer of organ fugues, pastoral chorus and choral fugue. *d.* of cholera in London 14 June 1872.

FLOYER, JOHN *(younger son of Rev. Wm. Floyer* 1746–1819, *V. of Stinsford, Dorset). b.* 26 April 1811; ed. at Winchester and Balliol coll. Ox., B.A. 1831; sheriff of Dorset 1844; M.P. for Dorset 1846–57 and 1864–85; contested Dorset, April 1857; chairman of Dorset quarter sessions. *d.* 5 Old palace yard, Westminster 4 July 1887.

FLUDE, THOMAS PETERS *(2 son of Jonathan Flude, town major of Berwick on Tweed).* Second lieut. R.A. 17 July 1817, col. 15 May 1855, col. commandant 11 Dec. 1868 to 1 Oct. 1877; general 1 Oct. 1877. *d.* Tweed house, Folkestone 13 July 1885 in 87 year.

FOGGO, GEORGE. *b.* London 14 April 1793; instructed in painting by Jean Baptist Regnault in Paris; worked with his brother James Foggo 1819–59; one of founders and hon. sec. of Soc. for obtaining free access to Museums; lithographer; published a set of lithographs from Raphael's cartoons 1828; *Catalogue of the pictures in the National Gallery* 1844 and the *Adventures of Sir J. Brook, Rajah of Sarawak* 1853; exhibited 7 pictures at R.A., 14 at B.I. and 36 at Suffolk st. 1816–64. *d.* London 26 Sep. 1869.

FOGGO, JAMES. *b.* London 11 June 1789; instructed by Jean Baptist Regnault in Paris; returned to London 1815; supported himself by teaching and portrait painting; from 1819 painted pictures in conjunction with his brother George Foggo for 40 years; well known as painters of altar pieces; exhibited a large picture "The Christian inhabitants of Parga preparing to emigrate"; exhibited their works with Haydon and others at the Pantheon, London 1843 etc.; exhibited 5 pictures at R.A., 8 at B.I. and 22 at Suffolk st. 1816–58; with his brother undertook care of exhibition of pictures at Pantheon Oxford st. London 1852. *d.* London 14 Sep. 1860.

FOLEY, THOMAS HENRY FOLEY, 4 Baron *(eld. son of 3 Baron Foley 1780–1833).* *b.* Hill st. Berkeley sq. London 11 Dec. 1808; M.P. for Worcestershire 5 Aug. 1830 to 16 April 1833; captain of corps of gentlemen at arms 1833–34, 1835–41, 1846–52, 1852–58, 1859–66 and 1868 to death; P.C. 1833; lord lieut. of Worcestershire. *d.* Paris 20 Nov. 1869, personalty sworn under £250,000, 22 Jany. 1870.

FOLEY, REV. DANIEL. *b.* about 1815; employed in shop of Patrick Grey, Tralee; educ. Trin. coll. Dublin, B.A. 1843, M.A. 1852, B.D. 1854, D.D. 1858; professor of Irish in univ. of Dublin 1849–61; prebendary of Kilbragh in Cashel cath. to death; R. of Templetuohy 1852 to death; lectured against disestablishment of Ch. of Ireland; author of *An English-Irish Dictionary, Dublin* 1855. *d.* Blackrock, Dublin 7 July 1874.

FOLEY, JOHN HENRY. *b.* Dublin 24 May 1818; student of the R.A. London 1835, A.R.A. 1849, R.A. 1858; his group of Iro and Bacchus exhibited 1840 purchased by the earl of Ellesmere; executed statues of Hampden and Selden for St. Stephen's hall, Westminster; executed group of Asia and figure of Prince Consort for Albert Memorial, Hyde park, Caractacus and Egeria for Mansion house, and statues of Canning, Harding and Outram for Calcutta; exhibited 49 works at R.A. and 8 at B.I. 1839–75. *d.* Hampstead 27 Aug. 1874. *bur.* St. Paul's cathedral 4 Sep., left his models to the Dublin Soc. and the bulk of his property to the Artists' Benevolent fund. *Journal of British Archæol. Assoc. xxxi,* 226–29 (1875); *Sandby's History of Royal Academy ii,* 315–17 (1862); *I.L.N. xxx,* 419 (1857), *portrait, lxv,* 236, 249, 254 (1874), *portrait.*

FOLJAMBE, GEORGE SAVILE. *b.* 4 June 1800; ed. at Eton and St. John's coll. Cam.; kept

FOLJAMBE, G. S. *(Con.)*
fox hounds in Notts. 1822–45 when he sold them for upwards of £3500; sheriff of Notts. *d.* Osberton near Worksop 18 Dec. 1869. *Sporting Review lxiii,* 12–14, 371 (1870).

FOLLETT, BRENT SPENCER (4 *son of Benjamin Follett of Topsham, Devon).* *b.* 1810; barrister L.I. 7 June 1833, bencher 3 Nov. 1851 to death, treasurer 1872; Q.C. 11 July 1851; M.P. for Bridgwater 1852–57; contested Cirencester, April 1859; chief registrar of Land Registry Office, London 18 Aug. 1862 to death; member of council of legal education, London. *d.* 23 Jany. 1887.

FOLSOM, ABBY H. *b.* England about 1792; went to the U.S. about 1837; became noted as an advocate of anti-slavery reform and for addresses at meetings of American anti-slavery society about 1842–5; author of *A letter from a member of the Boston bar to an Avaricious Landlord, Boston* 1851. (*m.* Mr. Folsom of Massachusetts). *d.* Rochester, New York 1867.

FONBLANQUE, ALBANY WILLIAM (3 *son of John de Grenier Fonblanque 1760–1838).* *b.* London 1793; a journalist on *Morning Chronicle, Times* and *Atlas;* on the *Examiner* 1826, manager and editor 1830–47, sole proprietor to 1860; head of statistical department of Board of Trade 1847 to death; a brilliant talker, a finished scholar and a student of music and art; author of *England under seven administrations* 3 vols. 1837. *d.* London 14 Oct. 1872. *Life,* ed. by E. B. de Fonblanque 1874; *Westminster Papers vii,* 21–23 (1874); *Graphic vi,* 442, 445 (1872), *portrait.*

FONBLANQUE, JOHN SAMUEL MARTIN DE GRENIER *(brother of the preceding).* *b.* Brook st. Grosvenor sq. London, March 1787; ed. at Charterhouse and Caius coll. Cam.; 2 lieut. 21 fusiliers 3 June 1810, 1 lieut. to 25 March 1817 when placed on h.p.; served in the American war, made prisoner at New Orleans; barrister L.I. 27 Nov. 1816; one of the 70 comrs. of bankruptcy 1817, comr. of Court of Bankruptcy 1830 to death; a founder of *The Jurist,* a quarterly journal of *jurisprudence and legislation* 1827; author with J. A. Paris of *Medical Jurisprudence* 3 vols. 1823. *d.* Brighton 3 Nov. 1865.

FOOTE, HENRY RICHARD. Entered navy 6 May 1830; captain 20 Oct. 1853; harbour manager and secretary Newport dock company 1854; retired captain 31 March 1866; retired admiral 9 Jany. 1880. *d.* Ellesmere house, Newport, Monmouthshire 23 Nov. 1885 aged 68.

FORAN, MOST REV. NICHOLAS. *b.* Waterford; ed. at Maynooth; pres. of St. John's college, Waterford short time; parish priest of Lismore; parish priest of Dungarvan to 1837; R.C. Bishop of Waterford and Lismore 23 May 1837 to death; consecrated 24 Aug. 1837. *d.* Dungarvan 18 May 1855 in 74 year.

FORBES, WALTER FORBES, 18 Baron. *b.* Crailing house, Roxburghshire 29 May 1798; ensign Coldstream guards 1814; commanded a company at defence of Hougoumont 18 June 1815; retired 1825; succeeded 4 May 1843; a great benefactor to St. Ninian's cathedral, Perth. *d.* Richmond, Surrey 1 May 1868, monument in Guards' chapel, Wellington barracks, London.

FORBES, RIGHT REV. ALEXANDER PENROSE (2 *son of John Hay Forbes, lord Medwyn 1776–1854*). *b.* Edinburgh 6 June 1817; educ. Glasgow univ. 1833 and Haileybury coll.; assistant collector Rajahmundry, India 1837; head assistant to the Sudder and Foujdarry Adawlut 1839–40; matric. from Brasenose coll. Oxf. 1840, Boden Sanskrit scholar 1841; B.A. 1844, M.A. 1846, D.C.L. 18 May 1848; C. of Aston Rowant, Oxf. 1844; C. of St. Thomas', Oxf. 1845; incumb. of Stonehaven, Kincardine 1846; V. of St. Saviour's, Leeds 1847, one of the first Tractarian churches; elected bishop of Brechin 21 Sep. 1847 when the seat of the bishoprick was removed from Brechin to Dundee, and he also became V. of St. Paul's, Dundee; censured by the college of bishops for his teaching on the real presence 15 March 1860; built St. Paul's cathedral, Dundee 1855 and founded sisterhood of St. Mary and St. Modwenna; author of *An explanation of the Thirty nine articles 2 vols. 1867–68* in which he was assisted by Dr. Pusey; *The prisoners of Craigmacaire 1852; The pious life of Helen Inglis 1854; Kalendars of Scottish saints 1872* and 20 other works. *d.* Castle hill, Dundee 8 Oct. 1875. *Mackey's Bishop Forbes (1888), portrait; Memoir of Alexander, bishop of Brechin, By Miss Skene (1876).*

FORBES, SIR CHARLES FERGUSSON. *b.* 1779; hospital assistant in army medical service, May 1798; served in Egypt, Gallicia and the Peninsula; retired with rank of deputy inspector general of hospitals 1864; M.D. Edinburgh 24 June 1808; L.R.C.P. 22 Dec. 1814, F.R.C.P. 10 July 1841; practised in London 1814 to death; physician Royal Westminster infirmary for diseases of the eye 1816, fell out with his colleage G. J. Guthrie 1827 when he resigned; fought a duel with Hale Thomson one of Guthrie's party, on Clapham common 29 Dec. 1827; F.L.S. 1822; K.C.H.

FORBES, SIR C. F. (*Con.*)

1837; knighted at St. James's palace 13 March 1844. *d.* 23 Argyll st. London 22 March 1852. *Munk's Roll of College of Physicians (1878) iii*, 129; *Medical Circular i*, 137 (1852).

FORBES, DAVID. Entered Bombay army 1819; lieut. col. 9 Bombay N.I. 23 Nov. 1841 to 25 May 1852; commandant at Aden 9 Jany. 1851 to 25 May 1852; col. 3 European regiment 1854 to death; M.G. 28 Nov. 1854. *d.* Upper Brunswick place, Brighton 2 April 1863.

FORBES, DAVID (*son of Edward Forbes of Oakhill, Isle of Man, banker*). *b.* Douglas 6 Sep. 1828; educ. Brentwood, Essex and Edin. univ.; superintendent of mining and metallurgical works at Espedal, Norway 1848–58; F.G.S. 1853 and one of secretaries 1871; F.R.S. 3 June 1856; partner with Evans and Askin, nickel smelters, Birmingham 1856; A.I.C.E. 1 Feb. 1853, mem. of council 1872–73; visited Bolivia, Peru, South Sea islands and Africa in search of mines and minerals 1857–66; foreign sec. of Iron and Steel Institute 1871–6; one of the first to apply the microscope to the study of rocks; wrote 58 papers on scientific subjects. *d.* 11 York place, Portman sq. London 5 Dec. 1876. *Quarterly Journal of Geol. Soc. xxxiii*, 41–8 (1877); *Min. of proc. of Instit. of C.E. xlix*, 270–75 (1877); *Journal of Iron and Steel Institute 1876 pp. 519–24.*

FORBES, DUNCAN. *b.* Kinnaird, Perthshire 28 April 1798; village school master of Straloch 1815; educ. Carmichael sch., Perth gram. sch. and St. Andrew's univ., M.A. 1823, LL.D. 1847; employed in Calcutta academy Nov. 1823 to 1826; assistant to Dr. John Borthwick Gilchrist, teacher of Hindustani and to Dr. Sandford Arnet 1826–37; professor of oriental languages, King's coll. London 1837–61; hon. fellow of King's coll. 1861; catalogued Persian MSS. in British Museum 1849–55; author of *The Hindustani Manual 1845; The history of chess from the time of the early invention of the game in India 1860; A grammar of the Bengali language 1861; A grammar of the Arabic language 1863* and other books. *d.* London 17 Aug. 1868. *Annual Report R. Asiatic Soc.*, May 1869 *pp. vii–viii.*

FORBES, EDWARD (2 *child of Edward Forbes of Douglas, Isle of Man, banker*). *b.* Douglas 12 Feb. 1815; ed. at univ. of Edin. 1831–36; naturalist to H.M.'s surveying ship Beacon, in the Levant 1841–42; professor of botany at King's college, London, Oct. 1842; F.G.S. 4 Dec. 1844, librarian and curator 1842–44,

FORBES, E. *(Con.)*

pres. 1853; F.R.S. 13 Feb. 1845; palæontologist at Museum of practical geology 1 Nov. 1844 to 1854; founded Club of the Metropolitan Red Lions 1845; professor of natural history in Univ. of Edin. April 1854 to death; published with Sylvanus Hanley *A History of British Mollusca* 4 vols. 1848–53; author of many books and papers on natural history. *d.* Wardie near Edinburgh 18 Nov. 1854. *J. H. Bennett's Memoir of E. Forbes* 1855; *Memoir of E. Forbes by G. Wilson and A. Geikie* 1861, *portrait*; *Sir A. Grant's Univ. of Edin. ii*, 434 (1884); *I.L.N. xxv*, 564, 566 (1854), *portrait*.

FORBES, FRANCIS REGINALD (2 *son of 6 Earl of Granard 1760–1837*). *b.* Moira castle, Ireland 17 Sep. 1791; attached to embassy at St. Petersburg, July 1812; minister plenipotentiary at Dresden 26 Nov. 1832; raised to rank of envoy extraordinary and minister plenipotentiary 2 May 1857, transferred to Rio de Janeiro 13 Dec. 1858; retired 2 Sep. 1859, pension granted him 1 Nov. 1859. *d.* Geneva 5 Nov. 1873.

FORBES, REV. GEORGE HAY *(brother of Right Rev. A. P. Forbes)*. *b.* 4 Aug. 1821; episcopal minister at Burntisland 1849 to death; founded and endowed the Pitsligo press at Burntisland, issued theological pamphlets, ancient liturgies and missals, and a periodical called *The Panoply* 1853–69, all of which he printed himself, the press was moved to Edinburgh, January 1884; author of *The goodness of God, Prize essay* 1849; *Doctrinal errors of the English prayer book* 1863. *d.* The Parsonage, Burntisland 7 Nov. 1875.

FORBES, HENRY. *b.* 1804; pupil of Smart, Hummel, Moscheles and Herz; organist of St. Luke's, Chelsea; his opera *The Fairy Oak* produced at Drury Lane 18 Oct. 1845; his cantata Ruth performed London 1847; conductor of Società Armonica 1827–50; composer of *National Psalmody* 1843. *d.* London 24 Nov. 1859.

FORBES, JAMES. *b.* Bridgend, Perthshire, May 1793; head gardener to Duke of Bedford at Woburn abbey, Beds. 37 years; A.L.S. 17 Jany. 1832; published *Hortus ericaceus Woburnensis* 1825; *Salicetum Woburnense* 1829; *Hortus Woburnensis* 1833; *Pinetum Woburnense* 1839. *d.* The Abbey Gardens, Woburn 6 July 1861. *Proc. of Linnœan Soc.* (1861) 104.

FORBES, JAMES DAVID *(youngest son of Sir Wm. Forbes, 7 Bart. 1773–1828)*. *b.* Edinburgh 20 April 1809; ed. at Univ. of Edin., LL.D. 1860; F.R.S. Edin. 1828, sec. 1840–51;

FORBES, J. D. *(Con.)*

F.R.S. 7 June 1832, Rumford medallist 1838 for discovery of polarisation of heat; a founder of British Association 1832; professor of natural philosophy in Univ. of Edin. 30 Jany. 1833, resigned April 1860; dean of Faculty of Arts 1837; granted civil list pension of £200, 14 Oct. 1845; surveyed Mer de Glace 1850; principal of St. Andrews 2 Dec. 1859 to Oct. 1868; author of *Travels through the Alps of Savoy with observations on glaciers* 1843 and of upwards of 149 articles in scientific transactions. *d.* Clifton hill house, Bristol 31 Dec. 1868. *Life and letters of J. D. Forbes* 1873; *Proc. of Royal Soc. xix*, 1–9 (1871); *Sir A. Grant's Univ. of Edin. ii*, 354–7 (1884); *Contemporary Review xxii*, 484–508 (1873).

FORBES, SIR JOHN (4 *son of Alexander Forbes of the Enzie, Banffshire)*. *b.* Cuttelbrae, Ruthven, Banffshire 18 Oct. 1787; ed. at Marischal coll. Aberdeen 1803–6 and Univ. of Edin., M.D. 1817; assistant surgeon R.N. 1807–16 when placed on h.p.; phys. at Penzance 1817–22, at Chichester 1822–40, in London 1840–59; F.R.S. 5 Feb. 1829; founded *British and Foreign medical review*, Jany. 1836, edited it 1836 to Oct. 1847, 48 numbers; phys. extraord. to Prince Consort, Aug. 1840 to 1859; phys. in ord. to H.M.'s Household, Feb. 1841 to 1859; F.R.C.S. Lond. 1845; knighted at Buckingham palace 8 Aug. 1853; author of *Original cases illustrating the use of the stethoscope* 1824; editor with A. Tweedie and J. Conolly of *Cyclopædia of practical medicine* 1833–35, 4 vols.; author of *A physician's holiday in Switzerland* 1848; *Sight seeing in Germany* 1856. *d.* Whitchurch near Reading 13 Nov. 1861. *E. A. Parke's Memoir of Sir John Forbes*; *Proc. of Royal Soc. xii*, 6–10 (1862).

FORBES, REV. JOHN. *b.* Dunkeld, Perthshire; educ. Perth academy and St. Andrew's univ., D.D. 1837; LL.D. of Glasgow univ. 1840; minister at Hope park chapel, Edinburgh 1826, at Outer-High church, Glasgow 18 Dec. 1828; left the Presbyterian ch. 24 May 1843; contributed to *The evidences of Revealed Religion* 1838; Free church minister of Free St. Paul's Glasgow 1843; author of *Differential and integral calculus; Three sermons on Lord's Day* 1831 and other books. *d.* Glasgow 25 Dec. 1874 aged 73. *Wylie's Disruption Worthies* (1881) 253–60; *John Smith's Our Scottish Clergy* (1848) 231–7.

FORBES, JOHN HAY (2 *son of Sir Wm. Forbes, 6 Bart., of Pitsligo 1739–1806)*. *b.* Edinburgh Sep. 1776; advocate 2 March 1799; sheriff depute of Perthshire 1807; judge of Court of

FORBES, J. H. *(Con.)*

Session with title of Lord Medwyn, Jany. 1825 to Oct. 1852; a lord of justiciary 16 Nov. 1830 to May 1849; edited *Thoughts concerning man's condition in this life and hopes in world to come, By Alexander Forbes, Baron Pitsligo* 1854. *d.* Edinburgh 25 July 1854. *J. Kay's Edinburgh Portraits ii,* 99 (1842), *portrait.*

FORBES, NATHANIEL. Entered Madras army 1782; col. 24 Madras N.I. 1820 or 1821 to death; L.G. 10 Jany. 1837. *d.* Sloane st. London 16 Aug. 1851.

FORBES, THOMAS JOHN. Second lieut. R.A. 6 March 1795; col. commandant 8 Dec. 1847 to death; general 16 Jany. 1859. *d.* Stoke-by-Nayland, Colchester 1 Feb. 1868 aged 87.

FORBES, WILLIAM. *b.* 1806; M.P. for Stirlingshire 1835–38 and 1841 to death. *d.* Callander house near Stirling 10 Feb. 1855.

FORBES, WILLIAM ALEXANDER (2 son of John Staats Forbes). *b.* Cheltenham 24 June 1855; educ. Kensington sch. and Winchester coll.; studied at Edin. univ. 1873 and univ. coll. London 1875–76; matric. St. John's coll. Cam. 1876, fellow; prosector to Zoological soc. of London, Dec. 1879 to death; lectured on comparative anatomy Charing Cross hospital medical sch.; wrote on the muscular structure and voice organs of birds; travelled in Pernambuco 1880 and in tropical Africa 1882 to investigate the fauna; author of *The collected papers of A. H. Garrod* 1881. *d.* Shonga on the Niger 14 Jany. 1883. *bur.* Wickham, Kent 1 April 1884. *F. E. Beddard's Collected Papers of W. A. Forbes* (1885).

FORBES, WILLIAM NAIRN (6 son of John Forbes of Blackford, co. Aberdeen). *b.* Blackford 3 April 1796; ed. at King's coll. old Aberdeen, univ. of Edin. and Addiscombe; 2 lieut. Bengal engineers 1816, col. 1 Aug. 1854 to death; M.G. 28 Nov. 1854; superintendent of mint machinery at Calcutta 1823; master of Calcutta mint 3 Feb. 1836 to death; built cathedral at Calcutta 1839–47; M.I.C.E. 1828. *d.* on board the 'Oriental' off the island of Tibble Teer on his way to England 1 May 1855. *Min. of proc. of Instit. of C.E. xx,* 138-40 (1861).

FORBES-LESLIE, JONATHAN (*youngest son of John Forbes of Blackford*). *b.* 1798; ensign 78 foot 19 Jany. 1814, lieut. col. 9 Nov. 1846 to 10 Dec. 1847 when he retired from the army; author of *Eleven years in Ceylon* 2 vols. 1840; *Recent disturbances and military executions in*

FORBES-LESLIE, J. *(Con.)*

Ceylon 1850; assumed name of Leslie after Forbes 1861. *d.* Rothienorman, Aberdeenshire 23 Dec. 1877. *Leslie's Family of Leslie* (1869) *iii,* 320.

FORD, CHARLES ERSKINE. *b.* 5 Jany. 1812; 2 lieut. R.E. 29 April 1829, col. 11 Oct. 1863, col. commandant 1 Oct. 1877 to death; general 1 Oct. 1877; placed on retired list 1 July 1881. *d.* Hampton court palace 27 July 1884.

FORD, REV. DAVID EVERARD (*son of Rev. David Ford, congregational minister*). *b.* Long Melford, Suffolk 13 Sep. 1797; congregational minister at Lymington, Hants. 1821–1841; visited stations of congregational union 1841–43; minister of Richmond chapel, Manchester 1843, resigned 1858; author of *Decapolis, or the individual obligation of christians to save souls* 1840, *fifth American ed.* 1848; *Chorazin* 1841; *Damascus* 1842; *Laodicea* 1844 and *Alarm in Zion* 1848; published music for psalms and hymns 1825–29 and *Rudiments of music* 1843. *d.* Bedford 23 Oct. 1875.

FORD, RICHARD (*eld. son of Sir Richard Ford, chief police magistrate of London, who d. 3 May 1806 aged 47*). *b.* Sloane st. London April 1796; ed. at Winchester and Trin. coll. Ox.; B.A. 1817, M.A. 1822; barrister L.I. 17 May 1822; resided in Spain 1830–34; settled at Heavitree near Exeter 1834; contributed to *Quarterly Review* 1836–57; author of *A handbook for travellers in Spain and readers at home* 2 vols. 1845, *new ed.* 2 vols. 1861; *Gatherings from Spain* 1846, *new ed.* 1861; had a fine collection of majolica ware. *d.* Heavitree 1 Sep. 1858. *Times 4 Sep.* 1858 *p.* 6, *col.* 5; *Waagen's Treasures of art ii,* 223-6 (1854); *Fraser's Mag. Oct.* 1858 *pp.* 422-4.

FORD, WILLIAM (*eld. son of Rev. Richard Wilbraham Ford, R. of Little Risington, Gloucs.*) *b.* 4 May 1812; ed. at Eton and King's coll. Cam., fellow; B.A. 1834, M.A. 1837; admitted solicitor 1836; partner in firm of Ranken and Co. London 1837; member of council of Incorporated Law Society 1860–76, vice pres. 1869–70, pres. 1870–71. *d.* Majori, South Italy 10 Jany. 1889.

FORDHAM, GEORGE (*son of James Fordham*). *b.* Cambridge 11 Sep. 1837; trained under R. Drewitt and E. Smith, and commenced his career at Brighton 1850; at the head of list of winning jockeys 1855–63, won 165 races 1862; won the Oaks 5 times, the Cambridgeshire 4 times, the Ascot cup 5 times, the 2000 guineas 3 times, the 1000 guineas 7 times; won the Derby on Sir Bevys 1879, won the

Grand prix de Paris 1867, 1868 and 1881, the French Derby 1861 and 1868, the French Oaks 1880; known as "the demon." *d.* Slough 12 Oct. 1887. *Baily's Mag. iii,* 183–8 (1861) *xlviii,* 277–9 (1888); *Illust. sporting news ii,* 301 (1863), *portrait; Illust. sp. and dr. news i,* 16 (1874), *portrait,* 24 *May 1884, portrait; Sporting Mirror ii,* 37–40 (1881), *portrait.*

FORDYCE, ALEXANDER DINGWALL. *b.* Aberdeen 4 March 1800; entered navy 12 June 1813; commander on h.p. 3 Sep. 1841; retired captain 14 July 1857; M.P. for Aberdeen 1847–52; author of *Outlines of naval routine* 1837. *d.* Aberdeen 16 July 1864. *Naval and military gazette 30 July 1864 p.* 483.

FORDYCE, CHARLES FRANCIS. *b.* 19 Dec. 1819; ensign 41 foot 17 Feb. 1838; major 47 foot 1852–55; A.Q.M.G. Canada 1855–57; military sec. to governor of Madras 1866–71, private sec. 1871–72; col. second battalion Gloucestershire regiment 7 Aug. 1884 to death; placed on retired list with hon. rank of general 1 July 1881; C.B. 2 Jany. 1857. *d.* Hayford, Torquay 23 Sep. 1887.

FORDYCE, GEORGE DINGWALL *(brother of Alexander Dingwall Fordyce).* *b.* 1808; advocate 1832, advocate depute; sheriff of Sutherland and Caithness 14 Aug. 1857 to 1875. *d.* Forres st. Edinburgh 7 Sep. 1875.

FORDYCE, JOHN. *b.* Ayton, Berwickshire; ensign 34 foot 18 Dec. 1828; lieut. col. 74 foot 10 July 1846 to death; killed in the action of Waterkloof, Caffraria 6 Nov. 1851. *The Christian Soldier* 1856; *W. R. King's Campaigning in Kaffirland* (1853) *p.* 146, *view of his death.*

FORDYCE, SIR JOHN *(son of James Fordyce).* *b.* 4 March 1806; 2 lieut. Bengal artillery 10 May 1822, col. commandant 5 April 1873 to death; L.G. 21 Jany. 1872; K.C.B. 24 May 1873. *d.* Colne house, Earl's Colne, Essex 26 Feb. 1877.

FORDYCE, WILLIAM DINGWALL. *b.* Rubilaw cottage, Aberdeen 31 March 1836; ed. at Univ. of Edin., M.A. 1859; advocate 1862; M.P. for Aberdeenshire 1866–68, for East Aberdeenshire 1868 to death. *d.* Brucklay Castle near Aberdeen 27 Nov. 1875.

FORESTER, JOHN GEORGE WELD, 2 Baron *(eld. child of 1 Baron Forester 1767–1828).* *b.* Sackville st. Piccadilly, London 9 Aug. 1801; M.P. for Wenlock 1826–28; captain of corps of gentlemen-at-arms 1841–46; P.C. 14 Sep. 1841; master of the Belvoir fox hounds 1830–

58. *d.* Willey park, Broseley, Shropshire 10 Oct. 1874. *Baily's Mag. xii,* 163–5 (1867), *portrait.*

FORESTER, GEORGE CECIL WELD FORESTER, 3 Baron *(brother of the preceding).* *b.* Sackville st. Piccadilly, London 10 May 1807; ed. at Westminster; cornet Royal horse guards 27 May 1824, lieut. col. 2 Sep. 1853 to 30 Sep. 1859; placed on retired list 1 Oct. 1877; general 1 Oct. 1877; M.P. for Wenlock 1828–74; controller of the household, March to Dec. 1852 and Feb. 1858 to July 1859. *d.* 3 Carlton gardens, London 14 Feb. 1886.

FORMBY, REV. HENRY (2 *son of Henry Greenhalgh Formby of Bury, Lancs.* 1789–1834). *b.* 1816; ed. at Clitheroe gr. sch. Charterhouse and Brasenose coll. Ox.; B.A. 1837, M.A. 1841; V. of Ruardean, Gloucs. 1844; received into R.C. church at St. Mary's college, Oscott 24 Jany. 1846; ordained priest at Oscott 18 Sep. 1847; priest at St. Chads, Birmingham and Wednesbury successively; resided at Dominican priory of St. Peter, Hinckley, Leics. about 1865 to death; edited for some years *The monthly magazine of the Holy Rosary,* n.s. 1873, &c.; author of *A visit to the East* 1843 and 40 other books. *d.* Normanton hall, Leics. 12 March 1884. *Gillow's English Catholics ii,* 309–13 (1885).

FORREST, SIR JAMES, 1 Baronet *(son of James Forrest of Edinburgh, writer to the signet 1744–1820).* *b.* 16 Oct. 1780; advocate 1803; lord provost of Edinburgh 1838; created a baronet 7 Aug. 1838; a ruling elder of established church of Scotland to 1843 when he joined the free church; grand master of grand lodge of freemasons in Scotland. *d.* Plymouth 5 April 1860.

FORREST, ROBERT. *b.* Carluke, Lanarkshire 1790; a stonemason in Clydesdale quarries; cut colossal figure of first Viscount Melville in centre of St. Andrew sq. Edinburgh; sculptor of statues of John Knox in Glasgow necropolis, and of Mr. Ferguson of Raith at Haddington 1843; opened his public exhibition of statuary on the Calton hill, Edinburgh 1832. *d.* Edinburgh 29 Dec. 1852. *W. Anderson's Scottish Nation iii,* 710 (1863); *Georgian Era iv,* 180 (1834).

FORREST, THOMAS. *b.* Burnwynd, Wilkieston, Midlothian 1805; studied under W. H. Lizars in Edinburgh; line engraver; many of his plates were published by Royal Assoc. for promotion of fine arts in Scotland; gave a complete set of his works 160 in number to Royal Scottish Academy 1884. *d.* Edinburgh 15 Oct. 1889.

FORRESTER, ALFRED HENRY (*son of Robert Forrester of 5 North gate, royal exchange, London, public notary*). *b.* London 10 Sep. 1804; apprentice to a notary in the city; connected with his brother Charles Robert Forrester (who *d.* 15 Jany. 1850 aged 47) in business about 1825–39; illustrated several of his brother's books in which the pseudonym of Alfred Crowquill was conjointly used by writer and artist, but afterwards it was used by the artist alone; contributed sketches to vols. 2, 3 and 4 of *Punch* 1842–3; member of staff of *Illustrated London News* from 1843; wrote and illustrated *A. Crowquill's Guide to watering places* 1839 and 25 other books; illustrated wholly or partly *Ups and Downs* 1823 and 32 other books. *d.* 3 Portland place north, Clapham road, London 26 May 1872. *Everitt's English caricaturists* (1886) 194, 368–71, 410; *Illustrated Review* 15 *June* 1872 *pp.* 737–42, *portrait; Bentley's Miscellany* (1846) *xix,* 87, 99, *portrait.*

FORRESTER, HENRY, stage name of Henry Frost. *b.* Capel near Dorking 9 April 1827; became an actor 1855; first appeared in London at Marylebone theatre as Korac in *Zembuca* 18 Dec. 1858; acted at Sadler's Wells 1861–64, at Princess's, Victoria, Surrey, Royalty, Lyceum; played Iago at Lyceum 14 Feb. 1876; played Daniel Druce in the provinces more than 300 times. *d.* Capel house, South Lambeth, London 9 April 1882. *Illust. sp. and dr. news v,* 31–3 (1876).

FORRESTER, JOSEPH JAMES, Baron de Forrester. *b.* Hull 27 May 1809; merchant and wine shipper at Oporto 1831 to death; surveyed river Douro with a view to improvement of its navigation, and published a map of it 1848, adopted by Portuguese government as a national work; author of *A word or two on port wine* 1844, anon., 8 editions, for which he received addresses of thanks from 102 parishes of the Upper Douro; *Oliveira Prize essay on Portugal* 1853, 2 ed. 1854; created Baron de Forrester for life by Queen of Portugal; F.S.A. 1 May 1856; drowned in the river Douro near a rapid called the Ponto do Cachuo 12 May 1861. *Memorials of Star club of London vol.* 1 (1855).

FORSAYETH, THOMAS (*son of Rev. John Forsayeth of Cork*). *b.* Cork 1798; ed. at Cork and Trin. coll. Dublin; called to Irish bar, Jany. 1824; went Munster circuit; recorder of Cork 1844 to death; Q.C. 6 July 1858. *d.* Merville, Queenstown, co. Cork 13 Oct. 1877. *J. R. O'Flanagan's Irish bar* (1879) 408.

FORSHALL, REV. JOSIAH (*eld. son of Samuel Forshall of Witney, Oxon.*) *b.* Witney 29 March

FORSHALL, REV. J. (*Con.*)
1795; ed. at Ex. coll. Ox., fell. of his coll. 30 June 1819 to 13 July 1826, assistant tutor 1820, tutor 1822–24; B.A. 1818, M.A. 1821; assist. keeper of MSS. in British Museum 1824, keeper 1827 to July 1837, secretary Feb. 1828–51; F.R.S. 12 June 1828; chaplain of Foundling Hospital 1829–59; edited *Catalogue of Arundel and Burney manuscripts in British Museum* 1834 and other catalogues; published *Gospel of St. John arranged* 1859, and other books; published with Sir F. Madden *The Holy Bible…in the earliest English versions made by John Wycliffe* 4 vols. 1850. *d.* 49 Woburn place, London 18 Dec. 1863. *R. Cowtan's Memories of the British Museum* (1872) 364–76.

FORSTER, REV. CHARLES. Ed. at Trin. coll. Dublin; P.C. of Ash, Kent 1834–38; one of the six preachers in Canterbury cathedral 1835 to death; R. of Stisted near Braintree, Essex 1838 to death; author of *Discourses on subjects of Scripture history* 1823; *The life of J. Jebb, bishop of Limerick* 1836; *The one primeval language* 1851 and other books. *d.* Stisted rectory 20 Aug. 1871 aged 84. *Braintree Advertiser* 30 *Aug.* 1871 *p.* 2.

FORSTER, FRANK. *b.* near Newcastle 1800; managed mines near Swansea, also in Lancs.; assistant of Robert Stephenson in his chief enterprises up to completion of Chester and Holyhead railway on which he was resident engineer of portion from near Conway to Holyhead; chief engineer to Metropolitan commission of sewers from its formation 1849 to 1852; M.I.C.E. 1845. *d.* Elm lodge, Kilburn, London 13 April 1852. *Min. of proc. of Instit. of C.E. xii,* 157 (1853).

FORSTER, SIR GEORGE, 2 Baronet. *b.* Baronstown Glebe, co. Louth 21 March 1796; called to bar in Ireland 1830; succeeded 4 Dec. 1843; M.P. for co. Monaghan 1852–65. *d.* Fitzwilliam sq. Dublin 4 April 1876.

FORSTER, REV. HENRY (*youngest son of Thomas Forster of St. Michael's, Oxford*). Matric. from New coll. Ox. 17 Nov. 1827 aged 18; B.A. 1832, M.A. 1834; esquire bedel in divinity in Univ. of Ox., Feb. 1832 to death when the office expired. *d.* Oxford 25 April 1857.

FORSTER, JOHN (*eld. child of Robert Forster of Newcastle, cattle dealer, who d. 1836*). *b.* Newcastle 2 April 1812; ed. at Newcastle gr. sch. and Univ. coll. London; student at I.T. 10 Nov. 1828, barrister 27 Jany. 1843; dramatic critic on the *True Sun* 1832; edited *Foreign quarterly review* 1842–3; edited *Daily News* 9 Feb. 1846 to Oct. 1846; edited *Examiner*

FORSTER, J. (*Con.*)

1847 to Dec. 1855; sec. to Lunacy commission 28 Dec. 1855 to Feb. 1861, comr. in Lunacy, Feb. 1861 to 1872; painted by Maclise as Kitely in Ben Jonson's Every man in his humour; bequeathed his collection of pictures, books, &c. to South Kensington Museum; author of *Lives of the statesmen of the Commonwealth* 5 vols. 1836–9; *The life and adventures of Oliver Goldsmith* 1848, new ed. 2 vols. 1854; *Life of Charles Dickens* 3 vols. 1872–4 and many other books. *d.* Palace gate, Kensington 1 Feb. 1876. *Catalogue of the Forster library* (1888) *i-xxii*; *Handbook of Forster and Dyce collections* (1877) 1–21; *Monthly Chronicle of north country lore*, Feb. 1888 pp. 49–54; *Madden's Life of Countess of Blessington* (1855) *ii*, 396–405; *T. Powell's Pictures of living authors* (1851) 193–200; *E. Yates's Recollections* (1884) *ii*, 161–3; *G.M., n.s. xvi*, 313–19 (1876); *Temple Bar xlvi*, 491–505 (1876); *I.L.N. vii*, 329 (1845), *portrait*; *Graphic xiii*, 179, 182, 188 (1876), *portrait*.

FORSTER, John. *b.* 1817; M.P. for Berwick 1853–57. *d.* 91 Victoria st. London 7 Jany. 1878.

FORSTER, John Cooper (*son of Mr. Forster of Lambeth, surgeon*). *b.* Mount st. Lambeth 13 Nov. 1823; ed. at King's coll. sch. and Guy's hospital; M.R.C.S. 1844, F.R.C.S. 1849, pres. 1884–5; M.B. London 1847; demonstrator of anatomy at Guy's 1850, assistant surgeon 1855, surgeon 1870–80; retired from practice 1885; the first to perform operation of gastrotomy in England 1858; author of *The surgical diseases of children* 1860, papers in Pathological and Clinical Society's Transactions and reports of cases in Guy's Hospital Reports. *d.* 29 Upper Grosvenor st. London 2 March 1886. *Guy's Hospital Reports vol. xiv*, 40–57 (1887).

FORSTER, Thomas Bowes. Entered Madras army 1818; col. 9 Madras N.I. 13 April 1855 to 1869; L.G. 3 July 1867. *d.* Burder Titley, Herefordshire 21 March 1870.

FORSTER, Thomas Emerson. *b.* Garrigill Gate, Northumberland 1802; resident viewer at Walker colliery, Northumberland 1823; engineer at Newcastle 1846 to death; M.I.C.E. 16 Feb. 1836; pres. of north of England institute of mining engineers 1866–68. *d.* Ellison place, Newcastle 7 March 1875. *Transactions of north of England institute of mining engineers, xxv*, 5–10 (1876); *Min. of proc. of Instit. of C.E. xliii*, 300–303 (1876).

FORSTER, Thomas Ignatius Maria (*eld. son of Thomas Furley Forster of Bishopsgate, London,*

FORSTER, T. I. M. (*Con.*)

Russia merchant 1761–1825). *b.* Bank of England, Threadneedle st. 9 Nov. 1789; studied at C.C. coll. Cam., M.B. 1818; left Cambridge for Edinburgh, Feb. 1816; discovered a comet 3 July 1819; joined Church of Rome about 1823; founded with Gompertz the Animals' Friend Society 1833; F.L.S. 1811; F.R.A.S.; author of *Observations on the brumal retreat of the swallow* 1808, 5 ed. 1817; *Researches about atmospheric phenomena* 1813, 3 ed. 1823 and 44 other books. *d.* Brussels 2 Feb. 1860. *Epistolarium Forsterianum* 2 vols. *Bruges* 1845–50, privately printed; *Recueil de ma vie, mes ouvrages, et mes pensées, opuscule philosophique*, 3 ed. Brussels 1837.

FORSTER, William (*son of Mr. Forster of Tottenham, land agent*). *b.* Tottenham 23 March 1784; minister of Society of Friends 1805; resided at Bradpole, Dorset 1816, afterwards at Norwich; spent 5 years on a mission to United States 1820–25; investigated condition of people in Ireland, Nov. 1846 to April 1847; presented an anti-slavery address to president of United States 1 Oct. 1853; author of *A Christian exhortation to sailors* 1813; *Recent intelligence from Van Diemen's Land* 1831; *A Salutation of Christian love* 1860. *d.* at house of Samuel Low near the Holston river, East Tennessee 27 Jany. 1854. *Memoirs of life of W. Forster edited by B. Seebohm* 2 vols. 1865; *Brief memoir of W. Forster by R. Charlton* 1867.

FORSTER, William Edward (*only child of the preceding*). *b.* Bradpole, Dorset 11 July 1818; ed. at the Friend's sch. Tottenham 1832–5; woollen manufacturer at Bradford with Wm. Fison 1842 to death; left Society of Friends 1850; contested Leeds, April 1859; M.P. for Bradford, Feb. 1861 to 1885, for central division of Bradford, Nov. 1885 to death; under sec. of state for colonies 25 Nov. 1865 to July 1866; P.C. 9 Dec. 1868; vice pres. of committee of council on education 16 Dec. 1868 to Feb. 1874; lord rector of Aberdeen Univ., installed 24 Nov. 1876; presented with freedom of city of Aberdeen 27 Nov. 1876; admitted to freedom of Clothworkers' Co. 5 June 1877; chief sec. of state for Ireland, April 1880 to May 1882. *d.* 80 Eccleston sq. London 5 April 1886. *bur.* at Burley-in-Wharfedale. *Life of W. E. Forster, By T. W. Reid* 1888, 2 *portraits*; *Illustrated Review vi*, 279–81; *Alpine Journal, May* 1886; *I.L.N. xlviii*, 313 (1866), *portrait, lxxvii*, 112 (1881), *portrait*.

FORSTER, William Frederick. Ensign 3 footguards 26 Aug. 1813; captain 97 foot 18 Aug. 1825 to 18 Feb. 1826 when placed

FORSTER, W. F. *(Con.)*

on h.p.; deputy adjutant general 27 Feb. 1855 to 1 July 1860; military sec. to Duke of Cambridge commander in chief 1 July 1860 to 1 Nov. 1871; colonel 81 foot 12 Feb. 1863 to death; general 6 Jany. 1874; K.H. 1833. *d.* 7 Chesterfield st. Mayfair, London 8 June 1879 aged 80.

FORSYTH, JAMES. *b.* 1838; entered Indian civil service; settlement officer and deputy comr. of Nimar; captain Bengal staff corps; author of *The sporting rifle and its projectiles* 1863; *The highlands of Central India, notes on their forests and wild tribes, natural history and sports* 1871. *d.* 38 Manchester st. Manchester sq. London 1 May 1871.

FORSYTH, SIR JOHN. Inspector general medical department, Bengal army 12 Nov. 1857; hon. phys. to the Queen 6 Sep. 1861 to death; C.B. 29 Aug. 1862; K.C.S.I. 24 May 1881. *d.* 51 Selborne road, West Brighton 14 Jany. 1883 in 84 year.

FORSYTH, SIR THOMAS DOUGLAS (10 *child of Thomas Forsyth of Liverpool, merchant). b.* Birkenhead 7 Oct. 1827; ed. at Sherborne, Rugby and Haileybury; entered Bengal civil service 1848; deputy comr. Umballa 1857; officiating comr. in Punjab 1860; comr. of Lahore 1863, of Jullundur 1865, of Umballa 1871, of Oudh 1872; additional member of governor general's council 1874; envoy on special mission to Burma 1875, retired 1878; C.B. 1860; K.C.S.I. 27 July 1874. *d.* Eastbourne 17 Dec. 1886.

FORSYTH, WILLIAM *(son of Morris Forsyth of Turriff, Aberdeenshire). b.* Turriff 24 Oct. 1818; ed. at Univs. of Aberdeen and Edin.; assistant to a country doctor; sub-editor of the *Inverness Courier* 1842; sub editor of *Aberdeen Herald* 1843; joined staff of *Aberdeen Journal* 1848, editor 1849 to death; member of Aberdeen school board; author of *The martyrdom of Kelavane* 1861; *Idylls and Lyrics* 1872 and other books. *d.* Richmond hill, Aberdeen 21 June 1879. *Memoir of W. Forsyth, By A. Walker* (1882).

FORT, RICHARD. *b.* Oakenshaw, Lancs. 15 March 1822; ed. at Eton and Ch. Ch. Ox.; sheriff of Lancs. 1854; contested Clitheroe 1853, M.P. for Clitheroe 1865–68. *d.* 24 Queen's gate gardens, London 2 July 1868.

FORTESCUE, HUGH FORTESCUE, 2 Earl *(eld. child of 1 Earl Fortescue* 1753–1841). *b.* 13 Feb. 1783; styled Viscount Ebrington 1789–1841; ed. at Eton and Brasenose coll. Ox., B.A. 1803, M.A. 1810; M.P. for Barnstaple

FORTESCUE, 2 Earl *(Con,)*

1804–7, for St. Mawes 1807–9, for Buckingham 1812–17, for Devon 1818–20, 1830 and 1831–32, for Tavistock 1820–30, for North Devon 15 Dec. 1832 to 1 March 1839 when summoned to House of Peers in his father's barony of Fortescue; col. of 1 Devon militia 20 May 1816 to death; F.R.S. 5 June 1817; lord lieut. of Ireland 1 March 1839 to 15 Sep. 1841; P.C. 1 March 1839; lord lieut. of Devon 1839 to death; lord steward of H.M.'s household 1846–50; parliamentary sec. of Poor law board 1847–51; K.G. 12 July 1856; author of *Memorandum of two conversations between Napoleon and Viscount Ebrington* 1814. *d.* at house of H. Ford, 25 Southernhay, Exeter 14 Sep. 1861. *Saunders's Portraits of Reformers* (1840) 135, *portrait; The Eton portrait gallery* (1876) 349–52.

FORTESCUE, GEORGE MATTHEW *(brother of the preceding). b.* Hill st. London 21 May 1791; ed. at Eton and Univ. of Edin.; M.P. for Hindon, Wilts. 1827–32. *d.* Boconnoc near Lostwithiel, Cornwall 24 Jany. 1877.

FORTESCUE, JOHN WILLIAM (2 *son of 2 Earl Fortescue* 1783–1861). *b.* 14 July 1819; M.P. for Barnstaple 1847–52. *d.* Madeira 25 Sep. 1859.

FORTESCUE, MATTHEW *(son of Joseph Fortescue of the Scots Greys). b.* 18 May 1805; ed. at Queen's coll. Cam., B.A. 1828, M.A. 1831; special pleader; barrister M.T. 22 Nov. 1839; judge of county court's circuit No. 58 (Devonshire) 8 Oct. 1857 to death. *d.* Oak park house, Dawlish 27 March 1883.

FORTUNE, ROBERT. *b.* Kelloe, Edrom, Berwickshire 16 Sep. 1813; superintendent of indoor-plant department in Royal Horticultural Society's garden at Chiswick, sent to China by the Society as collector 1842; curator of Chelsea botanical garden 1846–8; introduced tea-plant into north-west provinces of India 1851; author of *Three years' wanderings in the northern provinces of China* 1847; *Two visits to the tea countries of China and the British plantations in the Himalayas* 2 vols. 1853 and other books. *d.* 1 Gilston road, South Kensington, London 13 April 1880. *Field and Semple's Memoirs of botanic garden at Chelsea* (1878) 205–8.

FOSS, EDWARD *(eld. son of Edward Smith Foss of 36 Essex st. Strand, London, solicitor, who d. 13 May 1830 aged 74). b.* Gough sq. Fleet st. London 16 Oct. 1787; articled to his father 1804, partner with him 1811–30; student of Inner Temple 1822; under sheriff of

FOSS, E. *(Con.)*

London 1827–8; retired from practice 1840; F.S.A. 18 April 1822; one of founders of Incorporated Law Society 1827, pres. 1842–44; published *The grandeur of the law* 1843; *The judges of England* 9 vols. 1848–64; *Tabulæ Curiales* 1865; *Biographia Juridica* 1870. d. Frensham house, Addiscombe 27 July 1870. *Foss' Biographia Juridica* (1870) *pp. xii-xv.*

FOSTER, CHARLES JAMES. b. Bicester, Oxfordshire 24 Nov. 1820; went to United States 1847; edited Woodruff's *Trotting horses of America* 1868, 2 ed. 1875, also Bogardus's *Field cover and trap shooting* 1874; wrote for *The Spirit of the times* paper; established the *New York Sportsman* 1876; considered the best informed man in America on subject of racing. d. Astoria, New York 12 Sep. 1883.

FOSTER, EDWARD WARD *(son of Edward Foster, land steward to Sir R. Burdett).* b. in parish of All Saints, Derby 8 Nov. 1762; lieut. 20 regt. of foot; served in America, Holland and Egypt; retired 1805; miniature painter to the royal family with apartments in Round tower, Windsor; exhibited 22 landscapes at R.A. 1812–28; travelled in England as a portrait painter; invented machine for taking faces; author of *An elementary grammar of French language* 1837; *A chronological analysis of the Old and New Testament* 1850; *Chart of Histories of Rome, France and Britain* 1835; *Chronological Chart of History of British Empire* 1847; had grant of £60 a year from Bounty fund. d. Derby 12 March 1865. *J. B. Robinson's Derbyshire Gatherings* (1866) 81–4, *portrait.*

FOSTER, JAMES LANCELOT. b. York; edited *Yorkshire Gazette*, manager and publisher of it 1852–82; sheriff of York 1870–71. d. 15 Ogleforth, York 3 Dec. 1883 in 74 year.

FOSTER, JOHN *(son of Jonas Foster, yeoman).* b. Thornton, Yorkshire 20 Jany. 1798; established a worsted business at Low Fold near Queensbury 1819; removed to Cannon Mill, Great Horton 1832; built the Blackdike mill 1835; introduced power-looms into his works 1836; commenced using alpaca wool and mohair 1837; employed 3000 people and manufactured 15,000 packs of wool a year; retired 1869; purchased Hornby castle estate, Lancaster 1861. d. Prospect house, Queensbury 6 March 1879. *Fortunes made in business* ii, 1–107 (1884), *portrait.*

FOSTER, JOHN FREDERIC *(son of Rev. Dr. Frederick Wm. Foster, Moravian bishop).* b. Wyke near Halifax, Yorkshire 1795; ed. at a Moravian coll. and Queen's coll. Cam., B.A.

FOSTER, J. F. *(Con.)*

1817, M.A. 1821; barrister M.T. 1 June 1821; stipendiary mag. of Manchester, Aug. 1825 to April 1838; chairman of quarter sessions of hundred of Salford 9 April 1838 to death; recorder of Manchester 18 April 1839, resigned May. d. Alderley, Cheshire 9 April 1858. *G.M. iv*, 559–60 (1858); *Illust. news of the world ii,* 117 (1858), *portrait.*

FOSTER, PETER LE NEVE *(only son of Peter Le Neve Foster of Lenwade, Norfolk).* b. Lenwade 17 Aug. 1809; ed. at Norwich gr. sch. and Trin. hall, Cam., fellow 1830; 38 wrangler 1830; B.A. 1830, M.A. 1833; barrister M.T. 29 Jany. 1836; practised as a conveyancer 1836–53; sec. to Society of Arts 1853 to death; a founder of Photographic Soc. of London 1853; pres. of Quekett Microscopical Club; sec. of mechanical science section of British Association 13 years; author of *Photography* 1876. d. East hill, Wandsworth, London 21 Feb. 1879. *Journal of Soc. of Arts* (1879) *xxvii*, 316; *I.L.N. lxxiv*, 224 (1879), *portrait.*

FOSTER, THOMAS. Second lieut. R.E. 1 Sep. 1815, col. commandant 8 Feb. 1866 to death; general 8 June 1871. d. 5 Cleveland terrace, Hyde park, London 26 Aug. 1872 aged 76.

FOSTER, THOMAS CAMPBELL *(son of John Foster, proprietor and editor of Leeds Patriot paper).* b. Knaresbro', Yorkshire 6 Oct. 1813; sub-editor of *Liverpool Standard;* reporter for *The Times* in Houses of Parliament; made enquiries into the Rebecca riots and other important questions for *The Times;* special pleader 1842; barrister M.T. 30 Jany. 1846, bencher Jany. 1878; contested Sheffield 13 July 1865; revising barrister for west riding of Yorkshire 1868–75; recorder of Warwick 23 Dec. 1874 to death; Q.C. 25 June 1875; author of *Letters on the condition of the people of Ireland* 1845; *Treatise on the writ of Scire Facias* 1851 and other books. d 30 Orsett terrace, Hyde park, London 1 July 1882. *Biograph vol.* 1 (1882) *pp.* 293–326.

FOSTER, SIR WILLIAM, 1 Baronet *(younger son of Wm. Foster of Norwich 1762–1821).* b. 16 June 1798; attorney at Norwich 1820 to death; alderman of Norwich to death, sheriff 1832, mayor 1844; created baronet 3 Aug. 1838. d. St. Giles's st. Norwich 2 Dec. 1874.

FOTHERGILL, JOHN MILNER *(son of Mr. Fothergill of Morland, Westmoreland, surgeon).* b. Morland 11 April 1841; ed. at Univ. of Edin., M.D. 1865; practised at Morland, then at Leeds; M.R.C.P. 1872; phys. in London 1872 to death; author of *Digitalis, its modes of action and its uses* 1871; *The heart and its*

FOTHERGILL, J. M. *(Con.)*

diseases with their treatment 1872, 2 *ed.* 1879 and 20 other books. *d.* 3 Henrietta st. Cavendish sq. London 28 June 1888. *Midland medical miscellany ii*, 161–2 (1883), *portrait.*

FOULKES, REV. HENRY (2 *son of John Foulkes of Henllan, Denbighshire* 1736–1814). Matric. from Jesus coll. Ox. 10 July 1790 aged 17; B.A. 1794, M.A. 1797, B.D. 1804, D.D. 1817; fellow of Jesus coll. to 1817, principal 1817 to death; R. of Yelford, Oxon. 1815 to death; R. of Besselsleigh, Berks. and of Llandyssil, Cardigan 1817 to death. *d.* Jesus college 17 Sep. 1857.

FOULKES, WILLIAM DECIMUS INGLETT *(youngest son of Rev. Peter Foulkes, V. of Shebbear, Devon).* Ed. at Bedford gr. sch.; barrister M.T. 6 June 1871; a reporter on *The Law Journal Reports* 1875; edited *The Law Journal* newspaper 1879 to death; author of *An elementary view of the proceedings in an action in the supreme court* 1876, 3 *ed.* 1884; *A Generation of Judges. By Their Reporter* 1886; author with J. M. Lely of *The Judicature acts...with notes* 1875, 4 *ed.* 1883 and other books. *d.* 25 Half Moon st. Piccadilly, London 17 Feb. 1890 in 42 year.

FOUNTAIN, JOSEPH. Theatrical artist at Leeds many years; the pioneer of the now extensive industry of designing and printing theatrical posters. *d.* 31 Brunswick terrace, Leeds 11 Oct. 1887 in 60 year.

FOURACRES, CHARLES. *b.* Devonshire; enlisted in 1st Madras fusiliers; sub-engineer Godavery Delta irrigation works; engaged on Sone irrigation works 1869, resigned 1879; invented an excavator for which government gave him 10,000 rupees; invented the hydraulic-brake shutter for the Sone weir and the vertical-action bucket steam dredger 1878; engineer of the Seebpur engineering factory Calcutta 1879, retired 1884 when he was awarded a bonus of 15,000 rupees; M.I.C.E. 2 Dec. 1879. *d.* Bristol 14 July 1884. *Min. of proc. of Instit. of C.E. lxxviii*, 418–24 (1884).

FOURDRINIER, HENRY. *b.* Lombard st. London 11 Feb. 1766; succeeded his father as a paper maker and wholesale stationer; patented with his brother Sealy (who *d.* 1847) invention of paper making machine 1801, perfected their machine for making continuous paper 1807; became bankrupt 1810; £7000 voted by Parliament to Messrs. Fourdrinier as compensation for their loss by defective state of law of patents 8 May 1840. *d.* Mavesyn, Rydware, Staffs. 3 Sep. 1854. *G.M. xliv*, 102–103 (1855); *I.L.N. xxv*, 345, 354 (1854), *portrait.*

FOWKE, FRANCIS. *b.* Belfast, July 1823; 2 lieut. R.E. 18 June 1842, captain 17 Feb. 1854 to death; inspector of Science and Art department, London 1857, architect and engineer to same department; sec. to English commission attached to Paris exhibition 1855–57; designed Museum of science and art, Edinburgh, opened 19 May 1866; planned buildings for International Exhibition 1862; Albert hall was chiefly designed by him; author of *A description of the buildings at South Kensington for the reception of the Sheepshanks pictures* 1858; *Some account of the buildings designed for the International Exhibition of 1862*, 1861. *d.* The Museum, South Kensington 4 Dec. 1865, bust by Woolner in the Museum. *Papers on professional subjects, Corps. of R.E. xxv*, 9; *Min. of proc. of Instit. of C.E. xxx*, 468–70 (1866); *I.L.N. xl*, 431, 433 (1862), *portrait.*

FOWKE, SIR FREDERICK GUSTAVUS, 1 Baronet (3 *son of Sir Thomas Fowke, knt., who d. 30 Nov. 1786). b.* 24 Jany. 1782; created baronet 7 Feb. 1814. *d.* Leamington 17 May 1856.

FOWLER, CHARLES. *b.* Collumpton 17 May 1792; apprentice to a builder at Exeter; erected court of bankruptcy, Basinghall st. London; gained first premium in a design for London bridge 1822; rebuilt Covent Garden market 1829–30; built Hungerford market opened July 1833; restored Powderham castle, Devon; built churches at Charmouth, Buckley and Honiton and Devon county lunatic asylum at Exminster 1845. *d.* Great Marlow 26 Sep. 1867. *Pycroft's Art in Devon* (1883) *p.* 45.

FOWLER, FRANK. Lecturer in Willis' rooms, London; engaged on a London daily paper; lecturer in Sydney 1855; started the *Month*, first respectable magazine in Sydney, July 1857 last issue Dec. 1858; contested Sydney for legislative assembly receiving 2000 votes; edited a London newspaper; founded The Library Co. London 1860, sec. of it to death; author of *Southern lights and shadows* 1859 and other books. *d.* Oakley cottage, Hammersmith 22 Aug. 1863 aged 30. *Frank Fowler's Last Gleanings* (1864) *pp. vii-xvii.*

FOWLER, GEORGE. Formerly of Collumpton; author of *Three years in Russia* 2 vols. 1841; *Lives of the sovereigns of Russia* 1858; *Turkey, a history of the Ottoman empire* 1854; *History of the war between Turkey and Russia* 1855; *Mary Markland the cottager's daughter*, 2 *ed.* 1861. *d.* Victoria terrace, Bayswater, London 20 April 1858.

FOWLER, JOHN. *b.* Melksham, Wiltshire 11 July 1826; entered works of Gilke, Wilson

FOWLER, J. (Con.)

& Co. at Middlesbrough 1847; drained Hainault Forest, Essex by use of his patent drainage plough about 1851; invented with Jeremiah Head a steam plough which gained prize of £500 at Chester show of Royal Agricultural Society 1858; invented double engine tackle 1860; established with Kitson and Hewitson, manufacturing works at Hunslet, Leeds 1860. *d.* Ackworth, Yorkshire 4 Dec. 1864. *Trans. of Soc. of Engineers for 1868 pp. 299–318; Practical Mag.* (1875) 257–62, *portrait.*

FOWLER, SIR JOHN DICKENSON. Solicitor, High Bailiff of Burton upon Trent 1818; knighted by Prince Regent at Beaudesert 8 Nov. 1818 but never gazetted. *d.* Burton 5 Feb. 1839 aged 70 but name remained in Knightages to 1864.

FOWLER, LYDIA. *b.* Nantucket, Massachusetts 1823; a graduate of Syracuse medical college; the first female professor of obstetrics in America; lived in London 1863 to death; author of *Familiar lessons on phrenology and physiology* 1847; *Familiar lessons on astronomy* 1848; *The pet of the household and how to save it* 1865; *Heart melodies, poems* 1870 and 14 other books. (*m.* Lorenzo Niles Fowler of London, phrenologist). *d.* 62 St. Augustine's road, Camden sq. London 26 Jany. 1879.

FOWLER, RICHARD. *b.* London 28 Nov. 1765; ed. at Univ. of Edin., M.D. 1793; L.C.P. London 1796; practised at Salisbury from 1796; phys. to Salisbury infirmary 1796–1841; F.R.S. 1 April 1802; purchased and endowed ground for Salisbury and South Wiltshire museum to which he gave a large part of his books and collections 1862; author of *Some Observations on the mental state of the blind and deaf and dumb, Salisbury* 1843, 2 ed. 1860; *An attempt to detect the physiological process by which thinking is effected, Salisbury* 1849, 2 ed. 1852. *d.* Milford near Salisbury 13 April 1863 having attained a greater age than had any other member of the Royal Coll. of Phys. from its foundation. *Proc. of Royal Soc. xiii, pp. iii–v* (1864); *Munk's Roll,* 2 ed. vol. *ii*, p. 447.

FOX, CAROLINE (2 *dau. of Robert Were Fox* 1789–1877). *b.* Falmouth 24 May 1819; kept a journal from 1835 to 1871 which has rendered her celebrated; friend of John Sterling, John Stuart Mill and other eminent men. *d.* Penjerrick near Falmouth 12 Jany. 1871. *Memories of old friends, extracts from journals of Caroline Fox 1835 to 1871,* ed. by H. N. Pym 1881, *portrait,* 3 ed. 2 vols. 1882.

FOX, SIR CHARLES (*youngest son of Francis Fox of Derby, physician*). *b.* Derby 11 March 1810; assistant engineer on London and Birmingham

FOX, SIR C. (Con.)

railway 1830–35; a civil and consulting engineer in London 1857 to death; introduced the switch into railway practice 1838; erected with John Henderson the building for Great Exhibition in Hyde Park 1850–1; erected Crystal Palace, Sydenham 1852–54; carried out the East Kent and other railways; erected bridges over Thames at Barnes, Richmond, and Staines and many other large bridges; M.I.C.E. 13 Jany. 1838; knighted at Windsor Castle 23 Oct. 1851. *d.* Blackheath, Kent 14 June 1874. *Min. of proc. of Instit. of C.E. xxxix, 264–6* (1875); *Graphic ix, 15, 17* (1874), *portrait; Practical Mag. vi, 129–33, portrait.*

FOX, CHARLES (7 *son of Robert Were Fox of Falmouth*). *b.* Falmouth 22 Dec. 1797; partner in firm of G. C. and R. W. Fox and Co. merchants, Falmouth; partner in Perran foundry co., manager 1824–47; one of founders of royal Cornwall polytechnic soc. 1833, pres. 1871–72; with Sir Charles Lemon introduced man engines into Cornish mines 1842; pres. of Miners' Association of Cornwall and Devon 1861–63; pres. of royal geological soc. of Cornwall 1864–67. *d.* Trebah near Falmouth 18 April 1878. *Boase and Courtney's Bibl. Cornub.* 160–61, 1186; *Joseph Foster's Descendants of Francis Fox* (1872) 11.

FOX, CHARLES RICHARD (*natural son of 3 Baron Holland 1773–1840*). *b.* 6 Nov. 1796; in the navy 1809–13; ensign Grenadier guards 1815, captain 1830 to 1836 when placed on h.p.; A.D.C. to the Sovereign 1832–1846; surveyor general of Ordnance 5 Dec. 1832 to 12 Jany. 1835; general 6 March 1863; col. of 57 foot 5 Sep. 1865 to death; M.P. for Calne, Wilts. 1831–32, for Tavistock 1832–34, for Stroud 1835, for Tower Hamlets 1841–47; had finest private collection of Greek coins in the world, purchased by Royal Museum at Berlin 1873. *d.* 1 Addison road, Kensington, London 13 April 1873. *Numismatic Chronicle xiv, 16–19* (1874); *Waagen's Galleries of Art* (1857) 232–4; *I.L.N. lxii, 393, 451* (1873).

FOX, EBENEZER. *b.* England; chief reporter on the *Manchester Guardian* several years; went to Dunedin, New Zealand; on staff of *Otago Daily Times* 1862; confidential clerk and secretary to treasury New Zealand 1870 to death; wrote articles in *New Zealand Times* on denudation of the forests which attracted much attention. *d.* Wellington, Jany. 1886.

FOX, EDWARD. Author of *Poetical Tentatives, By Lynn Erith* 1854; *Pleasure paths of travel* 1857; *Amian and Bertha and other poems* 1858; drowned while bathing in the Avon at Keynsham, Somerset 9 Aug. 1862 aged 33.

FOX, HENRY HAWES. *b.* Bristol 5 Jany. 1788 ; ed. at Glasgow and St. John's coll. Cam. ; pres. of royal medical society, Edin. ; practised at Bristol 1811–32, phys. to infirmary there 1816–32 ; M.D. Cam. 1826 ; bought estate of Northwood, Gloucs. 1832 where he built an asylum for the insane ; originated a method of fire proof construction· now known as Fox and Barrett's. *d.* Northwood 12 Oct. 1851.

FOX, REV. JOHN *(son of Henry Fox of St. Bees, Cumberland).* *b.* St. Bees ; ed. at St. Bees ; matric. from Queen's coll. Ox. 4 Dec. 1794 aged 20, tabarder 1798, fellow 1808–27 ; B.A. 1798, M.A. 1812, B.D. 1827, D.D. 1827 ; master of Northleach sch. 1826–27 ; provost of Queen's coll. Ox. 1827 to death. *d.* Oxford 11 Aug. 1855. *bur.* Sherborne.

FOX, RICHARD MAXWELL. *b.* Raheny Glebe, co. Dublin 1816 ; M.P. for co. Longford 13 Aug. 1847 to death. *d.* St. Leonard's on Sea 26 April 1856.

FOX, ROBERT WERE *(brother of Charles Fox 1797–1878).* *b.* Falmouth 26 April 1789 ; made researches upon internal temperature of the earth from 1815, the first to prove that the heat increased with the depth ; a founder of Royal Polytechnic Soc. 1833 ; F.R.S. 9 June 1848 ; contributed 52 papers to scientific periodicals. *d.* Penjerrick near Falmouth 25 July 1877. *A catalogue of the works of R. W. Fox with A sketch of his life, By J. H. Collins, Truro* 1878 ; *Boase and Courtney's Bibl. Cornub.* i, 162–5 (1874), iii, 1188 (1882).

FOX, SACKVILLE WALTER LANE. *b.* 1800 ; M.P. for Helston 1831–34, for Beverley 1840– 41 and 1847–52, for Ipswich 1842–47. *d.* 22 Pall Mall, London 18 Aug. 1874.

FOX, SAMUEL. *b.* Bradwell, North Derbyshire 1815 ; a steel maker at Stockbridge near Sheffield ; patented Fox's paragon frame for umbrellas 6 April 1852 by which he made a fortune ; established large works at Lille, France ; chairman of Samuel Fox and Co., Stockbridge works, Deepcar near Sheffield to death. *d.* The Lodge, North Cliffe near Market Vᵗ ighton, Yorkshire 25 Feb. 1887.

FOX, SARAH HUSTLER *(only dau. of Wm. Hustler of Apple hall, Bradford, Yorkshire).* *b.* Apple hall 8 Aug. 1800. *(m.* 20 Dec. 1825 Charles Fox 1797–1878.) Author of *A metrical version of the book of Job* 1852–4 ; *Poems original and translated* 1863 ; *Catch who can, or hide and seek, original double acrostics* 1869. *d.* Trebah near Falmouth 19 Feb. 1882.

FOX, REV. WILLIAM JOHNSON. *b.* Uggeshall farm near Wrentham, Suffolk 1 March 1786 ; Independent minister at Fareham 1810 ; Unitarian minister at Chichester 1812–17 ; minister of Parliament court chapel, London 1817, of a chapel built for him in South place, Finsbury 1824–52 ; edited the *Monthly Repository* 1833 to 1836 ; a leading orator of the Anti-Corn-law League ; M.P. for Oldham 1847–52, 1852–57 and 1857–62 ; contested Oldham 1852 and 1857 ; author of *Lectures to the working classes* 4 vols. 1845–49 and 30 other books. *d.* 3 Sussex place, Regent's park, London 3 June 1864. *Memorial edition of collected works of W. J. Fox, vol.* 12 (1868) ; *John Evans's Lancashire authors* (1850) 92–96 ; *People's Journal iii,* 69 (1848), *portrait ; I.L.N. xii;* 298 (1848), *portrait.*

FOX, WILLIAM TILBURY *(son of Luther Owen Fox, M.D. of Broughton, Winchester).* *b.* 1836 ; ed. at Univ. coll. London ; M.B. London 1857, M.D. 1858 ; phys. accoucheur to Farringdon General Dispensary ; a specialist on dermatology ; phys. to skin departments of Charing Cross and University college hospitals ; one of editors of the *Lancet ;* author of *Skin diseases, their description, pathology, diagnosis and treatment* 1864, 3 ed. 1873 ; *Atlas of skin diseases* 1875–7 and 12 other books. *d.* Paris 7 June 1879. *bur.* Willesden cemetery 14 June.

FOX, WILSON. *b.* Wellington, Somerset 2 Nov. 1831 ; B.A. London 1850, M.B. 1854, M.D. 1855 ; phys. at Newcastle-under-Lyme 1859– 61 ; professor of pathological anatomy at Univ. coll. London 1861 ; assistant phys. Univ. coll. hospital 1862, phys. 1867 ; F.R.C.P. 1866 ; Holme professor of clinical medicine Univ. coll. hospital 1867 ; phys. extraord. to the Queen 16 Aug. 1869, phys. in ordinary 18 Dec. 1882 to death ; F.R.S. 6 June 1872 ; author of *On the diagnosis and treatment of the varieties of Dyspepsia* 1867, 3 ed. under the title of *The diseases of the stomach* 1872, and other books. *d.* Preston, Lancs. 3 May 1887. *bur.* Taunton 6 May, bust in shire hall, Taunton unveiled 25 Oct. 1888.

FRADELLE, HENRY JOSEPH. *b.* Lille, France 1778 ; historical painter in London from 1816 ; exhibited 11 pictures at R.A., 36 at B.I. and 2 at Suffolk st. gallery 1817–54. *d.* 36 Weymouth st. Portland place, London 14 March 1865.

FRAIL, JOHN FREDERICK. *b.* Shrewsbury 1 May 1804 ; hairdresser Shrewsbury ; a local actor ; electioneering agent to the Carlton club in Shropshire ; clerk of the course,

FRAIL, J. F. (Con.)

Shrewsbury 1843; organised many race meetings; entertained at dinner and presented with plate worth £350, 1854; town councillor 1854, mayor. *d.* Shrewsbury 9 March 1879. *Sporting Review xxxix*, 361–3 (1858); *Sporting Times* 24 July 1875 p. 396, *portrait; Illust. sp. and dr. news vi*, 403, 419 (1877), *portrait, x*, 620, 627 (1879), *portrait.*

FRANCATELLI, CHARLES ELMÉ. *b.* London 1805; studied cookery under Carème; chef to Earl of Chesterfield, Earl of Dudley, Lord Kinnaird and Rowland Errington successively; managed St. James's club, London; chief cook and maitre d'hotel to the Queen 1840–42; lessee of Coventry House club; chef at the Reform club 1854–61; managed St. James's hotel, Berkeley st. Piccadilly 1863–70, and Freemason's tavern, Great Queen st. 1870–76; author of *The modern cook* 1846, 12 ed. 1865 and other books. *d.* Eastbourne 10 Aug. 1876. *A. Hayward's Art of dining, new ed.* (1883) 75–6.

FRANCE, VEN. FRANCIS. Educ. at Shrewsbury and St. John's coll. Cam.; B.A. 1840, M.A. 1843, B.D. 1850; fellow tutor and pres. of his college; archdeacon of Ely, Dec. 1859 to death; author of *The example of Christ* 1861. *d.* Cambridge 14 April 1864.

FRANCILLON, JAMES (6 son of Francis Francillon of Harwich, Essex). *b.* 21 Nov. 1802; admitted attorney; conveyancing clerk to Messrs. Wilton at Gloucester 1824; barrister G.I. 20 Nov. 1833; judge of county courts, circuit 54 (Gloucestershire), March 1847 to death; author of *Lectures elementary and familiar on English law* 2 series 1860–1. *d.* of cholera at Lausanne 3 Sep. 1866.

FRANCIS, FRANCIS (son of Captain Morgan, R.N.) *b.* Seton, Devon 1822; changed his name from Morgan to Francis 1843; angling editor of *The Field* 25 years; established the Thames Rights defence association; suggested plan of the National fish-culture association; a member of the commission on oyster culture 1868–70; author of *Pickackifax, a novel in rhyme* 1854; *Newton Dogvane, a novel* 3 vols. 1859 and 14 other books. *d.* The Firs, Twickenham 24 Dec. 1886. *F. Francis's A Book on Angling*, 6 ed. (1887), *portrait; The Field* 1 Jany. 1887 p. 9, cols. 1–3.

FRANCIS, GEORGE (2 son of George Francis of Maidstone, Kent). *b.* 20 Aug. 1824; barrister G.I. 16 Jany. 1850, bencher 26 May 1880, treasurer 1886; recorder of Faversham, March 1864 to Nov. 1872; recorder of Canterbury,

FRANCIS, G. (Con.)

Nov. 1872 to Aug. 1883; master in Q.B. division, July 1878, master of supreme court of judicature 1879 to death. *d.* 12 Carlton hill, Maida vale, London 20 Jany. 1890.

FRANCIS, GEORGE GRANT (eld. son of John Francis of Swansea). *b.* Swansea, Jany. 1814; mayor of Swansea 1853–4; col. of 1st Glamorgan artillery volunteers raised by his exertions 1859; author of *The free grammar school Swansea*, Swansea 1849; *The smelting of copper in the Swansea district, privately printed Swansea* 1867, published 1881, and other books on Welsh history and topography. *d.* 9 Upper Phillimore place, Kensington, London 21 April 1882. *bur.* Swansea cemetery 26 April. *Athenæum 28 April 1882 pp.* 510–11.

FRANCIS, GEORGE HENRY. *b.* about 1817; edited *Morning Post, Atlas, Dublin Daily Express;* manager and assistant editor of the *Press;* edited *Morning Chronicle;* author of *Orators of the age* 1847 and other books. *d.* Paris 28 Aug. 1866.

FRANCIS, GEORGE WILLIAM. *b.* London 1800; edited *Magazine of science and school of arts* 5 vols. 1840–5; went to Australia 1849; director of Adelaide botanic garden to death; author of *Catalogue of British plants and ferns* 1835, 5 ed. 1840; *An analysis of British ferns* 1837, 5 ed. 1855; *Electrical experiments* 8 ed. 1855 and 8 other books. *d.* Adelaide 9 Aug. 1865.

FRANCIS, JAMES GOODALL. *b.* London 1819; went to Van Diemen's Land 1834; partner with Mr. Macpherson in a business at Hobart Town 1847; managed a branch business in Melbourne 1853; vice pres. of chamber of commerce N.S.W. 1856, pres. 1857; member for Richmond in Victorian legislative assembly 1859–74; comr. of trade and customs 1863–68; treasurer of Victoria 1870–71; prime minister 1872–74; passed a free education act 1874; member for Warrnambool in Victorian assembly 1878–82. *d.* Queenscliff, Victoria 25 Jany. 1884.

FRANCIS, JOHN. *b.* Lincolnshire 3 Sep. 1780; pupil of Francis Chantrey in London; executed by command of the Queen a bust in marble of Prince Albert 1844; exhibited 71 sculptures at the R.A. 1820–57. *d.* 56 Albany st. Regent's park, London 30 Aug. 1861.

FRANCIS, JOHN. *b.* Bermondsey, London 18 July 1811; junior clerk in office of the *Athenæum*, Sep. 1831, business manager and publisher of that paper 4 Oct. 1831 to death; did more than any man to procure repeal of duty

FRANCIS, J. (Con.)

on newspaper advertisements 1853, of stamp duty on newspapers 1855 and of the paper duty 1861. *d.* 20 Wellington st. Strand, London 6 April 1882. *John Francis, publisher of the Athenæum, By J. C. Francis (1888) i, 1–19, 45–7, 226, ii, 173 et seq. 545–50, portrait; H. J. Nicoll's Great Movements (1881) 269–339.*

FRANCIS, SIR PHILIP. *b.* 1822; barrister M.T. 21 Nov. 1845; judge of supreme consular court of the Levant and consul general at Constantinople 16 Sep. 1867 to death; knighted by patent 7 Dec. 1868; author of *The law of Charities* 1854; *The new common law procedure acts* 1854. *d.* on board H.M.S. Antelope between Besika and Smyrna 9 Aug. 1876. *Graphic xiv, 257, 261 (1876), portrait.*

FRANCKLYN, JOHN HENRY. *b.* 8 Jany. 1812; 2 lieut. R.A. 26 July 1831, col. commandant 20 Dec. 1878 to death; general 13 Nov. 1880; C.B. 2 Jany. 1857. *d.* The Wigwam, Dacres road, Forest hill 12 Feb. 1881.

FRANKLAND, CHARLES COLVILLE (3 *son of Rev. Roger Frankland, R. of Yarlington, Somerset, who d. 25 March 1826*). *b.* Bath 10 Feb. 1797; entered navy 13 Jany. 1813, captain 23 Nov. 1841; retired admiral 30 July 1875; published *Travels to and from Constantinople 2 vols.* 1829; *Narrative of a visit to the courts of Russia and Sweden 2 vols.* 1832. *d.* 2 Royal crescent, Bath 13 April 1876.

FRANKLIN, LADY JANE (2 *dau. of John Griffin of Bedford place, London*). *b.* 1792; travelled in the East, Van Diemen's Land and New Zealand 1828–44; the first lady who travelled overland from Melbourne to Sydney; sent out at her own expense to the Arctic regions 5 ships in search of her husband Sir John Franklin 1850–57; received gold medal of Royal Geog. Soc. 1860. (*m.* at Great Stanmore 5 Nov. 1828 John Franklin, captain R.N. who *d.* Victory point, King William Land 11 June 1847, his name is in the navy list down to April 1854); author of *A letter to Viscount Palmerston* 1857, 2 editions. She *d.* 45 Phillimore gardens, London 18 July 1875. *Graphic xi, 157, 163 (1875), portrait.*

FRANKLYN, GEORGE WOODROFFE. *b.* Bristol 1800; a merchant at Bristol; mayor of Bristol 1842–43; M.P. for Poole 1852–65. *d.* Lovel hill, Winkfield, Berks. 5 Nov. 1870.

FRANKS, SIR JOHN (2 *son of Thomas Franks of Ballymagooly, co. Cork 1729–87*). *b.* Loher Cannon near Tralee, co. Kerry 1769; ed. at

FRANKS, SIR J. (Con.)

Trin. coll. Dublin; B.A. 1788, M.A. 1791; called to Irish bar 1792; K.C. 25 Nov. 1822; one of judges of supreme court, Calcutta 1825–1834 when he resigned; knighted at Carlton house 20 April 1825; resided at Roebuck near Dublin 1835 to death; bencher of King's Inns, Dublin 1840. *d.* St. Bridgets, Clonkeagh, co. Dublin 11 Jany. 1852.

FRANKS, SIR THOMAS HARTE (2 *son of Wm. Franks of Carrig castle near Mallow, co. Cork*). Ensign 10 foot 7 July 1825, lieut. col. 28 March 1845 to 20 July 1858; commanded 4th infantry division during Indian mutiny 1858; M.G. 20 July 1858; C.B. 27 June 1846, K.C.B. 27 July 1858. *d.* Ibstone house, Tetsworth, Oxon. 5 Feb. 1862.

FRASER, ALEXANDER. *b.* Edinburgh 7 April 1786; painter in Edin. to 1813, in London 1813–59; painted the details and still life in David Wilkie's pictures for about 20 years; A.R.S.A. 1840; exhibited 32 pictures at R.A., 97 at B.I. and 37 at Suffolk st. gallery 1810–59. *d.* Wood Green, Middlesex 15 Feb. 1865.

FRASER, HASTINGS. Ensign 74 foot 9 April 1788; lieut. col. 86 foot 18 April 1805 to 31 Aug. 1826; col. 83 foot 30 Sep. 1835, col. 61 foot 1 Sep. 1848 to death; general 11 Nov. 1851; C.B. 4 June 1815. *d.* Bury st. St. James's, London 29 Sep. 1852 aged 81.

FRASER, SIR HUGH (*son of Wm. Fraser, commissary of Inverness*). Entered military service of H.E.I. Co. 1790; col. of 5 Madras N.I. 1 May 1834 to death; L.G. 23 Nov. 1841; K.C.B. 7 April 1832 for commanding troops at assault of Copaul Droog. *d.* Braclangwell, co. Cromarty 6 Oct. 1851 aged 78.

FRASER, RIGHT REV. JAMES (*eld. son of James Fraser of Prestbury, Gloucs.*) *b.* Prestbury 18 Aug. 1818; ed. at Bridgnorth and Shrewsbury; scholar of Lincoln coll. Ox. 1836; Ireland scholar 1839; B.A. 1840, M.A. 1842; fellow of Oriel coll. 1840–60, tutor 1842–47, subdean and librarian 1844; R. of Cholderton, Wiltshire 1847–60; select preacher at Oxford 1851, 1861, 1871, 1877 and 1885; R. of Ufton Nervet, Berkshire 1860–70; preb. of Salisbury 1861–70; bishop of Manchester 18 Jany. 1870 to death, consecrated at Manchester cathedral 25 March 1870. *d.* Bishop's Court, Higher Broughton, Manchester 22 Oct. 1885. *bur.* at Ufton Nervet. *Memoir of James Fraser. By Thomas Hughes, Q.C. 1887, portrait; J. W. Diggle's The Lancashire life of Bishop Fraser 1889, portrait; Dublin univ. mag. xcv, 452–64 (1880), portrait; Church portrait*

FRASER, RIGHT REV. J. (Con.)

gallery i, 47 (1880), portrait; Our Bishops and Deans. By Rev. F. Arnold ii, 119–30 (1875); Rev. C. M. Davies's Orthodox London 2 series (1874) 94–107, 393.

FRASER, JAMES BAILLIE (eld. son of Edward Satchell Fraser of Reelick, Inverness-shire). b. Reelick 11 June 1783; travelled in the Himalayas 1815, in Persia 1821–2; took charge of the Persian princes when they visited England 1835–6; author of Narrative of the Persian princes in London 2 vols. 1838; Travels in Koordistan, Mesopotamia, &c. 2 vols. 1840; The dark falcon, a tale of the Attruck 4 vols. 1844 and 14 other books. d. Reelick 24 Jany. 1856. G.M. xlv, 307–8 (1856).

FRASER, JAMES STUART (youngest son of Charles Fraser, col. Madras army, who d. 5 May 1795). b. Edinburgh 1 July 1783; lieut. 18 Madras N.I. 15 Dec. 1800; commandant at Pondicherry 1816–28; col. 36 Madras N.I. 26 Sep. 1835 to death; resident at Hyderabad 31 Dec. 1839 to 1852; general 2 June 1860. d. Twickenham park, Twickenham 22 Aug. 1869. H. Fraser's Memoir of J. S. Fraser (1885), portrait.

FRASER, SIR JOHN (3 son of Wm. Mackenzie Fraser, M.D. of Balnairn). b. Bath 1792; ed. at Eton; aide-de-camp and Persian interpreter to commander-in-chief in India; retired from army 1827; sec. to lord high comr. of Ionian Islands to 1854; K.C.M.G. 1853. d. Bath 26 Dec. 1864.

FRASER, JOHN FARQUHAR. Barrister L.I. 13 May 1817; judge of county courts, circuit 46 (Surrey), March 1847 to death; author of The reports of Sir E. Coke in 13 parts, 10 parts by J. F. F. 1826; resided at 104 Eaton place, Belgrave sq. London. d. Feb. 1865.

FRASER, PATRICK, Lord Fraser (son of Patrick Fraser of Perth, merchant). b. Pitlochry near Perth 1819; ed. at Perth gr. sch. and univ. of St. Andrews; called to the bar 1843; sheriff of Renfrewshire 3 Feb. 1862; LL.D. Edin. 1871; dean of Faculty of Advocates 16 Jany. 1878; Q.C. 1880; a lord of session with title of Lord Fraser 4 Feb. 1881 to death; lord ordinary in exchequer cases 15 Nov. 1881 to death; author of A treatise on the law of Scotland as applicable to the personal and domestic relations 2 vols. Edin. 1846; The conflict of laws in cases of divorce, Edin. 1860 and 5 other books; found dead in his study chair at Gattonside near Melrose 27 March 1889. Juridical Review i, 178–83 (1889), portrait.

FRASER, ROBERT SAMUEL. b. North Shields 26 Oct. 1829; apprentice to William Clark, engineer, Sunderland 1843; manager of the s.s. Chasseur floating factory in Balaclava harbour 1855–56 for the government; assistant to inspector of machinery in the Arsenal, Woolwich 1856; manager of royal gun factories, Woolwich 1859, deputy assist. superintendent 1866; invented the service gun known as the Fraser 1867 but since called the Woolwich gun and still in use; presented by government on two occasions with £5000 each time; changed spelling of his name from Frazer to Fraser 1866; M.I.C.E. 6 Dec. 1864. d. of consumption Arbory cottage, Sydenham road, Croydon 12 July 1884. Min. of proc. of Instit. of C.E. lxxviii, 424–9 (1884).

FRASER, REV. ROBERT WILLIAM (son of captain Robert Fraser). b. Perth 1810; licensed to preach by Edinburgh presbytery 1840; minister of parish of Burntisland 1843–7; minister of St. John's ch. Edin. 1847 to death; author of Moriah, or sketches of the sacred rites of ancient Israel, Edinburgh 1849 and many other books. d. 19 Lauriston st. Edinburgh 10 Sep. 1876. Scotsman 12 Sep. 1876 p. 4.

FRASER, THOMAS. Took a leading part in Parisian political life which he described in racy articles, sent to the Morning Chronicle 1835–55; sec. to Hudson Bay Co. London 1855. d. Florence 2 Nov. 1869. Newspaper Press 1 Dec. 1869 p. 15.

FRASER, THOMAS (son of vice admiral Alexander Fraser, who d. 29 Dec. 1829). b. May 1796; entered navy 11 Nov. 1811; commander 22 July 1826; captain on h.p. 23 Nov. 1841; V.A. on h.p. 1870. d. 19 Brighton place, Portobello 28 Oct. 1870. Crombie's Modern Athenians (1882), p. 139, portrait.

FRASER, MOST REV. WILLIAM. b. Scotland about 1790; R.C. vicar apostolic of Nova Scotia with title of bishop of Fanes 1821; devoted himself to Scottish members of his flock in Antigonish, northern part of the peninsula and neglected the Irish; the Pope divided province of Nova Scotia into two dioceses, Antigonish being united to Cape Breton and erected into diocese of Arishat with W. Fraser as titular bishop. d. Antigonish 4 Oct. 1857.

FRASER, REV. WILLIAM (eld. son of Wm. Fraser of St. George's, Southwark, London). Matric. from Worcester coll. Ox. 9 June 1841 aged 17; B.A. 1845, M.A. 1848, B.C.L. 1848, D.C.L. 1861; C. of Alton, Staffs. 1853–58, V. 1858 to death; P.C. of Cotton, Staffs. 1862 to death; author of Parish Sermons 2

FRASER, REV. W. (Con.)

series 1855-60; *A plain commentary of the Book of Psalms, chiefly founded on the Fathers* 2 vols. 1857 and other books. *d.* Alton vicarage 26 Nov. 1877.

FRASER, REV. WILLIAM. *b.* Cullen, Banffshire 1817; a master in Normal seminary, Glasgow; pastor of the Free Middle congregation, Paisley 1849 to death; LL.D. Glasgow 1872; member of Paisley school board; author of *The state of our educational enterprises* 1858; *Blending lights, or the relations of natural science, archæology and history to the Bible* 1873. *d.* Free Middle manse, Paisley 21 Sep. 1879. *Renfrewshire Independent* 27 Sep. 1879 p. 4.

FRASER, WILLIAM CHARLES. Entered Madras army 1797; col. 14 Madras N.I. 1848 to death; general 20 June 1854. *d.* Stanley place, Paddington, London 4 March 1859 aged 74.

FRAZER, JOHN JAMES, stage name of John James Fricker. Principal tenor singer in London 1843; went to the United States about 1851. *d.* Philadelphia 18 June 1863 in 59 year.

FREAKE, SIR CHARLES JAMES, 1 Baronet (*eld. son of Charles Freake of St. George's, Hanover sq. London*). *b.* 7 April 1814; contested Chelsea 17 Nov. 1868; built Cromwell road and other streets in Kensington; created baronet 23 May 1882. *d.* 1 Cromwell houses, Kensington, London 6 Oct. 1884.

FREDERICK, CHARLES (2 *son of lieut. colonel Thomas Frederick, who d. 28 May 1844 aged 80*). *b.* 7 May 1797; entered navy 5 June 1810; captain 23 Oct. 1842; member of Irish relief committee 1847; member of Board of Admiralty, June 1859; senior officer on coast of Ireland 31 March 1865 to 8 Oct. 1867; retired admiral 30 July 1875. *d.* 13 Victoria st. Westminster 23 Dec. 1875.

FREDERICK, EDWARD (*son of col. Charles Frederick*). *b.* 23 June 1784; entered Bombay army 1799; col. 10 Bombay N.I. 28 June 1838 to death; general 26 June 1860; C.B. 28 July 1838. *d.* Shawford house, Hants. 5 Dec. 1866.

FREEBURN, JAMES. *b.* parish of St. Cuthbert's, Midlothian 1808; enlisted in 7th battalion of R.A. 1825, serjeant-major April 1844, quartermaster of 10th battalion 1 April 1846 to 21 April 1856 when he retired with hon. rank of captain; invented an elaborate series of metal and wood fuzes for exploding live shells 1846, his fuzes were adopted in the army 1847. *d.* Plumstead, Woolwich 5 Aug. 1876.

FREEMAN, VEN. PHILIP (*son of Edmund Freeman of The Cedars, Combs, Suffolk*). *b.* The Cedars 3 Feb. 1818; ed. at Trin. coll. Cam., scholar 1835; Craven univ. scholar 1838; B.A. 1839, M.A. 1842; fellow of St. Peter's coll. 1842-53; principal of theological coll. Chichester 1846-55; canon and reader in theology in Cumbrae coll. Scotland 1855-58; V. of Thorverton, Devon 1858-74; preb. of Exeter 1861-64; canon of Exeter 1864 to death; archdeacon of Exeter, April 1865 to death; author of *Proportion in Gothic architecture* 1848; *The principles of divine service* 2 parts 1855-62 and 17 other books. *d.* 1 Northumberland terrace, Primrose hill, London 24 Feb. 1875 from effects of an accident at Chalk Farm railway station 18 Feb.

FREEMAN, SAMUEL. Engraver of portraits; worked chiefly in stipple; engraved numerous portraits and other illustrations for Rev. T. F. Dibdin's *Northern Gallery*, Jones's *National Gallery* and other books. *d.* 22 Jeffrey's st. Camden Town, London 27 Feb. 1857 aged 84.

FREEMAN, WILLIAM DEANE. Called to bar in Ireland 1817; Q.C. 17 Aug. 1841; assistant barrister for Galway to death. *d.* Galway 13 Oct. 1852. *Law magazine and law review ii,* 236-40 (1857).

FREEMAN, REV. JOSEPH JOHN. *b.* Thames st. London 7 Oct. 1794; Congregational minister at Chelmsford 21 May 1816; minister for London missionary soc. in Madagascar 1826-35; minister at Walthamstow 1836; one of foreign secretaries of London Missionary Soc. 1841 and home sec. 1846; visited missionary stations in Guiana and Jamaica 1842-43; took charge of Malagasy refugees when in England 1848; visited mission churches at the Cape and in the Mauritius 1849-51; author of *The Holy Bible in the Malagasy language* 1830; *A Tour to South Africa* 1851 and 9 other works. *d.* Homburg 8 Sep. 1851. *Congregational Year Book* (1852) pp. 215-16; *Waddington's Congregational history v,* 51-9 (1880).

FREER, JOHN CHARLES. *b.* Malta 1802; appeared on stage at Portsmouth about 1824; played at theatres in east of London with success; kept a public house in Shoreditch which failed; went to Philadelphia; appeared at Park theatre, New York as Richard III. 18 May 1839; lessee of Richmond hill theatre, New York; stage manager of Chatham theatre, New York 10 years. Cut his throat at a coffee house, Bridge court, Cannon row, Westminster bridge, London 24 Dec. 1857, *d.* Westminster hospital same day. *bur.* Working 30 Dec. *Theatrical times iii,* 89 (1848), *portrait; Era* 27 Dec. 1857 p. 11.

FREER, VEN. RICHARD LANE (son of Rev. Thomas Lane Freer, R. of Handsworth, Staffs., who d. 1835 aged 57). b. 1806; ed. at Westminster and Ch. Ch., Ox., B.A. 1828, D.D. 1858; R. of Bishopstone, Herefordshire 1830 to death; preb. of Hereford cath. 1847 to death; archdeacon of Hereford, April 1852 to death; prelector of Hereford cath. 1861 to death. d. Bishopstone rectory 11 Aug. 1863. *Memoir of Ven. R. L. Freer [by his widow], privately printed 1866, portrait.*

FREESTUN, SIR WILLIAM LOCKYER (2 son of Edward Freestun of Primrose hill, co. Waterford). b. May park, Waterford 1804; ensign 5 foot 4 June 1812; on the staff of British legion under Sir De Lacy Evans 1835–37; served on the staff in Syria as assistant adjutant general with rank of major 15 Dec. 1840 to 1842; M.P. for Weymouth 1847–59; knighted at St. James's palace 20 June 1860. d. 22 Gloucester sq. Hyde park, London 16 April 1862.

FREETH, SIR JAMES (youngest son of Sampson Freeth of Birmingham). b. Birmingham 1786; ensign royal staff corps 25 Dec. 1806, captain 1814 to 1830 when placed on h.p.; A.Q.M.G. 1826–1851, Q.M.G. 1 Feb. 1851 to 13 Aug. 1855; col. 64 foot 13 Aug. 1855 to death; general 9 March 1865; K.H. 1833; K.C.B. 10 Nov. 1862. d. 80 Coleshill st. Eaton sq. London 19 Jany. 1867.

FREILIGRATH, FERDINAND. b. Detmold, North Germany 17 June 1810; clerk in a bank at Amsterdam 1831–36; a merchant's clerk in City of London 1846–48; imprisoned at Düsseldorf 2 months in 1848 for publishing a poem entitled *The Dead to the Living* 1848; clerk in a bank in City of London 1851–67; naturalised in England 16 Oct. 1858; lived in Germany 1867 to death; a most popular modern German poet; his collected works were published in 6 vols. at Stuttgart 1877. d. Cannstadt near Stuttgart 17 March 1876. *W. Buchner's F. Freiligrath, ein Dichterleben 2 vols. (1882), 2 portraits.*

FREMANTLE, SIR CHARLES HOWE (2 son of admiral Sir Thomas Francis Fremantle 1765–1819). b. 1 June 1800; midshipman R.N. 12 Dec. 1812; captain 4 Aug. 1826; admiral superintendent in Balaklava 18 June 1855; commander-in-chief at Devonport, Oct. 1863 to Oct. 1866; admiral 9 Feb. 1864; K.C.B. 2 Jany. 1857, G.C.B. 13 March 1867. d. 57 Grosvenor st. London 25 May 1869.

FRENCH, Queen of the, MARIE AMELIE DE BOURBON (2 dau. of Ferdinand I. 1751–1825, king of the Two Sicilies). b. Caserte palace near Naples 26 April 1782. (m. at Palermo 25 Nov. 1809 Louis Philippe De Bourbon b. Paris 6 Oct. 1773 king of the French 1830–48, d. Claremont, Surrey 26 Aug. 1850); lived at Claremont, March 1848 to death. d. Claremont 24 March 1866. bur. in mausoleum at Weybridge 3 April. *Mrs. Challis's Illustrious women of France (1873) 215–320, portrait; I.L.N. xii, 147 (1848), portrait; G.M. i, 741–3 (1866).*

FRENCH, MOST REV. EDMUND (son of Rev. Dr. Ffrench, protestant warden of Galway). Educ. Trin. coll. Dublin; Catholic warden of Galway to 1831 when office was abolished; R.C. Bishop of Kilmacduagh and Kilfenora 26 July 1824 to death; consecrated 13 March 1825. d. Gort, co. Galway 14 July 1852.

FRENCH, FITZSTEPHEN (youngest son of Arthur French of French park, co. Roscommon, who d. 24 Nov. 1820). b. 7 Dec. 1801; ed. at Trin. coll. Dublin; M.P. for co. Roscommon 7 Dec. 1832 to death; col. Roscommon militia 23 Dec. 1854 to death; P.C. Ireland 1866; author of *The Question Are the Government entitled to the support of the Irish liberal members?* 1839. d. 68 Warwick sq. London 4 June 1873.

FRENCH, GEORGE (3 son of Arthur French of French park, co. Roscommon, M.P. for that county). b. 23 Nov. 1771; called to Irish bar 1795; K.C. 18 Feb. 1822; assistant barrister co. Longford; crown prosecutor Connaught circuit. d. Seamont, Malhide 26 Oct. 1860. *O. J. Burke's Anecdotes of Connaught circuit (1885) 278.*

FRENCH, GEORGE. Educ. at Shrewsbury and Caius coll. Cam.; barrister L.I. 11 June 1844; edited *The Equity Reports vol. 3*, 1853; judge of mixed courts at Sierra Leone 16 Aug. 1871; returned to England 1875; judge of supreme court for China at Shanghae 10 Dec. 1877; chief justice of supreme court for China and Japan at Shanghae 30 Oct. 1878 to death. d. Kobe, Japan 13 Nov. 1881.

FRENCH, GEORGE RUSSELL. b. London 1803; surveyor and architect to Ironmonger's Company; mem. of council and vice pres. of London and Middlesex Archæological Soc.; author of *Ancestry of Victoria and Albert* 1841; *Genealogical and biographical history of England* 1847 and other books. d. London 1 Nov. 1881.

FRENCH, GILBERT JAMES (son of James French of Edinburgh, shawl manufacturer). b. 4 Nicholson square, Edinburgh 18 April 1804; apprenticed to a draper in Edinburgh; partner

FRENCH, G. J. *(Con.)*

with John Cross, draper of Bolton, Lancashire; a church furnisher in Manchester road, Bolton; pres. of Bolton mechanics institution 1857–58; life member of Society of Antiquaries 9 Feb. 1860; author of *Practical remarks on some of the minor accessories to the service of the church* 1844; *The life and times of Samuel Crompton* 1859 and 9 other books. *d.* Newport sq. Bolton 4 May 1866.

FRENCH, HENRY JOHN. Ensign 90 foot 27 Aug. 1812; major 85 foot 23 May 1836 to 31 July 1846 when placed on h.p.; col. 80 foot 3 Sep. 1867 to death; L.G. 9 Aug. 1870. *d.* 17 Belgrave road, Eccleston sq. London 25 Jany. 1874 aged 77.

FRENCH, SYDNEY. Edited *Weekly Despatch;* acting editor of *Licensed Victuallers' Gazette* to death. *d.* Alresford house, Stansfield road, Stockwell 27 Oct. 1878 aged 42. *bur.* Kensal Green cemetery 1 Nov.

FRENCH, THOMAS. A jockey; rode St. Albans in the Great Metropolitan stakes 1861; won the Derby on Kingcraft 1870, on Favonius 1871; accomplished unprecedented feat of riding 6 winners in one day at Newmarket July meeting 1869. *d.* Newmarket 30 Aug. 1873 in 29 year. *Illust. sp. and dramatic news i,* 255, 256 (1874), *portrait; Baily's mag. xviii,* (1870), *portrait.*

FRERE, BARTHOLOMEW (5 *son of John Frere of Roydon, Norfolk, F.R.S.* 1740–1807). *b.* 30 Nov. 1776; ed. at Trin. coll. Cam., B.A. 1799, M.A. 1806; sec. of legation at Lisbon 1801; sec. of legation at Constantinople 1807–8, 1811–15 and 1817–20, minister plenipotentiary ad interim there 1815–17 and 1820–21; retired on pension Aug. 1821. *d.* 23 Old Burlington st. London 29 May 1851.

FRERE, GEORGE EDWARD (2 *son of Edward Frere of Llanelly, Brecknockshire*). *b.* 29 Jany. 1807; ed. at Charterhouse and Univ. of Edin.; barrister M.T. 8 Nov. 1851; F.R.S. 8 June 1837. *d.* Roydon hall near Diss, Norfolk 3 Dec. 1887.

FRERE, SIR HENRY BARTLE EDWARD, 1 Baronet (6 *son of Edward Frere of Llanelly*). *b.* Clydach, Brecknockshire 29 March 1815; entered Indian civil service 15 Jany. 1834; resident at Sattara 1 May 1847; comr. to Scinde 2 Dec. 1850; member of council at Calcutta 21 Dec. 1859; governor of Bombay 24 April 1862 to 6 March 1867; member of council of India 12 Nov. 1866; P.C. 4 Aug. 1873; presented with freedom of city of

FRERE, SIR H. B. E. *(Con.)*

London 16 July 1874; baronet 19 May 1876; governor of Cape of Good Hope 5 March 1877 to July 1880; K.C.B. 20 May 1859, G.C.B. 17 May 1876; G.C.S.I. 12 Feb. 1866; F.R.S. 3 May 1877; author of *Eastern Africa as a field for missionary labour* 1874 and other books. *d.* Wressil lodge, Wimbledon 29 May 1884. *bur.* St. Paul's cath. 5 June, statue erected on Thames embankment 1888. *G. B. Malleson's Recreations* (1872) 388–437; *Escott's Pillars of the empire* (1879) 92–7; *Army and navy mag. i,* 474–78 (1881), *portrait.*

FRERE, JAMES HATLEY (*brother of Bartholomew Frere* 1776–1851). *b.* 1779; introduced a phonetic system for teaching the blind to read about 1838; author of *A combined view of the prophecies of Daniel, Esdras and S. John* 1815; *The art of teaching to read by elementary sounds* 1840 and 10 other books. *d.* Shillington vicarage, Beds. 8 Dec. 1866.

FRERE, REV. JOHN ALEXANDER (3 *son of James Hatley Frere of army pay office* 1779–1866). *b.* 9 May 1814; ed. at Trin. coll. Cam., B.A. 1838, M.A. 1841; fellow, tutor and senior dean of his college 1840–47; Whitehall preacher 1847–8; Christian advocate of Univ. of Cam. 1848–50; V. of Shillington, Beds. 1853 to death; author of *On the incarnation* 1853 and other books. *d.* Achenkirch, Austrian Tyrol 27 Aug. 1877.

FRERE, PHILIP HOWARD (*eld. son of Wm. Frere* 1775–1836, *master of Downing coll. Cam.*) *b.* 1813; ed. at Eton and Trin. coll. Cam., B.A. 1836, M.A. 1839; fellow of Downing coll. 1837, tutor and bursar 1839; edited *Journal of Royal Agricultural Society* 1862 to death, in which he wrote many papers on agriculture. *d.* Panton house, Cambridge 12 May 1868.

FRESHFIELD, JAMES WILLIAM (*eld. son of James Freshfield of Chertsey, Surrey*). *b.* Windsor 1775; pensioner at Peterhouse coll. Cam.; admitted solicitor 1795; solicitor to Bank of England 1812–40; M.P. for Penryn and Falmouth 1830–32, 1835–41 and 1852–57; M.P. for Boston 1851–52; barrister G.I. 16 Nov. 1842; chairman of Surrey quarter sessions; sheriff of Surrey 1850; chairman of the Divorce Committee 1856–57; F.R.S. 10 April 1834; author of *County Rates* 1854. *d.* 6 Devonshire place, London 27 June 1864.

FREWEN, CHARLES HAY. *b.* 1813; M.P. for East Sussex 1846–57; sheriff of Leics. 1866. *d.* Cold Overton hall, Oakham 1 Sep. 1878.

FREWEN, THOMAS (*brother of preceding*). *b.* Cold Overton hall 26 Aug. 1811; M.P. for South Leics. 1835–36; sheriff of Sussex 1839. *d.* Brickwall house, Northiam 14 Oct. 1870.

FRISWELL, JAMES HAIN (*son of Wm. Friswell of 93 Wimpole st. London, attorney*). *b.* Newport, Shropshire 8 May 1825; founded in London the Friday Knights, a social society, January 1858, the name was changed to the Urban club 15 November 1858; edited *The Censor, a weekly review* 23 May to 7 November 1868; edited the Bayard series and the Gentle Life series; author of *The gentle life* 1864 anon., 21 *ed.* 1879, 2nd series 1868, 11 *ed.* 1879, and 34 other books. *d.* Fair home, Bexley Heath, Kent 12 March 1878. *Graphic 30 March* 1878 *pp.* 320, 332, *portrait; Pictorial World* 6 *April* 1878 *pp.* 82, 84, *portrait.*

FRITH, JOHN WHARTON. Ensign 12 foot 17 July 1804; lieut. col. 58 foot 1836–1842; inspecting field officer 30 Dec. 1842; col. 2 West India regiment 1860, col. 3 foot 1863 to death; L.G. 13 Aug. 1862. *d.* 85 Waterloo road, Dublin 8 Sep. 1864 aged 74.

FROME, EDWARD CHARLES. *b.* Gibraltar 7 Jany. 1802; 2 lieut. R.E. 1825, col. 1859, col. commandant 1871 to death; surveyor general of South Australia 1839–49, of Mauritius 1851–58; inspector general of engineers at head quarters 1868–9; lieut. governor of Guernsey 1 May 1869 to 30 April 1874; general 21 Nov. 1874; F.R.A.S.; author of *Outlines of the method of conducting a trigonometrical survey* 1840, 4 *ed.* 1873. *d.* Ewell, Surrey 12 Feb. 1890.

FROPIER, SIR GABRIEL PIERRE JULES. Member of legislative council of Mauritius; knighted by patent 31 Oct. 1862. *d.* 1882.

FROST, CHARLES (*son of Thomas Frost of Kingston-upon-Hull, solicitor*). *b.* Kingston-upon-Hull 1781 or 1782, solicitor there to death; solicitor to Hull dock company 33 years; F.S.A. 2 May 1822; pres. of Hull literary and philos. soc. 10 times; vice pres. of British Assoc. at Hull meeting 1853; author of *Notices relative to the early history of the town of Hull* 1827 and other books. *d.* Hull 5 Sep. 1862. *R. W. Corlass's Sketches of Hull authors* (1879) 33–4; *I.L.N. xxiii*, 225, 226 (1853), *portrait.*

FROST, JOHN (*son of John Frost of Mill st. Newport, Monmouthshire, publican*). Tailor and draper at Newport 1811, member of town council of Newport, magistrate 1835, mayor 1836; elected 1838 as delegate to represent Chartists of Monmouthshire at national convention of working classes which met in Lon-

FROST, J. (*Con.*)

don 4 Feb. 1839 and was dissolved 14 Sep.; led a large body of working men into Newport and attacked the Westgate hotel 4 Nov. 1839, tried at Monmouth 10 Dec. 1839, Frost, Williams and Jones sentenced to be hung, drawn and quartered 16 Jany. 1840 being the last persons in this country so sentenced, transported to Van Diemen's Land 1840, obtained a conditional pardon 1854, a free pardon May 1856; author of *The horrors of convict life* 1856. *d.* Stapleton near Bristol 29 July 1877 aged 93. *Gurney's Trial of John Frost for high treason* (1840); *W. C. Townsend's Modern state trials* (1850) i, 1–101; *The rise and fall of Chartism in Monmouthshire* (1840) *p.* 6 *et seq. portrait; Century Mag. xxiii*, 428 (1882), *portrait.*

FROST, WILLIAM EDWARD. *b.* Wandsworth, Surrey, Sep. 1810; student at the R.A. 1829; painter of portraits and allegorical pictures; A.R.A. Nov. 1846, R.A. 30 Dec. 1870 to June 1876 when he resigned; exhibited 77 pictures at R.A. and 33 at B.I. 1836–78. *d.* 40 Fitzroy sq. London 4 June 1877. *Sandby's History of Royal Academy* (1862) ii, 219–21; *Art Journal* (1849) *p.* 184, *portrait,* (1857) *pp.* 5–7, (1877) *pp.* 234, 280; *I.L.N. xxx*, 419, 420 (1857), *portrait, and lviii*, 61, 63 (1871), *portrait.*

FROUDE, VEN. ROBERT HURRELL (*son of Robert Froude of Walkhampton, Devon*). Matric. from Oriel coll. Ox. 28 Jany. 1788 aged 17, B.A. 1792, M.A. 1795; R. of Denbury, Devon 1798 to death; R. of Dartington, Devon 1799 to death; archdeacon of Totnes 30 May 1820 to death. *d.* Dartington 23 Feb. 1859.

FROUDE, WILLIAM (4 *son of the preceding*). *b.* Dartington parsonage 28 Nov. 1810; ed. at Westminster and Oriel coll. Ox., B.A. 1832, M.A. 1837; worked under I. K. Brunel on Bristol and Exeter railway 1837 to May 1844 when line was opened; lived at Paignton near Torquay 1859–67, at Chelston Cross, Torquay which he built, 1867 to death; conducted at the Admiralty establishment, Torquay, experiments on resistance and propulsion of ships 1870 to death; M.I.C.E. 1846, mem. of council 1877; F.R.S. 2 June 1870, royal medallist 1876. *d.* Admiralty house, Simon's Town, Cape of Good Hope 4 May 1879. *Min. of proc. of Instit. of C.E. lx*, 395–404 (1880); *Nature xx*, 148–50, 169–73 (1879); *Proc. of Royal Soc. xxix, pp.* ii-vi (1879); *Rev. T. Mozley's Reminiscences* (1882) ii, 14–17.

FRY, FRANCIS (2 *son of Joseph Storrs Fry* 1769–1835). *b.* Westbury-on-Trym near Bristol 28 Oct. 1803; partner in firm of J. S. Fry &

FRY, F. (*Con.*)

Sons, cocoa and chocolate manufactures, Bristol; a director of Bristol and Gloucester railway 1839–45, of Bristol and Exeter, South Devon and other railways; his collection of British bibles said to be finest in the world became property of the Bible Society, March 1890; F.S.A. 13 Feb. 1863; published *A description of the Great Bible* 1539, *and the six editions of Cranmer's Bible* 1540 *and* 1541 *printed by Grafton and Whitchurch* 1865 and 11 other books. *d.* Tower house, Cotham, Bristol 12 Nov. 1886. *A brief memoir of F. Fry. By his son T. Fry, privately printed* (1887), *portrait.*

FULCHER, GEORGE WILLIAMS. Bookseller, stationer and printer at Sudbury, Suffolk; started the *Sudbury Pocket Book* 1825, edited it 1825 to death; author of *The village paupers and other poems* 1845; *Life of Thomas Gainsborough* 1856 and other books. *d.* Sudbury 19 June 1855 in 60 year.

FULFORD, RIGHT REV. FRANCIS (2 *son of Baldwin Fulford of Great Fulford, Devon*). *b.* Sidmouth, Devon 3 June 1803; ed. at Tiverton gr. sch. and Ex. coll. Ox., fellow 1824–30; B.A. 1827, M.A. 1838, hon. D.D. 1850; R. of Trowbridge, Wilts. 1832–42; R. of Croydon, Cambs. 1842–45; min. of Curzon chapel, Hanover sq. London 1845–50; bishop of Montreal 19 July 1850 to death, consecrated in Westminster Abbey 25 July; metropolitan bishop of Canada 9 July 1860 to death; edited *Colonial church chronicle and missionary journal* 1848–50; author of *A course of plain sermons on the Church of England* 2 vols. 1837–40 and 10 other books. *d.* See house, Montreal 9 Sep. 1868. *F. Taylor's Last three bishops appointed by the Crown for the Anglican church of Canada* (1870) 23–130, *portrait; I.L.N. 24 Aug.* 1850 *p.* 168, *portrait,* 29 *Nov.* 1862 *pp.* 576, 587, *portrait.*

FULFORD, JOHN (*brother of the preceding*). *b.* 16 Feb. 1809; entered navy 1821; captain 1848; R.A. 1866; retired admiral 5 Aug. 1877. *d.* Bemerton, Salisbury 15 Feb. 1888.

FULLER, CHARLES FRANCIS. Sculptor at Florence; exhibited 28 sculptures at the R.A. 1859–75. *d.* Florence 10 March 1875 aged 45.

FULLER, FRANCIS. *b.* Coulsdon, Surrey 29 June 1807; surveyor to London, Brighton and South Coast railway 25 years; constructed line from Caterham Junction to Caterham at his own cost and without aid of act of parliament; promoted with Sir Henry Cole and Scott Russell the Great Exhibition of 1851; declined knighthood; managing director of

FULLER, F. (*Con.*)

Crystal Palace co. 1852; saw the race for the Derby at Epsom 1821–84, 64 years, a fact unparalleled in turf history; author of *Alexandra Park* 1873. *d.* 63 St. Aubyn's, Hove, Brighton 27 May 1887. *The Field 4 June* 1887 *p.* 769; *I.L.N. xix,* 487, 508 (1851), *portrait.*

FULLER, HENRY PETER. *b.* 1785; a surgeon in London 1807–59; a governor of St. George's hospital 1817 to death, visiting apothecary there 1819 to death, raised in 1830 sum of £20,000 for rebuilding the hospital, where one of the wards is named after him. *d.* Sarratt hall, Rickmansworth, Herts. 28 Aug. 1866.

FULLER, RIGHT REV. THOMAS BROCK. *b.* Kingston, Upper Canada 16 July 1810; R. of St. George's, Toronto 1853–67; archdeacon of Toronto 1867–75; bishop of Niagara 1875 to death. *d.* Bishophurst, Hamilton, Canada 17 Dec. 1884.

FULLERTON, LADY GEORGIANA CHARLOTTE (*younger dau. of 1 Earl Granville 1773–1846*). *b.* Tixall hall, Staffs. 23 Sep. 1812; admitted into R.C. church 29 March 1846; enrolled herself in the third order of St. Francis 1856; founded with Miss Taylor a religious community called the Poor Servants of the Mother of God Incarnate 1868; author of *Ellen Middleton, a tale* 3 vols. 1844; *Too strange not to be true, a tale* 3 vols. 1864 and 33 other books. (*m.* 13 July 1833 Alexander George Fullerton of Ballintoy castle, co. Antrim). *d.* Ayrfield, Bournemouth 19 Jany. 1885. *bur.* in cemetery of convent of Sacred Heart, Roehampton, Surrey 23 Jany. *Life of Lady Georgiana Fullerton, from the French of Mrs. Madame Augustus Craven. By H. J. Coleridge* (1888), *portrait.*

FULLERTON, JOHN (*son of Wm. Fullerton of Carstairs*). *b.* 16 Dec. 1775; an advocate Feb. 1798; a lord of session with title of Lord Fullerton 7 Feb. 1829 to Nov. 1853 when he retired. *d.* Edinburgh 3 Dec. 1853.

FULLOM, STEPHEN WATSON. edited *United Service Mag.* many years; resided at Torquay; author of *The King and the countess* 3 vols. 1849; *The great highway* 3 vols. 1854; *History of woman* 2 vols. 1855; *The last days of Jerusalem, a song* 1871 and 11 other books. *d.* in a cab at Liverpool 13 July 1872 aged 54.

FULTON, HAMILTON HENRY (*son of Hamilton Fulton, C.E., state engineer to North Carolina and Georgia 1819–29, who d. 1834*). *b.* Charles st. London 1813; pupil to his father 1829–39; M.I.C.E. 6 May 1845; an engineer in London from 1846; engineer of West London and Crystal palace railway, of Ryde and Ventnor

FULTON, H. H. *(Con.)*

railway, and of Salisbury and Dorset junction railway 1860 ; projected a railway bridge over the Severn 1863 and a scheme for Manchester ship canal 1882 ; author of *London Water Supply* 1869. *d.* Bedford house, Chiswick 10 Aug. 1886. *Min. of proc. of Instit. of C.E. lxxxvii,* 418–22 (1886).

FURLEY, ROBERT (3 *son of Robert Furley of Canterbury).* b. 1811 ; solicitor at Ashford, Kent 1832–69 ; F.S.A. 12 Jany. 1871 ; author of *A history of the Weald of Kent* 2 vols. 1871–74. *d.* Ashford, Kent 9 Sep. 1887.

FURNELL, MICHAEL CUDMORE. *b.* 1 July 1829 ; M.R.C.S. 1851, F.R.C.S. 1870 ; M.D. St. Andrews 1877 ; assistant surgeon H.E.I. Co. 7 Feb. 1855 ; surgeon to governor of Madras 1871–73 ; principal and professor of medicine, Medical college, Madras 1875–80 ; surgeon general Madras, April 1885 to death. *d.* Monte Carlo 24 May 1888.

FURNER, WILLIAM *(eld. son of John Furner of Brighton).* b. Brighton 1791 ; admitted attorney 1815 ; member of firm of Hill, Fitzburgh and Furner at Brighton 30 years ; comr. of bankrupts for Brighton district ; judge of local courts of request at Brighton and Shoreham 1840–47 ; judge of county courts, circuit 50 (Sussex), March 1847 to 20 Sep. 1877 when he resigned ; barrister G.I. 7 May 1851. *d.* 18 Palmeira sq. Brighton 25 Nov. 1877.

FURNESS, RICHARD *(son of Samuel Furness of Eyam, Derbyshire, farmer).* b. Eyam 2 Aug. 1791 ; a currier at Eyam 1813 ; schoolmaster in free school at Dore, Derbyshire 1821 ; author of *The Rag Bag* 1832 a satirical poem ; *Medicus-Magus, a poem in three cantos, Sheffield* 1836, title was afterwards altered to *The Astrologer. d.* Eyam 13 Dec. 1857. *The poetical works of R. Furness with a sketch of his life, By G. C. Holland, M.D.* (1858).

FURTADO, TERESA ELIZABETH *(dau. of Charles Furtado of London, professor of music, by Annie Flanagan).* b. 12 a.m. at 19 Edward st. Hampstead road, London 6 June 1845 ; made her début on the stage at New Royalty theatre 8 Feb. 1864 as Mercury in Burnand's burlesque *Ixion;* leading actress at Olympic theatre 1865–6, then at Adelphi theatre where she played Esmeralda in *Notre Dame* 10 April 1872. *(m.* 10 Aug. 1873 John Clarke, comedian, who *d.* 20 Feb. 1879 aged 49). *d.* 77 Mornington road, Regent's park, London 9 Aug. 1877. *Illust. sp. and dr. news* 17 Oct. 1874 *p.* 49, *portrait, and p.* 75 ; *Era* 12 *Aug.* 1877 *p.* 4, *col.* 2, 19 *Aug. p.* 5, *col.* 2.

FYDELL, SAMUEL RICHARD *(elder son of Thomas Fydell 1740–1812, M.P. for Boston).* b. Hardwicke hall near Chepstow 6 April 1771 ; receiver general for Lincolnshire 1794 to 1834 when office was abolished by Land tax amendment act 1834 and he declined pension offered him ; sheriff of Rutland 1840 ; lieut. col. of South Lincoln militia. *d.* Morcott hall, Rutland 1 Feb. 1868. *bur.* in family vault St. Botolph's church, Boston. *G.M. v,* 395 (1868).

FYFE, ANDREW *(eld. son of Andrew Fyfe of Edinburgh, anatomist 1754–1824).* b. 18 Jany. 1792 ; ed. at Univ. of Edin., M.D. 1814 ; fellow of college of surgeons Edin. 1818, pres. 1842–3 ; professor of chemistry in Univ. of Aberdeen 1844 to death ; author of *Elements of Chemistry* 2 vols. 1827, 3 ed. 1833. *d.* 4 Windsor st. Edinburgh 31 Dec. 1861.

FYFE, JAMES HAMILTON *(only son of John Fyfe of Edinburgh).* b. Edinburgh 1837 ; ed. at City of London school ; barrister M.T. 17 Nov. 1863 ; a reporter on *Edinburgh Express, Scotsman, Times;* assistant editor of *Pall Mall Gazette* 1867–71, of *Saturday Review* 1871 to about 1878 ; author of *Triumphs of invention and discovery* 1860 ; *British enterprise beyond the seas or our colonies* 1863 and other books. *d.* 35 Cathcart road, West Brompton, London 5 June 1880.

FYFE, WILLIAM BAXTER COLLIER. *b.* Dundee about 1836 ; studied at R.S.A. and in Paris ; painter in London 1863 to death ; exhibited 23 pictures at R.A., 2 at B.I. and 4 at Suffolk st. gallery 1866–79. *d.* 62 Abbey road, St. John's Wood, London 15 Sep. 1882.

FYFE, WILLIAM WALLACE *(eld. son of Peter Fyfe, R.N. of Dundee).* A contributor to the newspaper press ; promoter and manager of the Church and Country Newspaper Co., and of the Newspaper Press college at Dorchester about 1865, both schemes were unsuccessful and involved him in loss ; edited *The Provincial Souvenir, Paisley* 1846 ; author of *Agricultural science applied in practice* 1859 ; *Canada as a field for emigration* 1861 and 8 other books. *d.* Houndsgate, Nottingham 25 Sep. 1867. *Newspaper Press* 1 Oct. 1867 *p.* 205.

FYNMORE, JAMES. Midshipman R.N. at Trafalgar 1805 of which battle he was last survivor ; captain R.M. 1836–1848, hon. lieut. col. 28 Nov. 1854 to death. *d.* Blenheim grove, Rye lane, Peckham 15 April 1887 in 94 year. *Graphic xix,* 217 (1879), *portrait, xxxv,* 448 (1887), *portrait.*

FYSH, REV. FREDERICK. Ed. at Queen's coll. Cam. ; B.A. 1832, M.A. 1835 ; lived at 2

FYSH, REV. F. (*Con.*)

Duke st. Bath 1840–47, at 6 Lower terrace, Torquay 1856; author of *Catechism of the Apocalypse* 1844; *A Lyrical version of the Psalms* 2 vols. 1851; *Historia Apodeixis Horæ historicæ et chronologicæ* 5 vols. 1856 and 15 other books. *d.* 1867.

G

GABRIEL, MARY ANN VIRGINIA (*dau. of the succeeding*). *b.* Banstead, Surrey 7 Feb. 1825; composed several hundred songs, many of which became very popular; her operetta *Widows Bewitched* was performed at St. George's hall, London 13 Nov. 1867; composed 3 cantatas *Dreamland, Evangeline* and *Graziella.* (*m.* Nov: 1874 George Edward March of the Foreign office, London, who wrote most of her librettos). *d.* St. George's hospital, London 7 Aug. 1877 from compound fracture of the skull, result of carriage accident near Grosvenor hotel 5 Aug. *Lennox's Fashion then and now,* ii, 92–4 (1878); *Illust. sp. and dr. news* vi, 597, 620 (1877), *portrait.*

GABRIEL, ROBERT BURD. Cornet 2 dragoon guards 1797, captain 1805–1822 when placed on h.p.; M.G. 9 Nov. 1846; col. 7 dragoon guards 18 March 1853 to death; K.H. 1834; C.B. 19 July 1838. *d.* 7 Connaught place west, London 15 April 1853 aged 74.

GAGE, EDWARD THOMAS (2 son of 4 *Viscount Gage* 1791–1877). *b.* 28 Dec. 1825; 2 lieut. R.A. 1844, col. 1876, col. commandant 1887 to death; brigade major R.A. in Crimea 1854–55; commanded Woolwich district 1881–3; L.G. 1882; placed on retired list 1 April 1888; C.B. 13 March 1867. *d.* Clifton crescent, Folkestone 21 May 1889.

GAGE, SIR WILLIAM HALL (6 *son of general Thomas Gage* 1721–87). *b.* Park place, St. James's, London 2 Oct. 1777; entered navy 1789; captain 1797; commander in chief in East Indies 1825–30, on the Lisbon station 1834–37, at Devonport 1848–51; a lord of the Admiralty 1842–1846; admiral 1846; R.A. of United Kingdom 1853; V.A. of United Kingdom 1854; admiral of the Fleet 20 May 1862 to death; G.C.H. and K.B. 19 April 1834; G.C.B. 18 May 1860. *d.* Thurston, Suffolk 4 Jany. 1864.

GAINES, THOMAS. Last survivor of the 12 Bow street officers who under Sir Richard Birnie captured the Cato st. conspirators 23 Feb. 1820. *d.* Metropolitan asylum, Leavesdon, Herts. 4 Feb. 1879 aged nearly 90.

GAINSBOROUGH, CHARLES NOEL, 1 Earl of (*eld. son of Sir Gerard Noel Noel,* 2 *baronet* 1759–1838). *b.* 2 Oct. 1781; M.P. for Rutland 1808–14; succeeded his mother as 3 Baron Barham 12 April 1823; created Baron Noel, Viscount Campden and Earl of Gainsborough 16 Aug. 1841; married four times. *d.* 17 Prince's Gate, Hyde park, London 10 June 1866. *bur.* Teston church, Kent 19 June.

GAINSBOROUGH, CHARLES GEORGE NOEL, 2 Earl of. *b.* Edinburgh 5 Sep. 1818; M.P. for Rutland 1840–41; contested Rutland 1841 and co. Cork 1860; sheriff of Rutland 1848, lord lieutenant of Rutland 6 March 1867 to death; taken ill in a cab and *d.* University. college hospital, London 13 Aug. 1881.

GAIRDNER, JOHN (*eld. son of Robert Gairdner, captain Bengal artillery, who d.* 1795 *or* 1796). *b.* Mount Charles near Ayr 18 Sep. 1790; ed. at Univ. of Edin., M.D. 1811; phys. in Edin. 1813; F.C.S. Edin. 1813, pres. 1830–32; author of many papers in *Trans. of Medico-Chirurgical Soc. of Edin.* and in medical journals; his anonymous book *Burns and the Ayrshire Moderates* was privately printed 1883. *d.* 45 Northumberland st. Edinburgh 12 Dec. 1876. *The Scotsman* 14 *Dec.* 1876 *p.* 5.

GAIRDNER, WILLIAM (*brother of the preceding, b.* Mount Charles near Ayr 11 Nov. 1793; ed. at Univ. of Edin., M.D. 1813; phys. in London 1822–66; L.C.P. 1823; author of *Essay on the effects of Iodine on the human constitution* 1824, and *On Gout, its history, its causes and its cure* 1849, 4 ed. 1860. *d.* Avignon 28 April 1867.

GAIRDNER, WILLIAM JOHN. Entered Bengal army 1807; M.G. 1851; col. 63 Bengal N.I. 1852 to death; C.B. 3 April 1846. *d.* Strathtyrum house, St. Andrews 3 Feb. 1861 aged 71.

GAISFORD, VERY REV. THOMAS (*eld. son of John Gaisford of Iford, Wilts.*) *b.* Iford 22 Dec. 1779; commoner of Ch. Ch. Ox., Oct. 1797, student Dec. 1800; B.A. 1801, D.D. 1831; Regius professor of Greek at Oxford 29 Feb. 1812 to death; R. of Westwell, Oxon. 1815–47; preb. of Llandaff 1823 to death; preb. of St. Paul's 1823 to death; preb. of Worcester 1825–29; preb. of Durham 1829–31; dean of Ch. Ch. Ox. 10 Oct. 1831 to death; published *Poetæ Minores Græci* 4 vols. 1814–20 and 32 other classical and patristic works. *d.* the Deanery, Ch. Ch. Oxford 2 June 1855. *bur.* in nave of Ch. Ch. cathedral 9 June. *G.M. xliv,* 98–100 (1855).

GALBERRY, MOST REV. THOMAS. *b.* Naas, co. Kildare 1833; taken to Philadelphia 1836;

ordained R.C. priest 20 Dec. 1856; pres. of Villanova college; provincial of the Augustinian order 1874; bishop of Hartford 1876 to death; consecrated 19 March 1876. *d.* New York 10 Oct. 1878.

GALE, Charles James *(son of Charles Gale).* *b.* April 1805; barrister M.T. 1 June 1832; judge of county courts, circuit 51 (Hampshire), March 1847, of circuit 21 (Warwickshire) 1874 to Sep. 1874 when he retired on pension; author of *A treatise on the law of easements* 1839, 6 *ed.* 1888; published with Henry Davison *Reports in the court of Queen's Bench 1841–43*, 3 *vols.* 1841–43. *d.* Kitnocks, Botley near Southampton 5 Aug. 1876.

GALIGNANI, John Anthony *(eld. son of Giovanni Antonio Galignani of London, teacher of languages, who d. Paris 1821).* *b.* London 13 Oct. 1796; bookseller at Cambrai 1816; bookseller and publisher with his brother at 18 Rue Vivienne, Paris; *Galignani's Messenger* was founded by their father 1814 as a tri-weekly, it became a daily paper 1821; obtained denizenship Dec. 1830, never naturalised; removed to Rue de Rivoli 1855; knight of the Legion of Honour; gave with his brother between 5 and 6 million francs to charities of Paris. *d.* Paris 29 Dec. 1873. *I.L.N. lxiv*, 48 (1874), *portrait.*

GALIGNANI, William *(brother of the preceding).* *b.* London 10 March 1798; mayor of parish of Etiolles near Paris more than 20 years; erected with his brother a hospital for indigent English at Neuilly; obtained denizenship Dec. 1830, naturalised 1832; officer of Legion of Honour; bequeathed a site and funds for erection at Neuilly of the Retraite Galignani Frères for 100 inmates. *d.* 82 Faubourg St. Honoré, Paris 11 Dec. 1882, a fine sculpture of the two brothers by Chapu has been erected at Corbeil.

GALL, James. Member of firm of Gall and Inglis, publishers in George st. Edinburgh; master of Merchants' Co. Edin. 1850; author of *Gospel of St. John for the blind* 1835; *Philosophy of education* 1840 and other books. *d.* Edinburgh 3 Nov. 1874 aged 90. *Publishers' Circular* (1874) 866.

GALL, Richard Herbert. *b.* 10 Nov. 1815; ensign 3 foot 3 July 1835; major 14 light dragoons 1857–64 when placed on h.p.; A.D.C. to the Queen 8 June 1870 to death; lieut. governor of Chelsea hospital 1 March 1874 to death; C.B. 21 March 1859. *d.* Chelsea hospital 21 Feb. 1881.

GALLAGHER, Rev. Hugh P. *b.* Killygordan, Donegal 1815; went to the U.S. of A. 1837; ordained R.C. priest at Philadelphia 1840; pres. of Theological seminary Pittsburg 1844; founded and edited *Pittsburg Catholic;* theologian to first plenary council of Baltimore 1852; founded and edited *Catholic Standard* 1853; built many churches, schools and hospitals. *d.* San Francisco, March 1882.

GALLOWAY, Randolph Stewart, 9 Earl of. *b.* Coolhurst, Sussex 16 Sep. 1800; ed. at Harrow; M.P. for Cockermouth 1826–31; lord lieut. of Kirkcudbright to 1845, of Wigtonshire to 1851. *d.* Galloway house **near** Wigton 2 Jany. 1873.

GALLOWAY, Thomas *(son of Wm. Galloway of Symington, Lanarkshire, miller).* *b.* Symington 26 Feb. 1796; ed. at New Academy, Lanark, and Univ. of Edin., M.A. 1820; teacher of mathematics at Sandhurst 1823–33; register or actuary of Amicable Life Assurance Co. of London 1833 to death; F.R.A.S. 13 Feb. 1829; F.R.S. 18 Dec. 1834, member of council 1843 to death; author of many articles in *Encyclopædia Britannica, Edinburgh Review* and *Philosophical Mag. d.* 45 Torrington sq. London 1 Nov. 1851.

GALLOWAY, Thomas James. Ensign 15 foot 1821; lieut. col. 70 foot 1848–1863; brigadier general Bengal 1857–1861; col. 49 foot 1871–1874; col. 70 foot 7 Sep. 1874 to death; general 1 Oct. 1877. *d.* Kilmeague, Naas, Ireland 15 Sep. 1881 aged 81.

GALLWEY, Sir William Payne, 2 Baronet. *b.* 1807; succeeded 16 April 1831; M.P. for Thirsk, Yorkshire 1851–1880. *d.* Thirkleby park near Thirsk 19 Dec. 1881 in 74 year.

GALWAY, George Edward Arundell Monckton Arundel, 6 Viscount. *b.* Knutsford, Cheshire 1 March 1805; ed. at Harrow and Ch. Ch. Ox.; succeeded 1834; M.P. for East Retford 1847 to death; master of fox hounds in Notts. 1865 to death. *d.* Serlby hall, Notts. 6 Feb. 1876. *Baily's Mag. xix*, 171 (1871), *portrait.*

GALWEY, Sir Michael *(youngest son of James Galwey).* *b.* 1818; entered Madras army 1835; commandant 36 Madras N.I. 1865 to 1869; C.B. 26 July 1858, K.C.B. 2 June 1877; L.G. 1 Oct. 1877. *d.* London 22 July 1878.

GAMBIER, Sir Edward John (3 *son of Samuel Gambier 1752–1813, first comr. of the navy).* *b.* 1794; ed. at Eton and Trin. coll. Cam., B.A. 1817, M.A. 1820; barrister L.I. 7 Feb. 1822; a municipal corporation comr. 1833;

GAMBIER, SIR E. J. *(Con.)*

recorder of Prince of Wales Island 1834; puisne judge at Madras 28 Nov. 1836, chief justice 11 March 1842 to 1849; knighted at St. James's palace 6 Aug. 1834; author of *A treatise on parochial settlements* 1828, 2 ed. 1835. *d.* 22 Hyde park gate, Kensington, London 31 May 1879 in 86 year.

GAMBIER, GEORGE CORNISH. *b.* 1795; entered navy 18 June 1808; captain 4 June 1821; retired admiral 27 April 1863. *d.* Great Berkhampstead, Herts. 18 June 1879.

GAMBIER, ROBERT *(brother of the preceding)*. *b.* Wateringbury, Kent 3 Aug. 1791; entered navy 3 Aug. 1804; captain 6 June 1814; retired admiral 15 Jany. 1862. *d.* 7 Onslow sq. London 26 Jany. 1872.

GAMBIER, ROBERT FITZGERALD (2 *son of Sir James Gambier, F.R.S.*) *b.* Lisbon 21 Nov. 1803; entered navy 28 Feb. 1815; captain 9 Nov. 1846; retired admiral 1 Aug. 1877. *d.* 7 Crescent, Anglesey, Gosport 17 Oct. 1885.

GAMBLE, DOMINIC JACOTIN. *b.* 15 Aug. 1823; ensign 4 foot 19 April 1844; D.Q.M.G. New Zealand 1861–67; A.Q.M.G. Aldershot 1869–74; commanded forces in West Indies 1878–83; director general of military education 1887 to death; L.G. 1886?; C.B. 25 Feb. 1864. *d.* 58 Courtfield gardens, South Kensington, London 21 Nov. 1887.

GAMGEE, JOSEPH SAMPSON *(eld. son of Joseph Gamgee, veterinary surgeon)*. *b.* Leghorn 17 April 1828; M.R.C.S. 1854; surgeon to British Italian legion during Crimean war 1855; surgeon to Queen's hospital Birmingham 1857–81; invented several surgical appliances largely adopted; author of *Researches in pathological anatomy and clinical surgery* 1856 and 11 other books. *d.* 22 Broad st. Birmingham 18 Sep. 1886.

GAMMAGE, ROBERT GEORGE. *b.* Northampton; apprenticed to a coachbuilder; a Chartist lecturer 1842–4; Chartist sec. for Northampton district 1844; a shoemaker at Northampton 1844–8; removed to Birmingham 1848; mem. of paid executive of National Charter Assoc. 1853–4; M.R.C.S. 1864; assistant to Dr. Heath of Newcastle; practised at Sunderland; author of *History of the Chartist movement* 1854 and 20 other works. *d.* Northampton 7 Jany. 1888 aged 72.

GAMMON, FREDERIC THOMAS *(son of Rev. John Gammon, pres. of Bible Christian conference in London* 1859*)*. *b.* Somerset 1849; entered firm of S. W. Partridge & Co. of London,

GAMMON, F. T. *(Con.)*

publishers 1865, head of the firm 1883 to death; edited *British Workman, Band of Hope Review, Band of Mercy,* and other periodicals; author of *The canal boy who became president* [*G. A. Garfield*] 1881 and 4 other small books. *d.* St. Leonards-on-Sea 19 Sep. 1888.

GANDELL, REV. ROBERT (6 *son of Thomas Gandell of City of London*). *b.* London; matric. from St. John's coll. Ox. 5 Dec. 1839 aged 21; Michel scholar Queen's coll. 1843–5, fellow 1845–50; B.A. 1843, M.A. 1846; Kennicott scholar 1844, Pusey and Ellerton scholar 1845; tutor of Magdalen hall 1848–72; Laudian professor of Arabic 1861 to death; chaplain at C.C. coll. 1852–77; fellow of Hertford coll. 1874 to death; preb. of Wells 1874, canon of Wells 1880 to death; edited Lightfoot's *Horæ Hebraicæ et Talmudicæ* 4 vols. 1859; contributed commentaries on Amos, Nahum and Zephaniah to the Speaker's Commentary 1876. *d.* The Liberty, Wells 24 Oct. 1887. *bur.* Holywell cemetery, Oxford.

GAPE, JOSEPH. Entered navy 2 Aug. 1803; inspecting commander coast guard 1837 to 1841; captain 1841; admiral on h.p. 30 July 1875. *d.* 1 Upper Phillimore place, Kensington, London 12 March 1876 in 83 year.

GARBETT, REV. EDWARD (6 *son of Rev. James Garbett* 1775–1857, *preb. of Hereford*). *b.* Hereford 10 Dec. 1817; ed. at Hereford coll. and Brasenose coll. Ox., B.A. 1841, M.A. 1847; V. of St. Stephen's, Birmingham 1847–49; P.C. of St. Bartholomew's, Grays Inn road, London 1850–63; V. of Ch. Ch. Surbiton 1863–77; hon. canon of Winchester 1875; R. of Barcombe near Lewes 1877 to death; edited *The Record* 1854–67 and *The Christian Advocate* 1867–74; author of *The Soul's Life* 1863 and 30 other books. *d.* Barcombe rectory 11 Oct. 1887. *The Record* 14 and 21 Oct. 1887.

GARBETT, VEN. JAMES *(brother of the preceding)*. *b.* Hereford 1802; ed. at Brasenose coll. Ox., scholar 1819, fellow 1825–36, tutor 1827, junior dean 1832; B.A. 1822, M.A. 1825; Michel fellow of Queen's coll. 1824–5; Bampton lecturer 1842; professor of poetry in Univ. of Ox. 1842–52; R. of Clayton near Brighton 1835 to death; preb. of Chichester 1844; archdeacon of Chichester 28 April 1851 to death; author of *De Rei poeticæ idea* 1843; *Parochial Sermons* 2 vols. 1843–4 and 30 other books. *d.* 7 Belgrave place, Brighton 26 March 1879 in 78 year. *I.L.N. lxxiv,* 373 (1879), *portrait.*

GARD, RICHARD SOMMERS. *b.* North Tawton near Barnstaple 1797; sheriff of Devon 1854; contested Honiton, Devon 1852; M.P. for Exeter 1857–65. *d.* Court hall, Monkton near Honiton 16 Dec. 1868 in 72 year.

GARDEN, REV. FRANCIS *(son of Alexander Garden of Glasgow, merchant).* *b.* 1810; ed. at Glasgow and Trin. coll. Cam., B.A. 1833, M.A. 1836; P.C. of Holy Trinity, Blackheath 1840–44; Inc. of St. Paul's, Edin. 1845–49; C. of St. Stephen's, Westminster 1854–59; teacher of theology Queen's coll. London 1858–81; sub-dean of chapels royal St. James's and Whitehall, Nov. 1859 to death; edited *The Christian Remembrancer* from 1841; author of *Discourses on heavenly knowledge and love* 1848; *An outline of Logic* 1867, 2 ed. 1871 and 14 other books. *d.* 67 Victoria st. Westminster 11 May 1884.

GARDINER, ALLEN FRANCIS (5 *son of Samuel Gardiner of Coombe lodge, Oxfordshire* 1755–1827). *b.* Basildon parsonage, Berkshire 28 June 1794; entered navy 23 June 1810; commander 13 Sep. 1826; went to the Zulu country, South Africa 1834; laboured among the Indians of Chili 1838–43; founded Patagonian Missionary Soc. 1844; author of *Outlines of a plan for exploring the interior of Australia* 1833; *A voice from South America* 1847 and other books. *d.* Picton island, South America, probably 6 Sep. 1851, his remains were found 21 Jany. 1852. *Memoir of A. F. Gardiner, By J. W. Marsh* 1857, *portrait; The story of A. Gardiner, By J. W. Marsh* 1867, *portrait; C. M. Yonge's Pioneers and Founders* (1871) 255–84.

GARDINER, SIR JOHN *(son of John Gardiner, captain 3 foot).* *b.* 1777; ensign 3 foot 1791; commanded a brigade at battles of Nivelle 1813 and Orthes 1814; A.G. in Ireland 1823–1830; D.A.G. at the Horse Guards 1830–1841; col. of 61 foot 1840, of 50 foot 1844, of 6 foot 1849 to death; L.G. 23 Nov. 1841; K.C.B. 19 July 1838. *d.* 23 Eaton place, London 6 June 1851.

GARDINER, ROBERT *(son of Robert Hallowell of Bristol).* *b.* Bristol about 1782; went to the U.S. 1792; graduated at Harvard 1801; took surname of Gardiner 1802; lived at town of Gardiner, Maine 1803 to death, gave a church, a lyceum and a public library to Gardiner; pres. of Maine Historical Soc. 1846–55. *d.* Gardiner 22 March 1864.

GARDINER, SIR ROBERT WILLIAM *(brother of Sir John Gardiner* 1777–1851). *b.* 2 May 1781; 2 lieut. R.A. 7 April 1797, col. 24 Nov. 1839; A.D.C. to the Sovereign 22 July 1830

GARDINER, SIR R. W. *(Con.)*

to 23 Nov. 1841; governor and commander in chief at Gibraltar 21 Nov. 1848 to July 1855; col. commandant R.A. 22 March 1853 to death; general 28 Nov. 1854; K.C.B. 2 Jany. 1815, G.C.B. 21 June 1859; K.C.H. 1820; author of *Memoir of admiral Sir Graham Moore* 1844 and of 12 pamphlets on military organisation 1848–60. *d.* Melbourne lodge, Claremont, Esher, Surrey 26 June 1864.

GARDINER, WILLIAM. *b.* Dundee 1809; in shop of George Robertson, hosier, Dundee 1824–44; collected and sold many thousands of botanical specimens; sold many vols. of dried plants illustrative of the British Flora; A.L.S.; author of *Botanical rambles in Braemar, Dundee* 1845; *Twenty lessons on British mosses,* 4 ed. Dundee 1849, 2nd series 1849; *The Flora of Forfarshire* 1848. *d.* Dundee 21 June 1852. *W. Norrie's Dundee Celebrities* (1873) 139–144.

GARDINER, WILLIAM *(only son of Thomas Gardiner of Leicester, stocking manufacturer, who d. aged* 93). *b.* Leicester 15 March 1770; assistant to Coltman of Leicester, hosiery warehouseman; member of Acad. of St. Cecilia at Rome; published *Sacred Melodies* 6 vols. 1812; *The Music of Nature* 1832; *Music and Friends* 3 vols. 1838–53; *Sights in Italy* 1847. *d.* Leicester 16 Nov. 1853. *G.M. xli,* 92–95 (1854); *W. Gardiner's Poems with life, by his daughter* 1854; *Notes and Queries* 5 s. x, 169–71 (1878).

GARDNER, ALEXANDER. *b.* Paisley; printer, bookseller and publisher there 1829 to death; wrote religious books; author of *On lots, By G. A. Paisley* 1851. *d.* Greenhill cottage, Paisley 25 Aug. 1875 aged 76.

GARDNER, HENRY. Left by his will dated 24 July 1876 sum of £300,000 for benefit of the blind in England and Wales. *d.* 1 Westbourne terrace, Hyde park, London 9 January 1879.

GARDNER, JOHN. One of the best low comedians of his day; acted at City of London theatre 1850. *d.* 14 Queen st. Hoxton sq. London 5 May 1851 aged 51. *The Era* 11 May 1851 p. 12.

GARDNER, JOHN. *b.* Great Coggeshall, Essex 1804; apothecary in London 1829 to death, M.D. Giessen 1847; a founder of Royal college of chemistry 1844, sec. 1844–6; professor of chemistry and materia medica to General Apothecaries' Co.; introduced into England podophyllin and many other American drugs; L.R.C.P. Edin. 1860; translated and edited Liebig's *Familiar Letters on Chemistry* 1843, 2nd series 1844; author of *Household Medicine* 9 ed. 1878; *Longevity* 5 ed. 1878; *Hymns for*

GARDNER, J. *(Con.)*
the sick and convalescent 2 ed. 1879. *d.* 29 Lansdowne crescent, Notting hill, London 14 Nov. 1880.

GARDNER, MARTHA. *b.* 1776. *d.* 85 Grove st. Liverpool 10 March 1881 aged 104 years and 5 months. *Notes and Queries* 6 *s. iii*, 486 (1881).

GARDNER, RICHARD. *b.* Manchester 1813; ed. at Manchester sch., Charterhouse and Wadham coll. Ox., B.A. 1838; M.P. for Leicester 30 July 1847 but election declared void; M.P. for Leicester 9 July 1852 to death; author of some political pamphlets. *d.* 100 Eaton square, London 4 June 1856 aged 43.

GARDNER, WILLIAM. *b.* Ohio 1844; perfected the machine gun called after him 1876 which was introduced in the British service 1881; patented various improvements in fire-arms 1882–4; perfected an improved quick-firing cannon 1886. *d.* Henley lodge, St. Leonards-on-Sea 20 Jany. 1887.

GARDNER, WILLIAM HENRY (3 *son of* 1 *Baron Gardiner* 1742–1802). *b.* 6 Oct. 1774; 2 lieut. R.A. 18 Sep. 1793; col. commandant 1 April 1846 to death; general 20 June 1854. *d.* Bishopsteignton, Devon 15 Dec. 1856.

GARFIT, THOMAS. *b.* Boston 16 Oct. 1815; barrister M.T. 16 Jany. 1846; a banker at Boston; M.P. for Boston 1878–80 when unseated on petition. *d.* Boulogne 29 May 1883.

GARLAND, CHARLES (*son of Thomas Garland of Illogan, Cornwall* 1771–1827). *b.* Illogan 10 March 1813; edited *The Cornish Telegraph* weekly paper from first number 3 Jany. 1851 to 1853; edited *Pembrokeshire Herald* weekly paper from first number 5 Jany. 1844 to 1849; author of *Wings of the Dove* and 8 other poems in *The Pocket Album* 1831–2; *Outlines of scripture doctrine, and history* 1842. *d.* 2 Trewartha terrace, Penzance 17 Feb. 1875. *S. W. Christopher's Poets of Methodism* (1875) 467–70.

GARLAND, JOHN. Ensign 44 foot 14 March 1805; captain 73 foot 26 Nov. 1813 to 25 June 1817 when placed on h.p.; K.H. 1833. *d.* Lille, France 17 Jany. 1851.

GARLAND, JOHN BINGLEY (*son of George Garland, M.P. for Poole, d.* 1825). *b.* 1791; sheriff of Dorset 1828; gave 13 acres to Poole for a cemetery 1854; lived in Newfoundland many years, speaker of the first house of assembly there 1855 etc. *d.* Leeson house near Swanage, Dorset 12 Jany. 1875 aged 83. *I.L.N. lxvi*, 115 (1875).

GARLAND, THOMAS (*brother of Charles Garland* 1813–75). *b.* Bridge near Redruth, Cornwall, April 1804; edited *The Cornubian*, Falmouth weekly paper from first number 1 Oct. 1830 to 18 Dec. 1832; author of *Letters on the recent agitations in Wesleyan Methodism* 1852. *d.* Fairfield, Illogan 30 July 1865. *Memorials, literary and religious, of T. Garland* (1868); *S. W. Christopher's Poets of Methodism* (1875) 454–66.

GARNAULT, JOSEPH. Entered Madras army 1810; col. 29 Madras N.I. 11 Dec. 1848 to 1869; general 22 Feb. 1870. *d.* 14 Hesketh crescent, Torquay 15 May 1872.

GARNER, THOMAS. *b.* Birmingham 1789; pupil of Samuel Lines, engraver; a founder of the Antique Academy, Birmingham, which became Royal Birmingham Soc. of Artists; chiefly known by his plates in the *Art Journal*. *d.* Birmingham 14 July 1868.

GARNETT, ARTHUR WILLIAM (*younger son of Wm. Garnett* 1793–1873). *b.* 1 June 1829; lieut. Bengal engineers 1848, 2 captain 27 Aug. 1858 to death; designed and built Fort Garnett and other forts, barracks, &c. on the Punjab frontier; built the church at Kohat. *d.* Calcutta 1 May 1861. *bur.* St. Paul's cath. Calcutta where is monument, also monuments in church at Kohat and in church of Holy Trinity at Brompton.

GARNETT, JEREMIAH (*son of Wm. Garnett of Otley, Yorkshire, paper manufacturer*). *b.* Wharfside, Otley 2 Oct. 1793; in office of Wheeler's *Manchester Chronicle* about 1814–21; started with J. E. Taylor the *Manchester Guardian* 1821 of which he was printer, business manager and sole reporter, sole editor Jany. 1844 to 1861. *d.* Sale near Manchester 27 Sep. 1870. *Sphinx iii*, 349 (1870).

GARNETT, THOMAS (*brother of the preceding*). *b.* Otley 18 Jany. 1799; manager Low Moor cotton mill Clitheroe, Garnett & Horsfall 1828, afterwards sole proprietor; mayor of Clitheroe 1850; author of *Facts on the natural history of the salmon* 1867; *Essays in natural history and agriculture: edited by R. Garnett, privately printed* 1883. *d.* Low Moor 25 May 1878.

GARNETT, WILLIAM (2 *son of Thomas Garnett of Old Hutton, Kendal, who d.* 1793). *b.* London 13 Nov. 1793; deputy registrar of the land-tax 1819, registrar to 1841; assistant inspector general of stamps and taxes 1835, inspector general 1842; took a leading part in introduction of income tax in Great Britain 1842 and in Ireland 1853; author of *The guide to*

GARNETT, W. *(Con.)*

the property and income tax 1842; *The guide to the income tax laws as applicable to Ireland* 1853. *d.* 4 Argyll road, Kensington 30 Sep. 1873.

GARNETT, WILLIAM JAMES. *b.* Manchester 10 July 1818; ed. at Eton and Ch. Ch. Ox., B.A. 1841, M.A. 1844; barrister I.T. 1845; M.P. for Lancaster 1857–1864. *d.* Quernmore park near Lancaster 15 Sep. 1873.

GARNIER, VERY REV. THOMAS (2 *son of George Garnier of Rookesbury, Hants.*) *b.* 26 Feb. 1776; ed. at Winchester and Worcester coll. Ox.; fellow of All Souls coll. 1796; B.C.L. 1800, D.C.L. 1850; R. of Bishopstoke, Hants. 1807-69; preb. of Winchester, 1830–40; dean of Winchester 9 April 1840 to 1872; F.L.S. 1798. *d.* close of Winchester cathedral 29 June 1873. *Church of England photographic gallery* (1859) *part 7, portrait.*

GARNIER, VERY REV. THOMAS (2 *son of the preceding*). *b.* Bishopstoke rectory 15 April 1809; ed. at Winchester and Worc. coll. Ox.; B.A. 1830, B.C.L. 1833; rowed in first boat race with Cambridge 10 June 1829; fellow of All Souls coll. 1830; V. of Lewknor 1835–40; R. of Longford, Derbyshire 1840–49; chaplain of Lock hospital, London 1849–50; chaplain to Speaker of House of Commons 1849 to death; R. of Trinity ch. Marylebone 1850–59; dean of Ripon 29 Aug. 1859; dean of Lincoln 30 March 1860 to death; author of *Domestic duties, sermons* 1851 and other works. *d.* Deanery, Lincoln 7 Dec. 1863. *Illust. news of the world ix* (1862), *portrait; Some account of T. Garnier, B.C.L.* (1863).

GARRARD, THOMAS *(eld. son of Thomas Garrard of Lambourne, Berkshire*). *b.* 1787; chamberlain of Bristol 1822, city treasurer 1 Jany. 1836 to March 1856; author of *Edward Colston the philanthropist, his life and times, edited by S. G. Tovey, privately printed* 1852. *d.* Springfield place, Bath 18 Dec. 1859. *J. Latimer's Annals of Bristol* (1887), 80, 102, 348.

GARRETT, RHODA *(eld. dau. of Rev. John Fisher Garrett, P.C. of Elton, Derbyshire*). *b.* Eyam, Derbyshire 1841; partner with Agnes Garrett as house decorators in London to death; author of *Electoral disabilities of women* 1872; author with Agnes Garrett of *Suggestions for House decoration in painting woodwork and furniture* 1876. *d.* 2 Gower st. London 22 Nov. 1882 aged 41. *bur.* Rustington, Sussex 25 Nov.

GARRETT, RICHARD *(son of Richard Garrett, agricultural implement maker d. 1837*). *b.* about 1805; entered his father's works at an early age; became head of firm of Garrett and Sons, Leiston Works, Saxmundham, Suffolk 1836,

GARRETT, R. *(Con.)*

where 500 men were employed; manufactured patent steam engines, thrashing machines, corn and seed drilling and manuring machines, etc.; one of the founders of R. Agricultural soc. of England 1837, member of council; retired from active business 1855. *d.* Carlton house, Saxmundham 26 June 1866. *Journal of Agriculture, Sept.* 1866, *portrait; Farmer's Mag. July* 1857 *pp.* 1–2, *portrait.*

GARRETT, RICHARD *(son of the preceding*). *b.* at the Works house, Leiston, 22 July 1829; manager of Leiston works 1850, and partner with his father and brother 1853; invented improved thrashing machines 1859, and portable steam engines; farmer of 2000 acres in West Suffolk; breeder of horses and sheep 1869; an amateur prize fighter; A.I.C.E. 7 March 1854, member 30 Oct. 1877. *d.* 30 July 1884. *Min. of Proc. of Instit. of C.E. lxxviii,* 429–34 (1884).

GARRETT, SIR ROBERT *(eld. son of John Garrett of Ellington near Ramsgate*). *b.* 1794; ed. at Harrow; ensign 2 foot 6 March 1811; lieut. colonel 46 foot 16 May 1845 to 18 Aug. 1856 when placed on h.p.; commanded 4th division before Sebastopol 1855–1856; colonel of 4th West India regt. 1 April 1862, of 43 foot 14 Jany. 1866 to death; K.H. 1836; K.C.B. 2 Jany. 1857; L.G. 10 March 1866; service reward 10 Feb. 1855. *d.* 40 Pall Mall, London 13 June 1869. *Morning Post* 16 June 1869 *p.* 5.

GARROD, ALFRED HENRY *(eld. child of Sir Alfred Baring Garrod*). *b.* Charterhouse sq. London 18 May 1846; ed. at St. John's coll. Cam., scholar 1870, fellow 1873; B.A. 1872; prosector to Zoological Soc. London 1871 to death; professor of comparative anatomy at King's coll. London 1874–79; Fullerian professor of physiology, Royal Institution 5 April 1875 to death; F.R.S. 1 June 1876; author of many papers on zoology. *d.* 10 Harley st. London 17 Sep. 1879. *A. H. Garrod's Scientific Papers, edited by W. A. Forbes* (1881) *pp. ix-xxi, portrait; I.L.N. lxxv,* 424 (1879), *portrait.*

GARSIDE, REV. CHARLES BRIERLEY *(only son of Joseph Garside of Manchester, surgeon, who d. 21 May 1868 aged 78*). *b.* Manchester 6 April 1818; ed. at gr. sch. Manchester and Brasenose coll. Ox., B.A. 1841, M.A. 1844; C. of Tetbury, Gloucs. 1842; C. of Margaret st. chapel, London 1847; received into R.C. church 21 June 1850, ordained priest at Rome 23 Dec. 1854; assistant priest at St. Mary's, Chelsea 1857–61, at St. Aloysius, Somers Town 1861; author of *The impiety of bartering faith for opinion* 1850 and 6 other books. *d.* Posileppo near Naples 21 May 1876.

GARSTIN, EDWIN. Second lieut. Bengal engineers 6 May 1815, col. commandant 5 Dec. 1848 to death; general 1 March 1867. *d.* Bangalore 13 July 1871.

GARTLAND, MOST REV. FRANCIS XAVIER. *b.* Dublin 1805; ordained R.C. priest in Philadelphia 1832; assistant pastor of St. John's ch. Philadelphia 1832, pastor; vicar general of New York 1845; bishop of Savannah 1849 to death, consecrated 10 Sep. 1850. *d.* Savannah 20 Sep. 1854. *R. H. Clarke's Lives of deceased bishops of Catholic church in the United States* (1872) *ii*, 408–14.

GARVEY, MICHAEL ANGELO. Barrister M.T. 17 Nov. 1854; author of *The silent revolution, or future effects of steam* 1852; *A manual of human culture* 1866 and other books. *d.* 24 St. Augustine's road, Camden Town, London 1 Aug. 1877.

GARVOCK, SIR JOHN *(only son of major John Garvock who d. 14 March 1838 aged 67).* *b.* Kennington, Surrey 1817; ensign 10 foot 4 Sep. 1835; captain 31 foot 1843–55 when placed on h.p.; commanded Peshawur division of Bengal army 1863–65; commanded northern district of England 1866–67, southern district 1877 to death; col. of 89 foot 1870, of 10 foot 1874 to death; general 1 Oct. 1877; K.C.B. 5 Aug. 1864, G.C.B. 29 May 1875. *d.* 81 Queen's gate, South Kensington, London 10 Nov. 1878.

GARWOOD, REV. JOHN. Matric. from Magd. hall, Ox. 24 Oct. 1828 aged 23; B.A. 1832, M.A. 1835; P.C. of St. Mary, Spital sq. London 1832–46; clerical sec. to London city mission 1837–76; author of *The million-peopled city, London* 1853. *d.* 17 Cambridge road, Kilburn, London 6 Dec. 1889.

GASCOIGNE, ERNEST FREDERIC. *b.* May 1796; ensign 39 foot 2 May 1811; captain grenadier guards 7 Aug. 1840 to 15 Nov. 1850 when placed on h.p.; colonel of 69 foot 3 April 1858 to death; general 20 Jany. 1867; served in the Peninsula and American war. *d.* 14 Lowndes sq. London 18 July 1876.

GASCOYNE, CHARLES *(son of general Isaac Gascoyne, col. 54 foot).* *b.* 1805; ensign 54 foot 7 Dec. 1820; lieut. col. 94 foot 1839 to 1841, of 6 foot 1841 to 1842 when placed on h.p.; lieut. col. 72 foot 1845 to 1849 when placed on h.p.; col. 89 foot 1864; col. 72 foot 1870 to death; general 10 May 1872. *d.* 4 Chesterfield st. London 10 March 1881 aged 76.

GASELEE, STEPHEN *(eld. son of Sir Stephen Gaselee 1762–1839 judge of court of Common*

GASELEE, S. *(Con.)*

Pleas). *b.* 77 Upper Guilford st. London 1 Sep. 1807; ed. at Winchester and Balliol coll. Ox., B.A. 1828, M.A. 1832; barrister I.T. 16 June 1832; serjeant at law 2 Nov. 1840, treasurer of Serjeants' Inn 1866; contested Portsmouth 1855; M.P. for Portsmouth 1865 –68. *d.* 2 Cambridge sq. Hyde Park, London 20 Oct. 1883.

GASKELL, BENJAMIN *(elder son of Daniell Gaskell of Clifton Hall near Manchester who d 1787).* *b.* 28 Feb. 1781; ed. at Gateacre near Liverpool and Trin. coll. Cam.; M.P. for Maldon 1806, but unseated on petition; M.P. for Maldon 1812–26. *d.* Thornes house near Wakefield 21 Jany. 1856.

GASKELL, DANIEL. *b.* 11 Sep. 1782; M.P. for Wakefield 1832–37. *d.* Lupset hall, Wakefield 20 Dec. 1875.

GASKELL, ELIZABETH CLEGHORN *(dau. of Wm. Stevenson, keeper of records to Treasury in London, who d. 22 April 1829).* *b.* Lindsay row, Chelsea 29 Sep. 1810; ed. at Stratford-on-Avon; author of *Mary Barton, a tale of Manchester life* 2 *vols.* 1848 anon., translated into many languages; *Ruth, a novel* 3 *vols.* 1853; *North and South* 2 *vols.* 1855; *Life of Charlotte Bronte* 2 *vols.* 1857; *Sylvia's Lovers* 3 *vols.* 1863 and 14 other books. *(m.* 30 Aug. 1832 Rev. Wm. Gaskell 1805–84). *d.* Holybourne near Alton, Hants. 12 Nov. 1865. *bur.* Knutsford, Cheshire. *Dict. of Nat. Biog. xxi*, 49–54 (1890).

GASKELL, JAMES MILNES *(only child of Benjamin Gaskell 1781–1856).* *b.* 19 Oct. 1810; ed. at Eton and Ch. Ch. Ox.; M.P. for Wenlock 1832–1868; a lord of the Treasury 1841 to 11 March 1846. *d.* 28 Norfolk st. Park lane, London 5 Feb. 1873.

GASKELL, SAMUEL. Educ. at Manchester and Edinburgh; medical superintendent of Lancashire lunatic asylum 1840 where he carried out the non-restraint system; one of the medical comrs. in lunacy, Jany. 1849 to 1866. *d.* Walton, Surrey 30 March 1886 aged 79.

GASKELL, REV. WILLIAM *(eld. son of Wm. Gaskell of Latchford near Warrington, sail-canvas maker, who d. 15 March 1819).* *b.* Latchford 24 July 1805; ed. at Univ. of Glasgow, M.A. 1824; studied at Manchester college, York 1825–28; pastor of Cross st. chapel, Manchester 3 Aug. 1828 to death; sec. of York college, Manchester 1840–46; professor of English history, literature and composition in it 1846– 53 when it was moved to London; professor of literature in Unitarian home missionary board 1854–84, principal 1876–84; one of

GASKELL, REV. W. *(Con.)*

editors of *Unitarian Herald* 1861–75 ; author of *Temperance Rhymes* 1839 ; *Two lectures on the Lancashire dialect* 1844 and other books. *(m.* 30 Aug. 1832 Elizabeth Cleghorn Stevenson 1810–65). *d.* Plymouth Grove, Manchester 11 June 1884. *bur.* Unitarian Chapel yard, Knutsford 14 June. *Sir T. Baker's Memorials of a dissenting chapel* (1884) *pp.* 54, 153 ; *John Evans's Lancashire authors* (1876) 96–101.

GASKIN, REV. THOMAS. Educ. at St. John's coll. Cam. ; B.A. 1831, M.A. 1834 ; fellow of Jesus coll. about 1831–78 ; F.R.S. 21 March 1839 ; F.R.A.S. ; author of *The Solutions of geometrical problems* 1847 ; *The Solutions of trigonometrical problems* 1847 ; *Geometrical construction of a conic section* 1852. *d.* 7 Pittville lawn, Cheltenham 17 Feb. 1887 aged 76.

GASKOIN, GEORGE. M.R.C.S. 1838 ; L.S.A. 1841 ; house surgeon St. George's hospital 1839 ; practised in London 1838 to death ; K.C.Christ of Portugal ; K.C.Isabella la Catholica of Spain ; translated *The Medical works of Francisco de Villalobos* 1870 ; author of *On Psoriasis or Lepra* 1875 ; *Essay on the range of hereditary tendencies in health and in disease* 1882. *d.* The priory, Caerleon, Monmouth 5 Feb. 1887 aged 70.

GASKOIN, JOHN SAMUEL. *b.* Bagshot Sep. 1790 ; educ. St. George's hospital ; a specialist in skin diseases ; surgeon to George iv. and William iv. ; F.L.S. 1853. *d.* 32 Clarges st. May Fair, London 5 Oct. 1858. *Proc. of Med. and Chir. Soc. iii,* 48 (1861).

GASPEY, THOMAS *(son of Wm. Gaspey, lieut. R.N.) b.* Hoxton, London 31 March 1788 ; parliamentary reporter for *Morning Post* about 1808–24 ; sub-editor of *Courier* about 1824–28 ; edited *Sunday Times* 1828 ; edited evening edition of *Morning Chronicle* (in which 'Sketches by Boz' first appeared 1835) ; published *The mystery or forty years ago, a novel* 1820 anon. ; *The witch finder, or the wisdom of our ancestors* 3 vols. 1824 ; *The life and times of the good Lord Cobham* 2 vols. 1843 and many other books. *d.* Shooters' Hill, Kent 8 Dec. 1871. *Newspaper Press vi,* 40 (1872).

GASPEY, THOMAS WILLIAM *(son of the preceding).* Ph. Doc. of Heidelberg ; author of *Heidelberg and its castle* 1860 ; *The Rhine and the Rhine Lands* 1855. *d.* 4 Ordnance ter. Shooter's hill road, Kent 22 Dec. 1871 aged 53.

GASPEY, WILLIAM *(brother of the preceding). b.* Westminster 20 June 1812 ; author of *Lyrics and Meditations* 1850 and other books in prose and verse. *d.* 17 St. Ann's road, North Brixton 19 July 1888.

GASSIOT, JOHN PETER. *b.* London 2 April 1797 ; midshipman R.N. ; member of firm of Martinez, Gassiot & Co. wine merchants of London and Oporto ; chairman of committee of Kew observatory which he purchased for £10,000 and presented to Royal Soc. 1871 ; discovered dark bands, or stratification of electric discharge 1852 ; author of 44 papers in scientific periodicals ; F.R.S. 9 April 1840, founded the Scientific Relief fund. *d.* St. John's house, Ryde 15 Aug. 1877.

GASTINEAU, HENRY G. Studied at the R.A. ; joined Soc. of Painters in water-colours 1818, associate 1821, member 1823, exhibited 1818–75 ; exhibited 26 landscapes at R.A. and 3 at B.I. 1812–41. *d.* Norfolk lodge, Cold harbour lane, Camberwell 17 Jany. 1876 in 85 year.

GATLEY, ALFRED. *b.* Kerridge near Macclesfield 1816 ; studied at British Museum and R.A. ; sculptor in London 1841–52, at Rome 1852 to death ; exhibited 30 sculptures at R.A. 1841–52 ; exhibited a bas-relief of The overthrow of Pharaoh in the Red Sea, and statues of Echo and Night at International Exhibition, London 1862. *d.* Rome 28 June 1863. *Our sculptor friend, by Miss M. A. Sumner in Aunt Judy's Mag., Oct.* 1885 *pp.* 722–736.

GATHERCOLE, REV. MICHAEL AUGUSTUS. C. of Rilstone-in-Burnsall, Yorkshire 1832–5 ; C. of Cleasby, Yorkshire 1835–37 ; V. of Chatteris, Cambs. 1845–77 ; convicted at York assizes of publishing in *The Watchman* a libel imputing improper practices to the nuns at Darlington and Stockton, sentenced by Court of Queen's Bench to 3 months' imprisonment in the Marshalsea, London 24 Nov. 1838 ; edited *The Church Magazine* 6 vols. 1839–44 ; author of *Letters to a dissenting minister of the Congregational Independent denomination, containing remarks on the principles of that sect, and the author's reasons for leaving it. By L. S. E.* 1833 and 3 other books under initials of L. S. E. *d.* Manor house, Chatteris 11 Dec. 1886 aged 84.

GATTI, CARLO. *b.* Dongio, valley of Blenio, canton Ticino, Switzerland 27 July 1817 ; walked to Paris with 25 francs in his pocket 1829, sold roast chestnuts in the streets and a peculiar dough called goffre, in Paris 1829–47, and in London 1847–49 ; chocolate maker with Battista Bolla at 129 Holborn hill 1849 ; pastry cook at 33, 34 and 65 Great hall, Hungerford market ; built Hungerford hall, Villiers st. Strand 1851, pulled down for Charing Cross station 1862 ; an ice merchant at Caledonian road, King's Cross 1857 to death, imported ice from Norway. *d.* Dongio 6 Sep.

1878. *Penny pictorial news* 21 Sep. 1878 *pp.* 1, 3, *portrait; Graphic xviii,* 341 (1878), *portrait; Marcus Fall's London Town* (1880) *i,* 244–52.

GATTY, MARGARET *(youngest dau. of Rev. Alexander John Scott). b.* Burnham rectory, Essex 3 June 1809; edited *Aunt Judy's Mag.,* May 1866 to death; author of *Parables from nature* 5 vols. 1855–71; *Legendary tales* 1858; *Aunt Judy's Tales* 1859 and about 20 other books. *(m.* 8 July 1839 Alfred Gatty, D.D., V. of Ecclesfield, Yorkshire). *d.* Ecclesfield vicarage 4 Oct 1873. *Parables from nature* (1885) *ix-xxi; A. Gatty's A life at one living* (1884) 164–7; *I.L.N.* 18 *Oct.* 1873 *pp.* 369, 370, *portrait.*

GAUNTLETT, HENRY JOHN *(eld. son of Rev. Henry Gauntlett 1762–1833 V. of Olney, Bucks.) b.* Wellington, Salop 9 July 1805; organist of Olney ch. 1815–25, of St. Olaves, Southwark 1827–46; solicitor in London 1831–46; Mus. Doc. Canterbury 1842 being first instance of such a degree since Reformation; organist at Union chapel, Islington 1853–61, at All Saints Notting hill 1861–63, at St. Bartholomew's, Smithfield 1872 to death; edited *Musical world;* started *The Church Musician* 1850, edited it 1850–51; patented application of electricity to the organ 1852; published *Comprehensive tune books* 2 vols. 1851 and 65 other musical works. *d.* 15 St. Mary Abbott's terrace, Kensington 21 Feb. 1876. *I.L.N. lxviii,* 253, 254 (1876), *portrait.*

GAVIN, GEORGE O'HALLORAN. *b.* Limerick 1810; M.P. for Limerick 1858–1874. *d.* Kilfreacon court, Limerick 23 Oct. 1880.

GAVIN, HECTOR. L.R.C.S. Edin. 1835, F.R.C.S. 1838; M.D. Edin. 1836; M.R.C.S. Eng. 1843; Superintending inspector of General board of health 1851–53; phys. general to Post Office, London 1853; lecturer on forensic medicine at Charing Cross hospital; editor of *Journal of Public Health;* author of *On feigned and fictitious diseases of soldiers* 1843 and 4 other books; accidentally shot by his brother Wm. Gavin in his hut at Balaklava in the Crimea 21 April 1855 aged 39; Margaret his widow granted civil list pension of £50 15 Nov. 1856.

GAVIN, ROBERT (2 *son of Peter Gavin of Leith, merchant). b.* Leith 1827; A.R.S.A. 1854, R.S.A. 10 Feb. 1879; painted numerous Moorish pictures at Tangier; exhibited 5 pictures at the R.A. 1855–71. *d.* Cherry Bank, Newhaven near Edinburgh 6 Oct. 1883. *S. Armytage's Beautiful pictures by British artists pp.* 63–4.

GAWEN, JOHN CHARLES GAWEN ROBERTS. *b.* 25 Aug. 1787; captain R.N. 13 June 1815; retired admiral 4 Oct. 1862. *d.* Park st. Grosvenor square, London 21 Nov. 1874.

GAWLER, GEORGE *(son of Samuel Gawler, captain 73 foot, who d.* 1799 *aged* 25*). b.* 1796; ed. at Great Marlow; ensign 52 foot 4 Oct. 1810, major 1831–34 when placed on h.p.; led the forlorn hope at storming of Badajoz 6 April 1812; governor of South Australia 12 Oct. 1838 to 13 May 1841 when recalled; col. 9 Nov. 1846; K.H. 1837. *d.* Southsea 8 May 1869.

GAY, JOHN. *b.* Wellington, Somerset 1813; M.R.C.S. 1834; surgeon to Royal free hospital, London 1836–54; surgeon of Great Northern hospital 1856 to death; author of *On femoral rupture, its anatomy, pathology and surgery* 1848; *A memoir on indolent ulcers and their surgical treatment* 1855; *On varicose disease of the lower extremities* 1868; *On hœmorrhoidal disorders* 1882. *d.* 51 Belsize park, Hampstead 15 Sep. 1885. *Medical Circular ii,* 249–51 (1853), *portrait; Barker's Photographs of medical men ii,* 43 (1868), *portrait.*

GAYER, ARTHUR EDWARD *(eld. son of Edward Echlin Gayer, major 67 foot). b.* near Newcastle under Lyne 6 July 1801; ed. at Durham and Bath gr. schools and Trin. coll. Dublin, B.A. 1823, LL.B. and LL.D. 1830; called to Irish bar 1827; Q.C. 2 Nov. 1844; chancellor and vicar general of diocese of Ossory 1848, of Meath Jany. 1851, of Cashel June 1851; contested Univ. of Dublin, March 1857; an ecclesiastical comr. for Ireland 8 June 1859 to July 1869; edited *The Catholic Layman* 1851–57, reprinted in 8 vols. Dublin 1862; author of several pamphlets defending established church of Ireland, and of *Papal infallibility and supremacy tried by ecclesiastical history, scripture and reason* 1877. *d.* Abbotsleigh, Upper Norwood, Surrey 12 Jany. 1877. *A. E. Gayer's Memoirs of family of Gayer, privately printed* (1870).

GEACH, CHARLES *(son of George Geach of St. Austell, Cornwall). b.* St. Austell 1808; clerk in Bank of England, Birmingham 1826–36; manager of Birmingham and Midland bank 1836; purchased Park Gate iron manufacturing co. 1840 and Patent Shaft and Axle-tree co. 1840; made a fortune in railroad iron 1844–5; mayor of Birmingham 1847; M.P. for Coventry 8 April 1851 to death. *d.* 9 Park st. Westminster 1 Nov. 1854. *E. Edwards's Personal recollections of Birmingham* (1877) 125–31; *Min. of proc. of Instit. of C.E. xiv,* 148–51 (1855); *I.L.N. xxi,* 377, 378 (1852), *portrait.*

GEARY, STEPHEN. Architect and civil engineer at Hamilton place, New road, London; erected an octagonal structure with a colossal statue of George iv. on the top, in the centre of the 6 roads uniting at Battle Bridge 1831 when the name was changed to King's Cross; took out patents for artificial fuel, paving streets, water supply, obtaining motive power, and 3 other patents 1838–47; designed the first gin palace in London about 1830; founded the London Cemetery Co. 1838 for which he laid out Highgate cemetery, opened 20 May 1839. *d.* 19 Euston place, London 28 Aug. 1854 in 75 year. *A. W. Pugin's Contrasts (1841), plate xiv.*

GEDDES, JOHN. Ensign 27 foot 22 Dec. 1804, major 1825 to 1831 when placed on h.p.; col. 46 foot 13 Feb. 1860, col. 27 foot 24 April 1860 to death; L.G. 23 March 1861. *d.* 15 Salisbury road, Newington, Edinburgh 28 April 1869.

GEDEN, REV. JOHN DURY *(son of Rev. John Geden, Wesleyan minister).* *b.* Hastings 5 May 1822; assistant tutor of Richmond coll. Surrey 1847–51; tutor in sacred and classical languages at theological coll. Didsbury, Lancs. 1856–83; joint-editor of *London Quarterly Review* 1857; elected into the legal hundred 1868; member of Old Testament revision company 1870; hon. D.D. St. Andrews 1885; author of *Didsbury sermons in the Wesleyan college chapel* 1878. *d.* Didsbury 9 March 1886.

GEDGE, REV. SYDNEY *(youngest son of Peter Gedge of Bury St. Edmunds).* *b.* 1802; educ. Bury St. Edmunds' gram. sch. and St. Catharine's coll. Camb.; fellow 1825–27; B.A. 1824, M.A. 1827; C. of North Runcton, Norfolk 1827–35; second master king Edward's sch. Birmingham 1835–59; V. of All Saints, Northampton 1859–77; rural dean Northampton 1871–77; preacher and speaker for Ch. missionary soc. and hon. life governor; author of 4 single sermons 1856–69. *d.* Cromer 29 Aug. 1883, five of his sons became clergymen. *The Guardian 5 Sept. 1883 p. 1300.*

GEERAN or GUERIN, THOMAS. Enlisted in 71 regt. 3 March 1813, deserted 10 April; worked as a sawyer; settled at Brighton; professed to have been a son of Michael Geeran, farmer, born at Scariff co. Clare 14 May 1766 and to have served in 71 regt. abroad 1796–1819; made a living by relating his military adventures and dilating on his great age. *d.* infirmary of Brighton union 28 Oct. 1871 claiming to be 105. *Longevity, with Life of Thomas Geeran (1871), portrait; Thom's Human Longevity (1873) pp. 12, 131–54.*

GELDART, REV. EDMUND MARTIN *(2 son of Thomas Geldart of Thorpe, Norwich and of Hannah Ransome Geldart who was a writer of children's book and d. 1861).* *b.* Norwich 20 Jany. 1844; ed. at Ball. coll. Oxf., scholar 1863–67; B.A. 1867, M.A. 1873; assist. master Manchester gram. sch. 1867 and 1869–71; a teacher at Athens 1867–69; C. of All Saints, Manchester 1869–71; C. of St. George's ch. Everton 1871; minister of Hope st. unitarian chapel, Liverpool 1873–77; unitarian minister Croydon 1877–85; author of *Modern Greek in relation to ancient* 1870; *Faith and Freedom 14 sermons* 1881 and other works; left Newhaven on 10 April 1885 for Paris, supposed to have been lost during passage to Dieppe. *A son of Belial, autobiographical sketches by Nitram Tradleg i.e. M. Geldart (1883); Echoes of Truth ed. Mrs. Geldart (1886) with portrait.*

GELDART, REV. JAMES WILLIAM *(eld. son of Rev. James Geldart, R. of Kirk Deighton, Yorks. who d. 12 Nov. 1839 aged 79).* *b.* Swinnow hall, Wetherby 15 Feb. 1785; ed. at Beverley gr. sch. and Trin. hall, Cam., LL.B. 1806, LL.D. 1814; fell. of St. Catherine's hall 1808–9; fell. and tutor of Trin. hall 1809–20; Regius professor of civil law at Cam. 11 Dec. 1813 to 1847; R. of Kirk Deighton 1840 to death; author of a new ed. of *S. Halifax's Analysis of the civil law* 1836. *d.* Kirk Deighton rectory 16 Feb. 1876.

GELDART, THOMAS CHARLES. Barrister L.I. 9 May 1823; master of Trinity hall, Cam. 1852 to death; LL.D. by royal mandate 4 Jany. 1853; author with H. F. Maddock of *Reports of cases in court of vice-chancellor* 1829. *d.* the Master's lodge, Trinity hall, Cambridge 17 Sep. 1877 aged 80.

GELL, JOHN SHERBROOKE. Entered Bombay army 11 June 1839; commanded Bombay district 28 Oct. 1872 to 11 June 1877; M.G. 1 Oct. 1877. *d.* Downderry, Cornwall 16 July 1878.

GENDALL, JOHN. *b.* Exeter 1790; went to London with introduction to Sir John Soane; manager for Rudolph Ackermann, Strand, London, print seller; went on sketching tour in Normandy, gave illustrated description of tour at Exeter 6 Nov. 1862, his sketches published in *Picturesque tour of the Seine* 1821; exhibited 25 pictures at R.A. and 1 at B.I. 1818–63; his works chiefly views in Devonshire; settled at Exeter as an artist 1839. *d.* Cathedral yard, Exeter 1 March 1865 aged 75. *G. Pycroft's Art in Devonshire (1883) 50–54.*

GEAREY, SIR WILLIAM RICHARD POWLETT, 3 Baronet. *b.* Oxon-Heath, Tunbridge 13 Nov. 1810; succeeded his father 6 Aug. 1825; contested West Kent, Dec. 1832, M.P. for West Kent, Jany. 1835 to Feb. 1838. *d.* Oxon-Heath 19 Dec. 1877.

GEDDES, JAMES LORAINE. *b.* Edinburgh 19 March 1827; served in Bengal artillery about 1846–55; settled at Vinton, Benton co. U.S.A. 1857; private in 8th Iowa regiment Aug. 1861, brigadier general 5 June 1865; provost marshal of Memphis; captured Spanish fort during Mobile campaign; professor of military tactics at Iowa college of agriculture; wrote *The soldier's battle prayer, The stars and stripes,* and several other popular war-songs. *d.* Ames, Story co. Iowa 21 Feb. 1887.

GENESTE, REV. MAXIMILIAN (*4 son of Lewis Geneste of Kirk Bradden, Isle of Man*). Matric. from Queen's coll. Ox. 20 May 1820 aged 20; B.A. 1824, M.A. 1827; P.C. of Holy Trinity, West Cowes, Isle of Wight 1832 to death; author of *The parallel histories of Judah and Israel* 2 vols. 1843 and other books; translated Krümmacher's *Glance into the Kingdom of grace* 1837 and other books. *d.* Trafalgar house, Cowes 27 July 1860.

GEOGHEGAN, ARTHUR GERALD. Author of *The Monks of Kilcrea, By * * ** 1853, 3 ed. 1861 and other books; contributed to *The Nation* many years. *d.* 27 Addison road, London 29 Nov. 1889 aged nearly 80.

GEOGHEGAN, JOSEPH BRYAN. *b.* Oldfield road, Salford, Manchester 13 April 1815; manager of Victoria music hall, Bolton 1864 to death; proprietor of Star theatre, Hanley; author of *John Barleycorn* 1860; *The men of merry merry England* 1858; *Lancashire Witches,* and upwards of 200 other favourite songs. *d.* Bolton 21 Jany. 1889.

GEOGHEGAN, MOST REV. PATRICK BONAVENTURE. *b.* Dublin 1811; joined Franciscan order at Coimbra; the first resident R.C. priest at Port Phillip, New Holland 1839; vicar general of Melbourne 1848; bishop of Adelaide 1859 to death; consecrated 8 Sep. 1859. *d.* Kingston, Dublin 5 May 1865.

GEORGE, FREDERICK DARLEY. Cornet 11 light dragoons 1825; major 22 foot 1849–53 when placed on h.p.; D.A.G. Windward and Leeward Islands 1853–58; col. 76 foot 28 April 1875 to death; general 1 Oct. 1877; C.B. 4 July 1843. *d.* 67 Brunswick place, Brighton 2 June 1888 aged 80.

GEORGE, JOHN (*eld. son of John George of Dublin, merchant, who d. 1837*). *b.* Dublin 18 Nov. 1804; ed. at Frascati school and Trin. coll. Dublin; called to bar at King's Inns, Dublin 1826, bencher 1859; barrister G.I. 16 May 1827; Q.C. 2 Nov. 1844; M.P. for co. Wexford 1852–57 and 1859–66; solicitor general for Ireland, Feb. to July 1859; judge of court of Queen's Bench, Ireland, Nov. 1866 to death; P.C. Ireland 1866. *d.* 45 Fitzwilliam sq. Dublin 15 Dec. 1871.

GERARD, ROBERT TOLVER, 1 Baron. *b.* Sutton, Lancs. 12 May 1808; lieut. col. Lancashire yeomanry cavalry 1855, col. 1878 to death; A.D.C. to the Queen 23 March 1867 to death; sheriff of Lancs. 1859; created Baron Gerard of Bryn, Lancs. 18 Jany. 1876. *d.* 16 South st. Park lane, London 15 March 1887. *I.L.N.* lxviii, 61, 62 (1876), *portrait.*

GETTY, SAMUEL GIBSON. *b.* 30 Nov. 1817; M.P. for Belfast 1860–68. *d.* 60 Redcliffe gardens, London 15 Dec. 1877.

GIBB, ALEXANDER (*only son of John Gibb, C.E., who introduced use of Aberdeen granite in construction of public works*). *b.* Larbert, Stirlingshire 21 Sep. 1804; partner with his father at Aberdeen; built Victoria bridge over the Wear 1836, remarkable for its height and large spans; planned and carried out railway lines in North of Scotland; engineer of Great North of Scotland railway 1845 to death; lessee of Rubislaw quarries near Aberdeen; M.I.C.E. 9 Feb. 1830. *d.* Willowbank, Aberdeen 8 Aug. 1867. *Min. of proc. of Instit. of C.E.* xxvii, 587–89 (1868).

GIBB, SIR GEORGE DUNCAN, 4 Baronet (*eld. son of Thomas Gibb*). *b.* Montreal 25 Dec. 1821; educ. McGill coll., M.D. 1846; L.R.C.S. Ireland 1848; M.R.C.P. Lond. 1859; in practice at Montreal 1849–53; one of originators of St. Lawrence sch. of medicine and professor there; gave his collection of 1500 specimens to Natural History soc., Montreal 1853; founded Pathological soc., Montreal, president 1853; settled in London 1853; assist. physician Westminster hospital; assumed a disputed baronetage May 1867; discovered crystal of diabetic sugar 1854; the first to remove tumours from the larynx by the mouth 1864; author of *A treatise on whooping cough* 1854; *On diseases of throat and windpipe* 1860; *Life of Robert Gib* 2 vols. 1874 and 41 other works. *d.* 1 Bryanston st. Portman sq. London 16 Feb. 1876. *N. and Q.* 3 Ser. x 311, xii 274, 362, 421, 536 (1866–67), 4 Ser. i 37 (1868); *Morgan's Bibliotheca Canadensis* (1867) *pp.* 140–50.

GIBBES, SIR GEORGE SMITH (*son of Rev. George Gibbes, R. of Woodborough, Wilts.*) *b.* 1771; Commoner of Ex. coll. Ox.; B.A. 1792, M.A. 1795, M.B. 1796, M.D. 1799; fellow of Magd. coll. Ox.; candidate of coll. of physicians 1803, fellow 1804, Harveian orator 1817; physician to Bath general hospital 1804; physician extraord. to Queen Charlotte 1819; knighted by George iv. at Carlton house 10 May 1820; removed to Cheltenham about 1835, afterwards to Sidmouth; F.L.S. 21 May 1793; F.R.S. 18 Feb. 1796; author of *A treatise on the Bath waters* 1800 and other books. *d.* Sidmouth 23 June 1851. *bur.* family vault at Woodborough. *W. Munk's Roll* (1878) *iii*, 13.

GIBBONS, DAVID OCTAVIUS (*eld. child of Edward Augustus Gibbons, who d.* 20 *Aug.* 1834). *b.* 28 Oct. 1811; special pleader 1834; author of *A manual of the law of fixtures* 1836; *A treatise on the law of dilapidations and nuisances* 1838, 2 *ed.* 1849 and other books. *d.* 30 St. George's sq. London 23 Oct. 1876.

GIBBONS, SIR SILLS JOHN, 1 Baronet (*son of Richard Gibbons of Sittingbourne, Kent*). *b.* Chatham 1809; hop merchant in London; alderman for Castle Baynard ward 1862-75, sheriff 1865-6, lord mayor 1871-2; created baronet 11 March 1872. *d.* Hastings 11 Jany. 1876. *I.L.N. lix,* 457, 458 (1871), *portrait.*

GIBBS, SIR BENJAMIN THOMAS BRANDRETH (*youngest son of Thomas Gibbs of Ampthill, Beds.*) *b.* London 1821; steward of yard of R. Agricultural soc. 1839-42, hon. director 1843-74, vice president 1871-85; hon. sec. of Smithfield club 1843-85, presented with a silver candelabra 12 Dec. 1855; associated with agricultural sections of national exhibitions in London 1851 and 1862, in Paris 1855, 1867 and 1878, in Vienna 1873, in Philadelphia 1875; commander of order of Francis Joseph 1873; officer of Legion of honour 1878; knighted for his agricultural services, first person so rewarded, by the Queen at Windsor 27 Nov. 1878; sec. of Fisheries exhibition, London 1883; author of *The Smithfield club, a condensed history* 1857. *d.* Mossley house, Sinclair road, West Kensington park 2 June 1885. *Journ. of Royal Agric. Soc. xxi,* 611-20 (1885), *portrait; The Biograph, March* 1882 *pp.* 259-61; *I.L.N. xxvii,* 725-26 (1855), *portrait.*

GIBBS, JAMES (*son of Michael Gibbs of Walbrook, London, merchant*). *b.* 25 July 1825; *ed.* at Merchant Taylors' and Haileybury; entered Bombay civil service 1846; barrister I.T. 6 June 1864; judge of high court Bombay, Feb. 1866 to 1879; vice chancellor of Univ.

GIBBS, J. (*Con.*)
of Bombay 1870-79; mem. of governor general's council 10 May 1880 to 1885, pres. 1884; C.S.I. 1878; C.I.E. 1878. *d.* 58 Courtfield gardens, South Kensington, London 30 Oct. 1886.

GIBBS, JOSEPH. *b.* Staffordshire 1798; established extensive sawing and cutting works at Crayford Mills, Kent and London; invented "Gibbs' elbow joint" chiefly used for construction of inlaid floors; erected much machinery here and in Holland for manufacturing purposes and lifting water; M.I.C.E. 6 April 1852; author of *Considerations relative to sewage of London* 1849; *Cotton cultivation in its various details* 1862. *d.* 11 Feb. 1864. *Min. of proc. of Instit. of C.E. xxiv,* 528-31 (1865).

GIBBS, MATILDA BLANCHE (*youngest dau. of Sir Thomas Crawley-Boevey, 3 Baronet* 1769-1847). Founded St. Michael and All Angels' Home for Consumptives at Axbridge 1878, St. Michael's Home at Cheddar and St. John's Convalescent Home at Tyntesfield, all in Somerset. (*m.* 1 Aug. 1839 Wm. Gibbs 1790-1875). *d.* Tyntesfield 22 Sep. 1887 aged 69, personalty declared at £483,683 7s. 4d.

GIBBS, MRS. (*dau. of Mr. Graddon*). *b.* Taunton 1804; first sang at Vauxhall 1821, in Dublin 1823; first appeared in London at Drury Lane Oct. 1824 as Susanna in the *Marriage of Figaro;* second only to Miss Stephens in ballad singing and to Miss Paton in bravura singing; sang in New Orleans, Dec. 1835, in New York Nov. 1836, returned to England; reappeared in New York 1855 with an entertainment of song and anecdote entitled *The Lakes of Killarney.* (*m.* about 1827 Alexander Gibbs of firm of Graddon and Gibbs, pianoforte makers); date of death not known. *J. N. Ireland's Records of New York stage ii,* 180-1 (1867); *Cumberland's Minor Theatre vol. iii, portrait; Le Bal Costumé, polka composed by Mrs. Gibbs* (1854), *portrait.*

GIBBS, WILLIAM (2 *son of Antony Gibbs of Exeter, merchant* 1756-1815). *b.* 22 May 1790; partner with his elder brother as merchants in Cadiz and London, head of the firm on his brother's death 21 Aug. 1842; held for some years monoply of the guano islands; built the chapel at Keble college, Oxford, dedicated 25 April 1876. *d.* Tyntesfield near Bristol 3 April 1875, personalty sworn under £800,000, 2 Oct. 1875.

GIBSON, ALEXANDER. *b.* Laurencekirk, Kincardineshire 24 Oct. 1800; M.D. Edin.; assistant surgeon H.E.I.C. service 1825; passed

GIBSON, A. *(Con.)*

in Hindustani, Mahrati and Gujerati; superintendent of botanical garden at Dapuri 1838; conservator of forests in Bombay 1847–60; F.L.S. 19 April 1853;· author of *Forest Reports Bombay* 1849–55; *Bombay Flora* 1861; *A handbook to forests of Bombay* 1863. *d.* 16 Jany. 1867. *Proc. Linnean Soc.* (1866–67) *p.* 33.

GIBSON, ALEXANDER CRAIG. *b.* Harrington, Cumberland 17 March 1813; F.S.A.; L.M. Edin.; M.R.C.S. Eng. 1846; L.S.A. 1855; in practice at Branthwaite and Ullock 1841–43, at Coniston 1843–49, at Hawkshead 1849–57, at Bebington, Cheshire 1857–72; contributed to *Kendal Mercury, Tait's Mag.*, and to *Trans. of Historic Soc. of Lancashire and Cheshire;* author of *The old man, or ravings and ramblings round Coniston, Kendal* 1849; *The Folk-speech of Cumberland, stories and rhymes in dialect of West Border counties, Carlisle* 1869; wrote *The Lockerbie Lycke*, a ballad in Annandale dialect. *d.* Bebington 12 June 1874.

GIBSON, DAVID COOKE. *b.* Edinburgh 4 March 1827; artist in Edin. 1844–52, in London 1852 to death; exhibited 5 domestic pictures at the R.A. 1855–57; wrote *Angelo and Zelica* and other poems. *d.* London 5 Oct. 1856. *Struggles of a young artist, being a memoir of D. C. Gibson (anon. by W. Macduff)* 1858, *portrait.*

GIBSON, GEORGE STACEY *(only son of Wyatt George Gibson of Saffron Walden, Essex).* *b.* Saffron Walden 20 July 1818; senior partner in firm of Gibson, Tuke and Gibson, bankers, Saffron Walden; clerk of yearly meeting of Soc. of Friends; added six species to the British flora, described in the *Phytologist* 1842–51; F.L.S. 1847; author of *The Flora of Essex* 1862. *d.* Temperance hotel, 12 Bishopsgate st. without, London 5 April 1883. *Journal of Botany* 1883, *pp.* 161–65, *2 portraits.*

GIBSON, REV. JAMES. *b.* Crieff, Perthshire 31 Jany. 1799; educ. Glasgow univ.; licensed presbyterian minister 1820; travelled with Capt. Elliot in Portugal 1825; assistant in the College parish, Glasgow; built a ch. at Kingston, Glasgow, and was minister 1839–43; joined the Free church and had a chapel built for him at Kingston 1843; professor of systematic theology in Free ch. coll. Glasgow 1856; edited *Church of Scotland Mag.* 1834–37, and *Scottish Protestant vols. i, ii,* 1852; author of *Marriage affinity question* 1854; *The public worship of God* 1869 and other books. *d.* Glasgow 2 Nov. 1871. *Wylie's Disruption Worthies* (1876) 261–64, *portrait.*

GIBSON, JAMES. Called to bar in Ireland 1828; law adviser to general assembly of Irish presbyterian church; a comr. of national education in Ireland 1848 to death; chairman of Queen's co.; chairman of co. Donegal to 1879; M.P. for Belfast, Aug. 1837 to March 1838 when unseated on petition; Q.C. 30 Jany. 1869. *d.* 35 Mountjoy sq. Dublin 5 Feb. 1880.

GIBSON, SIR JAMES BROWN. *b.* 1805; ed. at Univ. of Edin., M.D. 1826; M.R.C.S. Eng. 1826; hospital assistant in the army 14 Dec. 1826, surgeon 2 July 1841; served in Crimean war; body surgeon to Duke of Cambridge 1855; director general of medical department 7 March 1860 to 30 March 1867 when placed on h.p.; hon. physician to the Queen 16 Aug. 1859 to death; C.B. 2 Jany. 1857, K.C.B. 28 March 1865. *d.* Rome 25 Feb. 1868.

GIBSON, JAMES YOUNG (4 *son of William Gibson of Edinburgh, merchant).* *b.* Edinburgh 19 Feb. 1826; educ. Edin. univ. and at divinity hall of United Presbyterian ch. 1847–52, licensed preacher 1853, at Melrose 1853–59; travelled in Egypt and Palestine 1865 and in Spain 1871–72; settled in London 1872, at Long Ditton near Surbiton 1884; corrected proofs of J. Duffield's *Don Quixote* 1881; translator and editor of *Journey to Parnassus by Miguel de Cervantes* 1883; *Numantia, a tragedy by Miguel de Cervantes* 1885. *d.* Granville hotel, Ramsgate 2 Oct. 1886. *bur.* Dean cemetery, Edin. *The Cid by J. Y. Gibson, ed. M. D. Gibson, memoir by Agnes Smith* 1887 *pp. xxiii-lv, portrait; Illust. sp. and dr. news xxvi,* 122 (1886).

GIBSON, JANE (2 *dau. of John Gibson of Oakbank near Glasgow).* *b.* Oakbank 22 May 1785; resided for many years in Edinburgh with Mrs. Grant of Laggan; founded the John Gibson bursaries in Glasgow Univ. at cost of £1000 in 1877. *d.* 9 Blythswood sq. Glasgow 25 Nov. 1887 aged 102 years and 6 months. *Glasgow Herald* 26 *Nov.* 1887 *p.* 4.

GIBSON, JOHN. *b.* Newcastle 1794; ornamental and house painter and enameller in glass; painted church windows in Newcastle and neighbourhood; formed a gallery of paintings; sheriff of Newcastle 1853–4. *d.* the Leazes ter. Newcastle 25 Nov. 1854. *Mackenzie's Hist. of Newcastle* (1827) *pp.* 345, 761.

GIBSON, JOHN *(son of a market gardener).* *b.* Gyffin near Conway 19 June 1790; removed to Liverpool 1799; sent to Royal Academy Psyche drawn by Zephyrs 1816; came to London 1817; arrived in Rome 20 Oct. 1817 staid there to 1844 where he studied under

GIBSON, J. *(Con.)*

Canova and Thorwalsden ; A.R.A. 1833, R.A. 1838 ; exhibited 33 works at R.A. 1816–64 ; his better known works are Mars and Cupid 1819, Hylas and the Nymphs 1826, Cupid tormenting the soul 1839, The Queen 1846, The tinted Venus 1854, Christ blessing little children 1862 ; revived the use of colour in statuary. *d.* Rome 27 Jany. 1866. *bur.* English cemetery, left £32,000 and the contents of his studio to the Royal Academy. *Lady Eastlake's Life of John Gibson* (1870), *portrait ; W. B. Scott's British school of sculpture* (1871) 109–22 ; *Sandby's History of Royal Academy ii,* 188–92 (1862) ; *Illust. news of the world iii* (1859), *portrait.*

NOTE.—The King of Bavaria placed his statue on the exterior of the Glyptothek at Munich and in the hall of the Walhalla near Ratisbon. There is a fine collection of about 20 casts from his best grouped statues at the Crystal Palace.

GIBSON, JOHN *(son of George Gibson of Leith, merchant).* *b.* Leith 15 Jany. 1796 ; ed. at high school and Univ. of Edin. ; writer to the Signet 1819 ; agent for the Buccleuch estates 1821 to death ; legal adviser to Sir Walter Scott 1821–32 ; deputy keeper of the privy seal 1850 ; treasurer to Society of writers to the signet ; published *Reminiscences of Sir Walter Scott* 1871. *d.* 29 Greenhill gardens, Edinburgh 14 Sep. 1877. *A Mackie's Review of the conduct of J. Gibson* (1823).

GIBSON, JOHN THOMAS. Entered Madras army 1800 ; M.G. 23 Nov. 1841; colonel 1 European regiment 27 Feb. 1842 to death. *d.* Kotagherry, Madras 30 June 1851.

GIBSON, SOLOMON *(younger brother of John Gibson, R.A.* 1790–1866). Passed his life in Liverpool ; modelled a small figure of Mercury when aged 16 which is his best work ; exhibited 2 sculptures at R.A. 1816–22 ; a Greek, Latin and Welsh scholar ; wrote many papers on ancient Welsh literature ; lived chiefly on the bounty of his brother ; fell down dead entering his hotel in Paris 29 Jany. 1866.

GIBSON, THOMAS MILNER *(son of Thomas Milner Gibson, major 37 foot, d.* 1807). *b.* Port of Spain, Trinidad 3 Sep. 1806 ; educ. Charterhouse 1819 and Trin. coll. Camb., B.A. 1830 ; M.P. Ipswich 1837–39 ; M.P. Manchester 1841–57 ; M.P. Ashton-under-Lyne 1857–68 ; a free trader 1837 and a prominent orator of Anti-corn law league ; V.P. of board of trade 1846–48 ; P.C. 8 July 1846 ; moved vote of censure on Palmerston for his law of conspiracy bill which caused resignation of ministry 19 Feb. 1858 ; presi-

GIBSON, T. M. *(Con.)*

dent of poor law board 1859 ; president of board of trade 1859–66 ; assumed additional surname of Milner 7 Feb. 1839 ; president of Assoc. for repeal of taxes on knowledge 1850, on repeal received testimonial 1 Oct. 1861 ; amateur yachtsman, navigating his own vessel, the last person who cruised in the Mediterranean with a pass from the dey of Algiers 1830. *(m.* 23 Feb. 1832 Susanna Arethusa only child of Rev. Sir T. G. Cullum, she was a leader in society and an advocate of mesmerism and spiritualism, *d.* Paris 23 Feb. 1885 aged 71). *d.* on board his yacht Resolute at Algiers 25 Feb. 1884. *bur.* Theberton churchyard 13 March. *G. H. Francis's Orators of the age* (1847) 294–300 ; *J. Evans's Lancashire authors* (1850) 101–5 ; *I.L.N.* 31 *Dec.* 1842 *p.* 541, *portrait,* 8 *March* 1884 *pp.* 217, 227, *portrait.*

GIBSON, REV. WILLIAM *(son of James Gibson of Ballymena, co. Antrim, merchant).* *b.* Ballymena 8 May 1808 ; Presbyterian minister of First Ballybay, co. Monaghan 1834 ; colleague of Rev. S. Hannay in Rosemary st. ch. Belfast 1840 ; professor of christian ethics in the assembly's coll. Belfast 1847 ; moderator of the general assembly 1859 ; author of *The position of the church of Ireland and the duty of presbyterians in reference to it* 1835 ; *The year of grace, a history of the Ulster revival of* 1859, *Edin.* 1860 ; chief founder of the *Banner of Ulster* newspaper 1842. *d.* Dublin 8 June 1867.

GIBSON, WILLIAM SIDNEY. *b.* Parson's Green, Fulham, Middlesex 1814 ; barrister L.I. 29 Jany. 1845 ; registrar of Newcastle upon Tyne district court of bankruptcy 1843 to 1870 when granted sum of £1000 on abolition of the court ; M.A. Durham 1857 ; F.S.A. 24 Feb. 1842 ; F.G.S. ; author of *The history of the monastery founded at Tynemouth* 2 *vols.* 1846–7 ; *Lord Lyndhurst In memoriam* 1865, *new ed.* 1869 and 11 other books. *d.* Grosvenor hotel, London 3 Jany. 1871. *bur.* in disused burial ground of the Old Priory, Tynemouth. *Colburn's New monthly mag. April* 1871 *p.* 244.

GIBSONE, JOHN CHARLES HOPE *(son of general D. A. Gibsone).* *b.* 21 May 1810 ; cornet 7 dragoon guards 1830, lieut. col. 1847–49 ; lieut. col. 17 light dragoons 1860–62 ; col. of 8 hussars 10 Dec. 1868, of 17 lancers 22 Sep. 1875 to death ; general 1 Oct. 1877. *d.* Redcross lodge, Leamington 18 July 1884.

GIFFARD, SIR GEORGE MARKHAM (4 *son of the succeeding).* *b.* Portsmouth dockyard 4 Nov. 1813 ; ed. at Winchester and New coll. Ox., fellow 1832 ; B.C.L. 1841 ; barrister L.I. 20 Nov. 1840 ; practised in court of chancery ;

GIFFARD, SIR G. M. *(Con.)*

Q.C. Jany. 1859, bencher of his inn 1859; vice chancellor March 1868; knighted at Windsor Castle 14 May 1868; a lord justice of appeal 1 Jany. 1869 to death; P.C. 4 Feb. 1869. *d.* 4 Princes gardens, Hyde park, London 13 July 1870. *Foss's Biographia Juridica* (1870) 299, 792; *I.L.N. lii,* 320 (1868), *portrait, lvii,* 107, 259 (1870).

GIFFARD, JOHN. *b.* 1766; entered navy 25 April 1780; captain 19 Oct. 1796; lieut. governor of royal naval college at Portsmouth 23 March 1807 to 12 Aug. 1819; admiral 23 Nov. 1841. *d.* Southampton 25 Sep. 1855.

GIFFARD, JOHN WALTER DE LONGUEVILLE *(eld. son of the succeeding). b.* 1817; ed. at Merton coll. Ox., B.A. and M.A. 1843; barrister I.T. 19 Nov. 1843; reported in V.C. Stuart's court 1852–70; judge of county courts, circuit 12 (West Riding of Yorkshire), 15 March 1875, of circuit 58 (Devonshire) March 1883 to death; author of *Reports of cases adjudged in court of chancery by Sir John Stuart 1858–1865,* 5 *vols.* 1860–71; author with John Smale of *Reports of cases adjudged in court of chancery by Sir John Stuart 1852–1857,* 3 *vols.* 1855–58. *d.* North Huish near Ivybridge, Devon 20 Oct. 1888.

GIFFARD, STANLEY LEES *(youngest son of John Giffard of Dromartin, co. Dublin 1747–1819). b.* Dublin 4 Aug. 1788; ed. at Trin. coll. Dublin, B.A. 1807, M.A. 1811; barrister M.T. 24 May 1811; edited *St. James's Chronicle* some years; edited *Standard* newspaper 1827 to death; contributed articles to *Quarterly Review* and *Blackwood's Mag. d.* Folkestone 6 Nov. 1858.

GIFFORD, ADAM *(eld. son of James Gifford, treasurer of the Merchant Co.) b.* Edinburgh 28 Feb. 1820; educ. Edinburgh institution 1832; apprenticed to a solicitor 1835, managing clerk; called to the Scotch bar 1849; advocate depute 1861; conducted the prosecution of Jessie M'Lauchlan in the Sandyford murder case 1863; sheriff of Orkney and Zetland 1865; a judge of court of session, with the title of Lord Gifford 28 Jany. 1870, resigned 25 Jany. 1881. *d.* Granton house, Edinburgh 20 Jany. 1887, left £80,000 to found lectureships on natural theology at Edinburgh, Glasgow, Aberdeen and St. Andrews.

GIFFORD, JAMES *(eld. son of James Gifford, unitarian writer 1740–1813). b.* Halifax, Nova Scotia 20 Nov. 1768; midshipman R.N. 1 Oct. 1783; captain 12 Aug. 1812 when he left the sea, rear admiral 1 Oct. 1846; spent his income in works of benevolence and in

GIFFORD, J. *(Con.)*

furthering cause of unitarianism; author of *The remonstrance of a unitarian addressed to the Bishop of St. Davids'* 1818, 2 ed. 1820; *Letter of a unitarian to the minister of St. James's church, Jersey* 1845. *d.* Mount Orgueil cottage near St. Helier, Jersey 20 Aug. 1853.

GILBART, JAMES WILLIAM. *b.* London 21 March 1794; clerk in a London bank 1813; cashier in a Birmingham office 1825–7; manager of branches of Provincial Bank of Ireland at Kilkenny and Waterford 1829–33; general manager of London and Westminster bank 1833–59 when he retired on pension of £1600, bank opened 10 March 1834; F.R.S. 18 June 1846; author of *A practical treatise on banking* 1827, 6 ed. 1856; *The history and principles of banking* 1834 and 14 other books republished in 6 vols. 1865. *d.* Brompton crescent, London 8 Aug. 1863. *J. W. Gilbart's Practical treatise on banking, vol. i* (1856), *portrait; Drawing room portrait gallery of eminent personages, 3rd series* (1860), *portrait.*

GILBERT, ANN *(eld. child of Rev. Isaac Taylor of Ongar 1759–1829). b.* opposite Islington ch. London 30 Jany. 1782; engraved small plates for Darton and Harvey's juvenile works; co-author with her sister Jane of *Original poems for infant minds* 2 vols. 1804–5; *Hymns for infant minds* 1810 and other books. *(m.* 24 Dec. 1813 Rev. Joseph Gilbert 1779–1852). *d.* College st. Nottingham 20 Dec. 1866. *Josiah Gilbert's Autobiography of Mrs. Gilbert* 2 vols. (1874), 2 *portraits.*

GILBERT, RIGHT REV. ASHURST TURNER *(son of Thomas Gilbert, captain R.M., who d. 14 Dec. 1844 aged 86). b.* near Burnham Beeches, Bucks. 14 May 1786; ed. at Manchester gr. sch. and Brasenose coll. Ox.; B.A. 1809, M.A. 1811, B.D. 1819, D.D. 1822; fellow of Brasenose 1811, principal 2 Feb. 1822 to Feb. 1842; vice chancellor of Ox. 1836–40; bishop of Chichester 24 Jany. 1842 to death, consecrated at Lambeth palace 27 Feb. 1842; inhibited Rev. John Purchas from carrying on ritualistic services at St. James's chapel, Brighton 14 Oct. 1868; author of 14 letters, sermons and charges. *d.* Episcopal palace, Chichester 21 Feb. 1870. *Manchester school register ii,* 221–4 (1868).

GILBERT, ELIZABETH MARGARETTA MARIA (2 *dau. of the preceding). b.* Oxford 7 Aug. 1826; became entirely blind April 1829; established work rooms for blind people at New Turnstile, Holborn, London, May 1854 which developed into Association for promoting the general welfare of the blind 1855; writer of fugitive

GILBERT, E. M. M. *(Con.)*

verses. *d.* 5 Stanhope place, Hyde park, London 7 Feb. 1885. *F. Martin's Elizabeth Gilbert and her works for the blind (1887), portrait.*

GILBERT, REV. JOSEPH. *b.* Wrangle, Lincs. 20 March 1779; Independent minister at Southend, Essex; classical tutor at Rotherham college; pastor of Nether chapel, Sheffield 1818; pastor of James st. chapel, Nottingham 1825, of Friar lane chapel, Nottingham 1828 to 1851; chairman of Congregational Union 1833; author of *The Christian Atonement, its basis, nature and bearings* 1836, 2 ed. 1852. *d.* Nottingham 12 Dec. 1852. *A biographical sketch of J. Gilbert, by his widow* 1853 pp. 1–150.

GILBERT, JOSEPH FRANCIS. Resided at Portsmouth 1813; resided at Chichester many years; painted many views in Sussex; exhibited 6 pictures at R.A., 5 at B.I. and 12 at Suffolk st. gallery 1813–53. *d.* London 25 Sep. 1855 in 64 year.

GILBERT, MISS. *b.* Hants.; pupil of J. S. Rarey the horse tamer 1859; kept a riding school in London; the best performer with the Queen's hounds; the chief subject of Landseer's picture called "The pretty horsebreaker." *d.* Dec. 1863. *I.L.N. xxxii,* 593, 594 (1858), *portrait; Baily's Mag. Feb.* 1864 p. 321.

GILBERT, RICHARD *(son of Robert Gilbert of St. John's sq. Clerkenwell, printer, who d.* 10 Jany. 1815 *aged* 51*). b.* St. John's sq. 1794; a printer with his brother in London 1815; head of firm of Gilbert and Rivington, printers 1830 to death; projected and edited *Clergyman's Almanack* 1818, *Gilbert's Clergyman's Almanack* 1835; author of *Liber Scholasticus* 1829, 2nd ed. entitled *The parents school and college guide* 1843; *The Clerical guide, or ecclesiastical directory* 1817 anon., 2 ed. 1821 anon., 3 ed. 1829, 4 ed. 1836. *d.* 70 Euston sq. London 26 Feb. 1852.

GILBERT, SIR WALTER RALEIGH, 1 Baronet *(3 son of Rev. Edmund Gilbert, R. of Helland, Cornwall, who d.* 1816*). b.* Bodmin 18 March 1785; entered Bengal army 1800; lieut. col. 39 Bengal N.I. 1824; col. 35 Bengal N.I. 1832; commanded divisions in first and second Sikh wars 1845–6 and 1849; col. 1 European regiment 1845 to death; member of council of India 3 April 1850 to death; L.G. 11 Nov. 1851; K.C.B. 3 April 1846, G.C.B. 9 June 1849; created baronet 31 Dec. 1850. *d.* Stevens' hotel, Bond st. London 10 May 1853, memorial obelisk erected on the Beacon, Bodmin 1856–7. *G.M. xxxix,* 652–3 (1853); *I.L.N. vii,* 269 (1845), *portrait, viii,* 269 (1846), *portrait, xxii,* 404, 483 (1853); *Bentley's Miscellany xxxiii,* 627–32 (1853).

GILBERT, WILLIAM. Entered Bombay army 1795; col. 21 Bombay N.I. 1 May 1824 to 17 Feb. 1852; col. 3 Bombay N.I. 17 Feb. 1852 to death; general 20 June 1854. *d.* Tweed near Lymington, Hants. 5 Nov. 1866 aged 85.

GILBERT, WILLIAM. Author of *On present system of rating for the poor in the metropolis* 1857; *De Profundis* 2 vols. 1864; *Sir Thomas Bramston* 3 vols. 1869; *King George's Middy* 1869; *Doctor Austin's Guests* 2 vols. 1866; *The City, an enquiry into the corporation, its livery companies* 1877 and 20 other books; some of his books are illustrated by his son W. S. Gilbert. *d.* The Close, Salisbury 3 Jany. 1889 in 86 year. *Contemporary Review xii,* 437–40 (1869).

GILBEY, ALFRED. *b.* Bishop Stortford, Herts. 23 Oct. 1833; with his elder brother Henry P. Gilbey, wine merchant, London 1847; in government civil service in the Crimea 1855; firm of William and A. Gilbey, wine merchants 357 Oxford st. London, established Feb. 1857; firm admitted 6 other partners all relatives; removed business to the Pantheon, Oxford st. 1867, wine and spirit business became largest in Great Britain; author with W. Gilbey of *Treatise on wines and spirits of the producing countries* 1869. *d.* Wooburn house, Wooburn, Bucks. 28 Nov. 1879, personalty sworn under £350,000, 23 Feb. 1880. *Wine Trade Review* 15 *Dec.* 1879 p. 599 *and* 15 *March* 1880 p. 107.

GILCHRIST, ALEXANDER *(son of James Gilchrist of Newington Green, London* 1783–1835*). b.* Newington Green 25 April 1828; ed. at Univ. college school; barrister M.T. 3 May 1850; author of *Life of William Etty, R.A.* 2 vols. 1855; *Life of William Blake, Pictor Ignotus* 2 vols. 1863; contributed to *Eclectic Review, Literary Review* and *Critic. d.* 6 Cheyne row, Chelsea 30 Nov. 1861. *A. Gilchrist's Life of W. Blake,* (2 ed. 1880) *ii,* 359–76.

GILCHRIST, ANNE *(dau. of John Parker Burrows, solicitor, d.* 1839*). b.* 7 Gower st. London 25 Feb. 1828; educ. under the Misses Cahusac at Highgate 1833; resided at Guildford and Chelsea 1828 etc.; in U.S. America 1876–79; friend of W. M. Rossetti 1862. *(m.* 4 Feb. 1851 the preceding); author of *Lost in the woods* 1864; *Secular ethics of a national education* 1872; *Mary Lamb* 1883; contributed to *Household Words* and *Blackwood's Mag. d.* Keat's corner, Well road, Hampstead 29 Nov. 1885. *Life and writings of Anne Gilchrist* (1887), *with portraits.*

GILDEA, VERY REV. GEORGE ROBERT. Educ. at Trin. coll. Dublin, B.A. 1827, M.A. 1832;

GILDEA, VERY REV. G. R. *(Con.)*

C. of Westport, Tuam 1826–28; C. of Kilmaine 1828–34; R. of Newport, Ireland 1834–44; R. of Kilmaine 1844–67; R. of Moylough 1867–73; provost of Tuam cathedral 1872 to death; author of *Reproductive relief spinning in the West of Ireland* 1849. *d.* 17 Alfred place, Thurloe sq. London 2 June 1887 in 84 year.

GILDERDALE, REV. JOHN. *b.* 1802; educ. Howden gram. sch. Essex and St. Catharine's hall, Camb., B.A. 1826, M.A. 1830, B.D. 1853, ad eundem Oxford 1847; C. of Huddersfield 1840–42; lecturer Halifax parish ch. Yorkshire 1842–47; principal of the Forest sch. Walthamstow 1848 to 1863; P.C. of Caundle Stourton, Dorset 1863; author of *An essay on natural religion and revelation* 1837; *A course of family prayer for one month* 1838; *A letter to Lord Brougham on national education* 1838. *d.* Caundle Stourton 25 Sep. 1864 aged 62.

GILES, REV. HENRY. *b.* Cranford, Wexford 1 Nov. 1809; Unitarian minister at Greenock 2 years, at Liverpool 3 years; went to America 1840 where he became a brilliant lecturer; author of *Lectures and essays* 2 vols. 1850; *Christian thought on life* 1850; *Human life in Shakespeare* 1868, all at Boston, U.S.A., and other books. *d.* Hyde park near Boston 10 July 1882.

GILES, JAMES WILLIAM. *b.* Glasgow 4 Jany. 1801; at age of 13 maintained his mother and sister by painting; taught classes in Aberdeen 1821; visited Italy; portrait and landscape painter; A.R.S.A. 1829; exhibited 2 works at R.A., 80 at B.I. and 13 at Suffolk st. 1830–68, and many at R. Scottish Academy; his picture 'The Weird Wife' is in the National gallery of Scotland. *d.* Bon Accord st. Aberdeen 6 Oct. 1870.

GILES, REV. JOHN ALLEN *(eld. son of Wm. Giles of Mark, Somerset).* *b.* Southwick house, Mark 26 Oct. 1808; ed. at Charterhouse and C.C. coll. Ox., scholar 1824, fellow 1832–33; double first class 1828; B.A. 1828, M.A. 1831, D.C.L. 1838; Vinerian scholar 1831; head master of Camberwell coll. sch. 1834–6; head master of City of London sch. 1836–40; C. of Bampton, Oxon. 1845–54; sentenced at Oxford assizes 6 March 1855 to a year's imprisonment in Oxford Castle for making a false entry in marriage register book of Bampton parish church, but released by royal warrant 4 June 1855; C. of Perivale, Mid. 1857–61; R. of Sutton, Surrey 1867 to death; published *Patres Ecclesiae Anglicanae* 34 vols. 1837–43; *Life and letters of Thomas Becket* 2 vols. 1846; *History of Bampton* 1847, 2 ed. 1848; *Christian*

GILES, REV. J. A. *(Con.)*

records on the age, authorship and authenticity of the *New Testament* 1854 which he suppressed, and 80 other books. *d.* Sutton rectory 24 Sep. 1884.

GILES, VEN. JOHN DOUGLAS *(eld. son of Robert Giles of Wedmore, Somerset).* Matric. from C.C. coll. Ox. 28 Nov. 1828 aged 16, exhibitioner 1828–32; B.A. 1832, M.A. 1836; V. of Swinstead, Lincs. 1840–50; R. of Belleau with Aby, Lincs. 1850–61; R. of Willoughby, Lincs. 1861 to death; archdeacon of Stow 1863 to death; precentor of Lincoln cath. April 1866 to death; author of *Village sermons* 1861. *d.* Willoughby rectory 5 Feb. 1867.

GILES-PULLER, CHRISTOPHER WILLIAM *(only son of Sir Christopher Puller 1773–1824, chief justice of supreme court of Calcutta).* *b.* London 16 June 1807; ed. at Eton and Ch. Ch. Ox., double first class 1828; barrister L.I. 23 Nov. 1832; practised in court of chancery 1832–41; with his mother founded and endowed church of St. Giles at High Cross near Standon, Herts., consecrated 6 Aug. 1847; contested Herts. 1852 and 1854; M.P. for Herts. 31 March 1857 to death; assumed additional name of Giles 1857. *d.* Youngsbury near Ware, Herts. 16 Feb. 1864.

GILFILLAN, REV. GEORGE (11 *child of Rev. Samuel Gilfillan* 1762–1826). *b.* Comrie, Perthshire 30 Jany. 1813; ed. at Glasgow coll.; licensed as a United Presbyterian minister 1835; minister of the School-Wynd ch. Dundee, March 1836 to death; a successful public lecturer; took an important part in political and religious meetings; author of *Hades or the Unseen, a sermon* 1843, *three editions; A gallery of literary portraits* 1845, *Second ser.* 1850, *Third ser.* 1854; *Life of Robert Burns* 1856; *History of a Man: By B. E. ed. by G. G., a semi-autobiographical romance* 1856; *British Poets* 6 vols. 1853–60; *Night, a poem* 1867 and about 100 other books. *d.* Arnhalt, Brechin 13 Aug. 1878. *bur.* Balgay cemetery, Dundee, the funeral procession being 2 miles long. *The lamps of the temple,* 3 ed. (1856) 242–68; *Our Scottish clergy* 2 series (1849) 368–78; *P. R. Drummond's Perthshire* (1879) 160–70.

GILFILLAN, JAMES *(brother of the preceding).* *b.* Comrie, Perthshire 11 May 1797; educ. Glasgow coll. 1808, and at the divinity hall of antiburgher synod, Edin.; United Secession ch. minister Stirling 24 Dec. 1822, resigned 1869; D.D. of Glasgow univ. 1866; author of *The Sabbath viewed in the light of reason, revelation and history* 1861. *d.* Portobello near Edinburgh 28 Jany. 1874.

GILL, THOMAS. b. 19 Feb. 1782; entered navy 15 Jany. 1794; captain 10 Jany. 1837, retired R.A. 8 April 1868; on 14 June 1803 in action with Lodi off St. Domingo severely wounded, voted a sword of 50 guineas by Patriotic Soc. d. Grove lodge, Pulteney road, Bath 27 Jany. 1874. *Athenæum 21 June 1862 pp. 823–4.*

GILL, WILLIAM JOHN (*son of Robert Gill, major Madras army*). b. Bangalore 10 Sep. 1843; ed. at Brighton college and R.M. academy, Woolwich; 2 lieut. R.E. 11 Nov. 1864, captain 21 Dec. 1877 to death; travelled in Persia with col. Valentine Baker 1873; contested Hackney 1874, Nottingham 1880; travelled in China and Tibet 1876–78; gold medallist of R.G.S. 26 May 1879; gold medallist of Paris geographical society 1880; author of *The river of golden sand* 2 vols. 1880; started from Suez for the desert 8 Aug. 1882, murdered by Bedouins at Wady Sudr 11 Aug. 1882. bur. in the crypt of St. Paul's cath. 6 April 1883, stained glass memorial window in Rochester cathedral. *W. J. Gill's River of golden sand, new ed.* (1883) pp. 19–66, *portrait*; *Graphic xxvi, 469* (1882), *portrait.*

GILLAN, REV. ROBERT (*son of Robert Gillan, minister at Hawick, Roxburgh, d. 7 May 1824*). b. Hawick 1800; educ. Edin. univ.; Presbyterian minister at Stamfordham, Northumberland 1830, at South Shields 1833, at Holytown, Lanarkshire 1837, at Wishaw 1842, at Abbotshall, Fifeshire 1843, at St. John's, Glasgow 1847 and at Inchinnan, Renfrewshire 1861 to death; D.D. of Glasgow univ. 1853; lecturer on pastoral theology at the Scottish universities; publicly entertained at Glasgow and presented with his portrait 11 Oct. 1870; moderator of general assembly 1873; author of *The Decalogue, a series of discourses* 1856. d. Inchinnan manse 1 Nov. 1879. *J. Smith's Our Scottish Clergy* (1848) 182–8; *H. Scott's Fasti ii, pt. 1, p. 269.*

GILLIES, MARGARET (2 dau. of William Gillies, merchant). b. Throgmorton st. London 7 Aug. 1803; educ. Edinburgh; had lessons in painting from F. Cruikshank in London, and from Hendrik and Ary Scheffer in Paris; Assoc. of Old Soc. of painters in water-colours 1852 and a constant contributor to its gallery; exhibited 101 subjects at R.A., 2 at B.I. and 8 at Suffolk st. 1832–61; some of her best known works are Past and present 1855, The heavens are telling 1856, Cercando Pace 1875; resided Church row, Hampstead, but d. The Warren, Crockham hill, Kent 20 July 1887. *Clayton's English Female artists* (1876) ii, 87–94; *Hays's Women of the Day* (1885) 77–78.

GILLIES, MARY (*sister of the preceding*). Author of *The voyage of the Constance* 1860; *The Carewes* 1861; *Great fun for our little friends* 1862; *More fun for little friends, by Harriet Myrtle* 1864. d. 1870.

GILLIES, ROBERT PIERCE (*son of Dr. Thomas Gillies d* 1808). b. at or near Arbroath 1788; educ. Edin. univ.: admitted advocate 1813; in pecuniary difficulties from 1813 to his decease; imprisoned for debt 1847–9; friend of Scott and Wordsworth; an early contributor to *Blackwood's Mag.;* called Kempferhausen in the *Noctes Ambrosianæ;* founder and editor of *Foreign Quarterly Review,* July 1827; resided in London 1827 and at Boulogne 1840–47; author of *Childe Alarique, a poet's reverie, by R. P. G.* 1814; *The confessions of Sir H. Longueville, by R. P. G.* 2 vols. 1814; *German stories* 3 vols. 1826; *Tales of a voyager to the Arctic Ocean* 6 vols. 1826–29; *Memoirs of a literary veteran* 3 vols. 1851. d. Kensington 28 Nov. 1858.

GILLIS, MOST REV. JAMES (*only child of Alexander Gillis of Fochabers, Elgin, who d. Nov. 1833*). b. Montreal 7 April 1802; founded St. Margaret's convent, Edinburgh for nuns of the Ursuline order 16 June 1835; coadjutor bishop of Eastern district of Scotland 28 July 1837; consecrated bishop of Limyra in partibus 22 July 1838; vicar apostolic of East of Scotland 24 May 1852 to death; introduced the Jesuits into his district 1859; author of *Facts relating to admission into catholic church of viscount and viscountess Feilding* 1850 and many letters and discourses. d. Greenhill near Edinburgh 24 Feb. 1864. *Gordon's Catholic mission in Scotland* (18) 480, *portrait; History of St. Margaret's convent, Edinburgh* (1886), *portrait; Morgan's Bibliotheca Canadensis* (1867) 151–3.

GILLKREST, JAMES. Hospital assistant in the army 1800; surgeon 43 foot 1804; inspector general 1845–46 when placed on retired list; author of *Cholera Gleanings, a family handbook* 1849; *Notes worth noticing relative to the Cholera* 1852, of a work on yellow fever which he presented to French Academy of Medicine, and of a monograph on yellow fever published in General Board of Health's second report on quarantine. d. St. Alban's place, Haymarket London 25 Dec. 1853.

GILLMAN, JOSEPH. b. Little Over near Derby 1759; fought under Rodney and Hood off Port Royal, Jamaica, April 1782, believed to have been last survivor of that battle; one of the foremost mutineers at the Nore, May-June 1797; one of forlorn hope at storming of Seringapatam 4 May 1799; received a com-

GILLMAN, J. *(Con.)*

pound fracture of both legs at Copenhagen 2 April 1801. *d.* Manchester 25 June 1855 in 96 year.

GILLOTT, JOSEPH. *b.* Sheffield 11 Oct. 1799; working cutler; removed to Birmingham 1821; adapted the press to the making of steel pens 1830, invented side slits and cross grinding of the points, sold the pens at 1s. each; established works at Graham st. Newhall hill 1859 where he employed 450 persons and sold his pens at 4d. the gross; formed a collection of paintings chiefly Turner's and Etty's, collection sold in 1873 for £170,000; collected violins which realised £4000; had a residence at Stanmore near London. *d.* Westbourne road, Edgbaston, Birmingham 5 Jany. 1873, personalty sworn under £250,000. *Practical Mag.* (1873) *i*, 322–5, *portrait*; *Mayhew's Shops of London* (1865) 98–100; *Edwards's Personal recollections of Birmingham* (1877) 89–100.

GILLOW, REV. JOHN *(youngest son of John Gillow of Elswick Grange)*. *b.* 27 Feb. 1814; ed. at Ushaw college, Durham, professor of mathematics there 1837–42, of natural philosophy 1842–50, of dogmatic theology 1850–59 and 1863 to death, of moral theology 1859–60; canon theologian of cathedral chapter of Hexham 1857; created D.D. by Pius ix, 1859; vice pres. of Ushaw college 1859 to death. *d.* Ushaw college 9 Aug. 1877. *J. Gillow's English Catholics ii*, 476–81 (1885).

GILLY, REV. WILLIAM STEPHEN *(son of Rev. Wm. Gilly, R. of Wanstead, Essex, who d. 23 Nov. 1837 aged 75)*. *b.* 28 Jany. 1789; ed. at Christ's hospital and Caius and St. Catharine's hall, Cam., B.A. 1812, M.A. 1817, D.D. 1833; R. of North Fambridge, Essex 1817; canon of Durham 1826; P.C. of St. Margaret's, Durham 1827–51; V. of Norham on the Tweed 1851 to death; canon residentiary of Durham 1853 to death; author of *The Spirit of the Gospel* 1818; *A memoir of Felix Neff* 1832, *many eds.*; *Our Protestant Forefathers* 1835, *many eds.*, and numerous other books. *d.* Norham 10 Sep. 1855. *G.M. xliv*, 437–39 (1855).

GILPIN, REV. BERNARD *(4 son of Rev. Wm. Gilpin, R. of Pulverbatch, Salop)*. *b.* Cheam, Surrey 26 Jany. 1803; ed. at Queen's coll. Cam., B.A. 1825, M.A. 1828; R. of St. Andrew, Hertford 15 Jany. 1829 to Oct. 1835 when he resigned and seceded from Church of England; preached for 35 years in a chapel at Port Vale Bengeo, Hertford, built for him by his followers. *d.* Pulverbatch 10 Jany. 1871. *Benson's Memorials of B. Gilpin* (1874), *with portrait.*

GILPIN, CHARLES *(son of James Gilpin of Bristol)*. *b.* Bristol 1815; publisher and bookseller in Bishopsgate st. London to 1853; common councilman London 1848; parliamentary sec. of Poor law board 28 June 1859 to 22 Feb. 1865; contested Perth 1852; M.P. for Northampton, April 1857 to death; chairman of National freehold land society. *d.* 10 Bedford sq. Holborn, London 8 Sep. 1874. *The drawing room portrait gallery of eminent personages 3rd series* (1860), *portrait*; *The statesmen of England* (1862) *No. 45, portrait*; *I.L.N. xxxiii*, 92, 94 (1858), *portrait, lxv*, 260, 273, 379 (1874), *portrait.*

GILPIN, HENRY DILWOOD *(son of Joshua Gilpin of Philadelphia 1765–1840)*. *b.* Lancaster 14 April 1801; ed. in England 1811–16; graduated at Univ. of Pennsylvania 1819; attorney in Philadelphia 1822 to death; attorney general of the U.S. 1840–1; edited *Atlantic Souvenir 7 vols.* 1826–32; published *Opinions of the attorney generals of the United States 2 vols., Washington* 1841 and other books. *d.* Philadelphia 29 Jany. 1860. *Memorials of H. D. Gilpin, Privately printed Philadelphia* (1860); *Appleton's American biography ii*, 659 (1887), *portrait.*

GILPIN, SIR RICHARD THOMAS, 1 Baronet *(only son of Richard Gilpin of Hockliffe grange, Leighton Buzzard, Beds., who d. 3 Jany. 1841)*. *b.* Manchester st. Manchester sq. London 12 Jany. 1801; ed. at Rugby and Christ's coll. Cam.; col. Bedfordshire militia 11 Sep. 1848 to death; sheriff of Beds. 1850; M.P. for Beds. 1851–80; created baronet 19 Feb. 1876. *d.* Hockliffe grange 8 April 1882.

GIOVANELLI, EDWARD, stage name of Edward Edwards. *b.* Clerkenwell, London, Aug. 1823; first appeared in London at Cabinet theatre 1839; proprietor of Highbury Barn gardens, Islington 21 May 1861 to 14 Oct. 1870 when he lost his dancing license after spending £35,000 on the property; built Alexandra theatre in the gardens, opened 20 May 1865; manager of Royal Alfred theatre opened 12 Nov. 1870. *d.* 6 Lady Somerset road, Kentish town, London 14 March 1881.

GIRAUD, HERBERT JOHN *(2 son of John Thomas Giraud, surgeon 1764–1836)*. *b.* Faversham, Kent 14 April 1817; educ. Edin. univ., M.D. 1840; entered service of H.E.I.C. 1842, professor of chemistry and botany 1845 and then principal of Grant Medical coll. Bombay; medical officer of Sir J. Jeejeeboy's hospital; chemical analyst to Bombay government; deputy inspector general of Bombay army

GIRAUD, H. J. *(Con.)*

medical service, retired 1868 ; dean of faculty of medicine, Bombay university 1863 ; writer of papers on botany and chemistry. *d.* Shanklin, Isle of Wight 12 Jany. 1888.

GIRAUD, RICHARD HERVÉ. *b.* Canterbury 1801 ; midshipman R.N. to 1815 ; solicitor in London 1822 to death ; a Freemason 1824 to death, founder and first master of the Huguenot lodge ; a director of French hospital, London 1829, sec., treasurer and deputy governor successively ; a founder of Huguenot Soc. of London, April 1885. *d.* 55 Doughty st. London 13 Oct. 1886.

GIRDLESTONE, REV. CHARLES *(2 son of Samuel Rainbow Girdlestone of London, barrister).* *b.* London 6 March 1797 ; ed. at Wadham coll. Ox., B.A. 1818, M.A. 1821 ; fell. of Balliol coll. 1818–26 ; C. of Hastings 1822–24 ; C. of Ferry Hincksey, Berks. 1824–26 ; select preacher at Ox. 1825 and 1830 ; V. of Sedgley, Staffs. 1826–37 ; R. of Alderley, Cheshire 1837–47 ; R. of Kingswinsford, Staffs. 1847–77 ; author of *The New Testament with a commentary* 2 vols. 1832–5 ; *The Holy Bible with a commentary* 4 vols. 1842, *new ed.* 6 vols. 1873 ; *The question of the day, By the Creature of an Hour* 1857, and 60 other books. *d.* Holywell house, Weston-super-Mare 28 April 1881.

GIRDLESTONE, REV. EDWARD *(brother of the preceding).* *b.* London 6 Sep. 1805 ; ed. at Balliol coll. Ox., scholar 1823–6, B.A. 1826, M.A. 1829 ; C. of Deane, Lancs. 1828, V. 1830–55 ; canon of Bristol 1854 ; V. of St. Nicholas with St. Leonard's, Bristol 1855–58 ; V. of Wapley, Gloucs. 1858–62 ; V. of Halberton, Devon 1862–72 ; V. of Olveston, Gloucs. 1872 to death ; author of *Sermons on Romanism and Tractarianism* 1851 ; *Remarks on Essays and Reviews* 1861 and 15 other books. *d.* Canon's house, Bristol 4 Dec. 1884. *Church of England photographic portrait gallery* (1859) *part* 6, *portrait ; Church Portrait Journal, Aug.* 1884 *pp.* 57–60, *portrait.*

GIRLING, MARY ANNE *(dau. of Mr. Clouting, farmer).* *b.* Little Glemham, Suffolk 27 April 1827 ; a wesleyan methodist ; believed that she was called to be a new incarnation of the Deity 1864 ; commenced preaching at 107 Bridge road, Battersea 1870, community named themselves The Children of God, but generally called Shakers ; removed to New Forest lodge, Hampshire 2 Jany. 1872 ; ejected for non-payment of rent 1873 and 1878 and suffered much hardship ; rented Tiptoe farm, Hordle. Lymington 1879 ; members expected

GIRLING, M. A. *(Con.)*

to live for ever and that Mrs. Girling would rule over the world. *(m.* George Stanton Girling a general dealer at Ipswich*).* *d.* Tiptoe farm 18 Sep. 1886. *Irish Monthly, Oct.* 1878 *pp.* 555–64 ; *Lymington Chronicle* 23 *and* 30 *Sept.* 1886.

GISBORNE, JOHN *(2 son of John Gisborne of Yoxall, Staffs.) b.* St. Helen's, Derby 26 Aug. 1770 ; ed. at Harrow and St. John's coll. Cam., B.A. 1792 ; author of *The Vales of Wever* 1797 ; *Reflections* 1833 and other poems. *d.* Pentrich, Derbyshire 17 June 1851. *A brief memoir of the life of John Gisborne with extracts from his diary* (1852).

GISBORNE, LIONEL. *b.* St. Petersburgh 1823 ; civil engineer ; worked for the government in Ireland 1842–52 ; practised in London 1852 to death ; brought forward a scheme for embankment of river Thames 1852 ; projected several of the long submarine telegraphs 1851 to death ; partner with Henry C. Forde ; A.I.C.E. 1852 ; author of *The Isthmus of Darien* 1853. *d.* Dartmouth st. Westminster 9 March 1861. *Min. of proc. of Instit. of C.E. xxi,* 586–92 (1862).

GISBORNE, THOMAS *(eld. son of Rev. Thomas Gisborne* 1758–1846*). b.* 1794 ; M.P. for Stafford 1830–32, for North Derbyshire 1832–37, for Carlow 1839–41, for Nottingham 1843–47 ; contested Totnes 1840, Newport and South Leics. 1841, Ipswich 1842, Nottingham 1847 and Kidderminster 1849 ; author of *Essays on Agriculture* 1854, and of speeches and pamphlets. *d.* Yoxall lodge, Staffs. 20 July 1852.

GIUGLINI, ANTONIO. *b.* Fanó, Italy 1827 ; sang at Her Majesty's theatre, London 1857–58 ; sang with much success in the provinces and abroad ; had a sweet and high tenor voice, the best since Tamberlik ; became insane 1862. *d.* in an asylum at Pesaro, Italy 12 Oct. 1865. *Illust. sporting news iv,* 553 (1865), *portrait.*

GLADSTONE, SIR JOHN, 1 Baronet *(eld. son of Thomas Gladstones of Leith, corn merchant* 1732–1809*). b.* Leith 11 Dec. 1764 ; corn merchant at Liverpool 1788–1843 when he retired ; M.P. for Lancaster 1818, for Woodstock 1820, for Berwick 1826–27 when unseated on petition ; dropped the final s in his name by r.l. 10 Feb. 1835 ; created baronet 18 July 1846 ; author of *Plain facts connected with the Corn laws* 1846 and other pamphlets. *d.* Fasque, Kincardineshire 7 Dec. 1851. *Fortunes made in business ii,* 111–36 (1884) ; *H. R. F. Bourne's English merchants ii,* 290–306 (1886).

GLADSTONE, JOHN NEILSON. *b.* 18 Jany. 1807; M.P. for Walsall 1841, for Ipswich 1842–7, for Devizes 1852–7 and 1859 to death; sheriff of Wilts. 1859. *d.* Bowden park, Wilts. 7 Feb. 1863. *I.L.N. xxii*, 197, 198 (1853), *portrait.*

GLADSTONE, MURRAY (6 *son of Robert Gladstone of Liverpool* 1773–1835). *b.* Liverpool 14 Feb. 1816; employed in making surveys for railways; a merchant at Calcutta 1844–50; established firm of Gladstone, Latham & Co. in Manchester 1850; erected an observatory at Penmaenmawr, North Wales; F.R.A.S. 11 May 1860. *d.* suddenly while walking along the shore at Penmaenmawr 23 Aug. 1875. *Monthly notices of R.A.S. xxxvi*, 142 (1876).

GLADSTONE, SIR THOMAS, 2 Baronet *(eld. son of Sir John Gladstone* 1764–1851). *b.* Annfield near Liverpool 25 July 1804; ed. at Eton and Ch. Ch. Ox., B.A. 1827, M.A. 1830; M.P. for Queenborough, Kent 1830–32, for Portarlington 1832–35, for Leicester 1835–37, for Ipswich 1842 but unseated on petition; lord lieut. of Kincardineshire; founded at Fasque, Kincardineshire a herd of pure-bred polled cattle. *d.* Fasque house 20 March 1889. *Fortunes made in business ii*, 137–40 (1884).

GLASGOW, JAMES CARR-BOYLE, 5 Earl of (2 *son of 4 Earl of Glasgow* 1766–1843). *b.* London 10 April 1792; served in the navy 1807–18, retired commander 5 Oct. 1867; assumed name of Carr before Boyle 2 Aug. 1823; contested Ayrshire 1837, M.P. for Ayrshire 1839–43; lord lieut. and sheriff principal of Renfrewshire 21 Oct. 1844; kept many racehorses 1819 to death, most of which were unnamed; won the Two thousand guineas and Doncaster Cup with General Peel 1864; master of Renfrewshire fox hounds. *d.* Hawkhead, Renfrewshire 11 March 1869. *Rice's British Turf* (1879) ii, 242–55; *Saddle and Sirloin, By the Druid. Part North* (1870) 26–32; *Baily's Mag. i*, 257–60 (1860), *portrait.*

GLASGOW, GEORGE FREDERICK BOYLE, 6 Earl of *(half-brother of the preceding).* *b.* 9 Oct. 1825; ed. at Ch. Ch. Ox., B.A. 1847, M.A. 1852; M.P. for Buteshire, Feb. to July 1865, contested Buteshire, July 1865; lord clerk register of Scotland 1879 to death; principal keeper of the Signet. *d.* 32 Palmerston place, Edinburgh 23 April 1890.

GLASS, JOSEPH. *b.* 1792; invented the chimney-sweeping machine now in use for which he received a silver medal and prize of £200 about 1828; author of *Chimney-sweeping described* 1834. *d.* Brixton, London 29 Dec. 1867.

GLASS, SIR RICHARD ATWOOD *(eld. son of Francis Glass of Bradford, Wilts.)* *b.* Bradford 3 July 1820; established with Kuper a wire-rope manufactory; introduced use of twisted iron wires in Dover and Calais cable as a protecting medium for submarine telegraphs 1852; made a length of 1250 miles of the Atlantic cable of 1858 which failed; partner in firm of Glass, Elliot and Co., Greenwich, firm was eventually absorbed in the Telegraph construction and maintenance co., managing director; knighted by patent 26 Nov. 1866; chairman of Anglo-American Telegraph company; M.P. for Bewdley 1868–69 when unseated on petition; A.I.C.E. 4 May 1858. *d.* Moorlands, Bitterne, Southampton 22 Dec. 1873. *I.L.N. xlix*, 545, 558 (1866), *portrait.*

GLASSE, FREDERICK HENRY HASTINGS. Entered navy 20 Nov. 1818; captain 9 Nov. 1846; R.A. 16 Sep. 1864, retired 1 April 1870; admiral 1 Aug. 1877; C.B. 2 Jany. 1857. *d.* Billacombe villa, Plymstock, South Devon 25 May 1884.

GLAZEBROOK, THOMAS KIRKLAND *(son of Rev. James Glazebrook* 1744–1803). *b.* Ashby-de-la-Zouch, Leics. 4 June 1780; glass manufacturer at Warrington; lived at Southport 1835 to death; F.L.S.; printed many songs and poems; author of *The first eclogue of Virgil translated into English verse* 1807; *A guide to Southport* 1809, 2 ed. 1826 and other books. *d.* Southport 17 Jany. 1855. *J. Kendrick's Warrington Worthies*, 2 ed. (1854) p. 6, *portrait.*

GLEIG, REV. GEORGE ROBERT *(son of Right Rev. George Gleig* 1753–1840, *primate of Scotch episcopalian church).* *b.* Stirling 20 April 1796; ed. at Glasgow univ. and Balliol coll. Ox., B.A. 1818, M.A. 1821; ensign 3 garrison battalion 1812; lieut. 85 foot 1813–16 when placed on h.p., sold out 1826; served in Peninsula 1813–14 and in American war; R. of Ivychurch, Kent 1822–80; chaplain of Chelsea hospital 1834–40; principal chaplain to the forces 1844–46, chaplain general 1846–75 when placed on h.p.; inspector general of military schools 1846–57; preb. of St. Paul's 29 Dec. 1848 to death; author of *The Subaltern* 1826; *The Chelsea pensioners* 1829; *The history of the British Empire in India* 4 vols. 1830–5; *Memoirs of the life of Warren Hastings* 3 vols. 1841 and 35 other books; the survivor of original contributors to *Blackwood's Mag.* and *Fraser's Mag. d.* Stratfield Turgis near Winchfield 9 July 1888. *Maclise Portrait Gallery* (1883) 267–70, *portrait; Colburn's New Monthly xlix*, 220–23 (1837), *portrait.*

GLENELG, Charles Grant, 1 Baron (*eld son of Charles Grant 1746-1823, M.P. for Invernesshire*). *b.* Kidderpore, Bengal 26 Oct. 1778; ed. at Magd. coll. Cam., fellow 1802, 4th wrangler and chancellor's medallist 1801; B.A. 1801, M.A. 1804, L.L.D. 1819; barrister L.I. 13 June 1807; M.P. for Fortrose burghs 1811-18, for Invernesshire 1818-35; a lord of the treasury 1813-19; chief sec. for Ireland 1818-1821; P.C. Ireland 1819; P.C. 28 May 1819; vice pres. of board of trade 1823, pres. 1827-28; treasurer of navy 1827-28; pres. of board of control 1830-34; sec. of state the colonies 1835-39; created Baron Glenelg of Glenelg, Inverness 11 May 1835; F.R.S. 27 May 1828. *d.* Cannes 23 April 1866.

GLENGALL, Richard Butler, 2 Earl of (*eld. child of 1 Earl of Glengall 1775-1819*). *b.* 29 May 1794; succeeded his father 30 Jany. 1819; colonel of South Tipperary artillery 21 Nov. 1826 to death; Irish representative peer 1 Sep. 1829 to death; wrote *The Irish tutor* 1823; *The follies of fashion, a comedy in 5 acts* 1830 and other dramatic works. *d.* Cowes, Isle of Wight 22 June 1858.

GLENNIE, George. Captain of the Royal and Ancient Golf club of St. Andrews; made celebrated score of 88 for King Wm. Fourth's medal at St. Andrews 1855 which was unbeaten until 1884; the George Glennie medal was instituted 1881, and presented by Royal Blackheath golf club to the St. Andrew's club. *d.* 3 St. Germain's place, Blackheath 26 March 1886 aged 68. *H. G. Hutchinson's Golf* (1890) 388-90, *portrait.*

GLENNY, George. *b.* 1 Nov. 1793; gained many prizes at flower shows; wrote a series of letters in *The British Luminary* 1820 of which he became editor; edited *Royal ladies' magazine and St. James's Archives*; started *Horticultural Journal* 1832; edited *Gardener's Gazette, Garden Journal, Practical Florist, Glenny's Journal, &c.*; started the Metropolitan Society of Florists and Amateurs 1832; author of *Cottage gardening* 1847; *The handy-book of gardening* 1858; *The properties of Flowers and plants* 1864 and other books. *d.* Gipsy Hill, Norwood, Surrey 17 May 1874. *Gardener's Mag. 23 May 1874 p. 269, portrait.*

GLEW, Edward Lees (*son of Thomas Faulkner Glew of Dublin, solicitor*). *b.* Dublin 3 March 1817; ed. at Trin. coll. Dublin; became a portrait painter; settled at Walsall; published *History of the borough and foreign of Walsall, Walsall* 1856; started a newspaper in Birmingham; resided at 53 Beaver st.

Glew, E. L. (*Con.*)
New York as a painter; removed to Philadelphia, then to Trenton, New Jersey. *d.* Newark, New Jersey 9 Oct. 1870. *Morning Advertiser 11 Oct. 1870 p. 3, col. 5.*

GLIDDON, George Robins. *b.* Devonshire 1809; resided in Egypt nearly 23 years; U.S. vice consul at Alexandria about 20 years; lectured in Boston, New York and Philadelphia on Egyptian antiquities; agent for Honduras interoceanic railway at time of his death; author of *A memoir on the cotton of Egypt* 1841; *Discourses on Egyptian archæology* 1841 and other books; author with J. C. Nott of *Types of Mankind* 1854, and edited L. F. A. Maury's *Indigenous races of the earth* 1857. *d.* Panama 16 Nov. 1857.

GLOUCESTER and EDINBURGH, Mary, Duchess of (*4 dau. of King George the Third 1738-1820*). *b.* 25 April 1776. (*m.* at Buckingham palace 22 July 1816 her cousin Prince William Frederick, 2 Duke of Gloucester and Edinburgh, *b.* 15 Jany. 1776, *d.* 30 Nov. 1834); ranger and keeper of Richmond new park 30 Oct. 1850 to death. *d.* Gloucester house, Park lane, London 30 April 1857. *H. Martineau's Biographical Sketches*, 4 ed. (1876) 21-9; *I.L.N. xxx*, 434, 465, 466 (1857), *portrait.*

GLOVER, Charles William. *b.* London, Feb. 1806; violinist in orchestras of Drury Lane and Covent Garden; musical director Queen's theatre, Tottenham st. 1832 etc.; composed Jeannette and Jeannot 1845, Cosin Harry a semi-comic song 1855, Tis hard to give the hand where the heart can never be 1853, and a very large number of pieces for the piano; ballads and songs. *d.* Caversham road, Kentish town, London 23 March 1863.

GLOVER, Edmund (*eld. son of Samuel Glover and Julia Glover, actress, who d. 16 July 1850*). *b.* England 1813; acted at Haymarket theatre, London, at Edinburgh 1841 where he played Richelieu, Rob Roy, etc.; engaged Jenny Lind in 1847 to sing in Edinburgh, Glasgow and Perth, cleared £3000; lessee of Prince's theatre, Glasgow 1848; manager of Paisley and Dunfermline theatres and of Greenock theatre in 1849; last appeared as Triplet in Edinburgh 25 May 1859; a good actor, dancer, fencer and pantomimist. *d.* 3 Gayfield place, Edinburgh 23 Oct. 1860. *Dibdin's Annals of Edinburgh stage* (1888) 380 *et seq.*

GLOVER, Edward Auchmuty (*eld. son of James Glover of Mount Glover, co. Cork*). Ed. at Trin. coll. Dublin, B.A. 1837; called to

GLOVER, E. A. *(Con.)*

bar in Ireland 1840 ; insolvent in Ireland 1849 ; barrister M.T. 30 Jany. 1852 ; contested Canterbury 18 Aug. 1854 ; contested Beverley 7 July 1852, M.P. for Beverley 28 March 1857 to 3 Aug. 1857 when unseated on petition ; sentenced at Central Criminal Court 13 April 1858 to 3 months' imprisonment in Newgate for having made false declaration as to his property, this was the last prosecution of the kind, the property qualification of M.P's. was abolished by 21 & 22 Vict. c. 26, 28 June 1858. *d.* 65 Denbigh st. Pimlico, London 17 March 1862 aged 45. *Annual Register* (1858) 69–71 ; *Wolferstan and Dew's Reports i*, 214–24 (1859).

GLOVER, SARAH ANN *(eld. dau. of Rev. Edward Glover, R. of St. Lawrence, Norwich).* Governess in family of Sir T. Fowell Buxton ; taught children at Norwich music on the Sol-faing mode 1815 ; founded the Tonic Sol-fa method 1840 which Rev. John Curwen modified and made popular 1844 ; entertained at a soirée in Jewin st. school-room, London 20 April 1855 ; author of *A manual of the Norwich Sol-fa system* 1845 ; *Manual of Tetrachordal system* 1850 ; resided 11 St. Owen st. Hereford ; portrait in Tonic Sol-fa coll. Forest Gate, Essex. *d.* Great Malvern 20 Oct. 1867 aged 82. *Memorials of J. Curwen* (1882) *pp. viii*, 49, 173.

GLOVER, VEN. GEORGE *(son of George Glover of Wigan).* *b.* 1778 ; ed. at Manchester sch. and Brasenose coll. Ox., B.A. 1801, M.A. 1811 ; R. of South Repps, Norfolk 1804 to death ; archdeacon of Sudbury 21 July 1823 to death ; V. of Gayton, Norfolk 1831 to death ; author of *A course of sermons* 2 vols. 1859. *d.* South Repps 4 May 1862, memorial brass on chancel floor of South Repps church. *Manchester School Register ii*, 196–8 (1868).

GLOVER, SIR JOHN HAWLEY *(son of rev. John Glover, English chaplain at Cologne).* Entered R.N. 1841 ; in expedition to the Niger under Dr. Baikie 1857–61 ; acting consul at Lagos 22 May to 21 Nov. 1863, colonial secretary 9 May 1864 and administrator of the settlement 19 Oct. 1866 to 1872 ; commissioner to friendly natives near the Gold coast 18 Aug. 1873 ; commanded 800 houssas in the march to Coomassie 1874, received thanks of both houses of parliament ; G.C.M.G. 8 May 1874 ; governor of Newfoundland Jany. 1876 to June 1881, and 17 Dec. 1883 to death ; retired captain 24 Nov. 1877 ; governor of the Leeward islands Dec. 1881 to 17 Dec. 1883. *d.* 35 Harley st. Cavendish sq. London 30 Sept. 1885. *I.L.N. lxiv.* 384, 386 (1874), *portrait.*

GLOVER, PERCY CLABON *(2 son of Rev. Richard Glover, vicar of St. Luke's, West Holloway).* *b.* Holy Trinity parsonage, Maidstone 14 May 1856 ; educ. Highgate and Worcester coll. Ox., B.A. 1880, M.A. 1883 ; founded the De Quincy soc. at his coll. 1878 ; served as tutor with various families in England and abroad ; his collar bone fractured playing Lacrosse at Dulwich 5 March 1888. *d.* of rheumatic fever at Addiscombe vicarage 1 April 1888. *Self Discipline, a memoir of P. C. Glover by Rev. Richard Glover* (1889), *with portrait.*

GLOVER, STEPHEN. Author of *The Peak guide,* Derby 1830 ; *The history and gazetteer of county of Derby,* ed. by Thomas Noble, vol. i, pt. i, 1831, vol. ii, pt. i, 1833, never finished ; assisted Thomas Bateman in his *Vestiges of the Antiquities of Derbyshire* 1848. *d.* 26 Dec. 1869. *bur.* Moreton, Cheshire.

GLOVER, STEPHEN *(brother of Charles W. Glover 1806–63).* *b.* London 1812 ; teacher of music, London ; composer of Merry is the Greenwood, a cavatina 1847 ; Beauty and the beast, chamber opera 1868 ; The dream is past 1837, What are the wild waves saying 1850, Stars of the summer night 1855, There is a sweet wild rose 1863, duets ; Annie on the Banks o' Dee 1857, Emigrants' Farewell 1850, songs ; and upwards of 1200 other works all of which commanded a sale. *d.* 71 Talbot road, Bayswater, London 7 Dec. 1870. *Grove's Music and Musicians* (1889) *iv*, 648–9.

GLOVER, WILLIAM. Ed. at Trin. coll. Dublin ; barrister M.T. 23 Jany. 1829 ; serjeant at law 19 June 1840 ; purchased *Morning Chronicle* from Duke of Newcastle, W. E. Gladstone and Sidney Herbert for £7500 in 1854, receiving from them £3000 a year for 3 years ; engaged with Napoleon III. to edit the paper in his interest 1855, brought actions against French government for breach of contract ; sold the paper to George Stiff 1860, it ceased 1862 ; author of *A practical treatise on the law of municipal corporations* 1836. *d.* 3 Gower st. Bedford sq. London 21 Dec. 1870. *Grant's Newspaper Press* (1871) *i*, 310–12.

GLOVER, WILLIAM HOWARD *(brother of Edmund Glover 1813–60).* *b.* Kilburn, London 6 June 1819 ; a violinist in Lyceum orchestra under Wagstaff 1834 ; with his mother founded Music and dramatic agency Soho sq. London ; gave a season of opera in Manchester with his own pupils ; gave annual monster concerts at St. James's hall and Drury Lane ; initiated performance of Beethoven's Pastoral Symphony with pictorial and choregraphic illustrations 1863, and of Israel in Egypt

GLOVER, W. H. (*Con.*)

1865; his cantata Tam o' Shanter produced at Philharmonic 4 July 1855; his opera Ruy Blas brought out at Covent Garden 24 Oct. 1861; musical critic on *Morning Post* 1849-65; conductor of Niblo's orchestra, New York 1868; *Palomita* operetta produced at Niblo's 1875. *d.* New York 28 Oct. 1875.

GLYN, HENRY CARR. *b.* 17 April 1829; entered navy 4 March 1844; captain 20 Aug. 1861; V.A. 9 June 1882; C.B. 29 May 1875. *d.* 32 Eaton place, London 16 Feb. 1884. *bur.* family vault, Stanbridge church 21 Feb. *Illust. sp. and dr. news xx*, 661 (1884), *portrait*; *I.L.N. lxxxiv*, 205 (1884), *portrait*.

GLYN, ISABELLA DALLAS (*dau. of Mr. Gearns, architect*). *b.* Edinburgh 22 May 1823; appeared at Manchester under her mother's maiden name Glyn 8 Nov. 1847 as Constance in *King John*; at Olympic, London as Lady Macbeth 26 Jany. 1848; played at Sadler's Wells 1848-51; gave her first Shakespearian reading Sep. 1851; appeared at Drury Lane as Bianca in *Fazio* 26 Dec. 1851, at St. James' 1854, at Standard 1855, at Sadler's Wells 1859, at Princess's 1867; gave recitals at Boston, U.S.A. 1870; gave Shakespeare readings at Steinway hall and St. James' hall 1878, 1879; a theatrical instructor; the latest adherent of the Kemble sch. of acting. *m.* (1) Edward Wills; *m.* (2) in Glasgow, Dec. 1853 and in London 12 July 1855 Eneas Sweetland Dallas *d.* 1879, divorced on her petition 10 May 1874, she was imprisoned at Holloway for contempt of court in declining to give up documents relating to her divorce case, released 28 June 1876. *d.* of cancer 13 Mount st. Grosvenor sq. London 18 May 1889. *The Duchess of Malfi, with a memoir of Miss Glyn* (1851) *pp.* 1-6, *portrait*; *Tallis's Dramatic Mag.* (1850) 37-40, 2 *portraits*; *Tallis's Drawing room table book* (1851) 1-2, *portrait, and parts* 7, 10, 12, 17, 21, 5 *portraits*; *The Players iii*, 391, 408 (1861), *portrait*.

GLYNN, HENRY RICHARD (*youngest son of John Glynn 1722-79, serjeant at law, M.P. for Middlesex*). *b.* 2 Sep. 1768; entered navy 19 May 1780; captain 10 April 1797; admiral 9 Nov. 1846, placed on half pay June 1851; mayor of Plymouth 1838. *d.* Bideford 20 July 1856.

GLYNN, JOSEPH (*son of James Glynn of Ouseburn iron foundry, Newcastle*). *b.* Hanover sq. Newcastle 6 Feb. 1799; designed and executed gas works for Berwick upon Tweed 1821; engineer to Butterley iron co. Derbyshire;

GLYNN, J. (*Con.*)

employed the water wheel or scoop wheel for draining marshes and fens by steam power; chairman of Eastern counties railway 2 years; M.I.C.E. 22 April 1828; member of Society of Arts 16 Nov. 1836; F.R.S. 8 Feb. 1838; author of *Rudimentary treatise on the construction of cranes* 1849, 4 ed. 1865. *d.* 28 Westbourne park villas, London 6 Feb. 1863.

GLYNNE, SIR STEPHEN RICHARD, 9 Baronet. *b.* Hawarden castle, Flintshire 22 Sep. 1807; succeeded 5 March 1815; ed. at Eton and Ch. Ch. Ox., B.A. 1828, M.A. 1831; M.P. for Flint district 1832-5, for Flintshire 1837-41 and 1842-47; lord lieut. of Flintshire 30 June 1845 to death; taken ill in street and *d.* Dr. Flack's surgery 56 High st. Shoreditch, London 17 June 1874. *Times* 18, 19, 20 *June* 1874.

GOAD, JOHN. *b.* Plymouth 20 Feb. 1825; known universally as the quarrier and worker of Devonshire marble having 4 large quarries near Plymouth, supplied all the polished marble for interior of the Oratory at Brompton, London 1854; found dead in his bed at his residence, Buckingham place, Stonehouse, Plymouth 25 Jany. 1886.

GOBAT, RIGHT REV. SAMUEL. *b.* Cremuse, canton Berne, Switzerland 26 Jany. 1799; studied at Bale, Paris and London; entered service of Church Missionary Soc., laboured in Abyssinia 1830-32; principal of Missionary college, Malta 1839; nominated bishop of Jerusalem by King of Prussia 1846; consecrated at Lambeth 5 July 1846; naturalised in England by act of parliament 9 & 10 Vict. c. 49, 13 Aug. 1846; author of *Journal of a three years residence in Abyssinia* 1847. *d.* Jerusalem 11 May 1879.

GODBY, CHRISTOPHER. Entered Bengal army 1805; col. 55 Bengal N.I. 1853 to death; L.G. 22 Nov. 1862; C.B. 21 May 1846. *d.* South bank, Batheaston 8 Dec. 1867 aged 77.

GODDARD, GEORGE BOUVERIE. *b.* Salisbury 25 Dec. 1832; self taught artist; spent 2 years in zoological gardens, London, studying animal life 1849-51; drew sporting subjects on wood for Punch; settled in London 1857; exhibited 19 paintings at R.A. and 2 at Suffolk st. 1856-79; chiefly an animal painter; his principle works were Lord Wolverton's blood hounds 1875, The struggle for existence 1879 now in Walker gallery, Liverpool, Love and War in the Abbotsbury swannery 1883. *d.* 37 Brook green, Hammersmith, London 6 March 1886.

GODFREY, ADOLPHUS FREDERICK (*son of the succeeding*). *b.* 1837; bandmaster of the Coldstream Guards Dec. 1863 to death; wrote many lancers, polkas, galops and quadrilles; confined in Peckham lunatic asylum, Surrey 1 June 1881. *d.* there 28 Aug. 1882.

GODFREY, CHARLES. *b.* Kingston, Surrey 22 Nov. 1790; bandmaster of Coldstream guards nearly 50 years; musician in ordinary to Wm. IV. 1831; editor and arranger of *Jullien's Military Band Journal* 1847. *d.* London 12 Dec. 1863.

GODKIN, JAMES. *b.* Gorey, co. Wexford 1806; pastor of dissenting ch. at Armagh 1834; missionary to Roman Catholics to 1845; went to London as a journalist 1847; established in Belfast *The Christian Patriot* 1849; editor of *Derry Standard;* editor of *Daily Express,* Dublin; member of Irish tenant league 1850; special commissioner of *Irish Times* to ascertain feeling of the farmers on land question 1869; granted civil list pension of £90, 5 April 1869; author of *A guide from the church of Rome to the church of Christ* 1836, 3 ed. 1845; *Ireland and her churches* 1867; *The land war in Ireland* 1870 and other books. *d.* Upper Norwood, Surrey 2 May 1879.

GODLEY, DENIS (*son of John Godley of Killigar, co. Leitrim*). *b.* 1823; ensign 74 highlanders 1839; sec. to governor general of Canada 1861–68; sec. to commission on Irish church temporalities 1869–81; sec. to Irish land commission 1881–88; C.B. 1881. *d.* Guardswell, Ascot 24 Jany. 1890.

GODLEY, JOHN ROBERT (*brother of the preceding*). *b.* 1814; ed. at Harrow and Christ church, Ox., B.A. 1836; proposed to emigrate one million Irish to Canada; contested Leitrim county 12 Aug. 1847; Canterbury colony, New Zealand, founded by him and E. G. Wakefield 1850, guided Canterbury 1850–52, agent in England 1854–56; commissioner of income tax Ireland 1853; assistant under secretary at war 1855–61; F.R.G.S.; author of *Letters from America* 2 vols. 1844; *Observations on an Irish poor law* 1847. *d.* 11 Gloucester place, Portman square, London 17 Nov. 1861. *Selection from writings and memoir by J. E. Fitzgerald* (1863) 1–32, *portrait*.

GODWIN, EDWARD WILLIAM. *b.* Old Market st. Bristol 26 May 1833; architect Bristol and then in partnership with Henry Crisp; removed to London 1862; built Northampton and Congleton town halls; assisted W. Burgess in his designs for new law courts London, and R. W. Eddis in his designs for parliament

GODWIN, E. W. (*Con.*)

houses Berlin; designed theatrical costumes for Hamlet, Claudian, Helena in Troas and the Bachelors 1886; F.S.A. 13 Feb. 1862; F.R.I.B.A.; a constant contributor to the *British Architect;* author of *Art furniture by W. Watt, from designs by E. W. Godwin* 1877; *Temple Bar illustrated* 1877; *A few notes on the architecture and costumes of Claudian* 1883 and other books. *d.* 6 Great College st. Westminster 6 Oct. 1886. *British Architect 15 Oct. 1886 pp. 347–48, portrait*.

GODWIN, GEORGE. *b.* Brompton, London 28 Jany.'1815; chief founder of Art Union of London 14 Feb. 1837, hon. sec.; author of *The last day,* a farce played at Olympic 28 Oct. 1840, and of several dramas; editor of *The Builder* Dec. 1842 to Oct. 1883; F.R.S. 7 March 1839; F.S.A. 13 Feb. 1838; vice pres. of R.I. of British Architects, gold medallist 1881, founded the Godwin bursary 1881; architect of St. Mary's ch. West Brompton and many other edifices; restored St. Mary's, Redcliffe, Bristol 1846–75; made a collection of ancient chairs, including Shakespeare's chair, sold 19 April 1888; author of *The churches of London* 2 vols. 1839; *A history of St. Paul's cathedral* 1837; *Facts and fancies* 1844; *History in Ruins, letters on history of architecture* 1853; *London Shadows* 1854; *Another blow for life* 1864. *d.* 6 Cromwell place, South Kensington 27 Jany. 1888. *Colburn's New Monthly Mag., vol. 167 p. 182, portrait*.

GODWIN, HENRY. Ensign 9 foot 30 Oct. 1799; lieut. col. 41 foot 26 July 1821; lieut. col. 87 foot 5 April 1827 to 25 June 1827, when placed on h.p.; employed in 6 several commands during Burmese war 1824–6; M.G. 9 Nov. 1846; recaptured Pegu Nov. 1852; col. 20 foot 25 Oct. 1853; C.B. 26 Dec. 1826, gazetted K.C.B. 9 Dec. 1853; author of *Burmah, Letters and papers written 1852–53,* 1854. *d.* Simla, Bengal 26 Oct. 1853 aged 69.

GODWIN, JOHN. *b.* Swansea; pupil of Sir James M'Adam; engineer to Ulster railway 1836–62; the first professor of engineering Queen's college, Belfast 1849; M.I.C.E. 24 June 1845. *d.* Tamnagharrie, co. Down 15 Jany. 1869.

GODWIN, REV. JOHN HENSLEY. *b.* Bristol 18 June 1809; educ. Highbury coll. 1833–36 and Edin. univ. 1836–37; congregational minister Old Meeting, Norwich 1837; resident and philosophical tutor Highbury coll. 1839; professor of New Testament exegesis, mental and moral philosophy and English, New coll. 1850–72; author of *Christian Baptism* 1845;

GODWIN, REV. J. H. *(Con.)*

Christian Faith 1852; *Translations of The Revelations* 1856, *St. Matthew* 1863, *St. Mark* 1869, *The Epistle to the Galatians* 1871 and *The Romans* 1873; a contributor to the *Contemporary Review* and the *Evangelical Mag.* *d.* 1 Belsize ter. Hampstead 26 Feb. 1889.

GODWIN, MARIANNE ELIZABETH. Caricaturist in London; signed her pictures with the word "Jack." *d.* University college hospital London 12 Aug. 1887 from her muslin dress catching fire at the ironing stove at her residence 13 Fitzroy sq. London.

GODWIN-AUSTEN, ROBERT ALFRED CLOYNE *(eld. son of Sir Henry Edmund Austen).* 1785–1871). *b.* Shalford house, Guildford 17 March 1808; ed. at Midhurst, Sussex and Oriel coll. Ox. fellow 1830, B.A. 1830; student of L.I. 1830; F.G.S. 19 March 1830, sec. 1843–4 and 1853–4; Wollaston medallist 1862; member of British Association 1846, pres. of geological section at Norwich 1868, and at Brighton 1872; F.R.S. 7 June 1849; made a splendid collection of palœozoic fossils in Cornwall which he presented to Jermyn st. Museum; took additional name of Godwin by royal license 1854; author of numerous papers on geology in scientific journals. *d.* Shalford house near Guildford 25 Nov. 1884. *Geological Mag. Jany.* 1885 *pp.* 1–10; *Proc. of Royal Soc. xxxviii, pp. ix–xiii* (1885); *Quarterly Journal of Geol. Soc. xli,* 37–9 (1885).

GOLD, CHARLES EMILIUS. Ensign 65 foot 20 March 1828; lieut. col. 30 Dec. 1845 to 15 June 1860; L.G. 27 Dec. 1868. *d.* Dover 29 July 1871 aged 68.

GOLD, WILLIAM GEORGE. Second lieut. royal staff corps 7 April 1825; lieut. col. of 53 foot 26 July 1844, of 4 foot 8 Dec. 1848 to 7 Sep. 1852, when placed on h.p.; col. of 32 foot 28 Aug. 1865, of 53 foot 2 Feb. 1867 to death; L.G. 29 March 1868. *d.* Garthmyl hall, Montgomeryshire 26 Dec. 1868 aged 68.

GOLDFINCH, SIR HENRY *(son of Henry Goldfinch of Peckham, Surrey).* *b.* London 1781; 2 lieut. R.E. 1 March 1790, col. 10 Jany. 1837, col. commandant 17 Feb. 1854 to death; L.G. 11 Nov. 1851; C.B. 4 June 1815, K.C.B. 6 April 1852. *d.* 11 Upper Wimpole st. London 21 Nov. 1854.

GOLDIE, GEORGE. *b.* Mornay house, Edinburgh 25 Oct. 1784; ed. at Univ. of Edin. M.D. 1808; L.R.C.P. London 1812; practised in London 1812 at Warminster, at York 1815 to about 1849; phys. to York county hospital 1822–33; took charge of cholera hospital at

GOLDIE, G. *(Con.)*

York during epidemic of cholera 1831; took an active part in agitation for Catholic emancipation; contributed to *British and Foreign Medical Review* and medical journals. *d.* Sheffield 2 May 1853. *J. Gillow's English Catholics ii,* 510–13 (1885).

GOLDIE, GEORGE *(son of the preceding).* *b.* York 1828; ed. at St. Cuthbert's coll. near Durham; pupil and afterwards partner of Messrs. Hatfield and Weightman of Sheffield, architects; practised in London; designed pro-cathedral at Kensington, cathedral at Sligo and many other Roman Catholic churches, convents, &c. in Great Britain and Ireland; A.R.I.B.A. *d.* 9 Kensington sq. London 1 March 1887.

GOLDIE, SIR GEORGE LEIGH. Cornet 6 dragoon guards 3 Sep. 1803; lieut. col. 11 foot 29 May 1835 to 26 Feb. 1841, when placed on h.p.; col. of 77 foot 22 Dec. 1854, of 35 foot 13 Feb. 1861 to death; general 6 Nov. 1862; C.B. 19 July 1838, K.C.B. 28 June 1861. *d.* Claremont Southampton 26 March 1863 aged 72.

GOLDING, BENJAMIN. *b.* Essex; ed. at St. Andrew's Univ., M.D. 6 Dec. 1823; L.R.C.P. London 4 June 1825; physician to West London infirmary, founded the Charing Cross hospital which was the infirmary rebuilt and renamed 1831, director of it to death; published *An historical account of St. Thomas's hospital, Southwark* 1819. *d.* The Boltons, West Brompton, London 21 June 1863 aged 69.

GOLDING, RICHARD. *b.* London 15 Aug. 1785; engraved B. West's Death of Nelson, book plates for Don Quixote and Gil Blas, Sir T. Lawrence's Princess Charlotte of Wales 1818, Westall's Princess Victoria, W. Fowler's Princess Victoria 1830 and Rubens' St. Ambrose refusing Theodosius admission into the Church; commenced engraving Maclise's A Peep into Futurity, for the Art Union 1842 which was still unfinished in 1852. *d.* in a poor lodging Stebbington st. St. Pancras, London 28 Dec. 1865. *bur.* Highgate cemetery, body exhumed Sep. 1866 on a suspicion that he had been poisoned by his doctor.

GOLDNEY, PHILIP *(2 son of Thomas Goldney of Clifton).* *b.* London 21 Nov. 1802; cadet H.E.I.C.S. 1821, capt. 11 June 1836; learned the native languages and Persian; collector and magistrate in Sind 1844; commissioner in charge of Fyzabad to 1857; lieut. col. 53 Bengal N.I. 1853–56, 22 Bengal N.I. 1856–57, 38 Bengal N.I. 1857 to death; shot by the mutineers on an island in the Gograh 9 June 1857.

GOLDSBROUGH, RICHARD. *b.* Shipley near Bradford, Yorks. 1821; wool merchant Bradford 1842; went to Adelaide, Australia, settled in Melbourne 1847 and became a dealer in wool, etc. 1848; in partnership with Edward Rowe and George Kirk 1853 as dealers in stations, stock and wool; amalgamated with Australian agency and banking corporation 1881 when the consolidated concern became a limited co. and himself chairman, capital 3 millions; steward of Victoria racing club from its foundation. *d.* Melbourne 8 April 1886.

GOLDSMID, ANNA MARIA *(sister of the succeeding).* Pupil of Thomas Campbell the poet, who gave her some of his manuscripts which she bequeathed to British Museum; gave large sums to charity, often anonymously; published many original pamphlets on education; translated L. Philippsohn's *The development of the religious idea in Judaism* 1855 and J. Cohen's *The Deicides, Analysis of the life of Jesus* 1872 and other books. *d.* 26 Cambridge sq. Hyde park, London 8 Feb. 1889 aged 84.

GOLDSMID, SIR FRANCIS HENRY, 2 Baronet *(2 son of Sir Isaac Lyon Goldsmid, 1 baronet 1778–1859).* *b.* Spital sq. London 1 May 1808; barrister L.I. 31 Jany. 1833, bencher 11 Jany. 1858; Q.C. 9 Jany. 1858, the first Jew called to the English bar and the first Jewish Q.C. and bencher; pres. of senate of Univ. coll. London, where is portrait of him by R. Lehmann; M.P. for Reading 11 Jany. 1860 to death; founded Jews' infant sch. 1841, now largest infant sch. in England; founded Anglo-Jewish Association 1871; author of many pamphlets. *d.* St. Thomas's hospital, London 2 May 1878 from effects of an accident at Waterloo station same day. *Memoir of Sir F. H. Goldsmid, by D. W. Marks and Albert Lowy, 2 ed. (1882), portrait.*

GOLDSMID, FREDERICK DAVID. *b.* London 1812; M.P. for Honiton 12 July 1865 to death. *d.* 20 Portman sq. London 18 March 1866, personalty sworn under £400,000 23 June 1866.

GOLDSMID, HENRY EDWARD *(son of Edward Goldsmid of Upper Harley st. London).* *b.* 9 May 1812; educ. Haileybury coll. where he learnt Persian and Hindustani; went to Bombay 1832; assistant revenue commissioner Tauna 1835 when he devised the revenue survey and assessment system which was applied to the whole of the lands in Bombay 1865–68 with great success; sec. to Bombay government in revenue department 1848 and chief sec. 1854. *d.* Cairo 3 Jany. 1855.

GOLDSMID, SIR ISAAC LYON, 1 Baronet *(eld. son of Asher Goldsmid of Finsbury sq. London who d. 1 Nov. 1822).* *b.* Bury st. St. Mary Axe, London 13 Jany. 1778; member of firm of Mocatta and Goldsmid, bullion brokers; treasurer of Univ. coll. hospital 1839–57; created baronet 15 Oct. 1841, being the first Jew so created; created Baron de Goldsmid and Da Palmeira of Portugal 1846; endowed chair of geology in Univ. coll. London, where is portrait of him by B. R. Faulkner; F.R.S. 13 March 1828. *d.* St. John's lodge, Regent's park, London 27 April 1859. *J. Picciotto's Sketches of Anglo-Jewish history* (1875) 249–56; *N. H. Nixon's History of North London hospital* (1882), 16–18; *Banker's Mag. June 1859, pp. 375–82, July 1859, pp. 449–57, April 1860, pp. 220–4.*

GOLDSMITH, GEORGE *(son of John Goldsmith, paymaster R.N.)* Entered navy 20 June 1821; captain 16 Sep. 1842; superintendent of Chatham dockyard 1856–61; admiral 30 July 1875; C.B. 4 Feb. 1856; granted Greenwich hospital pension 1866. *d.* 35 Victoria road, Old Charlton, Kent 2 July 1888 in 82 year.

GOLDSTUECKER, THEODOR. *b.* Königsberg, Prussia 18 Jany. 1821; Ph. D. Königsberg 1840; came to England 1850; contributed to *Chambers' Encyclopædia* 1862–68 and to *Westminster Review;* professor of Sanskrit in Univ. coll. London May 1852 to death; chief founder of Sanskrit Text Society 1866; pres. of Philological Soc. to death; author of *On the Mahâbhârata* 1868 and other books. *d.* 14 St. George's sq. Primrose hill, London 6 March 1872. *Goldstuecker's Literary Remains 2 vols.* (1879); *Trubner's Record vii,* 109, 145 (1872).

GOLIGHTLY, REV. CHARLES POURTALES *(2 son of William Golightly of Ham, Surrey).* *b.* 23 May 1807; educ. Eton and at Oriel. coll. Ox., B.A. 1828, M.A. 1830; C. of Penshurst, Kent 1828; C. of Littlemore, Oxford 1836; C. of Godalming, Surrey 1839–41; C. of Headington Quarry, Oxford 1849–58; C. of Marston, Ox. 1858–68; a prominent opponent of the ritualistic movement 1840; author of *Look at home or a short and easy method with the Roman Catholics* 1837; *Brief remarks upon No. 90 of the Tracts for the Times* 1841, and many other works against Ritualism. *d.* 6 Holywell st. Oxford 25 Dec. 1885. *E. M. Goulburn's Reminiscences of C. P. Golightly* (1886); *Mozley's Reminiscences ii,* 108–13 (1882).

GOLLOP, GEORGE TILLY *(elder son of Thomas Gollop of Sherborne 1745–93).* *b.* 11 Oct. 1791; ed. at Brasenose coll. Ox.; student of I.T. 1811; made a tour on the continent, riding

GOLLOP, G. T. *(Con.)*

from Holland to Vienna and on to Naples 1814 ; held the estate of Strode, Dorset 1793 to death 96 years ; published a vol. of translations of several poems of Schiller, and translations of Eichhorn's *Introduction to the New Testament* and *Introduction to the Old Testament*. *d.* Strode manor, Dorset 22 Feb. 1889.

GOMERSAL, EDWARD ALEXANDER *(son of a military officer)*. *b.* Gomersal near Leeds ; first appeared in London at Haymarket theatre 16 Sep. 1811 ; spoke the first words upon boards of new T.R. Windsor ; played Napoleon in *The Battle of Waterloo* at Astley's about 1817, acted same character in every amphitheatre in Great Britain ; proprietor with B. O. Conquest of Garrick theatre, Whitechapel to 4 Nov. 1846 when it was burned down ; is referred to in the *Bon Gaultier Ballads* and *The Newcomes*. *d.* Leeds 19 Oct. 1862 aged 74. *Era 26 Oct. 1862 p. 10, col. 4.*

GOMM, SIR WILLIAM MAYNARD (1 *son of lieut. col. William Gomme, killed* 1794). *b.* Barbadoes 10 Nov. 1784 ; gazetted ensign 9 regt. 24 May 1794 ; served in Holland 1799, Spain 1800, Hanover 1805, Baltic 1807, Peninsula 1808–9, 1810–14, at Quatre Bras and Waterloo 1815 ; lieut. col. of Coldstream guards 1836 ; K.C.B. 2 Jany. 1815, G.C.B. 21 June 1859 ; commander in Jamaica 1839–41 ; governor of Mauritius 1842–49 ; col. of 13 foot 10 March 1846, of Coldstream guards 15 Aug. 1863 to death ; commander in chief in India, Jany. 1851 to Dec. 1855, general 1854, field marshal 1 Jany. 1868 ; constable of Tower of London 31 Oct. 1872 to death ; knight of St. Anne of Russia 1815, of St. Vladimir 1874 ; author of *The story of Newcastle, Jamaica, etc.* 1864 ; five Field-marshal Gomm scholarships founded at Keble coll. Ox. by the will of his widow who *d.* 30 Nov. 1877 leaving £15,000 for the purpose. He *d.* Brighton 15 March 1875. *bur.* Ch. Ch. Rotherhithe. *I.L.N. lxi,* 412, 414 (1872), *portrait ; Graphic xi,* 315 (1875), *portrait ; Letters and Journals of Sir W. M. Gomm* (1881), *portrait*

NOTE.—The public house Sir William Gomm, 44 Abbeyfield road, Rotherhithe, London, is named after him.

GOMPERTZ, BENJAMIN *(son of Mr. Gompertz, diamond merchant)*. *b.* Bury st. London 5 March 1779 ; a stock broker ; president of Old Mathematical soc. of Crispin st. Spitalfields which became Astronomical soc. 1820, member of council 1821–31 ; F.R.S. 29 June 1819 ; F.R.A.S., member of council 1832, contributed to the complete catalogue of stars ; actuary of Alliance British and Foreign assurance Co. 1824–48 ; propounded the law of

GOMPERTZ, B. *(Con.)*

human mortality 1825 ; author of *The principles and application of imaginary quantities* 2 vols. 1817–18 ; *Hints on Porisms* 1850. *d.* 1 Kennington terrace, Vauxhall, London 14 July 1865. *Assurance Mag. April* 1866, *pp.* 1–20 ; *Walford's Insurance Cyclop. v,* 437–54 (1878).

GOMPERTZ, LEWIS *(younger brother of the preceding)*. Spent his life in enforcing kindness to animals ; a strict vegetarian and would never ride in a coach ; hon. sec. of soc. for prevention of cruelty to animals 1826–32 ; founded the Animals' Friend soc. 1832 ; edited *The Animals' Friend or the Progress of Humanity* 1846 ; invented shot proof ships, fortifications for reflecting the balls to the place fired from, a mechanical cure for apoplexy, and the expanding chuck which is now found attached to lathes in workshops ; author of *Mechanical inventions and suggestions on locomotion* 1850 ; *Fragments in defence of animals* 1852. *d.* 5 Kennington oval, London 2 Dec. 1861. *Fragments in defence of animals by L. Gompertz* (1852), *portrait.*

GOOCH, SIR DANIEL, 1 Baronet. (3 *son of John Gooch of Bedlington, Northumberland* 1783–1833). *b.* Bedlington 24 Aug. 1816 ; chief locomotive engineer to Great Western Railway Company 1837–1864, chairman Nov. 1866 to death ; M.P. for Cricklade 1865–85 ; comr. on Trades Union ; Chairman of Great Eastern Steamship Co. ; Chairman of Telegraph Construction and Maintenance Company ; one of purchasers of Great Eastern Steamship, with a view to her being employed in laying Atlantic cable, and this having been effected in 1866, created baronet 15 Nov. 1866, being first engineer made a baronet. *d.* Clewer park, Windsor 15 Oct. 1889. *Biograph, March to April* 1882 *pp.* 329–32 ; *Touchstone 29 March* 1879 *pp.* 1–2, *portrait ; Colburn's New monthly mag. cxvi,* 1390 (1879), *portrait.*

GOOCH, SIR EDWARD SHERLOCK, 6 Baronet. *b.* Holbecks, Suffolk 1802 ; M.P. for East Suffolk 19 Feb. 1846 to death ; provincial grand master of freemasons 1851 to death ; succeeded 18 Dec. 1851. *d.* Benacre hall, Suffolk 9 Nov. 1856.

GOOCH, REV. JOHN HENRY. *b.* Suffolk ; ed. at Trin. coll. Cam., scholar, 14 wrangler 1834, B.A. 1834, M.A. 1837 ; assist. master Wakefield proprietory sch. 1838–40 ; master of Heath gr. sch. Halifax 1840–61 ; Inc. of Stainland near Halifax 1841–60 ; author of *Church catechism expanded* 1851. *d.* 22 July 1861 aged 60. *T. Cox's History of Heath gr. sch.* (1879) 45, 77, *portrait.*

GOOCH, THOMAS LONGRIDGE *(eld. son of John Gooch). b.* London 1 Nov. 1808; pupil of George Stephenson 1823–29; made working drawings for Liverpool and Manchester railway 1827–8, resident engineer on it at Liverpool 1829–30, had charge of the Dart locomotive on opening of the line 1830; resident engineer on London and Birmingham line 1833; with G. Stephenson joint principal engineer of Manchester and Leeds line 1839–41 and alone 1841–44; with G. Stephenson and G. P. Bidder engineer of Trent valley line 1845; retired from business 1851; as an engineer second only to the Stephensons and Brunel; M.I.C.E. 3 June 1845. *d.* Team lodge, Gateshead 23 Nov. 1882. *Min. of proc. of Instit. of C.E. lxxii,* 300–8 (1883).

GOOCH, SIR THOMAS SHERLOCK, 5 Baronet. *b.* 2 Nov. 1767; M.P. for Suffolk 1806–30; succeeded his father 7 April 1826; chairman of Suffolk quarter sessions to 1843. *d.* Benacre hall, Suffolk 18 Dec. 1851.

GOOD, JOSEPH HENRY. *b.* Sambrook, Shropshire 18 Nov. 1775; articled to Sir John Sloane 1795–99; built Apps' Court park, Surrey and Horndean, Hampshire; surveyor to Thavies estate, Holborn, and parish of St. Andrew's, Holborn; surveyor to Armourers' co. 1819, built new hall Coleman st. 1840; architect to Royal Pavilion, Brighton 1822, to the commissioners for building new churches 1826; clerk of works to the Tower, Royal Mint, Fleet and King's bench prisons, etc. 1830 and Kensington palace 1831; F.R.I.B.A. 1834. *d.* Palace Green, Kensington 20 Nov. 1857.

GOOD, THOMAS SWORD. *b.* Berwick-upon-Tweed 4 Dec. 1789; a house painter, produced cheap portraits; a genre painter of domestic subjects; exhibited 19 pictures at R.A., 43 at B.I. and 2 at Suffolk st. 1820–34; his chief paintings are Coast scene with a fisherman 1833, The Newspaper, No News, and Study of a boy, all in the National gallery; J. W. Barnes of Durham has a large collection of his works. *d.* in a house on the Quay walls, Berwick 15 April 1872.

GOODALL, EDWARD. *b.* Leeds 17 Sept. 1795; self-taught, from 1811 practised engraving and painting; commenced engraving Turner's pictures 1823 and produced a long series; engraved Stanfield's The Castle of Ischia and F. Goodall's The Piper, for the Art Union of London; etched Maclise's Shakspeare's Seven Ages 1850; exhibited 2 engravings at R.A., 3 at B.I. and 8 at Suffolk st. 1822–41. *d.* 143 Hampstead road, London 11 April 1870.

GOODALL, FREDERICK TREVELYAN *(son of Frederick Goodall, R.A.)* Student at R.A., gold medal for his picture The return of Ulysses 1869; exhibited 17 pictures at R.A. 1868–71. *d.* Capri, Italy from an accident 11 April 1871 aged 23.

GOODALL, HOWARD *(brother of the preceding).* Exhibited at R.A., Nydia in the house of Glaucus 1870 and Capri girls winnowing 1873. *d.* Cairo 17 Jany. 1874 aged 24.

GOODALL, ISABELLA. *b.* Liverpool 10 Aug. 1851; appeared at Royal amphitheatre, Liverpool 1865 in *The Middy ashore;* appeared in London at Prince of Wales's theatre 15 April 1866 as Coralie in *A winning hazard;* burlesque actress at Strand theatre London several years. *d.* 124 Pentonville road, London 3 Feb. 1884. *bur.* Norwood cemetery 9 Feb. beside her mother, her sister Annie (actress *d.* 1 March 1877 aged 30), and her brother.

GOODALL, WALTER *(youngest son of Edward Goodall 1795–1870). b.* 6 Nov. 1830; studied at Somerset house and Royal academy; Assoc. of Soc. of Painters in water-colours 1853, mem. 1862; exhibited 3 drawings at R.A. 1852 and works at Royal Manchester Institution; his Lottery Ticket shown at Philadelphia Centennial exhib. 1876; made drawings from pictures in Vernon gallery for Art Union; published *Walter Goodall's Rustic Sketches. d.* Clapham near Bedford 14 May 1889.

GOODALL, WILLIAM. Whip of the Belvoir fox hounds 1837–42, huntsman 1842 to death. *d.* The Kennels near Belvoir 17 May 1859. *Scott and Sebright, By the Druid* (1862) 408–11; *Silk and Scarlet, By the Druid* (1859) 372, portrait; *Sporting Review xli,* 398–400 (1859).

GOODE, JOHN. Ensign 3 West India foot 5 Sep. 1811; lieut. 10 foot 10 Aug. 1826 to 20 Feb. 1835, captain on h.p. 20 Feb. 1835 to death; arrested at 218 Regent street, London 4 Nov. 1837 for making use of threatening gestures and language to Queen Victoria in the Birdcage walk same day, declared before the authorities that he was John the Second king of England, son of George iv. and Queen Caroline, and was born in Montague place, Blackheath; tried in Court of Queen's Bench for using seditious language to the Queen and sent to Bethlehem hospital as insane 18 Nov. 1837, moved to Broadmoor criminal lunatic asylum March 1864 where he *d.* from natural decay 10 Feb. 1883. *Times 6, 7, 20 Nov.* 1837.

GOODE, VERY REV. WILLIAM *(son of Rev. Wm. Goode 1762–1816, R. of St. Andrew's and St.*

GOODE, VERY REV. W. *(Con.)*
Ann's, Blackfriars, London). b. 10 Nov. 1801;
ed. at St. Paul's sch. and Trin. coll. Cam.,
B.A. 1825, M.A. 1828, D.D. 1860; C. of Ch.
Ch. Newgate st. London 1825–35; R. of St.
Antholin's, Watling st. 1835–49; R. of Allhallows, Thames st. 1849–56; Warburtonian
lecturer 1853–57; R. of St. Margaret, Lothbury 1856–60; dean of Ripon 10 May 1860
to death; edited *Christian Observer;* author of
A memoir of the Rev. W. Goode, 2 ed. 1828; *A
brief history of church rates,* 2 ed. 1838; *The
divine rule of faith and practice* 2 vols. 1842,
new ed. 3 vols. 1853, and 6 other books; found
dead in his bed at the Deanery, Ripon 13
Aug. 1868. *I.L.N. liii,* 187 (1868).

GOODENOUGH, JAMES GRAHAM *(son of Rev.
Edmund Goodenough 1785–1845, dean of Wells).*
b. Stoke hill near Guildford 3 Dec. 1830; ed.
at Westminster; naval cadet 7 May 1844,
captain 9 May 1863; captain of the Minotaur
1867–70; worked for the *Daily News* French
peasant relief fund 1870; naval attaché to all
maritime courts of Europe 1871–73; commodore of the Australian station 22 May 1873
to death; C.M.G. 28 May 1875; C.B. 29
May 1875. *d.* on board the Pearl about 500
miles from Sydney 20 Aug. 1875 from arrow
wounds received at Carlyon bay, island of
Santa Cruz 12 Aug. *bur.* St. Leonard's cemetery, north shore of Sydney harbour 24 Aug.,
bust by Prince Victor of Hohenlohe in painted
hall Greenwich hospital; the 'Goodenough
royal naval home' in Sydney was founded in
his honour. *Journal of Commodore Goodenough,*
edited with a memoir by his widow (1876), portrait; *H. A. Page's Leaders of men* (1880)
140–78; *Graphic xi,* 269 (1875), *portrait.*

GOODENOUGH, VEN. WILLIAM *(son of Rev.
Edmund Goodenough, V. of Swindon, Wilts.,
who d. 8 Nov. 1807 aged 62).* Ed. at Westminster; matric. at Ch. Ch. Ox. 9 June 1790
aged 17; kept a school at Ealing, Middlesex;
V. of Warkworth, Northumberlard 1811,
of Mareham le Fen, Lincs. 1818 to death;
archdeacon of Carlisle 20 June 1827 to death;
V. of Great Salkeld, Cumberland 1827 to
death. *d.* Mareham le Fen 13 Dec. 1854.

GOODEVE, JOSEPH (3 *son of John Goodeve of
Bury hall, Hants.)* b. Gosport, Hants. 1801;
barrister I.T. 28 Nov. 1829; wrote for *Westminster Review* and *Monthly Mag.;* professor
of English law at Presidency coll. Calcutta
1860; master in equity of supreme court of
Calcutta 1861; author of *The law of evidence
as administered in England and applied to India*
1862. *d.* Cook's Folly near Bristol 29 Jany.
1865. *bur.* Norwood cemetery, Surrey.

GOODEVE, LOUIS ARTHUR *(son of the preceding).* b. 11 Jany. 1841; ed. at Westminster
and Ch. Ch. Ox., junior student 1859–66;
B.A. 1862; barrister M.T. 9 June 1865;
practised at Calcutta; editor and sec. of
Bengal Law Reports 1868–70 and 1873; superintendent of law and jurisprudence Presidency
coll. Calcutta 1871; law lecturer Bristol Univ.
coll. 1878–80; author of *Railway passengers
and railway companies* 1877; *Modern law of real
property* 1883, 2 ed. 1885; *Modern law of personal property* 1887 and other books. *d.* Clayton villa, Clifton park, Clifton 13 March 1888.

GOODFELLOW, SAMUEL. Second lieut. Bombay engineers 1795, col. 29 July 1825 to
death; L.G. 11 Nov. 1851. *d.* 19 Fitzroy sq.
London 14 June 1860.

GOODFORD, REV. CHARLES OLD (2 *son of
Rev. John Goodford of Chilton Cantelo, Somerset
1784–1835).* b. Chilton Cantelo 15 July 1812;
ed. at Eton and King's coll. Cam., fellow to
1844; B.A. 1836, M.A. 1839, D.D. 1853;
assistant master at Eton 1835, head master
1853–62, provost 27 Jany. 1862 to death;
R. of Chilton Cantelo 1856 to death; edited
P. Terentii Afri Comœdiæ 1854. *d.* The lodge,
Eton 9 May 1884. *Lyte's Eton College* (1875)
475–8, 517, 519; *I.L.N.* 17 *May* 1884 *pp.*
465, 475, *portrait; Graphic* 7 *June* 1884 *pp.*
546, 549, *portrait.*

GOODLAKE, FRANCIS. Printer and publisher
of *The Times* 1858–1882 when he retired on
pension. *d.* Brixton 12 April 1890 in 68 year.

GOODLAKE, GERALD LITTLEHALES *(youngest
son of T. M. Goodlake of Letcombe, Berkshire
1807–77).* b. Wadley, Berkshire 14 May
1832; ed. at Eton; 2 lieut. 21 foot 14 June
1850; ensign Coldstream guards 27 June
1851, major 14 Aug. 1872 to 7 Aug. 1875
when placed on h.p.; D.A.Q.M.G. Crimea
1855–1856; A.D.C. to the Queen 1869–1879;
M.G. 11 Aug. 1879; V.C. 24 Feb. 1857; one
of the best all-round sportsmen of his time.
d. Denham fishery, Uxbridge 5 April 1890.
Baily's Mag. xxxii, 373 (1878), *portrait; Sporting Mirror ii,* 197–8 (1881), *portrait; Graphic*
26 *April* 1890 *p.* 533, *portrait.*

GOODMAN, SIR GEORGE *(son of Benjamin
Goodman of Leeds, who d. 10 June 1848 aged
85).* Woolstapler at Leeds and Bradford;
mayor of Leeds 1836, 1847 and 9 Nov. 1850
to 20 March 1852; represented Leeds at
Great Exhibition 1851; knighted at St.
James's palace 26 Feb. 1852; M.P. for Leeds
1852–1857. *d.* Roundhay near Leeds 13 Oct.
1859 aged 67. *R. V. Taylor's Biographia
Leodiensis* (1865) 477–80.

GOODSIR, JOHN (eld. son of John Goodsir of Anstruther, Fife, surgeon). b. Anstruther 14 March 1814; ed. at St. Andrews and Univ. of Edin.; L.C.S. Edin. 1836, curator of Museum 1841–43; curator of Museum in Univ. of Edin. 1845–46; professor of anatomy in Univ. of Edin. 1846 to Dec. 1866; author of Anatomical and pathological observations 1845; conducted Annals of anatomy and physiology, Nos. 1-3, 1850–53. d. South Cottage, Wardie near Edinburgh 6 March 1867. J. Goodsir's Anatomical memoirs, edited by W. Turner i, 1–191 (1868), portrait; Proc. of Royal Soc. xvi, 14–16 (1868).

GOODWIN, CHARLES WYCLIFFE (eld. son of Charles Goodwin of King's Lynn, Norfolk, solicitor). b. King's Lynn 1817; ed. at St. Cath. coll. Cam., B.A. 1838, M.A. 1842; barrister L.I. 14 Nov. 1848; edited the Literary Gazette 1871, The Parthenon 1872; assistant judge of supreme court for China and Japan 31 March 1865, acting judge 1869 and 22 May 1876 to death; wrote essays on Hieratic Papyri in Cambridge Essays 1858, and On the Mosaic Cosmogony in Essays and Reviews 1860. d. Shanghai 17 Jany. 1878.

GOODWIN, JOSIAH. Journalist in Devonshire; editor of Journal of Bath and West of England Soc. 1859–90, sec. 1866–83; assisted in editing Journal of Royal Agricultural Soc. 1863 etc. d. Bath 3 June 1890 aged 70. I.L.N. 14 June 1890 p. 741, portrait.

GOODWIN, THOMAS (brother of William Goodwin, music librarian, d. 1 April 1876). b. London 1799; landed in New York 24 Aug. 1827; music librarian New York. d. New York 28 June 1886. O. Mason's Sketches and Impressions from after dinner talk of T. Goodwin (1887) p. iii.

GOODWYN, HENRY. 2 lieut. Bengal engineers 18 Dec. 1823, lieut. col. 5 Dec. 1848, col. commandant 3 Aug. 1855 to death; general 14 July 1871; author of Memoir on the Taperchain suspension bridge, Calcutta 1844; The last Adam 1868; The book of the Revelation of Jesus Christ 1877. d. Bournemouth 8 Nov. 1886.

GOODWYN, JULIUS EDMUND (son of Wildman Goodwyn of Blackheath). b. 21 Feb. 1824; ensign 41 foot 5 Jany. 1844, lieut. col. 9 March 1855 to March 1866; brigadier general Bengal 14 March 1866 to 28 Feb. 1870; col. of 1 battalion Gloucestershire regiment 5 Nov. 1880, of 1 battalion Welsh regiment 20 Jany. 1883 to death; general 10 Jany. 1881; placed on retired list 1 July 1881; C.B. 2

GOODWYN, J. E. (Con.)

Jany. 1857; author of Antitypical parallels, or the kingdom of Israel and of Heaven, By Gershom 1866. d. Bath 4 March 1890.

GOOLD, WYNDHAM (youngest son of Thomas Goold of Dublin, master in chancery, who d. 16 July 1846). Ed. at Westminster school and Univ. of Dublin; called to Irish bar 1837; M.P. for co. Limerick 14 Dec. 1850 to death. d. London 27 Nov. 1854 in 40 year.

GORDON, EDWARD STRATHEARN GORDON, 1 Baron (eld. son of John Gordon, major 2 foot). b. Inverness 10 April 1814; ed. at royal academy, Inverness and Univ. of Edin.; LL.B. Glasgow and Edin.; called to bar in Scotland 1835; Q.C. 12 Nov. 1868; sheriff of Perthshire 26 July 1858 to 12 July 1866; solicitor general for Scotland 12 July 1866 to 28 Feb. 1867; lord advocate of Scotland 28 Feb. 1867 to Dec. 1868 and 26 Feb. 1874 to Oct. 1876; M.P. for Thetford 3 Dec. 1867 to 11 Nov. 1868 when borough was disfranchised; contested Glasgow and Aberdeen univs. 1868, M.P. for these univs. 1869–76; dean of faculty of advocates 1869–74; P.C. 17 March 1874; lord of appeal in ordinary 6 Oct. 1876 to death; created Baron Gordon of Drumearn, co. Stirling 6 Oct. 1876. d. Brussels 21 Aug. 1879. Journal of jurisprudence xxiii, 541–2 (1879).

GORDON, ADAM LINDSAY (son of Capt. Adam D. Gordon). b. Fayal in the Azores 1833; educ. Cheltenham coll. and Woolwich; in the mounted police, South Australia 1853; a horse breaker; member of the house of assembly, Victoria 1865; livery stable keeper Ballarat 1867; a steeple chaser; settled at Brighton near Melbourne 1869; failed in securing reversion to Esselmont estate, Scotland 1869; author of Sea spray and smoke drift 1867; Bush ballads and galloping rhymes 1870; Ashtaroth, a dramatic lyric; shot himself on the beach at Brighton 24 June 1870. J. H. Ross' Laureate of the Centaurs (1888), portrait; Poems ed. by Marcus Clarke (1887); Temple Bar, Feb. 1884 pp. 208–20.

GORDON, ALEXANDER (2 son of David Gordon, inventor of system of compressing gas, who d. about 1830). b. New York 5 May 1802; ed. at Univ. of Edin.; manager of the portable gas works in London until they were abolished about 1827; constructed many lighthouses, especially in the colonies; designed and erected the original great sea-light in an iron tower at Morant point, Jamaica, the first of many of a similar character 1842; founded with Sir George Cayley and others the Polytechnic

Institution, London 1838; A.I.C.E. 10 April 1827, M.I.C.E. 17 Feb. 1835; his widow Sarah Gordon granted civil list pension of £50, 20 Dec. 1872; author of *An historical and practical treatise upon elemental locomotion* 1832, 3 ed. 1836 and other books. *d.* Sandown, Isle of Wight 14 May 1868.

GORDON, SIR ALEXANDER CORNEWALL DUFF-3 Baronet *(elder son of Sir Wm. Duff-Gordon, 2 baronet 1772-1823).* *b.* Great Marylebone st. London 3 Feb. 1811; ed. at Eton; a senior clerk in Treasury 1854-56; sec. to chancellor of Exchequer 1854; a comr. of Board of Inland Revenue 1856; asst. gentleman usher of privy chamber to death; translated Von Ense's *Sketches of German life* 1847, *A. Weill's Village tales from Alsatia* 1847; translated with his wife Lady Lucy Duff-Gordon, L. Ranke's *Memoirs of the house of Brandenburg and history of Prussia* 3 vols. 1849. *d.* 4 Upper Eccleston st. Belgrave sq. London 27 Oct. 1872.

GORDON, SIR ALEXANDER HAMILTON- *(2 son of 4 Earl of Aberdeen 1784-1860).* *b.* 11 Dec. 1817; ed. at Harrow; ensign Grenadier guards 2 May 1834, captain 10 April 1849 to 17 Oct. 1856; D.Q.M.G. at head quarters 1855-60; brigadier general Dublin district 1861-66; commanded Bombay division 1867-70; col. 100 foot 5 July 1872 to death; general 1 Oct. 1877; placed on retired list 1 July 1881; C.B. 5 July 1855, K.C.B. 24 May 1873; M.P. for East Aberdeenshire 1875-85; author of *Remarks on national defences, volunteers and rifles* 1853; *An enquiry into the organization of the Army* 1875. *d.* 34 Lennox gardens, London 18 May 1890. *Pictorial World* 29 May 1890 p. 697, *portrait.*

GORDON, ARCHIBALD. Ed. at Univ. of Edin., M.D. 1834; assistant surgeon in army 28 June 1836, surgeon major 1854; principal medical officer of 2nd division in Crimea 1854-55; inspector general 9 March 1867 to 1 July 1870; C.B. 4 Feb. 1856; hon. surgeon to Queen 9 Aug. 1871 to death. *d.* West Hoathly, Sussex 3 Aug. 1886.

GORDON, CHARLES *(son of Francis Grant, captain R.N., who assumed name of Gordon 1768 and d. 1803).* Entered navy June 1796; captain 21 Dec. 1807; C.B. 4 July 1840; R.A. 23 Nov. 1841; admiral on half pay 20 Jany. 1858. *d.* Duke st. Bath 3 Oct. 1860 aged 79.

GORDON, CHARLES. Entered navy 19 June 1810; captain 17 April 1828; retired admiral 24 April 1865. *d.* Huntly, Aberdeenshire 19 May 1876.

GORDON, CHARLES GEORGE (4 *son of lieut. general Henry William Gordon d.* 1865). *b.* Woolwich 28 Jany. 1833; 2 lieut. R.E. 23 June 1852; lieut. col. 1 Oct. 1877 to death; served in Crimea 1854-56; went to China June 1860; commander of the 'Ever Victorious Army' in China 1863-64 when in 33 engagements he stamped out the Taiping rebellion, received from emperor yellow jacket and peacock's feather of a mandarin of first class, always known afterwards as Chinese Gordon; hon. C.B. 9 Dec. 1864; governor of equatorial provinces of Central Africa where he suppressed slavery 1874-76; created Pasha by Khedive of Egypt 1877; governor general of the Soudan, Darfour, the Equatorial provinces and the Red Sea littoral 1877-79; taken prisoner by King John of Abyssinia, Nov. 1879; private sec. to marquis of Ripon viceroy of India, May 1880; adviser of Chinese government in their relations with Russia, Sep. 1880; commander of troops in Mauritius 1881-82; M.G. 23 March 1882; commandant of colonial forces Cape of Good Hope 1882; author of *Colonel Gordon in Central Africa* 1881; *Reflections in Palestine* 1883; *General Gordon's Letters from Crimea, Danube and Armenia* 1884; sent by the English government to the Soudan to withdraw the garrisons and evacuate the country, arrived at Khartoum 18 Feb. 1884, besieged by the Mahdi 12 March; killed in the storming of Khartoum 26 Jany. 1885, *monu.* by Hamo Thornycroft erected in Trafalgar sq. 15 Oct. 1888, Gordon Boys' Home for homeless boys founded 1889. *A. E. Hake's Journals at Khartoum of C. G. Gordon* (1885); *A. Forbes' Chinese Gordon* (1886), *portrait; Events in life of C. G. Gordon, By Sir H. W. Gordon* (1886); *Letters of C. G. Gordon* (1888); *Chesney's Essays in modern military biography* (1874) 163-213; *D. C. Boulger's China iii,* 578-628 (1884), *portrait.*

GORDON, CHARLES WILLIAM. *b.* 19 March 1817; captain Madras cavalry; contested Berwick-on-Tweed, March 1857; M.P. for Berwick-on-Tweed, April 1859 to death. *d.* Pall Mall, London 15 June 1863.

GORDON, COSMO *(youngest son of Alexander Gordon, Lord Rockville 1739-92).* *b.* 28 Nov. 1777; ensign 71 foot 6 Dec. 1792; major 94 foot 12 Feb. 1807 to 20 July 1809; lieut. col. 63 foot 20 July 1809 to 1810 when placed on h.p.; granted service reward 1 July 1851; general 20 June 1854. *d.* Exton, Hants. 7 March 1867.

GORDON, DOUGLAS WILLIAM COPE (3 *son of* 10 *Marquis of Huntley 1792-1863).* *b.* 11

GORDON, D. W. C. (Con.)

Oct. 1851; lieut. Coldstream Guards 1871–1880; contested Hunts. 1874; M.P. for West Aberdeenshire 1876–80, for Hunts. 1880–85. d. Green Park chambers, 90 Piccadilly, London 4 Aug. 1888.

GORDON, ELIZABETH, Duchess of Gordon (dau. of Alexander Brodie, M.P. Elgin 1796–1802, d. 15 Jany. 1812). b. London 20 June 1794; owner of great wealth on father's death 1812. (m. 11 Dec. 1813 George Gordon, marquis of Huntley, who became 5 duke of Gordon 1827 and d. 28 May 1836); the unblushing vice she found in high quarters led her to make a renunciation of the world 1826; left the episcopal ch. and joined the Free ch. of Scotland and held an important position in the evangelical party 1847; a great patron of open air preaching. d. Huntly lodge, Strathbogie 31 Jany. 1864. A. M. Stuart's Life of duchess of Gordon (1865), portrait; Wylie's Disruption Worthies (1881) 271–78, portrait.

GORDON, GABRIEL. Ensign 60 foot 6 Jany. 1781, lieut. col. 9 March 1802 to 4 Jany. 1808 when placed on h.p.; col. 91 foot 19 April 1837 to death; general 9 Nov. 1846. d. Higher Ardwick lodge near Manchester 7 Aug. 1855 aged 92.

GORDON, GEORGE. b. Lucan co. Dublin 25 Feb. 1806; learnt gardening under his father 1820; with J. Colvill, King's road, Chelsea 1827; on staff of Horticultural Soc. Chiswick 18 Feb. 1828, foreman of the arboretum to his decease; A.L.S. 16 Feb. 1841; author with R. Glendenning of The Pinetum, 1858, supplement 1862, 2 ed. 1875, New ed. 1880. d. Kew 11 Oct. 1879; his herbarium purchased by Sir J. Hooker and given to royal gardens, Kew. Gardener's Chronicle xii, 569 (1879).

GORDON, GEORGE HUNTLY (son of Pryse Lockhart Gordon). educ. for the Scottish church; licensed to preach; transcribed manuscript of Waverley novels for the press in order that the secret of the authorship might not be betrayed; Sir Walter Scott wrote two sermons for him published under title of Religious discourses, By A Layman 1828, preface signed W.S. which Gordon sold for £250; clerk in the treasury, clerk in government stationery office 30 years; contributed much to Notes and Queries. d. Inverness 27 Dec. 1868 aged 72.

GORDON, GEORGE THOMAS. (2 son of Samuel Gordon, captain R.N.) b. 1807; entered navy 5 March 1818; captain 9 Nov. 1846; R.A. 28 Oct. 1864; retired 1 April 1870; admiral 1 Aug. 1877; K.H. 1837. d. Ingleden, Kent 30 July 1887.

GORDON, HENRY (brother of Charles Gordon who d. 3 Oct. 1860). Entered navy 18 May 1791; captain 8 April 1805; admiral on h.p. 21 Jany. 1854; mayor of Bath twice. d. Nelson place, Bath 14 Sep. 1855.

GORDON, SIR HENRY PERCY, 2 Baronet (only son of Sir James W. Gordon 1772–1851). b. 52 Upper Seymour st. London 1806; ed. at St. Peter's coll. Cam., fellow 1830; B.A. 1827, M.A. 1830; barrister L.I. 5 May 1831; F.R.S. 9 Dec. 1830. d. Blackhall, Aberdeenshire 29 July 1876.

GORDON, HENRY WILLIAM. Second lieut. R.A. 17 Aug. 1803; col. commandant 22 Feb. 1863 to death; L.G. 19 May 1863. d. Southampton 19 Sep. 1865 aged 79.

GORDON, SIR HENRY WILLIAM (brother of Charles George Gordon 1833–85). b. Blackheath, Kent 18 July 1818; ensign 59 foot Aug. 1835; entered ordnance department 1855; controller general Jany. 1870; commissary general Nov. 1875 to 9 July 1878 when he retired; C.B. 22 Jany. 1857, K.C.B. 6 Aug. 1877; author of Events in the life of Charles George Gordon 1886. d. Oat hall, Hayward's heath, Sussex 22 Oct. 1887. Graphic 26 Nov. 1887 pp. 581–82, portrait.

GORDON, SIR JAMES ALEXANDER. (eld. son of Charles Gordon of Wardhouse, Aberdeenshire). b. Kildrummie castle, Aberdeen 1782; entered navy 25 Nov. 1793; captain 16 May 1805; lost a leg at capture of French frigate "La Pomone" at Pelagosa 29 Nov. 1811; governor of royal naval hospital Plymouth 1827–32; superintendent of Chatham dockyard 1832–37; lieut. governor of Greenwich hospital 1 July 1840, governor 17 Oct. 1853 to death; admiral 21 Jany. 1854; admiral of the Fleet 30 Jany. 1868 to death; K.C.B. 2 Jany. 1851, G.C.B. 5 July 1855. d. Greenwich hospital 8 Jany. 1869. Macmillan's Mag. xix, 353–54 (1869); I.L.N. liv, 74, 165, 166 (1869), portrait.

GORDON, JAMES ALEXANDER. b. Middlesex; ed. at Univ. of Edin.; M.D. 24 June 1814; established The Quarterly Journal of Foreign Medicine and Surgery 1819, edited it; L.R.C.P. 16 April 1821, fellow 9 July 1836, Censor 1838; Assist. physician to London hospital 18 July 1827, physician 18 Nov. 1828 to Dec. 1844; retired from practice and lived at Dorking about 1846 to death; F.R.S. 2 April 1835. d. Dorking 18 April 1872 aged 78. Munk's Roll of royal college of physicians (1878) iii, 232.

GORDON, SIR JAMES DAVIDSON (son of Evelyn M. Gordon of the Bengal C.S.) Entered Bengal

GORDON, SIR J. D. *(Con.)*

C.S. 1854; private sec. to governor general of India Jany. 1866; resident Mysore and chief comr. of Coorg 1881–83 when he retired; K.C.S.I. 24 May 1881. *d.* 31 St. James's st. London 27 June 1889 aged 54. *bur.* Aston ch. near Knebworth 4 July.

GORDON, SIR JAMES WILLOUGHBY, 1 Baronet *(brother of Charles Gordon, who d. 3 Oct. 1860). b.* 21 Oct. 1772; ensign 66 foot 17 Oct. 1783; lieut. col. royal African corps 13 June 1808, col. 25 July 1810 to 27 Nov. 1815; Q.M.G. in the Peninsula 1811–12; Q.M.G. at head quarters 1812 to death; col. of 85 foot 27 Nov. 1815, of 23 foot 23 April 1823 to death; general 23 Nov. 1841; created baronet 5 Dec. 1818; G.C.H. 1825; G.C.B. 13 Sep. 1831; F.R.S. 11 June 1801. *d.* his residence near royal hospital, Chelsea 24 Jany. 1851.

GORDON, JOHN *(brother of 4 Earl of Aberdeen 1784–1860). b.* 1792; captain R.N. 31 Dec. 1818; retired admiral 23 March 1863. *d.* 28 Queen Anne st. Cavendish sq. London 11 Nov. 1869.

GORDON, SIR JOHN *(son of Samuel Gordon of Clonmel, co. Tipperary). b.* Clonmel 1798; general medical practitioner at Cork 1820 to death; mayor of Cork 1855; knighted by lord lieut. of Ireland 1855. *d.* Cork 29 Jany. 1871.

GORDON, JOHN SHEPHEARD. Publisher of *The Record* more than 50 years. *d.* 1 Albert road, Crouch hill near London 31 Oct. 1884 aged 76.

GORDON, SIR JOHN WATSON- *(eld. son of James Watson, captain R.A.) b.* Edinburgh 1788; leading portrait painter in Scotland 1823 to death; exhibited 123 portraits at R.A. London 1827–64; assumed name of Watson-Gordon by which he is always known; A.R.A. 1841, R.A. 11 Feb. 1851; pres. of R.S.A. March 1850 to death; knighted at St. James's palace 3 July 1850; limner to the Queen for Scotland 1850 to death. *d.* Catherine bank house, Edinburgh 1 June 1864, the Watson-Gordon professorship of fine art instituted in Univ. of Edin. 1879. *Sandby's Royal Academy ii,* 287–9 (1862); *Redgrave's Century of Painters ii,* 76–8 (1866); *I.L.N. xviii,* 219 (1851), *portrait.*

GORDON, SIR JOHN WILLIAM *(elder son of Thomas Gordon of Harperfield, Lanarkshire who d.* 1832). *b.* 1814; 2 lieut. R.E. 1 Dec. 1833; commanded R.E. in Crimea 1854–5; lieut. col. R.E. 1856–66; A.D.C. to the Queen 1855–66; D.A.G. at head quarters 1856–61; M.G. 3 Aug. 1866; inspector general of R.E.

GORDON, SIR J: W: *(Con.)*

1 June 1869 to death; C.B. 5 July 1855, K.C.B. 28 March 1865; A.I.C.E. 3 Feb. 1857; cut his throat at house of lieut. col. Hutchinson, Golfston, Westward Ho. Devon 8 Feb. 1870; full length portrait in head-quarter messroom of R.E. at Chatham. *Chesney's Essays in modern military biography* (1874) 154–62. *Min. of proc. of Instit. of C.E. xxxi,* 241–5 (1871); *I.L.N. lvi,* 211 (1870).

GORDON, JOSEPH. *b.* 1836; borough surveyor of Carlisle; designed many plans for draining large towns in North of England and Scotland; designed and carried out sewerage of Frankfort-on-Main 1886 and of other foreign cities; surveyor of Leicester 1880 where he greatly reduced the death rate; engineer to London county council 9 July 1889 to death; A.I.C.E. 1862; M.I.C.E. 1874. *d.* in an omnibus outside Eyre Arms tavern St. John's Wood, London 9 Nov. 1889. *bur.* Leicester cemetery 13 Nov.

GORDON, LADY LUCY DUFF- *(only child of John Austin 1790–1859). b.* Queen sq. Westminster 24 June 1821; left Unitarian ch. for ch. of England 1837. *(m.* 16 May 1840 Sir Alexander Cornewall Duff-Gordon, bart. 1811–72); intimate with Dickens, Thackeray, Eliot Warburton and others; visited Heinrich Heine in Paris 1854; lived in Egypt 1862 to decease; translated many works from German and French; author of *Letters from the Cape* in Galton's *Vacation Tourist* 1862–63, *pp.* 119–222; *Letters from Egypt* 1865. *d.* Cairo 14 July 1869. *Lady Duff-Gordon's Last letters from Egypt with a memoir by her daughter Mrs. Ross* (1875) *i-xl, portrait;* *Macmillan's Mag.* Sep. 1869 *pp.* 457–62; *Good Words* (1875) *pp.* 637–40.

GORDON, REV. OSBORNE (2 *son of George Gordon of Broseley, Salop). b.* Broseley 21 April 1813; educ. Bridgnorth sch. and Christ Church, Oxford; double first class in classics and mathematics; B.A. 1836, M.A. 1839, B.D. 1847; rhetoric reader to university 1845 and Greek reader 1846; proctor 1846–47; censor Christ Church 1846; university examiner 1848–52; select preacher 1849 and 1862; member hebdomadal council 1854, 1857; Prince of Wales became his pupil at Christ Church 1859; member of Oxford univ. commission 1877; R. of Easthampstead, Berks. 1860 to death; author of *Eusebii Pamphili historiæ ecclesiasticæ Annotationes variorum* 1842; *Considerations on improvement of examination statute* 1847. *d.* Easthampstead 25 May 1883. *G. Marshall's Osborne Gordon* (1885) *pp.* 1–72, *with portrait.*

GORDON, REV. ROBERT. *b.* Glencairn, Dumfriesshire 5 May 1786; educ. Edin. univ. to 1809 and at Marischal coll. Aberdeen D.D. 1823; presbyterian minister at Kinfauns, Perthshire 1816, at St. Cuthbert's chapel of ease, Edin. 1821, at Hope park chapel of ease 1824, at New North ch. 1825, at the High ch. 1830; moderator of general assembly 20 May 1841; joined Free ch. and was minister of Free High ch. Edin. 1843 to death; invented a self registering hygrometer; author of articles Euclid, geography and meteorology in *Edinburgh Encyclopædia;* wrote *Sermons* 1825; *Christ as made known to the Ancient Church* 4 *vols.* 1854–55. *d.* 14 Northumberland st. Edinburgh 21 Oct. 1853. *Wylie's Disruption Worthies* (1881) *pp.* 309–316; *Crombie's Modern Athenians* (1882) *p.* 19–21, *portrait.*

GORDON, SAMUEL ENDERBY (2 son of Henry *Wm. Gordon, col. commandant R.A. who d.* 19 *Sep.* 1865 *aged* 79). *b.* 14 Nov. 1824; 2 lieut. R.A. 19 June 1844; col. 23 Dec. 1875; director of artillery studies at Woolwich 1 May 1871 to 31 Oct. 1877; L.G. 23 May 1882; placed on retired list with hon. rank of general 1 Nov. 1882; C.B. 13 March 1867. *d.* Brook lodge, The Park, Cheltenham 5 Feb. 1883.

GORDON, WILLIAM (2 *son of George Gordon, Lord Haddo* 1764–91). *b.* 1785; midshipman R.N. 2 July 1797; captain 12 March 1810; V.A. 11 Feb. 1854; commander-in-chief at the Nore 1 July 1854 to 1 July 1857; M.P. for Aberdeenshire 1820–54; a lord of the Admiralty 8 Sep. 1841 to 17 Feb. 1846. *d.* Exmouth 3 Feb. 1858.

GORDON, WILLIAM. *b.* 26 June 1821; ensign 17 foot 20 July 1838; lieut. col. 15 Jany. 1861 to 1 April 1873; lieut. col. brigade depot 1 April 1873 to 14 April 1875 when placed on h.p.; A.A.G. 1 April 1870 to 31 March 1873; L.G. 29 April 1880; placed on retired list with hon. rank of general 1 July 1881; C.B. 20 May 1871. *d.* while grouse shooting on the hill of Correen, Aberdeenshire 14 Aug. 1883.

GORDON, WILLIAM ALEXANDER. Ensign 112 foot 2 Oct. 1794; captain 50 foot 23 Oct. 1806 to 26 Nov. 1818 when placed on h.p.; colonel 54 foot 15 Aug. 1850 to death; L.G. 11 Nov. 1851; C.B. 26 Sep. 1831. *d.* Nairn, Scotland 10 Aug. 1856 aged 87.

GORE, AUGUSTUS FREDERICK (*only son of Edward Gore* 1797–1879, *captain R.N.) b.* 1 Feb. 1826; colonial sec. Barbadoes 1867–74; lieut. governor of Tobago 29 Sep. 1877, of St. Vincent 5 Aug. 1880 to 1886; F.G.S. *d.* 21 Sep. 1887.

GORE, CATHERINE GRACE FRANCES (*dau. of C. Moody of East Retford, Nottinghamshire, wine merchant*). *b.* East Retford 1799. (*m.* 15 Feb. 1823 Charles Arthur Gore, lieut. and capt. 1 life guards, *d.* 1846). Resided in France 1832–35; her dramas *The School for Coquettes* produced at Haymarket theatre 1831 and *Quid pro Quo or the Days of Dupes*, a prize drama, at Haymarket 1844; author of *Theresa Marchmont, or the Maid of Honour* 1824; *Manners of the day, or Women as they are* 3 *vols.* 1830, greatly praised by Geo. IV.; *Mothers and daughters* 3 *vols.* 1831 anon.; *Cecil, or the Adventures of a Coxcomb* 3 *vols.* 1841 anon.; *The Royal Favourite* 3 *vols.* 1845 and 65 other works. *d.* Linwood, Lyndhurst, Hampshire 29 Jany. 1861. *bur.* Kensal Green cemetery 7 Feb. *New Monthly mag. xlix, pt. i,* 434–35 (1837), *portrait; I.L.N.* 16 Feb. 1861 *p.* 147, *portrait; R. H. Horne's New spirit of the age, i,* 232–39 (1844).

NOTE.—She was a ward of Sir John Dean Paul, her novel *The Banker's Wife* 1843 was dedicated to him, which is very curious as in it is described a swindling banker just like he turned out to be in 1855 when she lost £20,000.

GORE, SIR CHARLES STEPHEN (4 *son of* 2 *Earl of Arran* 1734–1809). *b.* 26 Dec. 1793; cornet 16 light dragoons 21 Oct. 1808; served in Peninsula and at Waterloo 1811–15; col. of 91 foot 8 Aug. 1855, of 6 foot 9 March 1861 to death; general Feb. 1863; lieut. governor of Chelsea hospital Dec. 1868 to death; C.B. 1838, K.C.B. 18 May 1860, G.C.B. 13 March 1867; K.H. 1836. *d.* Chelsea hospital 4 Sep. 1869. *Register and Mag. of Biog. Oct.* 1869 *p.* 198.

GORE, JOHN. Entered navy Sep. 1797; captain 27 July 1825; retired admiral 15 Dec. 1863. *d.* 9 York place, Clifton 7 Dec. 1869 aged 85.

GORE, MONTAGUE (*eld. son of Rev. Charles Gore of Barrow court, Somerset, who d.* 21 *April* 1841). Matric. from Ch. Ch. Ox. 8 May 1818 aged 18; student of L.I. 1821; M.P. for Devizes 1832–34, for Barnstaple 1841–47; author of 20 pamphlets on political and social subjects; translated Valentini's *Description of the seat of war in European Turkey* 1854. *d.* Chapel place, Vere st. London 5 Oct. 1864.

GORE, ROBERT (*brother of* 6 *Earl of Arran* 1801–84). *b.* 5 May 1810; entered navy 4 Sep. 1823; captain R.N. 9 Nov. 1846; M.P. for New Ross 1841–47; chargé d' affaires and consul general at Monte Video 23 Oct. 1846, at Buenos Ayres 29 Aug. 1851 to death. *d.* Monte Video 4 Aug. 1854.

GORE-LANGTON, WILLIAM HENRY. *b.* London 1802; M.P. for Bristol 1852–65. *d.* 2 Prince's Gate, London 16 May 1875.

GORE-LANGTON, WILLIAM HENRY POWELL. *b.* Burdrop, Wilts. 25 July 1824; M.P. for West Somerset 1851–59 and 1863 to death. *d.* Newton park near Bath 11 Dec. 1873.

GORHAM, REV. GEORGE CORNELIUS *(son of George James Gorham of St. Neots, Hunts. merchant).* *b.* St. Neots 21 Aug. 1787; ed. at St. Neots and Queen's coll. Cam., fellow 1809–27; 3rd wrangler and 2nd Smith's prizeman 1808; B.A. 1808, M.A. 1812, B.D. 1820; C. of Beckenham, Kent 1814–18; C. of Clapham, Surrey 1818–27; C. of St. Mary's chapel, Maidenhead 1840–42; C. of Fawley near Henley 1843–46; V. of St. Just in Penwith, Cornwall 1846–50; presented by Lord Chancellor Cottenham to vicarage of Brampford Speke near Exeter 2 Nov. 1847, but the Bishop of Exeter refused to institute him on account of his views on baptismal regeneration, the result was more than 2½ years' litigation at end of which Gorham was instituted by Sir H. J. Fust, judge of the court of arches; author of *The history and antiquities of Eynesbury and St. Neots* 2 *vols.* 1820 and many other books. *d.* Brampford Speke 19 June 1857; *Bentley's Miscellany xxvii*, 612–16 (1850), *portrait; I.L.N.* 25 May 1850 *p.* 373, *portrait.*

GORING, SIR HARRY DENT, 7 Baronet. *b.* Devonshire place, London 30 Dec. 1801; M.P. for Shoreham 1832–41; succeeded 26 March 1844; sheriff of Anglesea 1848. *d.* Hotel Windsor, Rue Rivoli, Paris 19 April 1859.

GORMANSTON, EDWARD ANTHONY JOHN PRESTON, 1 Baron *(eld. child of 12 Viscount Gormanston 1775–1860).* *b.* Dublin 3 June 1796; sheriff of co. Dublin 1845; created baron Gormanston of Whitewood co. Meath in peerage of U.K. 8 Dec. 1868. *d.* Gormanston castle, Balbriggan 28 Sep. 1876.

GORRIE, REV. PETER DOUGLAS. *b.* Glasgow 21 April 1813; went to U.S. of A. 1820; minister of Methodist Episcopal church; member of New York conference 1836 to death; author of *The churches and sects in the United States, New York* 1850; *Episcopal methodism as it was and is* 1852; *Black River Conference memorial* 2 *vols.* 1852–81 and other books. *d.* Potsdam, New York 12 Sep. 1884.

GORRINGE, HENRY HONEYCHURCH *(son of Rev. Mr. Gorringe of the Church of England).* *b.* Barbadoes 11 Aug. 1841; a common sailor in the U.S. Federal navy 1862; commanded

GORRINGE, H. H. *(Con.)*
sloop Portsmouth 1869–71; transported from Alexandria to New York an Egyptian obelisk 1879–80, erected it in Central Park, N.Y. 1880, total expense was 103,732 dollars; formed American ship-building co.; author of *Egyptian obelisks, New York* 1882, *Another ed.* 1885. *d.* New York 7 July 1885. *bur.* at Sparkhill on the Hudson.

GORTON, SANDFORD. Established the *Astronomical Register* Jany. 1863 and edited it to 1872, printed all the first volume himself at his own private printing press, Stamford villa, Downs Road, Clapton where he established an observatory; F.R.A.S. 8 June 1860. *d.* 38 Pembury road, Clapton 14 Feb. 1879 in 56 year. *Monthly notices of Royal Astronom. Soc. xl,* 194 (1880).

GOSFORD, ARCHIBALD ACHESON, 3 Earl of *(only son of 2 Earl of Gosford 1776–1849).* *b.* Portland place, London 20 Aug. 1806; ed. at Ch. Ch. Ox., B.A. 1828; M.P. for Armagh 1830–47; col. of Armagh militia 1834; created Baron Acheson of Clancairney, co. Armagh 18 Sep. 1847; succeeded 27 March 1849; K.P. 1855. *d.* 59 Grosvenor st. London 15 June 1864.

GOSLING, WILLIAM CLARKE FRANCIS. *b.* 9 Aug. 1822; 2 lieut. Madras artillery 11 June 1840; A.A.G. R.A. Madras 1868–73; col. R.A. 1 Aug. 1872 to death; L.G. 12 May 1882; hon. general 31 Dec. 1883. *d.* Folkestone 14 June 1885.

GOSS, MOST REV. ALEXANDER. *b.* Ormskirk, Lancs. 5 July 1814; ed. at St. Cuthbert's coll. Ushaw 1827–39; studied at English coll. Rome 1839–42; vice pres. of St. Edward's coll. Everton, Liverpool 16 Jany. 1843 (date of opening) to 21 June 1853; bishop of Gerra *in partibus.* and co-adjutor bishop of Liverpool 29 July 1853, bishop 25 Jany. 1856 to death, consecrated by Cardinal Wiseman 25 Sep. 1853; edited for Chetham Soc. *Abbot's Journal and The trials at Manchester in* 1694, 1864, and for Manx Soc. *The Chronicle of Man and the Sudreys* 2 *vols.* 1874. *d.* St. Edward's college 3 Oct. 1872. *bur.* St. Sepulchre's cemetery, Ford 8 Oct. *Gillow's English Catholics ii,* 535–40 (1885); *Brady's Episcopal Succession iii,* 418–22 (1877).

GOSS, SIR JOHN *(son of Joseph Goss of Fareham, Hants., organist).* *b.* Fareham 27 Dec. 1800; chorister of chapel royal, London 1811–16; pupil of Thomas Attwood 1816; organist of St. Luke's, Chelsea 9 Jany. 1825; professor of harmony Royal Academy 1827; organist

GOSS, SIR J. *(Con.)*

to St. Paul's 1838, resigned 1872 ; composer to the chapel royal 1856 ; knighted at Windsor Castle 19 March 1872·for his anthem on Prince of Wales' recovery "The Lord is my strength"; entertained at a banquet at Albion tavern, London 17 April 1872 ; Mus. D. of Cambridge 1876 ; writer of 'Cantate Domino' a canon sung at meeting of Concentores Sodales 13 Feb. 1824, 'Have mercy on me' an anthem 1833, 'If we believe that Jesus died' anthem for funeral of D. of Wellington 1852 ; author of *Introduction to Harmony* 1833 ; edited *Sacred Minstrel* 3 *vols.* 1833 ; ed. with W. Mercer *The Church Psalter with appropriate chants and tunes* 1855, *ten editions. d.* 15 Clarewood ter. Lambeth road, Brixton Rise 10 May 1880, his memorial tablet in crypt of St. Paul's was designed by John Belcher, unveiled 10 May 1886. *W. A. Barrett's English church composers* (1882) 173–8.

GOSSE, EMILY *(dau. of Wm. Bowes of Boston, Mass.) b.* London 9 Nov. 1806 ; one of the earliest workers in the East End of London ; author of *Abraham and his children* 1855 and of a series of popular religious tracts ; author with P. H. Gosse of *Seaside Pleasures* 1853, anon. *(m.* 1848 Philip Henry Gosse, he *d.* 1888). *d.* Barnsbury, London 9 Feb. 1857. *Memorials of Mrs. Gosse, By P. H. Gosse* (1857); *Tell Jesus, recollections of E. Gosse, By A. Shipton* (1858).

GOSSE, PHILIP HENRY *(son of Thomas Gosse of Worcester, miniature painter* 1765–1844). *b.* Worcester 6 April 1810 ; ed. at Poole and Blandford ; lived in Newfoundland 1827–35 ; collected birds and insects in Jamaica for British Museum 1844–46 ; lived at St. Marychurch, Torquay 1857 to death ; F.R.S. 5 June 1856 ; author of *The Canadian Naturalist* 1840 ; *The Aquarium* 1854 ; *Omphalos* 1857 ; *Actinologia Britannica* 1860 ; *A year at the shore* 1865 and 30 other books. *d.* Sandhurst villa, St. Marychurch, Torquay 23 Aug. 1888. *I.L.N.* 8 Sep. 1888 *p.* 279, *portrait ; Graphic* 22 *Sep.* 1888 *pp.* 314, 320, *portrait.*

GOSSELIN, GERARD (3 *son of Joshua Gosselin of St. Peter's Port, Guernsey* 1739–1813) *b.* St. Peter's Port 4 Feb. 1769 ; ensign 34 foot 27 Sep. 1787 ; captain 2 life guards 6 June 1794 ; governor of Halifax 1815 ; general 23 Nov. 1841. *d.* Mount Ospringe, Faversham, Kent 11 June 1859.

GOSSELIN, SIR THOMAS LE MARCHANT *(brother of the preceding). b.* St. Peter's Port, Guernsey 7 May 1765 ; entered navy 2 Aug. 1778 ;

GOSSELIN, SIR T. LE M. *(Con.)*

captain 23 July 1795 ; received thanks from both Houses of Parliament 1809 for embarking British army after battle of Corunna ; admiral 23 Nov. 1841. *d.* Jersey 27 Nov. 1857. *bur.* Bengeo church, Herts.

GOSSET, HENRY (2 *son of Matthew Gosset of Bagot, Jersey, d.* 1843). Entered navy 15 June 1809 ; captain 1 Jany. 1829 ; admiral on h.p. 12 Sep. 1865. *d.* Old Quebec st. Portman sq. London 1 March 1877 aged 82.

GOSSET, REV. ISAAC *(eld. son of Rev. Isaac Gosset, D.D., F.R.S., who d.* 1812). *b.* 1783 ; ed. at Exeter coll. Ox., B.A. 1804, M.A. 1807 ; C. of Windsor 1809–14 ; V. of Datchet 1814– 21 ; chaplain to royal household Windsor Castle 1818 to death ; V. of New Windsor 1821 to death. *d.* Windsor ? 11 Feb. 1855. *G.M.* April 1855 *p.* 435.

GOSSET, MONTAGUE (2 *son of Daniel Gosset of Tanner's End, Edmonton). b.* 1 July 1792 ; ed. at Broxbourne ; entered navy Nov. 1806 ; apprenticed to Mr. Stocker of Guy's hospital 1809–14 ; M.R.C.S. 1814, hon. F.R.C.S. 1843 ; practised in city of London 1820 to death ; communicated to the profession the only case of renal aneurism then detected 1829. *d.* 40 Broad st. buildings, city of London 21 Oct. 1854. *G.M. xlii,* 633–5 (1854).

GOSSET, SIR RALPH ALLEN *(only son of Sir William Gosset, serjeant at arms* 1835 *to death* 27 *March* 1848). Assistant serjeant at arms to the Queen, July 1836, deputy serjeant April 1854, serjeant at arms in ordinary 5 April 1875, retired Aug. 1885 ; had to employ force to prevent Mr. Bradlaugh re-entering the house 3 Aug. 1881 ; K.C.B. 11 Aug. 1885. *d.* The Wick, Richmond hill 27 Nov. 1885 aged 76. *I.L.N. lxxxvii,* 157, 582 (1885), 2 *portraits ; Times* 28 *Nov.* 1885 *p.* 10, 3 *Dec. p.* 8 ; *Guardian* 2 *Dec.* 1885 *p.* 1811.

GOTCH, REV. FREDERIC WILLIAM. *b.* Kettering 1807 ; pastor of baptist chapel at Boxmoor 1836–45 ; classical and mathematical tutor at Bristol college 1845, pres. 1868–82, hon. pres. 1882 to death ; B.A. Dublin 1839, M.A. 1842, LL.B. and LL.D. 1859 ; member of Old Testament revision committee ; author of *Revised English Bible, Genesis to Deuteronomy* 1877 ; edited *A supplement to Tischendorf's Reliquiae ex incendio ereptae codicis Cottoniani* 1881. *d.* 21 Pembroke road, Clifton 17 May 1890 in 83 year. *I.L.N.* 31 *May* 1890 *p.* 680, *portrait ; Pictorial World* 29 *May* 1890 *p.* 697, *portrait..*

GOTT, JOSEPH. *b.* Calverley near Leeds 1785; student of R. Academy, gold medallist for group of Jacob wrestling with the angel 1819; his namesake Benjamin Gott sent him to Rome where he lived nearly 40 years; exhibited 30 sculptures at R.A. and 7 at B.I. 1820–48; his principal works were executed for Armley house and ch. Leeds, the residence of his patron B. Gott. *d.* Rome Jany. 1860.

GOUDY, REV. ALEXANDER PORTER *(son of Andrew Goudy, presbyterian minister).* *b.* Bally-walter, co. Down, Feb. 1809; educ. Belfast coll. 1823; assist. presbyterian minister Strabane 1831 and minister 1833 to death; engaged in controversy with Archibald Boyd, afterwards dean of Exeter, on the merits of episcopacy 1839; aided in passing Marriages, Ireland, Act 7 & 8 Vict. c. 81, 1843; D.D. of Jefferson coll. U.S.A. 1851; moderator of general assembly of his ch. 1857; author of *Worship of the Presbyterian church* 1839. *d.* Dublin 14 Dec. 1858.

GOUGH, HUGH GOUGH, 1 Viscount (4 *son of George Gough of Woodstown, co. Limerick* 1751–1836). *b.* Woodstown 3 Nov. 1779; lieut. 78 highlanders 6 June 1795; served at Cape of Good Hope 1795, in West Indies 1796–1803, in Peninsula 1808–13 twice severely wounded; in Ireland 1819–26, in command of Mysore division of Madras army 1837–41; commander of troops in China 1841; commander in chief Madras 1841; commander in chief in India 11 Aug. 1843; routed the Mahratta army at Maharajpore 29 Dec. 1843; defeated the Sikhs at Mudki 18 Dec. 1845, at Ferozeshah 21–22 Dec. 1845, at Sobraon 10 Feb. 1846, at Ramnuggar 22 Nov. 1848, at Chillianwallah 13 Jany. 1849 and at Goojerat 21 Feb. 1849; col. 87 foot 15 March 1844, general 20 June 1854; col. in chief of 60 royal rifles 28 Jany. 1854 to death; col. royal horse guards 29 June 1855 to death; field marshal 9 Nov. 1862; knighted at Carlton house 4 Dec. 1815; C.B. 1815, K.C.B. 13 Sep. 1831, G.C.B. 14 Oct. 1841; created a baronet 23 Dec. 1842; received the thanks of parliament in 1842 and 1843 and of H.E.I.C. in 1842 and 1849; created Baron Gough 25 April 1846; cr. viscount Gough 15 June 1849 with a pension of £2000 to himself and next 2 heirs to title; K.P. 1857; P.C. 11 June 1859; K.C.S.I. 1861, G.C.S.I. 1861. *d.* St. Helen's near Booterstown, co. Dublin 2 March 1869. *bur.* Stillorgan ch. yard 9 March. *C. R. Low's Soldiers of the Victorian age* i, 222–59 (1880); *Shadwell's Life of Lord Clyde* (1881) i, 147 *et seq.*; *Register and Mag. of Biog.* i, 286–89, 522; *History of the campaign on the Sutlej* (1846) *p.* 11, *etc.*; *Nolan's British empire*

GOUGH, H. G., 1 Viscount. *(Con.)*
in India, ii, 663, *portrait; Dublin Univ. Mag.* xxxvi, 192–208, *portrait; I.L.N.* xiv, 265 (1849), *portrait,* liv, 274, 293 (1869), *portrait.*

GOUGH, ALEXANDER DICK. *b.* 3 Nov. 1804; pupil of Benjamin Wyatt 1823; superintended erection of Apsley house and D. of York's column 1834; partner with R. L. Roumieu 1836–48; made surveys for railways 1845–48; with Roumieu exhibited 19 works at R.A. 1837–49; built Islington literary and scientific institution 1837–38; rebuilt Old St. Pancras ch. in the Anglo-Norman style 1847–48 and many churches, schools and houses. *d.* 6 Second grove, Tollington park, London 8 Sep. 1871. *bur.* Highgate cemetery. *The Architect* 30 *Sept.* 1871 *p.* 173.

GOUGH, JOHN BALLANTINE or BARTHOLOMEW. *b.* Sandgate, Kent 22 Aug. 1817; went to America 1829; temperance lecturer 1843; lectured in England 1853–55, 1857–60 and 1878; M.A. of Amherst Univ.; author of *Orations delivered on various occasions* 1854; *Temperance gleanings* 1879; *Sunlight and shadow* 1881 and about 20 small books. *d.* of paralysis at Frankford, Philadelphia 18 Feb. 1886. *Autobiography of J. B. Gough* (1879), *portrait; Appleton's Cyclop. of American Biog.* ii, 692 (1887), *portrait; Drawing room portrait gallery 2nd series* (1859), *portrait; I.L.N.* xxv, 208, 209 (1854), *portrait.*

GOULBURN, EDWARD (3 *son of Munbee Goulburn of Portland place, London, who d.* 29 Nov. 1793 *aged* 36). *b.* 1787; cornet royal horse guards 1803, lieut. 1804–5 when he sold out having been prosecuted for libelling some of his brother officers in his book *The Blueviad, a satyrical poem* 1805; barrister M.T. 9 June 1815; a Welsh judge; recorder of Leicester to 1835, of Lincoln, and of Boston; serjeant at law 4 Feb. 1829, received patent of precedence after Serjeant Storks 1840; a comr. of Court of Bankruptcy 21 Oct. 1842 to 1868; contested Ipswich 1832, M.P. for Leicester 1835–37; author of *The pursuits of fashion, a satirical poem* 1809, anon., 4 ed. 1812; *Edward de Montfort* 3 vols. 1812. *d.* 5 Seymour st. Portman sq. London 24 Aug. 1868.

GOULBURN, FREDERICK *(youngest son of the succeeding).* *b.* 8 April 1818; ed. at Trin. coll. Cam.; barrister I.T. 26 Jany. 1844; comr. of customs 28 Jany. 1845; vice chairman of board of customs 1859, chairman 1875 to death; C.B. 10 July 1871. *d.* 57 Ennismore gardens, London 8 May 1878.

GOULBURN, HENRY *(brother of Edward Goulburn 1787–1868).* *b.* Marylebone, London 19

GOULBURN, H. *(Con.)*

March 1784; ed. at Trin. coll. Cam., B.A. 1805, M.A. 1808, hon. D.C.L. Ox. 1834; contested Horsham 1807, Univ. of Cam. 1826; M.P. for Horsham 1808–12, for St. Germans 1812–18, for West Looe 1818–26, for Armagh 1826–31, for Univ. of Cam. 1831 to death; under sec. of state for home department 1810–12, for the Colonies 1812–21; chief sec. for Ireland 1821–27; P.C. 10 Dec. 1821; chancellor of exchequer 1828–30 and 1841–46; sec. of state for home department 1834–35; conservative candidate for speakership of House of Commons 27 May 1839 when defeated by C. S. Lefevre by 18 votes; an ecclesiastical comr. for England 1845. *d.* Betchworth house near Dorking 12 Jany. 1856. *Portraits of eminent conservatives 2nd series* (1846), *portrait; G.M. xlv*, 183–4 (1856).

GOULD, Rev. George *(eld. son of George Gould of Bristol, tradesman).* *b.* Castle green, Bristol 20 Sep. 1818; clerk to a wine merchant 1832; articled to an accountant 1836; student of Bristol Baptist coll. Sep. 1838; pastor Lower Abbey st. Dublin 1841, at South st. chapel, Exeter 1846, at St. Mary's chapel, Norwich 1849 to decease; president of Baptist Union 1879; one of the founders of Anti-state church association 1844; author of *India, its history, religion and government* 1858; *Open communion and the baptists of Norwich* 1860 and 10 other works; edited *Church Examiner* 1852. *d.* Norwich 13 Feb. 1882. *Sermons and addresses with a memoir by G. P. Gould* (1884), *with portrait.*

GOULD, Gerald Francis. Attaché at Hanover 1 Jany. 1854; minister resident at Belgrade 3 March 1879; minister resident at Stuttgardt 16 April 1881 to death; C.B. 20 April 1880. *d.* Stuttgardt 5 Sep. 1883 aged 48.

GOULD, Most Rev. James Alpius. *b.* Cork 4 Nov. 1812; entered Augustinian order, educ. at Grantstown; ordained priest at Perugia 1835; arrived in Sydney, Feb. 1838; R.C. priest at Campbeltown near Sydney 1838–48; elected 9 July 1847 and consecrated the first bishop of the Port Philip settlement 8 Aug. 1848 which became the colony of Victoria 1 July 1851; archbishop of Melbourne 4 May 1874 to death. *d.* Brighton near Melbourne 11 June 1886.

GOULD, John. *b.* Lyme Regis 14 Sep. 1804; gardener Ripley castle, Yorkshire; taxidermist Zoological gardens, London 1827; travelled in Australia and adjoining islands 1838–40; F.R.S. 19 Jany. 1843; exhibited his collection of 5000 humming birds in Zoo-

GOULD, J. *(Con.)*

logical gardens 1851, sold to British Museum for £3000 in 1881; produced 41 folio volumes illustrated by 2999 plates; his chief works were *A Century of birds from the Himalayan mountains* 1832; *The birds of Europe* 5 vols. 1832–7; *The birds of Australia* 8 vols. 1848–69; *Monograph of the Trochilidæ* 1849–61; *The birds of Asia* 7 vols. 1850–83; *The birds of Great Britain* 5 vols. 1862–73; *The birds of New Guinea* 1875–80. *(m.* 1829 Elizabeth Coxen who assisted him in his writings and executed all his drawings, she *d.* Egham 15 Aug. 1841). *d.* 26 Charlotte st. Bedford sq. London 3 Feb. 1881. *I.L.N. xx*, 457 (1852), *portrait, lxxviii*, 220 (1881), *portrait; Zoologist v*, 109–15 (1881); *Nature xxiii*, 364–5, 491 (1881).

GOULDING, William *(eld. son of Joshua Goulding of Birr, King's co.)* *b.* 1817; a merchant at Cork and Dublin; contested Cork city, Feb. 1874; M.P. for Cork city 25 May 1876 to 24 March 1880. *d.* Summerhill house, Sidney place, Cork 8 Dec. 1884.

GOULSTON, James. An aeronaut known as Giuseppe Lunardini; fell from his balloon during an ascent from Belle Vue gardens, Manchester, and was killed at Stone breaks hill near Saddleworth, Yorkshire 3 June 1852.

GOURLAY, William Cameron. *b.* Edinburgh 1817; first appeared on stage at T.R. Edinburgh 18 May 1836 as Norval in Home's *Douglas;* the best actor of Bailie Nicol Jarvie in *Rob Roy* except Charles Mackay; manager of Victoria Temple, Edinburgh, changed the name to Royal Victoria theatre 4 Sep. 1848. *d.* 80 Great Western road, Glasgow 3 Feb. 1883.

GOURLIE, William. *b.* Glasgow, March 1815; educ. Glasgow univ.; partner with his father as a merchant; studied botany under Sir W. J. Hooker and Dr. J. H. Balfour; collected mosses, shells and fossil plants; member Edin. Botanical soc. 1836 and of Glasgow Philosophical soc. 1841; F.L.S. 1855. *d.* of cancer at his brother's house, Pollokshields, Glasgow 24 June 1856. *Proc. Linnœan soc.* (1857) *p. xxvii.*

GOVER, Charles E. *(son of Thomas Gover of Poplar, Middlesex).* Principal and sec. of Madras military male orphan asylum Egmore, Madras 1864; member R. Asiatic soc. 1868–71; fellow Anthropological soc.; wrote in *Journal Asiatic soc.* and in *Cornhill Mag.;* author of *Indian weights and measures, Madras* 1865; *The folk songs of Southern India, Madras* 1872. *d.* Madras 20 Sep. 1872.

GOW, JAMES. *b.* Soutar's Close, West Port, Dundee 16 March 1814; a weaver in Dundee; wrote many short poems in the *Dundee Chronicle*, *Tait's Mag.*, *Chambers's Journal* and *Hogg's Instructor;* published a collection of his pieces entitled *The lays of the loom;* wrote no new poem after 1847 so that he was frequently spoken of as the late James Gow and confused with James Gow the political agitator who *d.* 4 Oct. 1849. *d.* 29 Jany. 1872. *W. Norrie's Dundee Celebrities* (1873) 382–90.

GOWAN, GEORGE EDWARD. Second lieut. Bengal artillery 1 April 1806; col. commandant 3 July 1845 to death; A.D.C. to the Queen 19 June 1846 to 20 June 1854; commanded Ferozepore district 1849–52, Lahore division 1853–58; L.G. 27 Sep. 1859; C.B. 22 May 1843. *d.* Pen hill near Bath 19 Dec. 1865 aged 77.

GOWAN, OGLE ROBERT. *b.* co. Wexford, Ireland 1796; edited the *Antidote* 1822–25 and the *Sentinel* 1825–29, Dublin weekly papers; went to Canada 1829; commanded 2nd regiment of Leeds militia; during Mc Kenzie-Papineau rebellion of 1837–9, he was designated "the right arm of British power in America"; founder of Orange lodges of North America, grand master 20 years; a member of Canadian parliament 1834–41; edited the *Brockville Statesman* weekly paper 1829-51 and the *Patriot* and the *British Empire* 1851–55; author of *Orangeism, its origin and history* 3 vols. 1859. *d.* Toronto 21 Aug. 1876.

GOWANS, SIR JAMES. *b.* 1821; a railway contractor; constructed Bathgate railway, various sections of North British railway, 35 miles of Highland railway and other lines; laid down first tramway in Scotland sanctioned by Parliament; member of Edinburgh town council many years; chairman of executive committee of Edinburgh Exhibition 1886; knighted by the Queen at Holyrood palace 19 Aug. 1886; Lord Dean of Guild of Edinburgh 1886 to death; author of *Model dwelling-houses* 1886; *Edinburgh and its neighbourhood in the days of our grandfathers* 1886. *d.* 1 Blantyre terrace, Edinburgh 25 June 1890.

GOWANS, WILLIAM. *b.* Lismahagow, Scotland 29 March 1803; went to U.S.A. 1821; a gardener in New York 1825, afterwards a stonecutter, a stevedore and a vendor of newspapers; bookseller in New York 1828–37 and 1840 to death; book auctioneer 1837, issued 28 book catalogues 1842–70, his stock of books at his death numbered nearly 300,000 vols.; author of *Gowans' Bibliotheca Americana* 5 numbers 1845–69; *A catalogue of books on Freemasonry* 1858. *d.* New York 27 Nov. 1870. *Appleton's American Biography* (1887) *ii*, 698, *portrait*.

GOYDER, REV. DAVID GEORGE. *b.* Angel's court, Westminster 1 March 1796; educ. Westminster sch. 1805; apprenticed to a brush maker 1810 and to a printer 1814; schoolmaster to the Swedenborgians' soc. at Bristol 1821 and a minister 3 Nov. 1822; school organiser, inspector and missionary for the Swedenborgians 1825 etc.; lecturer on phrenology; author of *Swedenborg and his mission* 1853; *Lectures on Freemasonry* 1864; *The book of family worship* 1871 and 15 other books. *d.* Bradford, Yorkshire 2 July 1878 aged 82. *My battle for life, The autobiography of a phrenologist, by D. G. Goyder* (1857).

GRABHAM, JOHN. Entered British Museum 4 March 1833, second superintendent of Reading-room there 1850 to death; compiled *Index to Encyclopedia Metropolitana* 1842 and to *Townsend and Cattley's ed. of Foxes " Acts and Monuments"* 1849; edited and made additions to Bishop E. Maltby's *Greek Gradus* 3rd ed. 1850. *d.* 15 Noel st., Islington, London 9 Aug. 1858 aged 57.

GRACE, GEORGE FREDERICK *(youngest son of the succeeding).* *b.* Downend near Bristol 13 Dec. 1850; played many cricket matches as one of the Gloucestershire eleven; played in South *v.* North at Canterbury 1866; a good batsman and bowler, and one of the finest fieldsmen ever known at long-leg and cover-point. *d.* of pneumonia at Red Lion hotel, Basingstoke 22 Sep. 1880. *bur.* Downend ch. 27 Sep. *Sporting Mirror i*, 157–8 (1881), *portrait; Illust. sp. and dr. news, i*, 568, 570 (1874), *portrait, xiv*, 53 (1880), *portrait; Hants. and Berks. gazette 25 Sept. 1880, p. 5.*

GRACE, HENRY MILLS. *b.* Long Ashton, Somerset; L.S.A. 1829, M.R.C.S. 1830; surgeon to Royal Gloucs. hussars 1841 to death; father of the 5 Messrs. Grace; kept up West Gloucs. cricket club many years; founder & treasurer of Gloucestershire county cricket club; a right hand batsman but fielded and threw left. *d.* Downend 23 Dec. 1871 aged 63. *Lillywhite's Cricket Scores v*, 93 (1876).

GRACE, OLIVER DOWELL JOHN. *b.* Mantua house, Elphin 19 Oct. 1791; sheriff of Roscommon 1830; M.P. for co. Roscommon 1847–59. *d.* Mantua house 25 Jany. 1871.

GRAFTON, HENRY FITZROY, 5 Duke of. *b.* 10 Feb. 1790; ed. at Trin. coll. Cam., M.A. 1814; M.P. for Bury St. Edmunds 1818–30, for Thetford 1834–44; col. East Suffolk militia 1823–30, col. West Suffolk militia 1830–45; succeeded 28 Sep. 1844. *d.* Wakefield lodge, Northamptonshire 26 March 1863.

GRAFTON, WILLIAM HENRY FITZROY, 6 Duke of. *b.* Grosvenor place, London 4 Aug. 1819; M.P. for Thetford 1847–63; succeeded 26 March 1863. *d.* 4 Grosvenor place, London 21 May 1882. *Baily's Mag. xxxiv,* 311 (1879), *portrait.*

GRAFTON, FREDERICK WILLIAM. *b.* 1816; head of firm of F. W. Grafton & Co., calico printers of Broad Oak, Accrington and Manchester; owner of Heysham hall, Lancs.; M.P. for North-East Lancs. 1880–85. *d.* 7 Kensington palace gardens, London 27 Jany. 1890.

GRAHAM, CLEMENTINA STIRLING *(eldest dau. of Patrick Stirling of Pittendriech, who in 1802 took the surname of Graham).* *b.* Dundee, May 1782; an intimate friend of Francis Lord Jeffrey and Henry T. Lord Cockburn; lived partly in Edinburgh and partly at Duntrune, Forfarshire; her house was a meeting place for all literary persons; had great powers of personation and of disguising herself; author of *The Bee preserver, By Jonas de Gelieu, a translation* 1829, *another ed.* 1876; *Mystification, with poems and sketches, privately printed* 1859, *published* 1865, *4 ed.* 1869. *d.* Duntrune 22 Aug. 1877. *Mystification, 4 ed.* (1869) *p. i, etc., with portrait; W. Chambers's Stories of remarkable persons* (1878) 289–302; *John Leech and other papers, By John Brown, 2 ed.* (1882) 169–75.

GRAHAM, DAVID. *b.* London 8 Feb. 1808; admitted to New York bar; professor of law of pleading and practice in New York university 1838; author of *Practice of the supreme court of state of New York* 1832, *2 ed.* 1836; *An essay on New Trials* 1834; *A treatise on the Courts of law and equity in state of New York* 1839; edited *Smith's Chancery practice* 1842. *d.* Nice 27 May 1852.

GRAHAM, SIR FORTESCUE *(son of Richard Graham, lieut. col. R.M.)* *b.* Tintinhull near Yeovil 1794; 2 lieut. R.M. 17 Nov. 1808; A.D.C. to the Queen 10 July 1854 to 27 Feb. 1857; commanded Portsmouth division of R.M. 22 June 1855 to 20 Feb. 1857 and Plymouth division 1 June 1863 to 23 Aug. 1866; col. royal marine artillery 23 Aug. 1866 to 1 April 1870 when he retired on full pay; general 10 Nov. 1866; C.B. 5 July 1855, K.C.B. 28 March 1865. *d.* 69 Durnford st. Stonehouse, Plymouth 9 Oct. 1880.

GRAHAM, GEORGE (4 *son of Sir James Graham, 1 baronet* 1761–1824). *b.* 1801; military sec. at Bombay 1828–30; private sec. to his brother Sir James Graham 1831–34 and 1841–42;

registrar general of births, deaths, and marriages 1838–79. *d.* 31 Chapel st., Belgrave sq., London 20 May 1888.

GRAHAM, GEORGE FARQUHAR *(eld. son of lieut. col. Humphrey Graham).* *b.* Edinburgh 28 Dec. 1789; a self taught musician and violinist; sec. of first Edin. musical festival with G. Hogarth 1815; studied music in Italy; composed three well known songs, County Guy 1823, You never longed nor loved, and The mariner's song; wrote for the Encyclopædia Britannica the articles on music and the organ; author of *An account of the first Edinburgh musical festival* 1816; *An essay on the theory and practice of musical composition* 1838; *Ancient Scottish melodies a selection from the Skene M.S., By G. F. Graham and Finlay Dun* 1839; *The songs of Scotland, The biographical notices by G. F. Graham* 1848, *New ed.* 1884. *d.* Gilmore place, Edinburgh 12 March 1867.

GRAHAM, HENRY HOPE. *b.* 16 Sep. 1808; ensign 57 foot 1829; lieut. col. 59 foot 29 April 1853; superintending officer of recruiting 1860–67; general 1 Oct. 1877; col. of 77 foot 1875 to death; C.B. 1858. *d.* Somerset st. Portman sq., London 9 July 1886.

GRAHAM, JAMES GILLESPIE *(son of a poor man called Gillespie).* *b.* 1777; a working joiner. *(m.* Margaret Anne Græme, dau. of William Graham of Orchill, on whose death in 1825 he took the surname of Graham, she *d.* 1826); architect Edinburgh; laid out part of lower new town Edinburgh 1815; built, enlarged, and restored many residences for the Scotch nobility 1810, etc.; erected many churches and chapels 1813, etc.; introduced a purer gothic style into Scotland; great friend of A. W. Pugin from 1830, with him erected Victoria hall, Castle hill, Edinburgh for the meetings of the general assembly 1842–3; F.S.A. Scotland as James Gillespie 24 March 1817. *d.* York place, Edinburgh 21 March 1855. *Crombie's Modern Athenians* (1882), 141–43, *portrait.*

GRAHAM, SIR JAMES ROBERT GEORGE, 2 Baronet *(eld. son of Sir James Graham, 1 Baronet* 1761–1824). *b.* Naworth, Cumberland 1 June 1792; ed. at Westminster and Ch. Ch. Ox.; private sec. to Lord Montgomerie, British minister in Sicily; M.P. for Hull 1818, for St. Ives 1820–21, for Carlisle 1826–9, 1852–61, for Cumberland 1829–32, for East Cumberland 1832–7, for Pembroke 1838–41, for Dorchester 1841–7, for Ripon 1847–52; first lord of the Admiralty 25 Nov. 1830 to 11 June 1834, and 30 Dec. 1852 to Feb. 1855;

GRAHAM, SIR J. R. G. (Con.)

sec. of state for home department 6 Sep. 1841 to 6 July 1846; lord rector of Glasgow Univ.; ecclesiastical comr. Sep. 1846; K.C.B. 15 April 1854; F.R.S. 22 Dec. 1831; author of *Corn and currency, an address* 1826 and other pamphlets. *d.* Netherby near Carlisle 25 Oct. 1861. *bur.* north side of Arthuret church. *Life by T. M. Torrens 2 vols.* (1863), *portrait; H. Lonsdale's Worthies of Cumberland ii, 1 et seq.* (1868); *G. H. Francis's Orators of the age* (1847), 183–205; *D. O. Maddyn's Chiefs of parties ii,* 242–56 (1859); *Saddle and Sirloin By the Druid, Part North* (1870), 33–9.

GRAHAM, RIGHT REV. JOHN *(only son of John Graham, managing clerk to Thos. Griffith of The Bailey, city of Durham).* *b.* Claypath, city of Durham 23 Feb. 1794; ed. at Durham gr. sch. and Ch. coll. Cam., 4th wrangler 1816, Chancellor's medallist 1816. B.A. 1816, M.A. 1819; fell. of his coll. 1816; deacon 1818; preb. of Sanctæ Crucis in Linc. cath. 1828 and of Leighton Ecclesia 1834; master of Christ's coll. Cam. 1830–49, vice chancellor of the Univ. 1834 and 1840; chap. in ord. to Prince Albert 26 Jany. 1841; R. of Willingham, Cambs. 1843–8; bishop of Chester 11 March 1848 to death, consecrated in chapel royal, Whitehall 18 May 1848; clerk of the Closet to the Queen 25 Sep. 1849 to death; published *Sermons on the Commandments* 1826. *d.* the Palace, Chester 15 June 1865. *G.M. xix,* 240–42 (1865).

GRAHAM, JOHN MURRAY *(eld. son of Andrew Murray* 1782–1847). *b.* Aberdeenshire 15 Oct. 1809; educ. Edin. univ., M.A. 1828; advocate 1831; succeeded to part of estate of Thomas Graham, Lord Lynedoch 1859 and took his name of Graham; author of *A month's tour in Spain* 1867; *Memoir of General Lord Lynedoch* 1868, 2 ed. 1877; *An historical view of literature and art from accession of House of Hanover to Victoria* 1871, 2 ed. 1872; *Annals of the Viscount and the first and second Earls of Stair 2 vols.* 1875. *d.* Murray's hall, Perthshire 18 Jany. 1881. *Antiquary iii,* 136 (1881); *Academy* 29 Jany. 1881 *p.* 81.

GRAHAM, MONTAGU WILLIAM *(younger son of 3 Duke of Montrose* 1755–1836). *b.* 25 Grosvenor sq. London 2 Feb. 1807; M.P. for Grantham 1852–57, for Herefordshire 1858–65. *d.* Wilton st. Belgrave sq. London 21 June 1878.

GRAHAM, THOMAS *(eld. son of James Graham, merchant).* *b.* Glasgow 20 Dec. 1805; educ. Glasgow gram. sch. and univ., M.A. 1826; professor of chemistry, Andersonian Instit.

GRAHAM, T. *(Con).*

Glasgow 1830–37; professor at London univ. now Univ. coll. 1837–55; non-resident assayer of Royal Mint and master April 1855 to death; F.R.S. 25 Dec. 1836; F.G.S.; D.C.L. Oxf. 20 June 1855; discovered law of diffusion of gases, Keith medal R.S. Edin. 1834; discovered polybasic character of phosphoric acid, gold medal R.S. 1840; investigated transpirability of gases, gold medal 1850; speculated on constitution of phosphates and discovered diffusion of liquids, Copley medal 1862; a founder and first president Chemical Soc. 1840; a founder and first president Cavendish Soc. 1846; author of *Outlines of botany* 1841; *Elements of chemistry* 1842, 2 ed. 1847 and other books. *d.* 4 Gordon sq. London 16 Sep. 1869. *Walford's Portraits of living celebrities* (1859), *No. 8,. portrait; Proc. of Royal Soc. xviii, pp. xvii–xxvi* (1870); *Proc. of Royal Soc. Edin. vii,* 15 (1872); *S. Muspratt's Chemistry, i,* (1853), *portrait.*

GRAHAM, WILLIAM. Gretna Green post-boy; known by the sobriquet of "Carwinley;" important witness in celebrated Wakefield marriage case 24 March 1827. *d.* Carlisle 18 Dec. 1864 aged 79.

GRAHAM, WILLIAM. *b.* Dufton Wood near Appleby 1808; a successful wrestler; member of a large London firm; chiefly raced under pseudonyms, his 3 Oaks winners are registered as Regalia 1865 belonging to Mr. Harlock, and Formosa 1868 and Gamos 1870 to Mr. G. Jones; Sabinus was said to belong to Mr. Hessey, other names he used were Brown, Keswick, Fischer & Winchester; made £18,965 in 1868. *d.* 8 Holloway road, Highbury, London 19 Jany. 1876. *Baily's Mag. xxviii,* 126–30 (1876); *Bell's Life* 22 Jany. 1876 *p.* 6.

GRAHAM, REV. WILLIAM. *b.* Clough farm, co. Antrim 1810; presbyterian minister at Dundonald near Belfast 1836; missionary to the Jews at Damascus 1842, at Hamburg, at Bonn to 1883; D.D., M.R.I.A.; author of *The spirit of love, a commentary* 1857; *Fifty songs of Zion* 1857; *A practical commentary on the epistle to Titus* 1860; *Lectures on St. Paul's epistle to the Ephesians* 1870. *d.* Belfast 11 Dec. 1883.

GRAHAM, WILLIAM. *b.* 1816; M.P. for Glasgow 14 July 1865 to 26 Jany. 1874. *d.* Oakdene near Guildford 16 July 1885. *I.L.N. xlviii,* 144 (1866), *portrait.*

GRAHAM, REV. WILLIAM. Educ. Glasgow univ. D.D.; licentiate of United Presbyterian ch.; pastor of Mount Pleasant ch. Liverpool

GRAHAM, REV. W. (Con.)

1846–80; moderator of English Presbyterian synod 1877; professor of church history, Presbyterian coll., Guildford st., London 1880; author of *Memoirs of John Macfarlane* 1876. *d.* Acton West 26 Nov. 1887 aged 64. *bur.* Birkenhead 1 Dec. *Christian World* 1 *Dec.* 1887 *p.* 917.

GRAHAM-GILBERT, JOHN. *b.* Glasgow 1794; educ. R. Acad. sch. London 1818–21; portrait painter; in Italy 1823, 1826; exhibited 27 pictures at R.A. and 26 at B.I. 1820–64; settled in Edinburgh 1827, Glasgow 1834; R.S.A. 1829; painted Portrait of Walter Scott 1829, The pear tree wall 1844, Females at a fountain 1846. (*m.* 1834 Miss Gilbert of Yorkhill near Glasgow, and assumed the surname of Gilbert. She was also an artist, and on her death in 1877 left pictures to Corporation galleries at Glasgow). *d.* Yorkhill 4 June 1866.

GRAHAME, ROBERT. *b.* Stockwell st., Glasgow 1759; the leading democrat of the West of Scotland 1793; the first Lord Provost of Glasgow after enactment of Burgh Reform; leading partner of firm of Grahame and Mitchell of Glasgow, writers. *d.* Hatton hall, Northamptonshire 28 Dec. 1851.

GRAINGER, RICHARD. *b.* Newcastle upon Tyne 1796; ed. at St. Andrew's charity sch. there; apprenticed to a carpenter; erected Eldon square, Leazes terrace and crescent, the Arcade, Grey st., Grainger st., Market st., Clayton st. and Clayton st. west, all in Newcastle upon Tyne 1826–31; purchased the Elswick estate on the Tyne for £200,000. *d.* West Clayton st. Newcastle upon Tyne 4 July 1861. *Once a week*, v, 401–406 (1861).

GRAINGER, RICHARD DUGARD (*son of Edward Grainger of Birmingham, surgeon*). *b.* Birmingham 1801, ed. at gr. school there and Woolwich, at St. Thomas' and Webb st. sch.; M.R.C.S. 1822, F.R.C.S. 1843; kept a private anatomical school in Webb st. Borough, London 1822–42 when it was amalgamated with St. Thomas's hospital; professor of anatomy and physiology at St. Thomas's 1842–60; F.R.S. 22 Jany. 1846; delivered Hunterian oration 1848; a cholera inspector 1849; an inspector under the Burials Act 1853 to death; one of Childrens' employment comrs. 13 Feb. 1862; author of *Elements of general anatomy* 1829; *Observations on the spinal cord* 1837; *Observations on the cultivation of organic science* 1848; *Sanitary report on cholera* 1848–9. *d.* 6 Hornsey lane, Highgate 1 Feb. 1865. *bur.* Eltham 7 Feb. *Medical times and gazette,* i, 157–58 (1865).

GRAINGER, THOMAS. *b.* Gogar green, Ratho near Edinburgh 12 Nov. 1794; civil engineer and surveyor in Edin. 1816; executed the Monkland and Kirkintilloch railway 1824, the first in Scotland on which 'edge rails' were used; partner with Mr. Miller 1825–45; executed Paisley and Renfrew railway 1834, Arbroath and Forfar line 1835, Edinburgh, Leith and Newhaven line 183 ; Edinburgh, Perth and Dundee lines 1847; pres. of royal Scottish society of arts 2 years; M.I.C.E. 1829; F.R.S. Edin.; F.S.A. Edin. *d.* Stockton on Tees 25 July 1852 from injuries received in a collision of trains near Stockton on Tees 21 July. *Min. of proc. of Instit. of C.E. xii,* 159 (1853).

GRANARD, GEORGE ARTHUR HASTINGS FORBES, 7 Earl of. *b.* Chilton hall, Suffolk 5 Aug. 1833; succeeded 9 June 1837; attaché to legation at Dresden 1852–54; lord lieut. of Leitrim, Nov. 1856 to July 1872; K.P. 30 Jany. 1857. *d.* Castle Forbes, co. Longford 25 Aug. 1889. *I.L.N. xlii,* 181 (1862), *portrait.*

GRANGER, THOMAS COLPITTS (*eld. son of Joseph Granger of Durham*). Barrister I.T. 14 May 1830, bencher 1850; recorder of Hull 1847 to death; Q.C. 1850; contested city of Durham Jany. 1835 and July 1837; M.P. for city of Durham June 1841 to death; author of *A supplement to the statutes by Sir W. D. Evans* 1836; author with R. P. Tyrwhitt of *Reports of cases in the Court of Exchequer and Exchequer Chamber* 1835–37, 1 *vol.* 1837; author with James Manning of *Reports of cases in the Court of Common Pleas* 1840–45, 7 *vols.* 1841–46. *d.* York 13 Aug. 1852 aged 50. *bur.* in vaults of Temple church, London.

GRANT, SIR ALEXANDER, 8 Baronet (*elder son of Sir Robert Innes Grant, 7 baronet* 1794–1856). *b.* New York 13 Sep. 1826; ed. at Harrow and Balliol coll. Ox., scholar 1844–9, fellow 1849–60, hon. fellow 1882; B.A. 1849, M.A. 1852, D.C.L. 1860; examiner for Indian civil service 1855; inspector of schools in Madras 1859; professor of history and political economy in Elphinstone coll., Madras 1860, principal 1862; vice chancellor of Univ. of Bombay 1863–5 and 1865–8; director of public instruction in Bombay 1865; member of legislative council of Bombay 1868; vice chancellor and principal of Univ. of Edin. 6 July 1868 to death, installed 3 Nov. 1868; devised and carried out tercentenary festival 1884; F.R.S. Edin. 1869; author of *The story of the University of Edinburgh during its first three hundred years* 1884 and other books. *d.*

GRANT, SIR A. *(Con.)*
21 Landowne crescent, Edinburgh 30 Nov.
1884. *W. Hole's Quasi Cursores* (1884) 6, 7–17;
Trans. of Royal Soc. of Edin. (1885).

GRANT, SIR ALEXANDER CRAY, 6 Baronet
*(eld. son of Sir Alexander Grant, 5 baronet, who
d. 25 July 1825).* *b.* Bowring's Leigh, Devon
30 Nov. 1782; ed. at St. John's coll. Cam.;
member of colonial assembly of Jamaica
1810–11; M.P. for Tregony 1812–18, for
Lostwithiel 1818–26, for Aldborough 1826–
30, for Westbury 1830–32, for town of Cambridge 1840–43; contested Great Grimsby
1835 and Honiton 1837; chairman of committees of house of commons 1826–32; a
member of board of control for India 20
Dec. 1834 to 29 April 1835; a comr. for
auditing public accounts 1843 to death. *d.*
Somerset house,? London 29 Nov. 1854.

GRANT, VEN. ANTHONY *(youngest son of Thomas
Grant of Portsea).* *b.* 31 Jany. 1806; ed. at
Winchester and New coll. Ox., fellow 1825–
39; B.C.L. 1832, D.C.L. 1842; select
preacher 1852 and 1861; C. of Chelmsford
1836; V. of Romford, Essex 1838–62; V. of
Aylesford, Kent 1862–77; archdeacon of St.
Albans 1846 to death; archdeacon of Rochester 1863–82; canon of Rochester 1860 to
death; author of *The past and prospective extension of the gospel to the heathen* 1844, a
Bampton lecture which marked an epoch in
mission work. *An historical sketch of the Crimea*
1855 and other books. *d.* 11 Royal crescent,
Ramsgate 25 Nov. 1883.

GRANT, CHARLES. Second lieut. Bengal artillery 22 April 1819, col. 16 Feb. 1861, col.
commandant 11 Jany. 1868 to death; general
1 Oct. 1877; C.B. 9 June 1849. *d.* 3 Suffolk
sq., Cheltenham 13 Jany. 1882.

GRANT, COLESWORTHY. *b.* London 25 Oct.
1813; went to Calcutta 1832; well known as
an artist; professor of drawing Howrah engineering coll. 1849 and at Presidency engineering coll. Calcutta 185–; founded Calcutta
soc. for prevention of cruelty to animals, and
became hon. sec. 4 Oct. 1861; contributed
167 portrait sketches to the *India Review* and
other papers 1838–50; made 78 sketches of
Oriental heads; author of *Rough pencillings of
a rough trip to Rangoon in 1846,* Calcutta 1853;
Anglo-Indian domestic life 185–, anon.; *Rural
life-in Bengal, Letters from an Artist in India
to his sisters in England* 1860; *To the children
of Calcutta, On cruelty,* Calcutta 1872. *d.* Calcutta 31 May 1880. *P. C. Mittra's Life of C.
Grant* (1881), *portrait.*

GRANT, DAVID. *b.* Upper Banchory, Kincardineshire 1823; educ. Aberdeen univ.; schoolmaster Elgin; French master Oundle gram.
sch. Northamptonshire 1861; assist. master
Eccleshall coll. near Sheffield 1865; kept a
day sch. at Sheffield by which he was ruined
1880; private tutor Edinburgh 1880 to
death; author of *Metrical tales,* Sheffield 1880;
Lays and legends of the North, Edin. 1884; *A
book of ten songs with music* 1887. *d.* Edinburgh 1886. *D. H. Edwards' Modern Scotch
poets,* Brechin (1880).

GRANT, SIR FRANCIS *(4 son of Francis Grant
of Kilgraston, Perthshire, who d. 1819).* *b.*
Edinburgh 18 Jany. 1803; ed. at Harrow;
exhibited 253 portraits at R.A. 1834–79;
the fashionable portrait painter of the day
from 1840; A.R.A. 1842, R.A. 11 Feb. 1851,
pres. 1866; member of Belgian academy
1855; knighted at Buckingham Palace 24
March 1866; hon. D.C.L. Ox. 1870. *d.* The
Lodge, Melton Mowbray 5 Oct. 1878. *Illustrated Review,* v, 449–55, *portrait; J. Sherer's
Gallery of British artists,* ii, 1–3; *Sandby's
History of Royal Academy* ii, 295–7 (1862);
I.L.N. vi, 293 (1845), *portrait,* xviii, 219
(1851), *portrait,* xlviii, 232 (1866), *portrait.*

GRANT, GERTRUDE ELIZABETH. Author under
pseudonym of Gerald Grant of 3 novels
Coming home to roost 3 vols. 1872, *The old
✠ quarry* 3 vols. 1873, *The great gulf fixed* 3
vols. 1877. *d.* Göritz, Austria 29 Dec. 1882.

GRANT, JAMES. *b.* Elgin, Morayshire 1802;
a founder and editor of *Elgin Courier* 1827;
went to London 1833; conducted *London
Saturday Journal* 1839, *Grant's London Journal*
1840; editor of *Morning Advertiser* 1850–71,
of *Christian Standard* 1872; author of *The
great metropolis* 1836, 1837; *Random recollections of House of Commons and House of Lords*
2 vols. 1836, *second ser. called The British senate*
1838; *The metropolitan pulpit* 1839; *The
newspaper press, its origin, progress and present
position* 3 vols. 1871–72; *The Plymouth Brethren* 1875 and upwards of 30 other works. *d.*
35 Cornwall road, Bayswater, London 23 May
1879. *Bookseller, June* 1879 *p.* 510; *Licensed
Victuallers Almanac* (1862), *portrait; I.L.N.
lxxiv,* 561 (1879), *portrait.*

GRANT, JAMES. *b.* Glen Urquhart, Inverness-
shire 1840; educ. Aberdeen univ., M.A.;
studied law in Edinburgh; assistant to professor Cosmo Innes, whom he helped in his
books; worked under John Hill Burton and
professor Masson in publication of Scottish
privy council records; F.S.A.; author of

GRANT, J. *(Con.)*

History of the burgh and parish schools of Scotland, vol. 1, 1876, *vol.* 2 though completed not printed; *History of the university of Edinburgh, unprinted. d.* at his brother's residence 114 Bell terrace, Newcastle-on-Tyne 9 Aug. 1885.

GRANT, JAMES *(eld. son of John Grant, capt. 92 highlanders). b.* Edinburgh 1 Aug. 1822; resident in Newfoundland 1833–39; ensign 62 foot 1840, resigned 1843; with David Rhind architect, Edin. 1843; founder and sec. of National association for Vindication of Scottish rights 1852 which was ridiculed in *Punch;* an early volunteer; joined Roman Catholic ch. 1875; author of *The Romance of war 4 vols.* 1846–47; *Memorials of the castle of Edinburgh* 1850; *The adventures of an aide-de-camp 3 vols.* 1848; *Old and new Edinburgh 3 vols.* 1880; *Love's labour won 3 vols.* 1888 and about 60 other works. *d.* 25 Tavistock road, Westbourne park, London 5 May 1887.

GRANT, JAMES GREGOR. Lecturer for Northern Union of Mechanics' institutes; resided in Sunderland; wrote a series of stories on local legends for *Newcastle Weekly Chronicle;* author of *Madonna Pia and other poems 2 vols.* 1848. *d.* London 25 Dec. 1875.

GRANT, SIR JAMES HOPE *(youngest son of Francis Grant of Kilgraston, Perthshire). b.* 22 July 1808; cornet 9 lancers 29 Aug. 1826, lieut. col. 29 April 1850 to 26 Feb. 1858; colonel 4 hussars 18 Jany. 1861 to 6 Feb. 1865; col. 9 lancers 9 Feb. 1865 to death; general 23 April 1872, took an important part in suppression of Indian mutiny 1857–8; commanded British forces during Chinese war 1860; commander in chief at Madras 1861–5; quartermaster general at head quarters 1865–70; commanded division at Aldershot 1 Nov. 1870 to death; C.B. 24 Dec. 1842, K.C.B. 21 Jany. 1858, G.C.B. 9 Nov. 1860. *d.* at house of Baroness Gray, 42 Grosvenor gardens, London 7 March 1875. *C. R. Low's Soldiers of the Victorian age, ii,* 252–307 (1880); *Golden Hours* (1869) 818–32, *portrait; D. C. Boulger's History of China, iii,* 483 *et seq.* (1884); *I.L.N. lxvi,* 258, 273, 277, 278, 470 (1875), *portrait.*

GRANT, JAMES MACPHERSON. *b.* Alvie, Invernessshire 1822; went with his parents to New South Wales 1836; articled to Chambers and Thurlow, solicitors, Sydney 1841–47; solicitor 1847, partner with Mr. Thurlow; solicitor Melbourne 1854; member for Bendigo to legislative council Victoria, Nov. 1855, member for Sandhurst boroughs 1856, for Avoca 1859 to decease; V.P. of Board of

GRANT, J. M. *(Con.)*

lands and works 1861, president 1864–68, 1868–69, 1871–72; minister of justice 1875, 1877–80; chief sec. 1881–83; did much in settling the people on the public lands. *d.* Melbourne? 1 April 1885. *Men of the time in Australia, Victoria* (1878) 73.

GRANT, SIR JAMES ROBERT *(son of Duncan Grant of Mulochaird in Strathspey). b.* Forres co. Moray Feb. 1773; assistant surgeon 22 Jany. 1792; inspector general of army hospitals 14 July 1814; chief of medical department at Waterloo; received order of St. Anne of Russia from Emperor Alexander at Paris 1815; K.H. 1816; knighted by Prince Regent at Carlton house 18 March 1819; C.B. 16 Aug. 1850. *d.* Basford vicarage, Notts 10 Jany. 1864. *bur.* St. Mary's churchyard, Carlisle 18 Jany.

GRANT, JAMES WILLIAM *(son of Robert Grant). b.* Wester Elchies, Morayshire 12 Aug. 1788; writer H.E.I.C.S. 22 July 1805 in Bengal; retired 1849; detected the companion of Antares 23 July 1844 two years before Mitchel perceived the duplicity of the star; erected an observatory at Elchies 1849, where he placed the Trophy telescope purchased from great exhibition of 1851, this was sold to Mr. Aytoun in 1864; F. R. Astronom. Soc. 13 Jany. 1854. *d.* Wester Elchies 17 Sept. 1865.

GRANT, JOHN *(brother of Sir Francis Grant 1803–78). b.* 13 June 1798; master of Perthshire hounds 1836–41; chairman of Tay district board of salmon fishing; his residence Kilgraston house, Perthshire burnt 1872. *d.* London 20 Jany. 1873. *Babington's Fife foxhounds* (1883) 66, *portrait; Perthshire Constitutional* 22 Jany. 1873 *p.* 2.

GRANT, JOHN *(eld. son of Ewen Grant). b.* Glasgow 22 May 1819; assisted in Tithe commutation commission survey in Devon 1838; employed on Exeter and Yeovil railway 1845; assist. surveyor metropolitan commission of sewers April 1849, engineer 1852; assist. engineer metropolitan board of works 1856; superintended construction of numerous streets, sewers, pumping stations and the outfall works at Crossness; connected with construction of portions of Chelsea and Albert embankments; made successful experiments on use of portland cement 1858 etc.; M.I.C.E. 3 Dec. 1861, Telford medal 1880; reported on Artizans' dwellings, Glasgow 1877, Fish supply of London 1881, and on Sludge filter presses 1885. *d.* 48 Blessington road, Lee, Kent 24 March 1888. *Min. of proc. of Instit. of C.E. xcii,* 389–92 (1888).

GRANT, SIR JOHN THORNTON (*eld. son of Wm. Charles Grant, captain 92 foot, killed at Waterloo 18 June 1815*). *b.* Ireland 26 Dec. 1810; ensign 49 foot 28 April 1828, lieut. col. 22 Dec. 1854 to 3 Aug. 1860; lieut. col. 18 foot 3 Aug. 1860 to 28 May 1866 when placed on h.p.; brig. gen. Madras 1863–68, M.G. Bombay 1869–74; col. 94 foot 25 June 1879 to death; general 21 May 1880; C.B. 5 July 1855, K.C.B. 24 May 1881. *d.* Upton park, Slough 16 Jany. 1886.

GRANT, SIR LEWIS (*younger son of Duncan Grant of Mulochaird in Strathspey*). Ensign 95 foot 15 Feb. 1794; lieut. col. 70 foot 1804–24; governor of Bahama islands May 1820 to 1829; governor of Trinidad 5 Dec. 1831 to 9 June 1833; knighted at St. James's palace 13 Sep. 1831; K.C.H. 13 Sep. 1831; colonel 96 regt. 9 April 1839 to death; general 11 Nov. 1851. *d.* suddenly in an omnibus in Regent st. London 26 Jany. 1852 aged 70.

GRANT, PHILIP. Power loom weaver; very active in trying to further the cause of the Ten Hours' Bill 1825 etc.; edited the *Ten Hours' Advocate*, a periodical; Ten Hours' Bill passed 1874; author of *History of factory legislation*. *d.* Granville st. Upper Brook st. Chorlton-on-Medlock 4 April 1880. *Manchester Courier 7 April 1880 p. 6.*

GRANT, SIR RICHARD (*son of Richard Grant, H.M.'s proctor at Jamaica*). *b.* Kingston, Jamaica 1783; entered navy July 1798; captain 17 May 1828; R.A. on half pay 7 Feb. 1855; knighted by Earl Talbot, lord lieut. of Ireland 1820. *d.* Shawefield, Havant, Hants. 3 March 1859 aged 75.

GRANT, REV. ROBERT (*son of Thomas Grant of Sheerness, Kent*). Matric. from New coll. Ox. 15 Nov. 1815 aged 18, fellow 1815–28; B.C.L. 1823; V. of Bradford Abbas, Dorset 1828–86; preb. of Salisbury 1845 to death; author of *Lectures on the parable of the prodigal son* 1830; *Kapiolani and other poems* 1848; *Reminiscences of a clergyman during a ministry of forty years in a country parish* 1873. *d.* 11 Clarendon row, Southsea 15 Sep. 1887 in 91 year.

GRANT, ROBERT EDMOND (*7 son of Alexander Grant of Edinburgh, writer to the signet, d. 1808*). *b.* Argyle sq. Edin. 11 Nov. 1793; ed. at high school and univ. Edin., M.D. Edin. 1814; M.R.C.S. Edin. 1814; F.R.S. Edin. 1824; professor of comparative anatomy and zoology in univ. of London, June 1827 to death, lectured 5 times a week, never omitted a single lecture; Fullerian professor of physiology in royal institution 1837–40; Swiney

GRANT, R. E. (*Con.*)

lecturer on geology at British Museum 5 years; F.R.S. 4 Feb. 1836; styled the Cuvier of England; author of *An essay on the study of the animal kingdom* 1828, 2 ed. 1829; *Outlines of comparative anatomy* 1835–41, and papers in *Lancet*. *d.* 2 Euston grove, Euston sq. London 23 Aug. 1874, left all his property to Univ. coll. London. *Proc. of Royal society, xxiii, pp. vi–x* (1875); *Quarterly Journal of Geological society, xxxi,* 49–52.

GRANT, MOST REV. THOMAS (*2 son of Bernard Grant of Ackerson's Mill near Newry, quartermaster 82 foot, who d. May 1856 aged 69*). *b.* Ligny-les-Aires, France 5 Nov. 1816; entered St. Cuthbert's college, Ushaw, Durham 1 Jany. 1829; entered English college, Rome 1 Dec. 1836; created D.D. 27 Aug. 1841; priest 28 Nov. 1841; sec. to Cardinal Acton 1841–47 when he died; prorector of English college, Rome 13 April 1844, rector 13 Oct. 1844 to 27 June 1851; bishop of Southwark 27 June 1851 to death, consecrated in church of English college, Rome by Cardinal Fransoni 4 July 1851; author of *Meditations of the Sisters of Mercy before renewal of vows* 1874. *d.* the English college, Rome 1 June 1870. *bur.* in cemetery of orphanage at Norwood, Surrey. *Thomas Grant, bishop of Southwark, by Grace Ramsay* 1874, *with 2 portraits; Gillow's English Catholics, iii,* 5–11 (1887).

GRANT, SIR THOMAS TASSELL (*eld. son of Thomas Grant of Soberton, Hants.*) *b.* Portsea, Hants. 1795; entered naval service 1812; storekeeper Clarence victualling yard, Gosport 1828; controller of victualling and transport service Dec. 1850 to 1858; invented steam machinery for making biscuits 1829 for which he had parliamentary grant of £2000; invented a life buoy, a feathering paddle wheel, and Grant's patent fuel 1839 which is used in the navy; distilled fresh water from the sea 1849, the Wye with his apparatus sent to the Crimea produced 10,000 gallons daily 1855; K.C.B. 6 Sep. 1858; F.R.S. *d.* 20 Chester ter. Regent's park, London 15 Oct. 1859 aged 64. *Times 19 Oct. 1859 p. 7; G.M. Nov. 1859 p. 534.*

GRANT, WILLIAM (*brother of Most Rev. Thomas Grant 1816–70*). Professor at St. Peter's college, Agra 18— to death; started the *Agra Weekly Register*. *d.* Agra 20 May 1863.

GRANT, WILLIAM AUGUSTINE IGNATIUS. *b.* 1838; a Presbyterian; a member of Church of England; a Roman Catholic 1857–68; an Irvingite 1868–73; an extreme Ritualist 1873–80; a Roman Catholic again 1880 to death; a landscape painter, exhibited 1 picture at R.A. and 4 at B.I. 1862–64; lived at Peckham many years; one of the ablest controversialists of his day; author of *The Communion of Saints in the Church of God* 1867; *Apostolic Lordship and the interior life: a narrative of five years' communion with Catholic Apostolic Angels*, privately printed 1873, published under title of *Apostolic Lordship, or five years with the Irvingites: and why I left them* 1874; *The peoples' mass book, By a Layman of the Church of England* 1874 and other books. *d.* Clifton 21 May 1883. *Gillow's English Catholics iii*, 11–14 (1887).

GRANT, WILLIAM JAMES. *b.* Hackney, London 1829; student at R.A. 1844; exhibited 39 works at R.A. and 5 at B.I. 1847–66; some of his pictures were, Edward the Black Prince entertaining French King 1848, Samson and Delilah 1852, The morning of the duel 1860, The lady and the wasp 1866. *d.* London? 2 June 1866.

GRANT, SIR WILLIAM KEIR (*son of Archibald Keir of H.E.I.C.S.*) *b.* 1771; cornet 15 dragoons 30 May 1792; one of 8 officers who saved Francis II. Emperor of Germany from being taken prisoner by the French in the plains of Catau Cambresis 24 April 1794, received gold medal and was made knight of Maria Theresa; lieut. col. 22 light dragoons 3 Dec. 1800; served in India as adjutant general 1806–14; commander in chief and second member of council in Java 1815–16; served in India 1819–21; col. 8 dragoons 1 Feb. 1833 to 24 Aug. 1839, and of 2 dragoons 24 Aug. 1839 to death; general 23 Nov. 1841; K.C.H. 1821, G.C.H. 1835; K.C.B. 3 Dec. 1822; G.C. of Lion and Sun, Persia. *d.* 20 Chapel st. Belgrave sq. London 7 May 1852. *G.M. June* 1852 *pp.* 619–20; *Dod's Peerage* 1852 *p.* 258.

GRANTHAM, GEORGE. Entered Madras army 1823; col. 5 Madras N.I. 4 Nov. 1856–61; col. 39 Madras N.I. 1861–69; L.G. 6 March 1868; drowned in collision between steamers Mary and Normandy about 20 miles from the Needles, Isle of Wight 17 March 1870 aged 67. *Times* 18–26 *March* 1870.

GRANTHAM, REV. GEORGE PEIRCE (*son of George Grantham of firm of Gosling and Sharp, bankers, London*). *b.* Finsbury, London 11 Jany. 1833; educ. King's coll. Lond. and Univ. of Lond.; C. of Allhallows East, Exeter 1859–61; C. of Rame, Cornwall 1861–65; C. of Hotham 1865–67; senior C. of St. Saviour's, Leeds 1867–76; precentor and senior curate

of St. Michael's, Swanmore, Ryde 1876–79; V. of Llanbadoc near Usk 1879–81; C. of Holy Cross mission ch. Bedminster 1881–83; C. of St. Augustine, Kensington 1883; V. of Ston Easton with Farrington Gurney 1885; author of *Holy Songs* 1866; *The mysteries of holy church and other verses* 1871; *History of St. Saviour's, Leeds* 1872; *Carols for yule tide, with original music* 1877; editor of *Ecclesiastical Art Rev.* 1878. *d.* The Elms, Farrington Gurney 13 Oct. 1885. *bur.* Arnos vale cemetery, Bristol. *International Mag.,* Oct. 1885 *pp.* 110–11.

GRANTHAM, JOHN. Educ. Guy's and St. Thomas' hospitals; L.S.A. 1823; M.R.C.S. 21 Feb. 1823, hon. fellow 26 Aug. 1844; author of *Facts and observations on medicine and surgery* 1844. *d.* Crayford, Kent 14 Nov. 1873 in 73 year.

GRANTHAM, JOHN (2 *son of John Grantham, surveyor*). *b.* Croydon 1809; managing partner of firm of Mather, Dickson & Co.; one of founders of Polytechnic society, Liverpool; a naval architect and consulting engineer at Liverpool; planned and executed several of the largest iron sailing and steam ships; took out patents for screw propellers, and invented a system of sheathing iron built ships with copper; practised in London 1859 to death; constructed the first tramway in Copenhagen 1863; patented a steam tramway car; one of founders of Institution of naval architects Jany. 1860, member of council Jany. 1860 to death; A.I.C.E. 11 Feb. 1840, M.I.C.E. 29 Nov. 1864; author of *Iron as a material for ship building* 1842; *Iron ship building* 1858, 5 ed. 1868. *d.* Croydon 10 July 1874. *Min. of proc. of Instit. of C.E. xxxix*, 266–68 (1875).

GRANVILLE, AUGUSTUS BOZZI (3 *son of Carlo Bozzi, postmaster general Milan*). *b.* Milan 7 Oct. 1783; studied at Univ. of Pavia 1799–1802, M.D. 28 Aug. 1802; assistant surgeon in British navy March 1807, retired as surgeon on half pay 1813; assumed maternal name of Granville; M.R.C.S. Eng. 1813; L.R.C.P. 1817; studied at La Maternité, Paris, and qualified as an accoucher 1816–17; settled at 8 Saville row, London 1818; F.R.S. 1817; physician accoucher Westminster general dispensary 1819; introduced use of prussic acid for chest affections; established a West-end infirmary for young children; pres. of Westminster medical soc. 1829; visited Kissingen 1840–68 and set the fashion of drinking its waters; confidential friend of ex-king Joseph Bonaparte 1832–44; author of *St. Petersburg,*

GRANVILLE, A. B. (Con.)

a journal of travels 2 vols. 1828, 2 ed. 1829; The spas of Germany 2 vols. 1837, 2 ed. 1838; The spas of England and sea-bathing places 3 vols. 1841 and 31 other works. d. 20 Folkestone ter. Dover 3 March 1872. Autobiography of A. B. Granville (1874), portrait; Munk's Coll. of physicians, iii, 174-7 (1878); Physic and physicians, ii, 269-71 (1839).

GRATTAN, SIR EDMUND ARNOUT (son of Thomas C. Grattan 1792-1864). b. 1818; British consul at Boston for state of Massachusetts 4 Aug. 1848 to 1858; consul at Antwerp 11 Jany. 1858 to 1883; consul general for Belgium 28 Nov. 1883 to 1888; British commissioner Antwerp exhibition 1885; V.P. Royal Geog. soc. Antwerp; F.R.G.S.; knighted by patent 18 Nov. 1889. d. Ostend Aug. 1890 aged 72.

GRATTAN, HENRY PLUNKETT, stage name of Henry Willoughby Grattan Plunkett. b. Dublin 1808; made his dèbut at Milton st. theatre London in The Rake's Progress; author of The Minerali, or the dying gift, a drama by H. Plunkett, produced at Cobourg theatre; The Dumb Conscript produced at Astley's 1835; Faust or the Demon of the Drachenfels produced at Sadler's Wells 15 Sep. 1842; wrote the first few numbers of Punch with Henry Mayhew and 4 others 17 July 1841 et seq.; edited The Squib June to Dec. 1842 30 numbers; played Hamlet at Park theatre New York 11 May 1843; built the first theatre at Memphis; editor and owner of The Age newspaper; author of The Bottle, a poem, New York 1848; sometimes used name of Harry Plunkett as a stage name; founded the Actors' Fund; produced many plays; spent 23 years in America; author of The Fairy Circle, The Sisters, Glory, Orson and other pieces all produced in England. d. 25 Dec. 1889. bur. Fulham cemetery 30 Dec.

GRATTAN, MRS. HENRY PLUNKETT (dau. of Mr. M'Phain). b. London 1811; acted in the provinces and then at Garrick theatre, London; made first appearance in America at St. Charles theatre, New Orleans, as lady Anne in Richard iii, 1836; at the new Chatham theatre, America. was the original Madelon in the Carpenter of Rouen 16 Nov. 1840. m. (1) H. P. Grattan; sang in the role of Pollio in Norma at Adelphi, London Oct. 1842; m. (2) Mr. Barker; m. (3) Mr. Madison; returned to America, at Chatham theatre 8 July 1850, retook name of Mrs. Grattan when appearing as Amelia in Wild Oats; travelled throughout the United States and the West Indies playing chief roles in standard dramas; final

GRATTAN, MRS. H. P. (Con.)

engagement at Arch st. theatre, Philadelphia 18 Sept. 1876 in Led Astray. d. 101 West Twenty-ninth st. New York 14 Dec. 1876. Era 7 Jany. 1877 p. 5; The Squib 22 Oct. 1842 p. 92.

GRATTAN, JAMES (eld. son of right hon. Henry Grattan 1746-1820). b. 7 April 1787; cornet 20 light dragoons 9 Aug. 1810; lieut. 9 light dragoons 4 July 1811 to 18 Aug. 1814 when placed on h.p.; M.P. for co. Wicklow 1821-41; P.C. Ireland 1841. d. Tinnehinch, co. Carlow 21 Oct. 1854.

GRATTAN, JOHN. Ensign 18 foot 8 July 1813, lieut. col. 25 May 1853 to 31 July 1854 when placed on h.p.; col. 17 foot 1 May 1868 to death; L.G. 15 Sep. 1870; C.B. 24 Dec. 1842. d. Brussels 29 April 1871 aged 75.

GRATTAN, THOMAS COLLEY (son of Colley Grattan, solicitor). b. Dublin 1792; settled at Bordeaux 1818, Paris 1820?; proprietor and editor of The Paris monthly review Jany. 1822 to April 1823, 15 numbers; produced Ben Nazir the Saracen, a tragedy at Drury lane 21 May 1827; removed to Brussels 1828; British consul to state of Massachusetts 1839-46; assisted Lord Ashburton in treaty of Washington 1842; author of Highways and byways or Tales of the roadside 2 vols. 1823, second ser. 3 vols. 1825, third ser. 3 vols. 1827; The history of the Netherlands 1830; Legends of the Rhine 3 vols. 1832; Civilised America 2 vols. 1859, and about 15 other works. d. Jermyn st. London 4 July 1864. Dublin Univ. Mag. Dec. 1853, pp. 658-65, portrait; Colburn's New Monthly xxxii, 77-80 (1831), portrait.

GRATWICKE, WILLIAM GRATWICKE KINDLESIDES (son of rev. William Kindlesides, R. of Angmering, Sussex, who took name of Gratwicke, d. 1820). b. Angmering 1794; began racing 1825; won the Derby with Frederick 1825, with Merry Monarch 1845; won One thousand guineas and Oaks with Governess 1858. d. Ham near Arundel 5 Dec. 1862. Baily's Mag. iv, 55-9 (1862), portrait; Sporting Review xlix, 179-80 (1863); Sporting Times 11 July 1885, p. 2.

GRAVATT, WILLIAM (son of Wm. Gravatt lieut. col. R.E. who d. 13 June 1851 aged 80). b. Gravesend 14 July 1806; apprenticed to Bryan Donkin C.E. 1822; placed under I. K. Brunel; F.R.S. 1832, F.R.A.S. 1832; worked on the Thames tunnel 1826-32 when works stopped; engineer to Calder and Hebble navigation 1832; examined the county for original

GRAVATT, W. *(Con.)*

scheme of London and Dover railway 183-; invented a level which generally bears his name but which he called the 'dumpy,' also the level staff universally employed, and a pocket instrument called a nadir; traced the line for the Bristol and Exeter railway 75 miles in about a month 184-; printed "*Companion to the mountain barometer*," which was translated into Chinese; A.I.C.E. 1826, M.I.C.E. 1828. *d.* 15 Park st. Westminster 30 May 1866, having been poisoned by an overdose of morphia given inadvertently by his nurse. *Min. of proc. of Instit. of C.E. xxvi,* 565-75 (1867).

GRAVES, FRANCIS *(son of Robert Graves d. 1825 and grandson of Robert Graves of Catherine st. Strand, both of them printsellers).* *b.* 25 Dec. 1802; with A. Molteno of Pall Mall at age of 13, removed to M. Colnaghi's in Cockspur st. 1826; printseller with his brother, Henry Graves 1838 to death. *d.* 6 Pall Mall, London 15 Oct. 1859.

GRAVES, JAMES *(eld. son of rev. Richard Graves, R. of Coolcullen).* *b.* Kilkenny 11 Oct. 1815; educ. Trin. coll. Dublin; B.A. 1839; C. of Skeirke, Queen's county 1840-46; C. of St. Patrick's, Kilkenny 1846-54; R. of Maine 1854-60; V. of Kilsheelan, Clonmel 1860-66; R. of Inisnag near Kilkenny 1863 to decease; with J. G. A. Prim established Kilkenny archæological soc. 1849, which became R. Hist. and Archæol. assoc. of Ireland 1869; awarded civil list pension of £100, 19 June 1878; had finest collection of ferns in Ireland; edited *A Roll of the proceedings of the King's council in Ireland 1392-3, (Rolls Series 1877);* author of *A brief memoir of the Lady E. Fitzgerald, The Fair Geraldine* 1874; with G. A. Prim issued *History of cathedral church of St. Canice, Kilkenny* 1857. *d.* Inisnag 20 March 1886. *Journal R. Historical Assoc. of Ireland vii,* 465-69 (1887); *Academy* 25 Dec. 1886, *p.* 427.

GRAVES, REV. JOHN. Scholar of Christ's coll. Cam. 1852; B.A. 1855, M.A. 1858; lecturer in history Trinity coll. Battersea 1857-59; assist. master Kensington gram. sch. 1859-61; classical master Cheltenham coll. 1861-74; chaplain to H.M. at Kensington palace 1884 to death. *d.* Kensington palace 4 March 1888 aged 56.

GRAVES, JOHN CROSBIE. *b.* 19 Sep. 1820; cornet 3 Bombay cavalry 3 May 1837; lieut. col. Bombay cavalry 1866, col. 1878 to death; L.G. 7 May 1882; C.B. 14 Aug. 1868. *d.* Poonah 27 Nov. 1882.

GRAVES, JOHN THOMAS *(eld. son of John Crosbie Graves of Dublin, barrister).* *b.* Dublin 4 Dec. 1806; entered Trin. coll. Dublin 1823, classical gold medallist and B.A. 1827, M.A. 1832; incorporated in Oriel coll. Ox. 1830, M.A. 1831; barrister King's inns, Dublin 1830 and of Inner Temple 10 June 1831; professor of jurisprudence in Univ. coll. London 1839; examiner in laws in Univ. of London; F.R.S. 1839, member of council; assist. poor law commissioner 7 April 1846; poor law inspector 1847 to Feb. 1871; elucidated the subject of the logarithms of negative and imaginary quantities 1826, and sent contributions to *Philos. Trans., British Association Reports* and *Philos. Mag.;* bequeathed his mathematical library of 10,000 volumes and 5,000 pamphlets to Univ. coll. London. *d.* Cheltenham 29 March 1870. *Proc. of royal society, xix,* 27-28 (1871); *University coll. Gazette, vol. i, No. 12, pp.* 189-90.

GRAVES, JOHN WOODCOCK *(son of Joseph Graves, plumber).* *b.* Wigton, Cumberland 9 Feb. 1795; worked with his uncle Geo. Graves a sign painter at Cockermouth; connected with woollen mills at Caldbeck; landed at Hobart Town, Tasmania, June 1833; invented a machine for preparing New Zealand flax; author of the hunting song *D'ye ken John Peel with his coat so gray* 1824 and other poems. *d.* Liverpool st. Hobart Town 17 Aug. 1886. *Sidney Gilpin's Songs of Cumberland* (1866) 408-15; *I.S. and D. News* 30 *Oct.* 1886 *pp.* 182, 190.

NOTE.—John Peel, hunter died 1854. Graves wrote on hearing of the death of his friend 2 poems "Monody on John Peel" and "At the grave of John Peel."

GRAVES, REV. RICHARD HASTINGS *(son of Richard Graves, D.D., dean of Armagh 1763-1829).* *b.* 1791; educ. Trin. coll. Dublin, B.A. 1812, M.A. 1818, B.D. and D.D. 1828; R. of Brigown, Cloyne 1812; preb. of Cloyne 30 July 1832; edited *The whole works of Richard Graves, D.D.,* Dublin 4 vols. 1840; author of *Daniel's Great period of 2300 days discovered and determined* 1854; *Terminal synchronism of Daniel's two principal periods* 1858 and 10 other books. *d.* 118 Upper Leeson st. Dublin 26 Dec. 1877. *Cotton's Fasti Hibernici* (1878) *pp. xii,* 27.

GRAVES, ROBERT *(brother of Francis Graves 1802-59).* *b.* Tottenham court road, London 7 May 1798; pupil of John Romney, line engraver 1812; studied in the life school, Ship yard, Temple Bar; exhibited 25 engravings at R.A. and 13 at Suffolk st. 1824-73; member of Soc. of British Artists, Suffolk st.;

GRAVES, R. *(Con.)*

assoc. engraver of R.A. 1836 ; engraved Lord Byron after T. Phillips 1836, The Whiskey Still after Landseer 1842, the Hon. Mrs. Graham after Gainsborough 1866, the Blue Boy after Gainsborough 1868, and many other subjects besides engravings for books. *d.* 20 Grove ter. Highgate road, London 28 Feb. 1873. *I.L.N. 8 March* 1873 *p.* 235, *15 March pp.* 247, 249, *portrait ; Sandby's History of Royal Academy ii.* 222–3 (1862).

GRAVES, Robert James *(younger brother of Richard Hastings Graves* 1791–1877). *b.* Dublin 27 March 1797 ; ed. at Trin. coll. Dublin, B.A. 1815, M.B. 1818, M.D. 1841 ; spent 3 years visiting chief continental schools 1818–21 ; settled in Dublin 1821 ; one of founders of Park st. school of medicine 1821 ; one of physicians of Meath hospital 1821 ; professor of institutes of medicine to King and Queen's college of physicians in Ireland 1827, president 1843 and 1844 ; started with Robert Kane *Dublin Journal of medical science* 1832 and was one of the editors to his death ; F.R.S. 1849 ; substituted adequate nourishment and stimulants for the old lowering treatment in fevers ; author of *Clinical lectures* 1834–35, 1836–7 ; *A system of clinical medicine* 1843 ; *Clinical lectures* 1848, 2 ed. 2 vols. 1884, much praised by Trousseau the great French physician. *d.* 4 Merrion sq. south, Dublin 20 March 1853. *Studies in physiology and medicine, ed. by W. Stokes* (1863) *pp. ix-lxxiii, portrait ; Medical Times and Gazette, viii,* 1–5 (1854) ; *Dublin Univ. Mag. xix,* 260–73 (1842), *portrait.*

GRAVES, Samuel Robert *(2 son of William Graves of New Ross).* *b.* Blackwell lodge, co. Kilkenny 1818 ; merchant and shipowner at Liverpool ; chairman of Liverpool shipowners' association 1856 and local marine board 1856 ; mayor of Liverpool 1860–61 ; M.P. for Liverpool 15 July 1865 to death, on 19 Nov. 1868 polled 16,766 votes, largest number polled by any borough member ; commodore of Royal Mersey yacht club ; author of *A letter on National dangers* 1860 ; *A yachting cruise on the Baltic* 1863. *d.* Euston hotel, Euston sq. London 18 Jany. 1873, personalty sworn under £180,000. *I.L.N. l,* 165, 166 (1867), *portrait, lxii,* 91, 113, 114 (1873), *portrait.*

GRAVES, Thomas. Entered R.N. 9 March 1816 ; in the Adventure surveying vessel 1827 ; surveying in the Mediterranean 1832–50 ; captain 3 Aug. 1846 ; F.R.A.S., F.G.S. ; port officer Malta ; stabbed by a boatman in the street at Malta 29 Aug. 1856. *United Service Gazette* 6 Sept. 1856 *pp.* 5, 6, 8.

GRAVES-SAWLE, Sir Joseph Sawle, 1 Baronet *(son of admiral John Graves d.* 6 *May* 1811 *aged* 68). *b.* Exeter 10 Dec. 1793 ; took surname of Sawle by royal license 7 April 1815, took additional name of Graves by r.l. 30 Nov. 1827 ; cr. baronet 22 March 1836. *d.* Ashfield house, Honiton, Devon 13 Jany. 1865.

GRAY, John Gray, 16 Baron. *b.* Aberdeen 12 May 1798 ; succeeded 20 Aug. 1842 ; a representative peer for Scotland, March 1847 to death. *d.* 18 Champs Elysees, Paris 31 Jany. 1867.

GRAY, Rev. Andrew *(eld. son of William Gray, stocking-maker).* *b.* Aberdeen 2 Nov. 1805 ; educ. Marischal coll. 1820, M.A. 1824 ; presbyterian minister at Woodside near Aberdeen 1 Sept. 1831 ; minister of West church, Perth 14 July 1836 ; minister of the Free church, Perth 1843 to death ; convenor of Glasgow evangelisation committee 1855 ; author of *The present conflict between civil and ecclesiastical courts examined* 1839 ; *A catechism of the principles of the Free church* 1845 ; *Gospel contrasts and parallels* 1862, and some pamphlets. *d.* Perth 10 March 1861. *A. Candlish's Memoir of A Gray* (1862), *pp. ix-civ, portrait ; Wylie's Disruption Worthies* (1881) ; *J. Smith's Our Scottish Clergy* 3 ser. (1851), 281–8.

GRAY, Charles. *b.* Anstruther, Fifeshire 10 March 1782 ; second lieut. R.M. 10 Oct. 1804 ; capt. 9 April 1829 to 13 Nov. 1840, when he retired on full pay ; a founder of Musomanik soc. at Anstruther which existed 1813–17 ; Memb. of Soc. of Antiquaries of Scotland ; author of *Poems and songs, Cupar* 1811, 2 ed. *Edin.* 1814 ; *Lays and Lyrics* 1841 ; *A familiar epistle to P. M'Leod Edin.* 1845 ; contributed to *J. F. Wood's Songs of Scotland* 3 vols. 1848–9. *d.* Archibald place, Edinburgh 13 April 1851. *Wilson's Poets of Scotland ii,* 41–3 (1877) ; *Conolloy's Eminent Men of Fife* (1866) *p.* 207 ; *Whistle Binkie* (1878) *pp.* 28–32.

GRAY, David. *b.* Kirkaldy, Fifeshire ; professor of natural philosophy Marischal coll. Aberdeen 1845 to death. *d.* Aberdeen 10 Feb. 1856 aged 45.

GRAY, David *(eld. son of a hand-loom weaver).* *b.* Merkland, Kirkintilloch, Dumbartonshire 29 Jany. 1838 ; educ. Glasgow univ. ; private tutor ; sent verses to the *Glasgow Citizen ;* went to London 5 May 1860 and spent his first night in Hyde park, then lived in a garret with R. W. Buchanan ; befriended by Monckton Milnes (Lord Houghton) and Sydney Dobell ; returned to Merkland, Jany. 1861 ; in Sudbrook park hydropathic establishment, Richmond 1861 ; author of *The Luggie and*

GRAY, D. *(Con.)*

other poems 1862; *Poems, with memoirs by Lord Houghton and others* 1863, *another ed.* Glasgow 1874. *d.* of consumption and in poverty at Merkland 3 Dec. 1861. *David Gray and other essays by Robert W. Buchanan* (1868) *pp.* 63–174, *with portrait; J. G. Wilson's Poets of Scotland* (1877) ii, 485–88; *Cornhill Mag. ix,* 164–77 (1864).

GRAY, EDMUND DWYER (2 *son of Sir John Gray, M.P.* 1816–75). *b.* Dublin 29 Dec. 1845; stockbroker; connected with the *Freeman's Journal,* became manager on his father's death 1875, converted it into a limited co. 1887; proprietor of *Belfast Morning News;* contested Kilkenny 1875, M.P. Tipperary 1877–80, M.P. county Carlow 1880–85, M.P. St. Stephen's Green, Dublin 1885 to death, supported Mr. Parnell; lord mayor of Dublin 1880, organised a famine relief fund amounting to £180,000; high sheriff of Dublin 1882, sent to prison for 3 months for comments in *Freeman's Journal* on trial of Francis Hynes. *d.* Pembroke house, Upper Mount st. Dublin 27 March 1888. *Freeman's Journal* 28, 29 *March and* 2 *April* 1888; *Pall Mall Gazette* 28 March 1888 *p.* 10, *portrait.*

GRAY, EDWARD WILLIAM. *b.* 1787; cheese factor and mealman, Bartholomew st. Newbury, Berks. 1823; mayor of Newbury 1839–40; edited *The history of Newbury, including 28 parishes in Berks., also a Catalogue of Plants,* Speenhamland 1839. *d.* Woodspeen, Berks. 19 June 1860 aged 73. *N. and Q.* 4 ser. iii, 554, 607 (1869); *Money's Newbury* (1887) *pp.* 410, 552.

GRAY, GEORGE ROBERT (*youngest son of Samuel Frederick Gray, chemist d.* 1836). *b.* Chelsea 8 July 1809; educ. at Merchant Taylors' sch.; assistant zoological department British Museum 1831, assistant keeper 1869; F.R.S. 1866; author of *Entomology of Australia* 1833; *A list of the genera of birds* 1840, 2 ed. 1841, 3 ed. 1855; *Genera of birds* 3 vols. 1844–49; *Hand-list of the genera and species of birds* 1869–72 and 13 other books. *d.* London 5 May 1872. *Annals of Natural History* 4 ser. ix, 480 (1872).

GRAY, HENRY. F.R.C.S.; lecturer on anatomy St. George's hospital; took triennial prize of R. coll. surgeons 1849 for essay on anatomy of the eye; took triennial Astley Cooper prize of £300 for researches on the spleen 1853; resident Fellow Med. Chir. Soc. 1850; F.R.S. 1852; author of *Anatomy descriptive and surgical* 1858, 11 *ed.* 1887; *The pocket Gray or anatomist's vade mecum* 1879, 6 *ed.* 1886 and other books. *d.* of small pox 8 Wilton st.,

GRAY, H. *(Con.)*

Belgrave sq., London 8 June 1861 aged 36. *Proc. Royal Soc. xii, p. xi* (1863); *Proc. R. Med. Chir. Soc. iv.* 78–79 (1862).

GRAY, JOHN. *b.* Aberdeen 1805; educ. Gordon's hospital; with White and Whitmore, solicitors, London; barrister Middle Temple 26 Jany. 1838, bencher 1863; Q.C. 4 Nov. 1863; solicitor to the Treasury March 1871, conducted prosecution of Arthur Orton, the Tichborne claimant 1873; author of *Gray's Country Attorney's practice* 1836; *The Country Solicitor's practice* 1837; *Gray's Law of costs* 1853. *d.* 16 Gloucester road, Regent's Park, London 22 Jany. 1875 in his 68 year. *I.L.N. lxvi,* 109, 110 (1875), *portrait.*

GRAY, SIR JOHN (3 *son of John Gray*). *b.* Claremorris, co. Mayo 1816; M.D. practised in Dublin 1839; editor and part proprietor of Freeman's Journal 1841, sole proprietor 1850; indicted with D. O'Connell for conspiracy against the queen and imprisoned in Richmond bridewell Feb. to Sept. 1843; contested Monaghan 1852, M.P. Kilkenny city 1865 to death; knighted by the earl of Carlisle 30 June 1863 for his services in procuring water for Dublin from the Vartry river; declined to serve as lord mayor of Dublin 1868; originated movement which led to Gladstone's disestablishment of Irish church, and was presented with £3,500 Aug. 1863; author of *The Irish church establishment* 1866. *d.* Bath 9 April 1875. *bur.* Glasnevin cemetery, Dublin, marble statue erected in Sackville st. Dublin 1879. *I.L.N. xliii,* 248 (1863) *lxvi,* 379 (1875); *Medical Times* 17 *April* 1875, *p.* 431.

GRAY, JOHN EDWARD (*elder bro. of George Robert Gray* 1809–72). *b.* Walsall, Staffs. 12 Feb. 1800; educ. St. Bartholomew's and Middlesex hospitals; blackballed at Linnean soc. 1822, elected Fellow 1857; F. Entom. soc. 1824; assistant British Museum 1824, keeper of zoological department 31 March 1840, resigned Dec. 1874, edited many catalogues of the contents of his department; on natural history, zoology, social, educational and sanitary questions, wrote 1162 books, papers and memoirs 1824 to death; F.R.S. 1832, vice president; Dr. Philos. of Munich univ. 1852; author of *A hand catalogue of postage stamps* 1862, 2 ed. 1863; *Handbook of British waterweeds* 1864; *Lizards of Australia and New Zealand* 1867; *Synopsis of star fishes in British Museum* 1866 and other books. *d.* British Museum 7 March 1875. *Athenæum* 13 *March* 1875, *p.* 363; *Portraits of Men of Eminence* (1863), *portrait.*

GRAY, REV. JOHN HAMILTON (*only son of Robert Gray of Carntyre, Lanarks., who d.* 1833). *b.* Glasgow 29 Dec. 1800; ed. at Glasgow, Magd. coll., Ox. and Gottingen; B.A. Ox. 1824, M.A. Ox. 1826; member of Scottish bar 1824–28; a constant visitor to the continent and Italy; V. of Bolsover and Scarcliff, co. Derby 1833–66; rural dean of Chesterfield 1847; R. of Walton-le-Wald, co. Leicester 1866; author of *On the ordaining influence of the Holy Ghost* 1837; *Sermons in Rome during Lent* 1838, 1842; *Bolsover Castle* 1838 and other books. (*m.* 23 June 1829 Elizabeth Caroline eld. dau. of James Raymond Johnstone of Alva, co. Clackmannan, she was author of *Tour to the sepulchres of Etruria* 1841, 3 *ed.* 1843 and 3 other books, and *d.* 21 Feb. 1887 aged 87), he *d.* 91 Sloane st. London 20 April 1867. *bur.* crypt of Glasgow cath. *Autobiography of Rev. J. H. Gray* (1868), *portrait.*

GRAY, VENERABLE JOHN HENRY. Educ. Christ's coll. Camb.; B.A. 1847, M.A. 1850, LL.D. 1876; D.D. of Lambeth, March 1881; C. of Rothley, Leicester 1850–52; H.M. consular chaplain, Canton 1852–78; archdeacon of Hong Kong 1867–78; R. of Hunsdon, Herts. 1881–84; author of *China, a history of the laws, manners and customs of the people* 2 vols. 1878; *Walks in the city of Canton* 1875; *A journey round the world* 1879; contributed to the *London and China Express* a series of papers on Chinese customs 1889–90. *d.* St. Leonard's, Sussex 16 March 1890 aged 62.

GRAY, JOSEPH BOWERS (*eld. son of Joseph Gray of Chelmsford*). *b.* 1820; matric. from Magd. hall, Oxf. 24 Feb. 1848 aged 28; principal of Berwick college, Maine, U.S.; M.A. and D. Med. *d.* South Berwick 1 Nov. 1856 aged 39. *G.M. ii, 247* (1887).

GRAY, REV. JOSHUA TAYLOR (*5 son of Rev. J. Gray, pastor of College st. church, Northampton*). *b.* Devonport 9 Feb. 1809; educ. Mill Hill gram. sch. and Bristol coll.; Ph. D.; pastor at Cambridge; kept schools at North Brixton and at South Crescent, Bedford sq. London; pastor Wellington sq. ch. Hastings 1849; tutor in Stepney coll. 1850; author of *Exercises in logic* 1845; *Immortality, its real and alleged evidences* 1843, 2 *ed.* 1847. *d.* 1 Stuart villa, Sydenham road, Bristol 13 July 1854. *S. A. Swaine's Faithful men of Bristol coll.* (1884) *pp.* 315–17.

GRAY, LOUISA M. (*dau. of Rev. Thomas Gray of Freech, Inverurie*). Author of *Ada and Gerty, a story of school life,* Edin. 1875, 2 *ed.* 1878; *Mine own people* 1884; *Dunalton, the story of Jack and his guardians* 1886. *d.* Dec. 1888 or Jany. 1889.

GRAY, MARIA EMMA (*dau. of Henry Smith, lieut. R.N.*) *b.* Greenwich hospital, Kent 1787. (*m.* (1) 1810 Francis Edward Gray of Oporto and Blackheath, who *d.* 1814; *m.* (2) in 1826 John Edward Gray 1800–75, whom she assisted in his works, especially by her drawing); arranged Cuming collection of shells in British Museum; author of *Figures of molluscous animals for the use of students* 5 vols. 1842–74; arranged sets of algæ for schools to encourage study; bequeathed her collection of algæ to Cambridge univ. museum; the genus Grayemma was called after her 1866; her husband struck a bronze medal with their portraits on it 1863. *d.* 43 Russell sq. London 9 Dec. 1876. *Times 15 Dec.* 1876 *p.* 7.

GRAY, PAUL. *b.* Dublin; came to London 1863 aged 21; etched the large cartoons for new series of *Fun* 1863; supplied the illustrations to Kingsley's *Hereward the Wake* 1866; connected as an artist with *London Journal, London Society,* etc.; illustrated *Ghosts' wives* 1867 and *Idyllic pictures* 1867. *d.* Brighton 14 Nov. 1866 aged 24. *bur.* R.C. cemetery, Kensal green 17 Nov. *Daily Telegraph* 19 *Nov.* 1866 *p.* 5.

GRAY, PETER. *b.* Aberdeen 1807?; educ. Aberdeen univ.; studied mathematics and life contingencies; hon. mem. Institution of Actuaries; F.R. Astronom. Soc.; F.R. Micros. Soc.; consulting actuary to Railway accident mutual assurance soc. 1874; author of *Tables and Formulæ for the computation of life contingencies* 1849; *Tables for the formation of logarithms and anti-logarithms to* 12 *places* 1865, another *ed.* 1876; with H. A. Smith and W. Orchard *Assurance and annuity table on the Carlisle rate of mortality* 1851. *d.* 20 St. Augustine road, Camden sq. London 17 Jany. 1887. *Journ. of Instit. of Actuaries, xxvi, pt. i,* 301–2, 406; *Walford's Insurance Cyclopædia, v,* 540–41 (1878).

GRAY, RIGHT REV. ROBERT (*7 son of Dr. Robert Gray, bishop of Bristol, d.* 28 *Sep.* 1834 *aged* 70). *b.* Bishopwearmouth rectory, Durham 3 Oct. 1809; ed. at Univ. coll. Ox., B.A. 1831, M.A. 1834, created D.D. 1847; P.C. of Whitworth, Durham 1834; V. of Stockton on Tees, collated 30 Sep. 1845; hon. canon of Durham cath., collated 3 Oct. 1846; the first bishop of Capetown 28 June 1847 to death; consecrated 29 June 1847; resigned his bishopric in order to have the diocese divided into three parts 23 Nov. 1853; bishop of Cape Town and metropolitan of South Africa 6 Dec. 1853; deprived Rev. W. Long of Mowbray of his license for not attending a synod 1861, privy council reversed the sen-

GRAY, RIGHT REV. R. *(Con.)*

tence 1863; deposed J. W. Colenso, bishop of Natal for heresy 1863, privy council reversed the sentence 1865; author of *Journal of a visitation tour in Cape Town* 1850; *Journal of a visitation of the diocese of Natal* 1864; *Journal of a visitation of eastern portion of diocese of Capetown* 1866 and other books. *d.* Capetown 1 Sep. 1872. *bur.* Claremont ch. yard 3 Sep. *Life of R. Gray, bishop of Capetown* 2 vols. (1876); *Graphic, vi, 370, 372 (1872), portrait.*

GRAY, ROBERT *(son of Archibald Gray, merchant).* *b.* Dunbar, co. Haddington 15 Aug. 1825; clerk City of Glasgow bank 1845, agent of branch St. Vincent st., Glasgow 1871, inspector of branches to 1874; superintendent of branches, Bank of Scotland 1874, cashier Edinb. 1882 to death; a great student of ornithology; a founder of Nat. Hist. soc. of Glasgow 1851, treasurer 1854–6, sec. 1858–71; F.R.S. Edin. 1875, vice president 1882; sec. Royal Physical soc. Edin. 1877 which he reformed. *(m.* 8 April 1856 Elizabeth dau. of Thomas Anderson of Girvan, she made extensive geological collections and aided her husband in his ornithological pursuits); author of *The Birds of the West of Scotland* 1871. *d.* Bank of Scotland house, Edinburgh 18 Feb. 1887.

GRAY, VENERABLE ROBERT. Lindsay scholar of Hatfield hall, Durham, B.A. 1856, M.A. and B.D. 1864, D.D. 1871; C. of Leverbridge, Lancs. 1856–8; head master of gram. schs. at Simonstown and Georgetown, S. Africa 1858–63; head master of high sch. and inspector of schs. of St. Helena 1864–68; archdeacon of Pieter-Maritzburg 1868; dean of Pieter-Maritzburg 1869–70; chaplain of Martley union, Worcs. 1878–84; V. of Toller Porcorum, Dorset 1884 to death. *d.* Toller Porcorum about 15 Oct. 1887 in 56 year. *Times* 18 *Oct.* 1887 *p.* 6; *Guardian* 19 *Oct.* 1887 *p.* 1568.

GRAY, REV. ROBERT HENRY *(eld. son of Robert Gray of Brompton).* Matric. from Ch. Ch. Oxf. 13 May 1836 aged 18, student 1836–48, B.A. 1840, M.A. 1842; C. of Knowsley, Lancs. 1846–50; V. of Kirkby, Liverpool 1850–77; hon. canon of Chester cath. 1867; R. of Wolsingham, Durham 1877 to death; author of *Inspiration of Holy Scripture* 1859; *On the difficulties of the first chapter of Genesis* 1860 and other books. *d.* Wolsingham 19 May 1885 aged 67.

GRAY, THOMAS *(son of a schoolmaster at Westminster).* Clerk in marine department of board of trade at 30s. a week 1851, permanent assist. sec. 1867 to death; auditor of Mersey

GRAY, T. *(Con.)*

dock estate; especially clever in surveying steamships; author of *Rule of the road* 1867; *Diggles, a legend of the Victoria Docks, By Arthur de Cripp Elgate i.e. T. Gray* 1868; *Under the red ensign, or going to sea* 1878; *Fifty years of legislation in relation to the shipping trade and the safety of ships and seamen* 1887; C.B. 1885. *d.* Rokesby house, 23 St. Michael's road, Stockwell, Surrey 15 March 1890 aged 58. *Times* 18 *March* 1890 *p.* 5; *I.L.N.* 29 *March* 1890 *p.* 390, *portrait.*

GREAM, GEORGE THOMPSON *(son of Rev. Robert Gream, R. of Rotherfield, Sussex, d.* 1856). M.R.C.S. Eng. 1836; M.D. King's coll. Aberdeen 1850; M.R.C.P. Lond. 1859, F.R.C.P. 1867; F.K.Q.C.P. Ireland 1867; physician accoucheur to Princess of Wales 13 Jany. 1864; on the retirement of Sir C. Locock became the leading west-end practitioner in midwifery; author of *Remarks on diet of children* 1847; *Remarks on the employment of anœsthetic agents in midwifery* 1848. *d.* The Drive, Hove, Brighton 20 July 1888 aged 76. *Lancet* 28 *July* 1888 *p.* 189.

GREATHED, SIR EDWARD HARRIS *(eld. son of Edward Harris Greathed of Uddens near Wimborne, Dorset, d.* 1 *Dec.* 1840 *aged* 63). *b.* South Audley st. London 8 June 1812; ed. at Westminster 1825–9; ensign 8 foot 22 June 1832, lieut. col. 26 June 1858 to 28 Oct. 1859 when placed on h.p.; served in India 1846–59, commanded eastern district of England 1872–7; col. 108 foot 28 Jany. 1880 to death; general 1 July 1880; C.B. 1 Jany. 1858, K.C.B. 28 March 1865. *d.* Uddens 19 Nov. 1881. *Robertson's Memorial of Sir E. H. Greathed* (1885), *portrait.*

GREATHED, WILLIAM WILBERFORCE HARRIS *(brother of the preceding).* *b.* Paris 21 Dec. 1826; 2 lieut. Bengal Engineers 9 Dec. 1844, lieut. col. 1 July 1867; served during Indian mutiny 1857–8; assistant military sec. Horse Guards 1861–65; chief engineer 2 class D.P. works 7 Oct. 1870; constructed Agra canal from the Jumna, and Lower Ganges canal 1873; general 7 July 1868; C.B. 1860. *d.* London 29 Dec. 1878. *bur.* Hampreston ch. Dorset 4 Jany. 1879. *Memorial of life of W. W. H. Greathed* (1879), *portrait.*

GREATHEED, REV. SAMUEL STEPHENSON. Educ. at Trin. coll. Cam., scholar, fellow 1837; 4th wrangler 1835; B.A. 1835, M.A. 1838; C. of West Drayton, Middlesex 1840; R. of Corringham, Essex 1862 to death; composer of *The sequential book of church music* 1849; *Enoch's Prophecy* 1854 an oratorio; *The English*

GREATHEED, REV. S. S. (*Con.*)

Gradual 1871 and several other works in sacred music. *d.* Corringham 19 Jany. 1887 in 74 year.

GREATOREX, HENRY WELLINGTON (*son of Thomas Greatorex 1758–1831, organist of Westminster Abbey*). *b.* Burton-on-Trent 1816; ed. by his father; went to New York 1839, teacher of music there and organist of Calvary church; organist at St. Paul's chapel, New York; did much to advance the standard of sacred music; published *A collection of psalms and hymn tunes, chants, anthems, and sentences, Boston* 1851. *d.* Charleston, South Carolina, Sep. 1858.

GREAVES, CHARLES (*eld. son of Charles Greaves d.* 1829). *b.* Amwell, Herts. 19 Oct. 1816; articled to J. M. Rendel, civil engineer, Plymouth 1831–7; was in India 1842–7 when he made a survey for the Great Western railway of Bengal; engineer of East London waterworks 1851–75, in Oct. 1872 was presented with £1000 for his services in carrying out improved filter beds, pumping engines, etc. at cost of one million; engineer at Westminster chambers, Victoria st. London 1875–78; M.I.C.E. 2 May 1848; F.G.S.; F.R. Meteorol. soc. 1851, president 1879; had a meteorological observatory Surrey st. London 1878–83. *d.* Sunhill, Clevedon 4 Nov. 1883. *Min. of proc. of Instit. of C.E. lxxvi,* 355–59 (1884).

GREAVES, CHARLES SPRENGEL (*eld. son of Will. Greaves of Mayfield, Staffs. M.D.* 1771–1848). *b.* 18 July 1801; ed. at Rugby and Queen's coll. Ox., B.A. 1823, M.A. 1825; barrister L.I. 22 Nov. 1827, bencher 15 April 1850; Q.C. 28 Feb. 1850; one of secs. to criminal law commission 1878; author of *The proper time for the publication of Banns* 1867; *A review of the statutes, rubrics and canons relating to vestments* 1867; edited Sir W. O. Russell's *Treatise on crimes and misdemeanours* 2 vols., 3 ed. 1843, 3 vols. 4 ed. 1865. *d.* 11 Blandford sq. London 3 June 1881.

GREAVES, EDWARD. *b.* 21 Sep. 1803; a banker at Warwick; mayor of Warwick 1840; M.P. for Warwick 1852–65 and 1868–74. *d.* Avonside, Barford, Warwickshire 6 July 1879.

GREAVES, HENLEY GEORGE (*son of Geo. Greaves d.* 1860). *b.* 9 Oct. 1818; master of the Cottesmore hounds 1847–52, of the Essex 1853–58, of the Warwickshire 1858–61, of the Vale of White Horse 1861–63, of the old Berkshire 1863. *d.* Winslow, Bucks. 14 Aug. 1872.

GREAVES, RICHARD. Lieut. 7 foot 16 July 1812; major 34 foot 1828 to 21 Jany. 1837 when placed on h.p.; col. of 40 foot 15 Dec. 1851 to death; general 25 Oct. 1871. *d.* 69 Chester sq. London 22 May 1872 aged 79.

GREEN, REV. AARON LEVY (*youngest son of Levy Green*). *b.* Middlesex st. Aldgate, London, Aug. 1821; ed. at Talmud Torah sch.; minister of the Bristol congregation May 1838 to 1851; second reader of Greek synagogue, Duke st. Aldgate, March 1851; minister of old Portland st. branch synagogue 1855; hon. sec. to Jews' coll. Finsbury sq. 1852; a founder of Jewish assoc. for diffusion of religious knowledge 1860; a founder of Anglo Jewish assoc. 1871; a scholar in many languages; author of pamphlets; a writer in *The Jewish Chronicle* under name of Nemo 1853–83; seized with apoplexy in Cornhill, and on being taken to St. Bartholomew's hospital was found to be dead 11 March 1883. *Jewish Chronicle 16 March 1883 pp.* 9–13.

GREEN, SIR ANDREW PELLATT. Entered navy 14 April 1793; in the Harrier sloop at capture of Coxhaven 1813, and as a volunteer at Gluckstadt 1814; captain 12 April 1814, placed on h.p. 1820; naval A.D.C. to William iv. 1837 and to Victoria 1841; V.A. on h.p. 31 Jany. 1856; K.H. 1818, K.C.H. 24 Aug. 1832. *d.* 9 James st. Buckingham gate, London 26 Dec. 1858 aged 81.

GREEN, BENJAMIN RICHARD (*son of James Green, portrait painter 1771–1834*). *b.* London 1808; studied in R. Academy sch. and painted figures and landscapes; memb. Instit. of painters in water colours 1834; teacher of drawing and a lecturer; exhibited 40 works at R.A. and 38 at Suffolk st. 1832–62; sec. of Artists' Annuity Fund; author of *A numismatic atlas of ancient history* 1829; *A series of heads after the Antique* 1836; *A guide to pictorial perspective* 1851. *d.* London 5 Oct. 1876.

GREEN, BEVIS ELLERBY. Apprenticed to Mr. Hurst of Longman's 1807, a partner 1824 to June 1865 when he retired; was only remaining partner of the old firm of Longman, Hurst, Rees, Orme, Brown and Green, publishers Paternoster row. *d.* 5 Kensington palace gardens 24 Jany. 1869 aged 75, will proved March 1869 personalty under £200,000.

GREEN, CHARLES (*son of Thomas Green, fruiterer d.* 1850). *b.* 92 Goswell road, London 31 Jany. 1785; fruiterer with his father; made first balloon ascent from Green park, London 19 July 1821 using carburetted hydrogen gas; went up on the back of a pony 16 Aug. 1828; constructed Great Nassau balloon for

GREEN, C. (*Con.*)

Vauxhall gardens 1836; went in the Nassau from London to Nassau, Germany 7–8 Nov. 1836; ascended with Robert Cocking 24 July 1837 when Cocking in coming down in a parachute was killed; ascended to height of $5\frac{1}{4}$ miles 10 Sep. 1838; farewell and last of 527 voyages, at Vauxhall 13 Sep. 1852; invented the guide rope to regulate ascent and descent of balloon. *d.* Ariel villa, 51 Tufnell park road, Holloway, London 26 March 1870. *Mason's Aeronautica* (1838) 1–98, *portrait; Turnor's Astra Castra* (1865) 129 *etc.*, 2 *portraits; I.L.N.* 16 *April* 1870 *p.* 401, *portrait.*

GREEN, CHRISTOPHER. *b.* near Wisbeach 1820; rode for Mr. Willoughby, Ben Land and Earl Poulett 1850; a trainer at Littleport, Isle of Ely, removed to Newmarket 1859; won the Grand National on Abd-el-Kader 1850 and on Half Caste 1859. *d.* Wisbeach 26 Feb. 1874. *Illust. sporting and dramatic news,* i, 61–2 (1874), *portrait.*

GREEN, ELIZA S. CRAVEN (*dau. of Mr. Craven*). *b.* Leeds 1803; lived for sometime in Isle of Man and in Manchester, then returned to Leeds; a contributor of poetry and prose sketches to the *Phœnix* 1828, *Falcon* 1831, both Manchester magazines, to the *Odd-fellows' Magazine* 1841, *Leeds Intelligencer* 1816, *La Follet* 1846, *Hogg's Instructor* and *Chambers's Journal;* had a grant from queen's privy purse; author of *A legend of Mona,* Douglas 1825; *Sea weeds and heath flowers,* Douglas 1858, 2 *ed.;* edited *Flowers from the glen, By J. Waddington* 1862. *d.* Meanwood st., Little London, Leeds 11 March 1866. *Biographia Leodiensis* (1867), *Suppl.* 610; *W. Grainge's Poets of Yorkshire,* ii, 505.

GREEN, FRANK WILLIAM. Author of *Cherry and fair star,* burlesque at Surrey theatre 1874; *Jack and the beanstalk,* pantomime at Garrison theatre, Woolwich 1874; *Jack the giant killer,* pantomime Surrey theatre 1875; *Cinderella,* pantomime at Prince of Wales' theatre, Birmingham 1877; also wrote *Gulliver and the fair Persian, Lothair* for Theatre royal, Liverpool, and *Hop o' my Thumb* for T.R. Brighton. *d.* 5 Staple inn, Holborn, London 16 April 1884 aged 42.

GREEN, REV. HENRY (*son of a paper maker*). *b.* Penshurst, Kent 23 June 1801; educ. Glasgow univ., M.A. 1825; minister Presbyterian ch. Knutsford, Cheshire, Jany. 1827, resigned June 1872, also kept a school; one of founders of Holbein soc. 1868, member of council; a student of the early emblem

GREEN, REV. H. (*Con.*)

writers; author of *Sir I. Newton's Views on Trinitarian doctrine* 1856; *The cat in chancery,* Manchester 1858, anon.; *Knutsford and its traditions* 1859; edited 6 works for Holbein soc., and about 15 other books. *d.* Knutsford 9 Aug. 1873. *Unitarian Herald* 22 *Aug.* 1873.

GREEN, JOHN (*son of Mr. Green, agricultural implement maker*). *b.* Newton Fell house, Nafferton, Northumberland 20 June 1787; partner with his father, when they removed to Corbridge; removed to Newcastle, architect there 1821; designed and executed the chain bridge over the Tyne at Scotswood 1831; built bridges over the Tees and the Ouse, the theatre and Grey column at Newcastle, the Durham monument on Pensher hill, and churches at Stockton and Middlesbrough; M.I.C.E. 1840. *d.* Newcastle 30 Sep. 1852. *Minutes of proc. of Instit. of C.E.* xiii, 138–40 (1854).

GREEN, JOHN. Actor at old English opera house, London, and at Covent Garden; manager of the Cider Cellars in Maiden lane, Strand, London, and singer there; chairman and conductor of music at Evans' hall 43 King st. Covent Garden 1842–4; manager and proprietor in succession to W. C. Evans (who *d.* 1855) of Evans's hotel and music hall 1844 to 1865 when he sold it for £30,000 to a joint stock company which took possession 24 June 1865; gave evidence before committee on theatrical licences 1866; his theatrical portraits were sold at Christie's 22 July 1871; always known as Paddy Green; author of *Odds and Ends about Covent Garden* 1866. *d.* 6 Farm st. May Fair, London 12 Dec. 1874 aged 73. *House of Commons Papers,* xvi, 200–204 (1866).

GREEN, SIR JOHN. Vice consul at Nauplia 1 May 1835; agent and consul general for united principalities of Moldavia and Wallachia 12 Jany. 1867 to 16 Feb. 1874 when he retired on a pension; C.B. 25 Oct. 1865; knighted at Windsor Castle 7 July 1874. *d.* Marienbad 18 Sep. 1877 aged 69.

GREEN, JOHN (*son of John Green of Greenville, co. Kilkenny*). *b.* 1815; lieut. 5 light dragoons; lieut. 4 dragoon guards; M.P. co. Kilkenny 1847–65. *d.* London 16 June 1883.

GREEN, JOHN GEORGE. *b.* Buckden, Hunts.; gentleman usher to William iv. and Victoria 1832 to death; probably last surviving military officer who was on duty at Nelson's funeral in St. Paul's cathedral 9 Jany. 1806. *d.* in same room in which he was born at Buckden 5 Jany. 1882 aged 94.

GREEN, JOHN PHILIP (*only son of Rev. Henry Green*). *b.* 1830; ed. at Univ. college, London, B.A. London 1849, LL.B. 1853; barrister M.T. 17 Nov. 1856; went to Bombay 1862; judge of high court of judicature Bombay 22 Feb. 1873 to 1881; lived at or near Naples 1881 to death; edited *Bombay High Court Reports* 1862–65, 1870. *killed* by an earthquake at Casamicciola in the island of Ischia 28 July 1883.

GREEN, REV. JOHN RICHARD (*elder son of Richard Green of St. Aldates, Oxford, parish clerk of St. Mary the Virgin, d.* 1849). *b.* Oxford 12 Dec. 1837; educ. Magdalen coll. sch.; scholar of Jesus coll. 1853–60, B.A. 1860, M.A. 1862, hon. fellow 1877–83; LL.D. Edin. 1878; C. of St. Barnabas, King's sq. London 1860–3; C. of Holy Trinity, Hoxton 1863–6; P.C. of St. Philip, Stepney 1866–9; hon. librarian Lambeth palace 1869 to death; author of *A Short history of the English people* 1874, *numerous editions; History of the English people* 4 vols. 1877–80; *The making of England* 1881 and other books; edited *History primers* 6 vols. 1875–84; *Literature primers* 6 vols. 1875–9; *Classical writers* 7 vols. 1879–82. *d.* Mentone 7 March 1883. *The conquest of England, finished by Mrs. Green* (1883), *portrait; Contemporary Review xliii,* 732–46 (1883); *Fortnightly Review xxxiii,* 734–47 (1883); *Macmillan's Mag.* May 1883 *pp.* 59–74.

GREEN, JONATHAN. *b.* 1788; M.R.C.S. Eng. 7 Dec. 1810; M. D. Heidelberg 1834; F. R. Med. Chir. soc. 1835; surgeon R.N.; introduced and established fumigating baths 5 Bury st. St. James', London 1823; removed to 40 Great Marlborough st. 1825, but the baths were not successful; author of *The utility of fumigating baths* 1823; *A practical compendium of diseases of the skin* 1835 and other books. *d.* in the Charterhouse, London 23 Feb. 1864.

GREEN, JOSEPH HENRY (*only son of Joseph Green, merchant d.* 1833). *b.* London 1 Nov. 1791; M.R.C.S. 1815, member of council 1835, president 1849, 1858, delivered Hunterian orations 1840 and 1847; in practice at 22, then at 46 Lincoln's inn fields 1815–36; surgeon St. Thomas' hospital 1820–53, consulting surgeon 1853; gave sir Astley Cooper £1000 for half of his anatomical preparations 3 Aug. 1820; professor of anatomy R. C. Surgeons 1824, and Royal academy 1825–52; F.R.S. 1825; a great lithotomist, in 1827 he operated on 40 cases, with only one death; professor of surgery King's coll. London 1830–6; resided Hadley, Middlesex 1836 to death; D.C.L. Oxf. 9 June 1853;

the companion and friend of Coleridge; author of *The dissector's manual* 1820; *A manual of modern surgery* 1828; *Spiritual philosophy* 2 vols. 1865 and other works. *d.* The Mount, Hadley 13 Dec. 1863. *bur.* Highgate cemetery. *Spiritual Philosophy by J. H. Green, Memoir by J. Simon in i, pp. i-lx* (1865), *portrait; Waagen's Treasures of Art ii,* 458–61 (1854).

GREEN, RICHARD (*son of George Green, partner in firm of Green, Wigram and Green, owners of a line of East India ships*). *b.* Blackwall Dec. 1803; partner in his father's business, which on G. Green's death was dissolved; partner with his brother Henry Green, commenced a line of Australian ships 1850, and a line to China 1862; established a sailors' home 1830 and instituted a course of navigation for his officers and men; chairman of committee of Thames marine officers training ship 'Worcester.' *d.* at his sister's residence 7 Hanover ter. Regent's park, London 17 Jany. 1863; left the site and a perpetual endowment for Sailors' Home at Poplar; personalty sworn under £350,000 14 March 1863. *I.L.N. Jany.* 1863 *pp.* 120, 126, *portrait; Times* 20, 27 *Jany.* 11 *Feb.* 1863.

GREEN, RICHARD. *b.* Islington, March 1783; bookseller at Framlingham about 1824 to death; postmaster 1853 to death; author of *The history of Framlingham* 1834; *The strangers' guide to Framlingham* 1853, 3 *ed.* 1878. *d.* Framlingham 8 June 1873.

GREEN, ROBERT. A baritone vocalist at Canterbury and Oxford music halls London, where he appeared in selections from Offenbach and other composers 1865 etc.; sang at the Alhambra. *d.* Clayton hospital, Wakefield 14 March 1882 from hydrophobia.

GREEN, ROGER. *b.* Youghal, co. Cork 4 Nov. 1798; M.D. Edin., Aug. 1826; founded Youghal literary and scientific institution 1833. *d.* Youghal 4 Oct. 1851. *Medical Directory* 1852 *pp.* 661–2.

GREEN, THOMAS HIDEN. Kept cows and a milk shop in Cato st. Edgware road, London; betrayed Arthur Thistlewood and the 4 other conspirators to the government, they were arrested 23 Feb. 1820 and executed 1 May; changed his name from Hiden to Green; rewarded with a place in the stamping department Somerset house, and a retiring pension; murdered his landlord Louis Keyzor at Whitton near Hounslow 11 Oct. 1869, shot himself through the heart at 13 Keyzor place, Whitton same day aged 81. *Times* 14 *Oct.* 1869 *p.* 7.

GREEN, THOMAS HILL (*youngest son of Valentine Green, R. of Birkin, Yorkshire*). *b.* Birkin 7 April 1836; educ. Rugby 1850-5 and Ball. coll. Oxf., B.A. 1859, M.A. 1862, fellow 1860–82, senior dean 1865, ethical lecturer and tutor 1869, dean 1871-72, classical tutor 1875, Whyte professor of moral philosophy 21 Dec. 1877 to death; assist. commissioner on middle class schools 1864–6; set up a coffee tavern in St. Clement's, Oxford 1875; his character is described in Mrs. Ward's *Robert Elsmere* 1888 under the name of Mr. Gray; edited *The philosophical works of David Hume* 1874. *d.* at house of H. P. Symonds, F.R.C.S., 35 Beaumont st. Oxford 26 March 1882. *The works of T. H. Green* (1888), *memoir in iii, pp. xi-clxi, portrait; Macmillan's Mag.*, *May 1882 p.* 87.

GREEN, REV. THOMAS LOUIS (5 *son of John Green of Solihull, Warws.*) *b.* Stourbridge, Worcs. 1799; ed. at Sedgley Park sch. and Oscott coll.; R.C. priest at Tixall, Staffs. 1830–46; chaplain at St. Mary's priory, Princethorpe near Coventry 1848–58; chaplain to Lord Acton at Aldenham park near Bridgnorth 1860–82; created D.D. in Shrewsbury cath. 20 Oct. 1866; author of *The truth, the whole truth, and nothing but the truth, The Catholic Church vindicated* 2 vols. 1838–40 and 6 other books. *d.* Salter's hall, Newport, Salop 27 Feb. 1883. *Gillow's English Catholics iii, 27–32* (1887).

GREENALL, VEN. RICHARD (4 *son of Edward Greenall of Wilderspool near Warrington, Lancs. brewer and banker d. 20 Nov. 1835*). *b.* 11 May 1806; educ. Brasen. coll. Ox., B.A. 1828, M.A. 1831; P.C. of Stretton, Cheshire 1831 to death; rural dean 1839 to death; hon. canon of Chester 1865 to death; archdeacon of Chester 26 Sep. 1866 to death; author of sermons. *d.* Wilton house, Northwick, Cheshire 27 Nov. 1867.

GREENE, JOHN BAKER STAFFORD (*eld. son of John Alfred Greene, barrister of King's inns, Dublin*). *b.* 1833; B.A. and M.B. Trin. coll. Dublin 1853; M.R.C.S. Eng. 1853; assist. surgeon 1 foot 1854–56, served in Crimean campaign, present at Alma, Inkerman and Sebastopol; barrister of M.T. 7 June 1858; LL.B. London univ. 1859; a writer for periodicals; was with Sir Rich. M'Cormack's ambulance during siege of Paris 1870; author of *The Hebrew migration from Egypt* 1879, 2 ed. 1883; *Notes on Ireland* 1886. *d.* suddenly 13 Clements' inn, Strand, London 22 June 1888. *Times 26 June 1888 p.* 10.

GREENE, JOHN STOCK TURNER (*eld. son of Thomas Green of Bedford, Lancs.*) *b.* 12 Dec. 1803; ed. at Pemb. coll. Camb.; barrister M.T. 27 Nov. 1829; judge of county courts circuit No. 10 (Lancashire) March 1847 to March 1872. *d.* Southworth house near Wigan 16 June 1874.

GREENE, RICHARD WILSON (*son of Sir Jonas Greene, recorder of Dublin d.* 1828). *b.* Dublin 1792; ed. at Trin. coll. Dublin; called to bar in Ireland 1814; K.C. 13 July 1830; bencher of King's Inns 1834; first sergeant 23 May 1835; solicitor general for Ireland Nov. 1842 to Dec. 1845; attorney general Jany. to July 1846; received a patent of precedence 1851; a baron of court of exchequer in Ireland 1852–61; P.C. Ireland 1846; author of *A report of the King against W. O'Grady respecting office of clerk of the pleas* 1816; *A report of the trial of D. Waring for perjury* 1817. *d.* 49 Stephens green, Dublin 23 March 1861.

GREENE, THOMAS (*eld. son of Thomas Greene of Slyne, Lancs. 1737–1810*). *b.* 19 Jany. 1794; educ. Oriel. coll. Ox., B.A. 1814, M.A. 1817; barrister G.I. 12 May 1819, but never practised, bencher 1838 to death; M.P. for Lancaster 1824–52 and 1853-7; chairman of committees of house of commons 17 Sep. 1841 to 1847; sheriff of Lancashire 1823. *d.* Whittington hall, Westmoreland 8 Aug. 1872.

GREENE, THOMAS WEBB (2 *son of Thomas Webb Green of Lichfield d.* 10 *Jany.* 1842). *b.* 1804; ed. at Repton gr. sch. and Trin. hall, Cam., LL.B. 1833, LL.M. 1859; barrister M.T. 23 Nov. 1832, bencher 1858; Q.C. Jany. 1858; leader in V. C. Stuart's court 1868–75; member of council on law reporting 22 Feb. 1865, chairman to death. *d.* 9 Upper Wimpole st. London 14 Nov. 1875.

GREENHOW, EDWARD HEADLAM. *b.* North Shields 1814; practised with his father in North Shields and Tynemouth 1834–52; M.D. King's coll. Aberdeen 1852; F.R.C.P. Lond. 1859, censor 1880–81, Croonian lecturer 1875; settled in London 1853; lecturer on public health at St. Thomas' hospital 1855, the first appointment of the kind in England; physician Middlesex hospital 1870; a founder of Clinical soc. 1867, treasurer 1867–79, president 1879; F.R.S. 2 June 1870; retired to Reigate 1881; author of *On diphtheria* 1860; *On Addison's disease* 1866; *On bronchitis* 1878 and other works. *d.* of syncope at Charing Cross railway station 22 Nov. 1888. *Lancet 1 Dec.* 1888 *pp.* 1104–6.

GREENING, HENRY. *b.* Bromsgrove, Worcestershire 1809; articled to E. W. Oldaker of Pershore, solicitor; a special pleader about 1834; retired from practice 1880; author of *A collection of forms of declarations* 1837, 2 ed. 1852; edited Chitty's *Treatise on pleading,* 7 ed. 3 vols. 1844. *d.* St. Leonards-on-Sea 31 July 1881 in 72 year. *bur.* Highgate cemetery.

GREENOUGH, GEORGE BELLAS *(son of George Bellas, proctor Doctors' Commons, d. 12 July 1784).* *b.* 18 Jany. 1778; ed. at Eton; took name of Greenough after his grandfather 179–; entered Pemb. coll. Cam. 1795, resided 9 terms; active member of Royal Institution 1801–7, sec. several years; M.P. for Gatton, Surrey 1807–12; chief founder of Geological society 1807, president 1811–18, 1833–35; F.L.S. 1811; president R. Geog. soc. 1839, 1840; author of *A critical examination of the first principles of geology* 1819; *Memoirs of a geological map of England* 1820; *Addresses at meetings of Geological soc.* 1834, 1835, 1840; published *Geological map of England and Wales* 1819; *General sketch of physical and geological features of India, 9 sheets* 1854; *A physical and geological map of England and Wales* 1865. *d.* Naples 2 Aug. 1855, bust in Geol. soc. apartments, bequeathed his books and maps to Geological and R. Geographical societies. *Quarterly journal of Geological soc. xii, 26–34* (1856); *Journ. R. Geogr. soc. xxv, p. lxxxviii.*

GREENSTREET, JOHN. Entered Bengal army 1795; colonel 60 Bengal N.I. 1 May 1824 to death; general 20 June 1854. *d.* Frenchay near Bristol 9 April 1856 aged 74.

GREENWELL, DOROTHY *(only dau. of William Thomas Greenwell of Greenwell Ford, Durham 1777–1854).* *b.* Greenwell Ford 6 Dec. 1821; known as Dora Greenwell; lived with her mother at Durham 1847–65, resided 12 Great College st. Westminster 1874; author of *Poems* 1848; *Stories that might be true* 1850; *The patience of hope* 1860, *another ed.* 1863; *Songs of Salvation* 1873; *Lacordaire, a memoir* 1867; *Camera Obscura* 1876 and 12 other works. *d.* 8 Alma road, Clifton 29 March 1882. *W. Dorling's Memoirs of D. Greenwell* (1885).

GREENWOOD, GEORGE (2 *son of Wm. Greenwood of Brookwood park, Hants., d.* 1844 *aged* 80). *b.* 10 June 1799; ed. at Eton; cornet 2 life guards 1817, lieut. col. 1837 to 1840 when he retired; reduced weight of helmet from 8 lb. to 3 lb. 1840; the best breaker in of horses of his day; published *Hints on horsemanship* 1839, *new ed.* 1861, the best book on the subject ever done; *The tree lifter* 1844,

GREENWOOD, G. *(Con.)*
3 ed. 1876; *Rain and rivers, or Hutton and Playfair against Lyell and all comers* 1857, 2 ed. 1866. *d.* Brookwood park 3 Nov. 1875. *River terraces* (1877), *with memoir, pp. ix-xv.*

GREENWOOD, JOHN *(brother of the preceding).* *b.* 24 July 1800; ed. at Eton and Jesus coll. Cam., B.A. 1822, M.A. 1825; barrister L.I. and M.T. 8 Feb. 1828; Q.C. Dec. 1848; bencher of M.T. 1848; recorder of Portsmouth 1847–8, of Devonport Dec. 1848–51; assist. solicitor to the Treasury 1851 to June 1866, solicitor June 1866 to death; author of *The Law Journal, a digest of cases in the Law Journal and Reports* 1823; *The law of loan societies* 1846. *d.* 53 Chester sq. London 12 Feb. 1871. *I.L.N. lviii, 163, 315* (1871).

GREENWOOD, JOHN *(eld. son of Frederick Greenwood of Norton Conyers, Ripon).* *b.* Ryshworth hall, Yorkshire 20 Feb. 1830; educ. Eton and Christ Church, Ox., B.A. 1851; M.P. for Ripon 1857–65. *d.* 7 Chandos st. Cavendish sq. London 21 Feb. 1874.

GREENWOOD, JOHN BESWICKE *(eld. son of Abram Greenwood).* *b.* 1796; ed. at Eton and Caius coll. Cam., B.A. 1818, M.A. 1821; barrister L.I. 22 Nov. 1821; police magistrate at Clerkenwell court, London 1837 to May 1847; chairman of West Riding quarter sessions; author of *The early ecclesiastical history of Dewsbury* 1859. *d.* Moor house, Dewsbury 9 Oct. 1879. *I.L.N. x, 332* (1847), *portrait.*

GREENWOOD, THOMAS. *b.* 1790; ed. at St. John's coll. Cam., B.A. 1815, M.A. 1831; barrister G.I. 24 June 1817, bencher 1837 to death, treasurer 1841–2; fellow of Univ. of Durham, reader in history and polite literature there; author of *Cathedra Petri, a survey of the papal supremacy* 1843, *another ed.* 1856; *Position and prospects of the churches of Great Britain and Ireland with reference to the establishment of a Roman Catholic hierarchy* 1851. *d.* 14 Westbourne ter. Hyde Park, London 1 Nov. 1871.

GREENWOOD, THOMAS. *b.* Gildersome near Leeds; a machine and tool maker Leeds 1833; manager for Sir Peter Fairbairn at Leeds to 1856; constructed machinery for manufacture of the Enfield rifle and other war stores 1854; partner with John Batley at Leeds 1856; established a small arms manufactory in Russia 1871; A.I.C.E. 4 Feb. 1860. *d.* Gipsy hill near the Crystal palace 9 Feb. 1873. *bur.* Woodhouse cemetery, Leeds. *Minutes of proc. of Instit. of C.E. xxxviii, 311–13* (1874); *Leeds Times 15 Feb. 1873 p. 5.*

GREENWOOD, THOMAS LONGDON *(son of Thomas Greenwood who painted scenery for Tom and Jerry at Olympic theatre)*. *b.* 1806; druggist Clerkenwell; partner with Robert Plunkett Honner as managers of Sadler's wells 1839, acting manager May 1841, lessee 1842–44, partner there with Samuel Phelps 1844–60 when many Shakspeare's dramas were produced; director of Astleys; acting manager of Princesses; as the elder of the Brothers Grinn supplied pantomimes to metropolitan theatres; writer of *Jack Shepherd*, an adaptation; *Paul the Pilot; Is it the king?;* the pantomime *Harlequin Robin Hood* at Sadler's Wells 1844. *d.* Trinity sq. Brixton 10 May 1879. *Michael Williams' Some London theatres* (1883) 17–29; *Era* 18 *May* 1879 *p.* 5.

GREER, SAMUEL MACURDY *(eld. son of Rev. Thos. Greer, presbyterian minister at Dunboe)*. *b.* Springvale, co. Derry 1810; educ. Belfast acad. and Glasgow univ.; called to the Irish bar 1833; an originator of the tenant league 1850, which demanded the three F's, fixity of tenure, fair rents and free sale; contested co. Derry 1852, 1859, and Londonderry city 1860, 1865; M.P. for Londonderry 1857–59; recorder of Londonderry 1870–8; county court judge of Cavan and Leitrim 1878. *d.* 3 Gardiner's place, Dublin 3 Nov. 1880.

GREEY, EDWARD. *b.* Sandwich, Kent 1 Dec. 1835; capt. of R. Marines at storming of Pekin; in British legation in Japan; spent 6 years in the county and learnt the language; went to U.S. America 1868, was naturalized, manager of Brooklyn theatre; had a store in New York for sale of Japanese works of art; writer of 5 dramas *Mirah, Vendome, The third state, The College belles,* and *Uncle Abner;* author of 7 works in Japanese history, *Blue Jackets* 1871, *The Loyal Ronins* 1880, *Young Americans in Japan* 1882, *The wonderful city of Tokio* 1883, *The Golden lotus* 1883, *Bear Worshippers of Yezo* 1884, *A captive of love* 1886; shot himself New York city 1 Oct. 1888. *bur.* Woodland cemetery.

GREG, PERCY *(son of William Rathbone Greg 1809–81)*. *b.* Bury 1836; contributed to the *Manchester Guardian, Standard* and *Saturday Review;* a secularist and a spiritualist; author of *Shadows of the past* 1856 and *The spirit of enquiry* 1857, both by Lionel H. Holdreth; *Interleaves* 1875; *The Devil's Advocate* 1878; *Across the Zodiac* 2 vols. 1880; *Errant* 3 vols. 1880; *Ivey cousin and bride* 3 vols. 1881; *Sanguelac* 3 vols. 1883; *Without God, negative science and natural ethics* 1883; *The Verge of Night* 3 vols. 1885; *History of the United States*

GREG, P. *(Con.)*

to the reconstruction of the Union 2 vols. 1887. *d.* 16 Tedworth sq. London 24 Dec. 1889 in 54 years. *Manchester Guardian* 30 *Dec.* 1889 *p.* 8.

GREG, ROBERT HYDE *(son of Samuel Greg, mill owner, Wilmslow, Cheshire)*. *b.* King st. Manchester 24 Sept. 1795; educ. Edin. univ.; joined his father in business; an advocate of parliamentary reform and repeal of the corn laws; contested Macclesfield 1837; M.P. Manchester 1839–41; a practical and experimental farmer at Norcliffe, Cheshire and Coles park, Herts.; author of pamphlets on politics and farming. *d.* Norcliffe hall 21 Feb. 1875. *bur.* unitarian chapel, Wilmslow.

GREG, SAMUEL *(brother of the preceding)*. *b.* King st. Manchester 6 Sept. 1804; educ. at unitarian schools; studied and practised mesmerism 1831; mill owner at Lower House mill, Bollington near Macclesfield 1832–47; instituted the order of the silver cross as a reward for good conduct in young women 1836; entertained Kossuth at Mount Bollington 22 March 1857; author of *Scenes from the life of Jesus* 1854, 2 ed. 1869; *Letters on religious belief* 1856. *d.* Bollington 14 May 1876. *H. A. Page's Leaders of men* (1880) 264–77; *Good Words xviii,* 588–91 (1877); *A Layman's Legacy by S. Greg, with memoir* (1877) *pp.* 3–63.

GREG, WILLIAM RATHBONE *(brother of the preceding)*. *b.* Manchester 1809; educ. Edin. univ. 1826–8; manager of one of his father's mills at Bury 1828; mill owner at Bury 1832–50; a commissioner of board of customs 1856–64; comptroller of the stationary office 1864–77; author of *Sketches in Greece and Turkey* 1833; *The Creed of Christendom* 1851, 8 ed. 1883; *Political problems for our age and country* 1870; *Enigmas of life* 1872, 15 ed. 1883; *Mistaken aims and attainable ideals of the artizan classes* 1876 and 16 other books; in 1852 he wrote 12 articles for the four leading quarterlies. *d.* Park lodge, Park side, Wimbledon 15 Nov. 1881. *Macmillan's Mag., June* 1883 *pp.* 109–26.

GREGAN, JOHN EDGAR. *b.* Dumfries 18 Dec. 1813; studied architecture under Walter Newall and W. Thomas Atkinson; architect Manchester 1840 where he erected churches of St. John, Longsight, and St. John, Miles Platting, and bank for Sir B. Heywood & Co.; hon. sec. Royal Instit. Manchester; F.R.I.B.A. *d.* York place, Manchester 29 April 1855. *bur.* St. Michael's churchyard, Dumfries. *Builder, May* 1855 *p.* 222.

GREGER, MAX. *b.* Budapest 1821; original importer of Hungarian wines into England 1861; carried on business at 7 Mincing lane, London; resided in London 1863–80; introduced the wine flagon system 1872; dissolved partnership with C. W. Wilson 1 June 1881, business converted into limited liability co. capital £200,000 in 1881; given order of Gold Crown & Cross 1874; knight of order of Franz Joseph 1875; created Count de Budavolgy by the Emperor of Austria 1878. *d.* Villa Budavolgy, Budapest 19 April 1886 aged 66. *London Figaro 1 May 1886 p. 7, portrait; Wine Trade Review 15 May 1886 p. 278.*

GREGG, RIGHT REV. JOHN (6 *son of Richard Gregg of Cappa near Ennis, co. Clare*). *b.* Cappa 4 Aug. 1798; ed. at Trin. coll. Dublin, scholar 1822, B.A. 1825, M.A., B.D. and D.D. 1860; C. of French church, Portarlington 1826–8; V. of Kilsallaghan, Dublin 1828–36; chaplain of Bethesda chapel, Dublin 1836–9; minister of Trinity ch. Dublin 1839–62; archdeacon of Kildare 1857–62; bishop of Cork, Cloyne and Ross 13 Feb. 1862 to death; new cathedral of St. Finbarre, Cork built cost £100,000, 1870; one of the most earnest evangelical leaders of Irish ch.; author of *A missionary visit to Achill and Erris* 1850; *The life of faith, sermons and lectures* 2 series 1883–5 and 30 other addresses, charges, sermons and children's books. *d.* the Palace, Cork 26 May 1878. *bur.* Mount Jerome cemetery, Dublin. *Memorials of life of J. Gregg, D.D.* (1879), *portrait; I.L.N. lxxii, 519, 533 (1878), portrait.*

GREGG, REV. TRESHAM DAMES. Educ. Dublin univ., B.A. 1826, M.A. 1830, B.D. and D.D. 1853; chaplain of St. Nicholas within, Dublin; committed to Dublin bridewell for refusing to give bail in a convent case 3 May 1841, committal found to be illegal 8 May; author of *Free thoughts on protestant matters* 1846; *A methodization of the Hebrew verbs* 1852, 3 ed. 1861; *The life and death of Edward VI, a drama* 1857; *Mary Tudor, a drama* 1858; *The time of the restoration of all things* 1868 and 20 other books. *d.* Sandymount, Dublin 28 Oct. 1881 aged 82. *Authentic Report of case of Rev. T. D. Gregg* 1841.

GREGORY, BARNARD. *b.* 1796; editor of *The Satirist, or The Censor of the Times,* first number 10 April 1831, in connection with which paper he libelled and black mailed many persons, especially Charles, duke of Brunswick and Luneburg; imprisoned in 1839 and 1850 for libels; *The Satirist* suppressed 15 Dec. 1849 being No. 924; played Hamlet at Covent Garden 13 Feb. 1843 when there was a riot

GREGORY, B. *(Con.)*

headed by the Duke of Brunswick; acted at the Haymarket, Victoria and Strand theatres in 1846; author of four dramas; edited *The Penny Satirist* 10 vols. 1837–46. *d.* The Priory, 22 Aberdeen place, St. John's Wood, London 24 Nov. 1852. *The Theatre, Sep. 1878 pp. 117–21; The Town, ii, 515, 531 (1839).*

GREGORY, FRANCIS THOMAS *(son of Capt. Joshua Gregory of 78 highlanders*). Went to Western Australia 1829; assistant surveyor of W.A., explored the Murchison, Lyons and Gascoyne rivers 1857; sent by imperial government to north west coast in search of lands fit for growing cotton, when he discovered the Nicol bay pearl fisheries and the De Grey, Ashburton and Fortescue rivers 1861; surveyor general W.A.; noticed the existence of payable coal fields in Western Australia and made a geological map of the colony; assessing commissioner Queensland, then crown lands commissioner and postmaster general 188–, member legislative council 1879; F.R. Geog. Soc., gold medallist 1863; author with A. C. Gregory of *Journals of Australian explorations,* Brisbane 1884. *d.* Harlaxton estate, Queensland 24 Oct. 1888. *Times 12 Nov. 1888 p. 7; J. E. T. Wood's Hist. of discovery of Australia, ii, 409–32 (1865).*

GREGORY, GEORGE (2 *son of Rev. Wm. Gregory, R. of St. Andrews, Canterbury, who d. 13 Jany. 1803*). *b.* the Precincts, Canterbury 16 Aug. 1790; ed. at King's sch. Canterbury and Univ. of Edin.; M.D. 12 Sep. 1811; M.R.C.S. Eng. 2 July 1812; assist. surgeon to the forces in Mediterranean 1813–16 when placed on h.p.; L.R.C.P. 1816, F.R.C.P. 1839; practised in London 1816 to death; physician to small pox and vaccination hospital 1824 to death; author of *The Elements of the theory and practice of physic* 2 vols. 1820, 6 ed. 1846; *Lectures on the eruptive fevers* 1843. *d.* 6 Camden sq. Camden town, London 25 Jany. 1853. *Munk's College of physicians, iii, 152 (1878).*

GREGORY, RICHARD LEMMON. Librarian first at Choat's and then at Loder's at Brighton for many years; was a cricketer and a runner when aged 80; well known as Dick Gregory. *d.* his son's residence 8 Bond st. Brighton 13 May 1851 aged 84. *J. G. Bishop's A peep into the past, Brighton* (1880) 126–27.

GREGORY, WILLIAM (4 *son of James Gregory, professor of medicine 1753–1821*). *b.* Edinburgh 25 Dec. 1803; educ. Edin. univ.; pupil of Liebig at Giessen; professor of medicine and chemistry King's coll. Aberdeen 1839; professor of chemistry Edin. univ. 1844 to death;

GREGORY, W. (Con.)

edited many of Liebig's works 1839–51; introduced a process for making muriate of morphia which came into general use; author of *Outlines of chemistry* 1845, 2 ed. 1847, divided into 2 volumes 1853; *Letters to a candid enquirer on animal magnetism* 1851 and 8 other books. *d.* Princes st. Edinburgh 24 April 1858. *Proc. R. Soc. of Edin. iv,* 121–2 (1862); *S. Muspratt's Chemistry vol. i* (1853), *portrait.*

GREGSON, SAMUEL. *b.* Lancaster 1795; contested Lymington 1837; M.P. for Lancaster 1847, unseated on petition 1848; M.P. again 1852 to death; chairman of East India and China association; author of *Indian fibres* 1854. *d.* 32 Upper Harley st. London 8 Feb. 1865.

GREGSON, WILLIAM. *b.* Liverpool 1790; ed. at Brasen. coll. Ox., B.A. 1810, M.A. 1813; barrister L.I. 12 June 1815; private sec. to Sir Robert Peel; drafted bills for home office from 1820; under sec. of state for home dept. 3 Jany. 1834 to 18 April 1835; one of founders of Marlborough college 1843 and of Training college at Highbury 1850; one of earliest promoters of ragged school movement 1844. *d.* 12 Duke st. south, Edge hill, Liverpool, Feb. 1863.

GREIG, SIR HECTOR. *b.* 1789; superintendent of quarantine at Malta; chief sec. at Malta to 1854; C.M.G. 9 Feb. 1833, K.C.M.G. 26 Jany. 1839; *d.* 8 Ovington ter. Brompton, London 5 Oct. 1873.

GREIG, IRWIN MONTGOMERY. *b.* 24 June 1834; educ. at Addiscombe; 2 lieut. Bombay engineers 9 Dec. 1852, col. 1882–86; superintending engineer of southern division 1879, of northern division 1879, and of central division 1880–6; employed on irrigation works, and on construction of roads and bridges; was in the expedition into Arabia 1858; field engineer in Abyssinian campaign 1868; M.G. 6 Nov. 1886; A.I.C.E. Dec. 1873. *d.* 6 Hyde park mansions, London 4 July 1887. *Min. of Proc. of Instit. of C.E. xc,* 449–50 (1887).

GREIG, JOHN. *b.* Moffat, Dumfriesshire 6 Aug. 1779; went to western New York 1800 and studied law with Nathaniel W. Howell, admitted to the bar 1804 and was a partner with Howell till 1820; entertained all strangers of distinction at his residence; bore a striking resemblance to Sir W. Scott; regent of the state university 1825 and chancellor 1845 to death; representative to Congress 1841. *d.* Canandaigua, state of New York 1 April 1858.

GREIG, JOHN JAMES. Ensign 24 foot 15 May 1828, lieut. 1834 to 4 Aug. 1843 when placed on h.p.; head constable of Liverpool 1852, resigned 22 July 1881; C.B. 14 Oct. 1867. *d.* Bournemouth 2 or 4 Dec. 1882 aged 76.

GREIG, WORONZOW. Barrister I.T. 14 May 1830, went Northern circuit; one of secretaries of statistical soc.; F.R.S. *d.* Surrey lodge, Lambeth 20 Oct. 1865 aged 60.

GRELLIER, JAMES. Veterinary surgeon royal waggon train 16 May 1805 to 29 Dec. 1807 when placed on h.p.; proprietor and editor of the *Manx Sun* for many years from 1821. *d.* Hills house, Douglas, Isle of Man 9 May 1860 aged 83.

GRENFELL, JOHN PASCOE *(son of John Granville Grenfell of city of London).* *b.* Battersea 20 Sept. 1800; entered naval service of H.E.I.C. 1811; joined naval service of Chilian republic as a lieut. and took part in war of independence 1819–23; served in Brazilian war against Portugal 1823 and lost his right arm in action off Buenos Ayres 29 July 1826; commanded fleet on lakes of province of Rio Grande del Sol, defeated the rebels 1835–36 and was made a rear admiral 1844; consul general for Brazil in England, at Liverpool 1846–51 and 1852 to death; in command of Brazilian fleet in the war with Argentine republic, forced the passage of the Parana 1851; vice admiral 1852, admiral; had a pension for the loss of his arm. *d.* Prince's park, Liverpool 20 March 1869. *Register and Mag. of Biography, May* 1869, *pp.* 391–92; *I.L.N. xxi,* 492–93 (1852), *portrait.*

GRENFELL, SIDNEY. *b.* 1807; entered navy 25 June 1822; captain 15 Jany. 1850; R.A. 6 April 1860; retired admiral 21 March 1878; C.B. 13 March 1867. *d.* Castlepark, Exmouth 5 March 1884.

GRENVILLE, VERY REV. GEORGE NEVILLE (3 *son of 2 Baron Braybrook* 1750–1825). *b.* Stanlake, Berkshire 17 Aug. 1789; ed. at Eton and Trin. coll. Cam., M.A. 1810; master of Magdalen coll. Cam. 1813–53; R. of Hawarden, Flintshire 1814–34; vice chancellor of Cam. 1818; took surname of Grenville by r.l. 7 July 1825; chaplain in ord. to George iv. and Victoria; dean of Windsor 1846 to death. *d.* Butleigh court near Glastonbury 10 June 1854. *G.M. xlii,* 72–3 (1854).

GRENVILLE, RALPH NEVILLE *(eld. son of the preceding).* *b.* 27 Feb. 1817; ed. at Eton and Magd. coll. Camb., M.A. 1837; M.P. Wind-

GRENVILLE, R. N. *(Con.)*

sor 1841–7 as Ralph Neville ; M.P. East Somerset 1865–8 ; M.P. Mid Somerset 1868–78 ; a lord of the treasury 1846–7 ; took additional name of Grenville on death of his father 1854 ; sheriff of Somerset 1862 ; author of *Cathedrals* 1871. *d.* Butleigh court near Glastonbury 20 Aug. 1886.

GRESLEY, Rev. John Morewood *(son of Rev. Wm. Gresley 1760–1829, R. of Seale, Leics.)* *b.* 6 July 1816 ; ed. at St. Mary hall, Ox., B.A. 1840, M.A. 1845 ; C. of Seale 1841–7, R. of Seale 1847 to death ; master of Etwall hospital, Derby ; edited publications of Anastatic soc. from its foundation 1854 to 1859 when it was incorporated with the Ilam Anastatic drawing soc. ; author of *Plain sermons on present events* 1850–1. *d.* Overseale, Leics. 15 May 1866.

GRESLEY, Sir Thomas, 10 Baronet *(1 son of Rev. Sir William Nigel Gresley, 9 bart. d. 1847).* *b.* Nether Seal hall, Leics. 17 Jany. 1832 ; educ. Rugby ; cornet 1 dragoon guards 18 Jany. 1850, captain 1853–58 when he sold out ; aide-de-camp to lord lieut. of Ireland ; lieut. col. 1 bat. Derbyshire rifle volunteers 1860 ; M.P. South Derbyshire 21 Nov. 1868. *d.* Shipley hall, Derbyshire 18 Dec. 1868. *Reg. and Mag. of Biog. i,* 150, 356 (1869).

GRESLEY, Rev. William *(1 son of Richard Gresley of Stowe house, Staffs., barrister 1776–1850).* *b.* Kenilworth 16 March 1801 ; educ. Westminster and Ch. Ch. Oxf., student 1819, B.A. 1823, M.A. 1825 ; C. of Drayton-Bassett near Tamworth 1828–30 ; C. of St. Chad's, Lichfield 1830–7 ; preb. of Lichfield cath. 1840 to death ; P.C. of All Saints, Boyne Hill, Berks. 1857 to death ; an extreme high churchman ; author of *Ecclesiastes Anglicanus, a treatise on the art of preaching* 1835 ; *Portrait of an English churchman* 1838, 8 ed. 1839 ; *The siege of Lichfield* 1840 ; *Bernard Leslie, a tale 2 parts* 1842–59 ; *The ordinance of confession* 1851 ; *Thoughts on religion and philosophy* 1875 and 60 other books. *d.* Boyne hill 19 Nov. 1876. *Ch. of E. photographic portrait gallery* 1859, *portrait* 38 ; *Scepticism of the Nineteenth century* (1879), *memoir pp. v–xiii, portrait.*

GRESSWELL, Dan. *b.* Kelsey hall, Spilsby, Lincolnshire 13 May 1819 ; M.R.C. veterinary surgeons 1840 and fellow 1877 ; fellow of Veterinary Med. Assoc. 1840 ; settled at Louth, Lincolnshire, mayor 1871 ; a writer on Lactiferous glands, Paralysis in the horse, Arsenical poisoning, etc. *d.* Kelsey house, Louth 13 March 1883.

GRESWELL, Edward *(3 son of Rev. W. Parr Greswell 1765–1854).* *b.* Denton near Manchester 3 Aug. 1797 ; educ. Manchester gram. sch. 1811–15 ; scholar of Brasen. coll. Oxf. 1815 ; Lancash. scholar Corpus Christi 1816, took a double first 1819, B.A. 1819, M.A. 1822, B.D. 1830, tutor of his coll. 1822–34, fellow 1823 to death, vice president 1840–69 ; author of *Harmonia Evangelica* 1830, 5 ed. 1855 ; *Fasti temporis Catholici and Origines Kalendariæ* 4 vols. 1852 ; *Origines Kalendariæ Italicæ* 4 vols. 1854 ; *Origines Kalendariæ Hellenicæ* 6 vols. 1862 and 8 other books. *d.* Corpus Christi coll. 29 June 1869. *Smith's Manchester School register, iii,* 79–82 (1874) ; *Register and Mag. of Biog. ii,* 92–93 (1869).

GRESWELL, Rev. Richard *(brother of the preceding).* *b.* Denton 22 July 1800 ; educ. Worcester coll. Oxf., scholar 1818–24, took a double first 1822, B.A. 1822, M.A. 1825, B.D. 1836, tutor of his coll. 1822–53, fellow 1824–37, dean 1825, hon. fellow 1878 ; raised £250,000 for the National soc. 1843, etc. ; a founder of the Ashmolean soc. 1828 ; chairman of W. E. Gladstone's election committees 1847–56 ; F.R.S. 10 June 1830. *d.* 39 St. Giles', Oxford, on anniversary of his birth 22 July 1881. *Burgon's Lives of Twelve good men, ii,* 93–122 (1888).

GRESWELL, Rev. William *(2 son of the succeeding).* *b.* Denton about 1795 ; educ. Manchester sch. and Brasen. coll. Oxf., scholar 1815–17, B.A. 1818, fellow of Balliol 1818–38, M.A. 1820 ; C. of Disley, Cheshire ; R. of Kilve near Bridgewater 1837 to death ; author of *A popular view of correspondency between Mosaic ritual and the Christian religion* 1834 ; *A commentary on the order of the burial of the dead* 1836. *d.* Kilve rectory 6 Nov. 1876 aged 80. *Manchester School register, iii,* 78 (1874).

GRESWELL, Rev. William Parr *(son of John Greswell of Chester).* *b.* Tarvin, Cheshire 23 June 1765 ; C. of Blackley near Manchester 1789–91 ; inc. of Denton and Haughton near Manchester 1791, resigned 1853 ; kept a school at Denton ; author of *Annals of Parisian typography* 1818 ; *The monastery of St. Werburgh, a poem* 1823 ; *A view of the early Parisian Greek press 2 vols.* 1833. *d.* Denton 12 Jany. 1854, his library sold at Sotheby's Feb. 1855. *Manchester School Register, iii,* 77–78 (1874) ; *Booker's Denton (Chetham Soc. Miscell. vol. ii,* 1851) 109.

GRETTON, Rev. Frederick Edward *(youngest son of Rev. George Gretton, prebendary of Hereford).* *b.* 1803 or 1804 ; ed. at St. John's

GRETTON, REV. F. E. *(Con.)*

coll. Cam., fellow 1829, B.A. 1826, M.A. 1829, B.D. 1836 ; C. of Tickencote, Rutland and head master Stamford gram. sch. 1834–72 ; R. of St. Mary, Stamford 1847–64 ; select preacher at Cambridge 1861–2 ; author of *Elmsleiana Critica* 1833 ; *Parochial sermons* 1843 ; *Passages from English poetry with a Latin verse translation* 1873 and 15 other books. *d.* Oddington, Gloucs. 27 March 1890.

GREVILLE, FULKE SOUTHWELL GREVILLE-NUGENT, 1 Baron (*2 son of Algernon Greville of North Lodge, Herts.* 1791–1857). *b.* 17 Feb. 1821 ; col. of Westmeath militia 22 Aug. 1850 to death ; M.P. for co. Longford 1852–69 ; assumed additional surname of Nugent by r.l. 8 Aug. 1866 ; cr. Baron Greville of Clonyn, co. Westmeath, in peerage of the U.K. 15 Dec. 1869 ; lord lieutenant of Westmeath 27 March 1871 to death. *d.* Clonyn castle, Delvin 25 Jany. 1883.

GREVILLE, ALGERNON FREDERICK (*2 son of Charles Greville* 1762–1832). *b.* 29 Dec. 1798 ; ensign 1 foot guards 1814, present at Quatre Bras and Waterloo ; aide-de-camp to general Sir John Lambert and then to the Duke of Wellington until 1818 ; aide-de-camp to the Duke in the ordnance office 1819 ; private sec. to the Duke 1827–30, 1834–35, 1842 ; Bath and Gloucester king of arms 1830 to death. *d.* Hillingdon, Middlesex 15 Dec. 1864.

GREVILLE, CHARLES CAVENDISH FULKE (*brother of the preceding*). *b.* 2 April 1794, educ. Eton and Ch. Ch. Oxf., student 1810–14 ; page to George iii ; private sec. to earl of Bathurst 1814 ; sec. of Jamaica, performed the duties by a deputy ; clerk of privy council 1821, resigned May 1859 ; member of jockey club, managed racing establishment of Duke of York 1821–26 ; won the St. Leger with Mango 1837 ; kept a political diary 1818–60 which was published in 3 vols. 1874, 3 vols. 1885 and 2 vols. 1887, the first series was suppressed and reprinted in an expurgated edition ; author of many pamphlets. *d.* 16 Bruton st. London the residence of Earl Granville 18 Jany. 1865. *The Greville Memoirs,* i, pp. x-xi (1874) ; *Baily's Mag.* vii, 217–21 (1864), *portrait ; Sporting Rev.* xli, 138–43 (1859), *liii,* 75–80 (1865).

GREVILLE, HENRY WILLIAM (*younger brother of the preceding*). *b.* 28 Oct. 1801; educ. Westminster and Ch. Ch. Ox., B.A. 1823 ; present at Duchess of Richmond's ball at Brussels 15 June 1815 ; private sec. to Lord Francis Egerton chief sec. for Ireland 1828–30 ;

GREVILLE, H. W. *(Con.)*

precis writer to Viscount Palmerston 1834 ; first paid attache to British embassy in Paris 1835–44 ; kept a diary which was edited by Viscountess Enfield as *Leaves from the diary of H. Greville* 2 vols. 1883–4. *d.* 19 Queen st. Mayfair, London 12 Dec. 1872. *Leaves from the diary, second series* (1884) v-viii, *portrait.*

GREVILLE, ROBERT KAYE (1 son of *Rev. Robert Greville* 1760–1830, *R. of Edlaston, Derby*). *b.* Bishop Auckland, Durham 13 Dec. 1794 ; educ. in medicine in London and Edin.; member of Wernerian soc. 1816 ; F.R.S. Edin. 1821, LL.D. Glasgow 1824 ; lecturer on zoology and botany in Edin. ; made large collections of plants, insects, crustacea and mollusks ; collected 15,000 botanical specimens for Botanical soc. of Edin. 1837 ; his algæ went to the British museum, his insects to the univ. of Edin., his flowering plants to univ. of Glasgow, and his cryptogamic plants to Edin. botanic gardens ; fell into poverty and painted landscapes for a living ; author of *Scottish Cryptogamic flora* 6 vols. 1823–8 ; *Flora Edinensis* 1824 ; *Algæ Britannicæ* 1830 and 6 other books ; with W. J. Hooker he published *Icones filicum* 2 vols. 1829–31. *d.* Ormelie villa, Murrayfield near Edinburgh 4 June 1866. *Proc. Royal Soc. of Edin.* vi, 25–7 (1869) ; *Trans. Botanical Soc. Edin.* viii, 464.

GREY, CHARLES (*2 son of 2 Earl Grey* 1764–1845). *b.* Howick house, Bilton, Northumberland 15 March 1804 ; 2 lieut. rifle brigade 1820 ; lieut. col. 71 foot 1833–42 when placed on h.p. ; col. of 3 foot 1860, of 71 foot 1863 to death ; general 29 Aug. 1868 ; M.P. for Chipping Wycombe 1831–37 ; treasurer and private sec. to Prince Consort 10 Oct. 1849 to his death 14 Dec. 1861 ; private sec. to the Queen 3 March 1866 to death ; author of *Some account of the life of Charles, second Earl Grey* 1861 ; *The early years of the Prince Consort* 1867. *d.* St. James's palace, London 31 March 1870. *More leaves from a journal of a life in the Highlands* (1884) 67, *portrait ; I.L.N.* lvi, 386, 416 (1870), *portrait.*

GREY, SIR CHARLES EDWARD (*younger son of Ralph Wm. Grey of Backworth, Northumberland*). *b.* 1785 ; ed. at Univ. coll. Ox., B.A. 1806, M.A. 1810 ; fellow of Oriel coll. 1808 ; barrister L.I. 11 Feb. 1811 ; a bankruptcy commissioner 1817 ; judge of supreme court of Madras 17 May 1820 to 1825 ; knighted by George iv. at Carlton house 17 May 1820 ; chief justice of supreme court of Bengal 2 Feb. 1825 to 1832 ; a commissioner for affairs of Lower Canada 19 June 1835 to 1836 ; P.C. 1 July 1835 ; G.C.H. 1837 ; contested

GREY, SIR C. E. (*Con.*)

Tynemouth 1837, M.P. for Tynemouth 1838–41; governor of Barbadoes, St. Vincent, Trinidad and St. Lucia 24 Aug. 1841 to 1 Oct. 1846; governor of Jamaica 26 Sep. 1846 to Aug. 1853. *d.* Tunbridge Wells 1 June 1865.

GREY, SIR FREDERICK WILLIAM (3 *son of* 2 *Earl Grey* 1764–1845). *b.* 23 Aug. 1805; entered navy 18 Jany. 1819; captain 19 April 1828; rear admiral superintendent in the Bosphorus, Jany. 1855 to July 1856; a lord of the admiralty, June 1861 to June 1866, admiral 24 April 1865, retired 23 Aug. 1870; K.C.B. 2 Jany. 1857, G.C.B. 28 March 1865; author of *On the organization of the navy* 1860. *d.* Linwood near Staines 2 May 1878.

GREY, SIR GEORGE, 2 Baronet (*only son of Sir George Grey,* 1 *bart., d.* 3 Oct. 1828). *b.* Gibraltar 11 May 1799; educ. Oriel. coll. Oxf., B.A. 1821, M.A. 1824; barrister L.I. 2 May 1826; M.P. Devonport 1832–47; M.P. North Northumberland 1847–52; M.P. Morpeth 1853–74; under sec. of state, colonies 1834–5 and 1835–39; judge advocate general 1839–41; sec. of state home department 1846–52, 1855–8, and 1861–6; sec. of state colonies 1854–5; chancellor of duchy of Lancaster 1841 and 1859–61; P.C. 1 March 1839; ecclesiastical commissioner Feb. 1841; G.C.B. 31 March 1849; prevented the chartists under Smith O'Brien invading house of commons with their monster petition 10 April 1848; retired on a pension of £2,000. *d.* Fallodon, Northumberland 9 Sept. 1882. *M. Creighton's Memoir of Sir G. Grey* (1884), *portrait; I.L.N. xxii* 240 (1853), *xxxv* 586, 588 (1859), *lxxxi* 340 (1882), *portrait.*

GREY, REV. HENRY (*son of a medical man). b.* Alnwick, Northumberland 11 Feb. 1778; presbyterian minister of Stenton, East Lothian 1801 to 1813, of St. Cuthbert's chapel of ease, Edin. 1813, of the new North Church 1821, of St. Mary's 1825, of St. Mary's Free church 1843; president of Free church general assembly 1844; presented with a testimonial 1863, which was turned into the Grey scholarships in New coll. Edin.; had a conflict with Dr. Andrew Thompson on the Apocrypha 1829; author of *A catechism on baptism* 4 ed. 1842 and various pamphlets. *d.* Edinburgh 13 Jany. 1859. *C. M. Birrell's Thoughts in the evening of life* (1871), *portrait.*

GREY, SIR JOHN (*younger son of Charles Grey of Morwick, Northumberland*). Ensign 75 foot 18 July 1798; major 5 foot 1811–16 when placed on h.p.; served in India 1799 etc., in Peninsula 1806 etc.; held a divisional command in Bengal 1840–45, at head of left wing of army

GREY, SIR J. (*Con.*)

of Gwalior defeated the Mahratta army of 12,000 men at Punniar on 29 Dec. 1843; K.C.B. 2 May 1844; col. 73 foot 1846–9; col. 5 foot 1849 to death; commander in chief Bombay 30 Dec. 1850 to Nov. 1852; general 20 Feb. 1855. *d.* Morwick hall 19 Feb. 1856. *Canon's Records of 5th Fusiliers* (1838) 75 *etc.*

GREY, JOHN (*eld. child of George Grey of West Ord near Berwick, d.* 1793). *b.* Millfield Hill, Glendale, Aug. 1785; took part in agitation for Catholic emancipation and in struggle which preceded Reform bill of 1832; had charge of the Greenwich hospital estates in Northumberland and Cumberland 1833–63; made improvements in farming and in rearing cattle. *d.* Lipwood house on the Tyne near Haydon bridge 22 Jany. 1868. *Memoir of John Grey of Dilston* (1874); *Saddle and sirloin by the Druid* (1878) *pp.* 121–8, *portrait.*

GREY, RALPH WILLIAM (*son of R. W. Grey of Backworth house, Northumberland*). *b.* 1819; educ. Eton and Trin. coll. Cam., B.A. 1840; private sec. to Lord Sydenham governor general of Canada 1839; private sec. to Lord John Russell 1850; M.P. Tynemouth 1847–52; M.P. Liskeard 1854–9; parliamentary sec. poor law board 28 Jany. 1851 to 3 March 1852 and 1856–58; a commissioner of the customs 1859 to death; of Chipchase castle, Northumberland. *d.* Wimbledon 1 Oct. 1869.

GREY, SIR WILLIAM (4 *son of Rt. Rev. Edward Grey* 1782–1837, *bp. of Hereford). b.* 26 March 1818; matric from Ch. Ch. Ox. 19 May 1836; clerk in war office; at Haileybury coll. 1839–40; private sec. to Sir H. Maddock, dep. governor of Lower Bengal 1845; sec. of Bank of Bengal 1851–4; sec. to government of Bengal 1854–7; sec. to government of India in home department 1859, member of council of governor general 1862–7; lieut. governor of Bengal 1867 to Feb. 1871; governor of Jamaica, March 1874 to March 1877; K.C.S.I. 28 May 1870. *d.* Parkfield, Marldon near Torquay 15 May 1878.

GRIERSON, CRIGHTON. Second lieut. R.E. 1 June 1810, lieut. col. 1 April 1846 to 1 Sep. 1847 when placed on retired list; general 8 June 1871. *d.* 14 Sackville st. Piccadilly, London 7 Nov. 1871 aged 81.

GRIERSON, JAMES. *b.* 10 Oct. 1827; traffic manager Shrewsbury and Birmingham railway 1851; goods manager Great Western railway 1857 and general manager Oct. 1863 to death, by his management raised the stock from £47 to £135; author of *Railway rates, English and Foreign* 1886; his residence 4 Holland villas

GRIERSON, J. *(Con.)*

road, Kensington, damaged by fire 1887. *d.* Bridge house, Marlow 7 Oct. 1887. *bur.* Barnes cemetery 12 Oct. *London Figaro* 15 *Oct.* 1887 *p. 6, portrait; Herapath's Railway Journal* 15 *Oct.* 1887 *p.* 1064.

GRIESS, JOHN PETER. F.R.S. 4 June 1868; F.C.S.; of Burton on Trent. *d.* Bournemouth 30 Aug. 1888 aged 60.

GRIEVE, THOMAS *(son of John Henderson Grieve, scene painter).* *b.* Lambeth, London 11 June 1799; scene painter Covent Garden 1839, Drury Lane 1862; painted diorama of Overland Mail 1850; with W. Telbin and John Absolon painted panorama of Campaigns of Wellington 1852, and panoramas of the Ocean Mail, the Crimean War and the Arctic regions. *d.* 1 Palace road, Lambeth 16 April 1882.

GRIFFIES-WILLIAMS, WORSHIPFUL SIR ERASMUS HENRY, 2 Baronet *(2 son of Sir George Griffies-Williams, d. 28 March 1843).* *b.* Llwyn-y-Wormwood 22 July 1794; ed. at St. John's coll. Cam., B.A. 1818, M.A. 1821; R. of Rushall, Wilts. 1829 to death; R. of Marlborough 1830 to 1858; chancellor of St. David's cathedral 1858 to death; author of *A letter on the repeal of the corn laws* 1846; *The supremacy of the sovereign asserted* 1850. *d.* Llandovery 30 Nov. 1870.

GRIFFIES-WILLIAMS, SIR WATKIN LEWES, 3 Baronet *(brother of the preceding).* *b.* 1800; entered Madras army 12 June 1819; col. of 3 Madras light infantry 29 Jany. 1854 to 1869; general 25 July 1870. *d.* 38 Elgin road, Notting hill, London 23 May 1877.

GRIFFIN, CHARLES *(only son of R. Griffin of Glasgow, bookseller, d. Nov. 1832 aged 43).* *b.* London 1819; ed. at univ. of Glasgow; bookseller with John Joseph Griffin in Glasgow 1836–53 and in London 1847–53; bought the *Encyclopædia Metropolitana* for £5,000 about 1847; bookseller alone in Glasgow 1853–9; left Glasgow and managed London business 1859–61; partner with Henry Bohn in Stationers' hall court, Jany. 1861 to death. *d.* Combe lodge, Swanscombe, Kent 5 Aug. 1862. *Bookseller* 30 *Aug.* 1862 *p.* 561, 30 *Sept. p.* 616.

GRIFFIN, RIGHT REV. HENRY *(2 son of John Griffin, deputy registrar of deeds in Ireland).* *b.* Wexford 10 July 1786; entered Trin. coll. Dublin 1798; scholar 1802, fellow 1811–29, B.A. 1803, M.A. 1814; R. of Clonfeacle, Armagh to 1854; Bishop of Limerick, Ardfert and Aghadoe, consecrated 1 Jany. 1854. *d.* the university club, 17 Stephen's Greennorth, Dublin 5 April 1866. *bur.* Benburt, co. Tyrone.

GRIFFIN, JOHN JOSEPH. *b.* London 1802; bookseller, publisher and dealer in chemical apparatus at Glasgow to 1852, partly edited *Encyclopædia Metropolitana;* chemical apparatus dealer as J. J. Griffin & Sons, 22 Garrick st. Covent Garden, London 1852 to death; a founder of Chemical soc. 1840; devised new forms of chemical apparatus; author of *Chemical recreations* 1834, 10 ed. 1860; *Treatise on the blow pipe* 18—; *The chemical testing of wines and spirits* 1866, 2 ed. 1872 and other books. *d.* 31 Park road, Haverstock hill, London 9 June 1877. *Journ. Chemical soc. xxxiii,* 229 (1878).

GRIFFITH, EDWARD *(son of William Griffith of Stanwell, Middlesex).* *b.* 1790; educ. St. Paul's sch. 1800–1806; clerk of common pleas office; master of court of common pleas 1837 to death; F.R.S.; F.L.S.; F.S.A.; author of *General descriptions of the vertebrated animals, monkeys and lemurs* 1821; *The Animal kingdom* 15 vols. 1832 with other writers, and other books. *d.* 32 Fitzroy sq. London 8 Jany. 1858.

GRIFFITH, GEORGE *(son of John Wynne Griffith, M.P. of Garn near Rhyl, co. Denbigh, d. 1834).* *b.* 1790; barrister M.T. 26 Nov. 1830; recorder of Denbigh 1834 to death. *d.* Garn, Denbigh 23 April 1877 in 88 year.

GRIFFITH, GEORGE. Clerk in a corn merchant's office in Bewdley; author of *The free schools of Worcestershire* 1852; *Life of George Wilson* 1854; *The endowed schools of England and Ireland* 1864; *Going to markets and grammar schools, records in the Midland counties* 2 vols. 1870 and other books. *d.* Bewdley 1883. *J. R. Burton's Bewdley* (1883) 61.

GRIFFITH, HENRY DARBY *(youngest son of major general Darby Griffith of Pardworth house, Berks.)* *b.* 22 May 1810; ensign 4 foot 25 Nov. 1828; captain 2 dragoons 1839, lieut. col. 27 Aug. 1852; at battles of Balaklava, Inkerman and Tchernaya and siege and fall of Sebastopol; A.D.C. to the Queen 1855–66; col. 5 lancers 1 Jany. 1872 to death; general 1 Oct. 1877; C.B. 5 July 1855. *d.* Bushy Ruff house near Dover 17 Nov. 1887.

GRIFFITH, REV. JOHN. *b.* 1789 or 1790; ed. at Trin. coll. Cam., scholar, Bell's univ. scholar 1810, 8 wrangler 1812, B.A. 1812, M.A. 1815, B.D. 1822, D.D. 1831; fellow of Em. coll. 1814, tutor 1818–27; chaplain to Lord Amherst in China 1816, wrecked in the Alceste on Gaspar island 18 Nov. 1817; canon of Rochester 1827–72; V. of Aylesford, Kent 1830–32; V. of Boxley, Kent 1832–53; prosecuted Strahan, Paul and Bates bankers

GRIFFITH, REV. J. *(Con.)*

for having unlawfully disposed of deeds valued at £22,000, defendants sentenced to 14 years' transportation 26 Oct. 1855. *d.* 3 Bay's hill lawn, Cheltenham 29 May 1879.

GRIFFITH, JULIUS GEORGE. First lieut. Bombay artillery 27 May 1810, col. commandant 3 July 1845 to death; general 7 Sep. 1866. *d.* Boulogne 31 July 1872 in 81 year.

GRIFFITH, SIR RICHARD JOHN, 1 Baronet *(only son of Richard Griffith of Milicent, co. Kildare 1752–1820).* *b.* Hume st. Dublin 20 Sep. 1784; lieut. R. Irish Artill. 1799; inspector general of royal mines in Ireland 1809; mining engineer and professor of geology to Royal Dublin Soc. 1812; sole comr. for general valuation of land in Ireland 1827–68; deputy chairman of board of public works Ireland 1846, chairman 1854–64; F.G.S., Wollaston medallist 1854 for his geological map of Ireland; M.I.C.E. 1839; created baronet 20 April 1858; author of *Geological and mining report on the Leinster coal district* 1814. *d.* 2 Fitzwilliam place, Dublin 22 Sep. 1878. *Dublin Univ. Mag. lxxxiii,* 432–37 (1874), *portrait; Proc. of Royal Soc. of Edin. x,* 17–20 (1880); *Quarterly Journal of Geol. Soc. xxxv,* 39–41 (1879).

GRIFFITH, REV. THOMAS. Ed. at St. John's coll. Cam., B.A. 1822, M.A. 1832; min. of Ram's Epis. chap. Homerton 1830–72; prebendary of Sneating in St. Paul's cath. 1862–80; author of *The leading idea of christianity investigated* 1833; *Our baptismal standing* 1850; *Studies of the divine master* 1875 and 25 other books. *d.* 8 Clapton sq. Clapton 24 Aug. 1883.

GRIFFITH, REV. WILLIAM *(son of Rev. William Griffith d.* 1860). *b.* London 1806; Wesleyan M. minister 1828; connected with the issuing of the Fly sheets 1847; expelled by the Wesleyan Methodist conference in company with Rev. James Everett and Rev. Samuel Dunn 25 July 1849; minister of Methodist free churches 1857 to death. *d.* Derby 12 July 1883. *I.L.N. xv,* 187–8 (1849), *portrait; Christian World* 19 July 1883 p. 481.

GRIFFITH, WILLIAM DARLING *(son of A. F. Griffith, head of Longman's old book department).* *b.* 18 Oct. 1805; learnt bookselling with Hamilton, Adams and Co.; publisher St. Paul's churchyard to 1843; partner with E. C. Grant 1843 to 1856 as Grant and Griffith, booksellers; partner with Robert Farran, June 1856 to death. *d.* 6 York villa, Campden hill, London 20 Feb. 1877. *Bookseller, March* 1877 p. 218.

GRIFFITH, WILLIAM PETIT *(son of John William Griffith, architect, d.* 27 *Nov.* 1855 *aged* 65). *b.* 9 St. John's sq. Clerkenwell, London 7 July 1815; F.S.A. 12 May 1842; F.R.I.B.A. 14 June 1847; some of his work was the reparation of St. John ch. Clerkenwell 1845, the restoration of St. John's gate 1845–6, designing Cherrytree tavern, Clerkenwell 1852, the goldsmiths' and jewellers' annuity institution asylum 1853, designing the house of detention, Kingston-on-Thames; author of *The geometrical proportion of architecture* 1843; *Ancient Gothic churches* 3 parts 1847–52; *Suggestions for a more perfect period of gothic architecture* 1855. *d.* 3 Isledon road, Highbury, London 14 Sept. 1884.

GRIFFITHS, REV. DAVID. *b.* Glanmeilwch, Llangadoc, Carmarthenshire 20 Dec. 1792; schoolmaster Cwmaman 1811–12; in Madagascar as a missionary 1821–35 and 1838–42; established a church, day and night schools, a printing press and printed the New Testament 1831; condemned to death but sentence commuted to a fine 1839; pastor of congregational ch. Hay, Brecknockshire 1842; spent 5 years revising Madagascar scriptures 1852–7; author of *History of Madagascar, in Welsh; The Persecuted Christians of Madagascar* 1841 and works in the Malagasy tongue. *d.* Machynlleth, Montgomerys. 21 March 1863. *Rees and Thomas' Eglwysi Annybynol Cymru, iv,* 359–61.

GRIFFITHS, EVAN. *b.* Gellibeblig, Glamorganshire 1795; ed. at a college at Newport, Monmouth; pastor of churches in Gower; went to Swansea and translated Matthew Henry's commentary into Welsh, acting also as the printer and collecting subscriptions for the work 1828, etc.; author of *Welsh English dictionary, Abertawy* 1847 and many works in the Welsh language 1839–56. *d.* Swansea 31 Aug. 1873. *Rees and Thomas' Eglwysi Annybynol Cymru, iv.*

GRIFFITHS, FREDERICK AUGUSTUS. Ensign R.A. 13 Dec. 1813; major on retired full pay 28 Nov. 1854; author of *The Artillerists' manual and compendium of infantry exercise,* Woolwich 1839, 10 ed. 1868; *Notes on military law,* Woolwich 1841. *d.* St. Mary Bourne near Andover 25 March 1869 aged 73.

GRIFFITHS, FREDERICK CHARLES. Cornet 2 dragoon guards 17 June 1824; lieut. col. 10 dragoons 11 Nov. 1851, of 9 dragoons 25 May 1855, of 12 Lancers 14 Oct. 1856 to 12 Dec. 1857; M.G. 12 Dec. 1857. *d.* Westbourne place, Eaton sq. London 15 March 1858 aged 53.

GRIFFITHS, REV. JOHN (*son of Dr. John Griffiths, head master Rochester gr. sch.*) *b.* 1807; ed. at Wadham coll. Oxf., scholar 1824–30, B.A. 1827, M.A. 1833, B.D. and D.D. 1872, fellow 1830–54, subwarden 1837–54, hon. fellow 1868, warden 4 Nov. 1871 to Sep. 1881; keeper of the university archives 1857 to death; one of the four tutors who signed the protest against Newman's Tract xc. March 1841; sold his collection of rare engravings and etchings May 1883, Rembrandt's portrait of Dr. Arnold Tholinx went for £1510 the largest sum ever given for a print; author of *Laws of the Greek Accents* 1831, 5 *ed.* 1853; *An index to the wills in the Court of the Chancellor of Oxford* 1862 and other works. *d.* 63 St. Giles' street, Oxford 14 Aug. 1885.

GRIFFITHS, JOHN. *b.* Bod-Gwilym 21 Dec. 1821; apprentice to a grocer at Barmouth; went to London 1846; wrote for the Welsh press under name of Wmffra Edward; contributor to the *Banner Cymru* 1857 and was in its sole employment from 1860, known as Gohebydd Llandain, Y Gohebydd and Pobman. *d.* London? 13 Dec. 1877. *bur.* Llangollen cemetery. *Red Dragon, iv,* 385–93 (1883), *portrait.*

GRIFFITHS, RICHARD CLEWIN. *b.* 8 Sep. 1791; ed. at St. Thomas' and Guy's hospital; M.S.A. 1812; M.R.C.S. Eng. 1813; one of the first to combine the practice of medicine and surgery, retired from practice 1850; master of the Apothecaries' co. 1855 to death; helped to establish Zoological gardens 1827 and Botanical soc. 1839, public feeding of the animals introduced by him. *d.* 20 Gower st. London 5 Sep. 1881, portrait in parlour of Soc. of Apothecaries. *Times 13 Sept.* 1881 *p.* 9.

GRIFFITHS, ROBERT. *b.* Lleweny farm in Vale of Clywdd 13 Dec. 1805; pattern maker in an engine works, Birmingham, soon became foreman; engineer at Smethwick to 1845; had engineering works at Havre 1845–8 where the iron work for the Havre and Paris railways was manufactured; took out many patents 1835–78; experimented on rivet machines 1835, glass grinding 1836, making hexagon nuts 1837, machinery for making bolts and railway spikes and rivets 1845, atmospheric railways 1845–6, screw propellors 1847, and an electric hair brush to prevent hair turning white 1852; partner in Coppa colliery, Flintshire 1862. *d.* 107 Ledbury road, Bayswater, London 16 June 1883. *Engineering 29 June* 1883 *p.* 606.

GRIMALDI, STACEY (2 *son of Wm. Grimaldi of London* 1751–1830, *portrait painter*). *b.* 7

King st. St. James's sq. London 18 Oct. 1790; attorney and solicitor 1 Copthall court, city of London; engaged in many record and peerage cases; F.S.A. 1824; marquis Grimaldi in Italy 27 May 1830; lecturer at the Incorporated Law Soc. on the public records 1834, auditor there 1853; contributed to *Gent. Mag.* 1813–61; author of *A synopsis of the history of England* 1825, 2 *ed.* 1871; *Origines genealogicæ* 1828; *The genealogy of the family of Grimaldi* 1834 and 5 other books. *d.* Hernden house, Eastry, Kent 28 March 1863.

GRIMSHAW, JAMES. *b.* Bolton, Lancashire, 1846; light weight jockey, won 164 races in 1864, called the Pocket Hercules; took the Cesarewitch on Hartington 1862 and on Thalestris 1864; won the Newmarket Biennial on Kangaroo 1865, when lord Hastings gave £12,000 for the winner which ultimately was worked in a cab; gained the 1000 guineas with Hester and the St. Leger with Hawthornden 1870; rode in Germany and Austria 1871 to death. *d.* of cancer Pardubitz, Bohemia 12 Dec. 1888. *Baily's Mag. ix* (1864), *portrait; Illust. Sport. News, ii,* 333 (1863), *portrait, v,* 60, 264 (1866), *portrait; Times 20 Dec.* 1888 *p.* 5.

GRIMSHAW, WILLIAM. *b.* Greencastle, Londonderry 1782; went to Philadelphia, U.S. America 1815; author of *An Etymological dictionary* 1821, 2 *ed.* 1826; *Gentleman's Lexicon and Ladies' Lexicon* 1829; *Life of Napoleon; History of the United States* 1822 and many other books all published in Philadelphia. *d.* Philadelphia 1852.

GRIMSTON, REV. EDWARD HARBOTTLE (2 *son of 1 earl of Verulam, d.* 1845). *b.* 42 Grosvenor sq. London 2 April 1812; ed. at Ch. Ch. Oxf., B.A. 1831; fellow of All Souls 1834–42, M.A. 1838; M.P. St. Albans 1835–41; R. of Pebmarsh, Essex 1841 to death; R. of Great Henny, Essex 1845 to death; member of Marylebone cricket club, played at Lords to 1841, continued to play in county matches, one of the best style of players ever seen. *d.* Pebmarsh rectory 4 May 1881. *Lillywhite's Cricket Scores, ii,* 29 (1862).

GRIMSTON, REV. FRANCIS SYLVESTER (5 *son of 1 earl of Verulam, d.* 1845). *b.* Gorhambury near St. Albans 8 Dec. 1822; ed. at Harrow and Magd. coll. Camb., M.A. 1845; R. of Colne-Wake, Essex 1847 to decease; played at Lord's 3–4 Aug. 1838 in Eton *v.* Harrow, generally played in the country, a good wicket keeper. *d.* Colne-Wake 28 Oct. 1865. *Lillywhite's Cricket Scores, ii,* 467 (1862) *v, p. xv* (1876).

GRIMSTON, ROBERT (4 *son of* 1 *earl of Verulam, d.* 1845). *b.* 42 Grosvenor sq. London 18 Sept. 1816; ed. at Harrow and Ch. Ch. Oxf., B.A. 1838; barrister L.I. 21 Nov. 1843; director of Electric telegraph co. 1852, and connected with telegraph companies till his death; hon. treasurer and one of first members of I Zingari 1845, played at Lords 1838–52; assisted in formation of Surrey county eleven which began playing in Kennington oval then a market garden 1846; very successful against fast bowling; is described in Whyte Melville's novel *Captain Digby Grand* 2 vols. 1853. *d.* in his chair at Gorhambury 7 April 1884. *F. Gale's Life of R. Grimston* (1885), *portrait; Sporting Mirror, vii,* 165 (1884), *portrait.*

GRINFIELD, REV. EDWARD WILLIAM *(son of Thomas Grinfield, Moravian minister, Bristol). b.* 1785; ed. at Lincoln coll. Oxf., B.A. 1806, M.A. 1808; student of L.I. 1805, of I.T. 1806; minister of Laura chapel, Bath 1820; preacher at Kensington; founded and endowed with £1000 a lectureship on the Septuagint at Oxford 1859; author of *The doctrinal harmony of the New Testament* 1824; *Scholia Hellenistica in Novum Testamentum* 2 vols. 1848; *The Jesuit, historical sketch* 1851 and 20 other books. *d.* 6 Lower Brunswick place, Brighton 9 July 1864.

GRINFIELD, REV. THOMAS *(brother of the preceding). b.* Bath 1788; ed. at Trin. coll. Cam., B.A. 1811; C. of St. Sidwell's, Exeter; R. of Shirland, Derbyshire 9 May 1827 to death; C. of St. Mary-le-Port, Bristol 1847 to death; author of *Epistles and miscellaneous poems* 1815; *The visions of Patmos* 1827; *The history of preaching* 1880. *d.* Clifton 8 April 1870.

GRISI, GIULIA *(dau. of Gaetano Grisi an officer of engineers). b.* Milan 22 May 1812; sang at Milan 1829, Florence 1830 and Paris 1832; one of the greatest soprano vocalists; appeared at Her Majesty's theatre, London 22 April 1834 as Ninetta in *La Gazza Ladra;* prima donna at Her Majesty's 1834–41 and 1843–5, at Covent Garden 1846–61; last appeared on the stage at Her Majesty's 5 May 1866 as Lucrezia when she was hissed. *d.* Hotel du Nord, Berlin 29 Nov. 1869. *C. Heath's Beauties of the opera and ballet* (1845) *p.* 33, *portrait; H. S. Edwards's The Prima Donna, i,* 267–308 (1888); *The Mapleson memoirs, i* 89–94 (1888).

GRISSELL, THOMAS (1 *son of Thomas De la Garde Grissell of Stockwell, d.* 1863). *b.* London 4 Oct. 1801; ed. at St. Paul's sch.; partner with Henry Peto, builder 1825–30 when Peto died; partner with Sir Samuel Morton Peto, baronet 1830–47 when Sir S. M. Peto was

GRISSELL, T. *(Con.)*
elected M.P. Norwich; in business alone 1847–50; purchased Norbury park near Dorking 1850; A.I.C.E. 7 March 1843; F.S.A. 16 March 1843; F.H.S.; sheriff of Surrey 1854–55. *d.* Norbury park, Dorking 26 May 1874.

GROCOTT, JOHN COOPER. Attorney at Liverpool 1821 to death; sergeant at mace of the corporation; author of *Practice of the borough court of Liverpool, Liverpool* 1837, 2 *ed.* 1847; *Index to familiar quotations, Liverpool* 1854, 3 *ed.* 1866. *d.* 123 Park st. Liverpool 23 Feb. 1874 aged 81. *Law Times, lvi,* 325, 335 (1874).

GRONOW, REES HOWELL *(eld. son of Wm. Gronow of Swansea, d.* 1830). *b.* 7 May 1794; ed. at Eton; ensign 1 foot guards 24 Dec. 1812, lieut. 1815–21 when he sold out; served in Spain 1812–14, present at Waterloo; contested Grimsby 1831, M.P. for Stafford 1832, unseated 1833, contested Stafford 1835; one of the chief dandies of London 1814 etc., admitted at Almack's where he remembered introduction of quadrilles and waltzes 1813; author of *Reminiscences* 1862; *Recollections and anecdotes* 1863; *Celebrities of London and Paris* 1865; *Last recollections* 1866. *d.* Paris 20 Nov. 1865. *Reminiscences* (1862), *portrait.*

GROOME, VEN. ROBERT HINDES (2 *son of Rev. John Hindes Groome, R. of Earl Soham, d.* 1845 *aged* 68). *b.* Framlingham, Suffolk 18 Jany. 1810; ed. at Caius coll. Cam., B.A. 1832, M.A. 1836; C. of Tannington, Suffolk 1833; R. of Monk-Soham, Suffolk 1845 to death; hon. canon of Norwich 1858–71; archdeacon of Suffolk 1869, resigned 1887; edited *Christian Advocate Review* 1861–6; author of *How to read, a lecture* 1857. *d.* Monk-Soham 19 March 1889.

GROSE, REV. THOMAS (2 *son of Rev. John Grose, R. of Metteswell, Essex). b.* 1806; ed. at Clare hall, Cam., B.A. 1827, M.A. 1830; lecturer of St. John's, Wapping 1833; chaplain of Stepney union 1838; C. of St. Peter's, Cornhill 1839 to death; author of *A reply to the American Anti-theistical catechism* 1834; *Discipline of Church of England defended against W. Tiptaft* 1838. *d.* London 21 March 1867.

GROSSMITH, GEORGE. *b.* Reading 20 Aug. 1820; connected with the press, on staff of *Times* 35 years; first lectured on Wit and Humour at Reading 9 Dec. 1847; public reader and lecturer, travelled throughout the United Kingdom. *d.* of apoplexy, Savage club, Caledonian hotel, London 24 April 1880. *Illust. sp. and dr. news* 15 *May* (1880), *portrait.*

GROSVENOR, THOMAS (3 son of Thomas Grosvenor 1734–95, M.P. for Chester). b. 30 May 1764; ed. at Westminster; ensign 3 foot guards 1 Oct. 1779, captain 1793–1802; served in the Low Countries 1793–99, at Copenhagen 1807 and at Walcheren 1809; received the thanks of parliament 1 Feb. 1808; col. of 97 foot 25 Feb. 1807, of 65 foot 8 Feb. 1814 to death; general 12 Aug. 1819, field marshal 9 Nov. 1846; M.P. for Chester 1795–1826, for Stockbridge 1826–30. d. Mount Ararat near Richmond, Surrey 20 Jany. 1851.

GROTE, ARTHUR (younger bro. of the succeeding). b. Beckenham, Kent 29 Nov. 1814; of Bengal C.S. 1832; in revenue department 1853, retired 1868; president of Asiatic soc. of Bengal 1859–62, 1865; F.L.S., F.Z.S. d. 42 Ovington sq. London 4 Dec. 1886.

GROTE, GEORGE (1 son of George Grote 1762–1830, of city of London, banker). b. Clay hill near Beckenham 17 Nov. 1794; ed. at Sevenoaks and the Charterhouse; clerk in bank of Prescott, Grote & Co. 1810, partner in it 1816–43; one of founders of London university, opened 2 Oct. 1828, member of council 1828 to death; M.P. for city of London 1832–41; introduced motion in favor of the ballot 25 April 1833; F.G.S. 1843; D.C.L. Ox. 1853; V.C. of the university of London 1862; contested lord rectorship of univ. of Aberdeen 1866; author of History of Greece 12 vols. 1846–56, 4 ed. 10 vols. 1872; Plato and other companions of Socrates 3 vols. 1865, 2 ed. 1867 and other books. d. 12 Savile row, London 18 June 1871. bur. Westminster abbey 24 June. Personal history of G. Grote, by Mrs. Grote (1873), portrait; J. H. Friswell's Modern men of letters (1870) 183–94; Illustrated Review, vol. ii (1871) 33–37, portrait; Rev. P. Anton's Masters in history (1880) 63–119.

GROTE, HARRIET (dau. of Thomas Lewin of H.E.I.C.S., d. June 1843). b. the Ridgeway near Southampton 1 July 1792. (m. 5 March 1820 George Grote 1794–1871); educated herself to assist her husband in his literary work and managed his landed property for him; held receptions for foreigners and English politicians; a friend of Mendelssohn and Jenny Lind; known as the Queen of the Radicals; author of Memoir of life of Ary Scheffer 1860, 2 editions; Collected Papers 1862; The personal life of George Grote 1873. d. The Ridgeway, Shere near Guildford 29 Dec. 1878. Mrs. Grote, by Lady Eastlake (1880); Englishwoman's Domestic Mag. xvi, 120, 176 (1874).

GROTE, REV. JOHN (brother of George Grote 1794–1871). b. Beckenham 5 May 1813; ed.

GROTE, REV. J. (Con.)
at Trin. coll. Cam., B.A. 1835, M.A. 1838, fellow 1837 to death; V. of Trumpington near Cambridge 1847 to death; prof. of moral philos. in Univ. of Cam., May 1855 to death; author of Exploratio philosophica 1865, pt. i only; An examination of the utilitarian philosophy of J. S. Mill 1870. d. Trumpington vicarage 21 Aug. 1866.

GROUCOCK, RICHARD. b. Waters Upton, Salop; founded firm of Groucock and Copestake, warehousemen 5 Bow church yard, London 1826, they were joined by George Moore 1830. d. Waters Upton 26 July 1853 aged 51. D. Puseley's Commercial companion (1858) p. 46.

GROVE, WILLIAM (eld. son of Edward Grove of Stratton hall, Staffs.) b. 1796; ed. at Oriel coll. Ox., B.A. 1819, M.A. 1821; barrister L.I. 1 June 1821; police magistrate at Worship st. London 1834–40, at Greenwich and Woolich 1840–46. d. Union workhouse, Maidenhead 29 Jany. 1875.

GROVER, REV. HENRY MONTAGUE (eld. son of Harry Grover of Hemel Hempstead, Herts.) b. Watford, Herts. 1791; ed. at Peterhouse coll. Cam., LL.B. 1830; solicitor in Bedford row, London 1816–24; R. of Hitcham, Bucks. 16 Feb. 1833 to death; author of Anne Boleyn, a tragedy 1826; The history of the resurrection 1841. d. Hitcham rectory 20 Aug. 1866.

GROVES, ANTHONY NORRIS. b. Newton, Hampshire 1795; ed. at Trin. coll. Dublin; dentist at Plymouth 1813–6, at Exeter 1816–29; one of the founders of the Plymouth Brethren 1828; teacher of christianity at Bagdad 1829–33; travelling missionary in India 1833–4, 1836–48, 1849–52; author of Journal of a journey from London to Bagdad 1831; Journal of a residence at Bagdad 1837. d. 21 Paul st. Bristol 20 May 1853. Memoir of A. N. Groves, 3 ed. (1869).

GRUBB, EDWARD (2 son of Edward Grubb of Great Queen st. London). Barrister G.I. 11 Feb. 1828; clerk of records and writs in chancery 186– to death; a total abstainer 1833; author of Essays, analytical and philosophical, on the human mind, By E. G. 1845; Old and New Temperance advocacy, a speech 1858. d. 22 Gordon st. Gordon sq. London 8 June 1878 aged 77.

GRUBB, THOMAS. b. Kilkenny, Ireland 1800; a practical optician and manufacturer of reflectors in Dublin, made the Melbourne reflector 1867 the largest except the Parsonstown speculum then known; much consulted by

GRUBB, T. *(Con.)*

Lord Rosse and other astronomers; retired from business 1868; F.R.S. 2 June 1864; F.R.A.S. 1870; writer of many papers on microscopes and telescopes; M.R.I.A. 14 Jany. 1839. *d.* 141 Leinster road, Rathmines, Dublin 19 Sep. 1878.

GRUNDY, JAMES. *b.* New Radford, Nottingham 5 March 1824; professional bowler to earl of Leicester at Holkham 1847–51; bowler to the Marylebone club 1851–71; also a good batsman; landlord of Midland hotel, Carrington st. Nottingham 1869. *d.* Midland hotel, Nottingham 24 Nov. 1873. *Illust. sporting news, i,* 117 (1862), *portrait, iii,* 361 (1864), *portrait, v,* 457 (1866), *portrait; Bell's Life in London* 29 Dec. 1873 *p.* 4.

GRUNDY, JOHN CLOWES *(eld. son of John Grundy, cotton spinner).* *b.* Bolton, Lancs. 3 Aug. 1806; print seller Manchester; one of the best judges of engravings in England; patron of David Cox, S. Prout and others; in conjunction with Sir F. Moon published David Roberts' *Sketches in the Holy Land, Egypt, &c.* 1842–8. *d.* while on a visit to London 19 May 1867.

GRUNEISEN, CHARLES LEWIS *(son of Charles Gruneisen of Stuttgart).* *b.* Bloomsbury, London 2 Nov. 1806; special correspondent of *Morning Post* to Carlist army in Spain 1837–8, correspondent in Paris 1839–44 when he organised a pigeon express; organiser of the Italian opera at Covent Garden 1846, supported it till 1869; entrusted by Meyerbeer with the score of *Le Prophète* which was produced at Covent Garden 1849; musical critic for *Athenæum* 1868 to death; a founder and director of Conservative land soc. 1852, sec. 1853–72; author of *The opera and the press* 1869; *Sketches of Spain* 1874. *d.* 16 Surrey st. Strand, London 1 Nov. 1879.

GRYLLS, REV. HENRY *(3 son of Rev. Richard Gerveys Grylls* 1758–1841, *V. of St. Neot, Cornwall).* *b.* Helston, Cornwall 1 Feb. 1794; ed. at Ex. coll. Ox., B.A. 1816, M.A. 1821; V. of St. Neot 21 Dec. 1820 to death; author of *A selection of masonic prayers* 1844; *A descriptive sketch of the windows of St. Neot church* 1830, 4 *ed.* 1854; *A manual of private and domestic prayer* 1861. *d.* Helston 11 June 1862.

GRYLLS, MARY *(1 dau. of Rev. Charles Grylls* 1812–76, *V. of Lanhydrock, Cornwall).* *b.* Helston, Cornwall 15 Feb. 1836; author of *Death in the palace* 1861; *Helen and her cousins* 1863 and 4 other books all being anonymous. *d.* Lanhydrock 13 Nov. 1863.

GUBBINS, MARTIN RICHARD. *b.* 1812; of H.E.I.C.S. 1830; member of British commission in Oudh 1856–7; manager of intelligence department during the mutiny 1857–8; judge of supreme court of Agra 1858–63; author of *Reports upon the settlement of Zillah Etawah, Agra* 1844; *Accounts of the mutinies in Oudh* 1858, 3 *ed.* 1858; hanged himself at Somerset house, Clarendon place, Leamington 6 May 1863. *Royal Leamington Spa Courier* 9 *May* 1863 *p.* 10.

GUDGE, JAMES. Clerk of journals of house of commons 1835 to death. *d.* Westminster hospital, London 7 May 1857 aged 62, having tried to drown himself in the Thames 6 May.

GUERINT, SEBASTIAN FRANCIS *(son of Mr. Guerint a Swiss who was the first engine turner of watch cases in England).* *b.* 1791; appeared at Sadler's Wells theatre 23 April 1817 as Harlequin in *The yellow dwarf* to Grimaldi's clown; ballet master at the Olympic 1848; proprietor of exhibition of hydraulics and moving figures on site of old Savile house, Leicester sq.; acting manager at Royalty theatre 1869. *d.* 87 Charlotte st. Fitzroy sq. London 9 March 1870.

GUERNSEY, WELLINGTON. *b.* Mullingar, co. Westmeath 8 June 1817; studied music under Mercadante at Lisbon; an officer of engineers in war between Paraguay and Brazil and the U.S. of America 1865; war correspondent and journalist 40 years; writer of the words of upwards of 100 songs including Mary Blane and Alice, where art thou ?; composer of song I'll hang my harp on a willow tree 1845, a mass in B flat 1865 and 80 other pieces of music. *d.* London 13 Nov. 1885.

GUEST, EDWIN *(son of E. Guest).* *b.* 1802; ed. at Caius coll. Cam., fellow 1824; 11 wrangler 1824, B.A. 1824, M.A. 1827, LL.D. 1853; barrister L.I. 19 June 1828; master of Caius coll. 1852, resigned 14 Oct. 1880; V.C. of Univ. of Cam. 1854–5; F.R.S. 20 June 1839; founder of Philological soc., and sec. 1842, wrote many papers in *Transactions;* author of *A history of English rhythms* 2 vols. 1838, *new ed.* 1882; *Guest's Compendious Shorthand* 1883; *Origines Celticæ* 1883. *d.* Sandford park near Oxford 23 Nov. 1880 in 78 year. *Spectator* 4 Dec. 1880 *p.* 1551.

GUEST, JOHN *(son of James Guest, tailor).* *b.* Bridge-gate, Rotherham 5 May 1799; clerk at the Phœnix iron works; head of firm of Guest and Chrimes, brass founders 1847; a temperance advocate 1836; alderman of Rotherham 1871 and a benefactor to the town;

GUEST, J. *(Con.)*

F.S.A. 5 May 1874 ; author of *Relics and records of Rotherham* 1866 ; *Historic notices of Rotherham* 1879. *d.* Moorgate Grange, Rotherham 18 July 1880. *Hulbert's Annals of Almondbury* (1882) 438 ; *Sketches of the life of J. Guest, by T. Beggs* (1881), *portrait.*

GUEST, Sir Josiah John, 1 Baronet *(elder son of Thomas Guest of Dowlais near Merthyr Tydvil, manager of iron works, d.* 1807*).* *b.* Dowlais 2 Feb. 1785 ; general manager of Dowlais iron works 1815, owner of the works 1849 to death ; M.P. for Honiton 1826–31 ; contested Honiton 1831 ; M.P. for Merthyr 11 Dec. 1832 to death ; contested Glamorgan 1837 ; chairman of Taff Vale railway ; F.R.S. 10 June 1830 ; F.G.S. ; A.I.C.E. 1834 ; cr. Baronet 14 Aug. 1838. *d.* Dowlais 26 Nov. 1852. *Min. of proc. of Instit. of C.E. xii,* 163–5 (1853).

GUICCIOLI, Countess Teresa *(dau. of Count Gamba of Ravenna).* *b.* 1801. *(m.* 1818 Count Guiccioli of Ravenna) ; first met Lord Byron April 1819 at Venice ; separated from her husband and lived under protection of Byron Jany. 1820 to July 1823 ; *(m.* 1851 Hilaire marquis de Boissy, he was *b.* 1798, *d.* 26 Sep. 1866) ; visited England ; author of *Lord Byron jugé par les témoins de sa vie* 1869. *d.* Setimello near Florence, March 1873. *Mary R. Darby Smith's Recollections of la marquise de Boissy* (1878), *with 3 portraits.*

GUILFORD, Rev. Francis North, 6 Earl of. *b.* 17 Dec. 1772 ; master of St. Cross hospital, Winchester 9 Jany. 1808 to 1855, the Rolls court obliged him⁻ to give up part of the income in 1855 ; succeeded 14 Oct. 1827 ; R. of Old Alresford, New Alresford and Medstead 1797–1850 ; author of *Tract on the Epiphany* 1835. *d.* Waldershare park near Dover 29 Jany. 1861. *C. Beavan's Chancery Reports, xvi,* 435–69 (1854), *xviii,* 475–7, 601–8 (1855).

GUILFORD, Dudley Francis North, 7 Earl of. *b.* Weavering, Kent 14 July 1851 ; succeeded his grandfather 1861 ; cornet R. horse guards 1868, lieut. 1870, retired 1871 ; master of East Kent hounds 1872. *d.* Sydling court near Dorchester 19 Dec. 1885 from injuries received while hunting day before. *Baily's Mag. xxiii,* 125 (1873), *portrait.*

GUILLE, Very Rev. William *(son of Wm. Guille of Guernsey).* Matric. from Oriel coll. Ox. 15 Nov. 1810 aged 18, B.A. 1814, M.A. 1817 ; R. of St. Andrew's, Guernsey 1837–58 ; R. of St. Peter's Port, Guernsey 1858 to death ; dean of Guernsey 1858 to death. *d.* Guernsey 14 June 1869.

GUILLEMARD, Rev. William Henry *(son of Daniel Guillemard, silk merchant, Spitalfields).* *b.* Hackney 23 Nov. 1815 ; ed. at Pemb. coll. Cam., B.A. 1838, M.A. 1841, B.D. 1849, D.D. 1870 ; fellow of his coll. 1839 ; head master of Royal coll. Armagh 1848–69 ; V. of St. Mary the Less, Camb. 1869, resigned 1887 ; author of *The Greek Testament, Hebraistic edition* 1875 ; *Hebraisms in the Greek Testament, Camb.* 1879 an unfinished work. *d.* Waterbeach near Cambridge 2 Sep. 1887.

GUINNESS, Sir Benjamin Lee, 1 Baronet (3 *son of Arthur Guinness b.* 12 *March* 1768, *head of firm of Guinness & Co. brewers, Dublin, d. Beaumont house near Dublin 9 June* 1855). *b.* Dublin 1 Nov. 1798 ; lord mayor of Dublin 1851 ; sole proprietor of firm of Arthur Guinness & Co. 1857, developed the business which became largest in the world, it was made a limited liability co. 1886 with capital of £6,000,000 ; restored St. Patrick's cath. Dublin at cost of £150,000, 1860–67 ; LL.D. of univ. of Dublin 1863 ; M.P. for city of Dublin 17 July 1865 to death ; cr. baronet 15 April 1867. *d.* 27 Norfolk st. Park lane, London 19 May 1868. *bur.* Mount Jerome cemetery, Dublin 27 May, personalty sworn under £1,100,000, 8 Aug. 1868 ; bronze statue erected in St. Patrick's ch. yard Sep. 1875. *I.L.N. xlvi,* 207, 209 (1865), *portrait, lii,* 547 (1868) ; *Graphic xii,* 278, 293 (1875).

GUINNESS, Richard Samuel. *b.* Dublin 17 June 1797 ; head of firm of Guinness & Co. Dublin 1855 to death ; M.P. for Kinsale 1847–48, for Barnstaple 1855–57. *d.* Deepwell, Blackrock, co. Dublin 28 Aug. 1857.

GUION, Stephen Barker. *b.* U.S. of America 1820 ; went to Liverpool 1851 ; naturalised 18 Oct. 1858 ; started the Guion line of Atlantic steamers 1866 ; pres. of Liverpool Liberal association many years ; represented Exchange Ward in the Liverpool city council 1869 to Nov. 1885. *d.* Devonshire road, Prince's park, Liverpool 19 Dec. 1885.

GUISE, Sir John Wright, 3 Baronet (2 *son of Sir John Guise,* 1 *Bart.* 1733–94). *b.* Highnam court, Gloucs. 20 July 1777 ; ensign 70 foot 1794 ; ensign 3 foot guards 1795, first major 1814–21 ; served in Spain 1800, Egypt 1801 and in Peninsula 1812–14 ; K.C.B. 13 Sept. 1831, G.C.B. 10 Nov. 1862 ; succeeded his brother 23 July 1834 ; col. 85 foot 1 June 1847 to death ; general 11 Nov. 1851. *d.* Elmore court near Gloucester 1 April 1865.

GULL, Sir William Withey, 1 Baronet *(youngest son of John Gull, barge owner, d.* 1827*).*

GULL, SIR W. W. (Con.)

b. Colchester 31 Dec. 1815; M.B. London univ. 1841, M.D. 1846; F.R.C.P. Lond. 1848, censor 1859-61 and 1872-3, Gulstonian lecturer 1849, Harveian orator 1870; medical tutor Guy's hospital 1841, lecturer 1843-56, physician and lecturer 1856-65; Fullerian prof. of physiology, Royal Instit. 1847-9; D.C.L. Oxf. 1868, LL.D. Camb. 1880, and Edinb. 1884; F.R.S. 3 June 1869; attended Prince of Wales when ill from typhoid fever Nov. to Dec. 1871; cr. baronet 20 Jany. 1872; phys. in ordinary to P. of Wales 24 Feb. 1872; phys. in ordinary to the queen 1887; pres. of Clinical soc. of Lond. 1872; pre-eminent as a clinical physician, the first to describe disease known as myxoedema 1873. d. 74 Brook st. London 29 Jany. 1890. bur. Thorpe-le-Soken, Essex, left personalty £344,023 besides landed estates. Midland Medical miscell. iii, 97-8 (1884), portrait; I.L.N. lix, 612 (1871), portrait, and 1 Feb. 1890 p. 131, portrait.

GULLIVER, GEORGE. b. Banbury 4 June 1804; M.R.C.S. 1826, F.R.C.S. 1843; Hunterian professor of comparative anatomy 1861, Hunterian orator 1863; hospital assistant in army 17 May 1827; surgeon to R. horse guards 1843-53 when placed on h.p.; present at duel 1 July 1843 between Col. Fawcett and Lieut. Munro, tried for murder but acquitted; F.R.S. 7 March 1839; The Amicus of Dr. John Davy's two books The Angler and his friends 1855 and The Angler in the Lake district 1857; made researches on the blood, chyle, lymph, etc.; edited for the Sydenham soc. The works of William Hewson, F.R.S. 1846; Notes of researches in anatomy, etc. 1870, another ed. 1880. d. 3 Clovis ter. Canterbury 17 Nov. 1882. Biograph May-June 1882 pp. 388-92.

GULLY, JAMES MANBY. b. Kingston, Jamaica 14 March 1808; came to England 1814; M.D. of Edin. univ. 1829, M.R.C.S. Edin. 1829; physician in London 1830-42; edited Liverpool Medical Journal 1834; at Malvern as a practiser of hydropathy 1842 to 31 Dec. 1871; became very intimate with Mrs. C. D. T. Bravo and was one of the witnesses in the Bravo poison case July-Aug. 1876; his name removed from medical societies and Medical Register 1876; author of The water cure in chronic disease 1846, 13 ed. 1877; The lady of Belleisle, a drama produced at Drury lane 4 Dec. 1839; appears as Dr. Gullson in Chas. Reade's novel It is never too late to mend 1857. d. Orwell lodge, Bedford hill road, Balham, Surrey 27 March 1883. Palatine Note-book, iii, 215-6 (1883); The Balham Mystery (1876), 33 portrait.

GULLY, JOHN. b. Crown inn, Wick and Abson, Gloucs. 21 Aug. 1783; a butcher at Bath; fought Henry Pearce the 'Game Chicken' 8 Oct. 1805 when he was beaten; beat Bob Gregson the Lancashire giant 14 Oct. 1807, again 10 May 1808; declined title of champion of England 1808; landlord of the Plough inn 23 Carey st. Chancery lane, London 1808-10; bookmaker and owner of race horses from 1812; bought Mameluke from Lord Jersey in 1827 for £4200; won the St. Leger with Margrave 1832, the 2000 guineas with Ugly Buck 1844 and with Hermit 1854; the Derby with Pyrrhus the First 1846 and with Andover 1854; the Oaks with Mendicant 1846; M.P. for Pontefract 1832-7, contested Pontefract 1841; proprietor of Wingate colliery, Durham 1862. d. the North Bailey, city of Durham 9 March 1863. bur. Ackworth near Pontefract 14 March. H. D. Miles's Pugilistica, i, 182-91 (1880), portrait; W. Day's Reminiscences (1886) 53-70; Famous racing men (1882) 72-82; The Fancy, ii, 365-72 (1826), portrait; Rice's British Turf, i, 288-93 (1879).

GUNDRY, THOMAS. A miner in Cornwall; champion wrestler of Cornwall 25 years; beat the Devonshire champion twice; a carrier; was married 4 times. d. Stennack, Camborne 23 Oct. 1888 aged 70. The Cornishman 1 Nov. 1888 p. 3.

GUNN, ROBERT CAMPBELL. b. Cape of Good Hope 4 April 1808; assist. superintendent of convict prisons, Tasmania 1829; superintendent, police magistrate and coroner; sent collections of plants to Sir W. Hooker and W. Lindley, and mammals, birds, etc. to Dr. J. E. Gray; clerk to executive and legislative councils of Tasmania and private sec. to Sir John Franklin 1837-43; F.L.S. Jany. 1850; F.R.S. 1 June 1854; a commissioner to select site for capital of New Zealand, when Wellington was chosen 1864. d. Hobart Town 12 March 1881. Proc. Royal Soc. xxxiv, pp. xiii-xv (1883).

GUNNER, THOMAS (2 son of Wm. Gunner of Bishop's Waltham, Hants.) b. 23 Nov. 1815; ed. at Winchester and Trin. coll. Ox., B.A. 1838, M.A. 1840; barrister L.I. 27 Jany. 1842; recorder of Southampton, Oct. 1870 to death. d. Heathfield, Winchester 3 March 1883.

GUNNING, HENRY (1 son of Rev. Francis Gunning, V. of Newton near Cambridge, d. 1788). b. Newton 13 Feb. 1768 · ed. at Christ's coll. Cam., 5 wr. 1788, B.A. 1788, M.A. 1791; one of esquires bedells of the univ. 13 Oct. 1789, senior esquire bedell 1827 to death; mem. of town council of Cambridge 1835-41;

GUNNING, H. (Con.)

author of *Poll books of Cambridge* 7 vols. 1822–47; *The ceremonies in the senate house, Cambridge* 1836. *d.* Brighton 4 Jany. 1854. *Remisiscences of Cambridge, by H. Gunning* 2 vols. 1854, *portrait; G.M.* xli, 207–208 (1854).

GUNNING, JOHN. *b.* 1774; hospital assistant in the army Oct. 1793; surgeon to commander in chief through Peninsular war; surgeon in chief at Waterloo; inspector general 1 Feb. 1816, placed on h.p. 1 Oct. 1816; lived at Paris 1815 to death; C.B. 17 Aug. 1849. *d.* 52 Rue du Colisée, Paris 11 Jany. 1863. *Proc. of Med. and Chir. society,* iv, 207 (1864).

GUNNING, VEN. WILLIAM. Ed. at Ch. coll. Cam., LL.B. 1828; V. of Stowey near Bath 1839–51; preb. of Wells 24 Aug. 1840 to death; V. of Buckland Newton, Dorset 1851 to death; archdeacon of Bath, Aug. 1852 to death. *d.* Manila crescent, Weston-super-Mare 11 Oct. 1860 aged 64.

GUNSON, REV. WILLIAM MANDELL. Ed. at Bolton-Gate sch. near Mealsgate and Christ's coll. Cam., 28 wrangler and 1 class cl. trip. 1847, B.A. 1847, M.A. 1850, fellow of his coll. 1847, tutor 1851–70; drowned himself near the Knowe, Baggrew, Aspatria, Cumberland 30 Sep. 1881.

GUNTER, ROBERT. Confectioner at Berkeley sq. London 1819–44. *d.* Earl's court, Old Brompton 16 Oct. 1852 aged 69.

GUPPY, THOMAS RICHARD (2 son of Samuel Guppy of Bristol, merchant). *b.* Bristol 1797; a sugar refiner at Bristol about 1826–30; started with I. K. Brunel a company for constructing a railway from Bristol to London 1830 for which they got an act 1832; constructed with Brunel the 'Great Western' steamship which was launched 19 July 1837, ran from Bristol to New York 1838–46, became property of Royal mail steam packet company 1846 and was broken up 1857; invented the cellular system of ship building; constructed the Great Britain, launched 19 July 1843; assisted in the introduction of the screw propeller; manager of Cwmavon, Glamorgan, copper works 1844; practised at Naples 1849, a mechanical engineer there 1854; A.I.C.E. 3 May 1842, M.I.C.E. 19 Feb. 1878. *d.* Portici near Naples 28 June 1882. *Min. of proc. of Instit. of C.E.* lxix, 411–15 (1882).

GURDON, BRAMPTON. *b.* London 25 Sep. 1797; sheriff of Norfolk 1855; M.P. for West Norfolk 1857–65. *d.* 38 Hill st. Berkeley sq. London 28 April 1881.

GURDON, WILLIAM (4 son of lieut. col. Theophilus Thornhagh Gurdon of Letton, Norfolk 1764–1849). *b.* 1804; ed. at Eton and Downing coll. Cam., fellow 1838, B.A. 1826, M.A. 1829; barrister I.T. 3 July 1829; recorder of Bury St. Edmunds 185– to 1860; judge of county courts, circuit 38 (Essex), March 1847 to March 1871; author of *Our highways: what they are and what they might be; Bankruptcy for the million* 1862. *d.* Brantham court, Manningtree, Suffolk 12 Oct. 1884.

GURDON-REBOW, JOHN. *b.* London 1799; assumed additional name of Rebow 1835; sheriff of Essex 1853; M.P. for Colchester 1857–59 and 1865 to death. *d.* Wivenhoe park near Colchester 12 Oct. 1870.

GURNEY, ANNA (youngest child of Richard Gurney of Keswick near Norwich, d. 16 July 1811). *b.* 31 Dec. 1795; paralysed at 10 months old and deprived for ever of the use of her lower limbs; translated the *Anglo-Saxon Chronicle, By A Lady in the country* 1819; lived at Northrepps cottage near Cromer 1825 to death; travelled in Italy and Greece. *d.* Keswick near Norwich 6 June 1857. *bur.* in Overstrand church. *Journal of British Archæol. Assoc.* xiv, 187–9 (1858).

GURNEY, REV. ARCHER THOMPSON (son of Richard Gurney 1790–1843, vice-warden of stannaries of Devon). *b.* Tregony, Cornwall 15 July 1820; barrister of M.T. 8 May 1846; ordained C. of Holy Trinity, Exeter 1849; chaplain to Court chapel, Paris 1858–71; C. of Llangunider, Brecon 1882–3; author of *Turandot, Princess of China, a drama* 1836; *Songs of early summer* 1856; *Words of faith and cheer* 1874 and other books, besides songs and hymns. *d.* Castle hotel, 4 Northgate st. Bath 21 March 1887.

GURNEY, DANIEL (youngest son of John Gurney d. 1809). *b.* Earlham hall near Norwich 9 March 1791; partner in firm of Gurney & Co. bankers, Norwich 1820–80; F.S.A. 12 March 1818; sheriff of Norfolk 1853; author of *The record of the house of Gournay* 1848–58. *d.* North Runcton, Norfolk 14 June 1880.

GURNEY, EDMUND (3 son of John Hampden Gurney 1802–62). *b.* Hersham near Walton-on-Thames, Surrey 23 March 1847; ed. at Trin. coll. Cam., B.A. 1871, fellow 1872; resided at Harrow 1872–5; studied music 1872–5, medicine 1877–81 and law 1881–3; a founder of Soc. for Psychical research 1882 and a writer of numerous articles on the subject; a student of hypnotism 1887; author of *The power of sound* 1880; *Tertium Quid,*

GURNEY, E. *(Con.)*

chapters on disputed questions 2 *vols.* 1887; principal author of *Phantasms of the living* 1886. *d.* from taking an overdose of narcotic at the Royal Albion hotel, Brighton 23 June 1888. *Brighton Gazette 28 June 1888 p. 6.*

GURNEY, Sir Goldsworthy *(son of John Gurney of Trevorgus, Cornwall, d. 1823). b.* Treator near Padstow 14 Feb. 1793; surgeon at Wadebridge 1814, in London 1820; invented the steam jet 1820 and the oxy-hydrogen blow-pipe 1823; discovered Drummond light 1826; invented an instrument of musical glasses played as a piano; applied high pressure steam to a locomotive on the road from London to Bath 28 July 1829; invented Bude light 1839; introduced new mode of lighting house of commons 1839, superintendent of lighting and ventilation there 1854–63; knighted by patent 10 Aug. 1863. *d.* The Reeds near Bude 28 Feb. 1875.

GURNEY, Hudson *(brother of Anna Gurney 1775–1857). b.* Norwich 19 Jany. 1775; M.P. Shaftesbury 1812, unseated on petition; M.P. Newton, Isle of Wight 1816–31; F.S.A. 13 Feb. 1812, V.P. 1822–46; F.R.S. 15 Jany. 1818; sheriff of Norfolk 1835; purchased from Mrs. Woodward all S. Woodward's manuscripts, and printed the *Norfolk Topographer's Manual* 1842 and the *The history of Norwich castle* 1847; wrote *Cupid and Psyche: a mythological tale from the Golden Ass of Apuleius* 1799, 3 *ed.* 1801; printed privately a translation of Ariosto's *Orlando Furioso* 1843. *d.* Keswick hall near Norwich 9 Nov. 1864. *bur.* Intwood ch. yard, personalty sworn under £1,100,000, 24 Dec. 1864. *C. R. Smith's Retrospections, i, 242–45 (1883).*

GURNEY, Rev. John Hampden *(1 son of Sir John Gurney 1768–1845). b.* 12 Serjeant's inn, Fleet st. London 15 Aug. 1802; ed. at Trin. coll. Cam., B.A. 1824, M.A. 1827; C. of Lutterworth, Leics. 1827–44; R. of St. Mary's, Bryanston sq. London 6 Dec. 1847 to death; preb. of St. Pancras, St. Paul's cath. 1857 to death; author of *Historical sketches 1400–1546,* 1852; *St. Louis and Henry iv,* 1855; *God's heroes and the world's heroes* 1858. *d.* 63 Gloucester place, Portman sq. London 8 March 1862. *Church of England photographic portrait gallery* (1859) *p.* 40, *portrait.*

GURNEY, John Henry *(only son of Joseph John Gurney the philanthropist 1788–1847). b.* 1819; of firm of Gurneys, Birkbecks, Barclay and Buxton, bankers in the eastern counties; M.P. Lynn Regis 1854–65; an active partner in Overend, Gurney & Co. bill discounters,

GURNEY, J. H. *(Con.)*

London 1865, the firm suspended payment 10 May 1866 liabilities £11,000,000; presented his collections of birds to Norfolk and Norwich museum; author of *A sketch of the raptorial birds in the Norwich museum* 1872. *d.* Northrepps, Norfolk 21 April 1890. *I.L.N. xxvi,* 181 (1855), *portrait; Pictorial World* 8 *May* 1890 *p.* 598, *portrait.*

GURNEY, Rev. John Phillips. ed. at Queen's coll. Cam., B.A. 1823, M.A. 1834; chaplain of Black chapel, Great Waltham, Essex; V. of Great Canfield, Essex 22 Dec. 1822 to death; author of *The woman and the dragon, an exposition of twelfth chapter of Apocalypse* 1851; *The approaching fall of Rome* 1857. *d.* Great Canfield vicarage 9 March 1872.

GURNEY, Joseph *(eld. son of W. B. Gurney 1777–1855). b.* London 15 Oct. 1804; shorthand writer to houses of parliament 1849–72; treasurer of Religious Tract soc. and of Baptist coll. in Regent's park; author of *The annotated paragraph Bible, By J. G.* 2 *vols.* 1850–60; *The revised English Bible, Preface, By J. G.* 1877. *d.* Tynedale lodge, Wimbledon common, Surrey 12 Aug. 1879.

GURNEY, Russell *(brother of Rev. J. H. Gurney 1802–62). b.* Norwood, Surrey 2 Sep. 1804; ed. at Trin. coll. Cam., B.A. 1826; barrister I.T. 21 Nov. 1828, bencher 1845; Q.C. 1845; judge of sheriff's court and small debts court, city of London 1850; common serjeant of city of London, Jany. 1856; recorder of city of London 16 Dec. 1856, resigned Feb. 1878; M.P. Southampton, July 1865 to death; a comr. to inquire into disturbances in Jamaica Jany. 1866; P.C. 11 June 1866; F.R.S. 22 April 1875; prime warder of Fishmongers' co. 1876. *d.* 8 Kensington palace gardens 31 May 1878. *Times 1 June 1878 p.* 13, 6 *June p.* 7; *I.L.N. lxxii,* 589–90 (1878), *portrait.*

GURNEY, Samuel *(2 son of John Gurney, banker, d. 1809). b.* Earlham hall near Norwich 18 Oct. 1786; partner with Richardson and Overend, bill and money lenders, 14 Birchin lane, London 1807; firm became Overend, Gurney & Co. 1824; known as the bankers' banker; in 1856 the firm had deposits of eight millions, insolvent 1866; a patron of the colony of Liberia, his name given to a town in Gallenas 1851. *d.* Paris 5 June 1856. *bur.* Friends' cemet. Barking 19 June. *H. R. F. Bourne's English merchants ii,* 347–64 (1866); *I.L.N. xxix,* 16 (1856), *portrait.*

GURNEY, Samuel *(2 son of the preceding). b.* Upton, Essex 1816; partner in Overend, Guerney & Co. London; M.P. Penryn and

Falmouth 1857-65; sheriff of Surrey 1861; director of several telegraph companies; F.L.S. F.R.G.S. *d.* The Spa, Tunbridge Wells 4 April 1882 aged 66. *I.L.N. 24 July 1859 pp.* 92, 94, *portrait.*

GURNEY, WILLIAM BRODIE *(son of Joseph Gurney, shorthand writer, d.* 1815). *b.* Stamford hill, London 24 Dec. 1777; a public shorthand writer, reported many state trials 1806–20; shorthand writer to houses of parliament 1813; founded Sunday school union 1803, sec., treasurer, pres. 1803 to death; a founder and editor of *The Youth's magazine* 1805; lay preacher at London female penitentiary 1807; author of *A lecture to children and youth* 1848; edited *Brachygraphy by T. Gurney,* 15 ed. 1824, 16 *ed.* 1835. *d.* Denmark hill, Camberwell 25 March 1855. *W. H. Watson's First fifty years of the Sunday school* (1873) 69–75.

GÜTZLAFF, CARL FRIEDRICH AUGUST. *b.* Pyritz, Pomerania 8 July 1803; D.D.; sent to the East by Netherland missionary soc. 1827; went to Macao, China 1831; interpreter to British superintendency 1834; travelled in Japan 1837; Chinese sec. to British consulate, Canton 1844 to death; founded Christian union of Chinese to propogate the gospel 1840; visited England 1850; author of *The Journal of three voyages along the coast of China* 1834, 3 *ed.* 1840; *A sketch of Chinese history* 2 vols. 1834; *China opened* 2 vols. 1838 and many other works in Dutch, German, Latin, Siamese, Chinese and Japanese. *d.* Victoria, Hong Kong 9 Aug. 1851. *Allgemeine Deutsche Biographie, x,* 236–7 (1879).

GUTCH, JOHN MATHEW *(eld. son of Rev. John Gutch* 1746–1831, *chaplain of All Souls' coll. Ox.) b.* Oxford 1776; ed. at Christ's hospital; law stationer in Southampton buildings, Chancery lane to 1803; proprietor and printer of *Felix Farley's Bristol Journal* 1804–44; second-hand bookseller at Bristol; partner in Lavender's bank, Worcester 1823–48 when the bank failed; F.S.A. 1839; started with Robert Alexander the *Morning Journal,* London 6 Oct. 1828, last number 30 May 1830; wrote or edited *The Country Constitutional Guardian,* Bristol 1822–24 a monthly serial; edited *Poems of Geo. Withers* 3 vols. 1820 and works about Robin Hood 1847–66. *d.* Barbourne near Worcester 20 Sep. 1861.

GUTCH, JOHN WHEELEY GOUGH *(only child of the preceding). b.* Bristol 1809; M.R.C.S. 1830; practised in Florence; a queen's messenger 1850–61; contributed to *Felix Farley's Journal;* edited *The literary and scientific register*

1842–56. *d.* 38 Bloomsbury sq. London 30 April 1862. *F. O. List* (1862) *p.* 161.

GUTHRIE, CHARLES SETON (1 *son of George Dempster Guthrie of Scots Calder). b.* 1808; ed. at H.E.I.C. coll. Addiscombe; lieut. col. Bengal engineers 1855–57 when he retired; made a collection of 18,440 eastern coins, the largest ever brought together, which was offered to German government for £5,000; member of Numismatic soc. to death. *d.* 26 Dec. 1874. *Numismatic Chronicle Proceedings, xv,* 12 *(Dec.* 1875).

GUTHRIE, FREDERICK *(son of Alexander Guthrie of 54 New Bond st. London, tailor). b.* Bayswater, London 15 Oct. 1833; ed. at Univ. sch. and coll. London; B.A. London 1855, M.A.?; Ph. D. of Marburg univ. Prussia 1854; F.R.S. Edin. 1860; assist. prof. of chemistry Owen's coll. Manchester 1856–9 and at Edin. 1859–61; prof. of chemistry and physics R. coll. Mauritius 1861–7; lecturer and prof. Sch. of science, South Kensington 1869 to death; discovered the Approach caused by vibration 1870; F.R.S. 8 June 1871; founder of Physical soc. of London 1873, president 1884; author of *The Jew, a poem* 1863, *Logrono, a metric drama* 1877, both under name of Frederick Cerny; *Elements of heat* 1868; *The first book of knowledge* 1881, new ed. 1883. *d.* of cancer of the throat 24 St. James' sq. Notting hill, London 21 Oct. 1886. *Nature 4 Nov.* 1886 *pp.* 8–10.

GUTHRIE, GEORGE JAMES *(only son of Andrew Guthrie of Lower James st. Golden sq. London, chiropodist). b.* London 1 May 1785; M.R.C.S. 5 Feb. 1801, member of council 1824, president 1833, 41, 54; assist. surgeon to 29 regt. 1801; served in Canada 1803–8, the Peninsula 1808–14 and at Waterloo 1815; surgeon on half pay Sep. 1814; lectured on surgery in London 1816–45; the first in England who used a lithotrite for crushing a stone in the bladder 1816; founded infirmary for diseases of the eye 1816 which became R. Westminster ophthalmic hospital; assist. surgeon to Westminster hospital 1823, surgeon 1827–43; professor of anatomy and surgery 1828–31; F.R.S. 1827; author of *Lectures on the operative surgery of the eye* 1827; *On diseases and injuries of arteries, with their cure* 1830; *On the operation for extraction of a cataract from the eye* 1834; *Commentaries on the surgery of the war in Portugal, &c.* 6 ed. 1853. *d.* 4 Berkeley st. Berkeley sq. London 1 May 1856. *Lancet 15 June* 1850 *pp.* 726–36, *portrait; Pettigrew's Medical portrait gallery, iv,* (1840), *portrait; Medical Circular, iv,* 13–15, 33–34, (1854).

GUTHRIE, JAMES ALEXANDER (1 *son of David Charles Guthrie of Craigie, Dundee*). *b.* 8 Sep. 1823; ed. at Merchant Taylors' sch. and Wadham coll. Ox., B.A. 1845, M.A. 1852; merchant and banker 9 Idol lane, London as Chalmers and Guthrie; director of bank of England 1858–60, 1861–66, 1867–69 and 1870 to death. *d.* 78 Portland place, London 17 Jany. 1873.

GUTHRIE, REV. JOHN. Ed. at Trin. coll. Cam., scholar; 10 wrangler and B.A. 1817, M.A. 1820; R. of Thorpe, Notts. 1827; V. of Helmarton, Wilts. 1833; R. of Calstone-Willington 1833; V. of Calne, Wilts. 7 Feb. 1835 to death; preb. of Salisbury cath. 1852–8; canon residentiary Bristol cath. 1858 to death; author of *On the neglect of christian ordinances* 1855 and other pamphlets. *d.* Dorset house, Clifton 6 July 1865.

GUTHRIE, REV. THOMAS (6 *son of David Guthrie of Brechin, merchant, d. March* 1824). *b.* Brechin 12 July 1803; ed. at univ. of Edin. 1815–26, D.D. 1849; manager of his father's bank, Brechin 1827–9; minister of Arbirlot, Forfarshire 1830–37; a minister of Old Greyfriar's church, Edin. 1837 and of St. John's parish 1840–3; minister of Free St. John's ch. 1843–64; moderator of Free ch. general assembly 1862; presented with £5000, 20 Feb. 1865; F.R.S. Edin. 1869; ed. the *Sunday Mag.* 1864 to death; author of *The gospel in Ezekiel* 1856, circulated 50,000 copies; *The city, its sins and sorrows* 1857; *Studies of character from the Old Testament,* 2 series 1867–70 and about 30 lectures, sermons and tracts. *d.* Eversfield place, St. Leonard's on Sea 24 Feb. 1873. *bur.* Grange cemet. Edin. 28 Feb. *Autobiography of T. Guthrie* 2 vols. (1874–5), 3 *portraits; Crombie's Modern Athenians* (1882) 83–7, *portrait; Wylie's Disruption Worthies* (1881); *Illust. news of the world, viii* (1861), *portrait.*

NOTE.—He did more than any other man from 1847 onwards, to popularise ragged schools. Samuel Smiles in his Self-Help calls him The Apostle of the ragged school movement.

GUTTERIDGE, THOMAS (*son of Mr. Gutteridge, a wharfinger, London, then landlord of White Lion tavern, Birmingham*). L.S.A. 1826; M.R.C.S. 1827; surgeon Birmingham; professor of anatomy Soc. of Arts 1832, presented with 100 guineas 1842; G. F. Muntz found guilty of assaulting him in an anti-church rate riot at the Old Church, Birmingham 1837; opposed confirmation of Dr. James Prince Lee as bp. of Manchester in St. James' ch. Piccadilly, London 10 Jany. 1848; found guilty of libels on Dr. Lee at Warwick 6 April 1848;

GUTTERIDGE, T. (*Con.*)

author of *Church rates* 1842 and of 4 works on the corruptions and abuses in the Birmingham hospital 1844–51. *d.* Birmingham 3 May 1880. *Edgbastoniana, iii,* 34–6 (1883), *portrait; Langford's Modern Birmingham, i,* 13, 519 (1868).

GUTTERIDGE, WILLIAM. *b.* Chelmsford, Essex 1798; leader of band in the park theatre, Brussels 1815; leader at Birmingham theatre 1818; member of George iv. band and of William iv. band; resided in Brighton 1823 to death; organist of St. Peter's ch. 1828; conductor of Old Sacred Harmonic soc. 1828; had a music warehouse in Castle sq.; much patronised by Geo. iv. and Victoria. *d.* 55 London road, Brighton 23 Sept. 1872.

GUY, JOSEPH (2 *son of Joseph Guy of Bristol, schoolmaster*). *b.* 4 May 1784; ed. at Magd. hall, Oxf.; private tutor and schoolmaster; author of *Guy's New exercises in orthography* 1818; *Guy's Geographia Antiqua* 1830; *Royal Victoria spelling book* 1850; *Guy's New Speaker* 1852 and about 12 other school books all of which were often reprinted. *d.* 5 Eden place, Kentish Town, London 16 Jany. 1867. *Bookseller* 31 *Jany.* 1867 p. 11.

GUY, JOSEPH. *b.* Nottingham 30 July 1814; a baker; kept Carpenters' Arms inn, Mansfield road, Nottingham 1856 to death; first played at Lord's 25–26 June 1838 the Coronation match; after Pilch and Wenman the best batsman in England; had a benefit on Trent Bridge ground 4 Aug. 1856 when he cleared £165 9s. 6d. *d.* Nottingham 15 April 1873. *Lillywhite's Cricket Scores, ii,* 449 (1862), *v, page xv* (1876).

GUY, SIR PHILIP MELMOTH NELSON (*only son of Melmoth Guy of Kenton hall, Devon*). *b.* Sidmouth, Devon 1804; ensign 5 foot 23 Sep. 1824, lieut. colonel 21 May 1850 to 1 Sep. 1861; commanded third infantry brigade at siege and capture of Lucknow 5–28 March 1858; governor of Jersey 1 Oct. 1868 to 1 Oct. 1873; colonel of 55 foot 14 Dec. 1873 to death; general 1 Oct. 1877; C.B. 24 March 1858, K.C.B. 24 May 1873. *d.* Wiesbaden 10 March 1878.

GUY, WILLIAM AUGUSTUS. *b.* Chichester 1810; ed. Pemb. coll. Cam., M.B. 1837, M.L. 1838; F.R.C.P. Lond. 1844, Croonian lecturer 1861, Lumleian 1868 and Harveian 1875; professor of forensic medicine King's coll. Lond. 1838, dean of the medical faculty 1846, 1849, permanent dean 1850–58; edited *Journal Statistical soc.* 1852–6, hon. sec. 1843–68, president 1873–5; F.R.S. 7 June 1866, V.P. 1876–7;

GUY, W. A. (Con.)

author of *Principles of Forensic medicine* 1844, 4 *ed.* 1857; *Public Health* 2 *parts* 1870–74. *d.* 12 Gordon st. Gordon sq. London 10 Sept. 1885 in 76 year. *Barker's Photographs of medical men* (1865) 59–64, *portrait.*

GUYON, RICHARD DEBAUFRE (3 *son of John Guyon, commander R.N. d.* 1844). *b.* Walcot, Bath 31 March 1803; received a commission in Austrian army 1823, capt. 1827; became country gentleman in Hungary 1839; opposed Jellachich at the head of a section of the revolutionists of 1848, defeated him at Pakozd 29 Sept.; fled to Turkey, Aug. 1849; the first Christian who obtained rank of pacha and a Turkish military command without betraying his religion, known as Khourschid Pacha (the Sun); defeated by the Russians at battle of Kurekdere 5 or 6 Aug. 1854. *d.* of cholera at Scutari 13 Oct. 1856. *R. A. Kinglake's The patriot general Guyon* (1856), *portrait; E. H. Nolan's History of Russian war,* i, 294 (1855), *portrait.*

GWATKIN, EDWARD (*eld. son of Robert Lovell Gwatkin of Killiow, Cornwall* 1757–1843). Entered Bengal army 1804 and was in India to 1855; col. 31 Bengal N.I. 17 Nov. 1853 to death. *d.* at sea on board the 'Hotspur' near England 13 April 1855. *Boase's Collect. Cornub.* (1890) 307–8.

GWILT, JOHN SEBASTIAN (*son of the succeeding*). *b.* 1811; ed. at Westminster sch.; architect; assisted his father in *A project for a New National gallery* 1838 and with drawings for *An Encyclopædia of architecture* 1851. *d.* Hambledon, Henley on Thames 4 March 1890.

GWILT, JOSEPH (*younger son of George Gwilt, surveyor to county of Surrey, d.* 9 *Dec.* 1807). *b.* parish of St. George the Martyr, Southwark 11 Jany. 1784; ed. at St. Paul's sch.; surveyor to county of Surrey 1807–46; built Lee ch. Lewisham 1814, Markree Castle near Sligo 1843 and Ch. of St. Thomas, Charlton, Woolwich 1846; F.S.A. 1815, F.R.A.S. 1833; author of *A treatise on the equilibrium of arches* 1811, 3 *ed.* 1839; *Notitia architectonica Italiana* 1818; *Sciography or examples of shadows* 1822, 2 *ed.* 1824, the first English treatise on the subject; *An encyclopædia of architecture* 1842, 3 *ed.* 1859; translated *The Architecture of Vitruvius* 1826. *d.* South Hill, Henley-on-Thames 14 Sep. 1863. *Journal British Archæol. Assoc. xx,* 178–81 (1864).

GWYN, HOWEL (1 *son of William Gwyn of Abercrane, Brecon, d.* 1830). *b.* 24 June 1806;

GWYN. H. (Con.)

ed. at Trin. coll. Ox., B.A. 1829, M.A. 1832; contested Penryn 1841 and 1859, M.P. 1847–57; contested Barnstaple 1865; M.P. Brecknock 1866–8 when unseated; contested Brecon county 1875; sheriff of co. Glamorgan 1837, of co. Carmarthen 1838 and of co. Brecon 1842. *d.* Duffryn, Neath 25 Jany. 1888.

GYE, FREDERICK. *b.* 1781; printer with G. Balne, city of London 1806–36; made £30,000 in a state lottery; proprietor of London wine co. 1817–36 and of London genuine tea co. 1818–36; with William Hughes purchased Vauxhall gardens ,for £28,000, 1821, conducted them to 1840, had the Great Nassau balloon built for him 1836; M.P. Chippenham, Wilts. 1826–30. *d.* 2 Lansdowne st. Hove, Brighton 13 Feb. 1869.

GYE, FREDERICK (*son of the preceding*). *b.* Finchley, Middlesex 1810; acting manager for Mons. Jullien at Drury Lane 1847; business manager for E. Delafield at Covent Garden 1848; lessee of Covent Garden, Sep. 1849, house burnt down 5 March 1856; lessee of Drury Lane 1852; lessee of Lyceum theatre 1856–7; rebuilt Covent Garden at cost of £120,000, house reopened 15 April 1858; partner with J. H. Mapleson at Covent Garden 1869–70, sole proprietor and manager 1870 to death. *d.* Dytchley park, Charlbury, Oxon. 4 Dec. 1878 from effects of being accidentally shot near there 27 Nov. *bur.* Norwood cemetery 9 Dec. *I.S. and D. News* 24 *June* 1876 *pp.* 297, 302, *portrait; H. S. Edwards's Lyrical Drama,* i, 15–30 (1881); *The Mask* (1868), 97 *portrait; The Mapleson Memoirs, vol.* 1 *passim* (1888).

GYLL, SIR ROBERT (5 *son of Wm. Gyll* 1774–1806, *capt.* 2 *life guards*). *b.* London 11 July 1805; lieut. of yeomen of the guard 1830–40; knighted at St. James's palace 13 Sep. 1831. *d.* Cumbernauld lodge, Feltham hill, Middlesex 17 Aug. 1880.

H

HAAS, ERNST ANTON MAX. *b.* Coburg 18 April 1835; ed. at Univ. of Berlin, Ph. D.; assistant department of printed books British Museum 1866 to death; professor of Sanskrit Univ. coll. London, April 1876 to death; Alma his widow granted civil list pension of £80, 29 Jany. 1883; compiler of *Catalogue of Sanskrit and Pali books in the British museum* 1876. *d.* 11 Westbourne park road, London 3 July 1882.

HAAST, Sir John Francis Julius Von *(son of Mathias Haas of Bonn, Prussia, merchant).* *b.* Bonn 1 May 1824 ; ed. at Bonn univ. and Cologne univ. ; Ph. D. of Tübingen univ. 1862; D. Sc. Cambridge 1886; explored S.W. part of Nelson, New Zealand 1859 ; government geologist of province of Canterbury 1861 ; discovered the Southern Alps of N.Z. ; founded Canterbury museum at Christchurch 1866, director 1866 to death ; professor of geology Canterbury coll. Christchurch to death ; F.R.G.S., gold medallist 1884 ; F.R.S. 6 June 1867 ; C.M.G. 24 May 1883, K.C.M.G. 28 June 1886 ; author of *New Zealand scenery* 1877 ; *Geology of the provinces of Canterbury and Westland, Auckland* 1879. *d.* Wellington, N.Z. 15 Aug. 1887. *Proc. of Royal Geog. Soc. ix, 687–8* (1887).

HABERFIELD, Sir John Kerle *(son of Andrew Haberfield of Devonport).* *b.* Devonport 1785 ; attorney at Bristol 1810 to death ; mayor of Bristol 1838, 39, 46, 49, 50 and 51 ; knighted at St. James's Palace 26 March 1851 for zeal in promoting local subscriptions for Great Exhibition. *d.* 23 York crescent, Clifton 1 Jany. 1858. *I.L.N. xviii,* 618 (1851), *portrait.*

HABERSHON, Matthew. *b.* 1789 ; designed churches in Yorkshire 1824 &c. ; built Derby town hall ; went to Jerusalem to arrange for building the Anglican cath. 1842 ; received great gold medal for science and literature from king of Prussia 1844 ; author of *A dissertation on the prophetic scriptures* 1834, 2 ed. 1840 and other fanciful works on prophecy ; *The ancient half-timbered houses of England* 1836 and 6 other books. *d.* Bonner's hall, Victoria park, London 5 July 1852. *Dict. of Architecture, iv,* 1–2.

HABERSHON, Samuel Osborne. *b.* Rotherham 1825 ; ed. at Univ. coll. London ; M.B. London 1848, M.D. 1851 ; M.R.C.S. and L.S.A. 1848 ; M.R.C.P. 1851, F.R.C.P. 1856, Lumleian lecturer 1876, Harveian orator 1883, and V.P. 1887 ; pres. of Medical soc. of Lond. 1873 ; lecturer on materia medica at Guy's hospital 1856–73, on medicine 1873–7, physician 1866, resigned 1880 ; did much to elucidate abdominal diseases ; author of *Observations on diseases of alimentary canal, oesophagus, stomach, caecum and intestines* 1857, 3 ed. 1878 ; *On the diseases of the stomach* 1866, 3 ed. 1879. *d.* 70 Brook st. Grosvenor sq. London 22 Aug. 1889. *Lancet, ii,* 445, 880–82, 979 (1889).

HACK, Daniel Pryor *(elder son of Daniel Hack, high constable of Brighton).* *b.* Brighton 1794 ; apprenticed to a draper at Chelmsford 1808 ; imprisoned at Chelmsford for refusing to serve

Hack, D. P. *(Con.)*
in militia 1814 ; a draper at Brighton 1815–26 ; a minister among The Friends 1823 to death ; gave £500 to Brighton free library. *d.* 99 Trafalgar st. Brighton 7 March 1886. *The Annual Monitor for* 1887 *pp.* 99–122.

HACKBLOCK, William. M.P. for Reigate, Surrey 28 March 1857 to death. *d.* at his brother's house, Brockham Warren, Betchworth, Surrey 2 Jany. 1858 aged 52.

HACKETT, James Thomas. *b.* in south of Ireland 1805 ; surveyor ; member and sec. of London Astrological soc. 1826, the last survivor of the society ; reporter on *Herapath's Railway Journal* nearly 40 years ; railway correspondent to *The Times ;* author of *The student's assistant in astronomy and astrology* 1836. *d.* Park villa, Alexandra road, Friern Barnet 13 Feb. 1876. *Herapath's Railway Journal* 6 *May* 1876 *p.* 518 ; *Athenæum* 15 *Apl.* 1876 *pp.* 535–6.

HACKETT, John *(son of John Hackett, vice admiral).* *b.* 2 Oct. 1819 ; ed. at Sandhurst ; ensign 70 foot 17 Nov. 1837 ; deputy assistant Q.M.G. in Crimea 8 March 1854 to March 1855 ; major 76 foot 1866, lieut. col. 1872–76 ; commander of troops in West Indies 11 May 1878 to 1 April 1882 ; hon. M.G. 1 April 1882. *d.* West Brighton 1 Nov. 1890. *I.L.N.* 29 *Nov.* 1890 *p.* 680, *portrait.*

HACKETT, Sir William *(son of Bartholomew Hackett of Cork).* *b.* 1824 ; ed. at Stonyhurst and Trin. coll. Dublin, B.A. 1845 ; called to Irish bar 1845 ; barrister L.I. 21 Nov. 1851 ; Queen's advocate Gold Coast 1861, chief justice 1863, lieut. governor 1864 ; recorder of Prince of Wales Island 1866–75 ; knighted at Windsor Castle 12 Dec. 1866 ; chief justice of Fiji 1875–76 ; chief justice of Ceylon 20 Nov. 1876. *d.* Colombo, Ceylon 17 May 1877.

HACKETT, Sir William Bartholomew *(son of Bartholomew Hackett of Carrigaline, co. Cork).* *b.* Carrigaline 1800 ; a merchant at Cork, the largest manufacturer of leather in Ireland ; mayor of Cork 1852 ; knighted by Earl of Eglinton at opening of Irish National Exhibition at Cork 10 June 1852. *d.* 28 Jany. 1872.

HACKMAN, Rev. Alfred *(son of Thomas Hackman, vestry clerk of Fulham, Middlesex).* *b.* Fulham 8 April 1811 ; servitor at Ch. Ch. Ox. 25 Oct. 1832, B.A. 1837, M.A. 1840, chaplain Ch. Ch. 1837–73, precentor 1841–73 ; clerk Bodleian Lib. 1837, sub-librarian 1862–73 ; V. of Cowley, Oxon. 1842–44 ; V. of St. Paul's, Oxford 1844–71 ; author of *A catalogue of the collection of the Tanner MSS.* 1860. *d.* Thames Ditton, Surrey 18 Sep. 1874.

HADDAN, Rev. Arthur West (2 *son of Thomas Haddan, solicitor, d.* 1844 *aged* 63). *b.* Woodford, Essex 31 Aug. 1816 ; ed. at Brasn. coll. Ox. ; scholar of Trin. coll. 1835, fellow 1839, tutor 1842–57, Johnson theol. scholar 1839 ; B.A. 1837, M.A. 1840, B.D. 1847 ; C. of St. Mary the Virgin, Ox. 1841–42 ; contributed to *Guardian* 1846 to death ; one of secretaries to W. E. Gladstone's committee at Oxford elections 1847–65 ; R. of Barton on the Heath, Warws. 1857 to death ; hon. canon of Worcester 1870 to death ; author in conjunction with Dr. W. Stubbs of *Councils and ecclesiastical documents* 3 vols. 1869–71; for the Anglo-Catholic lib. he edited *The works of John Bramhall, Archbp. of Armagh* 5 vols. 1842–5 and *The Theological works of Herbert Thorndike* 6 vols. 1844–56. *d.* Barton 8 Feb. 1873. *Remains of Rev. A. W. Haddan, ed. by A. P. Forbes, Bp. of Brechin* (1876).

HADDAN, Thomas Henry *(brother of the preceding). b.* in city of London 1814 ; ed. at Brasenose coll. Ox. ; took a double first 1837, B.A. 1837, M.A. 1840, B.C.L. 1844 ; fellow of Ex. coll. 1837–43; Eldon scholar 1840 ; barrister I.T. 11 June 1841, equity draftsman and conveyancer ; Vinerian fellow Oxf. univ. 1847; *Guardian* newspaper projected in his chambers 6 New sq , first number issued 21 Jany. 1846, editor for a short time ; lectured on jurisdiction of court of chancery 1862 ; author of *Remarks on legal education* 1848. *d.* Vichy, France 5 Sept. 1873, body removed to Highgate cemet. *Law Times, lv* 384–5 (1873) *lvi,* 44.

HADDINGTON, Thomas Hamilton, 9 Earl of *(only son of 8 Earl of Haddington* 1753– 1828). *b.* Edinburgh 21 June 1780 ; ed. at Edin. univ. and Ch. Ch. Ox., B.A. 1801, M.A. 1815 ; known as Lord Binning 1780–1826 ; M.P. St. Germans 1802–6 ; M.P. Cockermouth Jany. to April 1807 ; M.P. Callington May 1807–1812 ; P.C. 29 July 1814 ; commissioner for management of affairs of India 1814–22; M.P. Michael 1814–18; M.P. for Rochester 1818–26; M.P. Yarmouth, June to Aug. 1826 ; cr. Baron Melros of Tynningham 24 July 1827 ; succeeded to earldom 17 March 1828 ; lord lieut. of Ireland 29 Dec. 1834 to 23 April 1835 ; received £30,674 1s. 8d. for surrender of office of keeper of Holyrood park 1843 ; first lord of the admiralty 8 Sep. 1841 to 13 Jany. 1846 ; lord privy seal 21 Jany. to 6 July 1846 ; K.T. 28 Oct. 1853. *d.* Tynningham house, Haddingtonshire 1 Dec. 1858. *Portraits of eminent conservatives and statesmen 2nd series* (1836–42), *portrait.*

HADFIELD, Charles *(son of Charles Hadfield). b.* Glossop, Derbyshire 14 Oct. 1821 ; house

HADFIELD, C. *(Con.)*

painter at Manchester ; edited *Weekly Wages* 1861 five numbers ; on staff of *Newcastle Chronicle* and lecturer for Northern Reform union 1861 ; editor of *Manchester City News* 1865–7, of *Warrington Examiner* and of *Salford Weekly News* 1880–3; author of two prize essays on Mechanics' institutions and The Homes of the working classes 1850, 1857. *d.* 3 Chester road, Stretford, Manchester 4 June 1884. *Manchester City News* 7, 14 *June* 1884.

HADFIELD, Elizabeth (2 *dau. of Peter Taylor of Hollingwood near Manchester).* A Friend ; author of *Sprays from the Hedgerows* 1850, *with portrait; Poetic weeds by E. H.* 1850. *(m.* George Hadfield), she *d.* Wetheral near Carlisle 23 March 1861 aged 43.

HADFIELD, George *(son of Robert Hadfield, merchant). b.* Sheffield 28 Dec. 1787; attorney at Manchester 1810–53; contested Bradford 1835 ; a founder of Anti-corn-law league 1841; principal promoter of the litigation as to Lady Hewley's charities 1833–42; M.P. for Sheffield 1852–74; helped in passing Common law procedure act 1854 ; author of the Qualification for offices abolition act 1866 ; author of *The expediency of relieving the bishops from attendance in parliament* 1870. *d.* Conyngham road, Victoria park, Manchester 21 April 1879, personalty sworn under £250,000, 28 June 1879. *James Griffin's Memories of the past* (1883) 264–311.

HADFIELD, Matthew Ellison (1 *son of Joseph Hadfield of Lees hall, Glossop, Derbyshire). b.* Lees hall 8 Sep. 1812 ; architect Sheffield 1838 to death ; contributed to revival of mediæval and Gothic architecture ; designed and built many churches etc. in Leeds and neighbourhood ; served 4 Dukes of Norfolk in succession ; F.R.I.B.A. May 1847 ; pres. of Sheffield sch. of art 1878–80. *d.* Knowle house, Sheffield 9 March 1885. *J. Gillow's English Catholics* (1887) *iii,* 79–82.

HADFIELD, William. *b.* 1806 ; first sec. of Buenos Ayres great southern railway ; sec. South American steam navigation co. ; merchant at Liverpool ; bankrupt 6 Nov. 1847 ; founded in London *The South American Journal and Brazil and River Plate Mail* 7 Nov. 1863, editor to death ; author of *Brazil, The River Plate and the Falkland islands* 1854. *d.* London 14 Aug. 1887.

HADLEY, Robert. *b.* England ; coach proprietor, and landlord of the English hotel 10 South st. St. Andrew st. Edinburgh 1844–51; a well known four-in-hand whip. *d.* Edinburgh 1851. *Crombie's Modern Athenians* (1882) 121, *portrait.*

HADLEY, SIMEON CHARLES. *b.* Cambridge, Gloucs. Nov. 1831; common councilman city of London 1861, alderman Castle Baynard ward 8 Nov. 1875, sheriff of London and Middlesex 1876, passed over for lord mayor 1883, resigned his alderman's gown 7 June 1884; miller of firm of J. and J. Hadley city flour mills Upper Thames st. London, the mills burnt down 10–12 Nov. 1872; bankrupt 1884, discharged 5 Dec. 1884; master of Bakers' co.; resided Cranbrook park, Ilford. *d.* at his lodgings, Kennington 15 May 1890. *I.L.N. lxix,* 485, 486 (1876), *portrait; Graphic xiv,* 451, 452 (1876), *portrait.*

HADOW, EDWARD ASH. *b.* 1831; ed. at Bristol sch. of medicine, and King's coll. London; M.B. London 1853; M.R.C.S. 1853; made researches on gun cotton and investigations into the constitution of the platinum bases; entirely devoted himself to chemistry; demonstrator of chemistry King's coll. London 1856 to death; editor of P. F. Hardwicke's *Manual of photography* 1864; F.C.S. *d.* London 11 Aug. 1866. *Lancet 25 Aug.* 1866 *p.* 224.

HADOW, ROBERT DOUGLAS (1 *son of Patrick Douglas Hadow of Sudbury priory, Middlesex, d.* 1876). *b.* 1846. *killed* by a fall of nearly 4,000 feet whilst descending the Matterhorn, Switzerland 14 July 1865. *bur.* north side of Zermatt churchyard. *E. Whymper's Ascent of the Matterhorn* (1880) 273–95.

HAGAN, SIR ROBERT (5 *son of John Hagan of Magherafelt, co. Londonderry). b.* Magherafelt 3 Nov. 1794; entered navy 22 Dec. 1807; served on coast of Spain 1813, on coast of Africa 1815–23 when he captured 40 slave ships; inspecting commander coast guard, Ireland 1838–43; captain 11 Jany. 1843; R.A. on half pay 22 Nov. 1862; knighted by Marquis of Normanby, in Ireland 1835. *d.* Pembroke road, Dublin 25 April 1863.

HAGART, CHARLES (*elder son of Thomas Campbell Hagart of Bantaskine, co. Stirling* 1784–1868). *b.* 23 June 1814; ed. at Eton.; cornet 7 hussars 15 June 1832, lieut. col. 31 Oct. 1851 to 13 May 1859 when placed on h.p.; C.B. 26 July 1858; commanded cavalry brigade in Indian mutiny 1857; colonel 11 hussars 19 Nov. 1871; colonel 7 hussars 19 Jany. 1873 to death; general 1 Oct. 1877. *d.* Eastbury manor, Compton near Guildford 30 July 1879.

HAGGARD, ELLA (1 *dau. of Bazett Doveton of Bombay C.S.). b.* Bombay 16 June 1819. (*m.*

HAGGARD, E. *(Con.)*
30 May 1844 William Meybohn Rider Haggard of Bradenham hall, Norfolk, *b.* 1817); author of *Myra, or the rose of the East* 1857; *Life and its author* 1890. *d.* Bradenham hall 9 Dec. 1889. *Life and its author* (1890), memoir, pp. 3–12, *portrait.*

HAGGARD, JOHN (3 *son of Wm. Henry Haggard of Bradenham hall, d.* 1837). *b.* Bradfield, Herts. 1794; ed. at Westminster and Trin. hall, Cam., LL.B. 1813, LL.D. 1818, fellow of his coll. 1815–20; fellow of college of doctors of law, London 3 Nov. 1818; chancellor of dioceses of Lincoln 1836 to death, of Winchester 1845 to death, and of Manchester 1847 to death; commissary for Surrey 1847 to death; author of *Reports of cases in Consistory court of London* 1789–1821, 2 vols. 1822; *Reports of cases in the court of Admiralty* 1822–1838, 3 vols. 1825–40; *Reports of cases in the Ecclesiastical courts* 1827–1833, 4 vols. 1829–33. *d.* Brighton 31 Oct. 1856 in 63 year. *Manchester Guardian 4 Nov.* 1856, *p.* 3.

HAGGARD, WILLIAM DEBONAIRE. Member British Archæol. Assoc. 1843, member of council 1848; F.S.A.; mem. R. Astronom. and Numismatic societies; author of *Observations on the standard of value* 1847; *Miscellaneous Papers* 1860. *d.* Durham villa, Kensington 4 April 1886 aged 79.

HAGHE, LOUIS R. I. *b.* Tournay, Belgium 17 March 1806; came to England 1824; partner with William Day in producing lithographic works, among them were David Roberts' Holy Land and Egypt 1842–8; member of New Soc. of Painters in water colours 1835, president 1873–84; exhibited 8 oil paintings at British Institution 1856–60; painted The council of war at Courtray 1854; published *Sketches in Belgium and Germany* 3 series 1840. *d.* 103 Stockwell road, Stockwell, London 9 March 1885. *Stationery trades journal, vi,* 144 (1885); *I.L.N. lxxxvi,* 327 (1885), *portrait.*

HAIG, ROBERT WOLSELEY. *b.* 1831; 2 lieut. R.A. 19 Dec. 1848, captain 9 May 1855 to death; brevet major 22 Oct. 1870; sec. to R.A. institute on Woolwich common; F.R.S. 6 June 1867. *d.* Woolwich 6 June 1872 aged 41.

HAIGH, REV. DANIEL HENRY (*son of George Haigh, calico printer). b.* Brinscall hall near Chorley 7 Aug. 1819; built great part of All Saints, Leeds at his own expense 1846; received into R.C. church 1 Jany. 1847, a priest 8 April 1848; spent £15,000 on erection and endowment St. Augustine's R.C. ch.

HAIGH, REV. D. H. (Con.)

Erdington near Birmingham 1848–50, missioner there to 1876; chief authority in England on Runic literature; author of *An essay on numismatic history of the East Angles.*, Leeds 1845; *The Anglo-Saxon sagas* 1861; *The conquest of Britain by the Saxons* 1861. *d.* Oscott coll. 10 May 1879. *Gillow's Bibl. Dict. of English Catholics iii*, 84–7 (1887).

HAILSTONE, EDWARD (*youngest son of Samuel Hailstone of Bradford, solicitor*). *b.* 1818; solicitor at Bradford 1841; law clerk to Leeds and Liverpool canal co. 40 years; F.S.A. 6 April 1843; accumulated manuscripts, books, &c. relating to Yorkshire which he left to the library of dean and chapter, York; author of *Catalogue of library of E. Hailstone* 1858; *Portraits of Yorkshire worthies with biographical notices* 2 vols. 1869. *d.* Walton hall near Wakefield 24 March 1890.

HAILSTONE, SAMUEL. *b.* Hoxton, London 1768; solicitor with John Hardy at Bradford, Yorks. 1791; leading authority on flora of Yorkshire; collected minerals and books; contrib. list of rare plants to Whitaker's History of Craven 1812, pp. 509–18; F.L.S. 1801. *d.* Horton hall, Bradford 26 Dec. 1851, his herbarium given to Yorkshire Philos. soc. is in the museum at York. *John James's Bradford* (1866) 316–18.

HAINES, REV. HERBERT (*son of John Haines, surgeon*). *b.* Hampstead 1 Sept. 1826; ed. at Ex. coll. Ox., B.A. 1849, M.A. 1851; C. of Delamere, Cheshire 1849; second master of College school, Gloucester 22 June 1850 to death; author of *A manual for the study of monumental brasses, By H. H.* 1848, 2 ed. 2 vols. 1861; *A guide to the cathedral church of Gloucester* 1867, 3 ed. 1885. *d.* College school, Gloucester 18 Sept. 1872.

HAINES, WILLIAM CLARKE. *b.* England 1807; a surgeon; a farmer near Geelong, Victoria 1848; member for South Grant in Victoria legislative council 1853, chief sec. 28 Nov. 1855 to 11 March 1857 and 29 April 1857 to 10 March 1858; spent 3 years in Europe 1858–61; member for Portland 1861 to death; treasurer of Victoria 14 Nov. 1861 to 27 June 1863. *d.* 1864.

HAINSSELIN, D. F. Sailor in British navy; supposed to be last survivor of Keppel's action 1778; also at celebrated relief of Gibraltar 1782; in the action with the French fleet off Plymouth in the Royal George 29 May and 1 June 1794, for which he had medal with two bars. *d.* Chapel st. Devonport 3 Sep. 1852 aged 92.

HAIRE, ROBERT. Called to Irish bar 1793; K.C. 7 Feb. 1835; resided at Armagh, co. Fermanagh. *d.* 3 March 1851.

HAITE, JOHN JAMES. Member of Soc. of British musicians; author of *The principles of natural harmony, founded upon the discovery of the true semitonic scale* 1855; *Violoncello tutor;* composer of many musical pieces including Favourite melodies as quintets 1865, Abraham's sacrifice a cantata 1871, David and Goliath an oratorio 1880, The song of the year. *d.* London, Oct. 1874.

HAKEWILL, ARTHUR WILLIAM (1 *son of James Hakewill* 1778–1843, *architect*). *b.* 1808; member Architectural soc.; architect, writer and lecturer; lectured on James Barry's painting at Soc. of Arts; author of *An apology for architectural monstrosities of London* 1835; *Plans of Thorpe - hall, Peterborough* 1851; *Modern tombs, or gleanings from the cemeteries of London* 1851. *d.* 19 June 1856.

HAKEWILL, EDWARD CHARLES (*youngest son of Henry Hakewill* 1771–1830, *architect*). *b.* 1812; designed churches at Stonham Aspall and Grundisburgh, Suffolk, South Hackney and St. James' Clapton; metropolitan district surveyor to 1867; M.R.I.B.A.; author of *The Temple, an essay on the Ark, the Tabernacle and the Temple of Jerusalem* 1851. *d.* Playford, Suffolk 9 Oct. 1872. *Builder 2 Nov.* 1872 *p.* 860.

HAKEWILL, JOHN HENRY (*brother of the preceding*). *b.* 1811; architect of Stowlangtofft hall, Suffolk, the hospital at Bury St. Edmunds, Erchfont ch. Wilts., and churches at Yarmouth; F.R.I.B.A. 1854; an originator of Architects' Benevolent Fund. *d.* 77 Inverness ter. Bayswater, London 30 Aug. 1880. *Builder 11 Sept.* 1880, *p.* 315.

HALCOMB, JOHN (*son of John Halcomb of Marlborough, coach proprietor*). *b.* 1790; barrister I.T. 13 June 1823; serjeant at law 19 Feb. 1840; contested Dover 1826, 1828, 1830, 1832 and 1841; M.P. for Dover 1833–35; contested Warwick 1835; author of *A report of the trials in the causes of Rowe versus Grenfell, &c.* 1826; *A practical measure of relief from the present system of the poor laws* 1826; *A practical treatise on passing private bills through both houses of parliament* 1836, 2 ed. 1838. *d.* New Radnor 3 Nov. 1852.

HALDANE, DANIEL RUTHERFORD (*son of James Alexander Haldane of Airthrey, co. Stirling*). *b.* 1824; ed. at Edin. univ., M.D. 1848, LL.D. 1884; F.R.C.P. Edin. 1852, afterwards sec. and president; F.R.S. Edin. 1867; lecturer

on medical jurisprudence Surgeons' hall, Edin.
then teacher of medicine; physician royal
infirmary, Edin. *d.* at 22 Charlotte sq. Edin.
12 April 1887 from effect of breaking his leg
25 Dec. 1886. *Scotsman 13 April 1887 p.* 6.

HALDANE, Rev. James Alexander *(youngest
son of Capt. James Haldane of Airthrey house,
co. Stirling, d. 30 June 1768). b.* Dundee 14
July 1768; ed. at Edin. univ. 1781–5; of
H.E.I.C. naval service 1785–94; established
soc. for propogating the Gospel at home 1797;
minister of Leith walk congregational ch.
Edin. 1799 to death; embraced Baptist senti-
ments 1808; took part in many religious controversies 1811–47; an itinerant preacher and
tract distributor in Scotland 1797 to death;
author of *A view of the social worship of the
first Christians* 1805, 2 ed. 1806; *The doctrine
of the Atonement* 1847, 5 ed. 1877, and 11
other books. *d.* Edinburgh 8 Feb. 1851. *A.
Haldane's Memoirs of R. and J. A. Haldane*
(1855), *portrait.*

HALDANE, Rev. Robert *(son of a farmer). b.*
Overtown, Lecropt, Perthshire 1772; ed. at
Glasgow univ.; presbyterian minister Drum-
melzier, Peebles 1807–9; professor of mathematics St. Andrews univ. 1807–20; minister
of St. Andrews parish, principal of St. Mary's
coll. and primarius professor of divinity 1820
to death; moderator of general assembly
1827 and chairman at the disruption in 1843;
F.R.S. Edin. *d.* St. Mary's coll. St. Andrews
9 March 1854.

HALDIMAND, William *(son of Anthony Francis Haldimand 1741–1817, merchant). b.* London 9 Sep. 1784; in business with his father;
director of bank of England 1809; M.P.
Ipswich 1820–26; settled at Denanton near
Lausanne 1828; erected hospital at Aix-les-
Bains 1829; gave £24,000 for a blind asylum
at Lausanne. *d.* Denanton 20 Sep. 1862. *W.
de la Rive's Vie de Haldimand.*

HALDON, Sir Laurence Palk, 1 Baron *(1
son of Sir Laurence Vaughan Palk, 3 baronet, d.
1860). b.* London 5 Jany. 1818; ed. at Eton;
M.P. South Devon 1854–68 and East Devon
1868–80; hon. col. 1 Devon A.V. 10 July
1868 to death; commodore Torquay yacht
club, built a harbour at Torquay; cr. baron
Haldon of Haldon, Devon 29 April 1880. *d.*
Haldon house near Exeter 23 March 1883.
Baily's Mag. xxxii, 187 (1878), *portrait.*

HALE, Charles B. *b.* Ballington, Essex 23
June 1819; made first appearance at Hereford
as Thessalus in *Alexander the Great* 8 Jany.

1837; first appeared in London at Olympic
theatre as Filch in *Beggars' Opera* 5 Oct. 1849;
first appeared at Broadway theatre, New York
7 May 1852 as Sam Warren in the *Poor
Relation;* a member of John Brougham's
theatre, New York 1868–9, played character
parts and old men. *d.* Morrisania, New York
11 Feb. 1876. *Appleton's Annual Cyclop. for
1876 p.* 618.

HALE, Charlotte France. *b.* London 8 Aug.
1830; first appeared at Surrey theatre as
Dick in *Oliver Twist* June 1838; made her
debut in New York at Astor place opera
house as Margaret Overreach in a *New Way
to pay Old Debts* 8 May 1852; played in Philadelphia, Baltimore, New Orleans and Montreal. *(m.* Charles B. Hale *d.* 1876), she *d.*
Cincinnati 6 Dec. 1865.

HALE, Joseph. Ensign Bombay army 4 Jany.
1821; lieut. col. 23 Bombay light infantry
1857–58; col. of 22 Bombay N.I. 1858–60, of
1 European regiment 1860–62, of 103 foot 30
Sep. 1862 to death; commanded Poona division 1860–62; L.G. 23 Feb. 1869. *d.* 11
Royal crescent, Bath 13 Feb. 1873.

HALE, Robert Blagden *(son of Robert Hale
Blagden Hale of Alderley, Gloucestershire, d.
1855). b.* 1807; ed. at C. C. coll. Ox.,
B.A. 1829; student of Lincoln's inn 1830;
M.P. for West Gloucs. 1836–57; sheriff of
Gloucester 1870. *d.* Alderley 22 July 1883.

HALE, Rev. Thomas Jacob John *(son of
Thomas Hale of Batheaston, Somerset). b.* 1789;
ed. at Queen's coll. Ox., B.A. 1812, M.A. 1815,
B. and D.D. 1826; successively chaplain at
Versailles, St. Germain-en-Laye and at the
British embassy in Paris 17 June 1851 to
death. *d.* Paris 25 April 1857.

HALE, Warren Stormes *(youngest son of
Edward Hale of Herts.) b.* 2 Feb. 1791; apprentice to his bro. Ford Hale, wax chandler,
London 1804; candle manufacturer 21 Cat-
eaton st. and Queen st. London, the first to
utilise animal and vegetable fatty acids in
England; member of common council city of
London 1826, deputy of Coleman st. ward
1850, alderman 1856, sheriff 1858–9, lord
mayor 1864–5; a founder of City of London
sch. 1837, chairman of the committee to death,
Warren Stormes Hale scholarship founded
1865; master of Co. of Tallow chandlers 1849,
1851. *d.* West Heath, Hampstead 23 Aug.
1872. *City Press* 24, 31 *Aug.,* 12 *Oct.* 1872;
I.L.N. xlv, 469 (1864), *portrait; Lord Mayor's
song for 9 Nov.* [on *W. S. Hales*] 1864.

HALE, VEN. WILLIAM HALE (*son of John Hale, surgeon, Lynn, Norfolk, d.* 1799). *b.* 12 Sep. 1795; ed. at Charterhouse sch. and Oriel coll. Ox., B.A. 1817, M.A. 1820; C. of St. Benet, Gracechurch st. London 1818; preacher at the Charterhouse 1823–42, master Feb. 1842 to death; domestic chaplain to Dr. C. J. Blomfield bishop of Chester and London 1824–8; prebendary of St. Paul's 1829–46, canon 1840 to death; archdeacon of St. Albans 1839–40, of Middlesex 1840–42 and of London 4 Nov. 1842 to death; R. of St. Giles, Cripplegate 1847–57; hon. curator of Lambeth palace library March 1869; arranged the records and documents at St. Paul's cath.; author of *A series of precedents illustrative of discipline of Church of England* 1847; *Some account of the history of the hospital of King James, founded by Thomas Sutton* 1854, anon.; *Some account of Christ's hospital* 1855 and edited 3 works for the Camden Soc. 1858–74. *d.* Master's lodge, Charterhouse 27 Nov. 1870. *bur.* in the nave of St. Paul's cath. 3 Dec. *The Church of England photographic portrait gallery* 1859, *portrait* 41.

HALES, MARY BARBARA FELICITAS (*dau. of Sir Edward Hales d. before* 1841). *b.* 1836; a ward in chancery; took the veil 1861 but obtaining a dispensation from Pius ix for her vows of poverty and obedience, returned to Hales place near Canterbury; commenced erecting a nunnery at Hales place, her trustees interfered, a lawsuit ensued, Hales place passed to the Jesuits who made the mansion into a college; a witness in the Tichborne case 1872. *d.* Sarre court, Kent 18 April 1885. *Times 24 April 1885 p.* 11.

HALES, ROBERT (*son of Mr. Hales of West Somerton near Yarmouth, farmer who was 6 feet 6 inches high, weighing 14 stone*). *b.* Somerton 2 May 1814; worked on board a Norfolk wherry and was then in the navy; known as the Norfolk giant, stood 7 feet 6 inches high and weighed 452 lbs.; exhibited in the U.S. of America 14 Dec. 1848 to Dec. 1850; landlord of Craven Head tavern, Drury Lane, London, Jany. 1851, became insolvent 22 Sep. 1855; introduced to the Queen at Buckingham palace 11 April 1851; spent some time in France; kept the Burgoyne arms, Langsett road, Sheffield 1861. *d.* Marine passage, Yarmouth 22 Nov. 1863. *bur.* West Somerton. *Wood's Giants and Dwarfs* (1868) 208; *I.L.N. xix,* 44 (1851), *portrait; Yarmouth Chronicle 28 Nov. 1863 p.* 8.

NOTE.—His sister Mary 7 feet 2 inches high and weighing 224 lbs., exhibited herself with her brother at New Bartholomew fair in Britannia Fields 1848. She *d.* in Guernsey.

HALFORD, FREDERIC WILLIAM. Secretary to the Reform club, Pall Mall, London 8 Aug. 1862 to 30 June 1887; author of *The Angel, an idyll* 1870. *d.* Hastings 6 May 1888 in 59 year.

HALFORD, SIR HENRY, 2 Baronet (*only son of Sir Henry Vaughan,* 1 *baronet* 1766–1844, *who assumed surname of Halford* 1809). *b.* London 22 April 1797; ed. at Westminster and Ch. Ch. Ox.; ensign 43 foot 5 March 1818; lieut. 33 foot 1821 to 8 Aug. 1822 when placed on h.p.; M.P. South Leicestershire, Dec. 1832 to 20 March 1857; attempted to ameliorate condition of framework knitters; made researches into *History of French revolution,* a work unpublished at his death. *d.* Wiston hall, Newton Harcourt, Leicestershire 22 May 1868. *I.L.N. lii,* 570 (1868); *Journal of British Archæol. Assoc. xxv,* 315 (1869).

HALIBURTON, JAMES (*son of James Haliburton who changed his name to Burton*). *b.* 22 Sep. 1788; ed. at Trin. coll. Cam., B.A. 1810, M.A. 1815; made geological survey in Egypt 1822; with John Gardner Wilkinson in Egypt 1824, with Edward W. Lane in 1826 and again in Egypt 1830–5; resumed name of Haliburton 1838; F.G.S. to 1841; author of *Excerpta Hieroglyphica,* 6 *lithograph plates, Cairo* 1825–9; *Collectanea Ægyptiaca* 63 *volumes MSS.* in Br. Museum. *d.* 10 Hamilton place, Newington, Edinburgh 22 Feb. 1862.

HALIBURTON, THOMAS CHANDLER (*only child of Wm. Otis Haliburton, justice of court of common pleas, Nova Scotia*). *b.* Windsor, Nova Scotia, Dec. 1796; ed. at gr. sch. and King's coll. Windsor; chief justice of court of common pleas, N.S. 1828–40, judge of supreme court 1 Jany. 1842 to Feb. 1856; M.P. for Launceston, England 29 April 1859 to 6 July 1865; author of *An historical account of Nova Scotia* 2 *vols.* 1829; *The Clockmaker, or sayings of Sam Slick* 3 *series* 1837, 1838, 1840; *The attaché, or Sam Slick in England* 4 *vols.* 1843–4 and 13 other books. *d.* Gordon house, Isleworth, Middlesex 27 Aug. 1865. *Bentley's Miscellany, xiv,* 81–94 (1843), *portrait; J. Grant's Public Characters, i,* 291–304 (1841); *Morgan's Bibliotheca Canadensis* (1867) 166–71; *The Critic, xviii,* 126 (1859), *portrait.*

HALIDAY, ALEXANDER HENRY. *b.* 21 Nov. 1806; ed. at Trin. coll. Dublin, gold medallist 1827; sheriff of Antrim 1843; edited with others *The natural history review* 7 vols. 1854–60; author of *Hymenoptera Britannica Oxyura* 1839; author with G. Busk of *Reports on Zoology* 1847. *d.* Villa Pisani near Lucca 13 July 1870. *I.L.N. lvii,* 155 (1870).

HALIDAY, Charles *(son of William Haliday of Dublin, apothecary).* b. 1789; a merchant in the bark trade Dublin 1813; member of Royal Irish academy Jany. 1847; director of bank of Ireland; consul for Greece; sec. of Chamber of commerce, Dublin; formed a considerable library; author of *An inquiry into the use of liquors in producing crime* 1830 and papers on the history of the port and commerce of Dublin 1854–73. d. Monkstown park near Dublin 14 Sep. 1866. *The Scandinavian kingdom of Dublin, by C. Haliday (1884) with memoir by J. P. Prendergast, pp. iii-cxxiii.*

HALIDAY, William Robert. b. 1809; ensign 75 foot 12 Feb. 1830; major 36 foot 1849 to 24 June 1862 when placed on h.p.; commandant and inspector general school of musketry at Hythe 16 Oct. 1867 to 1 Jany. 1873; L.G. 1 Oct. 1877. d. Hanover chambers, 23 Hanover sq. London 12 Feb. 1878.

HALIFAX, Charles Wood, 1 Viscount *(1 son of Sir Francis Lindley Wood 1771–1846, 2 baronet).* b. Pontefract 20 Dec. 1800; ed. at Eton and Oriel coll. Ox., B.A. 1821, M.A. 1824; student of Lincoln's inn 1822; M.P. Great Grimsby 1826–31, M.P. Wareham 1831, M.P. Halifax 1832–65, M.P. Ripon 1865–6; sec. to the treasury 1832–4, sec. to admiralty 1835–9; chancellor of exchequer 1846–52; P.C. 6 July 1846; president of board of control 1852–5; first lord of admiralty 1855–8; G.C.B. 19 June 1856; sec. of state India and president of council 1859–66; lord privy seal 1870–4; cr. Viscount Halifax of Monk Bretton, co. York 25 Feb. 1866; many of his speeches were printed 1839–53. d. Hickleton near Doncaster 8 Aug. 1885. *The British Cabinet in 1853 pp. 334–46; I.L.N. xviii, 129 (1851) portrait, lxxxvii, 181 (1885) portrait.*

HALKETT, Sir Alexander *(5 son of Sir John Wedderburn Halket 1720–93, 4 baronet).* b. 1773; 2 lieut. 23 foot 31 March 1790; lieut. col. of 93 foot 25 Aug. 1800, of 104 foot 3 May 1810 to 27 Oct. 1814; served in West Indies 1794–96, at Cape of Good Hope 1804; knighted by William iv. at St. James's palace 8 March 1837; K.C.H. 8 March 1837; general 23 Nov. 1841. d. Edinburgh 24 Aug. 1851.

HALKETT, Sir Colin *(1 son of major general Frederick Godar Halkett 1728–1803).* b. Venloo, Netherlands 7 Sep. 1774; ensign and lieut. Dutch foot guards 2 March 1792 to 27 April 1795; ensign 3 foot 3 Jany. 1799 to Feb. 1800; capt. 2 Dutch light infantry in British pay Feb. 1800 to 1802; lieut. col. commandant 2 bat. King's German legion 1803–12; served in the Peninsula and commanded a brigade at

HALKETT, Sir C. *(Con.)*

Waterloo; lieut. governor of Jersey 23 July 1821 to 7 Aug. 1830; commander in chief at Bombay 1831–2; col. of 95 foot 1823, of 71 foot 1829, of 31 foot 1838, and of 45 foot 1847 to death; lieut. governor Chelsea hospital 1848, governor 1849 to death; K.C.B. 2 Jany. 1815, G.C.B. 30 Dec. 1847; G.C.H. 1820; general 9 Nov. 1846. d. Chelsea hospital 24 Sep. 1856.

HALKETT, Sir Hugh *(brother of preceding).* b. Musselburgh near Edinburgh 30 Aug. 1783; ensign in Scotch brigade in Holland 1794; went to India as lieut. 1798, remained till 1801; major King's German legion 1805 with which he served in the Peninsula 1809–12; lieut. col. 22 Sep. 1812 to 24 May 1816, commanded first Hanoverian brigade in North Germany 1813–14; commanded 3 and 4 Hanoverian landwehr at Waterloo, when he took general Pierre J. E. Cambronne prisoner; served in the Hanoverian service 1817 to 1858 when he was made baron Von Halkett and voted his full pay as a pension 18 June 1858; C.B. 4 June 1815; G.C.H. 1851. d. Hanover 26 July 1863. *Leben des Freiherrn Hugh von Halkett, Stuttgart (1865).*

HALKETT, John. b. London 1768; governor of the Bahamas 5 Dec. 1801, of Tobago 27 Oct. 1803 to 1805; chairman of board of comrs. of West India accounts 1814–19; author of *Historical notes respecting the Indians of North America* 1823. d. Brighton, Nov. 1852.

HALKETT, John Craigie *(2 son of John Cornelius Craigie Halkett of Hall Hill, d. 1812).* Entered Bengal army; defended the fort of Khelat-i-Ghilzie in Afghanistan; lieut. col. 20 Bengal N.I. to 1861; retired M.G. 31 Dec. 1861; C.B. 24 Dec. 1842; served 35 years in India and fought in more than 100 battles. d. 59 Melville st. Edinburgh 5 Jany. 1870.

HALKETT, Samuel *(son of a brewer).* b. North Back of Canongate, Edinburgh 1814; ed. at Smith's Classical sch.; in business with Mr. Harrison 10 years; knew many of the European and Asiatic languages; keeper of library of Faculty of Advocates 1848 to death; commenced printing a catalogue 1860; made a Report on the Library, printed 1868; collected materials 1852–71 for a dictionary of anonymous English works published as *A dictionary of the anonymous and pseudonymous literature of Great Britain, By the late Samuel Halkett and the late Rev. John Laing,* 4 vols. *Edinburgh* 1882–8. d. 35 East Claremont st. Edin. 20 April 1871. *Edin. Evening Courant 21 April 1871 p. 8.*

HALL, Anna Maria *(dau. of Mr. Fielding). b.* Anne st. Dublin 6 Jany. 1800; edited *Juvenile Forget me not 1826–34, Sharpe's London Mag.* 1852–3, *St. James's Mag.* 1862–3; produced 3 dramas The French refugee 1836, The Groves of Blarney 1838 and Mabel's curse; granted civil list pension of £100, 10 Dec. 1868. *(m.* 20 Sep. 1824 Samuel Carter Hall 1800–89); author of *Sketches of Irish character* 3 vols. 1829; *Lights and shadows of Irish life* 3 vols. 1838; *Pilgrimages to English shrines* 1850; *A woman's story* 3 vols. 1857; *The Fight of Faith* 2 vols. 1869 and about 40 other works; with her husband wrote *Ireland, its scenery, characters, &c.* 3 vols. 1841–3 and other works. *d.* Devon lodge, East Moulsey, Surrey 30 Jany. 1881. *S. C. Hall's Retrospect of a long life,* ii, 251–2, 421–78 (1883), *portrait; Maclise Portrait gallery* (1883) 366–72, *portrait; Biograph, Jany.* 1882 *pp.* 104–14; *Illust. news of the world, viii* (1861), *portrait.*

HALL, Chambers. *b.* 1786; collector of drawings, bronzes, etc.; gave to Br. Museum 66 drawings by Thomas Girtin 1855 and to Univ. of Oxford drawings by Raphael, sketches by Hogarth, bronzes, &c. 1855; author of *The picture: a nosegay for amateurs...and all the craft, By C. H.* 1837. *d.* 16 Bury st. St. James', London 29 Aug. 1855.

HALL, Sir Charles (4 *son of John Hall of Manchester, merchant). b.* Manchester 14 April 1814; pupil of Lewis Duval the conveyancer, to whose practice he succeeded 1844; barrister M.T. 23 Nov. 1838, bencher 15 Jany. 1872; counsel in Bridgewater peerage case 1853, Shrewsbury peerage case 1857 and Allgood *v.* Blake 1872; said to have made £10,000 a year at the chancery bar, of which he was the head 1871–3; one of conveyancing counsel to court of chancery 1864 to Nov. 1873, vice chancellor 11 Nov. 1873; knighted at Windsor castle 12 Dec. 1873; a judge of high court of justice Nov. 1875, resigned 12 Sep. 1882. *d.* 8 Bayswater hill, London 12 Dec. 1883. *I.L.N. lxiii,* 485 (1873), *portrait.*

HALL, Charles Radclyffe. *b.* Congleton, Cheshire 1819; M.R.C.S. Eng. 1845; F.R.C.P. Edin. 1848; F.R.C.P. Lond. 1859; medical officer Manchester royal infirmary; physician Clifton; physician Bristol general hospital 1849, removed to Torquay 1850; consulting physician Torquay hospital for consumption 1851; president British Medical assoc. 1853 and 1860; physician Erith house institution, Torquay 1855, consulting physician 1864; author of *Torquay in its medical aspect* 1857; *Modern medicine, its aims and tendencies, Torquay* 1860 and of many papers in medical

HALL, C. R. *(Con.)* journals. *d.* Derwent house, Torquay 21 March 1879. *T. H. Barker's Photographs of Medical men* (1865) 133–37, *portrait.*

HALL, Collinson *(son of Collinson Hall, adapter of percussion cap to flint gun* 1818). *b.* 1800; farmer at Havering Atte Bower, Essex, 500 acres; a practical and experimental farmer using expensive manures; the first to use a steam threshing machine; a lecturer on farming; removed to Prince's gate farm, Navestock, Essex 1850; took out 11 patents for steam ploughs; one of the first to send country milk to London; erected a steam flour mill 1852; made a self propelling ploughing engine 1853. *d.* Dytchleys near Brentford at the residence of his son, April 1880. *Illust. Sporting and Dramatic News 17 April* 1880 *pp.* 101–2, *portrait.*

HALL, Edward Pickard *(son of John Vine Hall* 1774–1860). *b.* Worcester 4 June 1808; associated with his father in conducting *Maidstone Journal and Kentish Advertiser;* organist and choirmaster East Farleigh; a partner in the Oxford press 1853–84; a founder of Oxford Churchmen's Union; M.A. of Oxford univ. 6 March 1877; author of *The Oxford index to the authorised version of the Bible* 1877. *d.* Oxford 6 Nov. 1886. *The Bookseller 8 Jany.* 1887 *p.* 7.

HALL, Francis. *b.* Taunton 1785; went to U.S. of A. 1799; apprenticed to a printer; entered office of New York *Commercial Advertiser* 1811, part owner and co-editor 1813 to death; recording sec. of Methodist Missionary soc. 30 years; organized with others the first "pewed" Methodist church in New York about 1833; LL.D. Wesleyan Univ. 1854. *d.* New York 11 Aug. 1866.

HALL, Rev. Francis Russell *(son of Rev. Samuel Hall, Inc. of St. Peter's, Manchester, d.* 1814). *b.* Manchester 17 May 1788; ed. at St. John's coll. Cam., 10 wr. 1810, B.A. 1810, M.A. 1813, B.D. 1820, D.D. 1839; fellow of his coll. 1807–26; R. of St. Vigor's, Fulbourn, Cam. 20 Oct. 1826 to death; author of *Reasons for not contributing to circulate the Apocrypha* 1825; *Regeneration and baptism considered* 1832; *Hints to young clergymen* 1843. *d.* Fulbourn rectory 18 Nov. 1866.

HALL, Frederic Thomas. Solicitor at 15 Gray's inn square, London 1858 to death; author of *The Gospels consolidated with a copious index, by F. T. H.* 1869; *Alphabetical Harmony of the Gospels, by F. T. H.* 1877; *The pedigree of the devil* 1883. *d.* Wraysbury, Bucks. 15 July 1885 in 50 year.

HALL, Gage John. Ensign 105 foot 29 May 1783; lieut. col. 7 West India foot 3 Sep. 1807 to 4 June 1813; prisoner in France 1805–14; commanded the forces at Mauritius 1817–19; col. of 99 foot 25 March 1824, of 70 foot 30 Jany. 1832 to death; general 23 Nov. 1841. d. Elmfield house, Exeter 18 April 1854.

HALL, Harry. b. Cambridge; exhibited 10 paintings at R.A., 17 at B.I. and 26 at Suffolk st. 1838–75; painted winners of the Derby 43 consecutive years. d. High st. Newmarket 22 April 1882 in 68 year. *Graphic, xxv,* 528 (1882), *portrait.*

HALL, Henry. b. Dublin 4 June 1804; first appeared in London at Strand theatre 17 May 1836 as Iago in Dowling's burletta *Othello! (according to act of parliament)*, in which he made a great hit, he studied the part consisting of 20 lengths and as many pieces of music in 5 hours, this has been often cited as the most rapid act of study on record; played Old Weller in Moncrieff's drama *Sam Weller or the Pickwickians*, July 1837; manager of Strand theatre 1841–5; made his debut in America at Burton's theatre, New York 1854; stage manager of Laura Keene's theatre, New York. d. Cincinnati, Ohio 5 July 1858. *Tallis's Drawing room table book, part 7, portrait.*

HALL, Henry (4 son of Ven. Francis Hall, *archdeacon of Kilmacduagh*). b. 11 Sep. 1789; entered Bengal army 1804; raised a corps among a wild race of Imhairs in West of India whom he civilized by inducing them to abandon their habits of murder and infanticide; col. of 21 Bengal N.I. 21 Dec. 1844 to 1869; general 23 July 1866; C.B. 20 July 1838. d. Knockbrach lodge, Athenry, co. Galway 22 Aug. 1875.

HALL, Henry Bryan. b. London 11 March 1808; engraved all the portrait work in large works of the historical engraver to the Queen many years; went to New York 1850; illustrated many artistic and literary publications; engraved 12 portraits of Washington after different artists; in business with his 3 sons as engravers latterly. d. Morrisania, New York 28 April 1884.

HALL, Herbert Byng. Ensign 39 foot 10 Dec. 1824; captain 7 foot 1832; captain 62 foot 1833 to 20 Sep. 1833 when he sold out; attaché to staff of commander in chief of army of Queen of Spain some time; extra foreign service messenger on Constantinople station 4 Jany. 1855 to 30 Sep. 1858; foreign service

HALL, H. B. *(Con.)* messenger 24 Jany. 1859, retired on a pension 1 July 1882; author of *Spain and the seat of war in Spain* 1837; *Scenes at home and abroad* 1839; *The Queen's Messenger* 1865; *The adventures of a bric-a-brac hunter* 1868 and 13 other books. d. Glen Rock, Weston, Bath 25 April 1883 aged 78.

HALL, James *(youngest son of Sir James Hall, 4 baronet 1761–1832).* b. about 1800; exhibited 8 pictures at R.A. and 7 at B.I. 1835–54; painted portraits of Duke of Wellington 1838 and of Sir Walter Scott whose MS. of 'Waverley' he gave to Advocates' library at Edinburgh; F.G.S.; contested Taunton 1841 and 1842; author of some speculative letters on Binocular Perspective in the *Art Journal*, March pp. 89–90, and August pp. 245–6, 1852. d. Ashestiel, co. Selkirk 26 Oct. 1854.

HALL, James *(son of Samuel Hall, attorney).* b. Beverley, Yorkshire 1801; a well known sheep breeder; master of Holderness fox hounds 1847 to death; presented with his portrait and a silver dinner service at Beverley 1857. d. Scorbrough, E.R. Yorks. 19 July 1877. *F. Ross' Celebrities of Yorkshire worlds* (1878) 70–71.

HALL, Sir John (1 son of Rev. John Hall of *Stannington, Yorkshire).* b. Stannington 1779; consul and agent for maritime seignory of Papenburgh in East Friesland 1807; consul general for Hanover in the United Kingdom 1816–54; sheriff of Essex 1817; sec. to St. Katherine's Dock company 1824–53; K.C.H. 1831; knighted at St. James's palace 23 March 1831; author of *Plain statement of facts connected with St. Katharine's dock* 1824; *Letter on obstructions of river Thames* 1827. d. 6 Lansdowne crescent, Kensington park, London 21 Jany. 1861.

HALL, Sir John *(son of John Hall of Little Beck, Westmoreland).* b. Little Beck 1795; hospital assistant in army 24 June 1815; inspector general 28 March 1854 to 1 Jany. 1857 when placed on h.p.; served the campaigns of Flanders 1815, Kaffraria 1847 and 1851; principal medical officer throughout Crimean campaign 1854–56; M.D. St. Andrews 1845; K.C.B. 5 Feb. 1856; author of *Observations on the report of the sanitary commissioners in the Crimea* 1855 and 1856, 1857. d. Pisa, Italy 17 Jany. 1866. *Proc. of Med. and Chir. Soc. v,* 149, 165 (1867).

HALL, John *(son of John Hall of Weston Colville, Cambs., who d. 25 Aug. 1860 aged 93).* b. 1799; cornet 1 life guards 4 Sep. 1817,

HALL, J. *(Con.)*

lieut. col. 9 Nov. 1846 to 20 June 1854; col. 19 hussars 10 Feb. 1865 to death; general 10 Oct. 1870; M.P. for Buckingham 1845–57. *d.* 5 May 1872 in 74 year.

HALL, REV. JOHN. *b.* Preston 1796; ed. at Ushaw coll.; R.C. priest St. Michael's chapel, Macclesfield 17 April 1821 to 1841; erected St. Alban ch. Macclesfield from design by Pugin 1839–41; designed and erected St. Mary chapel, Congleton 1825–6; erected St. Gregory chapel, Bollington 1834; cr. D.D. by Pius ix. 1852; V.G. to bishop of Shrewsbury and provost of cathedral chapter to death. *d.* Macclesfield 1 Oct. 1876. *Gillow's English Catholics, iii,* 90–92 (1887).

HALL, JOHN EDWARD *(eld. son of Edward Hall of Acton, Middlesex).* *b.* 1837; ed. at Queen's coll. Ox., B.A. 1861, M.A. 1862; barrister L.I. 11 June 1862; reporter for the *Weekly Reporter;* reported in the Court of Appeal for the *Law Reports* 1875–84; a revising barrister 1880 to death; author of *Treatise on the law relating to profits à prendre and rights of common* 1871. *d.* 40 St. James's sq. Notting hill, London 11 Aug. 1886.

HALL, JOHN VINE. *b.* Diss, Norfolk 14 March 1774; a bookseller at Worcester 1804–1814; a stationer at Maidstone 1814–50; proprietor of the *Maidstone Journal and Kentish Advertiser;* lived in Kentish Town, London 1854 to death; published the *Sinner's Friend* 29 May 1821, this tract reached its 356 ed. before the author's death, it is said to have been translated into 30 languages and to have circulated more than 1,500,000 copies. *d.* Heath cottage, Kentish Town, London 22 Sep. 1860. *The Author of the Sinner's Friend, An autobiography* (1865), *portrait.*

HALL, JOSEPH. M.D. King's college, Aberdeen on Elphinstone foundation 1851; author of *Lancaster castle, its history and associations* 1843; *The doctor's guide to Canada; Handbook for merchant captains, a guide to the medicine chest.* *d.* 34 Terrace, Trinity sq. Tower hill, London 2 April 1854.

HALL, LEWIS ALEXANDER. Second lieut. R.E. 21 July 1810, col. commandant 3 Aug. 1863 to death; L.G. 3 Aug. 1863; author of *Astronomical observations made with Airy's Zenith sector* 1852. *d.* Southampton 16 March 1868 aged 74.

HALL, MARSHALL *(4 son of Robert Hall of Basford, Notts., cotton spinner* 1755–1827*).* *b.* Basford 18 Feb. 1790; ed. at Univ. of Edin.,

HALL, M. *(Con.)*

M.D. 1812; F.R.C.P. 1841, Gulstonian lecturer 1842, Croonian lecturer 1850–2; practised at Nottingham 1817–26, physician to general hospital there 1825–6; practised in London 1826–53, made £4000 a year; F.R.S. Edin. 1818; F.R.S. 5 April 1832, member of council 1850–52, but society refused to print account of many of his discoveries; member of Institute of France 1855; discovered the reflex function of the medulla oblongata and the medulla spinalis 1832; author of *On diagnosis* 1817, 3 ed. 1837; *An essay on the circulation of the blood* 1831; *Observations on blood letting* 1836; *Principles of the theory and practice of medicine* 1837; *On the diseases of the nervous system* 1841 and 20 other works. *d.* 37 King's road, Brighton 11 Aug. 1857. *Memoir by his widow Charlotte Hall* (1861), *portrait; Proc. of royal soc. ix,* 52–56 (1857); *J. F. Clarke's Autobiographical recollections* (1874) 327–30; *Pettigrew's Medical portrait gallery, iv* (1840), *portrait; C. Brown's Lives of Nottinghamshire Worthies* (1882) 350–52.

HALL, RICHARD. *b.* 1817; author of *A tale of the past, and other poems* 1850. *d.* 1866. *The Red Dragon, iv,* 223–30 (1883).

HALL, RICHARD. *b.* Cirencester, Gloucs. 1806, a land agent and surveyor there 1827 to about 1850; much engaged in purchasing land for railway companies; in London about 1850 to death; member of Institution of Surveyors 13 July 1868, president May 1870 to 1872; A.I.C.E. 5 Jany. 1861; helped to establish Agricultural coll. at Cirencester 1842; resided Baglan house, Glamorgan. *d.* Hillingdon Furze near Uxbridge 22 Feb. 1878. *Trans. Instit. of Surveyors, x,* 385–7 (1877–8).

HALL, ROBERT *(only child of Henry Hall of Bank lodge, Leeds* 1773–1859*).* *b.* Kirkgate, Leeds 15 Nov. 1801; commoner at Ch. Ch. Ox., B.A. 1823, M.A. 1826; barrister L.I. 20 Nov. 1828; deputy recorder of Leeds 1842; recorder of Doncaster 1845 to death; lecturer on common law at Inner Temple 1848–52; contested Leeds 1852, M.P. for Leeds 28 March 1857; author of *Mettray, a lecture on continental reformatories* 1854. *d.* Folkestone 26 May 1857. *bur.* Whitkirk church near Leeds, statue in Leeds town hall erected July 1861. *Taylor's Biographia Leodiensis* (1865) 466–71; *I.L.N. 27 June* 1857 *p.* 627, *portrait, xxxix,* 50 (1861).

NOTE.—He had all his arms and legs broken in a railway accident at the Leeds central station 3 Jany. 1855 for which he obtained a verdict of £4,500 damages from the Great Northern railway co.

HALL, ROBERT. *b.* Kingston, Upper Canada 1817; entered R.N. 27 May 1833; commander of Agamemnon one of first screw ships 1853; captain 24 June 1855; in expedition to Kertch 1855'; private sec. to D. of Somerset first lord of admiralty 1863; superintendent of Pembroke dockyard 1866; naval sec. to admiralty 1872 to death; C.B. 2 June 1869; retired captain 5 July 1872, retired V.A. 21 March 1878. *d.* 28 Craven hill gardens, London 11 June 1882.

HALL, SAMUEL. *b.* 1769; cobbler Sutton-in-Ashfield, Notts.; joined the quakers; known as the Sherwood Forest Patriarch; author of *A few remarks, among which are reasons why the Quakers suffer loss rather than serve in the army* 1797. *d.* Brookside cottage, Sutton-in-Ashfield 20 Aug. 1852 in 84 year. *Smith's Friends' Books, i,* 907 (1867); *Spencer T. Hall's Biographical Sketches* (1873) 211–28.

HALL, SAMUEL (*elder bro. of Marshall Hall 1790–1857*). *b.* Basford, Notts. 1781; took out patents in 1817 and 1823 for gassing lace and net, which were most successful, process still used; took out 20 other patents chiefly relating to steam engines and boilers. *d.* Morgan st. Tredegar sq. Bow, London 21 Nov. 1863. *W. Felkin's History of Hosiery* (1867) 300–6.

HALL, SAMUEL CARTER (4 *son of Robert Hall, lieut. col. of the Devon and Cornwall fencibles, d.* 1836). *b.* Geneva barracks near Waterford 9 May 1800; gallery reporter for *The New Times* 1823; edited the *Literary Observer* 1823; established the *Amulet* 1825 which he edited 1825–37; sub-edited and edited *New Monthly Mag.* 1830–36; started a newspaper called *The Town;* established *Art Union Journal* 15 Feb. 1839 which he edited to 1880; member of Soc. of Noviomagus 11 Dec. 1828, president 1855–81; barrister I.T. 30 April 1841; F.S.A. 7 April 1842; edited *Social Notes* 1877, 48 numbers; granted civil list person of £150, 28 April 1880; a spiritualist; author of *The baronial halls and picturesque edifices of England* 1848; *A book of memories of great men and women of the age* 1871, 2 ed. 1876; *Memoir of T. Moore* 1879; edited *The book of gems, poets and artists* 3 vols. 1836–8; and with his wife published about 340 volumes. (*m.* 20 Sep. 1824 Anna Maria Fielding). *d.* 24 Stanford road, Kensington, London 16 March 1889. *bur.* Addlestone ch. yard 23 March. *S. C. Hall's Retrospect of a long life* (1883), *portrait; I.L.N.* 30 *March* 1889 *p.* 407, *portrait; Illust. news of the world, viii* (1861), *portrait.*

HALL, REV. SAMUEL ROMILLY (*son of John Wesley Hall*). *b.* Bristol 1 Dec. 1812; ed. at Hoxton instit. 1835–7; Wesleyan Methodist minister 1837 to death, president of the conference 1868; author of *Memoirs of Mr. John Janeway* 1854; *Illustrative records of John Wesley and early Methodism* 1856; *A charge delivered to forty three junior preachers* 1869. *d.* Rosentein, Redland, Bristol 6 June 1876. *I.L.N. liii,* 200 (1868), *portrait; Nightingale's Life of S. R. Hall* (1879), *portrait.*

HALL, SPENCER. *b.* Ireland 1806; librarian Athenæum club, London 1833, collected a fine library of books of reference, retired May 1875; F.S.A. 13 May 1858; author of *Suggestions for classification of the library at the Athenæum* 1838; *Echyngham of Echyngham* 1850; *Documents from Simancas relating to reign of Elizabeth* 1865 and of papers on archæology. *d.* Tunbridge Wells 21 Aug. 1875, his library sold 26 June 1876.

HALL, SPENCER TIMOTHY (*son of Samuel Hall 1769–1852*). *b.* Sutton-in-Ashfield 16 Dec. 1812; stocking weaver 1823; printer and bookseller at Sutton 1836; co-editor of *Iris* newspaper and governor of Hillis hospital, Sheffield 1841; lecturer on mesmerism 1841; cured Harriet Martineau when she was given up by her physician 1844; homœopathic doctor at Derby 1852–66, at Plumgarths near Kendal 1866, at Burnley 1870, at Lytham 1880, at Blackpool 1881 to death; known as the Sherwood Forester; author of *The Sherwood Forester's Offering* 1841, the greater part of which he set up in type without manuscript; *The peak and the plain* 1853; *Biographical sketches of remarkable people* 1873. *d.* Alexandra road, South Shore, Blackpool 26 April 1885. *Blackpool Herald* 1 *May* 1885 *p.* 6.

HALL, SYDNEY (*son of C. H. Hall of 16 light dragoons*). *b.* Bury St. Edmunds 5 April 1813; engineer 1837, in partnership with J. C. Sherrard 1838–48; parliamentary surveyor for railways to 1847; constructed Chard and Bridgewater canal 1841–3; director of Patent fuel co. Swansea 1848–71; claimed to have discovered aniline dyes; engineer in London 1871–5; M.I.C.E. 4 April 1843. *d.* 34 Lansdowne road, London 30 Aug. 1884. *Min. of proc. of Instit. of C.E. lxxix,* 366–8 (1885).

HALL, REV. THOMAS GRAINGER. *b.* 1803; ed. at Magd. coll. Cam., 5 wrangler 1824; B.A. 1824, M.A. 1827; fellow and tutor of his coll. 1824–31; professor of mathematics King's coll. London 1844–74; prebendary of Wenlakesbarn in St. Paul's cath. 18 April 1845 to death; author of *An elementary treatise*

HALL, REV. T. G. *(Con.)*

on the differential and integral calculus 1834, 6 ed. 1863; *The elements of algebra* 1840, 2 ed. 1846; *Arithmetic for the use of schools, 2 parts* 1852–3. *d.* Kingshurst, Paignton, Devon 26 Aug. 1881.

HALL, THOMAS HENRY. *b.* 1796; ed. at Eton and King's coll. Cam., fellow, B.A. 1821, M.A. 1824; barrister L.I. 12 Nov. 1824; practised as equity draughtsman 5 years; F.R.S.; author of *Carmen Graecum. In obitum principissae Carolettae* 1818; *Carmen Latinum. Thebae Aegyptiacae* 1819. *d.* 16 Norfolk crescent, Hyde park, London 24 Dec. 1870.

HALL, THOMAS JAMES *(youngest son of Cossley Hall of Hyde hall, Jamaica). b.* Hyde hall, Jamaica 1788; ed. at Harrow; fellow commoner at Trin. coll. Cam., B.A. 1811, M.A. 1815; barrister M.T. 10 Feb. 1815.; judge advocate and advocate general of Jamaica 1819; joined the northern circuit 1824; comr. of bankruptcy in Liverpool; stipendiary magistrate of Liverpool (the first) 1836 to May 1839; chief magistrate at Bow st. London 1839 to 6 July 1864 when he retired; declined a knighthood and a baronetage. *d.* 20 Leamington road villas, Paddington 20 March 1876.

HALL, WILLIAM *(son of Mr. Hall of Birmingham, worker in fancy tortoise shell). b.* Bristol st. Birmingham 18 Janry. 1812; apprenticed to his father; landscape painter; mem. of Birmingham society of artists 1852, curator many years; an adviser of picture buyers who desired to form choice collections. *d.* King's Heath near Birmingham 24 April 1880. *W. Hall's Biography of David Cox* (1881), *preface.*

HALL, WILLIAM. Exhibited 7 landscapes at R.A. and 1 at Suffolk st. 1876–80. *d.* 23 Coleshill st. Eaton sq. London 17 June 1884 aged 61.

HALL, WILLIAM HENRY. An aeronaut; made many ascents from Manchester, Liverpool and Sheffield; ascended in Florence Nightingale balloon from the cricket ground, Newcastle-on-Tyne 15 Aug. 1859, balloon came down at Boldon 7 miles from Newcastle when he was thrown out and fell 120 feet. *d.* Newcastle infirmary 19 Aug. 1859 aged 39. *Times* 17 *Aug.* 1859 *p.* 10, 18 *Aug. p.* 9, 22 *Aug. p.* 10.

HALL, SIR WILLIAM HUTCHEON *(son of William Hall). b.* 1800; entered navy 24 Oct. 1811; commanded H.E.I.C. war steamer Nemesis 1839–43, being lent by the admiralty, served in Chinese war 1841–43 and was present in 21 engagements; known generally as Nemesis

HALL, SIR W. H. *(Con.)*

Hall; captain 22 Oct. 1844; F.R.S. 22 April 1847; served in Baltic during Russian war 1854–5; C.B. 5 July 1855, K.C.B. 13 March 1867; granted Greenwich hospital pension 9 Dec. 1871; retired admiral 11 Dec. 1875; inventor of Hall's patent anchor and of iron bilge-tanks; author of *Sailors' Homes, their origin and progress* 1852, 2 ed. 1854; *Our national defences* 1876. *d.* 48 Phillimore gardens, Campden hill, London 25 June 1878. *bur.* Mereworth, Kent 29 June. *O'Byrne* (1849) *p.* 444–6; *I.L.N. xxv,* 641, 642 (1854), *portrait.*

HALL, REV. WILLIAM JOHN. *b.* 1793; ed. at C. C. coll. Cam., B.A. 1821, M.A. 1824; priest in ordinary to H.M. chapel royal 1829 to death; minor prebend. St. Paul's cath. London, Second canon and senior cardinal 31 March 1826 to death; V. of Sandon, Herts. 20 Janry. 1829–33; R. of St. Benet with St. Peter, Paul's wharf, London 12 Janry. 1835 to 1851; V. of Tottenham, Middlesex 1851 to death; editor of *Christian remembrancer* and *Psalms and hymns* 1836 numerous editions; author of *The doctrine of purgatory* 1843. *d.* Beech house, High road, Tottenham 16 Dec. 1861.

HALL, SIR WILLIAM KING *(son of Dr. James Hall, R.N. d.* 1869). *b.* London 11 March 1816; entered R.N. 22 Sep. 1829; served in the Caffre war 1852–3, in the Baltic 1854–5, in Chinese war 1856–8; rear admiral superintendent Sheerness dockyard 1865–9; superintendent Devonport dockyard 1871–5; C.B. 3 July 1855, K.C.B. 20 May 1871; commander in chief at the Nore 1877–9; admiral 2 Aug. 1879, retired 3 Janry. 1881; great advocate of temperance in the navy. *d.* 38 Jermyn st. London 29 July 1886. *O'Byrne* (1849) *p.* 446.

HALL, WILLIAM SANDFORD *(eldest brother of Samuel Carter Hall* 1800–89). *b.* Cork 1795; ensign 18 foot 19 Dec. 1811; paymaster of 17 foot 10 July 1840, of 53 foot 2 Feb. 1849 to 19 Nov. 1852 when placed on h.p.; founded a Mechanics' institute at Cork; assist. editor of *United Service Mag.;* originated United Service Museum, Whitehall, London 1830. *d.* Peldon, Essex 26 Feb. 1876.

HALLAHAN, MARGARET MARY *(only child of Edmund Hallahan). b.* London 23 Janry. 1803; domestic servant to Madame Caulier, lace warehouse, Cheapside 1815; admitted to third order of St. Dominic 1834; founded a community of Dominican tertians in Spon. st. Coventry 28 March 1844 which she removed to Clifton, Bristol 1848 and to Stone, Staffs.

HALLAHAN, M. M. (Con.)

1854 where she erected the finest specimen of conventual buildings in England; went to Rome 1858; founded 4 other convents 1860–67, schools, 4 churches, orphanages and a hospital at Stone. *d.* Stone 11 May 1868. *Life of Mother M. M. Hallahan* (1869), *portrait; Gillow's English Catholics, iii,* 96–101 (1888).

HALLAM, HENRY *(son of John Hallam, dean of Bristol, d.* 1812*).* b. Windsor 9 July 1777; ed. at Eton and Ch. Ch. Ox., B.A. 1799, M.A. 1832, D.C.L. 1848; barrister I.T. 2 July 1802, bencher 1841; a commissioner of stamps 1806–26, retired on a pension of £500 a year which he resigned 1850; a founder 1834 and treasurer of Statistical soc.; F.S.A. 12 March 1801, V.P. 1824 to death; received one of two 50 guinea medals given by Geo. iv. for historical eminence 1830; author of *A view of the state of Europe during the middle ages* 2 vols. 1818; *The constitutional history of England, Hen. vii.-Geo. ii.* 2 vols. 1827; *Introduction to the literature of Europe in the 15th, 16th and 17th centuries* 4 vols. 1837–39. *d.* Penshurst, Kent 21 Jany. 1859. *H. Martineau's Biographical sketches* 4 ed. (1876) 393–401; *Maclise Portrait Gallery* (1883) 430–6, *portrait; Proc. of Royal Soc. x,* 12–18 (1860).

HALLARD, FREDERICK *(son of Mr. Hallard, professor of French at Edinburgh).* b. Edinburgh 1821; ed. at Avranches, Paris and at Edinburgh univ.; member of faculty of advocates 1814; reporter and editor of *The Scottish Jurist* 1829; sheriff substitute of Midlothian 1855 to death; author of *A proposal to facilitate the abolition of feudal conveyancing* 1860; *The Inferior Judge* 1869; *The catalogue question in the Advocates' library, a retrospect: By one of the defeated* 1872. *d.* 61 York place, Edinburgh 19 Jany. 1882. *Journal of Jurisprudence, xxvi,* 90–92 (1882).

HALLE, HUGHES R. P. FRASER *(eld. son of Joseph Halle, capt. 82 foot).* Head master of South Lambeth gr. sch. 33 years; LL.D.; author of *Critical letters on Scribbleomania, By R. F. Brancassine* 1842; *The Britannic censor of European philosophy* 1844; *Exact philosophy* 1848; *Letters relating to the Vale of Teign* 1851. *d.* 8 Lincoln terrace, Bullen road, Lavender hill 23 May 1886 aged 78 years.

HALLEWELL, EDMUND GILLING (2 son of *Rev. John Hallewell of Farnham, Yorks.)* b. Boroughbridge, Yorkshire 1796; ed. at Ripon; M.P. for Newry 1851–52; published a long series of letters on various questions of social and political economy in the *Gloucestershire Chronicle* and other newspapers under signature of 'A true Conservative.' *d.* Beauchamps near Gloucester 5 Nov. 1881.

HALLEWELL, EDMUND GILLING *(son of the preceding).* b. 1822; col. in the army 2 Nov. 1860; commandant Royal military coll. Sandhurst 1 April 1864 to death. *d.* Royal military college, Sandhurst 27 Nov. 1869.

HALLEY, REV. ROBERT (1 son of *Robert Hally of Blackheath, Kent, nurseryman).* b. Blackheath 13 Aug. 1796; ed. at Homerton academy, London 1816–21; pastor of the Independent ch. St. Neots, Hunts. 18 May 1822; classical tutor at Highbury college, London, college opened 5 Sep. 1826; D.D. Princetown college, New Jersey 1834; pastor of Mosley st. chapel, Manchester 1839–48 and of Cavendish st. chapel, Manchester 1848–57; chairman of congregational union of England and Wales for 1855; principal of and professor of theology in New college, London 1857–72; author of *An inquiry into the nature of the sacraments* 2 vols. 1844–51, 2 ed. 2 vols. 1854; *Lancashire: its puritanism and nonconformity* 2 vols. 1869, 2 ed. 1872. *d.* Batworth park near Arundel 18 Aug. 1876. *bur.* Abney park cemetery 24 Aug. *A short biography of Rev. Robert Halley, edited by Robert Halley, M.A.* (1879).

HALLIBURTON, SIR BRENTON. b. Halifax, Nova Scotia 3 Dec. 1773; capt. 7 fusiliers; admitted barrister 1803, bencher 1807, mem. of council 1816; judge of supreme court of Nova Scotia 1811, chief justice 1835; knighted by patent 13 April 1859; author of *Observations on the importance of the North American colonies to Great Britain* 1825, 2 ed. 1831; *Reflections on passing events, a poem* 1856, and letters in the *Halifax Recorder* on the American war, signed Anglo-American 1813. *d.* near Halifax 16 July 1860. *Memoir of Sir B. Halliburton, By Rev. G. W. Hill* (1864); *Morgan's Bibliotheca Canadensis* (1867) 173.

HALLIDAY, ANDREW *(son of Rev. Wm. Duff, d.* 1844*).* b. The Grange, Marnock, Banffshire early in 1830; ed. at Marischal coll. and univ. Aberdeen; went to London 1849; discarded name of Duff; contributed to *Morning Chronicle, People's Journal,* &c.; wrote the article 'Beggars' in *H. Mayhew's London Labour* 1851; a founder of the Savage club 1857, pres. 1857 to death; wrote a series of essays in *All the year round* 1861, &c., since collected into volumes called *Everyday papers* 2 vols. 1864, *Sunnyside papers* 1866 and *Town and country sketches* 1866; wrote with Frederick Lawrence burlesque of *Kenilworth* produced at Strand theatre 26 Dec. 1858, it ran for more than 100 nights; with Wm. Brough the *Area Belle* 1864 and other farces for Adelphi; wrote *The Great city* produced at Drury Lane 22 April

HALLIDAY, A. *(Con.)*

1867 which ran 102 nights; *For love or money* with which Vaudeville theatre opened 16 April 1870; *Little Emly* produced at Olympic theatre 9 Oct. 1869 which ran 200 nights; *Amy Robsart* produced at Drury Lane 24 Sep. 1870. *d.* 74 St. Augustine's road, Camden Town, London 10 April 1877. *Cartoon Portraits* (1873) 88–9, *portrait; Illust. Review, i,* 81–2 (1874), *portrait.*

HALLIDAY, MICHAEL FREDERICK. *b.* 1822; clerk in parliament office, house of lords 1839 to death; exhibited 8 pictures at R.A. and 1 at Suffolk st. 1853–66; his chief works were The measure for the wedding ring 1856 and Roma vivente e Roma morta 1866; an early member of the pre-Raphaelite sch.; one of first 8 who competed for Elcho shield at Wimbledon 1862. *d.* 30 Thurloe place, South Kensington, London 1 June 1869.

HALLIWELL, RICHARD BISSETT. *b.* Fitzroy st. Fitzroy sq. London 30 Nov. 1842; an engineer in London; amateur cricketer; a hard hitter and excellent wicket keeper; played in the Middlesex eleven and in the Gentlemen *v.* the Players; generally played under name of Bissett. *d.* 9 Nov. 1881.

HALLIWELL-PHILLIPPS, JAMES ORCHARD (*3 son of Thomas Halliwell*). *b.* Sloane st. Chelsea 21 June 1820; matric. from Trin. coll. Cam. 1837, removed to Jesus coll. 1838; LL.D. of Edin. univ. 1883; F.S.A. 14 Feb. 1839; F.R.S. 30 May 1839; projected Cambridge Antiquarian soc. and was the sec. 1840; settled with his father in London 1840; became connected with Shakespeare soc. 1840; accused of taking MSS. from library of Trin. coll. Cam. 1844; forbidden to enter Br. Museum library 10 Feb. 1845; presented his Shakespearian library to Univ. of Edin. Feb. 1872; bought theatre Stratford on Avon, March 1872; was the means of buying Shakespeare's residence New place, Stratford 1863, conveyed it to the corporation of Stratford by deed dated 8 April 1876; author of *Dictionary of archaic and provincial words* 1846, 10 ed. 1881; *Life of William Shakespeare* 1848; *Shakespeare* 16 vols. 1853–63; *Lithographed facsimiles of the Shakespearean quartos* 48 vols. 1862–71 of which there are only 15 complete sets. (*m.* 9 Aug. 1842 Henrietta E. M. eld. dau. of Sir Thomas Phillipps, baronet, she *d.* 25 March 1879); discontinued name of Halliwell and assumed name of Phillips by r.l. 29 Feb. 1872, prefixed former name of Halliwell to name of Phillips by deed inrolled in chancery 28 May 1879. *d.* Hollingbury Copse near Brighton 3 Jany. 1889. *I.L.N.* 12 *Jany.* 1889 *p.* 36, *portrait.*

HALLOWES, JOHN. Entered navy July 1803; captain 5 Dec. 1842; R.A. on half pay 20 May 1862; admiral on half pay 30 July 1875. *d.* Milton house near Portsmouth 11 Jany. 1883 aged 91.

HALLYBURTON, JOHN FREDERICK GORDON- (*3 son of 9th Marquis of Huntly, d.* 1853). *b.* 15 Aug. 1799; entered navy Feb. 1813, captain 4 Aug. 1836; G.C.H. 22 Aug. 1836; known as Lord J. F. Gordon from 1838; admiral on half pay 8 April 1868; assumed name of Hallyburton 1843; M.P. for Forfar 1841–52. *d.* Hallyburton house, Coupar Angus 29 Sep. 1878.

HALPIN, REV. ROBERT CRAWFORD. Boy volunteer in Canadian rebellion 1839; ensign 14 foot 1840; educ. Trin. coll. Dublin, B.A. 1843, M.A. 1868; chaplain in army 1849; served in Crimean campaign, medal, 4 clasps and Turkish medal; in China war 1860; chaplain to household brigade 1863, retired 1 July 1880; reward for distinguished service 1 April 1875; chaplain hospital for women Soho, London 1880. *d.* 22 Belsize sq. London 19 March 1889.

HALPINE, CHARLES GRAHAM (*son of Rev. Nicholas John Halpine 1790–1850, editor of the Dublin Evening Mail*). *b.* Oldcastle, co. Meath, Nov. 1829; ed. at Trin. coll. Dublin to 1846; emigrated to U.S. America 1851; assist. editor *Boston Post* 1852; editor *New York Leader* 1857; served in Federal army April 1861 to 1864; assist. adjutant general and colonel 1862; editor of *New York Citizen* 1864; registrar of the county of New York 1867; author under name of Miles O'Reilly of *Life and adventures of Private Miles O'Reilly* 1864; *Baked meats of the funeral by Private Miles O'Reilly* 1866. *d.* from taking undiluted chloroform at New York city 3 Aug. 1868. *Poetical works of C. G. Halpine* (1869), *portrait.*

HALSEY, THOMAS PLUMER (*1 son of Joseph T. W. Halsey of Gaddesden park, Herts. d.* 1818). *b.* 26 Jany. 1815; M.P. for co. Hertford, Jany. 1846 to death; *lost* in the 'Ercolano' steamer off Villa Franca on her way from Genoa to Marseilles 24 April 1854. *G.M.* xli, 649 (1854); *A.R.* 1854 *pp.* 68, 292.

HALSTED, FRANCIS. Printseller Bond st., then at 13 Rathbone place, Oxford st. London; great authority on Turner before Ruskin's era commenced; formed the collection of Liber Studiorum prints which Mr. Stokes bequeathed to Miss Mary Constance Clark; formed similar collections for J. L. Taylor proprietor of *Manchester Guardian,* and Sir John Hippesley. *d.* St. John's Wood, Aug. 1879 aged 72.

HALY, RIGHT REV. FRANCIS. *b.* Doonane parish, Queen's county 1781; ed. at Maynooth 1807–12; C. of Rathvilly 1812–3; administrator of Mountrath 1813–22; parish priest of Kilcock 1822; bp. of Kildare and Leighlin, consecrated 25 March 1838; visited Rome 1844. *d.* Carlow 19 Aug. 1855 aged 74, left his library to Carlow coll. *Comerford's Collections* (1883) 140–50, *portrait.*

HALY, SIR WILLIAM O'GRADY *(son of Aylmer Haly of Wadhurst castle, Sussex).* *b.* 1810; ensign 4 foot 17 June 1828; lieut. col. 38 foot 4 Feb. 1859 to 12 Jany. 1865; colonel of 106 foot 17 May 1874, of 47 foot 2 Nov. 1875 to death; served Eastern campaign of 1854–55; commanded forces in Canada 6 May 1873 to death; general 1 Oct. 1877; C.B. 5 July 1855, K.C.B. 29 May 1875. *d.* Halifax, Nova Scotia 19 March 1878.

HAMBLET, HENRY. Steward and practically manager of Garrick club 35 King st. Covent Garden, London for many years down to 17 May 1862. *d.* London 1863. *W. Ballantine's Experiences* (1883) 151; *Lord W. P. Lennox's My Recollections* (1874) i, 144.

HAMBLETON, REV. JOHN *(5 son of John Hambleton of St. Mary's, Wallingford).* *b.* 1799; ed. at St. Edm. hall, Ox., B.A. 1825, M.A. 1829; minister of Holloway episcopal chapel, Holloway road, London 1830 to death; author of *Christ the good physician, a sermon* 1829, 7 ed. 1847; *A brief history of the soul* 1833, 7 ed. 1847; *A help to preparation for death, judgment and eternity* 1839; *Seven lectures on the Bible as the word of God* 1861. *d.* 21 Compton ter. Upper st. Islington, London 22 Oct. 1865.

HAMBLIN, THOMAS SOWERBY. *b.* Pentonville, London 14 May 1800; ballet dancer Adelphi theatre at 6s. a week; first acted at Sadler's Wells 1819, at Drury Lane 26 Dec. 1819 as Truman in *George Barnwell;* appeared at Park theatre, New York as Hamlet, Oct. 1825; lessee of Bowery theatre, New York, Aug. 1830, theatre burnt 16 Sep. 1836; played at Covent Garden 1836–7; lessee of Bowery 1838, again burnt 1845, lessee again 1847 to death; lessee of Park theatre, New York 1848, theatre burnt 16 Dec. 1848; his chief characters were Hamlet, The Stranger, William Tell, Virginius, Rolla and Petruchio. *d.* of brain fever Broome st. New York 8 Jany. 1853, left 100,000 dollars. *Ireland's New York Stage,* i, 459–61 (1866); *Appleton's Cyclop. of American Biog.* iii, 55 (1887), *portrait.*

HAMEL, JOSEPH VON. *b.* Sarepta on the Volga 1788; member of Imperial academy of

HAMEL, J. V. *(Con.)*

sciences, St. Petersburgh 1828; ascended Mont Blanc when 3 of his guides perished 20 Aug. 1820; travelled and resided much in England from 1814 onwards; reported to his government on progress of science and arts in England; author of *England and Russia, the voyage of J. Tradescant to the White sea* 1854; *Historical account of Galvanic and electro-magnetic telegraph* 1859; *Bishop Watson and the electric telegraph* 1861 and works in Russian and German. *d.* Duke st. St. James', London 22 Sep. 1862. *G.M. xiii,* 510, 788 (1862).

HAMERTON, JOHN MILLET. Ensign 44 foot 31 Oct. 1792, lieut. col. 31 March 1814 to 24 Jany. 1816 when placed on h.p.; col. 55 foot 7 Dec. 1848 to death; general 20 June 1854; C.B. 22 June 1815. *d.* Orchardstown house near Clonmel 27 Jany. 1855 aged 77.

HAMILTON, ALEXANDER HAMILTON-DOUGLAS 10 Duke of *(elder son of 9 Duke of Hamilton 1740–1819).* *b.* St. James's sq. London 5 Oct. 1767; ed. at Ch. Ch. Ox., M.A. 1789; styled Marquis of Douglas 1799–1819; M.P. for Lancaster 1802–6; col. of royal Lanarkshire militia 1802–34; lord lieut. of Lanarkshire 13 Nov. 1803 to death; ambassador to St. Petersburgh 28 May 1806 to July 1812; P.C. 18 June 1806; called to House of Lords by writ in his father's barony of Dutton 4 Nov. 1806; F.R.S. 14 Jany. 1808; F.R.S. Edin., president; succeeded 16 Feb. 1819; lord high steward at coronations of Wm. iv. and of Victoria; K.G. 5 Feb. 1836. *d.* 12 Portman sq. London 18 Aug. 1852.

NOTE.—He cherished an idea that he was the legitimate King of Scotland; at his death his body was embalmed, deposited in a sarcophagus brought from the Pyramids of Egypt, and buried in a mausoleum 120 feet high which he had erected near Hamilton palace at cost of £130,000.

HAMILTON, WILLIAM ALEXANDER ANTHONY ARCHIBALD HAMILTON-DOUGLAS, 11 Duke of *(only son of the preceding).* *b.* Grosvenor place, London 18 Feb. 1811; Marquis of Douglas 1819–52; ed. at Ch. Ch. Oxf., B.A. 1832; col. 1 royal Lanark militia 23 Jany. 1834 to death; knight marischall of Scotland, June 1846; major commandant Glasgow yeomanry 1848–56; lord lieutenant of Lanarkshire, Aug. 1852 to death; grand master of freemasons of Scotland; lived chiefly at Paris and Baden. *d.* Paris 15 July 1863.

HAMILTON, ALEXANDER. *b.* 27 Jany. 1774; called to Irish bar 1795; K.C. 25 Nov. 1822. *d.* Oct. 1852.

HAMILTON, Ven. Anthony (2 *son of Ven. Anthony Hamilton 1739-1812, archdeacon of Colchester*). *b.* 12 July 1778; ed. at St. John's coll. Oxf., B.A. 1800, M.A. 1803; R. of Loughton, Essex 1805 to death; preb. of Warminster in Wells cath. 1810-27; chaplain in ord. to the Sovereign 1812-37; R. of St. Mary Le Bow with St. Pancras, Soper Lane and All Hallows, Honey Lane, London 1820 to death; archdeacon of Taunton and preb. of Milverton prima in Wells cath. 5 Dec. 1827 to death; precentor and first residentiary canon Lichfield cath. 1831 to 1850. *d.* Loughton rectory 10 Sep. 1851.

HAMILTON, Arthur Philip. Entered navy Oct. 1800; on 28 Sep. 1810 in a boat attack captured 2 brigs from under the battery of Pointe du Ché near Rochelle; captain 31 May 1816; retired admiral 4 Oct. 1862. *d.* 2 Dorset sq. London 2 Sep. 1877.

HAMILTON, Charles. *b.* 1801; ed. at Addiscombe; ensign Bengal army 27 Jany. 1818; lieut.-col. Bengal infantry 19 Jany. 1843, served in Gwalior campaign 1843, commanded 2 grenadier N.I. at battle of Maharajpore and same regt. in Sutlej campaign 1845-6 including actions of Moodkee and Ferozeshah and capture of Kote Kangra 1846; C.B. 22 May 1843; general 16 May 1872; retired 1 Oct. 1877. *d.* 19 Sussex gardens, London 27 Oct. 1889.

HAMILTON, Charles George Archibald (2 *son of 11 duke of Hamilton 1811-63*). *b.* Connaught place, London 18 May 1847; cornet 11 hussars 1866-69; served in German army at siege of Strasbourg 1870; his vagaries were the talk of Paris and the German spas about 1870; joined the Church of Rome 1885; resided at Biarritz 1876-86. *d.* Nice 2 May 1886, having been nursed by his intended wife Mdlle. Pignatelli. *bur.* in Hamilton palace mausoleum 12 May.

HAMILTON, Charles James (*elder son of Charles Powell Hamilton 1747-1825, admiral R.N.*) *b.* 29 July 1779; minister plenipo. to French court 3 March 1832 to 19 April 1833 at Buenos Ayres 5 July 1834; envoy extrad. and min. plen. at Rio Janiero 2 Oct. 1835 to 9 Feb. 1847 when he was pensioned. *d.* 15 Dec. 1856.

HAMILTON, Charles William. Entered Bengal army 1799; col. 40 Bengal N.I. 1850 to death; L.G. 11 Nov. 1851. *d.* Home Mead, Lymington 22 July 1866 aged 82.

HAMILTON, Claud (2 *son of James Hamilton, Viscount Hamilton 1786-1814*). *b.* Lower

Grosvenor st. London 27 July 1813; ed. at Harrow and Trin. coll. Cam.; M.P. for co. Tyrone 1835-37 and 1839-74; treasurer of the household 27 Feb. 1852 to Dec. 1852 and 26 Feb. 1858 to June 1859; P.C. 27 Feb. 1852; vice chamberlain of the household 10 July 1866 to Dec. 1868; lieut.-col. commandant Donegal militia 19 July 1867 to death. *d.* 83 Portland place, London 3 June 1884. *bur.* at Elton 12 June.

HAMILTON, Sir Edward, 1 Baronet (2 *son of Sir John Hamilton, 1 baronet, d. 1784*). *b.* 12 March 1772; entered navy 21 May 1799; cut out Spanish frigate 'Hermione' from port of Puerto Cabello 25 Oct. 1799, a feat unsurpassed in naval annals; captain 3 June 1797; knighted by patent 3 June 1800; received freedom of city of London 25 Oct. 1800; commanded royal yacht Mary 1806-19; K.C.B. 2 Jany. 1815; baronet 26 Jany. 1819; admiral 9 Nov. 1846. *d.* 17 Cumberland terrace, Regent's park, London 20 March 1851.

HAMILTON, Eliza Mary (5 *child of Archibald Hamilton of Dublin, attorney 1778-1819*). *b.* 4 April 1807; author of *Poems*, Dublin 1838. *d.* Dublin 14 May 1851.

HAMILTON, Elizabeth (*dau. of Sir W. S. Hamilton 1788-1856*). A promoter of university education of women in Scotland; wrote memoir of her father for *Encyclopædia Britannica*; author of *Microcosmus by H. Lotze, a translation* 1885. *d.* 30 Northampton park, Canonbury, London 2 March 1882 aged 42.

HAMILTON, Frederic Douglas- (5 *son of Capt. Augustus Barrington P. A. P. Hamilton*). *b.* 12 May 1815; attaché at Buenos Ayres 1834-6, at Rio de Janiero 1836, paid attaché there 1844; first paid attaché at Vienna 1852; sec. of legation at Stuttgardt 1853-8, at Athens 1859, at Frankfort 1859, at Stockholm 1862; chargé d'affaires and consul general at Quito, Equator 1867, minister resident and consul general there 1872, retired 17 Nov. 1883. *d.* Tunbridge Wells 15 May 1887.

HAMILTON, Sir Frederick William (*son of William Richard Hamilton 1777-1859*). *b.* 8 July 1815; page of honour to George iv. and William iv. 1826-31; ensign Grenadier guards 12 July 1831, adjutant 1836-46, lieut. col. 19 June 1860; col. 21 fusiliers 10 Jany. 1870 to death; general 21 Nov. 1876, retired 1881; served with the grenadier guards 1854-5, present at Alma, Balaklava and Inkerman; commanded divisions of the army in the trenches at Sebastopol; C.B. 29 Dec. 1856,

HAMILTON, SIR F. W. *(Con.)*

K.C.B. 24 May 1873; military attaché at Berlin 1860–62; V.P. of council on military education 1862–6; commander of forces in Scotland 1866–8; commanded brigade of guards 1868–70; author of *The origin and history of the First Grenadier guards* 3 vols. 1874–7. *d.* Pitcorthie, Fife 4 Oct. 1890. *I.L.N.* 18 Oct. 1890 *p.* 433, *portrait.*

HAMILTON, GEORGE ALEXANDER *(elder son of Rev. George Hamilton of Tyrellas, co. Down, who d. March 1833).* *b.* Tyrellas 29 Aug. 1802; ed. at Rugby, Trin. coll. Dublin, B.A. 1821, M.A. 1832, LL.B. and LL.D. 1851, and Trin. coll. Ox., B.A. 1822, D.C.L. 1853; contested city of Dublin 1826, 1830, 1832 and 1837; M.P. for city of Dublin 1835–7; M.P. for univ. of Dublin 1843–59; financial sec. of the Treasury, March to Dec. 1852, March 1858 to Jany. 1859, permanent sec. Jany. 1859; a comr. of church temporalities in Ireland 1870; P.C. 7 Aug. 1869. *d.* Kingstown near Dublin 17 Sep. 1871. *Portraits of eminent conservatives* 2 *series* (1846), *portrait; I.L.N. xxi,* 517, 518 (1852), *portrait.*

HAMILTON, HANS HENRY *(4 son of Henry Hamilton of Ballymacool, Meath).* *b.* 1801; ed. at Trin. coll. Dublin, B.A. 1820, M.A. 1832; called to Irish bar 1823; Q.C. 9 Nov. 1852; chairman of quarter sessions for co. Galway 1852–8, for co. Armagh 1858 to death. *d.* 28 Fitzwilliam place, Dublin 20 April 1875. *Irish Law Times, ix,* 208 (1875).

HAMILTON, VERY REV. HENRY PARR *(son of Alexander Hamilton of Edinburgh, M.D. 1739–1802).* *b.* 3 April 1794; ed. at Trin. coll. Cam.; 9th wrangler 1816, B.A. 1816, M.A. 1819; fell. of his coll. 1816; R. of Wath near Ripon 1830–50; P.C. of St. Mary the Great, Cam. 1833–44; rural dean 1847; dean of Salisbury 17 April 1850 to death; F.R.S. 17 Jany. 1828; F.R.A.S.; F.G.S.; author of *The principles of analytical geometry, Cambridge* 1826; *An analytical system of conic sections, Cambridge* 1828, 5 *ed.* 1843; *The church and the education question* 1848; *Scheme for the reform of their cathedral by the dean and chapter of Salisbury* 1855. *d.* the Deanery, the Close, Salisbury 7 Feb. 1880. *Monthly notices of Royal Astronom. Soc. xli,* 184–7 (1881).

HAMILTON, REV. JAMES *(son of Rev. William Hamilton 1780–1835, minister of St. Andrew's, Dundee).* *b.* Lonend, Paisley 27 Nov. 1814; ed. at Glasgow univ., B.A. 1835, and at Edin. univ., D.D.; assist. presbyterian minister St. George's ch. Edin. 1838, minister at Abernyte 1839, at Roxburgh ch. Edin. 1841, at National

HAMILTON, REV. J. *(Con.)*

Scotch ch. Regent sq. London 1841 to death; author of *Life in earnest* 1845; *Memoirs of Richard Williams* 1854; *A morning beside the lake of Galilee* 1863; *Excelsior, helps to progress* 6 vols. 1854; *Works* 6 vols. 1869–73; editor of *Presbyterian Messenger* 1849 and of *Evangelical Christendom* 1864. *d.* 48 Euston sq. London 24 Nov. 1867. *W. Arnot's Life of J. Hamilton* (1870), *portrait; Illust. news of the world, ix* (1862), *portrait.*

HAMILTON, REV. JAMES. *b.* county Kerry about 1813; ed. at Carlow coll., professor of classics there 1835 and of natural philosophy 1842–51; ordained priest 20 Dec. 1836; missioner in the parishes of Mountrath, Bagenalstown and Rathvilly to 1842, and in Tullow 1851–7; military chaplain at the Curragh camp Dec. 1857, at Woolwich, at Bermuda 1865–7, at Aldershot 1868–73, held rank as a major; delivered 4 lectures on the 'Structure of the Heavens' in the Rotunda, Dublin, Jany. 1856. *d.* at the house of his brother Dr. W. Hamilton at Tarbert 20 Dec. 1873. *Comerford's Collections* (1883) 214–24.

HAMILTON, JAMES. *b.* Ireland 1819; drawing master in Philadelphia; illustrated *Life of Rear admiral J. Paul Jones* 1845, Kane's *Arctic Explorations* 1856, *The Arabian Nights,* Coleridge's *Ancient Mariner,* and other popular works; painted many pictures especially marine views. *d.* 10 March 1878.

HAMILTON, SIR JAMES *(son of Rev. George Hamilton of Armagh).* *b.* Warrenpoint, co. Down 1815; ed. at Belfast academical instit.; chairman of Belfast harbour commission 1867 to death; knighted by lord lieut. earl Spencer, on opening of horticultural exhibition at Belfast 9 Aug. 1872. *d.* West view, Bangor, co. Down 26 Oct. 1882. *Times* 10 *Aug.* 1872, *p.* 12, 21 *Aug. p.* 7.

HAMILTON, SIR JAMES JOHN, 2 Baronet *(only son of Sir John Hamilton, 1 baronet, G.C.S.I. 1755–1835).* *b.* Londonderry 1 March 1802; ed. at Harrow and Ch. Ch. Ox., B.A. 1822; 2 lieut. rifle brigade 10 July 1823, served during Canadian rebellion 1837–8; major on h.p. 8 Oct. 1838, sold out May 1852; M.P. for Sudbury, Suffolk 25 July to Dec. 1837; contested Marylebone, July 1841 and July 1847; sheriff of Pembrokeshire 1857, of Tyrone 1859. *d.* 6 Portman sq. London 12 Jany. 1876. *I.L.N. lxviii,* 95, 215 (1876).

HAMILTON, JANET *(dau. of a shoemaker called Thomson).* *b.* Carshill, Shotts parish, Lanarkshire 12 Oct. 1795; a yarn spinner; learnt to write 1848; wrote for Cassell's *Working*

HAMILTON, J. *(Con.)*

Man's Friend 1849; became blind 1855; author of *Poems and songs* 1863; *Poems of purpose and sketches* 1865; *Poems and Ballads* 1868; *Poems, essay and sketches* 1880. (*m.* 1809 John Hamilton, shoemaker), she *d.* Langloan, Lanarkshire 27 Oct. 1873, Memorial fountain erected at Langloan. *Poems, sketches and essays by J. Hamilton* (1885), *portrait; Good Words, Feb.* 1884 *pp.* 118–24, *portrait.*

HAMILTON, SIR JOHN. *b.* Dover 1765; captain in H.M.'s packet service; communicated to admiral Duncan intelligence of the Dutch fleet being at sea which led to victory at Camperdown 11 Oct. 1797; knighted at St. James's palace 5 March 1845. *d.* at Capt. Luke Smithett's house, 17 Snargate st. Dover 1 Feb. 1858.

HAMILTON, JOHN. *b.* Dumfriesshire; a newspaper reporter at Preston; edited the *Aylesbury News* 7 years; formed a church at Aylesbury; edited the *Empire* in London, joint proprietor of it with George Thompson; edited the *Morning Star* to 1860; F.R.S. *d.* Howe villa, Windermere 14 Oct. 1860 aged 39.

HAMILTON, JOHN. *b.* 1809; M.R.C.S. Ireland, F.R.C.S. 1844, V.P. 1874; edited *The Dublin Journal of medical and chemical science* 1832; visiting surgeon Richmond hospital 1844–75; surgeon in ordinary to the queen 1874; governor of House of Industry hospitals 1875; president Dublin pathological soc.; author of *An essay on syphilitic sarcocele* 1849; *The restoration of a lost nose* 1864; *Lectures on syphilitic osteitis and periostitis* 1874. *d.* 14 Merrion sq. North, Dublin 2 Nov. 1875. *Medical Times* 13 *Nov.* 1875 *p.* 561.

HAMILTON, JOHN POTTER. Cornet Scotch Greys 1793; commanded a battalion at battle of Castalla, May 1813; lieut.-col. 83 foot 3 June 1813; captain 3 foot guards 1814, retired Aug. 1819; special commissioner to Colombia 10 Oct. 1823, signed treaty of amity 18 April 1825; K.H. 1836; author of *Travels through Colombia* 1827; *Reminiscences of an old sportsman* 2 vols. 1860. *d.* Bodleyfryd, Wrexham 28 Jany. 1873 aged 95.

HAMILTON, REV. JOSEPH HARRIMAN. Ed. at Trin. coll. Cam.; 27 wrangler and B.A. 1822, M.A. 1825; chaplain of his coll. 1824; C. of St. Michael, Chester sq. Pimlico, London 1848–71; prebendary of Chiswick in St. Paul's cath. 1859–72; R. of Frant, Sussex 1871 to 1879; canon residentiary of Rochester 1872 to death. *d.* the precincts, Rochester 17 Aug. 1881 aged 81.

HAMILTON, KER BAILLIE (4 *son of Ven. Charles Baillie-Hamilton* 1764–1820, *archdeacon of Cleveland*). *b.* 13 July 1804; entered H.E.I.C.S. 1822; clerk of council and acting colonial sec. Cape of Good Hope 1829; lieut. governor of Grenada 1846–52; administrator of Barbadoes and the Windward islands 1851–2; governor of Newfoundland 1852–5; governor in chief of Antigua and Leeward islands 1855 to Jany. 1863; C.B. 23 July 1862; retired 1867; author of *Our saddle horses* 1865. *d.* 43 Broadwater Down, Tunbridge Wells 6 Feb. 1889.

HAMILTON, NICHOLAS. Ensign 5 foot 15 June 1796; inspecting field officer 10 June 1813 to 11 Nov. 1851; colonel 82 foot 10 Dec. 1856 to death; L.G. 11 Jany. 1858. *d.* 35 Lower Bagot st. Dublin 13 Dec. 1859 in 78 year.

HAMILTON, RICHARD. *b.* 18 Dec. 1810; ensign 1 Madras N.I. 25 Aug. 1828, major 21 May 1858; lieut.-col. Madras staff corps 18 Feb. 1861, placed on retired list 18 Dec. 1880; general 23 Aug. 1884; C.B. 29 May 1875. *d.* Nethway, Torquay 1 March 1888.

HAMILTON, ROBERT DOUGLAS *(son of a stone mason and farmer).* *b.* Muirhead, Lanarkshire 16 Jany. 1783; ed. at Glasgow and Edin. universities; assist. surgeon in H.M. hospital ship 'Tromp' at Falmouth, April 1808 to Nov. 1809; surgeon at St. Mawes 1809–12; served as a surgeon with the army in the Peninsula; emigrated to U.S. America 1827; settled at Scarborough near Toronto, Upper Canada 1830; contributed to newspapers and periodicals under name of Guy Pollock; author of *Essays, Truro* 1812; *Craignethan castle. A poem, Edin.* 1817, anon.; *The principles of medicine, vol. i,* 1821; *Dr. Shaddow of Gostlington, By Mungo Coulter Goggle. d.* Scarborough 2 April 1857. *Morgan's Bibl. Canadensis* (1867) 174.

HAMILTON, SIR ROBERT NORTH COLLIE, 6 Baronet (1 *son of Sir Frederick Hamilton,* 5 *baronet, d.* 1853). *b.* Benares, India 7 April 1802; of H.E.I.C.S. 1819; judge of Benares March 1829; sec. to the government in N.W. provinces March 1842, and resident with Holkar at Indore 1844; governor general's agent for Central India 1854–9; served during the mutiny 1857–8; retired 1860; member of supreme council 1859–60; K.C.B. 18 May 1860; sheriff of Warwickshire 1866; contested S. Warwickshire 1868. *d.* Avon Cliffe, Stratford-on-Avon 31 May 1887.

HAMILTON, THOMAS. *b.* Edinburgh 1784; apprentice to his father a carpenter; architect

and builder at Edinburgh; designed Burns'
memorial at Alloway near Ayr 1818, completed
1823, Knox monument Glasgow 1825, Edinburgh high sch. 1825-9, George iv. bridge
1827, Ayr town buildings 1828, Burns' monument Edin. 1830, Dr. Guthrie's ch. 1840 and
the Martyrs' monument on the Calton hill
1844; author of *Observations on completing the
college of Edinburgh* 1816; *Report relative to
improvements on the earthern mound* 1830. *d.*
9 Howe st. Edinburgh 24 Feb. 1858. *Crombie's
Modern Athenians* (1882) 142-4, *portrait*.

HAMILTON, THOMAS. *b.* Longridge, parish of
Stonehouse, Lanarkshire 4 Feb. 1783; partner
with Robert and John Ogle at 37 Paternoster
row, London 1 Jany. 1808 to 1813; wholesale bookseller at 33 Paternoster row 1813-
50 when he retired, joined by Wm. Adams
1824, by Joseph Johnson Miles 1833; published some important books, chiefly religious,
the works of W. Jay of Bath, Rev. J. A.
James and Rev. C. Bradley; lived at Windmill place, Clapham common from 1850, *d.*
there 27 Dec. 1877. *bur.* Beddington churchyard 2 Jany. 1878. *Bookseller* (1878) *p.* 7.

HAMILTON, WALTER FERRIER (1 *son of Col.
John Hamilton of Cairn hill, Ayrshire). b.*
Cairn hill 31 May 1818; M.P. for Linlithgow-
shire 1859-65. *d.* Cathlow house, Torphichen,
Linlithgowshire 8 April 1872.

HAMILTON, RIGHT REV. WALTER KERR
(elder son of Ven. Anthony Hamilton 1778-
1851). *b.* London 16 Nov. 1808; ed. at Eton
and Ch. Ch. Ox., student 1827-32, B.A.
1831, M.A. 1833, D.D. 1854; fellow of
Merton 1832-42; C. of Wolvercot, Oxf.
1833; V. of St. Peter's-in-the-East, Oxf.
1837-41; canon of Salisbury, June 1841,
precentor 1843; bishop of Salisbury 27 March
1854 to death, consecrated at Lambeth 14
May; established a theological coll. at Salisbury 1861; an extreme high churchman, his
episcopal charge 1867 gave rise to discussion
in house of lords; author of *Morning and evening services for every day in the week* 1842;
Cathedral reform 1855; *A charge* 1867 to which
there were 9 published replies. *d.* the palace,
Salisbury 1 Aug. 1869. *W. K. Hamilton,
bishop of Salisbury, By H. P. Liddon* (1869);
Register and Mag. of Biog. ii, 143-4 (1869).

HAMILTON, WALTER RICHARD POLLOCK (4
*son of Alexander Hamilton of Inistioge, Ireland).
b.* 18 Aug. 1856; sub-lieut. 70 foot 28 Feb.
1874; with the Guide cavalry in Bèngal;
served in Jowaki-Afridi expedition 1877-8,
in Afghan campaign 1878, Victoria cross for

gallantry at Futtehabad 2 April 1879 when
as the last officer he had to assume command
of Guide cavalry; accompanied Sir Louis
Cavagnari to Kabul where he was killed 3
Sep. 1879. *Shadbolt's Afghan campaign, Biographical division* (1882) 98-100, *portrait*.

HAMILTON, SIR WILLIAM *(son of W. Hamilton). b.* 14 Feb. 1790; entered royal navy
1803; a prisoner of war in France 1805-14;
vice consul at Flushing and Middleburg 1817,
at Antwerp 1818, at Ostend 1818, at Nieuport
1820, at Boulogne 1822, consul there 28 June
1826 to 1 April 1873 when he retired on
pension; knighted by patent 21 Feb. 1873.
d. 113 Grande rue, Boulogne 14 Feb. 1877.
I.L.N. lxii, 369, 370 (1873), *portrait*.

HAMILTON, WILLIAM ALEXANDER BAILLIE-
(brother of Ker Baillie Hamilton 1804-89). *b.*
Normanby, Yorkshire 6 June 1803; entered
navy 28 Aug. 1816; captain 9 Aug. 1828;
private sec. to first lord of the Admiralty
1841, sec. of the Admiralty Jany. 1845 to
1855 when granted a pension of £1000;
comr. of patriotic fund 1865-81; admiral on
h.p. 12 Sep. 1865. *d.* Portree, Isle of Skye
1 Oct. 1881.

HAMILTON, WILLIAM BISHOP. *b.* London
1810; went to U.S. of A. 1827; traversed
Mississippi river on a flat boat giving dramatic performances at chief towns several
years; acted at Burton's Chambers st. theatre
New York; went to California 1851; lessee
of Jenny Lind theatre, San Francisco, afterwards of San Francisco Hall, the American
theatre and Metropolitan, all in San Francisco; returned to New York 1859. *d.* London 3 Dec. 1868.

HAMILTON, WILLIAM JOHN (1 *son of William
Richard Hamilton* 1777-1859). *b.* London 5
July 1805; ed. at Charterhouse and Univ. of
Gottingen; F.G.S. 1831, sec. 1832-54, pres.
1854, 1865-6; with H. Strickland explored
the Levant and the volcanic region of the
Katakekaumene 1835; went on horseback
through Asia Minor 1836; F.R.G.S., pres.
1837, 1841, 1842, 1847, founder's medallist
1843; F.R.S.; M.P. for Newport, Isle of
Wight 1841-47; director of Great Indian
peninsular railway 1849 to death; author of
Researches in Asia Minor, Pontus and Armenia
2 vols. 1842. *d.* 23 Chesham place, London
27 June 1867. *Quarterly Journal of Geol. Soc.
xxiv,* 29-33 (1867).

HAMILTON, WILLIAM RICHARD *(son of Rev.
Anthony Hamilton* 1739-1812, *archdeacon of
Colchester). b.* London 9 Jany. 1777; ed. at

HAMILTON, W. R. *(Con.)*

Harrow where he was lamed for life; sec. to lord Elgin at Constantinople 1799, sent to Egypt 1801 when he recovered the Rosetta stone from the French; aided in collecting and removing the Elgin marbles from Athens 1802; F.S.A. 1804, director 1809–10; under sec. of state for foreign affairs 1809–22; minister at Naples 1822–4; treasurer of Royal institution 1832–49; F.R.S.; a trustee of Br. Museum 1838–58; author of *Ægyptiaca or the ancient and modern state of Egypt* 1809; *Memorandum on the earl of Elgin's pursuits in Greece* 1811. *d.* 12 Bolton row, London 11 July 1859. *Chambers' Eminent Scotsmen, ii,* 229 (1869).

HAMILTON, SIR WILLIAM ROWAN (4 *child of Archibald Hamilton of Dublin, attorney* 1778– 1819). *b.* 29 Dominick st. Dublin at midnight 3–4 Aug. 1805; was acquainted with 9 languages in 1819; student of Trin. coll. Dublin 1823, B.A. 1827, M.A. 1837, LL.B. and LL.D. 1839; Andrews professor of astronomy, astronomer royal for Ireland and superintendent of Dublin observatory at Dunsink near Dublin 1827 to death; knighted by lord lieutenant Lord Mulgrave in library of Trin. coll. 15 Aug. 1835; M.R.I.A. 1832, president 1837; granted civil list pension of £200, 27 April 1844 which was continued to his widow; discovered conical refraction 1824; invented quaternions 1843; author of *Lectures on quaternions* 1853; *The elements of quaternions* 1866. *d.* Dunsink observatory 2 Sep. 1865. *R. P. Graves' Life of Sir W. R. Hamilton* 3 vols. 1882–89, *3 portraits; Dublin Univ. Mag., xix,* 94–110 (1842), *portrait; Proc. of Royal Soc. of Edin. v,* 473 (1866).

HAMILTON, SIR WILLIAM STIRLING, 3 Baronet *(elder son of Wm. Hamilton* 1758–90, *professor of anatomy in univ. of Glasgow).* *b.* Glasgow univ. 8 March 1788; ed. at Glasgow and Edin. univs.; student of Balliol coll. Ox. 1807, B.A. 1811, M.A. 1814; D.D. of Leyden 1840; called to Scottish bar 1813; styled himself a baronet, under the decision of an Edinburgh jury 1816; H.M.'s solicitor for Teinds in Scotland 1832; professor of universal history Univ. of Edin. 1821, professor of logic and metaphysics there 1836 to death; contributed articles on metaphysics to *Edinburgh Review* 1829–39; F.R.S. Edin., resigned 1835; published an edition of the works of Thomas Reid 1846 and of Dugald Steward 10 vols. 1854–8; author of *Discussions on philosophy and literature, education and university reform* 1852, 3 ed. 1866; *Lectures on metaphysics and logic* 4 vols. 1859–60, 2 ed. 1861–

HAMILTON, SIR W. S. *(Con.)*

66; a civil list pension granted to Lady Hamilton 13 Oct. 1849. *d.* 16 Great King st. Edinburgh 6 May 1856, his bust placed in senate hall of Edin. university Dec. 1867, his library of 9000 volumes purchased and given to Glasgow univ. *Veitch's Memoir of Sir W. Hamilton* (1869), *portrait; Sir W. Hamilton, By W. H. S. Monck* (1881); *De Quincey's Works, xvi,* 114–79 (1871); *Sir A. Grant's Story of Univ. of Edin. ii,* 332–35 (1884).

HAMLET, THOMAS. *b.* Boughton, Cheshire 1770; silver-smith and jeweller at 1 and 2 Princes st. Soho, London 1801–1841; built the Royal bazaar, British diorama and exhibition of works of art, opened at 73 Oxford st. about April 1828, it was burned down 27 May 1829, loss £50,000, rebuilt 1830 renamed the Queen's Bazaar 1834, converted it into the Princess's theatre at cost of £47,000 which opened with promenade concerts 30 Sep. 1840; bankrupt 20 March 1841; sold the theatre for £14,500; considered a millionaire at one time, but greatly reduced by being unable to recover on certain bonds of the Prince Regent and Duke of York. *d.* 5 Park place, St. James's, London 21 Feb. 1853.

HAMLEY, FRANCIS GILBERT *(eld. son of Joseph Hamley, d.* 1854). *b.* 1815; ensign 12 foot 7 Aug. 1835; major 50 foot 8 Jany. 1858 to 1873; governor general of South Australia 19 Feb. 1868 to 16 Feb. 1869; M.G. 9 Aug. 1873. *d.* Cheltenham 12 Jany. 1876.

HAMMACK, JOHN GEORGE *(younger son of John Hammack of London).* Timber merchant 30 Cannon st. road, Commercial road, London; surveyor in city of London; retained in almost every case coming under provisions of the Lands Clauses Consolidation act; returning officer for Tower Hamlets borough; chairman of city of London and Tower Hamlets cemetery co.; chairman of Ratcliff gas light co. 25 years; one of the two chief assistants of registrar general in taking census in 1861. *d.* Boxlands near Dorking 4 Oct. 1861 aged 70.

HAMMERSLEY, JAMES ASTBURY. *b.* Burslem, Staffs. 1815; exhibited 3 pictures at R.A., 3 at B.I. and 10 at Suffolk st. 1842–52; head master Manchester sch. of design 1849– 62; president Manchester acad. of fine arts 1857–61; among his paintings were Mountain and clouds, Loughrigg Fell 1850 in Manchester art gallery; The castle of Rosenau in the collection at Windsor; author of *The condition of the continental schools of art* 1850. *d.* Manchester about 1868.

HAMMICK, Sir Stephen Love, 1 Baronet *(eld. son of Stephen Hammick of Plymouth, alderman).* *b.* Plymouth 28 Feb. 1777; M.C.S. 1799; hon. fellow R.C.S. 1843; surgeon of Royal naval hospital at Plymouth 1803–29; surgeon extraordinary to George iv. 1820–30, to Wm. iv. 1830–37; practised 36 Cavendish sq. London 1829–56; baronet 25 July 1834; author of *Practical remarks on amputation, fractures and stricture of the urethra* 1830. *d.* The Crescent, Plymouth 15 June 1867.

HAMMILL, John *(only son of Martin Hammill of Liverpool).* *b.* 13 April 1803; ed. at Macclesfield gr. sch. and Trin. coll. Cam., B.A. 1825, M.A. 1832; barrister I.T. 30 Jany. 1832; one of boundary comrs. of boroughs 16 July 1835; comr. of bankruptcy in Liverpool 1840; police magistrate at Worship st. London 1847, at Marylebone Jany. 1860 to death. *d.* 34 Sussex gardens, Hyde park, London 30 July 1860.

HAMMOND, Edmund Hammond, 1 Baron (3 son of George Hammond, d. 1853). *b.* London 25 June 1802; ed. at Eton, Harrow and Univ. coll. Ox., B.A. 1823, M.A. 1826, scholar 1824–8, fellow 1828–46; clerk privy council office 1823–4; in foreign office 1824, chief of the oriental department 1830–41; permanent under sec. of state for foreign affairs 10 April 1854, retired 10 Oct. 1873 on his full pay of £2500; P.C. 11 June 1866; cr. baron Hammond of Kirk Ella, Kingston-on-Hull 22 Feb. 1874; assured Lord Granville that the world was profoundly at peace 27 June 1870, French and Prussian war broke out 15 July. *d.* Mentone, France 29 April 1890. *I.L.N. lxiii,* 413, 414 (1873), *portrait; Graphic* 24 *May* 1890 *p.* 583, *portrait.*

HAMMOND, Alfred William. Music seller and publisher at 9 New Bond st. and then at 214 Regent st. London 1850–62; projector, proprietor and many years editor of *Musical Standard,* No. 1, Aug. 2, 1862; composer of *As o'er the past my mem'ry strays,* a hymn 1857; *When all thy mercies O my God,* a hymn 1857. *d.* Belvedere near Erith, Kent 18 Dec. 1875.

HAMMOND, George *(younger son of William Hammond).* *b.* 1763; matric. from Merton coll. Ox. 16 March 1780 aged 17, B.A. 1784, M.A. 1788, D.C.L. 1810; sec. to David Hartley in Paris when conducting peace negotiations with France and America 1783; chargé d'affaires at Vienna 1788–90, at Madrid 1791; minister plenipo. to U.S. America 1791–5; under sec. foreign office, London 1795–1806, 1807–9; a comr. for British claims on France, Sep. 1814 to July 1828 when pen-

HAMMOND, G. *(Con.)*
sioned; connected with the *Anti-Jacobin* 1797 and the *Quarterly Rev.* 1809. *d.* 22 Portland place, London 22 April 1853 aged 90.

HAMMOND, James Lempriere. *b.* 1828; ed. at Trin. coll. Cam., B.A. 1852, M.A. 1855, fellow, tutor and bursar; executor of Dr. Wm. Whewell 1866 when he superintended the additions to Trin. coll., completed under Whewell's will at cost of £100,000 in 1868; assistant Endowed schools commissioner; assistant Charity commissioner for England and Wales; sec. to D. of Devonshire, chancellor of Cambridge; on the governing bodies of Christ's hospital and Westminster school; author of *Carmen Latinum. Cantab.* 1849. *d.* Clyde villa, Hammersmith, Middlesex 23 July 1880 in 52 year. *Times* 28, 30, 31 *July* 1880.

HAMMOND, John *(youngest son of Lempriere Hammond of Jersey).* *b.* 1801; solicitor general of Jersey 1848–58; bailiff of Jersey and pres. of The States 16 Feb. 1858 to death. *d.* Royal court house, Jersey 14 Feb. 1880.

HAMOND, Sir Graham Eden, 2 Baronet *(only son of Sir Andrew Snape Hamond 1738–1828, captain R.N., 1 baronet).* *b.* Newman st. London 30 Dec. 1779; entered R.N. 1785, captain 30 Nov. 1798; present at battle of Copenhagen 1801; knight commander of Tower and Sword 1825; commander in chief on South American station 1834–8; C.B. 4 June 1815, K.C.B. 13 Sep. 1831, G.C.B. 5 July 1855; admiral 22 Jany. 1847, admiral of the fleet 10 Nov. 1862. *d.* Norton lodge, Freshwater, Isle of Wight 20 Dec. 1862.

HAMOND, Horace Edward. Cornet 1 life guards 18 Feb. 1828, lieut. 1831, sold out 12 Sep. 1834; aide-de-camp to king of Hanover some time; precis writer to earl of Malmesbury sec. of state foreign affairs 28 Feb. 1852; consul at Cherbourg 1 April 1852 to death; K.H. *d.* 8 Feb. 1876.

HAMPDEN, John *(brother of Right Rev. R. D. Hampden).* *b.* 27 Oct. 1798; ed. at Univ. coll. Ox.; collector of pictures, coins and medals; collected materials for life of John Hampden the patriot. *d.* 4 Clarence ter. Warwick st. Leamington 13 Nov. 1860. *Numismatic Chronicle, xxi, Proceedings* 11–12 (1861).

HAMPDEN, John (1 son of Rev. John Hampden, R. of Hinton Martel, Dorset 1829–47). Matric. from St. Mary hall, Ox. 14 Feb. 1839 aged 19; author of *The rampart of steel or a fancys (sic) for a permanent coast militia and an army of reserve,* Canterbury 1852; *John Hampden's Monthly. The truth seeker's oracle and*

HAMPDEN, J. *(Con.)*

scriptural science review, Nos. 1–3 *May–July* 1876; *Description of J. Hampden's improvements in artillery* 1876; *The new manual of Biblical Cosmography* 1877; *The earth in its creation and the portion adapted to man's occupation* 1880; published *John Hampden's Circular map of the world* 1875; *John Hampden's Chronometrical Dial-plate* 1876; edited *Cosmos. A Geographical Review* 1883. *d.* from bronchitis at 3 Park st. Croydon 22 Jany. 1891. *Daily Graphic* 27 *Jany.* 1891 p. 6 col. 2.

NOTE.—He inserted an advertisement in *Scientific Opinion* 12 Jany. 1870 offering £500 to anyone proving that the earth is round. This challenge was accepted by Alfred Russel Wallace; Hampden and Wallace each deposited £500 in the hands of John Henry Walsh who decided in favour of Wallace as having "proved the curvature to and fro of the Bedford Level canal between Witney bridge and Welsh's dam (6 miles) to the extent of 5 feet more or less." Walsh paid the £1000 to Wallace 1 April 1870 although Hampden instructed him not to do so, Hampden brought an action against Walsh to recover his £500, which was tried in the Queen's Bench division 17 Jany. 1876 when the judges held that Hampden having demanded his deposit money back before it had been paid over by Walsh, was entitled to judgment. *Law Reports i, Q.B. division* (1876) 189-98; *Experimental proofs that the surface of standing water is not convex but horizontal with an examination of the question, Is the earth a globe or a plane? between J. Hampden and A. R. Wallace. By Parallax* [Samuel Birley Rowbotham] 1870.

HAMPDEN, RIGHT REV. RENN DICKSON *(eld. son of Renn Hampden, colonel of militia).* *b.* Barbadoes 29 March 1793; ed. at Oriel coll. Ox., double first class 1813, B.A. 1814, M.A. 1816, B.D. and D.D. 1833, fellow 1814–7, tutor 1832, Bampton lecturer 1832; C. of Newton near Bath 1816; principal of St. Mary hall, Ox., April 1833–48; professor of moral philosophy 1834–36; canon of Ch. Ch. Ox. and regius professor of divinity 17 Feb. 1836 to 1848; R. of Ewelme, Oxfs. 1836–48; bp. of Hereford 28 Dec. 1847 to death, his election opposed by 13 bishops and the dean of Hereford, consecrated at Lambeth palace 26 March 1848; author of *The Scholastic philosophy considered in its relation to Christian theology* 1833 and of essays, lectures, sermons and charges. *d.* 107 Eaton place, London 23 April 1868. *Memorials by his daughter* (1871), *portrait*; *Mozley's Reminiscences,* i, 350–86 (1882); *I.L.N. xii,* 22 (1848), *portrait.*

HAMPSON, JOHN. *b.* 1790; master of Bury st. academy, Manchester 1810–60; author of *The Monitory and Epistolary Exercise book for schools* 1841. *d.* Ardwick, Manchester, Oct. 1878 in 88 year.

HAMPTON, JOHN SOMERSET PAKINGTON, 1 Baron *(younger son of Wm. Russell of Powick court, Worcs., who d. 9 Dec. 1812).* *b.* Powick

HAMPTON, J. S. P. *(Con.)*

court 20 Feb. 1799; ed. at Eton and Oriel coll. Ox., D.C.L. 7 June 1853; assumed name of Pakington 1830; chairman of Worcs. quarter sessions 1834–54; M.P. for Droitwich 1837–74; sec. of state for the colonies 27 Feb. to Dec. 1852; P.C. 27 Feb. 1852; first lord of the admiralty Feb. 1858 to June 1859 and June 1866 to March 1867; sec. of state for war 8 March 1867 to Dec. 1868; first civil service commissioner Nov. 1875; baronet 13 July 1846; G.C.B. 15 June 1859; created Baron Hampton of Hampton Lovett and of Westwood, co. Worcester 6 March 1874. *d.* 9 Eaton sq. London 9 April 1880. *bur.* in family mausoleum Hampton Lovett church, Worcs. 15 April. *The drawing room portrait gallery of eminent personages, second series* 1859, *portrait*; *The statesmen of England* (1862), *portrait*; *I.L.N. xx,* 321 (1852), *xxi,* 237 (1852), *portrait.*

HAMPTON, RICHARD. *b.* Nancekuke down, Illogan, Cornwall 4 April 1782; a worker at a stamping mill; first preached at Redruth 1811; itinerated in Devon and Cornwall as a Wesleyan, known as the Cornish pilgrim preacher 1813–58. *d.* Porth Towan, Illogan 2 April 1858. *Foolish Dick, an autobiography of Richard Hampton* 1873, *portrait.*

HAMPTON, WILLIAM PHILIP. *b.* 21 Sep. 1810; ensign 30 Bengal N.I. 4 Nov. 1828, commandant 2 Bengal N.I. 1 Jany. 1864 to 1 March 1870; L.G. 1 Oct. 1877. *d.* 65 Haverstock hill, London 23 Jany. 1881.

HANBURY, BENJAMIN. *b.* Wolverhampton 13 May 1778; in Bank of England 1803–59; deacon of Congregational ch. Union st. London 1819–57; treasurer of Congregational Union 1831 to death; author of *An historical research concerning the Congregational church in England* 1820; *Historical memorials relating to the Independents* 3 vols. 1839–44; edited Hooker's *Ecclesiastical Polity* 3 vols. 1830. *d.* 16 Gloucester villas, Brixton, Surrey 12 Jany. 1864. *Evangelical Mag.* 1864 p. 166.

HANBURY, DANIEL *(1 son of Daniel Bell Hanbury of firm of Allen and Hanbury, chemists, Plough court, Lombard st. London).* *b.* London 11 Sep. 1825; partner in firm of Allen and Hanbury to 1870; student at Pharmaceutical soc. 1844, member 1857, examiner 1860–72; F.L.S. 1855, treasurer to death; F. Chem. soc. 21 Jany. 1858, and F.R. Micros. soc. 1867; F.R.S. 6 June 1867, member of council 1872–5; studied the materia medica of the Chinese; visited Greece and the Holy Land 1860; the cucurbitaceous genus Hanburya named after

HANBURY, D. *(Con.)*

him 1870; author with professor Friedrich
A. Flückiger of *Pharmacographia* 1874. *d.*
Clapham common, Surrey 24 March 1875.
Science papers. ed. by J. Ince 1876, *memoir pp.*
3–40, *portrait; Proc. of Royal soc. xxiv,* 2–3
(1876); *Nature, xi,* 428 (1875).

HANBURY, DANIEL BELL (1 *son of Capel Han-*
bury). b. 8 Feb. 1794; with Allen and Hanbury 1808, partner, retired 1868; an originator of Pharmaceutical soc. 1841, treasurer
1852–67; assisted to make index for *Pharma-*
cographia 1874. *d.* Hollywood, Clapham common 12 Feb. 1882. *Pharmaceutical Journal,*
xii, 698 (1881–82).

HANBURY, SIR JOHN (2 *son of Wm. Hanbury*
of Kelmarsh, Northamptonshire). b. Kelmarsh
1782; ed. at Eton; ensign 58 foot 20 July
1799; served in Egypt 1801, in Peninsula
1808–9, 1813–4, in Portugal 1826–7; major
grenadier guards 25 July 1821 to 22 July
1830; colonel 99 foot 6 Oct. 1851 to death;
general 20 June 1854; K.C.H. and K.B.
1832; K.C.B. 10 Nov. 1862. *d.* 15 Charles
st. Berkeley sq. London 7 June 1863.

HANBURY, ROBERT (2 *son of Osgood Hanbury*
of Holfield Grange, Essex 1765–1852). *b.* 2
July 1796; clerk with Truman, Buxton & Co.
brewers 1815, partner 1820, managing partner
of business in London and at Burton on Trent;
sheriff of Herts. 1854; had large gardens and
conservatories at Poles near Ware; built and
endowed Thundridge ch. Herts. 184– and
Christ Church, Ware 1858. *d.* Poles, Ware 20
Jany. 1884. *Licensed Victuallers' Gazette* 16
Jany. 1875 *pp.* 64, 67, *portrait; Licensed Vic-*
tuallers' Year Book 1876 *pp.* 83–5, *portrait.*

HANBURY, ROBERT CULLING (1 *son of the pre-*
ceding). b. London 19 March 1823; partner
in Truman, Hanbury and Co. brewers, London; M.P. for Middlesex 29 April 1857 to
death. *d.* 10 Upper Grosvenor st. London 29
March 1867. *bur.* in churchyard of Thundridge, Herts. *I.L.N. xxx,* 479 (1857), *portrait.*

HANCE, HENRY FLETCHER. *b.* Old Brompton,
London 4 Aug. 1827; entered Hong-kong
C.S. 1 Sep. 1844; 4 assistant in superintendency of trade at Hong-kong 1 May 1854,
1 assistant 1857; vice consul at Whampoa
near Canton 1861–78; consul Canton 1878,
1881, 1883; acting consul at Amoy, May
1886; spent his life in study of botany of
China. *d.* Amoy 22 June 1886, his herbarium
22,000 species offered to British Museum.

HANCOCK, ALBANY *(son of John Hancock,*
saddler, Newcastle-on-Tyne, d. 1812). *b.* Bridge

HANCOCK, A. *(Con.)*

End, Newcastle 24 Dec. 1806; solicitor Newcastle 1830–2; a founder of the Tyneside
Naturalists' Field club 1846; F.L.S. 1862;
wrote over 70 papers on birds, shells, mollusca, etc. 1836 etc., the first to examine
carefully the internal structures of mollusca
1843, gold medallist of Royal soc. 1858; with
J. Alder wrote *A monograph of the British*
Nudibranchiate mollusca 7 *parts* 1845–55. *d.* 4
St. Mary's ter. Newcastle 24 Oct. 1873.
Trans. Northumberland Nat. Hist. Soc. v, 118,
(1875), *portrait; Monthly Chronicle of North*
country lore, Dec. 1890 *pp.* 568–70, *portrait.*

HANCOCK, HENRY. Entered Bombay army
18 June 1819; adjutant general 1 May 1848
to 15 Sep. 1856; col. 19 Bombay N.I. 1856–
69; L.G. 30 March 1869. *d.* Friedenfels,
Upper Maize hill, St. Leonards on Sea, Sussex
30 Dec. 1872 aged 70.

HANCOCK, HENRY *(son of Samuel Hancock of*
London, merchant). b. Bread st. hill, London
6 Aug. 1809; M.R.C.S. 1834, F.R.C.S. 1843,
prof. of human anat. 1865, president 1872,
Hunterian orator 1873; house surgeon Westminster hospital, demonstrator of anatomy
1834–8; lecturer on anatomy and physiology
Charing Cross hospital 1838, assist. surgeon
1839, surgeon to 1875, lecturer on surgery;
surgeon Westminster ophthalmic hospital to
1875; the first to remove the os calcis and
retain the foot; author of *On the operation for*
strangulated hernia 1850; *On the operative sur-*
gery of the foot and ankle-joint 1873. *d.* Standen
house, Chute, Wilts. 1 Jany. 1880. *Medical*
Times 10 *Jany.* 1880 *p.* 53; *Lancet* (1853) *ii,*
578, *portrait.*

HANCOCK, JOHN *(brother of Albany Hancock*
1806–73). *b.* about 1808; saddler and ironmonger at Newcastle; formed finest collection
of British birds in the Kingdom and presented
it to Museum of Natural History Soc. Barras
bridge, Newcastle 1881; author of *A catalogue*
of the birds of Northumberland and Durham in
Natural History Trans. 1874 and of other
papers in same work and in Trans. of Tyneside
Naturalists' Field Club. *d.* 4 St. Mary's terrace,
Newcastle 11 Oct. 1890. *Monthly chronicle of*
North country lore, Dec. 1890 *pp.* 566–9, 2 *por-*
traits; Graphic 25 Oct. 1890 *p.* 460, *portrait.*

HANCOCK, SIR SAMUEL *(brother of Henry*
Hancock 1809–80). *b.* 3 June 1805; exon of
the yeomen of the guard 1832–47; knighted
at St. James's palace 12 May 1841. *d.* 5
Paragon buildings, Cheltenham 7 Aug. 1886.

HANCOCK, THOMAS (2 *son of James Hancock,*
timber merchant). b. Marlborough, Wilts. 8

HANCOCK, T. (Con.)

May 1786; invented the masticator by which india rubber was pressed into blocks or rolled into sheets 1820; india rubber manufacturer Goswell road, London 1821, works burnt down 11 April 1834, Manchester works burnt 1838; partner with Charles Macintosh maker of waterproof garments London and Manchester; patented vulcanised india rubber and vulcanite or ebonite 1843; took out 16 patents 1820–47. d. Woodberry vale, Stoke Newington 26 March 1865. *Personal Narrative of India-rubber manufacture in England, By T. Hancock* (1857), *portrait.*

HANCOCK, WALTER (*brother of the preceding*). b. Marlborough 16 June 1799; engineer Stratford, Essex; invented steam engine in which the cylinder and piston were replaced by flexible steam bags, ran it on the road from Stratford to London Feb. 1831, built 10 similar machines up to 1840; associated with Thomas Hancock in manufacture of india rubber 1841; author of *Narrative of twelve years experiments of steam carriages on common roads* 1838. d. West Ham, Essex 14 May 1852.

HANCOCK, WILLIAM NEILSON (2 son of Wm. John Hancock of Lisburn, Antrim). b. Castle st. Lisburn 1820; ed. at Dungannon and Trin. coll. Dublin, B.A. 1843, LL.B. 1846, LL.D. 1849; barrister King's inns 1844; Q.C. 1859; professor of political economy at Trin. coll.; professor of political economy and jurisprudence Queen's coll. Belfast; founded Statistical and social inquiry Soc. of Ireland 1847; sec. to Univ. of Dublin commission, Irish railway commission and other commissions; clerk of the Crown and Hanaper office, Dublin. d. at residence of Sir Wm. Thomson, Glasgow 10 July 1888. bur. Mount Jerome cemetery, Dublin 17 July.

HAND, GEORGE SUMNER. b. 1807; entered navy 5 Feb. 1821, captain 6 Sep. 1852, retired admiral 15 June 1879; C.B. 20 May 1859; F.R.G.S.; served in Ava 1825, West Indies 1829–31, on coast of Africa 1844–9. d. I. 4 The Albany, Piccadilly, London 1 Dec. 1883.

HANDLEY, JOHN. b. Stoke, Notts. 1807; a banker at Newark and Sleaford as Handley, Peacock & Co.; M.P. for Newark 1857–65; sheriff of Notts. 1869. d. North gate, Newark 8 Dec. 1880.

HANDYSIDE, ROBERT (*son of William Handyside, writer to the signet*). b. Edinburgh 1798; ed. at Univ. of Edin.; advocate at Scottish bar 1822; deputy of the lord advocate 1835; sheriff depute of co. Stirling 9 July 1840;

HANDYSIDE, R. (Con.)

solicitor general for Scotland 17 Jany. 1853; a lord of session and justiciary with courtesy title of Lord Handyside 15 Nov. 1853 to death. d. Kennet, Edinburgh 18 April 1858. *Journal of jurisprudence ii*, 245 (1858).

HANHAM, THOMAS BARNABAS (*youngest son of Rev. Sir James Hanham, 7 baronet, d. 2 April 1849, m. Eliza Dean dau. of William Patey, she d. Wimborne, Dorset 5 June 1877 aged 90*). b. 11 June 1825; sub-lieut. R.N. 6 Aug. 1845, lieut. 1847, retired 1864, commander 30 April 1879; Provincial S.G.W. of Dorset. d. Manston house, Blandford, Dorset 27 Nov. 1883, cremated Manston 4 Dec. when a masonic ritual was used which had not been employed in England during the century. m. as his third wife 1 Dec. 1868 Edith Mary widow of major John Swinburne 18 regt., she d. 30 July 1876.

NOTE.—He erected in the private grounds of Manston house a crematorium, and having disinterred the remains of his third wife and his mother, had them cremated there on the 8 and 9 Oct. 1882. These were the first cremations in England in modern times. *Times* 12 Oct. 1882 p. 4, 5 Dec. 1883 p. 7, 6 Dec. p. 7; *Trans. Cremation Soc.* 1885 p. 48 *with view of the Crematorium.*

HANKEY, SIR FREDERICK (3 son of John Hankey). Ensign 90 foot Sep. 1800; major of 50 foot 1808, of 2 Ceylon regiment 1809, of 15 foot 1815 to 25 March 1816 when placed on h.p.; sec. to order of St. Michael and St. George 17 Nov. 1818 to 20 June 1833; col. in the army 27 Nov. 1825, retired Aug. 1826; sec. to government of Malta 1825 to 1838; G.C.M.G. 4 May 1833 for his services in Malta. d. 7 Montagu sq. London 13 March 1855 aged 81.

HANKEY, HENRY AITCHISON (*son of John Peter Hankey*). b. 6 Oct. 1805; ensign 10 foot 26 June 1823; lieut. col. 1 dragoon guards 19 Jany. 1844 to 12 Nov. 1852; col. of 3 hussars 12 Jany. 1866, of 1 dragoon guards 1 Jany. 1872 to death; general 7 Dec. 1871. d. Cliff house, Sandgate 24 June 1886.

HANKEY, WILLIAM ALERS. b. London 15 Aug. 1771; ed. at univ. of Edin.; head of the firm of Hankeys & Co. bankers, 7 Fenchurch st. London; assisted in proceedings of Religious tract society 1801–1808; one of founders and conductors of British and foreign Bible society 1804, treasurer 1801–32; A.I.C.E. 1820, treasurer 1820–45; gave evidence on slavery before house of commons 1833; author of *Letters to Joseph Sturge relating to the Arcadia estate in Jamaica* 1838. d. 5 Hyde park gardens, London 23 March 1859. *Min. of proc. of Instit. of C.E. xx*, 134 (1861).

HANKINSON, Most Rev. Michael Adrian. *b.* Warrington 29 Sep. 1817; ordained priest at St. Edmund's Benedictine college, Douay 1841, sub-prior there to 1851, prior 1854–63; bishop of Port Louis, Mauritius 1863 to death, during which time an epidemic carried off one-sixth of the population in 3 years. *d.* Douay 21 Sep. 1870. *Gillow's English Catholics* (1888) *iii*, 111–2.

HANKINSON, Ven. Robert Edwards. *b.* 1798; ed. at C.C. coll. Cam., B.A. 1820, M.A. 1824; R. of Halesworth, Suffolk 1850–63; archdeacon of Norwich 1857 to death; R. of North Creake, Norfolk 1863 to death; author of *The Communion of believers, a course of lectures* 1838; *The call of Abraham, a Seatonian poem* 1841. *d.* North Creake 27 March 1868 aged 70.

HANLON, Thomas. *b.* Manchester 1836; first appeared in public as a gymnast at the Colosseum, Liverpool; organised with his 5 brothers gymnastic performances that have made them famous in Europe and America; performed in U.S. of America 1858–62 and 1865–6, in California, South America and Europe 1862–4; performed in London and at the Exposition in Paris 1867; committed suicide at Harrisburg, Pennsylvania 5 April 1868.

HANMER, John Hanmer, 1 Baron (1 *child of Thomas Hanmer* 1781–1818, *lieut.-col. Flintshire militia*). *b.* 22 Dec. 1809; ed. at Eton and Ch. Ch. Ox.; succeeded his grandfather as 3 baronet 1828; sheriff of Flintshire 1832; M.P. Shrewsbury 1832–37; M.P. Hull 1841–47; M.P. Flint district 1847–72; cr. Baron Hanmer of Hanmer and of Flint 1 Oct. 1872; author of *Poems on various subjects* 1836; *Fra Cipolla and other poems* 1839; *Sonnets* 1840; *A memoir of the family and parish of Hanmer* 1877. *d.* Knotley hall, Kent 8 March 1881. *St. Paul's, x,* 368–77 (1872); *I.L.N. lxi*, 340, 342 (1872), *portrait.*

HANMER, Henry (6 *child of Sir Thomas Hanmer, d.* 1828). *b.* 30 April 1789; cornet royal horse guards 6 Oct. 1808, major 1826 to 4 Dec. 1832; M.P. for Aylesbury 1832–36; sheriff of Bucks. 1854; K.H. 1837. *d.* Stockgrove near Leighton Buzzard 2 Feb. 1868.

HANN, James (*son of a colliery smith*). *b.* Washington, co. Durham 1799; engineer in a Tyne towing vessel; kept schools at Gateshead and at Friar's Green near Newcastle; accountant in office of Isaac Dodds, Gateshead; calculator in Nautical almanac office; writing master King's coll. sch. London and then mathematical master there to death;

Hann, J. (*Con.*)
A.I.C.E. 13 June 1843; author of *Mathematics for practical men* 1833; *A short treatise on the steam engine* 1847; *Examples on the integral calculus* 1850 and other works. *d.* King's coll. hospital, London 17 Aug. 1856.

HANNA, Rev. Samuel. *b.* Kellswater near Ballymena, co. Antrim 1772; ed. at Glasgow univ., M.A. 1789, D.D. 1818; presbyterian minister, Drumbo, co. Down 1795 and at Rosemary st. Belfast 1799 to death; professor of divinity and ch. history at Assembly's coll. Belfast 1817; moderator of synod of Ulster 1809; first moderator of the general presbyterian assembly 1840; author of single sermons and pamphlets. *d.* at residence of his son in law Rev. Dr. Denham, James st. Londonderry 23 April 1852. *bur.* Belfast 30 April, portrait in hall of Assembly's coll. Belfast. *Belfast News Letter 26 April* 1852 *p.* 2.

HANNA, Rev. William (*son of preceding*). *b.* Belfast 26 Nov. 1808; ed. at Glasgow univ., LL.D. 1852, and at Edin. univ., D.D. 1864; presbyterian minister East Kilbride near Glasgow 1835 and at Skirling, Peeblesshire 1837–43; minister of Free ch. Skirling 1843–50; colleague of Rev. Thos. Guthrie in St. John's Free ch. Edin. 1850–66; ed. of *North British Review;* author of *Memoirs of the life and writings of Thomas Chalmers, D.D.* 4 vols. 1849–52; *The Posthumous works of Thomas Chalmers* 9 vols. 1847; *Last days of our Lord's passion* 1862 which circulated 50,000 copies, and many other works. *d.* 77 Coleshill st. Eaton sq. London 24 May 1882. *Guardian, May* 1882 *p.* 760; *Scott's Fasti, vol. i, pt. i, p.* 229.

HANNAH, Rev. John (3 *son of a small coal dealer*). *b.* Lincoln 3 Nov. 1792; appointed Wesleyan Methodist minister 1814; went to America as representative to the Conferences 1824 and 1856; theological tutor at theological training institutions at Hoxton and Stoke Newington 1834–42; sec. of Conference 1840–2, 1854–8, president 1842 and 1851; theological tutor at Didsbury, Yorkshire 1843 to death; author of *Memoirs of Rev. D. Stowe* 1828; *Documents relating to British and Canadian conferences* 1860 and other works. *d.* Didsbury 29 Dec. 1867. *Introductory Lectures on Theology, By J. Hannah* (1875) *with Memoir by W. B. Pope pp.* 1–69; *J. Evans's Lancashire authors* (1876) 118–23; *I.L.N. i*, 200 (1842), *portrait.*

HANNAH, Ven. John (1 *son of the preceding*). *b.* Lincoln 16 July 1818; ed. at Brasen. coll. Ox. 1837; Lincoln scholar of Corpus Christi 1837–40, B.A. 1840, M.A. 1843, D.C.L. 1853; fellow of Lincoln 1840–4; Bampton lecturer

HANNAH, VEN. J. *(Con.)*

1863; rector of Edinburgh academy 1847–52; warden of Trinity coll. Glenalmond, Perth 1854–70; V. of Brighton 1870 to Dec. 1887 which he divided into 11 ecclesiastical districts; prebendary of Chichester 1874–76; archdeacon of Lewes 1876 to death; editor of *Poems and psalms by H. King, bishop of Chichester* 1843; *Poems by Sir H. Wotton and Sir W. Raleigh* 1845, 2 ed. 1875; author of *Discourse on the fall and its result* 1857 and other books. *d.* Brighton vicarage 1 June 1888. *Times 2 June 1888 p. 13, col. 6.*

HANNAN, JOHN. *b.* St. Giles's, London 29 Sep. 1817; a pugilist known as the Drury lane Irishman; beat Dan Dismore 6 June 1837, £25 a side; beaten by Tom Maley 30 Aug. 1838, £25 a side; beat John Walker 1 Nov. 1838, £25 a side, beat him again 2 April 1839 in 3 hours and 48 minutes, £50 a side; beaten by Byng Stocks 11 June 1839, £25 a side; beat Dick Forsey 14 April 1840, £25 a side; fought John Broome known as Young Ducrow £500 a side at New park farm near Bicester 26 Jany. 1841 when Broome won after 47 rounds in 79 minutes, the amount fought for was the largest since Ward and Cannon fought 1825. *d.* 7 King st. Soho, London 18 Oct. 1857. *Henning's Recollections of the prize ring* (1888) 101–111.

HANNAY, REV. ALEXANDER. *b.* Kirkcudbright 27 Feb. 1822; ed. at Glasgow univ.; D.D. of Yale univ. 1881; congregational minister Prince's st. ch. Dundee 1846 to 1862; minister City road ch. London 1862–6, at West Croydon 1866–70; sec. Colonial missionary soc.; sec. Congregational union of England and Wales 10 May 1870 to death; author of *The claims of the temperance movement on the churches* 1868; *How is England to be saved? An appeal to young men* 1877. *d.* Lincluden, Sunnyside road, Hornsey Rise 12 Nov. 1890. *I.L.N. 29 Nov. 1890 p. 678, portrait.*

HANNAY, JAMES (1 son of *David Hannay 1794–1864, banker, author of Ned Allen*). *b.* Dumfries 17 Feb. 1827; midshipman R.N. 1840–45; reporter on *Morning Chronicle* 1846; contributed to *Pasquin* a comic paper 1847; contested Dumfries burghs May 1857; editor of *Edinburgh Evening Courant* 1860–64; consul at Barcelona 13 July 1868 to death; author of *King Dobbs, Sketches in Ultramarine* 1849; *Blackwood v. Carlyle: a vindication, by a Carlylian* 1850; *Singleton Fontenoy, R.N.* 3 vols. 1850; *Satires and satirists: six lectures* 1854; *Sand and shells* 1854 which contains notices of his naval career; *Eustace Conyers* 3 vols. 1855;

HANNAY, J. *(Con.)*

Three hundred years of a Norman house, the barons of Gournay 1867; *Studies on Thackeray* 1869. *d.* Putchet, Barcelona 9 Jany. 1873. *Temple Bar, xxxviii,* 89–94 (1873), *xlix,* 234–47 (1877); *The Critic xvii,* 629 (1858), *portrait.*

NOTE.—He is described under the name of Eglinton Conyers in The Club and the Drawing Room by Cecil Hay 2 vols. 1870.

HANNAY, ROBERT (*son of James Hannay of Kirkcudbright*). *b.* Lock-Bank, Castle-Douglas 1789; ed. at gram. sch. Annan and at Ball. coll. Ox., B.A. 1812; member of Speculative soc.; advocate in Scotland 1814; visited libraries of the Vatican and Stockholm; gave evidence on British museum before house of commons 1836; author of *Address to Lord Hope on collecting and reporting decisions* 1821; *Defence of the usury laws* 1823; *History of the representation of England, drawn from records* 1831. *d.* Kew, Surrey 2 Feb. 1868. *Journal of Jurisprudence, xii,* 218 (1869); *Rep. on British Museum* (1836) 418–26.

HANNINGTON, RIGHT REV. JAMES (3 son of *Charles Smith Hannington, warehouseman*). *b.* Hurstpierpoint near Brighton 3 Sep. 1847; ed. at St. Mary hall, Ox., B.A. 1873, M.A. 1875, D.C.L. 1884; C. of Martinhoe and Trentishoe, Devon 1874–75; C. of St. George's, Hurstpierpoint 1875–82, 1883; missionary in Central Africa 1882–3; bishop of Eastern equatorial Africa, consecrated at Lambeth 24 June 1884; author of *Peril and adventure in Central Africa* 1886; headed an expedition to the Lake Victoria Nyanza 23 July 1885, murdered by order of Mwanga king of U-Ganda 29 Oct. 1885. *E. C. Dawson's James Hannington* (1887), *portrait.*

HANOVER, ERNEST AUGUSTUS, King of (5 son of *George III.*) *b.* Kew 6 June 1771; ed. at Univ. of Gottingen 1786–90; K.G. 2 June 1786, installed 28 May 1801; commanded first brigade of Hanoverian cavalry 1794, lost his left eye in battle of Tournay 10 May 1794; created Earl of Armagh and Duke of Cumberland and Teviotdale 24 April 1799; badly wounded in his apartments St. James's palace, London 31 May 1810 by his Italian valet Sellis who then cut his own throat; col. of 15 hussars 28 March 1801, of royal horse guards 22 Jany. 1827 to Nov. 1830; field marshal 26 Nov. 1813; served in campaigns of 1813–14; G.C.B. 2 Jany. 1815; G.C.H. 12 Aug. 1815; K.P. 20 Aug. 1821; king of Hanover 20 June 1837, immediately revoked the constitution, granted a new constitution 1840. *d.* Herrenhausen palace, Hanover 18 Nov. 1851. *C. A. Wilkinson's Court of King*

HANOVER, King of. *(Con.)*

Ernest 2 vols. (1886), *portrait ; Jesse's Memoirs of life of George III.* (1867) *iii,* 541–6 ; *Sir N. H. Nicolas's Orders of knighthood, iv* (1842), *portrait ; I.L.N. ii,* 410 (1843), *portrait ; Annual Register* (1833) 90–96.

HANOVER, GEORGE FREDERICK ALEXANDER CHARLES ERNEST AUGUSTUS, King of *(only son of preceding).* b. Berlin 27 May 1819 ; G.C.H. 1830 ; at cricket match at Windsor struck himself in eye while swinging round a long purse and blinded himself 1833 ; K.G. 15 Aug. 1835 ; lost sight of his other eye by Dr. Karl Gräfe of Berlin cutting through the optic nerve while operating June 1840 ; succeeded his father as Duke of Cumberland and King of Hanover 18 Nov. 1851, revoked constitution 1855 ; took part with Austria in Seven Weeks war 1866, Hanover incorporated with Prussia by royal decree 20 Sep. 1866 ; general in British army 27 May 1876 ; visited England 16 May to 17 June 1876. *d.* Rue de Presbourg, Paris 12 June 1878. *bur.* St. George's chapel, Windsor 25 June. *Allgemeine Deutsche Bio-graphie, viii,* 657–70 (1878) ; *Almanac de Gotha* (1853), *portrait ; Contemporary Review, xxxix,* 646–64 (1881) ; *Times* 13–26 June 1878 ; *I.L.N.* 25 June 1853 p. 508, *portrait.*

HANSELL, REV. EDWARD HALIFAX (4 *son of Peter Hansell, V. of Worstead, Norfolk, d.* 1841). *b.* St. Mary-in-the-Marsh, Norwich 6 Nov. 1814 ; ed. at Ball. coll. Ox. 1832 ; a demy of Magd. coll. 1832–47, fellow 1847–53 ; B.A. 1836, M.A. 1838, B.D. 1847 ; tutor of Merton coll. 1845–9 ; V.P. of Magd. college 1852, fellow, tutor and mathematical lecturer and prælector of theology there 1852–6 ; R. of East Ilsley, Berks. 1865 to death ; author of *Notes on the first essay in Essays and Reviews* 1850 ; *The sorrows of the Cross* 1880, 2 ed. 1881 ; ed. of *Codex A. B. D. Z. et Sinaiticus. Nov. Test. Græce.* 3 vols. 1864. *d.* East Ilsley 8 May 1884.

HANSLER, SIR JOHN JACOB (1 *son of John Jacob Hansler, Landaman of canton Zurich).* b. St. Martin's in the Fields, London 1788 ; knighted at St. James's palace 19 July 1837 being the first knight created by Victoria ; F.R.S. Jany. 1838 ; F.S.A. ; D.L. for Essex. *d.* 3 H. The Albany, Piccadilly, London 28 April 1867. *Dodd's Peerage* (1841) 167.

HANSOM, JOSEPH ALOYSIUS *(son of Henry Hansom of York, builder, who d.* 16 *Feb.* 1854 *aged* 75). *b.* York 26 Oct. 1803 ; architect with Edward Welch at Halifax 1828, they became bankrupt 25 April 1834 ; managed the bank, coal mines and estates of Dempster Hemming of Caldecote hall, Warws. ; regis-

HANSOM, J. A. *(Con.)*

tered a patent safety cab 23 Dec. 1834, sold his rights in it for £10,000 but money never paid, the principal of safety consisted in the suspended or cranked axle, the back seat for the driver was not in the original patent ; founded *The Builder* newspaper, No. 1 published 31 Dec. 1842 ; architect at Preston 1847–54, at Edinburgh, at Clifton, at Ramsgate, in London 1862–79 ; built the spire of St. Walburge's church, Preston 306 feet high, the loftiest in England since the Reformation ; designed church at Arundel for Duke of Norfolk. *d.* 399 Fulham road, London 29 June 1882. *Gillow's English Catholics, iii,* 115–20 (1888) ; *I.L.N. lxxxi,* 56 (1882), *portrait.*

HANSON, ALFRED *(eld. son of Joshua Flesher Hanson of Backwell, Somerset).* b. 29 June 1816 ; barrister M.T. 27 Jany. 1843 ; junior counsel to comrs. of customs, &c. 1853–65 ; revising barrister for London 1861–64 ; comptroller of legacy and succession duties at Somerset House, July 1865 to death ; author of *The Succession duty act, with decisions and notes* 1865 ; *The acts relating to probate legacy and succession duties, By A. H.* 1870, 3 ed. 1876 ; *The Revenue acts of 1880 and 1881 and Death duties* 1883. *d.* 1 Upper Westbourne terrace, London 6 Jany. 1886.

HANSON, SIR RICHARD DAVIES. *b.* London 6 Dec. 1805 ; solicitor 3 Philpot lane, London 1828 ; editor of the *Globe* and a writer for the *Morning Chronicle* 1828 ; asst. comr. in enquiry on crown lands Canada 1838 ; crown prosecutor Wellington, N.Z. 1840–6 ; advocate general South Australia 1851 ; attorney general 1856–57 ; attorney general and leader of government 1857–60 ; chief justice of supreme court Nov. 1861 to death ; knighted at Windsor Castle 9 July 1869 ; acting governor of S. Australia 1872–3 ; first chancellor of Adelaide univ. 1874 ; author of *The Jesus of history* 1869 ; *Letters to and from Rome, By V.S.C.* 1873 ; *The apostle Paul and the preaching of Christianity* 1875. *d.* Australia 4 March 1876. *I.L.N. lv,* 117 (1869), *portrait.*

HANSON, LOUISA. Widow of James Hanson, captain R.N. who was lost in the Brazen sloop of war off Newhaven, April 1800 when all on board were lost except one man. *d.* Marl house, Bexley, Kent 2 July 1884 aged 103. 47 *Rep. Registrar General* (1886) p. lxxxi.

HANSON, SAMUEL *(son of an orange merchant).* b. 47 Botolph lane, Eastcheap, London, Sep. 1804 ; the leading dealer in the green and dried fruit trade from about 1833, retired 1871, the firm commenced business in 1747 ;

a founder of Commercial Union Association 1862. d. Zurich, Switzerland 11 Feb. 1882. bur. Zurich. *City Press* 18 *Feb.* 1882 *p.* 4.

HANWELL, JOSEPH. b. about 1790; 2 lieut. R.A. 23 May 1806, captain 5 June 1835 to 10 April 1845 when he retired on full pay; L.G. 24 Aug. 1866. d. Belleville, Ontario, Canada 5 July 1873.

HARCOURT, CHARLES, stage name of Charles Parker Hillier. b. June 1838; made his first public appearance at St. James' theatre, London 30 March 1863 as Robert Audley in *Lady Audley's Secret;* lessee of Marylebone theatre 1871–2; played at most of the London theatres, one of best exponents of character of Mercutio; sec. of National dramatic academy Jany. 1880 to death; played Bashford in *The World* at Drury lane from 31 July 1880; while rehearsing at Haymarket theatre fell into the scene dock 18 Oct. 1880, d. Charing Cross hospital 27 Oct. 1880. *Graphic* 6 *Nov.* 1880 *pp.* 437, 438, 438, *portrait; Illust. sp. and dr. news* 6 *Nov.* 1880 *p.* 173, *portrait; W. H. Rideing's Dramatic Notes* (1881) *p.* 37.

HARCOURT, EGERTON VENABLES VERNON *(youngest son of Most Rev. Edward Vernon Harcourt 1757–1814, archbishop of York).* b. Rose castle, Cumberland 7 June 1803; ed. at Ch. Ch. Ox., student 1821–34; B.A. 1825, M.A. 1828; barrister I.T. 25 June 1830; principal registrar of province of York 1842 to death; registrar of diocese of York 1842 to death; gave sum of £9,000 to archbishop of York to form a fund for augmentation of poor livings in Yorkshire, distributed Feb. 1891. d. Whitwell hall, Yorkshire 19 Oct. 1883. *Proc. of Royal Geog. Soc. v,* 663 (1883).

HARCOURT, FRANCIS VERNON (10 *child of Most Rev. E. V. Harcourt).* b. Rose castle, Cumberland 7 Jany. 1801; ensign 1 foot guards 7 Sep. 1820, captain 1834 to 7 Aug. 1840 when placed on h.p.; col. in the army 9 Nov. 1846; M.P. for Isle of Wight 1852–57; sheriff of Sussex 1867; author of *Hints to young officers on military law and courts martial* 1833. d. Buxted park near Uckfield, Sussex 23 April 1880.

HARCOURT, FREDERICK EDWARD VERNON (5 *son of Most Rev. E. V. Harcourt).* b. May 1790; entered navy 13 Feb. 1803, captain 7 June 1814, retired admiral 20 May 1862; author of *The Protestant missionary's catechism* 1853; wrote Tracts for British Soc. for promoting principles of Reformation 1843 etc. d. 47 Cadogan place, London 30 April 1883.

HARCOURT, GEORGE SIMON (1 *son of John Simon Harcourt, M.P. Westbury).* b. 5 Feb. 1807; ed. at Eton; matric. at Ch. Ch. Ox. 1825; sheriff of Bucks. 1834; M.P. for Bucks. 1837–41. d. 35 St. George's sq. Belgravia, London 24 Oct. 1871.

HARCOURT, GEORGE GRANVILLE VENABLES (1 *son of Most Rev. E. V. Harcourt).* b. Sudbury 6 Aug. 1785; ed. at Westminster and Ch. Ch. Ox., student 1803–14; B.A. 1808, M.A. 1810; barrister L.I. 13 May 1817; M.P. for Lichfield 1806–30; M.P. for Oxfordshire 1831 to death; chancellor and commissary of diocese of York 1818 to death. · d. Strawberry hill, Twickenham 19 Dec. 1861. bur. in family vault at Stanton Harcourt 27 Dec. *Law Times xxxvii,* 122, 154 (1861).

NOTE.—By royal license dated 15 January 1831 the Archbishop of York and his issue took name of Harcourt, but in April 1840 G. G. Harcourt sent a letter to the *Times* stating that his name was G. H. Vernon.

HARCOURT, GRANVILLE (6 *son of Most Rev. E. V. Harcourt).* b. Rose castle, Cumberland 26 July 1792; ed. at Ch. Ch. Ox., student 1812–14; B.A. 1814, M.A. 1816; barrister L.I. 13 May 1817; M.P. for Aldborough, Yorkshire 1815–20; contested Retford 1830; M.P. for Retford 1831–47; chancellor of province of York to death. d. Grove hall, Retford 8 Dec. 1879.

HARCOURT, REV. LEVESON VENABLES VERNON (2 *son of Most Rev. E. V. Harcourt).* b. Sudbury 1788; ed. at Ch. Ch. Ox., student 1806–13; B.A. 1810, M.A. 1813; R. of Beckenham, Kent 1835–51; chancellor of York cath. 30 May 1827 to death; author of *The Doctrine of the deluge* 2 vols. 1838; *A remonstrance to the bishop of Exeter on his letter to Archbishop of Canterbury* 1850; *Lectures on the four gospels* 3 vols. 1851; *On connexion of chemistry with agriculture* 1855. d. 29 Portland place, London 26 July 1860.

HARCOURT, OCTAVIUS HENRY CYRIL VERNON (8 *son of Most Rev. E. V. Harcourt).* b. Rose castle, Cumberland 25 Dec. 1793; entered R.N. Aug. 1806; served in Egypt 1807, on coast of Spain 1809, in West Indies 1824–7; captain 7 Aug. 1827; surveyed coast of Central America and California 1834–6; V.A. on h.p. 4 June 1861; sheriff of Yorkshire 1848; built and endowed Healey ch. Yorkshire 1849. d. Swinton park, Yorkshire 14 Aug. 1863. *Leeds Mercury* 17 *Aug.* 1863 *p.* 3.

HARCOURT, REV. WILLIAM VENABLES VERNON (4 *son of Most Rev. E. V. Harcourt).* b. Sudbury, June 1789; served in R.N. on West India station 5 years; ed. at Ch. Ch. Ox.,

HARCOURT, REV. W. V. V. (Con.)

student 1807–15; B.A. 1811, M.A. 1814; V. of Bishopsthorpe, Yorks. 1814–24; R. of Etton, Yorks. 1816; R. of Nunburnholne, Yorks. 1816–8; preb. of North Newbald, York 6 Aug. 1821 to death; R. of Whildrake 1824–33; R. of Bolton Percy 1837–65; president Yorkshire Philos. soc. 1822; F.G.S. 1823; F.R.S. 1824; founder and general sec. of British Assoc. 1831, president 1839; founder of Yorkshire sch. for the blind and Castle Howard reformatory; studied the action of heat on inorganic bodies; author of *Symmetrical psalmody or portions of psalms translated into metrical stanzas* 1855; *What is truth? A poetical dialogue* 1869; *Sermons* 1873. *d.* Nuneham near Oxford 1 April 1871. *Quarterly Journal of geol. soc. xxviii*, 40 (1872).

HARDEN, JOHN WILLIAM (*youngest son of John Harden of Brathay hall, Westmoreland, d. 1847*). *b.* 11 Dec. 1809; ed. at gr. sch. Manchester and Univ. of Edin.; barrister I.T. 20 Nov. 1835; comr. of bankruptcy in Cheshire and North Wales; a revising barrister on northern circuit 1841; judge of county courts, circuit No. 7 (Lancashire) 1847 to death; author of *Scripture proofs on leading doctrines of the Gospel, By J. W. H.* 1873; *Questions on the leading doctrines of the Gospel* 1873. *d.* Bournemouth 16 April 1875.

HARDIMAN, JAMES. *b.* Westport, co. Mayo Feb. 1782; admitted solicitor 1814; subcommissioner of the Irish records 1830; member of R. Irish Academy and of Iberno-Celtic soc.; librarian to Queen's college, Galway 1849 to death; published *The history of the town and county of Galway* 1820; *Irish minstrelsy, or bardic remains of Ireland* 2 vols. 1831; edited R. O'Flaherty's *West Connaught* 1846. *d.* Galway 13 Nov. 1855.

HARDING, ANNE RAIKES. *b.* 1780; author of *Correction: a novel* 3 vols. 1818; *Decision: a tale* 3 vols. 1819; *The Refugees: an Irish tale* 3 vols. 1822; *Realities* 4 vols. 1825; *Dissipation: a novel* 4 vols. 1827; *Experience: a tale for all ages* 4 vols. 1828; *An epitome of universal history* 1848; *Sketches of the Highlands* 18— and other works all published anonymously; contributed to reviews and periodicals. (*m.* Thomas Harding of Bristol, merchant). *d.* at residence of her son in law Rev. William Kynaston Groves, Boulogne 27 April 1858. *G.M. June* 1858 *p.* 684.

HARDING, FRANCIS. *b.* 28 April 1799; entered navy 24 Jany. 1812, captain 23 Nov. 1841, retired V.A. 24 May 1867; served in Griper discovery ship 1824 in attempt to reach Repulse Bay. *d.* Cheltenham 2 Jany. 1875.

HARDING, FRANCIS PYM. Ensign 22 foot 16 March 1838, lieut.-col. 25 Sep. 1857 to 5 Dec. 1871 when placed on h.p.; commandant of Balaklava, Jany. 1855 to July 1856; M.G. 6 March 1868; C.B. 2 Jany. 1857. *d.* the Grove, Lymington, Hants. 25 Feb. 1875.

HARDING, SIR GEORGE JUDD. Second lieut. R.E. 1 Oct. 1802; served in Sicily, Spain and with the Prussian army 1812–18; colonel commandant R.E. 10 May 1859 to death; L.G. 23 Nov. 1858; C.B. 19 July 1838, K.C.B. 18 May 1860; governor of Guernsey 22 Nov. 1855 to 1 April 1859. *d.* Belmont lodge, Guernsey 5 July 1860 aged 72.

HARDING, GEORGE PERFECT (*son of Silvester Harding 1745–1809, artist and publisher*). Miniature painter, exhibited 20 pictures at R.A. and 2 at Suffolk st. 1802–40; made water colour copies of ancient historical portraits; a founder of the Granger soc. 1840, which collapsed in 1843; F.S.A. 1839–47; fell into pecuniary difficulties and sold his collections of drawings; published *Eighteen portraits of deans of Westminster* 1822–3; *Ancient paintings and brasses in the Abbey, Westminster* 1825; *Description of an account of the Princes of Wales* 1828. *d.* Hercules buildings, Lambeth 23 Dec. 1853. *G.M. May* 1854 *pp.* 548–49.

HARDING, JAMES DUFFIELD. *b.* Deptford 1798; exhibited 39 landscapes at R.A., 8 at B.I. and 17 at Suffolk st. 1811–58; Assoc. of Soc. of painters in water-colours 1820, member 1821; a successful teacher; made lithographic drawings for his *Sketches at home and abroad* 1836, published 1839; Louis Philippe sent him a service of Sevres china; invented papers of various tints and textures 1830 which were known as Harding's papers; invented lithotint 1841; author of *Lessons on art* 1849, 8 ed. 1867; *The principles and practice of art* 1845, another ed. 1876, and 8 other books; furnished the illustrations to 20 works. *d.* 15 Lonsdale terrace, Barnes, Surrey 4 Dec. 1863. *Art Journal* 1850 *p.* 181, *portrait*, 1856 *p.* 270, 1864 *p.* 89; *Encyclop. Brit.* 9 ed. *xi*, 473, *xiv*, 701; *I.L.N. xliii*, 656, 657 (1863), *portrait*.

HARDING, RIGHT REV. JOHN (3 *son of Wm. Harding, chief clerk transport office*). *b.* Queen sq. Bloomsbury, London 7 Jany. 1805; ed. at Westminster and Worcester coll. Ox., B.A. 1826, M.A. 1829, D.D. 1851; R. of St. Andrew-by-the-Wardrobe and St. Anne's, Blackfriars, London 1836–51; sec. of Pastoral aid soc.; bishop of Bombay 31 July 1851, consecrated at Lambeth 10 Aug., resigned

HARDING, RIGHT REV. J. *(Con.)*

April 1868; author of *Texts and thoughts for christian ministers* 1874 and charges and single sermons. *d.* St. Helens lodge, Ore near Hastings 18 June 1874. *I.L.N. lxiv*, 619 (1874).

HARDING, SIR JOHN DORNEY *(eld. son of Rev. John Harding, R. of Coyty and Coychurch, Glamorganshire).* *b.* Rockfield, Monmouthshire 1809; ed. at Charterhouse and at Oriel coll. Ox., B.A. 1830, M.A. 1833, D.C.L. 1837; student L.I. 1829, student I.T. 1833, barrister I.T. 20 Nov. 1835; advocate in Doctors' Commons 2 Nov. 1837; advocate general 5 March 1852–62 when he retired; knighted at St. James's palace 24 March 1852; bencher of his inn 1852, reader 1867; Q.C. Jany. 1858; author of *An essay on the influence of Welsh tradition upon European literature, By Sir J. D. H.* 1840. *d.* Sandywell asylum, Dowdeswell near Cheltenham 23 Nov. 1868. *Mozley's Reminiscences, ii,* 136–41 (1882).

HARDING, REV. THOMAS *(4 son of William Harding of St. Margaret's, Westminster).* *b.* 1806; ed. at Worcester coll. Ox., B.A. 1826, M.A. 1829; chaplain Bethlehem hospital 1831–3; V. of Bexley, Kent 9 Oct. 1833 to death; editor of H. Bullinger's *Five decades of Godlie sermons, Parker Soc.* 4 vols. 1849–52; author of *Justification by faith through the propitiation of Christ a safeguard for the times. Three sermons* 1868, and 17 single sermons. *d.* Bexley 12 Nov. 1874.

HARDING, WILLIAM *(3 son of Robert Harding of Upcott, Devon, d.* 1804). *b.* 16 Aug. 1792; ensign 5 foot 11 July 1811, lieut. 1813 to 25 March 1817 when placed on h.p.; served in Peninsula 1812 to end of the war; major on h.p. 14 Nov. 1826; F.G.S.; author of *History of Tiverton* 2 vols. 1845–7. *d.* Barnstaple 15 Jany. 1886.

HARDING, WYNDHAM *(brother of Sir J. D. Harding* 1809–68). *b.* 9 Aug. 1818; ed. at Rugby; worked on Manchester and Leeds railway 1836–38; sec. to Glasgow, Greenock and Paisley railway 1839, acting general manager to 1844; general superintendent of Bristol and Gloucester railway 1844–45; sec. to London and South Western railway Sep. 1848 to Oct. 1852; A.I.C.E. March 1846, member of council; F.R.S.; freighted at his own expense the first Australian emigrant ship which sailed from Southampton under superintendence of Mrs. Chisholm 184–; author of *Railways. The gauge question* 1845, 4 *ed.* 1846; *Alphabet of Colour* 1853. *d.* near Cheltenham 15 April 1885. *Min. of proc. of Instit. of C.E. xv,* 97–100 (1856).

HARDINGE, HENRY HARDINGE, 1 Viscount *(3 son of Rev. Henry Hardinge* 1754–1820, *R. of Stanhope, Durham).* *b.* Wrotham, Kent 30 March 1785; ensign Queen's Rangers, Upper Canada 1798; deputy quartermaster general in Portuguese army during Peninsular war 1809–14; lieut. col. 40 foot 12 April 1814; captain 1 foot guards 1814–27 when placed on h.p.; served campaign of 1815 with Prussian army as brigadier general; severely wounded at Ligny 16 June 1815, left hand amputated; M.P. for Durham 1820–30, for St. Germans 1830–31, for Newport, Cornwall 1831–32, for Launceston 1832–44; clerk of the ordnance 1823–27 and Jany. to May 1828; sec. of war 1828–30 and 1841–44; P.C. 30 May 1828; second to Duke of Wellington in his duel with the Earl of Winchelsea 21 March 1829; sec. of Ireland 30 July to 26 Nov. 1830 and 17 Dec. 1834 to 22 April 1835; col. of 97 foot 4 March 1833, of 57 foot 31 May 1843 to death; governor general of India 6 May 1844 to 12 Jany. 1848; present at battles of Moodkee, Ferozeshah and Sobraon; K.C.B. 5 Jany. 1815, G.C.B. 1 July 1844; .created Viscount Hardinge of Lahore and King's Newton, co. Derby 2 May 1846; granted pension of £5000 per annum by H.E.I. Co. 1846; master general of the Ordnance 5 March 1852; commander in chief 23 Sep. 1852 to 15 July 1856; general 20 June 1854, field marshal 2 Oct. 1855. *d.* South park near Tunbridge Wells 24 Sep. 1856, 2 portraits of him by Sir Francis Grant in National portrait gallery. *Portraits of eminent conservatives and statesmen 1 series* (1836), *portrait; T. Collins's Portraits and memoirs of eminent naval and military personages* (1847) *No. 1, portrait; W. C. Taylor's National portrait gallery, iii,* 130 (1847), *portrait; J. J. Briggs's History of Melbourne in the county of Derby,* 2 *ed.* (1852) 148–57, *portrait.*

HARDINGE, REV. SIR CHARLES, 2 Baronet *(son of Rev. Henry Hardinge of Hampton, Middlesex).* *b.* 22 March 1780; ed. at Univ. coll. Ox., B.A. 1801, M.A. 1804; R. of Crowhurst, Sussex 1804 to death; V. of Tunbridge, Kent 1809 to death; succeeded his uncle 5 Nov. 1826; author of *Plain discourses* 1821; *A practical exposition of the election of grace* 1847; *Baptismal regeneration* 1850. *d.* Boundes Park, Tunbridge Wells 3 Feb. 1864.

HARDINGE, RICHARD. *b.* 14 April 1790; 2 lieut. R.A. 23 May 1806, col. 1854 to 26 Oct. 1858; M.G. 26 Oct. 1858; K.H. 1825. *d.* 32 Hyde park sq. London 20 July 1864.

HARDMAN, EDWARD TOWNLEY. *b.* Drogheda 6 April 1845; ed. at R. coll. of science, Dublin; on staff of geological survey, Ireland 1870 and 1885; F.R.G.S. Ireland; F. Chem. soc.; went to Kimberley district, West Australia and reported on the mineral resources and the gold fields 1883–5, a range of mountains in West Australia named after him; wrote many papers in *Journal Geol. Soc. of Ireland* and *Proc. of Irish Acad.* from 1871 onward. *d.* Wicklow 30 April 1887. *Geological Mag.* (1887) *p.* 334.

HARDMAN, FREDERICK *(son of Joseph Hardman, merchant).* *b.* London 1814; lieut. in British legion in Spain 1834; *Times* foreign correspondent in Spain, Turkey, Russia, Italy and France 1850 to death; a regular contributor to *Blackwood's Mag.* from 1840; author of *The student of Salamanca* 1847, anon.; *The Spanish campaign in Morocco* 1860. *d.* Paris 6 Nov. 1874. *Times* 13 *Nov.* 1874 *p.* 6, 28 *Nov. p.* 10; *Graphic,* x, 512 (1874), *portrait.*

HARDMAN, JOHN *(son of John Hardman of Birmingham, metal button maker).* *b.* Birmingham 7 Aug. 1811; partner with his father; founded ecclesiastical metal works at Birmingham 1838, added stained-glass works 1845, in which business he enjoyed a practical monoply; founded in St. Chad's R.C. cathedral, Birmingham a choir for performance of the Gregorian chant which he superintended personally 18 years and endowed with sum of £1000. *d.* Pemberton villa, Clifton 29 May 1867. *bur.* in crypt of St. Chad's cathedral.

HARDMAN, JULIANA *(sister of the preceding).* *b.* 26 April 1813; ed. at Benedictine convent of Caverswall, Staffs.; made her religious profession 19 Aug. 1841 assuming the name of Mary; superioress of convent of Our Lady of Mercy at Handsworth near Birmingham (founded by her father) 6 Sep. 1841 to 1876 during which time 59 sisters were professed there; founded a convent of her institute at Nottingham 1844; built church of St. Mary's, Brougham st. Birmingham 1847. *d.* at the convent, Handsworth 24 March 1884.

HARDMAN, SIR WILLIAM *(only son of William Bridge Hardman of Chamber hall, Bury, Lancs.)* *b.* Bury 13 Aug. 1828; ed. Trin. coll. Cam., B.A. 1851, M.A. 1854; barrister I.T. 30 April 1852; recorder of Kingston-on-Thames, June 1875 to death; inspector of Woking convict prison; chairman Surrey sessions second court 1871–2, first court 1877 to death; contested East Surrey 1868; a founder of the Primrose league 1882, chairman of the grand council; knighted at Osborne 29 Dec. 1885; alderman of Surrey county council; editor of

Morning Post 1872 to death. *d.* St. Leonards on Sea 12 Sep. 1890. *bur.* Kingston cemetery 16 Sep. *I.L.N.* 20 *Sep.* 1890 *p.* 374, *portrait; Pictor. ' World* 25 *Sep.* 1890 *p.* 396, *portrait; Sell's World's Press* 1891 *p.* 85, *portrait.*

HARDWICK, VEN. CHARLES. *b.* Slingsby near Malton, Yorkshire 22 Sep. 1821; ed. at St. Cath. hall, Cam., B.A. 1844, M.A. 1847, B.D. 1859; Skrine fellow of his college 1845; Whitehall preacher 1851; prof. of divinity Queen's coll. Birmingham, March–Sep. 1853; divinity lecturer at King's coll. Cam. 1855 to death; christian advocate in univ. of Cam. 1855 to death; mem. of council of senate 1856 to death; archdeacon of Ely 1859; author of *A history of the Articles of religion, By C. H.* 1851, 3 ed. 1876; *History of Christian church, Middle Age* 1853, 3 *ed.* 1872; *Twenty sermons* 1853; *Christ and other masters, an inquiry into the contrast between Christianity and religious systems of ancient world* 4 parts 1855–9; edited works for Percy Soc. and for the University press; killed by falling over a precipice near the Port de Venasque in the Pyrenees 18 Aug. 1859. *bur.* Luchon cemetery 21 Aug. *Christ and other masters,* 2 *ed.* 1863, *with memoir; G.M.* vii, 419–21 (1859).

HARDWICK, CHARLES *(son of an innkeeper, d. 1835).* *b.* Preston 10 Sep. 1817; apprentice to a printer 1831; portrait painter Preston; member Pleasant Retreat lodge, Preston 1841, sec. 1845, chairman; grand master Manchester Unity of Odd-Fellows 1857–8; founder and V.P. of Manchester literary club; author of *History of the borough of Preston* 1857; *The history of Friendly societies* 1859, 2 *ed.* 1869; *Traditions, superstitions and folk-lore* 1872; *On some battlefields in Lancashire* 1882; editor of *Country Words, a North of England Mag.* 1866–7. *d.* Manchester 8 July 1889. *Quarterly Mag. of Odd-Fellows,* i, 321–6 (1858), *portrait; Academy* 20 *July* 1889 *p.* 39.

HARDWICK, JOHN (1 son of Thomas Hardwick 1752–1829, architect). *b.* 3 Dec. 1791; ed. at Ball. coll. Ox., fellow 1808–22; B.C.L. 1815, D.C.L. 1830; barrister L.I. 28 June 1816; stipendiary magistrate at Lambeth 1821, at High st. Marylebone 1840–1, at Great Marlborough st. 1841, retired March 1856; F.R.S. 5 April 1838. *d.* 101 Lansdowne place, Brighton 31 May 1875. *Law Times* 12 *June* 1875 *p.* 127; *I.L.N.* 9 Oct. 1847 *p.* 236, *portrait.*

HARDWICK, PHILIP *(brother of the preceding).* *b.* 9 Rathbone place, London 15 June 1792; ed. at Royal academy sch.; exhibited 23 drawings at R.A. 1807–44; architect London

HARDWICK, P. *(Con.)*

1819, some of his chief works were the St. Katharine's dock house 1827-8, the Goldsmiths' Co. hall 1829-35, Babraham house, Cambs. 1832, Euston station and hotel London 1834-9, Lincoln's inn hall and library 1842-5; F.S.A. 1824, member of council 1842; M.I.C.E. 13 April 1824; F.R.S. 8 Dec. 1831; M.I.B.A. 1834, V.P. 1839 and 1841; F.G.S. 1837; A.R.A. 1840, R.A. 1841; published *Drawings of the hall and library, Lincoln's inn, with text* 1842. *d.* at his son's residence, Westcombe lodge, Wimbledon common, Surrey 28 Dec. 1870. *Sandby's History of royal academy, ii,* 202 (1862).

HARDWICKE, CHARLES PHILIP YORKE, 4 Earl of *(eld. child of Admiral Sir Joseph Sydney Yorke, K.C.B. 1768-1831).* *b.* Sydney lodge, Southampton 2 April 1799; ed. at Harrow; midshipman R.N. 15 May 1815, captain 6 June 1825, admiral on h.p. 3 Dec. 1863; M.P. for Reigate 1831-32, for Cambs. 1832 to 18 Nov. 1834 when he succeeded his uncle as 4 Earl; lord lieut. of Cambs. 31 Dec. 1834 to death; LL.D. Cam. 1835, D.C.L. Ox. 1853; P.C. 27 Feb. 1852; postmaster general 1 March to 28 Dec. 1852; lord keeper of the privy seal 26 Feb. 1858 to 18 June 1859. *d.* Sydney lodge, Southampton 17 Sep. 1873. *J. Grant's Portraits of public characters, i,* 30-38 (1841); *Waagen's Galleries of art* (1857) 518-23; *I.L.N. ii,* 57 (1843), *portrait.*

HARDWICKE, ROBERT. *b.* Dyke near Bourn, Lincs., Sep. 1823; printer with Bateman near Lincoln's Inn Fields, London, at 26 Duke st. Piccadilly to 1856; publisher at 192 Piccadilly 1856 to death; one of founders of Quekett microscopical club 1865; F.L.S.; published *Hardwicke's Science Gossip* 1865 to death, and other periodicals. *d.* 192 Piccadilly, London 8 March 1875. *Publishers' Circular* (1875) *p.* 202.

HARDWICKE, WILLIAM. *b.* Bourne, Lincs. about 1817; ed. at Univ. coll. London and Paris; L.S.A. 1838, M.R.C.S. 1839; M.D. Univ. of Jena 1857; surgeon to St. Pancras royal general dispensary; deputy coroner for central Middlesex, May 1863, coroner 19 Nov. 1874 to death; medical officer of health for Paddington; author of *Life and health assurance for the working classes* 1864; *On the advantages of baths and wash-houses* 1874. *d.* Richmond villa, St. Mary's terrace, Paddington 15 April 1881. *bur.* Hendon ch. yard 20 April.

HARDY, BENJAMIN (3 *son of Samuel Hardy of Islington, London). b.* 1808; barrister G.I. 23 Nov. 1836; Q.C. 13 Dec. 1866; bencher of Lincoln's Inn 1867. *d.* 8 Upper Avenue road, St. John's Wood, London 30 July 1876.

HARDY, MISS ELIZABETH. *b.* Ireland 1794; author of *Michael Cassidy, or the cottage gardener. Thames Ditton,* 1845; *Owen Glendower, or the Prince in Wales: an historical romance* 2 vols. 1849; *The confessor: a jesuit tale of the times* 1854, all anonymous; imprisoned for a small debt 1852 and *d.* Queen's bench prison, London 9 May 1854 aged 60. *G.M. June* 1854 *p.* 670.

HARDY, JOHN *(eld. son of John Hardy of Horton, parish of Bradford, Yorkshire, who d.* 3 *June* 1806). *b.* 1773 or 1774; barrister M.T. 7 June 1799, admitted ad eundem at I.T. 1803, bencher 1840, reader 1850; chief steward of honour of Pontefract 1806-33; recorder of Leeds 1806-33; M.P. for Bradford 1832-37 and 1841-47; gave sum of £6000 for erection of churches at Bradford 1848. *d.* Dunstall hall, Staffs. 29 Sep. 1855.

HARDY, SIR JOHN, 1 Baronet *(eld. son of the preceding). b.* 23 Feb. 1809; ed. at Oriel coll. Ox., B.A. 1831, M.A. 1834; M.P. for Midhurst 1859, for Dartmouth 1860, for South Warwickshire 1868-74; created baronet 23 Feb. 1876. *d.* 22 South st. Park lane, London 9 July 1888.

HARDY, REV. JOHN FREDERIC. *b.* 1826; ed. Trin. coll. Cam., B.A. 1848, M.A. 1851, B.D. 1858; Fishmonger fellow of Sidney Sussex coll. 1855 to death; private tutor at Cam.; proctor 1854 and 1875; author of *Ascent of the Finster Aar Horn, in Peaks, Passes and Glaciers, Alpine Club* 1860 *pp.* 198-215; *Ascent of Ætna, ib.* 1860 *pp.* 280-89; *The Col du Sonadon from the top of the Col. to Chermontane. ib.* 1862 *i,* 252-8; *A visit to the Jökul's Glacier. ib.* 1862 *ii,* 429-41. *d.* Sidney Sussex coll. 27 March 1888.

HARDY, JOHN RICHARD (3 *son of Rev. Robert Hardy, V. of Walberton, Sussex). b.* 1807; ed. at Peterhouse, Cam., B.A. 1829; emigrated to New South Wales 1833; edited the *Australian* newspaper at Sydney; police magistrate of Yass, of Paramatta 1850; chief commissioner of the gold district, Bathurst 1851. *(m.* 1835 dau. of Sir Alfred Stephen, chief justice N.S.W.); probably dead. *I.L.N. xxi,* 9, 125 (1852).

HARDY, PETER *(brother of Sir Thomas Duffus Hardy* 1804-78). *b.* 17 Dec. 1813; actuary Mutual Assurance office 1837 and London Assurance office 1850; F.R.S. 1839; a founder of the Institute of actuaries 1848; had a large library; author of *The doctrine of simple and compound interest, annuities and reversions* 1839; *A new and general notation for life contingencies* 1840. *d.* Guilford st. London 23 April 1863. *Proc. of Royal soc. xiii, p. v* (1864).

HARDY, Rev. Robert Spence. *b.* Preston 1 July 1803; a printer at York 1819; Wesleyan missionary in Ceylon 1825–30, 1835–47, 1862–5; minister at Leeds 1865 to death; hon. mem. of R.A.S. 2 Feb. 1856; author of *On the connexion of the British government with the idolatry of Ceylon* 1834; *Notices of the Holy Land* 1835; *Eastern monachism, an account of the laws of the order of the Mendicants* 1850; *A manual of Budhism* 1853. *d.* Headingley near Leeds 16 April 1868. *Minutes of Conference* (1868) 25–7.

HARDY, Robert William Hale. Entered navy 1806; at capture of island of Java 1811, at siege of New Orleans 1815; lieut. 20 Feb. 1815 after which he did not go afloat; commander 21 Oct. 1861; F.R.A.S. 1849; author of *Travels in the interior of Mexico* 1829; *Incidental remarks on properties of light* 1856; *Deity as creator, sustainer and user. Prepared in fulfilment of the purpose of R. W. H. Hardy* 1874. *d.* Kilkenny house, Bath 30 July 1871 aged 77. *Monthly Notices R.A.S. xxxii*, 122 (1872).

HARDY, Samuel Little. *b.* 1815; L. and L.M.R.C.S. Ireland 1839 and fellow 1844; M.D. Glasgow 1840; licentiate K.Q.C.P. and L.M. 1852, fellow 1868; M.R.I.A. 1858; physician Pitt st. Instit. for diseases of children, Dublin; physician accoucheur Steevens' hospital; president Obstetrical soc. 1867; one of the first to recommend chloroform as a local anæsthetic; had a large obstetrical practice; author with A. H. Mac Clintock of *Practical observations on midwifery* 1848; contributed to Dublin medical journals 1845 &c. *d.* 9 Merrion sq. north, Dublin 29 Oct. 1868. *Medical Times 7 Nov.* 1868 *p.* 544.

HARDY, Sir Thomas Duffus (3 *son of Thomas Bartholomew Price Hardy, major R.A.*) *b.* Port Royal, Jamaica 22 May 1804; junior clerk in Public record office, Tower of London 1 Jany. 1819; assistant keeper of public records 1840, deputy keeper 15 July 1861 to death; knighted at Windsor Castle 9 July 1869; did much to render the records accessible to the public; instrumental in appointment of Historical MSS. commission 1869; edited *Description of the Close Rolls in the Tower* 1833 and six other works for the old Record commission; *A descriptive catalogue of MSS. relating to the history of Great Britain and Ireland* 3 vols. 1862–71 and other works for the Rolls series; author of *A catalogue of the Lords Chancellors, Keepers of the Great seal, &c.* 1843; *Life of Henry Lord Langdale* 1852. *d.* 126 Portsdown road, Maida vale, London 15 June 1878. *Times 17 June* 1878 *p.* 12 *col.* 6.

HARDY, Sir William (*brother of the preceding*). *b.* Jamaica 6 July 1807; clerk in Record office, Tower of London 1823; keeper of records of duchy of Lancaster 1830–68; assistant keeper in Record office, Fetter lane, London 1868 and deputy keeper 4 July 1878, resigned 27 Jany. 1886; reorganised the record office and commenced the commission for the destruction of valueless documents; F.S.A. 4 May 1837; placed on Historical MSS. commission 1878; knighted at Osborne 31 Dec. 1883; compiled *Charters of duchy of Lancaster* 1845; translated *A collection of the chronicles by J. de Waurin* 1858. *d.* Milton cottage, 71 St. Germain's road, Forest hill, London 17 March 1887. *Proc. of Soc. of Antiq. xi*, 369 (1887).

HARE, Sir John (2 *son of John Hare of Firfield near Bristol, floor cloth manufacturer*). *b.* 1784; partner in his father's business to 1840 when he retired; owner of the Cambria which saved the passengers and crew of Kent East Indiaman in the bay of Biscay 1 March 1825; knighted at St. James's palace 1 July 1840 on presenting address on queen's marriage; resided Brislington, Somerset. *d.* Hardelot castle près Tamar, Pas-de-Calais, France 2 Feb. 1865.

HARE, John Middleton (*son of Rev. Edward Hare, wesleyan minister, d.* 1818). Ed. at Woodhouse grove sch. near Leeds 1813; apprentice to James Nichols, printer, London, where he also served as a reader and editor; edited *Gem Annual* in succession to Tom Hood; sub-edited *The Sphynx* weekly paper for J. S. Buckingham 4 vols. 1827–8; assist. commissioner on popular education 1858; director of British Equitable life assurance co.; author of *An analysis and exposure of the government scheme of education* 1847; *Familiar colloquies between a father and his children* 1862. *Dead?*

HARE, Ven. Julius Charles (3 *son of Francis Hare-Naylor* 1753–1815). *b.* Valdagno near Vicenza 13 Sep. 1795; ed. at Bologna 1797–9 and Trin. coll. Cam., B.A. 1816, M.A. 1819; fell. of his coll. 1818, classical lecturer 1822; R. of Hurstmonceaux, Sussex 18 June 1832 to death; archdeacon of Lewes 10 April 1840 to death; preb. of Chichester, Jany. 1851 to death; chaplain to the Queen 13 June 1853 to death; translated with Connop Thirlwall *Niebuhr's History of Rome* 2 vols. 1828–32; author of *The mission of the Comforter, and other sermons* 2 vols. 1846, 3 ed. 1876 and other books; author with his brother A. W. Hare of *Guesses at Truth, By Two Brothers*, 1st series 1827, 2nd series 1848, new ed. 1871. *d.* Hurstmonceaux rectory 23 Jany. 1855. *A. J. C. Hare's Memorials of a quiet life* (1884) 2

HARE, VEN. J. C. (*Con.*)

vols.; *Sussex archæological collection*, iv, 125–208; *Quarterly Review*, xcvii, 1–28 (1855); *M. A. Lower's Worthies of Sussex* (1865) 255–6; *Guardian* 8 March 1882 pp. 349–50.

HARE, MARIA (*dau. of Rev. Oswald Leycester, rector of Stoke-upon-Terne, Salop*). *b.* Toft near Knutsford 22 Nov. 1798; good classical scholar; intimate acquaintance of Reginald Heber, bp. of Calcutta. (*m.* 2 June 1829 Rev. Augustus William Hare, rector of Alton Barnes *d.* Rome 18 Feb. 1834); author of *A true and sad story* 1862; wrote a portion of and collected materials for *Memorials of a Quiet Life;* lived in Hurstmonceaux parish near her brother in law the Rev. Julius Charles Hare from 1834 for many years. *d.* Holmhurst 13 Nov. 1870. *A. J. C. Hare's Memorials of a quiet life* (1884) 2 vols., 2 portraits; *C. Kegan Paul's Biographical Sketches* (1883) 71–92.

HARE, REV. ROBERT HENRY (5 son of Rev. Edward Hare, d. 1818). *b.* Mount Pleasant, Liverpool 3 March 1816; ed. at Woodhouse grove sch. 1824; apprentice to Christopher and Dove, leather factors, Darlington; Wesleyan Methodist minister at Hornsea 1838–40 and at 14 other places in north of England 1840–72. *d.* Chapel house, the Square, Dunstable 11 Oct. 1873. *J. M. Hare's Ministry of R. H. Hare* (1874), *portrait*.

HARENC, CHARLES JOSEPH (2 son of Benjamin Harenc of Foots Cray, Kent). Matric. from Ch. Ch. Ox. 8 Dec. 1829 aged 18, B.A. 1833; barrister I.T. 9 June 1837; played his first cricket match at Lord's 2 Aug. 1826; one of the best bowlers in England 1830–34; played as late as 1849. *d.* Costin st. Bedford 14 Dec. 1877. *Lillywhite's Cricket Scores*, i, 547 (1862).

HAREWOOD, HENRY LASCELLES, 3 Earl of. *b.* 11 June 1797; ensign 1 foot guards 1814, sold out 1831; lieut. Yorkshire hussar yeomanry 1820, major 1839–43;' col. of West Yorkshire hussars; M.P. for Northallerton, Yorkshire 1826–31; styled Viscount Lascelles 1839–41; succeeded as 3 Earl 24 Nov. 1841; lord lieut. of West Riding, Yorkshire 21 Jany. 1846 to death. *d.* Harewood house near Leeds 22 Feb. 1857 having fractured his skull while following the Bramham Moor foxhounds 24 Jany. *Taylor's Biographia Leodiensis* (1865) 463–6.

HARFORD, JOHN SCANDRETT (1 son of John Scandrett Harford of Blaise castle, Gloucs., banker, d. 1815). *b.* Bristol 8 Oct. 1785; ed. at Christ's coll. Cam.; D.C.L. of Ox. univ. 1822; the hero of Hannah More's *Cœlebs in*

HARFORD, J. S. (*Con.*)

search of a wife 1809; made a collection of pictures at Blaise castle 1815–7; gave the site of the castle of Lampeter for St. David's coll. 1822 of which he became visitor 1827; F.R.S. 29 May 1823; sheriff of Cardigan 1824; M.P. Cardigan 9 July 1841 to 18 April 1842; author of *The life of T. Burgess, bishop of Salisbury* 1840; *Life of Michael Angelo Buonarotti* 2 vols. 1857, 2 ed. 1858 and 8 other books. *d.* Blaise castle 16 April 1866. *Christian Observer, July* 1866 pp. 489–98; *Waagen's Treasures of art*, iii, 187–95 (1854).

HARFORD, SUMMERS. *b.* 1795; M.P. for Lewes 30 June 1841, unseated 21 March 1842; contested Brighton 5 May 1842; sheriff of Monmouth 1841. *d.* Haverfordwest, Pembrokeshire 2 June 1873.

HARGOOD, WILLIAM. *b.* 22 June 1801; entered navy 19 June 1813, captain 10 Jany. 1837, admiral on h.p. 15 Jany. 1869. *d.* North lodge, Worthing 8 July 1888.

HARGRAVE, JOHN FLETCHER (*son of Mr. Hargrave of Greenwich, ironmonger, d.* 1851). *b.* Greenwich 28 Dec. 1815; ed. at King's coll. London and Trin. coll. Cam., B.A. 1837, M.A. 1840; barrister L.I. 25 Jany. 1841; landed at Sydney, N.S.W. Feb. 1857, a district court judge 1 year, solicitor general Feb. to Oct. 1859, Nov. 1859 to April 1860, Aug. to Oct. 1863 and Feb. to June 1865; M.P. for East Camden 1859, for Wollongong 1859; attorney general 2 April 1860 to 31 July 1863; mem. of legislative council Oct. 1859; a puisne judge of supreme court 1865; primary judge in equity; first judge of divorce court 1873–84; edited vol. i. of 21st ed. of *Blackstone's Commentaries* 1843; many of his law lectures at Sydney Univ. were printed; author of *Treatise on the Thellusson act, 39 & 40 Geo. iii, c. 98, with practical observations upon trusts for accumulation* 1842. *d.* Rushcutters' Bay N.S.W. 23 Feb. 1885.

HARGRAVE, WILLIAM. *b.* Cork 1795; L.R.C.S. Ireland 1819, fellow 1825, president; M.B. Dublin univ. 1823; surgeon in sch. of college of surgeons, president; surgeon city of Dublin hospital; member of general medical council 10 May 1861, resigned 16 Feb. 1874; contributed to *Dublin Medical Press* and *Dublin Quarterly Journal;* author of *A system of operative surgery, Dublin* 1831. *d.* 56 Upper Mount st., Merrion sq. east, Dublin 24 Nov. 1874. *Medical Times* 5 Dec. 1874 p. 649.

HARGREAVE, CHARLES JAMES. *b.* Wortley near Leeds, Dec. 1820; ed. at Univ. coll.

HARGREAVE, C. J. *(Con.)*

London; L.L.B. London; professor of jurisprudence Univ. coll. 1843–9; barrister I.T. 7 June 1844, bencher 1851, master of the library 1865 and reader 1866; a commissioner of Incumbered estates court, Ireland 1849–58; judge of Landed estate court 1858 to death; Q.C. 1852; F.R.S. 18 April 1844, gold medallist; LL.D. of Dublin univ. 1852; author of *An essay on the resolution of algebraic equations*, Dublin 1866; wrote many mathematical papers in *Philos. Trans.* and other scientific periodicals. *d.* Bray near Dublin 23 April 1866. *Law Mag. and Law Rev.*, Aug. 1866 *pp.* 220–35.

HARGREAVES, HENRY. *b.* Manchester, Oct. 1807; with Butterworth and Brooks, calico printers, Manchester, and then a traveller for the firm to 1841; backed Alice Hawthorne for the Chester cup 1841, and commenced a racing career which lasted to 1870; won £40,000 on Ellington in Derby of 1856; purchased John Massey Stanley's stud 1856. *d.* 6 Cleveland sq. Bayswater, London 3 July 1887. *Baily's Mag.*, Aug. 1887 *pp.* 60–62; *Sporting Review*, *xxxix*, 298–9 (1858).

HARGROVE, WILLIAM *(youngest son of Ely Hargrove of Knaresborough 1741–1818).* *b.* Knaresborough 16 Oct. 1788; bought the *York Herald* 1813, edited it 13 July 1813 to 1848; member of common council York 1818, sheriff 1831; first sec. and treasurer Mechanics' Institute, York 1827; collected Roman and mediæval remains excavated in and near York, gave them to Yorkshire Philos. Soc. about 1852; author of *History and description of the ancient city of York* 2 vols., York 1818; *The York poetical miscellany* 1835; author with J. Hargrove of *A new guide to the city of York* 1842. *d.* St. Mary's, Bootham, York 24 Aug. 1862. *Effective Advertiser* 1 May 1886 *pp.* 25–31, *portrait*.

HARINGTON, REV. EDWARD CHARLES *(only son of Rev. Edward Harington of the Isle of Man, d.* 1811). *b.* Clifton 1804; ed. at Worcester coll. Ox., B.A. 1828, M.A. 1833; V. of St. David's, Exeter 1832–47; preb. of Ex. cath. 1845, chancellor 15 July 1847 to July 1880, canon residentiary 1856 to July 1880, spent £15,000 on repairing the cath.; a founder of Exeter diocesan training college 1840 where he taught for many years; always attended turning of first sod of every new railway in England; author of *Brief notes on the church of Scotland* 1843; *The reconsecration and reconciliation of churches* 1850 and 12 other books. *d.* The Close, Exeter 14 July 1881.

HARINGTON, SIR HENRY BYNG *(eld. son of Henry Hawes Harington of Madras).* *b.* 1808;

HARINGTON, SIR H. B. *(Con.)*

entered Bengal army 1824, transferred to Bengal civil service 1828; additional member of council, member of supreme council 13 June 1862; lieut. governor of North Western provinces of India 1863 to 1865; K.C.S.I. 24 May 1866. *d.* 70 Oxford terrace, London 7 Oct. 1871.

HARINGTON, REV. RICHARD *(2 son of Sir John Edward Harington, 8 bart., of Ridlington, co. Rutland 1760–1831).* *b.* 26 April 1800; ed. at Ch. Ch. Ox., B.A. 1821, M.A. 1824, B.D. and D.D. 1842; fellow of Brasenose coll. 1821–33, principal 1842 to death; R. of Olde, Northamptonshire 1833–42. *d.* High st. Oxford 13 Dec. 1853. *bur.* in Brasn. coll. chapel 20 Dec. *G.M.* xli, 206–207 (1854); *Correspondence between Dean of Manchester and the principal of Brasenose* 1846.

HARKER, DANIEL RICHARD. Toast master, city of London; retired a few years before his death. *d.* Osborn villas, Westgreen road, Tottenham, Nov. 1874 aged 70.

HARKNESS, ROBERT. *b.* Ormskirk, Lancs. 28 July 1816; ed. at Edin. univ. 1833–4; professor of geology Queen's coll. Cork 1853 to death; F.G.S.; F.R.S. Edin. 1854; F.R.S. 5 June 1856; did much to elucidate geology of Scotland; a writer of upwards of 60 scientific papers; author with H. A. Nicholson of *On the Coniston group* 1868. *d.* Imperial hotel, Dublin 4 Oct. 1878. *Quarterly journal of geol. soc.* xxxv, 41–4 (1879); *Geol. Mag.* (1878) 528, 574–76, *portrait*; *Proc. of royal soc. of Edin.* x, 31–3 (1880); *I.L.N.* lxxiii, 400 (1878), *portrait*.

HARLAND, AURELIUS *(son of Dr. Harland, d.* 1866). Ed. at Edin. univ., M.D. 1844; at Hong Kong 1844 to death; surgeon of Seaman's hospital; acquired Chinese and studied Chinese medicine and physiology; sent papers to R. Asiatic soc. *d.* Hong Kong 12 Sep. 1858, public monument in the Happy Valley. *H. Hance's Memoir of A. Harland* (1858); *S. Smiles' Men of Invention* (1884) 288–92.

HARLAND, REV. EDWARD *(2 son of Christopher Harland of Ashbourne, Derbyshire).* Matric. from Wadham coll. Ox. 16 June 1827 aged 17; B.A. 1831, M.A. 1836; C. of Sandon, Staffs. 1836–51; V. of Colwich, Staffs. 1851 to death; preb. of Lichfield cath. 1873 to death; author of *Index Sermonum* 1858; *A church psalter and hymnal* 1865, *Supplement* 1863. *d.* Rushton hall, Stafford 8 June 1890.

HARLAND, EDWARD JAMES *(brother of Aurelius Harland).* *b.* Scarborough, May 1831; pupil of R. Stephenson, Newcastle upon Tyne

HARLAND, E. J. *(Con.)*

1846–51; journeyman with J. and G. Thomson, Glasgow 1851; manager for Thomas Toward ship builder near Newcastle 1853; manager for R. Hickson & Co. Belfast 1854, purchased the business 1857, took in Mr. Woolff as a partner 1862; made improvements in length, flatness of bottom and squareness of bilge in build of ships, which became known as Belfast bottoms; built for the government the Lynx and Algerine gun vessels and the Hecla store and torpedo ship 3360 tons; built ships for all the great ocean lines. *d.* 1866. *S. Smiles' Men of Invention* (1884) 288–323.

HARLAND, JOHN (1 *son of John Harland, clock maker).* *b.* Hull 27 May 1806; compositor 1821–8; letter press printer; taught himself shorthand and made improvements in the system; chief of reporting staff of *Manchester Guardian* 1830–60; F.S.A.; an early member of the Rosicrucians; edited 14 volumes for Chetham soc.; author of *Historical account of Salley abbey, Yorkshire* 1853; *Ballads and songs of Lancashire* 1865, 2 *ed.* 1875; *Lancashire Lyrics* 1866; and with T. T. Wilkinson of *Lancashire folk lore* 1867. *d.* Brideoak st. Cheetham hill road, Manchester 23 April 1868. *bur.* Rusholme road cemetery. *Sketches of Hull authors, By R. W. Corlass* (1879) 35–9; *J. Harland and T. T. Wilkinson's Lancashire legends* (1873) memoir pp. xv–xxxv, with portrait.

HARLAND, REV. WILLIAM. *b.* Newton near Pickering, Yorkshire 1801; Primitive Methodist minister Hull 1828; sec. to committee of privileges, London 1857; edited *Primitive Methodist Mag.* and was editor superintendent of all works issued by the connexion; author of *The Primitive Methodist revival hymn book* 1861; *The Christian Cabinet illustrated almanack* (1860) *p.* 37; probably dead.

HARLE, WILLIAM LOCKEY *(son of Mr. Harle of Stockton).* *b.* York 1811; solicitor at Newcastle upon Tyne 1833 to death, in London 1848 to death; deputy recorder of Newcastle, member of the town council 1841–53 and 1858 to death, sheriff 1864, alderman 1868 to death; author of *A Career in the Commons* 1850, in which he set forth a complete programme of policy for liberals; *An argument on the inutility of the distinction between barrister and attorney* 1851. *d.* 30 Victoria sq. Newcastle 18 Jany. 1878. *Monthly chronicle of north country lore, Feb.* 1888 *p.* 49, *portrait; Sketch of that distinguished author, editor, lawyer and municipal patriot, Mr. W. L. H., edited by himself* (1854).

HARLECH, JOHN RALPH ORMSBY-GORE, 1 Baron *(eld. child of Wm. Ormsby-Gore, M.P. of*

HARLECH, J. R. O. *(Con.)*

Porkington, co. Salop 1779–1860). *b.* 3 June 1816; ed. at Eton and Ch. Ch. Ox., B.A. 1837, M.A. 1865; student of L.I. 1837; M.P. for Carnarvonshire 1837–41, for North Shropshire 1859–75; created Baron Harlech of Harlech, co. Merioneth 14 Jany. 1876. *d.* Boreham house near Chelmsford 15 June 1876. *Graphic, xiii,* 134, 138 (1876), *portrait.*

HARLEY, EDWARD *(eld. son of Edward Harley of Bristol, iron merchant).* *b.* Bristol 19 June 1808; ed. at Shrewsbury; solicitor at Bristol 1831 to death; deputy registrar of Bristol Court of Conscience (a borough court of record since time of Wm. iii.) 1 Jany. 1837, registrar Dec. 1843 to 1847 when the court was abolished by County Courts' Act 1846; joint registrar of Bristol county court 1847 to death; joint district registrar of the High Court 1875 to death. *d.* Condover Grange near Shrewsbury 25 Oct. 1888.

HARLEY, GEORGE. *b.* 1791; drawing master; exhibited 2 landscapes at R.A. and 1 at Suffolk st. 1817–65; drew in lithography some landscape drawings as 'Lessons in Landscape' for Rowney and Forster's series 1820–22; author of *A guide to landscape drawing in pencil and chalk* 1848, 3 *ed.* 1849. *d.* 32 Kelly st., St. Pancras, London 10 Jany. 1871.

HARLEY, JOHN PRITT *(son of John Harley, draper).* *bapt.* St. Martin-in-the-Fields, London 5 March 1786; apprentice to a linen draper 1801; acted in Kent and Sussex 1807–13; first appeared in London at English opera house as Marcelli in *The Devil's Bridge* 15 July 1815; played the chief parts at Drury Lane 1815–35, 1838, 1841–8, at St. James' theatre 1835, at Covent Garden 1838, 1840, at Princesses theatre 1850 to death; especially good in Shakespearean clowns; master and treasurer Drury Lane theatrical fund 1833 to death; made a collection of 300 walking sticks and canes. *d.* 14 Upper Gower st. London 22 Aug. 1858. *Illust. sp. and dr. news 13 Sep.* 1879 *pp.* 629–30; *Metropolitan Mag. xvii,* 126–32 (1836); *Oxberry's Dramatic Biography, i,* 69–77 (1825), *portrait; Planche's Extravaganzas ii,* 63 (1879), *portrait.*

HARLOWE, SARAH. *b.* London 1765; singer and actor at Sadler's Wells 1789; first appeared at Covent Garden in *The Fugitive* 4 Nov. 1790; played at the Haymarket 1792, at Drury Lane 1793, 1816, at English opera house 1794, at Royalty theatre 1797, retired 1826; a low comedy actress with a complete knowledge of the stage; her best parts were Lucy in *The Rivals* and the Widow Warren in

The Road to Ruin. d. 5 Albert place, Gravesend, Kent 2 Jany. 1852. *Oxberry's Dramatic Biog. iii,* 235–41 (1825), *portrait ; Mrs. C. B. Wilson's Our Actresses, i,* 91–3 (1844).

HARMAN, EDWARD ROBERT KING- (1 son of *Hon. Lawrence King-Harman of Rockingham, Roscommon, d.* 10 Oct. 1875). *b.* 3 April 1838 ; ed. at Eton 1847–50 ; ensign 60 rifles 1855, lieut. 1856 to 59 or 60 ; contested Longford co. 16 May 1870, contested Dublin city 18 Aug. 1870 ; M.P. Sligo co. 12 Jany. 1877 to 24 March 1880, contested Sligo co., April 1880 ; M.P. co. Dublin 1883–5, contested co. Dublin, Dec. 1885 ; M.P. Isle of Thanet division of Kent 1885 to death ; col. Roscommon militia 14 Aug. 1878 to death ; lord lieut. of Roscommon 1878 to death ; P.C. Ireland 1885 ; parliamentary under sec. for Ireland 8 April 1887 to death. *d.* Rockingham 10 June 1888. *Times* 11 *June* 1888 *p.* 9, 15 *June p.* 5 ; *Graphic, xxvii,* 296 (1883), *portrait.*

HARMAR, DAVID JAMES. Standard bearer of the Corps of Gentlemen at arms 31 Jany. 1848 to 30 Sep. 1872. *d.* 7 the Paragon, Bath 12 Oct. 1874 aged 59.

HARMER, JAMES *(son of a Spitalfields' weaver, d.* 1787). *b.* London 1777 ; attorney in London 1798–1833 when he relinquished his practice worth £4000 a year ; common councilman city of London 1826, alderman of ward of Farringdon without 1833–40 ; sheriff of London and Middlesex 1834 ; chief proprietor of the *Weekly Dispatch* which in 1835 circulated 32,000 weekly and he made £15,000 a year ; a founder of R. Free hospital, Greville st. 1828 ; resided at Ingress Park near Greenhithe which he built chiefly of the stone removed from old London Bridge ; author of *Murder of Mr. Steele : documents to show innocence of J. Holloway* 1807 ; *Account of case of G. Mathews who was convicted and pardoned* 1819 ; *The case of Edward Harris who was executed, facts to prove his innocence* 1825. *d.* at Adam Steele's house, Cricklewood, Middlesex 11 June 1853. *G.M. xl,* 201 (1853) ; *I.L.N. xxii,* 507 (1853) ; *Grant's Newspaper press, iii,* 41–42 (1872).

NOTE.—In 1840 he was the senior alderman below the chair, but was not elected Lord Mayor in consequence of his connexion with the *Weekly Dispatch* which then advocated advanced religious and political views.

HARNESS, SIR HENRY DRURY *(son of John Harness, M.D., comr. of transport board). b.* 29 April 1804 ; 2 lieut. R.A. 24 May 1827 ; instructor in fortification at Woolwich 1834–40 and professor of fortification 1844–5 ; instructor in surveying at Chatham 1840–44 ;

inspector of Welsh roads 1845 ; sec. to railway commission 1846 ; deputy master of the mint 1850–52 when he entirely reformed the working arrangements ; commissioner of public works in Ireland 1852–4 ; commanded engineers in India 1857–9, at Cawnpore, siege of Lucknow and at operations in Rohilkund and Oude ; director R. engineer establishment, Chatham 1860 ; managed cattle plague department of privy council 1866 ; C.B. 26 July 1858, K.C.B. 24 May 1873 ; col. commandant R.E. 15 June 1877 to death ; general 1 Oct. 1877 ; author of papers in *Papers of Corps of Engineers* 1844. *d.* Barton End, Headington, Oxford 10 Feb. 1883, portrait in mess of R.E. at Chatham. *Min. of Proc. of Instit. of C.E. lxxiii,* 378 (1883) ; *Monthly Notices of R.A.S. xliv,* 133–5 (1884) ; *T. B. Collinson's Memoir of Sir H. D. Harness* (1883), *portrait.*

HARNESS, REV. WILLIAM *(elder bro. of Sir H. D. Harness). b.* near Wickham, Hants. 14 March 1790 ; ed. at Harrow where in 1802 he made an acquaintance with Byron which he kept up ; at Christ's coll. Cam., B.A. 1812, M.A. 1816, Boyle lecturer 1822 ; C. of Hampstead 1823–6 ; incumb. Regent sq. chapel, London 1826–44 ; clerical registrar of privy council 1841 ; minister of Brompton chapel 1844–7 ; P.C. of All Saints, Knightsbridge 1849 to death, he raised the money for building this ch. ; editor of *The Works of Shakespeare 8 vols.* 1825 to which he prefixed a life ; author of *The life of Mary Russell Mitford* 1870 ; *killed* by falling down stairs at the deanery, Battle, Sussex 11 Nov. 1869. *L' Estrange's Life of Rev. W. Harness* (1871) ; *Reg. and Mag. of Biography,* Dec. 1869 *pp.* 308–9.

HARNETT, A. W. *(second son of Maurice Harnett of Milltown, co. Dublin). b.* about 1817 ; ed. by his father and at Trin. coll. Dublin ; barrister L.I. ; edited a paper in the south of Ireland some years ; edited *The Universal News* from date of first number Dec. 1860, the organ of more educated English Roman Catholics. *d.* St. John's Wood, London 6 June 1864. *Law Times, xxxix,* 452 (1864).

HARPER, REV. JAMES *(younger son of Rev. Alexander Harper). b.* Lanark 23 June 1795 ; ed. at Edin. univ.; D.D. of Jefferson coll. U.S. America 1843, D.D. of Glasgow univ. 1877 ; united secession minister at North Leith 1819 to death ; chairman of the synod 1840 ; professor of pastoral theology, secession ch. 1843–8 ; promoted the union of the secession and relief bodies 1848 ; professor of systematic theology 1848 ; moderator of united presby-

HARPER, REV. J. *(Con)*.

terian synod 1860 ; president of theological hall of united presbyterian ch. 1876 ; editor of *Edinburgh Theological Mag.* 1826 and *United Presbyterian Mag.* 1850. *d.* Leith Mount 13 April 1879. *Andrew Thomson's Life of J. Harper* (1880), *portrait ; John Smith's Our Scottish clergy, 3rd series* (1851) 338–45.

HARPER, THOMAS. *b.* Worcester 3 May 1787 ; trumpeter and horn player in the East India Co. volunteer band 1799, inspector of musical instruments to the Co. to his death ; principal trumpet Drury Lane and Lyceum opera house 1806 ; played at Birmingham festival 1820 ; trumpet at the Ancient Concerts, the Italian opera and Philharmonic concerts ; his imitation of the voice part in ' Let the bright Seraphin' was a great achievement of art ; author of A selection of favourite airs adapted for the Royal Kent bugle 1830 ; seized with illness at Exeter hall and *d.* at the house of his friend Joseph Surman, 9 Exeter hall, Strand, London 20 Jany. 1853. *Musical World* 29 Jany. 1853 p. 83 ; *W. W. Cazalet's Royal academy of music* (1854) 294 ; *Dramatic and musical review, iii,* 200 (1844).

HARPER, WILLIAM. *b.* Manchester 1806 ; yarn merchant Pall Mall, Manchester ; wrote the weekly trade article for the *Manchester Courier ;* author of *The Genius and other poems* 1840 ; *Cain and Abel, a dramatic poem, and minor pieces* Manchester 1844 ; *Memoir of Benjamin Braidley* 1848. *d.* Lever st. Lower Broughton, Manchester 30 Jany. 1857. *John Evans's Lancashire authors* (1876) 113–8 ; *R. W. Procter's Literary reminiscences* (1860) 121–5 ; *The Manchester Quarterly,* July 1889 *pp.* 248–53.

HARPUR, CHARLES. *b.* Windsor, New South Wales 1811; gold commissioner Araluen 1858–66 ; unsuccessful as an agriculturalist ; author of *The Bushrangers, a play in 5 acts,* Sydney 1853 ; *The Tower of the Dream,* Sydney 1865. *d.* Eurobodalla, N.S.W. 10 June 1868. *G. B. Barton's Poets of New South Wales (Sydney* (1866) 38–48.

HARRADEN, RICHARD BANKES *(son of Richard Harraden 1756–1838, engraver). b.* 1778 ; member of Soc. of British Artists 1824–49 ; exhibited 2 landscapes at B.I. and 21 at Suffolk st. 1823–30 ; made drawings for Costumes of the various orders in the university, Cambridge 1803, Cantabrigia Depicta. Cambridge 1809, History of university of Cambridge 1814, Illustrations of the university of Cambridge 1830, Views of all the colleges 1830. *d.* 18 Regent st. Cambridge 17 Nov. 1862. *R. Willis' Architectural Hist. of Cambridge* (1886) i, *pp. cxv–xviii.*

HARRAL, THOMAS. Edited *Suffolk Chronicle and Bury Gazette ;* author of *A monody on death of John Palmer with observations on London stage* 1798 ; *Ann Boleyn and Caroline of Brunswick compared* 1820 ; *Henry the eighth and George the fourth* 1820 ; *The apotheosis of Pitt, a masque.* Bury 1822 ; *Picturesque views of the Severn* 1824. *d.* Dorset st. Portman sq. London 31 Jany. 1853 at advanced age.

HARRILD, ROBERT. *b.* Bermondsey, London 1 Jany. 1780 ; printer ; manufacturer of printers' materials and a printers' engineer 1809 ; invented the composition balls and rollers for inking type 1810, soon universally adopted as the means of rapid printing ; preserved the printing press on which Benjamin Franklin had worked in London, it is now in patent office, Washington. *d.* Round hill villa, Sydenham, Kent 28 July 1853. *Bigmore and Wyman's Bibl. of printing, i,* 206, 232, 234, 306.

HARRINGTON, CHARLES STANHOPE, 4 Earl of *(eld. son of 3 Earl of Harrington 1753–1829). b.* 8 April 1780 ; styled Lord Petersham 1780–1829 ; ensign Coldstream guards 2 Dec. 1795 ; major Queen's Rangers 12 Feb. 1803 ; lieut. col. 3 West India regiment 25 June 1807 to 13 Aug. 1812 when placed on h.p. ; col. in the army 4 June 1814 ; a lord of the bedchamber 1812–29 ; succeeded as 4 Earl 5 Sep. 1829. *d.* Brighton 3 March 1851. *G.M. xxxv,* 547 (1851) ; *I.L.N. xviii,* 200 (1851).

NOTE.—As Lord Petersham he was a distinguished leader of fashion, and originated a vestment which long retained his name the Petersham great coat. He also wore hats of a peculiar shape. When young cut out his own clothes, made his own blacking. Lord Petersham's mixture was a favourite snuff. *H. Melton's Hints on Hats* (1865) *p.* 39 ; *J. Timb's English Eccentrics, i,* 56–7 (1866) ; *J. Ashton's Social England, ii,* 308–9 (1890), 2 *portraits.*

HARRINGTON, MARIA STANHOPE, Countess of *(dau. of Samuel T. Foote, theatrical manager, Plymouth and Exeter). b.* Plymouth 24 July 1797 ; appeared as Juliet at Plymouth theatre July 1810, at Covent Garden as Amanthis in *The Child of Nature* 26 May 1814 at which house she acted every season till 1825 ; first appeared at Drury Lane as Letitia Hardy in *The Belle's Stratagem* 9 March 1826 ; performed throughout the United Kingdom and in Paris ; had 2 children by Colonel Berkeley 1815 etc.; obtained £3000 damages from "Pea-Green" Hayne for breach of promise 22 Dec. 1824 ; retired from the stage at Birmingham 11 March 1831. *(m.* 7 April 1831 the preceding). *d.* 2 Richmond terrace, Whitehall, London 27 Dec. 1867. *Mrs. C. B. Wilson's Our Actresses, i,* 208–41 (1844), *portrait ; Oxberry's Dramatic Biog. i,* 33–46 (1825), *portrait ; Theatrical Inquisitor, vi,* 3–6 (1815), *portrait.*

HARRINGTON, LEICESTER FITZGERALD CHARLES STANHOPE, 5 Earl of (*brother of 4 Earl of Harrington* 1780-1851). *b.* Dublin barracks 2 Sep. 1784; cornet 1 life guards 25 Sep. 1799; major 47 foot 4 July 1816 to 26 June 1823 when placed on h.p.; served in Mahratta war 1817-18; col. in the army 10 Janv. 1837; C.B. 14 Oct. 1818; co-operated with Lord Byron and others in assisting the Greeks against the Turks 1823; knt. of Greek order of the Redeemer 30 April 1838. *d.* Harrington house, Kensington palace gardens, London 7 Sep. 1862. *T. Moore's Life of Byron* (1847) 585, 601 *etc.; Waagen's Galleries of art* (1857) 234-39.

HARRIOT, DAVID. Entered Bengal army 1803; colonel 6 Bengal light cavalry 1849 to death; C.B. 3 April 1846. *d.* Cheltenham 6 Sep. 1851 aged 68.

HARRIS, GEORGE FRANCIS ROBERT HARRIS, 3 Baron (*eld. child of 2 Baron Harris* 1782-1845). *b.* Belmont, Faversham, Kent 14 Aug. 1810; ed. at Eton and Ch. Ch. Ox., B.A. 1832, D.C.L. 1863; lieut. governor of Trinidad 5 May 1846, governor and commander in chief there 3 Nov. 1846; governor of Madras, Feb. 1854 to Janv. 1859; lord in waiting to the Queen 1860-63; chamberlain to Princess of Wales, March 1863; K.C.S.I. 25 June 1861, G.C.S.I. 24 May 1866. *d.* Belmont 23 Nov. 1872.

HARRIS, AUGUSTUS, stage name of Augustus Glossop (*son of Joseph Glossop who built the Coburg theatre, London* 1817 *and d. Jany.* 1835, *by Madame Feron, vocalist who d.* 7 *May* 1853). *b.* Portici, Naples 12 June 1825; light comedian at Bower saloon, Stangate, London; played at Princess's theatre 1843, managed the Princess's 24 Sep. 1859 to 16 Oct. 1862; stage manager of Royal Italian Opera, Covent Garden 1846 to death; stage director of royal opera, St. Petersburgh, held same post at Madrid, Paris, Berlin and Barcelona; lessee of Covent Garden during pantomime seasons of 1869-73. (*m.* 17 Feb. 1846 Maria Ann Bone, columbine at Princess's theatre); wrote *The Avalanche, a drama* 1854; *The little treasure, a comedy* 1855 and 11 other pieces; with E. Falconer *The Rose of Castile, an opera* 1857; *Satanella, an opera* 1858. *d.* 2 Bedford place, Holborn, London 19 April 1873. *The Mask* (1868) 97, *portrait; Entertainment Gazette* 15 *Jany.* 1887 *p.* 8; *Era* 27 *April* 1873 *p.* 4.

HARRIS, CHARLES. *b.* 19 Oct. 1817; ensign 27 Bengal N.I. 24 Sep. 1835, major 1860-62; lieut. col. Bengal staff corps 1866-77; L.G. 18 May 1881. *d.* 55 Sutherland gardens, Harrow road, London 1 March 1889.

HARRIS, RIGHT REV. CHARLES AMYAND (3 son of 2 Earl of Malmesbury 1778-1841). *b.* Christchurch, Hants. 4 Aug. 1813; ed. at Oriel coll. Ox., B.A. 1835, M.A. 1837; fellow of All Souls' coll. 1835-37; student at I.T. 1834; ordained deacon 1836; R. of Wilton, Wilts. 1840-48; preb. of Salisbury 1841-63; domestic chaplain to bishop of Salisbury 1841-68; P.C. of Rownhams, Southampton 1856-63; archdeacon of Wilts. 1863-68; V. of Bremhill-with-Highway, Wilts. 1863-68; bishop of Gibraltar 1868 to Oct. 1873, consecrated in Canterbury cath. 1 May 1868; author of *One rule and one mind, a sermon* 1841. *d.* Torquay 16 March 1874. *bur.* Bremhill 19 March.

HARRIS, CHRISTOPHER ARTHUR MOHUN (1 son of Isaac Donnithorne who assumed name of Harris, d. 1848). *b.* Barton Cliffe cottage, Hants. 14 Jany. 1801; ed. at Eton and at Geneva univ. 1816; foreign correspondent for *The Press* at Brussels 1854-6; a personal friend of Lord Beaconsfield 35 years; assumed name of Mohun, July 1878; kept hounds at Hayne to 1834; hereditary deputy ranger of Dartmoor; author of *Letters on the great political questions of the day, By Ismaël* 1852. *d.* Cross house, Bishops' Teignton, South Devon 30 Oct. 1887. *Boase's Collect. Cornub.* (1890) 319, 1710; *Baily's Mag. xlviii,* 343-5 (1888).

HARRIS, REV. DAVID. *b.* Fearn 1771; licensed by presbytery of Dundee 1 Dec. 1802; presbyterian minister Fearn 8 Sep. 1803 to death; author of *Account of the parish of Fearn* 18—. *d.* Riverside villa, Blair-gowrie 18 Oct. 1867 in 96 year. *H. Scott's Fasti Ecclesiæ Scoticanæ* (1871) *iii, pt. ii, p.* 832.

HARRIS, EDMUND ROBERT. Solicitor at Preston 1827 to death; left £285,000 to town of Preston for purposes of public utility, of this £105,000 was expended on the Harris free public library and museum and £100,000 on the Harris orphanage Oct. 1883. *d.* Whinfield, Lancs. 27 May 1877 aged 73.

HARRIS, SIR EDWARD ALFRED JOHN (2 son of 2 Earl of Malmesbury 1778-1841). *b.* Spring Gardens, London 20 May 1808; midshipman R.N. 1823, captain 23 Nov. 1841; M.P. for Christchurch 1844-52; consul general in Chili 1853-8; min. plenipo. at Berne 31 March 1858, envoy extraord. 16 Dec. 1859; envoy extraord. at Amsterdam 22 Aug. 1867 to 19 Nov. 1877 when retired on pension of £1300; R.A. 12 April 1862, admiral on h.p. 5 Aug. 1875; C.B. 15 June 1863, K.C.B. 13 July 1872. *d.* Sondling park near Hythe, Kent 17 July 1888

HARRIS, FRANCIS *(son of John Harris of Winchester place, Southwark, hat maker).* *b.* Winchester place 1 Dec. 1829 ; ed. at King's coll. London and Caius coll. Cam., B.A. 1852, M.B. 1854, M.D. 1859 ; M.R.C.P. 1857 ; demonstrator of morbid anatomy St. Bartholomew's hospital 1858–61, assistant phys. 1861–74 ; author of *On the nature of the substance found in the amyloid degeneration of various organs of the human body* 1859. *d.* 24 Cavendish sq. London 3 Sep. 1885. *bur.* churchyard of Brenchley, Kent. *Gee's Memoir of F. Harris ; St. Bartholomew's Hospital Reports* (1885) *xxxiii-viii.*

HARRIS, FURLONG ELIZABETH SHIPTON. *b.* 1822 ; author of *From Oxford to Rome, and how it fared with some who lately made the journey. By A Companion Traveller* 1847, 3 ed. 1847 ; *Rest in the church. By the author of From Oxford to Rome* 1848 ; *Via Dolorosa, the Catholic devotion of the stations. By the author, etc.* 1848. *d.* St. Martin's st. Wallingford 20 June 1852.

HARRIS, REV. GEORGE *(son of Abraham Harris, Unitarian minister at Swansea).* *b.* Maidstone, Kent 15 May 1794 ; matric. at Glasgow univ. Nov. 1812 ; a founder of Scottish Unitarian Assoc. July 1813, sec. 1813–16 ; minister of Renshaw st. chapel, Liverpool 1817–22 ; planned a Unitarian Christian Assoc. 1818 ; minister of Cloth Hall chapel, Bolton 1822, of Moor lane chapel, Bolton 1823–25 ; minister at Glasgow 1825–41, at Edinburgh 1841–45, of Hanover sq. chapel, Newcastle 1845 to death ; edited *The Christian Pioneer, Glasgow* 19 vols. 1826–45 ; author of *Unitarianism, the only religion which can become universal, Liverpool* 1818 ; *Christianity and Church of Irelandism, Glasgow* 1835, 15 ed. 1835 ; *The great business of life* 1847 and other books. *d.* Newcastle 24 Dec. 1859.

HARRIS, GEORGE *(eld. son of George Harris of Rugby).* *b.* Rugby 6 May 1809 ; ed. at Rugby and Trin. coll. Cam. ; barrister M.T. 13 Jany. 1843 ; acting judge Birmingham county court 2 years ; registrar of court of bankruptcy, Manchester 1862–8 ; the first suggester of the Historical MSS. commission 1857 ; V.P. Anthropological Instit. ; president Manchester Anthropological soc. ; F.S.A. 7 Feb. 1861 ; author of *The life of lord chancellor Hardwicke* 1847 ; *Civilization considered as a science* 1861 ; *The true theory of representation in a state* 1852 ; *The theory of the arts* 2 vols. 1869 ; *A philosophical treatise on nature and constitution of man* 2 vols. 1876. *d.* Iselipps manor, Northolt, Middlesex 15 Nov. 1890. *Times 22 Nov.* 1890 *p.* 8.

HARRIS, GEORGE FREDERIC *(eld. son of Joseph Harris of Liverpool).* *b.* 1813 ; ed. at Trin. coll. Cam., 3rd in classical tripos and B.A. 1835 ; fellow of his coll. ; assistant master at Harrow about 1840, lower master 1863 to Dec. 1868, a very popular master. *d.* Mountside, Harrow 7 May 1869 aged 57.

HARRIS, GEORGE FREDERICK. *b.* 1797 ; organist St. Lawrence, Jewry, city of London 1821 to death ; chorus master Drury Lane theatre 1836 ; founder and conductor of London Professional chorus soc. ; under name of Rudolph Nordmann published *The airs from Balfe's opera Satanella arranged for pianoforte duets* 1859 ; *Two hundred and fifty chants* 1862 and 45 other pieces. *d.* 19 Torrington sq. London, 25 Nov. 1867.

HARRIS, REV. JAMES. *b.* London 25 Aug. 1824 ; employed in a hosier's shop ; studied theology at Tronchiennes, Namur and Louvain in Belgium and at St. Beuno's coll. North Wales 1850–6 ; ordained priest 22 Sep. 1861 ; minister at St. Beuno's 1861, professor of ecclesiastical history 1862, of moral theology 1864–5 ; spiritual father and prefect of studies at St. Francis Xavier's coll. Liverpool 1865, superior of the coll. 1879 to death. *d.* Kentish Town, London 4 Dec. 1883. *Memoir of Father James Harris, By Thomas Harper* (1884).

HARRIS, REV. JOHN *(eld. son of a tailor and draper).* *b.* Ugborough, Devon 8 March 1802 ; minister of Congregational ch. at Epsom 1825 ; prof. of theology in Cheshunt coll. 1837 ; D.D. Brown univ. U.S.A. 1838 ; one of editors of *Biblical Review* 1846 ; principal of and prof. of theology in New coll. St. John's Wood, London 1850 to death, college opened 8 Oct. 1851 ; chairman of Congregational Union of England and Wales 1852 ; author of *The great teacher : characteristics of our Lord's ministry* 1835 ; *The Pre-Adamite earth* 1846 ; *The altar of the household* 1853, 11 ed. 1859 and other books. *d.* New college, London 21 Dec. 1856. *Congregational year book* (1858) 207–9.

HARRIS, JOHN. *b.* 1791 ; student royal academy ; employed in British museum 1820 ; artist, lithographer and copyist ; noted for his fac simile reproductions of wood engravings and block printing to supply deficiencies in imperfect books ; completed missing leaves for volumes in libraries of Lord Spencer, Thomas Grenville, British Museum, the Duke of Sussex and others ; made the illustrations for *Dibdin's Bibliotheca Spenceriana* 1814 and *Pettigrew's Bibliotheca Sussexiana* 1839. *d.* Croydon 28 Dec. 1873 aged 82. *Cowtan's British Museum* (1872) 334–8.

HARRIS, JOHN. *b.* 1807; prompter and stage director theatre royal, Belfast; manager and then lessee of Queen's theatre, Dublin 1845–51; lessee of theatre royal, Dublin 26 Dec. 1851 to death; his second season began 16 Oct. 1852 and ended 15 July 1854, 516 nights the longest season in annals of Irish stage; produced 12 of Shakespeare's plays May 1852 to Feb. 1855. (*m.* 184– Miss Julia Nicholl, well known actress); found drowned at Killiney Strand 13 March 1874. *bur.* from his residence 11 Waterloo road, Dublin, in Mount Jerome cemet. 19 March. *History of theatre royal, Dublin* (1870) 130–79; *Irish Times* 16 *March* 1874 *p.* 2, 17 *March p.* 2, 20 *March p.* 2.

HARRIS, JOHN (1 son of John Harris, miner, *d.* 23 *April* 1848). *b.* Six Chimneys' cottage, Bolennowe hill, Camborne, Cornwall 14 Oct. 1820; worked in Dolcoath mine 1832–57; scripture reader at Falmouth 1857 to death; local Wesleyan preacher; had grants from R. Literary fund 1872, 1875, and from R. Bounty fund 1877, 1881; author of *Lays from the mine, the moor and the mountain* 1853, 2 *ed.* 1856; *Luda, a lay of the Druids* 1868; *Tales and other poems* 1877; *My autobiography* 1882, *with portrait*, and other works; had prize of a gold watch for The Shakespeare tercentenary prize poem 1864. *d.* Killigrew ter. Falmouth 7 Jany. 1884. *bur.* Treslothan 10 Jany.

HARRIS, JOHN DOVE. *b.* Leicester 1809; mayor of Leicester 1850 and 1856; M.P. for Leicester 1857–59 and 1865–74. *d.* Ratcliff hall, Ratcliff on Wreake, Leics. 20 Nov. 1878. *I.L.N. xxxiii*, 92, 94 (1858), *portrait*.

HARRIS, JOSEPH. Entered Bengal army 1803; col. 3 Bengal N.I. 1846–58; col. 4 European infantry 1859 to death; L.G. 29 Aug. 1859. *d.* Carlton road, Maida vale, London 22 July 1861 aged 81.

HARRIS, JOSEPH JOHN. *b.* London 1799; organist of St. Olave's ch. Southwark 1823–28; organist at Blackburn 1828–31; singing master and assistant organist at Manchester collegiate ch. 1831, organist of Manchester cathedral 1848 to death; director of the Gentlemen's glee club, Manchester; published *A selection of psalm and hymn tunes, Southwark* 1827; *The cathedral daily service, Manchester* 1844; *The musical expression, a guide for parents* 1845. *d.* 242 Brunswick st. Oxford st. Manchester 10 Feb. 1869.

HARRIS, JOSIAH (*son of William Harris*). *b.* Mevagissey, Cornwall 6 May 1821; edited *The Bath Herald* 1848–52; *The Western Luminary, Exeter* 1854–5; *The Wolverhampton*

Journal 1855–6; *The Oxford University Herald* 1856; author of *The pulpit of Cornwall, By Ishmael,* 3 *numbers* 1859; *A tear and a floweret, Biography of J. W. Etheridge* 1871. *d.* Portmellon, Mevagissey 5 March 1888.

HARRIS, MATTHEW (*son of Peter Harris, builder, Athlone*). *b.* Roscommon 1826; a working bricklayer and slater; road contractor, architect, builder, contractor; a Fenian 1865–80; member of Land and National leagues, his speech about shooting landlords like partridges had a wide notoriety; M.P. East Galway, Dec. 1885 to death; by the special commission he was condemned as guilty of criminal conspiracy 1889. *d.* near Ballinasloe 14 April 1890. *Pall Mall Gazette* 15 *April* 1890 *p.* 6, *portrait*.

HARRIS, RICHARD. *b.* Leicester, Oct. 1777; in R. Phillips' printing office Leicester to 1793; served in the army 1797–1802; founded a manufactory of knitted shawls and fancy hosiery at Leicester 1802, had various partners and lastly his 2 sons; mayor of Leicester 1844–45; M.P. for Leicester 2 Sep. 1848 to 1 July 1852. *d.* Leicester 2 Feb. 1854. *T. Lomas' Memoir of R. Harris* (1855).

HARRIS, REV. ROBERT. *b.* Feb. 1764; ed. at Sid. Suss. coll. Cam., fellow, 10 wrangler 1786; B.A. 1786, M.A. 1789, B.D. 1797; incumb. of St. George's church, Preston, Sep. 1797 to death. *d.* Preston 6 Jany. 1862.

HARRIS, ROBERT (*son of James Harris of Wittersham hall, Kent*). *b.* 9 July 1809; entered navy 26 Jany. 1822; served in Excellent gunnery ship Portsmouth 1833–6; served in China 1840–1; captain 17 Oct. 1849; in the Illustrious training ship 1854–7 where he had charge of Sir J. Graham's novices; organised and introduced into the navy, naval cadets and boys' training ship system 1857–62; granted good service pension 2 April 1863. *d.* Southsea, Portsmouth 16 Jany. 1865.

HARRIS, THOMAS. *b.* 15 June 1810; called to Irish bar 1834; Q.C. 6 July 1858. *d.* 1 Nov. 1877.

HARRIS, SIR THOMAS NOEL (*son of Rev. Hamlyn Harris, R. of Whitewell, Rutland*). *b.* 1785; ensign 87 foot 5 Feb. 1801; captain 18 light dragoons 27 Aug. 1807, sold out 1808; served in all Blucher's actions 1813–14; brought to England first news of surrender of Paris, April 1814; lost his right arm at Waterloo; captain 1 dragoon guards 8 Sep. 1815 to 25 March 1816 when placed on h.p.; deputy adjutant general in Canada 22 July 1830 to

HARRIS, SIR T. N. *(Con.)*

14 Sep. 1832; chief magistrate at Gibraltar 1835; one of grooms of H.M.'s privy chamber to death; K.H. 1830; knighted at St. James's palace 28 April 1841. *d.* Updown, Eastry, Kent 23 March 1860.

HARRIS, WILLIAM. *b.* 1797; F.G.S. 1839; collected the organic remains found in the Kent chalk pits, especially the sponges and fishes; mapped the area of the cretaceous strata about Charing on the Ordnance map; traced the fossiliferous ironstone near Charing. *d.* Charing, Kent 13 May 1877 aged 80. *Geol. Mag., Aug.* 1877 *pp.* 381–82.

HARRIS, WILLIAM AUGUSTUS (1 *son of William Harris*). *b.* Bovey Tracey 1846; ed. at Blundell's sch. Tiverton and Ball. coll. Ox., scholar 1863–8, B.A. 1867; barrister I.I. 1 May 1871; called to American bar 1870; F.R.A.S. 11 Feb. 1870, member of Eclipse expedition to Sicily 1870; author of *Harris' Mining Laws* 1877. *d.* 49 Blessington road, Lee, Lewisham 28 Feb. 1880. *Monthly Notices of R. Astronom. Soc., Feb.* 1881 *pp.* 187–8.

HARRIS, WILLIAM CHARLES (*son of John Harris of Clapham, Surrey*). *b.* 1809; ensign 68 foot 12 June 1830, captain 19 Jany. 1838 to 5 Oct. 1838 when he sold out; chief constable of Hampshire 1843–56; assist. comr. of Metropolitan police 3 March 1856, retired Nov. 1881 on pension of £533 6s. 8d.; C.B. 12 July 1881; author of *A manual of drill for county and district constables* 1862. *d.* Eastdon house, Starcross, Devon 8 March 1887.

HARRIS, SIR WILLIAM SNOW (*only son of Thomas Harris, solicitor*). *b.* Plymouth 1 April 1791; ed. at Edin. univ.; surgeon in the militia; practised in Plymouth to 1824; invented method of arranging lightning conductors in ships 1820 which was employed in Russian navy, (Czar gave him a ring and vase), not used in English navy until 1843; knighted at St. James's palace 28 April 1847, and had a grant of £5000 in 1854; a founder of the Blue Friars and known as Brother Bacon clerk 17 May 1829; F.R.S. 2 June 1831, communicated papers on laws of electricity 1826, 1834, 1836 and 1839, Copley medal 1835, Bakerian lecturer 1839; civil list pension of £300 for services in cultivation of science 23 July 1841; scientific referee of government in electrical matters 1860; author of *On utility of fixing lightning conductors on ships* 1830; *On the nature of thunder storms* 1843; *Rudimentary treatises on Electricity* 1848, *Magnetism* 1852 and *Galvanism* 1856. *d.* 6 Windsor villas, Plymouth 22 Jany. 1867.

HARRIS, SIR W. S. *(Con.)*

Treatise on Frictional Electricity (1867), *memoir by C. Tomlinson; Wright's The Blue Friars* (1889) 73–74, *portrait; Encyclop. Brit. xi,* 493–4 (1880); *Proc. Royal Soc. xvi,* 18–22 (1868).

HARRISON, ARTHUR AYLETT (3 *son of Rev. Thomas Harrison, P.C. of Womenswould, Kent*). *b.* 1831; ed. at Trin. coll. Cam., B.A. 1853, M.B. 1858; phys. to Church Missionary station, Abbeokuta, West Africa; author of *Theory of heat* 1864. *d.* on board the 'Macgregor Laird' off Accra, Gold Coast, Africa 12 June 1864 aged 33.

HARRISON, BENJAMIN (4 *son of Benjamin Harrison 1734–97, treasurer of Guy's hospital*). *b.* West Ham, Essex 29 July 1771; treasurer of Guy's hospital 1797 to death; with Sir Astley Cooper separated Guy's from St. Thomas's 1825; deputy governor of Hudson's Bay and South Sea companies; chairman of Exchequer loan board; F.R.S.; F.S.A. *d.* West side, Clapham common 18 May 1856. *W. J. Cripps's Pedigree of family of Harrison, privately printed* 1881.

HARRISON, VEN. BENJAMIN (*eld. son of the preceding*). *b.* 26 Sep. 1808; ed. at Ch. Ch. Ox., student 1828–48; B.A. 1830, M.A. 1833; Kennicott Hebrew scholar 1831, Pusey and Ellerton Hebrew scholar 1832; select preacher at Ox. 1835–7; domestic chaplain to abp. of Canterbury 1843–8; canon of Canterbury and archdeacon of Maidstone 6 Dec. 1845 to death; F.S.A. 7 Dec. 1854; one of the revisers of Old Testament 1870–84, published 19 May 1885; author of Nos. 16, 17, 24 and 49 of *Tracts for the Times* 1841; *An Historical inquiry into the true interpretation of the rubrics* 1845; *Prophetic outlines of the Christian church and the Antichristian power* 1849 and 30 addresses, charges, lectures and single sermons. *d.* 7 Bedford sq. London 25 March 1887. *Proc. of Soc. of Antiq. xi,* 371 (1887).

HARRISON, SIR EDMUND STEPHEN (*son of Henry Holland Harrison*). *b.* 1810; clerk in privy council office 1826, chief clerk 1860–76; deputy clerk of the council 1860 to death; C.B. 2 April 1875; knighted at Windsor Castle 21 April 1880. *d.* 114 Harley st. London 21 Sep. 1882.

HARRISON, SIR GEORGE. *b.* Stonehaven, Kincardineshire 1812; clothier Edin. in partnership with Samuel Halkett 1839 then with his sons; sec. to Chamber of commerce 1856–63, chairman 1866–9; a founder of the Philosophical Institution; chairman Scottish trade

HARRISON, SIR G. (Con.)

protection soc. 1878–82; town councillor 1875, treasurer of the city 1879–82, lord provost Nov. 1882 to Nov. 1885; LL.D. of Edin. univ. 1884; knighted at Osborne 11 Aug. 1884; M.P. southern div. of Edin. Nov. 1885. d. 7 Whitehouse ter. Edinburgh 23 Dec. 1885. bur. Warriston cemet. 26 Dec. W. Hole's Quasi Cursores (1884) ix, xiv-xvii, portrait; The Scotsman 24 Dec. 1885 pp. 4, 5, 28 Dec. p. 5.

HARRISON, GEORGE HARRISON ROGERS. b. 1806; Blue Mantle pursuivant 15 Nov. 1831 to 6 July 1849; Windsor herald 6 July 1849 to death; F.S.A.; author of A genealogical account of the Maitland family 1869. d. Windsor house 288 Kennington park road, London 2 March 1880.

HARRISON, GEORGE HENRY DE STRABOLGIE NEVILLE PLANTAGENET- (only child of ·Marley Harrison of Waston, Yorkshire 1772–1822). b. 14 July 1817; general of brigade in Mexican army in Yucatan war 1843; brigadier general in Peruvian army 1844 and in Monte Video 1845; marshal general of the army of 'God and Liberty' of Corrientes in the Argentine republic 1845; general of cavalry in Danish army during Schleswig-Holstein war 1848; lieut. general of the German Confederation 1848; appointed marshal in Turkish army by the Sultan 1853; petitioned parliament for summons to parliament by his title of Duke of Lancaster as heir of the whole blood of Henry vi. 1858; travelled through nearly all the countries in Europe, Asia, Africa and America; not allowed access to British Museum library after 1850 because he claimed to be Duke of Lancaster; bankrupt 25 Oct. 1861, liabilities £6484, confined in Queen's prison, Southwark; worked from 1865 to death in the Public Record office on the rolls of the queen's bench and common pleas, making collections for family history, Rich. i. to Jas. i., left 30 folio volumes of MSS.; author of The history of Yorkshire, Wapentake of Gilling West 1879 price 15 guineas, of which he sold but 20 copies, it contains his pedigree and portrait; Petition of General Plantagenet-Harrison to house of lords touching the duchy of Lancaster 1858. d. about 18 July 1890.

HARRISON, JOHN. A life guardsman; one of the Cato st. conspirators 1820, was appointed to fire the King st. cavalry barracks; transported to Botany Bay 1820; became chief baker at Bathurst, N.S.W. Australia. d. before 1863. R. Therry's Reminiscences (2 ed. 1863) 96–98.

HARRISON, JOHN. b. 1808; M.R.C.S. 1832, F.R.C.S. 1843; house surgeon Lock hospital; house surgeon St. George's hospital, lecturer on surgical anatomy; author of The pathology of stricture of the urethra 1852, 2 ed. 1858; The pathology of venereal diseases 1860. d. 2 Albany courtyard, Piccadilly, London 3 Jany. 1870.

HARRISON, REV. JOHN. b. 1815; C. of Burslem 1854–58; C. of Rotherham 1858–60; C. of Sheffield 1860–63; C. of Pitsmoor, Sheffield 1863–67; V. of Fenwick near Doncaster 1867 to death; D.D. Edin. 1870; author of An answer to Dr. Pusey's challenge respecting the doctrine of the real presence 2 vols. 1871; The eastward position unscriptural and not primitive and catholic 1876 and 5 other books. d. Askern near Doncaster 26 Feb. 1883 aged 68.

HARRISON, JOHN GREGSON. L.S.A. 1828, M.R.C.S. Eng. 1829, M.D. Giessen 1842, F.R.C.P. Edin. 1845; medical officer to L. & N.W. railway many years, presented with a service of plate value 300 guineas March 1854; medical inspector of factories; surgeon 6 royal Lancashire militia 1 Sep. 1856 to death. d. Cheltenham 1 Dec. 1862 aged 56. I.L.N. 1 April 1854 p. 289, picture of service of plate.

HARRISON, JOSEPH. Head gardener to Lord Wharncliffe at Worley hall near Sheffield to 1837; started The Floricultural Cabinet and Florists' Magazine 1833, monthly mag., edited it 1833–55; a florist at Downham, Norfolk 1837, at Kingston, Surrey; edited The gardener's and forester's record 1833; The garden almanac 1842 etc.; The gardeners' and naturalists' almanac 1852; with J. Paxton The Horticultural register 1831. d. about 1858.

HARRISON, MARY (dau. of Wm. Rossiter of Stockport, Lancs., hat maker). b. Liverpool 1788; taught painting in Liverpool and Chester about 1818–29; lived in London 1829 to death; an original member of New Society of Painters in water-colours 1831; exhibited 20 flower pictures at R.A., 9 at B.I. and 20 at Suffolk st. 1833–63. (m. 1814 William Harrison, he was ruined and d. 1861), she d. Chesnut lodge, Hampstead 25 Nov. 1875. E. C. Clayton's English female artists, i, 411–15 (1876).

HARRISON, REV. MATTHEW (son of John Harrison of Appleby). Matric. from Queen's coll. Ox. 10 Oct. 1810 aged 18, fellow 1815–33; B.A. 1814, M.A. 1818; R. of Church Oakley, Hants. 1832 to death; author of The rise, progress and present structure of the English language 1848, 2 ed. Philadelphia 1856. d. Church Oakley 1 Jany. 1862.

HARRISON, ROBERT. Ed. at Trin. coll. Dublin, B.A. 1814, M.A. and M.B. 1824, M.D. 1837; L. and F.R.C.S. Ireland 1816; M. and F.R.C.S. Eng. 1815; professor of anatomy and physiology Trin. coll. 1844 to death; surgeon to Dr. Steevens' hospital and medical college, Dublin; author of *The Dublin Dissector* 2 vols. *Dublin* 1827; *The surgical anatomy of the arteries of the body* 2 vols. *Dublin* 1824, 4 *ed.* 1839. *d.* 1 Hume st. Dublin 23 April 1858. *Lancet, i,* 135–9 (1827–8); *Medical Directory* 1859 *p.* 973.

HARRISON, ROBERT ALEXANDER. *b.* Montreal 1833; called to Upper Canadian bar 1855, the first person called with honours; chief clerk of crown law department for Upper Canada 1854–59; Q.C. 1867; member of House of Commons 1867–72; chief justice of province of Ontario 8 Oct. 1875 to death; author of *A digest of all the cases in the Queen's Bench and Practice court for Upper Canada 1823–51, Toronto* 1852; *The statutes of practical utility* 1857; *The common law procedure act* 1856, 1858; *The municipal manual for Upper Canada* 1859, 4 *ed.* 1879; *The common law procedure act, Canada* 1870. *d.* Nov. 1878. *Morgan's Bibl. Canad.* (1867) 176–7.

HARRISON, SAMUEL (*youngest son of Rev. William Harrison, wesleyan minister*). *b.* Banwell, Somerset 1826; ed. Woodhouse grove 1834; apprentice to a printer, Sheffield; shorthand reporter to *Sheffield Times* to 1854; introduced type-high stereotype columns in newspapers; proprietor with Henry Pawson of *Sheffield Times* 1854–7, sole proprietor 1857, editor 1854–69; acquired the *Sheffield Iris*, the *Sheffield Mercury* and the *Sheffield Argus*, all of which were incorporated in the *Times;* author of *The Last Judgment, a poem in twelve books* 1857, *new ed.* 1862; *A complete history of the great flood at Sheffield* 1864. *d.* Oakvilla, Broombank, Sheffield 21 Feb. 1871. *Sheffield Times* 25 *Feb.* 1871 *p.* 8, 4 *March p.* 8.

HARRISON, SAMUEL BEALEY (*eld. son of John Harrison of Foxley Grove, Berkshire*). *b.* Manchester 4 March 1802; special pleader; barrister M.T. 15 June 1832; settled at Bronte, co. Halton, Canada as a miller and farmer 1837; called to bar of Upper Canada, Michs. term 1839, Q.C. 4 Jany. 1845, bencher of the Law society; judge of county court of county of York; represented Kingston in 1st parliament of United Canada 1841–43 and Kent in 2nd parliament 1843–45; mem. of executive council of Canada 1841–43; mem. of board of works 1841–44. *d.* Toronto 23 July 1867.

HARRISON, THOMAS. Educated for an architect; associated with Wm. Ruff in supplying racing intelligence to London and provincial papers; on staff of *Bell's Life in London* to 1860; on staff of *The Field* 1860 to death. *d.* 8 Lodge road, St. John's Wood, London 16 July 1882. *The Field* 22 *July* 1882 *p.* 134.

HARRISON, THOMAS ELLIOTT (*son of William Harrison, ship builder, Sunderland*). *b.* North End, Fulham, Middlesex 4 April 1808; pupil of William Chapman, C.E. to 1829; surveyed part of the line for London and Birmingham railway 1830 and Stanhope and Tyne railway 1832, and built the Victoria bridge over the Wear 170 feet high with arches of 160 feet span 1837–8; engineer with Robert Stephenson of high level bridge at Newcastle 1849; engineer in chief of York, Newcastle and Berwick line 1849 to death; designed and carried out the Jarrow docks at South Shields 1855–9, designed the Hartlepool docks; built York railway station 1877; M.I.C.E. 1834, pres. 1874. *d.* Newcastle 20 March 1888. *Min. of proc. of Instit. of C.E. xciv,* 301–13 (1888), *portrait.*

HARRISON, THOMAS RICHARD (*son of James Harrison, printer*). *b.* 3 May 1798; head of firm of Harrison & Sons, printers, St. Martin's lane, Charing Cross, London; partner with J. W. Parker; printer to the Foreign office and printer of *London Gazette. d.* 53 Russell sq. London 29 April 1869.

HARRISON, WILLIAM. *b.* Maryport, Cumberland, Oct. 1812; commander of merchant ships to 1842; connected with Cunard line of packets 1842–55 and crossed the Atlantic 180 times; app. commander of the Great Eastern Jany. 1856, conducted her from Deptford to Portland roads Sep. 1859; *drowned* off Southampton dock gates 21 Jany. 1860. *I.L.N.* 6 *Nov.* 1858, *portrait,* 4 *Feb.* 1860, *portrait; Drawing Room portrait gallery* (3 *Ser.* 1860), *portrait.*

HARRISON, WILLIAM (*only son of a coal merchant*). *b.* Marylebone, London 15 June 1813; ed. at Royal Academy of Music 1836–7; first appeared in London at Covent Garden 2 May 1839 as Henrique in Rooke's opera of *Henrique or the Love Pilgrim;* sang at Drury Lane 1843, the original Thaddeus in Balfe's *Bohemian girl* 27 Nov. 1843; played at Princess's 1849, at Haymarket 1851; toured through U.S. with Louisa Pyne 1854–57, they opened Lyceum theatre 21 Sep. 1857 and were lessees of Covent Garden 1858 to 19 March 1864, produced 10 new operas; sole manager of Her Majesty's theatre 8 Nov. 1864 to 16 March

1865; made his last appearance as Fritz in *Grand Duchess* at Liverpool, May 1868; had a tenor voice of remarkable purity and sweetness; translated Masse's operetta *Les noces de Jeannette* and produced it at Covent Garden as *The marriage of Georgette* in 1860. *(m.* 4 March 1839 Ellen dau. of Wm. Clifford, actor *d.* 156 Cambridge st. Pimlico, London 5 Jany. 1889), he *d.* Gaisford st. Kentish town, London 9 Nov. 1868. *Grove's Dict. of music, i,* 693 (1879); *Era* 15 *Nov.* 1868 *p.* 10; *Illust. news of the world, viii* (1861), *portrait; Reg. and Mag. of Biog. i,* 51–3 (1869).

NOTE.—He was the first to endeavour to establish English opera and in his undertakings lost £20,000. He produced more English operas than any of his successors have been able or willing to do.

HARRISON, REV. WILLIAM *(son of James Harrison of London). b.* 1797; ed. at Ch. Ch. Ox., B.A. 1820, M.A. 1823; V. of St. Oswald, Chester 1827 to death; master of King's sch. Chester; minor canon of Chester cath. 1839–73; author of *Sermons* 1859. *d.* St. Oswald 11 Feb. 1880 aged 83.

HARRISON, REV. WILLIAM (1 son of William Harrison, doctor, Bermondsey, Surrey). *b.* 1811; ed. at Ch. Ch. Ox., scholar 1829–32, B.A. 1832, M.A. 1835; R. of Birch, Essex 1848 to death; hon. canon of St. Albans 1877 to death; chaplain to Duchess of Cambridge 1879 to death; author of *Sermons on the commandments* 1841; *The tongue of time or language of a church clock* 1842, 3 ed. 1844; *Consecrated thoughts* 1843 and 15 other books. *d.* Birch rectory 1 July 1882.

HARRISON, WILLIAM *(son of Isaac Harrison, hat manufacturer). b.* Salford, Lancs. 11 Dec. 1802; lived at the Cape of Good Hope; settled in the Isle of Man 1845; member of House of Keys, March 1856 to 1867; chief founder of Manx Soc. 1858, edited for it *The Bibliotheca Monensis* 1861 and 11 other volumes; contributed to *Manchester Guardian. d.* Rock Mount near Peel 22 Nov. 1884.

HARRISON, WILLIAM FREDERICK *(eld. son of Mary Harrison* 1788–1875). *b.* Amiens, France March 1815; in New 3 per cent. office, Bank of England; painter, exhibited marine subjects. *d.* Goodwick, Pembrokeshire 3 Dec. 1880.

HARRISON, WILLIAM GEORGE. *b.* 1827; proper sizar of St. John's coll. Cam., 18 wrangler and B.A. 1850; known as Devil Harrison at Cambridge and by the bar; barrister I.T. 26 Jany. 1853, bencher 23 Nov. 1877; Q.C. 14 Feb. 1877; had a good many

pupils; a commercial lawyer; author with G. A. Cape of *The Joint stock companies' act* 1856. *d.* South lodge, Edgware 5 March 1883. *bur.* Highgate cemet. 10 March.

HARRISON, WILLIAM HENRY. Edited *The Humourist* 1831; author of *The Wreath of Beauty with other poems* 1816; *Montfort, a poem* 1818; *Tales of a Physician* 1829, 2 series 1831; *Christmas Tales* 1840; *The Fossil bride and other verses* 1868. *d.* 19 Beaufort st. Chelsea 5 March 1878 aged 83.

HARRISON, WILLIAM WATERS (1 son of Rev. William Harrison of Chester). *b.* 1827; ed. at Brasenose coll. Ox., scholar 1845–8; B.A. 1848, M.A. 1851; esquire bedel of law 7 Nov. 1848; esquire bedel of law and divinity May 1857 to death, the last of the old triumvirate of esquire bedels, the office abolished by the Statute De Bedellis 22 May 1856. *d.* Sarah Acland home, Oxford 2 March 1891. *G. V. Cox's Recollections of Oxford,* 2 ed. (1870) 253, 419–24.

HARROD, HENRY. *b.* Aylsham, Norfolk 30 Sep. 1817; attorney at Norwich 1838–62, at Marlborough 1862–64; sec. Norfolk and Norwich Archæol. soc. 12 years; a professional antiquary in London 1864 to death; F.S.A. 16 March 1854; author of *Gleanings among the castles and convents of Norfolk. Norwich* 1857; *Calendar of court rolls of borough of Colchester* 1865, and other works on Colchester and King's Lynn. *d.* 2 Rectory grove, Clapham, Surrey 24 Jany. 1871. *Proc. of Soc. of Antiq., 2nd series, v,* 141–43 (1871).

HARROWBY, DUDLEY RYDER, 2 Earl of. *b.* Army pay office, Whitehall, London 23 May 1798; known as lord Sandon 1809–47; ed. at Ch. Ch. Ox., B.A. 1820, M.A. 1832, D.C.L. 1848; M.P. Tiverton 1819–31, M.P. Liverpool 1831–47; sec. to the India board, Dec. 1830 to May 1831; ecclesiastical commissioner 1847–55; succeeded as 2 earl 26 Dec. 1847; chancellor of duchy of Lancaster 31 March to 7 Dec. 1855; P.C. 31 March 1855; lord keeper of privy seal 7 Dec. 1855 to Dec. 1857; K.G. 28 June 1859. *d.* Sandon house, Stone, Staffs. 19 Nov. 1882. *Graphic xxvi,* 605 (1882), *portrait; I.L.N. lxxxi,* 560 (1882), *portrait; Portraits of eminent conservatives* (2 ser. 1846), *portrait.*

HART, ALBAN J. H. *b.* 1798; ed. at Stonyhurst 1817; master Sedgley park sch.; teacher in a university in U.S. America; resided in St. Mary's coll. Oscott to which he presented his library; author of *The mind and its creations. New York* 1853; *My own language, or elements of English grammar. Baltimore* 1860;

HART, A. J. H. (*Con.*)

The hermit of the Alps, a poem in four Cantos, and other poems; Catholic psychology, or the philosophy of the human mind 1867. *d.* Worcester 13 April 1879 aged 81. *Gillow's English catholics, iii,* 152 (1887).

HART, SIR ANDREW SEARLE (*youngest son of Rev. George Vaughan Hart of Glenalla, Donegal*). *b.* Limerick 14 March 1811; ed. at Trinity coll. Dublin, B.A. 1833, M.A. 1839, LL.B. and LL.D. 1840; fellow of his coll. 1835, senior fellow 1858, vice provost 1876; member of general synod of Irish ch.; prof. of Real and personal property, King's inns, Dublin 4 June 1879; contributed to *Camb. and Dublin Math. Journal, Proc. of Irish Acad.* and *Quart. journal of mathematics;* knighted at Dublin castle by lord Carnarvon 25 Jany. 1886; author of *An elementary treatise on mechanics* 1844, 2 ed. 1847; *An elementary treatise on hydrostatics and hydrodynamics* 1846, 2 ed. 1850. *d.* at house of his brother in law G. V. Hart, Kilderry, co. Donegal 13 April 1890.

HART, CHARLES. *b.* 19 May 1797; ed. at R. Acad. of music; organist of Essex st. chapel, Strand, London, of St. Dunstan's, Stepney 1829–33, of Trinity ch. Mile End, and of St. George's, Beckenham; composer of *Anthems* 1830; *The Jubilate and Te Deum* 1832 which gained the Gresham gold medal Dec. 1831; *Omnipotence, a sacred oratorio,* which he conducted on first performance at Hanover sq. rooms 2 April 1839; *Sacred harmony, tunes from the most celebrated composers* 1841. *d.* 148 Bond st. London 29 March 1859. *Grove's Dict. of music, i,* 692 (1879).

HART, REV. GEORGE AUGUSTUS FREDERICK. Ed. at Trin. coll. Cam., B.A. 1820, M.A. 1823; V. of Arundel, Sussex 1844 to death; chaplain in ord. to the Queen 14 Dec. 1848 to death. *d.* Arundel 7 April 1873.

HART, SIR HENRY (*son of Richard Hart of Uckfield, Sussex*). *b.* Wilmington, Sussex 1781; entered navy March 1796, captain 1 Aug. 1811; sent on a mission to the Imaum of Muscat 1804; K.C.H. 25 Jany. 1836; knighted at St. James's palace 23 Feb. 1836; comr. of Greenwich hospital 14 Oct. 1845; retired R.A. 1 Oct. 1846. *d.* Royal hospital, Greenwich 23 Dec. 1856.

HART, HENRY GEORGE (3 *son of lieut. col. William Hart, d. Cape of Good Hope* 1848). *b.* 7 Sep. 1808; ensign 49 foot 1 April 1829, major 15 Dec. 1848 to 3 Feb. 1854 when placed on h.p.; aided by his wife brought out the *Quarterly Army list,* Feb. 1839, was then

HART, H. G. (*Con.*)

allowed access to official records, and in 1840 published *The New Annual Army list,* the Quarterly and Annual lists have since regularly appeared; poor law inspector Ireland 1845-6; major depot battalion 21 April 1854 to 1 Dec. 1856 and in 1856 suppressed a mutiny of North Tipperary militia; major on half pay 1 Dec. 1856 to death; L.G. 4 Dec. 1877. *d.* Biarritz, France 24 March 1878.

HART, HENRY WYATT (*eld. son of Rev. Cornelius Hart, V. of Old St. Pancras, London*). *b.* 1850; ed. at St. John's coll. Cam., B.A. 1873; barrister I.T. 25 April 1877; author of *Bankruptcy law and practice* 1880, 3 ed. 1887; with Ernest Eiloart *Interrogatories. Rules relating to the law of discovery and inspection* 1879. *d.* Aden, on his way home from Queensland 20 June 1886.

HART, JOHN. *b.* 1809; engaged in whaling and had a whaling establishment at Encounter bay, N.S.W. Australia; had flour mills at Port Adelaide, S. Australia 1846, Hart's flour commanding the highest price in the market; M.L.C. South Australia 1857, treasurer 21 Aug. to 1 Sep. 1857, 30 Sep. 1857 to 12 June 1858 and 15 July 1864 to 22 March 1865, chief secretary 4-15 July 1863, 23 Oct. 1865 to 27 March 1866 and 24 Sep. to 12 Oct. 1868, treasurer and premier 30 May 1870 to 10 Nov. 1871; C.M.G. 15 Jany. 1870; while presiding at meeting of Mercantile marine insurance co. in Adelaide he essayed to speak and *fell dead* 28 Jany. 1873. *Heaton's Australian Dictionary* (1879) 87, 153-5.

HART, SOLOMON ALEXANDER (*son of Samuel Hart, gold and silver worker, mezzotint engraver and teacher of Hebrew*). *b.* Plymouth, April 1806; student R. Acad. London, Aug. 1823; exhibited 121 pictures at R.A., 25 at B.I. and 34 at Suffolk st. 1826–80; A.R.A. 1835, R.A. 1840, professor of painting 1854–63, librarian of the institution 1865 to death; curator of painted hall, Greenwich; elected member of Athenæum 1845; some of his pictures were *The elevation of the Law* 1830 in Vernon gallery; *Lady Jane Grey at the place of her execution* 1839 in Plymouth guildhall; *Milton visiting Galileo in prison* 1847. *d.* 36 Fitzroy sq. London 11 June 1881. *A. Brodie's Reminiscences of S. A. Hart* (1882), *portrait; I.L.N. lxxviii,* 621 (1881), *portrait; G. Pycroft's Art in Devonshire* (1883) 55-58.

HART, REV. WILLIAM HENRY (*only son of Wm. Hart of Dorking, surgeon*). *b.* Dorking 6 Jany. 1831; ed. at Merchant Taylors' sch. 1839–49; Andrew's exh. to St. John's coll. Ox. 1849; Blount sch. of Trinity coll. 1850; demy of

HART, REV. W. H. (Con.)

Magdalen coll. 1850–61; B.A. 1853, M.A. 1856; assist. C. of Hawkhurst, Kent 1855 to 1860; resident chaplain to Soc. of Gray's Inn, Oct. 1860 to death. *d.* 5 Oct. 1861. *bur.* Brighton parochial cemetery. *J. R. Bloxam's Register of Magd. coll., vii,* 384–9 (1881).

HARTING, JAMES VINCENT (1 *son of James Harting of Hampstead, solicitor*). *b.* 1812; ed. at Downside coll. near Bath, and at London Univ. 1828–30; solicitor 24 Lincoln's inn fields 1836 to death; chiefly engaged in connection with Roman Catholic business, solicitor to Cardinal Newman, defended him in the Achilli case 31 Jany. 1852; gave evidence before parliamentary commission on convents 1871; F.S.A. 2 June 1864; author of *The holy hour* 1851. *d.* 2 Upper Montague st. Russell sq. London 30 Aug. 1883. *The Tablet lxii,* 382 (1883); *Gillow's English Catholics, iii,* 157–60 (1887).

HARTLAND, FREDERICK AUGUSTUS. *b.* 25 Dec. 1783; one of the best pantomimists, associated with Grimaldi at Sadler's Wells theatre 1802; struck on the head by a plank from a scaffold in Mount st. Westminster road, London 16 Aug. 1852, died on his way to St. Thomas' hospital, *bur.* St. Mary Newington ch. yard. *Era 22 Aug.* 1852 *p.* 12.

HARTLEY, HUMPHREY ROBERT. *b.* 24 Aug. 1794; ensign 57 foot 8 Oct. 1812, lieut. col. 12 April 1831 to 4 Sep. 1835 when placed on h.p.; M.G. 20 June 1854; introduced the first savings' bank in the British army at Madras 6 Nov. 1832, and libraries for non-commissioned officers. *d.* 27 Upper Berkeley st. Portman sq. London 7 Aug. 1854.

HARTLEY, JAMES. Large shipowner at Dublin; director of some of principal steam companies in the United Kingdom; *found dead* in his cabin on board the 'Nubia' between Ceylon and Suez 11 April 1857.

HARTLEY, JAMES (*son of John Hartley of Harborne, Staffs., d.* 1830). *b.* Dumbarton 1810; partner in Chance, Hartley & Co. glass makers, Smethwick; first to use sulphate of soda in crown glass; used a thimble instead of an iron bar in blowing glass; the first in England to make German sheet-glass; removed to Sunderland and erected glasshouses 1833; invented Hartley's patent rolled plate 1847 used in Great Exhibition building 1851, made from it a fortune; mayor of Sunderland 1851–3; M.P. Sunderland 1865–8; A.I.C.E. 5 May 1868. *d.* Ashbrooke hall, Sunderland 24 May 1886. *Min. of proc. of Instit. of C.E. lxxxv,* 409–12 (1887).

HARTLEY, JESSE (*son of a bridge master in N.R. Yorkshire*). *b.* near Pontefract 1780; apprentice to a mason; surveyor of the Liverpool docks 1824 to death, constructed or altered every dock there 1824–60; completed the Grosvenor bridge over the river Dee at Chester, which had the largest single span stone arch (200 feet) in existence at the time 1832. *d.* Bootle Marsh near Liverpool 24 Aug. 1860. *Min. of proc. of Instit. of C.E. xxxiii,* 219–22 (1872).

NOTE.—His son John Bernard Hartley who was *b.* 3 Sep. 1814 and *d.* 14 Dec. 1869, was joint surveyor of Liverpool docks with his father from July 1847.

HARTLEY, LEONARD LAWRIE (*only child of Archibald Campbell, surgeon, d. Bedale, Yorkshire 1837 by Mary dau. of Leonard Hartley*). *b.* 1816; assumed the name of Hartley by r.l. on 15 July 1841 after death of his uncle George Hartley of Middleton Tyas, Yorks.; collected a library of 60,000 volumes chiefly on topography, books sold for £9636 14s. 6d. June 1885. *d.* 138 Marina, St. Leonards on Sea 27 Dec. 1883, his heir at law advertised for 7 Feb. 1884. *Times 7 Feb.* 1884 *p.* 1.

HARTMAN, SIR JULIUS. *b.* 6 May 1774; captain artillery King's German Legion 9 Nov. 1803, major 12 April 1806 to 24 Feb. 1816 when placed on h.p.; re-entered Hanoverian service 1816, L.G. 1836; hon. K.C.B. 2 Jany. 1815; cr. a baron of Kingdom of Hanover by George V. King of Hanover 1855 or 1856, only baron he created. *d.* Hanover 7 June 1856. *Allgemeine Deutsche Biographie, x,* 688–91 (1879).

HARTNOLL, JOHN HOOPER. *b.* 1799 or 1800; mathematical master Greenwich hospital sch., retired on a pension; started *The Kentish Mercury* 1832, proprietor and editor to his decease; proprietor and editor of *Post Magazine and Insurance Monitor* 1839 and *Post Magazine Almanac and Insurance Directory* 1854; author of *The annual balance sheets of all the insurance companies, with a letter on the Joint Stock Companies' registration act* 1853, 2 ed. 1853. *d.* Bexley house, Greenwich 6 June 1870. *Newspaper Press, iv,* 174 (1870); *Kentish Mercury 11 June* 1870 *p.* 4.

HARTOG, NUMA EDWARD (1 *son of Alphonse Hartog, professor of French*). *b.* London 20 May 1846; ed. at Univ. coll. sch. and Univ. coll. London; B.A. and B.Sc. London 1864; foundation scholar of Trin. coll. Cam. 1866, senior wrangler 1869 the first Jew who won that distinction; admitted B.A. without taking usual oath 29 Jany. 1869; second Smith prizeman 1869, religious tests prevented him be-

HARTOG, N. E. *(Con.)*

coming fellow of his college; gave evidence before house of lords on religious tests 3 March 1871. *d.* of small pox Belsize sq. Hampstead, London 19 June 1871. *Times* 21, 22, 23 *June* 1871; *Jewish Chronicle* 23 *June* 1871.

HARTRIDGE, WILLIAM. Chairman of Bombay and Baroda railway co.; a common councilman for Broad st. ward, London to 1880; master of the Salter's Co. *d.* Addelam, Upper Deal, Kent 25 Jany. 1885 aged 76.

HARTSHORNE, REV. CHARLES HENRY *(only son of John Hartshorne of Liverpool, ironmaster).* *b.* Broseley, Shropshire 17 March 1802; ed. at Shrewsbury and St. John's coll. Cam., pensioner 4 Jany. 1821; B.A. 1825, M.A. 1828; C. of Benthall, Salop 1825–8; C. of Little Wenlock, Salop 1828–36; C. of Cogenhoe, Northamptonshire 1838–50, and R. of Holdenby 2 Nov. 1850 to death; a founder of British Archæol. Assoc. and Institute 1844 and a contributor to the journal; F.S.A.; author of *Ancient metrical Tales* 1829; *Salopia Antiqua* 1841; *Historical Memoirs of Northampton* 1848 and 20 other books. *d.* Holdenby rectory 11 March 1865. *Journal of B.A. Assoc. xxii,* 322–5 (1866).

HARTT, CHARLES FREDERIC *(son of James William Hartt).* *b.* Fredericton, New-Brunswick 23 Aug. 1840; ed. at Acacia coll. to 1860; went to St. John's 1860; geologist in the Thayer expedition to Brazil 1865, again in Brazil 1867, 1870, 1871, 1874, 1878; founded geological museum at Rio Janiero; student of Indian languages and folk lore; professor of natural history Vassar college 1868; professor of geology Cornell univ. 1868 to death; author of *Thayer expedition. Scientific results of a journal to Brazil. Boston* 1870; *Amazonian tortoise myths. Rio* 1875. *d.* of yellow fever, Rio Janiero 19 March 1878. *Nature* 13 *June* 1878 *pp.* 174–5; *Popular Science Monthly. New York, June* 1878 *pp.* 231–5, *portrait.*

HARTY, WILLIAM. *b.* 1781; ed. at Trin. coll. Dublin, B.A. 1801, M.B. 1804, M.D. 1830; F.K.Q.C. of P. 1824–27, censor 1826; physician to Dublin prisons 40 years; physician to King's hospital or Blue coat sch. Dublin 40 years; author of *Dysentery and its combinations* 1805; *An historic sketch of the contagious fever epidemic in Ireland* 1817–19. *Dublin* 1820; *Failure of the Reformation in Ireland. By a Protestant Layman. Dublin* 1837. *d.* Ballickmoyle, Queen's county 30 March 1854.

HARVEY, ALEXANDER. *b.* 1811; L.R.C.S. Edin. 1832, M.D. Edin. 1835; professor of materia medica Aberdeen univ.; consulting physician Aberdeen royal infirmary; author of *On the foetus in utero* 1849, 2 ed. 1886; *On a remarkable effect of cross breeding* 1851; *Trees and their nature, or the bud and its attributes* 1856; *Man's place unique in nature. By a University Professor* 1865; with A. D. Davidson *Syllabus of materia medica. Aberdeen* 1873, 8 ed. 1887. *d.* 16 Hanover ter. Ladbroke sq. London 25 April 1889.

HARVEY, BISSELL. Cornet 26 light dragoons 9 Nov. 1797; captain 1 foot 20 June 1811 to 25 Oct. 1821 when placed on h.p.; fort major Edinburgh castle 1822–40; inspecting field officer of Leeds recruiting district 24 Jany. 1840, of Glasgow recruiting district Dec. 1846 to Nov. 1847; lieut. col. 9 foot 5 Nov. 1847, retired same day; K.H. 1837. *d.* Whitby 6 Feb. 1854.

HARVEY, DANIEL WHITTLE (1 *son of Matthew Barnard Harvey of Witham, Essex).* *b.* Witham 1786; attorney at Feering house, Essex, at Witham and at Colchester 1807–1819; struck his own name off the rolls 1819; contested Colchester 1812 and 1818, M.P. Colchester 1818 to 1820; M.P. Colchester 14 July 1820, election declared void; M.P. Colchester 1826–34; M.P. Southwark 1835–40; registrar of metropolitan public carriages Feb. 1839; commissioner of city of London police Jany. 1840 to death; established the *Sunday Times* 20 Oct. 1822; proprietor of the *True Sun* 1833–7; established *Weekly True Sun* 1833, ran to 1839; commenced the *Statesman or Weekly True Sun* 5 Jany. 1840, ran to 27 Dec. 1840. *d.* 26 Old Jewry, city of London 24 Feb. 1863. *bur.* at Hackney unitarian chapel. *Newspaper Press* 1 *Sep.* 1869 *pp.* 192–3, *by Cyrus Redding; I.L.N.* 7 *March* 1863 *pp.* 253, 254, *portrait; G.M. May* 1863 *pp.* 662–3; *Times* 25 *Feb.* 1863 *p.* 5.

NOTE.—He was admitted a student of the Inner Temple 7 Nov. 1810, but the Benchers refused to call him to the bar in 1819 on account of more than one verdict having gone against him in actions affecting his character; at his request in 1821 they examined into the particulars of the charges brought against him, and came to a resolution that they saw no reason to alter their determination. In 1834 he procured a committee of the House of Commons to be appointed, at the head of which was Daniel O'Connell to examine the evidence and that committee reported in his favour, but the Benchers of the Inner Temple nevertheless refused to call him to the bar.—.No call of the House of Commons has been enforced since Harvey's motion on the pension list 19 April 1836.—.He was tried at the Guildhall, London 30 Oct. 1823 for a libel on George iv. in the *Sunday Times* 9 Feb. 1823, sentenced to pay a fine of £200 and to be imprisoned in the Marshalsea 3 months. *Reports of State Trials, n.s. ii,* 1-68 (1889).

HARVEY, REV. EDMUND GEORGE (1 *son of Rev. Wm. Woodis Harvey 1798–1864*). *b.* Penzance 20 Feb. 1828; ed. Queen's coll. Cam., B.A. 1850; R. of Truro 1860–5; V. of Mullion near Helston, Cornwall 1865 to death; author of *Our cruise in the Undine through France, Prussia, etc. By the Captain* 1854; *Mullyon, its history, scenery and antiquities* 1875 and other works, beside several small publications on music. *d.* Mullion 21 June 1884. *Boase and Courtney's Bibl. Cornub.* 211–12, 1219.

HARVEY, SIR EDWARD (*youngest son of John Harvey, captain R.N., killed on board the Brunswick 1 June 1794*). *b.* 3 March 1783; first class volunteer on board 'Brunswick' 1793; captain 18 April 1811; at bombardment of St. Jean d' Acre 1840; superintendent at Malta 1848–53; commander in chief at the Nore 1857–60; admiral 9 June 1860; awarded good service pension 21 May 1862; K.C.B. 28 June 1861, G.C.B. 28 March 1865. *d.* Walmer, Kent 4 May 1865.

HARVEY, ENOCH (*eld. son of Thomas Harvey of Liverpool, solicitor*). *b.* Mount Pleasant, Liverpool 1826; solicitor at Liverpool 1849 to death; member of Incorporated Law Soc. of Liverpool 1855 to death, pres. 1881–2; *killed at Mersey road station of Cheshire lines, Liverpool 1 Oct. 1890 in 65 year.*

HARVEY, SIR GEORGE (*son of a watchmaker*). *b.* St. Ninians, Stirlingshire, Feb. 1806; ed. in Trustees' academy, Edin. 1826–8; A.R.S.A. 1826, R.S.A. 1829, president 1864; F.R.S. Edin. 1867; knighted at Windsor castle 26 March 1867; exhibited 24 pictures at R.A. and 2 at Suffolk st. 1832–73; exhibited in Edinburgh institution and Scottish academy from 1826; among his pictures were Covenanters preaching 1829; Shakespeare before Sir Thomas Lucy 1837; and First reading of the Bible in the crypt of St. Paul's 1840; author of *Notes of the early history of the Royal Scottish Academy* 1870. *d.* 21 Regent ter. Edinburgh 22 Jany. 1876. *A. L. Simpson's Harvey's Celebrated paintings* (1870); *I.L.N. lxviii*, 157 (1876), *portrait; Graphic, xiii*, 161 (1876), *portrait.*

HARVEY, SIR GEORGE FREDERICK (*son of lieut.-gen. Sir John Harvey, K.C.B.*) *b.* 1809; entered Indian C.S. 1827; commissioner and political agent at Agra and Delhi during mutiny 1857–8; retired on annuity 1863; K.C.S.I. 24 May 1867. *d.* 122 Sloane st. London 4 Nov. 1884.

HARVEY, HENRY (*son of Sir Thomas Harvey, K.C.B., vice admiral, d.* 1841). *b.* 28 April

HARVEY, H. (*Con.*)
1812; entered R.N. 15 Dec. 1822 as first class volunteer; signal midshipman to Sir E. Codrington at battle of Navarino 20 Oct. 1827; captain 10 Dec. 1852, retired 24 April 1866; admiral 15 June 1879. *d.* Walmer 27 May 1887. *Times* 1 June 1887 p. 10.

HARVEY, SIR JOHN. *b.* 1778; ensign 80 foot 18 Sep. 1794; A.D.C. and military sec. to major general Dowdeswell in India 1803–6; D.A.G. in Upper Canada 1812–14; governor of New Brunswick 1837, of Newfoundland 20 July 1841, of Nova Scotia 26 June 1846 to death; col. of 59 foot 3 Dec. 1844 to death; L.G. 9 Nov. 1846; knighted at King's lodge, Windsor 15 Dec. 1824; K.C.H. 19 March 1837; K.C.B. 19 July 1838. *d.* Halifax, Nova Scotia 22 March 1852.

HARVEY, J. B. *b.* 1792; lessee of theatres at Guernsey, Jersey, Exeter, Devonport, Salisbury, Chelmsford and Weymouth. *d.* 96 St. Mary st. Weymouth 7 Sep. 1862 aged 70.

HARVEY, MARGARET (*dau. of John Harvey of Sunderland, surgeon*). *b.* 1768; resided at Newcastle; assisted in a ladies' school at Bishop Wearmouth, Durham 1818; author of *Monody on the princess Charlotte 1812; The lays of the minstrel's daughter. Newcastle* 1814; *Raymond de Percy: a romantic melodrame. Bishop Wearmouth* 1822, this was performed at Sunderland, April 1822. *d.* Bishop Wearmouth 18 June 1858.

HARVEY, REV. RICHARD. *b.* 1798; ed. at Eton and St. Cath. coll. Cam., B.A. 1818, M.A. 1821; R. of Hornsey 22 May 1829 to 1880, where he built three district churches; chaplain to Archbp. of York 1862–74; prebendary of Brownswood in St. Paul's cath. 1843–58; canon residentiary Gloucester cath. 1858 to death; chaplain in ordinary to the queen 18 June 1847 to death; author of *Hymns for young persons* [by *R. H.*] 1834, 2 ed. 1837; *Two sermons on keeping the Lord's Day* 1850. *d.* College green, Gloucester 27 June 1889. *bur.* same time as his wife at Gloucester cath. 2 July.

HARVEY, SIR ROBERT BATESON, 1 Baronet (*son of Robert Harvey of Langley park, Slough*). *b.* Langley park 17 Nov. 1825; ed. at Eton, matric. from Ch. Ch. Ox. 31 May 1844; a keen deerstalker; kept steeplechasers; M.P. Bucks. 1863–68 and 1874–85; cr. baronet 28 Nov. 1868; master of Norfolk harriers 1869. *d.* Langley park, Slough 23 March 1887. *Baily's Mag. xxvi*, 311–12 (1875), *portrait.*

HARVEY, SIR ROBERT JOHN (*eld. son of John Harvey of Thorpe near Norwich 1755–1842*).

HARVEY, SIR R. J. *(Con.)*

b. Thorpe 21 Feb. 1785; studied at Marburg, Leipsic, Hesse Cassel and Valenciennes; ensign 53 foot 8 Oct. 1803; studied at military college, High Wycombe 1807–9; served in Peninsular war, rode from Paris to Lisbon with despatches 1400 miles in 14 days; lieut.-col. on half pay 25 Oct. 1815; knighted by Prince Regent at Carlton house 6 Feb. 1817; C.B. 26 Sep. 1831; colonel of 2 West India regt. 15 June 1848 to death; general 17 July 1859; F.R.S., F.S.A. *d.* Mousehold heath near Norwich 18 June 1860. *Journal of British Archæol. Assoc. xvii,* 186–8 (1861).

HARVEY, SIR ROBERT JOHN HARVEY, 1 Baronet *(eld. son of the preceding). b.* 16 April 1817; sheriff of Norfolk 1863; M.P. for Thetford 12 July 1865 to 11 Nov. 1868 when it was disfranchised by Reform act of 1867; created baronet 8 Dec. 1868; shot himself with a pistol at Crown point hall, Norwich 19 July 1870.

HARVEY, THOMAS. *b.* Barnsley, Yorkshire 1812; ed. at Ackworth sch. 1822–5; chemist Leeds about 1837–67; in the West Indies enquiring into condition of negroes 1836–7; in Finland aiding the unarmed inhabitants 1856; visited Jamaica about the Gordon riots 1866; visited the Mennonites in Russia and aided them to emigrate to Canada 1867; went to Canada to see the Friends 1884; author with J. Sturge of *The West Indies* in 1837, 1838; with W. Brewin of *Jamaica in 1866, a narrative of a tour* 1867 and 12 pamphlets. *d.* Headingley near Leeds 25 Dec. 1884. *bur.* Adel near Leeds 29 Dec. *Times 30 Dec.* 1884 *p.* 4; *J. N. Nodal's Bibliography of Ackworth sch.* (1889) 12–13.

HARVEY, THOMAS HINGSTON (3 son of Rev. *William Woodis Harvey* 1798–1864). *b.* Penzance 26 Feb. 1831; solicitor at Truro 1855–63; practised at Constantinople 1863 to death; solicitor to the Pacha of Egypt; accompanied admiral Hobart to Syra in Crete to advise him on international law 1872; author of *The tourist's guide through Cornwall. Truro* 1861; *Harkylogy. Mr. T. Smitheram's account of Archæological Association* 1862. *d.* Pera, Constantinople 23 April 1872. *Boase and Courtney's Bibl. Cornub.* 213, 1220.

HARVEY, REV. WILLIAM (4 son of admiral Sir *Thomas Harvey, K.C.B.* 1775–1841). Matric. from Brasenose coll. Ox. 10 March 1842 aged 18; B.A. 1845, M.A. 1848; compiled *The active list of flag officers and captains of the Royal navy, with progress of officers from entrance into the service* 1861, 5 ed. 1865, *ed. by W. Arthur* 1868. *d.* Walmer, Kent 18 March 1865.

HARVEY, WILLIAM *(son of the keeper of the baths at Westgate). b.* Newcastle-upon-Tyne 13 July 1796; apprentice to Thomas Bewick 1810; studied drawing under B. R. Haydon and anatomy under Sir C. Bell 1817; wood engraver 1822–24, designer for copper plate and wood engravers 1824 to death; engraved on wood in imitation of copper plate, Haydon's Assassination of Dentatus, the most ambitious block which had been cut in England 1821; his masterpieces are his illustrations to *Northcote's Fables* 1828–33 and to *Lane's Thousand and one nights* 1838–40; he also illustrated 30 other works 1829–68. *d.* Prospect lodge, Richmond, Surrey 13 Jany. 1866. *Chatto's Treatise on wood engraving* (1861) 527–34; *I.L.N. xlviii,* 97 (1866), *portrait.*

HARVEY, WILLIAM. *b.* 1813 or 1814; a founder of Sussex Archæological Soc. 1846; had a cabinet of coins, chiefly of those found in Sussex; F.S.A. 3 March 1853. *d.* Lewes 22 April 1869. *Numismatic Chronicle, vol. x* (1870), *Proceedings p.* 13.

HARVEY, WILLIAM. Surgeon in London; hon. superintendent Islington reformatory; wrote many articles under pseudonym of Aleph in *The City Press;* author of *The old city and its highways and byways, By Aleph* 1865. *d.* 48 Lonsdale sq. Islington, London 18 March 1873 aged 77.

HARVEY, WILLIAM. *b.* 1807 or 1808; ed. at Guy's hospital; L.S.A. 1830; M.R.C.S. 1830, F.R.C.S. 1853; surgeon to Royal dispensary for diseases of the ear 1846 to death; F. Med. Chir. Soc. 1841; one of 3 chief aurists in London for many years; prescribed a diet for William Banting which reduced his weight from 202 lbs. to 156 lbs. 1862–3, and originated Banting; aural surgeon Great Northern hospital 186– to death; author of *The ear in health and disease, with remarks on treatment of deafness* 1854, 4 ed. 1865; *On rheumatism, gout and neuralgic headache* 1857, 4 ed. 1865; *On corpulence in relation to disease* 1872; *On deafness and noises in the ear,* 7 ed. 1876. *d.* 3 George st. Hanover sq. London 5 Dec. 1876. *Medical Times 23 Dec.* 1876 *p.* 717; *Proc. Med. Chir. Soc. viii,* 198–9 (1880).

HARVEY, WILLIAM HENRY *(son of Joseph Massey Harvey of Limerick, merchant, a quaker). b.* Summerville near Limerick 5 Feb. 1811; ed. at Ballitore school, Kildare 1824–7; M.D. Dublin univ. 1844; treasurer and registrar general at Cape of Good Hope 1836–42; became the chief authority on algæ; keeper of the Herbarium to univ. of Dublin 30 March 1844; professor of botany to Royal Dublin society; *bapt.* St. Mark's ch. Dublin 25 Feb. 1846; professor of botany in univ. of Dublin 1856; lecturer at Irish museum of industry about 1856; F.R.S. 3 June 1864; author of *Genera of South African plants, Capetown* 1838, 2 *ed.* 1868; *A manual of British Algæ* 1841; *Phycologia Britannica, a history of British sea-weeds* 4 vols. 1846–51; *The seaside book* 1849, 4 *ed.* 1857; *Phycologia Australica* 5 vols. 1858–63 and other books. *d.* Torquay 15 May 1866. *Memoir of W. H. Harvey* (1869), *portrait.*

HARVEY, Rev. WILLIAM WIGAN (2 *son of George Daniel Harvey, commissioner of bankruptcy*). *b.* Great Stanmore, Middlesex 1810; ed. at Eton and King's coll. Cam.; B.A. 1832, M.A. 1836, B.D. 1855; fellow of King's 1831, divinity lecturer 1836–44 and 1862–3, Tyrwhitt Hebrew scholar 1833; R. of Buckland, Herts. 1844–72; R. of Ewelme near Oxford, Dec. 1871 to death; author of *Ecclesiæ Anglicanæ Vindex Catholicus* 1841; *The history and theology of the three creeds* 1854; *Sancti Irenæi quæ supersunt Opera* 1857 and many sermons, pamphlets and reviews. *d.* Ewelme 7 May 1883. *Hansard's Debates, ccix,* 291–2, 772, 1153, 1673, 1720, 1946 (1872); *Annual Register* (1872) 34–6.

HARVEY, Rev. WILLIAM WOODIS. *b.* Alverton Vean, Penzance 15 June 1798; Wesleyan missionary in Hayti to 1824; servitor at Queen's coll. Cam., B.A. 1828, M.A. 1835; V. of Truro 1839–60; prebendary of Exeter 1859–64; author of *Sketches of Hayti* 1827 and of many single sermons. *d.* Torquay 6 Oct. 1864. *Boase and Courtney's Bibl. Cornub.* 213–15, 1220; *Boase's Collect. Cornub.* (1890) 332.

HARWOOD, CHARLES *(son of Rev. Thomas Harwood of Shepperton, Middlesex).* Barrister I.T. 20 June 1828; recorder of Shrewsbury, Dec. 1839 to death; judge of county courts, circuit 50 (Kent), March 1847 to death. *d.* The Leas, Folkestone 25 Sep. 1866.

HARWOOD, ISABELLA NEIL *(dau. of the succeeding).* *b.* 1838 or 1839; author of *Abbot's Cleve, a novel* 1864; *Carleton Grange* 1866; *Raymond's Heroine* 1867; *Kathleen* 1869; *The Heir expectant* 1870; author under pseudonym of Ross Neil of the plays *Lady Jane Grey. Inez or the bride of Portugal* 1871 (produced at Gaiety theatre, London under title of *Loyal Love* 13 Aug. 1887); *The Cid, The King and the Angel, Duke for a day* 1874; *Elfinella* (produced at Princess's theatre 1876). *Lord and Lady Russell* 1876, *Arabella Stuart. The heir of Lynne. Tasso* 1879; *Andrea the painter. Claudia's*

choice. Orestes. Pandora 1883. *d.* South Bank, Baldslow road, Hastings 29 May 1888. *Saturday Review* 2 *June* 1888 *p.* 644.

HARWOOD, PHILIP. *b.* Bristol 1809; articled to a solicitor; studied at Univ. of Edin.; pastor of Unitarian chapel, Bridport 1835; assistant minister at South place chapel, London 1841; sub-editor of *The Examiner,* of *The Spectator,* of the *Morning Chronicle* about 1849–54, of the *Saturday Review* from date of first number 3 Nov. 1855 and editor Aug. 1868 to Dec. 1883; author of *Materialism in religion: or religious forms and theological formulas* 1840; *History of the Irish rebellion of* 1798, 1844, 2 *ed.* 1848 and many lectures and sermons. *d.* South Bank, Baldslow road, Hastings 10 Dec. 1887. *Saturday Review* 17 *Dec.* 1887 *p.* 188.

HASELDEN, ADOLPHUS FREDERICK. *b.* 1817; Assoc. Pharmaceutical Soc. of Gt. Britain, member of council 1859, V.P. 1869, P. 1871–3, contributed many papers to the Journal; author of *A translation of the Pharmacopoeia Collegii regalis medicorum Londinensis* 1837; *Notes on the British Pharmacopoeia, showing additions* 1864. *d.* Shaftesbury cottage, Croydon 4 Feb. 1880. *The Pharmaceutical Journal* 7 *Feb.* 1880 *pp.* 624, 631.

HASELL, ELIZABETH JULIA (2 *dau. of Edward Williams Hasell of Dalemain near Penrith, Cumberland* 1796–1872). *b.* 17 Janry. 1830; taught herself Latin, Greek, Spanish and Portuguese; contributed to *Blackwood's Mag.* and *Quarterly Review* from about 1858; author of *The Rock, and other short lectures on passages of Holy Scripture* 1867; *Calderon* and *Tasso* in *Foreign Classics for English readers* 2 vols. 1879 and 1882; *Short family prayers* 1879, 2 *ed.* 1884; *Bible Partings* 1883; *Via Crucis or meditations for Passion and Easter Tide* 1884. *d.* Dalemain 14 Nov. 1887.

HASLAM, SAMUEL HOLKER. F.L.S. 1836; made a collection of plants and insects, which he gave to Natural Hist. Soc. of Kendal 1854. *d.* Woodhouse, Milnthorpe, Westmoreland 13 April 1856. *Proc. Linnean Soc.* 1856 *p.* xlii.

HASLEM, JOHN. *b.* Carrington near Manchester 1808; flower painter and figure painter; painted for Duke of Sussex a head of Lord Byron for presentation to King of Greece; exhibited 37 enamels at R.A. and 14 at Suffolk st. 1836–65; painted a set of enamels in imitation of Petitot, which were shown at South Kensington 1862 and 1865 as the work of Petitot; author of *The old Derby china factory* 1876. *d.* Derby 30 April 1884 aged 76.

HASSALL, RICHARD. M.R.C.S. 1844; M.D. St. Andrew's 1852; M.R.C.P. Lond. 1875; examining physician R. hospital for consumption Ventnor; in practice at 4 Suffolk place, Pall Mall, London; author of *Cholera, its nature and treatment* 1854; *Poisoning by chloride of zinc. d.* 60 St. George's sq. London 13 Dec. 1875. *I.L.N. lxviii*, 167 (1876).

HASSALL, WALTER WILLIS. Clerk to Mr. Foster, solicitor, Wells; reporter for *Dorset county chronicle*, Dorchester; resident reporter *Southern Times*, Weymouth; editor and proprietor with Mr. Atkins of *Weymouth Guardian* to death; while walking along railway at Weymouth knocked down by train and *killed* 23 Dec. 1868. *Newspaper Press, iii*, 59 (1869).

HASSARD, MICHAEL DOBBYN (*younger son of Richard Hassard, captain of Waterford militia*). *b.* Waterford, Oct. 1817; ed. at Waterford school and Trin. coll. Dublin, gold medallist 1838, B.A. 1852; M.P. for city of Waterford 1857–65; acted each session as chairman of committees; paid referee of House of Commons 1866 to death; sheriff of Waterford 1853. *d.* Glenville, co. Waterford 7 April 1869. *Reg. and mag. of biog., i*, 393 (1869).

HASTED, REV. HENRY (*son of an apothecary*). *b.* Bury St. Edmunds 17 Sep. 1771; ed. at Bury gr. sch. and Ch. coll. Cam., 6 wr. and B.A. 1793; fell. of his coll.; preacher of St. Mary's, Bury 1802–42; R. of Braiseworth, Suffolk 1812 to death; R. of Horninger, Suffolk 1814 to death; F.L.S. 1810; F.R.S. 1812; author of *A course of lectures for Lent. Bury* 1838; *Sermons for Lent and Easter* 1852. *d.* Bury St. Edmunds 26 Nov. 1852.

HASTIE, ALEXANDER (*son of Robert Hastie of Glasgow, merchant*). *b.* 1805; a merchant at Glasgow; lord provost 1846–48; M.P. for Glasgow 1847–57. *d.* 1864.

HASTIE, ARCHIBALD (*son of W. Hastie*). *b.* 1791; coach builder and East India agent in London; a director of the East India docks and chief manager of them; M.P. for Paisley 17 March 1836 to death; the owner of Burns' punch bowl, kept the anniversaries of the poet's birthday as high festivals. *d.* Edinburgh 9 Nov. 1857. *Times* 11 *Nov.* 1857 *p.* 12.

HASTINGS, HENRY WEYSFORD CHARLES PLANTAGENET MURE RAWDON HASTINGS, 4 Marquis of. *b.* Cavendish sq. London 22 July 1842; succeeded his bro. as 4 marquis 17 Jany. 1851; ed. at Eton; succeeded his mother in barony of Grey de Ruthyn 18 Nov. 1858; matric. from Ch. Ch. Ox. 1860; commenced

HASTINGS, Marquis of. (*Con.*)

horse racing 1862; purchased horses at unheard of prices and backed them for large amounts; trained his horses with John Day at Danebury; lost a fabulous sum on Kangaroo which he purchased in 1865 for £12,000 highest price ever paid for a race-horse; lost heavily on Lady Elizabeth in the Derby 1868; struck out the Earl from racing for the St. Leger 1868; lived most extravagantly and gambled; master of the Quorn hounds 1866; won the Cambridgeshire with Ackworth 1864, the 1000 guineas with Repulse 1866; lost £103,000 when Hermit won the Derby 1867. *d.* Grosvenor sq. London 10 Nov. 1868. *Reg. and mag. of biog., i*, 44–6 (1869); *Rice's Hist. of British Turf, i*, 354–91 (1879); *Baily's Mag. xi* 279–81 (1866), *portrait*; *Sporting Review, lx* 396–400 (1868), *lxi* 31–38 (1869).

HASTINGS, JACOB ASTLEY, 22 Baron (*eld. son of Sir Jacob Henry Astley, 5 baronet 1756–1817*). *b.* 13 Nov. 1797; M.P. for West Norfolk, Dec. 1832 to July 1837; contested West Norfolk 29 July 1837; summoned to parliament as Baron Hastings (the abeyance having been terminated in his favour) by writ dated 18 May 1841. *d.* of paralysis at 45 York terrace, Regent's park, London 27 Dec. 1859.

HASTINGS, JACOB HENRY DELAVAL ASTLEY, 23 Baron (*elder son of the preceding*). *b.* 21 May 1822; ed. at Eton and Ch. Ch. Ox.; cornet 2 life guards 17 March 1843, lieut. 28 Jany. 1848 to 23 May 1851 when he sold out; hon. col. Norfolk artillery militia 23 Jany. 1860 to death; master of the Eastern Norfolk hounds 1862 to death. *d.* Melton Constable, Norfolk 8 March 1871. *Baily's Mag. xix*, 287 (1871), *portrait*.

HASTINGS, SIR CHARLES (6 *son of Rev. James Hastings, who d.* 1856). *b.* Ludlow, Salop 11 Jany. 1794; ed. at Univ. of Edin. 1815, M.D. 1818; practised at Worcester 1818 to death; physician to Worcester infirmary to 16 Jany. 1862 when presented with piece of plate value 600 guineas; founded the Provincial (afterwards the British) medical and surgical association 19 July 1832, president 1856; knighted at St. James's palace 3 July 1850; published *A treatise on inflammation of the lungs* 1820; *Illustrations of the natural history of Worcestershire* 1834; founded *Midland medical and surgical reporter* 1828; member of general medical council 13 Nov. 1858 to 13 Nov. 1863. *d.* Barnard's Green near Malvern, Worcs. 30 July 1866. *Barker's Photographs of medical men* (1865) 17–22, *portrait*; *Lancet, ii*, 185–8 (1851), *portrait, ii*, 139 (1866).

HASTINGS, SIR CHARLES ABNEY-, 2 Baronet. *b.* 1 Oct. 1792; succeeded 30 Sep. 1823; assumed additional name of Abney; sheriff of Derbyshire 1825; M.P. for Leicester 1826–31. *d.* 6 Cavendish sq. London 30 July 1858.

HASTINGS, FRANCIS DECIMUS (*brother of Sir Charles Hastings 1794–1866*). *b.* 1795; entered navy 19 Aug. 1807, served in Syrian and Peninsula wars; B.A. of Trin. coll. Cam. 1828; captain 4 Nov. 1840; V.A. on half pay 2 Dec. 1865. *d.* Barbourne house, Worcester 21 May 1869. *Reg. and mag. of biog. ii, 42 (1869).*

HASTINGS, GEORGE FOWLER (*2 son of 11 Earl of Huntingdon 1779–1828*). *b.* 28 Nov. 1814; entered navy 3 Sep. 1824; in Chinese war 1841; captain 31 Jany. 1845; commanded the Curaçoa during Russian war; superintendent of Haslar hospital and Clarence victualling yard 1858–63; R.A. 27 April 1863, V.A. 10 Sep. 1869; C.B. 2 Jany. 1857; commander in chief in the Pacific 21 Nov. 1866 to 1 Nov. 1869; commander in chief at the Nore 11 Feb. 1873 to 11 Feb. 1876. *d.* 41 Stanhope gardens, London 21 March 1876.

HASTINGS, REV. HENRY JAMES (*brother of Sir Charles Hastings 1794–1866*). Ed. at Trin. coll. Cam., B.A. 1819, M.A. 1822; C. of Martley, Worcs. 1820–31 and 1851–56; R. of Areley Kings near Stourport 1831–56; R. of Martley 1856 to death; author of *Parochial sermons from Advent to Trinity Sunday* 1845; *The Indian mutinies a fresh motive for church missions* 1857; *A plea for the prayer book as it is, with remarks on its history* 1858 and other books. *d.* Martley rectory 12 May 1875.

HASTINGS, HUGH J. *b.* co. Fermanagh, Ireland 20 Aug. 1820; settled at Albany, New York 1831; reporter for the *Atlas* at Albany 1840; established the *Weekly Switch* at Albany 1843 and the *Knickerbocker* 1844; collector of port of Albany 1849–50; editor of *Commercial Advertiser* at New York 1868, proprietor 1875. *d.* from effect of a carriage accident, Monmouth Beach, New Jersey 12 Sep. 1883.

HASTINGS, JAMES. A tailor at Cheltenham; followed Lord Fitzhardinge's fox hounds 25 years on foot; on one occasion walked 72 miles in connexion with a hunt. *d.* 1851. *bur.* Charlton ch. yard. *Cecil's Records of the chase (1877) 190–2.*

HASTINGS, REV. JAMES (*son of James Hastings of Westminster*). Matric. from Wadham coll. Ox. 28 March 1776 aged 20; R. of Martley, Worcs. 1796 to death. *d.* the Tything, Worcester 10 July 1856 aged 100.

HASTINGS, JOANNA (*eld. child of the preceding*). *b.* Sutton Coldfield, Warwickshire 14 March 1782. *d.* Imperial villa, Great Malvern 12 March 1886 within 2 days of being 104.

HASTINGS, JOHN. *b.* 1805; M.D. Edin. 1840; L.R.C.P. Lond. 1847; author of *Pulmonary consumption treated with naphtha* 1843, 2 ed. 1845; *Treatise on the diseases of the larynx and the trachea* 1850; *An inquiry into the value of the excreta of reptiles in phthisis* 1862. *d.* 14 Albemarle st. Piccadilly, London 20 Dec. 1874.

HASTINGS, REV. JOHN DAVID. *b.* 1800; ed. at Trin. coll. Dublin, B.A. 1823, M.A. 1826; R. of Trowbridge, Wilts. 1841 to death; preb. of Salisbury cath. March 1860 to death; author of *The absolution of the church of Rome, not the absolution of the church of England* 1851; edited *Posthumous sermons. By Rev. George Crabbe* 1850. *d.* 13 April 1869. *Reg. and mag. of biog. i, 476 (1869).*

HASTINGS, SIR THOMAS (*brother of Joanna Hastings 1782–1886*). *b.* Whichford rectory, Warws. 3 July 1790; entered navy Sep. 1803; first lieut. of the Undaunted which took Napoleon to Elba, April 1814; captain 22 July 1830; in command of gunnery establishment on board H.M.S. Excellent 1832–45; superintendent of royal naval college at Portsmouth 1839–45; knighted at St. James's palace 5 June 1839 for his improvements in naval gunnery; principal storekeeper of the ordnance 25 July 1845 to May 1855 when office abolished; C.B. 22 Nov. 1850, K.C.B. 9 March 1859; retired admiral 2 April 1866. *d.* 7 Seymour st. Portman square, London 3 Jany. 1870. *O'Byrne (1849) 475–6.*

HATCH, REV. EDWIN (1 *son of Samuel Hatch*). *b.* Derby 4 Sep. 1835; ed. at King Edward's sch. Birmingham and at Pemb. coll. Ox., B.A. 1857, M.A. 1867; professor of classics Trinity coll. Toronto 1859–62; rector of high sch. Quebec 1862–7; vice prin. of St. Mary's hall, Ox. 1867–85, master of the schools 1868–9, 1873 and 1875; Bampton lecturer 1880, Grinfield lecturer on Septuagint 1882–84; D.D. of Edin. univ. 1883; R. of Purleigh, Essex 1883 to death; reader in ecclesiastical history, Ox. 1886 to death; author of *The organisation of the early christian churches* 1880; *The growth of church institutions* 1887; *Essays in Biblical Greek* 1889; *The influence of Greek ideas upon the Christian church* 1890; edited the *Official Gazette, Oxford* from 1870. *d.* 6 Canterbury road, Oxford 10 Nov. 1889. *Memorials of E. Hatch (1890), portrait; I.L.N. 23 Nov. 1889 pp. 647, 648, portrait.*

HATCH, George Cliffe. *b.* 11 Jany. 1820; ensign 57 Bengal N.I. 22 Aug. 1839, captain 19 April 1851; lieut. col. Bengal staff corps. 12 Dec. 1864; general 17 Aug. 1890. *d.* Cheltenham 11 Feb. 1891.

HATCH, Henry. Sole proprietor and lessee of Victoria theatre, Oxford 1868–72, of theatre royal, Oxford 1872 to death. *d.* 2 Cambridge villas, St. Mark's road, Notting hill, London 9 Oct. 1885 aged 69.

HATCH, Rev. Walter Mooney (4 *son of Samuel Hatch of Derby*). Matric. from New coll. Ox. 18 Oct. 1862 aged 19, fellow 1867–77; B.A. 1866, M.A. 1869; head warden St. Paul's coll. Stony Stratford 1870–5; warden of Knutsford coll. 1875, junior dean 1876; R. of Birchanger, Essex 1877 to death; editor of *Characteristics of A. A. Cooper 3 Earl of Shaftesbury* 1870; author of *Early Counsels, sermons* 1875; *The moral philosophy of Aristotle* 1879. *d.* Birchanger 2 Dec. 1877 aged 34.

HATCHARD, Right Rev. Thomas Goodwin (*son of Thomas Hatchard, publisher, d. 13 Nov. 1858*). *b.* 11 Sloane st. Chelsea 18 Sep. 1817; ed. at King's coll. Lon. and Brasenose coll. Ox.; B.A. 1841, M.A. 1845, D.D. 1869; C. of Windlesham, Surrey 1842–44; R. of Havant, Hants. 1846–56; R. of St. Nicholas, Guildford 1856–69; bishop of Mauritius 1869 to death, consecrated in Westminster abbey 24 Feb. 1869; author of *The German tree. A moral for the young* 1851; *The floweret gathered, a memoir of his daughter* 1858. *d.* of fever at Mauritius 28 Feb. 1870. *I.L.N. lvi*, 411 (1870); *Times* 31 *March* 1870 *p.* 9.

HATCHELL, John (2 *son of Henry Hatchell of Wexford*). *b.* Wexford 1783; ed. at Trin. coll. Dublin, B.A. 1804; called to Irish bar 1809; K.C. 7 Feb. 1835; bencher of King's Inns, Dublin 1846; solicitor general for Ireland 24 Dec. 1847, attorney general 23 Sep. 1850 to Feb. 1852; P.C. Ireland 1850; M.P. for Windsor 1850–52; comr. of insolvent debtors' court, Dublin, June 1854. *d.* Fortfield house near Dublin 14 Aug. 1870. *I.L.N. xvi*, 148 (1850), *portrait, lvii*, 226 (1870).

HATFIELD, Weston James (*son of Weston Hatfield, proprietor of Independent Press, Cambridge*). *b.* 1830; newspaper correspondent in Paris 1848; a founder of Permanent Building soc. Cambridge 1853; connected with the press in the Colonies from 1853; editor and proprietor of the *Cambridge Independent Press* and printer at Cambridge 1863 to death. *d.* 2 Poplar villas, Station road, Cambridge 14 Nov. 1871. *Newspaper Press* 1 *Dec.* 1871 *p.* 19.

HATHERLEY, William Page Wood, 1 Baron (2 *son of Sir Matthew Wood of Falcon sq., city of London, hop merchant 1768–1843*). *b.* Falcon sq. 29 Nov. 1801; ed. at Woodbridge, Bow and at Winchester 1812–1818; went to Trin. coll. Cam., Oct. 1820, scholar 1822, fellow 1824–30; 24 wrangler 1824; B.A. 1824, M.A. 1827, LL.D. 1864; barrister L.I. 27 Nov. 1827; engaged in parliamentary practice 1828–41; lived in Dean's yard, Westminster 1830–44; Q.C. Feb. 1845; M.P. for city of Oxford 1847–53; vice chancellor of county palatine of Lancaster 7 May 1849 to March 1851; solicitor general 28 March 1851 to Feb. 1852 and 28 Dec. 1852 to 10 Jany. 1853; knighted at Buckingham palace 14 April 1851; vice chancellor 10 Jany. 1853, lord justice of appeal 6 March 1868; P.C. 28 March 1868; lord chancellor 9 Dec. 1868 to 15 Oct. 1872 when he resigned; created Baron Hatherley of Down Hatherley, Gloucs. 8 Dec. 1868; F.R.S. 22 Dec. 1834, member of council, vice pres.; translated *Lord Bacon's Novum Organon* 1826. *d.* 31 Great George st. Westminster 10 July 1881. *bur.* in churchyard of Great Bealings, Suffolk 15 July. *A memoir of Baron Hatherley* 2 vols. 1883, 2 *portraits*; *The Crown of the road by Rev. C. Bullock* (1884) 191–224, *portrait*; *A generation of Judges* (1886) 139–46.

HATHERTON, Edward John Littleton, 1 Baron (*only son of Moreton Walhouse of Hatherton, Staffs.*) *b.* London 18 March 1791; ed. at Rugby and Brasenose coll. Ox., created D.C.L. 18 June 1817; assumed surname of Littleton on death of his grand uncle Sir Edward Littleton 4 Bart. 18 May 1812; chairman of Staffordshire and Worcestershire Canal co. 1812 to death; M.P. for Staffordshire 1812–32; M.P. for South Staffordshire 1832–5; president of Boundary commission 1831; liberal candidate for speakership of house of commons but defeated by 210 votes 29 Jany. 1833; chief sec. for Ireland 17 May 1833 to 17 Dec. 1834; his negotiations with O'Connell led to the break up of the Grey ministry Nov. 1834; cr. Baron Hatherton of Hatherton, Staffordshire 11 May 1835; lord lieut. of Staffs. 8 June 1854, resigned Sep. 1862; F.R.S.; author of *Memoir and correspondence relating to political occurences in June and July* 1834 (1872). *d.* Teddesley park, Penkridge, Staffs. 4 May 1863. *G.M. xv*, 101 (1863); *I.L.N. x*, 53 (1847), *portrait*; *Colburn's New Monthly Mag. June* 1863 *pp.* 176–82.

HATHERTON, Edward Richard Littleton, 2 Baron. *b.* Teddesley park 31 Dec. 1815; ed. at Eton; M.P. Walsall 1847–52; M.P.

HATHERTON, 2 Baron. (*Con.*)

South Staffordshire 1853–7; col. 2nd Stafford militia 5 Jany. 1852 to death; vice lieut. of Staffs. 1855; succeeded as 2 baron 1863; C.B. 24 May 1881. *d.* 22 Rutland gate, London 3 April 1888.

HATHORN, GEORGE. *b.* 17 Nov. 1803; entered navy 9 Aug. 1817; captain 4 Nov. 1840; admiral on half pay 14 July 1871. *d.* 14 Pencester road, Dover 29 Jany. 1876.

HATTERSLEY, ROBERT. A working engineer at Manchester; took out patents for type setting machines 1857, 62, 67, 72 and 75, machines shown at Great Exhibition 1862; his machines very much used especially in Liverpool; by his machine one man can produce in an hour 100 to 160 lines of minion news-work and justify the same. *d.* Manchester 13 Feb. 1889 aged 59.

HATTON, FRANK (*2 son of Joseph Hatton, journalist and author*). *b.* Horfield near Bristol 31 Aug. 1861; ed. at Marcq coll. near Lille 1874–6 and at King's coll. sch. 1876; mineral explorer and metallurgical chemist to British North Borneo co. 1881, employed in Borneo 1881 to death; contributed articles to various periodicals; when returning from pursuing an elephant was *killed* by accidental explosion of his own rifle on Segamah river 1 March 1883. *North Borneo, exploration and adventures on the Equator by F. Hatton, with Biographical sketch by J. Hatton* (1886), *portrait*; *Graphic, xxvii,* 469 (1883), *portrait*.

HATTON, JOHN LIPTROT. *b.* Concert st. Liverpool 12 Oct. 1809; played Blueskin in Jack Sheppard at Little Liver theatre, Liverpool; organist St. Nicholas, Chapel st. Liverpool; settled in London 1832; chorus master Drury Lane, London 1842–3, his operetta Queen of the Thames produced 25 Feb. 1843; his opera Pascal Bruno produced at Vienna 1843; sang at Hereford festival 1846; visited America 1848, 1850, playing and singing; conductor of Glee and Madrigal union, London 1850; conductor and composer at Princess' theatre for Charles Kean 1853–9 where he wrote music for 9 plays; accompanyist and conductor Ballad concerts, St. James' hall 1866–75; composer of the opera Rose or Love's Ransom, Covent Garden 1864; Robin Hood cantata 1856; Hezekiah sacred drama, Crystal palace 1877; The village blacksmith, and other part songs; Come back Annie 1862, Friar of orders grey, Good bye sweetheart 1855, Leather Bottél, Simon the cellarer 1847, Under the Greenwood tree 1856, songs; besides anthems,

HATTON, J. L. (*Con.*)

dance music, &c.; his name is attached to upward of 150 pieces of music; some of his pieces published with pseudonym of P. B. Czapek 1845 etc. *d.* Margate 20 Sep. 1886. *Illust. S. and D. News, xxvi,* 61 (1886), *portrait; Brown's Biog. Dict. of Music* (1886) 308; *Grove's Dict. of Musicians, i,* 697 (1887).

HATTON, VILLIERS FRANCIS. *b.* Dromana, co. Waterford 20 Aug. 1787; entered navy 1799; lost an arm in an action with a Danish sloop off the Coast of Norway 19 June 1808; captain 7 Feb. 1812, V.A. on half pay 27 Sep. 1855; M.P. for co. Wexford 1841–47; had pension of £300 a year for his wounds. *d.* 8 Feb. 1859. *G.M. March* 1859 *p.* 333.

HAUGHTON, REV. GEORGE DUNBAR (*2 son of Rev. John Haughton, R. of Middleton, Lancs. d. 1828*). *b.* Middleton 6 May 1807; ed. at Manchester sch. and Worcester coll. Ox., B.A. 1829; C. of Lockerley, Hants. 1876–82; editor of *Bath Express* from beginning; author of *On sex in the world to come* 1841; *The martyr-boy of Pistoja, a ballad* 1861. *d.* about 1888. *Manchester school reg. iii,* 165 (1874).

HAUGHTON, JAMES (*son of Samuel Pearson Haughton*). *b.* Carlow 5 May 1795; corn and flour merchant, Dublin 1817–50; a reformer; associated with O'Connell in the Repeal movement, with Wilberforce in the Anti-slavery meetings 1838, and with Father Mathew in advocating temperance; a unitarian 1834; author of *A plea for teetotalism and the Maine liquor law* 1855. *d.* 35 Eccles st. Dublin 20 Feb. 1873. *Memoir of J. Haughton by his son* (1877), *portrait*.

HAUGHTON, JOHN COLPOYS (*son of Richard H. Haughton*). *b.* Dublin 25 Nov. 1817; ed. at Shrewsbury; entered R.N. 30 March 1830, midshipman 1832–7; ensign 31 Bengal N.I. 9 Dec. 1837; in Afghan war 1839–42, adjutant of 4 Goorka regt. in Shah Soojah's service when he defended Char-ee-kar 5–11 Nov. 1841, with his right hand amputated and some of the muscle of his neck severed he had to ride to Cabul 14–16 Nov.; with the Ramghur battalion in 6 actions 1846–7; superintendent of penal settlement in Andaman islands 1859; commissioner of Cooch Behar and manager of the maharajah's estates 1865–73; retired 1873; C.S.I. 24 May 1866; L.G. 1 April 1882; author of *Char-ee-kar and service there with the 4 Goorkha regiment* 1867, *2 ed.* 1879. *d.* Ramsgate 17 Sep. 1887. *Sir V. Eyre's Kabul insurrection* (1879) *p.* 135 *et seq.; Times* 21 *Sep.* 1887 *p.* 10 col. 6.

HAUSSMANN, JOSEPHINE CONSTANTINE. *b.* Breslau 22 March 1791; served in Prussian army 1813–21; an artist in England. *d.* 23 New Ormond st. Queen sq. London 28 May 1881.

HAVELL, WILLIAM *(son of a drawing master at Reading).* *b.* Reading 9 Feb. 1782; painter in oils and water colours; exhibited 103 pictures at R.A., 42 at B.I. and 32 at Suffolk st. 1804–57; a foundation member of Soc. of painters in water-colours 1804, seceded 1813, rejoined in 1825; went with Lord Amherst's embassy to China as a draughtsman 1816; in India practising his profession 1817–25; lost his savings by failure of an Indian bank and became a pensioner on Turner fund of Royal Academy; his best known painting is 'Windsor' in South Kensington museum; published with Robert Havell *A series of views of Noblemen's seats* 1823. *d.* 3 High row, Kensington 16 Dec. 1857. *Redgrave's Dict. of Artists* (1878) 201; *Monkhouse's Earlier English Water-colour painters* (1890) 65, 91, 95, 119, 131.

HAVELOCK, CHARLES FREDERICK (4 *son of Wm. Havelock, ship builder, Sunderland).* *b.* Ingress park, Greenhithe, Kent 16 Oct. 1803; cornet 16 lancers 13 Dec. 1821, engaged in every battle in India from Bhurtpore 18 Jany. 1826 to Goojerat 21 Feb. 1849; major 53 foot 24 May 1846 to 27 July 1849 when placed on h.p.; brigadier general of the Irregular Osmanli cavalry 1854 to 1856. *d.* Titchfield, Hampshire 14 May 1868.

HAVELOCK, SIR HENRY *(brother of the preceding).* *b.* Ford hall, Bishop Wearmouth 5 April 1795; ed. at Charterhouse; student at Middle Temple 1813–14; 2 lieut. 95 regt. 30 July 1815; D.A.A.G. in Burmese war 1824–6; in first Afghan war and present at capture of Cabul, July 1839; aided Sir R. Sale at time of the Cabul rising and took part in siege of Jallálabád 1841; C.B. 4 Oct. 1842, K.C.B. 26 Sep. 1857; Persian interpreter to Sir Hugh Gough in Gwalior campaign 1843–4; in first Sikh war and present at Mudki, Ferozeshah and Sobraon 1845; D.A.G. of queen's troops, Bombay 1847; A.G. of queen's troops in India 1854; commanded a division in the Persian war 1856–7; commanded a column in the Indian mutiny and fought battle of Futtehpore 12 July 1857, defeated Nana Sahib 16 July and recaptured Cawnpore 17 July, relieved Lucknow 25–26 Sep.; M.G. 29 Sep. 1857; gazetted baronet 26 Nov. 1857; author of *Memoirs of the campaigns of Sir A. Campbell's army in Ava.* Serampore 1828; *Narrative of the war in Afghanistan 1838–39,* 2 vols. 1840. *d.* of diarrhœa, the Dilkoosha

HAVELOCK, SIR H. *(Con.)*

near Lucknow 24 Nov. 1857. *bur.* in the square of the Alumbagh, statue by Wm. Behnes in Trafalgar sq. London 1861. *Marsham's Memoirs of Sir H. Havelock* (1860), *portrait; R. M. Martin's Indian empire,* ii, *276* (1858–61), *portrait; Nolan's British empire in India,* ii, *751* (1858–60), *portrait; Landels' Baptist Worthies* (1884) 339–72, *portrait.*

HAVERFIELD, ROBERT ROSS. *b.* Bideford, Devon, Feb. 1819; went to Australia 1838; crossed the Mallee from lake Tyrell to lake Hindmarsh, Victoria; with A. M. Lloyd started the *Bendigo Advertiser* 1851, editor 1870 to death; explored the Darling country, N.S.W. and crossed from Menindie to Booligal on the Lachlan; crossed the Barrier ranges to the northern stations of S. Australia; sec. to Victorian royal commission to inquire about deaths of Burke and Wills 1861; arbitrator in assessment of runs in Oven's district 1860; started the *Riverene Herald* at Deniliquin 1863; sub-editor of *Age* in Melbourne. *d.* Sandhurst, Victoria 21 April 1889. *Times 5 June 1889 p. 10.*

HAVERGAL, FRANCES RIDLEY *(youngest child of Rev. W. H. Havergal 1793–1870).* *b.* Astley rectory, Worcs. 14 Dec. 1836; studied in Louisenschule at Düsseldorf 1852; wrote verses from the age of seven; engaged in religious and philanthropic work; author of *The ministry of song* 1871, 5 ed. 1874; *The four happy days* 1874, 15th thousand 1883; *Life chords* 1880; *Poetical works* 2 vols. 1884 and about 40 other books; wrote many popular hymns. *d.* Caswell bay road, Swansea 3 June 1879. *Memorials of F. R. Havergal by Her Sister* (1880), *portrait; Letters of F. R. Havergal* (1885); *J. E. Prescott's Hymns* (2 ed. 1886) 214–27; *C. Bullock's Crown of the Road* (1884) 135–90, *portrait.*

HAVERGAL, REV. FRANCIS TEBBS (5 *child of Rev. W. H. Havergal).* *b.* 27 Aug. 1829; bible clerk New coll. Ox.; B.A. 1852, M.A. 1857; vicar choral Hereford cath. 1853–74; V. of Pipe with Lyde, Herefordshire 1861–74 and V. of Upton Bishop 1874 to death; preb. of Hereford 1877 to death; author of *Fasti Herefordenses* 1869; *Memorials of Sir F. A. G. Ouseley* 1889 and other works. *d.* Upton Bishop 27 July 1890. *Guardian 6 Aug. 1890 p. 1233.*

HAVERGAL, REV. HENRY EAST (2 *child of Rev. W. H. Havergal).* *b.* Coaley, Gloucs. 22 July 1820; chorister New coll. Ox. 1828–34, bible clerk 1839; B.A. 1843, M.A. 1846; chaplain Ch. Ch. 1843 and at New coll. 1844–7; V. of Cople, Beds 1847 to death; built an

HAVERGAL, REV. H. E. (Con.)

F. organ, that being the note to which the voice extends; singer, double bass and trumpet performer; he published *Selections from the hymns of George Wither* 1846; *Tunes, chants and responses* 1865; *Forty-two chants* 1870, besides other works. *d.* Cople vicarage 12 Jany. 1875. *Record* 18, 20 *Jany.* 1875; *Choir* 23 *Jany.* 1875 p. 50.

HAVERGAL, MARIA VERNON GRAHAM (3 *child of Rev. W. H. Havergal*). *b.* Coaley, Gloucs. 15 Nov. 1821; engaged in philanthropic and religious works; author of *Pleasant fruits from the cottage and the class* 1871; *Memorials of Frances R. Havergal* 1880; *Outlines of the gentle life, Sketch of E. P. Shaw by her sister* 1887; she also edited many of Frances R. Havergal's works 1879–87. *d.* 3 Paragon villas, Weston-super-mare 22 June 1887. *bur.* Astley near Bewdley 28 June. *Autobiography of M. V. G. Havergal, Ed. by J. M. Crane* (1887), *portrait.*

HAVERGAL, REV. WILLIAM HENRY (*only son of Wm. Havergal of Chipping Wycombe, Bucks.* 1765–1854). *b.* Chipping Wycombe 18 Jany. 1793; ed. at Merchant Taylor's school and St. Edmund's hall, Ox., B.A. 1816, M.A. 1819; C. of Coaley, Gloucs. 1820–22; C. of Astley near Bewdley 1822–29; R. of Astley 1829–42; R. of St. Nicholas, Worcester 1845–60; hon. canon Worcester cath. 1845; V. of Shareshill, Staffs. 1860–70; endeavoured to restore metrical psalmody to its original purity; he composed *An evening service in E flat, and one hundred antiphonal chants* 1836; *Old church psalmody* 1847; his sacred song *Summertime is coming*, and his psalm tune *Evan*, are well known; author of *Sermons* 2 vols. 1853; *A history of the Old Hundredth psalm tune, New York* 1854 and other works. *d.* Pyrmont villa, Binswood ter. Leamington 19 April 1870. *bur.* Astley ch. yard 23 April. *Records of Rev. W. H. Havergal* (1882), 2 *portraits; Bullock's The Crown of the road* (1884) 243–302, 2 *portraits; Lymington's The pastor remembered* (1870) 43–54.

HAVERS, MARY ALICE. Exhibited 18 pictures at R.A. and 3 at Suffolk st. 1873–80, exhibited also at Manchester; many of her pictures were engraved and published. (*m.* Frederick Morgan). *d.* 11 Marlborough road, St. John's Wood, London 26 Aug. 1890. *I.L.N.* 6 *Sep.* 1890 p. 295, *portrait.*

HAVERTY, JOSEPH PATRICK. *b.* Galway 1794; member R. Hibernian academy; exhibited 17 portraits at R.A. and 8 at Suffolk st. 1835–58; among his pictures were the Limerick Piper,

HAVERTY, J. P. (Con.)

in Irish National gallery; Father Mathew receiving a repentent pledge-breaker 1844; his set of 3, Baptism, Confession and Confirmation were lent to Irish exhibition in London 1888; his portrait of D O'Connell belongs to Reform club, London. *d.* Dublin 1864. *Webb's Irish biography* (1878) 584.

HAVERTY, MARTIN. *b.* Mayo 1 Dec. 1809; ed. at Irish coll. Paris; on staff of *Freeman's Journal*, Dublin 1837–50; sub-librarian King's Inns, Dublin 1852–77; author of *Wanderings in Spain* 2 vols. 1844; *The history of Ireland* 1860, 2 ed. 1885. *d.* 5 Wells park, Fairview, Dublin 18 Jany. 1887. *Irish Law Times, xxi,* 49, 110 (1887).

HAVILAND, JOHN (*only son of John Haviland of Gundenham, Somerset, surgeon* 1754–1817). *b.* Bridgewater 2 Feb. 1785; ed. at Winchester and St. John's coll. Cam., 12 wr. 1807, B.A. 1807, M.A. 1810, M.L. 1812, M.D. 1817; fell. of his coll.; prof. of anatomy in Univ. of Cam. 1814–17, regius prof. of physic 7 March 1817 to death; physician to Addenbrooke's hospital, Cam. 1817–39 when he retired from practice; inceptor candidate of R.C.P. 1814, candidate 1817, fellow 30 Sep. 1818, delivered Harveian oration 1837. *d.* 21 Trumpington st. Cambridge 8 Jany. 1851. *bur.* at Fen Ditton near Cambridge. *Munk's College of physicians, iii,* 183 (1878).

HAVILAND, JOHN (*son of James Haviland of Taunton*). *b.* Gundenham, Somerset 15 Dec. 1792; pupil of James Elmes, architect; went to Russia to enter imperial corps of engineers 1815; went to United States 1816; M.R.I.B.A.; with Hugh Bridgport managed an architectural drawing sch. in Philadelphia; he planned the hall of justice, New York; the U.S. naval hospital, Norfolk, Va.; deaf and dumb asylum, Philadelphia; state insane asylum, Harrisburg; eastern penitentiary, Philadelphia, and the state penitentiaries of New Jersey, Missouri and Rhode island; author with H. Bridgport of *Builders' Assistant for carpenters. Baltimore* 3 *vols.* 1818. *d.* Philadelphia 28 March 1852. *G.M. xxxvii,* 629 (1852); *Appleton's American Biography, iii,* 118 (1887).

NOTE.—He introduced the plan of building the cells of prisons in lines radiating from a common centre, on the system advocated by Jeremy Bentham in his Panopticon.

HAVILAND-BURKE, EDMUND (*only son of Thomas W. A. Haviland-Burke* 1795–1852, *barrister*). *b.* 27 Jany. 1836; ed. at Eton; barrister L.I. 30 April 1860; equity draftsman and conveyancer; contested Christchurch,

HAVILAND-BURKE, E. (Con.)

Hants. 1865; M.P. Christchurch 1868–74. *d. co.* Dublin 17 June 1886. *Law Times, lxxxi,* 158 (1886).

HAVILLAND, JOHN VON SONNENTAG DE *(son of John Haviland* 1792–1852). *b.* U.S. America 1827; ed. at St. Petersburg; general in several foreign services; barrister I.T. 26 Jany. 1870; Rouge Croix pursuivant, Herald's coll. 16 Aug. 1866, York herald 20 March 1872 to death; changed spelling of his name to Havilland and resumed the prefix of de 1869; F.S.A. 1872; knight of justice of St. John of Jerusalem. *d.* Paignton, Devon 18 Sep. 1886. *bur.* Langford Budville, Somerset. *Proc. Soc. of Antiquaries, xi,* 376 (1885–7); *Law Times* 9 Oct. 1886 p. 391.

HAVILLAND, THOMAS FIOTT DE (1 *son of Sir Peter de Havilland, d.* 1821). *b.* Havilland hall, Guernsey 10 April 1775; ensign Madras engineers 3 May 1793; built the Jeybourg barracks, Guernsey 1812; civil engineer and architect for Madras presidency 1814; constructed the Mount road and the sea wall of Madras 1822; built the cathedral and St. Andrew's presbyterian ch. Madras; acting chief engineer 9 Feb. 1821; lieut.-col. 1 May 1824; retired 20 April 1825; author of *Report on Indian limestone* 1822. *d.* Beauvoir, Guernsey 23 Feb. 1866. *G.M. April* 1866 *p.* 603; *H. M. Vibart's Madras Engineers, ii,* 1–35 (1883).

HAWARDEN, CORNWALLIS MAUDE, 3 Viscount. *b.* 28 March 1780; succeeded his brother 26 Feb. 1807; created D.C.L. at Ox. 5 July 1810; a representative peer of Ireland 31 Oct. 1836 to death; a lord in waiting to the Queen 1841–46 and Feb. to Dec. 1852. *d.* Dundrum near Cashel 12 Oct. 1856.

HAWES, SIR BENJAMIN (1 *son of Benjamin Hawes of Russell sq. London, soapboiler* 1770–1860). *b.* London 19 March 1797; soap manufacturer in partnership with his father and uncle; M.P. Lambeth 1832–47; M.P. Kinsale 1848–52; under sec. of state for the colonies 6 July 1846 to 31 Oct. 1851; deputy secretary at war 31 Oct. 1851 to 1857 when office abolished; permanent under sec. of state for war department 1857 to death; K.C.B. 5 Feb. 1856; made the arrangement for the partnership between Sir W. F. Cooke and Sir C. Wheatstone the electricians 1837. *.d.* 9 Queen sq. Westminster 15 May 1862. *Francis' Orators of the age* (1847) 345–50; *G.M. xiii,* 101–3 (1862); *May's Law of parliament* (1883) 217.

HAWES, REV. THOMAS HENRY (1 *son of William Hawes of St. John's, Westminster).* Matric.

HAWES, REV. T. H. *(Con.)*

from Magd. hall, Ox. 9 July 1824 aged 18; B.A. 1828, M.A. 1834, D.D. 1839; scholar New coll. 1829–57, chaplain 1830–56; V. of Nether Stowey, Somerset 1849–57; R. of Burgh Castle, Norfolk 1857 to death; composer and editor of *Two penitential anthems.* Oxford 1849; *A morning and communion service.* Bristol 1855; *Congregational psalmody.* Wells 1855. *d.* Burgh Castle rectory 2 Feb. 1888.

HAWES, MARIA BILLINGTON (2 *dau. of William Hawes, musical composer* 1785–1846). *b.* Craven st. Strand, London 1816, Mrs. Billington was her godmother; first appeared at her father's annual concert 1832; sang at musical festival in Westminster abbey as second contralto 1838; her singing in the works of Pergolesi, Handel, Haydn, Spohr & Mendelssohn moved whole audiences to tears; principal contralto in first performance of Mendelssohn's Lobgesang 23 Sep. 1840 and in the Elijah 26 Aug. 1846; *O rest in the Lord* was written expressly for her by Mendelssohn; composer of *There be none of beauty's daughters, song* 1856; *O Lord thy mercies we proclaim, hymn* 1872 and 25 other compositions. (*m.* 1847 J. D. Merest), she *d.* a widow at St. John's park, Ryde, Isle of Wight 24 April 1886. *Musical Standard* 26 June 1886 *pp.* 406–7.

HAWES, WILLIAM *(son of Benjamin Hawes* 1770–1860). *b.* 23 May 1805; received testimonial 1841 for his efforts to amend laws relating to soap; member of Soc. of Arts 1849, chairman of council 5 times; treasurer of Royal Humane Society 1868 to death, this society was partly founded by Dr. William Hawes his grandfather in 1774; engaged in schemes for management of hospitals, workhouses and baths and washhouses; aided in amending bankruptcy laws, presented by merchants of city of London with a service of plate 1847; comr. of Exhibition of 1862, read before Soc. of Arts a series of papers on the Exhibition 1861–3. *d.* 17 Montague place, Russell sq. London 1 May 1885 aged 80. *Times* 8 *May* 1885 *p.* 11; *Journal of Soc. of Arts* 8 *May* 1885 *p.* 720.

HAWKE, EDWARD WILLIAM HARVEY HAWKE, 4 Baron. *b.* Womersley park, Pontefract 15 July 1799; ed. at Eton; succeeded 29 Nov. 1834; master of the Badsworth hounds 14 Sep. 1826 to 1866. *d.* Womersley park 8 Jany. 1869. *Baily's Mag. ix,* 163–66 (1864), *portrait.*

HAWKER, EDWARD *(son of James Hawker, captain R.N. d.* 1787). *b.* 1782; entered navy 1793; captain 6 June 1804; admiral on h.p.

HAWKER, E. *(Con.)*

17 Sep. 1853, pensioned 18 March 1858; a writer in *The Times* on naval matters under signature of A Flag Officer; author of *A letter to Wellington* 1840. *d.* Brighton 8 June 1860 aged 78.

HAWKER, HENRY SAMUEL (4 *son of general Sir Samuel Hawker*). *b.* 1816 or 1817; lieut. R.N. 6 March 1838, captain 9 July 1861, retired 12 Oct. 1868, retired admiral 15 July 1887. *d.* Buckingham palace road, London 11 May 1889 in 73 year.

HAWKER, PETER *(son of colonel Peter Ryves Hawker of Longparish, Hants., d. 6 Feb. 1790).* *b.* London 24 Dec. 1786; ed. at Eton; cornet 1 royal dragoons 1801; captain 14 light dragoons 14 Aug. 1804 to 18 March 1813 when he sold out owing to wound received at Talavera; lieut.-col. of North Hampshire militia 14 Nov. 1821 to death; published *Journal of a regimental officer during the recent campaign in Portugal and Spain* 1810; *Instructions to young sportsmen in all that relates to guns and shooting* 1814, 11 *ed.* 1857; made inventions and improvements in fire arms 1851 etc.; invented hand moulds to facilitate playing on keyed instruments, patented by him 1 Nov. 1820. *d.* 2 Dorset place, Dorset sq. London 7 Aug. 1853. *G.M. xl,* 313 (1853); *I.L.N. xix,* 534, 536 (1851), *portrait, xxiii,* 138 (1853).

HAWKER, REV. ROBERT STEPHEN (1 *son of Jacob Stephen Hawker, surgeon, Plymouth, then vicar of Stratton, d. 1845).* *b.* Stoke Damarel, Devon 3 Dec. 1804; ed. at Liskeard gram. sch.; articled to W. Jacobson, attorney, Plymouth; at Cheltenham gram. sch. and Pemb. coll. Ox. 1823, migrated to Magd. hall, B.A. 1828, M.A. 1836; won Newdigate prize for poem on Pompeii 27 June 1827; V. of Morwenstow 31 Dec. 1834 to death; instituted ruridecanal synods 1844; V. of Wellcombe 1850 to death; instituted weekly offertories and harvest thanksgivings; author of *Tendrils. By Reuben.* Cheltenham 1821; *Ecclesia.* Oxford 1840; *Echoes from Old Cornwall* 1846; *The quest of the Sangraal. Exeter* 1864 his best work; *Footprints of former men in far Cornwall* 1870; on the originality of his ballad *And shall Trelawny die?* there has been much discussion; delineated in Mortimer Collins' novel *Sweet and Twenty* 1875 as Canon Tremaine; in his last hours received into R.C. ch. *d.* 9 Lockyer st. Plymouth 15 Aug. 1875, his widow Pauline Mary granted civil list pension of £80, 13 Oct. 1880. *Lee's Memorials of Rev. R. S. Hawker* (1876), *portrait; Baring-Gould's The vicar of Morwenstow* (1876), *portrait,* 3 *ed.* 1876; *Poetical Works. Ed. J. G. Godwin* (1879),

HAWKER, REV. R. S. *(Con.)*

portrait; Boase and Courtney's Bibl. Cornub. i, 220-2, *iii,* 1222-3; *Gillow's English Catholics, iii,* 183-90 (1887).

HAWKER, SIR THOMAS. *b.* 1777; cornet 11 dragoons 12 May 1795; served in the Mediterranean and Spain 1805-15; lieut. col. 20 dragoons 2 Sep. 1808 to 1818; colonel of 6 dragoon guards 5 June 1839 to death; general 20 June 1854; K.C.H. 1837, knighted by William iv. at St. James's palace 1 March 1837. *d.* Fern villa, Lansdowne place, Clifton 13 June 1858.

HAWKES, MERVYN LANARK (4 *son of Sidney Milnes Hawkes*). *b.* 1861; an originator of League for abolition of House of Lords; a lecturer at Radical clubs; contested Eye 1885, Sheffield central division 1885, Hartlepool 1886; in Australia 1888-90; author of *A Primrose Dame, the story of an election. Bristol* 1886. *d.* of consumption at his father's house, Bruges, Belgium 17 Oct. 1890.

HAWKES, ROBERT. *b.* 1790; cornet Bengal army 30 July 1806, served during Mahratta war 1817-18; lieut. col. 9 Bengal light cavalry 1845 to 28 Nov. 1854; commanded at Lucknow 26 Jany. 1852 to 15 Nov. 1853; general 25 June 1870. *d.* 52 York terrace, Regent's park, London 18 Dec. 1876.

HAWKINS, ALFRED. *b.* England; shipping master of port of Quebec some years; author of *Hawkins's Picture of Quebec with historical recollections. Quebec* 1834; *The plan of the naval and military operations before Quebec, and death of Wolfe* 1842; *The Quebec directory and guide. Quebec* 1844. *d.* Quebec 30 June 1854.

HAWKINS, CÆSAR HENRY (3 *son of Rev. Edward Hawkins, R. of Kelston, Somerset, d.* 1805). *b.* Bisley, Gloucs. 19 Sep. 1798; ed. at Christ's hospital and St. George's hospital; M.R.C.S. 1821, F.R.C.S. 1843; taught anatomy in Hunterian school, Windmill st.; surgeon to St. George's hosp. 1829-61, consulting surgeon 1861; examiner at royal college of surgeons 1849-66, Hunterian orator 1849, pres. 1852, 1861; surgeon extraord. to the Queen 11 Nov. 1857, serjeant surgeon in ord. 25 Nov. 1862 to death; member of general medical council 4 July 1865 to 4 July 1870; F.R.S. 5 June 1856; popularised operations of ovariotomy and colotomy; author of *The Hunterian oration, presidential addresses and pathological and surgical writings* 2 vols. *privately printed* 1874. *d.* 26 Grosvenor st. London 20 July 1884. *Medical Times, ii,* 119 (1884); *I.L.N. lxxxv,* 133 (1884), *portrait.*

HAWKINS, EDWARD (1 *son of Edward Hawkins, banker, Macclesfield, d.* 1816). *b.* Macclesfield 5 May 1780; ed. Macclesfield gram. sch.; partner in Swansea bank and a manager of Neath Abbey copper works to 1807; F.L.S. 1806; made collection of books and prints relating to Chester; F.R.S. 1821, V.P., withdrew 1856; F.S.A. 1826, member of council 1828, chairman of executive committee 1853–9, V.P.; fellow Numismatic Soc. 1836, president; deputy keeper of antiquities British museum May 1825, keeper 1826 to Dec. 1860; formed collections of British medals and of 8000 English political caricatures, purchased by Br. Museum 1860 and 1868; author of *Description of the Anglo-Gallic coins in British Museum* 1826; *The silver coins of England* 1841, 3 ed. 1887; *Descriptive account of British Medals* 1852, Br. Museum refused to publish this as it contained political opinions, but revised and ed. by A. W. Franks and H. A. Grueber as *Medallic illustrations of history of Great Britain and Ireland* was published in 2 vols. 1885. *d.* 6 Lower Berkeley st. London 22 May 1867. *Proc. of Soc. of Antiquaries, iv,* 103–106 (1868); *Numismatic Chronicle Proceedings, vii,* 11–12 (1867).

HAWKINS, REV. EDWARD (*brother of Cæsar Henry Hawkins* 1798–1884). *b.* Bath 27 Feb. 1789; ed. at Elmore, Gloucs. 1796–1800, at Merchant Taylor's school 1801 to 1807; Andrew exhibitioner at St. John's coll. Ox. 1807; double 1st class 1811; tutor of his college 1812; B.A. 1811, M.A. 1814, B.D. and D.D. 1828; fellow of Oriel coll. Easter 1813 to 2 Feb. 1828, tutor 1819, select preacher 1820–1, 1824–5, 1830–1 and 1842–3; V. of St. Mary the Virgin, Oxford 1823–28; Whitehall preacher 1827–28; provost of Oriel coll. 2 Feb. 1828 to death, but resigned his active duties 3 Oct. 1874; canon of Rochester 2 Feb. 1828 to death; R. of Purleigh, Essex 2 Feb. 1828 to death; V. of Lamberhurst, Kent 1831–4; declined the vice-chancellorship 1840 and 1870; Bampton lecturer 1840; Ireland professor of exegesis of holy scripture 2 Nov. 1847 to 19 Oct. 1861; lived at Rochester 1875 to death; author of *A dissertation upon unauthoritative tradition as an introduction to Christian doctrines* 1819, reprinted 1889; *A manual for Christians after confirmation* 1826, 6 ed. 1839; *Discourses upon the historical scriptures of the Old Testament* 1833; *An inquiry into the uses of the means of attaining Christian truth, eight sermons* 1840, and about 30 other publications. *d.* the Precincts, Rochester 18 Nov. 1882. *bur.* in the cathedral cemetery 24 Nov. *J. W. Burgon's Lives of twelve good men* (1888) *i,* 376–475, *portrait; Quarterly Rev. clvi,* 305–52 (1883); *T. Mozley's Reminiscences, vol. i* (1882).

NOTE.—There is a fine portrait of him by Sir Francis Grant in Oriel common room.—.He was a great conservative and his opposition to any change in the tutorial system at Oriel occasioned the resignation of Newman, Richard Hurrell Froude, and Robert Wilberforce.

HAWKINS, REV. ERNEST (6 *son of Henry Hawkins of Lawrence End, parish of Kimpton, Herts., major H.E.I.C.*) *b.* Lawrence End 25 Jany. 1801; ed. at Ball. coll. Ox., B.A. 1824, M.A. 1827, B.D. 1839; fellow of Ex. coll. Ox. 26 Dec. 1831 to 29 July 1852; assistant sec. S.P.G. 1838, sec. 1843–64, the society greatly expanded under his management; preb. of St. Paul's 1844–64; minister of Curzon chapel, Mayfair, London 1850 to death; vice prin. of Bishop's coll. Cape Town, Feb. 1859; canon of Westminster 7 Nov. 1864 to death, installed 5 Dec. 1864; author of *Documents relating to the erection of bishoprics in the colonies* 1844, 4 ed. 1855; *Manual of prayer for working men and their families* 1855, 4 ed. 1856; *The book of Psalms with explanatory notes* 1857, 3 ed. 1865 and 14 other books. *d.* Dean's yard, Westminster 5 Oct. 1868. *bur.* Westminster abbey cloisters 12 Oct. *Boase's Exeter coll.* (1879) 130; *Chester's Westminster abbey* (1876) 518; *I.L.N.* 10 Oct. 1868 p. 363.

HAWKINS, FRANCIS (*brother of Rev. Edward Hawkins* 1789–1882). *b.* Bisley, Gloucs. 30 July 1794; ed. at Merchant Taylors' sch. 1805–12; probationary fellow of St. John's coll. Ox. 1812, Newdigate prizeman 1813; B.A. 1816, B.C.L. 1819, M.B. 1820, M.D. 1823; inceptor candidate of R.C.P. 1821, candidate 1823, fellow 30 Sep. 1824; phys. Middlesex hosp. 18 Dec. 1824 to 1858; prof. of theory and practice of medicine in King's coll. London 1831–6; phys. to royal household of William iv. 24 July 1830 to 1837; Gulstonian lecturer at coll. of phys. 1826, censor 1827, Croonian lecturer 1827–29, Lumleian lecturer 1832, 1834, 1840, 1841, Harveian orator 1848, an elect 14 Nov. 1850, consiliarius 1859–61, 1863–65 and 1869, registrar 30 Sep. 1829 to 1858; registrar of general council of Medical education and registration 25 Nov. 1858, retired 22 Dec. 1876; phys. to H.M.'s household in ordinary 13 Dec. 1861 to death; author of *Rheumatism and some diseases of the heart* 1826; edited *The Medical Register* 1859. *d.* 16 Ashley place, Victoria st. London 13 Dec. 1877. *Munk's College of physicians, iii,* 286 (1878); *Medical Times, ii,* 686 (1877).

HAWKINS, FRANCIS SPENCER. *b.* 1799; entered Bengal army 1817, M.G. 28 Nov. 1854; col. 2 Bengal N.I. 18 Feb. 1856 to death; C.B. 24 Dec. 1842. *d.* 32 Sussex gardens, Hyde park, London 3 June 1860 aged 61.

HAWKINS, GEORGE (son of George Hawkins, landscape painter). b. 1809; architectural draughtsman; exhibited 7 drawings at R.A. 1830–48; lithographer, worked for Day and Son, London; his chief work was a series of the Monastic ruins of Yorkshire, sketches by W. Richardson, description by E. Churton 2 vols. York 1844–56. d. 116 Camden road villas, Camden Town, London 6 Nov. 1852. Art Journal (1852) 375; G.M. xxxviii, 655 (1852).

HAWKINS, JOHN (son of Henry Hawkins, major H.E.I. Co.) b. Huntingdon 28 June 1791; ed. at Hitchin and Rugby; articled to Joseph Eade of Hitchin, Herts. solicitor; practised at Hitchin 1812 to death; steward of 28 manors at one time; a founder of the Hitchin Friendly Institution, May 1827; a trustee of nearly every charity in Hitchin. d. The Grange, Hitchin 22 March 1877. Law Journal, xii, 232–4 (1877).

HAWKINS, JOHN CROFT. b. 6 April 1798; entered navy 1811; entered marine service of H.E.I. Co. 1812; surveyed the Euphrates 1838; captain 21 Jany. 1839; commodore of Persian gulf squadron 1845–47; acting superintendent and commander in chief of Indian navy Aug. 1848 to 27 Jany. 1849; thrown out of his curricle and killed on the spot near his house in Colaba, Bombay 25 Aug. 1851.

HAWKINS, JOHN HEYWOOD (1 son of John Hawkins of Bignor park near Petworth, Sussex, d. Trewithen, Cornwall 4 July 1841). b. 1803; ed. at Eton and Trin. coll. Cam., B.A. 1825, M.A. 1828; sheriff of Sussex 1826; M.P. for St. Michael, Cornwall 1830–31, for Tavistock, Devon 1831–32, and for Newport, Isle of Wight 12 Dec. 1832 to 23 June 1841; F.R.S. d. Bignor park 27 June 1877 in 75 year.

HAWKINS, JOHN ISAAC (son of Isaac Hawkins of Taunton). b. Taunton 14 March 1772; ed. at Jersey coll. Pennsylvania; lived at village of Bordentown, New Jersey many years; started The journal of human nature and human progress; returned to England; patented a machine for taking likenesses in profile from size of life downwards; invented the claviole or finger keyed viol which imitated all the instruments of a band, patented in his father's name 1800; invented portable grand or cottage piano, patented in America and England 1800; consulting engineer in London 1816–49; invented Pentagraph for giving any number of copies of a letter, generally used until superseded by Wedgwood's carbonic manifold writer and copying presses; invented the ever-pointed pencil, the iridium-pointed gold pen 1823, and a method of condensing coffee;

HAWKINS, J. I. (Con.)
M.I.C.E. 27 April 1824; claimed to have made the first survey for a tunnel under the Thames 1808; went to U.S. of America 1849. d. Elizabeth Town, New Jersey 28 June 1855. Min. of proc. of Instit. of C.E. xxv, 512–14 (1866); Encyclop. Brit. xix, 75 (1885).

HAWKINS, MAJOR RHODE (3 son of Edward Hawkins 1780–1867). b. Nutfield, Surrey 4 Feb. 1820; travelling architect in expedition sent by Sir Charles Fellowes to Caria and Lycia 1844, The Harpy Tomb at Br. Museum was reconstructed from his drawings and measurements; architect to Committee of council on Education. d. Redlands near Dorking 19 Oct. 1884.

HAWKINS, SUSANNA (dau. of a blacksmith). b. near Ecclefechan, Annandale 1787; a herder of cattle, and dairymaid at Gillenbie; domestic servant; published fugitive poems in little volumes with paper covers, and hawked them herself in Scotland and England; author of The Poetical works of Susanna Hawkins. Dumfries 1829; Poems and songs, vol. ii, iii, iv, v, vi, vii, viii, ix, 1832, 1835, 1838, 1841, 1850, 1851, 1856 and 1861. d. Burnswark hill, Hoddam, Dumfriesshire 29 March 1868. Irving's Dict. of Scotsmen (1881) 206; Dumfries Courier 7 April 1868 p. 3.

HAWKINS, THOMAS (son of John Hawkins). b. Glastonbury 25 July 1810; F.G.S. 1831; a collector of fossils; his collection of Devon, Somerset and Dorset fossils, purchased by government for £3000 in 183–, is now in Natural History Museum, South Kensington; presented collections of saurian fossils to geological museums of Cambridge 1856 and Oxford 1874; author of Memoirs of Ichthyosauri and Plesiosauri 1834; The book of the great sea-dragons 1840; Prometheus 1850, reprinted 1887; My life and works 1 vol. only 1887. d. Ventnor, Isle of Wight 29 Oct. 1889. Times 31 Oct. 1889 p. 10.

HAWKINS, WALTER. b. London 1787; ed. at Hackney; Russian merchant and ship and insurance broker Finsbury circus, retired 1848; caused a medal to be struck in 1848 which he presented to young persons to encourage them in industry, courtesy and integrity; made a collection of 5000 medals and coins, which he left to the Royal United Service Instit. with £500; author of papers in Archæologia and Numismatic Chronicle; F.S.A. 1842; member Numismatic soc. 1836. d. 5 Leonard place, Kensington 27 Jany. 1862. Numismatic Chronicle Proceedings, ii, 18–19 (1862); Journal of British Archæol. Assoc. xix, 155–6 (1863).

HAWKINS, WILLIAM *(brother of John Hawkins 1791-1877). b.* 1789; ed. at Rugby; solicitor at Hertford 1821, at Hitchin 18— to death; delivered a lecture on Emigration, published by the Emigration comrs. 1833; circulated a series of letters under title of *Thoughts on agriculture. d.* Hitchin 6 May 1875.

HAWKSHAW, ANN *(dau. of Rev. James Jackson of Green Hamerton, Yorks.) b.* 1812. *(m.* 1835 Sir John Hawkshaw, C.E., F.R.S., he was *b.* Leeds 1811, living 1891); author of *Dionysius the Areopagite, poems* 1842; *Poems for my children* 1847; *Sonnets on Anglo-Saxon history* 1854; under name of Aunt Effie *Aunt Effie's Rhymes for little children* 1852; *Aunt Effie's Gift to the nursery* 1854, 2 ed. 1876. *d.* Belgrave mansions, Pimlico, London 29 April 1885. *J. Evans' Lancashire authors* (1876) 51.

HAWLEY, FREDERICK *(son of Benjamin Buck Hawley, capt.* 51 *foot, d.* 15 *July* 1838). *b.* Portsea 10 Jany. 1827; sec. Great Eastern steamship co. 1852; solicitor at 102 Chancery lane, London 1852; actor under name of Frederick Haywell 1855-85, first appeared Marylebone theatre as Florizel 5 March 1855; acted at Sadler's Wells 5 seasons, at Prince's theatre, Manchester many years; manager of T.R. Manchester; librarian Shakespeare memorial library, Stratford-on-Avon 17 May 1886 to death; made MS. catalogue of all editions of Shakespeare's plays in every language 1889; wrote 2 dramas *Found,* Theatre royal, Manchester 2 March 1874 and *Agnes of Bavaria,* Gaiety theatre, London 31 Oct. 1883; author of *The royal family of England, remarks on the royal succession* 1851. *d.* Stratford 13 March 1889. *bur.* Highgate cemet. 18 Mch. *Stratford-on-Avon Herald* 15 *March and* 26 *April* 1889.

HAWLEY, SIR JOSEPH HENRY, 3 Baronet *(eld. son of Sir Henry Hawley, 2 baronet 1776-1831). b.* Harley st. London 27 Oct. 1813; cornet 9 lancers 31 Aug. 1832, sold out 11 April 1834; visited Greece, the Mediterranean and Italy 1834 etc.; sheriff of Kent 1844; kept a racing stud 1844 to 19 July 1873 when he sold it for 23,575 guineas; won the Oaks with Miame 1847, the One thousand guineas with Aphrodite 1851, the Derby with Teddington 1851, Beadsman 1858, Musjid 1859, and Blue Gown 1868, the Two thousand guineas with Fitz Roland 1858, and the St. Leger with Pero Gomez 1869; won £100,000 on Beadsman 1858; collected a fine library at Leybourne grange near Maidstone. *d.* 34 Eaton Place, London 20 April 1875. *Rice's History of the British turf* (1879) ii, 232-41; *Baily's Mag. iii,* 1-5 (1861), *portrait; Sporting*

HAWLEY, SIR J. H. *(Con.)* *Review, xl,* 111-14 (1858), *lx,* 15-18 (1868); *Famous Racing Men, By Thormanby* (1882) 95-100; *Illust. sp. and dr. news, iii,* 93, 95, 112 (1875), *portrait.*

HAWTHORN, ROBERT *(eld. son of Robert Hawthorn, engineer of Walbottle colliery near Newcastle 50 years). b.* Dewley Burn near Walbottle 13 June 1796; machine maker at Forth Banks, Newcastle 1817 to death; invented a new slide rule for engineers 1832 which was generally adopted; applied fixed eccentrics in a locomotive engine 1835 which invention was much used; M.I.C.E. 13 Feb. 1839; description of the first class express engine made by R. and W. Hawthorn, Newcastle, see *Tredgold's Principles and practice of machinery of locomotive engines* 1850, *Ninth Paper pp.* 1-16 *with* 4 *plates. d.* 26 June 1867. *bur.* ch. yard of Newburn near Walbottle 2 July. *Min. of proc. of Instit. of C.E. xxvii,* 590-92 (1868).

HAWTREY, REV. EDWARD CRAVEN *(only son of Rev. Edward Hawtrey, V. of Burnham near Eton, d.* 1803). *b.* Burnham 7 May 1789; ed. at Eton 1799-1807; scholar of King's coll. Cam. 1807, fellow 1810; assistant master at Eton 1814-34, head master 1834-53, provost 12 Jany. 1853 to death, raised number of boys from 444 in 1835 to 777 in 1846, suppressed the Eton Montem 1847; R. of Ewhurst, Sussex 1835-53; R. of Eton 1853-4; V. of Mapledurham, Oxon. 1854 to death; a great linguist, known as the English Mezzofanti; printed privately *Il Trifoglio ovvero Scherzi Metrici d' un Inglese* 1839 and other poems. *d.* the Lodge, Eton college 27 Jany. 1862 the last person buried in Eton college chapel, monument erected in chapel 1878. *Lyte's History of Eton College* (1875) 404-73, *portrait; I.L.N. xl,* 202, 204 (1862), *portrait.*

HAWTREY, REV. STEPHEN THOMAS. *b.* 1808; ed. at Trin. coll. Cam., B.A. 1832, M.A. 1835; M.A. Oxford 1846; head math. master Eton coll. 1836-71; P.C. of Holy Trin. Windsor 1844-51; founded St. Mark's sch. Windsor 1851, warden 1871 to death; author of *St. Mark's school by the seaside in* 1861, 1861; *Reminiscences of a French Eton* 1867; *Introduction to the elements of Euclid* 1874, 4 ed. 1884 and other books. *d.* Church house, Windsor 29 Oct. 1886 in 79 year.

HAY, SIR ADAM, 7 Baronet. *b.* 14 Dec. 1795; M.P. for Lanark burghs 1820-30; succeeded 1 Nov. 1838. *d.* Cannes, France 18 Jany. 1867.

HAY, SIR ANDREW LEITH *(eld. son of general Alexander Leith Hay 1758-1838). b.* Aberdeen

HAY, SIR A. L. *(Con.)*

17 Feb. 1785; ensign 72 foot 8 Jany. 1806, served through Peninsular war 1808–14, served in the West Indies 1816–30; captain 2 foot 1817 to 30 Sep 1819 when placed on h.p.; M.P. for the Elgin burghs 1832–38 and 1841–47; contested Elgin burghs 1847 and city of Aberdeen 1852; clerk of the Ordnance 19 June 1834 to 22 Dec. 1834 and 18 April 1835 to 21 March 1838; K.H. 1834; governor of Bermuda 6 Feb. 1838 to 1 Nov. 1839 but never went to Bermuda; published *A narrative of the Peninsular war* 2 vols. 1831; *The castellated architecture of Aberdeenshire* 1849. *d.* Leith hall, Aberdeenshire 13 Oct. 1862.

HAY, CHARLES CRAWFORD. *b.* 1809; ensign 19 foot 27 June 1824, lieut.-col. 30 Aug. 1842 to 14 April 1854 when placed on h.p.; commandant and inspector general of school of musketry at Hythe 13 April 1860 to 16 Oct. 1867; colonel of 58 foot 25 Nov. 1864, of 93 foot 29 Aug. 1868 to death; L.G. 20 Jany. 1867. *d.* Freshwater, Isle of Wight 27 Sep. 1873.

HAY, CHARLES MURRAY. *b.* 1802; ensign Coldstream guards 1 Nov. 1821, major 25 April 1848 to 20 June 1854; col. 91 foot 9 March 1861 to death; L.G. 24 Aug. 1861. *d.* Lower Belgrave st. London 3 July 1864.

HAY, DAVID RAMSAY. *b.* Edinburgh, March 1798; a house decorator in Edin. about 1818 to death; decorated Abbotsford for Sir Walter Scott 1824, and hall of Soc. of Arts, London about 1846; F.R.S. Edin.; a founder of the Æsthetic Society, Edin. 1851; author of *The laws of harmonious colouring adapted to house painting* 1828, 6 ed. 1847; *The natural principles and analogy of the harmony of form* 1842; *The geometric beauty of the human figure defined* 1851 and 12 other books. *d.* Jordan Bank, Edinburgh 10 Sep. 1866.

HAY, SIR EDWARD HAY DRUMMOND *(eld. son of Edward Wm. Auriol Drummond Hay 1785–1845, consul general for Morocco).* *b.* 4 March 1815; entered colonial office 1834; governor of Virgin islands 1839–50; lieut. governor of St. Kitts 1850–54; governor of St. Helena 1854–63; knighted by patent 22 Aug. 1859; retired on a pension of £500, 1865. *d.* Lymington, Hants. 24 Jany. 1884.

HAY, GEORGE *(eld. son of 8 Marquis of Tweeddale 1787–1876).* *b.* Yester house, co. Haddington 26 April 1822; ed. at Trin. hall, Cam., M.A. 1845; M.P. for Totnes 5 Nov. 1855 to death; styled Earl of Gifford 1822–62. *d.* Dufferin lodge, Highgate, London 22 Dec. 1862.

HAY, JAMES. Cornet 16 lancers 10 June 1795, lieut. col. 18 Feb. 1813 to Feb. 1819 when placed on h.p.; lieut. col. 4 light dragoons 25 Dec. 1821 to 21 Nov. 1822 when placed on h.p.; lieut. col. 2 dragoon guards 22 July 1830 to 27 Oct. 1837 when placed on h.p.; colonel 79 highlanders 8 Feb. 1849 to death; L.G. 11 Nov. 1851; C.B. 4 June 1815. *d.* at his seat near Kilburn, co. Longford 25 Feb. 1854.

HAY, JAMES *(2 son of 7 Marquis of Tweeddale 1753–1804).* Ensign 52 foot 23 Jany. 1806; captain grenadier guards 26 March 1818 to 26 Nov. 1830 when placed on h.p.; colonel 86 foot 8 May 1854 to death; general 1 June 1862; chairman of Aberdeen railway company. *d.* Spa, Belgium 17 Aug. 1862.

HAY, JOHN *(brother of the preceding).* *b.* 1 April 1793; entered navy 4 Dec. 1804; lost his left arm at cutting out of some vessels in Hyères Bay 1807; captain 8 May 1816; C.B. 17 Feb. 1837; chairman of board of naval construction 1846; a lord of the admiralty 13 July 1846 to 30 Jany. 1850; captain superintendent of Devonport dockyard 9 Feb. 1850 to death; R.A. 25 Aug. 1851; M.P. for co. Haddington 1826–31; M.P. for Windsor 1847–50. *d.* St. Michael's terrace, Stoke, Plymouth 26 or 27 Aug. 1851. *bur.* Yeaster, co. Haddington.

HAY, JOHN BAKER PORTER. *b.* 1800; entered navy 28 Dec. 1811, captain 7 March 1842, retired R.A. 12 April 1862, retired admiral 30 July 1875. *d.* 14 Gloucester place, Brighton 14 Jany. 1886.

HAY, MARY CECIL *(dau. of Thomas William Hay, watchmaker, Shrewsbury).* *b.* Market sq. Shrewsbury 1840; resided at Chiswick, Middlesex and then at East Preston, Worthing; frequently visited Cornwall and introduced many Cornish incidents into her novels; author of *Hidden perils* 3 vols. 1873; *Old Myddleton's Money* 3 vols. 1874; *Nora's love test* 3 vols. 1876, 2 ed. 1878; *For her dear sake* 3 vols. 1880; *A wicked girl and other tales* 3 vols. 1886 and 10 other works of fiction. *d.* The Bay Trees, East Preston near Worthing 24 July 1886. *bur.* Highgate cemet. 29 July.

HAY, ROBERT *(4 son of Robert Hay of Whittingham, co. Haddington).* *b.* 6 Jany. 1799; a leading member of an archæological expedition in Egypt 1826–32, 49 large vols. of drawings made during this expedition by or for him were acquired by the British Museum, Dec. 1876; published *Illustrations of Cairo* 1840. *d.* Amisfield, East Lothian 4 Nov. 1863.

HAY, R. *(Con.)*

Additional MS. 31054 *in British Museum library, being part of his diary in Egypt; Catalogue of Egyptian antiquities belonging to R. Hay* 1869.

HAY, SIR ROBERT, 8 Baronet. *b.* 8 May 1825; succeeded his father 18 Jany. 1867; one of the neatest players of golf; with Willie Dunn played Tom Morris and Allan Robertson at North Berwick 1852; won medals at St. Andrews 1848, 1851, 1852, 1872, with 101, 110, 99 and 94; one of the best players in foursome matches. *d.* Lyons, France 30 May 1885. *Hutchinson's Golf (Badminton Lib.* 1890) 64, 362, 413, 415, 416, *portrait; Foster's Baronetage* (1883) 700.

HAY, ROBERT WILLIAM. *b.* 1786; ed. at Ch. Ch. Ox., B.A. 1807, M.A. 1809; private sec. to Viscount Melville first lord of the admiralty 1812–25; under sec. of state for Colonies 1825–1835; F.R.S. *d.* Malta 9 May 1861.

HAY, WILLIAM *(eld. son of Robert Hay of Lawfield and Spott, d.* 1844). *b.* 1794; ensign 52 foot 30 Jany. 1810; captain 5 dragoon guards 1 July 1824 to 12 Nov. 1829 when he sold out; inspecting superintendent of Metropolitan police 1839 and second commissioner 1850 to death; C.B. 25 Oct. 1851. *d.* 67 Cadogan place, Chelsea 29 Aug. 1855.

HAYDAY, JAMES. *b.* London 1796; appren- to Charles Marchant a vellum-binder, London; bookbinder at 31 Little Queen st. Lincoln's Inn Fields 1833–61; bound books so as to open freely; introduced Turkey morocco instead of the straight grained; his name attached to a book raised its value 25 per cent.; adjudicated bankrupt 10 June 1861. *d.* St. Leonards-on-Sea 19 March 1872. *Bookseller, April* 1872 *p.* 284.

HAYDEN, GEORGE THOMAS. Author of *An essay on the wear and tear of human life and the remedy. Dublin* 1846; *A dialogue on religious equality, or the road to the revival of christianity. Dublin* 1852. *d.* 82 Harcourt st. Dublin 30 July 1857.

HAYDN, JOSEPH TIMOTHY *(son of Thomas Haydn). b.* Ireland 1786 or 1787; ed. abroad; originated at Dublin the *Evening Mail* 1823 and the *Statesman and Patriot* 1828, edited them some years; connected with the *Limerick Times* 1837–9; contributed to London newspapers and periodicals; engaged in record department of admiralty to death; edited S. Lewis's *Topographical Dictionary 8 vols.* 1842–7; his name given to the Haydn series of works of reference 1841 etc.; author of *The Dictionary*

HAYDN, J. T. *(Con.)*

of Dates 1841, 19 *ed.* 1889; *The book of dignities* 1851, 2 *ed.* 1890; granted civil list pension of £25, 27 Dec. 1855. *d.* Crawley st. Oakley sq. London 17 Jany. 1856. *Westminster Review, Jany.* 1830 *p.* 91.

HAYDOCK, THOMAS *(2 son of George Haydock of The Tagg, Cottam, Lancs.) b.* 21 Feb. 1772; ed. at Douay coll. 1785–95; opened a school at 42 Allport st. Manchester 1797; publisher of R.C. books in Manchester 1799–1816; published an edition of the Douay Bible and Testament in numbers July 1811 to Sep. 1814, this is generally known as Haydock's Bible and was republished at Edinburgh and London 1845–8; publisher at Lower Ormond quay, Dublin many years, kept a school in Dublin; publisher at Liverpool about 1840, then at Preston. *d.* Preston 25 Aug. 1859. *Gillow's English Catholics, iii,* 226–30 (1888).

HAYDON, FRANK SCOTT *(eld. son of Benjamin Robert Haydon, historical painter* 1786–1846). *b.* London 12 Dec. 1822; junior clerk in Record office, London, Nov. 1845, senior clerk June 1860, assistant keeper May 1885 to death; author of *Calendar of the patent rolls of the reign of Edward I,* printed in the Appendices to the *Annual reports of the deputy keeper of the public records* 1881–88; edited *Eulogium historiarum sive temporis Chronicon ab orbe condito ad mccclxvi. Rolls Series* 1868; *shot himself* through the brain at Southey lodge, Kingston road, Wimbledon 29 Oct. 1887. *Times* 1 *Nov.* 1887 *p.* 11.

NOTE.—His mother who had been a widow named Mary Hymans, *m* B. R. Haydon 10 Oct. 1821, received a civil list pension of £50 July 4, 1846 and *d.* Heustridge villas, St. John's Wood, London 25 July 1854 aged 61.

HAYDON, FREDERICK WORDSWORTH *(2 son of B. R. Haydon* 1786–1846). *b.* London 14 Sep. 1827; in the navy; inspector of factories 1859–67 when dismissed, he then published a letter addressed to W. E. Gladstone entitled *Our officials at the home office* 1869; author of *Benjamin Robert Haydon. Correspondence and table-talk 2 vols.* 1876. *d.* Bethlehem hospital, London 12 Nov. 1886.

HAYDON, MICHAEL. Detective sergeant city of London; brought Austin Bidwell from Havanna in Bank of England forgery case; with Brett arrested the thieves in the South Eastern gold bullion robbery case 1855 and the thieves in the South Western gold dust robbery case 1851 and with Brett figures in Frith's Railway station 1862; retired on a pension 1879. *d.* 64 Devonshire road, Hackney 15 April 1880. *bur.* Highgate cemetery 21 April. *City Press* 21 *April* 1880 *p.* 5.

HAYE, Thomas Davey *(eld. son of George Haye, captain R.N. of Tavistock 1788–1852).* *b.* St. Heliers, Jersey 22 July 1838; ed. at Rugby; barrister M.T. 17 Nov. 1863, practised as a conveyancer; translated 2 works by H. A. Taine *English positivism* 1870 and *On Intelligence* 1871; author of *A fragment of an intended treatise on Suretyship* 1870. *d.* 7 Roydon villas, Clifton 10 March 1876. *bur.* in R.C. cemetery, Bristol. *Law Times, lx,* 405 (1876); *Boase and Courtney's Bibl. Cornub.* 224, 1225.

HAYES, Catherine. *b.* 4 Patrick st. Limerick 29 Oct. 1825; resided with Antonio Sapio of Dublin as his pupil 1839–42; studied under Garcia in Paris, and Ronconi in Milan 1842–5; made first appearance on stage at Marseilles opera house in *I Puritani* 10 May 1845; prima donna at La Scala, Milan 1845–6; sang in Vienna 1846, chief Italian cities 1846–49; first appeared in London at Royal Italian opera in *Linda di Chamouni* 10 April 1849; sang in United States, California, Sandwich islands and India 1851–6; sang at Jullien's concerts in Her Majesty's theatre, London 1857; had a soprano voice ascending to D. in alt.; a mare called after her Catherine Hayes won the Oaks 1853. *(m.* at St. George's, Hanover sq. London 8 Oct. 1857 William Avery Bushnell of Connecticut, U.S., he *d.* at Biaritz 2 July 1858 aged 35). *d.* at house of Henry Lee, Roccles, Upper Sydenham, Kent 11 Aug. 1861. *bur.* Kensal Green cemetery 17 Aug. *E. C. Clayton's Queens of song, ii,* 274–96 (1863); *Tallis's Drawing room table book* (1851) 33–35, *portrait; I.L.N. xix,* 285 (1851), *portrait; Dublin Univ. mag. xxxvi,* 584–95 (1850), *portrait.*

HAYES, Edmund *(eld. son of William Hayes of Millmount, co. Down, linen manufacturer).* *b.* Millmount 1804; ed. at Belfast academical instit. and Trin. coll. Dublin; B.A. 1825, LL.B. and LL.D. 1832; called to Irish bar 1827; Q.C. 9 Nov. 1852; law adviser to the crown 1852 and 1858; solicitor general 1858; judge of court of queen's bench Jany. 1859 to Nov. 1866 when he resigned; published *Crimes and punishment or a digest of the criminal. statute law of Ireland* 1842, 2 ed. 2 vols. 1843. *d.* Crinken house near Bray, Dublin 29 April 1867. *Irish Law Times, i,* 240 (1867).

HAYES, Sir Edmund Samuel, 3 Baronet. *b.* Dublin 2 July 1806; succeeded 16 Sep. 1827; M.P. for co. Donegal 17 May 1831 to death. *d.* 30 June 1860.

HAYES, Sir George (2 son of Sheedy Hayes, a West Indian proprietor). *b.* Judd place, Somers

HAYES, Sir G. *(Con.)*
Town, London 19 June 1805; ed. at Highgate and St. Edmund's R.C. college at Ware; articled to W. F. Patterson, solicitor, Leamington 1819–24; special pleader, went Midland circuit of which he became leader; barrister M.T. 29 Jany. 1830, sergeant at law Feb. or March 1856, received patent of precedence next after A. J. Stephens 22 Feb. 1861; recorder of Leicester, Dec. 1861 to Aug. 1868; justice of court of Queen's bench 24 Aug. 1868 to death; knighted at Windsor Castle 9 Dec. 1868; author of an Elegy in which he humorously lamented the extinction of John Doe and Richard Roe from the pleadings in ejectment 1854; seized with paralysis 19 Nov. 1869, *d.* Westminster palace hotel, London 24 Nov. 1869. *Law magazine and law review, xxix,* 114–25 (1870); *Reg. and mag. of biog. Dec.* 1869, 304–305.

HAYES, John. *b.* about 1786; portrait and historical painter; exhibited 77 pictures at R.A., 9 at B.I. and 1 at Suffolk st. gallery 1814–57, chiefly portraits. *d.* 51a Berners st. Oxford st. London 14 June 1866.

HAYES, John Boon. M.D. King's college, Aberdeen; M.R.C.S. 1848; lecturer on practical physiology and demonstrator of anatomy at University coll. London; assistant surgeon Bengal 4 Aug. 1855; author of *Lectures on histology and microscopical manipulation. d.* Calcutta 18 July 1856. *Indian Annals of Medical Science. Calcutta, iv,* 260 (1856).

HAYES, John Montagu *(son of John Hayes, R.A., C.B., who d. 7 April 1838).* *b.* 23 March 1816; entered navy 20 March 1829, captain 9 July 1855, retired V.A. 21 March 1878; C.B. 30 Nov. 1864. *d.* Charlton house, Southsea 3 April 1882.

HAYES, Michael Angelo *(son of Edward Hayes of Waterford, painter).* *b.* Waterford 1820; first exhibited in Dublin 1840; exhibited one picture at R.A. and 2 at Suffolk st. 1845–7; member of Royal Hibernian academy 1854, sec. March 1856 to 1857; associate member of New Soc. of Water-colours in London, a regular contributor to their exhibitions; marshal of city of Dublin; author of *The royal Hibernian academy, a glance at its management and proceedings* 1857; *found dead* in a watertank at his house 4 Salem place, Dublin 31 Dec. 1877.

HAYES, Timothy. *b.* Dublin 22 Sep. 1841; a jig dancer; went to the U.S. America where he invented the plan of dancing in clogs 1860 which was a great success; went to Europe with the Christy's Minstrels 186–, toured through U.S. dancing clog dances to tune of My Mary Ann, sometimes receiving 200 dollars a week, known as the father of clog dancers; danced Dick Sands (*b.* Birstall, Yorkshire 2 May 1840) for "the championship clog" and 1000 dollars and won 1863. *d.* Washington asylum, Worcester, U.S. 12 May 1877. *Public Opinion 21 July 1877 p. 77.*

HAYES, WILLIAM. *b.* 1827; a pugilist; beat Mike Madden in 185 rounds and 6 hours at Edenbridge for £100 a side 17 July 1849; beat Jack Jones in 72 rounds and 3 hours at Mildenhall for £200 a side 15 Nov. 1853; fought John Walker £200 a side 36 rounds in 2½ hours at Appledore 18 Dec. 1855, darkness came on, fight adjourned, money eventually drawn; beaten by Bob Travers in 78 rounds and 3 hours and 45 minutes for £100 a side 13 May 1857; fought 15 battles won 7. *d.* London 28 Jany. 1859. *bur.* Highgate 4 Feb. *Bell's Life in London 30 Jany. 1859 p. 6.*

HAYES, WILLIAM. Certificated conveyancer in London 1813; barrister M.T. 27 Nov. 1818; leading real property lawyer many years; conveyancing counsel of Court of Chancery 1861 to death; author of *An inquiry into the effect of limitations to heirs of the body in devises* 1824; *The concise conveyancer* 1830, 4 *ed.* 1882; *A short introduction to conveyancing* 1834, 5 *ed.* 2 *vols.* 1840; author with Thomas Jarman of *Concise forms of wills with practical notes* 1835, 9 *ed.* 1883. *d.* The Priory, Norwood, Surrey 31 Jany. 1871. *Law Times 11 Feb. 1871 p. 286.*

HAYES, WILLIAM. Solicitor at Cork; prominent figure at period of repeal and catholic emancipation movement; had a dispute during the election at Cork, Dec. 1826 with John Bric a R.C. barrister, they fought a duel at Donnybrook near Dublin 26 Dec. 1826 when Bric aged 36 was shot dead. *d.* Clarence terrace, Cork 1 Nov. 1886 aged 91. *Freeman's Journal 30 Dec. 1826 p. 1.*

HAYES, REV. WILLIAM. Ed. at C.C. coll. Cam.; M.A. by Abp. of Canterbury 13 Dec. 1843; assistant master in King's coll. sch. London 1837–79, hon. fellow of King's coll. 1879; chaplain of St. Katherine's hospital, Regent's park, London 1844 to death; author of *Questions adapted to the Rev. J. R. Major's Latin grammar* 1837. *d.* 31 St. Mark's crescent, Regent's park 31 March 1888.

HAYMAN, REV. SAMUEL *(eld. son of Matthew Hayman of South Abbey, Youghal, co. Cork).* *b.*

Youghal 27 July 1818; ed. Clonmel and Trin. coll. Dublin, B.A. 1839; C. of Glanworth 1841–47; C. of Youghal 1849–63; R. of Ardnageehy, Cork 1863–7; R. of Doneraile 1867–72; R. of Carrigaline, Cork 1872–5; R. of Douglas, Cork 1875 to death; canon of Cork 18— to death; author of *The handbook for Youghal, with historical annals of the town* 3 series. Youghal 1852; *Illustrated guide to the Blackwater and Ardmore* 1861; *About Footsteps, in twelve chapters* 1869; *Criteria, or the divine examen.* Dublin 1873 and many other books. *d.* Douglas rectory 15 Dec. 1876. *Journal of Royal Hist. and archæol. assoc. of Ireland 4 series, viii,* 165–70.

HAYNAU, JULIUS JAKOB, Baron Von. *b.* Cassel in Hesse 14 Oct. 1786; entered Austrian army 1801; field marshal lieutenant 1844; his flogging of women at capture of Brescia, North Italy 30 March 1849 gained him name of the "Hyæna of Brescia"; commander in chief of Austrian army in Hungary 1849–50, committed many cruelties; dismissed the service July 1850; visited London, assaulted at Barclay and Perkins' brewery 4 Sep. 1850 barely escaped alive, Austrian ambassador demanded reparation for the assault 22 Sep. but did not get any. *d.* Vienna 14 March 1853. *Life of Haynau, By Baron Schönhals, Gratz* 1852; *I.L.N. xv,* 373 (1849) portrait, *xvii,* 221 (1850) attack on; *Times* 5, 6, 11, 12, 16, 17, 18, 19, 23, 25, 27 *Sep. 1850.*

HAYNES, FREEMAN OLIVER *(eld. son of Henry Haynes, captain R.N.) b.* Clifton 1818; ed. at Paris and Caius coll. Cam., fellow, 15 wrangler 1840, B.A. 1840, M.A. 1843; barrister L.I. 6 May 1845; published *Outlines of equity.* Cambridge 1858, 5 *ed.* 1880. and other books. *d.* Donhead lodge, Wimbledon, Surrey 12 July 1880.

HAYNES, JOHN BISHOP. *b.* 1803; ed. at Guy's hospital; L.S.A. 1825, M.R.C.S. 1826, F.R.C.S. 1852; demonstrator of anatomy at Guy's; in practice at Whitchurch, Hants., settled at Evesham 1832, mayor of Evesham 1846; founder with Sir C. Hastings of Provincial medical association at Worcester 1832; author of *How to supply the agricultural labourer with good beer at a low price. Evesham* 1865. *d.* Battleton lodge, Evesham 17 Feb. 1873.

HAYNES, JOSEPH. *b.* Ireland 1788; an editor of *Morning Herald;* wrote two tragedies *Conscience* and *Mary Stuart* 1840. *d.* Norwood, Surrey 24 Jany. 1851 aged 63. *I.L.N. 22 Feb. 1851 p. 166.*

HAYNES, MATTHEW PRIESTMAN. b. Husband's Bosworth, Leicestershire; ed. St. Mary's coll. Oscott; teacher at St. Peter's R.C. sch. Birmingham; political orator in reform movement; a journalist; editor of *Mayo Telegraph* 1831; started *Penny Catholic Mag.* London 7 Sep. 1839 which came to an end in 1840; author of *An interesting account of the teetotal galas at Dyrham park* 1840; *The position of the Jews as affected by the return of Baron Leopold de Rothschild* 1847. *dead. Gillow's English Catholics, iii,* 231–2 (1887).

HAYNES, ROBERT *(eld. son of Richard Haynes of Barbadoes).* b. Barbadoes 1769; in militia during threatened French invasion 1805; received thanks of council and assembly of Barbadoes for his military services on occasion of Negro insurrection 1816; had local rank of lieut.-general; speaker of Barbadoes House of assembly 182–. *d.* Reading 18 April 1851 in 82 year.

HAYTER, SIR GEORGE *(son of Charles Hayter, miniature painter 1761–1835).* b. St. James' st. London 17 Dec. 1792; ed. at Royal academy; midshipman R.N. 1808; exhibited 48 pictures at R.A., 40 at B.I. and 1 at Suffolk st. 1809–59; painter of miniatures and portraits to Princess Charlotte and Prince Leopold 1815; received 200 guineas from British institution for his picture The Prophet Ezra 1815; studied in Rome 1816–19, in Paris 1826–31; member of academies of Parma, Florence, Bologna and Venice 1826; portrait and historical painter to Victoria 1837, and principal painter in ordinary 12 June 1841; knighted at St. James' palace 1 June 1842; some of his paintings were The duke of Wellington standing by his horse Copenhagen 1821; The trial of queen Caroline 1823; The trial of lord William Russell 1825; The queen on the throne in the house of lords 1838; The christening of the prince of Wales 1859; author of *An essay on colours,* in App. to *Hortus Ericœus Woburnensis* 1825. *d.* 238 Marylebone road, London 18 Jany. 1871. *Redgrave's Dict. of Artists* (1878) *p.* 205; *Art Journal, March* 1871 *p.* 79; *I.L.N. lviii,* 91 (1871); *Times* 23 *Jany.* 1871 *p.* 9.

HAYTER, SIR WILLIAM GOODENOUGH, 1 Baronet *(son of John Hayter of Winterbourne Stoke).* b. Winterbourne Stoke 28 Jany. 1792; ed. at Winchester and Trin. coll. Ox., B.A. 1814; barrister L.I. 23 Nov. 1819, bencher 15 April 1839, treasurer 1853; Q.C. 21 Feb. 1839, retired from practice 1839; M.P. for Wells 24 July 1837 to July 1865; judge advocate general 30 Dec. 1847 to 30 May 1849; P.C. 11 Feb. 1848; financial sec. to

HAYTER, SIR W. G. *(Con.)*
treasury 22 May 1849 to July 1850; parliamentary and patronage sec. July 1850 to March 1852 and Dec. 1852 to March 1858; cr. baronet 19 April 1858; a service of plate presented to him at Willis's rooms by lord Palmerston and 365 members of house of commons in remembrance of his services as Liberal "whip" 27 Feb. 1861; *found drowned* in a lake in grounds of South hill park, Easthampstead, Berkshire 26 Dec. 1878. *I.L.N. xvii,* 64 (1850), *portrait.*

HAYTHORNE, SIR EDMUND *(son of John Haythorne of Hill house, Gloucester).* b. Bristol 28 May 1818; ed. at Sandhurst; ensign 98 foot 12 May 1837, lieut. col. 12 May 1854, lieut. col. 1 foot 6 June 1855 to 26 June 1866 when placed on h.p.; brigadier general Chusan field force 1843, in Punjaub campaign 1848–9; served in the Crimea 1855; A.G. of British forces in Bengal 1860–65; K.C.B. 24 May 1873; col. 55 foot 11 March 1878; col. 37 foot 3 Feb. 1879 to death; general 15 March 1879. *d.* Silchester house near Reading 18 Oct. 1888. *I.L.N. 10 Nov.* 1888 *pp.* 546, 547, *portrait.*

HAYWARD, ABRAHAM (1 *son of Joseph Hayward of Wilton near Salisbury, author of The science of horticulture, d.* 1844). b. Kingsbury square, Wilton 22 Nov. 1801; ed. Tiverton gram. sch. 1811–17; admitted a solicitor 29 Oct. 1824; barrister I.T. 15 June 1832; founded *Law Magazine* 1828, editor 1828–44; contributed to *Edinburgh Rev.* 1844, *Quarterly Rev.* 1869, *Fraser,* etc.; Q.C. 22 Feb. 1845, but Inner Temple refused to elect him a bencher; a writer on the *Morning Chronicle* 1848, *Saturday Rev.* 1855, *Times* 1858; sec. poor law board Dec. 1854; a good and original talker and a social raconteur; drawn as Venom Tuft in *Ten thousand a year* 1841; author of *The statutes founded on the common law reports* 1832; *Faust, a dramatic poem, translated* 1833, 3 ed. 1855; *The art of dining* [*By A.H.*] 1852, 3 ed. 1883; *Lord Chesterfield and George Selwyn* 1854; *Biographical and critical essays* 5 vols. 1858–74; *Short rules for modern whist* [*By A.H.*] 1878; *Sketches of eminent statesmen and writers* 2 vols. 1880. *d.* 8 St. James st. 2 Feb. 1884. *bur.* Highgate cemet. 6 Feb. *Selections from Correspondence of A. Hayward* 2 vols. 1886; *H. R. F. Bourne's English newspapers ii,* 153, 246, 248, 400 (1887); *Vanity Fair* 27 *Nov.* 1875 *p.* 301, *portrait; Times* 4 *Feb.* 1884 *pp.* 8, 9; *I.L.N. lxxxiv,* 157 (1884), *portrait.*

HAYWARD, DANIEL. b. Mitcham, Surrey 25 Aug. 1808; gardener; played with Mitcham eleven from 1825 ; resided at Cambridge and was in the town eleven ; a showy and effective batsman and a fast field ; his first match at Lord's was Marylebone v. Cambridge 2, 3 July 1832 ; with M.C.C. 1841 ; one of Surrey eleven 1846. *d.* Cambridge 29 May 1852. *Lillywhite's Cricket scores ii,* 180 (1862) ; *Denison's Cricket* (1846), 32.

HAYWARD, HENRY. *b.* Broseley, Shropshire 1814 ; one of most remarkable violinists of the century ; pupil of Spagnoletti, but an accurate reproducer of Paganini's performances and known as the English Paganini ; first appeared Hanover sq. rooms, London 19 June 1839 ; played several times at Windsor Castle ; teacher and music seller at Wolverhampton 1839 to death ; published *Pizzicato rondo for the violin* 1850 ; *Hayward's Violin solos with pianoforte accompaniment 7 numbers* 1885 and other pieces. *d.* 12 Queen st. Wolverhampton 12 Nov. 1884. *The Musical Directory* (1886), *p. xix.*

HAYWARD, THOMAS (2 *son of Daniel Hayward* 1808–52). *b.* Chatteris near March, Cambs. 21 March 1835 ; gardener ; professional cricketer at Richmond, Yorkshire 1853, 1855 and 1856, at Newport, Pagnell 1854, at Bishop's Auckland 1857 and 1858 ; his first match at Lord's, United England eleven v. All England eleven 6, 7 June 1859 ; the best all-round cricketer in England ; made 200 in one innings at Cambridge 12 May 1859 ; one of the English eleven in America and Canada 1859, and in Australia 1864 ; had 2 benefits 21 May and 1 June 1868 ; keeper of All England ale stores, Cambridge 1875. *d.* Clarendon st. Cambridge 21 July 1876. *Lillywhite's Cricket scores vi,* 204 (1876), *vii, p. xiii* (1877) ; *Illust. Sporting News* (1862) 113, *portrait.* W. G. Grace's *Cricket* (1891) 107, *portrait,* 321.

HAZLETON, VICTOR ISAAC. Landlord of Duke's Arms and lessee of Bower saloon or theatre, Stangate, 43 Lambeth Upper Marsh, London 1851–75. *d.* London 14 June 1890.

HAZLEWOOD, COLIN HENRY. *b.* 1823 ; low comedian on Lincoln, York and Western circuits ; played at Surrey theatre 1851 ; at City of London theatre 10 years ; wrote for the weekly penny publications ; wrote a great number of dramas, farces and burlesques chiefly for the Britannia and Pavilion theatres for which he was paid at the rate of about 50s. an act ; thirty of his pieces printed in Lacy's Acting edition 1853–9. *d.* 44 Huntingdon st. Haggerston, London 31 May 1875. *Era Almanack* 1869 *pp.* 18, 45.

HEAD, CHARLES. In service of telegraph co. 1845 ; the largest bookmaker in the ring ; made £12,000 when Lozenge won the Cambridgeshire 1867 ; made the largest book on St. Leger of 1870 ; lost £10,000 when Glenlivat won Chester cup 1871 ; proprietor of Philharmonic theatre, Islington 1880, name changed to New Grand theatre 1882, lessee to 1885. *d.* 97b Regent st. London 26 May 1889. *Sporting Times* 24 Oct. 1874 *p.* 84, *portrait.*

HEAD, SIR EDMUND WALKER, 8 Baronet *(only son of Rev. Sir John Head, 7 baronet* 1773–1838). *b.* Wiarton place near Maidstone 16 Feb. 1805 ; ed. at Winchester and Oriel coll. Ox. ; B.A. 1827, M.A. 1830, D.C.L. 1862 ; fellow of Merton coll. 1830–37 ; assistant poor law comr. 1836, poor law comr. 1841–47 ; lieut. governor of New Brunswick 26 Oct. 1847 to Sep. 1854 ; governor general of Canada 19 Sep. 1854 to Oct. 1861 ; P.C. 27 Aug. 1857 ; K.C.B. 11 Dec. 1860 ; civil service comr. 29 April 1862 ; chairman of Hudson's Bay co. 1862 to death ; F.R.S. April 1863 ; author of *A Handbook of Spanish and French schools of painting* 1848 ; *Shall and Will or two chapters on auxiliary verbs* 1856, *new ed.* 1858 ; *Ballads and other poems* 1868 and other books. *d.* 29 Eaton sq. London 28 Jany. 1868. *Proc. of Royal Soc. xvi,* 71–8 (1868) ; *Appleton's Cyclop. of American Biog. iii,* 151 (1887), *portrait.*

HEAD, SIR FRANCIS BOND, 1 Baronet (4 *son of James Roper Head of the Hermitage near Rochester, d.* 1814). *b.* the Hermitage 1 Jany. 1793 ; 1 lieut. R.E. 13 March 1811 ; captain royal staff corps 1827 to 23 Dec. 1828 when placed on h.p., sold out 1838 ; lieut. governor of Canada, Nov. 1835 to Jany. 1838 ; K.C.H. 27 Nov. 1835 ; cr. baronet 14 July 1838 ; granted civil list pension of £100, 6 Oct. 1853 ; P.C. 20 Dec. 1867 ; author of *Bubbles from the Brunnen of Nassau* 1834, 7 ed. 1866 ; *A faggot of French sticks* 2 vols. 1851, 3 ed. 1855 ; *Descriptive essays contributed to the Quarterly Review* 2 vols. 1857 and many other books. *d.* Duppa's hall, Croydon 20 July 1875. *The speeches of Sir F. B. Head and a biographical sketch. Toronto* (1836) 15–20 ; *I.L.N. lxvii,* 109, 119 (1875), *portrait ; Graphic, xi,* 123 (1875), *portrait.*

HEAD, SIR GEORGE *(brother of the preceding). b.* the Hermitage near Rochester 1782 ; ed. at the Charterhouse ; captain West Kent militia 1808 ; a commissariat clerk 1809 ; served in the Peninsula 1809–14 ; asst. commissary general 25 Dec. 1814, placed on half pay 1823 ; deputy knight marshal at coronation of

HEAD, SIR G. *(Con.)*

William iv. 1831 ; knighted at St. James's palace 12 Oct. 1831 ; deputy knight marshal to Queen Victoria ; published *Forest scenery and incidents in the wilds of North America* 1829, 2 ed. 1838 ; *A home tour through the manufacturing districts of England in the summer of 1835*, 2 ed. 2 vols. 1840 ; *A home tour through various parts of the United Kingdom* 1832 ; *Rome, a tour of many days* 3 vols. 1849. *d.* Cockspur st. London 2 May 1855 aged 73. *Sir G. Head's Memoirs of an assistant commissary general* (1832).

HEAD, REV. HENRY ERSKINE *(brother of the preceding)*. *b.* 9 Jany. 1797 ; ed. at St. Mary hall, Ox., B.A. 1825, M.A. 1828 ; R. of Feniton, Devon 1838 to death ; had controversies with the bishops of Exeter and London and printed many books on these matters 1838–41 ; author of *Observations on early rising and early prayer* 1828 ; *Sermons on spiritual comfort and assurance* 1832 ; *Sermons on the first principles of the oracles of God* 1840 ; *Dialogues on the Apocalypse* 1841. *d.* Feniton 16 May 1860.

HEAD, JOHN *(eld. son of Jeremiah Head of Ipswich)*. *b.* Ipswich 8 Feb. 1832 ; erected pumping engines and pumps to supply city of Warsaw with water from the Vistula 1853 ; manager of works of Evans, Lilpop and Ran of Warsaw, engineers ; when on outbreak of war in 1854 all Englishmen were ordered to leave Russia, an exception was made in his favour ; partner of Messrs. Ransome at Ipswich 1857 to death ; author of *A few notes on the portable steam engine* 1877. *d.* Ipswich 19 May 1881. *Min. of proc. of Instit. of C.E. lxvii*, 397–99 (1882).

HEAD, WILLIAM. Huntsman to the Cheshire hounds to 1831 and the Donnington hounds from 1831 ; on retiring lived at Leicester and then at Kegworth, Leicestershire. *d.* Kegworth 19 Nov. 1865 in 85 year. *Sporting Review, Dec. 1865 pp.* 401–2.

HEADFORT, THOMAS TAYLOUR, 2 Marquis of *(elder son of 1 Marquis of Headfort 1757– 1829)*. *b.* 4 May 1787 ; ed. at Trin. coll. Cam., M.A. 1811 ; lord lieut. of Cavan 1831 to death ; col. of Meath militia 1831 to death ; cr. Baron Kenlis of Kenlis, co. Meath in peerage of U.K. 10 Sep. 1831 ; P.C. Ireland 1835 ; lord in waiting to the Queen 1837–41 ; K.P. 15 April 1839. *d.* Headfort house, Kells, co. Meath 6 Dec. 1870.

HEADLAM, EDWARD *(3 son of the succeeding)*. *b.* 1824 ; ed. at Durham gr. sch. and St. John's coll. Cam., fellow, 12th wrangler 1847, B.A. 1847, M.A. 1850 ; barrister I.T. 30 April

HEADLAM, E. *(Con.)*

1856 ; civil service comr. 1855 ; director of examinations 1876 to death. *d.* 24 Norfolk sq. Hyde park, London 26 Oct. 1882.

HEADLAM, VEN. JOHN *(son of Thomas Emerson Headlam of Gateshead)*. Matric. from Lincoln coll. Ox. 1 April 1786 aged 16, B.A. 1790, M.A. 1792 ; R. of Wycliffe, Yorkshire 1793 to death ; archdeacon of Richmond 30 Dec. 1826 to death ; chancellor of Ripon 1846 to death ; author of *Letters to the Rt. Hon. Robert Peel on prison labour* 2 vols. 1823–4 ; *Observations on church rates, tithes and church reform, Richmond* 1838, and of charges and single sermons. *d.* Wycliffe, Yorkshire 4 May 1854 aged 85.

HEADLAM, THOMAS EMERSON *(eld. son of preceding)*. *b.* Wycliffe rectory, Yorkshire 25 June 1813 ; ed. at Shrewsbury and Trin. coll. Cam., 16 wr. 1836, B.A. 1836, M.A. 1839 ; barrister I.T. 3 May 1839, bencher 1851, reader 1866, treasurer 1867 ; M.P. for Newcastle-on-Tyne 1847–74 ; carried through parliament the Trustee act 1850 ; Q.C. 1851 ; chancellor of diocese of Ripon May 1854, of Durham 1854 ; judge advocate general June 1859 to July 1866 ; P.C. 18 June 1859 ; F.R.G.S. ; edited *The practice of the high court of chancery by E. R. Daniell*, 2 ed. 1845, 3 ed. 1857 ; *Pleadings and practice of the high court of chancery by E. R. Daniell*, 2 ed. 1851 ; *A supplement to Daniell's Chancery practice* 1851 ; author of *The Trustees' Act* 1850, 3 ed. 1855. *d.* Calais 3 Dec. 1875. *I.L.N. lxvii*, 590, 629 (1875), *portrait.*

HEADLAND, EDWARD. *b.* Tonbridge 1803 ; ed. at St. George's hospital ; studied anatomy under Joshua Brookes ; L.S.A. 1823, M.R.C.S. 1848 ; in practice at Featherstone buildings, Holborn, at Guilford st. and at 6 Upper Portland place ; one of the first to claim payment for his services and not for physic ; the leading general practitioner of his time ; fellow and then president of Medical soc. of London where he took important part in the debates. *d.* 6 Upper Portland place, London 8 Dec. 1869. *J. F. Clarke's Autobiographical Recollections* (1874), 393–8.

HEADLAND, REV. EDWARD *(younger son of Edward Headland of Portland place, London)*. *b.* 1831 ; ed. at Caius coll. Cam., 14 wrangler 1855, B.A. 1855, M.A. 1859, fellow of his coll. ; C. of St. Mary's, Bury St. Edmunds 1855–57 ; C. of St. Marylebone church, London 1857–61 ; R. of Bincombe with Broadwey, Dorset 1861 ; author of *The happy sufferer. A narrative* 1860 ; *The epistles to the Thessalonians,*

HEADLAND, REV. E. (Con.)

Introduction by E. Headland 1863; *The truth and office of the Christian ministry* 1868. *d.* 6 Cavendish crescent, Bath 8 July 1876 aged 45.

HEADLAND, THOMAS HUGHES. Accompanied C. Dickens on his first American tour as secretary 1842; silversmith 13 Great Sutton st. Clerkenwell, London 1842–59; kept Sussex hotel at Eastbourne about 1869–72. *d.* Merton lodge, 17 Bolton road, Eastbourne 2 Jany. 1888 aged 82. *Forster's C. Dickens i, 278* (1872); *Eastbourne Chronicle 7 Jany. 1888 pp.* 4, 5.

HEADLEY, WINN CHARLES ALLANSON, 3 Baron. *b.* 25 June 1810; succeeded his uncle 1840; a representative peer for Ireland 26 Sep. 1868 to death. *d.* Ennismore gardens, Kensington, London 30 July 1877.

HEALD, HENRY GEORGE. *b.* 1822; well known to Sunday school teachers in all parts of the world; secretary of Church of England Sunday school institute 1855–72; lecturer at Sunday schools 1872 to death. *d.* 90 Albert road, Peckham Rye, Surrey 25 Nov. 1881 aged 59. *bur.* Brompton cemetery 30 Nov.

HEALD, JAMES (2 son of James Heald, merchant). *b.* Portwood near Stockport 1 March 1796; ed. Rochdale; in his father's business at Brinnington and Disley, Cheshire, became a partner and made a fortune; resided at Parr's Wood near Didsbury, Manchester 1825 to death; M.P. Stockport 1847–52; treasurer Wesleyan missionary soc., the most prominent layman in the connection and a preacher; founded and chiefly maintained Stockport infirmary. *d.* Parr's Wood 26 Oct. 1873. *bur.* Chapel-en-le-Frith, Derbyshire, personalty sworn under £350,000, 3 Jany. 1874. *Manchester Examiner 29 Oct. 1873 p.* 8.

HEALE, REV. EDMUND MARKHAM (2 *son of Markham Heale of Calne, Wilts.*) *b.* 12 May 1825; ed. at Merchant Taylors' sch. and Queen's coll. Ox., Boden Sanskrit scholar 1844, B.A. 1847, M.A. 1850; professor of classics in royal military coll. Sandhurst, June 1851 to 1859; C. of Woolavington, Somerset 1859–60; R. of Yelling near Huntingdon 1860 to death; author of *Manual of Geography* 1853, 3 *ed.* 1863. *d.* Yelling rectory 7 Dec. 1874.

HEALE, JAMES NEWTON. *b.* 1810; L.S.A. 1834; M.R.C.S. 1835, F.R.C.S. 1845, M.R.C.P. 1846; M.B. London 1850, M.D. 1850; phys. royal free hospital, London; phys. Hants. county hospital; author of *Treatise on vital causes* 1859; *A treatise on the physiological anatomy of the lungs* 1862. *d.* Hollington lodge near St. Leonards-on-Sea 16 April 1891.

HEALES, RICHARD (*son of an ironmonger*). *b.* London; apprentice to a coachmaker; went to Victoria, Australia 1842; a day labourer, became proprietor of his master's business; councillor for Gipps ward, Melbourne 1849; member of legislative assembly for East Bourke 1857 to death; chief sec. 26 Nov. 1860 to 14 Nov. 1861; president of board of lands and works and comr. of crown lands 27 June 1863 to death. *d.* Melbourne 19 June 1864.

HEAPHY, CHARLES (*son of Thomas Heaphy water colour painter* 1775–1835). *b.* 1818; draughtsman to New Zealand co. 1839, exploring in N.Z. 1839, road making 1843; draughtsman to N.Z. government Aug. 1848; commissioner Coromandel gold fields 1852; surveyor for government of N.Z. 1854, chief surveyor 1864; was in third Maori war, wounded 11 Feb. 1864, major in militia 11 Feb. 1864, V.C. 8 Feb. 1867; member N.Z. house of representatives 1867–70, comr. of government insurance and judge of native land courts 1878, retired June 1881; author of *Narrative of a residence in various parts of New Zealand* 1842. *d.* Brisbane 3 Aug. 1881 aged 63. *O'Byrne's Victoria Cross* (1880) 174.

HEAPHY, THOMAS (*brother of the preceding*). *b.* St. John's Wood, London 2 April 1813; assumed additional christian name of Frank, but dropped it before 1850; exhibited 51 pictures at R.A., 8 at B.I. and 36 at Suffolk st. 1831–74; member soc. of British Artists to 1867; among his best known paintings are Lord Burleigh showing his bride her new home 1865 and Lizzie Farren after Countess of Derby waiting at the prison bars with her father's breakfast 1872; visited Rome several times to investigate origin of likeness of Christ; author of *The likeness of Christ, an enquiry into the verisimilitude of the received likeness of our Blessed Lord* 1880, 2 *ed.* 1886; *A wonderful ghost story, Mr. Heaphy's own narrative* 1882. *d.* 46 Sussex st. Pimlico, London 7 Aug. 1873. *Bryan's Dict. of Painters, i, 636* (1886).

HEARD, JACOB or JAMES. *b.* 1799; went to Russia where he introduced the Lancaster schools; wrote a large number of Russian school books and several very popular novels; author of *A practical grammar of the Russian language.* St. Petersburg 1827; *Key to the themes contained in Heard's Russian grammar.* St. Petersburg 1827; *Phraseology of the Russian language.* St. Petersburg 1840; *An edition of Oliver Goldsmith's Vicar of Wakefield in Russian* 1846. *d.* 28 Sep. 1875.

HEARD, JOHN ISAAC. *b.* Kinsale, co. Cork 1787; ed. at Peterhouse coll. Cam., B.A. 1808; sheriff of Cork 1849; M.P. for Kinsale 1852 to 1859. *d.* Kinsale 1 Sep. 1862.

HEARDER, JONATHAN NASH *(eld. son of Jonathan Hearder).* *b.* Plymouth 24 Dec. 1809; practical chemist and electrician at Plymouth; devised improvements with induction coil and application of electricity to medical purposes; constructed an electro-dynamic coil 1846; patented improvements in submarine telegraph cables 1858; a popular lecturer in West of England; electrician to South Devon hospital; D.Sc., Ph.D., F.C.S.; became blind in 1831 but continued his researches in electricity; author of *Guide to the fishing of Plymouth and neighbourhood* 18—. *d.* 13 Princess sq. Plymouth 16 July 1876. *Boase and Courtney's Bibl. Cornub.* 225, 1225.

HEARN, PATRICK. Owner of 100 cabs, 20 omnibuses and 1000 barrows; known as the Wheel King of London. *d.* 20 Feb. 1889 aged 47.

HEARN, WILLIAM EDWARD *(son of Rev. W. E. Hearn, vicar of Killague).* *b.* Belturbet, co. Cavan 22 April 1826; ed. at Enniskillen and Trin. coll. Dublin, scholar 1845, B.A. 1847, LL.B., LL.D. and M.A. 1863; professor of Greek, Queen's coll. Galway 1849–54; first prof. of modern history, Melbourne univ. 1854–73, dean of the faculty of law 1873, chancellor May to Oct. 1886; called to the Irish bar 1853 and to bar of Victoria 1860; Q.C. 1886; member of legislative council for Central province 1878, introduced bills for the codification of the laws; author of *The Cassell prize essay on the condition of Ireland* 1851; *The government of England, its structure and its developement* 1867, 2 ed. 1887; *The Aryan household, its structure and its developement* 1879; *The theory of legal duties and rights* 1885. *d.* Melbourne 23 April 1888. *Men of the Time. Victoria* 1878 *p.* 86; *Australasian* 28 *April* 1888.

HEARNE, REV. DANIEL. *b.* Ireland; ed. at Maynooth; priest of St. Patrick's chapel, Manchester 1832, removed by Dr. Brown bishop of Liverpool 1846, his removal led to a series of brawls in the church 1846; brought an action for libel against Rev. Hugh Stowell 1840; stabbed in his arm and wrist while walking in the Corso, Rome, Aug. 1848; took charge of the mission at Bootle near Liverpool from 25 March 1849 to 5 Oct. 1851; went to U.S. America 1851; fell from the scaffolding of a church and was *killed* U.S. America about

HEARNE, REV. D. *(Con.)*
1852. *Gillow's English Catholics,* iii, 232–8 (1888); *Adolphus and Ellis Reports, xii,* 719–33 (1842).

HEARSEY, SIR JOHN BENNETT. *b.* 1793; entered Bengal army 14 Sep. 1808, commanded Presidency division 11 Aug. 1856 to 12 April 1861; L.G. 15 June 1862; col. 21 hussars 30 Sep. 1862 to death; C.B. 9 June 1849, K.C.B. 4 July 1857 for his services during Sepoy mutiny. *d.* Boulogne, France 23 Oct. 1865.

HEATH, CAROLINE *(dau. of Francis Heath).* *b.* July 1835; ed. at Miss Richardson's school, Blackheath; made her début at Princess's theatre, London 18 Sep. 1852 as Stella in Boucicault's *The Prima Donna;* played Ophelia at same house Jany. 1858, Cordelia 17 April 1858; played Juliet at Sadler's Wells 16 Sep. 1859 and Fiordelisa in Tom Taylor's *The Fool's Revenge,* Oct 1859; played The Queen of Spain in *Ruy Blas* at Princess's 27 Oct. 1860; acted in the provinces; played Jane Shore in W. G. Wills' drama *Jane Shore* at Princess's, Oct. 1876 to March 1877, in the provinces March to Dec. 1877 and at Princess's again; played Clotilde in *Fernande* at Court theatre 20 Sep. 1879; private reader to the Queen. *(m.* 31 July 1866 William Henry Barrett known as Wilson Barrett, actor). *d.* Worthing 26 July 1887. *Pascoe's Dramatic List,* 2 ed. (1880) 170–3; *I.L.N. xxxv,* 571, 584 (1859), *portrait, lxix,* 524 (1876); *Illust. Sport. and Dr. News, vi,* 59, 68–9, 84 (1876), *portrait; Theatre, iii,* 189 (1879), *portrait, ii,* 11 (1883); *The Players, i,* 1 (1860), *portrait.*

HEATH, CHRISTOPHER *(son of John Heath, dentist).* *b.* London 26 March 1802; ed. at St. Paul's sch. 1813–7; a dentist in London to 1835; angel or minister of the Irvingite or catholic apostolic ch. 14 Newman st. London 1835, removed to a new ch. in Gordon sq. 1853 where he was the angel to his death; latterly he was in receipt of £1000 a year; visited the branch churches on the continent. *d.* 28 Gordon sq. London 1 Nov. 1876. *Miller's Irvingism, i,* 152, 268, 318 (1878).

HEATH, REV. DUNBAR ISIDORE. *b.* 1816; ed. at Trin. coll. Cam., fellow 1840–7; 5 wrangler 1838, B.A. 1838, M.A. 1841; V. of Brading, Isle of Wight, Dec. 1846 to 6 June 1862 when deprived of his benefice by judicial committee of privy council for expressions derogatory to the 39 articles used in his sermons 1859; edited *Journal of Anthropology* 1870; author of *A brief account of the Scottish and Italian missions to the Anglo-Saxons* 1845; *The future human Kingdom of Christ, or man's heaven to be* this earth 2 vols. 1852–3; *Sermons on important subjects* 1860 and other books. *d.* Esher, Surrey 27 May 1888 aged 72. *A defence of my professional character, By D. I. Heath* [1862].

HEATH, GEORGE (1 son of a farmer). *b.* Gratton in Horton parish, Staffs. 9 March 1844; farm labourer, an apprentice to a carpenter to 1864; became consumptive 1864; known as the Moorland poet; author of *Preludes* 1865, *Second ed. called Simple poems* 1866; *Heart strains* 1866; *The poems of George Heath* (1870), *portrait; The poems of G. Heath* (1880), *portrait.* *d.* Gratton 5 May 1869. *Good Words* 1871 *pp.* 170–77, *portrait.*

HEATH, GEORGE CRAUFURD. Ed. at Eton and King's coll. Cam., B.A. 1807, M.A. 1810, fellow of King's coll. 1807 to death; F.R.S. *d.* 18 July 1860.

HEATH, GEORGE THOMAS. *b.* 1778; barrister I.T. 13 Nov. 1807; serjeant at law 22 Nov. 1830, received patent of precedence 1834; deputy judge of county court of Middlesex. *d.* 34 Montagu place, Russell sq. London 21 Jany. 1852.

HEATH, JOHN BENJAMIN (son of John Heath of Genoa, merchant). *b.* Genoa 6 June 1790; ed. at Harrow 1798–1806; fag to Lord Byron; consul general for Kingdom of Sardinia 10 May 1817–61, for Kingdom of Italy 1861 to death; a merchant and foreign banker in London to death; a director of Bank of England 1823–72, deputy governor 1843–4, governor 1846–7; master of Grocers company 1829; F.S.A. 12 Jany. 1832; F.R.S. 2 Feb. 1843; baron Heath in the Kingdom of Italy 26 May 1867; author of *Some account of the Company of Grocers* 1829, 2 ed. 1854. *d.* 66 Russell sq. London 16 Jany. 1879, personalty sworn under £250,000, 8 March 1879. *Proc. of Royal Soc. xxix,* 6 (1879); *Proc. of Soc. of Antiq. viii,* 101 (1881).

HEATH, REV. RICHARD FORD (only son of Richard Ford Heath of Uxbridge, Middlesex). *b.* 1833; matric. at Univ. of London 1850, B.A. 1853; matric. at Univ. of Oxford 17 Feb. 1873, B.A. 1876, M.A. 1879; C. of St. Philip and St. James, Oxford 1875–8; head master of Bideford gr. sch. 1879–80; V. of Bishopswood, Staffs. 1880 to death; author of *Albrecht Dürer and Titian* 2 vols. 1879 in *Illustrated biographies of Great Artists.* *d.* Bideford 11 March 1888 aged 55.

HEATH, THOMAS. *b.* Sutton in Ashfield, Notts. 10 Dec. 1808; played with the Nottingham eleven 1828–45; could throw a ball 107

yards; a good cover point and middle wicket; lacemaker, emigrated to France where he remained 1839–44; resided at Nottingham 1844 to death. *d.* while on a visit to Sutton 16 Oct. 1872. *bur.* Nottingham. *Lillywhite's Cricket Scores, ii,* 66 (1862), v, *p. xiv* (1876).

HEATHCOAT, JOHN (son of Francis Heathcoat of Long Whatton, Leics., farmer). *b.* Duffield near Derby 7 Aug. 1783; a setter up of hosiery and warp frames at Nottingham, at Hathern 1803, at Loughborough 1805; inventor of lace making machinery by patenting a bobbin net machine 1809 which he called Old Loughborough; partner with Charles Lacy 1809–16, partner with John Boden at Tiverton 1816–21; retired from business 1843; M.P. for Tiverton 12 Dec. 1832 to 23 April 1859; built British schools at Tiverton, opened 1843. *d.* Bollam house, Tiverton 18 Jany. 1861. *W. Felkin's History of Hosiery* (1867) 180–270, *portrait; Bevan's British manufacturing industries, Hosiery, By W. Felkin* (1877) 56–73; *Mozley's Reminiscences, i,* 239–42 (1885).

HEATHCOTE, ARTHUR (son of Sir Gilbert Heathcote 1773–1851). *b.* 22 June 1829; had private races in Durdans park; a perpetual steward of Epsom races to which he contributed an annual plate; master Surrey stag hounds to death. *d.* Durdans, Epsom 18 March 1869. *Sporting Rev. Feb. 1863 p.* 165, *portrait; Sporting Gazette 20 March 1869 p.* 199.

HEATHCOTE, EDMUND (3 son of Rev. Samuel Heathcote of Red house, Hursley, d. 27 Nov. 1846 aged 73). *b.* 1814; entered navy June 1827, captain 15 Dec. 1852; commander in chief at Queenstown 20 May 1871 to 1 Jany. 1874; V.A. 1 Jany. 1874, retired 30 Jany. 1879; retired admiral 15 June 1879. *d.* Fritham lodge, New Forest 29 Oct. 1881.

HEATHCOTE, SIR GILBERT, 4 Baronet (eld. son of Sir Gilbert Heathcote 3 baronet). *b.* Oct. 1773; succeeded 4 Dec. 1785; M.P. for Lincolnshire 1796–1807, for Rutland 1812–1841; won the Derby with Amato 1838. *d.* Durdans, Epsom 27 March 1851. *W. Day's Reminiscences* 2 ed. (1886) 155; *I.L.N. xviii,* 273 (1851); *Thoughts of a Lincolnshire freeholder. With a dialogue between Sir G. Heathcote and a Lincolnshire freeholder, 3 ed.* 1796.

HEATHCOTE, SIR HENRY (4 son of Sir William Heathcote, 3 bart., of Hursley park, Hants., M.P. 1746–1819). *b.* 20 Jany. 1777; entered navy 3 July 1790, captain 5 Feb. 1798; knighted 20 July 1819 at request of Sir Gore Ouseley and Mirza Abdul Hassan the Persian ambassador whom he conveyed to Persia 1808;

HEATHCOTE, SIR H. *(Con.)*

R.A. 27 May 1825, V.A. 10 Jany. 1837, admiral on h.p. 9 Nov. 1846; awarded a service pension 1 July 1851; published *Treatise on stay-sails, and the superiority of stay-sails invented by Sir H. Heathcote* 1824. *d.* Ingouville near Havre 16 Aug. 1851.

HEATHCOTE, SIR WILLIAM, 5 Baronet *(only son of Rev. Wm. Heathcote 1772–1802, preb. of Winchester).* *b.* Worting, Hants. 17 May 1801; ed. at Winchester and Oriel coll. Ox., B.A. 1821, B.C.L. 1824, D.C.L. 1830; fellow of All Souls coll. 1822–5, hon. fellow 1858; succeeded 22 Feb. 1825; M.P. for Hants. 1826–32, for North Hants. 1837–49 and for Oxford Univ. 1854–68; chairman of Hants. quarter sessions; P.C. 9 Aug. 1870. *d.* Hursley park near Winchester 18 Aug. 1881.

HEATHCOTE, REV. WILLIAM BEADON (3 *son of Rev. Gilbert Heathcote of Winchester).* bapt. at St. Thomas, Winchester 14 Jany. 1813; ed. at Winchester and New coll. Ox., fellow 1832–53; B.C.L. 1839, M.A. 1859; tutor and dean of canon law 1839, sub-warden 1840, bursar 1845, dean of civil law 1846; warden of Radley; precentor of Salisbury cath. 1854 to death; preb. of Salisbury cath. 1856 to death; V. of Sturminster Marshall 1858–62; R. of Compton Bassett 1862 to death; author of *The psalter with the Gregorian tones, By W. B. H.* 1845; *Harmonized Gregorian tones for the Psalter* 1849. *d.* London 21 Aug. 1862.

HEATHER, JOHN FRY. Mathematical master at royal military academy, Woolwich many years; lecturer at Royal Artillery Institute; author of *A treatise of mathematical instruments* 1849, 7 ed. 1864, new ed. 3 vols. 1871; *The elements of mathematical drawing* 1872 and other works. *d.* Stroud-green road, Finsbury park, London 13 Nov. 1886.

HEATHERINGTON, ALEXANDER. Opened in 1867 at Halifax, Nova Scotia, the International Mining agency; associated with the Canadian mines bureau 30 Moorgate st. London; started the *Mining Gazette*, No. 1 Halifax 10 Jany. 1868 and was the editor; F.G.S.; author of *The gold yield of Nova Scotia* 1860–9, continued as *The mining industries of Nova Scotia* 1870–4; *A practical guide for persons interested in gold fields of Nova Scotia* 1868. *d.* Toronto, Canada 8 March 1878. *Geological Mag. v*, 336 (1878).

HEATHORN, CATHERINE *(dau. of Robert Heathorn, brewer, Maidstone).* bapt. All Saints' ch. Maidstone 17 April 1783. *d.* at res. of her grand niece Mrs. A. E. Rowcroft 2 Craven place, Maidstone 2 Feb. 1888 aged nearly 105 years. *I.L.N.* 27 *Oct.* 1883 *p.* 416, *portrait*.

HEATON, CLEMENT *(son of Rev. James Heaton, wesleyan minister, d. 1862).* *b.* Bradford, Wilts. 1824; glass painter and designer, Warwick 1850; founded firm of Heaton and Butler, glass painters and church decorators, London 1857; his chief works were decorating Trinity coll. chapel, Cambridge, Eaton hall, the town halls at Rochdale and Manchester, and churches at Banbury, Ascot, West Newton and Sandringham. *d.* Feb. 1882.

HEATON, JOHN DEAKIN *(son of John Heaton, bookseller and printer, Leeds).* *b.* 7 Briggate, Leeds 23 Nov. 1817; ed. at Leeds gram. sch. 1830–4; studied at Leeds sch. of medicine 1835, at Caius coll. Cam. 1839, at Univ. coll. Lond. 1840 and in Paris 1842; M.B. Univ. of Lond. 1841, M.D. 1843, F.R.C.P. Lond. 1848; senior physician Leeds general infirmary 1843; lecturer on practice of medicine Leeds sch. of medicine 1844; physician Leeds infirmary 1850 to death; established Yorkshire college of Science 1874; member of Leeds Philosophical and literary soc. 1843, member of council 1845, president; mem. of Leeds sch. board 29 Nov. 1870. *d.* 2 East Parade, Leeds 28 March 1880. *Reid's Memoir of J. D. Heaton* (1883), *portrait*.

HEATON, MARY MARGARET *(eld. dau. of James Keymer, silk printer).* *b.* 15 May 1836. *(m.* 1863 Charles William Heaton, professor of chemistry);* contributed to *The Academy* 1869 to death; author of *Masterpieces of Flemish art* 1869; *History of life of Albrecht Dürer* 1870, 2 ed. 1881; *A concise history of painting* 1873; *Leonardo da Vinci and his works* 1874; *Happy springtime. With rhymes for mothers and children* 1874. *d.* St. Leonards-on-Sea 1 June 1883. *Academy 9 June* 1883 *p.* 408.

HEAVISIDES, HENRY. *b.* Darlington 29 Nov. 1791; journeyman printer at Stockton from 1814, presented with a public testimonial March 1847; contributed to periodicals; author of *Pleasures of home and other poems* 1837, 3 ed. 1849; *The minstrelsy of Britain, poetry and poets from Elizabeth to the present time.* Stockton 1860; *Courtship and marriage, their lights and shades* 1864; *The annals of Stockton-on-Tees, with biographical notices* 1865. *d.* before 1879. *Annals of Stockton* (1865) 176–80, *portrait*.

HEAVYSEGE, CHARLES. *b.* Liverpool 2 May 1816; went to Canada and took up his residence at Montreal 1853, worked in a machine shop; a reporter to the *Daily Witness*, Montreal 1860; author of *The revolt of Tartarus* 1852; *Saul, a drama [by C. H.]* 1857, 2 ed. 1859, contains 10,000 lines of verse; *Count*

HEAVYSEGE, C. *(Con.)*

Filippi or the unequal marriage, a drama 1860 ; *Jephthah's daughter* 1865 ; *Ode for tercentenary of Shakespeare's birth* 1864 ; *The Advocate, a novel* 1865. *d.* Montreal 1876. *The Atlantic Monthly*, Oct. 1865 *pp.* 412–18, 250–54 ; *The Canadian Monthly*, x, 127–34 ; *Morgan's Bibl. Canad.* 1867 *p.* 181.

HEBB, CHRISTOPHER HENRY. *b.* 1771 ; M.R.C.S. ; surgeon and apothecary at Worcester ; medical attendant to prince Lucien Bonaparte and his household at Thorngrove near Worcester ; one of the originators of Provincial medical and surgical association 1832 ; the first mayor of Worcester after the municipal reform act 1833, chairman of the charity trustees there to 1846 ; founded almshouses at Worcester for decayed aldermen and councillors and their widows 1853 ; translated Corvisart's *Diseases of the heart* ; published *An account of all the public charities in the city of Worcester that are under the management of the Worcester charity trustees* 1842, 3 ed. 1860. *d.* Britannia sq. Worcester 26 Oct. 1861 aged 90.

HEBDITCH, REV. SAMUEL *(son of a manufacturer)*. *b.* Lopen, Somerset 22 March 1821 ; ed. at Highbury coll. 1843–8 ; congregational minister at Ashburton 1848–53, Woolwich 1853–5, Bristol 1855–72 and Clapton park, Hackney 1872–85 ; minister Collins' st. congregational ch. Melbourne, Victoria 1880–81 ; organised the Young Christians' Band, London 1881 ; minister Brougham palace ch. North Adelaide, South Australia 1885 to death ; chairman Congregational union, S.A. 1887–8 ; a very successful preacher ; author of *Genuine revival, An address* 1872. *d.* Adelaide 5 May 1888. *Congregational Year Book* (1889) 181–6.

HEBERT, REV. CHARLES. Scholar of C.C.C. Cam. 1827 ; scholar of Trin. coll. 1828 ; 35 wrangler and first class in classics 1830 ; B.A. 1831, M.A. 1834, B.D. 1872, D.D. 1874 ; V. of Lechlade 1844–51 ; R. of Burslem 1851–58 ; V. and then R. of Lowestoft 1862–70 ; V. of Ambleside 1875–78 ; author of *Neology not true and truth not new* 1861 ; *On clerical subscription* 1862 ; *Faith and doubt* 1872 ; *The Lord's supper, uninspired teaching* 2 vols. 1879 ; *The New Testament scriptures, a translation of the six primary epistles* 1882. *d.* 1 Marine ter. Silloth, Cumb. 23 June 1890 in 83 year.

HECHT, EDOUARD *(son of Heinrich Hecht, musician, Frankfort)*. *b.* Dürkheim-on-the-Haardt, Rhenish Bavaria 28 Nov. 1832 ; came to England, Nov. 1854, settled at Manchester as a music master ; conductor of Manchester Liedertafel 1859–78, of St. Cecilia choral soc.

HECHT, E. *(Con.)*

1860 and of Stretford choral soc. 1879 ; chorus master for Sir Charles Hallé at his concerts 1870 and then sub-conductor ; lecturer on harmony and composition, Owen's coll. 1875 ; conductor of Bradford and Halifax musical soc. ; wrote *The charge of the light brigade, a chorus* ; *Impromptu for the pianoforte* 1872 ; *Eric the Dane, a cantata* 1882 and 23 other pieces of music. *d.* Ravenswood, Spath road, Palatine road, Didsbury, Manchester 6 March 1887. *Grove's Dict. of Music*, iv, 670 ; *Manchester Evening News* 7 March 1887.

HECKFORD, NATHANIEL *(son of Capt. N. Heckford)*. *b.* Calcutta 24 April 1842 ; student London hospital 1859 ; M.R.C.S. 1863 ; L.R.C.P. Edin. 1865, L.S.A. 1867 ; consulting surgeon Broad st. buildings, City of London 1863 ; established and endowed East London hospital for children and Dispensary for women, Ratcliff Cross 28 Jany. 1868, where he was the active surgeon to his death ; a good diagnoser and a brilliant operator ; revived the operation of paracentesis capitis ; sec. Beaumont medical soc.; author of very numerous medical papers. *d.* Ramsgate 14 Dec. 1871. *bur.* Woking. *Medical Times* 6 Jany. 1872 *p.* 25 ; *The story of the East London hospital for children. By Mrs. N. Heckford* 1887.

HEDLEY, OSWALD DODD *(son of Wm. Hedley of Wylam-on-Tyne)*. Author of a work entitled *Who invented the Locomotive engine* 1858, in which he claimed that his father William Hedley who had the direction of the Wylam colleries and *d.* 184–, invented the locomotive and took out a patent 13 March 1813. *d.* Beckenham, Kent 1 April 1882.

HEDLEY, THOMAS *(brother of the preceding)*. *b.* 1805 or 1808 ; barrister G.I. 29 Jany. 1831, went Northern circuit ; a coal owner at 75 Quay side, Newcastle. *d.* 66 Jesmond road, Newcastle-on-Tyne 5 Aug. 1877.

NOTE.—He left a legacy of £200,000 for purpose of founding and endowing the see of a bishop of the Reformed Anglican church for the county of Northumberland.

HEELIS, STEPHEN. *b.* 1811 ; solicitor. at Manchester 1826 to death ; promoted Manchester law association formed Dec. 1838, pres. of it 18— and 1867 ; alderman of Salford 1853–57, mayor 1855–57 ; declined knighthood 1857. *d.* Above Beck, Grasmere 26 Aug. 1871 aged 60. *Law Times*, li, 339, 356 (1871).

HEENAN, JOHN CAMEL *(son of Timothy Heenan, an Irishman)*. *b.* West Troy, New York 2 May 1835 ; a machinist at Benicia, California

HEENAN, J. C. *(Con.)*

1852-4 ; a miner 1854-7 ; went to New York 1857 ; fought John Morrissey for 5000 dollars a side and the championship of America at Long Point, Canada 20 Oct 1858 when Morrissey won in 11 rounds lasting 21 minutes ; proclaimed champion of America as Morrissey declined to fight again ; landed at Liverpool 16 Jany. 1860 ; fought Tom Sayers for £200 a side and the champion belt near Farnborough railway station on the borders of Hants and Surrey 17 April 1860, after fighting 37 rounds in 2 hours the referee left the ring, the battle was declared drawn and both men were presented with silver belts at the Alhambra, London 30 May 1860 ; sailed for New York 4 July 1860 ; returned to England 3 April 1862 ; fought Tom King for £1000 a side and the championship at Wadhurst, Kent 10 Dec. 1863 when King won in 24 rounds lasting 35 minutes ; always known as the "Benicia Boy," stood 6 feet 2½ inches, and weighed 260 pounds. *(m.* near New York 3 April 1859 Adah Isaacs Menken the actress, he obtained a divorce in Indiana 1862), he *d.* Green River Station, Wyoming Territory 28 Oct. 1873. *Modern Boxing by Pendragon* [Henry Sampson] (1878) 57-78 ; *W. E. Harding's Champions of the American prize ring* (1888) 12-14, *portrait ; H. D. Miles's Pugilistica* (1881) *iii, frontispiece, and pp.* 415-43, *portrait ; Illust. sporting news i,* 29, 41, 193 (1862), 3 *portrait.*

NOTE.—He is one of the characters in Edward Jenkins's novel *Lisa Lena* 2 vols. 1880. A poem entitled "The Combat of Sayerius and Heenanus, a lay of ancient London" appeared in Punch, April 28, 1860 ; the poem is a paraphrase of Lord Macaulay's lay "Horatius" in the "Lays of Ancient Rome"; the author of it was said to be William Makepeace Thackeray.

HEGINBOTHAM, HENRY. Mayor of Stockport, Cheshire twice ; author of *Stockport, ancient and modern* 1877. *d.* Stockport 26 April 1891.

HEINKE, JOHN WILLIAM *(son of a Pole, a coppersmith). b.* London 1816 ; established himself as a submarine engineer at 79 Great Portland st. London 1845 ; invented an improved diving dress and air pump, obtained medal at Great Exhibition of 1851 ; removed the vessels sunk in Sebastopol harbour 1856 ; reported on the possible raising of the Lutine frigate from off Terschelling 1858 ; recovered the watches stolen from Walker's shop, 63 Cornhill, and thrown over Blackfriar's bridge Feb. 1865 ; A.I.C.E. 2 Dec. 1856. *d.* 9 Regent's park villas, Regent's park, London 12 April 1870. *Min. of Proc. of I.C.E. xxxi,* 247-8 (1871).

HELLER, ROBERT, stage name of William Henry Palmer *(son of Henry Palmer, musician, Canterbury). b.* Canterbury 1830 ; ed. at R. Academy of music, London 1845-6, King's scholar ; appeared as a conjurer at Rochester ; landed in America 15 Sept. 1852, made his début as a conjurer at Museum, Albany N.Y. ; appeared in Chinese assembly room, Broadway, New York ; a teacher of Music in Washington D.C. under his own name of Palmer ; opened the French theatre No. 585 Broadway, New York, which he called Heller's Salle Diabolique 11 April 1864 ; gave performances in Polygraphic hall, King William st. London 27 Jany. to Feb. 1868 ; his half sister assisted him in his second-sight seances from 1868 ; visited Australia, Java, India and California ; opened the Globe theatre, New York as Heller's Wonder theatre 15 Nov. 1876 ; opened Fifth-avenue hall, New York 10 Dec. 1877, and Concert hall, Philadelphia 25 Nov. 1878 being his last appearance ; improved on Houdin and became a most finished clairvoyant entertainer ; composer of *Sophie galop,* New York 1863 and other pieces of music ; left nearly £80,000. *d.* Continental hotel, Philadelphia 28 Nov. 1878. *T. A. Brown's American stage* (1870) 168, *portrait ; W. I. Bishop's Second-sight explained, as exhibited by R. Houdin and R. Heller* (1880).

HELMORE, REV. HOLLOWAY. Chief of the Makololo Mission which started about middle of 1859 from coast of Africa for a journey of 1000 miles to the tribes on north of the Zambesi, this journey was accomplished 1859. *d.* Linyanti 21 April 1860. *Waddington's Congregational history v,* 229-64 (1880).

HELMORE, REV. THOMAS *(son of Thomas Helmore). b.* Kidderminster 7 May 1811 ; ed. at Magd. hall Ox., B.A. 1840, M.A. 1845 ; C. of St. Michael, Lichfield ; priest vicar in Lichfield cath. 1840-2 ; vice-principal of St. Mark's coll. Chelsea 1842-6 and precentor 1846, retired 1877 when National Soc. gave him a pension ; master of the choristers chapel royal St. James' 1846 to death ; priest in ordinary to the Queen 1847 to death ; R. of Beverstone, Gloucs. 1872, resigned 1872 ; precentor at Bedford chapel, Bloomsbury ; hon. precentor of Motett choir, and of London Gregorian choral association ; author and writer of *The psalter noted* 1849 ; *A manual of plain song* 1850 ; *Carols for Christmas tide set to ancient melodies* 1853 ; *A treatise on choir and chorus singing* 1855 ; *St. Mark's chant book* 1863 ; *A catechism of music* 1878 and other pieces of music. *d.* 72 St. George's sq. Pimlico, London 6 July 1890. *Pictorial World* 17 *July* 1890 *p.* 76, *portrait.*

HELPS, SIR ARTHUR (1 *son of Thomas Helps of Balham, Surrey*). *b.* Streatham, Surrey 10 July 1813; ed. at Eton and Trin. coll. Camb., B.A. 1835, M.A. 1839; D.C.L. of Oxford 8 June 1864; private sec. to Spring Rice (Lord Monteagle) chancellor of exchequer; private sec. to lord Morpeth chief sec. for Ireland 1839; comr. of French, Danish and Spanish claims; clerk of privy council 9 June 1860 to death; employed by Queen to revise Prince Albert's Speeches 1862, and with the preparation of Leaves of our Life in the Highlands 1868, and Mountain, Loch and Glen 1869; C.B. 30 June 1871, K.C.B. 18 July 1872; author of *Thoughts in the cloister and the crowds* 1835 anon.; *Catherine Douglas a drama* 1843 *anon.*; *Friends in council* 2 vols. 1847, *2nd series* 2 vols. 1857, *both anon.*; *The conquerors of the New World* 1848; *Spanish conquest in America* 4 vols. 1855–61; *Realmah a novel* 1868. *d.* 13 Lower Berkeley st. London 7 March 1875. *bur.* Streatham cemet. 12 March. His widow Bissel dau. of Capt. Edward Fuller granted civil list pension of £200, 4 May 1875. *Graphic 8 May 1875 pp.* 436, 450, *portrait.*

HEMANS, CHARLES ISIDORE (*youngest son of Felicia Dorothea Hemans, poetess 1793–1835*). *b.* 1817; settled in Rome and made Roman history and archæology his chief study; originated the *Roman Advertiser*, first English paper in Rome 1846; hon. sec. and librarian of English archæological soc. in Rome; author of *Catholic Italy* 1860; *The story of monuments in Rome* 2 *parts* 1864–5; *A history of christianity and sacred art* 3 vols. 1866–72: *d.* at Baths of Lucca 26 Oct. 1876. *Times 3 Nov. 1876 p. 9.*

HEMANS, GEORGE WILLOUGHBY (*brother of the preceding*). *b.* St. Asaph, Wales 27 Aug. 1814; ed. at military coll. Sarèze, France; pupil to Sir John Macneill, C.E., London; chief engineer of Midland G.W. railway, Ireland 1845–51; constructed a greater number of railways in Ireland than any other engineer 1845–53; railway and sewerage engineer in London 1854 to death; engineer in chief for province of Canterbury, N.Z. 1870 and then engineer in chief for N.Z. to his death; F.R.G.S., F.G.S.; A.I.C.E. 1837, M.I.C.E. 18 May 1845, member of council 1856, V.P. 1872–5; author with R. Hassard of *On the future water supply of London* 1866; seized with paralysis Sep. 1872 and never spoke again. *d.* 11 Roland gardens, South Kensington, London 29 Dec. 1885. *I.L.N. xix*, 208 (1851); *Min. of Proc. of C.E. lxxxv*, 394–99 (1886).

HEMING, DEMPSTER (*youngest son of George Heming of Weddington near Nuneaton, Warws.*)

HEMING, D. (*Con.*)

b. about 1778; ed. at Univ. of St. Andrews; barrister M.T. 27 May 1808; practised with great success at Madras; registrar of supreme court at Calcutta; contested North Warwickshire 26 Dec. 1832; sheriff of Warws. 1840; F.R.A.S. *d.* 7 Hubert terrace, Dover 24 Dec. 1874. *bur.* in family burial place in Warws.

NOTE.—He was the oldest barrister in the law list, his exact age was unknown to his relatives.

HEMPEL, CARL or CHARLES FREDERIC (*eld. son of the succeeding*). *b.* Truro, Sep. 1811; teacher of music at Truro, organist of St. Mary's ch. there 1844–57; introduced into Cornwall choral performances on a large scale; matric. from Magd. hall, Ox. 11 Feb. 1855, B.M. 15 Feb.; his oratorio The Seventh Seal performed at Oxford 19 March 1862, D.M. 20 March; organist and choirmaster St. John's episcopal ch. Perth 1857 to death; conductor of Perth choral union, and of the Euterpean soc.; printed portions of The Seventh Seal 1864 etc., and many pieces of light music. *d.* Perth 25 April 1867. *Boase and Courtney's Bibl. Cornub.* 227–8, 1226; *Boase's Collect. Cornub. p.* 349; *The Choir, v,* 360 (1867).

HEMPEL, CHARLES WILLIAM. *b.* Chelsea 28 Aug. 1777; played organ in King's German chapel, St. James' 1785; studied at Leipsic and Dresden 1793–4; organist of St. Mary's ch. Truro, May 1804 to 1844; removed to Exeter 1844; composer and writer of *Psalms from the New Version* 1805; *Sacred melodies* 1812; *A morning and evening service* 1820; *An introduction to the pianoforte* 1822; he also was author of *The Commercial tourist or gentleman traveller, a poem* 1822, 3 *ed.* 1832; a banker's clerk in London 1854–5. *d.* in the workhouse, Prince's road, Lambeth, London 14 March 1855. *Dictionary of Musicians, i,* 359–60 (1827).

HEMPHILL, ANDREW T. Ensign 29 foot 7 April 1825, lieut.-colonel 8 Dec. 1846 to 8 March 1848; lieut.-colonel 26 foot 8 March 1848 to 31 July 1860 when placed on h.p.; commander first infantry brigade at Dublin 1 July 1861 to death; M.G. 10 Nov. 1861. *d.* 11 Burlington road, Dublin 31 March 1863.

HEMPHILL, BARBARA (*youngest dau. of Rev. Patrick Hare, rector of Golden, Tipperary*). (*m.* John Hemphill of Rathkeany, Tipperary, who *d.* 26 Sep. 1833); author of *Lionel Deerhurst, or fashionable life under the Regency* 3 vols. 1846; *The priest's niece* 3 vols. 1855; *Freida the Jongler* 3 vols. 1857. *d.* Dublin 5 May 1858.

HEMSLEY, JOHN. Chairman of Implement committee of R. Agric. soc. of England 1876 to death, member of council 22 May 1874 to death ; a frequent judge of steam cultivation, implements, etc. at the annual meetings, steward of implements 1886 ; author of *Report on the trial of agricultural implements at Taunton* 1875. *d.* Shelton, Newark, Dec. 1888. *Agricultural Gazette* 1888.

HEMY, HENRY FREDERICK. *b.* Newcastle 12 Nov. 1818 ; resided Newcastle to 1885 ; removed to West Hartlepool 1885 ; pianist to the Earl of Ravensworth ; musical instructor at Ushaw coll. Durham ; engaged upon A history of the organ, when he died ; composer of upwards of 100 pieces of music including Drawing room melodies 1851 ; Melodies of the Tyne and Wear 1857 ; Thirteen sacred songs 1869 ; God save the Prince of Wales, song 1876 ; set to music a number of Longfellow's poems ; author of *The royal modern tutor for the pianoforte* 1854, copyright of which was sold for £500, 1867 and for £3000, 1879. *d.* suddenly at 10 Regent st. Hartlepool 10 June 1888. *bur.* Moor Edge cemet. Newcastle. *Northern Daily Mail* 11 *June* 1888 *p.* 3, 14 *June p.* 3.

HENCHY, DAVID O'CONNOR. *b.* Rutland sq. west, Dublin 1810 ; M.P. for co. Kildare 1852–59. *d.* 1 Dec. 1876.

HENDERSON, ALEXANDER. *b.* Aberdeenshire 1780 ; ed. at Univ. of Edin., M.D. 12 Sep. 1803 ; L.C.P. 22 Dec. 1808 ; resided at 6 Curzon st. London ; published *A sketch of the revolutions of medical science by P. J. G. Cabanis,* translated from the French 1806 ; *An examination of the imposture of Ann Moore the fasting woman of Tutbury* 1813 ; *The history of ancient and modern wines* 1824. *d.* Caskieben, Aberdeenshire 16 Sep. 1863. *Munk's Roll of Physicians, iii,* 69 (1878).

HENDERSON, ALEXANDER. *b.* 1828 or 1829 ; in service of Post office ; sec. to Edward Askew Sothern the comedian ; lessee and manager Prince of Wales' theatre, Liverpool 1861? to 8 Feb. 1868 ; lessee of Criterion theatre, London 1876–9 ; lessee of Folly theatre 1876–9 ; lessee of Globe theatre 1878–81 ; opened the Comedy theatre with *La Mascotte* comic opera 15 Oct. 1881, lessee to 1885 ; lessee of Avenue theatre 1885 to decease. (*m.* (1) Miss Moon of Liverpool ; *m.* (2) Lydia Thompson, actress). *d.* Prince of Wales' hotel, Cannes 1 Feb. 1886 aged 57. *bur.* 2 Feb. *The Era* 6 Feb. 1886 *p.* 8, 19 *Jany.* 1889 *p.* 16 ; *A. Brereton's Dramatic Notes* (1887) 15–17.

HENDERSON, ANDREW *(son of John Henderson of Shetland).* *b.* Liverpool 10 Jany. 1800 ; in the navy 1813–16 ; commanded ships for Palmer & Co. ; formed with Lord William Bentinck and Auber the East India steam navigation co. and the Assam co. ; commanded the India 1840 first steamer that went round the Cape ; conveyed first mails between Calcutta and Suez ; A.I.C.E. 1840 ; invented a bow and stern rudder. *d.* 20 Feb. 1868. *Min. of proc. of Instit. of C.E. xxx,* 472–75 (1870).

HENDERSON, REV. ANKETELL MATTHEW. *b.* Anketell grove, Monaghan, Ireland 1820 ; Wesleyan minister in Ireland 1841–52 ; Congregational minister at Cork 1852–6, at Claremont chapel, Pentonville, London 1856–65 ; wrote articles in the *Patriot,* the *British Quarterly* and the *London Quarterly Reviews* 1856–65 ; president of Congregational coll. Melbourne, Australia 1865 to death ; pastor of Collins' st. ch. 1866 to death, built a new ch. at cost of £23,000 which was opened free of debt 1868 ; an eloquent preacher ; preached in Theatre Royal during rebuilding of his church ; edited *The preacher's manual, By S. J. Sturtevant* 1866. *d.* in house of his nephew John Garvin, Toronto, Canada 23 June 1876. *Heaton's Australian Dictionary* (1879) 89 ; *Congregational Year Book* (1877) 374–76 ; *J. Jones' Sermon on death of A. M. Henderson* (1876).

HENDERSON, CHARLES COOPER *(younger son of John Henderson, amateur artist).* *b.* Abbey house, Chertsey 14 June 1803 ; ed. at Winchester ; studied for the bar ; painted sporting pictures and sketches, horses and coaching scenes, many of which were engraved and published by Messrs. Fores, London ; exhibited 2 pictures at R.A. 1840–8. *d.* Lower Halliford-on-Thames 21 Aug. 1877.

HENDERSON, REV. EBENEZER *(youngest son of George Henderson, agricultural labourer).* *b.* The Linn, parishes of Saline and Dunfermline 17 Nov. 1784 ; clock and watch maker 1794, kept cows, then a boot and shoemaker 1799 ; ed. at Robert Haldane's seminary, Edinburgh 1803–5 ; engaged founding Bible societies in Denmark, Sweden, Norway, Iceland and Russia 1805 etc. ; minister at Elsinore 1806–7, at Gothenburg 1807 ; formed first Congregational ch. in Sweden 6 Oct. 1811 ; visited Iceland and distributed Bibles 1814 ; at St. Petersburg printed the Bible in 10 dialects 1816, resided in Russia to 1825 ; tutor at Gosport, Hoxton and Highbury colleges 1825–50 ; minister Sheen Vale independent chapel, Mortlake, Surrey 1852–3 ; author of *Iceland, a residence in that island* 2 vols. 1818 ; *The Book of the Twelve minor Prophets translated*

HENDERSON, REV. E. *(Con.)*

1845; *The Vaudois, a tour to the valleys of Piedmont* 1845; *The Book of Isaiah translated* 1840, 2 *ed.* 1857 and many other works. *d.* Mortlake 16 May 1858. *Memoir of E. Henderson by Thalia S. Henderson* (1859), *portrait.*

HENDERSON, EBENEZER *(son of John Henderson, watch and clock maker).* *b.* Dunfermline, Feb. 1809; made an orrery and an astronomical clock 1827; clerk to his brother a tanner at St. Helens 1829; curator Liverpool Astronomical instit.; member of 13 scientific societies in England, LLD. of an American coll.; F.R.A.S.; received freedom of Elgin 1850 and of Dunfermline 1859; made a combination of wheels to show and check sidereal time 1850; restored old market cross of Dunfermline 1868 and queen Margaret's stone; author of *An historical treatise on horology* 1836; *A treatise on astronomy* 1843, 3 *ed.* 1848; *Life of James Ferguson* 1867, 2 *ed.* 1870; *The annals of Dunfermline and vicinity* 1879. *d.* Muckhart, Perthshire 2 Nov. 1879.

HENDERSON, GEORGE *(son of Capt. Henderson of 4 foot).* *b.* Newton, Aberdeenshire 4 June 1783; 2 lieut. R.E. March 1800; served in Ceylon 1803–12, in the Peninsula 1812–14; lieut.-col. R.E. 30 Dec. 1824, retired from the service 9 April 1825; general superintendent London and South Western railway co. 1830, a director to death; A.I.C.E. May 1837; chairman London Equitable gas co., and Southampton gas co. to death. *d.* 11 Anglesea place, Southampton 21 April 1855. *Proc. of Instit. of C.E. xv,* 100–101 (1856).

HENDERSON, GEORGE. *b.* 1785 or 1786; entered navy 1 March 1794; captain 1 Aug. 1811; retired admiral 1 Nov. 1860. *d.* Middle Deal, Kent 23 Jany. 1864 aged 78. *O'Byrne p.* 493.

HENDERSON, GEORGE AUGUSTUS. Ensign 2 foot 1 Oct. 1794; inspecting field officer of militia, Nova Scotia 24 Aug. 1815 to 10 Feb. 1817 when placed on h.p.; col. 59 foot 27 April 1852 to death; L.G. 20 June 1854; K.H. 1836. *d.* Kempsey, Worcs. 7 Sep. 1857 aged 78.

HENDERSON, GILBERT. *b.* Colquitt st. Liverpool 8 Aug. 1797; ed. at Brasenose coll. Ox., B.A. 1817; barrister L.I. 12 Nov. 1824; a leader on the northern circuit; recorder of Liverpool 24 July 1843 to death. *d.* Hyde park sq. London 5 Dec. 1861. *The Liverpool Courier* 7 Dec. 1861 *p.* 5.

HENDERSON, JAMES *(son of a labourer).* *b.* Scotland 1829; worked on a farm for 50s. a

HENDERSON, J. *(Con.)*

year 1843–5; butler to Mr. Grant Duff 1847–52; ed. at Surgeons' hall, Edin. 1855–8, surgeon 1858; M.D. of St. Andrew's univ. 1859; medical missionary Shanghai, China 1860–5, in charge of the Chinese hospital 1860–5; author of *Shanghai Hygiene, or hints for preservation of health in China* 1863; edited *Reports of the Chinese hospital, Shanghai* 1860–63. *d.* Nagasaki, Japan 30 July 1865. *Memorials of J. Henderson* (1868), *portrait; Good Words* (1878) 784–90.

HENDERSON, J. SCOTT. *b.* Berwickshire 1838; a banker at Paisley; edited the *Ayr Observer* some years, the *Times* and *Mirror* at Bristol, the *Edinburgh Courant* 1867–72 and the *Bullionist* in London; translated H. C. L. Von Sybel's *Clerical policy in the nineteenth century* 1875. *d.* Oaklands, St. Mark's road, Notting hill, London 18 Sep. 1883.

HENDERSON, JOHN *(son of John Henderson, gardener at Brechin castle).* *b.* Brechin 14 June 1804; carpenter Brechin; architect Edinburgh making a special study of gothic; designed and built many episcopal and other churches in Scotland 1831–65; Trinity college, Glenalmond, Perth with its decorated chapel is his best work 1847. *d.* 7 Greenhill park, Edinburgh 27 June 1865. *Dictionary of Architecture, iv,* 43.

HENDERSON, JOHN *(son of Robert Henderson, merchant and shipowner).* *b.* Borrowstounness, Linlithgowshire 1780; drysalter Glasgow; East India merchant London; gave from £30,000 to £40,000 a year to religious and charitable schemes; maintained several religious newspapers; spent £4000 in sending copy of a publication to all railway servants to tell them of the sinfulness of Sunday labour; stopped for sometime Sunday railway travelling in Scotland; maintained mission churches in Glasgow; a founder of Evangelical Alliance 1845. *d.* Park Inchinnan, Renfrewshire 1 May 1867. *Glasgow Daily Herald* 2 May 1867 *p.* 2.

HENDERSON, JOHN *(son of John Henderson the actor).* *b.* London 1822; apprenticed to Sanders the equestrian; performed as an equestrian artiste in every capital in Europe; returned to England 1862, equestrian director 1862 to death. *(m.* 1843 Agnes Selina Hengler). *d.* Ipswich 10 May 1867. *bur.* Highgate cemetery 3 July. *Illustrated sporting news, ii,* 428 (1862), *portrait, iv,* 641 (1865), *portrait; Era* 19 May 1867 *p.* 14 col. 3.

HENDERSON, JOHN *(brother of Charles Cooper Henderson 1803–77).* *b.* Adelphi ter. London

1797; ed. at Ball. coll. Ox., B.A. 1817, M.A.
1820; studied for the bar; spent his life in
collecting works of art, which he kept at his
residence 3 Montague st. Bloomsbury, London;
F.S.A. 11 March 1858; left to Univ. of
Oxford his Greek and Roman vases and
Egyptian antiquities, to British Museum his
water-colour drawings, enamels, porcelain,
glass, metal work, arms and MSS., to National
Gallery some water-colour drawings and paintings. *d.* 3 Montague st. London 20 Nov.
1878. *Waagen's Galleries of art* (1857) 202–
13; *Proc. of Soc. of Antiquaries*, viii, 105
(1881); *Academy 30 Nov. 1878 p. 531*; *Works
of art in pottery, glass and metal in collection of
J. Henderson 1868.*

HENDERSON, JOHN *(son of Gilbert Henderson).*
b. Durham 2 May 1811; ed. Durham gram.
sch.; carpet manufacturer and coal owner,
Durham; M.P. Durham city 1864–74; M.P.
Durham 5 Feb. 1874 but election declared
void. *d.* Bournemouth 4 April 1884. *Times*
10 *April* 1884 *p.* 7.

HENDERSON, JOHN IRVING. *b.* Dumfriesshire
1781; in R.N.; advocate of the Scotch bar
1812; sheriff substitute of Dundee district, of
Forfarshire 1832, resigned 1860. *d.* Black-
ness crescent, Dundee 24 Dec. 1860; his
daughter erected schools to his memory which
were opened by the Bishop of Brechin 2 Aug.
1862 but shortly afterwards finally closed.
Norrie's Dundee Celebrities (1873) 193; *Dundee
Advertiser 25 Dec. 1860 p. 3.*

HENDERSON, PETER. *b.* Pathhead near Edinburgh 25 June 1823; apprentice to a gardener
1839; went to U.S. America 1843; green-
house horticulturist Jersey City, and seedsman in New York, the largest business of its
kind in America; author of *Gardening for
profit* 1867, circulated 100,000 copies; *Practical floriculture* 1869; *Gardening for pleasure*
1875; *Henderson's Handbook of plants* 1881;
Garden and farm topics 1884; *How the farm
pays* 1884. *d.* Jersey City Heights, Jany.
1890. *Appleton's American Biog.* iii, 164 (1887).

HENDERSON, PETER LINDSAY. *b.* Glasgow
1831, ed. at high school there; master in the
merchant service; owner and manager of a
line of steamers between Copenhagen and
Germany 1857; established whale fisheries in
Iceland, using steamships with harpoon guns;
proprietor of the Greenwich and Poplar horse
ferry; A.I.C.E. 7 Feb. 1871. *d.* Woodfield,
Hendon 20 Feb. 1881. *Proc. of Instit. of C.E.
lxiv*, 341–2 (1881).

HENDERSON, WILLIAM (4 *son of William
Henderson, sheriff substitute of Caithness).* *b.*
Thurso 17 Jany. 1810; ed. at univ. of Edin.,
M.D. 1831; physician fever hospital, Edin.
1832; pathologist Royal infirmary, resigned
1845; made clinical studies on the heart and
blood vessels 1835–7; F.R.C.P. Edin. 1838;
professor of general pathology, Univ. of Edin.
1842, resigned 1869; adopted homœopathy
1845 when professor Syme, Sir John Forbes
and others withdrew from associating with
him, and he was expelled from the Med. Chir.
Soc. of Edin. in Dec. 1851, wrote many works
on homœopathy in reply to his adversaries
1845–53; author also of *Letter to lord provost
on charges against Queen's college 1840*; *A
dictionary of names of persons and places in Old
and New Testaments 1869. d.* 19 Ainslie place,
Edinburgh 1 April 1872. *Grant's University of
Edinburgh*, ii, 451 (1884); *British Journal of
Homœopathy*, xxx, 617–23 (1872).

HENDERSON, WILLIAM. Called to Irish bar
1825; Q.C. 26 May 1858. *d.* 1875.

HENDERSON, WILLIAM. *b.* Biggar, Lanarkshire 5 Aug. 1831; compositor with firm of
T. & A. Constable, Edinburgh; a type-music
printer with Novello, Ewer & Co. London
1860; partner with James Cossar Rait at 30
Penton st. Pentonville, and also with Montague Spalding, as type music printers 1861,
they acquired a world-wide reputation, they
moved to Winsley st. Oxford st. 1864, then
to Berners st., afterwards to 3 Marylebone
lane and Dyott house, Holborn; a composer
of some ability. *d.* suddenly at Ipswich 22
May 1891. *Stationery Trades Journal 30 May
1891 p. 254.*

HENDERSON, WILLIAM WILMOTT. Entered
navy May 1799, captain 9 Oct. 1815, R.A. 21
March 1851; commander in chief on south east
coast of America 19 July 1851 to 1 May 1854;
K.H. 13 Jany. 1835; C.B. 18 Dec. 1840. *d.*
at sea returning to England 12 July 1854.

HENDREN, MOST REV. JOSEPH WILLIAM. *b.*
Birmingham 19 Oct. 1791; received Franciscan habit 2 Aug. 1806; a teacher at Baddesley
school 1812–16; priest 28 Sep. 1815; a teacher
at Perthyre 1816–18, at Aston 1818–23;
president Baddesley academy 1823–26; served
mission at Abergavenny 1826–39; confessor
and spiritual director to the nuns and pensioners of Franciscan convent at Taunton
Lodge 1839–48; vicar apostolic of western
district, and bishop of Uranopolis in partibus
28 July 1848, consecrated at Clifton by bishop
Ullathorne 10 Sep. 1848; translated to newly
created See of Clifton 29 Sep. 1850; translated to See of Nottingham 27 June 1851,

HENDREN, MOST REV. J. W. (Con.)
resigned 26 Dec. 1852; bishop of Martyr-
opolis in partibus 25 Feb. 1853, resided at
Birmingham, May 1853 to death. *d.* Birmingham 14 Nov. 1866. *Gillow's English
Catholics, iii,* 266–7 (1887); *Brady's Episcopal
succession, iii,* 317, 333, 357, 406, 432 (1877).

HENDRICKEN, MOST REV. THOMAS FRANCIS.
b. Kilkenny, Ireland 5 May 1827; ed. at St.
Kyran's coll. Kilkenny and at Maynooth;
ordained in Dublin, R.C. priest 29 April 1853;
pastor at Winsted, Conn., U.S. America 1854;
pastor at Waterbury 1855–72 where he built
the church of the Immaculate Conception;
Pius ix. created him D.D. 1868; first bishop
of new diocese of Providence, R.I., consecrated
28 April 1872, built a cathedral and an episcopal residence. *d.* Providence 11 June 1886.
Appleton's American Biography, iii, 165 (1887).

HENEAGE, EDWARD (2 *son of George Robert
Heneage of Hainton, Lincolnshire, d.* 1833). *b.*
24 July 1802; M.P. for Great Grimsby 7
Jany. 1835 to 1 July 1852; contested Great
Grimsby 8 July 1852. *d.* Stag's End, Hemel
Hempstead 25 June 1880.

HENEAGE, GEORGE FIESCHI (*brother of preced-
ing*). *b.* 22 Nov. 1800; ed. at Trin. coll.
Cam., B.A. 1822, M.A. 1826; M.P. Great
Grimsby 1826–30; M.P. Lincoln 1831–4 and
1852–62; sheriff of Lincolnshire 1839. *d.*
Hainton 11 May 1868.

HENFREY, ARTHUR (3 *son of Henry Antram
Henfrey*). *b.* Aberdeen 1 Nov. 1819; studied
at St. Bartholomew's hospital; M.R.C.S. 1843;
lecturer on botany at Middlesex and St.
George's hospitals 1847; professor of botany
King's coll. 1853; F.L.S. 1844; F.R.S. 3 June
1852; edited *The Botanical Gazette* 3 *vols.* 1849–
51, the *Photographic Journal, vols.* 1, 2, 1853;
author of *Outlines of structural and physiological
botany* 1847; *The vegetation of Europe, its conditions and causes* 1852; *An elementary course
of botany* 1857, 4 *ed.* 1884, besides many
translations from the German and other books.
d. 12 Heathfield ter. Turnham green, Middlesex 7 Sep. 1859. *Proc. Royal Soc. x,* 18 (1860).

HENFREY, HENRY WILLIAM (*eld. son of preceding*). *b.* London 5 July 1852; ed. at
Brighton coll.; member Numismatic soc. 1868,
on council; contributed 12 papers to *Numismatic Chronicle;* member British Archæol.
Assoc. 1870 and wrote in its proceedings;
author of *A guide to the study of English coins*
1870, 2 *ed.* 1885; *Numismata Cromwelliana*
1877; edited *Henfrey's Journal,* St. Albans
1864. *d.* Widmore cottage, Bromley, Kent
31 July 1881. *Numismatic Chronicle, ii,* 21–2
(1882).

HENGLER, EDWARD HENRY (*son of Henry
Hengler, tight rope dancer of Vauxhall gardens*).
b. 1819; tight rope dancer; kept a riding
school with his brother John Milton Hengler
at Elizabeth st. Pembroke place, Liverpool.
d. Liverpool 8 Jany. 1865. *Era* 15 *Jany.*
1865 *p.* 14.

HENGLER, FREDERICK CHARLES (*brother of
the preceding*). *b.* Cambridge 1820; taught
the circus business by his father; violin and
trumpet player in James Wild's theatre,
Bradford 1841; business manager of Price and
Powell's circus, afterwards purchased the
circus with which he travelled; built circuses
in Liverpool 1857, Glasgow and Dublin 1863,
Hull 1866, Bristol 1867, Birmingham 1868
and London 1871; introduced spectacular
pieces played by children; taught riding to
several members of the royal family; a great
horse tamer and exhibitor of trained animals.
d. Cambridge house, 27 Fitzjohn's avenue,
Hampstead, Middlesex 28 Sep. 1887. *bur.*
Pauntley, Gloucestershire, left £59,665 2s. 5d.
Frost's Circus Life (1876) 48 *etc.*; *The Era* 15
Jany. 1865 *and* 1 *Oct.* 1887; *Judy* 13 *Dec.*
1882 *p.* 280, *portrait.*

NOTE.—His eldest son and successor Frederick
Charles Hengler was *b.* 4 Aug. 1855 and *d.* 7 May 1889.

HENLAND, HENRY. *b.* Germany 1778; scientific dealer in minerals in London 1807, having
purchased Old Humphrey's collection; supplied the British Museum with greater part of
their collection of minerals; formed a mineralogical cabinet for C. H. Turner of Rooks
Nest, Surrey, an account of which was printed
in 3 volumes with an atlas of 83 plates of
forms of crystals; foreign secretary Geological
soc. some years. *d.* Hastings 16 Nov. 1856.

HENLEY, JOSEPH WARNER (*only son of Joseph
Henley, merchant, London*). *b.* Putney, Surrey
3 March 1793; ed. at Fulham and Magd.
coll. Ox., B.A. 1815, M.A. 1834, hon. D.C.L.
1854; in his father's office 1815–17; M.P.
for Oxfordshire 1841–78; president of board
of trade 27 Feb. to 17 Dec. 1852 and 25 Feb.
1858 to March 1859; P.C. 27 Feb. 1852;
author of *A Conservative's opinion on the contagious diseases act.* Nottingham 1878. *d.* Water-
perry, Oxfordshire 8 Dec. 1884. *The drawing
room portrait gallery of eminent personages* 2
series (1859), *portrait; The statesmen of England*
(1862), *portrait; St. James' Mag.* March 1870
pp. 771–4, *portrait.*

HENLEY, WILLIAM THOMAS. *b.* Midhurst,
Sussex 1814; a leather dresser, a light porter
1829 and a dock labourer; a philosophical
instrument maker 1838; assisted Sir C.

HENLEY, W. T. *(Con.)*

Wheatstone and made his electrical apparatus 1836; took out 13 patents for improvements in electric telegraphs, &c. 1848–71; founded the British and Irish magnetic telegraph co.; made 14,000 miles of submarine cables; made electric light apparatus 1849; had manufactories at North Woolwich 1859 and iron works and colleries in Wales employing 2000 men and making a profit of £80,000 a year; failed for £500,000 in 1874; director of Henley's Telegraph works 1880 to death. *d.* Chesterton house, Plaistow, Essex 13 Dec. 1882. *bur.* Kensal green 18 Dec. *Times 15 Dec.* 1882 *p.* 5; *The·Electrician 23 Dec.* 1882 *p.* 136.

HENN, JONATHAN (2 *son of William Henn of Paradise, co. Clare, master of Irish court of chancery, d.* 1822). *b.* 1789; ed. at Lucan and at Trin. coll. Dublin, B.A. 1808; called to Irish bar 1811; went Connaught circuit, joined Munster circuit; defended D. O'Connell in the Repeal prosecutions 1843; K.C. 7 Feb. 1835; engaged for the Crown in the case of John Mitchell 1849; assistant barrister for co. of Donegal; retired from practice about 1850; a brilliant orator. *d.* Clifton villa, Bray, co. Dublin 22 July 1873. *J. R. O'Flanagan's Irish bar* (1879) 225–31; *Law mag. and law review, ii,* 233–35 (1857).

HENN, THOMAS RICE (3 *son of Thomas Rice Henn, Q.C., recorder of Galway*). *b.* Dublin 2 Nov. 1849; ed. at Windermere coll. and R. Milit. acad. Woolwich 1866; lieut. Bombay engineers 7 July 1869, commanded 2 company in Afghan war 1880; present in Bolan pass and at Candahar; brigade major R.E. 1879–80; *killed* while covering the retreat of the army at the battle of Maiwand 27 July 1880, window to his memory placed in Rochester cath. *Shadbolt's Afghan campaign. Biog. Division* (1882) 107–9, *portrait.*

HENN, WILLIAM *(brother of Jonathan Henn, d.* 1873). Called to Irish bar 1808; bencher of King's Inns, Dublin 1822, master in chancery 1822 to death. *d.* Dublin 8 March 1857. *O'Flanagan's Irish bar* (1879) 224.

HENNEDY, ROGER. *b.* Carrick-fergus near Belfast, Aug. 1809; a block cutter for calico printers; learnt to draw on stone and made designs for textiles; a teacher of botany at Glasgow 1848; in business with a partner 1851–7; professor of botany Andersonian univ. Glasgow 1863 to death; author of *The Clydesdale Flora, plants and ferns of the Clyde district, Glasgow* 1865, 4 ed. 1878. *d.* Whitehall near Bothwell, Lanarkshire 22 Oct. 1877.

HENNEN, JOHN *(son of John Hennen, M.D., d. Gibraltar 3 Nov.* 1828). M.R.C.S. Edin. 1820; M.D. Edin. 1821; M.R.C.P. Lond. 1843; in medical department of army 1824; physician R. Milit. asylum, Southampton 1828–40; in practice at 24 Upper Southwick st. Hyde park, London 1847; F. Med. and Chir. soc. 1844, librarian 1848–50, compiled an Index to the Society's Transactions 1851; translated C. J. Nitzsch' *System of christian doctrine* 1849; edited his father's *Sketches of medical topography of the Mediterranean* 1830. *d.* Tunbridge Wells, June 1871 aged 71. *Proc. Med. Chir. Soc. vii,* 38 (1875).

HENNESSY, WILLIAM MAUNSELL. *b.* Castle Gregory, co. Kerry 1829; resided for some time in U.S. America; in the Lunatic asylum office 1855; wrote for Irish newspapers; chief clerk Public Record office, Dublin 1868, assist. deputy keeper 1886 to his death; Todd professor R. Irish acad. 1822–4; the best Irish scholar of his day; contributed to *The Academy, La Revue Celtique,* etc.; edited *Chronicon Scotorum. A chronicle of Irish affairs* 1866; *The annals of Loch Cé. A chronicle of Irish affairs* 1871; J. Graves' *Pedigree of the White Knight* 1881; J. C. Mangan's *The poets and poetry of Munster* 1883 and many other works. *d.* 71 Pembroke road, Dublin 13 Jany. 1889. *Academy 26 Jany.* 1889 *p.* 56.

HENNIKER, JOHN HENNIKER-MAJOR, 4 Baron *(eld. son of 3 Baron Henniker* 1777–1832, *who in 1822 assumed additional surname of Major).* *b.* Stratford Green, Essex 3 Feb. 1801; ed. at St. John's coll. Cam.; barrister L.I. 28 May 1824; M.P. for East Suffolk 1832–47 and 1856 to 13 July 1866 when created Baron Hartismere of Hartismere, co. Suffolk; sheriff of Suffolk 1853; F.S.A. 16 Dec. 1852. *d.* 6 Grafton st. Bond st. London 16 April 1870. *I.L.N. xxx,* 479 (1857), *portrait.*

HENNIKER, ALDBOROUGH *(eld. son of Aldborough Brydges John Henniker of Catcott, Somerset* 1797–1880). *b.* 6 July 1821; ed. at the Charterhouse; barrister G.I. 1 May 1844, bencher 7 July 1874, treasurer 1877 to death; Q.C. 6 July 1874; member of council of legal education. *d.* 26 Leinster sq. Bayswater, London 28 Jany. 1880 from injuries received by falling down the staircase at King's Cross station of Metropolitan railway.

HENNIKER, REV. ROBERT *(brother of the preceding).* *b.* 1 June 1833; ed. at Trin. coll. Ox., Johnson's Theol. sch. 1856, B.A. 1856, M.A. 1860; C. of St. Michael, Alnwick 1858–60; P.C. of South Charlton near Alnwick 1860–69; head master of Rossall school

HENNIKER, REV. R. *(Con.)*

1869–75; V. of Frocester near Stroud 1875 to death; author of *Stories from English history for young children* 1861; *Trifles for travellers* 1864. *d.* Frocester vicarage 1 Feb. 1880.

HENNING, JOHN *(son of Samuel Henning, carpenter).* *b.* Paisley 2 May 1771; carpenter; modeller of wax figures 1800; a modeller at Glasgow; studied in Trustees' academy, Edin. 1802; went to London 1811; made models of the Parthenon and Phigaleian friezes with the missing parts restored 1811–23; made models in relief of cartoons of Raphael; exhibited 17 sculptures at R.A., 8 at B.I. and 37 at Suffolk st. 1816–52; executed busts of Princess Charlotte of Wales and Mrs. Siddons; a founder of Soc. of British Artists 1847; presented with freedom of Paisley 1846; executed the relievi on the gate at Hyde park corner and those on the Athenæum club. *d.* 17 Lower Belgrave place, Pimlico, London 8 April 1851. *bur.* St. Pancras cemet. Finchley.

HENNINGSEN, CHARLES FREDERICK *(son of a Suede).* *b.* England 1815; in Carlist army in Spain, lieut.-col. 1834; served in Russian army in Circassia; commander of fortress of Comorn under Kossuth in Hungary 1849; commander of the artillery under William Walker in Nicaragua, America 1856, major general; colonel of 3 regt. of Wise's brigade in Confederate army and served in Virginia; superintended construction of first Minié rifle made in U.S. America; author of *Revelations of Russia. Paris* 1845; *The most striking events of a twelve months' campaign with Zumalacarregui* 2 vols. 1836; *The White slave* 3 vols. 1845; *Personal recollections of Nicaragua,* and other works. *d.* Washington, D.C. 14 June 1877. *Appleton's American Biography, iii,* 169 (1887).

HENRADE, MARY *(3 dau. of Thomas Young of Melbourne, Australia).* *b.* 1842; appeared in original cast of *Our American Cousin* at Haymarket theatre, London 11 Nov. 1861; played at Lyceum theatre, Oct. 1864, and at chief west end theatres. *(m.* Stephen Demetrius Pitzipios a Greek merchant and general agent at 17 Throgmorton st. London). *d.* Duncroft house, 3 Grove end road, London 11 March 1876 aged 34. *Era* 19 March 1876 *p.* 10 *col.* 4.

HENRY, ALEXANDER. *b.* Loughbrickland, co. Down 1783; came from U.S. America and settled in Palace st. Manchester as an American house doing an export trade in cotton and woollen goods 1804; crossed the Atlantic 30 times; opened houses at Leeds, Huddersfield, Bradford, Leicester, Nottingham, Glasgow

HENRY, A. *(Con.)*

and Belfast; member of Anti-Corn law league 1838; M.P. South Lancashire 20 Dec. 1847 to June 1852; entertained Kossuth 1850; lost his sight many years before his death. *d.* Harrogate 4 Oct. 1862. *London Society* (*Nov.* 1880) 446–62; *Hunt's Merchant's Mag. xix,* 63–67 (1848), *xxxiv,* 36–45 (1856).

HENRY, CHAPLIN, assumed name of Henry Charles Stroud. *b.* 1826; bookseller; had a fine bass voice; attached to choir of Surrey chapel, Blackfriars road, London; an early member of Henry Leslie's choir 1856; chief bass at Foundling chapel; a singer at the banquets at the City of London halls; author of *O write me a song of my father, Ballad* 1869. *d.* Peckham 12 Jany. 1888. *Musical Times* 1 *Feb.* 1888 *p.* 92.

HENRY, GEORGE FITZGERALD *(brother of Sir Thomas Henry 1807–76).* *b.* 1827; entered service of P. and O.S.N. Co. 1847, commander on the China line, superintendent of service at Bombay; connected with Bank of Bombay and the Port Trust board; member of the Bombay corporation; thrown out of his carriage at Bombay and *killed* 23 Feb. 1877. *The Graphic* 5 *May* 1877 *pp.* 407, 408, *portrait.*

HENRY, JAMES (1 *son of Robert Henry, woollen draper).* *b.* Dublin 13 Dec. 1798; ed. at Trin. coll. Dublin, B.A. 1819, M.A. and M.B. 1822, M.D. 1832; a physician in Dublin with a large practice 1822–45 charging a five shilling fee instead of the usual guinea; from 1841 the study of Virgil became the object of his life, began walking through Europe with his wife and daughter making Virgilian researches 1846; wife Anne Jane dau. of John Patton *d.* Arco, Tyrol and was cremated; crossed the Alps 17 times; dau. Katharine Olivia *b.* 20 Nov. 1830 assistant to her father in his travels and studies, *d.* 7 Dec. 1872; author of *Miliaria accuratius descripta. Dublin* 1832; *The Eneis, books i and ii rendered into English blank Iambic by J. H.* 1845; *Notes of a twelve years' voyage of discovery in the first six books of the Eneis. Dresden* 1853; *Poems, chiefly philosophical. Dresden* 1856, *with a portrait; Thalia Petasata, a foot journey from Carlsruhe to Bassano. Dresden* 1859; *Æneidea, remarks on the Æneis, with collation of principal editions* 2 vols. 1873–9. *d.* Dalkey lodge, Dalkey near Dublin 14 July 1876. *The Academy* 12 *Aug.* 1876 *pp.* 162–3.

HENRY, JOHN. Entered Madras army 1800; col. 51 Madras N.I. 15 March 1842 to death; L.G. 3 Aug. 1855. *d.* Holles st. Cavendish sq. London 17 Dec. 1860.

HENRY, MICHAEL *(son of a merchant, d. April 1840).* b. Kennington, London 19 Feb. 1830; ed. at City of London sch. 1840–44; assisted in editing *Mechanics' Mag.* 1846–57; a patent agent in London 1857 to death; edited *Jewish Chronicle* 1868 to death; founded General Benevolent Assoc. 1847, hon. sec. to death; hon. sec. Stepney Jewish schools to death; A.I.C.E.; author of *The Inventor's almanac* 1858; *A defence of the present patent laws* 1866; his clothes caught fire when he was in his office 68 Fleet st., d. from the burns at 6 Argyle sq. Euston sq. London 16 June 1875. *bur.* Willesden cemet. 21 June. *Jewish Chronicle 25 June 1875 pp.* 205–6; *Times 18 June 1875 p.* 13, *19 June p.* 7.

HENRY, SIR THOMAS *(eld. son of David Henry of Stephens green, Dublin, government contractor).* b. Dublin 1807; ed. at Von Feinaigles sch. and at Trin. coll. Dublin, B.A. 1824, M.A. 1827; barrister M.T. 23 Jany. 1829; magistrate at Lambeth st. police court near Whitechapel, April 1840, removed to Bow st. 1846, chief mag. at Bow st. 6 July 1864 to death; knighted at Windsor castle 30 Nov. 1864. d. 23 Hanover sq. London 16 June 1876. *I.L.N. 14 March 1846 p.* 172, *portrait,* 24 *June* 1876 *p.* 623, 1 *July pp.* 3, 4, *portrait ; Graphic, xiii,* 614, 628 (1876), *portrait.*

HENRY, WALTER. b. Donegal, Ireland 1 Jany. 1791; ed. Trin. coll. Dublin; hospital assistant in 66 foot April 1811, served in the Peninsula to 1814, in Nepaulese war 1816–7, in St. Helena 1817–21, prepared bulletin of post mortem appearance of body of Napoleon; in Canada 1827–41; staff surgeon 1839, inspector general of hospitals in Canada 1852, retired 1856; wrote in periodicals under pseudonyms of Miles, Piscator, and Scrutator; author of *Trifles from my Portfolio, or recollections of 29 years military service, By a Staff Surgeon. Quebec* 2 vols. 1839; *Events of a military life* 2 *vols.* 1843. d. Belleville, Upper Canada 27 June 1860. *Morgan's Bibl. Canadensis* (1867) 182–3.

HENRY, WILLIAM ALEXANDER. b. Halifax, Nova Scotia 30 Dec. 1816; barrister N.S. Nov. 1840; Q.C. 1849; member of Nova Scotia Assembly 1840 for many years; mayor of Halifax; solicitor general 3 times; provincial secretary and attorney general; puisne judge of supreme court of Canada, Oct. 1875 to death. d. Ottawa 3 May 1888.

HENSLOW, REV. JOHN STEVENS (1 *son of John Prentis Henslow, solicitor, Enfield, d.* 1854). b. Rochester, Kent 6 Feb. 1796; ed. at free gram. sch. Rochester and St. John's coll. Cam., 16 wr. 1818, B.A. 1818, M.A. 1821;

HENSLOW, REV. J. S. *(Con.)* F.L.S. 1818; F.G.S. 1819; founded with Adam Sedgwick, the Cambridge Phil. Soc. 15 Nov. 1819; prof. of mineralogy at Cam. 1822 to March 1827; P.C. of St. Mary the Less, Cam. 1824–32; prof. of botany at Cam. June 1825 to death, his enthusiasm rendered botany popular, Darwin and others were his pupils; V. of Cholsey, Berks. 1832–7; R. of Hitcham, Suffolk 1837 to death; established study of botany in his schools; for tithe dinners substituted excursions; discovered beds of phosphatic nodules in the Suffolk Crag 1843 much used for manure; a founder of the Ipswich museum 1848; author of *Catalogue of British plants* 1829, 2 ed. 1835; *The principles of descriptive and physiological botany* 1836; *An account of Roman antiquities found at Rougham, Bury St. Edmunds* 1843; *A dictionary of botanical terms* 1856 and other books. d. Hitcham rectory house 16 May 1861, his collections divided between Ipswich, Cambridge and Kew museums. *Jenyns' Memoir of J. S. Henslow* (1862), *portrait; Popular Science Monthly, iii,* 159–72 (1873), *portrait; Longman's Mag. June 1883 pp.* 147–59.

HENSMAN, REV. JOHN *(son of Thomas Hensman of Birmingham).* b. Bedford 22 Sep. 1780; ed. at C.C. coll. Cam., 9 wr. 1801, B.A 1801, M.A. 1804; fellow of his coll. 1801; C. to Rev. Charles Simeon at Cam. 1801; C. of Wraxall, Somerset 1803–9; C. in charge of Clifton parish ch. Bristol 1809–22; C. of Dowry chapel, Clifton 1822–30; incumb. of Trinity ch. Hotwells 1830–44; P.C. of Christ Church, Clifton 1844–7; R. of Clifton 1847 to death; St. James' chapel, Clifton commonly known as the Hensman memorial church was consecrated Dec. 1862; hon. canon of Bristol cath. 1858; well known member of evangelical party; prime mover in building 4 churches in Clifton. d. Clifton hill 23 April 1864. *Bristol Times 30 April 1864 p.* 6.

HENSOM, GRAVENER. b. Nottingham 1785; engaged in hosiery trade and in point and bobbin net manufacture; had a practical knowledge of all kinds of looms; wandered about the coasts of England, Scotland and France discovering and exposing the tricks of the smugglers; imprisoned in Coldbath-fields prison for his connection with Luddite riots; gave evidence before parliamentary committee; author of *List of 100 inventions and alterations in the stocking and lace machines* 1828; *Civil, political and mechanical history of the frame-work knitting and lace trades* 1831 which was never finished. d. Broad st. Nottingham 15 Nov. 1852. *Felkin's History of hosiery* (1867) *pp. xv–xvii; Wylie's Nottingham* (1853) 234–5.

HENTY, EDWARD (6 son of Thomas Henty, land-owner and banker, West Tarring, Sussex, who went to Tasmania 1831). b. West Tarring, Sussex 10 March 1809; emigrated to Tasmania 1831; one of the three founders of the colony of Victoria, Australia; the first settler in Portland Bay, Victoria 19 Nov. 1834 where he had a whaling station; imported pure merino sheep 1835; ploughed the first land ever turned up in Victoria 1835; went inland and took up large sheep runs; member for Normanby in legislative assembly 1856–61; held Muntham station, Victoria. d. Offington, St. Kilda road, Melbourne 14 Aug. 1878. Times 28 Sep. 1878 p. 10; Men of the Time. Victorian Series (1878) 86–8; R. Henty's Australiana (1886) 26 etc.

HENTY, WILLIAM (brother of the preceding). b. England 1808; emigrated to Tasmania 1831; solicitor at Launceston, Tasmania; member of legislative assembly, Tasmania; colonial secretary, Tasmania 1857–62; returned and settled in England 1863; author of Our improvements in cottage husbandry. Launceston 1850. d. 12 Medina villas, Brighton 11 July 1881. Times 14 July 1881 p. 9.

HENWOOD, WILLIAM JORY (eld. son of John Henwood of Perran-wharf near Truro). b. Perran-wharf 16 Jany. 1805; clerk to Fox & Co. at Perran 1822–7; first went underground 1825; assay master and supervisor of tin for duchy of Cornwall 1832–8; Telford medallist of Instit. of C.E. for paper On pumping engines 1837; made special study of metalliferous deposits; F.G.S. 1828, Murchison medallist 27 Feb. 1875; F.R.S. 27 Feb. 1840; in charge of Gongo-Soco mines, Brazil 1843–53; reported on the metals in Kumaon and Gurhwal for Indian government 1855; president R. Instit. of Cornwall 1869–71, delivered three valuable addresses; author of On the metalliferous deposits of Cornwall and Devon. Subterranean temperature, Water and Electric currents, being vol. v. of Trans. R. Geol. Soc. of Cornwall 1843, and Observations on metalliferous deposits and on Subterranean temperature vol. vi. 1871, and other books and numerous papers. d. 3 Clarence place, Penzance 5 Aug. 1875. Boase and Courtney's Bibl. Cornub. 230–3, 1227; Times 10 Aug. 1875 p. 3 by W. P. Courtney.

HEPBURN, HENRY POOLE (1 son of Francis K. Hepburn, major general). b. 24 Jany. 1822; ensign Scots Fusilier guards 19 Feb. 1841, lieut.-col. 21 March 1874 to 10 Oct. 1874 when placed on h.p.; served in Crimean campaign 1854–5, wounded at battle of Alma, medal with 2 clasps, Turkish medal and 5

HEPBURN, H. P. (Con.)
class of Medjidie; L.G. 1 July 1881; C.B. 2 June 1869; maintained an orphanage for daughters of soldiers of the Scots guards. d. The Hooke, Chailey, Lewes 26 Oct. 1888. Times 29 Oct. 1888 p. 6.

HEPPEL, JOHN MORTIMER (eld. son of George Hastings Heppel of Taplow, Bucks., paper maker). b. Taplow 23 Dec. 1817; ed. at Merchant Taylor's sch. and London univ.; established with Moser an engineering factory at Aix la Chapelle, partnership dissolved 1847; chief engineer on Madras railway, May 1857 to 1861; engineer to Peruvian railway 1865; A.I.C.E. 20 April 1835, M.I.C.E. 11 Feb. 1851; invented a water meter and other pieces of mechanism. d. 2 Storey's gate, Westminster 21 March 1872. Min. of Proc. of C.E. xxxvi, 265–68 (1873).

HERAPATH, JOHN (son of a maltster). b. Bristol 30 May 1790; a maltster with his cousin William Herapath at Bristol; conducted a mathematical school, taking candidates for the navy 1815; Royal Soc. refused to publish his paper "A mathematical enquiry into the causes of heat, gases, gravitation, &c." 1820, which was then printed in Annals of Philosophy and a controversy with Royal Soc. ensued; mathematical tutor at Cranford, Middlesex 1820–32; removed to Kensington 1832; one of first advocates of atmospheric railway system 1839; part proprietor and manager Railway Magazine 1835, called The Railway magazine and Annals of Science 1836–39, then Herapath's Railway Journal, became sole proprietor; printed numerous mathematical papers; author of Mathematical physics 2 vols. 1847. d. Catford bridge, Lewisham, Kent 24 Feb. 1868. G.M. April 1868 pp. 544–5; Herapath's Railway Journal 29 Feb. 1868 p. 234.

HERAPATH, SPENCER (2 son of the preceding). b. 1822; ed. in a college in Indiana, U.S. America; connected with Herapath's Railway Journal; sec. to Admiral Laws manager Lancashire and Yorkshire railway; sec. of Sheffield, Barnsley and Wakefield railway to 1865; A.I.C.E. 5 March 1867; head of firm of Spencer Herapath & Co., stock brokers, London 1844; member of committee of Spanish bondholders; director of Buenos Ayres Great southern railway 11 Jany. 1868; F.G.S.; F.A.S.; F.S.S. d. 18 Upper Phillimore gardens, Kensington 13 March 1884. Min. of Proc. of C.E. lxxviii, 447–8 (1884).

HERAPATH, WILLIAM (son of Mr. Herapath of Bristol, maltster). b. Bristol 26 May 1796; a maltster, Bristol; one of the founders of the

HERAPATH, W. (*Con.*)

Bristol Medical sch. 1828, professor of chemistry there 1828; president of Bristol Political Union 1831; one of the founders of Chemical Soc. of Lond. 23 Feb. 1841; F.C.S.; employed as analytical chemist in cases of Mary Ann Burdock of Bristol 1835 and of W. Palmer of Rugeley 1856; member of Bristol town council 1833 and senior magistrate. *d.* Manor house, Old Park st. Bristol 13 Feb. 1868. *Gent. Mag.* v, 404, 544 (1868); *Herapath's Railway Journal* 22 Feb. 1868 *p.* 205.

HERAPATH, WILLIAM BIRD (1 *son of the preceding*). *b.* 1820; L.S.A. 1843, M.R.C.S. 1844; ed. at Univ. of London, M.B. 1844, M.D. 1851; surgeon Queen Elizabeth's hospital, Bristol; president Bristol microscopical soc.; F.R.S.; made many chemical and toxicological discoveries; contributed numerous papers to scientific journals; discoverer and manufacturer of artificial tourmalines; author of *A few words on the Bristol and Clifton Hotwells* 1854; *The handbook for visitors to the Bristol and Clifton Hotwells* 1864. *d.* 32 Old Market st. Bristol 12 Oct. 1868. *I.L.N.* 24 Oct. 1868 *p.* 411; *Times* 15 Oct. 1868 *p.* 5.

HERAUD, JOHN ABRAHAM (*son of Abraham Heraud, law stationer, d. 1846*). *b.* St. Andrew's, Holborn, London 5 July 1799; friend of Coleridge, Southey, Wordsworth and Carlyle; assistant editor of *Fraser's Mag.* 1830–3; edited *The Sunbeam* 1838–9, the *Monthly Mag.* 1839–42 and the *Christian monthly mag.*; contributor and dramatic critic to the *Athenæum* 1843–68; dramatic critic *Illust. London News* 1849–79; a brother of the Charterhouse 21 July 1873 to death; wrote *Videna*, a tragedy, Marylebone theatre 1854, *Wife and no Wife*, and *Medea*; author of *The legend of St. Loy* 1820; *The descent into hell* 1830, 2 ed. 1835; *The judgment of the flood* 1834, new ed. 1857; *The life and times of G. Savonarola* 1843; *The sibyl among the tombs* 1886. *d.* Charterhouse, Charterhouse sq. London 20 April 1887. *Athenæum* 23, 30 *April* (1887); *I.L.N.* 30 *April* 1887 *p.* 485.

HERBERT OF LEA, SIDNEY HERBERT, 1 Baron (*younger son of* 11 *Earl of Pembroke* 1759–1827). *b.* Richmond, Surrey 16 Sep. 1810; ed. at Harrow and Oriel coll. Ox., B.A. 1831; M.P. for South Wilts., Dec. 1832 to Jany. 1861; sec. of board of control Jany. to April 1835; joint sec. of the admiralty 10 Sep. 1841 to 13 Feb. 1845; sec. of state for war 4 Feb. 1845 to 6 July 1846, 29 Dec. 1852 to 8 Feb. 1855 and 18 June 1859 to July 1861; sec. of state for the colonies Feb. 1855 to 15 May 1855; P.C. 3 Feb. 1845;

HERBERT OF LEA, Baron (*Con.*)

first president National Volunteer assoc. 16 Nov. 1859; cr. Baron Herbert of Lea, Wilts. 15 Jany. 1861; made great sanitary reforms in the army; author of *Proposal for the better application of cathedral institutions to their intended use* 1849; *The conduct of the war. A speech* 1854; *Military education. A speech* 1856. *d.* Wilton house, Salisbury 2 Aug. 1861, his statue in front of war office, Pall Mall, London, unveiled 1 June 1867. *The British Cabinet in* 1853, 276–86; *H. Martineau's Biog. sketches* (1876) 78–90; *Fraser's Mag.* lxv, 198 (1861); *I.L.N.* iv, 136 (1844), *portrait*.

NOTE.—With Lord Lincoln afterwards the duke of Newcastle, he became interested in the *Morning Chronicle*, which was the organ of the Peelites from 21 Feb. 1848 under the editorship of John Douglas Cook.—.In the autumn of 1854 the paper was sold to Serjeant William Glover.—.Lord Herbert is said to have lost £116,000 in this undertaking.—.*Bourne's English newspapers*, ii, 152-8.

HERBERT, ALFRED (*son of Thomas Herbert, waterman*). Apprentice to a boat-builder; painter of coast scenes with fishing boats and figures and views in the reaches of the Thames; exhibited 14 pictures at R.A., 3 at B.I. and 26 at Suffolk st. 1844–60; obliged to sell his pictures to dealers at low prices; 2 of his pictures are at South Kensington. *d.* Jany. 1861. *Redgrave Dict. of Artists* (1878) 209; *Art Journal* 1861 *p.* 56.

HERBERT, ALGERNON (*youngest son of* 1 *Earl of Carnarvon* 1741–1811). *b.* 12 July 1792; ed. at Eton and Ch. Ch. Ox., removed to Exeter coll., B.A. 1813, M.A. 1825; fellow of Merton coll. 1814–31, subwarden 1826, dean 1828; barrister I.T. 27 Nov. 1818; published *Nimrod, a discourse upon certain passages of history and fable, By A. H.* part i. 1826, reprinted, remodelled and republished in 2 vols. 1828, a 3 vol. 1828, vol. 4 part i. 1829, part ii. 1830; *Britannia after the Romans, By the Hon. A. H.* 2 vols. 1836–41; *Cyclops Christianus, or an argument to disprove the antiquity of the Stonehenge and other Megalithic erections in England and Britanny* 1849. *d.* Ickleton, Cambs. 11 June 1855. *G.M.* xliv, 649–50 (1855).

HERBERT, CHARLES. *b.* 1783; entered Madras army 1803; colonel 16 Madras N.I. 29 June 1842 to death; general 26 April 1866; C.B. 20 July 1838. *d.* Morland lodge, Croydon 17 Jany. 1867 aged 84.

HERBERT, CHARLES. *b.* 1805; ensign 66 foot 10 Dec. 1825; lieut. col. 75 foot 2 June 1857 to 7 Dec. 1858; lieut. col. 54 foot 7 Dec. 1858 to 27 July 1866 when he retired on full pay; L.G. 1 Oct. 1877; C.B. 1 Jany. 1858. *d.* Boyle cottage, Thames Ditton 19 Sep. 1879.

HERBERT, SIR CHARLES LYON. M.D.; knighted at St. James's palace 19 Aug. 1836; (*m.* 1812 Anne dau. of Humphrey Jeffreys of Bristol, she *d.* Florence 28 Nov. 1860), he *d.* Lower Berkeley st. Manchester sq. London 1855.

HERBERT, CYRIL WISEMAN (*youngest son of John Rogers Herbert 1810–90*). *b.* Gloucester road, Old Brompton, London 30 Sep. 1847; godson of Cardinal Nicholas Wiseman; ed. in France, at St. Mary's coll. Oscott and King's coll. London; studied in Italy 1868; exhibited 5 pictures at R.A. 1870–5; some of his paintings were Homeward after labour. Roman cattle driven home 1870; Returning to the fold. Welsh sheep driven home 1874, in Walker art gallery, Liverpool; curator of antique school in Royal Academy 1882. *d.* The Chimes, Kilburn 2 July 1882. *Academy 8 July 1882 p. 38; Art Journal 1882 p. 256.*

HERBERT, DENNIS. Inspecting field officer of militia, Nova Scotia 28 Jany. 1808 to 17 March 1817 when placed on h.p.; general 20 June 1854. *d.* Exeter 19 Sep. 1861.

HERBERT, EDWARD CHARLES HUGH (*younger son of 2 Earl of Carnarvon 1772–1833*). *b.* 30 March 1802; M.P. for Callington, Cornwall 1831–32. *d.* 30 May 1852.

HERBERT, EDWARD GILBERT. Ed. at Univ. college, London; barrister L.I. 17 Nov. 1862; equity draftsman and conveyancer; lecturer on law at Univ. of London; brought out with other writers a volume of essays entitled *Religious Republics* 1869 in which he wrote *The Congregational Character* pp. 91–132; wrote on art in public journals. *d.* Nottingham 12 March 1871.

HERBERT, EDWARD HENRY CHARLES (*only son of E. C. H. Herbert 1802–52*). *b.* 1 Sep. 1837; ed. at Ball. coll. Ox., scholar 1855–61, B.A. 1859, M.A. 1865; 3 sec. of legation at Athens 16 Nov. 1868 to death; while on an excursion to the plains of Marathon, taken prisoner by Greek brigands and murdered at Oropos Sykamenos 21 April 1870, *bur.* Burghclere ch. yard 15 May. *Times* 14 *April* 1870 *p. 5, 7 May p. 12, 17 May p. 6; I.L.N. lvi,* 491, 557 (1870); *Parl. Papers* 1870 *and* 1871.

HERBERT, HENRY ARTHUR (*elder son of Charles John Herbert of Muckross abbey, co. Kerry, d. 1836*). *b.* Muckross 1815; ed. at Trin. coll. Cam.; M.P. for co. Kerry 9 Aug. 1847 to death; chief sec. to lord lieut. of Ireland, June 1857 to Feb. 1858; P.C. 25 June 1857; sheriff of Kerry 1836; lord lieut.

HERBERT, H. A. (*Con.*)
of Kerry 1853 to death; hon. colonel of Kerry militia 9 Jany. 1854 to death. *d.* Adare manor, Limerick 26 Feb. 1866. *I.L.N. xxv,* 616 (1854), *portrait.*

HERBERT, HENRY WILLIAM (*elder son of Hon. and Rev. William Herbert 1778–1847, dean of Manchester*). *b.* 10 Poland st. Oxford st. London 3 April 1807; ed. at Eton and at Caius coll. Cam., B.A. 1830; classical master in Rev. R. T. Huddart's sch. New York 1831–9; with A. D. Patterson established the *American Monthly Mag.* 1833; made much money but was improvident and quarrelled with his friends; lived at The Cedars on the Passaic 1846–58; author of *Cromwell, a novel* 2 vols. 1837; *The Roman traitor* 3 vols. 1846; *The knights of England, France and Scotland* 1852; *Memoirs of Henry VIII of England and his six wives* 1858; under the pseudonym of Frank Forester he wrote *My Shooting Box* 1846; *Frank Forester and his friends* 3 vols. 1849; *The Deerstalker* 1850; *Horse and horsemanship of the United States and British provinces* 2 vols. 1857 and other books; *shot himself* through the head at Stevens house, Broadway, New York 17 May 1858. *Judd's Life of F. Forester 2 vols.* (1882), *portrait; Picton's Life of F. Forester* (1881); *Appleton's American Biog. iii,* 179–80 (1877), *portrait.*

HERBERT, JOHN (*son of Wm. Herbert 1771–1851*), *librarian Guildhall library, city of London*). *b.* Walcot place, Lambeth 28 Feb. 1814; appeared as Romeo in the Catherine st. theatre 1831; a comic singer at Vauxhall, Cremorne and Rosherville 1833 etc.; played in dramatic companies at Brighton 1837–8, at York 1839–40, at Newcastle 1840, at Sadler's Wells 1841, at the Victoria 1843, at City of London 1844–7; a low comedian of much ability, his best character was Paulo in *Plot and Counterplot;* acted at Royal theatre, Edinburgh 1851–2. *d.* Edinburgh 6 April 1852. *Theatrical Times, ii,* 217, 226 (1847), *portrait; J. C. Dibdin's Edinburgh Stage* (1888) 434, 436.

HERBERT, JOHN MAURICE (*son of John Lawrence Herbert of New hall, Montgomeryshire*). *b.* 15 July 1808; ed. at cathedral school, Hereford and St. John coll. Cam., B.A. 1830, M.A. 1833; fellow of his college 1830–40; barrister L.I. 8 May 1835; assistant tithe and copyhold comr.; comr. for enfranchising assessionable manors of duchy of Cornwall; judge of county courts, circuit No. 24 (South Wales) 12 March 1847 to death; F.G.S. *d.* Rocklands near Ross 3 Nov. 1882. *I.L.N. lxxxi,* 569 (1882), *portrait; Red Dragon, iii,* 1 (1883), *portrait.*

HERBERT, JOHN ROGERS *(son of the controller of customs, Maldon, Essex)*. *b.* Maldon 23 Jany. 1810; student R. Acad. London 1826; exhibited 69 pictures at R.A., 26 at B.I. and 7 at Suffolk st. 1830–80; studied in Italy 1835; joined the Church of Rome 1840; A.R.A. 1841, R.A. 1846, retired 1886; a master of the School of design, Somerset house 1837; decorated the peers' robing room, house of lords with 9 pictures, the best being, Moses bringing the tables of the law, executed in the water glass process and taking 14 years to complete; commenced painting religious subjects with, Introduction of Christianity into Britain 1842; some of his best known works are, Sir Thomas More and his daughter 1844; The acquittal of the seven bishops 1846; Our Saviour subject to his parents at Nazareth 1847; Laborare est orare 1862; The sower of good seed 1865; The bay of Salamis 1869; The adoration of the Magi 1874. *d.* The Chimes, Kilburn 17 March 1890. *bur.* Kensal green. *Sandby's Hist. of R. Academy, ii,* 179–81 (1862); *Sherer's Gallery of British artists, i,* 39–46; *I.L.N.* 29 March 1890 p. 390, *portrait; Pictorial World 3 April 1890 pp.* 423, 441, *portrait; Times 20 March 1890 p.* 10.

HERBERT, SIR PERCY EGERTON (2 *son of 2 Earl of Powis* 1785–1848). *b.* Powis castle, Montgomeryshire 15 April 1822; ed. at Eton and Sandhurst; ensign 43 foot 17 Jany. 1840; served in Kaffir war 1851–3, Russian war 1854–6 and wounded at the Alma, Indian mutiny 1857–8; A.D.C. to the Queen 29 June 1855 to 28 Jany. 1868; lieut.-col. 82 foot 19 Feb. 1858 to 16 Nov. 1860 when placed on h.p.; deputy quartermaster general 1 Nov. 1860 to 28 April 1865; L.G. 22 Sep. 1875; colonel 74 highlanders April 1876; M.P. Ludlow 1854–60; M.P. South Shropshire 1865 to death; treasurer of H.M.'s household 27 Feb. 1867 to Dec. 1868; C.B. 5 July 1855, K.C.B. 2 June 1869; P.C. 19 March 1867. *d.* Styche, Market Drayton 7 Oct. 1876.

HERBERT, ST. LEGER ALGERNON (1 *son of Frederick Charles Herbert* 1819–68, *commander in navy*). *b.* Kingston, Canada 16 Aug. 1850; ed. at naval sch. New Cross, Kent and at Wadham coll. Ox., scholar 1869–74; in Canadian C.S. 1875–8; private sec. to Sir Garnet Wolseley in Cyprus 1878 and in South Africa 1879; at the storming of Sekokoeni's Mountain and for his services C.M.G. 1880; a correspondent of *The Times* from 1878; sec. to Sir F. Roberts in Africa, Feb. 1881; sec. to Transvaal commission 1881; special corres-

HERBERT, ST. L. A. *(Con.)* pondent for *Morning Post* in Egypt from Sep. 1883, shot through the leg at Tamai; on staff of Sir H. Stewart in Egypt 1884, *killed* at battle of Gubat near Metammeh in the Soudan 19 Jany. 1885; *monument* to memory of 7 journalists who died in Soudan, in crypt of St. Paul's. *Morning Post 29 Jany. 1885 p.* 5; *I.L.N. lxxxvi,* 171 (1885), *portrait.*

HERBERT, SIR THOMAS (2 *son of Richard Townshend Herbert of Cahirnane, M.P. co. Kerry* 1783–90). *b.* Cahirnane, Feb. 1793; entered navy 23 July 1803; captain 25 Nov. 1822; served in China during war operations in Canton river 1840–41; commodore on south east coast of America 11 Jany. 1847 to 21 June 1849; a junior lord of admiralty, Feb. to Dec. 1852; V.A. 8 Dec. 1857; sheriff of Kerry 1829; C.B. 29 June 1841, K.C.B. 14 Oct. 1841; M.P. for Dartmouth 1852–57. *d.* 74 Cadogan place, London 4 Aug. 1861.

HERBERT, REV. THOMAS MARTIN *(son of Thomas Herbert of Nottingham)*. *b.* Nottingham 18 Oct. 1835; ed. at Mill Hill sch., Spring Hill coll., Lancashire coll. and at Univ. coll. London, B.A. London, M.A.; congregational minister at Nether chapel, Sheffield to 1867, at Cheadle 1868–76; professor of philosophy and church history, Lancashire coll. 1876 to death; author of *The external relations of Congregationalism,* printed in Religious Republics 1869; *Difficulties in the way of religious education by the state* 1874; *The realistic assumptions of modern science* 1879. *d.* Ottringham near Manchester 28 Nov. 1877. *The Congregationalist, vii,* 33–40 (1878); *Congregational Year Book* (1879) 320–21.

HERBERT, WILLIAM. *b.* 1771; librarian Guildhall library, city of London 1828–45; author of *Antiquities of the inns of court and chancery* 1804; *Select views of London and its environs 2 vols.* 1804–5; *The history of the twelve great livery companies of London 2 vols.* 1836–7; with E. W. Brayley he wrote *Syr Reginalde or the Black tower, a romance* 1803; *History of Lambeth palace* 1806; with Robert Wilkinson *Londina illustrata 2 vols.* 1819–25. *d.* 40 Brunswick st. Haggerston, London 18 Nov. 1851.

HERBISON, DAVID *(son of an innkeeper, d.* 1827). *b.* Ballymena, co. Antrim 14 Oct. 1800; a hand loom linen weaver 1814–27 and 1830 to death; resided in Canada 1827–30; known as The Bard of Dunclug; author of *The fate of Mc. Quillan and O'Neill's daughter, poems, Belfast* 1841; *Midnight musings* 1848; *Woodland wanderings* 1858; *The Snow wreath*

HERBISON, D. (*Con.*)

1869, *with Autobiography of the author; The children of the year* 1876. *d.* Dunclug near Ballymena 26 May 1880, *monu.* at Ballymena. *Collected works of D. Herbison, ed. by Rev. D. Mc. Meekin* (1883), *with memoir.*

HERDMAN, ROBERT (4 *son of Rev. William Herdman, minister of Rattray, Perthshire, d.* 1838). *b.* Rattray 17 Sep. 1829; ed. at Madras coll. St. Andrews 1838, and at Univ. of St. Andrews; studied art in Trustees' acad. Edin. 1847 and in Italy 1854–6 and 1868; A.R. Scottish Acad. 1858, Academician 1863; portrait, figure and landscape painter; exhibited at R. Scottish Acad. 1850 to death; exhibited 32 pictures at R.A. Lond. and 2 at B.I. 1861–80; some of his paintings were, After the battle, a scene in covenanting times 1870, in National gallery, Scotland; Charles Edward seeking shelter in the house of an adherent 1876; Landless and homeless 1887; author of *Address to the students of the Board of manufacturers' Art School* 1888; *found dead* in his studio from heart disease, Edinburgh 10 Jany. 1888. *Times* 12 *Jany.* 1888 p. 6.

HERDMAN, WILLIAM GAWIN (*son of a corn merchant*). *b.* Liverpool 13 March 1805; art teacher Liverpool; member of Liverpool academy till 1857 when he was expelled for his opposition to pre-Raphaeliteism; established an Art school in Liverpool 1857; exhibited 5 pictures at R.A. and 1 at Suffolk st. 1834–61; the reformation of perspective occupied much of his time; the founder of shilling art-unions; F.S.A.; published *Views of Fleetwood-on-Wyre* 1838; *Studies from the folio of W. G. H.* 1838; *Pictorial relics of ancient Liverpool* 1843; *A treatise on the curvilinear perspective of nature* 1853; *Thoughts on speculative cosmology and the principles of art* 1870; *found dead* in his bed at 41 St. Domingo vale, Liverpool 29 March 1882. *Bryan's Dictionary of painters* (1886) 645; *Liverpool Mercury* 1 *April* 1882 p. 5.

HERING, GEORGE EDWARDS (*younger son of a German bookbinder*). *b.* London 1805; studied in Munich art sch. 1829 and in Italy 1830 etc.; landscape painter; exhibited 88 pictures at R.A., 86 at B.I. and 10 at Suffolk st. 1836–80; among his paintings were The ruins of the palace of the Cæsars at Rome 1836; Amalfi 1841 and Capri 18—, both in the Royal collection; Bridge over a stream 1847, in South Kensington museum; published *Sketches on the Danube, in Hungary and Transilvania* 1838; *The mountains and lakes in Switzerland, the Tyrol and Italy, twenty coloured lithographs* 1847. *d.* 45 Grove end road, St.

HERING, G. E. (*Con.*)

John's Wood, London 18 Dec. 1879, his wife a well known painter, exhibited landscapes 1853–8. *Art Journal, xxxii,* 83; *Clement and Hutton's Artists* (1879) 348.

HERIOT, FREDERICK LEWIS MAITLAND. *b.* 6 Feb. 1818; barrister 1839, advocate depute; sheriff of Forfarshire 21 Feb. 1862 to death; edited *The Scottish jurist, containing reports of cases decided in the courts of session. d.* Paris 7 March 1881. *Journal of Jurisprudence, xxv,* 204 (1881).

HERMAN, GEORGE FREDERIC. Joined British auxiliary legion in Spain as a captain in the Rifle corps 11 July 1835 and was present during all the fighting 1835–8, lieut.-col. 1 Oct. 1836; went out to Syria as assistant adjutant general on staff of Sir Charles Smith 1840 and served through Syrian campaign, receiving Sultan's gold medal; vice consul at Bengazi 31 March 1848; consul at Tripoli 1 Jany. 1852 and consul general there 26 March 1856 to 13 Jany. 1865, retired on a pension 18 July 1865. *d.* 2 Aug. 1873. *Foreign Office List* (1873) 111–12.

HERMON, EDWARD (*son of Richard Hermon*). *b.* London about 1821; member of firm of Horrocks, Miller and Co. cotton spinners, Preston; M.P. Preston 1868–81; gave money for prizes, for Essays on the prevention of explosions and accidents in coal mines 1874. *d.* Berkeley sq. London 6 May 1881, personalty sworn to be £588,000 on 25 June 1881, his pictures were sold for £37,116 4s. 6d. on 13 May 1882.

HERON, DENIS CAULFIELD (*eld. son of W. Heron*). *b.* Dublin 1826; ed. at St. Gregory's Downside and Trin. coll. Dublin, B.A. 1845, LL.B. and LL.D. 1857; obtained a university scholarship 1845 but precluded from enjoying it on account of being a Roman Catholic; called to Irish bar 1848; professor of jurisprudence in Queen's college, Galway 1849–59; Q.C. 4 July 1860; law adviser at Dublin Castle, April to July 1866; bencher of King's Inns 1872; M.P. for Tipperary 1870–74; third serjeant at law Oct. 1880 to death; author of *The constitutional history of the university of Dublin* 1847; *Should the tenant of land possess the property in the improvements made by him?* 1852; *An introduction to the history of jurisprudence* 1860; *The principles of jurisprudence* 1873. *d.* while salmon fishing on the river Corrib at Galway 15 April 1881. *bur.* Glasnevin cemetery, Dublin 19 April. *Case of D. C. Heron against the provost and senior fellows of Trinity college, Dublin* (1846).

HERON, Sir Joseph (*son of James Holt Heron, merchant*). *b.* Manchester 1809; ed. at Moravian sch. at Fairfield; admitted attorney and solicitor 1830; town clerk of Manchester, Dec. 1838 to death, an able administrator, instrumental in obtaining the act for the Thirlmere water scheme for Manchester 1879; knighted at Windsor castle 9 July 1869. *d.* Cannes, France 23 Dec. 1889. *Times 25 Dec. 1889 p.* 4; *Law Journal, xxv,* 14 (1890).

HERON, Matilda. *b.* Labby vale, Londonderry, Ireland 1 Dec. 1830; studied in Philadelphia, U.S. America under Peter Richings; first appeared at Walnut st. theatre as Bianca in *Fazio* 17 Feb. 1851; played at St. Louis 1852, in San Francisco 1853, in New York 1854 and 1857 when she acted as Camille her most successful character. (*m.* 24 Dec. 1857 Robert Stoepel, musical director, from whom she separated 1862, sued for a divorce March 1869); appeared at Lyceum, London as Rosalie Lee in *New Year's Eve* 1 April 1861 but met with little success; returned to U.S. America, made last appearance as Medea in April 1876; teacher of elocution New York 1876 to death; published *Camille. Adapted from the French of A. Dumas* [*by M. H.*] 1856; *Medea, a tragedy by G. J. B. E. W. Legouvé, translated* 1857. *d.* New York city 7 March 1877. *Appleton's American Biog. iii,* 184 (1887), *portrait; Soulé's Annals of San Francisco* (1855) 661, *portrait.*

HERON, Sir Robert, 2 Baronet (*only son of Thomas Heron of Chilham castle, Kent*). *b.* Newark 27 Nov. 1765; ed. at St. John's coll. Cam.; succeeded his uncle Sir ·R. Heron 18 Jany. 1805; came into large property on death of his uncle Rev. Robert Heron 19 Jany. 1813; M.P. Grimsby 1812–18; contested Lincolnshire 1818; M.P. Peterborough 1819–47; built the nave and tower of Stubton ch. Lincolnshire; author of *Notes. Grantham* 1850, *reprinted* 1851. *d.* Stubton hall near Newark 29 May 1854. *G.M. July 1854 pp.* 74–5.

HERRIES, Sir Charles John (*eld. son of succeeding*). *b.* 1815; ed. at Eton and Trin. coll. Cam., B.A. 1837, M.A. 1840; barrister I.T. 20 Nov. 1840; commissioner of excise 22 Nov. 1842; dep. chairman of board of inland revenue 1856, chairman 15 Aug. 1877, retired 1881 on a pension of £1353; C.B. 1871, K.C.B. 27 Oct. 1880; author of *Memoir of Rt. Hon. J. C. Herries* 2 vols. 1880. *d.* St. Julian's, Sevenoaks 14 March 1883. *Times 16 March 1870 p.* 8.

HERRIES, John Charles (*eld. son of Charles Herries of London, merchant, d.* 1819). *b.* Nov. 1778; ed. at Cheam and at Univ. of Leipsic; clerk in the treasury 5 July 1798; private sec. to Nicholas Vansittart when secretary of the treasury 1801–1802, to Spencer Perceval when prime minister 1810–12; secretary and registrar to order of the Bath, Jany. 1809, resigned 1822; comptroller of army accounts 1811; commissary in chief 1 Oct. 1811 to 24 Oct. 1816 when office was abolished and he retired on pension of £1350; auditor of the civil list 29 Oct. 1816 to 1821; financial sec. to the treasury 7 Feb. 1823 to 4 Sep. 1827; chancellor of the exchequer 17 Aug. 1827 to 26 Jany. 1828; P.C. 17 Aug. 1827; master of the mint 12 Feb. 1828 to 14 Dec. 1830; president of board of trade 2 Feb. 1830 to 22 Nov. 1830; secretary at war 16 Dec. 1834 to 20 April 1835; president of board of control 28 Feb. to Dec. 1852; member of the India board 28 Feb. 1852; M.P. for Harwich 1823–41; contested Ipswich 3 July 1841; M.P. for Stamford 1847–53; translated Frederick Gentz's work *On the state of Europe before and after the French revolution* 1803. *d.* St. Julian's, Sevenoaks 24 April 1855. *E. Herries' Memoir of J. C. Herries* 2 vols. 1880; *Portraits of eminent conservatives and statesmen* 2 series (1846); *I.L.N. xiv,* 269 (1849), *portrait.*

HERRIES, Sir William Lewis (*brother of the preceding*). *b.* Amiens, France 1785; cornet 19 dragoons 23 Jany. 1801; served in South America, at Walcheren, at siege of Flushing and in Peninsula; lost his leg before Bayonne 1814; permanent assistant quartermaster general 28 July 1814 to 31 July 1817 when placed on h.p.; chairman of board of comrs. for auditing public accounts; lieut.-col. on half pay 13 Aug. 1830 to 9 Nov. 1846; a comr. of Chelsea hospital; col. of 68 foot 17 April 1854 to death; L.G. 20 June 1854; K.C.H. 1826; knighted at Carlton house 29 May 1826; C.B. 19 July 1831. *d.* 14 Bolton st. Piccadilly, London 3 June 1857.

HERRING, John Frederick (*son of Mr. Herring, fringe maker, Newgate st. London*). *b.* Surrey 1795; coach painter at Doncaster 1814; driver of the Nelson coach from Wakefield to Lincoln 1814–6, then of the Doncaster and Halifax coach, and later on of the Highflyer coach between London and York; painted Filho da Puta the winner of the St. Leger 1815, and the winners for 32 years in succession; painted Mameluke the winner of the Derby 1827 and the winners for 18 years following; at Doncaster till 1830, at Six mile

HERRING, J. F. *(Con.)*

bottom, Newmarket 1830-33, settled at Camberwell 1833; exhibited 22 pictures at R.A., 44 at B.I. and 82 at Suffolk st. 1818-68; member of Soc. of British Artists 1841-52; animal painter to duchess of Kent; among his pictures were, A frugal meal, now in National gallery; A group of ducks, in the Glasgow gallery, and A black horse drinking from a trough, in National gallery, Dublin; many of his paintings were engraved, and published by Fores, Fuller and Graves; he published *The Horse, 12 plates. d.* Meopham park near Tunbridge Wells 23 Sep. 1865. *Memoir of J. F. Herring. Sheffield (1848), portrait; Scott and Sebright, By the Druid (1862) 88-93; I.L.N. xlvii, 360, 361 (1865), portrait.*

HERRING, PAUL, stage name of William Smith. *b.* 20 Sep. 1800; clown at Richardson's show playing 12 times a day and also taking part in the outside parade; acted Bob Logic in the original cast of *Tom and Jerry* at the royal amphitheatre 17 Sep. 1821; in H. Brading's dramatic co. at Albert saloon, Shepherd fields, London where he was the hero in *The imp of the devil's gorge* 1841; clown at Victoria theatre under Daniel Webster Osbaldiston; played clown last time at St. James' theatre 1859; pantaloon from 1859, played in *The White Cat* at Drury Lane 1877. *d.* 32 North st. Hercules buildings, Lambeth, London 18 Sep. 1878. *bur.* Tooting cemetery 25 Sep. *The Era 22 and 29 Sep.* 1878; *Illust. S. and D. News, ii,* 268 (1874); *Tinsley's Mag., July* 1883 *pp.* 72-6.

HERRING, RICHARD. *b.* 1829; paper agent and wholesale stationer Finsbury pavement, London; made a study of telegraphy; author of *Paper and paper making, ancient and modern* 1855, 3 ed. 1863; *A letter on the collection of rags for paper making* 1860; *A few personal recollections of the Rev. George Croly* 1861; *Mr. Herring and the telegraphs* 1874, 4 ed. 1875 and other books. *d.* 27 St. Mary's road, Islington 5 Oct. 1886. *The Bookseller 8 Oct.* 1886 *p.* 949.

HERSCHEL, SIR JOHN FREDERICK WILLIAM, 1 Baronet *(only child of Sir Friedrich Wilhelm Herschel, astronomer 1738-1822). b.* Slough, Bucks. 7 March 1792; ed. at Hitcham, Eton and St. John's coll. Cam., senior wrangler, Smith's prizeman and fellow of his coll. 1813; B.A. 1813, M.A. 1816; F.R.S. 27 May 1813, member of council, one of secretaries 1824-7, royal medallist 1833, 1836 and 1840; a founder of R. Astronomical soc. 1820, wrote the inaugural address, first foreign secretary

HERSCHEL, SIR J. F. W. *(Con.)*

1824-7, medallist 1826, 1836, president 1827; discovered 525 new nebulae; discovered double stars; made researches and discoveries in light, heat and photography, one of the greatest men since Sir Isaac Newton; K.H. 12 Oct. 1831; baronet 17 July 1838; lord rector of Marischal college, Aberdeen, March 1842; master of the mint 13 Dec. 1850, resigned Feb. 1855; president of British association at Cambridge meeting 1845; one of the 8 foreign members of Institute of France 23 July 1855; wrote upwards of 150 scientific papers; author of *Results of astronomical observations made 1834-8 at Cape of Good Hope being the completion of a survey of the heavens* 1847; *A manual of scientific enquiry, for the use of the navy* 1849, 5 ed. 1886; *Outlines of astronomy* 1849, 10 ed. 1869; *Familiar lectures on scientific subjects* 1866; *The Iliad of Homer translated into accentuated hexameters* 1866. *d.* Collingwood, Hawkhurst, Kent 11 May 1871. *bur.* Westminster abbey 19 May. *Dunkin's Obituary notices of astronomers (1879)* 47-85; *Martineau's Biog. sketches (1876)* 449-67; *Monthly notices R. Astronom. soc. xxxii,* 122-42 (1872); *Illust. News of World, ix* (1862), *portrait; Year book of facts (1846), portrait.*

HERSCHELL, HELEN S. *(dau. of William Mowbray of Edinburgh).* A Latin, Greek, Hebrew and German scholar; a friend of Rev. Edward Irving 1834-8. *(m.* 1831 the succeeding); wrote *The Bystander,* a series of papers in *The Christian Ladies' magazine;* author of *The child's help to self-examination and prayer* 1835; *The voice from the fire* 1839. *d.* Bonn, Germany 31 Dec. 1853. *bur.* Kensal green 12 Jany. 1854. *Far above rubies. Memoir of Helen S. Herschell* (1854).

HERSCHELL, REV. RIDLEY HAIM *(son of a Jew). b.* Strzelno, Prussian Poland 7 April 1807; ed. at Berlin univ. 1822; baptized in England by bishop of London 1830; missionary among the Jews; in charge of Lady Olivia Sparrow's schools and mission work at Leigh, Essex and Brampton, Hunts. 1835-8; opened an unsectarian chapel in London 1838, removed to Trinity chapel, John st. Edgware road 1846; a founder of British soc. for propagating gospel among Jews; one of first to establish school excursions; a founder of Evangelical Alliance 1845; author of *A brief sketch of the state and expectations of the Jews 3 ed.* 1834; *Plain reasons why I a Jew have become a catholic and not a Roman catholic* 1842; *A visit to my fatherland. Notes of a journey to Syria and Palestine* 1844; edited *The voice of Israel*

HERSCHELL, REV. R. H. *(Con.)*
conducted by Jews who believe that Jesus is the Messiah, vols. 1–2, 1845–7, and other books. *d.* Brighton 14 April 1864.

HERSEE, WILLIAM. *b.* Coldwaltham, Sussex 1786; a ploughman; bookseller with Cooper at Bunhill row, London 1813; accountant in Inland revenue office, London 1809–26; edited the *Warwick Advertiser* 1831 to March 1852; published *Poems, rural and domestic.* Chichester 1810; *The battle of Vittoria, a poem* 1813; *The spirit of the orders issued by the board of excise for the guidance of officers* 1829 and other books. *d.* Warwick 6 Aug. 1854.

HERSHON, PAUL ISAAC. *b.* Galicia 1817; early converted to christianity; a missionary for promoting christianity among the Jews in England; director of the house of industry for Jews at Jerusalem, and then of the model farm at Jaffa, retired 1859; author of *Extracts from the Talmud* 1860; *The Pentateuch according to the Talmud. Genesis* 1878; *A Talmudic miscellany* 1880; *Treasures of the Talmud* 1882; translated the New Testament into Judæo-Polish for the use of the Continental Jews. *d.* 9 Park avenue, Wood Green, Middlesex 14 Oct. 1888. *Times* 15 *Oct.* 1888 *p.* 10.

HERTFORD, MARIA SEYMOUR-CONWAY, Marchioness of *(dau. of the Marchese Fagniani an Italian).* *b.* 1771; known as Mie Mie; lived with George Selwyn as his adopted dau. at Matson hall, Gloucester 1779–91 when he died leaving her £30,000; a public singer. *(m.* 18 May 1798 Francis, Earl of Yarmouth who in 1822 became 3 Marquis of Hertford 1777–1842); travelled on the continent as the acknowledged mistress of Marshal Andoche Junot, duc d' Abrantes 1802–4; the 4th Duke of Queensberry ('Old Q') bequeathed to her by will in 1810 a sum of £100,000. *d.* 3 Rue Taitbout, Paris, March 1856 aged 85. *P. Fitzgerald's Kings and Queens of an hour, ii,* 355–70 (1883); *The Croker Papers, By L. J. Jennings, i,* 235–6 (1884).

HERTFORD, RICHARD SEYMOUR-CONWAY, 4 Marquis of *(elder son of 3 Marquis of Hertford 1777–1842).* *b.* 22 Feb. 1800; styled viscount Beauchamp 1800–22, earl of Yarmouth 1822–42; attaché of embassy at Paris 1817; cornet 2 dragoons 24 Feb. 1820, captain 25 March to 17 April 1823 when placed on h.p.; M.P. co. Antrim 1821–26; captain of Cape corps of cavalry 1823; attaché of embassy at Constantinople 1829; succeeded his father 1 March 1842; K.G. 19 Jany. 1846; commander of Legion of Honour for encouragement given to the arts 14 Nov. 1855; known by the nickname of Bagatelle. *d.* 6 Rue

HERTFORD, 4 Marquis of *(Con.)*
Lafitte, Paris 25 Aug. 1870. *bur.* Pere la Chaise cemetery, personalty sworn under £500,000, 8 July 1871. *Irish Reports. Common Law series, vi,* 196–220, 343–410 (1873); *Some professional recollections* [*By C. R. Williams*] (1883) 75–92; *Waagen's Treasures of art, ii,* 154–61 (1854); *Waagen's Galleries of art* (1857) 79–92; *Lippincott's Mag. xiii,* 191–6 (1874).

HERTFORD, FRANCIS HUGH GEORGE SEYMOUR, 5 Marquis of *(son of Sir George Francis Seymour, G.C.B.* 1787–1870). *b.* 11 Feb. 1812; ensign 3 foot guards 12 July 1827, captain 28 Nov. 1845 to 10 Dec. 1847; groom of the robes to the Queen 1837–70; state steward to lord lieut. of Ireland 1843–46; equerry to Prince Albert 1846–58, to the Queen 1858–70; deputy ranger of Windsor great park 1850–70; succeeded his cousin 25 Aug. 1870; lord chamberlain of the household 21 Feb. 1874 to 7 May 1879; P.C. 2 March 1874; general 10 Feb. 1876; G.C.B. 24 Jany. 1879. *d.* Ragley hall near Alcester, Warws. 25 Jany. 1884. *Graphic, xxix,* 100 (1884), *portrait; I.L.N. lxxxiv,* 97 (1884), *portrait.*

HERTSLET, LEWIS. *b.* Nov. 1787; sub-librarian in foreign office, London 5 Feb. 1801; librarian and keeper of the papers 6 Jany. 1810 to 20 Nov. 1857 when he retired on pension; superintendent of queen's messengers and comptroller of their accounts for three secretaries of state offices 30 June 1824 to 30 June 1854 when office abolished; author of *A complete collection of the treaties between Great Britain and foreign powers and of the laws concerning the same* 11 vols. 1827–66. *d.* 16 Great college st. Westminster, London 15 March 1870.

HERTZEN or GERTSEN, ALEKSANDR IVANO-VICH *(son of Mr. Yakovlef, d.* 1846). *b.* Moscow 1812; ed. at Moscow univ.; imprisoned in 1835, in Siberia 1835–7; editor of *Vladimir gazette* 1837; in office of minister of interior, Moscow 1840; in France, Switzerland and Italy 1846; came to England 1848, established a printing office in Paternoster row, edited the *Free Russian Press; The Polar Star; Kolokol* [*The Bell*], ed. by Iskander, 196 numbers 1857–63, it was afterwards published at Geneva; lost his influence by taking the side of the Polish insurgents; author of *Imprimerie Russe à Londres* 1855; *La France ou l' Angleterre. Par Iscander* 1858; *Le monde Russe et la Révolution* 2 parts 1860–62 and many other works in French, Russian and Polish. *d.* Paris 21 Jany. 1870. *Temple Bar, April* 1870 *pp.* 44–58, *by W. R. S. Ralston; A. Hertzen's My exile to Siberia* 2 vols. (1855).

HERVEY, ALFRED *(youngest son of 1 marquis of Bristol 1769–1859). b.* St. James' sq. London 25 June 1816; ed. at Eton and Trin. coll. Cam., M.A. 1837, LL.D. 1864; barrister I.T. 27 Jany. 1843; M.P. for Brighton 1842–57, for Bury St. Edmunds 1859–65; a lord of the treasury Dec. 1852 to Feb. 1855; keeper of privy seal to Prince of Wales 4 Feb. 1853 to 1855; receiver general of inland revenue 1871 to death. *d.* Lowndes st. London 15 April 1875. *I.L.N. lxvi,* 402 (1875).

HERVEY, ANDREW. Entered Bengal army 1805; col. 52 Bengal N.I. 8 March 1849 to death; L.G. 23 July 1861; C.B. 9 June 1849. *d.* England 14 June 1862.

HERVEY, AUGUSTUS HENRY CHARLES *(2 son of 2 marquis of Bristol 1800–64). b.* Ickworth park, Bury St. Edmunds 2 Aug. 1837; ed. at Eton and Trin. coll. Cam., M.A. 1859; attaché at St. Petersburg 31 July 1862, at Dresden 19 Feb. 1863, resigned 24 Jany. 1865; M.P. West Suffolk 8 Dec. 1864 to death. *d.* at res. of his brother 6 St. James' sq. London 28 May 1875.

HERVEY, THOMAS KIBBLE *(son of James Hervey of Manchester, drysalter). b.* Paisley 4 Feb. 1799; ed. at Manchester free gr. sch.; articled to Sharp, Eccles & Co. solicitors, Manchester; studied for the bar; at Trin. coll. Cam. 1818–20; edited the *Friendship's Offering* 1826–7; migrated to Paris 1827 but soon returned to London; edited *The Amaranth* 1839; a leading contributor to the *Athenæum* from 1828, editor 23 May 1846, resigned Dec. 1853; contributed to the *Art Journal* 1855–9. *(m.* 17 Oct. 1843 Eleanor Louisa dau. of George Conway Montagu, she is an author and poetess); author of *Australia with other poems* 1824; *The poetical sketch book* 1829; *The book of Christmas* 1837; *The English Helicon* 1841. *d.* Kentish town, London 27 Feb. 1859. *bur.* Highgate cemet. *The poems of T. K. Hervey, Ed. by Mrs. Hervey with a memoir* (1866), *portrait; Manchester sch. register,* iii, 284 (1874).

HERZ, JAMES. *b.* 1807; founder of the Cheque Bank opened Pall Mall east, London 23 July 1873, the payment of all cheques drawn being guaranteed by the Bank. *d.* Coburg hotel 14 Charles st. Grosvenor sq. London 23 Feb. 1880. *Times* 1 *April* 1873 *p.* 10, 25 *Sep. p.* 5, 26 *Sep. p.* 4; *Banker's Mag. xxxiii,* 651, 930 (1873).

HESKETH, SIR THOMAS GEORGE FERMOR, 5 Baronet. *b.* Rufford hall near Ormskirk, Lancs. 11 Jany. 1825; succeeded 10 Feb. 1843; sheriff of Lancs. 1848; lieut. col. commandant 2 royal Lancashire militia 1 March

HESKETH, SIR T. G. F, *(Con.)* 1852 to 25 Sep. 1872; M.P. for Preston 4 April 1862 to death; assumed name of Fermor by royal license 8 Nov. 1867. *d.* Rufford hall 20 Aug. 1872. *I.L.N. lxi,* 215, 571 (1872).

HESKETH-FLEETWOOD, SIR PETER, 1 Baronet *(3 son of Robert Hesketh of Rossall, Lancs. 1764–1824). b.* Wennington hall near Lancaster 9 May 1801; ed. at Trin. coll. Ox., B.A. 1823, M.A. 1826; sheriff of Lancashire 1830; assumed by r.l. additional name of Fleetwood, March 1831; M.P. for Preston 10 Dec. 1832 to July 1847; cr. a Baronet 20 July 1838; projected and commenced building town of Fleetwood, Lancashire on his estate at Rossall at mouth of river Wyre 1836; published a translation of Victor Hugo's *Last days of a condemned,* to which he prefixed *Observations on capital punishment* 1840. *d.* 127 Piccadilly, London 12 April 1866. *G.M.* i, 908 (1866); *I.L.N. xlviii,* 426 (1866); *Herald and genealogist,* iv, 371 (1866–7).

HESLEDEN, WILLIAM SMITH. *b.* 1773; Assoc. British Archæol. Assoc. 1845; wrote *An account of ancient earth works at Barton and on the site of the battle of Brunanburgh in the time of Athelstan;* published *A sketch of the properties of Sutton patent gravitated sails for windmills* 1807. *d.* Barton-upon-Humber 24 Dec. 1854. *Journ. B. Archæol. Assoc. xi,* 162 (1855).

HESLOP, REV. GEORGE HENRY *(1 son of Rev. Alfred Heslop of Keswick, Cumb.) b.* 1822; ed. at Queen's coll. Ox., scholar 1842–8, fellow 1848–51; B.A. 1846, M.A. 1846; head master of St. Bees gram. sch. 1854–79; hon. canon of Carlisle 1875; R. of Church Oakley, Hants. 1879 to death; one of the most exact and correct scholars of his time; in the Catena Classicorum series, Rivingtons, London, he edited *Demosthenes' Orationes publicae* 1868 and *Demosthenes' De Falsa legatione. d.* Oakley rectory, Basingstoke 30 Jany. 1887.

HESLOP, THOMAS PRETIOUS *(son of Mr. Heslop a Scotchman and major R.A.) b.* West Indies 1823; apprenticed to Thomas Underhill, M.D. of Tipton, Staffs.; studied at Universities of Dublin and Edin., M.D. Edin. 1848; M.R.C.P. 1859, F.R.C.P. 1872; practised at Birmingham 1848 to death, house physician general hospital 1848 to Jany. 1852; professor of physiology at Queen's college 1853–58 and senior phys. 1870–82; the chief consultant phys. in Midland counties many years; founded the Free hospital for children opened in Steel house lane, Birmingham 1861, the Women's hospital 1871 and the Skin and Lock hospital 1880; founded the Midland

Medical Society 1848; a trustee of Mason college 1873, president of the council 1884 to death, gave 11,000 volumes to the library; author of *The realities of medical attendance on the sick children of the poor.* Birmingham 1869; *The abuse of alcohol in the treatment of acute diseases* 1872. *d.* the Devil's Elbow, 3 miles south of Braemar 17 June 1885. *bur.* at Dublin 20 June. *Birmingham Weekly Post* 20 *June* 1885 *p.* 4 *col.* 7.

HESSEY, REV. FRANCIS (2 *son of James Augustus Hessey of St. Bride's, London*). *b.* 10 April 1816; ed. at Merchant Taylors and St. John's coll. Ox., scholar and fellow 1834-61; S.C.L. 1837, B.C.L. 1839, D.C.L. 1844; C. of Kentish town, London 1839-40; principal of Huddersfield coll. sch. 1840-43; head master of Kensington sch. 1843-53; V. of St. Barnabas, Kensington 1853 to Oct. 1881; author of *Hints to district visitors, By F. H.* 1858; *Confirmation questions* 1859, 7 *ed.* 1866, *Second series* 1862; *Catechetical lessons on book of Common prayer* 1868; *A few parochial sermons preached at St. Barnabas, Kensington* 1882. *d.* Midhurst, Sussex 10 Aug. 1882.

HETHERINGTON, REV. WILLIAM MAXWELL. *b.* in parish of Troqueer near Dumfries 4 June 1803; a gardiner; ed. at Edin. Univ. 1822; presbyterian minister of Torphichen, Linlithgow 1836-43; a free ch. minister to students at St. Andrews 1843-8; minister at St. Paul's, Edin. 1848; edited the *Free Church Magazine* 1844-8; professor of systematic theology in Glasgow Free Church coll. 1857; LL.D. and D.D. of an American university; author of *Twelve dramatic sketches founded on the pastoral poetry of Scotland* 1829; *The minister's family* 1838, 12 *ed.* 1880; *History of the Church of Scotland* 1842, 7 *ed.* 2 vols. 1852; *History of Westminster assembly of divines* 1843, 4 *ed.* 1878; *The anti-christian system or popery as predicted in Scripture* 1851. *d.* 23 May 1865. *bur.* Grange cemet. Edin. *Wylie's Disruption Worthies* (1881); *The apologetics of the Christian faith By W. H. Hetherington* 1867, *with a Memoir pp. xiii-xv; Scott's Fasti vol.* i, *pt.* i, *p.* 204.

HEWETSON, CHARLES. Entered Madras army 1811; col. 49 Madras N.I. 21 July 1861 to 1869; L.G. 25 June 1870. *d.* Madras 4 Feb. 1873.

HEWETT, SIR PRESCOTT GARDINER, 1 Baronet (*son of Wm. Nathan Wrighte Hewett of Bilham hall near Doncaster*). *b.* 3 July 1812; ed. at St. George's hospital and in Paris; M.R.C.S. 1836, hon. F.R.C.S. 1843, professor of human

anatomy and surgery, member of council 1867, vice pres. 1875, pres. 1876; surgeon extraord. to the Queen 14 Oct. 1867, sergeant surgeon extraord. 19 Feb. 1877; surgeon in ord. to Prince of Wales 10 March 1874; pres. of Clinical Soc. 1873; F.R.S. 4 June 1874; retired from practice Nov. 1883; created baronet 6 Aug. 1883. *d.* Chestnut lodge, Horsham, Sussex 19 June 1891. *bur.* Brompton cemetery, London 25 June.

HEWETT, SIR WILLIAM NATHAN WRIGHTE (2 *son of Dr. William Wrighte Hewett*). *b.* Brighton 12 Aug. 1834; entered the navy March 1847; shewed great presence of mind and courage in a battery before Sebastopol and at Inkerman 1854, lieut. 20 Oct.; V.C. 24 Feb. 1857; commodore and commander in chief on west coast of Africa during Ashantee war 1873-76, and present at capture of Coomassie; K.C.B. 31 March 1874, Ashantee medal with clasp; commander in chief in East Indies 1882-5; occupied Suez and seized the Canal 1882; defended Suakim 6 Feb. 1884, governor for the Khedive 10 Feb.; went on a mission to king John of Abyssinia, April 1884; commander of Channel squadron 18 March 1886 to 17 April 1888; known as the fighting admiral; K.C.S.I. 17 Nov. 1882. *d.* Haslar hospital, Portsmouth 13 May 1888. *Times* 15 *May* 1888 *p.* 8, 16 *May pp.* 11, 16, 18 *May p.* 5; *I.L.N. xxxix* 41 (1861), *portrait, lxxxiv* 172 (1884), *portrait.*

HEWITSON, WILLIAM CHAPMAN. *b.* Newcastle-upon-Tyne 9 Jany. 1806; ed. at York; land surveyor, sometime under George Stephenson on London and Birmingham railway, came into a fortune and gave up business; resided at Bristol, at Hampstead and from 1848 at Oatland's park, Surrey; made a study of birds' eggs and collected specimens in Norway 1833; made a collection of diurnal lepidoptera, paid travellers to search for them in all parts of the world and gave £350 for a single specimen 1848, etc.; member of Entomological soc. 1846, the Zoological 1859 and the Linnean 1862; author of *British Oology being illustrations of the eggs of British birds with figures of each species* Newcastle 3 *vols.* 1833-42; *Coloured illustrations of the eggs of British birds* 2 *vols.* 1846, 3 *ed.* 2 *vols.* 1856; *Illustrations of diurnal lepidoptera* 2 *vols.* 1863-78; *Description of* 100 *new species of hesperidiæ* 1867. *d.* Oatland's park 28 May 1878. *bur.* Walton-on-Thames. Left his lepidoptera, stuffed birds, pictures and water colours to Br. Museum, now in Cromwell road; his books and £30,000 to Nat. Hist. Soc. New-

HEWITSON, W. C. *(Con.)*

castle, and money to the Müller institute Bristol. *Academy 8 June* 1878 *p.* 512; *Nature xviii*, 196–7 (1878).

HEWITT, DANIEL CHANDLER. *b.* Scotland 1789; author of *New analysis of music, a theory of melody, harmony and modulation* 1828; *The true science of music* 1860 *and* 1864. *d.* London 1869.

HEWITT, JOHN. *b.* Lichfield 1807; organist St. Mary's ch. Lichfield; in war office, London; resided at Woolwich; wrote articles in magazines under name of Sylvanus Swanquill; author of *The tower of London, its history* 1841; *Ancient armour and weapons in Europe* 3 vols. 1855–60; *Official catalogue of the Tower armories* 1859; *Old Woolwich* 1860; *Handbook for the city of Lichfield* 1874, 2 ed. 1884 and other works. *d.* Lichfield 10 Jany. 1878. *bur.* in cathedral close 15 Jany. *Reliquary xviii*, 228–30 (1877–8).

HEWITT, WILLIAM HENRY. *b.* 1791; entered Bengal army 1806; col. 27 Bengal N.I. 1850 to death; L.G. 30 Dec. 1859. *d.* Westfield house, Bath 16 April 1863 aged 72.

HEWLETT, THOMAS (2 *son of Thomas Hewlett of Oxford*). *b.* Oxford 16 March 1845; of Magd. hall Ox., B. Mus. 22 June 1865; organist Duke of Buccleuch's chapel, Dalkeith; teacher and organist in Edin.; accompanyist Edin. Sacred harmonic soc.; organist Newington park ch. Edin.; wrote *Are other eyes, Madrigal* 1864; *The good old days, A Christmas song* 1865; *Introduction, offertoire and fuge for the organ* 1867; *Second offertoire for the organ* 1872 *and Third* 1872. *d.* 2 Hope park crescent, Edinburgh 1 April 1874.

HEWLETT, THOMAS GILLHAM. *b.* 1832; M.R.C.S. Eng. 1853; assist. surgeon Bombay army 20 Jany. 1854, surgeon 20 Jany. 1865; served during Indian mutiny 1857–8; deputy assay master Bombay mint; health officer Bombay when he organized the public health department; sanitary commissioner for Bombay presidency; deputy surgeon general Bombay 1 Nov. 1879; C.I.E. 1 Jany. 1878; author of *Reports on leprosy in the Bombay presidency* 1879; *Report on enteric fever* 1883. *d.* of heart disease at Finchley road station, Metropolitan railway 8 Oct. 1889. *Times* 29 *Oct.* 1889 *p.* 9, 31 *Oct. p.* 10.

HEWSON, REV. WILLIAM *(son of William Hewson, banker's clerk). b.* 12 April 1806. *bapt.* St. Margaret's, Westminster 29 Dec.; ed. at St. Paul's sch. and St. John's coll. Cam., B.A.

HEWSON, REV. W. *(Con.)*

1830, M.A. 1833; C. of Bishop Burton, Yorks. 1830–3; C. of Spofforth 1834–5; head master of Sherburn gram. sch. Yorks. 1835–8 and of St. Peter's sch. York 1838–47; P.C. of Goatland 1848 to death; author of *The key of David or the mystery of the 7 sealed books of Jewish prophecy* 1855; *The oblation and temple of Ezekiel's prophetic visions 5 parts* 1858; *Thy kingdom come* 1859; *Christianity in relation to Judaism and Heathenism* 1860; *The Hebrew and Greek scriptures compared with Oriental history, dialling, science and mythology 7 parts* 1870. *d.* 1 St. Hilda ter. Whitby 23 April 1870. *bur.* York cemet. *Smales' Whitby authors* (1867) 104, 171–6, 217; *Whitby Times* 29 *April* 1870 *p.* 4.

HEY, WILLIAM *(son of William Hey* 1772–1844 *surgeon). b.* Leeds 23 Dec. 1796; M.R.C.S., F.R.C.S.; succeeded his father at Leeds 1844; surgeon Leeds infirmary 1830–51, consulting surgeon 1864; a founder of Leeds school of medicine, and lecturer on surgery there 1831–57; president surgical section British Med. Assoc. at Leeds, July 1869; V.P. Leeds Philos. and Lit. Soc. 1835 and 1839. *d.* Gledhow Wood, Leeds 10 May 1875. *British Medical Journal*, i, 763 (1875).

HEY, VEN. WILLIAM *(son of Rev. Samuel Hey, vicar of Ockbrook, Derbyshire). b.* Ockbrook 1811; ed. at Sherborne and at St. John's coll. Cam., fellow 1836, B.A. 1834, M.A. 1837; head master St. Peter's sch. York 1844–64; V. of St. Helen, Stonegate 1854–77; preb. of Weighton, York cath. 1854–81 and succentor canonicorum 1871–81; canon residentiary of York cath. 1864; precentor and preb. of Duffield 1881; archdeacon of Cleveland 1874 to death; examining chaplain to Archbp. of York 1874; V. of St. Olave with St. Giles', York 1877 to death; select preacher Cam. 1879. *d.* The Residence, Minster yard, York 22 Nov. 1882. *Church portrait journal, Jany.* 1880 *pp.* 5–8, *portrait.*

HEYGATE, JAMES. *b.* West Haddow, Northampton; M.R.C.S. 1823, M.D. Edin. 1836; in practice at Hanslope, Bucks., at Derby 1837 to death; senior physician Derbyshire general infirmary; F.R.S.; V.P. British medical assoc.; author of *Tic douloureux, An essay* 1836 and of papers in medical journals. *d.* Little Eaton, Derby 4 Aug. 1872. *Medical Times* 31 *Aug.* 1872 *p.* 243.

HEYSHAM, THOMAS COULTHARD *(eld. son of Dr. John Heysham). b.* 1792; mayor of Carlisle 1839; J.P. for Cumberland; made extensive collections in entomology, ornithology and botany; his name given to some species of coleoptera. d. Fisher st. Carlisle 6 April 1857. *Carlisle Journal* 10 *April* 1857 *p.* 8, 17 *April p.* 8.

HEYTESBURY, WILLIAM A'COURT, 1 Baron (*eld. son of Sir William Pierce Ashe A'Court, 1 Baronet 1747–1817*). b. Salisbury 11 July 1779; ed. at Eton; sec. of legation at Naples 31 July 1801; sec. to special mission at Vienna 20 April 1807; first commissioner of affairs, Malta 1812; envoy extraord. to Barbary states 5 Jany. 1813, to Naples 5 July 1814 and to Spain 5 April 1822; ambassador to Portugal 22 Sep. 1824 and to Russia 5 April 1828, pensioned 18 Aug. 1832; succeeded as 2 baronet 22 July 1817; P.C. 30 Dec. 1817; G.C.B. 20 Sep. 1819; cr. baron Heytesbury of Heytesbury, Wilts. 23 Jany. 1828; nominated governor general of India 28 Jany. 1835 but the ministry resigned and he never took office; lord lieut. of Ireland 26 July 1844 to 11 July 1846; governor of the Isle of Wight to 1857. d. Heytesbury 31 May 1860. *F. O. List* (1860) 145; *I.L.N. v,* 60 (1844), *portrait; Eton portrait gallery* (1876) 346–8; *Waagen's Galleries of art* (1857) 386–90.

HEYTESBURY, WILLIAM HENRY ASHE A'COURT-HOLMES, 2 Baron (*son of the preceding*). b. London 1809; ed. at Eton and St. John's coll. Camb. M.A. 1831. m. 2 Oct. 1833 Elizabeth Woosley, eld. dau of Sir Leonard Worsley Holmes, bart., and assumed name of Holmes on 14 Oct.; M.P. for Isle of Wight 1837–47; succeeded as 2 Baron 31 May 1860. d. Heytesbury 21 April 1891.

HEYWOOD, SIR BENJAMIN, 1 Baronet (*eld. son of Nathaniel Heywood of Manchester, banker, d.* 1815). b. St. Ann's sq. Manchester 12 Dec. 1793; ed. at univ. of Glasgow 1809–11; banker at Manchester 1814, sole proprietor 1828, retired 1860; chief founder of Manchester mechanics' institution 1824, president 1824–44; M.P. for Lancashire 1831–1832; baronet 28 July 1838; F.R.S. 1843; gave £1000 toward Manchester public park 1844; vice pres. of British association at Manchester 1842 and 1861; author of *Address delivered at Manchester mechanics' institution* 1843. d. Claremont near Manchester 11 Aug. 1865. bur. St. John's Islam's o' the Height; personalty sworn under £400,000, 14 Oct. 1865. *Grindon's Manchester banks* (1877) 79–86; *T. Heywood's Memoir of Sir B. Heywood* (1888), *portrait.*

HEYWOOD, JOHN. b. 1804; hand loom weaver to 1837; a ruler to his brother Abel Heywood 1839–46; a stationer Deansgate st. Manchester from 1846, the largest copy book maker in the world, bookseller and newsagent, employed 120 hands; member of Manchester city council 1860–61; chairman of Chorlton guardians. d. Manchester 7 Oct. 1864. *The Bookseller* 26 *Feb.* 1861, *p.* 105.

HEYWOOD, JOHN (*son of the preceding*). b. 1832; errand boy in a solicitor's office; succeeded to his father's book, news and stationery establishment, Manchester 1864; made a central depot for the small local booksellers, and a book saloon for the exhibition of educational appliances; had 30,000 customers' names in his books, and employed 30 carts to distribute books and newspapers; his Excelsior printing and bookbinding works, Hulme hall road, Manchester, opened 4 July 1870; employed 750 workmen; printed a series of books called *J. Heywood's Pocket guides* 1869 etc., and many other works. d. The Grange, Derbyshire lane, Stretford, Manchester 10 May 1888. *Bookseller, June* 1888 *pp.* 573–4.

HEYWOOD, JOHN JOSEPH (*son of R. Heywood of Glencrutchery near Douglas*). b. 1789; first deemster or chief justice of Isle of Man 1821 to death. d. Bomahague, Douglas 26 May 1855 aged 66. bur. Kirk Onchar ch. yard. *Hardwicke's Annual Biog.* (1856) 355.

HEYWOOD, THOMAS (*brother of Sir B. Heywood*). b. Manchester 3 Sep. 1797; ed. at Manchester gram. sch. 1811; partner in Heywood, Bros. & Co. bankers, St. Ann's sq. Manchester, retired 1828; collected a remarkable library of local books at Swinton, they were sold Manchester 22–3 April 1835; boroughreeve of Salford 1826; sheriff of Herefordshire 1840; F.S.A.; member of council of Chetham soc. for which he edited The Norris Papers 1846 and 5 other works; author of *The earls of Derby and the verse writers of the 16th and 17th centuries. Manchester* 1826; *The most pleasant song of Lady Bessy* 1829. d. Hope End near Ledbury 20 Nov. 1866; his general library sold Manchester, Nov. 1868. *Manchester sch. reg. iii,* 74–6 (1874).

HEYWORTH, LAWRENCE (4 *son of Peter Heyworth, woollen manufacturer, d.* 1799). b. Greensnook, Bacup 1786; ed. at Hipperholme gram. sch. near Halifax 1799–1802; woollen manufacturer with his brothers at Bacup 1802; established business connections with Portuguese and Spanish 1805 and with South America 1808; in S. America 1809–16;

HEYWORTH, L. (Con.)

established agencies in Liverpool and Hamburg; firm became Heyworth, Brothers & Co., retired 1836; purchased Yew Tree estate near Liverpool 1819; chairman Liverpool Free trade association; M.P. Derby 1848–57; author of *On the corn laws and other legislative restrictions*, 7 ed. 1843; *On economic fiscal legislation* 1845; *The expansion of the suffrage and accession of blessings God has in store for all classes through the wise exercise of the franchise* 1861. *d.* Yew Tree, West Derby, Liverpool 19 April 1872. *I.L.N.* 22 *June* 1850 *pp.* 443–4, *portrait; Newbigging's Forest of Rossendale* (1868) 181–88.

HIBBERD, JAMES SHIRLEY *(son of a master mariner)*. *b.* St. Dunstan, Stepney, London 1825; apprentice to a bookseller at Stepney; editor of *Floral World* 1858, which he managed to 1875; editor *Gardener's Magazine* 1861 to death; a practical writer on agriculture, experimented on fruit trees and vegetables, especially on potatoes; temperance advocate and a vegetarian; a popular lecturer, lectured at Wylde's Great Globe; F.R.H.S.; author of *Brambles and Bayleaves. Essays* 1855, 3 ed. 1873; *Profitable gardening* 1863; *Familiar garden flowers* 5 vols. 1879–87; *Water-cresses without sewage* 1878 and 25 other books. *d.* 1 Priory road, The Green, Kew 16 Nov. 1890. *Gardener's Mag.* 22 *Nov.* 1890, *portrait; I.L.N.* 29 *Nov.* 1890 *p.* 678, *portrait.*

HIBBERD, SAMUEL. *b.* 1839; jockey; won the Cambridgeshire on Malacca 1856, Cesarewitch on Lecturer 1866, the Chester Cup on One Act in 1856 and on Dalby in 1865 and 1866. *d.* Newmarket 21 Feb. 1888. *Times* 29 *Feb.* 1888 *p.* 9.

HIBBERT, JOHN *(son of John Hibbert of Braywick lodge, Maidenhead, d. 1855)*. *b.* 29 Jany. 1811; ed. at Eton and King's coll. Cam., scholar, fellow; B.A. 1833, M.A. 1836; barrister I.T. 29 April 1836; chairman of Cookham board of guardians; built a ch. for the poor of the Maidenhead and Cookham union; founded and endowed a ward in Royal Windsor infirmary. *d.* Braywick lodge, Maidenhead 28 March 1888.

HIBBS, REV. RICHARD. *b.* 1812; ed. at St. John's coll. Cam., scholar; B.A. 1841, M.A. 1844; C. of Bishop Hatfield 1841–3; C. of Corton near Lowestoft 1843–8; teacher and preacher at Lowestoft 1848–52; C. of St. Paul's, Covent Garden 1852; assist. minister St. John's chapel, Edin. 1852–4, a controversy with the incumbent led him to establish the New Church of England chapel, St. Vincent

HIBBS, REV. R. (Con.)

st. Edin. 1854; C. of Market Lavington 1874–6; chaplain at Lisbon; chaplain at Rotterdam and Utrecht 1876–8; author of *The substance of a series of discourses on baptism* 1848; *Scottish episcopal Romanism, or popery without a pope* 1856; *Truth vindicated or some account of the New Church of England chapel* 1858, 4 ed. 1859; *Prussia and the poor, or the systematized relief of the poor at Elberfeld in contrast with that of England* 1876, 4 ed. 1883. *d.* 13 St. Lawrence road, North Kensington, London 26 March 1886. *Academy* 10 *April* 1886 *pp.* 255–6.

HICKEY, REV. WILLIAM *(eld. son of Rev. Ambrose Hickey, rector of Murragh, co. Cork 1796 to his death in 1826)*. *b.* 1787 or 1788; ed. at Trin. coll. Dublin 1804–5, B.A. 1809, M.A. 1832; pensioner St. John's coll. Cam. 7 March 1806, B.A. 1809; C. of Dunleckny, Leighlin 1811; V. of Bannow, Ferns 1820; founded an agricultural soc. on a farm of 40 acres; a founder of South Wexford agricultural soc., the first of its kind in Ireland; R. of Kilcormuick 1826; R. of Wexford 1831; R. of Mulrankin 1834 to death; endeavoured to improve the husbandry of small farms; author of *State of the poor in Ireland* 1817; member of R. Dublin soc., gold medallist; civil list pension of £80, 6 Oct. 1853; had pension from R. Literary fund; under the pseudonym of Martin Doyle he wrote *Hints to small farmers* 1830, *numerous editions; Hints on emigration to Upper Canada* 1831, 3 ed. 1834; *Practical gardening* 1833, 2 ed. 1836; *A cyclopædia of practical husbandry* 1839, *new editions* 1844, 1851; *The farmer's manual* 1868; with Edmund Murphy he conducted the *Irish Farmer's and Gardener's Magazine* 9 vols. 1834–42. *d.* Mulrankin 24 Oct. 1875. *Dublin Univ. Mag., April* 1840 *pp.* 374–6, *portrait; Wexford Independent* 27 *and* 30 *Oct.* 1875.

HICKLEY, VICTOR GRANT *(son of J. A. Hickley of Purbrook, Hants.)* *b.* 1823 or 1824; sublieut. R.N. 18 Aug. 1842; captain 1 April 1858, retired 8 June 1868; retired admiral 12 April 1886. *d.* Taunton railway station 27 Jany. 1888.

HICKLIN, JOHN. *b.* England; editor of *Nottingham Journal*, and of *Chester Courant*; author of *Church and state. Historic facts ancient and modern.* Torquay 1873; *Literary recreations. d.* 13 Jany. 1877.

HICKS, AGNES ROSS *(dau. of J. Ross of Campsie, Stirlingshire)*. *b.* 1850; ed. under Warwick

HICKS, A. R. *(Con.)*

Jordan, Mus. Bac. organist of St. Stephen's, Lewisham; soprano singer; first appeared in public at Public hall, Lee, Kent 1875; sang at St. James' hall, London, her old ballads being in much favor; well known by her singing of Gounod's 'Worker.' *(m.* George Hicks), she *d.* 32 Henrietta st. Covent Garden, London 13 March 1886. *bur.* Norwood cemet. 17 March. *The Era, March 1886 p.* 13.

HICKS, EDWARD *(only son of Edward Simpson of Lichfield).* b. 10 Aug. 1814; ed. at Charterhouse and C.C. coll. Cam., B.A. 1836; student of Inner Temple 1837; assumed surname of Hicks on succeeding his kinsman Rev. James Hicks 1835; sheriff of Cam. 1862; master of harriers; M.P. Cambs. 1879–85; contested Newmarket division 1885. *d.* Wilbraham Temple, Cambridge 13 Jany. 1889.

HICKS, SIR FRANCIS *(youngest son of John Hicks of Southwark, London).* b. Southwark 1821; treasurer of St. Thomas's hospital, London 1865 to death; knighted at St. James's palace 21 June 1871 on opening of new St. Thomas's hospital. *d.* Margate 1 Sep. 1877 in 57 year. *Times 4 Sep.* 1877 *p.* 9.

HICKS, GEORGE. Entered Bengal army 7 Sep. 1808; col. 70 Bengal N.I. 7 May 1854 to 1869; L.G. 28 Oct. 1868; C.B. 3 April 1846. *d.* 24 Oct. 1873.

HICKS, MARY *(dau. of John and Sarah Roden).* bapt. Broseley, Salop 14 Nov. 1773; she however said she was dau. of Samuel and Mary Roden and *bapt.* Broseley 15 Feb. 1767. *(m.* at Isleworth, John Hicks who *d.* 1848). *d.* Brentford workhouse 24 Nov. 1870 aged 97. *W. J. Thoms' Longevity* (1879) 236–42.

HICKS, NEWTON TREE *(son of Cecil Hicks, who d. 15 March* 1866). *b.* 4 Sep. 1811; appeared as Richard 3rd at Royalty theatre, London 1824; played at the Coburg, the New Brunswick and Surrey theatres; in the provinces 6 or 7 years; made the round of metropolitan theatres; known by sobriquet of Bravo or Brayvo Hicks; some of his characters were Fabian in *The Black Doctor;* Monte Christo at the Surrey, June 1848; Sir Thomas Clifford in *The Hunchback,* and Leopold in *The Jewess;* retired from the stage about 1863; lived in Hogarth's house, Hogarth lane, Chiswick. *d.* 21 Feb. 1873. *Theatrical Times, ii* 17 (1847), *portrait, iii* 209 (1848), *portrait; Era* 2 March 1873 *p.* 11.

NOTE.—His brother Cecil Hicks pianist at the Canterbury, Cambridge and Foresters' music halls, *d.* 19 Jany. 1888. *bur.* Ilford cemet. 29 Jany.

HICKS, WILLIAM. *b.* 29 April 1831; ensign 24 Bombay N.I. 3 March 1851; served in India in campaign of 1857–9, with Panjâb movable column, in Rohilkand campaign and under Lord Clyde; captain Bombay Staff Corps 29 Dec. 1861; brigade major in 1 div. in Abyssinian campaign 1867–8; lieut.-col. B.S.C. 29 Dec. 1875 to 1 July 1880; A.A.G. Bombay 3 Dec. 1877 to 1 July 1880; commander of Egyptian army in the Sûdân to suppress the Mahdi's revolt Feb. 1883 and known as Hicks Pasha, joined his troops at Khartûm, ascended the White Nile to Duem and advanced across the desert to El'Obeyd Sep. 1883, betrayed into an ambuscade and *killed* with most of his troops at the battle of Kashgil 4 Nov. 1883. *J. Colborne's With Hicks Pasha in the Soudan* (1884), *portrait; I.L.N. lxxxiii,* 521 (1883), *portrait; Graphic xxviii,* 529 (1883), *portrait.*

HICKS, WILLIAM ROBERT *(son of William Hicks, schoolmaster, Bodmin, d.* 1833). *b.* Bodmin 1 April 1808; schoolmaster Bodmin 1832–40; clerk of Bodmin board of guardians 1834; domestic superintendent Cornwall county lunatic asylum 1840–60, with the medical officers introduced a more humane treatment of the patients; mayor of Bodmin 1865; a well known story teller, familiar in London as the Yorick of the West; was a proficient in the Cornish and Devonshire dialects, and in miners' talk. *d.* Westheath, Bodmin 5 Sep. 1868. *Collier's W. R. Hicks, a memoir* (1888), *portrait.*

HICKSON, GEORGE BLAKE. Called to the bar in Ireland 1819; Q.C. 1 July 1837. *d.* 2 Aug. 1869.

HICKSON, WILLIAM EDWARD *(son of William Hickson, boot manufacturer, London).* b. 7 Jany. 1803; boot maker, partner with his father, retired 1840; a pioneer of national education and of popular musical culture; on the royal commission on condition of handloom weavers 1837, when he visited seats of industry in Great Britain and Ireland; studied national school systems in Holland, Belgium and Germany 1839; editor and proprietor of *Westminster Review, vols.* 34–45, 1840–52; author of *The singing master, instructions for teaching singing in schools and families, 3 parts* 1836; *Dutch and German schools* 1840; *Part singing or vocal harmony for choral societies, 4 parts* 1842; *Time and faith, an enquiry into the data of ecclesiastical history* 2 vols. 1857; *A musical gift containing 24 new songs* 1859. *d.* Fairseat, Sevenoaks, Kent 22 March 1870.

HIGGIN, RIGHT REV. WILLIAM (4 *son of John Higgin of Greenfield, governor of Lancaster*

HIGGIN, RIGHT REV. W. (Con.)

castle 1783–1833). b. Lancaster 27 Sep. 1793; ed. at Lancaster gram. sch., Manchester gram. sch., and Trin. coll. Cam., 13 wr. 1817, B.A. 1817; M.A. of Trin. coll. Dublin 1835, D.D. 1849; C. of Clifton 1817–20; chaplain Richmond general penitentiary, Dublin 1820–8; R. of Roscrea 1828–45; vicar general of Killaloe 1828–45; dean of Limerick, instituted 25 Jany. 1845; bishop of Limerick 1849; translated to Derry 7 Dec. 1853, enthroned 20 Dec.; comr. of national education 1853; an ecclesiastical comr. for Ireland 1866; author of *Ministerial fidelity and zeal. A sermon* 1839, and other sermons and charges 1849–67. d. the Palace, Londonderry 12 July 1867. bur. in ground of St. Columba cath. *Manchester school register, iii*, 62–5 (1874).

HIGGINBOTTOM, JOHN (son of a solicitor). b. Ashton under Lyne 14 June 1788; studied at Edin.; M.R.C.S. 1818, F.R.C.S. 1844; F.R.S. 3 June 1852; practised at Nottingham 1812 to death; temperance advocate, gave no alcohol to his patients; wrote in scientific journals on tritons, tadpoles and frogs 1850–62; author of *An essay on the application of lunar caustic in the case of wounds and ulcers* 1826, 3 ed. 1865; *Mothers, doctors and nurses. A dialogue on paralysis and apoplexy* 1850. d. St. Alban's villas, Gill st. Nottingham 7 April 1876. *The Lancet* 29 April 1876 p. 652.

HIGGINS, MOST REV. ANDREW. b. Killarney 1834; dean of Kerry; bishop of Kerry 5 Feb. 1882 to death. d. The palace, Kerry 1 May 1889. bur. in the cathedral 3 May. *Tablet* 4 May 1889 p. 702, 11 May p. 736.

HIGGINS, CHARLES. b. 1805 or 1806; M.D. Edin. 1825; knight of legion of honour; author of *Observations on climate, diet and medical treatment in France and England* 1835; *Notes sur l'emploi des alterants dans les maladies, aigues et chroniques. Paris* 1859. d. 212 Rue de Rivoli, Paris 27 July 1866.

HIGGINS, CHARLES LONGUET (1 son of John Higgins of Turvey abbey, Beds., d. 1846). b. Turvey abbey 30 Nov. 1806; pensioner of Trin. coll. Cam. 14 Nov. 1825; B.A. 1830, M.A. 1834; student of Lincoln's inn 16 Nov. 1830, withdrew his name 2 Nov. 1847; studied medicine at St. Bartholomew's 1836–8; in practice at Turvey 1838; visited Egypt and the Holy Land 1848; restored Turvey ch. 1852–4, built schools 1847, a village museum 1852 and better cottages 1849 etc.; projected a hymn book for general use in Ch. of England, and printed *Hymnology, a paper read*

HIGGINS, C. L. (Con.)

before the church congress Nottingham. *Oxford* 1871. d. Turvey 23 Jany. 1885. *J. W. Burgon's Lives of twelve good men* (1888) ii, 343–422.

HIGGINS, GEORGE GORE OUSELEY (2 son of Fitzgerald Higgins of Westport, co. Mayo). b. 15 Oct. 1818; ed. at Brussels and Trin. coll. Dublin; in C.S. in Jamaica; M.P. for Mayo 1850 to 1857; lieut.-col. North Mayo militia 5 Feb. 1855 to 1 Oct. 1861. d. 6 Wilton place, London 8 May 1874. *I.L.N. xvii*, 169 (1850), portrait.

HIGGINS, MATTHEW JAMES (only son of Matthew Higgins of Benown castle, Westmeath). b. Benown castle 4 Dec. 1810; ed. at Eton; matric. from New coll. Ox. 22 May 1828; went to British Guiana 1838 and 1846 where he owned an estate; contributed an article called 'Jacob Omnium the Merchant Prince' to *New Monthly Magazine*, Aug. 1845; agent for the British Association for the relief of the destitute Irish 1847; contested Westbury 31 July 1847; one of chief writers on *Morning Chronicle* 1848; contributed to *The Times* on all kinds of questions under pseudonym of Jacob Omnium, J.O., Civilian, Paterfamilias, West Londoner, A Belgravian Mother, Mother of six, A thirsty soul, John Barleycorn, Providus, and many others till 1863; contributed to the *Edinburgh Rev.*, the *Cornhill* and the *Pall Mall Gazette*; author of *Is cheap sugar the triumph of free trade? A letter to Lord J. Russell* 1847, *Second Letter* 1848, *Third Letter* 1848; *Light horse* 1855; *The story of the Mhow court-martial* 1864 and other books. d. Kingston house near Abingdon 14 Aug. 1868. bur. in R.C. cemet. Fulham 21 Aug. *Essays on social subjects by M. J. Higgins, with memoir by Sir W. S. Maxwell* (1875); *Cornhill, xviii*, 507–12 (1868); *The Mask* (1868), 42 portrait.

HIGGINS, THOMAS GORDON. b. 1789; Second lieut. R.A. 4 Oct. 1806, col. 20 June 1854 to 24 Jany. 1857, col. commandant 20 Sep. 1865 to death; L.G. 26 Dec. 1865; commandant of garrison of Quebec 5 years, presented with a piece of plate by inhabitants of Quebec 30 April 1853. d. 83 Sloane st. Chelsea 20 June 1871 aged 82. *I.L.N. xxii*, 341 (1853), picture of testimonial.

HIGGINSON, REV. EDWARD (eld. son of Rev. Edward Higginson, unitarian minister, d. 1832). b. Heaton Norris, Lancs. 9 Jany. 1807; ed. at Manchester coll. York 1823–8; unitarian minister Bowl alley lane chapel, Hull 1828–46, at Westgate chapel, Wakefield 1846–58, and at High st. chapel, Swansea 1858–76;

HIGGINSON, REV. E. *(Con.)*

president Royal Institution, South Wales 1877–9; author of *Orthodoxy and unbelief* 1832; *The sacrifice of Christ* 1833, 2 ed. 1848; *The spirit of the Bible* 2 vols. 1853–5, 2 ed. 1863; *Ecce Messias* 1871; with his wife Emily dau. of George Thomas he wrote *The fine arts in Italy* 1859. *d.* 2 Glanmore ter. Swansea 12 Feb. 1880. *Autobiographical sketch in Christian Reformer* (1856) 192, (1857) 528; *Christian Life* 21 Feb. 1880 *pp.* 86–7, *portrait.*

HIGGINSON, GEORGE POWELL. *b.* 1787; ensign 1 foot guards 6 Nov. 1805, captain 26 Oct. 1820 to 11 April 1834 when placed on h.p.; col. 94 foot 29 Jany. 1855 to death; general 9 Nov. 1862. *d.* Cannes 19 April 1866 aged 79.

HIGGINSON, SIR JAMES MACAULAY *(son of James Higginson, major 10 foot).* *b.* 1805; ed. at Trin. coll. Dublin; entered Bengal army 1824; private sec. to Lord Metcalfe in India, Jamaica and Canada 1835–46; governor of Antigua and the Leeward island 1846–50; governor of Mauritius 1 Oct. 1850 to 11 Sep. 1857; C.B. 1 March 1851, K.C.B. 2 Jany. 1857. *d.* Tulfaris, co. Wicklow 28 June 1885.

HIGGS, WILLIAM ALPHEUS (3 *son of William Higgs of Tiverton, Somerset).* *b.* Luckington near Frome 1838; head of firms of W. A. Higgs & Co. and Barber & Co. tea merchants, London; sheriff of London and Middlesex 1887–8; accompanied Lord mayor Polydore de Keyser to Belgium on his visit to his native country 1888; F.R.G.S.; of Willenhall park, New Barnet; a breeder of prize stock. *d.* suddenly at Hotel Victoria, Northumberland avenue, London when starting to attend lord mayor's ball 23 Dec. 1889. *City Press* 28 Dec. 1889 *p.* 5.

HIGHTON, EDWARD. *b.* Leicester 13 Aug. 1817; resident engineer of Taff Vale dock and railway 1845; telegraphic engineer to London and North Western railway co. 1846; A.I.C.E. 1847; received large gold medal of Society of Arts for his inventions in electric telegraphy 1849; author of *The electric telegraph, its history and progress* 1852; *Highton's Mathematical arrangement of code for telegraph purposes* 1857. *d.* 5 Gloucester road, Regent's park, London 13 Nov. 1859.

HIGHTON, REV. HENRY (1 *son of Henry Highton).* *b.* Leicester 19 Jany. 1816; ed. at Rugby and Queen's coll. Ox., B.A. 1837, M.A. 1840; Mitchel fell. of his coll. 1840–1; assistant master of Rugby 1841–56; principal of Cheltenham coll. March 1859 to 1862; silver

HIGHTON, REV. H. *(Con.)*

medallist of Soc. of Arts for paper on Telegraphy without insulation 1 May 1872; patented 4 improvements in galvanic batteries 1871–2 and 3 improvements in electric telegraphs 1873–4; invented artificial stone much used for paving and building; author of *A letter to Sir M. Montefiore on address presented by 1500 continental Jews* 1842; *A catechism of the Second Advent* 1851; *A revised translation of the New Testament* 1862; *Letter on repeal of the Act of uniformity* 1863; *Dean Stanley and Saint Socrates, the ethics of the philosopher and the philosophy of the divine* 1873. *d.* The Cedars, Putney 23 Dec. 1874.

HIGMAN, REV. JOHN PHILIPS. *b.* 1793; ed. at Trin. coll. Cam., 3rd wrangler 1816; B.A. 1816, M.A. 1819; fellow and tutor of his coll.; R. of Fakenham, Norfolk 1834 to death; F.R.S. 23 May 1820; F.R.A.S.; author of *A syllabus of the differential and integral calculus* 1826. *d.* Cambridge ter. Hyde park, London 7 Aug. 1855.

HIGSON, JOHN *(eld. son of Daniel Higson).* *b.* Whiteley Farm, Gorton, Lancs. 25 July 1825; ed. at Ardwick and Gorton old sch.; cashier of Victoria mills, Droylsden; cashier of Springhead spinning co. Droylsden; author of *The Gorton historical recorder or a history of the Mesne manor and its inhabitants* 1852; *A history of Droylsden* 1859; *Explosions in coal mines* 1878; commenced a newspaper at Droylsden which was a failure; contributed to *Ashton Reporter* under signature of H. *d.* Birch cottage, Lees near Oldham 13 Dec. 1871. *bur.* Droylsden ch. yard. *Procter's Manchester streets* (1874) 288–91; *Ashton Reporter* 16 Dec. 1871.

HILDIGE, JAMES GRAHAM. Ed. at Trin. coll. Dublin; M.R.C.S. Eng. 1852; L.K.Q.C.P.I. 1853; F.R.C.S.I. 1859; lecturer on ophthalmic surgery Carmichael sch. of medicine; author of *Medical sketches in Austria, Prussia and Italy, with remarks on the Campagna and the conquered provinces in Italy and Hungary.* Dublin 1859; writer of papers in medical journals. *d.* 7 Upper Merrion st. Dublin 14 May 1871.

HILDITCH, SIR EDWARD *(son of John Frederick Hilditch of Hammersmith).* *b.* 1805; studied at St. George's hospital; M.R.C.S. 1826; M.D. Aberdeen 1859; entered navy 1826, on West India station 1830–55; inspector general of hospitals and fleets 6 Feb. 1854 to 13 Jany. 1870 when he retired; in charge of Royal hospital, Plymouth 1855–61, of Greenwich hospital 1861–65; knighted at Windsor

HILDITCH, SIR E. (Con.)

castle 20 Nov. 1865; hon. physician to the Queen 1868 to death. d. 18 Arundel gardens, Bayswater, London 24 Aug. 1876.

HILDYARD, REV. JAMES (8 son of Rev. Wm. Hildyard 1762–1842, R. of Winstead in Holderness, Yorkshire). b. Winstead 11 April 1809; ed. at Shrewsbury 1820–29, was head of the sch. from 1826, headed a rebellion in the sch. known as the Beef Row, April 1829; pensioner at Ch. coll. Cam. Oct. 1829, Tancred divinity student 1829, sen. opt. in mathematics, second in the first class of the class. tripos and chancellor's medallist Jany. 1833; B.A. 1833, M.A. 1836, B.D. 1846; fellow of his coll. 1833 and classical lecturer and tutor; Cambridge preacher at Chapel royal, Whitehall 1843, 1844; senior proctor 1843; R. of Ingoldsby, Lincoln, June 1846 to death; author of M. A. Plauti Menæchmi cum notis 1836; Five sermons on the parable of the rich man and Lazarus 1841; The university system of private tuition examined 1844; Reply to the bishops in convocation, on Lord Ebury's motion for a revision of the liturgy. Signed Ingoldsby 1858, 4 ed. 2 vols. 1879. d. Ingoldsby 27 Aug. 1887. The Biograph, May 1881 pp. 472–77; William Smith's Old Yorkshire (1883) pp. 142–46, portrait; Church portrait journal, April 1877, 49–50, portrait.

HILDYARD, JOHN (brother of the preceding). b. 1796 or 1797; ed. at Shrewsbury, head boy there; went to St. John's coll. Cam., B.A. 1818, M.A. 1821; barrister L.I. 10 July 1821; recorder of Stamford, Grantham and Leicester 1835–54; judge of county courts, circuit 20 (Leicestershire), March 1847 to death. d. the King's hotel, Loughborough 13 Feb. 1855. bur. in Townshend vault, All Saints' church, Hertford 21 Feb.

NOTE.—His father lived to see 9 sons masters of arts in Cambridge university, and 6 of them fellows of their respective colleges.

HILDYARD, ROBERT CHARLES (brother of the preceding). b. Winstead 1800; ed. at Oakham sch. and Cath. hall, Cam., B.A. 1823, M.A. 1826, fellow of his coll.; barrister L.I. 25 May 1827; admitted ad eundem at I.T. 1833, bencher 1844, reader 1857; counsel to duchy of Lancaster to 1846; Q.C. 1845; M.P. for Whitehaven 28 July 1847 to death. d. 24 Lowndes st. London 7 Dec. 1857.

HILDYARD, THOMAS BLACKBORNE THOROTON- (son of colonel Thomas B. Thoroton-Hildyard of Flintham hall, Notts., d. 1830). b. 8 April 1821; ed. at Eton; matric. from Ch. Ch. Ox. 16 Oct. 1839; sheriff of Notts. 1862; M.P.

HILDYARD, T. B. T.- (Con.)

South Notts. 1846–52 and 1866–85; chairman Notts. quarter sessions 6 April 1874. d. 11 Moreton gardens, South Kensington 19 March 1888.

NOTE.—His fellow member for South Notts. 1874-85 George Storer d. Thornton hall, Notts. the same day 19 March.

HILDYARD, REV. WILLIAM (son of Rev. John Hildyard of Monk's Eleigh, Suffolk). Matric. from Trin. coll. Ox. 24 May 1808 aged 17, scholar 1812–5, B.A. 1812, M.A. 1817; assist. P.C. Beverley minster 1820; R. of Hameringham cum Scrayfield, Lincoln 1837–66; author of Thoughts on Sunday schools. Beverley 1827; Specimens of composition 1832; A manual of ancient geography for the use of schools 1835; A letter to the Rev. A. J. Carr respecting a sermon preached by him in St. John's chapel, Beverley 1843. d. Market Deeping, Lincs. 11 Feb. 1875. I.L.N. lxvi, 211 (1875).

HILES, JOHN. b. 1810; organist at Shrewsbury 1835–53, at Portsmouth 1853–60, and at Brighton 1860–74; organist Christ church, Gipsy hill, London 1874–81; author of A catechism for the pianoforte student 1871, 18 ed. 1882, circulated 65,000 copies; A complete dictionary of 12,500 musical terms 1871, 7 ed. 1882; Short Voluntaries for the organ 4 series 1854–75; Catechism of the organ 1876; revised The Amateur organist. By E. Travis 1872, and composed many pieces of music. d. 51 Elsham road, Kennington, London 4 Feb. 1882. Musical Directory (1883) p. xviii.

HILL, ROWLAND HILL, 2 Viscount (eld. son of John Hill 1769–1814, colonel in the army). b. 10 May 1800; ed. at Oriel coll. Ox., M.A. 1820; cornet royal horse guards 1820–24; M.P. for Shropshire 1821–32, for North Shropshire 1832–42; succeeded his grandfather as 4 baronet 21 May 1824, and his uncle as 2 viscount 10 Dec. 1842; lieut.-col. North Salop yeomanry cavalry 18 Aug. 1824; lord lieut. of Shropshire 20 Nov. 1845 to death; col. Shropshire militia 8 June 1849 to Aug. 1852. d. Hawkstone park, Salop 2 Jany. 1875. I.L.N. iv, 65 (1844), portrait.

HILL, REV. ALEXANDER (son of George Hill, D.D. 1750–1819, principal of St. Andrew's univ.) b. St. Andrews 19 July 1785; ed. at St. Andrews, B.A. 1804, D.D. 1828; licensed as a presbyterian preacher Sep. 1806; minister of Colmonell, Ayrshire 1815–16 and of Dailly 1816–40; professor of divinity Glasgow univ. 1840–62; moderator of the general assembly 1845; author of The practice in the

HILL, REV. A. (Con.)

judicatories of the church of Scotland 2 ed. 1830, 5 *ed.* 1851; *Practical hints to young ministers; Counsels regarding the pastoral office.* d. 24 Wellington sq. Ayr 27 Jany. 1867. *John Smith's Our Scottish Clergy 3rd series* (1851) 364–9; *Scott's Fasti ii, part i, p.* 108.

HILL, DAVID OCTAVIUS (*son of Thomas Hill, bookseller, Perth*). *b.* Perth 1802; studied under Andrew Wilson, Edin.; landscape painter; sec. Soc. of Arts, Edin. 1830, which became R. Scottish academy, sec. 1838–70; R.S.A.; the first to apply photography to portraiture and to use calotype; a commissioner of the board of manufactures 1850; originated Art Union of Edin. 183–, the first institution of the kind; exhibited 4 pictures at R.A., 1 at B.I. and 2 at Suffolk st. 1832–68 and many at R.S.A.; commenced in 1843 his picture, Signing the deed of demission, which contains 500 portraits, finished 1865, now in Free Ch. assembly hall, Edin.; published 60 pictures of the Scenery of the Land of Burns 1841. *d.* Edinburgh 17 May 1870. *Redgrave's Dictionary of Artists* (1878) 211; *Edinburgh Evening Courant* 18 May 1870 p. 8.

HILL, SIR DUDLEY . ST. LEGER (*eld. son of Dudley Hill*). *b.* co. Carlow 1790; ensign 82 foot 27 Aug. 1804; captain royal West India rangers 1810–14; major attached to Portuguese and Spanish army 1814 to 25 Dec. 1816 when placed on h.p.; major 95 foot 1823 to 19 Jany. 1826 when placed on h.p.; served in South America 1806–8 and in the Peninsula 1808–14, being wounded 7 times; K.T.S. 20 Nov. 1816; knighted 25 Nov. 1816; governor of St. Lucia 15 April 1834 to 21 Dec. 1847; general on staff in Bengal 10 April 1848 to death; colonel of 50 regt. 28 March 1849 to death; M.G. 23 Nov. 1841; C.B. 4 June 1815, K.C.B. 2 March 1848. *d.* Umballa, Bengal 21 Feb. 1851. *I.L.N. xviii,* 329 (1851).

HILL, EDWARD ROWLEY (*2 son of Hugh Hill 1770–1850, colonel battle axe guards, Dublin castle*). *b.* 29 Dec. 1795; ensign 43 foot 23 Feb. 1813; lieut. col. 1 West India regiment 1 Jany. 1847 to 7 Sep. 1855; lieut. col. 68 foot 7 Sep. 1855 to 10 Sep. 1858 when placed on h.p.; col. 5 foot 21 Feb. 1868 to death; general 1 Oct. 1877. *d.* Brighton 10 Sep. 1878.

HILL, EDWIN (*2 child of Thomas Wright Hill of Birmingham 1763–1851*). *b.* Birmingham 25 Nov. 1793; manager Fazeley st. rolling mills, Birmingham to 1827; with his bro. Sir Rowland Hill kept a school at Bruce castle, Tottenham 1827; supervisor of the stamps de-

HILL, E. (Con.)

partment, Somerset house 1840, remodelled the machinery in use, thus effecting a saving of many thousands a year; with W. De la Rue invented machine for folding envelopes 1840; author of *Principles of currency. Means of ensuring uniformity of value and adequacy of supply* 1856; *Criminal capitalists, pamphlets* 1870–2. *d.* 1 St. Mark's sq. Regent's park, London 6 Nov. 1876. *G. B. Hill's Life of Sir Rowland Hill* (1880) i, 37, ii, 99, 503.

HILL, ELLEN (*dau. of Mr. Shaw*). *b.* 1803; an actress of some note at the minor theatres; played leading business at the Royalty, the Marylebone and the City of London theatres; acted in a drama with the young Roscius, W. H. Betty and Charles Kean; retired from stage 1840. (*m.* William John Hill, leader and composer *d.* Dublin, Jany. 1851). *d.* London 9 Dec. 1866 aged 63. *Era 23 Dec.* 1866 p. 12.

HILL, GEORGE. *b.* co. Wexford 1809; printer; contributed articles on the scenery and antiquities of Wexford and Kilkenny to *Dublin Penny Journal,* illustrated by his own drawings; reporter to the *Waterford Mail, Wexford Independent, Drogheda Conservative, Liverpool Herald, Rochdale Pilot* and the *Bacup and Rossendale News.* d. Bacup, Lancs. 8 July 1869. *Newspaper Press 2 Aug.* 1869 p. 181.

HILL, GEORGE AUGUSTA (*5 son of 2 marquis of Downshire 1753–1801*). *b.* 9 Dec. 1801; lieut. royal horse guards 20 July 1820; captain 8 hussars 1825 to 6 July 1830 when placed on h.p.; M.P. for Carrickfergus 1831–2; sheriff of Donegal 1845; author of *Facts from Gweedore with useful hints to Donegal tourists. Dublin* 2 *parts* 1845, 3 *ed.* 1854. *d.* Ballyane house near Ramelton, co. Donegal 6 April 1879.

HILL, HENRY. *b.* Manchester 1807; first betted at Newmarket 1829; in partnership with John Gully; factotum for Lord George Bentinck for many years; cleared some thousands on Bloomsbury winning the Derby 1839; discovered the Running Rein fraud 1844; kept race horses; won heavily on Pyrrhus the First, winner of Derby 1846; won the Two Thousand with Pitsford 1850; with Rogerthorpe won Goodwood cup 1856; the largest better on the Derby except W. E. Davies the Leviathan; lost £40,000 in one year on the Stock Exchange; purchased Ackworth near Pomfret from John Gully. *d.* 52 Queen's gate ter. Kensington 1 Feb. 1881 aged 74. *Sporting Rev., April* 1858 *pp.* 295–8; *W. Day's Reminiscences* (1886) 63–76.

HILL, Rev. Henry Thomas. *b.* 1815; ed. at C.C. coll. Cam., B.A. 1837, M.A. 1840; P.C. of Lye, Worcs. 1839–43; C. of Wolverley 1843–51; R. of Felton 1851 to death; V. of Preston Wynne, Hereford 1858–76; diocesan inspector of schools 1870–72; preb. of Nonnington in Hereford cath. 1870 to death; author of *Church restoration, What is it? Whence is it?* 1864; *Thoughts on churches and church yards* 1856, 3 ed. 1862. *d.* Felton 11 Jany. 1882.

HILL, Sir Hugh (2 *son of James Hill of Graig, co. Cork* 1771–1850). *b.* Graig 1802; entered Trin. coll. Dublin, Nov. 1816, B.A. 1821; at King's Inns, Dublin; practised in London as a special pleader below the bar 1827–41; barrister M.T. 29 Jany. 1841, bencher Dec. 1851; Q.C. July 1851; serjeant at law May 1858; judge of court of Queen's Bench 29 May 1858 to 3 Dec. 1861; knighted at Buckingham palace 18 April 1859. *d.* Royal crescent hotel, Brighton 12 Oct. 1871.

HILL, Sir James (*eld. son of James Haylock Hill of Newbold Firs, Leamington*). *bapt.* at St. Thomas, Winchester 6 Feb. 1814; ed. at Winchester and New coll. Ox., B.A. 1836, M.A. 1840; fellow of his coll.; barrister I.T. 3 May 1839; second charity estate comr. 24 Oct. 1853, chief charity estate comr. 7 Dec. 1872 to death; knighted at Windsor castle 5 May 1873; published *A practical treatise on the law relating to trustees, their powers, duties, privileges and abilities* 1845. *d.* Folkestone 23 Oct. 1875. *Law Times,* lx, 60 (1875); *I.L.N.* lxvii, 447 (1875), lxviii, 22 (1876).

HILL, James Frederick. *b.* Norwich 1817; conductor; composer of *Old Friends met together, part song,* printed in J. P. Hullah's *The Singer's Library* 1859. *d.* St. Giles ter. Bethel st. Norwich 9 March 1877.

HILL, James John (*son of Daniel Hill of Birmingham*). *b.* Broad st. Birmingham 1810; ed. at Hazlewood sch.; pupil of John Vincent Barber of Birmingham, artist; a portrait painter in Birmingham to 1839; moved to London 1839; member of Society of British artists 1842; exhibited 10 pictures at R.A., 5 at B.I. and 109 at Suffolk st. 1842–80. *d.* Sutton house, West Hill, Highgate 27 Jany. 1882. *Birmingham Weekly Post* 4 Feb. 1882.

HILL, Sir John. *b.* 1774; entered navy 25 Sep. 1781, present in battle of the Nile; an agent for transports 24 March 1813–1819; captain 28 Oct. 1815; captain superintendent of victualling yard at Deptford 1820–1838; superintendent of dockyard at Sheerness 9

March 1838–41, at Deptford 11 Dec. 1841 to 16 April 1851; rear admiral 2 April 1851; knighted at St. James's palace 31 Aug. 1831. *d.* Walmer lodge, Deal 20 Jany. 1855 aged 81.

HILL, Rev. John (*son of John Hill of London*). *b.* 1787; ed. at St. Edmund hall, Ox., B.A. 1809, M.A. 1812, B.D. 1844; vice principal of his hall 1812–51; city lecturer at Oxford 1851; R. of Wyke Regis, Dorset 1851 to death; editor of *Artis Logicæ Rudimenta by H. Aldrich. With observations* 1849; author of a few sermons. *d.* Wyke Regis 22 Feb. 1855. *bur.* St. Peter's in the East, Oxford.

HILL, Rev. John Harwood (*son of Robert Hill of Leamington*). *b.* Louth, Lincs. 1809; pensioner Peter house, Cam. 30 June 1830, B.A. 1834; R. of Cranoe, Leics. 1837 to death, and V. of Welham 1841 to death; F.S.A. 12 Jany. 1871; local sec. Leicestershire Architect. and Archæol. Soc. and a contributor to its transactions; author of *The chronicle of the christian ages or records of events ecclesiastical, civil and military. Uppingham* 2 vols. 1859; *The history of the parish of Langton. Leicester* 1867; *The history of Market Harborough. Leicester* 1875. *d.* Cranoe rectory 3 Dec. 1886. *Proc. Soc. of Antiquaries,* xi, 371 (1885–7); *Academy* 18 Dec. 1886 p. 411.

HILL, Ven. Justly (*youngest son of colonel William Hill of St. Boniface, Isle of Wight*). *bapt.* Bonchurch, I. of W. 16 Dec. 1781; ed. at Winchester and New coll. Ox., scholar, B.A. 1805, M.A. 1808; fellow of his coll. 1802–20; R. of Shanklin and Bonchurch, Isle of Wight 1809 to death; R. of Tingewick, Bucks. 1818 to death; archdeacon and commissary of Buckingham 1825; author of *Two charges delivered to the clergy and churchwardens of the archdeaconry of Buckingham. Eton,* 2 ed. 1847, and other charges and sermons. *d.* Shanklin 18 March 1853.

HILL, Matthew Davenport (*eld. child of Thomas Wright Hill of Birmingham* 1763–1851). *b.* Suffolk st. Birmingham 6 Aug. 1792; ed. at Wolverhampton and in his father's school, Birmingham; assisted in his father's school to 1815; barrister L.I. 18 Nov. 1819, went Midland circuit, quitted it 1846; defended wife of Richard Carlile on charge of selling a libel 1820; leading counsel for Nottingham rioters 1831, for Canadian prisoners 1839, for Rebecca rioters 1843, and for D. O'Connell 1844; for the plaintiffs in Braintree ch. rate case 1848, for the crown in Dr. Hampden's case 1848; for many years in parliament and in the courts engaged in Baron de Bode's case; established with Bentham and Brougham the Soc. for Diffusion of useful knowledge, Jany. 1827; M.P. for Hull 1832–35; Q.C. 7 July 1834; recorder of Birmingham, April 1839, resigned Jany. 1866; one of commissioners of court of bankruptcy for Bristol district 24 March 1851 to 31 Dec. 1869 when office was abolished, granted sum of £1800; author of *Suggestions for repression of crime* 1857; *Our exemplars. Biographical sketches* 1861.   *d.* Heath house, Stapleton, Gloucs. 7 June 1872. *The Recorder of Birmingham, a memoir of M. D. Hill, By R. and F. D. Hill* (1878), *portrait; Law mag. and review, July* 1872 *pp.* 515–29.

HILL, REV. PASCOE GRENFELL (*son of major Thomas Hill*). *b.* Marazion; Cornwall 15 May 1804; ed. at Mill Hill sch. Middlesex and Trin. coll. Dublin, B.A. 1836; chaplain R.N. 1836–45; chaplain Westminster hospital 1852–7; R. of St. Edmund the King and martyr with St. Nicholas Acons, Lombard st. London 26 Jany. 1863 to death; the first to introduce a surpliced choir into a city ch.; author of *Fifty days on board a slave ship* 1843, 3 ed. 1853; *A voyage to the slave coasts* 1849; *A journey through Palestine* 1852; *Life of Napoleon* 3 vols. 1869. *d.* the rectory house 32 Finsbury sq. London 28 Aug. 1882. *bur.* Ilford cemetery. *City Press* 2 *Sep.* 1882 *p.* 5; *Boase & Courtney's Bibl. Cornub. i,* 240.

HILL, PERCY. *b.* 24 Dec. 1817; ensign 68 foot 26 June 1835; lieut. colonel rifle brigade 22 June 1855 to 6 March 1868; served in Russian war 1854–6 and in Indian mutiny 1857–8; L.G. 1 Oct. 1877; colonel 85 foot 27 Sep. 1879 to death; C.B. 26 July 1858. *d.* 24 April 1880.

HILL, REV. RICHARD HUMPHRY (*2 son of Rev. Richard Hill of Wolverton, Somerset*). *b.* Wolverton 21 Oct. 1824; chorister Magd. coll. Ox. 1834–42, demy 1842–51, matric. from Ex. coll. 2 June 1842; B.A. 1846, M.A. 1849, D.C.L. 1854; head master of Beaumaris gr. sch. 1850–64 and of Magd. coll. sch. Ox. Jany. 1865 to 23 July 1876 which he raised to the level of a first-rate public school; precentor and canon of Bangor 31 Dec. 1864 to death; R. of Stanway near Colchester 22 Dec. 1874 to death. *d.* Stanway rectory 26 Feb. 1891. *J. R. Bloxam's Register of Magdalen College, i* 219, *vii* 353–6.

HILL, SIR ROBERT CHAMBRE (4 *son of Sir John Hill of Hawkstone, Salop,* 3 *bart.* 1740–1824). *b.* 25 March 1778; ed. at Rugby; cornet royal horse guards 11 June 1794, lieut. colonel

13 May 1813 to 24 July 1823; knighted by the prince regent at Carlton house 29 May 1812; served in the Peninsula and at Waterloo; C.B. 22 June 1815.   *d.* Prees hall, Salop 5 March 1860. *The case of J. Jebb with charges against Sir R. Hill* (1830).

HILL, ROBERT GARDINER (*son of Robert Hill of Leamington*). *b.* Louth, Lincs. 26 Feb. 1811; M.R.C.S. 1834; L.C.P. Edin. 1859; resident house surgeon of Lincoln lunatic asylum July 1835; proprietor with Richard Sutton Harvey of Eastgate House private asylum, Lincoln 1840–63; presented with a testimonial at Lincoln 29 Oct. 1851 as the author and originator of the non-restraint system in lunacy; mayor of Lincoln 1852–3; F.S.A. 17 Feb. 1853; resident medical proprietor of Earl's Court house, Old Brompton, London, Oct. 1863 to death; author of *A concise history of the entire abolition of medical restraint in the treatment of the insane* 1857; *Lunacy, its past and its present* 1870. *d.* Earl's Court House, London 30 May 1878. *Robertson's Photographs of eminent medical men* (1868) *ii* 65–8, *portrait; Medical Circular* 7 *Sep.* 1853 *pp.* 187–9, *portrait, and* 23 *Nov. pp.* 522–3; *I.L.N.* 3 *Jany.* 1852 *pp.* 13–14, *view of testimonial.*

HILL, SIR ROWLAND (3 *son of Thomas Wright Hill* 1763–1851). *b.* Kidderminster 3 Dec. 1795; a teacher in his father's schools at Birmingham and Tottenham 1808–28; established the Hazelwood system of school management 1812; undertook the management of his father's money affairs from 1812; invented a rotatory printing press; sec. to the South Australian commission 1835–9; published *Post office reform, its importance and practicability* 1836; described his adhesive postage stamp 13 Feb. 1837; attached to the Treasury to introduce cheap postage 1839–42, dismissed by Sir R. Peel, Sep. 1842, penny postage established 10 Jany. 1840; director of London and Brighton railway 1843, chairman 1845–6, introduced system of express and excursion trains; presented by public subscription with £13,000, 17 June 1846; sec. to post-master-general Nov. 1846; permanent sec. of post office, April 1854 to 4 March 1864; had a grant from parliament of £20,000, 1864; F.R.S. 11 June 1857, member of council 1867; D.C.L. of Ox. 9 June 1864; K.C.B. 10 Feb. 1860; F.R.A.S.; presented with freedom of city of London 6 June 1879; author of *Home colonies, plan for extinction of pauperism* 1832; *Post office reform* 1837, 3 ed. 1837; *The state and prospects of penny postage* 1844; *Results of postal reform* 1864. *d.* Ber-

HILL, Sir R. *(Con.)*

tram house, Hampstead 27 Aug. 1879. *bur.* St. Paul's chapel, Westminster abbey 4 Sep. *G. B. Hill's Life of Sir R. Hill 2 vols.* 1880, *portrait; W. Lewin's Her Majesty's Mails (2 ed.* 1865) 168–97, *portrait; Walford's Photographic portraits,* No. 12, *April 1857, portrait; H. J. Nichol's Great movements* (1881) 189–220, *portrait.*

NOTE.—Sir R. Hill's statue at corner of Royal exchange, London, was unveiled 17 June 1882.—. Other statues have been erected at Kidderminster and Birmingham.

HILL, RIGHT REV. ROWLEY (3 *son of Sir George Hill,* 3 *bart.* 1804–45). *b.* 22 Feb. 1836; ed. at Christ's hospital, Lond. and Trin. coll. Cam., B.A. 1859, M.A. 1863; C. of Ch. Ch. Dover 1860–61; C. of St. Mary, Marylebone 1861–63; P.C. of St. Luke's, Marylebone 1863–68; R. of Frant, Sussex 1868–71; V. of St. Michael's, Chester sq. London 1871–73; V. of Sheffield 1873–77; preb. of York cath. 1876–77; bishop of Sodor and Man 17 July 1877 to death, consecrated in York Minster 24 Aug.; author of *Sunday school lessons: the collects* 1866, 2 *ed.* 1867; *Sunday school lessons: the gospels* 1866; *The titles of our Lord* 1870. *d.* 10 Hereford sq. Old Brompton, London 27 May 1887. *Church Portrait Journal* ii, 25 (1878), *portrait.*

HILL, THOMAS. *b.* 1794; at Royalty theatre; clown at Drury Lane, especially known in the pantomime of *Jack of Spades* under R. W. Elliston's management. *d.* 26 May 1851 aged 57. *bur.* St. Peter's ch. Walworth road. *Era* 8 *June* 1851 *p.* 11.

HILL, REV. THOMAS. *b.* 1808; ed. at Clare coll. Cam., B.A. 1830, M.A. 1833; assist. classical master of Mercer's sch. London 1832–50; P.C. of Holy Trin. Minories, London 1850 to death; author of *The harmony of the Latin and Greek languages* 1842; *The history of the parish of Holy Trinity Minories* 1851. *d.* 30 Little Trinity lane, London 13 Feb. 1865.

HILL, VEN. THOMAS. Ed. at Trin. coll. Cam., B.A. 1810, M.A. 1813, B.D. 1822; V. of Badgeworth, Gloucs. 1821; V. of Chesterfield, Derby 1822–46; archdeacon of Derby 4 Jany. 1847 to 1873; canon res. with prebendal stalls of Offley and Flixton annexed, in Lichfield cath. 1851–63; P.C. of Hasland, Derby 1851–63; author of *The doctrine of the Trinity* 1820; *Letters and memoirs of W. A. Shirley, bishop of Sodor and Man* 1849; *The life of L. Saunders* 1858. *d.* Harrogate 14 Sep. 1875.

HILL, THOMAS WRIGHT *(son of James Hill, baker and dealer in horse corn). b.* Kidderminster 24 April 1763; ed. at Kidderminster gram. sch.; apprentice to a brass founder; discovered the distinction between vocal and whisper letters; said to have edited the *Hazelwood Magazine* 1824–30; invented a system of philosophic short-hand; devised scheme for representation of minorities; a manufacturer of woollen stuffs; founded a school at Hill Top, Birmingham 1803, with his sons removed it to Hazelwood near Birmingham 1819 and to Bruce castle, Tottenham, Middlesex 1827; F.R. Astronom. Soc.; a volume of *Selections from his papers* was printed in 1860. *d.* Bruce terrace, Tottenham 13 June 1851. *M. D. Hill's Remains of T. W. Hill* (1859); *Edin. Rev. xli,* 315–35 (1825); *Monthly Notices R. Astronom. Soc.* 1852 *pp.* 90–93; *Life of Sir R. Hill* (1880) i, 2 *et seq., portrait.*

HILL, WILLIAM. *b.* 1806; salesman and book keeper with Daniel Lee & Co., calico printers, Manchester; mnemonicalist; author of *Fifteen lessons on the analogy and syntax of the English language* 1833; *The rational school grammar and entertaining class book; The complete English exposition and comprehensive spelling book; The educational monitor, which will enable the student to fix knowledge rapidly in the mind* 1847; *How to teach the alphabet in a few hours* 1865; *Memories for the million* 1875. *d.* Rose Bank, Patricroft near Salford 2 April 1881. *Gillow's English catholics,* iii, 310–11 (1887).

HILL, SIR WILLIAM *(son of Daniel Hill, member of council, Antigua). b.* 1805; entered military service of E.I.C. 1821; commanded garrison of 500 men at Pegu Pagoda, which he held against 6000 men 1852; commanded the Gwalior contingent 1853; commanded the Nizam's contingent during the Indian mutiny 1857; col. in the army 1859; retired with rank of M.G. 31 Dec. 1861; K.C.S.I. 24 May 1867. *d.* Southsea 20 Aug. 1886.

HILL, WILLIAM JOHN. Composer of *Our Saviour's farewell. A devotional canzonette* 1839. (*m.* Ellen Shaw *d.* 9 Dec. 1866 aged 63). *d.* Dublin, Jany. 1851.

HILL, WILLIAM JONES, stage name of William Hill Jones. *b.* 14 Jany. 1834; a musician; appeared as an actor at Court theatre, London 25 Jany. 1871 as Nicodemus Nobbs in *Turn him out,* as John Brodie in *Dotheboys' Hall,* as the manager in *Vesta's Temple* 14 Nov. 1872, in *The Happy Land* made up as Robert Lowe 3 March 1873, as Uncle Bopeddy in *The Wedding March* 15 Nov. 1873, in *Peacock's*

HILL, W. J. (*Con.*)

Holiday 16 April 1874; at the Criterion in *Betsy* 6 Aug. 1879; as Mr. Cattermole in *Private Secretary* at Prince's theatre 29 March 1884; as the Baillie in *Les cloches de Corneville* at Folly theatre Feb. 1878 to 1879; acted Irascible Fizzleton in *Nita's First* at Novelty up to 11 April 1888. *d.* Birchmore villa, 29 Ampthill sq. London 13 April 1888. *bur.* Highgate cemet. *Illust. Sport. and Dram. News, xiv,* 397 (1881), *portrait; Theatre, v,* 95 (1885), *portrait, xi,* 281 (1888); *Saturday Programme 25 Nov.* 1876 *pp.* 10–11, *portrait; Era* 14 *April* 1888 *p.* 8, 21 *April p.* 9.

HILLIER, GEORGE (*eld. son of William Hillier, commander R.N.*) *b.* Kennington 1815; made collections for the *History and antiquities of the Isle of Wight,* engraved the plates himself and printed part of it in his own house; discovered the Anglo-Saxon cemetery at Chessel Down and excavated the graves; author of *The topography of the Isle of Wight* 1850; *A narrative of the attempted escape of Charles I. from Carisbrook* 1852; *The sieges of Arundel castle* 1854; *The stranger's guide to Reading* 1859. *d.* Ryde, Isle of Wight 1 April 1866.

HILLIER, THOMAS. *b.* 1831; ed. at Univ. coll. London, M.B. Lond. 1845, B.A. 1849, M.D. 1855; M.R.C.S. 1852; F.R.C.P. 1867; resident medical officer Univ. coll. hospital; medical officer of health St. Pancras 12 years; physician hospital for sick children, Great Ormond st.; lectured on diseases of skin at University coll.; author of *Hand-book of skin diseases.* 1865; *Diseases of children* 1868 and other books. *d.* 32 Queen Anne st. London 7 Nov. 1868. *Medical Times 14 Nov.* 1868 *p.* 573; *Proc. Med. and Chir. Soc. vi,* 154 (1871).

HILLMAN, WILLIAM AUGUSTUS (*eld. son of William Hillman, surgeon R.N., d.* 1865). *b.* 1819; ed. at London univ.; M.R.C.S. 1841, F.R.C.S. 1845, student in human and comparative anatomy there 1841–4; assist. surgeon Westminster hospital and lecturer on physiology and general anatomy there 10 years; surgeon Westminster hospital 1869–71; author of *The study of physic and surgery* 1846. *d.* 2 Argyle st. Regent st. London 11 Dec. 1873. *Medical Times 20 Dec.* 1873 *p.* 705.

HILLS, JAMES. *b.* 1800; whip of the old Surrey hounds 7 seasons; first whip of Lord Ducie's hounds; huntsman of the Heythrop hounds at Heythrop near Didcot many years from 1835. *Scott and Sebright, By The Druid* (1862) 359–72, *portrait; Cecil's Records of the Chase* (1877) 163–7.

HILLS, TOM. *b.* 1793; huntsman of the Old Surrey hounds 1812–62; landlord of the Plough at Bletchingly. *d.* Feb. 1873. *Sporting Rev. June* 1859 *pp.* 394–7; *Baily's Mag. March* 1873 *pp.* 161–4.

HILLYAR, SIR CHARLES FARRELL (2 *son of Sir James Hillyar* 1769–1843, *rear admiral*). *b.* 1818; cadet R.N. 24 July 1828; served in South America 1837; severely wounded at Lagos 1851; captain 20 Feb. 1852; served at blockade of Sebastopol 1854–5; commander in chief in China 31 Aug. 1877 to 26 Sep. 1878; C.B. 2 June 1869, K.C.B. 21 June 1887; admiral 26 Sep. 1878, retired 9 June 1882. *d.* Torre house, Torpoint, Cornwall 14 Dec. 1888.

HILLYAR, ROBERT PURKIS. Inspector of hospitals and fleets 23 Nov. 1841; K.H. 1 Jany. 1837; C.B. 17 Aug. 1850. *d.* Little Green near Gosport 23 March 1855.

HILLYER, WILLIAM RICHARD (*son of an innkeeper*). *b.* Leybourne, Kent 5 March 1813; played with Town Malling club from 1830; first round armed bowler of his time, known as 'the best of all bowlers'; his balls took a curl and uprooted the middle stump; the finest short-slip ever seen; first played at Lord's 27 July 1835; practice bowler to Marylebone club to 1851; in his last match 7 June 1855 broke his thumb; had a benefit at the Oval 1858 which produced £300. *d.* Wheeler st. Maidstone 8 Jany. 1861. *bur.* Leybourne. *Lillywhite's Cricket Scores, ii,* 334 (1862), *vol. v, page xv* (1876).

HILLYERD, REV. SAMUEL JOHN (*son of Nicholas John Hillyerd*). *b.* 20 Feb. 1784; National schoolmaster Farnley Tyas, Yorks. to 1819; raised himself by education and was ordained as a literate 1819; C. of Denby Penistone, Yorks. 1819, C. of Farnley Tyas 1821, C. of Primrose hill, Great Horton, Bradford 1823; P.C. of Tattersall, Lincs. 1823–46; V. of Semperingham, Lincs. 1846 to death; a brilliant preacher. *d.* Semperingham 29 Juné 1861. *Hulbert's Suppl. Annals of Almondbury* (1885) 16; *Correspondence between C. G. Selleck and S. J. Hillyerd on universal salvation* (1835).

HILTON, HILDA. *b.* 1853; actress and vocalist; played with success in the provinces; acted at Criterion as Little Loo in *Orange Blossom* 1877; at Globe as Mrs. Honeyton in *The Happy Pair;* at the Strand as Ruth in *Ruth's Romance;* at the Gaiety as Juliana in *The Honeymoon* 1880; at the Princess' as Martha Gibbs in *All that glitters is not gold;* at Sadler's Wells 1881; at the Globe as Frou Frou; lessee of Opera Comique 1883 when she pro-

HILTON, H. *(Con.)*

duced *Bondage* 31 March; she wrote *Princess Carlo's plot* drama in 3 acts adapted from Ouida's *Afternoon*, brought out at Novelty theatre 31 Jany. 1887. *d.* Florence 13 June 1888 aged 35. *The Theatre* 1 *Aug.* 1881 *p.* 125, *portrait; Illust. Sport. and Dram. News* 8 *Jany.* 1881 *pp.* 401, 419, *portrait.*

HILTON, JOHN. *b.* Sible Hedingham, Essex 22 Sep. 1807; ed. at Chelmsford gr. sch. and Boulogne-sur-Mur; studied at Guy's 1824, M.R.C.S. 1827, F.R.C.S. 1843; demonstrator of anatomy at Guy's 1828, made dissections of the body which were reproduced in wax for Guy's museum, assist. surgeon 1844, full surgeon 1849; professor of surgery at R.C.S. 14 July 1859, president 1867; in practice at New Broad st., city of London; surgeon extraordinary to the queen 14 Oct. 1867; F.R.S. 10 Jany. 1839; author of *On rest and pain, a course of lectures* 1863, 3 *ed.* 1880; *Notes on the functional relations of portions of the cranium* 1855; *The Hunterian Oration* 1867. *d.* Hedingham house, Clapham common 14 Sep. 1878. *Proc. of Med. Chir. Soc. viii,* 388–90 (1875); *Medical Times, ii,* 422 (1878); *The Medical profession in all countries, i, No.* 17 (1873).

HIME, BENJAMIN. Musical publisher; vocal composer; wrote *I see them on their winding ways,* song 1830; *Let us hope for the best,* song 1835; *O the Forester's life is the life for me* 1855 and 20 other pieces. *d.* 30 Victoria st. Manchester 1871.

HINCHLIFF, JOHN ELY. *b.* 1777; chief assistant in studio of John Flaxman 1806–26; completed some of Flaxman's unfinished works 1826; exhibited 36 works at R.A. and 9 at B.I. 1814–49; among his sculptures were Christian and Apollyon 1815, Leonidas, Menelaus and Paris, and Theseus and Hippodamia; made many mural tablets and sepulchral monuments. *d.* Mornington place, 185 Hampstead road, London 23 Nov. 1867.

HINCHLIFF, JOHN JAMES *(son of the preceding).* *b.* 1805; in hydrographic department of admiralty; executed engravings for *Beattie's Castles and abbeys of England* 1842, and *Gastineau's Picturesque scenery of Wales* 1860. *d.* Walton-by-Clevedon, Somerset 16 Dec. 1875.

HINCHLIFF, THOMAS WOODBINE *(eld. son of Chamberlain Hinchliff).* *b.* 1826; president of Alpine club; F.R.G.S.; author of *Summer months among the Alps* 1857; *South American sketches* 1863; *Over the sea and far away, wanderings round the world* 1876. *d.* Aix les Bains, Savoy 8 May 1882. *Proc. of R. Geog. Soc. iv,* 424 (1882).

HINCKS, REV. EDWARD *(eld. son of Rev. Thomas Dix Hincks* 1767–1857). *b.* Cork 19 Aug. 1792; ed. at Trin. coll. Dublin, scholar 1810, B.A. 1812, M.A. 1817, B.D. 1823, D.D. 1829, fellow 1813–9; R. of Ardtrea 1819–26; R. of Killeleagh, co. Down 1826 to death; a pioneer in deciphering cuneiform inscriptions; studied Assyrian monuments 1846 and discovered the names of Sennacherib and Nebuchadnezzar; discovered conjointly with Sir H. C. Rawlinson the Persian cuneiform vowel system; the results of his investigations were printed in Trans. Royal Irish Acad. 1833–65; author of *Report to Trustees of British museum on cylinders and terra cotta tablets* 1854; *Letter on the Polyphony of Assyrio-Babylonian writings* 1863 and 25 other works; granted civil list pension of £100, 20 April 1854. *d.* Killeleagh 3 Dec. 1866. *Webb's Irish Biography* (1878) 251; *G.M. iii,* 122 (1867).

HINCKS, SIR FRANCIS *(brother of the preceding).* *b.* Cork 9 May 1807; ed. at Royal Belfast Institution; clerk to a shipowner, Belfast; went to Canada 1830, opened a warehouse in Toronto; founded and edited the *Toronto Examiner* 1838; member for county of Oxford in Canadian legislature, March 1841 to Nov. 1855; inspector general of public accounts 1842–3 and 1848–54; started the *Montreal Pilot* 1844; prime minister of Canada 1851–5; governor of Windward Islands 1855–62; governor of British Guiana 1862–9; C.B. 23 July 1862; K.C.M.G. 23 June 1869; finance minister for Dominion of Canada 1869–73; president of City Bank of Montreal 1874 which failed; editor of *Journal of Commerce,* Montreal; author of 5 pamphlets and of *Reminiscenses of my public life* 1884. *d.* Montreal 18 Aug. 1885. *Dublin Univ. Mag. vol.* 88, *p.* 534, *portrait; I.L.N. xxvii,* 413–14 (1855), *portrait; Morgan's Bibliotheca Canadensis* (1867) *p.* 186.

HINCKS, VEN. THOMAS *(son of the succeding).* *b.* 1796; R. of Finvoy, Connor to 1865; R. of Billy, Connor 1865 to death; archdeacon of Connor 1865 to death. *d.* the archdeaconry, Bushmills, co. Antrim 28 March 1882.

HINCKS, REV. THOMAS DIX *(son of Edward Hincks, d.* 1772). *b.* Bachelor's quay, Dublin 24 June 1767; ed. at Trin. coll. Dublin 1784–8 and at Hackney New coll. 1788–90; presbyterian minister Cork 1790; kept a school at Cork 1791–1803; lecturer on chemistry and natural philosophy, Royal Cork institution 1810–13; tutor Fermoy academy 1815–21; classical head master Belfast Academical Instit. 1821–36 and professor of Hebrew there 1822–49; LL.D. of Glasgow

HINCKS, REV. T. D. (Con.)

univ. 1834; author of *Letters occasioned by the circulation of Paine's Age of Reason* 1795, 2 ed. 1796; *An introduction to ancient geography* 1825, 7 ed. 1855; *Rudiments of Greek grammar* 1825 and other books. *d.* Murray's ter. Belfast 24 Feb. 1857. *bur.* Killeleagh.

HINCKS, REV. WILLIAM (*son of the preceding*). *b.* Cork, May 1794; presbyterian minister Cork 1815, at Exeter 1816–22 and at Renshaw st. Liverpool 1822–7; professor of natural philosophy at Manchester coll. York 1827–39; editor of *The Enquirer* 1842–9; professor of natural history, Queen's coll. Cork 1849–53 and at University coll. Toronto 1853–71; contributed to *Canadian Journal* 1854–65. *d.* Toronto 10 Sep. 1871. *Morgan's Bibl. Canad.* (1867) 186–7.

HIND, REV. JOHN. *b.* Cumberland 1796; sizar St. John's coll. Cam. 1813, scholar 1815, B.A. 1818, M.A. 1821; fellow of Sid. Suss. coll.; moderator 1822, 1823, 1826, examiner 1824, 1827; granted civil list pension of £100, 4 Oct. 1858; author of *The principles of the differential and integral calculus* 1827; *The elements of plane and spherical trigonometry* 5 ed. 1855; *The principles and practice of arithmetic* 1832, 8 ed. 1856. *d.* 22 Trumpington st. Cambridge 17 Dec. 1866. *Light Blue,* ii, 120 (1867).

HINDLEY, CHARLES. *b.* Fairfield 1800; classical and mathematical tutor Moravian establishment, Gracehill, Ireland to 1819; a cotton spinner 1819; a founder of the Aston and Dukinfield mechanics' instit. 1825; president of Peace soc.; contested Ashton-under-Lyne 14 Dec. 1832; contested Warrington 7 Jany. 1835; M.P. Ashton 9 Jany. 1835 to death. *d.* Dartmouth house, Queen st. Westminster 1 Dec. 1857. *Dr. Todd and the late member for Ashton. Fatal effects of the stimulating treatment of disease. By A. B. Granville* 1860.

HINDLIP, HENRY ALLSOPP, 1 Baron (3 *son of Samuel Allsopp of Burton on Trent, brewer* 1780–1838). *b.* 19 Feb. 1811; head of firm of Allsopp and Sons, brewers, Burton; M.P. for East Worcestershire 1874–80, contested it 1880; cr. a baronet 7 May 1880; cr. baron Hindlip of Hindlip in the co. of Worcester and of Alsop-en-le-Dale in the co. of Derby 15 Feb. 1886. *d.* Hindlip hall near Worcester 3 April 1887. *London Figaro* 9 *April* 1887 *p.* 4, *portrait.*

HINDMARCH, WILLIAM MATHEWSON (*son of Wm. Hindmarch of Sunderland, brewer*). *b.*

HINDMARCH, W. M. (*Con.*)

Fan quay near Sunderland 10 June 1803; articled to Thomas Collin of Sunderland, attorney; barrister G.I. 30 Jany. 1832, bencher 12 April 1862; Q.C. 5 Feb. 1862; attorney general of county palatine of Durham 7 Dec. 1861; recorder of York, Oct. 1865 to death; author of *A treatise on the law relating to patent privileges for the sole use of inventions* 1846; *Observations on the defects of the patent laws, with suggestions for reform* 1851. *d.* Aix la Chapelle 27 Aug. 1866. *Journal of B. A. Assoc. xxiii,* 307 (1867).

HINDMARSH, SIR JOHN. *b.* 1786; entered navy May 1793; served in Lord Howe's action and in battle of the Nile when though but a Midshipman he was in temporary command of the Bellerophon; captain 3 Sep. 1831; K.H. 4 May 1836; founded the colony of South Australia 28 Dec. 1836 and was governor to 16 July 1838; lieut. governor of Heligoland 28 Sep. 1840 to 7 March 1857; knighted at Buckingham palace 7 Aug. 1851; R.A. on half pay 31 Jany. 1856. *d.* Denbigh place, Belgravia, London 29 July 1860. *Heaton's Australian Dict. of Dates* (1879) 91.

HINDS, RIGHT REV. SAMUEL (*son of Abel Hinds of Barbadoes*). *b.* Barbadoes 1795; ed. at Charterhouse and Queen's coll. Ox.; B.A. 1815, M.A. 1818, B.D. and D.D. 1831; missionary to the Negroes of Barbadoes; principal of Codrington college Barbadoes; vice-principal of St. Alban hall Ox. 1827–31; domestic chaplain to archbishop Whately in Dublin 1831–3 and 1843; V. of Ardeley, Herts. 5 Feb. 1835 to March 1843; prebendary of St. Patrick's cathedral Dublin 1843; V. of united parishes of Castlenock, Clonsilla and Mullahidart 1843–8; dean of Carlisle 27 Sep. 1848; bishop of Norwich 26 Sep. 1849, consecrated at Lambeth 2 Dec. 1849, resigned 1857; author of *The history of the rise and progress of Christianity* 2 vols. 1828, 2 ed. 1846; *Sonnets and other poems* 1834; *The three temples of the one true God contrasted* 1830, 3 ed. 1857 and 25 other books. *d.* 40 Clarendon road, Notting hill, London 7 Feb. 1872. *I.L.N. xv,* 376 (1849), *portrait, lx,* 163, (1872).

HINGSTON, EDWARD PERON. *b.* about 1823; attended lectures at King's coll. Lond.; contributed to periodicals 1841–42; manager for professor Anderson the wizard of the north, acting manager for him at Covent Garden, Dec. 1855 to 5 March 1856 when house burnt; went with Anderson to America and Australia 1856–64; manager for Artemus Ward, American humorist in America and England 1864

HINGSTON, E. P. *(Con.)*

to Jany. 1867; managed "the Hall by the sea," Margate; stage manager at St. James's theatre 1870; lessee and manager of Opera Comique theatre, Oct. 1872 to Dec. 1873; manager at Criterion theatre 21 March 1874; edited many works by R. H. Newell, Mark Twain and Artemus Ward 1865–76; author of *The Siddons of Modern Italy, Adelaide Ristori* 1856; *The Genial Showman, Being reminiscences of Artemus Ward* 1870. *d.* Crowndale road, Camden town, London 9 June 1876. *Era* 18 *June* 1876 *p.* 10; *Illust. Sporting news, vi,* 473 (1867), *portrait.*

HINTON, JAMES (3 *child of Rev. John Howard Hinton* 1791–1873). *b.* Reading 1822; ed. at Harpenden; cashier at a woollen draper's shop in Whitechapel 1838–9; clerk in an insurance office in the city; M.R.C.S. 1848; assist. surgeon at Newport, Essex 1847; in the West Indies 1848–50; partner with Mr. Fisher in Bartholomew Close, London 1850–3; in practice at 18 Savile row, London 1853 to 1874; aural surgeon to Guy's hospital 1863; the chief aurist in London from date of Toynbee's death to March 1874 when he retired; author of *Man and his dwelling place* 1859, 3 *ed.* 1872; *Life in nature* 1862; *The mystery of pain* 1866, 3 *ed.* 1879; *Thoughts on health* 1871; *The question of aural surgery* 1874. *d.* St. Michael's, Madeira 16 Dec. 1875. *bur.* at Ponta Delgada in the island of Sao Miguel. *Life and letters of James Hinton, edited by Ellice Hopkins* (1878), *portrait; Graphic, xiii,* 99, 101 (1876), *portrait; Good Words* (1878) 784–90, *portrait.*

HINTON, REV. JOHN HOWARD *(son of Rev. James Hinton, congregational minister* 1761– 1823). *b.* Oxford 24 March 1791; ed. at Bristol coll. 1811–13 and at Edin. univ., M.A. 1816; baptist minister at Haverfordwest 1816–20, at Hosier st. chapel, Reading 1820– 37, at Devonshire sq. chapel, London 1837– 63, at Reading 1863–8; resided at Bristol 1868 to death; sec. of the Baptist Union many years; author of *The work of the Holy Spirit in conversion considered* 1830, 3 *ed.* 1841; *The epistle to the Hebrews freely rendered* 1843; *Athanasius, or Four books on immortality* 1849; *An exposition of the epistle to the Romans* 1863; author with his brother Rev. Isaac Taylor Hinton *d.* 1847 of *The history and topography of the United States* 2 vols. Boston 1834, 2 *ed.* New York 1853. *d.* 1 Redland terrace, Clifton, Bristol 17 Dec. 1873. *Baptist Handbook* (1875) 277–80; *I.L.N.* 10 *Jany.* 1874 *pp.* 35–6, *portrait; S. A. Swaine's Faithful Baptist men of Bristol coll.* (1884) 238.

HIRST, WILLIAM. *b.* near Huddersfield 1777; a cloth dresser and manufacturer at Leeds 1810; commenced finishing his goods by machinery 1813; introduced spinning mules, Lewis' machine and hydraulic presses into his works 1813–25; made a large fortune which he lost in 1825; freely communicated his improved process to the public and was called the father of the Yorkshire woollen trade; *d.* in poverty at Leeds 29 Aug. 1858. *Taylor's Biographia Leodiensis* (1865) 472–4.

HISLOP, REV. STEPHEN *(son of Stephen Hislop, mason).* *b.* Duns, Berwickshire 8 Sep. 1817; ed. at Edinburgh and Glasgow universities 1834–9; a tutor; sec. to Ladies' soc. for female education in India 1843; Free church of Scotland minister 1844; missionary to Nagpoor, Central India 1844–58 and 1861 to death; opened a school at Nagpoor 1846 which grew into Hislop coll.; studied the languages of the aboriginal tribes; made discoveries in geology and natural history; contributed papers to Royal Asiatic Soc. Journal 1835 etc. and to Quart. Journ. Geol. Soc. 1854–61; author of *Papers relating to the Aboriginal tribes of the central provinces* 1866; drowned in attempting to cross a stream 20 miles south of Nagpoor 4 Sep. 1863. *R. Hunter's Hist of Mission of Free Ch. to India* (1873) *pp.* 24, 384; *Quart. Journ. Geol. Soc.* 1864 *pp. xxxix-xl; G. Smith's Life of S. Hislop* (1889), *portrait.*

HITCHCOCK, RICHARD *(son of Rodney Hitchcock of Springvale, co. Cork, farmer, d. Aug.* 1853). *b.* Blennerville near Tralee, March 1825; devoted himself to the study of archæology of his native country, using his pen and pencil in their description; assistant librarian Trinity coll. Dublin; assistant to geological society of Ireland; contributed papers to proc. of Kilkenny Archæol. Soc.; *d.* Roundtown near Dublin 3 Dec. 1856.

HITCHIN, GEORGE. *b.* 1785; editor of the *Hampshire Chronicle* 1814 to death. *d.* High st. Winchester 2 May 1858. *Hampshire Chronicle* 8 *May* 1858 *pp.* 4, 5.

HITCHINS, BENJAMIN ROBERTSON. *b.* 1792; entered Madras army 1806; lieut. colonel 47 N.I. 12 May 1842 to 2 Jany. 1854; colonel 1 European regiment 2 Jany. 1854 to death; L.G. 26 Aug. 1866. *d.* Upper Norwood, Surrey 13 July 1867 aged 75.

HITCHMAN, FRANCIS. *b.* 1839; connected with *Western Morning News,* Plymouth; editor of *Manchester Courier;* assist. editor *Standard,* London; wrote for the reviews and magazines,

HITCHMAN, F. (Con.)

London; an active member of the Primrose League; author of *Pius the ninth. A biography* 1878; *The public life of the earl of Beaconsfield* 2 vols. 1879, 2 ed. 1881; *Eighteenth century studies. Essays* 1881; *Richard F. Burton, his life, travels and explorations* 2 vols. 1888. *d.* London, Dec. 1890.

HOARE, CHARLES (2 *son of Sir Richard Hoare of Barn Elms, Surrey, 1 bart. 1735–87*). *b.* 25 Aug. 1767; partner in banking house of Hoare & Co. 37 Fleet st. London, afterwards senior partner to death; F.S.A. Jany. 1792; built Luscombe house near Dawlish, Devon 179–; F.R.S. 1809. *d.* Luscombe house 16 Nov. 1851.

HOARE, CHARLES HUGH (3 *son of George Matthew Hoare, brewer, London*). *b.* 24 Oct. 1819; ed. at Rugby and Ex. coll. Ox., B.A. 1841; manager of his father's brewery and ultimately sole acting partner; member of All England Eleven; president and treasurer of Surrey cricket club; member of committee of Lord's. *d.* Romsey, Hants. 4 April 1869.

HOARE, VEN. CHARLES JAMES (3 *son of Henry Hoare, banker 1750–1828*). *b.* London 14 July 1781; admitted a pensioner at St. John's coll. Cam. 7 May 1799, 2 wr. and 2 Smith's pr. 1803, B.A. 1803, M.A. 1806; Lady Margaret fellow of his coll. 24 March 1806 to 4 July 1811; V. of Blandford Forum, Dorset 1807 to March 1821; V. of Godstone, Surrey, March 1821 to death; archdeacon of Winchester 10 Nov. 1829; canon residentiary of Winchester cath. 2 Dec. 1831; archdeacon of Surrey 14 Nov. 1847, resigned 1860; author of *The shipwreck of St. Paul. A Seatonian prize poem* 1808, 2 ed. 1860; *Sermons on the Christian character* 1821; *The holy scriptures, their nature, authority and use* 1845, 2 ed. 1857 and other books. *d.* Godstone 18 Jany. 1865.

HOARE, VERY REV. EDWARD NEWENHAM (4 *son of Rev. John Hoare, chancellor of St. Mary's and Vicar general of diocese of Limerick, d. 9 March 1813 aged 47*). *b.* 11 April 1802; archdeacon of Ardfert 23 Dec. 1836 to 1839; dean of Achonry 14 June 1839 to 1850; dean of Waterford 26 Nov. 1850 to death; edited *The Christian Herald, Dublin* 5 vols. 1830–5; author of *The tendency of the principles advocated in the Tracts for the Times considered* 1841; *Remarks on mis-statements as to scriptural education in Ireland* 1850; *Practical suggestions with view to removal of objections to the working of the national education system of education in Ireland* 1854. *d.* Lauranah villa, Hamlet road, Upper Norwood 1 Feb. 1877.

HOARE, EDWARD WALLIS (2 *son of Sir Edward Hoare, bart. 1745–1814*). *b.* Cork 4 May 1779; entered navy May 1790; when signal lieut. of the London condemned to death by the delegates of the mutineers at Spithead 1797; served in Egypt 1801, at Isle of France 1811; landed on island of Java and routed the enemy 5 June 1811; on half pay 13 Aug. 1812; captain 13 May 1847; admiral on half pay 9 June 1860. *d.* Upton near Ryde, Isle of Wight 6 Jany. 1870.

HOARE, REV. GEORGE TOOKER (2 *son of Ven. Charles James Hoare 1781–1865*). *b.* 27 July 1820; ed. at St. John's coll. Cam., B.A. 1843, M.A. 1847; P.C. of Tandridge, Surrey 1853–65; V. of Godstone, Surrey 1865 to death; edited *Dare and endure* 1868; author of *The village museum, or how we gather profit with pleasure* 1858; *A letter written for the people, hints on letter writing* 1860; *True stories of brave deeds* 1870. *d.* Aix la Chapelle 9 Aug. 1881.

HOARE, JOHN GURNEY (2 *son of Samuel Hoare, banker 1783–1847*). *b.* 7 May 1810; ed. at Trin. coll. Cam., B.A. 1832, M.A. 1835; banker Fleet st. London; president of Guy's hospital, Dec. 1867 to death. *d.* Biarritz, France 17 Feb. 1875. *I.L.N. lxvi,* 211, 259 (1875).

HOARE, JOSEPH (*brother of the preceding*). *b.* 21 March 1814; ed. at Trin. coll. Cam.; banker of firm of Hoare & Co. Fleet st.; M.P. Hull 30 April 1859 but unseated on petition Aug. 1859; contested Manchester 18 Nov. 1868; president Hampstead conservative assoc. *d.* Child's Hill house, Hampstead 21 Jany. 1886. *Times 25 Jany.* 1886 p. 7.

HOARE, REV. WILLIAM HENRY (2 *son of William Henry Hoare 1776–1819*). *b.* Penzance 31 Oct. 1809; ed. at St. John's coll. Cam.; 31 wr. 1831, B.A. 1831, M.A. 1834, fellow of his coll. 25 March 1833 to 1835; C. of All Saints, Southampton 1841; commissary to bishop of Newcastle, N.S.W. Australia; diocesan inspector of diocese of Chichester; founder and sec. of Worth clerical association; author of *Harmony of the Apocalypse with the prophecies of holy scriptures* 1848; *Outlines of ecclesiastical history before the Reformation* 1852, 2 ed. 1857; *The veracity of the book of Genesis, with the life of the inspired historian* 1860 and other books. *d.* Oakfield, Crawley, Sussex 22 Feb. 1888. *Boase and Courtney's Bibl. Cornub.* i, 244.

HOBART, AUGUSTUS CHARLES (3 *son of 6 earl of Buckinghamshire 1793–1885*). *b.* Walton-on-the-Wolds, Leics. 1 April 1822; ed. at

HOBART, A. C. *(Con.)*

Cheam; entered navy March 1835; employed in suppressing slave trade 1835–43; present during Russian war 1854–5; commanded mortar boats at attack on Sveaborg; attached to coast guard at Dingle, co. Kerry 1855–61; captain 23 May 1863 when he retired on h.p.; ran the blockade and carried cargoes into Wilmington and Charleston, U.S. America 1863–5; naval adviser to Sultan of Turkey 1867; suppressed the Cretan rebellion 1867; full admiral with title of Pasha 1869; reorganised Turkish fleet and manœuvred against the Russian ships in Black sea 1877; mushir or marshal of Turkish empire 8 Jany. 1881, first christian who ever held that dignity; name struck off British navy list 1867, 1877, restored 1874 and 1884 when he became retired V.A. 30 Oct. 1884; president of Turkish admiralty board; author of *Never caught, By Captain Roberts* 1867; *The torpedo scare* 1885. *d.* Milan, Italy 19 June 1886. *Sketches of my life, By Hobart Pasha* 1887, *portrait; Biographical Mag., No. 1, June 1877 pp. 35–45; I.L.N. lxx, 433, 435 (1877), portrait.*

HOBART, VERE HENRY *(brother of the preceding).* *b.* Welbourn, Lincs. 8 Dec. 1818; ed. at Cheam and Trin. coll. Ox., scholar 1836–42, B.A. 1840; clerk in board of trade 1842 to 1 Oct. 1863; known as lord Hobart from 1849; private sec. to Sir George Grey; sec. of states for colonies 1854–55; a writer in the press on Irish questions from 1850; with Mr. Foster, paymaster general, investigated and advised on Turkish finance 1861; director general of Ottoman bank to 1871; governor of presidency of Madras 14 March 1872 to death; author of *Essay on the Alabama claims* 1870; *Political essays* 1866, *Reprinted* 1877. *d.* of typhoid fever at Madras 27 April 1875. *Essays. With Biographical sketch by his widow* 2 vols. 1885, 2 *portraits.*

HOBBS, JOHN WILLIAM. *b.* Henley on Thames 1 Aug. 1799; chorister Canterbury cath.; tenor singer; sang at Norwich musical festival 1813; singer at King's and St. John's coll. Cam. and St. George's chapel Windsor; gentleman of the chapel royal, London 1827; lay vicar Westminster abbey 1836; well known glee singer; composer of Wake, Lady, Wake 1845; Phillis is my only joy 1848; For these and all Thy mercies, A grace 1851; When Delia sings 1862; The captive Greek girl and 70 other pieces. *d.* 20 Duppas Hill ter. Croydon 12 Jany. 1877.

HOBBS, THOMAS FRANCIS (1 son of Capt. Hobbs of Barnaby house, King's county). Second lieut. 21 foot 15 Jany. 1847, which regiment he

HOBBS, T. F. *(Con.)*

commanded at the attack on the Redan 18 June 1855; lieut. colonel 14 depot battalion 8 March 1859; lieut. col. 6 foot 6 Feb. 1863 to death; connected with the suppression of the outbreak in Jamaica, became of unsound mind 1866; author of *The subaltern's hand-book and guide to the military examination.* Belfast 1859; *threw himself overboard* from the 'Tyne' off the coast of Hayti 25 April 1866.

HOBBS, WILLIAM FISHER *(son of a yeoman).* *b.* White Colne, Essex 1809; farmer at Marks hall, Coggeshall 1831; grew improved and more productive wheat; famous for his pigs known as the Fisher Hobbs pigs; V.P. of Royal agricultural society to death; member of council of Smithfield club to death; a scientific farmer, using the best machinery. *d.* Boxted lodge near Colchester 11 Oct. 1866. *Min. of proc. of Instit. of C.E. xxvi,* 577–79 (1867).

HOBHOUSE, HENRY *(only son of Henry Hobhouse of Hadspen house, Somerset 1742–92).* *b.* Clifton 12 April 1776; ed. at Eton and Brasenose coll. Ox., B.A. 1797, M.A. 1799, D.C.L. 1827; barrister M.T. 23 Jany. 1801; solicitor to H.M. customs 1806–12; solicitor to the Treasury 1812–17; under sec. of state for home department 28 June 1817 to July 1827 when he resigned on a pension of £1000; keeper of the state papers 23 May 1826 to death; P.C. 28 June 1828; chairman of Somerset quarter sessions, resigned 1845; one of Ecclesiastical comrs. for England 1838 to death; commissioner of the records 10 June 1852 when he commenced a new system for their arrangement. *d.* Hadspen house, Somerset 13 April 1854. *G.M. xlii,* 79–80 (1854); *Times* 18 *April* 1854 *p.* 9.

HOBHOUSE, THOMAS BENJAMIN (5 son of Sir Benjamin Hobhouse, bart. 1757–1831). *b.* 19 June 1807; ed. at Ball. coll. Ox., B.A. 1828; contested Aylesbury 1835; M.P. Rochester 1837–41; contested Newark 1841; M.P. Lincoln 1848–52; contested Ipswich 1852. *d.* 31 Dec. 1876.

HOBLER, FRANCIS *(son of Francis Hobler, clerk to the lord mayor 1803–43 who d. 21 Jany. 1844 aged 78).* Solicitor in City of London 1817–60; solicitor to Licensed Victuallers Soc. 1837–60; solicitor for the Crown in trial of F. B. Courvoisier 18–20 June 1840; sec. of Numismatic Soc. of London; author of *Familiar exercises between an attorney and his articled clerk on the principles of the laws of real property* 1831, 2 ed. 1838; *Liber mercatoris or the merchant's manual, being a concise treatise on bills of exchange* 1838; *Records of Roman history as exhibited on the Roman coins* 2 vols. 1860.

HOBLYN, RICHARD DENNIS (1 *son of Rev. Richard Hoblyn 1771–1827, R. of All Saints, Colchester*). *b.* Colchester 9 April 1803; ed. at Tiverton gram. sch. and Ball. coll. Ox., B.A. 1824, M.A. 1828; ordained 1832, resigned clerical life; devoted himself to teaching and writing on education; author of *A dictionary of terms used in medicine and the collateral sciences* 1835, 11 ed. 1887; *A manual of the steam engine* 1842; *A dictionary of scientific terms* 1849. *d.* 22 Aug. 1886.

HOBLYN, THOMAS (*eld. son of Edward Hoblyn*). *b.* Liskeard 1778; chief clerk in H.M. treasury 1820–34; F.R.S. 27 June 1811; F.L.S. 4 March 1823; author of *Precepts for the use of Hoblyn's equalizer, the value in imperial measure equivalent to any value in wine measure* 1826; *Description of a method of founding a light-house on the Goodwin sands* 1851. *d.* White Barns, Herts. 6 Aug. 1860. *Boase and Courtney's Bibl. Cornub. i, 246, iii, 1232; Boase's Collect. Cornub. 370.*

HOBSON, FREDERICK. *b.* 1800; proprietor of *The Leeds Times* 1833 to death, and manager of the commercial department; joined by his son William Hobson. *d.* Woodhouse, Leeds 18 Feb. 1863. *Leeds Times 21 Feb. 1863 p. 4.*

HOBSON, JOHN. *b.* Leeds; musical director of the Christy (afterwards the Moore and Burgess) minstrels London for 12 years before his death; composer of The flight of the birds 1870; The man with the appetite 1880. *d.* 8 Appach road, Brixton 31 Jany. 1887.

HOBSON, MARTIN. *b.* 1833; chorus master at Alhambra palace, London; musical conductor to Bernard's opera company; composed many popular songs, among others The boys of merry England 1865; A norrible tale of the suicidal family 1865; Give me the man of honest heart 1867; O sing the song you used to sing 1872; I likes a drop of good beer 1875; Popular hymns, carols and sacred songs, arranged for pianoforte, 40 numbers 1875; Popular favourites arranged for the pianoforte, 153 numbers 1876–9, and 30 other pieces besides arranging many songs, etc. *d.* 3 Dec. 1880.

HOBSON, RICHARD. *b.* Whitehaven, Cumberland 1795; studied at St. George's hospital, London; at Queen's coll. Cam., M.B. 1825, M.D. 1830; settled in Leeds 1831; physician Leeds infirmary 1833–43; kept a pack of harriers; was intimate with C. Waterton from 1836; published *Charles Waterton, his home, habits and handiwork* 1866. *d.* 10 Park place, Leeds 29 Nov. 1868.

HOBSON, WILLIAM ROBERT (*only son of Capt. William Hobson, governor of New Zealand, d. 1842*). *b.* 1831; entered R.N. 1845; mate of the Rattlesnake in her expedition to Behring Straits as relieving ship to the Enterprise and Investigator 1853; lieut. 20 April 1855, served in Baltic campaign 1854–5; accompanied Capt. Francis L. M'Clintock in the Fox in search of Sir John Franklin 1857–9, in the sledge party April to June 1859, discovered 6 May 1859 in the cairn built by the crews of the Erebus and Terror the tin case containing the record that Sir John Franklin died 11 June 1847; captain 11 April 1866, retired 12 Aug. 1872. *d.* Pitminster near Taunton 11 Oct. 1880. *I.L.N. 15 Oct. 1859 p. 362–3, portrait.*

HOBY, REV. JAMES (*son of George Hoby, boot maker to George III., St. James' st. Piccadilly*). *b.* London 1788; ed. at Bristol Baptist coll. 1812; assist. minister at Maze Pond chapel to 1823; minister at Birmingham, Weymouth and Twickenham; visited United States as one of a deputation from the Baptist Union 1836; author of *Narrative of a visit to christian brethren in Hamburg, Copenhagen, etc.* 1844; *Memoir of William Yates, D.D. of Calcutta* 1847; *Anti-popery. A lecture* 1851. *d.* Caterham 20 Nov. 1871. *S. A. Swaine's Faithful Baptist men (1884) 242–3; Baptist Handbook 1872 p. 226.*

HOCHSCHILD, BARON CHARLES. Ambassador and minister plenipotentiary from Sweden in London 6 Nov. 1854 to death. *d.* 8 Sep. 1857.

HODDER, GEORGE. *b.* 1819; ed. at Christ's hospital; connected with Henry Mayhew in the initiation of *Punch* or the *London Charivari* 17 July 1841; connected with *Morning Post*; author of *Memories of my time, including personal reminiscences of eminent men* 1870; upset in a four-horse drag in Richmond park on 28 May 1870 when his skull was fractured, *d.* Richmond infirmary 31 July 1870. *Newspaper Press, iv, 175, 215 (1870); Times 4 Aug. 1870 p. 9.*

HODGE, JOHN. *b.* Scotland 10 April 1787; wholesale stationer and paper maker, firm being Spalding and Hodge, 145–7 Drury lane, London from 1810; largest house in England, probably in the world. *d.* 18 Gilston road, West Brompton, 15 Dec. 1865.

HODGES, EDWARD. *b.* Bristol 20 July 1796; organist of Clifton church, of St. James's ch. Bristol 1819, of St. Nicholas's ch. Bristol 1821–35; Mus. Bac. and Mus. Doc. Cam. 1825; went to Toronto, Canada 1835; went to U.S. of A. 1838; organist of Trinity ch. New York 1846–63; composed a morning

HODGES, E. (Con.)

and evening service and two anthems for re-opening of St. James's organ Bristol 2 May 1824, published 1825; published *An apology for church music and musical festivals, Bristol* 1834; *Canticles of the Church, New York* 1864. *d.* Clifton 1 Sep. 1876.

HODGES, REV. EDWARD RICHMOND. *b.* 1826; scripture reader in London; sent by Soc. for promoting Christianity among the Jews, as a missionary to Palestine; missionary in Algeria to 1856; minister of reformed episcopal church; author of *Ancient Egypt* 1851; edited Craik's *Principia Hebraica* 1863; Cory's *Ancient fragments of the Phœnician and other authors* 1876 and other books. *d.* Tollington park, Holloway, London 9 May 1881. *Academy* 18 *June* 1881 *p.* 454.

HODGES, SIR GEORGE FLOYD (*son of George Thomas Hodges of Limerick*). *b.* Old Abbey, Limerick 1792; ensign 61 foot 28 Aug. 1806; served in the Peninsula and at Waterloo 1810–15; adjutant recruiting district 5 May 1825 to 31 Dec. 1830 when placed on h.p.; commanded British and foreign legion in Portugal under Dom Pedro 1832; chargè d'affaires and consul general to Hanse Towns 31 July 1841 to 1860 when he retired on a pension; C.B. 1 March 1851, K.C.B. 6 Aug. 1860; author of *Narrative of the expedition to Portugal in 1832 under the orders of Dom Pedro* 2 *vols.* 1833; contributed many articles to periodicals. *d.* 60 Lansdowne place, Brighton 14 Dec. 1862.

HODGES, JAMES. *b.* Queenborough, Kent 6 April 1814; engineer, worked under contractor for Greenwich railway 1834; superintended construction of Shakespeare tunnel, Dover and blasting of Round cliff, Down 1842–3; resident engineer on Norfolk railway; contracted for 50 miles of Great Northern railway; superintended construction of Victoria bridge over the St. Lawrence 1853–60; engaged in manufacturing peat fuel in Canada 1862; constructed the Callao docks 1870–5; a great benefactor to Bagshot; author of *Construction of the great Victoria bridge in Canada* 1860. *d.* Perry hill, Bagshot, June 1879. *I.L.N.* 22 *Sep.* 1860 *p.* 266, *portrait; Engineering* 25 *June* 1879 *p.* 78.

HODGES, THOMAS LAW (*son of Thomas Hallett Hodges, d. 1801*). *b.* 3 June 1776; major West Kent regiment of militia; M.P. for Kent 1830–32; for West Kent 1832–41 and 1847–52; author of *Minutes of evidence before house of commons on emigration, and on state of the poor laws* 1833; *The use of Pearson's drain plough* 1833. *d.* Hemsted, Kent 14 May 1857.

HODGES, SIR WILLIAM (*eld. son of Wm. Hodges of Weymouth*). *b.* Melcombe Regis, Dorset 29 Sep. 1808; ed. at Salisbury and London Univ.; barrister I.T. 3 May 1833; a revising barrister for Devon and Cornwall 1837–57; recorder of Poole, Dorset Nov. 1846 to Nov. 1857; drafted the Public health act 1848; chief justice of the Cape colony, judge of vice admiralty court, and president of legislative council 9 Feb. 1858 to death; knighted at Buckingham palace 3 Feb. 1858; author of *Report of the case of the Queen v. Lumsdaine* 1839; *The law relating to the assessment of railways* 1842; *The statute law relating to railways* 1845; *A treatise on the law of railways* 1855, 7 *ed.* 2 *vols.* 1888; with G. Williams and F. L. Wollaston *Reports of cases in court of queen's bench* 1840 continued as *Term Reports* to 1841. *d.* Sea point house, Cape town 17 Aug. 1868.

HODGETTS, FOLEY JOHN HODGETTS. *b.* Prestwood near Stourbridge 17 July 1797; took name of Hodgetts before that of Foley by r.l. 4 April 1821; M.P. for Droitwich 1822–34; contested Droitwich 1835; M.P. for East Worcestershire 1847 to death. *d.* Prestwood house, Stafford 13 Nov. 1861.

HODGKIN, JOHN (2 *son of John Hodgkin of Tottenham, Middlesex, grammarian* 1766–1845). *b.* Pentonville, London 11 March 1800; barrister L.I. 22 Nov. 1825; practised as a conveyancer 1825–43; had numerous pupils; aimed at conciseness and brevity in documents; a preacher among the Friends, and a visitor to Ireland, France and America 1861; helped to prepare the Encumbered Estates act 1849; author of *Observations on the establishment of a General Register of titles* 1827. *d.* Bournemouth 3 July 1875. *bur.* Friends' ground, Winchmore hill, Middlesex.

HODGKIN, THOMAS (*brother of the preceding*). *b.* Tottenham, Middlesex 17 Aug. 1798; studied at Guy's hospital, in Paris and in Edin., M.D. Edin. 1823; settled in London; L.R.C.P.; curator of museum and professor of morbid anatomy, Guy's hospital; on senate of Univ. of London 1837 to death; a founder of Aborigines protection soc. 1838; F.R.G.S.; Hodgkin's disease is the name given to an enlargement of the lymphatic glands; author of *An essay on medical education* 1828; *Hints relative to the cholera in London* 1832; *Lectures on the morbid anatomy of the serous and mucous membranes* 2 *vols.* 1836–40; *Lectures on the means of promoting and preserving health* 1835, 2 *ed.* 1841; *Narrative of a journey to Morocco in 1863, with portrait of author* 1866 and 14 other works. *d.* while on a visit to Jaffa,

HODGKIN, T. *(Con.)*

Palestine 4 April 1866, Sir M. Montefiore erected an obelisk to his memory there. *Medical Times, i,* 403 (1866); *Proc. of Med. and Chir. Soc. v,* 250 (1867); *Barker's Photographs of Medical Men, ii,* 73–6 (1868), *portrait.*

HODGKINSON, EATON *(son of Mr. Hodgkinson of Anderton, parish of Great Budworth, Cheshire, farmer, d. 1795).* b. Anderton 26 Feb. 1789; ed. at Northwich gram. sch.; pawn broker, Salford, Manchester 1811; pupil of Dr. John Dalton of Manchester 1811; member of Manchester Lit. and Philos. society 1826, president 1848–50; F.R.S. 1841; professor of mechanical principles of engineering in Univ. coll. London 1847; hon. M.I.C.E. 1851; F.G.S.; experimented on strength and forms of iron beams and invented Hodgkinson's beam; his paper on Strength of pillars of cast iron in Philos. Trans. obtained for him Royal soc. royal medal 1841; edited *Practical essay on strength of cast iron, By T. Tredgold* 5 ed. 1860. d. Eaglesfield house, Higher Broughton near Manchester 18 June 1861. *Life of E. Hodgkinson in Memoirs Manchester Lit. and Philos. Soc. ii,* 145 (1861); *Proceedings of royal society, xii,* 11–13 (1862); *Minutes of Proc. of Instit. of C.E. xxi,* 542–45 (1862).

HODGKINSON, REV. GEORGE CHRISTOPHER. b. 1816; ed. at Trin. coll. Cam., 14 wrangler and B.A. 1837, M.A. 1842; principal R. Agric. coll. Cirencester; principal of York and Ripon Diocesan training institution to 1854; head master Louth gram. sch. 1854–76; sec. of National soc.; R. of Screveton, Notts. 1876 to death; an alpine climber; recommended use of aneroids in mountain expeditions; made astronomical observations on the summit of Mont Blanc; experimented on registering amount and intensity of sunshine; author of *The doctrine of the church. And the statement of G. C. Hodgkinson of the Training school, York in his defence* 1854; *Drops for the cup of uniformity, unity and peace* 1845. d. Car Colston, Notts. 25 April 1880.

HODGKINSON, SIR GEORGE EDMUND *(only son of George Hodgkinson).* b. Southwell, Notts. 1817; ship owner, ship and insurance agent, 74 Cornhill, London; at one time in partnership with Sir John Pirie, bart.; sheriff of London 1850–51, after the Queen's visit to the city 9 July 1851 was knighted at Buckingham palace 17 July 1851. d. Bournemouth 26 March 1886.

HODGKINSON, GROSVENOR. b. Newark upon Trent 12 Feb. 1818; solicitor at Newark 1839–70; M.P. for Newark 1859–74. d. Newark 14 Feb. 1881.

HODGSON, ANTHONY. b. Newcastle-upon-Tyne 1780; ed. at Crook hall coll. and at Ushaw; hatter Newcastle, and bookseller dealing chiefly in R.C. books; a great student of English R.C. history; contributed many articles to *Catholic Miscellany, Catholic Mag., Weekly Orthodox journal,* and *London and Dublin orthodox journal.* d. Newcastle 10 Feb. 1869. *Gillow's English Catholics iii,* 315–18 (1887).

HODGSON, BRIAN *(son of Brian Hodgson, innkeeper, Buxton, d. 1827).* bapt. Buxton 15 March 1767; partner in banking house of Hawkins, Mills & Co., Macclesfield 1787, the bank failed but paid 20s. in the pound; superintendent of Martello towers on coast of Essex, office abolished 1820; barrack master of the troops at Canterbury 1820–50. d. in Holland 31 Jany. 1858.

HODGSON, CHRISTOPHER *(eld. son of John Hodgson of Bishop Auckland, Durham).* b. Bartlett's buildings Holborn, London 1784; attorney and notary in Westminster 1805–71'; chapter clerk to dean and chapter of St. Paul's 1806; sec. to Abp. of Canterbury 1809; sec. to Bp. of London 1813; M.A. by Abp. of Canterbury 22 July 1820; sec. to governors of queen Anne's bounty 15 Feb. 1822, resigned Jany. 1871; sec. to Abp. of York 1826; treasurer to queen Anne's bounty 1839 to Jany. 1871; author of *Instructions for the use of candidates for holy orders* 1817, 9 ed. 1870; *An account of the augmentation of small livings by the Governors of the Bounty of Queen Anne* 2 parts 1826–35, 2 ed. 1845–56. d. Spring grove, Isleworth, Middlesex 7 Aug. 1874. *bur.* Norwood cemetery.

HODGSON, CHRISTOPHER PEMBERTON. b. 1821; resided in New South Wales 1840–45 and accompanied several exploring expeditions; vice consul at Pau, France 1851–5; vice consul at Caen 1857–9; consul at Nagasaki, Japan 1859, and at Hakodadi 1859–61; author of *Reminiscences of Australia* 1846; *El Ydaivur* 1849; *Pyrenaica, a history of the viscounts of Bèarn* 1855; *The Wanderer and other poems* 1849; *A residence at Nagasaki and Hakodadi* 1861. d. Pau 11 Oct. 1865.

HODGSON, EDMUND *(son of a bookseller in Wimpole st. London).* b. 1794; publisher with Robert Saunders at 39 Fleet st. London 1825–8; publisher at 192 Fleet st. 1829–55, at 2 Chancery lane 1856 to about 1867; pres. of Booksellers' Provident Institution. d. 102 Lower Tulse hill, Brixton 3 May 1875. *Publisher's Circular* (1875) 383–4.

HODGSON, REV. FRANCIS (2 son of Rev. James Hodgson, R. of Humber, co. Hereford, d. Oct. 1810). b. Croydon 16 Nov. 1781; ed. at Eton 1794-99, scholar King's coll. Cam. 1799; B.A. 1804, M.A. 1807, B.D. 1840; fellow and tutor of his college 1808-14; friend of lord Byron whom he visited at Newstead 1808, corresponded with lady Byron about her separation; C. of Bradden, Northamptonshire 1815-16; V. of Bakewell, Derbyshire 1816-40; archdeacon of Derby 9 Sep. 1836 to 30 Dec. 1840; P.C. of Edensor in Chatsworth park 1838-40; provost of Eton college 5 May 1840 to death; R. of Cottesford, Oxon. 1842 to death; published *The satires of Juvenal, A translation* 1807; *The Friends, a poem* 1818; *Mythology for versification* 1831; *Select portions of sacred history conveyed in sense for Latin verses* 1828, 2 ed. 1833; *Sacred lyrics adapted to Latin versification in the principal metres of Horace* 1842; made considerable contributions in Latin to the *Arundines Cami.* d. The Lodge, Eton college 29 Dec. 1852. bur. in college chapel 4 Jany. 1853. *Memoir of Rev. F. Hodgson by his son* 2 vols. 1878, *portrait; H. C. M. Lyte's History of Eton college* (1875) 413-73.

HODGSON, REV. FRANCIS. b. Duffield 13 Feb. 1805; settled at West Chester, Pa., U.S. America; minister of Methodist Episcopal ch. at Dauphin, Pa. 1828, at Philadelphia, New York, Hartford and New Haven; author of *Examination into the new system of divinity* 1829; *The ecclesiastical polity of Methodism defended; The Calvinistic doctrine of predestination examined and refuted* 1855. d. 16 April 1877. *Appleton's American biography, iii,* 225 (1887).

HODGSON, FREDERICK. b. 1795; a brewer and merchant at Barnstaple; M.P. for Barnstaple 1824-30, 1831-2 and 1837-47. d. Paris 30 March 1854. *E. Yates's Recollections, i,* 12 (1884).

HODGSON, HENRY (son of Robert Hodgson). b. Congleton, Cheshire 24 Feb. 1781; entered Bengal army 1798; col. 51 Bengal N.I. 5 June 1829 to 1841; col. 12 Bengal N.I. 1841 to death; L.G. 11 Nov. 1851. d. Passy, Paris 8 March 1855.

HODGSON, ISAAC. b. Bradford 15 Nov. 1828; a cricketer 1847; first played at Lord's 16 July 1860; with C. Lawrence at Glasgow put the England Eleven out for 20 runs 20 Sep. 1860; bowler to Manchester Broughton club 1862; right hand batsman, but bowled left, round armed, slow with a twist; a good player at Knurr and Spell; had a benefit at

HODGSON, I. (Con.)

Bradford 29 Aug. 1867; landlord of West End tavern, Lister hills, Bradford. d. Bradford 24 Nov. 1867. *Lillywhite's Cricket Scores vi,* 437-8 (1876).

HODGSON, JOHN STUDHOLME (2 son of John Hodgson 1757-1846, *general in the army*). b. Blake st. York May 1805; ed. at Woolwich; ensign 23 Bengal N.I. 3 Feb. 1822; served in campaign of 1845-6 and was wounded at Sobraon; raised first Sikh regt. embodied in British service which he commanded in second Sikh war 1848-9; as brigadier, organised Punjab irregular force 1850; in command of Peshawer frontier; lieut.-col. 12 Bengal N.I. 15 April 1858 to 1862; M.G. 23 July 1861; retired 1865. d. 10 Stanhope terrace, Hyde park, London 14 Jany. 1870.

HODGSON, JOSEPH (son of John Hodgson oj Birmingham, merchant). b. Penrith, Cumberland 1788; studied at St. Bartholomew's hospital; M.R.C.S. 1811, member of council 1849, examiner in surgery 1856-66, president 1864; in practice at King st. Cheapside 1811-18; edited *London Medical Rev.*; removed to Birmingham 1818; surgeon to general dispensary and general hospital to 1848; a founder of Birmingham eye infirmary 1824; returned to London 1849; examiner in surgery London univ.; president Medico-Chirur. Soc. 1851; very successful as a lithotomist; F.R.S. 14 April 1831; attended Sir Robert Peel on his death 2 July 1850; author of *A treatise on the diseases of arteries and veins* 1815 which was translated into German and Italian. d. 60 Westbourne ter. London 7 Feb. 1869. *Reg. and Mag. of Biog.* March 1869 pp. 211-2; *J. F. Clarke's Biog. Recollections* (1874) 331-5.

HODGSON, REV. JOSEPH LOWTHER (3 son of William Hodgson of Houghton house, Cumberland). b. 27 Sep. 1818; ed. at Pet. coll. Cam., B.A. 1840, M.A. 1844; P.C. of Wetheral with Warwick 1848 to death; hon. canon of Carlisle cath. 1858 to death; author of *A simple catechism of the Lord's prayer* 1851; *The village schools of Cumberland* 1857. d. Harber Grange near Carlisle 29 March 1861.

HODGSON, REV. JOSEPH STORDY (2 son of Joseph Hodgson). b. 1806; ed. at Caius coll. Cam., B.A. 1829, M.A. 1834; R. of Brinklow near Coventry 1840-58; R. of Aikton, Cumberland 1858-70; hon. canon of Carlisle cath. 1872, canon residentiary 1872 to death; author of *Considerations in phrenology* 1839 ;. *The duty of private judgment* 1844. d. The Abbey, Carlisle 24 Jany. 1879.

HODGSON, KIRKMAN DANIEL *(eld son of John Hodgson of the Elms, Hampstead, d.* 1858). *b.* London 1814; ed. at the Charterhouse 1826 etc.; partner in firm of Baring Brothers and Co. merchants; a director of Bank of England 1849–78, deputy governor 1862, governor 1863–4; M.P. for Bridport 1857–68, contested Penryn 1868; M.P. Bristol 1870 to 1878. *d.* Ash Grove, Sevenoaks 11 Sep. 1879, personalty sworn under £400,000 Nov. 1879.

HODGSON, MARY *(dau. of Thomas Hodgson* 1800–69). *b.* Bentham, Yorkshire 1835; ed. at Ackworth sch. near Pontefract 1846–50; student of Manchester sch. of Art 1874, and at Manchester Academy of art 1876; lady exhibitor 1882, associate 1884; landscape painter in oil and water colours; made studies of animals, especially of cats; author of *A plea for the Alliance, in verse* 1864; *Vegetarian receipts for Christmas time* 1883; illustrated H. Thompson's *History of Ackworth School* 1879 with 12 drawings. *d.* York 13 Sep. 1886. *J. H. Nodal's Bibliography of Ackworth school* (1889) 15, *portrait.*

HODGSON, RICHARD. *b.* Wimpole st. London 1804; partner in firm of Hodgson and Graves of Pall Mall, London, publishers to 1841; introduced many improvements in daguerreotype; built an observatory at Claybury in Essex 1852, removed it to Hawkwood near Chingford, Essex; F.R.A.S. 14 April 1848, mem. of council 12 Feb. 1858, hon. sec. 1863–67. *d.* Hawkwood 4 May 1872.

HODGSON, SIR ROBERT *(son of Robert Hodgson, speaker of house of assembly, Prince Edward island).* *b.* Charlotte town, Prince Edward island 1798; ed. at Collegiate sch. Windsor, Nova Scotia; admitted to bar of Nova Scotia and of Prince Edward island 1819; surrogate and judge of probate for P.E. island 1828, attorney general and advocate general 1828, president of legislative council 1840, and acting chief justice 1841; resigned all offices except surrogate and judge 1851; chief justice 1852, judge of vice admiralty court 1853; acting governor of P.E. island 1865, 1868 and 1873–4; lieut.-governor July 1874 to July 1879; knighted by patent 1 March 1869. *d.* Charlotte town 16 Sep. 1880.

HODGSON, STUDHOLME JOHN *(son of general John Hodgson* 1757–1846). *b.* 1 April 1805; ensign 50 regt. 30 Dec. 1819; served in 45, 39 and 19 regiments in Ceylon, India and the first Burmese war; commander of the forces in Ceylon 1865–69; commander of troops in Straits Settlement; administrator of civil

HODGSON, S. J. *(Con.)*

government of Ceylon; colonel 54 regt. 13 March 1868; colonel 4 regt. 21 Nov. 1876 to death; general 2 Feb. 1876; retired 1 Oct. 1877. *d.* Argyll hall, Torquay 31 Aug. 1890.

HODGSON, THOMAS. *b.* Lancaster, Jany. 1800; land surveyor, Lancaster 1821; made a survey of the county of Westmoreland 1823–5, concerning which he had a paper war with G. & J. Greenwood, map publishers; author of *Plan of the county of Westmoreland* 1828, another issue with the geological strata coloured by Adam Sedgwick is dated 1841. *d.* Lancaster 1869.

HODGSON, THOMAS. Master Badsworth hounds for 3 seasons, of Holderness hounds 16 seasons and of Quorn hounds 2 seasons; registrar of deeds, West Riding of Yorkshire. *d.* Snydale hall, May 1863 aged 70. *Sporting Rev., June* 1863 *pp.* 461–3.

HODGSON, WILLIAM. *b.* 1745; studied medicine and botany in Holland; M.D.; tried at Old Bailey 9 Dec. 1793 for proposing toast of The French Republic and comparing the king to a German hog butcher, imprisoned in Newgate 2 years; author of *The picture of the Times* 1795; *The commonwealth of reason* 1795; *The case of W. Hodgson now confined in Newgate* 1795; *A critical grammar of the French and English language* 1819; *Flora's cabinet in which the relation of chemistry to the flower garden is elucidated* 1835; *The life of Napoleon Bonaparte* 1841. *d.* Hemingford ter. Islington 2 March 1851 aged 106. *G.M. xxxv,* 560 (1851); *N. & Q.* 14 *June* 1884 *p.* 475.

HODGSON, WILLIAM BALLANTYNE *(son of William Hodgson a working printer).* *b.* Edinborough 6 Oct. 1815; matric. at Edin. univ. Nov. 1829; a lecturer on literature, education and phrenology in Fifeshire; sec. Mechanics' instit. Liverpool 1 June 1839; principal of Liverpool institute 1844; LL.D. of Glasgow univ. 11 March 1846; principal Chorlton high sch. Manchester 1847–51; lectured on economic science R. Instit. London 1854; assist. comr. of inquiry into primary education 1858; professor of commercial law Edin. univ. 17 July 1871; author of *Lectures on education* 1837; *The education of girls* 1864–6, 2 ed. 1869; *The true scope of economic science* 1870; *Turgot, his life, times and opinions* 1870 and other works. *d.* at Brussels while attending educational congress 24 Aug. 1880. *Meiklejohn's Life and letters of W. B. Hodgson* (1885), *portrait; Grant's University of Edinburgh, ii,* 466–9 (1884).

HODGSON, WILLIAM NICHOLSON *(eld. son of Joseph Hodgson)*. *b.* Carlisle 14 Aug. 1801; M.P. Carlisle 1847-52, 1857-9 and 1865-8; M.P. East Cumberland 1868 to death; sheriff of Cumberland 1863. *d.* 33 Duke st. St. James's, London 2 April 1876.

HODSON, VEN. GEORGE *(youngest son of Mr. Hodson of Carlisle)*. *b.* 1787; ed. at Trin. coll. Cam., B.A. 1810, of Magd. coll., M.A. 1813; Taxor of the university 1813; P.C. of Ch. Ch. Birmingham, Oct. 1824; archdeacon of Stafford, April 1829 to death; second residentiary canon and chancellor of Lichfield cath. 28 June 1833 to death; V. of St. Mary, Lichfield 1851 to death; author of *Twelve sermons on christian temper and experience* 1825; *Morning discourses at Christ Church, Birmingham* 1832; *The church of Rome's traffic in pardons* 1838; *The finished course* 1855. *d.* Riva on the Lago di Garda 13 Aug. 1855.

HODSON, GEORGE A. *(son of George A. Hodson, musical composer of numerous pieces)*. *b.* Dublin 1822; first appeared on stage at Bath about 1839; actor of Irish characters; played *Teddy the Tiler* at Covent Garden 1841; lessee of Cheltenham theatre; lessee of theatre royal, Gloucester to his death. *d.* Bath 27 June 1869. *Era 4 July 1869 p. 11 col. 4.*

HODSON, JAMES. *b.* Streat Place near Ditchling, Sussex 30 Oct. 1808; miller at Brighton; first played at Lord's 10 June 1839 when he was no-balled for being too high; round armed bowler; resided at Hunston near Chichester from 1856. *d.* 17 March 1880. *Lillywhite's Cricket scores, ii, 495 (1862).*

HODSON, MARGARET *(eld. dau. of Allen Holford of Davenham, by Margaret Wrench of Chester, authoress)*. *b.* 1778; author of *Wallace or the fight of Falkirk, a romance* 1809, 2 ed. 1810; *Poems* 1811; *Margaret of Anjou* 1816; *Warbeck of Wolfstein* 1820. *(m.* 16 Oct. 1820 Septimus Hodson, rector of Thrapston, Northamptonshire *d.* 12 Dec. 1833); a friend of Southey, Coleridge and Landor; also published *The lives of Vasco Nunez de Balboa and Francisco Pizarro from the Spanish of Don Manuel Josef Quintana* 1832. *d.* Sharrow cottage, Dawlish, Devon 11 Sep. 1852. *N. & Q. 2 S. i 113, 4 S. ix 534, x 94, xi 411.*

HODSON, WILLIAM STEPHEN RAIKES *(3 son of Ven. George Hodson 1787-1855, archdeacon of Stafford)*. *b.* Maisemore court near Gloucester 19 March 1821; ed. at Rugby and Trin. coll. Cam., B.A. 1844; entered H.E.I.C. service Sep. 1845; with the 2nd grenadiers engaged in Sikh war; adjutant of corps of guides 1847; assist. commissary at Umritsur in the

HODSON, W. S. R. *(Con.)*

Punjab 1849; commander of corps of guides Sep. 1852, removed 1855; two inquiries made as to his conduct, the last being favourable 1856; raised and commanded a regiment of irregular horse known throughout the mutiny of 1857 as Hodson's horse; managed the intelligence department 1857; pursued and captured the king of Delhi 21 Sep. 1857; captured and shot with his own hands the 3 princes of Delhi 22 Sep. 1857; shot by a native in the begum's palace at Lucknow 11 March 1858, *d.* Lucknow 12 March 1858. *Twelve years of a soldier's life in India, By W. R. Hodson* 1859; *Rev. G. H. Hodson's Hodson of Hodson's Horse* (1883); *R. B. Smith's Life of Lord Lawrence, i 309, ii 14, 538; Kaye and Malleson's Indian mutiny, vols. i-iv* (1888-89).

HOFFMEISTER, SIR WILLIAM CARTER *(son of Charles William Hoffmeister, collector of customs, Belfast)*. *b.* Portsmouth 6 July 1817; ed. at Glasgow univ., M.D. 1840; M.R.C.S. 1840, F.R.C.S. 1855; L.R.C.P. 1861; surgeon apothecary to the Queen at Osborne; surgeon Royal yacht squadron; knighted at Osborne 26 Aug. 1884. *d.* Clifton house, Cowes, Isle of Wight 29 July 1890.

HOGAN, JOHN *(son of a builder)*. *b.* Tallow, co. Waterford, Oct. 1800; with Sir Thomas Deane, architect Cork 1815-22; decorated R.C. chapel, Cork with 44 wooden figures of saints 1822; studied in Rome 1823-9; first works in marble, A shepherd boy 1824 and a Drunken Faun; retired to Ireland 1829; his 'Dead Christ' forms altar piece of R.C. chapel, Clarendon st. Dublin; patronised by R.C. clergy; made statues of D. O'Connell and others, and busts of Father Mathew, &c.; exhibited 4 sculptures at R.A. London 1833-50. *d.* Dublin 20 March 1858. His widow Cornelia granted civil list pension of £100, 4 Oct. 1858. *Dublin Univ. Mag. xxxv, 72 (1850), portrait; Art Journal, ii, 376 (1850), portrait.*

HOGAN, JOHN SHERIDAN. *b.* near Dublin 1815; sent to Toronto, Canada 1826; newsboy for *Canadian Wesleyan* 1826, foreman, then on staff of writers; studied law, attorney 1844 in practice at Hamilton; sent articles on Canadian politics to *Blackwood's Edin. Mag.* 1850; established *United Empire* newspaper at Toronto; accused of complicity in burning steamer Caroline, but discharged, brought a claim for indemnity which was not entertained; first prize for an essay on *Canada and her resources*, at Paris exhibition 1855; editor *Toronto Daily Colonist* 1856 and for some years; member for county of Grey in Canadian parliament 1857; *murdered near*

HOGAN, J. S. *(Con.)*

Toronto, Dec. 1859. *Morgan's Bibl. Canad.* (1867) 192 ; *Appleton's American Biog. iii,* 229 (1887).

HOGARTH, GEORGE. *b.* Edinburgh 1783 ; a writer to the signet ; a violinist and composer ; a contributor to *Edinburgh Courant ;* a writer on *Morning Chronicle,* London 1831, afterwards editor ; musical critic to *Daily News* 1846–66 and also to *Illust. London News ;* sec. to Philharmonic soc. 1850–64 ; compiled the *Houseland Narrative* 1850–61 ; author of *Musical history, biography and criticism* 1835 ; *Memoirs of the opera in Italy, France, Germany and England* 2 vols. 1851 ; his musical publications were *The musical herald* 2 vols. 1846 ; *School music arranged for three voices* 1852. *d.* at res. of his dau. Mrs. R. C. Roney, 10 Gloucester crescent, Regent's park, London 12 Feb. 1870. *Newspaper Press, iv* 81 (1870).

HOGARTH, MOST REV. WILLIAM. *b.* Dodding Green, Kendal, Westmoreland 25 March 1786 ; entered catholic college at Crook hall near Consett 29 Aug. 1796, this college was subsequently removed to Ushaw ; received tonsure and four minor orders at Durham 19 March 1807, ordained sub-deacon 2 April 1808, deacon 14 Dec. 1808, priest 20 Dec. 1809 ; a professor and general prefect at Ushaw college ; chaplain at Cliffe hall 31 Oct. 1816 to 9 Nov. 1824 ; transferred to the mission at Darlington 9 Nov. 1824 where he remained to death ; vicar general to bishops Briggs, Mostyn and Riddell ; vicar apostolic of the northern district, and bishop of Samosata in partibus 28 July 1848, consecrated in St. Cuthbert's chapel, Ushaw 24 Aug. 1848 ; bishop of Hexham and Newcastle 29 Sep. 1850 to death. *d.* Paradise row, Darlington 29 Jany. 1866. *bur.* St. Cuthbert's coll. Ushaw 6 Feb. *Brady's Episcopal succession, iii,* 346, 357, 410–13 (1877) ; *Gillow's English Catholics, iii,* 321–23 (1887).

HOGG, HENRY *(son of a manufacturer of hosiery).* *b.* Nottingham 1831 ; solicitor at Nottingham to death ; wrote a number of short poems in the *Christian Miscellany,* also wrote hymns and carols some of which he set to music ; published *Poems, Nottingham* 1852 ; *Songs for the Times* 1856. *d.* Nottingham 1874. *Wylie's Old and New Nottingham* (1853) 247.

HOGG, JAMES. *b.* Leitrim, Ireland ; contributed to *Dublin University Mag.* and *New York Albion ;* editor and proprietor of *New Brunswick Reporter* at Fredericton to death ; author of *Poems. St. John, N.B.* 1825 ; *Poems, religious, moral and sentimental. d.* Fredericton, New Brunswick 12 June 1866. *Morgan's Bibl. Canad.* (1867) 192.

HOGG, JAMES *(son of James Hogg). b.* near Edinburgh 26 March 1806 ; apprenticed to James Muirhead, printer, Edin. 1818 ; printer and publisher in Edin. 1837–58 ; edited *Hogg's Weekly Instructor,* first number 1 March 1845, title changed to *The Instructor* 1849, afterwards to *Titan,* last number Dec. 1859 altogether 29 vols. ; publisher in London 1858 to July 1867 ; published De Quincey's *Collected Works* 14 vols. 1857, new ed. 15 vols. 1862 ; *Churchman's Family Mag.* and *London Society* projected by his son Feb. 1862. *d.* The Acacia, Crescent road, St. John's, Kent 14 March 1888. *H. A. Page's [i.e. A. H. Japp's] Life of T. de Quincey* (1877) i 396, ii 1–33, 339 ; *Nicoll's Landmarks of English literature* (1883) 454–5.

HOGG, SIR JAMES WEIR, 1 Baronet *(eld. son of William Hogg of Lisburn, co. Antrim* 1754–1824). *b.* Stoneyford, co. Antrim 7 Sep. 1790 ; scholar of Trinity coll. Dublin 1808, B.A. 1810 ; student of Gray's inn, London 20 May 1811 ; went to Calcutta 1814, practised at the bar to 1822 ; registrar in supreme court, Calcutta 1822–33 ; returned to England, June 1833 with a large fortune ; M.P. Beverley 1835–47 ; M.P. Honiton 1847–57 ; director of H.E.I.C. 11 Sep. 1839, deputy chairman 1845–6, 1850–1 and 1851–2, chairman 1846–7 and 1852–3 ; cr. baronet 20 July 1846 ; member of council of India 21 Sep. 1858 to 1872, vice president 1860 ; P.C. 5 Feb. 1872. *d.* 11 Grosvenor crescent, London 27 May 1876, personalty sworn under £350,000, 8 July 1876. *I.L.N. iv,* 268 (1844), *portrait ; Times* 29 May 1876 *p.* 12.

HOGG, JOHN (2 *son of John Hogg of Norton house near Stockton on Tees, barrister, d.* 1840). *b.* 21 March 1800 ; ed. at Durham gr. sch. and St. Peter's coll. Cam., scholar 1820, B.A. 1822, M.A. 1827, fellow 1827 ; barrister I.T. 27 Jany. 1832 ; F.L.S. 1823 ; F.R.S. 20 June 1839 ; mem. of Royal Soc. of Lit. 1843, foreign sec. and vice pres. 1866 ; F.R.G.S., sec. 1849–50 ; author of *A catalogue of Sicilian plants* 1842 ; *Letters from abroad to a friend at Cambridge* 1844, and 40 articles in periodical publications. *d.* Norton house 16 Sep. 1869. *Proc. of Royal Geog. Soc. xiv,* 298–9.

HOGG, MARGARET *(dau. of Mr. Phillips of Langbridgemoor, Annandale, farmer). (m.* 28 April 1820 James Hogg 1770–1835 the Ettrick shepherd) ; friend of Sir Walter Scott ; received a present of £130 from Cincinnati 1853 ; civil list pension of £50, 3 Jany. 1854. *d.* Bellevue place, Linlithgow 15 Nov. 1870 aged about 80. *C. Rogers' Leaves from my autobiography* (1876) 256, 265–78.

HOGG, THOMAS JEFFERSON (*brother of John Hogg* 1800–69). *b.* Norton 24 May 1792; ed. at Durham gr. sch. and Univ. coll. Ox. from which he was expelled 25 March 1811 for declining to disavow a publication entitled *The necessity of Atheism* by Shelley; made acquaintance of Shelley at Oxford 1810, which he kept to his death 1822; barrister M.T. 28 Nov. 1817; a municipal corporation comr. for England and Wales 1833–34; revising barrister for Northumberland and Berwick 20 years; came into £2000 under Shelley's will in 1844; author of *Memoirs of Prince Alesy Haimatoff, Translated by John Brown, esq.* [*i.e. T. J. Hogg*], *A novel* 1813; *Two hundred and nine days, or the Journal of a traveller on the continent* 2 vols. 1827; *Life of P. B. Shelley* 2 vols 1858, never completed. *d.* 33 Clifton road, St. John's Wood, London 27 Aug. 1862. *Durham County Advertiser 5 Sept.* 1862 *p.* 5; *G.M. xiii,* 506, 643 (1862).

HOGGAN, JOHN (4 *son of major George Hoggan of Waterside, Dumfries*). *b.* 1790; entered Bengal army 1807; colonel 45 Bengal N.I. 11 July 1853 to death; M.G. 28 Nov. 1854; C.B. 9 June 1849. *d.* Delna, Bengal 13 Nov. 1861.

HOGGE, CHARLES. *b.* 1814; 2 lieut. Bengal artillery 11 Dec. 1829; colonel R.A. 20 Feb. 1860 to death; C.B. 17 June 1858. *d.* Erith 18 Sep. 1865.

HOGGINS, CHRISTOPHER ARGYLE. *b.* 1793; barrister M.T. 12 Feb. 1830; went northern circuit; Q.C. March 1850; bencher of his inn 1850. *d.* 3 Plowden buildings, Temple 19 June 1871.

HOLBERTON, VEN. ROBERT (*son of Robert Holberton of Torr house, Devon*). *b.* 1800; ed. at Ex. coll. Ox., B.A. 1821, M.A. 1825; R. of St. John, Antigua 1827–50; archdeacon of Antigua 1843–50; V. of Norbiton, Surrey 1850–75; C. of Walton-on-the-Hill 1876–8. *d.* Devon lodge, Kew 14 June 1886.

HOLCROFT, THOMAS (*son of Thomas Holcroft, dramatist* 1745–1809). Journalist in London 1822 to death; Paris correspondent for the *Morning Herald;* sec. to the Asiatic Society; edited an East Indian paper in India some years. *d.* 37 Woburn place, London 6 Feb. 1852. *G.M. xxxvii,* 425 (1852).

HOLDEN, GEORGE. *b.* 1800; professor of music; organist St. George's ch. Liverpool to death; composer of anthems, songs, etc.; wrote *Smiling Mirth. d.* 22 Rodney st. Liverpool 5 Dec. 1856.

HOLDEN, REV. GEORGE (*son of Rev. George Holden, master of Horton-in-Ribbesdale gram. sch.*) *b.* Horton 1783; ed. at univ. of Glasgow, B.A.; P.C. of Maghull near Liverpool 1811 to death; V. of Horton, 1821–5; author of *An attempt towards an improved version of the Proverbs* 1819; *The christian expositor or guide to the New Testament* 1830; *An essay on the angels of the church* 1862; and 13 other books. *d.* Maghull 19 March 1865; his library and half his property left to clergy of Ripon, library kept in palace at Ripon. *G.M. xviii,* 657 (1865).

HOLDEN, GEORGE. *b.* Walsall, Staffs. 29 Nov. 1821; beat C. Davis at Sutton Coldfield 24 Jany. 1843 in 73 rounds; beaten by Paddy Gill on Warwickshire Moor 29 Oct. 1844 in 21 rounds for £50; beat Bill Stevens at Calf Heath near Wolverhampton 14 July 1845 in 56 rounds for £25; beat Bob Smith at the Clock, Bickenhall 1 April 1846 in 84 rounds for £50; one of the gamest men who ever lived; licensed victualler, Wolverhampton; landlord of the Malt shovel inn, Walsall. *d.* Wood's Fold, New st. Walsall 4 Feb. 1889. *Sporting Life 9 Feb.* 1889 *p.* 7.

NOTE.—He had 3 brothers Jem, Ted and John all pugilists, his son George Holden, junior, also was well known, he fought Charley Linch, Jack Lead and Peter Morris in London.

HOLDEN, GEORGE KENYON. *b.* Worcester 1806; attorney and solicitor; emigrated to Sydney, Australia 1831; private sec. to Sir Richard Bourke 1831–7; crown prosecutor 1837; solicitor in practice at Sydney from 1838; member of legislative council 1861; examiner of titles 1862. *d.* Rockton, Sydney 16 April 1874. *Heaton's Australian Dict. of Dates* (1879) 94.

HOLDEN, REV. JOHN. *b.* Bonds, Garstang, Lancs. 6 May 1797; ed. at Stonyhurst and Oscott colleges 1812–25; priest 6 Oct. 1825; missioner at Thetford, Norfolk 1825–39; member of Soc. of Jesus 21 Feb. 1840; missioner at Spinkhill, Derbyshire 1842, at Lowergate, Clitheroe, Lancs. 1843 and at Lincoln 1847–59; procurator at St. Bruno's coll. St. Asaph 1859–61; author of *A discharge of grape shot against "Authorities to prove that Church of Rome prohibits reading of the Scriptures." By the Rev. T. D. Atkinson* 1826. *d.* Mount St. Mary coll. Spinkhill, Derbyshire 30 June 1861. *Gillow's English Catholics, iii,* 339–40 (1887).

HOLDEN, MOSES. *b.* Bolton 21 Nov. 1777; a landscape gardener, then a weaver; constructed an orrery and a magic lantern 1814–5;

HOLDEN, M. *(Con.)*

gave astronomical lectures in north of England from 1815; assisted in establishing Preston Institution; freedom of the borough given him 1834; published *A small celestial atlas or maps of the visible heavens in the latitude of Britain* 1818, 4 ed. 1840; *An almanac* 1835, &c. *d.* Preston 3 June 1864.

HOLDEN, HENRY. *b.* 1810; a butcher at Birmingham; landlord of the Rodney inn, Coleshill st. Birmingham about 1840; built a small music hall there, which became the leading one in the Midlands, built a large music hall there, and a brewery 1857, managed his hall down to 1863 or 1864. *d.* Lansdowne house, Malvern 27 Jany. 1880. *Era 1 Feb. 1880 p. 4.*

HOLDFORTH, JAMES *(son of Joseph Holdforth, silk manufacturer Leeds).* *b.* Leeds 14 June 1778; J.P. for Leeds 1836; mayor of Leeds Nov. 1838, first Roman catholic mayor since the Reformation; president of Leeds Catholic institute; supported a ragged school in Leeds. *d.* Burley hill, Leeds 13 July 1861. *Gillow's English Catholics iii,* 346–7 (1887); *Taylor's Biog. Leodiensis* (1865) 498.

HOLDING, FREDERICK *(son of Henry Holding, painter).* *b.* 1817; painter at Manchester; illustrated Southey's *Battle of Blenheim* 1864 and other books; scene painter Theatre royal and Prince's theatre, Manchester. *d.* 1874. *Manchester City News 3 May* 1890.

HOLDING, HENRY JAMES *(brother of preceding).* *b.* Salford, Lancs., Nov. 1833; a calico printer's pattern designer; a painter of marine and torrent scenery in oil and water colours; exhibited in Manchester, Liverpool and London; his chief works were, Finding the body of Rufus by the charcoal burners 1862 and Bettwys-y-Coed 1872. *d.* Paris 2 Aug. 1872.

HOLE, LEWIS *(son of Rev. Wm. Hole, archdeacon of Barnstaple, d. 26 Oct. 1791 aged 82).* *b.* Strodeley, Devon 16 Jany. 1779; entered R.N. 1793, first lieut. of the Revenge at Trafalgar; captain 4 Dec. 1813; retired R.A. 1 Oct. 1846; retired admiral 11 Feb. 1861. *d.* Newport near Barnstaple 16 July 1870. *I.L.N. lvii,* 131 (1870); *O'Byrne* (1849) 529.

HOLKER, SIR JOHN *(son of Samuel Holker of Bury, Lancs.)* *b.* Bury 24 March 1828; ed. at Bury gr. sch.; barrister G.I. 9 June 1854, bencher 15 April 1868, treasurer 1875; practised at Manchester 1854–64; removed to London 1864; Q.C. 21 Feb. 1868; much engaged in patent cases; M.P. Preston 1872–82; solicitor general 20 April 1874; knighted at

HOLKER, SIR J. *(Con.)*

Windsor Castle 12 Dec. 1874; attorney general 25 Nov. 1875 to May 1880, his income during 1875–77 was £22,000 a year; lord justice of court of appeal 14 Jany. 1882, resigned 19 May 1882. *d.* 46 Devonshire st. Portland place, London 24 May 1882. *bur.* St. Cuthbert's church, Lytham 30 May. *A generation of Judges, By Their Reporter* (1886) 119–27; *I.L.N. lxiv,* 493 (1874), *portrait; Times 25 May 1882 p. 9, cols. 3–4.*

HOLL, CHARLTON. *b.* 1805; entered Madras army 1820; colonel 15 Madras N.I. 11 July 1861 to 1864; general 1 Oct. 1877. *d.* 39 Royal crescent, Notting hill, London 4 Dec. 1878.

HOLL, FRANCIS *(4 son of William Holl, engraver 1771–1838).* *b.* Bayham st. Camden Town, London 23 March 1815; pupil of his father; engaged 25 years engraving pictures belonging to the Queen; exhibited 17 engravings at R.A. 1856–79; A.R.A. Jany. 1883; his principal works were, The Stocking Loom by A. Elmore, and The coming of age in the olden time, and The railway station, both by W. P. Frith; portraits of him by his son Frank Holl were exhibited at the R.A. 1868 and 1884. *d.* Elm house, Milford near Godalming 14 Jany. 1884. *bur.* Highgate cemetery 19 Jany.

HOLL, FRANCIS MONTAGUE, known as Frank Holl *(eld. son of the preceding).* *b.* 7 St. James's terrace, Kentish Town, London 4 July 1845; studied at R.A. schools, silver medallist 1862–3, gold medallist 1863, travelling student of R.A. 1868–9; worked for *The Graphic* 1874–6; portrait painter 1876 to death, painted 198 portraits including nearly all celebrated men of the day 1879–88; A.R.A. 19 June 1878, R.A. 29 March 1883; associate of Royal Soc. of painters in water-colours 26 March 1883. *d.* The Three Gables, 6 Fitzjohn's Avenue, London 31 July 1888. *Universal Review 15 Aug. 1888 pp. 478–93, portrait; Graphic 3 May 1879, portrait, and 11 Aug. 1888, portrait.*

HOLL, HENRY *(brother of Francis Holl 1815–84).* *b.* July 1811; first appeared on stage as prince Arthur in *King John* at Drury Lane 1828; acted in the provinces; for many years a member of Haymarket Co.; wrote for the stage *Grace Huntley,* Adelphi 1833, *Wapping Old Stairs,* Haymarket 18 Nov. 1837, *Louise or the White Scarf,* Victoria 1838, *The Forest keeper,* Drury Lane 15 Feb. 1860, and *Caught in a trap,* Princess's 8 Feb. 1860; a reader at Hanover square rooms about 1874; author of

HOLL, H. *(Con.)*

The King's mail 3 vols. 1863; *The Old house in Crosby square* 2 vols. 1863; *More secrets than one* 3 vols. 1864. *d.* 1 Horbury crescent, Notting hill, London 20 Nov. 1884. *Theatrical Times, iii,* 17, 50 (1848), *portrait; N. & Q.* 6 *S. x* 487 (1884).

HOLL, WILLIAM *(brother of the preceding).* *b.* Plaistow, Essex, Feb. 1807; pupil of his father; engraved many portraits for Lodge's Portraits 1834, Knight's Gallery of Portraits 1833–36, &c.; engraved W. P. Frith's An English Merrymaking, The village pastor, &c.; engraved pictures after J. Absolom, A. Elmore, B. West and others; F.G.S.; exhibited 22 engravings at R.A. 1860–71. *d.* 174 Adelaide road, Haverstock hill, London 30 Jany. 1871.

HOLLAND, HENRY EDWARD VASSALL, 4 Baron *(only son of 3 Baron Holland 1773–1840).* *b.* 7 March 1802; sec. of legation at Turin 24 July 1832, at Vienna 3 July 1835; minister plenipotentiary to Germanic confederation 17 April 1838, and to Florence 6 Dec. 1838 to 8 June 1846; succeeded 22 Oct. 1840; edited *Foreign reminiscences of Henry Richard* 3 Baron Holland 1850; *Memoirs of the Whig party, By H. R.* 3 Baron Holland 1852. *d.* Naples 18 Dec. 1859. *Saunders's Portraits of reformers* (1840) 191, *portrait.*

HOLLAND, CHARLES. *b.* 1802; M.D. Edin. 1824; L.R.C.S. Lond. 1828; F.R.S. 19 Jany. 1837; president Roy. Med. Soc. Edin. *d.* St. Chads, Lichfield 21 March 1876.

HOLLAND, EDWARD *(eld. son of Samuel Holland, merchant, London).* *b.* 1806; M.P. East Worcestershire 1835–7, contested E. Worcs. 4 Aug. 1837; contested East Gloucestershire 9 Jany. 1854; M.P. Evesham 1855–68. *d.* Dumbleton hall near Evesham 5 Jany. 1875.

HOLLAND, REV. FREDERICK WHITMORE. *b.* Dumbleton near Evesham 1837; ed. at Eton and Trin coll. Cam., B.A. 1860, M.A. 1864; V. of All Saints with St. Lawrence, Evesham 1872 to death; revisited the peninsula of Sinai in 1861 and 1865; joint hon. sec. of Palestine exploration fund 1866 to death; a founder of the Sinai survey fund, and accompanied Sir C. W. Wilson's expedition to Sinai 1868; again went to Sinai 1878; F.R. Geog. Soc. 1867, wrote many papers on Palestine in its Journal; author of *Sinai and Jerusalem, or scenes from Bible lands* 1870. *d.* on the Nissen, near Thun, Switzerland 27 Aug. 1880. *Proc. R. Geographical Soc. iii,* 670–1 (1881).

HOLLAND, GEORGE. *b.* Lambeth, London 6 Dec. 1791; clerk in a silk warehouse, London; appeared at Drury Lane in a small part 1817; first appeared at Bowery theatre, New York 12 Sep. 1827 as Jerry in *The Day after the Fair;* treasurer of the St. Charles theatre, New Orleans 1834; connected with Mitchell's Olympic theatre, New York 1843–9; with Wood and Christy's negro minstrels under an assumed name 1849–52; member of Wallack's Co. 1852–7; made his last appearance at Daly's Fifth Avenue theatre 15 May 1870; in his performances he brought in numerous eccentricities, ventriloquial diversions and imitations of men and animals. *d.* New York city 20 Dec. 1871; 15,000 dollars subscribed for his wife and family. *Thos. H. Morrell's Life of G. Holland* 1871; *Ireland's New York Stage, i* 560, *ii* 421, 620 (1866–7).

HOLLAND, GEORGE CALVERT. *b.* Pitsmoor, Sheffield 28 Feb. 1801; apprentice to a hairdresser; ed. at Edinburgh univ., M.D. 1827; in practice at Manchester 1829, removed to Sheffield; became a director of railways and banks and was ruined; resided in London 1849–51; returned to Sheffield as a homœopathic practitioner 1851; alderman of Sheffield 1862 to death; author of *The physiology of the fœtus, liver and spleen* 1831; *The vital statistics of Sheffield* 1843; *The nature and cure of consumption* 1850; *The domestic practice of homœopathy* 1859 and 15 other books; conducted *The Sheffield Homœopathic Lancet* 1853. *d.* Sheffield 7 March 1865. *G.M. xviii* 653 (1865).

HOLLAND, SIR HENRY, 1 Baronet *(son of Peter Holland of Knutsford, Cheshire, surgeon).* *b.* Knutsford 27 Oct. 1788; ed. at Newcastle upon Tyne 1799–1803, at Bristol 1804, and at Glasgow univ. 1804–6; studied medicine at Edin. Univ., M.D. 12 Sep. 1811; domestic physician to Caroline, princess of Wales 1814; L.R.C.P. 1816, F.R.C.P. 1828 and V.P., Gulstonian lecturer 1830, censor 1832, 1836 and 1842, consiliarius 1836, 1839, 1844–46, 1850–52 and 1869; physician extraordinary to William iv. 16 April 1835; one of H.M.'s physicians extraordinary 8 Aug. 1837; one of prince Albert's physicians extraordinary 1840; one of H.M.'s physicians in ordinary 22 Dec. 1852; cr. baronet 10 May 1853; F.G.S. 1809, F.R.S. 19 Jany. 1815; D.C.L. Ox. 1856; a manager of Royal Institution 4 Feb. 1861, president; author of *Travels in the Ionian islands, Albania, Thessaly, Macedonia* 1815, 2 *ed.* 2 vols. 1819; *Medical notes and reflections* 1839, 3 *ed.* 1855; *Recollections of past life* 1872, 2 *ed.* 1872 and 6 other books. *d.* 25 Brook st. Grosvenor sq. London 27 Oct. 1873. *Munk's*

HOLLAND, SIR H. (*Con.*)

Roll of Physicians, iii, 144–9 (1878); *Barker's Photographs of Medical men* (1865) 65–8, *portrait; J. F. Clarke's Autobiographical Recollections* (1874) 458–95; *Graphic, viii*, 460, 466 (1873), *portrait*.

NOTE.—His 2 wife Saba whom he *m.* 20 March 1834, *d.* 2 Nov. 1866, she wrote A memoir of her father the Rev. Sydney Smith 2 vols. 1855, 4 ed. 1855.

HOLLAND, JAMES *(son of a potter). b.* Burslem 17 Oct. 1800; painter of flowers on pottery and porcelain; went to London 1819; painter in water colours and oil; exhibited 32 pictures at R.A., 91 at B.I. and 108 at Suffolk st. 1815–67; Assoc. Soc. Painters in water colours 1835–43; member of Soc. of British Artists 1843–8; member Water Colour Soc. 1856; paid many visits abroad from 1830; drew for the *Landscape* and other annuals 1839 etc.; one of the finest colourists of the English school; his views in Venice fetch large prices; several of his pictures are at South Kensington. *d.* London 12 Feb. or Dec. 1870. *Redgrave's Dict. of Artists* (1878) 219; *Bryan's Dict. of painters, i*, 671 (1886).

HOLLAND, JOHN *(son of John Holland of Richmond hill, Handsworth, Yorkshire, optical instrument maker). b.* in Sheffield Park 14 March 1794; edited the *Sheffield Iris* 1825–32, the *Newcastle Courant* 1832–3; joint editor of *Sheffield Mercury* 1835–48; presented by ten gentlemen of Sheffield with an annuity of £100, 1870; author of *Sheffield Park, a descriptive poem. Sheffield* 1820; *The history of the town and parish of Worksop, Nottingham* 1826; *The Psalmists of Britain* 1843, and 15 other books; author with James Everett of *Memoirs of the life and writings of James Montgomery* 7 vols. 1854–6. *d.* in Sheffield Park 28 Dec. 1872. *W. Hudson's Life of John Holland* (1874), *portrait; Reliquary, xv*, 145.

HOLLAND, JOHN *(son of a house painter and picture dealer). b.* 15 Vernon st. Nottingham 14 Dec. 1829; a self taught artist; resided in Todmorden district, Lancs., then in London, afterwards at Trebray lodge, Tintagel, Cornwall; sent 3 pictures *The Storm, After the Storm*, and *The Wreckers* to the exhibition at the Nottingham Castle Art museum 1868; a most rapid painter, only excelled in speed by Smith the painter of waterfalls. *d.* Trebray lodge, Feb. 1886.

HOLLAND, REV. SAMUEL *(son of Nicholas Holland of Greenwich, Kent). b.* Greenwich 1772; ed. at St. Paul's sch. and at Worc. coll. Ox., B.A. 1792, M.A. 1795, M.B. 1796, M.D. 1799; candidate of college of physicians

HOLLAND, REV. S. (*Con.*)

30 Sep. 1799, fellow 30 Sep. 1800, censor 1803; physician to the Middlesex hospital 15 Jany. 1801 to 1806 when he quitted the profession; ordained deacon and priest 1806; R. of Poynings, Sussex 1806–46; R. of Beaudesert, Warcs. 1806 to death; preb. of Thorney, Chichester cath. 1817; precentor of Chicester cath. and preb. of Oving 1825 to death; author of *The preaching of the regular clergy, illustrated and defended* 1813, 6 ed. 1817 and of several sermons. *d.* 33 Regency square, Brighton 16 April 1857 aged 85. *Munk's Roll of Physicians, ii*, 470 (1878).

HOLLAND, REV. THOMAS AGAR *(eld son of the preceding). b.* 16 Jany. 1803; ed. at Westminster sch. and Worcester coll. Ox., B.A. 1825, M.A. 1828; V. of Oving, Sussex 1827–38; R. of Greatham, Hants. 1838–46; R. of Poynings, Sussex 1846 to death; author of *Dryburgh Abbey and other poems* 1826, 4 ed. 1884 and of a *History of Poynings* in the Trans. of Sussex Archæological Society for 1863. *d.* Poynings Rectory 18 Oct. 1888.

HOLLAND, THOMAS SEWARD. *b.* 1827; M.D. Edin. 1850; M.R.C.S. England 1850; assist. physician Renkioi hospital in the Dardanelles 1855–6; author of *Pathological anatomy considered in its relations to medical science* 1852, and papers in medical journals. *d.* at his lodgings, Lambeth 16 June 1856.

HOLLINGS, JAMES FRANCIS. *b.* 1806; second master proprietary sch. Leicester 1837; proprietor and editor of *Leicestershire Mercury* 7 years; member of town council Leicester, and Mayor; one of the founders of Leicester Literary and Philos. Soc., president several times; barrister M.T. 21 Nov. 1851; author of *The life of Gustavus Adolphus* 1838; *The life of Marcus Tullius Cicero* 1839; *The history of Leicester during the civil war* 1840; *Roman Leicester* 1855; *Lord Macaulay* 1860; *hanged himself* at Stonygate, Leicester 15 Sep. 1862. *Leicestershire Mercury* 20 Sep. 1862 p. 5.

HOLLINGWORTH, VEN. JOHN BANKS. *b.* 1779; ed. at Peterhouse, Cam., B.A. 1804, M.A. 1807, B.D. 1814; fellow of his coll. 1804; assistant preacher at Lincoln's Inn 1806; R. of St. Margaret, Lothbury and St. Christopher le Stocks, London 1814 to death; Norrisian professor of Div. at Cam. 1824–38; archdeacon of Huntingdon 25 Feb. 1828 to death; author of *Heads of lectures on divinity delivered in the university of Cambridge* 1825, 3 ed. 1835, and charges and sermons. *d.* Rectory house, St. Margaret's, Lothbury 9 Feb. 1856. *G.M. xlv*, 430–1 (1856).

HOLLINS, JOHN (*son of Thomas Hollins, a painter on glass*). *b.* Birmingham 1 June 1798; exhibited 101 pictures at R.A., 35 at B.I. and 6 at Suffolk st. 1819–55; removed to London 1822; studied in Italy 1825–7; A.R.A. 1842; historical, figure, and landscape painter, introduced portraits into some of his historical pictures. *d.* 47 Berners st., London 7 March 1855. *Redgrave's Dict. of Artists* (1878) 220; *Literary Gazette 17 March* 1855 *p.* 170.

HOLLINS, PETER (*eld. son of William Hollins, architect and sculptor 1754–1843*). *b.* Birmingham 1800; ed. as a sculptor and assisted his father; in Chantrey's studio; exhibited 44 pieces of sculpture at R.A. and 1 at Suffolk st. 1822–71; resided Old Bond st. London 1828–43, then returned to Birmingham where he erected statues of Sir R. Peel and Sir Rowland Hill; V.P. of Soc. of Arts, Birmingham. *d.* 17 Great Hampton st. Birmingham 16 Aug. 1886, portrait in Birmingham Art gallery.

HOLLINWORTH, JOHN IBBETSON. Entered navy June 1795; retired captain 3 April 1811; retired admiral 9 June 1860. *d.* Southsea 28 Dec. 1861 aged 79.

HOLLOND, REV. EDMUND (*eld. son of William Hollond of H.E.I.C.*) Ed. at Queen's coll. Cam., B.A. 1828, M.A. 1831; succeeded his uncle 1845; lord of manor of Middleton Austin; resided at Benhall lodge, Saxmundham, Suffolk; a great Evangelical; author of *Israel's pre-millenial future or the testimony of scripture as to Israel's return and what awaits him in his own land* 1875; patron of 8 livings. *d.* 33 Hyde park gardens, London 18 March 1884 in 83 year.

HOLLOND, ELLEN JULIA (*dau. of Thomas Teed of Stanmore hall, Middlesex*). *b.* Madras 1822. (*m.* 18 March 1840 Robert Hollond, M.P. for Hastings, *d.* 1877); her salon in Paris frequented by the leading liberals 1840–77; started the first crèche in London 1844; founded an English nurses' home in Paris with a branch at Nice; sat for the head of Monica in Ary Scheffer's picture of St. Augustine and his mother 1846; her portrait by Scheffer painted 1852 is in National gallery; author of *Channing, sa vie and ses œuvres* 1857; *La vie de village en Angleterre* 1862; *Les Quakers, études sur les premiers Amis et leur société* 1870. *d.* Stanmore hall 29 Nov. 1884. *Journal des Débats* 6 Dec. 1884.

HOLLOND, ROBERT (*youngest son of William Hollond of Grosvenor place, London, and Bengal*

HOLLOND, R. (*Con.*)

civil service, *d.* 14 Feb. 1836). *b.* 5 Jany. 1808; ed. at C.C. coll. Cam., B.A. 1828, M.A. 1831; barrister L.I. 24 Nov. 1834; M.P. for Hastings 1837–52; in company with Charles Green and Monck Mason made at his own expense a voyage in the Nassau balloon from London to Weilburg, Nassau 7–8 Nov. 1836; John Hollins painted a picture of the 3 persons with the balloon in the back ground 1836. *d.* Paris 26 Dec. 1877, personalty sworn under £350,000, 16 Feb. 1878. *Hatton Turnor's Astra Castra* (1865) 139–58; *Monck Mason's Aeronautica* (1838) 1–98, *portrait*.

HOLLOWAY, JAMES LEWIS (*son of Benjamin Holloway of Lee place, Charlbury, Oxon.*) *b.* 2 July 1824; M.R.C.S. and L.S.A. 1847; assistant surgeon 17 March 1848; principal medical officer at Cape of Good Hope; surgeon general 12 March 1882 to death; C.B. 27 Nov. 1879. *d.* Netley 19 April 1883.

HOLLOWAY, SIR THOMAS (*brother of the preceding*). *b.* 1810; 2 lieut. R.M. 17 March 1825; at siege of Sebastopol 1854–5; served in China 1857 when he was wounded; A.D.C. to the Queen 27 Feb. 1857 to 1 July 1863; colonel 2nd commandant R.M. 25 Feb. 1858, colonel commandant 21 Nov. 1859 to death; general 1 April 1870; C.B. 18 June 1858, K.C.B. 13 March 1867. *d.* Farlington near Portsmouth 21 July 1875.

HOLLOWAY, THOMAS (*son of Mr. Holloway, baker and publican*). *b.* Devonport 22 Sep. 1800; ed. at Camborne and Penzance; removed to London 1828; merchant and foreign agent 1836; commenced advertising his pills and ointment 15 Oct. 1837, was spending £50,000 a year in advertising 1883; directions for use of his medicines were printed in almost all known languages; at 244 Strand, London 1838, removed to 533 New Oxford st. 1867; employed 100 people; made a large fortune; built and endowed at cost of £700,000 Holloway coll. for ladies at Mount Lee, Egham hill, Surrey, opened 30 June 1866; erected a sanatorium for mentally afflicted of lower middle class, opened 15 June 1885. *d.* Tittenhurst, Sunninghill, Berks. 26 Dec. 1883. *I.L.N.* 5 *Jany.* 1884 *p.* 24, *portrait; Graphic* 5 *Jany.* 1884 *p.* 5, *portrait; Some memories as to the origin of Holloway coll.* (1886).

HOLM, JOHN DIEDERICK. A well known phrenologist; executor of J. G. Spurzheim the German phrenologist (*b.* 1776, *d.* 1832). *d.* High st. Highgate 24 Oct. 1856 aged 84.

HOLMAN, MRS. (*dau. of Mr. Lattimer*). *b.* England 1798; appeared at Charleston theatre

1817. (*m.* (1) 22 Aug. 1817 Joseph George Holman, actor, who *d.* 24 Aug. 1817, the writer of numerous plays); appeared in New York singing The soldier tired of war's alarms, and Bishop's Echo song 8 July 1817; (*m.* (2) March 1819 Isaac Star Clawson); (*m.* (3) in 1824 Charles W. Sandford, lawyer and general of militia); appeared at her husband's house, the Lafayette theatre, Oct. 1826; last played in Park theatre, New York as Maria in *Of age to-morrow*, June 1832. *d.* New York city 1 Sep. 1859. *T. A. Brown's American stage* (1870) 181; *Ireland's New York stage*, i, 290, 336 (1866).

HOLMAN, JAMES (*son of Mr. Holman of Fore st. Exeter, chemist and druggist*). *b.* Exeter 15 Oct. 1786; entered navy 7 Dec. 1798, lieut. 27 April 1807, served till Nov. 1810 when he was invalided and became totally blind; a naval knight of Windsor 29 Sep. 1812; travelled over greater part of Europe 1819-24 and round the world 1827-32; F.R.S.; author of *A narrative of a journey through France, Italy, Savoy, &c.* 1822, with portrait; *Travels through Russia, Siberia, Poland, Austria, &c.* 2 vols. 1825, with portrait, 4 ed. 2 vols. 1834. *d.* at his lodgings near the Minories, London 28 July 1857. *Reynolds' Miscellany, x* 9 (1853), *portrait; Proc. of Linnœan Soc.* (1858) 26–30; *People's Journal, iv*, 213, *portrait*.

HOLMAN, JOHN. Steeple chaser; won royal birthday steeple chase at Worcester on The Page 1843; bred a large number of successful steeple chasers. *d.* Cheltenham, Jany. 1888. *Baily's Mag., Feb.* 1888 *pp.* 488–9.

HOLME, BRYAN (*son of Wm. Holme of Thurland castle, Lancs.*) baptised at Tunstal, Lancs. 29 Dec. 1776; articled to John Baldwin of Lancaster, solicitor; admitted solicitor Jany. 1800; a managing clerk in office of Bleasdale and Alexander of Hatton court, London about 1803, a partner in the firm at Hatton court and New Inn 1806-16; partner with Alexander at New Inn 1816-21, with Frampton and Loftus 1821-36, with Loftus and Young 1836 to death; projected "The Law Institution," Chancery Lane 2 June 1825, which became "The Incorporated Law Society" by a new charter granted 5 June 1845; a whole length portrait of him by H. W. Pickersgill, R.A. was placed in the Society's hall about 1836. *d.* 13 Brunswick sq. London 15 July 1856. *Legal Observer 23 Aug.* 1856 *pp.* 281–5.

HOLME, THOMAS WINN (*son of Thomas Holme*). *b.* Kendal 3 March 1828; ed. at Ackworth sch. 1841-3, and at Manchester art sch.;

managed a woollen mill near Kendal, and then powder mills at Sedgwick, near Leven's Park; a painter; author of *Poems and prose* 1874. *d.* Kendal 20 May 1876. *Nodal's Bibliog of Ackworth sch.* (1889) 16.

HOLMES, ALFRED (*son of Thomas Holmes of Lincoln*). *b.* London 9 Nov. 1837; learnt the violin from his father; with his brother Henry Holmes made a series of concert tours in Belgium 1855, Germany 1856, Austria 1857, Sweden 1857-9, Denmark 1860, Holland 1861; settled in Paris 1864, where he established a quartet party; produced at St. Petersburg his symphony *Jeanne d' Arc* April 1868, which was performed in 1870 at Théâtre Italien, Paris, and at Crystal Palace, Sydenham 27 Feb. 1875; composed symphonies *The Youth of Shakespeare, The siege of Paris* 1870, *Robin Hood, Charles XII*, and *Romeo and Juliet*; an opera in 5 acts called *Inez de Castro* 1869; overtures *The Cid* and *The Muses; Two nocturnes for the violin and piano*, Leipzig 1857. *d.* Paris 4 March 1876. *I.L.N. lxviii*, 315 (1876), *portrait*.

HOLMES, REV. ARTHUR. Ed. at Shrewsbury and St. John's coll. Cam., Bell sch. 1856, Craven sch. 1856, B.A. 1859, M.A. 1862; fellow of his coll. 1860-62; C. of All Saint's, Cam. 1860-61; lecturer of St. John's coll. 1860-73 and of Clare coll. 1864-73; senior fellow and dean of Clare coll. 1873 to death; deputy public orator of Cam. 1867, Lady Margaret preacher 1868, select preacher 1868-69; Cambridge preacher at chapel royal 1869-71; general editor of the *Catena Classicorum* series 1867 etc.; published *The Midias of Demosthenes with notes* 1862; *Demosthenes De Corona* 1867; *The Nemeian odes of Pindar* 1867; cut his throat at Clare coll. Cambridge 17 April 1875. *Cambridge Chronicle 24 April* 1875 *p.* 6.

HOLMES, EDWARD. *b.* 1797; ed. at Enfield; apprenticed to R. B. Seeley, bookseller; studied music under Vincent Novello; taught the piano in schools; wrote musical criticisms for *The Atlas* from 1829 and later for *The Spectator*; wrote articles in *Fraser's Mag.* and *Musical Times*; author of *A ramble among the musicians of Germany* 1828, 3 ed. 18 ; *The life of Mozart* 1845; *Analytical and thematic index of Mozart's pianoforte works* 1852; *A critical essay on the Requiem of Mozart* 1854; *Life of H. Purcell. d.* 4 Sep. 1859.

HOLMES, JAMES. *b.* 1777; apprenticed to an engraver; member of Soc. of Painters in Water-colours 1813-22; assisted to establish

HOLMES, J. *(Con.)*

Soc. of British Artists, member 1829–50; also a miniature painter; 2 of his portraits of Lord Byron were engraved; a personal friend of George iv. *d.* Shropshire 24 Feb. 1860. *Redgrave's Dict. of Artists* (1878) 221.

HOLMES, JAMES. *b.* Exeter 1789 or 1790; ed. at Exeter gr. sch.; apprenticed to Thomas Besley of Exeter, printer 16 Sep. 1806; printer at 4 Took's court, Chancery lane, London, March 1825 to 1869; started the *Court Journal* with Henry Colburn 25 April 1829; bought *The Athenæum* for £200, 7 Jany. 1830, joint proprietor with C. W. Dilkie 20 Sep. 1831, printed it 1829–69. *d.* 4 July 1873. *bur.* Kensal green cemetery 11 July.

HOLMES, JOHN *(son of Nathaniel Holmes d. Derby 18 Dec.* 1840). *b.* Deptford, Kent 17 July 1800; bookseller Derby; temporary assistant MSS. department Br. Museum 15 Jany. 1830, senior assistant April 1837, assistant keeper 6 May 1850 to death; adviser of 4 earl of Ashburnham in formation of his collection of MSS. which was sold 1883–4; author of *A catalogue of manuscripts, maps, charts in the British Museum* 1844. *d.* 4 Park ter. Highgate, London 1 April 1854, his library sold 15 June 1854. *G.M. ii,* 87–8 (1854).

HOLMES, JOHN. *b.* Rossshire, Scotland, March 1789; emigrated to Nova Scotia 1803; sat in Nova Scotia assembly 1836–47, 1851–8, in legislative council 1858–67; senator in Dominion parliament 1867. *d.* 1870. *Appleton's American Biography iii,* 242 (1887).

HOLMES, REV. JOSEPH. *b.* 1789; ed. at Queen's coll. Cam., 3 wrangler 1812, B.A. 1812, M.A. 1815, B.D. 1840, fellow and tutor of his coll. to 1819; head master Leeds gram. sch. 1830–53; C. of Trinity ch. Leeds 1830–45; author of *The duty of a christian state to support a national church establishment* 1834. *d.* Leeds 14 June 1854. *Taylor's Biog. Leodiensis* (1865) 454–5.

HOLMES, REV. PETER (1 *son of Walter Holmes of Bickleigh, Plymouth*). *b.* Bickleigh 1815; ed. at Plymouth gram. sch. and at Magd. hall Ox., B.A. 1840, M.A. 1844, D.D. 1859; C. of Sheepstor, Devon 1840–3; head master Plymouth gram. sch. 1840–54; diocesan inspector of schools, deanery of Plympton 7 years; kept a private school at Plymouth; F.R.A.S. Dec. 1841; author of *Observations on the standard of doctrine in the Church of England* 1848; *Bishop Bull's Defensio fidei Nicœnæ. A translation* 2 vols. 1851–2; contributed to Anglo-Catholic library, Christian Remem-

HOLMES, REV. P. *(Con.)*

brancer, Kitto's Biblical Cyclopœdia, Clark's Ante-Nicene Christian library. *d.* Wellington villa, Mannamead, Plymouth 11 Oct. 1878; left a valuable library. *Academy ii,* 428 (1878).

HOLMES, ROBERT *(son of Mr. Holmes of Belfast). b.* Dublin 1765; ed. at Trin. coll. Dublin, B.A. 1787; called to bar in Ireland 1795; imprisoned some months, being suspected of complicity with his brother-in-law, Robert Emmet's rising 1803; had the largest practice in the Irish courts, made upwards of £100,000; refused offices of crown prosecutor, King's counsel, and solicitor general; author of *A demonstration of the necessity of the legislative union of Great Britain and Ireland* 1799; *The case of Ireland stated* 1847. *d.* 37 Eaton place, Belgrave sq. London 30 Nov. 1859. *Dublin Univ. Mag., Jany.* 1848 *pp.* 122–33, *portrait; O'Flanagan's Irish Bar* (1879) 273–87.

HOLMES, REV. SAMUEL *(son of John Holmes of Feversham, Kent). b.* 1826; ed. at Magd. hall, Ox., B.A. 1841, M.A. 1845; P.C. of Sidcup 1844–50; R. of North Cray 1850–5; V. of Huddersfield 1855–66; canon residentiary of Ripon cath. 1863 to death; V. of St. Paul, Dorking 1866–81; author of sermons. *d.* 18 Park parade, Harrogate 9 Nov. 1890.

HOLMES, WILLIAM (5 *son of Thomas Holmes of co. Sligo, brewer). b.* co. Sligo 1779; ed. at Trin. coll. Dublin, B.A. 1795; D.C.L. of Oxford univ. 5 July 1810; military sec. to Sir Thomas Hislop in West Indies; M.P. for Grampound 1808–12, for Tregony 1812–18, for Totnes 1819–20, for Bishop's Castle 1820–30, for Haslemere 1830–2; contested Ipswich 1835; M.P. Berwick on Tweed 1837–41; contested Stafford 1841; whipper-in to the Tory party 30 years; treasurer of the ordnance 1820–30; was close to Spencer Perceval when he was assasinated 1812 and near to Wm. Huskisson when he was killed 1830. *d.* Grafton st. Bond st. London 26 Jany. 1851. *Portraits of eminent conservatives 2nd series* (1846), *portrait.*

HOLMES, SIR WILLIAM HENRY (3 *son of Alexander Holmes of Athgarven, co. Kildare). b.* 1817; private sec. to Sir Henry Light when governor of Guiana 1838–47; provost marshal of Guiana 1847, adjutant general of militia there; comr. from Guiana to Paris exhibition 1855; knighted at Buckingham palace 4 April 1856; author of *Report of an expedition to explore a route to the gold fields of Caratal* 1857; *Free cotton, how and where to grow it* 1862. *d.* 5 Osborne villas, Stoke, Devonport 9 Aug. 1868.

HOLMES, WILLIAM HENRY. *b.* Sudbury, Derbyshire 8 Jany. 1812 ; student at R.A. of music 1822, sub-professor of pianoforte 1826, afterwards professor ; the teacher of W. S. Bennett, J. W. Davison, G. A. and W. Macfarren ; appeared as a pianist at Philharmonic Soc. concert 24 March 1851 ; composer of *The Elfin of the Lake, an opera* 1850, of very numerous pieces left in MS. and of 130 printed pieces for the piano 1835–81. *d.* 23 April 1885. *bur.* Brompton cemet. 27 April. *Cazalet's Hist. of R. Acad. of music* (1854) 295 ; *Grove's Dict. of music, i,* 744 (1879).

HOLMES, SIR WILLIAM RICHARD (*son of William Henry Holmes of Kilrea, co. Londonderry*). *b.* London 1821 ; entered consular service at Erzeroum, Oct. 1841 ; vice consul at Batoom, Asia Minor 17 March 1846 ; consul at Diarbekir 23 Nov. 1852 ; consul in Bosnia 12 Jany. 1860 ; British delegate to commission for pacification of Herzegovina 1861 ; knighted at Osborne 13 Aug. 1877 ; retired from the service 1 Sep. 1877 on a pension ; author of *Sketches on the shores of the Caspian* 1845. *d.* Yewhurst, Belvedere, Kent 19 Jany. 1882.

HOLMS, JOHN (*son of James Holms of Saucel Bank, Paisley*). *b.* Saucel Bank 21 Sep. 1830 ; partner in firm of W. Holms and Brothers, spinners, Glasgow ; M.P. Hackney, London 1868–85 ; a lord of the treasury April 1880 to May 1882 ; parliamentary sec. of board of trade 1882–5 ; author of *The British army in* 1875, *its administration and organization* 1875 ; *Our military difficulty. d.* 16 Cornwall gardens, Queen's gate, London 31 March 1891. *I.L.N. lxvi,* 199, 200 (1875), *portrait,* 11 *April* 1891 p. 467, *portrait.*

HOLROYD, EDWARD (3 *son of Sir George Sowley Holroyd* 1758–1831, *justice of court of Queen's Bench*). *b.* 24 July 1794 ; ed. at Charterhouse and Trin. coll. Cam. ; admitted at Gray's inn 26 Nov. 1812 ; special pleader under the bar 7 years ; barrister G.I. 26 April 1826 ; a comr. of bankrupts Nov. 1828 ; a comr. of bankruptcy court Oct. 1831 to 31 Dec. 1869 when granted sum of £2000 on abolition of office ; author of *Observations upon the case of A. Thornton tried for the murder of Mary Ashford* 1819. *d.* Elland lodge, Wimbledon 29 Jany. 1881.

HOLT, ALFRED HENRY (*son of Henry Josiah Holt, pugilist* 1792–1844). Reported prize fights for *The Era, Morning Advertiser, Bell's Life in London* and *Sportsman. d.* 20 Nov. 1865 aged 39. *bur.* Nunhead cemetery.

HOLT, DAVID. *b.* Chorlton upon Medlock, Manchester 13 Nov. 1828 ; assistant sec. of

Lancashire and Yorkshire railway co. to death ; author of *Poems, rural and miscellaneous* 1846 ; *Lays of hero worship and other poems* 1850 ; *Janus, Lake sonnets and other poems* 1853 ; *Poems* 1868. *d.* Altrincham, Cheshire 15 March 1880.

HOLT, ELISE. *b.* London 11 July 1847 ; appeared as a comic singer, Surrey gardens, London 1863 ; pupil of Mdlle. Louise, danseuse 1863, and came out at the Victoria theatre as a dancer, and then as Cupid 26 Dec. 1864 ; played in burlesques at the Strand theatre 1865–8 ; appeared at Olympic theatre, Boston, U.S. America in burlesque of *Lucretia Borgia* 21 Dec. 1868 and at Waverly theatre, New York 18 Feb. 1869 ; visited California ; (*m.* Henry Palmer). *d.* about 1873. *T. A. Brown's American stage* (1870) 182, *portrait.*

HOLT, THOMAS (*son of a wool merchant, Leeds*). *b.* Horbury, Yorkshire 1811 ; with his father at Leeds 1825–8, partner 1832 ; a wool buyer in London 1828–31 ; a wool buyer in Australia 1842–55 ; purchased large estates in Queensland and New South Wales ; member for Stanley boroughs in legislative assembly, N.S.W. 1856 and for Newtown to 1866 ; colonial treasurer 6 June to 25 Aug. 1856 ; member of legislative council 1868 ; member of council on education 1873 ; author of *Two speeches on the subject of education in New South Wales* 1857. *d.* Halcot, Bexley, Kent 5 Sep. 1888. *Heaton's Australian Dict. of dates* (1879) 95.

HOLT, THOMAS LITTLETON. *b.* 1794 or 1795 ; known as Raggedy Holt ; projected *Weekly Chronicle ;* proprietor of *Iron Times* started during the railway mania 1845 ; edited *Morning Chronicle ;* started many papers in London with G. A. A'Beckett ; projected *The Novel* newspaper ; started *Ryland's Iron trade circular* at Birmingham ; edited a weekly paper called *Chat* 1846 ; took an active part in popularising cheap literature and in the abolition of the paper duty ; advertisement duty repealed partly owing to him 1853 ; edited *The Sixpenny magazine* 1863 ; *John Horsleydown or the confessions of a thief* 1860. *d.* The Burrows, Hendon 14 Sep. 1879. *Reminiscences of an old Bohemian, ii,* 35–46 (1882).

HOLYOAKE-GOODRICKE, SIR FRANCIS LYTTELTON, 1 Baronet (*eld. son of Francis Holyoake of Tettenhall, Staffs.* 1766–1835). *b.* Tettenhall 13 Nov. 1797 ; ed. at St. John's coll. Cam., B.A. 1819 ; assumed name of Goodricke by r.l. 12 Dec. 1833 ; sheriff of Warwickshire 1834 ; M.P. for Stafford, Feb. to May 1835, for South Stafford, May 1835

HOLYOAKE-GOODRICKE, SIR F. L. (*Con.*)

to 1837; created baronet 31 March 1835; master of Quorn hounds in Leicestershire 1834–5; one of the very best riders after hounds of his time. *d.* Sherborne house, Malvern Wells 29 Dec. 1865. *Burke's Vicissitudes of families, ii,* 398–9 (1869).

HOMAN, SIR WILLIAM JACKSON, 1 Baronet (2 *son of Rev. Philip Homan*). *b.* 1771; cr. baronet 1 Aug. 1801. *d.* Dromeroe, Cappoquin, co. Waterford 2 March 1852 aged 80. *G.M. xxxvii,* 406 (1852).

HOME, COSPATRICK ALEXANDER RAMEY HOME, 11 Earl of (*eld. son of 10 Earl 1769–1841*). *b.* Dalkeith house, N.B. 27 Oct. 1799; attaché to embassy at St. Petersburgh 1822–3; précis writer in foreign office 1824–7; under sec. of state for foreign affairs 9 June 1828 to 25 Nov. 1830; succeeded 12 Oct. 1841; a Scotch representative peer 1842–74; keeper of great seal of Scotland May 1853; cr. baron Douglas of Douglas co. Lanark in peerage of the U.K. 11 June 1875. *d.* near the Hirsel, Coldstream, Berwick 4 July 1881. *bur.* in church of St. Brides at Douglas 12 July. *F.O. list* 1882 *p.* 213.

HOME, DANIEL DUNGLAS (*son of William Home of the family of the earl of Home*). *b.* near Edinburgh 20 March 1833; taken by his aunt to Greenville, Connecticut about 1842 where he became famous for his mysterious raps, guitar playing without hands, etc.; came to London April 1855 where he held private spiritual seances; held séances before emperor of the French, King of Prussia, and Queen of Holland 1857–8; expelled from Rome as a sorcerer Jany. 1864; gave a series of public readings in America 1864; founded in London with John Elliotson and S. C. Hall the Spiritual Athenæum, a society for the propagation of spiritualism 1866, lived as sec. at the Society's rooms 22 Sloane st.; assumed name of Lyon-Home on being adopted as her son by a widow named Jane Lyon, who gave him £30,000 and assigned to him a mortgage security of £30,000, both sums were restored to her by the Court of Chancery 22 May 1868; gave public readings in the provinces 1869–70; author of *Incidents in my life* 1863, *2nd series* 1872; *Lights and Shadows of Spiritualism* 1877. *d.* Auteuil, near Paris 21 June 1886. *bur.* at St. Germain-en-Laye. *Annual register* (1868) 187–206; *The Mask* (1868) 141–6, *portrait*; *T. A. Trollope's What I remember, i,* 376–81; *Nineteenth century, April* 1890 *pp.* 577–81.

NOTE.—Robert Browning's poem Mr. Sludge the medium is understood to be a study of Home.

HOME, DAVID MILNE (1 *son of admiral Sir David Milne, d.* 1845). *b.* 1804; ed. at Edin. univ., B.A. 1829, LL.D. 1870; called to Scotch bar 1831; advocate depute 1841; succeeded to the family estate and took name of Home 1845; F.R.G.S.; tried to prevent appointment of Dr. Robert Wallace of the Old Greyfriars to the professorship of church history 1873, one of the last "heresy hunts" in the Church of Scotland; author of *Our Social reforms needed in Scotland* 1867; *Scotch poor houses and English work houses* 1873; *The salmon Fisheries of Scotland* 1882. *d.* Milne Graden, Coldstream 19 Sep. 1890. *Times* 23 *Sep.* 1890.

HOME, FRANCIS (*eld. son of James Home, professor of materia medica in Univ. of Edin.*) *b.* Edin. 1800; ed. at high school and univ. of Edin.; advocate 1825; sheriff substitute of co. Kinross 1838 and of co. Linlithgow 1838 to death. *d.* Main's house near Linlithgow 20 Jany. 1882.

HOME, SIR JAMES EVERARD, 2 Baronet (*elder son of Sir Everard Home, 1 bart., serjeant surgeon to George III.*) *b.* 25 Oct. 1798; entered navy 10 April 1810; succeeded 31 Aug. 1832; captain 5 Dec. 1837; C.B. 24 Dec. 1842; captain of the "Calliope" 26 guns 28 Nov. 1850 to death; F.R.S. *d.* Sydney 2 Nov. 1853. *bur.* Camperdown cemetery, Sydney 4 Nov.

HOME, JOHN. Entered Bengal army 1803; colonel 57 Bengal native infantry 1854 to death; M.G. 20 June 1854. *d.* Weston, Bath 12 April 1860.

HOME, JOHN HOME (*son of John Home of Bassenleau, co. Berwick*). *b.* 1797; ensign 1 foot guards 19 Jany. 1813, lieut. col. 15 April 1845 to 1 April 1849 when placed on h.p.; L.G. 22 Sep. 1858; colonel 56 foot 17 Oct. 1859 to death. *d.* Pall Mall, London 22 April 1860.

HOME, NORTH DALRYMPLE. *b.* Long Ashton, Aug. 1856; ed. at Bristol gram. sch. at Montreux and Paris; engaged in London and Westminster bank 2 years; student R. Acad. of music; tenor singer in German Reed's Co.; played in W. S. Gilbert's *Ages Ago,* and in *The Friar* operetta by Comyns Carr 15 Dec. 1886. *d.* Clifton 3 July 1887. *The Era, July* 1887 *p.*

HOME, RICHARD. *b.* 1789; entered Bengal army 1804; colonel 43 Bengal N.I. 7 April 1851 to 1861; colonel 6 Bengal N.I. 1861 to death; M.G. 28 Nov. 1854. *d.* Brighton 19 April 1862 aged 73.

HOME, ROBERT *(eld. son of James Home, captain 30 foot).* b. Antigua 29 Dec. 1837; 1 lieut. R.E. 7 April 1856, major 25 Aug. 1873 to death; deputy assistant Q.M.G. at Aldershot 1865–70; commander of R.E. on the Ashantee expedition 1873; C.B. 31 March 1874; assistant Q.M.G. at head quarters 1 April 1876; sent to Turkey to report on defence of Constantinople 1876; British comr. for delimitation of boundaries of Bulgaria 1877; contributed to *Quarterly Rev.* and *Macmillan's Mag.;* translated Baron Stoffel's *Military Reports* 1872; author of *The law of recruiting* 1872 and *A précis of modern tactics* 1873 the best English book on the subject. d. 21 Regent's park terrace, London 29 Jany. 1879; Anne Josephine his widow (dau. of J. Hunt) granted civil list pension of £300, 21 April 1879. *Graphic xix,* 372 (1879), *portrait; I.L.N. lxxiv,* 185 (1879), *portrait.*

HOMER, JOHN JAMES. b. Wandsworth 1809; educated for a solicitor; proprietor of Dolphin tavern, Mare st. Hackney; was the means of abolishing a brewers' impost known as butt-money 1836; hon. treasurer of the London Licensed Victuallers' Protection Soc. 1838 to death; governor of Incorporated Soc. of Licensed victuallers 1850; doubled the size of the *Morning Advertiser* 1850; common councilman for ward of Cornhill 1866; contested Hackney 18 Nov. 1868; wine and spirit merchant 2 Royal Exchange buildings, London 1852 to death; author of *A summary of the laws relating to licensed victuallers* 1839; *Monarch fire and life insurance co., Scenes at the election for a director* 1852. d. at res. of his son-in-law Dr. William Slimon 4 York place, Bow road, London 3 March 1888. *Licensed Victuallers' Almanack* (1862) 95–9, *portrait; Licensed Victuallers' Year book* (1875) 70–1, *portrait.*

HONE, VEN. RICHARD BRINDLEY *(2 son of Joseph Terry Hone of Faringdon, Berks.)* b. 1805; ed. at Brasen. coll. Ox., B.A. 1827, M.A. 1831; R. of Halesowen, Worcs. 1836 to death; hon. canon of Worcester 10 Nov. 1845 to death, archdeacon 7 Nov. 1849 to death; author of *Lives of eminent christians* 4 vols. 1834–43, 19 charges and 41 New Year's addresses. d. Halesowen rectory 5 May 1881.

HONEY, GEORGE ALFRED *(mother Mrs. Down d. 27 Nov. 1881 aged 90).* b. 25 May 1823; call-boy Adelphi theatre 1841; made debut in London at Princess's theatre Nov. 1848 as Pan in *Midas;* member of Pyne and Harrison company at Covent Garden 1858 etc.; played in Macfarren's opera *Robin Hood* at Her Majesty's 1860; played Eccles in *Caste* at

Prince of Wales's 1867, 1871 and 1879; Graves in *Money* at Holborn 1869 and at Prince of Wales's 1872, 1875 and 1879; Our Mr. Jenkins in *The Two Roses* at Vaudeville 1870; visited U.S. of America 1878; seized with a fit of paralysis while performing at Prince of Wales's 1879. d. 127 Camden road, London 28 May 1880. *Pascoe's Dramatic List* (1880) 183–4; *Illust. Sport. and Dram. News,* x 468–9 (1879) *portrait, xiii* 281 (1880), *portrait, xvii* 125 (1882), *view of tomb; The Era* 30 May 1880 p. 6, 6 June p. 7; *Mr. and Mrs. Bancroft On and off the stage 7th ed.* (1889) 107, 156, 274, 281–3.

HONNER, MARIA *(dau. of Eugene Macarthy, actor, d. Dramatic coll. 1886 aged 78).* b. Enniskillen Ireland 21 Dec. 1812; played with Kean and Macready in Ireland; chief star at Pavilion theatre, London 1831–2; at Coburg theatre 1833, at Sadler's Wells 1838–43, at Surrey theatre 1845, at City of London theatre 1845; excellent in Shakespearean parts, in Julia, in the Hunchback, and other roles; *(m.* (1) 21 May 1836 Robert W. Honner 1809–52; *m.* (2) Frederick Morton, stage manager);* she d. 4 Jany. 1870. *Actors by gaslight 4 Aug.* 1838 *pp.* 121–2, *portrait; Theatrical Times 10 Oct.* 1846 *pp.* 137–8, *portrait.*

HONNER, ROBERT WILLIAM *(youngest son of John Honner of Soho, London, solicitor, d. about 1817).* b. 24 Percy st. Tottenham court road, London 18 Jany. 1809; apprenticed to Charles Leclercq, ballet master 1817–20; made his debut at Sans Pareil theatre in a ballet 1818; actor at Coburg 1825; stage manager at Surrey 1835–38, manager 1842–46; lessee of Sadler's Wells 1838–41 and of City of London theatre 1846; stage manager of Standard theatre 1848 to death. d. Nichols sq. Hackney road, London 31 Dec. 1852. *Theatrical Times 27 March* 1847 *pp.* 89–90, *portrait.*

HONNER, SIR ROBERT WILLIAM. Entered Bombay army 1820; lieut. 4 Bombay N.I. 1 May 1824, lieut. col. 15 Sep. 1855 to 1861; commander of Nussurabad 6 March 1858 to 24 Oct. 1862; commander of Scinde division 28 March 1863 to 26 May 1866, C.B. 21 Jany. 1858, K.C.B. 28 March 1865; M.G. 17 Sep. 1861. d. Lower Berkeley st., Portman sq., London 8 Nov. 1868.

HONY, VEN. WILLIAM EDWARD *(2 son of Rev. Wm. Hony, V. of Liskeard, Cornwall 1778–95).* b. Liskeard 7 Feb. 1788; fellow of Ex. coll. Ox. 30 June 1808 to 3 July 1827, B.A. 1811, M.A. 1812, B.D. 1823; V. of South Newing-

HONY, VEN. W. E. (Con.)

ton, Oxon. 24 Oct. 1818 to 1827; R. of Baverstock 4 June 1827 to death; preb. of Salisbury 29 July 1841; archdeacon of Salisbury 3 Aug. 1846 to death, and canon residentiary 1857 to death; F.G.S. 1831; author of *Church Rates* 1859. *d.* The Canonry, Salisbury 7 Jany. 1875. *I.L.N. lxvi* 403 (1875).

HORNYGOLD, WILLIAM. *b.* 1797; an artist; lived in parish of St. Clement Danes, London; known for his drawings of theatrical characters for the toy theatre, to which he added sketches of the scenery incidental to the pieces performed; his portrait of C. Kemble as Hen. viii. is No. 55 in Skelt's portraits: drew the illustrations for comic songs; fell down intoxicated outside the 'Fountain,' 4 Clare Market, London, taken to the Strand union workhouse, where he *d.* 12 Feb. 1867 aged 69. *J. Diprose's Some account of parish of St. Clement Danes i*, 165–6 (1868).

HONYMAN, SIR GEORGE ESSEX, 4 Baronet *(eld. son of Sir Ord Honyman, 3 Bart. 1794–1863).* *b.* Strawberry hill, Middlesex 22 Jany. 1819; pupil of Martineau, Malton and Trollope, solicitors, London 1838–40; pupil of Sir Fitzroy Kelly and David O. Gibbons, the special pleader 1840, etc.; practised as a pleader 1842–9; barrister M.T. 8 June 1849, bencher Nov. 1866; best commercial lawyer of his day; Q.C. 23 July 1866; sergeant at law 23 Jany. 1873; judge of court of common pleas 23 Jany. 1873, resigned 21 Feb. 1875. *d.* Tunbridge Wells 16 Sep. 1875. *Law mag. and law review i*, 122–27 (1875); *I.L.N. lxvii*, 319, 333, 566, (1875), *portrait*.

HONYWOOD, REV. PHILIP JAMES (3 *son of William Honywood of Siston, Kent).* *b.* 1809; matric. from Trin. coll. Ox. 29 May 1827 aged 18, B.A. 1831; R. of Markshall, Essex 23 Dec. 1838 to 1866; R. of Bradwell next Coggeshall, Essex 27 March 1840 to 1845; R. of Colne-Wake, Essex 1866 to death; kept beagles at Markshall 1851–3 which were always followed on foot, sold his hounds 1853; injured himself hunting on foot three days a week. *d.* Colne-Wake 19 Nov. 1874 aged 65. *Baily's Mag. xxix*, 150–5 (1877).

HOOD, SIR ALEXANDER, 2 Baronet *(only son of Alexander Hood, capt. R.N., slain on board his ship the 'Mars' 1798).* *b.* Wootton, Somerset 5 July 1793; ed. at Ex. coll. Ox., M.A. 1814; K.C.B. 22 May 1812 as proxy for his uncle Sir S. Hood; succeeded as 2 baronet 24 Dec. 1814; M.P. West Somerset 1847 to death. *d.* 43 Wimpole st. London 7 March 1851.

HOOD, CHARLES. *b.* 18 Sep. 1825; ed. at Sandhurst; ensign 3 foot 26 June 1844, captain 1851 to 8 Jany. 1856; led the ladder party in the attack on the Redan 8 Oct. 1855; major 58 foot 28 Jany. 1859, lieut. col. 23 Nov. 1860 to 23 May 1874 when placed on h.p.; placed on retired list with hon. rank of L.G. 1 July 1881. *d.* 8 Feb. 1883.

HOOD, CHARLES *(son of William Hood, an ironmaster 18 Earl st. Blackfriars).* *b.* 1805; ironmaster with his brother in London; made researches into chemistry of combustion of coal, silver medal of Soc. of Arts; F.R.S. 7 Dec. 1843; F.R.A.S.; F.S.S.; chairman of British home for incurables 1861–6; author of *A practical treatise on warming buildings by hot water, to which are added Remarks on ventilation* 1837, 5 ed. 1879. *d.* 10 Leinster gardens, Bayswater, London 10 Dec. 1889.

HOOD, REV. EDWIN PAXTON *(son of a sailor in the navy).* *b.* at house of bishop Porteous 34 Half Moon st. Piccadilly, London 24 Oct. 1820; began to lecture on temperance and peace about 1840; Congregational minister at North Nibley, Gloucs. 1852–7, at Offord road, Islington 1857–62 and 1873, at Queen sq. church, Brighton 1862–73, at Cavendish st. Manchester 1877 to 1880, at Falcon sq. Aldersgate st. London 1882 to death; editor of the *Eclectic and Congregational Review*, of the *Argonaut* and *The Preacher's Lantern*; author of *Old England* 1851; *William Wordsworth, a biography* 1856; *The Peerage of Poverty* 1 series 1859, 3 ed. 1859, 2 series 1861, 5 ed. 1870 and 50 other books. *d.* suddenly at Paris 12 June 1885. *Congregational Year-Book* (1886) 178–82.

HOOD, FRANCIS GROSVENOR (2 *son of lieut. col. Francis Wheler Hood, killed in action 2 March 1814).* *b.* 4 March 1809; ensign grenadier guards 30 April 1827, captain 31 Dec. 1841, major of 3 battalion 20 June 1854 to death; leading his battalion gallantly contributed to defeat of the enemy at battle of the Alma 20 Sep. 1854; *killed* in the trenches before Sebastopol 18 Oct. 1854. *Kinglake's Invasion of the Crimea* 6 ed. iii 220–2, 239 et seq. iv 442.

HOOD, PETER. *b.* Gateshead 1808; ed. at St. George's hospital; L.S.A. 1831, M.D. St. Andrews 1863; practised in London among the upper classes; discouraged the practice of blood letting; a keen sportsman, fly fisher and whist player; treasurer of Fisheries' preservation soc.; president West Herts. medical assoc.; author of *Practical observations on diseases fatal to children* 1845; *The successful treatment of scarlet fever* 1857; *A treatise on gout, rheumatism and the allied affections* 1871, 3 ed. 1885. *d.* Watford, Herts. 18 Sep. 1890. *Lancet* 27 Sep. 1890 *p.* 699.

HOOD, REV. SAMUEL. *b.* Devizes 27 Dec. 1782; received episcopal ordination at Stirling, May 1826; minister of congregation in Trinity house, Dundee 1826–37; restored episcopacy at Rothesay and was minister there 1838, helped to establish seven churches in his district; dean of diocese of Argyle and the Isles 1847 to death; D.D. by archbishop of Canterbury 1870. *d.* Rothesay 30 May 1872. *Norrie's Dundee celebrities* (1873) 392.

HOOD, SAMUEL. *b.* Moyle, co. Donegal 1800; emigrated to Philadelphia 1826, a member of the bar there; author of *Practical treatise on the laws relating to registers, registers' courts, guardians and trustees in Pennsylvania* 1847; *A practical treatise on the law of decedents in Pennsylvania* 1847; *A brief account of the Society of the Friendly Sons of St. Patrick* 1844. *d.* Philadelphia 1875.

HOOD, THOMAS *(only son of Thomas Hood the poet 1798–1845).* *b.* Lake house, Wanstead, Essex 19 Jany. 1835; granted a civil list pension of £50, 4 Oct. 1847; commoner at Pemb. coll. Ox. 1853; edited the *Liskeard Gazette* 1858–59; clerk in the war office 11 July 1860 to May 1865; edited a periodical called *Saturday Night* 1862; edited *Fun,* May 1865 to death; *Tom Hood's Comic Annual* first issued 1867; author of *Captain Master's children* 3 vols. 1865; *A golden heart* 3 vols. 1868; *Rules of rhyme, a guide to English versification* 1869 and many other books. *d.* Gloucester cottage, Peckham Rye, Surrey 20 Nov. 1874. *Poems by Thomas Hood the younger, with a memoir by his sister Frances Freeling Broderip* 1877; *Cartoon portraits* (1873) 64–65, *portrait; Illust. sporting news,* iv, 357 (1865), *portrait.*

HOOD, THOMAS H. COCKBURN. *b.* 1820; in Australia and New Zealand to 1877; inherited Walton hall, Kelso from a relative; author of *The Rutherfords of that ilk* 188–; *The house of Cockburn, with anecdotes of the times in which many of them played a part, Edin.* 1888, and of many scientific papers. *d.* Edinburgh 16 Jany. 1889. *The Bookseller* 6 *March* 1889 *p.* 228.

HOOD, SIR WILLIAM CHARLES *(only son of Dr. William Chamberlayne Hood, d. Berners st. hotel, London* 16 *Dec.* 1879 *aged* 89). *b.* South Lambeth 1824; ed. at Brighton and Trin. coll. Dublin; M.D. St. Andrews 1846; F.R.C.P. Edin. 1850; F.R.C.P. London 1863; treasurer of Bridewell and Bethlehem hospital July 1868 to death; lord chancellor's visitor in lunacy to death; knighted at Windsor castle 7 July 1868. *d.* Bridewell royal hospital, London 4 Jany. 1870.

HOOF, WILLIAM. *b.* 1788; a railway contractor. *d.* Madeley house, Kensington 11 Aug. 1855, leaving property exceeding half a million.

HOOK, ANNA DELICIA *(dau. of John Johnson, physician, Birmingham).* *b.* 1812; author of *Some Meditations for every day in the year* 1864; *The Cross of Christ* 1855 which was edited by her husband; *(m.* June 1829 Rev. Walter Farquhar Hook 1798–1875). *d.* 5 May 1871 aged 59 *bur.* churchyard of Mid Lavant near Chichester 11 May.

HOOK, VERY REV. WALTER FARQUHAR *(eld. child of Very Rev. James Hook 1771–1828, dean of Worcester).* *b.* Conduit st. London 13 March 1798; ed. at Hertford, Tiverton, Winchester, and Ch. Ch. Ox., B.A. 1821, M.A. 1824, B.D. and D.D. 1837, student of Ch. Ch. 1817; C. of Whippingham, Isle of Wight 1821–25; P.C. of Moseley near Birmingham 1826–31; chaplain in ord. to the sovereign 1827 to death; V. of Holy Trin. Coventry 1828 to 1837; preb. of Linc. cath. 1832 to 1859; select preacher univ. of Ox. 1833–34 and 1858–59; V. of Leeds 1837 to 1859; preached his famous sermon *Hear the Church* before the Queen 17 June 1838, 31 ed. 1841, circulated 100,000 copies; dean of Chichester 24 Feb. 1859 to death, installed 19 March 1859; F.R.S. 5 June 1862; author of *A Church Dictionary* 1842, 14 ed. 1887; *An ecclesiastical biography* 8 vols. 1845–52; *Lives of the archbishops of Canterbury* 12 *vols.* 1860–76 and about 70 other books. *d.* the deanery, Chichester 20 Oct. 1875, memorial church at Leeds consecrated 29 Jany. 1880. *Life and letters of W. F. Hook By W. R. W. Stephens* 2 vols. 1878; *Illust. news of the world,* iii (1859), *portrait; Dent's Birmingham* (1880) 427, *portrait; Graphic* xii, 447, 448 (1875), *portrait.*

HOOKER, SIR WILLIAM JACKSON *(son of Joseph Hooker of Exeter).* *b.* Norwich 6 July 1785; ed. at Norwich gram. sch.; travelled for scientific purposes 1806–14; F.L.S. 1806; F.R.S. 9 Jany. 1812; lived at Halesworth, Suffolk 1815–20; regius prof. of botany Glasgow 1820–41; K.H. 1836; knighted at St. James' palace 20 April 1836; director of royal gardens, Kew 1841 to death, chief agent in building the palm house and the temperate house, and a founder of the museum of economic botany; LL.D. of Glasgow; D.C.L. of Ox. 1845; author of *Exotic flora* 3 vols. 1823–7; *Icones plantarum* 10 vols. 1827–54; *The Botanical Mag.* 38 vols. 1827–65; *British flora* 2 vols. 1830–1, many editions; *Species filicum* 5 vols. 1846–64 and 35 other

HOOKER, SIR W. J. *(Con.)*

books and many papers. *d.* Kew 12 Aug. 1865. *Proc. of R. Soc. xv*, 25–30 (1867); *Proc. Med. and Chir. Soc. v*, 150, 162 (1867); *Jerdan's National Portrait gallery* (1834) *v, portrait; Taylor's National Portrait gallery ii*, 95, *portrait.*

HOOLE, ELIJAH *(son of Holland Hoole, shoe maker). b.* Manchester 3 Feb. 1798; ed. at Manchester gr. sch. 1809–13; Wesleyan methodist missionary in Madras 1820–8 during which time he published a number of translations in Tamil; a superintendent of schools in Ireland 1829–34; assistant sec. in London of Wesleyan Missionary Soc. 1834, one of the general secretaries 1836 to death; author of *Personal narrative of a mission to the south of India from 1820–8*, 1829, 2 *ed.* 1844; *The year-book of missions* 1847. *d.* 30 Russell sq. London 17 June 1872. *T. F. Smith's Manchester School Reg. iii, pt.* 1, *pp.* 45, 290.

HOOPER, EDWARD. *b.* 1795; officer in navy; first appeared at Drury Lane as Colonel Briton, Sep. 1826; acting manager at Olympic 1832; lessee of St. James's 1839; manager of Strand 1848; proprietor of Cambridge theatre to death. (*m.* Miss Brothers, she was *b.* 1800, first appeared at Drury Lane as Mrs. Haller 19 Feb. 1827 and was a well-known actress at St. James's theatre). *d.* Cambridge 27 Jany. 1865 aged 70.

HOOPER, EDWARD. *b.* London 24 May 1829; ed. in London; member of firm of Bobbett and Hooper, wood engravers 1850 to death; an originator of the American water colour soc.; exhibited water colours at the Academy of design; engraved illustrations for *Festivals of song, By F. Saunders* 1866. *d.* Brooklyn, New York 13 Dec. 1870.

HOOPER, FREDERIC EDWARD EDEN. *b.* 1842; clerk in the Admiralty, London; wrote many verses on Christmas and other cards; author of *The Indian revolt. A poem, part i*, 1858. *d.* 12 Feb. 1886.

HOOPER, GEORGE. *b.* Oxford 1824; a journalist in London 1848–86; helped to start *The Leader* weekly paper 1850; wrote for *The Globe* and *The Spectator;* edited *Bombay Gazette* at Bombay 1868–71; on staff of *Daily Telegraph*, London 1872–86; author of *The Italian campaigns of general Bonaparte* 1859; *Waterloo, the downfall of the first Napoleon* 1862, *new ed.* 1890; *The campaign of Sedan* 1887; *Wellington, a memoir* 1889. *d.* Southsea 15 May 1890. *I.L.N.* 31 *May* 1890 *p.* 680, *portrait; Pictorial World* 29 *May* 1890 *p.* 697, *portrait.*

HOOPER, JOHN. *b.* Oxford 1802; went to U.S. of America 1839 and devoted himself to natural science; made collection of marine algæ which he left to Long island historical soc. *d.* Brooklyn, New York 26 April 1869. *Appleton's American Biog. iii*, 252 (1887).

HOOPER, JOHN KINNERSLEY (3 *son of Richard Hooper of Queenhithe and Limpsfield, Surrey). b.* 1791; wine merchant as Richard Hooper and Sons, 20 Queenhithe, London to death; alderman of Queenhithe ward 1840 to death, sheriff 1842–43, lord mayor 1847–48; received the French national guard at the mansion house 23 Oct. 1848; pres. of St. Bartholomew's hospital. *d.* St. Leonards-on-Sea 17 April 1854. *I.L.N. xi*, 309 (1847), *portrait.*

HOOPER, WILLIAM. *b.* 1819; a chemist; manufacturer of india-rubber goods 7 Pall Mall East, London and at Mitcham, Surrey 1857–78; inventor and manufacturer of india rubber insulated telegraph cables which he patented 19 March 1868; founder of Hooper's Telegraph Co. in London 1870. *d.* Beechwood, Clapham common, Surrey 25 Sep. 1878. *Journal Soc. of Arts* 1 *Nov.* 1878 *p.* 964.

HOOPER, WILLIAM HULME. *b.* 1827; mate of the Plover, R.N. Nov. 1847 and lieut. 12 May 1849, in the expedition to search for Sir John Franklin, sailed from Plymouth 30 Jany. 1848, reached Port Providence 16 Oct. 1848, led a party along the coast as far as Cape Atcheen, learned the language of the natives, returned to England Oct. 1851; author of *Ten months among the tents of the Tuski, with incidents of an Arctic boat expedition in search of Sir John Franklin* 1853. *d.* Brompton, London 19 May 1854.

HOPE, ADRIAN (6 *son of 4 Earl of Hopetown* 1765–1823). *b.* Hopetown house, Linlithgowshire 3 March 1821; 2 lieut. 60 rifles 23 Nov. 1838, served in Kafir war 1851–3; major 1855; lieut. col. 93 Highlanders 25 Jany. 1856 to death; commanded brigade in Crimea 1854–5; C.B. 24 March 1858; *killed* in attack on fort at Rowas 14 April 1858. *Martin's Indian empire, ii*, 493 (1876), *portrait.*

HOPE, ALEXANDER JAMES BERESFORD BERESFORD— *(youngest son of Thomas Hope of Deepdene, Surrey* 1770–1831). *b.* 25 Jany. 1820; ed. at Harrow and Trin. coll. Cam., B.A. 1841, M.A. 1844, D.C.L. 1848, hon. LL.D. 1864; LL.D. Washington and Tennessee 1879, LL.D. Dublin 1881; M.P. for Maidstone 1841–52 and 1857–65; contested Univ. of Cam. 1859 and Stoke-upon-Trent 1862; M.P. for Stoke 1865–8, M.P. for Univ. of Cam. 1868 to death; bought St. Augustine's abbey,

HOPE, A. J. B. B.- *(Con.)*

Canterbury as a college for missionary clergy 1844; built All Saints' church, Margaret st. London 1849; joint owner of *Saturday Review* with John Douglas Cook 1855; took additional surname of Beresford 30 May 1854; P.C. 20 April 1880; possessed a collection of pictures and objects of art at 1 Connaught place, London; author of *Poems* 1843; *Essays* 1844; *The English cathedral of the nineteenth century* 1861; *A popular view of the American civil war* 1861, 3 ed. 1861; *Worship in the Church of England* 1874, 2 ed. 1875; *Strictly tied up* 3 vols. 1880, a novel, anon. 3 ed. 1881; *The Brandreths* 3 vols. 1882, a novel, and 24 other books. *d.* Bedgebury park, Cranbrook, Kent 20 Oct. 1887. *C. Brown's Life of Beaconsfield* (1882) i, 194, *portrait; Waagen's Galleries of art* (1857) 189-92; *I.L.N.* 16 May 1857 pp. 477, 479, *portrait.*

HOPE, ANNE (2 *dau. of John Williamson Fulton of Calcutta, merchant).* b. Calcutta 1809. *(m.* 10 March 1831 James Hope, physician 1801-41); joined Church of Rome, Nov. 1850; author of *The acts of the early martyrs* 1855; *The lives of the early martyrs* 1857; *Life of St. Philip Neri* 1859; *Conversion of the Teutonic race* 2 vols. 1872; *Franciscan martyrs in England* 1878; wrote many articles in *Dublin Review* 1872-9. *d.* St. Mary-church, Torquay 2 Feb. 1887. *Gillow's English Catholics iii,* 375.

HOPE, CHARLES, Lord Granton *(eld. son of John Hope of London, merchant* 1739-85). *b.* 29 June 1763; admitted advocate 11 Dec. 1784; a depute advocate 1786; sheriff of Orkney 5 June 1792; lord advocate June 1801 to Nov. 1804; M.P. for Dumfries district 1802-3, for city of Edin. 1803-4; a lord of session and lord justice clerk 20 Nov. 1804, assumed title of lord Granton; lord pres. of court of session 12 Nov. 1811 to 1841; P.C. Scotland 17 Aug. 1822, lord justice general Dec. 1836 to 1841; lieut. general of royal archers of Scotland; author of *Notes by the lord president on the subject of hearing counsel in the Inner House* 1826. *d.* Moray place, Edinburgh 30 Oct. 1851. *Omond's Lord Advocates of Scotland ii,* 205-23; *Kay's Original Portraits ii,* 246-55 (1885), 3 *portraits; Lockhart's Peter's Letters to his kinsfolk, ii,* 102-8 (1819).

HOPE, CHARLES WEBLEY. *b.* 21 April 1829; entered navy 1842; captain 15 May 1861; A.D.C. to the Queen 12 Feb. 1873 to 1 Aug. 1877; R.A. 1 Aug. 1877; superintendent of Devonport dockyard 1 Feb. 1879 to death; F.R.G.S.; author of *The education and training of naval officers* 1869. *d.* Devonport dockyard 13 Feb. 1880.

HOPE, REV. FREDERICK WILLIAM (2 *son of John Thomas Hope of Netley, Salop* 1761-1854). *b.* 37 Upper Seymour st. Portman sq. London 3 Jany. 1797; ed. at Ch. Ch. Ox., B.A. 1820, M.A. 1823, hon. D.C.L. 1855; C. of Frodesley, Salop 1823; F.R.S. to 1851 when he withdrew; F.L.S. 5 March 1822; one of founders of Zoological Soc. 1826, of Entomological Soc. 1833, president 1835-37; resided at Naples and Nice 1840-62; executed in 1849 a deed of gift giving his collection of fishes, crustacea, birds, shells, books and 230,000 engravings to Univ. of Oxford, his fishes, etc. were removed to the New Museum and his engravings to Radcliffe library 1861; founded and endowed a professorship of zoology in the Univ. of Ox. 1861; author of *Buprestidae* 1835; *The Coleopterist's Manual* 3 parts 1837-40 and of about 60 papers on entomological subjects. *d.* 37 Upper Seymour st. London 15 April 1862. *Journal British Archæol. Assoc. xix,* 157-62 (1863); *Proc. Linnæan society* (1862) 90-93; *J. O. Westwood's Thesaurus Entomologicus Oxon.* (1874) pp. xvii-xxiv.

HOPE, GEORGE (2 *son of Robert Hope, tenant farmer).* b. Fenton, East Lothian 2 Jany. 1811; farmer at Fenton Barns to 1875; did much to improve the agriculture of East Lothian, his farm was well-known in America and on the continent; gained a prize of £30 offered by the Anti-Cornlaw league for an essay on *Agriculture and the corn laws* 1842; contributed *Hindrances to agriculture from a tenant farmer's point of view* to Recess Studies, Edited by Sir A. Grant, Edinburgh 1870; contested Haddingtonshire 1865 and East Aberdeenshire 1875. *d.* Broadlands, Berwickshire 1 Dec. 1876. *Memoir of George Hope, By His Daughter* (1881).

HOPE, GEORGE WILLIAM (2 *son of general the hon. Sir Alexander Hope* 1769-1837). *b.* Blackheath 4 July 1808; ed. at Ch. Ch. Ox., B.A. 1828, M.A. 1830; barrister L.I. 28 Jany. 1831; M.P. for Weymouth 1837 to 1841 when unseated on petition; M.P. for Southampton 1842-6; M.P. for New Windsor 1859 to death; under sec. of state for the colonies 8 Sep. 1841 to 8 Jany. 1846. *d.* Luffness, Haddingtonshire 18 Oct. 1863. *I.L.N. vi,* 184 (1845), *portrait.*

HOPE, SIR HENRY *(eld. child of Charles Hope, captain R.N., d.* 10 Sep. 1808). *b.* 1787; entered navy 2 April 1798, captain 24 May 1808, captain of the Endymion May 1813, captured the American frigate President 15 Jany. 1815; C.B. 4 June 1815, K.C.B. 5 July 1855; A.D.C. to the sovereign 1831-46; admiral 20 Jany. 1858. *d.* Holly hill, Hants. 23 Sep. 1863.

HOPE, HENRY THOMAS *(eldest bro. of Alexander J. B. Hope 1820–87).* b. 1808; ed. at Trin. coll. Cam., M.A. 1829; M.P. East Looe 1830–2; M.P. Gloucester 1833–41 and 1847–52; a great patron of architectural art; erected a residence 116 Piccadilly, now known as the Junior Athenæum club; sold Trenant park, Cornwall and purchased Castle Blaney, Ireland; possessed a collection of marble statues, vases and Italian and Dutch pictures. d. 116 Piccadilly, London 4 Dec. 1862, personalty sworn under £300,000, 17 Jany. 1863. *Waagen's Treasures of Art,* ii, 112–24 (1854); *I.L.N. xxxii,* 352 (1858).

HOPE, SIR JAMES *(only son of Sir George Hope, K.C.B. 1767–1818).* b. 3 March 1808; entered royal naval college 1 Aug. 1820; captain 28 June 1838; commander in chief East Indies 25 Jany. 1859 to 8 Feb. 1862, in North America and West Indies 7 Jany. 1864 to 10 Jany. 1867, and at Portsmouth 25 Feb. 1869 to 1 March 1872; admiral 21 Jany. 1870, retired March 1878, admiral of the fleet 15 June 1879; principal naval A.D.C. to the Queen 8 Feb. 1873; C.B. 3 April 1846, K.C.B. 9 Nov. 1860, G.C.B. 28 March 1865; grand cross of legion of honour 1861. d. Carriden house, Bowness, Linlithgowshire 9 June 1881, portrait by Sydney Hodges in painted hall at Greenwich. *D. C. Boulger's History of China, vol. iii, passim* (1884).

HOPE, JAMES. b. 28 May 1803; writer to the signet 1828; deputy keeper of the signet 1828 to death. d. Avenel, Edinburgh 14 Feb. 1882. *Law Times, lxxii,* 305 (1882).

HOPE, SIR JAMES ARCHIBALD *(son of lieut.-col. Erskine Hope).* b. 1785; ensign 26 foot 12 Jany. 1800, captain 1805–14; captain 3 foot guards 25 July 1814, major 10 Jany. 1837 to 1 Nov. 1839, when placed on h.p.; M.G. on the staff in Lower Canada 1841–7; colonel 9 foot 18 Feb. 1848 to death; general 12 June 1859; K.C.B. 2 Jany. 1815, G.C.B. 28 June 1861. d. Balgowan house, Cheltenham 30 Dec. 1871.

HOPE, SIR JOHN, 11 Baronet. b. Pinkie house, Midlothian 13 April 1781; succeeded 26 June 1801; M.P. for Midlothian 1845 to death. d. 104 Gloucester terrace, Hyde park, London 5 June 1853. *bur.* Inveresk churchyard 11 June.

HOPE, JOHN *(eld. son of Charles Hope of Granton 1763–1851).* b. Edinburgh 26 May 1794; admitted advocate 23 Nov. 1816; solicitor general for Scotland Nov. 1822 to 1830; dean of faculty of advocates 17 Dec. 1830 to 1841; lord justice clerk 1841 to death; P.C. 17

HOPE, J. *(Con.)*

April 1844; author of *A letter to Francis Jeffery, Esq., editor of the Edinburgh Review, By an Anti-Reformist* 1811 and two other letters. d. 20 Moray place, Edinburgh 15 June 1858, *bur.* at Ormiston near Tranent; portraits in national gallery of Scotland, in the Parliament house and in Scottish national portrait gallery. *Crombie's Modern Athenians* (1882) 73–4, *portrait.*

HOPE, SACKETT. Entered navy 2 Nov. 1814; present at bombardment of St. Jean d' Acre 1840; captain 4 Nov. 1840; V.A. on half pay 2 April 1866; granted pension for wounds 7 Nov. 1843. d. 9 Widcomb crescent, Bath 25 May 1868.

HOPE, WILLIAM WILLIAMS *(youngest child of John Williams Hope of Amsterdam, banker 1757–1813).* b. 1802; reassumed name of Williams before that of Hope by r.l. 14 July 1826; purchased Rushton hall near Kettering for £140,000 in 1828, sold it for £165,000 Sep. 1854; sheriff of Northamptonshire 1832; lived latterly in Paris, built a large house at 131 Rue St. Dominique, Faubourg St. Germain, played a prominent part in Parisian society, noted for his eccentricity and his collection of diamonds; *found dead* in his bed at 131 Rue St. Dominique, Paris 21 Jany. 1855. *Gronow's Last Recollections* (1866) 129–33; *Boase's Collect. Cornub.* (1890) 1262–4.

HOPE-JOHNSTONE, JOHN JAMES (1 *son of Sir William Hope-Johnstone, G.C.B. 1766–1831).* b. 29 Nov. 1796; M.P. for co. Dumfries 1830–47, and 1857–65; keeper of Lockmaben; claimed dormant earldom of Annandale. d. Raehills, Dumfriesshire 11 July 1876.

HOPE-SCOTT, JAMES ROBERT *(3 son of general the hon. Sir Alexander Hope, G.C.B. 1769–1837).* b. Great Marlow, Bucks. 15 July 1812; ed. at Eton 1825–28 and at Ch. Ch. Ox., B.A. 1832, B.C.L. 1838, D.C.L. 1842; fellow of Merton 13 April 1833; commenced a friendship with W. E. Gladstone 1837 and corresponded with him on "The State in its relation with the Church" 1838; barrister I.T. 26 Jany. 1838, reader 1862; a promoter of Glenalmond college, Perthshire 1841; chancellor of diocese of Salisbury 1840 to 10 Feb. 1845; Q.C. April 1849; paid fees of £20,000 by London and north western railway for 25 bills 1860; received into R.C. church at Farm st. London 6 April 1851; lived at Abbotsford 1853 to death; assumed additional name of Scott 1853; spent winters of 1863–70 at the Villa Madonna Hyères which he bought 1859; visited by Queen Victoria at Abbotsford 22

HOPE-SCOTT, J. R. *(Con.)*

Aug. 1867; built church of Our Lady and St. Andrew at Galashiels at cost of £10,000, opened 2 Feb. 1858; purchased estate of Lochshiel for £24,000, 1855; author of *The bishopric of the United Church of England and Ireland at Jerusalem* 1841, 2 ed. 1842. *d.* 7 Hyde park place, London 29 April 1873. *bur.* in the vaults of St. Margaret's convent, Bruntsfield, Edin. 7 May. *Memoirs of J. R. Hope-Scott, By Robert Ornsby* 2 vols. 1884.

HOPETOUN, JOHN ALEXANDER HOPE, 6 Earl of *(only son of 5 earl of Hopetoun 1803–43).* *b.* Edinburgh 22 March 1831; ed. at Harrow; cornet and sub-lieut. 1 life guards 1851–2; succeeded 8 April 1843; lord lieut. of Linlithgowshire 30 Sep. 1863 to death. *d.* Florence 1 April 1873. *Baily's Mag. xvi,* 159–61 (1869), *portrait.*

HOPKINS, SIR FRANCIS, 2 Baronet *(only son of Sir F. J. Hopkins, M.P.)* *b.* Athboy, co. Meath 28 May 1813; succeeded 19 Sep. 1814; ed. at Eton, matric. from Ch. Ch. Ox. 27 June 1830; knight of the Burning Tower at the Eglinton tournament 28–30 Aug. 1839; sheriff of Westmeath 1855. *d.* Madeira 11 May 1860. *J. H. Nixon's Eglinton tournament p. 6 and plate xiv* (1843).

HOPKINS, REV. GERARD MANLEY *(1 son of Manley Hopkins of Stratford, Essex).* *b.* Essex 1845; ed. at Ball. coll. Ox., exhibitioner 1863–8, B.A. 1868; fellow of royal univ. of Ireland 1885 (which was created by letters patent 22 April 1880), professor of classical literature there 1885 to death; member of Society of Jesus about 1868. *d.* of typhoid fever at University college, Stephen's Green, Dublin 8 June 1889. *bur.* Glasnevin cemet. 11 June. *Freeman's Journal 10 June 1889 p. 5.*

HOPKINS, JOHN BAKER. *b.* London 10 April 1830; began his career as a journalist 1858; editor of *Atlas* paper; joint editor with Henry Hotze of *The Index,* English organ of Confederate States, No. i. 1 May 1862, at the end of the war the paper ceased; London correspondent to *Paris Correspondence Havas* 1864–8; on *Standard* paper Sep. 1865 to 1868; on *Law Journal* 1867; contributed to *Morning Post* and *Vanity Fair* under pseudonym of Esse quam videri; chief leader writer on *London Figaro,* July 1870; author of *The Yogi's daughter, a tragedy* 1854; *Elviré, a reminiscence of Paris* 1855; *Not at all nervous, a farce* 1860; *Making the worst of it, a novel* 2 vols. 1874; *Jack Oakum, a play* 1877; *The true history of Nihilism, a novel* 1880. *d.* 14 Russell road, Holloway 20 Dec. 1888. *Cartoon portraits* (1873) 140–43, *portrait.*

HOPKINS, RIGHT REV. JOHN HENRY. *b.* Dublin 30 Jany. 1792; emigrated to U.S. of A. 1801, an iron manufacturer in Pennsylvania 1810–17 when he failed; admitted to Pittsburgh bar 1817, practised to 1823; R. of Trinity ch. Pittsburgh 1824–31; assistant minister Trinity ch. Boston 1831; professor of divinity in theol. seminary of Massachusetts 1831; first bishop of Vermont 31 Oct. 1832; R. of St. Paul's, Burlington 1832–56; seventh presiding bishop of ch. in U.S. 1865, attended Lambeth conference 1867; D.C.L. Ox. 3 Dec. 1867; author of *Christianity vindicated* 1833; *Essay on Gothic architecture* 1836; *Twelve canzonets, words and music* 1839; *The history of the confessional* 1850, and 30 other books. *d.* Rock Point, Vermont 9 Jany. 1868. *A sketch book of American episcopate. By K. G. Batterson* (1878) 104–106; *Appleton's American Biog. iii,* 254–6 (1887).

HOPKINS, JOHN LARKIN. *b.* Westminster 25 Nov. 1819; chorister boy in the abbey; organist of Rochester cathedral 1841–56; Mus. Bac. Cam. 1842, Mus. Doc. 1857; organist of Trin. coll. Cam. 1856 to death; composed *Five glees and a madrigal* 1842, and *Cathedral Services in C flat and E flat* 1857; author of *A new vocal tutor* 1855. *d.* Ventnor, Isle of Wight 25 April 1873.

HOPKINS, SIR JOHN PAUL *(eld. son of Capt. John Hopkins, killed on board the "Bellerophon" in the battle of the Nile).* Ensign 43 foot 1804; served in the Peninsula and in campaign of 1815; major 98 foot 25 June 1829, retired 18 Oct. 1831; K.H. 1836; governor of military knights of Windsor 1865 to death; knighted at Windsor castle 11 Dec. 1867. *d.* Windsor 9 March 1875.

HOPKINS, WILLIAM *(only son of William Hopkins of Kingston, Derbyshire, farmer).* *b.* Kingston 2 Feb. 1793; farmed without success near Bury St. Edmunds; entered at Peterhouse, Cam. 1822, 7 wrangler 1827, B.A. 1827, M.A. 1830; a private tutor at Cam. from 1827 and known as the senior wrangler maker; esquire bedel of Univ. of Cam. 1827 to death; F.G.S. 18—, Wollaston medallist 1850, president 1851–3; pres. of British Assoc. at Hull 1853; F.R.S. 1 June 1837; author of *Elements of trigonometry* 1833; *An abstract of a memoir on physical geology* 1836. *d.* Parker's Piece, Cambridge 13 Oct. 1866, portrait in hall of Peterhouse. *Quarterly Journal of Geol. Soc. xxiii, pp. xxix-xxxii* (1867); *I.L.N. xxiii,* 225 (1853), *portrait.*

HOPKINS, REV. WILLIAM BONNER. Ed. at Gonville and Caius coll. Cam., second wrangler, second Smith's prizeman and B.A. 1844, M.A. 1847, B.D. 1854; fellow and tutor of St. Cath. hall 1848–54; V. of St. Peter, Wisbech 1854–66; V. of Littleport near Ely 1866 to death; hon. canon of Ely 1865 to death, rural dean 1868; Dean Stanley said he was "the incarnation of sound common sense"; author of *Apostolic missions. Five sermons preached before the university* 1853; *The words spoken by Christ upon the Cross. Seven sermons* 1866; *The position and duty of non-abstainers* 1874, 2 ed. 1875. *d.* Littleport vicarage 24 March 1890.

HOPKINSON, SIR CHARLES *(son of B. Hopkinson of Highbury park, Middlesex). b.* Grantham 1784; ed. at Woolwich; lieut. R.A. 1799; served in Mahratta war 1803; commanded the artillery against the Poligars and at Hyderabad; lieut.-col. 1824; commanded Madras artillery; served in war in Ava 1825; retired through deafness 1829; C.B. 1826; knighted by Wm. iv. at St. James's palace 26 April 1837; author of *Hints to cadets and others proceeding to India* 1850. *d.* 2a King st. St. James's sq. London 17 Dec. 1864.

HOPKINSON, WILLIAM *(son of Rev. Samuel Edmund Hopkinson, R. of Morton-cum-Haconby). b.* 1784; coroner for the Soke of Peterborough; solicitor at Bourn and Stamford; purchased Little Gidding manor, Hunts. 700 acres 1853 and restored the church to the Caroline style in which it had been left by Nicholas Ferrar in 1637. *d.* Stamford 1 Sep. 1865. *Rivington's Ecclesiastical Year-book* (1866) 334.

HOPLEY, EDWARD WILLIAM JOHN. *b.* 1816; painter of domestic subjects and portraits; exhibited 15 pictures at R.A., 26 at B.I. and 7 at Suffolk st. 1844–69; his picture, The birth of a pyramid, shown 1859; invented a trigonometrical system of facial measurement for the use of artists. *d.* 14 South Bank, Regent's Park, London 30 April 1869.

HOPPER, VEN. AUGUSTUS MACDONALD *(son of Walter Carles Hopper of Walworth, co. Durham). b.* 11 Aug. 1816; ed. at Shrewsbury and Trin. coll. Cam., B.A. 1839, M.A. 1842, fellow of St. John's 1841–5; R. of Starston, Norfolk 1845 to death; hon. canon of Norwich 1854–72; archdeacon of Norwich 1868 to death; author of *Two Charges* 1869 and 1870. *d.* Starston rectory 7 Jany. 1878.

HOPPER, CLARENCE *(son of Thomas Hopper of Reading, surgeon d.* 1856*). b.* Granthan, Wilts 17 May 1817; ed. at Reading gram. sch.; palæographer of British Archæol. Assoc. 1862; an expert in deciphering ancient

writings; employed in Record office; edited *London Chronicle of Hen. VII. and Hen. VIII.* 1859, and *Sir F. Drake's service against the Spaniards* 1863, in vols. 4 and 5 of Camden Miscellany; author of *A descriptive account of churchwardens' presentments Stratford-on-Avon* 1867; *A catalogue of books illustrative of Shakespeare* 1868. *d.* Brighton 10 June 1868. *Journal of B.A. Assoc. xxv,* 316 (1869).

HOPPER, THOMAS *(son of Mr. Hopper of Rochester, surveyor). b.* Rochester 6 July 1776; architect and surveyor 40 Connaught ter. London; made alterations at Carlton House, London 1807; surveyor of Essex 40 years; built Arthur's club, St. James's st., Atlas fire office, Cheapside and St. Mary's hospital, Paddington 1843; competed for erection of General Post Office 1820, for rebuilding of Royal Exchange 1839, and for Houses of parliament 1840; published *A letter to viscount Duncannon on competitors for building houses of parliament* 1837; *Designs for the houses of parliament* 1842. *d.* 1 Bayswater Hill, London 11 Aug. 1856.

HOPPUS, REV. JOHN *(only son of Rev. John Hoppus, independent minister, Yardley, Hastings). b.* London 1789; ed. at Rotherham and Univs. of Edin. and Glasgow, M.A. Glasgow 1823, LL.D. 1839; minister of independent chapel, Carter lane, London 1823–5; professor of the philosophy of mind and logic in London Univ. 1829–66; F.R.S. 20 May 1841; author of *An account of Lord Bacon's Novum Organum Scientiarum* 1827; *Sketches on the Continent in 1835* 2 vols. 1836; *The crisis of popular education* 1847 and 12 other books. *d.* 26 Camden st. Camden town, London 29 Jany. 1875. *Congregational Year-book* (1876) 341–3.

HORAN, EDWARD JOHN. *b.* Quebec, Canada 1817; ed. in the Seminary of Quebec, priest 1842, a director of the Seminary; principal of the normal sch. Quebec; bishop of Kingston 1858, resigned; assistant of the pontifical throne; present at Vatican council 1870. *d.* Canada 16 Feb. 1875. *Appleton's American Biog. iii,* 262 (1887).

HORAN, MARY AUSTIN. *b.* Ireland 1820; entered the Convent of Mercy, Dublin; assisted in founding the Institution of Mercy, New York 1846; first mistress of novices in St. Catherine's convent, New York and trainer of the early members; built St. Joseph's Industrial institute for children. *d.* New York city 14 June 1874. *Appleton's American Biog. iii,* 262 (1887).

HORDERN, REV. JOSEPH *(son of Rev. Joseph Hordern of Prestwich, Lancs.)* b. 1794; ed. at Brasenose coll. Ox., B.A. 1816, M.A. 1820; V. of Rostherne, Cheshire 1821–54; R. of Burton Agnes with Harpham, Yorks. 1854 to death; author of *Plain directions for reading to the sick* 1826, 4 ed. 1830; *Sermons* 1830; *The armour of light, sermons* 1851. d. Knutsford, Cheshire 12 Aug. 1876. *F. Ross' Celebrities of the Wolds* (1878) 76.

HORMAN, GEORGE HELIER *(son of Philip Horman of St. Saviour's, Jersey).* b. 1817; practised as a solicitor in Jersey, one of the six advocates of the royal court there 1848; Her Majesty's advocate general for Jersey 23 July 1866 to death; chairman of the Channel islands bank 1858–74. d. The Terrace, St. Heliers, Jersey 29 May 1879.

HORN, HENRY *(son of Frederick Jacob Horn of Mansfield, Nottinghamshire).* b. 23 Sep. 1806; ed. at M.T. school and St. John's coll. Ox., B.A. 1829, M.A. 1832; fellow of Magdalen coll. 1831–4; barrister M.T. 11 Jany. 1833; recorder of Hereford 1847 to death; edited *Woodfall's Practical treatise on law of landlord and tenant,* 7 ed. 1856; with E. T. Hurlstone published *Reports in court of exchequer upon writs of error to exchequer chamber* 2 vols. 1840; while attending the corpse of his father in law J. S. Gowland *shot himself in the head* at Cagebrook near Hereford 29 Nov. 1857. *Hereford Journal* 2 Dec. 1857 p. 5.

HORN, MARION *(dau. of Mr. Horton, manufacturer of silver plate ware).* b. Birmingham 1811; sang small parts in English operas and served as a substitute for Emma Romer; studied under Marco Bordogni in Paris; had a mezzo soprano voice; appeared as Cinderella at Old Park theatre, New York 16 Sep. 1836 and then as Rosina, Amina, and Susanna; sang in operas throughout United States; *(m.* 1839 Charles Edward Horn 1786–1849, the writer of Cherry Ripe 1825, and I know a bank 1830); taught in New York many of best known American singers. d. Morrisania co. Winchester, New York, Jany. 1887. *Ireland's New York Stage,* ii, 176 (1867).

HORN, ROBERT *(youngest son of William Horn, farmer).* b. Bridge of Allan, Stirlingshire 24 May 1810; ed. at Glasgow univ.; passed at Scotch bar 1834; hon. memb. Speculative Soc. Edin.; a commissioner of the board of manufacturers 1866; vice dean of Faculty of Advocates 1874 and dean 1876; helped in preparing *Catalogue of Faculty of Advocate's Library* 1873. d. 7 Randolph crescent, Edinburgh 2 Jany. 1878. *Journ. of Jurisprudence, xxii,* 93–7 (1878).

HORNBLOWER, JANE ELIZABETH *(dau. of William Roscoe 1753–1831 historian).* b. Liverpool 1797; *(m.* Francis Hornblower); author of *Poems* 1820; *Poems* 1821; *Poems* 1843. d. Liverpool 2 Aug. 1853.

HORNBY, EDMUND *(eld. son of Rev. Geoffry Hornby, R. of Winwick, Lancs. d. 1812).* b. 16 June 1773; ed. at Trin. coll. Cam., B.A. 1794, M.A. 1797; barrister I.T. 22 June 1798; chairman of Lancaster court of quarter sessions many years; M.P. for Preston 1812–26; sheriff of Westmoreland 1828. d. Dalton hall near Burton, Westmoreland 18 Nov. 1857.

HORNBY, EDMUND GEORGE *(son of the preceding).* b. 6 Nov. 1799; ed. at Eton and Trin. coll. Cam., M.A. 1820; M.P. for Warrington 1832–5; constable of Lancaster castle. d. Dalton hall 26 or 27 Feb. 1865.

HORNBY, LOUISA *(sister of Edmund Hornby 1773–1857).* b. Winwick 5 April 1788; author of *Bible Stories; Universal Reform; The Full Loom* and other books. d. Winwick 6 Jany. 1873.

HORNBY, SIR PHIPPS *(brother of the preceding).* b. Winwick 27 April 1785; ed. at Sunbury; entered navy 19 May 1797, captain 16 Feb. 1810; as commander of the Volage took part in action off Lissa 1811, gold medal; superintendent of royal naval hospital and victualling yard at Plymouth 1832 to 6 Jany. 1838; superintendent of Woolwich dockyard 6 Jany. 1838 to 16 Dec. 1841; controller general of the coastguard 16 Dec. 1841 to Nov. 1846; commander in chief in the Pacific 1847–50; a lord of the admiralty 28 Feb. to 30 Dec. 1852; admiral 25 June 1858; C.B. 4 June 1815, K.C.B. 6 April 1852, G.C.B. 28 June 1861. d. Little Green near Petersfield 19 March 1867.

HORNBY, ROBERT VERNON ATHERTON. b. Atherton 6 Nov. 1805; author of *Statistical account of Winwick* 1837; *Vale: a poem* 1854. d. Wansfell, Windermere 25 Aug. 1857.

HORNBY, WILLIAM HENRY *(3 son of John Hornby of Blackburn).* b. Blackburn 2 July 1805; founded the Brookhouse cotton mills, Blackburn 1828; first mayor of Blackburn 1851; M.P. Blackburn 1857–69 when he was unseated. d. Pool hall, Nantwich, Cheshire 5 Sep. 1884. *Puseley's Commercial Companion* (1858) 114–5.

HORNCASTLE, JAMES HENRY. b. London 26 May 1801; appeared as first witch in Macbeth at Drury Lane 1820; first appeared at Chestnut street theatre, Philadelphia 28 Jany. 1839;

HORNCASTLE, J. H. *(Con.)*

at National theatre, New York with Louisa Pyne's troupe 1854 and at Broadway theatre 1855; attached to Princess' theatre, London; musician, actor, author and composer; an annuitant on General theatrical fund. *d.* West Malvern 6 May 1869. *Ireland's New York stage, ii, 231, 629 (1867).*

HORNE, JAMES. *b.* 1790; experimented on steam locomotives on roads; F.R.S. 6 Feb. 1834; A.I.C.E. 20 Feb. 1835, auditor 1840; applied warming and ventilating apparatus to halls of the City companies. *d.* London 26 Oct. 1856. *Min. of Proc. Instit. of C.E. xvii,* 102 (1858).

HORNE, LENOX *(younger brother of the succeeding)*. Baritone singer at Surrey theatre under name of Mr. Lennox 1849–51; lecturer at the Polytechnic Institution London; wrote *Two heads are better than one, A farce,* produced at Lyceum theatre Dec. 1854; *The baronet abroad; The tale of a comet. d.* Clapham road, Kennington 20 Nov. 1874.

HORNE, RICHARD HENRY or HENGIST. *b.* London 31 Dec. 1802; ed. at Sandhurst; midshipman in Mexican navy, served in war against Spain 1829; edited the *Monthly Repository* July 1836 to June 1837; sub-comr. to report on employment of children in mines 1843; went with Wm. Howitt to Australia 1852; commander of the gold escort between Ballarat and Melbourne 1852; comr. of crown lands for the gold fields 1853–4; territorial magistrate 1855 &c.; took name of Hengist instead of Henry 1864; returned to England 1869; granted civil list pension of £50, 19 June 1874, and another of £50, 28 April 1880; author of *Cosmo de Medici* 1837, a tragedy; *The death of Marlowe* 1837, a tragedy; *The history of Napoleon* 2 vols. 1841, new ed. 1879; *Orion, an epic poem* 1843, 10 ed. 1874, the 1st, 2nd and 3rd eds. were issued at a farthing; *A new spirit of the age* 2 vols. 1844; *The poor artist* 1850, 2 ed. 1871; *Sithron the Star-stricken* 1883, and 15 other books. *d.* Margate 13 March 1884. *R. H. Horne's Australian facts and prospects* (1859) 1–44; *H. B. Forman's Our living poets* (1871) 427–46; *Athenæum* 22 March 1884 *pp.* 374–5; *I.L.N. lxxxiv,* 301 (1884), *portrait.*

HORNE, REV. THOMAS HARTWELL *(son of William Horne of London, barrister's clerk). b.* Chancery lane, London 20 Oct. 1780; ed. at Christ's hospital 1789–95; barrister's clerk 1796–1806; sec. to Joseph Butterworth, M.P. 1806–9; sub-librarian to Surrey institution 1809–23; C. of Ch. Ch. Newgate st. London

HORNE, REV. T. H. *(Con.)*

1819–25; senior assist. librarian British museum 1824–60; assist. minister at Welbeck chapel, London 1825–33; F.S.A. 1828; F.R.S.L.; B.D. Cambridge 1829, D.D. Univ. of Pennsylvania; preb. of St. Paul's 1831 to death; R. of St. Edmund the King with St. Nicholas Acons, Lombard st. 25 Nov. 1833 to death; author of *An introduction to the critical study and knowledge of the Holy Scriptures* 3 vols. 1818, 11 ed. 1860; *Outlines for the classification of a library submitted to the trustees of the British museum* 1825; *A compendious introduction to the study of the Bible* 1827, 10 ed. 1862; *Manual of parochial psalmody* 1829, 41 ed. 1861 and about 50 other books. *d.* 47 Bloomsbury sq. London 27 Jany. 1862. *G. M. Turpin's The Rev. T. H. Horne* (1862), *portrait; Reminiscences of T. H. Horne, By his daughter S. A. Cheyne* (1862); *Cowtan's Memories of British Museum* (1872) 105–9.

HORNE, SIR WILLIAM (2 *son of Rev. Thomas Horne, schoolmaster at Chiswick). b.* 1774; barrister L.I. 23 June 1798, bencher 6 Nov. 1818; comr. of bankrupts 1806–18; K.C. Nov. 1818; attorney general to queen Adelaide 24 July 1830; solicitor general 26 Nov. 1830 to 23 Nov. 1832, attorney general 26 Nov. 1832 to Feb. 1834; appointed a baron of the Exchequer but declined the office 1834; master in chancery 23 July 1839, resigned 1853; M.P. for Helston 1812–18, for Bletchingley 1831, for Newton, Isle of Wight 1831–2, for Marylebone 12 Dec. 1832 to 29 Dec. 1834; knighted by Wm. IV. at St. James's palace 24 Nov. 1830. *d.* 49 Upper Harley st. London 13 July 1860. *Mrs. Hardcastle's Life of Lord Campbell* (1881) *ii,* 18–41; *Lord Brougham's Life and times, iii,* 341–54, 426–9.

HORNEGOLD or HORNIGOLD, WILLIAM 1797–1867, artist. *See* Hornygold, W. *ante col.* 1523.

HORNER, LEONARD *(youngest son of John Horner of Edinburgh, linen merchant). b.* Edinburgh 17 Jany. 1785; ed. at high sch. and univ. of Edin.; partner in a branch of his father's business in London 1804–17; F.G.S. 1808, sec. 1810, pres. 1846 and 1860; F.R.S. 1813, vice pres. 1857; warden of London Univ. 1827–31; inspector under the Factories act 1833–60; published *Works of Francis Horner* 1843; *Memoirs of Francis Horner* 1848, 2 ed. 2 vols. 1853; a translation of Villari's *History of Savonarola* 1863. *d.* 60 Montague sq. London 5 March 1864. *Quarterly Journal of Geol. soc. xxi,* 30–40 (1865); *Proc. of Royal soc. xiv,* 5–10 (1865); *Macmillan's Mag. x,* 319–26 (1864).

HORRABIN, REV. RICHARD. *b.* Garstang near Preston; ed. at Old Hall Green coll.; chaplain Virginia st. chapel, Ratcliffe highway, London 1815–39, and 1841–54; chaplain St. Mary, Moor fields 1839–41; gave evidence before house of commons on education of lower orders 1816; published *The New Testament, ed. by Marlow J. F. Sidney and revised by the Rev. R. Horrabin* 1818. *d.* Houndsditch, London 13 Dec. 1859. *Gillow's English Catholics iii*, 403–4 (1887).

HORSBURGH, JOHN. *b.* Prestonpans near Edinburgh 1791; apprenticed to Robert Scott the engraver 1805; engraved several plates after J. M. W. Turner for *Scott's Poetical* and *Prose Works* and other publications; engraved several single plates including Prince Charlie reading a despatch and 2 portraits of Sir Walter Scott; undertook gratuitously duties of pastor in Scottish Baptist church. *d.* 16 Buccleuch place, Edinburgh 24 Sep. 1869. *Pastoral addresses of J. Horsburgh with memoir* 1869.

HORSEY, GEORGE (4 *son of Charles Horsey of St. John st., London). b.* 29 Sep. 1819; barrister G.I. 22 May 1850; equity draughtsman and conveyancer; author of *A practical analysis of the Trustees Act* 1850; *The probate and administration act* 1858; *The court of Probate acts* 3 ed. 1859; *Law of property and trustees relief act* 1860. *d.* Colne villa, New Southgate, Middlesex 16 Sep. 1889.

HORSFALL, THOMAS BERRY. *b.* Liverpool 1805; a merchant in Liverpool, mayor of Liverpool 1847–48; M.P. Derby 8 July 1852, unseated 9 March 1853; M.P. Liverpool 9 July 1853 to Nov. 1868; president Liverpool chamber of commerce on its foundation 1849. *d.* Torquay 22 Dec. 1878.

HORSFIELD, THOMAS. *b.* Bethlehem, Pennsylvania 12 May 1773; ed. Univ. of Pennsylvania, M.D. 1798; studied natural history in Java 1799–1819; in service of Dutch government in Java and Sumatra to 1811 and of H.E.I.Co. 1811–20; keeper of museum, India House, London 1820 to death; F.L.S. 1820; F.R.S. 1828; author of *Zoological Researches in Java* 1824; *Descriptive catalogue of Lepidoptera in the H.E.I.C. museum*, 2 parts 1828–9 and other books. *d.* Chalcott villas, Camden town, London 24 July 1859. *Proc. of Royal Society x*, 19–21 (1860); *Proc. Linnean Soc.* (1859–60) 25–6.

HORSFORD, SIR ALFRED HASTINGS (*son of general George Horsford, d.* 1840). *b.* Bath 3 April 1818; 2 lieut. rifle brigade 12 July

HORSFORD, SIR A. H. (*Con.*)
1833, lieut.-col. 9 March 1855 to 1 Jany. 1868, col. commandant 2 battalion 21 Nov. 1880 to death; served in Kaffir wars 1847–8 and 1852–3, Crimean war 1854–5 and Indian mutiny 1857–8; D.A.G. at horse guards 1860–6; brigadier general at Aldershot 1866–9; military sec. at Horse Guards 1874–80; col. 79 foot 17 March 1876, col. 14 foot 1 Jany. 1879 to death; general 1 Oct. 1877; placed on retired list 3 April 1883; C.B. 5 July 1855, K.C.B. 8 May 1860, G.C.B. 29 May 1875. *d.* Munlochy near Inverness 13 Sep. 1885. *bur.* Kensal Green cemetery 19 Sep.

HORSFORD, SIR ROBERT MARSH (*eld. son of Paul Horsford, chief justice of Antigua, d.* 1850). *b.* Boswell court, Lincoln's inn, London 1798; ed. at Winchester; matric. from Ex. coll. Ox. 7 Dec. 1816; barrister M.T. 17 May 1822; settled in island of Antigua, solicitor general there 1825–46, attorney general 1846 to Nov. 1847, chief justice 19 Nov. 1847, retired Aug. 1856; knighted at Buckingham palace 25 Jany. 1841; C.B. 15 Nov. 1852. *d.* 11 Delamere terrace, Westbourne park, London 23 May 1875.

HORSLEY, CHARLES EDWARD (*son of the succeeding*). *b.* 24 Queen's buildings, Knightsbridge, London 16 Dec. 1822; pupil of Moscheles, Hauptmann, Spohr and Mendelssohn; teacher of music in London 1846; organist of St. John's, Notting hill 19 Sep. 1853 to June 1857; went to Melbourne 1868, then to New York 1872, choir master St. John's chapel 1872 to death; composed for Liverpool Philharmonic Soc. two oratorios *David* 1849 and *Joseph* 1852; wrote the cantata *Comus* 1854; produced oratorio *Gideon* at Glasgow musical festival 1860; wrote an ode *Euterpe* for opening of Melbourne town hall 1870, and about 35 other pieces; author of *A text book of harmony* 1876. *d.* New York city 28 Feb. 1876.

HORSLEY, WILLIAM H. *b.* London 15 Nov. 1774; articled to Theodore Smith, pianist 1790–4; organist of Ely chapel, Holborn 1794–8; member of Royal Soc. of Musicians 15 June 1797; founded with J. W. Callcott the Concentores Sodales a club for encouragement of glee and canon writing, June 1798 which existed till 1847; assistant organist Asylum for female orphans about 1798, organist 1802–54; Mus. Bac. Oxford 18 June 1800; organist at Belgrave chapel, Halkin st. 1812–37 and at the Charterhouse 1838; had few equals as a composer of glees; published *Five collections of glees* 1801–27; *An introduc-*

HORSLEY, W. H. *(Con.)*

tion to the study of practical harmony and modulation 1847; *The musical treasury* 1853 and about 60 pieces of music; his best known glees were *By Celia's Arbour* 1807 and *Mine be a cot*. *d.* 1 High row, Kensington, London 12 June 1858. *G.M. lxxxiii*, 82, 565 (1813); *Grove's Dictionary of music, i,* 753-4 (1879).

HORSMAN, CHARLOTTE *(dau. of Mr. Gardiner)*. *b.* Dublin 1827; *(m.* 1847 Charles Horsman, actor *b.* Welchpool, Montgomeryshire 21 Oct. 1825); a prominent actress at Lyceum, Strand, Sadler's Wells and Holborn theatres; a member of the Pygmalion and Galatea co.; her last appearance was at Bradford as Meg Merrilies 14 May 1877. *d.* 2 William st. Bradford 4 June 1878. *bur.* Undercliffe cemet. 7 June. *The Era* 9 *June* 1878 *p.* 12.

HORSMAN, EDWARD *(son of William Horsman d.* 22 *March* 1845 *aged* 86). *b.* 8 Feb. 1807; ed. at Rugby and Trin. coll. Cam.; admitted advocate at Scottish bar 1832; M.P. Cockermouth Feb. 1836 to 1 July 1852; M.P. Stroud 29 June 1853 to Nov. 1868; M.P. Liskeard 11 May 1869 to death; fought a duel at Wormwood Scrubbs with James Bradshaw, M.P. 1840; comr. of Church Inquiry in Scotland; a lord of the Treasury June to Sep. 1841; chief sec. of state for Ireland March 1855, resigned May 1857; P.C. 10 March 1855; on 13 March 1866 Bright described Horsman as retiring "into his political cave of Adullam," hence his party became known as "the cave"; author of *Five speeches on ecclesiastical affairs* 1849. *d.* Biarritz 30 Nov. 1876. *H. D. Traill's The new Lucian* (1884) 183-401; *I.L.N. xxx,* 478 (1857), *portrait; Graphic xiv,* 592, 595 (1876), *portrait*.

HORT, SIR JOSIAH WILLIAM, 2 Baronet (1 *son of Sir John Hort d.* 1807). *b.* 6 July 1791; ed. at Trin. coll. Cam., M.A. 1812; succeeded 23 Oct. 1807; M.P. co. Kildare 1831-2. *d.* Ebury st. Eaton square, London 24 Aug. 1876.

HORT, SIR JOHN JOSIAH, 3 Baronet (1 *son of the preceding)*. *b.* Dublin 14 Jany. 1824; ensign 61 foot 20 Nov. 1840; captain 4 foot 27 May 1847, lieut.-col. 1 Feb. 1856 to 10 Nov. 1856 when placed on h.p.; lieut.-col. 36 foot 15 May 1857 to 28 Dec. 1866; lieut.-col. 44 foot 28 Dec. 1866 to 10 Nov. 1869 when placed on h.p.; lieut.-col. brigade depot 1 April 1873; L.G. 10 Aug. 1878; C.B. 24 May 1873; knight of Malta. *d.* 35 Merrion sq. east, Dublin 5 Jany. 1882. *The case of maltreatment by Capt. Hort, fourth King's own regiment, of lieut. A. V. D. Harris. Plymouth* 1851.

HORT, SIR WILLIAM FITZMAURICE JOSIAH, 4 Baronet *(brother of the preceding)*. *b.* Boulogne-sur-mer 28 Jany. 1827; ed. at R.M.A. Woolwich; called to bar in Ireland 1852; paid resident magistrate at Kilkenny 1858, at Tuam co. Galway 1858-83. *d.* St. Canice's cottage, Kilkenny 18 Sep. 1887.

HORWITZ, BERNARD. *b.* Grand Duchy of Mecklenburg 1807; learnt chess from Mendheim at Berlin; one of the 7 great Berlin players known as the Pleiades; spent sometime at Hamburg; lived in England about 1845 to death; took part in nearly all the tournaments held in England before 1862; author of *Chess studies and end-games systematically arranged* 1884; author with J. Kling of *Chess Studies* 1851 three editions, and of a periodical called *The Chess Player* 4 vols. 1851-3. *d.* 27 Parkhurst road, Bowes Park, London 29 Aug. 1885. *I.L.N. viii,* 100 (1846), *portrait; Chess Monthly, vii,* 8; *Fortnightly Review, Dec.* 1886 *p.* 754.

HORWOOD, ALFRED JOHN *(younger son of Thomas Horwood of the Middle Temple, London, conveyancer)*. *b.* Camberwell, Surrey 1821; barrister M.T. 22 Nov. 1844; inspector under royal commission on historical manuscripts 1869 to death; edited *Year books of the reign of Edward the First. Rolls Series* 1858; *A catalogue of the manuscripts belonging to Gray's inn* 1869; *A common place book of John Milton* 1876. *d.* 1 New Court, Temple, London 7 July 1881. *Law Times, lxxi,* 255 (1881).

HOSACK, JOHN (3 *son of John R. Hosack of Glenaher, Dumfriesshire)*. *b.* Glenaher 1809; barrister M.T. 29 Jany. 1841, bencher 22 April 1875; magistrate at Clerkenwell police court 5 June 1877 to death; author of *A treatise on the conflict of laws of England and Scotland* 1847; *The rights of British and neutral commerce as affected by recent royal declarations and orders in council* 1854; *Mary Queen of Scots and her accusers, London* 1869, 2 ed. 2 vols. *Edin.* 1870-4 and other books. *d.* 172 Finborough road, West Brompton, London 3 Nov. 1887. *bur.* Lytham, Lancs. 8 Nov.

HOSKEN, JAMES *(son of James Hosken, gunner in navy, d. Penryn* 20 *June* 1848 *aged* 92). *b.* Plymouth 6 Dec. 1798; midshipman R.N. 1810, lieut. 1828; captain of the Great Western specially built for ocean steam navigation 1837, she left Bristol 8 April 1838 and reached New York 23 April, made 64 voyages in Great Western; captain of the Great Britain 1844, made 3 or 4 trips to New York in her, she was stranded in Dundrum bay 22 Sep. 1846; harbour master, postmaster and chief

HOSKEN, J. *(Con.)*

magistrate at Labuan 1848–9 ; commanded the Belle-Isle hospital ship in the Baltic 1854– 5 ; captain R.N. 15 June 1857, retired 8 Jany. 1868, retired V.A. 2 Aug. 1879. *d.* 32 Highfield road, Ilfracombe 2 ·Jany. 1885. *Autobiographical Sketch. Edited by his widow. Privately printed 1889.*

HOSKING, WILLIAM *(eld. son of John Hosking, woollen manufacturer).* b. Buckfastleigh, Devon 26 Nov. 1800 ; apprenticed to a builder and surveyor in New South Wales ; articled to W. Jenkins of Red Lion square, London, architect 1820–23 ; exhibited 1 drawing at R.A. and 9 at Suffolk st. 1825–9 ; F.S.A. 11 Feb. 1830 ; F.I.B.A. 16 Jany. 1835, member of council 1842–3 ; engineer of Birmingham, Bristol and Thames Junction railway 1834 ; superintended formation of Abney Park cemetery, Stoke Newington, London 30 acres 1839–40 ; professor of Art of construction in King's coll. London 1840, and of Principles and practice of architecture 1841 to death ; an official referee under Metropolitan building act 3 Sep. 1844 to 1855 ; published *Preliminary essay on bridges* 1841, 2 ed. 1842 ; *Theory, practice and architecture of bridges* 1842 ; *Some observations upon the recent addition of a reading room to the British museum* 1858, he claimed to have suggested the Circular reading room for which Panizzi has the credit. *d.* 23 Woburn sq. London 2 Aug. 1861. *G. Pycroft's Art in Devonshire* (1883) 70 ; *The Builder* 17 *Aug.* 1861 *p.* 560.

HOSKINS, SAMUEL ELLIOTT *(son of Samuel Hoskins of Guernsey).* b. Guernsey Feb. 1799 ; ed. at Guy's and St. Thomas's hospitals 1818– 20 ; L.S.A. 1821 ; M.R.C.S. 1822 ; L.R.C.P. 1834, F.R.C.P. 1859 ; physician in Guernsey 1827–59 ; F.R.S. 25 May 1843 ; author of *A Stethoscopic Chart. Guernsey* 1830 ; *Home resorts for invalids in the climate of Guernsey* 1852 ; *Louis le Grand or Fontainebleau and Versailles, a comedy in three acts* 1852 ; *Charles the Second in the Channel Islands* 2 vols. 1854 ; and other books. *d.* York place, Candie road, Guernsey 12 Oct. 1888. *Lancet* 20 *Oct.* 1888 *p.* 797, 27 *Oct. p.* 845.

HOSKINS, WILLIAM *(3 son of Abraham Hoskins of Newton park, Derbyshire).* b. Norton, Derbyshire 1816 ; ed. at Camb. univ. ; ꜱ actor in the provinces 1834 ; member of Phelps's company at Sadler's Wells 1844 ; then at Olympic ; went to Australia 1856, played at Queen's theatre, Melbourne ; manager Ballarat theatre 1858, of Theatre royal, Melbourne 1863, and of Haymarket, Melbourne ; rebuilt Theatre Royal, Christ Church, New Zealand ;

HOSKINS, W. *(Con.)*

teacher of elocution, Melbourne 1884 to death ; *(m.* (1) 1850 Julia Harland, actress *d.* New Zealand ; *m.* (2) Florence Colville, actress, she *d.* about 1881 ; *m.* (3) Miss Bowman). *d.* Melbourne 28 Sep. 1886. *Tallis' Drawing-room Table book, Parts* 8 *and* 12, *two portraits ; Theatrical Times ii,* 297 (1847), *portrait ; Era* 13 *Oct.* 1886 *p.* 9.

HOSKYNS, CHANDOS WREN *(2 son of Sir Hungerford Hoskyns, 7 baronet* 1776–1862). b. Hereford 15 Feb. 1812 ; ed. at Shrewsbury and Balliol coll. Ox., B.A. 1834 ; barrister I.T. 4 May 1838 ; assumed additional surname of Wren by royal license 15 April 1837 ; a co-editor of Journal of R. Agricultural Soc. ; M.P. for Hereford 1869–74 ; contributed *Anomalies of Agriculture* and many other papers to *Agricultural Gazette* 1844, &c. ; author of *Talpa, or the chronicles of a clay farm* 1852, 4 ed. 1857 ; *Occasional Essays* 1866 ; *Systems of land tenure in various countries* 1870. *d.* 41 Eccleston sq. London 28 Nov. 1876. *Journal of the Royal Agricultural Soc.* 1877 *p. xli ; Agricultural Gazette* 4 *Dec.* 1876 *p.* 544.

HOTHAM, BEAUMONT HOTHAM, 3 Baron *(elder son of Beaumont Hotham* 1768–99, *captain Coldstream guards).* b. Lullingstone castle, Dartford, Kent 9 Aug. 1794 ; ed. at Westminster ; ensign Coldstream guards 27 June 1810, lieut. 25 Dec. 1813 to 14 Oct. 1819 when placed on h.p. ; succeeded his grandfather 4 March 1814 ; served in the Peninsula 1812–14 ; general 12 Jany. 1865 ; M.P. Leominster 1820–41 ; M.P. East Yorkshire 1841–68. *d.* Sand Hutton near York 13 Dec. 1870. *bur.* in family vault at South Dalton 20 Dec., personalty sworn under £500,000, 21 Jany. 1871.

HOTHAM, SIR CHARLES *(1 son of Hon. and Rev. Frederick Hotham* 1774–1854, *R. of Dennington, Suffolk).* b. Dennington 14 Jany. 1806 ; entered navy 6 Nov. 1818, captain 28 June 1833 ; served in South America 1845–6 ; K.C.B. 9 March 1846 ; commander in chief West coast of Africa 1846–9 ; min. plenipo. to Argentine Confederation 17 April 1852 ; lieut. governor of colony of Victoria 6 Dec. 1853, governor in chief there 1 Feb. 1855 to death. *d.* Toorak, Melbourne 31 Dec. 1855.

HOTHAM, WILLIAM *(eld. child of lieut.-col. George Hotham* 1770–1823). b. 30 July 1794 ; entered navy June 1803, commanded a flotilla in the river Po 1813–14 ; captain 4 April 1825 ; K.H. 25 Jany. 1836 ; retired on half pay 1 Oct. 1846 ; retired admiral 30 Nov. 1863. *d.* Clifton, York 22 Feb. 1873.

HOTTEN, JOHN CAMDEN, originally named John William Hotten (*son of Wm. Hotten of Clerkenwell, London, carpenter*). *b.* 45 St. John's sq. Clerkenwell 12 Sep. 1832; placed with John Petheram, bookseller 71 Chancery lane 1846; in the United States 1848–56; a bookseller and publisher at 151B Piccadilly, London 1856 to death, and at 74–5 Piccadilly 1863 to death; published *Dictionary of modern slang, cant and vulgar words* 1859; A. C. Swinburne's *Poems and ballads* 1866 which Moxon had withdrawn from circulation; the first to introduce into England the works of J. R. Lowell, Artemus Ward, O. W. Holmes, C. G. Leland and Bret Harte 1864 &c. *d.* 4 Maitland park villas, Haverstock hill, Hampstead 14 June 1873. *bur.* Highgate cemet. 21 June. *Bookseller* 31 *Aug.* 1873 *pp.* 491–3; *Boase and Courtney's Bibl. Cornub.* 255, 1237.

HOUGH, REV. GEORGE. *b.* London 1797; ordained 1824; studied Hebrew under Dr. Wolff 1836; C. of Earl's Heaton, Dewsbury 1827–8; V. of South Crosland near Huddersfield 1829 to death; originator and sec. of the Almondbury clerical soc. 1828–78; gave considerable sums to church works and charities; author of *Annual new year addresses to the parishioners of Almondbury* 1840–79; *A brief exposition of the book of Revelation. Huddersfield* 1878. *d.* South Crosland 6 June 1879. *Hulbert's Annals of Almondbury* (1882) 76, 306–12, 506–7.

HOUGH, WILLIAM. Entered Bengal army 1805; captain 48 Bengal N.I. to 1 Oct. 1840 when invalided; lieut. col. July 1864; author of *Case book of European and native courts martial. Calcutta* 1821; *On the E.I.Co.'s mutiny acts* 1838; *Chronological exposition of opinions of writers on military law* 1839; *A narrative of the army of the Indies in the expedition to Afghanistan* 1841; *Political and military events in British India* 2 vols. 1853. *d.* Tenterden st. Hanover sq. London 3 Jany. 1865 aged 75.

HOUGHTON, RICHARD MONCKTON MILNES, 1 Baron (*only son of Robert Pemberton Milnes, M.P.* 1784–1858). *b.* London 19 June 1809; ed. at Trin. coll. Cam., M.A. 1831, hon. fellow of his coll. April 1876; M.P. Pontefract 1837–63; D.C.L. Ox. 1854; cr. Baron Houghton of Great Houghton, Yorks. 20 Aug. 1863; F.R.S. 10 Dec. 1868; president Social Science congress, Aug. 1873; hon. LL.D. Edin. 23 April 1878; a trustee of British museum 1881; author of *Memorials of a tour in Greece* 1834; *Memorials of many scenes* 1840; *Poems legendary and historical* 1844; *Palm leaves* 1844; *Monographs, personal and social*

HOUGHTON, 1 Baron. (*Con.*)

1873. *d.* Vichy, France 11 Aug. 1885. *Reid's Life and letters of lord Houghton* 2 vols. 1890, 2 portraits; *Poetical works of lord Houghton* 2 vols. 1876, *portrait.*

HOUGHTON, ARTHUR BOYD (4 *son of Capt. M. Houghton of H.E.I.C. service*). *b.* 1836; illustrator of the *Graphic* and *Fun;* exhibited 10 pictures at R.A., 4 at B.I., and 3 at Suffolk st. 1861–72; associate of Soc. of painters in water colours 1871; illustrated *Dalziel's Arabian Nights* 1864–5; *Adventures of Don Quixote* 1866 and many other works; author of *The gods on peace and war, as applicable to the eastern struggle* 1877. *d.* 162 King Henry's road, South Hampstead, London 23 Nov. 1875. *Redgrave's Dictionary of artists* (1878) 225; *Art Journal* 1876 *p.* 47.

HOUGHTON, REV. HENRY HALL (3 *son of Jeremiah Houghton*). *b.* Dublin 10 Dec. 1823; ed. at Sherborne and at Pemb. coll. Ox., scholar 1841–5, B.A. 1845, M.A. 1848; clerk of Magdalen coll. 1847–68; C. of St. Peter's, Cheltenham 1849–52; with his uncle rev. John Hall, canon of Bristol, founded at Oxford the Canon Hall and Hall-Houghton prizes for knowledge of Greek Testament, Septuagint and Syriac versions 1868–71 at cost of £11,000; on death of his uncle took name of Hall 1871; gave Church Missionary soc. £4,500 for instruction of native young men in the scriptures; gave hospital for sick Jews at Jerusalem £3,000. *d.* Melmerby hall, Cumberland 4 Sep. 1889. *Record* 20 *Sept.* 1889 *p.* 922.

HOUGHTON, REV. WILLIAM (*son of Thomas Houghton, governor of Preston house of correction*). *b.* Preston 17 May 1812; C. of St. Sennen and St. Levan, Cornwall 1848–65; V. of Manaccan, Cornwall 1865 to death; author of *Calvinism scripturally examined* 1836; *Rationalism in the church of England* 1863 and 4 other books. *d.* Manaccan Vicarage 25 Dec. 1870. *Boase and Courtney's Bibl. Cornub.* i, 256.

HOULDSWORTH, JOHN. *b.* Whitehall, Glasgow 12 April 1807; one of the founders of the Coltness and Dalmellington iron works in Lanarkshire and Ayrshire about 1835; senior partner of various establishments for machine making, iron founding, cotton spinning and weaving; the last provost of burgh of Anderston before it was incorporated with Glasgow; A.I.C.E. 1844. *d.* Bath st. Glasgow 18 Oct. 1859. *Minutes of proc. of Instit. of C.E., xix,* 189 (1860).

HOULDSWORTH, THOMAS (2 *son of Henry Houldsworth of Gonalston, Notts.*) *b.* 13 Sep. 1771; a merchant and cotton spinner at Manchester and Pontefract; M.P. Pontefract 1818–30; M.P. Newton, Lancs. 1830–2; M.P. North Notts. 1832–52. *d.* Portland place, Manchester 1 Sep. 1852.

HOULSTON, THOMAS *(son of Edward Houlston of Wellington, Salop, printer).* *b.* 1804; traveller for his father 1821–35; bookseller at 154 Strand, London 1835–44; partner with John Stoneman at 65 Paternoster row 1844 to 5 April 1856 when the latter died aged 64; partner with Henry Wright at 65 Paternoster row 1857 to death. *d.* Ryde, Isle of Wight 28 Aug. 1869. *Bookseller, Nov.* 1869 *p.* 938; *Reg. and Mag. of Biog. Oct.* 1869 *p.* 204.

HOULTON, SIR GEORGE *(youngest son of Joseph Houlton of Farley castle near Bath, d.* 1806). *b.* Carmarthen 1791; ensign 43 foot 20 Nov. 1806, captain 2 Nov. 1815 to 25 March 1817 when placed on h.p.; received war medal and 10 clasps for service in Peninsular war 1808–14; ensign of yeomen of the guard 25 Sep. 1835 to death; knighted 1835 or 1838, but name never in *London Gazette. d.* Farley castle 16 Sep. 1862.

HOULTON, JOSEPH. *b.* 1789; M.R.C.S. 1811, M.D. Erlangen 1840; surgeon East Norfolk militia; practised at Saffron Walden 1817, at Lisson grove, London 1823; professor of botany to Medical botanical society; with J. Davies edited *The London medical and surgical journal* 1828; translated F. Magendie's *Formulary for preparation of new remedies* 1828. *d.* 12 Blomfield st. Westbourne terrace, London 14 Jany. 1861.

HOUSMAN, FRANCIS *(son of William Housman of St. John's Wood, London).* *b.* London 3 Jany. 1829; ed. at Merchant Taylor's sch. 1838 &c.; barrister L.I. 7 June 1852; recorder of Rangoon 1871 to death; author of *A selection of precedents in conveyancing* 1861. *d.* Calcutta 19 July 1873.

HOUSTON, JOHN ADAM. *b.* Gwydir castle near Llanwrst, Wales 25 Dec. 1812; ed. at Edin. sch. of design; studied in Paris and Germany; a portrait painter in London some years; exhibited 45 pictures at R.A., 21 at B.I. and 3 at Suffolk st. 1840–8; resided in Edin. from 1841 to 1858 when he began contributing to the Scottish academy; returned to London 1858; exhibited *Gallantry, London* 1859; *Lights and shadows of the wayside* 1861; *Prospero and Miranda, Edin.* 1865. *d.* 10 Upper Phillimore place, Kensington 2 Dec. 1884. *Art Journal* (1869) 69–71, 127.

HOUSTON, REV. THOMAS. *b.* Donegore 1803; teacher in a sch. at Leyhmore near Ballymena 1818; ed. at Academical instit. Belfast 1819; reformed presbyterian minister Knockbraken 8 April 1828 to death; took part in the Arian separation from the synod of Ulster; professor of theology in Reformed presbyterian Theological hall, Belfast 1855 to death; went to U.S. America 1856 where he took a D.D. degree; edited *The Covenanter* 1830; author of *A practical treatise on christian baptism, Paisley* 1853; *The dominion and glory of the Redeemer. Discourses* 1880 and 7 other books. *d.* Royal hospital, Belfast 27 March 1882. *bur.* Knockbraken 30 March. *Belfast News-Letter 28 March* 1882 *p.* 5.

HOUSTOUN, SIR ROBERT (5 *son of colonel Andrew Houstoun).* *b.* Jordan hill, co. Renfrew 1780; entered Bengal army 1794 and served 25 years; col. 9 regiment light cavalry 1 May 1824 to 1858; col. 4 European light cavalry 1858 to death; governor of Addiscombe coll. 10 years; general 20 June 1854; K.C.B. 10 March 1837. *d.* Torquay 5 April 1862.

HOUSTOUN, WALLACE *(son of the preceding).* *b.* 1811; entered navy 2 Dec. 1824; captain 23 July 1847; R.A. 5 May 1865, retired 1 April 1870; retired admiral 1 Aug. 1877. *d.* 42 Eaton sq. London 17 May 1891.

HOVELL, WILLIAM HILTON. *b.* Yarmouth 26 April 1786; a marine trader on coasts of Australia and New Zealand 1813–19; farmer at Narellan 1819; accompanied Hamilton Hume in his overland journey from Sydney to Port Philip 1824–5; one of the first settlers at Western Port 1826; resided at Goulburn from 1829; author of *Reply to " A brief statement in connection with an expedition from Lake George to Port Philip. By Hamilton Hume." Sydney* 1855. *d.* Sydney 1876. *Heaton's Australian Dict. of Dates* (1879) 97.

HOWARD DE-WALDEN, CHARLES AUGUSTUS ELLIS, 6 Baron *(elder son of C. Rose Ellis, 1 Baron Seaford 1771–1845).* *b.* London 5 June 1799; ed. at Eton 1811–14; succeeded his maternal great grandfather as 6 Baron 8 July 1803, claim admitted 1806; under sec. of state for foreign affairs 5 July 1824; envoy extraord. and min. plenipo. at Stockholm 2 Oct. 1832, at Lisbon 22 Nov. 1833 and at Brussels 10 Dec. 1846 to death; G.C.B. 19 July 1838; K.T.S. 1841; succeeded as 2 Baron Seaford 1 July 1845. *d.* Lesve chateau, Namur, Belgium 29 Aug. 1868.

HOWARD, OF GLOSSOP, EDWARD GEORGE FITZALAN HOWARD, 1 Baron (2 *son of 16*

HOWARD OF GLOSSOP, 1 Baron *(Con.)*
Duke of Norfolk 1791–1856). *b.* 21 St. James's
sq. London 20 Jany. 1818; ed. at Trin. coll.
Cam.; M.P. Horsham, Sep. 1848 to 1 July
1852; M.P. Arundel, July 1852 to Dec. 1868
when the borough was disfranchised; P.C. 8
July 1846; vice chamberlain 8 July 1846 to
Feb. 1852; had charge of the Norfolk estates
as trustee of his nephew 1861–8 and acted as
deputy earl marshal of England 4 Feb. 1861
to Dec. 1868; cr. baron Howard of Glossop 9
Dec. 1869; chairman of Catholic poor school
committee 1869–77. *d.* 19 Rutland gate,
London 1 Dec. 1883. *bur.* in R.C. church of
St. Charles of Borromeo at Hadfield near
Glossop 11 Dec. *Gillow's English Catholics, iii,*
422–6 (1887).

HOWARD, CHARLES WENTWORTH GEORGE (5
son of 6 Earl of Carlisle 1773–1848). *b.* Chiswick, Middlesex 27 March 1814; ed. at Eton
and Trin. coll. Cam., M.A. 1836; M.P. for
East Cumberland, July 1840 to death. *d.*
Holker house, Lancs. 11 April 1879.

HOWARD, EDWARD HENRY (3 *son of Very
Rev. H. E. J. Howard* 1795–1868). *b.* 7 June
1832; ed. at Eton 1844; entered navy 21
June 1845; served in the Baltic 1855; captain
16 Feb. 1864; naval attaché at maritime
courts of Europe, Sep. 1874 to Dec. 1876;
A.D.C. to the queen 1878–9; V.P. Ordnance
committee 1881–4; V.A. 26 Nov. 1885, retired
29 Nov. 1889. *d.* 16 Granville park, Lewisham, Kent 18 Jany. 1890. *Pictorial World,
xvi,* 147, 165 (1890), *portrait.*

HOWARD, FRANK *(son of Henry Howard* 1769–
1847, *R.A., professor of painting to R.A.) b.*
Poland st. London 1805; ed. at Ely; pupil
and assistant to Sir Thomas Lawrence, P.R.A.;
consulting designer and modellist to Storr and
Mortimer of London, silversmiths; exhibited
43 paintings at R.A., 26 at B.I. and 9 at
Suffolk st. 1824–46; obtained prize for "Una
coming to seek the assistance of Gloriana,"
Westminster hall competition 1843; removed
to Liverpool about 1847; published *The spirit
of the plays of Shakspeare, a series of outline
plates* 5 *vols.* 1827–33; author of *The sketcher's
manual* 1837, 7 ed. 1860; *The science of drawing* 1839–40. *d.* Liverpool 29 June 1866.

HOWARD, GREVILLE THEOPHILUS (2 *son of
17 Earl of Suffolk and Berkshire* 1804–76). *b.*
22 Dec. 1836; matric. from Ch. Ch. Ox. 30
May 1855; barrister L.I. 17 Nov. 1863;
commissioner in lunacy 17 June 1873 to 1877.
d. Castle Rising near Lynn, Norfolk 28 July
1880.

HOWARD, HENRY. *b.* 25 July 1802; ed. at
Harrow; M.P. Steyning 1824–6; M.P. Shoreham 1826–32; sheriff of Cumberland 1834.
d. Thornbury castle, Gloucester 7 Jany. 1875.

HOWARD, VERY REV. HENRY EDWARD JOHN
(youngest child of 5 Earl of Carlisle 1748–1825).
b. Castle Howard, Yorkshire 14 Dec. 1795;
ed. at Eton 1805–11 and Ch. Ch. Ox., B.A.
1818, M.A. 1822, B.D. 1834, D.D. 1838; V.
of Stainton, Yorks. 5 July 1820; succentor
of York cath. with stall of Holme annexed 27
Nov. 1822; R. of Slingsby 1823–33; V. of
Sutton in the Forest 1824–33; dean of Lichfield with R. of Tattenhill, Staffs. annexed 27
Nov. 1833 to death; R. of Donington, Salop
11 Feb. 1834 to death; author of *Translations
from Claudian* 1823; *The books of Genesis,
Exodus, Leviticus, Numbers and Deuteronomy
according to the lxx, translated with notes* 3 *vols.*
1855–7 and 5 other books. *d.* Donington
rectory 8 Oct. 1868. *Guardian* 14 *Oct.* 1868
p. 1148; *Burke's Portrait gallery, ii,* 99 (1833),
portrait.

HOWARD, HENRY THOMAS (2 *son of 16 earl of
Suffolk* 1776–1851). *b.* 16 Jany. 1808; M.P.
Cricklade, Wilts. 1841–7. *d.* Beauchamp near
Gloucester 29 Jany. 1851.

HOWARD, JAMES (2 *son of John Howard* 1790–
1878). *b.* Bedford 16 Oct. 1821; head of firm
of James and Frederick Howard, makers of
agricultural instruments at Britannia works,
Bedford 1851; member of R. Agric. Soc., on
council; member of Farmers' club; an originator and first president of Farmers' Alliance
1879; a promoter and director of Agricultural
hall, London 1861; M.P. Bedford 1868–74;
M.P. Bedfordshire 1880–5; mayor of Bedford
1863 and 1864; sheriff of Bedfordshire 1878;
champion of Tenant's rights 1873; farmed
Clapham farm estate, Bedford 1862; took out
upwards of 60 patents for agricultural
machinery; author of *Steam cultivation, its
history* 1862; *Agricultural implement manufacture, its rise and progress* 1879 and 20 other
works. *d.* Midland hotel, St. Pancras, London
25 Jany. 1889. *bur.* Clapham, Beds. 30 Jany.
Agricultural Gazette 28 *Jany.,* 4 *Feb.* 1889;
London Figaro 2 *Feb.* 1889 *p.* 10, *portrait;
Farmers' Mag. xviii,* 1–7 (1860), *portrait.*

HOWARD, JAMES KENNETH (4 *son of 16 earl of
Suffolk* 1776–1851). *b.* 5 March 1814; précis
writer to viscount Palmerston 1835–40 and
private sec. to him 6 Jany. 1840 to 2 Sep.
1841; M.P. Malmesbury 1841–52; commissioner of woods and forests March 1855 to
death. *d.* Hajelby near Newbury 7 Jany. 1882.

HOWARD, JOHN (*son of John Moore Howard, farmer*). *b.* Bedford 1790; builder and land speculator; erected the Britannia foundry for manufacture of agricultural implements about 1838; invented an improved plough 1839; made over his business to his sons 1851; mayor of Bedford 1858–61, 1863–4 and 1871. *d.* Caldwell priory 23 Dec. 1878. *Times* 24 *Dec.* 1878 *p.* 7, *col.* 6.

HOWARD, JOHN. *b.* Burnley Wood, Lancs. 24 June 1824; champion long distance jumper using dumb bells, jumped 28 feet 6 inches Chester race course 1854; jumped 29 feet 7 inches at Lancaster and leaped over a billiard table lengthwise for a wager 1854; the greatest pedestrian of his time, beat Bob Coates 120 yards, Hyde park, Sheffield 1839; beat John Flockton of Leeds 120 yards at Garrick Corner; beat John Walker the Delemere forest stag 120 yards for £25 at Bellevue, Manchester, when 25,000 paid for admission; beat Robert Low of Heywood 100 yards for £25 at Bellevue, time 9¾ seconds up hill; beat the Demon, J. Whitehead alias Clark of Oldham 110 yards for £50 at Bellevue. *d.* suddenly, Dublin hotel, Bradford 14 Oct. 1875. *Bell's Life* 16 *Oct.* 1875 *p.* 8; *Illust. Sporting News* (1862) 68, 76–7, 116, 3 *portraits.*

HOWARD, JOHN ELIOT (*son of Luke Howard, F.R.S.* 1772–1864). *b.* Plaistow, Essex 11 Dec. 1807; manufacturing chemist with his father at Stratford; studied history of febrifuge alkaloids; purchased a collection of specimens of Peruvian bark at Madrid 1858; mem. Pharmaceutical soc. 1853; F.L.S. 1857; F.R.S. 4 June 1874; V.P. Victoria institute; received thanks of government for his aid in cinchona cultivation in India 1876; author of *Eight lectures on the scriptural truths most opposed to Puseyism* 1845, 2 ed. 1847; *Illustrations of the Nueva Quinologia of Pavon* 1859–62; *The Quinology of the East India plantations* 3 *parts* 1869–76; *The Epistle to the Hebrews. A translation* 1872 and 9 other books. *d.* Lord's Mead, Tottenham, Middlesex 22 Nov. 1883. *Graphic* 29 *Dec.* 1883 *pp.* 634, 637, *portrait*; *Trans. Essex Field club*, iv, 8–11, *portrait*.

HOWARD, JOHN MORGAN (*eld. son of John J. Howard of Swansea*). *b.* Nov. 1837; barrister M.T. 30 April 1858, bencher 16 Nov. 1877; Q.C. 6 July 1874; an editor of the *New Reports* 1862 to 1865; contested Lambeth 1868, 1874 and 1880; M.P. for Camberwell, Dulwich division 1885–7; recorder of Guildford 15 March 1875 to death; judge of circuit No. 59 (Cornwall), Nov. 1887 to

HOWARD, J. M. (*Con.*)

death. *d.* Chelston Dene, Torquay 10 April 1891. *I.L.N.* 18 *April* 1891 *p.* 499, *portrait*; *Graphic x*, 223, 224 (1874), *portrait*.

HOWARD, LUKE (*son of Robert Howard, introducer of the Argand lamp, d. Jany.* 1812). *b.* London 28 Nov. 1772; apprentice to a chemist at Stockport 1786; chemist in London 1793, partner with William Allen 1796–1803; chemist at Stratford 1805; made observations on the clouds 1802 and first used the terms cirrus, cumulus and stratus and nimbus or rain cloud; kept a meteorological register from 1806; F.R.S. 1821; corresponded with Goethe 1822 who sent him a poem entitled *Howard's Ehrengedächtniss;* author of *A few notes on a letter to the Archbishops and on a charge relative to Joseph Lancaster's plan for education. By Eccletus* 1806; *The climate of London* 2 *vols.* 1818–20, 2 ed. 3 *vols.* 1833; *Essay on the modification of clouds* 1830, 3 *ed.* 1865; *Cowper's English version of the Odyssey with a commentary. By Outis* 1843; *Barometrographia, twenty years' variation of the barometer* 1847 and 10 other books. *d.* at res. of his son R. Howard, Bruce grove, Tottenham 21 March 1864. *Proc. Royal Soc. xiv*, 10–12 (1865); *J. Bell and T. Redwood's Pharmacy* (1880) 331.

HOWARD, PHILIP HENRY (*eld. son of Henry Howard of Corby castle near Carlisle* 1757–1842). *b.* Edinburgh 22 April 1801; ed. at Oscott coll. and Stonyhurst; M.P. for Carlisle 1830–47 and 1848–52 being the second Roman Catholic returned to parliament; F.S.A. 8 Dec. 1842; sheriff of Cumberland 1860; wrote miscellaneous poems and other articles in *Edinburgh Catholic Mag.* and other periodicals. *d.* Ventnor, Isle of Wight 1 Jany. 1883. *Gillow's English Catholics, iii*, 441–2 (1888).

HOWARD, SIR RALPH, 1 Baronet (*elder son of Hugh Howard, comr. of stamp office, d. 3 Nov.* 1840 *aged* 80). *b.* 1801; M.P. co. Wicklow 1829–47 and 1848–52; contested Evesham 1847; colonel of Wicklow militia 1 Oct. 1834 to 11 Dec. 1871; created baronet 26 July 1838. *d.* 15 Aug. 1873.

HOWARTH, REV. HENRY (*son of Wm. Howarth, of Manchester, bath-keeper*). *b.* Manchester 12 Jany. 1801; ed. at Manchester sch. and St. John's coll. Cam., fellow 1823–33; B.A. 1823, M.A. 1826, B.D. 1833; Hulsean lecturer 1835–36; R. of Meppershall, Beds. 1833–45; R. of St. George's, Hanover sq. London 1845 to death; chaplain in ord. to the Queen 14 May 1855 to death; author of *The*

HOWARTH, REV. H. *(Con.)*

truth and obligation of revealed religion. Discourses 1836 ; *Jesus of Nazareth, the Christ of God. Discourses* 1837 ; *The liturgy as it is. Sermons* 1843 and 11 other books. *d.* Tunbridge Wells 25 Aug. 1876. *I.L.N. xxiv*, 400 (1854), *portrait.*

HOWDEN, JOHN HOBART CARADOC 2 Baron *(only child of 1st Baron Howden 1762–1839). b.* Dublin 16 Oct. 1799 ; ensign Grenadier Guards 13 July 1815 ; A.D.C. to Duke of Wellington in Paris, to Viscount Beresford in Portugal, and to Sir Thomas Maitland in the Mediterranean ; major on half pay 9 June 1825 ; L.G. 26 Dec. 1859 ; sold out 29 Oct. 1861 ; M.P. for Dundalk 1830–31 ; succeeded his father as 2 Baron July 1839 ; attaché at Berlin 1824, at Paris 1825 ; wounded in battle of Navarino ; military commissioner with French army at siege of Antwerp 1832, and with Spanish Army in Portugal 1834 ; envoy extraord. and minister plenipo. to Brazil 25 Jany. 1847 to 1850 ; minister plenipo. to Spain 14 May 1850 to March 1858 ; K.C.B. 23 Feb. 1852, G.C.B. 5 March 1858 ; K.H. 1830 ; equerry to Duchess of Kent 1841 to 1861. *d.* Caradoc near Bayonne 9 Oct. 1873. *Foreign office list July* 1873 *p.* 117.

HOWDEN, JAMES ADAM. *b.* 1803 ; entered Madras army 1819, M.G. 28 Nov. 1854 ; colonel 52 Madras N.I. 28 June 1855 to death. *d.* Devonshire place, Portland place, London 22 March 1869.

HOWE, RICHARD WILLIAM PENN CURZON-HOWE 1 Earl *(only son of the hon. Penn Assheton Curzon 1757–97). b.* Gopsall house, Leics. 11 Dec. 1796 ; capt. Leics. regt. of yeomanry 21 May 1818, lieut.-col. 1831–60 ; succeeded his grandfather as 2 viscount and baron Curzon 21 March 1820 ; took name of Howe 7 July 1821 ; cr. Earl Howe 15 July 1821 ; G.C.H. 1830 ; lord chamberlain to queen Adelaide 1830–31, when he was dismissed by earl Grey the prime minister, again lord chamberlain 1834–49 ; P.C. 31 Jany. 1831 ; succeeded his mother as 2 baron Howe 3 Dec. 1835 ; vice lieut. co. Leicester 27 Oct. 1863. *d.* Curzon house, South Audley st., London 12 May 1870. *Portraits of eminent conservatives* (1836) 1 *Series, portrait* 23.

HOWE, GEORGE AUGUSTUS FREDERICK LOUIS CURZON HOWE, 2 Earl (1 *son of the preceding). b.* Brook st. London 16 Jany. 1821 ; styled viscount Curzon 1821–70 ; ed. at Eton ; matric. from Ch. Ch. Ox. 30 May 1838 ; cornet Leics. regt. of yeomanry 1838, lieut.-col. 15 Nov. 1860, lieut.-col. commandant 15

HOWE, 2 Earl of. *(Con.)*

March 1870 to death ; M.P. South Leics. 1857–70 ; master of the Atherstone hounds some years ; succeeded as 2 earl Howe 12 May 1870. *d.* Gopsall hall, Leics. 4 Feb. 1876, personalty sworn under £250,000, 13 May 1876. *I.L.N. lxviii*, 167, 479 (1876) ; *Baily's Mag. xii*, 217–8 (1867), *portrait.*

HOWE, JOSEPH *(son of John Howe 1752–1835, King's printer at Halifax, Nova Scotia). b.* in a cottage on banks of North-west Arm, Halifax 13 Dec. 1804 ; a printer 1817–27 ; editor and proprietor of a paper called the *Nova Scotian* 1828 ; M.P. for co. of Halifax, Nov. 1836 ; member of the executive council 1840 ; speaker of house of assembly 1840 ; provincial sec. 4 years ; sec. of state for lower provinces in Dominion of Canada 1870–3 ; governor of Nova Scotia, May 1873 ; author of *Speech on the importance to Great Britain of her North American colonies* 1851 ; *Confederation considered in relation to the interests of the empire* 1866 ; *The organization of the empire* 1866 and 4 other books. *d.* Halifax 1 June 1873. *W. Annand's Speeches and letters of Joseph Howe* 2 vols. (1858).

HOWE, WILLIAM. *b.* West Auckland, co. Durham 3 March 1814 ; a mechanic with R. Stephenson & Co., Newcastle ; perfected Williams' valve gear known as the link motion, in the form in which it has been universally applied to locomotives, Aug. 1842 ; invented the three-cylinder locomotive engine 1846 ; engineer at Stephenson's Clay Cross collieries and iron works Nov. 1846 to death ; designed the self-acting fence now universally used at top of colliery winding shafts ; M.I.M.E. 1860. *d.* Clay Cross, Chesterfield 16 Jany. 1879. *N. P. Burgh's Link motion* (1870) *pp. i-xvi ; D. K. Clark's Railway machinery* (1855) 26 ; *Engineer, xlvii*, 67 (1879).

HOWELL, ARTHUR *(eld. son of James Howell 1811–79, contra-bassist). b.* London 1836 ; contra-bassist and bass singer ; stage manager Carl Rosa opera co. ; went on an Australian tour with his wife 1879 ; *(m.* 1874 Rose Hersee, soprano opera and concert singer). *d.* 32 Lawford road, Kentish Town, London 16 April 1885.

HOWELL, FRANCIS *(brother of the preceding). b.* London 1834 ; wrote 2 oratorios *The Captivity* 1860, *The Land of Promise* 1870 and many songs and ballads. *d.* 1882.

HOWELL, JAMES. *b.* Plymouth 1811 ; student R. Acad. of music, June 1825 to Dec. 1830 ; learnt double-bass under signor Anfossi ; professor of double-bass at R. Acad. of music 1830 ; M.R.A.M. ; double-bass player at the Ancient

HOWELL, J. *(Con.)*

and Philharmonic concerts and R. Italian opera; the successor of Domenico Dragonetti as the best double-bass player 1846. *d.* London 5 Aug. 1879. *Cazalet's R. Acad. of Music* (1854) 296–7; *Grove's Dict. of Music, i,* 754 (1879).

HOWELL, JOHN. *b.* Old Lauriston, Edinburgh 1788; bookbinder in Thistle st. Edin., invented the 'plough' for cutting edges of books; polyartist, curiosity dealer and china and picture repairer at 22 Frederick st., then at 110 Rose st. Edin.; broke one of his legs while using a flying machine in Edin.; introduced manufacture of Pompeian plates for dentists; author of *An essay on the war-galleys of the ancients. Edin.* 1826; *The life and adventures of Alexander Selkirk. Edin.* 1829; edited *The life of Alexander Alexander. Edin.* 1830; wrote several of Wilson's *Tales of the Borders. d.* 110 Rose st. Edinburgh 4 April 1863. *Notes and Queries,* 3rd ser. *ii* 491, *iii* 19, 78, 379, 4th ser. *ii* 393, 500.

HOWELL, JOHN *(son of Mr. Howell, army packer, Mark Lane). b.* London 1807; apprentice to his father; chief clerk to Ellis and Everington, haberdashers, hosiers and silk mercers, 3 St. Paul's ch. yard, London 1835, admitted a partner 1841, firm became Ellis, Howell & Co. 1857 and in 1871 John Howell & Co. limited, with J. Howell as chairman to his death; gave evidence before three parliamentary committees on laws of limited liability 1851 etc.; author of *Partnership-law legislation and limited liability reviewed* 1869. *d.* Rutland house, Kingston on Thames 3 Nov. 1888. *Warehouseman and Drapers' Trade Journal* (1888) 345–6, *portrait,* and 1049–50.

HOWELL, MATTHEW. *b.* 14 Feb. 1796; appeared as the child in *Pizarro* with George Frederick Cooke at Liverpool; made first appearance in London at Sadler's Wells 1810; played at the Coburg; came out at Drury Lane as harlequin in pantomime of *The Flying Chest,* Dec. 1823 and was for more than 20 years the recognised harlequin there; last appeared as harlequin at the Marylebone in 1847; played pantaloon some years. *d.* 1 Dec. 1873.

HOWELL, SIR THOMAS *(son of Thomas Howell of Clapham common, Surrey). b.* London 1802; ed. at Charterhouse 1815–16; in business in London to 1855; director of contracts at War Office 1855–74; knighted at Windsor castle 27 June 1876; author of *A day of business in the port of London* 1850; *A few stray thoughts upon Shakspeare* 1867. *d.* 2 Uplands, St. Leonards-on-Sea 23 April 1883.

HOWELL, THOMAS JONES *(son of Thomas Bayly Howell 1768–1815, editor of the State Trials). b.* 24 Dec. 1793; edited a *Complete collection of State Trials* vols. 22–33, 1815–26; barrister L.I. 17 May 1822; judge advocate and judge of vice-admiralty court at Gibraltar 1822; sec. to comrs. of colonial inquiry 1830; comr. for West India Islands relief 1832; inspector of factories 1833. *d.* 6 Eaton place west, London 4 June 1858.

HOWELLS, REV. JOHN. *b.* 21 Sep. 1777; C. of Tipton, Staffs. 1803–37; P.C. of Holy Trinity, Coventry 1837 to death; author of *A selection of psalms, hymns, anthems and choruses for public and private use. Tipton* 1831. *d.* Coventry 31 Dec. 1856. *monu.* in Holy Trinity ch. which says *d.* 1 Jany. 1857. *I.L.N. xxxiv,* 260 (1859), *view of monu.*

HOWES, EDWARD (2 son of Rev. George Howes, R. of Spixworth, Norfolk). *b.* Spixworth 7 July 1813; ed. at St. Paul's sch. and Trin. coll. Cam., fellow 1836–42; B.A. 1835, M.A. 1838; barrister L.I. 7 June 1839; chairman of Norfolk quarter sessions 1848; M.P. East Norfolk 1859–68; M.P. South Norfolk 1868 to death; a church estates comr. 4 Aug. 1866; author of *King Richard II, Act* 3 Sc. 2 *with Greek version* in *Prolusiones Academicæ. Cantab.* 1834 *pp.* 25–29. *d.* Morningthorpe, Norfolk 26 March 1871.

HOWES, JOSEPH. Landlord of the Blue Boar and Wellington castle inns, Leicester; on his retirement lived at Evington lodge near Leicester. *d.* at residence of Mr. Read, Morledge st. Leicester 13 Dec. 1853 in 102 year. *Willis' Current Notes* (1856) 27.

HOWIE, VERY REV. JAMES. Dean of Cloyne 17 Jany. 1851 to death; R. of Farriley 23 Oct. 1851. *d.* Barnabrow house, Cloyne 6 Dec. 1884.

HOWITT, GEORGE. *b.* Old Lenton, Notts. 14 March 1843; fast left-hand, round-arm bowler; went to London 1860; played for Middlesex and then for Notts.; bowled W. G. Grace for a brace of ducks at Neath in 1868; a member of the ground staff at Lord's 1870; went a voyage to Australia for his health 1880. *d.* Nottingham 19 Dec. 1881. *W. G. Grace's Cricket* (1891) 329.

HOWITT, HERBERT CHARLTON *(younger son of William Howitt). b.* Esher, Feb. 1838; visited Australia with his father 1852–4; went to Canterbury, New Zealand, Nov. 1860; employed in an expedition to discover gold 1862 and then in cutting a horse track over the mountains between Christchurch and the

HOWITT, H. C. *(Con.)*

western coast 1 Jany. 1863 to death; *drowned in crossing the Brunner Lake 27 June 1863, his body was not found.* W. *Howitt's History of discovery in Australia*, ii, 443–58 (1865); *M. Howitt, an autobiography*, i, 277, ii, 133–6 (1889).

HOWITT, MARY *(dau. of Samuel Botham).* b. Coleford, Gloucs. 12 March 1799; wrote verse at an early age; *(m.* 16 April 1821 William Howitt 1792–1879); wrote many books with her husband 1827–64; civil list pension of £100, 21 April 1879; joined R.C. ch., received by the Pope 10 Jany. 1888; edited *The drawing room scrap book* 1832–54, and *Pictorial calendar of the seasons* 1854; translated *Frederika Bremer's Novels* 18 vols. 1842–63, works she then made known to English readers; author of *Sketches of natural history* 1834; *Little coin, much care* 1842; *The Heir of West Waylen* 1847; *A popular history of the United States* 2 vols. 1859; *M. Howitt's Illustrated library for the young* 1861, *two series; The cost of Caergwyn* 3 vols. 1864; *Tales for all seasons* 1881; her name is attached to upwards of 110 volumes. *d.* 38 Via Gregoriana, Rome 30 Jany. 1888. *M. Howitt's Life of Mary Howitt* (1889), *two portraits; Alaric Watts' Life*, ii, 1–15 (1884); *Graphic* 18 Feb. 1888 *p.* 168, *portrait*.

HOWITT, RICHARD *(son of Thomas Howitt of Heanor, Derbyshire, farmer).* b. Heanor 1799; chemist and druggist at Parliament st. Nottingham 1823–39; farming in Australia 1839–44; farmer near Southwell 1846 to death; author of *Antediluvian Sketches and other poems* 1830; *The Gipsy King and other poems* 1840; *Impressions of Australia Felix, notes of a voyage round the world, Australian poems, &c.* 1845; *Wasps' Honey, or poetic gold and gems of poetic thought* 1868. *d.* at his farm Edingley, Notts. 5 Feb. 1869. *bur.* in Friends' cemetery, Mansfield. *The Reliquary*, x 209–16, xi 17–22, 103–8, 141–4 (1869–71); *S. T. Hall's Biographical Sketches* (1873) 308–11.

HOWITT, WILLIAM *(brother of the preceding).* b. Heanor, Derbyshire 18 Dec. 1792; ed. at Ackworth sch. 1802–6; chemist and druggist Nottingham 1823–36; alderman of Nottingham 1833; resided at Esher 1836–9, at Heidelberg 1840–3, at Clapton 1843–8, St. John's Wood, London 1848–52, in Australia 1852–4, at Highgate 1854–66, at Esher again 1866–70, at Rome 1870 to death; a spiritualist, friend of D. D. Home, and contributor to *Spiritual Mag.;* civil list pension of £140, 19 June 1865; *(m.* 1821 Mary Botham 1799–1888); celebrated his golden wedding 16

HOWITT, W. *(Con.)*

April 1871; part proprietor of *People's Journal* 1847, edited *Howitt's Journal* 1847–8; translated *Peter Schlemihl's Wundersame Geschichte* 1843 and other works; in conjunction with his wife he wrote *The literature and romances of Northern Europe* 1852; *Stories of English and foreign life* 1853; *Ruined abbeys and castles of Great Britain* 1862–4; his own chief works were *The book of the seasons* 1831 which after being refused by 4 publishing houses ran to 7 editions; *The rural life of England* 2 vols. 1838; *Visits to remarkable places* 1840, second series 1842; *Rural and domestic life of Germany* 1842; *Land, labour and gold, or two years-in Victoria* 2 vols. 1855; *Popular history of England* 5 vols. 1856–62, seven editions; *The northern heights of London* 1869. *d.* 55 Via Sistina, Rome 3 March 1879. *R. H. Horne's New spirit of the age,* i 177–98 (1844), *portrait; S. C. Hall's Retrospect of a long life,* ii, 126–31 (1883); *The Naturalist,* iv 366–73 (1839), *portrait; I.L.N.* 29 March 1879 *pp.* 297, 298, *portrait*.

HOWLETT, REV. JOHN HENRY *(son of John Howlett).* b. 10 June 1781; ed. at Merchant Taylors' sch. 1796–1800 when he became Parkin's exhibitioner to Pemb. coll. Cam.; 14 wrangler and B.A. 1804, M.A. 1807; fellow of his coll. 1806–7; V. of Hollington, Sussex 25 Nov. 1812 to 1834; morning reader at chapel royal, Whitehall 1809 to death; R. of Foston, Leics. 30 April 1834 to death; founder and sec. of Kensington gram. sch. 1831; author of *Metrical chronology* 1824, 6 ed. 1865; *Instruction in reading the liturgy of the United church of England and Ireland* 1826, 3 ed. 1866. *d.* 9 Young st. Kensington, London 10 Oct. 1867.

HOWLETT, SAMUEL BURT *(only son of Samuel Howlett of Gracechurch st. London).* b. 10 July 1794; cadet and officer in corps of royal military surveyors and draughtsmen 1808 to 1817 when corps was reduced; assistant surveyor and draughtsman to board of ordnance 1824, chief military surveyor 1830, draughtsman in charge of plans, &c. in inspector general of fortifications office 1838–56; made improvements in mountain barometer and in the stadiometer used in school of musketry; invented an anemometer; author of *A treatise on perspective* 1828; *Tables for determining altitude with the mountain barometer* 1844; *Description of a barometer that requires no correction either for zero or for temperature* 1844. *d.* 46 Palace grove, New Bromley, Kent 24 Jany. 1874.

NOTE.—The words "In" and "Out" which are now seen on the doors of every public office were sug-

HOWLETT, S. B. *(Con.)*

gested by him; they were first used at the Bank of England in consequence of a written communication made by him to the authorities.

HOWLEY, SIR JOHN (1 *son of John Howley of Rich Hill, co. Limerick*). *b.* Rich Hill 1789; ed. at Oscott coll. and Trin. coll. Dublin; called to the Irish bar 1815; chairman of quarter sessions for co. Tipperary 1835–65; K.C. 13 July 1835, third serjeant Sept. 1843, second serjeant July 1848; queen's first serjeant in Ireland June 1851 to death; bencher of King's Inns 1843; knighted by lord lieut. at Dublin Castle 14 Aug. 1865. *d.* 32 Upper Fitzwilliam st. Dublin 13 Feb. 1866.

HOWLISON, ROBERT (2 *son of a miller at Channelkirk, Berwickshire*). Said to have been *b.* Channelkirk on Handsel Monday (Jany.) 1769, but no proof of this; ploughman, and then a shepherd. *d.* West Linton, Peebleshire 30 Oct. 1871 said to be 103. *W. J. Thoms' Longevity of Man* (1879) 186–92.

HOWORTH, REV. WILLIAM (2 *son of Rev. Wm. Howorth*). *b.* 1806; ed. at Caius coll. Cam., B.A. 1827, M.A. 1830; R. of Whitton with Thurleston, Suffolk 3 Nov. 1835 to death; hon. canon of Norwich cath. 1863 to death; author of *Sermons doctrinal and practical* 1839; *The Redeemer, a poem* 1840; *Life and the issue of it* 1869. *d.* Whitton rectory 13 Dec. 1875.

HOWS, JOHN WILLIAM STANHOPE. *b.* London 1797; appeared as Shylock, Park theatre, New York 16 Feb. 1834; professor of elocution, Columbia, Carolina 1843–57; dramatic critic *New York Albion* 7 years; author of *The practical elocutionist* 1849, 6 ed. 1856; *The Shakspearian reader* 1850, 3 ed. 1870; *Golden leaves from the British and American dramatic poets* 1865; *Golden leaves from the American poets* 1866; *The ladies' book of reading and recitations* 1870. *d.* New York city 27 July 1871. *Appleton's American Biog. iii,* 288 (1887).

HOWSON, FRANK. *b.* London 1817; in a lancer regt. fought in Carlist war in Spain 1836; an artist in Australia 1842; the father of opera in the colonies; manager and stage director for Anna Bishop when appearing in operas in Australia 1854–6; with his sons and daus. produced plays and operas at San Francisco 1866. *d.* Omaha, Nebraska 16 Sep. 1869.

HOWSON, JOHN (2 *son of the preceding*). *b.* Hobart Town, Tasmania 17 Nov. 1844; first appeared on the stage at Royal Victoria theatre, Sydney; left Australia with his family

HOWSON, J. *(Con.)*

for San Francisco 1866, played there 1866–9; first appeared in New York at Wood's Museum, Nov. 1869; played in the U.S. of A. 1869–77; first appeared in England at Brighton 3 Sep. 1877 as Commodore Patatras in *La Créole*, played same part at Folly theatre, London 15 Sep.; acted the Marquis in *Les Cloches de Corneville* at same house 23 Feb. 1878 and at the Globe July 1879. *d.* 16 Dec. 1888. *C. E. Pascoe's Dramatic List* (1880) 189–90.

HOWSON, REV. JOHN. *b.* Giggleswick, Yorkshire 1787; ed. at Trin. coll. Dublin, B.A. 1811, M.A. 1813; second master Giggleswick gr. school 1814 to death; F.L.S. 1822; author of *The gain of Godliness* 1840. *d.* Giggleswick 23 Jany. 1859.

HOWSON, VERY REV. JOHN SAUL *(son of the preceding*). *b.* Giggleswick 5 May 1816; ed. at Giggleswick gr. sch. and Trin. coll. Cam., B.A. 1837, M.A. 1840, D.D. 1862; senior classical master Liverpool collegiate institute 1845 and principal 1849–65; exam. chaplain to bishop of Ely 1866–73; V. of St. Peter's, Wisbech 1866–7; dean of Chester 12 June 1867 to death, continued the repairing of the cath. and reopened it 25 Jany. 1872; instrumental in building and endowing the King's sch., the Queen's sch. and the museum, Chester; a contributor to the *Quarterly Review, The Speaker's Commentary,* etc.; author of *Sunday evenings. Short sermons* 1849; *Sermons to schoolboys* 1858–66, 2 series; *The character of St. Paul* 1862, 4 ed. 1884; *The companions of St. Paul* 1871 and about 35 other works; with the Rev. J. Conybeare, *The life and epistles of St. Paul* 2 vols. 1852, many editions. *d.* Bournemouth 15 Dec. 1885. *bur:* the cloister garden, Chester 19 Dec. *I.L.N. lxxxvii* 667 (1885), *portrait; Guardian, Dec.* 1885 *pp.* 1892, 1951; *Times,* 16, 17, 18, 19, 21, 23, 31 *Dec.* 1885.

HOWTH, THOMAS ST. LAWRENCE, 3 Earl of. *b.* 16 Aug. 1803; succeeded his father 4 April 1822; vice admiral of province of Leinster; K.P. 22 July 1835; lord lieut. of co. Dublin 1851 to death; trained his horses with W. Day at Danebury, won the Chester cup with Peep o' Day Boy in 1848; a flat race rider 1830–50. *d.* Cannes 4 Feb. 1874. *W. Day's Reminiscences* (1886) 236–8; *Sporting Times* 12 *Sep.* 1885 *pp.* 2–3.

HOYLE, WILLIAM. *b.* valley of Rossendale, Lancs. 1831; a cotton spinner with his father at Brooksbottom near Bury, Lancs. 1851–9; cotton spinner at Tollington near Bury 1859 to death; a temperance reformer, a Good

HOYLE, W. (Con.)

Templar and a vegetarian; contested Dewsbury 1880; wrote an annual letter to *The Times* on the "national drink bill of successive years"; built a residence at Claremont near Bury; author of *Hoyle's Hymns and songs for temperance societies and bands of hope* 1869; *Our national resources and how they are wasted* 1871, four editions; *Crime in England and Wales in the nineteenth century* 1876 and of 13 other books. *d.* Southport, Lancs. 26 Feb. 1886. *Manchester Guardian* 1 March 1886 *p.* 8.

HOYLES, SIR HUGH WILLIAM (*son of Newman Wright Hoyles, colonial treasurer of Newfoundland*). *b.* St. John's, Newfoundland, Jany. 1814; called to bar in Nova Scotia and Newfoundland 1837; member of assembly there 1848; acting solicitor general of Newfoundland 1854, attorney general and leader of the government 1861; chief justice of Newfoundland 4 March 1865 to 1880; knighted by patent 13 Feb. 1869. *d.* 18 Morris st. Halifax, Nova Scotia 1 Feb. 1888.

HUARD, LOUIS. *b.* in South of France 1813; studied at Antwerp; came to London 1854 and was connected with Illust. London news till his death; exhibited 2 figure paintings at British institution 1857; illustrated *Souvenirs de la fête donnée aux artistes exposants* 1849; *Sir S. W. Baker's Cast up by the sea* 1869; *A. and E. Keary's The heroes of Asgard* 1871 and other books. *d.* 37 Onslow sq. London 19 Sep. 1874. *I.L.N.* 10 Oct. 1874 *p.* 345, *portrait.*

HUBBACK, CATHERINE ANNE (*dau. of admiral Sir Francis Wm. Austen, G.C.B.* 1774–1865). (*m.* 25 Aug. 1842 John Hubback 1811–85); author of *The younger sister* 3 vols. 1850; *The wife's sister* 3 vols. 1851; *Life and its lessons* 3 vols. 1851; *Malvern or the three marriages* 3 vols. 1855; *May and December, a tale* 3 vols. 1855; *The old vicarage* 3 vols. 1856; *Agnes Milbourne* 2 vols. 1856; *The Rival suitors* 3 vols. 1857; *The stage and the company* 3 vols. 1858; *The mistake of a life* 3 vols. 1863.

HUBBACK, JOHN (2 son of *Joseph Hubback of Berwick-on-Tweed*). *b.* Berwick-on-Tweed 1811; barrister I.T. 12 June 1835; author of *A treatise on the evidence of succession to real and personal property and peerages* 1844. *d.* Brislington, Somerset 24 Feb. 1885.

HUBBARD, JOHN GELLIBRAND, 1 Baron Addington (1 son of *John Hubbard, Russian merchant d.* 1847). *b.* 21 March 1805; ed. at Bordeaux 1816–20 in his father's business 1821; Russia merchant 4 St. Helen's place,

HUBBARD, J. G. (Con.)

London; director of Bank of England 1838–41; chairman public works loan commission 1853 to death; M.P. Buckingham 1859–68; defeated lord Palmerston's government in making a motion for an enquiry into the income tax 1861; M.P. city of London 1874–87; P.C. 6 Aug. 1874; F.R.G.S.; gave much attention to the income tax, the coinage, ecclesiastical affairs and education; built and endowed St. Alban's ch. Holborn, consecrated 26 Feb. 1863; cr. baron Addington of Addington, Bucks. 22 July 1887; author of *Vindication of a fixed duty on corn* 1842; *The currency and the country* 1843; *The church and church rates* 1861, 2 ed. 1861; *A census of religion. Denominational worship. The national church. Essays* 1882; *Gladstone on the income tax* 1885 and 10 other pamphlets. *d.* Addington manor, Winslow, Bucks. 28 Aug. 1889. *I.L.N.* lxiv, 551, 552 (1874), *portrait*; *Touchstone* 5 April 1879 *pp.* 1–2, *portrait.*

HUBBARD, THOMAS. *b.* 1789; framework knitter; obtained possession of some property in Nottinghamshire and under the impression that he was the heir at law retained the ownership 6 years, a will was then found giving the property to a person named Holland; Hubbard under the belief that the will was forged refused to give up the deeds of the estate, and in July 1856 was imprisoned for contempt of court; he remained in the debtors' prison, Nottingham till his *death* 23 Jany. 1864. *G.M. April* 1864 *p.* 534.

HUBBARDE, JAMES DIBDEN. *b.* 1803; proprietor of *Wakefield Journal* to 1850; connected with and editor of *Hampshire Advertiser* 1850 to death; president of Ornithological association; author of *Pencil notes of five days' tour from Wakefield to Matlock. By J. D. H.* 1839. *d.* Wick cottage, Avenue road, Southampton 28 Jany. 1870. *Newspaper Press* 1 *March* 1870 *p.* 82; *Hampshire Advertiser* 29 *Jany.* 1870 *pp.* 4, 5.

HUCKIN, REV. HENRY ROBERT (*son of John Huckin, fishmonger, Islington*). *b.* 11 Oct. 1841; ed. at Merchant Taylors' sch. 1850–60, Andrew's exhib. to St. John's coll. Ox. 1860; B.A. 1864, M.A. 1867, D.D. 1874; assist. master at Haileybury 1865–8; a master at M.T. sch. 1869–74; head master Repton gram. sch. March 1874 to death; Townsend lecturer St. Magnus-the-Martyr, city of London 1871–3; ed. of *Milton. Comus, Lycidas. With notes* 1871; author of *The analogy of religion. Dialogues founded upon Butler's Analogy of religion* 1873. *d.* Repton 30 July 1882.

HUDDART, FANNY *(niece of Mary Amelia Warner the actress, d.* 1854). A contralto singer, played the chief contralto parts in all the Italian operas and also in English operas, was the original Azucena when the English version of Il Trovatore was produced at Drury Lane May 1855; sang the contralto parts in Handel's and Mendelssohn's oratorios at Sacred harmonic society's concerts; played the leading roles in Shakespearean dramas and modern comedies; *(m.* John Russell of Covent Garden theatre). *d.* 28 June 1880. *Era* 4 *July* 1880 *p.* 6.

HUDDLESTON, SIR JOHN WALTER (1 *son of Thomas Huddleston, captain in merchant service). b.* Dublin 8 Sep. 1815; ed. Trin. coll. Dublin; barrister G.I. 7 May 1839; was with Cockburn in Rugeley poisoning case 1856; Q.C. June 1857; bencher of his inn 4 Nov. 1857; contested Worcester 1852, Shrewsbury 1857 and Kidderminster 1859 and 1861; M.P. Canterbury 1865-8; contested Norwich 1870, M.P. 1874-5; counsel to the admiralty and judge advocate of the Fleet Nov. 1865 to 22 Feb. 1875; serjeant at law and justice of court of common pleas 22 Feb. 1875, transferred to court of exchequer 12 May 1875; knighted at Windsor castle 13 May 1875; created the last baron of the exchequer; judge of queen's bench division of high court of justice 26 Feb. 1881; tried the libel action Belt *v.* Lawes lasting 43 days 1881-2; entertained by the French bar in Paris 1868. *d.* 43 Ennismore gardens, South Kensington 5 Dec. 1890, cremated at Woking 12 Dec. *Pump Court, i, frontispiece and p.* 135 (1884), *portrait; Vanity Fair xxxv,* 325 (1886); *I.L.N. lxvi,* 229 (1875), *portrait; Graphic* 13 *Dec.* 1890 *p.* 667, *portrait.*

HUDSON, ALFRED. *b.* 15 Nov. 1808; ed. Dublin univ., M.B. 1834, M.D. 1861; M.R.C.S. England 1834; F.K.Q.C.P. Ireland 1857, censor 1858-9; M.R.I.A.; physician Adelaide hospital, Dublin; a physician in ordinary to queen in Ireland 21 Jany. 1878; member of general council of medical education and registration of U.K. for Ireland 14 May 1877 to death; a contributor to *Dublin medical journal* and *Dublin quarterly journal;* author of *Lectures on the study of fever* 1867, *new ed.* 1872; edited W. Stokes' *A treatise on diseases of the chest* 1882. *d.* Loweville near Dublin 19 Nov. 1880. *Times* 23 *Nov.* 1880 *p.* 6; *Medical Times ii,* 660 (1880).

HUDSON, REV. CHARLES. Educ. at St. John's coll. Cam., B.A. 1851, M.A. 1854; chaplain in the Crimea 1854-6; C. of St. Mary's, Bridgnorth 1856-7; V. of Shillington, Lincs.

1859 to death; the best Alpine amateur climber of his time, organized the party of 7 who ascended Mont Blanc without guides 14-15 Aug. 1855; author of *An Ascent of Mont Blanc and two ascents of Monte Rosa* 1856; *Narrative of the accident on the Col de Miage in July* 1861 in *Peaks and Passes, i,* 208-24 (1862); *killed* by a fall while descending the Matterhorn 14 July 1865. *bur.* Zermatt. *E. Whymper's Ascent of the Matterhorn* (1880) 273-95; *Times* 20, 21, 22 *July* and 12 *Aug.* 1865.

HUDSON, CORRIE. *b.* 1822; clerk in legacy and succession duty department of inland revenue office 1845-72, a principal clerk 1872 to death; author of *A practical guide to the payment of legacy and succession duties* 1867, 7 ed. 1888. *A practical guide to making and proving wills and obtaining letters of administration* 1876, 2 ed. 1878. *d.* 67 Bessborough st. Pimlico, London 6 Nov. 1880.

HUDSON, VERY REV. EDWARD GUSTAVUS. Educated Dublin univ., B.A. 1810, M.A. 1813; dean of Armagh 1841 to death, patent dated 1 Sep. 1841, instituted 5 March 1842. *d.* Glenville, co. Cork 14 Aug. 1851.

HUDSON, GEORGE *(son of a farmer and constable, d.* 1806). *b.* Howsham near York, March 1800; apprentice to Bell and Nicholson, drapers, York 1815, a partner, firm became Nicholson and Hudson; originator and manager York banking co. 1833; chairman of York and West riding railway 1837, Newcastle and Darlington 1842, Midland 1843, Eastern counties 1846 and many other lines; known as the railway king; resided at Albert gate, Knightsbridge, London 1846-52 which he bought with sum of £15000 presented to him 1846; lord mayor of York 1837 and 1846; M.P. Sunderland 1845-59; many of his transactions in railway shares were of a questionable nature; the great fall in railway shares in 1847 ruined him; resided much abroad from 1852; committed to York castle by sheriff of Yorkshire for contempt of court of exchequer in not paying £23,989 5s., released 7 Oct. 1865; friends raised £4800 and invested it in an annuity for him 1868; entertained at a banquet in Sunderland 1869. *d.* 37 Churton st. Belgrave road, London 14 Dec. 1871. *bur.* Scrayingham, Yorks. 21 Dec. *Evans' Facts, failures and frauds* (1859) 6-73; *Lennox's Celebrities I have known* 2 *Ser. i,* 184-92 (1877); *Fraser's Mag. Aug.* 1847 *pp.* 215-22; *Richardson's The mysteries of Hudson's railway frauds* (1850); *Williams' Midland railway*

HUDSON, G. (*Con.*)

(1877) 99–124, 132; *I.L.N.* 6 *Sep.* 1845 *p.* 157, *portrait; Graphic* 27 *Aug.* 1881 *pp.* 223, 229, *portrait; Times* 16, 22 *Dec.* 1871.

HUDSON, JAMES. Assistant sec. to royal society 1829–38; secretary Royal agricultural society from its foundation 27 June 1838 to death. *d.* Norton terrace, Longsight near Manchester 28 June 1859 aged 55.

HUDSON, JAMES. *b.* Aungier st. Dublin, March 1811; student R. Dublin soc. 1821; articled to a portrait painter Dublin; an actor in the provinces; appeared at Hawkins st. theatre, Dublin 1834; came out at Drury Lane as Gratiano in *Merchant of Venice* 1841; played King Alfourite in *Planché's Fortunio* 17 April 1843; acted Rory O'More in *The Irish Post* at the Haymarket, expressly written for him by Planché 28 Feb. 1846; considered the successor of Tyrone Power (drowned in President 1841); made his American debut Wallnut st. theatre, Philadelphia as Pandeen O'Rafferty in *Born to good luck* 15 Oct. 1849; played in New York 1850; appeared in a drawing room entertainment with Anna Thillon; retired from the stage 1858. *d.* 6 March 1878. *bur.* Highgate cemet. 9 March. *Tallis' Drawing room Scrap book* (1851) 21–2; *Theatrical Times* ii, 233 (1847), *portrait; Planché's Extravaganzas* ii, 179, (1879), *portrait; Ireland's New York Stage* ii, 549–50; *Era Almanack* (1879) 39; *Era* 10 *March* 1878 *p.* 11.

HUDSON, SIR JAMES (*son of Harrington Hudson of Bessingby hall, Bridlington, Yorkshire*). *b.* 1810; ed. at Rugby, Westminster, Paris and Rome; assistant private sec. to Wm. IV. 1830–37; resident gentleman usher to queen Adelaide 21 Nov. 1831; known as "Hurry Hudson" from the speed with which he travelled to Italy to summon Peel home 1834; sec. of legation at Washington 1838, at the Hague 1843, at Rio de Janeiro 1845; envoy extraord. and min. plenipo. to Emperor of Brazil 14 May 1850, to Grand Duke of Tuscany 29 Aug. 1851, but did not proceed there; envoy extraord. and min. plenipo. to King of Sardinia 19 Jany. 1852 to 20 Oct. 1863 when he retired on a pension of £1300; C.B. 1 March 1851, K.C.B. 2 May 1855, G.C.B. 11 Aug. 1863. *d.* Strasburg 20 Sep. 1885 in 76 year. *F. Ross's Celebrities of Yorkshire Wolds* (1878); *Elliot's Sir J. Hudson and Earl Russell* 1886; *Times* 24 *Sep.* 1885 *p.* 7, *cols.* 3–5.

HUDSON, JOHN CORRIE (*son of Thomas Hudson of the Stamp office*). *b.* 1796; ed. St.

HUDSON, J. C. (*Con.*)

Paul's sch. 1804 etc.; an advanced liberal; chief clerk in legacy duty office, Somerset house?; friend of Horne Tooke, Godwin, Shelley, Hazlitt, Charles Lamb, T. Hood, and Hamilton Reynolds; author of *A letter on the cruelty of employing children in sweeping chimneys* in *The Pamphleteer xxii,* 407–30 (1823). *d.* April 1879. *Athenæum* i, 506 (1879).

HUDSON, ROBERT. *b.* 1801; F.G.S., F.L.S., F.Z.S., vice president; F.R.S. 10 April 1834; writer on Fossil shells, *Mag. Nat. Hist. ix,* 103–5 (1836); resided Clapham common. *d.* Bournemouth 9 Feb. 1883.

HUDSON, WILLIAM ELIOT (*son of a professional man*). An enthusiast about Irish antiquities and well known in Irish literary circles; took an active part in the publication of *The Citizen, a monthly journal,* Dublin 1840–1. *d.* south of Ireland July or Aug. 1853.

HUDSPETH, JOHN. *b.* Manchester 21 Nov. 1806; apprentice in a mercantile house; an actor at Manchester and in Scotland and Ireland; first appeared in London at Pavilion theatre 1839; played at Strand theatre when William Copeland rechristened it Punch's playhouse 1851; at Queen's theatre, Tottenham court road 3 years; a favourite in David Dump in *The Irish Rebellion. d.* 2 Oct. 1866. *Theatrical Times, iii,* 357, 366 (1848), *portrait; Era* 7 *Oct.* 1866 *p.* 11.

HUE, CLEMENT (*son of John Hue, merchant, St. Heliers, Jersey*). *b.* St. Heliers 1779; ed. at Abingdon and Pemb. coll. Ox.; B.A. 1801, M.A. 1803, M.B. 1804, M.D. 1807; fellow of his coll.; candidate of college of physicians 30 Sep. 1807, fellow 30 Sep. 1808, censor 1812, registrar 1815 to 4 Feb. 1824, Harveian orator 1829, elect 13 April 1835, consiliarius 1836; physician to Foundling hospital 1815–37, governor and vice pres. many years; physician to St. Bartholomew's hospital 23 May 1823 to 1861; registrar of national vaccine establishment 1824 to death. *d.* 9 Bedford sq. London 23 June 1861. *Munk's College of physicians, iii,* 66 (1878).

HÜFFER, FRANCIS or FRANZ (*son of a banker*). *b.* Münster 22 May 1845; ed. at Münster, Leipzig and Berlin; Ph. D. Göttingen, July 1869; came to London 1869; assistant editor of *The Academy* about 1871; editor of the *New Quarterly Mag.* about 1876; musical critic to *The Times,* April 1879 to death; naturalised 18 Jany. 1882; edited *The Musical Review* 1883, *The Musical World* 1886; author of *Richard Wagner and the music of the future*

HÜFFER, F. *(Con.)*

1874; *The Troubadours: a history of Provençal life and literature in the middle ages* 1878; *Half a century of music in England* 1889 and other books; edited a series of biographies of *The Great Musicians* 1881–4; wrote the libretti for A. C. Mackenzie's two operas produced at Drury Lane, *Colomba* 1883 and *The Troubadour* 1885. *d.* 90 Brook green, Hammersmith 19 Jany. 1889. *Grove's Dict. of music*, iv, 680, 819 (1888); *Times* 21, 25 *Jany.* 1889.

HUELIN, REV. ELIAS. *b.* 1786; French protestant clergyman; owner of house property in London; assistant chaplain at Brompton cemetery; resided 15 Paulton sq. Chelsea; *murdered* and robbed by Walter Miller at 25 Wellington square, Chelsea 9 May 1870 and *buried* there. Walter Miller who had also murdered the housekeeper Ann Boss at 15 Paulton sq. was executed at the Old Bailey 1 Aug. 1870. *Annual Register* (1870) *pp.* 47, 95.

HUGGENS, JOHN. *b.* 29 April 1776; founded Huggens's college, 40 almshouses and a chapel at Northfleet, Kent which he himself superintended. *d.* Crown quay, Sittingbourne, Kent 11 Aug. 1865. *bur.* Northfleet churchyard.

HUGGINS, HASTINGS CHARLES. Ed. at Trin. coll. Dublin; barrister I.T. 26 Jany. 1858; practised in Island of Nevis, Q.C. Nevis, solicitor general Nevis, speaker of House of Assembly; attorney general British Honduras 1861; stipendiary mag. British Guiana to death; author of *The laws of Nevis from 1681 to 1861 inclusive, with appendices and index* 1862. *d.* Georgetown, Demerara 27 March 1883.

HUGGINS, HORATIO JAMES *(eld. son of Horatio Nelson Huggins of the island of St. Vincent).* *b.* 1811; barrister L.I. 1838; acting attorney general St. Vincent 1857 and 1858; Queen's advocate at Sierra Leone 9 May 1863 to 1880, chief justice there 1876 to 1880; manufacturer of bottle washing machines at Pentonville and Hornsey 1881, bankrupt 18 Feb. 1882. *d.* Staplehay, Hornsey 20 Jany. 1886. *bur.* Bedford cemetery.

HUGGINS, SAMUEL. *b.* Deal, Kent 1811; lived at Liverpool most of his life; an architect from 1846; member of Liverpool Architectural Soc. 1849, president 1856–8, read a paper *On so-called restorations of our cathedral and abbey churches* 1871 which led to formation of Soc. for protection of ancient buildings 1877; published *Chart of the history of architecture* 1863; compiled *Catalogue of the Liverpool free public library* 1872. *d.* Christleton near Chester 10 Jany. 1885. *Biograph*, i, 406 (1879).

HUGGINS, WILLIAM *(brother of the preceding).* *b.* Liverpool 1820; member of Liverpool Academy; painter at Chester 1861 to death; his horses, cattle and poultry pictures were his best work; exhibited 31 pictures at R.A., 8 at B.I. and 1 at Suffolk st. 1842–75; exhibited many pictures at Liverpool, Manchester, Dublin, Edinburgh and Glasgow. *d.* Christleton near Chester 25 Feb. 1884. *Biograph*, *Feb.* 1882 *pp.* 217–23; *Liverpool Mercury* 28 *Feb.* 1884 *p.* 6.

NOTE.—His sister Sarah Huggins, a painter of flowers and fruit and then of architectural views in Chester and Liverpool, *d.* Liverpool, May 1869. *The Builder* 8 *May* 1869 *p.* 369.

HUGHES, CHRISTOPHER *(youngest son of Henry Hughes of Northampton, solicitor).* *b.* Northampton 1815; articled to Hughes and Britten of Northampton, solicitors; admitted Trinity term 1837; clerk of the peace for borough of Northampton 1858 to death; translated *The odes, epodes, Carmen seculare, and the first satire of Horace* 1867. *d.* 60 Waterloo, Northampton 20 Oct. 1877. *Law Times*, lxiv, 53 (1877).

HUGHES, REV. DAVID. *b.* Cefn-uchaf, Llanddeiniolen, Carnarvonshire 1813; B.A., M.A.; member of Bethel independent church, Arfon, began preaching 1832; studied at Hackney coll. and Glasgow univ.; ordained 14 Sep. 1841, pastor of two small congregations in Flintshire; pastor at St. Asaph 1845, at Manchester 1846, at Bangor 1846 and at Tredegar, Monmouthshire 1 Nov. 1855 to death; author of *Geiriadur Ysgrythyrol o Dduwinyddol, i.e. A scriptural and theological dictionary* 2 vols. 1852–55, 2 ed. 2 vols. 1876–9; contributed to the *Gwyddoniadur or Welsh Cyclopædia*; edited and enlarged *An English and Welsh dictionary. By T. Edwards of Caerfallwch* 1864. *d.* Tredegar 3 June 1872.

HUGHES, EDWARD. *b.* Ireland 1819; second master of lower school, Greenwich hospital 4 Nov. 1841 and head master of royal naval school there 1844 to death; A.I.C.E. 1848; F.R.A.S.; F.R.G.S.; author of *A manual of explanatory arithmetic* 1849, 2 ed. 1855; *Outlines of physical geography* 1849, 5 ed. 1855; *Geography for elementary schools* 1851, *new ed.* 1873; *Select English poetry* 1851, 5 ed. 1856 and other school books. *d.* Greenwich hospital 30 July 1859.

NOTE.—His widow Sarah, youngest dau. of James Oliphant Bell, M.D., granted civil list pension of £100, 18 June 1863, she *d.* 9 Jany. 1884 aged 68.

HUGHES, EDWIN *(son of a steel toy manufacturer).* *b.* Birmingham 2 Oct. 1813; member of Batty & Sons' circus; the best polander performer in England, the first to introduce turning round on his head without holding; had a company of his own at Donnybrook fair two years; at Cheltenham established Hughes' Great mammoth equestrian circus; appeared before the Queen at Drury Lane under A. Bunn's management 22 April 1847; retired after nine seasons with a handsome fortune 1847; the first to drive thirty-two horses in hand; the first to introduce camels and elephants in harness. *d.* Welby house, Lower Norwood, Surrey 7 Dec. 1867. *bur.* Smithdown cemet. Liverpool 12 Dec. *Era* 22 *Dec.* 1867 *p.* 6; *Frost's Circus life* (1876) 97, 216.

HUGHES, EDWIN (*eld. son of Edwin Hughes of The Farm, Smithdown road, Wavertree near Liverpool*). *b.* Dublin 1 Feb. 1837; articled to Avison and Pritt of Liverpool, solicitors; admitted Jany. 1858; went to America, joined Federal army in which he became major; served under Garibaldi in Italy; a solicitor in Liverpool 1869 to death; captain 1 Lancashire artillery volunteers 21 Jany. 1874 to death; member of council of Financial reform association. *d.* 13 Elm vale, Fairfield, Liverpool 12 May 1879. *bur.* Smithdown cemetery, Liverpool. *Law Times, lxvii,* 105 (1879).

HUGHES, FANNY. *b.* 1843; educated for a singer; an actress in comedies and burlesques at Strand theatre when under Mrs. Swanborough's management 1862–72; played Orozembo in L. S. Buckingham's burlesque *Pizarro, or the Leotard of Peru* 24 April 1862; played Anne Boleyn in Wm. Brough's extravaganza *The field of the cloth of gold,* produced 11 April 1868; (*m.* Edward Swanborough of the Strand theatre). *d.* 5 Neville st. Onslow gardens, London 12 Jany. 1888.

HUGHES, GEORGE EDWARD (1 son of John Hughes of Uffington, Berks.) *b.* Uffington 18 Sep. 1821; ed. at Rugby and Oriel coll. Ox., B.A. 1845, M.A. 1849, D.C.L. 1850; stroke of Ox. univ. crew of 7 oars which beat Camb. crew of 8 oars 1843; a student of Lincoln's inn 1848; member of college of doctors of law 12 Nov. 1850, practised in the ecclesiastical courts; member of Pen and Pencil club at Pau; violoncello player. *d.* Hoylake, Cheshire 2 May 1872. *Memoirs of a brother. By Thomas Hughes* (1873), *portrait.*

HUGHES, GEORGE MARTIN. *b.* Maidstone 1827; a solicitor; investigated Romano-British topography of the south of England; author of *A history of Windsor forest, Sunninghill and the Great park* 1890. *d.* Kingswick, Sunninghill, Berkshire 9 Sep. 1891.

HUGHES, HENRY GEORGE (*eld. son of James Hughes of Dublin, solicitor*). *b.* Capel st. Dublin 22 Aug. 1810; ed. at Trin. coll. Dublin; called to Irish bar, Nov. 1834; Q.C. 2 Nov. 1844; bencher of King's Inns 1850; solicitor general for Ireland 26 Sep. 1850 to Feb. 1852 and Feb. 1858 to July 1859; baron of court of exchequer July 1859 to death; contested Cavan 1855; M.P. for co. Longford 1856–7; author of *Practice of the Court of chancery, Ireland. Dublin* 1837. *d.* Bray, Wicklow 22 July 1872. *Irish law times, vi,* 404 (1872).

HUGHES, HUGH (*son of Thomas Hughes*). *b.* Pwllygwichiad. *bapt.* Llandudno 20 Feb. 1790; apprentice to an engraver in Liverpool; studied oil painting in London; exhibited 4 landscapes at B.I. and 6 at Suffolk st. 1827–51; spent 3 years at Meddiant working at his *Beauties of Cambria* 60 views published Carmarthen 1823, drew 58 of the views and engraved all of them; a printer at Carnarvon where he published *Y Papur Newydd Cymraeg;* expelled from Welsh Calvinistic ch. London for signing petition in favor of catholic emancipation 1828; joined the Independents, then the Plymouth brethren; had a controversy with Rev. Evan Evans and published pamphlets under name of Cristion 1832; author of *Hynafion Cymreig, a work on Welsh antiquities. Carmarthen* 1823 and other books in Welsh language. *d.* Great Malvern 11 March 1863. *Red Dragon, May* 1887 *xi* 457–66, 576 (1887).

HUGHES, REV. HUGH (*son of Mr. Hughes, deacon of independent church at Cororion*). *b.* Cilgeraint, Llandegai, Carnarvonshire 1805; pastor of independent churches at Rhos-y-lan, Tabor, and Llanystymdwy, at Jackson st. Manchester, at Capelhelyg, Chwilog and Abererch in Carnarvonshire; set up a printing-press at Abererch and edited *Yr Arweinydd* a penny monthly many years; pastor of the new church at Bethel, Aberdare 1859 to death; competed frequently and successfully at Eisteddfods; most voluminous Welsh writer of his day; author of *Rhesymeg. Wrexham* 1856; *d.* Aberdare 8 Dec. 1864. *J. T. Jones's Geiriadur Bywgraffydol, i,* 567–70.

HUGHES, REV. HUGH. Educ. at St. Peter's coll. Cam., B.D. 1842, D.D. 1847; R. of St. John, Clerkenwell, London 13 Dec. 1839 to death; author of *Female characters of holy writ, in a course of sermons.* 3 series 1845, 6, 7; *The remarkable scenes of the bible* 1860, *new ed.* 1879. *d.* 18 Chadwell st. Myddleton sq. London 1870.

HUGHES, REV. JAMES. *b.* Carlow, March 1810; R.C. priest June 1833; professor of

HUGHES, REV. J. (*Con.*)

natural philosophy St. Patrick's coll. Carlow 1835-6; in charge of Carlow classical academy; C. of Maryborough; C. of Kilcock 1837; dean of coll. of St. Patrick's 1841-55; administrator of Carlow parish 1855-8; priest in charge of Naas, Dec. 1858 to death; author of *A practical exposition of the ceremonies to be observed at solemn mass. Dublin* 1843; *The ceremonies of low mass,* 4 ed. 1858; *The ceremonies of high mass; Pontifical ceremonies. d.* Naas, May 1876. *M. Comerford's Collections of Kildare and Leighlin* (1883) 229.

HUGHES, JAMES STANNUS. L.R.C.S. Ireland 1838, F.R.C.S. 1844, examiner in surgery, joint professor of surgery, sec. of council; M.D. Queen's univ. 1864; surgeon Jervis st. hospital, Dublin; surgeon in ordinary to Dublin castle; edited *Sir H. Marsh's Clinical lectures* 1869; author of *On diseases of the prostate gland* 1863, 2 ed. 1870, and of contributions to *Dublin medical press* and *Dublin hospital gazette. d.* 1 Merrion sq. west, Dublin 1 June 1884. *Medical Times* 7 *June* 1884 *p.* 771.

HUGHES, JOHN (*only child of Rev. Thomas Hughes, canon of St. Paul's, d. 6 Jany. 1833 aged 77*). *b.* 2 Jany. 1790; ed. at Westminster and Oriel coll. Ox., B.A. 1812, M.A. 1815; author of the macaronic Oriel grace-cup song '*Exultet mater Oriel*'; author of *Pompeii* 1820, *an ode; An Itinerary of Provence and the Rhone with etchings by the author* 1822; *Lays of past days* 1850; edited *The Boscobel Tracts* 1830, 2 ed. 1857; published a song called *The small coal man* attacking Lord Durham, long attributed to Theodore Hook and R. H. Barham; wrote for the magazines under pseud. of Buller of Brasenose; celebrated in John Wilson's *Christopher in the tent* in the Noctes Ambrosianæ. *d.* 7 Boltons, West Brompton, London 13 Dec. 1857. *G.M. iv,* 225 (1858); *Miss Mitford's Recollections* (1859) 462-4.

HUGHES, REV. JOHN (*son of Hugh Hughes of Adwy'r Clawdd near Wrexham, carpenter*). *b.* Adwy'r Clawdd 11 Feb. 1796; a carpenter to 1815; began preaching in Calvinistic methodist church at Adwy'r 1813; kept a school at Wrexham to 1835; authorised as a regular preacher to visit all parts of Wales, Feb. 1821; ordained at Bala 17 June 1829; a flour merchant 1835-8; co-pastor of Welsh Calvinistic churches of Liverpool 1838 to death; author of *History of Welsh Calvinistic Methodism* 3 vols. *Wrexham* 1851-6 and other books in the Welsh language. *d.* Abergele 8 Aug. 1860. *Sermons of Rev. John Hughes, with memoir and portrait* (1862).

HUGHES, VEN. JOHN (*son of John Hughes of Llwyn Glas near Aberystwyth*). *b.* 1787; C. at Llandrillo yn Rhôs near Conway 1811-17; P.C. of Aberystwyth 16 May 1827 to death; V. of Llanbadern-Fawr 14 June 1834 to death; preb. of Nantgunllo in Brecon coll. ch. to death; archdeacon of Cardigan 1859 to death; most popular preacher of Church of England in Wales; author of *The domestic ruler's monitor* 1821; *Ruth and her kindred* 1839; *Esther and her people. Sermons* 1842 and other books. *d.* 1 Nov. 1860. *J. Hughes's Sermons with biography by his son. Liverpool* (1864).

HUGHES, MOST REV. JOHN (*son of Patrick Hughes, farmer, d.* 1837). *b.* Annalogham, co. Tyrone 24 June 1797; a gardener and day labourer in U.S. of America 1817-9; ed. at Mount St. Mary's coll. Emmitsburg, Maryland 1819-26; ordained R.C. priest 1825; minister at St. Augustine's 1825 and then at St. Joseph's churches, Philadelphia, built ch. of St. John there which he served 1832; coadjutor to bishop John Dubois of New York Jany. 1838 and succeeded him as bishop 1842; founded St. John's coll. at Fordham 1841; archbishop of New York 3 Oct. 1850 to death; one of the founders of the American coll. at Rome 1858; author of *Controversy between Rev. Messrs. Hughes and Breckenridge on the subject "Is the protestant religion the religion of Christ?" Philadelphia* 3 ed. 1833; *The church and the world. A lecture* 1850, and other theological works. *d.* New York city 3 Jany. 1864; remains removed from old cath. of St. Patrick to crypt beneath high altar in new cath. 30 Jany. 1883. *Hassard's Life of Most Rev. J. Hughes* (1866), *portrait; Clarke's Lives of bishops of catholic church in U.S. ii,* 73-125 (1872); *Appleton's American Biog. iii,* 303-5 (1887), *portrait; Complete works of J. Hughes. Ed. by L. Kehoe* 2 vols. 1866.

HUGHES, JOHN (*youngest son of Thomas Hughes, civil engineer*). *b.* Linlithgow near Edin. 1823; ed. at Marischal coll. Aberdeen; parliamentary reporter for *Evening Sun,* London 1842, for *Times* 1844, for *Morning Chronicle,* for *Daily News,* and for *Times* again to 1860; theatrical art critic for the *Era;* purchased the *West Surrey Times,* Godalming 1860 and removed it to Guildford where he edited it to his death. *d.* 18 High st. Guildford 2 Nov. 1868. *The Newspaper Press* 1 *Dec.* 1868 *p.* 18.

HUGHES, JOHN (*youngest son of William Hughes of Pen y Clawdd, Denbighshire*). *b.* 1805; ed. at univ. of Edin.; barrister I.T. 3 May 1839; sec. to commission for settlement of claims of Portuguese government on British legion

under Sir De L. Evans 1844–9; twice went
to Sweden for Overend, Gurney & Co. and
then to Copenhagen to claim money advanced
before Danish-German war; a Welsh scholar
and a writer on Cambrian archæology. *d.*
34 Abingdon villas, Kensington 11 July 1883.
Law Times 28 July 1883 p. 249.

HUGHES, JOHN, known as Ceiriog *(youngest
child of Richard Hughes).* *b.* Penbryn, Llanar-
mon-Dyffryn Ceiriog, Denbighshire 25 Sep.
1832; clerk in an office in London road,
Manchester 1849–65; stationmaster on the
Cambrian railway at Llanidloes 1865, at
Towyn 1870, at Trefeglwys 1871, at Caersws
1871 to death; won many prizes for poetry
at Eisteddfods; the best lyric poet of Wales;
author of *Oriau'r Hwyr (Evening Hours) Ruthyn*
1860, 2 *ed.* 1861 of which 25,000 copies were
sold and of 7 other vols. of poetry 1862–88;
wrote 50 songs for *Brinley Richards's Songs of
Wales* 1873, among them is 'God bless the
Prince of Wales.' *d.* Caersws, Montgomeryshire 23 April 1887. *Memoir of J. C. Hughes.
By Llyfrbryf i.e. Isaac Foulkes. Liverpool.*

HUGHES, JOHN CHARLES. *b.* Hatton garden,
London 23 Dec. 1789; appeared at Cheltenham 1806; manager Woolwich theatre; acted
at Richmond; at Drury Lane 1818; good in
old men and country clowns. *Theatrical
Inquisitor, Oct.* 1818 *pp.* 251–3, *portrait.*

HUGHES, RIGHT REV. JOSHUA *(son of Caleb
Hughes of Newport, Pembrokeshire).* *b.* Nevern,
Pembrokeshire 7 Oct. 1807; ed. at Ystrad-
meirig gr. sch. and St. David's coll. Lampeter;
C. of Aberystwith 1830; C. of St. David's,
Carmarthen; V. of Abergwilly to 1846; V.
of Llandingat 1846–70; D.D. Lambeth; bishop of St. Asaph 25 March 1870 to death,
consecrated 8 May 1870; author of several
charges, sermons and pamphlets, one of the
latter on *The University of Brecknock. By
Veritas,* was much discussed. *d.* Crieff, Perthshire 21 Jany. 1889. *I.L.N. lvi,* 449 (1870),
portrait, and 2 *Feb.* 1889 *pp.* 135, 158, *portrait.*

HUGHES, JULIO HENRY *(son of Henry Hughes,
proprietor of Exeter theatre, and grandson of Mr.
Hughes manager of Sadler's Wells).* *b.* in residence attached to Devonport theatre 1810;
under scene painter at Vauxhall gardens; held
a share in the Exeter, Devonport and Guernsey
theatres; first appeared in London at Pavilion
theatre under management of Mr. Gladstones;
leading actor at the Surrey 1840–6; played
at Princess's 1847, at Sadler's Wells. *d.* 11
Oct. 1872. *Theatrical Times, ii,* 129, 138,
portrait.

HUGHES, MARY *(dau. of Mr. Robson). (m.*
1817 Thomas Hughes of Dundee; went to
U.S. of America 1817; kept a school for
young ladies at Philadelphia 1818–39; with
her husband commenced farming at Doyles-
town, Buck county 1839; contributed to the
Church Tract Soc. London 1824; author of
The alchemist, a tale 1818; *The orphan girl*
1819; *The rebellious school girl* 1821; *The life
of W. Penn* 1822, another ed. Philadelphia
1828; *Pleasing and instructive stories* 1830;
Sickroom dialogues, 4 *ed.* 1836; *The twin
brothers* 1839; *Village dialogues* 1839. See
Hale's Woman's Record (1855) 845.

NOTE.—She also wrote Aunt Mary's tales, Orna-
ments discovered, Metamorphosis, Emma Mortimer,
The two schools, Julia Ormond, Buds and Blossoms,
The ivy wreath.

HUGHES, PHILIP. Conducted musical choirs
in Manchester and the neighbourhood; gave
much time to musical services of R.C. ch.;
composer of music to many hymns such as
*The hymn to St. Albans; The green boughs
meet; O turn to Jesus' Mother turn; Jesus,
dulcis memoria,* and others. *d.* West Gorton,
Manchester 10 Feb. 1880. *Gillow's English
catholics, iii,* 469 (1887).

HUGHES, ROBERT BALL *(brother of Julio
Henry Hughes* 1810–72). *b.* London 19 Jany.
1806; pupil of E. H. Bailey the sculptor 7
years; gained gold medal at R.A. 1823 for a
bas-relief, 'Pandora brought by Mercury to
Epimetheus,' exhibited 4 sculptures at R.A.
1822–8; went to U.S. of America 1829 where
his chief works were statue of Alexander
Hamilton for Merchants' Exchange, New
York, destroyed by fire 1835; bronze statue
of Nathaniel Bowditch now at Mount Auburn;
and monument to bishop Hobart in Trin. ch.
New York; sent a statue of Oliver Twist to
Great exhibition in London 1851; lectured
on art and made sketches on wood with a hot
iron. *d.* Boston 5 March 1868.

HUGHES, SAMUEL *(5 son of Richard Hughes,
barrister).* *b.* 1801; barrister I.T. 28 Jany.
1831; author with T. Coventry of *An analytical digested index to the common law reports*
1827; furnished an index and notes to *Sir B.
Shower's Reports of cases in court of king's bench*
1836. *d.* Skipper's hill, Mayfield, Sussex 29
Nov. 1887.

HUGHES, THOMAS *(brother of Robert Ball
Hughes* 1806–68). *b.* 3 Dec. 1808; studied
with E. H. Bailey, sculptor; first appeared at
Queen's theatre, London 1825; at the St.
James's theatre under Edward Hooper's man-
agement when he appeared in a series of

HUGHES, T. *(Con.)*

original parts 1839 ; broke his leg and was unable to resume his profession. *d.* London 7 Sep. 1857. *The Era* 13 *Sep.* 1857 *p.* 11.

HUGHES, THOMAS. Connected with the turf 40 years ; an early patron of Fred Archer the jockey ; won the Chester cup with Our Mary Ann 1870 ; the Shobden cup twice with Oxonian which he sold for £3000 ; retired from the turf 1886. *d.* Aldford near Eaton hall about 25 Feb. 1890.

HUGHES, THOMAS. *b.* Chester 1827 ; apprentice to a printer ; connected with the press at Plymouth ; partner in firm of Minshull and Hughes, booksellers, Eastgate row, Chester, retired 1880 ; sheriff of Chester 1873 ; F.S.A. 7 June 1866 ; had great knowledge of antiquities of Chester and its neighbourhood ; edited D. King's *The vale royal of England* 1852 ; *George Batenham's Ancient Chester* 1880 ; author of *The stranger's handbook to Chester* 1856, 2 *ed.* 1857. *d.* The Grove, Chester 30 May 1890. *The Bookseller* 6 *June* 1890 *p.* 584.

HUGHES, THOMAS ELLIOTT. *b.* 6 Jany. 1830 ; 2 lieut. Bengal artillery 8 June 1849 ; commander of a mountain train battery on N.W. frontier of India, present at storming of Laloo and capture of Umbeylah ; lieut.-colonel R.A. 16 Jany. 1875, colonel 24 Jany. 1880 to death ; M.G. 11 Feb. 1885 ; A.A.G., R.A. at head quarters 1878–82 ; director general of ordnance in India 1884–5. *d.* Simla 24 May 1886.

HUGHES, THOMAS FIOTT (1 *son of Rev. Thomas Smart Hughes, V. of Edgware, d.* 1847). Student attaché at Constantinople 16 May 1845 ; instrumental in raising the Bashi-Bazouks during the Crimean war 1854 ; consul at Erzeroom 29 May 1856 ; oriental sec. at Constantinople 6 Feb. 1859 ; commissioner for the dedicated monasteries in the United Principalities ; retired from public service on a pension of £700, 12 Nov. 1875 ; great linguist and eastern scholar ; translated Arabian Nights into Persian but not printed. *d.* Cheltenham 18 June 1887 aged 62.

HUGHES, SIR WALTER WATSON (3 *son of Thomas Hughes of Pittenweem, Fife). b.* 1803 ; master in mercantile marine ; settled in South Australia, engaged in mining and pastoral pursuits 1841 ; shared in expenses of exploring expeditions and was a promoter of several new industries ; 'father' of the Univ. of Adelaide ; knighted at Windsor castle 16 Dec. 1880 ; purchased Fan Court, Lyne near Chertsey, Surrey 1883. *d.* Fan Court 1 Jany. 1887.

HUGHES, WILLIAM (4 *son of Rev. Sir Robert Hughes, bart., d.* 1814). *b.* Maker vicarage, Cornwall 2 March 1803 ; barrister G.I. 11 June 1833 ; auditor of poor law union district of Cornwall and Devon ; author of *Practical instructions for drawing wills* 1833 ; *The practical angler. By Piscator* 1842 ; *The three students of Gray's inn, A novel* 1846 ; *The practice of conveyancing* 2 vols. 1856–7 and other books. *d.* 2 Millbay grove, Plymouth 20 Aug. 1861. *Boase and Courtney's Bibl. Cornub.* i, 258.

HUGHES, WILLIAM. *b.* 1817 ; assistant in library of Br. Museum, cataloguing the geographical collection 1841, resigned Dec. 1843 ; F.R.G.S. ; editor of *Maunder's Treasury of geography* 1856 ; author of *Atlas of constructive geography* 1841 ; *A class book of modern geography* 1859, 3 *ed.* 1885 ; *A class book of physical geography* 1861, 4 *ed.* 1886 ; *A treatise on the construction of maps,* 3 *ed.* 1864, and about 30 other school books. *d.* 198 Adelaide road, Hampstead, London 21 May 1876. *Cowtan's British Museum* (1872) 321–2.

HUGHES, WILLIAM BULKELEY. *b.* 26 July 1797 ; ed. at Harrow ; barrister L.I. 21 May 1824 ; M.P. for Carnarvon district of boroughs 1837–59 and 1865 to death ; sheriff of Anglesea 1861. *d.* Plas Coch near Llanfair, Isle of Anglesea 9 March 1882. *Law Times, lxxii,* 376 (1882).

HUGHES, WILLIAM EDWARD (2 *son of Michael Hughes of Sherdley hall, Lancs. d.* 1825). *b.* 16 July 1823 ; ed. at Eton 1838–42 ; member of Turf club ; a player at whist, picquet and billiards ; won a race with Sophistry ; known as Gentleman Hughes and as Little Hughes. *d.* Brussels 17 Dec. 1885. *Sporting Rev. Aug.* 1858 *pp.* 118–19.

HUGHES, WILLIAM HUGHES (*son of John Hewitt). b.* 1792 ; barrister L.I. 26 June 1827 ; contested Oxford 1832 and 1837 ; M.P. for Oxford 18 March 1833 to 18 July 1837 ; sheriff of Hants. ; assumed name of Hughes 25 May 1825 ; alderman of London 1832 ; contributed preface and notes to *J. L. De Lolme's The constitution of England* 1834. *d.* Ilkley Wells house, Yorkshire 10 Oct. 1874.

HUGHES, WILLIAM LITTLE (*son of Wm. Hughes of Dublin). b.* Dublin 1822 ; clerk in foreign press department of ministry of the interior, Paris about 1857, chief clerk to death ; a collector of works on Shakespeare in all languages ; translated and published *Les temps difficiles. Par C. Dickens* 1857 ; *Devereux. Par Sir E. B. Lytton* 1859 ; *Histoire d' une chandelle. Par M. Faraday* 1865 ; *Œuvres choisies d' Edgar*

Poe 1885 ; *Les aventures de Huck Finn. Par M. Twain* 1886 and other works. *d.* Paris 5 Jany. 1887.

HUGO, REV. THOMAS *(eld. son of Charles Hugo, M.D. of Taunton). b.* Taunton 1820 ; ed. at Worc. coll. Ox., B.A. 1842 ; C. of Walton-le-Dale, Lancs. 1842–44 ; V. of Halliwell, Lancs. 1850–52 ; V. of St. Botolph's, Bishopsgate 1852–58 ; P.C. of All Saints, Bishopsgate 1858–68 ; R. of West Hackney 1868 to death ; F.S.A. 24 Feb. 1853 ; founder of London and Middlesex archæol. soc. 1855 ; made collection of works of the Brothers Bewick of Newcastle, and had many of their wood-blocks ; contributed to *Hymns ancient and modern* 1860 ; author of *The charters of Cleeve abbey* 1856 ; *Varus, a tragedy* 1864 ; *The Bewick collector. A catalogue of the works of T. and J. Bewick* 1866 ; *The Bewick collector. A supplement* 1868 ; *Bewick's Woodcuts* 1870 and 15 other books. *d.* West Hackney rectory 31 Dec. 1876. *bur.* Highgate cemet. 6 Jany. 1877. *Guardian* 3 Jany. 1877 *p.* 12.

HUISH, MARK. *b.* 1808 ; sec. and general manager Glasgow and Greenock railway 1839 or 40, of grand junction railway 1841–45, of Liverpool and Manchester and Bolton railway 1845–46, and of London and north western railway 1846 to Nov. 1858 ; A.I.C.E. 6 April 1852. *d.* Combe Wood, Bonchurch 18 Jany. 1867. *Min. of proc. of Instit. of C.E.* xxvii, 600–602 (1868) ; *I.L.N.* xxxiii, 517–8 (1858), *portrait ; Railway Management. Two letters to G. C. Glyn by J. Whitehead and M. Huish* 1848.

HULBERT, CHARLES *(son of Thomas Hulbert of Hulbert Green near Cheadle, Cheshire). b.* Manchester 18 Feb. 1778 ; manager of print works at Middleton 1800 ; cotton manufacturer at Swinton near Manchester, then at Coleham near Shrewsbury 1803–13 ; bookseller and printer, Shrewsbury 1813–27 and at Hadnal near Shrewsbury 1827 to death ; printed *Salopian Mag.* 1815–7 ; his house and library burnt 7 Jany. 1839 ; author of *The select museum of the world* 4 vols. 1822–5 ; *The history of Salop* 1837 ; *Cheshire Antiquities* 1838 ; *Memoirs of seventy years of an eventful life* 1848–52, *with portrait,* and many other books. *d.* Hadnal near Shrewsbury 7 Oct. 1857. *Obituary of C. Hulbert. By C. A. Hulbert,* 2 ed. (1860) ; *Shrewsbury Chronicle* 6 Nov. 1857.

HULBERT, REV. CHARLES AUGUSTUS *(eld. son of the preceding). b.* Coleham near Shrewsbury 31 Dec. 1804 or 1805 ; ed. at Shrewsbury and Sid. Sus. coll. Cam., B.A. 1834, M.A.

1837 ; C. of St. Mary's, Islington 1834–9 ; P.C. of Slaithwaite, Yorkshire 1839–67 ; V. of Almondbury near Huddersfield 26 Feb. 1867 to death ; hon. canon of Ripon, Oct. 1866 to death ; author of *Poetical recreations* 1828 ; *Theotokos, or the song of the Virgin* 1842 ; *Annals of the church in Slaithwaite* 1864 ; *Annals of the church and parish of Almondbury* 1882, *Supplementary Annals* 1885, and other books ; (Mary his wife dau. of James Lacy of Islington *d.* 2 May 1884 aged 75). *d.* 5 March 1888. *C. A. Hulbert's Annals of Almondbury* (1883) 96, 592, *portrait ; Supplementary Annals* (1885) 62–8, *portrait of his wife.*

HULINE, JAMES. *b.* about 1816 ; played clown in pantomime of *The Maid and the Magpie,* at Princess's theatre, London, Dec. 1854 ; in pantomime of Harlequin and the House that Jack built, at Drury Lane Dec. 1861 ; in pantomime of Ladybird or Harlequin Lord Dundreary, at Astley's Dec. 1862 ; father of the well known brothers Huline clowns. *d.* 31 Jany. 1890. *Illust. sp. and dram. news* 19 Dec. 1874 *p.* 268, *portrait.*

HULL, REV. EDWARD. *b.* 1789 ; ed. at St. John's coll. Cam., B.A. 1810, M.A. 1814 ; minister of St. Mary's attached to Blind sch. Liverpool 1819–57 ; author of *The institution and abuses of ecclesiastical property* 1831 ; *The tractarian and the prayer book* 1853. *d.* Waterloo road, Liverpool 6 Jany. 1867.

HULL, ROBERT. *b.* 1795 ; M.R.C.S. 1816, Ext. L.R.C.P. ; M.D. Lambeth ; physician Norfolk and Norwich eye infirmary ; author of *Cursory notes on the morbid eye* 1840 ; *Essay on determination of blood to the head* 1842 ; *A few suggestions on consumption* 1849. *d.* St. Michael-at-Plea, Norwich 13 April 1856.

HULL, WILLIAM *(son of a small farmer). b.* Graffham, Hunts. 6 May 1820 ; ed. at Moravian settlements, Ockbrook near Derby, Wellhouse, Yorkshire, and Grace Hill near Ballymena, Ireland 1834–40 ; travelled in France, Germany and Holland 1841–4 ; an artist at Manchester 1844–70 ; exhibited at Manchester academy of fine arts, Royal Manchester Instit. and the Black and white exhibitions held 1877–80 ; illustrated R. Langton's *Charles Dickens and Rochester* 1880 ; settled at Rydal, Westmoreland 1870 and became known as The painter of Rydal. *d.* Rydal 15 March 1880. *bur.* Grasmere ch. yard. *Portfolio, Jany.* 1886 *pp.* 15, 21 ; *Papers of Manchester Literary Club* (1880) 308–10 ; *Catalogue of water colour drawing, etc. by W. Hull, exhibited at Manchester Lit. Club* 1886.

HULL, WILLIAM WINSTANLEY (*son of John Hull, M.D., botanist 1761–1843*). *b.* Blackburn 15 March 1794; ed. at Manchester and Macclesfield gr. schs. and Brasenose coll. Ox., fellow 1816–20; B.A. 1815, M.A. 1817; barrister L.I. 16 June 1820; practised at chancery bar to 1846; with his brother Rev. John Hull drew up a petition praying for revision of the liturgy, presented to House of Lords 26 May 1840; author of *Occasional papers on church matters* 1848; *A collection of prayers for household use, with some hymns and other poems* 1852; *A letter concerning the revision of the book of common prayer* 1860. *d.* The Knowle, Hazlewood, Derbyshire 28 Aug. 1873. *Manchester School Register, iii, 37, 289.*

HULLAH, JOHN PYKE. *b.* Worcester 27 June 1812; studied music under Wm. Horsley and at royal academy of music 1832; his opera *The Village Coquette* produced at St. James's theatre, London 5 Dec. 1836 ran for 60 nights; organist of Croydon church 1837; his operas *The Barbers of Bassora* and *The Outpost* produced at Covent Garden 1837 and 1838 were unsuccessful; formed classes at Exeter Hall for teaching music to large numbers of persons on Wilhelm's method 1841, his classes removed to St. Martin's hall, Oct. 1849, formally opened 11 Feb. 1850, burnt down 26 Aug. 1860; organist to the Charterhouse 1858 to death; composed music for Kingsley's songs *The Sands of Dee* and *The Three Fishers;* conducted concerts of R.A. of music 1870–3; bankrupt Oct. 1860; musical inspector of training schools for United Kingdom, March 1872; LL.D. Edin. 1876; granted civil list pension of £150, 13 Oct. 1880; edited *Part music* 2 vols. 1842–5, *another ed.* 1868; *The song book* 1866; author of *Wilhelm's Method of teaching singing* 1841, 3 ed. 1854; *A grammar of musical harmony* 1852; *A grammar of counterpoint* 1864 and about 100 pieces of music. *d.* 17 Grosvenor mansions, Victoria st. London 21 Feb. 1884. *bur.* Kensal green 26 Feb. *Life of John Hullah* (1886); *Dublin Univ. Mag. March* 1880 *pp.* 323–33, *portrait; I.L.N. i,* 69, 76 (1842) *portrait, x* 405 (1847), *xvi* 117 (1850); *Graphic xxix,* 229 (1884), *portrait.*

HULLETT, REV. JOHN. *b.* 1815; ed. at St. Cath. hall, Cam., B.A. 1838; P.C. of Allestree, Derby 1849 to death; author of *Sermons preached for the most part in the church of Allestree* 1858, *Second series* 1859; *The true light and other poems* 1861. *d.* Toft near Knutsford 25 April 1865.

HULME, FREDERICK WILLIAM (*son of an artist*). *b.* Swinton, Yorkshire 1816; landscape painter; teacher of drawing and painting in London;

HULME, F. W. (*Con.*)

exhibited 36 pictures at R.A., 5 at B.I. and 5 at Suffolk st. 1845–80; published *A graduated series of drawing copies on landscape subjects for use of schools* 4 parts 1850. *d.* 8 St. Alban's road, Kensington, London 14 Nov. 1884. *I.L.N. lxxxv,* 556 (1884), *portrait; Athenæum 22 Nov.* 1884 *p.* 666.

HULME, JOHN WALTER. Barrister M.T. 23 Jany. 1829; chief justice of Hong Kong 9 Feb. 1844 to Jany. or Feb. 1860. *d.* Brighton 1 March 1861 in 57 year.

HULTON, REV. CAMPBELL BASSET ARTHUR GREY (*4 son of Henry Hulton of Preston 1765–1831, treasurer of co. of Lancaster*). *b.* Ballalhick, Isle of Man 3 May 1813; ed. at Manchester sch. and Brasenose coll. Ox., scholar 1831–4; B.A. 1835, M.A. 1838; Ellerton theological prizeman 1837; C. of St. Mary's, Manchester 1839–44; Chetham's librarian at Manchester 1839–45; R. of St. Paul's, Manchester 1844–60; R. of Emberton, Bucks. 1860 to death; author of *A catechetical help to bishop Butler's Analogy* 1854, another ed. 1859 *d.* Emberton rectory 30 April 1878. *Manchester sch. register, iii,* 176 (1874).

HULTON, WILLIAM ADAM (*brother of the preceding*). *b.* Preston 18 Oct. 1802; ed. at Manchester gr. sch.; barrister I.T. 29 June 1827; treasurer of county Lancaster 1831–49; assessor of Lancaster Sheriff's Court to 1847; judge of county courts, circuit No. 5 (Bolton, &c.), 13 March 1847; judge of circuit No. 6 (Liverpool), 31 Dec. 1859; judge of circuit No. 4 (Preston, &c.) 1863 to April 1886; edited and printed with his own hands *A Pedigree of the Hulton family* about 1847; member of council of Chetham Soc. 1848, edited for the Soc. *The Coucher book, or chartulary of Whalley Abbey* 4 vols. 1847–50, *Documents relating to the Priory of Penwortham* 1853; author of *A treatise on the law of convictions with the statutes and forms applicable to summary convictions by justices of the peace* 1835. *d.* Hurst Grange near Preston 3 March 1887. *Law Times* 19 March 1887 *p.* 367.

HUMBER, WILLIAM. *b.* 1821; pupil of G. Watson 1835–39; one of Thomas Brassey's staff 1847–52; practised as civil engineer 1852 to death; A.I.C.E. 6 May 1856; author of *A complete treatise on cast and wrought iron bridge construction* 2 vols. 1857, 3 ed. 1870; *A record of the progress of modern engineering* 1863–66, 4 vols. 1870; *A handy book for the calculation of strains in girders* 1868, 4 ed. 1885; *A comprehensive treatise on the water supply of cities and towns* 1876. *d.* 1 Portland villas, Brixton hill, Surrey 14 April 1881.

HUMBERSTON, PHILIP STAPLETON (*only son of Philip Humberston of Chester*). *b.* 1812; ed. at Westminster; M.P. for Chester 1859–65; sheriff of Cheshire 1878; hon. col. of 2 volunteer battalion of Cheshire regiment 20 May 1876 to death; member of council of Royal Agricultural Soc., proposed the use of a special form of Farming agreements 1855. *d.* Glan-y-Wern near Denbigh 16 Jany. 1891.

HUMBERT, ALBERT JENKINS. *b.* 1822; partner with Charles Frederick Reeks, architect, designed Carlisle parade and Robertson terrace, Hastings, and rebuilt the church at Bodiam; had premium for designs for new government offices 1856; rebuilt Whippingham ch. Isle of Wight 1860; designed mausoleum of duchess of Kent 1861 and that of Prince Consort 1862, both at Frogmore near Windsor; designed and superintended rebuilding of Sandringham house for prince of Wales 1869–71; F.R.I.B.A. *d.* Castle Mona, Douglas, Isle of Man 24 Dec. 1877.

HUMBLE, REV. HENRY. Ed. at Univ. coll. Durham, B.A. 1837, M.A. 1842; C. of Newburn, Northumberland 1842–53; canon and precentor of St. Ninian's cath. Perth 1853 to death; author of *A letter to the bishop of St. Andrews on his recent charge* 1859; *The recent episcopal decisions. A review of the transactions at the episcopal synod* 1858; *Remarks on a debate in convocation in reference to the Scottish liturgy* 1862; *The rights of laymen in the church of Christ* 1870; *The administration of canon law, a review of proceedings in the case of Humble and others v. the bishop of St. Andrews* 1873. *d.* San Remo, Italy 7 Feb. 1876.

HUMBLE, REV. MICHAEL MAUGHAN. *b.* 1811; ed. at Em. coll. Cam., B.A. 1833, M.A. 1860; C. of Felton, Northumberland 1835–9; R. of Sutton cum Duckmanton, Derbyshire 2 July 1839 to death; author of *Methodistic Catholicism* 1852; *The church of England and the fathers* 1854; *Credenda* 1875; *Family Prayers* 1879. *d.* Sutton rectory 3 Feb. 1889.

HUMBLE, WILLIAM. *b.* 1797; M.D.; F.G.S.; author of *A practical treatise on sea bathing. Worthing* 1838; *Dictionary of geology and mineralogy* 1840, 3 ed. 1860. *d.* Cliff lodge, Ramsgate 23 April 1878.

HUMBY, ANNE (*dau. of Mr. Ayre of London, law stationer*). *b.* London 1800; first appeared on the stage at Hull as Rosina; appeared at Bath 4 Nov. 1818 as Rosetta in *Love in a village;* played at Dublin 1821–5; first appeared in London at Haymarket theatre 18 April 1825 as Cowslip in *The Agreeable Surprise;* played at Haymarket 1825–30, then at

Drury Lane; unrivalled as an actress of chambermaids, &c.; the original exponent of Polly Briggs in Douglas Jerrold's *Rent Day* 25 Jany. 1832, of Sophy Hawes in Jerrold's *Housekeeper* at the Haymarket 17 July 1833, of Chicken in Jerrold's *Time Works Wonders* at the Haymarket 26 April 1845, and of Lady Clutterbuck in Boucicault's *Used up* at the Haymarket 6 Feb. 1844, and was seen in the same character at Windsor castle 4 Jany. 1849; made her last appearance on the stage, at Lyceum theatre as a Damsel in Barbadoes in *Drop the Curtain* 28 Nov. 1849; (*m.* (1) about 1817 William Henry Humby actor in the Hull circuit, subsequently a dentist London 1831 to 1847, *d.* Guernsey 15 June 1850 aged 58; *m.* (2) 3 April 1854 at Episcopal chapel, St. Peter's, Hammersmith, Joseph Hammon of Bridge road, Hammersmith, builder then aged 43); she lived at 198 Piccadilly, London 1848–51, at 3 Castlenau cottages, Barnes 1854–60 or 61 and must be *dead*, but her name cannot be found in register of deaths at Somerset house between 1866 and 1887. *The Oddfellow, i,* 81 (1839).

HUME, REV. ABRAHAM (*son of Thomas F. Hume*). *b.* Hillsborough, co. Down 9 Feb. 1814; ed. at Royal Belfast coll., Glasgow univ., LL.B. and LL.D. 1851, and Trin. coll. Dublin; B.A. Dublin 1843, LL.D. Cam. 1856, D.C.L. Ox. 1857; C. of St. Augustines, Everton 1844–47; prof. of English literature in collegiate institution, Liverpool 1844–7; V. of Vauxhall, Liverpool 1847 to death; surveyed Chili and Peru for South American Missionary Soc. 1867; chief founder of Hist. Soc. of Lancs. and Cheshire 1848, pres. 1869–75; sec. of church congress at Liverpool 1869; sec. of British association at Liverpool 1870; vice chairman of Liverpool school board 1870–6; sec. of Liverpool bishopric committee 1873–80; hon. canon of Chester 1874–80, of Liverpool 1880 to death; F.S.A. 14 March 1844; author of *The learned societies and printing clubs of the United Kingdom* 1847, new ed. 1853; *Ancient Meols, or some account of the antiquities found on the sea-coast of Cheshire* 2 parts 1863–66 with portrait of author; *Remarks on the Irish dialect of the English language* 1878, and more than 100 other books. *d.* All Soul's vicarage, 6 Rupert lane, Liverpool 21 Nov. 1884. *J. C. Morley's Memoir of Rev. A. Hume, Liverpool* 1887; *Crockford's Clerical Directory* (1876) 474.

HUME, ALEXANDER (*son of Walter Hume, a retail trader*). *b.* Kelso 1 Feb. 1809; a strolling player in England 1822 or 1823; employed

HUME, A. *(Con.)*

by London agents of Berwick & Co. brewers, Edinburgh 1827–40; London agent for Messrs. Lane, brewers, Cork 1841–7; author of *Scottish songs* 1835; *English songs and ballads* 1838; *Songs and poems, chiefly Scottish* 1845. *d.* Northampton, May 1851. *Rogers's Modern Scottish Minstrel, ii,* 182–94 (1856).

HUME, ALEXANDER. *b.* Edinburgh 17 Feb. 1811; tenor singer in St. Paul's episcopal ch. Edin.; chorus master in theatre royal, Edin.; arranged musical manual for the Glassites; cabinet maker at Glasgow about 1855; very successful in setting tunes to Scottish lyrics and songs of his own; edited *The lyric gems of Scotland. Glasgow* 1856, to which he made 50 contributions. *d.* Glasgow 4 Feb. 1859.

HUME, ALEXANDER HAMILTON *(son of Andrew Hamilton Hume 1762–1849, Australian settler).* *b.* Paramatta, New South Wales 18 June 1797; with his brother John Kennedy Hume (shot by bush rangers Jany. 1840) discovered Bong Bong and Berrima, Aug. 1814; accompanied surveyor Meehan in the discovery of Goulburn plains 1817, rewarded with grant of 300 acres near Appin; made the first overland journey from Sydney to Port Philip 2 Oct. to 16 Dec. 1824, discovered the Hume now called Murray river 16 Nov. 1824, rewarded with grant of 1200 acres of land valued at half a crown an acre 1825; accompanied Charles Sturt in his Macquarie and Darling river expedition 1828–9; F.R.G.S. 1860; author of *A brief statement of an overland expedition from Lake George to Port Philip* 1855, 3 ed. 1874. *d.* Fort George, Yass, N.S.W. 19 April 1873, monumental pillar at Albury on the Murray. *Heaton's Australian Dictionary* (1879) 98; *Bonwick's Port Philip Settlement* (1883) 80–93, *portrait.*

HUME, SIR GUSTAVUS (2 son of *Rev. Robert Hume of Dublin, d.* 1849). *b.* 25 Feb. 1826; ensign 38 foot 30 May 1843, captain 21 Sep. 1852 to 22 June 1858 when placed on h.p.; served in Crimean war 1854–5 and in Indian mutiny 1857–8; assistant inspector of volunteers 1860–65; lieut.-col. in the army 17 March 1863; member of corps of gentlemen-at-arms, Dec. 1872, adjutant 1 Jany. 1876, lieut. 20 Nov. 1878 to death; a knight of Legion of Honour; knighted at Windsor Castle 1 Dec. 1880. *d.* 21 Royal York crescent, Clifton 16 June 1891.

HUME, JOHN ROBERT. *b.* Renfrewshire 1781 or 1782; received medical education at Glasgow 1795, 98 and 99, and at Edinburgh 1796–97; entered medical department of army,

HUME, J. R. *(Con.)*

inspector general 3 Dec. 1818 to 25 April 1821 when placed on h.p.; M.D. St. Andrews 12 Jany. 1816; L.R.C.P. London 22 Dec. 1819, F.R.C.P. 9 July 1836; settled in London; private physician to duke of Wellington many years; D.C.L. Ox. 13 June 1834; one of metropolitan comrs. in lunacy 1 Sep. 1836 to death; C.B. 16 Aug. 1850. *d.* 9 Curzon st. London 1 March 1857. *Munk's Coll. of physicians, iii,* 212 (1878).

HUME, JOSEPH *(son of James Hume of Montrose, shipmaster).* *b.* Montrose 22 Jany. 1777; apprenticed to a surgeon of Montrose 1790; M.R.C.S. Edin. 1796; M.R.C.S. Lond. 2 Feb. 1797; assistant surgeon in marine service of East India Co.; Persian interpreter in army during Mahratta war 1802–1807; commissary general 1807, resigned and returned to England with £40,000, 1808; M.P. Weymouth, Jany. 1812; M.P. Aberdeen district of burghs 1818–30; M.P. Middlesex 1830–37; M.P. Kilkenny 1837–41; contested Leeds 1841; M.P. Montrose district of burghs 1842 to death; leader of the radical party 30 years, he spoke longer and oftener than any other private member, many of his speeches were printed; lord rector of Univ. of Aberdeen 1824 and 1828; F.R.S.; F.R.A.S. *d.* Burnley hall, Norfolk 20 Feb. 1855. *bur.* Kensal Green cemetery. *Joseph Hume a memorial [a poem].* By *J. B. Hume* (1855); *H. Martineau's Biographical sketches,* 4 *ed.* (1876) 64–70; *Reminiscences of 50 years. By Mark Boyd* (1871) 281–92; *J. Grant's Memoir of Sir G. Sinclair* (1870) 66–79; *St. Stephens. By Mask* (1839) 198–210; *Saunders's Portraits of reformers* (1840), 55 *portrait; Fagan's Reform club* (1887) 29–31, *portrait.*

HUMFREY, LEBBEUS CHARLES *(eld. son of Rev. Lebbeus Charles Humfrey, R. of Laughton, Leics. d.* 1833). *b.* about 1798; ed. at Trin. coll. Cam., B.A. 1820, M.A. 1823; barrister L.I. 17 June 1823, bencher 1845; went Midland circuit of which he became leader; counsel to *Times* newspaper; Q.C. Feb. 1845; marble bust of him by E. H. Bailey exhibited at the R.A. 1852. *d.* 11 Great Queen st. Westminster 11 May 1852. *bur.* beneath chapel of Lincoln's inn. *G.M. xxxviii,* 95–6 (1852).

HUMPHERY, JOHN *(eld. son of John Humphery of Shadwell, London).* *b.* 30 May 1794; a wharfinger and merchant at Hay's wharf, Tooley st. Southwark; M.P. for Southwark 1832–52; governor of Irish Society 1843 to death; alderman of Aldgate ward 1835 to death; sheriff of London 1832–3, lord mayor

HUMPHERY, J. (Con.)

1842–3. d. Battersea Rise, north side of Clapham common 28 Sep. 1863. *I.L.N. ii*, 279 (1843), *portrait*.

HUMPHREY, THOMAS. *b.* Mitcham, Surrey 16 Jany. 1839; one of the best batsmen of his day, especially good at cutting, made 1000 runs during a season several times; played for Surrey many years; a first-class fieldsman especially at long-leg and long-on; had a benefit at Kennington Oval 26–28 July 1876. *d.* the Asylum, Brookwood, Surrey 3 Sep. 1878. *bur.* Woking cemet. 9 Sep. *Illust. sp. and dram. news, v*, 401, 402, 430 (1876), *portrait; Bell's Life in London 7 Sep. 1878 pp. 3, 4, and 14 Sep. p. 4; W. G. Grace's Cricket* (1891) 329–30.

HUMPHREYS, HENRY NOEL (*son of James Humphreys of Birmingham*). *b.* Birmingham 4 Jany. 1810; resided in Italy about 1828–40; illustrated *Westwood's British butterflies* 1841; *Loudon's British Wild Flowers* 1856 and other books; author of *The Coins of England* 1846; *The coin-collector's manual* 2 vols. 1847; *The origin and progress of the art of writing* 1853; *A history of the art of printing* 1867 and 20 other books. *d.* 7 Westbourne sq. London 10 June 1879. *Academy 21 June 1879 p. 550.*

HUMPHREYS, SIR JOHN (*son of John Humphreys of Upper Clapton, Middlesex*). *b.* Upper Clapton 1814; a solicitor and parliamentary agent in London 1842–59; coroner for East Middlesex 1859 to death; knighted at Osborne 18 Aug. 1881. *d.* 20 Devonshire st. Portland place, London 20 Nov. 1886.

HUMPHREYS, WILLIAM. *b.* Dublin 1794; learnt engraving from George Murray at Philadelphia; engraved small plates for annuals, &c.; returned to England 1822; engraved steel plate head of Queen Victoria on postage stamps, also head of Washington for U.S. stamps; engraved Murillo's Spanish peasant boy 1833, C. R Leslie's Sancho and the Duchess 1838, and other large plates. *d.* at Alfred Novello's residence, Villa Novella, Genoa 21 Jany. 1865. *W. S. Baker's American Engravers* (1875) 84–86.

HUMPHRY, JOSEPH. *b.* 1795 or 1796; barrister L.I. 6 July 1821; Q.C. 1846 to 28 Nov. 1850; master in chancery 28 Nov. 1850 to 8 Aug. 1860 when he retired. *d.* Brighton 18 Nov. 1861.

NOTE.—He was the last master in chancery appointed, the office was abolished in 1852 by 15 & 16 Vict. cap. 80 having been in existence since 1272.

HUMPHRY, REV. WILLIAM GILSON (*eld. son of Wm. Wood Humphry, barrister*). *b.* Sudbury, Suffolk 30 Jany. 1815; ed. at Shrewsbury, captain of the school; entered Trin. coll. Cam. 1833, Pitt scholar 1835, fellow 1839, senior classic and 27th wrangler 1837, B.A. 1837; proctor of Univ. of Cam. 1845–6, Hulsean lecturer 1849–51, Boyle lecturer 1857–9; exam. chaplain to bishop Blomfield of London 1847–55; V. of Northolt, Middlesex 1852–5; preb. of St. Paul's 1852 to death; V. of St. Martin-in-the-Fields, London 1855 to death; one of revisers of New Testament 1870; a treasurer of S.P.C.K. 30 years; author of *A commentary on the Acts of the Apostles* 1847, 2 ed. 1854; *An historical treatise on the book of common prayer* 1853, 6 ed. 1885; *A commentary on the revised version of the New Testament for English readers* 1882, 2 ed. 1888 and 20 other books. *d.* 6 St. Martin's place, Trafalgar sq. London 10 Jany. 1886.

HUMPIDGE, THOMAS SAMUEL. *b.* Gloucester 23 July 1853; ed. at Royal school of mines 1874, Jodrell scholar 1875; B. Sc. London 1875; Ph. D. Heidelberg 1878; science master Fellenberg instit. Hofwyl near Berne 1878; prof. of natural science Univ. coll. Aberystwyth, Sep. 1879 to death; made discoveries in the atomic weight of beryllium, towards the cost of which the Royal Soc. made grants, all his apparatus burnt in the college July 1885; sent papers to *Philos. Trans.* and *Proceedings;* translated H. Kolbe's *A short text-book of inorganic chemistry* 1884. *d.* The college, Aberystwyth 30 Nov. 1887. *Journal Chemical soc.* (1888) 513–18.

HUNGATE, WILLIAM ANNING. *b.* 7 Sep. 1786; entered navy 10 July 1803, lieut. on h.p. 2 March 1815 to death; claimed to be descended from and to be entitled to estates of the Hungate family of Yorkshire, brought actions of ejectment to obtain possession of estates 1831 and 1832 but failed; assumed title of baronet and was presented to Wm. iv. as Sir W. A. Hungate, by Earl of Denbigh 27 April 1831. *d.* 18 Feb. 1852.

HUNLOKE, SIR HENRY JOHN JOSEPH, 6 Baronet. *b.* 29 Sep. 1812; succeeded 19 June 1816; formed a menagerie of rare animals at Wingeworth hall, Derbyshire, which was sold by auction after his death. *d.* Grafton st. London 8 Feb. 1856.

HUNNUM, ROBERT (*son of Fenwick Hunnum, purveyor to the Lambton kennel*). *b.* Durham 1795; second horseman to Mr. Ralph John Lambton of Merton house, Durham 1809 and known by name of 'Mr. Ralph's Great Coat';

HUNNUM, R. *(Con.)*

second whip 1818; first whipper-in 1829 till the Lambton hounds were sold to Lord Suffield; a man of great courage and endurance; huntsman to Sir Matthew White Ridley in Northumberland 1843, whose hounds were sold by auction in London 30 June 1845 for £773, after which the hunt was kept up by subscription. *The Book of Sports, ii,* 42–6 (1843), *portrait; New Sporting Mag. v,* 4–5 (1833), *portrait.*

HUNT, ANDREW. *b.* Erdington near Birmingham 1790; pupil of Samuel Lines the enengraver; landscape painter and teacher of drawing at Liverpool; member of Liverpool Academy and exhibitor there. *d.* 31 Oxford st. 22 July 1861.

HUNT, EDWARD *(son of Thomas Hunt).* *b.* Hammersmith, Middlesex 29 Sep. 1829; ed. at Univ. coll. London, B.A. London 1850; assistant to Crace Calvert, royal institution laboratory, Manchester 1851; discovered process for distilling resin without decomposition 1857; took out patent for treatment of resin in making soap 1858; partner with Samuel Barlow and H. D. Pochin as Samuel Barlow & Co. in bleaching and dyeing works Stakehill near Middleton, Lancs. 1861 to death; F.C.S. Dec. 1851. *d.* Whalley range, Manchester 12 Aug. 1883. *Gillow's English Catholics, iii,* 476–7 (1887).

HUNT, ELLEN ST. JOHN. *b.* Norwich 27 Nov. 1837; a contributor to *The Bible class mag.* and to *The Sunday school teachers' mag.* under pseudonym of Ion; author of *Thoughts of sunshine in sorrow. By E.S.J.H.* 1862, *Second series* 1866. *d.* Norwich 11 March 1864. *Memoir pp. v-xlvii in Thoughts of sunshine* (1866).

HUNT, FREDERICK KNIGHT. *b.* Buckinghamshire, April 1814; employed in printing office of *Morning Herald* 1830; clerk to a barrister in the Temple 1830; sec. to London Anti-Corn-law league 1836; studied medicine at Middlesex hospital, M.R.C.S. 13 Nov. 1840; projected the *Medical Times* which he edited 28 Sep. 1839; surgeon of a union in Norfolk; sub-editor of *Illustrated London News;* sub-editor of *Pictorial Times;* edited Hunt's *London Journal* 1844; assistant editor *Daily News* Jany. 1846, and editor 1851 to death; author of *The book of art* 1846; *The Rhine, its scenery and associations* 1845; *The fourth estate, contributions towards a history of newspapers* 2 *vols.* 1850. *d.* Forest hill, Sydenham 18 Nov. 1854. *John Francis, publisher of the Athenæum. By J. C. Francis, i,* 224, 226, 410–13 (1888); *Diprose's St. Clements, i,* 245 (1868).

HUNT, REV. GEORGE *(son of Nehemiah Augustus Hunt of Plymouth).* *b.* 1789; ed. at Trin. coll. Ox., B.A. 1810, M.A. 1813; V. of Egg Buckland near Plymouth 26 May 1818 to death; F.R.S.; edited *Specimens of lithography as applied to eastern literature* 1819; translated *The book of Job* 1825; *Himyaric inscriptions of Hisn Ghoráb* 1848. *d.* Egg Buckland 20 Feb. 1861.

HUNT, GEORGE WARD *(eld. son of Rev. George Hunt of Buckhurst, Berks.)* *b.* Buckhurst 30 July 1825; ed. at Eton and Ch. Ch. Ox., B.A. 1848, M.A. 1851, D.C.L. 1870; barrister I.T. 21 Nov. 1851, bencher 23 May 1873; contested Northampton 1852 and 1857; M.P. for North Northamptonshire 16 Dec. 1857 to death; chairman of quarter sessions for Northamptonshire, April 1866; financial sec. to treasury, July 1866 to Feb. 1868; chancellor of the exchequer 29 Feb. to Dec. 1868; P.C. 29 Feb. 1868; first lord of the admiralty 21 Feb. 1874 to death. *d.* Homburg 29 July 1877. *bur.* Homburg 30 July. *C. Brown's Life of Beaconsfield, ii,* 93, 162 (1882), *portrait; Graphic 4 Aug.* 1877 *pp.* 99, 113, *portrait.*

HUNT, HENRY. Educ. at St. Bartholomew's hospital and Paris; M.R.C.P. 1840, F.R.C.P. 1859; fellow of Royal Med. Chir. Soc.; practised at 68 Brook st. Hanover sq. London from 1840; phys. to Dispensary for Children; author of *On the nature and treatment of tic-douloureux, sciatica and other neuralgic disorders* 1844; *On the severer forms of heartburn and indigestion* 1854. *d.* 25 May 1877 aged 75.

HUNT, SIR HENRY ARTHUR *(son of James Hunt of Westminster).* *b.* 1810; consulting surveyor to H.M. commissioners of works and buildings 1856–86; receiver-general for dean and chapter of Westminster to 1886; partner in firm of Hunt, Stephenson and Jones, surveyors, 45 Parliament st. Westminster; A.I.C.E. 4 March 1851; C.B. 5 Aug. 1871; knighted at Osborne 21 July 1876. *d.* The Lees, Folkestone 13 Jany. 1889.

HUNT, HOLDSWORTH *(youngest son of Wm. Chollwill Hunt, M.D. of Dartmouth).* *b.* Dartmouth 1806; ed. at Crediton and in Paris; barrister I.T. 12 June 1833, bencher 1865 to death, reader 1879, treasurer 1880; member of council of legal education; member of French Institute 1851. *d.* 20 Park crescent, Portland place, London 26 April 1883.

HUNT, JAMES *(son of Thomas Hunt 1802–51).* *b.* Swanage, Dorset 1833; Ph. D. of Giessen 1855 and M.D. 1867; succeeded his father as a specialist in curing stammering, had a house at Hastings where he received many patients; member of Ethnological soc. of London 1854,

HUNT, J. *(Con.)*

hon. sec. 1859–62, hon. fellow 1862 ; founded
Anthropological soc. of London 1863, president 1863–8, director 1867 ; edited *Anthropological Rev.* 1863 ; agitated for making Anthropology a department at British Assoc. meetings which was done in 1883 ; F.S.A. ; F.R.S.L.
1854 ; author of *A manual of the philosophy of
voice and speech* 1859 ; *Stammering and stuttering, their nature and treatment* 1861, 7 ed. 1870
and 7 other books. *d.* Ore Court near Hastings 29 Aug. 1869. *Reg. and mag. of biog.,
ii,* 198–200 (1869).

HUNT, JAMES HENRY LEIGH *(son of Rev. Isaac
Hunt, d. 1809 aged 57).* *b.* Southgate, Middlesex 19 Oct. 1784 ; ed. at Christ hospital 1792–
99 ; started with his brother John, *The Examiner* a weekly paper 1808, editor 1808–21 ;
edited a quarterly mag. called *The Reflector*
which ran to 4 numbers 1810 ; tried for a
libel in *The Examiner* on the prince regent,
and imprisoned in Surrey gaol 3 Feb. 1813 to
3 Feb. 1815 ; great friend of Byron, Shelley,
Keats, C. Lamb, T. Moore, J. Forster and T.
Carlyle ; edited *The Indicator*, Oct. 1820 to
1822, 77 numbers ; was in Italy 1822–5 ; edited
The Liberal 1822–3, 2 vols. ; *The Literary
Examiner*, 27 numbers ; *The Companion* 1828,
28 numbers ; *The Chat of the Week* 1830, 13
numbers ; *The Tatler* a daily sheet entirely
written by himself 4 Oct. 1830 to 13 Feb.
1832, 59 numbers ; *Leigh Hunt's London
Journal* 1834 to 26 Dec. 1835, and *The
Monthly Repository* July 1837 to March 1838 ;
produced *A Legend of Florence* at Covent
Garden 7 Feb. 1840 ; civil list pension of
£200, 4 Oct. 1847 ; published *Leigh Hunt's
Journal* 1850 to March 1851 ; author of *Lord
Byron and some of his contemporaries* 1828 ;
The Town 2 vols. 1848 ; *The autobiography of
L. Hunt* 1850, 3 vols. new ed. 1860 ; *Table
talk* 1851 and very numerous other books. *d.*
at res. of Charles W. Reynell, Chatfield house,
(now 84) High st. Putney, Surrey 28 Aug.
1859. *bur.* Kensal Green cemet. Sep., monument by Joseph Durham, A.R.A. placed on
the spot 19 Oct. 1869. *The Correspondence of
Leigh Hunt* 2 vols. (1862) ; *Leigh Hunt's Lord
Byron*, 2 ed. (1828) 55–408, *portrait ; W.
Howitt's Homes and haunts of British poets, ii,*
347–67 (1847) ; *T. H. Ward's English poets, 2
ed.* (1883) *iv,* 340–7 ; *J. A. Langford's Prison
books* (1861) 316–33, *portrait ; Maclise Portrait
Gallery* (1883) 242–56, *portrait ; L. Hutton's
Literary landmarks of London, 4 ed.* (1888)
144–9 ; *F. E. Baines' Hampstead* (1890) 358,
portrait.

NOTE.—He is drawn in *Bleak House* 1853 as Harold
Skimpole and in A. W. Pinero's play *Lady Bountiful*

HUNT, J. H. L. *(Con.)*

1891 as Roderick Heron. His dau. Julia Trelawney
Leigh Hunt was granted civil list pension of £75, 19
April 1861 and *d.* Hammersmith 3 Feb. 1872.

HUNT, REV. JOHN HIGGS. *b.* 1780 ; ed. at
Charterhouse and Trin. coll. Cam., B.A. 1801,
M.A. 1804 ; edited *The Critical Review*, reviewed Byron's *Hours of Idleness* in it Sep.
1807 ; V. of Weedon Beck, Northamptonshire
20 March 1823 to death ; published *Tasso's
Jerusalem delivered, with notes and occasional
illustrations* 2 vols. 1818, reprinted in E. Sanford's *The works of the British poets*, vols. 48,
49 (1819) ; said to have written a work upon
Cosmo the Great. *d.* Weedon Beck 17 Nov.
1859.

HUNT, JOSEPH. Kept a tavern in London ; a
public singer at Naval Coffee house, St. Martin's lane, London ; William Probert and
John Thurtell murdered William Weare at
Gill's hill lane near Elstree, Herts. 24 Oct.
1823, Hunt was found guilty as an accessory
before the murder and sentenced to death 7
Jany. 1824 but eventually transported for
life ; court keeper of assize court, Bathurst,
N.S.W. 1839–59 ; living at Bathurst 1859 ;
father of a famous female singer living in
1864. *Narrative of murder of Mr. W. Weare,
the confession of Hunt and the execution of
Thurtell* (1824), *portrait.*

NOTE.—John Thurtell was hanged at Hertford 9
Jany. 1824, Wm. Probert escaped by turning King's
evidence, but was hanged at the Old Bailey 20 June
1825 for horse-stealing ; Thurtell's gig used by him in
going to Gill's hill lane, was exhibited in a piece called
The Gamblers produced at the Surrey theatre, Jany.
1824.

HUNT, ROBERT *(son of Robert Hunt lost in
H.M.S. Mocheron 1807).* *b.* Plymouth Dock
(now Devonport) 6 Sep. 1807 ; studied medicine in London ; chemist and druggist Chapel
st. Penzance 1833–4 ; sec. of Royal Cornwall
Polytechnic soc. 1840–5, pres. 1859 ; keeper
of the mining records office 1845 till it was
abolished 1883 ; lecturer on mechanical science
in Royal school of mines 1851–3, lecturer on
experimental physics 1853 ; F.R.S. 1 June
1854 ; The Miners' Assoc. of Cornwall and
Devon was instituted at a meeting called by
him 1859 and opened 1861 ; a comr. on
inquiry on quantity of coal remaining 1866 ;
made researches on solar rays, electrical phenomena in mineral veins and photography ;
edited Ure's *Dictionary of arts, manufactures
and mines* 1859, 1867 and 1875, *three editions ;*
author of *A popular treatise on the art of photography* 1841 ; *Researches on light* 1844, 2 ed.
1854 ; *Elementary physics* 1851, new ed. 1855 ;
Popular romances of West of England 2 vols.

HUNT, R. (Con.)

1865; *British mining* 1884, 2 *ed.* 1887; compiler and editor of annual blue books on Mineral statistics 1855–84. *d.* 26 St. Leonard's ter. Chelsea 17 Oct. 1887. *Boase and Courtney's Bibl. Cornub.* 259–60, 1238; *Athenæum* 22 *Oct.* 1887 *pp.* 541–2; *Times* 20 *Oct.* 1887 *p.* 5.

HUNT, THOMAS. *b.* Dorset 1802; ed. at Winchester and Trin. coll. Cam.; invented a method of curing stammering, which he practised at 224 Regent st. London 1827 to death; Sir John Forbes sent him pupils 1828–51; his pupils subscribed for his bust in marble which was modelled by Joseph Durham and exhibited in the R.A. 1849. *d.* Godlingstone near Swanage, Dorset 18 Aug. 1851. *James Hunt's Treatise on stammering, with memoir of T. Hunt* (1854) 27–69, *portrait; Fraser's Mag. July* 1859 *pp.* 1–14, *By Charles Kingsley.*

HUNT, THOMAS NEWMAN. *b.* 1806; merchant of firm of Newman, Hunt & Co. 12 New Broad st. city of London; a director of Bank of England 1856–83, deputy governor 1866–7, governor 1867–9; chairman of Public works loan commission. *d.* 79 Portland place, London 17 Jany. 1884.

HUNT, THORNTON LEIGH (*eld. son of J. H. Leigh Hunt* 1784–1859). *b.* London 10 Sep. 1810; studied drawing and painting; subeditor of *The Constitutional*, morning paper 15 Sep. 1836 which lasted to 1 July 1837; edited the *North Cheshire Reformer* at Chester; *The Argus* at Glasgow to 1840; one of chief contributors to *Spectator* 1840–60; one of founders of *Leader* 1850; one of chief contributors to *Globe;* on the *Daily Telegraph* as acting editor 1855–72; author of *The Foster Brother* 1845; *The rationale of railway administration* 1846; *Unity of the iron network, the argument for the break of guage* 1846; edited his father's *Autobiography* 1860, *Works* 1860, and *Correspondence* 1862. *d.* 41 Victoria road, Kilburn, Middlesex 25 June 1873. *Athenæum* 28 *June* 1873 *p.* 825; *Bourne's English newspapers,* ii, 98, 235, 241, 267 (1887).

HUNT, VERE DAWSON DE VERE (*son of Vere Hunt*). *b.* 7 July 1829; captain inland transport corps; author of *The horse and its master, with hints on breeding, breaking, etc.* 1859; *England's horses for peace and war* 1874. *d.* 9 Dec. 1878.

HUNT, WILLIAM. *b.* 1766; ed. at Rugby and King's coll. Cam., scholar 1784, fellow 1787 to death; B.A. 1789, M.A. 1792; barrister L.I. 27 June 1794; went Norfolk circuit,

HUNT, W. (Con.)

leader of it long time; assessor to the vice chancellor in the university courts 1805 to death; recorder of Tamworth (the last) 1817–42. *d.* King's college, Cambridge 6 Jany. 1852.

HUNT, WILLIAM (*son of Thomas Hunt*). *b.* Bath 1801; in business with his brother at Bath; a great supporter of Reform 1832; one of first members of Bath reformed corporation 1836, alderman 1841–7, 1848 to death; mayor of Bath 1840, 47, 54, 67 and 73; presented with a silver salver and his portrait 16 June 1869; J.P. for Bath 2 Sep. 1847 to death. *d.* 72 Pulteney st. Bath 17 Sep. 1885. *Keene's Bath Journal* 19 *Sep.* 1885 *p.* 4.

HUNT, VERY REV. WILLIAM. *b.* East Hendred, Berks. 15 June 1803; ordained priest 1830; professor at St. Edmund's coll. Ware 1830–2; missioner at Southampton 1832–41; minister St. James' chapel, Spanish place, Manchester sq. London 1842, resigned 1883; provost of the chapter of Westminster 1865. *d.* 6 Spanish place 9 Jany. 1889.

HUNT, WILLIAM GEORGE LENNON. *b.* 1842; a baritone; before he was 21 he had appeared in 20 different operas in Madrid; musical composer, dramatist, author; director of Philharmonic soc. of Madrid; consul at Loanda, South Africa 10 June 1878 to death. *d.* Loanda 30 Aug. 1879. *Illust. sp. and dr. news, xii,* 101, 102 (1879), *portrait.*

HUNT, WILLIAM HENRY (*son of John Hunt, tinplate worker*). *b.* 8 Old Belton st. (now Endell st.), Long Acre, London 28 March 1790; apprenticed to John Varley, artist 1804–11; painted in oils 1807–24, in water colours 1824–63; associate exhibitor of Watercolour soc. 1824, member 1826; member of Amsterdam royal academy 1856; exhibited 14 pictures at R.A., 6 at B.I. and 1 at Suffolk st. 1807–29; his *Roses in a Jar* in the Wade collection 1872 sold for five hundred guineas. *d.* 62 Stanhope st. Hampstead road, London 10 Feb. 1864. *Redgrave's Century of painters,* ii, 502–9 (1866); *Fraser's Mag. lxxii,* 525–36 (1865).

HUNTER, ADAM. *b.* Greenock 20 June 1791; ed. at Glasgow and Edin. univs., M.D. Edin. 1813; physician Edin. 1815 to death; F.R.S. Edin. 1839; made a report to Scottish national insurance co. on the lives insured; author of *The fruits of amalgamation exhibited in the correspondence of a Palladium policy holder with C. Jellicoe.* Edin. 1865. *d.* 18 Abercromby place, Edinburgh 24 June 1870. *Proc. Royal Soc. of Edin. vii,* 240–2 (1872).

HUNTER, SIR CLAUDIUS STEPHEN, 1 Baronet (*younger son of Henry Hunter of Beech hill, Berks., barrister 1739–89*). *b.* Beech hill 24 Feb. 1775; student of the Inner Temple; solicitor in London 1797 to Jany. 1811; alderman of ward of Bassishaw, Sep. 1804 to 1835; alderman of ward of Bridge without 1835 to death; lieut. col. of Royal east regiment of London militia 1806 and col. of royal west regt. 10 Jany. 1810 to death; sheriff of London 1808–9, lord mayor 1811–12 when he revived ancient ceremonies; created baronet 11 Dec. 1812; hon. D.C.L. Ox. 23 June 1819; president of London Life association 1835 to death. *d.* Mortimer hill, Berkshire 20 April 1851. *European Mag. lxii,* 177–84 (1812), *portrait; G.M. xxxvi,* 88–90 (1851); *Thornbury's London, i,* 116, 329–30, (1872).

HUNTER, SIR CLAUDIUS STEPHEN PAUL, 2 Baronet. *b.* Ghazepore, East Indies 21 Sep. 1825; ed. at Eton and St. John's coll. Ox., B.A. 1849, M.A. 1850; student of Inner Temple 1848; succeeded his grandfather 20 April 1851; captain royal London militia 1846–50; founder of 1st Berkshire volunteer regt. and capt. commandant 31 March 1860, lieut.-col. 2 Nov. 1872 to Dec. 1885; sheriff of Berks. 1860. *d.* Mortimer hill near Reading 7 Jany. 1890.

HUNTER, GEORGE. Entered Bengal army 1800; colonel 1 European regt. of light infantry 1843 to death; L.G. 11 Nov. 1851; C.B. 26 Dec. 1826. *d.* Bridge of Allan, Stirlingshire 11 Nov. 1854.

HUNTER, VEN. JAMES (*son of John Hunter*). *b.* Barnstaple 1817; clerk to Charles Roberts, solicitor, Barnstaple; a master in Tavistock sch.; ed. at Ch. Miss. coll. Islington to 1843; archdeacon of Cumberland, Rupert's Land 1854–67; V. of St. Matthew, Bayswater, London 1867 to death; M.A. 1855 and D.D. 1876 by Archbishop of Canterbury; author of *The Book of common prayer, Translated into the language of the Cree Indians* 1859; *The gospels of St. Matthew, St. Mark and St. John in Cree; The faith and duty of a christian in Cree;* with J. Mason and others *The Bible translated into the language of the Knisteneaux or Cree North American Indians* 2 parts 1861–2. *d.* 52 Leinster sq. London 12 Feb. 1882. *bur.* Highgate cemet. 18 Feb.

HUNTER, JAMES. *b.* Muirkirk, Ayrshire 1818; manager Coltness iron works 1839 and then a partner (Houldsworth & Co.), retired 1885, increased the works from 2 to 12 furnaces; the Coltness brand of iron became known all

HUNTER, J. (*Con.*)

over the world; D.L. for Ayrshire; A.I.C.E. 4 April 1854. *d.* Newman's House by Motherwell, Edinburgh 5 Oct. 1886. *Min. of Proc. I.C.E. lxxxix,* 494–5 (1887).

HUNTER, REV. JOHN (*youngest son of Rev. Andrew Hunter, minister of Tron ch. Edin., d. 1809*). *b.* Edin. 1788; presbyterian minister of Swinton, Berwickshire 1814–32; assistant minister of Tron ch. Edin. after a contest with the kirk session which was decided in house of lords Oct. 1832, minister of Tron ch. to death; D.D. of univ. of Edin. 29 May 1847. *d.* 9 Regent ter. Edinburgh 21 June 1866. *Crombie's Modern Athenians* (1882) 27–8, *portrait; Scott's Fasti, i part i, p.* 61.

HUNTER, JOHN (*son of professor Andrew Hunter*). In a writer's office copying law papers at 3d. a page; a writer to the signet 1826; auditor of court of session to 1866; author of *Miscellanies in verse. By N.R. i.e. J. Hunter* 1843. *d.* Craigcrook 3 Dec. 1869. *Journal of jurisprudence, xiv,* 42–5 (1870).

HUNTER, JOHN (*only son of John Hunter, physician*). *b.* Belfast 23 March 1843; ed. at Queen's coll. Belfast and Queen's univ., B.A. 1863, M.A. 1864; assistant professor of chemistry Queen's coll. 1865–70; professor of mathematics and natural philosophy King's coll. Windsor, Nova Scotia 1870–1; accompanied the Deep Sea dredging expedition in H.M.S. Porcupine 1869; made researches on the absorption of gases by charcoal, the absorption of mixed vapours, pressure of absorption and the composition of sea water. *d.* Enniscrone, Mayo 13 Sep. 1872. *Proc. of royal soc. of Edin. viii,* 322–4 (1875).

HUNTER, JOHN (2 *son of John Hunter, d. 3 Dec.* 1869). Advocate 1857; sheriff substitute of Peebleshire 1868 to death; member of Speculative soc. *d.* Kingsmuir, Peebles 29 Sep. 1872. *Journal of Jurisprudence, xvi,* 603–5 (1872).

HUNTER, JOHN CHARLES. *b.* 20 Aug. 1799; L.S.A. 1821; M.R.C.S. 1821; L.R.C.P. 1863; inspector National Vaccine establishment; author of 63rd vol. of the Family library *Sketches of imposture, deception and credulity* 1837. *d.* 30 Wilton place, Belgrave sq. London 19 Dec. 1871.

HUNTER, JOHN KELSO. *b.* Dunkeith, Ayrshire 15 Dec. 1802; a herd boy; shoemaker at Kilmarnock; removed to Glasgow; painted and exhibited portrait of himself at R.A. London 1847; author of *The retrospect of an*

HUNTER, J. K. *(Con.)*

artist's life 1868; *Life studies of character* 1871, containing facts about Robert Burns; *Memorials of west country men and manners. d.* Pollokshields near Glasgow 3 Feb. 1873. *Times* 6 *Feb.* 1873 *p.* 7.

HUNTER, REV. JOSEPH *(son of Michael Hunter of Sheffield, cutler* 1759–1831*). b.* Sheffield 6 Feb. 1783; minister of a Presbyterian congregation at Bath 1809–33; a sub-comr. of public records in London 1833, an assistant keeper of the first class 1838 to death; F.S.A., mem. of council and vice pres. 1855; author of *Hallamshire. The history of the parish of Sheffield* 1819, new ed. by Rev. A. Gatty 1869; *South Yorkshire. The history of the deanery of Doncaster* 2 vols. 1828–31; *The diary of Ralph Thoresby, F.R.S.* 2 vols. 1830 and 30 other books; his library was sold at Sothebys, Dec. 1861 for £1105; his MS. collections were purchased by Br. Museum 1862. *d.* 30 Torrington sq. London 9 May 1861. *bur.* Ecclesfield near Sheffield 15 May. *A brief memoir* [*by Sylvester Hunter*] 1861, *privately printed; Proc. of Soc. of Antiquaries, ii,* 106–8 (1861).

HUNTER, JOSEPH. *b.* Scarborough 21 Oct. 1857; became known in the match County Eleven *v.* Surrey at Sheffield 15 July 1878; member of Yorkshire Eleven 1881; played against Australian team in 1883; member of Shaw's English team in Australia 1884; had no superior as a wicket keeper; wicket keeper to the Yorkshire Eleven to 1889. *d.* at his residence the Wheat Sheaf hotel, Rotherham 4 Jany. 1891. *Illust. S. and D. News, xxiii,* 661, 662 (1885), *portrait.*

HUNTER, ROBERT *(only child of an East India merchant, d.* 1793*). b.* near Edinburgh 8 July 1791; ed. at High sch. Edin. to 1804 and at Edin. univ.; member of Scottish bar 1814; sheriff of Buteshire 1837 to death; sheriff of Dumbartonshire 1853 to death; author of *A treatise on the law of landlord and tenant. Edin.* 1833, 4 ed. 2 vols. 1876. *d.* 67 Northumberland st. Edinburgh 23 Dec. 1871. *Crombie's Modern Athenians* (1882) 16, *portrait; Journal of Jurisprudence, xvi,* 93–6 (1872).

HUNTER, ROBERT HOPE ALSTON *(3 son of Rev. William Hunter). b.* 1805; hospital assistant in army 10 Jany. 1827; surgeon of 57 regt. at Madras 1843–47; surgeon major 30 July 1847; placed on h.p. 10 Feb. 1852; author of *Statistical review of the climate of the principal stations for European troops in the Bombay presidency; The medical history of the queen's royal regiment during the campaign in Afghanistan. d.* Dollar 22 June 1867. *Medical Times* 3 *Aug.* 1867 *pp.* 135–6.

HUNTER, ROWLAND. *b.* 1774; extensive bookseller at 72 St. Paul's churchyard (where he succeeded his uncle Joseph Johnson) 1815–36. *d.* the Charterhouse 18 Jany. 1864.

HUNTER, WALTER. *b.* parish of Newbattle near Edin. 1772; worked as a millwright under Watt and Rennie; adapted steam power to move dredging buckets and ladders; partner with Wm. English as millwrights and engineers at 28 High st. south, Bow, London 1807 or 1808 to death; M.I.C.E. 1827. *d.* Bow 8 Feb. 1852. *Minutes of proc. of Instit. of C.E. xii,* 161 (1853).

HUNTER, WILLIAM *(son of Andrew Hunter of Bury St. Edmunds). b.* Bury St. Edmunds; of 76 Coleman st. City of London; member of ward of Coleman st. London 1823 and alderman 1843 to death, sheriff 1844–5, lord mayor 1851–52. *d.* 13 Westbourne terrace, Hyde park, London 22 Sep. 1856 aged 75. *I.L.N. xix,* 605 (1851), *portrait.*

HUNTER, WILLIAM FREDERICK. *b.* 1841; ed. at Edin. univ., M.A., LL.B.; at Heidelberg and Berlin univ., D.C.L.; examiner in law, Edin. univ.; advocate in Scotland 1865; barrister L.I. 30 April 1875; inherited Hafton estate, Argyleshire on death of his brother; wrote article on *Canon Law* in Encyclop. Brit. v. 15–22 (1876). *d.* Madeira 28 April 1880. *Journal of Jurisprudence, xxiv,* 320–1 (1880).

HUNTER-BLAIR, SIR DAVID, 3 Baronet. *b.* Edinburgh 1777; midshipman H.M.S. Hyacinth; succeeded his brother 24 May 1800; col. of Ayrshire militia during the war; convener of Ayrshire 1822 to 1855; vice lieut. of Ayrshire 1822 to death. *d.* Blairquhan, Ayr 26 Dec. 1857.

HUNTER-BLAIR, JAMES *(1 son of preceding). b.* Milton, Ayrshire 22 March 1817; ensign Scots fusilier guards 24 April 1835, captain 31 March 1848 to death; M.P. Ayrshire 22 July 1852 to death; *killed* when commanding his battalion at Inkerman 5 Nov. 1854.

HUNTINGDON, FRANCIS POWER PLANTAGENET HASTINGS, 13 Earl of *(eld. child of 12 Earl of Huntingdon* 1808–75*). b.* Gaultier cottage, Waterford 4 Dec. 1841; styled Lord Hastings 1841–75; matric. from Ch. Ch. Ox. 20 Jany. 1860; succeeded 13 Sep. 1875; master of harriers at Whitechurch, Waterford 1867–8, of fox hounds 1868–71; master of the Ormond and King's county hunt 1872–5 and of the King's county alone from 1875, the Land League ultimately mobbed his hounds and he sold the pack to a Canadian;

HUNTINGDON, 13 Earl of. *(Con.)*
speculated in land in Florida and visited that country. *d.* Shanavogue, King's county 20 May 1885. *Baily's Mag. xxxi,* 63–4 (1878), *portrait, xliv,* 295 (1885).

HUNTINGFORD, REV. HENRY *(son of Rev. Thomas Huntingford, master of Warminster school, Wilts.)* *b.* Warminster 19 Sep. 1787; ed. at Winchester and New coll. Ox., fellow 1807–14; fellow of Winchester 5 April 1814 to his death; B.C.L. 1814; prebendary of Colwall in Hereford cath. Dec. 1817; R. of Hampton Bishop, Herefordshire 1822 to death; canon residentiary of Hereford cath. 1822 to death; master of Ledbury hospital, Hereford 1867; published *Pindari Carmina juxta examplar Heynianum...et Lexicon Pindaricum ex integro Dammii opere etymologico excerptum* 1814, *another ed.* 1821; translated *Romanist Conversations [By B. Pictet]* 1826. *d.* Goodrest, Great Malvern 2 Nov. 1867. *bur.* Hampton Bishop. *F. T. Havergal's Fasti Herefordenses* (1869) 61.

HUNTLY, GEORGE GORDON, 9 Marquis of *(only son of 4 Earl of Aboyne 1726–94).* *b.* Edinburgh 28 June 1761; ensign 1 foot guards; lieut. col. 35 foot April 1789 to 15 June 1789; captain Coldstream guards 15 June 1789 to 1792 when he sold out; col. of Aberdeenshire militia 1798 to death; succeeded his father as 5 Earl of Aboyne 28 Dec. 1794; a representative peer of Scotland 1796–1815; cr. baron Meldrum of Morven, co. Aberdeen in peerage of the U.K. 11 Aug. 1815; K.T. 10 May 1827; succeeded as 9 marquis of Huntly by decision of House of Lords 22 June 1838 on death of his kinsman the 8 Marquis 28 May 1836. *d.* 24 Chapel st. Grosvenor sq. London 17 June 1853.

HUNTLY, CHARLES GORDON, 10 Marquis of *(eld. child of the preceding).* *b.* Orton near Peterborough 11 Jany. 1792; styled Lord Strathaven 1792–1853; ed. at St. John's coll. Cam., M.A. 1812; M.P. East Grinstead 1818–30; M.P. Hunts. 1830–31, contested Hunts. 1831; lord lieut. of Aberdeenshire 14 Feb. 1861 to death. *d.* Orton Longueville near Peterborough 17 Sep. 1863.

HUNTLEY, SIR HENRY VERE *(3 son of Rev. Richard Huntley of Boxwell court, Gloucs. 1776–1831).* *b.* 1795; entered navy 10 March 1809; accompanied Napoleon to St. Helena in the Northumberland 8 Aug. to 15 Oct. 1815; employed in suppressing slave trade 1826–37; commander 28 June 1838; lieut. gov. of settlements on river Gambia 23 Dec. 1839; lieut. gov. of Prince Edward's Island

HUNTLEY, SIR H. V. *(Con.)*
20 Aug. 1841 to 26 Oct. 1847; knighted by patent 9 Oct. 1841; consul at Loanda, Aug. 1858; consul at Santos, Brazil, May 1862 to death; author of *Peregrine scramble, or thirty years' adventures of a bluejacket* 2 vols. 1849; *Observation on free trade policy in connection with the Sugar act* 1846; *Seven years' service on the Slave coast* 2 vols. 1850; *California, its gold and its inhabitants* 2 vols. 1856. *d.* Santos, Brazil 7 May 1864.

HUNTLEY, JOHN. *b.* London 25 March 1805; a packer of bale goods; went to U.S. America 1832; prompter Richmond hill theatre, New York; acted in Baltimore, Philadelphia, Richmond, Cincinnati and Pittsburg, when he first undertook old men characters; stage manager for Ludlow and Smith at St. Louis 1848–53; travelled in America as an actor, prompter and manager 1853–63. *Brown's American stage* (1870) 190.

HUNTLEY, REV. RICHARD WEBSTER *(brother of Sir H. V. Huntley).* *b.* 1793; ed. at Oriel coll. Ox., B.A. 1815, M.A. 1819; fellow of All Souls 1815–31, proctor 1824; V. of Alderbury, Salop 20 Jany. 1829 to death; R. of Boxwell and Leighterton 3 Dec. 1831 to death; one of the 3 priests who opposed Dr. R. D. Hampden's election to bishopric of Hereford, both in Bow ch. 11 Jany. 1848 and in the queen's bench 1 Feb.; rural dean of Hawkesbury and Bitton 1840–51; author of *A letter to the archbishop of Canterbury on the ecclesiastical commission and the suppression of a bishoprick in North Wales* 1843; *A glossary of the Cotswold dialect illustrated by examples from ancient authors.* Gloucester 1868. *d.* Boxwell court, Gloucs. 4 April 1857. *The Year of the Church. By R. W. Huntley* (1860). *Memoir pp. vii–xviii.*

HURDIS, JAMES HENRY *(elder son of James Hurdis, poet 1763–1801).* *b.* 1800 probably at Bishopston, Berks.; ed. at Southampton; spent a few years in France; articled to Charles Heath the engraver; lived at Newick near Lewes; etched many portraits of local notabilities and views of buildings in Sussex, some of which are in the Sussex Archæological Society's collections; a friend of George Cruikshank. *d.* Southampton 30 Nov. 1857. *M. A. Lower's Worthies of Sussex* (1865) 170.

HURDLE, SIR THOMAS *(son of James Hurdle).* *b.* 1797; 2 lieut. R.M. 24 April 1812, lieut. col. 15 Aug. 1853; served at Navarino 1827, in Greece 1828, commanded brigade of R.M. in Crimea 1854–6; aide-de-camp to the queen 1855–7; col. commandant 20 Feb. 1857; retired on full pay 17 Nov. 1859; hon. major

HURDLE, SIR T. (*Con.*)
general 2 Dec. 1859 ; C.B. 5 July 1855,
K.C.B. 2 June 1877. *d.* Porchester, Fareham,
7 June 1889.

HURLSTONE, EDWIN TYRRELL. *b.* 1806 ;
barrister I.T. 31 Jany. 1834, went South-
Eastern circuit ; a revising barrister to death ;
author with John Gordon of *Exchequer Reports*
1854–56, 2 *vols.* 1855–56 ; with J. P. Norman
of *Reports of cases in the courts of Exchequer
and Exchequer Chamber* 1856–62, 7 *vols.* 1857–
62 ; with F. J. Coltman of *Reports of cases in
the Courts of Exchequer and Exchequer Chamber*
1862–65, 3 *vols.* 1863–66 and other Reports.
d. Thanet place, Temple, London 29 Sep. 1881.

HURLSTONE, FREDERICK YEATES (1 *son of
Thomas Yeates Hurlstone a proprietor of the
Morning Chronicle*). *b.* London 1800 or 1801 ;
pupil of Sir W. Beechey and Sir T. Lawrence ;
student of the R.A. 1820, silver medallist
1822, gold medallist 1823 ; exhibited 37 pictures at R.A., 19 at B.I. and 326 at Suffolk
st. 1821–70 ; member of Society of British
artists 1831, president 1835 and 1840 to
death ; awarded a gold medal at Paris exhibition 1855 ; 11 of his best works were
re-exhibited at Soc. of British Artists 1870 ;
author with others of *Protest against the Report
from the committee of the National gallery* 1855 ;
(*m.* 1836 Jane Coral an artist, who exhibited
6 pictures at R.A. and 23 at Suffolk st. 1846–
56 and *d.* 2 Oct. 1858) ; he *d.* 9 Chester st.
Belgrave sq. London 10 June 1869.

HURMAN, WILLIAM. Studied at Univ. coll.
London ; pupil of Robert Liston ; M.R.C.S.
1846 ; house surgeon Univ. coll. hospital ; in
practice at Windsor, Brighton and London ;
surgeon to 3rd Middlesex militia 11 Aug.
1865 to death ; one of the best known men
in the hunting, coaching and racing world ;
originator of the Badminton club, 100 Piccadilly, London 1876. *d.* 83 Grand parade,
Brighton, Dec. 1883. *Baily's Mag. Jany.*
1884 *pp.* 429–30.

HURST, REV. BLYTHE. *b.* Winlaton, Durham
6 July 1801 ; a blacksmith at Winlaton ;
ordained by Bishop Maltby at Auckland
castle, July 1842 ; C. of Alston, Cumberland
1844–6 ; V. of Collierley near Newcastle 1854
to death ; taught himself French, Latin,
Greek, Hebrew, Syriac and Arabic ; published
Four sermons, Christianity no priestcraft 1840.
d. Collierley 24 June 1882. *Newcastle Weekly
Chronicle* 1 July 1882 *p.* 7 col. 5 ; *I.L.N. lxxxi*,
56 (1882), *portrait.*

HURST, DANIEL. *b.* 1802 or 1803 ; publisher
with Henry Blackett at 13 Great Marlborough
st. London 1854 to death. *d.* Mitcham, Surrey 6 July 1870.

HURST, SAMUEL. *b.* Stalybridge, Lancashire
1832 ; champion wrestler of Lancashire ;
known as " The Stalybridge Infant " ; 6 feet
2½ inches high and 15 stone in weight ;
matched with J. C. Heenan 1860 but engagement fell through ; fought Tom Paddock for
£200 a side near Aldermaston, Berkshire 5
Nov. 1860 when Hurst won in 5 rounds and
obtained the champion belt ; broke his leg by
a fall 19 Nov. 1860 ; fought James Mace for
£200 a side on one of the islands up the river
Medway 18 June 1861 when Mace won in 8
rounds lasting 50 minutes and obtained the
belt ; kept the Wilton Arms tavern 4 Mayes
st. Manchester about 1861–5, the Glass House
tavern, Oldham road, Manchester about 1865–
70. *d.* Mayfield cottage, Manchester 22 May
1882. *Illust. sporting news* (1862) 249, *portrait ;
F. W. J. Henning's Some recollections of the
prize ring* (1888) 140–9.

HURST, REV. THOMAS (*son of Joseph Hurst*).
b. Lancashire about 1775 ; ordained a priest
at Lisbon ; priest in the English coll. at Lisbon
when used for secular education 1807, professor 1813, procurator of the restored college
1834 to death ; a minister in the British and
Portuguese hospitals in Lisbon 1807–14 ;
confessor to the Bridgettine nuns at Lisbon.
d. Lisbon 31 March 1855. *Gillow's English
Catholics iii*, 490–1 (1887).

HUSBAND, WILLIAM (*eld. son of James Husband, surveyor for Lloyd's Register at Falmouth
d.* 1857). *b.* Mylor near Falmouth 13 Oct.
1822 ; apprenticed to Harvey & Co. of Hayle,
Cornwall, engineers 1839–43 ; mechanical
engineer in charge of steam machinery on
drainage works Haarlem lake, Holland 1845–
9, planned and erected the half-weg engine,
the lake when drained added 47,000 acres of
rich soil to Holland ; manager of business of
firm of Harvey & Co. in London 1852–4, and
at Hayle 1854–63, a partner 1863 to death ;
patented balance valve for water-work purposes, four-beat pump valve, Husband's oscillating cylinder stamps, &c. ; M.I.C.E. 1 May
1866 ; originated 8th Cornwall artillery
volunteers 1860, captain 2 April 1860 to 6
May 1865. *d.* 26 Sion hill, Clifton 10 April
1887. *bur.* St. Erth, Cornwall 16 April. *Min.
of proc. of Instit. of C.E.* (1887) *lxxxix* 470–3.

HUSENBETH, REV. FREDERICK CHARLES
(*son of Frederick Charles Husenbeth of Bristol,
wine-merchant*). *b.* Bristol 30 May 1796 ; ed.

HUSENBETH, REV. F. C. (Con.)
at Sedgly Park sch. Staffs. and St. Mary's coll. Oscott; ordained R.C. priest 25 Feb. 1820; chaplain at Cossey hall, Norfolk 7 July 1820; missioner of St. Walstan's chapel, Cossey 1841 to death; grand vicar of the Midland district 1827; created D.D. by Pius ix. 7 July 1850; provost of the chapter and vicar-general of diocese of Northampton 24 June 1852; wrote 1305 articles under initials of F.C.H. in *Notes and Queries* 4 Feb. 1854 to 2 Nov. 1872; published *Breviarium Romanum suis locis interpositis officiis sanctorum Angliæ* 4 vols. 1830; *The Missal for the use of the laity* 1837; *Emblems of Saints by which they are distinguished in works of art* 1850, 3 ed. 1882; *The Holy Bible translated from the Latin Vulgate* 2 vols. 1853 and 50 other books. *d.* the presbytery adjoining St. Walstan's chapel at Cossey 31 Oct. 1872. *Gillow's English Catholics* (1887) iii, 492–507.

HUSK, WILLIAM HENRY. *b.* London 4 Nov. 1814; clerk to Manning and Dalston and their successors, solicitors, London 1833–86; member of Sacred Harmonic Soc. Oct. 1834, hon. librarian 1853–82 when society was dissolved, wrote prefaces to word-books of Oratorios performed at Society's concerts; author of *Catalogue of library of Sacred Harmonic Society* 1862, new ed. 1872; *Account of the musical celebrations on St. Cecilia's day in the 16th, 17th, and 18th centuries* 1857; edited *Songs of the Nativity* [1866]; wrote many articles in Grove's *Dictionary of Music.* *d.* 20 Westmoreland place, Pimlico, London 12 Aug. 1887.

HUSKISSON, SAMUEL (3 son of *Wm. Huskisson of Oxley, Staffs*). *b.* 1773; cornet 29 light dragoons 17 May 1799; served in Bengal 1799–1803; major 8 foot 4 July 1805; lieut.-col. 1 West India reg. 28 May 1807; lieut.-col. 9 garrison batallion 25 Sep. 1807 to May 1808; lieut.-col. 67 foot 16 June 1808 to 8 July 1824; general 11 Nov. 1851. *d.* 10 Mount st. Grosvenor sq. London 30 Dec. 1854.

HUSSEY, REV. JAMES MC.CONNELL (5 son of *William Hussey of Glasgow*). *b.* 1819 or 1820; ed. at Exeter coll. Ox., B.A. 1843, M.A. 1857; C. of Atherstone, Warwickshire 1846–8; P.C. of St. James, Kennington, London 1848–54; afternoon preacher at the Foundling hospital 1854–61; V. of Ch. Ch. North Brixton 1855 to death; hon. canon of Rochester Jany. 1878 to death; rural dean of Kennington 1879–87 and 1889 to death; D.D. by archbp. of Canterbury Jany. 1881; author of *Joy for the sorrowful or comfort in*

HUSSEY, REV. J. MC.C. (Con.)
sickness 1855, 2 ed. 1856; *Home. An essay* 1878; *Scandal and scandal-mongers* 1879. *d.* Ch. Ch. vicarage, Cancel road, Vassal road, Brixton 19 May 1891. *Daily Graphic* 22 May 1891 p. 9, portrait.

HUSSEY, REV. ROBERT (4 son of *Rev. Wm. Hussey, R. of Sandhurst, Kent*). *b.* 7 Oct. 1801; ed. at Westminster (King's scholar 1816) and Ch. Ch. Ox., student 1821–46; double first class 1824, B.A. 1825, M.A. 1827, B.D. 1837; Greek reader 1832, censor and librarian 1835, catechist 1836, select preacher 1831 and 1846, proctor 1836, Whitehall preacher 1841–3; regius prof. of ecclesiastical history in univ. of Ox. 23 April 1842 to death; P.C. of Binsey near Oxford 1845 to death; author of *An essay on the ancient weights and money* 1836; *An account of the Roman road from Alchester to Dorchester* 1841; *Sermons, mostly academical* 1849; edited the histories of *Socrates* 1844, *Evagrius* 1844, *Bœda* 1846 and *Sozomen* 3 vols. 1860 and 15 other works. *d.* Beaumont st. Oxford 2 Dec. 1856. *bur.* Sandford on Thames. *The Rise of the Papal power. Ed. by Jacob Ley* (1863), Memoir pp. viii–xxvii.

HUTCHESON, CHARLES. *b.* Scotland 1792; taught music in Glasgow; published *Christian Vespers, Glasgow* 1832, containing Hymn tunes harmonised in 3 and 4 parts, and An essay on church music. *d.* Glasgow 1856.

HUTCHESON, FRANCIS DEANE. *b.* 1800; entered navy 13 Oct. 1813; captain 23 Nov. 1841; retired admiral 30 July 1875. *d.* 76 Shaftesbury road, West Hammersmith 21 Dec. 1875.

HUTCHESSON, THOMAS. *b.* 1781; 2 lieut. R.A. 1 Dec. 1797; colonel 1 batt. R.A. 23 Nov. 1841 to 30 Aug. 1854; col. commandant 30 Aug. 1854 to death; L.G. 14 June 1856. *d.* Clarence lawn, Dover 28 Aug. 1857.

HUTCHINS, EDWARD JOHN (*eld. son of Edward Hutchins of Briton Ferry, co. Glamorgan*). *b.* 1809; ed. at Charterhouse and St. John's coll. Cam.; M.P. Penryn 23 Jany. 1840 to 23 June 1841; M.P. Lymington 30 April 1850 to 20 March 1857; contested Southampton 2 July 1841 and Poole 31 July 1847. *d.* Hastings 11 Feb. 1876. *I.L.N.* lxviii, 215 (1876).

HUTCHINSON, CHARLES HENRY. Second lieut. Madras artillery 13 June 1834 and colonel 9 June 1868 to 5 Feb. 1870 when he retired on full pay; M.G. 5 Feb. 1870. *d.* 20 Westbourne park, London 27 Oct. 1873.

HUTCHINSON, CHARLES WATERLOO. *b.* 18 June 1824; 2 lieut. Bengal engineers 9 June 1843; col. R.E. 1 April 1874, col. comandant 17 Dec. 1881 to death; general 28 Nov. 1885; placed on unemployed supernumerary list 16 Sep. 1886; author of *Specimens of various vernacular characters passing through the post office in India, photozincographed. Calcutta* 1877. *d.* 13 Kildare gardens, Bayswater, London 27 March 1890.

HUTCHINSON, GEORGE ROWAN. Second lieut. R.E. 29 May 1832, captain 13 Dec. 1847 to death; superintendent of new harbour works at Holyhead, *killed* by explosion of powder there 25 Feb. 1851 though half a mile from where it took place. *A.R.* (1864) 14.

HUTCHINSON, JOHN. *b.* Newcastle 1811; ed. at London univ.; assistant phys. to Hospital for consumption, Brompton; author of *The spirometer and stethoscope and scale-balance, their use in discriminating diseases of the chest and their value in life-offices* 1852. *d.* Fiji, Sandwich islands, July 1861.

HUTCHINSON, JOHN DYSON. *b.* Halifax, Yorkshire 6 July 1822; ed. at Hipperholme gram. sch.; in business at Halifax, retired 1870; mayor of Halifax 1868 and 1871; M.P. Halifax 21 Feb. 1877, accepted the Chiltern hundreds Aug. 1882. *d.* 25 Redcliffe sq. South Kensington, London 25 Aug. 1882.

HUTCHINSON, WILLIAM EVANS. *b.* 1806; superintendent of Midland counties line to July 1840; a director of Midland railway 1837 and chairman 1864–70; presented with a testimonial at a complimentary dinner 20 Dec. 1870. *d.* Oadby hall, Leicester 6 Dec. 1882. *F. S. Williams' Midland railway* (1888) 181–4, 195, 236, 243.

HUTCHISON, REV. ÆNEAS BARKLY *(eld. son of Robert Hutchison of London, merchant). b.* London 1819; ed. at Queen's coll. Cam., B.D. 1855, B.D. Oxford 1856; P.C. of St. James, Devonport 21 Aug. 1850 to death; author of *Memorials of the abbey of Dundrennan, Galloway* 1857; *A monograph of the history of St. Mary, Callington* 1861. *d.* Harrogate 25 Dec. 1866.

HUTCHISON, REV. WILLIAM [ANTONY] *(son of George Hutchison, a cashier in Bank of England, who d. 1833). b.* London 27 Sep. 1822; ed. at Trin. coll. Cam. 1843–5; received into R.C. church at Birmingham 21 Dec. 1845, confirmed by bishop Walsh, receiving name of Antony 29 Dec. 1845; ordained priest 15 Aug. 1847; a member of the Oratory, London, to the institution of which he largely con-

HUTCHISON, REV. W. *(Con.)*

tributed 1849 to death; established ragged schools and other charities; author of *Loreto and Nazareth : two lectures containing the result of personal investigation of the two sanctuaries* 1863. *d.* The Oratory, Brompton 12 July 1863. *Gillow's English Catholics, iii*, 511–4 (1887).

NOTE.—He left by his will dated 7 July 1860 all his property to the Brompton oratory, will disputed by his brother in law Dr. Alfred Smee but its validity affirmed in case of Knox *v.* Smee, Court of Probate 1864. *Annual Register* (1864) 232-41.

HUTCHISON, REV. WILLIAM CORSTON (2 *son of Robert Hutchison of Fincham, Norfolk).* Matric. from Worcester coll. Ox. 6 May 1841 aged 19; Curate of St. Mary's, Devonport 1848–50; Curate of St. Endellion, Cornwall 1850–1; joined Church of Rome Aug. 1851; lived chiefly abroad rest of his life; tutor to Prince Imperial of France; a member of the third order of St. Francis; a chevalier of Holy Cross of Jerusalem; private chamberlain to Pius ix. and Leo xiii.; had a great share in production of Dr. Fa di Bruno's *Catholic Belief. d.* Holly Place, Hampstead 9 Sep. 1883 aged 63. *bur.* Leytonstone cemet. *Gillow's English Catholics, iii*, 514–5 (1887).

HUTH, FREDERICK. *b.* Hanover 1777; settled at Corunna, landed in England 1809, naturalized by act 59 Geo. iii. cap. 90 (1819); founded house of F. Huth and Co. merchants, City of London 1816; one of most eminent merchants of City of London; had order of Charles iii. of Spain. *d.* 33 Upper Harley st. London 14 Jany. 1864, personalty sworn under £500,000, 5 March.

HUTH, HENRY (3 *son of the preceding). b.* London 1815; ed. at Rusden's sch. Leith hill, Surrey to 1833; travelled in Germany, France and the U.S. of A. 1836–9; joined a firm in Mexico 1840; in a firm at Hamburg 1844–9; merchant in London 1849 to death; purchased books at all the important sales, also daily at chief booksellers; with the single exception of Lord Spencer had finest private library then known; member of Philobiblon Society 1863, of Roxburgh club 1866; treasurer and pres. of royal hospital for incurables 1861; printed *Ancient ballads and broadsides* 1867; *Inedited poetical miscellanies* 1584–1700. 1870; *Fugitive Tracts* 1493–1700. 2 vols. 1875 and other books. *d.* 30 Prince's gate, London 10 Dec. 1878. *bur.* Bolney ch. yard, Sussex. *Times* 14 Dec. 1878 *p.* 9; *Athenæum* 21 Dec. 1878 *p.* 803; *Academy* 21 Dec. 1878 *p.* 583; *The Huth library. A catalogue of books, manuscripts, letters and engravings, collected by H. Huth 5 vols.* (1880).

HUTHERSAL, Rev. Cort *(son of John Huthersal of Ardwick green, Manchester, schoolmaster).* Ed. at Manchester school and St. John's coll. Cam., B.A. 1818, M.A. 1821; C. of St. Mary's, Manchester; C. of All Saints, Leamington to about 1837, lived at Leamington rest of his life; author of *Synopsis of the various administrations for the government of England from the year 1756 to 1842. London 1842, anon. d.* Leamington 14 Sep. 1859.

HUTHWAITE, Sir Edward *(eld. son of William Huthwaite, draper, Nottingham).* bapt. St. Peter's, Nottingham 24 June 1793; ed. at military academy Woolwich; second lieut. Bengal artillery 12 Nov. 1810, lieut.-col. 3 July 1845, col. commandant 23 Jany. 1854 to death; L.G. 6 March 1868; C.B. 3 April 1846, K.C.B. 2 June 1869; served in India 1810 to his death, and was present at Sobraon, Chillianwalla and Goojrat. *d.* Sherwood, Nynee Tal, India 5 April 1873. *I.L.N. lxii,* 475 (1873).

HUTHWAITE, Henry. *b.* 1769; entered Bengal army 1795; colonel 15 Bengal N.I. 1837–52; colonel 42 Bengal N.I. 1852 to death; L.G. 11 Nov. 1851. *d.* Hoveringham, Notts. 5 Dec. 1853.

HUTT, Sir George *(son of Richard Hutt of Appley Towers, Ryde, Isle of Wight).* *b.* 1809; lieut. Bombay artillery 28 Sep. 1827, major 12 Sep. 1855 to 9 Nov. 1858 when he retired; served during Scinde and Afghan campaigns 1839–44, in Persia 1857, and Indian mutiny 1857–8; M.G. 18 Jany. 1859; sec. to comrs. of Chelsea hospital 6 March 1865 to 13 March 1885; C.B. 26 Feb. 1846, K.C.B. 21 June 1887; edited *Papers illustrative of the history of the royal hospital at Chelsea* 1872. *d.* Appley Towers, Ryde, Isle of Wight 27 Sep. 1889. *Times* 31 Oct. 1889 *p.* 10.

HUTT, Richard. *b.* 1803; assistant to George Cawthorne of the circulating library 24 Cockspur st., London May 1825, managed the business for the widow 1833–50, and was partner with her son 1850–74 when the latter retired. *d.* 24 Cockspur st. 8 Nov. 1876 aged 73. *Bookseller* Dec. 1876 *p.* 1143; *Publisher's Circular* Dec. 1876 *p.* 920.

Note:—This was the first circulating library in London, it was commenced at 132 Strand in 1740 by Wright, who was succeeded by Batho. John Bell next became the proprietor of the business and was followed by G. Cawthorne who removed to Cockspur st. in 1807.

HUTT, Sir William *(brother of Sir George Hutt, 1809–89).* *b.* 2 Chester place, Lambeth, Surrey 6 Oct. 1801; ed. at St. Mary's hall, Ox. Feb. to Aug. 1820 and at Trin. coll. Cam.,

HUTT, Sir W. *(Con.)*
B.A. 1827, M.A. 1831; M.P. Hull 1832–41; M.P. Gateshead 1841–74; V.P. of board of trade and paymaster general 22 Feb. 1860 to Nov. 1865; P.C. 22 Feb. 1860; negotiated a treaty of commerce between Great Britain and Austria 27 Feb. 1865 etc.; member of mixed commission at Vienna to examine into Austrian Tariff 1 March 1865; K.C.B. 27 Nov. 1865. *d.* Appley Towers, Ryde, Isle of Wight 24 Nov. 1882.

HUTTON, Edward. *b.* 1797; L.R.C.S. Ireland 1819, F.R.C.S. 1824, president 1852, sec. June 1853 to June 1865; M.B. Dublin 1822, M.D. 1842; president of pathological society of Dublin; M.R.I.A.; contributed to *Dublin medical journal* and other periodicals. *d.* 5 Merrion square south, Dublin 24 Nov. 1865.

HUTTON, Frederick. *b.* 1801; entered navy 28 Jany. 1813; captain 3 July 1844; governor of Ascension 12 Nov. 1846; R.A. 1 April 1863. *d.* Tunbridge Wells 6 March 1866.

HUTTON, George. Entered Madras army 1811; colonel 22 Madras N.I. 1860 to death; M.G. 4 July 1856. *d.* Vizianagram, Madras 28 Aug. 1861.

HUTTON, Henry. Called to the bar in Ireland 1822, Q.C. 7 Feb. 1849; chairman of quarter sessions, co. Roscommon to death. *d.* 1859.

HUTTON, Rev. Henry *(son of lieut. general Henry Hutton, d. 1827).* *b.* Moate, Westmeath 1808; ed. at Wad. coll. Ox., B.A. 1830, M.A. 1833; C. of Lidlington, Beds. 1832; P.C. of Woburn, Beds. 1834–49; chaplain to duke of Bedford 1839; R. of St. Paul's, Covent Garden, London 1849 to death; author of *Lectures, doctrinal, explanatory and practical on the English liturgy. Woburn 1848; An account of the charitable institutions in parish of Saint Paul, Covent Garden 1858. d.* 7 Henrietta st. Covent Garden 23 June 1863. *Sermons on the Lord's Prayer. By H. Hutton* (1863), *Memoir pp. i-xlviii.*

HUTTON, James Frederick *(son of Wm. M. Hutton).* *b.* London 1826; an African merchant and manufacturer of cotton goods at Manchester; Belgian consul at Manchester 11 Aug. 1887 to death; pres. of Manchester chamber of commerce; F.R.G.S.; M.P. for North division of Manchester 1885 to 1886. *d.* Cairo 1 March 1890.

HUTTON, Rev. Peter. *b.* Holbeck near Leeds 29 June 1811; ed. at Benedictine college, Ampleforth; studied at Univ. of Louvain 1836–9; ordained priest 24 Sep. 1839; pres.

of St. Peter's college, Prior Park near Bath, and professor of Latin and Greek there Sep. 1839 to July 1841; entered the Order of Charity at Loughborough, Leics. 5 July 1841; rector of the college of Order of Charity near village of Ratcliffe-on-the-Wreak near Leicester 23 Nov. 1844, vice pres. 2 July 1850, pres. 1 Nov. 1851 to death; translated all the Latin and Greek authors read in the schools at Ratcliffe. *d.* Ratcliffe college 2 Sep. 1880. *J. Hirst's Brief memoir of Father Hutton. Market Weighton, St. William's press* (1886); *Gillow's English Catholics, iii,* 517–21 (1887).

HUTTON, ROBERT HOWARD (*son of Robert Hutton*). *b.* Soulby, Westmoreland 26 July 1840; farmer Milnthorpe 1863–9; bone setter at 74 Gloucester place, Portman sq. London 1871–9, at 36 Queen Anne st. Cavendish sq. 1879 to death; had an extensive practice and made much money; a well known huntsman at Melton Mowbray. *d.* University coll. hospital, London from taking laudanum in error for a black draught 16 July 1887.

NOTE.—His uncle Richard Hutton was a bone setter at Wyndham place, Crawford st. London for many years and *d.* Gilling lodge, Watford 6 Jany. 1871 aged 70. Among his successful cures were the Hon. Spencer Ponsonby in 1865 and George Moore the philanthropist in 1869.

HUTTON, REV. WYNDHAM MADDEN (*son of Rev. John Hutton of Granby, Notts.*) Matric. from St. Edmund hall, Ox. 7 July 1849 aged 18; at St. Bees 1854; V. of St. Paul, Tipton, Staffs. 1861–9; V. of Kirk-Christ-Lezayre, Isle of Man 1869–77; V. of Twyford with Hungarton and Thorpe-Satchville, Leics. 1877 to death; author of *Poems. By A member of the university of Oxford. Oxford* 1851; *Gottfried's pilgrimage: an allegory* 1866, 3 ed. 1868; *Bertha's Dream and other tales. Frome Selwood* 1868; *The unconquered island. Ramsay* 1873. *d.* Hungarton vicarage 18 Jany. 1882.

HUY, JOHN. Acting manager of Court theatre, London under Marie Litton, Jany. 1871 to March 1875 and under John Hare, March 1875 to 19 July 1879; acting manager of St. James's theatre, London under John Hare and W. H. Kendall 4 Oct. 1879 to 21 July 1888; ruptured his liver by falling on the stone stairs at his residence 3 Langham place, Regent st. London 29 Nov. 1891. *d.* 30 Nov. 1891 aged 57. *The Era 5 Dec. 1891 p. 9 col. 4.*

HUYSHE, ALFRED (*youngest son of Rev. John Huyshe of Exeter 1772–1851*). *b.* 1811; ed. at Addiscombe; 2 lieut. Bengal artillery 13

Dec. 1827; col. R.A. 29 April 1861 to 31 Oct. 1867; inspector general of artillery in India 1867–73; general 1 Oct. 1877; C.B. 2 June 1877. *d.* 46 Onslow sq. London 25 Feb. 1880 in 69 year. *Graphic xxii,* 196 (1880), *portrait.*

HUYSHE, GEORGE (*brother of the preceding*). *b.* 1804; ensign 13 Bengal N.I. 22 March 1820; col. Bengal infantry 15 Nov. 1853; general 19 Feb. 1872; C.B. 27 Sep. 1843. *d.* Guernsey 6 Oct. 1881.

HUYSHE, GEORGE LIGHTFOOT (2 *son of the preceding*). *b.* 1839; ensign rifle brigade 18 April 1856, capt. 19 Dec. 1862; served with 83 regt. in Indian mutiny 1857–9, in pursuit of Tantia Topee 1858–9, medal; on Sir G. Wolseley's staff on Red river expedition 1870; D.A.A.G. on Sir Garnet Wolseley's staff; author of *The Red river expedition* 1871; with H. Brackenbury of *Fanti and Ashanti* 1873. *d.* Prah-su, Ashantee 18 Jany. 1874. *Graphic, ix,* 218, 229 (1874), *portrait.*

HYDE, EDGAR (*youngest son of Rev. Henry Woodd Cock Hyde of Camberwell, Surrey*). *b.* 27 May 1829; ed. at St. Paul's sch. and C.C. coll. Ox., junior math. scholar 1847–57, fellow 1857–68; B.A. 1851, M.A. 1854; barrister I.T. 11 June 1862; practised at Calcutta 1862–71; edited *Reports of cases in Court of judicature at Fort William, Calcutta* 1864; author of *The Indian succession act, with introduction and synopsis* 1865. *d.* Folkestone 27 Jany. 1891.

HYDE, GEORGE HOOTON (*son of Rev. George Hooton Hyde, R. of Wareham, Dorset*). *b.* 1798; 2 lieut. R.A. 7 July 1817, captain 18 Aug. 1843 to 14 Jany. 1852 when he retired on full pay; general 1 Oct. 1877. *d.* 13 Albert place, Victoria road, Kensington, London 8 March 1879.

HYDE, HENRY (*brother of Edgar Hyde 1829–91*). *b.* St. Giles, Camberwell 1825; ed. Addiscombe to 1844; 2 lieut. Bengal engineers 7 June 1844; engaged in forming Cis-Sutlej states roads 1847; at siege of Mooltan and battle of Goojrat 1849; raised the Pathan companies of the sappers 1858; deputy consulting engineer railway department, N.W. provinces and Bengal 1859–60; inspector general of public works accounts, Bengal 1861; master of Calcutta mint Jany. 1862 to Jany. 1876, superintended paper currency department 1862–70; president Asiatic soc. Calcutta; inspector general of stores, India office, London 1876 to death; retired from royal engineers 17 Feb. 1878; hon. major

HYDE, H. *(Con.)*

general 17 Feb. 1878. *d.* Burntwood, Caterham, Surrey 23 Oct. 1887. *Min. of Proc. of I.C.E. xci*, 462–6 (1888).

HYDE, REV. JOHN. *b.* London 26 Feb. 1833; joined the Church of the Latter day saints 1849, preached Mormonism in France 1852, went to Salt Lake city 1853, lectured against Mormonism in the Sandwich islands and the United States of America and England 1855–6; *bapt.* by Dr. Jonathan Bayley in Argyle sq. ch. London and became a Swedenborgian 1858; minister at Brightlingsea 1859–61, at Derby 1861–6, and at Manchester 1866 to death; president of the New Jerusalem Church conference in London three times; author of *Mormonism, its leaders and designs. New York* 1857; *Swedenborg, the man of the age* 1859; *The serpent that beguiled Eve* 1862; *The doctrine of substitution* 1880, *new ed.* 1882; wrote under pseud. of A Bible Student *Our eternal homes* 1864, *several editions; Bible Photographs, a contrast between righteousness and wickedness* 1865 and other books. *d.* Milford, Derbyshire 18 Aug. 1875. *Intellectual Repository, Oct.* 1875 *pp.* 468–77; *Publishers' Circular* 1 *Sep.* 1875 *pp.* 635–6; *I.L.N. lxv*, 229, 230 (1874), *portrait.*

HYDES, JOHN P. Best known actor in New Zealand where he first appeared as Chizzler in the farce of *But-However* 23 April 1849; built Duke of Edinburgh theatre at Hokilika; held every position in the profession from checktaker to proprietor; great burlesque actor; appeared at Maguire's opera house, San Francisco as Pauline in burlesque of *Lady of Lyons* 30 April 1859. *d.* Melbourne early in 1883.

HYETT, WILLIAM HENRY *(eld. son of Rev. Henry Cay Adams of Shrewsbury, d. 1808). b.* 2 Sep. 1795; ed. at Westminster, matric. from Ch Ch. Ox. 21 Oct. 1813; swam across the Hellespont from Sestos to Abydos in 1 hour and 50 minutes; assumed name of Hyett upon succeeding to estates of Benjamin Hyett 1815; M.P. Stroud 13 Dec. 1832 to 30 Dec. 1834; made experiments on growth of trees by watering with chymical solutions; taught mechanical drawing in his schools at Painswick; founder of Gloucestershire eye institution 1866; made translations from Horace, Goethe, Victor Hugo and Filicaja which he privately printed; F.R.S. *d.* Painswick house, Gloucs. 10 March 1877. *Times* 13 *March* 1877 *p.* 10.

HYLAND, MOST REV. THOMAS RAYMOND. *b.* Dublin 3 Nov. 1837; entered Dominican order at Tallaght, Feb. 1856; ordained priest

HYLAND, MOST REV. T. R. *(Con.)*

in Rome 22 Dec. 1864; consecrated bishop of Euria, in partibus, in Rome 30 April 1882 and appointed coadjutor archbishop of Trinidad, West Indies. *d.* Trinidad 9 Oct. 1884.

HYLES, WILLIAM *(eld. son of Georges Hyles of Canute castle hotel, Southampton). b.* 1843; proprietor of the York music hall, Southampton from its foundation 1873 to death. *d.* Royal York hotel, above Bar, Southampton 30 Aug. 1878.

HYLTON, WILLIAM GEORGE HYLTON JOLIFFE, 1 Baron *(elder child of Rev. Wm. John Hylton of Merstham, Surrey d. 31 Jany. 1835). b.* Little Argyle st. London 7 Dec. 1800; cornet 15 hussars 10 April 1817; captain 29 foot 22 April 1824 to 24 June 1824 when placed on h.p.; cr. baronet 20 Aug. 1821; M.P. Petersfield 1830–34, 1841–66; under sec. of state for home department March 1852 to Dec. 1852; parliamentary sec. to treasury March 1858 to June 1859; P.C. 18 June 1859; whip to conservative party in house of commons; created baron Hylton of Hylton, co. Durham and of Petersfield, Hants. 16 July 1866. *d.* Merstham house, Redhill, Surrey 1 June 1876. *I.L.N. xxxii* 312 (1858) *portrait, li* 609, 610 (1867) *portrait, lxviii* 575 (1876).

HYMAN, REV. ORLANDO HAYDON BRIDGMAN (1 son of Simon Hyman of Devonport). *b.* 1814; ed. at Wadham coll. Ox., scholar 1830–5, senior fellow 1835 to death; B.A. 1834, M.A. 1840; a well known Greek scholar; had a remarkably tenacious memory, tore up his books when he had read them. *d.* Porchester place, Oxford sq., London 9 Dec. 1878. *Times* 18 *Dec.* 1878 *p.* 11; *N. and Q.* 5 *Series xi*, 201–2 (1879).

HYMERS, REV. JOHN *(son of a farmer). b.* Ormsby in Cleveland, Yorkshire 20 July 1803; a sizar at St. John's coll. Cam. 1822; 2 wrangler 1826, B.A. 1826, B.D. 1836, D.D. 1841; fellow of his coll. 1827, assistant tutor 1829, tutor 1832, senior fellow 1838–52, pres. 1848–52; lady Margaret preacher in Univ. of Cam. 1841–52; R. of Brandesburton in Holderness, Yorkshire 1852 to death; F.R.S. 31 May 1838; author of *The theory of Equations* 1837, 3 *ed.* 1858; *The Integral Calculus* 1844; *A treatise on spherical trigonometry* 1841 and other books; left nearly all his property to found a gram. sch. at Hull, but bequest invalid under statute of mortmain, his brother Robert Hymers gave £50,000 for same purpose Jany. 1891. *d.* Brandesburton 7 April 1887. *F. Ross's Celebrities of the Yorkshire wolds* (1878) *p.* 84.

INDEX.

INDEX.

This Index contains references to the most important, curious and interesting facts, to be found in the pages of this work.

B

CLUBS (Con.)

Lowtonian, secretary of 635.

Manchester literary founded 1330.

Metropolitan red lions founded 1077.

Pitt, president of 972.

Political economy founded 578.

Quekett microscopical, founder 1331, president 1090.

Raleigh founded 410.

Red house at Battersea 73.

Reform, chairmen 207, 977, chef 1097, erected 181, founded 654, 977, member expelled 363, secretaries 717, 1280.

Savage founded 1294.

Star, memorials of 1083.

Travellers' erected 181.

Tyneside Naturalists' Field founded 39, 1314.

Urban founded 1109.

Victoria yacht founded 10.

Coach drivers, Cotton 729, Herring 1446.

Coach proprietors, Barber 156, Chaplin 591, Hadley 1272, Halcomb 1276.

Coaches, coachmakers 68, revival of coaching 70.

Coal, Bidder's safety lamp for mines 272, coal exchange opened 927, coal factor 927, combustion of 1524, machine for weighing invented 888, quantity still remaining in England 1592, Small coal man, a political song 1573.

Coates, Robert d. 1848 known as Romeo Coates, his widow 367.

Coats, Chesterfield the 605, Petersham the 1344.

Cock fighting 112.

Cocking, Robert killed 1837, aeronaut 1223.

Coins, collectors of, Bergne 253, Borrell 341, Christmas 617, Coats 657, Cuff 780, Fox 1094, Guthrie 1264, Harvey 1368, Hawkins E. 1387, Hawkins W. 1390, Henfrey 1427.

Colenso, William John d. 1883 bishop of Natal, deposed by bishop Gray 1219.

Coleoptera, Brackenridge's collection 372, Brightwell's collection 400.

Coleridge, Samuel Taylor d. 1834 poet, Cottle's recollections of 728, literary cookery with reference to matters attributed to 377.

Colleges.

Agricultural at Cirencester established 1288.

College of arms, report on 233.

College of doctors of law 1571.

Crook hall removed to Ushaw 228.

Didsbury near Manchester founded 358.

Exeter diocesan founded 1337.

London coll. of divinity at Kilburn 348.

Manchester new coll. removed to London 361.

Marlborough founded 357, 1235.

St. Columba, Beresford's gift to 251.

St. John's hall, Highbury, principal 348.

Training at Highbury founded 1235.

Collier, a poetical 1005.

Collieries, Clay cross 1556, self acting fence for winding shafts 1556.

Colonies, Secretaries of state for colonies, Aberdeen 6, Cardwell 543, Glenelg 1157, Grey 1241, Herbert 1437, Hobart 1487, Pakington 1312, Stanley 863.

Colston, Edward d. 1721 merchant, life of 1125.

Columbine, Boleno 328.

Coming K., The authors of 221.

Commons, House of, best dressed man in 932, call of the house, the last 1364, clerk 1022, chiltern hundreds refused to a member 510, member expelled 934, person committed to custody of serjeant at arms 677, seat from which member hears thanks given him, remains his while member 1003, speakers 935, 1008, speakership, contests for 1191, 1376, thanks given to celebrated men 1003, 1039.

Compasses, Caithness gravitation compass 512, method of compensating errors invented 168.

Compensation refused by government to Douglas 904.

Concerts, of ancient music 290, promenade 770, 1308.

Confectioner, Gunter 1259.

Confessional unmasked, The 455.

Conjurors, Anderson 63, 1482, Blitz 314, Eagle 950, Heller 1418.

Conservatory at Surrey zoological gardens 7.

Control, board of, See Board of Control col. 1626.

Conveyancer, Hodgkin 1492.

Convicts, Buckley the convict 465, how convicts are made 555.

Cooke, Sir W. F. d. 1879, electrician 705, partner with Wheatstone 1383.

Cooks and cookery, Francatelli 1097, Kettner's manual 805.

Cooper, Sir Astley Preston d. 1841, his anatomical preparations 1225, life 708.

Cooper, Thompson, F.S.A. author 708.

Copper, Cwmavon copper works, Glamorgan 1259, Kapunda mine, South Australia 944, smelting copper in Swansea district 1098.

Coppin, George b. 1819, actor & theatrical manager 416.

Copybooks, Darnell's 817, largest maker of in the world 1458.

Coral, Jane d. 1858, painter 1601.

Cork, bishop of 851, great exhibition at 842, lord lieutenant 1038, St. Finbarre cath. 1233, water works 246.

Cork, Cloyne and Ross, bishops of 1060, 1233.

Corn, corn merchant 1378, drilling machines 1126, grinding corn, improvements in 353.

Corn. Anti-corn law league, A B C of the 98, founders of 98, 1272, final meeting 98, lecturers, members of and speakers 11, 361, 659, 1096, 1141, meeting in Covent Garden 397, secretary 1589.

Cornwall, assay master 1435, Cornish drolls 346, duchy, enquiry into revenues of 700, fauna 731, folk lore 731, glossary of words 731, Pendeen church built 36, Sunday sch. teacher the first 205, typhus fever 550.

Coromandel, the seven pagodas 557.

Corona Borealis, discovery of a new star in 288.

Coroners' inquests 615.

Corsets, corset à la Venus 477.

Costumes peculiar worn by F. Boott 340.

Cotehele house, Cornwall, account of 691.

Cottage allotment system 578.

Cotton, machinery exported 794, spinning machines, improvements in 325.

Cotton spinners, Armitage 83, Ashworth 97, 98, Bazley 202, Bright 399, Brook 414, Callender 517, Crompton 767, Cross 771, Fielden 1043 bis., Garnett 1124, Greg 1232, Hall 1287, Holms 1517, Hornby 1538, Horrocks 1444, Houldsworth 1549, Hoyle 1562, Hulbert 1579, Hutton 1608.

County Guy, a song 1196.

Coursers, Campbell 530, Etwall 1000.

Coursing, Ashdown hill meetings 752, Craven 752.

Courvoisier, F. Benjamin hanged 1840, his trial 1488.

E

F

Fruit dealer, Hanson 1322.
Fuel, Grant's patent 1206.
Fungi, collection of 790.
Furniture, collection of 255.
Fust, Sir Herbert Jenner *d.* 1852, judge of court of arches 1185.

G

Gaelic, dictionary 86, lexicographer 86.
Galvanism used to explode gunpowder in blowing down Round Downcliff 779.
Galway, bishop of 443.
Gambler, Ball-Hughes 147.
Games and gaming, law on 383.
Gardeners, Dale Jas. 801, Dale Joseph 802, Forbes 1077, Fortune 1088, Gordon 1179, Harrison 1354.
Garibaldi, Giuseppe *d.* 1882 patriot, British volunteer officers with 944.
Garston near Liverpool, coal drops at 800.
Garter, knights of the, Aberdeen 7, Ailesbury 31, Albert 38, Anglesey 70, Camden 521, Canning 537, Cleveland 647, Derby 863, Derby 863, Devonshire 869, Exeter 1010, Fitzwilliam 1064, Fortescue 1088, Hanover, king of 1321, Hertford 1449.
Garter, a knight of, allowed to retain the Thistle 7.
Gas, coal gas manufacture 643, engineers 1002, gas light and coke co. 1002, lime purifiers 643, oxide of iron used for purification 1002, polytechnic gas fire 119, portable gas 1176, system of compressing 1176, water meter 643.
Gasses, absorption of by charcoal 1596, law of diffusion of discovered 1198, transpirability of 1198.
Gentlemen at arms, a dignity to be had by purchase 473, corps of gentlemen at arms 1585.
Geographers, Findlay 1047, Laurie 1047, Purdy 1047, Van Kenlen 1047.
Geologists, Ansted 73, Boase 322, Buckland 462, Clarke 636, Daintree 800, Davidson 824, De La Beche 849, Evans 1001, Gray 1219, Greenough 1229, Hawkins 1390, Henland 1428, Henwood 1435, Hunt 1592, Turner 1428.
Geology, geological museum 849, geological soc. Bigsby's gold medal 275, geological survey 849, mineral veins, electrical phenomena in 1592.
George III. *d.* 1820, compared to a German hog butcher 1498, dau. Mary duchess of Gloucester 1158, his boot maker 1490, master of chapel royal to 114, pistol boy to 829.
George IV. *d.* 1830, Carlton house alterations at 1536, coronation at 948, coronation, cupbearer at 8, coronation, pugilists engaged to act as pages 224, Croly's life of 766, his bonds not paid 1308, his friends 1515, his jockey Chifney 608, 609, libels on 1364, 1591, visit to Ireland 463.
Germany, Francis II. at Catau Cambresis 1207, Kissingen, fashion set of drinking its waters 1208.
Ghosts, micrometer 494, origin and nature of 459.
Giants, Bethune 264, Cross 762, Hales 1279.
Gilbert, William Schwenck *b.* 1836 dramatist, as an illustrator 1146.
Gillray, James *d.* 1815, his caricatures 777, 1005.
Gipsies, advocate 745, Borrow's books about 342, friend 745, kings of 320 *bis.*, school for at Yetholm 134.
Giraffes exhibited 770.

Girtin, Thomas *d.* 1802 panorama painter, drawings by 1283.
Gladstone, William Ewart *b.* 1809, action for libel against 963, election committee at Oxford 1271, election committees 1238, his friend Hope-Scott 1532.
Glasgow, Anderson's univ. 778, 1000, 1009, Anderston incorporated with 1548, Chalmers and the Tron ch. 681, churches, scheme for building twenty 534, 681, Dollar institution 755, Dunlop st. theatre 43, Fir park 1009, John st. ch. built 66, manufactory of pure bread at 369, provident bank the first 1009, royal exchange 1009, sabbath sch. 681, statue of lord Clyde 657, temple of magic 63.
Glasgow University, Buchanan bursaries 459, Buchanan prizes instituted 459, Clark scholarships 626, lord rectors 426, 803, 863, 971, 973, 1027.
Glass, crown glass made with sulphate of soda 1361, cylindrical, machine for cutting 638, French glass 638, German sheet glass 1361, glass blower, a 392, Hartley's rolled plate 1361, thimble used instead of iron bar in blowing 1361.
Glass, designers and painters on, Baillie 128, Clarke 632, Cottingham 727, Heaton 1414.
Glass manufacturers, Glazebrook 1156, Hardman 1329, Hartley 1361.
Gloucester, British ragged schools founded 361, eye institution founded 1611, Sunday sch. the first 24, tea total soc. founded 361.
Gloucester, William Frederick *d.* 1834, duke of 1158.
Gloucestershire lord lieutenant 1062.
Glovers, Allcroft 49, Dent 861.
Glue, method of drying 557.
God save the king, the anthem of 627.
Goddard, Arabella *b.* 1836, pianist 833.
Godwin, William *d.* 1836, his wife 621.
Goethe, Johann Wolfgan von *d.* 1832, poem by 1554.
Goffres sold in the streets 1130.
Gold, automatic weighing machine for 730, bullion robbery 1396, cause of high price of 701, chemically pure made 1042, dust robbery 1396, gold thread manufacture 377, gold medal specially struck 550.
Golfers and golfing, Glennie 1157, Hay 1395, score of 88 *col.* 1157.
Gorham, Rev. G. C. *d.* 1857, his case 121, 1185.
Gothic architecture, revival of 886, 953.
Governesses, An appeal on behalf of, a poem 3.
Grace, For these and all thy mercies 1487.
Grahamstown, bishop of 727.
Grant, Mrs. Anne *d.* 1838, of Laggan 1140.
Granton harbour constructed 457.
Graphitic acid discovered 409.
Gravesend town pier 630.
Gray, Sir John *d.* 1875, M.P. 1216, his trial 1061.
Greece, coins of discovered 341, committee for in London 427, Englishmen who fought in 1049, swimming across Hellespont 1611.
Greenock, Comet steamboat boiler exploded 432.
Greenwich hospital, Bellot's monument 235, estates 1242, governors 13, 799, 1180, sixpenny revenue 1048.
Gretna green post boy 1198.
Griffith, Rev. William *d.* 1883, expelled Wesleyan ministry 939, 1245.
Groves, Anthony Norris *d.* 1853, missionary 1252, preacher in Dublin 691, tutor in his family 749.
Guano islands, monopoly of 1138.
Guernsey, bailiff of 546.
Gunpowder manufactories 610, 793.

Hose frames, circular invented 83, *See also* Stocking frames.

Hot blast, invention of 134.

Houghton, Richard Monckton Milnes *d.* 1885, first baron 1547, befriends D. Gray poet 1214-5.

Houlton, Sir George *d.* 1862, knighted 1835 or 1836 but objecting to pay the fees for registration he was never registered. There was an erroneous impression in existence that members of H.M. household were exempt from paying fees.

Hounds, masters of, Arkwright 83, Barnett 173, Beaufort 212, Bedford 218, Bentinck 248, Berkeley 254, Bessborough 261, Chaplin 591, Cope 714, Drake 915, Ducie 922, Farquharson 1023, Fenwick-Bisset 1034, Fitzhardinge, Earl of 1062, Fitzhardinge, Baron 1062, Fitzwilliam 1066, Foljambe 1073, Forester 1081, Galway 1118, Grant 1204, Greaves 1221, Guilford 1255, Hall 1286, Harris 1346, Harvey 1366, Hastings, marquis of 1372, Hastings, baron 1372, Hawke 1384, Heathcote 1412, Hicks 1461, Hobson 1489, Hodgson 1498, Holyoake-Goodricke 1519, Honywood 1523, Hood 1525, Howe 1556, Huntingdon 1598, Lambton 1588, Ridley 1589, Suffield 1589.

House decorators, Garrett 1125, Hay 1393.

Huddersfield, Convalescent home founded 414.

Hudson bay co., secretary 1102.

Hull, adventures of James Acland at 10, convent of our Lord of Mercy 679, grammar school founded 1612.

Hulsean lecturer, the first, Benson 245.

Hume, Joseph *d.* 1855, M.P. 1586, his private secretary 679, speech wilfully misreported 677.

Humming birds, Gould's collection of 1191.

Hungate family estates 1588.

Hunter, John *d.* 1793 surgeon, his coffin 462.

Hunting, D' ye ken John Peel, a song 1212, on foot 1373, 1523.

Hunting parsons, Anderson 65, Honywood 1523.

Huntsmen, Ayris 114, Bartlett 186, Carter 561, Christian 615, Davis 829, Goodall 1172, Head 1405, Hills J. 1477, Hills T. 1478, Hunnum 1588.

Huskisson, William *killed* 1830 statesman, person present at his death 1516.

Hussars, The Eleventh, crack regiment 542.

Hydraulic engineer, Beardmore 209.

Hydropathy, practiser of 1257.

Hydrostatic beds invented 90.

Hygrometer, a self registering 1183.

Hymns, ancient and modern, originator of 136, ancient and modern, writers in 948, hymns as a substitute for Dr. Watts 684, invalids hymn book 981, Just as I am without one plea 981, Much in sorrow, oft in woe 685, My God and Father while I stray 981.

Hymn tunes, Burnham 628, Joyful 276, Kilmarnock 901, Pembroke 628, Queenborough 628.

Hymn writer, Havergal 1380-81.

Hypnotism 378, 1260.

I

Ice merchant, Gatti 1130.

Iceland, Iceland and its volcanoes, large picture of 770, Icelandic dictionary 643.

Ilford, pleistocene mammalia found at 376.

I know a bank, a duet 1537.

I'll hang my harp on a willow tree, a song 1254.

Illuminated manuscripts, Bragge's collection 378, copying of 725.

Impostors, Ady 25, Aitken 36, Fletcher 1069.

Imprisoned eight years for refusing to give up deeds 1564.

Income tax introduced 1124.

India, Arnold medals in the Punjab 88, commander in chief 73, cinchona cultivation 1553, Delhi princes shot 1500, Euphrates route 604, flora of 66, fossil mammalia 574, Ganges canal 574, governors general Amherst 56, Canning 537, Dalhousie 803, Elgin 973, Ellenborough 975 and Hardinge 1328, Great Indian peninsular railway 592, Hobson-Jobson a glossary of colloquial words 485, Hodson's horse 1500, irrigation scheme 592, Indian church aid association founded 412, Kutchery technicalities 553, land revenue of N.W. provinces 286, Mhow court martial 756, Nagpore annexed 803, Nilagiris, collection of their arms, dresses, etc. 388, order of star of 537, Oudh annexed 803, Pathan companies raised 1610, Pegu annexed 803, Punjaub annexed 803, railway system initiated 254-55, Sanscrit proverbs 557, sec. of state Cranborne, afterwards marquis of Salisbury, 954 and Wood 1281, Sikh regt. the first 1496, Syrian route to 604, Telegu proverbs 557, tea plant introduced 1088, vernacular characters passing through post office 1605.

India, Bangalore, Cubbon park and statue 778.

India, Bengal, middle class schools 728, stud department 873.

India, Bombay, conservator of forests 1139, Elphinstone coll. 989, gas introduced 792, reformatory school of industry founded 468.

India, Calcutta, bishop Cotton 728, cathedral 1079, Calcutta journal established 461, drainage and water works 629, mint 1079, 1610, schools for native females of higher class established 264.

India, Madras, army commander of 73, female school of industry 612.

India rubber, manufacturers 1528, masticator invented for 1315, vulcanised india rubber 1315, waterproof garments 1315.

Initialism, *See also* Names and Pseudonyms.

A., H. A. S. *i.e.* Henry Adams Sergison Atwood 106.

A., S. A. *i.e.* Alexander Stewart Allen 48.

B., A. C. *i.e.* Arthur Coke Burnell 485.

B., B. H. *i.e.* Bertha H. Buxton 503.

B., A. E. *i.e.* Andrew Edmund Brae 377.

B., C. *i.e.* Cordelia Georgiana Budd 466.

B., E. *i.e.* Mrs. E. Babington 981.

B., E. S. *i.e.* Edwyn Sherard Burnaby 483.

B., F. C. *i.e.* Francis Capper Brooke 415.

B., G. C. *i.e.* George Clement Boase 321.

B., J. a friend of the Aborigines Protection Soc. *i.e.* John Burtt 495.

B., W. *i.e.* William Borrows 343.

B., W. *i.e.* William Brinton 402.

B., W. C. *i.e.* William Corbett Burder 476.

C. *i.e.* James Crossley 773.

C., C. *i.e.* Charles Chorley 614.

C., E. J. M. *i.e.* Edward James Mortimer Collins 680.

C., F. *i.e.* Frances Collins 679.

C., F. D. *i.e.* Frances Dorothy Cartwright 565.

C., F. L. *i.e.* Frederick Leigh Colvile 687.

C., F. P. *i.e.* F. Percy Cotton 679.

C., J. *i.e.* James Clay 640.

C., R. H. *i.e.* Robert Henry Clive 653.

C., W. L. *i.e.* William Lucas Collins 682.

IRELAND *(Con.)*

Ireland, Belfast, Belfast bottoms 1339, horticultural exhibition 1302.

Ireland, Dublin, crown and hanaper office 1315, exhibition 814.

Ireland, chief secretaries, Bexley 268, Carlisle 548, Cavendish 575, Derby 1863, Ellesmere 976, Forster 1086, Goulburn 1191, Glenelg 1157, Hardinge 1328, Hobhouse 427, Horsman 1543, Stanley 863, Walhouse or Littleton 1376.

Ireland, lord chancellors, Blackburne 296, Brady 377, Brewster 394, Brooke 418 and Campbell 526·

Ireland, lords lieutenants, Anglesey 71, Carlisle 548, Clarendon 623, De Grey 848, Eglinton 971, Fortescue 1088, Haddington 1271, Heytesbury 1457.

Irish scholars, Connellan O. 693, Connellan T. 693, Doudney 901, Foley 1073, Hennessy 1430.

Iron manufactory, blowing machine 551, cold blast pig 75, Coltness' brand of iron 1595, fan blast 351, Hodgkinson's beams 1493, hopper and spout kilns invented 342, iron chain cables invented 438, wrought iron rails, patent for 287.

Iron masters, Beale 205, Bolckow 327, Crawshay 756, Fletcher 1069, Geach 1132, Guest 1255, Harley 1340, Hood 1524, Houldsworth 1548, 1595.

Irving, Rev. Edward *d.* 1834 presbyterian, his friend 1448.

Irving, John Henry Brodribb *b.* 1838 actor, first appearance 830.

Isle of Wight, governor 1008, history of 1477.

Italy, British Italian legion 483, Italian antiquities, Disney collection 882.

J

Jaffa, model farm at 1449.

Jamaica, insurrection of the slaves 731.

Japanese scholar, Greey 1231.

Javelin men, fine paid for not providing them 80.

Jeannette and Jeannot, a song 1158.

Jerdan, William *d.* 1869 journalist, originated Literary gazette 669.

Jerrold, Douglas William *d.* 1857 dramatist, Housekeeper 1584, Rent day 1584, Time works wonders 1584.

Jersey, the six advocates of the royal court 1537.

Jerusalem, Anglican cathedral 1269, bishops of 159, 1162, hospital for sick jews 1548, house of industry at 1449.

Jesus Christ, likenesses of 1408.

Jews, Bevis Marks congregation 866, board of deputies 668, committee of seven elders 668, great synagogue, London 668, first called to the bar 1167, first created baronet 1168, jewish board of guardians 42, 668, jews' coll. London 982, ministers in London 866, united synagogue London 668.

Jim Crow sung in England 938.

Jockeys, Bullock 471, Butler 499, Chaloner 585, Chapple 593, Charlton 596, Chifney S. 608, Chifney W. 609, Constable 696, Day J. 840, Day J. B. 841, Day S. 841, Ede 956, Flatman 1067, Fordham 1080, French 1107 rode six winners in one day 1107, Green 1223, Grimshaw 1248, Hibberd 1459.

Jon Duan, authors of 221.

Jordan, Mrs. Dorothy *d.* 1816 actress, her sons 1056, 1057 *bis.*

Judge removed from office, Boothby B. 339.

Jumping, Howard the jumper 1553, jumping 29 ft. 7 in. col. 1553, over a billiard table 1553.

Junot, Andoche *d.* 1813 duc d'Abrantes, his mistress 1449.

Juggler, Allock 54.

Jullien, Louis G. Antoine J. *d.* 1860 composer, concerts at Covent garden 882, concerts at Surrey gardens 770, opera at Drury Lane 1268.

Junius, authorship of his letters 732, 945, his hand writing 579.

K

Kaleidoscope invented 394.

Kashmiri scholar 989.

Kean, Charles John *d.* 1868 actor, his secretary 513.

Kean, Edmund *d.* 1833 actor, his stage director 1034.

Keats, John *d.* 1821 poet, his friend 1591.

Kelly, Colonel, the Fenian, rescue of 53.

Kent, fossils of 1351.

Kent, Edward Augustus *d.* 1820 duke of, conspiracy to shoot 465.

Kent, Victoria M. L. *d.* 1861 duchess of, comptrollers of her household 696, 732, mausoleum built 1583.

Kerry, bishop of 968, lord lieutenant 1439.

Kew, observatory given up 854, observatory given to Royal soc. 1130.

Kew gardens, Bentham collection of books at 247. Champion's collection of plants 589, director of 1526.

Keyser, Polydore de, lord mayor of London 1465.

Keythorpe hall, Leicestershire, built 257.

Keyzor, Louis, murdered in 1869 at Whitton 1226.

Khol-rabi introduced 762.

Kildare and Leighlin, bishop of 1297.

Killala, bishops of 1031, 1060.

Kilmacduagh, bishop of 1106.

Kilmore, bishops of 444, 560, 815.

Kincardineshire, lords lieutenant 79, 1155.

King's-champion 948.

Kingsley, Charles *d.* 1875 V. of Eversley, music for his songs 1581.

Kinrossshire lord lieutenant 13.

Kirkcudbright lord lieutenant 1118.

Kiva, a ride to 484.

Knaresborough, history of 521.

Knights and knighthood, first knight created by Victoria 1321, knighthood declined by Brown 431, Carr 557, Cattermole 572, Fairbairn 1015, Fuller 1111, Hall 1291 and Heelis 1416, name still in knightage forty six years after death 1093, prefix Sir assumed 429, prefix Sir not used 588, refusal to pay the knightage fees 665.

Knights bachelor, A'Beckett 5, Agar 27, Alderson E. H. 40, Alderson J. 40, Allan 48, Amphlett 58, Anderson C. G. 60, Anderson G. W. 61, Anderson J. E. 62, Archibald 82, Armitage 83, Arney 87, Arrow 90, Arthur 91, Ashworth 97, Atherton 101, Atkinson H. E. 103, Atkinson J. 104, Austen 108, Awdry 111, Back 119, Bain 181, Baker 137, Bannerman 153, Bardsley 160, Barry C. 181, Barry R. 183, Bayly 201, Bell 231, Bellairs 232, Benedict 238, Bennett 244, Benson 245, Bent 246, Betham 262, Bethune 264, Biddlecombe 272, Bignold 275, Bishop 290, Bisset 291, Blaikie 301, Boag 321, Bodkin 324, Bogle 325, Bouch 346, Bovill 354, Bowring 362, Boxall 364, Brady A. 376, Brady F. 377, Brancker 380, Brand

Khondistan, human sacrifices in 532.
Knurr and spell player 1495.
Kossuth, Louis *b.* 1802, banquet to 69, entertained by Henry 1432, his friends 837, 1232.

L

Laboratories 941.
Lace, gassing of 1289, machine for making 83, made from mohair 287, manufacturers of 287, 1412, Old Loughborough machine 1412, patent for making 275.

Lacrosse player, Glover 1160.
Ladies' faces, enamelling of 770.
Laing, Rev. John *d.* 1880, librarian 1282.
Lamb, Charles *d.* 1834 essayist, attacked by cholera 93, his friends 487, 1591.
Lambeth, degrees 557, 1494, palace librarian 1225.
Lamps, Argand introduced 1554, lamp of life, invention and explosion of 10.
Lampeter castle turned into St. David's college 1336.
Lancaster duchy, chancellors of 6, 133, 623, 1241, 1358, duke of, claimant to the title 1353, records 1334.
Lanarkshire, lords lieutenant 226, 976, 1298 *bis.*
Land surveyor, Hodgson 1498.
Langalibalele, Caffre chief, treatment of 673.
Latin, hexameter verses, machine for composing 627.
Laurie, Sir Peter *d.* 1861, lord mayor 26, 27.
Lavalette, Antoine M. C., comte de *d.* 1830, his escape 897.
Law, common law procedure act 1272, inns of court commission 675, John Doe and Richard Roe 1398, king's bench filazer 18, large incomes made at the bar 451, law courts commission 675, law courts, design for 478, law courts, opening of the new 848, papers copied at three pence a page 1596, qualification for offices abolition act 1272, refusal to call to the bar 1364.
Law, Incorporated Law Society, law institute projected 1513, incorporated law soc., charter of 1513, presidents 330, 494, 635, 918, 1080, 1089.
Law, William John *d.* 1869 barrister, on route of Hannibal over Alps 984.
Lawrence, Sir Thomas *d.* 1830 P.R.A., funeral of 318, his assistant 1004.
Leamington, county library 988, music hall 988.
Leather manufacturer, Hackett 1270.
Lecturers, Bellew 234, Dawson 837, Gilfillan 1148, Gordon-Cumming 785, Grossmith 1250.
Lee, James Prince *d.* 1869 bp. of Manchester, his confirmation opposed 1265.
Leechdoms 661.
Leeds, musical festivals 725, St. Saviour's vicar of 1075.
Leicester, Mount St. Bernard abbey 476.
Leinster, Augustus Frederick *d.* 1874 third duke of, his son 1059.
Lemon, Mark *d.* 1870, dramatised the Chimes 4.
Leopold I. *d.* 1865 king of the Belgians, his equerry 796, master of his household 796.
Leopold, prince *d.* 1884, duke of Albany 38.
Lepidoptera, collections of 900, 1454, specimen costing £350 *col.* 1454.
Letter copying machines, pentagraph 1389, Wedgwood's manifold writer 1389.
Letters refused, the writer liable for the postage 26.
Letters, vocal and whisper 1476.
Leucocythemia or white cell blood discovered 242.
Lever, Charles James *d.* 1872 novelist, illustrators of his works 444.
Lewes, George Henry *d.* 1878 philosopher, Mary Ann Cross 771, studentships founded in his name 771.
Lewin, Thomas *d.* 1843 of H.E.I.C.S. 1251.
Librarians, Atkinson 104, Bandinel 150, Bradshaw 375, Brayley E. Wedlake 387, Brayley E. William 387, Brimley 401, Brough 424, Caulfield 573, Cochrane 660, Coxe 743, Crestadoro 758, Dalton 808, Deutsch 867, Edwards 965, Halkett 1282, Hall 1290, Hennen 1430, Herbert 1440, 1442, Hertslet 1450, Hitchcock 1484, Holmes 1515, Horne 1540, Hulton 1582.

LONDON (*Con.*)

guildhall librarian 39,

guild of St. Luke founded 391,

Guy's hospital separated from St. Thomas's 1352,

halls in city warmed and ventilated 1539,

Hancock's steam carriages 1315,

Highgate cemetery laid out 1133,

Holborn-viaduct opened 574,

Hotels, Claridge's 624, Freemasons' tavern 1097, Hampshire hog tavern 695, Mivart's 624, St. Albans 373 and St. James' 1097,

Hungerford market opened 1092, pulled down 1130,

Hyde park corner arch built 494,

Hyde park, relievi on the entrance gate 1431,

Kensington gram. sch. founded 1560,

Kensington palace, chaplains at 168, 1211, gardener 37,

Kensington South, fountains in exhibition garden 811, museum, Foster's pictures and books 1085,

King's college charter 409,

King's Weighhouse chapel 280,

Knightsbridge, memorials of 830,

Lambeth bridge opened 169,

Lambeth ragged sch. opened 212,

land registry office, registrar of 1074,

Leicester sq. Savile house exhibition of hydraulic figures 1254,

lent oratorios 323,

life in London by Pierce Egan 778,

Lincoln's inn hall and library foundation stone laid 451, finished 1331,

London bridge, account of 548, design for 1092, drawings of 701, stones of old bridge used to build Ingress park 1341,

London Pneumatic despatch Co., iron tubes for 180,

London university founded 1251,

lord mayor in 1852 had no procession or dinner 581,

lord mayor's carriage, paintings on 135,

lord mayor's show, Grace Darling's boat 816,

lord mayors, Allen 53, Besley 261, Carroll 559, Carter 562, Challis 582, Combe 687, Copeland 716, Cubitt 780, Curtis 793, Duke 927, Farncomb 1022, Finnis 1050, Gibbons 1137, Hale 1278, Hooper 1528, Humphery 1586, Hunter 1595, Hunter 1598, Laurie 26 and Moon 1253,

lord mayorship not granted 1273,

Manchester new college president 992,

marble arch, bassi relievi on 130,

Marshalsea, prisoners in 873, 1130,

Middle Temple chrysanthemum exhibition 802, library 945,

metropolitan board of works, last of original members 808,

metropolitan cattle market built 474,

metropolitan improvement commission 669,

Middlesex hospital, Cropper's devise to 768,

Mincing lane, the millionare of 725,

mint, master of 1198, mint works reformed 1342,

national gallery, director of 364,

national Scottish church, Covent Garden 784,

Nelson's column, bas reliefs on 544,

Newgate, governor of 441,

Nunhead cemetery laid out 474,

Pantheon exhibition of pictures 1073, turned into wine vaults 1146,

Pimlico district created 779,

LONDON (*Con.*)

police commissioner of city 1364,

queen's college teacher of theology 1121,

ragged school founded 9,

Regent's park, electric wire laid in 835, ice accident 885,

remembrancer of city 723,

Romano-British remains, collection of 130,

St. Alban's, Holborn built 1564,

St. Clement Danes parish, account of 881,

St. George in the East, disturbances at 51,

St. James' chapel royal, master of choristers 1418,

St. John's gate restored 1246,

St. Katharine docks opened 35,

St. Martin's hall burnt 1581,

St. Mary Magdalen ch. Munster sq. built 555,

St. Mary's hospital built 1536,

St. Michael's, Cornhill, registers of 605,

St. Pancras parish divided into 20 incumbencies 802,

St. Paul's cathedral, painted windows 439, person buried in 596,

St. Paul's, Covent garden, charitable institutions 1608

St. Paul's, Knightsbridge, erected 786,

St. Peter's, Newington, built 581,

St. Thomas' hospital opened 1461,

secondary of the city 849,

sewerage works 1204,

Smithfield market, enquiry into 505,

Soane museum curator 334,

Soho square bazaar established 419,

Somers Town, abbé Carrón's school 502,

Southwark, bishops of 667, 811, 1206,

stamps department Somerset house remodelled 1470,

surpliced choir the first in the city 1473,

Thames defences 553,

Thames embankment 1154, 1204,

Thames tunnel 1390, engineer of 207,

theatres See Theatres,

tower of London, catholic memories of 703, constables of 689, 798, 1169, deputy lieut. office abolished 864, persons committed to 51, 653, tower subway opened 169,

traders' tavern tokens 482,

trees, planting of 802,

Trinity house, master of 39,

University coll. diseased structures, drawings of 560, gymnasium 611,

University hall Gordon sq. 654,

Vauxhall, bridge foundation stone laid 453, embankment made 779, Holy Trinity ch. built 248,

Victoria docks formed 272,

Walworth, Clayton schools 642,

West London infirmary renamed Charing Cross hospital 1166,

Whitechapel ch. rebuilt 707,

wool exchange erected 765,

yeomen of the guard, exon of 1314,

York college commenced 1128,

zoological gardens, Regent's park, established 1247, animals fed in public 1247,

zoological gardens, the Surrey 7, 770.

Londonderry, lords lieutenant 839, 1036, Magee college 769.

Looms, power looms 1089.

Long, Rev. W. deprived of his license by Bp. of Capetown 1218.

M

MAGAZINES (Con.)

Gallery of terrors proprietor 4.
Gardener's chronicle founded 879.
Gardener's magazine editor 1459.
Gentleman's magazine, editors 451, 1066, proprietor 372.
Germ, The 682.
Ghost proprietor 4.
Hardwicke's science gossip commenced 1331.
Hazlewood magazine editor 1476.
Hebrew christian editor 832.
Hogg's weekly instructor editor 1502.
Household words, proprietors 372, discontinued 872.
Howitt's journal editor 1560.
Hunt's London journal editor 1589.
Hunt's yachting magazine founded 10.
Illustrated London magazine 84.
Intelligencer founded at Belleville 239.
Journal of health and disease, editor 994.
Journal of industry started 930.
Journal of London institution commenced 424.
Journal of morbid anatomy, editor 1025.
Journal of philosophy founded 629.
Journal of royal agricultural society, editor 1108.
Journal of statistical society, editor 1266.
Jurist founded 1074.
Laboratory, The, started 424.
Law magazine founded 1402.
Leigh Hunt's journal published 1591.
Leigh Hunt's London journal, editor 1591.
Leisure moments, editor 781.
Literary gazette originated 669.
Literary news, Sydney, editor 5.
Liverpool lion commenced 425.
Liverpool medical journal editor 1257.
London magazine started 141, editor 878.
London medical and surgical journal editors 994, 1549.
London medical repository editor 936.
London medical review editor 1496.
London photographic society journal editor 870.
London quarterly review editor 1133.
London society projected 1502.
Lover, proprietor 4.
Magazine of science and school of arts, editor 1098.
Mirth, editor 507.
Month commenced 1092.
Monthly magazine editor 1437.
Monthly magazine of holy rosary, editor 1082.
Monthly repository editors 1539, 1591.
Montreal medical gazette founded 122.
Museum criticum established 315.
Musical world editors 833, 1131.
National miscellany founded 84.
Natural history review editor 791.
Nautical magazine commenced 215.
New monthly magazine, editor 1289, sold 33.
New monthly magazine and humorist commenced 161.
New quarterly review founded 498, editor 1568.
North British review editors 1318.
Notes and Queries editor 898, writer in 1603.
Numismatic journal started 37.
Once a week editor 805.
Orchestra editor 1022.

MAGAZINES (Con.)

Oriental herald and colonial review commenced 461.
Panoply, The, founded 1077.
Penny catholic magazine started 1401, published 433.
People's journal proprietors 1560.
People's penny picture proprietor 4.
Photographic art journal projected 853.
Phrenological journal editor 742.
Political letters issued 556.
Political magazine commenced 556.
Poor Richard's journal proprietor 4.
Porcupine founded 715.
Portfolio started 10, 11.
Post magazine and insurance monitor proprietor 1362.
Preacher's lantern editor 1524.
Primitive methodist magazine commenced 350.
Prison proverbs commenced 11.
Quarterly journal of foreign medicine and surgery established 1180.
Quarterly mining review editor 993.
Quarterly review founded 764.
Railway magazine proprietor 1436.
Rambler, publisher 488.
Reflector, editor 1591.
Retrospective review, contributor to 773.
Royal ladies' magazine editor 1157.
St. James' magazine editor 1283.
Saturday night editor 1525.
Saturday review, contributors to 787, 805, editor 700.
Scripture magazine editor 555.
Sharpe's London magazine editor 1283.
Social notes editor 1289.
Sock and buskin editor 1022.
Sphynx begun 461.
Sporting review editor 546.
Squib, The editor of 1209.
Statistical journal editors 1070.
Student begun 34.
Sunbeam, editor 1437.
Sunday magazine editor 1265.
Ten hours advocate 1205.
Terrific penny magazine proprietor 4.
Theological critic established 88.
Thief, proprietor 4.
Tonic sol-fa reporter started 795.
Tract magazine editor 771.
Unitarian herald commenced 208, editor 1129.
United service magazine originated 669, editor 1112.
Westminster review, contributor to 1168, proprietor 1462.
Willis's current notes, editor 482.
Winter wreath begun 614.
Young England founded 249.
Youth's magazine founded 1263.
Zoist established 980.
Magic, history of 378, lectures on 424.
Magic lanterns made 609, slides for 609.
Magnetism, animal 378, 686, discoveries in 168.
Maidstone, Charles museum 594.
Mail coaches, Edinburgh to Aberdeen 49.
Majuba hill, battle of 677.
Malagasy scholars, Freeman 1104, Griffiths 1246.
Malt, malster, a 1436, raising and conveying of malt 534.

Malta, knights of, Arbuthnot 78, Bowyer 363, Hort 1543.

Man, most popular man in the three kingdoms 971.

Man, Isle of, Baume's property left to 196.

Manchester, Athenæum 773, banquet to W. Harrison Ainsworth 33, botanical guide 504, carbolic acid, manufacture of 520, chartist riots 83, Chetham soc. 773, Chetham library 773, Geological soc. founded 280, great exhibition 842, incorporated law assoc. 773, Kersal moor great meeting 658, law assoc. 1416, library of local books 1458, Lunardini's fall from a balloon 1192, Manchester coll. at Manchester and London 100, Manchester political union 658, New college removed to London 361, observatory at 361, Owen's coll. endowment of professorships 263 and trustees of 1026, Peterloo meeting 150, 681, rescue of Kelly the Fenian 53, royal institution founded 519, ship canal 1113, Thirlmere water scheme 1445, theatre royal 519, unity of odd fellows, grand master 1330, York college 1128.

Mandarin, Gordon 1178.

Manuscripts, Ashburnham collection 1515, Bragge's illuminated 378, historical commission on 1333.

Map makers, Arrowsmith 91, Cruchley 777.

Marble quarrier, Goad 1162.

March, George Edward of the Foreign office, writer of librettos 1115.

Margate, hall by the sea, manager 1483.

Marlborough college founded 1040, re-organized 728.

Marriages, four times married 105, 878, four times repeated 540, five times married 823, remarkable consanguineous marriage 12.

Martineau, Harriet d. 1876 author, cured by mesmerism 1290.

Marryat, Capt. Frederick d. 1848 novelist, Peter Simple 370.

Mary Blane, a song 1254.

Mastodon fossils 755.

Matamoros, Manuel a prisoner in Spain 7.

Matthews, Charles d. 1835 actor, his gallery of theatrical portraits 943.

Mathematician, Hamilton 1307.

Matterhorn, Switzerland, deaths on 902, 1566.

Mayhew, Henry d. 1887 author, a writer in Punch 1209.

Maynooth, synod at 781.

Mayor who paid fine not to serve, Barber 156.

Mazzini, Guiseppe d. 1872 political agitator, his friend 837.

Meats preserved, cases for 1008.

Meath, bishop of 498, lord lieutenant 1048.

Mecca, Bicknell's pilgrimage to the shrine of Mohammed 271.

Medals, for young persons for industry 1390, gold medal specially struck 550.

Medicine, Aldersgate st. sch. 732, clinical lectures established 276, college of physicians, president 40, fevers, modern treatment of 1213, Fleming's tincture 1067, name removed from medical register 1257, physician charging a five shilling fee 1432, podophyllin introduced 1122, practical teaching at the bedside 276, prussic acid used for chest affections 1208, scarlatina, its treatment 432, spirometer, use of 1605.

Medulla oblongata, reflex function of 1288.

Memory, systems of acquiring 1476, teacher of the art of 239.

Men, handsome men, Boyle 368, D'Orsay 899.

Menageries, Atkins 290, Batty 195, Bostock 345, Cross 770, Exeter change 770, King's Mews menagerie 770,

MENAGERIES *(Con.)*

Knowsley park 863, Liverpool 102, Regent's park 1247, Surrey Zoological gardens 7, 770, Wingeworth hall 1588, Wombwell, painted show cloth for 670 *See also* Zoological gardens.

Mendelssohn-Bartholdy, Felix d. 1847, works performed at Windsor 39, his friend 1251, Lobgesang first performed 1384.

Mer de Glace surveyed 1078.

Merest, J. D. *m.* Maria B. Hawes 1384.

Mesmerism, Harriet Martineau cured by 1290, London mesmeric infirmary 979-80, Zoist 980.

Mesmerists, Ashburner 93, Braid 378, Elliotson 979, Esdaile 997, Gibson 1142, Hall 1290.

Metallic solutions, insect life in 772.

Meteorology, account of meteorites 1071, Greave's observatory 1221, meteorologists 418, 429, meteorological department of board of trade 1064, meteorological registers 1554, self recording instruments invented 415.

Mexico, Tampico city taken 597.

Meyerbeer, Jacob d. 1864 composer, Le Prophete produced in London 1253.

Microscopes, achromatic 216, cheap and good 811, used for study of rocks 1076.

Middle level, commission on the 862.

Middlesborough, Albert park 327, first mayor 327.

Midwifery, use of anæsthetics 1220.

Milk, country milk sent to London 1284.

Mill, John Stuart d. 1873 philosopher, his friend 1093.

Milier, Hugh d. 1856 geologist, his dau. 823, old red sandstone 871.

Millers, Catt 571, Hadley 1273.

Milton, John d. 1674 poet, Fall of Adam 1010, his complace book 1544, Milton prize at St. Paul's sch. 632, Paradise lost, the prototype of 161.

Mind, power of over body 378.

Mine be a cot, a glee 1543.

Miniatures, on marble 558, painters of 725.

Minerals, cadmium sulphate of 570, collections of 416, 552, greenockite 570.

Mines and Mining, accidents in, life saving apparatus 125, Brunton's endless cloth 455, calciner, Brunton's 454, fuse, Brunton's 455, man engines 1094, oscillating cylinder stamps 1602, safety cage invented 115.

Mint, The, assay master 1042, coins made with mathematical precision 1042, commission of enquiry 667, Ipswich mints 1055, masters of 645, 935, 1446, 1448, models for coins 1042, pure gold 1042.

Miraculous healing 91.

Mitchell, John d. 1875 Irish politician, his prosecution 1429.

Mohair used 1089.

Modeller, Henning 1431.

Mollusca, internal structure of 1314.

Moneyers, Company of, provosts of 103, 104, dissolved 104.

Moneyrea where there is one God and no devil 304.

Mont Blanc, ascents of by Alison 47, Auldjo 107, Barry 182, Fellows 1033, Hamel 1298 and Hudson 1566, ascent of without guides 1566, astronomical observations made on summit 1493, fatalities on, Arkwright 82, Balfour 143 and Hamel 1298.

Moon, Sir Francis G. d. 1871, print seller 1253.

Moore, George d. 1876, philanthropist 1252, limb set by Hutton 1609.

Moore, Thomas d. 1852 poet, his friends 828, 1591.

Moray, Ross and Caithness, bishop of 958.

Morocco, emperor of, medical mission to 442.

Morphia, muriate of 1235.

Mortmain, statute of, the hospitals exempt from provisions of 768.

Moths, sugaring for 900.

Mount Sinai, the position of determined 223.

Mount Vesuvius, large picture of 770.

Mozart, Johann C. W. A. *d.* 1791 composer, Don Giovanni produced in England 114.

Muller, George *b.* 1805 a Prussian, founder of orphan houses 749.

Munich, Gibson's statues at 1141.

Muntz, George Frederick *d.* 1857 M.P., libelled by Gutteridge 1265.

Mural paintings by fictile vitrification 528.

Murchison, Sir Robert I. *d.* 1871 geologist, Dick's assistance to him 871.

Murderers, Barthelémy 185, Green 1226, Mc Lauchlan 1143, Miller 1569, Thurtell 1592.

Murray, James A. H. his New English dictionary 674.

Music, Bass' act on street musicians 189, catalogue of 1011, Concentores sodales 1187, conducting with a baton 724, contrapuntist soc. 1072, free chant 774, Hullah classes for teaching 1581, library of 1000, musical glasses 1261, music librarian 1175, musician the first knighted 290, new code staff notation 751, publishers 665, 676, 749, 823, 1309, reading from the score 628, Società Armonica 1077, sol-faing system 1159, thorough bass 492, tonic sol-fa system and coll. 795, type music printer 1426, Vogler's system of cadences 1072, writer on 992.

Music Halls, Cider cellars 1224, Collins' 681, Evans' 1224, Hungerford hall built 1130, Lansdowne proprietor 681, Marylebone proprietor 681, Mogul singing at 680, Royal, musical director 722, Weston's, musical director 722, York at Southampton 1612.

Musical composers, Bache 118, Benedict 238, Bennett 244, Bexfield 268, Bilby 276, Blockley 314, Blagrove 301, Blewitt 312, Calkin 516, Calcott W. 517, Callcott W. H. 517, Campana 525, Cianchetti 621, Coote 713, Corri 722, Costa 724, D'Albert 801, Davison 833, Dempster 856, Dibdin 871, Donaldson 893, Dougal 901, Dunne 940, Ellerton 976, Ellis 983, Elvey 991, Fawcett J. 1028, Fawcett J. 1028, Fish 1051, Fitzwilliam 1065, Flowers 1072, Forbes 1077, Gabriel 1115, Glover C. W. 1158, Glover S. 1160, Glover W. H. 1160, Godfrey A. F. and C. 1163, Goss 1186, Graham 1196, Greatheed 1220, Gutteridge 1266, Haite 1276, Harper 1343, Hart 1359, Hatton 1377, Havergal 1381, Hecht 1415, Helmore 1418, Hempel 1420, Hemy 1421, Hickson 1462, Hill J. F. 1471, Hill W. J. 1476, Hime 1479, Hobson 1489, Holmes A. 1514, Holmes W. H. 1517, Horn 1537, Horsley C. E. 1542, Horsley W. H. 1542, Howell 1556, Hughes 1576, Hullah 1581, Hume 1585, Hutcheson 1604, Lodge 976, Mackenzie 1569, Stoepel 1445, *See also* Pianists.

Muskets, stadiometer improved 1560.

Myriorama, invention of 627.

Myxoedema first described 1257.

N

Names, Fancy.

    Admiral, The fighting *i.e.* Sir W. N. W. Hewett 1454.

    Apostle of ragged school movement *i.e.* T. Guthrie 1265.

    Arsenic Sal *i.e.* Sarah Chesham 603.

NAMES, FANCY *(Con.)*

Attorney General for unstamped newspapers *i.e.* George Edmonds 960.

Auchterless John Pounds *i.e.* James Beattie 210.

Bagatelle *i.e.* Richard 4 marquis of Hertford 1449.

Bankers' Bankers *i.e.* Overend, Gurney & Co. 1262.

Bard of Dunclug, The *i.e.* David Herbison 1442.

Bendigo *i.e.* William Thompson 237, 573.

Bishop of Bond street, The *i.e.* William Bishop 291.

Blacksmith, The learned *i.e.* Elihu Burritt 491.

Bowlers, The best of all *i.e.* W. R. Hillyer 1478.

Brassey *i.e.* John Leechman 237, 573.

Calculating phenomenon, The *i.e.* George P. Bidder 271-72.

Cornish Pilgrim, The *i.e.* Richard Hampton 1312.

Cure, The perfect *i.e.* James Hurst Stead 312.

Cuvier of England *i.e.* Robert Edmond Grant 1206.

Delemere forest stag *i.e.* John Walker 1553.

Demon, The *i.e.* George Fordham 1080.

Demon pedestrian *i.e.* J. Whitehead 1553.

Dick, Foolish *i.e.* Richard Hampton 1312.

Dragon, The *i.e.* Bindon Blood 315.

Dutch Sam *i.e.* Elias Samuels 224.

English Horace Vernet *i.e.* Thomas Jones Barker 165.

Flower of Haddington, The *i.e.* Jane Baillie Welsh 549.

Fordham of Amateurs *i.e.* George Matthews Lde 956.

Game Chicken *i.e.* Henry Pearce 1258.

Genial Showman, The *i.e.* Charles Farrar Browne 443.

Gipsy's Friend, The *i.e.* Rev. James Crabb 745.

Hyæna of Brescia *i.e.* J. J. Baron Von Haynau 1400.

Iron king of Wales *i.e.* Robert Thompson Crawshay 756.

Kempferhausen *i.e.* Robert Pierce Gillies 1150.

King of Pine Growers *i.e.* James Dale 801.

King Richard *i.e.* Richard Tapper Cadbury 509.

Lancashire Giant *i.e.* Bob Gregson 1258.

Leviathan, The *i.e.* William Edmond Davies 829.

Lyndhurst of the Turf *i.e.* John Barham Day 841.

Mezzofanti, The English *i.e.* Edward C. Hawtrey 1392.

Moorland poet, The *i.e.* George Heath 1411.

Mr. Ralph's Great coat *i.e.* Robert Hunnum 1588.

Old Q' *i.e.* William 4 duke of Queensberry 1449.

Paganini, The English *i.e.* Henry Hayward 1403.

Perfect Cure, The *i.e.* James Hurst Stead 312.

Pocket Hercules, The *i.e.* James Grimshaw 1248.

Prisoner's friend, The *i.e.* Abraham Beal 205.

Queen of the Radicals *i.e.* Harriet Grote 1251.

Right arm of British power in America *i.e.* Ogle Robert Gowan 1193.

Roscius, The Young *i.e.* William Henry West Betty 265.

Rydal, The painter of *i.e.* William Hull 1580.

Senior wrangler maker, The *i.e.* William Hopkins 1534.

Sherwood forest patriarch *i.e.* Samuel Hall 1289.

Sherwood forester *i.e.* Spencer Timothy Hall 1290.

Stalybridge infant *i.e.* Samuel Hurst 1602.

True Conservative, A *i.e.* Edmund Gilling Hallewell 1293.

University Corporal *i.e.* Joseph Dornford 898.

Vampire, The *i.e.* Bindon Blood 315.

Wheel king of London *i.e.* Patrick Hearn 1409.

Yorick of the West, The *i.e.* William R. Hicks 1462.

Yorkshire woollen trade, Father of *i.e.* W. Hirst 1484.

Names, Titles, etc. Changed, Given and Taken, *See also* Actors' Stage Names and Pseudonyms.

Addington, Baron *i.e.* John G. Hubbard 1563.

Angell Cherry *i.e.* John Benedict Angell 70.

Anson, George *i.e.* George Adams 72.

Arundell, Thomas *i.e.* Thomas Arundell Tagg 92.

Baker, William *i.e.* William Wingfield 138.

Barclay, Capt. *i.e.* Robert B. Barclay Allardice 48.

Barlow, Sir William Owen *i.e.* William Owen 169.

Barr, Blithe Jamie *i.e.* James Barr 175.

Barrett-Lennard, Sir Thomas *i.e.* Thomas Thomas 178.

Beaconsfield, Earl of *i.e.* Benjamin Disraeli 203.

Beauregard, Countess de *i.e.* Elizabeth Hargett 214.

Becher, William *i.e.* William Wrixon 215.

Behram Pacha *i.e.* Robert Cannon 537.

Beke, Charles T. *i.e.* Charles Tilstone Beck 223.

Bellew, Thomas A. Grattan *i.e.* T. A. Bellew 234-5.

Belper, Baron *i.e.* Edward Strutt 236.

Bernard, Herman Hedwig *i.e.* H. Bernard 255.

Berri, Duchesse de *i.e.* Amy Brown 258.

Bethune, C. R. Drinkwater *i.e.* C. R. Bethune 264.

Binning, Lord *i.e.* Thomas H. earl of Haddington 1271.

Booker-Blakemore, Thomas W. *i.e.* T. W. Booker 335.

Bottomley-Firth, J. F. *i.e.* J. F. Bottomley 1050.

Bouchier, Barton *i.e.* Barton Boucher 347.

Boyd, William *i.e.* W. Keown 367.

Brabazon, Luke *i.e.* Luke Higgins 371.

Brancepeth, Baron *i.e.* G. H. Russell-Boyne 370.

Brand-Trevor, H. O. *i.e.* H. O. Brand, baron Dacre 798.

Bravo, Charles D. T. *i.e.* Charles D. Turner 384.

Brinckman, Sir T. H. L. *i.e.* Sir T. H. L. Broadhead 401.

Brocket, Stanes Brockett *i.e.* Stanes B. Chamberlayne 407.

Broke, Sir A. B. de Capell *i.e.* Sir A. B. de Capell Brooke 410.

Broke, Signal *i.e.* Charles Acton Broke 411.

Bromley, Sir George *i.e.* Sir George Smith 413.

Bromley-Davenport, William *i.e.* W. Davenport-Bromley 413.

Bronte, Duchess of *i.e.* Charlotte Mary Hood 413.

Bronte, Patrick *i.e.* Patrick Prunty 414.

Brooke, John Brooke Johnson *i.e.* John B. Johnson 417.

Bruce, Sir James L. Knight *i.e.* Sir James L. Knight 451.

Buckley-Mathew, Sir G. Benvenuto *i.e.* Sir George Byam Mathew 465.

Budavolgy, Count de *i.e.* Max Greger 1233.

Burton, James *i.e.* James Haliburton 1280.

Byng, Poodle *i.e.* Gerald Frederick Byng 505.

Calverley, Charles S. *i.e.* Charles S. Blayds 518.

Capua, Princess of *i.e.* Penelope Smyth 540.

Carington, Robert John, Baron Carington *i.e.* Robert J. Smith 546.

Carr-Boyle, James, earl of Glasgow *i.e.* James Carr 1155.

Champain, Sir J. N. Bateman *i.e.* Sir J. N. Champain 589.

Chetham-Strode, Sir E. *i.e.* Sir E. Chetham 606.

Cholmley, Sir George *i.e.* Sir George Strickland 613.

Christopher, Robert Adam *i.e.* Robert A. Dundas 618.

Christopher, R. A. Nisbet Hamilton *i.e.* Robert A. Christopher 618.

Clarges, Sir Richard Goddard *i.e.* Sir R. G. Hare 624.

Clark, D'Orsay *i.e.* Edward Rawson Clark 625.

Clark, Little *i.e.* William H. Clark 630.

Clark, Waterloo *i.e.* John Clark 627.

Clarke, Lame *i.e.* John Clarke 633.

Clark-Kennedy, Sir A. Kennedy *i.e.* Sir A. Kennedy Clark 630.

Clarke-Jervoise, Sir Samuel *i.e.* Sir Samuel Clarke 637.

Clarke-Travers, Sir W. H. St. Lawrence *i.e.* Sir W. H. St. Lawrence Clarke 637.

Cockayne-Cust, H. F. *i.e.* H. F. Cust 797.

Cockburn-Campbell, Sir A. T. *i.e.* Sir A. T. Cockburn 664.

Coffin, Rev. John *i.e.* Rev. John Pine 667.

Colley, Sir George Pomeroy Pomeroy *i.e.* Sir G. Pomeroy Colley 677.

Collins, Mortimer *i.e.* Edward J. Mortimer Collins 679.

Combe, Richard Thomas *i.e.* Richard Thomas Maddison 688.

Cooper, Wilbye *i.e.* John Wilbye Cooper 711.

Corbaux, Fanny *i.e.* Marie F. C. Doetter Corbaux 717.

Corbett, Joseph *i.e.* Joseph Plymley 718.

Corbett-Winder, Uvedale *i.e.* Uvedale Corbett 718.

Courten, Comtesse de *i.e.* Alphonsina Marie de St. Amand 358.

Cowell-Stepney, Sir John Stepney *i.e.* Sir John Stepney Cowell 736.

Crackanthorpe, Christopher *i.e.* Christopher Cookson 746.

Cradock, Rev. Edward Hartopp *i.e.* Edward Hartopp Grove 747.

Cresswell, Francis *i.e.* Francis Easterby 757.

Crompton-Stansfield, William Rookes *i.e.* William R. Crompton 767.

Crosse, Thomas Bright *i.e.* Thomas B. Ikin 772.

Cuffe, Sir Richard *i.e.* Sir R. Wheeler 780.

Cumming-Bruce, C. L. *i.e.* C. L. Cumming 785.

D'Aeth, William *i.e.* G. W. Hughes 799.

Dalling and Bulwer, baron *i.e.* W. H. L. E. Bulwer 806.

Davies, James *i.e.* James Banks 827.

Davis, Pope *i.e.* John Philip Davis 831.

Dawson-Damer, G. L. *i.e.* G. L. Dawson 839.

De Beauvoir, Sir J. E. *i.e.* Sir J. E. Browne 844.

De Grey, T. P. *i.e.* T. P. Weddell 848.

De Havilland, John V. S. *i.e.* J. V. S. Haviland 1383.

De La Saussaye, Sir R. *i.e.* Sir R. Sausse 852.

De Lisle, A. L. M. Phillipps *i.e.* A. L. M. Phillipps 854.

Denison, John *i.e.* Johe Wilkinson 858.

De Porquet, L. P. R. F. *i.e.* L. P. R. Fenwick 862.

De Quincey, Thomas *i.e.* Thomas Quincey 862.

De Trafford, Sir T. J. *i.e.* Sir T. J. Trafford 867.

Dinorben, Baron *i.e.* W. L. Hughes 881.

Dinsdale, Frederick *i.e.* F. Trotter 881.

Dod, Charles R. P. *i.e.* C. R. P. Dodd 887.

Dollond, George *i.e.* George Huggins 891.

Domvile, Charles *i.e.* Charles Pocklington 892.

Drake, Sir T. T. Fuller-Eliott *i.e.* Sir T. T. Fuller 915.

Duckett, Sir George *i.e.* Sir G. Jackson 923.

Dunbar, George *i.e.* George Orr 928.

Dundas, Sir J. W. Deans *i.e.* Sir J. W. Deans 933.

Dunlop, Alexander Murray *i.e.* A. Dunlop 937.

NAMES, TITLES, ETC. *(Con.)*

Dunlop, Alexander Colquhoun Stirling Murray *i.e.* A. Murray Dunlop 937.

Dyce-Sombre, David O. *i.e.* David O. Dyce 946.

Eardley, Sir Culling E. *i.e.* Sir C. E. Smith 951.

East, Sir E. G. Clayton *i.e.* Sir E. G. Clayton 952.

Eastwood, Thomas S. *i.e.* Thomas Smith Badger 122.

Egerton, John Hume *i.e.* J. H. Cust 970.

Ellacombe, Henry T. *i.e.* Henry T. Ellicombe 975.

Ellerton, John L. *i.e.* John L. Lodge 976.

Ellis, Andrew Ellis *i.e.* A. Ellis De Vezian 986.

Ellis-McTaggart, Francis *i.e.* F. Ellis 987.

Erle-Drax, J. S. W. Sawbridge *i.e.* J. S. W. Sawbridge 995.

Eversley, Charles S., viscount *i.e.* C. Shaw-Lefevre 1007.

Fairholt, F. W. *i.e.* F. W. Fahrholz 1015.

Fane, H. E. Hamlyn *i.e.* H. E. Fane 1019.

Farnborough, Thomas, baron *i.e.* Sir T. E. May 1021

Fenwick, Edward M. *i.e.* E. M. Reid 1034.

Fenwick-Bisset, M. *i.e.* M. Fenwick 1034.

Ferguson, J. F. *i.e.* J. F. Jaquemain 1035.

Ferguson-Davie, Sir H. R. *i.e.* Sir H. R. Ferguson 1037.

Fermor-Hesketh, Sir T. G. *i.e.* Sir T. G. Hesketh 1038

Fish, The Golden *i.e.* Thomas Liversedge Fish 1051.

Fitzball, Edward *i.e.* Edward Ball 1056.

Fitzgerald, John *i.e.* John Purcell 1058.

Fitzwilliam, C. W. Wentworth *i.e.* C. W. Fitzwilliam 1064.

Fitzwilliam, Ellen *i.e.* E. Chaplin 1065.

Fitzwilliam, Fanny E. *i.e.* F. E. Copeland 1065.

Fleetwood, Sir P. Hesketh *i.e.* Sir P. Hesketh 1067.

Fleming, Ann C. *i.e.* A. C. Knight 1067.

Forbes-Leslie, Jonathan *i.e.* Jonathan Forbes 1079.

Francis, Francis *i.e.* Francis Morgan 1097.

Fraser, Robert S. *i.e.* Robert S. Frazer 1102.

Gardiner, Robert *i.e.* Robert Hallowell 1121.

Giles-Puller, Christopher W. *i.e.* C. W. Giles 1148.

Gladstone, Sir John *i.e.* Sir John Gladstones 1154.

Godwin-Austen, Robert A. C. *i.e.* Robert A. C. Austen 1165.

Gordon, Chinese *i.e.* Charles George Gordon 1178.

Gordon, Francis *i.e.* Francis Grant 1177.

Gough, Frederick, Baron Calthorpe *i.e.* F. Calthorpe 518.

Graham, James Gillespie *i.e.* James Gillespie 1196.

Graham-Gilbert, John *i.e.* John Gilbert 1199.

Granton, Lord *i.e.* Charles Hope 1529.

Granville, Augustus Bozzi *i.e.* Augustus Bozzi 1208.

Gratwicke, William *i.e.* William Kindlesides 1210.

Graves-Sawle, Sir Joseph S. *i.e.* Sir Joseph S. Sawle 1214.

Green, Thomas Hiden *i.e.* Thomas Hiden 1226.

Greenhough, George Bellas *i.e.* George Bellas 1229.

Grenville, George Neville *i.e.* George Neville 1236.

Grenville, Ralph Neville *i.e.* Ralph Neville 1237.

Gurdon-Rebow, John *i.e.* John Gurdon 1260.

Halford, Sir Henry *i.e.* Sir Henry Vaughan 1280.

Haliburton, James *i.e.* James Burton 1280.

Hall, Nemesis *i.e.* Sir William H. Hall 1291.

Halliday, Andrew *i.e.* Andrew Halliday Duff 1294.

Halliwell-Phillipps James Orchard *i.e.* J. O. Phillipps 1295.

NAMES, TITLES, ETC. *(Con).*

Hallyburton, John F. Gordon *i.e.* John F. Gordon 1296.

Hampden, Augustus E. Hobart, Earl of Buckinghamshire *i.e.* Augustus E. Hobart 461.

Harrington, Earl of *i.e.* Lord Petersham 1344.

Harris, Christopher Arthur Mohun *i.e.* C. A. Harris 1346.

Harris, Isaac *i.e.* Isaac Donnithorne 1346.

Harrison, Devil *i.e.* William G. Harrison 1357.

Hartismere, Baron *i.e.* John H. M. Henniker 1430.

Hartley, Leonard Lawrie *i.e.* Leonard L. Campbell 1362.

Hastings, Sir Charles Abney *i.e.* Sir Charles Hastings 1373.

Hatherley, Baron *i.e.* Sir William P. Wood 1376.

Hayne, Pea-Green *i.e.* Joseph Hayne 538, 1344.

Hertford, Francis, marquis of *i.e.* the Earl of Yarmouth 1449.

Hesketh, Sir T. G. Fermor *i.e.* Sir T. G. Hesketh 1451

Hesketh-Fleetwood, Sir P. *i.e.* Sir P. Hesketh 1452.

Heytesbury, W. H. A'Court-Holmes 2 baron *i.e.* W. H. A'Court Heytesbury 2 baron 1457.

Hick, Edward *i.e.* Edward Simpson 1461.

Hicks Pasha *i.e.* William Hicks 1462.

Hindlip, Henry A., Baron *i.e.* H. A. Allsopp 1481.

Hodgetts, Foley John Hodgetts *i.e.* J. H. Foley 1492.

Holyoake-Goodricke, Sir F. L. *i.e.* Sir F. L. Holyoake 1518.

Hobart Pasha *i.e.* A. C. Hobart 1487.

Holt, Raggedy *i.e.* Thomas L. Holt 1518.

Home, David Milne *i.e.* David Milne 1520.

Hope, William Williams *i.e.* William Hope 1532.

Horne, Richard Hengist *i.e.* Richard Henry Horne 1539.

Hoskyns, Chandos Wren *i.e.* Chandos Hoskyns 1546.

Hotten, John Camden *i.e.* John William Hotten 1547.

Houghton, Henry Hall *i.e.* Henry Houghton 1548.

Howard de Walden, Charles A. E. Baron *i.e.* Charles A. Ellis 1550.

Howard, Miss *i.e.* Elizabeth Hargett 214.

Howland, Baron *i.e.* Francis R. Bedford 218.

Howe, Richard Penn Curzon *i.e.* Richard P. Curzon 1555.

Hudson, Hurry *i.e.* Sir James Hudson 1567.

Hughes, Edward Hughes Ball *i.e.* E. H. Ball 147.

Hughes, Gentleman *i.e.* William Edward Hughes 1578

Hughes, Little *i.e.* William Edward Hughes 1578.

Hughes, William Hughes *i.e.* William Hughes Hewitt 1578.

Humphreys, Alexander *i.e.* Alexander Alexander 42.

Hutchinson, Lavalette *i.e.* John, Earl of Donoughmore 897.

Hyett, William Henry *i.e.* William Henry Adams 1611.

Jerviswood, Lord *i.e.* C. Baillie Hamilton 129.

Kenlis, Baron *i.e.* Thomas T. marquis of Headfort 1405.

Khourschid Pasha *i.e.* Richard Debaufre Guyon 1267.

Lyon-Home, Daniel Dunglas *i.e.* D. D. Home 1519.

Maclae, Walter *i.e.* Walter Ewing 1009.

Manor, Lord *i.e.* G. Dundas 933.

Maurice, Leon d. 1826 *i.e.* lord Maurice Drummond de Melfort 827.

Medwyn, Lord *i.e.* J. H. Forbes 1078.

Meredyth, Baron *i.e.* W. M. S. Baron Athlumney 102

Milan, Count of *i.e.* Sir H. J. Caldwell 515.

Names, Titles, Etc. *(Con.)*

Milner-Gibson, Thomas *i.e.* Thomas Gibson 1141.

Montalbo, Countess de *i.e.* Josephine Benoite 358.

Myddleton, Robert *i.e.* Robert Biddulph 273.

Noel-Fearn, Henry *i.e.* Rev. H. Christmas 617.

Nicholls, Charlotte *i.e.* Charlotte Bronte 413.

Nugent, Fulke Southwell Greville- *i.e.* Fulke Southwell Greville 1239.

Osborne, George H. *i.e.* George 6 earl of Aberdeen 8.

Osborne, Ralph Bernal *i.e.* Ralph Bernal 255.

Pakington, John Somerset *i.e.* John Somerset Russell 1311.

Paget, Baron *i.e.* H. P. Anglesey 71.

Pyndar, John R. Beachamp *i.e.* John, earl Beauchamp 211.

Richardson-Currer, Henry *i.e.* Henry Richardson 790.

Ridley-Colborne, Nicholas W. *i.e.* Nicholas W. Ridley 669.

Russell-Boyne, Gustavus H. earl Brancepeth *i.e.* G. H. Boyne 369-70.

Sackville West, G. J. *i.e.* G. J. West 852.

Seymour-Vesey-Fitzgerald, Sir W. R. *i.e.* Sir W. R. Fitzgerald 1060.

Solly-Flood, Frederick *i.e.* Frederick Solly 1071.

Stanley, Henry Morton *i.e.* John Rowlands 242.

Stewart, The Abbé *i.e.* Stewart Drummond 475.

Vernon family, The, took name of Harcourt 1324.

Watson-Gordon, Sir J. *i.e.* Sir John Gordon 1181.

Weddell, Thomas P. 2 earl de Grey *i.e.* T. P. Robinson 848.

Yarde Buller, John *i.e.* John Buller Yarde 620.

Napoleon I. *d.* 1821, conveyed to St. Helena 663, exhumation of his body 42, medical attendant at St. Helena 89, on board Bellerophon 914, person present at his death 764, post mortem appearance of his body 1433, representations of him in dramas 1169, visitor at Elba 746, visitors at St. Helena 56, 1088, went in the Undaunted to Elba 1374.

Napoleon III. *d.* 1873, escape from Ham 932, his mistress the countess de Beauregard 214, subsidizes the Morning Chronicle 1160.

Nash, John *d.* 1835, architect 847.

Nassau, first bishop of 572.

Natal, bishop of 673, Majuba hill, battle of 677.

National Debt, money left for reduction of 844.

National Gallery, Wynn Ellis pictures 987.

Natural history, Bowerbank's collection of 357.

Naturalists, Audubon 107, Burchell 475.

Naturalisations, Albano 37, Albert, prince 38, Aldridge 42, Appold 78, Arntz 90, Bates 192, Batthyany 194, Baume 196, Beyer 268, Bianconi 269, Biber 269, Cavagnari 575, Chatelain 598, Costa 724, Crestadoro 758, Dallmeyer 806, Dellagana 854, Freiligrath 1105, Huth 1606.

Nature printing 372.

Navarino, battle of 665.

Navy, anchor, Hall's patent 1292, armour plating of ships 623, 675, bilge-tank, an iron 1292, boys' training ships 1350, captains by order in council 119, Cowper Cole's system 675, feats of daring 1300, first screw frigate 1046, forces of the enemy 1048, Graham's novices 1350, Keppel's action, last survivor of 1275, mounting guns on ships 675, nautical almanac office 1317, naval cadets 1350, pay office abolished 878, round war ships 972, screw ship the first 1289, target for defence of ships 583.

Nebuchadnezzar, king of Babylon, his name found on a monument 1480.

Negro minstrels, Buckley minstrels 464, Christy minstrels 1399, 1489, Moor and Burgess 1489.

Nelson, Horatio *killed* 1805 admiral, officer at his funeral 1224.

Newcastle, bishop of 581, chartist disturbances 1044, chemical soc. 622, literary and philosophical soc. 622, typographical soc. 20, Walker alkali works 622.

Newmarket, middle park plate founded 312, school for jockeys 1031.

Newman, John Henry *d.* 1889 cardinal, Achilli case 1361, his solicitor 1361, resigned fellowship 1388, tract ninety 1247.

Newport, bishop of 439, chartist riots 1110.

Newsagent, Berger 252.

Newspaper correspondents, Borrow G. H. 342, Bower H. E. tried for murder 356, Boweryem G. 358, Bowlby, T. W. 359, Cameron 524, Morton Saville *killed* in Paris 356.

Newspapers, church and country newspaper co. 1114, early papers, collection of 482, newspaper press college 1114, stamp duty on 1099.

Newspapers, *See also* Magazines.

Academy founded 77, assistant editor 1568.

Albion, New York, founded 186.

Anglo-Saxon, Boston, established 186.

Antidote, Dublin, editor 1193.

Athenæum commenced 461, editors 878, 884, 898, 1451, manager 1098, owners 103, 1515, dramatic critic 1437, musical critic 1253.

Atlas editors 1098, 1533.

Australian town and country journal commenced 243.

Banner of Ulster founded 1142.

Bath express editor 1378.

Belfast morning news, proprietor 1215.

Bell's life in London, proprietor 644, editors 907, 908.

Bombay standard commenced 468.

Britannia founded 732.

British luminary, editor 1157.

Builder founded 1322, editor 1164.

Bullionist, editors 1002, 1424.

Cambridge independent press, proprietor 1375.

Catholic layman, Dublin, editor 1132.

Censor, editor 1109.

Cerberus established 709.

Chat, editor 1518.

Chat of the week, editor 1591.

Christian advocate, editor 1120.

Christian observer, editor 1173.

Commercial gazette founded 243.

Companion, The, editor 1591.

Constitutional, sub-editor 1593.

Cornish telegraph, editor 1123.

Cornubian, editor 1124.

Country, The, established 741.

County courts chronicle established 741.

Court journal started 1515.

Daily express, Dublin, editor 1163.

Daily News, editors 872, 1084, 1589, manager 878, musical critic 1501, parliamentary reporter 1574.

Daily telegraph, acting editor 1593.

Dundee guardian commenced 468.

Edinburgh courant, editor 1424.

Edinburgh evening courant, editor 1319.

Elgin courier founded 1202.

Empire, proprietors 1303.

Poor servants of the Mother of God incarnate 1112.

Poplin manufacturer, Atkinson 104.

Population, census of 1023.

Porcelain manufacturers, Blore 317, Copeland 716.

Portland cement, experiments on 1204.

Portugal, Dom Pedro's expedition to 1491, sum given to sufferers by Massena's invasion 763.

Positivist, Baxter 197.

Post office, adhesive stamps introduced 1474, cheap postage introduced 1474, ocean penny postage 375, parcels post established 1027, penny postage established 1474, physician general 1131, stamps, designs for 583, stamps invented at Dundee 583, stamp perforator 81.

Postmasters General, Canning 536, Clanricarde 622, Colchester 670, Conyngham 698, Elgin 973, Fawcett 1027, Hardwicke 1331.

Potato, potato sowing machine 1055, potato spirit 240.

Potters, Dillwyn 880, Doulton 904.

Power loom, invention of 565.

Prayer, healing by means of 472.

Press prosecutions, Dolby 891, Drakard 914, Finlay 1048, Hobhouse 427.

Presses, screw and side lever 528.

Preston, Lancashire, money left to 1346, St. Walburge's ch. spire 1322.

Pretenders, *See* Claimants 1632.

Prime ministers, Aberdeen 6, Derby 863, Disraeli 203, Grey 1555, Palmerston 1564.

Primrose day, first kept 204, primrose league, founders of 1329.

Prince consort created 39, *See also* Albert 1621.

Print dealers, Colnaghi 684, Evans 1002, Graves 1211, Halsted 1296.

Printers, Applegath 77, Clay 640, Clowes 655, Cox & Son 742, Cox & Wyman 742, Dunkin 936, Gardner 1122, Gilbert 1145, Harrild 1344, Harrison 1356, Heavysides 1414, Holmes 1515, Howe 1556.

Printing, ball and roller 77, bank note machine 77, Bigg's charity for printers 275, cast words, use of 239, colour printing machine 77, composition balls and printing roller 895, 1344, Cowper's machines 738, Figgins type founder 1045, Franklin's printing press 1344, ink distributing machine 739, inking rollers first used 198, machinery, improvements in 895, machinery for printing and composing type 239, nature printing 372, printing press, four cylinder 77, 739, printing press, steam 77, printing presses, Applegath's 738, 739, Cowper's 738 and Walter's 738, queen's printers' patent 610, rotatory printing press 1474, silk printing 77, type founder 261, type-high stereotype columns in newspapers 1355, type setting machine 1377, type setting without copy 1290, typographical gazetteer 729, vertical machine 77.

Printing presses, private, Botfield 346, Gorton 1186.

Prisons and Prisoners, chaplain 640, diseases and mortality of 345, improved prisons 1382, prisoners of war, hospital for 486, treadmill invented 779.

Private secretary, a comedy 1477.

Privy councillor, nominated but not sworn in 590.

Privy seal, lords keeper of the, Buccleugh 457, Buckingham 460, Clanricarde 621, Clarendon 623, Disraeli 203, Ellenborough 975, Haddington 1271, Halifax 1281, Hardwicke 1331, Harrowby 1358.

Probate and divorce court, Cresswell judge 758, established 758.

Probate duty, large amount 779.

Probert, William *hanged* 1825 for horse stealing 1592.

Property, real property commission 409.

Provision merchants, Budgett 467 and Finnis 1050.

Psalms, free chant system of reciting 774.

Pseudonyms, *See also* Actors' stage names 1619, **Initialism** 1648, Names 1665 and Novels 1675.

* * * *i.e.* Arthur Gerald Geoghegan 1135.

Alazon *i.e.* Richard William Barnes 172.

Aleph *i.e.* William Harvey 1368.

Amicus Curiæ *i.e.* John Payne Collier 677.

Anglo-American *i.e.* Sir Brenton Halliburton 1294.

Anti-Reformist *i.e.* John Hope 1532.

Asiatic Liberal, An *i.e.* George Burges 477.

Atkinson, Isaac *i.e.* James Anderson 62.

Augur *i.e.* Henry Mort Feist 1032.

Aunt Effie *i.e.* Ann Hawkshaw 1391.

Aunt Lucy *i.e.* Lucy Elizabeth Bather 193.

Auntie B. *i.e.* Bertha H. Buxton 503.

Author of "Contrasts" *i.e.* William Gilbert 590.

Author of "Handbook of fictitious names" *i.e.* Ralph Thomas 426.

Ayrton, J. C. *i.e.* Mary Francis Chapman 592.

B., H. *i.e.* John Doyle 911.

Balance, A *i.e.* Thomas Binney 281.

Barleycorn, John *i.e.* Matthew James Higgins 1464.

Barnard de Burgh *i.e.* Barnabas Brough 424.

Beaujolais *i.e.* Hans Busk 498.

Beemaster *i.e.* Rev. John Cumming 784.

Bell, Acton *i.e.* Anne Bronte 413.

Bell, Currer *i.e.* Charlotte Bronte 413.

Bell, Ellis *i.e.* Emily Bronte 413.

Belgravian Mother, A *i.e.* Matthew J. Higgins 1464.

Bellew, John C. M. *i.e.* John Chippendale Montesquieu Higgin 234.

Bernhardt, J. Karl *i.e.* Thomas Crampton 751.

Bible student, A *i.e.* John Hyde 1611.

Blackmantle, Bernard *i.e.* Charles Molloy 1062.

Brancassine, R. F. *i.e.* Hughes Halle 1293.

Britannicus *i.e.* Thomas Brittain 404.

Brooke, Arthur *i.e.* John Chalk Claris 624.

Brother, A *i.e.* George Clement Boase 321.

Brother and Sister *i.e.* Frances Collins and F. **Percy** Cotton 679.

Brown, John *i.e.* T. J. Hogg 1503.

Brown Redivivus, Thomas *i.e.* Caroline Frances **Cornwallis** 722.

Buller of Brasenose *i.e.* John Hughes 1573.

Byron's Ghost *i.e.* G. R. Wythen Baxter 198.

C., V. S. *i.e.* Sir Richard D. Hanson 1322.

Captain of the Undine *i.e.* Edmund G. Harvey 1365.

Carwinley *i.e.* William Graham 1198.

Ceiriog *i.e.* John Hughes 1575.

Censor *i.e.* George Caldwell 514.

Cerny, Frederick *i.e.* Frederick Guthrie 1264.

Childers *i.e.* George Caldwell 514.

Civilian *i.e.* Matthew James Higgins 1464.

Claribel *i.e.* Charlotte Alington Barnard 170.

Cock of the Steeple, The *i.e.* Alexander Birnie 288.

Cœlebs *i.e.* Edward Augustus Carlyon 550.

Comyne, Alexander de *i.e.* Charles T. Browne 443.

Conway, Hugh *i.e.* Frederick John Fargus 1021.

Cornelie de B, Baronne *i.e.* Clara de Chatelain 598.

Cotton, Robert Turner *i.e.* Mortimer Collins 680.

Country Curate, A *i.e.* Rev. Erskine Neale 245.

Cousin Kate *i.e.* Catherine Douglas Bell 227.

Craven *i.e.* John William Carleton 546.
Creature of an Hour *i.e.* Charles Girdlestone 1153.
Cristion *i.e.* Hugh Hughes 1572.
Croker, Thomas Crofton *i.e.* Marianne Croker 765.
Crowquill, Alfred *i.e.* A. H. and C. R. Forrester 1083.
Czapek, P. B. *i.e.* John Liptrot Hatton 1378.
D. A. Y. *i.e.* David Elisha Davy 834.
Daly, John *i.e.* John Bessemeres 260.
Denarius *i.e.* Sir Henry Cole 671.
Detector *i.e.* Francis Burdett Courtenay 733.
Dewdrop *i.e.* Cordelia Georgiana Budd 466.
Dixon, Gerald *i.e.* William Jerrold Dixon 885.
Dolores *i.e.* Ellen Dickson 876.
Doyle, Martin *i.e.* William Hickey 1460.
Druid, The *i.e.* Henry Hall Dixon 883.
Dubois, Alfred *i.e.* James Stuart Bowes 358.
Eccletus *i.e.* Luke Howard 1554.
Edwards, Mr. *i.e.* George Matthews Ede 956.
Elgate, Arthur de Cripp *i.e.* Thomas Gray 1220.
Eliot, George *i.e.* Mary Ann Evans 771.
Englishman, A *i.e.* William Whittaker Barry 183.
Eos Glan Twrch *i.e.* John Edwards 966.
Ephemera *i.e.* Edward Fitzgibbon 1060-61.
Erith, Lynn *i.e.* Edward Fox 1094.
Esse quam videri *i.e.* John Baker Hopkins 1533.
Ex-Madras Civilian *i.e.* James Dewar Bourdillon 349.
Father Thomas *i.e.* Thomas Doyle 913.
Felix, Nicholas *i.e.* Nicholas Wanostrocht 1032.
Fiat Justitia *i.e.* Rev. Thomas Binney 280.
Fisher, P. *i.e.* William Andrew Chatto 600.
Flag Officer, A *i.e.* Edward Hawker 1385.
Florenz *i.e.* Charlotte Elliot 978.
Forester, Frank *i.e.* Henry William Herbert 1440.
Fpaid, I. D. *i.e.* John Evans 1004.
Gentleman in Black, The *i.e.* Charles Clarke 631.
Gershom *i.e.* Julius Edmund Goodwyn 1175.
Goggle, Mungo Coulter *i.e.* Robert D. Hamilton 1304.
Gohebydd Llandain *i.e.* John Griffiths 1247.
Grant, Gerald *i.e.* Gertrude Elizabeth Grant 1202.
Grinn, The Brothers *i.e.* E. L. Blanchard and Thomas L. Greenwood 1231.
Henry, D. S. *i.e.* Henry Dircks 881.
Hertfordshire incumbent, An *i.e.* Joseph Williams Blakesley 305.
Hieover Harry *i.e.* Charles Bindley 277.
Hogg, Nathan *i.e.* Thomas Baird 134.
Holdreth, Lionel H. *i.e.* Percy Greg 1231.
Holt, Sestertius *i.e.* William White Cooper 713.
Hotspur *i.e.* Henry Buck 460.
Hotspur *i.e.* Henry Mort Feist 1032.
Ianthe *i.e.* Charlotte Mary Bacon 120.
Ingoldsby *i.e.* James Hildyard 1467.
Ion *i.e.* Ellen St. John Hunt 1589.
Ishmael *i.e.* Josiah Harris 1349.
Ismael *i.e.* Christopher A. M. Harris 1346.
Iskander *i.e.* Aleksandr I. Hertzen 1450.
Jack *i.e.* Marianne Elizabeth Godwin 1165.
Jones, T. Percy *i.e.* William Edmondstone Aytoun 116
Junius Redivivus *i.e.* William Bridges Adams 19.
Knot, Maple *i.e.* Ebenezer Clemo 645.
L. S. E. *i.e.* Michael Augustus Gathercole 1130.
Lady, A *i.e.* Charlotte Susan Maria Bury 496.

Lady in the Country *i.e.* Anna Gurney 1260.
Layman, A *i.e.* Thomas Carlyle 550.
Layman, A *i.e.* John Sibbald Edison 959.
Layman, A *i.e.* Sir Walter Scott 1179.
Layman, A Protestant *i.e.* William Harty 1363.
Layman of the church of England, A *i.e.* W. A. L. Grant 1207.
Lee, Gibbons *i.e.* William Bennett 244.
Lewes, Walton *i.e.* Jeremiah Bowen 356.
Libertas *i.e.* Peter Brown 437.
Libra *i.e.* Edward Brotherton 423.
Manchester manufacturer *i.e.* Richard Cobden 659.
Martel, Charles *i.e.* Thomas Delf 853.
Member of University of Oxford *i.e.* W. M. Hutton 1609.
Miles *i.e.* Henry Walter 1433.
Mother of Six *i.e.* Matthew James Higgins 1464.
Myfyr Morganwg *i.e.* Evan Davies 826.
Myrtle, Harriet *i.e.* Mary Gillies 1150.
Neil, Ross *i.e.* Isabella N. Harwood 1369.
Nemo *i.e.* Aaron Levy Green 1222.
Nimrod *i.e.* Charles James Apperley 76.
Nordmann, Rudolph *i.e.* George F. Harris 1348.
Old Follower of Sir H. D. Chad's *i.e.* Montagu Burrows 580.
Oliver, Stephen the younger *i.e.* William Andrew Chatto 600.
Omnium, Jacob *i.e.* Matthew James Higgins 1464.
O'Reilly, Miles *i.e.* Charles Graham Halpine 1296.
Outis *i.e.* Luke Howard 1554.
Owl, the figure of an *i.e.* Clement Henry Bennett 240.
Oxford Divine, A *i.e.* Henry Bellenden Bulteel 472.
P——. P——. poet laureate *i.e.* George Daniel 811.
Page, H. A. *i.e.* A. H. Japp 1502.
Pamphilius *i.e.* David Mitchell Aird 34.
Parallax *i.e.* Samuel Birley Rowbotham 1311.
Pariah, A *i.e.* Caroline Frances Cornwallis 722.
Parley, Peter *i.e.* Samuel Clark 628.
Paterfamilias *i.e.* Matthew James Higgins 1464.
Phiz *i.e.* Hablot Knight Browne 443.
Pilgrim *i.e.* Edward Brotherton 423.
Piscator *i.e.* William Hughes 1578.
Piscator *i.e.* Henry Walter 1433.
Pobman *i.e.* John Griffiths 1247.
Pollock, Guy *i.e.* Robert Douglas Hamilton 1304.
Powdavie *i.e.* Peter Robert Drummond 921.
Providus *i.e.* Matthew James Higgins 1464.
Punjabee *i.e.* William Delafield Arnold 88.
Quid *i.e.* Robert Allan Fitzgerald 1059.
Reader in British Museum *i.e.* Andrea Crestadoro 758
Reuben *i.e.* Robert Stephen Hawker 1385.
Roberts, Captain *i.e.* A. C. Hobart 1487.
Rustum *i.e.* Sir Henry Lindesay Bethune 264.
Santa Croce, Rosalia *i.e.* Clara de Chatelain 598.
Scriblerus Redivivus *i.e.* Edward Caswall 569.
Scrutator *i.e.* Walter Henry 1433.
Search, John *i.e.* Thomas Binney 281.
Septuagenarian, A. *i.e.* James Booth 337.
Sister Mary Theresa *i.e.* Frances Ball 145.
Slick, Sam *i.e.* Thomas Chandler Haliburton 1280.
Smitheram, T. *i.e.* Thomas H. Harvey 1367.
Sparks, Timothy *i.e.* Charles Dickens 443.

Railway contractors, Brassey 384, Brotherhood 423, Crawley 756, Cubitt J. 779, Cubitt Sir W. 779, Dargan 814, Eassie 952, Fairbank 1050, Gowans 1193, Hoof 1526.

Ramhurst gunpowder mills 610.

Rams, steam 914.

Ramsay, G. M. R. Dalhousie d. 1880, first baron 804.

Raphael d. 1520 Raffaello Sanzio, drawings by 1283.

Rarey, John S. d. 1866, horse tamer 1145.

Ravenstone castle, Wigtonshire, purchased 343.

Rawlinson, Sir Henry Creswicke b. 1810, discovers cuneiform vowel system 1480.

Reading, look and say method of learning 795, phonetic method of teaching 711.

Readers, public, Bellew 234, 973, Dickens 872, Holl 1506.

Reaping machine, Bell's 230.

Rebecca riots 1090, 1472.

Records, public, account of 709, arrangement of 1488, destruction of valueless documents 1334, made accessible to public 1333, record commission 709.

Reform Bill, boundary act 747, Croker's opposition to 764, Roman catholic peer voted against reform bill 92, tenant at will clause 460.

Reform league, president of 206, the league dissolved 206.

Reform solicitor, the 4.

Refraction, conical, discovered 1307.

Religious communities, collection of works of instructions authorised by 648.

Religious Denominations.

Associate presbytery of Ireland founded 456.

Baptists, college in Regent's park 825, immersion in the harbour of St. John, New Brunswick 928, missionary soc. 741.

Barkerites at Newcastle 164.

Bible christian minister 1119.

Brentonites at Bath 390.

Bulteelers at Oxford 472.

Caffin's religious society at Blackheath 511.

Campbellites in America 526.

Catholic apostolic church, Albury ch. at 919, Albury, consultation at 541, angel 1410, apostles 85, 541, 550, 906, 919, apostolic lordship 1207, bishop of Scotland 321, Gordon square ch. opened 382, 1410, Irving 541, Newman st. ch. 541.

Children of God founded 1153.

Church of Christ at Finchingfield 296.

Church of England See also Ritualism 1691, baptismal regeneration 1185, bishop excommunicated 673, bishop resigned 106, ch. defence association founded 208, ch. congresses originated 208, ch. extension association founded 32, ch. of E. in Wales, the most popular preacher 1574, ch. rates, Braintree case 733, clergyman, oldest in England 964, court of arches 1185, crisis or the signs of the times, a sermon 99, election of bp. Hampden opposed by 13 bishops 1311, guilds commenced 586, harvest thanksgivings instituted 1385, hear the church, a sermon 1526, holy orders relinquished by Bellew 234, Clark 629 and Hoblyn 1489, liturgy, petition to parliament for reform of 1581, living of great value 817, priestly absolution, letters on 276, register books, false entries in 1147, ruri-decanal synods instituted 1385, weekly offertories instituted 1385.

Congregational Union of England and Wales 296.

Darbyism originated 813.

Disciples of Christ in America 526.

RELIGIOUS DENOMINATIONS (Con.)

Episcopal church of Scotland, primate 1156.

Freethinking Christians in London 96.

French protestant church 820.

Friends, deputation to emperor of Russia 595, missionaries 1086, origin of 718, plea for liberty of conscience 595, tent meetings 540.

Girlingites in the New Forest 1153.

Glassites, musical manual for 1585.

Irvingites, See Catholic Apostolic church col. 1689.

Jews, college 1222, converts from Judaism 1449, first jew a senior wrangler 1362, rabbi 1222, synagogues in London 1222, Talmud Torah sch. 1222.

Latter day Saints or Mormonites 1611.

Moravian bishop 1089.

Mormonism, account of 423, mormonism and its author 569, mormonites at Salt Lake city 1611.

New Jerusalem church or Swedenborgians 1611.

Plymouth Brethren, Ball R. 145, Congleton, Baron 691, founders of 1252, history of 1202, Orchard st. chapel London 691, Welbeck st. chapel London 691, works on the doctrine of 769.

Presbyterian church, The English 62, 158.

Presbyterian ch. in Scotland, a heresy hunt 1520, first missionary to India 924, See also Row 1691.

Presbyterian Free ch. minister 1453.

Primitive Methodists Connection founded 350, 655.

Reformed Anglican church bishopric 1416.

Reformed Episcopal church minister 1491.

Reformed Presbyterian minister 1550.

Roman Catholics, Brompton oratory 802, 1012, Jesuits obtain Hales place 1279, London oratory 802, mayor, the first roman catholic 1505, Moorfield's chapel ceiling and altarpiece 28, oratory London 1605, parliament, second member sent to 1554, St. George's cathedral built 913, scholarships could not be held by 1444, society of Jesus, ordo compiled 395, solicitor, the first admitted 177.

Roman Catholic church, converts to, Anstey 74, Badeley 121, Bellasis 233, Bellew 234, Bowden 355, Bowring 362, Bowyer 363, Burder 476, Burns 488, Caswall 569, Chatterton 599, Coffin 667, Dalgairns 802, Digby 878, Dodsworth 890, Elmsley 988, Estcourt 998, Faber 1012, Fielding 1150, Flowers 1072, Formby 1082, Forster 1086, Fullerton 1112, Garside 1126, Gilpin 1151, Grant 1203, Haigh 1274, Hamilton 1299, Hawker 1385, Herbert 1441, Hope 1529, Hope-Scott 1532, Hopkins 1533, Howitt 1599, Hutchison W. A. 1605, Hutchison W. C. 1606.

Sandemanian ch. 1020.

Seventh day Baptists 294.

Shakers in London 1153.

Swedenborgians, account of 423, church in London 1611, minister 1194.

Unitarians, home missionary board founded 208, works on unitarianism 1144.

United presbyterian church founded 1343.

United secession church minister 1342.

Welsh calvinist ch. London, expels a member 1572.

Welsh calvinist methodist ch. ministers 1573.

Wesleyan Methodists, Bunting Methodism 474, 475, Didsbury theological instit. 776, 777, Fletcher the imposter 1069, fly sheet controversy 939, 1007, 1245, Kingswood sch. 776, persons expelled 350, 1007, Wesley banner 939, Woodhouse Grove sch. 776.

Religious services in theatres 406.

Religious Tract Soc., its publications 771.

Royal Society Fellows *(Con.)*

Horner 1540, Horsfield 1541, Hoskins 1545, Houghton 1547, Howard J. E. 1553, Howard L. 1554, Hume 1586, Hunt G. 1590, Hunt R. 1592, Hunter 1594, Hyett 1611, Hymers 1612, Quin 940, Wood 1376.

Royal warrant 1147.

Rugby, rebellion at 731.

Rugeley poisoning case 1565.

Runic literature 1275.

Rural deans, account of 812.

Ruskin, John *b.* 1819 art critic, employs J. W. Bunny 474.

Russia, blank passes in 104, Lancaster schools introduced 1408, Mennonites emigrate to Canada 1367, peace with 737, Sebastopol, siege of 479.

Russia, St. Petersburg, Baird works founded 133, Alexander column bas reliefs 133, St. Nicholas bridge built 133.

S

Sabbath question, collection of books on the 742.

Sacred heart, society of the 797.

Sailors homes established 1226, 1292.

St. Albans, Harriet Beauclerk *d.* 1837 duchess of, Spanish dances composed for 310.

St. Andrew's university, principal 394 and rector 76, only place where degree can be obtained without residence 285.

St. Helens foundries 800.

St. John of Jerusalem, order of 429, prior of 948.

Safe maker, Chubb 618.

Salford, first member of parliament 423, Peel park given to 29.

Salisbury, bishop of 858, Blackmore museum 299, Salisbury and south Wiltshire museum 1093.

Salmon, killing fifty two in fifty five hours 1061.

Salvage committee, the first formed 348.

Sands, Dick *b.* 1840 clog dancer 1399.

Sandwich islands, king and queen of in England 317, 505.

San Remo, climate of 820.

Sanskrit scholars, Brown 430, Goldstuecker 1168, Haas 1268.

Saws and sawing, endless band machine 1009, inventions and improvements in saws 882.

Sax horns, improvements in 882.

Scandinavian scholar, Barclay 159.

Scene painters, Bough 347, Danson 812, Fenton 1034, Greenwood 1231, Telbin 1243.

Scheffer, Ary *d.* 1858 painter, his model for Monica 1511

Schools, agricultural 961, farm sch. system 1070, Fellenberg's system of industrial schools 507, Hazelwood system of management 1474, school excursions established 1448, seven pupils drowned 1070.

Sciography or examples of shadows 1267.

Scotland, Aberdeen, Udney sch. near 291, baronial architecture 455, church courts 700, churches, scheme for building two hundred 534, congregational union founded 320, education of women 1300, etymological dictionary of the language 755, Ferguson bequest founded 1035, Glasgow, first provost of 1199, Glenalmond coll. 1319, 1424, 1532, great seal, keeper of 1519, historiographer royal 409, 494, jesuits introduced 1150, legitimate king of 1298,

Scotland *(Con.)*

Lockmaben, keeper of 1532, locomotive engine the first 551, lunacy commission 744, poor, board of supervision 47, premier earl on union roll 753, Roman catholic bp. 1150, Rothesay, episcopacy restored in 1525, royal archers 1529, royal assoc. for promoting fine arts 755, secretary of state 804, Sunday travelling stopped 1424, Tay bridge, fall of 346, tramway the first 1193, Wellington school for criminals 644.

Scott, Sir Walter *d.* 1832, Abbotsford 317, 1393, 1532, Greig much like him 1235, his library 660, his friends 1150, 1502, his legal adviser 1141, sermons by 1179, Waverley, authorship of 25, Waverley, MS. of 1286, Waverley novels, printing of 738, Waverley novels, transcriber of 1179, works purchased by Black 292.

Screw propellers, experiments with 453.

Scullers, Bagshawe 126, Bates 192, Casamajor 567, Chambers J. G. 586, Chambers R. 587, Clasper 637, Coombes 707.

Sculptors, Behnes 223, Brodie 408, Burnard 484, Campbell 534, Carew 544, Durham 943, Earle 951, Fillans 1045, Foley 1073, Forrest 1082, Francis 1098. Fuller 1111, Gatley 1130, Gibson J. 1140, Gibson S. 1141, Gott 1189, Henning 1431, Hinchliff 1479, Hogan 1500, Hollins 1511, Hughes 1576.

Sea, deep sea dredging 1596, sea water, composition of 1596.

Secularist, Greg 1231.

Selby, St. James' ch. erected 107.

Selkirk, Alexander *d.* 1723 prototype of Robinson Crusoe, life of 1557.

Sellis *d.* 1810 attempts to murder Duke of Cumberland 1320.

Selwyn, George Augustus *d.* 1791 M.P., his adopted dau. 1449.

Sennacherib *d.* 680 B.C. king of Assyria, his name discovered on a monument 1480.

Serjeants at law, Adams 16, Alderson 40, Allen 52, Amphlett 58, Archibald 82, Bellasis 233, Bovill 354, Burke 480, Byles 504, Campbell 526, Channell 590, Clarke 635, Cleasby 643, Cox 741, Cresswell 758, Cross 770, Crowder 774, Doyley 913, Erle 954, Gaselee 1128, Glover 1160, Glynn 1161, Goulburn 1190, Halcomb 1276, Hayes 1398, Heath 1411, Hill 1471, Honyman 1523, Huddleston 1565, Storks 1190, peer made a serjeant 526.

Sermons remarkable 99, 472, 1526.

Serpents, serpent myths 712, worship of 842.

Sewage, method of utilising 113.

Sewing machine, Singer, original suggestion for the 214, introduced to Bombay 792.

Sextant, improved 831, protracting pocket 132.

Shaftesbury, Anthony A. *d.* 1885 seventh earl, his colleagues 1052.

Shakespeare, William *d.* 1616, before St. Thomas Lucy 1365, catalogue of plays in all languages 1391, chair 1164, clowns, representations of 690, dramas produced at Sadler's Wells 1231, New Place purchased 1295, no deerstalker 371, literary cookery with reference to matters attributed to 377, Shakspeare soc. 1295, Stratford library, librarian 1391, tercentenary 1071, 1349, twelve plays produced in Dublin 1349, works in all languages, collection of 1578.

Shakespeare, William, editions of his works, The Cambridge 629, Cassell's illustrated 631, Clarke's edition 631, Collier's editions 678, Collier's reported forgeries 677, facsimile of the quartos 1295, Harness' edition 1342, Perkin's folio 678.

SOCIETIES (Con.)

Botanical of Edinburgh founded 144.
British and foreign bible, founded 1316.
British and foreign sch. soc. training coll. 793.
British and foreign temperance founded 681.
British artists established 1515, president 1601.
British, for propogating gospel among Jews 1448.
British madrigal conductor 719.
Cambridge antiquarian projected 1295, founded 723.
Cambridge philosophical founded 1434.
Cambridge university musical founded 948.
Camden founded 451.
Cavendish founded 1198.
Cavendish philogical and chemical members 580.
Celtic union originated 536.
Chemical, London, founded 361, 1198, 1228, 1244, 1437.
Chetham projected 724, 773.
Christian instruction originated 296.
Colonial missionary founded 280.
Communist propaganda founded 169.
Congregational union merged in Missionary Soc. 9.
Conservative land founded 1253.
Contrapuntists founded 1072.
Corresponding founded 217.
Coventry labourers' and artisans' established 385.
De Quincey founded 1160.
Dublin historical originated 231.
Dublin, models left to 1073.
Dublin university zoological and botanical founded 146
English church union founded 391.
Entomological founded 783, 1530.
Epidemilogical, chief founder 117.
Ethnological 299, 434, 755.
Evening sketching founded 584.
Fanny Wright founded 818.
Farmers' alliance originated 1552.
Folk lore founded 713.
Freed slaves aid originated 795.
Friends of Italy founded 96.
Geological, foundation of 29, 1229.
Godists advocated 161.
Granger founded 1326.
Graphic society of artists founded 406.
Harleian founded 605.
Historical of Lancashire and Cheshire founded 1584.
Holbein founded 1223, publications 99.
Home missionary originated 9.
Horticultural, collector for in Brazil 893, sec. of 247.
Huguenot founded 1153.
Hunterian president 734.
Ilam Anastatic drawing and Anastatic soc. 1237.
Incorporated law instituted 1513.
India reform founded 874.
Juridical, sec. of 625.
Kilkenny archæological established 1211.
Lambeth chemical established 783.
League of universal brotherhood developed 491.
Legal discussion founded 157.
Liberal registration, sec. of 717.
Linnean, black ball J. E. Gray 1216.
London and Middlesex archæological founded 1579.
London astrological, last survivor of 1270.

SOCIETIES (Con.)

London city mission, sec. 1127.
London corresponding chairman 281.
London organ school founded 626.
London professional chorus founded 1348.
London surgical home formed 432.
Manx established 1357.
Mathematical president 1169.
Metaphysical, a member of 649.
Metropolitan soc. of florists and amateurs started 1157
Microscopical founded 357.
Middlesex archæological founded 352.
Midland medical founded 1453.
Moslem missionary fonnded 87.
Motett founded 946.
Musomanik, at Anstruther founded 1214.
National founded 730, money raised for 1238.
Natural history, Glasgow, founded 1219.
New British and foreign dissolved 488.
Newcastle literary and philosophical founded 232.
Northumberland and Durham natural history founded 39.
Numismatic first meeting 37.
Odontological first president 565.
Oxford churchmen's union founded 1284.
Paleontographical founded 357.
Parker secretary and librarian 113.
Patagonian missionary founded 1121.
Patriotic, rewards by 1056.
Peace, first congress 491.
Penzance natural history and antiquarian curator 731
People's international league founded 96.
Pharmaceutical originated 1313, founded 228.
Philharmonic, chief originator of 114, 725.
Philobiblon secretary 853.
Philological founded 1254, member of 674.
Philological school, principal of 2.
Photographic founded 1090.
Phrenological founded 688, 979.
Physical of London founded 1264.
Plinian, Edinburgh, founded 134.
Polytechnic, Liverpool, founded 1208.
Prayer book and homily founded 467.
Psychological founded 741.
Ray founded 357.
Record first president 773.
Religious book and tract founded 959.
Royal agricultural of England founded 1126, sec. 1567
Royal Birmingham soc. of artists founded 1124.
Royal college of chemistry founded 1122.
Royal Cornwall polytechnic founders 1094, 1095.
Royal general theatrical fund founded 737.
Royal geographical founded 410, 427.
Royal geological of Cornwall curator 731.
Royal historical first council 605.
Royal horticultural gardens at Chiswick 1088.
Royal medical and chirurgical presidents 23, 790, 980.
Royal physical, Edinburgh, reformed 1219, president 670.
Royal society of literature founded 117, sec. 572.
Sacred harmonic founded 393, conductor 725, dissolved 1603.
Sanskrit text 1168.

T

Waterford, Sir Henry de la Poer *d.* 1859, 3rd marquis, at Eglinton tournament 970.

Waterford and Lismore, bishop of 1075.

Waterton, Charles *d.* 1865 naturalist, his friend 1489.

Weare, William *murdered* 1823 by Thurtell 1592.

Weather, daily forecasts of 1064.

Weatherhead, Hume, an author 793.

Weaver, Duncan 930.

Wedding, golden, Howitt 1559.

Weights and measures, uniform throughout the world 438.

Wellington, Arthur, duke of *d.* 1852, anthem for his funeral 1187, death of 582, duel with earl of Winchelsea 1328, funeral car made 155, his physician 1586, his private sec. 1239, letter to from Joseph Ady 26.

Welsh scholars, Edwards J. 966, Edwards L. 966, Edwards R. 967, Edwards T. 967, Evans E. 1002, Evans J. 1004, Griffiths 1246, Hughes 1575.

West Indies, Jamaica, great sea light at Morant point 1176.

Westmeath lord lieutenant 1239.

Westminster, cartoon exhibition 639, clock in Westminster palace 861, hospital 768, school, arms over doorway 844.

Westminster abbey, burials in 657, 873, registers 605, stone arches painted 650.

Weybridge, Surrey, mortuary chapel of Orleans family 856, 1106.

Whale fisheries, establishment 1360, harpoon gun used 1425.

Wharfingers, Farncomb 1022, Humphery 1586.

What to eat, drink and avoid 782.

Whately, Richard *d.* 1863 arch-bp. of Dublin, edited The Cautions for the Times 1060.

What's in a name 489.

Wheat improved 1488.

Wheatstone, Sir Charles *d.* 1875 physicist, partner with Cooke 705, 1383, the maker of his electrical apparatus 1429.

Wheel, invention of a friction 382.

Whewell, William *d.* 1866 master of Trinity coll. Cambridge, his bequest to the coll. 1310.

Whist, blue peter or call for trumps invented 248, laws of 550, 640.

Whist players, Baldwin 640, Barnes 173, Bentinck 248, Bowyer 363, Brittain 404, Buckle 463, Clay 640, Hood 1524, Hughes 1578.

White, Arthur, attempted to shoot Charles Buxton 503.

White, Henry Kirke *d.* 1806 poet, Much in sorrow, oft in woe 685.

Wigan, Lancashire, cotton mill the first 800.

Wilberforce, Robert Isaac *d.* 1857 of Oriel coll., resigned fellowship 1388.

Wilhelm, Guillaume L. B. *d.* 1842 composer, method of teaching music 1581.

William iv. *d.* 1837, Mrs. Jordan 853, his dau. Sophia 853, sham baronet presented to 1588, sons 1056, 1057 *bis.*

Wills, in perogative office Dublin, index to 263, longest on record 779.

Wills proved for large amounts.

£50,000 *col.* 275.
£59,000 *col.* 1428.
£70,000 *col.* 12.
£80,000 *cols.* 1070, 1418.
£100,000 *col.* 188.
£140,000 *cols.* 108, 649.

WILLS (*Con.*)

£160,000 *cols.* 284, 299.
£180,000 *cols.* 80, 715, 1213.
£200,000 *cols.* 505, 732, 1222.
£250,000 *cols.* 48, 427, 433, 480, 504, 525, 578, 622, 648, 863, 941, 1073, 1151, 1272, 1411, 1556.
£280,000 *col.* 792.
£283,000 *col.* 198.
£300,000 *cols.* 8, 76, 217, 227, 477, 753, 786, 1122, 1531.
£344,023 *col.* 1257.
£350,000 *cols.* 96, 205, 217 *bis.*, 318, 575, 971, 974, 1146, 1226, 1407, 1502, 1512.
£370,000 *col.* 420.
£400,000 *cols.* 83, 94, 110, 221, 1167, 1457, 1497.
£483,000 *col.* 1138.
£500,000 *cols.* 698, 931, 942, 1450, 1526, 1546, 1606.
£503,000 *col.* 1043.
£542,000 *col.* 707.
£588,000 *col.* 1444.
£600,000 *cols.* 192, 218, 987, 1051.
£700,000 *col.* 733.
£800,000 *cols.* 83, 407, 773, 1138.
£900,000 *col.* 441.
£910,000 *col.* 457.
£1,000,000 *col.* 779.
£1,026,000 *col.* 923.
£1,098,000 *col.* 197.
£1,100,000 *cols.* 1256, 1261.
£1,190,000 *col.* 134.
£1,200,000 *col.* 756.
£1,300,000 *col.* 1043.
£1,500,000 *col.* 162.
£1,700,000 *col.* 949.
£2,000,000 *cols.* 134, 756.
£3,200,000 *col.* 384.
£3,540,000 *col.* 867.

Wilson, Sir Robert Thomas *d.* 1849 general, escape of Lavalette 897.

Wiltshire lord lieutenant 31.

Wimpole hall, Cambridgeshire, frescoes at 498.

Winchester, Cranbury cricket ground 586, Cranbury stables 586, St. Cross hospital and earl of Guildford 1255.

Winchelsea, Sussex, history of 712.

Wind instruments, catechism of 632.

Windmills, self regulating sails invented 779.

Window tax repealed 535.

Windsor castle, governor of 38.

Windsor, Old, novitiate at Beaumont lodge 635.

Wines, British largest maker of 289, Douro river, survey of 1083, port, a word or two on 1083, Hungarian introduced 1233, wine flagon system 1233.

Wine merchants, Gassiot 1130, Gilbey 1146, Hooper 1528, Husenbeth 1602, Max Greger 1233.

Wire drawing, drilled gems used in 406.

Wire walker, Diavolo 870.

Wiseman, Nicholas P. S. *d.* 1865 cardinal, his coadjutor archbp. 995, his godson 1439.

Wizards, *See* Conjurors 1634.

Wolff, Joseph *d.* 1862 missionary, teaches Hebrew 1547.

Wood carver, Davy 835.

Woods and Forests, etc., first commissioner of, Canning 536, Carlisle 548, Fitzroy 1063, Hobhouse 427, Howard 1552.

X

Y

Z